YOUTH BIBLE
CATHOLIC EDITION

NEW REVISED STANDARD VERSION
CATHOLIC EDITION

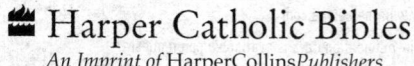

Harper Catholic Bibles
An Imprint of HarperCollins*Publishers*

Curriculum Division

LIVE

New Revised Standard Version Bible: Catholic Edition

Harper Catholic Bibles
An Imprint of HarperCollins*Publishers*

Visit the NRSV website at www.nrsv.net.

Visit Our Sunday Visitor's website at www.osv.com.

Produced with the assistance of The Livingstone Corporation (www.Livingstonecorp.com). Project staff includes Linda Taylor, Linda Washington, Jake Barton, and Joel Bartlett.

Additional design by Ralph Fowler.

Interior typesetting by Blue Heron Bookcraft, Battle Ground, WA.

Printed in China.

The following *nihil obstat* and *imprimatur* apply to ancillary material only.

Nihil Obstat	Imprimatur
Rev. Dr. S. R. Olds, S.T.D.	Most Reverend Thomas Wenski
Censor Librorum	Bishop of Orlando
February 18, 2010	February 18, 2010

The following *imprimatur* applies to the New Revised Standard Version Bible: Catholic Edition.

Imprimatur	Imprimatur
Most Rev. Daniel E. Pilarczyk	Canadian Conference of Catholic Bishops
President, National Conference of Catholic Bishops	Ottawa, October 15, 1991
Washington, DC, September 12, 1991	

Our Sunday Visitor Curriculum Division website: http://osvcurriculum.com

HarperCollins books may be purchased for educational, business, or sales promotional use. For information please write: Special Markets Department, HarperCollins Publishers, 10 East 53rd Street, New York, NY 10022.

HarperCollins website: http://www.harpercollins.com

Library of Congress cataloging-in-publication data is available upon request.

ISBN 978–0–06–177724–0

Item #CU4904

13 14 15 16 17   RRD   10 9 8 7 6 5 4 3 2

ACKNOWLEDGMENTS

THE FOLLOWING PEOPLE CONTRIBUTED TO THE LIVE BIBLE CATHOLIC EDITION:

Our Sunday Visitor Curriculum Division

Gabrielle Cash, Imar DaCunha, Denise Bates Enos, Sabrina Magnuson, Steve Paradis

HarperCollins*Publishers*

Marlene Baer, Suzanne Quist

Group Publishing, Inc.

Patty Anderson, Craig Cable, Pam Clifford, Scott Kinner, Jim Knowles, Karl Leuthauser, Joani Schultz, Jeff Storm, Rebecca Tolle, Kelli B. Trujillo, Roxanne Wieman, Tim Willms

Writers and Reviewers

Jenny Baker, Mike DeVries, Denise Bates Enos, Andrew Hodges, Amie Hollmann, Mikal Keefer, Shawn Keefer, Maureen Kelly, Joy-Elizabeth Lawrence, Justin Lawrence, Mariette Martineau, James Miller, Kristin Peach, Christina Schofield, Alison Tarka, Jason Tarka, Kelli B. Trujillo, Jeff White, Dean Woodbeck

Student Artists, Photographers, Poets, and Writers

Student illustrations, photographs, poems, and writings featured in LIVE are the copyrighted property of their creators, named on page A4. All rights reserved.

STUDENT CONTRIBUTORS

Akerley, Rachel: 107, 532, 767, 886, 1269
Allen, Josh: 337
Anderson, Gabe: 361, 577, 1502
Bardenhagen, Amy: 1493
Bedol, Lacy: 66, 425
Bernard, Jesse: 373, 414, 969, 1148, 1472
Blackson, Jordan: 199
Blum, Katie: 1436
Brantl, Joy: 17, 930
Brown, Rachel: 1112
Bukowiecki, Mateusz: 1140
Burton, Kim: 761, 1424, 1466
Carlson, Cady: 1332
Carter, John: 619, 803, 852
Celedonia, Justin: 1256
Colasuonno, Leah: 222, 325, 359
Crest, Angelique: 227
Cuevas, Ezequiel: 539
Dawes, Justin: 168, 607, 1456
Dobbs, Amy: 457
Douglas, Kate: 73, 93, 1053, 1071, 1231, 1232, 1251, 1356, 1478, 1495, 1498
Duckett, Katie: 515, 1387, 1406
Eatman, Amanda: 1446
Engle, Eric: 1484
Figura, Delia Blaise: 498, 1276
Ford, Rachel: 448
Frazier, Aieryon: 656
Furey, Rebekah: 193, 204
Gager, Allie: 45, 504, 1096, 1210
German, Eliza: 272, 285, 329, 502, 644, 1003, 1450
Gills, Amari: 622
Glenn, Alicia: 1144
Goldstein, Jill: 895
Gordon, Imani: 124
Goswick, Clay: 497, 571, 909, 918, 1060, 1173
Graham, Michelle: 925
Hamilton, Paul: 482

Hastings, Anna: 151, 269
Hiland, Lexi: 29, 36, 51, 53, 282, 317, 348, 406, 482, 929, 974, 1271
Hostert, Rachel: 129, 195, 308, 313, 493, 625, 647, 897, 904, 921, 1111, 1293, 1343
Houtchen, Megan: 749, 1362
Hoxie, Krista: 1487
Hubbard, Maggie: 75, 163, 171, 314, 511, 735, 809, 1163, 1321, 1448, 1462
Jauch, Daniel: 1340
John 3:16 Mission FYC: 522
Johnson, Lucy: 756, 867, 1058
Jones, Jessica: 52, 114, 174, 206, 325, 383, 746, 1049, 1214, 1418, 1501
Jordan, Lauren: 334, 381
Jozwiak, Michelle: 350, 378, 421, 486, 1336, 1504
K., Rose: 587, 822
Katchuk, Morgan: 236, 704, 736, 883, 1362, 1483
Katheder, Charlotte: 437, 468, 498, 520, 589, 621, 724, 782, 856, 1458, 1470
Katheder, Marshall: 91, 813, 1213
Kenerson, Becca: 769, 1101
Kidwell, Mallory: 689, 1086, 1301, 1442
Klink, Christy: A6, 78, 139, 147, 180, 247, 568, 653, 731, 815, 952, 961, 1023, 1515
Knollenberg, Emily: 473
Kwiatkowski, Katelyn: 1426
Lawrence, Jennifer: 517, 718, 1318, 1350
LeBlanc, Andrena: 559
Lezotte, Sharon: 293
Lyons, Bailey: 1119
Maddox, Rachel: 672
Martin, Acacia: 922
Martin, Josi: 326
Miller, Hannah: 460, 1487

Modlin, Chris: 1030, 1039
Montiel, Marvin Jorge: 156
Nappa, Tony: A12, 189, 574, 764, 993, 1189
Nelson, Caitlin: 341
Novak, Rebecca: 1328
Paradis, Jason: 548, 723, 791
Paratore, Vito: 248, 703
Perry, Samantha: A20, 1384
Peterson, Samantha: A19, 177
Phillips, Hilary: 500, 1368
Piner, Andrea: 1198
Price, Tasha: 786
Ramsey, Tyler: 1347
Reed, Randy: 119, 294, 459, 1380
Riling, Chrissy: 136, 686, 1259
Russell, Adelee: 1308, 1399
Schoettler, Megan: 776, 785, 794, 829, 1000, 1353, 1396, 1408
Sicher, Kristin: 63, 611, 1218
Smith, Bailey: 231, 626
Smith, Melissa: 1029, 1458
Smith, Rakay: 535
Snook, Sarah: 977
Stage, Ashly: 1438
Steckroth, Shelby: 384, 659, 1068
Stein, Katie: 120, 261, 1223
Stevens, Ariana: 353
Thomas, Mia: 1392
Thomas, Rosa: 22
Tolentino, Orchid: 593, 700
Verburg, Amanda: 938
Wallis, Erica: 54, 584, 685, 753, 1136, 1180, 1500
White, Talitha: 98, 416
Williamson, Ricky: 955
Willms, Catherine: 540, 754, 758, 1018, 1171, 1187, 1401, 1444
Yancey, Taylor-Quinn: 676, 874, 1006, 1036, 1152

CONTENTS

ALPHABETICAL LISTING OF THE BIBLE BOOKS

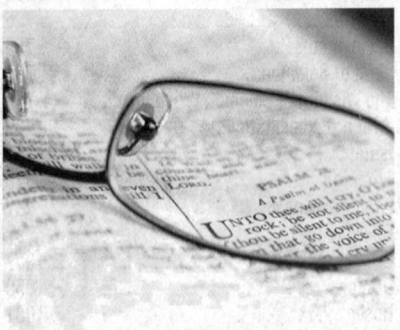

Psalm 28—© Christy Klink, 18

FEATURES GUIDE

> "For the word of God is living and active." (Hebrews 4.12)

This is your Bible...

It's the living Word of God.

It will speak directly to your real life. In these pages, you'll discover and get to know the one true God of the universe—the God who created you and loves you passionately.

God tugging at your heart...

As you read God's Word, you'll feel God tugging at your heart, challenging the way you live your life, relentlessly pursuing an ever deepening relationship with you. You'll get a true sense of how real, how close, how present God is in every moment of your life.

Your faith will come to life...

You'll catch God's vision for you and for the planet—you'll feel God's love and compassion for his people. You'll sense God's purpose for his people, the Church. Your faith will come to life.

Encountering God...

As God's Word permeates every part of your life—your world, your family, your parish, your friendships, your school, your interests, your very self—you'll encounter God in ways you may not have expected. You'll start to know deeply and personally that God is the one and only true God. He's real, passionate, relentless, compassionate, creative, and challenging.

WHAT'S INSIDE

The Bible—this collection of historical books, poems, worship songs, prophecies, gospels, and personal letters—was inspired by God. It's God's expression of himself—his expression of love to you. And an important part of faith in God is expressing yourself in return. In these pages you'll find challenges to **Express Yourself**. In these Express Yourself features, you'll make this Bible your own, expressing your thoughts, feelings, or questions by writing right on these pages, doodling, pasting pictures, and more. You'll respond to God's Word with other creative expressions like art, poetry, photography, graphic design, or journaling.

Sometimes expressing yourself honestly means asking God hard questions—tackling doubts, untangling confusions, authentically facing the hard parts of faith. Dealing with these **Real Questions** is important. You'll find several frank discussions of some sticky issues throughout this Bible. And you'll also find plenty of **Creative Space** in here to write down your own questions or doubts and to come up with your own creative expressions of faith—prayers, lists, song lyrics—whatever you want to say. So go ahead—make this Bible your own. Draw in it. Write in it. Express yourself.

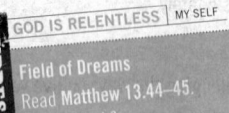

EXPRESS YOURSELF

GOD IS RELENTLESS | MY SELF

Field of Dreams
Read Matthew 13.44–45.

Slick, huh?

If you were certain a treasure was hidden in a tumble-down house, wouldn't you cash out your savings and run up a couple of credit cards in a scramble to buy the property?

What looked like an idiotic move to the neighborhood ("Did you hear what he *paid* for that shack?") would prove shrewd the moment you hauled out a box of gold or stuck a pipe in the ground and hit the oil field you knew was there.

Nailing down a sure thing— every investor's dream.

So why don't you do it?

Either you believe that Jesus was serious about this whole heaven and eternal life thing, or you don't. And if you *do*, then there simply no way to hang on to your current li and also live the one he has in mind for yo Sorry—you can't serve two masters. That not how it works.

If Jesus is

REAL QUESTIONS

RQ

I used to have a really strong faith, but now I wonder sometimes if God really cares or if God even exists at all. What do I do with these doubts?

It feels good to have the answers—to be confident, assured, ready for anything. And if we *don't* have an answer, we can find out nearly anything we want to know instantly, at the click of a mouse.

But even though we affirm our belief at every Mass during the Creed, some things—like faith—can't be so easily explained or instantly summarized. We all have doubts. And sometimes when we search for answers, the ones we find just don't make sense.

Let's just admit it. Sometimes our grasp on our faith feels shaky at best. Sometimes we followers of Christ feel a lot like Thomas, who famously declared, "Unless I see the mark of the nails in his hands, and put my finger in the mark of th and my hand in his side. (John 20.25). On and con

CREATIVE SPACE

Faith is much more than just expressing your thoughts and feelings—and it's a lot more than just holding on to a certain set of beliefs. Faith is something we live. It's something we express through our actions—our choices in relationships, our willingness to step out of our comfort zone, our decision to speak the truth about Jesus to others.

So we've got some challenges for you—specific ways you can put your faith into action, things that will help you grow closer to God and impact your world for him. We've called these ideas **Try This**—because they will prompt you not only to read Scripture, but to put it into practice in ways that fit your real, everyday life.

We also challenge you to get personal and real with yourself and Scripture with **Reality Check**. Here, Scripture is connected to your life and Church teachings and how you can care for yourself, your immediate family, the human family, and our planet.

Putting faith into action can be really tough, so just in case you need some inspiration along the way, we've included true stories of people **Just Like You**—men and women from different faiths, different backgrounds, different countries, and different times in history who chose to live vibrantly for Jesus, no matter

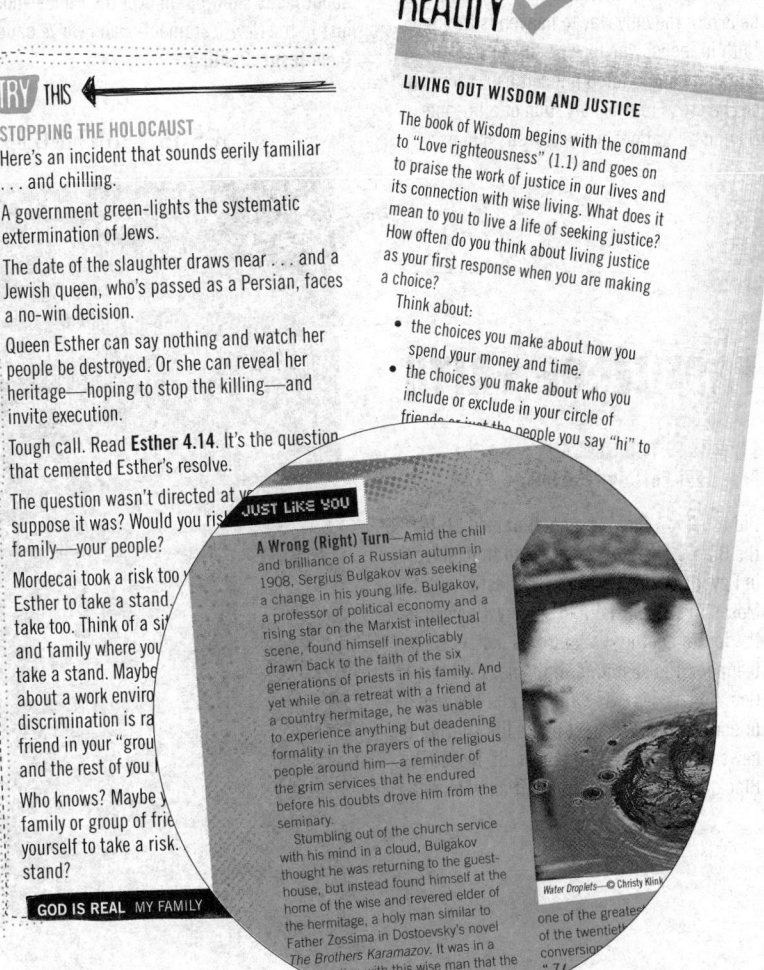

TRY THIS

STOPPING THE HOLOCAUST

Here's an incident that sounds eerily familiar . . . and chilling.

A government green-lights the systematic extermination of Jews.

The date of the slaughter draws near . . . and a Jewish queen, who's passed as a Persian, faces a no-win decision.

Queen Esther can say nothing and watch her people be destroyed. Or she can reveal her heritage—hoping to stop the killing—and invite execution.

Tough call. Read **Esther 4.14**. It's the question that cemented Esther's resolve.

The question wasn't directed at y[ou], suppose it was? Would you ris[k] family—your people?

Mordecai took a risk too [and] Esther to take a stand. [...] take too. Think of a si[...] and family where yo[...] take a stand. Maybe [...] about a work enviro[...] discrimination is ra[...] friend in your "grou[p...] and the rest of you [...]

Who knows? Maybe y[...] family or group of frie[...] yourself to take a risk[...] stand?

GOD IS REAL MY FAMILY

REALITY ✔

LIVING OUT WISDOM AND JUSTICE

The book of Wisdom begins with the command to "Love righteousness" (1.1) and goes on to praise the work of justice in our lives and its connection with wise living. What does it mean to you to live a life of seeking justice? How often do you think about living justice as your first response when you are making a choice?

Think about:

- the choices you make about how you spend your money and time.
- the choices you make about who you include or exclude in your circle of frie[nds or just the] people you say "hi" to

JUST LIKE YOU

A Wrong (Right) Turn—Amid the chill and brilliance of a Russian autumn in 1908, Sergius Bulgakov was seeking a change in his young life. Bulgakov, a professor of political economy and a rising star on the Marxist intellectual scene, found himself inexplicably drawn back to the faith of the six generations of priests in his family. And yet while on a retreat with a friend at a country hermitage, he was unable to experience anything but deadening formality in the prayers of the religious people around him—a reminder of the grim services that he endured before his doubts drove him from the seminary.

Stumbling out of the church service with his mind in a cloud, Bulgakov thought he was returning to the guest-house, but instead found himself at the home of the wise and revered elder of the hermitage, a holy man similar to Father Zossima in Dostoevsky's novel *The Brothers Karamazov*. It was in a [conv]ersation with this wise man that the [at]heist's change finally came. [...] continue down hi[s...]

one of the greate[st...] of the twentie[th...] conversio[n...] "7[...]

Water Droplets—© Christy Klink

what circumstances came their way. **Profile of Faith** spotlights Catholic saints, religious, and laypeople who serve as witnesses to living the values of the Scriptures.

"God abides in those who confess that Jesus is the Son of God, and they abide in God." (1 John 4.15)

At the heart of true faith is a living relationship with Jesus. Following Jesus starts with being honest with yourself: you're a sinner—we *all* are. We all do things that fall short of the best God wants for us. But God doesn't leave you hanging. God sent Jesus to show us how to live and reconcile us to the Father. A central part of our faith is believing the only way to heaven is through faith in Jesus, who took on the sins of all humanity and offered himself as a sacrifice on the cross for the salvation of all people. Having a relationship with Jesus means personally trusting him, following his guidance for your life, and getting to know him better through prayer and his Word. Not only will you spend eternity with him in heaven, but you also make him your number-one priority— and your best friend—here on earth. With the help of the Holy Spirit, you choose to live for him. This Bible will help you do that.

But as you read it, you may wonder at times, "What in the *world* does this have to do with Jesus?" It can be difficult sometimes to see how things like laws or prophecies or ancient letters relate to your friendship with Jesus in the here and now. So we point out for you some of the important places where truths about Jesus show up all over the Bible—not just in the New Testament—and we've called them **Jesus Sighting**.

JESUS SIGHTING

He stood a hair's breadth away from the presence and power of the living God. A curtain stood between them, literally a piece of cloth separating the infinite and the finite. The high priest alone could pull aside the sheet and step inside, presenting the only flawed human heart allowed to stand before the One whose very appearance could kill a person.

Moses put the stone tablets of the Ten Commandments in the wooden box overlaid with pure gold known as the Ark of the Covenant. The Ark was kept in a tent made of curtains, the tabernacle. God's presence was there.

One curtain mattered most. Between the Ark and the rest of the world was a curtain that kept an unclean people out of the presence of a perfect God. Even later in the Scriptures, when most of the curtains of the tabernacle described in Exodus 26 were replaced by the stone walls of the Temple, this one curtain remained, reminding the world that people aren't meant to get that close to God.

Now skip ahead nearly two thousand years after Moses. When Jesus was crucified, a strange thing happened. The curtain in the Temple was ̶̶̶̶̶̶ (see Matthew ̶̶̶̶̶̶

PROFILE OF FAITH

ST. MOSES THE BLACK:
Freedom Through Faith

Did you know there is a saint named St. Moses the Black? Like the people freed from slavery in Egypt with Moses of the Old Testament, St. Moses the Black endured slavery. He lived in the fourth century A.D. and was a slave as a teenager. His search for happiness led him to God, and Moses was baptized and became a priest. He spent the rest of his life sharing the news of God's love with others. St. Moses the Black is the patron saint of African Americans.

As a Catholic, you may also wonder why we believe the things we do or why we celebrate the seven sacraments. Scripture is the place where theologians and bishops look first and last as they develop doctrines and beliefs that are part of Tradition. In fact, we know that both Scripture and Tradition are God's Revelation to us. All teachings of the Church flow from the Word of God and bring us back to it. You'll see how in **It's Tradition**.

Think of the Bible as a tour guide or a map on your lifelong faith journey. To help chart your course, you'll find a helpful introductory section on the opening page of each book that also includes the who, what, when, and where of the book. **Path of Discipleship** connects important matters of faith revealed in the book to living the life of true discipleship today.

As you'll see in the pages that follow, LIVE takes great care to be anything but boring. Compelling quotes are given from a wide range of sources—not just from famous dead people. **Text Messages** supply the facts that make for a deeper understanding of what you're reading, and every now and then they'll hand you a factoid that's just fun to know.

TEXT MESSAGE

If you have older brothers and sisters and think they always get the best deal, take some comfort in Genesis 48.13–14. Though Jacob blessed both Manasseh, the older, and Ephraim, the younger, he crossed his hands and blessed Ephraim with his right hand. That made Ephraim's blessing more important.

This information has been scanned and is free of all known viruses. Please forward to all your friends.

It's Tradition

SACRAMENTS OF HEALING

Read **James 5.13**. Here James tells his community to call the elders to pray and anoint the sick with oil, and if they have sinned their sins will be forgiven. Then he encourages them to tell their sins to one another and pray for each other.

Forgiveness of sins and healing the sick were a significant part of Jesus' mission.

"If only we could be a bit more like Him, the world would be transformed."
—U2's Bono

PATH OF DISCIPLESHIP

What's your place in the family? Not your birth order, but "your position"? Are you the family hero, the clown, the leader, the easygoing one? Do you appreciate (or at least tolerate) the gifts and quirks of family members?

What's going on in your family life right now? Is your family hurting or is everyone getting along, helping out, having fun? Would you say you are a religious, faithful, or spiritual family because you pray together, talk about God, read Scripture, celebrate the sacraments, work for justice, and reach out to those in need? Or are you all too busy just *surviving* to spend time on your faith?

FEATURES GUIDE

MAKE CONTACT

Upload your faith expressions to **Learner.CalltoDiscipleship.com**—we'll post your photos, poems, sketches—whatever writings and images that honestly reflect how God is speaking to you.

Think of it as an online gallery showing how God's revealing himself through teens like you and teens, well . . . not like you.

Up on a Roof—© Tony Nappa, 17

Call to Discipleship

When it comes to faith, we're all seeking and growing and struggling and changing. We're not the finished product yet. We're what some in the book business would call a "rough edit"—a work in progress. It's the idea behind Philippians 1.6b: "The one who began a good work among you will bring it to completion by the day of Jesus Christ."

And one of the keys to growing in faith is being part of a community. You'll find one at **Learner.CalltoDiscipleship.com**—a website where you can post your thoughts and questions, chat about important issues, and upload photos, art, and other creative expressions of faith.

http://Learner.CalltoDiscipleship.com

PREFACE TO
THE NEW REVISED STANDARD VERSION
CATHOLIC EDITION

This Catholic edition of the New Revised Standard Version of the Bible has been authorized by the National Conference of Catholic Bishops in the U.S.A. and by the National Council of the Churches of Christ in the U.S.A. It has received the ecclesiastical approval of the Catholic Bishops of both the United States and Canada. The undersigned, who prepared this edition, is a member of the Revised Standard Version Bible Translation Committee as well as an active member and past president of the Catholic Biblical Association of America.

Roman Catholics are already familiar with the accuracy and elegance of the New Revised Standard Version, first published in 1990. It has previously appeared in two major types of edition: an edition of the Old and New Testaments alone, the Bible of most Protestants; and an edition of the Old and New Testaments with the Apocryphal/Deuterocanonical Books placed between the two Testaments. The text of the latter edition received the Imprimatur (official approbation) of the United States and Canadian Catholic Bishops. The New Revised Standard Version is truly an ecumenical translation, for it was produced by Roman Catholic, Eastern Orthodox, Protestant, and Jewish scholars. Because of this Catholic presence no change in the translation was requested for this edition. The only exceptions are the Book of Esther, which exists in two different forms that are explained below, and the Book of Daniel, which includes the deuterocanonical portions that are listed below.

Regarding the number of the books of the Old Testament canon and their arrangement, however, Protestants and Jews on the one hand, and Roman Catholics and Orthodox Christians on the other, hold different beliefs. From the time of the Reformation in the sixteenth century, Protestants have adopted the Jewish canon of the Old Testament, which was established by the rabbis at the end of the first century of the Common Era. This canon includes only those books that were written in Hebrew and Aramaic. In addition to these books, however, Roman Catholics, following the ancient tradition of the Christian church, also hold the Deuterocanonical Books of the Old Testament to be sacred and inspired, and therefore canonical. Protestants and Jews call these books Apocrypha, a word that means "hidden or concealed," an inappropriate title for works that were part of the Greek Old Testament (the Septuagint) from pre-Christian times. The Roman Catholic canon, which was fixed by the time of the Council of Hippo in 393 and reaffirmed by the two Councils of Carthage in 397 and 419, was formally defined by the Council of Trent in 1546. This canon contains seven Deuterocanonical Books: Tobit, Judith, the Wisdom of Solomon, Sirach (the Wisdom of Ben Sira, also known as Ecclesiasticus), Baruch including the Letter of Jeremiah as chapter 6, and 1 and 2 Maccabees; and extra portions of two other books: the Additions to Esther; and the Prayer of Azariah and the Song of the Three Jews inserted between verses 23 and 24 of Daniel 3, Susanna as Daniel 13, and Bel and the Dragon as Daniel 14. Over and above these books and extra portions, the Bible of Greek and Slavonic Orthodox Christians includes 1 Esdras, the Prayer of Manasseh, Psalm 151, and 3 Maccabees. The Slavonic Bible also contains 2 Esdras, and an appendix to the Greek Bible includes 4 Maccabees.

Several of the Deuterocanonical Books were written originally in Hebrew or Aramaic, the rest in Greek. More than two-thirds of the Book of Sirach is now extant in Hebrew, and four fragments of the Book of Tobit in Hebrew and Aramaic were recovered from Qumran Cave IV. It seems certain that Judith and the additions to Daniel were also written originally in Hebrew. Hebrew is the original language of the prose parts of Baruch; the poetic parts were composed in Greek. The Wisdom of Solomon was written completely in Greek. The original language of 1 Maccabees was Hebrew while 2 Maccabees was composed in Greek.

The Book of Esther has two different forms: the short Hebrew original; and the longer Greek version that contains one hundred and seven additional verses comprising six distinct portions, A through F. It is the translation of the entire Greek version that appears in the Deuterocanonical section of the New Revised Standard Version. In this Catholic edition, however, the translation of the Greek portions has been inserted at the appropriate places of the translation of the Hebrew form of the book. Some of the Greek portions apparently had a Hebrew origin; the others were written in Greek.

What is distinctive about this Catholic edition—as well as every other edition published by Roman Catholics—is that the Deuterocanonical Books and portions are placed in their proper order among the other books of the Old Testament. Thus, Tobit, Judith, the long form of Esther, and 1 and 2 Maccabees are found among the so-called historical books directly after Nehemiah. The Wisdom of Solomon and the Book of Sirach follow after the Song of Solomon among the wisdom books. Because Baruch, the well-known secretary of Jeremiah, is said to be the author of the work that bears his name, the book is placed after Jeremiah and Lamentations. This order of books comes from the Latin Vulgate translated by St. Jerome in the late fourth and early fifth centuries. It is essentially the same order as that found in the fourth-century Codex Vaticanus, one of the oldest extant manuscripts of the Septuagint.

Roman Catholics will welcome this edition of the New Revised Standard Version of the Bible for personal reading and study as well as liturgical usage. Based on the latest manuscript discoveries and critical editions, it offers the fruits of the best biblical scholarship in the idiom of today while being sensitive to the contemporary concern for inclusive language when referring to human beings.

Alexander A. Di Lella, O.F.M.
Andrews-Kelly-Ryan
Distinguished Professor of Biblical Studies
The Catholic University of America

September 30, 1992
Feast of St. Jerome

TO THE READER

This preface is addressed to you by the Committee of translators, who wish to explain, as briefly as possible, the origin and character of our work. The publication of our revision is yet another step in the long, continual process of making the Bible available in the form of the English language that is most widely current in our day. To summarize in a single sentence: the New Revised Standard Version of the Bible is an authorized revision of the Revised Standard Version, published in 1952, which was a revision of the American Standard Version, published in 1901, which, in turn, embodied earlier revisions of the King James Version, published in 1611.

In the course of time, the King James Version came to be regarded as the "Authorized Version." With good reason it has been termed "the noblest monument of English prose," and it has entered, as no other book has, into the making of the personal character and the public institutions of the English-speaking peoples. We owe to it an incalculable debt.

Yet the King James Version has serious defects. By the middle of the nineteenth century, the development of biblical studies and the discovery of many biblical manuscripts more ancient than those on which the King James Version was based made it apparent that these defects were so many as to call for revision. The task was begun, by authority of the Church of England, in 1870. The (British) Revised Version of the Bible was published in 1881–85; and the American Standard Version, its variant embodying the preferences of the American scholars associated with the work, was published, as was mentioned above, in 1901. In 1928 the copyright of the latter was acquired by the International Council of Religious Education and thus passed into the ownership of the churches of the United States and Canada that were associated in this council through their boards of education and publication.

The Council appointed a committee of scholars to have charge of the text of the American Standard Version and to undertake inquiry concerning the need for further revision. After studying the questions of whether revision should be undertaken and, if so, what its nature and extent should be, in 1937 the Council authorized a revision. The scholars who served as members of the Committee worked in two sections, one dealing with the OT and one with the NT. In 1946 the Revised Standard Version of the NT was published. The publication of the Revised Standard Version of the Bible, containing the OT and NT, took place on September 30, 1952. A translation of the Apocryphal/Deuterocanonical Books of the OT followed in 1957. In 1977 this collection was issued in an expanded edition containing three additional texts received by Eastern Orthodox communions (3 and 4 Maccabees and Psalm 151). Thereafter the Revised Standard Version gained the distinction of being officially authorized for use by all major Christian churches: Protestant, Anglican, Roman Catholic, and Eastern Orthodox.

The Revised Standard Version Bible Committee is a continuing body, comprising about thirty members, both men and women. Ecumenical in representation, it includes scholars affiliated with various Protestant denominations as well as several Roman Catholic members, an Eastern Orthodox member, and a Jewish member who serves in the OT section. For a period of time the Committee included several members from Canada and from England.

Because no translation of the Bible is perfect or acceptable to all groups of readers, and because discoveries of older manuscripts and further investigation of linguistic features of the text continue to become available, renderings of the Bible have proliferated. During the years following the publication of the Revised Standard Version, twenty-six other English translations and revisions of the Bible were produced by committees and by individual scholars—not to mention twenty-five other translations and revisions of the NT alone. One of the latter was the second edition of the RSV NT, issued in 1971, twenty-five years after its initial publication.

Following the publication of the RSV OT in 1952, significant advances were made in the discovery and interpretation of documents in Semitic languages related to Hebrew. In addition to the information that had become available in the late 1940s from the Dead Sea texts of Isaiah and Habakkuk, subsequent acquisitions from the same area brought to light many other early copies of all the books of the Hebrew scriptures (except Esther), though most of these copies are fragmentary. During the same period early Greek manuscript copies of books of the NT also became available.

In order to take these discoveries into account, along with recent studies of documents in Semitic languages related to Hebrew, in 1974 the Policies Committee of the Revised Standard Version, which is a standing committee of the National Council of the Churches of Christ in the U.S.A., authorized the preparation of a revision of the entire RSV Bible.

For the OT the Committee has made use of the *Biblia Hebraica Stuttgartensia* (1977; ed. sec. emendata, 1983). This is an edition of the Hebrew and Aramaic text as current early in the Christian era and fixed by Jewish scholars (the "Masoretes") of the sixth to the ninth centuries. The vowel signs, which were added by the Masoretes, are accepted in the main, but where a more probable and convincing reading can be obtained by assuming different vowels, this has been done. No notes are given in such cases, because the vowel points are less ancient and reliable than the consonants. When an alternative reading given by the Masoretes is translated in a footnote, it is identified by the words "Another reading is."

Departures from the consonantal text of the best manuscripts have been made only where it seems clear that errors in copying had been made before the text was standardized. Most of the corrections adopted are based on the ancient versions (translations into Greek, Aramaic, Syriac, and Latin), which were made prior to the time of the work of the Masoretes and which therefore may reflect earlier forms of the Hebrew text. In such instances a footnote specifies the version or versions from which the correction has been derived and also gives a translation of the Masoretic Text. Where it was deemed appropriate to do so, information is supplied in footnotes from subsidiary Jewish traditions concerning other textual readings (the *Tiqqune Sopherim*, "emendations of the scribes"). These are identified in the footnotes as "Ancient Heb tradition."

Occasionally it is evident that the text has suffered in transmission and that none of the versions provides a satisfactory restoration. Here we can only follow the best judgment of competent scholars as to the most probable reconstruction of the original text. Such reconstructions are indicated in footnotes by the abbreviation Cn ("Correction"), and a translation of the Masoretic Text is added.

For the Apocryphal/Deuterocanonical Books of the OT the Committee has made use of a number of texts. For most of these books the basic Greek text from which the present translation was made is the edition of the Septuagint prepared by Alfred Rahlfs and published by the Württemberg Bible Society (Stuttgart, 1935). For several of the books the more recently published individual volumes of the Göttingen Septuagint project were utilized. For the book of Tobit it was decided to follow the form of the Greek text found in Codex Sinaiticus (supported as it is by evidence from Qumran); where this text is defective, it was supplemented and corrected by other Greek manuscripts. For the three Additions to Daniel (namely, Susanna, the Prayer of Azariah and the Song of the Three Jews, and Bel and the Dragon) the Committee continued to use the Greek version attributed to Theodotion (the so-called Theodotion-Daniel). In translating Ecclesiasticus (Sirach), although constant reference was made to the Hebrew fragments of a large portion of this book (those discovered at Qumran and Masada as well as those recovered from the Cairo Geniza), the Committee generally followed the Greek text (including verse numbers) published by Joseph Ziegler in the Göttingen Septuagint (1965). But in many places the Committee has translated the Hebrew text when this provides a reading that is clearly superior to the Greek; the Syriac and Latin versions were also consulted throughout and occasionally adopted. The basic text adopted in rendering 2 Esdras is the Latin version given in *Biblia Sacra*, edited by Robert Weber (Stuttgart, 1971). This was supplemented by consulting the Latin text as edited by R. L. Bensly (1895) and by Bruno Violet (1910) as well as by taking into account the several Oriental versions of 2 Esdras, namely, the Syriac, Ethiopic, Arabic (two forms, referred to as Arabic 1 and Arabic 2), Armenian, and Georgian versions. Finally, since the Additions to the Book of Esther are disjointed and quite unintelligible as they stand in most editions of the Apocrypha, we have provided them with their original context by translating the whole of the Greek version of Esther from Robert Hanhart's Göttingen edition (1983).

For the NT the Committee has based its work on the most recent edition of *The Greek New Testament*, prepared by an interconfessional and international committee and published by the United Bible Societies (1966; 3d ed. corrected, 1983; information concerning changes to be introduced into the critical apparatus of the forthcoming 4th edition was available to the Committee). As in that edition, double brackets are used to enclose a few passages that are generally regarded to be later additions to the text, but that we have retained because of their evident antiquity and their importance in the textual tradition. Only in very rare instances have we replaced the text or the punctuation of the Bible Societies' edition by an alternative that seemed to us to be superior. Here and there in the footnotes the phrase "Other ancient authorities read" identifies alternative readings preserved by Greek manuscripts and early versions. In both OT and NT, alternative renderings of the text are indicated by the word "Or."

As for the style of English adopted for the present revision, among the mandates given to the Committee in 1980 by the Division of Education and Ministry of the National Council of Churches of Christ (which now holds the copyright of the RSV Bible) was the directive to continue in the tradition of the King James Bible, but to introduce such changes as are warranted on the basis of accuracy, clarity, euphony, and current English usage. Within the constraints set by the original texts and by the mandates of the Division, the Committee has followed the maxim "As literal as possible, as free as necessary." As a consequence, the New Revised Standard Version (NRSV) remains essentially a literal translation. Paraphrastic renderings have been adopted only sparingly, and then chiefly to compensate for a deficiency in the English language—the lack of a common-gender third-person singular pronoun.

During the almost half a century since the publication of the RSV, many in the churches have become sensitive to the danger of linguistic sexism arising from the inherent bias of the English language toward the masculine gender, a bias that in the case of the Bible has often restricted or obscured the meaning of the original text. The mandates from the Division specified that, in references to men and women, masculine-oriented language should be eliminated as far as this can be done without altering passages that reflect the historical situation of ancient patriarchal culture. As can be appreciated, more than once the Committee found that the several mandates stood in tension and even in conflict. The various concerns had to be balanced case by case in order to provide a faithful and acceptable rendering without using contrived English. Only very occasionally has the pronoun "he" or "him" been retained in passages where the reference may have been to a woman as well as to a man, for example, in several legal texts in Leviticus and Deuteronomy. In such instances of formal, legal language, the options of either putting the passage in the plural or of introducing additional nouns to avoid masculine pronouns in English seemed to the Committee to obscure the historic structure and literary character of the original. In the vast majority of cases, however, inclusiveness has been attained by simple rephrasing or by introducing plural forms when this does not distort the meaning of the passage. Of course, in narrative and in parable no attempt was made to generalize the sex of individual persons.

Another aspect of style will be detected by readers who compare the more stately English rendering of the OT with the less formal rendering adopted for the NT. For example, the traditional distinction between "shall" and "will" in English has been retained in the OT as appropriate in rendering a document that embodies what may be termed the classic form of Hebrew, while in the

NT the abandonment of such distinctions in the usage of the future tense in English reflects the more colloquial nature of the Koine Greek used by most NT authors except when they are quoting the OT.

Careful readers will notice that here and there in the OT the word LORD (or in certain cases GOD) is printed in capital letters. This represents the traditional manner in English versions of rendering the divine name, the "tetragrammaton" (see the text notes on Exodus 3.14–15), following the precedent of the ancient Greek and Latin translators and the long-established practice in the reading of the Hebrew scriptures in the synagogue. Although it is almost if not quite certain that the name was originally pronounced "Yahweh," this pronunciation was not indicated when the Masoretes added vowel sounds to the consonantal Hebrew text. To the four consonants YHWH of the divine name, which had come to be regarded as too sacred to be pronounced, they attached vowel signs indicating that in its place should be read the Hebrew word *Adonai*, meaning "Lord" (or *Elohim*, meaning "God"). Ancient Greek translators employed the word *Kyrios* ("Lord") for the name. The Vulgate likewise used the Latin word *Dominus* ("Lord"). The form "Jehovah" is of late medieval origin; it is a combination of the consonants of the divine name and the vowels attached to it by the Masoretes but belonging to an entirely different word. Although the American Standard Version (1901) had used "Jehovah" to render the tetragrammaton (the sound of y being represented by *j* and the sound of w by *v*, as in Latin), for two reasons the Committees that produced the RSV and the NRSV returned to the more familiar usage of the King James Version. (1) The word "Jehovah" does not accurately represent any form of the divine name ever used in Hebrew. (2) The use of any proper name for the one and only God, as though there were other gods from whom the true God had to be distinguished, began to be discontinued in Judaism before the Christian era and is inappropriate for the universal faith of the Christian church.

It will be seen that in the Psalms and in other prayers addressed to God the archaic second-person singular pronouns ("thee, thou, thine") and verb forms ("art, hast, hadst") are no longer used. Although some readers may regret this change, it should be pointed out that in the original languages neither the OT nor the NT makes any linguistic distinction between addressing a human being and addressing the deity. Furthermore, in the tradition of the King James Version one will not expect to find the use of capital letters for pronouns that refer to the deity—such capitalization is an unnecessary innovation that has only recently been introduced into a few English translations of the Bible. Finally, we have left to the discretion of the licensed publishers such matters as section headings, cross-references, and clues to the pronunciation of proper names.

This new version seeks to preserve all that is best in the English Bible as it has been known and used through the years. It is intended for use in public reading and congregational worship as well as in private study, instruction, and meditation. We have resisted the temptation to introduce terms and phrases that merely reflect current moods, and have tried to put the message of the scriptures in simple, enduring words and expressions that are worthy to stand in the great tradition of the King James Bible and its predecessors.

In traditional Judaism and Christianity, the Bible has been more than a historical document to be preserved or a classic of literature to be cherished and admired; it is recognized as the unique record of God's dealings with people over the ages. The OT sets forth the call of a special people to enter into covenant relation with the God of justice and steadfast love and to bring God's law to the nations. The NT records the life and work of Jesus Christ, the one in whom "the Word became flesh," as well as describes the rise and spread of the early Christian church. The Bible carries its full message not to those who regard it simply as a noble literary heritage of the past or who wish to use it to enhance political purposes and advance otherwise desirable goals, but to all persons and communities who read it so that they may discern and understand what God is saying to them. That message must not be disguised in phrases that are no longer clear or hidden under words that have changed or lost their meaning; it must be presented in language that is direct and plain and meaningful to people today. It is the hope and prayer of the translators that this version of the Bible may continue to hold a large place in congregational life and to speak to all readers, young and old alike, helping them to understand and believe and respond to its message.

For the Committee,
Bruce M. Metzger

Tree of Life—© Samantha Peterson, 16

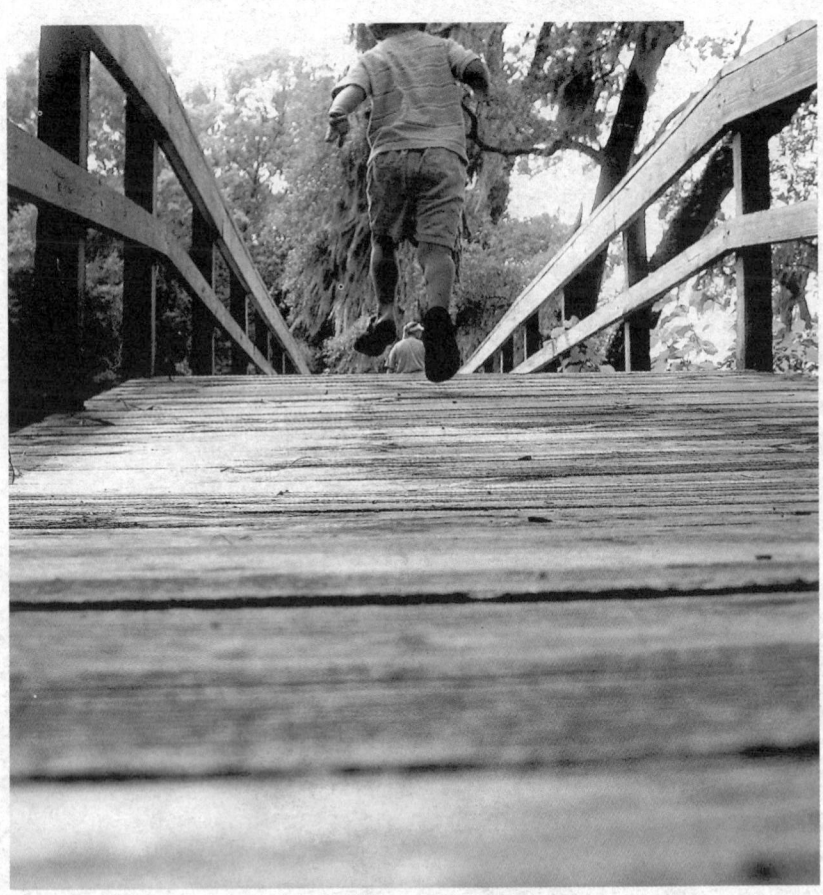
Become Like a Child, and You Shall Enter the Kingdom of God—© Samantha Perry, 18

OLD
testament

In the beginning...

LIVE

... START HERE

GENESIS
GOD AT THE STARTING LINE

Messy Faith

"Why are we here?" Everybody's wondered it. And at the start of Genesis, you'll find some answers. When there was nothing, God decided there should be something. And that something included you. God wanted to share his infinite love with you and all of humanity. This is how our Sacred Scripture begins. The Nicene Creed and the Apostles' Creed also profess our belief in God's role as Creator (see *Catechism of the Catholic Church* 279).

But the universe and the human race aren't the only things God launches in Genesis. The history of faith begins in these pages, starting with Abraham. Because of Abraham's faith, God promises Abraham descendants and land.

The stories that follow about the Patriarchs—Abraham, Isaac, Jacob, and Jacob's sons—show us what real faith looked like at its very beginning.

And to be honest, it doesn't look too good. Dig a little deeper into Genesis and you'll discover that the lives of these founders of our faith are the exact opposite of what you might expect. The men and women described in the next fifty chapters aren't always noble and heroic. In fact, they lie, cheat, steal, betray, get tricked, pick favorites, act violently, hate passionately, behave arrogantly, and just generally embarrass themselves.

The kind of faith we find in Genesis is real, not refined. Gritty, not polished. It reveals the human side of our struggle to become closer to God. Genesis shows us raw faith. It's faith that can get really messy, crowded by doubts, temptation, and failure—and it's faith that persists, inspired by the Spirit and strengthened by stubborn belief, desperate repentance, and unwavering trust. It's real faith for real people . . . like *you*.

> *"Science can purify religion from error and superstition. Religion can purify science from idolatry and false absolutes."*
>
> —Pope John Paul II

WHO Moses was traditionally considered the author, but modern scholars generally agree that the book is the result of three different sources.

WHAT A book of stories and religious traditions from the early history of ancient Israel, including the story of God's first interactions with creation and humans and the formation of the community of chosen people.

WHEN The events written about took place from prehistoric times to ca. 1300 B.C. The book was written and edited over a period of time, probably from ca. 900 to ca. 500 B.C.

WHERE Various locations including Ur (Iraq), Canaan (Palestine/Israel), and Egypt.

PATH OF DISCIPLESHIP

In Genesis 22, God told Abraham to sacrifice his son Isaac. Unlike the god Molech, a popular deity in Abraham's day who required child sacrifices, Abraham's God was different. And here Abraham's God put him to the ultimate test: Would Abraham keep from God his only son? **SPOILER ALERT:** At the last minute God spared Isaac.

Centuries later, on another hill in the Holy Land, God would give *his* Son as a sacrifice for humanity. He paid the cost that he would not require of us. God's love for us is matchless; he loves us more than we could *ever* love him (see CCC 211).

How can you apply this lesson of sacrifice to your life? It's not about giving things up, but about giving your complete trust and loyalty to God.

1 Six Days of Creation and the Sabbath

In the beginning when God created[a] the heavens and the earth, [2]the earth was a formless void and darkness covered the face of the deep, while a wind from God[b] swept over the face of the waters. [3]Then God said, "Let there be light"; and there was light. [4]And God saw that the light was good; and God separated the light from the darkness. [5]God called the light Day, and the darkness he called Night. And there was evening and there was morning, the first day.

6 And God said, "Let there be a dome in the midst of the waters, and let it separate the waters from the waters." [7]So God made the dome and separated the waters that were under the dome from the waters that were above the dome. And it was so. [8]God called the dome Sky. And there was evening and there was morning, the second day.

9 And God said, "Let the waters under the sky be gathered together into one place, and let the dry land appear." And it was so. [10]God called the dry land Earth, and the waters that were gathered together he called Seas. And God saw that it was good. [11]Then God said, "Let the earth put forth vegetation: plants yielding seed, and fruit trees of every kind on earth that bear fruit with the seed in it." And it was so. [12]The earth brought forth vegetation: plants yielding seed of every kind, and trees of every kind bearing fruit with the seed in it. And God saw that it was good. [13]And there was evening and there was morning, the third day.

14 And God said, "Let there be lights in the dome of the sky to separate the day from the night; and let them be for signs and for seasons and for days and years, [15]and let them be lights in the dome of the sky to give light upon the earth." And it was so. [16]God made the two great lights—the greater light to rule the day and the lesser light to rule the night—and the stars. [17]God set them in the dome of the sky to give light upon the earth, [18]to rule over the day and over the night, and to separate the light from the darkness. And God saw that it was good. [19]And there was evening and there was morning, the fourth day.

20 And God said, "Let the waters bring forth swarms of living creatures, and let birds fly above the earth across the dome of the sky." [21]So God created the great sea monsters and every living creature that moves, of every kind, with which the waters swarm, and every winged bird of every kind. And God saw that it was good. [22]God blessed them, saying, "Be fruitful and multiply and fill the waters in the seas, and let birds multiply on the earth." [23]And there was evening and there was morning, the fifth day.

24 And God said, "Let the earth bring forth living creatures of every kind: cattle and creeping things and wild animals of the earth of every kind." And it was so. [25]God made the wild animals of the earth of every kind, and the cattle of every kind, and everything that creeps upon the ground of every kind. And God saw that it was good.

26 Then God said, "Let us make humankind[c] in our image, according to our likeness; and let them have dominion over the fish of the sea, and over the birds of the air, and over the cattle, and over all the wild animals of the earth,[d] and over every creeping thing that creeps upon the earth."

27 So God created humankind[c] in his image,
    in the image of God he created them;[e]
    male and female he created them.

[28]God blessed them, and God said to them, "Be fruitful and multiply, and fill the earth and subdue it; and have dominion over the fish of the sea and over the birds of the air and over every living thing that moves upon the earth." [29]God said, "See, I have given you every plant yielding seed that is upon the face of all the earth, and every tree with seed in its fruit; you shall have them for food. [30]And to every beast of the earth, and to every bird of the air, and to everything that creeps on the earth, everything that has the breath of life, I have given every green plant for food." And it was so. [31]God saw everything that he had made, and indeed, it was very good. And there was evening and there was morning, the sixth day.

2 Thus the heavens and the earth were finished, and all their multitude. [2]And on the seventh day God finished the work that he had done, and he rested on the seventh day from all the work that he had done. [3]So God blessed the seventh day and hallowed it, because on it God rested from all the work that he had done in creation.

4 These are the generations of the heavens and the earth when they were created.

Another Account of the Creation

In the day that the LORD[f] God made the earth and the heavens, [5]when no plant of the field was yet in the earth and no herb of the field had yet sprung up—for the LORD God had not

---

a Or *when God began to create* or *In the beginning God created* b Or *while the spirit of God* or *while a mighty wind* c Heb *adam* d Syr: Heb *and over all the earth* e Heb *him* f Heb YHWH, as in other places where "LORD" is spelled with capital letters (see also Ex 3.14–15 with notes).

caused it to rain upon the earth, and there was no one to till the ground; 6but a stream would rise from the earth, and water the whole face of the ground— 7then the LORD God formed man from the dust of the ground,a and breathed into his nostrils the breath of life; and the man became a living being. 8And the LORD God planted a garden in Eden, in the east; and there he put the man whom he had formed. 9Out of the ground the LORD God made to grow every tree that is pleasant to the sight and good for food, the tree of life also in the midst of the garden, and the tree of the knowledge of good and evil.

10 A river flows out of Eden to water the garden, and from there it divides and becomes four branches. 11The name of the first is Pishon; it is the one that flows around the whole land of Havilah, where there is gold; 12and the gold of that land is good; bdellium and onyx stone are there. 13The name of the second river is Gihon; it is the one that flows around the whole land of Cush. 14The name of the third river is Tigris, which flows east of Assyria. And the fourth river is the Euphrates.

15 The LORD God took the man and put him in the garden of Eden to till it and keep it. 16And the LORD God commanded the man, "You may freely eat of every tree of the garden; 17but of the tree of the knowledge of good and evil you shall not eat, for in the day that you eat of it you shall die."

18 Then the LORD God said, "It is not good that the man should be alone; I will make him a helper as his partner." 19So out of the ground the LORD God formed every animal of the field and every bird of the air, and brought them to the man to see what he would call them; and whatever the man called every living creature, that was its name. 20The man gave names to all cattle, and to the birds of the air, and to every animal of the field; but for the manb there was not found a helper as his partner. 21So the LORD God caused a deep sleep to fall upon the man, and he slept; then he took one of his ribs and closed up its place with flesh. 22And the rib that the LORD God had taken from the man he made into a woman and brought her to the man. 23Then the man said,

"This at last is bone of my bones
        and flesh of my flesh;
this one shall be called Woman,c
        for out of Mand this one was taken."

24Therefore a man leaves his father and his mother and clings to his wife, and they become

a Or formed a man (Heb adam) of dust from the ground (Heb adamah)
b Or for Adam c Heb ishshah d Heb ish

LECTIO DIVINA

Translation: "divine reading." *Lectio divina* might sound complicated, but it's really quite user-friendly. It's a practice that dates back to twelfth-century monks and is still used today. In some ways it's like eating: take a bite, chew it, savor the taste, and digest it! It's a way of praying with Scripture that can help you learn, ponder, listen, and pray. You can try it by yourself or do it with others. In fact, you can use *lectio divina* with any part of this Bible. Give it a try.

Go somewhere quiet where you can read without interruptions. Light the area with candles—enough so you can see the words in this Bible. Take a deep breath. When you feel free of most distractions, you're ready to begin.

Take a bite. Read **Genesis 1.26–27** out loud (remember, you aren't really alone). Read it more than once, focusing on different words and what they mean to you each time you read the verses. Listen to the words. Taste the power and beauty of the words as you say them.

Chew it. Let yourself settle on a word or phrase. Why might the Holy Spirit have highlighted this particular selection for you? Ponder.

Savor it. Open your heart. Dare to have a dialogue with God. Start speaking to God and don't forget to listen to God's part of the conversation.

Digest it. Once you chew and swallow food, you don't have to consciously do much more in the digestion process. The same is true here. Just allow the words to feed your spirit. Be at peace in God's presence.

If you want to share your experience and learn about others' experiences, drop in at **Learner.CalltoDiscipleship.com** and tell others what happened when you tried *lectio divina*.

an said to the serpent, "We may eat of the fruit of the trees in the garden; ³but God said, 'You shall not eat of the fruit of the tree that is in the middle of the garden, nor shall you touch it, or you shall die.' " ⁴But the serpent said to the woman, "You will not die; ⁵for God knows that when you eat of it your eyes will be opened, and you will be like God,ᵃ knowing good and evil." ⁶So when the woman saw that the tree was good for food, and that it was a delight to the eyes, and that the tree was to be desired to make one wise, she took of its fruit and ate; and she also gave some to her husband, who was with her, and he ate. ⁷Then the eyes of both were opened, and they knew that they were naked; and they sewed fig leaves together and made loincloths for themselves.

8 They heard the sound of the LORD God walking in the garden at the time of the evening breeze, and the man and his wife hid themselves from the presence of the LORD God among the trees of the garden. ⁹But the LORD God called to the man, and said to him, "Where are you?" ¹⁰He said, "I heard the sound of you in the garden, and I was afraid, because I was naked; and I hid myself." ¹¹He said, "Who told you that you were naked? Have you eaten from the tree of which I commanded you not to eat?" ¹²The man said, "The woman whom you gave to be with me, she gave me fruit from the tree, and I ate." ¹³Then the LORD God said to the woman, "What is this that you have done?" The woman said, "The serpent tricked me, and I ate." ¹⁴The LORD God said to the serpent,

"Because you have done this,
    cursed are you among all animals
    and among all wild creatures;
upon your belly you shall go,
    and dust you shall eat
    all the days of your life.
¹⁵ I will put enmity between you and the
        woman,
    and between your offspring and hers;
he will strike your head,
    and you will strike his heel."
¹⁶To the woman he said,
"I will greatly increase your pangs in
        childbearing;
    in pain you shall bring forth children,
yet your desire shall be for your husband,
    and he shall rule over you."
¹⁷And to the manᵇ he said,
"Because you have listened to the voice of
        your wife,
    and have eaten of the tree
about which I commanded you,
    'You shall not eat of it,'

one flesh. ²⁵And the man and his wife were both naked, and were not ashamed.

3 The First Sin and Its Punishment

Now the serpent was more crafty than any other wild animal that the LORD God had made. He said to the woman, "Did God say, 'You shall not eat from any tree in the garden'?" ²The wom-

a Or gods b Or to Adam

cursed is the ground because of you;
in toil you shall eat of it all the days of
your life;
18 thorns and thistles it shall bring forth for
you;
and you shall eat the plants of the field.
19 By the sweat of your face
you shall eat bread
until you return to the ground,
for out of it you were taken;
you are dust,
and to dust you shall return."

20 The man named his wife Eve,*a* because she was the mother of all living. 21And the LORD God made garments of skins for the man*b* and for his wife, and clothed them.

22 Then the LORD God said, "See, the man has become like one of us, knowing good and evil; and now, he might reach out his hand and take also from the tree of life, and eat, and live forever"— 23therefore the LORD God sent him forth from the garden of Eden, to till the ground from which he was taken. 24He drove out the man; and at the east of the garden of Eden he placed the cherubim, and a sword flaming and turning to guard the way to the tree of life.

4 Cain Murders Abel

Now the man knew his wife Eve, and she conceived and bore Cain, saying, "I have produced*c* a man with the help of the LORD." 2Next she bore his brother Abel. Now Abel was a keeper of sheep, and Cain a tiller of the ground. 3In the course of time Cain brought to the LORD an offering of the fruit of the ground, 4and Abel for his part brought of the firstlings of his flock, their fat portions. And the LORD had regard for Abel and his offering, 5but for Cain and his offering he had no regard. So Cain was very angry, and his countenance fell. 6The LORD said to Cain, "Why are you angry, and why has your countenance fallen? 7If you do well, will you not be accepted? And if you do not do well, sin is lurking at the door; its desire is for you, but you must master it."

8 Cain said to his brother Abel, "Let us go out to the field."*d* And when they were in the field, Cain rose up against his brother Abel, and killed him. 9Then the LORD said to Cain, "Where is your brother Abel?" He said, "I do not know; am I my brother's keeper?" 10And the LORD said, "What have you done? Listen; your brother's blood is crying out to me from the ground! 11And now you are cursed from the ground, which has opened its mouth to receive your brother's blood from your hand. 12When you till the ground, it will no longer yield to you its strength; you will be a fugitive and a wanderer on the earth." 13Cain said to the LORD, "My punishment is greater than I can bear! 14Today you have driven me away from the soil, and I shall be hidden from your face; I shall be a fugitive and a wanderer on the earth, and anyone who meets me may kill me." 15Then the LORD said to him, "Not so!*e* Whoever kills Cain will suffer a sevenfold vengeance." And the LORD put a mark on Cain, so that no one who came upon him would kill him. 16Then Cain went away from the presence of the LORD, and settled in the land of Nod,*f* east of Eden.

Beginnings of Civilization

17 Cain knew his wife, and she conceived and bore Enoch; and he built a city, and named it Enoch after his son Enoch. 18To Enoch was born Irad; and Irad was the father of Mehujael, and Mehujael the father of Methushael, and Methushael the father of Lamech. 19Lamech took two wives; the name of the one was Adah, and the name of the other Zillah. 20Adah bore Jabal; he was the ancestor of those who live in tents and have livestock. 21His brother's name was Jubal; he was the ancestor of all those who play the lyre and pipe. 22Zillah bore Tubal-cain, who made all kinds of bronze and iron tools. The sister of Tubal-cain was Naamah.

23 Lamech said to his wives:
"Adah and Zillah, hear my voice;
you wives of Lamech, listen to what I say:
I have killed a man for wounding me,
a young man for striking me.
24 If Cain is avenged sevenfold,
truly Lamech seventy-sevenfold."

25 Adam knew his wife again, and she bore a son and named him Seth, for she said, "God has appointed*g* for me another child instead of Abel, because Cain killed him." 26To Seth also a son was born, and he named him Enosh. At that time people began to invoke the name of the LORD.

5 Adam's Descendants to Noah and His Sons

This is the list of the descendants of Adam. When God created humankind,*h* he made them*i* in the likeness of God. 2Male and female he created them, and he blessed them and named them "Humankind"*h* when they were created.

3 When Adam had lived one hundred thirty years, he became the father of a son in his like-

---

a In Heb *Eve* resembles the word for *living* *b* Or *for Adam* *c* The verb in Heb resembles the word for *Cain* *d* Sam Gk Syr Compare Vg: MT lacks *Let us go out to the field* *e* Gk Syr Vg: Heb *Therefore* *f* That is *Wandering* *g* The verb in Heb resembles the word for *Seth* *h* Heb *adam* *i* Heb *him* ness, according to his image, and named him Seth. ⁴The days of Adam after he became the father of Seth were eight hundred years; and he had other sons and daughters. ⁵Thus all the days that Adam lived were nine hundred thirty years; and he died.

6 When Seth had lived one hundred five years, he became the father of Enosh. ⁷Seth lived after the birth of Enosh eight hundred seven years, and had other sons and daughters. ⁸Thus all the days of Seth were nine hundred twelve years; and he died.

9 When Enosh had lived ninety years, he became the father of Kenan. ¹⁰Enosh lived after the birth of Kenan eight hundred fifteen years, and had other sons and daughters. ¹¹Thus all the days of Enosh were nine hundred five years; and he died.

12 When Kenan had lived seventy years, he became the father of Mahalalel. ¹³Kenan lived after the birth of Mahalalel eight hundred and forty years, and had other sons and daughters. ¹⁴Thus all the days of Kenan were nine hundred and ten years; and he died.

15 When Mahalalel had lived sixty-five years, he became the father of Jared. ¹⁶Mahalalel lived after the birth of Jared eight hundred thirty years, and had other sons and daughters. ¹⁷Thus all the days of Mahalalel were eight hundred ninety-five years; and he died.

18 When Jared had lived one hundred sixty-two years he became the father of Enoch. ¹⁹Jared lived after the birth of Enoch eight hundred years, and had other sons and daughters. ²⁰Thus all the days of Jared were nine hundred sixty-two years; and he died.

21 When Enoch had lived sixty-five years, he became the father of Methuselah. ²²Enoch walked with God after the birth of Methuselah three hundred years, and had other sons and daughters. ²³Thus all the days of Enoch were three hundred sixty-five years. ²⁴Enoch walked with God; then he was no more, because God took him.

25 When Methuselah had lived one hundred eighty-seven years, he became the father of Lamech. ²⁶Methuselah lived after the birth of Lamech seven hundred eighty-two years, and had other sons and daughters. ²⁷Thus all the days of Methuselah were nine hundred sixty-nine years; and he died.

28 When Lamech had lived one hundred eighty-two years, he became the father of a son; ²⁹he named him Noah, saying, "Out of the ground that the LORD has cursed this one shall bring us relief from our work and from the toil of our hands." ³⁰Lamech lived after the birth of Noah five hundred ninety-five years, and had other sons and daughters. ³¹Thus all the days of Lamech were seven hundred seventy-seven years; and he died.

32 After Noah was five hundred years old, Noah became the father of Shem, Ham, and Japheth.

6 The Wickedness of Humankind

When people began to multiply on the face of the ground, and daughters were born to them, ²the sons of God saw that they were fair; and they took wives for themselves of all that they chose. ³Then the LORD said, "My spirit shall not abide*ᵃ* in mortals forever, for they are flesh; their days shall be one hundred twenty years." ⁴The Nephilim were on the earth in those days—and also afterward—when the sons of God went in to the daughters of humans, who bore children to them. These were the heroes that were of old, warriors of renown.

5 The LORD saw that the wickedness of humankind was great in the earth, and that every inclination of the thoughts of their hearts was only evil continually. ⁶And the LORD was sorry that he had made humankind on the earth, and it grieved him to his heart. ⁷So the LORD said, "I will blot out from the earth the human beings I have created—people together with animals and creeping things and birds of the air, for I am sorry that I have made them." ⁸But Noah found favor in the sight of the LORD.

Noah Pleases God

9 These are the descendants of Noah. Noah was a righteous man, blameless in his generation; Noah walked with God. ¹⁰And Noah had three sons, Shem, Ham, and Japheth.

11 Now the earth was corrupt in God's sight, and the earth was filled with violence. ¹²And God saw that the earth was corrupt; for all flesh had corrupted its ways upon the earth. ¹³And God said to Noah, "I have determined to make an end of all flesh, for the earth is filled with violence because of them; now I am going to destroy them along with the earth. ¹⁴Make yourself an ark of cypress*ᵃ* wood; make rooms in the ark, and cover it inside and out with pitch. ¹⁵This is how you are to make it: the length of the ark three hundred cubits, its width fifty cubits, and its height thirty cubits. ¹⁶Make a roof*ᵇ* for the ark, and finish it to a cubit above; and put the door of the ark in its side; make it with lower, second, and third decks. ¹⁷For my part, I am going to bring a flood of waters on the earth, to destroy from under heaven all flesh in which is the breath of life; everything that is

a Meaning of Heb uncertain *b* Or *window*

on the earth shall die. [18]But I will establish my covenant with you; and you shall come into the ark, you, your sons, your wife, and your sons' wives with you. [19]And of every living thing, of all flesh, you shall bring two of every kind into the ark, to keep them alive with you; they shall be male and female. [20]Of the birds according to their kinds, and of the animals according to their kinds, of every creeping thing of the ground according to its kind, two of every kind shall come in to you, to keep them alive. [21]Also take with you every kind of food that is eaten, and store it up; and it shall serve as food for you and for them." [22]Noah did this; he did all that God commanded him.

7 The Great Flood

Then the LORD said to Noah, "Go into the ark, you and all your household, for I have seen that you alone are righteous before me in this generation. [2]Take with you seven pairs of all clean animals, the male and its mate; and a pair of the animals that are not clean, the male and its mate; [3]and seven pairs of the birds of the air also, male and female, to keep their kind alive on the face of all the earth. [4]For in seven days I will send rain on the earth for forty days and forty nights; and every living thing that I have made I will blot out from the face of the ground." [5]And Noah did all that the LORD had commanded him.

[6] Noah was six hundred years old when the flood of waters came on the earth. [7]And Noah with his sons and his wife and his sons' wives went into the ark to escape the waters of the flood. [8]Of clean animals, and of animals that are not clean, and of birds, and of everything that creeps on the ground, [9]two and two, male and female, went into the ark with Noah, as God had commanded Noah. [10]And after seven days the waters of the flood came on the earth.

[11] In the six hundredth year of Noah's life, in the second month, on the seventeenth day of the month, on that day all the fountains of the great deep burst forth, and the windows of the heavens were opened. [12]The rain fell on the earth forty days and forty nights. [13]On the very same day Noah with his sons, Shem and Ham and Japheth, and Noah's wife and the three wives of his sons entered the ark, [14]they and every wild animal of every kind, and all domestic animals of every kind, and every creeping thing that creeps on the earth, and every bird of every kind—every bird, every winged creature. [15]They went into the ark with Noah, two and two of all flesh in which there was the breath of life. [16]And those that entered, male and female of all flesh, went in as God had commanded him; and the LORD shut him in.

[17] The flood continued forty days on the earth; and the waters increased, and bore up the ark, and it rose high above the earth. [18]The waters swelled and increased greatly on the earth; and the ark floated on the face of the waters. [19]The waters swelled so mightily on the earth that all the high mountains under the whole heaven were covered; [20]the waters swelled above the mountains, covering them fifteen cubits deep. [21]And all flesh died that moved on the earth, birds, domestic animals, wild animals, all swarming creatures that swarm on the earth, and all human beings; [22]everything on dry land in whose nostrils was the breath of life died. [23]He blotted out every living thing that was on the face of the ground, human beings and animals and creeping things and birds of the air; they were blotted out from the earth. Only Noah was left, and those that were with him in the ark. [24]And

TEXT MESSAGE

Noah's boat described in Genesis 6.15 would have been huge for its time—about 450 feet long, the length of one and a half football fields. That's five times as long as the *Mayflower*, in which the Pilgrims sailed to North America in 1620. And it's more than half as long as the *Titanic*.

This information has been scanned and is free of all known viruses. Please forward to all your friends.

Imagination

I'm usually doodling during class. I *am* listening—I'm just drawing tiny shoes *while* I listen. I get about a dozen drawn before my mind goes blank and I run out of great new shoe ideas. So I start repeating them, and they begin to look alike. No matter how hard I try, inevitably I run out of new ideas.

Is it true that no two snowflakes are the same? That fingerprints never repeat? How does God do this amazing task of making new things? I've got three siblings and we're completely different—short, tall, hefty, trim, funny, geeky. Yet there's still this mysterious thread that connects us to our parents. Read **Genesis 2.23–24**. From the very beginning of time God had this great idea called *family*. Each and every family is created by him—through marriage, biology, and adoption—with its own combination of individuality and commonality.

We are also part of the human family, and we are responsible for promoting the common good of all members of our human family (see CCC 2203). Catholic social teaching also outlines our responsibilities by addressing the various needs and rights of our human family.

Doodle a portrait of your immediate family. What do you have in common with your parents? Your siblings? What distinguishes you from the others? What resemblance do you bear to your Father, God? How can people tell you belong to *his* family?

---

the waters swelled on the earth for one hundred fifty days.

8 The Flood Subsides

But God remembered Noah and all the wild animals and all the domestic animals that were with him in the ark. And God made a wind blow over the earth, and the waters subsided; ²the fountains of the deep and the windows of the heavens were closed, the rain from the heavens was restrained, ³and the waters gradually receded from the earth. At the end of one hundred fifty days the waters had abated; ⁴and in the seventh month, on the seventeenth day of the month, the ark came to rest on the mountains of Ararat. ⁵The waters continued to abate until the tenth month; in the tenth month, on the first day of the month, the tops of the mountains appeared.

6 At the end of forty days Noah opened the window of the ark that he had made ⁷and sent out the raven; and it went to and fro until the waters were dried up from the earth. ⁸Then he sent out the dove from him, to see if the waters had subsided from the face of the ground; ⁹but the dove found no place to set its foot, and it returned to him to the ark, for the waters were still on the face of the whole earth. So he put out his hand and took it and brought it into the ark with him. ¹⁰He waited another seven days, and again he sent out the dove from the ark; ¹¹and the dove came back to him in the evening, and there in its beak was a freshly plucked olive leaf; so Noah knew that the waters had subsided from the earth. ¹²Then he waited another seven days, and sent out the dove; and it did not return to him any more.

13 In the six hundred first year, in the first month, on the first day of the month, the waters were dried up from the earth; and Noah removed the covering of the ark, and looked, and saw that the face of the ground was drying. ¹⁴In the second month, on the twenty-seventh day of the month, the earth was dry. ¹⁵Then God said to Noah, ¹⁶"Go out of the ark, you and your wife, and your sons and your sons' wives with you. ¹⁷Bring out with you every living thing that is with you of all flesh—birds and animals and every creeping thing that creeps on the earth—so that they may abound on the earth, and be fruitful and multiply on the earth." ¹⁸So Noah went out with his sons and his wife and his sons' wives. ¹⁹And every animal, every creeping thing, and every bird, everything that moves on the earth, went out of the ark by families.

God's Promise to Noah

20 Then Noah built an altar to the LORD, and took of every clean animal and of every clean bird, and offered burnt offerings on the altar. ²¹And when the LORD smelled the pleasing odor, the LORD said in his heart, "I will never again curse the ground because of humankind, for the inclination of the human heart is evil from youth; nor will I ever again destroy every living creature as I have done.

²² As long as the earth endures,
  seedtime and harvest, cold and heat,
  summer and winter, day and night,
    shall not cease."

9 The Covenant with Noah

God blessed Noah and his sons, and said to them, "Be fruitful and multiply, and fill the earth. [2]The fear and dread of you shall rest on every animal of the earth, and on every bird of the air, on everything that creeps on the ground, and on all the fish of the sea; into your hand they are delivered. [3]Every moving thing that lives shall be food for you; and just as I gave you the green plants, I give you everything. [4]Only, you shall not eat flesh with its life, that is, its blood. [5]For your own lifeblood I will surely require a reckoning: from every animal I will require it and from human beings, each one for the blood of another, I will require a reckoning for human life.

[6] Whoever sheds the blood of a human,
    by a human shall that person's blood be
       shed;
  for in his own image
    God made humankind.

[7]And you, be fruitful and multiply, abound on the earth and multiply in it."

[8] Then God said to Noah and to his sons with him, [9]"As for me, I am establishing my covenant with you and your descendants after you, [10]and with every living creature that is with you, the birds, the domestic animals, and every animal of the earth with you, as many as came out of the ark.[a] [11]I establish my covenant with you, that never again shall all flesh be cut off by the waters of a flood, and never again shall there be a flood to destroy the earth." [12]God said, "This is the sign of the covenant that I make between me and you and every living creature that is with you, for all future generations: [13]I have set my bow in the clouds, and it shall be a sign of the covenant between me and the earth. [14]When I bring clouds over the earth and the bow is seen in the clouds, [15]I will remember my covenant that is between me and you and every living creature of all flesh; and the waters shall never again become a flood to destroy all flesh. [16]When the bow is in the clouds, I will see it and remember the everlasting covenant between God and every living creature of all flesh that is on the earth." [17]God said to Noah, "This is the sign of the covenant that I have established between me and all flesh that is on the earth."

Noah and His Sons

18 The sons of Noah who went out of the ark were Shem, Ham, and Japheth. Ham was the father of Canaan. [19]These three were the sons of Noah; and from these the whole earth was peopled.

20 Noah, a man of the soil, was the first to plant a vineyard. [21]He drank some of the wine and became drunk, and he lay uncovered in his tent. [22]And Ham, the father of Canaan, saw the nakedness of his father, and told his two brothers outside. [23]Then Shem and Japheth took a garment, laid it on both their shoulders, and walked backward and covered the nakedness of their father; their faces were turned away, and they did not see their father's nakedness. [24]When Noah awoke from his wine and knew what his youngest son had done to him, [25]he said,

  "Cursed be Canaan;
    lowest of slaves shall he be to his
       brothers."
[26]He also said,
  "Blessed by the LORD my God be Shem;
    and let Canaan be his slave.
[27] May God make space for[b] Japheth,
    and let him live in the tents of Shem;
    and let Canaan be his slave."

28 After the flood Noah lived three hundred fifty years. [29]All the days of Noah were nine hundred fifty years; and he died.

10 Nations Descended from Noah

These are the descendants of Noah's sons, Shem, Ham, and Japheth; children were born to them after the flood.

2 The descendants of Japheth: Gomer, Magog, Madai, Javan, Tubal, Meshech, and Tiras. [3]The descendants of Gomer: Ashkenaz, Riphath, and Togarmah. [4]The descendants of Javan: Elishah, Tarshish, Kittim, and Rodanim.[c] [5]From these the coastland peoples spread. These are the descendants of Japheth[d] in their lands, with their own language, by their families, in their nations.

6 The descendants of Ham: Cush, Egypt, Put, and Canaan. [7]The descendants of Cush: Seba, Havilah, Sabtah, Raamah, and Sabteca. The descendants of Raamah: Sheba and Dedan. [8]Cush became the father of Nimrod; he was the first on earth to become a mighty warrior. [9]He was a mighty hunter before the LORD; therefore it is said, "Like Nimrod a mighty hunter before the LORD." [10]The beginning of his kingdom was Babel, Erech, and Accad, all of them in the land of Shinar. [11]From that land he went into Assyria, and built Nineveh, Rehoboth-ir, Calah, and [12]Resen between Nineveh and Calah; that is the great city. [13]Egypt became the father of Ludim, Anamim, Lehabim, Naphtuhim, [14]Pathrusim, Casluhim, and Caphtorim, from which the Philistines come.[e]

15 Canaan became the father of Sidon his firstborn, and Heth, [16]and the Jebusites, the

---

a Gk: Heb adds *every animal of the earth*   b Heb *yapht*, a play on *Japheth*   c Heb Mss Sam Gk See 1 Chr 1.7: MT *Dodanim*   d Compare verses 20, 31. Heb lacks *These are the descendants of Japheth*   e Cn: Heb *Casluhim, from which the Philistines come, and Caphtorim*

Amorites, the Girgashites, [17]the Hivites, the Arkites, the Sinites, [18]the Arvadites, the Zemarites, and the Hamathites. Afterward the families of the Canaanites spread abroad. [19]And the territory of the Canaanites extended from Sidon, in the direction of Gerar, as far as Gaza, and in the direction of Sodom, Gomorrah, Admah, and Zeboiim, as far as Lasha. [20]These are the descendants of Ham, by their families, their languages, their lands, and their nations.

21 To Shem also, the father of all the children of Eber, the elder brother of Japheth, children were born. [22]The descendants of Shem: Elam, Asshur, Arpachshad, Lud, and Aram. [23]The descendants of Aram: Uz, Hul, Gether, and Mash. [24]Arpachshad became the father of Shelah; and Shelah became the father of Eber. [25]To Eber were born two sons: the name of the one was Peleg,[a] for in his days the earth was divided, and his brother's name was Joktan. [26]Joktan became the father of Almodad, Sheleph, Hazarmaveth, Jerah, [27]Hadoram, Uzal, Diklah, [28]Obal, Abimael, Sheba, [29]Ophir, Havilah, and Jobab; all these were the descendants of Joktan. [30]The territory in which they lived extended from Mesha in the direction of Sephar, the hill country of the east. [31]These are the descendants of Shem, by their families, their languages, their lands, and their nations.

32 These are the families of Noah's sons, according to their genealogies, in their nations; and from these the nations spread abroad on the earth after the flood.

11 The Tower of Babel

Now the whole earth had one language and the same words. [2]And as they migrated from the east,[b] they came upon a plain in the land of Shinar and settled there. [3]And they said to one another, "Come, let us make bricks, and burn them thoroughly." And they had brick for stone, and bitumen for mortar. [4]Then they said, "Come, let us build ourselves a city, and a tower with its top in the heavens, and let us make a name for ourselves; otherwise we shall be scattered abroad upon the face of the whole earth." [5]The LORD came down to see the city and the tower, which mortals had built. [6]And the LORD said, "Look, they are one people, and they have all one language; and this is only the beginning of what they will do; nothing that they propose to do will now be impossible for them. [7]Come, let us go down, and confuse their language there, so that they will not understand one another's speech." [8]So the LORD scattered them abroad from there over the face

of all the earth, and they left off building the city. [9]Therefore it was called Babel, because there the LORD confused[c] the language of all the earth; and from there the LORD scattered them abroad over the face of all the earth.

Descendants of Shem

10 These are the descendants of Shem. When Shem was one hundred years old, he became the father of Arpachshad two years after the flood; [11]and Shem lived after the birth of Arpachshad five hundred years, and had other sons and daughters.

12 When Arpachshad had lived thirty-five years, he became the father of Shelah; [13]and Arpachshad lived after the birth of Shelah four hundred three years, and had other sons and daughters.

14 When Shelah had lived thirty years, he became the father of Eber; [15]and Shelah lived after the birth of Eber four hundred three years, and had other sons and daughters.

16 When Eber had lived thirty-four years, he became the father of Peleg; [17]and Eber lived after the birth of Peleg four hundred thirty years, and had other sons and daughters.

18 When Peleg had lived thirty years, he became the father of Reu; [19]and Peleg lived after the birth of Reu two hundred nine years, and had other sons and daughters.

20 When Reu had lived thirty-two years, he became the father of Serug; [21]and Reu lived after the birth of Serug two hundred seven years, and had other sons and daughters.

22 When Serug had lived thirty years, he became the father of Nahor; [23]and Serug lived after the birth of Nahor two hundred years, and had other sons and daughters.

24 When Nahor had lived twenty-nine years, he became the father of Terah; [25]and Nahor lived after the birth of Terah one hundred nineteen years, and had other sons and daughters.

26 When Terah had lived seventy years, he became the father of Abram, Nahor, and Haran.

Descendants of Terah

27 Now these are the descendants of Terah. Terah was the father of Abram, Nahor, and Haran; and Haran was the father of Lot. [28]Haran died before his father Terah in the land of his birth, in Ur of the Chaldeans. [29]Abram and Nahor took wives; the name of Abram's wife was Sarai, and the name of Nahor's wife was Milcah. She was the daughter of Haran the father

a That is Division b Or migrated eastward c Heb balal, meaning to confuse of Milcah and Iscah. ³⁰Now Sarai was barren; she had no child.

31 Terah took his son Abram and his grandson Lot son of Haran, and his daughter-in-law Sarai, his son Abram's wife, and they went out together from Ur of the Chaldeans to go into the land of Canaan; but when they came to Haran, they settled there. ³²The days of Terah were two hundred five years; and Terah died in Haran.

12 The Call of Abram

Now the Lᴏʀᴅ said to Abram, "Go from your country and your kindred and your father's house to the land that I will show you. ²I will make of you a great nation, and I will bless you, and make your name great, so that you will be a blessing. ³I will bless those who bless you, and the one who curses you I will curse; and in you all the families of the earth shall be blessed."ᵃ

4 So Abram went, as the Lᴏʀᴅ had told him; and Lot went with him. Abram was seventy-five years old when he departed from Haran. ⁵Abram took his wife Sarai and his brother's son Lot, and all the possessions that they had gathered, and the persons whom they had acquired in Haran; and they set forth to go to the land of Canaan. When they had come to the land of Canaan, ⁶Abram passed through the land to the place at Shechem, to the oakᵇ of Moreh. At that time the Canaanites were in the land. ⁷Then the Lᴏʀᴅ appeared to Abram, and said, "To your offspringᶜ I will give this land." So he built there an altar to the Lᴏʀᴅ, who had appeared to him. ⁸From there he moved on to the hill country on the east of Bethel, and pitched his tent, with Bethel on the west and Ai on the east; and there he built an altar to the Lᴏʀᴅ and invoked the name of the Lᴏʀᴅ. ⁹And Abram journeyed on by stages toward the Negeb.

Abram and Sarai in Egypt

10 Now there was a famine in the land. So Abram went down to Egypt to reside there as an alien, for the famine was severe in the land. ¹¹When he was about to enter Egypt, he said to his wife Sarai, "I know well that you are a woman beautiful in appearance; ¹²and when the Egyptians see you, they will say, 'This is his wife'; then they will kill me, but they will let you live. ¹³Say you are my sister, so that it may go well with me because of you, and that my life may be spared on your account." ¹⁴When Abram entered Egypt the Egyptians saw that the woman was very beautiful. ¹⁵When the officials of Pharaoh saw her, they praised her to Pharaoh. And the woman was taken into Pharaoh's house. ¹⁶And for her sake he dealt well with Abram; and he had sheep, oxen, male donkeys, male and female slaves, female donkeys, and camels.

17 But the Lᴏʀᴅ afflicted Pharaoh and his house with great plagues because of Sarai,

---

a Or by you all the families of the earth shall bless themselves b Or terebinth c Heb seed

Addiction?

Freshman year of college = independence.

Well, independence and a ton of late-night phone calls . . . from the parental units. Sometimes it's one of them, sometimes it's both of them; most of the time, it's the same old questions.

Studying hard? Yep.

Eating healthy? Uh-huh.

Love interest? Um, no.

Every day check-ins. Sometimes they call more than once. Every topic of conversation has been exhausted.

Parents are obsessed with their kids, working hard to manage a rowdy family.

The Bible is a story of someone even more relentless in pursuit of a relationship with a loved one: God—longing to know us, at great cost to himself and with little thanks.

Check out **Genesis 17.1–16**. God's calls to humanity started forever ago. He hasn't stopped calling, despite busy signals, dropped calls, and angry disconnects.

Even back with Abraham, he had his thoughts on us—on me and on you—conceiving every possible way he could take us in as members of the family.

Think of that someone in your life or family who has loved you like crazy. Submit your story about that person and upload a photo at **Learner.CalltoDiscipleship.com**. How does this person's love show you something about God's relentless passion for a relationship with you?

Abram's wife. ¹⁸So Pharaoh called Abram, and said, "What is this you have done to me? Why did you not tell me that she was your wife? ¹⁹Why did you say, 'She is my sister,' so that I took her for my wife? Now then, here is your wife, take her, and be gone." ²⁰And Pharaoh gave his men orders concerning him; and they set him on the way, with his wife and all that he had.

a Heb *seed* b Or *terebinths*

13 Abram and Lot Separate

So Abram went up from Egypt, he and his wife, and all that he had, and Lot with him, into the Negeb.

2 Now Abram was very rich in livestock, in silver, and in gold. ³He journeyed on by stages from the Negeb as far as Bethel, to the place where his tent had been at the beginning, between Bethel and Ai, ⁴to the place where he had made an altar at the first; and there Abram called on the name of the LORD. ⁵Now Lot, who went with Abram, also had flocks and herds and tents, ⁶so that the land could not support both of them living together; for their possessions were so great that they could not live together, ⁷and there was strife between the herders of Abram's livestock and the herders of Lot's livestock. At that time the Canaanites and the Perizzites lived in the land.

8 Then Abram said to Lot, "Let there be no strife between you and me, and between your herders and my herders; for we are kindred. ⁹Is not the whole land before you? Separate yourself from me. If you take the left hand, then I will go to the right; or if you take the right hand, then I will go to the left." ¹⁰Lot looked about him, and saw that the plain of the Jordan was well watered everywhere like the garden of the LORD, like the land of Egypt, in the direction of Zoar; this was before the LORD had destroyed Sodom and Gomorrah. ¹¹So Lot chose for himself all the plain of the Jordan, and Lot journeyed eastward; thus they separated from each other. ¹²Abram settled in the land of Canaan, while Lot settled among the cities of the Plain and moved his tent as far as Sodom. ¹³Now the people of Sodom were wicked, great sinners against the LORD.

14 The LORD said to Abram, after Lot had separated from him, "Raise your eyes now, and look from the place where you are, northward and southward and eastward and westward; ¹⁵for all the land that you see I will give to you and to your offspring^a forever. ¹⁶I will make your offspring like the dust of the earth; so that if one can count the dust of the earth, your offspring also can be counted. ¹⁷Rise up, walk through the length and the breadth of the land, for I will give it to you." ¹⁸So Abram moved his tent, and came and settled by the oaks^b of Mamre, which are at Hebron; and there he built an altar to the LORD.

14 Lot's Captivity and Rescue

In the days of King Amraphel of Shinar, King Arioch of Ellasar, King Chedorlaomer of Elam, and King Tidal of Goiim, ²these kings made war with King Bera of Sodom, King Birsha of Gomorrah, King Shinab of Admah, King Shemeber of Zeboiim, and the king of Bela (that is, Zoar). ³All these joined forces in the Valley of Siddim (that is, the Dead Sea).ᵈ ⁴Twelve years they had served Chedorlaomer, but in the thirteenth year they rebelled. ⁵In the fourteenth year Chedorlaomer and the kings who were with him came and subdued the Rephaim in Ashteroth-karnaim, the Zuzim in Ham, the Emim in Shaveh-kiriathaim, ⁶and the Horites in the hill country of Seir as far as El-paran on the edge of the wilderness; ⁷then they turned back and came to En-mishpat (that is, Kadesh), and subdued all the country of the Amalekites, and also the Amorites who lived in Hazazon-tamar. ⁸Then the king of Sodom, the king of Gomorrah, the king of Admah, the king of Zeboiim, and the king of Bela (that is, Zoar) went out, and they joined battle in the Valley of Siddim ⁹with King Chedorlaomer of Elam, King Tidal of Goiim, King Amraphel of Shinar, and King Arioch of Ellasar, four kings against five. ¹⁰Now the Valley of Siddim was full of bitumen pits; and as the kings of Sodom and Gomorrah fled, some fell into them, and the rest fled to the hill country. ¹¹So the enemy took all the goods of Sodom and Gomorrah, and all their provisions, and went their way; ¹²they also took Lot, the son of Abram's brother, who lived in Sodom, and his goods, and departed.

13 Then one who had escaped came and told Abram the Hebrew, who was living by the oaksᵇ of Mamre the Amorite, brother of Eshcol and of Aner; these were allies of Abram. ¹⁴When Abram heard that his nephew had been taken captive, he led forth his trained men, born in his house, three hundred eighteen of them, and went in pursuit as far as Dan. ¹⁵He divided his forces against them by night, he and his servants, and routed them and pursued them to Hobah, north of Damascus. ¹⁶Then he brought back all the goods, and also brought back his nephew Lot with his goods, and the women and the people.

Abram Blessed by Melchizedek

17 After his return from the defeat of Chedorlaomer and the kings who were with him, the king of Sodom went out to meet him at the Valley of Shaveh (that is, the King's Valley). ¹⁸And King Melchizedek of Salem brought out bread and wine; he was priest of God Most High.ᶜ ¹⁹He blessed him and said,

"Blessed be Abram by God Most High,ᶜ
    maker of heaven and earth;

²⁰ and blessed be God Most High,ᶜ
    who has delivered your enemies into
        your hand!"

And Abram gave him one-tenth of everything. ²¹Then the king of Sodom said to Abram, "Give me the persons, but take the goods for yourself." ²²But Abram said to the king of Sodom, "I have sworn to the LORD, God Most High,ᶜ maker of heaven and earth, ²³that I would not take a thread or a sandal-thong or anything that is yours, so that you might not say, 'I have made Abram rich.' ²⁴I will take nothing but what the young men have eaten, and the share of the men who went with me—Aner, Eshcol, and Mamre. Let them take their share."

15 God's Covenant with Abram

After these things the word of the LORD came to Abram in a vision, "Do not be afraid, Abram, I am your shield; your reward shall be very great." ²But Abram said, "O Lord GOD, what will you give me, for I continue childless, and the heir of my house is Eliezer of Damascus?"ᵈ ³And Abram said, "You have given me no offspring, and so a slave born in my house is to be my heir." ⁴But the word of the LORD came to him, "This man shall not be your heir; no one but your very own issue shall be your heir." ⁵He brought him outside and said, "Look toward heaven and count the stars, if you are able to count them." Then he said to him, "So shall your descendants be." ⁶And he believed the LORD; and the LORDᵉ reckoned it to him as righteousness.

7 Then he said to him, "I am the LORD who brought you from Ur of the Chaldeans, to give you this land to possess." ⁸But he said, "O Lord GOD, how am I to know that I shall possess it?" ⁹He said to him, "Bring me a heifer three years old, a female goat three years old, a ram three years old, a turtledove, and a young pigeon." ¹⁰He brought him all these and cut them in two, laying each half over against the other; but he did not cut the birds in two. ¹¹And when birds of prey came down on the carcasses, Abram drove them away.

12 As the sun was going down, a deep sleep fell upon Abram, and a deep and terrifying darkness descended upon him. ¹³Then the LORDᵉ said to Abram, "Know this for certain, that your offspring shall be aliens in a land that is not theirs, and shall be slaves there, and they shall be oppressed for four hundred years; ¹⁴but I will bring judgment on the nation that they serve, and afterward they shall come out with great possessions. ¹⁵As for yourself, you shall go to your ancestors in peace; you shall be

a Heb *Salt Sea* b Or *terebinths* c Heb *El Elyon* d Meaning of Heb uncertain e Heb *he* buried in a good old age. ¹⁶And they shall come back here in the fourth generation; for the iniquity of the Amorites is not yet complete."

17 When the sun had gone down and it was dark, a smoking fire pot and a flaming torch passed between these pieces. ¹⁸On that day the LORD made a covenant with Abram, saying, "To your descendants I give this land, from the river of Egypt to the great river, the river Euphrates, ¹⁹the land of the Kenites, the Kenizzites, the Kadmonites, ²⁰the Hittites, the Perizzites, the Rephaim, ²¹the Amorites, the Canaanites, the Girgashites, and the Jebusites."

16 The Birth of Ishmael

Now Sarai, Abram's wife, bore him no children. She had an Egyptian slave-girl whose name was Hagar, ²and Sarai said to Abram, "You see that the LORD has prevented me from bearing children; go in to my slave-girl; it may be that I shall obtain children by her." And Abram listened to the voice of Sarai. ³So, after Abram had lived ten years in the land of Canaan, Sarai, Abram's wife, took Hagar the Egyptian, her slave-girl, and gave her to her husband Abram as a wife. ⁴He went in to Hagar, and she conceived; and when she saw that she had conceived, she looked with contempt on her mistress. ⁵Then Sarai said to Abram, "May the wrong done to me be on you! I gave my slave-girl to your embrace, and when she saw that she had conceived, she looked on me with contempt. May the LORD judge between you and me!" ⁶But Abram said to Sarai, "Your slave-girl is in your power; do to her as you please." Then Sarai dealt harshly with her, and she ran away from her.

7 The angel of the LORD found her by a spring of water in the wilderness, the spring on the way to Shur. ⁸And he said, "Hagar, slave-girl of Sarai, where have you come from and where are you going?" She said, "I am running away from my mistress Sarai." ⁹The angel of the LORD said to her, "Return to your mistress, and submit to her." ¹⁰The angel of the LORD also said to her, "I will so greatly multiply your offspring that they cannot be counted for multitude." ¹¹And the angel of the LORD said to her,

"Now you have conceived and shall bear a
    son;
you shall call him Ishmael,^a
for the LORD has given heed to your
    affliction.
¹² He shall be a wild ass of a man,
    with his hand against everyone,
    and everyone's hand against him;

and he shall live at odds with all his kin."
¹³So she named the LORD who spoke to her, "You are El-roi";^b for she said, "Have I really seen God and remained alive after seeing him?"^c ¹⁴Therefore the well was called Beer-la-hai-roi;^d it lies between Kadesh and Bered.

15 Hagar bore Abram a son; and Abram named his son, whom Hagar bore, Ishmael. ¹⁶Abram was eighty-six years old when Hagar bore him^e Ishmael.

17 The Sign of the Covenant

When Abram was ninety-nine years old, the LORD appeared to Abram, and said to him, "I am God Almighty;^f walk before me, and be blameless. ²And I will make my covenant between me and you, and will make you exceedingly numerous." ³Then Abram fell on his face; and God said to him, ⁴"As for me, this is my covenant with you: You shall be the ancestor of a multitude of nations. ⁵No longer shall your name be Abram,^c but your name shall be Abraham;^h for I have made you the ancestor of a multitude of nations. ⁶I will make you exceedingly fruitful; and I will make nations of you, and kings shall come from you. ⁷I will establish my covenant between me and you, and your offspring after you throughout their generations, for an everlasting covenant, to be God to you and to your offspringⁱ after you. ⁸And I will give to you, and to your offspring after you, the land where you are now an alien, all the land of Canaan, for a perpetual holding; and I will be their God."

9 God said to Abraham, "As for you, you shall keep my covenant, you and your offspring after you throughout their generations. ¹⁰This is my covenant, which you shall keep, between me and you and your offspring after you: Every male among you shall be circumcised. ¹¹You shall circumcise the flesh of your foreskins, and it shall be a sign of the covenant between me and you. ¹²Throughout your generations every male among you shall be circumcised when he is eight days old, including the slave born in your house and the one bought with your money from any foreigner who is not of your offspring. ¹³Both the slave born in your house and the one bought with your money must be circumcised. So shall my covenant be in your flesh an everlasting covenant. ¹⁴Any uncircumcised male who is not circumcised in the flesh of his foreskin shall be cut off from his people; he has broken my covenant."

15 God said to Abraham, "As for Sarai your wife, you shall not call her Sarai, but Sarah

---

a That is *God hears* b Perhaps *God of seeing* or *God who sees* c Meaning of Heb uncertain d That is *the Well of the Living One who sees me* e Heb *Abram* f Traditional rendering of Heb *El Shaddai* g That is *exalted ancestor* h Here taken to mean *ancestor of a multitude* i Heb *seed*

Wonder—© Joy Brantl, 17

shall be her name. 16I will bless her, and moreover I will give you a son by her. I will bless her, and she shall give rise to nations; kings of peoples shall come from her." 17Then Abraham fell on his face and laughed, and said to himself, "Can a child be born to a man who is a hundred years old? Can Sarah, who is ninety years old, bear a child?" 18And Abraham said to God, "O that Ishmael might live in your sight!" 19God said, "No, but your wife Sarah shall bear you a son, and you shall name him Isaac.*a* I will establish my covenant with him as an everlasting covenant for his offspring after him. 20As for Ishmael, I have heard you; I will bless him and make him fruitful and exceedingly numerous; he shall be the father of twelve princes, and I will make him a great nation. 21But my covenant I will establish with Isaac, whom Sarah shall bear to you at this season next year." 22And when he had finished talking with him, God went up from Abraham.

23 Then Abraham took his son Ishmael and all the slaves born in his house or bought with his money, every male among the men of Abraham's house, and he circumcised the flesh of their foreskins that very day, as God had said to him. 24Abraham was ninety-nine years old when he was circumcised in the flesh of his foreskin. 25And his son Ishmael was thirteen years old when he was circumcised in the flesh

of his foreskin. 26That very day Abraham and his son Ishmael were circumcised; 27and all the men of his house, slaves born in the house and those bought with money from a foreigner, were circumcised with him.

18 A Son Promised to Abraham and Sarah

The LORD appeared to Abraham*b* by the oaks*c* of Mamre, as he sat at the entrance of his tent in the heat of the day. 2He looked up and saw three men standing near him. When he saw them, he ran from the tent entrance to meet them, and bowed down to the ground. 3He said, "My lord, if I find favor with you, do not pass by your servant. 4Let a little water be brought, and wash your feet, and rest yourselves under the tree. 5Let me bring a little bread, that you may refresh yourselves, and after that you may pass on—since you have come to your servant." So they said, "Do as you have said." 6And Abraham hastened into the tent to Sarah, and said, "Make ready quickly three measures*d* of choice flour, knead it, and make cakes." 7Abraham ran to the herd, and took a calf, tender and good, and gave it to the servant, who hastened to prepare it. 8Then he took curds and milk and the calf that he had prepared, and set it before them; and he stood by them under the tree while they ate.

9 They said to him, "Where is your wife Sar-

a That is *he laughs* *b* Heb *him* *c* Or *terebinths* *d* Heb *seahs* ah?" And he said, "There, in the tent." ¹⁰Then one said, "I will surely return to you in due season, and your wife Sarah shall have a son." And Sarah was listening at the tent entrance behind him. ¹¹Now Abraham and Sarah were old, advanced in age; it had ceased to be with Sarah after the manner of women. ¹²So Sarah laughed to herself, saying, "After I have grown old, and my husband is old, shall I have pleasure?" ¹³The Lord said to Abraham, "Why did Sarah laugh, and say, 'Shall I indeed bear a child, now that I am old?' ¹⁴Is anything too wonderful for the Lord? At the set time I will return to you, in due season, and Sarah shall have a son." ¹⁵But Sarah denied, saying, "I did not laugh"; for she was afraid. He said, "Oh yes, you did laugh."

Judgment Pronounced on Sodom

16 Then the men set out from there, and they looked toward Sodom; and Abraham went with them to set them on their way. ¹⁷The Lord said, "Shall I hide from Abraham what I am about to do, ¹⁸seeing that Abraham shall become a great and mighty nation, and all the nations of the earth shall be blessed in him?ᵃ ¹⁹No, for I have chosenᵇ him, that he may charge his children and his household after him to keep the way of the Lord by doing righteousness and justice; so that the Lord may bring about for Abraham what he has promised him." ²⁰Then the Lord said, "How great is the outcry against Sodom and Gomorrah and how very grave their sin! ²¹I must go down and see whether they have done altogether according to the outcry that has come to me; and if not, I will know."

22 So the men turned from there, and went toward Sodom, while Abraham remained standing before the Lord.ᶜ ²³Then Abraham came near and said, "Will you indeed sweep away the righteous with the wicked? ²⁴Suppose there are fifty righteous within the city; will you then sweep away the place and not forgive it for the fifty righteous who are in it? ²⁵Far be it from you to do such a thing, to slay the righteous with the wicked, so that the righteous fare as the wicked! Far be that from you! Shall not the Judge of all the earth do what is just?" ²⁶And the Lord said, "If I find at Sodom fifty righteous in the city, I will forgive the whole place for their sake." ²⁷Abraham answered, "Let me take it upon myself to speak to the Lord, I who am but dust and ashes. ²⁸Suppose five of the fifty righteous are lacking? Will you destroy the whole city for lack of five?" And he said, "I will not destroy it if I find forty-five there." ²⁹Again

he spoke to him, "Suppose forty are found there." He answered, "For the sake of forty I will not do it." ³⁰Then he said, "Oh do not let the Lord be angry if I speak. Suppose thirty are found there." He answered, "I will not do it, if I find thirty there." ³¹He said, "Let me take it upon myself to speak to the Lord. Suppose twenty are found there." He answered, "For the sake of twenty I will not destroy it." ³²Then he said, "Oh do not let the Lord be angry if I speak just once more. Suppose ten are found there." He answered, "For the sake of ten I will not destroy it." ³³And the Lord went his way, when he had finished speaking to Abraham; and Abraham returned to his place.

19 The Depravity of Sodom

The two angels came to Sodom in the evening, and Lot was sitting in the gateway of Sodom. When Lot saw them, he rose to meet them, and bowed down with his face to the ground. ²He said, "Please, my lords, turn aside to your servant's house and spend the night, and wash your feet; then you can rise early and go on your way." They said, "No; we will spend the night in the square." ³But he urged them strongly; so they turned aside to him and entered his house; and he made them a feast, and baked unleavened bread, and they ate. ⁴But before they lay down, the men of the city, the men of Sodom, both young and old, all the people to the last man, surrounded the house; ⁵and they called to Lot, "Where are the men who came to you tonight? Bring them out to us, so that we may know them." ⁶Lot went out of the door to the men, shut the door after him, ⁷and said, "I beg you, my brothers, do not act so wickedly. ⁸Look, I have two daughters who have not known a man; let me bring them out to you, and do to them as you please; only do nothing to these men, for they have come under the shelter of my roof." ⁹But they replied, "Stand back!" And they said, "This fellow came here as an alien, and he would play the judge! Now we will deal worse with you than with them." Then they pressed hard against the man Lot, and came near the door to break it down. ¹⁰But the men inside reached out their hands and brought Lot into the house with them, and shut the door. ¹¹And they struck with blindness the men who were at the door of the house, both small and great, so that they were unable to find the door.

Sodom and Gomorrah Destroyed

12 Then the men said to Lot, "Have you anyone else here? Sons-in-law, sons, daughters,

---

a Or *and all the nations of the earth shall bless themselves by him* b Heb *known* c Another ancient tradition reads *while the Lord remained standing before Abraham* or anyone you have in the city—bring them out of the place. ¹³For we are about to destroy this place, because the outcry against its people has become great before the LORD, and the LORD has sent us to destroy it." ¹⁴So Lot went out and said to his sons-in-law, who were to marry his daughters, "Up, get out of this place; for the LORD is about to destroy the city." But he seemed to his sons-in-law to be jesting.

15 When morning dawned, the angels urged Lot, saying, "Get up, take your wife and your two daughters who are here, or else you will be consumed in the punishment of the city." ¹⁶But he lingered; so the men seized him and his wife and his two daughters by the hand, the LORD being merciful to him, and they brought him out and left him outside the city. ¹⁷When they had brought them outside, they*ᵃ said, "Flee for your life; do not look back or stop anywhere in the Plain; flee to the hills, or else you will be consumed." ¹⁸And Lot said to them, "Oh, no, my lords; ¹⁹your servant has found favor with you, and you have shown me great kindness in saving my life; but I cannot flee to the hills, for fear the disaster will overtake me and I die. ²⁰Look, that city is near enough to flee to, and it is a little one. Let me escape there—is it not a little one?—and my life will be saved!" ²¹He said to him, "Very well, I grant you this favor too, and will not overthrow the city of which you have spoken. ²²Hurry, escape there, for I can do nothing until you arrive there." Therefore the city was called Zoar.ᵇ ²³The sun had risen on the earth when Lot came to Zoar.

24 Then the LORD rained on Sodom and Gomorrah sulfur and fire from the LORD out of heaven; ²⁵and he overthrew those cities, and all the Plain, and all the inhabitants of the cities, and what grew on the ground. ²⁶But Lot's wife, behind him, looked back, and she became a pillar of salt.

27 Abraham went early in the morning to the place where he had stood before the LORD; ²⁸and he looked down toward Sodom and Gomorrah and toward all the land of the Plain and saw the smoke of the land going up like the smoke of a furnace.

29 So it was that, when God destroyed the cities of the Plain, God remembered Abraham, and sent Lot out of the midst of the overthrow, when he overthrew the cities in which Lot had settled.

The Shameful Origin of Moab and Ammon

30 Now Lot went up out of Zoar and settled in the hills with his two daughters, for he was

a Gk Syr Vg: Heb *he* *b* That is *Little*

TRY THIS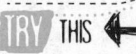

THE NO-WIN SITUATION

Read **Genesis 22.1–19**. Now put down your cell phone—it's too late to call Family Services to rush over for an intervention.

What was God *doing* here? He'd promised Abraham a son and a long lineage. Descendants like sand on a beach, like stars in the sky. Uncountable.

And now here's God insisting that Abraham take Isaac's life.

What was Abraham feeling as he raised the knife, as he recognized fear and betrayal in Isaac's eyes? God put Abraham into the ultimate no-win situation: obey God or save Isaac. There was no room for misunderstanding, no middle ground. Choose—that was the challenge.

Abraham chose God.

Abraham's faith was unshakable (see CCC 145), but God spared him the consequence of obedience . . . but not until the knife sliced toward Isaac's heart did an angel intervene.

This isn't a side of God we talk about much—a God who demands loyalty and obedience and subjects a heartbroken father to a grueling test. But God *is* God—and you aren't. He can demand whatever he wants from you or challenge you any way he chooses without explanation. But just as your parents make demands you don't like or understand, you know they have your best interests at heart. God does everything out of pure love for you, so even though you don't understand all the challenges thrown your way, trust that God knows best.

And God does challenge you. And like Abraham, the challenge involves your family. He insists that you *love* them . . . even when they're not particularly lovable.

Today—right now—who's the member of your family most difficult to love? To sacrificially serve? Decide now—right now—to nurture that wounded or distant relationship. Write down one step you'll take to make it happen.

GOD IS CHALLENGING MY FAMILY

afraid to stay in Zoar; so he lived in a cave with his two daughters. ³¹And the firstborn said to the younger, "Our father is old, and there is lay last night with my father; let us make him drink wine tonight also; then you go in and lie with him, so that we may preserve offspring through our father." 35So they made their father drink wine that night also; and the younger rose, and lay with him; and he did not know when she lay down or when she rose. 36Thus both the daughters of Lot became pregnant by their father. 37The firstborn bore a son, and named him Moab; he is the ancestor of the Moabites to this day. 38The younger also bore a son and named him Ben-ammi; he is the ancestor of the Ammonites to this day.

20 Abraham and Sarah at Gerar

From there Abraham journeyed toward the region of the Negeb, and settled between Kadesh and Shur. While residing in Gerar as an alien, 2Abraham said of his wife Sarah, "She is my sister." And King Abimelech of Gerar sent and took Sarah. 3But God came to Abimelech in a dream by night, and said to him, "You are about to die because of the woman whom you have taken; for she is a married woman." 4Now Abimelech had not approached her; so he said, "Lord, will you destroy an innocent people? 5Did he not himself say to me, 'She is my sister'? And she herself said, 'He is my brother.' I did this in the integrity of my heart and the innocence of my hands." 6Then God said to him in the dream, "Yes, I know that you did this in the integrity of your heart; furthermore it was I who kept you from sinning against me. Therefore I did not let you touch her. 7Now then, return the man's wife; for he is a prophet, and he will pray for you and you shall live. But if you do not restore her, know that you shall surely die, you and all that are yours."

8 So Abimelech rose early in the morning, and called all his servants and told them all these things; and the men were very much afraid. 9Then Abimelech called Abraham, and said to him, "What have you done to us? How have I sinned against you, that you have brought such great guilt on me and my kingdom? You have done things to me that ought not to be done." 10And Abimelech said to Abraham, "What were you thinking of, that you did this thing?" 11Abraham said, "I did it because I thought, There is no fear of God at all in this place, and they will kill me because of my wife. 12Besides, she is indeed my sister, the daughter of my father but not the daughter of my mother; and she became my wife. 13And when God caused me to wander from my father's house, I said to her, 'This is the kindness you must do me: at every place to which we come, say of me, He is my brother.' " 14Then Abimelech took sheep and oxen, and male and female slaves,

not a man on earth to come in to us after the manner of all the world. 32Come, let us make our father drink wine, and we will lie with him, so that we may preserve offspring through our father." 33So they made their father drink wine that night; and the firstborn went in, and lay with her father; he did not know when she lay down or when she rose. 34On the next day, the firstborn said to the younger, "Look, I and gave them to Abraham, and restored his wife Sarah to him. ¹⁵Abimelech said, "My land is before you; settle where it pleases you." ¹⁶To Sarah he said, "Look, I have given your brother a thousand pieces of silver; it is your exoneration before all who are with you; you are completely vindicated." ¹⁷Then Abraham prayed to God; and God healed Abimelech, and also healed his wife and female slaves so that they bore children. ¹⁸For the Lord had closed fast all the wombs of the house of Abimelech because of Sarah, Abraham's wife.

21 The Birth of Isaac

The Lord dealt with Sarah as he had said, and the Lord did for Sarah as he had promised. ²Sarah conceived and bore Abraham a son in his old age, at the time of which God had spoken to him. ³Abraham gave the name Isaac to his son whom Sarah bore him. ⁴And Abraham circumcised his son Isaac when he was eight days old, as God had commanded him. ⁵Abraham was a hundred years old when his son Isaac was born to him. ⁶Now Sarah said, "God has brought laughter for me; everyone who hears will laugh with me." ⁷And she said, "Who would ever have said to Abraham that Sarah would nurse children? Yet I have borne him a son in his old age."

Hagar and Ishmael Sent Away

8 The child grew, and was weaned; and Abraham made a great feast on the day that Isaac was weaned. ⁹But Sarah saw the son of Hagar the Egyptian, whom she had borne to Abraham, playing with her son Isaac.ᵃ ¹⁰So she said to Abraham, "Cast out this slave woman with her son; for the son of this slave woman shall not inherit along with my son Isaac." ¹¹The matter was very distressing to Abraham on account of his son. ¹²But God said to Abraham, "Do not be distressed because of the boy and because of your slave woman; whatever Sarah says to you, do as she tells you, for it is through Isaac that offspring shall be named for you. ¹³As for the son of the slave woman, I will make a nation of him also, because he is your offspring." ¹⁴So Abraham rose early in the morning, and took bread and a skin of water, and gave it to Hagar, putting it on her shoulder, along with the child, and sent her away. And she departed, and wandered about in the wilderness of Beer-sheba.

15 When the water in the skin was gone, she cast the child under one of the bushes. ¹⁶Then she went and sat down opposite him a good way off, about the distance of a bowshot; for she said, "Do not let me look on the death of the child." And as she sat opposite him, she lifted up her voice and wept. ¹⁷And God heard the voice of the boy; and the angel of God called to Hagar from heaven, and said to her, "What troubles you, Hagar? Do not be afraid; for God has heard the voice of the boy where he is. ¹⁸Come, lift up the boy and hold him fast with your hand, for I will make a great nation of him." ¹⁹Then God opened her eyes and she saw a well of water. She went, and filled the skin with water, and gave the boy a drink.

20 God was with the boy, and he grew up; he lived in the wilderness, and became an expert with the bow. ²¹He lived in the wilderness of Paran; and his mother got a wife for him from the land of Egypt.

Abraham and Abimelech Make a Covenant

22 At that time Abimelech, with Phicol the commander of his army, said to Abraham, "God is with you in all that you do; ²³now therefore swear to me here by God that you will not deal falsely with me or with my offspring or with my posterity, but as I have dealt loyally with you, you will deal with me and with the land where you have resided as an alien." ²⁴And Abraham said, "I swear it."

25 When Abraham complained to Abimelech about a well of water that Abimelech's servants had seized, ²⁶Abimelech said, "I do not know who has done this; you did not tell me, and I have not heard of it until today." ²⁷So Abraham took sheep and oxen and gave them to Abimelech, and the two men made a covenant. ²⁸Abraham set apart seven ewe lambs of the flock. ²⁹And Abimelech said to Abraham, "What is the meaning of these seven ewe lambs that you have set apart?" ³⁰He said, "These seven ewe lambs you shall accept from my hand, in order that you may be a witness for me that I dug this well." ³¹Therefore that place was called Beer-sheba;ᵇ because there both of them swore an oath. ³²When they had made a covenant at Beer-sheba, Abimelech, with Phicol the commander of his army, left and returned to the land of the Philistines. ³³Abrahamᶜ planted a tamarisk tree in Beer-sheba, and called there on the name of the Lord, the Everlasting God.ᵈ ³⁴And Abraham resided as an alien many days in the land of the Philistines.

22 The Command to Sacrifice Isaac

After these things God tested Abraham. He said to him, "Abraham!" And he said, "Here I am." ²He said, "Take your son, your only son Isaac, whom you love, and go to the land of Moriah,

a Gk Vg: Heb lacks *with her son Isaac* b That is *Well of seven* or *Well of the oath* c Heb *He* d Or *the Lord, El Olam* and offer him there as a burnt offering on one of the mountains that I shall show you." ³So Abraham rose early in the morning, saddled his donkey, and took two of his young men with him, and his son Isaac; he cut the wood for the burnt offering, and set out and went to the place in the distance that God had shown him. ⁴On the third day Abraham looked up and saw the place far away. ⁵Then Abraham said to his young men, "Stay here with the donkey; the boy and I will go over there; we will worship, and then we will come back to you." ⁶Abraham took the wood of the burnt offering and laid it on his son Isaac, and he himself carried the fire and the knife. So the two of them walked on together. ⁷Isaac said to his father Abraham, "Father!" And he said, "Here I am, my son." He said, "The fire and the wood are here, but where is the lamb for a burnt offering?" ⁸Abraham said, "God himself will provide the lamb for a burnt offering, my son." So the two of them walked on together.

9 When they came to the place that God had shown him, Abraham built an altar there and laid the wood in order. He bound his son Isaac, and laid him on the altar, on top of the wood. ¹⁰Then Abraham reached out his hand and took the knife to kill*ª* his son. ¹¹But the angel of the Lord called to him from heaven, and said, "Abraham, Abraham!" And he said, "Here I am." ¹²He said, "Do not lay your hand on the boy or do anything to him; for now I know that you fear God, since you have not withheld your son, your only son, from me." ¹³And Abraham looked up and saw a ram, caught in a thicket by its horns. Abraham went and took the ram and offered it up as a burnt offering instead of his son. ¹⁴So Abraham called that place "The Lord

Love—© Rosa Thomas, 16

will provide";*ᵇ* as it is said to this day, "On the mount of the Lord it shall be provided."*ᶜ*

15 The angel of the Lord called to Abraham a second time from heaven, ¹⁶and said, "By myself I have sworn, says the Lord: Because you have done this, and have not withheld your son, your only son, ¹⁷I will indeed bless you, and I will make your offspring as numerous as the stars of heaven and as the sand that is on the seashore. And your offspring shall possess the gate of their enemies, ¹⁸and by your offspring shall all the nations of the earth gain blessing for themselves, because you have obeyed my voice." ¹⁹So Abraham returned to his young men, and they arose and went together to Beer-sheba; and Abraham lived at Beer-sheba.

The Children of Nahor

20 Now after these things it was told Abraham, "Milcah also has borne children, to your brother Nahor: ²¹Uz the firstborn, Buz his brother, Kemuel the father of Aram, ²²Chesed, Hazo, Pildash, Jidlaph, and Bethuel." ²³Bethuel became the father of Rebekah. These eight Milcah bore to Nahor, Abraham's brother. ²⁴Moreover, his concubine, whose name was Reumah, bore Tebah, Gaham, Tahash, and Maacah.

23 Sarah's Death and Burial

Sarah lived one hundred twenty-seven years; this was the length of Sarah's life. ²And Sarah died at Kiriath-arba (that is, Hebron) in the land of Canaan; and Abraham went in to mourn for Sarah and to weep for her. ³Abraham rose up from beside his dead, and said to the Hittites, ⁴"I am a stranger and an alien residing among you; give me property among you for a burying place, so that I may bury my dead out of my sight." ⁵The Hittites answered Abraham, ⁶"Hear us, my lord; you are a mighty prince among us. Bury your dead in the choicest of our burial places; none of us will withhold from you any burial ground for burying your dead." ⁷Abraham rose and bowed to the Hittites, the people of the land. ⁸He said to them, "If you are willing that I should bury my dead out of my sight, hear me, and entreat for me Ephron son of Zohar, ⁹so that he may give me the cave of Machpelah, which he owns; it is at the end of his field. For the full price let him give it to me in your presence as a possession for a burying place." ¹⁰Now Ephron was sitting among the Hittites; and Ephron the Hittite answered Abraham in the hearing of the Hittites, of all who went in at the gate of his city, ¹¹"No,

a Or *to slaughter* *b* Or *will see;* Heb traditionally transliterated *Jehovah Jireh* *c* Or *he shall be seen* my lord, hear me; I give you the field, and I give you the cave that is in it; in the presence of my people I give it to you; bury your dead." ¹²Then Abraham bowed down before the people of the land. ¹³He said to Ephron in the hearing of the people of the land, "If you only will listen to me! I will give the price of the field; accept it from me, so that I may bury my dead there." ¹⁴Ephron answered Abraham, ¹⁵"My lord, listen to me; a piece of land worth four hundred shekels of silver—what is that between you and me? Bury your dead." ¹⁶Abraham agreed with Ephron; and Abraham weighed out for Ephron the silver that he had named in the hearing of the Hittites, four hundred shekels of silver, according to the weights current among the merchants.

17 So the field of Ephron in Machpelah, which was to the east of Mamre, the field with the cave that was in it and all the trees that were in the field, throughout its whole area, passed ¹⁸to Abraham as a possession in the presence of the Hittites, in the presence of all who went in at the gate of his city. ¹⁹After this, Abraham buried Sarah his wife in the cave of the field of Machpelah facing Mamre (that is, Hebron) in the land of Canaan. ²⁰The field and the cave that is in it passed from the Hittites into Abraham's possession as a burying place.

24 The Marriage of Isaac and Rebekah

Now Abraham was old, well advanced in years; and the LORD had blessed Abraham in all things. ²Abraham said to his servant, the oldest of his house, who had charge of all that he had, "Put your hand under my thigh ³and I will make you swear by the LORD, the God of heaven and earth, that you will not get a wife for my son from the daughters of the Canaanites, among whom I live, ⁴but will go to my country and to my kindred and get a wife for my son Isaac." ⁵The servant said to him, "Perhaps the woman may not be willing to follow me to this land; must I then take your son back to the land from which you came?" ⁶Abraham said to him, "See to it that you do not take my son back there. ⁷The LORD, the God of heaven, who took me from my father's house and from the land of my birth, and who spoke to me and swore to me, 'To your offspring I will give this land,' he will send his angel before you, and you shall take a wife for my son from there. ⁸But if the woman is not willing to follow you, then you will be free from this oath of mine; only you must not take my son back there." ⁹So the servant put his hand under the thigh of Abraham his master and swore to him concerning this matter.

10 Then the servant took ten of his master's camels and departed, taking all kinds of choice gifts from his master; and he set out and went to Aram-naharaim, to the city of Nahor. ¹¹He made the camels kneel down outside the city by the well of water; it was toward evening, the time when women go out to draw water. ¹²And he said, "O LORD, God of my master Abraham, please grant me success today and show steadfast love to my master Abraham. ¹³I am standing here by the spring of water, and the daughters of the townspeople are coming out to draw water. ¹⁴Let the girl to whom I shall say, 'Please offer your jar that I may drink,' and who shall say, 'Drink, and I will water your camels'—let her be the one whom you have appointed for your servant Isaac. By this I shall know that you have shown steadfast love to my master."

15 Before he had finished speaking, there was Rebekah, who was born to Bethuel son of Milcah, the wife of Nahor, Abraham's brother, coming out with her water jar on her shoulder. ¹⁶The girl was very fair to look upon, a virgin, whom no man had known. She went down to the spring, filled her jar, and came up. ¹⁷Then the servant ran to meet her and said, "Please let me sip a little water from your jar." ¹⁸"Drink, my lord," she said, and quickly lowered her jar upon her hand and gave him a drink. ¹⁹When she had finished giving him a drink, she said, "I will draw for your camels also, until they have finished drinking." ²⁰So she quickly emptied her jar into the trough and ran again to the well to draw, and she drew for all his camels. ²¹The man gazed at her in silence to learn whether or not the LORD had made his journey successful.

22 When the camels had finished drinking, the man took a gold nose-ring weighing a half shekel, and two bracelets for her arms weighing ten gold shekels, ²³and said, "Tell me whose daughter you are. Is there room in your father's house for us to spend the night?" ²⁴She said to him, "I am the daughter of Bethuel son of Milcah, whom she bore to Nahor." ²⁵She added, "We have plenty of straw and fodder and a place to spend the night." ²⁶The man bowed his head and worshiped the LORD ²⁷and said, "Blessed be the LORD, the God of my master Abraham, who has not forsaken his steadfast love and his faithfulness toward my master. As for me, the LORD has led me on the way to the house of my master's kin."

28 Then the girl ran and told her mother's household about these things. ²⁹Rebekah had a brother whose name was Laban; and Laban ran out to the man, to the spring. ³⁰As soon as he had seen the nose-ring, and the bracelets on his sister's arms, and when he heard the words of his sister Rebekah, "Thus the man spoke to

me," he went to the man; and there he was, standing by the camels at the spring. [31]He said, "Come in, O blessed of the LORD. Why do you stand outside when I have prepared the house and a place for the camels?" [32]So the man came into the house; and Laban unloaded the camels, and gave him straw and fodder for the camels, and water to wash his feet and the feet of the men who were with him. [33]Then food was set before him to eat; but he said, "I will not eat until I have told my errand." He said, "Speak on."

[34] So he said, "I am Abraham's servant. [35]The LORD has greatly blessed my master, and he has become wealthy; he has given him flocks and herds, silver and gold, male and female slaves, camels and donkeys. [36]And Sarah my master's wife bore a son to my master when she was old; and he has given him all that he has. [37]My master made me swear, saying, 'You shall not take a wife for my son from the daughters of the Canaanites, in whose land I live; [38]but you shall go to my father's house, to my kindred, and get a wife for my son.' [39]I said to my master, 'Perhaps the woman will not follow me.' [40]But he said to me, 'The LORD, before whom I walk, will send his angel with you and make your way successful. You shall get a wife for my son from my kindred, from my father's house. [41]Then you will be free from my oath, when you come to my kindred; even if they will not give her to you, you will be free from my oath.'

[42] "I came today to the spring, and said, 'O LORD, the God of my master Abraham, if now you will only make successful the way I am going! [43]I am standing here by the spring of water; let the young woman who comes out to draw, to whom I shall say, "Please give me a little water from your jar to drink," [44]and who will say to me, "Drink, and I will draw for your camels also"—let her be the woman whom the LORD has appointed for my master's son.'

[45] "Before I had finished speaking in my heart, there was Rebekah coming out with her water jar on her shoulder; and she went down to the spring, and drew. I said to her, 'Please let me drink.' [46]She quickly let down her jar from her shoulder, and said, 'Drink, and I will also water your camels.' So I drank, and she also watered the camels. [47]Then I asked her, 'Whose daughter are you?' She said, 'The daughter of Bethuel, Nahor's son, whom Milcah bore to him.' So I put the ring on her nose, and the bracelets on her arms. [48]Then I bowed my head and worshiped the LORD, and blessed the LORD, the God of my master Abraham, who had led me by the right way to obtain the daughter of my master's kinsman for his son. [49]Now then, if you will deal loyally and truly with my master, tell me; and if not, tell me, so that I may turn either to the right hand or to the left."

[50] Then Laban and Bethuel answered, "The thing comes from the LORD; we cannot speak to you anything bad or good. [51]Look, Rebekah is before you, take her and go, and let her be the wife of your master's son, as the LORD has spoken."

[52] When Abraham's servant heard their words, he bowed himself to the ground before the LORD. [53]And the servant brought out jewelry of silver and of gold, and garments, and gave them to Rebekah; he also gave to her brother and to her mother costly ornaments. [54]Then he and the men who were with him ate and drank, and they spent the night there. When they rose in the morning, he said, "Send me back to my master." [55]Her brother and her mother said, "Let the girl remain with us a while, at least ten days; after that she may go." [56]But he said to them, "Do not delay me, since the LORD has made my journey successful; let me go that I may go to my master." [57]They said, "We will call the girl, and ask her." [58]And they called Rebekah, and said to her, "Will you go with this man?" She said, "I will." [59]So they sent away their sister Rebekah and her nurse along with Abraham's servant and his men. [60]And they blessed Rebekah and said to her,

"May you, our sister, become
thousands of myriads;
may your offspring gain possession
of the gates of their foes."

[61]Then Rebekah and her maids rose up, mounted the camels, and followed the man; thus the servant took Rebekah, and went his way.

[62] Now Isaac had come from[a] Beer-lahai-roi, and was settled in the Negeb. [63]Isaac went out in the evening to walk[b] in the field; and looking up, he saw camels coming. [64]And Rebekah looked up, and when she saw Isaac, she slipped quickly from the camel, [65]and said to the servant, "Who is the man over there, walking in the field to meet us?" The servant said, "It is my master." So she took her veil and covered herself. [66]And the servant told Isaac all the things that he had done. [67]Then Isaac brought her into his mother Sarah's tent. He took Rebekah, and she became his wife; and he loved her. So Isaac was comforted after his mother's death.

---

a Syr Tg: Heb *from coming to* *b* Meaning of Heb word is uncertain

25 Abraham Marries Keturah

Abraham took another wife, whose name was Keturah. ²She bore him Zimran, Jokshan, Medan, Midian, Ishbak, and Shuah. ³Jokshan was the father of Sheba and Dedan. The sons of Dedan were Asshurim, Letushim, and Leummim. ⁴The sons of Midian were Ephah, Epher, Hanoch, Abida, and Eldaah. All these were the children of Keturah. ⁵Abraham gave all he had to Isaac. ⁶But to the sons of his concubines Abraham gave gifts, while he was still living, and he sent them away from his son Isaac, eastward to the east country.

The Death of Abraham

7 This is the length of Abraham's life, one hundred seventy-five years. ⁸Abraham breathed his last and died in a good old age, an old man and full of years, and was gathered to his people. ⁹His sons Isaac and Ishmael buried him in the cave of Machpelah, in the field of Ephron son of Zohar the Hittite, east of Mamre, ¹⁰the field that Abraham purchased from the Hittites. There Abraham was buried, with his wife Sarah. ¹¹After the death of Abraham God blessed his son Isaac. And Isaac settled at Beer-lahai-roi.

Ishmael's Descendants

12 These are the descendants of Ishmael, Abraham's son, whom Hagar the Egyptian, Sarah's slave-girl, bore to Abraham. ¹³These are the names of the sons of Ishmael, named in the order of their birth: Nebaioth, the firstborn of Ishmael; and Kedar, Adbeel, Mibsam, ¹⁴Mishma, Dumah, Massa, ¹⁵Hadad, Tema, Jetur, Naphish, and Kedemah. ¹⁶These are the sons of Ishmael and these are their names, by their villages and by their encampments, twelve princes according to their tribes. ¹⁷(This is the length of the life of Ishmael, one hundred thirty-seven years; he breathed his last and died, and was gathered to his people.) ¹⁸They settled from Havilah to Shur, which is opposite Egypt in the direction of Assyria; he settled down*ᵃ* alongside of*ᵇ* all his people.

The Birth and Youth of Esau and Jacob

19 These are the descendants of Isaac, Abraham's son: Abraham was the father of Isaac, ²⁰and Isaac was forty years old when he married Rebekah, daughter of Bethuel the Aramean of Paddan-aram, sister of Laban the Aramean. ²¹Isaac prayed to the LORD for his wife, because she was barren; and the LORD granted his prayer, and his wife Rebekah conceived. ²²The children struggled together within her; and she said, "If it is to be this way, why do I live?"*ᶜ* So she went to inquire of the LORD. ²³And the LORD said to her,

"Two nations are in your womb,
  and two peoples born of you shall be
    divided;
the one shall be stronger than the other,
  the elder shall serve the younger."

²⁴When her time to give birth was at hand, there were twins in her womb. ²⁵The first came out red, all his body like a hairy mantle; so they named him Esau. ²⁶Afterward his brother came out, with his hand gripping Esau's heel; so he was named Jacob.*ᵈ* Isaac was sixty years old when she bore them.

27 When the boys grew up, Esau was a skillful hunter, a man of the field, while Jacob was a quiet man, living in tents. ²⁸Isaac loved Esau, because he was fond of game; but Rebekah loved Jacob.

Esau Sells His Birthright

29 Once when Jacob was cooking a stew, Esau came in from the field, and he was famished. ³⁰Esau said to Jacob, "Let me eat some of that red stuff, for I am famished!" (Therefore he was called Edom.*ᵉ*) ³¹Jacob said, "First sell me your birthright." ³²Esau said, "I am about to die; of what use is a birthright to me?" ³³Jacob said, "Swear to me first."*ᶠ* So he swore to him, and sold his birthright to Jacob. ³⁴Then Jacob gave Esau bread and lentil stew, and he ate and drank, and rose and went his way. Thus Esau despised his birthright.

26 Isaac and Abimelech

Now there was a famine in the land, besides the former famine that had occurred in the days of Abraham. And Isaac went to Gerar, to King Abimelech of the Philistines. ²The LORD appeared to Isaac*ᵍ* and said, "Do not go down to Egypt; settle in the land that I shall show you. ³Reside in this land as an alien, and I will be with you, and will bless you; for to you and to your descendants I will give all these lands, and I will fulfill the oath that I swore to your father Abraham. ⁴I will make your offspring as numerous as the stars of heaven, and will give to your offspring all these lands; and all the nations of the earth shall gain blessing for themselves through your offspring, ⁵because Abraham obeyed my voice and kept my charge, my commandments, my statutes, and my laws."

6 So Isaac settled in Gerar. ⁷When the men

---

a Heb *he fell* *b* Or *down in opposition to* *c* Syr: Meaning of Heb uncertain *d* That is *He takes by the heel* or *He supplants* *e* That is *Red*
f Heb *today* *g* Heb *him*

of the place asked him about his wife, he said, "She is my sister"; for he was afraid to say, "My wife," thinking, "or else the men of the place might kill me for the sake of Rebekah, because she is attractive in appearance." 8When Isaac had been there a long time, King Abimelech of the Philistines looked out of a window and saw him fondling his wife Rebekah. 9So Abimelech called for Isaac, and said, "So she is your wife! Why then did you say, 'She is my sister'?" Isaac said to him, "Because I thought I might die because of her." 10Abimelech said, "What is this you have done to us? One of the people might easily have lain with your wife, and you would have brought guilt upon us." 11So Abimelech warned all the people, saying, "Whoever touches this man or his wife shall be put to death."

12 Isaac sowed seed in that land, and in the same year reaped a hundredfold. The LORD blessed him, 13and the man became rich; he prospered more and more until he became very wealthy. 14He had possessions of flocks and herds, and a great household, so that the Philistines envied him. 15(Now the Philistines had stopped up and filled with earth all the wells that his father's servants had dug in the days of his father Abraham.) 16And Abimelech said to Isaac, "Go away from us; you have become too powerful for us."

17 So Isaac departed from there and camped in the valley of Gerar and settled there. 18Isaac dug again the wells of water that had been dug in the days of his father Abraham; for the Philistines had stopped them up after the death of Abraham; and he gave them the names that his father had given them. 19But when Isaac's servants dug in the valley and found there a well of spring water, 20the herders of Gerar quarreled with Isaac's herders, saying, "The water is ours." So he called the well Esek,ᵃ because they contended with him. 21Then they dug another well, and they quarreled over that one also; so he called it Sitnah.ᵇ 22He moved from there and dug another well, and they did not quarrel over

it; so he called it Rehoboth,ᶜ saying, "Now the LORD has made room for us, and we shall be fruitful in the land."

23 From there he went up to Beer-she-ba. 24And that very night the LORD appeared to him and said, "I am the God of your father Abraham; do not be afraid, for I am with you and will bless you and make your offspring numerous for my servant Abraham's sake." 25So he built an altar there, called on the name of the LORD, and pitched his tent there. And there Isaac's servants dug a well.

26 Then Abimelech went to him from Gerar, with Ahuzzath his adviser and Phicol the commander of his army. 27Isaac said to them, "Why have you come to me, seeing that you hate me and have sent me away from you?" 28They said, "We see plainly that the LORD has been with you; so we say, let there be an oath between you and us, and let us make a covenant with you 29so that you will do us no harm, just as we have not touched you and have done to you nothing but good and have sent you away in peace. You are now the blessed of the LORD." 30So he made them a feast, and they ate and drank. 31In the morning they rose early and exchanged oaths; and Isaac set them on their way, and they departed from him in peace. 32That same day Isaac's servants came and told him about the well that they had dug, and said to him, "We have found water!" 33He called it Shibah;ᵈ therefore the name of the city is Beer-shebaᵉ to this day.

Esau's Hittite Wives

34 When Esau was forty years old, he married Judith daughter of Beeri the Hittite, and Basemath daughter of Elon the Hittite; 35and they made life bitter for Isaac and Rebekah.

27 Isaac Blesses Jacob

When Isaac was old and his eyes were dim so that he could not see, he called his elder son Esau and said to him, "My son"; and he answered, "Here I am." 2He said, "See, I am old; I do not know the day of my death. 3Now then, take your weapons, your quiver and your bow, and go out to the field, and hunt game for me. 4Then prepare for me savory food, such as I like, and bring it to me to eat, so that I may bless you before I die."

5 Now Rebekah was listening when Isaac spoke to his son Esau. So when Esau went to the field to hunt for game and bring it, 6Rebekah said to her son Jacob, "I heard your father say to your brother Esau, 7'Bring me game, and pre-

---

ᵃ That is Contention ᵇ That is Enmity ᶜ That is Broad places or Room ᵈ A word resembling the word for oath ᵉ That is Well of the oath or Well of seven pare for me savory food to eat, that I may bless you before the LORD before I die.' ⁸Now therefore, my son, obey my word as I command you. ⁹Go to the flock, and get me two choice kids, so that I may prepare from them savory food for your father, such as he likes; ¹⁰and you shall take it to your father to eat, so that he may bless you before he dies." ¹¹But Jacob said to his mother Rebekah, "Look, my brother Esau is a hairy man, and I am a man of smooth skin. ¹²Perhaps my father will feel me, and I shall seem to be mocking him, and bring a curse on myself and not a blessing." ¹³His mother said to him, "Let your curse be on me, my son; only obey my word, and go, get them for me." ¹⁴So he went and got them and brought them to his mother; and his mother prepared savory food, such as his father loved. ¹⁵Then Rebekah took the best garments of her elder son Esau, which were with her in the house, and put them on her younger son Jacob; ¹⁶and she put the skins of the kids on his hands and on the smooth part of his neck. ¹⁷Then she handed the savory food, and the bread that she had prepared, to her son Jacob.

18 So he went in to his father, and said, "My father"; and he said, "Here I am; who are you, my son?" ¹⁹Jacob said to his father, "I am Esau your firstborn. I have done as you told me; now sit up and eat of my game, so that you may bless me." ²⁰But Isaac said to his son, "How is it that you have found it so quickly, my son?" He answered, "Because the LORD your God granted me success." ²¹Then Isaac said to Jacob, "Come near, that I may feel you, my son, to know whether you are really my son Esau or not." ²²So Jacob went up to his father Isaac, who felt him and said, "The voice is Jacob's voice, but the hands are the hands of Esau." ²³He did not recognize him, because his hands were hairy like his brother Esau's hands; so he blessed him. ²⁴He said, "Are you really my son Esau?" He answered, "I am." ²⁵Then he said, "Bring it to me, that I may eat of my son's game and bless you." So he brought it to him, and he ate; and he brought him wine, and he drank. ²⁶Then his father Isaac said to him, "Come near and kiss me, my son." ²⁷So he came near and kissed him; and he smelled the smell of his garments, and blessed him, and said,

"Ah, the smell of my son
    is like the smell of a field that the LORD
    has blessed.
²⁸ May God give you of the dew of heaven,
    and of the fatness of the earth,
    and plenty of grain and wine.
²⁹ Let peoples serve you,

and nations bow down to you.
Be lord over your brothers,
    and may your mother's sons bow down
    to you.
Cursed be everyone who curses you,
    and blessed be everyone who blesses
    you!"

Esau's Lost Blessing

30 As soon as Isaac had finished blessing Jacob, when Jacob had scarcely gone out from the presence of his father Isaac, his brother Esau came in from his hunting. ³¹He also prepared savory food, and brought it to his father. And he said to his father, "Let my father sit up and eat of his son's game, so that you may bless me." ³²His father Isaac said to him, "Who are you?" He answered, "I am your firstborn son, Esau." ³³Then Isaac trembled violently, and said, "Who was it then that hunted game and brought it to me, and I ate it all[a] before you came, and I have blessed him?—yes, and blessed he shall be!" ³⁴When Esau heard his father's words, he cried out with an exceedingly great and bitter cry, and said to his father, "Bless me, me also, father!" ³⁵But he said, "Your brother came deceitfully, and he has taken away your blessing." ³⁶Esau said, "Is he not rightly named Jacob?[b] For he has supplanted me these two times. He took away my birthright; and look, now he has taken away my blessing." Then he said, "Have you not reserved a blessing for me?" ³⁷Isaac answered Esau, "I have already made him your lord, and I have given him all his brothers as servants, and with grain and wine I have sustained him. What then can I do for you, my son?" ³⁸Esau said to his father, "Have you only one blessing, father? Bless me, me also, father!" And Esau lifted up his voice and wept.

39 Then his father Isaac answered him:
"See, away from[c] the fatness of the earth
    shall your home be,
    and away from[d] the dew of heaven on
    high.
⁴⁰ By your sword you shall live,
    and you shall serve your brother;
but when you break loose,[e]
    you shall break his yoke from your neck."

Jacob Escapes Esau's Fury

41 Now Esau hated Jacob because of the blessing with which his father had blessed him, and Esau said to himself, "The days of mourning for my father are approaching; then I will kill my brother Jacob." ⁴²But the words of her elder son Esau were told to Rebekah; so she sent and

a Cn: Heb of all b That is He supplants or He takes by the heel c Or See, of d Or and of e Meaning of Heb uncertain called her younger son Jacob and said to him, "Your brother Esau is consoling himself by planning to kill you. ⁴³Now therefore, my son, obey my voice; flee at once to my brother Laban in Haran, ⁴⁴and stay with him a while, until your brother's fury turns away— ⁴⁵until your brother's anger against you turns away, and he forgets what you have done to him; then I will send, and bring you back from there. Why should I lose both of you in one day?"

46 Then Rebekah said to Isaac, "I am weary of my life because of the Hittite women. If Jacob marries one of the Hittite women such as these, one of the women of the land, what good will my life be to me?"

28 Then Isaac called Jacob and blessed him, and charged him, "You shall not marry one of the Canaanite women. ²Go at once to Paddan-aram to the house of Bethuel, your mother's father; and take as wife from there one of the daughters of Laban, your mother's brother. ³May God Almighty*ᵃ* bless you and make you fruitful and numerous, that you may become a company of peoples. ⁴May he give to you the blessing of Abraham, to you and to your offspring with you, so that you may take possession of the land where you now live as an alien—land that God gave to Abraham." ⁵Thus Isaac sent Jacob away; and he went to Paddan-aram, to Laban son of Bethuel the Aramean, the brother of Rebekah, Jacob's and Esau's mother.

Esau Marries Ishmael's Daughter

6 Now Esau saw that Isaac had blessed Jacob and sent him away to Paddan-aram to take a wife from there, and that as he blessed him he charged him, "You shall not marry one of the Canaanite women," ⁷and that Jacob had obeyed his father and his mother and gone to Paddan-aram. ⁸So when Esau saw that the Canaanite women did not please his father Isaac, ⁹Esau went to Ishmael and took Mahalath daughter of Abraham's son Ishmael, and sister of Nebaioth, to be his wife in addition to the wives he had.

Jacob's Dream at Bethel

10 Jacob left Beer-sheba and went toward Haran. ¹¹He came to a certain place and stayed there for the night, because the sun had set. Taking one of the stones of the place, he put it under his head and lay down in that place. ¹²And he dreamed that there was a ladder*ᵇ* set up on the earth, the top of it reaching to heaven; and the angels of God were ascending and descending on it. ¹³And the Lord stood beside him*ᶜ* and said, "I am the Lord, the God of Abraham your father and the God of Isaac; the land on which you lie I will give to you and to your offspring; ¹⁴and your offspring shall be like the dust of the earth, and you shall spread abroad to the west and to the east and to the north and to the south; and all the families of the earth shall be blessed*ᵈ* in you and in your offspring. ¹⁵Know that I am with you and will keep you wherever you go, and will bring you back to this land; for I will not leave you until I have done what I have promised you." ¹⁶Then Jacob woke from his sleep and said, "Surely the Lord is in this place—and I did not know it!" ¹⁷And he was afraid, and said, "How awesome is this place! This is none other than the house of God, and this is the gate of heaven."

18 So Jacob rose early in the morning, and he took the stone that he had put under his head and set it up for a pillar and poured oil on the top of it. ¹⁹He called that place Bethel;*ᵉ* but the name of the city was Luz at the first. ²⁰Then Jacob made a vow, saying, "If God will be with me, and will keep me in this way that I go, and will give me bread to eat and clothing to wear, ²¹so that I come again to my father's house in peace, then the Lord shall be my God, ²²and this stone, which I have set up for a pillar, shall be God's house; and of all that you give me I will surely give one-tenth to you."

29 Jacob Meets Rachel
Then Jacob went on his journey, and came to the land of the people of the east. ²As he looked, he saw a well in the field and three flocks of sheep lying there beside it; for out of that well the flocks were watered. The stone on the well's mouth was large, ³and when all the flocks were gathered there, the shepherds would roll the stone from the mouth of the well, and water the sheep, and put the stone back in its place on the mouth of the well.

4 Jacob said to them, "My brothers, where do you come from?" They said, "We are from Haran." ⁵He said to them, "Do you know Laban son of Nahor?" They said, "We do." ⁶He said to them, "Is it well with him?" "Yes," they replied, "and here is his daughter Rachel, coming with the sheep." ⁷He said, "Look, it is still broad daylight; it is not time for the animals to be gathered together. Water the sheep, and go, pasture them." ⁸But they said, "We cannot until all the flocks are gathered together, and the stone is rolled from the mouth of the well; then we water the sheep."

9 While he was still speaking with them, Rachel came with her father's sheep; for she

---

a Traditional rendering of Heb *El Shaddai* *b* Or *stairway* or *ramp* *c* Or *stood above it* *d* Or *shall bless themselves* *e* That is *House of God* kept them. ¹⁰Now when Jacob saw Rachel, the daughter of his mother's brother Laban, and the sheep of his mother's brother Laban, Jacob went up and rolled the stone from the well's mouth, and watered the flock of his mother's brother Laban. ¹¹Then Jacob kissed Rachel, and wept aloud. ¹²And Jacob told Rachel that he was her father's kinsman, and that he was Rebekah's son; and she ran and told her father.

13 When Laban heard the news about his sister's son Jacob, he ran to meet him; he embraced him and kissed him, and brought him to his house. Jacob*ᵃ* told Laban all these things, ¹⁴and Laban said to him, "Surely you are my bone and my flesh!" And he stayed with him a month.

Jacob Marries Laban's Daughters

15 Then Laban said to Jacob, "Because you are my kinsman, should you therefore serve me for nothing? Tell me, what shall your wages be?" ¹⁶Now Laban had two daughters; the name of the elder was Leah, and the name of the younger was Rachel. ¹⁷Leah's eyes were lovely,ᵇ and Rachel was graceful and beautiful. ¹⁸Jacob loved Rachel; so he said, "I will serve you seven years for your younger daughter Rachel." ¹⁹Laban said, "It is better that I give her to you than that I should give her to any other man; stay with me." ²⁰So Jacob served seven

years for Rachel, and they seemed to him but a few days because of the love he had for her.

21 Then Jacob said to Laban, "Give me my wife that I may go in to her, for my time is completed." ²²So Laban gathered together all the people of the place, and made a feast. ²³But in the evening he took his daughter Leah and brought her to Jacob; and he went in to her. ²⁴(Laban gave his maid Zilpah to his daughter Leah to be her maid.) ²⁵When morning came, it was Leah! And Jacob said to Laban, "What is this you have done to me? Did I not serve with you for Rachel? Why then have you deceived me?" ²⁶Laban said, "This is not done in our country—giving the younger before the firstborn. ²⁷Complete the week of this one, and we will give you the other also in return for serving me another seven years." ²⁸Jacob did so, and completed her week; then Laban gave him his daughter Rachel as a wife. ²⁹(Laban gave his maid Bilhah to his daughter Rachel to be her maid.) ³⁰So Jacob went in to Rachel also, and he loved Rachel more than Leah. He served Labanᶜ for another seven years.

31 When the LORD saw that Leah was unloved, he opened her womb; but Rachel was barren. ³²Leah conceived and bore a son, and she named him Reuben;ᵈ for she said, "Because the LORD has looked on my affliction; surely now my husband will love me." ³³She conceived again and bore a son, and said, "Be-

a Heb He *b* Meaning of Heb uncertain *c* Heb him *d* That is *See, a son*

Grow—© Lexi Hiland, 16

said, "This time I will praise[c] the LORD"; therefore she named him Judah; then she ceased bearing.

30 When Rachel saw that she bore Jacob no children, she envied her sister; and she said to Jacob, "Give me children, or I shall die!" ²Jacob became very angry with Rachel and said, "Am I in the place of God, who has withheld from you the fruit of the womb?" ³Then she said, "Here is my maid Bilhah; go in to her, that she may bear upon my knees and that I too may have children through her." ⁴So she gave him her maid Bilhah as a wife; and Jacob went in to her. ⁵And Bilhah conceived and bore Jacob a son. ⁶Then Rachel said, "God has judged me, and has also heard my voice and given me a son"; therefore she named him Dan.[d] ⁷Rachel's maid Bilhah conceived again and bore Jacob a second son. ⁸Then Rachel said, "With mighty wrestlings I have wrestled[e] with my sister, and have prevailed"; so she named him Naphtali.

9 When Leah saw that she had ceased bearing children, she took her maid Zilpah and gave her to Jacob as a wife. ¹⁰Then Leah's maid Zilpah bore Jacob a son. ¹¹And Leah said, "Good fortune!" so she named him Gad.[f] ¹²Leah's maid Zilpah bore Jacob a second son. ¹³And Leah said, "Happy am I! For the women will call me happy"; so she named him Asher.[g]

14 In the days of wheat harvest Reuben went and found mandrakes in the field, and brought them to his mother Leah. Then Rachel said to Leah, "Please give me some of your son's mandrakes." ¹⁵But she said to her, "Is it a small matter that you have taken away my husband? Would you take away my son's mandrakes also?" Rachel said, "Then he may lie with you tonight for your son's mandrakes." ¹⁶When Jacob came from the field in the evening, Leah went out to meet him, and said, "You must come in to me; for I have hired you with my son's mandrakes." So he lay with her that night. ¹⁷And God heeded Leah, and she conceived and bore Jacob a fifth son. ¹⁸Leah said, "God has given me my hire[h] because I gave my maid to my husband"; so she named him Issachar. ¹⁹And Leah conceived again, and she bore Jacob a sixth son. ²⁰Then Leah said, "God has endowed me with a good dowry; now my husband will honor[i] me, because I have borne him six sons"; so she named him Zebulun. ²¹Afterwards she bore a daughter, and named her Dinah.

22 Then God remembered Rachel, and God heeded her and opened her womb. ²³She conceived and bore a son, and said, "God has taken away my reproach"; ²⁴and she named him

cause the LORD has heard[a] that I am hated, he has given me this son also"; and she named him Simeon. ³⁴Again she conceived and bore a son, and said, "Now this time my husband will be joined[b] to me, because I have borne him three sons"; therefore he was named Levi. ³⁵She conceived again and bore a son, and

a Heb shama b Heb lawah c Heb hodah d That is He judged e Heb niphtal f That is Fortune g That is Happy h Heb sakar i Heb zabal

Joseph,[a] saying, "May the LORD add to me another son!"

Jacob Prospers at Laban's Expense

25 When Rachel had borne Joseph, Jacob said to Laban, "Send me away, that I may go to my own home and country. [26]Give me my wives and my children for whom I have served you, and let me go; for you know very well the service I have given you." [27]But Laban said to him, "If you will allow me to say so, I have learned by divination that the LORD has blessed me because of you; [28]name your wages, and I will give it." [29]Jacob said to him, "You yourself know how I have served you, and how your cattle have fared with me. [30]For you had little before I came, and it has increased abundantly; and the LORD has blessed you wherever I turned. But now when shall I provide for my own household also?" [31]He said, "What shall I give you?" Jacob said, "You shall not give me anything; if you will do this for me, I will again feed your flock and keep it: [32]let me pass through all your flock today, removing from it every speckled and spotted sheep and every black lamb, and the spotted and speckled among the goats; and such shall be my wages. [33]So my honesty will answer for me later, when you come to look into my wages with you. Every one that is not speckled and spotted among the goats and black among the lambs, if found with me, shall be counted stolen." [34]Laban said, "Good! Let it be as you have said." [35]But that day Laban removed the male goats that were striped and spotted, and all the female goats that were speckled and spotted, every one that had white on it, and every lamb that was black, and put them in charge of his sons; [36]and he set a distance of three days' journey between himself and Jacob, while Jacob was pasturing the rest of Laban's flock.

37 Then Jacob took fresh rods of poplar and almond and plane, and peeled white streaks in them, exposing the white of the rods. [38]He set the rods that he had peeled in front of the flocks in the troughs, that is, the watering places, where the flocks came to drink. And since they bred when they came to drink, [39]the flocks bred in front of the rods, and so the flocks produced young that were striped, speckled, and spotted. [40]Jacob separated the lambs, and set the faces of the flocks toward the striped and the completely black animals in the flock of Laban; and he put his own droves apart, and did not put them with Laban's flock. [41]Whenever the stronger of the flock were breeding, Jacob laid the rods in the troughs before the eyes of the flock, that they might breed among the rods, [42]but for the feebler of the flock he did not lay them there; so the feebler were Laban's, and the stronger Jacob's. [43]Thus the man grew exceedingly rich, and had large flocks, and male and female slaves, and camels and donkeys.

31 Jacob Flees with Family and Flocks

Now Jacob heard that the sons of Laban were saying, "Jacob has taken all that was our father's; he has gained all this wealth from what belonged to our father." [2]And Jacob saw that Laban did not regard him as favorably as he did before. [3]Then the LORD said to Jacob, "Return to the land of your ancestors and to your kindred, and I will be with you." [4]So Jacob sent and called Rachel and Leah into the field where his flock was, [5]and said to them, "I see that your father does not regard me as favorably as he did before. But the God of my father has been with me. [6]You know that I have served your father with all my strength; [7]yet your father has cheated me and changed my wages ten times, but God did not permit him to harm me. [8]If he said, 'The speckled shall be your wages,' then all the flock bore speckled; and if he said, 'The striped shall be your wages,' then all the flock bore striped. [9]Thus God has taken away the livestock of your father, and given them to me.

10 "During the mating of the flock I once had a dream in which I looked up and saw that the male goats that leaped upon the flock were striped, speckled, and mottled. [11]Then the angel of God said to me in the dream, 'Jacob,' and I said, 'Here I am!' [12]And he said, 'Look up and see that all the goats that leap on the flock are striped, speckled, and mottled; for I have seen all that Laban is doing to you. [13]I am the God of Bethel,[b] where you anointed a pillar and made a vow to me. Now leave this land at once and return to the land of your birth.' " [14]Then Rachel and Leah answered him, "Is there any portion or inheritance left to us in our father's house? [15]Are we not regarded by him as foreigners? For he has sold us, and he has been using up the money given for us. [16]All the property that God has taken away from our father belongs to us and to our children; now then, do whatever God has said to you."

17 So Jacob arose, and set his children and his wives on camels; [18]and he drove away all his livestock, all the property that he had gained, the livestock in his possession that he had acquired in Paddan-aram, to go to his father Isaac in the land of Canaan.

19 Now Laban had gone to shear his sheep,

a That is He adds   b Cn: Meaning of Heb uncertain

and Rachel stole her father's household gods. [20]And Jacob deceived Laban the Aramean, in that he did not tell him that he intended to flee. [21]So he fled with all that he had; starting out he crossed the Euphrates,*a* and set his face toward the hill country of Gilead.

Laban Overtakes Jacob

22 On the third day Laban was told that Jacob had fled. [23]So he took his kinsfolk with him and pursued him for seven days until he caught up with him in the hill country of Gilead. [24]But God came to Laban the Aramean in a dream by night, and said to him, "Take heed that you say not a word to Jacob, either good or bad."

25 Laban overtook Jacob. Now Jacob had pitched his tent in the hill country, and Laban with his kinsfolk camped in the hill country of Gilead. [26]Laban said to Jacob, "What have you done? You have deceived me, and carried away my daughters like captives of the sword. [27]Why did you flee secretly and deceive me and not tell me? I would have sent you away with mirth and songs, with tambourine and lyre. [28]And why did you not permit me to kiss my sons and my daughters farewell? What you have done is foolish. [29]It is in my power to do you harm; but the God of your father spoke to me last night, saying, 'Take heed that you speak to Jacob neither good nor bad.' [30]Even though you had to go because you longed greatly for your father's house, why did you steal my gods?" [31]Jacob answered Laban, "Because I was afraid, for I thought that you would take your daughters from me by force. [32]But anyone with whom you find your gods shall not live. In the presence of our kinsfolk, point out what I have that is yours, and take it." Now Jacob did not know that Rachel had stolen the gods.*b*

33 So Laban went into Jacob's tent, and into Leah's tent, and into the tent of the two maids, but he did not find them. And he went out of Leah's tent, and entered Rachel's. [34]Now Rachel had taken the household gods and put them in the camel's saddle, and sat on them. Laban felt all about in the tent, but did not find them. [35]And she said to her father, "Let not my lord be angry that I cannot rise before you, for the way of women is upon me." So he searched, but did not find the household gods.

36 Then Jacob became angry, and upbraided Laban. Jacob said to Laban, "What is my offense? What is my sin, that you have hotly pursued me? [37]Although you have felt about through all my goods, what have you found of all your household goods? Set it here before my kinsfolk and your kinsfolk, so that they may decide between us two. [38]These twenty years I have been with you; your ewes and your female goats have not miscarried, and I have not eaten the rams of your flocks. [39]That which was torn by wild beasts I did not bring to you; I bore the loss of it myself; of my hand you required it, whether stolen by day or stolen by night. [40]It was like this with me: by day the heat consumed me, and the cold by night, and my sleep fled from my eyes. [41]These twenty years I have been in your house; I served you fourteen years for your two daughters, and six years for your flock, and you have changed my wages ten times. [42]If the God of my father, the God of Abraham and the Fear*c* of Isaac, had not been on my side, surely now you would have sent me away empty-handed. God saw my affliction and the labor of my hands, and rebuked you last night."

Laban and Jacob Make a Covenant

43 Then Laban answered and said to Jacob, "The daughters are my daughters, the children are my children, the flocks are my flocks, and all that you see is mine. But what can I do today about these daughters of mine, or about their children whom they have borne? [44]Come now, let us make a covenant, you and I; and let it be a witness between you and me." [45]So Jacob took a stone, and set it up as a pillar. [46]And Jacob said to his kinsfolk, "Gather stones," and they took stones, and made a heap; and they ate there by the heap. [47]Laban called it Jegar-sahadutha:*d* but Jacob called it Galeed.*e* [48]Laban said, "This heap is a witness between you and me today." Therefore he called it Galeed, [49]and the pillar*f* Mizpah,*g* for he said, "The LORD watch between you and me, when we are absent one from the other. [50]If you ill-treat my daughters, or if you take wives in addition to my daughters, though no one else is with us, remember that God is witness between you and me."

51 Then Laban said to Jacob, "See this heap and see the pillar, which I have set between you and me. [52]This heap is a witness, and the pillar is a witness, that I will not pass beyond this heap to you, and you will not pass beyond this heap and this pillar to me, for harm. [53]May the God of Abraham and the God of Nahor"—the God of their father—"judge between us." So Jacob swore by the Fear*c* of his father Isaac, [54]and Jacob offered a sacrifice on the height and called his kinsfolk to eat bread; and they ate bread and tarried all night in the hill country.

[55]*h* Early in the morning Laban rose up, and

---

a Heb *the river* *b* Heb *them* *c* Meaning of Heb uncertain *d* In Aramaic *The heap of witness* *e* In Hebrew *The heap of witness* *f* Compare Sam: MT lacks *the pillar* *g* That is *Watchpost* *h* Ch 32.1 in Heb kissed his grandchildren and his daughters and blessed them; then he departed and returned home.

32 Jacob went on his way and the angels of God met him; [2]and when Jacob saw them he said, "This is God's camp!" So he called that place Mahanaim.[a]

Jacob Sends Presents to Appease Esau

3 Jacob sent messengers before him to his brother Esau in the land of Seir, the country of Edom, [4]instructing them, "Thus you shall say to my lord Esau: Thus says your servant Jacob, 'I have lived with Laban as an alien, and stayed until now; [5]and I have oxen, donkeys, flocks, male and female slaves; and I have sent to tell my lord, in order that I may find favor in your sight.' "

6 The messengers returned to Jacob, saying, "We came to your brother Esau, and he is coming to meet you, and four hundred men are with him." [7]Then Jacob was greatly afraid and distressed; and he divided the people that were with him, and the flocks and herds and camels, into two companies, [8]thinking, "If Esau comes to the one company and destroys it, then the company that is left will escape."

9 And Jacob said, "O God of my father Abraham and God of my father Isaac, O LORD who said to me, 'Return to your country and to your kindred, and I will do you good,' [10]I am not worthy of the least of all the steadfast love and all the faithfulness that you have shown to your servant, for with only my staff I crossed this Jordan; and now I have become two companies. [11]Deliver me, please, from the hand of my brother, from the hand of Esau, for I am afraid of him; he may come and kill us all, the mothers with the children. [12]Yet you have said, 'I will surely do you good, and make your offspring as the sand of the sea, which cannot be counted because of their number.' "

13 So he spent that night there, and from what he had with him he took a present for his brother Esau, [14]two hundred female goats and twenty male goats, two hundred ewes and twenty rams, [15]thirty milch camels and their colts, forty cows and ten bulls, twenty female donkeys and ten male donkeys. [16]These he delivered into the hand of his servants, every drove by itself, and said to his servants, "Pass on ahead of me, and put a space between drove and drove." [17]He instructed the foremost, "When Esau my brother meets you, and asks you, 'To whom do you belong? Where are you going? And whose are these ahead of you?' [18]then you shall say, 'They belong to your ser-

a Here taken to mean *Two camps*

REAL QUESTIONS

I used to have a really strong faith, but now I wonder sometimes if God really cares or if God even exists at all. What do I do with these doubts?

It feels good to have the answers—to be confident, assured, ready for anything. And if we *don't* have an answer, we can find out nearly anything we want to know instantly, at the click of a mouse.

But even though we affirm our belief at every Mass during the Creed, some things—like faith—can't be so easily explained or instantly summarized. We all have doubts. And sometimes when we search for answers, the ones we find just don't make sense.

Let's just admit it. Sometimes our grasp on our faith feels shaky at best. Sometimes we followers of Christ feel a lot like Thomas, who famously declared, "Unless I see the mark of the nails in his hands, and put my finger in the mark of the nails and my hand in his side, I will not believe" (John 20.25). On the outside we're smiling and confident, but on the inside we're desperate for proof.

But is seeing always believing? What would it really take to make your doubts disappear? Even if you had the answers, would it be enough to help you cross the bridge of doubt toward belief? Are your doubts genuine, or are they a way of keeping you at a comfortable distance from the risky, courageous way of living Jesus wants from you? Can you believe even in the middle of doubt? Can you say along with a man whose faith was wavering, "I believe; help my unbelief!" (Mark 9.24)?

Find some Creative Space in this Bible and write your thoughts on these issues, maybe adding some real questions of your own. Then explore more in the verses below, or talk to someone about your real questions.

(Want to explore more? Read Judges 6–7; Mark 9.14–29; John 20.24–29; and 1 Corinthians 1.18–25; 3.18–19.)

vant Jacob; they are a present sent to my lord Esau; and moreover he is behind us.'" [19]He likewise instructed the second and the third and all who followed the droves, "You shall say the same thing to Esau when you meet him, [20]and you shall say, 'Moreover your servant Jacob is behind us.'" For he thought, "I may appease him with the present that goes ahead of me, and afterwards I shall see his face; perhaps he will accept me." [21]So the present passed on ahead of him; and he himself spent that night in the camp.

Jacob Wrestles at Peniel

22 The same night he got up and took his two wives, his two maids, and his eleven children, and crossed the ford of the Jabbok. [23]He took them and sent them across the stream, and likewise everything that he had. [24]Jacob was left alone; and a man wrestled with him until daybreak. [25]When the man saw that he did not prevail against Jacob, he struck him on the hip socket; and Jacob's hip was put out of joint as he wrestled with him. [26]Then he said, "Let me go, for the day is breaking." But Jacob said, "I will not let you go, unless you bless me." [27]So he said to him, "What is your name?" And he said, "Jacob." [28]Then the man[a] said, "You shall no longer be called Jacob, but Israel,[b] for you have striven with God and with humans,[c] and have prevailed." [29]Then Jacob asked him, "Please tell me your name." But he said, "Why is it that you ask my name?" And there he blessed him. [30]So Jacob called the place Peniel,[d] saying, "For I have seen God face to face, and yet my life is preserved." [31]The sun rose upon him as he passed Penuel, limping because of his hip. [32]Therefore to this day the Israelites do not eat the thigh muscle that is on the hip socket, because he struck Jacob on the hip socket at the thigh muscle.

33 Jacob and Esau Meet

Now Jacob looked up and saw Esau coming, and four hundred men with him. So he divided the children among Leah and Rachel and the two maids. [2]He put the maids with their children in front, then Leah with her children, and Rachel and Joseph last of all. [3]He himself went on ahead of them, bowing himself to the ground seven times, until he came near his brother.

4 But Esau ran to meet him, and embraced him, and fell on his neck and kissed him, and they wept. [5]When Esau looked up and saw the women and children, he said, "Who are these

with you?" Jacob said, "The children whom God has graciously given your servant." [6]Then the maids drew near, they and their children, and bowed down; [7]Leah likewise and her children drew near and bowed down; and finally Joseph and Rachel drew near, and they bowed down. [8]Esau said, "What do you mean by all this company that I met?" Jacob answered, "To find favor with my lord." [9]But Esau said, "I have enough, my brother; keep what you have for yourself." [10]Jacob said, "No, please; if I find favor with you, then accept my present from my hand; for truly to see your face is like seeing the face of God—since you have received me with such favor. [11]Please accept my gift that is brought to you, because God has dealt graciously with me, and because I have everything I want." So he urged him, and he took it.

12 Then Esau said, "Let us journey on our way, and I will go alongside you." [13]But Jacob said to him, "My lord knows that the children are frail and that the flocks and herds, which are nursing, are a care to me; and if they are overdriven for one day, all the flocks will die. [14]Let my lord pass on ahead of his servant, and I will lead on slowly, according to the pace of the cattle that are before me and according to the pace of the children, until I come to my lord in Seir."

15 So Esau said, "Let me leave with you some of the people who are with me." But he said, "Why should my lord be so kind to me?" [16]So Esau returned that day on his way to Seir. [17]But Jacob journeyed to Succoth,[e] and built himself a house, and made booths for his cattle; therefore the place is called Succoth.

Jacob Reaches Shechem

18 Jacob came safely to the city of Shechem, which is in the land of Canaan, on his way from Paddan-aram; and he camped before the city. [19]And from the sons of Hamor, Shechem's father, he bought for one hundred pieces of money[f] the plot of land on which he had pitched his tent. [20]There he erected an altar and called it El-Elohe-Israel.[g]

34 The Rape of Dinah

Now Dinah the daughter of Leah, whom she had borne to Jacob, went out to visit the women of the region. [2]When Shechem son of Hamor the Hivite, prince of the region, saw her, he seized her and lay with her by force. [3]And his soul was drawn to Dinah daughter of Jacob; he loved the girl, and spoke tenderly to her. [4]So

a Heb he   b That is The one who strives with God or God strives   c Or with divine and human beings   d That is The face of God   e That is Booths
f Heb one hundred qesitah   g That is God, the God of Israel

"We may ignore, but we can nowhere evade the presence of God. The world is crowded with Him. He walks everywhere incognito."

—*C.S. Lewis,*
in his book Letters to Malcolm

Chaos—© Lexi Hiland, 16

Shechem spoke to his father Hamor, saying, "Get me this girl to be my wife."

5 Now Jacob heard that Shechem[a] had defiled his daughter Dinah; but his sons were with his cattle in the field, so Jacob held his peace until they came. ⁶And Hamor the father of Shechem went out to Jacob to speak with him, ⁷just as the sons of Jacob came in from the field. When they heard of it, the men were indignant and very angry, because he had committed an outrage in Israel by lying with Jacob's daughter, for such a thing ought not to be done.

8 But Hamor spoke with them, saying, "The heart of my son Shechem longs for your daughter; please give her to him in marriage. ⁹Make marriages with us; give your daughters to us, and take our daughters for yourselves. ¹⁰You shall live with us; and the land shall be open to you; live and trade in it, and get property in it." ¹¹Shechem also said to her father and to her brothers, "Let me find favor with you, and whatever you say to me I will give. ¹²Put the marriage present and gift as high as you like, and I will give whatever you ask me; only give me the girl to be my wife."

13 The sons of Jacob answered Shechem and his father Hamor deceitfully, because he had defiled their sister Dinah. ¹⁴They said to them, "We cannot do this thing, to give our sister to one who is uncircumcised, for that would be a disgrace to us. ¹⁵Only on this condition will we consent to you: that you will become as we are and every male among you be circumcised. ¹⁶Then we will give our daughters to you, and we will take your daughters for ourselves, and we will live among you and

become one people. ¹⁷But if you will not listen to us and be circumcised, then we will take our daughter and be gone."

18 Their words pleased Hamor and Hamor's son Shechem. ¹⁹And the young man did not delay to do the thing, because he was delighted with Jacob's daughter. Now he was the most honored of all his family. ²⁰So Hamor and his son Shechem came to the gate of their city and spoke to the men of their city, saying, ²¹"These people are friendly with us; let them live in the land and trade in it, for the land is large enough for them; let us take their daughters in marriage, and let us give them our daughters. ²²Only on this condition will they agree to live among us, to become one people: that every male among us be circumcised as they are circumcised. ²³Will not their livestock, their property, and all their animals be ours? Only let us agree with them, and they will live among us." ²⁴And all who went out of the city gate heeded Hamor and his son Shechem; and every male was circumcised, all who went out of the gate of his city.

Dinah's Brothers Avenge Their Sister

25 On the third day, when they were still in pain, two of the sons of Jacob, Simeon and Levi, Dinah's brothers, took their swords and came against the city unawares, and killed all the males. ²⁶They killed Hamor and his son Shechem with the sword, and took Dinah out of Shechem's house, and went away. ²⁷And the other sons of Jacob came upon the slain, and plundered the city, because their sister had been defiled. ²⁸They took their flocks and their herds, their donkeys, and whatever was in the city and in the field. ²⁹All their wealth, all their little ones and their wives, all that was in the houses, they captured and made their prey. ³⁰Then Jacob said to Simeon and Levi, "You have brought trouble on me by making me odious to the inhabitants of the land, the Canaanites and the Perizzites; my numbers are few, and if they gather themselves against me and attack me, I shall be destroyed, both I and my household." ³¹But they said, "Should our sister be treated like a whore?"

35 Jacob Returns to Bethel

God said to Jacob, "Arise, go up to Bethel, and settle there. Make an altar there to the God who appeared to you when you fled from your brother Esau." ²So Jacob said to his household and to all who were with him, "Put away the foreign gods that are among you, and purify yourselves, and change your clothes; ³then

a Heb *he*

come, let us go up to Bethel, that I may make an altar there to the God who answered me in the day of my distress and has been with me wherever I have gone." ⁴So they gave to Jacob all the foreign gods that they had, and the rings that were in their ears; and Jacob hid them under the oak that was near Shechem.

5 As they journeyed, a terror from God fell upon the cities all around them, so that no one pursued them. ⁶Jacob came to Luz (that is, Bethel), which is in the land of Canaan, he and all the people who were with him, ⁷and there he built an altar and called the place El-bethel,ᵃ because it was there that God had revealed himself to him when he fled from his brother. ⁸And Deborah, Rebekah's nurse, died, and she was buried under an oak below Bethel. So it was called Allon-bacuth.ᵇ

9 God appeared to Jacob again when he came from Paddan-aram, and he blessed him. ¹⁰God said to him, "Your name is Jacob; no longer shall you be called Jacob, but Israel shall be your name." So he was called Israel. ¹¹God said to him, "I am God Almighty:ᶜ be fruitful and multiply; a nation and a company of nations shall come from you, and kings shall spring from you. ¹²The land that I gave to Abraham and Isaac I will give to you, and I will give the land to your offspring after you." ¹³Then God went up from him at the place where he had spoken with him. ¹⁴Jacob set up a pillar in the place where he had spoken with him, a pillar of stone; and he poured out a drink offering on it, and poured oil on it. ¹⁵So Jacob called the place where God had spoken with him Bethel.

The Birth of Benjamin and the Death of Rachel

16 Then they journeyed from Bethel; and when they were still some distance from Ephrath, Rachel was in childbirth, and she had hard labor. ¹⁷When she was in her hard labor, the midwife said to her, "Do not be afraid; for now you will have another son." ¹⁸As her soul was departing (for she died), she named him Ben-oni;ᵈ but his father called him Benjamin.ᵉ ¹⁹So Rachel died, and she was buried on the way to Ephrath (that is, Bethlehem), ²⁰and Jacob set up a pillar at her grave; it is the pillar of Rachel's tomb, which is there to this day. ²¹Israel journeyed on, and pitched his tent beyond the tower of Eder.

22 While Israel lived in that land, Reuben went and lay with Bilhah his father's concubine; and Israel heard of it.

Now the sons of Jacob were twelve. ²³The sons of Leah: Reuben (Jacob's firstborn), Simeon, Levi, Judah, Issachar, and Zebulun. ²⁴The sons of Rachel: Joseph and Benjamin. ²⁵The sons of Bilhah, Rachel's maid: Dan and Naphtali. ²⁶The sons of Zilpah, Leah's maid: Gad and Asher. These were the sons of Jacob who were born to him in Paddan-aram.

The Death of Isaac

27 Jacob came to his father Isaac at Mamre, or Kiriath-arba (that is, Hebron), where Abraham and Isaac had resided as aliens. ²⁸Now the days of Isaac were one hundred eighty years. ²⁹And Isaac breathed his last; he died and was gathered to his people, old and full of days; and his sons Esau and Jacob buried him.

36 Esau's Descendants

These are the descendants of Esau (that is, Edom). ²Esau took his wives from the Canaanites: Adah daughter of Elon the Hittite, Oholibamah daughter of Anah sonᶠ of Zibeon the Hivite, ³and Basemath, Ishmael's daughter, sister of Nebaioth. ⁴Adah bore Eliphaz to Esau; Basemath bore Reuel; ⁵and Oholibamah bore Jeush, Jalam, and Korah. These are the sons of Esau who were born to him in the land of Canaan.

6 Then Esau took his wives, his sons, his daughters, and all the members of his household, his cattle, all his livestock, and all the property he had acquired in the land of Canaan; and he moved to a land some distance from his brother Jacob. ⁷For their possessions were too great for them to live together; the land where they were staying could not support them because of their livestock. ⁸So Esau settled in the hill country of Seir; Esau is Edom.

9 These are the descendants of Esau, ancestor of the Edomites, in the hill country of Seir. ¹⁰These are the names of Esau's sons: Eliphaz son of Adah the wife of Esau; Reuel, the son of Esau's wife Basemath. ¹¹The sons of Eliphaz were Teman, Omar, Zepho, Gatam, and Kenaz. ¹²(Timna was a concubine of Eliphaz, Esau's son; she bore Amalek to Eliphaz.) These were the sons of Adah, Esau's wife. ¹³These were the sons of Reuel: Nahath, Zerah, Shammah, and Mizzah. These were the sons of Esau's wife, Basemath. ¹⁴These were the sons of Esau's wife Oholibamah, daughter of Anah sonᵍ of Zibeon: she bore to Esau Jeush, Jalam, and Korah.

Clans and Kings of Edom

15 These are the clansʰ of the sons of Esau. The sons of Eliphaz the firstborn of Esau: the

---

a That is God of Bethel b That is Oak of weeping c Traditional rendering of Heb El Shaddai d That is Son of my sorrow e That is Son of the right hand or Son of the South f Sam Gk Syr: Heb daughter g Gk Syr: Heb daughter h Or chiefs clans[a] Teman, Omar, Zepho, Kenaz, [16]Korah, Gatam, and Amalek; these are the clans[a] of Eliphaz in the land of Edom; they are the sons of Adah. [17]These are the sons of Esau's son Reuel: the clans[a] Nahath, Zerah, Shammah, and Mizzah; these are the clans[a] of Reuel in the land of Edom; they are the sons of Esau's wife Basemath. [18]These are the sons of Esau's wife Oholibamah: the clans[a] Jeush, Jalam, and Korah; these are the clans[a] born of Esau's wife Oholibamah, the daughter of Anah. [19]These are the sons of Esau (that is, Edom), and these are their clans.[a]

20 These are the sons of Seir the Horite, the inhabitants of the land: Lotan, Shobal, Zibeon, Anah, [21]Dishon, Ezer, and Dishan; these are the clans[a] of the Horites, the sons of Seir in the land of Edom. [22]The sons of Lotan were Hori and Heman; and Lotan's sister was Timna. [23]These are the sons of Shobal: Alvan, Manahath, Ebal, Shepho, and Onam. [24]These are the sons of Zibeon: Aiah and Anah; he is the Anah who found the springs[b] in the wilderness, as he pastured the donkeys of his father Zibeon. [25]These are the children of Anah: Dishon and Oholibamah daughter of Anah. [26]These are the sons of Dishon: Hemdan, Eshban, Ithran, and Cheran. [27]These are the sons of Ezer: Bilhan, Zaavan, and Akan. [28]These are the sons of Dishan: Uz and Aran. [29]These are the clans[a] of the Horites: the clans[a] Lotan, Shobal, Zibeon, Anah, [30]Dishon, Ezer, and Dishan; these are the clans[a] of the Horites, clan by clan[c] in the land of Seir.

31 These are the kings who reigned in the land of Edom, before any king reigned over the Israelites. [32]Bela son of Beor reigned in Edom, the name of his city being Dinhabah. [33]Bela died, and Jobab son of Zerah of Bozrah succeeded him as king. [34]Jobab died, and Husham of the land of the Temanites succeeded him as king. [35]Husham died, and Hadad son of Bedad, who defeated Midian in the country of Moab, succeeded him as king, the name of his city being Avith. [36]Hadad died, and Samlah of Masrekah succeeded him as king. [37]Samlah died, and Shaul of Rehoboth on the Euphrates succeeded him as king. [38]Shaul died, and Baalhanan son of Achbor succeeded him as king. [39]Baal-hanan son of Achbor died, and Hadar succeeded him as king, the name of his city being Pau; his wife's name was Mehetabel, the daughter of Matred, daughter of Me-zahab.

40 These are the names of the clans[a] of Esau, according to their families and their localities by their names: the clans[a] Timna, Al-vah, Jetheth, [41]Oholibamah, Elah, Pinon, [42]Kenaz, Teman, Mibzar, [43]Magdiel, and Iram; these are the clans[a] of Edom (that is, Esau, the father of Edom), according to their settlements in the land that they held.

37 Joseph Dreams of Greatness

Jacob settled in the land where his father had lived as an alien, the land of Canaan. [2]This is the story of the family of Jacob.

Joseph, being seventeen years old, was shepherding the flock with his brothers; he was a helper to the sons of Bilhah and Zilpah, his father's wives; and Joseph brought a bad report of them to their father. [3]Now Israel loved Joseph more than any other of his children, because he was the son of his old age; and he had made him a long robe with sleeves.[d] [4]But when his brothers saw that their father loved him more than all his brothers, they hated him, and could not speak peaceably to him.

5 Once Joseph had a dream, and when he told it to his brothers, they hated him even more. [6]He said to them, "Listen to this dream that I dreamed. [7]There we were, binding sheaves in the field. Suddenly my sheaf rose and stood upright; then your sheaves gathered around it, and bowed down to my sheaf." [8]His brothers said to him, "Are you indeed to reign over us? Are you indeed to have dominion over us?" So they hated him even more because of his dreams and his words.

9 He had another dream, and told it to his brothers, saying, "Look, I have had another dream: the sun, the moon, and eleven stars were bowing down to me." [10]But when he told it to his father and to his brothers, his father rebuked him, and said to him, "What kind of dream is this that you have had? Shall we indeed come, I and your mother and your brothers, and bow to the ground before you?" [11]So his brothers were jealous of him, but his father kept the matter in mind.

Joseph Is Sold by His Brothers

12 Now his brothers went to pasture their father's flock near Shechem. [13]And Israel said to Joseph, "Are not your brothers pasturing the flock at Shechem? Come, I will send you to them." He answered, "Here I am." [14]So he said to him, "Go now, see if it is well with your brothers and with the flock; and bring word back to me." So he sent him from the valley of Hebron.

He came to Shechem, [15]and a man found him wandering in the fields; the man asked

a Or chiefs b Meaning of Heb uncertain c Or chief by chief d Traditional rendering (compare Gk): a coat of many colors; meaning of Heb uncertain him, "What are you seeking?" ¹⁶"I am seeking my brothers," he said; "tell me, please, where they are pasturing the flock." ¹⁷The man said, "They have gone away, for I heard them say, 'Let us go to Dothan.' " So Joseph went after his brothers, and found them at Dothan. ¹⁸They saw him from a distance, and before he came near to them, they conspired to kill him. ¹⁹They said to one another, "Here comes this dreamer. ²⁰Come now, let us kill him and throw him into one of the pits; then we shall say that a wild animal has devoured him, and we shall see what will become of his dreams." ²¹But when Reuben heard it, he delivered him out of their hands, saying, "Let us not take his life." ²²Reuben said to them, "Shed no blood; throw him into this pit here in the wilderness, but lay no hand on him"—that he might rescue him out of their hand and restore him to his father. ²³So when Joseph came to his brothers, they stripped him of his robe, the long robe with sleeves*a* that he wore; ²⁴and they took him and threw him into a pit. The pit was empty; there was no water in it.

25 Then they sat down to eat; and looking up they saw a caravan of Ishmaelites coming from Gilead, with their camels carrying gum, balm, and resin, on their way to carry it down to Egypt. ²⁶Then Judah said to his brothers, "What profit is it if we kill our brother and conceal his blood? ²⁷Come, let us sell him to the Ishmaelites, and not lay our hands on him, for he is our brother, our own flesh." And his brothers agreed. ²⁸When some Midianite traders passed by, they drew Joseph up, lifting him out of the pit, and sold him to the Ishmaelites for twenty pieces of silver. And they took Joseph to Egypt.

29 When Reuben returned to the pit and saw that Joseph was not in the pit, he tore his clothes. ³⁰He returned to his brothers, and said, "The boy is gone; and I, where can I turn?" ³¹Then they took Joseph's robe, slaughtered a goat, and dipped the robe in the blood. ³²They had the long robe with sleeves*a* taken to their father, and they said, "This we have found; see now whether it is your son's robe or not." ³³He recognized it, and said, "It is my son's robe! A wild animal has devoured him; Joseph is without doubt torn to pieces." ³⁴Then Jacob tore his garments, and put sackcloth on his loins, and mourned for his son many days. ³⁵All his sons and all his daughters sought to comfort him; but he refused to be comforted, and said, "No, I shall go down to Sheol to my son, mourning." Thus his father bewailed him. ³⁶Meanwhile the Midianites had sold him in Egypt to Potiphar,

one of Pharaoh's officials, the captain of the guard.

38 Judah and Tamar

It happened at that time that Judah went down from his brothers and settled near a certain Adullamite whose name was Hirah. ²There Judah saw the daughter of a certain Canaanite whose name was Shua; he married her and went in to her. ³She conceived and bore a son; and he named him Er. ⁴Again she conceived and bore a son whom she named Onan. ⁵Yet again she bore a son, and she named him Shelah. She*b* was in Chezib when she bore him. ⁶Judah took a wife for Er his firstborn; her name was Tamar. ⁷But Er, Judah's firstborn, was wicked in the sight of the Lord, and the Lord put him to death. ⁸Then Judah said to Onan, "Go in to your brother's wife and perform the duty of a brother-in-law to her; raise up offspring for your brother." ⁹But since Onan knew that the offspring would not be his, he spilled his semen on the ground whenever he went in to his brother's wife, so that he would not give offspring to his brother. ¹⁰What he did was displeasing in the sight of the Lord, and he put him to death also. ¹¹Then Judah said to his daughter-in-law Tamar, "Remain a widow in your father's house until my son Shelah grows up"—for he feared that he too would die, like his brothers. So Tamar went to live in her father's house.

12 In course of time the wife of Judah, Shua's daughter, died; when Judah's time of mourning was over,*c* he went up to Timnah to his sheepshearers, he and his friend Hirah the Adullamite. ¹³When Tamar was told, "Your father-in-law is going up to Timnah to shear his sheep," ¹⁴she put off her widow's garments, put on a veil, wrapped herself up, and sat down at the entrance to Enaim, which is on the road to Timnah. She saw that Shelah was grown up, yet she had not been given to him in marriage. ¹⁵When Judah saw her, he thought

a See note on 37.3   *b* Gk: Heb *He*   *c* Heb *when Judah was comforted* her to be a prostitute, for she had covered her face. [16]He went over to her at the roadside, and said, "Come, let me come in to you," for he did not know that she was his daughter-in-law. She said, "What will you give me, that you may come in to me?" [17]He answered, "I will send you a kid from the flock." And she said, "Only if you give me a pledge, until you send it." [18]He said, "What pledge shall I give you?" She replied, "Your signet and your cord, and the staff that is in your hand." So he gave them to her, and went in to her, and she conceived by him. [19]Then she got up and went away, and taking off her veil she put on the garments of her widowhood.

20 When Judah sent the kid by his friend the Adullamite, to recover the pledge from the woman, he could not find her. [21]He asked the townspeople, "Where is the temple prostitute who was at Enaim by the wayside?" But they said, "No prostitute has been here." [22]So he returned to Judah, and said, "I have not found her; moreover the townspeople said, 'No prostitute has been here.' " [23]Judah replied, "Let her keep the things as her own, otherwise we will be laughed at; you see, I sent this kid, and you could not find her."

24 About three months later Judah was told, "Your daughter-in-law Tamar has played the whore; moreover she is pregnant as a result of whoredom." And Judah said, "Bring her out, and let her be burned." [25]As she was being brought out, she sent word to her father-in-law, "It was the owner of these who made me pregnant." And she said, "Take note, please, whose these are, the signet and the cord and the staff." [26]Then Judah acknowledged them and said, "She is more in the right than I, since I did not give her to my son Shelah." And he did not lie with her again.

27 When the time of her delivery came, there were twins in her womb. [28]While she was in labor, one put out a hand; and the midwife took and bound on his hand a crimson thread, saying, "This one came out first." [29]But just then he drew back his hand, and out came his brother; and she said, "What a breach you have made for yourself!" Therefore he was named Perez.[a] [30]Afterward his brother came out with the crimson thread on his hand; and he was named Zerah.[b]

39 Joseph and Potiphar's Wife

Now Joseph was taken down to Egypt, and Potiphar, an officer of Pharaoh, the captain of the guard, an Egyptian, bought him from the Ishmaelites who had brought him down there. [2]The LORD was with Joseph, and he became a successful man; he was in the house of his Egyptian master. [3]His master saw that the LORD was with him, and that the LORD caused all that he did to prosper in his hands. [4]So Joseph found favor in his sight and attended him; he made him overseer of his house and put him in charge of all that he had. [5]From the time that he made him overseer in his house and over all that he had, the LORD blessed the Egyptian's house for Joseph's sake; the blessing of the LORD was on all that he had, in house and field. [6]So he left all that he had in Joseph's charge; and, with him there, he had no concern for anything but the food that he ate.

Now Joseph was handsome and good-looking. [7]And after a time his master's wife cast her eyes on Joseph and said, "Lie with me." [8]But he refused and said to his master's wife, "Look, with me here, my master has no concern about anything in the house, and he has put everything that he has in my hand. [9]He is not greater in this house than I am, nor has he kept back anything from me except yourself, because you are his wife. How then could I do this great wickedness, and sin against God?" [10]And although he spoke to Joseph day after day, he would not consent to lie beside her or to be with her. [11]One day, however, when he went into the house to do his work, and while no one else was in the house, [12]she caught hold of his garment, saying, "Lie with me!" But he left his garment in her hand, and fled and ran outside. [13]When she saw that he had left his garment in her hand and had fled outside, [14]she called out to the members of her household and said to them, "See, my husband[c] has brought among us a Hebrew to insult us! He came in to me to lie with me, and I cried out with a loud voice; [15]and when he heard me raise my voice and cry out, he left his garment beside me, and fled outside." [16]Then she kept his garment by her until his master came home, [17]and she told him the same story, saying, "The Hebrew servant, whom you have brought among us, came in to me to insult me; [18]but as soon as I raised my voice and cried out, he left his garment beside me, and fled outside."

19 When his master heard the words that his wife spoke to him, saying, "This is the way your servant treated me," he became enraged. [20]And Joseph's master took him and put him into the prison, the place where the king's prisoners were confined; he remained there in prison. [21]But the LORD was with Joseph and showed him steadfast love; he gave him favor in the sight of the chief jailer. [22]The chief jailer

---

a That is *A breach*   *b* That is *Brightness*; perhaps alluding to the crimson thread   *c* Heb *he* committed to Joseph's care all the prisoners who were in the prison, and whatever was done there, he was the one who did it. 23The chief jailer paid no heed to anything that was in Joseph's care, because the LORD was with him; and whatever he did, the LORD made it prosper.

40 The Dreams of Two Prisoners

Some time after this, the cupbearer of the king of Egypt and his baker offended their lord the king of Egypt. 2Pharaoh was angry with his two officers, the chief cupbearer and the chief baker, 3and he put them in custody in the house of the captain of the guard, in the prison where Joseph was confined. 4The captain of the guard charged Joseph with them, and he waited on them; and they continued for some time in custody. 5One night they both dreamed—the cupbearer and the baker of the king of Egypt, who were confined in the prison—each his own dream, and each dream with its own meaning. 6When Joseph came to them in the morning, he saw that they were troubled. 7So he asked Pharaoh's officers, who were with him in custody in his master's house, "Why are your faces downcast today?" 8They said to him, "We have had dreams, and there is no one to interpret them." And Joseph said to them, "Do not interpretations belong to God? Please tell them to me."

9 So the chief cupbearer told his dream to Joseph, and said to him, "In my dream there was a vine before me, 10and on the vine there were three branches. As soon as it budded, its blossoms came out and the clusters ripened into grapes. 11Pharaoh's cup was in my hand; and I took the grapes and pressed them into Pharaoh's cup, and placed the cup in Pharaoh's hand." 12Then Joseph said to him, "This is its interpretation: the three branches are three days; 13within three days Pharaoh will lift up your head and restore you to your office; and you shall place Pharaoh's cup in his hand, just as you used to do when you were his cupbearer. 14But remember me when it is well with you; please do me the kindness to make mention of me to Pharaoh, and so get me out of this place. 15For in fact I was stolen out of the land of the Hebrews; and here also I have done nothing that they should have put me into the dungeon."

16 When the chief baker saw that the interpretation was favorable, he said to Joseph, "I also had a dream: there were three cake baskets on my head, 17and in the uppermost basket there were all sorts of baked food for Pharaoh, but the birds were eating it out of the basket on my head." 18And Joseph answered,

"This is its interpretation: the three baskets are three days; 19within three days Pharaoh will lift up your head—from you!—and hang you on a pole; and the birds will eat the flesh from you."

20 On the third day, which was Pharaoh's birthday, he made a feast for all his servants, and lifted up the head of the chief cupbearer and the head of the chief baker among his servants. 21He restored the chief cupbearer to his cupbearing, and he placed the cup in Pharaoh's hand; 22but the chief baker he hanged, just as Joseph had interpreted to them. 23Yet the chief cupbearer did not remember Joseph, but forgot him.

41 Joseph Interprets Pharaoh's Dream

After two whole years, Pharaoh dreamed that he was standing by the Nile, 2and there came up out of the Nile seven sleek and fat cows, and they grazed in the reed grass. 3Then seven other cows, ugly and thin, came up out of the Nile after them, and stood by the other cows on the bank of the Nile. 4The ugly and thin cows ate up the seven sleek and fat cows. And Pharaoh troubled; so he sent and called for all the magicians of Egypt and all its wise men. Pharaoh told them his dreams, but there was no one who could interpret them to Pharaoh.

9 Then the chief cupbearer said to Pharaoh, "I remember my faults today. ¹⁰Once Pharaoh was angry with his servants, and put me and the chief baker in custody in the house of the captain of the guard. ¹¹We dreamed on the same night, he and I, each having a dream with its own meaning. ¹²A young Hebrew was there with us, a servant of the captain of the guard. When we told him, he interpreted our dreams to us, giving an interpretation to each according to his dream. ¹³As he interpreted to us, so it turned out; I was restored to my office, and the baker was hanged."

14 Then Pharaoh sent for Joseph, and he was hurriedly brought out of the dungeon. When he had shaved himself and changed his clothes, he came in before Pharaoh. ¹⁵And Pharaoh said to Joseph, "I have had a dream, and there is no one who can interpret it. I have heard it said of you that when you hear a dream you can interpret it." ¹⁶Joseph answered Pharaoh, "It is not I; God will give Pharaoh a favorable answer." ¹⁷Then Pharaoh said to Joseph, "In my dream I was standing on the banks of the Nile; ¹⁸and seven cows, fat and sleek, came up out of the Nile and fed in the reed grass. ¹⁹Then seven other cows came up after them, poor, very ugly, and thin. Never had I seen such ugly ones in all the land of Egypt. ²⁰The thin and ugly cows ate up the first seven fat cows, ²¹but when they had eaten them no one would have known that they had done so, for they were still as ugly as before. Then I awoke. ²²I fell asleep a second time*a* and I saw in my dream seven ears of grain, full and good, growing on one stalk, ²³and seven ears, withered, thin, and blighted by the east wind, sprouting after them; ²⁴and the thin ears swallowed up the seven good ears. But when I told it to the magicians, there was no one who could explain it to me."

25 Then Joseph said to Pharaoh, "Pharaoh's dreams are one and the same; God has revealed to Pharaoh what he is about to do. ²⁶The seven good cows are seven years, and the seven good ears are seven years; the dreams are one. ²⁷The seven lean and ugly cows that came up after them are seven years, as are the seven empty ears blighted by the east wind. They are seven years of famine. ²⁸It is as I told Pharaoh; God has shown to Pharaoh what he is about to do. ²⁹There will come seven years of great plenty throughout all the land of Egypt. ³⁰After them

awoke. ⁵Then he fell asleep and dreamed a second time; seven ears of grain, plump and good, were growing on one stalk. ⁶Then seven ears, thin and blighted by the east wind, sprouted after them. ⁷The thin ears swallowed up the seven plump and full ears. Pharaoh awoke, and it was a dream. ⁸In the morning his spirit was

a Gk Syr Vg: Heb lacks *I fell asleep a second time*

there will arise seven years of famine, and all the plenty will be forgotten in the land of Egypt; the famine will consume the land. ³¹The plenty will no longer be known in the land because of the famine that will follow, for it will be very grievous. ³²And the doubling of Pharaoh's dream means that the thing is fixed by God, and God will shortly bring it about. ³³Now therefore let Pharaoh select a man who is discerning and wise, and set him over the land of Egypt. ³⁴Let Pharaoh proceed to appoint overseers over the land, and take one-fifth of the produce of the land of Egypt during the seven plenteous years. ³⁵Let them gather all the food of these good years that are coming, and lay up grain under the authority of Pharaoh for food in the cities, and let them keep it. ³⁶That food shall be a reserve for the land against the seven years of famine that are to befall the land of Egypt, so that the land may not perish through the famine."

Joseph's Rise to Power

37 The proposal pleased Pharaoh and all his servants. ³⁸Pharaoh said to his servants, "Can we find anyone else like this—one in whom is the spirit of God?" ³⁹So Pharaoh said to Joseph, "Since God has shown you all this, there is no one so discerning and wise as you. ⁴⁰You shall be over my house, and all my people shall order themselves as you command; only with regard to the throne will I be greater than you." ⁴¹And Pharaoh said to Joseph, "See, I have set you over all the land of Egypt." ⁴²Removing his signet ring from his hand, Pharaoh put it on Joseph's hand; he arrayed him in garments of fine linen, and put a gold chain around his neck. ⁴³He had him ride in the chariot of his second-in-command; and they cried out in front of him, "Bow the knee!"ᵃ Thus he set him over all the land of Egypt. ⁴⁴Moreover Pharaoh said to Joseph, "I am Pharaoh, and without your consent no one shall lift up hand or foot in all the land of Egypt." ⁴⁵Pharaoh gave Joseph the name Zaphenath-paneah; and he gave him Asenath daughter of Potiphera, priest of On, as his wife. Thus Joseph gained authority over the land of Egypt.

46 Joseph was thirty years old when he entered the service of Pharaoh king of Egypt. And Joseph went out from the presence of Pharaoh, and went through all the land of Egypt. ⁴⁷During the seven plenteous years the earth produced abundantly. ⁴⁸He gathered up all the food of the seven years when there was plentyᵇ in the land of Egypt, and stored up food in the cities; he stored up in every city the food from the fields around it. ⁴⁹So Joseph stored up grain in such abundance—like the sand of the sea—that he stopped measuring it; it was beyond measure.

50 Before the years of famine came, Joseph had two sons, whom Asenath daughter of Potiphera, priest of On, bore to him. ⁵¹Joseph named the firstborn Manasseh,ᶜ "For," he said, "God has made me forget all my hardship and all my father's house." ⁵²The second he named Ephraim,ᵈ "For God has made me fruitful in the land of my misfortunes."

53 The seven years of plenty that prevailed in the land of Egypt came to an end; ⁵⁴and the seven years of famine began to come, just as Joseph had said. There was famine in every country, but throughout the land of Egypt there was bread. ⁵⁵When all the land of Egypt was famished, the people cried to Pharaoh for bread. Pharaoh said to all the Egyptians, "Go to Joseph; what he says to you, do." ⁵⁶And since the famine had spread over all the land, Joseph opened all the storehouses,ᵉ and sold to the Egyptians, for the famine was severe in the land of Egypt. ⁵⁷Moreover, all the world came to Joseph in Egypt to buy grain, because the famine became severe throughout the world.

42 Joseph's Brothers Go to Egypt

When Jacob learned that there was grain in Egypt, he said to his sons, "Why do you keep looking at one another? ²I have heard," he said, "that there is grain in Egypt; go down and buy grain for us there, that we may live and not die." ³So ten of Joseph's brothers went down to buy grain in Egypt. ⁴But Jacob did not send Joseph's brother Benjamin with his brothers, for he feared that harm might come to him. ⁵Thus the sons of Israel were among the other people who came to buy grain, for the famine had reached the land of Canaan.

6 Now Joseph was governor over the land; it was he who sold to all the people of the land. And Joseph's brothers came and bowed themselves before him with their faces to the ground. ⁷When Joseph saw his brothers, he recognized them, but he treated them like strangers and spoke harshly to them. "Where do you come from?" he said. They said, "From the land of Canaan, to buy food." ⁸Although Joseph had recognized his brothers, they did not recognize him. ⁹Joseph also remembered the dreams that he had dreamed about them. He said to them, "You are spies; you have come to see the nakedness of the land!" ¹⁰They said

---

a *Abrek*, apparently an Egyptian word similar in sound to the Hebrew word meaning *to kneel*   b Sam Gk: MT *the seven years that were*   c That is *Making to forget*   d From a Hebrew word meaning *to be fruitful*   e Gk Vg Compare Syr: Heb *opened all that was in* (or, *among*) *them* to him, "No, my lord; your servants have come to buy food. ¹¹We are all sons of one man; we are honest men; your servants have never been spies." ¹²But he said to them, "No, you have come to see the nakedness of the land!" ¹³They said, "We, your servants, are twelve brothers, the sons of a certain man in the land of Canaan; the youngest, however, is now with our father, and one is no more." ¹⁴But Joseph said to them, "It is just as I have said to you; you are spies! ¹⁵Here is how you shall be tested: as Pharaoh lives, you shall not leave this place unless your youngest brother comes here! ¹⁶Let one of you go and bring your brother, while the rest of you remain in prison, in order that your words may be tested, whether there is truth in you; or else, as Pharaoh lives, surely you are spies." ¹⁷And he put them all together in prison for three days.

18 On the third day Joseph said to them, "Do this and you will live, for I fear God: ¹⁹if you are honest men, let one of your brothers stay here where you are imprisoned. The rest of you shall go and carry grain for the famine of your households, ²⁰and bring your youngest brother to me. Thus your words will be verified, and you shall not die." And they agreed to do so. ²¹They said to one another, "Alas, we are paying the penalty for what we did to our brother; we saw his anguish when he pleaded with us, but we would not listen. That is why this anguish has come upon us." ²²Then Reuben answered them, "Did I not tell you not to wrong the boy? But you would not listen. So now there comes a reckoning for his blood." ²³They did not know that Joseph understood them, since he spoke with them through an interpreter. ²⁴He turned away from them and wept; then he returned and spoke to them. And he picked out Simeon and had him bound before their eyes. ²⁵Joseph then gave orders to fill their bags with grain, to return every man's money to his sack, and to give them provisions for their journey. This was done for them.

Joseph's Brothers Return to Canaan

26 They loaded their donkeys with their grain, and departed. ²⁷When one of them opened his sack to give his donkey fodder at the lodging place, he saw his money at the top of the sack. ²⁸He said to his brothers, "My money has been put back; here it is in my sack!" At this they lost heart and turned trembling to one another, saying, "What is this that God has done to us?"

29 When they came to their father Jacob in the land of Canaan, they told him all that had happened to them, saying, ³⁰"The man, the lord of the land, spoke harshly to us, and charged us with spying on the land. ³¹But we

said to him, 'We are honest men, we are not spies. ³²We are twelve brothers, sons of our father; one is no more, and the youngest is now with our father in the land of Canaan.' ³³Then the man, the lord of the land, said to us, 'By this I shall know that you are honest men: leave one of your brothers with me, take grain for the famine of your households, and go your way. ³⁴Bring your youngest brother to me, and I shall know that you are not spies but honest men. Then I will release your brother to you, and you may trade in the land.' "

35 As they were emptying their sacks, there in each one's sack was his bag of money. When they and their father saw their bundles of money, they were dismayed. ³⁶And their father Jacob said to them, "I am the one you have bereaved of children: Joseph is no more, and Simeon is no more, and now you would take Benjamin. All this has happened to me!" ³⁷Then Reuben said to his father, "You may kill my two sons if I do not bring him back to you. Put him in my hands, and I will bring him back to you." ³⁸But he said, "My son shall not go down with you, for his brother is dead, and he alone is left. If harm should come to him on the journey that you are to make, you would bring down my gray hairs with sorrow to Sheol."

43 The Brothers Come Again, Bringing Benjamin

Now the famine was severe in the land. ²And when they had eaten up the grain that they had brought from Egypt, their father said to them, "Go again, buy us a little more food." ³But Judah said to him, "The man solemnly warned us, saying, 'You shall not see my face unless your brother is with you.' ⁴If you will send our brother with us, we will go down and buy you food; ⁵but if you will not send him, we will not go down, for the man said to us, 'You shall not see my face, unless your brother is with you.' " ⁶Israel said, "Why did you treat me so badly as to tell the man that you had another brother?" ⁷They replied, "The man questioned us carefully about ourselves and our kindred, saying, 'Is your father still alive? Have you another brother?' What we told him was in answer to these questions. Could we in any way know that he would say, 'Bring your brother down'?" ⁸Then Judah said to his father Israel, "Send the boy with me, and let us be on our way, so that we may live and not die—you and we and also our little ones. ⁹I myself will be surety for him; you can hold me accountable for him. If I do not bring him back to you and set him before you, then let me bear the blame forever. ¹⁰If we had not delayed, we would now have returned twice."

Beautiful—© Allie Gager, 15

11 Then their father Israel said to them, "If it must be so, then do this: take some of the choice fruits of the land in your bags, and carry them down as a present to the man—a little balm and a little honey, gum, resin, pistachio nuts, and almonds. 12Take double the money with you. Carry back with you the money that was returned in the top of your sacks; perhaps it was an oversight. 13Take your brother also, and be on your way again to the man; 14may God Almighty*a* grant you mercy before the man, so that he may send back your other brother and Benjamin. As for me, if I am bereaved of my children, I am bereaved." 15So the men took the present, and they took double the money with them, as well as Benjamin. Then they went on their way down to Egypt, and stood before Joseph.

16 When Joseph saw Benjamin with them, he said to the steward of his house, "Bring the men into the house, and slaughter an animal and make ready, for the men are to dine with me at noon." 17The man did as Joseph said, and brought the men to Joseph's house. 18Now the men were afraid because they were brought to Joseph's house, and they said, "It is because of the money, replaced in our sacks the first time, that we have been brought in, so that he may have an opportunity to fall upon us, to make slaves of us and take our donkeys." 19So they went up to the steward of Joseph's house and spoke with him at the entrance to the house. 20They said, "Oh, my lord, we came down the first time to buy food; 21and when we came to the lodging place we opened our sacks, and there was each one's money in the top of his sack, our money in full weight. So we have brought it back with us. 22Moreover we have brought down with us additional money to buy food. We do not know who put our money in our sacks." 23He replied, "Rest assured, do not be afraid; your God and the God of your father must have put treasure in your sacks for you; I received your money." Then he brought Simeon out to them. 24When the steward*b* had brought the men into Joseph's house, and given them water, and they had washed their feet, and when he had given their donkeys fodder, 25they made the present ready for Joseph's coming at noon, for they had heard that they would dine there.

26 When Joseph came home, they brought him the present that they had carried into the house, and bowed to the ground before him. 27He inquired about their welfare, and said, "Is your father well, the old man of whom you spoke? Is he still alive?" 28They said, "Your servant our father is well; he is still alive." And they bowed their heads and did obeisance. 29Then he looked up and saw his brother

a Traditional rendering of Heb *El Shaddai* *b* Heb *the man*

And You Thought Your Family Was Dysfunctional . . .

Consider Joseph. His brothers kidnapped and abused him. Sold him into slavery. Denied their crimes—and got away with it.

For a while.

A "chance" encounter in Egypt revealed the truth: God was working through Joseph's horrible family situation the entire time. Read **Genesis 45.1–21** and **50.20**. It's the dramatic reconciliation scene—and an example of *major* forgiveness. Happy ending. Roll credits.

And yet . . .

If God had this outcome in mind all along—get Joseph to Egypt, prompt Egypt to stockpile grain for an upcoming famine, keep the Israelites from starving—then why didn't God just *do* that? Why put Joseph through so much grief along the way?

Maybe it's to point us to another truth: good can come out of family chaos and pain. God *can* help us through splintered situations—if we let him. We may not see the results today, tomorrow, or even in this generation. But God is real, and he's working through imperfect family situations.

Which raises a question: How is God working in and through *your* family?

Take a long-lens view back through several generations. Where has your family's faith journey gone over the years? How is a real God doing real work through real people—your people?

Look for a pattern. When you think you see it, post your thoughts about it on **Learner.CalltoDiscipleship.com**. The rest of us want to see what God's been up to in your family. After all, we're *all* a part of God's family.

Benjamin, his mother's son, and said, "Is this your youngest brother, of whom you spoke to me? God be gracious to you, my son!" ³⁰With that, Joseph hurried out, because he was overcome with affection for his brother, and he was about to weep. So he went into a private room and wept there. ³¹Then he washed his face and

a Gk Compare Vg: Heb lacks *Why have you stolen my silver cup?*

came out; and controlling himself he said, "Serve the meal." ³²They served him by himself, and them by themselves, and the Egyptians who ate with him by themselves, because the Egyptians could not eat with the Hebrews, for that is an abomination to the Egyptians. ³³When they were seated before him, the firstborn according to his birthright and the youngest according to his youth, the men looked at one another in amazement. ³⁴Portions were taken to them from Joseph's table, but Benjamin's portion was five times as much as any of theirs. So they drank and were merry with him.

44 Joseph Detains Benjamin

Then he commanded the steward of his house, "Fill the men's sacks with food, as much as they can carry, and put each man's money in the top of his sack. ²Put my cup, the silver cup, in the top of the sack of the youngest, with his money for the grain." And he did as Joseph told him. ³As soon as the morning was light, the men were sent away with their donkeys. ⁴When they had gone only a short distance from the city, Joseph said to his steward, "Go, follow after the men; and when you overtake them, say to them, 'Why have you returned evil for good? Why have you stolen my silver cup?ᵃ ⁵Is it not from this that my lord drinks? Does he not indeed use it for divination? You have done wrong in doing this.' "

6 When he overtook them, he repeated these words to them. ⁷They said to him, "Why does my lord speak such words as these? Far be it from your servants that they should do such a thing! ⁸Look, the money that we found at the top of our sacks, we brought back to you from the land of Canaan; why then would we steal silver or gold from your lord's house? ⁹Should it be found with any one of your servants, let him die; moreover the rest of us will become my lord's slaves." ¹⁰He said, "Even so; in accordance with your words, let it be: he with whom it is found shall become my slave, but the rest of you shall go free." ¹¹Then each one quickly lowered his sack to the ground, and each opened his sack. ¹²He searched, beginning with the eldest and ending with the youngest; and the cup was found in Benjamin's sack. ¹³At this they tore their clothes. Then each one loaded his donkey, and they returned to the city.

14 Judah and his brothers came to Joseph's house while he was still there; and they fell to the ground before him. ¹⁵Joseph said to them, "What deed is this that you have done? Do you not know that one such as I can practice divi-

nation?" [16]And Judah said, "What can we say to my lord? What can we speak? How can we clear ourselves? God has found out the guilt of your servants; here we are then, my lord's slaves, both we and also the one in whose possession the cup has been found." [17]But he said, "Far be it from me that I should do so! Only the one in whose possession the cup was found shall be my slave; but as for you, go up in peace to your father."

Judah Pleads for Benjamin's Release

18 Then Judah stepped up to him and said, "O my lord, let your servant please speak a word in my lord's ears, and do not be angry with your servant; for you are like Pharaoh himself. [19]My lord asked his servants, saying, 'Have you a father or a brother?' [20]And we said to my lord, 'We have a father, an old man, and a young brother, the child of his old age. His brother is dead; he alone is left of his mother's children, and his father loves him.' [21]Then you said to your servants, 'Bring him down to me, so that I may set my eyes on him.' [22]We said to my lord, 'The boy cannot leave his father, for if he should leave his father, his father would die.' [23]Then you said to your servants, 'Unless your youngest brother comes down with you, you shall see my face no more.' [24]When we went back to your servant my father we told him the words of my lord. [25]And when our father said, 'Go again, buy us a little food,' [26]we said, 'We cannot go down. Only if our youngest brother goes with us, will we go down; for we cannot see the man's face unless our youngest brother is with us.' [27]Then your servant my father said to us, 'You know that my wife bore me two sons; [28]one left me, and I said, Surely he has been torn to pieces; and I have never seen him since. [29]If you take this one also from me, and harm comes to him, you will bring down my gray hairs in sorrow to Sheol.' [30]Now therefore, when I come to your servant my father and the boy is not with us, then, as his life is bound up in the boy's life, [31]when he sees that the boy is not with us, he will die; and your servants will bring down the gray hairs of your servant our father with sorrow to Sheol. [32]For your servant became surety for the boy to my father, saying, 'If I do not bring him back to you, then I will bear the blame in the sight of my father all my life.' [33]Now therefore, please let your servant remain as a slave to my lord in place of the boy; and let the boy go back with his brothers. [34]For how can I go back to my father if the boy is not with me? I fear to see the suffering that would come upon my father."

45 Joseph Reveals Himself to His Brothers

Then Joseph could no longer control himself before all those who stood by him, and he cried out, "Send everyone away from me." So no one stayed with him when Joseph made himself known to his brothers. [2]And he wept so loudly that the Egyptians heard it, and the household of Pharaoh heard it. [3]Joseph said to his brothers, "I am Joseph. Is my father still alive?" But his brothers could not answer him, so dismayed were they at his presence.

4 Then Joseph said to his brothers, "Come closer to me." And they came closer. He said, "I am your brother, Joseph, whom you sold into Egypt. [5]And now do not be distressed, or angry with yourselves, because you sold me here; for God sent me before you to preserve life. [6]For the famine has been in the land these two years; and there are five more years in which there will be neither plowing nor harvest. [7]God sent me before you to preserve for you a remnant on earth, and to keep alive for you many survivors. [8]So it was not you who sent me here, but God; he has made me a father to Pharaoh, and lord of all his house and ruler over all the land of Egypt. [9]Hurry and go up to my father and say to him, 'Thus says your son Joseph, God has made me lord of all Egypt; come down to me, do not delay. [10]You shall settle in the land of Goshen, and you shall be near me, you and your children and your children's children, as well as your flocks, your herds, and all that you have. [11]I will provide for you there—since there are five more years of famine to come—so that you and your household, and all that you have, will not come to poverty.' [12]And now your eyes and the eyes of my brother Benjamin see that it is my own mouth that speaks to you. [13]You must tell my father how greatly I am honored in Egypt, and all that you have seen. Hurry and bring my father down here." [14]Then he fell upon his brother Benjamin's neck and wept, while Benjamin wept upon his neck. [15]And he kissed all his brothers and wept upon them; and after that his brothers talked with him.

16 When the report was heard in Pharaoh's house, "Joseph's brothers have come," Pharaoh and his servants were pleased. [17]Pharaoh said to Joseph, "Say to your brothers, 'Do this: load your animals and go back to the land of Canaan. [18]Take your father and your households and come to me, so that I may give you the best of the land of Egypt, and you may enjoy the fat of the land.' [19]You are further charged to say, 'Do this: take wagons from the land of Egypt for your little ones and for your wives, and bring your father, and come. [20]Give no

thought to your possessions, for the best of all the land of Egypt is yours.' "

21 The sons of Israel did so. Joseph gave them wagons according to the instruction of Pharaoh, and he gave them provisions for the journey. ²²To each one of them he gave a set of garments; but to Benjamin he gave three hundred pieces of silver and five sets of garments. ²³To his father he sent the following: ten donkeys loaded with the good things of Egypt, and ten female donkeys loaded with grain, bread, and provision for his father on the journey. ²⁴Then he sent his brothers on their way, and as they were leaving he said to them, "Do not quarrel*^a* along the way."

25 So they went up out of Egypt and came to their father Jacob in the land of Canaan. ²⁶And they told him, "Joseph is still alive! He is even ruler over all the land of Egypt." He was stunned; he could not believe them. ²⁷But when they told him all the words of Joseph that he had said to them, and when he saw the wagons that Joseph had sent to carry him, the spirit of their father Jacob revived. ²⁸Israel said, "Enough! My son Joseph is still alive. I must go and see him before I die."

46 Jacob Brings His Whole Family to Egypt

When Israel set out on his journey with all that he had and came to Beer-sheba, he offered sacrifices to the God of his father Isaac. ²God spoke to Israel in visions of the night, and said, "Jacob, Jacob." And he said, "Here I am." ³Then he said, "I am God,*^b* the God of your father; do not be afraid to go down to Egypt, for I will make of you a great nation there. ⁴I myself will go down with you to Egypt, and I will also bring you up again; and Joseph's own hand shall close your eyes."

5 Then Jacob set out from Beer-sheba; and the sons of Israel carried their father Jacob, their little ones, and their wives, in the wagons that Pharaoh had sent to carry him. ⁶They also took their livestock and the goods that they had acquired in the land of Canaan, and they came into Egypt, Jacob and all his offspring with him, ⁷his sons, and his sons' sons with him, his daughters, and his sons' daughters; all his offspring he brought with him into Egypt.

8 Now these are the names of the Israelites, Jacob and his offspring, who came to Egypt. Reuben, Jacob's firstborn, ⁹and the children of Reuben: Hanoch, Pallu, Hezron, and Carmi. ¹⁰The children of Simeon: Jemuel, Jamin, Ohad, Jachin, Zohar, and Shaul,*^c* the son of a Canaanite woman. ¹¹The children of Levi: Gershon, Kohath, and Merari. ¹²The children

of Judah: Er, Onan, Shelah, Perez, and Zerah (but Er and Onan died in the land of Canaan); and the children of Perez were Hezron and Hamul. ¹³The children of Issachar: Tola, Puvah, Jashub,*^d* and Shimron. ¹⁴The children of Zebulun: Sered, Elon, and Jahleel ¹⁵(these are the sons of Leah, whom she bore to Jacob in Paddan-aram, together with his daughter Dinah; in all his sons and his daughters numbered thirty-three). ¹⁶The children of Gad: Ziphion, Haggi, Shuni, Ezbon, Eri, Arodi, and Areli. ¹⁷The children of Asher: Imnah, Ishvah, Ishvi, Beriah, and their sister Serah. The children of Beriah: Heber and Malchiel ¹⁸(these are the children of Zilpah, whom Laban gave to his daughter Leah; and these she bore to Jacob— sixteen persons). ¹⁹The children of Jacob's wife Rachel: Joseph and Benjamin. ²⁰To Joseph in the land of Egypt were born Manasseh and Ephraim, whom Asenath daughter of Potiphera, priest of On, bore to him. ²¹The children of Benjamin: Bela, Becher, Ashbel, Gera, Naaman, Ehi, Rosh, Muppim, Huppim, and Ard ²²(these are the children of Rachel, who were born to Jacob—fourteen persons in all). ²³The children of Dan: Hashum.*^e* ²⁴The children of Naphtali: Jahzeel, Guni, Jezer, and Shillem ²⁵(these are the children of Bilhah, whom Laban gave to his daughter Rachel, and these she bore to Jacob—seven persons in all). ²⁶All the persons belonging to Jacob who came into Egypt, who were his own offspring, not including the wives of his sons, were sixty-six persons in all. ²⁷The children of Joseph, who were born to him in Egypt, were two; all the persons of the house of Jacob who came into Egypt were seventy.

Jacob Settles in Goshen

28 Israel*^f* sent Judah ahead to Joseph to lead the way before him into Goshen. When they came to the land of Goshen, ²⁹Joseph made ready his chariot and went up to meet his father Israel in Goshen. He presented himself to him, fell on his neck, and wept on his neck a good while. ³⁰Israel said to Joseph, "I can die now, having seen for myself that you are still alive." ³¹Joseph said to his brothers and to his father's household, "I will go up and tell Pharaoh, and will say to him, 'My brothers and my father's household, who were in the land of Canaan, have come to me. ³²The men are shepherds, for they have been keepers of livestock; and they have brought their flocks, and their herds, and all that they have.' ³³When Pharaoh calls you, and says, 'What is your occupation?' ³⁴you shall say, 'Your servants have been keep-

---

a Or *be agitated* *b* Heb *the God* *c* Or *Saul* *d* Compare Sam Gk Num 26.24; 1 Chr 7.1: MT *Iob* *e* Gk: Heb *Hushim* *f* Heb *He* ers of livestock from our youth even until now, both we and our ancestors'—in order that you may settle in the land of Goshen, because all shepherds are abhorrent to the Egyptians."

47 So Joseph went and told Pharaoh, "My father and my brothers, with their flocks and herds and all that they possess, have come from the land of Canaan; they are now in the land of Goshen." ²From among his brothers he took five men and presented them to Pharaoh. ³Pharaoh said to his brothers, "What is your occupation?" And they said to Pharaoh, "Your servants are shepherds, as our ancestors were." ⁴They said to Pharaoh, "We have come to reside as aliens in the land; for there is no pasture for your servants' flocks because the famine is severe in the land of Canaan. Now, we ask you, let your servants settle in the land of Goshen." ⁵Then Pharaoh said to Joseph, "Your father and your brothers have come to you. ⁶The land of Egypt is before you; settle your father and your brothers in the best part of the land; let them live in the land of Goshen; and if you know that there are capable men among them, put them in charge of my livestock."

7 Then Joseph brought in his father Jacob, and presented him before Pharaoh, and Jacob blessed Pharaoh. ⁸Pharaoh said to Jacob, "How many are the years of your life?" ⁹Jacob said to Pharaoh, "The years of my earthly sojourn are one hundred thirty; few and hard have been the years of my life. They do not compare with the years of the life of my ancestors during their long sojourn." ¹⁰Then Jacob blessed Pharaoh, and went out from the presence of Pharaoh. ¹¹Joseph settled his father and his brothers, and granted them a holding in the land of Egypt, in the best part of the land, in the land of Rameses, as Pharaoh had instructed. ¹²And Joseph provided his father, his brothers, and all his father's household with food, according to the number of their dependents.

The Famine in Egypt
13 Now there was no food in all the land, for the famine was very severe. The land of Egypt and the land of Canaan languished because of the famine. ¹⁴Joseph collected all the money to be found in the land of Egypt and in the land of Canaan, in exchange for the grain that they bought; and Joseph brought the money into Pharaoh's house. ¹⁵When the money from the land of Egypt and from the land of Canaan was spent, all the Egyptians came to Joseph, and said, "Give us food! Why should we die before your eyes? For our money is gone." ¹⁶And Joseph answered, "Give me your livestock, and I will give you food in exchange for your

TEXT MESSAGE

If you have older brothers and sisters and think they always get the best deal, take some comfort in Genesis 48.13–14. Though Jacob blessed both Manasseh, the older, and Ephraim, the younger, he crossed his hands and blessed Ephraim with his right hand. That made Ephraim's blessing more important.

This information has been scanned and is free of all known viruses. Please forward to all your friends.

livestock, if your money is gone." ¹⁷So they brought their livestock to Joseph; and Joseph gave them food in exchange for the horses, the flocks, the herds, and the donkeys. That year he supplied them with food in exchange for all their livestock. ¹⁸When that year was ended, they came to him the following year, and said to him, "We can not hide from my lord that our money is all spent; and the herds of cattle are my lord's. There is nothing left in the sight of my lord but our bodies and our lands. ¹⁹Shall we die before your eyes, both we and our land? Buy us and our land in exchange for food. We with our land will become slaves to Pharaoh; just give us seed, so that we may live and not die, and that the land may not become desolate."

20 So Joseph bought all the land of Egypt for Pharaoh. All the Egyptians sold their fields,

because the famine was severe upon them; and the land became Pharaoh's. [21]As for the people, he made slaves of them[a] from one end of Egypt to the other. [22]Only the land of the priests he did not buy; for the priests had a fixed allowance from Pharaoh, and lived on the allowance that Pharaoh gave them; therefore they did not sell their land. [23]Then Joseph said to the people, "Now that I have this day bought you and your land for Pharaoh, here is seed for you; sow the land. [24]And at the harvests you shall give one-fifth to Pharaoh, and four-fifths shall be your own, as seed for the field and as food for yourselves and your households, and as food for your little ones." [25]They said, "You have saved our lives; may it please my lord, we will be slaves to Pharaoh." [26]So Joseph made it a statute concerning the land of Egypt, and it stands to this day, that Pharaoh should have the fifth. The land of the priests alone did not become Pharaoh's.

The Last Days of Jacob

27 Thus Israel settled in the land of Egypt, in the region of Goshen; and they gained possessions in it, and were fruitful and multiplied exceedingly. [28]Jacob lived in the land of Egypt seventeen years; so the days of Jacob, the years of his life, were one hundred forty-seven years.

29 When the time of Israel's death drew near, he called his son Joseph and said to him, "If I have found favor with you, put your hand under my thigh and promise to deal loyally and truly with me. Do not bury me in Egypt. [30]When I lie down with my ancestors, carry me out of Egypt and bury me in their burial place." He answered, "I will do as you have said." [31]And he said, "Swear to me"; and he swore to him. Then Israel bowed himself on the head of his bed.

48 Jacob Blesses Joseph's Sons

After this Joseph was told, "Your father is ill." So he took with him his two sons, Manasseh and Ephraim. [2]When Jacob was told, "Your son Joseph has come to you," he[b] summoned his strength and sat up in bed. [3]And Jacob said to Joseph, "God Almighty[c] appeared to me at Luz in the land of Canaan, and he blessed me, [4]and said to me, 'I am going to make you fruitful and increase your numbers; I will make of you a company of peoples, and will give this land to your offspring after you for a perpetual holding.' [5]Therefore your two sons, who were born to you in the land of Egypt before I came to you in Egypt, are now mine; Ephraim and Manasseh shall be mine, just as Reuben and Simeon are.

[6]As for the offspring born to you after them, they shall be yours. They shall be recorded under the names of their brothers with regard to their inheritance. [7]For when I came from Paddan, Rachel, alas, died in the land of Canaan on the way, while there was still some distance to go to Ephrath; and I buried her there on the way to Ephrath" (that is, Bethlehem).

8 When Israel saw Joseph's sons, he said, "Who are these?" [9]Joseph said to his father, "They are my sons, whom God has given me here." And he said, "Bring them to me, please, that I may bless them." [10]Now the eyes of Israel were dim with age, and he could not see well. So Joseph brought them near him; and he kissed them and embraced them. [11]Israel said to Joseph, "I did not expect to see your face; and here God has let me see your children also." [12]Then Joseph removed them from his father's knees,[d] and he bowed himself with his face to the earth. [13]Joseph took them both, Ephraim in his right hand toward Israel's left, and Manasseh in his left hand toward Israel's right, and brought them near him. [14]But Israel stretched out his right hand and laid it on the head of Ephraim, who was the younger, and his left hand on the head of Manasseh, crossing his hands, for Manasseh was the firstborn. [15]He blessed Joseph, and said,

"The God before whom my ancestors
            Abraham and Isaac walked,
    the God who has been my shepherd all my
            life to this day,
[16]   the angel who has redeemed me from all
            harm, bless the boys;
    and in them let my name be perpetuated,
            and the name of my ancestors
            Abraham and Isaac;
    and let them grow into a multitude on the
            earth."

17 When Joseph saw that his father laid his right hand on the head of Ephraim, it displeased him; so he took his father's hand, to remove it from Ephraim's head to Manasseh's head. [18]Joseph said to his father, "Not so, my father! Since this one is the firstborn, put your right hand on his head." [19]But his father refused, and said, "I know, my son, I know; he also shall become a people, and he also shall be great. Nevertheless his younger brother shall be greater than he, and his offspring shall become a multitude of nations." [20]So he blessed them that day, saying,

    "By you[e] Israel will invoke blessings, saying,
    'God make you[e] like Ephraim and like
            Manasseh.' "

---

a Sam Gk Compare Vg: MT *He removed them to the cities* b Heb *Israel* c Traditional rendering of Heb *El Shaddai* d Heb *from his knees*
e *you* here is singular in Heb

So he put Ephraim ahead of Manasseh. ²¹ Then Israel said to Joseph, "I am about to die, but God will be with you and will bring you again to the land of your ancestors. ²² I now give to you one portion*a* more than to your brothers, the portion*a* that I took from the hand of the Amorites with my sword and with my bow."

49 Jacob's Last Words to His Sons

Then Jacob called his sons, and said: "Gather around, that I may tell you what will happen to you in days to come.

² Assemble and hear, O sons of Jacob;
   listen to Israel your father.

³ Reuben, you are my firstborn,
   my might and the first fruits of my vigor,
   excelling in rank and excelling in power.

⁴ Unstable as water, you shall no longer excel
   because you went up onto your father's
      bed;
   then you defiled it—you*b* went up onto
      my couch!

⁵ Simeon and Levi are brothers;
   weapons of violence are their swords.

⁶ May I never come into their council;
   may I not be joined to their company—
for in their anger they killed men,
   and at their whim they hamstrung oxen.

⁷ Cursed be their anger, for it is fierce,
   and their wrath, for it is cruel!
I will divide them in Jacob,
   and scatter them in Israel.

⁸ Judah, your brothers shall praise you;
   your hand shall be on the neck of your
      enemies;
   your father's sons shall bow down before
      you.

⁹ Judah is a lion's whelp;
   from the prey, my son, you have gone up.
He crouches down, he stretches out like a
      lion,
   like a lioness—who dares rouse him up?

¹⁰ The scepter shall not depart from Judah,
   nor the ruler's staff from between his
      feet,
until tribute comes to him;*c*
   and the obedience of the peoples is his.

¹¹ Binding his foal to the vine
      and his donkey's colt to the choice vine,
   he washes his garments in wine
      and his robe in the blood of grapes;

¹² his eyes are darker than wine,
   and his teeth whiter than milk.

¹³ Zebulun shall settle at the shore of the
      sea;
   he shall be a haven for ships,
      and his border shall be at Sidon.

¹⁴ Issachar is a strong donkey,
   lying down between the sheepfolds;

¹⁵ he saw that a resting place was good,
      and that the land was pleasant;
   so he bowed his shoulder to the burden,
      and became a slave at forced labor.

¹⁶ Dan shall judge his people
   as one of the tribes of Israel.

¹⁷ Dan shall be a snake by the roadside,
      a viper along the path,
   that bites the horse's heels
      so that its rider falls backward.

¹⁸ I wait for your salvation, O Lᴏʀᴅ.

¹⁹ Gad shall be raided by raiders,
   but he shall raid at their heels.

²⁰ Asher's*d* food shall be rich,
   and he shall provide royal delicacies.

²¹ Naphtali is a doe let loose
   that bears lovely fawns.*e*

²² Joseph is a fruitful bough,
   a fruitful bough by a spring;
   his branches run over the wall.*f*

²³ The archers fiercely attacked him;
   they shot at him and pressed him hard.

²⁴ Yet his bow remained taut,
      and his arms*g* were made agile
   by the hands of the Mighty One of Jacob,
      by the name of the Shepherd, the Rock of
         Israel,

²⁵ by the God of your father, who will help
      you,

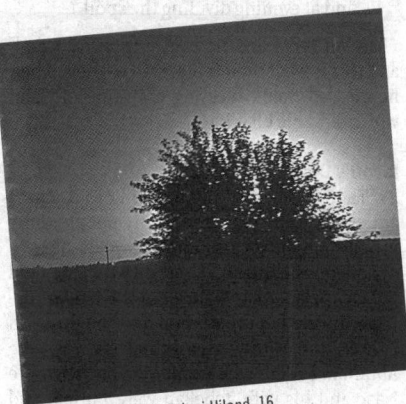

Light of the World—© Lexi Hiland, 16

---

a Or *mountain slope* (Heb *shekem*, a play on the name of the town and district of Shechem)   *b* Gk Syr Tg: Heb *he*   *c* Or *until Shiloh comes* or *until he comes to Shiloh* or (with Syr) *until he comes to whom it belongs*   *d* Gk Vg Syr: Heb *From Asher*   *e* Or *that gives beautiful words*   *f* Meaning of Heb uncertain   *g* Heb *the arms of his hands*

What No One Wants to Take a Picture Of—© Jessica Jones, 17

by the Almighty^a who will bless you
with blessings of heaven above,
blessings of the deep that lies beneath,
blessings of the breasts and of the womb.
²⁶ The blessings of your father
are stronger than the blessings of the
eternal mountains,
the bounties^b of the everlasting hills;
may they be on the head of Joseph,
on the brow of him who was set apart
from his brothers.

²⁷ Benjamin is a ravenous wolf,
in the morning devouring the prey,
and at evening dividing the spoil."

28 All these are the twelve tribes of Israel,
and this is what their father said to them when
he blessed them, blessing each one of them
with a suitable blessing.

Jacob's Death and Burial

29 Then he charged them, saying to them, "I
am about to be gathered to my people. Bury
me with my ancestors—in the cave in the field
of Ephron the Hittite, ³⁰in the cave in the field
at Machpelah, near Mamre, in the land of Canaan, in the field that Abraham bought from
Ephron the Hittite as a burial site. ³¹There
Abraham and his wife Sarah were buried; there
Isaac and his wife Rebekah were buried; and
there I buried Leah— ³²the field and the cave

that is in it were purchased from the Hittites."
³³When Jacob ended his charge to his sons, he
drew up his feet into the bed, breathed his last,
and was gathered to his people.

50 Then Joseph threw himself on his father's face and wept over him and kissed him.
²Joseph commanded the physicians in his
service to embalm his father. So the physicians embalmed Israel; ³they spent forty days
in doing this, for that is the time required for
embalming. And the Egyptians wept for him
seventy days.

4 When the days of weeping for him were
past, Joseph addressed the household of Pharaoh, "If now I have found favor with you, please
speak to Pharaoh as follows: ⁵My father made
me swear an oath; he said, 'I am about to die.
In the tomb that I hewed out for myself in the
land of Canaan, there you shall bury me.' Now
therefore let me go up, so that I may bury my
father; then I will return." ⁶Pharaoh answered,
"Go up, and bury your father, as he made you
swear to do."

7 So Joseph went up to bury his father.
With him went up all the servants of Pharaoh,
the elders of his household, and all the elders
of the land of Egypt, ⁸as well as all the household of Joseph, his brothers, and his father's
household. Only their children, their flocks,
and their herds were left in the land of Goshen.
⁹Both chariots and charioteers went up with

---

a Traditional rendering of Heb *Shaddai*   *b* Cn Compare Gk: Heb *of my progenitors to the boundaries* him. It was a very great company. [10]When they came to the threshing floor of Atad, which is beyond the Jordan, they held there a very great and sorrowful lamentation; and he observed a time of mourning for his father seven days. [11]When the Canaanite inhabitants of the land saw the mourning on the threshing floor of Atad, they said, "This is a grievous mourning on the part of the Egyptians." Therefore the place was named Abel-mizraim;[a] it is beyond the Jordan. [12]Thus his sons did for him as he had instructed them. [13]They carried him to the land of Canaan and buried him in the cave of the field at Machpelah, the field near Mamre, which Abraham bought as a burial site from Ephron the Hittite. [14]After he had buried his father, Joseph returned to Egypt with his brothers and all who had gone up with him to bury his father.

Joseph Forgives His Brothers

15 Realizing that their father was dead, Joseph's brothers said, "What if Joseph still bears a grudge against us and pays us back in full for all the wrong that we did to him?" [16]So they approached[b] Joseph, saying, "Your father gave this instruction before he died, [17]'Say to Joseph: I beg you, forgive the crime of your brothers and the wrong they did in harming

you.' Now therefore please forgive the crime of the servants of the God of your father." Joseph wept when they spoke to him. [18]Then his brothers also wept,[c] fell down before him, and said, "We are here as your slaves." [19]But Joseph said to them, "Do not be afraid! Am I in the place of God? [20]Even though you intended to do harm to me, God intended it for good, in order to preserve a numerous people, as he is doing today. [21]So have no fear; I myself will provide for you and your little ones." In this way he reassured them, speaking kindly to them.

Joseph's Last Days and Death

22 So Joseph remained in Egypt, he and his father's household; and Joseph lived one hundred ten years. [23]Joseph saw Ephraim's children of the third generation; the children of Machir son of Manasseh were also born on Joseph's knees.

24 Then Joseph said to his brothers, "I am about to die; but God will surely come to you, and bring you up out of this land to the land that he swore to Abraham, to Isaac, and to Jacob." [25]So Joseph made the Israelites swear, saying, "When God comes to you, you shall carry up my bones from here." [26]And Joseph died, being one hundred ten years old; he was embalmed and placed in a coffin in Egypt.

a That is *mourning* (or *meadow*) *of Egypt* *b* Gk Syr: Heb *they commanded* *c* Cn: Heb *also came*

Self—© Lexi Hiland, 16

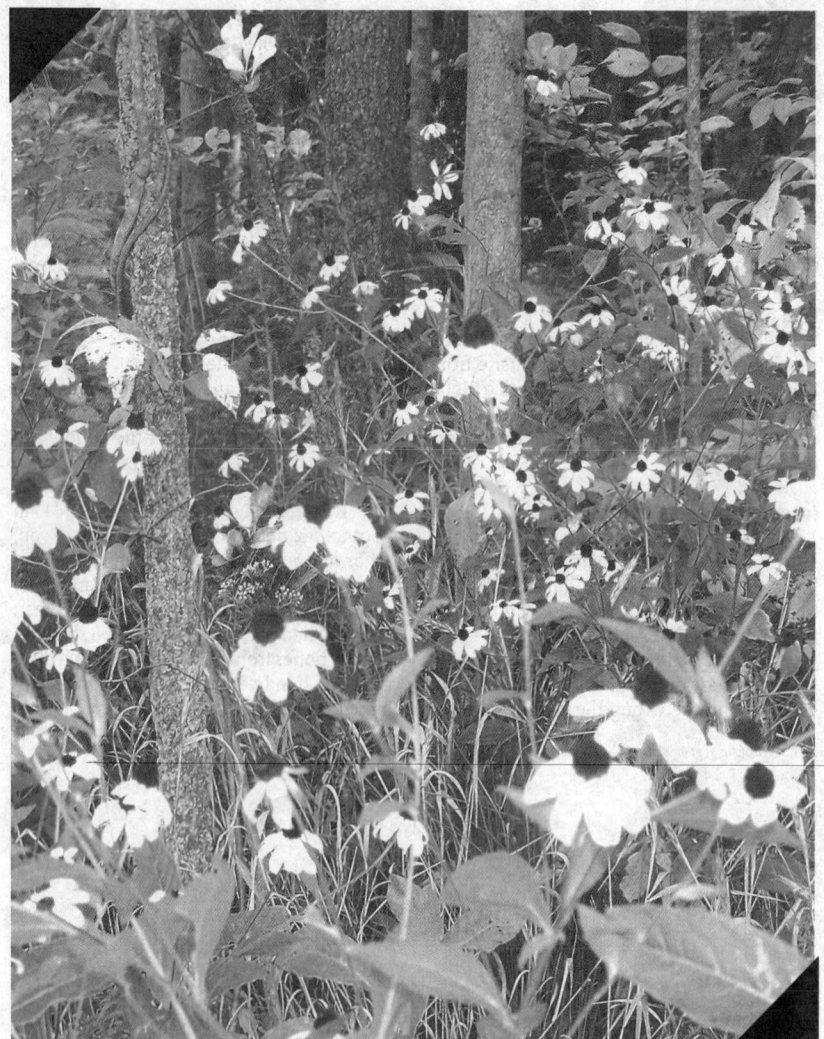

Untitled—© Erica Wallis, 17

EXODUS

GOD OR GODS?

Implicated

It doesn't look good when a former member of the royal household comes home to tell you that . . .

    (a) he's of the same race as your slaves, and

    (b) he and God are on *their* side.

It especially doesn't look good if you're Pharaoh and you've set yourself up as the hawk god Heru in human form. This kind of thing shouldn't happen to a god, and you have to keep up appearances.

Unfortunately for Pharaoh, appearances prove incorrect. God versus Pharaoh just isn't a fair fight. After a deluge of frogs, a river turned to blood, total darkness for three days, and other displays of God's power, Moses and God's people (the Israelites) finally flee captivity in Egypt. Soon, though, the Israelites get antsy and make an idol to worship. At this point, most readers of Exodus pause, groan, roll their eyes, and yell, "You idiots!"

Don't they know yet that God is the only true God? That these other so-called gods are totally fake and powerless? Don't they *get* it?

But if we read the Ten Commandments God gave his people through Moses, we're forced to pause again, this time with a heavy, awful feeling in our stomach.

We're just like them.

We idolize actors and athletes. We take charge of our own lives and shove God into a corner. We spend our time as we please. We obsess about getting more and more stuff. We disrespect our parents. The list goes on . . . and on . . . and on.

Exodus isn't just about the ancient Israelites. It's about *us.*

"The Ten Commandments state what is required in the love of God and love of neighbor. The first three concern love of God, and the other seven love of neighbor."
—Catechism of the Catholic Church 2067

WHO Moses has often been considered the author of Exodus, but modern scholars generally agree that the book is a combination of three different sources.

WHAT God delivers the Israelites from slavery in Egypt and makes them his people forever through a covenant of law and presence.

WHEN There is disagreement about when the events in Exodus took place; two possible dates are ca. 1270 B.C. and ca. 1446 B.C.

WHERE Egypt, then Saudi Arabia and Mt. Sinai (Mt. Horeb)

PATH OF DISCIPLESHIP

The Jewish people celebrate an annual holiday called Shavuot to remember God's giving the Ten Commandments to Moses. It's a celebration of the truth that God doesn't leave his people in the dark—he speaks to us! And God's communication didn't stop on Mt. Sinai. Jesus, called the "Word" (John 1.1), lived on earth as God's most profound communication to humanity. Jesus fulfilled the covenant between God and humankind, dying for our sins and rising to new life, one with God and the Holy Spirit in the Trinity (see CCC 292, 778). Read the words of Jesus; get to know him for yourself. Reflect on the message and the meaning. Listen closely—he's speaking to *you.*

1 These are the names of the sons of Israel who came to Egypt with Jacob, each with his household: [2]Reuben, Simeon, Levi, and Judah, [3]Issachar, Zebulun, and Benjamin, [4]Dan and Naphtali, Gad and Asher. [5]The total number of people born to Jacob was seventy. Joseph was already in Egypt. [6]Then Joseph died, and all his brothers, and that whole generation. [7]But the Israelites were fruitful and prolific; they multiplied and grew exceedingly strong, so that the land was filled with them.

The Israelites Are Oppressed

8 Now a new king arose over Egypt, who did not know Joseph. [9]He said to his people, "Look, the Israelite people are more numerous and more powerful than we. [10]Come, let us deal shrewdly with them, or they will increase and, in the event of war, join our enemies and fight against us and escape from the land." [11]Therefore they set taskmasters over them to oppress them with forced labor. They built supply cities, Pithom and Rameses, for Pharaoh. [12]But the more they were oppressed, the more they multiplied and spread, so that the Egyptians came to dread the Israelites. [13]The Egyptians became ruthless in imposing tasks on the Israelites, [14]and made their lives bitter with hard service in mortar and brick and in every kind of field labor. They were ruthless in all the tasks that they imposed on them.

15 The king of Egypt said to the Hebrew midwives, one of whom was named Shiphrah and the other Puah, [16]"When you act as midwives to the Hebrew women, and see them on the birthstool, if it is a boy, kill him; but if it is a girl, she shall live." [17]But the midwives feared God; they did not do as the king of Egypt commanded them, but they let the boys live. [18]So the king of Egypt summoned the midwives and said to them, "Why have you done this, and allowed the boys to live?" [19]The midwives said to Pharaoh, "Because the Hebrew women are not like the Egyptian women; for they are vigorous and give birth before the midwife comes to them." [20]So God dealt well with the midwives; and the people multiplied and became very strong. [21]And because the midwives feared God, he gave them families. [22]Then Pharaoh commanded all his people, "Every boy that is born to the Hebrews[a] you shall throw into the Nile, but you shall let every girl live."

2 Birth and Youth of Moses

Now a man from the house of Levi went and married a Levite woman. [2]The woman conceived and bore a son; and when she saw that he was a fine baby, she hid him three months. [3]When she could hide him no longer she got a papyrus basket for him, and plastered it with bitumen and pitch; she put the child in it and placed it among the reeds on the bank of the river. [4]His sister stood at a distance, to see what would happen to him.

5 The daughter of Pharaoh came down to bathe at the river, while her attendants walked beside the river. She saw the basket among the reeds and sent her maid to bring it. [6]When she opened it, she saw the child. He was crying, and she took pity on him. "This must be one of the Hebrews' children," she said. [7]Then his sister said to Pharaoh's daughter, "Shall I go and get you a nurse from the Hebrew women to nurse the child for you?" [8]Pharaoh's daughter said to her, "Yes." So the girl went and called the child's mother. [9]Pharaoh's daughter said to her, "Take this child and nurse it for me, and I will give you your wages." So the woman took the child and nursed it. [10]When the child grew up, she brought him to Pharaoh's daughter, and she took him as her son. She named him Moses,[b] "because," she said, "I drew him out[c] of the water."

Moses Flees to Midian

11 One day, after Moses had grown up, he went out to his people and saw their forced labor. He saw an Egyptian beating a Hebrew, one of his kinsfolk. [12]He looked this way and that, and seeing no one he killed the Egyptian and hid him in the sand. [13]When he went out the next day, he saw two Hebrews fighting; and he said to the one who was in the wrong, "Why do you strike your fellow Hebrew?" [14]He answered, "Who made you a ruler and judge over us? Do you mean to kill me as you killed the Egyptian?" Then Moses was afraid and thought, "Surely the thing is known." [15]When Pharaoh heard of it, he sought to kill Moses.

But Moses fled from Pharaoh. He settled in the land of Midian, and sat down by a well. [16]The priest of Midian had seven daughters. They came to draw water, and filled the troughs to water their father's flock. [17]But some shepherds came and drove them away. Moses got up and came to their defense and watered their flock. [18]When they returned to their father Reuel, he said, "How is it that you have come back so soon today?" [19]They said, "An Egyptian helped us against the shepherds; he even drew water for us and watered the flock." [20]He said to his daughters, "Where is he? Why did you leave the man? Invite him to break bread."

a Sam Gk Tg: Heb lacks *to the Hebrews* b Heb *Mosheh* c Heb *mashah*

²¹Moses agreed to stay with the man, and he gave Moses his daughter Zipporah in marriage. ²²She bore a son, and he named him Gershom; for he said, "I have been an alien*a* residing in a foreign land."

23 After a long time the king of Egypt died. The Israelites groaned under their slavery, and cried out. Out of the slavery their cry for help rose up to God. ²⁴God heard their groaning, and God remembered his covenant with Abraham, Isaac, and Jacob. ²⁵God looked upon the Israelites, and God took notice of them.

3 Moses at the Burning Bush

Moses was keeping the flock of his father-in-law Jethro, the priest of Midian; he led his flock beyond the wilderness, and came to Horeb, the mountain of God. ²There the angel of the LORD appeared to him in a flame of fire out of a bush; he looked, and the bush was blazing, yet it was not consumed. ³Then Moses said, "I must turn aside and look at this great sight, and see why the bush is not burned up." ⁴When the LORD saw that he had turned aside to see, God called to him out of the bush, "Moses, Moses!" And he said, "Here I am." ⁵Then he said, "Come no closer! Remove the sandals from your feet, for the place on which you are standing is holy ground." ⁶He said further, "I am the God of your father, the God of Abraham, the God of Isaac, and the God of Jacob." And Moses hid his face, for he was afraid to look at God.

7 Then the LORD said, "I have observed the misery of my people who are in Egypt; I have heard their cry on account of their taskmasters. Indeed, I know their sufferings, ⁸and I have come down to deliver them from the Egyptians, and to bring them up out of that land to a good and broad land, a land flowing with milk and honey, to the country of the Canaanites, the Hittites, the Amorites, the Perizzites, the Hivites, and the Jebusites. ⁹The cry of the Israelites has now come to me; I have also seen how the Egyptians oppress them. ¹⁰So come, I will send you to Pharaoh to bring my people, the Israelites, out of Egypt." ¹¹But Moses said to God, "Who am I that I should go to Pharaoh, and bring the Israelites out of Egypt?" ¹²He said, "I will be with you; and this shall be the sign for you that it is I who sent you: when you have brought the people out of Egypt, you shall worship God on this mountain."

The Divine Name Revealed

13 But Moses said to God, "If I come to the Israelites and say to them, 'The God of your an-

cestors has sent me to you,' and they ask me, 'What is his name?' what shall I say to them?" ¹⁴God said to Moses, "I AM WHO I AM."*b* He said further, "Thus you shall say to the Israelites, 'I AM has sent me to you.' " ¹⁵God also said to Moses, "Thus you shall say to the Israelites, 'The LORD,*c* the God of your ancestors, the God of Abraham, the God of Isaac, and the God of Jacob, has sent me to you':

This is my name forever,

and this my title for all generations.

¹⁶Go and assemble the elders of Israel, and say to them, 'The LORD, the God of your ancestors, the God of Abraham, of Isaac, and of Jacob, has appeared to me, saying: I have given heed to you and to what has been done to you in Egypt. ¹⁷I declare that I will bring you up out of the misery of Egypt, to the land of the Canaanites, the Hittites, the Amorites, the Perizzites, the Hivites, and the Jebusites, a land flowing

---

a Heb *ger b* Or *I AM WHAT I AM* or *I WILL BE WHAT I WILL BE c* The word "LORD" when spelled with capital letters stands for the divine name, YHWH, which is here connected with the verb *hayah*, "to be" with milk and honey.' ¹⁸They will listen to your voice; and you and the elders of Israel shall go to the king of Egypt and say to him, 'The LORD, the God of the Hebrews, has met with us; let us now go a three days' journey into the wilderness, so that we may sacrifice to the LORD our God.' ¹⁹I know, however, that the king of Egypt will not let you go unless compelled by a mighty hand.ᵃ ²⁰So I will stretch out my hand and strike Egypt with all my wonders that I will perform in it; after that he will let you go. ²¹I will bring this people into such favor with the Egyptians that, when you go, you will not go empty-handed; ²²each woman shall ask her neighbor and any woman living in the neighbor's house for jewelry of silver and of gold, and clothing, and you shall put them on your sons and on your daughters; and so you shall plunder the Egyptians."

4 Moses' Miraculous Power

Then Moses answered, "But suppose they do not believe me or listen to me, but say, 'The LORD did not appear to you.' " ²The LORD said to him, "What is that in your hand?" He said, "A staff." ³And he said, "Throw it on the ground." So he threw the staff on the ground, and it became a snake; and Moses drew back from it. ⁴Then the LORD said to Moses, "Reach out your hand, and seize it by the tail"—so he reached out his hand and grasped it, and it became a staff in his hand— ⁵"so that they may believe that the LORD, the God of their ancestors, the God of Abraham, the God of Isaac, and the God of Jacob, has appeared to you."

6 Again, the LORD said to him, "Put your hand inside your cloak." He put his hand into his cloak; and when he took it out, his hand was leprous,ᵇ as white as snow. ⁷Then God said, "Put your hand back into your cloak"—so he put his hand back into his cloak, and when he took it out, it was restored like the rest of his body— ⁸"If they will not believe you or heed the first sign, they may believe the second sign. ⁹If they will not believe even these two signs or heed you, you shall take some water from the Nile and pour it on the dry ground; and the water that you shall take from the Nile will become blood on the dry ground."

10 But Moses said to the LORD, "O my Lord, I have never been eloquent, neither in the past nor even now that you have spoken to your servant; but I am slow of speech and slow of tongue." ¹¹Then the LORD said to him, "Who gives speech to mortals? Who makes them mute or deaf, seeing or blind? Is it not I, the LORD? ¹²Now go, and I will be with your mouth and teach you what you are to speak." ¹³But he said, "O my Lord, please send someone else." ¹⁴Then the anger of the LORD was kindled against Moses and he said, "What of your brother Aaron the Levite? I know that he can speak fluently; even now he is coming out to meet you, and when he sees you his heart will be glad. ¹⁵You shall speak to him and put the words in his mouth; and I will be with your mouth and with his mouth, and will teach you what you shall do. ¹⁶He indeed shall speak for you to the people; he shall serve as a mouth for you, and you shall serve as God for him. ¹⁷Take in your hand this staff, with which you shall perform the signs."

Moses Returns to Egypt

18 Moses went back to his father-in-law Jethro and said to him, "Please let me go back to my kindred in Egypt and see whether they are still living." And Jethro said to Moses, "Go in peace." ¹⁹The LORD said to Moses in Midian, "Go back to Egypt; for all those who were seeking your life are dead." ²⁰So Moses took his wife and his sons, put them on a donkey, and went back to the land of Egypt; and Moses carried the staff of God in his hand.

21 And the LORD said to Moses, "When you go back to Egypt, see that you perform before Pharaoh all the wonders that I have put in your power; but I will harden his heart, so that he will not let the people go. ²²Then you shall say to Pharaoh, 'Thus says the LORD: Israel is my firstborn son. ²³I said to you, "Let my son go that he may worship me." But you refused to let him go; now I will kill your firstborn son.' "

24 On the way, at a place where they spent the night, the LORD met him and tried to kill him. ²⁵But Zipporah took a flint and cut off her son's foreskin, and touched Moses'ᶜ feet with it, and said, "Truly you are a bridegroom of blood to me!" ²⁶So he let him alone. It was then she said, "A bridegroom of blood by circumcision."

27 The LORD said to Aaron, "Go into the wilderness to meet Moses." So he went; and he met him at the mountain of God and kissed him. ²⁸Moses told Aaron all the words of the LORD with which he had sent him, and all the signs with which he had charged him. ²⁹Then Moses and Aaron went and assembled all the elders of the Israelites. ³⁰Aaron spoke all the words that the LORD had spoken to Moses, and performed the signs in the sight of the people. ³¹The people believed; and when they heard that the LORD had given heed to the Israelites and that he had seen their misery, they bowed down and worshiped.

---

a Gk Vg: Heb no, not by a mighty hand   b A term for several skin diseases; precise meaning uncertain   c Heb his

5 Bricks without Straw

Afterward Moses and Aaron went to Pharaoh and said, "Thus says the LORD, the God of Israel, 'Let my people go, so that they may celebrate a festival to me in the wilderness.' " ²But Pharaoh said, "Who is the LORD, that I should heed him and let Israel go? I do not know the LORD, and I will not let Israel go." ³Then they said, "The God of the Hebrews has revealed himself to us; let us go a three days' journey into the wilderness to sacrifice to the LORD our God, or he will fall upon us with pestilence or sword." ⁴But the king of Egypt said to them, "Moses and Aaron, why are you taking the people away from their work? Get to your labors!" ⁵Pharaoh continued, "Now they are more numerous than the people of the land*a* and yet you want them to stop working!" ⁶That same day Pharaoh commanded the taskmasters of the people, as well as their supervisors, ⁷"You shall no longer give the people straw to make bricks, as before; let them go and gather straw for themselves. ⁸But you shall require of them the same quantity of bricks as they have made previously; do not diminish it, for they are lazy; that is why they cry, 'Let us go and offer sacrifice to our God.' ⁹Let heavier work be laid on them; then they will labor at it and pay no attention to deceptive words."

10 So the taskmasters and the supervisors of the people went out and said to the people, "Thus says Pharaoh, 'I will not give you straw. ¹¹Go and get straw yourselves, wherever you can find it; but your work will not be lessened in the least.' " ¹²So the people scattered throughout the land of Egypt, to gather stubble for straw. ¹³The taskmasters were urgent, saying, "Complete your work, the same daily assignment as when you were given straw." ¹⁴And the supervisors of the Israelites, whom Pharaoh's taskmasters had set over them, were beaten, and were asked, "Why did you not finish the required quantity of bricks yesterday and today, as you did before?"

15 Then the Israelite supervisors came to Pharaoh and cried, "Why do you treat your servants like this? ¹⁶No straw is given to your servants, yet they say to us, 'Make bricks!' Look how your servants are beaten! You are unjust to your own people."*b* ¹⁷He said, "You are lazy, lazy; that is why you say, 'Let us go and sacrifice to the LORD.' ¹⁸Go now, and work; for no straw shall be given you, but you shall still deliver the same number of bricks." ¹⁹The Israelite supervisors saw that they were in trouble when they were told, "You shall not lessen your daily number of bricks." ²⁰As they left Pharaoh, they came upon Moses and Aaron who were waiting to meet them. ²¹They said to them, "The LORD look upon you and judge! You have brought us into bad odor with Pharaoh and his officials, and have put a sword in their hand to kill us."

22 Then Moses turned again to the LORD

---

a Sam: Heb *The people of the land are now many*   *b* Gk Compare Syr Vg: Heb *beaten, and the sin of your people* land in which they resided as aliens. [5]I have also heard the groaning of the Israelites whom the Egyptians are holding as slaves, and I have remembered my covenant. [6]Say therefore to the Israelites, 'I am the LORD, and I will free you from the burdens of the Egyptians and deliver you from slavery to them. I will redeem you with an outstretched arm and with mighty acts of judgment. [7]I will take you as my people, and I will be your God. You shall know that I am the LORD your God, who has freed you from the burdens of the Egyptians. [8]I will bring you into the land that I swore to give to Abraham, Isaac, and Jacob; I will give it to you for a possession. I am the LORD.' " [9]Moses told this to the Israelites; but they would not listen to Moses, because of their broken spirit and their cruel slavery.

10 Then the LORD spoke to Moses, [11]"Go and tell Pharaoh king of Egypt to let the Israelites go out of his land." [12]But Moses spoke to the LORD, "The Israelites have not listened to me; how then shall Pharaoh listen to me, poor speaker that I am?"[c] [13]Thus the LORD spoke to Moses and Aaron, and gave them orders regarding the Israelites and Pharaoh king of Egypt, charging them to free the Israelites from the land of Egypt.

The Genealogy of Moses and Aaron

14 The following are the heads of their ancestral houses: the sons of Reuben, the firstborn of Israel: Hanoch, Pallu, Hezron, and Carmi; these are the families of Reuben. [15]The sons of Simeon: Jemuel, Jamin, Ohad, Jachin, Zohar, and Shaul,[d] the son of a Canaanite woman; these are the families of Simeon. [16]The following are the names of the sons of Levi according to their genealogies: Gershon,[e] Kohath, and Merari, and the length of Levi's life was one hundred thirty-seven years. [17]The sons of Gershon:[e] Libni and Shimei, by their families. [18]The sons of Kohath: Amram, Izhar, Hebron, and Uzziel, and the length of Kohath's life was one hundred thirty-three years. [19]The sons of Merari: Mahli and Mushi. These are the families of the Levites according to their genealogies. [20]Amram married Jochebed his father's sister and she bore him Aaron and Moses, and the length of Amram's life was one hundred thirty-seven years. [21]The sons of Izhar: Korah, Nepheg, and Zichri. [22]The sons of Uzziel: Mishael, Elzaphan, and Sithri. [23]Aaron married Elisheba, daughter of Amminadab and sister of Nahshon, and she bore him Nadab, Abihu, Eleazar, and Ithamar. [24]The sons of Korah: Assir, Elkanah, and Abiasaph; these are the families

and said, "O LORD, why have you mistreated this people? Why did you ever send me? [23]Since I first came to Pharaoh to speak in your name, he has mistreated this people, and you have done nothing at all to deliver your people."

6 Israel's Deliverance Assured

Then the LORD said to Moses, "Now you shall see what I will do to Pharaoh: Indeed, by a mighty hand he will let them go; by a mighty hand he will drive them out of his land."

2 God also spoke to Moses and said to him: "I am the LORD. [3]I appeared to Abraham, Isaac, and Jacob as God Almighty,[a] but by my name 'The LORD'[b] I did not make myself known to them. [4]I also established my covenant with them, to give them the land of Canaan, the

a Traditional rendering of Heb *El Shaddai* b Heb YHWH; see note at 3.15 c Heb *me? I am uncircumcised of lips* d Or *Saul* e Also spelled *Gershom*; see 2.22

of the Korahites. 25Aaron's son Eleazar married one of the daughters of Putiel, and she bore him Phinehas. These are the heads of the ancestral houses of the Levites by their families.

26 It was this same Aaron and Moses to whom the LORD said, "Bring the Israelites out of the land of Egypt, company by company." 27It was they who spoke to Pharaoh king of Egypt to bring the Israelites out of Egypt, the same Moses and Aaron.

Moses and Aaron Obey God's Commands

28 On the day when the LORD spoke to Moses in the land of Egypt, 29he said to him, "I am the LORD; tell Pharaoh king of Egypt all that I am speaking to you." 30But Moses said in the LORD's presence, "Since I am a poor speaker,ᵃ why would Pharaoh listen to me?"

7 The LORD said to Moses, "See, I have made you like God to Pharaoh, and your brother Aaron shall be your prophet. 2You shall speak all that I command you, and your brother Aaron shall tell Pharaoh to let the Israelites go out of his land. 3But I will harden Pharaoh's heart, and I will multiply my signs and wonders in the land of Egypt. 4When Pharaoh does not listen to you, I will lay my hand upon Egypt and bring my people the Israelites, company by company, out of the land of Egypt by great acts of judgment. 5The Egyptians shall know that I am the LORD, when I stretch out my hand against Egypt and bring the Israelites out from among them." 6Moses and Aaron did so; they did just as the LORD commanded them. 7Moses was eighty years old and Aaron eighty-three when they spoke to Pharaoh.

Aaron's Miraculous Rod

8 The LORD said to Moses and Aaron, 9"When Pharaoh says to you, 'Perform a wonder,' then you shall say to Aaron, 'Take your staff and throw it down before Pharaoh, and it will become a snake.' " 10So Moses and Aaron went to Pharaoh and did as the LORD had commanded; Aaron threw down his staff before Pharaoh and his officials, and it became a snake. 11Then Pharaoh summoned the wise men and the sorcerers; and they also, the magicians of Egypt, did the same by their secret arts. 12Each one threw down his staff, and they became snakes; but Aaron's staff swallowed up theirs. 13Still Pharaoh's heart was hardened, and he would not listen to them, as the LORD had said.

The First Plague: Water Turned to Blood

14 Then the LORD said to Moses, "Pharaoh's heart is hardened; he refuses to let the people go. 15Go to Pharaoh in the morning, as he is going out to the water; stand by at the river bank to meet him, and take in your hand the staff that was turned into a snake. 16Say to him, 'The LORD, the God of the Hebrews, sent me to you to say, "Let my people go, so that they may worship me in the wilderness." But until now you have not listened. 17Thus says the LORD, "By this you shall know that I am the LORD." See, with the staff that is in my hand I will strike the water that is in the Nile, and it shall be turned to blood. 18The fish in the river shall die, the river itself shall stink, and the Egyptians shall be unable to drink water from the Nile.' " 19The LORD said to Moses, "Say to Aaron, 'Take your staff and stretch out your hand over the waters of Egypt—over its rivers, its canals, and its ponds, and all its pools of water—so that they may become blood; and there shall be blood throughout the whole land of Egypt, even in vessels of wood and in vessels of stone.' "

20 Moses and Aaron did just as the LORD commanded. In the sight of Pharaoh and of his officials he lifted up the staff and struck the water in the river, and all the water in the river was turned into blood, 21and the fish in the river died. The river stank so that the Egyptians could not drink its water, and there was blood throughout the whole land of Egypt. 22But the magicians of Egypt did the same by their secret arts; so Pharaoh's heart remained hardened, and he would not listen to them, as the LORD had said. 23Pharaoh turned and went into his house, and he did not take even this to heart. 24And all the Egyptians had to dig along the Nile for water to drink, for they could not drink the water of the river.

25 Seven days passed after the LORD had struck the Nile.

8ᵇ The Second Plague: Frogs

Then the LORD said to Moses, "Go to Pharaoh and say to him, 'Thus says the LORD: Let my people go, so that they may worship me. 2If you refuse to let them go, I will plague your whole country with frogs. 3The river shall swarm with frogs; they shall come up into your palace, into your bedchamber and your bed, and into the houses of your officials and of your people,ᶜ and into your ovens and your kneading bowls. 4The frogs shall come up on you and on your people and on all your officials.' " 5ᵈ And the LORD said to Moses, "Say to Aaron, 'Stretch out your hand with your staff over the rivers, the canals, and the pools, and make frogs come up on the land of Egypt.' " 6So Aaron stretched out his hand over the waters of Egypt; and the

---

a Heb *am uncircumcised of lips*; see 6.12 b Ch 7.26 in Heb c Gk: Heb *upon your people* d Ch 8.1 in Heb frogs came up and covered the land of Egypt. [7]But the magicians did the same by their secret arts, and brought frogs up on the land of Egypt.

8 Then Pharaoh called Moses and Aaron, and said, "Pray to the LORD to take away the frogs from me and my people, and I will let the people go to sacrifice to the LORD." [9]Moses said to Pharaoh, "Kindly tell me when I am to pray for you and for your officials and for your people, that the frogs may be removed from you and your houses and be left only in the Nile." [10]And he said, "Tomorrow." Moses said, "As you say! So that you may know that there is no one like the LORD our God, [11]the frogs shall leave you and your houses and your officials and your people; they shall be left only in the Nile." [12]Then Moses and Aaron went out from Pharaoh; and Moses cried out to the LORD concerning the frogs that he had brought upon Pharaoh.[a] [13]And the LORD did as Moses requested: the frogs died in the houses, the courtyards, and the fields. [14]And they gathered them together in heaps, and the land stank. [15]But when Pharaoh saw that there was a respite, he hardened his heart, and would not listen to them, just as the LORD had said.

The Third Plague: Gnats

16 Then the LORD said to Moses, "Say to Aaron, 'Stretch out your staff and strike the dust of the earth, so that it may become gnats throughout the whole land of Egypt.' " [17]And they did so; Aaron stretched out his hand with his staff and struck the dust of the earth, and gnats came on humans and animals alike; all the dust of the earth turned into gnats throughout the whole land of Egypt. [18]The magicians tried to produce gnats by their secret arts, but they could not. There were gnats on both humans and animals. [19]And the magicians said to Pharaoh, "This is the finger of God!" But Pharaoh's heart was hardened, and he would not listen to them, just as the LORD had said.

The Fourth Plague: Flies

20 Then the LORD said to Moses, "Rise early in the morning and present yourself before Pharaoh, as he goes out to the water, and say to him, 'Thus says the LORD: Let my people go, so that they may worship me. [21]For if you will not let my people go, I will send swarms of flies on you, your officials, and your people, and into your houses; and the houses of the Egyptians shall be filled with swarms of flies; so also the land where they live. [22]But on that day I will set apart the land of Goshen, where my people live, so that no swarms of flies shall be there,

that you may know that I the LORD am in this land. [23]Thus I will make a distinction[b] between my people and your people. This sign shall appear tomorrow.' " [24]The LORD did so, and great swarms of flies came into the house of Pharaoh and into his officials' houses; in all of Egypt the land was ruined because of the flies.

25 Then Pharaoh summoned Moses and Aaron, and said, "Go, sacrifice to your God within the land." [26]But Moses said, "It would not be right to do so; for the sacrifices that we offer to the LORD our God are offensive to the Egyptians. If we offer in the sight of the Egyptians sacrifices that are offensive to them, will they not stone us? [27]We must go a three days' journey into the wilderness and sacrifice to the LORD our God as he commands us." [28]So Pharaoh said, "I will let you go to sacrifice to the LORD your God in the wilderness, provided you do not go very far away. Pray for me." [29]Then Moses said, "As soon as I leave you, I will pray to the LORD that the swarms of flies may depart tomorrow from Pharaoh, from his officials, and from his people; only do not let Pharaoh again deal falsely by not letting the people go to sacrifice to the LORD."

30 So Moses went out from Pharaoh and prayed to the LORD. [31]And the LORD did as Moses asked: he removed the swarms of flies from Pharaoh, from his officials, and from his people; not one remained. [32]But Pharaoh hardened his heart this time also, and would not let the people go.

9 The Fifth Plague: Livestock Diseased

Then the LORD said to Moses, "Go to Pharaoh, and say to him, 'Thus says the LORD, the God of the Hebrews: Let my people go, so that they may worship me. [2]For if you refuse to let them go and still hold them, [3]the hand of the LORD will strike with a deadly pestilence your livestock in the field: the horses, the donkeys, the camels, the herds, and the flocks. [4]But the LORD will make a distinction between the livestock of Israel and the livestock of Egypt, so that nothing shall die of all that belongs to the Israelites.' " [5]The LORD set a time, saying, "Tomorrow the LORD will do this thing in the land." [6]And on the next day the LORD did so; all the livestock of the Egyptians died, but of the livestock of the Israelites not one died. [7]Pharaoh inquired and found that not one of the livestock of the Israelites was dead. But the heart of Pharaoh was hardened, and he would not let the people go.

---

a Or *frogs, as he had agreed with Pharaoh* *b* Gk Vg: Heb *will set redemption*

The Sixth Plague: Boils

8 Then the LORD said to Moses and Aaron, "Take handfuls of soot from the kiln, and let Moses throw it in the air in the sight of Pharaoh. ⁹It shall become fine dust all over the land of Egypt, and shall cause festering boils on humans and animals throughout the whole land of Egypt." ¹⁰So they took soot from the kiln, and stood before Pharaoh, and Moses threw it in the air, and it caused festering boils on humans and animals. ¹¹The magicians could not stand before Moses because of the boils, for the boils afflicted the magicians as well as all the Egyptians. ¹²But the LORD hardened the heart of Pharaoh, and he would not listen to them, just as the LORD had spoken to Moses.

The Seventh Plague: Thunder and Hail

13 Then the LORD said to Moses, "Rise up early in the morning and present yourself before Pharaoh, and say to him, 'Thus says the LORD, the God of the Hebrews: Let my people go, so that they may worship me. ¹⁴For this time I will send all my plagues upon you yourself, and upon your officials, and upon your people, so that you may know that there is no one like me in all the earth. ¹⁵For by now I could have stretched out my hand and struck you and your people with pestilence, and you would have been cut off from the earth. ¹⁶But this is why I have let you live: to show you my power, and to make my name resound through all the earth. ¹⁷You are still exalting yourself against my people, and will not let them go. ¹⁸Tomorrow at this time I will cause the heaviest hail to fall that has ever fallen in Egypt from the day it was founded until now. ¹⁹Send, therefore, and have your livestock and everything that you have in the open field brought to a secure place; every human or animal that is in the open field and is not brought under shelter will die when the hail comes down upon them.' " ²⁰Those officials of Pharaoh who feared the word of the LORD hurried their slaves and livestock off to a secure place. ²¹Those who did not regard the word of the LORD left their slaves and livestock in the open field.

22 The LORD said to Moses, "Stretch out your hand toward heaven so that hail may fall on the whole land of Egypt, on humans and animals and all the plants of the field in the land of Egypt." ²³Then Moses stretched out his staff toward heaven, and the LORD sent thunder and hail, and fire came down on the earth. And the LORD rained hail on the land of Egypt; ²⁴there was hail with fire flashing continually in the midst of it, such heavy hail as had never fallen in all the land of Egypt since it became a nation. ²⁵The hail struck down everything that was in the open field throughout all the land of Egypt, both human and animal; the hail also struck down all the plants of the field, and shattered every tree in the field. ²⁶Only in the land of Goshen, where the Israelites were, there was no hail.

27 Then Pharaoh summoned Moses and Aaron, and said to them, "This time I have sinned; the LORD is in the right, and I and my people are in the wrong. ²⁸Pray to the LORD! Enough of God's thunder and hail! I will let you go; you need stay no longer." ²⁹Moses said to him, "As soon as I have gone out of the city, I will stretch out my hands to the LORD; the thunder will cease, and there will be no more hail, so that you may know that the earth is the LORD's. ³⁰But as for you and your officials, I know that you do not yet fear the LORD God." ³¹(Now the flax and the barley were ruined, for the barley was in the ear and the flax was in bud. ³²But the wheat and the spelt were not ruined, for they are late in coming up.) ³³So Moses left Pharaoh, went out of the city, and stretched out his hands to the LORD; then the thunder and the hail ceased, and the rain no longer poured down on the earth. ³⁴But when Pharaoh saw that the rain and the hail and the thunder had ceased, he sinned once more and hardened his heart, he and his officials. ³⁵So the heart of Pharaoh was hardened, and he would not let the Israelites go, just as the LORD had spoken through Moses.

10 The Eighth Plague: Locusts

Then the LORD said to Moses, "Go to Pharaoh; for I have hardened his heart and the heart of his officials, in order that I may show these signs of mine among them, ²and that you may tell your children and grandchildren how

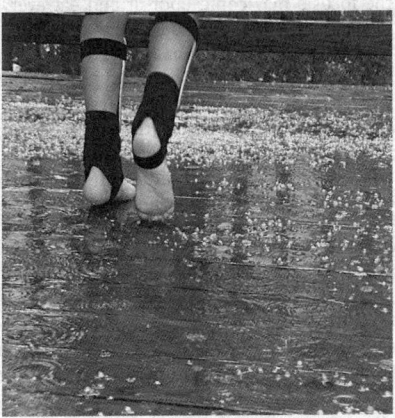

Dance for Joy—© Kristin Sicher, 15

I have made fools of the Egyptians and what signs I have done among them—so that you may know that I am the LORD."

3 So Moses and Aaron went to Pharaoh, and said to him, "Thus says the LORD, the God of the Hebrews, 'How long will you refuse to humble yourself before me? Let my people go, so that they may worship me. ⁴For if you refuse to let my people go, tomorrow I will bring locusts into your country. ⁵They shall cover the surface of the land, so that no one will be able to see the land. They shall devour the last remnant left you after the hail, and they shall devour every tree of yours that grows in the field. ⁶They shall fill your houses, and the houses of all your officials and of all the Egyptians—something that neither your parents nor your grandparents have seen, from the day they came on earth to this day.' " Then he turned and went out from Pharaoh.

7 Pharaoh's officials said to him, "How long shall this fellow be a snare to us? Let the people go, so that they may worship the LORD their God; do you not yet understand that Egypt is ruined?" ⁸So Moses and Aaron were brought back to Pharaoh, and he said to them, "Go, worship the LORD your God! But which ones are to go?" ⁹Moses said, "We will go with our young and our old; we will go with our sons and daughters and with our flocks and herds, because we have the LORD's festival to celebrate." ¹⁰He said to them, "The LORD indeed will be with you, if ever I let your little ones go with you! Plainly, you have some evil purpose in mind. ¹¹No, never! Your men may go and worship the LORD, for that is what you are asking." And they were driven out from Pharaoh's presence.

12 Then the LORD said to Moses, "Stretch out your hand over the land of Egypt, so that the locusts may come upon it and eat every plant in the land, all that the hail has left." ¹³So Moses stretched out his staff over the land of Egypt, and the LORD brought an east wind upon the land all that day and all that night; when morning came, the east wind had brought the locusts. ¹⁴The locusts came upon all the land of Egypt and settled on the whole country of Egypt, such a dense swarm of locusts as had never been before, nor ever shall be again. ¹⁵They covered the surface of the whole land, so that the land was black; and they ate all the plants in the land and all the fruit of the trees that the hail had left; nothing green was left, no tree, no plant in the field, in all the land of Egypt. ¹⁶Pharaoh hurriedly summoned Moses and Aaron and said, "I have sinned against the LORD your God, and against you. ¹⁷Do

forgive my sin just this once, and pray to the LORD your God that at the least he remove this deadly thing from me." ¹⁸So he went out from Pharaoh and prayed to the LORD. ¹⁹The LORD changed the wind into a very strong west wind, which lifted the locusts and drove them into the Red Sea;ᵃ not a single locust was left in all the country of Egypt. ²⁰But the LORD hardened Pharaoh's heart, and he would not let the Israelites go.

The Ninth Plague: Darkness

21 Then the LORD said to Moses, "Stretch out your hand toward heaven so that there may be darkness over the land of Egypt, a darkness that can be felt." ²²So Moses stretched out his hand toward heaven, and there was dense darkness in all the land of Egypt for three days. ²³People could not see one another, and for three days they could not move from where they were; but all the Israelites had light where they lived. ²⁴Then Pharaoh summoned Moses, and said, "Go, worship the LORD. Only your flocks and your herds shall remain behind. Even your children may go with you." ²⁵But Moses said, "You must also let us have sacrifices and burnt offerings to sacrifice to the LORD our God. ²⁶Our livestock also must go with us; not a hoof shall be left behind, for we must choose some of them for the worship of the LORD our God, and we will not know what to use to worship the LORD until we arrive there." ²⁷But the LORD hardened Pharaoh's heart, and he was unwilling to let them go. ²⁸Then Pharaoh said to him, "Get away from me! Take care that you do not see my face again, for on the day you see my face you shall die." ²⁹Moses said, "Just as you say! I will never see your face again."

11 Warning of the Final Plague

The LORD said to Moses, "I will bring one more plague upon Pharaoh and upon Egypt; afterwards he will let you go from here; indeed, when he lets you go, he will drive you away. ²Tell the people that every man is to ask his neighbor and every woman is to ask her neighbor for objects of silver and gold." ³The LORD gave the people favor in the sight of the Egyptians. Moreover, Moses himself was a man of great importance in the land of Egypt, in the sight of Pharaoh's officials and in the sight of the people.

4 Moses said, "Thus says the LORD: About midnight I will go out through Egypt. ⁵Every firstborn in the land of Egypt shall die, from the firstborn of Pharaoh who sits on his throne to the firstborn of the female slave who

_a_ Or _Sea of Reeds_

is behind the handmill, and all the firstborn of the livestock. ⁶Then there will be a loud cry throughout the whole land of Egypt, such as has never been or will ever be again. ⁷But not a dog shall growl at any of the Israelites—not at people, not at animals—so that you may know that the LORD makes a distinction between Egypt and Israel. ⁸Then all these officials of yours shall come down to me, and bow low to me, saying, 'Leave us, you and all the people who follow you.' After that I will leave." And in hot anger he left Pharaoh.

9 The LORD said to Moses, "Pharaoh will not listen to you, in order that my wonders may be multiplied in the land of Egypt." ¹⁰Moses and Aaron performed all these wonders before Pharaoh; but the LORD hardened Pharaoh's heart, and he did not let the people of Israel go out of his land.

12 The First Passover Instituted

The LORD said to Moses and Aaron in the land of Egypt: ²This month shall mark for you the beginning of months; it shall be the first month of the year for you. ³Tell the whole congregation of Israel that on the tenth of this month they are to take a lamb for each family, a lamb for each household. ⁴If a household is too small for a whole lamb, it shall join its closest neighbor in obtaining one; the lamb shall be divided in proportion to the number of people who eat of it. ⁵Your lamb shall be without blemish, a year-old male; you may take it from the sheep or from the goats. ⁶You shall keep it until the fourteenth day of this month; then the whole assembled congregation of Israel shall slaughter it at twilight. ⁷They shall take some of the blood and put it on the two doorposts and the lintel of the houses in which they eat it. ⁸They shall eat the lamb that same night; they shall eat it roasted over the fire with unleavened bread and bitter herbs. ⁹Do not eat any of it raw or boiled in water, but roasted over the fire, with its head, legs, and inner organs. ¹⁰You shall let none of it remain until the morning; anything that remains until the morning you shall burn. ¹¹This is how you shall eat it: your loins girded, your sandals on your feet, and your staff in your hand; and you shall eat it hurriedly. It is the passover of the LORD. ¹²For I will pass through the land of Egypt that night, and I will strike down every firstborn in the land of Egypt, both human beings and animals; on all the gods of Egypt I will execute judgments: I am the LORD. ¹³The blood shall be a sign for you on the houses where you live: when I see the blood, I will pass over you, and no plague shall destroy you when I strike the land of Egypt.

PROFILE OF FAITH

ST. MOSES THE BLACK:
Freedom Through Faith

Did you know there is a saint named St. Moses the Black? Like the people freed from slavery in Egypt with Moses of the Old Testament, St. Moses the Black endured slavery. He lived in the fourth century A.D. and was a slave as a teenager. His search for happiness led him to God, and Moses was baptized and became a priest. He spent the rest of his life sharing the news of God's love with others. St. Moses the Black is the patron saint of African Americans.

14 This day shall be a day of remembrance for you. You shall celebrate it as a festival to the LORD; throughout your generations you shall observe it as a perpetual ordinance. ¹⁵Seven days you shall eat unleavened bread; on the first day you shall remove leaven from your houses, for whoever eats leavened bread from the first day until the seventh day shall be cut off from Israel. ¹⁶On the first day you shall hold a solemn assembly, and on the seventh day a solemn assembly; no work shall be done on those days; only what everyone must eat, that alone may be prepared by you. ¹⁷You shall observe the festival of unleavened bread, for on this very day I brought your companies out of the land of Egypt: you shall observe this day throughout your generations as a perpetual ordinance. ¹⁸In the first month, from the evening of the fourteenth day until the evening of the twenty-first day, you shall eat unleavened bread. ¹⁹For seven days no leaven shall be found in your houses; for whoever eats what is leavened shall be cut off from the congregation of Israel, whether an alien or a native of the land. ²⁰You shall eat nothing leavened; in all your settlements you shall eat unleavened bread.

21 Then Moses called all the elders of Israel and said to them, "Go, select lambs for your families, and slaughter the passover lamb. ²²Take a bunch of hyssop, dip it in the blood that is in the basin, and touch the lintel and the two doorposts with the blood in the basin. None of you shall go outside the door of your

Presence—© Lacy Bedol, 16

house until morning. ²³For the LORD will pass through to strike down the Egyptians; when he sees the blood on the lintel and on the two doorposts, the LORD will pass over that door and will not allow the destroyer to enter your houses to strike you down. ²⁴You shall observe this rite as a perpetual ordinance for you and your children. ²⁵When you come to the land that the LORD will give you, as he has promised, you shall keep this observance. ²⁶And when your children ask you, 'What do you mean by this observance?' ²⁷you shall say, 'It is the passover sacrifice to the LORD, for he passed over the houses of the Israelites in Egypt, when he struck down the Egyptians but spared our houses.' " And the people bowed down and worshiped.

28 The Israelites went and did just as the LORD had commanded Moses and Aaron.

The Tenth Plague: Death of the Firstborn

29 At midnight the LORD struck down all the firstborn in the land of Egypt, from the firstborn of Pharaoh who sat on his throne to the firstborn of the prisoner who was in the dungeon, and all the firstborn of the livestock. ³⁰Pharaoh arose in the night, he and all his officials and all the Egyptians; and there was a loud cry in Egypt, for there was not a house without someone dead. ³¹Then he summoned Moses and Aaron in the night, and said, "Rise up, go away from my people, both you and the Israelites! Go, worship the LORD, as you said. ³²Take your flocks and your herds, as you said, and be gone. And bring a blessing on me too!"

The Exodus: From Rameses to Succoth

33 The Egyptians urged the people to hasten their departure from the land, for they said, "We shall all be dead." ³⁴So the people took their dough before it was leavened, with their kneading bowls wrapped up in their cloaks on their shoulders. ³⁵The Israelites had done as Moses told them; they had asked the Egyptians for jewelry of silver and gold, and for clothing, ³⁶and the LORD had given the people favor in the sight of the Egyptians, so that they let them have what they asked. And so they plundered the Egyptians.

37 The Israelites journeyed from Rameses to Succoth, about six hundred thousand men on foot, besides children. ³⁸A mixed crowd also went up with them, and livestock in great numbers, both flocks and herds. ³⁹They baked unleavened cakes of the dough that they had brought out of Egypt; it was not leavened, because they were driven out of Egypt and could not wait, nor had they prepared any provisions for themselves.

40 The time that the Israelites had lived in Egypt was four hundred thirty years. ⁴¹At the end of four hundred thirty years, on that very

day, all the companies of the Lord went out from the land of Egypt. ⁴²That was for the Lord a night of vigil, to bring them out of the land of Egypt. That same night is a vigil to be kept for the Lord by all the Israelites throughout their generations.

Directions for the Passover

43 The Lord said to Moses and Aaron: This is the ordinance for the passover: no foreigner shall eat of it, ⁴⁴but any slave who has been purchased may eat of it after he has been circumcised; ⁴⁵no bound or hired servant may eat of it. ⁴⁶It shall be eaten in one house; you shall not take any of the animal outside the house, and you shall not break any of its bones. ⁴⁷The whole congregation of Israel shall celebrate it. ⁴⁸If an alien who resides with you wants to celebrate the passover to the Lord, all his males shall be circumcised; then he may draw near to celebrate it; he shall be regarded as a native of the land. But no uncircumcised person shall eat of it; ⁴⁹there shall be one law for the native and for the alien who resides among you.

50 All the Israelites did just as the Lord had commanded Moses and Aaron. ⁵¹That very day the Lord brought the Israelites out of the land of Egypt, company by company.

13 The Lord said to Moses: ²Consecrate to me all the firstborn; whatever is the first to open the womb among the Israelites, of human beings and animals, is mine.

The Festival of Unleavened Bread

3 Moses said to the people, "Remember this day on which you came out of Egypt, out of the house of slavery, because the Lord brought you out from there by strength of hand; no leavened bread shall be eaten. ⁴Today, in the month of Abib, you are going out. ⁵When the Lord brings you into the land of the Canaanites, the Hittites, the Amorites, the Hivites, and the Jebusites, which he swore to your ancestors to give you, a land flowing with milk and honey, you shall keep this observance in this month. ⁶Seven days you shall eat unleavened bread, and on the seventh day there shall be a festival to the Lord. ⁷Unleavened bread shall be eaten for seven days; no leavened bread shall be seen in your possession, and no leaven shall be seen among you in all your territory. ⁸You shall tell your child on that day, 'It is because of what the Lord did for me when I came out of Egypt.' ⁹It shall serve for you as a sign on your hand and as a reminder on your forehead, so that the teaching of the Lord may be on your lips; for with a strong hand the Lord

brought you out of Egypt. ¹⁰You shall keep this ordinance at its proper time from year to year.

The Consecration of the Firstborn

11 "When the Lord has brought you into the land of the Canaanites, as he swore to you and your ancestors, and has given it to you, ¹²you shall set apart to the Lord all that first opens the womb. All the firstborn of your livestock that are males shall be the Lord's. ¹³But every firstborn donkey you shall redeem with a sheep; if you do not redeem it, you must break its neck. Every firstborn male among your children you shall redeem. ¹⁴When in the future your child asks you, 'What does this mean?' you shall answer, 'By strength of hand the Lord brought us out of Egypt, from the house of slavery. ¹⁵When Pharaoh stubbornly refused to let us go, the Lord killed all the firstborn in the land of Egypt, from human firstborn to the firstborn of animals. Therefore I sacrifice to the Lord every male that first opens the womb, but every firstborn of my sons I redeem.' ¹⁶It shall serve as a sign on your hand and as an emblem[a] on your forehead that by strength of hand the Lord brought us out of Egypt."

The Pillars of Cloud and Fire

17 When Pharaoh let the people go, God did not lead them by way of the land of the Philistines, although that was nearer; for God thought, "If the people face war, they may change their minds and return to Egypt." ¹⁸So God led the people by the roundabout way of the wilderness toward the Red Sea.[b] The Israelites went up out of the land of Egypt prepared for battle. ¹⁹And Moses took with him the bones of Joseph who had required a solemn oath of the Israelites, saying, "God will surely take notice of you, and then you must carry my bones with you from here." ²⁰They set out from Succoth, and camped at Etham, on the edge of the wilderness. ²¹The Lord went in front of them in a pillar of cloud by day, to lead them along the way, and in a pillar of fire by night, to give them light, so that they might travel by day and by night. ²²Neither the pillar of cloud by day nor the pillar of fire by night left its place in front of the people.

14 Crossing the Red Sea

Then the Lord said to Moses: ²Tell the Israelites to turn back and camp in front of Pi-ha-hiroth, between Migdol and the sea, in front of Baal-zephon; you shall camp opposite it, by the sea. ³Pharaoh will say of the Israelites, "They are wandering aimlessly in the land; the

---

a Or *as a frontlet*; meaning of Heb uncertain b Or *Sea of Reeds* wilderness has closed in on them." ⁴I will harden Pharaoh's heart, and he will pursue them, so that I will gain glory for myself over Pharaoh and all his army; and the Egyptians shall know that I am the LORD. And they did so.

5 When the king of Egypt was told that the people had fled, the minds of Pharaoh and his officials were changed toward the people, and they said, "What have we done, letting Israel leave our service?" ⁶So he had his chariot made ready, and took his army with him; ⁷he took six hundred picked chariots and all the other chariots of Egypt with officers over all of them. ⁸The LORD hardened the heart of Pharaoh king of Egypt and he pursued the Israelites, who were going out boldly. ⁹The Egyptians pursued them, all Pharaoh's horses and chariots, his chariot drivers and his army; they overtook them camped by the sea, by Pi-hahiroth, in front of Baal-zephon.

10 As Pharaoh drew near, the Israelites looked back, and there were the Egyptians advancing on them. In great fear the Israelites cried out to the LORD. ¹¹They said to Moses, "Was it because there were no graves in Egypt that you have taken us away to die in the wilderness? What have you done to us, bringing us out of Egypt? ¹²Is this not the very thing we told you in Egypt, 'Let us alone and let us serve the Egyptians'? For it would have been better for us to serve the Egyptians than to die in the wilderness." ¹³But Moses said to the people, "Do not be afraid, stand firm, and see the deliverance that the LORD will accomplish for you today; for the Egyptians whom you see today you shall never see again. ¹⁴The LORD will fight for you, and you have only to keep still."

15 Then the LORD said to Moses, "Why do you cry out to me? Tell the Israelites to go forward. ¹⁶But you lift up your staff, and stretch out your hand over the sea and divide it, that the Israelites may go into the sea on dry ground. ¹⁷Then I will harden the hearts of the Egyptians so that they will go in after them; and so I will gain glory for myself over Pharaoh and all his army, his chariots, and his chariot drivers. ¹⁸And the Egyptians shall know that I am the LORD, when I have gained glory for myself over Pharaoh, his chariots, and his chariot drivers."

19 The angel of God who was going before the Israelite army moved and went behind them; and the pillar of cloud moved from in front of them and took its place behind them. ²⁰It came between the army of Egypt and the army of Israel. And so the cloud was there with the darkness, and it lit up the night; one did not come near the other all night.

21 Then Moses stretched out his hand over the sea. The LORD drove the sea back by a strong east wind all night, and turned the sea into dry land; and the waters were divided. ²²The Israelites went into the sea on dry ground, the waters forming a wall for them on their right and on their left. ²³The Egyptians pursued, and went into the sea after them, all of Pharaoh's horses, chariots, and chariot drivers. ²⁴At the morning watch the LORD in the pillar of fire and cloud looked down upon the Egyptian army, and threw the Egyptian army into panic. ²⁵He clogged*ᵃ* their chariot wheels so that they turned with difficulty. The Egyptians said, "Let us flee from the Israelites, for the LORD is fighting for them against Egypt."

The Pursuers Drowned

26 Then the LORD said to Moses, "Stretch out your hand over the sea, so that the water may come back upon the Egyptians, upon their chariots and chariot drivers." ²⁷So Moses stretched out his hand over the sea, and at dawn the sea returned to its normal depth. As the Egyptians fled before it, the LORD tossed the Egyptians into the sea. ²⁸The waters returned and covered the chariots and the chariot drivers, the entire army of Pharaoh that had followed them into the sea; not one of them remained. ²⁹But the Israelites walked on dry ground through the sea, the waters forming a wall for them on their right and on their left.

30 Thus the LORD saved Israel that day from the Egyptians; and Israel saw the Egyptians dead on the seashore. ³¹Israel saw the great work that the LORD did against the Egyptians. So the people feared the LORD and believed in the LORD and in his servant Moses.

15 The Song of Moses

Then Moses and the Israelites sang this song to the LORD:

"I will sing to the LORD, for he has
triumphed gloriously;
horse and rider he has thrown into the sea.
2 The LORD is my strength and my might,ᵇ
and he has become my salvation;
this is my God, and I will praise him,
my father's God, and I will exalt him.
3 The LORD is a warrior;
the LORD is his name.

4 "Pharaoh's chariots and his army he cast
into the sea;
his picked officers were sunk in the Red
Sea.ᶜ
5 The floods covered them;

---

a Sam Gk Syr: MT *removed*   *b* Or *song*   *c* Or *Sea of Reeds*

they went down into the depths like a
stone.
6 Your right hand, O LORD, glorious in
power—
your right hand, O LORD, shattered the
enemy.
7 In the greatness of your majesty you
overthrew your adversaries;
you sent out your fury, it consumed them
like stubble.
8 At the blast of your nostrils the waters piled
up,
the floods stood up in a heap;
the deeps congealed in the heart of the
sea.
9 The enemy said, 'I will pursue, I will overtake,
I will divide the spoil, my desire shall
have its fill of them.
I will draw my sword, my hand shall
destroy them.'
10 You blew with your wind, the sea covered
them;
they sank like lead in the mighty waters.

11 "Who is like you, O LORD, among the gods?
Who is like you, majestic in holiness,
awesome in splendor, doing wonders?
12 You stretched out your right hand,
the earth swallowed them.

13 "In your steadfast love you led the people
whom you redeemed;
you guided them by your strength to your
holy abode.
14 The peoples heard, they trembled;
pangs seized the inhabitants of Philistia.
15 Then the chiefs of Edom were dismayed;
trembling seized the leaders of Moab;
all the inhabitants of Canaan melted away.
16 Terror and dread fell upon them;
by the might of your arm, they became
still as a stone
until your people, O LORD, passed by,
until the people whom you acquired
passed by.
17 You brought them in and planted them
on the mountain of your own
possession,
the place, O LORD, that you made your
abode,
the sanctuary, O LORD, that your hands
have established.
18 The LORD will reign forever and ever."

19 When the horses of Pharaoh with his
chariots and his chariot drivers went into
the sea, the LORD brought back the waters of
the sea upon them; but the Israelites walked
through the sea on dry ground.

a Or *Sea of Reeds* *b* That is *Bitterness*

TEXT MESSAGE

Ever do the "wave" at a sports event? You may not realize it, but Moses invented the cheer. Every time he lifted his arms, his "team" would start winning (Exodus 17.10–13).

This information has been scanned and is free of all known viruses. Please forward to all your friends.

The Song of Miriam
20 Then the prophet Miriam, Aaron's sister, took a tambourine in her hand; and all the women went out after her with tambourines and with dancing. 21 And Miriam sang to them:
"Sing to the LORD, for he has triumphed
gloriously;
horse and rider he has thrown into the sea."

Bitter Water Made Sweet
22 Then Moses ordered Israel to set out from the Red Sea,*a* and they went into the wilderness of Shur. They went three days in the wilderness and found no water. 23 When they came to Marah, they could not drink the water of Marah because it was bitter. That is why it was called Marah.*b* 24 And the people complained against Moses, saying, "What shall we drink?" 25 He

GOOD STUFF

There's a Tex-Mex restaurant in my town. I love eating there, even though I never know what to expect. Placing an order is more like making a suggestion.

Prayer feels like that to me sometimes. God often answers in a way I would never have thought or even wanted. But I keep coming back for more, 'cause in the end it always winds up being good stuff.

Read **Exodus 16**. The Israelites are famished. God doesn't wow them with an all-you-can-eat kosher buffet, but he does provide real food they can sink their teeth into. I'm guessing quail and manna weren't the menu choice of the day (and all the days to follow), but God proved himself faithful.

I have to admit, I'm always a little shocked when God answers prayer in a real and tangible way. How has God been real to you? How's he answered a prayer in a way you can really sink your teeth into?

Fasting, which is when we forgo a meal in order to clear our minds of all worldly concerns, can be a part of prayer. It's a small sacrifice we make to show our reverence for God and to acknowledge the sacrifice that he made for us in his Son Jesus. (Want to know more? See the *Catechism of the Catholic Church* 2043.)

The great pray-ers of the Church often fasted. They knew fasting prepared them for deeper prayer. Fasting leaves more space for God to enter into a conversation with us. We are called to fast on Ash Wednesday and each Friday in Lent. On those days, once we reach the age of eighteen, we are to eat only one full meal and two smaller meals that together don't exceed the size of the full meal.

Try a different kind of fasting while thinking about Exodus 16. Fast from the technology that distracts us so often: put away the laptop, the cell phone, the game player. Spend that time focusing on God. Try it on a regular basis and feel your friendship with God grow.

GOD IS REAL MY CHURCH

cried out to the LORD; and the LORD showed him a piece of wood;[a] he threw it into the water, and the water became sweet.

a Or *a tree* b Heb *he*

There the LORD[b] made for them a statute and an ordinance and there he put them to the test. 26 He said, "If you will listen carefully to the voice of the LORD your God, and do what is right in his sight, and give heed to his commandments and keep all his statutes, I will not bring upon you any of the diseases that I brought upon the Egyptians; for I am the LORD who heals you."

27 Then they came to Elim, where there were twelve springs of water and seventy palm trees; and they camped there by the water.

16 Bread from Heaven

The whole congregation of the Israelites set out from Elim; and Israel came to the wilderness of Sin, which is between Elim and Sinai, on the fifteenth day of the second month after they had departed from the land of Egypt. 2 The whole congregation of the Israelites complained against Moses and Aaron in the wilderness. 3 The Israelites said to them, "If only we had died by the hand of the LORD in the land of Egypt, when we sat by the fleshpots and ate our fill of bread; for you have brought us out into this wilderness to kill this whole assembly with hunger."

4 Then the LORD said to Moses, "I am going to rain bread from heaven for you, and each day the people shall go out and gather enough for that day. In that way I will test them, whether they will follow my instruction or not. 5 On the sixth day, when they prepare what they bring in, it will be twice as much as they gather on other days." 6 So Moses and Aaron said to all the Israelites, "In the evening you shall know that it was the LORD who brought you out of the land of Egypt, 7 and in the morning you shall see the glory of the LORD, because he has heard your complaining against the LORD. For what are we, that you complain against us?" 8 And Moses said, "When the LORD gives you meat to eat in the evening and your fill of bread in the morning, because the LORD has heard the complaining that you utter against him— what are we? Your complaining is not against us but against the LORD."

9 Then Moses said to Aaron, "Say to the whole congregation of the Israelites, 'Draw near to the LORD, for he has heard your complaining.' " 10 And as Aaron spoke to the whole congregation of the Israelites, they looked toward the wilderness, and the glory of the LORD appeared in the cloud. 11 The LORD spoke to Moses and said, 12 "I have heard the complaining of the Israelites; say to them, 'At twilight you shall eat meat, and in the morning you

shall have your fill of bread; then you shall know that I am the LORD your God.' "

13 In the evening quails came up and covered the camp; and in the morning there was a layer of dew around the camp. ¹⁴When the layer of dew lifted, there on the surface of the wilderness was a fine flaky substance, as fine as frost on the ground. ¹⁵When the Israelites saw it, they said to one another, "What is it?"ᵃ For they did not know what it was. Moses said to them, "It is the bread that the LORD has given you to eat. ¹⁶This is what the LORD has commanded: 'Gather as much of it as each of you needs, an omer to a person according to the number of persons, all providing for those in their own tents.' " ¹⁷The Israelites did so, some gathering more, some less. ¹⁸But when they measured it with an omer, those who gathered much had nothing over, and those who gathered little had no shortage; they gathered as much as each of them needed. ¹⁹And Moses said to them, "Let no one leave any of it over until morning." ²⁰But they did not listen to Moses; some left part of it until morning, and it bred worms and became foul. And Moses was angry with them. ²¹Morning by morning they gathered it, as much as each needed; but when the sun grew hot, it melted.

22 On the sixth day they gathered twice as much food, two omers apiece. When all the leaders of the congregation came and told Moses, ²³he said to them, "This is what the LORD has commanded: 'Tomorrow is a day of solemn rest, a holy sabbath to the LORD; bake what you want to bake and boil what you want to boil, and all that is left over put aside to be kept until morning.' " ²⁴So they put it aside until morning, as Moses commanded them; and it did not become foul, and there were no worms in it. ²⁵Moses said, "Eat it today, for today is a sabbath to the LORD; today you will not find it in the field. ²⁶Six days you shall gather it; but on the seventh day, which is a sabbath, there will be none."

27 On the seventh day some of the people went out to gather, and they found none. ²⁸The LORD said to Moses, "How long will you refuse to keep my commandments and instructions? ²⁹See! The LORD has given you the sabbath, therefore on the sixth day he gives you food for two days; each of you stay where you are; do not leave your place on the seventh day." ³⁰So the people rested on the seventh day.

31 The house of Israel called it manna; it was like coriander seed, white, and the taste of it was like wafers made with honey. ³²Moses said, "This is what the LORD has commanded:

'Let an omer of it be kept throughout your generations, in order that they may see the food with which I fed you in the wilderness, when I brought you out of the land of Egypt.' " ³³And Moses said to Aaron, "Take a jar, and put an omer of manna in it, and place it before the LORD, to be kept throughout your generations." ³⁴As the LORD commanded Moses, so Aaron placed it before the covenant,ᵇ for safekeeping. ³⁵The Israelites ate manna forty years, until they came to a habitable land; they ate manna, until they came to the border of the land of Canaan. ³⁶An omer is a tenth of an ephah.

17 Water from the Rock

From the wilderness of Sin the whole congregation of the Israelites journeyed by stages, as the LORD commanded. They camped at Rephidim, but there was no water for the people to drink. ²The people quarreled with Moses, and said, "Give us water to drink." Moses said to them, "Why do you quarrel with me? Why do you test the LORD?" ³But the people thirsted there for water; and the people complained against Moses and said, "Why did you bring us out of Egypt, to kill us and our children and livestock with thirst?" ⁴So Moses cried out to the LORD, "What shall I do with this people? They are almost ready to stone me." ⁵The LORD said to Moses, "Go on ahead of the people, and take some of the elders of Israel with you; take in your hand the staff with which you struck the Nile, and go. ⁶I will be standing there in front of you on the rock at Horeb. Strike the rock, and water will come out of it, so that the people may drink." Moses did so, in the sight of the elders of Israel. ⁷He called the place Massahᶜ and Meribah,ᵈ because the Israelites quarreled and tested the LORD, saying, "Is the LORD among us or not?"

Amalek Attacks Israel and Is Defeated

8 Then Amalek came and fought with Israel at Rephidim. ⁹Moses said to Joshua, "Choose some men for us and go out, fight with Amalek. Tomorrow I will stand on the top of the hill with the staff of God in my hand." ¹⁰So Joshua did as Moses told him, and fought with Amalek, while Moses, Aaron, and Hur went up to the top of the hill. ¹¹Whenever Moses held up his hand, Israel prevailed; and whenever he lowered his hand, Amalek prevailed. ¹²But Moses' hands grew weary; so they took a stone and put it under him, and he sat on it. Aaron and Hur held up his hands, one on one side, and the other on the other side; so his hands were

a Or "It is manna" (Heb man hu, see verse 31) b Or treaty or testimony; Heb eduth c That is Test d That is Quarrel steady until the sun set. ¹³And Joshua defeated Amalek and his people with the sword.

14 Then the Lord said to Moses, "Write this as a reminder in a book and recite it in the hearing of Joshua: I will utterly blot out the remembrance of Amalek from under heaven." ¹⁵And Moses built an altar and called it, The Lord is my banner. ¹⁶He said, "A hand upon the banner of the Lord!ᵃ The Lord will have war with Amalek from generation to generation."

18 Jethro's Advice

Jethro, the priest of Midian, Moses' father-in-law, heard of all that God had done for Moses and for his people Israel, how the Lord had brought Israel out of Egypt. ²After Moses had sent away his wife Zipporah, his father-in-law Jethro took her back, ³along with her two sons. The name of the one was Gershom (for he said, "I have been an alienᵇ in a foreign land"), ⁴and the name of the other, Eliezerᶜ (for he said, "The God of my father was my help, and delivered me from the sword of Pharaoh"). ⁵Jethro, Moses' father-in-law, came into the wilderness where Moses was encamped at the mountain of God, bringing Moses' sons and wife to him. ⁶He sent word to Moses, "I, your father-in-law Jethro, am coming to you, with your wife and her two sons." ⁷Moses went out to meet his father-in-law; he bowed down and kissed him; each asked after the other's welfare, and they went into the tent. ⁸Then Moses told his father-in-law all that the Lord had done to Pharaoh and to the Egyptians for Israel's sake, all the hardship that had beset them on the way, and how the Lord had delivered them. ⁹Jethro rejoiced for all the good that the Lord had done to Israel, in delivering them from the Egyptians.

10 Jethro said, "Blessed be the Lord, who has delivered you from the Egyptians and from Pharaoh. ¹¹Now I know that the Lord is greater than all gods, because he delivered the people from the Egyptians,ᵈ when they dealt arrogantly with them." ¹²And Jethro, Moses' father-in-law, brought a burnt offering and sacrifices to God; and Aaron came with all the elders of Israel to eat bread with Moses' father-in-law in the presence of God.

13 The next day Moses sat as judge for the people, while the people stood around him from morning until evening. ¹⁴When Moses' father-in-law saw all that he was doing for the people, he said, "What is this that you are doing for the people? Why do you sit alone, while all the people stand around you from morning until evening?" ¹⁵Moses said to his father-in-law, "Because the people come to me to inquire of God. ¹⁶When they have a dispute, they come to me and I decide between one person and another, and I make known to them the statutes and instructions of God." ¹⁷Moses' father-in-law said to him, "What you are doing is not good. ¹⁸You will surely wear yourself out, both you and these people with you. For the task is too heavy for you; you cannot do it alone. ¹⁹Now listen to me. I will give you counsel, and God be with you! You should represent the people before God, and you should bring their cases before God; ²⁰teach them the statutes and instructions and make known to them the way they are to go and the things they are to do. ²¹You should also look for able men among all the people, men who fear God, are trustworthy, and hate dishonest gain; set such men over them as officers over thousands, hundreds, fifties, and tens. ²²Let them sit as judges for the people at all times; let them bring every important case to you, but decide every minor case themselves. So it will be easier for you, and they will bear the burden with you. ²³If you do this, and God so commands you, then you will be able to endure, and all these people will go to their home in peace."

24 So Moses listened to his father-in-law and did all that he had said. ²⁵Moses chose able men from all Israel and appointed them as heads over the people, as officers over thousands, hundreds, fifties, and tens. ²⁶And they judged the people at all times; hard cases they brought to Moses, but any minor case they decided themselves. ²⁷Then Moses let his father-in-law depart, and he went off to his own country.

19 The Israelites Reach Mount Sinai

On the third new moon after the Israelites had gone out of the land of Egypt, on that very day, they came into the wilderness of Sinai. ²They had journeyed from Rephidim, entered the wilderness of Sinai, and camped in the wilderness; Israel camped there in front of the mountain. ³Then Moses went up to God; the Lord called to him from the mountain, saying, "Thus you shall say to the house of Jacob, and tell the Israelites: ⁴You have seen what I did to the Egyptians, and how I bore you on eagles' wings and brought you to myself. ⁵Now therefore, if you obey my voice and keep my covenant, you shall be my treasured possession out of all the peoples. Indeed, the whole earth is mine, ⁶but you shall be for me a priestly

---

ᵃ Cn: Meaning of Heb uncertain   ᵇ Heb ger   ᶜ Heb Eli, my God; ezer, help   ᵈ The clause because . . . Egyptians has been transposed from verse 10 kingdom and a holy nation. These are the words that you shall speak to the Israelites."

7 So Moses came, summoned the elders of the people, and set before them all these words that the LORD had commanded him. ⁸The people all answered as one: "Everything that the LORD has spoken we will do." Moses reported the words of the people to the LORD. ⁹Then the LORD said to Moses, "I am going to come to you in a dense cloud, in order that the people may hear when I speak with you and so trust you ever after."

The People Consecrated

When Moses had told the words of the people to the LORD, ¹⁰the LORD said to Moses: "Go to the people and consecrate them today and tomorrow. Have them wash their clothes ¹¹and prepare for the third day, because on the third day the LORD will come down upon Mount Sinai in the sight of all the people. ¹²You shall set limits for the people all around, saying, 'Be careful not to go up the mountain or to touch the edge of it. Any who touch the mountain shall be put to death. ¹³No hand shall touch them, but they shall be stoned or shot with arrows;ᵃ whether animal or human being, they shall not live.' When the trumpet sounds a long blast, they may go up on the mountain." ¹⁴So Moses went down from the mountain to the people. He consecrated the people, and they washed their clothes. ¹⁵And he said to the people, "Prepare for the third day; do not go near a woman."

16 On the morning of the third day there was thunder and lightning, as well as a thick cloud on the mountain, and a blast of a trumpet so loud that all the people who were in the camp trembled. ¹⁷Moses brought the people out of the camp to meet God. They took their stand at the foot of the mountain. ¹⁸Now Mount Sinai was wrapped in smoke, because the LORD had descended upon it in fire; the smoke went up like the smoke of a kiln, while the whole mountain shook violently. ¹⁹As the blast of the trumpet grew louder and louder, Moses would speak and God would answer him in thunder. ²⁰When the LORD descended upon Mount Sinai, to the top of the mountain, the LORD summoned Moses to the top of the mountain, and Moses went up. ²¹Then the LORD said to Moses, "Go down and warn the people not to break through to the LORD to look; otherwise many of them will perish. ²²Even the priests who approach the LORD must consecrate themselves or the LORD will break out against them." ²³Moses said to the

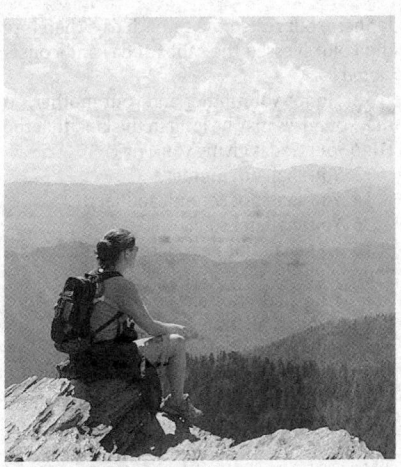

Gatlinburg—© Kate Douglas, 17

LORD, "The people are not permitted to come up to Mount Sinai; for you yourself warned us, saying, 'Set limits around the mountain and keep it holy.' " ²⁴The LORD said to him, "Go down, and come up bringing Aaron with you; but do not let either the priests or the people break through to come up to the LORD; otherwise he will break out against them." ²⁵So Moses went down to the people and told them.

20 The Ten Commandments

Then God spoke all these words:

2 I am the LORD your God, who brought you out of the land of Egypt, out of the house of slavery; ³you shall have no other gods beforeᵇ me.

4 You shall not make for yourself an idol, whether in the form of anything that is in heaven above, or that is on the earth beneath, or that is in the water under the earth. ⁵You shall not bow down to them or worship them; for I the LORD your God am a jealous God, punishing children for the iniquity of parents, to the third and the fourth generation of those who reject me, ⁶but showing steadfast love to the thousandth generationᶜ of those who love me and keep my commandments.

7 You shall not make wrongful use of the name of the LORD your God, for the LORD will not acquit anyone who misuses his name.

8 Remember the sabbath day, and keep it holy. ⁹Six days you shall labor and do all your work. ¹⁰But the seventh day is a sabbath to the LORD your God; you shall not do any work— you, your son or your daughter, your male or female slave, your livestock, or the alien resident in your towns. ¹¹For in six days the LORD made heaven and earth, the sea, and all that is

a Heb lacks *with arrows* *b* Or *besides* *c* Or *to thousands* in them, but rested the seventh day; therefore the LORD blessed the sabbath day and consecrated it.

12 Honor your father and your mother, so that your days may be long in the land that the LORD your God is giving you.

13 You shall not murder.*a*

14 You shall not commit adultery.

15 You shall not steal.

16 You shall not bear false witness against your neighbor.

17 You shall not covet your neighbor's house; you shall not covet your neighbor's wife, or male or female slave, or ox, or donkey, or anything that belongs to your neighbor.

18 When all the people witnessed the thunder and lightning, the sound of the trumpet, and the mountain smoking, they were afraid*b* and trembled and stood at a distance, 19and said to Moses, "You speak to us, and we will listen; but do not let God speak to us, or we will die." 20Moses said to the people, "Do not be afraid; for God has come only to test you and to put the fear of him upon you so that you do not sin." 21Then the people stood at a distance, while Moses drew near to the thick darkness where God was.

The Law concerning the Altar

22 The LORD said to Moses: Thus you shall say to the Israelites: "You have seen for yourselves that I spoke with you from heaven. 23You shall not make gods of silver alongside me, nor shall you make for yourselves gods of gold. 24You need make for me only an altar of earth and sacrifice on it your burnt offerings and your offerings of well-being, your sheep and your oxen; in every place where I cause my name to be remembered I will come to you and bless you. 25But if you make for me an altar of stone, do not build it of hewn stones; for if you use a chisel upon it you profane it. 26You shall not go up by steps to my altar, so that your nakedness may not be exposed on it."

21 The Law concerning Slaves

These are the ordinances that you shall set before them:

2 When you buy a male Hebrew slave, he shall serve six years, but in the seventh he shall go out a free person, without debt. 3If he comes in single, he shall go out single; if he comes in married, then his wife shall go out with him. 4If his master gives him a wife and she bears him sons or daughters, the wife and her children shall be her master's and he shall go out alone. 5But if the slave declares, "I love

my master, my wife, and my children; I will not go out a free person," 6then his master shall bring him before God.*c* He shall be brought to the door or the doorpost; and his master shall pierce his ear with an awl; and he shall serve him for life.

7 When a man sells his daughter as a slave, she shall not go out as the male slaves do. 8If she does not please her master, who designated her for himself, then he shall let her be redeemed; he shall have no right to sell her to a foreign people, since he has dealt unfairly with her. 9If he designates her for his son, he shall deal with her as with a daughter. 10If he takes another wife to himself, he shall not diminish the food, clothing, or marital rights of the first wife.*d* 11And if he does not do these three things for her, she shall go out without debt, without payment of money.

The Law concerning Violence

12 Whoever strikes a person mortally shall be put to death. 13If it was not premeditated, but came about by an act of God, then I will appoint for you a place to which the killer may flee. 14But if someone willfully attacks and kills another by treachery, you shall take the killer from my altar for execution.

15 Whoever strikes father or mother shall be put to death.

16 Whoever kidnaps a person, whether that person has been sold or is still held in possession, shall be put to death.

17 Whoever curses father or mother shall be put to death.

18 When individuals quarrel and one strikes the other with a stone or fist so that the injured party, though not dead, is confined to bed, 19but recovers and walks around outside with the help of a staff, then the assailant shall be free of liability, except to pay for the loss of time, and to arrange for full recovery.

20 When a slaveowner strikes a male or female slave with a rod and the slave dies immediately, the owner shall be punished. 21But if the slave survives a day or two, there is no punishment; for the slave is the owner's property.

22 When people who are fighting injure a pregnant woman so that there is a miscarriage, and yet no further harm follows, the one responsible shall be fined what the woman's husband demands, paying as much as the judges determine. 23If any harm follows, then you shall give life for life, 24eye for eye, tooth for tooth, hand for hand, foot for foot, 25burn for burn, wound for wound, stripe for stripe.

26 When a slaveowner strikes the eye of a

a Or kill *b* Sam Gk Syr Vg; MT *they saw* *c* Or *to the judges* *d* Heb *of her*

Path—© Maggie Hubbard, 15

male or female slave, destroying it, the owner shall let the slave go, a free person, to compensate for the eye. ²⁷If the owner knocks out a tooth of a male or female slave, the slave shall be let go, a free person, to compensate for the tooth.

Laws concerning Property

28 When an ox gores a man or a woman to death, the ox shall be stoned, and its flesh shall not be eaten; but the owner of the ox shall not be liable. ²⁹If the ox has been accustomed to gore in the past, and its owner has been warned but has not restrained it, and it kills a man or a woman, the ox shall be stoned, and its owner also shall be put to death. ³⁰If a ransom is imposed on the owner, then the owner shall pay whatever is imposed for the redemption of the victim's life. ³¹If it gores a boy or a girl, the owner shall be dealt with according to this same rule. ³²If the ox gores a male or female slave, the owner shall pay to the slaveowner thirty shekels of silver, and the ox shall be stoned.

33 If someone leaves a pit open, or digs a pit and does not cover it, and an ox or a donkey falls into it, ³⁴the owner of the pit shall make restitution, giving money to its owner, but keeping the dead animal.

35 If someone's ox hurts the ox of another, so that it dies, then they shall sell the live ox and divide the price of it; and the dead animal they shall also divide. ³⁶But if it was known that the ox was accustomed to gore in the past, and its owner has not restrained it, the owner shall restore ox for ox, but keep the dead animal.

22ᵃ Laws of Restitution

When someone steals an ox or a sheep, and slaughters it or sells it, the thief shall pay five oxen for an ox, and four sheep for a sheep.ᵇ The thief shall make restitution, but if unable to do so, shall be sold for the theft. ⁴When the animal, whether ox or donkey or sheep, is found alive in the thief's possession, the thief shall pay double.

2ᶜ If a thief is found breaking in, and is beaten to death, no bloodguilt is incurred; ³but if it happens after sunrise, bloodguilt is incurred.

5 When someone causes a field or vineyard to be grazed over, or lets livestock loose to graze in someone else's field, restitution shall be made from the best in the owner's field or vineyard.

6 When fire breaks out and catches in thorns so that the stacked grain or the standing grain or the field is consumed, the one who started the fire shall make full restitution.

7 When someone delivers to a neighbor money or goods for safekeeping, and they are stolen from the neighbor's house, then the thief, if caught, shall pay double. ⁸If the thief

a Ch 21.37 in Heb *b* Verses 2, 3, and 4 rearranged thus: 3b, 4, 2, 3a *c* Ch 22.1 in Heb

Did you know that neglecting to "Honor your father and your mother" could have dire consequences? According to Israelite law, if a child didn't honor his or her parents, the child could be put to death (Exodus 21.17). And you thought being grounded was tough!

Fact

This information has been scanned and is free of all known viruses. Please forward to all your friends.

is not caught, the owner of the house shall be brought before God,[a] to determine whether or not the owner had laid hands on the neighbor's goods.

9 In any case of disputed ownership involving ox, donkey, sheep, clothing, or any other loss, of which one party says, "This is mine," the case of both parties shall come before God;[a] the one whom God condemns[b] shall pay double to the other.

10 When someone delivers to another a donkey, ox, sheep, or any other animal for safekeeping, and it dies or is injured or is carried off, without anyone seeing it, [11]an oath before the LORD shall decide between the two of them that the one has not laid hands on the property of the other; the owner shall accept the oath, and no restitution shall be made.

[12]But if it was stolen, restitution shall be made to its owner. [13]If it was mangled by beasts, let it be brought as evidence; restitution shall not be made for the mangled remains.

14 When someone borrows an animal from another and it is injured or dies, the owner not being present, full restitution shall be made. [15]If the owner was present, there shall be no restitution; if it was hired, only the hiring fee is due.

Social and Religious Laws

16 When a man seduces a virgin who is not engaged to be married, and lies with her, he shall give the bride-price for her and make her his wife. [17]But if her father refuses to give her to him, he shall pay an amount equal to the bride-price for virgins.

18 You shall not permit a female sorcerer to live.

19 Whoever lies with an animal shall be put to death.

20 Whoever sacrifices to any god, other than the LORD alone, shall be devoted to destruction.

21 You shall not wrong or oppress a resident alien, for you were aliens in the land of Egypt. [22]You shall not abuse any widow or orphan. [23]If you do abuse them, when they cry out to me, I will surely heed their cry; [24]my wrath will burn, and I will kill you with the sword, and your wives shall become widows and your children orphans.

25 If you lend money to my people, to the poor among you, you shall not deal with them as a creditor; you shall not exact interest from them. [26]If you take your neighbor's cloak in pawn, you shall restore it before the sun goes down; [27]for it may be your neighbor's only clothing to use as cover; in what else shall that person sleep? And if your neighbor cries out to me, I will listen, for I am compassionate.

28 You shall not revile God, or curse a leader of your people.

29 You shall not delay to make offerings from the fullness of your harvest and from the outflow of your presses.[c]

The firstborn of your sons you shall give to me. [30]You shall do the same with your oxen and with your sheep: seven days it shall remain with its mother; on the eighth day you shall give it to me.

31 You shall be people consecrated to me; therefore you shall not eat any meat that is mangled by beasts in the field; you shall throw it to the dogs.

a Or *before the judges* *b* Or *the judges condemn* *c* Meaning of Heb uncertain

23 Justice for All

You shall not spread a false report. You shall not join hands with the wicked to act as a malicious witness. 2You shall not follow a majority in wrongdoing; when you bear witness in a lawsuit, you shall not side with the majority so as to pervert justice; 3nor shall you be partial to the poor in a lawsuit.

4 When you come upon your enemy's ox or donkey going astray, you shall bring it back. 5 When you see the donkey of one who hates you lying under its burden and you would hold back from setting it free, you must help to set it free.a

6 You shall not pervert the justice due to your poor in their lawsuits. 7Keep far from a false charge, and do not kill the innocent and those in the right, for I will not acquit the guilty. 8You shall take no bribe, for a bribe blinds the officials, and subverts the cause of those who are in the right.

9 You shall not oppress a resident alien; you know the heart of an alien, for you were aliens in the land of Egypt.

Sabbatical Year and Sabbath

10 For six years you shall sow your land and gather in its yield; 11but the seventh year you shall let it rest and lie fallow, so that the poor of your people may eat; and what they leave the wild animals may eat. You shall do the same with your vineyard, and with your olive orchard.

12 Six days you shall do your work, but on the seventh day you shall rest, so that your ox and your donkey may have relief, and your homeborn slave and the resident alien may be refreshed. 13Be attentive to all that I have said to you. Do not invoke the names of other gods; do not let them be heard on your lips.

The Annual Festivals

14 Three times in the year you shall hold a festival for me. 15You shall observe the festival of unleavened bread; as I commanded you, you shall eat unleavened bread for seven days at the appointed time in the month of Abib, for in it you came out of Egypt.

No one shall appear before me empty-handed. 16 You shall observe the festival of harvest, of the first fruits of your labor, of what you sow in the field. You shall observe the festival of ingathering at the end of the year, when you gather in from the field the fruit of your labor. 17Three times in the year all your males shall appear before the Lord GOD.

18 You shall not offer the blood of my sacrifice with anything leavened, or let the fat of my festival remain until the morning.

19 The choicest of the first fruits of your ground you shall bring into the house of the LORD your God.

You shall not boil a kid in its mother's milk.

The Conquest of Canaan Promised

20 I am going to send an angel in front of you, to guard you on the way and to bring you to the place that I have prepared. 21Be attentive to him and listen to his voice; do not rebel against him, for he will not pardon your transgression; for my name is in him.

22 But if you listen attentively to his voice and do all that I say, then I will be an enemy to your enemies and a foe to your foes.

23 When my angel goes in front of you, and brings you to the Amorites, the Hittites, the Perizzites, the Canaanites, the Hivites, and the Jebusites, and I blot them out, 24you shall not bow down to their gods, or worship them, or follow their practices, but you shall utterly demolish them and break their pillars in pieces. 25You shall worship the LORD your God, and Ib will bless your bread and your water; and I will take sickness away from among you. 26No one shall miscarry or be barren in your land; I will fulfill the number of your days. 27I will send my terror in front of you, and will throw into confusion all the people against whom you shall come, and I will make all your enemies turn their backs to you. 28And I will send the pestilencec in front of you, which shall drive out the Hivites, the Canaanites, and the Hittites from before you. 29I will not drive them out from before you in one year, or the land would become desolate and the wild animals would multiply against you. 30Little by little I will drive them out from before you, until you have increased and possess the land. 31I will set your borders from the Red Sead to the sea of the Philistines, and from the wilderness to the Euphrates; for I will hand over to you the inhabitants of the land, and you shall drive them out before you. 32You shall make no covenant with them and their gods. 33They shall not live in your land, or they will make you sin against me; for if you worship their gods, it will surely be a snare to you.

24 The Blood of the Covenant

Then he said to Moses, "Come up to the LORD, you and Aaron, Nadab, and Abihu, and seventy of the elders of Israel, and worship at a distance. 2Moses alone shall come near the LORD;

---

a Meaning of Heb uncertain   b Gk Vg: Heb he   c Or hornets: Meaning of Heb uncertain   d Or Sea of Reeds

Music to the Ears—© Christy Klink, 18

but the others shall not come near, and the people shall not come up with him."

3 Moses came and told the people all the words of the Lord and all the ordinances; and all the people answered with one voice, and said, "All the words that the Lord has spoken we will do." ⁴And Moses wrote down all the words of the Lord. He rose early in the morning, and built an altar at the foot of the mountain, and set up twelve pillars, corresponding to the twelve tribes of Israel. ⁵He sent young men of the people of Israel, who offered burnt offerings and sacrificed oxen as offerings of well-being to the Lord. ⁶Moses took half of the blood and put it in basins, and half of the blood he dashed against the altar. ⁷Then he took the book of the covenant, and read it in the hearing of the people; and they said, "All that the Lord has spoken we will do, and we will be obedient." ⁸Moses took the blood and dashed it on the people, and said, "See the blood of the covenant that the Lord has made with you in accordance with all these words."

On the Mountain with God

9 Then Moses and Aaron, Nadab, and Abihu, and seventy of the elders of Israel went up, ¹⁰and they saw the God of Israel. Under his feet there was something like a pavement of sapphire stone, like the very heaven for clearness. ¹¹God*ᵍ* did not lay his hand on the chief men of the people of Israel; also they beheld God, and they ate and drank.

12 The Lord said to Moses, "Come up to me on the mountain, and wait there; and I will give you the tablets of stone, with the law and the commandment, which I have written for their instruction." ¹³So Moses set out with his assistant Joshua, and Moses went up into the mountain of God. ¹⁴To the elders he had said, "Wait here for us, until we come to you again; for Aaron and Hur are with you; whoever has a dispute may go to them."

15 Then Moses went up on the mountain, and the cloud covered the mountain. ¹⁶The glory of the Lord settled on Mount Sinai, and the cloud covered it for six days; on the seventh day he called to Moses out of the cloud. ¹⁷Now the appearance of the glory of the Lord was like a devouring fire on the top of the mountain in the sight of the people of Israel. ¹⁸Moses entered the cloud, and went up on the mountain. Moses was on the mountain for forty days and forty nights.

25 Offerings for the Tabernacle

The Lord said to Moses: ²Tell the Israelites to take for me an offering; from all whose hearts prompt them to give you shall receive the offering for me. ³This is the offering that you shall receive from them: gold, silver, and bronze, ⁴blue, purple, and crimson yarns and fine linen, goats' hair, ⁵tanned rams' skins, fine leather,*ᵇ* acacia wood, ⁶oil for the lamps, spices for the anointing oil and for the fragrant incense, ⁷onyx stones and gems to be set in the ephod and for the breastpiece. ⁸And have them make me a sanctuary, so that I may dwell among them. ⁹In accordance with all that I show you concerning the pattern of the tabernacle and of all its furniture, so you shall make it.

The Ark of the Covenant

10 They shall make an ark of acacia wood; it shall be two and a half cubits long, a cubit and a half wide, and a cubit and a half high. ¹¹You shall overlay it with pure gold, inside and outside you shall overlay it, and you shall make a molding of gold upon it all around. ¹²You shall cast four rings of gold for it and put them on its four feet, two rings on the one side of it, and two rings on the other side. ¹³You shall make poles of acacia wood, and overlay them with gold. ¹⁴And you shall put the poles into the rings on the sides of the ark, by which to carry the ark. ¹⁵The poles shall remain in the rings of the ark; they shall not be taken from it. ¹⁶You shall put into the ark the covenant*ᶜ* that I shall give you.

17 Then you shall make a mercy seat*ᵈ* of pure gold; two cubits and a half shall be its length, and a cubit and a half its width. ¹⁸You shall make two cherubim of gold; you shall make them of hammered work, at the two ends of the mercy seat.*ᵉ* ¹⁹Make one cherub at the

a Heb *He* b Meaning of Heb uncertain c Or *treaty, or testimony*; Heb *eduth* d Or *a cover* e Or *the cover* one end, and one cherub at the other; of one piece with the mercy seat[a] you shall make the cherubim at its two ends. [20]The cherubim shall spread out their wings above, overshadowing the mercy seat[a] with their wings. They shall face one to another; the faces of the cherubim shall be turned toward the mercy seat.[a] [21]You shall put the mercy seat[a] on the top of the ark; and in the ark you shall put the covenant[b] that I shall give you. [22]There I will meet with you, and from above the mercy seat,[a] from between the two cherubim that are on the ark of the covenant,[b] I will deliver to you all my commands for the Israelites.

The Table for the Bread of the Presence

23 You shall make a table of acacia wood, two cubits long, one cubit wide, and a cubit and a half high. [24]You shall overlay it with pure gold, and make a molding of gold around it. [25]You shall make around it a rim a handbreadth wide, and a molding of gold around the rim. [26]You shall make for it four rings of gold, and fasten the rings to the four corners at its four legs. [27]The rings that hold the poles used for carrying the table shall be close to the rim. [28]You shall make the poles of acacia wood, and overlay them with gold, and the table shall be carried with these. [29]You shall make its plates and dishes for incense, and its flagons and bowls with which to pour drink offerings; you shall make them of pure gold. [30]And you shall set the bread of the Presence on the table before me always.

The Lampstand

31 You shall make a lampstand of pure gold. The base and the shaft of the lampstand shall be made of hammered work; its cups, its calyxes, and its petals shall be of one piece with it; [32]and there shall be six branches going out of its sides, three branches of the lampstand out of one side of it and three branches of the lampstand out of the other side of it; [33]three cups shaped like almond blossoms, each with calyx and petals, on one branch, and three cups shaped like almond blossoms, each with calyx and petals, on the other branch—so for the six branches going out of the lampstand. [34]On the lampstand itself there shall be four cups shaped like almond blossoms, each with its calyxes and petals. [35]There shall be a calyx of one piece with it under the first pair of branches, a calyx of one piece with it under the next pair of branches, and a calyx of one piece with it under the last pair of branches—so for the six branches that go out of the lampstand. [36]Their calyxes and their branches shall be of one piece with it, the whole of it one hammered piece of pure gold. [37]You shall make the seven lamps for it; and the lamps shall be set up so as to give light on the space in front of it. [38]Its snuffers and trays shall be of pure gold. [39]It, and all these utensils, shall be made from a talent of pure gold. [40]And see that you make them according to the pattern for them, which is being shown you on the mountain.

26 The Tabernacle

Moreover you shall make the tabernacle with ten curtains of fine twisted linen, and blue, purple, and crimson yarns; you shall make them with cherubim skillfully worked into them. [2]The length of each curtain shall be twenty-eight cubits, and the width of each curtain four cubits; all the curtains shall be of the same size. [3]Five curtains shall be joined to one another; and the other five curtains shall be joined to one another. [4]You shall make loops of blue on the edge of the outermost curtain in the first set; and likewise you shall make loops on the edge of the outermost curtain in the second set. [5]You shall make fifty loops on the one curtain, and you shall make fifty loops on the edge of the curtain that is in the second set; the loops shall be opposite one another. [6]You shall make fifty clasps of gold, and join the curtains to one another with the clasps, so that the tabernacle may be one whole.

7 You shall also make curtains of goats' hair for a tent over the tabernacle; you shall make eleven curtains. [8]The length of each curtain shall be thirty cubits, and the width of each curtain four cubits; the eleven curtains shall be of the same size. [9]You shall join five curtains by themselves, and six curtains by themselves, and the sixth curtain you shall double over at the front of the tent. [10]You shall make fifty loops on the edge of the curtain that is outermost in one set, and fifty loops on the edge of the curtain that is outermost in the second set.

11 You shall make fifty clasps of bronze, and put the clasps into the loops, and join the tent together, so that it may be one whole. [12]The part that remains of the curtains of the tent, the half curtain that remains, shall hang over the back of the tabernacle. [13]The cubit on the one side, and the cubit on the other side, of what remains in the length of the curtains of the tent, shall hang over the sides of the tabernacle, on this side and that side, to cover it. [14]You shall make for the tent a covering of tanned rams' skins and an outer covering of fine leather.[c]

a Or the cover b Or treaty, or testimony; Heb eduth c Meaning of Heb uncertain

The Framework

15 You shall make upright frames of acacia wood for the tabernacle. ¹⁶Ten cubits shall be the length of a frame, and a cubit and a half the width of each frame. ¹⁷There shall be two pegs in each frame to fit the frames together; you shall make these for all the frames of the tabernacle. ¹⁸You shall make the frames for the tabernacle: twenty frames for the south side; ¹⁹and you shall make forty bases of silver under the twenty frames, two bases under the first frame for its two pegs, and two bases under the next frame for its two pegs; ²⁰and for the second side of the tabernacle, on the north side twenty frames, ²¹and their forty bases of silver, two bases under the first frame, and two bases under the next frame; ²²and for the rear of the tabernacle westward you shall make six frames. ²³You shall make two frames for corners of the tabernacle in the rear; ²⁴they shall be separate beneath, but joined at the top, at the first ring; it shall be the same with both of them; they shall form the two corners. ²⁵And so there shall be eight frames, with their bases of silver, sixteen bases; two bases under the first frame, and two bases under the next frame.

26 You shall make bars of acacia wood, five for the frames of the one side of the tabernacle, ²⁷and five bars for the frames of the other side of the tabernacle, and five bars for the frames of the side of the tabernacle at the rear westward. ²⁸The middle bar, halfway up the frames, shall pass through from end to end. ²⁹You shall overlay the frames with gold, and shall make their rings of gold to hold the bars; and you shall overlay the bars with gold. ³⁰Then you shall erect the tabernacle according to the plan for it that you were shown on the mountain.

The Curtain

31 You shall make a curtain of blue, purple, and crimson yarns, and of fine twisted linen; it shall be made with cherubim skillfully worked into it. ³²You shall hang it on four pillars of acacia overlaid with gold, which have hooks of gold and rest on four bases of silver. ³³You shall hang the curtain under the clasps, and bring the ark of the covenant*a* in there, within the curtain; and the curtain shall separate for you the holy place from the most holy. ³⁴You shall put the mercy seat*b* on the ark of the covenant*a* in the most holy place. ³⁵You shall set the table outside the curtain, and the lampstand on the south side of the tabernacle opposite the table; and you shall put the table on the north side.

36 You shall make a screen for the entrance of the tent, of blue, purple, and crimson yarns, and of fine twisted linen, embroidered with needlework. ³⁷You shall make for the screen five pillars of acacia, and overlay them with gold; their hooks shall be of gold, and you shall cast five bases of bronze for them.

27 The Altar of Burnt Offering

You shall make the altar of acacia wood, five cubits long and five cubits wide; the altar shall be square, and it shall be three cubits high. ²You shall make horns for it on its four corners; its horns shall be of one piece with it, and you shall overlay it with bronze. ³You shall make pots for it to receive its ashes, and shovels and basins and forks and firepans; you shall make all its utensils of bronze. ⁴You shall also make for it a grating, a network of bronze; and on the net you shall make four bronze rings at its four corners. ⁵You shall set it under the ledge of the altar so that the net shall extend halfway down the altar. ⁶You shall make poles for the altar, poles of acacia wood, and overlay them with bronze; ⁷the poles shall be put through the rings, so that the poles shall be on the two sides of the altar when it is carried. ⁸You shall make it hollow, with boards. They shall be made just as you were shown on the mountain.

The Court and Its Hangings

9 You shall make the court of the tabernacle. On the south side the court shall have hangings of fine twisted linen one hundred cubits long for that side; ¹⁰its twenty pillars and their twenty bases shall be of bronze, but the hooks of the pillars and their bands shall be of silver. ¹¹Likewise for its length on the north side there shall be hangings one hundred cubits long, their pillars twenty and their bases twenty, of bronze, but the hooks of the pillars and their bands shall be of silver. ¹²For the width of the court on the west side there shall be fifty cubits of hangings, with ten pillars and ten bases. ¹³The width of the court on the front to the east shall be fifty cubits. ¹⁴There shall be fifteen cubits of hangings on the one side, with three pillars and three bases. ¹⁵There shall be fifteen cubits of hangings on the other side, with three pillars and three bases. ¹⁶For the gate of the court there shall be a screen twenty cubits long, of blue, purple, and crimson yarns, and of fine twisted linen, embroidered with needlework; it shall have four pillars and with them four bases. ¹⁷All the pillars around the court shall be banded with silver; their hooks shall be of silver, and their bases of bronze. ¹⁸The length of the court shall

a Or *treaty,* or *testimony;* Heb *eduth*   *b* Or *the cover* be one hundred cubits, the width fifty, and the height five cubits, with hangings of fine twisted linen and bases of bronze. ¹⁹All the utensils of the tabernacle for every use, and all its pegs and all the pegs of the court, shall be of bronze.

The Oil for the Lamp

20 You shall further command the Israelites to bring you pure oil of beaten olives for the light, so that a lamp may be set up to burn regularly. ²¹In the tent of meeting, outside the curtain that is before the covenant,ᵃ Aaron and his sons shall tend it from evening to morning before the LORD. It shall be a perpetual ordinance to be observed throughout their generations by the Israelites.

28 Vestments for the Priesthood

Then bring near to you your brother Aaron, and his sons with him, from among the Israelites, to serve me as priests—Aaron and Aaron's sons, Nadab and Abihu, Eleazar and Ithamar. ²You shall make sacred vestments for the glorious adornment of your brother Aaron. ³And you shall speak to all who have ability, whom I have endowed with skill, that they make Aaron's vestments to consecrate him for my priesthood. ⁴These are the vestments that they shall make: a breastpiece, an ephod, a robe, a checkered tunic, a turban, and a sash. When they make these sacred vestments for your brother Aaron and his sons to serve me as priests, ⁵they shall use gold, blue, purple, and crimson yarns, and fine linen.

The Ephod

6 They shall make the ephod of gold, of blue, purple, and crimson yarns, and of fine twisted linen, skillfully worked. ⁷It shall have two shoulder-pieces attached to its two edges, so that it may be joined together. ⁸The decorated band on it shall be of the same workmanship and materials, of gold, of blue, purple, and crimson yarns, and of fine twisted linen. ⁹You shall take two onyx stones, and engrave on them the names of the sons of Israel, ¹⁰six of their names on the one stone, and the names of the remaining six on the other stone, in the order of their birth. ¹¹As a gem-cutter engraves signets, so you shall engrave the two stones with the names of the sons of Israel; you shall mount them in settings of gold filigree. ¹²You shall set the two stones on the shoulder-pieces of the ephod, as stones of remembrance for the sons of Israel; and Aaron shall bear their names before the LORD on his two shoulders for remembrance. ¹³You shall make settings

ᵃ Or treaty, or testimony; Heb eduth

JESUS SIGHTING

He stood a hair's breadth away from the presence and power of the living God. A curtain stood between them, literally a piece of cloth separating the infinite and the finite. The high priest alone could pull aside the sheet and step inside, presenting the only flawed human heart allowed to stand before the One whose very appearance could kill a person.

Moses put the stone tablets of the Ten Commandments in the wooden box overlaid with pure gold known as the Ark of the Covenant. The Ark was kept in a tent made of curtains, the tabernacle. God's presence was there.

One curtain mattered most. Between the Ark and the rest of the world was a curtain that kept an unclean people out of the presence of a perfect God. Even later in the Scriptures, when most of the curtains of the tabernacle described in Exodus 26 were replaced by the stone walls of the Temple, this one curtain remained, reminding the world that people aren't meant to get that close to God.

Now skip ahead nearly two thousand years after Moses. When Jesus was crucified, a strange thing happened. The curtain in the Temple was ripped in half (see Matthew 27.51). Everyone who knows what the curtain was for knows what this tear means: the barrier that kept humanity separated from God is gone. Now anyone—man, woman, or child; religious leader or screwed-up sinner; wealthy celebrity or dirt-poor nobody— can approach God without fear. Now an encounter with the holy God is available . . . to *everyone.*

Jesus shows us that everyone is called to friendship with God, and we are called to come together. Solidarity is one of the guiding principles of our faith in Catholic social teaching, which says: "We are one human family. We are our brothers' and sisters' keepers, wherever they may be" (from the United States Conference of Catholic Bishops).

of gold filigree, [14]and two chains of pure gold, twisted like cords; and you shall attach the corded chains to the settings.

The Breastplate

15 You shall make a breastpiece of judgment, in skilled work; you shall make it in the style of the ephod; of gold, of blue and purple and crimson yarns, and of fine twisted linen you shall make it. [16]It shall be square and doubled, a span in length and a span in width. [17]You shall set in it four rows of stones. A row of carnelian,[a] chrysolite, and emerald shall be the first row; [18]and the second row a turquoise, a sapphire,[b] and a moonstone; [19]and the third row a jacinth, an agate, and an amethyst; [20]and the fourth row a beryl, an onyx, and a jasper; they shall be set in gold filigree. [21]There shall be twelve stones with names corresponding to the names of the sons of Israel; they shall be like signets, each engraved with its name, for the twelve tribes. [22]You shall make for the breastpiece chains of pure gold, twisted like cords; [23]and you shall make for the breastpiece two rings of gold, and put the two rings on the two edges of the breastpiece. [24]You shall put the two cords of gold in the two rings at the edges of the breastpiece; [25]the two ends of the two cords you shall attach to the two settings, and so attach it in front to the shoulder-pieces of the ephod. [26]You shall make two rings of gold, and put them at the two ends of the breastpiece, on its inside edge next to the ephod. [27]You shall make two rings of gold, and attach them in front to the lower part of the two shoulder-pieces of the ephod, at its joining above the decorated band of the ephod. [28]The breastpiece shall be bound by its rings to the rings of the ephod with a blue cord, so that it may lie on the decorated band of the ephod, and so that the breastpiece shall not come loose from the ephod. [29]So Aaron shall bear the names of the sons of Israel in the breastpiece of judgment on his heart when he goes into the holy place, for a continual remembrance before the Lord. [30]In the breastpiece of judgment you shall put the Urim and the Thummim, and they shall be on Aaron's heart when he goes in before the Lord; thus Aaron shall bear the judgment of the Israelites on his heart before the Lord continually.

Other Priestly Vestments

31 You shall make the robe of the ephod all of blue. [32]It shall have an opening for the head in the middle of it, with a woven binding around the opening, like the opening in a coat of mail,[c]

so that it may not be torn. [33]On its lower hem you shall make pomegranates of blue, purple, and crimson yarns, all around the lower hem, with bells of gold between them all around— [34]a golden bell and a pomegranate alternating all around the lower hem of the robe. [35]Aaron shall wear it when he ministers, and its sound shall be heard when he goes into the holy place before the Lord, and when he comes out, so that he may not die.

36 You shall make a rosette of pure gold, and engrave on it, like the engraving of a signet, "Holy to the Lord." [37]You shall fasten it on the turban with a blue cord; it shall be on the front of the turban. [38]It shall be on Aaron's forehead, and Aaron shall take on himself any guilt incurred in the holy offering that the Israelites consecrate as their sacred donations; it shall always be on his forehead, in order that they may find favor before the Lord.

39 You shall make the checkered tunic of fine linen, and you shall make a turban of fine linen, and you shall make a sash embroidered with needlework.

40 For Aaron's sons you shall make tunics and sashes and headdresses; you shall make them for their glorious adornment. [41]You shall put them on your brother Aaron, and on his sons with him, and shall anoint them and ordain them and consecrate them, so that they may serve me as priests. [42]You shall make for them linen undergarments to cover their naked flesh; they shall reach from the hips to the thighs; [43]Aaron and his sons shall wear them when they go into the tent of meeting, or when they come near the altar to minister in the holy place; or they will bring guilt on themselves and die. This shall be a perpetual ordinance for him and for his descendants after him.

29 The Ordination of the Priests

Now this is what you shall do to them to consecrate them, so that they may serve me as priests. Take one young bull and two rams without blemish, [2]and unleavened bread, unleavened cakes mixed with oil, and unleavened wafers spread with oil. You shall make them of choice wheat flour. [3]You shall put them in one basket and bring them in the basket, and bring the bull and the two rams. [4]You shall bring Aaron and his sons to the entrance of the tent of meeting, and wash them with water. [5]Then you shall take the vestments, and put on Aaron the tunic and the robe of the ephod, and the ephod, and the breastpiece, and gird him with the decorated band of the ephod; [6]and you shall set the turban on his head, and put

---

a The identity of several of these stones is uncertain b Or lapis lazuli c Meaning of Heb uncertain the holy diadem on the turban. [7]You shall take the anointing oil, and pour it on his head and anoint him. [8]Then you shall bring his sons, and put tunics on them, [9]and you shall gird them with sashes[a] and tie headdresses on them; and the priesthood shall be theirs by a perpetual ordinance. You shall then ordain Aaron and his sons.

10 You shall bring the bull in front of the tent of meeting. Aaron and his sons shall lay their hands on the head of the bull, [11]and you shall slaughter the bull before the LORD, at the entrance of the tent of meeting, [12]and shall take some of the blood of the bull and put it on the horns of the altar with your finger, and all the rest of the blood you shall pour out at the base of the altar. [13]You shall take all the fat that covers the entrails, and the appendage of the liver, and the two kidneys with the fat that is on them, and turn them into smoke on the altar. [14]But the flesh of the bull, and its skin, and its dung, you shall burn with fire outside the camp; it is a sin offering.

15 Then you shall take one of the rams, and Aaron and his sons shall lay their hands on the head of the ram, [16]and you shall slaughter the ram, and shall take its blood and dash it against all sides of the altar. [17]Then you shall cut the ram into its parts, and wash its entrails and its legs, and put them with its parts and its head, [18]and turn the whole ram into smoke on the altar; it is a burnt offering to the LORD; it is a pleasing odor, an offering by fire to the LORD.

19 You shall take the other ram; and Aaron and his sons shall lay their hands on the head of the ram, [20]and you shall slaughter the ram, and take some of its blood and put it on the lobe of Aaron's right ear and on the lobes of the right ears of his sons, and on the thumbs of their right hands, and on the big toes of their right feet, and dash the rest of the blood against all sides of the altar. [21]Then you shall take some of the blood that is on the altar, and some of the anointing oil, and sprinkle it on Aaron and his vestments and on his sons and his sons' vestments with him; then he and his vestments shall be holy, as well as his sons and his sons' vestments.

22 You shall also take the fat of the ram, the fat tail, the fat that covers the entrails, the appendage of the liver, the two kidneys with the fat that is on them, and the right thigh (for it is a ram of ordination), [23]and one loaf of bread, one cake of bread made with oil, and one wafer, out of the basket of unleavened bread that is before the LORD; [24]and you shall place all these on the palms of Aaron and on the palms

a Gk: Heb *sashes, Aaron and his sons*

The Next Time You're in Rome...

No trip to Rome is complete without a visit to the Vatican, the home of our Holy Father and the physical heart of our faith. If you're lucky enough to travel to Vatican City, don't miss the Sistine Chapel. But instead of staring up, soaking in the majesty of Michelangelo's ceiling, check out the floor.

It's amazing: a mosaic of stone and glass paste arranged in a mind-boggling design sometime before 1455—and every bit as creative as Michelangelo's ceiling overhead.

Both creations are in a church building. Both are dedicated to God's glory. But although Michelangelo is celebrated, the floor crew has long since been forgotten.

Read **Exodus 31.1–11**. The artists God tapped to direct tabernacle construction didn't do it alone. Hundreds, maybe thousands, of God's people cheerfully helped. They just didn't get any billing.

But so what? The point wasn't recognition. It was to creatively honor a creative God. And, working together, they did exactly that.

So join them. Creatively contribute to your church's liturgies. Craft a visual work of art, sing in your choir, write a song, proclaim the Word, or decorate your church building to mark a feast day or one of the seasons of the Church year.

Your God is creative. Your parish's worship can be the same.

Like a child's latest drawing hung on the refrigerator door by a delighted parent, your gift *will* be appreciated. Prized. Valued not for the skill—or lack of it—but for the heart behind it. Valued by God himself.

So get busy. Create. Participate. Worship. Post your effort at **Learner.CalltoDiscipleship.com**.

of his sons, and raise them as an elevation offering before the LORD. [25]Then you shall take them from their hands, and turn them into smoke on the altar on top of the burnt offering of pleasing odor before the LORD; it is an offering by fire to the LORD.

shall be a perpetual ordinance for Aaron and his sons from the Israelites, for this is an offering; and it shall be an offering by the Israelites from their sacrifice of offerings of well-being, their offering to the LORD.

29 The sacred vestments of Aaron shall be passed on to his sons after him; they shall be anointed in them and ordained in them. [30]The son who is priest in his place shall wear them seven days, when he comes into the tent of meeting to minister in the holy place.

31 You shall take the ram of ordination, and boil its flesh in a holy place; [32]and Aaron and his sons shall eat the flesh of the ram and the bread that is in the basket, at the entrance of the tent of meeting. [33]They themselves shall eat the food by which atonement is made, to ordain and consecrate them, but no one else shall eat of them, because they are holy. [34]If any of the flesh for the ordination, or of the bread, remains until the morning, then you shall burn the remainder with fire; it shall not be eaten, because it is holy.

35 Thus you shall do to Aaron and to his sons, just as I have commanded you; through seven days you shall ordain them. [36]Also every day you shall offer a bull as a sin offering for atonement. Also you shall offer a sin offering for the altar, when you make atonement for it, and shall anoint it, to consecrate it. [37]Seven days you shall make atonement for the altar, and consecrate it, and the altar shall be most holy; whatever touches the altar shall become holy.

The Daily Offerings

38 Now this is what you shall offer on the altar: two lambs a year old regularly each day. [39]One lamb you shall offer in the morning, and the other lamb you shall offer in the evening; [40]and with the first lamb one-tenth of a measure of choice flour mixed with one-fourth of a hin of beaten oil, and one-fourth of a hin of wine for a drink offering. [41]And the other lamb you shall offer in the evening, and shall offer with it a grain offering and its drink offering, as in the morning, for a pleasing odor, an offering by fire to the LORD. [42]It shall be a regular burnt offering throughout your generations at the entrance of the tent of meeting before the LORD, where I will meet with you, to speak to you there. [43]I will meet with the Israelites there, and it shall be sanctified by my glory; [44]I will consecrate the tent of meeting and the altar; Aaron also and his sons I will consecrate, to serve me as priests. [45]I will dwell among the Israelites, and I will be their God. [46]And they shall know that I am the LORD their God, who brought them out of the land of Egypt that I might dwell among them; I am the LORD their God.

26 You shall take the breast of the ram of Aaron's ordination and raise it as an elevation offering before the LORD; and it shall be your portion. [27]You shall consecrate the breast that was raised as an elevation offering and the thigh that was raised as an elevation offering from the ram of ordination, from that which belonged to Aaron and his sons. [28]These things

30 The Altar of Incense

You shall make an altar on which to offer incense; you shall make it of acacia wood. ²It shall be one cubit long, and one cubit wide; it shall be square, and shall be two cubits high; its horns shall be of one piece with it. ³You shall overlay it with pure gold, its top, and its sides all around and its horns; and you shall make for it a molding of gold all around. ⁴And you shall make two golden rings for it; under its molding on two opposite sides of it you shall make them, and they shall hold the poles with which to carry it. ⁵You shall make the poles of acacia wood, and overlay them with gold. ⁶You shall place it in front of the curtain that is above the ark of the covenant,*[a]* in front of the mercy seat*[b]* that is over the covenant,*[a]* where I will meet with you. ⁷Aaron shall offer fragrant incense on it; every morning when he dresses the lamps he shall offer it, ⁸and when Aaron sets up the lamps in the evening, he shall offer it, a regular incense offering before the Lord throughout your generations. ⁹You shall not offer unholy incense on it, or a burnt offering, or a grain offering; and you shall not pour a drink offering on it. ¹⁰Once a year Aaron shall perform the rite of atonement on its horns. Throughout your generations he shall perform the atonement for it once a year with the blood of the atoning sin offering. It is most holy to the Lord.

The Half Shekel for the Sanctuary

11 The Lord spoke to Moses: ¹²When you take a census of the Israelites to register them, at registration all of them shall give a ransom for their lives to the Lord, so that no plague may come upon them for being registered. ¹³This is what each one who is registered shall give: half a shekel according to the shekel of the sanctuary (the shekel is twenty gerahs), half a shekel as an offering to the Lord. ¹⁴Each one who is registered, from twenty years old and upward, shall give the Lord's offering. ¹⁵The rich shall not give more, and the poor shall not give less, than the half shekel, when you bring this offering to the Lord to make atonement for your lives. ¹⁶You shall take the atonement money from the Israelites and shall designate it for the service of the tent of meeting; before the Lord it will be a reminder to the Israelites of the ransom given for your lives.

The Bronze Basin

17 The Lord spoke to Moses: ¹⁸You shall make a bronze basin with a bronze stand for washing.

a Or treaty, or testimony; Heb *eduth b Or the cover c* Heb *it*

IT'S TRADITION

GOLDEN OLDIE

In the twenty-first century, things seem to go out-of-date so quickly—that "smart" phone you just bought is already obsolete now that the company has introduced a "new and improved" version, and the trendy shirt you paid way too much for is already out of style.

But some things are meant to last, and that includes the Old Testament. Here's what the *Catechism* has to say: "The Old Testament is an indispensable part of Sacred Scripture. Its books are divinely inspired and retain a permanent value [cf. *Dei verbum* 14], for the Old Covenant has never been revoked" (CCC 121).

You shall put it between the tent of meeting and the altar, and you shall put water in it; ¹⁹with the water*[c]* Aaron and his sons shall wash their hands and their feet. ²⁰When they go into the tent of meeting, or when they come near the altar to minister, to make an offering by fire to the Lord, they shall wash with water, so that they may not die. ²¹They shall wash their hands and their feet, so that they may not die: it shall be a perpetual ordinance for them, for him and for his descendants throughout their generations.

The Anointing Oil and Incense

22 The Lord spoke to Moses: ²³Take the finest spices: of liquid myrrh five hundred shekels, and of sweet-smelling cinnamon half as much, that is, two hundred fifty, and two hundred fifty of aromatic cane, ²⁴and five hundred of cassia—measured by the sanctuary shekel—and a hin of olive oil; ²⁵and you shall make of these a sacred anointing oil blended as by the perfumer; it shall be a holy anointing oil. ²⁶With it you shall anoint the tent of meeting and the ark of the covenant,*[a]* ²⁷and the table and all its utensils, and the lampstand and its utensils, and the altar of incense, ²⁸and the altar of burnt offering with all its utensils, and the basin with its stand; ²⁹you shall consecrate them, so that they may be most holy; whatever touches them will become holy. ³⁰You shall anoint Aaron and his sons, and consecrate them, in order that they may serve me as priests. ³¹You shall say to the Israelites, "This shall be my holy anointing

oil throughout your generations. [32]It shall not be used in any ordinary anointing of the body, and you shall make no other like it in composition; it is holy, and it shall be holy to you. [33]Whoever compounds any like it or whoever puts any of it on an unqualified person shall be cut off from the people."

34 The LORD said to Moses: Take sweet spices, stacte, and onycha, and galbanum, sweet spices with pure frankincense (an equal part of each), [35]and make an incense blended as by the perfumer, seasoned with salt, pure and holy; [36]and you shall beat some of it into powder, and put part of it before the covenant[a] in the tent of meeting where I shall meet with you; it shall be for you most holy. [37]When you make incense according to this composition, you shall not make it for yourselves; it shall be regarded by you as holy to the LORD. [38]Whoever makes any like it to use as perfume shall be cut off from the people.

31 Bezalel and Oholiab

The LORD spoke to Moses: [2]See, I have called by name Bezalel son of Uri son of Hur, of the tribe of Judah: [3]and I have filled him with divine spirit,[b] with ability, intelligence, and knowledge in every kind of craft, [4]to devise artistic designs, to work in gold, silver, and bronze, [5]in cutting stones for setting, and in carving wood, in every kind of craft. [6]Moreover, I have appointed with him Oholiab son of Ahisamach, of the tribe of Dan; and I have given skill to all the skillful, so that they may make all that I have commanded you: [7]the tent of meeting, and the ark of the covenant,[a] and the mercy seat[c] that is on it, and all the furnishings of the tent, [8]the table and its utensils, and the pure lampstand with all its utensils, and the altar of incense, [9]and the altar of burnt offering with all its utensils, and the basin with its stand, [10]and the finely worked vestments, the holy vestments for the priest Aaron and the vestments of his sons, for their service as priests, [11]and the anointing oil and the fragrant incense for the holy place. They shall do just as I have commanded you.

The Sabbath Law

12 The LORD said to Moses: [13]You yourself are to speak to the Israelites: "You shall keep my sabbaths, for this is a sign between me and you throughout your generations, given in order that you may know that I, the LORD, sanctify you. [14]You shall keep the sabbath, because it is holy for you; everyone who profanes it shall

be put to death; whoever does any work on it shall be cut off from among the people. [15]Six days shall work be done, but the seventh day is a sabbath of solemn rest, holy to the LORD; whoever does any work on the sabbath day shall be put to death. [16]Therefore the Israelites shall keep the sabbath, observing the sabbath throughout their generations, as a perpetual covenant. [17]It is a sign forever between me and the people of Israel that in six days the LORD made heaven and earth, and on the seventh day he rested, and was refreshed."

The Two Tablets of the Covenant

18 When God[d] finished speaking with Moses on Mount Sinai, he gave him the two tablets of the covenant,[a] tablets of stone, written with the finger of God.

32 The Golden Calf

When the people saw that Moses delayed to come down from the mountain, the people gathered around Aaron, and said to him, "Come, make gods for us, who shall go before us; as for this Moses, the man who brought us up out of the land of Egypt, we do not know what has become of him." [2]Aaron said to them, "Take off the gold rings that are on the ears of your wives, your sons, and your daughters, and bring them to me." [3]So all the people took off the gold rings from their ears, and brought them to Aaron. [4]He took the gold from them, formed it in a mold,[e] and cast an image of a calf; and they said, "These are your gods, O Israel, who brought you up out of the land of Egypt!" [5]When Aaron saw this, he built an altar before it; and Aaron made proclamation and said, "Tomorrow shall be a festival to the LORD." [6]They rose early the next day, and offered burnt offerings and brought sacrifices of well-being; and the people sat down to eat and drink, and rose up to revel.

7 The LORD said to Moses, "Go down at once! Your people, whom you brought up out of the land of Egypt, have acted perversely; [8]they have been quick to turn aside from the way that I commanded them; they have cast for themselves an image of a calf, and have worshiped it and sacrificed to it, and said, 'These are your gods, O Israel, who brought you up out of the land of Egypt!' " [9]The LORD said to Moses, "I have seen this people, how stiffnecked they are. [10]Now let me alone, so that my wrath may burn hot against them and I may consume them; and of you I will make a great nation."

a Or treaty, or testimony; Heb eduth   b Or with the spirit of God   c Or the cover   d Heb he   e Or fashioned it with a graving tool; Meaning of Heb uncertain

11 But Moses implored the LORD his God, and said, "O LORD, why does your wrath burn hot against your people, whom you brought out of the land of Egypt with great power and with a mighty hand? [12]Why should the Egyptians say, 'It was with evil intent that he brought them out to kill them in the mountains, and to consume them from the face of the earth'? Turn from your fierce wrath; change your mind and do not bring disaster on your people. [13]Remember Abraham, Isaac, and Israel, your servants, how you swore to them by your own self, saying to them, 'I will multiply your descendants like the stars of heaven, and all this land that I have promised I will give to your descendants, and they shall inherit it forever.' " [14]And the LORD changed his mind about the disaster that he planned to bring on his people.

15 Then Moses turned and went down from the mountain, carrying the two tablets of the covenant[a] in his hands, tablets that were written on both sides, written on the front and on the back. [16]The tablets were the work of God, and the writing was the writing of God, engraved upon the tablets. [17]When Joshua heard the noise of the people as they shouted, he said to Moses, "There is a noise of war in the camp." [18]But he said,

"It is not the sound made by victors,
    or the sound made by losers;
it is the sound of revelers that I hear."

[19]As soon as he came near the camp and saw the calf and the dancing, Moses' anger burned hot, and he threw the tablets from his hands and broke them at the foot of the mountain. [20]He took the calf that they had made, burned it with fire, ground it to powder, scattered it on the water, and made the Israelites drink it.

21 Moses said to Aaron, "What did this people do to you that you have brought so great a sin upon them?" [22]And Aaron said, "Do not let the anger of my lord burn hot; you know the people, that they are bent on evil. [23]They said to me, 'Make us gods, who shall go before us; as for this Moses, the man who brought us up out of the land of Egypt, we do not know what has become of him.' [24]So I said to them, 'Whoever has gold, take it off'; so they gave it to me, and I threw it into the fire, and out came this calf!"

25 When Moses saw that the people were running wild (for Aaron had let them run wild, to the derision of their enemies), [26]then Moses stood in the gate of the camp, and said, "Who is on the LORD's side? Come to me!" And all the sons of Levi gathered around him. [27]He said to them, "Thus says the LORD, the God of Israel, 'Put your sword on your side, each of you! Go

Accept No Substitutes
Read Exodus 32.1–33.6.

Okay . . . so what's with the cow? It's easy to mock people whose response to uncertainty was to sculpt a gold statue of a cow.

But consider the Israelites' position. Behind them: certain slavery. In front: a barren, dangerous unknown. Their leader had disappeared up a mountain. And God had lapsed into a hollow silence.

No one knows if the statue was a symbol of Baal, a god borrowed from the Canaanites, or was intended as a here-and-now symbol of the true God. Either way, it was a bad idea.

They'd built an idol—a substitute for the real thing. God's people on the plains of Sinai had opted for a visible god rather than trusting an invisible God.

That's precisely the tendency of God's people today, actually. We practically worship sports figures, celebrities, and music groups. We even get a little too reverential about name-brand clothes, cars, and personal electronics.

There's nothing wrong with admiring a performer's talent or enjoying nice clothes or possessions. But when those things become a substitute for trusting God, they become nothing more than idols.

Using craft clay, sculpt something you believe is an idol—a substitute for engaging the living, powerful God. When you've finished, take a photo and post it on **Learner.CalltoDiscipleship.com**. Then prayerfully smash the idol—and engage with God.

back and forth from gate to gate throughout the camp, and each of you kill your brother, your friend, and your neighbor.' " [28]The sons of Levi did as Moses commanded, and about three thousand of the people fell on that day. [29]Moses said, "Today you have ordained yourselves[b] for the service of the LORD, each one at the cost of a son or a brother, and so have brought a blessing on yourselves this day."

30 On the next day Moses said to the peo-

---

a Or treaty, or testimony; Heb eduth b Gk Vg Compare Tg: Heb Today ordain yourselves you have written." [33]But the LORD said to Moses, "Whoever has sinned against me I will blot out of my book. [34]But now go, lead the people to the place about which I have spoken to you; see, my angel shall go in front of you. Nevertheless, when the day comes for punishment, I will punish them for their sin."

35 Then the LORD sent a plague on the people, because they made the calf—the one that Aaron made.

33 The Command to Leave Sinai

The LORD said to Moses, "Go, leave this place, you and the people whom you have brought up out of the land of Egypt, and go to the land of which I swore to Abraham, Isaac, and Jacob, saying, 'To your descendants I will give it.' [2]I will send an angel before you, and I will drive out the Canaanites, the Amorites, the Hittites, the Perizzites, the Hivites, and the Jebusites. [3]Go up to a land flowing with milk and honey; but I will not go up among you, or I would consume you on the way, for you are a stiff-necked people."

4 When the people heard these harsh words, they mourned, and no one put on ornaments. [5]For the LORD had said to Moses, "Say to the Israelites, 'You are a stiff-necked people; if for a single moment I should go up among you, I would consume you. So now take off your ornaments, and I will decide what to do to you.' " [6]Therefore the Israelites stripped themselves of their ornaments, from Mount Horeb onward.

The Tent outside the Camp

7 Now Moses used to take the tent and pitch it outside the camp, far off from the camp; he called it the tent of meeting. And everyone who sought the LORD would go out to the tent of meeting, which was outside the camp. [8]Whenever Moses went out to the tent, all the people would rise and stand, each of them, at the entrance of their tents and watch Moses until he had gone into the tent. [9]When Moses entered the tent, the pillar of cloud would descend and stand at the entrance of the tent, and the LORD would speak with Moses. [10]When all the people saw the pillar of cloud standing at the entrance of the tent, all the people would rise and bow down, all of them, at the entrance of their tent. [11]Thus the LORD used to speak to Moses face to face, as one speaks to a friend. Then he would return to the camp; but his young assistant, Joshua son of Nun, would not leave the tent.

Moses' Intercession

12 Moses said to the LORD, "See, you have said to me, 'Bring up this people'; but you have not

ple, "You have sinned a great sin. But now I will go up to the LORD; perhaps I can make atonement for your sin." [31]So Moses returned to the LORD and said, "Alas, this people has sinned a great sin; they have made for themselves gods of gold. [32]But now, if you will only forgive their sin—but if not, blot me out of the book that let me know whom you will send with me. Yet you have said, 'I know you by name, and you have also found favor in my sight.' [13]Now if I have found favor in your sight, show me your ways, so that I may know you and find favor in your sight. Consider too that this nation is your people." [14]He said, "My presence will go with you, and I will give you rest." [15]And he said to him, "If your presence will not go, do not carry us up from here. [16]For how shall it be known that I have found favor in your sight, I and your people, unless you go with us? In this way, we shall be distinct, I and your people, from every people on the face of the earth."

17 The LORD said to Moses, "I will do the very thing that you have asked; for you have found favor in my sight, and I know you by name." [18]Moses said, "Show me your glory, I pray." [19]And he said, "I will make all my goodness pass before you, and will proclaim before you the name, 'The LORD';[a] and I will be gracious to whom I will be gracious, and will show mercy on whom I will show mercy. [20]But," he said, "you cannot see my face; for no one shall see me and live." [21]And the LORD continued, "See, there is a place by me where you shall stand on the rock; [22]and while my glory passes by I will put you in a cleft of the rock, and I will cover you with my hand until I have passed by; [23]then I will take away my hand, and you shall see my back; but my face shall not be seen."

34 Moses Makes New Tablets

The LORD said to Moses, "Cut two tablets of stone like the former ones, and I will write on the tablets the words that were on the former tablets, which you broke. [2]Be ready in the morning, and come up in the morning to Mount Sinai and present yourself there to me, on the top of the mountain. [3]No one shall come up with you, and do not let anyone be seen throughout all the mountain; and do not let flocks or herds graze in front of that mountain." [4]So Moses cut two tablets of stone like the former ones; and he rose early in the morning and went up on Mount Sinai, as the LORD had commanded him, and took in his hand the two tablets of stone. [5]The LORD descended in the cloud and stood with him there, and proclaimed the name, "The LORD."[a] [6]The LORD passed before him, and proclaimed,

"The LORD, the LORD,
 a God merciful and gracious,
 slow to anger,
 and abounding in steadfast love and
    faithfulness,

[7] keeping steadfast love for the thousandth
    generation,[b]
 forgiving iniquity and transgression and
    sin,
 yet by no means clearing the guilty,
 but visiting the iniquity of the parents
    upon the children
 and the children's children,
 to the third and the fourth generation."

[8]And Moses quickly bowed his head toward the earth, and worshiped. [9]He said, "If now I have found favor in your sight, O Lord, I pray, let the Lord go with us. Although this is a stiff-necked people, pardon our iniquity and our sin, and take us for your inheritance."

The Covenant Renewed

10 He said: I hereby make a covenant. Before all your people I will perform marvels, such as have not been performed in all the earth or in any nation; and all the people among whom you live shall see the work of the LORD; for it is an awesome thing that I will do with you.

11 Observe what I command you today. See, I will drive out before you the Amorites, the Canaanites, the Hittites, the Perizzites, the Hivites, and the Jebusites. [12]Take care not to make a covenant with the inhabitants of the land to which you are going, or it will become a snare among you. [13]You shall tear down their altars, break their pillars, and cut down their sacred poles[c] [14](for you shall worship no other god, because the LORD, whose name is Jealous, is a jealous God). [15]You shall not make a covenant with the inhabitants of the land, for when they prostitute themselves to their gods and sacrifice to their gods, someone among them will invite you, and you will eat of the sacrifice. [16]And you will take wives from among their daughters for your sons, and their daughters who prostitute themselves to their gods will make your sons also prostitute themselves to their gods.

17 You shall not make cast idols.

18 You shall keep the festival of unleavened bread. Seven days you shall eat unleavened bread, as I commanded you, at the time appointed in the month of Abib; for in the month of Abib you came out from Egypt.

19 All that first opens the womb is mine, all your male[d] livestock, the firstborn of cow and sheep. [20]The firstborn of a donkey you shall redeem with a lamb, or if you will not redeem it you shall break its neck. All the firstborn of your sons you shall redeem.

No one shall appear before me empty-handed.

21 Six days you shall work, but on the sev-

---

a Heb YHWH; see note at 3.15 b Or for thousands c Heb Asherim d Gk Theodotion Vg Tg: Meaning of Heb uncertain enth day you shall rest; even in plowing time and in harvest time you shall rest. ²²You shall observe the festival of weeks, the first fruits of wheat harvest, and the festival of ingathering at the turn of the year. ²³Three times in the year all your males shall appear before the Lord God, the God of Israel. ²⁴For I will cast out nations before you, and enlarge your borders; no one shall covet your land when you go up to appear before the Lord your God three times in the year.

25 You shall not offer the blood of my sacrifice with leaven, and the sacrifice of the festival of the passover shall not be left until the morning.

26 The best of the first fruits of your ground you shall bring to the house of the Lord your God.

You shall not boil a kid in its mother's milk.

27 The Lord said to Moses: Write these words; in accordance with these words I have made a covenant with you and with Israel. ²⁸He was there with the Lord forty days and forty nights; he neither ate bread nor drank water. And he wrote on the tablets the words of the covenant, the ten commandments.ᵃ

The Shining Face of Moses

29 Moses came down from Mount Sinai. As he came down from the mountain with the two tablets of the covenantᵇ in his hand, Moses did not know that the skin of his face shone because he had been talking with God. ³⁰When Aaron and all the Israelites saw Moses, the skin of his face was shining, and they were afraid to come near him. ³¹But Moses called to them; and Aaron and all the leaders of the congregation returned to him, and Moses spoke with them. ³²Afterward all the Israelites came near, and he gave them in commandment all that the Lord had spoken with him on Mount Sinai. ³³When Moses had finished speaking with them, he put a veil on his face; ³⁴but whenever Moses went in before the Lord to speak with him, he would take the veil off, until he came out; and when he came out, and told the Israelites what he had been commanded, ³⁵the Israelites would see the face of Moses, that the skin of his face was shining; and Moses would put the veil on his face again, until he went in to speak with him.

35 Sabbath Regulations

Moses assembled all the congregation of the Israelites and said to them: These are the things that the Lord has commanded you to do:

2 Six days shall work be done, but on the seventh day you shall have a holy sabbath of solemn rest to the Lord; whoever does any work on it shall be put to death. ³You shall kindle no fire in all your dwellings on the sabbath day.

Preparations for Making the Tabernacle

4 Moses said to all the congregation of the Israelites: This is the thing that the Lord has commanded: ⁵Take from among you an offering to the Lord; let whoever is of a generous heart bring the Lord's offering: gold, silver, and bronze; ⁶blue, purple, and crimson yarns, and fine linen; goats' hair, ⁷tanned rams' skins, and fine leather;ᶜ acacia wood, ⁸oil for the light, spices for the anointing oil and for the fragrant incense, ⁹and onyx stones and gems to be set in the ephod and the breastpiece.

10 All who are skillful among you shall come and make all that the Lord has commanded: the tabernacle, ¹¹its tent and its covering, its clasps and its frames, its bars, its pillars, and its bases; ¹²the ark with its poles, the mercy seat,ᵈ and the curtain for the screen; ¹³the table with its poles and all its utensils, and the bread of the Presence; ¹⁴the lampstand also for the light, with its utensils and its lamps, and the oil for the light; ¹⁵and the altar of incense, with its poles, and the anointing oil and the fragrant incense, and the screen for the entrance, the entrance of the tabernacle; ¹⁶the altar of burnt offering, with its grating of bronze, its poles, and all its utensils, the basin with its stand; ¹⁷the hangings of the court, its pillars and its bases, and the screen for the gate of the court; ¹⁸the pegs of the tabernacle and the pegs of the court, and their cords; ¹⁹the finely worked vestments for ministering in the holy place, the holy vestments for the priest Aaron, and the vestments of his sons, for their service as priests.

Offerings for the Tabernacle

20 Then all the congregation of the Israelites withdrew from the presence of Moses. ²¹And they came, everyone whose heart was stirred, and everyone whose spirit was willing, and brought the Lord's offering to be used for the tent of meeting, and for all its service, and for the sacred vestments. ²²So they came, both men and women; all who were of a willing heart brought brooches and earrings and signet rings and pendants, all sorts of gold objects, everyone bringing an offering of gold to the Lord. ²³And everyone who possessed blue or purple or crimson yarn or fine linen or goats' hair or tanned rams' skins or fine leather,ᶜ brought them. ²⁴Everyone who could make

---

a Heb words b Or treaty, or testimony; Heb eduth c Meaning of Heb uncertain d Or the cover

SAFE IN YOUR HANDS.

Safe in Your Hands

Take me in your palm, Lord,
And I'll wave fronds of palms
To adore.
I trust the path that you've laid.
I know that in love I was made
So I feel safe in your hands.
So I'll press mine together
And know that I am safe.

Safe in Your Hands—© Marshall Katheder, 19

an offering of silver or bronze brought it as the Lord's offering; and everyone who possessed acacia wood of any use in the work, brought it. 25All the skillful women spun with their hands, and brought what they had spun in blue and purple and crimson yarns and fine linen; 26all the women whose hearts moved them to use their skill spun the goats' hair. 27And the leaders brought onyx stones and gems to be set in the ephod and the breastpiece, 28and spices and oil for the light, and for the anointing oil, and for the fragrant incense. 29All the Israelite men and women whose hearts made them willing to bring anything for the work that the Lord had commanded by Moses to be done, brought it as a freewill offering to the Lord.

Bezalel and Oholiab

30 Then Moses said to the Israelites: See, the Lord has called by name Bezalel son of Uri son of Hur, of the tribe of Judah; 31he has filled him with divine spirit,*a* with skill, intelligence, and knowledge in every kind of craft, 32to devise artistic designs, to work in gold, silver, and bronze, 33in cutting stones for setting, and in carving wood, in every kind of craft. 34And he has inspired him to teach, both him and Oholiab son of Ahisamach, of the tribe of Dan. 35He has filled them with skill to do every kind of work done by an artisan or by a designer or by an embroiderer in blue, purple, and crimson yarns, and in fine linen, or by a weaver—by any sort of artisan or skilled designer.

36 Bezalel and Oholiab and every skillful one to whom the Lord has given skill and understanding to know how to do any work in the construction of the sanctuary shall work in accordance with all that the Lord has commanded.

2 Moses then called Bezalel and Oholiab and every skillful one to whom the Lord had given skill, everyone whose heart was stirred to come to do the work; 3and they received from Moses all the freewill offerings that the Israelites had brought for doing the work on the sanctuary. They still kept bringing him freewill offerings every morning, 4so that all the artisans who were doing every sort of task on the sanctuary came, each from the task being performed, 5and said to Moses, "The people are bringing much more than enough for doing the work that the Lord has commanded us to do." 6So Moses gave command, and word was proclaimed throughout the camp: "No man or woman is to make anything else as an offering for the sanctuary." So the people were restrained from bringing; 7for what they had already brought was more than enough to do all the work.

Construction of the Tabernacle

8 All those with skill among the workers made the tabernacle with ten curtains; they were made of fine twisted linen, and blue, purple, and crimson yarns, with cherubim skillfully worked into them. 9The length of each curtain was twenty-eight cubits, and the width of each curtain four cubits; all the curtains were of the same size.

10 He joined five curtains to one another, and the other five curtains he joined to one another. 11He made loops of blue on the edge of the outermost curtain of the first set; likewise he made them on the edge of the outermost curtain of the second set; 12he made fifty loops on the one curtain, and he made fifty loops on the edge of the curtain that was in the second set; the loops were opposite one another. 13And he made fifty clasps of gold, and joined the curtains one to the other with clasps; so the tabernacle was one whole.

14 He also made curtains of goats' hair for a tent over the tabernacle; he made eleven curtains. 15The length of each curtain was thirty cubits, and the width of each curtain four cubits; the eleven curtains were of the same size. 16He joined five curtains by themselves, and six curtains by themselves. 17He made fifty loops on the edge of the outermost curtain of the one set, and fifty loops on the edge of the other connecting curtain. 18He made fifty clasps of bronze to join the tent together so that it might be one whole. 19And he made for the tent a covering of tanned rams' skins and an outer covering of fine leather.*b*

20 Then he made the upright frames for the tabernacle of acacia wood. 21Ten cubits was the length of a frame, and a cubit and a half the width of each frame. 22Each frame had two pegs for fitting together; he did this for all the frames of the tabernacle. 23The frames for the tabernacle he made in this way: twenty frames for the south side; 24and he made forty bases of silver under the twenty frames, two bases under the first frame for its two pegs, and two bases under the next frame for its two pegs. 25For the second side of the tabernacle, on the north side, he made twenty frames 26and their forty bases of silver, two bases under the first frame and two bases under the next frame. 27For the rear of the tabernacle westward he made six frames. 28He made two frames for corners of the tabernacle in the rear. 29They were separate beneath, but joined at the top, at

a Or *the spirit of God*   *b* Meaning of Heb uncertain

The Steeple—© Kate Douglas, 17

the first ring; he made two of them in this way, for the two corners. ³⁰There were eight frames with their bases of silver: sixteen bases, under every frame two bases.

31 He made bars of acacia wood, five for the frames of the one side of the tabernacle, ³²and five bars for the frames of the other side of the tabernacle, and five bars for the frames of the tabernacle at the rear westward. ³³He made the middle bar to pass through from end to end halfway up the frames. ³⁴And he overlaid the frames with gold, and made rings of gold for them to hold the bars, and overlaid the bars with gold.

35 He made the curtain of blue, purple, and crimson yarns, and fine twisted linen, with cherubim skillfully worked into it. ³⁶For it he made four pillars of acacia, and overlaid them with gold; their hooks were of gold, and he cast for them four bases of silver. ³⁷He also made a screen for the entrance to the tent, of blue, purple, and crimson yarns, and fine twisted linen, embroidered with needlework; ³⁸and its five pillars with their hooks. He overlaid their capitals and their bases with gold, but their five bases were of bronze.

37 Making the Ark of the Covenant

Bezalel made the ark of acacia wood; it was two and a half cubits long, a cubit and a half wide, and a cubit and a half high. ²He overlaid it with pure gold inside and outside, and made a molding of gold around it. ³He cast for it four rings of gold for its four feet, two rings on its one side and two rings on its other side. ⁴He made poles of acacia wood, and overlaid them with gold, ⁵and put the poles into the rings on the sides of the ark, to carry the ark. ⁶He made a mercy seat*a* of pure gold; two cubits and a half was its length, and a cubit and a half its width. ⁷He made two cherubim of hammered gold; at the two ends of the mercy seat*b* he made them, ⁸one cherub at the one end, and one cherub at the other end; of one piece with the mercy seat*b* he made the cherubim at its two ends. ⁹The cherubim spread out their wings above, overshadowing the mercy seat*b* with their wings. They faced one another; the faces of the cherubim were turned toward the mercy seat.*b*

Making the Table for the Bread of the Presence

10 He also made the table of acacia wood, two cubits long, one cubit wide, and a cubit and a half high. ¹¹He overlaid it with pure gold, and made a molding of gold around it. ¹²He made around it a rim a handbreadth wide, and made a molding of gold around the rim. ¹³He cast for it four rings of gold, and fastened the rings to the four corners at its four legs. ¹⁴The rings that

a Or *a cover* *b* Or *the cover*

held the poles used for carrying the table were close to the rim. ¹⁵He made the poles of acacia wood to carry the table, and overlaid them with gold. ¹⁶And he made the vessels of pure gold that were to be on the table, its plates and dishes for incense, and its bowls and flagons with which to pour drink offerings.

Making the Lampstand

17 He also made the lampstand of pure gold. The base and the shaft of the lampstand were made of hammered work; its cups, its calyxes, and its petals were of one piece with it. ¹⁸There were six branches going out of its sides, three branches of the lampstand out of one side of it and three branches of the lampstand out of the other side of it; ¹⁹three cups shaped like almond blossoms, each with calyx and petals, on one branch, and three cups shaped like almond blossoms, each with calyx and petals, on the other branch—so for the six branches going out of the lampstand. ²⁰On the lampstand itself there were four cups shaped like almond blossoms, each with its calyxes and petals. ²¹There was a calyx of one piece with it under the first pair of branches, a calyx of one piece with it under the next pair of branches, and a calyx of one piece with it under the last pair of branches. ²²Their calyxes and their branches were of one piece with it, the whole of it one hammered piece of pure gold. ²³He made its seven lamps and its snuffers and its trays of pure gold. ²⁴He made it and all its utensils of a talent of pure gold.

Making the Altar of Incense

25 He made the altar of incense of acacia wood, one cubit long, and one cubit wide; it was square, and was two cubits high; its horns were of one piece with it. ²⁶He overlaid it with pure gold, its top, and its sides all around, and its horns; and he made for it a molding of gold all around, ²⁷and made two golden rings for it under its molding, on two opposite sides of it, to hold the poles with which to carry it. ²⁸And he made the poles of acacia wood, and overlaid them with gold.

Making the Anointing Oil and the Incense

29 He made the holy anointing oil also, and the pure fragrant incense, blended as by the perfumer.

38 Making the Altar of Burnt Offering

He made the altar of burnt offering also of acacia wood; it was five cubits long, and five cubits wide; it was square, and three cubits high. ²He

made horns for it on its four corners; its horns were of one piece with it, and he overlaid it with bronze. ³He made all the utensils of the altar, the pots, the shovels, the basins, the forks, and the firepans: all its utensils he made of bronze. ⁴He made for the altar a grating, a network of bronze, under its ledge, extending halfway down. ⁵He cast four rings on the four corners of the bronze grating to hold the poles; ⁶he made the poles of acacia wood, and overlaid them with bronze. ⁷And he put the poles through the rings on the sides of the altar, to carry it with them; he made it hollow, with boards.

8 He made the basin of bronze with its stand of bronze, from the mirrors of the women who served at the entrance to the tent of meeting.

Making the Court of the Tabernacle

9 He made the court; for the south side the hangings of the court were of fine twisted linen, one hundred cubits long; ¹⁰its twenty pillars and their twenty bases were of bronze, but the hooks of the pillars and their bands were of silver. ¹¹For the north side there were hangings one hundred cubits long; its twenty pillars and their twenty bases were of bronze, but the hooks of the pillars and their bands were of silver. ¹²For the west side there were hangings fifty cubits long, with ten pillars and ten bases; the hooks of the pillars and their bands were of silver. ¹³And for the front to the east, fifty cubits. ¹⁴The hangings for one side of the gate were fifteen cubits, with three pillars and three bases. ¹⁵And so for the other side; on each side of the gate of the court were hangings of fifteen cubits, with three pillars and three bases. ¹⁶All the hangings around the court were of fine twisted linen. ¹⁷The bases for the pillars were of bronze, but the hooks of the pillars and their bands were of silver; the overlaying of their capitals was also of silver, and all the pillars of the court were banded with silver. ¹⁸The screen for the entrance to the court was embroidered with needlework in blue, purple, and crimson yarns and fine twisted linen. It was twenty cubits long and, along the width of it, five cubits high, corresponding to the hangings of the court. ¹⁹There were four pillars; their four bases were of bronze, their hooks of silver, and the overlaying of their capitals and their bands of silver. ²⁰All the pegs for the tabernacle and for the court all around were of bronze.

Materials of the Tabernacle

21 These are the records of the tabernacle, the tabernacle of the covenant,ᵃ which were drawn

a Or treaty, or testimony; Heb eduth

up at the commandment of Moses, the work of the Levites being under the direction of Ithamar son of the priest Aaron. ²² Bezalel son of Uri son of Hur, of the tribe of Judah, made all that the LORD commanded Moses; ²³ and with him was Oholiab son of Ahisamach, of the tribe of Dan, engraver, designer, and embroiderer in blue, purple, and crimson yarns, and in fine linen.

24 All the gold that was used for the work, in all the construction of the sanctuary, the gold from the offering, was twenty-nine talents and seven hundred thirty shekels, measured by the sanctuary shekel. ²⁵ The silver from those of the congregation who were counted was one hundred talents and one thousand seven hundred seventy-five shekels, measured by the sanctuary shekel; ²⁶ a beka a head (that is, half a shekel, measured by the sanctuary shekel), for everyone who was counted in the census, from twenty years old and upward, for six hundred three thousand, five hundred fifty men. ²⁷ The hundred talents of silver were for casting the bases of the sanctuary, and the bases of the curtain; one hundred bases for the hundred talents, a talent for a base. ²⁸ Of the thousand seven hundred seventy-five shekels he made hooks for the pillars, and overlaid their capitals and made bands for them. ²⁹ The bronze that was contributed was seventy talents, and two thousand four hundred shekels; ³⁰ with it he made the bases for the entrance of the tent of meeting, the bronze altar and the bronze grating for it and all the utensils of the altar, ³¹ the bases all around the court, and the bases of the gate of court, all the pegs of the tabernacle, and all the pegs around the court.

39 Making the Vestments for the Priesthood

Of the blue, purple, and crimson yarns they made finely worked vestments, for ministering in the holy place; they made the sacred vestments for Aaron; as the LORD had commanded Moses.

2 He made the ephod of gold, of blue, purple, and crimson yarns, and of fine twisted linen. ³ Gold leaf was hammered out and cut into threads to work into the blue, purple, and crimson yarns and into the fine twisted linen, in skilled design. ⁴ They made for the ephod shoulder-pieces, joined to it at its two edges. ⁵ The decorated band on it was of the same materials and workmanship, of gold, of blue, purple, and crimson yarns, and of fine twisted linen; as the LORD had commanded Moses.

6 The onyx stones were prepared, enclosed

"The great danger for family life, in the midst of any society whose idols are pleasure, comfort, and independence, lies in the fact that people close their hearts and become selfish."

—Pope John Paul II

in settings of gold filigree and engraved like the engravings of a signet, according to the names of the sons of Israel; ⁷ He set them on the shoulder-pieces of the ephod, to be stones of remembrance for the sons of Israel; as the LORD had commanded Moses.

8 He made the breastpiece, in skilled work, like the work of the ephod, of gold, of blue, purple, and crimson yarns, and of fine twisted linen. ⁹ It was square; the breastpiece was made double, a span in length and a span in width when doubled. ¹⁰ They set in it four rows of stones. A row of carnelian,^a chrysolite, and emerald was the first row; ¹¹ and the second row, a turquoise, a sapphire,^b and a moonstone; ¹² and the third row, a jacinth, an agate, and an amethyst; ¹³ and the fourth row, a beryl, an onyx, and a jasper; they were enclosed in settings of gold filigree. ¹⁴ There were twelve stones with names corresponding to the names of the sons of Israel; they were like signets, each engraved with its name, for the twelve tribes. ¹⁵ They made on the breastpiece chains of pure gold, twisted like cords; ¹⁶ and they made two settings of gold filigree and two gold rings, and put the two rings on the two edges of the breastpiece; ¹⁷ and they put the two cords of gold in the two rings at the edges of the breastpiece. ¹⁸ Two ends of the two cords they had attached to the two settings of filigree; in this way they attached it in front to the shoulder-pieces of the ephod. ¹⁹ Then they made two rings of gold, and put them at the two ends of the breastpiece, on its inside edge next to the ephod. ²⁰ They made two rings of gold, and attached them in front to the lower part of the two shoulder-pieces of the ephod, at its joining above the decorated band of the ephod. ²¹ They bound the breastpiece by its rings to the rings of the ephod with a blue cord, so that it should lie on the decorated band of the ephod, and that the breastpiece should not come loose from the ephod; as the LORD had commanded Moses.

22 He also made the robe of the ephod wo-

---

^a The identification of several of these stones is uncertain   ^b Or *lapis lazuli*

ven all of blue yarn; 23and the opening of the robe in the middle of it was like the opening in a coat of mail,ᵃ with a binding around the opening, so that it might not be torn. 24On the lower hem of the robe they made pomegranates of blue, purple, and crimson yarns, and of fine twisted linen. 25They also made bells of pure gold, and put the bells between the pomegranates on the lower hem of the robe all around, between the pomegranates; 26a bell and a pomegranate, a bell and a pomegranate all around on the lower hem of the robe for ministering; as the LORD had commanded Moses.

27 They also made the tunics, woven of fine linen, for Aaron and his sons, 28and the turban of fine linen, and the headdresses of fine linen, and the linen undergarments of fine twisted linen, 29and the sash of fine twisted linen, and of blue, purple, and crimson yarns, embroidered with needlework; as the LORD had commanded Moses.

30 They made the rosette of the holy diadem of pure gold, and wrote on it an inscription, like the engraving of a signet, "Holy to the LORD." 31They tied to it a blue cord, to fasten it on the turban above; as the LORD had commanded Moses.

The Work Completed

32 In this way all the work of the tabernacle of the tent of meeting was finished; the Israelites had done everything just as the LORD had commanded Moses. 33Then they brought the tabernacle to Moses, the tent and all its utensils, its hooks, its frames, its bars, its pillars, and its bases; 34the covering of tanned rams' skins and the covering of fine leather,ᵃ and the curtain for the screen; 35the ark of the covenantᵇ with its poles and the mercy seat;ᶜ 36the table with all its utensils, and the bread of the Presence; 37the pure lampstand with its lamps set on it and all its utensils, and the oil for the light; 38the golden altar, the anointing oil and the fragrant incense, and the screen for the entrance of the tent; 39the bronze altar, and its grating of bronze, its poles, and all its utensils; the basin with its stand; 40the hangings of the court, its pillars, and its bases, and the screen for the gate of the court, its cords, and its pegs; and all the utensils for the service of the tabernacle, for the tent of meeting; 41the finely worked vestments for ministering in the holy place, the sacred vestments for the priest Aaron, and the vestments of his sons to serve as priests. 42The Israelites had done all of the work just as the LORD had commanded Moses. 43When Moses saw that they had done all the work just as the LORD had commanded, he blessed them.

40 The Tabernacle Erected and Its Equipment Installed

The LORD spoke to Moses: 2On the first day of the first month you shall set up the tabernacle of the tent of meeting. 3You shall put in it the ark of the covenant,ᵇ and you shall screen the ark with the curtain. 4You shall bring in the table, and arrange its setting; and you shall bring in the lampstand, and set up its lamps. 5You shall put the golden altar for incense before the ark of the covenant,ᵇ and set up the screen for the entrance of the tabernacle. 6You shall set the altar of burnt offering before the entrance of the tabernacle of the tent of meeting,

---

ᵃ Meaning of Heb uncertain ᵇ Or *treaty*, or *testimony*; Heb *eduth* ᶜ Or *the cover*

⁷and place the basin between the tent of meeting and the altar, and put water in it. ⁸You shall set up the court all around, and hang up the screen for the gate of the court. ⁹Then you shall take the anointing oil, and anoint the tabernacle and all that is in it, and consecrate it and all its furniture, so that it shall become holy. ¹⁰You shall also anoint the altar of burnt offering and all its utensils, and consecrate the altar, so that the altar shall be most holy. ¹¹You shall also anoint the basin with its stand, and consecrate it. ¹²Then you shall bring Aaron and his sons to the entrance of the tent of meeting, and shall wash them with water, ¹³and put on Aaron the sacred vestments, and you shall anoint him and consecrate him, so that he may serve me as priest. ¹⁴You shall bring his sons also and put tunics on them, ¹⁵and anoint them, as you anointed their father, that they may serve me as priests: and their anointing shall admit them to a perpetual priesthood throughout all generations to come.

16 Moses did everything just as the Lord had commanded him. ¹⁷In the first month in the second year, on the first day of the month, the tabernacle was set up. ¹⁸Moses set up the tabernacle; he laid its bases, and set up its frames, and put in its poles, and raised up its pillars; ¹⁹and he spread the tent over the tabernacle, and put the covering of the tent over it; as the Lord had commanded Moses. ²⁰He took the covenant*ᵃ* and put it into the ark, and put the poles on the ark, and set the mercy seat*ᵇ* above the ark; ²¹and he brought the ark into the tabernacle, and set up the curtain for screening, and screened the ark of the covenant;*ᵃ* as the Lord had commanded Moses. ²²He put the table in the tent of meeting, on the north side of the tabernacle, outside the curtain, ²³and set

the bread in order on it before the Lord; as the Lord had commanded Moses. ²⁴He put the lampstand in the tent of meeting, opposite the table on the south side of the tabernacle, ²⁵and set up the lamps before the Lord; as the Lord had commanded Moses. ²⁶He put the golden altar in the tent of meeting before the curtain, ²⁷and offered fragrant incense on it; as the Lord had commanded Moses. ²⁸He also put in place the screen for the entrance of the tabernacle. ²⁹He set the altar of burnt offering at the entrance of the tabernacle of the tent of meeting, and offered on it the burnt offering and the grain offering as the Lord had commanded Moses. ³⁰He set the basin between the tent of meeting and the altar, and put water in it for washing, ³¹with which Moses and Aaron and his sons washed their hands and their feet. ³²When they went into the tent of meeting, and when they approached the altar, they washed; as the Lord had commanded Moses. ³³He set up the court around the tabernacle and the altar, and put up the screen at the gate of the court. So Moses finished the work.

The Cloud and the Glory

34 Then the cloud covered the tent of meeting, and the glory of the Lord filled the tabernacle. ³⁵Moses was not able to enter the tent of meeting because the cloud settled upon it, and the glory of the Lord filled the tabernacle. ³⁶Whenever the cloud was taken up from the tabernacle, the Israelites would set out on each stage of their journey; ³⁷but if the cloud was not taken up, then they did not set out until the day that it was taken up. ³⁸For the cloud of the Lord was on the tabernacle by day, and fire was in the cloud*ᶜ* by night, before the eyes of all the house of Israel at each stage of their journey.

a Or *treaty*, or *testimony*; Heb *eduth* *b* Or *the cover* *c* Heb *it*

Life—© Talitha White, 17

LEVITICUS

NEXT TO GODLINESS

"I'm Supposed to Do *What?*"

Have you ever met anyone whose favorite book of the Bible is Leviticus? Probably not—and that makes sense. It's a book of ancient laws. However, throughout the laws regulating the early Israelites' sacrificial, ritual, and festival practices as well as everyday activities with regard to food, sex, and being a good neighbor runs a constant theme that is just as relevant today: God's people are called to be holy, because God is holy.

Some of these laws sound pointless or bizarre to us in the twenty-first century, but God didn't just pick these out of a hat. They were chosen to represent holiness to the Israelites in the time they were written. God called his people to live differently than the nations surrounding them—and they demonstrated that difference through an intense focus on inner righteousness and outward purity.

We're no longer bound by the laws of a sacrificial system or cleanliness rituals as a basis for our Catholic faith. But that doesn't give us license to write off Leviticus. By reading this book, you'll get a picture of God's passionate desire for holiness in his people, you'll be confronted by your inability to be sinless, you'll see a reflection of your own constant wandering away from God, and you'll be inspired to line up your inner spiritual life and outward actions with the perfect, loving will of your Creator.

Not sure how to toe that line? Let the Church be your loving guide. The doors are always open.

> *"God created us, every human being, for greater things—to love and be loved."*
> —Bl. Mother Teresa of Calcutta

WHO This book, like the others in the Pentateuch (the first five books of the Old Testament), was developed over time by a series of people or groups.

WHAT An ordered collection of God's laws concerning ceremonial purity and personal holiness to teach the people and the priests how to worship and be holy

WHEN The events occurred after the Exodus during the Israelites' time at Mt. Sinai ca. 1300 B.C. The laws, however, were not completed until much later, ca. 600 B.C.

WHERE The Sinai Peninsula

PATH OF DISCIPLESHIP

If you lived in ancient times and sinned, you'd take a sheep or goat to the temple. The priest would kill the animal and sprinkle its blood around the altar, then set fire to a portion of the offering. Through this process, the priest would have purified you from your sin, "and you shall be forgiven" (see Leviticus 5.8–10).

In 1 John, we are reminded that "God's love was revealed among us in this way: God sent his only Son into the world so that we might live through him. In this is love, not that we loved God but that he loved us and sent his Son to be the atoning sacrifice for our sins" (4.9–10).

During the Eucharist, we are reminded of Jesus' sacrifice on the cross, the ultimate expression of his love for us.

Right with God? The sacrifice has changed, but God hasn't.

1 The Burnt Offering

The Lord summoned Moses and spoke to him from the tent of meeting, saying: ²Speak to the people of Israel and say to them: When any of you bring an offering of livestock to the Lord, you shall bring your offering from the herd or from the flock.

3 If the offering is a burnt offering from the herd, you shall offer a male without blemish; you shall bring it to the entrance of the tent of meeting, for acceptance in your behalf before the Lord. ⁴You shall lay your hand on the head of the burnt offering, and it shall be acceptable in your behalf as atonement for you. ⁵The bull shall be slaughtered before the Lord; and Aaron's sons the priests shall offer the blood, dashing the blood against all sides of the altar that is at the entrance of the tent of meeting. ⁶The burnt offering shall be flayed and cut up into its parts. ⁷The sons of the priest Aaron shall put fire on the altar and arrange wood on the fire. ⁸Aaron's sons the priests shall arrange the parts, with the head and the suet, on the wood that is on the fire on the altar; ⁹but its entrails and its legs shall be washed with water. Then the priest shall turn the whole into smoke on the altar as a burnt offering, an offering by fire of pleasing odor to the Lord.

10 If your gift for a burnt offering is from the flock, from the sheep or goats, your offering shall be a male without blemish. ¹¹It shall be slaughtered on the north side of the altar before the Lord, and Aaron's sons the priests shall dash its blood against all sides of the altar. ¹²It shall be cut up into its parts, with its head and its suet, and the priest shall arrange them on the wood that is on the fire on the altar; ¹³but the entrails and the legs shall be washed with water. Then the priest shall offer the whole and turn it into smoke on the altar; it is a burnt offering, an offering by fire of pleasing odor to the Lord.

14 If your offering to the Lord is a burnt offering of birds, you shall choose your offering from turtledoves or pigeons. ¹⁵The priest shall bring it to the altar and wring off its head, and turn it into smoke on the altar; and its blood shall be drained out against the side of the altar. ¹⁶He shall remove its crop with its contents[a] and throw it at the east side of the altar, in the place for ashes. ¹⁷He shall tear it open by its wings without severing it. Then the priest shall turn it into smoke on the altar, on the wood that is on the fire; it is a burnt offering, an offering by fire of pleasing odor to the Lord.

2 Grain Offerings

When anyone presents a grain offering to the Lord, the offering shall be of choice flour; the worshiper shall pour oil on it, and put frankincense on it, ²and bring it to Aaron's sons the priests. After taking from it a handful of the choice flour and oil, with all its frankincense, the priest shall turn this token portion into smoke on the altar, an offering by fire of pleasing odor to the Lord. ³And what is left of the grain offering shall be for Aaron and his sons, a most holy part of the offerings by fire to the Lord.

4 When you present a grain offering baked in the oven, it shall be of choice flour: unleavened cakes mixed with oil, or unleavened wafers spread with oil. ⁵If your offering is grain prepared on a griddle, it shall be of choice flour mixed with oil, unleavened; ⁶break it in pieces, and pour oil on it; it is a grain offering. ⁷If your offering is grain prepared in a pan, it shall be made of choice flour in oil. ⁸You shall bring to the Lord the grain offering that is prepared in any of these ways; and when it is presented to the priest, he shall take it to the altar. ⁹The priest shall remove from the grain offering its token portion and turn this into smoke on the altar, an offering by fire of pleasing odor to the Lord. ¹⁰And what is left of the grain offering shall be for Aaron and his sons; it is a most holy part of the offerings by fire to the Lord.

11 No grain offering that you bring to the Lord shall be made with leaven, for you must not turn any leaven or honey into smoke as an offering by fire to the Lord. ¹²You may bring them to the Lord as an offering of choice products, but they shall not be offered on the altar for a pleasing odor. ¹³You shall not omit from your grain offerings the salt of the covenant with your God; with all your offerings you shall offer salt.

14 If you bring a grain offering of first fruits to the Lord, you shall bring as the grain offering of your first fruits coarse new grain from fresh ears, parched with fire. ¹⁵You shall add oil to it and lay frankincense on it; it is a grain offering. ¹⁶And the priest shall turn a token portion of it into smoke—some of the coarse grain and oil with all its frankincense; it is an offering by fire to the Lord.

3 Offerings of Well-Being

If the offering is a sacrifice of well-being, if you offer an animal of the herd, whether male or female, you shall offer one without blemish before the Lord. ²You shall lay your hand on

---

a Meaning of Heb uncertain

the head of the offering and slaughter it at the entrance of the tent of meeting; and Aaron's sons the priests shall dash the blood against all sides of the altar. ³You shall offer from the sacrifice of well-being, as an offering by fire to the LORD, the fat that covers the entrails and all the fat that is around the entrails; ⁴the two kidneys with the fat that is on them at the loins, and the appendage of the liver, which he shall remove with the kidneys. ⁵Then Aaron's sons shall turn these into smoke on the altar, with the burnt offering that is on the wood on the fire, as an offering by fire of pleasing odor to the LORD.

6 If your offering for a sacrifice of well-being to the LORD is from the flock, male or female, you shall offer one without blemish. ⁷If you present a sheep as your offering, you shall bring it before the LORD ⁸and lay your hand on the head of the offering. It shall be slaughtered before the tent of meeting, and Aaron's sons shall dash its blood against all sides of the altar. ⁹You shall present its fat from the sacrifice of well-being, as an offering by fire to the LORD: the whole broad tail, which shall be removed close to the backbone, the fat that covers the entrails, and all the fat that is around the entrails; ¹⁰the two kidneys with the fat that is on them at the loins, and the appendage of the liver, which you shall remove with the kidneys. ¹¹Then the priest shall turn these into smoke on the altar as a food offering by fire to the LORD.

12 If your offering is a goat, you shall bring it before the LORD ¹³and lay your hand on its head; it shall be slaughtered before the tent of meeting; and the sons of Aaron shall dash its blood against all sides of the altar. ¹⁴You shall present as your offering from it, as an offering by fire to the LORD, the fat that covers the entrails, and all the fat that is around the entrails; ¹⁵the two kidneys with the fat that is on them at the loins, and the appendage of the liver, which you shall remove with the kidneys. ¹⁶Then the priest shall turn these into smoke on the altar as a food offering by fire for a pleasing odor.

All fat is the LORD's. ¹⁷It shall be a perpetual statute throughout your generations, in all your settlements: you must not eat any fat or any blood.

4 Sin Offerings

The LORD spoke to Moses, saying, ²Speak to the people of Israel, saying: When anyone sins unintentionally in any of the LORD's commandments about things not to be done, and does any one of them:

3 If it is the anointed priest who sins, thus bringing guilt on the people, he shall offer for the sin that he has committed a bull of the herd without blemish as a sin offering to the LORD. ⁴He shall bring the bull to the entrance of the tent of meeting before the LORD and lay his hand on the head of the bull; the bull shall be slaughtered before the LORD. ⁵The anointed priest shall take some of the blood of the bull and bring it into the tent of meeting. ⁶The priest shall dip his finger in the blood and sprinkle some of the blood seven times before the LORD in front of the curtain of the sanctuary. ⁷The priest shall put some of the blood on the horns of the altar of fragrant incense that is in the tent of meeting before the LORD; and the rest of the blood of the bull he shall pour out at the base of the altar of burnt offering, which is at the entrance of the tent of meeting. ⁸He shall remove all the fat from the bull of sin offering: the fat that covers the entrails and all the fat that is around the entrails; ⁹the two kidneys with the fat that is on them at the loins; and the appendage of the liver, which he shall remove with the kidneys, ¹⁰just as these are removed from the ox of the sacrifice of well-being. The priest shall turn them into smoke upon the altar of burnt offering. ¹¹But the skin of the bull and all its flesh, as well as its head, its legs, its entrails, and its dung— ¹²all the rest of the bull—he shall carry out to a clean place outside the camp, to the ash heap, and shall burn it on a wood fire; at the ash heap it shall be burned.

13 If the whole congregation of Israel errs unintentionally and the matter escapes the notice of the assembly, and they do any one of the things that by the LORD's commandments ought not to be done and incur guilt; ¹⁴when the sin that they have committed becomes known, the assembly shall offer a bull of the herd for a sin offering and bring it before the tent of meeting. ¹⁵The elders of the congregation shall lay their hands on the head of the bull before the LORD, and the bull shall be slaughtered before the LORD. ¹⁶The anointed priest shall bring some of the blood of the bull into the tent of meeting, ¹⁷and the priest shall dip his finger in the blood and sprinkle it seven times before the LORD, in front of the curtain. ¹⁸He shall put some of the blood on the horns of the altar that is before the LORD in the tent of meeting; and the rest of the blood he shall pour out at the base of the altar of burnt offering that is at the entrance of the tent of meeting. ¹⁹He shall remove all its fat and turn it into smoke on the altar. ²⁰He shall do with the bull just as is done with the bull of sin offering; he shall do the same with this. The priest shall make atonement for them, and they shall be forgiven. ²¹He shall carry the bull outside the

camp, and burn it as he burned the first bull; it is the sin offering for the assembly.

22 When a ruler sins, doing unintentionally any one of all the things that by commandments of the LORD his God ought not to be done and incurs guilt, 23 once the sin that he has committed is made known to him, he shall bring as his offering a male goat without blemish. 24 He shall lay his hand on the head of the goat; it shall be slaughtered at the spot where the burnt offering is slaughtered before the LORD; it is a sin offering. 25 The priest shall take some of the blood of the sin offering with his finger and put it on the horns of the altar of burnt offering, and pour out the rest of its blood at the base of the altar of burnt offering. 26 All its fat he shall turn into smoke on the altar, like the fat of the sacrifice of well-being.

Thus the priest shall make atonement on his behalf for his sin, and he shall be forgiven.

27 If anyone of the ordinary people among you sins unintentionally in doing any one of the things that by the LORD's commandments ought not to be done and incurs guilt, 28 when the sin that you have committed is made known to you, you shall bring a female goat without blemish as your offering, for the sin that you have committed. 29 You shall lay your hand on the head of the sin offering; and the sin offering shall be slaughtered at the place of the burnt offering. 30 The priest shall take some of its blood with his finger and put it on the horns of the altar of burnt offering, and he shall pour out the rest of its blood at the base of the altar. 31 He shall remove all its fat, as the fat is removed from the offering of well-being, and the priest shall turn it into smoke on the altar for a pleasing odor to the LORD. Thus the priest shall make atonement on your behalf, and you shall be forgiven.

32 If the offering you bring as a sin offering is a sheep, you shall bring a female without blemish. 33 You shall lay your hand on the head of the sin offering; and it shall be slaughtered as a sin offering at the spot where the burnt offering is slaughtered. 34 The priest shall take some of the blood of the sin offering with his finger and put it on the horns of the altar of burnt offering, and pour out the rest of its blood at the base of the altar. 35 You shall remove all its fat, as the fat of the sheep is removed from the sacrifice of well-being, and the priest shall turn it into smoke on the altar, with the offerings by fire to the LORD. Thus the priest shall make atonement on your behalf for the sin that you have committed, and you shall be forgiven.

5 When any of you sin in that you have heard a public adjuration to testify and—though able to testify as one who has seen or learned of the matter—do not speak up, you are subject to punishment. 2 Or when any of you touch any unclean thing—whether the carcass of an unclean beast or the carcass of unclean livestock or the carcass of an unclean swarming thing—and are unaware of it, you have become unclean, and are guilty. 3 Or when you touch human uncleanness—any uncleanness by which one can become unclean—and are unaware of it, when you come to know it, you shall be guilty. 4 Or when any of you utter aloud a rash oath for a bad or a good purpose, whatever people utter in an oath, and are unaware of it, when you come to know it, you shall in any of these be guilty. 5 When you realize your guilt in any of these, you shall confess the sin

that you have committed. ⁶And you shall bring to the LORD, as your penalty for the sin that you have committed, a female from the flock, a sheep or a goat, as a sin offering; and the priest shall make atonement on your behalf for your sin.

7 But if you cannot afford a sheep, you shall bring to the LORD, as your penalty for the sin that you have committed, two turtledoves or two pigeons, one for a sin offering and the other for a burnt offering. ⁸You shall bring them to the priest, who shall offer first the one for the sin offering, wringing its head at the nape without severing it. ⁹He shall sprinkle some of the blood of the sin offering on the side of the altar, while the rest of the blood shall be drained out at the base of the altar; it is a sin offering. ¹⁰And the second he shall offer for a burnt offering according to the regulation. Thus the priest shall make atonement on your behalf for the sin that you have committed, and you shall be forgiven.

11 But if you cannot afford two turtledoves or two pigeons, you shall bring as your offering for the sin that you have committed one-tenth of an ephah of choice flour for a sin offering; you shall not put oil on it or lay frankincense on it, for it is a sin offering. ¹²You shall bring it to the priest, and the priest shall scoop up a handful of it as its memorial portion, and turn this into smoke on the altar, with the offerings by fire to the LORD; it is a sin offering. ¹³Thus the priest shall make atonement on your behalf for whichever of these sins you have committed, and you shall be forgiven. Like the grain offering, the rest shall be for the priest.

Offerings with Restitution

14 The LORD spoke to Moses, saying: ¹⁵When any of you commit a trespass and sin unintentionally in any of the holy things of the LORD, you shall bring, as your guilt offering to the LORD, a ram without blemish from the flock, convertible into silver by the sanctuary shekel; it is a guilt offering. ¹⁶And you shall make restitution for the holy thing in which you were remiss, and shall add one-fifth to it and give it to the priest. The priest shall make atonement on your behalf with the ram of the guilt offering, and you shall be forgiven.

17 If any of you sin without knowing it, doing any of the things that by the LORD's commandments ought not to be done, you have incurred guilt, and are subject to punishment. ¹⁸You shall bring to the priest a ram without blemish from the flock, or the equivalent, as a guilt offering; and the priest shall make atone-

ment on your behalf for the error that you committed unintentionally, and you shall be forgiven. ¹⁹It is a guilt offering; you have incurred guilt before the LORD.

6ᵃ The LORD spoke to Moses, saying: ²When any of you sin and commit a trespass against the LORD by deceiving a neighbor in a matter of a deposit or a pledge, or by robbery, or if you have defrauded a neighbor, ³or have found something lost and lied about it—if you swear falsely regarding any of the various things that one may do and sin thereby— ⁴when you have sinned and realize your guilt, and would restore what you took by robbery or by fraud or the deposit that was committed to you, or the lost thing that you found, ⁵or anything else about which you have sworn falsely, you shall repay the principal amount and shall add one-fifth to it. You shall pay it to its owner when you realize your guilt. ⁶And you shall bring to the priest, as your guilt offering to the LORD, a ram without blemish from the flock, or its equivalent, for a guilt offering. ⁷The priest shall make atonement on your behalf before the LORD, and you shall be forgiven for any of the things that one may do and incur guilt thereby.

Instructions concerning Sacrifices

8ᵇ The LORD spoke to Moses, saying: ⁹Command Aaron and his sons, saying: This is the ritual of the burnt offering. The burnt offering itself shall remain on the hearth upon the altar all night until the morning, while the fire on the altar shall be kept burning. ¹⁰The priest shall put on his linen vestments after putting on his linen undergarments next to his body; and he shall take up the ashes to which the fire has reduced the burnt offering on the altar, and place them beside the altar. ¹¹Then he shall take off his vestments and put on other garments, and carry the ashes out to a clean place outside the camp. ¹²The fire on the altar shall be kept burning; it shall not go out. Every morning the priest shall add wood to it, lay out the burnt offering on it, and turn into smoke the fat pieces of the offerings of well-being. ¹³A perpetual fire shall be kept burning on the altar; it shall not go out.

14 This is the ritual of the grain offering: The sons of Aaron shall offer it before the LORD, in front of the altar. ¹⁵They shall take from it a handful of the choice flour and oil of the grain offering, with all the frankincense that is on the offering, and they shall turn its memorial portion into smoke on the altar as a pleasing odor to the LORD. ¹⁶Aaron and his sons shall eat what is left of it; it shall be eaten

a Ch 5.20 in Heb b Ch 6.1 in Heb

as unleavened cakes in a holy place; in the court of the tent of meeting they shall eat it. [17]It shall not be baked with leaven. I have given it as their portion of my offerings by fire; it is most holy, like the sin offering and the guilt offering. [18]Every male among the descendants of Aaron shall eat of it, as their perpetual due throughout your generations, from the LORD's offerings by fire; anything that touches them shall become holy.

19 The LORD spoke to Moses, saying: [20]This is the offering that Aaron and his sons shall offer to the LORD on the day when he is anointed: one-tenth of an ephah of choice flour as a regular offering, half of it in the morning and half in the evening. [21]It shall be made with oil on a griddle; you shall bring it well soaked, as a grain offering of baked[a] pieces, and you shall present it as a pleasing odor to the LORD. [22]And so the priest, anointed from among Aaron's descendants as a successor, shall prepare it; it is the LORD's—a perpetual due—to be turned entirely into smoke. [23]Every grain offering of a priest shall be wholly burned; it shall not be eaten.

24 The LORD spoke to Moses, saying: [25]Speak to Aaron and his sons, saying: This is the ritual of the sin offering. The sin offering shall be slaughtered before the LORD at the spot where the burnt offering is slaughtered; it is most holy. [26]The priest who offers it as a sin offering shall eat of it; it shall be eaten in a holy place, in the court of the tent of meeting. [27]Whatever touches its flesh shall become holy; and when any of its blood is spattered on a garment, you shall wash the bespattered part in a holy place. [28]An earthen vessel in which it was boiled shall be broken; but if it is boiled in a bronze vessel, that shall be scoured and rinsed in water. [29]Every male among the priests shall eat of it; it is most holy. [30]But no sin offering shall be eaten from which any blood is brought into the tent of meeting for atonement in the holy place; it shall be burned with fire.

7 This is the ritual of the guilt offering. It is most holy; [2]at the spot where the burnt offering is slaughtered, they shall slaughter the guilt offering, and its blood shall be dashed against all sides of the altar. [3]All its fat shall be offered: the broad tail, the fat that covers the entrails, [4]the two kidneys with the fat that is on them at the loins, and the appendage of the liver, which shall be removed with the kidneys. [5]The priest shall turn them into smoke on the altar as an offering by fire to the LORD; it is a guilt offering. [6]Every male among the priests shall eat of it; it shall be eaten in a holy place; it is most holy.

7 The guilt offering is like the sin offering, there is the same ritual for them; the priest who makes atonement with it shall have it. [8]So, too, the priest who offers anyone's burnt offering shall keep the skin of the burnt offering that he has offered. [9]And every grain offering baked in the oven, and all that is prepared in a pan or on a griddle, shall belong to the priest who offers it. [10]But every other grain offering, mixed with oil or dry, shall belong to all the sons of Aaron equally.

Further Instructions

11 This is the ritual of the sacrifice of the offering of well-being that one may offer to the LORD. [12]If you offer it for thanksgiving, you shall offer with the thank offering unleavened cakes mixed with oil, unleavened wafers spread with oil, and cakes of choice flour well soaked in oil. [13]With your thanksgiving sacrifice of well-being you shall bring your offering with cakes of leavened bread. [14]From this you shall offer one cake from each offering, as a gift to the LORD; it shall belong to the priest who dashes the blood of the offering of well-being. [15]And the flesh of your thanksgiving sacrifice of well-being shall be eaten on the day it is offered; you shall not leave any of it until morning. [16]But if the sacrifice you offer is a votive offering or a freewill offering, it shall be eaten on the day that you offer your sacrifice, and what is left of it shall be eaten the next day; [17]but what is left of the flesh of the sacrifice shall be burned up on the third day. [18]If any of the flesh of your sacrifice of well-being is eaten on the third day, it shall not be acceptable, nor shall it be credited to the one who offers it; it shall be an abomination, and the one who eats of it shall incur guilt.

19 Flesh that touches any unclean thing shall not be eaten; it shall be burned up. As for other flesh, all who are clean may eat such flesh. [20]But those who eat flesh from the LORD's sacrifice of well-being while in a state of uncleanness shall be cut off from their kin. [21]When any one of you touches any unclean thing—human uncleanness or an unclean animal or any unclean creature—and then eats flesh from the LORD's sacrifice of well-being, you shall be cut off from your kin.

22 The LORD spoke to Moses, saying: [23]Speak to the people of Israel, saying: You shall eat no fat of ox or sheep or goat. [24]The fat of an animal that died or was torn by wild animals may be put to any other use, but you must

[a] Meaning of Heb uncertain

not eat it. 25If any one of you eats the fat from an animal of which an offering by fire may be made to the LORD, you who eat it shall be cut off from your kin. 26You must not eat any blood whatever, either of bird or of animal, in any of your settlements. 27Any one of you who eats any blood shall be cut off from your kin.

28 The LORD spoke to Moses, saying: 29Speak to the people of Israel, saying: Any one of you who would offer to the LORD your sacrifice of well-being must yourself bring to the LORD your offering from your sacrifice of well-being. 30Your own hands shall bring the LORD's offering by fire; you shall bring the fat with the breast, so that the breast may be raised as an elevation offering before the LORD. 31The priest shall turn the fat into smoke on the altar, but the breast shall belong to Aaron and his sons. 32And the right thigh from your sacrifices of well-being you shall give to the priest as an offering; 33the one among the sons of Aaron who offers the blood and fat of the offering of well-being shall have the right thigh for a portion. 34For I have taken the breast of the elevation offering, and the thigh that is offered, from the people of Israel, from their sacrifices of well-being, and have given them to Aaron the priest and to his sons, as a perpetual due from the people of Israel. 35This is the portion allotted to Aaron and to his sons from the offerings made by fire to the LORD, once they have been brought forward to serve the LORD as priests; 36these the LORD commanded to be given them, when he anointed them, as a perpetual due from the people of Israel throughout their generations.

37 This is the ritual of the burnt offering, the grain offering, the sin offering, the guilt offering, the offering of ordination, and the sacrifice of well-being, 38which the LORD commanded Moses on Mount Sinai, when he commanded the people of Israel to bring their offerings to the LORD, in the wilderness of Sinai.

8 The Rites of Ordination

The LORD spoke to Moses, saying: 2Take Aaron and his sons with him, the vestments, the anointing oil, the bull of sin offering, the two rams, and the basket of unleavened bread; 3and assemble the whole congregation at the entrance of the tent of meeting. 4And Moses did as the LORD commanded him. When the congregation was assembled at the entrance of the tent of meeting, 5Moses said to the congregation, "This is what the LORD has commanded to be done."

6 Then Moses brought Aaron and his sons forward, and washed them with water. 7He put the tunic on him, fastened the sash around him, clothed him with the robe, and put the ephod on him. He then put the decorated band of the ephod around him, tying the ephod to him with it. 8He placed the breastpiece on him, and in the breastpiece he put the Urim and the Thummim. 9And he set the turban on his head, and on the turban, in front, he set the golden ornament, the holy crown, as the LORD commanded Moses.

10 Then Moses took the anointing oil and anointed the tabernacle and all that was in it, and consecrated them. [11]He sprinkled some of it on the altar seven times, and anointed the altar and all its utensils, and the basin and its base, to consecrate them. [12]He poured some of the anointing oil on Aaron's head and anointed him, to consecrate him. [13]And Moses brought forward Aaron's sons, and clothed them with tunics, and fastened sashes around them, and tied headdresses on them, as the Lord commanded Moses.

14 He led forward the bull of sin offering; and Aaron and his sons laid their hands upon the head of the bull of sin offering, [15]and it was slaughtered. Moses took the blood and with his finger put some on each of the horns of the altar, purifying the altar; then he poured out the blood at the base of the altar. Thus he consecrated it, to make atonement for it. [16]Moses took all the fat that was around the entrails, and the appendage of the liver, and the two kidneys with their fat, and turned them into smoke on the altar. [17]But the bull itself, its skin and flesh and its dung, he burned with fire outside the camp, as the Lord commanded Moses.

18 Then he brought forward the ram of burnt offering. Aaron and his sons laid their hands on the head of the ram, [19]and it was slaughtered. Moses dashed the blood against all sides of the altar. [20]The ram was cut into its parts, and Moses turned into smoke the head and the parts and the suet. [21]And after the entrails and the legs were washed with water, Moses turned into smoke the whole ram on the altar; it was a burnt offering for a pleasing odor, an offering by fire to the Lord, as the Lord commanded Moses.

22 Then he brought forward the second ram, the ram of ordination. Aaron and his sons laid their hands on the head of the ram, [23]and it was slaughtered. Moses took some of its blood and put it on the lobe of Aaron's right ear and on the thumb of his right hand and on the big toe of his right foot. [24]After Aaron's sons were brought forward, Moses put some of the blood on the lobes of their right ears and on the thumbs of their right hands and on the big toes of their right feet; and Moses dashed the rest of the blood against all sides of the altar. [25]He took the fat—the broad tail, all the fat that was around the entrails, the appendage of the liver, and the two kidneys with their fat—and the right thigh. [26]From the basket of unleavened bread that was before the Lord, he took one cake of unleavened bread, one cake of bread with oil, and one wafer, and placed them on the fat and on the right thigh. [27]He placed all these on the palms of Aaron and on the palms of his sons, and raised them as an elevation offering before the Lord. [28]Then Moses took them from their hands and turned them into smoke on the altar with the burnt offering. This was an ordination offering for a pleasing odor, an offering by fire to the Lord. [29]Moses took the breast and raised it as an elevation offering before the Lord; it was Moses' portion of the ram of ordination, as the Lord commanded Moses.

30 Then Moses took some of the anointing oil and some of the blood that was on the altar and sprinkled them on Aaron and his vestments, and also on his sons and their vestments. Thus he consecrated Aaron and his vestments, and also his sons and their vestments.

31 And Moses said to Aaron and his sons, "Boil the flesh at the entrance of the tent of meeting, and eat it there with the bread that is in the basket of ordination offerings, as I was commanded, 'Aaron and his sons shall eat it'; [32]and what remains of the flesh and the bread you shall burn with fire. [33]You shall not go outside the entrance of the tent of meeting for seven days, until the day when your period of ordination is completed. For it will take seven days to ordain you; [34]as has been done today, the Lord has commanded to be done to make atonement for you. [35]You shall remain at the entrance of the tent of meeting day and night for seven days, keeping the Lord's charge so that you do not die; for so I am commanded." [36]Aaron and his sons did all the things that the Lord commanded through Moses.

9 Aaron's Priesthood Inaugurated

On the eighth day Moses summoned Aaron and his sons and the elders of Israel. [2]He said to Aaron, "Take a bull calf for a sin offering and a ram for a burnt offering, without blemish, and offer them before the Lord. [3]And say to the people of Israel, 'Take a male goat for a sin offering; a calf and a lamb, yearlings without blemish, for a burnt offering; [4]and an ox and a ram for an offering of well-being to sacrifice before the Lord; and a grain offering mixed with oil. For today the Lord will appear to you.' " [5]They brought what Moses commanded to the front of the tent of meeting; and the whole congregation drew near and stood before the Lord. [6]And Moses said, "This is the thing that the Lord commanded you to do, so that the glory of the Lord may appear to you." [7]Then Moses said to Aaron, "Draw near to the altar and sacrifice your sin offering and your burnt offering, and make atonement for yourself and for the people; and sacrifice the offering of the people, and make atonement for them; as the Lord has commanded."

8 Aaron drew near to the altar, and slaughtered the calf of the sin offering, which was for himself. [9]The sons of Aaron presented the blood to him, and he dipped his finger in the blood and put it on the horns of the altar; and the rest of the blood he poured out at the base of the altar. [10]But the fat, the kidneys, and the appendage of the liver from the sin offering he turned into smoke on the altar, as the Lord commanded Moses; [11]and the flesh and the skin he burned with fire outside the camp.

12 Then he slaughtered the burnt offering. Aaron's sons brought him the blood, and he dashed it against all sides of the altar. [13]And they brought him the burnt offering piece by piece, and the head, which he turned into smoke on the altar. [14]He washed the entrails and the legs and, with the burnt offering, turned them into smoke on the altar.

15 Next he presented the people's offering. He took the goat of the sin offering that was for the people, and slaughtered it, and presented it as a sin offering like the first one. [16]He presented the burnt offering, and sacrificed it according to regulation. [17]He presented the grain offering, and, taking a handful of it, he turned it into smoke on the altar, in addition to the burnt offering of the morning.

18 He slaughtered the ox and the ram as a sacrifice of well-being for the people. Aaron's sons brought him the blood, which he dashed against all sides of the altar, [19]and the fat of the ox and of the ram—the broad tail, the fat that covers the entrails, the two kidneys and the fat on them,[a] and the appendage of the liver. [20]They first laid the fat on the breasts, and the fat was turned into smoke on the altar; [21]and the breasts and the right thigh Aaron raised as an elevation offering before the Lord, as Moses had commanded.

22 Aaron lifted his hands toward the people and blessed them; and he came down after sacrificing the sin offering, the burnt offering, and the offering of well-being. [23]Moses and Aaron entered the tent of meeting, and then came out and blessed the people; and the glory of the Lord appeared to all the people. [24]Fire came out from the Lord and consumed the burnt offering and the fat on the altar; and when all the people saw it, they shouted and fell on their faces.

10 Nadab and Abihu

Now Aaron's sons, Nadab and Abihu, each took his censer, put fire in it, and laid incense on it;

and they offered unholy fire before the Lord, such as he had not commanded them. [2]And fire came out from the presence of the Lord and consumed them, and they died before the Lord. [3]Then Moses said to Aaron, "This is what the Lord meant when he said,

'Through those who are near me
  I will show myself holy,
and before all the people
  I will be glorified.' "
And Aaron was silent.

4 Moses summoned Mishael and Elzaphan, sons of Uzziel the uncle of Aaron, and said to them, "Come forward, and carry your kinsmen away from the front of the sanctuary to a place outside the camp." [5]They came forward and carried them by their tunics out of the camp, as Moses had ordered. [6]And Moses said to Aaron and to his sons Eleazar and Ithamar, "Do not dishevel your hair, and do not tear your vestments, or you will die and wrath will strike all the congregation; but your kindred, the whole house of Israel, may mourn the burning that the Lord has sent. [7]You shall not go outside the entrance of the tent of meeting, or you will die; for the anointing oil of the Lord is on you." And they did as Moses had ordered.

8 And the Lord spoke to Aaron: [9]Drink no wine or strong drink, neither you nor your sons, when you enter the tent of meeting, that you may not die; it is a statute forever throughout your generations. [10]You are to distinguish between the holy and the common, and between the unclean and the clean; [11]and you are to teach the people of Israel all the statutes that the Lord has spoken to them through Moses.

12 Moses spoke to Aaron and to his remaining sons, Eleazar and Ithamar: Take the grain offering that is left from the Lord's offerings

Fire—© Rachel Akerley, 16

a Gk: Heb *the broad tail, and that which covers, and the kidneys* by fire, and eat it unleavened beside the altar, for it is most holy; 13you shall eat it in a holy place, because it is your due and your sons' due, from the offerings by fire to the Lord; for so I am commanded. 14But the breast that is elevated and the thigh that is raised, you and your sons and daughters as well may eat in any clean place; for they have been assigned to you and your children from the sacrifices of the offerings of well-being of the people of Israel. 15The thigh that is raised and the breast that is elevated they shall bring, together with the offerings by fire of the fat, to raise for an elevation offering before the Lord; they are to be your due and that of your children forever, as the Lord has commanded.

16 Then Moses made inquiry about the goat of the sin offering, and—it had already been burned! He was angry with Eleazar and Ithamar, Aaron's remaining sons, and said, 17"Why did you not eat the sin offering in the sacred area? For it is most holy, and God*a* has given it to you that you may remove the guilt of the congregation, to make atonement on their behalf before the Lord. 18Its blood was not brought into the inner part of the sanctuary. You should certainly have eaten it in the sanctuary, as I commanded." 19And Aaron spoke to Moses, "See, today they offered their sin offering and their burnt offering before the Lord; and yet such things as these have befallen me! If I had eaten the sin offering today, would it have been agreeable to the Lord?" 20And when Moses heard that, he agreed.

11 Clean and Unclean Foods

The Lord spoke to Moses and Aaron, saying to them: 2Speak to the people of Israel, saying:

From among all the land animals, these are the creatures that you may eat. 3Any animal that has divided hoofs and is cleft-footed and chews the cud—such you may eat. 4But among those that chew the cud or have divided hoofs, you shall not eat the following: the camel, for even though it chews the cud, it does not have divided hoofs; it is unclean for you. 5The rock badger, for even though it chews the cud, it does not have divided hoofs; it is unclean for you. 6The hare, for even though it chews the cud, it does not have divided hoofs; it is unclean for you. 7The pig, for even though it has divided hoofs and is cleft-footed, it does not chew the cud; it is unclean for you. 8Of their flesh you shall not eat, and their carcasses you shall not touch; they are unclean for you.

9 These you may eat, of all that are in the waters. Everything in the waters that has fins and scales, whether in the seas or in the streams—such you may eat. 10But anything in the seas or the streams that does not have fins and scales, of the swarming creatures in the waters and among all the other living creatures that are in the waters—they are detestable to you 11and detestable they shall remain. Of their flesh you shall not eat, and their carcasses you shall regard as detestable. 12Everything in the waters that does not have fins and scales is detestable to you.

13 These you shall regard as detestable among the birds. They shall not be eaten; they are an abomination: the eagle, the vulture, the osprey, 14the buzzard, the kite of any kind; 15every raven of any kind; 16the ostrich, the nighthawk, the sea gull, the hawk of any kind; 17the little owl, the cormorant, the great owl, 18the water hen, the desert owl,*b* the carrion vulture, 19the stork, the heron of any kind, the hoopoe, and the bat.*c*

20 All winged insects that walk upon all fours are detestable to you. 21But among the winged insects that walk on all fours you may eat those that have jointed legs above their feet, with which to leap on the ground. 22Of them you may eat: the locust according to its kind, the bald locust according to its kind, the cricket according to its kind, and the grasshopper according to its kind. 23But all other winged insects that have four feet are detestable to you.

Unclean Animals

24 By these you shall become unclean; whoever touches the carcass of any of them shall be unclean until the evening, 25and whoever carries any part of the carcass of any of them shall wash his clothes and be unclean until the evening. 26Every animal that has divided hoofs but is not cleft-footed or does not chew the cud is unclean for you; everyone who touches one of them shall be unclean. 27All that walk on their paws, among the animals that walk on all fours, are unclean for you; whoever touches the carcass of any of them shall be unclean until the evening, 28and the one who carries the carcass shall wash his clothes and be unclean until the evening; they are unclean for you.

29 These are unclean for you among the creatures that swarm upon the earth: the weasel, the mouse, the great lizard according to its kind, 30the gecko, the land crocodile, the lizard, the sand lizard, and the chameleon. 31These are unclean for you among all that swarm; whoever touches one of them when they are dead shall be unclean until the eve-

a Heb *he* *b* Or *pelican* *c* Identification of several of the birds in verses 13–19 is uncertain ning. ³²And anything upon which any of them falls when they are dead shall be unclean, whether an article of wood or cloth or skin or sacking, any article that is used for any purpose; it shall be dipped into water, and it shall be unclean until the evening, and then it shall be clean. ³³And if any of them falls into any earthen vessel, all that is in it shall be unclean, and you shall break the vessel. ³⁴Any food that could be eaten shall be unclean if water from any such vessel comes upon it; and any liquid that could be drunk shall be unclean if it was in any such vessel. ³⁵Everything on which any part of the carcass falls shall be unclean; whether an oven or stove, it shall be broken in pieces; they are unclean, and shall remain unclean for you. ³⁶But a spring or a cistern holding water shall be clean, while whatever touches the carcass in it shall be unclean. ³⁷If any part of their carcass falls upon any seed set aside for sowing, it is clean; ³⁸but if water is put on the seed and any part of their carcass falls on it, it is unclean for you.

39 If an animal of which you may eat dies, anyone who touches its carcass shall be unclean until the evening. ⁴⁰Those who eat of its carcass shall wash their clothes and be unclean until the evening; and those who carry the carcass shall wash their clothes and be unclean until the evening.

41 All creatures that swarm upon the earth are detestable; they shall not be eaten. ⁴²Whatever moves on its belly, and whatever moves on all fours, or whatever has many feet, all the creatures that swarm upon the earth, you shall not eat; for they are detestable. ⁴³You shall not make yourselves detestable with any creature that swarms; you shall not defile yourselves with them, and so become unclean. ⁴⁴For I am the LORD your God; sanctify yourselves therefore, and be holy, for I am holy. You shall not defile yourselves with any swarming creature that moves on the earth. ⁴⁵For I am the LORD who brought you up from the land of Egypt, to be your God; you shall be holy, for I am holy.

46 This is the law pertaining to land animal and bird and every living creature that moves through the waters and every creature that swarms upon the earth, ⁴⁷to make a distinction between the unclean and the clean, and between the living creature that may be eaten and the living creature that may not be eaten.

12 Purification of Women after Childbirth

The LORD spoke to Moses, saying: ²Speak to the people of Israel, saying:

If a woman conceives and bears a male child, she shall be ceremonially unclean seven days; as at the time of her menstruation, she shall

REAL QUESTIONS

Why are so many supposedly religious people total hypocrites? It's not just famous pastors or politicians; it's everyone everywhere. How am I supposed to convince my friends to believe in Jesus when so many Christians are such bad examples?

RQ

Abraham and David not only make the list when it comes to Greatest Bible Heroes of All Time—they make the Outstanding Hypocrites list too. The Bible, like the world today, is packed full of hypocrites.

Hypocrisy in others can really tick us off. It's so infuriating when someone drags Jesus' name through the mud! But when we're feeling so spiritually self-assured, it's only a matter of time until we too find our faces in the mud at the bottom of sin's slippery slope. When we see glaring hypocrisy in others, Jesus doesn't let *us* off the hook. Check out these stinging words: "Why do you see the speck in your neighbor's eye, but do not notice the log in your own eye?" (Matthew 7.3). Although we can't make up for others' mistakes, we *can* choose to let people know that, even though we fall, God's grace still catches us.

Can you forgive hypocrites who've done damage to the name of Christ? Are you willing to take a harsh look in the mirror and scrutinize your own life? Do you have the guts to live honestly, openly admitting your faults and failings instead of putting up a front of religious perfection? Can you stop pointing fingers and focus on God's priorities instead— "to do justice, and to love kindness, and to walk humbly with your God" (Micah 6.8)?

Find some Creative Space in the Bible and write your thoughts on these issues, maybe adding some real questions of your own. Then explore more in the verses below, or talk to someone about your real questions.

(Want to explore more? Read Genesis 20; 2 Samuel 11–12; Matthew 6.1–18; 7.1–5; and 1 Peter 2.1.)

6 When the days of her purification are completed, whether for a son or for a daughter, she shall bring to the priest at the entrance of the tent of meeting a lamb in its first year for a burnt offering, and a pigeon or a turtledove for a sin offering. ⁷He shall offer it before the LORD, and make atonement on her behalf; then she shall be clean from her flow of blood. This is the law for her who bears a child, male or female. ⁸If she cannot afford a sheep, she shall take two turtledoves or two pigeons, one for a burnt offering and the other for a sin offering; and the priest shall make atonement on her behalf, and she shall be clean.

13 Leprosy, Varieties and Symptoms

The LORD spoke to Moses and Aaron, saying:

2 When a person has on the skin of his body a swelling or an eruption or a spot, and it turns into a leprous*ᵃ* disease on the skin of his body, he shall be brought to Aaron the priest or to one of his sons the priests. ³The priest shall examine the disease on the skin of his body, and if the hair in the diseased area has turned white and the disease appears to be deeper than the skin of his body, it is a leprous*ᵃ* disease; after the priest has examined him he shall pronounce him ceremonially unclean. ⁴But if the spot is white in the skin of his body, and appears no deeper than the skin, and the hair in it has not turned white, the priest shall confine the diseased person for seven days. ⁵The priest shall examine him on the seventh day, and if he sees that the disease is checked and the disease has not spread in the skin, then the priest shall confine him seven days more. ⁶The priest shall examine him again on the seventh day, and if the disease has abated and the disease has not spread in the skin, the priest shall pronounce him clean; it is only an eruption; and he shall wash his clothes, and be clean. ⁷But if the eruption spreads in the skin after he has shown himself to the priest for his cleansing, he shall appear again before the priest. ⁸The priest shall make an examination, and if the eruption has spread in the skin, the priest shall pronounce him unclean; it is a leprous*ᵃ* disease.

9 When a person contracts a leprous*ᵃ* disease, he shall be brought to the priest. ¹⁰The priest shall make an examination, and if there is a white swelling in the skin that has turned the hair white, and there is quick raw flesh in the swelling, ¹¹it is a chronic leprous*ᵃ* disease in the skin of his body. The priest shall pronounce him unclean; he shall not confine him, for he is unclean. ¹²But if the disease breaks out in the skin, so that it covers all the skin of

be unclean. ³On the eighth day the flesh of his foreskin shall be circumcised. ⁴Her time of blood purification shall be thirty-three days; she shall not touch any holy thing, or come into the sanctuary, until the days of her purification are completed. ⁵If she bears a female child, she shall be unclean two weeks, as in her menstruation; her time of blood purification shall be sixty-six days.

a A term for several skin diseases; precise meaning uncertain the diseased person from head to foot, so far as the priest can see, [13]then the priest shall make an examination, and if the disease has covered all his body, he shall pronounce him clean of the disease; since it has all turned white, he is clean. [14]But if raw flesh ever appears on him, he shall be unclean; [15]the priest shall examine the raw flesh and pronounce him unclean. Raw flesh is unclean, for it is a leprous[a] disease. [16]But if the raw flesh again turns white, he shall come to the priest; [17]the priest shall examine him, and if the disease has turned white, the priest shall pronounce the diseased person clean. He is clean.

18 When there is on the skin of one's body a boil that has healed, [19]and in the place of the boil there appears a white swelling or a reddish-white spot, it shall be shown to the priest. [20]The priest shall make an examination, and if it appears deeper than the skin and its hair has turned white, the priest shall pronounce him unclean; this is a leprous[a] disease, broken out in the boil. [21]But if the priest examines it and the hair on it is not white, nor is it deeper than the skin but has abated, the priest shall confine him seven days. [22]If it spreads in the skin, the priest shall pronounce him unclean; it is diseased. [23]But if the spot remains in one place and does not spread, it is the scar of the boil; the priest shall pronounce him clean.

24 Or, when the body has a burn on the skin and the raw flesh of the burn becomes a spot, reddish-white or white, [25]the priest shall examine it. If the hair in the spot has turned white and it appears deeper than the skin, it is a leprous[a] disease; it has broken out in the burn, and the priest shall pronounce him unclean. This is a leprous[a] disease. [26]But if the priest examines it and the hair in the spot is not white, and it is no deeper than the skin but has abated, the priest shall confine him seven days. [27]The priest shall examine him the seventh day; if it is spreading in the skin, the priest shall pronounce him unclean. This is a leprous[a] disease. [28]But if the spot remains in one place and does not spread in the skin but has abated, it is a swelling from the burn, and the priest shall pronounce him clean; for it is the scar of the burn.

29 When a man or woman has a disease on the head or in the beard, [30]the priest shall examine the disease. If it appears deeper than the skin and the hair in it is yellow and thin, the priest shall pronounce him unclean; it is an itch, a leprous[a] disease of the head or the beard. [31]If the priest examines the itching disease, and it appears no deeper than the skin and there is no black hair in it, the priest shall confine the person with the itching disease for seven days. [32]On the seventh day the priest shall examine the itch; if the itch has not spread, and there is no yellow hair in it, and the itch appears to be no deeper than the skin, [33]he shall shave, but the itch he shall not shave. The priest shall confine the person with the itch for seven days more. [34]On the seventh day the priest shall examine the itch; if the itch has not spread in the skin and it appears to be no deeper than the skin, the priest shall pronounce him clean. He shall wash his clothes and be clean. [35]But if the itch spreads in the skin after he was pronounced clean, [36]the priest shall examine him. If the itch has spread in the skin, the priest need not seek for the yellow hair; he is unclean. [37]But if in his eyes the itch is checked, and black hair has grown in it, the itch is healed, he is clean; and the priest shall pronounce him clean.

38 When a man or a woman has spots on the skin of the body, white spots, [39]the priest shall make an examination, and if the spots on the skin of the body are of a dull white, it is a rash that has broken out on the skin; he is clean.

40 If anyone loses the hair from his head, he is bald but he is clean. [41]If he loses the hair from his forehead and temples, he has baldness of the forehead but he is clean. [42]But if there is on the bald head or the bald forehead a reddish-white diseased spot, it is a leprous[a] disease breaking out on his bald head or his bald forehead. [43]The priest shall examine him; if the diseased swelling is reddish-white on his bald head or on his bald forehead, which resembles a leprous[a] disease in the skin of the body, [44]he is leprous,[a] he is unclean. The priest shall pronounce him unclean; the disease is on his head.

45 The person who has the leprous[a] disease shall wear torn clothes and let the hair of his head be disheveled; and he shall cover his upper lip and cry out, "Unclean, unclean." [46]He shall remain unclean as long as he has the disease; he is unclean. He shall live alone; his dwelling shall be outside the camp.

47 Concerning clothing: when a leprous[a] disease appears in it, in woolen or linen cloth, [48]in warp or woof of linen or wool, or in a skin or in anything made of skin, [49]if the disease shows greenish or reddish in the garment, whether in warp or woof or in skin or in anything made of skin, it is a leprous[a] disease and shall be shown to the priest. [50]The priest shall examine the disease, and put the diseased ar-

[a] A term for several skin diseases; precise meaning uncertain

ticle aside for seven days. ⁵¹He shall examine the disease on the seventh day. If the disease has spread in the cloth, in warp or woof, or in the skin, whatever be the use of the skin, this is a spreading leprous*a* disease; it is unclean. ⁵²He shall burn the clothing, whether diseased in warp or woof, woolen or linen, or anything of skin, for it is a spreading leprous*a* disease; it shall be burned in fire.

53 If the priest makes an examination, and the disease has not spread in the clothing, in warp or woof or in anything of skin, ⁵⁴the priest shall command them to wash the article in which the disease appears, and he shall put it aside seven days more. ⁵⁵The priest shall examine the diseased article after it has been washed. If the diseased spot has not changed color, though the disease has not spread, it is unclean; you shall burn it in fire, whether the leprous*a* spot is on the inside or on the outside.

56 If the priest makes an examination, and the disease has abated after it is washed, he shall tear the spot out of the cloth, in warp or woof, or out of skin. ⁵⁷If it appears again in the garment, in warp or woof, or in anything of skin, it is spreading; you shall burn with fire that in which the disease appears. ⁵⁸But the cloth, warp or woof, or anything of skin from which the disease disappears when you have washed it, shall then be washed a second time, and it shall be clean.

59 This is the ritual for a leprous*a* disease in a cloth of wool or linen, either in warp or woof, or in anything of skin, to decide whether it is clean or unclean.

14 Purification of Lepers and Leprous Houses

The LORD spoke to Moses, saying: ²This shall be the ritual for the leprous*a* person at the time of his cleansing:

He shall be brought to the priest; ³the priest shall go out of the camp, and the priest shall make an examination. If the disease is healed in the leprous*a* person, ⁴the priest shall command that two living clean birds and cedarwood and crimson yarn and hyssop be brought for the one who is to be cleansed. ⁵The priest shall command that one of the birds be slaughtered over fresh water in an earthen vessel. ⁶He shall take the living bird with the cedarwood and the crimson yarn and the hyssop, and dip them and the living bird in the blood of the bird that was slaughtered over the fresh water. ⁷He shall sprinkle it seven times upon the one who is to be cleansed of the leprous*a* disease; then he shall pronounce him clean, and he shall let the living bird go into the open field. ⁸The one who is to be cleansed shall wash his clothes, and shave off all his hair, and bathe himself in water, and he shall be clean. After that he shall come into the camp, but shall live outside his tent seven days. ⁹On the seventh day he shall shave all his hair: of head, beard, eyebrows; he shall shave all his hair. Then he shall wash his clothes, and bathe his body in water, and he shall be clean.

10 On the eighth day he shall take two male lambs without blemish, and one ewe lamb in its first year without blemish, and a grain offering of three-tenths of an ephah of choice flour mixed with oil, and one log*b* of oil. ¹¹The priest who cleanses shall set the person to be cleansed, along with these things, before the LORD, at the entrance of the tent of meeting. ¹²The priest shall take one of the lambs, and offer it as a guilt offering, along with the log*b* of oil, and raise them as an elevation offering before the LORD. ¹³He shall slaughter the lamb in the place where the sin offering and the burnt offering are slaughtered in the holy place; for the guilt offering, like the sin offering, belongs to the priest: it is most holy. ¹⁴The priest shall take some of the blood of the guilt offering and put it on the lobe of the right ear of the one to be cleansed, and on the thumb of the right hand, and on the big toe of the right foot. ¹⁵The priest shall take some of the log*b* of oil and pour it into the palm of his own left hand, ¹⁶and dip his right finger in the oil that is in his left hand and sprinkle some oil with his finger seven times before the LORD. ¹⁷Some of the oil that remains in his hand the priest shall put on the lobe of the right ear of the one to be cleansed, and on the thumb of the right hand, and on the big toe of the right foot, on top of the blood of the guilt offering. ¹⁸The rest of the oil that is in the priest's hand he shall put on the head of the one to be cleansed. Then the priest shall make atonement on his behalf before the LORD: ¹⁹the priest shall offer the sin offering, to make atonement for the one to be cleansed from his uncleanness. Afterward he shall slaughter the burnt offering; ²⁰and the priest shall offer the burnt offering and the grain offering on the altar. Thus the priest shall make atonement on his behalf and he shall be clean.

21 But if he is poor and cannot afford so much, he shall take one male lamb for a guilt offering to be elevated, to make atonement on his behalf, and one-tenth of an ephah of choice flour mixed with oil for a grain offering and a log*b* of oil; ²²also two turtledoves or two pi-

---

a A term for several skin diseases; precise meaning uncertain *b* A liquid measure geons, such as he can afford, one for a sin offering and the other for a burnt offering. ²³On the eighth day he shall bring them for his cleansing to the priest, to the entrance of the tent of meeting, before the LORD; ²⁴and the priest shall take the lamb of the guilt offering and the log*ᵃ* of oil, and the priest shall raise them as an elevation offering before the LORD. ²⁵The priest shall slaughter the lamb of the guilt offering and shall take some of the blood of the guilt offering, and put it on the lobe of the right ear of the one to be cleansed, and on the thumb of the right hand, and on the big toe of the right foot. ²⁶The priest shall pour some of the oil into the palm of his own left hand, ²⁷and shall sprinkle with his right finger some of the oil that is in his left hand seven times before the LORD. ²⁸The priest shall put some of the oil that is in his hand on the lobe of the right ear of the one to be cleansed, and on the thumb of the right hand, and the big toe of the right foot, where the blood of the guilt offering was placed. ²⁹The rest of the oil that is in the priest's hand he shall put on the head of the one to be cleansed, to make atonement on his behalf before the LORD. ³⁰And he shall offer, of the turtledoves or pigeons such as he can afford, ³¹one*ᵇ* for a sin offering and the other for a burnt offering, along with a grain offering; and the priest shall make atonement before the LORD on behalf of the one being cleansed. ³²This is the ritual for the one who has a leprous*ᶜ* disease, who cannot afford the offerings for his cleansing.

33 The LORD spoke to Moses and Aaron, saying:

34 When you come into the land of Canaan, which I give you for a possession, and I put a leprous*ᶜ* disease in a house in the land of your possession, ³⁵the owner of the house shall come and tell the priest, saying, "There seems to me to be some sort of disease in my house." ³⁶The priest shall command that they empty the house before the priest goes to examine the disease, or all that is in the house will become unclean; and afterward the priest shall go in to inspect the house. ³⁷He shall examine the disease; if the disease is in the walls of the house with greenish or reddish spots, and if it appears to be deeper than the surface, ³⁸the priest shall go outside to the door of the house and shut up the house seven days. ³⁹The priest shall come again on the seventh day and make an inspection; if the disease has spread in the walls of the house, ⁴⁰the priest shall command that the stones in which the disease appears be taken out and thrown into an unclean

place outside the city. ⁴¹He shall have the inside of the house scraped thoroughly, and the plaster that is scraped off shall be dumped in an unclean place outside the city. ⁴²They shall take other stones and put them in the place of those stones, and take other plaster and plaster the house.

43 If the disease breaks out again in the house, after he has taken out the stones and scraped the house and plastered it, ⁴⁴the priest shall go and make inspection; if the disease has spread in the house, it is a spreading leprous*ᶜ* disease in the house; it is unclean. ⁴⁵He shall have the house torn down, its stones and timber and all the plaster of the house, and taken outside the city to an unclean place. ⁴⁶All who enter the house while it is shut up shall be

ᵃ A liquid measure   ᵇ Gk Syr: Heb afford, ³¹such as he can afford, one   ᶜ A term for several skin diseases; precise meaning uncertain

Sunflower—© Jessica Jones, 17

unclean until the evening; [47] and all who sleep in the house shall wash their clothes; and all who eat in the house shall wash their clothes.

48 If the priest comes and makes an inspection, and the disease has not spread in the house after the house was plastered, the priest shall pronounce the house clean; the disease is healed. [49] For the cleansing of the house he shall take two birds, with cedarwood and crimson yarn and hyssop, [50] and shall slaughter one of the birds over fresh water in an earthen vessel, [51] and shall take the cedarwood and the hyssop and the crimson yarn, along with the living bird, and dip them in the blood of the slaughtered bird and the fresh water, and sprinkle the house seven times. [52] Thus he shall cleanse the house with the blood of the bird, and with the fresh water, and with the living bird, and with the cedarwood and hyssop and crimson yarn; [53] and he shall let the living bird go out of the city into the open field; so he shall make atonement for the house, and it shall be clean.

54 This is the ritual for any leprous[a] disease: for an itch, [55] for leprous[a] diseases in clothing and houses, [56] and for a swelling or an eruption or a spot, [57] to determine when it is unclean and when it is clean. This is the ritual for leprous[a] diseases.

15 Concerning Bodily Discharges

The LORD spoke to Moses and Aaron, saying: [2] Speak to the people of Israel and say to them:

When any man has a discharge from his member,[b] his discharge makes him ceremonially unclean. [3] The uncleanness of his discharge is this: whether his member[b] flows with his discharge, or his member[b] is stopped from discharging, it is uncleanness for him. [4] Every bed on which the one with the discharge lies shall be unclean; and everything on which he sits shall be unclean. [5] Anyone who touches his bed shall wash his clothes, and bathe in water, and be unclean until the evening. [6] All who sit on anything on which the one with the discharge has sat shall wash their clothes, and bathe in water, and be unclean until the evening. [7] All who touch the body of the one with the discharge shall wash their clothes, and bathe in water, and be unclean until the evening. [8] If the one with the discharge spits on persons who are clean, then they shall wash their clothes, and bathe in water, and be unclean until the evening. [9] Any saddle on which the one with the discharge rides shall be unclean. [10] All who touch anything that was under him shall be unclean until the evening, and all who carry such a thing shall wash their clothes, and bathe in water, and be unclean until the evening. [11] All those whom the one with the discharge touches without his having rinsed his hands in water shall wash their clothes, and bathe in water, and be unclean until the evening. [12] Any earthen vessel that the one with the discharge touches shall be broken; and every vessel of wood shall be rinsed in water.

13 When the one with a discharge is cleansed of his discharge, he shall count seven days for his cleansing; he shall wash his clothes and bathe his body in fresh water, and he shall be clean. [14] On the eighth day he shall take two turtledoves or two pigeons and come before the LORD to the entrance of the tent of meeting and give them to the priest. [15] The priest shall offer them, one for a sin offering and the other for a burnt offering; and the priest shall make atonement on his behalf before the LORD for his discharge.

16 If a man has an emission of semen, he shall bathe his whole body in water, and be unclean until the evening. [17] Everything made of cloth or of skin on which the semen falls shall be washed with water, and be unclean until the evening. [18] If a man lies with a woman and has an emission of semen, both of them shall bathe in water, and be unclean until the evening.

19 When a woman has a discharge of blood that is her regular discharge from her body, she shall be in her impurity for seven days, and whoever touches her shall be unclean until the evening. [20] Everything upon which she lies during her impurity shall be unclean; everything also upon which she sits shall be unclean. [21] Whoever touches her bed shall wash his clothes, and bathe in water, and be unclean

---

a A term for several skin diseases; precise meaning uncertain *b* Heb *flesh* until the evening. 22Whoever touches anything upon which she sits shall wash his clothes, and bathe in water, and be unclean until the evening; 23whether it is the bed or anything upon which she sits, when he touches it he shall be unclean until the evening. 24If any man lies with her, and her impurity falls on him, he shall be unclean seven days; and every bed on which he lies shall be unclean.

25 If a woman has a discharge of blood for many days, not at the time of her impurity, or if she has a discharge beyond the time of her impurity, all the days of the discharge she shall continue in uncleanness; as in the days of her impurity, she shall be unclean. 26Every bed on which she lies during all the days of her discharge shall be treated as the bed of her impurity; and everything on which she sits shall be unclean, as in the uncleanness of her impurity. 27Whoever touches these things shall be unclean, and shall wash his clothes, and bathe in water, and be unclean until the evening. 28If she is cleansed of her discharge, she shall count seven days, and after that she shall be clean. 29On the eighth day she shall take two turtledoves or two pigeons and bring them to the priest at the entrance of the tent of meeting. 30The priest shall offer one for a sin offering and the other for a burnt offering; and the priest shall make atonement on her behalf before the Lord for her unclean discharge.

31 Thus you shall keep the people of Israel separate from their uncleanness, so that they do not die in their uncleanness by defiling my tabernacle that is in their midst.

32 This is the ritual for those who have a discharge: for him who has an emission of semen, becoming unclean thereby, 33for her who is in the infirmity of her period, for anyone, male or female, who has a discharge, and for the man who lies with a woman who is unclean.

16 The Day of Atonement

The Lord spoke to Moses after the death of the two sons of Aaron, when they drew near before the Lord and died. 2The Lord said to Moses:

Tell your brother Aaron not to come just at any time into the sanctuary inside the curtain before the mercy seat*a* that is upon the ark, or he will die; for I appear in the cloud upon the mercy seat. *a* 3Thus shall Aaron come into the holy place: with a young bull for a sin offering and a ram for a burnt offering. 4He shall put on the holy linen tunic, and shall have the linen undergarments next to his body, fasten the linen sash, and wear the linen turban; these are the holy vestments. He shall bathe his body in water, and then put them on. 5He shall take from the congregation of the people of Israel two male goats for a sin offering, and one ram for a burnt offering.

6 Aaron shall offer the bull as a sin offering for himself, and shall make atonement for himself and for his house. 7He shall take the two goats and set them before the Lord at the entrance of the tent of meeting; 8and Aaron shall cast lots on the two goats, one lot for the Lord and the other lot for Azazel.*b* 9Aaron shall present the goat on which the lot fell for the Lord, and offer it as a sin offering; 10but the goat on which the lot fell for Azazel*b* shall be presented alive before the Lord to make atonement over it, that it may be sent away into the wilderness to Azazel.*b*

11 Aaron shall present the bull as a sin offering for himself, and shall make atonement for himself and for his house; he shall slaughter the bull as a sin offering for himself. 12He shall take a censer full of coals of fire from the altar before the Lord, and two handfuls of crushed sweet incense, and he shall bring it inside the curtain 13and put the incense on the fire before the Lord, that the cloud of the incense may cover the mercy seat*a* that is upon the covenant,*c* or he will die. 14He shall take some of the blood of the bull, and sprinkle it with his finger on the front of the mercy seat,*c* and before the mercy seat*c* he shall sprinkle the blood with his finger seven times.

15 He shall slaughter the goat of the sin offering that is for the people and bring its blood inside the curtain, and do with its blood as he did with the blood of the bull, sprinkling it upon the mercy seat*a* and before the mercy seat.*a* 16Thus he shall make atonement for the sanctuary, because of the uncleannesses of the people of Israel, and because of their transgressions, all their sins; and so he shall do for the tent of meeting, which remains with them in the midst of their uncleannesses. 17No one shall be in the tent of meeting from the time he enters to make atonement in the sanctuary until he comes out and has made atonement for himself and for his house and for all the assembly of Israel. 18Then he shall go out to the altar that is before the Lord and make atonement on its behalf, and shall take some of the blood of the bull and of the blood of the goat, and put it on each of the horns of the altar. 19He shall sprinkle some of the blood on it with his finger seven times, and cleanse it and hallow it from the uncleannesses of the people of Israel.

20 When he has finished atoning for the holy place and the tent of meeting and the al-

a Or *the cover* *b* Traditionally rendered *a scapegoat* *c* Or *treaty*, or *testament*; Heb *eduth* tar, he shall present the live goat. 21Then Aaron shall lay both his hands on the head of the live goat, and confess over it all the iniquities of the people of Israel, and all their transgressions, all their sins, putting them on the head of the goat, and sending it away into the wilderness by means of someone designated for the task.*a* 22The goat shall bear on itself all their iniquities to a barren region; and the goat shall be set free in the wilderness.

23 Then Aaron shall enter the tent of meeting, and shall take off the linen vestments that he put on when he went into the holy place, and shall leave them there. 24He shall bathe his body in water in a holy place, and put on his vestments; then he shall come out and offer his burnt offering and the burnt offering of the people, making atonement for himself and for the people. 25The fat of the sin offering he shall turn into smoke on the altar. 26The one who sets the goat free for Azazel*b* shall wash his clothes and bathe his body in water, and afterward may come into the camp. 27The bull of the sin offering and the goat of the sin offering, whose blood was brought in to make atonement in the holy place, shall be taken outside the camp; their skin and their flesh and their dung shall be consumed in fire. 28The one who burns them shall wash his clothes and bathe his body in water, and afterward may come into the camp.

29 This shall be a statute to you forever: In the seventh month, on the tenth day of the month, you shall deny yourselves,*c* and shall do no work, neither the citizen nor the alien who resides among you. 30For on this day atonement shall be made for you, to cleanse you; from all your sins you shall be clean before the LORD. 31It is a sabbath of complete rest to you, and you shall deny yourselves;*c* it is a statute forever. 32The priest who is anointed and consecrated as priest in his father's place shall make atonement, wearing the linen vestments, the holy vestments. 33He shall make atonement for the sanctuary, and he shall make atonement for the tent of meeting and for the altar, and he shall make atonement for the priests and for all the people of the assembly. 34This shall be an everlasting statute for you, to make atonement for the people of Israel once in the year for all their sins. And Moses did as the LORD had commanded him.

17 The Slaughtering of Animals

The LORD spoke to Moses:

2 Speak to Aaron and his sons and to all the people of Israel and say to them: This is what the LORD has commanded. 3If anyone of the house of Israel slaughters an ox or a lamb or a goat in the camp, or slaughters it outside the camp, 4and does not bring it to the entrance of the tent of meeting, to present it as an offering to the LORD before the tabernacle of the LORD, he shall be held guilty of bloodshed; he has shed blood, and he shall be cut off from the people. 5This is in order that the people of Israel may bring their sacrifices that they offer in the open field, that they may bring them to the LORD, to the priest at the entrance of the tent of meeting, and offer them as sacrifices of well-being to the LORD. 6The priest shall dash the blood against the altar of the LORD at the entrance of the tent of meeting, and turn the fat into smoke as a pleasing odor to the LORD, 7so that they may no longer offer their sacrifices for goat-demons, to whom they prostitute themselves. This shall be a statute forever to them throughout their generations.

8 And say to them further: Anyone of the house of Israel or of the aliens who reside among them who offers a burnt offering or sacrifice, 9and does not bring it to the entrance of the tent of meeting, to sacrifice it to the LORD, shall be cut off from the people.

Eating Blood Prohibited

10 If anyone of the house of Israel or of the aliens who reside among them eats any blood, I will set my face against that person who eats blood, and will cut that person off from the people. 11For the life of the flesh is in the blood; and I have given it to you for making atonement for your lives on the altar; for, as life, it is the blood that makes atonement. 12Therefore I have said to the people of Israel: No person among you shall eat blood, nor shall any alien who resides among you eat blood. 13And anyone of the people of Israel, or of the aliens who reside among them, who hunts down an animal or bird that may be eaten shall pour out its blood and cover it with earth.

14 For the life of every creature—its blood is its life; therefore I have said to the people of Israel: You shall not eat the blood of any creature, for the life of every creature is its blood; whoever eats it shall be cut off. 15All persons, citizens or aliens, who eat what dies of itself or what has been torn by wild animals, shall wash their clothes, and bathe themselves in water, and be unclean until the evening; then they shall be clean. 16But if they do not wash themselves or bathe their body, they shall bear their guilt.

a Meaning of Heb uncertain   *b* Traditionally rendered a *scapegoat*   *c* Or *shall fast*

18 Sexual Relations

The LORD spoke to Moses, saying:

2 Speak to the people of Israel and say to them: I am the LORD your God. [3]You shall not do as they do in the land of Egypt, where you lived, and you shall not do as they do in the land of Canaan, to which I am bringing you. You shall not follow their statutes. [4]My ordinances you shall observe and my statutes you shall keep, following them: I am the LORD your God. [5]You shall keep my statutes and my ordinances; by doing so one shall live: I am the LORD.

6 None of you shall approach anyone near of kin to uncover nakedness: I am the LORD. [7]You shall not uncover the nakedness of your father, which is the nakedness of your mother; she is your mother, you shall not uncover her nakedness. [8]You shall not uncover the nakedness of your father's wife; it is the nakedness of your father. [9]You shall not uncover the nakedness of your sister, your father's daughter or your mother's daughter, whether born at home or born abroad. [10]You shall not uncover the nakedness of your son's daughter or of your daughter's daughter, for their nakedness is your own nakedness. [11]You shall not uncover the nakedness of your father's wife's daughter, begotten by your father, since she is your sister. [12]You shall not uncover the nakedness of your father's sister; she is your father's flesh. [13]You shall not uncover the nakedness of your mother's sister, for she is your mother's flesh. [14]You shall not uncover the nakedness of your father's brother, that is, you shall not approach his wife; she is your aunt. [15]You shall not uncover the nakedness of your daughter-in-law: she is your son's wife; you shall not uncover her nakedness. [16]You shall not uncover the nakedness of your brother's wife; it is your brother's nakedness. [17]You shall not uncover the nakedness of a woman and her daughter, and you shall not take[a] her son's daughter or her daughter's daughter to uncover her nakedness; they are your[b] flesh; it is depravity. [18]And you shall not take[a] a woman as a rival to her sister, uncovering her nakedness while her sister is still alive.

19 You shall not approach a woman to uncover her nakedness while she is in her menstrual uncleanness. [20]You shall not have sexual relations with your kinsman's wife, and defile yourself with her. [21]You shall not give any of your offspring to sacrifice them[c] to Molech, and so profane the name of your God: I am the LORD. [22]You shall not lie with a male as with a woman; it is an abomination. [23]You shall not have sexual relations with any animal and de-

a Or *marry* b Gk: Heb lacks *your* c Heb *to pass them over*

JESUS SIGHTING

A final guttural grunt came from the bull as the old man slit its throat. He collected the warm blood in a dish. The old man dipped one wrinkled finger in the steaming liquid, then splattered the blood on the cloth covering the Ark—the holy, golden box that symbolized God's presence with his people.

Two goats were brought before the old man; one was slaughtered, just like the bull. And as with the bull, its blood was sprinkled onto the Ark.

But the third animal—the leftover goat—had a different fate. His neck was safe from the knife. Instead, the priest simply placed his hands on the goat's head, and then the goat was led away and sent into the wilderness.

This was the original "scapegoat." In the midst of the blood and gore of animal sacrifices, **Leviticus 16.6–22** describes this scapegoat—the creature upon whom the priest symbolically placed all of the people's sins. This "lucky" animal who avoided death got the unlucky job of carrying the burden of their sins far, far away.

Sounds eerily familiar, doesn't it? A bit like Jesus, making his way up the hill with the cross, carrying not just a rough, heavy beam of wood, but also the weight of everyone's sins—every single one of them—on his shoulders. John the Baptist called him "the Lamb of God who takes away the sin of the world" (John 1.29). But we can also call him the *true scapegoat*—for he carried away our sin and guilt eternally through his death and Resurrection. By his rising to new life, we can have the hope of a new life strengthened by God's grace.

JS

file yourself with it, nor shall any woman give herself to an animal to have sexual relations with it: it is perversion.

24 Do not defile yourselves in any of these ways, for by all these practices the nations I am casting out before you have defiled themselves. ²⁵Thus the land became defiled; and I punished it for its iniquity, and the land vomited out its inhabitants. ²⁶But you shall keep my statutes and my ordinances and commit none of these abominations, either the citizen or the alien who resides among you ²⁷(for the inhabitants of the land, who were before you, committed all of these abominations, and the land became defiled); ²⁸otherwise the land will vomit you out for defiling it, as it vomited out the nation that was before you. ²⁹For whoever commits any of these abominations shall be cut off from their people. ³⁰So keep my charge not to commit any of these abominations that were done before you, and not to defile yourselves by them: I am the LORD your God.

19 Ritual and Moral Holiness

The LORD spoke to Moses, saying:

2 Speak to all the congregation of the people of Israel and say to them: You shall be holy, for I the LORD your God am holy. ³You shall each revere your mother and father, and you shall keep my sabbaths: I am the LORD your God. ⁴Do not turn to idols or make cast images for yourselves: I am the LORD your God.

5 When you offer a sacrifice of well-being to the LORD, offer it in such a way that it is acceptable in your behalf. ⁶It shall be eaten on the same day you offer it, or on the next day; and anything left over until the third day shall be consumed in fire. ⁷If it is eaten at all on the third day, it is an abomination; it will not be acceptable. ⁸All who eat it shall be subject to punishment, because they have profaned what is holy to the LORD; and any such person shall be cut off from the people.

9 When you reap the harvest of your land, you shall not reap to the very edges of your field, or gather the gleanings of your harvest. ¹⁰You shall not strip your vineyard bare, or gather the fallen grapes of your vineyard; you shall leave them for the poor and the alien: I am the LORD your God.

11 You shall not steal; you shall not deal falsely; and you shall not lie to one another. ¹²And you shall not swear falsely by my name, profaning the name of your God: I am the LORD.

13 You shall not defraud your neighbor; you shall not steal; and you shall not keep for yourself the wages of a laborer until morning. ¹⁴You shall not revile the deaf or put a stumbling block before the blind; you shall fear your God: I am the LORD.

15 You shall not render an unjust judgment; you shall not be partial to the poor or defer to the great: with justice you shall judge your neighbor. ¹⁶You shall not go around as a slanderer*a* among your people, and you shall not profit by the blood*b* of your neighbor: I am the LORD.

17 You shall not hate in your heart anyone of your kin; you shall reprove your neighbor, or you will incur guilt yourself. ¹⁸You shall not take vengeance or bear a grudge against any of your people, but you shall love your neighbor as yourself: I am the LORD.

19 You shall keep my statutes. You shall not let your animals breed with a different kind; you shall not sow your field with two kinds of seed; nor shall you put on a garment made of two different materials.

20 If a man has sexual relations with a woman who is a slave, designated for another man but not ransomed or given her freedom, an inquiry shall be held. They shall not be put to death, since she has not been freed; ²¹but he shall bring a guilt offering for himself to the LORD, at the entrance of the tent of meeting, a ram as guilt offering. ²²And the priest shall make atonement for him with the ram of guilt offering before the LORD for his sin that he committed; and the sin he committed shall be forgiven him.

23 When you come into the land and plant all kinds of trees for food, then you shall regard their fruit as forbidden;*c* three years it shall be forbidden*d* to you, it must not be eaten. ²⁴In the fourth year all their fruit shall be set apart for rejoicing in the LORD. ²⁵But in the fifth year you may eat of their fruit, that their yield may be increased for you: I am the LORD your God.

26 You shall not eat anything with its blood. You shall not practice augury or witchcraft. ²⁷You shall not round off the hair on your temples or mar the edges of your beard. ²⁸You shall not make any gashes in your flesh for the dead or tattoo any marks upon you: I am the LORD.

29 Do not profane your daughter by making her a prostitute, that the land not become prostituted and full of depravity. ³⁰You shall keep my sabbaths and reverence my sanctuary: I am the LORD.

31 Do not turn to mediums or wizards; do not seek them out, to be defiled by them: I am the LORD your God.

---

a Meaning of Heb uncertain *b* Heb *stand against the blood* *c* Heb *as their uncircumcision* *d* Heb *uncircumcision*

MY JESUS

Upon this lonely road I walk; the cross
Is heavy on my back. Unceasing thoughts
Of sin, of guilt and shame my mind exhaust.
And by this anguish to my God I'm brought.

Eyes filled with love meet mine and touch my core.
With dust beneath His feet, He pushes past
To spread His arms of love so I may soar.
His hand may tremble, but His spirit's fast.

Hearts pained He soothed, yet none did His console.
The feet of friends He washed, but His none clean.
His arms were spread so I may live life whole.
And beaten, bruised His love forever will reign.

His place none take—He paid my sin in whole.
And Oh, the beauty when my Lord saved my soul.

My Jesus: A Formal Sonnet—© Randy Reed, 18

Day's End—© Katie Stein, 15

32 You shall rise before the aged, and defer to the old; and you shall fear your God: I am the Lord.

33 When an alien resides with you in your land, you shall not oppress the alien. 34The alien who resides with you shall be to you as the citizen among you; you shall love the alien as yourself, for you were aliens in the land of Egypt: I am the Lord your God.

35 You shall not cheat in measuring length, weight, or quantity. 36You shall have honest balances, honest weights, an honest ephah, and an honest hin: I am the Lord your God, who brought you out of the land of Egypt. 37You shall keep all my statutes and all my ordinances, and observe them: I am the Lord.

20 Penalties for Violations of Holiness

The Lord spoke to Moses, saying: 2Say further to the people of Israel:

Any of the people of Israel, or of the aliens who reside in Israel, who give any of their offspring to Molech shall be put to death; the people of the land shall stone them to death. 3I myself will set my face against them, and will cut them off from the people, because they have given of their offspring to Molech, defiling my sanctuary and profaning my holy name. 4And if the people of the land should ever close their eyes to them, when they give of their offspring to Molech, and do not put them to

death, 5I myself will set my face against them and against their family, and will cut them off from among their people, them and all who follow them in prostituting themselves to Molech.

6 If any turn to mediums and wizards, prostituting themselves to them, I will set my face against them, and will cut them off from the people. 7Consecrate yourselves therefore, and be holy; for I am the Lord your God. 8Keep my statutes, and observe them; I am the Lord; I sanctify you. 9All who curse father or mother shall be put to death; having cursed father or mother, their blood is upon them.

10 If a man commits adultery with the wife of*a* his neighbor, both the adulterer and the adulteress shall be put to death. 11The man who lies with his father's wife has uncovered his father's nakedness; both of them shall be put to death; their blood is upon them. 12If a man lies with his daughter-in-law, both of them shall be put to death; they have committed perversion, their blood is upon them. 13If a man lies with a male as with a woman, both of them have committed an abomination; they shall be put to death; their blood is upon them. 14If a man takes a wife and her mother also, it is depravity; they shall be burned to death, both he and they, that there may be no depravity among you. 15If a man has sexual relations with an animal, he shall be put to death;

a Heb repeats *if a man commits adultery with the wife of*

and you shall kill the animal. ¹⁶If a woman approaches any animal and has sexual relations with it, you shall kill the woman and the animal; they shall be put to death, their blood is upon them.

17 If a man takes his sister, a daughter of his father or a daughter of his mother, and sees her nakedness, and she sees his nakedness, it is a disgrace, and they shall be cut off in the sight of their people; he has uncovered his sister's nakedness, he shall be subject to punishment. ¹⁸If a man lies with a woman having her sickness and uncovers her nakedness, he has laid bare her flow and she has laid bare her flow of blood; both of them shall be cut off from their people. ¹⁹You shall not uncover the nakedness of your mother's sister or of your father's sister, for that is to lay bare one's own flesh; they shall be subject to punishment. ²⁰If a man lies with his uncle's wife, he has uncovered his uncle's nakedness; they shall be subject to punishment; they shall die childless. ²¹If a man takes his brother's wife, it is impurity; he has uncovered his brother's nakedness; they shall be childless.

22 You shall keep all my statutes and all my ordinances, and observe them, so that the land to which I bring you to settle in may not vomit you out. ²³You shall not follow the practices of the nation that I am driving out before you. Because they did all these things, I abhorred them. ²⁴But I have said to you: You shall inherit their land, and I will give it to you to possess, a land flowing with milk and honey. I am the Lord your God; I have separated you from the peoples. ²⁵You shall therefore make a distinction between the clean animal and the unclean, and between the unclean bird and the clean; you shall not bring abomination on yourselves by animal or by bird or by anything with which the ground teems, which I have set apart for you to hold unclean. ²⁶You shall be holy to me; for I the Lord am holy, and I have separated you from the other peoples to be mine.

27 A man or a woman who is a medium or a wizard shall be put to death; they shall be stoned to death, their blood is upon them.

21 The Holiness of Priests

The Lord said to Moses: Speak to the priests, the sons of Aaron, and say to them:

No one shall defile himself for a dead person among his relatives, ²except for his nearest kin: his mother, his father, his son, his daughter, his brother; ³likewise, for a virgin sister, close to him because she has had no husband, he may defile himself for her. ⁴But he shall not defile himself as a husband among his people and so profane himself. ⁵They shall not make bald spots upon their heads, or shave off the edges of their beards, or make any gashes in their flesh. ⁶They shall be holy to their God, and not profane the name of their God; for they offer the Lord's offerings by fire, the food of their God; therefore they shall be holy. ⁷They shall not marry a prostitute or a woman who has been defiled; neither shall they marry a woman divorced from her husband. For they are holy to their God, ⁸and you shall treat them as holy, since they offer the food of your God; they shall be holy to you, for I the Lord, I who sanctify you, am holy. ⁹When the daughter of a priest profanes herself through prostitution, she profanes her father; she shall be burned to death.

10 The priest who is exalted above his fellows, on whose head the anointing oil has been poured and who has been consecrated to wear the vestments, shall not dishevel his hair, nor tear his vestments. ¹¹He shall not go where there is a dead body; he shall not defile himself even for his father or mother. ¹²He shall not go outside the sanctuary and thus profane the sanctuary of his God; for the consecration of the anointing oil of his God is upon him: I am the Lord. ¹³He shall marry only a woman who is a virgin. ¹⁴A widow, or a divorced woman, or a woman who has been defiled, a prostitute, these he shall not marry. He shall marry a virgin of his own kin, ¹⁵that he may not profane his offspring among his kin; for I am the Lord; I sanctify him.

16 The Lord spoke to Moses, saying: ¹⁷Speak to Aaron and say: No one of your offspring throughout their generations who has a blemish may approach to offer the food of his God. ¹⁸For no one who has a blemish shall draw near, one who is blind or lame, or one who has a mutilated face or a limb too long, ¹⁹or one who has a broken foot or a broken hand, ²⁰or a hunchback, or a dwarf, or a man with a blemish in his eyes or an itching disease or scabs or crushed testicles. ²¹No descendant of Aaron the priest who has a blemish shall come near to offer the Lord's offerings by fire; since he has a blemish, he shall not come near to offer the food of his God. ²²He may eat the food of his God, of the most holy as well as of the holy. ²³But he shall not come near the curtain or approach the altar, because he has a blemish, that he may not profane my sanctuaries; for I am the Lord; I sanctify them. ²⁴Thus Moses spoke to Aaron and to his sons and to all the people of Israel.

22 The Use of Holy Offerings

The Lord spoke to Moses, saying: ²Direct Aaron and his sons to deal carefully with the sacred donations of the people of Israel, which

TEXT MESSAGE

They may not have had government welfare programs to help those in need in Old Testament times, but the Israelites were careful to take care of the poor. Farmers were told to leave grain in their field and grapes in their vineyards, so that poor people and travelers would have something to eat (Leviticus 19.9–10).

This information has been scanned and is free of all known viruses. Please forward to all your friends.

they dedicate to me, so that they may not profane my holy name; I am the LORD. ³Say to them: If anyone among all your offspring throughout your generations comes near the sacred donations, which the people of Israel dedicate to the LORD, while he is in a state of uncleanness, that person shall be cut off from my presence: I am the LORD. ⁴No one of Aaron's offspring who has a leprous^a disease or suffers a discharge may eat of the sacred donations until he is clean. Whoever touches anything made unclean by a corpse or a man who has had an emission of semen, ⁵and whoever touches any swarming thing by which he may be made unclean or any human being by whom he may be made unclean—whatever his uncleanness may be— ⁶the person who touches any such shall be unclean until evening and

shall not eat of the sacred donations unless he has washed his body in water. ⁷When the sun sets he shall be clean; and afterward he may eat of the sacred donations, for they are his food. ⁸That which died or was torn by wild animals he shall not eat, becoming unclean by it: I am the LORD. ⁹They shall keep my charge, so that they may not incur guilt and die in the sanctuary^b for having profaned it: I am the LORD; I sanctify them.

10 No lay person shall eat of the sacred donations. No bound or hired servant of the priest shall eat of the sacred donations; ¹¹but if a priest acquires anyone by purchase, the person may eat of them; and those that are born in his house may eat of his food. ¹²If a priest's daughter marries a layman, she shall not eat of the offering of the sacred donations; ¹³but if a priest's daughter is widowed or divorced, without offspring, and returns to her father's house, as in her youth, she may eat of her father's food. No lay person shall eat of it. ¹⁴If a man eats of the sacred donation unintentionally, he shall add one-fifth of its value to it, and give the sacred donation to the priest. ¹⁵No one shall profane the sacred donations of the people of Israel, which they offer to the LORD, ¹⁶causing them to bear guilt requiring a guilt offering, by eating their sacred donations: for I am the LORD; I sanctify them.

Acceptable Offerings

17 The LORD spoke to Moses, saying: ¹⁸Speak to Aaron and his sons and all the people of Israel and say to them: When anyone of the house of Israel or of the aliens residing in Israel presents an offering, whether in payment of a vow or as a freewill offering that is offered to the LORD as a burnt offering, ¹⁹to be acceptable in your behalf it shall be a male without blemish, of the cattle or the sheep or the goats. ²⁰You shall not offer anything that has a blemish, for it will not be acceptable in your behalf.

21 When anyone offers a sacrifice of well-being to the LORD, in fulfillment of a vow or as a freewill offering, from the herd or from the flock, to be acceptable it must be perfect; there shall be no blemish in it. ²²Anything blind, or injured, or maimed, or having a discharge or an itch or scabs—these you shall not offer to the LORD or put any of them on the altar as offerings by fire to the LORD. ²³An ox or a lamb that has a limb too long or too short you may present for a freewill offering; but it will not be accepted for a vow. ²⁴Any animal that has its testicles bruised or crushed or torn or cut, you shall not offer to the LORD; such you shall not

a A term for several skin diseases; precise meaning uncertain b Vg: Heb *incur guilt for it and die in it* do within your land, [25]nor shall you accept any such animals from a foreigner to offer as food to your God; since they are mutilated, with a blemish in them, they shall not be accepted in your behalf.

26 The Lord spoke to Moses, saying: [27]When an ox or a sheep or a goat is born, it shall remain seven days with its mother, and from the eighth day on it shall be acceptable as the Lord's offering by fire. [28]But you shall not slaughter, from the herd or the flock, an animal with its young on the same day. [29]When you sacrifice a thanksgiving offering to the Lord, you shall sacrifice it so that it may be acceptable in your behalf. [30]It shall be eaten on the same day; you shall not leave any of it until morning: I am the Lord.

31 Thus you shall keep my commandments and observe them: I am the Lord. [32]You shall not profane my holy name, that I may be sanctified among the people of Israel: I am the Lord; I sanctify you, [33]I who brought you out of the land of Egypt to be your God: I am the Lord.

23 Appointed Festivals

The Lord spoke to Moses, saying: [2]Speak to the people of Israel and say to them: These are the appointed festivals of the Lord that you shall proclaim as holy convocations, my appointed festivals.

The Sabbath, Passover, and Unleavened Bread

3 Six days shall work be done; but the seventh day is a sabbath of complete rest, a holy convocation; you shall do no work: it is a sabbath to the Lord throughout your settlements.

4 These are the appointed festivals of the Lord, the holy convocations, which you shall celebrate at the time appointed for them. [5]In the first month, on the fourteenth day of the month, at twilight,[a] there shall be a passover offering to the Lord, [6]and on the fifteenth day of the same month is the festival of unleavened bread to the Lord; seven days you shall eat unleavened bread. [7]On the first day you shall have a holy convocation; you shall not work at your occupations. [8]For seven days you shall present the Lord's offerings by fire; on the seventh day there shall be a holy convocation: you shall not work at your occupations.

The Offering of First Fruits

9 The Lord spoke to Moses: [10]Speak to the people of Israel and say to them: When you enter the land that I am giving you and you reap its harvest, you shall bring the sheaf of the first fruits of your harvest to the priest. [11]He shall raise the sheaf before the Lord, that you may find acceptance; on the day after the sabbath the priest shall raise it. [12]On the day when you raise the sheaf, you shall offer a lamb a year old, without blemish, as a burnt offering to the Lord. [13]And the grain offering with it shall be two-tenths of an ephah of choice flour mixed with oil, an offering by fire of pleasing odor to the Lord; and the drink offering with it shall be of wine, one-fourth of a hin. [14]You shall eat no bread or parched grain or fresh ears until that very day, until you have brought the offering of your God: it is a statute forever throughout your generations in all your settlements.

The Festival of Weeks

15 And from the day after the sabbath, from the day on which you bring the sheaf of the elevation offering, you shall count off seven weeks; they shall be complete. [16]You shall count until the day after the seventh sabbath, fifty days; then you shall present an offering of new grain to the Lord. [17]You shall bring from your settlements two loaves of bread as an elevation offering, each made of two-tenths of an ephah; they shall be of choice flour, baked with leaven, as first fruits to the Lord. [18]You shall present with the bread seven lambs a year old without blemish, one young bull, and two rams; they shall be a burnt offering to the Lord, along with their grain offering and their drink offerings, an offering by fire of pleasing odor to the Lord. [19]You shall also offer one male goat for a sin offering, and two male lambs a year old as a sacrifice of well-being. [20]The priest shall raise them with the bread of the first fruits as an elevation offering before the Lord, together with the two lambs; they shall be holy to the Lord for the priest. [21]On that same day you shall make proclamation; you shall hold a holy convocation; you shall not work at your occupations. This is a statute forever in all your settlements throughout your generations.

22 When you reap the harvest of your land, you shall not reap to the very edges of your field, or gather the gleanings of your harvest; you shall leave them for the poor and for the alien: I am the Lord your God.

The Festival of Trumpets

23 The Lord spoke to Moses, saying: [24]Speak to the people of Israel, saying: In the seventh month, on the first day of the month, you shall observe a day of complete rest, a holy convocation commemorated with trumpet blasts.

a Heb between the two evenings

God Is Real—© Imani Gordon, 11

25You shall not work at your occupations; and you shall present the LORD's offering by fire.

The Day of Atonement

26 The LORD spoke to Moses, saying: 27Now, the tenth day of this seventh month is the day of atonement; it shall be a holy convocation for you: you shall deny yourselves*a* and present the LORD's offering by fire; 28and you shall do no work during that entire day; for it is a day of atonement, to make atonement on your behalf before the LORD your God. 29For anyone who does not practice self-denial*b* during that entire day shall be cut off from the people. 30And anyone who does any work during that entire day, such a one I will destroy from the midst of the people. 31You shall do no work: it is a statute forever throughout your generations in all your settlements. 32It shall be to you a sabbath of complete rest, and you shall deny yourselves;*a* on the ninth day of the month at evening, from evening to evening you shall keep your sabbath.

The Festival of Booths

33 The LORD spoke to Moses, saying: 34Speak to the people of Israel, saying: On the fifteenth day of this seventh month, and lasting seven days, there shall be the festival of booths*c* to the LORD. 35The first day shall be a holy convocation; you shall not work at your occupations. 36Seven days you shall present the LORD's offerings by fire; on the eighth day you shall observe a holy convocation and present the LORD's offerings by fire; it is a solemn assembly; you shall not work at your occupations.

37 These are the appointed festivals of the LORD, which you shall celebrate as times of holy convocation, for presenting to the LORD offerings by fire—burnt offerings and grain offerings, sacrifices and drink offerings, each on its proper day— 38apart from the sabbaths of the LORD, and apart from your gifts, and apart from all your votive offerings, and apart from

all your freewill offerings, which you give to the LORD.

39 Now, the fifteenth day of the seventh month, when you have gathered in the produce of the land, you shall keep the festival of the LORD, lasting seven days; a complete rest on the first day, and a complete rest on the eighth day. 40On the first day you shall take the fruit of majestic*d* trees, branches of palm trees, boughs of leafy trees, and willows of the brook; and you shall rejoice before the LORD your God for seven days. 41You shall keep it as a festival to the LORD seven days in the year; you shall keep it in the seventh month as a statute forever throughout your generations. 42You shall live in booths for seven days; all that are citizens in Israel shall live in booths, 43so that your generations may know that I made the people of Israel live in booths when I brought them out of the land of Egypt: I am the LORD your God.

44 Thus Moses declared to the people of Israel the appointed festivals of the LORD.

24 The Lamp

The LORD spoke to Moses, saying: 2Command the people of Israel to bring you pure oil of beaten olives for the lamp, that a light may be kept burning regularly. 3Aaron shall set it up in the tent of meeting, outside the curtain of the covenant,*e* to burn from evening to morning before the LORD regularly; it shall be a statute forever throughout your generations. 4He shall set up the lamps on the lampstand of pure gold*f* before the LORD regularly.

The Bread for the Tabernacle

5 You shall take choice flour, and bake twelve loaves of it; two-tenths of an ephah shall be in each loaf. 6You shall place them in two rows, six in a row, on the table of pure gold.*g* 7You shall put pure frankincense with each row, to be a token offering for the bread, as an offering by fire to the LORD. 8Every sabbath day Aaron shall set them in order before the LORD regularly as a commitment of the people of Israel, as a covenant forever. 9They shall be for Aaron and his descendants, who shall eat them in a holy place, for they are most holy portions for him from the offerings by fire to the LORD, a perpetual due.

Blasphemy and Its Punishment

10 A man whose mother was an Israelite and whose father was an Egyptian came out among the people of Israel; and the Israelite woman's

---

a Or *shall fast* *b* Or *does not fast* *c* Or *tabernacles:* Heb *succoth* *d* Meaning of Heb uncertain *e* Or *treaty,* or *testament;* Heb *eduth*
f Heb *pure lampstand* *g* Heb *pure table*

son and a certain Israelite began fighting in the camp. [11]The Israelite woman's son blasphemed the Name in a curse. And they brought him to Moses—now his mother's name was Shelomith, daughter of Dibri, of the tribe of Dan— [12]and they put him in custody, until the decision of the LORD should be made clear to them.

13 The LORD said to Moses, saying: [14]Take the blasphemer outside the camp; and let all who were within hearing lay their hands on his head, and let the whole congregation stone him. [15]And speak to the people of Israel, saying: Anyone who curses God shall bear the sin. [16]One who blasphemes the name of the LORD shall be put to death; the whole congregation shall stone the blasphemer. Aliens as well as citizens, when they blaspheme the Name, shall be put to death. [17]Anyone who kills a human being shall be put to death. [18]Anyone who kills an animal shall make restitution for it, life for life. [19]Anyone who maims another shall suffer the same injury in return: [20]fracture for fracture, eye for eye, tooth for tooth; the injury inflicted is the injury to be suffered. [21]One who kills an animal shall make restitution for it; but one who kills a human being shall be put to death. [22]You shall have one law for the alien and for the citizen: for I am the LORD your God. [23]Moses spoke thus to the people of Israel; and they took the blasphemer outside the camp, and stoned him to death. The people of Israel did as the LORD had commanded Moses.

25 The Sabbatical Year

The LORD spoke to Moses on Mount Sinai, saying: [2]Speak to the people of Israel and say to them: When you enter the land that I am giving you, the land shall observe a sabbath for the LORD. [3]Six years you shall sow your field, and six years you shall prune your vineyard, and gather in their yield; [4]but in the seventh year there shall be a sabbath of complete rest for the land, a sabbath for the LORD: you shall not sow your field or prune your vineyard. [5]You shall not reap the aftergrowth of your harvest or gather the grapes of your unpruned vine: it shall be a year of complete rest for the land. [6]You may eat what the land yields during its sabbath—you, your male and female slaves, your hired and your bound laborers who live with you; [7]for your livestock also, and for the wild animals in your land all its yield shall be for food.

The Year of Jubilee

8 You shall count off seven weeks[a] of years, seven times seven years, so that the period of

a Or sabbaths

REALITY

CLEAN LIVING

Sure, Leviticus has a lot of rules, but those were rules for a time when the world was perceived as dangerous, and those dangers were largely misunderstood. Think of Leviticus as a guidebook for navigating through a dirty, hazardous place full of hidden perils—with directives aimed at keeping people clean and safe.

Sadly, there are places in the world today that aren't much safer or cleaner than they were five thousand years ago. One way we can live out our faith is by showing compassion toward those whose lives are compromised by poverty, ignorance, or circumstance. We too are called to help those less fortunate or unable to help themselves by meeting their physical needs through the following corporal works of mercy:

- Feeding the hungry
- Giving drink to the thirsty
- Clothing the naked
- Providing shelter for the homeless
- Visiting the sick
- Bringing justice to the captives
- Burying the dead

Helping the body is great, but we are also called to tend to the spirit. The spiritual works of mercy are:

- Instructing the innocent
- Counseling the doubtful
- Admonishing sinners
- Bearing wrongs patiently
- Forgiving offenses willingly
- Comforting the afflicted
- Praying for the living and the dead

Being Catholic isn't just something we do when we attend Mass on Sunday. Being Catholic is who we are, what we believe, and how we act 24-7. Showing compassion toward all is woven into the very fabric of our faith.

harvest the unpruned vines. [12]For it is a jubilee; it shall be holy to you: you shall eat only what the field itself produces.

13 In this year of jubilee you shall return, every one of you, to your property. [14]When you make a sale to your neighbor or buy from your neighbor, you shall not cheat one another. [15]When you buy from your neighbor, you shall pay only for the number of years since the jubilee; the seller shall charge you only for the remaining crop years. [16]If the years are more, you shall increase the price, and if the years are fewer, you shall diminish the price; for it is a certain number of harvests that are being sold to you. [17]You shall not cheat one another, but you shall fear your God; for I am the LORD your God.

18 You shall observe my statutes and faithfully keep my ordinances, so that you may live on the land securely. [19]The land will yield its fruit, and you will eat your fill and live on it securely. [20]Should you ask, "What shall we eat in the seventh year, if we may not sow or gather in our crop?" [21]I will order my blessing for you in the sixth year, so that it will yield a crop for three years. [22]When you sow in the eighth year, you will be eating from the old crop; until the ninth year, when its produce comes in, you shall eat the old. [23]The land shall not be sold in perpetuity, for the land is mine; with me you are but aliens and tenants. [24]Throughout the land that you hold, you shall provide for the redemption of the land.

25 If anyone of your kin falls into difficulty and sells a piece of property, then the next of kin shall come and redeem what the relative has sold. [26]If the person has no one to redeem it, but then prospers and finds sufficient means to do so, [27]the years since its sale shall be computed and the difference shall be refunded to the person to whom it was sold, and the property shall be returned. [28]But if there are not sufficient means to recover it, what was sold shall remain with the purchaser until the year of jubilee; in the jubilee it shall be released, and the property shall be returned.

29 If anyone sells a dwelling house in a walled city, it may be redeemed until a year has elapsed since its sale; the right of redemption shall be one year. [30]If it is not redeemed before a full year has elapsed, a house that is in a walled city shall pass in perpetuity to the purchaser, throughout the generations; it shall not be released in the jubilee. [31]But houses in villages that have no walls around them shall be classed as open country; they may be redeemed, and they shall be released in the jubilee. [32]As for the cities of the Levites, the Levites shall forever have the right of redemption

seven weeks of years gives forty-nine years. [9]Then you shall have the trumpet sounded loud; on the tenth day of the seventh month—on the day of atonement—you shall have the trumpet sounded throughout all your land. [10]And you shall hallow the fiftieth year and you shall proclaim liberty throughout the land to all its inhabitants. It shall be a jubilee for you: you shall return, every one of you, to your property and every one of you to your family. [11]That fiftieth year shall be a jubilee for you: you shall not sow, or reap the aftergrowth, or of the houses in the cities belonging to them. 33Such property as may be redeemed from the Levites—houses sold in a city belonging to them—shall be released in the jubilee; because the houses in the cities of the Levites are their possession among the people of Israel. 34But the open land around their cities may not be sold; for that is their possession for all time.

35 If any of your kin fall into difficulty and become dependent on you,*a* you shall support them; they shall live with you as though resident aliens. 36Do not take interest in advance or otherwise make a profit from them, but fear your God; let them live with you. 37You shall not lend them your money at interest taken in advance, or provide them food at a profit. 38I am the LORD your God, who brought you out of the land of Egypt, to give you the land of Canaan, to be your God.

39 If any who are dependent on you become so impoverished that they sell themselves to you, you shall not make them serve as slaves. 40They shall remain with you as hired or bound laborers. They shall serve with you until the year of the jubilee. 41Then they and their children with them shall be free from your authority; they shall go back to their own family and return to their ancestral property. 42For they are my servants, whom I brought out of the land of Egypt; they shall not be sold as slaves are sold. 43You shall not rule over them with harshness, but shall fear your God. 44As for the male and female slaves whom you may have, it is from the nations around you that you may acquire male and female slaves. 45You may also acquire them from among the aliens residing with you, and from their families that are with you, who have been born in your land; and they may be your property. 46You may keep them as a possession for your children after you, for them to inherit as property. These you may treat as slaves, but as for your fellow Israelites, no one shall rule over the other with harshness.

47 If resident aliens among you prosper, and if any of your kin fall into difficulty with one of them and sell themselves to an alien, or to a branch of the alien's family, 48after they have sold themselves they shall have the right of redemption; one of their brothers may redeem them, 49or their uncle or their uncle's son may redeem them, or anyone of their family who is of their own flesh may redeem them; or if they prosper they may redeem themselves. 50They shall compute with the purchaser the total from the year when they sold themselves to the alien until the jubilee year; the price of the sale shall be applied to the number of years: the time they were with the owner shall be rated as the time of a hired laborer. 51If many years remain, they shall pay for their redemption in proportion to the purchase price; 52and if few years remain until the jubilee year, they shall compute thus: according to the years involved they shall make payment for their redemption. 53As a laborer hired by the year they shall be under the alien's authority, who shall not, however, rule with harshness over them in your sight. 54And if they have not been redeemed in any of these ways, they and their children with them shall go free in the jubilee year. 55For to me the people of Israel are servants; they are my servants whom I brought out from the land of Egypt: I am the LORD your God.

26 Rewards for Obedience

You shall make for yourselves no idols and erect no carved images or pillars, and you shall not place figured stones in your land, to worship at them; for I am the LORD your God. 2You shall keep my sabbaths and reverence my sanctuary: I am the LORD.

3 If you follow my statutes and keep my commandments and observe them faithfully, 4I will give you your rains in their season, and the land shall yield its produce, and the trees of the field shall yield their fruit. 5Your threshing shall overtake the vintage, and the vintage shall overtake the sowing; you shall eat your bread to the full, and live securely in your land. 6And I will grant peace in the land, and you shall lie down, and no one shall make you afraid; I will remove dangerous animals from the land, and no sword shall go through your land. 7You shall give chase to your enemies, and they shall fall before you by the sword. 8Five of you shall give chase to a hundred, and a hundred of you shall give chase to ten thousand; your enemies shall fall before you by the sword. 9I will look with favor upon you and make you fruitful and multiply you; and I will maintain my covenant with you. 10You shall eat old grain long stored, and you shall have to clear out the old to make way for the new. 11I will place my dwelling in your midst, and I shall not abhor you. 12And I will walk among you, and will be your God, and you shall be my people. 13I am the LORD your God who brought you out of the land of Egypt, to be their slaves no more; I have broken the bars of your yoke and made you walk erect.

Penalties for Disobedience

14 But if you will not obey me, and do not observe all these commandments, 15if you spurn

a Meaning of Heb uncertain

my statutes, and abhor my ordinances, so that you will not observe all my commandments, and you break my covenant, ¹⁶I in turn will do this to you: I will bring terror on you; consumption and fever that waste the eyes and cause life to pine away. You shall sow your seed in vain, for your enemies shall eat it. ¹⁷I will set my face against you, and you shall be struck down by your enemies; your foes shall rule over you, and you shall flee though no one pursues you. ¹⁸And if in spite of this you will not obey me, I will continue to punish you sevenfold for your sins. ¹⁹I will break your proud glory, and I will make your sky like iron and your earth like copper. ²⁰Your strength shall be spent to no purpose: your land shall not yield its produce, and the trees of the land shall not yield their fruit.

21 If you continue hostile to me, and will not obey me, I will continue to plague you sevenfold for your sins. ²²I will let loose wild animals against you, and they shall bereave you of your children and destroy your livestock; they shall make you few in number, and your roads shall be deserted.

23 If in spite of these punishments you have not turned back to me, but continue hostile to me, ²⁴then I too will continue hostile to you: I myself will strike you sevenfold for your sins. ²⁵I will bring the sword against you, executing vengeance for the covenant; and if you withdraw within your cities, I will send pestilence among you, and you shall be delivered into enemy hands. ²⁶When I break your staff of bread, ten women shall bake your bread in a single oven, and they shall dole out your bread by weight; and though you eat, you shall not be satisfied.

27 But if, despite this, you disobey me, and continue hostile to me, ²⁸I will continue hostile to you in fury; I in turn will punish you myself sevenfold for your sins. ²⁹You shall eat the flesh of your sons, and you shall eat the flesh of your daughters. ³⁰I will destroy your high places and cut down your incense altars; I will heap your carcasses on the carcasses of your idols. I will abhor you. ³¹I will lay your cities waste, will make your sanctuaries desolate, and I will not smell your pleasing odors. ³²I will devastate the land, so that your enemies who come to settle in it shall be appalled at it. ³³And you I will scatter among the nations, and I will unsheathe the sword against you; your land shall be a desolation, and your cities a waste.

34 Then the land shall enjoy*a* its sabbath years as long as it lies desolate, while you are in the land of your enemies; then the land shall rest, and enjoy*a* its sabbath years. ³⁵As long as

it lies desolate, it shall have the rest it did not have on your sabbaths when you were living on it. ³⁶And as for those of you who survive, I will send faintness into their hearts in the lands of their enemies; the sound of a driven leaf shall put them to flight, and they shall flee as one flees from the sword, and they shall fall though no one pursues. ³⁷They shall stumble over one another, as if to escape a sword, though no one pursues; and you shall have no power to stand against your enemies. ³⁸You shall perish among the nations, and the land of your enemies shall devour you. ³⁹And those of you who survive shall languish in the land of your enemies because of their iniquities; also they shall languish because of the iniquities of their ancestors.

40 But if they confess their iniquity and the iniquity of their ancestors, in that they committed treachery against me and, moreover, that they continued hostile to me— ⁴¹so that I, in turn, continued hostile to them and brought them into the land of their enemies; if then their uncircumcised heart is humbled and they make amends for their iniquity, ⁴²then will I remember my covenant with Jacob; I will remember also my covenant with Isaac and also my covenant with Abraham, and I will remember the land. ⁴³For the land shall be deserted by them, and enjoy*a* its sabbath years by lying desolate without them, while they shall make amends for their iniquity, because they dared to spurn my ordinances, and they abhorred my statutes. ⁴⁴Yet for all that, when they are in the land of their enemies, I will not spurn them, or abhor them so as to destroy them utterly and break my covenant with them; for I am the LORD their God; ⁴⁵but I will remember in their favor the covenant with their ancestors whom I brought out of the land of Egypt in the sight of the nations, to be their God: I am the LORD.

46 These are the statutes and ordinances and laws that the LORD established between himself and the people of Israel on Mount Sinai through Moses.

27 Votive Offerings

The LORD spoke to Moses, saying: ²Speak to the people of Israel and say to them: When a person makes an explicit vow to the LORD concerning the equivalent for a human being, ³the equivalent for a male shall be: from twenty to sixty years of age the equivalent shall be fifty shekels of silver by the sanctuary shekel. ⁴If the person is a female, the equivalent is thirty shekels. ⁵If the age is from five to twenty years of age, the equivalent is twenty shekels for a

a Or *make up for*

male and ten shekels for a female. ⁶If the age is from one month to five years, the equivalent for a male is five shekels of silver, and for a female the equivalent is three shekels of silver. ⁷And if the person is sixty years old or over, then the equivalent for a male is fifteen shekels, and for a female ten shekels. ⁸If any cannot afford the equivalent, they shall be brought before the priest and the priest shall assess them; the priest shall assess them according to what each one making a vow can afford.

9 If it concerns an animal that may be brought as an offering to the Lord, any such that may be given to the Lord shall be holy. ¹⁰Another shall not be exchanged or substituted for it, either good for bad or bad for good; and if one animal is substituted for another, both that one and its substitute shall be holy. ¹¹If it concerns any unclean animal that may not be brought as an offering to the Lord, the animal shall be presented before the priest. ¹²The priest shall assess it: whether good or bad, according to the assessment of the priest, so it shall be. ¹³But if it is to be redeemed, one-fifth must be added to the assessment.

14 If a person consecrates a house to the Lord, the priest shall assess it: whether good or bad, as the priest assesses it, so it shall stand. ¹⁵And if the one who consecrates the house wishes to redeem it, one-fifth shall be added to its assessed value, and it shall revert to the original owner.

16 If a person consecrates to the Lord any inherited landholding, its assessment shall be in accordance with its seed requirements: fifty shekels of silver to a homer of barley seed. ¹⁷If the person consecrates the field as of the year of jubilee, that assessment shall stand; ¹⁸but if the field is consecrated after the jubilee, the priest shall compute the price for it according to the years that remain until the year of jubilee, and the assessment shall be reduced. ¹⁹And if the one who consecrates the field wishes to redeem it, then one-fifth shall be added to its assessed value, and it shall revert to the original owner; ²⁰but if the field is not redeemed, or if it has been sold to someone else, it shall no longer be redeemable. ²¹But when the field is released in the jubilee, it shall be holy to the Lord as a devoted field; it becomes the priest's holding. ²²If someone consecrates to the Lord a field that has been purchased, which is not a part of the inherited landholding, ²³the priest shall compute for it the proportionate assessment up to the year of jubilee, and the assessment shall be paid as of that day, a sacred donation to the Lord. ²⁴In the year of jubilee the field shall return to the one from whom it was bought, whose holding the land is. ²⁵All assessments shall be by the sanctuary shekel: twenty gerahs shall make a shekel.

26 A firstling of animals, however, which as a firstling belongs to the Lord, cannot be consecrated by anyone; whether ox or sheep, it is the Lord's. ²⁷If it is an unclean animal, it shall be ransomed at its assessment, with one-fifth

Endless—© Rachel Hostert, 18

added; if it is not redeemed, it shall be sold at its assessment.

28 Nothing that a person owns that has been devoted to destruction for the LORD, be it human or animal, or inherited landholding, may be sold or redeemed; every devoted thing is most holy to the LORD. 29 No human beings who have been devoted to destruction can be ransomed; they shall be put to death.

30 All tithes from the land, whether the seed from the ground or the fruit from the tree, are the LORD's; they are holy to the LORD.

31 If persons wish to redeem any of their tithes, they must add one-fifth to them. 32 All tithes of herd and flock, every tenth one that passes under the shepherd's staff, shall be holy to the LORD. 33 Let no one inquire whether it is good or bad, or make substitution for it; if one makes substitution for it, then both it and the substitute shall be holy and cannot be redeemed.

34 These are the commandments that the LORD gave to Moses for the people of Israel on Mount Sinai.

"WHEN A BOOK LEAVES YOUR HANDS, IT BELONGS TO GOD. HE MAY USE IT TO SAVE A FEW SOULS OR TO TRY A FEW OTHERS, BUT I THINK THAT FOR THE WRITER TO WORRY IS TO TAKE OVER GOD'S BUSINESS."

—Writer Flannery O'Connor

NUMBERS

SOUND OFF

Travelogue

Quick—describe your most recent family vacation in twenty-five words: *Sunburns. Too many cans of soda. Laughter. Mosquitoes. Family fights. Dull hours in the car. Best pizza ever. Late-night talks. Movies. Swimming. Skiing. Games.*

Some people keep journals when they travel to sum up the good—and not so good—memories of the experience. That's basically the gist of the story of Numbers. The Israelites kept a log of who they were, where they came from, where they stayed, and how they would draw the borders of their final settlement, the Promised Land.

Numbers also records some of the personal struggles they endured: fear of starvation and drought, quibbles with their leadership, and fear of the battles that lay ahead when they moved into an occupied territory. Numbers is essentially a travelogue, journal, photo album, genealogy, and plan for settling the land all rolled into one.

Behind the events in Numbers lies the reality that God will deliver on his promises. Always. Even when kings of foreign lands declare war on God's people or beg prophets to speak against them, God's will is done. Now *that's* not a bad thing to have on record.

> "The Lord has turned all our sunsets into sunrise."
> —St. Clement of Alexandria

WHO Developed over time by a series of people or groups, parts probably existed in oral form for some time before being written down.

WHAT Although Numbers gets its name because there is arithmetic in it and a census to count the Israelites, it is important because it traces their liturgical and ritual activity back to its beginnings.

WHEN The events took place during the time that the Israelites were wandering in the desert in the 1200s or 1400s B.C.

WHERE The Sinai Peninsula and northward toward what is now Israel and Palestine

PATH OF DISCIPLESHIP

Numbers 12.8 says that God spoke face-to-face with Moses, unlike any of the other prophets. Moses had a special, personal connection to God—so special that he could stand in God's holy presence. It was a rare privilege that many people still long for.

Jesus opens the same possibility up to us. Through him, humanity was given the opportunity for a relationship with God like the one that Moses had, face-to-face. We don't have to communicate to God through someone else. Jesus, who is both God and human, invites us—his disciples—to stand in God's presence and to deepen and strengthen our relationship with Father, Son, and Holy Spirit. It's up to us to accept the invitation.

1 The First Census of Israel

The LORD spoke to Moses in the wilderness of Sinai, in the tent of meeting, on the first day of the second month, in the second year after they had come out of the land of Egypt, saying: 2Take a census of the whole congregation of Israelites, in their clans, by ancestral houses, according to the number of names, every male individually; 3from twenty years old and upward, everyone in Israel able to go to war. You and Aaron shall enroll them, company by company. 4A man from each tribe shall be with you, each man the head of his ancestral house. 5These are the names of the men who shall assist you:

From Reuben, Elizur son of Shedeur.
6 From Simeon, Shelumiel son of Zurishaddai.
7 From Judah, Nahshon son of Amminadab.
8 From Issachar, Nethanel son of Zuar.
9 From Zebulun, Eliab son of Helon.
10 From the sons of Joseph:
from Ephraim, Elishama son of Ammihud;
from Manasseh, Gamaliel son of Pedahzur.
11 From Benjamin, Abidan son of Gideoni.
12 From Dan, Ahiezer son of Ammishaddai.
13 From Asher, Pagiel son of Ochran.
14 From Gad, Eliasaph son of Deuel.
15 From Naphtali, Ahira son of Enan.

16These were the ones chosen from the congregation, the leaders of their ancestral tribes, the heads of the divisions of Israel.

17 Moses and Aaron took these men who had been designated by name, 18and on the first day of the second month they assembled the whole congregation together. They registered themselves in their clans, by their ancestral houses, according to the number of names from twenty years old and upward, individually, 19as the LORD commanded Moses. So he enrolled them in the wilderness of Sinai.

20 The descendants of Reuben, Israel's firstborn, their lineage, in their clans, by their ancestral houses, according to the number of names, individually, every male from twenty years old and upward, everyone able to go to war: 21those enrolled of the tribe of Reuben were forty-six thousand five hundred.

22 The descendants of Simeon, their lineage, in their clans, by their ancestral houses, those of them that were numbered, according to the number of names, individually, every male from twenty years old and upward, everyone able to go to war: 23those enrolled of the tribe of Simeon were fifty-nine thousand three hundred.

24 The descendants of Gad, their lineage, in their clans, by their ancestral houses, according to the number of the names, from twenty years old and upward, everyone able to go to war: 25those enrolled of the tribe of Gad were forty-five thousand six hundred fifty.

26 The descendants of Judah, their lineage, in their clans, by their ancestral houses, according to the number of names, from twenty years old and upward, everyone able to go to war: 27those enrolled of the tribe of Judah were seventy-four thousand six hundred.

28 The descendants of Issachar, their lineage, in their clans, by their ancestral houses, according to the number of names, from twenty years old and upward, everyone able to go to war: 29those enrolled of the tribe of Issachar were fifty-four thousand four hundred.

30 The descendants of Zebulun, their lineage, in their clans, by their ancestral houses, according to the number of names, from twenty years old and upward, everyone able to go to war: 31those enrolled of the tribe of Zebulun were fifty-seven thousand four hundred.

32 The descendants of Joseph, namely, the descendants of Ephraim, their lineage, in their clans, by their ancestral houses, according to the number of names, from twenty years old and upward, everyone able to go to war: 33those enrolled of the tribe of Ephraim were forty thousand five hundred.

34 The descendants of Manasseh, their lineage, in their clans, by their ancestral houses, according to the number of names, from twenty years old and upward, everyone able to go to war: 35those enrolled of the tribe of Manasseh were thirty-two thousand two hundred.

36 The descendants of Benjamin, their lineage, in their clans, by their ancestral houses, according to the number of names, from twenty years old and upward, everyone able to go to war: 37those enrolled of the tribe of Benjamin were thirty-five thousand four hundred.

38 The descendants of Dan, their lineage, in their clans, by their ancestral houses, according to the number of names, from twenty years old and upward, everyone able to go to war: 39those enrolled of the tribe of Dan were sixty-two thousand seven hundred.

40 The descendants of Asher, their lineage, in their clans, by their ancestral houses, according to the number of names, from twenty years old and upward, everyone able to go to war: 41those enrolled of the tribe of Asher were forty-one thousand five hundred.

42 The descendants of Naphtali, their lineage, in their clans, by their ancestral houses, according to the number of names, from twenty years old and upward, everyone able to go to war: 43those enrolled of the tribe of Naphtali were fifty-three thousand four hundred.

44 These are those who were enrolled, whom Moses and Aaron enrolled with the help of the leaders of Israel, twelve men, each representing his ancestral house. ⁴⁵So the whole number of the Israelites, by their ancestral houses, from twenty years old and upward, everyone able to go to war in Israel— ⁴⁶their whole number was six hundred three thousand five hundred fifty. ⁴⁷The Levites, however, were not numbered by their ancestral tribe along with them.

48 The LORD had said to Moses: ⁴⁹Only the tribe of Levi you shall not enroll, and you shall not take a census of them with the other Israelites. ⁵⁰Rather you shall appoint the Levites over the tabernacle of the covenant,ᵃ and over all its equipment, and over all that belongs to it; they are to carry the tabernacle and all its equipment, and they shall tend it, and shall camp around the tabernacle. ⁵¹When the tabernacle is to set out, the Levites shall take it down; and when the tabernacle is to be pitched, the Levites shall set it up. And any outsider who comes near shall be put to death. ⁵²The other Israelites shall camp in their respective regimental camps, by companies; ⁵³but the Levites shall camp around the tabernacle of the covenant,ᵃ that there may be no wrath on the congregation of the Israelites; and the Levites shall perform the guard duty of the tabernacle of the covenant.ᵃ ⁵⁴The Israelites did so; they did just as the LORD commanded Moses.

2 The Order of Encampment and Marching

The LORD spoke to Moses and Aaron, saying: ²The Israelites shall camp each in their respective regiments, under ensigns by their ancestral houses; they shall camp facing the tent of meeting on every side. ³Those to camp on the east side toward the sunrise shall be of the regimental encampment of Judah by companies. The leader of the people of Judah shall be Nahshon son of Amminadab, ⁴with a company as enrolled of seventy-four thousand six hundred. ⁵Those to camp next to him shall be the tribe of Issachar. The leader of the Issacharites shall be Nethanel son of Zuar, ⁶with a company as enrolled of fifty-four thousand four hundred. ⁷Then the tribe of Zebulun: The leader of the Zebulunites shall be Eliab son of Helon, ⁸with a company as enrolled of fifty-seven thousand four hundred. ⁹The total enrollment of the camp of Judah, by companies, is one hundred eighty-six thousand four hundred. They shall set out first on the march.

10 On the south side shall be the regimental encampment of Reuben by companies. The

leader of the Reubenites shall be Elizur son of Shedeur, ¹¹with a company as enrolled of forty-six thousand five hundred. ¹²And those to camp next to him shall be the tribe of Simeon. The leader of the Simeonites shall be Shelumiel son of Zurishaddai, ¹³with a company as enrolled of fifty-nine thousand three hundred. ¹⁴Then the tribe of Gad: The leader of the Gadites shall be Eliasaph son of Reuel, ¹⁵with a company as enrolled of forty-five thousand six hundred fifty. ¹⁶The total enrollment of the camp of Reuben, by companies, is one hundred fifty-one thousand four hundred fifty. They shall set out second.

17 The tent of meeting, with the camp of the Levites, shall set out in the center of the camps; they shall set out just as they camp, each in position, by their regiments.

18 On the west side shall be the regimen-

ᵃ Or treaty, or testimony; Heb eduth

PROFILE OF FAITH
CÉSAR E. CHÁVEZ: Farm Workers Freedom Fighter

César Chávez was born in 1927 in Yuma, Arizona. During the Great Depression, his family lost everything and moved to California to find migrant field work.

At that time, migrant workers were treated poorly and labored for very low wages—if they were paid at all. Since many were in the United States illegally, they had nowhere to turn when their employers abused them.

Chávez began organizing workers to campaign for better pay and working conditions, which led to the creation of the National Farm Workers Association (NFWA). He worked tirelessly to bring justice to the poor until his death in 1993.

The lifework of Chávez embodies many of the principles of Catholic social teaching, including the life and dignity of the human person, the option for the poor and vulnerable, the dignity of work, and the rights of workers.

tal encampment of Ephraim by companies. The leader of the people of Ephraim shall be Elishama son of Ammihud, ¹⁹ with a company as enrolled of forty thousand five hundred. ²⁰Next to him shall be the tribe of Manasseh. The leader of the people of Manasseh shall be Gamaliel son of Pedahzur, ²¹with a company as enrolled of thirty-two thousand two hundred. ²²Then the tribe of Benjamin: The leader of the Benjaminites shall be Abidan son of Gideoni, ²³with a company as enrolled of thirty-five thousand four hundred. ²⁴The total enrollment of the camp of Ephraim, by companies, is one hundred eight thousand one hundred. They shall set out third on the march.

25 On the north side shall be the regimental encampment of Dan by companies. The leader of the Danites shall be Ahiezer son of Ammishaddai, ²⁶with a company as enrolled of sixty-two thousand seven hundred. ²⁷Those to camp next to him shall be the tribe of Asher. The leader of the Asherites shall be Pagiel son of Ochran, ²⁸with a company as enrolled of forty-one thousand five hundred. ²⁹Then the tribe of Naphtali: The leader of the Naphtalites shall be Ahira son of Enan, ³⁰with a company as enrolled of fifty-three thousand four hundred. ³¹The total enrollment of the camp of Dan is one hundred fifty-seven thousand six hundred. They shall set out last, by companies.^a

32 This was the enrollment of the Israelites by their ancestral houses; the total enrollment in the camps by their companies was six hundred three thousand five hundred fifty. ³³Just as the LORD had commanded Moses, the Levites were not enrolled among the other Israelites.

34 The Israelites did just as the LORD had commanded Moses: They camped by regiments, and they set out the same way, everyone by clans, according to ancestral houses.

3 The Sons of Aaron

This is the lineage of Aaron and Moses at the time when the LORD spoke with Moses on Mount Sinai. ²These are the names of the sons of Aaron: Nadab the firstborn, and Abihu, Eleazar, and Ithamar; ³these are the names of the sons of Aaron, the anointed priests, whom he ordained to minister as priests. ⁴Nadab and Abihu died before the LORD when they offered unholy fire before the LORD in the wilderness of Sinai, and they had no children. Eleazar and Ithamar served as priests in the lifetime of their father Aaron.

The Duties of the Levites

5 Then the LORD spoke to Moses, saying: ⁶Bring the tribe of Levi near, and set them before Aaron the priest, so that they may assist him. ⁷They shall perform duties for him and for the whole

a Compare verses 9, 16, 24: Heb by their regiments

congregation in front of the tent of meeting, doing service at the tabernacle; [8]they shall be in charge of all the furnishings of the tent of meeting, and attend to the duties for the Israelites as they do service at the tabernacle. [9]You shall give the Levites to Aaron and his descendants; they are unreservedly given to him from among the Israelites. [10]But you shall make a register of Aaron and his descendants; it is they who shall attend to the priesthood, and any outsider who comes near shall be put to death.

11 Then the Lord spoke to Moses, saying: [12]I hereby accept the Levites from among the Israelites as substitutes for all the firstborn that open the womb among the Israelites. The Levites shall be mine, [13]for all the firstborn are mine; when I killed all the firstborn in the land of Egypt, I consecrated for my own all the firstborn in Israel, both human and animal; they shall be mine. I am the Lord.

A Census of the Levites

14 Then the Lord spoke to Moses in the wilderness of Sinai, saying: [15]Enroll the Levites by ancestral houses and by clans. You shall enroll every male from a month old and upward. [16]So Moses enrolled them according to the word of the Lord, as he was commanded. [17]The following were the sons of Levi, by their names: Gershon, Kohath, and Merari. [18]These are the names of the sons of Gershon by their clans: Libni and Shimei. [19]The sons of Kohath by their clans: Amram, Izhar, Hebron, and Uzziel. [20]The sons of Merari by their clans: Mahli and Mushi. These are the clans of the Levites, by their ancestral houses.

21 To Gershon belonged the clan of the Libnites and the clan of the Shimeites; these were the clans of the Gershonites. [22]Their enrollment, counting all the males from a month old and upward, was seven thousand five hundred. [23]The clans of the Gershonites were to camp behind the tabernacle on the west, [24]with Eliasaph son of Lael as head of the ancestral house of the Gershonites. [25]The responsibility of the sons of Gershon in the tent of meeting was to be the tabernacle, the tent with its covering, the screen for the entrance of the tent of meeting, [26]the hangings of the court, the screen for the entrance of the court that is around the tabernacle and the altar, and its cords—all the service pertaining to these.

27 To Kohath belonged the clan of the Amramites, the clan of the Izharites, the clan of the Hebronites, and the clan of the Uzzielites; these are the clans of the Kohathites. [28]Counting all the males, from a month old and upward, there were eight thousand six hundred, attending to the duties of the sanctuary. [29]The clans of the Kohathites were to camp on the south side of the tabernacle, [30]with Elizaphan son of Uzziel as head of the ancestral house of the clans of the Kohathites. [31]Their responsibility was to be the ark, the table, the lampstand, the altars, the vessels of the sanctuary with which the priests minister, and the screen—all the service pertaining to these. [32]Eleazar son of Aaron the priest was to be chief over the leaders of the Levites, and to have oversight of those who had charge of the sanctuary.

33 To Merari belonged the clan of the Mahlites and the clan of the Mushites: these are the clans of Merari. [34]Their enrollment, counting all the males from a month old and upward, was six thousand two hundred. [35]The head of the ancestral house of the clans of Merari was Zuriel son of Abihail; they were to camp on the north side of the tabernacle. [36]The responsibility assigned to the sons of Merari was to be the frames of the tabernacle, the bars, the pillars, the bases, and all their accessories—all the service pertaining to these; [37]also the pillars of the court all around, with their bases and pegs and cords.

38 Those who were to camp in front of the tabernacle on the east—in front of the tent of meeting toward the east—were Moses and Aaron and Aaron's sons, having charge of the rites within the sanctuary, whatever had to be done for the Israelites; and any outsider who came near was to be put to death. [39]The total enrollment of the Levites whom Moses and Aaron enrolled at the commandment of the Lord, by their clans, all the males from a month old and upward, was twenty-two thousand.

The Redemption of the Firstborn

40 Then the Lord said to Moses: Enroll all the firstborn males of the Israelites, from a month old and upward, and count their names. [41]But you shall accept the Levites for me—I am the Lord—as substitutes for all the firstborn among the Israelites, and the livestock of the Levites as substitutes for all the firstborn among the livestock of the Israelites. [42]So Moses enrolled all the firstborn among the Israelites, as the Lord commanded him. [43]The total enrollment, all the firstborn males from a month old and upward, counting the number of names, was twenty-two thousand two hundred seventy-three.

44 Then the Lord spoke to Moses, saying: [45]Accept the Levites as substitutes for all the firstborn among the Israelites, and the livestock of the Levites as substitutes for their livestock; and the Levites shall be mine. I am the Lord. [46]As the price of redemption of the

two hundred seventy-three of the firstborn of the Israelites, over and above the number of the Levites, ⁴⁷you shall accept five shekels apiece, reckoning by the shekel of the sanctuary, a shekel of twenty gerahs. ⁴⁸Give to Aaron and his sons the money by which the excess number of them is redeemed. ⁴⁹So Moses took the redemption money from those who were over and above those redeemed by the Levites; ⁵⁰from the firstborn of the Israelites he took the money, one thousand three hundred sixty-five shekels, reckoned by the shekel of the sanctuary; ⁵¹and Moses gave the redemption money to Aaron and his sons, according to the word of the Lord, as the Lord had commanded Moses.

4 The Kohathites

The Lord spoke to Moses and Aaron, saying: ²Take a census of the Kohathites separate from the other Levites, by their clans and their ancestral houses, ³from thirty years old up to fifty years old, all who qualify to do work relating to the tent of meeting. ⁴The service of the Kohathites relating to the tent of meeting concerns the most holy things.

5 When the camp is to set out, Aaron and his sons shall go in and take down the screening curtain, and cover the ark of the covenant*ᵃ* with it; ⁶then they shall put on it a covering of fine leather,*ᵇ* and spread over that a cloth all of blue, and shall put its poles in place. ⁷Over the table of the bread of the Presence they shall spread a blue cloth, and put on it the plates, the dishes for incense, the bowls, and the flagons for the drink offering; the regular bread also shall be on it; ⁸then they shall spread over them a crimson cloth, and cover it with a covering of fine leather,*ᵇ* and shall put its poles in place. ⁹They shall take a blue cloth, and cover the lampstand for the light, with its lamps, its snuffers, its trays, and all the vessels for oil with which it is supplied; ¹⁰and they shall put it with all its utensils in a covering of fine leather,*ᵇ* and put it on the carrying frame. ¹¹Over the golden altar they shall spread a blue cloth, and cover it with a covering of fine leather,*ᵇ* and shall put its poles in place; ¹²and they shall take all the utensils of the service that are used in the sanctuary, and put them in a blue cloth, and cover them with a covering of fine leather,*ᵇ* and put them on the carrying frame. ¹³They shall take away the ashes from the altar, and spread a purple cloth over it; ¹⁴and they shall put on it all the utensils of the altar, which are used for the service there, the firepans, the forks, the shovels, and the basins, all the utensils of the altar; and they shall spread on it a covering of fine leather,*ᵇ* and shall put its poles in place. ¹⁵When Aaron and his sons have finished covering the sanctuary and all the furnishings of the sanctuary, as the camp sets out, after that the Kohathites shall come to carry these, but they must not touch the holy things, or they will die. These are the things of the tent of meeting that the Kohathites are to carry.

16 Eleazar son of Aaron the priest shall have charge of the oil for the light, the fragrant incense, the regular grain offering, and the anointing oil, the oversight of all the tabernacle and all that is in it, in the sanctuary and in its utensils.

17 Then the Lord spoke to Moses and Aaron, saying: ¹⁸You must not let the tribe of the clans of the Kohathites be destroyed from among the Levites. ¹⁹This is how you must deal with them in order that they may live and not die when they come near to the most holy things: Aaron and his sons shall go in and assign each to a particular task or burden. ²⁰But the Kohathites*ᶜ* must not go in to look on the holy things even for a moment; otherwise they will die.

The Gershonites and Merarites

21 Then the Lord spoke to Moses, saying: ²²Take a census of the Gershonites also, by their ancestral houses and by their clans; ²³from thirty years old up to fifty years old you shall enroll them, all who qualify to do work in the tent of meeting. ²⁴This is the service of the clans of the Gershonites, in serving and bearing burdens: ²⁵They shall carry the curtains of the tabernacle, and the tent of meeting with its covering, and the outer covering of fine leather*ᵇ* that is on top of it, and the screen for

Broken Bridge—© Chrissy Riling, 16

a Or *treaty*, or *testimony*; Heb *eduth* *b* Meaning of Heb uncertain *c* Heb *they* the entrance of the tent of meeting, ²⁶and the hangings of the court, and the screen for the entrance of the gate of the court that is around the tabernacle and the altar, and their cords, and all the equipment for their service; and they shall do all that needs to be done with regard to them. ²⁷All the service of the Gershonites shall be at the command of Aaron and his sons, in all that they are to carry, and in all that they have to do; and you shall assign to their charge all that they are to carry. ²⁸This is the service of the clans of the Gershonites relating to the tent of meeting, and their responsibilities are to be under the oversight of Ithamar son of Aaron the priest.

29 As for the Merarites, you shall enroll them by their clans and their ancestral houses; ³⁰from thirty years old up to fifty years old you shall enroll them, everyone who qualifies to do the work of the tent of meeting. ³¹This is what they are charged to carry, as the whole of their service in the tent of meeting: the frames of the tabernacle, with its bars, pillars, and bases, ³²and the pillars of the court all around with their bases, pegs, and cords, with all their equipment and all their related service; and you shall assign by name the objects that they are required to carry. ³³This is the service of the clans of the Merarites, the whole of their service relating to the tent of meeting, under the hand of Ithamar son of Aaron the priest.

Census of the Levites

34 So Moses and Aaron and the leaders of the congregation enrolled the Kohathites, by their clans and their ancestral houses, ³⁵from thirty years old up to fifty years old, everyone who qualified for work relating to the tent of meeting; ³⁶and their enrollment by clans was two thousand seven hundred fifty. ³⁷This was the enrollment of the clans of the Kohathites, all who served at the tent of meeting, whom Moses and Aaron enrolled according to the commandment of the LORD by Moses.

38 The enrollment of the Gershonites, by their clans and their ancestral houses, ³⁹from thirty years old up to fifty years old, everyone who qualified for work relating to the tent of meeting— ⁴⁰their enrollment by their clans and their ancestral houses was two thousand six hundred thirty. ⁴¹This was the enrollment of the clans of the Gershonites, all who served at the tent of meeting, whom Moses and Aaron enrolled according to the commandment of the LORD.

42 The enrollment of the clans of the Merarites, by their clans and their ancestral houses, ⁴³from thirty years old up to fifty years old, everyone who qualified for work relating to the tent of meeting— ⁴⁴their enrollment by their clans was three thousand two hundred. ⁴⁵This is the enrollment of the clans of the Merarites, whom Moses and Aaron enrolled according to the commandment of the LORD by Moses.

46 All those who were enrolled of the Levites, whom Moses and Aaron and the leaders of Israel enrolled, by their clans and their ancestral houses, ⁴⁷from thirty years old up to fifty years old, everyone who qualified to do the work of service and the work of bearing burdens relating to the tent of meeting, ⁴⁸their enrollment was eight thousand five hundred eighty. ⁴⁹According to the commandment of the LORD through Moses they were appointed to their several tasks of serving or carrying; thus they were enrolled by him, as the LORD commanded Moses.

5 Unclean Persons

The LORD spoke to Moses, saying: ²Command the Israelites to put out of the camp everyone who is leprous,ᵃ or has a discharge, and everyone who is unclean through contact with a corpse; ³you shall put out both male and female, putting them outside the camp; they must not defile their camp, where I dwell among them. ⁴The Israelites did so, putting them outside the camp; as the LORD had spoken to Moses, so the Israelites did.

Confession and Restitution

5 The LORD spoke to Moses, saying: ⁶Speak to the Israelites: When a man or a woman wrongs another, breaking faith with the LORD, that person incurs guilt ⁷and shall confess the sin that has been committed. The person shall make full restitution for the wrong, adding one-fifth to it, and giving it to the one who was wronged. ⁸If the injured party has no next of kin to whom restitution may be made for the wrong, the restitution for wrong shall go to the LORD for the priest, in addition to the ram of atonement with which atonement is made for the guilty party. ⁹Among all the sacred donations of the Israelites, every gift that they bring to the priest shall be his. ¹⁰The sacred donations of all are their own; whatever anyone gives to the priest shall be his.

Concerning an Unfaithful Wife

11 The LORD spoke to Moses, saying: ¹²Speak to the Israelites and say to them: If any man's wife goes astray and is unfaithful to him, ¹³if a

---

a A term for several skin diseases; precise meaning uncertain man has had intercourse with her but it is hidden from her husband, so that she is undetected though she has defiled herself, and there is no witness against her since she was not caught in the act; [14]if a spirit of jealousy comes on him, and he is jealous of his wife who has defiled herself; or if a spirit of jealousy comes on him, and he is jealous of his wife, though she has not defiled herself; [15]then the man shall bring his wife to the priest. And he shall bring the offering required for her, one-tenth of an ephah of barley flour. He shall pour no oil on it and put no frankincense on it, for it is a grain offering of jealousy, a grain offering of remembrance, bringing iniquity to remembrance.

16 Then the priest shall bring her near, and set her before the Lord; [17]the priest shall take holy water in an earthen vessel, and take some of the dust that is on the floor of the tabernacle and put it into the water. [18]The priest shall set the woman before the Lord, dishevel the woman's hair, and place in her hands the grain offering of remembrance, which is the grain offering of jealousy. In his own hand the priest shall have the water of bitterness that brings the curse. [19]Then the priest shall make her take an oath, saying, "If no man has lain with you, if you have not turned aside to uncleanness while under your husband's authority, be immune to this water of bitterness that brings the curse. [20]But if you have gone astray while under your husband's authority, if you have defiled yourself and some man other than your husband has had intercourse with you," [21]—let the priest make the woman take the oath of the curse and say to the woman—"the Lord make you an execration and an oath among your people, when the Lord makes your uterus drop, your womb discharge; [22]now may this water that brings the curse enter your bowels and make your womb discharge, your uterus drop!" And the woman shall say, "Amen. Amen."

23 Then the priest shall put these curses in writing, and wash them off into the water of bitterness. [24]He shall make the woman drink the water of bitterness that brings the curse, and the water that brings the curse shall enter her and cause bitter pain. [25]The priest shall take the grain offering of jealousy out of the woman's hand, and shall elevate the grain offering before the Lord and bring it to the altar; [26]and the priest shall take a handful of the grain offering, as its memorial portion, and turn it into smoke on the altar, and afterward shall make the woman drink the water. [27]When he has made her drink the water, then, if she has defiled herself and has been unfaithful to her husband, the water that brings the curse shall enter into her and cause bitter pain, and her womb shall discharge, her uterus drop, and the woman shall become an execration among her people. [28]But if the woman has not defiled herself and is clean, then she shall be immune and be able to conceive children.

29 This is the law in cases of jealousy, when a wife, while under her husband's authority, goes astray and defiles herself, [30]or when a spirit of jealousy comes on a man and he is jealous of his wife; then he shall set the woman before the Lord, and the priest shall apply this entire law to her. [31]The man shall be free from iniquity, but the woman shall bear her iniquity.

6 The Nazirites

The Lord spoke to Moses, saying: [2]Speak to the Israelites and say to them: When either men or women make a special vow, the vow of a nazirite,[a] to separate themselves to the Lord, [3]they shall separate themselves from wine and strong drink; they shall drink no wine vinegar or other vinegar, and shall not drink any grape juice or eat grapes, fresh or dried. [4]All their days as nazirites[b] they shall eat nothing that is produced by the grapevine, not even the seeds or the skins.

5 All the days of their nazirite vow no razor shall come upon the head; until the time is completed for which they separate themselves to the Lord, they shall be holy; they shall let the locks of the head grow long.

6 All the days that they separate themselves to the Lord they shall not go near a corpse. [7]Even if their father or mother, brother or sister, should die, they may not defile themselves; because their consecration to God is upon the head. [8]All their days as nazirites[b] they are holy to the Lord.

9 If someone dies very suddenly nearby, defiling the consecrated head, then they shall shave the head on the day of their cleansing; on the seventh day they shall shave it. [10]On the eighth day they shall bring two turtledoves or two young pigeons to the priest at the entrance of the tent of meeting, [11]and the priest shall offer one as a sin offering and the other as a burnt offering, and make atonement for them, because they incurred guilt by reason of the corpse. They shall sanctify the head that same day, [12]and separate themselves to the Lord for their days as nazirites,[b] and bring a male lamb a year old as a guilt offering. The former time shall be void, because the consecrated head was defiled.

a That is one separated or one consecrated b That is those separated or those consecrated

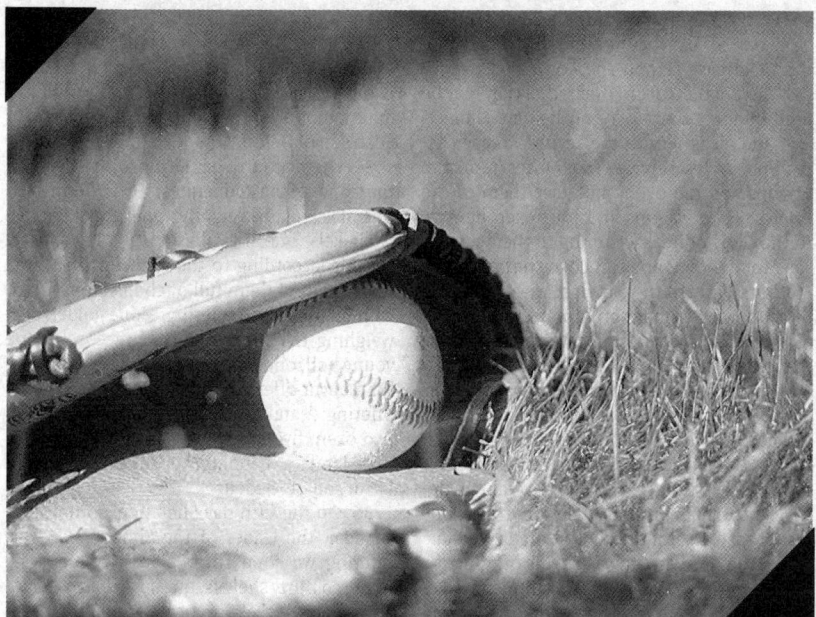

Baseball—© Christy Klink, 18

13 This is the law for the nazirites*a* when the time of their consecration has been completed: they shall be brought to the entrance of the tent of meeting, 14and they shall offer their gift to the LORD, one male lamb a year old without blemish as a burnt offering, one ewe lamb a year old without blemish as a sin offering, one ram without blemish as an offering of well-being, 15and a basket of unleavened bread, cakes of choice flour mixed with oil and unleavened wafers spread with oil, with their grain offering and their drink offerings. 16The priest shall present them before the LORD and offer their sin offering and burnt offering, 17and shall offer the ram as a sacrifice of well-being to the LORD, with the basket of unleavened bread; the priest also shall make the accompanying grain offering and drink offering. 18Then the nazirites*a* shall shave the consecrated head at the entrance of the tent of meeting, and shall take the hair from the consecrated head and put it on the fire under the sacrifice of well-being. 19The priest shall take the shoulder of the ram, when it is boiled, and one unleavened cake out of the basket, and one unleavened wafer, and shall put them in the palms of the nazirites,*a* after they have shaved the consecrated head. 20Then the priest shall elevate them as an elevation offering before the LORD; they are a holy portion for the priest, together with the breast that is elevated and the thigh that is offered. After that the nazirites*a* may drink wine.

21 This is the law for the nazirites*a* who take a vow. Their offering to the LORD must be in accordance with the nazirite*b* vow, apart from what else they can afford. In accordance with whatever vow they take, so they shall do, following the law for their consecration.

The Priestly Benediction

22 The LORD spoke to Moses, saying: 23Speak to Aaron and his sons, saying, Thus you shall bless the Israelites: You shall say to them,
24 The LORD bless you and keep you;
25 the LORD make his face to shine upon you, and be gracious to you;
26 the LORD lift up his countenance upon you, and give you peace.
27 So they shall put my name on the Israelites, and I will bless them.

7 Offerings of the Leaders

On the day when Moses had finished setting up the tabernacle, and had anointed and consecrated it with all its furnishings, and had anointed and consecrated the altar with all its utensils, 2the leaders of Israel, heads of their ancestral houses, the leaders of the tribes, who were over those who were enrolled, made offerings. 3They brought their offerings before the LORD, six covered wagons and twelve oxen,

a That is *those separated* or *those consecrated*   *b* That is *one separated* or *one consecrated* a wagon for every two of the leaders, and for each one an ox; they presented them before the tabernacle. 4Then the LORD said to Moses: 5Accept these from them, that they may be used in doing the service of the tent of meeting, and give them to the Levites, to each according to his service. 6So Moses took the wagons and the oxen, and gave them to the Levites. 7Two wagons and four oxen he gave to the Gershonites, according to their service; 8and four wagons and eight oxen he gave to the Merarites, according to their service, under the direction of Ithamar son of Aaron the priest. 9But to the Kohathites he gave none, because they were charged with the care of the holy things that had to be carried on the shoulders.

10 The leaders also presented offerings for the dedication of the altar at the time when it was anointed; the leaders presented their offering before the altar. 11The LORD said to Moses: They shall present their offerings, one leader each day, for the dedication of the altar.

12 The one who presented his offering the first day was Nahshon son of Amminadab, of the tribe of Judah; 13his offering was one silver plate weighing one hundred thirty shekels, one silver basin weighing seventy shekels, according to the shekel of the sanctuary, both of them full of choice flour mixed with oil for a grain offering; 14one golden dish weighing ten shekels, full of incense; 15one young bull, one ram, one male lamb a year old, for a burnt offering; 16one male goat for a sin offering; 17and for the sacrifice of well-being, two oxen, five rams, five male goats, and five male lambs a year old. This was the offering of Nahshon son of Amminadab.

18 On the second day Nethanel son of Zuar, the leader of Issachar, presented an offering; 19he presented for his offering one silver plate weighing one hundred thirty shekels, one silver basin weighing seventy shekels, according to the shekel of the sanctuary, both of them full of choice flour mixed with oil for a grain offering; 20one golden dish weighing ten shekels, full of incense; 21one young bull, one ram, one male lamb a year old, as a burnt offering; 22one male goat as a sin offering; 23and for the sacrifice of well-being, two oxen, five rams, five male goats, and five male lambs a year old. This was the offering of Nethanel son of Zuar.

24 On the third day Eliab son of Helon, the leader of the Zebulunites: 25his offering was one silver plate weighing one hundred thirty shekels, one silver basin weighing seventy shekels, according to the shekel of the sanctuary, both of them full of choice flour mixed with oil for a grain offering; 26one golden dish weighing ten shekels, full of incense; 27one young bull, one ram, one male lamb a year old, for a burnt offering; 28one male goat for a sin offering; 29and for the sacrifice of well-being, two oxen, five rams, five male goats, and five male lambs a year old. This was the offering of Eliab son of Helon.

30 On the fourth day Elizur son of Shedeur, the leader of the Reubenites: 31his offering was one silver plate weighing one hundred thirty shekels, one silver basin weighing seventy shekels, according to the shekel of the sanctuary, both of them full of choice flour mixed with oil for a grain offering; 32one golden dish weighing ten shekels, full of incense; 33one young bull, one ram, one male lamb a year old, for a burnt offering; 34one male goat for a sin offering; 35and for the sacrifice of well-being, two oxen, five rams, five male goats, and five male lambs a year old. This was the offering of Elizur son of Shedeur.

36 On the fifth day Shelumiel son of Zurishaddai, the leader of the Simeonites: 37his offering was one silver plate weighing one hundred thirty shekels, one silver basin weighing seventy shekels, according to the shekel of the sanctuary, both of them full of choice flour mixed with oil for a grain offering; 38one golden dish weighing ten shekels, full of incense; 39one young bull, one ram, one male lamb a year old, for a burnt offering; 40one male goat for a sin offering; 41and for the sacrifice of well-being, two oxen, five rams, five male goats, and five male lambs a year old. This was the offering of Shelumiel son of Zurishaddai.

42 On the sixth day Eliasaph son of Deuel, the leader of the Gadites: 43his offering was one silver plate weighing one hundred thirty shekels, one silver basin weighing seventy shekels, according to the shekel of the sanctuary, both of them full of choice flour mixed with oil for a grain offering; 44one golden dish weighing ten shekels, full of incense; 45one young bull, one ram, one male lamb a year old, for a burnt offering; 46one male goat for a sin offering; 47and for the sacrifice of well-being, two oxen, five rams, five male goats, and five male lambs a year old. This was the offering of Eliasaph son of Deuel.

48 On the seventh day Elishama son of Ammihud, the leader of the Ephraimites: 49his offering was one silver plate weighing one hundred thirty shekels, one silver basin weighing seventy shekels, according to the shekel of the sanctuary, both of them full of choice flour mixed with oil for a grain offering; 50one golden dish weighing ten shekels, full of incense; 51one young bull, one ram, one male lamb a year old, for a burnt offering; 52one male goat for a sin offering; 53and for the sacrifice of well-

being, two oxen, five rams, five male goats, and five male lambs a year old. This was the offering of Elishama son of Ammihud.

54 On the eighth day Gamaliel son of Pedahzur, the leader of the Manassites: 55his offering was one silver plate weighing one hundred thirty shekels, one silver basin weighing seventy shekels, according to the shekel of the sanctuary, both of them full of choice flour mixed with oil for a grain offering; 56one golden dish weighing ten shekels, full of incense; 57one young bull, one ram, one male lamb a year old, for a burnt offering; 58one male goat for a sin offering; 59and for the sacrifice of well-being, two oxen, five rams, five male goats, and five male lambs a year old. This was the offering of Gamaliel son of Pedahzur.

60 On the ninth day Abidan son of Gideoni, the leader of the Benjaminites: 61his offering was one silver plate weighing one hundred thirty shekels, one silver basin weighing seventy shekels, according to the shekel of the sanctuary, both of them full of choice flour mixed with oil for a grain offering; 62one golden dish weighing ten shekels, full of incense; 63one young bull, one ram, one male lamb a year old, for a burnt offering; 64one male goat for a sin offering; 65and for the sacrifice of well-being, two oxen, five rams, five male goats, and five male lambs a year old. This was the offering of Abidan son of Gideoni.

66 On the tenth day Ahiezer son of Ammishaddai, the leader of the Danites: 67his offering was one silver plate weighing one hundred thirty shekels, one silver basin weighing seventy shekels, according to the shekel of the sanctuary, both of them full of choice flour mixed with oil for a grain offering; 68one golden dish weighing ten shekels, full of incense; 69one young bull, one ram, one male lamb a year old, for a burnt offering; 70one male goat for a sin offering; 71and for the sacrifice of well-being, two oxen, five rams, five male goats, and five male lambs a year old. This was the offering of Ahiezer son of Ammishaddai.

72 On the eleventh day Pagiel son of Ochran, the leader of the Asherites: 73his offering was one silver plate weighing one hundred thirty shekels, one silver basin weighing seventy shekels, according to the shekel of the sanctuary, both of them full of choice flour mixed with oil for a grain offering; 74one golden dish weighing ten shekels, full of incense; 75one young bull, one ram, one male lamb a year old, for a burnt offering; 76one male goat for a sin offering; 77and for the sacrifice of well-being, two oxen, five rams, five male goats, and five male lambs a year old. This was the offering of Pagiel son of Ochran.

78 On the twelfth day Ahira son of Enan, the leader of the Naphtalites: 79his offering was one silver plate weighing one hundred thirty shekels, one silver basin weighing seventy shekels, according to the shekel of the sanctuary, both of them full of choice flour mixed with oil for a grain offering; 80one golden dish weighing ten shekels, full of incense; 81one young bull, one ram, one male lamb a year old, for a burnt offering; 82one male goat for a sin offering; 83and for the sacrifice of well-being, two oxen, five rams, five male goats, and five male lambs a year old. This was the offering of Ahira son of Enan.

84 This was the dedication offering for the altar, at the time when it was anointed, from the leaders of Israel: twelve silver plates, twelve silver basins, twelve golden dishes, 85each silver plate weighing one hundred thirty shekels and each basin seventy, all the silver of the ves-

TEXT MESSAGE

What do you call a person who grows a beard, watches what he eats, and never cuts his hair? A Nazirite. Nazirites were men who took a special vow to dedicate their lives to God (Numbers 6.2–8). Priests, deacons, religious, and laypeople of faith still profess vows and dedicate their lives to God today.

This information has been scanned and is free of all known viruses. Please forward to all your friends.

sels two thousand four hundred shekels according to the shekel of the sanctuary, ⁸⁶the twelve golden dishes, full of incense, weighing ten shekels apiece according to the shekel of the sanctuary, all the gold of the dishes being one hundred twenty shekels; ⁸⁷all the livestock for the burnt offering twelve bulls, twelve rams, twelve male lambs a year old, with their grain offering; and twelve male goats for a sin offering; ⁸⁸and all the livestock for the sacrifice of well-being twenty-four bulls, the rams sixty, the male goats sixty, the male lambs a year old sixty. This was the dedication offering for the altar, after it was anointed.

89 When Moses went into the tent of meeting to speak with the LORD,ᵃ he would hear the voice speaking to him from above the mercy seatᵇ that was on the ark of the covenantᶜ from between the two cherubim; thus it spoke to him.

8 The Seven Lamps

The LORD spoke to Moses, saying: ²Speak to Aaron and say to him: When you set up the lamps, the seven lamps shall give light in front of the lampstand. ³Aaron did so; he set up its lamps to give light in front of the lampstand, as the LORD had commanded Moses. ⁴Now this was how the lampstand was made, out of hammered work of gold. From its base to its flowers, it was hammered work; according to the pattern that the LORD had shown Moses, so he made the lampstand.

Consecration and Service of the Levites

5 The LORD spoke to Moses, saying: ⁶Take the Levites from among the Israelites and cleanse them. ⁷Thus you shall do to them, to cleanse them: sprinkle the water of purification on them, have them shave their whole body with a razor and wash their clothes, and so cleanse themselves. ⁸Then let them take a young bull and its grain offering of choice flour mixed with oil, and you shall take another young bull for a sin offering. ⁹You shall bring the Levites before the tent of meeting, and assemble the whole congregation of the Israelites. ¹⁰When you bring the Levites before the LORD, the Israelites shall lay their hands on the Levites, ¹¹and Aaron shall present the Levites before the LORD as an elevation offering from the Israelites, that they may do the service of the LORD. ¹²The Levites shall lay their hands on the heads of the bulls, and he shall offer the one for a sin offering and the other for a burnt offering to the LORD, to make atonement for the Levites. ¹³Then you shall have the Levites stand before Aaron and his sons, and you shall present them as an elevation offering to the LORD.

14 Thus you shall separate the Levites from among the other Israelites, and the Levites shall be mine. ¹⁵Thereafter the Levites may go in to do service at the tent of meeting, once you have cleansed them and presented them as an elevation offering. ¹⁶For they are unreservedly given to me from among the Israelites; I have taken them for myself, in place of all that open the womb, the firstborn of all the Israelites. ¹⁷For all the firstborn among the Israelites are mine, both human and animal. On the day that I struck down all the firstborn in the land of Egypt I consecrated them for myself, ¹⁸but I have taken the Levites in place of all the firstborn among the Israelites. ¹⁹Moreover, I have given the Levites as a gift to Aaron and his sons from among the Israelites, to do the service for the Israelites at the tent of meeting, and to make atonement for the Israelites, in order that there may be no plague among the Israelites for coming too close to the sanctuary.

20 Moses and Aaron and the whole congregation of the Israelites did with the Levites accordingly; the Israelites did with the Levites just as the LORD had commanded Moses concerning them. ²¹The Levites purified themselves from sin and washed their clothes; then Aaron presented them as an elevation offering before the LORD, and Aaron made atonement for them to cleanse them. ²²Thereafter the Levites went in to do their service in the tent of meeting in attendance on Aaron and his sons. As the LORD had commanded Moses concerning the Levites, so they did with them.

23 The LORD spoke to Moses, saying: ²⁴This applies to the Levites: from twenty-five years

---

a Heb him b Or the cover c Or treaty, or testimony; Heb eduth old and upward they shall begin to do duty in the service of the tent of meeting; [25]and from the age of fifty years they shall retire from the duty of the service and serve no more. [26]They may assist their brothers in the tent of meeting in carrying out their duties, but they shall perform no service. Thus you shall do with the Levites in assigning their duties.

9 The Passover at Sinai

The Lord spoke to Moses in the wilderness of Sinai, in the first month of the second year after they had come out of the land of Egypt, saying: [2]Let the Israelites keep the passover at its appointed time. [3]On the fourteenth day of this month, at twilight,[a] you shall keep it at its appointed time; according to all its statutes and all its regulations you shall keep it. [4]So Moses told the Israelites that they should keep the passover. [5]They kept the passover in the first month, on the fourteenth day of the month, at twilight,[a] in the wilderness of Sinai. Just as the Lord had commanded Moses, so the Israelites did. [6]Now there were certain people who were unclean through touching a corpse, so that they could not keep the passover on that day. They came before Moses and Aaron on that day, [7]and said to him, "Although we are unclean through touching a corpse, why must we be kept from presenting the Lord's offering at its appointed time among the Israelites?" [8]Moses spoke to them, "Wait, so that I may hear what the Lord will command concerning you."

[9] The Lord spoke to Moses, saying: [10]Speak to the Israelites, saying: Anyone of you or your descendants who is unclean through touching a corpse, or is away on a journey, shall still keep the passover to the Lord. [11]In the second month on the fourteenth day, at twilight,[a] they shall keep it; they shall eat it with unleavened bread and bitter herbs. [12]They shall leave none of it until morning, nor break a bone of it; according to all the statute for the passover they shall keep it. [13]But anyone who is clean and is not on a journey, and yet refrains from keeping the passover, shall be cut off from the people for not presenting the Lord's offering at its appointed time; such a one shall bear the consequences for the sin. [14]Any alien residing among you who wishes to keep the passover to the Lord shall do so according to the statute of the passover and according to its regulation; you shall have one statute for both the resident alien and the native.

The Cloud and the Fire

15 On the day the tabernacle was set up, the cloud covered the tabernacle, the tent of the covenant;[b] and from evening until morning it was over the tabernacle, having the appearance of fire. [16]It was always so: the cloud covered it by day[c] and the appearance of fire by night. [17]Whenever the cloud lifted from over the tent, then the Israelites would set out; and in the place where the cloud settled down, there the Israelites would camp. [18]At the command of the Lord the Israelites would set out, and at the command of the Lord they would camp. As long as the cloud rested over the tabernacle, they would remain in camp. [19]Even when the cloud continued over the tabernacle many days, the Israelites would keep the charge of the Lord, and would not set out. [20]Sometimes the cloud would remain a few days over the tabernacle, and according to the command of the Lord they would remain in camp; then according to the command of the Lord they would set out. [21]Sometimes the cloud would remain from evening until morning; and when the cloud lifted in the morning, they would set out, or if it continued for a day and a night, when the cloud lifted they would set out. [22]Whether it was two days, or a month, or a longer time, that the cloud continued over the tabernacle, resting upon it, the Israelites would remain in camp and would not set out; but when it lifted they would set out. [23]At the command of the Lord they would camp, and at the command of the Lord they would set out. They kept the charge of the Lord, at the command of the Lord by Moses.

10 The Silver Trumpets

The Lord spoke to Moses, saying: [2]Make two silver trumpets; you shall make them of hammered work; and you shall use them for summoning the congregation, and for breaking camp. [3]When both are blown, the whole congregation shall assemble before you at the entrance of the tent of meeting. [4]But if only one is blown, then the leaders, the heads of the tribes of Israel, shall assemble before you. [5]When you blow an alarm, the camps on the east side shall set out; [6]when you blow a second alarm, the camps on the south side shall set out. An alarm is to be blown whenever they are to set out. [7]But when the assembly is to be gathered, you shall blow, but you shall not sound an alarm. [8]The sons of Aaron, the priests, shall blow the trumpets; this shall be a perpetual institution for you throughout your generations. [9]When you go to war in your land against the

---

a Heb *between the two evenings* b Or *treaty*, or *testimony*; Heb *eduth* c Gk Syr Vg: Heb lacks *by day* adversary who oppresses you, you shall sound an alarm with the trumpets, so that you may be remembered before the LORD your God and be saved from your enemies. [10]Also on your days of rejoicing, at your appointed festivals, and at the beginnings of your months, you shall blow the trumpets over your burnt offerings and over your sacrifices of well-being; they shall serve as a reminder on your behalf before the LORD your God: I am the LORD your God.

Departure from Sinai

11 In the second year, in the second month, on the twentieth day of the month, the cloud lifted from over the tabernacle of the covenant.[a] [12]Then the Israelites set out by stages from the wilderness of Sinai, and the cloud settled down in the wilderness of Paran. [13]They set out for the first time at the command of the LORD by Moses. [14]The standard of the camp of Judah set out first, company by company, and over the whole company was Nahshon son of Amminadab. [15]Over the company of the tribe of Issachar was Nethanel son of Zuar; [16]and over the company of the tribe of Zebulun was Eliab son of Helon.

17 Then the tabernacle was taken down, and the Gershonites and the Merarites, who carried the tabernacle, set out. [18]Next the standard of the camp of Reuben set out, company by company; and over the whole company was Elizur son of Shedeur. [19]Over the company of the tribe of Simeon was Shelumiel son of Zurishaddai, [20]and over the company of the tribe of Gad was Eliasaph son of Deuel.

21 Then the Kohathites, who carried the holy things, set out; and the tabernacle was set up before their arrival. [22]Next the standard of the Ephraimite camp set out, company by company, and over the whole company was Elishama son of Ammihud. [23]Over the company of the tribe of Manasseh was Gamaliel son of Pedahzur, [24]and over the company of the tribe of Benjamin was Abidan son of Gideoni.

25 Then the standard of the camp of Dan, acting as the rear guard of all the camps, set out, company by company, and over the whole company was Ahiezer son of Ammishaddai.

[26]Over the company of the tribe of Asher was Pagiel son of Ochran, [27]and over the company of the tribe of Naphtali was Ahira son of Enan. [28]This was the order of march of the Israelites, company by company, when they set out.

29 Moses said to Hobab son of Reuel the Midianite, Moses' father-in-law, "We are setting out for the place of which the LORD said, 'I will give it to you'; come with us, and we will treat you well; for the LORD has promised good to Israel." [30]But he said to him, "I will not go, but I will go back to my own land and to my kindred." [31]He said, "Do not leave us, for you know where we should camp in the wilderness, and you will serve as eyes for us. [32]Moreover, if you go with us, whatever good the LORD does for us, the same we will do for you."

33 So they set out from the mount of the LORD three days' journey with the ark of the covenant of the LORD going before them three days' journey, to seek out a resting place for them, [34]the cloud of the LORD being over them by day when they set out from the camp.

35 Whenever the ark set out, Moses would say,

"Arise, O LORD, let your enemies be
        scattered,
    and your foes flee before you."
[36]And whenever it came to rest, he would say,
"Return, O LORD of the ten thousand
        thousands of Israel."[b]

11 Complaining in the Desert

Now when the people complained in the hearing of the LORD about their misfortunes, the LORD heard it and his anger was kindled. Then the fire of the LORD burned against them, and consumed some outlying parts of the camp. [2]But the people cried out to Moses; and Moses prayed to the LORD, and the fire abated. [3]So that place was called Taberah,[c] because the fire of the LORD burned against them.

4 The rabble among them had a strong craving; and the Israelites also wept again, and said, "If only we had meat to eat! [5]We remember the fish we used to eat in Egypt for nothing, the cucumbers, the melons, the leeks, the onions, and the garlic; [6]but now our strength is dried up, and there is nothing at all but this manna to look at."

7 Now the manna was like coriander seed, and its color was like the color of gum resin. [8]The people went around and gathered it, ground it in mills or beat it in mortars, then boiled it in pots and made cakes of it; and the taste of it was like the taste of cakes baked with

---

a Or treaty, or testimony; Heb eduth   b Meaning of Heb uncertain   c That is Burning oil. ⁹When the dew fell on the camp in the night, the manna would fall with it.

10 Moses heard the people weeping throughout their families, all at the entrances of their tents. Then the Lord became very angry, and Moses was displeased. ¹¹So Moses said to the Lord, "Why have you treated your servant so badly? Why have I not found favor in your sight, that you lay the burden of all this people on me? ¹²Did I conceive all this people? Did I give birth to them, that you should say to me, 'Carry them in your bosom, as a nurse carries a sucking child, to the land that you promised on oath to their ancestors'? ¹³Where am I to get meat to give to all this people? For they come weeping to me and say, 'Give us meat to eat!' ¹⁴I am not able to carry all this people alone, for they are too heavy for me. ¹⁵If this is the way you are going to treat me, put me to death at once—if I have found favor in your sight—and do not let me see my misery."

The Seventy Elders

16 So the Lord said to Moses, "Gather for me seventy of the elders of Israel, whom you know to be the elders of the people and officers over them; bring them to the tent of meeting, and have them take their place there with you. ¹⁷I will come down and talk with you there; and I will take some of the spirit that is on you and put it on them; and they shall bear the burden of the people along with you so that you will not bear it all by yourself. ¹⁸And say to the people: Consecrate yourselves for tomorrow, and you shall eat meat; for you have wailed in the hearing of the Lord, saying, 'If only we had meat to eat! Surely it was better for us in Egypt.' Therefore the Lord will give you meat, and you shall eat. ¹⁹You shall eat not only one day, or two days, or five days, or ten days, or twenty days, ²⁰but for a whole month—until it comes out of your nostrils and becomes loathsome to you—because you have rejected the Lord who is among you, and have wailed before him, saying, 'Why did we ever leave Egypt?' " ²¹But Moses said, "The people I am with number six hundred thousand on foot; and you say, 'I will give them meat, that they may eat for a whole month'! ²²Are there enough flocks and herds to slaughter for them? Are there enough fish in the sea to catch for them?" ²³The Lord said to Moses, "Is the Lord's power limited?ᵈ Now you shall see whether my word will come true for you or not."

24 So Moses went out and told the people the words of the Lord; and he gathered seventy elders of the people, and placed them all around the tent. ²⁵Then the Lord came down

in the cloud and spoke to him, and took some of the spirit that was on him and put it on the seventy elders; and when the spirit rested upon them, they prophesied. But they did not do so again.

26 Two men remained in the camp, one named Eldad, and the other named Medad, and the spirit rested on them; they were among those registered, but they had not gone out to the tent, and so they prophesied in the camp. ²⁷And a young man ran and told Moses, "Eldad and Medad are prophesying in the camp." ²⁸And Joshua son of Nun, the assistant of Moses, one of his chosen men,ᵇ said, "My lord Moses, stop them!" ²⁹But Moses said to him, "Are you jealous for my sake? Would that all the Lord's people were prophets, and that the Lord would put his spirit on them!" ³⁰And Moses and the elders of Israel returned to the camp.

The Quails

31 Then a wind went out from the Lord, and it brought quails from the sea and let them fall beside the camp, about a day's journey on this side and a day's journey on the other side, all around the camp, about two cubits deep on the ground. ³²So the people worked all that day and night and all the next day, gathering the quails; the least anyone gathered was ten homers; and they spread them out for themselves all around the camp. ³³But while the meat was still between their teeth, before it was consumed, the anger of the Lord was kindled against the people, and the Lord struck the people with a very great plague. ³⁴So that place was called Kibroth-hattaavah,ᶜ because there they buried the people who had the craving. ³⁵From Kibroth-hattaavah the people journeyed to Hazeroth.

12 Aaron and Miriam Jealous of Moses

While they were at Hazeroth, Miriam and Aaron spoke against Moses because of the Cushite woman whom he had married (for he had indeed married a Cushite woman); ²and they said, "Has the Lord spoken only through Moses? Has he not spoken through us also?" And the Lord heard it. ³Now the man Moses was very humble,ᵈ more so than anyone else on the face of the earth. ⁴Suddenly the Lord said to Moses, Aaron, and Miriam, "Come out, you three, to the tent of meeting." So the three of them came out. ⁵Then the Lord came down in a pillar of cloud, and stood at the entrance of the tent, and called Aaron and Miriam; and they both came forward. ⁶And he said, "Hear my words:

---

a Heb Lord's hand too short? b Or of Moses from his youth c That is Graves of craving d Or devout

When there are prophets among you,
I the LORD make myself known to them
in visions;
I speak to them in dreams.
⁷ Not so with my servant Moses;
he is entrusted with all my house.
⁸ With him I speak face to face— clearly, not
in riddles;
and he beholds the form of the LORD.
Why then were you not afraid to speak against
my servant Moses?" ⁹And the anger of the LORD
was kindled against them, and he departed.

10 When the cloud went away from over the
tent, Miriam had become leprous,ᵃ as white as
snow. And Aaron turned towards Miriam and
saw that she was leprous. ¹¹Then Aaron said to
Moses, "Oh, my lord, do not punish usᵇ for a
sin that we have so foolishly committed. ¹²Do
not let her be like one stillborn, whose flesh is
half consumed when it comes out of its mother's womb." ¹³And Moses cried to the LORD,
"O God, please heal her." ¹⁴But the LORD said
to Moses, "If her father had but spit in her face,
would she not bear her shame for seven days?
Let her be shut out of the camp for seven days,
and after that she may be brought in again."
¹⁵So Miriam was shut out of the camp for sev-
en days; and the people did not set out on the
march until Miriam had been brought in again.
¹⁶After that the people set out from Hazeroth,
and camped in the wilderness of Paran.

13 Spies Sent into Canaan

The LORD said to Moses, ²"Send men to spy out
the land of Canaan, which I am giving to the Israelites; from each of their ancestral tribes you
shall send a man, every one a leader among
them." ³So Moses sent them from the wilderness of Paran, according to the command
of the LORD, all of them leading men among
the Israelites. ⁴These were their names: From
the tribe of Reuben, Shammua son of Zaccur;
⁵from the tribe of Simeon, Shaphat son of
Hori; ⁶from the tribe of Judah, Caleb son of Jephunneh; ⁷from the tribe of Issachar, Igal son
of Joseph; ⁸from the tribe of Ephraim, Hoshea
son of Nun; ⁹from the tribe of Benjamin, Palti
son of Raphu; ¹⁰from the tribe of Zebulun,
Gaddiel son of Sodi; ¹¹from the tribe of Joseph
(that is, from the tribe of Manasseh), Gaddi son
of Susi; ¹²from the tribe of Dan, Ammiel son of
Gemalli; ¹³from the tribe of Asher, Sethur son
of Michael; ¹⁴from the tribe of Naphtali, Nahbi
son of Vophsi; ¹⁵from the tribe of Gad, Geuel
son of Machi. ¹⁶These were the names of the
men whom Moses sent to spy out the land.

And Moses changed the name of Hoshea son of
Nun to Joshua.

17 Moses sent them to spy out the land of
Canaan, and said to them, "Go up there into
the Negeb, and go up into the hill country,
¹⁸and see what the land is like, and whether the
people who live in it are strong or weak, whether they are few or many, ¹⁹and whether the
land they live in is good or bad, and whether
the towns that they live in are unwalled or fortified, ²⁰and whether the land is rich or poor,
and whether there are trees in it or not. Be
bold, and bring some of the fruit of the land."
Now it was the season of the first ripe grapes.

21 So they went up and spied out the land
from the wilderness of Zin to Rehob, near
Lebo-hamath. ²²They went up into the Negeb,
and came to Hebron; and Ahiman, Sheshai,
and Talmai, the Anakites, were there. (Hebron
was built seven years before Zoan in Egypt.)
²³And they came to the Wadi Eshcol, and cut
down from there a branch with a single cluster
of grapes, and they carried it on a pole between
two of them. They also brought some pomegranates and figs. ²⁴That place was called the
Wadi Eshcol,ᶜ because of the cluster that the Israelites cut down from there.

The Report of the Spies

25 At the end of forty days they returned from
spying out the land. ²⁶And they came to Moses
and Aaron and to all the congregation of the Israelites in the wilderness of Paran, at Kadesh;
they brought back word to them and to all the
congregation, and showed them the fruit of
the land. ²⁷And they told him, "We came to the
land to which you sent us; it flows with milk
and honey, and this is its fruit. ²⁸Yet the people
who live in the land are strong, and the towns
are fortified and very large; and besides, we saw
the descendants of Anak there. ²⁹The Amalekites live in the land of the Negeb; the Hittites,
the Jebusites, and the Amorites live in the hill
country; and the Canaanites live by the sea, and
along the Jordan."

30 But Caleb quieted the people before Moses, and said, "Let us go up at once and occupy
it, for we are well able to overcome it." ³¹Then
the men who had gone up with him said, "We
are not able to go up against this people, for
they are stronger than we." ³²So they brought
to the Israelites an unfavorable report of the
land that they had spied out, saying, "The land
that we have gone through as spies is a land
that devours its inhabitants; and all the people that we saw in it are of great size. ³³There
we saw the Nephilim (the Anakites come from

ᵃ A term for several skin diseases; precise meaning uncertain ᵇ Heb *do not lay sin upon us* ᶜ That is *Cluster* the Nephilim); and to ourselves we seemed like grasshoppers, and so we seemed to them."

14 The People Rebel

Then all the congregation raised a loud cry, and the people wept that night. ²And all the Israelites complained against Moses and Aaron; the whole congregation said to them, "Would that we had died in the land of Egypt! Or would that we had died in this wilderness! ³Why is the LORD bringing us into this land to fall by the sword? Our wives and our little ones will become booty; would it not be better for us to go back to Egypt?" ⁴So they said to one another, "Let us choose a captain, and go back to Egypt."

5 Then Moses and Aaron fell on their faces before all the assembly of the congregation of the Israelites. ⁶And Joshua son of Nun and Caleb son of Jephunneh, who were among those who had spied out the land, tore their clothes ⁷and said to all the congregation of the Israelites, "The land that we went through as spies is an exceedingly good land. ⁸If the LORD is pleased with us, he will bring us into this land and give it to us, a land that flows with milk and honey. ⁹Only, do not rebel against the LORD; and do not fear the people of the land, for they are no more than bread for us; their protection is removed from them, and the LORD is with us; do not fear them." ¹⁰But the whole congregation threatened to stone them.

Then the glory of the LORD appeared at the tent of meeting to all the Israelites. ¹¹And the LORD said to Moses, "How long will this people despise me? And how long will they refuse to believe in me, in spite of all the signs that I have done among them? ¹²I will strike them with pestilence and disinherit them, and I will make of you a nation greater and mightier than they."

Moses Intercedes for the People

13 But Moses said to the LORD, "Then the Egyptians will hear of it, for in your might you brought up this people from among them, ¹⁴and they will tell the inhabitants of this land. They have heard that you, O LORD, are in the midst of this people; for you, O LORD, are seen face to face, and your cloud stands over them and you go in front of them, in a pillar of cloud by day and in a pillar of fire by night. ¹⁵Now if you kill this people all at one time, then the nations who have heard about you will say, ¹⁶'It is because the LORD was not able to bring this people into the land he swore to give them that he has slaughtered them in the wilderness.' ¹⁷And now, therefore, let the power of the LORD be great in the way that you promised when you spoke, saying,

¹⁸ 'The LORD is slow to anger,
   and abounding in steadfast love,
   forgiving iniquity and transgression,

Shadows—© Christy Klink, 18

but by no means clearing the guilty,
visiting the iniquity of the parents
upon the children
to the third and the fourth generation.'
[19]Forgive the iniquity of this people according to the greatness of your steadfast love, just as you have pardoned this people, from Egypt even until now."

20 Then the LORD said, "I do forgive, just as you have asked; [21]nevertheless—as I live, and as all the earth shall be filled with the glory of the LORD— [22]none of the people who have seen my glory and the signs that I did in Egypt and in the wilderness, and yet have tested me these ten times and have not obeyed my voice, [23]shall see the land that I swore to give to their ancestors; none of those who despised me shall see it. [24]But my servant Caleb, because he has a different spirit and has followed me wholeheartedly, I will bring into the land into which he went, and his descendants shall possess it. [25]Now, since the Amalekites and the Canaanites live in the valleys, turn tomorrow and set out for the wilderness by the way to the Red Sea."[a]

An Attempted Invasion is Repulsed

26 And the LORD spoke to Moses and to Aaron, saying: [27]How long shall this wicked congregation complain against me? I have heard the complaints of the Israelites, which they complain against me. [28]Say to them, "As I live," says the LORD, "I will do to you the very things I heard you say: [29]your dead bodies shall fall in this very wilderness; and of all your number, included in the census, from twenty years old and upward, who have complained against me, [30]not one of you shall come into the land in which I swore to settle you, except Caleb son of Jephunneh and Joshua son of Nun. [31]But your little ones, who you said would become booty, I will bring in, and they shall know the land that you have despised. [32]But as for you, your dead bodies shall fall in this wilderness. [33]And your children shall be shepherds in the wilderness for forty years, and shall suffer for your faithlessness, until the last of your dead bodies lies in the wilderness. [34]According to the number of the days in which you spied out the land, forty days, for every day a year, you shall bear your iniquity, forty years, and you shall know my displeasure." [35]I the LORD have spoken; surely I will do thus to all this wicked congregation gathered together against me: in this wilderness they shall come to a full end, and there they shall die.

36 And the men whom Moses sent to spy out the land, who returned and made all the congregation complain against him by bringing a bad report about the land— [37]the men who brought an unfavorable report about the land died by a plague before the LORD. [38]But Joshua son of Nun and Caleb son of Jephunneh alone remained alive, of those men who went to spy out the land.

39 When Moses told these words to all the Israelites, the people mourned greatly. [40]They rose early in the morning and went up to the heights of the hill country, saying, "Here we are. We will go up to the place that the LORD has promised, for we have sinned." [41]But Moses said, "Why do you continue to transgress the command of the LORD? That will not succeed. [42]Do not go up, for the LORD is not with you; do not let yourselves be struck down before your enemies. [43]For the Amalekites and the Canaanites will confront you there, and you shall fall by the sword; because you have turned back from following the LORD, the LORD will not be with you." [44]But they presumed to go up to the heights of the hill country, even though the ark of the covenant of the LORD, and Moses, had not left the camp. [45]Then the Amalekites and the Canaanites who lived in that hill country came down and defeated them, pursuing them as far as Hormah.

15 Various Offerings

The LORD spoke to Moses, saying: [2]Speak to the Israelites and say to them: When you come into the land you are to inhabit, which I am giving you, [3]and you make an offering by fire to the LORD from the herd or from the flock—whether a burnt offering or a sacrifice, to fulfill a vow or as a freewill offering or at your appointed festivals—to make a pleasing odor for the LORD, [4]then whoever presents such an offering to the LORD shall present also a grain offering, one-tenth of an ephah of choice flour, mixed with one-fourth of a hin of oil. [5]Moreover, you shall offer one-fourth of a hin of wine as a drink offering with the burnt offering or the sacrifice, for each lamb. [6]For a ram, you shall offer a grain offering, two-tenths of an ephah of choice flour mixed with one-third of a hin of oil; [7]and as a drink offering you shall offer one-third of a hin of wine, a pleasing odor to the LORD. [8]When you offer a bull as a burnt offering or a sacrifice, to fulfill a vow or as an offering of well-being to the LORD, [9]then you shall present with the bull a grain offering, three-tenths of an ephah of choice flour, mixed with half a hin of oil, [10]and you shall present as a drink offering half a hin of wine, as an offering by fire, a pleasing odor to the LORD.

a Or *Sea of Reeds*

11 Thus it shall be done for each ox or ram, or for each of the male lambs or the kids. ¹²According to the number that you offer, so you shall do with each and every one. ¹³Every native Israelite shall do these things in this way, in presenting an offering by fire, a pleasing odor to the LORD. ¹⁴An alien who lives with you, or who takes up permanent residence among you, and wishes to offer an offering by fire, a pleasing odor to the LORD, shall do as you do. ¹⁵As for the assembly, there shall be for both you and the resident alien a single statute, a perpetual statute throughout your generations; you and the alien shall be alike before the LORD. ¹⁶You and the alien who resides with you shall have the same law and the same ordinance.

17 The LORD spoke to Moses, saying: ¹⁸Speak to the Israelites and say to them: After you come into the land to which I am bringing you, ¹⁹whenever you eat of the bread of the land, you shall present a donation to the LORD. ²⁰From your first batch of dough you shall present a loaf as a donation; you shall present it just as you present a donation from the threshing floor. ²¹Throughout your generations you shall give to the LORD a donation from the first of your batch of dough.

22 But if you unintentionally fail to observe all these commandments that the LORD has spoken to Moses— ²³everything that the LORD has commanded you by Moses, from the day the LORD gave commandment and thereafter, throughout your generations— ²⁴then if it was done unintentionally without the knowledge of the congregation, the whole congregation shall offer one young bull for a burnt offering, a pleasing odor to the LORD, together with its grain offering and its drink offering, according to the ordinance, and one male goat for a sin offering. ²⁵The priest shall make atonement for all the congregation of the Israelites, and they shall be forgiven; it was unintentional, and they have brought their offering, an offering by fire to the LORD, and their sin offering before the LORD, for their error. ²⁶All the congregation of the Israelites shall be forgiven, as well as the aliens residing among them, because the whole people was involved in the error.

27 An individual who sins unintentionally shall present a female goat a year old for a sin offering. ²⁸And the priest shall make atonement before the LORD for the one who commits an error, when it is unintentional, to make atonement for the person, who then shall be forgiven. ²⁹For both the native among the Israelites and the alien residing among them—you shall have the same law for anyone who acts in error. ³⁰But whoever acts high-handedly, whether a native or an alien, affronts the LORD, and shall be cut off from among the people. ³¹Because of having despised the word of the LORD and broken his commandment, such a person shall be utterly cut off and bear the guilt.

Penalty for Violating the Sabbath

32 When the Israelites were in the wilderness, they found a man gathering sticks on the sabbath day. ³³Those who found him gathering sticks brought him to Moses, Aaron, and to the whole congregation. ³⁴They put him in custody, because it was not clear what should be done to him. ³⁵Then the LORD said to Moses, "The man shall be put to death; all the congregation shall stone him outside the camp." ³⁶The whole congregation brought him outside the camp and stoned him to death, just as the LORD had commanded Moses.

Fringes on Garments

37 The LORD said to Moses: 38Speak to the Israelites, and tell them to make fringes on the corners of their garments throughout their generations and to put a blue cord on the fringe at each corner. 39You have the fringe so that, when you see it, you will remember all the commandments of the LORD and do them, and not follow the lust of your own heart and your own eyes. 40So you shall remember and do all my commandments, and you shall be holy to your God. 41I am the LORD your God, who brought you out of the land of Egypt, to be your God: I am the LORD your God.

16 Revolt of Korah, Dathan, and Abiram

Now Korah son of Izhar son of Kohath son of Levi, along with Dathan and Abiram sons of Eliab, and On son of Peleth—descendants of Reuben—took 2two hundred fifty Israelite men, leaders of the congregation, chosen from the assembly, well-known men,*a* and they confronted Moses. 3They assembled against Moses and against Aaron, and said to them, "You have gone too far! All the congregation are holy, every one of them, and the LORD is among them. So why then do you exalt yourselves above the assembly of the LORD?" 4When Moses heard it, he fell on his face. 5Then he said to Korah and all his company, "In the morning the LORD will make known who is his, and who is holy, and who will be allowed to approach him; the one whom he will choose he will allow to approach him. 6Do this: take censers, Korah and all your*b* company, 7and tomorrow put fire in them, and lay incense on them before the LORD; and the man whom the LORD chooses shall be the holy one. You Levites have gone too far!" 8Then Moses said to Korah, "Hear now, you Levites! 9Is it too little for you that the God of Israel has separated you from the congregation of Israel, to allow you to approach him in order to perform the duties of the LORD's tabernacle, and to stand before the congregation and serve them? 10He has allowed you to approach him, and all your brother Levites with you; yet you seek the priesthood as well! 11Therefore you and all your company have gathered together against the LORD. What is Aaron that you rail against him?"

12 Moses sent for Dathan and Abiram sons of Eliab; but they said, "We will not come! 13Is it too little that you have brought us up out of a land flowing with milk and honey to kill us in the wilderness, that you must also lord it over us? 14It is clear you have not brought us into a land flowing with milk and honey, or given us an inheritance of fields and vineyards. Would you put out the eyes of these men? We will not come!"

15 Moses was very angry and said to the LORD, "Pay no attention to their offering. I have not taken one donkey from them, and I have not harmed any one of them." 16And Moses said to Korah, "As for you and all your company, be present tomorrow before the LORD, you and they and Aaron; 17and let each one of you take his censer, and put incense on it, and each one of you present his censer before the LORD, two hundred fifty censers; you also, and Aaron, each his censer." 18So each man took his censer, and they put fire in the censers and laid incense on them, and they stood at the entrance of the tent of meeting with Moses and Aaron. 19Then Korah assembled the whole congregation against them at the entrance of the tent of meeting. And the glory of the LORD appeared to the whole congregation.

20 Then the LORD spoke to Moses and to Aaron, saying: 21Separate yourselves from this congregation, so that I may consume them in a moment. 22They fell on their faces, and said, "O God, the God of the spirits of all flesh, shall one person sin and you become angry with the whole congregation?"

23 And the LORD spoke to Moses, saying: 24Say to the congregation: Get away from the dwellings of Korah, Dathan, and Abiram. 25So Moses got up and went to Dathan and Abiram; the elders of Israel followed him. 26He said to the congregation, "Turn away from the tents of these wicked men, and touch nothing of theirs, or you will be swept away for all their sins." 27So they got away from the dwellings of Korah, Dathan, and Abiram; and Dathan and Abiram came out and stood at the entrance of their tents, together with their wives, their children, and their little ones. 28And Moses said, "This is how you shall know that the LORD has sent me to do all these works; it has not been of my own accord: 29If these people die a natural death, or if a natural fate comes on them, then the LORD has not sent me. 30But if the LORD creates something new, and the ground opens its mouth and swallows them up, with all that belongs to them, and they go down alive into Sheol, then you shall know that these men have despised the LORD."

31 As soon as he finished speaking all these words, the ground under them was split apart. 32The earth opened its mouth and swallowed them up, along with their households—everyone who belonged to Korah and all their goods. 33So they with all that belonged to

---

a Cn: Heb *and they confronted Moses, and two hundred fifty men . . . well-known men* *b* Heb *his*

Silence

The distance between us
So close, yet so far away
I hear You calling, "Come, my child."
You know my name
You know my every thought
Silence.
How is it You're always with me,
Yet sometimes, I can't feel a thing?
Never condemning. Never forsaking.
You're too powerful for words
So gentle all the same
Silence.
You know me more
Than I know myself
There's no need to say a word
You simply are I AM
Don't speak. He's waiting.
Silence.

Silence—© Anna Hastings, 16

them went down alive into Sheol; the earth closed over them, and they perished from the midst of the assembly. [34]All Israel around them fled at their outcry, for they said, "The earth will swallow us too!" [35]And fire came out from the LORD and consumed the two hundred fifty men offering the incense.

36[a] Then the LORD spoke to Moses, saying: [37]Tell Eleazar son of Aaron the priest to take the censers out of the blaze; then scatter the fire far and wide. [38]For the censers of these sinners have become holy at the cost of their lives. Make them into hammered plates as a covering for the altar, for they presented them before the LORD and they became holy. Thus they shall be a sign to the Israelites. [39]So Eleazar the priest took the bronze censers that had been presented by those who were burned; and they were hammered out as a covering for the altar— [40]a reminder to the Israelites that no outsider, who is not of the descendants of Aaron, shall approach to offer incense before the LORD, so as not to become like Korah and his company—just as the LORD had said to him through Moses.

41 On the next day, however, the whole congregation of the Israelites rebelled against Moses and against Aaron, saying, "You have killed the people of the LORD." [42]And when the congregation had assembled against them, Moses and Aaron turned toward the tent of meeting, the cloud had covered it and the glory of the LORD appeared. [43]Then Moses and Aaron came to the front of the tent of meeting, [44]and the LORD spoke to Moses, saying, [45]"Get away from this congregation, so that I may consume them in a moment." And they fell on their faces. [46]Moses said to Aaron, "Take your censer, put fire on it from the altar and lay incense on it, and carry it quickly to the congregation and make atonement for them. For wrath has gone out from the LORD; the plague has begun." [47]So Aaron took it as Moses had ordered, and ran into the middle of the assembly, where the plague had already begun among the people. He put on the incense, and made atonement for the people. [48]He stood between the dead and the living; and the plague was stopped. [49]Those who died by the plague were fourteen thousand seven hundred, besides those who died in the affair of Korah. [50]When the plague was stopped, Aaron returned to Moses at the entrance of the tent of meeting.

17 [b] The Budding of Aaron's Rod
The LORD spoke to Moses, saying: [2]Speak to the Israelites, and get twelve staffs from them, one for each ancestral house, from all the leaders of their ancestral houses. Write each man's name on his staff, [3]and write Aaron's name on the staff of Levi. For there shall be one staff for the head of each ancestral house. [4]Place them in the tent of meeting before the covenant,[c] where I meet with you. [5]And the staff of the man whom I choose shall sprout; thus I will put a stop to the complaints of the Israelites that they continually make against you. [6]Moses spoke to the Israelites; and all their leaders gave him staffs, one for each leader, according to their ancestral houses, twelve staffs; and the staff of Aaron was among theirs. [7]So Moses placed the staffs before the LORD in the tent of the covenant.[c]

8 When Moses went into the tent of the covenant[c] on the next day, the staff of Aaron for the house of Levi had sprouted. It put forth buds, produced blossoms, and bore ripe almonds. [9]Then Moses brought out all the staffs from before the LORD to all the Israelites; and they looked, and each man took his staff. [10]And the LORD said to Moses, "Put back the staff of Aaron before the covenant,[c] to be kept as a warning to rebels, so that you may make an end of their complaints against me, or else they will die." [11]Moses did so; just as the LORD commanded him, so he did.

12 The Israelites said to Moses, "We are perishing; we are lost, all of us are lost! [13]Everyone who approaches the tabernacle of the LORD will die. Are we all to perish?"

18 Responsibility of Priests and Levites
The LORD said to Aaron: You and your sons and your ancestral house with you shall bear responsibility for offenses connected with the sanctuary, while you and your sons alone shall bear responsibility for offenses connected with the priesthood. [2]So bring with you also your brothers of the tribe of Levi, your ancestral tribe, in order that they may be joined to you, and serve you while you and your sons with you are in front of the tent of the covenant.[c] [3]They shall perform duties for you and for the whole tent. But they must not approach either the utensils of the sanctuary or the altar, otherwise both they and you will die. [4]They are attached to you in order to perform the duties of the tent of meeting, for all the service of the tent; no outsider shall approach you. [5]You yourselves shall perform the duties of the sanctuary and the duties of the altar, so that wrath may never again come upon the Israelites. [6]It is I who now take your brother Levites from among the Israelites; they are now yours as a

a Ch 17.1 in Heb b Ch 17.16 in Heb c Or treaty, or testimony; Heb eduth gift, dedicated to the LORD, to perform the service of the tent of meeting. [7]But you and your sons with you shall diligently perform your priestly duties in all that concerns the altar and the area behind the curtain. I give your priesthood as a gift;[a] any outsider who approaches shall be put to death.

The Priests' Portion

8 The LORD spoke to Aaron: I have given you charge of the offerings made to me, all the holy gifts of the Israelites; I have given them to you and to your sons as a priestly portion due you in perpetuity. [9]This shall be yours from the most holy things, reserved from the fire: every offering of theirs that they render to me as a most holy thing, whether grain offering, sin offering, or guilt offering, shall belong to you and your sons. [10]As a most holy thing you shall eat it; every male may eat it; it shall be holy to you. [11]This also is yours: I have given to you, together with your sons and daughters, as a perpetual due, whatever is set aside from the gifts of all the elevation offerings of the Israelites; everyone who is clean in your house may eat them. [12]All the best of the oil and all the best of the wine and of the grain, the choice produce that they give to the LORD, I have given to you. [13]The first fruits of all that is in their land, which they bring to the LORD, shall be yours; everyone who is clean in your house may eat of it. [14]Every devoted thing in Israel shall be yours. [15]The first issue of the womb of all creatures, human and animal, which is offered to the LORD, shall be yours; but the firstborn of human beings you shall redeem, and the firstborn of unclean animals you shall redeem. [16]Their redemption price, reckoned from one month of age, you shall fix at five shekels of silver, according to the shekel of the sanctuary (that is, twenty gerahs). [17]But the firstborn of a cow, or the firstborn of a sheep, or the firstborn of a goat, you shall not redeem; they are holy. You shall dash their blood on the altar, and shall turn their fat into smoke as an offering by fire for a pleasing odor to the LORD; [18]but their flesh shall be yours, just as the breast that is elevated and as the right thigh are yours. [19]All the holy offerings that the Israelites present to the LORD I have given to you, together with your sons and daughters, as a perpetual due; it is a covenant of salt forever before the LORD for you and your descendants as well. [20]Then the LORD said to Aaron: You shall have no allotment in their land, nor shall you have any share among them; I am your share and your possession among the Israelites.

a Heb *as a service of gift*

REAL QUESTIONS

RQ

Why does God seem so distant? Some days I feel close to God, but other days God seems miles away.

Can you relate to the erratic emotions expressed in the Psalms? Sometimes God feels as close as your breath; sometimes it's as if he's vacated the universe. Sometimes you're warm, happy, worshiping. Other times you feel angry, abandoned, bitter, alone.

Feelings can be unpredictable, but they don't have to rock your faith. Throughout Sacred Scripture, God assures us again and again of his changeless commitment to his people. In Hebrews, we hear echoes of God's Old Testament encouragement: "I will never leave you or forsake you" (13.5). In Romans, Paul says that death, life, angels, demons, fears, worries, and even the powers of hell can't keep God's love away (8.38). And if that weren't enough, Paul even says that Christ "dwells" in us (see Romans 8.9–11). How much closer could God get?

God's presence may not always feel like the warm glow of a campfire, but he continually reveals himself in unexpected ways. Are you looking? How does God's presence go ignored in your daily routine? How can you remind yourself of your connection to Christ?

Do feelings of distance drive you away from God or motivate you to dive deeper into his presence? Is God the one who is distant, or is it you? No matter how we feel, Jesus is really present to us, and most especially in the sacraments.

Find some Creative Space in the Bible and write your thoughts on these issues, maybe adding some real questions of your own. Then explore more in the verses below, or talk to your parish pastor or director of religious education about your real questions.

(Want to explore more? Read Deuteronomy 31.6; Psalm 139.7–12; and Romans 8.31–39.)

25 Then the LORD spoke to Moses, saying: 26You shall speak to the Levites, saying: When you receive from the Israelites the tithe that I have given you from them for your portion, you shall set apart an offering from it to the LORD, a tithe of the tithe. 27It shall be reckoned to you as your gift, the same as the grain of the threshing floor and the fullness of the wine press. 28Thus you also shall set apart an offering to the LORD from all the tithes that you receive from the Israelites; and from them you shall give the LORD's offering to the priest Aaron. 29Out of all the gifts to you, you shall set apart every offering due to the LORD; the best of all of them is the part to be consecrated. 30Say also to them: When you have set apart the best of it, then the rest shall be reckoned to the Levites as produce of the threshing floor, and as produce of the wine press. 31You may eat it in any place, you and your households; for it is your payment for your service in the tent of meeting. 32You shall incur no guilt by reason of it, when you have offered the best of it. But you shall not profane the holy gifts of the Israelites, on pain of death.

19 Ceremony of the Red Heifer

The LORD spoke to Moses and Aaron, saying: 2This is a statute of the law that the LORD has commanded: Tell the Israelites to bring you a red heifer without defect, in which there is no blemish and on which no yoke has been laid. 3You shall give it to the priest Eleazar, and it shall be taken outside the camp and slaughtered in his presence. 4The priest Eleazar shall take some of its blood with his finger and sprinkle it seven times towards the front of the tent of meeting. 5Then the heifer shall be burned in his sight; its skin, its flesh, and its blood, with its dung, shall be burned. 6The priest shall take cedarwood, hyssop, and crimson material, and throw them into the fire in which the heifer is burning. 7Then the priest shall wash his clothes and bathe his body in water, and afterwards he may come into the camp; but the priest shall remain unclean until evening. 8The one who burns the heifer*a* shall wash his clothes in water and bathe his body in water; he shall remain unclean until evening. 9Then someone who is clean shall gather up the ashes of the heifer, and deposit them outside the camp in a clean place; and they shall be kept for the congregation of the Israelites for the water for cleansing. It is a purification offering. 10The one who gathers the ashes of the heifer shall wash his clothes and be unclean until evening.

21 To the Levites I have given every tithe in Israel for a possession in return for the service that they perform, the service in the tent of meeting. 22From now on the Israelites shall no longer approach the tent of meeting, or else they will incur guilt and die. 23But the Levites shall perform the service of the tent of meeting, and they shall bear responsibility for their own offenses; it shall be a perpetual statute throughout your generations. But among the Israelites they shall have no allotment, 24because I have given to the Levites as their portion the tithe of the Israelites, which they set apart as an offering to the LORD. Therefore I have said of them that they shall have no allotment among the Israelites.

a Heb *it*

This shall be a perpetual statute for the Israelites and for the alien residing among them. [11]Those who touch the dead body of any human being shall be unclean seven days. [12]They shall purify themselves with the water on the third day and on the seventh day, and so be clean; but if they do not purify themselves on the third day and on the seventh day, they will not become clean. [13]All who touch a corpse, the body of a human being who has died, and do not purify themselves, defile the tabernacle of the LORD; such persons shall be cut off from Israel. Since water for cleansing was not dashed on them, they remain unclean; their uncleanness is still on them.

14 This is the law when someone dies in a tent: everyone who comes into the tent, and everyone who is in the tent, shall be unclean seven days. [15]And every open vessel with no cover fastened on it is unclean. [16]Whoever in the open field touches one who has been killed by a sword, or who has died naturally,[a] or a human bone, or a grave, shall be unclean seven days. [17]For the unclean they shall take some ashes of the burnt purification offering, and running water shall be added in a vessel; [18]then a clean person shall take hyssop, dip it in the water, and sprinkle it on the tent, on all the furnishings, on the persons who were there, and on whoever touched the bone, the slain, the corpse, or the grave. [19]The clean person shall sprinkle the unclean ones on the third day and on the seventh day, thus purifying them on the seventh day. Then they shall wash their clothes and bathe themselves in water, and at evening they shall be clean. [20]Any who are unclean but do not purify themselves, those persons shall be cut off from the assembly, for they have defiled the sanctuary of the LORD. Since the water for cleansing has not been dashed on them, they are unclean.

21 It shall be a perpetual statute for them. The one who sprinkles the water for cleansing shall wash his clothes, and whoever touches the water for cleansing shall be unclean until evening. [22]Whatever the unclean person touches shall be unclean, and anyone who touches it shall be unclean until evening.

20 The Waters of Meribah

The Israelites, the whole congregation, came into the wilderness of Zin in the first month, and the people stayed in Kadesh. Miriam died there, and was buried there.

2 Now there was no water for the congregation; so they gathered together against Moses and against Aaron. [3]The people quarreled with Moses and said, "Would that we had died when our kindred died before the LORD! [4]Why have you brought the assembly of the LORD into this wilderness for us and our livestock to die here? [5]Why have you brought us up out of Egypt, to bring us to this wretched place? It is no place for grain, or figs, or vines, or pomegranates; and there is no water to drink." [6]Then Moses and Aaron went away from the assembly to the entrance of the tent of meeting; they fell on their faces, and the glory of the LORD appeared to them. [7]The LORD spoke to Moses, saying: [8]Take the staff, and assemble the congregation, you and your brother Aaron, and command the rock before their eyes to yield its water. Thus you shall bring water out of the rock for them; thus you shall provide drink for the congregation and their livestock.

9 So Moses took the staff from before the LORD, as he had commanded him. [10]Moses and Aaron gathered the assembly together before the rock, and he said to them, "Listen, you rebels, shall we bring water for you out of this rock?" [11]Then Moses lifted up his hand and struck the rock twice with his staff; water came out abundantly, and the congregation and their livestock drank. [12]But the LORD said to Moses and Aaron, "Because you did not trust in me, to show my holiness before the eyes of the Israelites, therefore you shall not bring this assembly into the land that I have given them." [13]These are the waters of Meribah,[b] where the people of Israel quarreled with the LORD, and by which he showed his holiness.

Passage through Edom Refused

14 Moses sent messengers from Kadesh to the king of Edom, "Thus says your brother Israel: You know all the adversity that has befallen us: [15]how our ancestors went down to Egypt, and we lived in Egypt a long time; and the Egyptians oppressed us and our ancestors; [16]and when we cried to the LORD, he heard our voice, and sent an angel and brought us out of Egypt; and here we are in Kadesh, a town on the edge of your territory. [17]Now let us pass through your land. We will not pass through field or vineyard, or drink water from any well; we will go along the King's Highway, not turning aside to the right hand or to the left until we have passed through your territory."

18 But Edom said to him, "You shall not pass through, or we will come out with the sword against you." [19]The Israelites said to him, "We will stay on the highway; and if we drink of your water, we and our livestock, then we will pay for it. It is only a small matter; just let us pass

_a_ Heb lacks _naturally_   _b_ That is _Quarrel_

Waterfall—© Marvin Jorge Montiel, 22

stroyed them and their towns; so the place was called Hormah.[b]

4 From Mount Hor they set out by the way to the Red Sea,[c] to go around the land of Edom; but the people became impatient on the way. [5]The people spoke against God and against Moses, "Why have you brought us up out of Egypt to die in the wilderness? For there is no food and no water, and we detest this miserable food." [6]Then the LORD sent poisonous[d] serpents among the people, and they bit the people, so that many Israelites died. [7]The people came to Moses and said, "We have sinned by speaking against the LORD and against you; pray to the LORD to take away the serpents from us." So Moses prayed for the people. [8]And the LORD said to Moses, "Make a poisonous[e] serpent, and set it on a pole; and everyone who is bitten shall look at it and live." [9]So Moses made a serpent of bronze, and put it upon a pole; and whenever a serpent bit someone, that person would look at the serpent of bronze and live.

The Journey to Moab

10 The Israelites set out, and camped in Oboth. [11]They set out from Oboth, and camped at Iye-abarim, in the wilderness bordering Moab toward the sunrise. [12]From there they set out, and camped in the Wadi Zered. [13]From there they set out, and camped on the other side of the Arnon, in[f] the wilderness that extends from the boundary of the Amorites; for the Arnon is the boundary of Moab, between Moab and the Amorites. [14]Wherefore it is said in the Book of the Wars of the LORD,

"Waheb in Suphah and the wadis.
The Arnon [15]and the slopes of the wadis
that extend to the seat of Ar,
and lie along the border of Moab."[g]

16 From there they continued to Beer;[h] that is the well of which the LORD said to Moses, "Gather the people together, and I will give them water." [17]Then Israel sang this song:

"Spring up, O well!—Sing to it!—
[18] the well that the leaders sank,
that the nobles of the people dug,
with the scepter, with the staff."

From the wilderness to Mattanah, [19]from Mattanah to Nahaliel, from Nahaliel to Bamoth, [20]and from Bamoth to the valley lying in the region of Moab by the top of Pisgah that overlooks the wasteland.[i]

King Sihon Defeated

21 Then Israel sent messengers to King Sihon of the Amorites, saying, [22]"Let me pass

through on foot." [20]But he said, "You shall not pass through." And Edom came out against them with a large force, heavily armed. [21]Thus Edom refused to give Israel passage through their territory; so Israel turned away from them.

The Death of Aaron

22 They set out from Kadesh, and the Israelites, the whole congregation, came to Mount Hor. [23]Then the LORD said to Moses and Aaron at Mount Hor, on the border of the land of Edom, [24]"Let Aaron be gathered to his people. For he shall not enter the land that I have given to the Israelites, because you rebelled against my command at the waters of Meribah. [25]Take Aaron and his son Eleazar, and bring them up Mount Hor; [26]strip Aaron of his vestments, and put them on his son Eleazar. But Aaron shall be gathered to his people,[a] and shall die there." [27]Moses did as the LORD had commanded; they went up Mount Hor in the sight of the whole congregation. [28]Moses stripped Aaron of his vestments, and put them on his son Eleazar; and Aaron died there on the top of the mountain. Moses and Eleazar came down from the mountain. [29]When all the congregation saw that Aaron had died, all the house of Israel mourned for Aaron thirty days.

21 The Bronze Serpent

When the Canaanite, the king of Arad, who lived in the Negeb, heard that Israel was coming by the way of Atharim, he fought against Israel and took some of them captive. [2]Then Israel made a vow to the LORD and said, "If you will indeed give this people into our hands, then we will utterly destroy their towns." [3]The LORD listened to the voice of Israel, and handed over the Canaanites; and they utterly de-

---

a Heb lacks *to his people* *b* Heb *Destruction* *c* Or *Sea of Reeds* *d* Or *fiery*; Heb *seraphim* *e* Or *fiery*; Heb *seraph* *f* Gk: Heb *which is in*
g Meaning of Heb uncertain *h* That is *Well* *i* Or *Jeshimon*

through your land; we will not turn aside into field or vineyard; we will not drink the water of any well; we will go by the King's Highway until we have passed through your territory." 23But Sihon would not allow Israel to pass through his territory. Sihon gathered all his people together, and went out against Israel to the wilderness; he came to Jahaz, and fought against Israel. 24Israel put him to the sword, and took possession of his land from the Arnon to the Jabbok, as far as to the Ammonites; for the boundary of the Ammonites was strong. 25Israel took all these towns, and Israel settled in all the towns of the Amorites, in Heshbon, and in all its villages. 26For Heshbon was the city of King Sihon of the Amorites, who had fought against the former king of Moab and captured all his land as far as the Arnon. 27Therefore the ballad singers say,

"Come to Heshbon, let it be built;
    let the city of Sihon be established.
28 For fire came out from Heshbon,
    flame from the city of Sihon.
It devoured Ar of Moab,
    and swallowed up*a* the heights of the
        Arnon.
29 Woe to you, O Moab!
    You are undone, O people of Chemosh!
He has made his sons fugitives,
    and his daughters captives,
    to an Amorite king, Sihon.
30 So their posterity perished
    from Heshbon*b* to Dibon,
    and we laid waste until fire spread to
        Medeba."*c*

31 Thus Israel settled in the land of the Amorites. 32Moses sent to spy out Jazer; and they captured its villages, and dispossessed the Amorites who were there.

King Og Defeated

33 Then they turned and went up the road to Bashan; and King Og of Bashan came out against them, he and all his people, to battle at Edrei. 34But the LORD said to Moses, "Do not be afraid of him; for I have given him into your hand, with all his people, and all his land. You shall do to him as you did to King Sihon of the Amorites, who ruled in Heshbon." 35So they killed him, his sons, and all his people, until there was no survivor left; and they took possession of his land.

22 Balak Summons Balaam to Curse Israel
The Israelites set out, and camped in the plains of Moab across the Jordan from Jericho. 2Now

Balak son of Zippor saw all that Israel had done to the Amorites. 3Moab was in great dread of the people, because they were so numerous; Moab was overcome with fear of the people of Israel. 4And Moab said to the elders of Midian, "This horde will now lick up all that is around us, as an ox licks up the grass of the field." Now Balak son of Zippor was king of Moab at that time. 5He sent messengers to Balaam son of Beor at Pethor, which is on the Euphrates, in the land of Amaw,*d* to summon him, saying, "A people has come out of Egypt; they have spread over the face of the earth, and they have settled next to me. 6Come now, curse this people for me, since they are stronger than I; perhaps I shall be able to defeat them and drive them from the land; for I know that whomever you bless is blessed, and whomever you curse is cursed."

7 So the elders of Moab and the elders of Midian departed with the fees for divination in their hand; and they came to Balaam, and gave him Balak's message. 8He said to them, "Stay here tonight, and I will bring back word to you, just as the LORD speaks to me"; so the officials of Moab stayed with Balaam. 9God came to Balaam and said, "Who are these men with you?" 10Balaam said to God, "King Balak son of Zippor of Moab, has sent me this message: 11'A people has come out of Egypt and has spread over the face of the earth; now come, curse them for me; perhaps I shall be able to fight against them and drive them out.' " 12God said to Balaam, "You shall not go with them; you shall not curse the people, for they are blessed." 13So Balaam rose in the morning, and said to the officials of Balak, "Go to your own land, for the LORD has refused to let me go with you." 14So the officials of Moab rose and went to Balak, and said, "Balaam refuses to come with us."

15 Once again Balak sent officials, more numerous and more distinguished than these. 16They came to Balaam and said to him, "Thus says Balak son of Zippor: 'Do not let anything hinder you from coming to me; 17for I will surely do you great honor, and whatever you say to me I will do; come, curse this people for me.' " 18But Balaam replied to the servants of Balak, "Although Balak were to give me his house full of silver and gold, I could not go beyond the command of the LORD my God, to do less or more. 19You remain here, as the others did, so that I may learn what more the LORD may say to me." 20That night God came to Balaam and said to him, "If the men have come

a Gk: Heb *and the lords of* *b* Gk: Heb *we have shot at them; Heshbon has perished* *c* Compare Sam Gk: Meaning of MT uncertain *d* Or *land of his kinsfolk*

to summon you, get up and go with them; but do only what I tell you to do." ²¹So Balaam got up in the morning, saddled his donkey, and went with the officials of Moab.

Balaam, the Donkey, and the Angel

22 God's anger was kindled because he was going, and the angel of the LORD took his stand in the road as his adversary. Now he was riding on the donkey, and his two servants were with him. ²³The donkey saw the angel of the LORD standing in the road, with a drawn sword in his hand; so the donkey turned off the road, and went into the field; and Balaam struck the donkey, to turn it back onto the road. ²⁴Then the angel of the LORD stood in a narrow path between the vineyards, with a wall on either side. ²⁵When the donkey saw the angel of the LORD, it scraped against the wall, and scraped Balaam's foot against the wall; so he struck it again. ²⁶Then the angel of the LORD went ahead, and stood in a narrow place, where there was no way to turn either to the right or to the left. ²⁷When the donkey saw the angel of the LORD, it lay down under Balaam; and Balaam's anger was kindled, and he struck the donkey with his staff. ²⁸Then the LORD opened the mouth of the donkey, and it said to Balaam, "What have I done to you, that you have struck me these three times?" ²⁹Balaam said to the donkey, "Because you have made a fool of me! I wish I had a sword in my hand! I would kill you right now!" ³⁰But the donkey said to Balaam, "Am I not your donkey, which you have ridden all your life to this day? Have I been in the habit of treating you this way?" And he said, "No."

31 Then the LORD opened the eyes of Balaam, and he saw the angel of the LORD standing in the road, with his drawn sword in his hand; and he bowed down, falling on his face. ³²The angel of the LORD said to him, "Why have you struck your donkey these three times? I have come out as an adversary, because your way is perverse*a* before me. ³³The donkey saw me, and turned away from me these three times. If it had not turned away from me, surely just now I would have killed you and let it live." ³⁴Then Balaam said to the angel of the LORD, "I have sinned, for I did not know that you were standing in the road to oppose me. Now therefore, if it is displeasing to you, I will return home." ³⁵The angel of the LORD said to Balaam, "Go with the men; but speak only what I tell you to speak." So Balaam went on with the officials of Balak.

36 When Balak heard that Balaam had come, he went out to meet him at Ir-moab, on the boundary formed by the Arnon, at the farthest point of the boundary. ³⁷Balak said to Balaam, "Did I not send to summon you? Why did you not come to me? Am I not able to honor you?" ³⁸Balaam said to Balak, "I have come to you now, but do I have power to say just anything? The word God puts in my mouth, that is what I must say." ³⁹Then Balaam went with Balak, and they came to Kiriath-huzoth. ⁴⁰Balak sacrificed oxen and sheep, and sent them to Balaam and to the officials who were with him.

Balaam's First Oracle

41 On the next day Balak took Balaam and brought him up to Bamoth-baal; and from there he could see part of the people of Israel.*b*

23 ¹Then Balaam said to Balak, "Build me seven altars here, and prepare seven bulls and seven rams for me." ²Balak did as Balaam had said; and Balak and Balaam offered a bull and a ram on each altar. ³Then Balaam said to Balak, "Stay here beside your burnt offerings while I go aside. Perhaps the LORD will come to meet me. Whatever he shows me I will tell you." And he went to a bare height.

4 Then God met Balaam; and Balaam said to him, "I have arranged the seven altars, and have offered a bull and a ram on each altar." ⁵The LORD put a word in Balaam's mouth, and said, "Return to Balak, and this is what you must say." ⁶So he returned to Balak,*c* who was standing beside his burnt offerings with all the officials of Moab. ⁷Then Balaam*d* uttered his oracle, saying:

"Balak has brought me from Aram,
    the king of Moab from the eastern
        mountains:
'Come, curse Jacob for me;
    Come, denounce Israel!'
⁸ How can I curse whom God has not cursed?
    How can I denounce those whom the
        LORD has not denounced?
⁹ For from the top of the crags I see him,
    from the hills I behold him.
Here is a people living alone,
    and not reckoning itself among the
        nations!
¹⁰ Who can count the dust of Jacob,
    or number the dust-cloud*e* of Israel?
Let me die the death of the upright,
    and let my end be like his!"

11 Then Balak said to Balaam, "What have you done to me? I brought you to curse my enemies, but now you have done nothing but bless them." ¹²He answered, "Must I not take care to say what the LORD puts into my mouth?"

a Meaning of Heb uncertain *b* Heb lacks *of Israel* *c* Heb *him* *d* Heb *he* *e* Or *fourth part*

Balaam's Second Oracle

13 So Balak said to him, "Come with me to another place from which you may see them; you shall see only part of them, and shall not see them all; then curse them for me from there." ¹⁴So he took him to the field of Zophim, to the top of Pisgah. He built seven altars, and offered a bull and a ram on each altar. ¹⁵Balaam said to Balak, "Stand here beside your burnt offerings, while I meet the LORD over there." ¹⁶The LORD met Balaam, put a word into his mouth, and said, "Return to Balak, and this is what you shall say." ¹⁷When he came to him, he was standing beside his burnt offerings with the officials of Moab. Balak said to him, "What has the LORD said?" ¹⁸Then Balaam uttered his oracle, saying:

"Rise, Balak, and hear;
>   listen to me, O son of Zippor:
¹⁹ God is not a human being, that he should
>   lie,
>   or a mortal, that he should change his
>   mind.
Has he promised, and will he not do it?
>   Has he spoken, and will he not fulfill it?
²⁰ See, I received a command to bless;
>   he has blessed, and I cannot revoke it.
²¹ He has not beheld misfortune in Jacob;
>   nor has he seen trouble in Israel.
The LORD their God is with them,
>   acclaimed as a king among them.
²² God, who brings them out of Egypt,
>   is like the horns of a wild ox for them.
²³ Surely there is no enchantment against
>   Jacob,
>   no divination against Israel;
now it shall be said of Jacob and Israel,
>   'See what God has done!'
²⁴ Look, a people rising up like a lioness,
>   and rousing itself like a lion!
It does not lie down until it has eaten the
>   prey
>   and drunk the blood of the slain."

25 Then Balak said to Balaam, "Do not curse them at all, and do not bless them at all." ²⁶But Balaam answered Balak, "Did I not tell you, 'Whatever the LORD says, that is what I must do'?"

27 So Balak said to Balaam, "Come now, I will take you to another place; perhaps it will please God that you may curse them for me from there." ²⁸So Balak took Balaam to the top of Peor, which overlooks the wasteland.ᵃ ²⁹Balaam said to Balak, "Build me seven altars here, and prepare seven bulls and seven rams for me." ³⁰So Balak did as Balaam had said, and offered a bull and a ram on each altar.

a Or overlooks Jeshimon

24 Balaam's Third Oracle

Now Balaam saw that it pleased the LORD to bless Israel, so he did not go, as at other times, to look for omens, but set his face toward the wilderness. ²Balaam looked up and saw Israel camping tribe by tribe. Then the spirit of God came upon him, ³and he uttered his oracle, saying:

Running Back

A running back's job is to take the football through lines of defenders. He stands a pretty good chance of getting pummeled by several big guys, but his job is to keep going. A running back is the model of persistence.

Read **Numbers 24.1–14**. Here a king named Balak has asked a prophet named Balaam to curse the Israelites so they won't overrun Balak's people and land. Instead, Balaam repeats everything that God tells him, which is exactly what Balak doesn't want to hear. Balaam is like a running back, and the ball is God's Word. He's going to get it through no matter who stands in the way, even a powerful king.

God relentlessly gives the messages he wants to give, even if they're not what we want to hear. God will bring about his will in the world—and in our lives—even when we try to get in the way.

Have you ever felt as though God was trying to tell you something? Did you resist his message? Ignore it? Stuff it down? Or did you receive it, believe it, accept it, embrace it?

Go to Mass a little early or stay a bit afterward and spend a few minutes in quiet reflection. Think about how God has pursued you relentlessly with his love, his presence, and his Word. And during Mass, listen to the readings—the Word of God—and ask God to help you stay open to what he wants you to do with your life.

and his seed shall have abundant water,
his king shall be higher than Agag,
and his kingdom shall be exalted.
8 God who brings him out of Egypt,
is like the horns of a wild ox for him;
he shall devour the nations that are his foes
and break their bones.
He shall strike with his arrows.*c*
9 He crouched, he lay down like a lion,
and like a lioness; who will rouse him
up?
Blessed is everyone who blesses you,
and cursed is everyone who curses you."

10 Then Balak's anger was kindled against Balaam, and he struck his hands together. Balak said to Balaam, "I summoned you to curse my enemies, but instead you have blessed them these three times. 11 Now be off with you! Go home! I said, 'I will reward you richly,' but the LORD has denied you any reward." 12 And Balaam said to Balak, "Did I not tell your messengers whom you sent to me, 13 'If Balak should give me his house full of silver and gold, I would not be able to go beyond the word of the LORD, to do either good or bad of my own will; what the LORD says, that is what I will say'? 14 So now, I am going to my people; let me advise you what this people will do to your people in days to come."

Balaam's Fourth Oracle

15 So he uttered his oracle, saying:
"The oracle of Balaam son of Beor,
the oracle of the man whose eye is clear,*a*
16 the oracle of one who hears the words of
God,
and knows the knowledge of the Most
High,*d*
who sees the vision of the Almighty,*b*
who falls down, but with his eyes
uncovered:
17 I see him, but not now;
I behold him, but not near—
a star shall come out of Jacob,
and a scepter shall rise out of Israel;
it shall crush the borderlands*e* of Moab,
and the territory*f* of all the Shethites.
18 Edom will become a possession,
Seir a possession of its enemies,*g*
while Israel does valiantly.
19 One out of Jacob shall rule,
and destroy the survivors of Ir."

20 Then he looked on Amalek, and uttered his oracle, saying:
"First among the nations was Amalek,
but its end is to perish forever."

"The oracle of Balaam son of Beor,
the oracle of the man whose eye is clear,*a*
4 the oracle of one who hears the words of
God,
who sees the vision of the Almighty,*b*
who falls down, but with eyes uncovered:
5 how fair are your tents, O Jacob,
your encampments, O Israel!
6 Like palm groves that stretch far away,
like gardens beside a river,
like aloes that the LORD has planted,
like cedar trees beside the waters.
7 Water shall flow from his buckets,

a Or *closed* or *open* *b* Traditional rendering of Heb *Shaddai* *c* Meaning of Heb uncertain *d* Or *of Elyon* *e* Or *forehead* *f* Some Mss read *skull* *g* Heb *Seir, its enemies, a possession*

21 Then he looked on the Kenite, and uttered his oracle, saying:

"Enduring is your dwelling place,
  and your nest is set in the rock;
22 yet Kain is destined for burning.
  How long shall Asshur take you away
    captive?"

23 Again he uttered his oracle, saying:

"Alas, who shall live when God does this?
24   But ships shall come from Kittim
  and shall afflict Asshur and Eber;
    and he also shall perish forever."

25 Then Balaam got up and went back to his place, and Balak also went his way.

25 Worship of Baal of Peor

While Israel was staying at Shittim, the people began to have sexual relations with the women of Moab. 2These invited the people to the sacrifices of their gods, and the people ate and bowed down to their gods. 3Thus Israel yoked itself to the Baal of Peor, and the LORD's anger was kindled against Israel. 4The LORD said to Moses, "Take all the chiefs of the people, and impale them in the sun before the LORD, in order that the fierce anger of the LORD may turn away from Israel." 5And Moses said to the judges of Israel, "Each of you shall kill any of your people who have yoked themselves to the Baal of Peor."

6 Just then one of the Israelites came and brought a Midianite woman into his family, in the sight of Moses and in the sight of the whole congregation of the Israelites, while they were weeping at the entrance of the tent of meeting. 7When Phinehas son of Eleazar, son of Aaron the priest, saw it, he got up and left the congregation. Taking a spear in his hand, 8he went after the Israelite man into the tent, and pierced the two of them, the Israelite and the woman, through the belly. So the plague was stopped among the people of Israel. 9Nevertheless those that died by the plague were twenty-four thousand.

10 The LORD spoke to Moses, saying: 11"Phinehas son of Eleazar, son of Aaron the priest, has turned back my wrath from the Israelites by manifesting such zeal among them on my behalf that in my jealousy I did not consume the Israelites. 12Therefore say, 'I hereby grant him my covenant of peace. 13It shall be for him and for his descendants after him a covenant of perpetual priesthood, because he was zealous for his God, and made atonement for the Israelites.' "

14 The name of the slain Israelite man, who was killed with the Midianite woman, was Zim-ri son of Salu, head of an ancestral house belonging to the Simeonites. 15The name of the Midianite woman who was killed was Cozbi daughter of Zur, who was the head of a clan, an ancestral house in Midian.

16 The LORD said to Moses, 17"Harass the Midianites, and defeat them; 18for they have harassed you by the trickery with which they deceived you in the affair of Peor, and in the affair of Cozbi, the daughter of a leader of Midian, their sister; she was killed on the day of the plague that resulted from Peor."

26 A Census of the New Generation

After the plague the LORD said to Moses and to Eleazar son of Aaron the priest, 2"Take a census of the whole congregation of the Israelites, from twenty years old and upward, by their ancestral houses, everyone in Israel able to go to war." 3Moses and Eleazar the priest spoke with them in the plains of Moab by the Jordan opposite Jericho, saying, 4"Take a census of the people,*a* from twenty years old and upward," as the LORD commanded Moses.

The Israelites, who came out of the land of Egypt, were:

5 Reuben, the firstborn of Israel. The descendants of Reuben: of Hanoch, the clan of the Hanochites; of Pallu, the clan of the Palluites; 6of Hezron, the clan of the Hezronites; of Carmi, the clan of the Carmites. 7These are the clans of the Reubenites; the number of those enrolled was forty-three thousand seven hundred thirty. 8And the descendants of Pallu: Eliab. 9The descendants of Eliab: Nemuel, Dathan, and Abiram. These are the same Dathan and Abiram, chosen from the congregation, who rebelled against Moses and Aaron in the company of Korah, when they rebelled against the LORD, 10and the earth opened its mouth and swallowed them up along with Korah, when that company died, when the fire devoured two hundred fifty men; and they became a warning. 11Notwithstanding, the sons of Korah did not die.

12 The descendants of Simeon by their clans: of Nemuel, the clan of the Nemuelites; of Jamin, the clan of the Jaminites; of Jachin, the clan of the Jachinites; 13of Zerah, the clan of the Zerahites; of Shaul, the clan of the Shaulites.*b* 14These are the clans of the Simeonites, twenty-two thousand two hundred.

15 The children of Gad by their clans: of Zephon, the clan of the Zephonites; of Haggi, the clan of the Haggites; of Shuni, the clan of the Shunites; 16of Ozni, the clan of the Oznites; of Eri, the clan of the Erites; 17of Arod, the clan

of the Arodites; of Areli, the clan of the Arelites. [18]These are the clans of the Gadites: the number of those enrolled was forty thousand five hundred.

19 The sons of Judah: Er and Onan; Er and Onan died in the land of Canaan. [20]The descendants of Judah by their clans were: of Shelah, the clan of the Shelanites; of Perez, the clan of the Perezites; of Zerah, the clan of the Zerahites. [21]The descendants of Perez were: of Hezron, the clan of the Hezronites; of Hamul, the clan of the Hamulites. [22]These are the clans of Judah: the number of those enrolled was seventy-six thousand five hundred.

23 The descendants of Issachar by their clans: of Tola, the clan of the Tolaites; of Puvah, the clan of the Punites; [24]of Jashub, the clan of the Jashubites; of Shimron, the clan of the Shimronites. [25]These are the clans of Issachar: sixty-four thousand three hundred enrolled.

26 The descendants of Zebulun by their clans: of Sered, the clan of the Seredites; of Elon, the clan of the Elonites; of Jahleel, the clan of the Jahleelites. [27]These are the clans of the Zebulunites; the number of those enrolled was sixty thousand five hundred.

28 The sons of Joseph by their clans: Manasseh and Ephraim. [29]The descendants of Manasseh: of Machir, the clan of the Machirites; and Machir was the father of Gilead; of Gilead, the clan of the Gileadites. [30]These are the descendants of Gilead: of Iezer, the clan of the Iezerites; of Helek, the clan of the Helekites; [31]and of Asriel, the clan of the Asrielites; and of Shechem, the clan of the Shechemites; [32]and of Shemida, the clan of the Shemidaites; and of Hepher, the clan of the Hepherites. [33]Now Zelophehad son of Hepher had no sons, but daughters: and the names of the daughters of Zelophehad were Mahlah, Noah, Hoglah, Milcah, and Tirzah. [34]These are the clans of Manasseh; the number of those enrolled was fifty-two thousand seven hundred.

35 These are the descendants of Ephraim according to their clans: of Shuthelah, the clan of the Shuthelahites; of Becher, the clan of the Becherites; of Tahan, the clan of the Tahanites. [36]And these are the descendants of Shuthelah: of Eran, the clan of the Eranites. [37]These are the clans of the Ephraimites: the number of those enrolled was thirty-two thousand five hundred. These are the descendants of Joseph by their clans.

38 The descendants of Benjamin by their clans: of Bela, the clan of the Belaites; of Ashbel, the clan of the Ashbelites; of Ahiram, the clan of the Ahiramites; [39]of Shephupham, the clan of the Shuphamites; of Hupham, the clan of the Huphamites. [40]And the sons of Bela were Ard and Naaman: of Ard, the clan of the Ardites; of Naaman, the clan of the Naamites. [41]These are the descendants of Benjamin by their clans; the number of those enrolled was forty-five thousand six hundred.

42 These are the descendants of Dan by their clans: of Shuham, the clan of the Shuhamites. These are the clans of Dan by their clans. [43]All the clans of the Shuhamites: sixty-four thousand four hundred enrolled.

44 The descendants of Asher by their families: of Imnah, the clan of the Imnites; of Ishvi, the clan of the Ishvites; of Beriah, the clan of the Beriites. [45]Of the descendants of Beriah: of Heber, the clan of the Heberites; of Malchiel, the clan of the Malchielites. [46]And the name of the daughter of Asher was Serah. [47]These are the clans of the Asherites: the number of those enrolled was fifty-three thousand four hundred.

48 The descendants of Naphtali by their clans: of Jahzeel, the clan of the Jahzeelites; of Guni, the clan of the Gunites; [49]of Jezer, the clan of the Jezerites; of Shillem, the clan of the Shillemites. [50]These are the Naphtalites[a] by their clans: the number of those enrolled was forty-five thousand four hundred.

51 This was the number of the Israelites enrolled: six hundred and one thousand seven hundred thirty.

52 The Lord spoke to Moses, saying: [53]To these the land shall be apportioned for inheritance according to the number of names. [54]To a large tribe you shall give a large inheritance, and to a small tribe you shall give a small inheritance; every tribe shall be given its inheritance according to its enrollment. [55]But the land shall be apportioned by lot; according to the names of their ancestral tribes they shall inherit. [56]Their inheritance shall be apportioned according to lot between the larger and the smaller.

57 This is the enrollment of the Levites by their clans: of Gershon, the clan of the Gershonites; of Kohath, the clan of the Kohathites; of Merari, the clan of the Merarites. [58]These are the clans of Levi: the clan of the Libnites, the clan of the Hebronites, the clan of the Mahlites, the clan of the Mushites, the clan of the Korahites. Now Kohath was the father of Amram. [59]The name of Amram's wife was Jochebed daughter of Levi, who was born to Levi in Egypt; and she bore to Amram: Aaron, Moses, and their sister Miriam. [60]To Aaron were born Nadab, Abihu, Eleazar, and Ithamar.

a Heb *clans of Naphtali*

Road—© Maggie Hubbard, 15

61 But Nadab and Abihu died when they offered unholy fire before the LORD. 62 The number of those enrolled was twenty-three thousand, every male one month old and upward; for they were not enrolled among the Israelites because there was no allotment given to them among the Israelites.

63 These were those enrolled by Moses and Eleazar the priest, who enrolled the Israelites in the plains of Moab by the Jordan opposite Jericho. 64 Among these there was not one of those enrolled by Moses and Aaron the priest, who had enrolled the Israelites in the wilderness of Sinai. 65 For the LORD had said of them, "They shall die in the wilderness." Not one of them was left, except Caleb son of Jephunneh and Joshua son of Nun.

27 The Daughters of Zelophehad

Then the daughters of Zelophehad came forward. Zelophehad was son of Hepher son of Gilead son of Machir son of Manasseh son of Joseph, a member of the Manassite clans. The names of his daughters were: Mahlah, Noah, Hoglah, Milcah, and Tirzah. 2 They stood before Moses, Eleazar the priest, the leaders, and all the congregation, at the entrance of the tent of meeting, and they said, 3 "Our father died in the wilderness; he was not among the company of those who gathered themselves together against the LORD in the company of Korah, but

died for his own sin; and he had no sons. 4 Why should the name of our father be taken away from his clan because he had no son? Give to us a possession among our father's brothers."

5 Moses brought their case before the LORD. 6 And the LORD spoke to Moses, saying: 7 The daughters of Zelophehad are right in what they are saying; you shall indeed let them possess an inheritance among their father's brothers and pass the inheritance of their father on to them. 8 You shall also say to the Israelites, "If a man dies, and has no son, then you shall pass his inheritance on to his daughter. 9 If he has no daughter, then you shall give his inheritance to his brothers. 10 If he has no brothers, then you shall give his inheritance to his father's brothers. 11 And if his father has no brothers, then you shall give his inheritance to the nearest kinsman of his clan, and he shall possess it. It shall be for the Israelites a statute and ordinance, as the LORD commanded Moses."

Joshua Appointed Moses' Successor

12 The LORD said to Moses, "Go up this mountain of the Abarim range, and see the land that I have given to the Israelites. 13 When you have seen it, you also shall be gathered to your people, as your brother Aaron was, 14 because you rebelled against my word in the wilderness of Zin when the congregation quarreled with me.ᵃ You did not show my holiness before

a Heb lacks *with me*

their eyes at the waters." (These are the waters of Meribath-kadesh in the wilderness of Zin.) [15]Moses spoke to the LORD, saying, [16]"Let the LORD, the God of the spirits of all flesh, appoint someone over the congregation [17]who shall go out before them and come in before them, who shall lead them out and bring them in, so that the congregation of the LORD may not be like sheep without a shepherd." [18]So the LORD said to Moses, "Take Joshua son of Nun, a man in whom is the spirit, and lay your hand upon him; [19]have him stand before Eleazar the priest and all the congregation, and commission him in their sight. [20]You shall give him some of your authority, so that all the congregation of the Israelites may obey. [21]But he shall stand before Eleazar the priest, who shall inquire for him by the decision of the Urim before the LORD; at his word they shall go out, and at his word they shall come in, both he and all the Israelites with him, the whole congregation." [22]So Moses did as the LORD commanded him. He took Joshua and had him stand before Eleazar the priest and the whole congregation; [23]he laid his hands on him and commissioned him—as the LORD had directed through Moses.

28 Daily Offerings

The LORD spoke to Moses, saying: [2]Command the Israelites, and say to them: My offering, the food for my offerings by fire, my pleasing odor, you shall take care to offer to me at its appointed time. [3]And you shall say to them, This is the offering by fire that you shall offer to the LORD: two male lambs a year old without blemish, daily, as a regular offering. [4]One lamb you shall offer in the morning, and the other lamb you shall offer at twilight;[a] [5]also one-tenth of an ephah of choice flour for a grain offering, mixed with one-fourth of a hin of beaten oil. [6]It is a regular burnt offering, ordained at Mount Sinai for a pleasing odor, an offering by fire to the LORD. [7]Its drink offering shall be one-fourth of a hin for each lamb; in the sanctuary you shall pour out a drink offering of strong drink to the LORD. [8]The other lamb you shall offer at twilight[a] with a grain offering and a drink offering like the one in the morning;

a Heb *between the two evenings*

you shall offer it as an offering by fire, a pleasing odor to the LORD.

Sabbath Offerings

9 On the sabbath day: two male lambs a year old without blemish, and two-tenths of an ephah of choice flour for a grain offering, mixed with oil, and its drink offering— [10]this is the burnt offering for every sabbath, in addition to the regular burnt offering and its drink offering.

Monthly Offerings

11 At the beginnings of your months you shall offer a burnt offering to the LORD: two young bulls, one ram, seven male lambs a year old without blemish; [12]also three-tenths of an ephah of choice flour for a grain offering, mixed with oil, for each bull; and two-tenths of choice flour for a grain offering, mixed with oil, for the one ram; [13]and one-tenth of choice flour mixed with oil as a grain offering for every lamb—a burnt offering of pleasing odor, an offering by fire to the LORD. [14]Their drink offerings shall be half a hin of wine for a bull, one-third of a hin for a ram, and one-fourth of a hin for a lamb. This is the burnt offering of every month throughout the months of the year. [15]And there shall be one male goat for a sin offering to the LORD; it shall be offered in addition to the regular burnt offering and its drink offering.

Offerings at Passover

16 On the fourteenth day of the first month there shall be a passover offering to the LORD. [17]And on the fifteenth day of this month is a festival; seven days shall unleavened bread be eaten. [18]On the first day there shall be a holy convocation. You shall not work at your occupations. [19]You shall offer an offering by fire, a burnt offering to the LORD: two young bulls, one ram, and seven male lambs a year old; see that they are without blemish. [20]Their grain offering shall be of choice flour mixed with oil: three-tenths of an ephah shall you offer for a bull, and two-tenths for a ram; [21]one-tenth shall you offer for each of the seven lambs; [22]also one male goat for a sin offering, to make atonement for you. [23]You shall offer these in addition to the burnt offering of the morning, which belongs to the regular burnt offering. [24]In the same way you shall offer daily, for seven days, the food of an offering by fire, a pleasing odor to the LORD; it shall be offered in addition to the regular burnt offering and its drink offering. [25]And on the seventh day you

shall have a holy convocation; you shall not work at your occupations.

Offerings at the Festival of Weeks

26 On the day of the first fruits, when you offer a grain offering of new grain to the LORD at your festival of weeks, you shall have a holy convocation; you shall not work at your occupations. 27You shall offer a burnt offering, a pleasing odor to the LORD: two young bulls, one ram, seven male lambs a year old. 28Their grain offering shall be of choice flour mixed with oil, three-tenths of an ephah for each bull, two-tenths for one ram, 29one-tenth for each of the seven lambs; 30with one male goat, to make atonement for you. 31In addition to the regular burnt offering with its grain offering, you shall offer them and their drink offering. They shall be without blemish.

29 Offerings at the Festival of Trumpets

On the first day of the seventh month you shall have a holy convocation; you shall not work at your occupations. It is a day for you to blow the trumpets, 2and you shall offer a burnt offering, a pleasing odor to the LORD: one young bull, one ram, seven male lambs a year old without blemish. 3Their grain offering shall be of choice flour mixed with oil, three-tenths of one ephah for the bull, two-tenths for the ram, 4and one-tenth for each of the seven lambs; 5with one male goat for a sin offering, to make atonement for you. 6These are in addition to the burnt offering of the new moon and its grain offering, and the regular burnt offering and its grain offering, and their drink offerings, according to the ordinance for them, a pleasing odor, an offering by fire to the LORD.

Offerings on the Day of Atonement

7 On the tenth day of this seventh month you shall have a holy convocation, and deny yourselves;a you shall do no work. 8You shall offer a burnt offering to the LORD, a pleasing odor: one young bull, one ram, seven male lambs a year old. They shall be without blemish. 9Their grain offering shall be of choice flour mixed with oil, three-tenths of an ephah for the bull, two-tenths for the one ram, 10one-tenth for each of the seven lambs; 11with one male goat for a sin offering, in addition to the sin offering of atonement, and the regular burnt offering and its grain offering, and their drink offerings.

Offerings at the Festival of Booths

12 On the fifteenth day of the seventh month you shall have a holy convocation; you shall not work at your occupations. You shall celebrate a festival to the LORD seven days. 13You shall offer a burnt offering, an offering by fire, a pleasing odor to the LORD: thirteen young bulls, two rams, fourteen male lambs a year old. They shall be without blemish. 14Their grain offering shall be of choice flour mixed with oil, three-tenths of an ephah for each of the thirteen bulls, two-tenths for each of the two rams, 15and one-tenth for each of the fourteen lambs; 16also one male goat for a sin offering, in addition to the regular burnt offering, its grain offering and its drink offering.

17 On the second day: twelve young bulls, two rams, fourteen male lambs a year old without blemish, 18with the grain offering and the drink offerings for the bulls, for the rams, and for the lambs, as prescribed in accordance with their number; 19also one male goat for a sin offering, in addition to the regular burnt offering and its grain offering, and their drink offerings.

20 On the third day: eleven bulls, two rams, fourteen male lambs a year old without blemish, 21with the grain offering and the drink offerings for the bulls, for the rams, and for the lambs, as prescribed in accordance with their number; 22also one male goat for a sin offering, in addition to the regular burnt offering and its grain offering and its drink offering.

23 On the fourth day: ten bulls, two rams, fourteen male lambs a year old without blemish, 24with the grain offering and the drink offerings for the bulls, for the rams, and for the lambs, as prescribed in accordance with their number; 25also one male goat for a sin offering, in addition to the regular burnt offering, its grain offering and its drink offering.

26 On the fifth day: nine bulls, two rams, fourteen male lambs a year old without blemish, 27with the grain offering and the drink offerings for the bulls, for the rams, and for the lambs, as prescribed in accordance with their number; 28also one male goat for a sin offering, in addition to the regular burnt offering and its grain offering and its drink offering.

29 On the sixth day: eight bulls, two rams, fourteen male lambs a year old without blemish, 30with the grain offering and the drink offerings for the bulls, for the rams, and for the lambs, as prescribed in accordance with their number; 31also one male goat for a sin offering, in addition to the regular burnt offering, its grain offering, and its drink offerings.

32 On the seventh day: seven bulls, two rams, fourteen male lambs a year old without blemish, 33with the grain offering and the

a Or and fast

drink offerings for the bulls, for the rams, and for the lambs, as prescribed in accordance with their number; [34]also one male goat for a sin offering, besides the regular burnt offering, its grain offering, and its drink offering.

35 On the eighth day you shall have a solemn assembly; you shall not work at your occupations. [36]You shall offer a burnt offering, an offering by fire, a pleasing odor to the LORD: one bull, one ram, seven male lambs a year old without blemish, [37]and the grain offering and the drink offerings for the bull, for the ram, and for the lambs, as prescribed in accordance with their number; [38]also one male goat for a sin offering, in addition to the regular burnt offering and its grain offering and its drink offering.

39 These you shall offer to the LORD at your appointed festivals, in addition to your votive offerings and your freewill offerings, as your burnt offerings, your grain offerings, your drink offerings, and your offerings of well-being.

40[a] So Moses told the Israelites everything just as the LORD had commanded Moses.

30 Vows Made by Women

Then Moses said to the heads of the tribes of the Israelites: This is what the LORD has commanded. [2]When a man makes a vow to the LORD, or swears an oath to bind himself by a pledge, he shall not break his word; he shall do according to all that proceeds out of his mouth.

3 When a woman makes a vow to the LORD, or binds herself by a pledge, while within her father's house, in her youth, [4]and her father hears of her vow or her pledge by which she has bound herself, and says nothing to her; then all her vows shall stand, and any pledge by which she has bound herself shall stand. [5]But if her father expresses disapproval to her at the time that he hears of it, no vow of hers, and no pledge by which she has bound herself, shall stand; and the LORD will forgive her, because her father had expressed to her his disapproval.

6 If she marries, while obligated by her vows or any thoughtless utterance of her lips by which she has bound herself, [7]and her husband hears of it and says nothing to her at the time that he hears, then her vows shall stand, and her pledges by which she has bound herself shall stand. [8]But if, at the time that her husband hears of it, he expresses disapproval to her, then he shall nullify the vow by which she was obligated, or the thoughtless utter-

ance of her lips, by which she bound herself; and the LORD will forgive her. [9](But every vow of a widow or of a divorced woman, by which she has bound herself, shall be binding upon her.) [10]And if she made a vow in her husband's house, or bound herself by a pledge with an oath, [11]and her husband heard it and said nothing to her, and did not express disapproval to her, then all her vows shall stand, and any pledge by which she bound herself shall stand. [12]But if her husband nullifies them at the time that he hears them, then whatever proceeds out of her lips concerning her vows, or concerning her pledge of herself, shall not stand. Her husband had nullified them, and the LORD will forgive her. [13]Any vow or any binding oath to deny herself,[b] her husband may allow to stand, or her husband may nullify. [14]But if her husband says nothing to her from day to day,[c] then he validates all her vows, or all her pledges, by which she is obligated; he has validated them, because he said nothing to her at the time that he heard of them. [15]But if he nullifies them some time after he has heard of them, then he shall bear her guilt.

16 These are the statutes that the LORD commanded Moses concerning a husband and his wife, and a father and his daughter while she is still young and in her father's house.

31 War against Midian

The LORD spoke to Moses, saying, [2]"Avenge the Israelites on the Midianites; afterward you shall be gathered to your people." [3]So Moses said to the people, "Arm some of your number for the war, so that they may go against Midian, to execute the LORD's vengeance on Midian. [4]You shall send a thousand from each of the tribes of Israel to the war." [5]So out of the thousands of Israel, a thousand from each tribe were conscripted, twelve thousand armed for battle. [6]Moses sent them to the war, a thousand from each tribe, along with Phinehas son of Eleazar the priest,[d] with the vessels of the sanctuary and the trumpets for sounding the alarm in his hand. [7]They did battle against Midian, as the LORD had commanded Moses, and killed every male. [8]They killed the kings of Midian: Evi, Rekem, Zur, Hur, and Reba, the five kings of Midian, in addition to others who were slain by them; and they also killed Balaam son of Beor with the sword. [9]The Israelites took the women of Midian and their little ones captive; and they took all their cattle, their flocks, and all their goods as booty. [10]All their towns where they had settled, and all their encampments, they burned, [11]but they took all the

---

a Ch 30.1 in Heb   b Or to fast   c Or from that day to the next   d Gk: Heb adds to the war spoil and all the booty, both people and animals. ¹²Then they brought the captives and the booty and the spoil to Moses, to Eleazar the priest, and to the congregation of the Israelites, at the camp on the plains of Moab by the Jordan at Jericho.

Return from the War

13 Moses, Eleazar the priest, and all the leaders of the congregation went to meet them outside the camp. ¹⁴Moses became angry with the officers of the army, the commanders of thousands and the commanders of hundreds, who had come from service in the war. ¹⁵Moses said to them, "Have you allowed all the women to live? ¹⁶These women here, on Balaam's advice, made the Israelites act treacherously against the LORD in the affair of Peor, so that the plague came among the congregation of the LORD. ¹⁷Now therefore, kill every male among the little ones, and kill every woman who has known a man by sleeping with him. ¹⁸But all the young girls who have not known a man by sleeping with him, keep alive for yourselves. ¹⁹Camp outside the camp seven days; whoever of you has killed any person or touched a corpse, purify yourselves and your captives on the third and on the seventh day. ²⁰You shall purify every garment, every article of skin, everything made of goats' hair, and every article of wood."

21 Eleazar the priest said to the troops who had gone to battle: "This is the statute of the law that the LORD has commanded Moses: ²²gold, silver, bronze, iron, tin, and lead— ²³everything that can withstand fire, shall be passed through fire, and it shall be clean. Nevertheless it shall also be purified with the water for purification; and whatever cannot withstand fire, shall be passed through the water. ²⁴You must wash your clothes on the seventh day, and you shall be clean; afterward you may come into the camp."

Disposition of Captives and Booty

25 The LORD spoke to Moses, saying, ²⁶"You and Eleazar the priest and the heads of the ancestral houses of the congregation make an inventory of the booty captured, both human and animal. ²⁷Divide the booty into two parts, between the warriors who went out to battle and all the congregation. ²⁸From the share of the warriors who went out to battle, set aside as tribute for the LORD, one item out of every five hundred, whether persons, oxen, donkeys, sheep, or goats. ²⁹Take it from their half and give it to Eleazar the priest as an offering to the LORD. ³⁰But from the Israelites' half you shall take one out of every fifty, whether per-

sons, oxen, donkeys, sheep, or goats—all the animals—and give them to the Levites who have charge of the tabernacle of the LORD."

31 Then Moses and Eleazar the priest did as the LORD had commanded Moses:

32 The booty remaining from the spoil that the troops had taken totaled six hundred seventy-five thousand sheep, ³³seventy-two thousand oxen, ³⁴sixty-one thousand donkeys, ³⁵and thirty-two thousand persons in all, women who had not known a man by sleeping with him.

36 The half-share, the portion of those who had gone out to war, was in number three hundred thirty-seven thousand five hundred sheep and goats, ³⁷and the LORD's tribute of sheep and goats was six hundred seventy-five. ³⁸The oxen were thirty-six thousand, of which the LORD's tribute was seventy-two. ³⁹The donkeys were thirty thousand five hundred, of which the LORD's tribute was sixty-one. ⁴⁰The persons were sixteen thousand, of which the LORD's tribute was thirty-two persons. ⁴¹Moses gave the tribute, the offering for the LORD, to Eleazar the priest, as the LORD had commanded Moses.

42 As for the Israelites' half, which Moses separated from that of the troops, ⁴³the congregation's half was three hundred thirty-seven thousand five hundred sheep and goats, ⁴⁴thirty-six thousand oxen, ⁴⁵thirty thousand five hundred donkeys, ⁴⁶and sixteen thousand persons. ⁴⁷From the Israelites' half Moses took one of every fifty, both of persons and of animals, and gave them to the Levites who had charge of the tabernacle of the LORD; as the LORD had commanded Moses.

48 Then the officers who were over the thousands of the army, the commanders of

REFUGE

In ninth grade, I permed my hair—big mistake.

Where does a nearsighted, skinny adolescent kid with braces and unusually disastrous hair turn for comfort? My place was my family. Everyone in my family loved me for me—not my looks.

Numbers 35.6 tells about God's plan for people with regrets. Jewish law said if you kill somebody, you die. And often the victim's family was more than ready to carry out the sentence.

"But what happens if it was an accident?" a nervous and sweaty guy anxiously wondered. God established cities of refuge to be places where accidental killers could run for protection until a proper trial could be arranged.

Stuff like that doesn't happen every day, but I often find myself running for cover from some stupid mistake, regret, or embarrassment. Where do you race to when things heat up and you're badly in need of understanding? Friends? Family? God? Is it possible for *you* to be that kind of escape for others?

Who in your family needs a refuge right now—who's hurting, tired, stressed, ignored, alone, frustrated, isolated, overworked, or underappreciated? Determine one tangible way you will be a refuge for that family member today.

GOD IS COMPASSIONATE MY FAMILY

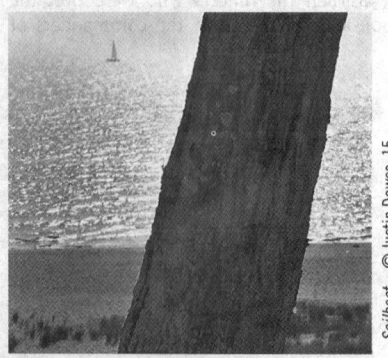

Sailboat—© Justin Dawes, 15

thousands and the commanders of hundreds, approached Moses, ⁴⁹and said to Moses, "Your servants have counted the warriors who are under our command, and not one of us is missing. ⁵⁰And we have brought the Lord's offering, what each of us found, articles of gold, armlets and bracelets, signet rings, earrings, and pendants, to make atonement for ourselves before the Lord." ⁵¹Moses and Eleazar the priest received the gold from them, all in the form of crafted articles. ⁵²And all the gold of the offering that they offered to the Lord, from the commanders of thousands and the commanders of hundreds, was sixteen thousand seven hundred fifty shekels. ⁵³(The troops had all taken plunder for themselves.) ⁵⁴So Moses and Eleazar the priest received the gold from the commanders of thousands and of hundreds, and brought it into the tent of meeting as a memorial for the Israelites before the Lord.

32 Conquest and Division of Transjordan

Now the Reubenites and the Gadites owned a very great number of cattle. When they saw that the land of Jazer and the land of Gilead was a good place for cattle, ²the Gadites and the Reubenites came and spoke to Moses, to Eleazar the priest, and to the leaders of the congregation, saying, ³"Ataroth, Dibon, Jazer, Nimrah, Heshbon, Elealeh, Sebam, Nebo, and Beon— ⁴the land that the Lord subdued before the congregation of Israel—is a land for cattle; and your servants have cattle." ⁵They continued, "If we have found favor in your sight, let this land be given to your servants for a possession; do not make us cross the Jordan."

6 But Moses said to the Gadites and to the Reubenites, "Shall your brothers go to war while you sit here? ⁷Why will you discourage the hearts of the Israelites from going over into the land that the Lord has given them? ⁸Your fathers did this, when I sent them from Kadesh-barnea to see the land. ⁹When they went up to the Wadi Eshcol and saw the land, they discouraged the hearts of the Israelites from going into the land that the Lord had given them. ¹⁰The Lord's anger was kindled on that day and he swore, saying, ¹¹'Surely none of the people who came up out of Egypt, from twenty years old and upward, shall see the land that I swore to give to Abraham, to Isaac, and to Jacob, because they have not unreservedly followed me— ¹²none except Caleb son of Jephunneh the Kenizzite and Joshua son of Nun, for they have unreservedly followed the Lord.' ¹³And the Lord's anger was kindled against Israel, and he made them wander in the wilderness for forty years, until all the generation that had done evil in the sight of the Lord had disappeared. ¹⁴And now you, a brood of sinners, have risen in place of your fathers, to increase the Lord's fierce anger against Israel! ¹⁵If you turn away from following him, he will again abandon them in the wilderness; and you will destroy all this people."

16 Then they came up to him and said, "We will build sheepfolds here for our flocks, and towns for our little ones, ¹⁷but we will take up arms as a vanguard*ᵃ* before the Israelites, until we have brought them to their place. Meanwhile our little ones will stay in the fortified towns because of the inhabitants of the land. ¹⁸We will not return to our homes until all the Israelites have obtained their inheritance. ¹⁹We will not inherit with them on the other side of the Jordan and beyond, because our inheritance has come to us on this side of the Jordan to the east."

20 So Moses said to them, "If you do this—if you take up arms to go before the Lord for the war, ²¹and all those of you who bear arms cross the Jordan before the Lord, until he has driven out his enemies from before him ²²and the land is subdued before the Lord—then after that you may return and be free of obligation to the Lord and to Israel, and this land shall be your possession before the Lord. ²³But if you do not do this, you have sinned against the Lord; and be sure your sin will find you out. ²⁴Build towns for your little ones, and folds for your flocks; but do what you have promised."

25 Then the Gadites and the Reubenites said to Moses, "Your servants will do as my lord commands. ²⁶Our little ones, our wives, our flocks, and all our livestock shall remain there in the towns of Gilead; ²⁷but your servants will cross over, everyone armed for war, to do battle for the Lord, just as my lord orders."

28 So Moses gave command concerning them to Eleazar the priest, to Joshua son of Nun, and to the heads of the ancestral houses of the Israelite tribes. ²⁹And Moses said to them, "If the Gadites and the Reubenites, everyone armed for battle before the Lord, will cross over the Jordan with you and the land shall be subdued before you, then you shall give them the land of Gilead for a possession; ³⁰but if they will not cross over with you armed, they shall have possessions among you in the land of Canaan." ³¹The Gadites and the Reubenites answered, "As the Lord has spoken to your servants, so we will do. ³²We will cross over armed before the Lord into the land of Canaan, but the possession of our inheritance shall remain with us on this side of*ᵇ* the Jordan."

33 Moses gave to them—to the Gadites and to the Reubenites and to the half-tribe of Manasseh son of Joseph—the kingdom of King Sihon of the Amorites and the kingdom of King Og of Bashan, the land and its towns, with the territories of the surrounding towns.

³⁴And the Gadites rebuilt Dibon, Ataroth, Aroer, ³⁵Atroth-shophan, Jazer, Jogbehah, ³⁶Beth-nimrah, and Beth-haran, fortified cities, and folds for sheep. ³⁷And the Reubenites rebuilt Heshbon, Elealeh, Kiriathaim, ³⁸Nebo, and Baal-meon (some names being changed), and Sibmah; and they gave names to the towns that they rebuilt. ³⁹The descendants of Machir son of Manasseh went to Gilead, captured it, and dispossessed the Amorites who were there; ⁴⁰so Moses gave Gilead to Machir son of Manasseh, and he settled there. ⁴¹Jair son of Manasseh went and captured their villages, and renamed them Havvoth-jair.*ᶜ* ⁴²And Nobah went and captured Kenath and its villages, and renamed it Nobah after himself.

33 The Stages of Israel's Journey from Egypt

These are the stages by which the Israelites went out of the land of Egypt in military formation under the leadership of Moses and Aaron. ²Moses wrote down their starting points, stage by stage, by command of the Lord; and these are their stages according to their starting places. ³They set out from Rameses in the first month, on the fifteenth day of the first month; on the day after the passover the Israelites went out boldly in the sight of all the Egyptians, ⁴while the Egyptians were burying all their firstborn, whom the Lord had struck down among them. The Lord executed judgments even against their gods.

5 So the Israelites set out from Rameses, and camped at Succoth. ⁶They set out from Succoth, and camped at Etham, which is on the edge of the wilderness. ⁷They set out from Etham, and turned back to Pi-hahiroth, which faces Baal-zephon; and they camped before Migdol. ⁸They set out from Pi-hahiroth, passed through the sea into the wilderness, went a three days' journey in the wilderness of Etham, and camped at Marah. ⁹They set out from Marah and came to Elim; at Elim there were twelve springs of water and seventy palm trees, and they camped there. ¹⁰They set out from Elim and camped by the Red Sea.*ᵈ* ¹¹They set out from the Red Sea*ᵈ* and camped in the wilderness of Sin. ¹²They set out from the wilderness of Sin and camped at Dophkah. ¹³They set out from Dophkah and camped at Alush. ¹⁴They set out from Alush and camped at Rephidim, where there was no water for the people to drink. ¹⁵They set out from Rephidim and camped in the wilderness of Sinai. ¹⁶They set out from the wilderness of Sinai and camped at Kibroth-hattaavah. ¹⁷They set out

ᵃ Cn: Heb *hurrying* *ᵇ* Heb *beyond* *ᶜ* That is *the villages of Jair* *ᵈ* Or *Sea of Reeds* from Kibroth-hattaavah and camped at Haze-roth. 18They set out from Hazeroth and camped at Rithmah. 19They set out from Rithmah and camped at Rimmon-perez. 20They set out from Rimmon-perez and camped at Libnah. 21They set out from Libnah and camped at Rissah. 22They set out from Rissah and camped at Ke-helathah. 23They set out from Kehelathah and camped at Mount Shepher. 24They set out from Mount Shepher and camped at Hara-dah. 25They set out from Haradah and camped at Makheloth. 26They set out from Makheloth and camped at Tahath. 27They set out from Tahath and camped at Terah. 28They set out from Terah and camped at Mithkah. 29They set out from Mithkah and camped at Hash-monah. 30They set out from Hashmonah and camped at Moseroth. 31They set out from Mo-seroth and camped at Bene-jaakan. 32They set out from Bene-jaakan and camped at Hor-haggidgad. 33They set out from Hor-haggidgad and camped at Jotbathah. 34They set out from Jotbathah and camped at Abronah. 35They set out from Abronah and camped at Ezion-geber. 36They set out from Ezion-geber and camped in the wilderness of Zin (that is, Kadesh). 37They set out from Kadesh and camped at Mount Hor, on the edge of the land of Edom.

38 Aaron the priest went up Mount Hor at the command of the LORD and died there in the fortieth year after the Israelites had come out of the land of Egypt, on the first day of the fifth month. 39Aaron was one hundred twenty-three years old when he died on Mount Hor.

40 The Canaanite, the king of Arad, who lived in the Negeb in the land of Canaan, heard of the coming of the Israelites.

41 They set out from Mount Hor and camped at Zalmonah. 42They set out from Zal-monah and camped at Punon. 43They set out from Punon and camped at Oboth. 44They set out from Oboth and camped at Iye-abarim, in the territory of Moab. 45They set out from Iyim and camped at Dibon-gad. 46They set out from Dibon-gad and camped at Almon-diblathaim. 47They set out from Almon-diblathaim and camped in the mountains of Abarim, before Nebo. 48They set out from the mountains of Abarim and camped in the plains of Moab by the Jordan at Jericho; 49they camped by the Jor-dan from Beth-jeshimoth as far as Abel-shittim in the plains of Moab.

Directions for the Conquest of Canaan

50 In the plains of Moab by the Jordan at Jeri-cho, the LORD spoke to Moses, saying: 51Speak to the Israelites, and say to them: When you cross over the Jordan into the land of Canaan, 52you shall drive out all the inhabitants of the land from before you, destroy all their figured stones, destroy all their cast images, and de-molish all their high places. 53You shall take possession of the land and settle in it, for I have given you the land to possess. 54You shall ap-portion the land by lot according to your clans; to a large one you shall give a large inheritance, and to a small one you shall give a small inheri-tance; the inheritance shall belong to the per-son on whom the lot falls; according to your ancestral tribes you shall inherit. 55But if you do not drive out the inhabitants of the land from before you, then those whom you let re-main shall be as barbs in your eyes and thorns in your sides; they shall trouble you in the land where you are settling. 56And I will do to you as I thought to do to them.

34 The Boundaries of the Land

The LORD spoke to Moses, saying: 2Command the Israelites, and say to them: When you enter the land of Canaan (this is the land that shall fall to you for an inheritance, the land of Ca-naan, defined by its boundaries), 3your south sector shall extend from the wilderness of Zin along the side of Edom. Your southern bound-ary shall begin from the end of the Dead Sea*a* on the east; 4your boundary shall turn south of the ascent of Akrabbim, and cross to Zin, and its outer limit shall be south of Kadesh-barnea; then it shall go on to Hazar-addar, and cross to Azmon; 5the boundary shall turn from Azmon to the Wadi of Egypt, and its termination shall be at the Sea.

6 For the western boundary, you shall have the Great Sea and its*b* coast; this shall be your western boundary.

7 This shall be your northern boundary: from the Great Sea you shall mark out your line to Mount Hor; 8from Mount Hor you shall mark it out to Lebo-hamath, and the outer limit of the boundary shall be at Zedad; 9then the boundary shall extend to Ziphron, and its end shall be at Hazar-enan; this shall be your northern boundary.

10 You shall mark out your eastern bound-ary from Hazar-enan to Shepham; 11and the boundary shall continue down from Shepham to Riblah on the east side of Ain; and the boundary shall go down, and reach the east-ern slope of the sea of Chinnereth; 12and the boundary shall go down to the Jordan, and its end shall be at the Dead Sea.*a* This shall be your land with its boundaries all around.

13 Moses commanded the Israelites, say-

a Heb *Salt Sea*   *b* Syr: Heb lacks *its*

ing: This is the land that you shall inherit by lot, which the LORD has commanded to give to the nine tribes and to the half-tribe; [14]for the tribe of the Reubenites by their ancestral houses and the tribe of the Gadites by their ancestral houses have taken their inheritance, and also the half-tribe of Manasseh; [15]the two tribes and the half-tribe have taken their inheritance beyond the Jordan at Jericho eastward, toward the sunrise.

Tribal Leaders

16 The LORD spoke to Moses, saying: [17]These are the names of the men who shall apportion the land to you for inheritance: the priest Eleazar and Joshua son of Nun. [18]You shall take one leader of every tribe to apportion the land for inheritance. [19]These are the names of the men: Of the tribe of Judah, Caleb son of Jephunneh. [20]Of the tribe of the Simeonites, Shemuel son of Ammihud. [21]Of the tribe of Benjamin, Elidad son of Chislon. [22]Of the tribe of the Danites a leader, Bukki son of Jogli. [23]Of the Josephites: of the tribe of the Manassites a leader, Hanniel son of Ephod, [24]and of the tribe of the Ephraimites a leader, Kemuel son of Shiphtan. [25]Of the tribe of the Zebulunites a leader, Eli-zaphan son of Parnach. [26]Of the tribe of the Issacharites a leader, Paltiel son of Azzan. [27]And of the tribe of the Asherites a leader, Ahihud son of Shelomi. [28]Of the tribe

of the Naphtalites a leader, Pedahel son of Ammihud. [29]These were the ones whom the LORD commanded to apportion the inheritance for the Israelites in the land of Canaan.

35 Cities for the Levites

In the plains of Moab by the Jordan at Jericho, the LORD spoke to Moses, saying: [2]Command the Israelites to give, from the inheritance that they possess, towns for the Levites to live in; you shall also give to the Levites pasture lands surrounding the towns. [3]The towns shall be theirs to live in, and their pasture lands shall be for their cattle, for their livestock, and for all their animals. [4]The pasture lands of the towns, which you shall give to the Levites, shall reach from the wall of the town outward a thousand cubits all around. [5]You shall measure, outside the town, for the east side two thousand cubits, for the south side two thousand cubits, for the west side two thousand cubits, and for the north side two thousand cubits, with the town in the middle; this shall belong to them as pasture land for their towns.

6 The towns that you give to the Levites shall include the six cities of refuge, where you shall permit a slayer to flee, and in addition to them you shall give forty-two towns. [7]The towns that you give to the Levites shall total forty-eight, with their pasture lands. [8]And as for the towns that you shall give from the possession of the

God's Reflection—© Maggie Hubbard, 15

Israelites, from the larger tribes you shall take many, and from the smaller tribes you shall take few; each, in proportion to the inheritance that it obtains, shall give of its towns to the Levites.

Cities of Refuge

9 The LORD spoke to Moses, saying: 10Speak to the Israelites, and say to them: When you cross the Jordan into the land of Canaan, 11then you shall select cities to be cities of refuge for you, so that a slayer who kills a person without intent may flee there. 12The cities shall be for you a refuge from the avenger, so that the slayer may not die until there is a trial before the congregation.

13 The cities that you designate shall be six cities of refuge for you: 14you shall designate three cities beyond the Jordan, and three cities in the land of Canaan, to be cities of refuge. 15These six cities shall serve as refuge for the Israelites, for the resident or transient alien among them, so that anyone who kills a person without intent may flee there.

Concerning Murder and Blood Revenge

16 But anyone who strikes another with an iron object, and death ensues, is a murderer; the murderer shall be put to death. 17Or anyone who strikes another with a stone in hand that could cause death, and death ensues, is a murderer; the murderer shall be put to death. 18Or anyone who strikes another with a weapon of wood in hand that could cause death, and death ensues, is a murderer; the murderer shall be put to death. 19The avenger of blood is the one who shall put the murderer to death; when they meet, the avenger of blood shall execute the sentence. 20Likewise, if someone pushes another from hatred, or hurls something at another, lying in wait, and death ensues, 21or in enmity strikes another with the hand, and death ensues, then the one who struck the blow shall be put to death; that person is a murderer; the avenger of blood shall put the murderer to death, when they meet.

22 But if someone pushes another suddenly without enmity, or hurls any object without lying in wait, 23or, while handling any stone that could cause death, unintentionally*a* drops it on another and death ensues, though they were not enemies, and no harm was intended, 24then the congregation shall judge between the slayer and the avenger of blood, in accordance with these ordinances; 25and the congregation shall rescue the slayer from the avenger of blood. Then the congregation shall send the slayer back to the original city of refuge. The slayer shall live in it until the death of the high priest who was anointed with the holy oil. 26But if the slayer shall at any time go outside the bounds of the original city of refuge, 27and is found by the avenger of blood outside the bounds of the city of refuge, and is killed by the avenger, no bloodguilt shall be incurred. 28For the slayer must remain in the city of refuge until the death of the high priest; but after the death of the high priest the slayer may return home.

29 These things shall be a statute and ordinance for you throughout your generations wherever you live.

30 If anyone kills another, the murderer shall be put to death on the evidence of witnesses; but no one shall be put to death on the testimony of a single witness. 31Moreover you shall accept no ransom for the life of a murderer who is subject to the death penalty; a murderer must be put to death. 32Nor shall you accept ransom for one who has fled to a city of refuge, enabling the fugitive to return to live in the land before the death of the high priest. 33You shall not pollute the land in which you live; for blood pollutes the land, and no expiation can be made for the land, for the blood that is shed in it, except by the blood of the one who shed it. 34You shall not defile the land in which you live, in which I also dwell; for I the LORD dwell among the Israelites.

36 Marriage of Female Heirs

The heads of the ancestral houses of the clans of the descendants of Gilead son of Machir son of Manasseh, of the Josephite clans, came forward and spoke in the presence of Moses and the leaders, the heads of the ancestral houses of the Israelites; 2they said, "The LORD commanded my lord to give the land for inheritance by lot to the Israelites; and my lord was commanded by the LORD to give the inheritance of our brother Zelophehad to his daughters. 3But if they are married into another Israelite tribe, then their inheritance will be

a Heb *without seeing*

taken from the inheritance of our ancestors and added to the inheritance of the tribe into which they marry; so it will be taken away from the allotted portion of our inheritance. ⁴And when the jubilee of the Israelites comes, then their inheritance will be added to the inheritance of the tribe into which they have married; and their inheritance will be taken from the inheritance of our ancestral tribe."

5 Then Moses commanded the Israelites according to the word of the Lᴏʀᴅ, saying, "The descendants of the tribe of Joseph are right in what they are saying. ⁶This is what the Lᴏʀᴅ commands concerning the daughters of Zelophehad, 'Let them marry whom they think best; only it must be into a clan of their father's tribe that they are married, ⁷so that no inheritance of the Israelites shall be transferred from one tribe to another; for all Israelites shall retain the inheritance of their ancestral tribes. ⁸Every daughter who possesses an inheritance in any tribe of the Israelites shall marry one from the clan of her father's tribe, so that all Israelites may continue to possess their ancestral inheritance. ⁹No inheritance shall be transferred from one tribe to another; for each of the tribes of the Israelites shall retain its own inheritance.' "

10 The daughters of Zelophehad did as the Lᴏʀᴅ had commanded Moses. ¹¹Mahlah, Tirzah, Hoglah, Milcah, and Noah, the daughters of Zelophehad, married sons of their father's brothers. ¹²They were married into the clans of the descendants of Manasseh son of Joseph, and their inheritance remained in the tribe of their father's clan.

13 These are the commandments and the ordinances that the Lᴏʀᴅ commanded through Moses to the Israelites in the plains of Moab by the Jordan at Jericho.

TEXT MESSAGE

Today, if a person kills someone, a trial is held to determine guilt or innocence and sentencing. In Old Testament times, such a person could be put to death. To protect people who accidentally killed, Numbers 35.6–28 tells of six cities of refuge where someone could go to be safe from the victim's relatives. But if the killer left the city, the dead person's family could take revenge.

This information has been scanned and is free of all known viruses. Please forward to all your friends.

You Never Know What's Around the Corner—© Jessica Jones, 17

DEUTERONOMY

ENCORE! REPEATING THE LAW ONCE MORE

A Moment to Remember

Standing on a cliff looking ahead to the land they'd longed for, the Israelites must have been anxious to complete the last leg of their journey. But Moses knew that before they took that final step, he needed to remind them of all God had done for them and go back over God's laws that would rule their land. This review essentially served as the constitution for their new country.

At first their constitution reads like a rule book. It sounds like long lists of everything forbidden. The people were to remain pure, offer the appropriate sacrifices, and obey God. At first glance, it'd be easy to suspect that the God behind this book is a cosmic police officer. But at the heart of Deuteronomy is the emphasis that the Israelites would never have made it without God's blessing and protection. They'd received bread in the desert when they were hungry and guidance when they were lost. Their constitution would forever remind them not to seek out other gods. It would never let them forget that the true God of heaven loved them enough to set them free. Jesus didn't forget either. In fact, he referenced Deuteronomy when he was tempted on the mountain (see Matthew 4.10).

> *"It is wonderful that God rained manna on our fathers and they were fed with daily food from heaven. And so it is written: Man ate the bread of angels."*
>
> —St. Ambrose

WHO Developed over time by different people or groups. The writing influence of one person or group that appears here continues through 2 Kings.

WHAT Couched in three sermons or speeches of Moses, Deuteronomy is a book of law. In it, Moses makes clear to the Israelites what they need to do to live as God's people.

WHEN The events in Deuteronomy probably took place toward the end of the 1200s or the 1400s B.C., at the end of the forty years of wandering in the desert. It was probably not composed in this form before 500 B.C.

WHERE The Sinai Peninsula and modern-day Israel and Palestine

PATH OF DISCIPLESHIP

Deuteronomy retells the story of how God provided bread from heaven, called manna, in the desert. The book notes that "one does not live by bread alone, but by every word that comes from the mouth of the LORD" (8.3). When we are afraid that we have nothing to depend on, God is here for us. When we're empty and hungry for purpose and meaning in life, God is the nourishment we need.

Jesus said, "I am the bread of life. Whoever comes to me will never be hungry" (John 6.35). When we have a friendship with Jesus, he is the miraculous manna that sustains us, fills us, strengthens us, feeds us. Jesus meets our most essential need: connection with our Creator. We celebrate that connection each time we come to the table at Mass, where we are nourished in word and sacrament. How else do you connect with the Father, Son, and Holy Spirit?

1 Events at Horeb Recalled

These are the words that Moses spoke to all Israel beyond the Jordan—in the wilderness, on the plain opposite Suph, between Paran and Tophel, Laban, Hazeroth, and Di-zahab. [2](By the way of Mount Seir it takes eleven days to reach Kadesh-barnea from Horeb.) [3]In the fortieth year, on the first day of the eleventh month, Moses spoke to the Israelites just as the Lord had commanded him to speak to them. [4]This was after he had defeated King Sihon of the Amorites, who reigned in Heshbon, and King Og of Bashan, who reigned in Ashtaroth and[g] in Edrei. [5]Beyond the Jordan in the land of Moab, Moses undertook to expound this law as follows:

6 The Lord our God spoke to us at Horeb, saying, "You have stayed long enough at this mountain. [7]Resume your journey, and go into the hill country of the Amorites as well as into the neighboring regions—the Arabah, the hill country, the Shephelah, the Negeb, and the seacoast—the land of the Canaanites and the Lebanon, as far as the great river, the river Euphrates. [8]See, I have set the land before you; go in and take possession of the land that I[b] swore to your ancestors, to Abraham, to Isaac, and to Jacob, to give to them and to their descendants after them."

Appointment of Tribal Leaders

9 At that time I said to you, "I am unable by myself to bear you. [10]The Lord your God has multiplied you, so that today you are as numerous as the stars of heaven. [11]May the Lord, the God of your ancestors, increase you a thousand times more and bless you, as he has promised you! [12]But how can I bear the heavy burden of your disputes all by myself? [13]Choose for each of your tribes individuals who are wise, discerning, and reputable to be your leaders." [14]You answered me, "The plan you have proposed is a good one." [15]So I took the leaders of your tribes, wise and reputable individuals, and installed them as leaders over you, commanders of thousands, commanders of hundreds, commanders of fifties, commanders of tens, and officials, throughout your tribes. [16]I charged your judges at that time: "Give the members of your community a fair hearing, and judge rightly between one person and another, whether citizen or resident alien. [17]You must not be partial in judging: hear out the small and the great alike; you shall not be intimidated by anyone, for the judgment is God's. Any case that is too hard for you, bring to me, and I will hear it." [18]So I charged you at that time with all the things that you should do.

Israel's Refusal to Enter the Land

19 Then, just as the Lord our God had ordered us, we set out from Horeb and went through all that great and terrible wilderness that you saw, on the way to the hill country of the Amorites, until we reached Kadesh-barnea. [20]I said to you, "You have reached the hill country of the Amorites, which the Lord our God is giving us. [21]See, the Lord your God has given the land to you; go up, take possession, as the Lord, the God of your ancestors, has promised you; do not fear or be dismayed."

22 All of you came to me and said, "Let us send men ahead of us to explore the land for us and bring back a report to us regarding the route by which we should go up and the cities we will come to." [23]The plan seemed good to me, and I selected twelve of you, one from each tribe. [24]They set out and went up into the hill country, and when they reached the Valley of Eshcol they spied it out [25]and gathered some of the land's produce, which they brought down to us. They brought back a report to us, and said, "It is a good land that the Lord our God is giving us."

26 But you were unwilling to go up. You rebelled against the command of the Lord your God; [27]you grumbled in your tents and said, "It is because the Lord hates us that he has brought us out of the land of Egypt, to hand us over to the Amorites to destroy us. [28]Where are we headed? Our kindred have made our hearts melt by reporting, 'The people are stronger and taller than we; the cities are large and fortified up to heaven! We actually saw there the offspring of the Anakim!' " [29]I said to you, "Have no dread or fear of them. [30]The Lord your God, who goes before you, is the one who will fight for you, just as he did for you in Egypt before your very eyes, [31]and in the wilderness, where you saw how the Lord your God carried you, just as one carries a child, all the way that you traveled until you reached this place. [32]But in spite of this, you have no trust in the Lord your God, [33]who goes before you on the way to seek out a place for you to camp, in fire by night, and in the cloud by day, to show you the route you should take."

The Penalty for Israel's Rebellion

34 When the Lord heard your words, he was wrathful and swore: [35]"Not one of these—not one of this evil generation—shall see the good land that I swore to give to your ancestors,

---

a Gk Syr Vg Compare Josh 12.4: Heb lacks and   b Sam Gk: MT the Lord

³⁶except Caleb son of Jephunneh. He shall see it, and to him and to his descendants I will give the land on which he set foot, because of his complete fidelity to the LORD." ³⁷Even with me the LORD was angry on your account, saying, "You also shall not enter there. ³⁸Joshua son of Nun, your assistant, shall enter there; encourage him, for he is the one who will secure Israel's possession of it. ³⁹And as for your little ones, who you thought would become booty, your children, who today do not yet know right from wrong, they shall enter there; to them I will give it, and they shall take possession of it. ⁴⁰But as for you, journey back into the wilderness, in the direction of the Red Sea."ᵃ

41 You answered me, "We have sinned against the LORD! We are ready to go up and fight, just as the LORD our God commanded us." So all of you strapped on your battle gear, and thought it easy to go up into the hill country. ⁴²The LORD said to me, "Say to them, 'Do not go up and do not fight, for I am not in the midst of you; otherwise you will be defeated by your enemies.' " ⁴³Although I told you, you would not listen. You rebelled against the command of the LORD and presumptuously went up into the hill country. ⁴⁴The Amorites who lived in that hill country then came out against you and chased you as bees do. They beat you down in Seir as far as Hormah. ⁴⁵When you returned and wept before the LORD, the LORD would neither heed your voice nor pay you any attention.

The Desert Years
46 After you had stayed at Kadesh as many days as you did, ¹we journeyed back into the wilderness, in the direction of the Red Sea,ᵃ as the LORD had told me and skirted Mount Seir for many days. ²Then the LORD said to me: ³"You have been skirting this hill country long enough. Head north, ⁴and charge the people as follows: You are about to pass through the territory of your kindred, the descendants of Esau, who live in Seir. They will be afraid of you, so, be very careful ⁵not to engage in battle with them, for I will not give you even so much as a foot's length of their land, since I have given Mount Seir to Esau as a possession. ⁶You shall purchase food from them for money, so that you may eat; and you shall also buy water from them for money, so that you may drink. ⁷Surely the LORD your God has blessed you in all your undertakings; he knows your going through this great wilderness. These forty years the LORD your God has been with you; you have lacked nothing." ⁸So we passed by our kin, the

ᵃ Or *Sea of Reeds*

REALITY

CHOOSE WITH CONVICTION

You may do a lot of things as a family, including attending Mass, but how you nurture and sustain your relationship with the triune God is entirely your own.

Check out what **Deuteronomy 4.39–40** says.

Just like listening to your parents can have positive results, choosing to follow God's commandments can enrich your life. Think about it. Once you make a choice and take action, the impact you have on others is out of your control. So whether you choose to obey and serve God or you choose another way of living, it's your choice. There's power in how you choose to live. Joshua knew about this when he said:

"Now if you are unwilling to serve the LORD, then choose this day whom you will serve, whether the gods your ancestors served in the region beyond the River or the gods of the Amorites in whose land you are living; but as for me and my household, we will serve the LORD" (Joshua 24.15).

Think about a choice you need to make—one involving action that can affect the people living in your house. Pray about it and then choose with conviction. Take notice of how people are affected by the single choice that you have made. Have you served the Lord in your house? Did you animate others to follow God?

Tree of Life—© Samantha Peterson, 16

descendants of Esau who live in Seir, leaving behind the route of the Arabah, and leaving behind Elath and Ezion-geber.

When we had headed out along the route of the wilderness of Moab, ⁹the LORD said to me: "Do not harass Moab or engage them in battle, for I will not give you any of its land as a possession, since I have given Ar as a possession to the descendants of Lot." ¹⁰(The Emim—a large and numerous people, as tall as the Anakim—had formerly inhabited it. ¹¹Like the Anakim, they are usually reckoned as Rephaim, though the Moabites call them Emim. ¹²Moreover, the Horim had formerly inhabited Seir, but the descendants of Esau dispossessed them, destroying them and settling in their place, as Israel has done in the land that the LORD gave them as a possession.) ¹³"Now then, proceed to cross over the Wadi Zered."

So we crossed over the Wadi Zered. ¹⁴And the length of time we had traveled from Kadesh-barnea until we crossed the Wadi Zered was thirty-eight years, until the entire generation of warriors had perished from the camp, as the LORD had sworn concerning them. ¹⁵Indeed, the LORD's own hand was against them, to root them out from the camp, until all had perished.

¹⁶Just as soon as all the warriors had died off from among the people, ¹⁷the LORD spoke to me, saying, ¹⁸"Today you are going to cross the boundary of Moab at Ar. ¹⁹When you approach the frontier of the Ammonites, do not harass them or engage them in battle, for I will not give the land of the Ammonites to you as a possession, because I have given it to the descendants of Lot." ²⁰(It also is usually reckoned as a land of Rephaim. Rephaim formerly inhabited it, though the Ammonites call them Zamzummim, ²¹a strong and numerous people, as tall as the Anakim. But the LORD destroyed them from before the Ammonites so that they could dispossess them and settle in their place. ²²He did the same for the descendants of Esau, who live in Seir, by destroying the Horim before them so that they could dispossess them and settle in their place even to this day. ²³As for the Avvim, who had lived in settlements in the vicinity of Gaza, the Caphtorim, who came from Caphtor, destroyed them and settled in their place.) ²⁴"Proceed on your journey and cross the Wadi Arnon. See, I have handed over to you King Sihon the Amorite of Heshbon, and his land. Begin to take possession by engaging him in battle. ²⁵This day I will begin to put the dread and fear of you upon the peoples everywhere under heaven; when they hear report of you, they will tremble and be in anguish because of you."

Defeat of King Sihon

26 So I sent messengers from the wilderness of Kedemoth to King Sihon of Heshbon with the following terms of peace: ²⁷"If you let me pass through your land, I will travel only along the road; I will turn aside neither to the right nor to the left. ²⁸You shall sell me food for money, so that I may eat, and supply me water for money, so that I may drink. Only allow me to pass through on foot— ²⁹just as the descendants of Esau who live in Seir have done for me and likewise the Moabites who live in Ar—until I cross the Jordan into the land that the LORD our God is giving us." ³⁰But King Sihon of Heshbon was not willing to let us pass through, for the LORD your God had hardened his spirit and made his heart defiant in order to hand him over to you, as he has now done.

31 The LORD said to me, "See, I have begun to give Sihon and his land over to you. Begin now to take possession of his land." ³²So when Sihon came out against us, he and all his people for battle at Jahaz, ³³the LORD our God gave him over to us; and we struck him down, along with his offspring and all his people. ³⁴At that time we captured all his towns, and in each town we utterly destroyed men, women, and children. We left not a single survivor. ³⁵Only the livestock we kept as spoil for ourselves, as well as the plunder of the towns that we had captured. ³⁶From Aroer on the edge of the Wadi Arnon (including the town that is in the wadi itself) as far as Gilead, there was no citadel too high for us. The LORD our God gave everything to us. ³⁷You did not encroach, however, on the land of the Ammonites, avoiding the whole upper region of the Wadi Jabbok as well as the towns of the hill country, just as[a] the LORD our God had charged.

3 Defeat of King Og

When we headed up the road to Bashan, King Og of Bashan came out against us, he and all his people, for battle at Edrei. ²The LORD said to me, "Do not fear him, for I have handed him over to you, along with his people and his land. Do to him as you did to King Sihon of the Amorites, who reigned in Heshbon." ³So the LORD our God also handed over to us King Og of Bashan and all his people. We struck him down until not a single survivor was left. ⁴At that time we captured all his towns; there was no citadel that we did not take from them—sixty towns, the whole region of Argob, the kingdom of Og in

a Gk Tg: Heb and all

Bashan. [5]All these were fortress towns with high walls, double gates, and bars, besides a great many villages. [6]And we utterly destroyed them, as we had done to King Sihon of Heshbon, in each city utterly destroying men, women, and children. [7]But all the livestock and the plunder of the towns we kept as spoil for ourselves.

8 So at that time we took from the two kings of the Amorites the land beyond the Jordan, from the Wadi Arnon to Mount Hermon [9](the Sidonians call Hermon Sirion, while the Amorites call it Senir), [10]all the towns of the tableland, the whole of Gilead, and all of Bashan, as far as Salecah and Edrei, towns of Og's kingdom in Bashan. [11](Now only King Og of Bashan was left of the remnant of the Rephaim. In fact his bed, an iron bed, can still be seen in Rabbah of the Ammonites. By the common cubit it is nine cubits long and four cubits wide.) [12]As for the land that we took possession of at that time, I gave to the Reubenites and Gadites the territory north of Aroer,[a] that is on the edge of the Wadi Arnon, as well as half the hill country of Gilead with its towns, [13]and I gave to the half-tribe of Manasseh the rest of Gilead and all of Bashan, Og's kingdom. (The whole region of Argob: all that portion of Bashan used to be called a land of Rephaim; [14]Jair the Manassite acquired the whole region of Argob as far as the border of the Geshurites and the Maacathites, and he named them—that is, Bashan—after himself, Havvoth-jair,[b] as it is to this day.) [15]To Machir I gave Gilead. [16]And to the Reubenites and the Gadites I gave the territory from Gilead as far as the Wadi Arnon, with the middle of the wadi as a boundary, and up to the Jabbok, the wadi being boundary of the Ammonites; [17]the Arabah also, with the Jordan and its banks, from Chinnereth down to the sea of the Arabah, the Dead Sea,[c] with the lower slopes of Pisgah on the east.

18 At that time, I charged you as follows: "Although the Lord your God has given you this land to occupy, all your troops shall cross over armed as the vanguard of your Israelite kin. [19]Only your wives, your children, and your livestock—I know that you have much livestock—shall stay behind in the towns that I have given to you. [20]When the Lord gives rest to your kindred, as to you, and they too have occupied the land that the Lord your God is giving them beyond the Jordan, then each of you may return to the property that I have given to you." [21]And I charged Joshua as well at that time, saying: "Your own eyes have seen everything that the Lord your God has done to these two kings; so the Lord will do to all the king-

doms into which you are about to cross. [22]Do not fear them, for it is the Lord your God who fights for you."

Moses Views Canaan from Pisgah

23 At that time, too, I entreated the Lord, saying: [24]"O Lord God, you have only begun to show your servant your greatness and your might; what god in heaven or on earth can perform deeds and mighty acts like yours! [25]Let me cross over to see the good land beyond the Jordan, that good hill country and the Lebanon." [26]But the Lord was angry with me on your account and would not heed me. The Lord said to me, "Enough from you! Never speak to me of this matter again! [27]Go up to the top of Pisgah and look around you to the west, to the north, to the south, and to the east. Look well,

[a] Heb *territory from Aroer*   [b] That is *Settlement of Jair*   [c] Heb *Salt Sea*

Putting on the Mask—© Christy Klink, 18

for you shall not cross over this Jordan. ²⁸But charge Joshua, and encourage and strengthen him, because it is he who shall cross over at the head of this people and who shall secure their possession of the land that you will see." ²⁹So we remained in the valley opposite Beth-peor.

4 Moses Commands Obedience

So now, Israel, give heed to the statutes and ordinances that I am teaching you to observe, so that you may live to enter and occupy the land that the LORD, the God of your ancestors, is giving you. ²You must neither add anything to what I command you nor take away anything from it, but keep the commandments of the LORD your God with which I am charging you. ³You have seen for yourselves what the LORD did with regard to the Baal of Peor—how the LORD your God destroyed from among you everyone who followed the Baal of Peor, ⁴while those of you who held fast to the LORD your God are all alive today.

5 See, just as the LORD my God has charged me, I now teach you statutes and ordinances for you to observe in the land that you are about to enter and occupy. ⁶You must observe them diligently, for this will show your wisdom and discernment to the peoples, who, when they hear all these statutes, will say, "Surely this great nation is a wise and discerning people!" ⁷For what other great nation has a god so near to it as the LORD our God is whenever we call to him? ⁸And what other great nation has statutes and ordinances as just as this entire law that I am setting before you today?

9 But take care and watch yourselves closely, so as neither to forget the things that your eyes have seen nor to let them slip from your mind all the days of your life; make them known to your children and your children's children— ¹⁰how you once stood before the LORD your God at Horeb, when the LORD said to me, "Assemble the people for me, and I will let them hear my words, so that they may learn to fear me as long as they live on the earth, and may teach their children so"; ¹¹you approached and stood at the foot of the mountain while the mountain was blazing up to the very heavens, shrouded in dark clouds. ¹²Then the LORD spoke to you out of the fire. You heard the sound of words but saw no form; there was only a voice. ¹³He declared to you his covenant, which he charged you to observe, that is, the ten commandments;ᵃ and he wrote them on two stone tablets. ¹⁴And the LORD charged me at that time to teach you statutes and ordinances for you to observe in the land that you are about to cross into and occupy.

15 Since you saw no form when the LORD spoke to you at Horeb out of the fire, take care and watch yourselves closely, ¹⁶so that you do not act corruptly by making an idol for yourselves, in the form of any figure—the likeness of male or female, ¹⁷the likeness of any animal that is on the earth, the likeness of any winged bird that flies in the air, ¹⁸the likeness of anything that creeps on the ground, the likeness of any fish that is in the water under the earth. ¹⁹And when you look up to the heavens and see the sun, the moon, and the stars, all the host of heaven, do not be led astray and bow down to them and serve them, things that the LORD your God has allotted to all the peoples everywhere under heaven. ²⁰But the LORD has taken you and brought you out of the iron-smelter, out of Egypt, to become a people of his very own possession, as you are now.

21 The LORD was angry with me because of you, and he vowed that I should not cross the Jordan and that I should not enter the good land that the LORD your God is giving for your possession. ²²For I am going to die in this land without crossing over the Jordan, but you are going to cross over to take possession of that good land. ²³So be careful not to forget the covenant that the LORD your God made with you, and not to make for yourselves an idol in the form of anything that the LORD your God has forbidden you. ²⁴For the LORD your God is a devouring fire, a jealous God.

25 When you have had children and children's children, and become complacent in the land, if you act corruptly by making an idol in the form of anything, thus doing what is evil

ᵃ Heb *the ten words*

in the sight of the LORD your God, and provoking him to anger, 26I call heaven and earth to witness against you today that you will soon utterly perish from the land that you are crossing the Jordan to occupy; you will not live long on it, but will be utterly destroyed. 27The LORD will scatter you among the peoples; only a few of you will be left among the nations where the LORD will lead you. 28There you will serve other gods made by human hands, objects of wood and stone that neither see, nor hear, nor eat, nor smell. 29From there you will seek the LORD your God, and you will find him if you search after him with all your heart and soul. 30In your distress, when all these things have happened to you in time to come, you will return to the LORD your God and heed him. 31Because the LORD your God is a merciful God, he will neither abandon you nor destroy you; he will not forget the covenant with your ancestors that he swore to them.

32 For ask now about former ages, long before your own, ever since the day that God created human beings on the earth; ask from one end of heaven to the other: has anything so great as this ever happened or has its like ever been heard of? 33Has any people ever heard the voice of a god speaking out of a fire, as you have heard, and lived? 34Or has any god ever attempted to go and take a nation for himself from the midst of another nation, by trials, by signs and wonders, by war, by a mighty hand and an outstretched arm, and by terrifying displays of power, as the LORD your God did for you in Egypt before your very eyes? 35To you it was shown so that you would acknowledge that the LORD is God; there is no other besides him. 36From heaven he made you hear his voice to discipline you. On earth he showed you his great fire, while you heard his words coming out of the fire. 37And because he loved your ancestors, he chose their descendants after them. He brought you out of Egypt with his own presence, by his great power, 38driving out before you nations greater and mightier than yourselves, to bring you in, giving you their land for a possession, as it is still today. 39So acknowledge today and take to heart that the LORD is God in heaven above and on the earth beneath; there is no other. 40Keep his statutes and his commandments, which I am commanding you today for your own well-being and that of your descendants after you, so that you may long remain in the land that the LORD your God is giving you for all time.

Cities of Refuge East of the Jordan

41 Then Moses set apart on the east side of the Jordan three cities 42to which a homicide could flee, someone who unintentionally kills another person, the two not having been at enmity before; the homicide could flee to one of these cities and live: 43Bezer in the wilderness on the tableland belonging to the Reubenites, Ramoth in Gilead belonging to the Gadites, and Golan in Bashan belonging to the Manassites.

Transition to the Second Address

44 This is the law that Moses set before the Israelites. 45These are the decrees and the statutes and ordinances that Moses spoke to the Israelites when they had come out of Egypt, 46beyond the Jordan in the valley opposite Beth-peor, in the land of King Sihon of the Amorites, who reigned at Heshbon, whom Moses and the Israelites defeated when they came out of Egypt. 47They occupied his land and the land of King Og of Bashan, the two kings of the Amorites on the eastern side of the Jordan: 48from Aroer, which is on the edge of the Wadi Arnon, as far as Mount Sirion*a* (that is, Hermon), 49together with all the Arabah on the east side of the Jordan as far as the Sea of the Arabah, under the slopes of Pisgah.

5 The Ten Commandments

Moses convened all Israel, and said to them:

Hear, O Israel, the statutes and ordinances that I am addressing to you today; you shall learn them and observe them diligently. 2The LORD our God made a covenant with us at Horeb. 3Not with our ancestors did the LORD make this covenant, but with us, who are all of us here alive today. 4The LORD spoke with you face to face at the mountain, out of the fire. 5(At that time I was standing between the LORD and you to declare to you the words*b* of the LORD; for you were afraid because of the fire and did not go up the mountain.) And he said:

6 I am the LORD your God, who brought you out of the land of Egypt, out of the house of slavery; 7you shall have no other gods before*c* me.

8 You shall not make for yourself an idol, whether in the form of anything that is in heaven above, or that is on the earth beneath, or that is in the water under the earth. 9You shall not bow down to them or worship them; for I the LORD your God am a jealous God, punishing children for the iniquity of parents, to the third and fourth generation of those who reject me, 10but showing steadfast love to the thousandth generation*d* of those who love me and keep my commandments.

a Syr: Heb *Sion* *b* Q Mss Sam Gk Syr Vg Tg: MT *word* *c* Or *besides* *d* Or *to thousands*

11 You shall not make wrongful use of the name of the Lord your God, for the Lord will not acquit anyone who misuses his name.

12 Observe the sabbath day and keep it holy, as the Lord your God commanded you. [13]Six days you shall labor and do all your work. [14]But the seventh day is a sabbath to the Lord your God; you shall not do any work—you, or your son or your daughter, or your male or female slave, or your ox or your donkey, or any of your livestock, or the resident alien in your towns, so that your male and female slave may rest as well as you. [15]Remember that you were a slave in the land of Egypt, and the Lord your God brought you out from there with a mighty hand and an outstretched arm; therefore the Lord your God commanded you to keep the sabbath day.

16 Honor your father and your mother, as the Lord your God commanded you, so that your days may be long and that it may go well with you in the land that the Lord your God is giving you.

17 You shall not murder.[a]

18 Neither shall you commit adultery.

19 Neither shall you steal.

20 Neither shall you bear false witness against your neighbor.

21 Neither shall you covet your neighbor's wife.

Neither shall you desire your neighbor's house, or field, or male or female slave, or ox, or donkey, or anything that belongs to your neighbor.

Moses the Mediator of God's Will

22 These words the Lord spoke with a loud voice to your whole assembly at the mountain, out of the fire, the cloud, and the thick darkness, and he added no more. He wrote them on two stone tablets, and gave them to me. [23]When you heard the voice out of the darkness, while the mountain was burning with fire, you approached me, all the heads of your tribes and your elders; [24]and you said, "Look, the Lord our God has shown us his glory and greatness, and we have heard his voice out of the fire. Today we have seen that God may speak to someone and the person may still live. [25]So now why should we die? For this great fire will consume us; if we hear the voice of the Lord our God any longer, we shall die. [26]For who is there of all flesh that has heard the voice of the living God speaking out of fire, as we have, and remained alive? [27]Go near, you yourself, and hear all that the Lord our God will say. Then

tell us everything that the Lord our God tells you, and we will listen and do it."

28 The Lord heard your words when you spoke to me, and the Lord said to me: "I have heard the words of this people, which they have spoken to you; they are right in all that they have spoken. [29]If only they had such a mind as this, to fear me and to keep all my commandments always, so that it might go well with them and with their children forever! [30]Go say to them, 'Return to your tents.' [31]But you, stand here by me, and I will tell you all the commandments, the statutes and the ordinances, that you shall teach them, so that they may do them in the land that I am giving them to possess." [32]You must therefore be careful to do as the Lord your God has commanded you; you shall not turn to the right or to the left. [33]You must follow exactly the path that the Lord your God has commanded you, so that you may live, and that it may go well with you, and that you may live long in the land that you are to possess.

6 The Great Commandment

Now this is the commandment—the statutes and the ordinances—that the Lord your God charged me to teach you to observe in the land that you are about to cross into and occupy, [2]so that you and your children and your children's children may fear the Lord your God all the days of your life, and keep all his decrees and his commandments that I am commanding you, so that your days may be long. [3]Hear therefore, O Israel, and observe them diligently, so that it may go well with you, and so that you may multiply greatly in a land flowing with milk and honey, as the Lord, the God of your ancestors, has promised you.

4 Hear, O Israel: The Lord is our God, the Lord alone.[b] [5]You shall love the Lord your God with all your heart, and with all your soul, and with all your might. [6]Keep these words that I am commanding you today in your heart. [7]Recite them to your children and talk about them when you are at home and when you are away, when you lie down and when you rise. [8]Bind them as a sign on your hand, fix them as an emblem[c] on your forehead, [9]and write them on the doorposts of your house and on your gates.

Caution against Disobedience

10 When the Lord your God has brought you into the land that he swore to your ancestors, to Abraham, to Isaac, and to Jacob, to give you—a land with fine, large cities that you did not build, [11]houses filled with all sorts of

---

a Or kill *b* Or *The Lord our God is one Lord,* or *The Lord our God, the Lord is one,* or *The Lord is our God, the Lord is one* *c* Or *as a frontlet* goods that you did not fill, hewn cisterns that you did not hew, vineyards and olive groves that you did not plant—and when you have eaten your fill, ¹²take care that you do not forget the LORD, who brought you out of the land of Egypt, out of the house of slavery. ¹³The LORD your God you shall fear; him you shall serve, and by his name alone you shall swear. ¹⁴Do not follow other gods, any of the gods of the peoples who are all around you, ¹⁵because the LORD your God, who is present with you, is a jealous God. The anger of the LORD your God would be kindled against you and he would destroy you from the face of the earth.

16 Do not put the LORD your God to the test, as you tested him at Massah. ¹⁷You must diligently keep the commandments of the LORD your God, and his decrees, and his statutes that he has commanded you. ¹⁸Do what is right and good in the sight of the LORD, so that it may go well with you, and so that you may go in and occupy the good land that the LORD swore to your ancestors to give you, ¹⁹thrusting out all your enemies from before you, as the LORD has promised.

20 When your children ask you in time to come, "What is the meaning of the decrees and the statutes and the ordinances that the LORD our God has commanded you?" ²¹then you shall say to your children, "We were Pharaoh's slaves in Egypt, but the LORD brought us out of Egypt with a mighty hand. ²²The LORD displayed before our eyes great and awesome signs and wonders against Egypt, against Pharaoh and all his household. ²³He brought us out from there in order to bring us in, to give us the land that he promised on oath to our ancestors. ²⁴Then the LORD commanded us to observe all these statutes, to fear the LORD our God, for our lasting good, so as to keep us alive, as is now the case. ²⁵If we diligently observe this entire commandment before the LORD our God, as he has commanded us, we will be in the right."

7 A Chosen People

When the LORD your God brings you into the land that you are about to enter and occupy, and he clears away many nations before you—the Hittites, the Girgashites, the Amorites, the Canaanites, the Perizzites, the Hivites, and the Jebusites, seven nations mightier and more numerous than you— ²and when the LORD your God gives them over to you and you defeat them, then you must utterly destroy them. Make no covenant with them and show them no mercy. ³Do not intermarry with them, giving your daughters to their sons or taking their

daughters for your sons, ⁴for that would turn away your children from following me, to serve other gods. Then the anger of the LORD would be kindled against you, and he would destroy you quickly. ⁵But this is how you must deal with them: break down their altars, smash their pillars, hew down their sacred poles,ᵃ and burn their idols with fire. ⁶For you are a people holy to the LORD your God; the LORD your God has chosen you out of all the peoples on earth to be his people, his treasured possession.

7 It was not because you were more numerous than any other people that the LORD set his heart on you and chose you—for you were the

JESUS SIGHTING

In Jesus' day, rabbis would give one another quizzes in order to study the law. The little question-and-answer tests would measure how well they knew the Scriptures.

There are around 620 different commands in the Old Testament, which makes for quite a long multiple-choice quiz! Jesus once was asked which commandment is the most important (see Matthew 22.36–40). Out of all the possible answers, Jesus selected a command from **Deuteronomy 6.4–9**, the passage known as the Shema (the Hebrew word for "listen" at the start of the passage). Here God commands us to love him above all else. Jesus' answer gives us a glimpse into who he really is—not some score-keeping, rule-obsessed deity ready to whack your hand with a ruler when you misbehave. Rather, Jesus shows us that behind all of these seemingly nitpicky laws in Deuteronomy is a loving God. More important than the details of all these laws is their true purpose: bringing people into a loving relationship with a holy God.

That's good news whenever it feels as though life is a test. At the heart of life's challenges is a God who is not as concerned about outward formalities as he is about our love.

a Heb *Asherim*

fewest of all peoples. [8]It was because the LORD loved you and kept the oath that he swore to your ancestors, that the LORD has brought you out with a mighty hand, and redeemed you from the house of slavery, from the hand of Pharaoh king of Egypt. [9]Know therefore that the LORD your God is God, the faithful God who maintains covenant loyalty with those who love him and keep his commandments, to a thousand generations, [10]and who repays in their own person those who reject him. He does not delay but repays in their own person those who reject him. [11]Therefore, observe diligently the commandment—the statutes and the ordinances—that I am commanding you today.

Blessings for Obedience

[12] If you heed these ordinances, by diligently observing them, the LORD your God will maintain with you the covenant loyalty that he swore to your ancestors; [13]he will love you, bless you, and multiply you; he will bless the fruit of your womb and the fruit of your ground, your grain and your wine and your oil, the increase of your cattle and the issue of your flock, in the land that he swore to your ancestors to give you. [14]You shall be the most blessed of peoples, with neither sterility nor barrenness among you or your livestock. [15]The LORD will turn away from you every illness; all the dread diseases of Egypt that you experienced, he will not inflict on you, but he will lay them on all who hate you. [16]You shall devour all the peoples that the LORD your God is giving over to you, showing them no pity; you shall not serve their gods, for that would be a snare to you.

[17] If you say to yourself, "These nations are more numerous than I; how can I dispossess them?" [18]do not be afraid of them. Just remember what the LORD your God did to Pharaoh and to all Egypt, [19]the great trials that your eyes saw, the signs and wonders, the mighty hand and the outstretched arm by which the LORD your God brought you out. The LORD your God will do the same to all the peoples of whom you are afraid. [20]Moreover, the LORD your God will send the pestilence[a] against them, until even the survivors and the fugitives are destroyed. [21]Have no dread of them, for the LORD your God, who is present with you, is a great and awesome God. [22]The LORD your God will clear away these nations before you little by little; you will not be able to make a quick end of them, otherwise the wild animals would become too numerous for you. [23]But the LORD your God will give them over to you, and throw them into great panic, until they are destroyed.

[24]He will hand their kings over to you and you shall blot out their name from under heaven; no one will be able to stand against you, until you have destroyed them. [25]The images of their gods you shall burn with fire. Do not covet the silver or the gold that is on them and take it for yourself, because you could be ensnared by it; for it is abhorrent to the LORD your God. [26]Do not bring an abhorrent thing into your house, or you will be set apart for destruction like it. You must utterly detest and abhor it, for it is set apart for destruction.

8 A Warning Not to Forget God in Prosperity

This entire commandment that I command you today you must diligently observe, so that you may live and increase, and go in and occupy the land that the LORD promised on oath to your ancestors. [2]Remember the long way that the LORD your God has led you these forty years in the wilderness, in order to humble you, testing you to know what was in your heart, whether or not you would keep his commandments. [3]He humbled you by letting you hunger, then by feeding you with manna, with which neither you nor your ancestors were acquainted, in order to make you understand that one does not live by bread alone, but by every word that comes from the mouth of the LORD.[b] [4]The clothes on your back did not wear out and your feet did not swell these forty years. [5]Know then in your heart that as a parent disciplines a child so the LORD your God disciplines you. [6]Therefore keep the commandments of the LORD your God, by walking in his ways and by fearing him. [7]For the LORD your God is bringing you into a good land, a land with flowing streams, with springs and underground waters welling up in valleys and hills, [8]a land of wheat and barley, of vines and fig trees and pomegranates, a land of olive trees and honey, [9]a land where you may eat bread without scarcity, where you will lack nothing, a land whose stones are iron and from whose hills you may mine copper. [10]You shall eat your fill and bless the LORD your God for the good land that he has given you.

[11] Take care that you do not forget the LORD your God, by failing to keep his commandments, his ordinances, and his statutes, which I am commanding you today. [12]When you have eaten your fill and have built fine houses and live in them, [13]and when your herds and flocks have multiplied, and your silver and gold is multiplied, and all that you have is multiplied, [14]then do not exalt yourself, forgetting the LORD your God, who brought you out of

---

a Or *hornets*: Meaning of Heb uncertain   *b* Or *by anything that the LORD decrees* the land of Egypt, out of the house of slavery, [15]who led you through the great and terrible wilderness, an arid wasteland with poisonous[a] snakes and scorpions. He made water flow for you from flint rock, [16]and fed you in the wilderness with manna that your ancestors did not know, to humble you and to test you, and in the end to do you good. [17]Do not say to yourself, "My power and the might of my own hand have gotten me this wealth." [18]But remember the LORD your God, for it is he who gives you power to get wealth, so that he may confirm his covenant that he swore to your ancestors, as he is doing today. [19]If you do forget the LORD your God and follow other gods to serve and worship them, I solemnly warn you today that you shall surely perish. [20]Like the nations that the LORD is destroying before you, so shall you perish, because you would not obey the voice of the LORD your God.

9 The Consequences of Rebelling against God

Hear, O Israel! You are about to cross the Jordan today, to go in and dispossess nations larger and mightier than you, great cities, fortified to the heavens, [2]a strong and tall people, the offspring of the Anakim, whom you know. You have heard it said of them, "Who can stand up to the Anakim?" [3]Know then today that the LORD your God is the one who crosses over before you as a devouring fire; he will defeat them and subdue them before you, so that you may dispossess and destroy them quickly, as the LORD has promised you.

4 When the LORD your God thrusts them out before you, do not say to yourself, "It is because of my righteousness that the LORD has brought me in to occupy this land"; it is rather because of the wickedness of these nations that the LORD is dispossessing them before you. [5]It is not because of your righteousness or the uprightness of your heart that you are going in to occupy their land; but because of the wickedness of these nations the LORD your God is dispossessing them before you, in order to fulfill the promise that the LORD made on oath to your ancestors, to Abraham, to Isaac, and to Jacob.

6 Know, then, that the LORD your God is not giving you this good land to occupy because of your righteousness; for you are a stubborn people. [7]Remember and do not forget how you provoked the LORD your God to wrath in the wilderness; you have been rebellious against the LORD from the day you came out of the land of Egypt until you came to this place.

a Or fiery; Heb seraph

TRY THIS

DOES IT MATTER?

I was talking to myself while driving home. I do that. That night I was praying/complaining. *My life stinks. What's the deal, God?*

I'd been praying, serving, reading, seeking. Doing the right things. Shouldn't life have been going, well, *better*?

Why had God given me abilities that were going unused? Why was my dating life so painfully uneventful? I'd been seeking God's guidance at every turn. Why was my life turning out this way?

His answer was obvious. Not audible, but discernible.

"Does it matter?"

Huh? I was stunned and silenced.

We serve God because he is God, not because of all he does for us. He is kind through and through, but his generosity is to be cherished, not expected and taken for granted. We aren't entitled to have our life turn out just as we please. Read **Deuteronomy 6.5**—he commands love and respect because of who he is, *not* what he does for us.

For the next week, pray the prayer of St. Ignatius when you wake up in the morning and when you go to bed at night. Ask for God's guidance and then listen to God dwelling within your heart. If you notice something powerful happening in your relationship with God, let us know about it at **Learner.CalltoDiscipleship.com**.

PRAYER OF ST. IGNATIUS OF LOYOLA

Dear Lord,
teach me to be generous;
teach me to serve you as you deserve;
to give, and not to count the cost;
to fight, and not to heed the wounds;
to labor, and not to seek to rest;
to give of myself, and not to ask for reward,
except the reward of knowing that I am doing your will.

GOD IS ONE AND ONLY MY INTERESTS

8 Even at Horeb you provoked the LORD to wrath, and the LORD was so angry with you that he was ready to destroy you. [9]When I went up the mountain to receive the stone tablets, the tablets of the covenant that the LORD made with you, I remained on the mountain forty

heaven; and I will make of you a nation mightier and more numerous than they."

15 So I turned and went down from the mountain, while the mountain was ablaze; the two tablets of the covenant were in my two hands. ¹⁶Then I saw that you had indeed sinned against the LORD your God, by casting for yourselves an image of a calf; you had been quick to turn from the way that the LORD had commanded you. ¹⁷So I took hold of the two tablets and flung them from my two hands, smashing them before your eyes. ¹⁸Then I lay prostrate before the LORD as before, forty days and forty nights; I neither ate bread nor drank water, because of all the sin you had committed, provoking the LORD by doing what was evil in his sight. ¹⁹For I was afraid that the anger that the LORD bore against you was so fierce that he would destroy you. But the LORD listened to me that time also. ²⁰The LORD was so angry with Aaron that he was ready to destroy him, but I interceded also on behalf of Aaron at that same time. ²¹Then I took the sinful thing you had made, the calf, and burned it with fire and crushed it, grinding it thoroughly, until it was reduced to dust; and I threw the dust of it into the stream that runs down the mountain.

22 At Taberah also, and at Massah, and at Kibroth-hattaavah, you provoked the LORD to wrath. ²³And when the LORD sent you from Kadesh-barnea, saying, "Go up and occupy the land that I have given you," you rebelled against the command of the LORD your God, neither trusting him nor obeying him. ²⁴You have been rebellious against the LORD as long as he has^a known you.

25 Throughout the forty days and forty nights that I lay prostrate before the LORD when the LORD intended to destroy you, ²⁶I prayed to the LORD and said, "Lord GOD, do not destroy the people who are your very own possession, whom you redeemed in your greatness, whom you brought out of Egypt with a mighty hand. ²⁷Remember your servants, Abraham, Isaac, and Jacob; pay no attention to the stubbornness of this people, their wickedness and their sin, ²⁸otherwise the land from which you have brought us might say, 'Because the LORD was not able to bring them into the land that he promised them, and because he hated them, he has brought them out to let them die in the wilderness.' ²⁹For they are the people of your very own possession, whom you brought out by your great power and by your outstretched arm."

days and forty nights; I neither ate bread nor drank water. ¹⁰And the LORD gave me the two stone tablets written with the finger of God; on them were all the words that the LORD had spoken to you at the mountain out of the fire on the day of the assembly. ¹¹At the end of forty days and forty nights the LORD gave me the two stone tablets, the tablets of the covenant. ¹²Then the LORD said to me, "Get up, go down quickly from here, for your people whom you have brought from Egypt have acted corruptly. They have been quick to turn from the way that I commanded them; they have cast an image for themselves." ¹³Furthermore the LORD said to me, "I have seen that this people is indeed a stubborn people. ¹⁴Let me alone that I may destroy them and blot out their name from under

a Sam Gk: MT *I have*

10 The Second Pair of Tablets

At that time the LORD said to me, "Carve out two tablets of stone like the former ones, and come up to me on the mountain, and make an ark of wood. ²I will write on the tablets the words that were on the former tablets, which you smashed, and you shall put them in the ark." ³So I made an ark of acacia wood, cut two tablets of stone like the former ones, and went up the mountain with the two tablets in my hand. ⁴Then he wrote on the tablets the same words as before, the ten commandments*a* that the LORD had spoken to you on the mountain out of the fire on the day of the assembly; and the LORD gave them to me. ⁵So I turned and came down from the mountain, and put the tablets in the ark that I had made; and there they are, as the LORD commanded me.

6 (The Israelites journeyed from Beeroth-bene-jaakan*b* to Moserah. There Aaron died, and there he was buried; his son Eleazar succeeded him as priest. ⁷From there they journeyed to Gudgodah, and from Gudgodah to Jotbathah, a land with flowing streams. ⁸At that time the LORD set apart the tribe of Levi to carry the ark of the covenant of the LORD, to stand before the LORD to minister to him, and to bless in his name, to this day. ⁹Therefore Levi has no allotment or inheritance with his kindred; the LORD is his inheritance, as the LORD your God promised him.)

10 I stayed on the mountain forty days and forty nights, as I had done the first time. And once again the LORD listened to me. The LORD was unwilling to destroy you. ¹¹The LORD said to me, "Get up, go on your journey at the head of the people, that they may go in and occupy the land that I swore to their ancestors to give them."

The Essence of the Law

12 So now, O Israel, what does the LORD your God require of you? Only to fear the LORD your God, to walk in all his ways, to love him, to serve the LORD your God with all your heart and with all your soul, ¹³and to keep the commandments of the LORD your God*c* and his decrees that I am commanding you today, for your own well-being. ¹⁴Although heaven and the heaven of heavens belong to the LORD your God, the earth with all that is in it, ¹⁵yet the LORD set his heart in love on your ancestors alone and chose you, their descendants after them, out of all the peoples, as it is today. ¹⁶Circumcise, then, the foreskin of your heart, and do not be stubborn any longer. ¹⁷For the LORD your God is God of gods and Lord of lords, the great God, mighty and awesome, who is not partial· and takes no bribe, ¹⁸who executes justice for the orphan and the widow, and who loves the strangers, providing them food and clothing. ¹⁹You shall also love the stranger, for you were strangers in the land of Egypt. ²⁰You shall fear the LORD your God; him alone you shall worship; to him you shall hold fast, and by his name you shall swear. ²¹He is your praise; he is your God, who has done for you these great and awesome things that your own eyes have seen. ²²Your ancestors went down to Egypt seventy persons; and now the LORD your God has made you as numerous as the stars in heaven.

11 Rewards for Obedience

You shall love the LORD your God, therefore, and keep his charge, his decrees, his ordinances, and his commandments always. ²Remember today that it was not your children (who have not known or seen the discipline of the LORD your God), but it is you who must acknowledge his greatness, his mighty hand and his outstretched arm, ³his signs and his deeds that he did in Egypt to Pharaoh, the king of Egypt, and to all his land; ⁴what he did to the Egyptian army, to their horses and chariots, how he made the water of the Red Sea*d* flow over them as they pursued you, so that the LORD has destroyed them to this day; ⁵what he did to you in the wilderness, until you came to this place; ⁶and what he did to Dathan and Abiram, sons of Eliab son of Reuben, how in the midst of all Israel the earth opened its mouth and swallowed them up, along with their households, their tents, and every living being in their company; ⁷for it is your own eyes that have seen every great deed that the LORD did.

8 Keep, then, this entire commandment that I am commanding you today, so that you may have strength to go in and occupy the land that you are crossing over to occupy, ⁹and so that you may live long in the land that the LORD swore to your ancestors to give them and to their descendants, a land flowing with milk and honey. ¹⁰For the land that you are about to enter to occupy is not like the land of Egypt, from which you have come, where you sow your seed and irrigate by foot like a vegetable garden. ¹¹But the land that you are crossing over to occupy is a land of hills and valleys, watered by rain from the sky, ¹²a land that the LORD your God looks after. The eyes of the LORD your God are always on it, from the beginning of the year to the end of the year.

13 If you will only heed his every command-

---

a Heb *the ten words*   *b* Or *the wells of the Bene-jaakan*   *c* Q Ms Gk Syr: MT lacks *your God*   *d* Or *Sea of Reeds* ment[a] that I am commanding you today—loving the LORD your God, and serving him with all your heart and with all your soul— [14]then he[b] will give the rain for your land in its season, the early rain and the later rain, and you will gather in your grain, your wine, and your oil; [15]and he[b] will give grass in your fields for your livestock, and you will eat your fill. [16]Take care, or you will be seduced into turning away, serving other gods and worshiping them, [17]for then the anger of the LORD will be kindled against you and he will shut up the heavens, so that there will be no rain and the land will yield no fruit; then you will perish quickly off the good land that the LORD is giving you.

18 You shall put these words of mine in your heart and soul, and you shall bind them as a sign on your hand, and fix them as an emblem[c] on your forehead. [19]Teach them to your children, talking about them when you are at home and when you are away, when you lie down and when you rise. [20]Write them on the doorposts of your house and on your gates, [21]so that your days and the days of your children may be multiplied in the land that the LORD swore to your ancestors to give them, as long as the heavens are above the earth.

22 If you will diligently observe this entire commandment that I am commanding you, loving the LORD your God, walking in all his ways, and holding fast to him, [23]then the LORD will drive out all these nations before you, and you will dispossess nations larger and mightier than yourselves. [24]Every place on which you set foot shall be yours; your territory shall extend from the wilderness to the Lebanon and from the River, the river Euphrates, to the Western Sea. [25]No one will be able to stand against you; the LORD your God will put the fear and dread of you on all the land on which you set foot, as he promised you.

26 See, I am setting before you today a blessing and a curse: [27]the blessing, if you obey the commandments of the LORD your God that I am commanding you today; [28]and the curse, if you do not obey the commandments of the LORD your God, but turn from the way that I am commanding you today, to follow other gods that you have not known.

29 When the LORD your God has brought you into the land that you are entering to occupy, you shall set the blessing on Mount Gerizim and the curse on Mount Ebal. [30]As you know, they are beyond the Jordan, some distance to the west, in the land of the Canaanites who live in the Arabah, opposite Gilgal, beside the oak[d] of Moreh.

31 When you cross the Jordan to go in to occupy the land that the LORD your God is giving you, and when you occupy it and live in it, [32]you must diligently observe all the statutes and ordinances that I am setting before you today.

12 Pagan Shrines to Be Destroyed

These are the statutes and ordinances that you must diligently observe in the land that the LORD, the God of your ancestors, has given you to occupy all the days that you live on the earth. 2 You must demolish completely all the places where the nations whom you are about to dispossess served their gods, on the mountain heights, on the hills, and under every leafy tree. [3]Break down their altars, smash their pillars, burn their sacred poles[e] with fire, and hew down the idols of their gods, and thus blot out their name from their places. [4]You shall not worship the LORD your God in such ways. [5]But you shall seek the place that the LORD your God will choose out of all your tribes as his habitation to put his name there. You shall go there, [6]bringing there your burnt offerings and your sacrifices, your tithes and your donations, your votive gifts, your freewill offerings, and the firstlings of your herds and flocks. [7]And you shall eat there in the presence of the LORD your God, you and your households together, rejoicing in all the undertakings in which the LORD your God has blessed you.

8 You shall not act as we are acting here today, all of us according to our own desires, [9]for you have not yet come into the rest and the possession that the LORD your God is giving you. [10]When you cross over the Jordan and live in the land that the LORD your God is allotting to you, and when he gives you rest from your enemies all around so that you live in safety, [11]then you shall bring everything that I command you to the place that the LORD your God will choose as a dwelling for his name: your burnt offerings and your sacrifices, your tithes and your donations, and all your choice votive gifts that you vow to the LORD. [12]And you shall rejoice before the LORD your God, you together with your sons and your daughters, your male and female slaves, and the Levites who reside in your towns (since they have no allotment or inheritance with you).

A Prescribed Place of Worship

13 Take care that you do not offer your burnt offerings at any place you happen to see. [14]But

a Compare Gk: Heb *my commandments* b Sam Gk Vg: MT I c Or *as a frontlet* d Gk Syr: Compare Gen 12.6; Heb *oaks* or *terebinths*
e Heb *Asherim*

Up on a Roof—© Tony Nappa, 17

only at the place that the LORD will choose in one of your tribes—there you shall offer your burnt offerings and there you shall do everything I command you.

15 Yet whenever you desire you may slaughter and eat meat within any of your towns, according to the blessing that the LORD your God has given you; the unclean and the clean may eat of it, as they would of gazelle or deer. 16 The blood, however, you must not eat; you shall pour it out on the ground like water. 17 Nor may you eat within your towns the tithe of your grain, your wine, and your oil, the firstlings of your herds and your flocks, any of your votive gifts that you vow, your freewill offerings, or your donations; 18 these you shall eat in the presence of the LORD your God at the place that the LORD your God will choose, you together with your son and your daughter, your male and female slaves, and the Levites resident in your towns, rejoicing in the presence of the LORD your God in all your undertakings. 19 Take care that you do not neglect the Levite as long as you live in your land.

20 When the LORD your God enlarges your territory, as he has promised you, and you say, "I am going to eat some meat," because you wish to eat meat, you may eat meat whenever you have the desire. 21 If the place where the LORD your God will choose to put his name is too far from you, and you slaughter as I have

commanded you any of your herd or flock that the LORD has given you, then you may eat within your towns whenever you desire. 22 Indeed, just as gazelle or deer is eaten, so you may eat it; the unclean and the clean alike may eat it. 23 Only be sure that you do not eat the blood; for the blood is the life, and you shall not eat the life with the meat. 24 Do not eat it; you shall pour it out on the ground like water. 25 Do not eat it, so that all may go well with you and your children after you, because you do what is right in the sight of the LORD. 26 But the sacred donations that are due from you, and your votive gifts, you shall bring to the place that the LORD will choose. 27 You shall present your burnt offerings, both the meat and the blood, on the altar of the LORD your God; the blood of your other sacrifices shall be poured out beside*a* the altar of the LORD your God, but the meat you may eat.

28 Be careful to obey all these words that I command you today,*b* so that it may go well with you and with your children after you forever, because you will be doing what is good and right in the sight of the LORD your God.

Warning against Idolatry

29 When the LORD your God has cut off before you the nations whom you are about to enter to dispossess them, when you have dispossessed them and live in their land, 30 take care

a Or *on* *b* Gk Sam Syr: MT lacks *today*

done for their gods. They would even burn their sons and their daughters in the fire to their gods. ³²ᵃ You must diligently observe everything that I command you; do not add to it or take anything from it.

13ᵇ If prophets or those who divine by dreams appear among you and promise you omens or portents, ²and the omens or the portents declared by them take place, and they say, "Let us follow other gods" (whom you have not known) "and let us serve them," ³you must not heed the words of those prophets or those who divine by dreams; for the LORD your God is testing you, to know whether you indeed love the LORD your God with all your heart and soul. ⁴The LORD your God you shall follow, him alone you shall fear, his commandments you shall keep, his voice you shall obey, him you shall serve, and to him you shall hold fast. ⁵But those prophets or those who divine by dreams shall be put to death for having spoken treason against the LORD your God—who brought you out of the land of Egypt and redeemed you from the house of slavery—to turn you from the way in which the LORD your God commanded you to walk. So you shall purge the evil from your midst.

6 If anyone secretly entices you—even if it is your brother, your father's son orᶜ your mother's son, or your own son or daughter, or the wife you embrace, or your most intimate friend—saying, "Let us go worship other gods," whom neither you nor your ancestors have known, ⁷any of the gods of the peoples that are around you, whether near you or far away from you, from one end of the earth to the other, ⁸you must not yield to or heed any such persons. Show them no pity or compassion and do not shield them. ⁹But you shall surely kill them; your own hand shall be first against them to execute them, and afterwards the hand of all the people. ¹⁰Stone them to death for trying to turn you away from the LORD your God, who brought you out of the land of Egypt, out of the house of slavery. ¹¹Then all Israel shall hear and be afraid, and never again do any such wickedness.

12 If you hear it said about one of the towns that the LORD your God is giving you to live in, ¹³that scoundrels from among you have gone out and led the inhabitants of the town astray, saying, "Let us go and worship other gods," whom you have not known, ¹⁴then you shall inquire and make a thorough investigation. If the charge is established that such an abhorrent thing has been done among you, ¹⁵you shall put the inhabitants of that town to the

that you are not snared into imitating them, after they have been destroyed before you: do not inquire concerning their gods, saying, "How did these nations worship their gods? I also want to do the same." ³¹You must not do the same for the LORD your God, because every abhorrent thing that the LORD hates they have

ᵃ Ch 13.1 in Heb ᵇ Ch 13.2 in Heb ᶜ Sam Gk Compare Tg: MT lacks *your father's son or* sword, utterly destroying it and everything in it—even putting its livestock to the sword. [16]All of its spoil you shall gather into its public square; then burn the town and all its spoil with fire, as a whole burnt offering to the Lord your God. It shall remain a perpetual ruin, never to be rebuilt. [17]Do not let anything devoted to destruction stick to your hand, so that the Lord may turn from his fierce anger and show you compassion, and in his compassion multiply you, as he swore to your ancestors, [18]if you obey the voice of the Lord your God by keeping all his commandments that I am commanding you today, doing what is right in the sight of the Lord your God.

14 Pagan Practices Forbidden

You are children of the Lord your God. You must not lacerate yourselves or shave your forelocks for the dead. [2]For you are a people holy to the Lord your God; it is you the Lord has chosen out of all the peoples on earth to be his people, his treasured possession.

Clean and Unclean Foods

3 You shall not eat any abhorrent thing. [4]These are the animals you may eat: the ox, the sheep, the goat, [5]the deer, the gazelle, the roebuck, the wild goat, the ibex, the antelope, and the mountain-sheep. [6]Any animal that divides the hoof and has the hoof cleft in two, and chews the cud, among the animals, you may eat. [7]Yet of those that chew the cud or have the hoof cleft you shall not eat these: the camel, the hare, and the rock badger, because they chew the cud but do not divide the hoof; they are unclean for you. [8]And the pig, because it divides the hoof but does not chew the cud, is unclean for you. You shall not eat their meat, and you shall not touch their carcasses.

9 Of all that live in water you may eat these: whatever has fins and scales you may eat. [10]And whatever does not have fins and scales you shall not eat; it is unclean for you.

11 You may eat any clean birds. [12]But these are the ones that you shall not eat: the eagle, the vulture, the osprey, [13]the buzzard, the kite of any kind; [14]every raven of any kind; [15]the ostrich, the nighthawk, the sea gull, the hawk of any kind; [16]the little owl and the great owl, the water hen [17]and the desert owl,[a] the carrion vulture and the cormorant, [18]the stork, the heron of any kind; the hoopoe and the bat.[b] [19]And all winged insects are unclean for you; they shall not be eaten. [20]You may eat any clean winged creature.

21 You shall not eat anything that dies of itself; you may give it to aliens residing in your towns for them to eat, or you may sell it to a foreigner. For you are a people holy to the Lord your God.

You shall not boil a kid in its mother's milk.

Regulations concerning Tithes

22 Set apart a tithe of all the yield of your seed that is brought in yearly from the field. [23]In the presence of the Lord your God, in the place that he will choose as a dwelling for his name, you shall eat the tithe of your grain, your wine, and your oil, as well as the firstlings of your herd and flock, so that you may learn to fear the Lord your God always. [24]But if, when the Lord your God has blessed you, the distance is so great that you are unable to transport it, because the place where the Lord your God will choose to set his name is too far away from you, [25]then you may turn it into money. With the money secure in hand, go to the place that the Lord your God will choose; [26]spend the money for whatever you wish—oxen, sheep, wine, strong drink, or whatever you desire. And you shall eat there in the presence of the Lord your God, you and your household rejoicing together. [27]As for the Levites resident in your towns, do not neglect them, because they have no allotment or inheritance with you.

28 Every third year you shall bring out the full tithe of your produce for that year, and store it within your towns; [29]the Levites, because they have no allotment or inheritance with you, as well as the resident aliens, the orphans, and the widows in your towns, may come and eat their fill so that the Lord your God may bless you in all the work that you undertake.

15 Laws concerning the Sabbatical Year

Every seventh year you shall grant a remission of debts. [2]And this is the manner of the remission: every creditor shall remit the claim that is held against a neighbor, not exacting it of a neighbor who is a member of the community, because the Lord's remission has been proclaimed. [3]Of a foreigner you may exact it, but you must remit your claim on whatever any member of your community owes you. [4]There will, however, be no one in need among you, because the Lord is sure to bless you in the land that the Lord your God is giving you as a possession to occupy, [5]if only you will obey the Lord your God by diligently observing this entire commandment that I command you today. [6]When the Lord your God has blessed you, as he promised you, you will lend to many na-

---

a Or *pelican* b Identification of several of the birds in verses 12–18 is uncertain tions, but you will not borrow; you will rule over many nations, but they will not rule over you.

7 If there is among you anyone in need, a member of your community in any of your towns within the land that the LORD your God is giving you, do not be hard-hearted or tight-fisted toward your needy neighbor. 8You should rather open your hand, willingly lending enough to meet the need, whatever it may be. 9Be careful that you do not entertain a mean thought, thinking, "The seventh year, the year of remission, is near," and therefore view your needy neighbor with hostility and give nothing; your neighbor might cry to the LORD against you, and you would incur guilt. 10Give liberally and be ungrudging when you do so, for on this account the LORD your God will bless you in all your work and in all that you undertake. 11Since there will never cease to be some in need on the earth, I therefore command you, "Open your hand to the poor and needy neighbor in your land."

12 If a member of your community, whether a Hebrew man or a Hebrew woman, is sold*a* to you and works for you six years, in the seventh year you shall set that person free. 13And when you send a male slave*b* out from you a free person, you shall not send him out empty-handed. 14Provide liberally out of your flock, your threshing floor, and your wine press, thus giving to him some of the bounty with which the LORD your God has blessed you. 15Remember that you were a slave in the land of Egypt, and the LORD your God redeemed you; for this reason I lay this command upon you today. 16But if he says to you, "I will not go out from you," because he loves you and your household, since he is well off with you, 17then you shall take an awl and thrust it through his earlobe into the door, and he shall be your slave*c* forever.

You shall do the same with regard to your female slave.*d*

18 Do not consider it a hardship when you send them out from you free persons, because for six years they have given you services worth the wages of hired laborers; and the LORD your God will bless you in all that you do.

The Firstborn of Livestock

19 Every firstling male born of your herd and flock you shall consecrate to the LORD your God; you shall not do work with your firstling ox nor shear the firstling of your flock. 20You shall eat it, you together with your household, in the presence of the LORD your God year by year at the place that the LORD will choose. 21But if it has any defect—any serious defect, such as lameness or blindness—you shall not sacrifice it to the LORD your God; 22within your towns you may eat it, the unclean and the clean alike, as you would a gazelle or deer. 23Its blood, however, you must not eat; you shall pour it out on the ground like water.

16 The Passover Reviewed

Observe the month*e* of Abib by keeping the passover to the LORD your God, for in the month of Abib the LORD your God brought you out of Egypt by night. 2You shall offer the passover sacrifice to the LORD your God, from the flock and the herd, at the place that the LORD will choose as a dwelling for his name. 3You must not eat with it anything leavened. For seven days you shall eat unleavened bread with it—the bread of affliction—because you came out of the land of Egypt in great haste, so that all the days of your life you may remember the day of your departure from the land of Egypt. 4No leaven shall be seen with you in all your territory for seven days; and none of the meat of what you slaughter on the evening of the first day shall remain until morning. 5You are not permitted to offer the passover sacrifice within any of your towns that the LORD your God is giving you. 6But at the place that the LORD your God will choose as a dwelling for his name, only there shall you offer the passover sacrifice, in the evening at sunset, the time of day when you departed from Egypt. 7You shall cook it and eat it at the place that the LORD your God will choose; the next morning you may go back to your tents. 8For six days you shall continue to eat unleavened bread, and on the seventh day there shall be a solemn assembly for the LORD your God, when you shall do no work.

The Festival of Weeks Reviewed

9 You shall count seven weeks; begin to count the seven weeks from the time the sickle is first put to the standing grain. 10Then you shall keep the festival of weeks to the LORD your God, contributing a freewill offering in proportion to the blessing that you have received from the LORD your God. 11Rejoice before the LORD your God—you and your sons and your daughters, your male and female slaves, the Levites resident in your towns, as well as the strangers, the orphans, and the widows who are among you—at the place that the LORD your God will choose as a dwelling for his name. 12Remember that you were a slave in Egypt, and diligently observe these statutes.

---

a Or *sells himself or herself* *b* Heb *him* *c* Or *bondman* *d* Or *bondwoman* *e* Or *new moon*

The Festival of Booths Reviewed

13 You shall keep the festival of booths[a] for seven days, when you have gathered in the produce from your threshing floor and your wine press. [14]Rejoice during your festival, you and your sons and your daughters, your male and female slaves, as well as the Levites, the strangers, the orphans, and the widows resident in your towns. [15]Seven days you shall keep the festival to the LORD your God at the place that the LORD will choose; for the LORD your God will bless you in all your produce and in all your undertakings, and you shall surely celebrate.

16 Three times a year all your males shall appear before the LORD your God at the place that he will choose: at the festival of unleavened bread, at the festival of weeks, and at the festival of booths.[a] They shall not appear before the LORD empty-handed; [17]all shall give as they are able, according to the blessing of the LORD your God that he has given you.

Municipal Judges and Officers

18 You shall appoint judges and officials throughout your tribes, in all your towns that the LORD your God is giving you, and they shall render just decisions for the people. [19]You must not distort justice; you must not show partiality; and you must not accept bribes, for a bribe blinds the eyes of the wise and subverts the cause of those who are in the right. [20]Justice, and only justice, you shall pursue, so that you may live and occupy the land that the LORD your God is giving you.

Forbidden Forms of Worship

21 You shall not plant any tree as a sacred pole[b] beside the altar that you make for the LORD your God; [22]nor shall you set up a stone pillar—things that the LORD your God hates.

17 You must not sacrifice to the LORD your God an ox or a sheep that has a defect, anything seriously wrong; for that is abhorrent to the LORD your God.

2 If there is found among you, in one of your towns that the LORD your God is giving you, a man or woman who does what is evil in the sight of the LORD your God, and transgresses his covenant [3]by going to serve other gods and worshiping them—whether the sun or the moon or any of the host of heaven, which I have forbidden— [4]and if it is reported to you or you hear of it, and you make a thorough inquiry, and the charge is proved true that such an abhorrent thing has occurred in Israel, [5]then you shall bring out to your gates that

The World Through My Sister's Eyeglasses
—© Rebekah Furey, 16

man or that woman who has committed this crime and you shall stone the man or woman to death. [6]On the evidence of two or three witnesses the death sentence shall be executed; a person must not be put to death on the evidence of only one witness. [7]The hands of the witnesses shall be the first raised against the person to execute the death penalty, and afterward the hands of all the people. So you shall purge the evil from your midst.

Legal Decisions by Priests and Judges

8 If a judicial decision is too difficult for you to make between one kind of bloodshed and another, one kind of legal right and another, or one kind of assault and another—any such matters of dispute in your towns—then you shall immediately go up to the place that the LORD your God will choose, [9]where you shall consult with the levitical priests and the judge who is in office in those days; they shall announce to you the decision in the case. [10]Carry out exactly the decision that they announce to you from the place that the LORD will choose, diligently observing everything they instruct you. [11]You must carry out fully the law that they interpret for you or the ruling that they announce to you; do not turn aside from the decision that they announce to you, either to the right or to the left. [12]As for anyone who presumes to disobey the priest appointed to minister there to the LORD your God, or the judge, that person shall die. So you shall purge the evil from Israel. [13]All the people will hear and be afraid, and will not act presumptuously again.

Limitations of Royal Authority

14 When you have come into the land that

---

a Or *tabernacles*; Heb *succoth* b Heb *Asherah*

the LORD your God is giving you, and have taken possession of it and settled in it, and you say, "I will set a king over me, like all the nations that are around me," [15]you may indeed set over you a king whom the LORD your God will choose. One of your own community you may set as king over you; you are not permitted to put a foreigner over you, who is not of your own community. [16]Even so, he must not acquire many horses for himself, or return the people to Egypt in order to acquire more horses, since the LORD has said to you, "You must never return that way again." [17]And he must not acquire many wives for himself, or else his heart will turn away; also silver and gold he must not acquire in great quantity for himself. [18]When he has taken the throne of his kingdom, he shall have a copy of this law written for him in the presence of the levitical priests. [19]It shall remain with him and he shall read in it all the days of his life, so that he may learn to fear the LORD his God, diligently observing all the words of this law and these statutes, [20]neither exalting himself above other members of the community nor turning aside from the commandment, either to the right or to the left, so that he and his descendants may reign long over his kingdom in Israel.

18 Privileges of Priests and Levites

The levitical priests, the whole tribe of Levi, shall have no allotment or inheritance within Israel. They may eat the sacrifices that are the LORD's portion[a] [2]but they shall have no inheritance among the other members of the community; the LORD is their inheritance, as he promised them.

3 This shall be the priests' due from the people, from those offering a sacrifice, whether an ox or a sheep: they shall give to the priest the shoulder, the two jowls, and the stomach. [4]The first fruits of your grain, your wine, and your oil, as well as the first of the fleece of your sheep, you shall give him. [5]For the LORD your God has chosen Levi[b] out of all your tribes, to stand and minister in the name of the LORD, him and his sons for all time.

6 If a Levite leaves any of your towns, from wherever he has been residing in Israel, and comes to the place that the LORD will choose (and he may come whenever he wishes), [7]then he may minister in the name of the LORD his God, like all his fellow-Levites who stand to minister there before the LORD. [8]They shall have equal portions to eat, even though they have income from the sale of family possessions.[a]

Child-Sacrifice, Divination, and Magic Prohibited

9 When you come into the land that the LORD your God is giving you, you must not learn to imitate the abhorrent practices of those nations. [10]No one shall be found among you who makes a son or daughter pass through fire, or who practices divination, or is a soothsayer, or an augur, or a sorcerer, [11]or one who casts spells, or who consults ghosts or spirits, or who seeks oracles from the dead. [12]For whoever does these things is abhorrent to the LORD; it is because of such abhorrent practices that the LORD your God is driving them out before you. [13]You must remain completely loyal to the LORD your God. [14]Although these nations that you are about to dispossess do give heed to soothsayers and diviners, as for you, the LORD your God does not permit you to do so.

A New Prophet Like Moses

15 The LORD your God will raise up for you a prophet[c] like me from among your own people; you shall heed such a prophet.[d] [16]This is what you requested of the LORD your God at Horeb on the day of the assembly when you said: "If I hear the voice of the LORD my God any more, or ever again see this great fire, I will die." [17]Then the LORD replied to me: "They are right in what they have said. [18]I will raise up for them a prophet[c] like you from among their own people; I will put my words in the mouth of the prophet,[e] who shall speak to them everything that I command. [19]Anyone who does not heed the words that the prophet[f] shall speak in my name, I myself will hold accountable. [20]But any prophet who speaks in the name of other gods, or who presumes to speak in my name a word that I have not commanded the prophet to speak—that prophet shall die." [21]You may say to yourself, "How can we recognize a word that the LORD has not spoken?" [22]If a prophet speaks in the name of the LORD but the thing does not take place or prove true, it is a word that the LORD has not spoken. The prophet has spoken it presumptuously; do not be frightened by it.

19 Laws concerning the Cities of Refuge

When the LORD your God has cut off the nations whose land the LORD your God is giving you, and you have dispossessed them and settled in their towns and in their houses, [2]you shall set apart three cities in the land that the LORD your God is giving you to possess. [3]You shall calculate the distances[g] and divide into

---

a Meaning of Heb uncertain b Heb him c Or prophets d Or such prophets e Or mouths of the prophets f Heb he g Or prepare roads to them

PROFILE OF FAITH

"Grant me chastity and self-control, but please not yet."

Would you ever guess that a guy who prayed like that would become a saint? Probably not, but it happened. He might not have realized it during his misspent youth in North Africa in the fourth century A.D., but St. Augustine was destined to become one of the most important and influential leaders of our faith.

Augustine was a self-centered, pleasure-seeking youth who lived for the thrill of the moment, relying on his wit and intellect to carry him along. He achieved fame and fortune in adulthood, but felt only misery; something was missing.

It wasn't until he found the answer to true happiness in Scripture that he realized that what he sought was a relationship with God. He devoted the rest of his life to God and the Church.

St. Augustine's experiences are lasting testimonies to the eloquent truth expressed to God in his *Confessions:* "Our heart is restless until it rests in you." St. Augustine's intelligent analysis of our faith and inspiring writings helped to shape many aspects of Church Tradition. His feast day is August 28.

Delicance—© Rachel Hostert, 18

---

three regions the land that the LORD your God gives you as a possession, so that any homicide can flee to one of them.

4 Now this is the case of a homicide who might flee there and live, that is, someone who has killed another person unintentionally when the two had not been at enmity before: [5]Suppose someone goes into the forest with another to cut wood, and when one of them swings the ax to cut down a tree, the head slips from the handle and strikes the other person who then dies; the killer may flee to one of these cities and live. [6]But if the distance is too great, the avenger of blood in hot anger might pursue and overtake and put the killer to death, although a death sentence was not deserved, since the two had not been at enmity before. [7]Therefore I command you: You shall set apart three cities.

8 If the LORD your God enlarges your territory, as he swore to your ancestors—and he will give you all the land that he promised your ancestors to give you, [9]provided you diligently observe this entire commandment that I command you today, by loving the LORD your God and walking always in his ways—then you shall add three more cities to these three, [10]so that the blood of an innocent person may not be shed in the land that the LORD your God is giving you as an inheritance, thereby bringing bloodguilt upon you.

11 But if someone at enmity with another lies in wait and attacks and takes the life of that person, and flees into one of these cities, [12]then the elders of the killer's city shall send to have the culprit taken from there and handed over to the avenger of blood to be put to death. [13]Show no pity; you shall purge the guilt of innocent blood from Israel, so that it may go well with you.

Property Boundaries

14 You must not move your neighbor's boundary marker, set up by former genera-

If the military had had chaplains in Old Testament times, they would not have performed many weddings for soldiers. That's because engaged men didn't have to serve in the military (Deuteronomy 20.7). And newly married men were exempt from military duty for a year (Deuteronomy 24.5)!

This information has been scanned and is free of all known viruses. Please forward to all your friends.

tions, on the property that will be allotted to you in the land that the LORD your God is giving you to possess.

Law concerning Witnesses

15 A single witness shall not suffice to convict a person of any crime or wrongdoing in connection with any offense that may be committed. Only on the evidence of two or three witnesses shall a charge be sustained. ¹⁶If a malicious witness comes forward to accuse someone of wrongdoing, ¹⁷then both parties to the dispute shall appear before the LORD, before the priests and the judges who are in office in those days, ¹⁸and the judges shall make a thorough inquiry. If the witness is a false witness, having testified falsely against another, ¹⁹then you shall do to the false witness just as the false witness had meant to do to the other. So you

shall purge the evil from your midst. ²⁰The rest shall hear and be afraid, and a crime such as this shall never again be committed among you. ²¹Show no pity: life for life, eye for eye, tooth for tooth, hand for hand, foot for foot.

20 Rules of Warfare

When you go out to war against your enemies, and see horses and chariots, an army larger than your own, you shall not be afraid of them; for the LORD your God is with you, who brought you up from the land of Egypt. ²Before you engage in battle, the priest shall come forward and speak to the troops, ³and shall say to them: "Hear, O Israel! Today you are drawing near to do battle against your enemies. Do not lose heart, or be afraid, or panic, or be in dread of them; ⁴for it is the LORD your God who goes with you, to fight for you against your enemies, to give you victory." ⁵Then the officials shall address the troops, saying, "Has anyone built a new house but not dedicated it? He should go back to his house, or he might die in the battle and another dedicate it. ⁶Has anyone planted a vineyard but not yet enjoyed its fruit? He should go back to his house, or he might die in the battle and another be first to enjoy its fruit. ⁷Has anyone become engaged to a woman but not yet married her? He should go back to his house, or he might die in the battle and another marry her." ⁸The officials shall continue to address the troops, saying, "Is anyone afraid or disheartened? He should go back to his house, or he might cause the heart of his comrades to melt like his own." ⁹When the officials have finished addressing the troops, then the commanders shall take charge of them.

10 When you draw near to a town to fight against it, offer it terms of peace. ¹¹If it accepts your terms of peace and surrenders to you, then all the people in it shall serve you at forced labor. ¹²If it does not submit to you peacefully, but makes war against you, then you shall besiege it; ¹³and when the LORD your God gives it into your hand, you shall put all its males to the sword. ¹⁴You may, however, take as your booty the women, the children, livestock, and everything else in the town, all its spoil. You may enjoy the spoil of your enemies, which the LORD your God has given you. ¹⁵Thus you shall treat all the towns that are very far from you, which are not towns of the nations here. ¹⁶But as for the towns of these peoples that the LORD your God is giving you as an inheritance, you must not let anything that breathes remain alive. ¹⁷You shall annihilate them—the Hittites and the Amorites, the Canaanites and the Perizzites, the Hivites and the Jebusites—just as the LORD your God has commanded, ¹⁸so that

they may not teach you to do all the abhorrent things that they do for their gods, and you thus sin against the LORD your God.

19 If you besiege a town for a long time, making war against it in order to take it, you must not destroy its trees by wielding an ax against them. Although you may take food from them, you must not cut them down. Are trees in the field human beings that they should come under siege from you? 20You may destroy only the trees that you know do not produce food; you may cut them down for use in building siegeworks against the town that makes war with you, until it falls.

21 Law concerning Murder by Persons Unknown

If, in the land that the LORD your God is giving you to possess, a body is found lying in open country, and it is not known who struck the person down, 2then your elders and your judges shall come out to measure the distances to the towns that are near the body. 3The elders of the town nearest the body shall take a heifer that has never been worked, one that has not pulled in the yoke; 4the elders of that town shall bring the heifer down to a wadi with running water, which is neither plowed nor sown, and shall break the heifer's neck there in the wadi. 5Then the priests, the sons of Levi, shall come forward, for the LORD your God has chosen them to minister to him and to pronounce blessings in the name of the LORD, and by their decision all cases of dispute and assault shall be settled. 6All the elders of that town nearest the body shall wash their hands over the heifer whose neck was broken in the wadi, 7and they shall declare: "Our hands did not shed this blood, nor were we witnesses to it. 8Absolve, O LORD, your people Israel, whom you redeemed; do not let the guilt of innocent blood remain in the midst of your people Israel." Then they will be absolved of bloodguilt. 9So you shall purge the guilt of innocent blood from your midst, because you must do what is right in the sight of the LORD.

Female Captives

10 When you go out to war against your enemies, and the LORD your God hands them over to you and you take them captive, 11suppose you see among the captives a beautiful woman whom you desire and want to marry, 12and so you bring her home to your house: she shall shave her head, pare her nails, 13discard her captive's garb, and shall remain in your house a full month, mourning for her father and moth-

er; after that you may go in to her and be her husband, and she shall be your wife. 14But if you are not satisfied with her, you shall let her go free and not sell her for money. You must not treat her as a slave, since you have dishonored her.

The Right of the Firstborn

15 If a man has two wives, one of them loved and the other disliked, and if both the loved and the disliked have borne him sons, the firstborn being the son of the one who is disliked, 16then on the day when he wills his possessions to his sons, he is not permitted to treat the son of the loved as the firstborn in preference to the son of the disliked, who is the firstborn. 17He must acknowledge as firstborn the son of the one who is disliked, giving him a double portion*a* of all that he has; since he is the first issue of his virility, the right of the firstborn is his.

Rebellious Children

18 If someone has a stubborn and rebellious son who will not obey his father and mother, who does not heed them when they discipline him, 19then his father and his mother shall take hold of him and bring him out to the elders of his town at the gate of that place. 20They shall say to the elders of his town, "This son of ours is stubborn and rebellious. He will not obey us. He is a glutton and a drunkard." 21Then all the men of the town shall stone him to death. So you shall purge the evil from your midst; and all Israel will hear, and be afraid.

Miscellaneous Laws

22 When someone is convicted of a crime punishable by death and is executed, and you hang him on a tree, 23his corpse must not remain all night upon the tree; you shall bury him that same day, for anyone hung on a tree is under God's curse. You must not defile the land that the LORD your God is giving you for possession.

22

You shall not watch your neighbor's ox or sheep straying away and ignore them; you shall take them back to their owner. 2If the owner does not reside near you or you do not know who the owner is, you shall bring it to your own house, and it shall remain with you until the owner claims it; then you shall return it. 3You shall do the same with a neighbor's donkey; you shall do the same with a neighbor's garment; and you shall do the same with anything else that your neighbor loses and you find. You may not withhold your help.

a Heb *two-thirds*

4 You shall not see your neighbor's donkey or ox fallen on the road and ignore it; you shall help to lift it up.

5 A woman shall not wear a man's apparel, nor shall a man put on a woman's garment; for whoever does such things is abhorrent to the Lord your God.

6 If you come on a bird's nest, in any tree or on the ground, with fledglings or eggs, with the mother sitting on the fledglings or on the eggs, you shall not take the mother with the young. 7 Let the mother go, taking only the young for yourself, in order that it may go well with you and you may live long.

8 When you build a new house, you shall make a parapet for your roof; otherwise you might have bloodguilt on your house, if anyone should fall from it.

9 You shall not sow your vineyard with a second kind of seed, or the whole yield will have to be forfeited, both the crop that you have sown and the yield of the vineyard itself.

10 You shall not plow with an ox and a donkey yoked together.

11 You shall not wear clothes made of wool and linen woven together.

12 You shall make tassels on the four corners of the cloak with which you cover yourself.

Laws concerning Sexual Relations

13 Suppose a man marries a woman, but after going in to her, he dislikes her 14 and makes up charges against her, slandering her by saying, "I married this woman; but when I lay with her, I did not find evidence of her virginity." 15 The father of the young woman and her mother shall then submit the evidence of the young woman's virginity to the elders of the city at the gate. 16 The father of the young woman shall say to the elders: "I gave my daughter in marriage to this man but he dislikes her; 17 now he has made up charges against her, saying, 'I did not find evidence of your daughter's virginity.' But here is the evidence of my daughter's virginity." Then they shall spread out the cloth before the elders of the town. 18 The elders of that town shall take the man and punish him; 19 they shall fine him one hundred shekels of silver (which they shall give to the young woman's father) because he has slandered a virgin of Israel. She shall remain his wife; he shall not be permitted to divorce her as long as he lives.

20 If, however, this charge is true, that evidence of the young woman's virginity was not found, 21 then they shall bring the young woman out to the entrance of her father's house and the men of her town shall stone her to death, because she committed a disgraceful act in Israel by prostituting herself in her father's house. So you shall purge the evil from your midst.

22 If a man is caught lying with the wife of another man, both of them shall die, the man who lay with the woman as well as the woman. So you shall purge the evil from Israel.

23 If there is a young woman, a virgin already engaged to be married, and a man meets her in the town and lies with her, 24 you shall bring both of them to the gate of that town and stone them to death, the young woman because she did not cry for help in the town and the man because he violated his neighbor's wife. So you shall purge the evil from your midst.

25 But if the man meets the engaged woman in the open country, and the man seizes her and lies with her, then only the man who lay with her shall die. 26 You shall do nothing to the young woman; the young woman has not committed an offense punishable by death, because this case is like that of someone who attacks and murders a neighbor. 27 Since he found her in the open country, the engaged woman may have cried for help, but there was no one to rescue her.

28 If a man meets a virgin who is not engaged, and seizes her and lies with her, and they are caught in the act, 29 the man who lay with her shall give fifty shekels of silver to the young woman's father, and she shall become his wife. Because he violated her he shall not be permitted to divorce her as long as he lives.

30ᵃ A man shall not marry his father's wife, thereby violating his father's rights.ᵇ

23 Those Excluded from the Assembly

No one whose testicles are crushed or whose penis is cut off shall be admitted to the assembly of the Lord.

2 Those born of an illicit union shall not be admitted to the assembly of the Lord. Even to the tenth generation, none of their descendants shall be admitted to the assembly of the Lord.

3 No Ammonite or Moabite shall be admitted to the assembly of the Lord. Even to the tenth generation, none of their descendants shall be admitted to the assembly of the Lord, 4 because they did not meet you with food and water on your journey out of Egypt, and because they hired against you Balaam son of Beor, from Pethor of Mesopotamia, to curse you. 5 (Yet the Lord your God refused to heed Balaam; the Lord your God turned the curse

---

a Ch 23.1 in Heb   b Heb *uncovering his father's skirt*

living it

Living it is knowing you have a purpose.

Living it is knowing there is a God who loves you

And knowing you're perfect in His eyes.

Living it is waking up every day having faith

And knowing anything is possible.

Living it is knowing that He sent His only Son

So you can have eternal life.

Living it is knowing that through Him you can share it with others.

Living it is knowing your eternity is in good hands in the end.

Living It—© Jordan Blackson, 16

into a blessing for you, because the Lord your God loved you.) [6]You shall never promote their welfare or their prosperity as long as you live.

7 You shall not abhor any of the Edomites, for they are your kin. You shall not abhor any of the Egyptians, because you were an alien residing in their land. [8]The children of the third generation that are born to them may be admitted to the assembly of the Lord.

Sanitary, Ritual, and Humanitarian Precepts

9 When you are encamped against your enemies you shall guard against any impropriety.

10 If one of you becomes unclean because of a nocturnal emission, then he shall go outside the camp; he must not come within the camp. [11]When evening comes, he shall wash himself with water, and when the sun has set, he may come back into the camp.

12 You shall have a designated area outside the camp to which you shall go. [13]With your utensils you shall have a trowel; when you relieve yourself outside, you shall dig a hole with it and then cover up your excrement. [14]Because the Lord your God travels along with your camp, to save you and to hand over your enemies to you, therefore your camp must be holy, so that he may not see anything indecent among you and turn away from you.

15 Slaves who have escaped to you from their owners shall not be given back to them. [16]They shall reside with you, in your midst, in any place they choose in any one of your towns, wherever they please; you shall not oppress them.

17 None of the daughters of Israel shall be a temple prostitute; none of the sons of Israel shall be a temple prostitute. [18]You shall not bring the fee of a prostitute or the wages of a male prostitute[a] into the house of the Lord your God in payment for any vow, for both of these are abhorrent to the Lord your God.

19 You shall not charge interest on loans to another Israelite, interest on money, interest on provisions, interest on anything that is lent. [20]On loans to a foreigner you may charge interest, but on loans to another Israelite you may not charge interest, so that the Lord your God may bless you in all your undertakings in the land that you are about to enter and possess.

21 If you make a vow to the Lord your God, do not postpone fulfilling it; for the Lord your God will surely require it of you, and you would incur guilt. [22]But if you refrain from vowing, you will not incur guilt. [23]Whatever your lips utter you must diligently perform, just as you have freely vowed to the Lord your God with your own mouth.

24 If you go into your neighbor's vineyard, you may eat your fill of grapes, as many as you wish, but you shall not put any in a container.

25 If you go into your neighbor's standing grain, you may pluck the ears with your hand, but you shall not put a sickle to your neighbor's standing grain.

24 Laws concerning Marriage and Divorce

Suppose a man enters into marriage with a woman, but she does not please him because he finds something objectionable about her, and so he writes her a certificate of divorce, puts it in her hand, and sends her out of his house; she then leaves his house [2]and goes off to become another man's wife. [3]Then suppose the second man dislikes her, writes her a bill of divorce, puts it in her hand, and sends her out of his house (or the second man who married her dies); [4]her first husband, who sent her away, is not permitted to take her again to be his wife after she has been defiled; for that would be abhorrent to the Lord, and you shall not bring guilt on the land that the Lord your God is giving you as a possession.

Miscellaneous Laws

5 When a man is newly married, he shall not go out with the army or be charged with any related duty. He shall be free at home one year, to be happy with the wife whom he has married.

6 No one shall take a mill or an upper millstone in pledge, for that would be taking a life in pledge.

7 If someone is caught kidnaping another Israelite, enslaving or selling the Israelite, then that kidnaper shall die. So you shall purge the evil from your midst.

8 Guard against an outbreak of a leprous[b] skin disease by being very careful; you shall carefully observe whatever the levitical priests instruct you, just as I have commanded them. [9]Remember what the Lord your God did to Miriam on your journey out of Egypt.

10 When you make your neighbor a loan of any kind, you shall not go into the house to take the pledge. [11]You shall wait outside, while the person to whom you are making the loan brings the pledge out to you. [12]If the person is poor, you shall not sleep in the garment given you as[c] the pledge. [13]You shall give the pledge back by sunset, so that your neighbor may sleep in the cloak and bless you; and it will be to your credit before the Lord your God.

14 You shall not withhold the wages of

---

a Heb *a dog* b A term for several skin diseases; precise meaning uncertain c Heb lacks *the garment given you as* poor and needy laborers, whether other Israelites or aliens who reside in your land in one of your towns. [15]You shall pay them their wages daily before sunset, because they are poor and their livelihood depends on them; otherwise they might cry to the LORD against you, and you would incur guilt.

16 Parents shall not be put to death for their children, nor shall children be put to death for their parents; only for their own crimes may persons be put to death.

17 You shall not deprive a resident alien or an orphan of justice; you shall not take a widow's garment in pledge. [18]Remember that you were a slave in Egypt and the LORD your God redeemed you from there; therefore I command you to do this.

19 When you reap your harvest in your field and forget a sheaf in the field, you shall not go back to get it; it shall be left for the alien, the orphan, and the widow, so that the LORD your God may bless you in all your undertakings. [20]When you beat your olive trees, do not strip what is left; it shall be for the alien, the orphan, and the widow.

21 When you gather the grapes of your vineyard, do not glean what is left; it shall be for the alien, the orphan, and the widow. [22]Remember that you were a slave in the land of Egypt; therefore I am commanding you to do this.

25 Suppose two persons have a dispute and enter into litigation, and the judges decide between them, declaring one to be in the right and the other to be in the wrong. [2]If the one in the wrong deserves to be flogged, the judge shall make that person lie down and be beaten in his presence with the number of lashes proportionate to the offense. [3]Forty lashes may be given but not more; if more lashes than these are given, your neighbor will be degraded in your sight.

4 You shall not muzzle an ox while it is treading out the grain.

Levirate Marriage

5 When brothers reside together, and one of them dies and has no son, the wife of the deceased shall not be married outside the family to a stranger. Her husband's brother shall go in to her, taking her in marriage, and performing the duty of a husband's brother to her, [6]and the firstborn whom she bears shall succeed to the name of the deceased brother, so that his name may not be blotted out of Israel. [7]But if the man has no desire to marry his brother's widow, then his brother's widow shall go up to the elders at the gate and say, "My husband's brother refuses to perpetuate his brother's

name in Israel; he will not perform the duty of a husband's brother to me." [8]Then the elders of his town shall summon him and speak to him. If he persists, saying, "I have no desire to marry her," [9]then his brother's wife shall go up to him in the presence of the elders, pull his sandal off his foot, spit in his face, and declare, "This is what is done to the man who does not build up his brother's house." [10]Throughout Israel his family shall be known as "the house of him whose sandal was pulled off."

Various Commands

11 If men get into a fight with one another, and the wife of one intervenes to rescue her husband from the grip of his opponent by reaching out and seizing his genitals, [12]you shall cut off her hand; show no pity.

13 You shall not have in your bag two kinds of weights, large and small. [14]You shall not have in your house two kinds of measures, large and small. [15]You shall have only a full and honest weight; you shall have only a full and honest measure, so that your days may be long in the land that the LORD your God is giving you. [16]For all who do such things, all who act dishonestly, are abhorrent to the LORD your God.

17 Remember what Amalek did to you on your journey out of Egypt, [18]how he attacked you on the way, when you were faint and weary, and struck down all who lagged behind you; he did not fear God. [19]Therefore when the LORD your God has given you rest from all your enemies on every hand, in the land that the LORD your God is giving you as an inheritance to possess, you shall blot out the remembrance of Amalek from under heaven; do not forget.

26 ### First Fruits and Tithes
When you have come into the land that the LORD your God is giving you as an inheritance to possess, and you possess it, and settle in it, [2]you shall take some of the first of all the fruit of the ground, which you harvest from the land that the LORD your God is giving you, and you shall put it in a basket and go to the place that

> "It doesn't matter if I hit a home run. It doesn't matter if we win a game... Whatever happens at the end of the day, as long as I glorify His name, that's what it's all about."
>
> —Albert Pujols, major league baseball MVP

the LORD your God will choose as a dwelling for his name. ³You shall go to the priest who is in office at that time, and say to him, "Today I declare to the LORD your God that I have come into the land that the LORD swore to our ancestors to give us." ⁴When the priest takes the basket from your hand and sets it down before the altar of the LORD your God, ⁵you shall make this response before the LORD your God: "A wandering Aramean was my ancestor; he went down into Egypt and lived there as an alien, few in number, and there he became a great nation, mighty and populous. ⁶When the Egyptians treated us harshly and afflicted us, by imposing hard labor on us, ⁷we cried to the LORD, the God of our ancestors; the LORD heard our voice and saw our affliction, our toil, and our oppression. ⁸The LORD brought us out of Egypt with a mighty hand and an outstretched arm, with a terrifying display of power, and with signs and wonders; ⁹and he brought us into this place and gave us this land, a land flowing with milk and honey. ¹⁰So now I bring the first of the fruit of the ground that you, O LORD, have given me." You shall set it down before the LORD your God and bow down before the LORD your God. ¹¹Then you, together with the Levites and the aliens who reside among you, shall celebrate with all the bounty that the LORD your God has given to you and to your house.

12 When you have finished paying all the tithe of your produce in the third year (which is the year of the tithe), giving it to the Levites, the aliens, the orphans, and the widows, so that they may eat their fill within your towns, ¹³then you shall say before the LORD your God: "I have removed the sacred portion from the house, and I have given it to the Levites, the resident aliens, the orphans, and the widows, in accordance with your entire commandment that you commanded me; I have neither transgressed nor forgotten any of your commandments: ¹⁴I have not eaten of it while in mourning; I have not removed any of it while I was unclean; and I have not offered any of it to the dead. I have obeyed the LORD my God, doing just as you commanded me. ¹⁵Look down from your holy habitation, from heaven, and bless your people Israel and the ground that you have given us, as you swore to our ancestors—a land flowing with milk and honey."

Concluding Exhortation

16 This very day the LORD your God is commanding you to observe these statutes and ordinances; so observe them diligently with all your heart and with all your soul. ¹⁷Today you have obtained the LORD's agreement: to be your God; and for you to walk in his ways, to keep his statutes, his commandments, and his ordinances, and to obey him. ¹⁸Today the LORD has obtained your agreement: to be his treasured people, as he promised you, and to keep his commandments; ¹⁹for him to set you high above all nations that he has made, in praise and in fame and in honor; and for you to be a people holy to the LORD your God, as he promised.

27 The Inscribed Stones and Altar on Mount Ebal

Then Moses and the elders of Israel charged all the people as follows: Keep the entire commandment that I am commanding you today. ²On the day that you cross over the Jordan into the land that the LORD your God is giving you, you shall set up large stones and cover them with plaster. ³You shall write on them all the words of this law when you have crossed over, to enter the land that the LORD your God is giving you, a land flowing with milk and honey, as the LORD, the God of your ancestors, promised you. ⁴So when you have crossed over the Jordan, you shall set up these stones, about which I am commanding you today, on Mount Ebal, and you shall cover them with plaster. ⁵And you shall build an altar there to the LORD your God, an altar of stones on which you have not used an iron tool. ⁶You must build the altar of the LORD your God of unhewn*a* stones. Then offer up burnt offerings on it to the LORD your God, ⁷make sacrifices of well-being, and eat them there, rejoicing before the LORD your God. ⁸You shall write on the stones all the words of this law very clearly.

9 Then Moses and the levitical priests spoke to all Israel, saying: Keep silence and hear, O Israel! This very day you have become the people of the LORD your God. ¹⁰Therefore obey the LORD your God, observing his commandments and his statutes that I am commanding you today.

Twelve Curses

11 The same day Moses charged the people as follows: ¹²When you have crossed over the Jordan, these shall stand on Mount Gerizim for the blessing of the people: Simeon, Levi, Judah, Issachar, Joseph, and Benjamin. ¹³And these shall stand on Mount Ebal for the curse: Reuben, Gad, Asher, Zebulun, Dan, and Naphtali. ¹⁴Then the Levites shall declare in a loud voice to all the Israelites:

a Heb *whole*

15 "Cursed be anyone who makes an idol or casts an image, anything abhorrent to the LORD, the work of an artisan, and sets it up in secret." All the people shall respond, saying, "Amen!"

16 "Cursed be anyone who dishonors father or mother." All the people shall say, "Amen!"

17 "Cursed be anyone who moves a neighbor's boundary marker." All the people shall say, "Amen!"

18 "Cursed be anyone who misleads a blind person on the road." All the people shall say, "Amen!"

19 "Cursed be anyone who deprives the alien, the orphan, and the widow of justice." All the people shall say, "Amen!"

20 "Cursed be anyone who lies with his father's wife, because he has violated his father's rights."*a* All the people shall say, "Amen!"

21 "Cursed be anyone who lies with any animal." All the people shall say, "Amen!"

22 "Cursed be anyone who lies with his sister, whether the daughter of his father or the daughter of his mother." All the people shall say, "Amen!"

23 "Cursed be anyone who lies with his mother-in-law." All the people shall say, "Amen!"

24 "Cursed be anyone who strikes down a neighbor in secret." All the people shall say, "Amen!"

25 "Cursed be anyone who takes a bribe to shed innocent blood." All the people shall say, "Amen!"

26 "Cursed be anyone who does not uphold the words of this law by observing them." All the people shall say, "Amen!"

28 Blessings for Obedience

If you will only obey the LORD your God, by diligently observing all his commandments that I am commanding you today, the LORD your God will set you high above all the nations of the earth; 2all these blessings shall come upon you and overtake you, if you obey the LORD your God:

3 Blessed shall you be in the city, and blessed shall you be in the field.

4 Blessed shall be the fruit of your womb, the fruit of your ground, and the fruit of your livestock, both the increase of your cattle and the issue of your flock.

5 Blessed shall be your basket and your kneading bowl.

6 Blessed shall you be when you come in, and blessed shall you be when you go out.

7 The LORD will cause your enemies who rise against you to be defeated before you; they shall come out against you one way, and flee before you seven ways. 8The LORD will command the blessing upon you in your barns, and in all that you undertake; he will bless you in the land that the LORD your God is giving you. 9The LORD will establish you as his holy people,

---

a Heb *uncovered his father's skirt*

Untitled—© Rebekah Furey, 16

as he has sworn to you, if you keep the commandments of the LORD your God and walk in his ways. [10] All the peoples of the earth shall see that you are called by the name of the LORD, and they shall be afraid of you. [11] The LORD will make you abound in prosperity, in the fruit of your womb, in the fruit of your livestock, and in the fruit of your ground in the land that the LORD swore to your ancestors to give you. [12] The LORD will open for you his rich storehouse, the heavens, to give the rain of your land in its season and to bless all your undertakings. You will lend to many nations, but you will not borrow. [13] The LORD will make you the head, and not the tail; you shall be only at the top, and not at the bottom—if you obey the commandments of the LORD your God, which I am commanding you today, by diligently observing them, [14] and if you do not turn aside from any of the words that I am commanding you today, either to the right or to the left, following other gods to serve them.

Warnings against Disobedience

15 But if you will not obey the LORD your God by diligently observing all his commandments and decrees, which I am commanding you today, then all these curses shall come upon you and overtake you:

16 Cursed shall you be in the city, and cursed shall you be in the field.

17 Cursed shall be your basket and your kneading bowl.

18 Cursed shall be the fruit of your womb, the fruit of your ground, the increase of your cattle and the issue of your flock.

19 Cursed shall you be when you come in, and cursed shall you be when you go out.

20 The LORD will send upon you disaster, panic, and frustration in everything you attempt to do, until you are destroyed and perish quickly, on account of the evil of your deeds, because you have forsaken me. [21] The LORD will make the pestilence cling to you until it has consumed you off the land that you are entering to possess. [22] The LORD will afflict you with consumption, fever, inflammation, with fiery heat and drought, and with blight and mildew; they shall pursue you until you perish. [23] The sky over your head shall be bronze, and the earth under you iron. [24] The LORD will change the rain of your land into powder, and only dust shall come down upon you from the sky until you are destroyed.

25 The LORD will cause you to be defeated before your enemies; you shall go out against them one way and flee before them seven ways. You shall become an object of horror to all the kingdoms of the earth. [26] Your corpses shall be food for every bird of the air and animal of the earth, and there shall be no one to frighten them away. [27] The LORD will afflict you with the boils of Egypt, with ulcers, scurvy, and itch, of which you cannot be healed. [28] The LORD will afflict you with madness, blindness, and confusion of mind; [29] you shall grope about at

noon as blind people grope in darkness, but you shall be unable to find your way; and you shall be continually abused and robbed, without anyone to help. 30You shall become engaged to a woman, but another man shall lie with her. You shall build a house, but not live in it. You shall plant a vineyard, but not enjoy its fruit. 31Your ox shall be butchered before your eyes, but you shall not eat of it. Your donkey shall be stolen in front of you, and shall not be restored to you. Your sheep shall be given to your enemies, without anyone to help you. 32Your sons and daughters shall be given to another people, while you look on; you will strain your eyes looking for them all day but be powerless to do anything. 33A people whom you do not know shall eat up the fruit of your ground and of all your labors; you shall be continually abused and crushed, 34and driven mad by the sight that your eyes shall see. 35The Lord will strike you on the knees and on the legs with grievous boils of which you cannot be healed, from the sole of your foot to the crown of your head. 36The Lord will bring you, and the king whom you set over you, to a nation that neither you nor your ancestors have known, where you shall serve other gods, of wood and stone. 37You shall become an object of horror, a proverb, and a byword among all the peoples where the Lord will lead you.

38 You shall carry much seed into the field but shall gather little in, for the locust shall consume it. 39You shall plant vineyards and dress them, but you shall neither drink the wine nor gather the grapes, for the worm shall eat them. 40You shall have olive trees throughout all your territory, but you shall not anoint yourself with the oil, for your olives shall drop off. 41You shall have sons and daughters, but they shall not remain yours, for they shall go into captivity. 42All your trees and the fruit of your ground the cicada shall take over. 43Aliens residing among you shall ascend above you higher and higher, while you shall descend lower and lower. 44They shall lend to you but you shall not lend to them; they shall be the head and you shall be the tail.

45 All these curses shall come upon you, pursuing and overtaking you until you are destroyed, because you did not obey the Lord your God, by observing the commandments and the decrees that he commanded you. 46They shall be among you and your descendants as a sign and a portent forever.

47 Because you did not serve the Lord your God joyfully and with gladness of heart for the abundance of everything, 48therefore you shall serve your enemies whom the Lord will send against you, in hunger and thirst, in nakedness and lack of everything. He will put an iron yoke on your neck until he has destroyed you. 49The Lord will bring a nation from far away, from the end of the earth, to swoop down on you like an eagle, a nation whose language you do not understand, 50a grim-faced nation showing no respect to the old or favor to the young. 51It shall consume the fruit of your livestock and the fruit of your ground until you are destroyed, leaving you neither grain, wine, and oil, nor the increase of your cattle and the issue of your flock, until it has made you perish. 52It shall besiege you in all your towns until your high and fortified walls, in which you trusted, come down throughout your land; it shall besiege you in all your towns throughout the land that the Lord your God has given you. 53In the desperate straits to which the enemy siege reduces you, you will eat the fruit of your womb, the flesh of your own sons and daughters whom the Lord your God has given you. 54Even the most refined and gentle of men among you will begrudge food to his own brother, to the wife whom he embraces, and to the last of his remaining children, 55giving to none of them any of the flesh of his children whom he is eating, because nothing else remains to him, in the desperate straits to which the enemy siege will reduce you in all your towns. 56She who is the most refined and gentle among you, so gentle and refined that she does not venture to set the sole of her foot on the ground, will begrudge food to the husband whom she embraces, to her own son, and to her own daughter, 57begrudging even the afterbirth that comes out from between her thighs, and the children that she bears, because she is eating them in secret for lack of anything else, in the desperate straits to which the enemy siege will reduce you in your towns.

58 If you do not diligently observe all the words of this law that are written in this book, fearing this glorious and awesome name, the Lord your God, 59then the Lord will overwhelm both you and your offspring with severe and lasting afflictions and grievous and lasting maladies. 60He will bring back upon you all the diseases of Egypt, of which you were in dread, and they shall cling to you. 61Every other malady and affliction, even though not recorded in the book of this law, the Lord will inflict on you until you are destroyed. 62Although once you were as numerous as the stars in heaven, you shall be left few in number, because you did not obey the Lord your God. 63And just as the Lord took delight in making you prosperous and numerous, so the Lord will take delight in bringing you to ruin and destruction; you shall be plucked off the land that

you are entering to possess. ⁶⁴The LORD will scatter you among all peoples, from one end of the earth to the other; and there you shall serve other gods, of wood and stone, which neither you nor your ancestors have known. ⁶⁵Among those nations you shall find no ease, no resting place for the sole of your foot. There the LORD will give you a trembling heart, failing eyes, and a languishing spirit. ⁶⁶Your life shall hang in doubt before you; night and day you shall be in dread, with no assurance of your life. ⁶⁷In the morning you shall say, "If only it were evening!" and at evening you shall say, "If only it were morning!"—because of the dread that your heart shall feel and the sights that your eyes shall see. ⁶⁸The LORD will bring you back in ships to Egypt, by a route that I promised you would never see again; and there you shall offer yourselves for sale to your enemies as male and female slaves, but there will be no buyer.

29ᵃ These are the words of the covenant that the LORD commanded Moses to make with the Israelites in the land of Moab, in addition to the covenant that he had made with them at Horeb.

The Covenant Renewed in Moab

2ᵇ Moses summoned all Israel and said to them: You have seen all that the LORD did before your eyes in the land of Egypt, to Pharaoh and to all his servants and to all his land, ³the great trials that your eyes saw, the signs, and those great wonders. ⁴But to this day the LORD has not given you a mind to understand, or eyes to see, or ears to hear. ⁵I have led you forty years in the wilderness. The clothes on your back have not worn out, and the sandals on your feet have not worn out; ⁶you have not eaten bread, and you have not drunk wine or

Foundation—© Jessica Jones, 17

strong drink—so that you may know that I am the LORD your God. ⁷When you came to this place, King Sihon of Heshbon and King Og of Bashan came out against us for battle, but we defeated them. ⁸We took their land and gave it as an inheritance to the Reubenites, the Gadites, and the half-tribe of Manasseh. ⁹Therefore diligently observe the words of this covenant, in order that you may succeedᶜ in everything that you do.

10 You stand assembled today, all of you, before the LORD your God—the leaders of your tribes,ᵈ your elders, and your officials, all the men of Israel, ¹¹your children, your women, and the aliens who are in your camp, both those who cut your wood and those who draw your water— ¹²to enter into the covenant of the LORD your God, sworn by an oath, which the LORD your God is making with you today; ¹³in order that he may establish you today as his people, and that he may be your God, as he promised you and as he swore to your ancestors, to Abraham, to Isaac, and to Jacob. ¹⁴I am making this covenant, sworn by an oath, not only with you who stand here with us today before the LORD our God, ¹⁵but also with those who are not here with us today. ¹⁶You know how we lived in the land of Egypt, and how we came through the midst of the nations through which you passed. ¹⁷You have seen their detestable things, the filthy idols of wood and stone, of silver and gold, that were among them. ¹⁸It may be that there is among you a man or woman, or a family or tribe, whose heart is already turning away from the LORD our God to serve the gods of those nations. It may be that there is among you a root sprouting poisonous and bitter growth. ¹⁹All who hear the words of this oath and bless themselves, thinking in their hearts, "We are safe even though we go our own stubborn ways" (thus bringing disaster on moist and dry alike)ᵉ— ²⁰the LORD will be unwilling to pardon them, for the LORD's anger and passion will smoke against them. All the curses written in this book will descend on them, and the LORD will blot out their names from under heaven. ²¹The LORD will single them out from all the tribes of Israel for calamity, in accordance with all the curses of the covenant written in this book of the law. ²²The next generation, your children who rise up after you, as well as the foreigner who comes from a distant country, will see the devastation of that land and the afflictions with which the LORD has afflicted it— ²³all its soil burned out by sulfur and salt, nothing planted, nothing

a Ch 28.69 in Heb b Ch 29.1 in Heb c Or *deal wisely* d Gk Syr: Heb *your leaders, your tribes* e Meaning of Heb uncertain sprouting, unable to support any vegetation, like the destruction of Sodom and Gomorrah, Admah and Zeboiim, which the LORD destroyed in his fierce anger— ²⁴they and indeed all the nations will wonder, "Why has the LORD done thus to this land? What caused this great display of anger?" ²⁵They will conclude, "It is because they abandoned the covenant of the LORD, the God of their ancestors, which he made with them when he brought them out of the land of Egypt. ²⁶They turned and served other gods, worshiping them, gods whom they had not known and whom he had not allotted to them; ²⁷so the anger of the LORD was kindled against that land, bringing on it every curse written in this book. ²⁸The LORD uprooted them from their land in anger, fury, and great wrath, and cast them into another land, as is now the case." ²⁹The secret things belong to the LORD our God, but the revealed things belong to us and to our children forever, to observe all the words of this law.

30 God's Fidelity Assured

When all these things have happened to you, the blessings and the curses that I have set before you, if you call them to mind among all the nations where the LORD your God has driven you, ²and return to the LORD your God, and you and your children obey him with all your heart and with all your soul, just as I am commanding you today, ³then the LORD your God will restore your fortunes and have compassion on you, gathering you again from all the peoples among whom the LORD your God has scattered you. ⁴Even if you are exiled to the ends of the world,ᵃ from there the LORD your God will gather you, and from there he will bring you back. ⁵The LORD your God will bring you into the land that your ancestors possessed, and you will possess it; he will make you more prosperous and numerous than your ancestors.

6 Moreover, the LORD your God will circumcise your heart and the heart of your descendants, so that you will love the LORD your God with all your heart and with all your soul, in order that you may live. ⁷The LORD your God will put all these curses on your enemies and on the adversaries who took advantage of you. ⁸Then you shall again obey the LORD, observing all his commandments that I am commanding you today, ⁹and the LORD your God will make you abundantly prosperous in all your undertakings, in the fruit of your body, in the fruit of your livestock, and in the fruit of your soil. For the LORD will again take delight in pros-

pering you, just as he delighted in prospering your ancestors, ¹⁰when you obey the LORD your God by observing his commandments and decrees that are written in this book of the law, because you turn to the LORD your God with all your heart and with all your soul.

Exhortation to Choose Life

11 Surely, this commandment that I am commanding you today is not too hard for you, nor is it too far away. ¹²It is not in heaven, that you should say, "Who will go up to heaven for us, and get it for us so that we may hear it and observe it?" ¹³Neither is it beyond the sea, that you should say, "Who will cross to the other side of the sea for us, and get it for us so that we may hear it and observe it?" ¹⁴No, the word is very near to you; it is in your mouth and in your heart for you to observe.

15 See, I have set before you today life and prosperity, death and adversity. ¹⁶If you obey the commandments of the LORD your Godᵇ that I am commanding you today, by loving the LORD your God, walking in his ways, and observing his commandments, decrees, and ordinances, then you shall live and become numerous, and the LORD your God will bless you in the land that you are entering to possess. ¹⁷But if your heart turns away and you do not hear, but are led astray to bow down to other gods and serve them, ¹⁸I declare to you today that you shall perish; you shall not live long in the land that you are crossing the Jordan to enter and possess. ¹⁹I call heaven and earth to witness against you today that I have set before you life and death, blessings and curses. Choose life so that you and your descendants may live, ²⁰loving the LORD your God, obeying him, and holding fast to him; for that means life to you and length of days, so that you may live in the land that the LORD swore to give to your ancestors, to Abraham, to Isaac, and to Jacob.

31 Joshua Becomes Moses' Successor

When Moses had finished speaking allᶜ these words to all Israel, ²he said to them: "I am now one hundred twenty years old. I am no longer able to get about, and the LORD has told me, 'You shall not cross over this Jordan.' ³The LORD your God himself will cross over before you. He will destroy these nations before you, and you shall dispossess them. Joshua also will cross over before you, as the LORD promised. ⁴The LORD will do to them as he did to Sihon and Og, the kings of the Amorites, and to their land, when he destroyed them. ⁵The LORD will

---

a Heb *of heaven*   b Gk: Heb lacks *If you obey the commandments of the LORD your God*   c Q Ms Gk: MT *Moses went and spoke* give them over to you and you shall deal with them in full accord with the command that I have given to you. [6]Be strong and bold; have no fear or dread of them, because it is the LORD your God who goes with you; he will not fail you or forsake you."

7 Then Moses summoned Joshua and said to him in the sight of all Israel: "Be strong and bold, for you are the one who will go with this people into the land that the LORD has sworn to their ancestors to give them; and you will put them in possession of it. [8]It is the LORD who goes before you. He will be with you; he will not fail you or forsake you. Do not fear or be dismayed."

The Law to Be Read Every Seventh Year

9 Then Moses wrote down this law, and gave it to the priests, the sons of Levi, who carried the ark of the covenant of the LORD, and to all the elders of Israel. [10]Moses commanded them: "Every seventh year, in the scheduled year of remission, during the festival of booths,[a] [11]when all Israel comes to appear before the LORD your God at the place that he will choose, you shall read this law before all Israel in their hearing. [12]Assemble the people—men, women, and children, as well as the aliens residing in your towns—so that they may hear and learn to fear the LORD your God and to observe diligently all the words of this law, [13]and so that their children, who have not known it, may hear and learn to fear the LORD your God, as long as you live in the land that you are crossing over the Jordan to possess."

Moses and Joshua Receive God's Charge

14 The LORD said to Moses, "Your time to die is near; call Joshua and present yourselves in the tent of meeting, so that I may commission him." So Moses and Joshua went and presented themselves in the tent of meeting, [15]and the LORD appeared at the tent in a pillar of cloud; the pillar of cloud stood at the entrance to the tent.

16 The LORD said to Moses, "Soon you will lie down with your ancestors. Then this people will begin to prostitute themselves to the foreign gods in their midst, the gods of the land into which they are going; they will forsake me, breaking my covenant that I have made with them. [17]My anger will be kindled against them in that day. I will forsake them and hide my face from them; they will become easy prey, and many terrible troubles will come upon them. In that day they will say, 'Have not these troubles come upon us because our God

is not in our midst?' [18]On that day I will surely hide my face on account of all the evil they have done by turning to other gods. [19]Now therefore write this song, and teach it to the Israelites; put it in their mouths, in order that this song may be a witness for me against the Israelites. [20]For when I have brought them into the land flowing with milk and honey, which I promised on oath to their ancestors, and they have eaten their fill and grown fat, they will turn to other gods and serve them, despising me and breaking my covenant. [21]And when many terrible troubles come upon them, this song will confront them as a witness, because it will not be lost from the mouths of their descendants. For I know what they are inclined to do even now, before I have brought them into the land that I promised them on oath." [22]That very day Moses wrote this song and taught it to the Israelites.

23 Then the LORD commissioned Joshua son of Nun and said, "Be strong and bold, for you shall bring the Israelites into the land that I promised them; I will be with you."

24 When Moses had finished writing down in a book the words of this law to the very end, [25]Moses commanded the Levites who carried the ark of the covenant of the LORD, saying, [26]"Take this book of the law and put it beside the ark of the covenant of the LORD your God; let it remain there as a witness against you. [27]For I know well how rebellious and stubborn you are. If you already have been so rebellious toward the LORD while I am still alive among you, how much more after my death! [28]Assemble to me all the elders of your tribes and your officials, so that I may recite these words in their hearing and call heaven and earth to witness against them. [29]For I know that after my death you will surely act corruptly, turning aside from the way that I have commanded you. In time to come trouble will befall you, because you will do what is evil in the sight of the LORD, provoking him to anger through the work of your hands."

The Song of Moses

30 Then Moses recited the words of this song, to the very end, in the hearing of the whole assembly of Israel:

32 Give ear, O heavens, and I will speak;
　　let the earth hear the words of my
　　　　mouth.
2 　May my teaching drop like the rain,
　　my speech condense like the dew;
　like gentle rain on grass,
　　like showers on new growth.

a Or tabernacles; Heb succoth

³ For I will proclaim the name of the LORD;
    ascribe greatness to our God!

⁴ The Rock, his work is perfect,
    and all his ways are just.
  A faithful God, without deceit,
    just and upright is he;
⁵ yet his degenerate children have dealt
    falsely with him,ᵃ
  a perverse and crooked generation.
⁶ Do you thus repay the LORD,
    O foolish and senseless people?
  Is not he your father, who created you,
    who made you and established you?
⁷ Remember the days of old,
    consider the years long past;
  ask your father, and he will inform you;
    your elders, and they will tell you.
⁸ When the Most Highᵇ apportioned the
    nations,
    when he divided humankind,
  he fixed the boundaries of the peoples
    according to the number of the gods;ᶜ
⁹ the LORD's own portion was his people,
    Jacob his allotted share.

¹⁰ He sustainedᵈ him in a desert land,
    in a howling wilderness waste;
  he shielded him, cared for him,
    guarded him as the apple of his eye.
¹¹ As an eagle stirs up its nest,
    and hovers over its young;
  as it spreads its wings, takes them up,
    and bears them aloft on its pinions,
¹² the LORD alone guided him;
    no foreign god was with him.
¹³ He set him atop the heights of the land,
    and fed him withᵉ produce of the field;
  he nursed him with honey from the crags,
    with oil from flinty rock;
¹⁴ curds from the herd, and milk from the
    flock,
    with fat of lambs and rams;
  Bashan bulls and goats,
    together with the choicest wheat—
    you drank fine wine from the blood of
    grapes.
¹⁵ Jacob ate his fill;ᶠ
    Jeshurun grew fat, and kicked.
  You grew fat, bloated, and gorged!
  He abandoned God who made him,
    and scoffed at the Rock of his salvation.
¹⁶ They made him jealous with strange gods,
    with abhorrent things they provoked
    him.
¹⁷ They sacrificed to demons, not God,
    to deities they had never known,

    to new ones recently arrived,
    whom your ancestors had not feared.
¹⁸ You were unmindful of the Rock that bore
    you;ᵍ
  you forgot the God who gave you birth.

¹⁹ The LORD saw it, and was jealous;ʰ
    he spurnedⁱ his sons and daughters.
²⁰ He said: I will hide my face from them,
    I will see what their end will be;
  for they are a perverse generation,
    children in whom there is no
    faithfulness.
²¹ They made me jealous with what is no god,
    provoked me with their idols.
  So I will make them jealous with what is no
    people,
    provoke them with a foolish nation.
²² For a fire is kindled by my anger,
    and burns to the depths of Sheol;
  it devours the earth and its increase,
    and sets on fire the foundations of the
    mountains.
²³ I will heap disasters upon them,
    spend my arrows against them:
²⁴ wasting hunger,
    burning consumption,
    bitter pestilence.
  The teeth of beasts I will send against them,
    with venom of things crawling in the
    dust.
²⁵ In the street the sword shall bereave,
    and in the chambers terror,
  for young man and woman alike,
    nursing child and old gray head.
²⁶ I thought to scatter themʲ
    and blot out the memory of them from
    humankind;
²⁷ but I feared provocation by the enemy,
    for their adversaries might
    misunderstand
  and say, "Our hand is triumphant;
    it was not the LORD who did all this."

²⁸ They are a nation void of sense;
    there is no understanding in them.
²⁹ If they were wise, they would understand
    this;
    they would discern what the end would be.

DEUTERONOMY 32

a Meaning of Heb uncertain b Traditional rendering of Heb *Elyon* c Q Ms Compare Gk Tg: MT *the Israelites* d Sam Gk Compare Tg: MT *found* e Sam Gk Syr Tg: MT *he ate* f Q Mss Sam Gk: MT lacks *Jacob ate his fill* g Or *that begot you* h Q Mss Gk: MT lacks *was jealous* i Cn: Heb *he spurned because of provocation* j Gk: Meaning of Heb uncertain

30 How could one have routed a thousand,
    and two put a myriad to flight,
unless their Rock had sold them,
    the Lord had given them up?
31 Indeed their rock is not like our Rock;
    our enemies are fools.*a*
32 Their vine comes from the vinestock of
    Sodom,
    from the vineyards of Gomorrah;
their grapes are grapes of poison,
    their clusters are bitter;
33 their wine is the poison of serpents,
    the cruel venom of asps.

34 Is not this laid up in store with me,
    sealed up in my treasuries?
35 Vengeance is mine, and recompense,
    for the time when their foot shall slip;
because the day of their calamity is at hand,
    their doom comes swiftly.*c*

36 Indeed the Lord will vindicate his people,
    have compassion on his servants,
when he sees that their power is gone,
    neither bond nor free remaining.
37 Then he will say: Where are their gods,
    the rock in which they took refuge,
38 who ate the fat of their sacrifices,
    and drank the wine of their libations?
Let them rise up and help you,
    let them be your protection!

39 See now that I, even I, am he;
    there is no god besides me.
I kill and I make alive;
    I wound and I heal;
    and no one can deliver from my hand.
40 For I lift up my hand to heaven,
    and swear: As I live forever,
41 when I whet my flashing sword,
    and my hand takes hold on judgment;
I will take vengeance on my adversaries,
    and will repay those who hate me.
42 I will make my arrows drunk with blood,
    and my sword shall devour flesh—
with the blood of the slain and the captives,
    from the long-haired enemy.

43 Praise, O heavens,*b* his people,
    worship him, all you gods!*c*
For he will avenge the blood of his
    children,*d*
    and take vengeance on his adversaries;
he will repay those who hate him,*c*
    and cleanse the land for his people.*e*

44 Moses came and recited all the words of this song in the hearing of the people, he and Joshua*f* son of Nun. 45 When Moses had finished reciting all these words to all Israel, 46 he said to them: "Take to heart all the words that I am giving in witness against you today; give them as a command to your children, so that they may diligently observe all the words of this law. 47 This is no trifling matter for you, but rather your very life; through it you may live long in the land that you are crossing over the Jordan to possess."

Moses' Death Foretold

48 On that very day the Lord addressed Moses as follows: 49 "Ascend this mountain of the Abarim, Mount Nebo, which is in the land of Moab, across from Jericho, and view the land of Canaan, which I am giving to the Israelites for a possession; 50 you shall die there on the mountain that you ascend and shall be gathered to your kin, as your brother Aaron died on Mount Hor and was gathered to his kin; 51 because both of you broke faith with me among the Israelites at the waters of Meribath-kadesh in the wilderness of Zin, by failing to maintain my holiness among the Israelites. 52 Although you may view the land from a distance, you shall not enter it—the land that I am giving to the Israelites."

33 Moses' Final Blessing on Israel

This is the blessing with which Moses, the man of God, blessed the Israelites before his death. 2 He said:

    The Lord came from Sinai,
        and dawned from Seir upon us;*g*
    he shone forth from Mount Paran.
    With him were myriads of holy ones;*h*
        at his right, a host of his own.*i*
3 Indeed, O favorite among*j* peoples,
    all his holy ones were in your charge;
they marched at your heels,
    accepted direction from you.
4 Moses charged us with the law,
    as a possession for the assembly of Jacob.
5 There arose a king in Jeshurun,
    when the leaders of the people
        assembled—
    the united tribes of Israel.

6 May Reuben live, and not die out,
    even though his numbers are few.

7 And this he said of Judah:
    O Lord, give heed to Judah,
    and bring him to his people;
    strengthen his hands for him,*k*
    and be a help against his adversaries.

---

a Gk: Meaning of Heb uncertain *b* Q Ms Gk: MT *nations* *c* Q Ms Gk: MT lacks this line *d* Q Ms Gk: MT *his servants* *e* Q Ms Sam Gk Vg: MT *his land his people* *f* Sam Gk Syr Vg: MT *Hoshea* *g* Gk Syr Vg Compare Tg: Heb *upon them* *h* Cn Compare Gk Sam Syr Vg: MT *He came from Ribeboth-kadesh* *i* Cn Compare Gk: meaning of Heb uncertain *j* Or *O lover of the* *k* Cn: Heb *with his hands he contended*

⁸And of Levi he said:
   Give to Levi*ᵃ* your Thummim,
      and your Urim to your loyal one,
   whom you tested at Massah,
      with whom you contended at the waters
         of Meribah;
⁹ who said of his father and mother,
      "I regard them not";
   he ignored his kin,
      and did not acknowledge his children.
   For they observed your word,
      and kept your covenant.
¹⁰ They teach Jacob your ordinances,
      and Israel your law;
   they place incense before you,
      and whole burnt offerings on your altar.
¹¹ Bless, O Lᴏʀᴅ, his substance,
      and accept the work of his hands;
   crush the loins of his adversaries,
      of those that hate him, so that they do
         not rise again.

¹²Of Benjamin he said:
   The beloved of the Lᴏʀᴅ rests in safety—
      the High God*ᵇ* surrounds him all day long—
         the beloved*ᶜ* rests between his shoulders.

¹³And of Joseph he said:
   Blessed by the Lᴏʀᴅ be his land,
      with the choice gifts of heaven above,
      and of the deep that lies beneath;
¹⁴ with the choice fruits of the sun,
      and the rich yield of the months;
¹⁵ with the finest produce of the ancient
         mountains,
      and the abundance of the everlasting
         hills;
¹⁶ with the choice gifts of the earth and its
         fullness,
      and the favor of the one who dwells on
         Sinai.*ᵈ*
   Let these come on the head of Joseph,
      on the brow of the prince among his
         brothers.
¹⁷ A firstborn*ᵉ* bull—majesty is his!
      His horns are the horns of a wild ox;
   with them he gores the peoples,
      driving them to*ᶠ* the ends of the earth;
   such are the myriads of Ephraim,
      such are the thousands of Manasseh.

¹⁸And of Zebulun he said:
   Rejoice, Zebulun, in your going out;
      and Issachar, in your tents.
¹⁹ They call peoples to the mountain;
      there they offer the right sacrifices;
   for they suck the affluence of the seas
      and the hidden treasures of the sand.

²⁰And of Gad he said:
   Blessed be the enlargement of Gad!
      Gad lives like a lion;
      he tears at arm and scalp.
²¹ He chose the best for himself,
      for there a commander's allotment was
         reserved;
   he came at the head of the people,
      he executed the justice of the Lᴏʀᴅ,
      and his ordinances for Israel.

²²And of Dan he said:
   Dan is a lion's whelp
      that leaps forth from Bashan.

²³And of Naphtali he said:
   O Naphtali, sated with favor,
      full of the blessing of the Lᴏʀᴅ,
      possess the west and the south.

²⁴And of Asher he said:
   Most blessed of sons be Asher;
      may he be the favorite of his brothers,
      and may he dip his foot in oil.
²⁵ Your bars are iron and bronze;
      and as your days, so is your strength.

²⁶ There is none like God, O Jeshurun,
      who rides through the heavens to your
         help,
      majestic through the skies.
²⁷ He subdues the ancient gods,*ᵍ*
      shatters*ʰ* the forces of old;*ⁱ*
   he drove out the enemy before you,
      and said, "Destroy!"
²⁸ So Israel lives in safety,
      untroubled is Jacob's abode*ʲ*
   in a land of grain and wine,
      where the heavens drop down dew.
²⁹ Happy are you, O Israel! Who is like you,
      a people saved by the Lᴏʀᴅ,
   the shield of your help,
      and the sword of your triumph!
   Your enemies shall come fawning to
         you,
      and you shall tread on their backs.

34 Moses Dies and Is Buried in the Land of Moab

Then Moses went up from the plains of Moab to Mount Nebo, to the top of Pisgah, which is opposite Jericho, and the Lᴏʀᴅ showed him the whole land: Gilead as far as Dan, ²all Naphtali, the land of Ephraim and Manasseh, all the land of Judah as far as the Western Sea, ³the Negeb, and the Plain—that is, the valley of Jericho, the city of palm trees—as far as Zoar. ⁴The Lᴏʀᴅ said to him, "This is the land of which I

a Q Ms Gk: MT lacks *Give to Levi* *b* Heb *above him* *c* Heb *he* *d* Cn: Heb *in the bush* *e* Q Ms Gk Syr Vg: MT *His firstborn* *f* Cn: Heb *the peoples, together* *g* Or *The eternal God is a dwelling place* *h* Cn: Heb *from underneath* *i* Or *the everlasting arms* *j* Or *fountain* swore to Abraham, to Isaac, and to Jacob, saying, 'I will give it to your descendants'; I have let you see it with your eyes, but you shall not cross over there." ⁵Then Moses, the servant of the Lord, died there in the land of Moab, at the Lord's command. ⁶He was buried in a valley in the land of Moab, opposite Beth-peor, but no one knows his burial place to this day. ⁷Moses was one hundred twenty years old when he died; his sight was unimpaired and his vigor had not abated. ⁸The Israelites wept for Moses in the plains of Moab thirty days; then the period of mourning for Moses was ended.

9 Joshua son of Nun was full of the spirit of wisdom, because Moses had laid his hands on him; and the Israelites obeyed him, doing as the Lord had commanded Moses.

10 Never since has there arisen a prophet in Israel like Moses, whom the Lord knew face to face. ¹¹He was unequaled for all the signs and wonders that the Lord sent him to perform in the land of Egypt, against Pharaoh and all his servants and his entire land, ¹²and for all the mighty deeds and all the terrifying displays of power that Moses performed in the sight of all Israel.

JOSHUA

GOD OF THE FEARFUL

Big Enough

Sometimes when we encounter people in the Bible, they can seem so *different*. They belong to another time and place, totally removed from the world in which we live. But nothing could be further from the truth. Their stories aren't "once upon a time" fables or fairy tales. The Scriptures were written by real people, in real places, at real times—wrestling with what it meant to be followers of God. The stories are filled with doubt and despair, victory and failure. In short, they are about real life.

The story of Joshua appears to be about victory, but just below the surface lies another message. Three times in the first nine verses God needs to remind Joshua to "be strong and courageous." Why would God have to remind Joshua of this *three times*? Perhaps it's because this is not a story of Joshua the strong and courageous, but rather Joshua the fearful.

Maybe you've had those kinds of moments as well. Rather than being filled with courage and strength, you're racked by questions and fear. *Am I good enough? Do I measure up? What if I fail?* God's response to Joshua is the same message God has for you and me. He welcomes our doubts. He embraces our fears and our questions. He's big enough for all of them. He can handle them. And he can be our source of courage in the midst of our confusion. Faith leaves room for questions and doubts, but God is big enough to fill the space.

"We must remember God more often than we draw breath."
—St. Gregory Nazianzen

WHO The book, named for one of the central characters, was written over a period of time by people who knew his story.

WHAT A story about Israel's conquest and division of the Promised Land among the Israelite tribes, and a reflection on its religious meaning

WHEN The book's central event—the invasion of Canaan—took place between 1200 and 1400 B.C. Most of the book was written in 7 B.C. and edited in 5 B.C.

WHERE Canaan (modern-day Israel and Palestine)

PATH OF DISCIPLESHIP

Somehow we've been sold the idea that questioning God means we lack faith. We're told that we need to face every challenge with "faith," meaning that we should have no fears, no questions, and no reservations. But this kind of thinking doesn't square with what the Bible says. Godly people, even Jesus himself, at times expressed genuine fears and apprehensions to God.

The night before Jesus died, he was in a garden, praying, "Remove this cup from me; yet, not what I want, but what you want" (Mark 14.36). Jesus was expressing real anxiety, asking if there was some other way to accomplish God's plan for the world.

Jesus' example in prayer is compelling. He refused to put on a brave face before God. He was *real*. A life of prayer is a "habit of being in the presence" of God (see *Catechism of the Catholic Church* 2565). Real prayer demands the intimacy of honesty. When we make it our habit to live in the presence of God, we can be honest about our feelings. God expects nothing less.

1 God's Commission to Joshua

After the death of Moses the servant of the LORD, the LORD spoke to Joshua son of Nun, Moses' assistant, saying, [2]"My servant Moses is dead. Now proceed to cross the Jordan, you and all this people, into the land that I am giving to them, to the Israelites. [3]Every place that the sole of your foot will tread upon I have given to you, as I promised to Moses. [4]From the wilderness and the Lebanon as far as the great river, the river Euphrates, all the land of the Hittites, to the Great Sea in the west shall be your territory. [5]No one shall be able to stand against you all the days of your life. As I was with Moses, so I will be with you; I will not fail you or forsake you. [6]Be strong and courageous; for you shall put this people in possession of the land that I swore to their ancestors to give them. [7]Only be strong and very courageous, being careful to act in accordance with all the law that my servant Moses commanded you; do not turn from it to the right hand or to the left, so that you may be successful wherever you go. [8]This book of the law shall not depart out of your mouth; you shall meditate on it day and night, so that you may be careful to act in accordance with all that is written in it. For then you shall make your way prosperous, and then you shall be successful. [9]I hereby command you: Be strong and courageous; do not be frightened or dismayed, for the LORD your God is with you wherever you go."

Preparations for the Invasion

10 Then Joshua commanded the officers of the people, [11]"Pass through the camp, and command the people: 'Prepare your provisions; for in three days you are to cross over the Jordan, to go in to take possession of the land that the LORD your God gives you to possess.' "

12 To the Reubenites, the Gadites, and the half-tribe of Manasseh Joshua said, [13]"Remember the word that Moses the servant of the LORD commanded you, saying, 'The LORD your God is providing you a place of rest, and will give you this land.' [14]Your wives, your little ones, and your livestock shall remain in the land that Moses gave you beyond the Jordan. But all the warriors among you shall cross over armed before your kindred and shall help them, [15]until the LORD gives rest to your kindred as well as to you, and they too take possession of the land that the LORD your God is giving them. Then you shall return to your own land and take possession of it, the land that

Moses the servant of the LORD gave you beyond the Jordan to the east."

16 They answered Joshua: "All that you have commanded us we will do, and wherever you send us we will go. [17]Just as we obeyed Moses in all things, so we will obey you. Only may the LORD your God be with you, as he was with Moses! [18]Whoever rebels against your orders and disobeys your words, whatever you command, shall be put to death. Only be strong and courageous."

2 Spies Sent to Jericho

Then Joshua son of Nun sent two men secretly from Shittim as spies, saying, "Go, view the land, especially Jericho." So they went, and entered the house of a prostitute whose name was Rahab, and spent the night there. [2]The king of Jericho was told, "Some Israelites have come here tonight to search out the land." [3]Then the king of Jericho sent orders to Rahab, "Bring out the men who have come to you, who entered your house, for they have come only to search out the whole land." [4]But the woman took the two men and hid them. Then she said, "True, the men came to me, but I did not know where they came from. [5]And when it was time to close the gate at dark, the men went out. Where the men went I do not know. Pursue them quickly, for you can overtake them." [6]She had, however, brought them up to the roof and hidden them with the stalks of flax that she had laid out on the roof. [7]So the men pursued them on the way to the Jordan as far as the fords. As soon as the pursuers had gone out, the gate was shut.

8 Before they went to sleep, she came up to them on the roof [9]and said to the men: "I know that the LORD has given you the land, and that dread of you has fallen on us, and that all the inhabitants of the land melt in fear before you. [10]For we have heard how the LORD dried up the water of the Red Sea[a] before you when you came out of Egypt, and what you did to the two kings of the Amorites that were beyond the Jordan, to Sihon and Og, whom you utterly destroyed. [11]As soon as we heard it, our hearts melted, and there was no courage left in any of us because of you. The LORD your God is indeed God in heaven above and on earth below. [12]Now then, since I have dealt kindly with you, swear to me by the LORD that you in turn will deal kindly with my family. Give me a sign of good faith [13]that you will spare my father and mother, my brothers and sisters, and all who belong to them, and deliver our lives from death." [14]The men said to her, "Our life for

---

a Or *Sea of Reeds*

yours! If you do not tell this business of ours, then we will deal kindly and faithfully with you when the LORD gives us the land."

15 Then she let them down by a rope through the window, for her house was on the outer side of the city wall and she resided within the wall itself. ¹⁶She said to them, "Go toward the hill country, so that the pursuers may not come upon you. Hide yourselves there three days, until the pursuers have returned; then afterward you may go your way." ¹⁷The men said to her, "We will be released from this oath that you have made us swear to you ¹⁸if we invade the land and you do not tie this crimson cord in the window through which you let us down, and you do not gather into your house your father and mother, your brothers, and all your family. ¹⁹If any of you go out of the doors of your house into the street, they shall be responsible for their own death, and we shall be innocent; but if a hand is laid upon any who are with you in the house, we shall bear the responsibility for their death. ²⁰But if you tell this business of ours, then we shall be released from this oath that you made us swear to you." ²¹She said, "According to your words, so be it." She sent them away and they departed. Then she tied the crimson cord in the window.

22 They departed and went into the hill country and stayed there three days, until the pursuers returned. The pursuers had searched all along the way and found nothing. ²³Then the two men came down again from the hill country. They crossed over, came to Joshua son of Nun, and told him all that had happened to them. ²⁴They said to Joshua, "Truly the LORD has given all the land into our hands; moreover all the inhabitants of the land melt in fear before us."

3 Israel Crosses the Jordan

Early in the morning Joshua rose and set out from Shittim with all the Israelites, and they came to the Jordan. They camped there before crossing over. ²At the end of three days the officers went through the camp ³and commanded the people, "When you see the ark of the covenant of the LORD your God being carried by the levitical priests, then you shall set out from your place. Follow it, ⁴so that you may know the way you should go, for you have not passed this way before. Yet there shall be a space between you and it, a distance of about two thousand cubits; do not come any nearer to it." ⁵Then Joshua said to the people, "Sanctify yourselves; for tomorrow the LORD will do wonders among you." ⁶To the priests Joshua said, "Take up the ark of the covenant, and pass on in front of the people." So they took up the ark of the covenant and went in front of the people.

7 The LORD said to Joshua, "This day I will begin to exalt you in the sight of all Israel, so that they may know that I will be with you as I was with Moses. ⁸You are the one who shall command the priests who bear the ark of the covenant, 'When you come to the edge of the waters of the Jordan, you shall stand still in the Jordan.' " ⁹Joshua then said to the Israelites, "Draw near and hear the words of the LORD your God." ¹⁰Joshua said, "By this you shall know that among you is the living God who without fail will drive out from before you the Canaanites, Hittites, Hivites, Perizzites, Girgashites, Amorites, and Jebusites: ¹¹the ark of the covenant of the Lord of all the earth is going to pass before you into the Jordan. ¹²So now select twelve men from the tribes of Israel, one from each tribe. ¹³When the soles of the feet of the priests who bear the ark of the LORD, the Lord of all the earth, rest

Expecting the Unexpected

Jason McElwain was the seventeen-year-old manager of his school's basketball team. Though he loved basketball, he'd never actually played in a real high-school game. Why? Jason had autism. But on senior night, his coach put him in . . . and the unexpected happened. Jason nailed six 3-point shots and a 2-pointer. *No one* could have predicted what Jason would accomplish in that game. When the last buzzer sounded, Jason was carried off the court—the school's most unlikely hero.

If you were to choose one person who could impact your hometown for God like no other, who would it be? Would it be the captain of the football team? Would it be the best-looking cheerleader? Or would it be someone totally unexpected? A quiet seventh-grader? A determined grandfather? The school's librarian? How about one of the "bad girls" or "bad boys" from school? That's who God used.

Read **Joshua 2.9–12**. During crunch time, God used Rahab—a prostitute—to protect two Israelite spies. Why did she do it? She tells us why herself: reread **Joshua 2.11**.

Rahab knew God was real and risked her life for that belief. Will you take a risk for God? How can you put it all on the line, because you're confident in God's reality? How can you allow God to work through *you* in unexpected ways? Sometimes God even works through personal desires like Rahab's desire to protect her family.

Grab a journal or find some Creative Space in this Bible to write a poem or song to God. Express your thoughts about how God used Rahab and how he may want to use you. Explore ways that God uses unexpected people to do unprecedented things. Then post your poem or song on **Learner.CalltoDiscipleship.com**.

---

in the waters of the Jordan, the waters of the Jordan flowing from above shall be cut off; they shall stand in a single heap."

14 When the people set out from their tents to cross over the Jordan, the priests bearing the ark of the covenant were in front of the peo-

a Heb *Salt Sea*

---

ple. ¹⁵Now the Jordan overflows all its banks throughout the time of harvest. So when those who bore the ark had come to the Jordan, and the feet of the priests bearing the ark were dipped in the edge of the water, ¹⁶the waters flowing from above stood still, rising up in a single heap far off at Adam, the city that is beside Zarethan, while those flowing toward the sea of the Arabah, the Dead Sea,ª were wholly cut off. Then the people crossed over opposite Jericho. ¹⁷While all Israel were crossing over on dry ground, the priests who bore the ark of the covenant of the LORD stood on dry ground in the middle of the Jordan, until the entire nation finished crossing over the Jordan.

4 Twelve Stones Set Up at Gilgal

When the entire nation had finished crossing over the Jordan, the LORD said to Joshua: ²"Select twelve men from the people, one from each tribe, ³and command them, 'Take twelve stones from here out of the middle of the Jordan, from the place where the priests' feet stood, carry them over with you, and lay them down in the place where you camp tonight.' " ⁴Then Joshua summoned the twelve men from the Israelites, whom he had appointed, one from each tribe. ⁵Joshua said to them, "Pass on before the ark of the LORD your God into the middle of the Jordan, and each of you take up a stone on his shoulder, one for each of the tribes of the Israelites, ⁶so that this may be a sign among you. When your children ask in time to come, 'What do those stones mean to you?' ⁷then you shall tell them that the waters of the Jordan were cut off in front of the ark of the covenant of the LORD. When it crossed over the Jordan, the waters of the Jordan were cut off. So these stones shall be to the Israelites a memorial forever."

8 The Israelites did as Joshua commanded. They took up twelve stones out of the middle of the Jordan, according to the number of the tribes of the Israelites, as the LORD told Joshua, carried them over with them to the place where they camped, and laid them down there. ⁹(Joshua set up twelve stones in the middle of the Jordan, in the place where the feet of the priests bearing the ark of the covenant had stood; and they are there to this day.)

10 The priests who bore the ark remained standing in the middle of the Jordan, until everything was finished that the LORD commanded Joshua to tell the people, according to all that Moses had commanded Joshua. The people crossed over in haste. ¹¹As soon as all the people had finished crossing over, the ark of

the LORD, and the priests, crossed over in front of the people. ¹²The Reubenites, the Gadites, and the half-tribe of Manasseh crossed over armed before the Israelites, as Moses had ordered them. ¹³About forty thousand armed for war crossed over before the LORD to the plains of Jericho for battle.

14 On that day the LORD exalted Joshua in the sight of all Israel; and they stood in awe of him, as they had stood in awe of Moses, all the days of his life.

15 The LORD said to Joshua, ¹⁶"Command the priests who bear the ark of the covenant,ᵃ to come up out of the Jordan." ¹⁷Joshua therefore commanded the priests, "Come up out of the Jordan." ¹⁸When the priests bearing the ark of the covenant of the LORD came up from the middle of the Jordan, and the soles of the priests' feet touched dry ground, the waters of the Jordan returned to their place and overflowed all its banks, as before.

19 The people came up out of the Jordan on the tenth day of the first month, and they camped in Gilgal on the east border of Jericho. ²⁰Those twelve stones, which they had taken out of the Jordan, Joshua set up in Gilgal, ²¹saying to the Israelites, "When your children ask their parents in time to come, 'What do these stones mean?' ²²then you shall let your children know, 'Israel crossed over the Jordan here on dry ground.' ²³For the LORD your God dried up the waters of the Jordan for you until you crossed over, as the LORD your God did to the Red Sea,ᵇ which he dried up for us until we crossed over, ²⁴so that all the peoples of the earth may know that the hand of the LORD is mighty, and so that you may fear the LORD your God forever."

5 The New Generation Circumcised

When all the kings of the Amorites beyond the Jordan to the west, and all the kings of the Canaanites by the sea, heard that the LORD had dried up the waters of the Jordan for the Israelites until they had crossed over, their hearts melted, and there was no longer any spirit in them, because of the Israelites.

2 At that time the LORD said to Joshua, "Make flint knives and circumcise the Israelites a second time." ³So Joshua made flint knives, and circumcised the Israelites at Gibeath-haaraloth.ᶜ ⁴This is the reason why Joshua circumcised them: all the males of the people who came out of Egypt, all the warriors, had died during the journey through the wilderness after they had come out of Egypt. ⁵Although all the people who came out had been circumcised, yet all the people born on the journey through the wilderness after they had come out of Egypt had not been circumcised. ⁶For the Israelites traveled forty years in the wilderness, until all the nation, the warriors who came out of Egypt, perished, not having listened to the voice of the LORD. To them the LORD swore that he would not let them see the land that he had sworn to their ancestors to give us, a land flowing with milk and honey. ⁷So it was their children, whom he raised up in their place, that Joshua circumcised; for they were uncircumcised, because they had not been circumcised on the way.

8 When the circumcising of all the nation was done, they remained in their places in the camp until they were healed. ⁹The LORD said to Joshua, "Today I have rolled away from you the disgrace of Egypt." And so that place is called Gilgalᵈ to this day.

The Passover at Gilgal

10 While the Israelites were camped in Gilgal they kept the passover in the evening on the fourteenth day of the month in the plains of Jericho. ¹¹On the day after the passover, on that very day, they ate the produce of the land, unleavened cakes and parched grain. ¹²The manna ceased on the day they ate the produce of the land, and the Israelites no longer had manna; they ate the crops of the land of Canaan that year.

Joshua's Vision

13 Once when Joshua was by Jericho, he looked up and saw a man standing before him with a drawn sword in his hand. Joshua went to him and said to him, "Are you one of us, or one of our adversaries?" ¹⁴He replied, "Neither; but as commander of the army of the LORD I have now come." And Joshua fell on his face to the earth and worshiped, and he said to him, "What do you command your servant, my lord?" ¹⁵The commander of the army of the LORD said to Joshua, "Remove the sandals from your feet, for the place where you stand is holy." And Joshua did so.

6 Jericho Taken and Destroyed

Now Jericho was shut up inside and out because of the Israelites; no one came out and no one went in. ²The LORD said to Joshua, "See, I have handed Jericho over to you, along with its king and soldiers. ³You shall march around the city, all the warriors circling the city once. Thus you shall do for six days, ⁴with seven priests bearing seven trumpets of rams' horns before the ark. On the seventh day you shall march around the city seven times, the priests blow-

---

ᵃ Or *treaty*, or *testimony*; Heb *eduth* ᵇ Or *Sea of Reeds* ᶜ That is *the Hill of the Foreskins* ᵈ Related to Heb *galal* to roll

REALITY ✓

WAR AND PEACE

The Bible is filled with stories of war. Joshua fought a battle at Jericho. Read **Joshua 5.13–6.27**. Christians went to war at the time of the Crusades. Over and over again we have seen and been involved in civil and world wars.

If Jesus came to bring peace, how can his disciples justify war? We can't. We live with it. We tolerate war when there's no doubt that people and countries are in danger and will incur grave and lasting damage; when we've tried everything else; or when we have a strong belief that the intended result of the fighting will bring about peace, not more bloodshed. As Catholics we are urged to pray and to act so the world will be free from war (see CCC 2307–2309).

What can you do to promote peace? Consider becoming genuinely informed, writing to your political leaders, or participating in a prayer for peace. Since unjust systems and oppression are often the causes of war, act to promote justice. On a smaller scale, there are always the little wars you encounter every day at home, school, or work. How can you help make peace in those situations?

ing the trumpets. ⁵When they make a long blast with the ram's horn, as soon as you hear the sound of the trumpet, then all the people shall shout with a great shout; and the wall of the city will fall down flat, and all the people shall charge straight ahead." ⁶So Joshua son of Nun summoned the priests and said to them, "Take up the ark of the covenant, and have seven priests carry seven trumpets of rams' horns in front of the ark of the LORD." ⁷To the people he said, "Go forward and march around the city; have the armed men pass on before the ark of the LORD."

8 As Joshua had commanded the people, the seven priests carrying the seven trumpets of rams' horns before the LORD went forward, blowing the trumpets, with the ark of the cov-

enant of the LORD following them. ⁹And the armed men went before the priests who blew the trumpets; the rear guard came after the ark, while the trumpets blew continually. ¹⁰To the people Joshua gave this command: "You shall not shout or let your voice be heard, nor shall you utter a word, until the day I tell you to shout. Then you shall shout." ¹¹So the ark of the LORD went around the city, circling it once; and they came into the camp, and spent the night in the camp.

12 Then Joshua rose early in the morning, and the priests took up the ark of the LORD. ¹³The seven priests carrying the seven trumpets of rams' horns before the ark of the LORD passed on, blowing the trumpets continually. The armed men went before them, and the rear guard came after the ark of the LORD, while the trumpets blew continually. ¹⁴On the second day they marched around the city once and then returned to the camp. They did this for six days.

15 On the seventh day they rose early, at dawn, and marched around the city in the same manner seven times. It was only on that day that they marched around the city seven times. ¹⁶And at the seventh time, when the priests had blown the trumpets, Joshua said to the people, "Shout! For the LORD has given you the city. ¹⁷The city and all that is in it shall be devoted to the LORD for destruction. Only Rahab the prostitute and all who are with her in her house shall live because she hid the messengers we sent. ¹⁸As for you, keep away from the things devoted to destruction, so as not to covet*ᵃ* and take any of the devoted things and make the camp of Israel an object for destruction, bringing trouble upon it. ¹⁹But all silver and gold, and vessels of bronze and iron, are sacred to the LORD; they shall go into the treasury of the LORD." ²⁰So the people shouted, and the trumpets were blown. As soon as the people heard the sound of the trumpets, they raised a great shout, and the wall fell down flat; so the people charged straight ahead into the city and captured it. ²¹Then they devoted to destruction by the edge of the sword all in the city, both men and women, young and old, oxen, sheep, and donkeys.

22 Joshua said to the two men who had spied out the land, "Go into the prostitute's house, and bring the woman out of it and all who belong to her, as you swore to her." ²³So the young men who had been spies went in and brought Rahab out, along with her father, her mother, her brothers, and all who belonged to her—they brought all her kindred

a Gk: Heb *devote to destruction* Compare 7.21

out—and set them outside the camp of Israel. [24]They burned down the city, and everything in it; only the silver and gold, and the vessels of bronze and iron, they put into the treasury of the house of the Lord. [25]But Rahab the prostitute, with her family and all who belonged to her, Joshua spared. Her family[a] has lived in Israel ever since. For she hid the messengers whom Joshua sent to spy out Jericho.

26 Joshua then pronounced this oath, saying,

"Cursed before the Lord be anyone who tries
    to build this city—this Jericho!
At the cost of his firstborn he shall lay its foundation,
    and at the cost of his youngest he shall set up its gates!"

27 So the Lord was with Joshua; and his fame was in all the land.

7 The Sin of Achan and Its Punishment

But the Israelites broke faith in regard to the devoted things: Achan son of Carmi son of Zabdi son of Zerah, of the tribe of Judah, took some of the devoted things; and the anger of the Lord burned against the Israelites.

2 Joshua sent men from Jericho to Ai, which is near Beth-aven, east of Bethel, and said to them, "Go up and spy out the land." And the men went up and spied out Ai. [3]Then they returned to Joshua and said to him, "Not all the people need go up; about two or three thousand men should go up and attack Ai. Since they are so few, do not make the whole people toil up there." [4]So about three thousand of the people went up there; and they fled before the men of Ai. [5]The men of Ai killed about thirty-six of them, chasing them from outside the gate as far as Shebarim and killing them on the slope. The hearts of the people melted and turned to water.

6 Then Joshua tore his clothes, and fell to the ground on his face before the ark of the Lord until the evening, he and the elders of Israel; and they put dust on their heads. [7]Joshua said, "Ah, Lord God! Why have you brought this people across the Jordan at all, to hand us over to the Amorites so as to destroy us? Would that we had been content to settle beyond the Jordan! [8]O Lord, what can I say, now that Israel has turned their backs to their enemies! [9]The Canaanites and all the inhabitants of the land will hear of it, and surround us, and cut off our name from the earth. Then what will you do for your great name?"

10 The Lord said to Joshua, "Stand up! Why have you fallen upon your face? [11]Israel has sinned; they have transgressed my covenant that I imposed on them. They have taken some of the devoted things; they have stolen, they have acted deceitfully, and they have put them among their own belongings. [12]Therefore the Israelites are unable to stand before their enemies; they turn their backs to their enemies, because they have become a thing devoted for destruction themselves. I will be with you no more, unless you destroy the devoted things from among you. [13]Proceed to sanctify the people, and say, 'Sanctify yourselves for tomorrow; for thus says the Lord, the God of Israel, "There are devoted things among you, O Israel; you will be unable to stand before your enemies until you take away the devoted things from among you." [14]In the morning therefore you shall come forward tribe by tribe. The tribe that the Lord takes shall come near by clans, the clan that the Lord takes shall come near by households, and the household that the Lord takes shall come near one by one. [15]And the one who is taken as having the devoted things shall be burned with fire, together with all that he has, for having transgressed the covenant of the Lord, and for having done an outrageous thing in Israel.' "

16 So Joshua rose early in the morning, and brought Israel near tribe by tribe, and the tribe of Judah was taken. [17]He brought near the clans of Judah, and the clan of the Zerahites was taken; and he brought near the clan of the Zerahites, family by family,[b] and Zabdi was taken. [18]And he brought near his household one by one, and Achan son of Carmi son of Zabdi son of Zerah, of the tribe of Judah, was taken. [19]Then Joshua said to Achan, "My son, give glory to the Lord God of Israel and make confession to him. Tell me now what you have done; do not hide it from me." [20]And Achan answered Joshua, "It is true; I am the one who sinned against the Lord God of Israel. This is what I did: [21]when I saw among the spoil a beautiful mantle from Shinar, and two hundred shekels of silver, and a bar of gold weighing fifty shekels, then I coveted them and took them. They now lie hidden in the ground inside my tent, with the silver underneath."

22 So Joshua sent messengers, and they ran to the tent; and there it was, hidden in his tent with the silver underneath. [23]They took them out of the tent and brought them to Joshua and all the Israelites; and they spread them out before the Lord. [24]Then Joshua and all Israel with him took Achan son of Zerah, with the silver, the mantle, and the bar of gold, with his sons and daughters, with his oxen, donkeys, and

a Heb She b Mss Syr: MT man by man

sheep, and his tent and all that he had; and they brought them up to the Valley of Achor. [25]Joshua said, "Why did you bring trouble on us? The LORD is bringing trouble on you today." And all Israel stoned him to death; they burned them with fire, cast stones on them, [26]and raised over him a great heap of stones that remains to this day. Then the LORD turned from his burning anger. Therefore that place to this day is called the Valley of Achor.[a]

8 Ai Captured by a Stratagem and Destroyed

Then the LORD said to Joshua, "Do not fear or be dismayed; take all the fighting men with you, and go up now to Ai. See, I have handed over to you the king of Ai with his people, his city, and his land. [2]You shall do to Ai and its king as you did to Jericho and its king; only its spoil and its livestock you may take as booty for yourselves. Set an ambush against the city, behind it."

3 So Joshua and all the fighting men set out to go up against Ai. Joshua chose thirty thousand warriors and sent them out by night [4]with the command, "You shall lie in ambush against the city, behind it; do not go very far from the city, but all of you stay alert. [5]I and all the people who are with me will approach the city. When they come out against us, as before, we shall flee from them. [6]They will come out after us until we have drawn them away from the city; for they will say, 'They are fleeing from us, as before.' While we flee from them, [7]you shall rise up from the ambush and seize the city; for the LORD your God will give it into your hand. [8]And when you have taken the city, you shall set the city on fire, doing as the LORD has ordered; see, I have commanded you." [9]So Joshua sent them out; and they went to the place of ambush, and lay between Bethel and Ai, to the west of Ai; but Joshua spent that night in the camp.[b]

10 In the morning Joshua rose early and mustered the people, and went up, with the elders of Israel, before the people to Ai. [11]All the fighting men who were with him went up, and drew near before the city, and camped on the north side of Ai, with a ravine between them and Ai. [12]Taking about five thousand men, he set them in ambush between Bethel and Ai, to the west of the city. [13]So they stationed the forces, the main encampment that was north of the city and its rear guard west of the city. But Joshua spent that night in the valley. [14]When the king of Ai saw this, he and all his people, the inhabitants of the city, hurried out early in the morning to the meeting place facing the Arabah to meet Israel in battle; but he

did not know that there was an ambush against him behind the city. [15]And Joshua and all Israel made a pretense of being beaten before them, and fled in the direction of the wilderness. [16]So all the people who were in the city were called together to pursue them, and as they pursued Joshua they were drawn away from the city. [17]There was not a man left in Ai or Bethel who did not go out after Israel; they left the city open, and pursued Israel.

18 Then the LORD said to Joshua, "Stretch out the sword that is in your hand toward Ai; for I will give it into your hand." And Joshua stretched out the sword that was in his hand toward the city. [19]As soon as he stretched out his hand, the troops in ambush rose quickly out of their place and rushed forward. They entered the city, took it, and at once set the city on fire. [20]So when the men of Ai looked back, the smoke of the city was rising to the sky. They had no power to flee this way or that, for the people who fled to the wilderness turned back against the pursuers. [21]When Joshua and all Israel saw that the ambush had taken the city and that the smoke of the city was rising, then they turned back and struck down the men of Ai. [22]And the others came out from the city against them; so they were surrounded by Israelites, some on one side, and some on the other; and Israel struck them down until no one was left who survived or escaped. [23]But the king of Ai was taken alive and brought to Joshua.

24 When Israel had finished slaughtering all the inhabitants of Ai in the open wilderness where they pursued them, and when all of them to the very last had fallen by the edge of the sword, all Israel returned to Ai, and attacked it with the edge of the sword. [25]The total of those who fell that day, both men and women, was twelve thousand—all the people of Ai. [26]For Joshua did not draw back his hand, with which he stretched out the sword, until he had utterly destroyed all the inhabitants of Ai. [27]Only the livestock and the spoil of that city Israel took as their booty, according to the word of the LORD that he had issued to Joshua. [28]So Joshua burned Ai, and made it forever a heap of ruins, as it is to this day. [29]And he hanged the king of Ai on a tree until evening; and at sunset Joshua commanded, and they took his body down from the tree, threw it down at the entrance of the gate of the city, and raised over it a great heap of stones, which stands there to this day.

Joshua Renews the Covenant

30 Then Joshua built on Mount Ebal an altar to the LORD, the God of Israel, [31]just as Moses the

a That is *Trouble* b Heb *among the people*

servant of the Lord had commanded the Israelites, as it is written in the book of the law of Moses, "an altar of unhewn[a] stones, on which no iron tool has been used"; and they offered on it burnt offerings to the Lord, and sacrificed offerings of well-being. [32]And there, in the presence of the Israelites, Joshua[b] wrote on the stones a copy of the law of Moses, which he had written. [33]All Israel, alien as well as citizen, with their elders and officers and their judges, stood on opposite sides of the ark in front of the levitical priests who carried the ark of the covenant of the Lord, half of them in front of Mount Gerizim and half of them in front of Mount Ebal, as Moses the servant of the Lord had commanded at the first, that they should bless the people of Israel. [34]And afterward he read all the words of the law, blessings and curses, according to all that is written in the book of the law. [35]There was not a word of all that Moses commanded that Joshua did not read before all the assembly of Israel, and the women, and the little ones, and the aliens who resided among them.

9 The Gibeonites Save Themselves by Trickery

Now when all the kings who were beyond the Jordan in the hill country and in the lowland all along the coast of the Great Sea toward Lebanon—the Hittites, the Amorites, the Canaanites, the Perizzites, the Hivites, and the Jebusites—heard of this, [2]they gathered together with one accord to fight Joshua and Israel.

3 But when the inhabitants of Gibeon heard what Joshua had done to Jericho and to Ai, [4]they on their part acted with cunning: they went and prepared provisions,[c] and took worn-out sacks for their donkeys, and wineskins, worn-out and torn and mended, [5]with worn-out, patched sandals on their feet, and worn-out clothes; and all their provisions were dry and moldy. [6]They went to Joshua in the camp at Gilgal, and said to him and to the Israelites, "We have come from a far country; so now make a treaty with us." [7]But the Israelites said to the Hivites, "Perhaps you live among us; then how can we make a treaty with you?" [8]They said to Joshua, "We are your servants." And Joshua said to them, "Who are you? And where do you come from?" [9]They said to him, "Your servants have come from a very far country, because of the name of the Lord your God; for we have heard a report of him, of all that he did in Egypt, [10]and of all that he did to the two kings of the Amorites who were beyond the Jordan, King Sihon of Heshbon, and King Og of Bashan who lived in Ashtaroth. [11]So our elders and all the

inhabitants of our country said to us, 'Take provisions in your hand for the journey; go to meet them, and say to them, "We are your servants; come now, make a treaty with us." ' [12]Here is our bread; it was still warm when we took it from our houses as our food for the journey, on the day we set out to come to you, but now, see, it is dry and moldy; [13]these wineskins were new when we filled them, and see, they are burst; and these garments and sandals of ours are worn out from the very long journey." [14]So the leaders[d] partook of their provisions, and did not ask direction from the Lord. [15]And Joshua made peace with them, guaranteeing their lives by a treaty; and the leaders of the congregation swore an oath to them.

16 But when three days had passed after they had made a treaty with them, they heard that they were their neighbors and were living among them. [17]So the Israelites set out and reached their cities on the third day. Now their cities were Gibeon, Chephirah, Beeroth, and Kiriath-jearim. [18]But the Israelites did not attack them, because the leaders of the congregation had sworn to them by the Lord, the God of Israel. Then all the congregation murmured against the leaders. [19]But all the leaders said to all the congregation, "We have sworn to them by the Lord, the God of Israel, and now we must not touch them. [20]This is what we will do to them: We will let them live, so that wrath may not come upon us, because of the oath that we swore to them." [21]The leaders said to them, "Let them live." So they became hewers of wood and drawers of water for all the congregation, as the leaders had decided concerning them.

22 Joshua summoned them, and said to

a Heb *whole* *b* Heb *he* *c* Cn: Meaning of Heb uncertain *d* Gk: Heb *men*

Untitled—© Leah Colasuonno, 15

them, "Why did you deceive us, saying, 'We are very far from you,' while in fact you are living among us? ²³Now therefore you are cursed, and some of you shall always be slaves, hewers of wood and drawers of water for the house of my God." ²⁴They answered Joshua, "Because it was told to your servants for a certainty that the LORD your God had commanded his servant Moses to give you all the land, and to destroy all the inhabitants of the land before you; so we were in great fear for our lives because of you, and did this thing. ²⁵And now we are in your hand: do as it seems good and right in your sight to do to us." ²⁶This is what he did for them: he saved them from the Israelites; and they did not kill them. ²⁷But on that day Joshua made them hewers of wood and drawers of water for the congregation and for the altar of the LORD, to continue to this day, in the place that he should choose.

10 The Sun Stands Still

When King Adoni-zedek of Jerusalem heard how Joshua had taken Ai, and had utterly destroyed it, doing to Ai and its king as he had done to Jericho and its king, and how the inhabitants of Gibeon had made peace with Israel and were among them, ²heᵃ became greatly frightened, because Gibeon was a large city, like one of the royal cities, and was larger than Ai, and all its men were warriors. ³So King Adoni-zedek of Je-

rusalem sent a message to King Hoham of Hebron, to King Piram of Jarmuth, to King Japhia of Lachish, and to King Debir of Eglon, saying, ⁴"Come up and help me, and let us attack Gibeon; for it has made peace with Joshua and with the Israelites." ⁵Then the five kings of the Amorites—the king of Jerusalem, the king of Hebron, the king of Jarmuth, the king of Lachish, and the king of Eglon—gathered their forces, and went up with all their armies and camped against Gibeon, and made war against it.

6 And the Gibeonites sent to Joshua at the camp in Gilgal, saying, "Do not abandon your servants; come up to us quickly, and save us, and help us; for all the kings of the Amorites who live in the hill country are gathered against us." ⁷So Joshua went up from Gilgal, he and all the fighting force with him, all the mighty warriors. ⁸The LORD said to Joshua, "Do not fear them, for I have handed them over to you; not one of them shall stand before you." ⁹So Joshua came upon them suddenly, having marched up all night from Gilgal. ¹⁰And the LORD threw them into a panic before Israel, who inflicted a great slaughter on them at Gibeon, chased them by the way of the ascent of Beth-horon, and struck them down as far as Azekah and Makkedah. ¹¹As they fled before Israel, while they were going down the slope of Beth-horon, the LORD threw down huge stones from heaven

ᵃ Heb they

on them as far as Azekah, and they died; there were more who died because of the hailstones than the Israelites killed with the sword.

12 On the day when the LORD gave the Amorites over to the Israelites, Joshua spoke to the LORD; and he said in the sight of Israel,

"Sun, stand still at Gibeon,
and Moon, in the valley of Aijalon."
13 And the sun stood still, and the moon stopped,
until the nation took vengeance on their enemies.

Is this not written in the Book of Jashar? The sun stopped in midheaven, and did not hurry to set for about a whole day. 14There has been no day like it before or since, when the LORD heeded a human voice; for the LORD fought for Israel.

15 Then Joshua returned, and all Israel with him, to the camp at Gilgal.

Five Kings Defeated

16 Meanwhile, these five kings fled and hid themselves in the cave at Makkedah. 17And it was told Joshua, "The five kings have been found, hidden in the cave at Makkedah." 18Joshua said, "Roll large stones against the mouth of the cave, and set men by it to guard them; 19but do not stay there yourselves; pursue your enemies, and attack them from the rear. Do not let them enter their towns, for the LORD your God has given them into your hand." 20When Joshua and the Israelites had finished inflicting a very great slaughter on them, until they were wiped out, and when the survivors had entered into the fortified towns, 21all the people returned safe to Joshua in the camp at Makkedah; no one dared to speak*a* against any of the Israelites.

22 Then Joshua said, "Open the mouth of the cave, and bring those five kings out to me from the cave." 23They did so, and brought the five kings out to him from the cave, the king of Jerusalem, the king of Hebron, the king of Jarmuth, the king of Lachish, and the king of Eglon. 24When they brought the kings out to Joshua, Joshua summoned all the Israelites, and said to the chiefs of the warriors who had gone with him, "Come near, put your feet on the necks of these kings." Then they came near and put their feet on their necks. 25And Joshua said to them, "Do not be afraid or dismayed; be strong and courageous; for thus the LORD will do to all the enemies against whom you fight." 26Afterward Joshua struck them down and put them to death, and he hung them on five trees. And they hung on the trees until evening. 27At sunset Joshua commanded, and they took

them down from the trees and threw them into the cave where they had hidden themselves; they set large stones against the mouth of the cave, which remain to this very day.

28 Joshua took Makkedah on that day, and struck it and its king with the edge of the sword; he utterly destroyed every person in it; he left no one remaining. And he did to the king of Makkedah as he had done to the king of Jericho.

29 Then Joshua passed on from Makkedah, and all Israel with him, to Libnah, and fought against Libnah. 30The LORD gave it also and its king into the hand of Israel; and he struck it with the edge of the sword, and every person in it; he left no one remaining in it; and he did to its king as he had done to the king of Jericho.

31 Next Joshua passed on from Libnah, and all Israel with him, to Lachish, and laid siege to it, and assaulted it. 32The LORD gave Lachish into the hand of Israel, and he took it on the second day, and struck it with the edge of the sword, and every person in it, as he had done to Libnah.

33 Then King Horam of Gezer came up to help Lachish; and Joshua struck him and his people, leaving him no survivors.

34 From Lachish Joshua passed on with all Israel to Eglon; and they laid siege to it, and assaulted it; 35and they took it that day, and struck it with the edge of the sword; and every person in it he utterly destroyed that day, as he had done to Lachish.

36 Then Joshua went up with all Israel from Eglon to Hebron; they assaulted it, 37and took it, and struck it with the edge of the sword, and its king and its towns, and every person in it; he left no one remaining, just as he had done to Eglon, and utterly destroyed it with every person in it.

38 Then Joshua, with all Israel, turned back to Debir and assaulted it, 39and he took it with its king and all its towns; they struck them with the edge of the sword, and utterly destroyed every person in it; he left no one remaining; just as he had done to Hebron, and as he had done to Libnah and its king, so he did to Debir and its king.

40 So Joshua defeated the whole land, the hill country and the Negeb and the lowland and the slopes, and all their kings; he left no one remaining, but utterly destroyed all that breathed, as the LORD God of Israel commanded. 41And Joshua defeated them from Kadesh-barnea to Gaza, and all the country of Goshen, as far as Gibeon. 42Joshua took all these kings and their land at one time, because the LORD God of Israel fought for Israel. 43Then Joshua returned, and all Israel with him, to the camp at Gilgal.

a Heb *moved his tongue*

11 The United Kings of Northern Canaan Defeated

When King Jabin of Hazor heard of this, he sent to King Jobab of Madon, to the king of Shimron, to the king of Achshaph, ²and to the kings who were in the northern hill country, and in the Arabah south of Chinneroth, and in the lowland, and in Naphoth-dor on the west, ³to the Canaanites in the east and the west, the Amorites, the Hittites, the Perizzites, and the Jebusites in the hill country, and the Hivites under Hermon in the land of Mizpah. ⁴They came out, with all their troops, a great army, in number like the sand on the seashore, with very many horses and chariots. ⁵All these kings joined their forces, and came and camped together at the waters of Merom, to fight with Israel.

6 And the LORD said to Joshua, "Do not be afraid of them, for tomorrow at this time I will hand over all of them, slain, to Israel; you shall hamstring their horses, and burn their chariots with fire." ⁷So Joshua came suddenly upon them with all his fighting force, by the waters of Merom, and fell upon them. ⁸And the LORD handed them over to Israel, who attacked them and chased them as far as Great Sidon and Misrephoth-maim, and eastward as far as the valley of Mizpeh. They struck them down, until they had left no one remaining. ⁹And Joshua did to them as the LORD commanded him; he hamstrung their horses, and burned their chariots with fire.

10 Joshua turned back at that time, and took Hazor, and struck its king down with the sword. Before that time Hazor was the head of all those kingdoms. ¹¹And they put to the sword all who were in it, utterly destroying them; there was no one left who breathed, and he burned Hazor with fire. ¹²And all the towns of those kings, and all their kings, Joshua took, and struck them with the edge of the sword, utterly destroying them, as Moses the servant of the LORD had commanded. ¹³But Israel burned none of the towns that stood on mounds except Hazor, which Joshua did burn. ¹⁴All the spoil of these towns, and the livestock, the Israelites took for their booty; but all the people they struck down with the edge of the sword, until they had destroyed them, and they did not leave any who breathed. ¹⁵As the LORD had commanded his servant Moses, so Moses commanded Joshua, and so Joshua did; he left nothing undone of all that the LORD had commanded Moses.

Summary of Joshua's Conquests

16 So Joshua took all that land: the hill country and all the Negeb and all the land of Goshen and the lowland and the Arabah and the hill country of Israel and its lowland, ¹⁷from Mount Halak, which rises toward Seir, as far as Baal-gad in the valley of Lebanon below Mount Hermon. He took all their kings, struck them down, and put them to death. ¹⁸Joshua made war a long time with all those kings. ¹⁹There was not a town that made peace with the Israelites, except the Hivites, the inhabitants of Gibeon; all were taken in battle. ²⁰For it was the LORD's doing to harden their hearts so that they would come against Israel in battle, in order that they might be utterly destroyed, and might receive no mercy, but be exterminated, just as the LORD had commanded Moses.

21 At that time Joshua came and wiped out the Anakim from the hill country, from Hebron, from Debir, from Anab, and from all the hill country of Judah, and from all the hill country of Israel; Joshua utterly destroyed them with their towns. ²²None of the Anakim was left in the land of the Israelites; some remained only in Gaza, in Gath, and in Ashdod. ²³So Joshua took the whole land, according to all that the LORD had spoken to Moses; and Joshua gave it for an inheritance to Israel according to their tribal allotments. And the land had rest from war.

12 The Kings Conquered by Moses

Now these are the kings of the land, whom the Israelites defeated, whose land they occupied beyond the Jordan toward the east, from the Wadi Arnon to Mount Hermon, with all the Arabah eastward: ²King Sihon of the Amorites who lived at Heshbon, and ruled from Aroer, which is on the edge of the Wadi Arnon, and from the middle of the valley as far as the river Jabbok, the boundary of the Ammonites, that is, half of Gilead, ³and the Arabah to the Sea of Chinneroth eastward, and in the direction of Beth-jeshimoth, to the sea of the Arabah, the Dead Sea,ᵃ southward to the foot of the slopes of Pisgah; ⁴and King Ogᵇ of Bashan, one of the last of the Rephaim, who lived at Ashtaroth and at Edrei ⁵and ruled over Mount Hermon and Salecah and all Bashan to the boundary of the Geshurites and the Maacathites, and over half of Gilead to the boundary of King Sihon of Heshbon. ⁶Moses, the servant of the LORD, and the Israelites defeated them; and Moses the servant of the LORD gave their land for a possession to the Reubenites and the Gadites and the half-tribe of Manasseh.

a Heb *Salt Sea* b Gk: Heb *the boundary of King Og*

The Kings Conquered by Joshua

7 The following are the kings of the land whom Joshua and the Israelites defeated on the west side of the Jordan, from Baal-gad in the valley of Lebanon to Mount Halak, that rises toward Seir (and Joshua gave their land to the tribes of Israel as a possession according to their allotments, 8 in the hill country, in the lowland, in the Arabah, in the slopes, in the wilderness, and in the Negeb, the land of the Hittites, Amorites, Canaanites, Perizzites, Hivites, and Jebusites):

9	the king of Jericho	one
	the king of Ai, which is next to Bethel	one
10	the king of Jerusalem	one
	the king of Hebron	one
11	the king of Jarmuth	one
	the king of Lachish	one
12	the king of Eglon	one
	the king of Gezer	one
13	the king of Debir	one
	the king of Geder	one
14	the king of Hormah	one
	the king of Arad	one
15	the king of Libnah	one
	the king of Adullam	one
16	the king of Makkedah	one
	the king of Bethel	one
17	the king of Tappuah	one
	the king of Hepher	one
18	the king of Aphek	one
	the king of Lasharon	one
19	the king of Madon	one
	the king of Hazor	one
20	the king of Shimron-meron	one
	the king of Achshaph	one
21	the king of Taanach	one
	the king of Megiddo	one
22	the king of Kedesh	one
	the king of Jokneam in Carmel	one
23	the king of Dor in Naphath-dor	one
	the king of Goiim in Galilee,ᵃ	one
24	the king of Tirzah	one

thirty-one kings in all.

13 The Parts of Canaan Still Unconquered

Now Joshua was old and advanced in years; and the Lᴏʀᴅ said to him, "You are old and advanced in years, and very much of the land still remains to be possessed. 2 This is the land that still remains: all the regions of the Philistines, and all those of the Geshurites 3 (from the Shihor, which is east of Egypt, northward to the boundary of Ekron, it is reckoned as Canaanite; there are five rulers of the Philistines, those of Gaza, Ashdod, Ashkelon, Gath, and Ekron), and those of the Avvim 4 in the south; all the land

a Gk: Heb *Gilgal*

SEARCHING FOR A HOME

Imagine this. You are in a place with no running water. Your food is what you can scavenge or steal. The only belongings you have fit in your backpack. In this new "homeland" it's almost impossible to find a job. When you do, your pay is below minimum wage and in a dangerous or unhealthy environment. The citizens of this new place look down on you and call you names.

Or perhaps you're a refugee. You and your family have fled the comfort and stability of your home, because you were afraid for your lives. You have walked miles and miles, and now you are crushed together in a refugee camp; you haven't had a bath or shower in weeks. You are housed in small tents. There are thousands of tents, many inhabited by people you do not trust. There is an airlift of food being dropped. You hope someone in your family gets there soon enough to bring food back to camp.

Our own concerns for a home and a homeland remind us that all human beings not only need but deserve the conditions necessary for proper human growth as a promise of God.

Think about this recent statement:

From its founding to the present, the United States remains a nation of immigrants grounded in the firm belief that newcomers offer new energy, hope and cultural diversity. Our common faith in Jesus Christ moves us to search for ways that favor a spirit of solidarity. It is a faith that transcends borders and bids us to overcome all forms of discrimination and violence, so that we may build relationships that are just and loving.

—From "Strangers No Longer: Together on the Journey of Hope," a pastoral letter concerning migration, from the Catholic Bishops of Mexico and the United States Want to explore more? Read **Joshua 22.1–5.**

of the Canaanites, and Mearah that belongs to the Sidonians, to Aphek, to the boundary of the Amorites, ⁵and the land of the Gebalites, and all Lebanon, toward the east, from Baal-gad below Mount Hermon to Lebo-hamath, ⁶all the inhabitants of the hill country from Lebanon to Misrephoth-maim, even all the Sidonians. I will myself drive them out from before the Israelites; only allot the land to Israel for an inheritance, as I have commanded you. ⁷Now therefore divide this land for an inheritance to the nine tribes and the half-tribe of Manasseh."

The Territory East of the Jordan

8 With the other half-tribe of Manasseh*ᵃ* the Reubenites and the Gadites received their inheritance, which Moses gave them, beyond the Jordan eastward, as Moses the servant of the LORD gave them: ⁹from Aroer, which is on the edge of the Wadi Arnon, and the town that is in the middle of the valley, and all the tableland from*ᵇ* Medeba as far as Dibon; ¹⁰and all the cities of King Sihon of the Amorites, who reigned in Heshbon, as far as the boundary of the Ammonites; ¹¹and Gilead, and the region of the Geshurites and Maacathites, and all Mount Hermon, and all Bashan to Salecah; ¹²all the kingdom of Og in Bashan, who reigned in Ashtaroth and in Edrei (he alone was left of the survivors of the Rephaim); these Moses had defeated and driven out. ¹³Yet the Israelites did not drive out the Geshurites or the Maacathites; but Geshur and Maacath live within Israel to this day.

14 To the tribe of Levi alone Moses gave no inheritance; the offerings by fire to the LORD God of Israel are their inheritance, as he said to them.

The Territory of Reuben

15 Moses gave an inheritance to the tribe of the Reubenites according to their clans. ¹⁶Their territory was from Aroer, which is on the edge of the Wadi Arnon, and the town that is in the middle of the valley, and all the tableland by Medeba; ¹⁷with Heshbon, and all its towns that are in the tableland; Dibon, and Bamoth-baal, and Beth-baal-meon, ¹⁸and Jahaz, and Kedemoth, and Mephaath, ¹⁹and Kiriathaim, and Sibmah, and Zereth-shahar on the hill of the valley, ²⁰and Beth-peor, and the slopes of Pisgah, and Beth-jeshimoth, ²¹that is, all the towns of the tableland, and all the kingdom of King Sihon of the Amorites, who reigned in Heshbon, whom Moses defeated with the leaders of Midian, Evi and Rekem and Zur and Hur and Reba, as princes of Sihon, who lived in the

land. ²²Along with the rest of those they put to death, the Israelites also put to the sword Balaam son of Beor, who practiced divination. ²³And the border of the Reubenites was the Jordan and its banks. This was the inheritance of the Reubenites according to their families with their towns and villages.

The Territory of Gad

24 Moses gave an inheritance also to the tribe of the Gadites, according to their families. ²⁵Their territory was Jazer, and all the towns of Gilead, and half the land of the Ammonites, to Aroer, which is east of Rabbah, ²⁶and from Heshbon to Ramath-mizpeh and Betonim, and from Mahanaim to the territory of Debir,*ᶜ* ²⁷and in the valley Beth-haram, Beth-nimrah, Succoth, and Zaphon, the rest of the kingdom of King Sihon of Heshbon, the Jordan and its banks, as far as the lower end of the Sea of Chinnereth, eastward beyond the Jordan. ²⁸This is the inheritance of the Gadites according to their clans, with their towns and villages.

The Territory of the Half-Tribe of Manasseh (East)

29 Moses gave an inheritance to the half-tribe of Manasseh; it was allotted to the half-tribe of the Manassites according to their families. ³⁰Their territory extended from Mahanaim, through all Bashan, the whole kingdom of King Og of Bashan, and all the settlements of Jair, which are in Bashan, sixty towns, ³¹and half of Gilead, and Ashtaroth, and Edrei, the towns of the kingdom of Og in Bashan; these were allotted to the people of Machir son of Manasseh according to their clans—for half the Machirites.

32 These are the inheritances that Moses distributed in the plains of Moab, beyond the Jordan east of Jericho. ³³But to the tribe of Levi Moses gave no inheritance; the LORD God of Israel is their inheritance, as he said to them.

14 The Distribution of Territory West of the Jordan

These are the inheritances that the Israelites received in the land of Canaan, which the priest Eleazar, and Joshua son of Nun, and the heads of the families of the tribes of the Israelites distributed to them. ²Their inheritance was by lot, as the LORD had commanded Moses for the nine and one-half tribes. ³For Moses had given an inheritance to the two and one-half tribes beyond the Jordan; but to the Levites he gave no inheritance among them. ⁴For the people of Joseph were two tribes, Manasseh and Ephraim; and no portion was given to the

---

a Cn: Heb With it *b* Compare Gk: Heb lacks *from* *c* Gk Syr Vg: Heb Lidebir

EVEN THOUGH I WILL STUMBLE

Even though I will stumble
on this path in front of me
just hold onto my hand,
be my hope and my strength.
If I walk across the mountains
and everything's at ease
I still need You oh Lord
to be my guide in this life.
And so be my God.
Won't You lead me through
the darkness and be the light of my life?
Lead me on, everlasting King,
oh be my shepherd, be there for me
'cause I am Yours.
Lord, I will trust in You.
Everything's in Your hands.
I will have faith in You, Almighty God.
You have my heart and my life.
I am Yours forever.

Even Though I Will Stumble—© Angelique Crest, 17

When we think of a nation, we think of a united territory. But when the Israelites conquered Canaan, they really only conquered parts of it at first. So they divided the land among the twelve tribes before they really controlled it (Joshua 17.11–13). Later, individual tribes conquered cities to unite their areas.

This information has been scanned and is free of all known viruses. Please forward to all your friends.

Levites in the land, but only towns to live in, with their pasture lands for their flocks and herds. ⁵The Israelites did as the LORD commanded Moses; they allotted the land.

Hebron Allotted to Caleb

6 Then the people of Judah came to Joshua at Gilgal; and Caleb son of Jephunneh the Kenizzite said to him, "You know what the LORD said to Moses the man of God in Kadesh-barnea concerning you and me. ⁷I was forty years old when Moses the servant of the LORD sent me from Kadesh-barnea to spy out the land; and I brought him an honest report. ⁸But my companions who went up with me made the heart of the people melt; yet I wholeheartedly followed the LORD my God. ⁹And Moses swore on that day, saying, 'Surely the land on which

your foot has trodden shall be an inheritance for you and your children forever, because you have wholeheartedly followed the LORD my God.' ¹⁰And now, as you see, the LORD has kept me alive, as he said, these forty-five years since the time that the LORD spoke this word to Moses, while Israel was journeying through the wilderness; and here I am today, eighty-five years old. ¹¹I am still as strong today as I was on the day that Moses sent me; my strength now is as my strength was then, for war, and for going and coming. ¹²So now give me this hill country of which the LORD spoke on that day; for you heard on that day how the Anakim were there, with great fortified cities; it may be that the LORD will be with me, and I shall drive them out, as the LORD said."

13 Then Joshua blessed him, and gave Hebron to Caleb son of Jephunneh for an inheritance. ¹⁴So Hebron became the inheritance of Caleb son of Jephunneh the Kenizzite to this day, because he wholeheartedly followed the LORD, the God of Israel. ¹⁵Now the name of Hebron formerly was Kiriath-arba;ᵃ this Arba wasᵇ the greatest man among the Anakim. And the land had rest from war.

15 The Territory of Judah

The lot for the tribe of the people of Judah according to their families reached southward to the boundary of Edom, to the wilderness of Zin at the farthest south. ²And their south boundary ran from the end of the Dead Sea,ᶜ from the bay that faces southward; ³it goes out southward of the ascent of Akrabbim, passes along to Zin, and goes up south of Kadesh-barnea, along by Hezron, up to Addar, makes a turn to Karka, ⁴passes along to Azmon, goes out by the Wadi of Egypt, and comes to its end at the sea. This shall be your south boundary. ⁵And the east boundary is the Dead Sea,ᶜ to the mouth of the Jordan. And the boundary on the north side runs from the bay of the sea at the mouth of the Jordan; ⁶and the boundary goes up to Beth-hoglah, and passes along north of Beth-arabah; and the boundary goes up to the Stone of Bohan, Reuben's son; ⁷and the boundary goes up to Debir from the Valley of Achor, and so northward, turning toward Gilgal, which is opposite the ascent of Adummim, which is on the south side of the valley; and the boundary passes along to the waters of En-shemesh, and ends at En-rogel; ⁸then the boundary goes up by the valley of the son of Hinnom at the southern slope of the Jebusites (that is, Jerusalem); and the boundary goes up to the top of the mountain that lies over against the valley of Hinnom,

---

a That is the city of Arba b Heb lacks this Arba was c Heb Salt Sea on the west, at the northern end of the valley of Rephaim; ⁹then the boundary extends from the top of the mountain to the spring of the Waters of Nephtoah, and from there to the towns of Mount Ephron; then the boundary bends around to Baalah (that is, Kiriath-jearim); ¹⁰and the boundary circles west of Baalah to Mount Seir, passes along to the northern slope of Mount Jearim (that is, Chesalon), and goes down to Beth-shemesh, and passes along by Timnah; ¹¹the boundary goes out to the slope of the hill north of Ekron, then the boundary bends around to Shikkeron, and passes along to Mount Baalah, and goes out to Jabneel; then the boundary comes to an end at the sea. ¹²And the west boundary was the Mediterranean with its coast. This is the boundary surrounding the people of Judah according to their families.

Caleb Occupies His Portion

13 According to the commandment of the LORD to Joshua, he gave to Caleb son of Jephunneh a portion among the people of Judah, Kiriath-arba,ᵃ that is, Hebron (Arba was the father of Anak). ¹⁴And Caleb drove out from there the three sons of Anak: Sheshai, Ahiman, and Talmai, the descendants of Anak. ¹⁵From there he went up against the inhabitants of Debir; now the name of Debir formerly was Kiriath-sepher. ¹⁶And Caleb said, "Whoever attacks Kiriath-sepher and takes it, to him I will give my daughter Achsah as wife." ¹⁷Othniel son of Kenaz, the brother of Caleb, took it; and he gave him his daughter Achsah as wife. ¹⁸When she came to him, she urged him to ask her father for a field. As she dismounted from her donkey, Caleb said to her, "What do you wish?" ¹⁹She said to him, "Give me a present; since you have set me in the land of the Negeb, give me springs of water as well." So Caleb gave her the upper springs and the lower springs.

The Towns of Judah

20 This is the inheritance of the tribe of the people of Judah according to their families. ²¹The towns belonging to the tribe of the people of Judah in the extreme south, toward the boundary of Edom, were Kabzeel, Eder, Jagur, ²²Kinah, Dimonah, Adadah, ²³Kedesh, Hazor, Ithnan, ²⁴Ziph, Telem, Bealoth, ²⁵Hazor-hadattah, Kerioth-hezron (that is, Hazor), ²⁶Amam, Shema, Moladah, ²⁷Hazar-gaddah, Heshmon, Beth-pelet, ²⁸Hazar-shual, Beer-sheba, Biziothiah, ²⁹Baalah, Iim, Ezem, ³⁰Eltolad, Chesil, Hormah, ³¹Ziklag, Madmannah, Sansannah, ³²Lebaoth, Shilhim, Ain, and Rimmon: in all, twenty-nine towns, with their villages.

ᵃ That is the city of Arba

33 And in the lowland, Eshtaol, Zorah, Ashnah, ³⁴Zanoah, En-gannim, Tappuah, Enam, ³⁵Jarmuth, Adullam, Socoh, Azekah, ³⁶Shaaraim, Adithaim, Gederah, Gederothaim: fourteen towns with their villages.

37 Zenan, Hadashah, Migdal-gad, ³⁸Dilan, Mizpeh, Jokthe-el, ³⁹Lachish, Bozkath, Eglon, ⁴⁰Cabbon, Lahmam, Chitlish, ⁴¹Gederoth, Beth-dagon, Naamah, and Makkedah: sixteen towns with their villages.

42 Libnah, Ether, Ashan, ⁴³Iphtah, Ashnah, Nezib, ⁴⁴Keilah, Achzib, and Mareshah: nine towns with their villages.

45 Ekron, with its dependencies and its villages; ⁴⁶from Ekron to the sea, all that were near Ashdod, with their villages.

47 Ashdod, its towns and its villages; Gaza, its towns and its villages; to the Wadi of Egypt, and the Great Sea with its coast.

48 And in the hill country, Shamir, Jattir, Socoh, ⁴⁹Dannah, Kiriath-sannah (that is, Debir), ⁵⁰Anab, Eshtemoh, Anim, ⁵¹Goshen, Holon, and Giloh: eleven towns with their villages.

52 Arab, Dumah, Eshan, ⁵³Janim, Beth-tappuah, Aphekah, ⁵⁴Humtah, Kiriath-arba (that is, Hebron), and Zior: nine towns with their villages.

55 Maon, Carmel, Ziph, Juttah, ⁵⁶Jezreel, Jokdeam, Zanoah, ⁵⁷Kain, Gibeah, and Timnah: ten towns with their villages.

58 Halhul, Beth-zur, Gedor, ⁵⁹Maarath, Beth-anoth, and Eltekon: six towns with their villages.

60 Kiriath-baal (that is, Kiriath-jearim) and Rabbah: two towns with their villages.

61 In the wilderness, Beth-arabah, Middin, Secacah, ⁶²Nibshan, the City of Salt, and En-gedi: six towns with their villages.

63 But the people of Judah could not drive out the Jebusites, the inhabitants of Jerusalem; so the Jebusites live with the people of Judah in Jerusalem to this day.

16 The Territory of Ephraim

The allotment of the Josephites went from the Jordan by Jericho, east of the waters of Jericho, into the wilderness, going up from Jericho into the hill country to Bethel; ²then going from Bethel to Luz, it passes along to Ataroth, the territory of the Archites; ³then it goes down westward to the territory of the Japhletites, as far as the territory of Lower Beth-horon, then to Gezer, and it ends at the sea.

4 The Josephites—Manasseh and Ephraim—received their inheritance.

5 The territory of the Ephraimites by their families was as follows: the boundary of their inheritance on the east was Ataroth-addar as far

as Upper Beth-horon, ⁶and the boundary goes from there to the sea; on the north is Michmethath; then on the east the boundary makes a turn toward Taanath-shiloh, and passes along beyond it on the east to Janoah, ⁷then it goes down from Janoah to Ataroth and to Naarah, and touches Jericho, ending at the Jordan. ⁸From Tappuah the boundary goes westward to the Wadi Kanah, and ends at the sea. Such is the inheritance of the tribe of the Ephraimites by their families, ⁹together with the towns that were set apart for the Ephraimites within the inheritance of the Manassites, all those towns with their villages. ¹⁰They did not, however, drive out the Canaanites who lived in Gezer: so the Canaanites have lived within Ephraim to this day but have been made to do forced labor.

17 The Other Half-Tribe of Manasseh (West)

Then allotment was made to the tribe of Manasseh, for he was the firstborn of Joseph. To Machir the firstborn of Manasseh, the father of Gilead, were allotted Gilead and Bashan, because he was a warrior. ²And allotments were made to the rest of the tribe of Manasseh, by their families, Abiezer, Helek, Asriel, Shechem, Hepher, and Shemida; these were the male descendants of Manasseh son of Joseph, by their families.

3 Now Zelophehad son of Hepher son of Gilead son of Machir son of Manasseh had no sons, but only daughters; and these are the names of his daughters: Mahlah, Noah, Hoglah, Milcah, and Tirzah. ⁴They came before the priest Eleazar and Joshua son of Nun and the leaders, and said, "The LORD commanded Moses to give us an inheritance along with our male kin." So according to the commandment of the LORD he gave them an inheritance among the kinsmen of their father. ⁵Thus there fell to Manasseh ten portions, besides the land of Gilead and Bashan, which is on the other side of the Jordan, ⁶because the daughters of Manasseh received an inheritance along with his sons. The land of Gilead was allotted to the rest of the Manassites.

7 The territory of Manasseh reached from Asher to Michmethath, which is east of Shechem; then the boundary goes along southward to the inhabitants of En-tappuah. ⁸The land of Tappuah belonged to Manasseh, but the town of Tappuah on the boundary of Manasseh belonged to the Ephraimites. ⁹Then the boundary went down to the Wadi Kanah. The towns here, to the south of the wadi, among the towns of Manasseh, belong to Ephraim. Then the boundary of Manasseh goes along the north side of the wadi and ends at the sea. ¹⁰The land to the south is Ephraim's and that to the north is Manasseh's, with the sea forming its boundary; on the north Asher is reached, and on the east Issachar. ¹¹Within Issachar and Asher, Manasseh had Beth-shean and its villages, Ibleam and its villages, the inhabitants of Dor and its villages, the inhabitants of En-dor and its villages, the inhabitants of Taanach and its villages, and the inhabitants of Megiddo and its villages (the third is Naphath).ᵃ ¹²Yet the Manassites could not take possession of those towns; but the Canaanites continued to live in that land. ¹³But when the Israelites grew strong, they put the Canaanites to forced labor, but did not utterly drive them out.

The Tribe of Joseph Protests

14 The tribe of Joseph spoke to Joshua, saying, "Why have you given me but one lot and one portion as an inheritance, since we are a numerous people, whom all along the LORD has blessed?" ¹⁵And Joshua said to them, "If you are a numerous people, go up to the forest, and clear ground there for yourselves in the land of the Perizzites and the Rephaim, since the hill country of Ephraim is too narrow for you." ¹⁶The tribe of Joseph said, "The hill country is not enough for us; yet all the Canaanites who live in the plain have chariots of iron, both those in Beth-shean and its villages and those in the Valley of Jezreel." ¹⁷Then Joshua said to the house of Joseph, to Ephraim and Manasseh, "You are indeed a numerous people, and have great power; you shall not have one lot only, ¹⁸but the hill country shall be yours, for though it is a forest, you shall clear it and possess it to its farthest borders; for you shall drive out the Canaanites, though they have chariots of iron, and though they are strong."

18 The Territories of the Remaining Tribes

Then the whole congregation of the Israelites assembled at Shiloh, and set up the tent of meeting there. The land lay subdued before them.

2 There remained among the Israelites seven tribes whose inheritance had not yet been apportioned. ³So Joshua said to the Israelites, "How long will you be slack about going in and taking possession of the land that the LORD, the God of your ancestors, has given you? ⁴Provide three men from each tribe, and I will send them out that they may begin to go throughout the land, writing a description of it with a view to their inheritances. Then come back to me. ⁵They shall divide it into seven portions, Judah continuing in its territory on the south,

---

a Meaning of Heb uncertain

and the house of Joseph in their territory on the north. ⁶You shall describe the land in seven divisions and bring the description here to me; and I will cast lots for you here before the Lᴏʀᴅ our God. ⁷The Levites have no portion among you, for the priesthood of the Lᴏʀᴅ is their heritage; and Gad and Reuben and the half-tribe of Manasseh have received their inheritance beyond the Jordan eastward, which Moses the servant of the Lᴏʀᴅ gave them."

8 So the men started on their way; and Joshua charged those who went to write the description of the land, saying, "Go throughout the land and write a description of it, and come back to me; and I will cast lots for you here before the Lᴏʀᴅ in Shiloh." ⁹So the men went and traversed the land and set down in a book a description of it by towns in seven divisions; then they came back to Joshua in the camp at Shiloh, ¹⁰and Joshua cast lots for them in Shiloh before the Lᴏʀᴅ; and there Joshua apportioned the land to the Israelites, to each a portion.

The Territory of Benjamin

11 The lot of the tribe of Benjamin according to its families came up, and the territory allotted to it fell between the tribe of Judah and the tribe of Joseph. ¹²On the north side their boundary began at the Jordan; then the boundary goes up to the slope of Jericho on the north, then up through the hill country westward; and it ends at the wilderness of Beth-aven. ¹³From there the boundary passes along southward in the direction of Luz, to the slope of Luz (that is, Bethel), then the boundary goes down to Ataroth-addar, on the mountain that lies south of Lower Beth-horon. ¹⁴Then the boundary goes in another direction, turning on the western side southward from the mountain that lies to the south, opposite Beth-horon, and it ends at Kiriath-baal (that is, Kiriath-jearim), a town belonging to the tribe of Judah. This forms the western side. ¹⁵The southern side begins at the outskirts of Kiriath-jearim; and the boundary goes from there to Ephron,ᵃ to the spring of the Waters of Nephtoah; ¹⁶then the boundary goes down to the border of the mountain that overlooks the valley of the son of Hinnom, which is at the north end of the valley of Rephaim; and it then goes down the valley of Hinnom, south of the slope of the Jebusites, and downward to En-rogel; ¹⁷then it bends in a northerly direction going on to En-shemesh, and from there goes to Geliloth, which is opposite the ascent of Adummim; then it goes down to the Stone of Bohan, Reuben's son; ¹⁸and passing on to the north of the slope of Beth-arabahᵇ it goes down to the Arabah; ¹⁹then the boundary passes on to the north of the slope of Beth-hoglah; and the boundary ends at the northern bay of the Dead Sea,ᶜ at the south end of the Jordan: this is the southern border. ²⁰The Jordan forms its boundary on the eastern side. This is the inheritance of the tribe of Benjamin, according to its families, boundary by boundary all around.

21 Now the towns of the tribe of Benjamin according to their families were Jericho, Beth-hoglah, Emek-keziz, ²²Beth-arabah, Zemaraim, Bethel, ²³Avvim, Parah, Ophrah, ²⁴Chephar-ammoni, Ophni, and Geba— twelve towns with their villages: ²⁵Gibeon, Ramah, Beeroth, ²⁶Mizpeh, Chephirah, Mozah, ²⁷Rekem, Irpeel, Taralah, ²⁸Zela, Haeleph, Jebusᵈ (that is, Jerusalem), Gibeahᵉ and Kiriath-jearimᶠ—fourteen towns with their villages. This is the inheritance of the tribe of Benjamin according to its families.

19 The Territory of Simeon

The second lot came out for Simeon, for the tribe of Simeon, according to its families; its inheritance lay within the inheritance of the tribe of Judah. ²It had for its inheritance Beersheba, Sheba, Moladah, ³Hazar-shual, Balah, Ezem, ⁴Eltolad, Bethul, Hormah, ⁵Ziklag, Beth-marcaboth, Hazar-susah, ⁶Beth-lebaoth, and Sharuhen—thirteen towns with their villages; ⁷Ain, Rimmon, Ether, and Ashan—four towns with their villages; ⁸together with all the villages all around these towns as far as Baalath-beer, Ramah of the Negeb. This was the inheritance of the tribe of Simeon according to its families. ⁹The inheritance of the tribe of Simeon formed part of the territory of Judah; because the portion of the tribe of Judah was

Mission Boy—© Bailey Smith, 17

ᵃ Cn See 15.9. Heb *westward* ᵇ Gk: Heb *to the slope over against the Arabah* ᶜ Heb *Salt Sea* ᵈ Gk Syr Vg: Heb *the Jebusite* ᵉ Heb *Gibeath* ᶠ Gk: Heb *Kiriath*

[11]then its boundary goes up westward, and on to Maralah, and touches Dabbesheth, then the wadi that is east of Jokneam; [12]from Sarid it goes in the other direction eastward toward the sunrise to the boundary of Chisloth-tabor; from there it goes to Daberath, then up to Japhia; [13]from there it passes along on the east toward the sunrise to Gath-hepher, to Eth-kazin, and going on to Rimmon it bends toward Neah; [14]then on the north the boundary makes a turn to Hannathon, and it ends at the valley of Iphtah-el; [15]and Kattath, Nahalal, Shimron, Idalah, and Bethlehem—twelve towns with their villages. [16]This is the inheritance of the tribe of Zebulun, according to its families—these towns with their villages.

The Territory of Issachar

17 The fourth lot came out for Issachar, for the tribe of Issachar, according to its families. [18]Its territory included Jezreel, Chesulloth, Shunem, [19]Hapharaim, Shion, Anaharath, [20]Rabbith, Kishion, Ebez, [21]Remeth, En-gannim, En-haddah, Beth-pazzez; [22]the boundary also touches Tabor, Shahazumah, and Beth-shemesh, and its boundary ends at the Jordan—sixteen towns with their villages. [23]This is the inheritance of the tribe of Issachar, according to its families—the towns with their villages.

The Territory of Asher

24 The fifth lot came out for the tribe of Asher according to its families. [25]Its boundary included Helkath, Hali, Beten, Achshaph, [26]Allammelech, Amad, and Mishal; on the west it touches Carmel and Shihor-libnath, [27]then it turns eastward, goes to Beth-dagon, and touches Zebulun and the valley of Iphtah-el northward to Beth-emek and Neiel; then it continues in the north to Cabul, [28]Ebron, Rehob, Hammon, Kanah, as far as Great Sidon; [29]then the boundary turns to Ramah, reaching to the fortified city of Tyre; then the boundary turns to Hosah, and it ends at the sea; Mahalab,[a] Achzib, [30]Ummah, Aphek, and Rehob—twenty-two towns with their villages. [31]This is the inheritance of the tribe of Asher according to its families—these towns with their villages.

The Territory of Naphtali

32 The sixth lot came out for the tribe of Naphtali, for the tribe of Naphtali, according to its families. [33]And its boundary ran from Heleph, from the oak in Zaanannim, and Adami-nekeb, and Jabneel, as far as Lakkum; and it ended at the Jordan; [34]then the boundary turns westward to Aznoth-tabor, and goes from there to Hukkok,

too large for them, the tribe of Simeon obtained an inheritance within their inheritance.

The Territory of Zebulun

10 The third lot came up for the tribe of Zebulun, according to its families. The boundary of its inheritance reached as far as Sarid;

a Cn Compare Gk: Heb *Mehebel*

touching Zebulun at the south, and Asher on the west, and Judah on the east at the Jordan. 35The fortified towns are Ziddim, Zer, Hammath, Rakkath, Chinnereth, 36Adamah, Ramah, Hazor, 37Kedesh, Edrei, En-hazor, 38Iron, Migdal-el, Horem, Beth-anath, and Beth-shemesh—nineteen towns with their villages. 39This is the inheritance of the tribe of Naphtali according to its families—the towns with their villages.

The Territory of Dan

40 The seventh lot came out for the tribe of Dan, according to its families. 41The territory of its inheritance included Zorah, Eshtaol, Ir-shemesh, 42Shaalabbin, Aijalon, Ithlah, 43Elon, Timnah, Ekron, 44Eltekeh, Gibbethon, Baalath, 45Jehud, Bene-berak, Gath-rimmon, 46Me-jarkon, and Rakkon at the border opposite Joppa. 47When the territory of the Danites was lost to them, the Danites went up and fought against Leshem, and after capturing it and putting it to the sword, they took possession of it and settled in it, calling Leshem, Dan, after their ancestor Dan. 48This is the inheritance of the tribe of Dan, according to their families—these towns with their villages.

Joshua's Inheritance

49 When they had finished distributing the several territories of the land as inheritances, the Israelites gave an inheritance among them to Joshua son of Nun. 50By command of the LORD they gave him the town that he asked for, Timnath-serah in the hill country of Ephraim; he rebuilt the town, and settled in it.

51 These are the inheritances that the priest Eleazar and Joshua son of Nun and the heads of the families of the tribes of the Israelites distributed by lot at Shiloh before the LORD, at the entrance of the tent of meeting. So they finished dividing the land.

20 The Cities of Refuge

Then the LORD spoke to Joshua, saying, 2"Say to the Israelites, 'Appoint the cities of refuge, of which I spoke to you through Moses, 3so that anyone who kills a person without intent or by mistake may flee there; they shall be for you a refuge from the avenger of blood. 4The slayer shall flee to one of these cities and shall stand at the entrance of the gate of the city, and explain the case to the elders of that city; then the fugitive shall be taken into the city, and given a place, and shall remain with them. 5And if the avenger of blood is in pursuit, they shall not give up the slayer, because the neighbor was killed by mistake, there having been no enmity between them before. 6The slayer shall remain in that city until there is a trial before the congregation, until the death of the one who is high priest at the time: then the slayer may return home, to the town in which the deed was done.' "

7 So they set apart Kedesh in Galilee in the hill country of Naphtali, and Shechem in the hill country of Ephraim, and Kiriath-arba (that is, Hebron) in the hill country of Judah. 8And beyond the Jordan east of Jericho, they appointed Bezer in the wilderness on the tableland, from the tribe of Reuben, and Ramoth in Gilead, from the tribe of Gad, and Golan in Bashan, from the tribe of Manasseh. 9These were the cities designated for all the Israelites, and for the aliens residing among them, that anyone who killed a person without intent could flee there, so as not to die by the hand of the avenger of blood, until there was a trial before the congregation.

21 Cities Allotted to the Levites

Then the heads of the families of the Levites came to the priest Eleazar and to Joshua son of Nun and to the heads of the families of the tribes of the Israelites; 2they said to them at Shiloh in the land of Canaan, "The LORD commanded through Moses that we be given towns to live in, along with their pasture lands for our livestock." 3So by command of the LORD the Israelites gave to the Levites the following towns and pasture lands out of their inheritance.

4 The lot came out for the families of the Kohathites. So those Levites who were descendants of Aaron the priest received by lot thirteen towns from the tribes of Judah, Simeon, and Benjamin.

5 The rest of the Kohathites received by lot ten towns from the families of the tribe of Ephraim, from the tribe of Dan, and the half-tribe of Manasseh.

6 The Gershonites received by lot thirteen towns from the families of the tribe of Issachar, from the tribe of Asher, from the tribe of Naphtali, and from the half-tribe of Manasseh in Bashan.

7 The Merarites according to their families received twelve towns from the tribe of Reuben, the tribe of Gad, and the tribe of Zebulun.

8 These towns and their pasture lands the Israelites gave by lot to the Levites, as the LORD had commanded through Moses.

9 Out of the tribe of Judah and the tribe of Simeon they gave the following towns mentioned by name, 10which went to the descendants of Aaron, one of the families of the Kohathites who belonged to the Levites, since the lot fell to them first. 11They gave them Kiriath-arba (Arba being the father of Anak), that is Hebron, in the hill country of Judah, along with the pasture lands around it. 12But the

fields of the town and its villages had been given to Caleb son of Jephunneh as his holding.

13 To the descendants of Aaron the priest they gave Hebron, the city of refuge for the slayer, with its pasture lands, Libnah with its pasture lands, [14]Jattir with its pasture lands, Eshtemoa with its pasture lands, [15]Holon with its pasture lands, Debir with its pasture lands, [16]Ain with its pasture lands, Juttah with its pasture lands, and Beth-shemesh with its pasture lands—nine towns out of these two tribes. [17]Out of the tribe of Benjamin: Gibeon with its pasture lands, Geba with its pasture lands, [18]Anathoth with its pasture lands, and Almon with its pasture lands—four towns. [19]The towns of the descendants of Aaron—the priests—were thirteen in all, with their pasture lands.

20 As to the rest of the Kohathites belonging to the Kohathite families of the Levites, the towns allotted to them were out of the tribe of Ephraim. [21]To them were given Shechem, the city of refuge for the slayer, with its pasture lands in the hill country of Ephraim, Gezer with its pasture lands, [22]Kibzaim with its pasture lands, and Beth-horon with its pasture lands—four towns. [23]Out of the tribe of Dan: Elteke with its pasture lands, Gibbethon with its pasture lands, [24]Aijalon with its pasture lands, Gath-rimmon with its pasture lands—four towns. [25]Out of the half-tribe of Manasseh: Taanach with its pasture lands, and Gath-rimmon with its pasture lands—two towns. [26]The towns of the families of the rest of the Kohathites were ten in all, with their pasture lands.

27 To the Gershonites, one of the families of the Levites, were given out of the half-tribe of Manasseh, Golan in Bashan with its pasture lands, the city of refuge for the slayer, and Beeshterah with its pasture lands—two towns. [28]Out of the tribe of Issachar: Kishion with its pasture lands, Daberath with its pasture lands, [29]Jarmuth with its pasture lands, En-gannim with its pasture lands—four towns. [30]Out of the tribe of Asher: Mishal with its pasture lands, Abdon with its pasture lands, [31]Helkath with its pasture lands, and Rehob with its pasture lands—four towns. [32]Out of the tribe of Naphtali: Kedesh in Galilee with its pasture lands, the city of refuge for the slayer, Hammoth-dor with its pasture lands, and Kartan with its pasture lands—three towns. [33]The towns of the several families of the Gershonites were in all thirteen, with their pasture lands.

34 To the rest of the Levites—the Merarite families—were given out of the tribe of Zebulun: Jokneam with its pasture lands, Kartah with its pasture lands, [35]Dimnah with its pasture lands, Nahalal with its pasture lands—four towns. [36]Out of the tribe of Reuben: Bezer with its pasture lands, Jahzah with its pasture lands, [37]Kedemoth with its pasture lands, and Mephaath with its pasture lands—four towns. [38]Out of the tribe of Gad: Ramoth in Gilead with its pasture lands, the city of refuge for the slayer, Mahanaim with its pasture lands, [39]Heshbon with its pasture lands, Jazer with its pasture lands—four towns in all. [40]As for the towns of the several Merarite families, that is, the remainder of the families of the Levites, those allotted to them were twelve in all.

41 The towns of the Levites within the holdings of the Israelites were in all forty-eight towns with their pasture lands. [42]Each of these towns had its pasture lands around it; so it was with all these towns.

43 Thus the LORD gave to Israel all the land that he swore to their ancestors that he would give them; and having taken possession of it, they settled there. [44]And the LORD gave them rest on every side just as he had sworn to their ancestors; not one of all their enemies had withstood them, for the LORD had given all their enemies into their hands. [45]Not one of all the good promises that the LORD had made to the house of Israel had failed; all came to pass.

22 The Eastern Tribes Return to Their Territory

Then Joshua summoned the Reubenites, the Gadites, and the half-tribe of Manasseh, [2]and said to them, "You have observed all that Moses the servant of the LORD commanded you, and have obeyed me in all that I have commanded you; [3]you have not forsaken your kindred these many days, down to this day, but have been careful to keep the charge of the LORD your God. [4]And now the LORD your God has given rest to your kindred, as he promised them; therefore turn and go to your tents in the land where your possession lies, which Moses the servant of the LORD gave you on the other side of the Jordan. [5]Take good care to observe the commandment and instruction that Moses the servant of the LORD commanded you, to love the LORD your God, to walk in all his ways, to keep his commandments, and to hold fast to him, and to serve him with all your heart and with all your soul." [6]So Joshua blessed them and sent them away, and they went to their tents.

7 Now to the one half of the tribe of Manasseh Moses had given a possession in Bashan; but to the other half Joshua had given a possession beside their fellow Israelites in the land west of the Jordan. And when Joshua sent them away to their tents and blessed them, [8]he said to them, "Go back to your tents with much wealth, and with very much livestock, with silver, gold, bronze, and iron, and

with a great quantity of clothing; divide the spoil of your enemies with your kindred." [9]So the Reubenites and the Gadites and the half-tribe of Manasseh returned home, parting from the Israelites at Shiloh, which is in the land of Canaan, to go to the land of Gilead, their own land of which they had taken possession by command of the LORD through Moses.

A Memorial Altar East of the Jordan

10 When they came to the region[a] near the Jordan that lies in the land of Canaan, the Reubenites and the Gadites and the half-tribe of Manasseh built there an altar by the Jordan, an altar of great size. [11]The Israelites heard that the Reubenites and the Gadites and the half-tribe of Manasseh had built an altar at the frontier of the land of Canaan, in the region[b] near the Jordan, on the side that belongs to the Israelites. [12]And when the people of Israel heard of it, the whole assembly of the Israelites gathered at Shiloh, to make war against them.

13 Then the Israelites sent the priest Phinehas son of Eleazar to the Reubenites and the Gadites and the half-tribe of Manasseh, in the land of Gilead, [14]and with him ten chiefs, one from each of the tribal families of Israel, every one of them the head of a family among the clans of Israel. [15]They came to the Reubenites, the Gadites, and the half-tribe of Manasseh, in the land of Gilead, and they said to them, [16]"Thus says the whole congregation of the LORD, 'What is this treachery that you have committed against the God of Israel in turning away today from following the LORD, by building yourselves an altar today in rebellion against the LORD? [17]Have we not had enough of the sin at Peor from which even yet we have not cleansed ourselves, and for which a plague came upon the congregation of the LORD, [18]that you must turn away today from following the LORD! If you rebel against the LORD today, he will be angry with the whole congregation of Israel tomorrow. [19]But now, if your land is unclean, cross over into the LORD's land where the LORD's tabernacle now stands, and take for yourselves a possession among us; only do not rebel against the LORD, or rebel against us[c] by building yourselves an altar other than the altar of the LORD our God. [20]Did not Achan son of Zerah break faith in the matter of the devoted things, and wrath fell upon all the congregation of Israel? And he did not perish alone for his iniquity!' "

21 Then the Reubenites, the Gadites, and the half-tribe of Manasseh said in answer to the heads of the families of Israel, [22]"The

a Or to Geliloth b Or at Geliloth c Or make rebels of us

Declarations

Do you ever get sick of political speeches? Those speeches with every word carefully crafted to keep everyone happy, to get everybody's vote, and to offend the fewest number of people? The strange thing is that in speeches like that it's basically impossible to figure out what the person is actually *saying*.

Not so with Joshua.

Read Joshua 24.14–15. You can almost hear the theme music swell as Joshua declares that not only will *he* obey God, but so will his wife. And his kids. And servants. And, presumably, his goats.

Joshua says it like it is.

If only *we* had that caliber of confidence. We mumble our way through the renewal of our baptismal promises or the creed at Mass every Sunday. Shouldn't they be words we proclaim loudly and with enthusiasm? We know from experience how quickly our passion for following God fades.

But what if, on behalf of your entire family, you *could* declare that your family will serve God—and God only?

Before you answer, consider: What would need to change? What would you start doing? Quit doing?

Jot down three of the more significant consequences below:

-
-
-

Got them? That's called counting the cost, and sincerely following God *always* costs something.

Share your list with your family and, without naming names, report how the conversation goes at Learner.CalltoDiscipleship.com. We'll be looking to hear from you.

Strong at Heart—© Morgan Katchuk, 14

LORD, God of gods! The LORD, God of gods! He knows; and let Israel itself know! If it was in rebellion or in breach of faith toward the LORD, do not spare us today ²³for building an altar to turn away from following the LORD; or if we did so to offer burnt offerings or grain offerings or offerings of well-being on it, may the LORD himself take vengeance. ²⁴No! We did it from fear that in time to come your children might say to our children, 'What have you to do with the LORD, the God of Israel? ²⁵For the LORD has made the Jordan a boundary between us and you, you Reubenites and Gadites; you have no portion in the LORD.' So your children might make our children cease to worship the LORD. ²⁶Therefore we said, 'Let us now build an altar, not for burnt offering, nor for sacrifice, ²⁷but to be a witness between us and you, and between the generations after us, that we do perform the service of the LORD in his presence with our burnt offerings and sacrifices and offerings of well-being; so that your children may never say to our children in time to come, "You have no portion in the LORD." ' ²⁸And we thought, If this should be said to us or to our descendants in time to come, we could say, 'Look at this copy of the altar of the LORD, which our ancestors made, not for burnt offerings, nor for sacrifice, but to be a witness between us and you.' ²⁹Far be it from us that we should rebel against the LORD, and turn away

this day from following the LORD by building an altar for burnt offering, grain offering, or sacrifice, other than the altar of the LORD our God that stands before his tabernacle!"

30 When the priest Phinehas and the chiefs of the congregation, the heads of the families of Israel who were with him, heard the words that the Reubenites and the Gadites and the Manassites spoke, they were satisfied. ³¹The priest Phinehas son of Eleazar said to the Reubenites and the Gadites and the Manassites, "Today we know that the LORD is among us, because you have not committed this treachery against the LORD; now you have saved the Israelites from the hand of the LORD."

32 Then the priest Phinehas son of Eleazar and the chiefs returned from the Reubenites and the Gadites in the land of Gilead to the land of Canaan, to the Israelites, and brought back word to them. ³³The report pleased the Israelites; and the Israelites blessed God and spoke no more of making war against them, to destroy the land where the Reubenites and the Gadites were settled. ³⁴The Reubenites and the Gadites called the altar Witness;[a] "For," said they, "it is a witness between us that the LORD is God."

23 Joshua Exhorts the People

A long time afterward, when the LORD had given rest to Israel from all their enemies all

a Cn Compare Syr: Heb lacks *Witness*

around, and Joshua was old and well advanced in years, [2]Joshua summoned all Israel, their elders and heads, their judges and officers, and said to them, "I am now old and well advanced in years; [3]and you have seen all that the LORD your God has done to all these nations for your sake, for it is the LORD your God who has fought for you. [4]I have allotted to you as an inheritance for your tribes those nations that remain, along with all the nations that I have already cut off, from the Jordan to the Great Sea in the west. [5]The LORD your God will push them back before you, and drive them out of your sight; and you shall possess their land, as the LORD your God promised you. [6]Therefore be very steadfast to observe and do all that is written in the book of the law of Moses, turning aside from it neither to the right nor to the left, [7]so that you may not be mixed with these nations left here among you, or make mention of the names of their gods, or swear by them, or serve them, or bow yourselves down to them, [8]but hold fast to the LORD your God, as you have done to this day. [9]For the LORD has driven out before you great and strong nations; and as for you, no one has been able to withstand you to this day. [10]One of you puts to flight a thousand, since it is the LORD your God who fights for you, as he promised you. [11]Be very careful, therefore, to love the LORD your God. [12]For if you turn back, and join the survivors of these nations left here among you, and intermarry with them, so that you marry their women and they yours, [13]know assuredly that the LORD your God will not continue to drive out these nations before you; but they shall be a snare and a trap for you, a scourge on your sides, and thorns in your eyes, until you perish from this good land that the LORD your God has given you.

14 "And now I am about to go the way of all the earth, and you know in your hearts and souls, all of you, that not one thing has failed of all the good things that the LORD your God promised concerning you; all have come to pass for you, not one of them has failed. [15]But just as all the good things that the LORD your God promised concerning you have been fulfilled for you, so the LORD will bring upon you all the bad things, until he has destroyed you from this good land that the LORD your God has given you. [16]If you transgress the covenant of the LORD your God, which he enjoined on you, and go and serve other gods and bow down to them, then the anger of the LORD will be kindled against you, and you shall perish quickly from the good land that he has given to you."

24 The Tribes Renew the Covenant

Then Joshua gathered all the tribes of Israel to Shechem, and summoned the elders, the heads, the judges, and the officers of Israel; and they presented themselves before God. [2]And Joshua said to all the people, "Thus says the LORD, the God of Israel: Long ago your ancestors—Terah and his sons Abraham and Nahor—lived beyond the Euphrates and served other gods. [3]Then I took your father Abraham from beyond the River and led him through all the land of Canaan and made his offspring many. I gave him Isaac; [4]and to Isaac I gave Jacob and Esau. I gave Esau the hill country of Seir to possess, but Jacob and his children went down to Egypt. [5]Then I sent Moses and Aaron, and I plagued Egypt with what I did in its midst; and afterwards I brought you out. [6]When I brought your ancestors out of Egypt, you came to the sea; and the Egyptians pursued your ancestors with chariots and horsemen to the Red Sea.[a] [7]When they cried out to the LORD, he put darkness between you and the Egyptians, and made the sea come upon them and cover them; and your eyes saw what I did to Egypt. Afterwards you lived in the wilderness a long time. [8]Then I brought you to the land of the Amorites, who lived on the other side of the Jordan; they fought with you, and I handed them over to you, and you took possession of their land, and I destroyed them before you. [9]Then King Balak son of Zippor of Moab, set out to fight against Israel. He sent and invited Balaam son of Beor to curse you, [10]but I would not listen to Balaam; therefore he blessed you; so I rescued you out of his hand. [11]When you went over the Jordan and came to Jericho, the citizens of Jericho fought against you, and also the Amorites, the Perizzites, the Canaanites, the Hittites, the Girgashites, the Hivites, and the Jebusites; and I handed them over to you. [12]I sent the hornet[b] ahead of you, which drove out before you the two kings of the Amorites; it was not by your sword or by your bow. [13]I gave you a land on which you had not labored, and towns that you had not built, and you live in them; you eat the fruit of vineyards and olive-yards that you did not plant.

14 "Now therefore revere the LORD, and serve him in sincerity and in faithfulness; put away the gods that your ancestors served beyond the River and in Egypt, and serve the LORD. [15]Now if you are unwilling to serve the LORD, choose this day whom you will serve, whether the gods your ancestors served in the region beyond the River or the gods of the Amorites in whose land you are living; but as for me and my household, we will serve the LORD."

a Or *Sea of Reeds*   b Meaning of Heb uncertain

PROFILE OF FAITH

Miguel Pro was born in Guadalupe, Zacatecas, on January 13, 1891. The Mexican Revolution, which resulted in a massive wave of anti-Catholicism, began when he was a teenager and studying to be a Jesuit. He studied in Mexico until 1914, when governmental anti-Catholicism forced the Jesuits to flee to Los Gatos, California. From there Miguel went to study in Granada, Spain; later he went to Nicaragua and Belgium.

In Belgium, because of his easy rapport with workers, Miguel was assigned to study the Catholic labor movement. He was ordained in Belgium in 1925. His superiors sent him back to his homeland, where the 1917 Constitution of Mexico was being rigorously enforced. The Constitution forbade Catholic education, religious orders, public worship, and many of the basic civil rights of clergy and religious, who were not allowed to vote or comment on public affairs in the press.

Fr. Miguel served a parish that was forced to go "underground." He celebrated the Eucharist in secret and administered the other sacraments to small groups of Catholics. He was arrested and martyred for defying the anti-Catholic laws and government of his homeland. Before the firing squad was ordered to shoot, Pro raised his arms and shouted the defiant cry of the revolutionary Cristeros, *Viva Cristo Rey!*—"Long live Christ the King!" He was beatified in 1988.

16 Then the people answered, "Far be it from us that we should forsake the LORD to serve other gods; 17for it is the LORD our God who brought us and our ancestors up from the land of Egypt, out of the house of slavery, and who did those great signs in our sight. He protected us along all the way that we went, and among all the peoples through whom we passed; 18and the LORD drove out before us all the peoples, the Amorites who lived in the land. Therefore we also will serve the LORD, for he is our God."

19 But Joshua said to the people, "You cannot serve the LORD, for he is a holy God. He is a jealous God; he will not forgive your transgressions or your sins. 20If you forsake the LORD and serve foreign gods, then he will turn and do you harm, and consume you, after having done you good." 21And the people said to Joshua, "No, we will serve the LORD!" 22Then Joshua said to the people, "You are witnesses against yourselves that you have chosen the LORD, to serve him." And they said, "We are witnesses." 23He said, "Then put away the foreign gods that are among you, and incline your hearts to the LORD, the God of Israel." 24The people said to Joshua, "The LORD our God we will serve, and him we will obey." 25So Joshua made a covenant with the people that day, and made statutes and ordinances for them at Shechem. 26Joshua wrote these words in the book of the law of God; and

he took a large stone, and set it up there under the oak in the sanctuary of the LORD. 27Joshua said to all the people, "See, this stone shall be a witness against us; for it has heard all the words of the LORD that he spoke to us; therefore it shall be a witness against you, if you deal falsely with your God." 28So Joshua sent the people away to their inheritances.

Death of Joshua and Eleazar

29 After these things Joshua son of Nun, the servant of the LORD, died, being one hundred ten years old. 30They buried him in his own inheritance at Timnath-serah, which is in the hill country of Ephraim, north of Mount Gaash.

31 Israel served the LORD all the days of Joshua, and all the days of the elders who outlived Joshua and had known all the work that the LORD did for Israel.

32 The bones of Joseph, which the Israelites had brought up from Egypt, were buried at Shechem, in the portion of ground that Jacob had bought from the children of Hamor, the father of Shechem, for one hundred pieces of money;*a* it became an inheritance of the descendants of Joseph.

33 Eleazar son of Aaron died; and they buried him at Gibeah, the town of his son Phinehas, which had been given him in the hill country of Ephraim.

a Heb one hundred qesitah

JUDGES

A BAD DAY...OVER AND OVER AND OVER AGAIN

The Dark Days of Israel

Rampant lust. Child sacrifice. Prostitution. War and bloodshed. Sound familiar, like it's ripped from CNN?

The sad fact is that these are straight out of Israel's history during the time of Judges. If you flip to the left in your Bible, you'll find some books filled with great high points. (Those covenants with Abraham and Moses are pretty huge.) The book of Judges, on the other hand, can unquestionably be called Israel's "dark ages."

When the story begins, Israel has forgotten all that God has done and is worshiping other gods (see the first two chapters for an overview). To call his people back from idolatry, God raises up judges. But these judges weren't like Judge Judy—they were more like military leaders fighting for the future of their country.

Though the book of Judges dives into some dark themes, there is still light. The message of God's undying love for his people is clear: God will do whatever it takes to call us back to him. Judges also shows us that God will use anything or anybody to do his work. Check out Samson's story as an example (Judges 14–16). Samson is deeply flawed and messed up; to be brutally honest, he ain't the best-dressed person in the pew! But the message of Judges is one we need to learn from—that even though we may forget God, God never forgets us!

"Actions speak louder than words. . . . It is useless for a man to flaunt his knowledge of the law if he undermines its teaching by his actions."

—St. Anthony of Padua

WHO The authors and editors are unknown, but they were probably persons very familiar with Deuteronomy.

WHAT A series of stories about sin, forgiveness, and reconciliation in Israel's life with God, told through the Israelite leaders, or judges, whom God used to deliver the chosen people from their sin

WHEN The events occurred after the conquest of Canaan and before the period of the kings (ca. 1200–1000 B.C.). It may have been written during the reign of King David, in the years 1000–970 B.C.

WHERE Israel

PATH OF DISCIPLESHIP

Judges shows why remembering God is so important. Throughout Israel's history, God called on his people to remember the great and awesome things he had done. But they seemed to *forget*, over . . . and over . . . and over.

What about us? Are there things that God has done that we should be remembering? Well, for starters, there is no greater thing that we can recall than the life and death of Jesus. Every Sunday we remember and give thanks through words, actions, and songs when we celebrate the Eucharist. It's good to really remember, to really say those words and think about them. Otherwise, we can let them become rote or "boring," or we just plain old forget what they mean—to us and for us.

Unlike the people in Judges, let's remember over . . . and over . . . and over again and give thanks for the great things God has done for us.

1

Israel's Failure to Complete the Conquest of Canaan

After the death of Joshua, the Israelites inquired of the LORD, "Who shall go up first for us against the Canaanites, to fight against them?" ²The LORD said, "Judah shall go up. I hereby give the land into his hand." ³Judah said to his brother Simeon, "Come up with me into the territory allotted to me, that we may fight against the Canaanites; then I too will go with you into the territory allotted to you." So Simeon went with him. ⁴Then Judah went up and the LORD gave the Canaanites and the Perizzites into their hand; and they defeated ten thousand of them at Bezek. ⁵They came upon Adoni-bezek at Bezek, and fought against him, and defeated the Canaanites and the Perizzites. ⁶Adoni-bezek fled; but they pursued him, and caught him, and cut off his thumbs and big toes. ⁷Adoni-bezek said, "Seventy kings with their thumbs and big toes cut off used to pick up scraps under my table; as I have done, so God has paid me back." They brought him to Jerusalem, and he died there.

8 Then the people of Judah fought against Jerusalem and took it. They put it to the sword and set the city on fire. ⁹Afterward the people of Judah went down to fight against the Canaanites who lived in the hill country, in the Negeb, and in the lowland. ¹⁰Judah went against the Canaanites who lived in Hebron (the name of Hebron was formerly Kiriath-arba); and they defeated Sheshai and Ahiman and Talmai.

11 From there they went against the inhabitants of Debir (the name of Debir was formerly Kiriath-sepher). ¹²Then Caleb said, "Whoever attacks Kiriath-sepher and takes it, I will give him my daughter Achsah as wife." ¹³And Othniel son of Kenaz, Caleb's younger brother, took it; and he gave him his daughter Achsah as wife. ¹⁴When she came to him, she urged him to ask her father for a field. As she dismounted from her donkey, Caleb said to her, "What do you wish?" ¹⁵She said to him, "Give me a present; since you have set me in the land of the Negeb, give me also Gulloth-mayim."ᵃ So Caleb gave her Upper Gulloth and Lower Gulloth.

16 The descendants of Hobabᵇ the Kenite, Moses' father-in-law, went up with the people of Judah from the city of palms into the wilderness of Judah, which lies in the Negeb near Arad. Then they went and settled with the Amalekites.ᶜ ¹⁷Judah went with his brother Simeon, and they defeated the Canaanites who inhabited Zephath, and devoted it to destruction. So the city was called Hormah. ¹⁸Judah took

Gaza with its territory, Ashkelon with its territory, and Ekron with its territory. ¹⁹The LORD was with Judah, and he took possession of the hill country, but could not drive out the inhabitants of the plain, because they had chariots of iron. ²⁰Hebron was given to Caleb, as Moses had said; and he drove out from it the three sons of Anak. ²¹But the Benjaminites did not drive out the Jebusites who lived in Jerusalem; so the Jebusites have lived in Jerusalem among the Benjaminites to this day.

22 The house of Joseph also went up against Bethel; and the LORD was with them. ²³The house of Joseph sent out spies to Bethel (the name of the city was formerly Luz). ²⁴When the spies saw a man coming out of the city, they said to him, "Show us the way into the city, and we will deal kindly with you." ²⁵So he showed them the way into the city; and they put the city to the sword, but they let the man and all his family go. ²⁶So the man went to the land of the Hittites and built a city, and named it Luz; that is its name to this day.

27 Manasseh did not drive out the inhabitants of Beth-shean and its villages, or Taanach and its villages, or the inhabitants of Dor and its villages, or the inhabitants of Ibleam and its villages, or the inhabitants of Megiddo and its villages; but the Canaanites continued to live in that land. ²⁸When Israel grew strong, they put the Canaanites to forced labor, but did not in fact drive them out.

29 And Ephraim did not drive out the Canaanites who lived in Gezer; but the Canaanites lived among them in Gezer.

30 Zebulun did not drive out the inhabitants of Kitron, or the inhabitants of Nahalol; but the Canaanites lived among them, and became subject to forced labor.

31 Asher did not drive out the inhabitants of Acco, or the inhabitants of Sidon, or of Ahlab, or of Achzib, or of Helbah, or of Aphik, or of Rehob; ³²but the Asherites lived among the Canaanites, the inhabitants of the land; for they did not drive them out.

33 Naphtali did not drive out the inhabitants of Beth-shemesh, or the inhabitants of Beth-anath, but lived among the Canaanites, the inhabitants of the land; nevertheless the inhabitants of Beth-shemesh and of Beth-anath became subject to forced labor for them.

34 The Amorites pressed the Danites back into the hill country; they did not allow them to come down to the plain. ³⁵The Amorites continued to live in Har-heres, in Aijalon, and in Shaalbim, but the hand of the house of Joseph rested heavily on them, and they became

---

a That is *Basins of Water* *b* Gk: Heb lacks *Hobab* *c* See 1 Sam 15.6: Heb *people* subject to forced labor. 36The border of the Amorites ran from the ascent of Akrabbim, from Sela and upward.

2 Israel's Disobedience

Now the angel of the Lord went up from Gilgal to Bochim, and said, "I brought you up from Egypt, and brought you into the land that I had promised to your ancestors. I said, 'I will never break my covenant with you. 2For your part, do not make a covenant with the inhabitants of this land; tear down their altars.' But you have not obeyed my command. See what you have done! 3So now I say, I will not drive them out before you; but they shall become adversaries[a] to you, and their gods shall be a snare to you." 4When the angel of the Lord spoke these words to all the Israelites, the people lifted up their voices and wept. 5So they named that place Bochim,[b] and there they sacrificed to the Lord.

Death of Joshua

6 When Joshua dismissed the people, the Israelites all went to their own inheritances to take possession of the land. 7The people worshiped the Lord all the days of Joshua, and all the days of the elders who outlived Joshua, who had seen all the great work that the Lord had done for Israel. 8Joshua son of Nun, the servant of the Lord, died at the age of one hundred ten years. 9So they buried him within the bounds of his inheritance in Timnath-heres, in the hill country of Ephraim, north of Mount Gaash. 10Moreover, that whole generation was gathered to their ancestors, and another generation grew up after them, who did not know the Lord or the work that he had done for Israel.

Israel's Unfaithfulness

11 Then the Israelites did what was evil in the sight of the Lord and worshiped the Baals; 12and they abandoned the Lord, the God of their ancestors, who had brought them out of the land of Egypt; they followed other gods, from among the gods of the peoples who were all around them, and bowed down to them; and they provoked the Lord to anger. 13They abandoned the Lord, and worshiped Baal and the Astartes. 14So the anger of the Lord was kindled against Israel, and he gave them over to plunderers who plundered them, and he sold them into the power of their enemies all around, so that they could no longer withstand their enemies. 15Whenever they marched out, the hand of the Lord was against them to bring misfortune, as the Lord had warned them and sworn to them; and they were in great distress.

a OL Vg Compare Gk: Heb sides b That is Weepers

16 Then the Lord raised up judges, who delivered them out of the power of those who plundered them. 17Yet they did not listen even to their judges; for they lusted after other gods and bowed down to them. They soon turned aside from the way in which their ancestors had walked, who had obeyed the commandments of the Lord; they did not follow their example. 18Whenever the Lord raised up judges for them, the Lord was with the judge, and he delivered them from the hand of their enemies all the days of the judge; for the Lord would be moved to pity by their groaning because of those who persecuted and oppressed them. 19But whenever the judge died, they would relapse and behave worse than their ancestors, following other gods, worshiping them and bowing down to them. They would not drop

any of their practices or their stubborn ways. ²⁰So the anger of the LORD was kindled against Israel; and he said, "Because this people have transgressed my covenant that I commanded their ancestors, and have not obeyed my voice, ²¹I will no longer drive out before them any of the nations that Joshua left when he died." ²²In order to test Israel, whether or not they would take care to walk in the way of the LORD as their ancestors did, ²³the LORD had left those nations, not driving them out at once, and had not handed them over to Joshua.

3 Nations Remaining in the Land

Now these are the nations that the LORD left to test all those in Israel who had no experience of any war in Canaan ²(it was only that successive generations of Israelites might know war, to teach those who had no experience of it before): ³the five lords of the Philistines, and all the Canaanites, and the Sidonians, and the Hivites who lived on Mount Lebanon, from Mount Baal-hermon as far as Lebo-hamath. ⁴They were for the testing of Israel, to know whether Israel would obey the commandments of the LORD, which he commanded their ancestors by Moses. ⁵So the Israelites lived among the Canaanites, the Hittites, the Amorites, the Perizzites, the Hivites, and the Jebusites; ⁶and they took their daughters as wives for themselves, and their own daughters they gave to their sons; and they worshiped their gods.

Othniel

7 The Israelites did what was evil in the sight of the LORD, forgetting the LORD their God, and worshiping the Baals and the Asherahs. ⁸Therefore the anger of the LORD was kindled against Israel, and he sold them into the hand of King Cushan-rishathaim of Aram-naharaim; and the Israelites served Cushan-rishathaim eight years. ⁹But when the Israelites cried out to the LORD, the LORD raised up a deliverer for the Israelites, who delivered them, Othniel son of Kenaz, Caleb's younger brother. ¹⁰The spirit of the LORD came upon him, and he judged Israel; he went out to war, and the LORD gave King Cushan-rishathaim of Aram into his hand; and his hand prevailed over Cushan-rishathaim. ¹¹So the land had rest forty years. Then Othniel son of Kenaz died.

Ehud

12 The Israelites again did what was evil in the sight of the LORD; and the LORD strengthened King Eglon of Moab against Israel, because they had done what was evil in the sight of the LORD.

¹³In alliance with the Ammonites and the Amalekites, he went and defeated Israel; and they took possession of the city of palms. ¹⁴So the Israelites served King Eglon of Moab eighteen years.

15 But when the Israelites cried out to the LORD, the LORD raised up for them a deliverer, Ehud son of Gera, the Benjaminite, a left-handed man. The Israelites sent tribute by him to King Eglon of Moab. ¹⁶Ehud made for himself a sword with two edges, a cubit in length; and he fastened it on his right thigh under his clothes. ¹⁷Then he presented the tribute to King Eglon of Moab. Now Eglon was a very fat man. ¹⁸When Ehud had finished presenting the tribute, he sent the people who carried the tribute on their way. ¹⁹But he himself turned back at the sculptured stones near Gilgal, and said, "I have a secret message for you, O king." So the king said,ᵃ "Silence!" and all his attendants went out from his presence. ²⁰Ehud came to him, while he was sitting alone in his cool roof chamber, and said, "I have a message from God for you." So he rose from his seat. ²¹Then Ehud reached with his left hand, took the sword from his right thigh, and thrust it into Eglon'sᵇ belly; ²²the hilt also went in after the blade, and the fat closed over the blade, for he did not draw the sword out of his belly; and the dirt came out.ᶜ ²³Then Ehud went out into the vestibule,ᵈ and closed the doors of the roof chamber on him, and locked them.

24 After he had gone, the servants came. When they saw that the doors of the roof chamber were locked, they thought, "He must be relieving himselfᵉ in the cool chamber." ²⁵So they waited until they were embarrassed. When he still did not open the doors of the roof chamber, they took the key and opened them. There was their lord lying dead on the floor.

26 Ehud escaped while they delayed, and passed beyond the sculptured stones, and escaped to Seirah. ²⁷When he arrived, he sounded the trumpet in the hill country of Ephraim; and the Israelites went down with him from the hill country, having him at their head. ²⁸He said to them, "Follow after me; for the LORD has given your enemies the Moabites into your hand." So they went down after him, and seized the fords of the Jordan against the Moabites, and allowed no one to cross over. ²⁹At that time they killed about ten thousand of the Moabites, all strong, able-bodied men; no one escaped. ³⁰So Moab was subdued that day under the hand of Israel. And the land had rest eighty years.

a Heb he said   b Heb his   c With Tg Vg: Meaning of Heb uncertain   d Meaning of Heb uncertain   e Heb covering his feet

Shamgar

31 After him came Shamgar son of Anath, who killed six hundred of the Philistines with an oxgoad. He too delivered Israel.

4 Deborah and Barak

The Israelites again did what was evil in the sight of the LORD, after Ehud died. ²So the LORD sold them into the hand of King Jabin of Canaan, who reigned in Hazor; the commander of his army was Sisera, who lived in Harosheth-ha-goiim. ³Then the Israelites cried out to the LORD for help; for he had nine hundred chariots of iron, and had oppressed the Israelites cruelly twenty years.

4 At that time Deborah, a prophetess, wife of Lappidoth, was judging Israel. ⁵She used to sit under the palm of Deborah between Ramah and Bethel in the hill country of Ephraim; and the Israelites came up to her for judgment. ⁶She sent and summoned Barak son of Abinoam from Kedesh in Naphtali, and said to him, "The LORD, the God of Israel, commands you, 'Go, take position at Mount Tabor, bringing ten thousand from the tribe of Naphtali and the tribe of Zebulun. ⁷I will draw out Sisera, the general of Jabin's army, to meet you by the Wadi Kishon with his chariots and his troops; and I will give him into your hand.' " ⁸Barak said to her, "If you will go with me, I will go; but if you will not go with me, I will not go." ⁹And she said, "I will surely go with you; nevertheless, the road on which you are going will not lead to your glory, for the LORD will sell Sisera into the hand of a woman." Then Deborah got up and went with Barak to Kedesh. ¹⁰Barak summoned Zebulun and Naphtali to Kedesh; and ten thousand warriors went up behind him; and Deborah went up with him.

11 Now Heber the Kenite had separated from the other Kenites,ᵃ that is, the descendants of Hobab the father-in-law of Moses, and had encamped as far away as Elon-bezaanannim, which is near Kedesh.

12 When Sisera was told that Barak son of Abinoam had gone up to Mount Tabor, ¹³Sisera called out all his chariots, nine hundred chariots of iron, and all the troops who were with him, from Harosheth-ha-goiim to the Wadi Kishon. ¹⁴Then Deborah said to Barak, "Up! For this is the day on which the LORD has given Sisera into your hand. The LORD is indeed going out before you." So Barak went down from Mount Tabor with ten thousand warriors following him. ¹⁵And the LORD threw Sisera and all his chariots and all his army into a panicᵇ before Barak; Sisera got down from his chariot and fled away on foot, ¹⁶while Barak pursued the chariots and the army to Harosheth-ha-goiim. All the army of Sisera fell by the sword; no one was left.

17 Now Sisera had fled away on foot to the tent of Jael wife of Heber the Kenite; for there was peace between King Jabin of Hazor and the clan of Heber the Kenite. ¹⁸Jael came out to meet Sisera, and said to him, "Turn aside, my lord, turn aside to me; have no fear." So

a Heb *from the Kain* b Heb adds *to the sword*; compare verse 16

Special Delivery

Just a guess: you don't own a wool fleece or a sheep you could grab one from in a pinch. But Gideon did—and God willingly communicated through that everyday object (sheep's wool) lying around Gideon's place. Read **Judges 6.36–40** for the details.

How does God communicate with you?

Yeah, sure. Scripture. Nature. Homilies. Friends. Yada, yada. That's all good and not to be discounted . . . but how does God communicate with you in *unusual* ways? *Creative* ways? How does God nudge you? Where in life do you catch him winking in your direction? Through the encouraging word of an old friend who slips back into your life? In a chirping sparrow outside your window that brings to mind a reassuring Scripture? Through a movie scene with a powerful, redemptive message? In a sudden sense of peace, as if God's shadow has drifted across you?

God is all about relationships, and if he's your friend, expect to hear from him. Be looking for it.

What's God saying to you these days? What's he revealing about who he's made you to be? What he's made you to do? Where is he looking for you to serve? To reflect his glory?

Big questions.

Feeling adventurous? Grab a can of spray paint and look for a place that your inner graffiti artist can use for self-expression, for instance, a giant piece of wood or cardboard or a bedroom wall you're looking to repaint. (Make sure it's okay with your parents!)

Start praying and painting at the same time. Ask God one or more of those big questions, and ask for him to help you see his answers in what you draw or write. And remember to post a photo of your painting on **Learner.CalltoDiscipleship.com**.

he turned aside to her into the tent, and she covered him with a rug. ¹⁹Then he said to her, "Please give me a little water to drink; for I am thirsty." So she opened a skin of milk and gave him a drink and covered him. ²⁰He said to her, "Stand at the entrance of the tent, and if anybody comes and asks you, 'Is anyone here?' say, 'No.'" ²¹But Jael wife of Heber took a tent peg, and took a hammer in her hand, and went softly to him and drove the peg into his temple, until it went down into the ground—he was lying fast asleep from weariness—and he died. ²²Then, as Barak came in pursuit of Sisera, Jael went out to meet him, and said to him, "Come, and I will show you the man whom you are seeking." So he went into her tent; and there was Sisera lying dead, with the tent peg in his temple.

23 So on that day God subdued King Jabin of Canaan before the Israelites. ²⁴Then the hand of the Israelites bore harder and harder on King Jabin of Canaan, until they destroyed King Jabin of Canaan.

5 The Song of Deborah

Then Deborah and Barak son of Abinoam sang on that day, saying:

² "When locks are long in Israel,
when the people offer themselves
willingly—
bless*a* the LORD!

³ "Hear, O kings; give ear, O princes;
to the LORD I will sing,
I will make melody to the LORD, the God
of Israel.

⁴ "LORD, when you went out from Seir,
when you marched from the region of
Edom,
the earth trembled,
and the heavens poured,
the clouds indeed poured water.
⁵ The mountains quaked before the LORD,
the One of Sinai,
before the LORD, the God of Israel.

⁶ "In the days of Shamgar son of Anath,
in the days of Jael, caravans ceased
and travelers kept to the byways.
⁷ The peasantry prospered in Israel,
they grew fat on plunder,
because you arose, Deborah,
arose as a mother in Israel.
⁸ When new gods were chosen,
then war was in the gates.
Was shield or spear to be seen
among forty thousand in Israel?
⁹ My heart goes out to the commanders of
Israel
who offered themselves willingly among
the people.
Bless the LORD.

a Or You who offer yourselves willingly among the people, bless

10 "Tell of it, you who ride on white donkeys,
  you who sit on rich carpets*a*
  and you who walk by the way.
11 To the sound of musicians*a* at the watering
    places,
  there they repeat the triumphs of the
    LORD,
  the triumphs of his peasantry in Israel.

"Then down to the gates marched the
    people of the LORD.

12 "Awake, awake, Deborah!
  Awake, awake, utter a song!
Arise, Barak, lead away your captives,
  O son of Abinoam.
13 Then down marched the remnant of the
    noble;
  the people of the LORD marched down
    for him*b* against the mighty.
14 From Ephraim they set out*c* into the valley,*d*
  following you, Benjamin, with your kin;
  from Machir marched down the
    commanders,
  and from Zebulun those who bear the
    marshal's staff;
15 the chiefs of Issachar came with Deborah,
  and Issachar faithful to Barak;
  into the valley they rushed out at his heels.
Among the clans of Reuben
  there were great searchings of heart.
16 Why did you tarry among the sheepfolds,
  to hear the piping for the flocks?
Among the clans of Reuben
  there were great searchings of heart.
17 Gilead stayed beyond the Jordan;
  and Dan, why did he abide with the ships?
Asher sat still at the coast of the sea,
  settling down by his landings.
18 Zebulun is a people that scorned death;
  Naphtali too, on the heights of the field.

19 "The kings came, they fought;
  then fought the kings of Canaan,
at Taanach, by the waters of Megiddo;
  they got no spoils of silver.
20 The stars fought from heaven,
  from their courses they fought against
    Sisera.
21 The torrent Kishon swept them away,
  the onrushing torrent, the torrent Kishon.
March on, my soul, with might!

22 "Then loud beat the horses' hoofs
  with the galloping, galloping of his steeds.

23 "Curse Meroz, says the angel of the LORD,
  curse bitterly its inhabitants,
because they did not come to the help of
  the LORD,
to the help of the LORD against the
  mighty.

24 "Most blessed of women be Jael,
  the wife of Heber the Kenite,
  of tent-dwelling women most blessed.
25 He asked water and she gave him milk,
  she brought him curds in a lordly bowl.
26 She put her hand to the tent peg
  and her right hand to the workmen's
    mallet;
she struck Sisera a blow,
  she crushed his head,
  she shattered and pierced his temple.
27 He sank, he fell,
  he lay still at her feet;
at her feet he sank, he fell;
  where he sank, there he fell dead.

28 "Out of the window she peered,
  the mother of Sisera gazed*e* through the
    lattice:
'Why is his chariot so long in coming?
  Why tarry the hoofbeats of his chariots?'
29 Her wisest ladies make answer,
  indeed, she answers the question herself:
30 'Are they not finding and dividing the
    spoil?—
  A girl or two for every man;
spoil of dyed stuffs for Sisera,
  spoil of dyed stuffs embroidered,
  two pieces of dyed work embroidered for
    my neck as spoil?'

31 "So perish all your enemies, O LORD!
  But may your friends be like the sun as it
    rises in its might."

And the land had rest forty years.

6 The Midianite Oppression

The Israelites did what was evil in the sight of the LORD, and the LORD gave them into the hand of Midian seven years. 2The hand of Midian prevailed over Israel; and because of Midian the Israelites provided for themselves hiding places in the mountains, caves and strongholds. 3For whenever the Israelites put in seed, the Midianites and the Amalekites and the people of the east would come up against them. 4They would encamp against them and destroy the produce of the land, as far as the neighborhood of Gaza, and leave no sustenance in Israel, and no sheep or ox or donkey. 5For they and their livestock would come up, and they would even bring their tents, as thick as locusts; neither they nor their camels could be counted; so they wasted the land as they came in. 6Thus Israel was greatly impoverished because of Mid-

---

a Meaning of Heb uncertain *b* Gk: Heb *me* *c* Cn: Heb *From Ephraim their root* *d* Gk: Heb *in Amalek* *e* Gk Compare Tg: Heb *exclaimed* ian; and the Israelites cried out to the LORD for help.

7 When the Israelites cried to the LORD on account of the Midianites, [8]the LORD sent a prophet to the Israelites; and he said to them, "Thus says the LORD, the God of Israel: I led you up from Egypt, and brought you out of the house of slavery; [9]and I delivered you from the hand of the Egyptians, and from the hand of all who oppressed you, and drove them out before you, and gave you their land; [10]and I said to you, 'I am the LORD your God; you shall not pay reverence to the gods of the Amorites, in whose land you live.' But you have not given heed to my voice."

The Call of Gideon

11 Now the angel of the LORD came and sat under the oak at Ophrah, which belonged to Joash the Abiezrite, as his son Gideon was beating out wheat in the wine press, to hide it from the Midianites. [12]The angel of the LORD appeared to him and said to him, "The LORD is with you, you mighty warrior." [13]Gideon answered him, "But sir, if the LORD is with us, why then has all this happened to us? And where are all his wonderful deeds that our ancestors recounted to us, saying, 'Did not the LORD bring us up from Egypt?' But now the LORD has cast us off, and given us into the hand of Midian." [14]Then the LORD turned to him and said, "Go in this might of yours and deliver Israel from the hand of Midian; I hereby commission you." [15]He responded, "But sir, how can I deliver Israel? My clan is the weakest in Manasseh, and I am the least in my family." [16]The LORD said to him, "But I will be with you, and you shall strike down the Midianites, every one of them." [17]Then he said to him, "If now I have found favor with you, then show me a sign that it is you who speak with me. [18]Do not depart from here until I come to you, and bring out my present, and set it before you." And he said, "I will stay until you return."

19 So Gideon went into his house and prepared a kid, and unleavened cakes from an ephah of flour; the meat he put in a basket, and the broth he put in a pot, and brought them to him under the oak and presented them. [20]The angel of God said to him, "Take the meat and the unleavened cakes, and put them on this rock, and pour out the broth." And he did so. [21]Then the angel of the LORD reached out the tip of the staff that was in his hand, and touched the meat and the unleavened cakes; and fire sprang up from the rock and consumed the meat and the unleavened cakes; and the angel of the LORD vanished from his sight. [22]Then Gideon perceived that it was the angel of the LORD; and Gideon said, "Help me, Lord GOD! For I have seen the angel of the LORD face to face." [23]But the LORD said to him, "Peace be to you; do not fear, you shall not die." [24]Then Gideon built an altar there to the LORD, and called it, The LORD is peace. To this day it still stands at Ophrah, which belongs to the Abiezrites.

25 That night the LORD said to him, "Take your father's bull, the second bull seven years old, and pull down the altar of Baal that belongs to your father, and cut down the sacred pole[a] that is beside it; [26]and build an altar to the LORD your God on the top of the stronghold here, in proper order; then take the second bull, and offer it as a burnt offering with the wood of the sacred pole[a] that you shall cut down." [27]So Gideon took ten of his servants, and did as the LORD had told him; but because he was too afraid of his family and the townspeople to do it by day, he did it by night.

Gideon Destroys the Altar of Baal

28 When the townspeople rose early in the morning, the altar of Baal was broken down, and the sacred pole[a] beside it was cut down, and the second bull was offered on the altar that had been built. [29]So they said to one another, "Who has done this?" After searching and inquiring, they were told, "Gideon son of Joash did it." [30]Then the townspeople said to Joash, "Bring out your son, so that he may die, for he has pulled down the altar of Baal and cut down the sacred pole[a] beside it." [31]But Joash said to all who were arrayed against him, "Will you contend for Baal? Or will you defend his cause? Whoever contends for him shall be put to death by morning. If he is a god, let him contend for himself, because his altar has been pulled down." [32]Therefore on that day Gideon[b] was called Jerubbaal, that is to say, "Let Baal contend against him," because he pulled down his altar.

33 Then all the Midianites and the Amalekites and the people of the east came together, and crossing the Jordan they encamped in the Valley of Jezreel. [34]But the spirit of the LORD took possession of Gideon; and he sounded the trumpet, and the Abiezrites were called out to follow him. [35]He sent messengers throughout all Manasseh, and they too were called out to follow him. He also sent messengers to Asher, Zebulun, and Naphtali, and they went up to meet them.

The Sign of the Fleece

36 Then Gideon said to God, "In order to see whether you will deliver Israel by my hand, as

a Heb Asherah b Heb he

you have said, [37]I am going to lay a fleece of wool on the threshing floor; if there is dew on the fleece alone, and it is dry on all the ground, then I shall know that you will deliver Israel by my hand, as you have said." [38]And it was so. When he rose early next morning and squeezed the fleece, he wrung enough dew from the fleece to fill a bowl with water. [39]Then Gideon said to God, "Do not let your anger burn against me, let me speak one more time; let me, please, make trial with the fleece just once more; let it be dry only on the fleece, and on all the ground let there be dew." [40]And God did so that night. It was dry on the fleece only, and on all the ground there was dew.

The Compartmentalizing of Life—© Christy Klink, 18

7 Gideon Surprises and Routs the Midianites

Then Jerubbaal (that is, Gideon) and all the troops that were with him rose early and encamped beside the spring of Harod; and the camp of Midian was north of them, below*a* the hill of Moreh, in the valley.

2 The LORD said to Gideon, "The troops with you are too many for me to give the Midianites into their hand. Israel would only take the credit away from me, saying, 'My own hand has delivered me.' [3]Now therefore proclaim this in the hearing of the troops, 'Whoever is fearful and trembling, let him return home.'" Thus Gideon sifted them out;*b* twenty-two thousand returned, and ten thousand remained.

4 Then the LORD said to Gideon, "The troops are still too many; take them down to the water and I will sift them out for you there. When I say, 'This one shall go with you,' he shall go with you; and when I say, 'This one shall not go with you,' he shall not go." [5]So he brought the troops down to the water; and the LORD said to Gideon, "All those who lap the water with their tongues, as a dog laps, you shall put to one side; all those who kneel down to drink, putting their hands to their mouths,*c* you shall put to the other side." [6]The number of those that lapped was three hundred; but all the rest of the troops knelt down to drink water. [7]Then the LORD said to Gideon, "With the three hundred that lapped I will deliver you, and give the Midianites into your hand. Let all the others go to their homes." [8]So he took the jars of the troops from their hands,*d* and their trumpets; and he sent all the rest of Israel back to their own tents, but retained the three hundred. The camp of Midian was below him in the valley.

9 That same night the LORD said to him, "Get up, attack the camp; for I have given it into your hand. [10]But if you fear to attack, go down to the camp with your servant Purah; [11]and you shall hear what they say, and afterward your hands shall be strengthened to attack the camp." Then he went down with his servant Purah to the outposts of the armed men that were in the camp. [12]The Midianites and the Amalekites and all the people of the east lay along the valley as thick as locusts; and their camels were without number, countless as the sand on the seashore. [13]When Gideon arrived, there was a man telling a dream to his comrade; and he said, "I had a dream, and in it a cake of barley bread tumbled into the camp of Midian, and came to the tent, and struck it so that it fell; it turned upside down, and the tent collapsed." [14]And his comrade answered, "This is no other than the sword of Gideon son of Joash, a man of Israel; into his hand God has given Midian and all the army."

15 When Gideon heard the telling of the dream and its interpretation, he worshiped; and he returned to the camp of Israel, and said, "Get up; for the LORD has given the army of Midian into your hand." [16]After he divided the three hundred men into three companies, and put trumpets into the hands of all of them, and empty jars, with torches inside the jars, [17]he said to them, "Look at me, and do the same; when I come to the outskirts of the camp, do as I do. [18]When I blow the trumpet, I and all who are with me, then you also blow the trumpets around the whole camp, and shout, 'For the LORD and for Gideon!'"

19 So Gideon and the hundred who were with him came to the outskirts of the camp at

a Heb from b Cn: Heb home, and depart from Mount Gilead" c Heb places the words *putting their hands to their mouths* after the word *lapped* in verse 6 d Cn: Heb *So the people took provisions in their hands*

Untitled—© Vito Paratore, 18

the beginning of the middle watch, when they had just set the watch; and they blew the trumpets and smashed the jars that were in their hands. ²⁰So the three companies blew the trumpets and broke the jars, holding in their left hands the torches, and in their right hands the trumpets to blow; and they cried, "A sword for the LORD and for Gideon!" ²¹Every man stood in his place all around the camp, and all the men in camp ran; they cried out and fled. ²²When they blew the three hundred trumpets, the LORD set every man's sword against his fellow and against all the army; and the army fled as far as Beth-shittah toward Zererah,^a as far as the border of Abel-meholah, by Tabbath. ²³And the men of Israel were called out from Naphtali and from Asher and from all Manasseh, and they pursued after the Midianites.

24 Then Gideon sent messengers throughout all the hill country of Ephraim, saying, "Come down against the Midianites and seize the waters against them, as far as Beth-barah, and also the Jordan." So all the men of Ephraim were called out, and they seized the waters as far as Beth-barah, and also the Jordan. ²⁵They captured the two captains of Midian, Oreb and Zeeb; they killed Oreb at the rock of Oreb, and Zeeb they killed at the wine press of Zeeb, as they pursued the Midianites. They brought the heads of Oreb and Zeeb to Gideon beyond the Jordan.

8 Gideon's Triumph and Vengeance

Then the Ephraimites said to him, "What have you done to us, not to call us when you went to fight against the Midianites?" And they upbraided him violently. ²So he said to them, "What have I done now in comparison with you? Is not the gleaning of the grapes of Ephraim better than the vintage of Abiezer? ³God has given into your hands the captains of Midian, Oreb and Zeeb; what have I been able to do in comparison with you?" When he said this, their anger against him subsided.

4 Then Gideon came to the Jordan and crossed over, he and the three hundred who were with him, exhausted and famished.^b ⁵So he said to the people of Succoth, "Please give some loaves of bread to my followers, for they are exhausted, and I am pursuing Zebah and Zalmunna, the kings of Midian." ⁶But the officials of Succoth said, "Do you already have in your possession the hands of Zebah and Zalmunna, that we should give bread to your army?" ⁷Gideon replied, "Well then, when the LORD has given Zebah and Zalmunna into my hand, I will trample your flesh on the thorns of the wilderness and on briers." ⁸From there he went up to Penuel, and made the same request of them; and the people of Penuel answered him as the people of Succoth had answered. ⁹So he said to the people of Penuel, "When I

a Another reading is *Zeredah* *b* Gk: Heb *pursuing*

come back victorious, I will break down this tower."

10 Now Zebah and Zalmunna were in Karkor with their army, about fifteen thousand men, all who were left of all the army of the people of the east; for one hundred twenty thousand men bearing arms had fallen. [11]So Gideon went up by the caravan route east of Nobah and Jogbehah, and attacked the army; for the army was off its guard. [12]Zebah and Zalmunna fled; and he pursued them and took the two kings of Midian, Zebah and Zalmunna, and threw all the army into a panic.

13 When Gideon son of Joash returned from the battle by the ascent of Heres, [14]he caught a young man, one of the people of Succoth, and questioned him; and he listed for him the officials and elders of Succoth, seventy-seven people. [15]Then he came to the people of Succoth, and said, "Here are Zebah and Zalmunna, about whom you taunted me, saying, 'Do you already have in your possession the hands of Zebah and Zalmunna, that we should give bread to your troops who are exhausted?' " [16]So he took the elders of the city and he took thorns of the wilderness and briers and with them he trampled[a] the people of Succoth. [17]He also broke down the tower of Penuel, and killed the men of the city.

18 Then he said to Zebah and Zalmunna, "What about the men whom you killed at Tabor?" They answered, "As you are, so were they, every one of them; they resembled the sons of a king." [19]And he replied, "They were my brothers, the sons of my mother; as the LORD lives, if you had saved them alive, I would not kill you." [20]So he said to Jether his firstborn, "Go kill them!" But the boy did not draw his sword, for he was afraid, because he was still a boy. [21]Then Zebah and Zalmunna said, "You come and kill us; for as the man is, so is his strength." So Gideon proceeded to kill Zebah and Zalmunna; and he took the crescents that were on the necks of their camels.

Gideon's Idolatry

22 Then the Israelites said to Gideon, "Rule over us, you and your son and your grandson also; for you have delivered us out of the hand of Midian." [23]Gideon said to them, "I will not rule over you, and my son will not rule over you; the LORD will rule over you." [24]Then Gideon said to them, "Let me make a request of you; each of you give me an earring he has taken as booty." (For the enemy[b] had golden earrings, because they were Ishmaelites.) [25]"We will willingly give them," they answered. So they spread a garment, and each threw into it an earring he had taken as booty. [26]The weight of the golden earrings that he requested was one thousand seven hundred shekels of gold (apart from the crescents and the pendants and the purple garments worn by the kings of Midian, and the collars that were on the necks of their camels). [27]Gideon made an ephod of it and put it in his town, in Ophrah; and all Israel prostituted themselves to it there, and it became a snare to Gideon and to his family. [28]So Midian was subdued before the Israelites, and they lifted up their heads no more. So the land had rest forty years in the days of Gideon.

Death of Gideon

29 Jerubbaal son of Joash went to live in his own house. [30]Now Gideon had seventy sons, his own offspring, for he had many wives. [31]His concubine who was in Shechem also bore him a son, and he named him Abimelech. [32]Then Gideon son of Joash died at a good old age, and was buried in the tomb of his father Joash at Ophrah of the Abiezrites.

33 As soon as Gideon died, the Israelites relapsed and prostituted themselves with the Baals, making Baal-berith their god. [34]The Israelites did not remember the LORD their God, who had rescued them from the hand of all their enemies on every side; [35]and they did not exhibit loyalty to the house of Jerubbaal (that is, Gideon) in return for all the good that he had done to Israel.

9 Abimelech Attempts to Establish a Monarchy

Now Abimelech son of Jerubbaal went to Shechem to his mother's kinsfolk and said to them and to the whole clan of his mother's family, [2]"Say in the hearing of all the lords of Shechem, 'Which is better for you, that all seventy of the sons of Jerubbaal rule over you, or that one rule over you?' Remember also that I am your bone and your flesh." [3]So his mother's kinsfolk spoke all these words on his behalf in the hearing of all the lords of Shechem; and their hearts inclined to follow Abimelech, for they said, "He is our brother." [4]They gave him seventy pieces of silver out of the temple of Baal-berith with which Abimelech hired worthless and reckless fellows, who followed him. [5]He went to his father's house at Ophrah, and killed his brothers the sons of Jerubbaal, seventy men, on one stone; but Jotham, the youngest son of Jerubbaal, survived, for he hid himself. [6]Then all the lords of Shechem and all Beth-millo came together, and they went and

a With verse 7, Compare Gk: Heb *he taught*   b Heb *they*

made Abimelech king, by the oak of the pillar*a* at Shechem.

The Parable of the Trees

7 When it was told to Jotham, he went and stood on the top of Mount Gerizim, and cried aloud and said to them, "Listen to me, you lords of Shechem, so that God may listen to you.

8 The trees once went out
to anoint a king over themselves.
So they said to the olive tree,
'Reign over us.'
9 The olive tree answered them,
'Shall I stop producing my rich oil
by which gods and mortals are honored,
and go to sway over the trees?'
10 Then the trees said to the fig tree,
'You come and reign over us.'
11 But the fig tree answered them,
'Shall I stop producing my sweetness
and my delicious fruit,
and go to sway over the trees?'
12 Then the trees said to the vine,
'You come and reign over us.'
13 But the vine said to them,
'Shall I stop producing my wine
that cheers gods and mortals,
and go to sway over the trees?'
14 So all the trees said to the bramble,
'You come and reign over us.'
15 And the bramble said to the trees,
'If in good faith you are anointing me
king over you,
then come and take refuge in my shade;
but if not, let fire come out of the bramble
and devour the cedars of Lebanon.'

16 "Now therefore, if you acted in good faith and honor when you made Abimelech king, and if you have dealt well with Jerubbaal and his house, and have done to him as his actions deserved— 17for my father fought for you, and risked his life, and rescued you from the hand of Midian; 18but you have risen up against my father's house this day, and have killed his sons, seventy men on one stone, and have made Abimelech, the son of his slave woman, king over the lords of Shechem, because he is your kinsman— 19if, I say, you have acted in good faith and honor with Jerubbaal and with his house this day, then rejoice in Abimelech, and let him also rejoice in you; 20but if not, let fire come out from Abimelech, and devour the lords of Shechem, and Beth-millo; and let fire come out from the lords of Shechem, and from Beth-millo, and devour Abimelech." 21Then Jotham ran away and fled, going to Beer, where he remained for fear of his brother Abimelech.

The Downfall of Abimelech

22 Abimelech ruled over Israel three years. 23But God sent an evil spirit between Abimelech and the lords of Shechem; and the lords of Shechem dealt treacherously with Abimelech. 24This happened so that the violence done to the seventy sons of Jerubbaal might be avenged*b* and their blood be laid on their brother Abimelech, who killed them, and on the lords of Shechem, who strengthened his hands to kill his brothers. 25So, out of hostility to him, the lords of Shechem set ambushes on the mountain tops. They robbed all who passed by them along that way; and it was reported to Abimelech.

26 When Gaal son of Ebed moved into Shechem with his kinsfolk, the lords of Shechem put confidence in him. 27They went out into the field and gathered the grapes from their vineyards, trod them, and celebrated. Then they went into the temple of their god, ate and drank, and ridiculed Abimelech. 28Gaal son of Ebed said, "Who is Abimelech, and who are we of Shechem, that we should serve him? Did not the son of Jerubbaal and Zebul his officer serve the men of Hamor father of Shechem? Why then should we serve him? 29If only this people were under my command! Then I would remove Abimelech; I would say*c* to him, 'Increase your army, and come out.' "

30 When Zebul the ruler of the city heard the words of Gaal son of Ebed, his anger was kindled. 31He sent messengers to Abimelech at Arumah,*d* saying, "Look, Gaal son of Ebed and his kinsfolk have come to Shechem, and they are stirring up*e* the city against you. 32Now therefore, go by night, you and the troops that are with you, and lie in wait in the fields. 33Then early in the morning, as soon as the sun rises, get up and rush on the city; and when he and the troops that are with him come out against you, you may deal with them as best you can."

a Cn: Meaning of Heb uncertain *b* Heb *might come* *c* Gk: Heb *and he said* *d* Cn See 9.41. Heb *Tormah* *e* Cn: Heb *are besieging*

34 So Abimelech and all the troops with him got up by night and lay in wait against Shechem in four companies. ³⁵When Gaal son of Ebed went out and stood in the entrance of the gate of the city, Abimelech and the troops with him rose from the ambush. ³⁶And when Gaal saw them, he said to Zebul, "Look, people are coming down from the mountain tops!" And Zebul said to him, "The shadows on the mountains look like people to you." ³⁷Gaal spoke again and said, "Look, people are coming down from Tabbur-erez, and one company is coming from the direction of Elon-meonenim."ª ³⁸Then Zebul said to him, "Where is your boastᵇ now, you who said, 'Who is Abimelech, that we should serve him?' Are not these the troops you made light of? Go out now and fight with them." ³⁹So Gaal went out at the head of the lords of Shechem, and fought with Abimelech. ⁴⁰Abimelech chased him, and he fled before him. Many fell wounded, up to the entrance of the gate. ⁴¹So Abimelech resided at Arumah; and Zebul drove out Gaal and his kinsfolk, so that they could not live on at Shechem.

42 On the following day the people went out into the fields. When Abimelech was told, ⁴³he took his troops and divided them into three companies, and lay in wait in the fields. When he looked and saw the people coming out of the city, he rose against them and killed them. ⁴⁴Abimelech and the company that wasᶜ with him rushed forward and stood at the entrance of the gate of the city, while the two companies rushed on all who were in the fields and killed them. ⁴⁵Abimelech fought against the city all that day; he took the city, and killed the people that were in it; and he razed the city and sowed it with salt.

46 When all the lords of the Tower of Shechem heard of it, they entered the stronghold of the temple of El-berith. ⁴⁷Abimelech was told that all the lords of the Tower of Shechem were gathered together. ⁴⁸So Abimelech went up to Mount Zalmon, he and all the troops that were with him. Abimelech took an ax in his hand, cut down a bundle of brushwood, and took it up and laid it on his shoulder. Then he said to the troops with him, "What you have seen me do, do quickly, as I have done." ⁴⁹So every one of the troops cut down a bundle and following Abimelech put it against the stronghold, and they set the stronghold on fire over them, so that all the people of the Tower of Shechem also died, about a thousand men and women.

50 Then Abimelech went to Thebez, and encamped against Thebez, and took it. ⁵¹But there was a strong tower within the city, and all the men and women and all the lords of the city fled to it and shut themselves in; and they went to the roof of the tower. ⁵²Abimelech came to the tower, and fought against it, and came near to the entrance of the tower to burn it with fire. ⁵³But a certain woman threw an upper millstone on Abimelech's head, and crushed his skull. ⁵⁴Immediately he called to the young man who carried his armor and said to him, "Draw your sword and kill me, so people will not say about me, 'A woman killed him.' " So the young man thrust him through, and he died. ⁵⁵When the Israelites saw that Abimelech was dead, they all went home. ⁵⁶Thus God repaid Abimelech for the crime he committed against his father in killing his seventy brothers; ⁵⁷and God also made all the wickedness of the people of Shechem fall back on their heads, and on them came the curse of Jotham son of Jerubbaal.

10 Tola and Jair

After Abimelech, Tola son of Puah son of Dodo, a man of Issachar, who lived at Shamir in the hill country of Ephraim, rose to deliver Israel. ²He judged Israel twenty-three years. Then he died, and was buried at Shamir.

3 After him came Jair the Gileadite, who judged Israel twenty-two years. ⁴He had thirty sons who rode on thirty donkeys; and they had thirty towns, which are in the land of Gilead, and are called Havvoth-jair to this day. ⁵Jair died, and was buried in Kamon.

Oppression by the Ammonites

6 The Israelites again did what was evil in the sight of the LORD, worshiping the Baals and the Astartes, the gods of Aram, the gods of Sidon, the gods of Moab, the gods of the Ammonites, and the gods of the Philistines. Thus they abandoned the LORD, and did not worship him. ⁷So the anger of the LORD was kindled against Israel, and he sold them into the hand of the Philistines and into the hand of the Ammonites, ⁸and they crushed and oppressed the Israelites that year. For eighteen years they oppressed all the Israelites that were beyond the Jordan in the land of the Amorites, which is in Gilead. ⁹The Ammonites also crossed the Jordan to fight against Judah and against Benjamin and against the house of Ephraim; so that Israel was greatly distressed.

10 So the Israelites cried to the LORD, saying, "We have sinned against you, because we have abandoned our God and have worshiped the Baals." ¹¹And the LORD said to the Israelites, "Did I not deliver youᵈ from the Egyptians and from the Amorites, from the Ammonites and

---

ª That is Diviners' Oak ᵇ Heb mouth ᶜ Vg and some Gk Mss: Heb companies that were ᵈ Heb lacks Did I not deliver you from the Philistines? [12]The Sidonians also, and the Amalekites, and the Maonites, oppressed you; and you cried to me, and I delivered you out of their hand. [13]Yet you have abandoned me and worshiped other gods; therefore I will deliver you no more. [14]Go and cry to the gods whom you have chosen; let them deliver you in the time of your distress." [15]And the Israelites said to the LORD, "We have sinned; do to us whatever seems good to you; but deliver us this day!" [16]So they put away the foreign gods from among them and worshiped the LORD; and he could no longer bear to see Israel suffer.

17 Then the Ammonites were called to arms, and they encamped in Gilead; and the Israelites came together, and they encamped at Mizpah. [18]The commanders of the people of Gilead said to one another, "Who will begin the fight against the Ammonites? He shall be head over all the inhabitants of Gilead."

11 Jephthah

Now Jephthah the Gileadite, the son of a prostitute, was a mighty warrior. Gilead was the father of Jephthah. [2]Gilead's wife also bore him sons; and when his wife's sons grew up, they drove Jephthah away, saying to him, "You shall not inherit anything in our father's house; for you are the son of another woman." [3]Then Jephthah fled from his brothers and lived in the land of Tob. Outlaws collected around Jephthah and went raiding with him.

4 After a time the Ammonites made war against Israel. [5]And when the Ammonites made war against Israel, the elders of Gilead went to bring Jephthah from the land of Tob. [6]They said to Jephthah, "Come and be our commander, so that we may fight with the Ammonites." [7]But Jephthah said to the elders of Gilead, "Are you not the very ones who rejected me and drove me out of my father's house? So why do you come to me now when you are in trouble?" [8]The elders of Gilead said to Jephthah, "Nevertheless, we have now turned back to you, so that you may go with us and fight with the Ammonites, and become head over us, over all the inhabitants of Gilead." [9]Jephthah said to the elders of Gilead, "If you bring me home again to fight with the Ammonites, and the LORD gives them over to me, I will be your head." [10]And the elders of Gilead said to Jephthah, "The LORD will be witness between us; we will surely do as you say." [11]So Jephthah went with the elders of Gilead, and the people made him head and commander over them; and Jephthah spoke all his words before the LORD at Mizpah.

12 Then Jephthah sent messengers to the king of the Ammonites and said, "What is there between you and me, that you have come to me to fight against my land?" [13]The king of the Ammonites answered the messengers of Jephthah, "Because Israel, on coming from Egypt, took away my land from the Arnon to the Jabbok and to the Jordan; now therefore restore it peaceably." [14]Once again Jephthah sent messengers to the king of the Ammonites [15]and said to him: "Thus says Jephthah: Israel did not take away the land of Moab or the land of the Ammonites, [16]but when they came up from Egypt, Israel went through the wilderness to the Red Sea[a] and came to Kadesh. [17]Israel then sent messengers to the king of Edom, saying, 'Let us pass through your land'; but the king of Edom would not listen. They also sent to the king of Moab, but he would not consent. So Israel remained at Kadesh. [18]Then they journeyed through the wilderness, went around the land of Edom and the land of Moab, arrived on the east side of the land of Moab, and camped on the other side of the Arnon. They did not enter the territory of Moab, for the Arnon was the boundary of Moab. [19]Israel then sent messengers to King Sihon of the Amorites, king of Heshbon; and Israel said to him, 'Let us pass through your land to our country.' [20]But Sihon did not trust Israel to pass through his territory; so Sihon gathered all his people together, and encamped at Jahaz, and fought with Israel. [21]Then the LORD, the God of Israel, gave Sihon and all his people into the hand of Israel, and they defeated them; so Israel occupied all the land of the Amorites, who inhabited that country. [22]They occupied all the territory of the Amorites from the Arnon to the Jabbok and from the wilderness to the Jordan. [23]So now the LORD, the God of Israel, has conquered the Amorites for the benefit of his people Israel. Do you intend to take their place? [24]Should you not possess what your god Chemosh gives you to possess? And should we not be the ones to possess everything that the LORD our God has conquered for our benefit? [25]Now are you any better than King Balak son of Zippor of Moab? Did he ever enter into conflict with Israel, or did he ever go to war with them? [26]While Israel lived in Heshbon and its villages, and in Aroer and its villages, and in all the towns that are along the Arnon, three hundred years, why did you not recover them within that time? [27]It is not I who have sinned against you, but you are the one who does me wrong by making war on me. Let the LORD, who is judge, decide today for the Israelites or for the Ammonites." [28]But the king of the Ammonites did not heed the message that Jephthah sent him.

a Or Sea of Reeds

"Remember this. When people choose to withdraw far from a fire, the fire continues to give warmth, but they grow cold. When people choose to withdraw far from light, the light continues to be bright in itself, but they are in darkness. This is also the case when people withdraw from God."

—St. Augustine

Jephthah's Vow

29 Then the spirit of the LORD came upon Jephthah, and he passed through Gilead and Manasseh. He passed on to Mizpah of Gilead, and from Mizpah of Gilead he passed on to the Ammonites. ³⁰And Jephthah made a vow to the LORD, and said, "If you will give the Ammonites into my hand, ³¹then whoever comes out of the doors of my house to meet me, when I return victorious from the Ammonites, shall be the LORD's, to be offered up by me as a burnt offering." ³²So Jephthah crossed over to the Ammonites to fight against them; and the LORD gave them into his hand. ³³He inflicted a massive defeat on them from Aroer to the neighborhood of Minnith, twenty towns, and as far as Abel-keramim. So the Ammonites were subdued before the people of Israel.

TEXT MESSAGE

Have you ever made a promise you later regretted? Judge Jephthah did. He promised to sacrifice the first thing that came out of his house after battle. Jephthah may have expected to see an animal, since houses in that day often included space for livestock. But when his only daughter appeared, he tore his clothes in sorrow (Judges 11.30–40).

This information has been scanned and is free of all known viruses. Please forward to all your friends.

Jephthah's Daughter

34 Then Jephthah came to his home at Mizpah; and there was his daughter coming out to meet him with timbrels and with dancing. She was his only child; he had no son or daughter except her. ³⁵When he saw her, he tore his clothes, and said, "Alas, my daughter! You have brought me very low; you have become the cause of great trouble to me. For I have opened my mouth to the LORD, and I cannot take back my vow." ³⁶She said to him, "My father, if you have opened your mouth to the LORD, do to me according to what has gone out of your mouth, now that the LORD has given you vengeance against your enemies, the Ammonites." ³⁷And she said to her father, "Let this thing be done for me: Grant me two months, so that I may go and wander*a* on the mountains, and bewail my virginity, my companions and I." ³⁸"Go," he said and sent her away for two months. So she departed, she and her companions, and bewailed her virginity on the mountains. ³⁹At the end of two months, she returned to her father, who did with her according to the vow he had made. She had never slept with a man. So there arose an Israelite custom that ⁴⁰for four days every year the daughters of Israel would go out to lament the daughter of Jephthah the Gileadite.

12 Intertribal Dissension

The men of Ephraim were called to arms, and they crossed to Zaphon and said to Jephthah, "Why did you cross over to fight against the Ammonites, and did not call us to go with you? We will burn your house down over you!" ²Jephthah said to them, "My people and I were engaged in conflict with the Ammonites who oppressed us*b* severely. But when I called you, you did not deliver me from their hand. ³When I saw that you would not deliver me, I took my life in my hand, and crossed over against the Ammonites, and the LORD gave them into my hand. Why then have you come up to me this day, to fight against me?" ⁴Then Jephthah gathered all the men of Gilead and fought with Ephraim; and the men of Gilead defeated Ephraim, because they said, "You are fugitives from Ephraim, you Gileadites—in the heart of Ephraim and Manasseh."*c* ⁵Then the Gileadites took the fords of the Jordan against the Ephraimites. Whenever one of the fugitives of Ephraim said, "Let me go over," the men of Gilead would say to him, "Are you an Ephraimite?" When he said, "No," ⁶they said to him, "Then say Shibboleth," and he said, "Sibboleth," for he could not pronounce it right. Then they

---

a Cn: Heb *go down* b Gk OL, Syr H: Heb lacks *who oppressed us*
c Meaning of Heb uncertain: Gk omits *because . . . Manasseh*

seized him and killed him at the fords of the Jordan. Forty-two thousand of the Ephraimites fell at that time.

7 Jephthah judged Israel six years. Then Jephthah the Gileadite died, and was buried in his town in Gilead.*ᵃ*

Ibzan, Elon, and Abdon

8 After him Ibzan of Bethlehem judged Israel. ⁹He had thirty sons. He gave his thirty daughters in marriage outside his clan and brought in thirty young women from outside for his sons. He judged Israel seven years. ¹⁰Then Ibzan died, and was buried at Bethlehem.

11 After him Elon the Zebulunite judged Israel; and he judged Israel ten years. ¹²Then Elon the Zebulunite died, and was buried at Aijalon in the land of Zebulun.

13 After him Abdon son of Hillel the Pirathonite judged Israel. ¹⁴He had forty sons and thirty grandsons, who rode on seventy donkeys; he judged Israel eight years. ¹⁵Then Abdon son of Hillel the Pirathonite died, and was buried at Pirathon in the land of Ephraim, in the hill country of the Amalekites.

13 The Birth of Samson

The Israelites again did what was evil in the sight of the Lord, and the Lord gave them into the hand of the Philistines forty years.

2 There was a certain man of Zorah, of the tribe of the Danites, whose name was Manoah. His wife was barren, having borne no children. ³And the angel of the Lord appeared to the woman and said to her, "Although you are barren, having borne no children, you shall conceive and bear a son. ⁴Now be careful not to drink wine or strong drink, or to eat anything unclean, ⁵for you shall conceive and bear a son. No razor is to come on his head, for the boy shall be a nazirite*ᵇ* to God from birth. It is he who shall begin to deliver Israel from the hand of the Philistines." ⁶Then the woman came and told her husband, "A man of God came to me, and his appearance was like that of an angel*ᶜ* of God, most awe-inspiring; I did not ask him where he came from, and he did not tell me his name; ⁷but he said to me, 'You shall conceive and bear a son. So then drink no wine or strong drink, and eat nothing unclean, for the boy shall be a nazirite*ᵇ* to God from birth to the day of his death.' "

8 Then Manoah entreated the Lord, and said, "O Lord, I pray, let the man of God whom you sent come to us again and teach us what we are to do concerning the boy who will be born." ⁹God listened to Manoah, and the angel of God came again to the woman as she sat in the field; but her husband Manoah was not with her. ¹⁰So the woman ran quickly and told her husband, "The man who came to me the other day has appeared to me." ¹¹Manoah got up and followed his wife, and came to the man and said to him, "Are you the man who spoke to this woman?" And he said, "I am." ¹²Then Manoah said, "Now when your words come true, what is to be the boy's rule of life; what is he to do?" ¹³The angel of the Lord said to Manoah, "Let the woman give heed to all that I said to her. ¹⁴She may not eat of anything that comes from the vine. She is not to drink wine or strong drink, or eat any unclean thing. She is to observe everything that I commanded her."

15 Manoah said to the angel of the Lord, "Allow us to detain you, and prepare a kid for you." ¹⁶The angel of the Lord said to Manoah, "If you detain me, I will not eat your food; but if you want to prepare a burnt offering, then offer it to the Lord." (For Manoah did not know that he was the angel of the Lord.) ¹⁷Then Manoah said to the angel of the Lord, "What is your name, so that we may honor you when your words come true?" ¹⁸But the angel of the Lord said to him, "Why do you ask my name? It is too wonderful."

19 So Manoah took the kid with the grain offering, and offered it on the rock to the Lord, to him who works*ᵈ* wonders.*ᵉ* ²⁰When the flame went up toward heaven from the altar, the angel of the Lord ascended in the flame of the altar while Manoah and his wife looked on; and they fell on their faces to the ground. ²¹The angel of the Lord did not appear again to Manoah and his wife. Then Manoah realized that it was the angel of the Lord. ²²And Manoah said to his wife, "We shall surely die, for we have seen God." ²³But his wife said to him, "If the Lord had meant to kill us, he would not have accepted a burnt offering and a grain offering at our hands, or shown us all these things, or now announced to us such things as these."

24 The woman bore a son, and named him Samson. The boy grew, and the Lord blessed him. ²⁵The spirit of the Lord began to stir him in Mahaneh-dan, between Zorah and Eshtaol.

14 Samson's Marriage

Once Samson went down to Timnah, and at Timnah he saw a Philistine woman. ²Then he came up, and told his father and mother, "I saw a Philistine woman at Timnah; now get her for me as my wife." ³But his father and mother

---

a Gk: Heb *in the towns of Gilead* *b* That is *one separated* or *one consecrated* *c* Or *the angel* *d* Gk Vg: Heb *and working* *e* Heb *wonders, while Manoah and his wife looked on* said to him, "Is there not a woman among your kin, or among all our[a] people, that you must go to take a wife from the uncircumcised Philistines?" But Samson said to his father, "Get her for me, because she pleases me." 4His father and mother did not know that this was from the LORD; for he was seeking a pretext to act against the Philistines. At that time the Philistines had dominion over Israel.

5 Then Samson went down with his father and mother to Timnah. When he came to the vineyards of Timnah, suddenly a young lion roared at him. 6The spirit of the LORD rushed on him, and he tore the lion apart barehanded as one might tear apart a kid. But he did not tell his father or his mother what he had done. 7Then he went down and talked with the woman, and she pleased Samson. 8After a while he returned to marry her, and he turned aside to see the carcass of the lion, and there was a swarm of bees in the body of the lion, and honey. 9He scraped it out into his hands, and went on, eating as he went. When he came to his father and mother, he gave some to them, and they ate it. But he did not tell them that he had taken the honey from the carcass of the lion.

10 His father went down to the woman, and Samson made a feast there as the young men were accustomed to do. 11When the people saw him, they brought thirty companions to be with him. 12Samson said to them, "Let me now put a riddle to you. If you can explain it to me within the seven days of the feast, and find it out, then I will give you thirty linen garments and thirty festal garments. 13But if you cannot explain it to me, then you shall give me thirty linen garments and thirty festal garments." So they said to him, "Ask your riddle; let us hear it." 14He said to them,

"Out of the eater came something to eat.
Out of the strong came something sweet."
But for three days they could not explain the riddle.

15 On the fourth[b] day they said to Samson's wife, "Coax your husband to explain the riddle to us, or we will burn you and your father's house with fire. Have you invited us here to impoverish us?" 16So Samson's wife wept before him, saying, "You hate me; you do not really love me. You have asked a riddle of my people, but you have not explained it to me." He said to her, "Look, I have not told my father or my mother. Why should I tell you?" 17She wept before him the seven days that their feast lasted; and because she nagged him, on the seventh day he told her. Then she explained the riddle to her people. 18The men of the town said to him on the seventh day before the sun went down,

"What is sweeter than honey?
What is stronger than a lion?"
And he said to them,

"If you had not plowed with my heifer,
you would not have found out my riddle."
19Then the spirit of the LORD rushed on him, and he went down to Ashkelon. He killed thirty men of the town, took their spoil, and gave the festal garments to those who had explained the riddle. In hot anger he went back to his father's house. 20And Samson's wife was given to his companion, who had been his best man.

15 Samson Defeats the Philistines

After a while, at the time of the wheat harvest, Samson went to visit his wife, bringing along a kid. He said, "I want to go into my wife's room." But her father would not allow him to go in. 2Her father said, "I was sure that you had rejected her; so I gave her to your companion. Is not her younger sister prettier than she? Why not take her instead?" 3Samson said to them, "This time, when I do mischief to the Philistines, I will be without blame." 4So Samson went and caught three hundred foxes, and took some torches; and he turned the foxes[c] tail to tail, and put a torch between each pair of tails. 5When he had set fire to the torches, he let the foxes go into the standing grain of the Philistines, and burned up the shocks and the standing grain, as well as the vineyards and[d] olive groves. 6Then the Philistines asked, "Who has done this?" And they said, "Samson, the son-in-law of the Timnite, because he has taken Samson's wife and given her to his companion." So the Philistines came up, and burned her and her father. 7Samson said to them, "If this is what you do, I swear I will not stop until I have taken revenge on you." 8He struck them down hip and thigh with great slaughter; and he went down and stayed in the cleft of the rock of Etam.

9 Then the Philistines came up and encamped in Judah, and made a raid on Lehi. 10The men of Judah said, "Why have you come up against us?" They said, "We have come up to bind Samson, to do to him as he did to us." 11Then three thousand men of Judah went down to the cleft of the rock of Etam, and they said to Samson, "Do you not know that the Philistines are rulers over us? What then have you done to us?" He replied, "As they did to me, so I have done to them." 12They said to him, "We have come down to bind you, so that we may give you into the hands of the Philistines." Samson answered them, "Swear to me that you yourselves will not attack me." 13They said to him, "No, we will only bind you and give you

---

a Cn: Heb *my* b Gk Syr: Heb *seventh* c Heb *them* d Gk Tg Vg: Heb lacks *and*

One End, One Beginning—Hannah More had had enough. Engaged to the wealthy William Turner for over six years (since she was twenty-two), Hannah became convinced that, despite her great love for him, he was unwilling to set a date for the wedding. Swallowing her pride and enduring the heartache, she did the unthinkable for a woman of her age and standing in eighteenth-century England: she broke off their engagement. Yet this unfortunate end to the relationship eventually had a happy consequence for Hannah and, by extension, for slaves throughout the British Commonwealth.

Her ex-fiancé, Mr. Turner, partially in apology for leading her on for so long, set Hannah up with an annual income of £200 (about $30,000 today). This guaranteed money allowed Hannah to do what she really wanted with her life: write. First she wrote plays; then soon after she penned influential articles and tracts against the slave trade in the British Empire.

Trusting in God and powerfully appealing to Scripture and the best instincts of women and men in London and the countryside, Hannah More and friends such as William

Wilberforce and William Pitt were able to abolish, first, the British slave trade in 1817 and, finally, slavery itself in 1833 (thirty years before America's Emancipation Proclamation). She was young, she was single, and she was a woman in an era dominated by men—but none of these factors held her back. Through faith in God, Hannah More turned a bad breakup into a chance to change the world!

---

into their hands; we will not kill you." So they bound him with two new ropes, and brought him up from the rock.

14 When he came to Lehi, the Philistines came shouting to meet him; and the spirit of the LORD rushed on him, and the ropes that were on his arms became like flax that has caught fire, and his bonds melted off his hands. [15]Then he found a fresh jawbone of a donkey, reached down and took it, and with it he killed a thousand men. [16]And Samson said,
"With the jawbone of a donkey,
  heaps upon heaps,
with the jawbone of a donkey
  I have slain a thousand men."
[17]When he had finished speaking, he threw away the jawbone; and that place was called Ramath-lehi.[a]

18 By then he was very thirsty, and he called on the LORD, saying, "You have granted this great victory by the hand of your servant. Am I now to die of thirst, and fall into the hands of the uncircumcised?" [19]So God split open the hollow place that is at Lehi, and water came from it. When he drank, his spirit returned, and he revived. Therefore it was named En-hakkore,[b] which is at Lehi to this day. [20]And he judged Israel in the days of the Philistines twenty years.

16 Samson and Delilah

Once Samson went to Gaza, where he saw a prostitute and went in to her. [2]The Gazites were told,[c] "Samson has come here." So they circled around and lay in wait for him all night at the city gate. They kept quiet all night, thinking, "Let us wait until the light of the morning; then we will kill him." [3]But Samson lay only until midnight. Then at midnight he rose up, took hold of the doors of the city gate and the two posts, pulled them up, bar and all, put them on his shoulders, and carried them to the top of the hill that is in front of Hebron.

4 After this he fell in love with a woman in the valley of Sorek, whose name was Delilah. [5]The lords of the Philistines came to her and said

---

a That is *The Hill of the Jawbone* b That is *The Spring of the One who Called* c Gk: Heb lacks *were told* mocked me and told me lies; please tell me how you could be bound." [11] He said to her, "If they bind me with new ropes that have not been used, then I shall become weak, and be like anyone else." [12] So Delilah took new ropes and bound him with them, and said to him, "The Philistines are upon you, Samson!" (The men lying in wait were in an inner chamber.) But he snapped the ropes off his arms like a thread.

13 Then Delilah said to Samson, "Until now you have mocked me and told me lies; tell me how you could be bound." He said to her, "If you weave the seven locks of my head with the web and make it tight with the pin, then I shall become weak, and be like anyone else." [14] So while he slept, Delilah took the seven locks of his head and wove them into the web,[a] and made them tight with the pin. Then she said to him, "The Philistines are upon you, Samson!" But he awoke from his sleep, and pulled away the pin, the loom, and the web.

15 Then she said to him, "How can you say, 'I love you,' when your heart is not with me? You have mocked me three times now and have not told me what makes your strength so great." [16] Finally, after she had nagged him with her words day after day, and pestered him, he was tired to death. [17] So he told her his whole secret, and said to her, "A razor has never come upon my head; for I have been a nazirite[b] to God from my mother's womb. If my head were shaved, then my strength would leave me; I would become weak, and be like anyone else."

18 When Delilah realized that he had told her his whole secret, she sent and called the lords of the Philistines, saying, "This time come up, for he has told his whole secret to me." Then the lords of the Philistines came up to her, and brought the money in their hands. [19] She let him fall asleep on her lap; and she called a man, and had him shave off the seven locks of his head. He began to weaken,[c] and his strength left him. [20] Then she said, "The Philistines are upon you, Samson!" When he awoke from his sleep, he thought, "I will go out as at other times, and shake myself free." But he did not know that the LORD had left him. [21] So the Philistines seized him and gouged out his eyes. They brought him down to Gaza and bound him with bronze shackles; and he ground at the mill in the prison. [22] But the hair of his head began to grow again after it had been shaved.

Samson's Death

23 Now the lords of the Philistines gathered to offer a great sacrifice to their god Dagon, and to

to her, "Coax him, and find out what makes his strength so great, and how we may overpower him, so that we may bind him in order to subdue him; and we will each give you eleven hundred pieces of silver." [6] So Delilah said to Samson, "Please tell me what makes your strength so great, and how you could be bound, so that one could subdue you." [7] Samson said to her, "If they bind me with seven fresh bowstrings that are not dried out, then I shall become weak, and be like anyone else." [8] Then the lords of the Philistines brought her seven fresh bowstrings that had not dried out, and she bound him with them. [9] While men were lying in wait in an inner chamber, she said to him, "The Philistines are upon you, Samson!" But he snapped the bowstrings, as a strand of fiber snaps when it touches the fire. So the secret of his strength was not known.

10 Then Delilah said to Samson, "You have

---

a Compare Gk: in verses 13–14, Heb lacks *and make it tight . . . into the web* b That is *one separated* or *one consecrated* c Gk: Heb *She began to torment him* rejoice; for they said, "Our god has given Samson our enemy into our hand." [24]When the people saw him, they praised their god; for they said, "Our god has given our enemy into our hand, the ravager of our country, who has killed many of us." [25]And when their hearts were merry, they said, "Call Samson, and let him entertain us." So they called Samson out of the prison, and he performed for them. They made him stand between the pillars; [26]and Samson said to the attendant who held him by the hand, "Let me feel the pillars on which the house rests, so that I may lean against them." [27]Now the house was full of men and women; all the lords of the Philistines were there, and on the roof there were about three thousand men and women, who looked on while Samson performed.

28 Then Samson called to the Lord and said, "Lord God, remember me and strengthen me only this once, O God, so that with this one act of revenge I may pay back the Philistines for my two eyes."[a] [29]And Samson grasped the two middle pillars on which the house rested, and he leaned his weight against them, his right hand on the one and his left hand on the other. [30]Then Samson said, "Let me die with the Philistines." He strained with all his might; and the house fell on the lords and all the people who were in it. So those he killed at his death were more than those he had killed during his life. [31]Then his brothers and all his family came down and took him and brought him up and buried him between Zorah and Eshtaol in the tomb of his father Manoah. He had judged Israel twenty years.

17 Micah and the Levite
There was a man in the hill country of Ephraim whose name was Micah. [2]He said to his mother, "The eleven hundred pieces of silver that were taken from you, about which you uttered a curse, and even spoke it in my hearing,—that silver is in my possession; I took it; but now I will return it to you."[b] And his mother said, "May my son be blessed by the Lord!" [3]Then he returned the eleven hundred pieces of silver to his mother; and his mother said, "I consecrate the silver to the Lord from my hand for my son, to make an idol of cast metal." [4]So when he returned the money to his mother, his mother took two hundred pieces of silver, and gave it to the silversmith, who made it into an idol of cast metal; and it was in the house of Micah. [5]This man Micah had a shrine, and he made an ephod and teraphim, and installed one of his sons, who became his priest. [6]In

those days there was no king in Israel; all the people did what was right in their own eyes.

7 Now there was a young man of Bethlehem in Judah, of the clan of Judah. He was a Levite residing there. [8]This man left the town of Bethlehem in Judah, to live wherever he could find a place. He came to the house of Micah in the hill country of Ephraim to carry on his work.[c] [9]Micah said to him, "From where do you come?" He replied, "I am a Levite of Bethlehem in Judah, and I am going to live wherever I can find a place." [10]Then Micah said to him, "Stay with me, and be to me a father and a priest, and I will give you ten pieces of silver a year, a set of clothes, and your living."[d] [11]The Levite agreed to stay with the man; and the young man became to him like one of his sons. [12]So Micah installed the Levite, and the young man became his priest, and was in the house of Micah. [13]Then Micah said, "Now I know that the Lord will prosper me, because the Levite has become my priest."

18 The Migration of Dan
In those days there was no king in Israel. And in those days the tribe of the Danites was seeking for itself a territory to live in; for until then no territory among the tribes of Israel had been allotted to them. [2]So the Danites sent five valiant men from the whole number of their clan, from Zorah and from Eshtaol, to spy out the land and to explore it; and they said to them, "Go, explore the land." When they came to the hill country of Ephraim, to the house of Micah, they stayed there. [3]While they were at Micah's house, they recognized the voice of the young Levite; so they went over and asked him, "Who brought you here? What are you doing in this place? What is your business here?" [4]He said to them, "Micah did such and such for me, and he hired me, and I have become his priest." [5]Then they said to him, "Inquire of God that we may know whether the mission we are undertaking will succeed." [6]The priest replied, "Go in peace. The mission you are on is under the eye of the Lord."

7 The five men went on, and when they came to Laish, they observed the people who were there living securely, after the manner of the Sidonians, quiet and unsuspecting, lacking[e] nothing on earth, and possessing wealth.[f] Furthermore, they were far from the Sidonians and had no dealings with Aram.[g] [8]When they came to their kinsfolk at Zorah and Eshtaol, they said to them, "What do you report?" [9]They said, "Come, let us go up against them; for we

---

a Or *so that I may be avenged upon the Philistines for one of my two eyes* *b* The words *but now I will return it to you* are transposed from the end of verse 3 in Heb *c* Or *Ephraim, continuing his journey* *d* Heb *living, and the Levite went* *e* Cn Compare 18.10: Meaning of Heb uncertain *f* Meaning of Heb uncertain *g* Symmachus: Heb *with anyone*

REALITY ✓

WHO IS THE LEADER?

Read **Judges 21.25**. The last verse of Judges

WHO IS THE LEADER?

Read **Judges 21.25**. The last verse of Judges
attempts to "explain" why the situations in
this book kept recurring: there was no common
good; the people were simply on their own,
doing "what was right in their own eyes." There
was increasingly no collective "people," nothing
but individuals "doing their own thing."

There is an almost tedious repetition of the
same pattern time after time: the Israelites fail
to keep the covenant; God is angry; they are
afflicted; they repent; God sends a leader who
unites them, calls for a deepened relationship
with God, and leads them to victory. And the
cycle begins all over again. Actually it becomes
a downward spiral, as in the gruesome story of
the Levite in **Judges 19.1–30**.

The underlying question of Joshua and
Judges is whether the Israelites can realize
that God is their true leader. Political games,
intertribal jealousies, and disobedience to the
ways of God introduce chaos into a divinely
ordered creation. To forget that is to live in
perilous times, then and now.

- In what ways do we as a Catholic
  "people" act for the "common good" as
  we stand in society and the world today?
- Can you see similarities or differences
  between what was going on in the Old
  Testament and what's happening today?

have seen the land, and it is very good. Will you
do nothing? Do not be slow to go, but enter
in and possess the land. [10]When you go, you
will come to an unsuspecting people. The land
is broad—God has indeed given it into your
hands—a place where there is no lack of anything on earth."

[11] Six hundred men of the Danite clan,
armed with weapons of war, set out from Zorah and Eshtaol, [12]and went up and encamped at Kiriath-jearim in Judah. On this account
that place is called Mahaneh-dan[a] to this day;
it is west of Kiriath-jearim. [13]From there they
passed on to the hill country of Ephraim, and
came to the house of Micah.

14 Then the five men who had gone to spy
out the land (that is, Laish) said to their comrades, "Do you know that in these buildings
there are an ephod, teraphim, and an idol of
cast metal? Now therefore consider what you
will do." [15]So they turned in that direction and
came to the house of the young Levite, at the
home of Micah, and greeted him. [16]While the
six hundred men of the Danites, armed with
their weapons of war, stood by the entrance
of the gate, [17]the five men who had gone to
spy out the land proceeded to enter and take
the idol of cast metal, the ephod, and the teraphim.[b] The priest was standing by the entrance
of the gate with the six hundred men armed
with weapons of war. [18]When the men went
into Micah's house and took the idol of cast
metal, the ephod, and the teraphim, the priest
said to them, "What are you doing?" [19]They said
to him, "Keep quiet! Put your hand over your
mouth, and come with us, and be to us a father
and a priest. Is it better for you to be priest to the
house of one person, or to be priest to a tribe
and clan in Israel?" [20]Then the priest accepted
the offer. He took the ephod, the teraphim, and
the idol, and went along with the people.

21 So they resumed their journey, putting
the little ones, the livestock, and the goods in
front of them. [22]When they were some distance
from the home of Micah, the men who were in
the houses near Micah's house were called out,
and they overtook the Danites. [23]They shouted
to the Danites, who turned around and said to
Micah, "What is the matter that you come with
such a company?" [24]He replied, "You take my
gods that I made, and the priest, and go away,
and what have I left? How then can you ask
me, 'What is the matter?' " [25]And the Danites
said to him, "You had better not let your voice
be heard among us or else hot-tempered fellows will attack you, and you will lose your life
and the lives of your household." [26]Then the
Danites went their way. When Micah saw that
they were too strong for him, he turned and
went back to his home.

The Danites Settle in Laish

27 The Danites, having taken what Micah had
made, and the priest who belonged to him,
came to Laish, to a people quiet and unsuspecting, put them to the sword, and burned
down the city. [28]There was no deliverer, because it was far from Sidon and they had no
dealings with Aram.[c] It was in the valley that

a That is *Camp of Dan* *b* Compare 17.4, 5; 18.14: Heb *teraphim and the cast metal* *c* Cn Compare verse 7: Heb *with anyone*

Angelic—© Katie Stein, 15

belongs to Beth-rehob. They rebuilt the city, and lived in it. 29They named the city Dan, after their ancestor Dan, who was born to Israel; but the name of the city was formerly Laish. 30Then the Danites set up the idol for themselves. Jonathan son of Gershom, son of Moses,ᵃ and his sons were priests to the tribe of the Danites until the time the land went into captivity. 31So they maintained as their own Micah's idol that he had made, as long as the house of God was at Shiloh.

19 The Levite's Concubine

In those days, when there was no king in Israel, a certain Levite, residing in the remote parts of the hill country of Ephraim, took to himself a concubine from Bethlehem in Judah. 2But his concubine became angry withᵇ him, and she went away from him to her father's house at Bethlehem in Judah, and was there some four months. 3Then her husband set out after her, to speak tenderly to her and bring her back. He had with him his servant and a couple of donkeys. When he reachedᶜ her father's house, the girl's father saw him and came with joy to meet him. 4His father-in-law, the girl's father, made him stay, and he remained with him three days; so they ate and drank, and heᵈ stayed there. 5On the fourth day they got up early in the morning, and he prepared to go; but the girl's father said to his son-in-law, "Fortify yourself with a bit of food, and after that you may go." 6So the two men sat and ate and drank together; and the girl's father said to the man, "Why not spend the night and enjoy yourself?" 7When the man got up to go, his father-in-law kept urging him until he spent the night there again. 8On the fifth day he got up early in the morning to leave; and the girl's father said, "Fortify yourself." So they lingeredᵉ until the day declined, and the two of them ate and drank.ᶠ 9When the man with his concubine and his servant got up to leave, his father-in-law, the girl's father, said to him, "Look, the day has worn on until it is almost evening. Spend the night. See, the day has drawn to a close. Spend the night here and enjoy yourself. Tomorrow you can get up early in the morning for your journey, and go home."

10 But the man would not spend the night; he got up and departed, and arrived opposite Jebus (that is, Jerusalem). He had with him a couple of saddled donkeys, and his concubine was with him. 11When they were near Jebus, the day was far spent, and the servant said to his master, "Come now, let us turn aside to this city of the Jebusites, and spend the night in it." 12But his master said to him, "We will not turn aside

ᵃ Another reading is *son of Manasseh* ᵇ Gk OL: Heb *prostituted herself against* ᶜ Gk: Heb *she brought him to* ᵈ Compare verse 7 and Gk: Heb *they* ᵉ Cn: Heb *Linger* ᶠ Gk: Heb lacks *and drank* into a city of foreigners, who do not belong to the people of Israel; but we will continue on to Gibeah." [13]Then he said to his servant, "Come, let us try to reach one of these places, and spend the night at Gibeah or at Ramah." [14]So they passed on and went their way; and the sun went down on them near Gibeah, which belongs to Benjamin. [15]They turned aside there, to go in and spend the night at Gibeah. He went in and sat down in the open square of the city, but no one took them in to spend the night.

16 Then at evening there was an old man coming from his work in the field. The man was from the hill country of Ephraim, and he was residing in Gibeah. (The people of the place were Benjaminites.) [17]When the old man looked up and saw the wayfarer in the open square of the city, he said, "Where are you going and where do you come from?" [18]He answered him, "We are passing from Bethlehem in Judah to the remote parts of the hill country of Ephraim, from which I come. I went to Bethlehem in Judah; and I am going to my home.[a] Nobody has offered to take me in. [19]We your servants have straw and fodder for our donkeys, with bread and wine for me and the woman and the young man along with us. We need nothing more." [20]The old man said, "Peace be to you. I will care for all your wants; only do not spend the night in the square." [21]So he brought him into his house, and fed the donkeys; they washed their feet, and ate and drank.

Gibeah's Crime

22 While they were enjoying themselves, the men of the city, a perverse lot, surrounded the house, and started pounding on the door. They said to the old man, the master of the house, "Bring out the man who came into your house,

so that we may have intercourse with him." [23]And the man, the master of the house, went out to them and said to them, "No, my brothers, do not act so wickedly. Since this man is my guest, do not do this vile thing. [24]Here are my virgin daughter and his concubine; let me bring them out now. Ravish them and do whatever you want to them; but against this man do not do such a vile thing." [25]But the men would not listen to him. So the man seized his concubine, and put her out to them. They wantonly raped her, and abused her all through the night until the morning. And as the dawn began to break, they let her go. [26]As morning appeared, the woman came and fell down at the door of the man's house where her master was, until it was light.

27 In the morning her master got up, opened the doors of the house, and when he went out to go on his way, there was his concubine lying at the door of the house, with her hands on the threshold. [28]"Get up," he said to her, "we are going." But there was no answer. Then he put her on the donkey; and the man set out for his home. [29]When he had entered his house, he took a knife, and grasping his concubine he cut her into twelve pieces, limb by limb, and sent her throughout all the territory of Israel. [30]Then he commanded the men whom he sent, saying, "Thus shall you say to all the Israelites, 'Has such a thing ever happened[b] since the day that the Israelites came up from the land of Egypt until this day? Consider it, take counsel, and speak out.' "

20 The Other Tribes Attack Benjamin

Then all the Israelites came out, from Dan to Beer-sheba, including the land of Gilead, and the congregation assembled in one body before the LORD at Mizpah. [2]The chiefs of all the people, of all the tribes of Israel, presented themselves in the assembly of the people of God, four hundred thousand foot-soldiers bearing arms. [3](Now the Benjaminites heard that the people of Israel had gone up to Mizpah.) And the Israelites said, "Tell us, how did this criminal act come about?" [4]The Levite, the husband of the woman who was murdered, answered, "I came to Gibeah that belongs to Benjamin, I and my concubine, to spend the night. [5]The lords of Gibeah rose up against me, and surrounded the house at night. They intended to kill me, and they raped my concubine until she died. [6]Then I took my concubine and cut her into pieces, and sent her throughout the whole extent of Israel's territory; for

a Gk Compare 19.29. Heb *to the house of the LORD*   b Compare Gk: Heb [30]*And all who saw it said, "Such a thing has not happened or been seen* they have committed a vile outrage in Israel. ⁷So now, you Israelites, all of you, give your advice and counsel here."

8 All the people got up as one, saying, "We will not any of us go to our tents, nor will any of us return to our houses. ⁹But now this is what we will do to Gibeah: we will go up*ᵃ* against it by lot. ¹⁰We will take ten men of a hundred throughout all the tribes of Israel, and a hundred of a thousand, and a thousand of ten thousand, to bring provisions for the troops, who are going to repay*ᵇ* Gibeah of Benjamin for all the disgrace that they have done in Israel." ¹¹So all the men of Israel gathered against the city, united as one.

12 The tribes of Israel sent men through all the tribe of Benjamin, saying, "What crime is this that has been committed among you? ¹³Now then, hand over those scoundrels in Gibeah, so that we may put them to death, and purge the evil from Israel." But the Benjaminites would not listen to their kinsfolk, the Israelites. ¹⁴The Benjaminites came together out of the towns to Gibeah, to go out to battle against the Israelites. ¹⁵On that day the Benjaminites mustered twenty-six thousand armed men from their towns, besides the inhabitants of Gibeah. ¹⁶Of all this force, there were seven hundred picked men who were left-handed; every one could sling a stone at a hair, and not miss. ¹⁷And the Israelites, apart from Benjamin, mustered four hundred thousand armed men, all of them warriors.

18 The Israelites proceeded to go up to Bethel, where they inquired of God, "Which of us shall go up first to battle against the Benjaminites?" And the Lord answered, "Judah shall go up first."

19 Then the Israelites got up in the morning, and encamped against Gibeah. ²⁰The Israelites went out to battle against Benjamin; and the Israelites drew up the battle line against them at Gibeah. ²¹The Benjaminites came out of Gibeah, and struck down that day twenty-two thousand of the Israelites. ²³*ᶜ* The Israelites went up and wept before the Lord until the evening; and they inquired of the Lord, "Shall we again draw near to battle against our kinsfolk the Benjaminites?" And the Lord said, "Go up against them." ²²The Israelites took courage, and again formed the battle line in the same place where they had formed it on the first day.

24 So the Israelites advanced against the Benjaminites the second day. ²⁵Benjamin moved out against them from Gibeah the second day, and struck down eighteen thousand of the Israelites, all of them armed men. ²⁶Then all the Isra-

elites, the whole army, went back to Bethel and wept, sitting there before the Lord; they fasted that day until evening. Then they offered burnt offerings and sacrifices of well-being before the Lord. ²⁷And the Israelites inquired of the Lord (for the ark of the covenant of God was there in those days, ²⁸and Phinehas son of Eleazar, son of Aaron, ministered before it in those days), saying, "Shall we go out once more to battle against our kinsfolk the Benjaminites, or shall we desist?" The Lord answered, "Go up, for tomorrow I will give them into your hand."

29 So Israel stationed men in ambush around Gibeah. ³⁰Then the Israelites went up against the Benjaminites on the third day, and set themselves in array against Gibeah, as before. ³¹When the Benjaminites went out against the army, they were drawn away from the city. As before they began to inflict casualties on the troops, along the main roads, one of which goes up to Bethel and the other to Gibeah, as well as in the open country, killing about thirty men of Israel. ³²The Benjaminites thought, "They are being routed before us, as previously." But the Israelites said, "Let us retreat and draw them away from the city toward the roads." ³³The main body of the Israelites drew back its battle line to Baal-tamar, while those Israelites who were in ambush rushed out of their place west*ᵈ* of Geba. ³⁴There came against Gibeah ten thousand picked men out of all Israel, and the battle was fierce. But the Benjaminites did not realize that disaster was close upon them.

35 The Lord defeated Benjamin before Israel; and the Israelites destroyed twenty-five thousand one hundred men of Benjamin that day, all of them armed.

36 Then the Benjaminites saw that they were defeated.*ᵉ*

The Israelites gave ground to Benjamin, because they trusted to the troops in ambush that they had stationed against Gibeah. ³⁷The troops in ambush rushed quickly upon Gibeah. Then they put the whole city to the sword. ³⁸Now the agreement between the main body of Israel and the men in ambush was that when they sent up a cloud of smoke out of the city ³⁹the main body of Israel should turn in battle. But Benjamin had begun to inflict casualties on the Israelites, killing about thirty of them; so they thought, "Surely they are defeated before us, as in the first battle." ⁴⁰But when the cloud, a column of smoke, began to rise out of the city, the Benjaminites looked behind them—and there was the whole city going up

---

ᵃ Gk: Heb lacks *we will go up*   *ᵇ* Compare Gk: Meaning of Heb uncertain   *ᶜ* Verses 22 and 23 are transposed   *ᵈ* Gk Vg: Heb *in the plain*   *ᵉ* This sentence is continued by verse 45.

in smoke toward the sky! ⁴¹Then the main body of Israel turned, and the Benjaminites were dismayed, for they saw that disaster was close upon them. ⁴²Therefore they turned away from the Israelites in the direction of the wilderness; but the battle overtook them, and those who came out of the city*ᵃ* were slaughtering them in between.*ᵇ* ⁴³Cutting down*ᶜ* the Benjaminites, they pursued them from Nohah*ᵈ* and trod them down as far as a place east of Gibeah. ⁴⁴Eighteen thousand Benjaminites fell, all of them courageous fighters. ⁴⁵When they turned and fled toward the wilderness to the rock of Rimmon, five thousand of them were cut down on the main roads, and they were pursued as far as Gidom, and two thousand of them were slain. ⁴⁶So all who fell that day of Benjamin were twenty-five thousand arms-bearing men, all of them courageous fighters. ⁴⁷But six hundred turned and fled toward the wilderness to the rock of Rimmon, and remained at the rock of Rimmon for four months. ⁴⁸Meanwhile, the Israelites turned back against the Benjaminites, and put them to the sword—the city, the people, the animals, and all that remained. Also the remaining towns they set on fire.

21 The Benjaminites Saved from Extinction

Now the Israelites had sworn at Mizpah, "No one of us shall give his daughter in marriage to Benjamin." ²And the people came to Bethel, and sat there until evening before God, and they lifted up their voices and wept bitterly. ³They said, "O LORD, the God of Israel, why has it come to pass that today there should be one tribe lacking in Israel?" ⁴On the next day, the people got up early, and built an altar there, and offered burnt offerings and sacrifices of well-being. ⁵Then the Israelites said, "Which of all the tribes of Israel did not come up in the assembly to the LORD?" For a solemn oath had been taken concerning whoever did not come up to the LORD to Mizpah, saying, "That one shall be put to death." ⁶But the Israelites had compassion for Benjamin their kin, and said, "One tribe is cut off from Israel this day. ⁷What shall we do for wives for those who are left, since we have sworn by the LORD that we will not give them any of our daughters as wives?"

⁸ Then they said, "Is there anyone from the tribes of Israel who did not come up to the LORD to Mizpah?" It turned out that no one from Jabesh-gilead had come to the camp, to the assembly. ⁹For when the roll was called among the people, not one of the inhabitants of Jabesh-gilead was there. ¹⁰So the congregation sent twelve thousand soldiers there and commanded them, "Go, put the inhabitants of Jabesh-gilead to the sword, including the women and the little ones. ¹¹This is what you shall do; every male and every woman that has lain with a male you shall devote to destruction." ¹²And they found among the inhabitants of Jabesh-gilead four hundred young virgins who had never slept with a man and brought them to the camp at Shiloh, which is in the land of Canaan.

13 Then the whole congregation sent word to the Benjaminites who were at the rock of Rimmon, and proclaimed peace to them. ¹⁴Benjamin returned at that time; and they gave them the women whom they had saved alive of the women of Jabesh-gilead; but they did not suffice for them.

15 The people had compassion on Benjamin because the LORD had made a breach in the tribes of Israel. ¹⁶So the elders of the congregation said, "What shall we do for wives for those who are left, since there are no women left in Benjamin?" ¹⁷And they said, "There must be heirs for the survivors of Benjamin, in order that a tribe may not be blotted out from Israel. ¹⁸Yet we cannot give any of our daughters to them as wives." For the Israelites had sworn, "Cursed be anyone who gives a wife to Benjamin." ¹⁹So they said, "Look, the yearly festival of the LORD is taking place at Shiloh, which is north of Bethel, on the east of the highway that goes up from Bethel to Shechem, and south of Lebonah." ²⁰And they instructed the Benjaminites, saying, "Go and lie in wait in the vineyards, ²¹and watch; when the young women of Shiloh come out to dance in the dances, then come out of the vineyards and each of you carry off a wife for himself from the young women of Shiloh, and go to the land of Benjamin. ²²Then if their fathers or their brothers come to complain to us, we will say to them, 'Be generous and allow us to have them; because we did not capture in battle a wife for each man. But neither did you incur guilt by giving your daughters to them.' " ²³The Benjaminites did so; they took wives for each of them from the dancers whom they abducted. Then they went and returned to their territory, and rebuilt the towns, and lived in them. ²⁴So the Israelites departed from there at that time by tribes and families, and they went out from there to their own territories.

25 In those days there was no king in Israel; all the people did what was right in their own eyes.

---

a Compare Vg and some Gk Mss: Heb *cities* *b* Compare Syr: Meaning of Heb uncertain *c* Gk: Heb *Surrounding* *d* Gk: Heb *pursued them at their resting place*

RUTH

THERE ARE *NO* OUTSIDERS

God's Family Looks a Little Different

We all know what it feels like to be an outsider at times. A different skin color makes us stand out sometimes. Or maybe we talk differently. Or maybe our family background is different. Or maybe *we're* just different.

Ruth was all those things.

After her husband died, she was forced to make a decision: go back home to her people and their religion or travel with her mother-in-law to a land where she would be the outsider. She chose to be the outsider.

Living in a culture that devalued women—especially women without husbands—Ruth was up against the steepest odds. Ruth felt the sting of sexism and the bite of racism. Ruth knew how hard sorrow could hit. But there was something about Ruth that wouldn't allow hatred to stop her. Ruth found strength in God greater than any sorrow. And in the end, Ruth learned that a person's value is not found in the externals. Value comes from God—and God welcomes *all* people.

Have you been there? Judged because of the color of your skin or because you look different? Or maybe because your family life is beyond crazy? Read through Ruth, and the message of God's wholehearted love for all people will shine through. There can never be someone who is too messed up, too hurt, or too different for God. There are *no* outsiders in God's family.

WHO The author is unknown.

WHAT A short story about Ruth the Moabite, her marriage to Boaz, and her place in the family line of David and Jesus

WHEN Scripture scholars historically place the setting of the story during the time of the Judges (1200–1050 B.C.). It was written later, probably soon after David died (965 B.C.).

WHERE From Moab (modern-day Jordan) to Judah (modern-day Israel and Palestine)

> *"I want to spend my heaven doing good on earth."*
> —St. Thérèse of Lisieux

 ## PATH OF DISCIPLESHIP

The book of Ruth is about choice, community, commitment, and risk. After her husband died, Ruth chose to remain with her mother-in-law. She could have gone back to her roots, but she took a big risk and began to live with Naomi and her community. Ruth trusted deeply in God's love for her. Jesus asked his disciples to leave everything and follow him. Like Ruth, they were faced with choices and risks as they entered new communities.

Each year at the Easter Vigil, the Church welcomes new members (catechumens and candidates) into our community of faith through the Rite of Christian Initiation of Adults. Some of these people have left behind families and faith communities to join us. Will you be like Boaz and step out to welcome them? Can you welcome new people into your school or onto a sports team? Perhaps Ruth's story can inspire you and may even help you have faith when *you* join a new group.

1 Elimelech's Family Goes to Moab

In the days when the judges ruled, there was a famine in the land, and a certain man of Bethlehem in Judah went to live in the country of Moab, he and his wife and two sons. ²The name of the man was Elimelech and the name of his wife Naomi, and the names of his two sons were Mahlon and Chilion; they were Ephrathites from Bethlehem in Judah. They went into the country of Moab and remained there. ³But Elimelech, the husband of Naomi, died, and she was left with her two sons. ⁴These took Moabite wives; the name of the one was Orpah and the name of the other Ruth. When they had lived there about ten years, ⁵both Mahlon and Chilion also died, so that the woman was left without her two sons and her husband.

Naomi and Her Moabite Daughters-in-Law

6 Then she started to return with her daughters-in-law from the country of Moab, for she had heard in the country of Moab that the LORD had considered his people and given them food. ⁷So she set out from the place where she had been living, she and her two daughters-in-law, and they went on their way to go back to the land of Judah. ⁸But Naomi said to her two daughters-in-law, "Go back each of you to your mother's house. May the LORD deal kindly with you, as you have dealt with the dead and with me. ⁹The LORD grant that you may find security, each of you in the house of your husband." Then she kissed them, and they wept aloud. ¹⁰They said to her, "No, we will return with you to your people." ¹¹But Naomi said, "Turn back, my daughters, why will you go with me? Do I still have sons in my womb that they may become your husbands? ¹²Turn back, my daughters, go your way, for I am too old to have a husband. Even if I thought there was hope for me, even if I should have a husband tonight and bear sons, ¹³would you then wait until they were grown? Would you then refrain from marrying? No, my daughters, it has been far more bitter for me than for you, because the hand of the LORD has turned against me." ¹⁴Then they wept aloud again. Orpah kissed her mother-in-law, but Ruth clung to her.

15 So she said, "See, your sister-in-law has gone back to her people and to her gods; return after your sister-in-law." ¹⁶But Ruth said,

"Do not press me to leave you
   or to turn back from following you!
Where you go, I will go;
   Where you lodge, I will lodge;
your people shall be my people,
   and your God my God.
¹⁷ Where you die, I will die—
   there will I be buried.
May the LORD do thus and so to me,
   and more as well,
if even death parts me from you!"

¹⁸When Naomi saw that she was determined to go with her, she said no more to her.

19 So the two of them went on until they came to Bethlehem. When they came to Bethlehem, the whole town was stirred because of them; and the women said, "Is this Naomi?" ²⁰She said to them,

"Call me no longer Naomi,ᵃ
   call me Mara,ᵇ
for the Almightyᶜ has dealt bitterly
      with me.
²¹ I went away full,
   but the LORD has brought me back
         empty;
why call me Naomi
   when the LORD has dealt harshly
         withᵈ me,
   and the Almightyᶜ has brought calamity
         upon me?"

22 So Naomi returned together with Ruth the Moabite, her daughter-in-law, who came back with her from the country of Moab. They came to Bethlehem at the beginning of the barley harvest.

2 Ruth Meets Boaz

Now Naomi had a kinsman on her husband's side, a prominent rich man, of the family of Elimelech, whose name was Boaz. ²And Ruth the Moabite said to Naomi, "Let me go to the field and glean among the ears of grain, behind someone in whose sight I may find favor." She said to her, "Go, my daughter." ³So she went. She came and gleaned in the field behind the reapers. As it happened, she came to the part of the field belonging to Boaz, who was of the family of Elimelech. ⁴Just then Boaz came from Bethlehem. He said to the reapers, "The LORD be with you." They answered, "The LORD bless you." ⁵Then Boaz said to his servant who was in charge of the reapers, "To whom does this young woman belong?" ⁶The servant who was in charge of the reapers answered, "She is the Moabite who came back with Naomi from the country of Moab. ⁷She said, 'Please, let me glean and gather among the sheaves behind the reapers.' So she came, and she has been on her feet from early this morning until now, without resting even for a moment."ᵉ

8 Then Boaz said to Ruth, "Now listen, my

ᵃ That is *Pleasant* ᵇ That is *Bitter* ᶜ Traditional rendering of Heb *Shaddai* ᵈ Or *has testified against* ᵉ Compare Gk Vg: Meaning of Heb uncertain daughter, do not go to glean in another field or leave this one, but keep close to my young women. [9]Keep your eyes on the field that is being reaped, and follow behind them. I have ordered the young men not to bother you. If you get thirsty, go to the vessels and drink from what the young men have drawn." [10]Then she fell prostrate, with her face to the ground, and said to him, "Why have I found favor in your sight, that you should take notice of me, when I am a foreigner?" [11]But Boaz answered her, "All that you have done for your mother-in-law since the death of your husband has been fully told me, and how you left your father and mother and your native land and came to a people that you did not know before. [12]May the LORD reward you for your deeds, and may you have a full reward from the LORD, the God of Israel, under whose wings you have come for refuge!" [13]Then she said, "May I continue to find favor in your sight, my lord, for you have comforted me and spoken kindly to your servant, even though I am not one of your servants."

14 At mealtime Boaz said to her, "Come here, and eat some of this bread, and dip your morsel in the sour wine." So she sat beside the reapers, and he heaped up for her some parched grain. She ate until she was satisfied, and she had some left over. [15]When she got up to glean, Boaz instructed his young men, "Let her glean even among the standing sheaves, and do not reproach her. [16]You must also pull out some handfuls for her from the bundles, and leave them for her to glean, and do not rebuke her."

17 So she gleaned in the field until evening. Then she beat out what she had gleaned, and it was about an ephah of barley. [18]She picked it up and came into the town, and her mother-in-law saw how much she had gleaned. Then she took out and gave her what was left over after she herself had been satisfied. [19]Her mother-in-law said to her, "Where did you glean today? And where have you worked? Blessed be the man who took notice of you." So she told her mother-in-law with whom she had worked, and said, "The name of the man with whom I worked today is Boaz." [20]Then Naomi said to her daughter-in-law, "Blessed be he by the LORD, whose kindness has not forsaken the living or the dead!" Naomi also said to her, "The man is a relative of ours, one of our nearest kin."[a] [21]Then Ruth the Moabite said, "He even said to me, 'Stay close by my servants, until they have finished all my harvest.'" [22]Naomi said to Ruth, her daughter-in-law, "It is better, my daughter, that you go out with his young

a Or one with the right to redeem

women, otherwise you might be bothered in another field." [23]So she stayed close to the young women of Boaz, gleaning until the end of the barley and wheat harvests; and she lived with her mother-in-law.

3 Ruth and Boaz at the Threshing Floor

Naomi her mother-in-law said to her, "My daughter, I need to seek some security for you, so that it may be well with you. [2]Now here is our kinsman Boaz, with whose young women you have been working. See, he is winnowing barley tonight at the threshing floor. [3]Now wash and anoint yourself, and put on your best clothes and go down to the threshing floor; but do not make yourself known to the

REALITY ✔

WHERE'S GOD?

"Anytime, anyplace, anywhere" was the message in the yearbook. It was a pledge from one friend to another to "be there" no matter what. Will it be honored over the years through crises, marriages, children, deaths, and plain old everyday difficulties?

Unlike in most books of the Bible, God never speaks and God is not quoted in Ruth. Yet God is present in every one of the relationships, which makes the story of Ruth so beloved. The lesson? God's activity is an everyday affair.

So it is in all of our lives, especially in relationships of dedication and trust, where God not only is present but impacts our lives in ways we often see in only the rearview mirror. God is here in our families and in our true friendships.

- Can you recall how a friend has been God-with-you?
- Is there something unique to the relationship between friends that allows for God's presence?
- What does it take to be a friend "anytime, anyplace, anywhere"?

man until he has finished eating and drinking. ⁴When he lies down, observe the place where he lies; then, go and uncover his feet and lie down; and he will tell you what to do." ⁵She said to her, "All that you tell me I will do."

6 So she went down to the threshing floor and did just as her mother-in-law had instructed her. ⁷When Boaz had eaten and drunk, and he was in a contented mood, he went to lie down at the end of the heap of grain. Then she came stealthily and uncovered his feet, and lay down. ⁸At midnight the man was startled, and turned over, and there, lying at his feet, was a woman! ⁹He said, "Who are you?" And she answered, "I am Ruth, your servant; spread your cloak over your servant, for you are next-of-kin."ᵃ ¹⁰He said, "May you be blessed by the

Lᴏʀᴅ, my daughter; this last instance of your loyalty is better than the first; you have not gone after young men, whether poor or rich. ¹¹And now, my daughter, do not be afraid, I will do for you all that you ask, for all the assembly of my people know that you are a worthy woman. ¹²But now, though it is true that I am a near kinsman, there is another kinsman more closely related than I. ¹³Remain this night, and in the morning, if he will act as next-of-kinᵃ for you, good; let him do it. If he is not willing to act as next-of-kinᵃ for you, then, as the Lᴏʀᴅ lives, I will act as next-of-kinᵃ for you. Lie down until the morning."

14 So she lay at his feet until morning, but got up before one person could recognize another; for he said, "It must not be known that the woman came to the threshing floor." ¹⁵Then he said, "Bring the cloak you are wearing and hold it out." So she held it, and he measured out six measures of barley, and put it on her back; then he went into the city. ¹⁶She came to her mother-in-law, who said, "How did things go with you,ᵇ my daughter?" Then she told her all that the man had done for her, ¹⁷saying, "He gave me these six measures of barley, for he said, 'Do not go back to your mother-in-law empty-handed.' " ¹⁸She replied, "Wait, my daughter, until you learn how the matter turns out, for the man will not rest, but will settle the matter today."

4 The Marriage of Boaz and Ruth

No sooner had Boaz gone up to the gate and sat down there than the next-of-kin,ᵃ of whom Boaz had spoken, came passing by. So Boaz said, "Come over, friend; sit down here." And he went over and sat down. ²Then Boaz took ten men of the elders of the city, and said, "Sit down here"; so they sat down. ³He then said to the next-of-kin,ᵃ "Naomi, who has come back from the country of Moab, is selling the parcel of land that belonged to our kinsman Elimelech. ⁴So I thought I would tell you of it, and say: Buy it in the presence of those sitting here, and in the presence of the elders of my people. If you will redeem it, redeem it; but if you will not, tell me, so that I may know; for there is no one prior to you to redeem it, and I come after you." So he said, "I will redeem it." ⁵Then Boaz said, "The day you acquire the field from the hand of Naomi, you are also acquiring Ruthᶜ the Moabite, the widow of the dead man, to maintain the dead man's name on his inheritance." ⁶At this, the next-of-kinᵃ said, "I cannot redeem it for myself without damaging my

ᵃ Or one with the right to redeem   ᵇ Or "Who are you,   ᶜ OL Vg: Heb from the hand of Naomi and from Ruth

CRY OUT

Sometimes You're the only one I can talk to
You're the only one who knows why these tears fall
Sometimes I wonder why I should even bother
Then I remember to call on my Heavenly Father

When I fall down, You pick me up
When I'm on my knees, You comfort me
I cry out to You, Lord
Are You listening?
Because I need You here with me

If I'm the only one left standing in this crowd
Help me have faith in You, openly and avowed
Take me by the hand and lead me back home
I'm stuck inside a world that I call my own

When I fall down, You pick me up
When I'm on my knees, You comfort me
I cry out to You, Lord
Are You listening?
Because I need You here with me

Can You see the tension in my veins
Trapped behind the glass of these window panes
Crying out to You, oh Lord, rescue me
Take me home to You where I have security

When I fall down, You pick me up
When I'm on my knees, You comfort me
I cry out to You, Lord
Are You listening?
Because I need You here with me
Oh, Lord, I need You here with me

Cry Out—© Anna Hastings, 17

own inheritance. Take my right of redemption yourself, for I cannot redeem it."

7 Now this was the custom in former times in Israel concerning redeeming and exchanging: to confirm a transaction, the one took off a sandal and gave it to the other; this was the manner of attesting in Israel. [8]So when the next-of-kin[a] said to Boaz, "Acquire it for yourself," he took off his sandal. [9]Then Boaz said to the elders and all the people, "Today you are witnesses that I have acquired from the hand of Naomi all that belonged to Elimelech and all that belonged to Chilion and Mahlon. [10]I have also acquired Ruth the Moabite, the wife of Mahlon, to be my wife, to maintain the dead man's name on his inheritance, in order that the name of the dead may not be cut off from his kindred and from the gate of his native place; today you are witnesses." [11]Then all the people who were at the gate, along with the elders, said, "We are witnesses. May the LORD make the woman who is coming into your house like Rachel and Leah, who together built up the house of Israel. May you produce children in Ephrathah and bestow a name in Bethlehem; [12]and, through the children that the LORD will give you by this young woman, may your house be like the house of Perez, whom Tamar bore to Judah."

The Genealogy of David

13 So Boaz took Ruth and she became his wife. When they came together, the LORD made her conceive, and she bore a son. [14]Then the women said to Naomi, "Blessed be the LORD, who has not left you this day without next-of-kin;[a] and may his name be renowned in Israel! [15]He shall be to you a restorer of life and a nourisher of your old age; for your daughter-in-law who loves you, who is more to you than seven sons, has borne him." [16]Then Naomi took the child and laid him in her bosom, and became his nurse. [17]The women of the neighborhood gave him a name, saying, "A son has been born to Naomi." They named him Obed; he became the father of Jesse, the father of David.

18 Now these are the descendants of Perez: Perez became the father of Hezron, [19]Hezron of Ram, Ram of Amminadab, [20]Amminadab of Nahshon, Nahshon of Salmon, [21]Salmon of Boaz, Boaz of Obed, [22]Obed of Jesse, and Jesse of David.

a Or one with the right to redeem

> "To touch God a little with our mind is a great blessing, to grasp him is impossible."
>
> —St. Augustine

1 SAMUEL

WHAT REALLY MATTERS

The Faith of God

People often talk about "having faith" in God. But doesn't it seem as if the God they describe is far off, completely removed from the "real" world—like he's this unseen force that's "out there" somewhere?

But what if that message isn't quite right?

What if God *is* intimately involved in *this* world?

What if God is always present, always active in the reality in which you and I live? What if this God actually has faith in *you*? What if this God believes in *you*? What difference could this reality make in your life?

The book of 1 Samuel is about this kind of God—an ever present, ever active Creator. It's about a God who sees something inside each and every human being, something far deeper than what we often see in each other. Just ask Samuel, who got a front-row seat and a first-class lesson about the kinds of people God chooses to use. While Samuel was looking at the stature of a person when he was choosing Israel's king, God was looking for something much deeper. You see, we judge a person's worth based on his or her exterior—on what someone has, what someone looks like, or what someone does. Yet God sees the interior—he sees who someone really *is*. He sees something so much bigger than we do.

When you look in the mirror, what do you see? When you look at others, what do you see? When God looks at humanity, he sees his creation. Loved. Valued. God believes in you. He has faith that you can be what he created you to be, and he is at work to help you along in the process.

"God is not only true, but Truth itself."
—Pope Leo XIII

WHO The books of 1 and 2 Samuel were shaped from fragments of many narratives. The authors and editors are unknown.

WHAT A theological history of God's interaction with God's chosen people during the rise of the kingdom of Israel from a theocracy (Yahweh is the "King") to a monarchy (the reigns of Saul and David)

WHEN The events in 1 and 2 Samuel took place ca. 1050–970 B.C.

WHERE Modern-day Israel and Palestine and the surrounding region

PATH OF DISCIPLESHIP

If there's one thing we learn in 1 Samuel, it is this: God messes up all the "rules" we set up for how life should work. Popularity, achievement, prestige—all the things society values—don't appear to have much currency in God's economy. Jesus continued the rule-breaking tradition that God established in the Old Testament. He had a habit of breaking the assigned "rules" of the religious leaders, and it drove them crazy.

During Jesus' time, people were strictly labeled either "in" or "out." Those who were "out" were rejected and labeled "sinners" by the religious elite. But Jesus ripped up those labels.

As a disciple of Jesus, are you committed to breaking the "rules"? Think of someone in your life who was rejected by others. Can you befriend that person? Jesus did, and calls you—his disciple—to do the same.

When God Began Creating—© Eliza German, 20

TRY THIS

CATERPILLARS

I was walking through a parking lot toward my car when I saw a fat, hairy caterpillar poking along. Hmmmm. *Parking lots aren't a good place for caterpillars*, I thought as I continued on my way.

I was haunted as I started my engine. So I stopped. And even though I hate touching wiggling, gross things, I moved the furry guy to a grassy area where he might stand a chance. There is something about squished caterpillars that is just *wrong*. Like how they never fulfill their destiny of becoming a butterfly and they never know what it's like to fly.

Read **1 Samuel 1.1–8**. That's how Hannah was feeling. She felt destined to be a mom, but her dreams were squashed. Again and again. She wanted a child . . . desperately. She knew she would be an awesome mom. It was her calling—and anything less seemed really depressing. She prayed tirelessly, but nothing happened. Until . . .

Sometimes it's hard to recognize God in a world so off its tracks, but I'm told that God is compassionate, and I tend to agree, because he can hardly ever sit tight when someone cries out to him in gut-wrenching despair. He gets cracking.

SPOILER ALERT: Read **1 Samuel 1.9–20** to find how God came through for Hannah's family. Then think about the times in your life when God has had compassion on you—times when he's gotten you out of harm's way and prevented you or your dreams from being squashed. Or how about ways God has shown compassion to your family members? Pray as you watch, and praise God for what he's doing.

GOD IS COMPASSIONATE MY FAMILY

1 Samuel's Birth and Dedication

There was a certain man of Ramathaim, a Zuphite[a] from the hill country of Ephraim, whose name was Elkanah son of Jeroham son of Elihu son of Tohu son of Zuph, an Ephraimite. [2]He had two wives; the name of the one was Hannah, and the name of the other Peninnah. Peninnah had children, but Hannah had no children.

3 Now this man used to go up year by year from his town to worship and to sacrifice to the LORD of hosts at Shiloh, where the two sons of Eli, Hophni and Phinehas, were priests of the LORD. [4]On the day when Elkanah sacrificed, he would give portions to his wife Peninnah and to all her sons and daughters; [5]but to Hannah he gave a double portion,[b] because he loved her, though the LORD had closed her womb. [6]Her rival used to provoke her severely, to irritate her, because the LORD had closed her womb. [7]So it went on year by year; as often as she went up to the house of the LORD, she used to provoke her. Therefore Hannah wept and would not eat. [8]Her husband Elkanah said to her, "Hannah, why do you weep? Why do you not eat? Why is your heart sad? Am I not more to you than ten sons?"

9 After they had eaten and drunk at Shiloh, Hannah rose and presented herself before the LORD.[c] Now Eli the priest was sitting on the seat beside the doorpost of the temple of the LORD. [10]She was deeply distressed and prayed to the LORD, and wept bitterly. [11]She made this vow: "O LORD of hosts, if only you will look on the misery of your servant, and remember me, and not forget your servant, but will give to your servant a male child, then I will set him before you as a nazirite[d] until the day of his death. He shall drink neither wine nor intoxicants,[e] and no razor shall touch his head."

12 As she continued praying before the LORD, Eli observed her mouth. [13]Hannah was praying silently; only her lips moved, but her voice was not heard; therefore Eli thought she was drunk. [14]So Eli said to her, "How long will you make a drunken spectacle of yourself? Put away your wine." [15]But Hannah answered, "No, my lord, I am a woman deeply troubled; I have drunk neither wine nor strong drink, but I have been pouring out my soul before the LORD. [16]Do not regard your servant as a worthless woman, for I have been speaking out of my great anxiety and vexation all this time."

a Compare Gk and 1 Chr 6.35–36: Heb *Ramathaim-zophim*
b Syr: Meaning of Heb uncertain c Gk: Heb lacks *and presented herself before the* LORD d That is *one separated* or *one consecrated*
e Cn Compare Gk Q Ms 1.22: MT *then I will give him to the* LORD *all the days of his life*

¹⁷Then Eli answered, "Go in peace; the God of Israel grant the petition you have made to him." ¹⁸And she said, "Let your servant find favor in your sight." Then the woman went to her quarters,^a ate and drank with her husband,^b and her countenance was sad no longer.^c

19 They rose early in the morning and worshiped before the Lᴏʀᴅ; then they went back to their house at Ramah. Elkanah knew his wife Hannah, and the Lᴏʀᴅ remembered her. ²⁰In due time Hannah conceived and bore a son. She named him Samuel, for she said, "I have asked him of the Lᴏʀᴅ."

21 The man Elkanah and all his household went up to offer to the Lᴏʀᴅ the yearly sacrifice, and to pay his vow. ²²But Hannah did not go up, for she said to her husband, "As soon as the child is weaned, I will bring him, that he may appear in the presence of the Lᴏʀᴅ, and remain there forever; I will offer him as a nazirite^d for all time."^{e 23}Her husband Elkanah said to her, "Do what seems best to you, wait until you have weaned him; only—may the Lᴏʀᴅ establish his word."^f So the woman remained and nursed her son, until she weaned him. ²⁴When she had weaned him, she took him up with her, along with a three-year-old bull,^g an ephah of flour, and a skin of wine. She brought him to the house of the Lᴏʀᴅ at Shiloh; and the child was young. ²⁵Then they slaughtered the bull, and they brought the child to Eli. ²⁶And she said, "Oh, my lord! As you live, my lord, I am the woman who was standing here in your presence, praying to the Lᴏʀᴅ. ²⁷For this child I prayed; and the Lᴏʀᴅ has granted me the petition that I made to him. ²⁸Therefore I have lent him to the Lᴏʀᴅ; as long as he lives, he is given to the Lᴏʀᴅ."

She left him there for^h the Lᴏʀᴅ.

2 Hannah's Prayer

Hannah prayed and said,

"My heart exults in the Lᴏʀᴅ;
   my strength is exalted in my God.ⁱ
My mouth derides my enemies,
   because I rejoice in my^j victory.

² "There is no Holy One like the Lᴏʀᴅ,
   no one besides you;
   there is no Rock like our God.
³ Talk no more so very proudly,
   let not arrogance come from your mouth;
for the Lᴏʀᴅ is a God of knowledge,
   and by him actions are weighed.
⁴ The bows of the mighty are broken,

but the feeble gird on strength.
⁵ Those who were full have hired themselves
   out for bread,
   but those who were hungry are fat with
     spoil.
The barren has borne seven,
   but she who has many children is forlorn.
⁶ The Lᴏʀᴅ kills and brings to life;
   he brings down to Sheol and raises up.
⁷ The Lᴏʀᴅ makes poor and makes rich;
   he brings low, he also exalts.
⁸ He raises up the poor from the dust;
   he lifts the needy from the ash heap,
to make them sit with princes
   and inherit a seat of honor.^k
For the pillars of the earth are the Lᴏʀᴅ's,
   and on them he has set the world.

⁹ "He will guard the feet of his faithful ones,
   but the wicked shall be cut off in darkness;
   for not by might does one prevail.
¹⁰ The Lᴏʀᴅ! His adversaries shall be shattered;
   the Most High^l will thunder in heaven.
The Lᴏʀᴅ will judge the ends of the earth;
   he will give strength to his king,
   and exalt the power of his anointed."

Eli's Wicked Sons

11 Then Elkanah went home to Ramah, while the boy remained to minister to the Lᴏʀᴅ, in the presence of the priest Eli.

12 Now the sons of Eli were scoundrels; they had no regard for the Lᴏʀᴅ ¹³or for the duties of the priests to the people. When anyone offered sacrifice, the priest's servant would come, while the meat was boiling, with a three-pronged fork in his hand, ¹⁴and he would thrust it into the pan, or kettle, or caldron, or pot; all that the fork brought up the priest would take for himself.^m This is what they did at Shiloh to all the Israelites who came there. ¹⁵Moreover, before the fat was burned, the priest's servant would come and say to the one who was sacrificing, "Give meat for the priest to roast; for he will not accept boiled meat from you, but only raw." ¹⁶And if the man said to him, "Let them burn the fat first, and then take whatever you wish," he would say, "No, you must give it now; if not, I will take it by force." ¹⁷Thus the sin of the young men was very great in the sight of the Lᴏʀᴅ; for they treated the offerings of the Lᴏʀᴅ with contempt.

The Child Samuel at Shiloh

18 Samuel was ministering before the Lᴏʀᴅ, a boy wearing a linen ephod. ¹⁹His mother used

a Gk: Heb *went her way* b Gk: Heb lacks *and drank with her husband* c Gk: Meaning of Heb uncertain d That is *one separated* or *one consecrated* e Cn Compare Q Ms: MT lacks *I will offer him as a nazirite for all time* f MT: Q Ms Gk Compare Syr *that which goes out of your mouth* g Q Ms Gk Syr: MT *three bulls* h Gk (Compare Q Ms) and Gk at 2.11: MT *And he* (that is, Elkanah) *worshiped there before* i Gk: Heb *the Lᴏʀᴅ* j Q Ms: MT *your* k Gk (Compare Q Ms) adds *He grants the vow of the one who vows, and blesses the years of the just* l Cn Heb *against him he* m Gk Syr Vg: Heb *with it*

REALITY ✔

IT'S COMPLICATED: BEING HUMAN

The people God chooses are not perfect—not by any stretch of the imagination—but they are complicated! The characters in 1 Samuel are no exception. As you read this book, try to zero in on the major personalities presented. Which of them would you choose to be your friend? Which one would you trust? Which one would you go on a camping trip with? Trust with your laptop?

Take a careful look at the complex personalities in the stories in 1 Samuel, especially those of Samuel and Saul. Good lives with evil. Honesty sits with dishonesty. Strength shows a weak side. Who are the major characters in your own life? How willing are you to recognize and accept their complex personalities?

to make for him a little robe and take it to him each year, when she went up with her husband to offer the yearly sacrifice. ²⁰Then Eli would bless Elkanah and his wife, and say, "May the LORD repay*a* you with children by this woman for the gift that she made to*b* the LORD"; and then they would return to their home.

21 And*c* the LORD took note of Hannah; she conceived and bore three sons and two daughters. And the boy Samuel grew up in the presence of the LORD.

Prophecy against Eli's Household

22 Now Eli was very old. He heard all that his sons were doing to all Israel, and how they lay with the women who served at the entrance to the tent of meeting. ²³He said to them, "Why do you do such things? For I hear of your evil dealings from all these people. ²⁴No, my sons; it is not a good report that I hear the people of the LORD spreading abroad. ²⁵If one person sins against another, someone can intercede for the sinner with the LORD;*d* but if someone

sins against the LORD, who can make intercession?" But they would not listen to the voice of their father; for it was the will of the LORD to kill them.

26 Now the boy Samuel continued to grow both in stature and in favor with the LORD and with the people.

27 A man of God came to Eli and said to him, "Thus the LORD has said, 'I revealed*e* myself to the family of your ancestor in Egypt when they were slaves*f* to the house of Pharaoh. ²⁸I chose him out of all the tribes of Israel to be my priest, to go up to my altar, to offer incense, to wear an ephod before me; and I gave to the family of your ancestor all my offerings by fire from the people of Israel. ²⁹Why then look with greedy eye*g* at my sacrifices and my offerings that I commanded, and honor your sons more than me by fattening yourselves on the choicest parts of every offering of my people Israel?' ³⁰Therefore the LORD the God of Israel declares: 'I promised that your family and the family of your ancestor should go in and out before me forever'; but now the LORD declares: 'Far be it from me; for those who honor me I will honor, and those who despise me shall be treated with contempt. ³¹See, a time is coming when I will cut off your strength and the strength of your ancestor's family, so that no one in your family will live to old age. ³²Then in distress you will look with greedy eye*h* on all the prosperity that shall be bestowed upon Israel; and no one in your family shall ever live to old age. ³³The only one of you whom I shall not cut off from my altar shall be spared to weep out his*i* eyes and grieve his*j* heart; all the members of your household shall die by the sword.*k* ³⁴The fate of your two sons, Hophni and Phinehas, shall be the sign to you—both of them shall die on the same day. ³⁵I will raise up for myself a faithful priest, who shall do according to what is in my heart and in my mind. I will build him a sure house, and he shall go in and out before my anointed one forever. ³⁶Everyone who is left in your family shall come to implore him for a piece of silver or a loaf of bread, and shall say, Please put me in one of the priest's places, that I may eat a morsel of bread.' "

3 Samuel's Calling and Prophetic Activity

Now the boy Samuel was ministering to the LORD under Eli. The word of the LORD was rare in those days; visions were not widespread.

2 At that time Eli, whose eyesight had begun to grow dim so that he could not see, was

a Q Ms Gk: MT *give* *b* Q Ms Gk: MT *for the petition that she asked of* *c* Q Ms Gk: MT *When* *d* Gk Compare Q Ms: MT *another, God will mediate for him* *e* Gk Tg Syr: Heb *Did I reveal* *f* Q Ms Gk: MT lacks *slaves* *g* Q Ms Gk: MT *then kick* *h* Q Ms Gk: MT *will kick* *i* Q Ms Gk: MT *your* *j* Q Ms Gk: Heb *your* *k* Q Ms See Gk: MT *die like mortals* lying down in his room; ³the lamp of God had not yet gone out, and Samuel was lying down in the temple of the LORD, where the ark of God was. ⁴Then the LORD called, "Samuel! Samuel!"ᵃ and he said, "Here I am!" ⁵and ran to Eli, and said, "Here I am, for you called me." But he said, "I did not call; lie down again." So he went and lay down. ⁶The LORD called again, "Samuel!" Samuel got up and went to Eli, and said, "Here I am, for you called me." But he said, "I did not call, my son; lie down again." ⁷Now Samuel did not yet know the LORD, and the word of the LORD had not yet been revealed to him. ⁸The LORD called Samuel again, a third time. And he got up and went to Eli, and said, "Here I am, for you called me." Then Eli perceived that the LORD was calling the boy. ⁹Therefore Eli said to Samuel, "Go, lie down; and if he calls you, you shall say, 'Speak, LORD, for your servant is listening.' " So Samuel went and lay down in his place.

10 Now the LORD came and stood there, calling as before, "Samuel! Samuel!" And Samuel said, "Speak, for your servant is listening." ¹¹Then the LORD said to Samuel, "See, I am about to do something in Israel that will make both ears of anyone who hears of it tingle. ¹²On that day I will fulfill against Eli all that I have spoken concerning his house, from beginning to end. ¹³For I have told him that I am about to punish his house forever, for the iniquity that he knew, because his sons were blaspheming God,ᵇ and he did not restrain them. ¹⁴Therefore I swear to the house of Eli that the iniquity of Eli's house shall not be expiated by sacrifice or offering forever."

15 Samuel lay there until morning; then he opened the doors of the house of the LORD. Samuel was afraid to tell the vision to Eli. ¹⁶But Eli called Samuel and said, "Samuel, my son." He said, "Here I am." ¹⁷Eli said, "What was it that he told you? Do not hide it from me. May God do so to you and more also, if you hide anything from me of all that he told you." ¹⁸So Samuel told him everything and hid nothing from him. Then he said, "It is the LORD; let him do what seems good to him."

19 As Samuel grew up, the LORD was with him and let none of his words fall to the ground. ²⁰And all Israel from Dan to Beersheba knew that Samuel was a trustworthy prophet of the LORD. ²¹The LORD continued to appear at Shiloh, for the LORD revealed himself to Samuel at Shiloh by the word of the LORD.

4 ¹And the word of Samuel came to all Israel.

The Ark of God Captured

In those days the Philistines mustered for war against Israel,ᶜ and Israel went out to battle against them;ᵈ they encamped at Ebenezer, and the Philistines encamped at Aphek. ²The Philistines drew up in line against Israel, and when the battle was joined,ᵉ Israel was defeated by the Philistines, who killed about four thousand men on the field of battle. ³When the troops came to the camp, the elders of Israel said, "Why has the LORD put us to rout today before the Philistines? Let us bring the ark of the covenant of the LORD here from Shiloh, so that he may come among us and save us from the power of our enemies." ⁴So the people sent to Shiloh, and brought from there the ark of the covenant of the LORD of hosts, who is enthroned on the cherubim. The two sons of Eli, Hophni and Phinehas, were there with the ark of the covenant of God.

5 When the ark of the covenant of the LORD came into the camp, all Israel gave a mighty shout, so that the earth resounded. ⁶When the Philistines heard the noise of the shouting, they said, "What does this great shouting in the camp of the Hebrews mean?" When they learned that the ark of the LORD had come to the camp, ⁷the Philistines were afraid; for they said, "Gods haveᶠ come into the camp." They also said, "Woe to us! For nothing like this has happened before. ⁸Woe to us! Who can deliver us from the power of these mighty gods? These are the gods who struck the Egyptians with every sort of plague in the wilderness. ⁹Take courage, and be men, O Philistines, in order not to become slaves to the Hebrews as they have been to you; be men and fight."

10 So the Philistines fought; Israel was defeated, and they fled, everyone to his home. There was a very great slaughter, for there fell of Israel thirty thousand foot soldiers. ¹¹The ark of God was captured; and the two sons of Eli, Hophni and Phinehas, died.

Death of Eli

12 A man of Benjamin ran from the battle line, and came to Shiloh the same day, with his clothes torn and with earth upon his head. ¹³When he arrived, Eli was sitting upon his seat by the road watching, for his heart trembled for the ark of God. When the man came into the city and told the news, all the city cried out. ¹⁴When Eli heard the sound of the outcry, he said, "What is this uproar?" Then the man came quickly and told Eli. ¹⁵Now Eli was ninety-eight years old and his eyes were set,

---

a Q Ms Gk See 3.10: MT *the LORD called Samuel*   *b* Another reading is *for themselves*   *c* Gk: Heb lacks *In those days the Philistines mustered for war against Israel*   *d* Gk: Heb *against the Philistines*   *e* Meaning of Heb uncertain   *f* Or *A god has* so that he could not see. [16]The man said to Eli, "I have just come from the battle; I fled from the battle today." He said, "How did it go, my son?" [17]The messenger replied, "Israel has fled before the Philistines, and there has also been a great slaughter among the troops; your two sons also, Hophni and Phinehas, are dead, and the ark of God has been captured." [18]When he mentioned the ark of God, Eli[a] fell over backward from his seat by the side of the gate; and his neck was broken and he died, for he was an old man, and heavy. He had judged Israel forty years.

19 Now his daughter-in-law, the wife of Phinehas, was pregnant, about to give birth. When she heard the news that the ark of God was captured, and that her father-in-law and her husband were dead, she bowed and gave birth; for her labor pains overwhelmed her. [20]As she was about to die, the women attending her said to her, "Do not be afraid, for you have borne a son." But she did not answer or give heed. [21]She named the child Ichabod, meaning, "The glory has departed from Israel," because the ark of God had been captured and because of her father-in-law and her husband. [22]She said, "The glory has departed from Israel, for the ark of God has been captured."

5 The Philistines and the Ark

When the Philistines captured the ark of God, they brought it from Ebenezer to Ashdod; [2]then the Philistines took the ark of God and brought it into the house of Dagon and placed it beside Dagon. [3]When the people of Ashdod rose early the next day, there was Dagon, fallen on his face to the ground before the ark of the Lord. So they took Dagon and put him back in his place. [4]But when they rose early on the next morning, Dagon had fallen on his face to the ground before the ark of the Lord, and the head of Dagon and both his hands were lying cut off upon the threshold; only the trunk of[b] Dagon was left to him. [5]This is why the priests of Dagon and all who enter the house of Dagon do not step on the threshold of Dagon in Ashdod to this day.

6 The hand of the Lord was heavy upon the people of Ashdod, and he terrified and struck them with tumors, both in Ashdod and in its territory. [7]And when the inhabitants of Ashdod saw how things were, they said, "The ark of the God of Israel must not remain with us; for his hand is heavy on us and on our god Dagon." [8]So they sent and gathered together all the lords of the Philistines, and said, "What shall we do with the ark of the God of Israel?" The inhabitants of Gath replied, "Let the ark of God be moved on to us."[c] So they moved the ark of the God of Israel to Gath.[d] [9]But after they had brought it to Gath,[e] the hand of the Lord was against the city, causing a very great panic; he struck the inhabitants of the city, both young and old, so that tumors broke out on them. [10]So they sent the ark of the God of Israel[f] to Ekron. But when the ark of God came to Ekron, the people of Ekron cried out, "Why[g] have they brought around to us[h] the ark of the God of Israel to kill us[i] and our[i] people?" [11]They sent therefore and gathered together all the lords of the Philistines, and said, "Send away the ark of the God of Israel, and let it return to its own place, that it may not kill us and our people." For there was a deathly panic[j] throughout the whole city. The hand of God was very heavy there; [12]those who did not die were stricken with tumors, and the cry of the city went up to heaven.

6 The Ark Returned to Israel

The ark of the Lord was in the country of the Philistines seven months. [2]Then the Philistines called for the priests and the diviners and said, "What shall we do with the ark of the Lord? Tell us what we should send with it to its place." [3]They said, "If you send away the ark of the God of Israel, do not send it empty, but by all means return him a guilt offering. Then you will be healed and will be ransomed;[k] will not his hand then turn from you?" [4]And they said, "What is the guilt offering that we shall return

a Heb *he* b Heb lacks *the trunk of* c Gk Compare Q Ms: MT They answered, "Let the ark of the God of Israel be brought around to Gath."
d Gk: Heb lacks *to Gath* e Q Ms: MT lacks *to Gath* f Q Ms Gk: MT lacks *of Israel* g Q Ms Gk: MT lacks *Why* h Heb *me* i Heb *my* j Q Ms reads *a panic from the Lord* k Q Ms Gk: MT *and it will be known to you*

to him?" They answered, "Five gold tumors and five gold mice, according to the number of the lords of the Philistines; for the same plague was upon all of you and upon your lords. 5So you must make images of your tumors and images of your mice that ravage the land, and give glory to the God of Israel; perhaps he will lighten his hand on you and your gods and your land. 6Why should you harden your hearts as the Egyptians and Pharaoh hardened their hearts? After he had made fools of them, did they not let the people go, and they departed? 7Now then, get ready a new cart and two milch cows that have never borne a yoke, and yoke the cows to the cart, but take their calves home, away from them. 8Take the ark of the Lord and place it on the cart, and put in a box at its side the figures of gold, which you are returning to him as a guilt offering. Then send it off, and let it go its way. 9And watch; if it goes up on the way to its own land, to Beth-shemesh, then it is he who has done us this great harm; but if not, then we shall know that it is not his hand that struck us; it happened to us by chance."

10 The men did so; they took two milch cows and yoked them to the cart, and shut up their calves at home. 11They put the ark of the Lord on the cart, and the box with the gold mice and the images of their tumors. 12The cows went straight in the direction of Beth-she-mesh along one highway, lowing as they went; they turned neither to the right nor to the left, and the lords of the Philistines went after them as far as the border of Beth-shemesh.

13 Now the people of Beth-shemesh were reaping their wheat harvest in the valley. When they looked up and saw the ark, they went with rejoicing to meet it.*a* 14The cart came into the field of Joshua of Beth-shemesh, and stopped there. A large stone was there; so they split up the wood of the cart and offered the cows as a burnt offering to the Lord. 15The Levites took down the ark of the Lord and the box that was beside it, in which were the gold objects, and set them upon the large stone. Then the people of Beth-shemesh offered burnt offerings and presented sacrifices on that day to the Lord. 16When the five lords of the Philistines saw it, they returned that day to Ekron.

17 These are the gold tumors, which the Philistines returned as a guilt offering to the Lord: one for Ashdod, one for Gaza, one for Ashkelon, one for Gath, one for Ekron; 18also the gold mice, according to the number of all the cities of the Philistines belonging to the five lords, both fortified cities and unwalled villages. The great stone, beside which they set down the ark of the Lord, is a witness to this day in the field of Joshua of Beth-shemesh.

The Ark at Kiriath-jearim

19 The descendants of Jeconiah did not rejoice with the people of Beth-shemesh when they greeted*b* the ark of the Lord; and he killed seventy men of them.*c* The people mourned because the Lord had made a great slaughter among the people. 20Then the people of Beth-shemesh said, "Who is able to stand before the Lord, this holy God? To whom shall he go so that we may be rid of him?" 21So they sent messengers to the inhabitants of Kiriath-jearim, saying, "The Philistines have returned the ark of the Lord. Come down and take it up to you." 7 1And the people of Kiriath-jearim came and took up the ark of the Lord, and brought it to the house of Abinadab on the hill. They consecrated his son, Eleazar, to have charge of the ark of the Lord.

2 From the day that the ark was lodged at Kiriath-jearim, a long time passed, some twenty years, and all the house of Israel lamented*d* after the Lord.

Samuel as Judge

3 Then Samuel said to all the house of Israel, "If you are returning to the Lord with all your heart, then put away the foreign gods and the Astartes from among you. Direct your heart to the Lord, and serve him only, and he will deliver you out of the hand of the Philistines." 4So Israel put away the Baals and the Astartes, and they served the Lord only.

5 Then Samuel said, "Gather all Israel at Mizpah, and I will pray to the Lord for you." 6So they gathered at Mizpah, and drew water and poured it out before the Lord. They fasted that day, and said, "We have sinned against the Lord." And Samuel judged the people of Israel at Mizpah.

7 When the Philistines heard that the people of Israel had gathered at Mizpah, the lords of the Philistines went up against Israel. And when the people of Israel heard of it they were afraid of the Philistines. 8The people of Israel said to Samuel, "Do not cease to cry out to the Lord our God for us, and pray that he may save us from the hand of the Philistines." 9So Samuel took a sucking lamb and offered it as a whole burnt offering to the Lord; Samuel cried out to the Lord for Israel, and the Lord answered him. 10As Samuel was offering up the burnt offering, the Philistines drew near to attack Isra-

---

a Gk: Heb *rejoiced to see it* *b* Gk: Heb *And he killed some of the people of Beth-shemesh, because they looked into* *c* Heb *killed seventy men, fifty thousand men* *d* Meaning of Heb uncertain el; but the LORD thundered with a mighty voice that day against the Philistines and threw them into confusion; and they were routed before Israel. [11]And the men of Israel went out of Mizpah and pursued the Philistines, and struck them down as far as beyond Beth-car.

12 Then Samuel took a stone and set it up between Mizpah and Jeshanah,[a] and named it Ebenezer;[b] for he said, "Thus far the LORD has helped us." [13]So the Philistines were subdued and did not again enter the territory of Israel; the hand of the LORD was against the Philistines all the days of Samuel. [14]The towns that the Philistines had taken from Israel were restored to Israel, from Ekron to Gath; and Israel recovered their territory from the hand of the Philistines. There was peace also between Israel and the Amorites.

15 Samuel judged Israel all the days of his life. [16]He went on a circuit year by year to Bethel, Gilgal, and Mizpah; and he judged Israel in all these places. [17]Then he would come back to Ramah, for his home was there; he administered justice there to Israel, and built there an altar to the LORD.

8 Israel Demands a King

When Samuel became old, he made his sons judges over Israel. [2]The name of his firstborn son was Joel, and the name of his second, Abijah; they were judges in Beer-sheba. [3]Yet his sons did not follow in his ways, but turned aside after gain; they took bribes and perverted justice.

4 Then all the elders of Israel gathered together and came to Samuel at Ramah, [5]and said to him, "You are old and your sons do not follow in your ways; appoint for us, then, a king to govern us, like other nations." [6]But the thing displeased Samuel when they said, "Give us a king to govern us." Samuel prayed to the LORD, [7]and the LORD said to Samuel, "Listen to the voice of the people in all that they say to you; for they have not rejected you, but they have rejected me from being king over them. [8]Just as they have done to me,[c] from the day I brought them up out of Egypt to this day, forsaking me and serving other gods, so also they are doing to you. [9]Now then, listen to their voice; only—you shall solemnly warn them, and show them the ways of the king who shall reign over them."

10 So Samuel reported all the words of the LORD to the people who were asking him for a king. [11]He said, "These will be the ways of the king who will reign over you: he will take your sons and appoint them to his chariots and to

be his horsemen, and to run before his chariots; [12]and he will appoint for himself commanders of thousands and commanders of fifties, and some to plow his ground and to reap his harvest, and to make his implements of war and the equipment of his chariots. [13]He will take your daughters to be perfumers and cooks and bakers. [14]He will take the best of your fields and vineyards and olive orchards and give them to his courtiers. [15]He will take one-tenth of your grain and of your vineyards and give it to his officers and his courtiers. [16]He will take your male and female slaves, and the best of your cattle[d] and donkeys, and put them to his work. [17]He will take one-tenth of your flocks, and you shall be his slaves. [18]And in that day you will cry out because of your king, whom you have chosen for yourselves; but the LORD will not answer you in that day."

Israel's Request for a King Granted

19 But the people refused to listen to the voice of Samuel; they said, "No! but we are determined to have a king over us, [20]so that we also may be like other nations, and that our king may govern us and go out before us and fight our battles." [21]When Samuel had heard all the words of the people, he repeated them in the ears of the LORD. [22]The LORD said to Samuel, "Listen to their voice and set a king over them." Samuel then said to the people of Israel, "Each of you return home."

9 Saul Chosen to Be King

There was a man of Benjamin whose name was Kish son of Abiel son of Zeror son of Becorath son of Aphiah, a Benjaminite, a man of wealth. [2]He had a son whose name was Saul, a handsome young man. There was not a man among the people of Israel more handsome than he; he stood head and shoulders above everyone else.

3 Now the donkeys of Kish, Saul's father, had strayed. So Kish said to his son Saul, "Take one of the boys with you; go and look for the donkeys." [4]He passed through the hill country of Ephraim and passed through the land of Shalishah, but they did not find them. And they passed through the land of Shaalim, but they were not there. Then he passed through the land of Benjamin, but they did not find them.

5 When they came to the land of Zuph, Saul said to the boy who was with him, "Let us turn back, or my father will stop worrying about the donkeys and worry about us." [6]But he said to him, "There is a man of God in this town; he is a man held in honor. Whatever he says always comes true. Let us go there now; perhaps he

a Gk Syr: Heb *Shen*   b That is *Stone of Help*   c Gk: Heb lacks *to me*   d Gk: Heb *young men* will tell us about the journey on which we have set out." [7]Then Saul replied to the boy, "But if we go, what can we bring the man? For the bread in our sacks is gone, and there is no present to bring to the man of God. What have we?" [8]The boy answered Saul again, "Here, I have with me a quarter shekel of silver; I will give it to the man of God, to tell us our way." [9](Formerly in Israel, anyone who went to inquire of God would say, "Come, let us go to the seer"; for the one who is now called a prophet was formerly called a seer.) [10]Saul said to the boy, "Good; come, let us go." So they went to the town where the man of God was.

11 As they went up the hill to the town, they met some girls coming out to draw water, and said to them, "Is the seer here?" [12]They answered, "Yes, there he is just ahead of you. Hurry; he has come just now to the town, because the people have a sacrifice today at the shrine. [13]As soon as you enter the town, you will find him, before he goes up to the shrine to eat. For the people will not eat until he comes, since he must bless the sacrifice; afterward those eat who are invited. Now go up, for you will meet him immediately." [14]So they went up to the town. As they were entering the town, they saw Samuel coming out toward them on his way up to the shrine.

15 Now the day before Saul came, the LORD had revealed to Samuel: [16]"Tomorrow about this time I will send to you a man from the land of Benjamin, and you shall anoint him to be ruler over my people Israel. He shall save my people from the hand of the Philistines; for I have seen the suffering of[a] my people, because their outcry has come to me." [17]When Samuel saw Saul, the LORD told him, "Here is the man of whom I spoke to you. He it is who shall rule over my people." [18]Then Saul approached Samuel inside the gate, and said, "Tell me, please, where is the house of the seer?" [19]Samuel answered Saul, "I am the seer; go up before me to the shrine, for today you shall eat with me, and in the morning I will let you go and will tell you all that is on your mind. [20]As for your donkeys that were lost three days ago, give no further thought to them, for they have been found. And on whom is all Israel's desire fixed, if not on you and on all your ancestral house?" [21]Saul answered, "I am only a Benjaminite, from the least of the tribes of Israel, and my family is the humblest of all the families of the tribe of Benjamin. Why then have you spoken to me in this way?"

22 Then Samuel took Saul and his servant-boy and brought them into the hall, and gave them a place at the head of those who had been invited, of whom there were about thirty. [23]And Samuel said to the cook, "Bring the portion I gave you, the one I asked you to put aside." [24]The cook took up the thigh and what went with it[b] and set them before Saul. Samuel said, "See, what was kept is set before you. Eat; for it is set[c] before you at the appointed time, so that you might eat with the guests."[d]

JESUS SIGHTING

Jealousy and coveting—wanting what others have—are such strong inclinations that even one of the Ten Commandments forbids them. But who would guess that the Israelites would go so far as to covet their neighbors' *government*? Maybe being surrounded by wealthy nations ruled by heroic kings was all it took to make them insist on a monarchy for themselves.

Read **1 Samuel 8.4–9**. Here the Hebrews ask for the same thing that everyone else has: a human ruler. God rightly sees what will happen. Any ruler other than God is going to go wrong . . . *way* wrong.

It's no mistake that Jesus is called the Son of David over and over again in the New Testament (see Matthew 9.27 for an example). The genealogy of Jesus (found in Matthew 1) traces his family tree back to the faithful kings of Israel. In his day, the Israelites were still waiting for the one true king to take the throne. Jesus stepped in to finally be the king worthy of ruling in God's name.

Lots of things contend for the thrones of our lives. Pseudo-kings—money, dating relationships, obsessions over sports or music, or celebrity worship—are happy to rule us. And if we're honest, we often *do* give these things power in our lives—the power to influence how we act, speak, dress, and think.

But only *Jesus*, the true King of kings, should be on the throne of our hearts.

---

a Gk: Heb lacks *the suffering of* b Meaning of Heb uncertain c Q Ms Gk: MT *it was kept* d Cn: Heb *it was kept for you, saying, I have invited the people*

So Saul ate with Samuel that day. 25When they came down from the shrine into the town, a bed was spread for Saul[a] on the roof, and he lay down to sleep.[b] 26Then at the break of dawn[c] Samuel called to Saul upon the roof, "Get up, so that I may send you on your way." Saul got up, and both he and Samuel went out into the street.

Samuel Anoints Saul

27 As they were going down to the outskirts of the town, Samuel said to Saul, "Tell the boy to go on before us, and when he has passed on, stop here yourself for a while, that I may make **10** known to you the word of God." 1Samuel took a vial of oil and poured it on his head, and kissed him; he said, "The LORD has anointed you ruler over his people Israel. You shall reign over the people of the LORD and you will save them from the hand of their enemies all around. Now this shall be the sign to you that the LORD has anointed you ruler[d] over his heritage: 2When you depart from me today you will meet two men by Rachel's tomb in the territory of Benjamin at Zelzah; they will say to you, 'The donkeys that you went to seek are found, and now your father has stopped worrying about them and is worrying about you, saying: What shall I do about my son?' 3Then you shall go on from there further and come to the oak of Tabor; three men going up to God at Bethel will meet you there, one carrying three kids, another carrying three loaves of bread, and another carrying a skin of wine. 4They will greet you and give you two loaves of bread, which you shall accept from them. 5After that you shall come to Gibeath-elohim,[e] at the place where the Philistine garrison is; there, as you come to the town, you will meet a band of prophets coming down from the shrine with harp, tambourine, flute, and lyre playing in front of them; they will be in a prophetic frenzy. 6Then the spirit of the LORD will possess you, and you will be in a prophetic frenzy along with them and be turned into a different person. 7Now when these signs meet you, do whatever you see fit to do, for God is with you. 8And you shall go down to Gilgal ahead of me; then I will come down to you to present burnt offerings and offer sacrifices of well-being. Seven days you shall wait, until I come to you and show you what you shall do."

Saul Prophesies

9 As he turned away to leave Samuel, God gave him another heart; and all these signs were ful-filled that day. 10When they were going from there[f] to Gibeah,[g] a band of prophets met him; and the spirit of God possessed him, and he fell into a prophetic frenzy along with them. 11When all who knew him before saw how he prophesied with the prophets, the people said to one another, "What has come over the son of Kish? Is Saul also among the prophets?" 12A man of the place answered, "And who is their father?" Therefore it became a proverb, "Is Saul also among the prophets?" 13When his prophetic frenzy had ended, he went home.[h]

14 Saul's uncle said to him and to the boy, "Where did you go?" And he replied, "To seek the donkeys; and when we saw they were not to be found, we went to Samuel." 15Saul's uncle said, "Tell me what Samuel said to you." 16Saul said to his uncle, "He told us that the donkeys had been found." But about the matter of the kingship, of which Samuel had spoken, he did not tell him anything.

Saul Proclaimed King

17 Samuel summoned the people to the LORD at Mizpah 18and said to them,[i] "Thus says the LORD, the God of Israel, 'I brought up Israel out of Egypt, and I rescued you from the hand of the Egyptians and from the hand of all the kingdoms that were oppressing you.' 19But today you have rejected your God, who saves you from all your calamities and your distresses; and you have said, 'No! but set a king over us.' Now therefore present yourselves before the LORD by your tribes and by your clans."

20 Then Samuel brought all the tribes of Israel near, and the tribe of Benjamin was taken by lot. 21He brought the tribe of Benjamin near by its families, and the family of the Matrites was taken by lot. Finally he brought the family of the Matrites near man by man,[j] and Saul the son of Kish was taken by lot. But when they sought him, he could not be found. 22So they inquired again of the LORD, "Did the man come here?"[k] and the LORD said, "See, he has hidden himself among the baggage." 23Then they ran and brought him from there. When he took his stand among the people, he was head and shoulders taller than any of them. 24Samuel said to all the people, "Do you see the one whom the LORD has chosen? There is no one like him among all the people." And all the people shouted, "Long live the king!"

25 Samuel told the people the rights and duties of the kingship; and he wrote them in a book and laid it up before the LORD. Then Samuel sent all the people back to their homes.

---

a Gk: Heb *and he spoke with Saul* *b* Gk: Heb lacks *and he lay down to sleep* *c* Gk: Heb *and they arose early and at break of dawn* *d* Gk: Heb lacks *over his people Israel. You shall . . . anointed you ruler* *e* Or *the Hill of God* *f* Gk: Heb *they came there* *g* Or *the hill* *h* Cn: Heb *he came to the shrine* *i* Heb *to the people of Israel* *j* Gk: Heb lacks *Finally . . . man by man* *k* Gk: Heb *Is there yet a man to come here?*

²⁶Saul also went to his home at Gibeah, and with him went warriors whose hearts God had touched. ²⁷But some worthless fellows said, "How can this man save us?" They despised him and brought him no present. But he held his peace.

Now Nahash, king of the Ammonites, had been grievously oppressing the Gadites and the Reubenites. He would gouge out the right eye of each of them and would not grant Israel a deliverer. No one was left of the Israelites across the Jordan whose right eye Nahash, king of the Ammonites, had not gouged out. But there were seven thousand men who had escaped from the Ammonites and had entered Jabesh-gilead.ᵃ

11 Saul Defeats the Ammonites

About a month later,ᵇ Nahash the Ammonite went up and besieged Jabesh-gilead; and all the men of Jabesh said to Nahash, "Make a treaty with us, and we will serve you." ²But Nahash the Ammonite said to them, "On this condition I will make a treaty with you, namely that I gouge out everyone's right eye, and thus put disgrace upon all Israel." ³The elders of Jabesh said to him, "Give us seven days' respite that we may send messengers through all the territory of Israel. Then, if there is no one to save us, we will give ourselves up to you." ⁴When the messengers came to Gibeah of Saul, they reported the matter in the hearing of the people; and all the people wept aloud.

5 Now Saul was coming from the field behind the oxen; and Saul said, "What is the matter with the people, that they are weeping?" So they told him the message from the inhabitants of Jabesh. ⁶And the spirit of God came upon Saul in power when he heard these words, and his anger was greatly kindled. ⁷He took a yoke of oxen, and cut them in pieces and sent them throughout all the territory of Israel by messengers, saying, "Whoever does not come out after Saul and Samuel, so shall it be done to his oxen!" Then the dread of the LORD fell upon the people, and they came out as one. ⁸When he mustered them at Bezek, those from Israel were three hundred thousand, and those from Judah seventyᶜ thousand. ⁹They said to the messengers who had come, "Thus shall you say to the inhabitants of Jabesh-gilead: 'Tomorrow, by the time the sun is hot, you shall have deliverance.' " When the messengers came and told the inhabitants of Jabesh, they rejoiced. ¹⁰So the inhabitants of Jabesh said, "Tomorrow we will give ourselves up to

you, and you may do to us whatever seems good to you." ¹¹The next day Saul put the people in three companies. At the morning watch they came into the camp and cut down the Ammonites until the heat of the day; and those who survived were scattered, so that no two of them were left together.

12 The people said to Samuel, "Who is it that said, 'Shall Saul reign over us?' Give them to us so that we may put them to death." ¹³But Saul said, "No one shall be put to death this day, for today the LORD has brought deliverance to Israel."

14 Samuel said to the people, "Come, let us go to Gilgal and there renew the kingship." ¹⁵So all the people went to Gilgal, and there they made Saul king before the LORD in Gilgal. There they sacrificed offerings of well-being before the LORD, and there Saul and all the Israelites rejoiced greatly.

TEXT MESSAGE

Modern military recruiters might not have much luck enlisting volunteers if they used Saul's methods in 1 Samuel 11.7. He cut two oxen into pieces and gave the pieces to messengers to carry around the country to mobilize people for war. (The act symbolized uniting all the people.) The approach worked for Saul; his army walloped the Ammonites (1 Samuel 11.11).

This information has been scanned and is free of all known viruses. Please forward to all your friends.

ᵃ Q Ms Compare Josephus, *Antiquities* VI.v.1 (68–71): MT lacks *Now Nahash . . . entered Jabesh-gilead.* ᵇ Q Ms Gk: MT lacks *About a month later* ᶜ Q Ms Gk: MT *thirty*

Living Water—© Lexi Hiland, 16

12 Samuel's Farewell Address

Samuel said to all Israel, "I have listened to you in all that you have said to me, and have set a king over you. ²See, it is the king who leads you now; I am old and gray, but my sons are with you. I have led you from my youth until this day. ³Here I am; testify against me before the LORD and before his anointed. Whose ox have I taken? Or whose donkey have I taken? Or whom have I defrauded? Whom have I oppressed? Or from whose hand have I taken a bribe to blind my eyes with it? Testify against me*ᵃ* and I will restore it to you." ⁴They said, "You have not defrauded us or oppressed us or taken anything from the hand of anyone." ⁵He said to them, "The LORD is witness against you, and his anointed is witness this day, that you have not found anything in my hand." And they said, "He is witness."

6 Samuel said to the people, "The LORD is witness, who*ᵇ* appointed Moses and Aaron and brought your ancestors up out of the land of Egypt. ⁷Now therefore take your stand, so that I may enter into judgment with you before the LORD, and I will declare to you*ᶜ* all the saving deeds of the LORD that he performed for you and for your ancestors. ⁸When Jacob went into Egypt and the Egyptians oppressed them,*ᵈ* then your ancestors cried to the LORD and the LORD sent Moses and Aaron, who brought forth your ancestors out of Egypt, and settled them in this place. ⁹But they forgot the LORD their God; and he sold them into the hand of Sisera, commander of the army of King Jabin of*ᵉ* Hazor, and into the hand of the Philistines, and into

the hand of the king of Moab; and they fought against them. ¹⁰Then they cried to the LORD, and said, 'We have sinned, because we have forsaken the LORD, and have served the Baals and the Astartes; but now rescue us out of the hand of our enemies, and we will serve you.' ¹¹And the LORD sent Jerubbaal and Barak,*ᶠ* and Jephthah, and Samson,*ᵍ* and rescued you out of the hand of your enemies on every side; and you lived in safety. ¹²But when you saw that King Nahash of the Ammonites came against you, you said to me, 'No, but a king shall reign over us,' though the LORD your God was your king. ¹³See, here is the king whom you have chosen, for whom you have asked; see, the LORD has set a king over you. ¹⁴If you will fear the LORD and serve him and heed his voice and not rebel against the commandment of the LORD, and if both you and the king who reigns over you will follow the LORD your God, it will be well; ¹⁵but if you will not heed the voice of the LORD, but rebel against the commandment of the LORD, then the hand of the LORD will be against you and your king.*ʰ* ¹⁶Now therefore take your stand and see this great thing that the LORD will do before your eyes. ¹⁷Is it not the wheat harvest today? I will call upon the LORD, that he may send thunder and rain; and you shall know and see that the wickedness that you have done in the sight of the LORD is great in demanding a king for yourselves." ¹⁸So Samuel called upon the LORD, and the LORD sent thunder and rain that day; and all the people greatly feared the LORD and Samuel.

19 All the people said to Samuel, "Pray to the LORD your God for your servants, so that we may not die; for we have added to all our sins the evil of demanding a king for ourselves." ²⁰And Samuel said to the people, "Do not be afraid; you have done all this evil, yet do not turn aside from following the LORD, but serve the LORD with all your heart; ²¹and do not turn aside after useless things that cannot profit or save, for they are useless. ²²For the LORD will not cast away his people, for his great name's sake, because it has pleased the LORD to make you a people for himself. ²³Moreover as for me, far be it from me that I should sin against the LORD by ceasing to pray for you; and I will instruct you in the good and the right way. ²⁴Only fear the LORD, and serve him faithfully with all your heart; for consider what great things he has done for you. ²⁵But if you still do wickedly, you shall be swept away, both you and your king."

a Gk: Heb lacks *Testify against me* *b* Gk: Heb lacks *is witness, who* *c* Gk: Heb lacks *and I will declare to you* *d* Gk: Heb lacks *and the Egyptians oppressed them* *e* Gk: Heb lacks *King Jabin of* *f* Gk Syr: Heb *Bedan* *g* Gk: Heb *Samuel* *h* Heb: Heb *and your ancestors*

13 Saul's Unlawful Sacrifice

Saul was . . .[a] years old when he began to reign; and he reigned . . . and two[b] years over Israel.

2 Saul chose three thousand out of Israel; two thousand were with Saul in Michmash and the hill country of Bethel, and a thousand were with Jonathan in Gibeah of Benjamin; the rest of the people he sent home to their tents. 3 Jonathan defeated the garrison of the Philistines that was at Geba; and the Philistines heard of it. And Saul blew the trumpet throughout all the land, saying, "Let the Hebrews hear!" 4 When all Israel heard that Saul had defeated the garrison of the Philistines, and also that Israel had become odious to the Philistines, the people were called out to join Saul at Gilgal.

5 The Philistines mustered to fight with Israel, thirty thousand chariots, and six thousand horsemen, and troops like the sand on the seashore in multitude; they came up and encamped at Michmash, to the east of Beth-aven. 6 When the Israelites saw that they were in distress (for the troops were hard pressed), the people hid themselves in caves and in holes and in rocks and in tombs and in cisterns. 7 Some Hebrews crossed the Jordan to the land of Gad and Gilead. Saul was still at Gilgal, and all the people followed him trembling.

8 He waited seven days, the time appointed by Samuel; but Samuel did not come to Gilgal, and the people began to slip away from Saul.[c] 9 So Saul said, "Bring the burnt offering here to me, and the offerings of well-being." And he offered the burnt offering. 10 As soon as he had finished offering the burnt offering, Samuel arrived; and Saul went out to meet him and salute him. 11 Samuel said, "What have you done?" Saul replied, "When I saw that the people were slipping away from me, and that you did not come within the days appointed, and that the Philistines were mustering at Michmash, 12 I said, 'Now the Philistines will come down upon me at Gilgal, and I have not entreated the favor of the LORD'; so I forced myself, and offered the burnt offering." 13 Samuel said to Saul, "You have done foolishly; you have not kept the commandment of the LORD your God, which he commanded you. The LORD would have established your kingdom over Israel forever, 14 but now your kingdom will not continue; the LORD has sought out a man after his own heart; and the LORD has appointed him to be ruler over his people, because you have not kept what the LORD commanded you." 15 And Samuel left and went on his way

from Gilgal.[d] The rest of the people followed Saul to join the army; they went up from Gilgal toward Gibeah of Benjamin.[e]

Preparations for Battle

Saul counted the people who were present with him, about six hundred men. 16 Saul, his son Jonathan, and the people who were present with them stayed in Geba of Benjamin; but the Philistines encamped at Michmash. 17 And raiders came out of the camp of the Philistines in three companies; one company turned toward Ophrah, to the land of Shual, 18 another company turned toward Beth-horon, and another company turned toward the mountain[f] that looks down upon the valley of Zeboim toward the wilderness.

19 Now there was no smith to be found throughout all the land of Israel; for the Philistines said, "The Hebrews must not make swords or spears for themselves"; 20 so all the Israelites went down to the Philistines to sharpen their plowshares, mattocks, axes, or sickles;[g] 21 The charge was two-thirds of a shekel[h] for the plowshares and for the mattocks, and one-third of a shekel for sharpening the axes and for setting the goads.[i] 22 So on the day of the battle neither sword nor spear was to be found in the possession of any of the people with Saul and Jonathan; but Saul and his son Jonathan had them.

Jonathan Surprises and Routs the Philistines

23 Now a garrison of the Philistines had gone out to the pass of Michmash.

14

1 One day Jonathan son of Saul said to the young man who carried his armor, "Come, let us go over to the Philistine garrison on the other side." But he did not tell his father. 2 Saul was staying in the outskirts of Gibeah under the pomegranate tree that is at Migron; the troops that were with him were about six hundred men, 3 along with Ahijah son of Ahitub, Ichabod's brother, son of Phinehas son of Eli, the priest of the LORD in Shiloh, carrying an ephod. Now the people did not know that Jonathan had gone. 4 In the pass,[j] by which Jonathan tried to go over to the Philistine garrison, there was a rocky crag on one side and a rocky crag on the other; the name of the one was Bozez, and the name of the other Seneh. 5 One crag rose on the north in front of Michmash, and the other on the south in front of Geba.

6 Jonathan said to the young man who carried his armor, "Come, let us go over to the

---

a The number is lacking in the Heb text (the verse is lacking in the Septuagint). b Two is not the entire number; something has dropped out. c Heb him d Gk: Heb went up from Gilgal to Gibeah of Benjamin e Gk: Heb lacks The rest . . . of Benjamin f Cn Compare Gk: Heb toward the border g Gk: Heb plowshare h Heb was a pim i Cn: Meaning of Heb uncertain j Heb Between the passes garrison of these uncircumcised; it may be that the LORD will act for us; for nothing can hinder the LORD from saving by many or by few." [7]His armor-bearer said to him, "Do all that your mind inclines to.[g] I am with you; as your mind is, so is mine."[b] [8]Then Jonathan said, "Now we will cross over to those men and will show ourselves to them. [9]If they say to us, 'Wait until we come to you,' then we will stand still in our place, and we will not go up to them. [10]But if they say, 'Come up to us,' then we will go up; for the LORD has given them into our hand. That will be the sign for us." [11]So both of them showed themselves to the garrison of the Philistines; and the Philistines said, "Look, Hebrews are coming out of the holes where they have hidden themselves." [12]The men of the garrison hailed Jonathan and his armor-bearer, saying, "Come up to us, and we will show you something." Jonathan said to his armor-bearer, "Come up after me; for the LORD has given them into the hand of Israel." [13]Then Jonathan climbed up on his hands and feet, with his armor-bearer following after him. The Philistines[c] fell before Jonathan, and his armor-bearer, coming after him, killed them. [14]In that first slaughter Jonathan and his armor-bearer killed about twenty men within an area about half a furrow long in an acre[d] of land. [15]There was a panic in the camp, in the field, and among all the people; the garrison and even the raiders trembled; the earth quaked; and it became a very great panic.

16 Saul's lookouts in Gibeah of Benjamin were watching as the multitude was surging back and forth.[e] [17]Then Saul said to the troops that were with him, "Call the roll and see who has gone from us." When they had called the roll, Jonathan and his armor-bearer were not there. [18]Saul said to Ahijah, "Bring the ark[f] of God here." For at that time the ark[f] of God went with the Israelites. [19]While Saul was talking to the priest, the tumult in the camp of the Philistines increased more and more; and Saul said to the priest, "Withdraw your hand." [20]Then Saul and all the people who were with him rallied and went into the battle; and every sword was against the other, so that there was very great confusion. [21]Now the Hebrews who previously had been with the Philistines and had gone up with them into the camp turned and joined the Israelites who were with Saul and Jonathan. [22]Likewise, when all the Israelites who had gone into hiding in the hill country of Ephraim heard that the Philistines were fleeing, they too followed closely after them in the battle. [23]So the LORD gave Israel the victory that day.

The battle passed beyond Beth-aven, and the troops with Saul numbered altogether about ten thousand men. The battle spread out over the hill country of Ephraim.

Saul's Rash Oath

24 Now Saul committed a very rash act on that day.[g] He had laid an oath on the troops, saying, "Cursed be anyone who eats food before it is evening and I have been avenged on my enemies." So none of the troops tasted food. [25]All the troops[h] came upon a honeycomb; and there was honey on the ground. [26]When the troops came upon the honeycomb, the honey was dripping out; but they did not put their hands to their mouths, for they feared the oath. [27]But Jonathan had not heard his father charge the troops with the oath; so he extended the staff that was in his hand, and dipped the tip of it in the honeycomb, and put his hand to his mouth; and his eyes brightened. [28]Then one of the soldiers said, "Your father strictly charged the troops with an oath, saying, 'Cursed be anyone who eats food this day.' And so the troops are faint." [29]Then Jonathan said, "My father has troubled the land; see how my eyes have brightened because I tasted a little of this honey. [30]How much better if today the troops had eaten freely of the spoil taken from their enemies; for now the slaughter among the Philistines has not been great."

31 After they had struck down the Philistines that day from Michmash to Aijalon, the troops were very faint; [32]so the troops flew upon the spoil, and took sheep and oxen and calves, and slaughtered them on the ground; and the troops ate them with the blood. [33]Then it was reported to Saul, "Look, the troops are sinning against the LORD by eating with the blood." And he said, "You have dealt treacherously; roll a large stone before me here."[i] [34]Saul said, "Disperse yourselves among the troops, and say to them, 'Let all bring their oxen or their sheep, and slaughter them here, and eat; and do not sin against the LORD by eating with the blood.' " So all of the troops brought their oxen with them that night, and slaughtered them there. [35]And Saul built an altar to the LORD; it was the first altar that he built to the LORD.

Jonathan in Danger of Death

36 Then Saul said, "Let us go down after the Philistines by night and despoil them until the

---

a Gk: Heb *Do all that is in your mind. Turn* b Gk: Heb lacks *so is mine* c Heb *They* d Heb *yoke* e Gk: Heb *they went and there* f Gk *the ephod* g Gk: Heb *The Israelites were distressed that day* h Heb *land* i Gk: Heb *me this day* morning light; let us not leave one of them." They said, "Do whatever seems good to you." But the priest said, "Let us draw near to God here." ³⁷So Saul inquired of God, "Shall I go down after the Philistines? Will you give them into the hand of Israel?" But he did not answer him that day. ³⁸Saul said, "Come here, all you leaders of the people; and let us find out how this sin has arisen today. ³⁹For as the LORD lives who saves Israel, even if it is in my son Jonathan, he shall surely die!" But there was no one among all the people who answered him. ⁴⁰He said to all Israel, "You shall be on one side, and I and my son Jonathan will be on the other side." The people said to Saul, "Do what seems good to you." ⁴¹Then Saul said, "O LORD God of Israel, why have you not answered your servant today? If this guilt is in me or in my son Jonathan, O LORD God of Israel, give Urim; but if this guilt is in your people Israel,ᵃ give Thummim." And Jonathan and Saul were indicated by the lot, but the people were cleared. ⁴²Then Saul said, "Cast the lot between me and my son Jonathan." And Jonathan was taken.

43 Then Saul said to Jonathan, "Tell me what you have done." Jonathan told him, "I tasted a little honey with the tip of the staff that was in my hand; here I am, I will die." ⁴⁴Saul said, "God do so to me and more also; you shall surely die, Jonathan!" ⁴⁵Then the people said to Saul, "Shall Jonathan die, who has accom-

plished this great victory in Israel? Far from it! As the LORD lives, not one hair of his head shall fall to the ground; for he has worked with God today." So the people ransomed Jonathan, and he did not die. ⁴⁶Then Saul withdrew from pursuing the Philistines; and the Philistines went to their own place.

Saul's Continuing Wars

47 When Saul had taken the kingship over Israel, he fought against all his enemies on every side—against Moab, against the Ammonites, against Edom, against the kings of Zobah, and against the Philistines; wherever he turned he routed them. ⁴⁸He did valiantly, and struck down the Amalekites, and rescued Israel out of the hands of those who plundered them.

49 Now the sons of Saul were Jonathan, Ishvi, and Malchishua; and the names of his two daughters were these: the name of the firstborn was Merab, and the name of the younger, Michal. ⁵⁰The name of Saul's wife was Ahinoam daughter of Ahimaaz. And the name of the commander of his army was Abner son of Ner, Saul's uncle; ⁵¹Kish was the father of Saul, and Ner the father of Abner was the son of Abiel.

52 There was hard fighting against the Philistines all the days of Saul; and when Saul saw any strong or valiant warrior, he took him into his service.

ᵃ Vg Compare Gk: Heb ⁴¹Saul said to the LORD, the God of Israel

Out of Egypt—© Eliza German, 20

ANOINTING

Throughout history, priests, prophets, and kings were anointed with oil to set them apart from the rest of society in their special roles. Read **1 Samuel 16.13**.

Today, anointing serves the same purpose. In Baptism, we are anointed; we are set apart and given our job description as priests, prophets, and kings for this world. As priests, our job is to offer prayer and worship to God; as prophets, to always speak the truth; as kings, to lead others to God through our example.

We are anointed with oil at Confirmation—setting us apart as people sealed with the gifts of the Holy Spirit. Priests and bishops are anointed—setting them apart for special service in the Church. Even altars and the walls of church buildings are anointed—setting them apart for sacred use.

The word "Christ" means "anointed one." As one of Christ's disciples, for what special purpose has God anointed you?

15 Saul Defeats the Amalekites but Spares Their King

Samuel said to Saul, "The LORD sent me to anoint you king over his people Israel; now therefore listen to the words of the LORD. ²Thus says the LORD of hosts, 'I will punish the Amalekites for what they did in opposing the Israelites when they came up out of Egypt. ³Now go and attack Amalek, and utterly destroy all that they have; do not spare them, but kill both man and woman, child and infant, ox and sheep, camel and donkey.' "

4 So Saul summoned the people, and numbered them in Telaim, two hundred thousand foot soldiers, and ten thousand soldiers of Judah. ⁵Saul came to the city of the Amalekites and lay in wait in the valley. ⁶Saul said to the Kenites, "Go! Leave! Withdraw from among the Amalekites, or I will destroy you with them; for you showed kindness to all the people of Israel when they came up out of Egypt." So the Kenites withdrew from the Amalekites. ⁷Saul defeated the Amalekites, from Havilah as far as Shur, which is east of Egypt. ⁸He took King Agag of the Amalekites alive, but utterly destroyed all the people with the edge of the sword. ⁹Saul and the people spared Agag, and the best of the sheep and of the cattle and of the fatlings, and the lambs, and all that was valuable, and would not utterly destroy them; all that was despised and worthless they utterly destroyed.

Saul Rejected as King

10 The word of the LORD came to Samuel: ¹¹"I regret that I made Saul king, for he has turned back from following me, and has not carried out my commands." Samuel was angry; and he cried out to the LORD all night. ¹²Samuel rose early in the morning to meet Saul, and Samuel was told, "Saul went to Carmel, where he set up a monument for himself, and on returning he passed on down to Gilgal." ¹³When Samuel came to Saul, Saul said to him, "May you be blessed by the LORD; I have carried out the command of the LORD." ¹⁴But Samuel said, "What then is this bleating of sheep in my ears, and the lowing of cattle that I hear?" ¹⁵Saul said, "They have brought them from the Amalekites; for the people spared the best of the sheep and the cattle, to sacrifice to the LORD your God; but the rest we have utterly destroyed." ¹⁶Then Samuel said to Saul, "Stop! I will tell you what the LORD said to me last night." He replied, "Speak."

17 Samuel said, "Though you are little in your own eyes, are you not the head of the tribes of Israel? The LORD anointed you king over Israel. ¹⁸And the LORD sent you on a mission, and said, 'Go, utterly destroy the sinners, the Amalekites, and fight against them until they are consumed.' ¹⁹Why then did you not obey the voice of the LORD? Why did you swoop down on the spoil, and do what was evil in the sight of the LORD?" ²⁰Saul said to Samuel, "I have obeyed the voice of the LORD, I have gone on the mission on which the LORD sent me, I have brought Agag the king of Amalek, and I have utterly destroyed the Amalekites. ²¹But from the spoil the people took sheep and cattle, the best of the things devoted to destruction, to sacrifice to the LORD your God in Gilgal." ²²And Samuel said,

"Has the LORD as great delight in burnt
offerings and sacrifices,
as in obedience to the voice of the LORD?
Surely, to obey is better than sacrifice,
and to heed than the fat of rams.
²³ For rebellion is no less a sin than
divination,
and stubbornness is like iniquity and
idolatry.
Because you have rejected the word of the
LORD,

he has also rejected you from being king."

24 Saul said to Samuel, "I have sinned; for I have transgressed the commandment of the LORD and your words, because I feared the people and obeyed their voice. [25]Now therefore, I pray, pardon my sin, and return with me, so that I may worship the LORD." [26]Samuel said to Saul, "I will not return with you; for you have rejected the word of the LORD, and the LORD has rejected you from being king over Israel." [27]As Samuel turned to go away, Saul caught hold of the hem of his robe, and it tore. [28]And Samuel said to him, "The LORD has torn the kingdom of Israel from you this very day, and has given it to a neighbor of yours, who is better than you. [29]Moreover the Glory of Israel will not recant[a] or change his mind; for he is not a mortal, that he should change his mind." [30]Then Saul[b] said, "I have sinned; yet honor me now before the elders of my people and before Israel, and return with me, so that I may worship the LORD your God." [31]So Samuel turned back after Saul; and Saul worshiped the LORD.

32 Then Samuel said, "Bring Agag king of the Amalekites here to me." And Agag came to him haltingly.[c] Agag said, "Surely this is the bitterness of death."[d] [33]But Samuel said,

"As your sword has made women childless,
  so your mother shall be childless among
      women."

And Samuel hewed Agag in pieces before the LORD in Gilgal.

34 Then Samuel went to Ramah; and Saul went up to his house in Gibeah of Saul. [35]Samuel did not see Saul again until the day of his death, but Samuel grieved over Saul. And the LORD was sorry that he had made Saul king over Israel.

16 David Anointed as King

The LORD said to Samuel, "How long will you grieve over Saul? I have rejected him from being king over Israel. Fill your horn with oil and set out; I will send you to Jesse the Bethlehemite, for I have provided for myself a king among his sons." [2]Samuel said, "How can I go? If Saul hears of it, he will kill me." And the LORD said, "Take a heifer with you, and say, 'I have come to sacrifice to the LORD.' [3]Invite Jesse to the sacrifice, and I will show you what you shall do; and you shall anoint for me the one whom I name to you." [4]Samuel did what the LORD commanded, and came to Bethlehem. The elders of the city came to meet him trembling, and said, "Do you come peaceably?" [5]He said, "Peaceably; I have come to sacrifice to the LORD; sanctify yourselves and come with me to the sacrifice." And he sanctified Jesse and his sons and invited them to the sacrifice.

6 When they came, he looked on Eliab and thought, "Surely the LORD's anointed is now before the LORD."[e] [7]But the LORD said to Samuel, "Do not look on his appearance or on the height of his stature, because I have rejected him; for the LORD does not see as mortals see; they look on the outward appearance, but the LORD looks on the heart." [8]Then Jesse called Abinadab, and made him pass before Samuel. He said, "Neither has the LORD chosen this one." [9]Then Jesse made Shammah pass by. And he said, "Neither has the LORD chosen this one." [10]Jesse made seven of his sons pass before Samuel, and Samuel said to Jesse, "The LORD has not chosen any of these." [11]Samuel said to Jesse, "Are all your sons here?" And he said, "There remains yet the youngest, but he is keeping the sheep." And Samuel said to Jesse, "Send and bring him; for we will not sit down until he comes here." [12]He sent and brought him in. Now he was ruddy, and had beautiful eyes, and was handsome. The LORD said, "Rise and anoint him; for this is the one." [13]Then Samuel took the horn of oil, and anointed him in the presence of his brothers; and the spirit of the LORD came mightily upon David from that day forward. Samuel then set out and went to Ramah.

David Plays the Lyre for Saul

14 Now the spirit of the LORD departed from Saul, and an evil spirit from the LORD tormented him. [15]And Saul's servants said to him, "See now, an evil spirit from God is tormenting you. [16]Let our lord now command the servants who attend you to look for someone who is skillful in playing the lyre; and when the evil spirit from God is upon you, he will play it, and you will feel better." [17]So Saul said to his servants, "Provide for me someone who can play well, and bring him to me." [18]One of the young men answered, "I have seen a son of Jesse the Bethlehemite who is skillful in playing, a man of valor, a warrior, prudent in speech, and a man of good presence; and the LORD is with him." [19]So Saul sent messengers to Jesse, and said, "Send me your son David who is with the sheep." [20]Jesse took a donkey loaded with bread, a skin of wine, and a kid, and sent them by his son David to Saul. [21]And David came to Saul, and entered his service. Saul loved him greatly, and he became his armor-

---

a Q Ms Gk: MT *deceive*　*b* Heb *he*　*c* Cn Compare Gk: Meaning of Heb uncertain　*d* Q Ms Gk: MT *Surely the bitterness of death is past*　*e* Heb *him*

Slam-dunking would have been easy for Goliath, who was nine foot four. His head would have been just a few inches below the basketball rim. But he was still no match for David, who was good at "long shots" (1 Samuel 17.41–54).

Fact

This information has been scanned and is free of all known viruses. Please forward to all your friends.

---

the Philistines a champion named Goliath, of Gath, whose height was six[a] cubits and a span. [5]He had a helmet of bronze on his head, and he was armed with a coat of mail; the weight of the coat was five thousand shekels of bronze. [6]He had greaves of bronze on his legs and a javelin of bronze slung between his shoulders. [7]The shaft of his spear was like a weaver's beam, and his spear's head weighed six hundred shekels of iron; and his shield-bearer went before him. [8]He stood and shouted to the ranks of Israel, "Why have you come out to draw up for battle? Am I not a Philistine, and are you not servants of Saul? Choose a man for yourselves, and let him come down to me. [9]If he is able to fight with me and kill me, then we will be your servants; but if I prevail against him and kill him, then you shall be our servants and serve us." [10]And the Philistine said, "Today I defy the ranks of Israel! Give me a man, that we may fight together." [11]When Saul and all Israel heard these words of the Philistine, they were dismayed and greatly afraid.

12 Now David was the son of an Ephrathite of Bethlehem in Judah, named Jesse, who had eight sons. In the days of Saul the man was already old and advanced in years.[b] [13]The three eldest sons of Jesse had followed Saul to the battle; the names of his three sons who went to the battle were Eliab the firstborn, and next to him Abinadab, and the third Shammah. [14]David was the youngest; the three eldest followed Saul, [15]but David went back and forth from Saul to feed his father's sheep at Bethlehem. [16]For forty days the Philistine came forward and took his stand, morning and evening.

17 Jesse said to his son David, "Take for your brothers an ephah of this parched grain and these ten loaves, and carry them quickly to the camp to your brothers; [18]also take these ten cheeses to the commander of their thousand. See how your brothers fare, and bring some token from them."

19 Now Saul, and they, and all the men of Israel, were in the valley of Elah, fighting with the Philistines. [20]David rose early in the morning, left the sheep with a keeper, took the provisions, and went as Jesse had commanded him. He came to the encampment as the army was going forth to the battle line, shouting the war cry. [21]Israel and the Philistines drew up for battle, army against army. [22]David left the things in charge of the keeper of the baggage, ran to the ranks, and went and greeted his brothers. [23]As he talked with them, the champion, the Philistine of Gath, Goliath by name, came up out of the ranks of the Philistines,

---

bearer. [22]Saul sent to Jesse, saying, "Let David remain in my service, for he has found favor in my sight." [23]And whenever the evil spirit from God came upon Saul, David took the lyre and played it with his hand, and Saul would be relieved and feel better, and the evil spirit would depart from him.

17 David and Goliath

Now the Philistines gathered their armies for battle; they were gathered at Socoh, which belongs to Judah, and encamped between Socoh and Azekah, in Ephes-dammim. [2]Saul and the Israelites gathered and encamped in the valley of Elah, and formed ranks against the Philistines. [3]The Philistines stood on the mountain on the one side, and Israel stood on the mountain on the other side, with a valley between them. [4]And there came out from the camp of

---

a MT: Q Ms Gk *four* *b* Gk Syr: Heb *among men*

and spoke the same words as before. And David heard him.

24 All the Israelites, when they saw the man, fled from him and were very much afraid. [25]The Israelites said, "Have you seen this man who has come up? Surely he has come up to defy Israel. The king will greatly enrich the man who kills him, and will give him his daughter and make his family free in Israel." [26]David said to the men who stood by him, "What shall be done for the man who kills this Philistine, and takes away the reproach from Israel? For who is this uncircumcised Philistine that he should defy the armies of the living God?" [27]The people answered him in the same way, "So shall it be done for the man who kills him."

28 His eldest brother Eliab heard him talking to the men; and Eliab's anger was kindled against David. He said, "Why have you come down? With whom have you left those few sheep in the wilderness? I know your presumption and the evil of your heart; for you have come down just to see the battle." [29]David said, "What have I done now? It was only a question." [30]He turned away from him toward another and spoke in the same way; and the people answered him again as before.

31 When the words that David spoke were heard, they repeated them before Saul; and he sent for him. [32]David said to Saul, "Let no one's heart fail because of him; your servant will go and fight with this Philistine." [33]Saul said to David, "You are not able to go against this Philistine to fight with him; for you are just a boy, and he has been a warrior from his youth." [34]But David said to Saul, "Your servant used to keep sheep for his father; and whenever a lion or a bear came, and took a lamb from the flock, [35]I went after it and struck it down, rescuing the lamb from its mouth; and if it turned against me, I would catch it by the jaw, strike it down, and kill it. [36]Your servant has killed both lions and bears; and this uncircumcised Philistine shall be like one of them, since he has defied the armies of the living God." [37]David said, "The LORD, who saved me from the paw of the lion and from the paw of the bear, will save me from the hand of this Philistine." So Saul said to David, "Go, and may the LORD be with you!"

38 Saul clothed David with his armor; he put a bronze helmet on his head and clothed him with a coat of mail. [39]David strapped Saul's sword over the armor, and he tried in vain to walk, for he was not used to them. Then David said to Saul, "I cannot walk with these; for I am not used to them." So David removed them. [40]Then he took his staff in his hand, and chose five smooth stones from the wadi, and put them in his shepherd's bag, in the pouch; his sling was in his hand, and he drew near to the Philistine.

41 The Philistine came on and drew near to David, with his shield-bearer in front of him. [42]When the Philistine looked and saw David, he disdained him, for he was only a youth, ruddy and handsome in appearance. [43]The Philistine said to David, "Am I a dog, that you come to me with sticks?" And the Philistine cursed David by his gods. [44]The Philistine said to David, "Come to me, and I will give your flesh to the birds of the air and to the wild animals of the field." [45]But David said to the Philistine, "You come to me with sword and spear and javelin; but I come to you in the name of the LORD of hosts, the God of the armies of Israel, whom you have defied. [46]This very day the LORD will deliver you into my hand, and I will strike you down and cut off your head; and I will give the dead bodies of the Philistine army this very day to the birds of the air and to the wild animals of the earth, so that all the earth may know that there is a God in Israel, [47]and that all this assembly may know that the LORD does not save by sword and spear; for the battle is the LORD's and he will give you into our hand."

48 When the Philistine drew nearer to meet David, David ran quickly toward the battle line to meet the Philistine. [49]David put his hand in his bag, took out a stone, slung it, and struck the Philistine on his forehead; the stone sank into his forehead, and he fell face down on the ground.

50 So David prevailed over the Philistine with a sling and a stone, striking down the Philistine and killing him; there was no sword in David's hand. [51]Then David ran and stood over the Philistine; he grasped his sword, drew it out of its sheath, and killed him; then he cut off his head with it.

When the Philistines saw that their champion was dead, they fled. [52]The troops of Israel and Judah rose up with a shout and pursued the Philistines as far as Gath[a] and the gates of Ekron, so that the wounded Philistines fell on the way from Shaaraim as far as Gath and Ekron. [53]The Israelites came back from chasing the Philistines, and they plundered their camp. [54]David took the head of the Philistine and brought it to Jerusalem; but he put his armor in his tent.

55 When Saul saw David go out against the Philistine, he said to Abner, the commander of the army, "Abner, whose son is this young man?" Abner said, "As your soul lives, O king, I

_a_ Gk Syr: Heb _Gai_

do not know." ⁵⁶The king said, "Inquire whose son the stripling is." ⁵⁷On David's return from killing the Philistine, Abner took him and brought him before Saul, with the head of the Philistine in his hand. ⁵⁸Saul said to him, "Whose son are you, young man?" And David answered, "I am the son of your servant Jesse the Bethlehemite."

18 Jonathan's Covenant with David

When Davidᵃ had finished speaking to Saul, the soul of Jonathan was bound to the soul of David, and Jonathan loved him as his own soul. ²Saul took him that day and would not let him return to his father's house. ³Then Jonathan made a covenant with David, because he loved him as his own soul. ⁴Jonathan stripped himself of the robe that he was wearing, and gave it to David, and his armor, and even his sword and his bow and his belt. ⁵David went out and was successful wherever Saul sent him; as a result, Saul set him over the army. And all the people, even the servants of Saul, approved.

6 As they were coming home, when David returned from killing the Philistine, the women came out of all the towns of Israel, singing and dancing, to meet King Saul, with tambourines, with songs of joy, and with musical instruments.ᵇ ⁷And the women sang to one another as they made merry,

"Saul has killed his thousands,
and David his ten thousands."

⁸Saul was very angry, for this saying displeased him. He said, "They have ascribed to David ten thousands, and to me they have ascribed thousands; what more can he have but the kingdom?" ⁹So Saul eyed David from that day on.

Saul Tries to Kill David

10 The next day an evil spirit from God rushed upon Saul, and he raved within his house, while David was playing the lyre, as he did day by day. Saul had his spear in his hand; ¹¹and Saul threw the spear, for he thought, "I will pin David to the wall." But David eluded him twice.

12 Saul was afraid of David, because the LORD was with him but had departed from Saul. ¹³So Saul removed him from his presence, and made him a commander of a thousand; and David marched out and came in, leading the army. ¹⁴David had success in all his undertakings; for the LORD was with him. ¹⁵When Saul saw that he had great success, he stood in awe of him. ¹⁶But all Israel and Judah loved David; for it was he who marched out and came in leading them.

David Marries Michal

17 Then Saul said to David, "Here is my elder daughter Merab; I will give her to you as a wife; only be valiant for me and fight the LORD's battles." For Saul thought, "I will not raise a hand against him; let the Philistines deal with him." ¹⁸David said to Saul, "Who am I and who are my kinsfolk, my father's family in Israel, that I should be son-in-law to the king?" ¹⁹But at the time when Saul's daughter Merab should have been given to David, she was given to Adriel the Meholathite as a wife.

20 Now Saul's daughter Michal loved David. Saul was told, and the thing pleased him. ²¹Saul thought, "Let me give her to him that she may be a snare for him and that the hand of the Philistines may be against him." Therefore Saul said to David a second time,ᶜ "You shall now be my son-in-law." ²²Saul commanded his servants, "Speak to David in private and say, 'See, the king is delighted with you, and all his servants love you; now then, become the king's son-in-law.' " ²³So Saul's servants reported these words to David in private. And David said, "Does it seem to you a little thing to become the king's son-in-law, seeing that I am a poor man and of no repute?" ²⁴The servants of Saul told him, "This is what David said." ²⁵Then Saul said, "Thus shall you say to David, 'The king desires no marriage present except a hundred foreskins of the Philistines, that he may be avenged on the king's enemies.' " Now Saul planned to make David fall by the hand of the Philistines. ²⁶When his servants told David these words, David was well pleased to be the king's son-in-law. Before the time had expired, ²⁷David rose and went, along with his men, and killed one hundredᵈ of the Philistines; and David brought their foreskins, which were given in full number to the king, that he might become the king's son-in-law. Saul gave him his daughter Michal as a wife. ²⁸But when Saul realized that the LORD was with David, and that Saul's daughter Michal loved him, ²⁹Saul was still more afraid of David. So Saul was David's enemy from that time forward.

30 Then the commanders of the Philistines came out to battle; and as often as they came out, David had more success than all the servants of Saul, so that his fame became very great.

19 Jonathan Intercedes for David

Saul spoke with his son Jonathan and with all his servants about killing David. But Saul's son Jonathan took great delight in David. ²Jonathan told David, "My father Saul is trying to kill

---

a Heb he b Or triangles, or three-stringed instruments c Heb by two d Gk Compare 2 Sam 3.14: Heb two hundred you; therefore be on guard tomorrow morning; stay in a secret place and hide yourself. [31]I will go out and stand beside my father in the field where you are, and I will speak to my father about you; if I learn anything I will tell you." [4]Jonathan spoke well of David to his father Saul, saying to him, "The king should not sin against his servant David, because he has not sinned against you, and because his deeds have been of good service to you; [5]for he took his life in his hand when he attacked the Philistine, and the LORD brought about a great victory for all Israel. You saw it, and rejoiced; why then will you sin against an innocent person by killing David without cause?" [6]Saul heeded the voice of Jonathan; Saul swore, "As the LORD lives, he shall not be put to death." [7]So Jonathan called David and related all these things to him. Jonathan then brought David to Saul, and he was in his presence as before.

Michal Helps David Escape from Saul

8 Again there was war, and David went out to fight the Philistines. He launched a heavy attack on them, so that they fled before him. [9]Then an evil spirit from the LORD came upon Saul, as he sat in his house with his spear in his hand, while David was playing music. [10]Saul sought to pin David to the wall with the spear; but he eluded Saul, so that he struck the spear into the wall. David fled and escaped that night.

11 Saul sent messengers to David's house to keep watch over him, planning to kill him in the morning. David's wife Michal told him, "If you do not save your life tonight, tomorrow you will be killed." [12]So Michal let David down through the window; he fled away and escaped. [13]Michal took an idol[a] and laid it on the bed; she put a net[b] of goats' hair on its head, and covered it with the clothes. [14]When Saul sent messengers to take David, she said, "He is sick." [15]Then Saul sent the messengers to see David for themselves. He said, "Bring him up to me in the bed, that I may kill him." [16]When the messengers came in, the idol[c] was in the bed, with the covering[b] of goats' hair on its head. [17]Saul said to Michal, "Why have you deceived me like this, and let my enemy go, so that he has escaped?" Michal answered Saul, "He said to me, 'Let me go; why should I kill you?' "

David Joins Samuel in Ramah

18 Now David fled and escaped; he came to Samuel at Ramah, and told him all that Saul had done to him. He and Samuel went and settled at Naioth. [19]Saul was told, "David is at

TRY THIS

B.F.F.

You won't find a stronger or deeper friendship than the one between David and Jonathan. Just read **1 Samuel 20.16–17** to see how close they were.

They were friends, as God created friendship to be. Jesus wants that kind of friendship with us too. He wants the kind of friendship that keeps intimate secrets, the kind that fights the same enemies, or a friendship that's so deep it hurts to be apart.

Find some Creative Space in this Bible and make a list of ten things you do with your best friend. Think about how those things make you feel. How do those things enrich your relationship? How can you make sure you also nurture your relationship with Jesus?

GOD IS PASSIONATE MY FRIENDS

Naioth in Ramah." [20]Then Saul sent messengers to take David. When they saw the company of the prophets in a frenzy, with Samuel standing in charge of[b] them, the spirit of God came upon the messengers of Saul, and they also fell into a prophetic frenzy. [21]When Saul was told, he sent other messengers, and they also fell into a frenzy. Saul sent messengers again the third time, and they also fell into a frenzy. [22]Then he himself went to Ramah. He came to the great well that is in Secu;[d] he asked, "Where are Samuel and David?" And someone said, "They are at Naioth in Ramah." [23]He went there, toward Naioth in Ramah; and the spirit of God came upon him. As he was going, he fell into a prophetic frenzy, until he came to Naioth in Ramah. [24]He too stripped off his clothes, and he too fell into a frenzy before Samuel. He lay naked all that day and all that night. Therefore it is said, "Is Saul also among the prophets?"

20 The Friendship of David and Jonathan
David fled from Naioth in Ramah. He came before Jonathan and said, "What have I done? What is my guilt? And what is my sin against your father that he is trying to take my life?" [2]He said to him, "Far from it! You shall not die. My father does nothing either great or small without disclosing it to me; and why should my father hide this from me? Never!" [3]But David also swore, "Your father knows well that

---

a Heb *took the teraphim* *b* Meaning of Heb uncertain *c* Heb *the teraphim* *d* Gk reads *to the well of the threshing floor on the bare height* you like me; and he thinks, 'Do not let Jonathan know this, or he will be grieved.' But truly, as the LORD lives and as you yourself live, there is but a step between me and death." ⁴Then Jonathan said to David, "Whatever you say, I will do for you." ⁵David said to Jonathan, "Tomorrow is the new moon, and I should not fail to sit with the king at the meal; but let me go, so that I may hide in the field until the third evening. ⁶If your father misses me at all, then say, 'David earnestly asked leave of me to run to Bethlehem his city; for there is a yearly sacrifice there for all the family.' ⁷If he says, 'Good!' it will be well with your servant; but if he is angry, then know that evil has been determined by him. ⁸Therefore deal kindly with your servant, for you have brought your servant into a sacred covenant*ᵃ* with you. But if there is guilt in me, kill me yourself; why should you bring me to your father?" ⁹Jonathan said, "Far be it from you! If I knew that it was decided by my father that evil should come upon you, would I not tell you?" ¹⁰Then David said to Jonathan, "Who will tell me if your father answers you harshly?" ¹¹Jonathan replied to David, "Come, let us go out into the field." So they both went out into the field.

12 Jonathan said to David, "By the LORD, the God of Israel! When I have sounded out my father, about this time tomorrow, or on the third day, if he is well disposed toward David, shall I not then send and disclose it to you? ¹³But if my father intends to do you harm, the LORD do so to Jonathan, and more also, if I do not disclose it to you, and send you away, so that you may go in safety. May the LORD be with you, as he has been with my father. ¹⁴If I am still alive, show me the faithful love of the LORD; but if I die,ᵇ ¹⁵never cut off your faithful love from my house, even if the LORD were to cut off every one of the enemies of David from the face of the earth." ¹⁶Thus Jonathan made a covenant with the house of David, saying, "May the LORD seek out the enemies of David." ¹⁷Jonathan made David swear again by his love for him; for he loved him as he loved his own life.

18 Jonathan said to him, "Tomorrow is the new moon; you will be missed, because your place will be empty. ¹⁹On the day after tomorrow, you shall go a long way down; go to the place where you hid yourself earlier, and remain beside the stone there.ᵇ ²⁰I will shoot three arrows to the side of it, as though I shot at a mark. ²¹Then I will send the boy, saying, 'Go, find the arrows.' If I say to the boy, 'Look, the arrows are on this side of you, collect them,' then you are to come, for, as the LORD lives, it is safe for you and there is no danger. ²²But if I say to the young man, 'Look, the arrows are beyond you,' then go; for the LORD has sent you away. ²³As for the matter about which you and I have spoken, the LORD is witnessᶜ between you and me forever."

24 So David hid himself in the field. When the new moon came, the king sat at the feast to eat. ²⁵The king sat upon his seat, as at other times, upon the seat by the wall. Jonathan stood, while Abner sat by Saul's side; but David's place was empty.

26 Saul did not say anything that day; for he thought, "Something has befallen him; he is not clean, surely he is not clean." ²⁷But on the second day, the day after the new moon, David's place was empty. And Saul said to his son Jonathan, "Why has the son of Jesse not come to the feast, either yesterday or today?" ²⁸Jonathan answered Saul, "David earnestly asked leave of me to go to Bethlehem; ²⁹he said, 'Let me go; for our family is holding a sacrifice in the city, and my brother has commanded me to be there. So now, if I have found favor in your sight, let me get away, and see my brothers.' For this reason he has not come to the king's table."

30 Then Saul's anger was kindled against Jonathan. He said to him, "You son of a perverse, rebellious woman! Do I not know that you have chosen the son of Jesse to your own shame, and to the shame of your mother's nakedness? ³¹For as long as the son of Jesse lives upon the earth, neither you nor your kingdom shall be established. Now send and bring him to me, for he shall surely die." ³²Then Jonathan answered his father Saul, "Why should he be put to death? What has he done?" ³³But Saul threw his spear at him to strike him; so Jonathan knew that it was the decision of his father to put David to death. ³⁴Jonathan rose from the table in fierce anger and ate no food on the second day of the month, for he was grieved for David, and because his father had disgraced him.

35 In the morning Jonathan went out into the field to the appointment with David, and with him was a little boy. ³⁶He said to the boy, "Run and find the arrows that I shoot." As the boy ran, he shot an arrow beyond him. ³⁷When the boy came to the place where Jonathan's arrow had fallen, Jonathan called after the boy and said, "Is the arrow not beyond you?" ³⁸Jonathan called after the boy, "Hurry, be quick, do not linger." So Jonathan's boy gathered up the arrows and came to his master. ³⁹But the boy knew nothing; only Jonathan and David knew the arrangement. ⁴⁰Jonathan gave his weapons to the boy and said to him, "Go and carry them

a Heb *a covenant of the* LORD   *b* Meaning of Heb uncertain   *c* Gk: Heb lacks *witness* to the city." ⁴¹As soon as the boy had gone, David rose from beside the stone heap*g* and prostrated himself with his face to the ground. He bowed three times, and they kissed each other, and wept with each other; David wept the more.*b* ⁴²Then Jonathan said to David, "Go in peace, since both of us have sworn in the name of the Lord, saying, 'The Lord shall be between me and you, and between my descendants and your descendants, forever.' " He got up and left; and Jonathan went into the city.*c*

21*d* David and the Holy Bread

David came to Nob to the priest Ahimelech. Ahimelech came trembling to meet David, and said to him, "Why are you alone, and no one with you?" ²David said to the priest Ahimelech, "The king has charged me with a matter, and said to me, 'No one must know anything of the matter about which I send you, and with which I have charged you.' I have made an appointment*e* with the young men for such and such a place. ³Now then, what have you at hand? Give me five loaves of bread, or whatever is here." ⁴The priest answered David, "I have no ordinary bread at hand, only holy bread—provided that the young men have kept themselves from women." ⁵David answered the priest, "Indeed women have been kept from us as always when I go on an expedition; the vessels of the young men are holy even when it is a common journey; how much more today will their vessels be holy?" ⁶So the priest gave him the holy bread; for there was no bread there except the bread of the Presence, which is removed from before the Lord, to be replaced by hot bread on the day it is taken away.

7 Now a certain man of the servants of Saul was there that day, detained before the Lord; his name was Doeg the Edomite, the chief of Saul's shepherds.

8 David said to Ahimelech, "Is there no spear or sword here with you? I did not bring my sword or my weapons with me, because the king's business required haste." ⁹The priest said, "The sword of Goliath the Philistine, whom you killed in the valley of Elah, is here wrapped in a cloth behind the ephod; if you will take that, take it, for there is none here except that one." David said, "There is none like it; give it to me."

David Flees to Gath

10 David rose and fled that day from Saul; he went to King Achish of Gath. ¹¹The servants of Achish said to him, "Is this not David the king of the land? Did they not sing to one another of him in dances,

'Saul has killed his thousands,
  and David his ten thousands'?"

¹²David took these words to heart and was very much afraid of King Achish of Gath. ¹³So he changed his behavior before them; he pretended to be mad when in their presence.*f* He scratched marks on the doors of the gate, and let his spittle run down his beard. ¹⁴Achish said to his servants, "Look, you see the man is mad; why then have you brought him to me? ¹⁵Do I lack madmen, that you have brought this fellow to play the madman in my presence? Shall this fellow come into my house?"

22 David and His Followers at Adullam

David left there and escaped to the cave of Adullam; when his brothers and all his father's house heard of it, they went down there to him. ²Everyone who was in distress, and everyone who was in debt, and everyone who was discontented gathered to him; and he became captain over them. Those who were with him numbered about four hundred.

3 David went from there to Mizpeh of Moab. He said to the king of Moab, "Please let my father and mother come*g* to you, until I know what God will do for me." ⁴He left them with the king of Moab, and they stayed with him all the time that David was in the stronghold. ⁵Then the prophet Gad said to David, "Do not remain in the stronghold; leave, and go into the land of Judah." So David left, and went into the forest of Hereth.

Never Too Young—© Sharon Lezotte, 17

a Gk: Heb *from beside the south*   *b* Vg: Meaning of Heb uncertain
c This sentence is 21.1 in Heb   *d* Ch 21.2 in Heb   *e* Q Ms Vg
Compare Gk: Meaning of MT uncertain   *f* Heb *in their hands*
g Syr Vg: Heb *come out*

"

Through prayer, God reveals Himself to me, little by little—it's like talking to a friend and gradually learning more about them.

Religion article for newspaper—© Randy Reed, 18

"

Saul Slaughters the Priests at Nob

6 Saul heard that David and those who were with him had been located. Saul was sitting at Gibeah, under the tamarisk tree on the height, with his spear in his hand, and all his servants were standing around him. 7Saul said to his servants who stood around him, "Hear now, you Benjaminites; will the son of Jesse give every one of you fields and vineyards, will he make you all commanders of thousands and commanders of hundreds? 8Is that why all of you have conspired against me? No one discloses to me when my son makes a league with the son of Jesse, none of you is sorry for me or discloses to me that my son has stirred up my servant against me, to lie in wait, as he is doing today." 9Doeg the Edomite, who was in charge of Saul's servants, answered, "I saw the son of Jesse coming to Nob, to Ahimelech son of Ahitub; 10he inquired of the LORD for him, gave him provisions, and gave him the sword of Goliath the Philistine."

11 The king sent for the priest Ahimelech son of Ahitub and for all his father's house, the priests who were at Nob; and all of them came to the king. 12Saul said, "Listen now, son of Ahitub." He answered, "Here I am, my lord." 13Saul said to him, "Why have you conspired against me, you and the son of Jesse, by giving him bread and a sword, and by inquiring of God for him, so that he has risen against me, to lie in wait, as he is doing today?"

14 Then Ahimelech answered the king, "Who among all your servants is so faithful as David? He is the king's son-in-law, and is quick*a* to do your bidding, and is honored in your house. 15Is today the first time that I have inquired of God for him? By no means! Do not let the king impute anything to his servant or to any member of my father's house; for your servant has known nothing of all this, much or little." 16The king said, "You shall surely die, Ahimelech, you and all your father's house." 17The king said to the guard who stood around him, "Turn and kill the priests of the LORD, because their hand also is with David; they knew that he fled, and did not disclose it to me." But the servants of the king would not raise their hand to attack the priests of the LORD. 18Then the king said to Doeg, "You, Doeg, turn and attack the priests." Doeg the Edomite turned and attacked the priests; on that day he killed eighty-five who wore the linen ephod. 19Nob, the city of the priests, he put to the sword; men and women, children and infants, oxen, donkeys, and sheep, he put to the sword.

20 But one of the sons of Ahimelech son of Ahitub, named Abiathar, escaped and fled after David. 21Abiathar told David that Saul had killed the priests of the LORD. 22David said to Abiathar, "I knew on that day, when Doeg the Edomite was there, that he would surely tell Saul. I am responsible*b* for the lives of all your father's house. 23Stay with me, and do not be afraid; for the one who seeks my life seeks your life; you will be safe with me."

23 David Saves the City of Keilah

Now they told David, "The Philistines are fighting against Keilah, and are robbing the threshing floors." 2David inquired of the LORD, "Shall I go and attack these Philistines?" The LORD said to David, "Go and attack the Philistines and save Keilah." 3But David's men said to him, "Look, we are afraid here in Judah; how much more then if we go to Keilah against the armies of the Philistines?" 4Then David inquired of the LORD again. The LORD answered him, "Yes, go down to Keilah; for I will give the Philistines into your hand." 5So David and his men went to Keilah, fought with the Philistines, brought away their livestock, and dealt them a heavy defeat. Thus David rescued the inhabitants of Keilah.

6 When Abiathar son of Ahimelech fled to David at Keilah, he came down with an ephod in his hand. 7Now it was told Saul that David had come to Keilah. And Saul said, "God has given*c* him into my hand; for he has shut himself in by entering a town that has gates and bars." 8Saul summoned all the people to war, to go down to Keilah, to besiege David and his men. 9When David learned that Saul was plotting evil against him, he said to the priest Abiathar, "Bring the ephod here." 10David said, "O LORD, the God of Israel, your servant has heard that Saul seeks to come to Keilah, to destroy the city on my account. 11And now, will*d* Saul come down as your servant has heard? O LORD, the God of Israel, I beseech you, tell your servant." The LORD said, "He will come down." 12Then David said, "Will the men of Keilah surrender me and my men into the hand of Saul?" The LORD said, "They will surrender you." 13Then David and his men, who were about six hundred, set out and left Keilah; they wandered wherever they could go. When Saul was told that David had escaped from Keilah, he gave up the expedition. 14David remained in the strongholds in the wilderness, in the hill country of the Wilderness of Ziph. Saul sought him every day, but the LORD*e* did not give him into his hand.

a Heb *and turns aside* *b* Gk Vg: Meaning of Heb uncertain *c* Gk Tg: Heb *made a stranger of* *d* Q Ms Compare Gk: MT *Will the men of Keilah surrender me into his hand? Will* *e* Q Ms Gk: MT *God*

David Eludes Saul in the Wilderness

15 David was in the Wilderness of Ziph at Horesh when he learned that*a* Saul had come out to seek his life. ¹⁶Saul's son Jonathan set out and came to David at Horesh; there he strengthened his hand through the LORD.*b* ¹⁷He said to him, "Do not be afraid; for the hand of my father Saul shall not find you; you shall be king over Israel, and I shall be second to you; my father Saul also knows that this is so." ¹⁸Then the two of them made a covenant before the LORD; David remained at Horesh, and Jonathan went home.

19 Then some Ziphites went up to Saul at Gibeah and said, "David is hiding among us in the strongholds of Horesh, on the hill of Hachilah, which is south of Jeshimon. ²⁰Now, O king, whenever you wish to come down, do so; and our part will be to surrender him into the king's hand." ²¹Saul said, "May you be blessed by the LORD for showing me compassion! ²²Go and make sure once more; find out exactly where he is, and who has seen him there; for I am told that he is very cunning. ²³Look around and learn all the hiding places where he lurks, and come back to me with sure information. Then I will go with you; and if he is in the land, I will search him out among all the thousands of Judah." ²⁴So they set out and went to Ziph ahead of Saul.

David and his men were in the wilderness of Maon, in the Arabah to the south of Jeshimon. ²⁵Saul and his men went to search for him. When David was told, he went down to the rock and stayed in the wilderness of Maon. When Saul heard that, he pursued David into the wilderness of Maon. ²⁶Saul went on one side of the mountain, and David and his men on the other side of the mountain. David was hurrying to get away from Saul, while Saul and his men were closing in on David and his men to capture them. ²⁷Then a messenger came to Saul, saying, "Hurry and come; for the Philistines have made a raid on the land." ²⁸So Saul stopped pursuing David, and went against the Philistines; therefore that place was called the Rock of Escape.*c* ²⁹*d* David then went up from there, and lived in the strongholds of En-gedi.

24 David Spares Saul's Life

When Saul returned from following the Philistines, he was told, "David is in the wilderness of En-gedi." ²Then Saul took three thousand chosen men out of all Israel, and went to look for David and his men in the direction of the Rocks of the Wild Goats. ³He came to the sheepfolds beside the road, where there was a cave; and Saul went in to relieve himself.*e* Now David and his men were sitting in the innermost parts of the cave. ⁴The men of David said to him, "Here is the day of which the LORD said to you, 'I will give your enemy into your hand, and you shall do to him as it seems good to you.'" Then David went and stealthily cut off a corner of Saul's cloak. ⁵Afterward David was stricken to the heart because he had cut off a corner of Saul's cloak. ⁶He said to his men, "The LORD forbid that I should do this thing to my lord, the LORD's anointed, to raise my hand against him; for he is the LORD's anointed." ⁷So David scolded his men severely and did not permit them to attack Saul. Then Saul got up and left the cave, and went on his way.

8 Afterwards David also rose up and went out of the cave and called after Saul, "My lord the king!" When Saul looked behind him, David bowed with his face to the ground, and did obeisance. ⁹David said to Saul, "Why do you listen to the words of those who say, 'David seeks to do you harm'? ¹⁰This very day your eyes have seen how the LORD gave you into my hand in the cave; and some urged me to kill you, but I spared*f* you. I said, 'I will not raise my hand against my lord; for he is the LORD's anointed.' ¹¹See, my father, see the corner of your cloak in my hand; for by the fact that I cut off the corner of your cloak, and did not kill you, you may know for certain that there is no wrong or treason in my hands. I have not sinned against you, though you are hunting me to take my life. ¹²May the LORD judge between me and you! May the LORD avenge me on you; but my hand shall not be against you. ¹³As the ancient proverb says, 'Out of the wicked comes forth wickedness'; but my hand shall not be against you. ¹⁴Against whom has the king of Israel come out? Whom do you pursue? A dead dog? A single flea? ¹⁵May the LORD therefore be judge, and give sentence between me and you. May he see to it, and plead my cause, and vindicate me against you."

16 When David had finished speaking these words to Saul, Saul said, "Is this your voice, my son David?" Saul lifted up his voice and wept. ¹⁷He said to David, "You are more righteous than I; for you have repaid me good, whereas I have repaid you evil. ¹⁸Today you have explained how you have dealt well with me, in that you did not kill me when the LORD put me into your hands. ¹⁹For who has ever found an enemy, and sent the enemy safely away? So may the LORD reward you with good for what

---

a Or *saw that* *b* Compare Q Ms Gk: MT *God* *c* Or *Rock of Division*; meaning of Heb uncertain *d* Ch 24.1 in Heb *e* Heb *to cover his feet* *f* Gk Syr Tg Vg: Heb *it* (my eye) *spared* you have done to me this day. [20]Now I know that you shall surely be king, and that the kingdom of Israel shall be established in your hand. [21]Swear to me therefore by the LORD that you will not cut off my descendants after me, and that you will not wipe out my name from my father's house." [22]So David swore this to Saul. Then Saul went home; but David and his men went up to the stronghold.

25 Death of Samuel

Now Samuel died; and all Israel assembled and mourned for him. They buried him at his home in Ramah.

Then David got up and went down to the wilderness of Paran.

David and the Wife of Nabal

[2]There was a man in Maon, whose property was in Carmel. The man was very rich; he had three thousand sheep and a thousand goats. He was shearing his sheep in Carmel. [3]Now the name of the man was Nabal, and the name of his wife Abigail. The woman was clever and beautiful, but the man was surly and mean; he was a Calebite. [4]David heard in the wilderness that Nabal was shearing his sheep. [5]So David sent ten young men; and David said to the young men, "Go up to Carmel, and go to Nabal, and greet him in my name. [6]Thus you shall salute him: 'Peace be to you, and peace be to your house, and peace be to all that you have. [7]I hear that you have shearers; now your shepherds have been with us, and we did them no harm, and they missed nothing, all the time they were in Carmel. [8]Ask your young men, and they will tell you. Therefore let my young men find favor in your sight; for we have come on a feast day. Please give whatever you have at hand to your servants and to your son David.' "

[9]When David's young men came, they said all this to Nabal in the name of David; and then they waited. [10]But Nabal answered David's servants, "Who is David? Who is the son of Jesse? There are many servants today who are breaking away from their masters. [11]Shall I take my bread and my water and the meat that I have butchered for my shearers, and give it to men who come from I do not know where?" [12]So David's young men turned away, and came back and told him all this. [13]David said to his men, "Every man strap on his sword!" And every one of them strapped on his sword; David also strapped on his sword; and about four hundred men went up after David, while two hundred remained with the baggage.

[14]But one of the young men told Abigail, Nabal's wife, "David sent messengers out of the wilderness to salute our master; and he shouted insults at them. [15]Yet the men were very good to us, and we suffered no harm, and we never missed anything when we were in the fields, as long as we were with them; [16]they were a wall to us both by night and by day, all the while we were with them keeping the sheep. [17]Now therefore know this and consider what you should do; for evil has been decided against our master and against all his house; he is so ill-natured that no one can speak to him."

[18]Then Abigail hurried and took two hundred loaves, two skins of wine, five sheep ready dressed, five measures of parched grain, one hundred clusters of raisins, and two hundred cakes of figs. She loaded them on donkeys [19]and said to her young men, "Go on ahead of me; I am coming after you." But she did not tell her husband Nabal. [20]As she rode on the donkey and came down under cover of the mountain, David and his men came down toward her; and she met them. [21]Now David had said, "Surely it was in vain that I protected all that this fellow has in the wilderness, so that nothing was missed of all that belonged to him; but he has returned me evil for good. [22]God do so to David[a] and more also, if by morning I leave so much as one male of all who belong to him."

[23]When Abigail saw David, she hurried and alighted from the donkey, and fell before David on her face, bowing to the ground. [24]She fell at his feet and said, "Upon me alone, my lord, be the guilt; please let your servant speak in your ears, and hear the words of your servant. [25]My lord, do not take seriously this ill-natured fellow, Nabal; for as his name is, so is he; Nabal[b] is his name, and folly is with him; but I, your servant, did not see the young men of my lord, whom you sent.

[26]"Now then, my lord, as the LORD lives, and as you yourself live, since the LORD has restrained you from bloodguilt and from taking vengeance with your own hand, now let your enemies and those who seek to do evil to my lord be like Nabal. [27]And now let this present that your servant has brought to my lord be given to the young men who follow my lord. [28]Please forgive the trespass of your servant; for the LORD will certainly make my lord a sure house, because my lord is fighting the battles of the LORD; and evil shall not be found in you so long as you live. [29]If anyone should rise up to pursue you and to seek your life, the life of my lord shall be bound in the bundle of the liv-

---

a Gk Compare Syr: Heb *the enemies of David* b That is *Fool* ing under the care of the LORD your God; but the lives of your enemies he shall sling out as from the hollow of a sling. [30]When the LORD has done to my lord according to all the good that he has spoken concerning you, and has appointed you prince over Israel, [31]my lord shall have no cause of grief, or pangs of conscience, for having shed blood without cause or for having saved himself. And when the LORD has dealt well with my lord, then remember your servant."

32 David said to Abigail, "Blessed be the LORD, the God of Israel, who sent you to meet me today! [33]Blessed be your good sense, and blessed be you, who have kept me today from bloodguilt and from avenging myself by my own hand! [34]For as surely as the LORD the God of Israel lives, who has restrained me from hurting you, unless you had hurried and come to meet me, truly by morning there would not have been left to Nabal so much as one male." [35]Then David received from her hand what she had brought him; he said to her, "Go up to your house in peace; see, I have heeded your voice, and I have granted your petition."

36 Abigail came to Nabal; he was holding a feast in his house, like the feast of a king. Nabal's heart was merry within him, for he was very drunk; so she told him nothing at all until the morning light. [37]In the morning, when the wine had gone out of Nabal, his wife told him these things, and his heart died within him; he became like a stone. [38]About ten days later the LORD struck Nabal, and he died.

39 When David heard that Nabal was dead, he said, "Blessed be the LORD who has judged the case of Nabal's insult to me, and has kept back his servant from evil; the LORD has returned the evildoing of Nabal upon his own head." Then David sent and wooed Abigail, to make her his wife. [40]When David's servants came to Abigail at Carmel, they said to her, "David has sent us to you to take you to him as his wife." [41]She rose and bowed down, with her face to the ground, and said, "Your servant is a slave to wash the feet of the servants of my lord." [42]Abigail got up hurriedly and rode away on a donkey; her five maids attended her. She went after the messengers of David and became his wife.

43 David also married Ahinoam of Jezreel; both of them became his wives. [44]Saul had given his daughter Michal, David's wife, to Palti son of Laish, who was from Gallim.

26 David Spares Saul's Life a Second Time

Then the Ziphites came to Saul at Gibeah, saying, "David is in hiding on the hill of Hachilah, which is opposite Jeshimon."[a] [2]So Saul rose and went down to the Wilderness of Ziph, with three thousand chosen men of Israel, to seek David in the Wilderness of Ziph. [3]Saul encamped on the hill of Hachilah, which is opposite Jeshimon[a] beside the road. But David remained in the wilderness. When he learned that Saul had come after him into the wilderness, [4]David sent out spies, and learned that Saul had indeed arrived. [5]Then David set out and came to the place where Saul had encamped; and David saw the place where Saul lay, with Abner son of Ner, the commander of his army. Saul was lying within the encampment, while the army was encamped around him.

6 Then David said to Ahimelech the Hittite, and to Joab's brother Abishai son of Zeruiah, "Who will go down with me into the camp to Saul?" Abishai said, "I will go down with you." [7]So David and Abishai went to the army by night; there Saul lay sleeping within the encampment, with his spear stuck in the ground at his head; and Abner and the army lay around him. [8]Abishai said to David, "God has given your enemy into your hand today; now therefore let me pin him to the ground with one stroke of the spear; I will not strike him twice." [9]But David said to Abishai, "Do not destroy him; for who can raise his hand against the LORD's anointed, and be guiltless?" [10]David said, "As the LORD lives, the LORD will strike him down; or his day will come to die; or he will go down into battle and perish. [11]The LORD forbid that I should raise my hand against the LORD's anointed; but now take the spear that is at his head, and the water jar, and let us go." [12]So David took the spear that was at Saul's head and the water jar, and they went away. No one saw it, or knew it, nor did anyone awake; for they were all asleep, because a deep sleep from the LORD had fallen upon them.

13 Then David went over to the other side, and stood on top of a hill far away, with a great distance between them. [14]David called to the army and to Abner son of Ner, saying, "Abner!

a Or *opposite the wasteland*

Will you not answer?" Then Abner replied, "Who are you that calls to the king?" [15]David said to Abner, "Are you not a man? Who is like you in Israel? Why then have you not kept watch over your lord the king? For one of the people came in to destroy your lord the king. [16]This thing that you have done is not good. As the Lord lives, you deserve to die, because you have not kept watch over your lord, the Lord's anointed. See now, where is the king's spear, or the water jar that was at his head?"

17 Saul recognized David's voice, and said, "Is this your voice, my son David?" David said, "It is my voice, my lord, O king." [18]And he added, "Why does my lord pursue his servant? For what have I done? What guilt is on my hands? [19]Now therefore let my lord the king hear the words of his servant. If it is the Lord who has stirred you up against me, may he accept an offering; but if it is mortals, may they be cursed before the Lord, for they have driven me out today from my share in the heritage of the Lord, saying, 'Go, serve other gods.' [20]Now therefore, do not let my blood fall to the ground, away from the presence of the Lord; for the king of Israel has come out to seek a single flea, like one who hunts a partridge in the mountains."

21 Then Saul said, "I have done wrong; come back, my son David, for I will never harm you again, because my life was precious in your sight today; I have been a fool, and have made a great mistake." [22]David replied, "Here is the spear, O king! Let one of the young men come over and get it. [23]The Lord rewards everyone for his righteousness and his faithfulness; for the Lord gave you into my hand today, but I would not raise my hand against the Lord's anointed. [24]As your life was precious today in my sight, so may my life be precious in the sight of the Lord, and may he rescue me from all tribulation." [25]Then Saul said to David, "Blessed be you, my son David! You will do many things and will succeed in them." So David went his way, and Saul returned to his place.

27 David Serves King Achish of Gath

David said in his heart, "I shall now perish one day by the hand of Saul; there is nothing better for me than to escape to the land of the Philistines; then Saul will despair of seeking me any longer within the borders of Israel, and I shall escape out of his hand." [2]So David set out and went over, he and the six hundred men who were with him, to King Achish son of Maoch of Gath. [3]David stayed with Achish at Gath, he and his troops, every man with his household, and David with his two wives, Ahinoam of Jezreel,

and Abigail of Carmel, Nabal's widow. [4]When Saul was told that David had fled to Gath, he no longer sought for him.

5 Then David said to Achish, "If I have found favor in your sight, let a place be given me in one of the country towns, so that I may live there; for why should your servant live in the royal city with you?" [6]So that day Achish gave him Ziklag; therefore Ziklag has belonged to the kings of Judah to this day. [7]The length of time that David lived in the country of the Philistines was one year and four months.

8 Now David and his men went up and made raids on the Geshurites, the Girzites, and the Amalekites; for these were the landed settlements from Telam[a] on the way to Shur and on to the land of Egypt. [9]David struck the land, leaving neither man nor woman alive, but took away the sheep, the oxen, the donkeys, the camels, and the clothing, and came back to Achish. [10]When Achish asked, "Against whom[b] have you made a raid today?" David would say, "Against the Negeb of Judah," or "Against the Negeb of the Jerahmeelites," or, "Against the Negeb of the Kenites." [11]David left neither man nor woman alive to be brought back to Gath, thinking, "They might tell about us, and say, 'David has done so and so.' " Such was his practice all the time he lived in the country of the Philistines. [12]Achish trusted David, thinking, "He has made himself utterly abhorrent to his people Israel; therefore he shall always be my servant."

28

In those days the Philistines gathered their forces for war, to fight against Israel. Achish said to David, "You know, of course, that you and your men are to go out with me in the army." [2]David said to Achish, "Very well, then you shall know what your servant can do." Achish said to David, "Very well, I will make you my bodyguard for life."

Saul Consults a Medium

3 Now Samuel had died, and all Israel had mourned for him and buried him in Ramah, his own city. Saul had expelled the mediums and the wizards from the land. [4]The Philistines assembled, and came and encamped at Shunem. Saul gathered all Israel, and they encamped at Gilboa. [5]When Saul saw the army of the Philistines, he was afraid, and his heart trembled greatly. [6]When Saul inquired of the Lord, the Lord did not answer him, not by dreams, or by Urim, or by prophets. [7]Then Saul said to his servants, "Seek out for me a woman who is a medium, so that I may go to her and inquire of her." His servants said to him, "There is a medium at Endor."

a Compare Gk 15.4: Heb *from of old*   b Q Ms Gk Vg: MT lacks *whom*

If you think it's not manly to cry, read 1 Samuel 30.3–4. When they found their town burned and their families carted off into captivity, David and his army cried so much that they were too weak to cry anymore.

This information has been scanned and is free of all known viruses. Please forward to all your friends.

8 So Saul disguised himself and put on other clothes and went there, he and two men with him. They came to the woman by night. And he said, "Consult a spirit for me, and bring up for me the one whom I name to you." ⁹The woman said to him, "Surely you know what Saul has done, how he has cut off the mediums and the wizards from the land. Why then are you laying a snare for my life to bring about my death?" ¹⁰But Saul swore to her by the LORD, "As the LORD lives, no punishment shall come upon you for this thing." ¹¹Then the woman said, "Whom shall I bring up for you?" He answered, "Bring up Samuel for me." ¹²When the woman saw Samuel, she cried out with a loud voice; and the woman said to Saul, "Why have you deceived me? You are Saul!" ¹³The king said to her, "Have no fear; what do you see?" The woman said to Saul, "I see a divine being*

a Or *a god; or gods*

coming up out of the ground." ¹⁴He said to her, "What is his appearance?" She said, "An old man is coming up; he is wrapped in a robe." So Saul knew that it was Samuel, and he bowed with his face to the ground, and did obeisance.

15 Then Samuel said to Saul, "Why have you disturbed me by bringing me up?" Saul answered, "I am in great distress, for the Philistines are warring against me, and God has turned away from me and answers me no more, either by prophets or by dreams; so I have summoned you to tell me what I should do." ¹⁶Samuel said, "Why then do you ask me, since the LORD has turned from you and become your enemy? ¹⁷The LORD has done to you just as he spoke by me; for the LORD has torn the kingdom out of your hand, and given it to your neighbor, David. ¹⁸Because you did not obey the voice of the LORD, and did not carry out his fierce wrath against Amalek, therefore the LORD has done this thing to you today. ¹⁹Moreover the LORD will give Israel along with you into the hands of the Philistines; and tomorrow you and your sons shall be with me; the LORD will also give the army of Israel into the hands of the Philistines."

20 Immediately Saul fell full length on the ground, filled with fear because of the words of Samuel; and there was no strength in him, for he had eaten nothing all day and all night. ²¹The woman came to Saul, and when she saw that he was terrified, she said to him, "Your servant has listened to you; I have taken my life in my hand, and have listened to what you have said to me. ²²Now therefore, you also listen to your servant; let me set a morsel of bread before you. Eat, that you may have strength when you go on your way." ²³He refused, and said, "I will not eat." But his servants, together with the woman, urged him; and he listened to their words. So he got up from the ground and sat on the bed. ²⁴Now the woman had a fatted calf in the house. She quickly slaughtered it, and she took flour, kneaded it, and baked unleavened cakes. ²⁵She put them before Saul and his servants, and they ate. Then they rose and went away that night.

29 The Philistines Reject David

Now the Philistines gathered all their forces at Aphek, while the Israelites were encamped by the fountain that is in Jezreel. ²As the lords of the Philistines were passing on by hundreds and by thousands, and David and his men were passing on in the rear with Achish, ³the commanders of the Philistines said, "What are these Hebrews doing here?" Achish said to the commanders of the Philistines, "Is this not David, the servant of King Saul of Israel, who has been with me now for days and years? Since he deserted to me I have found no fault in him to this day." ⁴But the commanders of the Philistines were angry with him; and the commanders of the Philistines said to him, "Send the man back, so that he may return to the place that you have assigned to him; he shall not go down with us to battle, or else he may become an adversary to us in the battle. For how could this fellow reconcile himself to his lord? Would it not be with the heads of the men here? ⁵Is this not David, of whom they sing to one another in dances,

'Saul has killed his thousands,
  and David his ten thousands'?"

6 Then Achish called David and said to him, "As the LORD lives, you have been honest, and to me it seems right that you should march out and in with me in the campaign; for I have found nothing wrong in you from the day of your coming to me until today. Nevertheless the lords do not approve of you. ⁷So go back now; and go peaceably; do nothing to displease the lords of the Philistines." ⁸David said to Achish, "But what have I done? What have you found in your servant from the day I entered your service until now, that I should not go and fight against the enemies of my lord the king?" ⁹Achish replied to David, "I know that you are as blameless in my sight as an angel of God; nevertheless, the commanders of the Philistines have said, 'He shall not go up with us to the battle.' ¹⁰Now then rise early in the morning, you and the servants of your lord who came with you, and go to the place that I appointed for you. As for the evil report, do not take it to heart, for you have done well before me.ᵃ Start early in the morning, and leave as soon as you have light." ¹¹So David set out with his men early in the morning, to return to the land of the Philistines. But the Philistines went up to Jezreel.

30 David Avenges the Destruction of Ziklag

Now when David and his men came to Ziklag on the third day, the Amalekites had made a raid on the Negeb and on Ziklag. They had attacked Ziklag, burned it down, ²and taken captive the women and allᵇ who were in it, both small and great; they killed none of them, but carried them off, and went their way. ³When David and his men came to the city, they found it burned down, and their wives and sons and daughters taken captive. ⁴Then David and the people who were with him raised their voices and wept, until they had no more strength to weep. ⁵David's two wives also had been taken captive, Ahinoam of Jezreel, and Abigail the widow of Nabal of Carmel. ⁶David was in great danger; for the people spoke of stoning him, because all the people were bitter in spirit for their sons and daughters. But David strengthened himself in the LORD his God.

7 David said to the priest Abiathar son of Ahimelech, "Bring me the ephod." So Abiathar brought the ephod to David. ⁸David inquired of the LORD, "Shall I pursue this band? Shall I overtake them?" He answered him, "Pursue; for you shall surely overtake and shall surely rescue." ⁹So David set out, he and the six hundred men who were with him. They came to the Wadi Besor, where those stayed who were left behind. ¹⁰But David went on with the pursuit, he and four hundred men; two hundred stayed behind, too exhausted to cross the Wadi Besor.

11 In the open country they found an Egyptian, and brought him to David. They gave him bread and he ate; they gave him water to drink; ¹²they also gave him a piece of fig cake and two clusters of raisins. When he had eaten, his spirit revived; for he had not eaten bread or drunk water for three days and three nights. ¹³Then David said to him, "To whom do you belong? Where are you from?" He said, "I am a young man of Egypt, servant to an Amalekite. My master left me behind because I fell sick three days ago. ¹⁴We had made a raid on the Negeb of the Cherethites and on that which belongs to Judah and on the Negeb of Caleb; and we burned Ziklag down." ¹⁵David said to him, "Will you take me down to this raiding party?" He said, "Swear to me by God that you will not kill me, or hand me over to my master, and I will take you down to them."

16 When he had taken him down, they were spread out all over the ground, eating and drinking and dancing, because of the great amount of spoil they had taken from the land of the Philistines and from the land of Judah. ¹⁷David attacked them from twilight until the evening of the next day. Not one of them escaped, except four hundred young men, who mounted camels and fled. ¹⁸David recovered all that the Amalekites had taken; and David rescued his two wives. ¹⁹Nothing was missing, whether small or great, sons or daughters, spoil or anything that had been taken; David brought back everything. ²⁰David also captured all the flocks and herds, which were driven ahead of the other cattle; people said, "This is David's spoil."

21 Then David came to the two hundred

ᵃ Gk: Heb lacks *and go to the place . . . done well before me*   ᵇ Gk: Heb lacks *and all* men who had been too exhausted to follow David, and who had been left at the Wadi Besor. They went out to meet David and to meet the people who were with him. When David drew near to the people he saluted them. [22]Then all the corrupt and worthless fellows among the men who had gone with David said, "Because they did not go with us, we will not give them any of the spoil that we have recovered, except that each man may take his wife and children, and leave." [23]But David said, "You shall not do so, my brothers, with what the LORD has given us; he has preserved us and handed over to us the raiding party that attacked us. [24]Who would listen to you in this matter? For the share of the one who goes down into the battle shall be the same as the share of the one who stays by the baggage; they shall share alike." [25]From that day forward he made it a statute and an ordinance for Israel; it continues to the present day.

26 When David came to Ziklag, he sent part of the spoil to his friends, the elders of Judah, saying, "Here is a present for you from the spoil of the enemies of the LORD"; [27]it was for those in Bethel, in Ramoth of the Negeb, in Jattir, [28]in Aroer, in Siphmoth, in Eshtemoa, [29]in Racal, in the towns of the Jerahmeelites, in the towns of the Kenites, [30]in Hormah, in Borashan, in Athach, [31]in Hebron, all the places where David and his men had roamed.

31 The Death of Saul and His Sons

Now the Philistines fought against Israel; and the men of Israel fled before the Philistines, and many fell[a] on Mount Gilboa. [2]The Philistines overtook Saul and his sons; and the Philistines killed Jonathan and Abinadab and Malchishua, the sons of Saul. [3]The battle pressed hard upon Saul; the archers found him, and he was badly wounded by them. [4]Then Saul said to his armor-bearer, "Draw your sword and thrust me through with it, so that these uncircumcised may not come and thrust me through, and make sport of me." But his armor-bearer was unwilling; for he was terrified. So Saul took his own sword and fell upon it. [5]When his armor-bearer saw that Saul was dead, he also fell upon his sword and died with him. [6]So Saul and his three sons and his armor-bearer and all his men died together on the same day. [7]When the men of Israel who were on the other side of the valley and those beyond the Jordan saw that the men of Israel had fled and that Saul and his sons were dead, they forsook their towns and fled; and the Philistines came and occupied them.

8 The next day, when the Philistines came to strip the dead, they found Saul and his three sons fallen on Mount Gilboa. [9]They cut off his head, stripped off his armor, and sent messengers throughout the land of the Philistines to carry the good news to the houses of their idols and to the people. [10]They put his armor in the temple of Astarte;[b] and they fastened his body to the wall of Beth-shan. [11]But when the inhabitants of Jabesh-gilead heard what the Philistines had done to Saul, [12]all the valiant men set out, traveled all night long, and took the body of Saul and the bodies of his sons from the wall of Beth-shan. They came to Jabesh and burned them there. [13]Then they took their bones and buried them under the tamarisk tree in Jabesh, and fasted seven days.

a Heb *and they fell slain* b Heb plural

2 SAMUEL

GOD'S RELENTLESS LOVE

When You Really Mess Up . . .

Have you ever wondered where exactly we've gotten some of our images of who God is? For some people, God is like some cosmic record keeper of rights and wrongs. With this kind of God, no matter what you do, you're never quite good enough—you never quite measure up to God's ideal. And if you ever mess up in a big way, then you're loaded with so much guilt, darkness, and isolation that it's like you're totally beyond hope of a perfect God really *loving* you.

Perhaps you know exactly what this feels like.

This kind of thinking has a tremendous influence on how we live in our relationship with God, doesn't it? Maybe even more than we realize. If we were truly honest with ourselves, we would have to admit that much of what we do in our "faith" is just an attempt to please this record-keeping God so he will keep loving us.

But is this really how God *is*? Is this really what "faith" should be?

The book of 2 Samuel shows us that such a simplistic view of our relationship with God doesn't cut it. In it we find King David at his finest . . . and at his worst. Lusting, having an affair with a married woman who becomes pregnant, then setting up a murder to cover his tracks—major stuff. Yet the one thing that remains consistent throughout the entire story is the relentless love of God. God didn't turn a blind eye to David's sin. But God didn't turn his back on David either. He had a purpose for David, and in his love and mercy he worked through David's shortcomings to accomplish it. Despite David's sins, God's love remained steady, strong, and true. God just loved David. Period.

And so it is with *you* as well. God's love for you is relentless. And God is utterly committed to accomplishing his purpose for you.

WHO The books of 1 and 2 Samuel were shaped from fragments of many narratives. The authors and editors are unknown.

WHAT A historical record of David's kingship, God's promises to David, and the consequences of David's sin

WHEN The events in 1 and 2 Samuel took place ca. 1050–970 B.C.

WHERE Jerusalem begins to take center stage in 2 Samuel as the "City of David" (2 Samuel 5.7).

"We praise thee, O God; we acknowledge thee to be the Lord."
—St. Caesarius of Arles

PATH OF DISCIPLESHIP

When David tried to cover up and hide away his sin, God didn't let it happen. God pursued David by sending the prophet Nathan to confront him. God didn't let David toss away his authentic faith. Instead, God helped David confess the wrong he'd done and restored David's relationship with him.

During Mass, we confess our sins to God and to our brothers and sisters standing with us. If you think about it, that's kind of an unusual scene in today's society: people admitting *out loud and in front of other people* that they have failed. God wants to make all things new again. You. Me. All creation. Every inch of it. This is God's relentless pursuit: to bring love and peace.

This pursuit has a name. His name is Jesus. He challenges us to turn away from sin and live faithfully in relationship with him.

1 David Mourns for Saul and Jonathan

After the death of Saul, when David had returned from defeating the Amalekites, David remained two days in Ziklag. ²On the third day, a man came from Saul's camp, with his clothes torn and dirt on his head. When he came to David, he fell to the ground and did obeisance. ³David said to him, "Where have you come from?" He said to him, "I have escaped from the camp of Israel." ⁴David said to him, "How did things go? Tell me!" He answered, "The army fled from the battle, but also many of the army fell and died; and Saul and his son Jonathan also died." ⁵Then David asked the young man who was reporting to him, "How do you know that Saul and his son Jonathan died?" ⁶The young man reporting to him said, "I happened to be on Mount Gilboa; and there was Saul leaning on his spear, while the chariots and the horsemen drew close to him. ⁷When he looked behind him, he saw me, and called to me. I answered, 'Here sir.' ⁸And he said to me, 'Who are you?' I answered him, 'I am an Amalekite.' ⁹He said to me, 'Come, stand over me and kill me; for convulsions have seized me, and yet my life still lingers.' ¹⁰So I stood over him, and killed him, for I knew that he could not live after he had fallen. I took the crown that was on his head and the armlet that was on his arm, and I have brought them here to my lord."

11 Then David took hold of his clothes and tore them; and all the men who were with him did the same. ¹²They mourned and wept, and fasted until evening for Saul and for his son Jonathan, and for the army of the Lord and for the house of Israel, because they had fallen by the sword. ¹³David said to the young man who had reported to him, "Where do you come from?" He answered, "I am the son of a resident alien, an Amalekite." ¹⁴David said to him, "Were you not afraid to lift your hand to destroy the Lord's anointed?" ¹⁵Then David called one of the young men and said, "Come here and strike him down." So he struck him down and he died. ¹⁶David said to him, "Your blood be on your head; for your own mouth has testified against you, saying, 'I have killed the Lord's anointed.' "

17 David intoned this lamentation over Saul and his son Jonathan. ¹⁸(He ordered that The Song of the Bow[a] be taught to the people of Judah; it is written in the Book of Jashar.) He said:

¹⁹ Your glory, O Israel, lies slain upon your
    high places!
    How the mighty have fallen!
²⁰ Tell it not in Gath,

proclaim it not in the streets of Ashkelon;
or the daughters of the Philistines will
    rejoice,
    the daughters of the uncircumcised will
        exult.

²¹ You mountains of Gilboa,
    let there be no dew or rain upon you,
    nor bounteous fields![b]
For there the shield of the mighty was
    defiled,
    the shield of Saul, anointed with oil no
        more.

²² From the blood of the slain,
    from the fat of the mighty,
the bow of Jonathan did not turn back,
    nor the sword of Saul return empty.

²³ Saul and Jonathan, beloved and lovely!
    In life and in death they were not divided;
they were swifter than eagles,
    they were stronger than lions.

²⁴ O daughters of Israel, weep over Saul,
    who clothed you with crimson, in luxury,
    who put ornaments of gold on your
        apparel.

²⁵ How the mighty have fallen
    in the midst of the battle!

Jonathan lies slain upon your high places.
²⁶   I am distressed for you, my brother
        Jonathan;
greatly beloved were you to me;
    your love to me was wonderful,
    passing the love of women.

²⁷ How the mighty have fallen,
    and the weapons of war perished!

2 David Anointed King of Judah

After this David inquired of the Lord, "Shall I go up into any of the cities of Judah?" The Lord said to him, "Go up." David said, "To which shall I go up?" He said, "To Hebron." ²So David went up there, along with his two wives, Ahinoam of Jezreel, and Abigail the widow of Nabal of Carmel. ³David brought up the men who were with him, every one with his household; and they settled in the towns of Hebron. ⁴Then the people of Judah came, and there they anointed David king over the house of Judah.

When they told David, "It was the people of Jabesh-gilead who buried Saul," ⁵David sent messengers to the people of Jabesh-gilead, and said to them, "May you be blessed by the Lord, because you showed this loyalty to Saul your lord, and buried him! ⁶Now may the Lord show steadfast love and faithfulness to you!

a Heb that The Bow b Meaning of Heb uncertain

And I too will reward you because you have done this thing. [7]Therefore let your hands be strong, and be valiant; for Saul your lord is dead, and the house of Judah has anointed me king over them."

Ishbaal King of Israel

8 But Abner son of Ner, commander of Saul's army, had taken Ishbaal[a] son of Saul, and brought him over to Mahanaim. [9]He made him king over Gilead, the Ashurites, Jezreel, Ephraim, Benjamin, and over all Israel. [10]Ishbaal,[a] Saul's son, was forty years old when he began to reign over Israel, and he reigned two years. But the house of Judah followed David. [11]The time that David was king in Hebron over the house of Judah was seven years and six months.

The Battle of Gibeon

12 Abner son of Ner, and the servants of Ishbaal[a] son of Saul, went out from Mahanaim to Gibeon. [13]Joab son of Zeruiah, and the servants of David, went out and met them at the pool of Gibeon. One group sat on one side of the pool, while the other sat on the other side of the pool. [14]Abner said to Joab, "Let the young men come forward and have a contest before us." Joab said, "Let them come forward." [15]So they came forward and were counted as they passed by, twelve for Benjamin and Ishbaal[a] son of Saul, and twelve of the servants of David. [16]Each grasped his opponent by the head, and thrust his sword in his opponent's side; so they fell down together. Therefore that place was called Helkath-hazzurim,[b] which is at Gibeon. [17]The battle was very fierce that day; and Abner and the men of Israel were beaten by the servants of David.

18 The three sons of Zeruiah were there, Joab, Abishai, and Asahel. Now Asahel was as swift of foot as a wild gazelle. [19]Asahel pursued Abner, turning neither to the right nor to the left as he followed him. [20]Then Abner looked back and said, "Is it you, Asahel?" He answered, "Yes, it is." [21]Abner said to him, "Turn to your right or to your left, and seize one of the young men, and take his spoil." But Asahel would not turn away from following him. [22]Abner said again to Asahel, "Turn away from following me; why should I strike you to the ground? How then could I show my face to your brother Joab?" [23]But he refused to turn away. So Abner struck him in the stomach with the butt of his spear, so that the spear came out at his back. He fell there, and died where he lay. And all those who came to the place where Asahel had fallen and died, stood still.

24 But Joab and Abishai pursued Abner. As the sun was going down they came to the hill of Ammah, which lies before Giah on the way to the wilderness of Gibeon. [25]The Benjaminites rallied around Abner and formed a single band; they took their stand on the top of a hill. [26]Then Abner called to Joab, "Is the sword to keep devouring forever? Do you not know that the end will be bitter? How long will it be before you order your people to turn from the pursuit of their kinsmen?" [27]Joab said, "As God lives, if you had not spoken, the people would have continued to pursue their kinsmen, not stopping until morning." [28]Joab sounded the trumpet and all the people stopped; they no longer pursued Israel or engaged in battle any further.

29 Abner and his men traveled all that night through the Arabah; they crossed the Jordan, and, marching the whole forenoon,[c] they came to Mahanaim. [30]Joab returned from the pursuit of Abner; and when he had gathered all the people together, there were missing of David's servants nineteen men besides Asahel. [31]But the servants of David had killed of Benjamin three hundred sixty of Abner's men. [32]They took up Asahel and buried him in the tomb of his father, which was at Bethlehem. Joab and his men marched all night, and the day broke upon them at Hebron.

TEXT MESSAGE

Saul's shield (2 Samuel 1.21) would have been made of leather. If the shield was not anointed with oil, it would dry up, crack, and fall apart.

This information has been scanned and is free of all known viruses. Please forward to all your friends.

a Gk Compare 1 Chr 8.33; 9.39: Heb Ish-bosheth, "man of shame" b That is Field of Sword-edges c Meaning of Heb uncertain

3 Abner Defects to David

There was a long war between the house of Saul and the house of David; David grew stronger and stronger, while the house of Saul became weaker and weaker.

2 Sons were born to David at Hebron: his firstborn was Amnon, of Ahinoam of Jezreel; 3 his second, Chileab, of Abigail the widow of Nabal of Carmel; the third, Absalom son of Maacah, daughter of King Talmai of Geshur; 4 the fourth, Adonijah son of Haggith; the fifth, Shephatiah son of Abital; 5 and the sixth, Ithream, of David's wife Eglah. These were born to David in Hebron.

6 While there was war between the house of Saul and the house of David, Abner was making himself strong in the house of Saul. 7 Now Saul had a concubine whose name was Rizpah daughter of Aiah. And Ishbaal*a* said to Abner, "Why have you gone in to my father's concubine?" 8 The words of Ishbaal*b* made Abner very angry; he said, "Am I a dog's head for Judah? Today I keep showing loyalty to the house of your father Saul, to his brothers, and to his friends, and have not given you into the hand of David; and yet you charge me now with a crime concerning this woman. 9 So may God do to Abner and so may he add to it! For just what the LORD has sworn to David, that will I accomplish for him, 10 to transfer the kingdom from the house of Saul, and set up the throne of David over Israel and over Judah, from Dan to Beer-sheba." 11 And Ishbaal*a* could not answer Abner another word, because he feared him.

12 Abner sent messengers to David at Hebron,*c* saying, "To whom does the land belong? Make your covenant with me, and I will give you my support to bring all Israel over to you." 13 He said, "Good; I will make a covenant with you. But one thing I require of you: you shall never appear in my presence unless you bring Saul's daughter Michal when you come to see me." 14 Then David sent messengers to Saul's son Ishbaal,*d* saying, "Give me my wife Michal, to whom I became engaged at the price of one hundred foreskins of the Philistines." 15 Ishbaal*d* sent and took her from her husband Paltiel the son of Laish. 16 But her husband went with her, weeping as he walked behind her all the way to Bahurim. Then Abner said to him, "Go back home!" So he went back.

17 Abner sent word to the elders of Israel, saying, "For some time past you have been seeking David as king over you. 18 Now then bring it about; for the LORD has promised David: Through my servant David I will save my people Israel from the hand of the Philistines, and from all their enemies." 19 Abner also spoke directly to the Benjaminites; then Abner went to tell David at Hebron all that Israel and the whole house of Benjamin were ready to do.

20 When Abner came with twenty men to David at Hebron, David made a feast for Abner and the men who were with him. 21 Abner said to David, "Let me go and rally all Israel to my lord the king, in order that they may make a covenant with you, and that you may reign over all that your heart desires." So David dismissed Abner, and he went away in peace.

Abner Is Killed by Joab

22 Just then the servants of David arrived with Joab from a raid, bringing much spoil with them. But Abner was not with David at Hebron, for David*e* had dismissed him, and he had gone away in peace. 23 When Joab and all the army that was with him came, it was told Joab, "Abner son of Ner came to the king, and he has dismissed him, and he has gone away in peace." 24 Then Joab went to the king and said, "What have you done? Abner came to you; why did you dismiss him, so that he got away? 25 You know that Abner son of Ner came to deceive you, and to learn your comings and goings and to learn all that you are doing."

26 When Joab came out from David's presence, he sent messengers after Abner, and they brought him back from the cistern of Sirah; but David did not know about it. 27 When Abner returned to Hebron, Joab took him aside in the gateway to speak with him privately, and there he stabbed him in the stomach. So he died for shedding*f* the blood of Asahel, Joab's*g* brother. 28 Afterward, when David heard of it, he said, "I and my kingdom are forever guiltless before the LORD for the blood of Abner son of Ner. 29 May the guilt*h* fall on the head of Joab, and on all his father's house; and may the house of Joab never be without one who has a discharge, or who is leprous,*i* or who holds a spindle, or who falls by the sword, or who lacks food!" 30 So Joab and his brother Abishai murdered Abner because he had killed their brother Asahel in the battle at Gibeon.

31 Then David said to Joab and to all the people who were with him, "Tear your clothes, and put on sackcloth, and mourn over Abner." And King David followed the bier. 32 They buried Abner at Hebron. The king lifted up his voice and wept at the grave of Abner, and all the people wept. 33 The king lamented for Abner, saying,

---

a Heb *And he* *b* Gk Compare 1 Chr 8.33; 9.39: Heb *Ish-bosheth,* "man of shame" *c* Gk: Heb *where he was* *d* Heb *Ish-bosheth* *e* Heb *he* *f* Heb lacks *shedding* *g* Heb *his* *h* Heb *May it* *i* A term for several skin diseases; precise meaning uncertain

"Should Abner die as a fool dies?
³⁴ Your hands were not bound,
　　your feet were not fettered;
　as one falls before the wicked
　　you have fallen."

And all the people wept over him again. ³⁵Then all the people came to persuade David to eat something while it was still day; but David swore, saying, "So may God do to me, and more, if I taste bread or anything else before the sun goes down!" ³⁶All the people took notice of it, and it pleased them; just as everything the king did pleased all the people. ³⁷So all the people and all Israel understood that day that the king had no part in the killing of Abner son of Ner. ³⁸And the king said to his servants, "Do you not know that a prince and a great man has fallen this day in Israel? ³⁹Today I am powerless, even though anointed king; these men, the sons of Zeruiah, are too violent for me. The LORD pay back the one who does wickedly in accordance with his wickedness!"

4 Ishbaal Assassinated

When Saul's son Ishbaal^a heard that Abner had died at Hebron, his courage failed, and all Israel was dismayed. ²Saul's son had two captains of raiding bands; the name of the one was Baanah, and the name of the other Rechab. They were sons of Rimmon a Benjaminite from Beeroth—for Beeroth is considered to belong to Benjamin. ³(Now the people of Beeroth had fled to Gittaim and are there as resident aliens to this day).

4 Saul's son Jonathan had a son who was crippled in his feet. He was five years old when the news about Saul and Jonathan came from Jezreel. His nurse picked him up and fled; and, in her haste to flee, it happened that he fell and became lame. His name was Mephibosheth.^b

5 Now the sons of Rimmon the Beerothite, Rechab and Baanah, set out, and about the heat of the day they came to the house of Ishbaal,^c while he was taking his noonday rest. ⁶They came inside the house as though to take wheat, and they struck him in the stomach; then Rechab and his brother Baanah escaped.^d ⁷Now they had come into the house while he was lying on his couch in his bedchamber; they attacked him, killed him, and beheaded him. Then they took his head and traveled by way of the Arabah all night long. ⁸They brought the head of Ishbaal^c to David at Hebron and said to the king, "Here is the head of Ishbaal,^c son of Saul, your enemy, who sought your life; the LORD has avenged my lord the king this day on Saul and on his offspring."

9 David answered Rechab and his brother Baanah, the sons of Rimmon the Beerothite, "As the LORD lives, who has redeemed my life out of every adversity, ¹⁰when the one who told me, 'See, Saul is dead,' thought he was bringing good news, I seized him and killed him at Ziklag—this was the reward I gave him for his news. ¹¹How much more then, when wicked men have killed a righteous man on his bed in his own house! And now shall I not require his blood at your hand, and destroy you from the earth?" ¹²So David commanded the young men, and they killed them; they cut off their hands and feet, and hung their bodies beside the pool at Hebron. But the head of Ishbaal^c they took and buried in the tomb of Abner at Hebron.

5 David Anointed King of All Israel

Then all the tribes of Israel came to David at Hebron, and said, "Look, we are your bone and flesh. ²For some time, while Saul was king over us, it was you who led out Israel and brought it in. The LORD said to you: It is you who shall be shepherd of my people Israel, you who shall be ruler over Israel." ³So all the elders of Israel came to the king at Hebron; and King David made a covenant with them at Hebron before the LORD, and they anointed David king over Israel. ⁴David was thirty years old when he began to reign, and he reigned forty years. ⁵At Hebron he reigned over Judah seven years and six months; and at Jerusalem he reigned over all Israel and Judah thirty-three years.

Jerusalem Made Capital of the United Kingdom

6 The king and his men marched to Jerusalem against the Jebusites, the inhabitants of the land, who said to David, "You will not come in here, even the blind and the lame will turn you back"—thinking, "David cannot come in here." ⁷Nevertheless David took the stronghold of Zion, which is now the city of David. ⁸David had said on that day, "Whoever would strike down the Jebusites, let him get up the water shaft to attack the lame and the blind, those whom David hates."^e Therefore it is said,

---

a Heb lacks *Ishbaal* b In 1 Chr 8.34 and 9.40, *Merib-baal* c Heb *Ish-bosheth* d Meaning of Heb of verse 6 uncertain e Another reading is *those who hate David* their idols there, and David and his men carried them away.

22 Once again the Philistines came up, and were spread out in the valley of Rephaim. [23]When David inquired of the LORD, he said, "You shall not go up; go around to their rear, and come upon them opposite the balsam trees. [24]When you hear the sound of marching in the tops of the balsam trees, then be on the alert; for then the LORD has gone out before you to strike down the army of the Philistines." [25]David did just as the LORD had commanded him; and he struck down the Philistines from Geba all the way to Gezer.

6 David Brings the Ark to Jerusalem

David again gathered all the chosen men of Israel, thirty thousand. [2]David and all the people with him set out and went from Baale-judah, to bring up from there the ark of God, which is called by the name of the LORD of hosts who is enthroned on the cherubim. [3]They carried the ark of God on a new cart, and brought it out of the house of Abinadab, which was on the hill. Uzzah and Ahio,[c] the sons of Abinadab, were driving the new cart [4]with the ark of God;[d] and Ahio[c] went in front of the ark. [5]David and all the house of Israel were dancing before the LORD with all their might, with songs[e] and lyres and harps and tambourines and castanets and cymbals.

6 When they came to the threshing floor of Nacon, Uzzah reached out his hand to the ark of God and took hold of it, for the oxen shook it. [7]The anger of the LORD was kindled against Uzzah; and God struck him there because he reached out his hand to the ark;[f] and he died there beside the ark of God. [8]David was angry because the LORD had burst forth with an outburst upon Uzzah; so that place is called Perez-uzzah,[g] to this day. [9]David was afraid of the LORD that day; he said, "How can the ark of the LORD come into my care?" [10]So David was unwilling to take the ark of the LORD into his care in the city of David; instead David took it to the house of Obed-edom the Gittite. [11]The ark of the LORD remained in the house of Obed-edom the Gittite three months; and the LORD blessed Obed-edom and all his household.

12 It was told King David, "The LORD has blessed the household of Obed-edom and all that belongs to him, because of the ark of God." So David went and brought up the ark of God from the house of Obed-edom to the city of David with rejoicing; [13]and when those who bore the ark of the LORD had gone six paces, he sacri-

Columbine Flower—© Rachel Hostert, 18

"The blind and the lame shall not come into the house." [9]David occupied the stronghold, and named it the city of David. David built the city all around from the Millo inward. [10]And David became greater and greater, for the LORD, the God of hosts, was with him.

11 King Hiram of Tyre sent messengers to David, along with cedar trees, and carpenters and masons who built David a house. [12]David then perceived that the LORD had established him king over Israel, and that he had exalted his kingdom for the sake of his people Israel.

13 In Jerusalem, after he came from Hebron, David took more concubines and wives; and more sons and daughters were born to David. [14]These are the names of those who were born to him in Jerusalem: Shammua, Shobab, Nathan, Solomon, [15]Ibhar, Elishua, Nepheg, Japhia, [16]Elishama, Eliada, and Eliphelet.

Philistine Attack Repulsed

17 When the Philistines heard that David had been anointed king over Israel, all the Philistines went up in search of David; but David heard about it and went down to the stronghold. [18]Now the Philistines had come and spread out in the valley of Rephaim. [19]David inquired of the LORD, "Shall I go up against the Philistines? Will you give them into my hand?" The LORD said to David, "Go up; for I will certainly give the Philistines into your hand." [20]So David came to Baal-perazim, and David defeated them there. He said, "The LORD has burst forth against[a] my enemies before me, like a bursting flood." Therefore that place is called Baal-perazim.[b] [21]The Philistines abandoned

---

a Heb *paraz* *b* That is *Lord of Bursting Forth* *c* Or *and his brother* *d* Compare Gk: Heb *and brought it out of the house of Abinadab, which was on the hill with the ark of God* *e* Q Ms Gk 1 Chr 13.8: Heb *fir trees* *f* 1 Chr 13.10 Compare Q Ms: Meaning of Heb uncertain *g* That is *Bursting Out Against Uzzah* ficed an ox and a fatling. ¹⁴David danced before the LORD with all his might; David was girded with a linen ephod. ¹⁵So David and all the house of Israel brought up the ark of the LORD with shouting, and with the sound of the trumpet.

16 As the ark of the LORD came into the city of David, Michal daughter of Saul looked out of the window, and saw King David leaping and dancing before the LORD; and she despised him in her heart.

17 They brought in the ark of the LORD, and set it in its place, inside the tent that David had pitched for it; and David offered burnt offerings and offerings of well-being before the LORD. ¹⁸When David had finished offering the burnt offerings and the offerings of well-being, he blessed the people in the name of the LORD of hosts, ¹⁹and distributed food among all the people, the whole multitude of Israel, both men and women, to each a cake of bread, a portion of meat,ᵃ and a cake of raisins. Then all the people went back to their homes.

20 David returned to bless his household. But Michal the daughter of Saul came out to meet David, and said, "How the king of Israel honored himself today, uncovering himself today before the eyes of his servants' maids, as any vulgar fellow might shamelessly uncover himself!" ²¹David said to Michal, "It was before the LORD, who chose me in place of your father and all his household, to appoint me as prince over Israel, the people of the LORD, that I have danced before the LORD. ²²I will make myself yet more contemptible than this, and I will be abased in my own eyes; but by the maids of whom you have spoken, by them I shall be held in honor." ²³And Michal the daughter of Saul had no child to the day of her death.

7 God's Covenant with David

Now when the king was settled in his house, and the LORD had given him rest from all his enemies around him, ²the king said to the prophet Nathan, "See now, I am living in a house of cedar, but the ark of God stays in a tent." ³Nathan said to the king, "Go, do all that you have in mind; for the LORD is with you."

4 But that same night the word of the LORD came to Nathan: ⁵Go and tell my servant David: Thus says the LORD: Are you the one to build me a house to live in? ⁶I have not lived in a house since the day I brought up the people of Israel from Egypt to this day, but I have been moving about in a tent and a tabernacle. ⁷Wherever I have moved about among all the people of Israel, did I ever speak a word with any of the tribal

leadersᵇ of Israel, whom I commanded to shepherd my people Israel, saying, "Why have you not built me a house of cedar?" ⁸Now therefore thus you shall say to my servant David: Thus says the LORD of hosts: I took you from the pasture, from following the sheep to be prince over my people Israel; ⁹and I have been with you wherever you went, and have cut off all your enemies from before you; and I will make for you a great name, like the name of the great ones of the earth. ¹⁰And I will appoint a place for my people Israel and will plant them, so that they may live in their own place, and be disturbed no more; and evildoers shall afflict them no more, as formerly, ¹¹from the time that I appointed judges over my people Israel; and I will give you rest from all your enemies. Moreover the LORD declares to you that the LORD will make you a house. ¹²When your days are fulfilled and you lie down with your ancestors, I will raise up your offspring after you, who shall come forth from your body, and I will establish his kingdom. ¹³He shall build a house for my name, and I will establish the throne of his kingdom forever. ¹⁴I will be a father to him, and he shall be a son to me. When he commits iniquity, I will punish him with a rod such as mortals use, with blows inflicted by human beings. ¹⁵But I will not takeᶜ my steadfast love from him, as I took it from Saul, whom I put away from before you. ¹⁶Your house and your kingdom shall be made sure forever before me;ᵈ your throne shall be established forever. ¹⁷In accordance with all these words and with all this vision, Nathan spoke to David.

David's Prayer

18 Then King David went in and sat before the LORD, and said, "Who am I, O Lord GOD, and what is my house, that you have brought me thus far? ¹⁹And yet this was a small thing in your eyes, O Lord GOD; you have spoken also of your servant's house for a great while to come. May this be instruction for the people,ᵉ O Lord GOD! ²⁰And what more can David say to you? For you know your servant, O Lord GOD! ²¹Because of your promise, and according to your own heart, you have wrought all this greatness, so that your servant may know it. ²²Therefore you are great, O LORD God; for there is no one like you, and there is no God besides you, according to all that we have heard with our ears. ²³Who is like your people, like Israel? Is there anotherᶠ nation on earth whose God went to redeem it as a people, and to make a name for himself, doing great and awesome

ᵃ Vg: Meaning of Heb uncertain ᵇ Or *any of the tribes* ᶜ Gk Syr Vg 1 Chr 17.13: Heb *shall not depart* ᵈ Gk Heb Mss: MT *before you*; Compare 2 Sam 7.26, 29 ᵉ Meaning of Heb uncertain ᶠ Gk: Heb *one* things for them,[a] by driving out[b] before his people nations and their gods?[c] [24]And you established your people Israel for yourself to be your people forever; and you, O LORD, became their God. [25]And now, O LORD God, as for the word that you have spoken concerning your servant and concerning his house, confirm it forever; do as you have promised. [26]Thus your name will be magnified forever in the saying, 'The LORD of hosts is God over Israel'; and the house of your servant David will be established before you. [27]For you, O LORD of hosts, the God of Israel, have made this revelation to your servant, saying, 'I will build you a house'; therefore your servant has found courage to pray this prayer to you. [28]And now, O Lord GOD, you are God, and your words are true, and you have promised this good thing to your servant; [29]now therefore may it please you to bless the house of your servant, so that it may continue forever before you; for you, O Lord GOD, have spoken, and with your blessing shall the house of your servant be blessed forever."

8 David's Wars

Some time afterward, David attacked the Philistines and subdued them; David took Methegammah out of the hand of the Philistines.

[2] He also defeated the Moabites and, making them lie down on the ground, measured them off with a cord; he measured two lengths of cord for those who were to be put to death, and one length[d] for those who were to be spared. And the Moabites became servants to David and brought tribute.

[3] David also struck down King Hadadezer son of Rehob of Zobah, as he went to restore his monument[e] at the river Euphrates. [4]David took from him one thousand seven hundred horsemen, and twenty thousand foot soldiers. David hamstrung all the chariot horses, but left enough for a hundred chariots. [5]When the Arameans of Damascus came to help King Hadadezer of Zobah, David killed twenty-two thousand men of the Arameans. [6]Then David put garrisons among the Arameans of Damascus; and the Arameans became servants to David and brought tribute. The LORD gave victory to David wherever he went. [7]David took the gold shields that were carried by the servants of Hadadezer, and brought them to Jerusalem. [8]From Betah and from Berothai, towns of Hadadezer, King David took a great amount of bronze.

[9] When King Toi of Hamath heard that David had defeated the whole army of Hadadezer, [10]Toi sent his son Joram to King David, to greet him and to congratulate him because he had fought against Hadadezer and defeated him. Now Hadadezer had often been at war with Toi. Joram brought with him articles of silver, gold, and bronze; [11]these also King David dedicated to the LORD, together with the silver and gold that he dedicated from all the nations he subdued, [12]from Edom, Moab, the Ammonites, the Philistines, Amalek, and from the spoil of King Hadadezer son of Rehob of Zobah.

13 David won a name for himself. When he returned, he killed eighteen thousand Edomites[f] in the Valley of Salt. [14]He put garrisons in Edom; throughout all Edom he put garrisons, and all the Edomites became David's servants. And the LORD gave victory to David wherever he went.

David's Officers

15 So David reigned over all Israel; and David administered justice and equity to all his people. [16]Joab son of Zeruiah was over the army; Jehoshaphat son of Ahilud was recorder; [17]Zadok son of Ahitub and Ahimelech son of Abiathar were priests; Seraiah was secretary; [18]Benaiah son of Jehoiada was over[g] the Cherethites and the Pelethites; and David's sons were priests.

9 David's Kindness to Mephibosheth

David asked, "Is there still anyone left of the house of Saul to whom I may show kindness for Jonathan's sake?" [2]Now there was a servant of the house of Saul whose name was Ziba, and he was summoned to David. The king said to him, "Are you Ziba?" And he said, "At your service!" [3]The king said, "Is there anyone remaining of the house of Saul to whom I may show the kindness of God?" Ziba said to the king, "There remains a son of Jonathan; he is crippled in his feet." [4]The king said to him, "Where is he?" Ziba said to the king, "He is in the house of Machir son of Ammiel, at Lo-debar." [5]Then King David sent and brought him from the house of Machir son of Ammiel, at Lo-debar. [6]Mephibosheth[h] son of Jonathan son of Saul came to David, and fell on his face and did obeisance. David said, "Mephibosheth!"[h] He answered, "I am your servant." [7]David said to him, "Do not be afraid, for I will show you kindness for the sake of your father Jonathan; I will restore to you all the land of your grandfather Saul, and you yourself shall eat at my table always." [8]He did obeisance and said, "What is your servant, that you should look upon a dead dog such as I?"

a Heb you b Gk 1 Chr 17.21: Heb for your land c Cn: Heb before your people, whom you redeemed for yourself from Egypt, nations and its gods d Heb one full length e Compare 1 Sam 15.12 and 2 Sam 18.18 f Gk: Heb returned from striking down eighteen thousand Arameans g Syr Tg Vg 20.23; 1 Chr 18.17: Heb lacks was over h Or Merib-baal : See 4.4 note

PROFILE OF FAITH

Dorothy Day's passion for peace and practice of justice embodied Catholic social teaching in action.

Day used her gifts as a writer to be a voice for the poor, the lonely, the immigrants, and the homeless. She marched, she fasted, she protested, and she spent time in jail—all in the name of Christ, who calls us to feed the hungry, clothe the naked, and welcome the stranger.

In 1933, she established the *Catholic Worker* newspaper, which was distributed in the streets of New York City for a penny a copy. The newspaper grew into something much bigger than Day had ever imagined, and the Catholic Worker movement was born. Within three short years—during the Great Depression—thirty-three Catholic Worker houses of hospitality sprang up throughout the United States.

Unfortunately, many of the conditions that caused Dorothy Day to start the Catholic Worker movement still exist. Today, thousands of volunteers support more than 185 Catholic Worker houses throughout the United States, Canada, Mexico, and Europe. These volunteers make it *their* business to live in community, provide hospitality to the homeless, and follow a path of nonviolence. And the *Catholic Worker* newspaper? It still sells for a penny a copy.

If your path to discipleship is calling you to serve like Dorothy Day, make it *your* business to find out more about the Catholic Worker movement at **Learner.CalltoDiscipleship.com**. While there, post a note to let us know about your passion for peace and the practice of justice.

---

9 Then the king summoned Saul's servant Ziba, and said to him, "All that belonged to Saul and to all his house I have given to your master's grandson. ¹⁰You and your sons and your servants shall till the land for him, and shall bring in the produce, so that your master's grandson may have food to eat; but your master's grandson Mephibosheth*a* shall always eat at my table." Now Ziba had fifteen sons and twenty servants. ¹¹Then Ziba said to the king, "According to all that my lord the king commands his servant, so your servant will do." Mephibosheth*a* ate at David's*b* table, like one of the king's sons. ¹²Mephibosheth*a* had a young son whose name was Mica. And all who lived in Ziba's house became Mephibosheth's*c* servants. ¹³Mephibosheth*a* lived in Jerusalem, for he always ate at the king's table. Now he was lame in both his feet.

10 The Ammonites and Arameans Are Defeated

Some time afterward, the king of the Ammonites died, and his son Hanun succeeded him. ²David said, "I will deal loyally with Hanun son of Nahash, just as his father dealt loyally with me." So David sent envoys to console him concerning his father. When David's envoys came into the land of the Ammonites, ³the princes of the Ammonites said to their lord Hanun, "Do you really think that David is honoring your father just because he has sent messengers with condolences to you? Has not David sent his envoys to you to search the city, to spy it out, and to overthrow it?" ⁴So Hanun seized David's envoys, shaved off half the beard of each, cut off their garments in the middle at their hips, and sent them away. ⁵When David was told, he sent to meet them, for the men were greatly ashamed. The king said, "Remain at Jericho until your beards have grown, and then return."

6 When the Ammonites saw that they had become odious to David, the Ammonites sent and hired the Arameans of Beth-rehob and the Arameans of Zobah, twenty thousand foot soldiers, as well as the king of Maacah, one thousand men, and the men of Tob, twelve thousand men. ⁷When David heard of it, he sent Joab and all the army with the warriors. ⁸The Ammonites came out and drew up in battle array at the entrance of the gate; but the Arameans of Zobah and of Rehob, and the men of Tob and Maacah, were by themselves in the open country.

---

a Or *Merib-baal:* See 4.4 note *b* Gk: Heb *my* *c* Or *Merib-baal's:* See 4.4 note

9 When Joab saw that the battle was set against him both in front and in the rear, he chose some of the picked men of Israel, and arrayed them against the Arameans; [10]the rest of his men he put in the charge of his brother Abishai, and he arrayed them against the Ammonites. [11]He said, "If the Arameans are too strong for me, then you shall help me; but if the Ammonites are too strong for you, then I will come and help you. [12]Be strong, and let us be courageous for the sake of our people, and for the cities of our God; and may the LORD do what seems good to him." [13]So Joab and the people who were with him moved forward into battle against the Arameans; and they fled before him. [14]When the Ammonites saw that the Arameans fled, they likewise fled before Abishai, and entered the city. Then Joab returned from fighting against the Ammonites, and came to Jerusalem.

15 But when the Arameans saw that they had been defeated by Israel, they gathered themselves together. [16]Hadadezer sent and brought out the Arameans who were beyond the Euphrates; and they came to Helam, with Shobach the commander of the army of Hadadezer at their head. [17]When it was told David, he gathered all Israel together, and crossed the Jordan, and came to Helam. The Arameans arrayed themselves against David and fought with him. [18]The Arameans fled before Israel; and David killed of the Arameans seven hundred chariot teams, and forty thousand horsemen,[a] and wounded Shobach the commander of their army, so that he died there. [19]When all the kings who were servants of Hadadezer saw that they had been defeated by Israel, they made peace with Israel, and became subject to them. So the Arameans were afraid to help the Ammonites any more.

11 David Commits Adultery with Bathsheba

In the spring of the year, the time when kings go out to battle, David sent Joab with his officers and all Israel with him; they ravaged the Ammonites, and besieged Rabbah. But David remained at Jerusalem.

2 It happened, late one afternoon, when David rose from his couch and was walking about on the roof of the king's house, that he saw from the roof a woman bathing; the woman was very beautiful. [3]David sent someone to inquire about the woman. It was reported, "This is Bathsheba daughter of Eliam, the wife of Uriah the Hittite." [4]So David sent messengers to get her, and she came to him, and he lay with her. (Now she was purifying herself after her period.) Then she returned to her house. [5]The woman conceived; and she sent and told David, "I am pregnant."

6 So David sent word to Joab, "Send me Uriah the Hittite." And Joab sent Uriah to David. [7]When Uriah came to him, David asked how Joab and the people fared, and how the war was going. [8]Then David said to Uriah, "Go down to your house, and wash your feet." Uriah went out of the king's house, and there followed him a present from the king. [9]But Uriah slept at the entrance of the king's house with all the servants of his lord, and did not go down to his house. [10]When they told David, "Uriah did not go down to his house," David said to Uriah, "You have just come from a journey. Why did you not go down to your house?" [11]Uriah said to David, "The ark and Israel and Judah remain in booths;[b] and my lord Joab and the servants of my lord are camping in the open field; shall I then go to my house, to eat and to drink, and to lie with my wife? As you live, and as your soul lives, I will not do such a thing." [12]Then David said to Uriah, "Remain here today also, and tomorrow I will send you back." So Uriah remained in Jerusalem that day. On the next day, [13]David invited him to eat and drink in his presence and made him drunk; and in the evening he went out to lie on his couch with the servants of his lord, but he did not go down to his house.

David Has Uriah Killed

14 In the morning David wrote a letter to Joab, and sent it by the hand of Uriah. [15]In the letter he wrote, "Set Uriah in the forefront of the hardest fighting, and then draw back from him, so that he may be struck down and die." [16]As Joab was besieging the city, he assigned Uriah to the place where he knew there were valiant warriors. [17]The men of the city came out and fought with Joab; and some of the servants of David among the people fell. Uriah the Hittite was killed as well. [18]Then Joab sent and told David all the news about the fighting; [19]and he instructed the messenger, "When you have finished telling the king all the news about the fighting, [20]then, if the king's anger rises, and if he says to you, 'Why did you go so near the city to fight? Did you not know that they would shoot from the wall? [21]Who killed Abimelech son of Jerubbaal?[c] Did not a woman throw an upper millstone on him from the wall, so that he died at Thebez? Why did you go so near the wall?' then you shall say, 'Your servant Uriah the Hittite is dead too.' "

22 So the messenger went, and came and

---

a 1 Chr 19.18 and some Gk Mss read *foot soldiers* b Or *at Succoth* c Gk Syr Judg 7.1: Heb *Jerubbesheth* told David all that Joab had sent him to tell. ²³The messenger said to David, "The men gained an advantage over us, and came out against us in the field; but we drove them back to the entrance of the gate. ²⁴Then the archers shot at your servants from the wall; some of the king's servants are dead; and your servant Uriah the Hittite is dead also." ²⁵David said to the messenger, "Thus you shall say to Joab, 'Do not let this matter trouble you, for the sword devours now one and now another; press your attack on the city, and overthrow it.' And encourage him."

26 When the wife of Uriah heard that her husband was dead, she made lamentation for him. ²⁷When the mourning was over, David sent and brought her to his house, and she became his wife, and bore him a son.

Nathan Condemns David

But the thing that David had done displeased **12** the LORD, ¹and the LORD sent Nathan to David. He came to him, and said to him, "There were two men in a certain city, the one rich and the other poor. ²The rich man had very many flocks and herds; ³but the poor man had nothing but one little ewe lamb, which he had bought. He brought it up, and it grew up with him and with his children; it used to eat of his meager fare, and drink from his cup, and lie in his bosom, and it was like a daughter to him. ⁴Now there came a traveler to the rich man, and he was loath to take one of his own flock or herd to prepare for the wayfarer who had come to him, but he took the poor man's lamb, and prepared that for the guest who had come to him." ⁵Then David's anger was greatly kindled against the man. He said to Nathan, "As the LORD lives, the man who has done this deserves to die; ⁶he shall restore the lamb fourfold, because he did this thing, and because he had no pity."

7 Nathan said to David, "You are the man! Thus says the LORD, the God of Israel: I anointed you king over Israel, and I rescued you from the hand of Saul; ⁸I gave you your master's house, and your master's wives into your bosom, and gave you the house of Israel and of Judah; and if that had been too little, I would have added as much more. ⁹Why have you despised the word of the LORD, to do what is evil in his sight? You have struck down Uriah the Hittite with the sword, and have taken his wife to be your wife, and have killed him with the sword of the Ammonites. ¹⁰Now therefore the sword shall never depart from your house, for you have despised me, and have taken the wife of Uriah the Hittite to be your wife. ¹¹Thus says the LORD: I will raise up trouble against you from within your own house; and I will take

Through the Trees—© Rachel Hostert, 18

your wives before your eyes, and give them to your neighbor, and he shall lie with your wives in the sight of this very sun. ¹²For you did it secretly; but I will do this thing before all Israel, and before the sun." ¹³David said to Nathan, "I have sinned against the LORD." Nathan said to David, "Now the LORD has put away your sin; you shall not die. ¹⁴Nevertheless, because by

Sun—© Maggie Hubbard, 15

this deed you have utterly scorned the LORD,ᵃ the child that is born to you shall die." ¹⁵Then Nathan went to his house.

Bathsheba's Child Dies

The LORD struck the child that Uriah's wife bore to David, and it became very ill. ¹⁶David therefore pleaded with God for the child; David fasted, and went in and lay all night on the ground. ¹⁷The elders of his house stood beside him, urging him to rise from the ground; but he would not, nor did he eat food with them. ¹⁸On the seventh day the child died. And the servants of David were afraid to tell him that the child was dead; for they said, "While the child was still alive, we spoke to him, and he did not listen to us; how then can we tell him the child is dead? He may do himself some harm." ¹⁹But when David saw that his servants were whispering together, he perceived that the child was dead; and David said to his servants, "Is the child dead?" They said, "He is dead."

20 Then David rose from the ground, washed, anointed himself, and changed his clothes. He went into the house of the LORD, and worshiped; he then went to his own house; and when he asked, they set food before him and he ate. ²¹Then his servants said to him, "What is this thing that you have done? You fasted and wept for the child while it was alive; but when the child died, you rose and ate food." ²²He said, "While the child was still alive, I fasted and wept; for I said, 'Who knows? The LORD may be gracious to me, and the child may live.' ²³But now he is dead; why should I fast? Can I bring him back again? I shall go to him, but he will not return to me."

Solomon Is Born

24 Then David consoled his wife Bathsheba, and went to her, and lay with her; and she bore a son, and he named him Solomon. The LORD loved him, ²⁵and sent a message by the prophet Nathan; so he named him Jedidiah,ᵇ because of the LORD.

The Ammonites Crushed

26 Now Joab fought against Rabbah of the Ammonites, and took the royal city. ²⁷Joab sent messengers to David, and said, "I have fought against Rabbah; moreover, I have taken the water city. ²⁸Now, then, gather the rest of the people together, and encamp against the city, and take it; or I myself will take the city, and it will be called by my name." ²⁹So David gathered all the people together and went to Rabbah, and fought against it and took it. ³⁰He took the crown of Milcomᶜ from his head; the weight of it was a talent of gold, and in it was a precious stone; and it was placed on David's head. He also brought forth the spoil of the city, a very great amount. ³¹He brought out the people who were in it, and set them to work with saws and iron picks and iron axes, or sent them to the brickworks. Thus he did to all the cities of the Ammonites. Then David and all the people returned to Jerusalem.

13 Amnon and Tamar

Some time passed. David's son Absalom had a beautiful sister whose name was Tamar; and David's son Amnon fell in love with her. ²Amnon was so tormented that he made himself ill because of his sister Tamar, for she was a virgin and it seemed impossible to Amnon to do anything to her. ³But Amnon had a friend whose name was Jonadab, the son of David's brother Shimeah; and Jonadab was a very crafty man. ⁴He said to him, "O son of the king, why are you so haggard morning after morning? Will you not tell me?" Amnon said to him, "I love Tamar, my brother Absalom's sister." ⁵Jonadab said to him, "Lie down on your bed, and pretend to be ill; and when your father comes to see you, say to him, 'Let my sister Tamar come and give me something to eat, and prepare the food in my sight, so that I may see it and eat it from her hand.' " ⁶So Amnon lay down, and pretended to be ill; and when the king came to see him, Amnon said to the king, "Please let my sister Tamar come and make a couple of cakes in my sight, so that I may eat from her hand."

7 Then David sent home to Tamar, saying, "Go to your brother Amnon's house, and prepare food for him." ⁸So Tamar went to her

---

a Ancient scribal tradition: Compare 1 Sam 25.22 note: Heb *scorned the enemies of the* LORD *b* That is *Beloved of the* LORD *c* Gk See 1 Kings 11.5, 33: Heb *their kings* brother Amnon's house, where he was lying down. She took dough, kneaded it, made cakes in his sight, and baked the cakes. [9]Then she took the pan and set them[a] out before him, but he refused to eat. Amnon said, "Send out everyone from me." So everyone went out from him. [10]Then Amnon said to Tamar, "Bring the food into the chamber, so that I may eat from your hand." So Tamar took the cakes she had made, and brought them into the chamber to Amnon her brother. [11]But when she brought them near him to eat, he took hold of her, and said to her, "Come, lie with me, my sister." [12]She answered him, "No, my brother, do not force me; for such a thing is not done in Israel; do not do anything so vile! [13]As for me, where could I carry my shame? And as for you, you would be as one of the scoundrels in Israel. Now therefore, I beg you, speak to the king; for he will not withhold me from you." [14]But he would not listen to her; and being stronger than she, he forced her and lay with her.

15 Then Amnon was seized with a very great loathing for her; indeed, his loathing was even greater than the lust he had felt for her. Amnon said to her, "Get out!" [16]But she said to him, "No, my brother;[b] for this wrong in sending me away is greater than the other that you did to me." But he would not listen to her. [17]He called the young man who served him and said, "Put this woman out of my presence, and bolt the door after her." [18](Now she was wearing a long robe with sleeves; for this is how the virgin daughters of the king were clothed in earlier times.[c]) So his servant put her out, and bolted the door after her. [19]But Tamar put ashes on her head, and tore the long robe that she was wearing; she put her hand on her head, and went away, crying aloud as she went.

20 Her brother Absalom said to her, "Has Amnon your brother been with you? Be quiet for now, my sister; he is your brother; do not take this to heart." So Tamar remained, a desolate woman, in her brother Absalom's house. [21]When King David heard of all these things, he became very angry, but he would not punish his son Amnon, because he loved him, for he was his firstborn.[d] [22]But Absalom spoke to Amnon neither good nor bad; for Absalom hated Amnon, because he had raped his sister Tamar.

Absalom Avenges the Violation of His Sister

23 After two full years Absalom had sheepshearers at Baal-hazor, which is near Ephraim, and Absalom invited all the king's sons. [24]Absalom came to the king, and said, "Your ser-vant has sheepshearers; will the king and his servants please go with your servant?" [25]But the king said to Absalom, "No, my son, let us not all go, or else we will be burdensome to you." He pressed him, but he would not go but gave him his blessing. [26]Then Absalom said, "If not, please let my brother Amnon go with us." The king said to him, "Why should he go with you?" [27]But Absalom pressed him until he let Amnon and all the king's sons go with him. Absalom made a feast like a king's feast.[e] [28]Then Absalom commanded his servants, "Watch when Amnon's heart is merry with wine, and when I say to you, 'Strike Amnon,' then kill him. Do not be afraid; have I not myself commanded you? Be courageous and valiant." [29]So the servants of Absalom did to Amnon as Absalom had commanded. Then all the king's sons rose, and each mounted his mule and fled.

30 While they were on the way, the report came to David that Absalom had killed all the king's sons, and not one of them was left. [31]The king rose, tore his garments, and lay on the ground; and all his servants who were standing by tore their garments. [32]But Jonadab, the son of David's brother Shimeah, said, "Let not my lord suppose that they have killed all the young men the king's sons; Amnon alone is dead. This has been determined by Absalom from the day Amnon[f] raped his sister Tamar. [33]Now therefore, do not let my lord the king take it to heart, as if all the king's sons were dead; for Amnon alone is dead."

34 But Absalom fled. When the young man who kept watch looked up, he saw many people coming from the Horonaim road[g] by the side of the mountain. [35]Jonadab said to the king, "See, the king's sons have come; as your servant said, so it has come about." [36]As soon as he had finished speaking, the king's sons arrived, and raised their voices and wept; and the king and all his servants also wept very bitterly.

37 But Absalom fled, and went to Talmai son of Ammihud, king of Geshur. David mourned for his son day after day. [38]Absalom, having fled to Geshur, stayed there three years. [39]And the heart of[h] the king went out, yearning for Absalom; for he was now consoled over the death of Amnon.

14

Absalom Returns to Jerusalem

Now Joab son of Zeruiah perceived that the king's mind was on Absalom. [2]Joab sent to Tekoa and brought from there a wise woman. He said to her, "Pretend to be a mourner; put on mourning garments, do not anoint your-

---

a Heb and poured b Cn Compare Gk Vg: Meaning of Heb uncertain c Cn: Heb were clothed in robes d Q Ms Gk: MT lacks but he would not punish . . . firstborn e Gk Compare Q Ms: MT lacks Absalom made a feast like a king's feast f Heb he g Cn Compare Gk: Heb the road behind him h Q Ms Gk: MT And David self with oil, but behave like a woman who has been mourning many days for the dead. ³Go to the king and speak to him as follows." And Joab put the words into her mouth.

4 When the woman of Tekoa came to the king, she fell on her face to the ground and did obeisance, and said, "Help, O king!" ⁵The king asked her, "What is your trouble?" She answered, "Alas, I am a widow; my husband is dead. ⁶Your servant had two sons, and they fought with one another in the field; there was no one to part them, and one struck the other and killed him. ⁷Now the whole family has risen against your servant. They say, 'Give up the man who struck his brother, so that we may kill him for the life of his brother whom he murdered, even if we destroy the heir as well.' Thus they would quench my one remaining ember, and leave to my husband neither name nor remnant on the face of the earth."

8 Then the king said to the woman, "Go to your house, and I will give orders concerning you." ⁹The woman of Tekoa said to the king, "On me be the guilt, my lord the king, and on my father's house; let the king and his throne be guiltless." ¹⁰The king said, "If anyone says anything to you, bring him to me, and he shall never touch you again." ¹¹Then she said, "Please, may the king keep the Lord your God in mind, so that the avenger of blood may kill no more, and my son not be destroyed." He said, "As the Lord lives, not one hair of your son shall fall to the ground."

12 Then the woman said, "Please let your servant speak a word to my lord the king." He said, "Speak." ¹³The woman said, "Why then have you planned such a thing against the people of God? For in giving this decision the king convicts himself, inasmuch as the king does not bring his banished one home again. ¹⁴We must all die; we are like water spilled on the ground, which cannot be gathered up. But God will not take away a life; he will devise plans so as not to keep an outcast banished forever from his presence.ᵃ ¹⁵Now I have come to say this to my lord the king because the people have made me afraid; your servant thought, 'I will speak to the king; it may be that the king will perform the request of his servant. ¹⁶For the king will hear, and deliver his servant from the hand of the man who would cut both me and my son off from the heritage of God.' ¹⁷Your servant thought, 'The word of my lord the king will set me at rest'; for my lord the king is like the angel of God, discerning good and evil. The Lord your God be with you!"

18 Then the king answered the woman, "Do not withhold from me anything I ask you." The woman said, "Let my lord the king speak." ¹⁹The king said, "Is the hand of Joab with you in all this?" The woman answered and said, "As surely as you live, my lord the king, one cannot turn right or left from anything that my lord the king has said. For it was your servant Joab who commanded me; it was he who put all these words into the mouth of your servant. ²⁰In order to change the course of affairs your servant Joab did this. But my lord has wisdom like the wisdom of the angel of God to know all things that are on the earth."

21 Then the king said to Joab, "Very well, I grant this; go, bring back the young man Absalom." ²²Joab prostrated himself with his face to the ground and did obeisance, and blessed the king; and Joab said, "Today your servant knows that I have found favor in your sight, my lord the king, in that the king has granted the request of his servant." ²³So Joab set off, went to Geshur, and brought Absalom to Jerusalem. ²⁴The king said, "Let him go to his own house; he is not to come into my presence." So Absalom went to his own house, and did not come into the king's presence.

David Forgives Absalom

25 Now in all Israel there was no one to be praised so much for his beauty as Absalom; from the sole of his foot to the crown of his head there was no blemish in him. ²⁶When he cut the hair of his head (for at the end of every year he used to cut it; when it was heavy on him, he cut it), he weighed the hair of his head, two hundred shekels by the king's weight. ²⁷There were born to Absalom three sons, and one daughter whose name was Tamar; she was a beautiful woman.

28 So Absalom lived two full years in Jerusalem, without coming into the king's presence. ²⁹Then Absalom sent for Joab to send him to the king; but Joab would not come to him. He sent a second time, but Joab would not come. ³⁰Then he said to his servants, "Look, Joab's field is next to mine, and he has barley there; go and set it on fire." So Absalom's servants set the field on fire. ³¹Then Joab rose and went to Absalom at his house, and said to him, "Why have your servants set my field on fire?" ³²Absalom answered Joab, "Look, I sent word to you: Come here, that I may send you to the king with the question, 'Why have I come from Geshur? It would be better for me to be there still.' Now let me go into the king's presence; if there is guilt in me, let him kill me!" ³³Then Joab went to the king and told him; and he summoned

ᵃ Meaning of Heb uncertain

Absalom. So he came to the king and prostrated himself with his face to the ground before the king; and the king kissed Absalom.

15 Absalom Usurps the Throne

After this Absalom got himself a chariot and horses, and fifty men to run ahead of him. ²Absalom used to rise early and stand beside the road into the gate; and when anyone brought a suit before the king for judgment, Absalom would call out and say, "From what city are you?" When the person said, "Your servant is of such and such a tribe in Israel," ³Absalom would say, "See, your claims are good and right; but there is no one deputed by the king to hear you." ⁴Absalom said moreover, "If only I were judge in the land! Then all who had a suit or cause might come to me, and I would give them justice." ⁵Whenever people came near to do obeisance to him, he would put out his hand and take hold of them, and kiss them. ⁶Thus Absalom did to every Israelite who came to the king for judgment; so Absalom stole the hearts of the people of Israel.

7 At the end of four*ᵃ* years Absalom said to the king, "Please let me go to Hebron and pay the vow that I have made to the LORD. ⁸For your servant made a vow while I lived at Geshur in Aram: If the LORD will indeed bring me back to Jerusalem, then I will worship the LORD in Hebron."*ᵇ* ⁹The king said to him, "Go in peace." So he got up, and went to Hebron. ¹⁰But Absa-

lom sent secret messengers throughout all the tribes of Israel, saying, "As soon as you hear the sound of the trumpet, then shout: Absalom has become king at Hebron!" ¹¹Two hundred men from Jerusalem went with Absalom; they were invited guests, and they went in their innocence, knowing nothing of the matter. ¹²While Absalom was offering the sacrifices, he sent for*ᶜ* Ahithophel the Gilonite, David's counselor, from his city Giloh. The conspiracy grew in strength, and the people with Absalom kept increasing.

David Flees from Jerusalem

13 A messenger came to David, saying, "The hearts of the Israelites have gone after Absalom." ¹⁴Then David said to all his officials who were with him at Jerusalem, "Get up! Let us flee, or there will be no escape for us from Absalom. Hurry, or he will soon overtake us, and bring disaster down upon us, and attack the city with the edge of the sword." ¹⁵The king's officials said to the king, "Your servants are ready to do whatever our lord the king decides." ¹⁶So the king left, followed by all his household, except ten concubines whom he left behind to look after the house. ¹⁷The king left, followed by all the people; and they stopped at the last house. ¹⁸All his officials passed by him; and all the Cherethites, and all the Pelethites, and all the six hundred Gittites who had followed him from Gath, passed on before the king.

a Gk Syr: Heb *forty* *b* Gk Mss: Heb lacks *in Hebron* *c* Or *he sent*

Guided by Light—© Lexi Hiland, 16

19 Then the king said to Ittai the Gittite, "Why are you also coming with us? Go back, and stay with the king; for you are a foreigner, and also an exile from your home. 20You came only yesterday, and shall I today make you wander about with us, while I go wherever I can? Go back, and take your kinsfolk with you; and may the LORD show[a] steadfast love and faithfulness to you." 21But Ittai answered the king, "As the LORD lives, and as my lord the king lives, wherever my lord the king may be, whether for death or for life, there also your servant will be." 22David said to Ittai, "Go then, march on." So Ittai the Gittite marched on, with all his men and all the little ones who were with him. 23The whole country wept aloud as all the people passed by; the king crossed the Wadi Kidron, and all the people moved on toward the wilderness.

24 Abiathar came up, and Zadok also, with all the Levites, carrying the ark of the covenant of God. They set down the ark of God, until the people had all passed out of the city. 25Then the king said to Zadok, "Carry the ark of God back into the city. If I find favor in the eyes of the LORD, he will bring me back and let me see both it and the place where it stays. 26But if he says, 'I take no pleasure in you,' here I am, let him do to me what seems good to him." 27The king also said to the priest Zadok, "Look,[b] go back to the city in peace, you and Abiathar,[c] with your two sons, Ahimaaz your son, and Jonathan son of Abiathar. 28See, I will wait at the fords of the wilderness until word comes from you to inform me." 29So Zadok and Abiathar carried the ark of God back to Jerusalem, and they remained there.

30 But David went up the ascent of the Mount of Olives, weeping as he went, with his head covered and walking barefoot; and all the people who were with him covered their heads and went up, weeping as they went. 31David was told that Ahithophel was among the conspirators with Absalom. And David said, "O LORD, I pray you, turn the counsel of Ahithophel into foolishness."

Hushai Becomes David's Spy

32 When David came to the summit, where God was worshiped, Hushai the Archite came to meet him with his coat torn and earth on his head. 33David said to him, "If you go on with me, you will be a burden to me. 34But if you return to the city and say to Absalom, 'I will be your servant, O king; as I have been your father's servant in time past, so now I will be your servant,' then you will defeat for me the counsel of Ahithophel. 35The priests Zadok and Abiathar will be with you there. So whatever you hear from the king's house, tell it to the priests Zadok and Abiathar. 36Their two sons are with them there, Zadok's son Ahimaaz and Abiathar's son Jonathan; and by them you shall report to me everything you hear." 37So Hushai, David's friend, came into the city, just as Absalom was entering Jerusalem.

16 David's Adversaries

When David had passed a little beyond the summit, Ziba the servant of Mephibosheth[d] met him, with a couple of donkeys saddled, carrying two hundred loaves of bread, one hundred bunches of raisins, one hundred of summer fruits, and one skin of wine. 2The king said to Ziba, "Why have you brought these?" Ziba answered, "The donkeys are for the king's household to ride, the bread and summer fruit for the young men to eat, and the wine is for those to drink who faint in the wilderness." 3The king said, "And where is your master's son?" Ziba said to the king, "He remains in Jerusalem; for he said, 'Today the house of Israel will give me back my grandfather's kingdom.'" 4Then the king said to Ziba, "All that belonged to Mephibosheth[d] is now yours." Ziba said, "I do obeisance; let me find favor in your sight, my lord the king."

Shimei Curses David

5 When King David came to Bahurim, a man of the family of the house of Saul came out whose name was Shimei son of Gera; he came out cursing. 6He threw stones at David and at all the servants of King David; now all the people and all the warriors were on his right and on his left. 7Shimei shouted while he cursed, "Out! Out! Murderer! Scoundrel! 8The LORD has avenged on all of you the blood of the house of Saul, in whose place you have reigned; and the LORD has given the kingdom into the hand of your son Absalom. See, disaster has overtaken you; for you are a man of blood."

9 Then Abishai son of Zeruiah said to the king, "Why should this dead dog curse my lord the king? Let me go over and take off his head." 10But the king said, "What have I to do with you, you sons of Zeruiah? If he is cursing because the LORD has said to him, 'Curse David,' who then shall say, 'Why have you done so?'" 11David said to Abishai and to all his servants, "My own son seeks my life; how much more now may this Benjaminite! Let him alone, and let him curse; for the LORD has bidden him. 12It may be that the LORD will look on my dis-

a Gk Compare 2.6: Heb lacks may the LORD show   b Gk: Heb Are you a seer or Do you see?   c Cn: Heb lacks and Abiathar   d Or Merib-baal: See 4.4 note tress,[a] and the LORD will repay me with good for this cursing of me today." [13]So David and his men went on the road, while Shimei went along on the hillside opposite him and cursed as he went, throwing stones and flinging dust at him. [14]The king and all the people who were with him arrived weary at the Jordan;[b] and there he refreshed himself.

The Counsel of Ahithophel

15 Now Absalom and all the Israelites[c] came to Jerusalem; Ahithophel was with him. [16]When Hushai the Archite, David's friend, came to Absalom, Hushai said to Absalom, "Long live the king! Long live the king!" [17]Absalom said to Hushai, "Is this your loyalty to your friend? Why did you not go with your friend?" [18]Hushai said to Absalom, "No; but the one whom the LORD and this people and all the Israelites have chosen, his I will be, and with him I will remain. [19]Moreover, whom should I serve? Should it not be his son? Just as I have served your father, so I will serve you."

20 Then Absalom said to Ahithophel, "Give us your counsel; what shall we do?" [21]Ahithophel said to Absalom, "Go in to your father's concubines, the ones he has left to look after the house; and all Israel will hear that you have made yourself odious to your father, and the hands of all who are with you will be strengthened." [22]So they pitched a tent for Absalom upon the roof; and Absalom went in to his father's concubines in the sight of all Israel. [23]Now in those days the counsel that Ahithophel gave was as if one consulted the oracle[d] of God; so all the counsel of Ahithophel was esteemed, both by David and by Absalom.

17 Moreover Ahithophel said to Absalom, "Let me choose twelve thousand men, and I will set out and pursue David tonight. [2]I will come upon him while he is weary and discouraged, and throw him into a panic; and all the people who are with him will flee. I will strike down only the king, [3]and I will bring all the people back to you as a bride comes home to her husband. You seek the life of only one man,[e] and all the people will be at peace." [4]The advice pleased Absalom and all the elders of Israel.

The Counsel of Hushai

5 Then Absalom said, "Call Hushai the Archite also, and let us hear too what he has to say." [6]When Hushai came to Absalom, Absalom said to him, "This is what Ahithophel has said; shall we do as he advises? If not, you tell us." [7]Then Hushai said to Absalom, "This time the coun-

sel that Ahithophel has given is not good." [8]Hushai continued, "You know that your father and his men are warriors, and that they are enraged, like a bear robbed of her cubs in the field. Besides, your father is expert in war; he will not spend the night with the troops. [9]Even now he has hidden himself in one of the pits, or in some other place. And when some of our troops[f] fall at the first attack, whoever hears it will say, 'There has been a slaughter among the troops who follow Absalom.' [10]Then even the valiant warrior, whose heart is like the heart of a lion, will utterly melt with fear; for all Israel knows that your father is a warrior, and that those who are with him are valiant warriors. [11]But my counsel is that all Israel be gathered to you, from Dan to Beer-sheba, like the sand

---

a Gk Vg: Heb iniquity b Gk: Heb lacks at the Jordan c Gk: Heb all the people, the men of Israel d Heb word e Gk: Heb like the return of the whole (is) the man whom you seek f Gk Mss: Heb some of them by the sea for multitude, and that you go to battle in person. [12]So we shall come upon him in whatever place he may be found, and we shall light on him as the dew falls on the ground; and he will not survive, nor will any of those with him. [13]If he withdraws into a city, then all Israel will bring ropes to that city, and we shall drag it into the valley, until not even a pebble is to be found there." [14]Absalom and all the men of Israel said, "The counsel of Hushai the Archite is better than the counsel of Ahithophel." For the LORD had ordained to defeat the good counsel of Ahithophel, so that the LORD might bring ruin on Absalom.

Hushai Warns David to Escape

15 Then Hushai said to the priests Zadok and Abiathar, "Thus and so did Ahithophel counsel Absalom and the elders of Israel; and thus and so I have counseled. [16]Therefore send quickly and tell David, 'Do not lodge tonight at the fords of the wilderness, but by all means cross over; otherwise the king and all the people who are with him will be swallowed up.' " [17]Jonathan and Ahimaaz were waiting at Enrogel; a servant-girl used to go and tell them, and they would go and tell King David; for they could not risk being seen entering the city. [18]But a boy saw them, and told Absalom; so both of them went away quickly, and came to the house of a man at Bahurim, who had a well in his courtyard; and they went down into it. [19]The man's wife took a covering, stretched it over the well's mouth, and spread out grain on it; and nothing was known of it. [20]When Absalom's servants came to the woman at the house, they said, "Where are Ahimaaz and Jonathan?" The woman said to them, "They have crossed over the brook[a] of water." And when they had searched and could not find them, they returned to Jerusalem.

21 After they had gone, the men came up out of the well, and went and told King David. They said to David, "Go and cross the water quickly; for thus and so has Ahithophel counseled against you." [22]So David and all the people who were with him set out and crossed the Jordan; by daybreak not one was left who had not crossed the Jordan.

23 When Ahithophel saw that his counsel was not followed, he saddled his donkey and went off home to his own city. He set his house in order, and hanged himself; he died and was buried in the tomb of his father.

24 Then David came to Mahanaim, while Absalom crossed the Jordan with all the men of Israel. [25]Now Absalom had set Amasa over

a Meaning of Heb uncertain

the army in the place of Joab. Amasa was the son of a man named Ithra the Ishmaelite,[a] who had married Abigal daughter of Nahash, sister of Zeruiah, Joab's mother. [26]The Israelites and Absalom encamped in the land of Gilead.

27 When David came to Mahanaim, Shobi son of Nahash from Rabbah of the Ammonites, and Machir son of Ammiel from Lo-debar, and Barzillai the Gileadite from Rogelim, [28]brought beds, basins, and earthen vessels, wheat, barley, meal, parched grain, beans and lentils,[b] [29]honey and curds, sheep, and cheese from the herd, for David and the people with him to eat; for they said, "The troops are hungry and weary and thirsty in the wilderness."

18 The Defeat and Death of Absalom

Then David mustered the men who were with him, and set over them commanders of thousands and commanders of hundreds. [2]And David divided the army into three groups:[c] one third under the command of Joab, one third under the command of Abishai son of Zeruiah, Joab's brother, and one third under the command of Ittai the Gittite. The king said to the men, "I myself will also go out with you." [3]But the men said, "You shall not go out. For if we flee, they will not care about us. If half of us die, they will not care about us. But you are worth ten thousand of us;[d] therefore it is better that you send us help from the city." [4]The king said to them, "Whatever seems best to you I will do." So the king stood at the side of the gate, while all the army marched out by hundreds and by thousands. [5]The king ordered Joab and Abishai and Ittai, saying, "Deal gently for my sake with the young man Absalom." And all the people heard when the king gave orders to all the commanders concerning Absalom.

6 So the army went out into the field against Israel; and the battle was fought in the forest of Ephraim. [7]The men of Israel were defeated there by the servants of David, and the slaughter there was great on that day, twenty thousand men. [8]The battle spread over the face of all the country; and the forest claimed more victims that day than the sword.

9 Absalom happened to meet the servants of David. Absalom was riding on his mule, and the mule went under the thick branches of a great oak. His head caught fast in the oak, and he was left hanging[e] between heaven and earth, while the mule that was under him went on. [10]A man saw it, and told Joab, "I saw Absalom hanging in an oak." [11]Joab said to the man who told him, "What, you saw him! Why then did you not

strike him there to the ground? I would have been glad to give you ten pieces of silver and a belt." [12]But the man said to Joab, "Even if I felt in my hand the weight of a thousand pieces of silver, I would not raise my hand against the king's son; for in our hearing the king commanded you and Abishai and Ittai, saying: For my sake protect the young man Absalom! [13]On the other hand, if I had dealt treacherously against his life[f] (and there is nothing hidden from the king), then you yourself would have stood aloof." [14]Joab said, "I will not waste time like this with you." He took three spears in his hand, and thrust them into the heart of Absalom, while he was still alive in the oak. [15]And ten young men, Joab's armor-bearers, surrounded Absalom and struck him, and killed him.

16 Then Joab sounded the trumpet, and the troops came back from pursuing Israel, for Joab restrained the troops. [17]They took Absalom, threw him into a great pit in the forest, and raised over him a very great heap of stones. Meanwhile all the Israelites fled to their homes. [18]Now Absalom in his lifetime had taken and set up for himself a pillar that is in the King's Valley, for he said, "I have no son to keep my name in remembrance"; he called the pillar by his own name. It is called Absalom's Monument to this day.

David Hears of Absalom's Death

19 Then Ahimaaz son of Zadok said, "Let me run, and carry tidings to the king that the LORD has delivered him from the power of his enemies." [20]Joab said to him, "You are not to carry tidings today; you may carry tidings another day, but today you shall not do so, because the king's son is dead." [21]Then Joab said to a Cushite, "Go, tell the king what you have seen." The Cushite bowed before Joab, and ran. [22]Then Ahimaaz son of Zadok said again to Joab, "Come what may, let me also run after the Cushite." And Joab said, "Why will you run, my son, seeing that you have no reward[g] for the tidings?" [23]"Come what may," he said, "I will run." So he said to him, "Run." Then Ahimaaz ran by the way of the Plain, and outran the Cushite.

24 Now David was sitting between the two gates. The sentinel went up to the roof of the gate by the wall, and when he looked up, he saw a man running alone. [25]The sentinel shouted and told the king. The king said, "If he is alone, there are tidings in his mouth." He kept coming, and drew near. [26]Then the sentinel saw another man running; and the sentinel called to the gatekeeper and said, "See, another man

---

a 1 Chr 2.17: Heb Israelite b Heb and lentils and parched grain c Gk: Heb sent forth the army d Gk Vg Symmachus: Heb for now there are ten thousand such as we e Gk Syr Tg: Heb was put f Another reading is at the risk of my life g Meaning of Heb uncertain running alone!" The king said, "He also is bringing tidings." [27]The sentinel said, "I think the running of the first one is like the running of Ahimaaz son of Zadok." The king said, "He is a good man, and comes with good tidings."

[28] Then Ahimaaz cried out to the king, "All is well!" He prostrated himself before the king with his face to the ground, and said, "Blessed be the LORD your God, who has delivered up the men who raised their hand against my lord the king." [29]The king said, "Is it well with the young man Absalom?" Ahimaaz answered, "When Joab sent your servant,[a] I saw a great tumult, but I do not know what it was." [30]The king said, "Turn aside, and stand here." So he turned aside, and stood still.

[31] Then the Cushite came; and the Cushite said, "Good tidings for my lord the king! For the LORD has vindicated you this day, delivering you from the power of all who rose up against you." [32]The king said to the Cushite, "Is it well with the young man Absalom?" The Cushite answered, "May the enemies of my lord the king, and all who rise up to do you harm, be like that young man."

David Mourns for Absalom

[33b] The king was deeply moved, and went up to the chamber over the gate, and wept; and as he went, he said, "O my son Absalom, my son, my son Absalom! Would I had died instead of you, O Absalom, my son, my son!"

19 It was told Joab, "The king is weeping and mourning for Absalom." [2]So the victory that day was turned into mourning for all the troops; for the troops heard that day, "The king is grieving for his son." [3]The troops stole into the city that day as soldiers steal in who are ashamed when they flee in battle. [4]The king covered his face, and the king cried with a loud voice, "O my son Absalom, O Absalom, my son, my son!" [5]Then Joab came into the house to the king, and said, "Today you have covered with shame the faces of all your officers who have saved your life today, and the lives of your sons and your daughters, and the lives of your wives and your concubines, [6]for love of those who hate you and for hatred of those who love you. You have made it clear today that commanders and officers are nothing to you; for I perceive that if Absalom were alive and all of us were dead today, then you would be pleased. [7]So go out at once and speak kindly to your servants; for I swear by the LORD, if you do not go, not a man will stay with you this night; and this will be worse for you than any disaster that has come upon you from your youth until now."

[8]Then the king got up and took his seat in the gate. The troops were all told, "See, the king is sitting in the gate"; and all the troops came before the king.

David Recalled to Jerusalem

Meanwhile, all the Israelites had fled to their homes. [9]All the people were disputing throughout all the tribes of Israel, saying, "The king delivered us from the hand of our enemies, and saved us from the hand of the Philistines; and now he has fled out of the land because of Absalom. [10]But Absalom, whom we anointed over us, is dead in battle. Now therefore why do you say nothing about bringing the king back?"

[11] King David sent this message to the priests Zadok and Abiathar, "Say to the elders of Judah, 'Why should you be the last to bring the king back to his house? The talk of all Israel has come to the king.[c] [12]You are my kin, you are my bone and my flesh; why then should you be the last to bring back the king?' [13]And say to Amasa, 'Are you not my bone and my flesh? So may God do to me, and more, if you are not the commander of my army from now on, in place of Joab.' " [14]Amasa[d] swayed the hearts of all the people of Judah as one, and they sent word to the king, "Return, both you and all your servants." [15]So the king came back to the Jordan; and Judah came to Gilgal to meet the king and to bring him over the Jordan.

[16] Shimei son of Gera, the Benjaminite, from Bahurim, hurried to come down with the people of Judah to meet King David; [17]with him were a thousand people from Benjamin. And Ziba, the servant of the house of Saul, with his fifteen sons and his twenty servants, rushed down to the Jordan ahead of the king, [18]while the crossing was taking place,[e] to bring over the king's household, and to do his pleasure.

David's Mercy to Shimei

Shimei son of Gera fell down before the king, as he was about to cross the Jordan, [19]and said to the king, "May my lord not hold me guilty or remember how your servant did wrong on the day my lord the king left Jerusalem; may the king not bear it in mind. [20]For your servant knows that I have sinned; therefore, see, I have come this day, the first of all the house of Joseph to come down to meet my lord the king." [21]Abishai son of Zeruiah answered, "Shall not Shimei be put to death for this, because he cursed the LORD's anointed?" [22]But David said, "What have I to do with you, you sons of Zeruiah, that you should today become an adversary to me? Shall anyone be put to death in Israel this

---

a Heb *the king's servant, your servant* *b* Ch 19.1 in Heb *c* Gk: Heb *to the king, to his house* *d* Heb *He* *e* Cn: Heb *the ford crossed* day? For do I not know that I am this day king over Israel?" ²³The king said to Shimei, "You shall not die." And the king gave him his oath.

David and Mephibosheth Meet

24 Mephibosheth*a* grandson of Saul came down to meet the king; he had not taken care of his feet, or trimmed his beard, or washed his clothes, from the day the king left until the day he came back in safety. ²⁵When he came from Jerusalem to meet the king, the king said to him, "Why did you not go with me, Mephibosheth?"*a* ²⁶He answered, "My lord, O king, my servant deceived me; for your servant said to him, 'Saddle a donkey for me,*b* so that I may ride on it and go with the king.' For your servant is lame. ²⁷He has slandered your servant to my lord the king. But my lord the king is like the angel of God; do therefore what seems good to you. ²⁸For all my father's house were doomed to death before my lord the king; but you set your servant among those who eat at your table. What further right have I, then, to appeal to the king?" ²⁹The king said to him, "Why speak any more of your affairs? I have decided: you and Ziba shall divide the land." ³⁰Mephibosheth*a* said to the king, "Let him take it all, since my lord the king has arrived home safely."

David's Kindness to Barzillai

31 Now Barzillai the Gileadite had come down from Rogelim; he went on with the king to the Jordan, to escort him over the Jordan. ³²Barzillai was a very aged man, eighty years old. He had provided the king with food while he stayed at Mahanaim, for he was a very wealthy man. ³³The king said to Barzillai, "Come over with me, and I will provide for you in Jerusalem at my side." ³⁴But Barzillai said to the king, "How many years have I still to live, that I should go up with the king to Jerusalem? ³⁵Today I am eighty years old; can I discern what is pleasant and what is not? Can your servant taste what he eats or what he drinks? Can I still listen to the voice of singing men and singing women? Why then should your servant be an added burden to my lord the king? ³⁶Your servant will go a little way over the Jordan with the king. Why should the king recompense me with such a reward? ³⁷Please let your servant return, so that I may die in my own town, near the graves of my father and my mother. But here is your servant Chimham; let him go over with my lord the king; and do for him whatever seems good to you." ³⁸The king answered, "Chimham shall go over with me, and I will do for him whatever seems good to you; and all that you desire of me I will do for you." ³⁹Then all the people crossed over the Jordan, and the king crossed over; the king kissed Barzillai and blessed him, and he returned to his own home. ⁴⁰The king went on to Gilgal, and Chimham went on with him; all the people of Judah, and also half the people of Israel, brought the king on his way.

a Or Merib-baal: See 4.4 note *b* Gk Syr Vg: Heb *said, 'I will saddle a donkey for myself*

41 Then all the people of Israel came to the king, and said to him, "Why have our kindred the people of Judah stolen you away, and brought the king and his household over the Jordan, and all David's men with him?" 42All the people of Judah answered the people of Israel, "Because the king is near of kin to us. Why then are you angry over this matter? Have we eaten at all at the king's expense? Or has he given us any gift?" 43But the people of Israel answered the people of Judah, "We have ten shares in the king, and in David also we have more than you. Why then did you despise us? Were we not the first to speak of bringing back our king?" But the words of the people of Judah were fiercer than the words of the people of Israel.

20 The Rebellion of Sheba

Now a scoundrel named Sheba son of Bichri, a Benjaminite, happened to be there. He sounded the trumpet and cried out,

"We have no portion in David,
    no share in the son of Jesse!
Everyone to your tents, O Israel!"

2So all the people of Israel withdrew from David and followed Sheba son of Bichri; but the people of Judah followed their king steadfastly from the Jordan to Jerusalem.

3 David came to his house at Jerusalem; and the king took the ten concubines whom he had left to look after the house, and put them in a house under guard, and provided for them, but did not go in to them. So they were shut up until the day of their death, living as if in widowhood.

4 Then the king said to Amasa, "Call the men of Judah together to me within three days, and be here yourself." 5So Amasa went to summon Judah; but he delayed beyond the set time that had been appointed him. 6David said to Abishai, "Now Sheba son of Bichri will do us more harm than Absalom; take your lord's servants and pursue him, or he will find fortified cities for himself, and escape from us." 7Joab's men went out after him, along with the Cherethites, the Pelethites, and all the warriors; they went out from Jerusalem to pursue Sheba son of Bichri. 8When they were at the large stone that is in Gibeon, Amasa came to meet them. Now Joab was wearing a soldier's garment and over it was a belt with a sword in its sheath fastened at his waist; as he went forward it fell out. 9Joab said to Amasa, "Is it well with you, my brother?" And Joab took Amasa by the beard with his right hand to kiss him. 10But Amasa did not notice the sword in Joab's hand; Joab struck him in the belly so that his entrails poured out on the ground, and he died. He did not strike a second blow.

Then Joab and his brother Abishai pursued Sheba son of Bichri. 11And one of Joab's men took his stand by Amasa, and said, "Whoever favors Joab, and whoever is for David, let him follow Joab." 12Amasa lay wallowing in his blood on the highway, and the man saw that all the people were stopping. Since he saw that all who came by him were stopping, he carried Amasa from the highway into a field, and threw a garment over him. 13Once he was removed from the highway, all the people went on after Joab to pursue Sheba son of Bichri.

14 Sheba*a* passed through all the tribes of Israel to Abel of Beth-maacah;*b* and all the Bichrites*c* assembled, and followed him inside. 15Joab's forces*d* came and besieged him in Abel of Beth-maacah; they threw up a siege ramp against the city, and it stood against the rampart. Joab's forces were battering the wall to break it down. 16Then a wise woman called from the city, "Listen! Listen! Tell Joab, 'Come here, I want to speak to you.' " 17He came near her; and the woman said, "Are you Joab?" He answered, "I am." Then she said to him, "Listen to the words of your servant." He answered, "I am listening." 18Then she said, "They used to say in the old days, 'Let them inquire at Abel'; and so they would settle a matter. 19I am one of those who are peaceable and faithful in Israel; you seek to destroy a city that is a mother in Israel; why will you swallow up the heritage of the LORD?" 20Joab answered, "Far be it from me, far be it, that I should swallow up or destroy! 21That is not the case! But a man of the hill country of Ephraim, called Sheba son of Bichri, has lifted up his hand against King David; give him up alone, and I will withdraw from the city." The woman said to Joab, "His head shall be thrown over the wall to you." 22Then the woman went to all the people with her wise plan. And they cut off the head of Sheba son of Bichri, and threw it out to Joab. So he blew the trumpet, and they dispersed from the city, and all went to their homes, while Joab returned to Jerusalem to the king.

23 Now Joab was in command of all the army of Israel;*e* Benaiah son of Jehoiada was in command of the Cherethites and the Pelethites; 24Adoram was in charge of the forced labor; Jehoshaphat son of Ahilud was the recorder; 25Sheva was secretary; Zadok and Abiathar were priests; 26and Ira the Jairite was also David's priest.

---

a Heb He b Compare 20.15: Heb and Beth-maacah c Compare Gk Vg: Heb Berites d Heb They e Cn: Heb Joab to all the army, Israel

HOME

Forever is Your kindness,
Forever is Your grace,
Forever You have loved me,
Though I have never seen Your face.
I have knocked upon Your door,
And You have welcomed me with love.
Who knew I had a special Friend
In the heavens up above?
When the time arrives
For You to call my name,
My soul will fly towards You,
And I will never be the same.
For then I'll live forever
With the Father that loves me so,
And when I enter those pearly gates
I would know,
I am finally home.

Home—© Jessica Jones, 17

Untitled—© Leah Colasuonno, 15

HOME

Forever is Your kindness,
Forever is Your grace,
Forever You have loved me,
Though I have never seen Your face.
I have knocked upon Your door,
And You have welcomed me with love.
Who knew I had a special Friend
In the heavens up above?
When the time arrives
For You to call my name,
My soul will fly towards You,
And I will never be the same.
For then I'll live forever
With the Father that loves me so,
And when I enter those pearly gates
I would know,
I am finally home.

Silhouette of God's Grace—© Josi Martin, 17

21 David Avenges the Gibeonites

Now there was a famine in the days of David for three years, year after year; and David inquired of the LORD. The LORD said, "There is bloodguilt on Saul and on his house, because he put the Gibeonites to death." ²So the king called the Gibeonites and spoke to them. (Now the Gibeonites were not of the people of Israel, but of the remnant of the Amorites; although the people of Israel had sworn to spare them, Saul had tried to wipe them out in his zeal for the people of Israel and Judah.) ³David said to the Gibeonites, "What shall I do for you? How shall I make expiation, that you may bless the heritage of the LORD?" ⁴The Gibeonites said to him, "It is not a matter of silver or gold between us and Saul or his house; neither is it for us to put anyone to death in Israel." He said, "What do you say that I should do for you?" ⁵They said to the king, "The man who consumed us and planned to destroy us, so that we should have no place in all the territory of Israel— ⁶let seven of his sons be handed over to us, and we will impale them before the LORD at Gibeon on the mountain of the LORD."ᵃ The king said, "I will hand them over."

7 But the king spared Mephibosheth,ᵇ the son of Saul's son Jonathan, because of the oath of the LORD that was between them, between David and Jonathan son of Saul. ⁸The king took the two sons of Rizpah daughter of Aiah, whom she bore to Saul, Armoni and Mephibosheth;ᵇ and the five sons of Merabᶜ daughter of Saul, whom she bore to Adriel son of Barzillai the Meholathite; ⁹he gave them into the hands of the Gibeonites, and they impaled them on the mountain before the LORD. The seven of them perished together. They were put to death in the first days of harvest, at the beginning of barley harvest.

10 Then Rizpah the daughter of Aiah took sackcloth, and spread it on a rock for herself, from the beginning of harvest until rain fell on them from the heavens; she did not allow the birds of the air to come on the bodiesᵈ by day, or the wild animals by night. ¹¹When David was told what Rizpah daughter of Aiah, the concubine of Saul, had done, ¹²David went and took the bones of Saul and the bones of his son Jonathan from the people of Jabesh-gilead, who had stolen them from the public square of Beth-shan, where the Philistines had hung them up, on the day the Philistines killed Saul on Gilboa. ¹³He brought up from there the bones of Saul and the bones of his son Jonathan; and they gathered the bones of those who had been impaled. ¹⁴They buried the bones of Saul and of his son Jonathan in the land of Benjamin in Zela, in the tomb of his father Kish; they did all that the king commanded. After that, God heeded supplications for the land.

a Cn Compare Gk and 21.9: Heb *at Gibeah of Saul, the chosen of the LORD* *b* Or *Merib-baal*: See 4.4 note *c* Two Heb Mss Syr Compare Gk: MT *Michal* *d* Heb *them*

Exploits of David's Men

15 The Philistines went to war again with Israel, and David went down together with his servants. They fought against the Philistines, and David grew weary. 16Ishbi-benob, one of the descendants of the giants, whose spear weighed three hundred shekels of bronze, and who was fitted out with new weapons,*a* said he would kill David. 17But Abishai son of Zeruiah came to his aid, and attacked the Philistine and killed him. Then David's men swore to him, "You shall not go out with us to battle any longer, so that you do not quench the lamp of Israel."

18 After this a battle took place with the Philistines, at Gob; then Sibbecai the Hushathite killed Saph, who was one of the descendants of the giants. 19Then there was another battle with the Philistines at Gob; and Elhanan son of Jaare-oregim, the Bethlehemite, killed Goliath the Gittite, the shaft of whose spear was like a weaver's beam. 20There was again war at Gath, where there was a man of great size, who had six fingers on each hand, and six toes on each foot, twenty-four in number; he too was descended from the giants. 21When he taunted Israel, Jonathan son of David's brother Shimei, killed him. 22These four were descended from the giants in Gath; they fell by the hands of David and his servants.

22 David's Song of Thanksgiving

David spoke to the LORD the words of this song on the day when the LORD delivered him from the hand of all his enemies, and from the hand of Saul. 2He said:

The LORD is my rock, my fortress, and my
  deliverer,
3 my God, my rock, in whom I take refuge,
my shield and the horn of my salvation,
 my stronghold and my refuge,
 my savior; you save me from violence.
4 I call upon the LORD, who is worthy to be
  praised,
 and I am saved from my enemies.

5 For the waves of death encompassed me,
 the torrents of perdition assailed me;
6 the cords of Sheol entangled me,
 the snares of death confronted me.

7 In my distress I called upon the LORD;
 to my God I called.
From his temple he heard my voice,
 and my cry came to his ears.

8 Then the earth reeled and rocked;
 the foundations of the heavens trembled
 and quaked, because he was angry.
9 Smoke went up from his nostrils,

and devouring fire from his mouth;
 glowing coals flamed forth from him.
10 He bowed the heavens, and came down;
 thick darkness was under his feet.
11 He rode on a cherub, and flew;
 he was seen upon the wings of the wind.
12 He made darkness around him a canopy,
 thick clouds, a gathering of water.
13 Out of the brightness before him
 coals of fire flamed forth.
14 The LORD thundered from heaven;
 the Most High uttered his voice.
15 He sent out arrows, and scattered them
  —lightning, and routed them.
16 Then the channels of the sea were seen,
 the foundations of the world were laid
  bare
at the rebuke of the LORD,
 at the blast of the breath of his nostrils.

17 He reached from on high, he took me,
 he drew me out of mighty waters.
18 He delivered me from my strong enemy,
 from those who hated me;
 for they were too mighty for me.
19 They came upon me in the day of my calamity,
 but the LORD was my stay.
20 He brought me out into a broad place;
 he delivered me, because he delighted
  in me.

21 The LORD rewarded me according to my
  righteousness;
 according to the cleanness of my hands
  he recompensed me.
22 For I have kept the ways of the LORD,
 and have not wickedly departed from my
  God.
23 For all his ordinances were before me,
 and from his statutes I did not turn aside.
24 I was blameless before him,
 and I kept myself from guilt.
25 Therefore the LORD has recompensed me
  according to my righteousness,
 according to my cleanness in his sight.

26 With the loyal you show yourself loyal;
 with the blameless you show yourself
  blameless;
27 with the pure you show yourself pure,
 and with the crooked you show yourself
  perverse.
28 You deliver a humble people,
 but your eyes are upon the haughty to
  bring them down.
29 Indeed, you are my lamp, O LORD,
 the LORD lightens my darkness.
30 By you I can crush a troop,
 and by my God I can leap over a wall.

a Heb *was belted anew*

31 This God—his way is perfect;
>> the promise of the LORD proves true;
>> he is a shield for all who take refuge in
>> him.

32 For who is God, but the LORD?
>> And who is a rock, except our God?
33 The God who has girded me with strength[a]
>> has opened wide my path.[b]
34 He made my[c] feet like the feet of deer,
>> and set me secure on the heights.
35 He trains my hands for war,
>> so that my arms can bend a bow of bronze.
36 You have given me the shield of your
>> salvation,
>> and your help[d] has made me great.
37 You have made me stride freely,
>> and my feet do not slip;
38 I pursued my enemies and destroyed them,
>> and did not turn back until they were
>> consumed.
39 I consumed them; I struck them down, so
>> that they did not rise;
>> they fell under my feet.
40 For you girded me with strength for the
>> battle;
>> you made my assailants sink under me.
41 You made my enemies turn their backs to me,
>> those who hated me, and I destroyed
>> them.
42 They looked, but there was no one to save
>> them;
>> they cried to the LORD, but he did not
>> answer them.
43 I beat them fine like the dust of the earth,
>> I crushed them and stamped them down
>> like the mire of the streets.

44 You delivered me from strife with the
>> peoples;[e]
>> you kept me as the head of the nations;
>> people whom I had not known served me.
45 Foreigners came cringing to me;
>> as soon as they heard of me, they obeyed
>> me.
46 Foreigners lost heart,
>> and came trembling out of their
>> strongholds.

47 The LORD lives! Blessed be my rock,
>> and exalted be my God, the rock of my
>> salvation,
48 the God who gave me vengeance
>> and brought down peoples under me,
49 who brought me out from my enemies;
>> you exalted me above my adversaries,
>> you delivered me from the violent.

50 For this I will extol you, O LORD, among the
>> nations,
>> and sing praises to your name.
51 He is a tower of salvation for his king,
>> and shows steadfast love to his anointed,
>> to David and his descendants forever.

23 The Last Words of David

Now these are the last words of David:
>> The oracle of David, son of Jesse,
>> the oracle of the man whom God
>> exalted,[f]
>> the anointed of the God of Jacob,
>> the favorite of the Strong One of Israel:

2 The spirit of the LORD speaks through me,
>> his word is upon my tongue.
3 The God of Israel has spoken,
>> the Rock of Israel has said to me:
>> One who rules over people justly,
>> ruling in the fear of God,
4 is like the light of morning,
>> like the sun rising on a cloudless morning,
>> gleaming from the rain on the grassy
>> land.

5 Is not my house like this with God?
>> For he has made with me an everlasting
>> covenant,
>> ordered in all things and secure.
>> Will he not cause to prosper
>> all my help and my desire?
6 But the godless are[g] all like thorns that are
>> thrown away;
>> for they cannot be picked up with the
>> hand;
7 to touch them one uses an iron bar
>> or the shaft of a spear.
>> And they are entirely consumed in fire on
>> the spot.[h]

David's Mighty Men

8 These are the names of the warriors whom David had: Josheb-basshebeth a Tahchemonite; he was chief of the Three;[i] he wielded his spear[j] against eight hundred whom he killed at one time.

9 Next to him among the three warriors was Eleazar son of Dodo son of Ahohi. He was with David when they defied the Philistines who were gathered there for battle. The Israelites withdrew, 10but he stood his ground. He struck down the Philistines until his arm grew weary, though his hand clung to the sword. The LORD brought about a great victory that day. Then the people came back to him—but only to strip the dead.

11 Next to him was Shammah son of Agee,

---

a Q Ms Gk Syr Vg Compare Ps 18.32: MT *God is my strong refuge* b Meaning of Heb uncertain c Another reading is *his* d Q Ms: MT *your answering* e Gk: Heb *from strife with my people* f Q Ms: MT *who was raised on high* g Heb *But worthlessness* h Heb *in sitting* i Gk Vg Compare 1 Chr 11.11: Meaning of Heb uncertain j 1 Chr 11.11: Meaning of Heb uncertain the Hararite. The Philistines gathered together at Lehi, where there was a plot of ground full of lentils; and the army fled from the Philistines. [12]But he took his stand in the middle of the plot, defended it, and killed the Philistines; and the LORD brought about a great victory.

13 Towards the beginning of harvest three of the thirty[a] chiefs went down to join David at the cave of Adullam, while a band of Philistines was encamped in the valley of Rephaim. [14]David was then in the stronghold; and the garrison of the Philistines was then at Bethlehem. [15]David said longingly, "O that someone would give me water to drink from the well of Bethlehem that is by the gate!" [16]Then the three warriors broke through the camp of the Philistines, drew water from the well of Bethlehem that was by the gate, and brought it to David. But he would not drink of it; he poured it out to the LORD, [17]for he said, "The LORD forbid that I should do this. Can I drink the blood of the men who went at the risk of their lives?" Therefore he would not drink it. The three warriors did these things.

18 Now Abishai son of Zeruiah, the brother of Joab, was chief of the Thirty.[b] With his spear he fought against three hundred men and killed them, and won a name beside the Three. [19]He was the most renowned of the Thirty,[c] and became their commander; but he did not attain to the Three.

20 Benaiah son of Jehoiada was a valiant warrior[d] from Kabzeel, a doer of great deeds; he struck down two sons of Ariel[e] of Moab. He also went down and killed a lion in a pit on a day when snow had fallen. [21]And he killed an Egyptian, a handsome man. The Egyptian had a spear in his hand; but Benaiah went against him with a staff, snatched the spear out of the Egyptian's hand, and killed him with his own spear. [22]Such were the things Benaiah son of Jehoiada did, and won a name beside the three warriors. [23]He was renowned among the Thirty, but he did not attain to the Three. And David put him in charge of his bodyguard.

24 Among the Thirty were Asahel brother of Joab; Elhanan son of Dodo of Bethlehem; [25]Shammah of Harod; Elika of Harod; [26]Helez the Paltite; Ira son of Ikkesh of Tekoa; [27]Abiezer of Anathoth; Mebunnai the Hushathite; [28]Zalmon the Ahohite; Maharai of Netophah; [29]Heleb son of Baanah of Netophah; Ittai son of Ribai of Gibeah of the Benjaminites; [30]Benaiah of Pirathon; Hiddai of the torrents of Gaash; [31]Abi-albon the Arbathite; Azmaveth of Bahurim; [32]Eliahba of Shaalbon; the sons

A Man and Woman's Love Given from God—© Eliza German, 20

of Jashen: Jonathan [33]son of[f] Shammah the Hararite; Ahiam son of Sharar the Hararite; [34]Eliphelet son of Ahasbai of Maacah; Eliam son of Ahithophel the Gilonite; [35]Hezro[g] of Carmel; Paarai the Arbite; [36]Igal son of Nathan of Zobah; Bani the Gadite; [37]Zelek the Ammonite; Naharai of Beeroth, the armor-bearer of Joab son of Zeruiah; [38]Ira the Ithrite; Gareb the Ithrite; [39]Uriah the Hittite—thirty-seven in all.

24 David's Census of Israel and Judah

Again the anger of the LORD was kindled against Israel, and he incited David against them, saying, "Go, count the people of Israel and Judah." [2]So the king said to Joab and the commanders of the army,[h] who were with him, "Go through all the tribes of Israel, from Dan to Beer-sheba, and take a census of the people, so that I may know how many there are." [3]But Joab said to the king, "May the LORD your God increase the number of the people a hundredfold, while the eyes of my lord the king can still see it! But why does my lord the king want to do this?" [4]But the king's word prevailed against Joab and the commanders of the army. So Joab and the commanders of the army went out from the presence of the king to take a census of the people of Israel. [5]They crossed the Jordan, and began from[i] Aroer and from the city that is in the middle of the valley, toward Gad and on to Jazer. [6]Then they came to Gilead, and to Kadesh in the land of the Hittites;[j] and they came to Dan, and from Dan[k] they went around to Sidon, [7]and came to the fortress of Tyre and to all the cities of the Hivites and Canaanites; and they went out to the Negeb of Judah at Beer-sheba.

a Heb adds head b Two Heb Mss Syr: MT Three c Syr Compare 1 Chr 11.25: Heb Was he the most renowned of the Three? d Another reading is the son of Ish-hai e Gk: Heb lacks sons of f Gk: Heb lacks son of g Another reading is Hezrai h 1 Chr 21.2 Gk: Heb to Joab the commander of the army i Gk Mss: Heb encamped in Aroer south of j Gk: Heb to the land of Tahtim-hodshi k Cn Compare Gk: Heb they came to Dan-jaan and

[8]So when they had gone through all the land, they came back to Jerusalem at the end of nine months and twenty days. [9]Joab reported to the king the number of those who had been recorded: in Israel there were eight hundred thousand soldiers able to draw the sword, and those of Judah were five hundred thousand.

Judgment on David's Sin

[10] But afterward, David was stricken to the heart because he had numbered the people. David said to the LORD, "I have sinned greatly in what I have done. But now, O LORD, I pray you, take away the guilt of your servant; for I have done very foolishly." [11]When David rose in the morning, the word of the LORD came to the prophet Gad, David's seer, saying, [12]"Go and say to David: Thus says the LORD: Three things I offer[a] you; choose one of them, and I will do it to you." [13]So Gad came to David and told him; he asked him, "Shall three[b] years of famine come to you on your land? Or will you flee three months before your foes while they pursue you? Or shall there be three days' pestilence in your land? Now consider, and decide what answer I shall return to the one who sent me." [14]Then David said to Gad, "I am in great distress; let us fall into the hand of the LORD, for his mercy is great; but let me not fall into human hands."

15 So the LORD sent a pestilence on Israel from that morning until the appointed time; and seventy thousand of the people died, from Dan to Beer-sheba. [16]But when the angel stretched out his hand toward Jerusalem to destroy it, the LORD relented concerning the evil, and said to the angel who was bringing destruction among the people, "It is enough; now stay your hand." The angel of the LORD was then by the thresh-ing floor of Araunah the Jebusite. [17]When David saw the angel who was destroying the people, he said to the LORD, "I alone have sinned, and I alone have done wickedly; but these sheep, what have they done? Let your hand, I pray, be against me and against my father's house."

David's Altar on the Threshing Floor

18 That day Gad came to David and said to him, "Go up and erect an altar to the LORD on the threshing floor of Araunah the Jebusite." [19]Following Gad's instructions, David went up, as the LORD had commanded. [20]When Araunah looked down, he saw the king and his servants coming toward him; and Araunah went out and prostrated himself before the king with his face to the ground. [21]Araunah said, "Why has my lord the king come to his servant?" David said, "To buy the threshing floor from you in order to build an altar to the LORD, so that the plague may be averted from the people." [22]Then Araunah said to David, "Let my lord the king take and offer up what seems good to him; here are the oxen for the burnt offering, and the threshing sledges and the yokes of the oxen for the wood. [23]All this, O king, Araunah gives to the king." And Araunah said to the king, "May the LORD your God respond favorably to you."

24 But the king said to Araunah, "No, but I will buy them from you for a price; I will not offer burnt offerings to the LORD my God that cost me nothing." So David bought the threshing floor and the oxen for fifty shekels of silver. [25]David built there an altar to the LORD, and offered burnt offerings and offerings of well-being. So the LORD answered his supplication for the land, and the plague was averted from Israel.

a Or hold over *b* 1 Chr 21.12 Gk: Heb seven

"The thing you have to worry about when you talk about your faith publicly is that people think you're going to be a hypocrite. Now, we all make mistakes. We all make dumb decisions. We all do stupid things that we wish we hadn't done, but if you have a faith, then you ought to be willing to acknowledge it."

—Lou Holtz, college football analyst on ESPN and former head football coach at Notre Dame University

1 KINGS
MONEY, SEX, POWER...AND FAILURE

Like Father, Like Son?

In terms of biblical characters, Solomon is a giant. Only eclipsed by his father, David, as a great ruler, the third king of Israel saw his kingdom grow to levels of prosperity that no one had ever dreamed of. Israel had become a superpower. But isn't there a saying about too much of a good thing . . . ?

Though Solomon had many good traits (like being the wisest person on earth), moderation was *not* one of them! He had seven hundred wives, major bling, wealth that made the world envious, and a building project that would have made Donald Trump blush. Yet in the end he lost sight of what was truly important. Solomon's story shows us what happens when *things* take control over our lives: we lose our judgment and become nothing more than consumers. God gives gifts for us to enjoy, but our lives become a wreck when those gifts are never enough.

What about you? Is there some urge inside of you that just wants *more*? More power, more friends, more money, more gadgets, more everything? The mark of those who follow Jesus is that they look for and find total satisfaction in the Kingdom of Jesus, not in the material kingdom of this world.

WHO Shaped by a final author or editor from many fragments whose authors are unknown.

WHAT The book gives a record of Solomon's reign, the division of Israel into two nations, the downward spiral of God's people, and the rise of the prophet Elijah. It also highlights that being faithful to God results in blessing, and infidelity can result in the deterioration of the nation.

WHEN The events in 1 Kings took place ca. 971–846 B.C. Likely written between 586 and 539 B.C.

WHERE The events of 1 Kings 1–11 center on Jerusalem. In 1 Kings 12, the nation splits into two kingdoms: the larger northern kingdom of Israel and the smaller southern kingdom of Judah.

> *"To one who has faith, no explanation is necessary. To one without faith, no explanation is possible."*
> —St. Thomas Aquinas

PATH OF DISCIPLESHIP

The greatest achievement under Solomon's reign was the building of the Temple—the earthly house of God. It was a magnificent house of worship, where God promised to meet his people in a unique way (see 1 Kings 9.3). The Temple became the center of life for the Jews.

You've probably heard the phrase, "You are a temple of the Holy Spirit." Have you ever stopped to think about it? The Holy Spirit dwells in *you*. What an awesome image Paul gave us (see 1 Corinthians 6.19–20). And it's true! In Baptism, the Holy Spirit comes to live in us.

The Israelites had a great respect for the Temple because God dwelt there. How about you? Do you have great respect for the temple of your body? Do you do the things necessary to keep it healthy? On the other hand, do you make your body a false god? Do you worship the temple and not God dwelling within?

1 The Struggle for the Succession

King David was old and advanced in years; and although they covered him with clothes, he could not get warm. ²So his servants said to him, "Let a young virgin be sought for my lord the king, and let her wait on the king, and be his attendant; let her lie in your bosom, so that my lord the king may be warm." ³So they searched for a beautiful girl throughout all the territory of Israel, and found Abishag the Shunammite, and brought her to the king. ⁴The girl was very beautiful. She became the king's attendant and served him, but the king did not know her sexually.

5 Now Adonijah son of Haggith exalted himself, saying, "I will be king"; he prepared for himself chariots and horsemen, and fifty men to run before him. ⁶His father had never at any time displeased him by asking, "Why have you done thus and so?" He was also a very handsome man, and he was born next after Absalom. ⁷He conferred with Joab son of Zeruiah and with the priest Abiathar, and they supported Adonijah. ⁸But the priest Zadok, and Benaiah son of Jehoiada, and the prophet Nathan, and Shimei, and Rei, and David's own warriors did not side with Adonijah.

9 Adonijah sacrificed sheep, oxen, and fatted cattle by the stone Zoheleth, which is beside En-rogel, and he invited all his brothers, the king's sons, and all the royal officials of Judah, ¹⁰but he did not invite the prophet Nathan or Benaiah or the warriors or his brother Solomon.

11 Then Nathan said to Bathsheba, Solomon's mother, "Have you not heard that Adonijah son of Haggith has become king and our lord David does not know it? ¹²Now therefore come, let me give you advice, so that you may save your own life and the life of your son Solomon. ¹³Go in at once to King David, and say to him, 'Did you not, my lord the king, swear to your servant, saying: Your son Solomon shall succeed me as king, and he shall sit on my throne? Why then is Adonijah king?' ¹⁴Then while you are still there speaking with the king, I will come in after you and confirm your words."

15 So Bathsheba went to the king in his room. The king was very old; Abishag the Shunammite was attending the king. ¹⁶Bathsheba bowed and did obeisance to the king, and the king said, "What do you wish?" ¹⁷She said to him, "My lord, you swore to your servant by the Lord your God, saying: Your son Solomon shall succeed me as king, and he shall sit on my throne. ¹⁸But now suddenly Adonijah has become king, though you, my lord the king, do not know it. ¹⁹He has sacrificed oxen, fatted cattle, and sheep in abundance, and has invited all the children of the king, the priest Abiathar, and Joab the commander of the army; but your servant Solomon he has not invited. ²⁰But you, my lord the king—the eyes of all Israel are on you to tell them who shall sit on the throne of my lord the king after him. ²¹Otherwise it will come to pass, when my lord the king sleeps with his ancestors, that my son Solomon and I will be counted offenders."

22 While she was still speaking with the king, the prophet Nathan came in. ²³The king was told, "Here is the prophet Nathan." When he came in before the king, he did obeisance to the king, with his face to the ground. ²⁴Nathan said, "My lord the king, have you said, 'Adonijah shall succeed me as king, and he shall sit on my throne'? ²⁵For today he has gone down and has sacrificed oxen, fatted cattle, and sheep in abundance, and has invited all the king's children, Joab the commander^a of the army, and the priest Abiathar, who are now eating and drinking before him, and saying, 'Long live King Adonijah!' ²⁶But he did not invite me, your servant, and the priest Zadok, and Benaiah son of Jehoiada, and your servant Solomon. ²⁷Has this thing been brought about by my lord the king and you have not let your servants know who should sit on the throne of my lord the king after him?"

The Accession of Solomon

28 King David answered, "Summon Bathsheba to me." So she came into the king's presence, and stood before the king. ²⁹The king swore, saying, "As the Lord lives, who has saved my life from every adversity, ³⁰as I swore to you by the Lord, the God of Israel, 'Your son Solomon shall succeed me as king, and he shall sit on my throne in my place,' so will I do this day." ³¹Then Bathsheba bowed with her face to the ground, and did obeisance to the king, and said, "May my lord King David live forever!"

32 King David said, "Summon to me the priest Zadok, the prophet Nathan, and Benaiah son of Jehoiada." When they came before the king, ³³the king said to them, "Take with you the servants of your lord, and have my son Solomon ride on my own mule, and bring him down to Gihon. ³⁴There let the priest Zadok and the prophet Nathan anoint him king over Israel; then blow the trumpet, and say, 'Long live King Solomon!' ³⁵You shall go up following him. Let him enter and sit on my throne;

---

a Gk: Heb the commanders

he shall be king in my place; for I have appointed him to be ruler over Israel and over Judah." [36]Benaiah son of Jehoiada answered the king, "Amen! May the LORD, the God of my lord the king, so ordain. [37]As the LORD has been with my lord the king, so may he be with Solomon, and make his throne greater than the throne of my lord King David."

38 So the priest Zadok, the prophet Nathan, and Benaiah son of Jehoiada, and the Cherethites and the Pelethites, went down and had Solomon ride on King David's mule, and led him to Gihon. [39]There the priest Zadok took the horn of oil from the tent and anointed Solomon. Then they blew the trumpet, and all the people said, "Long live King Solomon!" [40]And all the people went up following him, playing on pipes and rejoicing with great joy, so that the earth quaked at their noise.

41 Adonijah and all the guests who were with him heard it as they finished feasting. When Joab heard the sound of the trumpet, he said, "Why is the city in an uproar?" [42]While he was still speaking, Jonathan son of the priest Abiathar arrived. Adonijah said, "Come in, for you are a worthy man and surely you bring good news." [43]Jonathan answered Adonijah, "No, for our lord King David has made Solomon king; [44]the king has sent with him the priest Zadok, the prophet Nathan, and Benaiah son of Jehoiada, and the Cherethites and the Pelethites; and they had him ride on the king's mule; [45]the priest Zadok and the prophet Nathan have anointed him king at Gihon; and they have gone up from there rejoicing, so that the city is in an uproar. This is the noise that you heard. [46]Solomon now sits on the royal throne. [47]Moreover the king's servants came to congratulate our lord King David, saying, 'May God make the name of Solomon more famous than yours, and make his throne greater than your throne.' The king bowed in worship on the bed [48]and went on to pray thus, 'Blessed be the LORD, the God of Israel, who today has granted one of my offspring[a] to sit on my throne and permitted me to witness it.' "

49 Then all the guests of Adonijah got up trembling and went their own ways. [50]Adonijah, fearing Solomon, got up and went to grasp the horns of the altar. [51]Solomon was informed, "Adonijah is afraid of King Solomon; see, he has laid hold of the horns of the altar, saying, 'Let King Solomon swear to me first that he will not kill his servant with the sword.' " [52]So Solomon responded, "If he proves to be a worthy man, not one of his hairs shall fall to the ground; but if wickedness is found in him, he shall die." [53]Then King Solomon sent to have him brought down from the altar. He came to do obeisance to King Solomon; and Solomon said to him, "Go home."

2 David's Instruction to Solomon

When David's time to die drew near, he charged his son Solomon, saying: [2]"I am about to go the way of all the earth. Be strong, be courageous, [3]and keep the charge of the LORD your God, walking in his ways and keeping his statutes, his commandments, his ordinances, and his testimonies, as it is written in the law of Moses, so that you may prosper in all that you do and wherever you turn. [4]Then the LORD will establish his word that he spoke concerning me: 'If your heirs take heed to their way, to walk before me in faithfulness with all their heart and with all their soul, there shall not fail you a successor on the throne of Israel.'

5 "Moreover you know also what Joab son

TEXT MESSAGE

The books of 1 and 2 Kings are important not just for the stories they tell, but because they provide background information for seventeen other books in the Old Testament. Many of the prophets with their own books—including Isaiah, Jeremiah, Ezekiel, Daniel, Hosea, Amos, Obadiah, Micah, Haggai, and Zechariah— ministered during the time period covered in Kings.

Fact

This information has been scanned and is free of all known viruses. Please forward to all your friends.

---

[a] Gk: Heb *one*

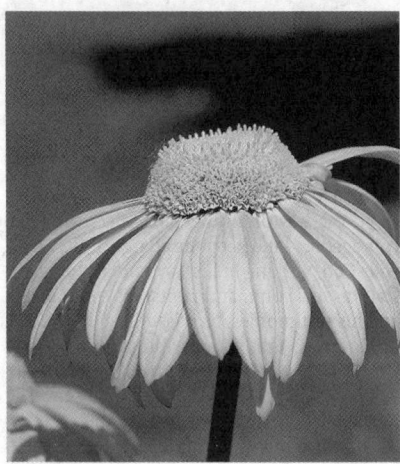

Stand Out—© Lauren Jordan, 18

of Zeruiah did to me, how he dealt with the two commanders of the armies of Israel, Abner son of Ner, and Amasa son of Jether, whom he murdered, retaliating in time of peace for blood that had been shed in war, and putting the blood of war on the belt around his waist, and on the sandals on his feet. 6 Act therefore according to your wisdom, but do not let his gray head go down to Sheol in peace. 7 Deal loyally, however, with the sons of Barzillai the Gileadite, and let them be among those who eat at your table; for with such loyalty they met me when I fled from your brother Absalom. 8 There is also with you Shimei son of Gera, the Benjaminite from Bahurim, who cursed me with a terrible curse on the day when I went to Mahanaim; but when he came down to meet me at the Jordan, I swore to him by the Lord, 'I will not put you to death with the sword.' 9 Therefore do not hold him guiltless, for you are a wise man; you will know what you ought to do to him, and you must bring his gray head down with blood to Sheol."

Death of David

10 Then David slept with his ancestors, and was buried in the city of David. 11 The time that David reigned over Israel was forty years; he reigned seven years in Hebron, and thirty-three years in Jerusalem. 12 So Solomon sat on the throne of his father David; and his kingdom was firmly established.

Solomon Consolidates His Reign

13 Then Adonijah son of Haggith came to Bathsheba, Solomon's mother. She asked, "Do you come peaceably?" He said, "Peaceably." 14 Then he said, "May I have a word with you?"

She said, "Go on." 15 He said, "You know that the kingdom was mine, and that all Israel expected me to reign; however, the kingdom has turned about and become my brother's, for it was his from the Lord. 16 And now I have one request to make of you; do not refuse me." She said to him, "Go on." 17 He said, "Please ask King Solomon—he will not refuse you—to give me Abishag the Shunammite as my wife." 18 Bathsheba said, "Very well; I will speak to the king on your behalf."

19 So Bathsheba went to King Solomon, to speak to him on behalf of Adonijah. The king rose to meet her, and bowed down to her; then he sat on his throne, and had a throne brought for the king's mother, and she sat on his right. 20 Then she said, "I have one small request to make of you; do not refuse me." And the king said to her, "Make your request, my mother; for I will not refuse you." 21 She said, "Let Abishag the Shunammite be given to your brother Adonijah as his wife." 22 King Solomon answered his mother, "And why do you ask Abishag the Shunammite for Adonijah? Ask for him the kingdom as well! For he is my elder brother; ask not only for him but also for the priest Abiathar and for Joab son of Zeruiah!" 23 Then King Solomon swore by the Lord, "So may God do to me, and more also, for Adonijah has devised this scheme at the risk of his life! 24 Now therefore as the Lord lives, who has established me and placed me on the throne of my father David, and who has made me a house as he promised, today Adonijah shall be put to death." 25 So King Solomon sent Benaiah son of Jehoiada; he struck him down, and he died.

26 The king said to the priest Abiathar, "Go to Anathoth, to your estate; for you deserve death. But I will not at this time put you to death, because you carried the ark of the Lord God before my father David, and because you shared in all the hardships my father endured." 27 So Solomon banished Abiathar from being priest to the Lord, thus fulfilling the word of the Lord that he had spoken concerning the house of Eli in Shiloh.

28 When the news came to Joab—for Joab had supported Adonijah though he had not supported Absalom—Joab fled to the tent of the Lord and grasped the horns of the altar. 29 When it was told King Solomon, "Joab has fled to the tent of the Lord and now is beside the altar," Solomon sent Benaiah son of Jehoiada, saying, "Go, strike him down." 30 So Benaiah came to the tent of the Lord and said to him, "The king commands, 'Come out.'" But he said, "No, I will die here." Then Benaiah brought the king word again, saying, "Thus said Joab, and thus he answered me." 31 The king replied to

him, "Do as he has said, strike him down and bury him; and thus take away from me and from my father's house the guilt for the blood that Joab shed without cause. 32The LORD will bring back his bloody deeds on his own head, because, without the knowledge of my father David, he attacked and killed with the sword two men more righteous and better than himself, Abner son of Ner, commander of the army of Israel, and Amasa son of Jether, commander of the army of Judah. 33So shall their blood come back on the head of Joab and on the head of his descendants forever; but to David, and to his descendants, and to his house, and to his throne, there shall be peace from the LORD forevermore." 34Then Benaiah son of Jehoiada went up and struck him down and killed him; and he was buried at his own house near the wilderness. 35The king put Benaiah son of Jehoiada over the army in his place, and the king put the priest Zadok in the place of Abiathar.

36 Then the king sent and summoned Shimei, and said to him, "Build yourself a house in Jerusalem, and live there, and do not go out from there to any place whatever. 37For on the day you go out, and cross the Wadi Kidron, know for certain that you shall die; your blood shall be on your own head." 38And Shimei said to the king, "The sentence is fair; as my lord the king has said, so will your servant do." So Shimei lived in Jerusalem many days.

39 But it happened at the end of three years that two of Shimei's slaves ran away to King Achish son of Maacah of Gath. When it was told Shimei, "Your slaves are in Gath," 40Shimei arose and saddled a donkey, and went to Achish in Gath, to search for his slaves; Shimei went and brought his slaves from Gath. 41When Solomon was told that Shimei had gone from Jerusalem to Gath and returned, 42the king sent and summoned Shimei, and said to him, "Did I not make you swear by the LORD, and solemnly adjure you, saying, 'Know for certain that on the day you go out and go to any place whatever, you shall die'? And you said to me, 'The sentence is fair; I accept.' 43Why then have you not kept your oath to the LORD and the commandment with which I charged you?" 44The king also said to Shimei, "You know in your own heart all the evil that you did to my father David; so the LORD will bring back your evil on your own head. 45But King Solomon shall be blessed, and the throne of David shall be established before the LORD forever." 46Then the king commanded Benaiah son of Jehoiada; and he went out and struck him down, and he died.

So the kingdom was established in the hand of Solomon.

3 Solomon's Prayer for Wisdom

Solomon made a marriage alliance with Pharaoh king of Egypt; he took Pharaoh's daughter and brought her into the city of David, until he had finished building his own house and the house of the LORD and the wall around Jerusalem. 2The people were sacrificing at the high places, however, because no house had yet been built for the name of the LORD.

3 Solomon loved the LORD, walking in the statutes of his father David; only, he sacrificed and offered incense at the high places. 4The king went to Gibeon to sacrifice there, for that was the principal high place; Solomon used to offer a thousand burnt offerings on that altar. 5At Gibeon the LORD appeared to Solomon in a dream by night; and God said, "Ask what I should give you." 6And Solomon said, "You have shown great and steadfast love to your servant my father David, because he walked before you in faithfulness, in righteousness, and in uprightness of heart toward you; and you have kept for him this great and steadfast love, and have given him a son to sit on his throne today. 7And now, O LORD my God, you have made your servant king in place of my father David, although I am only a little child; I do not know how to go out or come in. 8And your servant is in the midst of the people whom you have chosen, a great people, so numerous they cannot be numbered or counted. 9Give your servant therefore an understanding mind to govern your people, able to discern between good and evil; for who can govern this your great people?"

10 It pleased the Lord that Solomon had asked this. 11God said to him, "Because you have asked this, and have not asked for yourself long life or riches, or for the life of your enemies, but have asked for yourself understanding to discern what is right, 12I now do according to your word. Indeed I give you a wise and discerning mind; no one like you has been before you and no one like you shall arise after you. 13I give you also what you have not asked, both riches and honor all your life; no other king shall compare with you. 14If you will walk in my ways, keeping my statutes and my commandments, as your father David walked, then I will lengthen your life."

15 Then Solomon awoke; it had been a dream. He came to Jerusalem where he stood before the ark of the covenant of the LORD. He offered up burnt offerings and offerings of well-being, and provided a feast for all his servants.

GIFT OF THE SPIRIT: WISDOM

Did you ever wish that you could be the one chosen by some wonderful magic person to have all your wishes—or at least that one big one—granted? Imagine wishing for what you most wanted in the whole world . . . and getting it! It would be awesome.

Well, it happened to Solomon. He asked for wisdom. He got it. And for a while he used it wisely, but not forever.

During the sacrament of Confirmation, we receive the gift of wisdom, along with six other gifts: understanding, right judgment, courage, knowledge, reverence, and wonder and awe. Gifts are meant to be opened and used. Once you receive them, the gifts of the Holy Spirit are permanent. You never lose them, but you have to use them to get the benefit for yourself and others.

The gift of wisdom gives you the power to see things from God's perspective. Think about that. Seeing from God's perspective means looking at situations through God's eyes, not just from your own viewpoint. You use this gift and develop it when you think about God's presence, action, and guidance in your life. That kind of thinking helps you make wise decisions.

The gifts of the Holy Spirit are like having special superpowers—the gift of wisdom is the ability to love the things that are of God.

You have that gift. Be aware of it. Use it daily for God's purposes and for the good of others. If you do, you won't end up like Solomon!

Solomon's Wisdom in Judgment

16 Later, two women who were prostitutes came to the king and stood before him. 17The one woman said, "Please, my lord, this woman and I live in the same house; and I gave birth while she was in the house. 18Then on the third day after I gave birth, this woman also gave birth. We were together; there was no one else with us in the house, only the two of us were in the house. 19Then this woman's son died in the night, because she lay on him. 20She got up in the middle of the night and took my son from beside me while your servant slept. She laid him at her breast, and laid her dead son at my breast. 21When I rose in the morning to nurse my son, I saw that he was dead; but when I looked at him closely in the morning, clearly it was not the son I had borne." 22But the other woman said, "No, the living son is mine, and the dead son is yours." The first said, "No, the dead son is yours, and the living son is mine." So they argued before the king.

23 Then the king said, "The one says, 'This is my son that is alive, and your son is dead'; while the other says, 'Not so! Your son is dead, and my son is the living one.' " 24So the king said, "Bring me a sword," and they brought a sword before the king. 25The king said, "Divide the living boy in two; then give half to the one, and half to the other." 26But the woman whose son was alive said to the king—because compassion for her son burned within her—"Please, my lord, give her the living boy; certainly do not kill him!" The other said, "It shall be neither mine nor yours; divide it." 27Then the king responded: "Give the first woman the living boy; do not kill him. She is his mother." 28All Israel heard of the judgment that the king had rendered; and they stood in awe of the king, because they perceived that the wisdom of God was in him, to execute justice.

4 Solomon's Administrative Officers

King Solomon was king over all Israel, 2and these were his high officials: Azariah son of Zadok was the priest; 3Elihoreph and Ahijah sons of Shisha were secretaries; Jehoshaphat son of Ahilud was recorder; 4Benaiah son of Jehoiada was in command of the army; Zadok and Abiathar were priests; 5Azariah son of Nathan was over the officials; Zabud son of Nathan was priest and king's friend; 6Ahishar was in charge of the palace; and Adoniram son of Abda was in charge of the forced labor.

7 Solomon had twelve officials over all Israel, who provided food for the king and his household; each one had to make provision for one month in the year. 8These were their names: Ben-hur, in the hill country of Ephraim; 9Ben-deker, in Makaz, Shaalbim, Beth-shemesh, and Elon-beth-hanan; 10Ben-hesed, in Arubboth (to him belonged Socoh and all the land of Hepher); 11Ben-abinadab, in all Naphath-dor (he had Taphath, Solomon's daughter, as his wife); 12Baana son of Ahilud, in Taanach, Megiddo, and all Beth-shean, which is beside Zarethan below Jezreel, and from Beth-shean to Abel-meholah, as far as

the other side of Jokmeam; ¹³Ben-geber, in Ramoth-gilead (he had the villages of Jair son of Manasseh, which are in Gilead, and he had the region of Argob, which is in Bashan, sixty great cities with walls and bronze bars); ¹⁴Ahinadab son of Iddo, in Mahanaim; ¹⁵Ahimaaz, in Naphtali (he had taken Basemath, Solomon's daughter, as his wife); ¹⁶Baana son of Hushai, in Asher and Bealoth; ¹⁷Jehoshaphat son of Paruah, in Issachar; ¹⁸Shimei son of Ela, in Benjamin; ¹⁹Geber son of Uri, in the land of Gilead, the country of King Sihon of the Amorites and of King Og of Bashan. And there was one official in the land of Judah.

Magnificence of Solomon's Rule

20 Judah and Israel were as numerous as the sand by the sea; they ate and drank and were happy. ²¹^a Solomon was sovereign over all the kingdoms from the Euphrates to the land of the Philistines, even to the border of Egypt; they brought tribute and served Solomon all the days of his life.

22 Solomon's provision for one day was thirty cors of choice flour, and sixty cors of meal, ²³ten fat oxen, and twenty pasture-fed cattle, one hundred sheep, besides deer, gazelles, roebucks, and fatted fowl. ²⁴For he had dominion over all the region west of the Euphrates from Tiphsah to Gaza, over all the kings west of the Euphrates; and he had peace on all sides. ²⁵During Solomon's lifetime Judah and Israel lived in safety, from Dan even to Beer-sheba, all of them under their vines and fig trees. ²⁶Solomon also had forty thousand stalls of horses for his chariots, and twelve thousand horsemen. ²⁷Those officials supplied provisions for King Solomon and for all who came to King Solomon's table, each one in his month; they let nothing be lacking. ²⁸They also brought to the required place barley and straw for the horses and swift steeds, each according to his charge.

Fame of Solomon's Wisdom

29 God gave Solomon very great wisdom, discernment, and breadth of understanding as vast as the sand on the seashore, ³⁰so that Solomon's wisdom surpassed the wisdom of all the people of the east, and all the wisdom of Egypt. ³¹He was wiser than anyone else, wiser than Ethan the Ezrahite, and Heman, Calcol, and Darda, children of Mahol; his fame spread throughout all the surrounding nations. ³²He composed three thousand proverbs, and his songs numbered a thousand and five. ³³He would speak of trees, from the cedar that is in

In the Beginning God Created—© Josh Allen, 29 (youth leader)

the Lebanon to the hyssop that grows in the wall; he would speak of animals, and birds, and reptiles, and fish. ³⁴People came from all the nations to hear the wisdom of Solomon; they came from all the kings of the earth who had heard of his wisdom.

5^b Preparations and Materials for the Temple

Now King Hiram of Tyre sent his servants to Solomon, when he heard that they had anointed him king in place of his father; for Hiram had always been a friend to David. ²Solomon sent word to Hiram, saying, ³"You know that my father David could not build a house for the name of the LORD his God because of the warfare with which his enemies surrounded him, until the LORD put them under the soles of his feet.^c ⁴But now the LORD my God has given me rest on every side; there is neither adversary nor misfortune. ⁵So I intend to build a house for the name of the LORD my God, as the LORD said to my father David, 'Your son, whom I will set on your throne in your place, shall build the house for my name.' ⁶Therefore command that cedars from the Lebanon be cut for me. My servants will join your servants, and I will give you whatever wages you set for your servants; for you know that there is no one among us who knows how to cut timber like the Sidonians."

7 When Hiram heard the words of Solomon, he rejoiced greatly, and said, "Blessed be the LORD today, who has given to David a wise son to be over this great people." ⁸Hiram sent word to Solomon, "I have heard the message that you have sent to me; I will fulfill all your

a Ch 5.1 in Heb   *b* Ch 5.15 in Heb   *c* Gk Tg Vg: Heb *my feet* or *his feet* needs in the matter of cedar and cypress timber. [9]My servants shall bring it down to the sea from the Lebanon; I will make it into rafts to go by sea to the place you indicate. I will have them broken up there for you to take away. And you shall meet my needs by providing food for my household." [10]So Hiram supplied Solomon's every need for timber of cedar and cypress. [11]Solomon in turn gave Hiram twenty thousand cors of wheat as food for his household, and twenty cors of fine oil. Solomon gave this to Hiram year by year. [12]So the LORD gave Solomon wisdom, as he promised him. There was peace between Hiram and Solomon; and the two of them made a treaty.

[13] King Solomon conscripted forced labor out of all Israel; the levy numbered thirty thousand men. [14]He sent them to the Lebanon, ten thousand a month in shifts; they would be a month in the Lebanon and two months at home; Adoniram was in charge of the forced labor. [15]Solomon also had seventy thousand laborers and eighty thousand stonecutters in the hill country, [16]besides Solomon's three thousand three hundred supervisors who were over the work, having charge of the people who did the work. [17]At the king's command, they quarried out great, costly stones in order to lay the foundation of the house with dressed stones. [18]So Solomon's builders and Hiram's builders and the Gebalites did the stonecutting and prepared the timber and the stone to build the house.

6 Solomon Builds the Temple

In the four hundred eightieth year after the Israelites came out of the land of Egypt, in the fourth year of Solomon's reign over Israel, in the month of Ziv, which is the second month, he began to build the house of the LORD. [2]The house that King Solomon built for the LORD was sixty cubits long, twenty cubits wide, and thirty cubits high. [3]The vestibule in front of the nave of the house was twenty cubits wide, across the width of the house. Its depth was ten cubits in front of the house. [4]For the house he made windows with recessed frames.[a] [5]He also built a structure against the wall of the house, running around the walls of the house, both the nave and the inner sanctuary; and he made side chambers all around. [6]The lowest story[b] was five cubits wide, the middle one was six cubits wide, and the third was seven cubits wide; for around the outside of the house he made offsets on the wall in order that the supporting beams should not be inserted into the walls of the house.

[7] The house was built with stone finished at the quarry, so that neither hammer nor ax nor any tool of iron was heard in the temple while it was being built.

[8] The entrance for the middle story was on the south side of the house: one went up by winding stairs to the middle story, and from the middle story to the third. [9]So he built the house, and finished it; he roofed the house with beams and planks of cedar. [10]He built the structure against the whole house, each story[c] five cubits high, and it was joined to the house with timbers of cedar.

[11] Now the word of the LORD came to Solomon, [12]"Concerning this house that you are building, if you will walk in my statutes, obey my ordinances, and keep all my commandments by walking in them, then I will establish my promise with you, which I made to your father David. [13]I will dwell among the children of Israel, and will not forsake my people Israel."

[14] So Solomon built the house, and finished it. [15]He lined the walls of the house on the inside with boards of cedar; from the floor of the house to the rafters of the ceiling, he covered them on the inside with wood; and he covered the floor of the house with boards of cypress. [16]He built twenty cubits of the rear of the house with boards of cedar from the floor to the rafters, and he built this within as an inner sanctuary, as the most holy place. [17]The house, that is, the nave in front of the inner sanctuary, was forty cubits long. [18]The cedar within the house had carvings of gourds and open flowers; all was cedar, no stone was seen. [19]The inner sanctuary he prepared in the innermost part of the house, to set there the ark of the covenant of the LORD. [20]The interior of the inner sanctuary was twenty cubits long, twenty cubits wide, and twenty cubits high; he overlaid it with pure gold. He also overlaid the altar with cedar.[d] [21]Solomon overlaid the inside of the house with pure gold, then he drew chains of gold across, in front of the inner sanctuary, and overlaid it with gold. [22]Next he overlaid the whole house with gold, in order that the whole house might be perfect; even the whole altar that belonged to the inner sanctuary he overlaid with gold.

The Furnishings of the Temple

[23] In the inner sanctuary he made two cherubim of olivewood, each ten cubits high. [24]Five cubits was the length of one wing of the cherub, and five cubits the length of the other wing of the cherub; it was ten cubits from the tip of one wing to the tip of the other. [25]The other cherub also measured ten cubits; both cherubim had

a Gk: Meaning of Heb uncertain b Gk: Heb *structure* c Heb lacks *each story* d Meaning of Heb uncertain the same measure and the same form. ²⁶The height of one cherub was ten cubits, and so was that of the other cherub. ²⁷He put the cherubim in the innermost part of the house; the wings of the cherubim were spread out so that a wing of one was touching the one wall, and a wing of the other cherub was touching the other wall; their other wings toward the center of the house were touching wing to wing. ²⁸He also overlaid the cherubim with gold.

29 He carved the walls of the house all around about with carved engravings of cherubim, palm trees, and open flowers, in the inner and outer rooms. ³⁰The floor of the house he overlaid with gold, in the inner and outer rooms.

31 For the entrance to the inner sanctuary he made doors of olivewood; the lintel and the doorposts were five-sided.ᵃ ³²He covered the two doors of olivewood with carvings of cherubim, palm trees, and open flowers; he overlaid them with gold, and spread gold on the cherubim and on the palm trees.

33 So also he made for the entrance to the nave doorposts of olivewood, four-sided each, ³⁴and two doors of cypress wood; the two leaves of the one door were folding, and the two leaves of the other door were folding. ³⁵He carved cherubim, palm trees, and open flowers, overlaying them with gold evenly applied upon the carved work. ³⁶He built the inner court with three courses of dressed stone to one course of cedar beams.

37 In the fourth year the foundation of the house of the LORD was laid, in the month of Ziv. ³⁸In the eleventh year, in the month of Bul, which is the eighth month, the house was finished in all its parts, and according to all its specifications. He was seven years in building it.

7 Solomon's Palace and Other Buildings

Solomon was building his own house thirteen years, and he finished his entire house.

2 He built the House of the Forest of the Lebanon one hundred cubits long, fifty cubits wide, and thirty cubits high, built on four rows of cedar pillars, with cedar beams on the pillars. ³It was roofed with cedar on the forty-five rafters, fifteen in each row, which were on the pillars. ⁴There were window frames in the three rows, facing each other in the three rows. ⁵All the doorways and doorposts had four-sided frames, opposite, facing each other in the three rows.

6 He made the Hall of Pillars fifty cubits long and thirty cubits wide. There was a porch in front with pillars, and a canopy in front of them.

ᵃ Meaning of Heb uncertain

7 He made the Hall of the Throne where he was to pronounce judgment, the Hall of Justice, covered with cedar from floor to floor.

8 His own house where he would reside, in the other court back of the hall, was of the same construction. Solomon also made a house like this hall for Pharaoh's daughter, whom he had taken in marriage.

9 All these were made of costly stones, cut according to measure, sawed with saws, back and front, from the foundation to the coping, and from outside to the great court. ¹⁰The foundation was of costly stones, huge stones, stones of eight and ten cubits. ¹¹There were costly stones above, cut to measure, and cedarwood. ¹²The great court had three courses of dressed stone to one layer of cedar beams all around; so had the inner court of the house of the LORD, and the vestibule of the house.

Products of Hiram the Bronzeworker

13 Now King Solomon invited and received Hiram from Tyre. ¹⁴He was the son of a widow of the tribe of Naphtali, whose father, a man of

Tyre, had been an artisan in bronze; he was full of skill, intelligence, and knowledge in working bronze. He came to King Solomon, and did all his work.

15 He cast two pillars of bronze. Eighteen cubits was the height of the one, and a cord of twelve cubits would encircle it; the second pillar was the same.[a] [16]He also made two capitals of molten bronze, to set on the tops of the pillars; the height of the one capital was five cubits, and the height of the other capital was five cubits. [17]There were nets of checker work with wreaths of chain work for the capitals on the tops of the pillars; seven[b] for the one capital, and seven[b] for the other capital. [18]He made the columns with two rows around each latticework to cover the capitals that were above the pomegranates; he did the same with the other capital. [19]Now the capitals that were on the tops of the pillars in the vestibule were of lily-work, four cubits high. [20]The capitals were on the two pillars and also above the rounded projection that was beside the latticework; there were two hundred pomegranates in rows all around; and so with the other capital. [21]He set up the pillars at the vestibule of the temple; he set up the pillar on the south and called it Jachin; and he set up the pillar on the north and called it Boaz. [22]On the tops of the pillars was lily-work. Thus the work of the pillars was finished.

23 Then he made the molten sea; it was round, ten cubits from brim to brim, and five cubits high. A line of thirty cubits would encircle it completely. [24]Under its brim were panels all around it, each of ten cubits, surrounding the sea; there were two rows of panels, cast when it was cast. [25]It stood on twelve oxen, three facing north, three facing west, three facing south, and three facing east; the sea was set on them. The hindquarters of each were toward the inside. [26]Its thickness was a handbreadth; its brim was made like the brim of a cup, like the flower of a lily; it held two thousand baths.[c]

27 He also made the ten stands of bronze; each stand was four cubits long, four cubits wide, and three cubits high. [28]This was the construction of the stands: they had borders; the borders were within the frames; [29]on the borders that were set in the frames were lions, oxen, and cherubim. On the frames, both above and below the lions and oxen, there were wreaths of beveled work. [30]Each stand had four bronze wheels and axles of bronze; at the four corners were supports for a basin. The supports were cast with wreaths at the side of each. [31]Its

opening was within the crown whose height was one cubit; its opening was round, as a pedestal is made; it was a cubit and a half wide. At its opening there were carvings; its borders were four-sided, not round. [32]The four wheels were underneath the borders; the axles of the wheels were in the stands; and the height of a wheel was a cubit and a half. [33]The wheels were made like a chariot wheel; their axles, their rims, their spokes, and their hubs were all cast. [34]There were four supports at the four corners of each stand; the supports were of one piece with the stands. [35]On the top of the stand there was a round band half a cubit high; on the top of the stand, its stays and its borders were of one piece with it. [36]On the surfaces of its stays and on its borders he carved cherubim, lions, and palm trees, where each had space, with wreaths all around. [37]In this way he made the ten stands; all of them were cast alike, with the same size and the same form.

38 He made ten basins of bronze; each basin held forty baths,[c] each basin measured four cubits; there was a basin for each of the ten stands. [39]He set five of the stands on the south side of the house, and five on the north side of the house; he set the sea on the southeast corner of the house.

40 Hiram also made the pots, the shovels, and the basins. So Hiram finished all the work that he did for King Solomon on the house of the LORD: [41]the two pillars, the two bowls of the capitals that were on the tops of the pillars, the two latticeworks to cover the two bowls of the capitals that were on the tops of the pillars; [42]the four hundred pomegranates for the two latticeworks, two rows of pomegranates for each latticework, to cover the two bowls of the capitals that were on the pillars; [43]the ten stands, the ten basins on the stands; [44]the one sea, and the twelve oxen underneath the sea.

45 The pots, the shovels, and the basins, all these vessels that Hiram made for King Solomon for the house of the LORD were of burnished bronze. [46]In the plain of the Jordan the king cast them, in the clay ground between Succoth and Zarethan. [47]Solomon left all the vessels unweighed, because there were so many of them; the weight of the bronze was not determined.

48 So Solomon made all the vessels that were in the house of the LORD: the golden altar, the golden table for the bread of the Presence, [49]the lampstands of pure gold, five on the south side and five on the north, in front of the inner sanctuary; the flowers, the lamps, and the tongs, of gold; [50]the cups, snuffers, basins,

---

a Cn: Heb *and a cord of twelve cubits encircled the second pillar* ; Compare Jer 52.21   *b* Heb: Gk *a net*   *c* A Heb measure of volume

The Barn—© Caitlin Nelson, 13

dishes for incense, and firepans, of pure gold; the sockets for the doors of the innermost part of the house, the most holy place, and for the doors of the nave of the temple, of gold.

51 Thus all the work that King Solomon did on the house of the LORD was finished. Solomon brought in the things that his father David had dedicated, the silver, the gold, and the vessels, and stored them in the treasuries of the house of the LORD.

8 Dedication of the Temple

Then Solomon assembled the elders of Israel and all the heads of the tribes, the leaders of the ancestral houses of the Israelites, before King Solomon in Jerusalem, to bring up the ark of the covenant of the LORD out of the city of David, which is Zion. ²All the people of Israel assembled to King Solomon at the festival in the month Ethanim, which is the seventh month. ³And all the elders of Israel came, and the priests carried the ark. ⁴So they brought up the ark of the LORD, the tent of meeting, and all the holy vessels that were in the tent; the priests and the Levites brought them up. ⁵King Solomon and all the congregation of Israel, who had assembled before him, were with him before the ark, sacrificing so many sheep and oxen that they could not be counted or numbered. ⁶Then the priests brought the ark of the covenant of the LORD to its place, in the inner sanctuary of the house, in the most holy place, underneath the wings of the cherubim. ⁷For

the cherubim spread out their wings over the place of the ark, so that the cherubim made a covering above the ark and its poles. ⁸The poles were so long that the ends of the poles were seen from the holy place in front of the inner sanctuary; but they could not be seen from outside; they are there to this day. ⁹There was nothing in the ark except the two tablets of stone that Moses had placed there at Horeb, where the LORD made a covenant with the Israelites, when they came out of the land of Egypt. ¹⁰And when the priests came out of the holy place, a cloud filled the house of the LORD, ¹¹so that the priests could not stand to minister because of the cloud; for the glory of the LORD filled the house of the LORD.

12 Then Solomon said,
"The LORD has said that he would dwell in
thick darkness.
¹³ I have built you an exalted house,
a place for you to dwell in forever."

Solomon's Speech

14 Then the king turned around and blessed all the assembly of Israel, while all the assembly of Israel stood. ¹⁵He said, "Blessed be the LORD, the God of Israel, who with his hand has fulfilled what he promised with his mouth to my father David, saying, ¹⁶'Since the day that I brought my people Israel out of Egypt, I have not chosen a city from any of the tribes of Israel in which to build a house, that my name might be there; but I chose David to be over my

people Israel.' [17] My father David had it in mind to build a house for the name of the LORD, the God of Israel. [18] But the LORD said to my father David, 'You did well to consider building a house for my name; [19] nevertheless you shall not build the house, but your son who shall be born to you shall build the house for my name.' [20] Now the LORD has upheld the promise that he made; for I have risen in the place of my father David; I sit on the throne of Israel, as the LORD promised, and have built the house for the name of the LORD, the God of Israel. [21] There I have provided a place for the ark, in which is the covenant of the LORD that he made with our ancestors when he brought them out of the land of Egypt."

Solomon's Prayer of Dedication

22 Then Solomon stood before the altar of the LORD in the presence of all the assembly of Israel, and spread out his hands to heaven. [23] He said, "O LORD, God of Israel, there is no God like you in heaven above or on earth beneath, keeping covenant and steadfast love for your servants who walk before you with all their heart, [24] the covenant that you kept for your servant my father David as you declared to him; you promised with your mouth and have this day fulfilled with your hand. [25] Therefore, O LORD, God of Israel, keep for your servant my father David that which you promised him, saying, 'There shall never fail you a successor before me to sit on the throne of Israel, if only your children look to their way, to walk before me as you have walked before me.' [26] Therefore, O God of Israel, let your word be con-

firmed, which you promised to your servant my father David.

27 "But will God indeed dwell on the earth? Even heaven and the highest heaven cannot contain you, much less this house that I have built! [28] Regard your servant's prayer and his plea, O LORD my God, heeding the cry and the prayer that your servant prays to you today; [29] that your eyes may be open night and day toward this house, the place of which you said, 'My name shall be there,' that you may heed the prayer that your servant prays toward this place. [30] Hear the plea of your servant and of your people Israel when they pray toward this place; O hear in heaven your dwelling place; heed and forgive.

31 "If someone sins against a neighbor and is given an oath to swear, and comes and swears before your altar in this house, [32] then hear in heaven, and act, and judge your servants, condemning the guilty by bringing their conduct on their own head, and vindicating the righteous by rewarding them according to their righteousness.

33 "When your people Israel, having sinned against you, are defeated before an enemy but turn again to you, confess your name, pray and plead with you in this house, [34] then hear in heaven, forgive the sin of your people Israel, and bring them again to the land that you gave to their ancestors.

35 "When heaven is shut up and there is no rain because they have sinned against you, and then they pray toward this place, confess your name, and turn from their sin, because you punish[a] them, [36] then hear in heaven, and forgive the sin of your servants, your people Israel, when you teach them the good way in which they should walk; and grant rain on your land, which you have given to your people as an inheritance.

37 "If there is famine in the land, if there is plague, blight, mildew, locust, or caterpillar; if their enemy besieges them in any[b] of their cities; whatever plague, whatever sickness there is; [38] whatever prayer, whatever plea there is from any individual or from all your people Israel, all knowing the afflictions of their own hearts so that they stretch out their hands toward this house; [39] then hear in heaven your dwelling place, forgive, act, and render to all whose hearts you know—according to all their ways, for only you know what is in every human heart— [40] so that they may fear you all the days that they live in the land that you gave to our ancestors.

41 "Likewise when a foreigner, who is not

a Or when you answer   b Gk Syr: Heb in the land

of your people Israel, comes from a distant land because of your name [42]—for they shall hear of your great name, your mighty hand, and your outstretched arm—when a foreigner comes and prays toward this house, [43]then hear in heaven your dwelling place, and do according to all that the foreigner calls to you, so that all the peoples of the earth may know your name and fear you, as do your people Israel, and so that they may know that your name has been invoked on this house that I have built.

[44] "If your people go out to battle against their enemy, by whatever way you shall send them, and they pray to the LORD toward the city that you have chosen and the house that I have built for your name, [45]then hear in heaven their prayer and their plea, and maintain their cause.

[46] "If they sin against you—for there is no one who does not sin—and you are angry with them and give them to an enemy, so that they are carried away captive to the land of the enemy, far off or near; [47]yet if they come to their senses in the land to which they have been taken captive, and repent, and plead with you in the land of their captors, saying, 'We have sinned, and have done wrong; we have acted wickedly'; [48]if they repent with all their heart and soul in the land of their enemies, who took them captive, and pray to you toward their land, which you gave to their ancestors, the city that you have chosen, and the house that I have built for your name; [49]then hear in heaven your dwelling place their prayer and their plea, maintain their cause [50]and forgive your people who have sinned against you, and all their transgressions that they have committed against you; and grant them compassion in the sight of their captors, so that they may have compassion on them [51](for they are your people and heritage, which you brought out of Egypt, from the midst of the iron-smelter). [52]Let your eyes be open to the plea of your servant, and to the plea of your people Israel, listening to them whenever they call to you. [53]For you have separated them from among all the peoples of the earth, to be your heritage, just as you promised through Moses, your servant, when you brought our ancestors out of Egypt, O Lord GOD."

Solomon Blesses the Assembly

[54] Now when Solomon finished offering all this prayer and this plea to the LORD, he arose from facing the altar of the LORD, where he had knelt with hands outstretched toward heaven;

[55]he stood and blessed all the assembly of Israel with a loud voice:

[56] "Blessed be the LORD, who has given rest to his people Israel according to all that he promised; not one word has failed of all his good promise, which he spoke through his servant Moses. [57]The LORD our God be with us, as he was with our ancestors; may he not leave us or abandon us, [58]but incline our hearts to him, to walk in all his ways, and to keep his commandments, his statutes, and his ordinances, which he commanded our ancestors. [59]Let these words of mine, with which I pleaded before the LORD, be near to the LORD our God day and night, and may he maintain the cause of his servant and the cause of his people Israel, as each day requires; [60]so that all the peoples of the earth may know that the LORD is God; there is no other. [61]Therefore devote yourselves completely to the LORD our God, walking in his statutes and keeping his commandments, as at this day."

Solomon Offers Sacrifices

[62] Then the king, and all Israel with him, offered sacrifice before the LORD. [63]Solomon offered as sacrifices of well-being to the LORD twenty-two thousand oxen and one hundred twenty thousand sheep. So the king and all the people of Israel dedicated the house of the LORD. [64]The same day the king consecrated the middle of the court that was in front of the house of the LORD; for there he offered the burnt offerings and the grain offerings and the fat pieces of the sacrifices of well-being, because the bronze altar that was before the LORD was too small to receive the burnt offerings and the grain offerings and the fat pieces of the sacrifices of well-being.

[65] So Solomon held the festival at that time, and all Israel with him—a great assembly, people from Lebo-hamath to the Wadi of Egypt—before the LORD our God, seven days.[a] [66]On the eighth day he sent the people away; and they blessed the king, and went to their tents, joyful and in good spirits because of all the goodness that the LORD had shown to his servant David and to his people Israel.

9 God Appears Again to Solomon

When Solomon had finished building the house of the LORD and the king's house and all that Solomon desired to build, [2]the LORD appeared to Solomon a second time, as he had appeared to him at Gibeon. [3]The LORD said to him, "I have heard your prayer and your plea, which you made before me; I have consecrat-

a Compare Gk: Heb *seven days and seven days, fourteen days* ed this house that you have built, and put my name there forever; my eyes and my heart will be there for all time. ⁴As for you, if you will walk before me, as David your father walked, with integrity of heart and uprightness, doing according to all that I have commanded you, and keeping my statutes and my ordinances, ⁵then I will establish your royal throne over Israel forever, as I promised your father David, saying, 'There shall not fail you a successor on the throne of Israel.'

6 "If you turn aside from following me, you or your children, and do not keep my commandments and my statutes that I have set before you, but go and serve other gods and worship them, ⁷then I will cut Israel off from the land that I have given them; and the house that I have consecrated for my name I will cast out of my sight; and Israel will become a proverb and a taunt among all peoples. ⁸This house will become a heap of ruins;ᵃ everyone passing by it will be astonished, and will hiss; and they will say, 'Why has the LORD done such a thing to this land and to this house?' ⁹Then they will say, 'Because they have forsaken the LORD their God, who brought their ancestors out of the land of Egypt, and embraced other gods, worshiping them and serving them; therefore the LORD has brought this disaster upon them.' "

10 At the end of twenty years, in which Solomon had built the two houses, the house of the LORD and the king's house, ¹¹King Hiram of Tyre having supplied Solomon with cedar and cypress timber and gold, as much as he desired, King Solomon gave to Hiram twenty cities in the land of Galilee. ¹²But when Hiram came from Tyre to see the cities that Solomon had given him, they did not please him. ¹³Therefore he said, "What kind of cities are these that you have given me, my brother?" So they are called the land of Cabulᵇ to this day. ¹⁴But Hiram had sent to the king one hundred twenty talents of gold.

Other Acts of Solomon

15 This is the account of the forced labor that King Solomon conscripted to build the house of the LORD and his own house, the Millo and the wall of Jerusalem, Hazor, Megiddo, Gezer ¹⁶(Pharaoh king of Egypt had gone up and captured Gezer and burned it down, had killed the Canaanites who lived in the city, and had given it as dowry to his daughter, Solomon's wife; ¹⁷so Solomon rebuilt Gezer), Lower Beth-horon, ¹⁸Baalath, Tamar in the wilderness, within the land, ¹⁹as well as all of Solomon's storage cities, the cities for his chariots, the cities for his cavalry, and whatever Solomon desired to build, in Jerusalem, in Lebanon, and in all the land of his dominion. ²⁰All the people who were left of the Amorites, the Hittites, the Perizzites, the Hivites, and the Jebusites, who were not of the people of Israel— ²¹their descendants who were still left in the land, whom the Israelites were unable to destroy completely—these Solomon conscripted for slave labor, and so they are to this day. ²²But of the Israelites Solomon made no slaves; they were the soldiers, they were his officials, his commanders, his captains, and the commanders of his chariotry and cavalry.

23 These were the chief officers who were over Solomon's work: five hundred fifty, who had charge of the people who carried on the work.

24 But Pharaoh's daughter went up from the city of David to her own house that Solomon had built for her; then he built the Millo.

25 Three times a year Solomon used to offer up burnt offerings and sacrifices of well-being on the altar that he built for the LORD, offering incenseᶜ before the LORD. So he completed the house.

Solomon's Commercial Activity

26 King Solomon built a fleet of ships at Ezion-geber, which is near Eloth on the shore of the Red Sea,ᵈ in the land of Edom. ²⁷Hiram sent his servants with the fleet, sailors who were familiar with the sea, together with the servants of Solomon. ²⁸They went to Ophir, and imported from there four hundred twenty talents of gold, which they delivered to King Solomon.

10 Visit of the Queen of Sheba

When the queen of Sheba heard of the fame of Solomon (fame due toᵉ the name of the LORD), she came to test him with hard questions. ²She came to Jerusalem with a very great retinue, with camels bearing spices, and very much gold, and precious stones; and when she came to Solomon, she told him all that was on her mind. ³Solomon answered all her questions; there was nothing hidden from the king that he could not explain to her. ⁴When the queen of Sheba had observed all the wisdom of Solomon, the house that he had built, ⁵the food of his table, the seating of his officials, and the attendance of his servants, their clothing, his valets, and his burnt offerings that he offered at the house of the LORD, there was no more spirit in her.

ᵃ Syr Old Latin: Heb *will become high* ᵇ Perhaps meaning *a land good for nothing* ᶜ Gk: Heb *offering incense with it that was* ᵈ Or *Sea of Reeds* ᵉ Meaning of Heb uncertain

6 So she said to the king, "The report was true that I heard in my own land of your accomplishments and of your wisdom, [7]but I did not believe the reports until I came and my own eyes had seen it. Not even half had been told me; your wisdom and prosperity far surpass the report that I had heard. [8]Happy are your wives![a] Happy are these your servants, who continually attend you and hear your wisdom! [9]Blessed be the LORD your God, who has delighted in you and set you on the throne of Israel! Because the LORD loved Israel forever, he has made you king to execute justice and righteousness." [10]Then she gave the king one hundred twenty talents of gold, a great quantity of spices, and precious stones; never again did spices come in such quantity as that which the queen of Sheba gave to King Solomon.

11 Moreover, the fleet of Hiram, which carried gold from Ophir, brought from Ophir a great quantity of almug wood and precious stones. [12]From the almug wood the king made supports for the house of the LORD, and for the king's house, lyres also and harps for the singers; no such almug wood has come or been seen to this day.

13 Meanwhile King Solomon gave to the queen of Sheba every desire that she expressed, as well as what he gave her out of Solomon's royal bounty. Then she returned to her own land, with her servants.

14 The weight of gold that came to Solomon in one year was six hundred sixty-six talents of gold, [15]besides that which came from the traders and from the business of the merchants, and from all the kings of Arabia and the governors of the land. [16]King Solomon made two hundred large shields of beaten gold; six hundred shekels of gold went into each large shield. [17]He made three hundred shields of beaten gold; three minas of gold went into each shield; and the king put them in the House of the Forest of Lebanon. [18]The king also made a great ivory throne, and overlaid it with the finest gold. [19]The throne had six steps. The top of the throne was rounded in the back, and on each side of the seat were arm rests and two lions standing beside the arm rests, [20]while twelve lions were standing, one on each end of a step on the six steps. Nothing like it was ever made in any kingdom. [21]All King Solomon's drinking vessels were of gold, and all the vessels of the House of the Forest of Lebanon were of pure gold; none were of silver—it was not considered as anything in the days of Solomon. [22]For the king had a fleet of ships of Tarshish at sea with the fleet of Hi-

a Gk Syr: Heb men

JESUS SIGHTING

Imagine you are Solomon trying to fill your father's shoes. David was a heroic, successful, effective, faithful, beloved, legendary king. But now it's your turn.

No pressure, right?

So you start strong. You pray for wisdom and soon prove to the world you're way ahead of your peers in that department. With wisdom comes respect, and with respect comes connections . . . and glory! Soon you're trading up and down the Mediterranean with other kingdoms, making yourself and your people extremely wealthy.

Read **1 Kings 11.1–13**. Solomon came to trust his wealth more than God. His wealth and false pride led him away from God to his downfall and the downfall of the kingdom.

Jesus uses this image of Solomon in his glory as an illustration in the Sermon on the Mount (Matthew 6.28–34). Jesus' listeners knew Solomon's story. They got the point. "No one can serve two masters . . . you cannot serve God and wealth" (6.24).

Jesus was reminding them to trust God first. Today, we need to keep trusting God and to stop looking for other people or things to replace God. The rest will come. What you really need you will have, because God takes care of those things better than we can ourselves.

In the Sermon on the Mount Jesus reminds us not to worry, but to be happy and secure . . . no matter what we have or don't have. If God provides for those who have no means to provide for themselves, surely we can trust him to provide what we need.

ram. Once every three years the fleet of ships of Tarshish used to come bringing gold, silver, ivory, apes, and peacocks.*

23 Thus King Solomon excelled all the kings of the earth in riches and in wisdom. 24The whole earth sought the presence of Solomon to hear his wisdom, which God had put into his mind. 25Every one of them brought a present, objects of silver and gold, garments, weaponry, spices, horses, and mules, so much year by year.

26 Solomon gathered together chariots and horses; he had fourteen hundred chariots and twelve thousand horses, which he stationed in the chariot cities and with the king in Jerusalem. 27The king made silver as common in Jerusalem as stones, and he made cedars as numerous as the sycamores of the Shephelah. 28Solomon's import of horses was from Egypt and Kue, and the king's traders received them from Kue at a price. 29A chariot could be imported from Egypt for six hundred shekels of silver, and a horse for one hundred fifty; so through the king's traders they were exported to all the kings of the Hittites and the kings of Aram.

11 Solomon's Errors

King Solomon loved many foreign women along with the daughter of Pharaoh: Moabite, Ammonite, Edomite, Sidonian, and Hittite women, 2from the nations concerning which the Lord had said to the Israelites, "You shall not enter into marriage with them, neither shall they with you; for they will surely incline your heart to follow their gods"; Solomon clung to these in love. 3Among his wives were seven hundred princesses and three hundred concubines; and his wives turned away his heart. 4For when Solomon was old, his wives turned away his heart after other gods; and his heart was not true to the Lord his God, as was the heart of his father David. 5For Solomon followed Astarte the goddess of the Sidonians, and Milcom the abomination of the Ammonites. 6So Solomon did what was evil in the sight of the Lord, and did not completely follow the Lord, as his father David had done. 7Then Solomon built a high place for Chemosh the abomination of Moab, and for Molech the abomination of the Ammonites, on the mountain east of Jerusalem. 8He did the same for all his foreign wives, who offered incense and sacrificed to their gods.

9 Then the Lord was angry with Solomon, because his heart had turned away from the Lord, the God of Israel, who had appeared to him twice, 10and had commanded him concerning this matter, that he should not follow other gods; but he did not observe what the Lord commanded. 11Therefore the Lord said to Solomon, "Since this has been your mind and you have not kept my covenant and my statutes that I have commanded you, I will surely tear the kingdom from you and give it to your servant. 12Yet for the sake of your father David I will not do it in your lifetime; I will tear it out of the hand of your son. 13I will not, however, tear away the entire kingdom; I will give one tribe to your son, for the sake of my servant David and for the sake of Jerusalem, which I have chosen."

Adversaries of Solomon

14 Then the Lord raised up an adversary against Solomon, Hadad the Edomite; he was of the royal house in Edom. 15For when David was in Edom, and Joab the commander of the army went up to bury the dead, he killed every male in Edom 16(for Joab and all Israel remained there six months, until he had eliminated every male in Edom); 17but Hadad fled to Egypt with some Edomites who were servants of his father. He was a young boy at that time. 18They set out from Midian and came to Paran; they took people with them from Paran and came to Egypt, to Pharaoh king of Egypt, who gave him a house, assigned him an allowance of food, and gave him land. 19Hadad found great favor in the sight of Pharaoh, so that he gave him his sister-in-law for a wife, the sister of Queen Tahpenes. 20The sister of Tahpenes gave birth by him to his son Genubath, whom Tahpenes weaned in Pharaoh's house; Genubath was in Pharaoh's house among the children of Pharaoh. 21When Hadad heard in Egypt that David slept with his ancestors and that Joab the commander of the army was dead, Hadad said to Pharaoh, "Let me depart, that I may go to my own country." 22But Pharaoh said to him, "What do you lack with me that you now seek to go to your own country?" And he said, "No, do let me go."

23 God raised up another adversary against Solomon,* Rezon son of Eliada, who had fled from his master, King Hadadezer of Zobah. 24He gathered followers around him and became leader of a marauding band, after the slaughter by David; they went to Damascus, settled there, and made him king in Damascus. 25He was an adversary of Israel all the days of Solomon, making trouble as Hadad did; he despised Israel and reigned over Aram.

Jeroboam's Rebellion

26 Jeroboam son of Nebat, an Ephraimite of Zeredah, a servant of Solomon, whose

a Or *baboons* *b* Heb *him*

mother's name was Zeruah, a widow, rebelled against the king. ²⁷The following was the reason he rebelled against the king. Solomon built the Millo, and closed up the gap in the wall*ᵃ* of the city of his father David. ²⁸The man Jeroboam was very able, and when Solomon saw that the young man was industrious he gave him charge over all the forced labor of the house of Joseph. ²⁹About that time, when Jeroboam was leaving Jerusalem, the prophet Ahijah the Shilonite found him on the road. Ahijah had clothed himself with a new garment. The two of them were alone in the open country ³⁰when Ahijah laid hold of the new garment he was wearing and tore it into twelve pieces. ³¹He then said to Jeroboam: Take for yourself ten pieces; for thus says the Lᴏʀᴅ, the God of Israel, "See, I am about to tear the kingdom from the hand of Solomon, and will give you ten tribes. ³²One tribe will remain his, for the sake of my servant David and for the sake of Jerusalem, the city that I have chosen out of all the tribes of Israel. ³³This is because he has*ᵇ* forsaken me, worshiped Astarte the goddess of the Sidonians, Chemosh the god of Moab, and Milcom the god of the Ammonites, and has*ᵇ* not walked in my ways, doing what is right in my sight and keeping my statutes and my ordinances, as his father David did. ³⁴Nevertheless I will not take the whole kingdom away from him but will make him ruler all the days of his life, for the sake of my servant David whom I chose and who did keep my commandments and my statutes; ³⁵but I will take the kingdom away from his son and give it to you—that is, the ten tribes. ³⁶Yet to his son I will give one tribe, so that my servant David may always have a lamp before me in Jerusalem, the city where I have chosen to put my name. ³⁷I will take you, and you shall reign over all that your soul desires; you shall be king over Israel. ³⁸If you will listen to all that I command you, walk in my ways, and do what is right in my sight by keeping my statutes and my commandments, as David my servant did, I will be with you, and will build you an enduring house, as I built for David, and I will give Israel to you. ³⁹For this reason I will punish the descendants of David, but not forever." ⁴⁰Solomon sought therefore to kill Jeroboam; but Jeroboam promptly fled to Egypt, to King Shishak of Egypt, and remained in Egypt until the death of Solomon.

Death of Solomon

41 Now the rest of the acts of Solomon, all that he did as well as his wisdom, are they not written in the Book of the Acts of Solomon? ⁴²The time that Solomon reigned in Jerusalem over all Israel was forty years. ⁴³Solomon slept with his ancestors and was buried in the city of his father David; and his son Rehoboam succeeded him.

12 The Northern Tribes Secede

Rehoboam went to Shechem, for all Israel had come to Shechem to make him king. ²When Jeroboam son of Nebat heard of it (for he was still in Egypt, where he had fled from King Solomon), then Jeroboam returned from*ᶜ* Egypt. ³And they sent and called him; and Jeroboam and all the assembly of Israel came and said to Rehoboam, ⁴"Your father made our yoke heavy. Now therefore lighten the hard service

a Heb lacks *in the wall*   *b* Gk Syr Vg: Heb *they have*   *c* Gk Vg Compare 2 Chr 10.2: Heb *lived in*

Untitled—© Lexi Hiland, 16

of your father and his heavy yoke that he placed on us, and we will serve you." [5]He said to them, "Go away for three days, then come again to me." So the people went away.

6 Then King Rehoboam took counsel with the older men who had attended his father Solomon while he was still alive, saying, "How do you advise me to answer this people?" [7]They answered him, "If you will be a servant to this people today and serve them, and speak good words to them when you answer them, then they will be your servants forever." [8]But he disregarded the advice that the older men gave him, and consulted with the young men who had grown up with him and now attended him. [9]He said to them, "What do you advise that we answer this people who have said to me, 'Lighten the yoke that your father put on us'?" [10]The young men who had grown up with him said to him, "Thus you should say to this people who spoke to you, 'Your father made our yoke heavy, but you must lighten it for us'; thus you should say to them, 'My little finger is thicker than my father's loins. [11]Now, whereas my father laid on you a heavy yoke, I will add to your yoke. My father disciplined you with whips, but I will discipline you with scorpions.' "

12 So Jeroboam and all the people came to Rehoboam the third day, as the king had said, "Come to me again the third day." [13]The king answered the people harshly. He disregarded the advice that the older men had given him [14]and spoke to them according to the advice of the young men, "My father made your yoke heavy, but I will add to your yoke; my father disciplined you with whips, but I will discipline you with scorpions." [15]So the king did not lis-

ten to the people, because it was a turn of affairs brought about by the LORD that he might fulfill his word, which the LORD had spoken by Ahijah the Shilonite to Jeroboam son of Nebat.

16 When all Israel saw that the king would not listen to them, the people answered the king,

"What share do we have in David?
　We have no inheritance in the son of Jesse.
　To your tents, O Israel!
　Look now to your own house, O David."
So Israel went away to their tents. [17]But Rehoboam reigned over the Israelites who were living in the towns of Judah. [18]When King Rehoboam sent Adoram, who was taskmaster over the forced labor, all Israel stoned him to death. King Rehoboam then hurriedly mounted his chariot to flee to Jerusalem. [19]So Israel has been in rebellion against the house of David to this day.

First Dynasty: Jeroboam Reigns over Israel

20 When all Israel heard that Jeroboam had returned, they sent and called him to the assembly and made him king over all Israel. There was no one who followed the house of David, except the tribe of Judah alone.

21 When Rehoboam came to Jerusalem, he assembled all the house of Judah and the tribe of Benjamin, one hundred eighty thousand chosen troops to fight against the house of Israel, to restore the kingdom to Rehoboam son of Solomon. [22]But the word of God came to Shemaiah the man of God: [23]Say to King Rehoboam of Judah, son of Solomon, and to all the house of Judah and Benjamin, and to the rest of the people, [24]"Thus says the LORD, You shall not go up or fight against your kindred the people of Israel. Let everyone go home, for this thing is from me." So they heeded the word of the LORD and went home again, according to the word of the LORD.

Jeroboam's Golden Calves

25 Then Jeroboam built Shechem in the hill country of Ephraim, and resided there; he went out from there and built Penuel. [26]Then Jeroboam said to himself, "Now the kingdom may well revert to the house of David. [27]If this people continues to go up to offer sacrifices in the house of the LORD at Jerusalem, the heart of this people will turn again to their master, King Rehoboam of Judah; they will kill me and return to King Rehoboam of Judah." [28]So the king took counsel, and made two calves of gold. He said to the people, [a] "You have gone up

a Gk: Heb *to them*

to Jerusalem long enough. Here are your gods, O Israel, who brought you up out of the land of Egypt." [29]He set one in Bethel, and the other he put in Dan. [30]And this thing became a sin, for the people went to worship before the one at Bethel and before the other as far as Dan.[a] [31]He also made houses[b] on high places, and appointed priests from among all the people, who were not Levites. [32]Jeroboam appointed a festival on the fifteenth day of the eighth month like the festival that was in Judah, and he offered sacrifices on the altar; so he did in Bethel, sacrificing to the calves that he had made. And he placed in Bethel the priests of the high places that he had made. [33]He went up to the altar that he had made in Bethel on the fifteenth day in the eighth month, in the month that he alone had devised; he appointed a festival for the people of Israel, and he went up to the altar to offer incense.

13 A Man of God from Judah

While Jeroboam was standing by the altar to offer incense, a man of God came out of Judah by the word of the Lord to Bethel [2]and proclaimed against the altar by the word of the Lord, and said, "O altar, altar, thus says the Lord: 'A son shall be born to the house of David, Josiah by name; and he shall sacrifice on you the priests of the high places who offer incense on you, and human bones shall be burned on you.' " [3]He gave a sign the same day, saying, "This is the sign that the Lord has spoken: 'The altar shall be torn down, and the ashes that are on it shall be poured out.' " [4]When the king heard what the man of God cried out against the altar at Bethel, Jeroboam stretched out his hand from the altar, saying, "Seize him!" But the hand that he stretched out against him withered so that he could not draw it back to himself. [5]The altar also was torn down, and the ashes poured out from the altar, according to the sign that the man of God had given by the word of the Lord. [6]The king said to the man of God, "Entreat now the favor of the Lord your God, and pray for me, so that my hand may be restored to me." So the man of God entreated the Lord; and the king's hand was restored to him, and became as it was before. [7]Then the king said to the man of God, "Come home with me and dine, and I will give you a gift." [8]But the man of God said to the king, "If you give me half your kingdom, I will not go in with you; nor will I eat food or drink water in this place. [9]For thus I was commanded by the word of the Lord: You shall not eat food, or drink water, or return by the way that you came." [10]So he went another way, and did not return by the way that he had come to Bethel.

11 Now there lived an old prophet in Bethel. One of his sons came and told him all that the man of God had done that day in Bethel; the words also that he had spoken to the king, they told to their father. [12]Their father said to them, "Which way did he go?" And his sons showed him the way that the man of God who came from Judah had gone. [13]Then he said to his sons, "Saddle a donkey for me." So they saddled a donkey for him, and he mounted it. [14]He went after the man of God, and found him sitting under an oak tree. He said to him, "Are you the man of God who came from Judah?" He answered, "I am." [15]Then he said to him, "Come home with me and eat some food." [16]But he said, "I cannot return with you, or go in with you; nor will I eat food or drink water with you in this place; [17]for it was said to me by the word of the Lord: You shall not eat food or drink water there, or return by the way that you came." [18]Then the other[c] said to him, "I also am a prophet as you are, and an angel spoke to me by the word of the Lord: Bring him back with you into your house so that he may eat food and drink water." But he was deceiving him. [19]Then the man of God[c] went back with him, and ate food and drank water in his house.

20 As they were sitting at the table, the word of the Lord came to the prophet who had brought him back; [21]and he proclaimed to the man of God who came from Judah, "Thus says the Lord: Because you have disobeyed the word of the Lord, and have not kept the commandment that the Lord your God commanded you, [22]but have come back and have eaten food and drunk water in the place of which he said to you, 'Eat no food, and drink no water,' your body shall not come to your ancestral tomb." [23]After the man of God[c] had eaten food and had drunk, they saddled for him a donkey belonging to the prophet who had brought him back. [24]Then as he went away, a lion met him on the road and killed him. His body was thrown in the road, and the donkey stood beside it; the lion also stood beside the body. [25]People passed by and saw the body thrown in the road, with the lion standing by the body. And they came and told it in the town where the old prophet lived.

26 When the prophet who had brought him back from the way heard of it, he said, "It is the man of God who disobeyed the word of the Lord; therefore the Lord has given him to the lion, which has torn him and killed him

---

a Compare Gk: Heb *went to the one as far as Dan* b Gk Vg Compare 13.32: Heb *a house* c Heb *he*

Serenity—© Michelle Jozwiak, 18

according to the word that the LORD spoke to him." ²⁷Then he said to his sons, "Saddle a donkey for me." So they saddled one, ²⁸and he went and found the body thrown in the road, with the donkey and the lion standing beside the body. The lion had not eaten the body or attacked the donkey. ²⁹The prophet took up the body of the man of God, laid it on the donkey, and brought it back to the city,ᵃ to mourn and to bury him. ³⁰He laid the body in his own grave; and they mourned over him, saying, "Alas, my brother!" ³¹After he had buried him, he said to his sons, "When I die, bury me in the grave in which the man of God is buried; lay my bones beside his bones. ³²For the saying that he proclaimed by the word of the LORD against the altar in Bethel, and against all the houses of the high places that are in the cities of Samaria, shall surely come to pass."

33 Even after this event Jeroboam did not turn from his evil way, but made priests for the high places again from among all the people; any who wanted to be priests he consecrated for the high places. ³⁴This matter became sin to the house of Jeroboam, so as to cut it off and to destroy it from the face of the earth.

14 Judgment on the House of Jeroboam

At that time Abijah son of Jeroboam fell sick. ²Jeroboam said to his wife, "Go, disguise yourself, so that it will not be known that you are the wife of Jeroboam, and go to Shiloh; for the prophet Ahijah is there, who said of me that I should be king over this people. ³Take with you ten loaves, some cakes, and a jar of honey, and go to him; he will tell you what shall happen to the child."

4 Jeroboam's wife did so; she set out and went to Shiloh, and came to the house of Ahijah. Now Ahijah could not see, for his eyes were dim because of his age. ⁵But the LORD said to Ahijah, "The wife of Jeroboam is coming to inquire of you concerning her son; for he is sick. Thus and thus you shall say to her."

When she came, she pretended to be another woman. ⁶But when Ahijah heard the sound of her feet, as she came in at the door, he said, "Come in, wife of Jeroboam; why do you pretend to be another? For I am charged with heavy tidings for you. ⁷Go, tell Jeroboam, 'Thus says the LORD, the God of Israel: Because I exalted you from among the people, made you leader over my people Israel, ⁸and tore the kingdom away from the house of David to give it to you; yet you have not been like my servant David, who kept my commandments and followed me with all his heart, doing only that which was right in my sight, ⁹but you have done evil above all those who were before you and have gone and made for yourself other gods, and cast images, provoking me to anger, and have thrust me behind your back; ¹⁰therefore, I will bring evil upon the house of Jeroboam. I will cut off from Jeroboam every male, both bond and free in Israel, and will consume the house of Jeroboam, just as one

ᵃ Gk: Heb *he came to the town of the old prophet*

burns up dung until it is all gone. ¹¹Anyone belonging to Jeroboam who dies in the city, the dogs shall eat; and anyone who dies in the open country, the birds of the air shall eat; for the LORD has spoken.' ¹²Therefore set out, go to your house. When your feet enter the city, the child shall die. ¹³All Israel shall mourn for him and bury him; for he alone of Jeroboam's family shall come to the grave, because in him there is found something pleasing to the LORD, the God of Israel, in the house of Jeroboam. ¹⁴Moreover the LORD will raise up for himself a king over Israel, who shall cut off the house of Jeroboam today, even right now!ᵃ

15 "The LORD will strike Israel, as a reed is shaken in the water; he will root up Israel out of this good land that he gave to their ancestors, and scatter them beyond the Euphrates, because they have made their sacred poles,ᵇ provoking the LORD to anger. ¹⁶He will give Israel up because of the sins of Jeroboam, which he sinned and which he caused Israel to commit."

17 Then Jeroboam's wife got up and went away, and she came to Tirzah. As she came to the threshold of the house, the child died. ¹⁸All Israel buried him and mourned for him, according to the word of the LORD, which he spoke by his servant the prophet Ahijah.

Death of Jeroboam
19 Now the rest of the acts of Jeroboam, how he warred and how he reigned, are written in the Book of the Annals of the Kings of Israel. ²⁰The time that Jeroboam reigned was twenty-two years; then he slept with his ancestors, and his son Nadab succeeded him.

Rehoboam Reigns over Judah
21 Now Rehoboam son of Solomon reigned in Judah. Rehoboam was forty-one years old when he began to reign, and he reigned seventeen years in Jerusalem, the city that the LORD had chosen out of all the tribes of Israel, to put his name there. His mother's name was Naamah the Ammonite. ²²Judah did what was evil in the sight of the LORD; they provoked him to jealousy with their sins that they committed, more than all that their ancestors had done. ²³For they also built for themselves high places, pillars, and sacred polesᵇ on every high hill and under every green tree; ²⁴there were also male temple prostitutes in the land. They committed all the abominations of the nations that the LORD drove out before the people of Israel.

25 In the fifth year of King Rehoboam, King Shishak of Egypt came up against Jerusalem; ²⁶he took away the treasures of the house of

the LORD and the treasures of the king's house; he took everything. He also took away all the shields of gold that Solomon had made; ²⁷so King Rehoboam made shields of bronze instead, and committed them to the hands of the officers of the guard, who kept the door of the king's house. ²⁸As often as the king went into the house of the LORD, the guard carried them and brought them back to the guardroom.

29 Now the rest of the acts of Rehoboam, and all that he did, are they not written in the Book of the Annals of the Kings of Judah? ³⁰There was war between Rehoboam and Jeroboam continually. ³¹Rehoboam slept with his ancestors and was buried with his ancestors in the city of David. His mother's name was Naamah the Ammonite. His son Abijam succeeded him.

15 Abijam Reigns over Judah: Idolatry and War
Now in the eighteenth year of King Jeroboam son of Nebat, Abijam began to reign over Judah. ²He reigned for three years in Jerusalem. His mother's name was Maacah daughter of Abishalom. ³He committed all the sins that his father did before him; his heart was not true to the LORD his God, like the heart of his father David. ⁴Nevertheless for David's sake the LORD his God gave him a lamp in Jerusalem, setting up his son after him, and establishing Jerusalem; ⁵because David did what was right in the sight of the LORD, and did not turn aside from anything that he commanded him all the days of his life, except in the matter of Uriah the Hittite. ⁶The war begun between Rehoboam and Jeroboam continued all the days of his life. ⁷The rest of the acts of Abijam, and all that he did, are they not written in the Book of the Annals of the Kings of Judah? There was war between Abijam and Jeroboam. ⁸Abijam slept with his ancestors, and they buried him in the city of David. Then his son Asa succeeded him.

Asa Reigns over Judah
9 In the twentieth year of King Jeroboam of Israel, Asa began to reign over Judah; ¹⁰he reigned forty-one years in Jerusalem. His mother's name was Maacah daughter of Abishalom. ¹¹Asa did what was right in the sight of the LORD, as his father David had done. ¹²He put away the male temple prostitutes out of the land, and removed all the idols that his ancestors had made. ¹³He also removed his mother Maacah from being queen mother, because she had made an abominable image for Asherah; Asa cut down her image and burned it

ᵃ Meaning of Heb uncertain ᵇ Heb *Asherim*

at the Wadi Kidron. [14]But the high places were not taken away. Nevertheless the heart of Asa was true to the LORD all his days. [15]He brought into the house of the LORD the votive gifts of his father and his own votive gifts—silver, gold, and utensils.

Alliance with Aram against Israel

16 There was war between Asa and King Baasha of Israel all their days. [17]King Baasha of Israel went up against Judah, and built Ramah, to prevent anyone from going out or coming in to King Asa of Judah. [18]Then Asa took all the silver and the gold that were left in the treasures of the house of the LORD and the treasures of the king's house, and gave them into the hands of his servants. King Asa sent them to King Ben-hadad son of Tabrimmon son of Hezion of Aram, who resided in Damascus, saying, [19]"Let there be an alliance between me and you, like that between my father and your father: I am sending you a present of silver and gold; go, break your alliance with King Baasha of Israel, so that he may withdraw from me." [20]Ben-hadad listened to King Asa, and sent the commanders of his armies against the cities of Israel. He conquered Ijon, Dan, Abel-beth-maacah, and all Chinneroth, with all the land of Naphtali. [21]When Baasha heard of it, he stopped building Ramah and lived in Tirzah. [22]Then King Asa made a proclamation to all Judah, none was exempt: they carried away the stones of Ramah and its timber, with which Baasha had been building; with them King Asa built Geba of Benjamin and Mizpah. [23]Now the rest of all the acts of Asa, all his power, all that he did, and the cities that he built, are they not written in the Book of the Annals of the Kings of Judah? But in his old age he was diseased in his feet. [24]Then Asa slept with his ancestors, and was buried with his ancestors in the city of his father David; his son Jehoshaphat succeeded him.

Nadab Reigns over Israel

25 Nadab son of Jeroboam began to reign over Israel in the second year of King Asa of Judah; he reigned over Israel two years. [26]He did what was evil in the sight of the LORD, walking in the way of his ancestor and in the sin that he caused Israel to commit. 27 Baasha son of Ahijah, of the house of Issachar, conspired against him; and Baasha struck him down at Gibbethon, which belonged to the Philistines; for Nadab and all Israel were laying siege to Gibbethon. [28]So Baasha killed Nadab[a] in the third year of King Asa of Judah, and succeeded him. [29]As soon as he was king, he killed all the house of Jeroboam; he left to the house of Jeroboam not one that breathed, until he had destroyed it, according to the word of the LORD that he spoke by his servant Ahijah the Shilonite— [30]because of the sins of Jeroboam that he committed and that he caused Israel to commit, and because of the anger to which he provoked the LORD, the God of Israel.

31 Now the rest of the acts of Nadab, and all that he did, are they not written in the Book of the Annals of the Kings of Israel? [32]There was war between Asa and King Baasha of Israel all their days.

Second Dynasty: Baasha Reigns over Israel

33 In the third year of King Asa of Judah, Baasha son of Ahijah began to reign over all Israel at Tirzah; he reigned twenty-four years. [34]He did what was evil in the sight of the LORD, walking in the way of Jeroboam and in the sin that he caused Israel to commit.

16 The word of the LORD came to Jehu son of Hanani against Baasha, saying, [2]"Since I exalted you out of the dust and made you leader over my people Israel, and you have walked in the way of Jeroboam, and have caused my people Israel to sin, provoking me to anger with their sins, [3]therefore, I will consume Baasha and his house, and I will make your house like the house of Jeroboam son of Nebat. [4]Anyone belonging to Baasha who dies in the city the dogs shall eat; and anyone of his who dies in the field the birds of the air shall eat."

5 Now the rest of the acts of Baasha, what he did, and his power, are they not written in the Book of the Annals of the Kings of Israel? [6]Baasha slept with his ancestors, and was buried at Tirzah; and his son Elah succeeded him. [7]Moreover the word of the LORD came by the prophet Jehu son of Hanani against Baasha and his house, both because of all the evil that he did in the sight of the LORD, provoking him to anger with the work of his hands, in being like the house of Jeroboam, and also because he destroyed it.

Elah Reigns over Israel

8 In the twenty-sixth year of King Asa of Judah, Elah son of Baasha began to reign over Israel in Tirzah; he reigned two years. [9]But his servant Zimri, commander of half his chariots, conspired against him. When he was at Tirzah, drinking himself drunk in the house of Arza, who was in charge of the palace at Tirzah, [10]Zimri came in and struck him down and

a Heb *him*

I know now that because God is by my side and I have a wonderful set of family and friends there to help me when I stumble that I can, and will, get through it.

Every person feels insignificant at some point in their life, but look at David. He was a shepherd, not a big, strong warrior—and that's why God chose him. It's not the outward strength that makes the person; it's their unstoppable heart and mind-set that pushes them to do more, even if it seems impossible.

killed him, in the twenty-seventh year of King Asa of Judah, and succeeded him.

11 When he began to reign, as soon as he had seated himself on his throne, he killed all the house of Baasha; he did not leave him a single male of his kindred or his friends. [12]Thus Zimri destroyed all the house of Baasha, according to the word of the LORD, which he spoke against Baasha by the prophet Jehu— [13]because of all the sins of Baasha and the sins of his son Elah that they committed, and that they caused Israel to commit, provoking the LORD God of Israel to anger with their idols. [14]Now the rest of the acts of Elah, and all that he did, are they not written in the Book of the Annals of the Kings of Israel?

Third Dynasty: Zimri Reigns over Israel

15 In the twenty-seventh year of King Asa of Judah, Zimri reigned seven days in Tirzah. Now the troops were encamped against Gibbethon, which belonged to the Philistines, [16]and the troops who were encamped heard it said, "Zimri has conspired, and he has killed the king"; therefore all Israel made Omri, the commander of the army, king over Israel that day in the camp. [17]So Omri went up from Gibbethon, and all Israel with him, and they besieged Tirzah. [18]When Zimri saw that the city was taken, he went into the citadel of the king's house; he burned down the king's house over himself with fire, and died— [19]because of the sins that he committed, doing evil in the sight of the LORD, walking in the way of Jeroboam, and for the sin that he committed, causing Israel to sin. [20]Now the rest of the acts of Zimri, and the conspiracy that he made, are they not written in the Book of the Annals of the Kings of Israel?

Fourth Dynasty: Omri Reigns over Israel

21 Then the people of Israel were divided into two parts; half of the people followed Tibni son of Ginath, to make him king, and half followed Omri. [22]But the people who followed Omri overcame the people who followed Tibni son of Ginath; so Tibni died, and Omri became king. [23]In the thirty-first year of King Asa of Judah, Omri began to reign over Israel; he reigned for twelve years, six of them in Tirzah.

Samaria the New Capital

24 He bought the hill of Samaria from Shemer for two talents of silver; he fortified the hill, and called the city that he built, Samaria, after the name of Shemer, the owner of the hill.

25 Omri did what was evil in the sight of the LORD; he did more evil than all who were be-fore him. [26]For he walked in all the way of Jeroboam son of Nebat, and in the sins that he caused Israel to commit, provoking the LORD, the God of Israel, to anger by their idols. [27]Now the rest of the acts of Omri that he did, and the power that he showed, are they not written in the Book of the Annals of the Kings of Israel? [28]Omri slept with his ancestors, and was buried in Samaria; his son Ahab succeeded him.

Ahab Reigns over Israel

29 In the thirty-eighth year of King Asa of Judah, Ahab son of Omri began to reign over Israel; Ahab son of Omri reigned over Israel in Samaria twenty-two years. [30]Ahab son of Omri did evil in the sight of the LORD more than all who were before him.

Ahab Marries Jezebel and Worships Baal

31 And as if it had been a light thing for him to walk in the sins of Jeroboam son of Nebat, he took as his wife Jezebel daughter of King Ethbaal of the Sidonians, and went and served Baal, and worshiped him. [32]He erected an altar for Baal in the house of Baal, which he built in Samaria. [33]Ahab also made a sacred pole.[g] Ahab did more to provoke the anger of the LORD, the God of Israel, than had all the kings of Israel who were before him. [34]In his days Hiel of Bethel built Jericho; he laid its foundation at the cost of Abiram his firstborn, and set up its gates at the cost of his youngest son Segub, according to the word of the LORD, which he spoke by Joshua son of Nun.

17 Elijah Predicts a Drought

Now Elijah the Tishbite, of Tishbe[b] in Gilead, said to Ahab, "As the LORD the God of Israel lives, before whom I stand, there shall be neither dew nor rain these years, except by my word." [2]The word of the LORD came to him, saying, [3]"Go from here and turn eastward, and hide yourself by the Wadi Cherith, which is east of the Jordan. [4]You shall drink from the wadi, and I have commanded the ravens to feed you there." [5]So he went and did according to the word of the LORD; he went and lived by the Wadi Cherith, which is east of the Jordan. [6]The ravens brought him bread and meat in the morning, and bread and meat in the evening; and he drank from the wadi. [7]But after a while the wadi dried up, because there was no rain in the land.

The Widow of Zarephath

8 Then the word of the LORD came to him, saying, [9]"Go now to Zarephath, which belongs

---

a Heb Asherah b Gk: Heb of the settlers

to Sidon, and live there; for I have commanded a widow there to feed you." ¹⁰So he set out and went to Zarephath. When he came to the gate of the town, a widow was there gathering sticks; he called to her and said, "Bring me a little water in a vessel, so that I may drink." ¹¹As she was going to bring it, he called to her and said, "Bring me a morsel of bread in your hand." ¹²But she said, "As the Lᴏʀᴅ your God lives, I have nothing baked, only a handful of meal in a jar, and a little oil in a jug; I am now gathering a couple of sticks, so that I may go home and prepare it for myself and my son, that we may eat it, and die." ¹³Elijah said to her, "Do not be afraid; go and do as you have said; but first make me a little cake of it and bring it to me, and afterwards make something for yourself and your son. ¹⁴For thus says the Lᴏʀᴅ the God of Israel: The jar of meal will not be emptied and the jug of oil will not fail until the day that the Lᴏʀᴅ sends rain on the earth." ¹⁵She went and did as Elijah said, so that she as well as he and her household ate for many days. ¹⁶The jar of meal was not emptied, neither did the jug of oil fail, according to the word of the Lᴏʀᴅ that he spoke by Elijah.

Elijah Revives the Widow's Son

17 After this the son of the woman, the mistress of the house, became ill; his illness was so severe that there was no breath left in him. ¹⁸She then said to Elijah, "What have you against me, O man of God? You have come to me to bring my sin to remembrance, and to cause the death of my son!" ¹⁹But he said to her, "Give me your son." He took him from her bosom, carried him up into the upper chamber where he was lodging, and laid him on his own bed. ²⁰He cried out to the Lᴏʀᴅ, "O Lᴏʀᴅ my God, have you brought calamity even upon the widow with whom I am staying, by killing her son?" ²¹Then he stretched himself upon the child three times, and cried out to the Lᴏʀᴅ, "O Lᴏʀᴅ my God, let this child's life come into him again." ²²The Lᴏʀᴅ listened to the voice of Elijah; the life of the child came into him again, and he revived. ²³Elijah took the child, brought him down from the upper chamber into the house, and gave him to his mother; then Elijah said, "See, your son is alive." ²⁴So the woman said to Elijah, "Now I know that you are a man of God, and that the word of the Lᴏʀᴅ in your mouth is truth."

18 Elijah's Message to Ahab

After many days the word of the Lᴏʀᴅ came to Elijah, in the third year of the drought,ᵃ saying, "Go, present yourself to Ahab; I will send

ᵃ Heb lacks *of the drought*

REALITY ✔

WAITING PRAYER

Elijah was in deep trouble, and he knew it. Ever had that happen? Like Elijah, have you ever gotten in trouble for trying to do the right thing? Or maybe you've gotten in trouble the old-fashioned way—for doing something you totally knew was wrong.

Right or wrong, when you're in deep trouble, you're scared, confused, and maybe even really angry. You can feel things churning around in your guts and in your head.

When this happens, do what Elijah did: "Go out and stand on the mountain before the Lᴏʀᴅ, for the Lᴏʀᴅ is about to pass by" (1 Kings 19.11). For Elijah, the Lord passed by as "a sound of sheer silence" (9.12).

The prayer of being still (standing) and waiting is a different kind of prayer than what you probably are used to. In times of trouble, don't you usually pray with a lot of words and promises? You know, "Dear God, please, please, get me out of this, and if you, do I will . . ."

Being still in prayer is a tough kind of prayer, because in the silence you have to listen—*really* listen—to yourself and to what God might be telling you. It might become the prayer of an examination of your conscience. Or it might remain a silent listening prayer in which you hear God say, "Trust me. In the end, all will be well."

rain on the earth." ²So Elijah went to present himself to Ahab. The famine was severe in Samaria. ³Ahab summoned Obadiah, who was in charge of the palace. (Now Obadiah revered the Lᴏʀᴅ greatly; ⁴when Jezebel was killing off the prophets of the Lᴏʀᴅ, Obadiah took a hundred prophets, hid them fifty to a cave, and provided them with bread and water.) ⁵Then Ahab said to Obadiah, "Go through the land to all the springs of water and to all the wadis; perhaps we may find grass to keep the horses and mules alive, and not lose some of the animals."

⁶So they divided the land between them to pass through it; Ahab went in one direction by himself, and Obadiah went in another direction by himself.

7 As Obadiah was on the way, Elijah met him; Obadiah recognized him, fell on his face, and said, "Is it you, my lord Elijah?" ⁸He answered him, "It is I. Go, tell your lord that Elijah is here." ⁹And he said, "How have I sinned, that you would hand your servant over to Ahab, to kill me? ¹⁰As the LORD your God lives, there is no nation or kingdom to which my lord has not sent to seek you; and when they would say, 'He is not here,' he would require an oath of the kingdom or nation, that they had not found you. ¹¹But now you say, 'Go, tell your lord that Elijah is here.' ¹²As soon as I have gone from you, the spirit of the LORD will carry you I know not where; so, when I come and tell Ahab and he cannot find you, he will kill me, although I your servant have revered the LORD from my youth. ¹³Has it not been told my lord what I did when Jezebel killed the prophets of the LORD, how I hid a hundred of the LORD's prophets fifty to a cave, and provided them with bread and water? ¹⁴Yet now you say, 'Go, tell your lord that Elijah is here'; he will surely kill me." ¹⁵Elijah said, "As the LORD of hosts lives, before whom I stand, I will surely show myself to him today." ¹⁶So Obadiah went to meet Ahab, and told him; and Ahab went to meet Elijah.

17 When Ahab saw Elijah, Ahab said to him, "Is it you, you troubler of Israel?" ¹⁸He answered, "I have not troubled Israel; but you have, and your father's house, because you have forsaken the commandments of the LORD and followed the Baals. ¹⁹Now therefore have all Israel assemble for me at Mount Carmel, with the four hundred fifty prophets of Baal and the four hundred prophets of Asherah, who eat at Jezebel's table."

Elijah's Triumph over the Priests of Baal

20 So Ahab sent to all the Israelites, and assembled the prophets at Mount Carmel. ²¹Elijah then came near to all the people, and said, "How long will you go limping with two different opinions? If the LORD is God, follow him; but if Baal, then follow him." The people did not answer him a word. ²²Then Elijah said to the people, "I, even I only, am left a prophet of the LORD; but Baal's prophets number four hundred fifty. ²³Let two bulls be given to us; let them choose one bull for themselves, cut it in pieces, and lay it on the wood, but put no fire to it; I will prepare the other bull and lay it on the wood, but put no fire to it. ²⁴Then you call on the name of your god and I will call on the name

of the LORD; the god who answers by fire is indeed God." All the people answered, "Well spoken!" 25Then Elijah said to the prophets of Baal, "Choose for yourselves one bull and prepare it first, for you are many; then call on the name of your god, but put no fire to it." 26So they took the bull that was given them, prepared it, and called on the name of Baal from morning until noon, crying, "O Baal, answer us!" But there was no voice, and no answer. They limped about the altar that they had made. 27At noon Elijah mocked them, saying, "Cry aloud! Surely he is a god; either he is meditating, or he has wandered away, or he is on a journey, or perhaps he is asleep and must be awakened." 28Then they cried aloud and, as was their custom, they cut themselves with swords and lances until the blood gushed out over them. 29As midday passed, they raved on until the time of the offering of the oblation, but there was no voice, no answer, and no response.

30 Then Elijah said to all the people, "Come closer to me"; and all the people came closer to him. First he repaired the altar of the LORD that had been thrown down; 31Elijah took twelve stones, according to the number of the tribes of the sons of Jacob, to whom the word of the LORD came, saying, "Israel shall be your name"; 32with the stones he built an altar in the name of the LORD. Then he made a trench around the altar, large enough to contain two measures of seed. 33Next he put the wood in order, cut the bull in pieces, and laid it on the wood. He said, "Fill four jars with water and pour it on the burnt offering and on the wood." 34Then he said, "Do it a second time"; and they did it a second time. Again he said, "Do it a third time"; and they did it a third time, 35so that the water ran all around the altar, and filled the trench also with water.

36 At the time of the offering of the oblation, the prophet Elijah came near and said, "O LORD, God of Abraham, Isaac, and Israel, let it be known this day that you are God in Israel, that I am your servant, and that I have done all these things at your bidding. 37Answer me, O LORD, answer me, so that this people may know that you, O LORD, are God, and that you have turned their hearts back." 38Then the fire of the LORD fell and consumed the burnt offering, the wood, the stones, and the dust, and even licked up the water that was in the trench. 39When all the people saw it, they fell on their faces and said, "The LORD indeed is God; the LORD indeed is God." 40Elijah said to them, "Seize the prophets of Baal; do not let one of them escape." Then they seized them; and Elijah brought them down to the Wadi Kishon, and killed them there.

The Drought Ends

41 Elijah said to Ahab, "Go up, eat and drink; for there is a sound of rushing rain." 42So Ahab went up to eat and to drink. Elijah went up to the top of Carmel; there he bowed himself down upon the earth and put his face between his knees. 43He said to his servant, "Go up now, look toward the sea." He went up and looked, and said, "There is nothing." Then he said, "Go again seven times." 44At the seventh time he said, "Look, a little cloud no bigger than a person's hand is rising out of the sea." Then he said, "Go say to Ahab, 'Harness your chariot and go down before the rain stops you.' " 45In a little while the heavens grew black with clouds and wind; there was a heavy rain. Ahab rode off and went to Jezreel. 46But the hand of the LORD was on Elijah; he girded up his loins and ran in front of Ahab to the entrance of Jezreel.

19 Elijah Flees from Jezebel

Ahab told Jezebel all that Elijah had done, and how he had killed all the prophets with the sword. 2Then Jezebel sent a messenger to Elijah, saying, "So may the gods do to me, and more also, if I do not make your life like the life of one of them by this time tomorrow." 3Then he was afraid; he got up and fled for his life, and came to Beer-sheba, which belongs to Judah; he left his servant there.

4 But he himself went a day's journey into the wilderness, and came and sat down under a solitary broom tree. He asked that he might die: "It is enough; now, O LORD, take away my life, for I am no better than my ancestors." 5Then he lay down under the broom tree and fell asleep. Suddenly an angel touched him and said to him, "Get up and eat." 6He looked, and there at his head was a cake baked on hot stones, and a jar of water. He ate and drank, and lay down again. 7The angel of the LORD came a second time, touched him, and said, "Get up and eat, otherwise the journey will be too much for you." 8He got up, and ate and drank; then he went in the strength of that food forty days and forty nights to Horeb the mount of God. 9At that place he came to a cave, and spent the night there.

Then the word of the LORD came to him, saying, "What are you doing here, Elijah?" 10He answered, "I have been very zealous for the LORD, the God of hosts; for the Israelites have forsaken your covenant, thrown down your altars, and killed your prophets with the sword. I alone am left, and they are seeking my life, to take it away."

Elijah Meets God at Horeb

11 He said, "Go out and stand on the mountain before the LORD, for the LORD is about to

pass by." Now there was a great wind, so strong that it was splitting mountains and breaking rocks in pieces before the LORD, but the LORD was not in the wind; and after the wind an earthquake, but the LORD was not in the earthquake; [12]and after the earthquake a fire, but the LORD was not in the fire; and after the fire a sound of sheer silence. [13]When Elijah heard it, he wrapped his face in his mantle and went out and stood at the entrance of the cave. Then there came a voice to him that said, "What are you doing here, Elijah?" [14]He answered, "I have been very zealous for the LORD, the God of hosts; for the Israelites have forsaken your covenant, thrown down your altars, and killed your prophets with the sword. I alone am left, and they are seeking my life, to take it away." [15]Then the LORD said to him, "Go, return on your way to the wilderness of Damascus; when you arrive, you shall anoint Hazael as king over Aram. [16]Also you shall anoint Jehu son of Nimshi as king over Israel; and you shall anoint Elisha son of Shaphat of Abel-meholah as prophet in your place. [17]Whoever escapes from the sword of Hazael, Jehu shall kill; and whoever escapes from the sword of Jehu, Elisha shall kill. [18]Yet I will leave seven thousand in Israel, all the knees that have not bowed to Baal, and every mouth that has not kissed him."

Elisha Becomes Elijah's Disciple

19 So he set out from there, and found Elisha son of Shaphat, who was plowing. There were twelve yoke of oxen ahead of him, and he was with the twelfth. Elijah passed by him and threw his mantle over him. [20]He left the oxen, ran after Elijah, and said, "Let me kiss my father and my mother, and then I will follow you." Then Elijah[a] said to him, "Go back again; for what have I done to you?" [21]He returned from following him, took the yoke of oxen, and slaughtered them; using the equipment from the oxen, he boiled their flesh, and gave it to the people, and they ate. Then he set out and followed Elijah, and became his servant.

20 Ahab's Wars with the Arameans

King Ben-hadad of Aram gathered all his army together; thirty-two kings were with him, along with horses and chariots. He marched against Samaria, laid siege to it, and attacked it. [2]Then he sent messengers into the city to King Ahab of Israel, and said to him: "Thus says Ben-hadad: [3]Your silver and gold are mine; your fairest wives and children also are mine." [4]The king of Israel answered, "As you say, my lord, O king, I am yours, and all that I have."

[5]The messengers came again and said: "Thus says Ben-hadad: I sent to you, saying, 'Deliver to me your silver and gold, your wives and children'; [6]nevertheless I will send my servants to you tomorrow about this time, and they shall search your house and the houses of your servants, and lay hands on whatever pleases them,[b] and take it away."

7 Then the king of Israel called all the elders of the land, and said, "Look now! See how this man is seeking trouble; for he sent to me for my wives, my children, my silver, and my gold; and I did not refuse him." [8]Then all the elders and all the people said to him, "Do not listen or consent." [9]So he said to the messengers of Ben-hadad, "Tell my lord the king: All that you first demanded of your servant I will do; but this thing I cannot do." The messengers left and brought him word again. [10]Ben-hadad sent to him and said, "The gods do so to me, and more also, if the dust of Samaria will provide a handful for each of the people who follow me." [11]The king of Israel answered, "Tell him: One who puts on armor should not brag like one who takes it off." [12]When Ben-hadad heard this message—now he had been drinking with the kings in the booths—he said to his men, "Take your positions!" And they took their positions against the city.

Prophetic Opposition to Ahab

13 Then a certain prophet came up to King Ahab of Israel and said, "Thus says the LORD, Have you seen all this great multitude? Look, I will give it into your hand today; and you shall know that I am the LORD." [14]Ahab said, "By whom?" He said, "Thus says the LORD, By the young men who serve the district governors." Then he said, "Who shall begin the battle?" He answered, "You." [15]Then he mustered the young men who served the district governors, two hundred thirty-two; after them he mustered all the people of Israel, seven thousand.

16 They went out at noon, while Ben-hadad was drinking himself drunk in the booths, he and the thirty-two kings allied with him. [17]The young men who served the district governors went out first. Ben-hadad had sent out scouts,[c] and they reported to him, "Men have come out from Samaria." [18]He said, "If they have come out for peace, take them alive; if they have come out for war, take them alive."

19 But these had already come out of the city: the young men who served the district governors, and the army that followed them. [20]Each killed his man; the Arameans fled and Israel pursued them, but King Ben-hadad

---

a Heb *he* b Gk Syr Vg: Heb *you* c Heb lacks *scouts*

Come Home To Me—© Leah Colasuonno, 15

of Aram escaped on a horse with the cavalry. [21]The king of Israel went out, attacked the horses and chariots, and defeated the Arameans with a great slaughter.

22 Then the prophet approached the king of Israel and said to him, "Come, strengthen yourself, and consider well what you have to do; for in the spring the king of Aram will come up against you."

The Arameans Are Defeated

23 The servants of the king of Aram said to him, "Their gods are gods of the hills, and so they were stronger than we; but let us fight against them in the plain, and surely we shall be stronger than they. [24]Also do this: remove the kings, each from his post, and put commanders in place of them; [25]and muster an army like the army that you have lost, horse for horse, and chariot for chariot; then we will fight against them in the plain, and surely we shall be stronger than they." He heeded their voice, and did so.

26 In the spring Ben-hadad mustered the Arameans and went up to Aphek to fight against Israel. [27]After the Israelites had been mustered and provisioned, they went out to engage them; the people of Israel encamped opposite them like two little flocks of goats, while the Arameans filled the country. [28]A man of God approached and said to the king of Israel, "Thus says the LORD: Because the Arame-

ans have said, 'The LORD is a god of the hills but he is not a god of the valleys,' therefore I will give all this great multitude into your hand, and you shall know that I am the LORD." [29]They encamped opposite one another seven days. Then on the seventh day the battle began; the Israelites killed one hundred thousand Aramean foot soldiers in one day. [30]The rest fled into the city of Aphek; and the wall fell on twenty-seven thousand men that were left.

Ben-hadad also fled, and entered the city to hide. [31]His servants said to him, "Look, we have heard that the kings of the house of Israel are merciful kings; let us put sackcloth around our waists and ropes on our heads, and go out to the king of Israel; perhaps he will spare your life." [32]So they tied sackcloth around their waists, put ropes on their heads, went to the king of Israel, and said, "Your servant Ben-hadad says, 'Please let me live.' " And he said, "Is he still alive? He is my brother." [33]Now the men were watching for an omen; they quickly took it up from him and said, "Yes, Ben-hadad is your brother." Then he said, "Go and bring him." So Ben-hadad came out to him; and he had him come up into the chariot. [34]Ben-hadad[a] said to him, "I will restore the towns that my father took from your father; and you may establish bazaars for yourself in Damascus, as my father did in Samaria." The king of Israel responded,[b] "I will let you go on those terms." So he made a treaty with him and let him go.

a Heb *He* *b* Heb lacks *The king of Israel responded*

A Prophet Condemns Ahab

35 At the command of the LORD a certain member of a company of prophets[a] said to another, "Strike me!" But the man refused to strike him. ³⁶Then he said to him, "Because you have not obeyed the voice of the LORD, as soon as you have left me, a lion will kill you." And when he had left him, a lion met him and killed him. ³⁷Then he found another man and said, "Strike me!" So the man hit him, striking and wounding him. ³⁸Then the prophet departed, and waited for the king along the road, disguising himself with a bandage over his eyes. ³⁹As the king passed by, he cried to the king and said, "Your servant went out into the thick of the battle; then a soldier turned and brought a man to me, and said, 'Guard this man; if he is missing, your life shall be given for his life, or else you shall pay a talent of silver.' ⁴⁰While your servant was busy here and there, he was gone." The king of Israel said to him, "So shall your judgment be; you yourself have decided it." ⁴¹Then he quickly took the bandage away from his eyes. The king of Israel recognized him as one of the prophets. ⁴²Then he said to him, "Thus says the LORD, 'Because you have let the man go whom I had devoted to destruction, therefore your life shall be for his life, and your people for his people.'" ⁴³The king of Israel set out toward home, resentful and sullen, and came to Samaria.

21 Naboth's Vineyard

Later the following events took place: Naboth the Jezreelite had a vineyard in Jezreel, beside the palace of King Ahab of Samaria. ²And Ahab said to Naboth, "Give me your vineyard, so that I may have it for a vegetable garden, because it is near my house; I will give you a better vineyard for it; or, if it seems good to you, I will give you its value in money." ³But Naboth said to Ahab, "The LORD forbid that I should give you my ancestral inheritance." ⁴Ahab went home resentful and sullen because of what Naboth the Jezreelite had said to him; for he had said, "I will not give you my ancestral inheritance." He lay down on his bed, turned away his face, and would not eat.

5 His wife Jezebel came to him and said, "Why are you so depressed that you will not eat?" ⁶He said to her, "Because I spoke to Naboth the Jezreelite and said to him, 'Give me your vineyard for money; or else, if you prefer, I will give you another vineyard for it'; but he answered, 'I will not give you my vineyard.'" ⁷His wife Jezebel said to him, "Do you now govern Israel? Get up, eat some food, and be cheerful; I will give you the vineyard of Naboth the Jezreelite."

8 So she wrote letters in Ahab's name and sealed them with his seal; she sent the letters to the elders and the nobles who lived with Naboth in his city. ⁹She wrote in the letters, "Proclaim a fast, and seat Naboth at the head of the assembly; ¹⁰seat two scoundrels opposite him, and have them bring a charge against him, saying, 'You have cursed God and the king.' Then take him out, and stone him to death." ¹¹The men of his city, the elders and the nobles who lived in his city, did as Jezebel had sent word to them. Just as it was written in the letters that she had sent to them, ¹²they proclaimed a fast and seated Naboth at the head of the assembly. ¹³The two scoundrels came in and sat opposite him; and the scoundrels brought a charge against Naboth, in the presence of the people, saying, "Naboth cursed God and the king." So they took him outside the city, and stoned him to death. ¹⁴Then they sent to Jezebel, saying, "Naboth has been stoned; he is dead."

15 As soon as Jezebel heard that Naboth had been stoned and was dead, Jezebel said to Ahab, "Go, take possession of the vineyard of Naboth the Jezreelite, which he refused to give you for money; for Naboth is not alive, but dead." ¹⁶As soon as Ahab heard that Naboth was dead, Ahab set out to go down to the vineyard of Naboth the Jezreelite, to take possession of it.

Elijah Pronounces God's Sentence

17 Then the word of the LORD came to Elijah the Tishbite, saying: ¹⁸Go down to meet King Ahab of Israel, who rules[b] in Samaria; he is now in the vineyard of Naboth, where he has gone to take possession. ¹⁹You shall say to him, "Thus says the LORD: Have you killed, and also taken possession?" You shall say to him, "Thus says the LORD: In the place where dogs licked up the blood of Naboth, dogs will also lick up your blood."

20 Ahab said to Elijah, "Have you found me, O my enemy?" He answered, "I have found you. Because you have sold yourself to do what is evil in the sight of the LORD, ²¹I will bring disaster on you; I will consume you, and will cut off from Ahab every male, bond or free, in Israel; ²²and I will make your house like the house of Jeroboam son of Nebat, and like the house of Baasha son of Ahijah, because you have provoked me to anger and have caused Israel to sin. ²³Also concerning Jezebel the LORD said, 'The dogs shall eat Jezebel within the bounds of Jezreel.' ²⁴Anyone belonging to Ahab who dies in the city the dogs shall eat; and anyone of his who dies in the open country the birds of the air shall eat."

a Heb of the sons of the prophets b Heb who is

25 (Indeed, there was no one like Ahab, who sold himself to do what was evil in the sight of the LORD, urged on by his wife Jezebel. 26He acted most abominably in going after idols, as the Amorites had done, whom the LORD drove out before the Israelites.)

27 When Ahab heard those words, he tore his clothes and put sackcloth over his bare flesh; he fasted, lay in the sackcloth, and went about dejectedly. 28Then the word of the LORD came to Elijah the Tishbite: 29"Have you seen how Ahab has humbled himself before me? Because he has humbled himself before me, I will not bring the disaster in his days; but in his son's days I will bring the disaster on his house."

22 Joint Campaign with Judah against Aram

For three years Aram and Israel continued without war. 2But in the third year King Jehoshaphat of Judah came down to the king of Israel. 3The king of Israel said to his servants, "Do you know that Ramoth-gilead belongs to us, yet we are doing nothing to take it out of the hand of the king of Aram?" 4He said to Jehoshaphat, "Will you go with me to battle at Ramoth-gilead?" Jehoshaphat replied to the king of Israel, "I am as you are; my people are your people, my horses are your horses."

5 But Jehoshaphat also said to the king of Israel, "Inquire first for the word of the LORD." 6Then the king of Israel gathered the prophets together, about four hundred of them, and said to them, "Shall I go to battle against Ramoth-gilead, or shall I refrain?" They said, "Go up; for the LORD will give it into the hand of the king." 7But Jehoshaphat said, "Is there no other prophet of the LORD here of whom we may inquire?" 8The king of Israel said to Jehoshaphat, "There is still one other by whom we may inquire of the LORD, Micaiah son of Imlah; but I hate him, for he never prophesies anything favorable about me, but only disaster." Jehoshaphat said, "Let the king not say such a thing." 9Then the king of Israel summoned an officer and said, "Bring quickly Micaiah son of Imlah." 10Now the king of Israel and King Jehoshaphat of Judah were sitting on their thrones, arrayed in their robes, at the threshing floor at the entrance of the gate of Samaria; and all the prophets were prophesying before them. 11Zedekiah son of Chenaanah made for himself horns of iron, and he said, "Thus says the LORD: With these you shall gore the Arameans until they are destroyed." 12All the prophets were prophesying the same and saying, "Go up

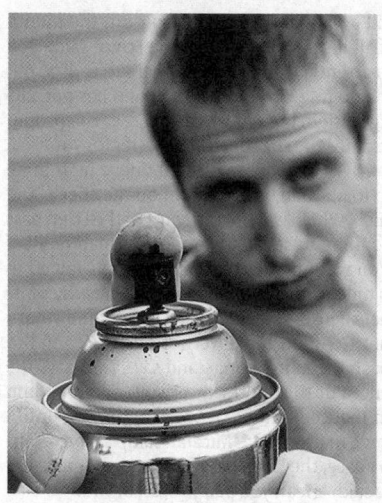

Untitled—© Gabe Anderson, 13

to Ramoth-gilead and triumph; the LORD will give it into the hand of the king."

Micaiah Predicts Failure

13 The messenger who had gone to summon Micaiah said to him, "Look, the words of the prophets with one accord are favorable to the king; let your word be like the word of one of them, and speak favorably." 14But Micaiah said, "As the LORD lives, whatever the LORD says to me, that I will speak."

15 When he had come to the king, the king said to him, "Micaiah, shall we go to Ramoth-gilead to battle, or shall we refrain?" He answered him, "Go up and triumph; the LORD will give it into the hand of the king." 16But the king said to him, "How many times must I make you swear to tell me nothing but the truth in the name of the LORD?" 17Then Micaiah*a* said, "I saw all Israel scattered on the mountains, like sheep that have no shepherd; and the LORD said, 'These have no master; let each one go home in peace.' " 18The king of Israel said to Jehoshaphat, "Did I not tell you that he would not prophesy anything favorable about me, but only disaster?"

19 Then Micaiah*a* said, "Therefore hear the word of the LORD: I saw the LORD sitting on his throne, with all the host of heaven standing beside him to the right and to the left of him. 20And the LORD said, 'Who will entice Ahab, so that he may go up and fall at Ramoth-gilead?' Then one said one thing, and another said another, 21until a spirit came forward and stood before the LORD, saying, 'I will entice him.' 22'How?' the LORD asked him. He replied, 'I

a Heb *he*

will go out and be a lying spirit in the mouth of all his prophets.' Then the LORD[a] said, 'You are to entice him, and you shall succeed; go out and do it.' 23So you see, the LORD has put a lying spirit in the mouth of all these your prophets; the LORD has decreed disaster for you."

24 Then Zedekiah son of Chenaanah came up to Micaiah, slapped him on the cheek, and said, "Which way did the spirit of the LORD pass from me to speak to you?" 25Micaiah replied, "You will find out on that day when you go in to hide in an inner chamber." 26The king of Israel then ordered, "Take Micaiah, and return him to Amon the governor of the city and to Joash the king's son, 27and say, 'Thus says the king: Put this fellow in prison, and feed him on reduced rations of bread and water until I come in peace.' " 28Micaiah said, "If you return in peace, the LORD has not spoken by me." And he said, "Hear, you peoples, all of you!"

Defeat and Death of Ahab

29 So the king of Israel and King Jehoshaphat of Judah went up to Ramoth-gilead. 30The king of Israel said to Jehoshaphat, "I will disguise myself and go into battle, but you wear your robes." So the king of Israel disguised himself and went into battle. 31Now the king of Aram had commanded the thirty-two captains of his chariots, "Fight with no one small or great, but only with the king of Israel." 32When the captains of the chariots saw Jehoshaphat, they said, "It is surely the king of Israel." So they turned to fight against him; and Jehoshaphat cried out. 33When the captains of the chariots saw that it was not the king of Israel, they turned back from pursuing him. 34But a certain man drew his bow and unknowingly struck the king of Israel between the scale armor and the breastplate; so he said to the driver of his chariot, "Turn around, and carry me out of the battle, for I am wounded." 35The battle grew hot that day, and the king was propped up in his chariot facing the Arameans, until at evening he died; the blood from the wound had flowed into the bottom of the chariot. 36Then about sunset a shout went through the army, "Every man to his city, and every man to his country!"

37 So the king died, and was brought to Samaria; they buried the king in Samaria. 38They washed the chariot by the pool of Samaria; the dogs licked up his blood, and the prostitutes

washed themselves in it,[b] according to the word of the LORD that he had spoken. 39Now the rest of the acts of Ahab, and all that he did, and the ivory house that he built, and all the cities that he built, are they not written in the Book of the Annals of the Kings of Israel? 40So Ahab slept with his ancestors; and his son Ahaziah succeeded him.

Jehoshaphat Reigns over Judah

41 Jehoshaphat son of Asa began to reign over Judah in the fourth year of King Ahab of Israel. 42Jehoshaphat was thirty-five years old when he began to reign, and he reigned twenty-five years in Jerusalem. His mother's name was Azubah daughter of Shilhi. 43He walked in all the way of his father Asa; he did not turn aside from it, doing what was right in the sight of the LORD; yet the high places were not taken away, and the people still sacrificed and offered incense on the high places. 44Jehoshaphat also made peace with the king of Israel.

45 Now the rest of the acts of Jehoshaphat, and his power that he showed, and how he waged war, are they not written in the Book of the Annals of the Kings of Judah? 46The remnant of the male temple prostitutes who were still in the land in the days of his father Asa, he exterminated.

47 There was no king in Edom; a deputy was king. 48Jehoshaphat made ships of the Tarshish type to go to Ophir for gold; but they did not go, for the ships were wrecked at Ezion-geber. 49Then Ahaziah son of Ahab said to Jehoshaphat, "Let my servants go with your servants in the ships," but Jehoshaphat was not willing. 50Jehoshaphat slept with his ancestors and was buried with his ancestors in the city of his father David; his son Jehoram succeeded him.

Ahaziah Reigns over Israel

51 Ahaziah son of Ahab began to reign over Israel in Samaria in the seventeenth year of King Jehoshaphat of Judah; he reigned two years over Israel. 52He did what was evil in the sight of the LORD, and walked in the way of his father and mother, and in the way of Jeroboam son of Nebat, who caused Israel to sin. 53He served Baal and worshiped him; he provoked the LORD, the God of Israel, to anger, just as his father had done.

a Heb *he* *b* Heb lacks *in it*

READ ON

2 KINGS

KISS THE LAND GOOD-BYE

Idolatry Is Not Your Friend

The story started so promising in 1 Kings: a kingdom with untold riches, a ruler who was the son of the beloved David, and a Temple where God took up residence! But by the time we turn a few pages to 2 Kings, things have crashed and burned. Wars and revolt now rule the land.

What happened? In a word: *idolatry*.

God wanted his people to worship him *only* (see Exodus 19–20). Yet when we read 2 Kings, Israel and Judah are out in the backyard putting the finishing touches on their altars to other gods. But don't think they woke up one morning and just suddenly decided to ditch the true God for a membership in the "god-of-the-month club." It was a slow process.

Idolatry usually starts small—like spending a little too much time with a boyfriend or girlfriend; playing games all through the night; studying a little too much. None of these things is inherently evil. But when they cause our relationship with God to grow cold, then we know that idolatry has struck.

This is what happened to Israel and Judah in 2 Kings. Read it through and notice that the theme of idolatry keeps popping up over and over and over again. Also, notice how persistent God is. Second Kings shows us that no matter how much we turn from God, he is relentless in calling us back!

> **"Nothing is politically right which is morally wrong."**
> —Daniel O'Connell, nineteenth-century Irish Catholic liberator

WHO Shaped from many fragments, by an unknown, author or editor

WHAT A historical account of Israel and Judah's many idolatrous kings, the bold actions of Elijah's successor, Elisha, and the eventual defeat and enslavement of God's people

WHEN The events in 2 Kings took place ca. 853–562 B.C.; likely written between 586 and 539 B.C.

WHERE Israel (the northern kingdom) and Judah (the southern kingdom)

PATH OF DISCIPLESHIP

Could you imagine if every political speech ended with, "For the kingdom, the power, and the glory are yours, now and forever"? That was not exactly the line on the lips of some of the leaders in 2 Kings.

Power meant importance and prestige. Leaders like Elijah and Elisha did their best to remind the people in Israel and Judah that power belonged to God. They could not separate their faith and their politics. Then, along came Jesus who was most powerful when he put others first. He taught us servant leadership. He didn't wear a T-shirt that said, "It's all about me." He gave the glory to God. He could not separate his faith and politics either.

If we are true disciples of Jesus, we *can't* separate our political beliefs and actions from our call to discipleship. In fact, discipleship demands that we take our roles as servant leaders into our communities, into the streets, into our families, and into our groups of friends. Dare to be different from the people in 2 Kings. Make a T-shirt that says, "For the kingdom, the power, and the glory are yours, now and forever." Put it on. Live it. Wear it out. See how you can change the world.

1

Elijah Denounces Ahaziah

After the death of Ahab, Moab rebelled against Israel.

2 Ahaziah had fallen through the lattice in his upper chamber in Samaria, and lay injured; so he sent messengers, telling them, "Go, inquire of Baal-zebub, the god of Ekron, whether I shall recover from this injury." ³But the angel of the LORD said to Elijah the Tishbite, "Get up, go to meet the messengers of the king of Samaria, and say to them, 'Is it because there is no God in Israel that you are going to inquire of Baal-zebub, the god of Ekron?' ⁴Now therefore thus says the LORD, 'You shall not leave the bed to which you have gone, but you shall surely die.' " So Elijah went.

5 The messengers returned to the king, who said to them, "Why have you returned?" ⁶They answered him, "There came a man to meet us, who said to us, 'Go back to the king who sent you, and say to him: Thus says the LORD: Is it because there is no God in Israel that you are sending to inquire of Baal-zebub, the god of Ekron? Therefore you shall not leave the bed to which you have gone, but shall surely die.' " ⁷He said to them, "What sort of man was he who came to meet you and told you these things?" ⁸They answered him, "A hairy man, with a leather belt around his waist." He said, "It is Elijah the Tishbite."

9 Then the king sent to him a captain of fifty with his fifty men. He went up to Elijah, who was sitting on the top of a hill, and said to him, "O man of God, the king says, 'Come down.' " ¹⁰But Elijah answered the captain of fifty, "If I am a man of God, let fire come down from heaven and consume you and your fifty." Then fire came down from heaven, and consumed him and his fifty.

11 Again the king sent to him another captain of fifty with his fifty. He went up*ᵃ* and said to him, "O man of God, this is the king's order: Come down quickly!" ¹²But Elijah answered them, "If I am a man of God, let fire come down from heaven and consume you and your fifty." Then the fire of God came down from heaven and consumed him and his fifty.

13 Again the king sent the captain of a third fifty with his fifty. So the third captain of fifty went up, and came and fell on his knees before Elijah, and entreated him, "O man of God, please let my life, and the life of these fifty servants of yours, be precious in your sight. ¹⁴Look, fire came down from heaven and consumed the two former captains of fifty men with their fifties; but now let my life be pre-cious in your sight." ¹⁵Then the angel of the LORD said to Elijah, "Go down with him; do not be afraid of him." So he set out and went down with him to the king, ¹⁶and said to him, "Thus says the LORD: Because you have sent messengers to inquire of Baal-zebub, the god of Ekron,—is it because there is no God in Israel to inquire of his word?—therefore you shall not leave the bed to which you have gone, but you shall surely die."

Death of Ahaziah

17 So he died according to the word of the LORD that Elijah had spoken. His brother,*ᵇ* Jehoram succeeded him as king in the second year of King Jehoram son of Jehoshaphat of Judah, because Ahaziah had no son. ¹⁸Now the rest of the acts of Ahaziah that he did, are they not written in the Book of the Annals of the Kings of Israel?

2

Elijah Ascends to Heaven

Now when the LORD was about to take Elijah up to heaven by a whirlwind, Elijah and Elisha were on their way from Gilgal. ²Elijah said to Elisha, "Stay here; for the LORD has sent me as far as Bethel." But Elisha said, "As the LORD lives, and as you yourself live, I will not leave you." So they went down to Bethel. ³The company of prophets*ᶜ* who were in Bethel came out to Elisha, and said to him, "Do you know that today the LORD will take your master away from you?" And he said, "Yes, I know; keep silent."

4 Elijah said to him, "Elisha, stay here; for the LORD has sent me to Jericho." But he said, "As the LORD lives, and as you yourself live, I will not leave you." So they came to Jericho. ⁵The company of prophets*ᶜ* who were at Jericho drew near to Elisha, and said to him, "Do you know that today the LORD will take your master away from you?" And he answered, "Yes, I know; be silent."

6 Then Elijah said to him, "Stay here; for the LORD has sent me to the Jordan." But he said, "As the LORD lives, and as you yourself live, I will not leave you." So the two of them went on. ⁷Fifty men of the company of prophets*ᶜ* also went, and stood at some distance from them, as they both were standing by the Jordan. ⁸Then Elijah took his mantle and rolled it up, and struck the water; the water was parted to the one side and to the other, until the two of them crossed on dry ground.

9 When they had crossed, Elijah said to Elisha, "Tell me what I may do for you, before I am taken from you." Elisha said, "Please let me inherit a double share of your spirit." ¹⁰He

---

a Gk Compare verses 9, 13: Heb *He answered*   *b* Gk Syr: Heb lacks *His brother*   *c* Heb *sons of the prophets* responded, "You have asked a hard thing; yet, if you see me as I am being taken from you, it will be granted you; if not, it will not." ¹¹As they continued walking and talking, a chariot of fire and horses of fire separated the two of them, and Elijah ascended in a whirlwind into heaven. ¹²Elisha kept watching and crying out, "Father, father! The chariots of Israel and its horsemen!" But when he could no longer see him, he grasped his own clothes and tore them in two pieces.

Elisha Succeeds Elijah

13 He picked up the mantle of Elijah that had fallen from him, and went back and stood on the bank of the Jordan. ¹⁴He took the mantle of Elijah that had fallen from him, and struck the water, saying, "Where is the LORD, the God of Elijah?" When he had struck the water, the water was parted to the one side and to the other, and Elisha went over.

15 When the company of prophets*ᵃ* who were at Jericho saw him at a distance, they declared, "The spirit of Elijah rests on Elisha." They came to meet him and bowed to the ground before him. ¹⁶They said to him, "See now, we have fifty strong men among your servants; please let them go and seek your master; it may be that the spirit of the LORD has caught him up and thrown him down on some mountain or into some valley." He responded, "No, do not send them." ¹⁷But when they urged him until he was ashamed, he said, "Send them." So they sent fifty men who searched for three days but did not find him. ¹⁸When they came back to him (he had remained at Jericho), he said to them, "Did I not say to you, Do not go?"

Elisha Performs Miracles

19 Now the people of the city said to Elisha, "The location of this city is good, as my lord sees; but the water is bad, and the land is unfruitful." ²⁰He said, "Bring me a new bowl, and put salt in it." So they brought it to him. ²¹Then he went to the spring of water and threw the salt into it, and said, "Thus says the LORD, I have made this water wholesome; from now on neither death nor miscarriage shall come from it." ²²So the water has been wholesome to this day, according to the word that Elisha spoke.

23 He went up from there to Bethel; and while he was going up on the way, some small boys came out of the city and jeered at him, saying, "Go away, baldhead! Go away, baldhead!" ²⁴When he turned around and saw them, he cursed them in the name of the LORD. Then two she-bears came out of the woods and

a Heb *sons of the prophets*

JESUS SIGHTING

Elijah has quite a track record: spitefully teasing the false prophets of Baal, parting the Jordan River, making the rain stop, calling for wet wood to burst into flame, and standing closer to God than anyone since Moses. Read the dramatic grand finale of Elijah's life in **2 Kings 2.9–12**. These kinds of things will get you talked about. That's why both Judaism and Christianity hail Elijah as one of the greatest prophets of the Hebrew Scriptures.

People talked about Elijah quite a bit in Jesus' day too. After Elijah ascended into heaven, the Jews waited in anticipation for his return. In later tradition they even set out an empty chair at their circumcisions and a cup of wine for him at Passover in hopes that he would join them. Why? They believed that the return of Elijah meant the promised Savior would be close on his heels.

Elijah did not come back to earth to pave the way for the Messiah. Instead, John the Baptist, a man who had many symbolic similarities to this Old Testament prophet, came (see Matthew 17.10–13). But the real Old Testament Elijah actually *did* show up, just a bit later. When Jesus took his three closest friends up to a mountaintop, Jesus' appearance was awesomely transformed—his clothes became dazzling white—and then Elijah and Moses appeared and spoke with him (see Mark 9.2–8).

Elijah's "return" to earth during this amazing moment with Jesus is filled with powerful symbolism. It affirmed that Jesus *was* the promised Messiah and the fulfillment of the Old Testament prophecies—the hope the world was waiting for. Elijah's amazing departure to heaven, escorted by a chariot of fire (as recorded in 2 Kings 2.1–12) is nothing compared to the glory of Elijah having this amazing role in revealing Jesus as the true Savior for humanity.

JS

mauled forty-two of the boys. ²⁵From there he went on to Mount Carmel, and then returned to Samaria.

3 Jehoram Reigns over Israel

In the eighteenth year of King Jehoshaphat of Judah, Jehoram son of Ahab became king over Israel in Samaria; he reigned twelve years. ²He did what was evil in the sight of the LORD, though not like his father and mother, for he removed the pillar of Baal that his father had made. ³Nevertheless he clung to the sin of Jeroboam son of Nebat, which he caused Israel to commit; he did not depart from it.

War with Moab

4 Now King Mesha of Moab was a sheep breeder, who used to deliver to the king of Israel one hundred thousand lambs, and the wool of one hundred thousand rams. ⁵But when Ahab died, the king of Moab rebelled against the king of Israel. ⁶So King Jehoram marched out of Samaria at that time and mustered all Israel. ⁷As he went he sent word to King Jehoshaphat of Judah, "The king of Moab has rebelled against me; will you go with me to battle against Moab?" He answered, "I will; I am with you, my people are your people, my horses are your horses." ⁸Then he asked, "By which way shall we march?" Jehoram answered, "By the way of the wilderness of Edom."

9 So the king of Israel, the king of Judah, and the king of Edom set out; and when they had made a roundabout march of seven days, there was no water for the army or for the animals that were with them. ¹⁰Then the king of Israel said, "Alas! The LORD has summoned us, three kings, only to be handed over to Moab." ¹¹But Jehoshaphat said, "Is there no prophet of the LORD here, through whom we may inquire of the LORD?" Then one of the servants of the king of Israel answered, "Elisha son of Shaphat, who used to pour water on the hands of Elijah, is here." ¹²Jehoshaphat said, "The word of the LORD is with him." So the king of Israel and Jehoshaphat and the king of Edom went down to him.

13 Elisha said to the king of Israel, "What have I to do with you? Go to your father's prophets or to your mother's." But the king of Israel said to him, "No; it is the LORD who has summoned us, three kings, only to be handed over to Moab." ¹⁴Elisha said, "As the LORD of hosts lives, whom I serve, were it not that I have regard for King Jehoshaphat of Judah, I would give you neither a look nor a glance. ¹⁵But get me a musician." And then, while the musician was playing, the power of the LORD came on him. ¹⁶And he said, "Thus says the LORD, 'I will make this wadi full of pools.' ¹⁷For thus says the LORD, 'You shall see neither wind nor rain, but the wadi shall be filled with water, so that you shall drink, you, your cattle, and your animals.' ¹⁸This is only a trifle in the sight of the LORD, for he will also hand Moab over to you. ¹⁹You shall conquer every fortified city and every choice city; every good tree you shall fell, all springs of water you shall stop up, and every good piece of land you shall ruin with stones." ²⁰The next day, about the time of the morning offering, suddenly water began to flow from the direction of Edom, until the country was filled with water.

21 When all the Moabites heard that the kings had come up to fight against them, all who were able to put on armor, from the youngest to the oldest, were called out and were drawn up at the frontier. ²²When they rose early in the morning, and the sun shone upon the water, the Moabites saw the water opposite them as red as blood. ²³They said, "This is blood; the kings must have fought together, and killed one another. Now then, Moab, to the spoil!" ²⁴But when they came to the camp of Israel, the Israelites rose up and attacked the Moabites, who fled before them; as they entered Moab they continued the attack.^a ²⁵The cities they overturned, and on every good piece of land everyone threw a stone, until it was covered; every spring of water they stopped up, and every good tree they felled. Only at Kir-hareseth did the stone walls remain, until the slingers surrounded and attacked it. ²⁶When the king of Moab saw that the battle was going against him, he took with him seven hundred swordsmen to break through, opposite the king of Edom; but they could not. ²⁷Then he took his firstborn son who was to succeed him, and offered him as a burnt offering on the wall. And great wrath came upon Israel, so they withdrew from him and returned to their own land.

4 Elisha and the Widow's Oil

Now the wife of a member of the company of prophets^b cried to Elisha, "Your servant my husband is dead; and you know that your servant feared the LORD, but a creditor has come to take my two children as slaves." ²Elisha said to her, "What shall I do for you? Tell me, what do you have in the house?" She answered, "Your servant has nothing in the house, except a jar of oil." ³He said, "Go outside, borrow vessels from all your neighbors, empty vessels and

---

a Compare Gk Syr: Meaning of Heb uncertain   b Heb *the sons of the prophets* not just a few. 4Then go in, and shut the door behind you and your children, and start pouring into all these vessels; when each is full, set it aside." 5So she left him and shut the door behind her and her children; they kept bringing vessels to her, and she kept pouring. 6When the vessels were full, she said to her son, "Bring me another vessel." But he said to her, "There are no more." Then the oil stopped flowing. 7She came and told the man of God, and he said, "Go sell the oil and pay your debts, and you and your children can live on the rest."

Elisha Raises the Shunammite's Son

8 One day Elisha was passing through Shunem, where a wealthy woman lived, who urged him to have a meal. So whenever he passed that way, he would stop there for a meal. 9She said to her husband, "Look, I am sure that this man who regularly passes our way is a holy man of God. 10Let us make a small roof chamber with walls, and put there for him a bed, a table, a chair, and a lamp, so that he can stay there whenever he comes to us."

11 One day when he came there, he went up to the chamber and lay down there. 12He said to his servant Gehazi, "Call the Shunammite woman." When he had called her, she stood before him. 13He said to him, "Say to her, Since you have taken all this trouble for us, what may be done for you? Would you have a word spoken on your behalf to the king or to the commander of the army?" She answered, "I live among my own people." 14He said, "What then may be done for her?" Gehazi answered, "Well, she has no son, and her husband is old." 15He said, "Call her." When he had called her, she stood at the door. 16He said, "At this season, in due time, you shall embrace a son." She replied, "No, my lord, O man of God; do not deceive your servant."

17 The woman conceived and bore a son at that season, in due time, as Elisha had declared to her.

18 When the child was older, he went out one day to his father among the reapers. 19He complained to his father, "Oh, my head, my head!" The father said to his servant, "Carry him to his mother." 20He carried him and brought him to his mother; the child sat on her lap until noon, and he died. 21She went up and laid him on the bed of the man of God, closed the door on him, and left. 22Then she called to her husband, and said, "Send me one of the servants and one of the donkeys, so that I may quickly go to the man of God and come back again." 23He said, "Why go to him today? It is neither new moon nor sabbath." She said, "It will be all right." 24Then she saddled the don-

MIRACLES

Check out **2 Kings 4.1–44.** It reads like a word collage of Elisha's extraordinary and miraculous deeds. You can't help but think, "Amazing!" "Incredible!" and maybe even, "You've got to be kidding me!"

It's pretty jaw-dropping stuff. In no time at all, Elisha is responsible for a miraculous oil filling empty vessels, a childless couple being granted a son, a person being raised from the dead, and a multitude being fed from so little. "Awesome" doesn't even begin to cover it.

Miracles are signs or wonders that can only be caused by the power of God. Miracles invite faith. They are not meant to be a sideshow or evidence of some kind of magic. In both the Old Testament and the New, miracles occur for the "little ones"—the least among us—and they are almost always for regular and daily needs: freedom, hope, life, and restoration. Jesus' miracles are signs of the Kingdom of God. The miracles of Elisha are a foreshadowing of what is to come (see *Catechism of the Catholic Church* 547–548).

key and said to her servant, "Urge the animal on; do not hold back for me unless I tell you." 25So she set out, and came to the man of God at Mount Carmel.

When the man of God saw her coming, he said to Gehazi his servant, "Look, there is the Shunammite woman; 26run at once to meet her, and say to her, Are you all right? Is your husband all right? Is the child all right?" She answered, "It is all right." 27When she came to the man of God at the mountain, she caught hold of his feet. Gehazi approached to push her away. But the man of God said, "Let her alone, for she is in bitter distress; the Lord has hidden it from me and has not told me." 28Then she said, "Did I ask my lord for a son? Did I not say, Do not mislead me?" 29He said to Gehazi, "Gird up your loins, and take my staff in your hand, and go. If you meet anyone, give no greeting, and if anyone greets you, do not answer; and lay my staff on the face of the child."

NO STRINGS ATTACHED

The HIV/AIDS pandemic is one of the most urgent health crises of our day, especially on the continent of Africa.

What is *your* role in this crisis? Do you think you have one?

Keep that question in mind as you read **2 Kings 5.1–14**. It tells of a foreign army commander, Naaman, who sought to be healed of leprosy by the prophet Elisha. Elisha showed God's compassion by telling him to wash in the Jordan River. Naaman cooperated and was completely healed! This story reveals God's great compassion even for those who do not know him. God cares about the physical, emotional, and social needs of all human beings.

There are many ways you can show God's compassion to those in desperate need *with no strings attached*. Get some friends together and research how you can fight HIV/AIDS by finding links on **Learner.CalltoDiscipleship.com**.

Discuss what you find with your friends. *Then take action!* When you've made a plan, *do it*, and write about your experience on **Learner.CalltoDiscipleship.com**.

GOD IS COMPASSIONATE MY FRIENDS

---

30 Then the mother of the child said, "As the Lord lives, and as you yourself live, I will not leave without you." So he rose up and followed her. 31 Gehazi went on ahead and laid the staff on the face of the child, but there was no sound or sign of life. He came back to meet him and told him, "The child has not awakened."

32 When Elisha came into the house, he saw the child lying dead on his bed. 33 So he went in and closed the door on the two of them, and prayed to the Lord. 34 Then he got up on the bed[a] and lay upon the child, putting his mouth upon his mouth, his eyes upon his eyes, and his hands upon his hands; and while he lay bent over him, the flesh of the child became warm. 35 He got down, walked once to and fro in the room, then got up again and bent over him; the child sneezed seven times, and the child opened his eyes. 36 Elisha[b] summoned Gehazi and said, "Call the Shunammite woman." So he called her. When she came to him, he said, "Take your son." 37 She came and fell at his feet, bowing to the ground; then she took her son and left.

Elisha Purifies the Pot of Stew

38 When Elisha returned to Gilgal, there was a famine in the land. As the company of prophets was[c] sitting before him, he said to his servant, "Put the large pot on, and make some stew for the company of prophets."[d] 39 One of them went out into the field to gather herbs; he found a wild vine and gathered from it a lapful of wild gourds, and came and cut them up into the pot of stew, not knowing what they were. 40 They served some for the men to eat. But while they were eating the stew, they cried out, "O man of God, there is death in the pot!" They could not eat it. 41 He said, "Then bring some flour." He threw it into the pot, and said, "Serve the people and let them eat." And there was nothing harmful in the pot.

Elisha Feeds One Hundred Men

42 A man came from Baal-shalishah, bringing food from the first fruits to the man of God: twenty loaves of barley and fresh ears of grain in his sack. Elisha said, "Give it to the people and let them eat." 43 But his servant said, "How can I set this before a hundred people?" So he repeated, "Give it to the people and let them eat, for thus says the Lord, 'They shall eat and have some left.'" 44 He set it before them, they ate, and had some left, according to the word of the Lord.

5 The Healing of Naaman

Naaman, commander of the army of the king of Aram, was a great man and in high favor with his master, because by him the Lord had given victory to Aram. The man, though a mighty warrior, suffered from leprosy.[e] 2 Now the Arameans on one of their raids had taken a young girl captive from the land of Israel, and she served Naaman's wife. 3 She said to her mistress, "If only my lord were with the prophet who is in Samaria! He would cure him of his leprosy."[e] 4 So Naaman[b] went in and told his lord just what the girl from the land of Israel had said. 5 And the king of Aram said, "Go then, and I will send along a letter to the king of Israel."

He went, taking with him ten talents of silver, six thousand shekels of gold, and ten sets of garments. 6 He brought the letter to the king of Israel, which read, "When this letter reaches you, know that I have sent to you my servant Naaman, that you may cure him of his leprosy."[e] 7 When the king of Israel read the letter,

---

a Heb lacks *on the bed* b Heb *he* c Heb *sons of the prophets were* d Heb *sons of the prophets* e A term for several skin diseases; precise meaning uncertain he tore his clothes and said, "Am I God, to give death or life, that this man sends word to me to cure a man of his leprosy?[a] Just look and see how he is trying to pick a quarrel with me."

8 But when Elisha the man of God heard that the king of Israel had torn his clothes, he sent a message to the king, "Why have you torn your clothes? Let him come to me, that he may learn that there is a prophet in Israel." 9So Naaman came with his horses and chariots, and halted at the entrance of Elisha's house. 10Elisha sent a messenger to him, saying, "Go, wash in the Jordan seven times, and your flesh shall be restored and you shall be clean." 11But Naaman became angry and went away, saying, "I thought that for me he would surely come out, and stand and call on the name of the LORD his God, and would wave his hand over the spot, and cure the leprosy![a] 12Are not Abana[b] and Pharpar, the rivers of Damascus, better than all the waters of Israel? Could I not wash in them, and be clean?" He turned and went away in a rage. 13But his servants approached and said to him, "Father, if the prophet had commanded you to do something difficult, would you not have done it? How much more, when all he said to you was, 'Wash, and be clean'?" 14So he went down and immersed himself seven times in the Jordan, according to the word of the man of God; his flesh was restored like the flesh of a young boy, and he was clean.

15 Then he returned to the man of God, he and all his company; he came and stood before him and said, "Now I know that there is no God in all the earth except in Israel; please accept a present from your servant." 16But he said, "As the LORD lives, whom I serve, I will accept nothing!" He urged him to accept, but he refused. 17Then Naaman said, "If not, please let two mule-loads of earth be given to your servant; for your servant will no longer offer burnt offering or sacrifice to any god except the LORD. 18But may the LORD pardon your servant on one count: when my master goes into the house of Rimmon to worship there, leaning on my arm, and I bow down in the house of Rimmon, when I do bow down in the house of Rimmon, may the LORD pardon your servant on this one count." 19He said to him, "Go in peace."

Gehazi's Greed

But when Naaman had gone from him a short distance, 20Gehazi, the servant of Elisha the man of God, thought, "My master has let that Aramean Naaman off too lightly by not accepting from him what he offered. As the LORD lives, I will run after him and get something out of him." 21So Gehazi went after Naaman. When Naaman saw someone running after him, he jumped down from the chariot to meet him and said, "Is everything all right?" 22He replied, "Yes, but my master has sent me to say, 'Two members of a company of prophets[c] have just come to me from the hill country of Ephraim; please give them a talent of silver and two changes of clothing.' " 23Naaman said, "Please accept two talents." He urged him, and tied up two talents of silver in two bags, with two changes of clothing, and gave them to two of his servants, who carried them in front of Gehazi.[d] 24When he came to the citadel, he took the bags[e] from them, and stored them inside; he dismissed the men, and they left.

25 He went in and stood before his master; and Elisha said to him, "Where have you been, Gehazi?" He answered, "Your servant has not gone anywhere at all." 26But he said to him, "Did I not go with you in spirit when someone left his chariot to meet you? Is this a time to accept money and to accept clothing, olive orchards and vineyards, sheep and oxen, and male and female slaves? 27Therefore the leprosy[a] of Naaman shall cling to you, and to your descendants forever." So he left his presence leprous,[a] as white as snow.

6 The Miracle of the Ax Head

Now the company of prophets[c] said to Elisha, "As you see, the place where we live under your charge is too small for us. 2Let us go to the Jordan, and let us collect logs there, one for each of us, and build a place there for us to live." He answered, "Do so." 3Then one of them said, "Please come with your servants." And he answered, "I will." 4So he went with them. When they came to the Jordan, they cut down trees. 5But as one was felling a log, his ax head fell into the water; he cried out, "Alas, master! It was borrowed." 6Then the man of God said, "Where did it fall?" When he showed him the place, he cut off a stick, and threw it in there, and made the iron float. 7He said, "Pick it up." So he reached out his hand and took it.

The Aramean Attack Is Thwarted

8 Once when the king of Aram was at war with Israel, he took counsel with his officers. He said, "At such and such a place shall be my camp." 9But the man of God sent word to the king of Israel, "Take care not to pass this place, because the Arameans are going down there." 10The king of Israel sent word to the place of

---

a A term for several skin diseases; precise meaning uncertain *b* Another reading is *Amana* *c* Heb *sons of the prophets* *d* Heb *him*
e Heb lacks *the bags*

which the man of God spoke. More than once or twice he warned such a place[a] so that it was on the alert.

11 The mind of the king of Aram was greatly perturbed because of this; he called his officers and said to them, "Now tell me who among us sides with the king of Israel?" 12Then one of his officers said, "No one, my lord king. It is Elisha, the prophet in Israel, who tells the king of Israel the words that you speak in your bedchamber." 13He said, "Go and find where he is; I will send and seize him." He was told, "He is in Dothan." 14So he sent horses and chariots there and a great army; they came by night, and surrounded the city.

15 When an attendant of the man of God rose early in the morning and went out, an army with horses and chariots was all around the city. His servant said, "Alas, master! What shall we do?" 16He replied, "Do not be afraid, for there are more with us than there are with them." 17Then Elisha prayed: "O LORD, please open his eyes that he may see." So the LORD opened the eyes of the servant, and he saw; the mountain was full of horses and chariots of fire all around Elisha. 18When the Arameans[b] came down against him, Elisha prayed to the LORD, and said, "Strike this people, please, with blindness." So he struck them with blindness as Elisha had asked. 19Elisha said to them, "This is not the way, and this is not the city; follow me, and I will bring you to the man whom you seek." And he led them to Samaria.

20 As soon as they entered Samaria, Elisha said, "O LORD, open the eyes of these men so that they may see." The LORD opened their eyes, and they saw that they were inside Samaria. 21When the king of Israel saw them he said to Elisha, "Father, shall I kill them? Shall I kill them?" 22He answered, "No! Did you capture with your sword and your bow those whom you want to kill? Set food and water before them so that they may eat and drink; and let them go to their master." 23So he prepared for them a great feast; after they ate and drank, he sent them on their way, and they went to their master. And the Arameans no longer came raiding into the land of Israel.

Ben-hadad's Siege of Samaria

24 Some time later King Ben-hadad of Aram mustered his entire army; he marched against Samaria and laid siege to it. 25As the siege continued, famine in Samaria became so great that a donkey's head was sold for eighty shekels of silver, and one-fourth of a kab of dove's dung for five shekels of silver. 26Now as the king of Israel was walking on the city wall, a woman cried out to him, "Help, my lord king!" 27He said, "No! Let the LORD help you. How can I help you? From the threshing floor or from the wine press?" 28But then the king asked her, "What is your complaint?" She answered, "This woman said to me, 'Give up your son; we will eat him today, and we will eat my son tomorrow.' 29So we cooked my son and ate him. The next day I said to her, 'Give up your son and we will eat him.' But she has hidden her son." 30When the king heard the words of the woman he tore his clothes—now since he was walking on the city wall, the people could see that he had sackcloth on his body underneath—31and he said, "So may God do to me, and more, if the head of Elisha son of Shaphat stays on his shoulders today." 32So he dispatched a man from his presence.

Now Elisha was sitting in his house, and the elders were sitting with him. Before the messenger arrived, Elisha said to the elders, "Are you aware that this murderer has sent someone to take off my head? When the messenger comes, see that you shut the door and hold it closed against him. Is not the sound of his master's feet behind him?" 33While he was still speaking with them, the king[c] came down to him and said, "This trouble is from the LORD! Why should I hope in the LORD any longer?" 7 1But Elisha said, "Hear the word of the LORD: thus says the LORD, Tomorrow about this time a measure of choice meal shall be sold for a shekel, and two measures of barley for a shekel, at the gate of Samaria." 2Then the captain on whose hand the king leaned said to the man of God, "Even if the LORD were to make windows in the sky, could such a thing happen?" But he said, "You shall see it with your own eyes, but you shall not eat from it."

The Arameans Flee

3 Now there were four leprous[d] men outside the city gate, who said to one another, "Why should we sit here until we die? 4If we say, 'Let us enter the city,' the famine is in the city, and we shall die there; but if we sit here, we shall also die. Therefore, let us desert to the Aramean camp; if they spare our lives, we shall live; and if they kill us, we shall but die." 5So they arose at twilight to go to the Aramean camp; but when they came to the edge of the Aramean camp, there was no one there at all. 6For the Lord had caused the Aramean army to hear the sound of chariots, and of horses, the sound of a great army, so that they said to one another, "The king of Israel has hired the kings of the

---

a Heb warned it b Heb they c See 7.2: Heb messenger d A term for several skin diseases; precise meaning uncertain

Hittites and the kings of Egypt to fight against us." [7]So they fled away in the twilight and abandoned their tents, their horses, and their donkeys leaving the camp just as it was, and fled for their lives. [8]When these leprous[a] men had come to the edge of the camp, they went into a tent, ate and drank, carried off silver, gold, and clothing, and went and hid them. Then they came back, entered another tent, carried off things from it, and went and hid them.

9 Then they said to one another, "What we are doing is wrong. This is a day of good news; if we are silent and wait until the morning light, we will be found guilty; therefore let us go and tell the king's household." [10]So they came and called to the gatekeepers of the city, and told them, "We went to the Aramean camp, but there was no one to be seen or heard there, nothing but the horses tied, the donkeys tied, and the tents as they were." [11]Then the gatekeepers called out and proclaimed it to the king's household. [12]The king got up in the night, and said to his servants, "I will tell you what the Arameans have prepared against us. They know that we are starving; so they have left the camp to hide themselves in the open country, thinking, 'When they come out of the city, we shall take them alive and get into the city.' " [13]One of his servants said, "Let some men take five of the remaining horses, since those left here will suffer the fate of the whole multitude of Israel that have perished already;[b] let us send and find out." [14]So they took two mounted men, and the king sent them after the Aramean army, saying, "Go and find out." [15]So they went after them as far as the Jordan; the whole way was littered with garments and equipment that the Arameans had thrown away in their haste. So the messengers returned, and told the king.

16 Then the people went out, and plundered the camp of the Arameans. So a measure of choice meal was sold for a shekel, and two measures of barley for a shekel, according to the word of the LORD. [17]Now the king had appointed the captain on whose hand he leaned to have charge of the gate; the people trampled him to death in the gate, just as the man of God had said when the king came down to him. [18]For when the man of God had said to the king, "Two measures of barley shall be sold for a shekel, and a measure of choice meal for a shekel, about this time tomorrow in the gate of Samaria," [19]the captain had answered the man of God, "Even if the LORD were to make windows in the sky, could such a thing happen?" And he had answered, "You shall see it

> "The Spirit is truly the dwelling of the saints, and the saints are for the Spirit a place where he dwells as in his own home, since they offer themselves as a dwelling place for God and are called his temple."
>
> —St. Basil, *De Spiritu Sancto*

with your own eyes, but you shall not eat from it." [20]It did indeed happen to him; the people trampled him to death in the gate.

8 The Shunammite Woman's Land Restored

Now Elisha had said to the woman whose son he had restored to life, "Get up and go with your household, and settle wherever you can; for the LORD has called for a famine, and it will come on the land for seven years." [2]So the woman got up and did according to the word of the man of God; she went with her household and settled in the land of the Philistines seven years. [3]At the end of the seven years, when the woman returned from the land of the Philistines, she set out to appeal to the king for her house and her land. [4]Now the king was talking with Gehazi the servant of the man of God, saying, "Tell me all the great things that Elisha has done." [5]While he was telling the king how Elisha had restored a dead person to life, the woman whose son he had restored to life appealed to the king for her house and her land. Gehazi said, "My lord king, here is the woman, and here is her son whom Elisha restored to life." [6]When the king questioned the woman, she told him. So the king appointed an official for her, saying, "Restore all that was hers, together with all the revenue of the fields from the day that she left the land until now."

Death of Ben-hadad

7 Elisha went to Damascus while King Ben-hadad of Aram was ill. When it was told him, "The man of God has come here," [8]the king said to Hazael, "Take a present with you and go to meet the man of God. Inquire of the LORD through him, whether I shall recover from this illness." [9]So Hazael went to meet him, taking a present with him, all kinds of goods of Damascus, forty camel loads. When he entered and stood before him, he said, "Your son King Ben-hadad of Aram has sent me to you, saying, 'Shall I recover from this illness?' " [10]Elisha said to him, "Go, say to him, 'You shall

---

[a] A term for several skin diseases; precise meaning uncertain   [b] Compare Gk Syr Vg: Meaning of Heb uncertain

certainly recover'; but the LORD has shown me that he shall certainly die." [11] He fixed his gaze and stared at him, until he was ashamed. Then the man of God wept. [12] Hazael asked, "Why does my lord weep?" He answered, "Because I know the evil that you will do to the people of Israel; you will set their fortresses on fire, you will kill their young men with the sword, dash in pieces their little ones, and rip up their pregnant women." [13] Hazael said, "What is your servant, who is a mere dog, that he should do this great thing?" Elisha answered, "The LORD has shown me that you are to be king over Aram." [14] Then he left Elisha, and went to his master Ben-hadad,[a] who said to him, "What did Elisha say to you?" And he answered, "He told me that you would certainly recover." [15] But the next day he took the bed-cover and dipped it in water and spread it over the king's face, until he died. And Hazael succeeded him.

Jehoram Reigns over Judah

16 In the fifth year of King Joram son of Ahab of Israel,[b] Jehoram son of King Jehoshaphat of Judah began to reign. [17] He was thirty-two years old when he became king, and he reigned eight years in Jerusalem. [18] He walked in the way of the kings of Israel, as the house of Ahab had done, for the daughter of Ahab was his wife. He did what was evil in the sight of the LORD. [19] Yet the LORD would not destroy Judah, for the sake of his servant David, since he had promised to give a lamp to him and to his descendants forever.

20 In his days Edom revolted against the rule of Judah, and set up a king of their own. [21] Then Joram crossed over to Zair with all his chariots. He set out by night and attacked the Edomites and their chariot commanders who had surrounded him;[c] but his army fled home. [22] So Edom has been in revolt against the rule of Judah to this day. Libnah also revolted at the same time. [23] Now the rest of the acts of Joram, and all that he did, are they not written in the Book of the Annals of the Kings of Judah? [24] So Joram slept with his ancestors, and was buried with them in the city of David; his son Ahaziah succeeded him.

Ahaziah Reigns over Judah

25 In the twelfth year of King Joram son of Ahab of Israel, Ahaziah son of King Jehoram of Judah began to reign. [26] Ahaziah was twenty-two years old when he began to reign; he reigned one year in Jerusalem. His mother's name was Athaliah, a granddaughter of King Omri of Is-

rael. [27] He also walked in the way of the house of Ahab, doing what was evil in the sight of the LORD, as the house of Ahab had done, for he was son-in-law to the house of Ahab.

28 He went with Joram son of Ahab to wage war against King Hazael of Aram at Ramoth-gilead, where the Arameans wounded Joram. [29] King Joram returned to be healed in Jezreel of the wounds that the Arameans had inflicted on him at Ramah, when he fought against King Hazael of Aram. King Ahaziah son of Jehoram of Judah went down to see Joram son of Ahab in Jezreel, because he was wounded.

9 Anointing of Jehu

Then the prophet Elisha called a member of the company of prophets[d] and said to him, "Gird up your loins; take this flask of oil in your hand, and go to Ramoth-gilead. [2] When you arrive, look there for Jehu son of Jehoshaphat, son of Nimshi; go in and get him to leave his companions, and take him into an inner chamber. [3] Then take the flask of oil, pour it on his head, and say, 'Thus says the LORD: I anoint you king over Israel.' Then open the door and flee; do not linger."

4 So the young man, the young prophet, went to Ramoth-gilead. [5] He arrived while the commanders of the army were in council, and he announced, "I have a message for you, commander." "For which one of us?" asked Jehu. "For you, commander." [6] So Jehu[e] got up and went inside; the young man poured the oil on his head, saying to him, "Thus says the LORD the God of Israel: I anoint you king over the people of the LORD, over Israel. [7] You shall strike down the house of your master Ahab, so that I may avenge on Jezebel the blood of my servants the prophets, and the blood of all the servants of the LORD. [8] For the whole house of Ahab shall perish; I will cut off from Ahab every male, bond or free, in Israel. [9] I will make the house of Ahab like the house of Jeroboam son of Nebat, and like the house of Baasha son of Ahijah. [10] The dogs shall eat Jezebel in the territory of Jezreel, and no one shall bury her." Then he opened the door and fled.

11 When Jehu came back to his master's officers, they said to him, "Is everything all right? Why did that madman come to you?" He answered them, "You know the sort and how they babble." [12] They said, "Liar! Come on, tell us!" So he said, "This is just what he said to me: 'Thus says the LORD, I anoint you king over Israel.' " [13] Then hurriedly they all took their cloaks and spread them for him on the bare[c] steps;

a Heb lacks Ben-hadad b Gk Syr: Heb adds Jehoshaphat being king of Judah, c Meaning of Heb uncertain d Heb sons of the prophets e Heb he

Encounter Life—© Jesse Bernard, 17

and they blew the trumpet, and proclaimed, "Jehu is king."

Joram of Israel Killed

14 Thus Jehu son of Jehoshaphat son of Nimshi conspired against Joram. Joram with all Israel had been on guard at Ramoth-gilead against King Hazael of Aram; ¹⁵but King Joram had returned to be healed in Jezreel of the wounds that the Arameans had inflicted on him, when he fought against King Hazael of Aram. So Jehu said, "If this is your wish, then let no one slip out of the city to go and tell the news in Jezreel." ¹⁶Then Jehu mounted his chariot and went to Jezreel, where Joram was lying ill. King Ahaziah of Judah had come down to visit Joram.

17 In Jezreel, the sentinel standing on the tower spied the company of Jehu arriving, and said, "I see a company." Joram said, "Take a horseman; send him to meet them, and let him say, 'Is it peace?' " ¹⁸So the horseman went to meet him; he said, "Thus says the king, 'Is it peace?' " Jehu responded, "What have you to do with peace? Fall in behind me." The sentinel reported, saying, "The messenger reached them, but he is not coming back." ¹⁹Then he sent out a second horseman, who came to them and said, "Thus says the king, 'Is it peace?' " Jehu answered, "What have you to do with peace? Fall in behind me." ²⁰Again the sentinel reported, "He reached them, but he is not coming back. It looks like the driving of Jehu son of Nimshi; for he drives like a maniac."

21 Joram said, "Get ready." And they got his chariot ready. Then King Joram of Israel and King Ahaziah of Judah set out, each in his chariot, and went to meet Jehu; they met him at the property of Naboth the Jezreelite. ²²When Joram saw Jehu, he said, "Is it peace, Jehu?" He answered, "What peace can there be, so long as the many whoredoms and sorceries of your mother Jezebel continue?" ²³Then Joram reined about and fled, saying to Ahaziah, "Treason, Ahaziah!" ²⁴Jehu drew his bow with all his strength, and shot Joram between the shoulders, so that the arrow pierced his heart; and he sank in his chariot. ²⁵Jehu said to his aide Bidkar, "Lift him out, and throw him on the plot of ground belonging to Naboth the Jezreelite; for remember, when you and I rode side by side behind his father Ahab how the LORD uttered this oracle against him: ²⁶'For the blood of Naboth and for the blood of his children that I saw yesterday, says the LORD, I swear I will repay you on this very plot of ground.' Now therefore lift him out and throw him on the plot of ground, in accordance with the word of the LORD."

Ahaziah of Judah Killed

27 When King Ahaziah of Judah saw this, he fled in the direction of Beth-haggan. Jehu pursued him, saying, "Shoot him also!" And they shot him^a in the chariot at the ascent to Gur,

---

a Syr Vg Compare Gk: Heb lacks *and they shot him*

which is by Ibleam. Then he fled to Megiddo, and died there. 28His officers carried him in a chariot to Jerusalem, and buried him in his tomb with his ancestors in the city of David.

29 In the eleventh year of Joram son of Ahab, Ahaziah began to reign over Judah.

Jezebel's Violent Death

30 When Jehu came to Jezreel, Jezebel heard of it; she painted her eyes, and adorned her head, and looked out of the window. 31As Jehu entered the gate, she said, "Is it peace, Zimri, murderer of your master?" 32He looked up to the window and said, "Who is on my side? Who?" Two or three eunuchs looked out at him. 33He said, "Throw her down." So they threw her down; some of her blood spattered on the wall and on the horses, which trampled on her. 34Then he went in and ate and drank; he said, "See to that cursed woman and bury her; for she is a king's daughter." 35But when they went to bury her, they found no more of her than the skull and the feet and the palms of her hands. 36When they came back and told him, he said, "This is the word of the LORD, which he spoke by his servant Elijah the Tishbite, 'In the territory of Jezreel the dogs shall eat the flesh of Jezebel; 37the corpse of Jezebel shall be like dung on the field in the territory of Jezreel, so that no one can say, This is Jezebel.' "

10 Massacre of Ahab's Descendants

Now Ahab had seventy sons in Samaria. So Jehu wrote letters and sent them to Samaria, to the rulers of Jezreel,ᵃ to the elders, and to the guardians of the sons ofᵇ Ahab, saying, 2"Since your master's sons are with you and you have at your disposal chariots and horses, a fortified city, and weapons, 3select the son of your master who is the best qualified, set him on his father's throne, and fight for your master's house." 4But they were utterly terrified and said, "Look, two kings could not withstand him; how then can we stand?" 5So the steward of the palace, and the governor of the city, along with the elders and the guardians, sent word to Jehu: "We are your servants; we will do anything you say. We will not make anyone king; do whatever you think right." 6Then he wrote them a second letter, saying, "If you are on my side, and if you are ready to obey me, take the heads of your master's sons and come to me at Jezreel tomorrow at this time." Now the king's sons, seventy persons, were with the leaders of the city, who were charged with their upbringing. 7When the letter reached them, they took the king's sons and killed them, seventy persons; they put their heads in baskets and sent them to him at Jezreel. 8When the messenger came and told him, "They have brought the heads of the king's sons," he said, "Lay them in two heaps at the entrance of the gate until the morning." 9Then in the morning when he went out, he stood and said to all the people, "You are innocent. It was I who conspired against my master and killed him; but who struck down all these? 10Know then that there shall fall to the earth nothing of the word of the LORD, which the LORD spoke concerning the house of Ahab; for the LORD has done what he said through his servant Elijah." 11So Jehu killed all who were left of the house of Ahab in Jezreel, all his leaders, close friends, and priests, until he left him no survivor.

12 Then he set out and went to Samaria. On the way, when he was at Beth-eked of the Shepherds, 13Jehu met relatives of King Ahaziah of Judah and said, "Who are you?" They answered, "We are kin of Ahaziah; we have come down to visit the royal princes and the sons of the queen mother." 14He said, "Take them alive." They took them alive, and slaughtered them at the pit of Beth-eked, forty-two in all; he spared none of them.

15 When he left there, he met Jehonadab son of Rechab coming to meet him; he greeted him, and said to him, "Is your heart as true to mine as mine is to yours?"ᶜ Jehonadab answered, "It is." Jehu said,ᵈ "If it is, give me your hand." So he gave him his hand. Jehu took him up with him into the chariot. 16He said, "Come

a Or of the city; Vg Compare Gk   b Gk: Heb lacks of the sons of   c Gk: Heb Is it right with your heart, as my heart is with your heart?   d Gk: Heb lacks Jehu said with me, and see my zeal for the LORD." So he[a] had him ride in his chariot. [17]When he came to Samaria, he killed all who were left to Ahab in Samaria, until he had wiped them out, according to the word of the LORD that he spoke to Elijah.

Slaughter of Worshipers of Baal

18 Then Jehu assembled all the people and said to them, "Ahab offered Baal small service; but Jehu will offer much more. [19]Now therefore summon to me all the prophets of Baal, all his worshipers, and all his priests; let none be missing, for I have a great sacrifice to offer to Baal; whoever is missing shall not live." But Jehu was acting with cunning in order to destroy the worshipers of Baal. [20]Jehu decreed, "Sanctify a solemn assembly for Baal." So they proclaimed it. [21]Jehu sent word throughout all Israel; all the worshipers of Baal came, so that there was no one left who did not come. They entered the temple of Baal, until the temple of Baal was filled from wall to wall. [22]He said to the keeper of the wardrobe, "Bring out the vestments for all the worshipers of Baal." So he brought out the vestments for them. [23]Then Jehu entered the temple of Baal with Jehonadab son of Rechab; he said to the worshipers of Baal, "Search and see that there is no worshiper of the LORD here among you, but only worshipers of Baal." [24]Then they proceeded to offer sacrifices and burnt offerings.

Now Jehu had stationed eighty men outside, saying, "Whoever allows any of those to escape whom I deliver into your hands shall forfeit his life." [25]As soon as he had finished presenting the burnt offering, Jehu said to the guards and to the officers, "Come in and kill them; let no one escape." So they put them to the sword. The guards and the officers threw them out, and then went into the citadel of the temple of Baal. [26]They brought out the pillar[b] that was in the temple of Baal, and burned it. [27]Then they demolished the pillar of Baal, and destroyed the temple of Baal, and made it a latrine to this day.

28 Thus Jehu wiped out Baal from Israel. [29]But Jehu did not turn aside from the sins of Jeroboam son of Nebat, which he caused Israel to commit—the golden calves that were in Bethel and in Dan. [30]The LORD said to Jehu, "Because you have done well in carrying out what I consider right, and in accordance with all that was in my heart have dealt with the house of Ahab, your sons of the fourth generation shall sit on the throne of Israel." [31]But Jehu was not careful to follow the law of the LORD the God of Israel with all his heart; he did not turn from the sins of Jeroboam, which he caused Israel to commit.

Death of Jehu

32 In those days the LORD began to trim off parts of Israel. Hazael defeated them throughout the territory of Israel: [33]from the Jordan eastward, all the land of Gilead, the Gadites, the Reubenites, and the Manassites, from Aroer, which is by the Wadi Arnon, that is, Gilead and Bashan. [34]Now the rest of the acts of Jehu, all that he did, and all his power, are they not written in the Book of the Annals of the Kings of Israel? [35]So Jehu slept with his ancestors, and they buried him in Samaria. His son Jehoahaz succeeded him. [36]The time that Jehu reigned over Israel in Samaria was twenty-eight years.

11 Athaliah Reigns over Judah

Now when Athaliah, Ahaziah's mother, saw that her son was dead, she set about to destroy all the royal family. [2]But Jehosheba, King Joram's daughter, Ahaziah's sister, took Joash son of Ahaziah, and stole him away from among the king's children who were about to be killed; she put[c] him and his nurse in a bedroom. Thus she[d] hid him from Athaliah, so that he was not killed; [3]he remained with her six years, hidden in the house of the LORD, while Athaliah reigned over the land.

Jehoiada Anoints the Child Joash

4 But in the seventh year Jehoiada summoned the captains of the Carites and of the guards and had them come to him in the house of the LORD. He made a covenant with them and put them under oath in the house of the LORD; then he showed them the king's son. [5]He commanded them, "This is what you are to do: one-third of you, those who go off duty on the sabbath and guard the king's house [6](another third being at the gate Sur and a third at the gate behind the guards), shall guard the palace; [7]and your two divisions that come on duty in force on the sabbath and guard the house of the LORD[e] [8]shall surround the king, each with weapons in hand; and whoever approaches the ranks is to be killed. Be with the king in his comings and goings."

9 The captains did according to all that the priest Jehoiada commanded; each brought his men who were to go off duty on the sabbath, with those who were to come on duty

---

a Gk Syr Tg: Heb *they*   b Gk Syr Tg: Heb *pillars*   c With 2 Chr 22.11: Heb lacks *she put*   d Gk Syr Vg Compare 2 Chr 22.11: Heb *they*
e Heb *the LORD to the king*

on the sabbath, and came to the priest Jehoiada. [10]The priest delivered to the captains the spears and shields that had been King David's, which were in the house of the LORD; [11]the guards stood, every man with his weapons in his hand, from the south side of the house to the north side of the house, around the altar and the house, to guard the king on every side. [12]Then he brought out the king's son, put the crown on him, and gave him the covenant;[a] they proclaimed him king, and anointed him; they clapped their hands and shouted, "Long live the king!"

Death of Athaliah

13 When Athaliah heard the noise of the guard and of the people, she went into the house of the LORD to the people; [14]when she looked, there was the king standing by the pillar, according to custom, with the captains and the trumpeters beside the king, and all the people of the land rejoicing and blowing trumpets. Athaliah tore her clothes and cried, "Treason! Treason!" [15]Then the priest Jehoiada commanded the captains who were set over the army, "Bring her out between the ranks, and kill with the sword anyone who follows her." For the priest said, "Let her not be killed in the house of the LORD." [16]So they laid hands on her; she went through the horses' entrance to the king's house, and there she was put to death.

17 Jehoiada made a covenant between the LORD and the king and people, that they should be the LORD's people; also between the king and the people. [18]Then all the people of the land went to the house of Baal, and tore it down; his altars and his images they broke in pieces, and they killed Mattan, the priest of Baal, before the altars. The priest posted guards over the house of the LORD. [19]He took the captains, the Carites, the guards, and all the people of the land; then they brought the king down from the house of the LORD, marching through the gate of the guards to the king's house. He took his seat on the throne of the kings. [20]So all the people of the land rejoiced; and the city was quiet after Athaliah had been killed with the sword at the king's house.

21[b] Jehoash[c] was seven years old when he began to reign.

12 The Temple Repaired

In the seventh year of Jehu, Jehoash began to reign; he reigned forty years in Jerusalem. His mother's name was Zibiah of Beer-sheba. [2]Jehoash did what was right in the sight of the LORD all his days, because the priest Jehoiada

instructed him. [3]Nevertheless the high places were not taken away; the people continued to sacrifice and make offerings on the high places.

4 Jehoash said to the priests, "All the money offered as sacred donations that is brought into the house of the LORD, the money for which each person is assessed—the money from the assessment of persons—and the money from the voluntary offerings brought into the house of the LORD, [5]let the priests receive from each of the donors; and let them repair the house wherever any need of repairs is discovered." [6]But by the twenty-third year of King Jehoash the priests had made no repairs on the house. [7]Therefore King Jehoash summoned the priest Jehoiada with the other priests and said to them, "Why are you not repairing the house? Now therefore do not accept any more money from your donors but hand it over for the repair of the house." [8]So the priests agreed that they would neither accept more money from the people nor repair the house.

9 Then the priest Jehoiada took a chest, made a hole in its lid, and set it beside the altar on the right side as one entered the house of the LORD; the priests who guarded the threshold put in it all the money that was brought into the house of the LORD. [10]Whenever they saw that there was a great deal of money in the chest, the king's secretary and the high priest went up, counted the money that was found in the house of the LORD, and tied it up in bags. [11]They would give the money that was weighed out into the hands of the workers who had the oversight of the house of the LORD; then they paid it out to the carpenters and the builders who worked on the house of the LORD, [12]to the masons and the stonecutters, as well as to buy timber and quarried stone for making repairs on the house of the LORD, as well as for any outlay for repairs of the house. [13]But for the house of the LORD no basins of silver, snuffers, bowls, trumpets, or any vessels of gold, or of silver, were made from the money that was brought into the house of the LORD, [14]for that was given to the workers who were repairing the house of the LORD with it. [15]They did not ask an accounting from those into whose hand they delivered the money to pay out to the workers, for they dealt honestly. [16]The money from the guilt offerings and the money from the sin offerings was not brought into the house of the LORD; it belonged to the priests.

Hazael Threatens Jerusalem

17 At that time King Hazael of Aram went up, fought against Gath, and took it. But when

---

a Or *treaty* or *testimony*; Heb *eduth* *b* Ch 12.1 in Heb *c* Another spelling is *Joash*; see verse 19

Hazael set his face to go up against Jerusalem, [18]King Jehoash of Judah took all the votive gifts that Jehoshaphat, Jehoram, and Ahaziah, his ancestors, the kings of Judah, had dedicated, as well as his own votive gifts, all the gold that was found in the treasuries of the house of the LORD and of the king's house, and sent these to King Hazael of Aram. Then Hazael withdrew from Jerusalem.

Death of Joash

19 Now the rest of the acts of Joash, and all that he did, are they not written in the Book of the Annals of the Kings of Judah? [20]His servants arose, devised a conspiracy, and killed Joash in the house of Millo, on the way that goes down to Silla. [21]It was Jozacar son of Shimeath and Jehozabad son of Shomer, his servants, who struck him down, so that he died. He was buried with his ancestors in the city of David; then his son Amaziah succeeded him.

13 Jehoahaz Reigns over Israel

In the twenty-third year of King Joash son of Ahaziah of Judah, Jehoahaz son of Jehu began to reign over Israel in Samaria; he reigned seventeen years. [2]He did what was evil in the sight of the LORD, and followed the sins of Jeroboam son of Nebat, which he caused Israel to sin; he did not depart from them. [3]The anger of the LORD was kindled against Israel, so that he gave them repeatedly into the hand of King Hazael of Aram, then into the hand of Ben-hadad son of Hazael. [4]But Jehoahaz entreated the LORD, and the LORD heeded him; for he saw the oppression of Israel, how the king of Aram oppressed them. [5]Therefore the LORD gave Israel a savior, so that they escaped from the hand of the Arameans; and the people of Israel lived in their homes as formerly. [6]Nevertheless they did not depart from the sins of the house of Jeroboam, which he caused Israel to sin, but walked[a] in them; the sacred pole[b] also remained in Samaria. [7]So Jehoahaz was left with an army of not more than fifty horsemen, ten chariots and ten thousand footmen; for the king of Aram had destroyed them and made them like the dust at threshing. [8]Now the rest of the acts of Jehoahaz and all that he did, including his might, are they not written in the Book of the Annals of the Kings of Israel? [9]So Jehoahaz slept with his ancestors, and they buried him in Samaria; then his son Joash succeeded him.

Jehoash Reigns over Israel

10 In the thirty-seventh year of King Joash of Judah, Jehoash son of Jehoahaz began to reign over Israel in Samaria; he reigned sixteen years. [11]He also did what was evil in the sight of the LORD; he did not depart from all the sins of Jeroboam son of Nebat, which he caused Israel to sin, but he walked in them. [12]Now the rest of the acts of Joash, and all that he did, as well as the might with which he fought against King Amaziah of Judah, are they not written in the Book of the Annals of the Kings of Israel? [13]So Joash slept with his ancestors, and Jeroboam sat upon his throne; Joash was buried in Samaria with the kings of Israel.

Death of Elisha

14 Now when Elisha had fallen sick with the illness of which he was to die, King Joash of Israel went down to him, and wept before him, crying, "My father, my father! The chariots of Israel and its horsemen!" [15]Elisha said to him,

a Gk Syr Tg Vg: Heb _he walked_ b Heb _Asherah_

Fade Away—© Michelle Jozwiak, 18

"Take a bow and arrows"; so he took a bow and arrows. [16]Then he said to the king of Israel, "Draw the bow"; and he drew it. Elisha laid his hands on the king's hands. [17]Then he said, "Open the window eastward"; and he opened it. Elisha said, "Shoot"; and he shot. Then he said, "The LORD's arrow of victory, the arrow of victory over Aram! For you shall fight the Arameans in Aphek until you have made an end of them." [18]He continued, "Take the arrows"; and he took them. He said to the king of Israel, "Strike the ground with them"; he struck three times, and stopped. [19]Then the man of God was angry with him, and said, "You should have struck five or six times; then you would have struck down Aram until you had made an end of it, but now you will strike down Aram only three times."

20 So Elisha died, and they buried him. Now bands of Moabites used to invade the land in the spring of the year. [21]As a man was being buried, a marauding band was seen and the man was thrown into the grave of Elisha; as soon as the man touched the bones of Elisha, he came to life and stood on his feet.

Israel Recaptures Cities from Aram

22 Now King Hazael of Aram oppressed Israel all the days of Jehoahaz. [23]But the LORD was gracious to them and had compassion on them; he turned toward them, because of his covenant with Abraham, Isaac, and Jacob, and would not destroy them; nor has he banished them from his presence until now.

24 When King Hazael of Aram died, his son Ben-hadad succeeded him. [25]Then Jehoash son of Jehoahaz took again from Ben-hadad son of Hazael the towns that he had taken from his father Jehoahaz in war. Three times Joash defeated him and recovered the towns of Israel.

14 Amaziah Reigns over Judah

In the second year of King Joash son of Joahaz of Israel, King Amaziah son of Joash of Judah, began to reign. [2]He was twenty-five years old when he began to reign, and he reigned twenty-nine years in Jerusalem. His mother's name was Jehoaddin of Jerusalem. [3]He did what was right in the sight of the LORD, yet not like his ancestor David; in all things he did as his father Joash had done. [4]But the high places were not removed; the people still sacrificed and made offerings on the high places. [5]As soon as the royal power was firmly in his hand he killed his servants who had murdered his father the king. [6]But he did not put to death the children of the murderers; according to what is written in the book of the law of Moses, where the LORD commanded, "The parents shall not be put to death for the children, or the children be put to death for the parents; but all shall be put to death for their own sins."

7 He killed ten thousand Edomites in the Valley of Salt and took Sela by storm; he called it Jokthe-el, which is its name to this day.

8 Then Amaziah sent messengers to King Jehoash son of Jehoahaz, son of Jehu, of Israel, saying, "Come, let us look one another in the face." [9]King Jehoash of Israel sent word to King Amaziah of Judah, "A thornbush on Lebanon sent to a cedar on Lebanon, saying, 'Give your daughter to my son for a wife'; but a wild animal of Lebanon passed by and trampled down the thornbush. [10]You have indeed defeated Edom, and your heart has lifted you up. Be content with your glory, and stay at home; for why

should you provoke trouble so that you fall, you and Judah with you?"

11 But Amaziah would not listen. So King Jehoash of Israel went up; he and King Amaziah of Judah faced one another in battle at Beth-shemesh, which belongs to Judah. [12]Judah was defeated by Israel; everyone fled home. [13]King Jehoash of Israel captured King Amaziah of Judah son of Jehoash, son of Ahaziah, at Beth-shemesh; he came to Jerusalem, and broke down the wall of Jerusalem from the Ephraim Gate to the Corner Gate, a distance of four hundred cubits. [14]He seized all the gold and silver, and all the vessels that were found in the house of the LORD and in the treasuries of the king's house, as well as hostages; then he returned to Samaria.

15 Now the rest of the acts that Jehoash did, his might, and how he fought with King Amaziah of Judah, are they not written in the Book of the Annals of the Kings of Israel? [16]Jehoash slept with his ancestors, and was buried in Samaria with the kings of Israel; then his son Jeroboam succeeded him.

17 King Amaziah son of Joash of Judah lived fifteen years after the death of King Jehoash son of Jehoahaz of Israel. [18]Now the rest of the deeds of Amaziah, are they not written in the Book of the Annals of the Kings of Judah? [19]They made a conspiracy against him in Jerusalem, and he fled to Lachish. But they sent after him to Lachish, and killed him there. [20]They brought him on horses; he was buried in Jerusalem with his ancestors in the city of David. [21]All the people of Judah took Azariah, who was sixteen years old, and made him king to succeed his father Amaziah. [22]He rebuilt Elath and restored it to Judah, after King Amaziah[a] slept with his ancestors.

Jeroboam II Reigns over Israel

23 In the fifteenth year of King Amaziah son of Joash of Judah, King Jeroboam son of Joash of Israel began to reign in Samaria; he reigned forty-one years. [24]He did what was evil in the sight of the LORD; he did not depart from all the sins of Jeroboam son of Nebat, which he caused Israel to sin. [25]He restored the border of Israel from Lebo-hamath as far as the Sea of the Arabah, according to the word of the LORD, the God of Israel, which he spoke by his servant Jonah son of Amittai, the prophet, who was from Gath-hepher. [26]For the LORD saw that the distress of Israel was very bitter; there was no one left, bond or free, and no one to help Israel. [27]But the LORD had not said that he would blot out the name of Israel from under heaven,

so he saved them by the hand of Jeroboam son of Joash.

28 Now the rest of the acts of Jeroboam, and all that he did, and his might, how he fought, and how he recovered for Israel Damascus and Hamath, which had belonged to Judah, are they not written in the Book of the Annals of the Kings of Israel? [29]Jeroboam slept with his ancestors, the kings of Israel; his son Zechariah succeeded him.

15 Azariah Reigns over Judah

In the twenty-seventh year of King Jeroboam of Israel King Azariah son of Amaziah of Judah began to reign. [2]He was sixteen years old when he began to reign, and he reigned fifty-two years in Jerusalem. His mother's name was Jecoliah of Jerusalem. [3]He did what was right in the sight of the LORD, just as his father Amaziah had done. [4]Nevertheless the high places were not taken away; the people still sacrificed and made offerings on the high places. [5]The LORD struck the king, so that he was leprous[b] to the day of his death, and lived in a separate house. Jotham the king's son was in charge of the palace, governing the people of the land. [6]Now the rest of the acts of Azariah, and all that he did, are they not written in the Book of the Annals of the Kings of Judah? [7]Azariah slept with his ancestors; they buried him with his ancestors in the city of David; his son Jotham succeeded him.

Zechariah Reigns over Israel

8 In the thirty-eighth year of King Azariah of Judah, Zechariah son of Jeroboam reigned over Israel in Samaria six months. [9]He did what was evil in the sight of the LORD, as his ancestors had done. He did not depart from the sins of Jeroboam son of Nebat, which he caused Israel to sin. [10]Shallum son of Jabesh conspired against him, and struck him down in public and killed him, and reigned in place of him. [11]Now the rest of the deeds of Zechariah are written in the Book of the Annals of the Kings of Israel. [12]This was the promise of the LORD that he gave to Jehu, "Your sons shall sit on the throne of Israel to the fourth generation." And so it happened.

Shallum Reigns over Israel

13 Shallum son of Jabesh began to reign in the thirty-ninth year of King Uzziah of Judah; he reigned one month in Samaria. [14]Then Menahem son of Gadi came up from Tirzah and came to Samaria; he struck down Shallum son of Jabesh in Samaria and killed him; he reigned

a Heb the king b A term for several skin diseases; precise meaning uncertain in place of him. 15Now the rest of the deeds of Shallum, including the conspiracy that he made, are written in the Book of the Annals of the Kings of Israel. 16At that time Menahem sacked Tiphsah, all who were in it and its territory from Tirzah on; because they did not open it to him, he sacked it. He ripped open all the pregnant women in it.

Menahem Reigns over Israel

17 In the thirty-ninth year of King Azariah of Judah, Menahem son of Gadi began to reign over Israel; he reigned ten years in Samaria. 18He did what was evil in the sight of the LORD; he did not depart all his days from any of the sins of Jeroboam son of Nebat, which he caused Israel to sin. 19King Pul of Assyria came against the land; Menahem gave Pul a thousand talents of silver, so that he might help him confirm his hold on the royal power. 20Menahem exacted the money from Israel, that is, from all the wealthy, fifty shekels of silver from each one, to give to the king of Assyria. So the king of Assyria turned back, and did not stay there in the land. 21Now the rest of the deeds of Menahem, and all that he did, are they not written in the Book of the Annals of the Kings of Israel? 22Menahem slept with his ancestors, and his son Pekahiah succeeded him.

Pekahiah Reigns over Israel

23 In the fiftieth year of King Azariah of Judah, Pekahiah son of Menahem began to reign over Israel in Samaria; he reigned two years. 24He did what was evil in the sight of the LORD; he did not turn away from the sins of Jeroboam son of Nebat, which he caused Israel to sin. 25Pekah son of Remaliah, his captain, conspired against him with fifty of the Gileadites, and attacked him in Samaria, in the citadel of the palace along with Argob and Arieh; he killed him, and reigned in place of him. 26Now the rest of the deeds of Pekahiah, and all that he did, are written in the Book of the Annals of the Kings of Israel.

Pekah Reigns over Israel

27 In the fifty-second year of King Azariah of Judah, Pekah son of Remaliah began to reign over Israel in Samaria; he reigned twenty years. 28He did what was evil in the sight of the LORD; he did not depart from the sins of Jeroboam son of Nebat, which he caused Israel to sin.

29 In the days of King Pekah of Israel, King Tiglath-pileser of Assyria came and captured Ijon, Abel-beth-maacah, Janoah, Kedesh, Hazor, Gilead, and Galilee, all the land of Naphtali; and he carried the people captive to Assyria. 30Then Hoshea son of Elah made a conspiracy against Pekah son of Remaliah, attacked him, and killed him; he reigned in place of him, in the twentieth year of Jotham son of Uzziah. 31Now the rest of the acts of Pekah, and all that he did, are written in the Book of the Annals of the Kings of Israel.

Jotham Reigns over Judah

32 In the second year of King Pekah son of Remaliah of Israel, King Jotham son of Uzziah of Judah began to reign. 33He was twenty-five years old when he began to reign and reigned sixteen years in Jerusalem. His mother's name was Jerusha daughter of Zadok. 34He did what was right in the sight of the LORD, just as his father Uzziah had done. 35Nevertheless the high places were not removed; the people still sacrificed and made offerings on the high places. He built the upper gate of the house of the LORD. 36Now the rest of the acts of Jotham, and all that he did, are they not written in the Book of the Annals of the Kings of Judah? 37In those days the LORD began to send King Rezin of Aram and Pekah son of Remaliah against Judah. 38Jotham slept with his ancestors, and was buried with his ancestors in the city of David, his ancestor; his son Ahaz succeeded him.

16 Ahaz Reigns over Judah

In the seventeenth year of Pekah son of Remaliah, King Ahaz son of Jotham of Judah began to reign. 2Ahaz was twenty years old when he began to reign; he reigned sixteen years in Jerusalem. He did not do what was right in the sight of the LORD his God, as his ancestor David had done, 3but he walked in the way of the kings of Israel. He even made his son pass through fire, according to the abominable practices of the nations whom the LORD drove out before the people of Israel. 4He sacrificed and made offerings on the high places, on the hills, and under every green tree.

5 Then King Rezin of Aram and King Pekah son of Remaliah of Israel came up to wage war on Jerusalem; they besieged Ahaz but could not conquer him. 6At that time the king of Edom*a* recovered Elath for Edom,*b* and drove the Judeans from Elath; and the Edomites came to Elath, where they live to this day. 7Ahaz sent messengers to King Tiglath-pileser of Assyria, saying, "I am your servant and your son. Come up, and rescue me from the hand of the king of Aram and from the hand of the king of Israel, who are attacking me." 8Ahaz also took the silver and gold found in the house of the

a Cn: Heb King Rezin of Aram b Cn: Heb Aram

Reflections—© Lauren Jordan, 18

LORD and in the treasures of the king's house, and sent a present to the king of Assyria. [9]The king of Assyria listened to him; the king of Assyria marched up against Damascus, and took it, carrying its people captive to Kir; then he killed Rezin.

10 When King Ahaz went to Damascus to meet King Tiglath-pileser of Assyria, he saw the altar that was at Damascus. King Ahaz sent to the priest Uriah a model of the altar, and its pattern, exact in all its details. [11]The priest Uriah built the altar; in accordance with all that King Ahaz had sent from Damascus, just so did the priest Uriah build it, before King Ahaz arrived from Damascus. [12]When the king came from Damascus, the king viewed the altar. Then the king drew near to the altar, went up on it, [13]and offered his burnt offering and his grain offering, poured his drink offering, and dashed the blood of his offerings of well-being against the altar. [14]The bronze altar that was before the LORD he removed from the front of the house, from the place between his altar and the house of the LORD, and put it on the north side of his altar. [15]King Ahaz commanded the priest Uriah, saying, "Upon the great altar offer the morning burnt offering, and the evening grain offering, and the king's burnt offering, and his grain offering, with the burnt offering of all the people of the land, their grain offering, and their drink offering; then dash against it all the blood of the burnt offering, and all the

blood of the sacrifice; but the bronze altar shall be for me to inquire by." [16]The priest Uriah did everything that King Ahaz commanded.

17 Then King Ahaz cut off the frames of the stands, and removed the laver from them; he removed the sea from the bronze oxen that were under it, and put it on a pediment of stone. [18]The covered portal for use on the sabbath that had been built inside the palace, and the outer entrance for the king he removed from[a] the house of the LORD. He did this because of the king of Assyria. [19]Now the rest of the acts of Ahaz that he did, are they not written in the Book of the Annals of the Kings of Judah? [20]Ahaz slept with his ancestors, and was buried with his ancestors in the city of David; his son Hezekiah succeeded him.

17 Hoshea Reigns over Israel

In the twelfth year of King Ahaz of Judah, Hoshea son of Elah began to reign in Samaria over Israel; he reigned nine years. [2]He did what was evil in the sight of the LORD, yet not like the kings of Israel who were before him. [3]King Shalmaneser of Assyria came up against him; Hoshea became his vassal, and paid him tribute. [4]But the king of Assyria found treachery in Hoshea; for he had sent messengers to King So of Egypt, and offered no tribute to the king of Assyria, as he had done year by year; therefore the king of Assyria confined him and imprisoned him.

a Cn: Heb lacks *from*

Israel Carried Captive to Assyria

5 Then the king of Assyria invaded all the land and came to Samaria; for three years he besieged it. ⁶In the ninth year of Hoshea the king of Assyria captured Samaria; he carried the Israelites away to Assyria. He placed them in Halah, on the Habor, the river of Gozan, and in the cities of the Medes.

7 This occurred because the people of Israel had sinned against the LORD their God, who had brought them up out of the land of Egypt from under the hand of Pharaoh king of Egypt. They had worshiped other gods ⁸and walked in the customs of the nations whom the LORD drove out before the people of Israel, and in the customs that the kings of Israel had introduced.ᵃ ⁹The people of Israel secretly did things that were not right against the LORD their God. They built for themselves high places at all their towns, from watchtower to fortified city; ¹⁰they set up for themselves pillars and sacred polesᵇ on every high hill and under every green tree; ¹¹there they made offerings on all the high places, as the nations did whom the LORD carried away before them. They did wicked things, provoking the LORD to anger; ¹²they served idols, of which the LORD had said to them, "You shall not do this." ¹³Yet the LORD warned Israel and Judah by every prophet and every seer, saying, "Turn from your evil ways and keep my commandments and my statutes, in accordance with all the law that I commanded your ancestors and that I sent to you by my servants the prophets." ¹⁴They would not listen but were stubborn, as their ancestors had been, who did not believe in the LORD their God. ¹⁵They despised his statutes, and his covenant that he made with their ancestors, and the warnings that he gave them. They went after false idols and became false; they followed the nations that were around them, concerning whom the LORD had commanded them that they should not do as they did. ¹⁶They rejected all the commandments of the LORD their God and made for themselves cast images of two calves; they made a sacred pole,ᶜ worshiped all the host of heaven, and served Baal. ¹⁷They made their sons and their daughters pass through fire; they used divination and augury; and they sold themselves to do evil in the sight of the LORD, provoking him to anger. ¹⁸Therefore the LORD was very angry with Israel and removed them out of his sight; none was left but the tribe of Judah alone.

19 Judah also did not keep the commandments of the LORD their God but walked in the customs that Israel had introduced. ²⁰The LORD rejected all the descendants of Israel; he punished them and gave them into the hand of plunderers, until he had banished them from his presence.

21 When he had torn Israel from the house of David, they made Jeroboam son of Nebat king. Jeroboam drove Israel from following the LORD and made them commit great sin. ²²The people of Israel continued in all the sins that Jeroboam committed; they did not depart from them ²³until the LORD removed Israel out of his sight, as he had foretold through all his servants the prophets. So Israel was exiled from their own land to Assyria until this day.

Assyria Resettles Samaria

24 The king of Assyria brought people from Babylon, Cuthah, Avva, Hamath, and Sepharvaim, and placed them in the cities of Samaria in place of the people of Israel; they took possession of Samaria, and settled in its cities. ²⁵When they first settled there, they did not worship the LORD; therefore the LORD sent lions among them, which killed some of them. ²⁶So the king of Assyria was told, "The nations that you have carried away and placed in the cities of Samaria do not know the law of the god of the land; therefore he has sent lions among them; they are killing them, because they do not know the law of the god of the land." ²⁷Then the king of Assyria commanded, "Send there one of the priests whom you carried away from there; let himᵈ go and live there, and teach them the law of the god of the land." ²⁸So one of the priests whom they had carried away from Samaria came and lived in Bethel; he taught them how they should worship the LORD.

29 But every nation still made gods of its own and put them in the shrines of the high places that the people of Samaria had made, every nation in the cities in which they lived; ³⁰the people of Babylon made Succoth-benoth, the people of Cuth made Nergal, the people of Hamath made Ashima; ³¹the Avvites made Nibhaz and Tartak; the Sepharvites burned their children in the fire to Adrammelech and Anammelech, the gods of Sepharvaim. ³²They also worshiped the LORD and appointed from among themselves all sorts of people as priests of the high places, who sacrificed for them in the shrines of the high places. ³³So they worshiped the LORD but also served their own gods, after the manner of the nations from among whom they had been carried away. ³⁴To this day they continue to practice their former customs.

ᵃ Meaning of Heb uncertain ᵇ Heb *Asherim* ᶜ Heb *Asherah* ᵈ Syr Vg: Heb *them*

They do not worship the Lord and they do not follow the statutes or the ordinances or the law or the commandment that the Lord commanded the children of Jacob, whom he named Israel. [35]The Lord had made a covenant with them and commanded them, "You shall not worship other gods or bow yourselves to them or serve them or sacrifice to them, [36]but you shall worship the Lord, who brought you out of the land of Egypt with great power and with an outstretched arm; you shall bow yourselves to him, and to him you shall sacrifice. [37]The statutes and the ordinances and the law and the commandment that he wrote for you, you shall always be careful to observe. You shall not worship other gods; [38]you shall not forget the covenant that I have made with you. You shall not worship other gods, [39]but you shall worship the Lord your God; he will deliver you out of the hand of all your enemies." [40]They would not listen, however, but they continued to practice their former custom.

41 So these nations worshiped the Lord, but also served their carved images; to this day their children and their children's children continue to do as their ancestors did.

18 Hezekiah's Reign over Judah

In the third year of King Hoshea son of Elah of Israel, Hezekiah son of King Ahaz of Judah began to reign. [2]He was twenty-five years old when he began to reign; he reigned twenty-nine years in Jerusalem. His mother's name was Abi daughter of Zechariah. [3]He did what was right in the sight of the Lord just as his ancestor David had done. [4]He removed the high places, broke down the pillars, and cut down the sacred pole.[a] He broke in pieces the bronze serpent that Moses had made, for until those days the people of Israel had made offerings to it; it was called Nehushtan. [5]He trusted in the Lord the God of Israel; so that there was no one like him among all the kings of Judah after him, or among those who were before him. [6]For he held fast to the Lord; he did not depart from following him but kept the commandments that the Lord commanded Moses. [7]The Lord was with him; wherever he went, he prospered. He rebelled against the king of Assyria and would not serve him. [8]He attacked the Philistines as far as Gaza and its territory, from watchtower to fortified city.

9 In the fourth year of King Hezekiah, which was the seventh year of King Hoshea son of Elah of Israel, King Shalmaneser of Assyria came up against Samaria, besieged it, [10]and at the end of three years, took it. In the sixth year

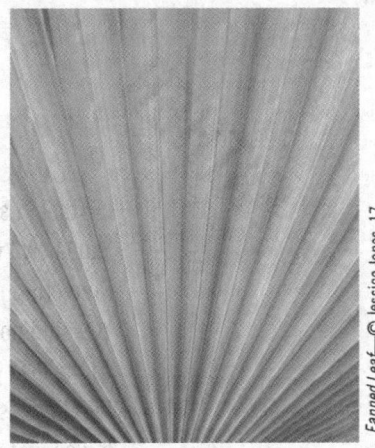

of Hezekiah, which was the ninth year of King Hoshea of Israel, Samaria was taken. [11]The king of Assyria carried the Israelites away to Assyria, settled them in Halah, on the Habor, the river of Gozan, and in the cities of the Medes, [12]because they did not obey the voice of the Lord their God but transgressed his covenant—all that Moses the servant of the Lord had commanded; they neither listened nor obeyed.

Sennacherib Invades Judah

13 In the fourteenth year of King Hezekiah, King Sennacherib of Assyria came up against all the fortified cities of Judah and captured them. [14]King Hezekiah of Judah sent to the king of Assyria at Lachish, saying, "I have done wrong; withdraw from me; whatever you impose on me I will bear." The king of Assyria demanded of King Hezekiah of Judah three hundred talents of silver and thirty talents of gold. [15]Hezekiah gave him all the silver that was found in the house of the Lord and in the treasuries of the king's house. [16]At that time Hezekiah stripped the gold from the doors of the temple of the Lord, and from the doorposts that King Hezekiah of Judah had overlaid and gave it to the king of Assyria. [17]The king of Assyria sent the Tartan, the Rabsaris, and the Rabshakeh with a great army from Lachish to King Hezekiah at Jerusalem. They went up and came to Jerusalem. When they arrived, they came and stood by the conduit of the upper pool, which is on the highway to the Fuller's Field. [18]When they called for the king, there came out to them Eliakim son of Hilkiah, who was in charge of the palace, and Shebnah the secretary, and Joah son of Asaph, the recorder.

19 The Rabshakeh said to them, "Say to

a Heb *Asherah*

FATHER

"Father" I say, running into your arms—
You knew I needed you and you were right there,
Protecting me from all those harms.
You said no one could compare
To the love you have for me,
And I guess you were right—
It was just so hard for me to see.
Now there's perfect sight:
You are a father to the fatherless
And that you will always be.
I love your realness,
And that you love me.
You give me what I need,
You always know what's wrong.
With you I don't have to plead and plead—
All I have to do is be strong.
With your help nothing is impossible,
And I can do all things.
I shall stay prayerful,
Always in the mornings,
And in the afternoon.
I love you so much,
It's like to this world I am immune…
Yet here I am friendless,
But God, you are the father to the fatherless!

Father—© Shelby Steckroth, 15

Hezekiah: Thus says the great king, the king of Assyria: On what do you base this confidence of yours? 20Do you think that mere words are strategy and power for war? On whom do you now rely, that you have rebelled against me? 21See, you are relying now on Egypt, that broken reed of a staff, which will pierce the hand of anyone who leans on it. Such is Pharaoh king of Egypt to all who rely on him. 22But if you say to me, 'We rely on the LORD our God,' is it not he whose high places and altars Hezekiah has removed, saying to Judah and to Jerusalem, 'You shall worship before this altar in Jerusalem'? 23Come now, make a wager with my master the king of Assyria: I will give you two thousand horses, if you are able on your part to set riders on them. 24How then can you repulse a single captain among the least of my master's servants, when you rely on Egypt for chariots and for horsemen? 25Moreover, is it without the LORD that I have come up against this place to destroy it? The LORD said to me, Go up against this land, and destroy it."

26 Then Eliakim son of Hilkiah, and Shebnah, and Joah said to the Rabshakeh, "Please speak to your servants in the Aramaic language, for we understand it; do not speak to us in the language of Judah within the hearing of the people who are on the wall." 27But the Rabshakeh said to them, "Has my master sent me to speak these words to your master and to you, and not to the people sitting on the wall, who are doomed with you to eat their own dung and to drink their own urine?"

28 Then the Rabshakeh stood and called out in a loud voice in the language of Judah, "Hear the word of the great king, the king of Assyria! 29Thus says the king: 'Do not let Hezekiah deceive you, for he will not be able to deliver you out of my hand. 30Do not let Hezekiah make you rely on the LORD by saying, The LORD will surely deliver us, and this city will not be given into the hand of the king of Assyria.' 31Do not listen to Hezekiah; for thus says the king of Assyria: 'Make your peace with me and come out to me; then every one of you will eat from your own vine and your own fig tree, and drink water from your own cistern, 32until I come and take you away to a land like your own land, a land of grain and wine, a land of bread and vineyards, a land of olive oil and honey, that you may live and not die. Do not listen to Hezekiah when he misleads you by saying, The LORD will deliver us. 33Has any of the gods of the nations ever delivered its land out of the hand of the king of Assyria? 34Where are the gods of Hamath and Arpad? Where are the gods of

Sepharvaim, Hena, and Ivvah? Have they delivered Samaria out of my hand? 35Who among all the gods of the countries have delivered their countries out of my hand, that the LORD should deliver Jerusalem out of my hand?' "

36 But the people were silent and answered him not a word, for the king's command was, "Do not answer him." 37Then Eliakim son of Hilkiah, who was in charge of the palace, and Shebna the secretary, and Joah son of Asaph, the recorder, came to Hezekiah with their clothes torn and told him the words of the Rabshakeh.

19 Hezekiah Consults Isaiah

When King Hezekiah heard it, he tore his clothes, covered himself with sackcloth, and went into the house of the LORD. 2And he sent Eliakim, who was in charge of the palace, and Shebna the secretary, and the senior priests, covered with sackcloth, to the prophet Isaiah son of Amoz. 3They said to him, "Thus says Hezekiah, This day is a day of distress, of rebuke, and of disgrace; children have come to the birth, and there is no strength to bring them forth. 4It may be that the LORD your God heard all the words of the Rabshakeh, whom his master the king of Assyria has sent to mock the living God, and will rebuke the words that the LORD your God has heard; therefore lift up your prayer for the remnant that is left." 5When the servants of King Hezekiah came to Isaiah, 6Isaiah said to them, "Say to your master, 'Thus says the LORD: Do not be afraid because of the words that you have heard, with which the servants of the king of Assyria have reviled me. 7I myself will put a spirit in him, so that he shall hear a rumor and return to his own land; I will cause him to fall by the sword in his own land.' "

Sennacherib's Threat

8 The Rabshakeh returned, and found the king of Assyria fighting against Libnah; for he had heard that the king had left Lachish. 9When the king*a* heard concerning King Tirhakah of Ethiopia,*b* "See, he has set out to fight against you," he sent messengers again to Hezekiah, saying, 10"Thus shall you speak to King Hezekiah of Judah: Do not let your God on whom you rely deceive you by promising that Jerusalem will not be given into the hand of the king of Assyria. 11See, you have heard what the kings of Assyria have done to all lands, destroying them utterly. Shall you be delivered? 12Have the gods of the nations delivered them, the nations that my predecessors destroyed, Gozan, Haran, Re-

a Heb *he* *b* Or *Nubia*; Heb *Cush*

zeph, and the people of Eden who were in Telassar? ¹³Where is the king of Hamath, the king of Arpad, the king of the city of Sepharvaim, the king of Hena, or the king of Ivvah?"

Hezekiah's Prayer

14 Hezekiah received the letter from the hand of the messengers and read it; then Hezekiah went up to the house of the Lord and spread it before the Lord. ¹⁵And Hezekiah prayed before the Lord, and said: "O Lord the God of Israel, who are enthroned above the cherubim, you are God, you alone, of all the kingdoms of the earth; you have made heaven and earth. ¹⁶Incline your ear, O Lord, and hear; open your eyes, O Lord, and see; hear the words of Sennacherib, which he has sent to mock the living God. ¹⁷Truly, O Lord, the kings of Assyria have laid waste the nations and their lands, ¹⁸and have hurled their gods into the fire, though

they were no gods but the work of human hands—wood and stone—and so they were destroyed. ¹⁹So now, O Lord our God, save us, I pray you, from his hand, so that all the kingdoms of the earth may know that you, O Lord, are God alone."

20 Then Isaiah son of Amoz sent to Hezekiah, saying, "Thus says the Lord, the God of Israel: I have heard your prayer to me about King Sennacherib of Assyria. ²¹This is the word that the Lord has spoken concerning him:

> She despises you, she scorns you—
>   virgin daughter Zion;
> she tosses her head—behind your back,
>   daughter Jerusalem.

²² "Whom have you mocked and reviled?
>   Against whom have you raised your voice
> and haughtily lifted your eyes?
>   Against the Holy One of Israel!
²³ By your messengers you have mocked the
>   Lord,
>   and you have said, 'With my many
>   chariots
> I have gone up the heights of the
>   mountains,
>   to the far recesses of Lebanon;
> I felled its tallest cedars,
>   its choicest cypresses;
> I entered its farthest retreat,
>   its densest forest.
²⁴ I dug wells
>   and drank foreign waters,
> I dried up with the sole of my foot
>   all the streams of Egypt.'
²⁵ "Have you not heard
>   that I determined it long ago?
> I planned from days of old
>   what now I bring to pass,
> that you should make fortified cities
>   crash into heaps of ruins,
²⁶ while their inhabitants, shorn of strength,
>   are dismayed and confounded;
> they have become like plants of the field
>   and like tender grass,
> like grass on the housetops,
>   blighted before it is grown.

²⁷ "But I know your rising*ᵃ* and your sitting,
>   your going out and coming in,
>   and your raging against me.
²⁸ Because you have raged against me
>   and your arrogance has come to my ears,
> I will put my hook in your nose
>   and my bit in your mouth;
> I will turn you back on the way
>   by which you came.

---

a Gk Compare Isa 37.27 Q Ms: MT lacks *rising*

29 "And this shall be the sign for you: This year you shall eat what grows of itself, and in the second year what springs from that; then in the third year sow, reap, plant vineyards, and eat their fruit. ³⁰The surviving remnant of the house of Judah shall again take root downward, and bear fruit upward; ³¹for from Jerusalem a remnant shall go out, and from Mount Zion a band of survivors. The zeal of the LORD of hosts will do this.

32 "Therefore thus says the LORD concerning the king of Assyria: He shall not come into this city, shoot an arrow there, come before it with a shield, or cast up a siege ramp against it. ³³By the way that he came, by the same he shall return; he shall not come into this city, says the LORD. ³⁴For I will defend this city to save it, for my own sake and for the sake of my servant David."

Sennacherib's Defeat and Death

35 That very night the angel of the LORD set out and struck down one hundred eighty-five thousand in the camp of the Assyrians; when morning dawned, they were all dead bodies. ³⁶Then King Sennacherib of Assyria left, went home, and lived at Nineveh. ³⁷As he was worshiping in the house of his god Nisroch, his sons Adrammelech and Sharezer killed him with the sword, and they escaped into the land of Ararat. His son Esar-haddon succeeded him.

20 Hezekiah's Illness

In those days Hezekiah became sick and was at the point of death. The prophet Isaiah son of Amoz came to him, and said to him, "Thus says the LORD: Set your house in order, for you shall die; you shall not recover." ²Then Hezekiah turned his face to the wall and prayed to the LORD: ³"Remember now, O LORD, I implore you, how I have walked before you in faithfulness with a whole heart, and have done what is good in your sight." Hezekiah wept bitterly. ⁴Before Isaiah had gone out of the middle court, the word of the LORD came to him: ⁵"Turn back, and say to Hezekiah prince of my people, Thus says the LORD, the God of your ancestor David: I have heard your prayer, I have seen your tears; indeed, I will heal you; on the third day you shall go up to the house of the LORD. ⁶I will add fifteen years to your life. I will deliver you and this city out of the hand of the king of Assyria; I will defend this city for my own sake and for my servant David's sake." ⁷Then Isaiah said, "Bring a lump of figs. Let them take it and apply it to the boil, so that he may recover."

8 Hezekiah said to Isaiah, "What shall be the sign that the LORD will heal me, and that I shall go up to the house of the LORD on the third day?" ⁹Isaiah said, "This is the sign to you from the LORD, that the LORD will do the thing that he has promised: the shadow has now advanced ten intervals; shall it retreat ten intervals?" ¹⁰Hezekiah answered, "It is normal for the shadow to lengthen ten intervals; rather let the shadow retreat ten intervals." ¹¹The prophet Isaiah cried to the LORD; and he brought the shadow back the ten intervals, by which the sunᵃ had declined on the dial of Ahaz.

Envoys from Babylon

12 At that time King Merodach-baladan son of Baladan of Babylon sent envoys with letters and a present to Hezekiah, for he had heard that Hezekiah had been sick. ¹³Hezekiah welcomed them;ᵇ he showed them all his treasure house, the silver, the gold, the spices, the precious oil, his armory, all that was found in his storehouses; there was nothing in his house or in all his realm that Hezekiah did not show them. ¹⁴Then the prophet Isaiah came to King Hezekiah, and said to him, "What did these men say? From where did they come to you?" Hezekiah answered, "They have come from a far country, from Babylon." ¹⁵He said, "What have they seen in your house?" Hezekiah answered, "They have seen all that is in my house; there is nothing in my storehouses that I did not show them."

16 Then Isaiah said to Hezekiah, "Hear the word of the LORD: ¹⁷Days are coming when all that is in your house, and that which your ancestors have stored up until this day, shall be carried to Babylon; nothing shall be left, says the LORD. ¹⁸Some of your own sons who are born to you shall be taken away; they shall be eunuchs in the palace of the king of Babylon." ¹⁹Then Hezekiah said to Isaiah, "The word of the LORD that you have spoken is good." For he thought, "Why not, if there will be peace and security in my days?"

Death of Hezekiah

20 The rest of the deeds of Hezekiah, all his power, how he made the pool and the conduit and brought water into the city, are they not written in the Book of the Annals of the Kings of Judah? ²¹Hezekiah slept with his ancestors; and his son Manasseh succeeded him.

21 Manasseh Reigns over Judah

Manasseh was twelve years old when he began to reign; he reigned fifty-five years in Je-

---

a Syr See Isa 38.8 and Tg: Heb it b Gk Vg Syr: Heb When Hezekiah heard about them rusalem. His mother's name was Hephzibah. [2]He did what was evil in the sight of the LORD, following the abominable practices of the nations that the LORD drove out before the people of Israel. [3]For he rebuilt the high places that his father Hezekiah had destroyed; he erected altars for Baal, made a sacred pole,[a] as King Ahab of Israel had done, worshiped all the host of heaven, and served them. [4]He built altars in the house of the LORD, of which the LORD had said, "In Jerusalem I will put my name." [5]He built altars for all the host of heaven in the two courts of the house of the LORD. [6]He made his son pass through fire; he practiced soothsaying and augury, and dealt with mediums and with wizards. He did much evil in the sight of the LORD, provoking him to anger. [7]The carved image of Asherah that he had made he set in the house of which the LORD said to David and to his son Solomon, "In this house, and in Jerusalem, which I have chosen out of all the tribes of Israel, I will put my name forever; [8]I will not cause the feet of Israel to wander any more out of the land that I gave to their ancestors, if only they will be careful to do according to all that I have commanded them, and according to all the law that my servant Moses commanded them." [9]But they did not listen; Manasseh misled them to do more evil than the nations had done that the LORD destroyed before the people of Israel.

10 The LORD said by his servants the prophets, [11]"Because King Manasseh of Judah has committed these abominations, has done things more wicked than all that the Amorites did, who were before him, and has caused Judah also to sin with his idols; [12]therefore thus says the LORD, the God of Israel, I am bringing upon Jerusalem and Judah such evil that the ears of everyone who hears of it will tingle. [13]I will stretch over Jerusalem the measuring line for Samaria, and the plummet for the house of Ahab; I will wipe Jerusalem as one wipes a dish, wiping it and turning it upside down. [14]I will cast off the remnant of my heritage, and give them into the hand of their enemies; they shall become a prey and a spoil to all their enemies, [15]because they have done what is evil in my sight and have provoked me to anger, since the day their ancestors came out of Egypt, even to this day."

16 Moreover Manasseh shed very much innocent blood, until he had filled Jerusalem from one end to another, besides the sin that he caused Judah to sin so that they did what was evil in the sight of the LORD.

17 Now the rest of the acts of Manasseh, all that he did, and the sin that he committed, are they not written in the Book of the Annals of the Kings of Judah? [18]Manasseh slept with his ancestors, and was buried in the garden of his house, in the garden of Uzza. His son Amon succeeded him.

Amon Reigns over Judah

19 Amon was twenty-two years old when he began to reign; he reigned two years in Jerusalem. His mother's name was Meshullemeth daughter of Haruz of Jotbah. [20]He did what was evil in the sight of the LORD, as his father Manasseh had done. [21]He walked in all the way in which his father walked, served the idols that his father served, and worshiped them; [22]he abandoned the LORD, the God of his ancestors, and did not walk in the way of the LORD. [23]The servants of Amon conspired against him, and killed the king in his house. [24]But the people of the land killed all those who had conspired against King Amon, and the people of the land made his son Josiah king in place of him. [25]Now the rest of the acts of Amon that he did, are they not written in the Book of the Annals of the Kings of Judah? [26]He was buried in his tomb in the garden of Uzza; then his son Josiah succeeded him.

22 Josiah Reigns over Judah

Josiah was eight years old when he began to reign; he reigned thirty-one years in Jerusalem. His mother's name was Jedidah daughter of Adaiah of Bozkath. [2]He did what was right in the sight of the LORD, and walked in all the way of his father David; he did not turn aside to the right or to the left.

Hilkiah Finds the Book of the Law

3 In the eighteenth year of King Josiah, the king sent Shaphan son of Azaliah, son of Meshullam, the secretary, to the house of the LORD, saying, [4]"Go up to the high priest Hilkiah, and have him count the entire sum of the money that has been brought into the house of the LORD, which the keepers of the threshold have collected from the people; [5]let it be given into the hand of the workers who have the oversight of the house of the LORD; let them give it to the workers who are at the house of the LORD, repairing the house, [6]that is, to the carpenters, to the builders, to the masons; and let them use it to buy timber and quarried stone to repair the house. [7]But no accounting shall be asked from them for the money that is delivered into their hand, for they deal honestly."

8 The high priest Hilkiah said to Shaphan

the secretary, "I have found the book of the law in the house of the LORD." When Hilkiah gave the book to Shaphan, he read it. ⁹Then Shaphan the secretary came to the king, and reported to the king, "Your servants have emptied out the money that was found in the house, and have delivered it into the hand of the workers who have oversight of the house of the LORD." ¹⁰Shaphan the secretary informed the king, "The priest Hilkiah has given me a book." Shaphan then read it aloud to the king.

11 When the king heard the words of the book of the law, he tore his clothes. ¹²Then the king commanded the priest Hilkiah, Ahikam son of Shaphan, Achbor son of Micaiah, Shaphan the secretary, and the king's servant Asaiah, saying, ¹³"Go, inquire of the LORD for me, for the people, and for all Judah, concerning the words of this book that has been found; for great is the wrath of the LORD that is kindled against us, because our ancestors did not obey the words of this book, to do according to all that is written concerning us."

14 So the priest Hilkiah, Ahikam, Achbor, Shaphan, and Asaiah went to the prophetess Huldah the wife of Shallum son of Tikvah, son of Harhas, keeper of the wardrobe; she resided in Jerusalem in the Second Quarter, where they consulted her. ¹⁵She declared to them, "Thus says the LORD, the God of Israel: Tell the man who sent you to me, ¹⁶Thus says the LORD, I will indeed bring disaster on this place and on its inhabitants—all the words of the book that the king of Judah has read. ¹⁷Because they have abandoned me and have made offerings to other gods, so that they have provoked me to anger with all the work of their hands, therefore my wrath will be kindled against this place, and it will not be quenched. ¹⁸But as to the king of Judah, who sent you to inquire of the LORD, thus shall you say to him, Thus says the LORD, the God of Israel: Regarding the words that you have heard, ¹⁹because your heart was penitent, and you humbled yourself before the LORD, when you heard how I spoke against this place, and against its inhabitants, that they should become a desolation and a curse, and because you have torn your clothes and wept before me, I also have heard you, says the LORD. ²⁰Therefore, I will gather you to your ancestors, and you shall be gathered to your grave in peace; your eyes shall not see all the disaster that I will bring on this place." They took the message back to the king.

23 Josiah's Reformation

Then the king directed that all the elders of Judah and Jerusalem should be gathered to him. ²The king went up to the house of the LORD, and with him went all the people of Judah, all the inhabitants of Jerusalem, the priests, the prophets, and all the people, both small and great; he read in their hearing all the words of the book of the covenant that had been found in the house of the LORD. ³The king stood by the pillar and made a covenant before the LORD, to follow the LORD, keeping his commandments, his decrees, and his statutes, with all his heart and all his soul, to perform the words of this covenant that were written in this book. All the people joined in the covenant.

4 The king commanded the high priest Hilkiah, the priests of the second order, and the guardians of the threshold, to bring out of the temple of the LORD all the vessels made for Baal, for Asherah, and for all the host of heaven; he burned them outside Jerusalem in the fields of the Kidron, and carried their ashes to Bethel. ⁵He deposed the idolatrous priests whom the kings of Judah had ordained to make offerings in the high places at the cities of Judah and around Jerusalem; those also who made offerings to Baal, to the sun, the moon, the constellations, and all the host of the heavens. ⁶He brought out the image of*ᵃ* Asherah from the house of the LORD, outside Jerusalem, to the Wadi Kidron, burned it at the Wadi Kidron, beat it to dust and threw the dust of it upon the graves of the common people. ⁷He broke down the houses of the male temple prostitutes that were in the house of the LORD, where the women did weaving for Asherah. ⁸He brought all the priests out of the towns of Judah, and defiled the high places where the priests had made offerings, from Geba to Beer-sheba; he broke down the high places of the gates that were at the entrance of the gate of Joshua the governor of the city, which were on the left at the gate of the city. ⁹The priests of the high places, however, did not come up to the altar of the LORD in Jerusalem, but ate unleavened bread among their kindred. ¹⁰He defiled Topheth, which is in the valley of Ben-hinnom, so that no one would make a son or a daughter pass through fire as an offering to Molech. ¹¹He removed the horses that the kings of Judah had dedicated to the sun, at the entrance to the house of the LORD, by the chamber of the eunuch Nathan-melech, which was in the precincts;ᵇ then he burned the chariots of the sun with fire. ¹²The altars on the roof of the upper chamber of Ahaz, which the kings of Judah had made, and the altars that Manasseh had made in the two courts of the house of the LORD, he pulled down from there and broke in pieces, and threw the rubble into the Wadi Kidron. ¹³The king defiled the high places that were east of Jerusalem, to the south of the Mount of Destruction, which King Solomon of Israel had built for Astarte the abomination of the Sidonians, for Chemosh the abomination of Moab, and for Milcom the abomination of the Ammonites. ¹⁴He broke the pillars in pieces, cut down the sacred poles,ᶜ and covered the sites with human bones.

15 Moreover, the altar at Bethel, the high place erected by Jeroboam son of Nebat, who caused Israel to sin—he pulled down that altar along with the high place. He burned the high place, crushing it to dust; he also burned the sacred pole.ᵈ ¹⁶As Josiah turned, he saw the tombs there on the mount; and he sent and took the bones out of the tombs, and burned them on the altar, and defiled it, according to the word of the LORD that the man of God proclaimed,ᵉ when Jeroboam stood by the altar at the festival; he turned and looked up at the tomb of the man of God who had predicted these things. ¹⁷Then he said, "What is that monument that I see?" The people of the city told him, "It is the tomb of the man of God who came from Judah and predicted these things that you have done against the altar at Bethel." ¹⁸He said, "Let him rest; let no one move his bones." So they let his bones alone, with the bones of the prophet who came out of Samaria. ¹⁹Moreover, Josiah removed all the shrines of the high places that were in the towns of Samaria, which kings of Israel had made, provoking the LORD to anger; he did to them just as he had done at Bethel. ²⁰He slaughtered on the altars all the priests of the high places who were there, and burned human bones on them. Then he returned to Jerusalem.

The Passover Celebrated

21 The king commanded all the people, "Keep the passover to the LORD your God as prescribed in this book of the covenant." ²²No such passover had been kept since the days of the judges who judged Israel, even during all the days of the kings of Israel and of the kings of Judah; ²³but in the eighteenth year of King Josiah this passover was kept to the LORD in Jerusalem.

24 Moreover Josiah put away the mediums, wizards, teraphim,ᶠ idols, and all the abominations that were seen in the land of Judah and in Jerusalem, so that he established the words of the law that were written in the book that the priest Hilkiah had found in the house of the LORD. ²⁵Before him there was no king like him,

---

a Heb lacks *image of* *b* Meaning of Heb uncertain *c* Heb *Asherim* *d* Heb *Asherah* *e* Gk: Heb *proclaimed, who had predicted these things* *f* Or *household gods*

PROFILE OF FAITH

Hezekiah was a good king. He was like most of us: sometimes good, sometimes bad. Kind of *normal*.

God continues to use normal people—average Joes and Janes—as his instruments today. At the age of six, Robert Emmet Judge lost his father to an illness. Later, he worked shining shoes at New York's Penn Station, across the street from St. Francis of Assisi Church. He was so inspired by the work of the friars that he entered the Franciscan seminary when he was fifteen. He was ordained in his late twenties and took the religious name Mychal.

As a priest, Fr. Mychal struggled with alcoholism, but with the help of Alcoholics Anonymous he regained his sobriety. In addition to helping others with addiction, Fr. Mychal ministered to the homeless, people with AIDS, immigrants—basically anyone in need of help.

On September 11, 2001, the World Trade Center in New York City was hit by hijacked jetliners. Fr. Mychal, then chaplain of the New York City Fire Department, went straight to the scene. Rudy Guiliani, then the mayor of New York, asked him to pray. He anointed people in the streets before going into the North Tower, where he continued to minister to the victims and the rescuers.

At 9:59 A.M., the South Tower collapsed and debris flew into the lobby of the North Tower, striking and killing Fr. Mychal. The image of Fr. Mychal being carried out of the North Tower by firefighters is one of the most famous from that dark September day. His body bag was labeled "Victim 0001."

---

who turned to the LORD with all his heart, with all his soul, and with all his might, according to all the law of Moses; nor did any like him arise after him.

26 Still the LORD did not turn from the fierceness of his great wrath, by which his anger was kindled against Judah, because of all the provocations with which Manasseh had provoked him. 27The LORD said, "I will remove Judah also out of my sight, as I have removed Israel; and I will reject this city that I have chosen, Jerusalem, and the house of which I said, My name shall be there."

Josiah Dies in Battle

28 Now the rest of the acts of Josiah, and all that he did, are they not written in the Book of the Annals of the Kings of Judah? 29In his days Pharaoh Neco king of Egypt went up to the king of Assyria to the river Euphrates. King Josiah went to meet him; but when Pharaoh Neco met him at Megiddo, he killed him. 30His servants carried him dead in a chariot from Megiddo, brought him to Jerusalem, and buried him in his own tomb. The people of the land took Jehoahaz son of Josiah, anointed him, and made him king in place of his father.

Reign and Captivity of Jehoahaz

31 Jehoahaz was twenty-three years old when he began to reign; he reigned three months in Jerusalem. His mother's name was Hamutal daughter of Jeremiah of Libnah. 32He did what was evil in the sight of the LORD, just as his ancestors had done. 33Pharaoh Neco confined him at Riblah in the land of Hamath, so that he might not reign in Jerusalem, and imposed tribute on the land of one hundred talents of silver and a talent of gold. 34Pharaoh Neco made Eliakim son of Josiah king in place of his father Josiah, and changed his name to Jehoiakim. But he took Jehoahaz away; he came to Egypt, and died there. 35Jehoiakim gave the silver and the gold to Pharaoh, but he taxed the land in order to meet Pharaoh's demand for money. He exacted the silver and the gold from the people of the land, from all according to their assessment, to give it to Pharaoh Neco.

Jehoiakim Reigns over Judah

36 Jehoiakim was twenty-five years old when he began to reign; he reigned eleven years in Jerusalem. His mother's name was Zebidah daughter of Pedaiah of Rumah. 37He did what was evil in the sight of the LORD, just as all his ancestors had done.

24 Judah Overrun by Enemies

In his days King Nebuchadnezzar of Babylon came up; Jehoiakim became his servant for three years; then he turned and rebelled against him. 2The LORD sent against him bands of the

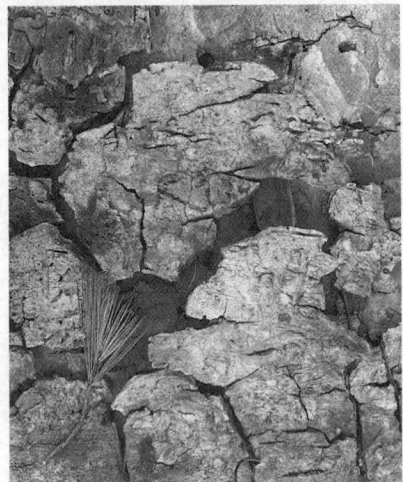

Capture of Jerusalem

13 He carried off all the treasures of the house of the LORD, and the treasures of the king's house; he cut in pieces all the vessels of gold in the temple of the LORD, which King Solomon of Israel had made, all this as the LORD had foretold. [14]He carried away all Jerusalem, all the officials, all the warriors, ten thousand captives, all the artisans and the smiths; no one remained, except the poorest people of the land. [15]He carried away Jehoiachin to Babylon; the king's mother, the king's wives, his officials, and the elite of the land, he took into captivity from Jerusalem to Babylon. [16]The king of Babylon brought captive to Babylon all the men of valor, seven thousand, the artisans and the smiths, one thousand, all of them strong and fit for war. [17]The king of Babylon made Mattaniah, Jehoiachin's uncle, king in his place, and changed his name to Zedekiah.

Zedekiah Reigns over Judah

18 Zedekiah was twenty-one years old when he began to reign; he reigned eleven years in Jerusalem. His mother's name was Hamutal daughter of Jeremiah of Libnah. [19]He did what was evil in the sight of the LORD, just as Jehoiakim had done. [20]Indeed, Jerusalem and Judah so angered the LORD that he expelled them from his presence.

The Fall and Captivity of Judah

25 Zedekiah rebelled against the king of Babylon. [1]And in the ninth year of his reign, in the tenth month, on the tenth day of the month, King Nebuchadnezzar of Babylon came with all his army against Jerusalem, and laid siege to it; they built siegeworks against it all around. [2]So the city was besieged until the eleventh year of King Zedekiah. [3]On the ninth day of the fourth month the famine became so severe in the city that there was no food for the people of the land. [4]Then a breach was made in the city wall;[a] the king with all the soldiers fled[b] by night by the way of the gate between the two walls, by the king's garden, though the Chaldeans were all around the city. They went in the direction of the Arabah. [5]But the army of the Chaldeans pursued the king, and overtook him in the plains of Jericho; all his army was scattered, deserting him. [6]Then they captured the king and brought him up to the king of Babylon at Riblah, who passed sentence on him. [7]They slaughtered the sons of Zedekiah before his eyes, then put out the eyes of Zedekiah; they bound him in fetters and took him to Babylon.

Chaldeans, bands of the Arameans, bands of the Moabites, and bands of the Ammonites; he sent them against Judah to destroy it, according to the word of the LORD that he spoke by his servants the prophets. [3]Surely this came upon Judah at the command of the LORD, to remove them out of his sight, for the sins of Manasseh, for all that he had committed, [4]and also for the innocent blood that he had shed; for he filled Jerusalem with innocent blood, and the LORD was not willing to pardon. [5]Now the rest of the deeds of Jehoiakim, and all that he did, are they not written in the Book of the Annals of the Kings of Judah? [6]So Jehoiakim slept with his ancestors; then his son Jehoiachin succeeded him. [7]The king of Egypt did not come again out of his land, for the king of Babylon had taken over all that belonged to the king of Egypt from the Wadi of Egypt to the River Euphrates.

Reign and Captivity of Jehoiachin

8 Jehoiachin was eighteen years old when he began to reign; he reigned three months in Jerusalem. His mother's name was Nehushta daughter of Elnathan of Jerusalem. [9]He did what was evil in the sight of the LORD, just as his father had done.

10 At that time the servants of King Nebuchadnezzar of Babylon came up to Jerusalem, and the city was besieged. [11]King Nebuchadnezzar of Babylon came to the city, while his servants were besieging it; [12]King Jehoiachin of Judah gave himself up to the king of Babylon, himself, his mother, his servants, his officers, and his palace officials. The king of Babylon took him prisoner in the eighth year of his reign.

a Heb lacks *wall* *b* Gk Compare Jer 39.4; 52.7: Heb lacks *the king* and lacks *fled*

8 In the fifth month, on the seventh day of the month—which was the nineteenth year of King Nebuchadnezzar, king of Babylon—Nebuzaradan, the captain of the bodyguard, a servant of the king of Babylon, came to Jerusalem. 9He burned the house of the LORD, the king's house, and all the houses of Jerusalem; every great house he burned down. 10All the army of the Chaldeans who were with the captain of the guard broke down the walls around Jerusalem. 11Nebuzaradan the captain of the guard carried into exile the rest of the people who were left in the city and the deserters who had defected to the king of Babylon—all the rest of the population. 12But the captain of the guard left some of the poorest people of the land to be vinedressers and tillers of the soil.

13 The bronze pillars that were in the house of the LORD, as well as the stands and the bronze sea that were in the house of the LORD, the Chaldeans broke in pieces, and carried the bronze to Babylon. 14They took away the pots, the shovels, the snuffers, the dishes for incense, and all the bronze vessels used in the temple service, 15as well as the firepans and the basins. What was made of gold the captain of the guard took away for the gold, and what was made of silver, for the silver. 16As for the two pillars, the one sea, and the stands, which Solomon had made for the house of the LORD, the bronze of all these vessels was beyond weighing. 17The height of the one pillar was eighteen cubits, and on it was a bronze capital; the height of the capital was three cubits; latticework and pomegranates, all of bronze, were on the capital all around. The second pillar had the same, with the latticework.

18 The captain of the guard took the chief priest Seraiah, the second priest Zephaniah, and the three guardians of the threshold; 19from the city he took an officer who had been in command of the soldiers, and five men of the king's council who were found in the city; the secretary who was the commander of the army who mustered the people of the land; and sixty men of the people of the land who were found in the city. 20Nebuzaradan the captain of the guard took them, and brought them to the king of Babylon at Riblah. 21The king of Babylon struck them down and put them to death at Riblah in the land of Hamath. So Judah went into exile out of its land.

Gedaliah Made Governor of Judah

22 He appointed Gedaliah son of Ahikam son of Shaphan as governor over the people who remained in the land of Judah, whom King Nebuchadnezzar of Babylon had left. 23Now when all the captains of the forces and their men heard that the king of Babylon had appointed Gedaliah as governor, they came with their men to Gedaliah at Mizpah, namely, Ishmael son of Nethaniah, Johanan son of Kareah, Seraiah son of Tanhumeth the Netophathite, and Jaazaniah son of the Maacathite. 24Gedaliah swore to them and their men, saying, "Do not be afraid because of the Chaldean officials; live in the land, serve the king of Babylon, and it shall be well with you." 25But in the seventh month, Ishmael son of Nethaniah son of Elishama, of the royal family, came with ten men; they struck down Gedaliah so that he died, along with the Judeans and Chaldeans who were with him at Mizpah. 26Then all the people, high and low,*a* and the captains of the forces set out and went to Egypt; for they were afraid of the Chaldeans.

Jehoiachin Released from Prison

27 In the thirty-seventh year of the exile of King Jehoiachin of Judah, in the twelfth month, on the twenty-seventh day of the month, King Evil-merodach of Babylon, in the year that he began to reign, released King Jehoiachin of Judah from prison; 28he spoke kindly to him, and gave him a seat above the other seats of the kings who were with him in Babylon. 29So Jehoiachin put aside his prison clothes. Every day of his life he dined regularly in the king's presence. 30For his allowance, a regular allowance was given him by the king, a portion every day, as long as he lived.

a Or *young and old*

"Maybe we should simply be asking ourselves what is missing in the world and why, instead of what is missing in our confined little private lives and why. Perhaps we ought to be asking ourselves what we are doing to make things better for other people rather than what we are doing to make things better for ourselves."

—Joan D. Chittister, Benedictine sister

1 CHRONICLES

A HOPE-INSPIRING HISTORY

God's Story

There's a dangerous idea out there that the Old Testament is just some sort of unimportant prelude to the New Testament—to the really important stuff. And then there's the tendency to misunderstand Old Testament Judaism, boiling it down to a faith based upon works (good deeds and rule following) and not upon the gift of God's grace.

Nothing could be further from the truth.

In grace, God chose the nation of Israel to be his people, and this was before he ever gave them the law—the rules for right living laid out in books like Exodus and Deuteronomy. In love, God made a covenant with them—a promise that they would be his people and he would be their God. The law was given to help the people respond to God's love through outward action.

God's covenant with his people is a covenant of grace and love: it is an enduring covenant that lasts through the ups and downs of Israel's traumatic history recorded in Chronicles. The history within the pages of this book is not merely a prelude to the "real story"—to Jesus. Instead, it is an integral part of the arc of God's story that spans time, from the beginning, through the New Testament, and even up to today.

First Chronicles was written to God's people after they'd returned from captivity in a foreign land. So the events recorded here weren't some boring history book for them—they were a vital source of hope, a record of God's faithfulness, a reminder of God's promises, and a tribute to God's grace.

And in 1 Chronicles, we see God's people faced with a challenge over and over again. Though God had chosen them as his people, they also needed to choose him. Would they make him their God? Would they worship him alone? Would they live faithfully as God's people?

These are not merely questions of the past. These are questions for us today, for God's people living in God's story in the here and now.

WHO The author is not known for certain, but is usually called the Chronicler.

WHAT A historical record of the story of God's people from Adam to King David

WHEN Part of a larger work, which may have included Ezra and Nehemiah, written ca. 450–400 B.C. The events span the period of time from the start of recorded history to 538 B.C.

WHERE Israel

"He that takes truth for his guide, and duty for his end, may safely trust to God's providence to lead him aright."
—Blaise Pascal

PATH OF DISCIPLESHIP

The book of 1 Chronicles was a written reminder that God had chosen the nation of Israel to be his people. Being the people of God was not meant to be some elite position, as if they were better than the rest of the world. Rather, they were meant to be a conduit through which the entire world would be blessed.

When Jesus walked the earth, he invited others to follow him. It was an invitation to a different way of living. At the Last Supper, Jesus gave us a wonderful example of what it means to follow him. He washed the feet of his disciples and charged them to go out and do likewise (see John 13.1–17). It was an invitation to actually follow Jesus and to walk as he did. He extends that invitation to *you*—to walk as a child of the light, as a companion and servant.

1   From Adam to Abraham

Adam, Seth, Enosh; [2]Kenan, Mahalalel, Jared; [3]Enoch, Methuselah, Lamech; [4]Noah, Shem, Ham, and Japheth.

5 The descendants of Japheth: Gomer, Magog, Madai, Javan, Tubal, Meshech, and Tiras. [6]The descendants of Gomer: Ashkenaz, Diphath,[a] and Togarmah. [7]The descendants of Javan: Elishah, Tarshish, Kittim, and Rodanim.[b]

8 The descendants of Ham: Cush, Egypt, Put, and Canaan. [9]The descendants of Cush: Seba, Havilah, Sabta, Raama, and Sabteca. The descendants of Raamah: Sheba and Dedan. [10]Cush became the father of Nimrod; he was the first to be a mighty one on the earth.

11 Egypt became the father of Ludim, Anamim, Lehabim, Naphtuhim, [12]Pathrusim, Casluhim, and Caphtorim, from whom the Philistines come.[c]

13 Canaan became the father of Sidon his firstborn, and Heth, [14]and the Jebusites, the Amorites, the Girgashites, [15]the Hivites, the Arkites, the Sinites, [16]the Arvadites, the Zemarites, and the Hamathites.

17 The descendants of Shem: Elam, Asshur, Arpachshad, Lud, Aram, Uz, Hul, Gether, and Meshech.[d] [18]Arpachshad became the father of Shelah; and Shelah became the father of Eber. [19]To Eber were born two sons: the name of the one was Peleg (for in his days the earth was divided), and the name of his brother Joktan. [20]Joktan became the father of Almodad, Sheleph, Hazarmaveth, Jerah, [21]Hadoram, Uzal, Diklah, [22]Ebal, Abimael, Sheba, [23]Ophir, Havilah, and Jobab; all these were the descendants of Joktan.

24 Shem, Arpachshad, Shelah; [25]Eber, Peleg, Reu; [26]Serug, Nahor, Terah; [27]Abram, that is, Abraham.

From Abraham to Jacob

28 The sons of Abraham: Isaac and Ishmael. [29]These are their genealogies: the firstborn of Ishmael, Nebaioth; and Kedar, Adbeel, Mibsam, [30]Mishma, Dumah, Massa, Hadad, Tema, [31]Jetur, Naphish, and Kedemah. These are the sons of Ishmael. [32]The sons of Keturah, Abraham's concubine: she bore Zimran, Jokshan, Medan, Midian, Ishbak, and Shuah. The sons of Jokshan: Sheba and Dedan. [33]The sons of Midian: Ephah, Epher, Hanoch, Abida, and Eldaah. All these were the descendants of Keturah.

34 Abraham became the father of Isaac. The sons of Isaac: Esau and Israel. [35]The sons of Esau: Eliphaz, Reuel, Jeush, Jalam, and Korah. [36]The sons of Eliphaz: Teman, Omar, Zephi, Gatam, Kenaz, Timna, and Amalek. [37]The sons of Reuel: Nahath, Zerah, Shammah, and Mizzah.

38 The sons of Seir: Lotan, Shobal, Zibeon, Anah, Dishon, Ezer, and Dishan. [39]The sons of Lotan: Hori and Homam; and Lotan's sister was Timna. [40]The sons of Shobal: Alian, Manahath, Ebal, Shephi, and Onam. The sons of Zibeon: Aiah and Anah. [41]The sons of Anah: Dishon. The sons of Dishon: Hamran, Eshban, Ithran, and Cheran. [42]The sons of Ezer: Bilhan, Zaavan, and Jaakan.[e] The sons of Dishan:[f] Uz and Aran.

43 These are the kings who reigned in the land of Edom before any king reigned over the Israelites: Bela son of Beor, whose city was called Dinhabah. [44]When Bela died, Jobab son of Zerah of Bozrah succeeded him. [45]When Jobab died, Husham of the land of the Temanites succeeded him. [46]When Husham died, Hadad son of Bedad, who defeated Midian in the country of Moab, succeeded him; and the name of his city was Avith. [47]When Hadad died, Samlah of Masrekah succeeded him. [48]When Samlah died, Shaul[g] of Rehoboth on the Euphrates succeeded him. [49]When Shaul[g] died, Baal-hanan son of Achbor succeeded him. [50]When Baal-hanan died, Hadad succeeded him; the name of his city was Pai, and his wife's name Mehetabel daughter of Matred, daughter of Me-zahab. [51]And Hadad died.

The clans[h] of Edom were: clans[h] Timna, Aliah,[i] Jetheth, [52]Oholibamah, Elah, Pinon, [53]Kenaz, Teman, Mibzar, [54]Magdiel, and Iram; these are the clans[h] of Edom.

2   The Sons of Israel and the Descendants of Judah

These are the sons of Israel: Reuben, Simeon, Levi, Judah, Issachar, Zebulun, [2]Dan, Joseph, Benjamin, Naphtali, Gad, and Asher. [3]The sons of Judah: Er, Onan, and Shelah; these three the Canaanite woman Bath-shua bore to him. Now Er, Judah's firstborn, was wicked in the sight of the LORD, and he put him to death. [4]His daughter-in-law Tamar also bore him Perez and Zerah. Judah had five sons in all.

5 The sons of Perez: Hezron and Hamul. [6]The sons of Zerah: Zimri, Ethan, Heman, Calcol, and Dara,[j] five in all. [7]The sons of Carmi: Achar, the troubler of Israel, who transgressed in the matter of the devoted thing; [8]and Ethan's son was Azariah.

9 The sons of Hezron, who were born to him: Jerahmeel, Ram, and Chelubai. [10]Ram became the father of Amminadab, and Am-

---

a Gen 10.3 *Ripath*; See Gk Vg   b Gen 10.4 *Dodanim*; See Syr Vg   c Heb *Casluhim, from which the Philistines come, Caphtorim*; See Am 9.7, Jer 47.4   d *Mash* in Gen 10.23   e Or *and Akan*; See Gen 36.27   f See 1.38: Heb *Dishon*   g Or *Saul*   h Or *chiefs*   i Or *Alvah*; See Gen 36.40   j Or *Darda*; Compare Syr Tg some Gk Mss; See 1 Kings 4.31

minadab became the father of Nahshon, prince of the sons of Judah. ¹¹Nahshon became the father of Salma, Salma of Boaz, ¹²Boaz of Obed, Obed of Jesse. ¹³Jesse became the father of Eliab his firstborn, Abinadab the second, Shimea the third, ¹⁴Nethanel the fourth, Raddai the fifth, ¹⁵Ozem the sixth, David the seventh; ¹⁶and their sisters were Zeruiah and Abigail. The sons of Zeruiah: Abishai, Joab, and Asahel, three. ¹⁷Abigail bore Amasa, and the father of Amasa was Jether the Ishmaelite.

18 Caleb son of Hezron had children by his wife Azubah, and by Jerioth; these were her sons: Jesher, Shobab, and Ardon. ¹⁹When Azubah died, Caleb married Ephrath, who bore him Hur. ²⁰Hur became the father of Uri, and Uri became the father of Bezalel.

21 Afterward Hezron went in to the daughter of Machir father of Gilead, whom he married when he was sixty years old; and she bore him Segub; ²²and Segub became the father of Jair, who had twenty-three towns in the land of Gilead. ²³But Geshur and Aram took from them Havvoth-jair, Kenath and its villages, sixty towns. All these were descendants of Machir, father of Gilead. ²⁴After the death of Hezron, in Caleb-ephrathah, Abijah wife of Hezron bore him Ashhur, father of Tekoa.

25 The sons of Jerahmeel, the firstborn of Hezron: Ram his firstborn, Bunah, Oren, Ozem, and Ahijah. ²⁶Jerahmeel also had another wife, whose name was Atarah; she was the mother of Onam. ²⁷The sons of Ram, the firstborn of Jerahmeel: Maaz, Jamin, and Eker. ²⁸The sons of Onam: Shammai and Jada. The sons of Shammai: Nadab and Abishur. ²⁹The name of Abishur's wife was Abihail, and she bore him Ahban and Molid. ³⁰The sons of Nadab: Seled and Appaim; and Seled died childless. ³¹The son*ᵃ* of Appaim: Ishi. The son*ᵃ* of Ishi: Sheshan. The son*ᵃ* of Sheshan: Ahlai. ³²The sons of Jada, Shammai's brother: Jether and Jonathan; and Jether died childless. ³³The sons of Jonathan: Peleth and Zaza. These were the descendants of Jerahmeel. ³⁴Now Sheshan had no sons, only daughters; but Sheshan had an Egyptian slave, whose name was Jarha. ³⁵So Sheshan gave his daughter in marriage to his slave Jarha; and she bore him Attai. ³⁶Attai became the father of Nathan, and Nathan of Zabad. ³⁷Zabad became the father of Ephlal, and Ephlal of Obed. ³⁸Obed became the father of Jehu, and Jehu of Azariah. ³⁹Azariah became the father of Helez, and Helez of Eleasah. ⁴⁰Eleasah became the father of Sismai, and Sismai of Shallum. ⁴¹Shallum became the father of Jekamiah, and Jekamiah of Elishama.

42 The sons of Caleb brother of Jerahmeel: Mesha*ᵇ* his firstborn, who was father of Ziph. The sons of Mareshah father of Hebron. ⁴³The sons of Hebron: Korah, Tappuah, Rekem, and Shema. ⁴⁴Shema became father of Raham, father of Jorkeam; and Rekem became the father of Shammai. ⁴⁵The son of Shammai: Maon;

a Heb *sons* *b* Gk reads *Mareshah*

and Maon was the father of Beth-zur. ⁴⁶Ephah also, Caleb's concubine, bore Haran, Moza, and Gazez; and Haran became the father of Gazez. ⁴⁷The sons of Jahdai: Regem, Jotham, Geshan, Pelet, Ephah, and Shaaph. ⁴⁸Maacah, Caleb's concubine, bore Sheber and Tirhanah. ⁴⁹She also bore Shaaph father of Madmannah, Sheva father of Machbenah and father of Gibea; and the daughter of Caleb was Achsah. ⁵⁰These were the descendants of Caleb.

The sons*a* of Hur the firstborn of Ephrathah: Shobal father of Kiriath-jearim, ⁵¹Salma father of Bethlehem, and Hareph father of Beth-gader. ⁵²Shobal father of Kiriath-jearim had other sons: Haroeh, half of the Menuhoth. ⁵³And the families of Kiriath-jearim: the Ithrites, the Puthites, the Shumathites, and the Mishraites; from these came the Zorathites and the Eshtaolites. ⁵⁴The sons of Salma: Bethlehem, the Netophathites, Atroth-beth-joab, and half of the Manahathites, the Zorites. ⁵⁵The families also of the scribes that lived at Jabez: the Tirathites, the Shimeathites, and the Sucathites. These are the Kenites who came from Hammath, father of the house of Rechab.

3 Descendants of David and Solomon

These are the sons of David who were born to him in Hebron: the firstborn Amnon, by Ahinoam the Jezreelite; the second Daniel, by Abigail the Carmelite; ²the third Absalom, son of Maacah, daughter of King Talmai of Geshur; the fourth Adonijah, son of Haggith; ³the fifth Shephatiah, by Abital; the sixth Ithream, by his wife Eglah; ⁴six were born to him in Hebron, where he reigned for seven years and six months. And he reigned thirty-three years in Jerusalem. ⁵These were born to him in Jerusalem: Shimea, Shobab, Nathan, and Solomon, four by Bath-shua, daughter of Ammiel; ⁶then Ibhar, Elishama, Eliphelet, ⁷Nogah, Nepheg, Japhia, ⁸Elishama, Eliada, and Eliphelet, nine. ⁹All these were David's sons, besides the sons of the concubines; and Tamar was their sister.

10 The descendants of Solomon: Rehoboam, Abijah his son, Asa his son, Jehoshaphat his son, ¹¹Joram his son, Ahaziah his son, Joash his son, ¹²Amaziah his son, Azariah his son, Jotham his son, ¹³Ahaz his son, Hezekiah his son, Manasseh his son, ¹⁴Amon his son, Josiah his son. ¹⁵The sons of Josiah: Johanan the firstborn, the second Jehoiakim, the third Zedekiah, the fourth Shallum. ¹⁶The descendants of Jehoiakim: Jeconiah his son, Zedekiah his son; ¹⁷and the sons of Jeconiah, the captive: Shealtiel his son, ¹⁸Malchiram, Pedaiah, Shenazzar, Jekamiah, Hoshama, and Nedabiah; ¹⁹The sons of Pedaiah: Zerubbabel and Shimei; and the sons of Zerubbabel: Meshullam and Hananiah, and Shelomith was their sister; ²⁰and Hashubah, Ohel, Berechiah, Hasadiah, and Jushab-hesed, five. ²¹The sons of Hananiah: Pelatiah and Jeshaiah, his son*b* Rephaiah, his son*b* Arnan, his son*b* Obadiah, his son*b* Shecaniah. ²²The son*c* of Shecaniah: Shemaiah. And the sons of Shemaiah: Hattush, Igal, Bariah, Neariah, and Shaphat, six. ²³The sons of Neariah: Elioenai, Hizkiah, and Azrikam, three. ²⁴The sons of Elioenai: Hodaviah, Eliashib, Pelaiah, Akkub, Johanan, Delaiah, and Anani, seven.

4 Descendants of Judah

The sons of Judah: Perez, Hezron, Carmi, Hur, and Shobal. ²Reaiah son of Shobal became the father of Jahath, and Jahath became the father of Ahumai and Lahad. These were the families of the Zorathites. ³These were the sons*d* of Etam: Jezreel, Ishma, and Idbash; and the name of their sister was Hazzelelponi, ⁴and Penuel was the father of Gedor, and Ezer the father of Hushah. These were the sons of Hur, the firstborn of Ephrathah, the father of Bethlehem. ⁵Ashhur father of Tekoa had two wives, Helah and Naarah; ⁶Naarah bore him Ahuzzam, Hepher, Temeni, and Haahashtari.*e* These were the sons of Naarah. ⁷The sons of Helah: Zereth, Izhar,*f* and Ethnan. ⁸Koz became the father of Anub, Zobebah, and the families of Aharhel son of Harum. ⁹Jabez was honored more than his brothers; and his mother named him Jabez, saying, "Because I bore him in pain." ¹⁰Jabez called on the God of Israel, saying, "Oh that you would bless me and enlarge my border, and that your hand might be with me, and that you would keep me from hurt and harm!" And God granted what he asked. ¹¹Chelub the brother of Shuhah became the father of Mehir, who was the father of Eshton. ¹²Eshton became the father of Beth-rapha, Paseah, and Tehinnah the father of Ir-nahash. These are the men of Recah. ¹³The sons of Kenaz: Othniel and Seraiah; and the sons of Othniel: Hathath and Meonothai.*g* ¹⁴Meonothai became the father of Ophrah; and Seraiah became the father of Joab father of Ge-harashim,*h* so-called because they were artisans. ¹⁵The sons of Caleb son of Jephunneh: Iru, Elah, and Naam; and the son*c* of Elah: Kenaz. ¹⁶The sons of Jehallelel: Ziph, Ziphah, Tiria, and Asarel. ¹⁷The sons of Ezrah: Jether, Mered, Epher, and Jalon. These are the sons of Bithiah, daughter

---

a Gk Vg: Heb son b Gk Compare Syr Vg: Heb sons of c Heb sons d Gk Compare Vg: Heb the father e Or Ahashtari f Another reading is Zohar g Gk Vg: Heb lacks and Meonothai h That is Valley of artisans of Pharaoh, whom Mered married;[a] and she conceived and bore[b] Miriam, Shammai, and Ishbah father of Eshtemoa. [18]And his Judean wife bore Jered father of Gedor, Heber father of Soco, and Jekuthiel father of Zanoah. [19]The sons of the wife of Hodiah, the sister of Naham, were the fathers of Keilah the Garmite and Eshtemoa the Maacathite. [20]The sons of Shimon: Amnon, Rinnah, Ben-hanan, and Tilon. The sons of Ishi: Zoheth and Ben-zoheth. [21]The sons of Shelah son of Judah: Er father of Lecah, Laadah father of Mareshah, and the families of the guild of linen workers at Beth-ashbea; [22]and Jokim, and the men of Cozeba, and Joash, and Saraph, who married into Moab but returned to Lehem[c] (now the records[d] are ancient). [23]These were the potters and inhabitants of Netaim and Gederah; they lived there with the king in his service.

Descendants of Simeon

24 The sons of Simeon: Nemuel, Jamin, Jarib, Zerah, Shaul;[e] [25]Shallum was his son, Mibsam his son, Mishma his son. [26]The sons of Mishma: Hammuel his son, Zaccur his son, Shimei his son. [27]Shimei had sixteen sons and six daughters; but his brothers did not have many children, nor did all their family multiply like the Judeans. [28]They lived in Beer-sheba, Moladah, Hazar-shual, [29]Bilhah, Ezem, Tolad, [30]Bethuel, Hormah, Ziklag, [31]Beth-marcaboth, Hazar-susim, Beth-biri, and Shaaraim. These were their towns until David became king. [32]And their villages were Etam, Ain, Rimmon, Tochen, and Ashan, five towns, [33]along with all their villages that were around these towns as far as Baal. These were their settlements. And they kept a genealogical record.

34 Meshobab, Jamlech, Joshah son of Amaziah, [35]Joel, Jehu son of Joshibiah son of Seraiah son of Asiel, [36]Elioenai, Jaakobah, Jeshohaiah, Asaiah, Adiel, Jesimiel, Benaiah, [37]Ziza son of Shiphi son of Allon son of Jedaiah son of Shimri son of Shemaiah— [38]these mentioned by name were leaders in their families, and their clans increased greatly. [39]They journeyed to the entrance of Gedor, to the east side of the valley, to seek pasture for their flocks, [40]where they found rich, good pasture, and the land was very broad, quiet, and peaceful; for the former inhabitants there belonged to Ham. [41]These, registered by name, came in the days of King Hezekiah of Judah, and attacked their tents and the Meunim who were found there, and exterminated them to this day, and settled in their place, because there was pasture there for their flocks. [42]And some of them, five hundred men of the Simeonites, went to Mount Seir, having as their leaders Pelatiah, Neariah, Rephaiah, and Uzziel, sons of Ishi; [43]they destroyed the remnant of the Amalekites that had escaped, and they have lived there to this day.

5 Descendants of Reuben

The sons of Reuben the firstborn of Israel. (He was the firstborn, but because he defiled his father's bed his birthright was given to the sons of Joseph son of Israel, so that he is not enrolled in the genealogy according to the birthright; [2]though Judah became prominent among his brothers and a ruler came from him, yet the birthright belonged to Joseph.) [3]The sons of Reuben, the firstborn of Israel: Hanoch, Pallu, Hezron, and Carmi. [4]The sons of Joel: Shemaiah his son, Gog his son, Shimei

---

TEXT MESSAGE

Genealogies (family histories), like the one in 1 Chronicles 1–9, are common in the Old Testament. In fact, there are about two dozen of them there, of which the Chronicles genealogy is the longest. Unlike modern genealogies, Old Testament lists included only important people, not everyone who descended from the original person.

Fact

This information has been scanned and is free of all known viruses. Please forward to all your friends.

---

a The clause: *These are . . . married* is transposed from verse 18
b Heb lacks *and bore* c Vg Compare Gk: Heb *and Jashubi-lahem*
d Or *matters* e Or *Saul*

his son, [5]Micah his son, Reaiah his son, Baal his son, [6]Beerah his son, whom King Tilgath-pilneser of Assyria carried away into exile; he was a chieftain of the Reubenites. [7]And his kindred by their families, when the genealogy of their generations was reckoned: the chief, Jeiel, and Zechariah, [8]and Bela son of Azaz, son of Shema, son of Joel, who lived in Aroer, as far as Nebo and Baal-meon. [9]He also lived to the east as far as the beginning of the desert this side of the Euphrates, because their cattle had multiplied in the land of Gilead. [10]And in the days of Saul they made war on the Hagrites, who fell by their hand; and they lived in their tents throughout all the region east of Gilead.

Descendants of Gad

11 The sons of Gad lived beside them in the land of Bashan as far as Salecah: [12]Joel the chief, Shapham the second, Janai, and Shaphat in Bashan. [13]And their kindred according to their clans: Michael, Meshullam, Sheba, Jorai, Jacan, Zia, and Eber, seven. [14]These were the sons of Abihail son of Huri, son of Jaroah, son of Gilead, son of Michael, son of Jeshishai, son of Jahdo, son of Buz; [15]Ahi son of Abdiel, son of Guni, was chief in their clan; [16]and they lived in Gilead, in Bashan and in its towns, and in all the pasture lands of Sharon to their limits. [17]All of these were enrolled by genealogies in the days of King Jotham of Judah, and in the days of King Jeroboam of Israel.

18 The Reubenites, the Gadites, and the half-tribe of Manasseh had valiant warriors, who carried shield and sword, and drew the bow, expert in war, forty-four thousand seven hundred sixty, ready for service. [19]They made war on the Hagrites, Jetur, Naphish, and Nodab; [20]and when they received help against them, the Hagrites and all who were with them were given into their hands, for they cried to God in the battle, and he granted their entreaty because they trusted in him. [21]They captured their livestock: fifty thousand of their camels, two hundred fifty thousand sheep, two thousand donkeys, and one hundred thousand captives. [22]Many fell slain, because the war was of God. And they lived in their territory until the exile.

The Half-Tribe of Manasseh

23 The members of the half-tribe of Manasseh lived in the land; they were very numerous from Bashan to Baal-hermon, Senir, and Mount Hermon. [24]These were the heads of their clans: Epher,[a] Ishi, Eliel, Azriel, Jeremi-ah, Hodaviah, and Jahdiel, mighty warriors, famous men, heads of their clans. [25]But they transgressed against the God of their ancestors, and prostituted themselves to the gods of the peoples of the land, whom God had destroyed before them. [26]So the God of Israel stirred up the spirit of King Pul of Assyria, the spirit of King Tilgath-pilneser of Assyria, and he carried them away, namely, the Reubenites, the Gadites, and the half-tribe of Manasseh, and brought them to Halah, Habor, Hara, and the river Gozan, to this day.

6[b] Descendants of Levi

The sons of Levi: Gershom,[c] Kohath, and Merari. [2]The sons of Kohath: Amram, Izhar, Hebron, and Uzziel. [3]The children of Amram: Aaron, Moses, and Miriam. The sons of Aaron: Nadab, Abihu, Eleazar, and Ithamar. [4]Eleazar became the father of Phinehas, Phinehas of Abishua, [5]Abishua of Bukki, Bukki of Uzzi, [6]Uzzi of Zerahiah, Zerahiah of Meraioth, [7]Meraioth of Amariah, Amariah of Ahitub, [8]Ahitub of Zadok, Zadok of Ahimaaz, [9]Ahimaaz of Azariah, Azariah of Johanan, [10]and Johanan of Azariah (it was he who served as priest in the house that Solomon built in Jerusalem). [11]Azariah became the father of Amariah, Amariah of Ahitub, [12]Ahitub of Zadok, Zadok of Shallum, [13]Shallum of Hilkiah, Hilkiah of Azariah, [14]Azariah of Seraiah, Seraiah of Jehozadak; [15]and Jehozadak went into exile when the LORD sent Judah and Jerusalem into exile by the hand of Nebuchadnezzar.

16[d] The sons of Levi: Gershom, Kohath, and Merari. [17]These are the names of the sons of Gershom: Libni and Shimei. [18]The sons of Kohath: Amram, Izhar, Hebron, and Uzziel. [19]The sons of Merari: Mahli and Mushi. These are the clans of the Levites according to their ancestry. [20]Of Gershom: Libni his son, Jahath his son, Zimmah his son, [21]Joah his son, Iddo his son, Zerah his son, Jeatherai his son. [22]The sons of Kohath: Amminadab his son, Korah his son, Assir his son, [23]Elkanah his son, Ebiasaph his son, Assir his son, [24]Tahath his son, Uriel his son, Uzziah his son, and Shaul his son. [25]The sons of Elkanah: Amasai and Ahimoth, [26]Elkanah his son, Zophai his son, Nahath his son, [27]Eliab his son, Jeroham his son, Elkanah his son. [28]The sons of Samuel: Joel[e] his firstborn, the second Abijah.[f] [29]The sons of Merari: Mahli, Libni his son, Shimei his son, Uzzah his son, [30]Shimea his son, Haggiah his son, and Asaiah his son.

a Gk Vg: Heb and Epher   b Ch 5.27 in Heb   c Heb Gershon, variant of Gershom; See 6.16   d Ch 6.1 in Heb   e Gk Syr Compare verse 33 and 1 Sam 8.2: Heb lacks Joel   f Heb reads Vashni, and Abijah for the second Abijah, taking the second as a proper name

Musicians Appointed by David

31 These are the men whom David put in charge of the service of song in the house of the Lord, after the ark came to rest there. ³²They ministered with song before the tabernacle of the tent of meeting, until Solomon had built the house of the Lord in Jerusalem; and they performed their service in due order. ³³These are the men who served; and their sons were: Of the Kohathites: Heman, the singer, son of Joel, son of Samuel, ³⁴son of Elkanah, son of Jeroham, son of Eliel, son of Toah, ³⁵son of Zuph, son of Elkanah, son of Mahath, son of Amasai, ³⁶son of Elkanah, son of Joel, son of Azariah, son of Zephaniah, ³⁷son of Tahath, son of Assir, son of Ebiasaph, son of Korah, ³⁸son of Izhar, son of Kohath, son of Levi, son of Israel; ³⁹and his brother Asaph, who stood on his right, namely, Asaph son of Berechiah, son of Shimea, ⁴⁰son of Michael, son of Baaseiah, son of Malchijah, ⁴¹son of Ethni, son of Zerah, son of Adaiah, ⁴²son of Ethan, son of Zimmah, son of Shimei, ⁴³son of Jahath, son of Gershom, son of Levi. ⁴⁴On the left were their kindred the sons of Merari: Ethan son of Kishi, son of Abdi, son of Malluch, ⁴⁵son of Hashabiah, son of Amaziah, son of Hilkiah, ⁴⁶son of Amzi, son of Bani, son of Shemer, ⁴⁷son of Mahli, son of Mushi, son of Merari, son of Levi; ⁴⁸and their kindred the Levites were appointed for all the service of the tabernacle of the house of God.

49 But Aaron and his sons made offerings on the altar of burnt offering and on the altar of incense, doing all the work of the most holy place, to make atonement for Israel, according to all that Moses the servant of God had commanded. ⁵⁰These are the sons of Aaron: Eleazar his son, Phinehas his son, Abishua his son, ⁵¹Bukki his son, Uzzi his son, Zerahiah his son, ⁵²Meraioth his son, Amariah his son, Ahitub his son, ⁵³Zadok his son, Ahimaaz his son.

Settlements of the Levites

54 These are their dwelling places according to their settlements within their borders: to the sons of Aaron of the families of Kohathites—for the lot fell to them first— ⁵⁵to them they gave Hebron in the land of Judah and its surrounding pasture lands, ⁵⁶but the fields of the city and its villages they gave to Caleb son of Jephunneh. ⁵⁷To the sons of Aaron they gave the cities of refuge: Hebron, Libnah with its pasture lands, Jattir, Eshtemoa with its pasture lands, ⁵⁸Hilen*a* with its pasture lands, Debir with its pasture lands, ⁵⁹Ashan with its pasture lands, and Beth-shemesh with its pas-

a Other readings Hilez, Holon; See Josh 21.15

ture lands. ⁶⁰From the tribe of Benjamin, Geba with its pasture lands, Alemeth with its pasture lands, and Anathoth with its pasture lands. All their towns throughout their families were thirteen.

61 To the rest of the Kohathites were given by lot out of the family of the tribe, out of the half-tribe, the half of Manasseh, ten towns. ⁶²To the Gershomites according to their families were allotted thirteen towns out of the tribes of Issachar, Asher, Naphtali, and Manasseh in Bashan. ⁶³To the Merarites according to their families were allotted twelve towns out of the tribes of Reuben, Gad, and Zebulun. ⁶⁴So the people of Israel gave the Levites the towns with their pasture lands. ⁶⁵They

also gave them by lot out of the tribes of Judah, Simeon, and Benjamin these towns that are mentioned by name.

66 And some of the families of the sons of Kohath had towns of their territory out of the tribe of Ephraim. [67]They were given the cities of refuge: Shechem with its pasture lands in the hill country of Ephraim, Gezer with its pasture lands, [68]Jokmeam with its pasture lands, Beth-horon with its pasture lands, [69]Aijalon with its pasture lands, Gath-rimmon with its pasture lands; [70]and out of the half-tribe of Manasseh, Aner with its pasture lands, and Bileam with its pasture lands, for the rest of the families of the Kohathites.

71 To the Gershomites: out of the half-tribe of Manasseh: Golan in Bashan with its pasture lands and Ashtaroth with its pasture lands; [72]and out of the tribe of Issachar: Kedesh with its pasture lands, Daberath[a] with its pasture lands, [73]Ramoth with its pasture lands, and Anem with its pasture lands; [74]out of the tribe of Asher: Mashal with its pasture lands, Abdon with its pasture lands, [75]Hukok with its pasture lands, and Rehob with its pasture lands; [76]and out of the tribe of Naphtali: Kedesh in Galilee with its pasture lands, Hammon with its pasture lands, and Kiriathaim with its pasture lands. [77]To the rest of the Merarites out of the tribe of Zebulun: Rimmono with its pasture lands, Tabor with its pasture lands, [78]and across the Jordan from Jericho, on the east side of the Jordan, out of the tribe of Reuben: Bezer in the steppe with its pasture lands, Jahzah with its pasture lands, [79]Kedemoth with its pasture lands, and Mephaath with its pasture lands; [80]and out of the tribe of Gad: Ramoth in Gilead with its pasture lands, Mahanaim with its pasture lands, [81]Heshbon with its pasture lands, and Jazer with its pasture lands.

7 Descendants of Issachar

The sons[b] of Issachar: Tola, Puah, Jashub, and Shimron, four. [2]The sons of Tola: Uzzi, Rephaiah, Jeriel, Jahmai, Ibsam, and Shemuel, heads of their ancestral houses, namely of Tola, mighty warriors of their generations, their number in the days of David being twenty-two thousand six hundred. [3]The son[c] of Uzzi: Izrahiah. And the sons of Izrahiah: Michael, Obadiah, Joel, and Isshiah, five, all of them chiefs; [4]and along with them, by their generations, according to their ancestral houses, were units of the fighting force, thirty-six thousand, for they had many wives and sons. [5]Their kindred belonging to all the fami-

a Or Dobrath b Syr Compare Vg: Heb And to the sons c Heb sons lies of Issachar were in all eighty-seven thousand mighty warriors, enrolled by genealogy.

Descendants of Benjamin

6 The sons of Benjamin: Bela, Becher, and Jediael, three. ⁷The sons of Bela: Ezbon, Uzzi, Uzziel, Jerimoth, and Iri, five, heads of ancestral houses, mighty warriors; and their enrollment by genealogies was twenty-two thousand thirty-four. ⁸The sons of Becher: Zemirah, Joash, Eliezer, Elioenai, Omri, Jeremoth, Abijah, Anathoth, and Alemeth. All these were the sons of Becher; ⁹and their enrollment by genealogies, according to their generations, as heads of their ancestral houses, mighty warriors, was twenty thousand two hundred. ¹⁰The sons of Jediael: Bilhan. And the sons of Bilhan: Jeush, Benjamin, Ehud, Chenaanah, Zethan, Tarshish, and Ahishahar. ¹¹All these were the sons of Jediael according to the heads of their ancestral houses, mighty warriors, seventeen thousand two hundred, ready for service in war. ¹²And Shuppim and Huppim were the sons of Ir, Hushim the son*ᵃ* of Aher.

Descendants of Naphtali

13 The descendants of Naphtali: Jahziel, Guni, Jezer, and Shallum, the descendants of Bilhah.

Descendants of Manasseh

14 The sons of Manasseh: Asriel, whom his Aramean concubine bore; she bore Machir the father of Gilead. ¹⁵And Machir took a wife for Huppim and for Shuppim. The name of his sister was Maacah. And the name of the second was Zelophehad; and Zelophehad had daughters. ¹⁶Maacah the wife of Machir bore a son, and she named him Peresh; the name of his brother was Sheresh; and his sons were Ulam and Rekem. ¹⁷The son*ᵃ* of Ulam: Bedan. These were the sons of Gilead son of Machir, son of Manasseh. ¹⁸And his sister Hammolecheth bore Ishhod, Abiezer, and Mahlah. ¹⁹The sons of Shemida were Ahian, Shechem, Likhi, and Aniam.

Descendants of Ephraim

20 The sons of Ephraim: Shuthelah, and Bered his son, Tahath his son, Eleadah his son, Tahath his son, ²¹Zabad his son, Shuthelah his son, and Ezer and Elead. Now the people of Gath, who were born in the land, killed them, because they came down to raid their cattle. ²²And their father Ephraim mourned many days, and his brothers came to comfort him. ²³Ephraim*ᵇ* went in to his wife, and she conceived and bore a son; and he named him Beriah, because disaster*ᶜ* had befallen his house. ²⁴His daughter was Sheerah, who built both Lower and Upper Beth-horon, and Uzzen-sheerah. ²⁵Rephah was his son, Resheph his son, Telah his son, Tahan his son, ²⁶Ladan his son, Ammihud his son, Elishama his son, ²⁷Nun*ᵈ* his son, Joshua his son. ²⁸Their possessions and settlements were Bethel and its towns, and eastward Naaran, and westward Gezer and its towns, Shechem and its towns, as far as Ayyah and its towns; ²⁹also along the borders of the Manassites, Beth-shean and its towns, Taanach and its towns, Megiddo and its towns, Dor and its towns. In these lived the sons of Joseph son of Israel.

Descendants of Asher

30 The sons of Asher: Imnah, Ishvah, Ishvi, Beriah, and their sister Serah. ³¹The sons of Beriah: Heber and Malchiel, who was the father of Birzaith. ³²Heber became the father of Japhlet, Shomer, Hotham, and their sister Shua. ³³The sons of Japhlet: Pasach, Bimhal, and Ashvath. These are the sons of Japhlet. ³⁴The sons of Shemer: Ahi, Rohgah, Hubbah, and Aram. ³⁵The sons of Helem*ᵉ* his brother: Zophah, Imna, Shelesh, and Amal. ³⁶The sons of Zophah: Suah, Harnepher, Shual, Beri, Imrah, ³⁷Bezer, Hod, Shamma, Shilshah, Ithran, and Beera. ³⁸The sons of Jether: Jephunneh, Pispa, and Ara. ³⁹The sons of Ulla: Arah, Hanniel, and Rizia. ⁴⁰All of these were men of Asher, heads of ancestral houses, select mighty warriors, chief of the princes. Their number enrolled by genealogies, for service in war, was twenty-six thousand men.

8 Descendants of Benjamin

Benjamin became the father of Bela his firstborn, Ashbel the second, Aharah the third, ²Nohah the fourth, and Rapha the fifth. ³And Bela had sons: Addar, Gera, Abihud,*ᶠ* ⁴Abishua, Naaman, Ahoah, ⁵Gera, Shephuphan, and Huram. ⁶These are the sons of Ehud (they were heads of ancestral houses of the inhabitants of Geba, and they were carried into exile to Manahath): ⁷Naaman,*ᵍ* Ahijah, and Gera, that is, Heglam,*ʰ* who became the father of Uzza and Ahihud. ⁸And Shaharaim had sons in the country of Moab after he had sent away his wives Hushim and Baara. ⁹He had sons by his wife Hodesh: Jobab, Zibia, Mesha, Malcam, ¹⁰Jeuz, Sachia, and Mirmah. These were his sons, heads of ancestral houses. ¹¹He also had sons by Hushim: Abitub and Elpaal. ¹²The sons of

---

a Heb *sons* *b* Heb *He* *c* Heb *beraah* *d* Here spelled *Non;* see Ex 33.11 *e* Or *Hotham;* see 7.32 *f* Or *father of Ehud;* see 8.6 *g* Heb *and Naaman* *h* Or *he carried them into exile*

Elpaal: Eber, Misham, and Shemed, who built Ono and Lod with its towns, [13]and Beriah and Shema (they were heads of ancestral houses of the inhabitants of Aijalon, who put to flight the inhabitants of Gath); [14]and Ahio, Shashak, and Jeremoth. [15]Zebadiah, Arad, Eder, [16]Michael, Ishpah, and Joha were sons of Beriah. [17]Zebadiah, Meshullam, Hizki, Heber, [18]Ishmerai, Izliah, and Jobab were the sons of Elpaal. [19]Jakim, Zichri, Zabdi, [20]Elienai, Zillethai, Eliel, [21]Adaiah, Beraiah, and Shimrath were the sons of Shimei. [22]Ishpan, Eber, Eliel, [23]Abdon, Zichri, Hanan, [24]Hananiah, Elam, Anthothijah, [25]Iphdeiah, and Penuel were the sons of Shashak. [26]Shamsherai, Shehariah, Athaliah, [27]Jaareshiah, Elijah, and Zichri were the sons of Jeroham. [28]These were the heads of ancestral houses, according to their generations, chiefs. These lived in Jerusalem.

29 Jeiel[a] the father of Gibeon lived in Gibeon, and the name of his wife was Maacah. [30]His firstborn son: Abdon, then Zur, Kish, Baal,[b] Nadab, [31]Gedor, Ahio, Zecher, [32]and Mikloth, who became the father of Shimeah. Now these also lived opposite their kindred in Jerusalem, with their kindred. [33]Ner became the father of Kish, Kish of Saul,[c] Saul[c] of Jonathan, Malchishua, Abinadab, and Esh-baal; [34]and the son of Jonathan was Merib-baal; and Merib-baal became the father of Micah. [35]The sons of Micah: Pithon, Melech, Tarea, and Ahaz. [36]Ahaz became the father of Jehoaddah; and Jehoaddah became the father of Alemeth, Azmaveth, and Zimri; Zimri became the father of Moza. [37]Moza became the father of Binea; Raphah was his son, Eleasah his son, Azel his son. [38]Azel had six sons, and these are their names: Azrikam, Bocheru, Ishmael, Sheariah, Obadiah, and Hanan; all these were the sons of Azel. [39]The sons of his brother Eshek: Ulam his firstborn, Jeush the second, and Eliphelet the third. [40]The sons of Ulam were mighty warriors, archers, having many children and grandchildren, one hundred fifty. All these were Benjaminites.

9 So all Israel was enrolled by genealogies; and these are written in the Book of the Kings of Israel. And Judah was taken into exile in Babylon because of their unfaithfulness. [2]Now the first to live again in their possessions in their towns were Israelites, priests, Levites, and temple servants.

Inhabitants of Jerusalem after the Exile

3 And some of the people of Judah, Benjamin, Ephraim, and Manasseh lived in Jerusalem: [4]Uthai son of Ammihud, son of Omri, son of

Imri, son of Bani, from the sons of Perez son of Judah. [5]And of the Shilonites: Asaiah the firstborn, and his sons. [6]Of the sons of Zerah: Jeuel and their kin, six hundred ninety. [7]Of the Benjaminites: Sallu son of Meshullam, son of Hodaviah, son of Hassenuah, [8]Ibneiah son of Jeroham, Elah son of Uzzi, son of Michri, and Meshullam son of Shephatiah, son of Reuel, son of Ibnijah; [9]and their kindred according to their generations, nine hundred fifty-six. All these were heads of families according to their ancestral houses.

Priestly Families

10 Of the priests: Jedaiah, Jehoiarib, Jachin, [11]and Azariah son of Hilkiah, son of Meshullam, son of Zadok, son of Meraioth, son of Ahitub, the chief officer of the house of God; [12]and Adaiah son of Jeroham, son of Pashhur, son of Malchijah, and Maasai son of Adiel, son of Jahzerah, son of Meshullam, son of Meshillemith, son of Immer; [13]besides their kindred, heads of their ancestral houses, one thousand seven hundred sixty, qualified for the work of the service of the house of God.

Levitical Families

14 Of the Levites: Shemaiah son of Hasshub, son of Azrikam, son of Hashabiah, of the sons of Merari; [15]and Bakbakkar, Heresh, Galal, and Mattaniah son of Mica, son of Zichri, son of Asaph; [16]and Obadiah son of Shemaiah, son of Galal, son of Jeduthun, and Berechiah son of Asa, son of Elkanah, who lived in the villages of the Netophathites.

17 The gatekeepers were: Shallum, Akkub, Talmon, Ahiman; and their kindred Shallum was the chief, [18]stationed previously in the king's gate on the east side. These were the gatekeepers of the camp of the Levites. [19]Shallum son of Kore, son of Ebiasaph, son of Korah, and his kindred of his ancestral house, the Korahites, were in charge of the work of the service, guardians of the thresholds of the tent, as their ancestors had been in charge of the camp of the LORD, guardians of the entrance. [20]And Phinehas son of Eleazar was chief over them in former times; the LORD was with him. [21]Zechariah son of Meshelemiah was gatekeeper at the entrance of the tent of meeting. [22]All these, who were chosen as gatekeepers at the thresholds, were two hundred twelve. They were enrolled by genealogies in their villages. David and the seer Samuel established them in their office of trust. [23]So they and their descendants were in charge of the gates of the house of the LORD, that is, the house of the tent, as guards.

---

a Compare 9.35: Heb lacks *Jeiel* *b* Gk Ms adds *Ner* ; Compare 8.33 and 9.36 *c* Or *Shaul*

24The gatekeepers were on the four sides, east, west, north, and south; 25and their kindred who were in their villages were obliged to come in every seven days, in turn, to be with them; 26for the four chief gatekeepers, who were Levites, were in charge of the chambers and the treasures of the house of God. 27And they would spend the night near the house of God; for on them lay the duty of watching, and they had charge of opening it every morning.

28 Some of them had charge of the utensils of service, for they were required to count them when they were brought in and taken out. 29Others of them were appointed over the furniture, and over all the holy utensils, also over the choice flour, the wine, the oil, the incense, and the spices. 30Others, of the sons of the priests, prepared the mixing of the spices, 31and Mattithiah, one of the Levites, the firstborn of Shallum the Korahite, was in charge of making the flat cakes. 32Also some of their kindred of the Kohathites had charge of the rows of bread, to prepare them for each sabbath.

33 Now these are the singers, the heads of ancestral houses of the Levites, living in the chambers of the temple free from other service, for they were on duty day and night. 34These were heads of ancestral houses of the Levites, according to their generations; these leaders lived in Jerusalem.

a Compare 8.35: Heb lacks *and Ahaz*

The Family of King Saul

35 In Gibeon lived the father of Gibeon, Jeiel, and the name of his wife was Maacah. 36His firstborn son was Abdon, then Zur, Kish, Baal, Ner, Nadab, 37Gedor, Ahio, Zechariah, and Mikloth; 38and Mikloth became the father of Shimeam; and these also lived opposite their kindred in Jerusalem, with their kindred. 39Ner became the father of Kish, Kish of Saul, Saul of Jonathan, Malchishua, Abinadab, and Esh-baal; 40and the son of Jonathan was Merib-baal; and Merib-baal became the father of Micah. 41The sons of Micah: Pithon, Melech, Tahrea, and Ahaz;*a* 42and Ahaz became the father of Jarah, and Jarah of Alemeth, Azmaveth, and Zimri; and Zimri became the father of Moza. 43Moza became the father of Binea; and Rephaiah was his son, Eleasah his son, Azel his son. 44Azel had six sons, and these are their names: Azrikam, Bocheru, Ishmael, Sheariah, Obadiah, and Hanan; these were the sons of Azel.

10 Death of Saul and His Sons

Now the Philistines fought against Israel; and the men of Israel fled before the Philistines, and fell slain on Mount Gilboa. 2The Philistines overtook Saul and his sons; and the Philistines killed Jonathan and Abinadab and Malchishua, sons of Saul. 3The battle pressed hard on

Guided By Light—© Lexi Hiland, 16

Saul; and the archers found him, and he was wounded by the archers. ⁴Then Saul said to his armor-bearer, "Draw your sword, and thrust me through with it, so that these uncircumcised may not come and make sport of me." But his armor-bearer was unwilling, for he was terrified. So Saul took his own sword and fell on it. ⁵When his armor-bearer saw that Saul was dead, he also fell on his sword and died. ⁶Thus Saul died; he and his three sons and all his house died together. ⁷When all the men of Israel who were in the valley saw that the army*ᵃ* had fled and that Saul and his sons were dead, they abandoned their towns and fled; and the Philistines came and occupied them.

8 The next day when the Philistines came to strip the dead, they found Saul and his sons fallen on Mount Gilboa. ⁹They stripped him and took his head and his armor, and sent messengers throughout the land of the Philistines to carry the good news to their idols and to the people. ¹⁰They put his armor in the temple of their gods, and fastened his head in the temple of Dagon. ¹¹But when all Jabesh-gilead heard everything that the Philistines had done to Saul, ¹²all the valiant warriors got up and took away the body of Saul and the bodies of his sons, and brought them to Jabesh. Then they buried their bones under the oak in Jabesh, and fasted seven days.

13 So Saul died for his unfaithfulness; he was unfaithful to the Lord in that he did not keep the command of the Lord; moreover, he had consulted a medium, seeking guidance, ¹⁴and did not seek guidance from the Lord.

Therefore the Lord*ᵇ* put him to death and turned the kingdom over to David son of Jesse.

11 David Anointed King of All Israel

Then all Israel gathered together to David at Hebron and said, "See, we are your bone and flesh. ²For some time now, even while Saul was king, it was you who commanded the army of Israel. The Lord your God said to you: It is you who shall be shepherd of my people Israel, you who shall be ruler over my people Israel." ³So all the elders of Israel came to the king at Hebron, and David made a covenant with them at Hebron before the Lord. And they anointed David king over Israel, according to the word of the Lord by Samuel.

Jerusalem Captured

4 David and all Israel marched to Jerusalem, that is Jebus, where the Jebusites were, the inhabitants of the land. ⁵The inhabitants of Jebus said to David, "You will not come in here." Nevertheless David took the stronghold of Zion, now the city of David. ⁶David had said, "Whoever attacks the Jebusites first shall be chief and commander." And Joab son of Zeruiah went up first, so he became chief. ⁷David resided in the stronghold; therefore it was called the city of David. ⁸He built the city all around, from the Millo in complete circuit; and Joab repaired the rest of the city. ⁹And David became greater and greater, for the Lord of hosts was with him.

David's Mighty Men and Their Exploits

10 Now these are the chiefs of David's warriors, who gave him strong support in his kingdom, together with all Israel, to make him king, according to the word of the Lord concerning Israel. ¹¹This is an account of David's mighty warriors: Jashobeam, son of Hachmoni,*ᶜ* was chief of the Three;*ᵈ* he wielded his spear against three hundred whom he killed at one time.

12 And next to him among the three warriors was Eleazar son of Dodo, the Ahohite. ¹³He was with David at Pas-dammim when the Philistines were gathered there for battle. There was a plot of ground full of barley. Now the people had fled from the Philistines, ¹⁴but he and David took their stand in the middle of the plot, defended it, and killed the Philistines; and the Lord saved them by a great victory.

15 Three of the thirty chiefs went down to the rock to David at the cave of Adullam, while the army of Philistines was encamped in the valley of Rephaim. ¹⁶David was then in the

---

a Heb *they* *b* Heb *he* *c* Or *a Hachmonite* *d* Compare 2 Sam 23.8: Heb *Thirty* or *captains* stronghold; and the garrison of the Philistines was then at Bethlehem. [17]David said longingly, "O that someone would give me water to drink from the well of Bethlehem that is by the gate!" [18]Then the Three broke through the camp of the Philistines, and drew water from the well of Bethlehem that was by the gate, and they brought it to David. But David would not drink of it; he poured it out to the LORD, [19]and said, "My God forbid that I should do this. Can I drink the blood of these men? For at the risk of their lives they brought it." Therefore he would not drink it. The three warriors did these things.

20 Now Abishai,[a] the brother of Joab, was chief of the Thirty.[b] With his spear he fought against three hundred and killed them, and won a name beside the Three. [21]He was the most renowned[c] of the Thirty,[b] and became their commander; but he did not attain to the Three.

22 Benaiah son of Jehoiada was a valiant man[d] of Kabzeel, a doer of great deeds; he struck down two sons of[e] Ariel of Moab. He also went down and killed a lion in a pit on a day when snow had fallen. [23]And he killed an Egyptian, a man of great stature, five cubits tall. The Egyptian had in his hand a spear like a weaver's beam; but Benaiah went against him with a staff, snatched the spear out of the Egyptian's hand, and killed him with his own spear. [24]Such were the things Benaiah son of Jehoiada did, and he won a name beside the three warriors. [25]He was renowned among the Thirty, but he did not attain to the Three. And David put him in charge of his bodyguard.

26 The warriors of the armies were Asahel brother of Joab, Elhanan son of Dodo of Bethlehem, [27]Shammoth of Harod,[f] Helez the Pelonite, [28]Ira son of Ikkesh of Tekoa, Abiezer of Anathoth, [29]Sibbecai the Hushathite, Ilai the Ahohite, [30]Maharai of Netophah, Heled son of Baanah of Netophah, [31]Ithai son of Ribai of Gibeah of the Benjaminites, Benaiah of Pirathon, [32]Hurai of the wadis of Gaash, Abiel the Arbathite, [33]Azmaveth of Baharum, Eliahba of Shaalbon, [34]Hashem[g] the Gizonite, Jonathan son of Shagee the Hararite, [35]Ahiam son of Sachar the Hararite, Eliphal son of Ur, [36]Hepher the Mecherathite, Ahijah the Pelonite, [37]Hezro of Carmel, Naarai son of Ezbai, [38]Joel the brother of Nathan, Mibhar son of Hagri, [39]Zelek the Ammonite, Naharai of Beeroth, the armor-bearer of Joab son of Zeruiah, [40]Ira the Ithrite, Gareb the Ithrite, [41]Uriah the Hittite, Zabad son of Ahlai, [42]Adina son of Shiza the Reubenite, a leader of the Reubenites, and thirty with him, [43]Hanan son of Maacah, and Joshaphat the Mithnite, [44]Uzzia the Ashterathite, Shama and Jeiel sons of Hotham the Aroerite, [45]Jediael son of Shimri, and his brother Joha the Tizite, [46]Eliel the Mahavite, and Jeribai and Joshaviah sons of Elnaam, and Ithmah the Moabite, [47]Eliel, and Obed, and Jaasiel the Mezobaite.

12 David's Followers in the Wilderness

The following are those who came to David at Ziklag, while he could not move about freely because of Saul son of Kish; they were among the mighty warriors who helped him in war. [2]They were archers, and could shoot arrows and sling stones with either the right hand or the left; they were Benjaminites, Saul's kindred. [3]The chief was Ahiezer, then Joash, both sons of Shemaah of Gibeah; also Jeziel and Pelet sons of Azmaveth; Beracah, Jehu of Anathoth, [4]Ishmaiah of Gibeon, a warrior among the Thirty and a leader over the Thirty; Jeremiah,[h] Jahaziel, Johanan, Jozabad of Gederah, [5]Eluzai,[i] Jerimoth, Bealiah, Shemariah, Shephatiah the Haruphite; [6]Elkanah, Isshiah, Azarel, Joezer, and Jashobeam, the Korahites; [7]and Joelah and Zebadiah, sons of Jeroham of Gedor.

8 From the Gadites there went over to David at the stronghold in the wilderness mighty and experienced warriors, expert with shield and spear, whose faces were like the faces of lions, and who were swift as gazelles on the mountains: [9]Ezer the chief, Obadiah second, Eliab third, [10]Mishmannah fourth, Jeremiah fifth, [11]Attai sixth, Eliel seventh, [12]Johanan eighth, Elzabad ninth, [13]Jeremiah tenth, Machbannai eleventh. [14]These Gadites were officers of the army, the least equal to a hundred and the greatest to a thousand. [15]These are the men who crossed the Jordan in the first month, when it was overflowing all its banks, and put to flight all those in the valleys, to the east and to the west.

16 Some Benjaminites and Judahites came to the stronghold to David. [17]David went out to meet them and said to them, "If you have come to me in friendship, to help me, then my heart will be knit to you; but if you have come to betray me to my adversaries, though my hands have done no wrong, then may the God of our ancestors see and give judgment." [18]Then the spirit came upon Amasai, chief of the Thirty, and he said,

a Gk Vg Tg Compare 2 Sam 23.18: Heb Abshai b Syr: Heb Three c Compare 2 Sam 23.19: Heb more renowned among the two d Syr: Heb the son of a valiant man e See 2 Sam 23.20: Heb lacks sons of f Compare 2 Sam 23.25: Heb the Harorite g Compare Gk and 2 Sam 23.32: Heb the sons of Hashem h Heb verse 5 i Heb verse 6

"We are yours, O David;
  and with you, O son of Jesse!
Peace, peace to you,
  and peace to the one who helps you!
  For your God is the one who helps you."

Then David received them, and made them officers of his troops.

19 Some of the Manassites deserted to David when he came with the Philistines for the battle against Saul. (Yet he did not help them, for the rulers of the Philistines took counsel and sent him away, saying, "He will desert to his master Saul at the cost of our heads.") [20] As he went to Ziklag these Manassites deserted to him: Adnah, Jozabad, Jediael, Michael, Jozabad, Elihu, and Zillethai, chiefs of the thousands in Manasseh. [21] They helped David against the band of raiders,[a] for they were all warriors and commanders in the army. [22] Indeed from day to day people kept coming to David to help him, until there was a great army, like an army of God.

David's Army at Hebron

23 These are the numbers of the divisions of the armed troops who came to David in Hebron to turn the kingdom of Saul over to him, according to the word of the LORD. [24] The people of Judah bearing shield and spear numbered six thousand eight hundred armed troops. [25] Of the Simeonites, mighty warriors, seven thousand one hundred. [26] Of the Levites four thousand six hundred. [27] Jehoiada, leader of the house of Aaron, and with him three thousand seven hundred. [28] Zadok, a young warrior, and twenty-two commanders from his own ancestral house. [29] Of the Benjaminites, the kindred of Saul, three thousand, of whom the majority had continued to keep their allegiance to the house of Saul. [30] Of the Ephraimites, twenty thousand eight hundred, mighty warriors, notables in their ancestral houses. [31] Of the half-tribe of Manasseh, eighteen thousand, who were expressly named to come and make David king. [32] Of Issachar, those who had understanding of the times, to know what Israel ought to do, two hundred chiefs, and all their kindred under their command. [33] Of Zebulun, fifty thousand seasoned troops, equipped for battle with all the weapons of war, to help David[b] with singleness of purpose. [34] Of Naphtali, a thousand commanders, with whom there were thirty-seven thousand armed with shield and spear. [35] Of the Danites, twenty-eight thousand six hundred equipped for battle. [36] Of Asher, forty thousand seasoned troops ready for battle. [37] Of the Reubenites and Gadites and the half-tribe of Manasseh from beyond the Jordan, one hundred twenty thousand armed with all the weapons of war.

38 All these, warriors arrayed in battle order, came to Hebron with full intent to make David king over all Israel; likewise all the rest of Israel were of a single mind to make David king. [39] They were there with David for three days, eating and drinking, for their kindred

a Or *as officers of his troops* *b* Gk: Heb lacks *David* had provided for them. [40]And also their neighbors, from as far away as Issachar and Zebulun and Naphtali, came bringing food on donkeys, camels, mules, and oxen—abundant provisions of meal, cakes of figs, clusters of raisins, wine, oil, oxen, and sheep, for there was joy in Israel.

13 The Ark Brought from Kiriath-jearim

David consulted with the commanders of the thousands and of the hundreds, with every leader. [2]David said to the whole assembly of Israel, "If it seems good to you, and if it is the will of the LORD our God, let us send abroad to our kindred who remain in all the land of Israel, including the priests and Levites in the cities that have pasture lands, that they may come together to us. [3]Then let us bring again the ark of our God to us; for we did not turn to it in the days of Saul." [4]The whole assembly agreed to do so, for the thing pleased all the people.

5 So David assembled all Israel from the Shihor of Egypt to Lebo-hamath, to bring the ark of God from Kiriath-jearim. [6]And David and all Israel went up to Baalah, that is, to Kiriath-jearim, which belongs to Judah, to bring up from there the ark of God, the LORD, who is enthroned on the cherubim, which is called by his[a] name. [7]They carried the ark of God on a new cart, from the house of Abinadab, and Uzzah and Ahio[b] were driving the cart. [8]David and all Israel were dancing before God with all their might, with song and lyres and harps and tambourines and cymbals and trumpets.

9 When they came to the threshing floor of Chidon, Uzzah put out his hand to hold the ark, for the oxen shook it. [10]The anger of the LORD was kindled against Uzzah; he struck him down because he put out his hand to the ark; and he died there before God. [11]David was angry because the LORD had burst out against Uzzah; so that place is called Perez-uzzah[c] to this day. [12]David was afraid of God that day; he said, "How can I bring the ark of God into my care?" [13]So David did not take the ark into his care into the city of David; he took it instead to the house of Obed-edom the Gittite. [14]The ark of God remained with the household of Obed-edom in his house three months, and the LORD blessed the household of Obed-edom and all that he had.

14 David Established at Jerusalem

King Hiram of Tyre sent messengers to David, along with cedar logs, and masons and carpenters to build a house for him. [2]David then perceived that the LORD had established him as king over Israel, and that his kingdom was highly exalted for the sake of his people Israel.

3 David took more wives in Jerusalem, and David became the father of more sons and daughters. [4]These are the names of the children whom he had in Jerusalem: Shammua, Shobab, and Nathan; Solomon, [5]Ibhar, Elishua, and Elpelet; [6]Nogah, Nepheg, and Japhia; [7]Elishama, Beeliada, and Eliphelet.

Defeat of the Philistines

8 When the Philistines heard that David had been anointed king over all Israel, all the Philistines went up in search of David; and David heard of it and went out against them. [9]Now the Philistines had come and made a raid in the valley of Rephaim. [10]David inquired of God, "Shall I go up against the Philistines? Will you give them into my hand?" The LORD said to him, "Go up, and I will give them into your hand." [11]So he went up to Baal-perazim, and David defeated them there. David said, "God has burst out[d] against my enemies by my hand, like a bursting flood." Therefore that place is called Baal-perazim.[e] [12]They abandoned their gods there, and at David's command they were burned.

13 Once again the Philistines made a raid in the valley. [14]When David again inquired of God, God said to him, "You shall not go up after them; go around and come on them opposite the balsam trees. [15]When you hear the sound of marching in the tops of the balsam trees, then go out to battle; for God has gone out before you to strike down the army of the Philistines." [16]David did as God had commanded him, and they struck down the Philistine army from Gibeon to Gezer. [17]The fame of David went out into all lands, and the LORD brought the fear of him on all nations.

15 The Ark Brought to Jerusalem

David[f] built houses for himself in the city of David, and he prepared a place for the ark of God and pitched a tent for it. [2]Then David commanded that no one but the Levites were to carry the ark of God, for the LORD had chosen them to carry the ark of the LORD and to minister to him forever. [3]David assembled all Israel in Jerusalem to bring up the ark of the LORD to its place, which he had prepared for it. [4]Then David gathered together the descendants of Aaron and the Levites: [5]of the sons of Kohath, Uriel the chief, with one hundred twenty of his kindred; [6]of the sons of Merari, Asaiah the chief, with two hundred twenty of his kindred; [7]of the sons of Gershom, Joel the chief,

---

a Heb lacks his b Or and his brother c That is Bursting Out Against Uzzah d Heb paraz e That is Lord of Bursting Out f Heb He with one hundred thirty of his kindred; [8]of the sons of Elizaphan, Shemaiah the chief, with two hundred of his kindred; [9]of the sons of Hebron, Eliel the chief, with eighty of his kindred; [10]of the sons of Uzziel, Amminadab the chief, with one hundred twelve of his kindred.

11 David summoned the priests Zadok and Abiathar, and the Levites Uriel, Asaiah, Joel, Shemaiah, Eliel, and Amminadab. [12]He said to them, "You are the heads of families of the Levites; sanctify yourselves, you and your kindred, so that you may bring up the ark of the Lord, the God of Israel, to the place that I have prepared for it. [13]Because you did not carry it the first time,[a] the Lord our God burst out against us, because we did not give it proper care." [14]So the priests and the Levites sanctified themselves to bring up the ark of the Lord, the God of Israel. [15]And the Levites carried the ark of God on their shoulders with the poles, as Moses had commanded according to the word of the Lord.

16 David also commanded the chiefs of the Levites to appoint their kindred as the singers to play on musical instruments, on harps and lyres and cymbals, to raise loud sounds of joy. [17]So the Levites appointed Heman son of Joel; and of his kindred Asaph son of Berechiah; and of the sons of Merari, their kindred, Ethan son of Kushaiah; [18]and with them their kindred of the second order, Zechariah, Jaaziel, Shemiramoth, Jehiel, Unni, Eliab, Benaiah, Maaseiah, Mattithiah, Eliphelehu, and Mikneiah, and the gatekeepers Obed-edom and Jeiel. [19]The singers Heman, Asaph, and Ethan were to sound bronze cymbals; [20]Zechariah, Aziel, Shemiramoth, Jehiel, Unni, Eliab, Maaseiah, and Benaiah were to play harps according to Alamoth; [21]but Mattithiah, Eliphelehu, Mikneiah, Obed-edom, Jeiel, and Azaziah were to lead with lyres according to the Sheminith. [22]Chenaniah, leader of the Levites in music, was to direct the music, for he understood it. [23]Berechiah and Elkanah were to be gatekeepers for the ark. [24]Shebaniah, Joshaphat, Nethanel, Amasai, Zechariah, Benaiah, and Eliezer, the priests, were to blow the trumpets before the ark of God. Obed-edom and Jehiah also were to be gatekeepers for the ark.

25 So David and the elders of Israel, and the commanders of the thousands, went to bring up the ark of the covenant of the Lord from the house of Obed-edom with rejoicing. [26]And because God helped the Levites who were carrying the ark of the covenant of the Lord, they sacrificed seven bulls and seven rams. [27]David was clothed with a robe of fine linen, as also

a Meaning of Heb uncertain

were all the Levites who were carrying the ark, and the singers, and Chenaniah the leader of the music of the singers; and David wore a linen ephod. [28] So all Israel brought up the ark of the covenant of the LORD with shouting, to the sound of the horn, trumpets, and cymbals, and made loud music on harps and lyres.

29 As the ark of the covenant of the LORD came to the city of David, Michal daughter of Saul looked out of the window, and saw King David leaping and dancing; and she despised him in her heart.

16 The Ark Placed in the Tent

They brought in the ark of God, and set it inside the tent that David had pitched for it; and they offered burnt offerings and offerings of well-being before God. [2] When David had finished offering the burnt offerings and the offerings of well-being, he blessed the people in the name of the LORD; [3] and he distributed to every person in Israel—man and woman alike—to each a loaf of bread, a portion of meat,[a] and a cake of raisins.

4 He appointed certain of the Levites as ministers before the ark of the LORD, to invoke, to thank, and to praise the LORD, the God of Israel. [5] Asaph was the chief, and second to him Zechariah, Jeiel, Shemiramoth, Jehiel, Mattithiah, Eliab, Benaiah, Obed-edom, and Jeiel, with harps and lyres; Asaph was to sound the cymbals, [6] and the priests Benaiah and Jahaziel were to blow trumpets regularly, before the ark of the covenant of God.

David's Psalm of Thanksgiving

7 Then on that day David first appointed the singing of praises to the LORD by Asaph and his kindred.

8 O give thanks to the LORD, call on his
    name,
  make known his deeds among the
    peoples.
9 Sing to him, sing praises to him,
  tell of all his wonderful works.
10 Glory in his holy name;
  let the hearts of those who seek the LORD
    rejoice.
11 Seek the LORD and his strength,
  seek his presence continually.
12 Remember the wonderful works he has
    done,
  his miracles, and the judgments he
    uttered,
13 O offspring of his servant Israel,[b]
  children of Jacob, his chosen ones.

14 He is the LORD our God;
  his judgments are in all the earth.
15 Remember his covenant forever,
  the word that he commanded, for a
    thousand generations,
16 the covenant that he made with Abraham,
  his sworn promise to Isaac,
17 which he confirmed to Jacob as a statute,
  to Israel as an everlasting covenant,
18 saying, "To you I will give the land of
    Canaan
  as your portion for an inheritance."

19 When they were few in number,
  of little account, and strangers in the
    land,[c]
20 wandering from nation to nation,
  from one kingdom to another people,
21 he allowed no one to oppress them;
  he rebuked kings on their account,
22 saying, "Do not touch my anointed ones;
  do my prophets no harm."

23 Sing to the LORD, all the earth.
  Tell of his salvation from day to day.
24 Declare his glory among the nations,
  his marvelous works among all the
    peoples.
25 For great is the LORD, and greatly to be
    praised;
  he is to be revered above all gods.
26 For all the gods of the peoples are idols,
  but the LORD made the heavens.
27 Honor and majesty are before him;
  strength and joy are in his place.

28 Ascribe to the LORD, O families of the
    peoples,
  ascribe to the LORD glory and strength.
29 Ascribe to the LORD the glory due his name;
  bring an offering, and come before him.
  Worship the LORD in holy splendor;
30   tremble before him, all the earth.
  The world is firmly established; it shall
    never be moved.
31 Let the heavens be glad, and let the earth
    rejoice,
  and let them say among the nations,
    "The LORD is king!"
32 Let the sea roar, and all that fills it;
  let the field exult, and everything in it.
33 Then shall the trees of the forest sing for joy
  before the LORD, for he comes to judge
    the earth.
34 O give thanks to the LORD, for he is good;
  for his steadfast love endures forever.

35 Say also:
  "Save us, O God of our salvation,

a Compare Gk Syr Vg: Meaning of Heb uncertain b Another reading is Abraham (compare Ps 105.6) c Heb in it

and gather and rescue us from among
the nations,
that we may give thanks to your holy name,
and glory in your praise.
36 Blessed be the Lord, the God of Israel,
from everlasting to everlasting."
Then all the people said "Amen!" and praised
the Lord.

Regular Worship Maintained

37 David left Asaph and his kinsfolk there before the ark of the covenant of the Lord to minister regularly before the ark as each day required, 38and also Obed-edom and his*a* sixty-eight kinsfolk; while Obed-edom son of Jeduthun and Hosah were to be gatekeepers. 39And he left the priest Zadok and his kindred the priests before the tabernacle of the Lord in the high place that was at Gibeon, 40to offer burnt offerings to the Lord on the altar of burnt offering regularly, morning and evening, according to all that is written in the law of the Lord that he commanded Israel. 41With them were Heman and Jeduthun, and the rest of those chosen and expressly named to render thanks to the Lord, for his steadfast love endures forever. 42Heman and Jeduthun had with them trumpets and cymbals for the music, and instruments for sacred song. The sons of Jeduthun were appointed to the gate.

43 Then all the people departed to their homes, and David went home to bless his household.

17 God's Covenant with David

Now when David settled in his house, David said to the prophet Nathan, "I am living in a house of cedar, but the ark of the covenant of the Lord is under a tent." 2Nathan said to David, "Do all that you have in mind, for God is with you."

3 But that same night the word of the Lord came to Nathan, saying: 4Go and tell my servant David: Thus says the Lord: You shall not build me a house to live in. 5For I have not lived in a house since the day I brought out Israel to this very day, but I have lived in a tent and a tabernacle.*b* 6Wherever I have moved about among all Israel, did I ever speak a word with any of the judges of Israel, whom I commanded to shepherd my people, saying, Why have you not built me a house of cedar? 7Now therefore thus you shall say to my servant David: Thus says the Lord of hosts: I took you from the pasture, from following the sheep, to be ruler over my people Israel; 8and I have been with you wherever you went, and have cut off

all your enemies before you; and I will make for you a name, like the name of the great ones of the earth. 9I will appoint a place for my people Israel, and will plant them, so that they may live in their own place, and be disturbed no more; and evildoers shall wear them down no more, as they did formerly, 10from the time that I appointed judges over my people Israel; and I will subdue all your enemies.

Moreover I declare to you that the Lord will build you a house. 11When your days are fulfilled to go to be with your ancestors, I will raise up your offspring after you, one of your own sons, and I will establish his kingdom. 12He shall build a house for me, and I will establish his throne forever. 13I will be a father to him, and he shall be a son to me. I will not take my steadfast love from him, as I took it from him who was before you, 14but I will confirm him in my house and in my kingdom forever, and his throne shall be established forever. 15In accordance with all these words and all this vision, Nathan spoke to David.

David's Prayer

16 Then King David went in and sat before the Lord, and said, "Who am I, O Lord God, and what is my house, that you have brought me thus far? 17And even this was a small thing in your sight, O God; you have also spoken of your servant's house for a great while to come. You regard me as someone of high rank,*c* O Lord God! 18And what more can David say to you for honoring your servant? You know your servant. 19For your servant's sake, O Lord, and according to your own heart, you have done all these great deeds, making known all these great things. 20There is no one like you, O Lord, and there is no God besides you, according to all that we have heard with our ears. 21Who is like your people Israel, one nation on the earth whom God went to redeem to be his people, making for yourself a name for great and terrible things, in driving out nations before your people whom you redeemed from Egypt? 22And you made your people Israel to be your people forever; and you, O Lord, became their God.

23 "And now, O Lord, as for the word that you have spoken concerning your servant and concerning his house, let it be established forever, and do as you have promised. 24Thus your name will be established and magnified forever in the saying, 'The Lord of hosts, the God of Israel, is Israel's God'; and the house of your servant David will be established in your presence. 25For you, my God, have revealed to your

---

a Gk Syr Vg: Heb *their* *b* Gk 2 Sam 7.6: Heb *but I have been from tent to tent and from tabernacle* *c* Meaning of Heb uncertain servant that you will build a house for him; therefore your servant has found it possible to pray before you. 26And now, O LORD, you are God, and you have promised this good thing to your servant; 27therefore may it please you to bless the house of your servant, that it may continue forever before you. For you, O LORD, have blessed and are blessed*a* forever."

18 David's Kingdom Established and Extended

Some time afterward, David attacked the Philistines and subdued them; he took Gath and its villages from the Philistines.

2 He defeated Moab, and the Moabites became subject to David and brought tribute.

3 David also struck down King Hadadezer of Zobah, toward Hamath,*b* as he went to set up a monument at the river Euphrates. 4David took from him one thousand chariots, seven thousand cavalry, and twenty thousand foot soldiers. David hamstrung all the chariot horses, but left one hundred of them. 5When the Arameans of Damascus came to help King Hadadezer of Zobah, David killed twenty-two thousand Arameans. 6Then David put garrisons*c* in Aram of Damascus; and the Arameans became subject to David, and brought tribute. The LORD gave victory to David wherever he went. 7David took the gold shields that were carried by the servants of Hadadezer, and brought them to Jerusalem. 8From Tibhath and from Cun, cities of Hadadezer, David took a vast quantity of bronze; with it Solomon made the bronze sea and the pillars and the vessels of bronze.

9 When King Tou of Hamath heard that David had defeated the whole army of King Hadadezer of Zobah, 10he sent his son Hadoram to King David, to greet him and to congratulate him, because he had fought against Hadadezer and defeated him. Now Hadadezer had often been at war with Tou. He sent all sorts of articles of gold, of silver, and of bronze; 11these also King David dedicated to the LORD, together with the silver and gold that he had carried off from all the nations, from Edom, Moab, the Ammonites, the Philistines, and Amalek.

12 Abishai son of Zeruiah killed eighteen thousand Edomites in the Valley of Salt. 13He put garrisons in Edom; and all the Edomites became subject to David. And the LORD gave victory to David wherever he went.

David's Administration

14 So David reigned over all Israel; and he administered justice and equity to all his people.

"Oh, mighty secrets of God! Never should I weary of trying to explain them if I thought it possible to succeed! I would write a thousand foolish things that one might be to the point, if only it might make us praise God more."

—St. Teresa of Avila

15Joab son of Zeruiah was over the army; Jehoshaphat son of Ahilud was recorder; 16Zadok son of Ahitub and Ahimelech son of Abiathar were priests; Shavsha was secretary; 17Benaiah son of Jehoiada was over the Cherethites and the Pelethites; and David's sons were the chief officials in the service of the king.

19 Defeat of the Ammonites and Arameans

Some time afterward, King Nahash of the Ammonites died, and his son succeeded him. 2David said, "I will deal loyally with Hanun son of Nahash, for his father dealt loyally with me." So David sent messengers to console him concerning his father. When David's servants came to Hanun in the land of the Ammonites, to console him, 3the officials of the Ammonites said to Hanun, "Do you think, because David

---

a Or *and it is blessed*   *b* Meaning of Heb uncertain   *c* Gk Vg 2 Sam 8.6 Compare Syr: Heb lacks *garrisons*

Majestic—© Jesse Bernard, 17

him advanced toward the Arameans for battle; and they fled before him. ¹⁵When the Ammonites saw that the Arameans fled, they likewise fled before Abishai, Joab's brother, and entered the city. Then Joab came to Jerusalem.

16 But when the Arameans saw that they had been defeated by Israel, they sent messengers and brought out the Arameans who were beyond the Euphrates, with Shophach the commander of the army of Hadadezer at their head. ¹⁷When David was informed, he gathered all Israel together, crossed the Jordan, came to them, and drew up his forces against them. When David set the battle in array against the Arameans, they fought with him. ¹⁸The Arameans fled before Israel; and David killed seven thousand Aramean charioteers and forty thousand foot soldiers, and also killed Shophach the commander of their army. ¹⁹When the servants of Hadadezer saw that they had been defeated by Israel, they made peace with David, and became subject to him. So the Arameans were not willing to help the Ammonites any more.

20 Siege and Capture of Rabbah

In the spring of the year, the time when kings go out to battle, Joab led out the army, ravaged the country of the Ammonites, and came and besieged Rabbah. But David remained at Jerusalem. Joab attacked Rabbah, and overthrew it. ²David took the crown of Milcom*ᵃ* from his head; he found that it weighed a talent of gold, and in it was a precious stone; and it was placed on David's head. He also brought out the booty of the city, a very great amount. ³He brought out the people who were in it, and set them to work*ᵇ* with saws and iron picks and axes.*ᶜ* Thus David did to all the cities of the Ammonites. Then David and all the people returned to Jerusalem.

Exploits against the Philistines

4 After this, war broke out with the Philistines at Gezer; then Sibbecai the Hushathite killed Sippai, who was one of the descendants of the giants; and the Philistines were subdued. ⁵Again there was war with the Philistines; and Elhanan son of Jair killed Lahmi the brother of Goliath the Gittite, the shaft of whose spear was like a weaver's beam. ⁶Again there was war at Gath, where there was a man of great size, who had six fingers on each hand, and six toes on each foot, twenty-four in number; he also was descended from the giants. ⁷When he taunted Israel, Jonathan son of Shimea, David's brother, killed him. ⁸These were descend-

has sent consolers to you, that he is honoring your father? Have not his servants come to you to search and to overthrow and to spy out the land?" ⁴So Hanun seized David's servants, shaved them, cut off their garments in the middle at their hips, and sent them away; ⁵and they departed. When David was told about the men, he sent messengers to them, for they felt greatly humiliated. The king said, "Remain at Jericho until your beards have grown, and then return."

6 When the Ammonites saw that they had made themselves odious to David, Hanun and the Ammonites sent a thousand talents of silver to hire chariots and cavalry from Mesopotamia, from Aram-maacah and from Zobah. ⁷They hired thirty-two thousand chariots and the king of Maacah with his army, who came and camped before Medeba. And the Ammonites were mustered from their cities and came to battle. ⁸When David heard of it, he sent Joab and all the army of the warriors. ⁹The Ammonites came out and drew up in battle array at the entrance of the city, and the kings who had come were by themselves in the open country.

10 When Joab saw that the line of battle was set against him both in front and in the rear, he chose some of the picked men of Israel and arrayed them against the Arameans; ¹¹the rest of his troops he put in the charge of his brother Abishai, and they were arrayed against the Ammonites. ¹²He said, "If the Arameans are too strong for me, then you shall help me; but if the Ammonites are too strong for you, then I will help you. ¹³Be strong, and let us be courageous for our people and for the cities of our God; and may the Lord do what seems good to him." ¹⁴So Joab and the troops who were with

a Gk Vg See 1 Kings 11.5, 33: MT *of their king*   *b* Compare 2 Sam 12.31: Heb *and he sawed*   *c* Compare 2 Sam 12.31: Heb *saws* ed from the giants in Gath; they fell by the hand of David and his servants.

21 The Census and Plague

Satan stood up against Israel, and incited David to count the people of Israel. ²So David said to Joab and the commanders of the army, "Go, number Israel, from Beer-sheba to Dan, and bring me a report, so that I may know their number." ³But Joab said, "May the LORD increase the number of his people a hundredfold! Are they not, my lord the king, all of them my lord's servants? Why then should my lord require this? Why should he bring guilt on Israel?" ⁴But the king's word prevailed against Joab. So Joab departed and went throughout all Israel, and came back to Jerusalem. ⁵Joab gave the total count of the people to David. In all Israel there were one million one hundred thousand men who drew the sword, and in Judah four hundred seventy thousand who drew the sword. ⁶But he did not include Levi and Benjamin in the numbering, for the king's command was abhorrent to Joab.

7 But God was displeased with this thing, and he struck Israel. ⁸David said to God, "I have sinned greatly in that I have done this thing. But now, I pray you, take away the guilt of your servant; for I have done very foolishly." ⁹The LORD spoke to Gad, David's seer, saying, ¹⁰"Go and say to David, 'Thus says the LORD: Three things I offer you; choose one of them, so that I may do it to you.' " ¹¹So Gad came to David and said to him, "Thus says the LORD, 'Take your choice: ¹²either three years of famine; or three months of devastation by your foes, while the sword of your enemies overtakes you; or three days of the sword of the LORD, pestilence on the land, and the angel of the LORD destroying throughout all the territory of Israel.' Now decide what answer I shall return to the one who sent me." ¹³Then David said to Gad, "I am in great distress; let me fall into the hand of the LORD, for his mercy is very great; but let me not fall into human hands."

14 So the LORD sent a pestilence on Israel; and seventy thousand persons fell in Israel. ¹⁵And God sent an angel to Jerusalem to destroy it; but when he was about to destroy it, the LORD took note and relented concerning the calamity; he said to the destroying angel, "Enough! Stay your hand." The angel of the LORD was then standing by the threshing floor of Ornan the Jebusite. ¹⁶David looked up and saw the angel of the LORD standing between earth and heaven, and in his hand a drawn sword stretched out over Jerusalem. Then David and the elders, clothed in sackcloth, fell on their faces. ¹⁷And David said to God, "Was it not I who gave the command to count the people? It is I who have sinned and done very wickedly. But these sheep, what have they done? Let your hand, I pray, O LORD my God, be against me and against my father's house; but do not let your people be plagued!"

David's Altar and Sacrifice

18 Then the angel of the LORD commanded Gad to tell David that he should go up and erect an altar to the LORD on the threshing floor of Ornan the Jebusite. ¹⁹So David went up following Gad's instructions, which he had spoken in the name of the LORD. ²⁰Ornan turned and saw the angel; and while his four sons who were with him hid themselves, Ornan continued to thresh wheat. ²¹As David came to Ornan, Ornan looked and saw David; he went out from the threshing floor, and did obeisance to David with his face to the ground. ²²David said to Ornan, "Give me the site of the threshing floor that I may build on it an altar to the LORD— give it to me at its full price—so that the plague may be averted from the people." ²³Then Ornan said to David, "Take it; and let my lord the king do what seems good to him; see, I present the oxen for burnt offerings, and the threshing sledges for the wood, and the wheat for a grain offering. I give it all." ²⁴But King David said to Ornan, "No; I will buy them for the full price. I will not take for the LORD what is yours, nor offer burnt offerings that cost me nothing." ²⁵So David paid Ornan six hundred shekels of gold by weight for the site. ²⁶David built there an altar to the LORD and presented burnt offerings and offerings of well-being. He called upon the LORD, and he answered him with fire from heaven on the altar of burnt offering. ²⁷Then the LORD commanded the angel, and he put his sword back into its sheath.

The Place Chosen for the Temple

28 At that time, when David saw that the LORD had answered him at the threshing floor of Ornan the Jebusite, he made his sacrifices there. ²⁹For the tabernacle of the LORD, which Moses had made in the wilderness, and the altar of burnt offering were at that time in the high place at Gibeon; ³⁰but David could not go before it to inquire of God, for he was afraid of

22 the sword of the angel of the LORD. ¹Then David said, "Here shall be the house of the LORD God and here the altar of burnt offering for Israel."

David Prepares to Build the Temple

2 David gave orders to gather together the aliens who were residing in the land of Israel, and he set stonecutters to prepare dressed

Thea Bowman was the granddaughter of a slave. As a child, she converted to Catholicism, and as an adult she chose a life as a Franciscan Sister of Perpetual Adoration. As a black religious sister in a predominantly white world, Sr. Thea was able to cross societal boundaries and share her cultural and spiritual gifts while learning and lifting up the cultural gifts of others. Throughout her adult life, she embraced Catholicism and religious life without abandoning the beautiful gift of her "blackness." It was her life's mission to share her rich cultural heritage and spirituality in song, prayer, teaching, and preaching.

Thea is remembered as a teacher, evangelist, catechist, and especially as an inspirer and pioneer. She was a leader in the movement encouraging black Catholics to express their cultural roots inside the Catholic Church. She earned a doctorate in English literature at the Catholic University of America in Washington, D.C., and went on to found the Institute of Black Studies at Xavier University in New Orleans, where she helped men and women, black and white, understand what it means to be a black Catholic. Black Catholic leaders say that the world and especially the Church are different—and better—because of the work she did.

I Love Jesus—© Talitha White, 16

In her most public act before she died of bone cancer in 1990 at age fifty-two, she made a powerful plea for renewed black Catholic evangelization efforts before the U.S. bishops at their summer meeting. At her invitation following her talk, the bishops crossed arms, linked hands, and joined her in song. Some swayed. Others wept.

In an interview with Mike Wallace on *60 Minutes,* she said, "I think the difference between me and some people is that I'm content to do my little bit. Sometimes people think they have to do big things in order to make change. But if each one would light a candle we'd have a tremendous light."

stones for building the house of God. ³David also provided great stores of iron for nails for the doors of the gates and for clamps, as well as bronze in quantities beyond weighing, ⁴and cedar logs without number—for the Sidonians and Tyrians brought great quantities of cedar to David. ⁵For David said, "My son Solomon is young and inexperienced, and the house that is to be built for the LORD must be exceedingly magnificent, famous and glorified throughout all lands; I will therefore make preparation for it." So David provided materials in great quantity before his death.

David's Charge to Solomon and the Leaders

6 Then he called for his son Solomon and charged him to build a house for the LORD, the God of Israel. ⁷David said to Solomon, "My son, I had planned to build a house to the name of the LORD my God. ⁸But the word of the LORD came to me, saying, 'You have shed much blood and have waged great wars; you shall not build a house to my name, because you have shed so much blood in my sight on the earth. ⁹See, a son shall be born to you; he shall be a man of peace. I will give him peace from all his enemies on every side; for his name shall

be Solomon,[a] and I will give peace[b] and quiet to Israel in his days. [10]He shall build a house for my name. He shall be a son to me, and I will be a father to him, and I will establish his royal throne in Israel forever.' [11]Now, my son, the Lord be with you, so that you may succeed in building the house of the Lord your God, as he has spoken concerning you. [12]Only, may the Lord grant you discretion and understanding, so that when he gives you charge over Israel you may keep the law of the Lord your God. [13]Then you will prosper if you are careful to observe the statutes and the ordinances that the Lord commanded Moses for Israel. Be strong and of good courage. Do not be afraid or dismayed. [14]With great pains I have provided for the house of the Lord one hundred thousand talents of gold, one million talents of silver, and bronze and iron beyond weighing, for there is so much of it; timber and stone too I have provided. To these you must add more. [15]You have an abundance of workers: stonecutters, masons, carpenters, and all kinds of artisans without number, skilled in working [16]gold, silver, bronze, and iron. Now begin the work, and the Lord be with you."

17 David also commanded all the leaders of Israel to help his son Solomon, saying, [18]"Is not the Lord your God with you? Has he not given you peace on every side? For he has delivered the inhabitants of the land into my hand; and the land is subdued before the Lord and his people. [19]Now set your mind and heart to seek the Lord your God. Go and build the sanctuary of the Lord God so that the ark of the covenant of the Lord and the holy vessels of God may be brought into a house built for the name of the Lord."

23 Families of the Levites and Their Functions

When David was old and full of days, he made his son Solomon king over Israel.

2 David assembled all the leaders of Israel and the priests and the Levites. [3]The Levites, thirty years old and upward, were counted, and the total was thirty-eight thousand. [4]"Twenty-four thousand of these," David said, "shall have charge of the work in the house of the Lord, six thousand shall be officers and judges, [5]four thousand gatekeepers, and four thousand shall offer praises to the Lord with the instruments that I have made for praise." [6]And David organized them in divisions corresponding to the sons of Levi: Gershon,[c] Kohath, and Merari.

7 The sons of Gershon[d] were Ladan and Shimei. [8]The sons of Ladan: Jehiel the chief, Zetham, and Joel, three. [9]The sons of Shimei: Shelomoth, Haziel, and Haran, three. These were the heads of families of Ladan. [10]And the sons of Shimei: Jahath, Zina, Jeush, and Beriah. These four were the sons of Shimei. [11]Jahath was the chief, and Zizah the second; but Jeush and Beriah did not have many sons, so they were enrolled as a single family.

12 The sons of Kohath: Amram, Izhar, Hebron, and Uzziel, four. [13]The sons of Amram: Aaron and Moses. Aaron was set apart to consecrate the most holy things, so that he and his sons forever should make offerings before the Lord, and minister to him and pronounce blessings in his name forever; [14]but as for Moses the man of God, his sons were to be reckoned among the tribe of Levi. [15]The sons of Moses: Gershom and Eliezer. [16]The sons of Gershom: Shebuel the chief. [17]The sons of Eliezer: Rehabiah the chief; Eliezer had no other sons, but the sons of Rehabiah were very numerous. [18]The sons of Izhar: Shelomith the chief. [19]The sons of Hebron: Jeriah the chief, Amariah the second, Jahaziel the third, and Jekameam the fourth. [20]The sons of Uzziel: Micah the chief and Isshiah the second.

21 The sons of Merari: Mahli and Mushi. The sons of Mahli: Eleazar and Kish. [22]Eleazar died having no sons, but only daughters; their kindred, the sons of Kish, married them. [23]The sons of Mushi: Mahli, Eder, and Jeremoth, three.

24 These were the sons of Levi by their ancestral houses, the heads of families as they were enrolled according to the number of the names of the individuals from twenty years old and upward who were to do the work for the service of the house of the Lord. [25]For David said, "The Lord, the God of Israel, has given rest to his people; and he resides in Jerusalem forever. [26]And so the Levites no longer need to carry the tabernacle or any of the things for its service"— [27]for according to the last words of David these were the number of the Levites from twenty years old and upward— [28]"but their duty shall be to assist the descendants of Aaron for the service of the house of the Lord, having the care of the courts and the chambers, the cleansing of all that is holy, and any work for the service of the house of God; [29]to assist also with the rows of bread, the choice flour for the grain offering, the wafers of unleavened bread, the baked offering, the offering mixed with oil, and all measures of quantity or size. [30]And they shall stand every morning, thanking and praising the Lord, and likewise

a Heb Shelomoh b Heb shalom c Or Gershom; See 1 Chr 6.1, note, and 23.15 d Vg Compare Gk Syr: Heb to the Gershonite at evening, [31] and whenever burnt offerings are offered to the LORD on sabbaths, new moons, and appointed festivals, according to the number required of them, regularly before the LORD. [32] Thus they shall keep charge of the tent of meeting and the sanctuary, and shall attend the descendants of Aaron, their kindred, for the service of the house of the LORD."

24 Divisions of the Priests

The divisions of the descendants of Aaron were these. The sons of Aaron: Nadab, Abihu, Eleazar, and Ithamar. [2] But Nadab and Abihu died before their father, and had no sons; so Eleazar and Ithamar became the priests. [3] Along with Zadok of the sons of Eleazar, and Ahimelech of the sons of Ithamar, David organized them according to the appointed duties in their service. [4] Since more chief men were found among the sons of Eleazar than among the sons of Ithamar, they organized them under sixteen heads of ancestral houses of the sons of Eleazar, and eight of the sons of Ithamar. [5] They organized them by lot, all alike, for there were officers of the sanctuary and officers of God among both the sons of Eleazar and the sons of Ithamar. [6] The scribe Shemaiah son of Nethanel, a Levite, recorded them in the presence of the king, and the officers, and Zadok the priest, and Ahimelech son of Abiathar, and the heads of ancestral houses of the priests and of the Levites; one ancestral house being chosen for Eleazar and one chosen for Ithamar.

7 The first lot fell to Jehoiarib, the second to Jedaiah, [8] the third to Harim, the fourth to Seorim, [9] the fifth to Malchijah, the sixth to Mijamin, [10] the seventh to Hakkoz, the eighth to Abijah, [11] the ninth to Jeshua, the tenth to Shecaniah, [12] the eleventh to Eliashib, the twelfth to Jakim, [13] the thirteenth to Huppah, the fourteenth to Jeshebeab, [14] the fifteenth to Bilgah, the sixteenth to Immer, [15] the seventeenth to Hezir, the eighteenth to Happizzez, [16] the nineteenth to Pethahiah, the twentieth to Jehezkel, [17] the twenty-first to Jachin, the twenty-second to Gamul, [18] the twenty-third to Delaiah, the twenty-fourth to Maaziah. [19] These had as their appointed duty in their service to enter the house of the LORD according to the procedure established for them by their ancestor Aaron, as the LORD God of Israel had commanded him.

Other Levites

20 And of the rest of the sons of Levi: of the sons of Amram, Shubael; of the sons of Shubael, Jehdeiah. [21] Of Rehabiah: of the sons of Rehabiah, Isshiah the chief. [22] Of the Izharites, Shelomoth; of the sons of Shelomoth, Jahath. [23] The sons of Hebron:[a] Jeriah the chief,[b] Amariah the second, Jahaziel the third, Jekameam the fourth. [24] The sons of Uzziel, Micah; of the sons of Micah, Shamir. [25] The brother of Micah, Isshiah; of the sons of Isshiah, Zechariah. [26] The sons of Merari: Mahli and Mushi. The sons of Jaaziah: Beno.[c] [27] The sons of Merari: of Jaaziah, Beno,[c] Shoham, Zaccur, and Ibri. [28] Of Mahli: Eleazar, who had no sons. [29] Of Kish, the sons of Kish: Jerahmeel. [30] The sons of Mushi: Mahli, Eder, and Jerimoth. These were the sons of the Levites according to their ancestral houses. [31] These also cast lots corresponding to their kindred, the descendants of Aaron, in the presence of King David, Zadok, Ahimelech, and the heads of ancestral houses of the priests and of the Levites, the chief as well as the youngest brother.

25 The Temple Musicians

David and the officers of the army also set apart for the service the sons of Asaph, and of Heman, and of Jeduthun, who should prophesy with lyres, harps, and cymbals. The list of those who did the work and of their duties was: [2] Of the sons of Asaph: Zaccur, Joseph, Nethaniah, and Asarelah, sons of Asaph, under the direction of Asaph, who prophesied under the direction of the king. [3] Of Jeduthun, the sons of Jeduthun: Gedaliah, Zeri, Jeshaiah, Shimei,[d] Hashabiah, and Mattithiah, six, under the direction of their father Jeduthun, who prophesied with the lyre in thanksgiving and praise to the LORD. [4] Of Heman, the sons of Heman: Bukkiah, Mattaniah, Uzziel, Shebuel, and Jerimoth, Hananiah, Hanani, Eliathah, Giddalti, and Romamti-ezer, Joshbekashah, Mallothi, Hothir, Mahazioth. [5] All these were the sons of Heman the king's seer, according to the promise of God to exalt him; for God had given Heman fourteen sons and three daughters. [6] They were all under the direction of their father for the music in the house of the LORD with cymbals, harps, and lyres for the service of the house of God. Asaph, Jeduthun, and Heman were under the order of the king. [7] They and their kindred, who were trained in singing to the LORD, all of whom were skillful, numbered two hundred eighty-eight. [8] And they cast lots for their duties, small and great, teacher and pupil alike.

9 The first lot fell for Asaph to Joseph; the second to Gedaliah, to him and his brothers and his sons, twelve; [10] the third to Zaccur, his sons and his brothers, twelve; [11] the fourth to Izri, his sons and his brothers, twelve; [12] the

---

a See 23.19: Heb lacks *Hebron* b See 23.19: Heb lacks *the chief* c Or *his son*: Meaning of Heb uncertain d One Ms: Gk: MT lacks *Shimei*

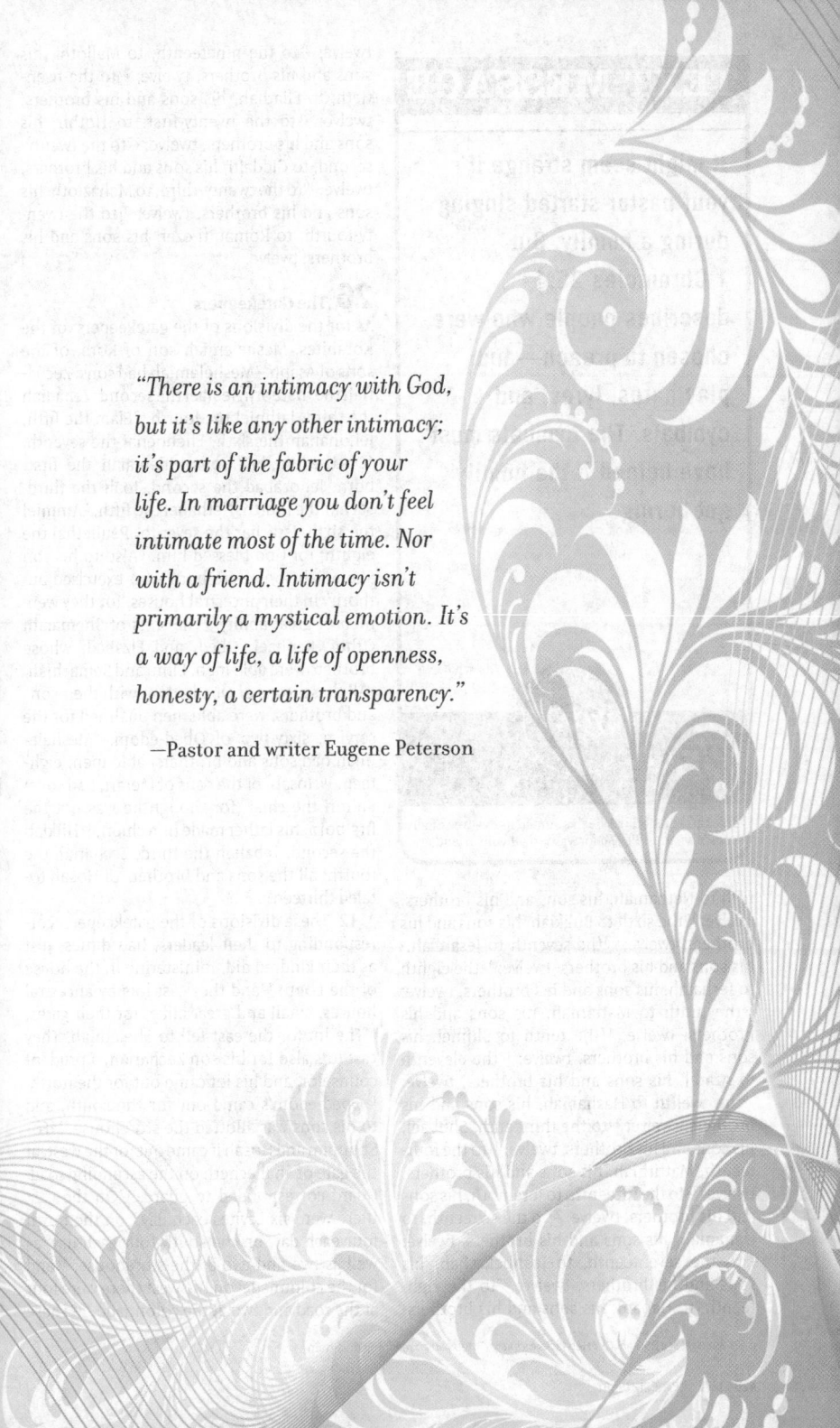

"There is an intimacy with God, but it's like any other intimacy; it's part of the fabric of your life. In marriage you don't feel intimate most of the time. Nor with a friend. Intimacy isn't primarily a mystical emotion. It's a way of life, a life of openness, honesty, a certain transparency."

—Pastor and writer Eugene Peterson

twelve; [26]to the nineteenth, to Mallothi, his sons and his brothers, twelve; [27]to the twentieth, to Eliathah, his sons and his brothers, twelve; [28]to the twenty-first, to Hothir, his sons and his brothers, twelve; [29]to the twenty-second, to Giddalti, his sons and his brothers, twelve; [30]to the twenty-third, to Mahazioth, his sons and his brothers, twelve; [31]to the twenty-fourth, to Romamti-ezer, his sons and his brothers, twelve.

26 The Gatekeepers

As for the divisions of the gatekeepers: of the Korahites, Meshelemiah son of Kore, of the sons of Asaph. [2]Meshelemiah had sons: Zechariah the firstborn, Jediael the second, Zebadiah the third, Jathniel the fourth, [3]Elam the fifth, Jehohanan the sixth, Eliehoenai the seventh. [4]Obed-edom had sons: Shemaiah the firstborn, Jehozabad the second, Joah the third, Sachar the fourth, Nethanel the fifth, [5]Ammiel the sixth, Issachar the seventh, Peullethai the eighth; for God blessed him. [6]Also to his son Shemaiah sons were born who exercised authority in their ancestral houses, for they were men of great ability. [7]The sons of Shemaiah: Othni, Rephael, Obed, and Elzabad, whose brothers were able men, Elihu and Semachiah. [8]All these, sons of Obed-edom with their sons and brothers, were able men qualified for the service; sixty-two of Obed-edom. [9]Meshelemiah had sons and brothers, able men, eighteen. [10]Hosah, of the sons of Merari, had sons: Shimri the chief (for though he was not the firstborn, his father made him chief), [11]Hilkiah the second, Tebaliah the third, Zechariah the fourth: all the sons and brothers of Hosah totaled thirteen.

12 These divisions of the gatekeepers, corresponding to their leaders, had duties, just as their kindred did, ministering in the house of the LORD; [13]and they cast lots by ancestral houses, small and great alike, for their gates. [14]The lot for the east fell to Shelemiah. They cast lots also for his son Zechariah, a prudent counselor, and his lot came out for the north. [15]Obed-edom's came out for the south, and to his sons was allotted the storehouse. [16]For Shuppim and Hosah it came out for the west, at the gate of Shallecheth on the ascending road. Guard corresponded to guard. [17]On the east there were six Levites each day,[b] on the north four each day, on the south four each day, as well as two and two at the storehouse; [18]and for the colonnade[c] on the west there were four at the road and two at the colonnade.[c] [19]These

fifth to Nethaniah, his sons and his brothers, twelve; [13]the sixth to Bukkiah, his sons and his brothers, twelve; [14]the seventh to Jesarelah,[a] his sons and his brothers, twelve; [15]the eighth to Jeshaiah, his sons and his brothers, twelve; [16]the ninth to Mattaniah, his sons and his brothers, twelve; [17]the tenth to Shimei, his sons and his brothers, twelve; [18]the eleventh to Azarel, his sons and his brothers, twelve; [19]the twelfth to Hashabiah, his sons and his brothers, twelve; [20]to the thirteenth, Shubael, his sons and his brothers, twelve; [21]to the fourteenth, Mattithiah, his sons and his brothers, twelve; [22]to the fifteenth, to Jeremoth, his sons and his brothers, twelve; [23]to the sixteenth, to Hananiah, his sons and his brothers, twelve; [24]to the seventeenth, to Joshbekashah, his sons and his brothers, twelve; [25]to the eighteenth, to Hanani, his sons and his brothers, were the divisions of the gatekeepers among the Korahites and the sons of Merari.

The Treasurers, Officers, and Judges

20 And of the Levites, Ahijah had charge of the treasuries of the house of God and the treasuries of the dedicated gifts. 21 The sons of Ladan, the sons of the Gershonites belonging to Ladan, the heads of families belonging to Ladan the Gershonite: Jehieli.*

22 The sons of Jehieli, Zetham and his brother Joel, were in charge of the treasuries of the house of the Lord. 23 Of the Amramites, the Izharites, the Hebronites, and the Uzzielites: 24 Shebuel son of Gershom, son of Moses, was chief officer in charge of the treasuries. 25 His brothers: from Eliezer were his son Rehabiah, his son Jeshaiah, his son Joram, his son Zichri, and his son Shelomoth. 26 This Shelomoth and his brothers were in charge of all the treasuries of the dedicated gifts that King David, and the heads of families, and the officers of the thousands and the hundreds, and the commanders of the army, had dedicated. 27 From booty won in battles they dedicated gifts for the maintenance of the house of the Lord. 28 Also all that Samuel the seer, and Saul son of Kish, and Abner son of Ner, and Joab son of Zeruiah had dedicated—all dedicated gifts were in the care of Shelomoth* and his brothers.

29 Of the Izharites, Chenaniah and his sons were appointed to outside duties for Israel, as officers and judges. 30 Of the Hebronites, Hashabiah and his brothers, one thousand seven hundred men of ability, had the oversight of Israel west of the Jordan for all the work of the Lord and for the service of the king. 31 Of the Hebronites, Jerijah was chief of the Hebronites. (In the fortieth year of David's reign search was made, of whatever genealogy or family, and men of great ability among them were found at Jazer in Gilead.) 32 King David appointed him and his brothers, two thousand seven hundred men of ability, heads of families, to have the oversight of the Reubenites, the Gadites, and the half-tribe of the Manassites for everything pertaining to God and for the affairs of the king.

27 The Military Divisions

This is the list of the people of Israel, the heads of families, the commanders of the thousands and the hundreds, and their officers who served the king in all matters concerning the divisions that came and went, month after month throughout the year, each division numbering twenty-four thousand:

2 Jashobeam son of Zabdiel was in charge of the first division in the first month; in his division were twenty-four thousand. 3 He was

a The Hebrew text of verse 21 is confused *b* Gk Compare 26.28: Heb *Shelomith*

Untitled—© Michelle Jozwiak, 18

a descendant of Perez, and was chief of all the commanders of the army for the first month. 4Dodai the Ahohite was in charge of the division of the second month; Mikloth was the chief officer of his division. In his division were twenty-four thousand. 5The third commander, for the third month, was Benaiah son of the priest Jehoiada, as chief; in his division were twenty-four thousand. 6This is the Benaiah who was a mighty man of the Thirty and in command of the Thirty; his son Ammizabad was in charge of his division.*a* 7Asahel brother of Joab was fourth, for the fourth month, and his son Zebadiah after him; in his division were twenty-four thousand. 8The fifth commander, for the fifth month, was Shamhuth, the Izrahite; in his division were twenty-four thousand. 9Sixth, for the sixth month, was Ira son of Ikkesh the Tekoite; in his division were twenty-four thousand. 10Seventh, for the seventh month, was Helez the Pelonite, of the Ephraimites; in his division were twenty-four thousand. 11Eighth, for the eighth month, was Sibbecai the Hushathite, of the Zerahites; in his division were twenty-four thousand. 12Ninth, for the ninth month, was Abiezer of Anathoth, a Benjaminite; in his division were twenty-four thousand. 13Tenth, for the tenth month, was Maharai of Netophah, of the Zerahites; in his division were twenty-four thousand. 14Eleventh, for the eleventh month, was Benaiah of Pirathon, of the Ephraimites; in his division were twenty-four thousand. 15Twelfth, for the twelfth month, was Heldai the Netophathite, of Othniel; in his division were twenty-four thousand.

Leaders of Tribes

16 Over the tribes of Israel, for the Reubenites, Eliezer son of Zichri was chief officer; for the Simeonites, Shephatiah son of Maacah; 17for Levi, Hashabiah son of Kemuel; for Aaron, Zadok; 18for Judah, Elihu, one of David's brothers; for Issachar, Omri son of Michael; 19for Zebulun, Ishmaiah son of Obadiah; for Naphtali, Jerimoth son of Azriel; 20for the Ephraimites, Hoshea son of Azaziah; for the half-tribe of Manasseh, Joel son of Pedaiah;

21for the half-tribe of Manasseh in Gilead, Iddo son of Zechariah; for Benjamin, Jaasiel son of Abner; 22for Dan, Azarel son of Jeroham. These were the leaders of the tribes of Israel. 23David did not count those below twenty years of age, for the LORD had promised to make Israel as numerous as the stars of heaven. 24Joab son of Zeruiah began to count them, but did not finish; yet wrath came upon Israel for this, and the number was not entered into the account of the Annals of King David.

Other Civic Officials

25 Over the king's treasuries was Azmaveth son of Adiel. Over the treasuries in the country, in the cities, in the villages and in the towers, was Jonathan son of Uzziah. 26Over those who did the work of the field, tilling the soil, was Ezri son of Chelub. 27Over the vineyards was Shimei the Ramathite. Over the produce of the vineyards for the wine cellars was Zabdi the Shiphmite. 28Over the olive and sycamore trees in the Shephelah was Baal-hanan the Gederite. Over the stores of oil was Joash. 29Over the herds that pastured in Sharon was Shitrai the Sharonite. Over the herds in the valleys was Shaphat son of Adlai. 30Over the camels was Obil the Ishmaelite. Over the donkeys was Jehdeiah the Meronothite. Over the flocks was Jaziz the Hagrite. 31All these were stewards of King David's property.

32 Jonathan, David's uncle, was a counselor, being a man of understanding and a scribe; Jehiel son of Hachmoni attended the king's sons. 33Ahithophel was the king's counselor, and Hushai the Archite was the king's friend. 34After Ahithophel came Jehoiada son of Benaiah, and Abiathar. Joab was commander of the king's army.

28 Solomon Instructed to Build the Temple

David assembled at Jerusalem all the officials of Israel, the officials of the tribes, the officers of the divisions that served the king, the commanders of the thousands, the commanders of the hundreds, the stewards of all the property and cattle of the king and his sons, together with the palace officials, the mighty warriors, and all the warriors. 2Then King David rose to his feet and said: "Hear me, my brothers and my people. I had planned to build a house of rest for the ark of the covenant of the LORD, for the footstool of our God; and I made preparations for building. 3But God said to me, 'You shall not build a house for my name, for you are a warrior and have shed blood.' 4Yet the

---

a Gk Vg: Heb *Ammizabad was his division*

LORD God of Israel chose me from all my ancestral house to be king over Israel forever; for he chose Judah as leader, and in the house of Judah my father's house, and among my father's sons he took delight in making me king over all Israel. ⁵And of all my sons, for the LORD has given me many, he has chosen my son Solomon to sit upon the throne of the kingdom of the LORD over Israel. ⁶He said to me, 'It is your son Solomon who shall build my house and my courts, for I have chosen him to be a son to me, and I will be a father to him. ⁷I will establish his kingdom forever if he continues resolute in keeping my commandments and my ordinances, as he is today.' ⁸Now therefore in the sight of all Israel, the assembly of the LORD, and in the hearing of our God, observe and search out all the commandments of the LORD your God; that you may possess this good land, and leave it for an inheritance to your children after you forever.

9 "And you, my son Solomon, know the God of your father, and serve him with single mind and willing heart; for the LORD searches every mind, and understands every plan and thought. If you seek him, he will be found by you; but if you forsake him, he will abandon you forever. ¹⁰Take heed now, for the LORD has chosen you to build a house as the sanctuary; be strong, and act."

11 Then David gave his son Solomon the plan of the vestibule of the temple, and of its houses, its treasuries, its upper rooms, and its inner chambers, and of the room for the mercy seat;ᵃ ¹²and the plan of all that he had in mind: for the courts of the house of the LORD, all the surrounding chambers, the treasuries of the house of God, and the treasuries for dedicated gifts; ¹³for the divisions of the priests and of the Levites, and all the work of the service in the house of the LORD; for all the vessels for the service in the house of the LORD, ¹⁴the weight of gold for all golden vessels for each service, the weight of silver vessels for each service, ¹⁵the weight of the golden lampstands and their lamps, the weight of gold for each lampstand and its lamps, the weight of silver for a lampstand and its lamps, according to the use of each in the service, ¹⁶the weight of gold for each table for the rows of bread, the silver for the silver tables, ¹⁷and pure gold for the forks, the basins, and the cups; for the golden bowls and the weight of each; for the silver bowls and the weight of each; ¹⁸for the altar of incense made of refined gold, and its weight; also his plan for the golden chariot of the cherubim

that spread their wings and covered the ark of the covenant of the LORD.

19 "All this, in writing at the LORD's direction, he made clear to me—the plan of all the works."

20 David said further to his son Solomon, "Be strong and of good courage, and act. Do not be afraid or dismayed; for the LORD God, my God, is with you. He will not fail you or forsake you, until all the work for the service of the house of the LORD is finished. ²¹Here are the divisions of the priests and the Levites for all the service of the house of God; and with you in all the work will be every volunteer who has skill for any kind of service; also the officers and all the people will be wholly at your command."

29 Offerings for Building the Temple

King David said to the whole assembly, "My son Solomon, whom alone God has chosen, is young and inexperienced, and the work is great; for the templeᵇ will not be for mortals but for the LORD God. ²So I have provided for the house of my God, so far as I was able, the gold for the things of gold, the silver for the things of silver, and the bronze for the things of bronze, the iron for the things of iron, and wood for the things of wood, besides great quantities of onyx and stones for setting, antimony, colored stones, all sorts of precious stones, and marble in abundance. ³Moreover, in addition to all that I have provided for the holy house, I have a treasure of my own of gold and silver, and because of my devotion to the house of my God I give it to the house of my God: ⁴three thousand talents of gold, of the gold of Ophir, and seven thousand talents of refined silver, for overlaying the walls of the house, ⁵and for all the work to be done by artisans, gold for the things of gold and silver for the things of silver. Who then will offer willingly, consecrating themselves today to the LORD?"

6 Then the leaders of ancestral houses made their freewill offerings, as did also the leaders of the tribes, the commanders of the thousands and of the hundreds, and the officers over the king's work. ⁷They gave for the service of the house of God five thousand talents and ten thousand darics of gold, ten thousand talents of silver, eighteen thousand talents of bronze, and one hundred thousand talents of iron. ⁸Whoever had precious stones gave them to the treasury of the house of the LORD, into the care of Jehiel the Gershonite. ⁹Then the people rejoiced because these had

a Or the cover b Heb fortress

given willingly, for with single mind they had offered freely to the LORD; King David also rejoiced greatly.

David's Praise to God

10 Then David blessed the LORD in the presence of all the assembly; David said: "Blessed are you, O LORD, the God of our ancestor Israel, forever and ever. [11]Yours, O LORD, are the greatness, the power, the glory, the victory, and the majesty; for all that is in the heavens and on the earth is yours; yours is the kingdom, O LORD, and you are exalted as head above all. [12]Riches and honor come from you, and you rule over all. In your hand are power and might; and it is in your hand to make great and to give strength to all. [13]And now, our God, we give thanks to you and praise your glorious name.

14 "But who am I, and what is my people, that we should be able to make this freewill offering? For all things come from you, and of your own have we given you. [15]For we are aliens and transients before you, as were all our ancestors; our days on the earth are like a shadow, and there is no hope. [16]O LORD our God, all this abundance that we have provided for building you a house for your holy name comes from your hand and is all your own. [17]I know, my God, that you search the heart, and

take pleasure in uprightness; in the uprightness of my heart I have freely offered all these things, and now I have seen your people, who are present here, offering freely and joyously to you. [18]O LORD, the God of Abraham, Isaac, and Israel, our ancestors, keep forever such purposes and thoughts in the hearts of your people, and direct their hearts toward you. [19]Grant to my son Solomon that with single mind he may keep your commandments, your decrees, and your statutes, performing all of them, and that he may build the temple[a] for which I have made provision."

20 Then David said to the whole assembly, "Bless the LORD your God." And all the assembly blessed the LORD, the God of their ancestors, and bowed their heads and prostrated themselves before the LORD and the king. [21]On the next day they offered sacrifices and burnt offerings to the LORD, a thousand bulls, a thousand rams, and a thousand lambs, with their libations, and sacrifices in abundance for all Israel; [22]and they ate and drank before the LORD on that day with great joy.

Solomon Anointed King

They made David's son Solomon king a second time; they anointed him as the LORD's prince, and Zadok as priest. [23]Then Solomon

a Heb fortress

sat on the throne of the LORD, succeeding his father David as king; he prospered, and all Israel obeyed him. 24All the leaders and the mighty warriors, and also all the sons of King David, pledged their allegiance to King Solomon. 25The LORD highly exalted Solomon in the sight of all Israel, and bestowed upon him such royal majesty as had not been on any king before him in Israel.

Summary of David's Reign

26 Thus David son of Jesse reigned over all Israel. 27The period that he reigned over Israel was forty years; he reigned seven years in Hebron, and thirty-three years in Jerusalem. 28He died in a good old age, full of days, riches, and honor; and his son Solomon succeeded him. 29Now the acts of King David, from first to last, are written in the records of the seer Samuel, and in the records of the prophet Nathan, and in the records of the seer Gad, 30with accounts of all his rule and his might and of the events that befell him and Israel and all the kingdoms of the earth.

Unseen—© Lacy Bedol, 16

"Since I had *given myself* to
Jesus in order to please Him and
comfort Him, I must not oblige
Him to do *my will* instead of His."
—St. Thérèse of Lisieux

2 CHRONICLES

RETURNING HOME AGAIN

More Than Just "I'm Sorry"

The books of 1 and 2 Chronicles are similar to a homecoming. They were written for people who had lived in exile, away from their home for many years, wondering if they would ever see their land again.

Living away from home is painful. The memories of how things were or how they should be clash against the backdrop of how things are, creating a hunger and a yearning for home.

Repentance in the Bible means way more than merely feeling sorry for what you've done. *Shuv*, a Hebrew word for "repent," carries with it the idea of "returning." In this sense, to repent is to return, to come home again.

When God calls his people to repent in 2 Chronicles 7.11–18, he isn't just telling them to feel sorry for what they have done in the past. He's inviting them to come home again—to live the life of harmony with God they were created to live.

Perhaps you know what this yearning to be home is like. Perhaps you feel it is impossible to ever go "home" to God, that there's simply too much that has gone wrong. Repent. *Shuv*. Come home again. God is waiting.

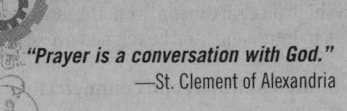

"Prayer is a conversation with God."
—St. Clement of Alexandria

WHO The author is not known for certain, but is usually called the Chronicler.

WHAT A historical account of the story of Israel from the reign of Solomon to the return from exile in Babylon to the land of Israel

WHEN The books of 1 and 2 Chronicles were part of a larger work, which may have included Ezra and Nehemiah, written ca. 450–400 B.C. The events in 1 and 2 Chronicles span the period from the start of recorded history to 538 B.C.

WHERE Israel

PATH OF DISCIPLESHIP

Jesus was eating dinner with his disciples one night when he said, "I am the way, and the truth, and the life. No one comes to the Father except through me" (John 14.6). Jesus made an incredibly profound statement here. He was saying that *he* was going to be the way to come home again. *If you want to live in harmony with God, then imitate the way I live.*

Just as God called his people to repent in 2 Chronicles 7.14, he calls us to turn from our old way of living and to live as Jesus did. Each year on Ash Wednesday, we are signed with ashes and hear the words "Repent, and believe in the good news" (Mark 1.15). It's our invitation to begin a Lenten journey back to God. Through prayer, fasting, and almsgiving (giving money or goods to the poor), we have a chance to reflect on our relationship with God and the Church as we prepare to celebrate our homecoming with the renewal of our baptismal promises on Easter.

SIGNS OF THE TIMES

Why did the author of Chronicles write the history over again? Isn't once enough? It seems as if he may have had two reasons. First, he retold the story not simply to repeat it endlessly, but to help the Israelites at that time to reinterpret faith for their new day and time.

New times, different cultures, progress in science and technology, to name a few things, call us to make something new of what has been given to us. But the new cannot be disconnected from the Church's history and tradition. Reading the "signs of the times" without the light of Scripture, Tradition, and Church history can hurt our faith more than help it.

Second, the writer of Chronicles placed great emphasis on the history of worship as a commitment and encounter between God and the people.

Without a community of prayer, faith becomes nothing more than what an individual values. The history of Israel, the early Church, and the Church today live this truth. Ours is not a "whatever floats your boat" type of faith; we assemble at liturgy not as individuals, but as a community. Without a people of faith, there is no faith.

1 Solomon Requests Wisdom

Solomon son of David established himself in his kingdom; the LORD his God was with him and made him exceedingly great.

2 Solomon summoned all Israel, the commanders of the thousands and of the hundreds, the judges, and all the leaders of all Israel, the heads of families. ³Then Solomon, and the whole assembly with him, went to the high place that was at Gibeon; for God's tent of meeting, which Moses the servant of the LORD had made in the wilderness, was there. ⁴(But David had brought the ark of God up from Kiriath-jearim to the place that David had prepared for it; for he had pitched a tent for it in Jerusalem.) ⁵Moreover the bronze altar that

Bezalel son of Uri, son of Hur, had made, was there in front of the tabernacle of the LORD. And Solomon and the assembly inquired at it. ⁶Solomon went up there to the bronze altar before the LORD, which was at the tent of meeting, and offered a thousand burnt offerings on it.

7 That night God appeared to Solomon, and said to him, "Ask what I should give you." ⁸Solomon said to God, "You have shown great and steadfast love to my father David, and have made me succeed him as king. ⁹O LORD God, let your promise to my father David now be fulfilled, for you have made me king over a people as numerous as the dust of the earth. ¹⁰Give me now wisdom and knowledge to go out and come in before this people, for who can rule this great people of yours?" ¹¹God answered Solomon, "Because this was in your heart, and you have not asked for possessions, wealth, honor, or the life of those who hate you, and have not even asked for long life, but have asked for wisdom and knowledge for yourself that you may rule my people over whom I have made you king, ¹²wisdom and knowledge are granted to you. I will also give you riches, possessions, and honor, such as none of the kings had who were before you, and none after you shall have the like." ¹³So Solomon came from*ᵃ* the high place at Gibeon, from the tent of meeting, to Jerusalem. And he reigned over Israel.

Solomon's Military and Commercial Activity

14 Solomon gathered together chariots and horses; he had fourteen hundred chariots and twelve thousand horses, which he stationed in the chariot cities and with the king in Jerusalem. ¹⁵The king made silver and gold as common in Jerusalem as stone, and he made cedar as plentiful as the sycamore of the Shephelah. ¹⁶Solomon's horses were imported from Egypt and Kue; the king's traders received them from Kue at the prevailing price. ¹⁷They imported from Egypt, and then exported, a chariot for six hundred shekels of silver, and a horse for one hundred fifty; so through them these were exported to all the kings of the Hittites and the kings of Aram.

2ᵇ Preparations for Building the Temple

Solomon decided to build a temple for the name of the LORD, and a royal palace for himself. ² ᶜ Solomon conscripted seventy thousand laborers and eighty thousand stonecutters in the hill country, with three thousand six hundred to oversee them.

a Gk Vg: Heb *to* *b* Ch 1.18 in Heb *c* Ch 2.1 in Heb

Alliance with Huram of Tyre

3 Solomon sent word to King Huram of Tyre: "Once you dealt with my father David and sent him cedar to build himself a house to live in. ⁴I am now about to build a house for the name of the LORD my God and dedicate it to him for offering fragrant incense before him, and for the regular offering of the rows of bread, and for burnt offerings morning and evening, on the sabbaths and the new moons and the appointed festivals of the LORD our God, as ordained forever for Israel. ⁵The house that I am about to build will be great, for our God is greater than other gods. ⁶But who is able to build him a house, since heaven, even highest heaven, cannot contain him? Who am I to build a house for him, except as a place to make offerings before him? ⁷So now send me an artisan skilled to work in gold, silver, bronze, and iron, and in purple, crimson, and blue fabrics, trained also in engraving, to join the skilled workers who are with me in Judah and Jerusalem, whom my father David provided. ⁸Send me also cedar, cypress, and algum timber from Lebanon, for I know that your servants are skilled in cutting Lebanon timber. My servants will work with your servants ⁹to prepare timber for me in abundance, for the house I am about to build will be great and wonderful. ¹⁰I will provide for your servants, those who cut the timber, twenty thousand cors of crushed wheat, twenty thousand cors of barley, twenty thousand baths*ᵈ* of wine, and twenty thousand baths of oil."

11 Then King Huram of Tyre answered in a letter that he sent to Solomon, "Because the LORD loves his people he has made you king over them." ¹²Huram also said, "Blessed be the LORD God of Israel, who made heaven and earth, who has given King David a wise son, endowed with discretion and understanding, who will build a temple for the LORD, and a royal palace for himself.

13 "I have dispatched Huram-abi, a skilled artisan, endowed with understanding, ¹⁴the son of one of the Danite women, his father a Tyrian. He is trained to work in gold, silver, bronze, iron, stone, and wood, and in purple, blue, and crimson fabrics and fine linen, and to do all sorts of engraving and execute any design that may be assigned him, with your artisans, the artisans of my lord, your father David. ¹⁵Now, as for the wheat, barley, oil, and wine, of which my lord has spoken, let him send them to his servants. ¹⁶We will cut whatever timber you need from Lebanon, and bring it to you as rafts by sea to Joppa; you will take it up to Jerusalem."

17 Then Solomon took a census of all the aliens who were residing in the land of Israel, after the census that his father David had taken; and there were found to be one hundred fifty-three thousand six hundred. ¹⁸Seventy thousand of them he assigned as laborers, eighty thousand as stonecutters in the hill country, and three thousand six hundred as overseers to make the people work.

3 Solomon Builds the Temple

Solomon began to build the house of the LORD in Jerusalem on Mount Moriah, where the LORD had appeared to his father David, at the place that David had designated, on the threshing floor of Ornan the Jebusite. ²He began to build on the second day of the second month of the fourth year of his reign. ³These are Solomon's measurements*ᵇ* for building the house of God: the length, in cubits of the old standard, was sixty cubits, and the width twenty cubits. ⁴The vestibule in front of the nave of the house was twenty cubits long, across the width of the house;*ᶜ* and its height was one hundred twenty cubits. He overlaid it on the inside with pure gold. ⁵The nave he lined with cypress, covered it with fine gold, and made palms and chains on it. ⁶He adorned the house with settings of precious stones. The gold was gold from Parvaim. ⁷So he lined the house with gold—its beams, its thresholds, its walls, and its doors; and he carved cherubim on the walls.

8 He made the most holy place; its length, corresponding to the width of the house, was twenty cubits, and its width was twenty cubits; he overlaid it with six hundred talents of fine gold. ⁹The weight of the nails was fifty shekels of gold. He overlaid the upper chambers with gold.

10 In the most holy place he made two carved cherubim and overlaid*ᵈ* them with gold. ¹¹The wings of the cherubim together extended twenty cubits: one wing of the one, five cubits long, touched the wall of the house, and its other wing, five cubits long, touched the wing of the other cherub; ¹²and of this cherub, one wing, five cubits long, touched the wall of the house, and the other wing, also five cubits long, was joined to the wing of the first cherub. ¹³The wings of these cherubim extended twenty cubits; the cherubim*ᵉ* stood on their feet, facing the nave. ¹⁴And Solomon*ᶠ* made the curtain of blue and purple and crimson fabrics and fine linen, and worked cherubim into it.

---

a A Hebrew measure of volume *b* Syr: Heb *foundations* *c* Compare 1 Kings 6.3: Meaning of Heb uncertain *d* Heb *they overlaid* *e* Heb *they* *f* Heb *he*

15 In front of the house he made two pillars thirty-five cubits high, with a capital of five cubits on the top of each. [16]He made encircling[a] chains and put them on the tops of the pillars; and he made one hundred pomegranates, and put them on the chains. [17]He set up the pillars in front of the temple, one on the right, the other on the left; the one on the right he called Jachin, and the one on the left, Boaz.

4 Furnishings of the Temple

He made an altar of bronze, twenty cubits long, twenty cubits wide, and ten cubits high. [2]Then he made the molten sea; it was round, ten cubits from rim to rim, and five cubits high. A line of thirty cubits would encircle it completely. [3]Under it were panels all around, each of ten cubits, surrounding the sea; there were two rows of panels, cast when it was cast. [4]It stood on twelve oxen, three facing north, three facing west, three facing south, and three facing east; the sea was set on them. The hindquarters of each were toward the inside. [5]Its thickness was a handbreadth; its rim was made like the rim of a cup, like the flower of a lily; it held three thousand baths.[b] [6]He also made ten basins in which to wash, and set five on the right side, and five on the left. In these they were to rinse what was used for the burnt offering. The sea was for the priests to wash in.

7 He made ten golden lampstands as prescribed, and set them in the temple, five on the south side and five on the north. [8]He also made ten tables and placed them in the temple, five on the right side and five on the left. And he made one hundred basins of gold. [9]He made the court of the priests, and the great court, and doors for the court; he overlaid their doors with bronze. [10]He set the sea at the southeast corner of the house.

11 And Huram made the pots, the shovels, and the basins. Thus Huram finished the work that he did for King Solomon on the house of God: [12]the two pillars, the bowls, and the two capitals on the top of the pillars; and the two latticeworks to cover the two bowls of the capitals that were on the top of the pillars; [13]the four hundred pomegranates for the two latticeworks, two rows of pomegranates for each latticework, to cover the two bowls of the capitals that were on the pillars. [14]He made the stands, the basins on the stands, [15]the one sea, and the twelve oxen underneath it. [16]The pots, the shovels, the forks, and all the equipment for these Huram-abi made of burnished bronze for King Solomon for the house of the LORD. [17]In the plain of the Jordan the king cast

a Cn: Heb in the inner sanctuary   b A Hebrew measure of volume them, in the clay ground between Succoth and Zeredah. [18]Solomon made all these things in great quantities, so that the weight of the bronze was not determined.

19 So Solomon made all the things that were in the house of God: the golden altar, the tables for the bread of the Presence, [20]the lampstands and their lamps of pure gold to burn before the inner sanctuary, as prescribed; [21]the flowers, the lamps, and the tongs, of purest gold; [22]the snuffers, basins, ladles, and firepans, of pure gold. As for the entrance to the temple: the inner doors to the most holy place and the doors of the nave of the temple were of gold.

5 Thus all the work that Solomon did for the house of the Lord was finished. Solomon brought in the things that his father David had dedicated, and stored the silver, the gold, and all the vessels in the treasuries of the house of God.

The Ark Brought into the Temple

2 Then Solomon assembled the elders of Israel and all the heads of the tribes, the leaders of the ancestral houses of the people of Israel, in Jerusalem, to bring up the ark of the covenant of the Lord out of the city of David, which is Zion. [3]And all the Israelites assembled before the king at the festival that is in the seventh month. [4]And all the elders of Israel came, and the Levites carried the ark. [5]So they brought up the ark, the tent of meeting, and all the holy vessels that were in the tent; the priests and the Levites brought them up. [6]King Solomon and all the congregation of Israel, who had assembled before him, were before the ark, sacrificing so many sheep and oxen that they could not be numbered or counted. [7]Then the priests brought the ark of the covenant of the Lord to its place, in the inner sanctuary of the house, in the most holy place, underneath the wings of the cherubim. [8]For the cherubim spread out their wings over the place of the ark, so that the cherubim made a covering above the ark and its poles. [9]The poles were so long that the ends of the poles were seen from the holy place in front of the inner sanctuary; but they could not be seen from outside; they are there to this day. [10]There was nothing in the ark except the two tablets that Moses put there at Horeb, where the Lord made a covenant[a] with the people of Israel after they came out of Egypt.

11 Now when the priests came out of the holy place (for all the priests who were present had sanctified themselves, without regard to their divisions), [12]all the levitical singers, Asaph, Heman, and Jeduthun, their sons and kindred, arrayed in fine linen, with cymbals, harps, and lyres, stood east of the altar with one hundred twenty priests who were trumpeters. [13]It was the duty of the trumpeters and singers to make themselves heard in unison in praise and thanksgiving to the Lord, and when the song was raised, with trumpets and cymbals and other musical instruments, in praise to the Lord,

"For he is good,
     for his steadfast love endures forever,"
the house, the house of the Lord, was filled with a cloud, [14]so that the priests could not stand to minister because of the cloud; for the glory of the Lord filled the house of God.

6 Dedication of the Temple
Then Solomon said, "The Lord has said that he would reside in thick darkness. [2]I have built you an exalted house, a place for you to reside in forever."

3 Then the king turned around and blessed all the assembly of Israel, while all the assembly of Israel stood. [4]And he said, "Blessed be the Lord, the God of Israel, who with his hand has fulfilled what he promised with his mouth to my father David, saying, [5]'Since the day that I brought my people out of the land of Egypt, I have not chosen a city from any of the tribes of Israel in which to build a house, so that my name might be there, and I chose no one as ruler over my people Israel; [6]but I have chosen Jerusalem in order that my name may be there, and I have chosen David to be over my people Israel.' [7]My father David had it in mind to build a house for the name of the Lord, the God of Israel. [8]But the Lord said to my father David, 'You did well to consider building a house for my name; [9]nevertheless you shall not build the house, but your son who shall be born to you shall build the house for my name.' [10]Now the Lord has fulfilled his promise that he made; for I have succeeded my father David, and sit on the throne of Israel, as the Lord promised, and have built the house for the name of the Lord, the God of Israel. [11]There I have set the ark, in which is the covenant of the Lord that he made with the people of Israel."

Solomon's Prayer of Dedication

12 Then Solomon[b] stood before the altar of the Lord in the presence of the whole assembly of Israel, and spread out his hands. [13]Solomon had made a bronze platform five cubits long, five cubits wide, and three cubits high, and had set it in the court; and he stood on it.

a Heb lacks *a covenant* b Heb *he*

Then he knelt on his knees in the presence of the whole assembly of Israel, and spread out his hands toward heaven. [14]He said, "O Lord, God of Israel, there is no God like you, in heaven or on earth, keeping covenant in steadfast love with your servants who walk before you with all their heart— [15]you who have kept for your servant, my father David, what you promised to him. Indeed, you promised with your mouth and this day have fulfilled with your hand. [16]Therefore, O Lord, God of Israel, keep for your servant, my father David, that which you promised him, saying, 'There shall never fail you a successor before me to sit on the throne of Israel, if only your children keep to their way, to walk in my law as you have walked before me.' [17]Therefore, O Lord, God of Israel, let your word be confirmed, which you promised to your servant David.

18 "But will God indeed reside with mortals on earth? Even heaven and the highest heaven cannot contain you, how much less this house that I have built! [19]Regard your servant's prayer and his plea, O Lord my God, heeding the cry and the prayer that your servant prays to you. [20]May your eyes be open day and night toward this house, the place where you promised to set your name, and may you heed the prayer that your servant prays toward this place. [21]And hear the plea of your servant and of your people Israel, when they pray toward this place; may you hear from heaven your dwelling place; hear and forgive.

22 "If someone sins against another and is required to take an oath and comes and swears before your altar in this house, [23]may you hear from heaven, and act, and judge your servants, repaying the guilty by bringing their conduct on their own head, and vindicating those who are in the right by rewarding them in accordance with their righteousness.

24 "When your people Israel, having sinned against you, are defeated before an enemy but turn again to you, confess your name, pray and plead with you in this house, [25]may you hear from heaven, and forgive the sin of your people Israel, and bring them again to the land that you gave to them and to their ancestors.

26 "When heaven is shut up and there is no rain because they have sinned against you, and then they pray toward this place, confess your name, and turn from their sin, because you punish them, [27]may you hear in heaven, forgive the sin of your servants, your people Israel, when you teach them the good way in which they should walk; and send down rain upon your land, which you have given to your people as an inheritance.

28 "If there is famine in the land, if there is plague, blight, mildew, locust, or caterpillar; if their enemies besiege them in any of the settlements of the lands; whatever suffering, whatever sickness there is; [29]whatever prayer, whatever plea from any individual or from all your people Israel, all knowing their own suffering and their own sorrows so that they stretch out their hands toward this house; [30]may you hear from heaven, your dwelling place, forgive, and render to all whose heart you know, according to all their ways, for only you know the human heart. [31]Thus may they fear you and walk in your ways all the days that they live in the land that you gave to our ancestors.

32 "Likewise when foreigners, who are not of your people Israel, come from a distant land because of your great name, and your mighty hand, and your outstretched arm, when they come and pray toward this house, [33]may you hear from heaven your dwelling place, and do whatever the foreigners ask of you, in order that all the peoples of the earth may know your name and fear you, as do your people Israel, and that they may know that your name has been invoked on this house that I have built.

34 "If your people go out to battle against their enemies, by whatever way you shall send them, and they pray to you toward this city that you have chosen and the house that I have built for your name, [35]then hear from heaven their prayer and their plea, and maintain their cause.

36 "If they sin against you—for there is no one who does not sin—and you are angry with them and give them to an enemy, so that they are carried away captive to a land far or near; [37]then if they come to their senses in the land to which they have been taken captive, and repent, and plead with you in the land of their captivity, saying, 'We have sinned, and have done wrong; we have acted wickedly'; [38]if they repent with all their heart and soul in the land of their captivity, to which they were taken captive, and pray toward their land, which you gave to their ancestors, the city that you have chosen, and the house that I have built for your name, [39]then hear from heaven your dwelling place their prayer and their pleas, maintain their cause and forgive your people who have sinned against you. [40]Now, O my God, let your eyes be open and your ears attentive to prayer from this place.

41 "Now rise up, O Lord God, and go to your
resting place,
you and the ark of your might.
Let your priests, O Lord God, be clothed
with salvation,
and let your faithful rejoice in your
goodness.

⁴² O Lᴏʀᴅ God, do not reject your anointed
one.
Remember your steadfast love for your
servant David."

7 Solomon Dedicates the Temple

When Solomon had ended his prayer, fire came down from heaven and consumed the burnt offering and the sacrifices; and the glory of the Lᴏʀᴅ filled the temple. ²The priests could not enter the house of the Lᴏʀᴅ, because the glory of the Lᴏʀᴅ filled the Lᴏʀᴅ's house. ³When all the people of Israel saw the fire come down and the glory of the Lᴏʀᴅ on the temple, they bowed down on the pavement with their faces to the ground, and worshiped and gave thanks to the Lᴏʀᴅ, saying,

"For he is good,
for his steadfast love endures forever."

4 Then the king and all the people offered sacrifice before the Lᴏʀᴅ. ⁵King Solomon offered as a sacrifice twenty-two thousand oxen and one hundred twenty thousand sheep. So the king and all the people dedicated the house of God. ⁶The priests stood at their posts; the Levites also, with the instruments for music to the Lᴏʀᴅ that King David had made for giving thanks to the Lᴏʀᴅ—for his steadfast love endures forever—whenever David offered praises by their ministry. Opposite them the priests sounded trumpets; and all Israel stood.

7 Solomon consecrated the middle of the court that was in front of the house of the Lᴏʀᴅ; for there he offered the burnt offerings and the fat of the offerings of well-being because the bronze altar Solomon had made could not hold the burnt offering and the grain offering and the fat parts.

8 At that time Solomon held the festival for seven days, and all Israel with him, a very great congregation, from Lebo-hamath to the Wadi of Egypt. ⁹On the eighth day they held a solemn assembly; for they had observed the dedication of the altar seven days and the festival seven days. ¹⁰On the twenty-third day of the seventh month he sent the people away to their homes, joyful and in good spirits because of the goodness that the Lᴏʀᴅ had shown to David and to Solomon and to his people Israel.

11 Thus Solomon finished the house of the Lᴏʀᴅ and the king's house; all that Solomon had planned to do in the house of the Lᴏʀᴅ and in his own house he successfully accomplished.

God's Second Appearance to Solomon

12 Then the Lᴏʀᴅ appeared to Solomon in the night and said to him: "I have heard your

a The word *you* in this verse is plural

Feelin' Smaller Every Day

Have you ever been to a magnificent building? Maybe a giant cathedral, a historic public building, or a museum? Or have you ever stood in an open field at night and seen the Milky Way? How does it make you feel? Small, maybe, or insignificant next to the millions of stars, years of world history, masses of people, tons of marble, or numbers of stories?

When Solomon finally finished building God's Temple, it was glorious. Read **2 Chronicles 7.1–10**, the story of the Temple's dedication. Imagine how the people attending the ceremony felt as they saw God's presence fill the Temple. What do you think their experiences were like?

Use some Creative Space in this Bible to write a fictional first-person account of the Temple's dedication. Describe the emotions and sensations that accompanied the ceremony. What can you learn about God's majesty from a fictional character sharing real human emotions? When you're finished, share your writing with others on **Learner.CalltoDiscipleship.com**.

prayer, and have chosen this place for myself as a house of sacrifice. ¹³When I shut up the heavens so that there is no rain, or command the locust to devour the land, or send pestilence among my people, ¹⁴if my people who are called by my name humble themselves, pray, seek my face, and turn from their wicked ways, then I will hear from heaven, and will forgive their sin and heal their land. ¹⁵Now my eyes will be open and my ears attentive to the prayer that is made in this place. ¹⁶For now I have chosen and consecrated this house so that my name may be there forever; my eyes and my heart will be there for all time. ¹⁷As for you, if you walk before me, as your father David walked, doing according to all that I have commanded you and keeping my statutes and my ordinances, ¹⁸then I will establish your royal throne, as I made covenant with your father David saying, 'You shall never lack a successor to rule over Israel.'

19 "But if you*ᵃ* turn aside and forsake my

statutes and my commandments that I have set before you, and go and serve other gods and worship them, [20]then I will pluck you[a] up from the land that I have given you;[a] and this house, which I have consecrated for my name, I will cast out of my sight, and will make it a proverb and a byword among all peoples. [21]And regarding this house, now exalted, everyone passing by will be astonished, and say, 'Why has the LORD done such a thing to this land and to this house?' [22]Then they will say, 'Because they abandoned the LORD the God of their ancestors who brought them out of the land of Egypt, and they adopted other gods, and worshiped them and served them; therefore he has brought all this calamity upon them.' "

8 Various Activities of Solomon

At the end of twenty years, during which Solomon had built the house of the LORD and his own house, [2]Solomon rebuilt the cities that Huram had given to him, and settled the people of Israel in them.

[3] Solomon went to Hamath-zobah, and captured it. [4]He built Tadmor in the wilderness and all the storage towns that he built in Hamath. [5]He also built Upper Beth-horon and Lower Beth-horon, fortified cities, with walls, gates, and bars, [6]and Baalath, as well as all Solomon's storage towns, and all the towns for his chariots, the towns for his cavalry, and whatever Solomon desired to build, in Jerusalem, in Lebanon, and in all the land of his dominion. [7]All the people who were left of the Hittites, the Amorites, the Perizzites, the Hivites, and the Jebusites, who were not of Israel, [8]from their descendants who were still left in the land, whom the people of Israel had not destroyed—these Solomon conscripted for forced labor, as is still the case today. [9]But of the people of Israel Solomon made no slaves for his work; they were soldiers, and his officers, the commanders of his chariotry and cavalry. [10]These were the chief officers of King Solomon, two hundred fifty of them, who exercised authority over the people.

[11] Solomon brought Pharaoh's daughter from the city of David to the house that he had built for her, for he said, "My wife shall not live in the house of King David of Israel, for the places to which the ark of the LORD has come are holy."

[12] Then Solomon offered up burnt offerings to the LORD on the altar of the LORD that he had built in front of the vestibule, [13]as the duty of each day required, offering according to the commandment of Moses for the sab-

a Heb them

baths, the new moons, and the three annual festivals—the festival of unleavened bread, the festival of weeks, and the festival of booths. [14]According to the ordinance of his father David, he appointed the divisions of the priests for their service, and the Levites for their offices of praise and ministry alongside the priests as the duty of each day required, and the gatekeepers in their divisions for the several gates; for so David the man of God had commanded. [15]They did not turn away from what the king had commanded the priests and Levites regarding anything at all, or regarding the treasuries.

16 Thus all the work of Solomon was accomplished from[a] the day the foundation of the house of the Lord was laid until the house of the Lord was finished completely.

17 Then Solomon went to Ezion-geber and Eloth on the shore of the sea, in the land of Edom. [18]Huram sent him, in the care of his servants, ships and servants familiar with the sea. They went to Ophir, together with the servants of Solomon, and imported from there four hundred fifty talents of gold and brought it to King Solomon.

9 Visit of the Queen of Sheba

When the queen of Sheba heard of the fame of Solomon, she came to Jerusalem to test him with hard questions, having a very great retinue and camels bearing spices and very much gold and precious stones. When she came to Solomon, she discussed with him all that was on her mind. [2]Solomon answered all her questions; there was nothing hidden from Solomon that he could not explain to her. [3]When the queen of Sheba had observed the wisdom of Solomon, the house that he had built, [4]the food of his table, the seating of his officials, and the attendance of his servants, and their clothing, his valets, and their clothing, and his burnt offerings[b] that he offered at the house of the Lord, there was no more spirit left in her.

5 So she said to the king, "The report was true that I heard in my own land of your accomplishments and of your wisdom, [6]but I did not believe the[c] reports until I came and my own eyes saw it. Not even half of the greatness of your wisdom had been told to me; you far surpass the report that I had heard. [7]Happy are your people! Happy are these your servants, who continually attend you and hear your wisdom! [8]Blessed be the Lord your God, who has delighted in you and set you on his throne as king for the Lord your God. Because your God loved Israel and would establish them forever, he has made you king over them, that you may execute justice and righteousness." [9]Then she gave the king one hundred twenty talents of gold, a very great quantity of spices, and precious stones: there were no spices such as those that the queen of Sheba gave to King Solomon.

10 Moreover the servants of Huram and the servants of Solomon who brought gold from Ophir brought algum wood and precious stones. [11]From the algum wood, the king made steps[d] for the house of the Lord and for the king's house, lyres also and harps for the singers; there never was seen the like of them before in the land of Judah.

12 Meanwhile King Solomon granted the queen of Sheba every desire that she expressed, well beyond what she had brought to the king. Then she returned to her own land, with her servants.

Solomon's Great Wealth

13 The weight of gold that came to Solomon in one year was six hundred sixty-six talents of gold, [14]besides that which the traders and merchants brought; and all the kings of Arabia and the governors of the land brought gold and silver to Solomon. [15]King Solomon made two hundred large shields of beaten gold; six hundred shekels of beaten gold went into each large shield. [16]He made three hundred shields of beaten gold; three hundred shekels of gold went into each shield; and the king put them in the House of the Forest of Lebanon. [17]The king also made a great ivory throne, and overlaid it with pure gold. [18]The throne had six steps and a footstool of gold, which were attached to the throne, and on each side of the seat were arm rests and two lions standing beside the arm rests, [19]while twelve lions were standing, one on each end of a step on the six steps. The like of it was never made in any kingdom. [20]All King Solomon's drinking vessels were of gold, and all the vessels of the House of the Forest of Lebanon were of pure gold; silver was not considered as anything in the days of Solomon. [21]For the king's ships went to Tarshish with the servants of Huram; once every three years the ships of Tarshish used to come bringing gold, silver, ivory, apes, and peacocks.[e]

22 Thus King Solomon excelled all the kings of the earth in riches and in wisdom. [23]All the kings of the earth sought the presence of Solomon to hear his wisdom, which God had put into his mind. [24]Every one of them brought a present, objects of silver and gold, garments, weaponry, spices, horses, and mules, so much

year by year. ²⁵Solomon had four thousand stalls for horses and chariots, and twelve thousand horses, which he stationed in the chariot cities and with the king in Jerusalem. ²⁶He ruled over all the kings from the Euphrates to the land of the Philistines, and to the border of Egypt. ²⁷The king made silver as common in Jerusalem as stone, and cedar as plentiful as the sycamore of the Shephelah. ²⁸Horses were imported for Solomon from Egypt and from all lands.

Death of Solomon

29 Now the rest of the acts of Solomon, from first to last, are they not written in the history of the prophet Nathan, and in the prophecy of Ahijah the Shilonite, and in the visions of the seer Iddo concerning Jeroboam son of Nebat? ³⁰Solomon reigned in Jerusalem over all Israel forty years. ³¹Solomon slept with his ancestors and was buried in the city of his father David; and his son Rehoboam succeeded him.

10 The Revolt against Rehoboam

Rehoboam went to Shechem, for all Israel had come to Shechem to make him king. ²When Jeroboam son of Nebat heard of it (for he was in Egypt, where he had fled from King Solomon), then Jeroboam returned from Egypt. ³They sent and called him; and Jeroboam and all Israel came and said to Rehoboam, ⁴"Your father made our yoke heavy. Now therefore lighten the hard service of your father and his heavy yoke that he placed on us, and we will serve you." ⁵He said to them, "Come to me again in three days." So the people went away.

6 Then King Rehoboam took counsel with the older men who had attended his father Solomon while he was still alive, saying, "How do you advise me to answer this people?" ⁷They answered him, "If you will be kind to this people and please them, and speak good words to them, then they will be your servants forever." ⁸But he rejected the advice that the older men gave him, and consulted the young men who had grown up with him and now attended him. ⁹He said to them, "What do you advise that we answer this people who have said to me, 'Lighten the yoke that your father put on us'?" ¹⁰The young men who had grown up with him said to him, "Thus should you speak to the people who said to you, 'Your father made our yoke heavy, but you must lighten it for us'; tell them, 'My little finger is thicker than my father's loins. ¹¹Now, whereas my father laid on you a heavy yoke, I will add to your yoke. My father disciplined you with whips, but I will discipline you with scorpions.' "

12 So Jeroboam and all the people came to Rehoboam the third day, as the king had said, "Come to me again the third day." ¹³The king answered them harshly. King Rehoboam rejected the advice of the older men; ¹⁴he spoke to them in accordance with the advice of the young men, "My father made your yoke heavy, but I will add to it; my father disciplined you with whips, but I will discipline you with scorpions." ¹⁵So the king did not listen to the people, because it was a turn of affairs brought about by God so that the Lord might fulfill his word, which he had spoken by Ahijah the Shilonite to Jeroboam son of Nebat.

16 When all Israel saw that the king would not listen to them, the people answered the king,

"What share do we have in David?
    We have no inheritance in the son of
        Jesse.
Each of you to your tents, O Israel!
    Look now to your own house, O David."

So all Israel departed to their tents. ¹⁷But Rehoboam reigned over the people of Israel who were living in the cities of Judah. ¹⁸When King Rehoboam sent Hadoram, who was taskmaster over the forced labor, the people of Israel stoned him to death. King Rehoboam hurriedly mounted his chariot to flee to Jerusalem. ¹⁹So Israel has been in rebellion against the house of David to this day.

11 Judah and Benjamin Fortified

When Rehoboam came to Jerusalem, he assembled one hundred eighty thousand chosen troops of the house of Judah and Benjamin to fight against Israel, to restore the kingdom to Rehoboam. ²But the word of the Lord came to Shemaiah the man of God: ³Say to King Rehoboam of Judah, son of Solomon, and to all Israel in Judah and Benjamin, ⁴"Thus says the Lord: You shall not go up or fight against your kindred. Let everyone return home, for this thing is from me." So they heeded the word of the Lord and turned back from the expedition against Jeroboam.

5 Rehoboam resided in Jerusalem, and he built cities for defense in Judah. ⁶He built up Bethlehem, Etam, Tekoa, ⁷Beth-zur, Soco, Adullam, ⁸Gath, Mareshah, Ziph, ⁹Adoraim, Lachish, Azekah, ¹⁰Zorah, Aijalon, and Hebron, fortified cities that are in Judah and in Benjamin. ¹¹He made the fortresses strong, and put commanders in them, and stores of food, oil, and wine. ¹²He also put large shields and spears in all the cities, and made them very strong. So he held Judah and Benjamin.

Priests and Levites Support Rehoboam

13 The priests and the Levites who were in all Israel presented themselves to him from

Waiting for Birds—© Charlotte Katheder, 16

all their territories. [14]The Levites had left their common lands and their holdings and had come to Judah and Jerusalem, because Jeroboam and his sons had prevented them from serving as priests of the LORD, [15]and had appointed his own priests for the high places, and for the goat-demons, and for the calves that he had made. [16]Those who had set their hearts to seek the LORD God of Israel came after them from all the tribes of Israel to Jerusalem to sacrifice to the LORD, the God of their ancestors. [17]They strengthened the kingdom of Judah, and for three years they made Rehoboam son of Solomon secure, for they walked for three years in the way of David and Solomon.

Rehoboam's Marriages

18 Rehoboam took as his wife Mahalath daughter of Jerimoth son of David, and of Abihail daughter of Eliab son of Jesse. [19]She bore him sons: Jeush, Shemariah, and Zaham. [20]After her he took Maacah daughter of Absalom, who bore him Abijah, Attai, Ziza, and Shelomith. [21]Rehoboam loved Maacah daughter of Absalom more than all his other wives and concubines (he took eighteen wives and sixty concubines, and became the father of twenty-eight sons and sixty daughters). [22]Rehoboam appointed Abijah son of Maacah as chief prince

among his brothers, for he intended to make him king. [23]He dealt wisely, and distributed some of his sons through all the districts of Judah and Benjamin, in all the fortified cities; he gave them abundant provisions, and found many wives for them.

12 Egypt Attacks Judah

When the rule of Rehoboam was established and he grew strong, he abandoned the law of the LORD, he and all Israel with him. [2]In the fifth year of King Rehoboam, because they had been unfaithful to the LORD, King Shishak of Egypt came up against Jerusalem [3]with twelve hundred chariots and sixty thousand cavalry. A countless army came with him from Egypt—Libyans, Sukkiim, and Ethiopians.[a] [4]He took the fortified cities of Judah and came as far as Jerusalem. [5]Then the prophet Shemaiah came to Rehoboam and to the officers of Judah, who had gathered at Jerusalem because of Shishak, and said to them, "Thus says the LORD: You abandoned me, so I have abandoned you to the hand of Shishak." [6]Then the officers of Israel and the king humbled themselves and said, "The LORD is in the right." [7]When the LORD saw that they humbled themselves, the word of the LORD came to Shemaiah, saying: "They have humbled themselves; I will not destroy them,

a Or *Nubians*; Heb *Cushites*

but I will grant them some deliverance, and my wrath shall not be poured out on Jerusalem by the hand of Shishak. [8]Nevertheless they shall be his servants, so that they may know the difference between serving me and serving the kingdoms of other lands."

9 So King Shishak of Egypt came up against Jerusalem; he took away the treasures of the house of the LORD and the treasures of the king's house; he took everything. He also took away the shields of gold that Solomon had made; [10]but King Rehoboam made in place of them shields of bronze, and committed them to the hands of the officers of the guard, who kept the door of the king's house. [11]Whenever the king went into the house of the LORD, the guard would come along bearing them, and would then bring them back to the guardroom. [12]Because he humbled himself the wrath of the LORD turned from him, so as not to destroy them completely; moreover, conditions were good in Judah.

Death of Rehoboam

13 So King Rehoboam established himself in Jerusalem and reigned. Rehoboam was forty-one years old when he began to reign; he reigned seventeen years in Jerusalem, the city that the LORD had chosen out of all the tribes of Israel to put his name there. His mother's name was Naamah the Ammonite. [14]He did evil, for he did not set his heart to seek the LORD.

15 Now the acts of Rehoboam, from first to last, are they not written in the records of the prophet Shemaiah and of the seer Iddo, recorded by genealogy? There were continual wars between Rehoboam and Jeroboam. [16]Rehoboam slept with his ancestors and was buried in the city of David; and his son Abijah succeeded him.

13 Abijah Reigns over Judah

In the eighteenth year of King Jeroboam, Abijah began to reign over Judah. [2]He reigned for three years in Jerusalem. His mother's name was Micaiah daughter of Uriel of Gibeah.

Now there was war between Abijah and Jeroboam. [3]Abijah engaged in battle, having an army of valiant warriors, four hundred thousand picked men; and Jeroboam drew up his line of battle against him with eight hundred thousand picked mighty warriors. [4]Then Abijah stood on the slope of Mount Zemaraim that is in the hill country of Ephraim, and said, "Listen to me, Jeroboam and all Israel! [5]Do you not know that the LORD God of Israel gave the kingship over Israel forever to David and his sons by a covenant of salt? [6]Yet Jeroboam son of Nebat, a servant of Solomon son of David, rose up and rebelled against his lord; [7]and certain worthless scoundrels gathered around him and defied Rehoboam son of Solomon, when Rehoboam was young and irresolute and could not withstand them.

8 "And now you think that you can withstand the kingdom of the LORD in the hand of the sons of David, because you are a great multitude and have with you the golden calves that Jeroboam made as gods for you. [9]Have you not driven out the priests of the LORD, the descendants of Aaron, and the Levites, and made priests for yourselves like the peoples of other lands? Whoever comes to be consecrated with a young bull or seven rams becomes a priest of what are no gods. [10]But as for us, the LORD is our God, and we have not abandoned him. We have priests ministering to the LORD who are descendants of Aaron, and Levites for their service. [11]They offer to the LORD every morning and every evening burnt offerings and fragrant incense, set out the rows of bread on the table of pure gold, and care for the golden lampstand so that its lamps may burn every evening; for we keep the charge of the LORD our God, but you have abandoned him. [12]See, God is with us at our head, and his priests have their battle trumpets to sound the call to battle against you. O Israelites, do not fight against the LORD, the God of your ancestors; for you cannot succeed."

13 Jeroboam had sent an ambush around to come on them from behind; thus his troops[a] were in front of Judah, and the ambush was behind them. [14]When Judah turned, the battle was in front of them and behind them. They cried out to the LORD, and the priests blew the trumpets. [15]Then the people of Judah raised the battle shout. And when the people of Judah shouted, God defeated Jeroboam and all Israel before Abijah and Judah. [16]The Israelites fled before Judah, and God gave them into their hands. [17]Abijah and his army defeated them with great slaughter; five hundred thousand picked men of Israel fell slain. [18]Thus the Israelites were subdued at that time, and the people of Judah prevailed, because they relied on the LORD, the God of their ancestors. [19]Abijah pursued Jeroboam, and took cities from him: Bethel with its villages and Jeshanah with its villages and Ephron[b] with its villages. [20]Jeroboam did not recover his power in the days of Abijah; the LORD struck him down, and he died. [21]But Abijah grew strong. He took four-

teen wives, and became the father of twenty-two sons and sixteen daughters. ²²The rest of the acts of Abijah, his behavior and his deeds, are written in the story of the prophet Iddo.

14ᵃ Asa Reigns

So Abijah slept with his ancestors, and they buried him in the city of David. His son Asa succeeded him. In his days the land had rest for ten years. ²ᵇ Asa did what was good and right in the sight of the LORD his God. ³He took away the foreign altars and the high places, broke down the pillars, hewed down the sacred poles,ᶜ ⁴and commanded Judah to seek the LORD, the God of their ancestors, and to keep the law and the commandment. ⁵He also removed from all the cities of Judah the high places and the incense altars. And the kingdom had rest under him. ⁶He built fortified cities in Judah while the land had rest. He had no war in those years, for the LORD gave him peace. ⁷He said to Judah, "Let us build these cities, and surround them with walls and towers, gates and bars; the land is still ours because we have sought the LORD our God; we have sought him, and he has given us peace on every side." So they built and prospered. ⁸Asa had an army of three hundred thousand from Judah, armed with large shields and spears, and two hundred eighty thousand troops from Benjamin who carried shields and drew bows; all these were mighty warriors.

Ethiopian Invasion Repulsed

9 Zerah the Ethiopianᵈ came out against them with an army of a million men and three hundred chariots, and came as far as Mareshah. ¹⁰Asa went out to meet him, and they drew up their lines of battle in the valley of Zephathah at Mareshah. ¹¹Asa cried to the LORD his God, "O LORD, there is no difference for you between helping the mighty and the weak. Help us, O LORD our God, for we rely on you, and in your name we have come against this multitude. O LORD, you are our God; let no mortal prevail against you." ¹²So the LORD defeated the Ethiopiansᵉ before Asa and before Judah, and the Ethiopiansᵉ fled. ¹³Asa and the army with him pursued them as far as Gerar, and the Ethiopiansᵉ fell until no one remained alive; for they were broken before the LORD and his army. The people of Judahᶠ carried away a great quantity of booty. ¹⁴They defeated all the cities around Gerar, for the fear of the LORD was on them. They plundered all the cities; for there was much plunder in them. ¹⁵They also attacked the tents of those who had livestock,ᵍ

> "If the Christian church loses this generation, it will be not because we didn't entertain them, but because we didn't dare them...didn't actually challenge them to think about how they live."
>
> —Shane Claiborne, *The Irresistible Revolution*

and carried away sheep and goats in abundance, and camels. Then they returned to Jerusalem.

15

The spirit of God came upon Azariah son of Oded. ²He went out to meet Asa and said to him, "Hear me, Asa, and all Judah and Benjamin: The LORD is with you, while you are with him. If you seek him, he will be found by you, but if you abandon him, he will abandon you. ³For a long time Israel was without the true God, and without a teaching priest, and without law; ⁴but when in their distress they turned to the LORD, the God of Israel, and sought him, he was found by them. ⁵In those times it was not safe for anyone to go or come, for great disturbances afflicted all the inhabitants of the lands. ⁶They were broken in pieces, nation against nation and city against city, for God troubled them with every sort of distress. ⁷But you, take courage! Do not let your hands be weak, for your work shall be rewarded."

8 When Asa heard these words, the prophecy of Azariah son of Oded,ʰ he took courage, and put away the abominable idols from all the land of Judah and Benjamin and from the towns that he had taken in the hill country of Ephraim. He repaired the altar of the LORD that was in front of the vestibule of the house of the LORD.ⁱ ⁹He gathered all Judah and Benjamin, and those from Ephraim, Manasseh, and Simeon who were residing as aliens with them, for great numbers had deserted to him from Israel when they saw that the LORD his God was with him. ¹⁰They were gathered at Jerusalem in the third month of the fifteenth year of the reign of Asa. ¹¹They sacrificed to the LORD on that day, from the booty that they had brought, seven hundred oxen and seven thousand sheep. ¹²They entered into a covenant to seek the LORD, the God of their ancestors, with all their heart and with all their soul. ¹³Whoever would not seek the LORD, the God of Israel, should be put to death, whether young or old, man or woman. ¹⁴They took an oath to the

---

a Ch 13.23 in Heb b Ch 14.1 in Heb c Heb *Asherim* d Or *Nubian*; Heb *Cushite* e Or *Nubians*; Heb *Cushites* f Heb *They* g Meaning of Heb uncertain h Compare Syr Vg: Heb *the prophecy, the prophet Obed* i Heb *the vestibule of the LORD*

LORD with a loud voice, and with shouting, and with trumpets, and with horns. [15]All Judah rejoiced over the oath; for they had sworn with all their heart, and had sought him with their whole desire, and he was found by them, and the LORD gave them rest all around.

16 King Asa even removed his mother Maacah from being queen mother because she had made an abominable image for Asherah. Asa cut down her image, crushed it, and burned it at the Wadi Kidron. [17]But the high places were not taken out of Israel. Nevertheless the heart of Asa was true all his days. [18]He brought into the house of God the votive gifts of his father and his own votive gifts—silver, gold, and utensils. [19]And there was no more war until the thirty-fifth year of the reign of Asa.

16 Alliance with Aram Condemned

In the thirty-sixth year of the reign of Asa, King Baasha of Israel went up against Judah, and built Ramah, to prevent anyone from going out or coming into the territory of[a] King Asa of Judah. [2]Then Asa took silver and gold from the treasures of the house of the LORD and the king's house, and sent them to King Ben-hadad of Aram, who resided in Damascus, saying, [3]"Let there be an alliance between me and you, like that between my father and your father; I am sending to you silver and gold; go, break your alliance with King Baasha of Israel, so that he may withdraw from me." [4]Ben-hadad listened to King Asa, and sent the commanders of his armies against the cities of Israel. They conquered Ijon, Dan, Abel-maim, and all the store-cities of Naphtali. [5]When Baasha heard of it, he stopped building Ramah, and let his work cease. [6]Then King Asa brought all Judah, and they carried away the stones of Ramah and its timber, with which Baasha had been building, and with them he built up Geba and Mizpah.

7 At that time the seer Hanani came to King Asa of Judah, and said to him, "Because you relied on the king of Aram, and did not rely on the LORD your God, the army of the king of Aram has escaped you. [8]Were not the Ethiopians[b] and the Libyans a huge army with exceedingly many chariots and cavalry? Yet because you relied on the LORD, he gave them into your hand. [9]For the eyes of the LORD range throughout the entire earth, to strengthen those whose heart is true to him. You have done foolishly in this; for from now on you will have wars." [10]Then Asa was angry with the seer, and put him in the stocks, in prison, for he was in a rage with him

because of this. And Asa inflicted cruelties on some of the people at the same time.

Asa's Disease and Death

11 The acts of Asa, from first to last, are written in the Book of the Kings of Judah and Israel. [12]In the thirty-ninth year of his reign Asa was diseased in his feet, and his disease became severe; yet even in his disease he did not seek the LORD, but sought help from physicians. [13]Then Asa slept with his ancestors, dying in the forty-first year of his reign. [14]They buried him in the tomb that he had hewn out for himself in the city of David. They laid him on a bier that had been filled with various kinds of spices prepared by the perfumer's art; and they made a very great fire in his honor.

17 Jehoshaphat's Reign

His son Jehoshaphat succeeded him, and strengthened himself against Israel. [2]He placed forces in all the fortified cities of Judah, and set garrisons in the land of Judah, and in the cities of Ephraim that his father Asa had taken. [3]The LORD was with Jehoshaphat, because he walked in the earlier ways of his father;[c] he did not seek the Baals, [4]but sought the God of his father and walked in his commandments, and not according to the ways of Israel. [5]Therefore the LORD established the kingdom in his hand. All Judah brought tribute to Jehoshaphat, and he had great riches and honor. [6]His heart was courageous in the ways of the LORD; and furthermore he removed the high places and the sacred poles[d] from Judah.

7 In the third year of his reign he sent his officials, Ben-hail, Obadiah, Zechariah, Nethanel, and Micaiah, to teach in the cities of Judah. [8]With them were the Levites, Shemaiah, Nethaniah, Zebadiah, Asahel, Shemiramoth, Jehonathan, Adonijah, Tobijah, and Tobadonijah; and with these Levites, the priests Elishama and Jehoram. [9]They taught in Judah, having the book of the law of the LORD with them; they went around through all the cities of Judah and taught among the people.

10 The fear of the LORD fell on all the kingdoms of the lands around Judah, and they did not make war against Jehoshaphat. [11]Some of the Philistines brought Jehoshaphat presents, and silver for tribute; and the Arabs also brought him seven thousand seven hundred rams and seven thousand seven hundred male goats. [12]Jehoshaphat grew steadily greater. He built fortresses and storage cities in Judah. [13]He carried out great works in the cities of Judah. He had soldiers, mighty warriors, in

a Heb lacks the territory of b Or Nubians; Heb Cushites c Another reading is his father David d Heb Asherim

Jerusalem. ¹⁴This was the muster of them by ancestral houses: Of Judah, the commanders of the thousands: Adnah the commander, with three hundred thousand mighty warriors, ¹⁵and next to him Jehohanan the commander, with two hundred eighty thousand, ¹⁶and next to him Amasiah son of Zichri, a volunteer for the service of the Lord, with two hundred thousand mighty warriors. ¹⁷Of Benjamin: Eliada, a mighty warrior, with two hundred thousand armed with bow and shield, ¹⁸and next to him Jehozabad with one hundred eighty thousand armed for war. ¹⁹These were in the service of the king, besides those whom the king had placed in the fortified cities throughout all Judah.

18 Micaiah Predicts Failure

Now Jehoshaphat had great riches and honor; and he made a marriage alliance with Ahab. ²After some years he went down to Ahab in Samaria. Ahab slaughtered an abundance of sheep and oxen for him and for the people who were with him, and induced him to go up against Ramoth-gilead. ³King Ahab of Israel said to King Jehoshaphat of Judah, "Will you go with me to Ramoth-gilead?" He answered him, "I am with you, my people are your people. We will be with you in the war."

4 But Jehoshaphat also said to the king of Israel, "Inquire first for the word of the Lord." ⁵Then the king of Israel gathered the prophets together, four hundred of them, and said to them, "Shall we go to battle against Ramoth-gilead, or shall I refrain?" They said, "Go up; for God will give it into the hand of the king." ⁶But Jehoshaphat said, "Is there no other prophet of the Lord here of whom we may inquire?" ⁷The king of Israel said to Jehoshaphat, "There is still one other by whom we may inquire of the Lord, Micaiah son of Imlah; but I hate him, for he never prophesies anything favorable about me, but only disaster." Jehoshaphat said, "Let the king not say such a thing." ⁸Then the king of Israel summoned an officer and said, "Bring quickly Micaiah son of Imlah." ⁹Now the king of Israel and King Jehoshaphat of Judah were sitting on their thrones, arrayed in their robes; and they were sitting at the threshing floor at the entrance of the gate of Samaria; and all the prophets were prophesying before them. ¹⁰Zedekiah son of Chenaanah made for himself horns of iron, and he said, "Thus says the Lord: With these you shall gore the Arameans until they are destroyed." ¹¹All the prophets were prophesying the same and saying, "Go up

a Heb *he*

to Ramoth-gilead and triumph; the Lord will give it into the hand of the king."

12 The messenger who had gone to summon Micaiah said to him, "Look, the words of the prophets with one accord are favorable to the king; let your word be like the word of one of them, and speak favorably." ¹³But Micaiah said, "As the Lord lives, whatever my God says, that I will speak."

14 When he had come to the king, the king said to him, "Micaiah, shall we go to Ramoth-gilead to battle, or shall I refrain?" He answered, "Go up and triumph; they will be given into your hand." ¹⁵But the king said to him, "How many times must I make you swear to tell me nothing but the truth in the name of the Lord?" ¹⁶Then Micaiah*ᵃ* said, "I saw all Israel scattered on the mountains, like sheep with-

Defeat and Death of Ahab

28 So the king of Israel and King Jehoshaphat of Judah went up to Ramoth-gilead. 29The king of Israel said to Jehoshaphat, "I will disguise myself and go into battle, but you wear your robes." So the king of Israel disguised himself, and they went into battle. 30Now the king of Aram had commanded the captains of his chariots, "Fight with no one small or great, but only with the king of Israel." 31When the captains of the chariots saw Jehoshaphat, they said, "It is the king of Israel." So they turned to fight against him; and Jehoshaphat cried out, and the LORD helped him. God drew them away from him, 32for when the captains of the chariots saw that it was not the king of Israel, they turned back from pursuing him. 33But a certain man drew his bow and unknowingly struck the king of Israel between the scale armor and the breastplate; so he said to the driver of his chariot, "Turn around, and carry me out of the battle, for I am wounded." 34The battle grew hot that day, and the king of Israel propped himself up in his chariot facing the Arameans until evening; then at sunset he died.

19 King Jehoshaphat of Judah returned in safety to his house in Jerusalem. 2Jehu son of Hanani the seer went out to meet him and said to King Jehoshaphat, "Should you help the wicked and love those who hate the LORD? Because of this, wrath has gone out against you from the LORD. 3Nevertheless, some good is found in you, for you destroyed the sacred poles[b] out of the land, and have set your heart to seek God."

The Reforms of Jehoshaphat

4 Jehoshaphat resided at Jerusalem; then he went out again among the people, from Beer-sheba to the hill country of Ephraim, and brought them back to the LORD, the God of their ancestors. 5He appointed judges in the land in all the fortified cities of Judah, city by city, 6and said to the judges, "Consider what you are doing, for you judge not on behalf of human beings but on the LORD's behalf; he is with you in giving judgment. 7Now, let the fear of the LORD be upon you; take care what you do, for there is no perversion of justice with the LORD our God, or partiality, or taking of bribes."

8 Moreover in Jerusalem Jehoshaphat appointed certain Levites and priests and heads of families of Israel, to give judgment for the LORD and to decide disputed cases. They had their seat at Jerusalem. 9He charged them: "This is how you shall act: in the fear of the LORD, in faithfulness, and with your whole

out a shepherd; and the LORD said, 'These have no master; let each one go home in peace.' " 17The king of Israel said to Jehoshaphat, "Did I not tell you that he would not prophesy anything favorable about me, but only disaster?"

18 Then Micaiah[a] said, "Therefore hear the word of the LORD: I saw the LORD sitting on his throne, with all the host of heaven standing to the right and to the left of him. 19And the LORD said, 'Who will entice King Ahab of Israel, so that he may go up and fall at Ramoth-gilead?' Then one said one thing, and another said another, 20until a spirit came forward and stood before the LORD, saying, 'I will entice him.' The LORD asked him, 'How?' 21He replied, 'I will go out and be a lying spirit in the mouth of all his prophets.' Then the LORD[a] said, 'You are to entice him, and you shall succeed; go out and do it.' 22So you see, the LORD has put a lying spirit in the mouth of these your prophets; the LORD has decreed disaster for you."

23 Then Zedekiah son of Chenaanah came up to Micaiah, slapped him on the cheek, and said, "Which way did the spirit of the LORD pass from me to speak to you?" 24Micaiah replied, "You will find out on that day when you go in to hide in an inner chamber." 25The king of Israel then ordered, "Take Micaiah, and return him to Amon the governor of the city and to Joash the king's son; 26and say, 'Thus says the king: Put this fellow in prison, and feed him on reduced rations of bread and water until I return in peace.' " 27Micaiah said, "If you return in peace, the LORD has not spoken by me." And he said, "Hear, you peoples, all of you!"

a Heb *he* *b* Heb *Asheroth*

heart; ¹⁰whenever a case comes to you from your kindred who live in their cities, concerning bloodshed, law or commandment, statutes or ordinances, then you shall instruct them, so that they may not incur guilt before the LORD and wrath may not come on you and your kindred. Do so, and you will not incur guilt. ¹¹See, Amariah the chief priest is over you in all matters of the LORD; and Zebadiah son of Ishmael, the governor of the house of Judah, in all the king's matters; and the Levites will serve you as officers. Deal courageously, and may the LORD be with the good!"

20 Invasion from the East

After this the Moabites and Ammonites, and with them some of the Meunites,ᵃ came against Jehoshaphat for battle. ²Messengersᵇ came and told Jehoshaphat, "A great multitude is coming against you from Edom,ᶜ from beyond the sea; already they are at Hazazon-tamar" (that is, En-gedi). ³Jehoshaphat was afraid; he set himself to seek the LORD, and proclaimed a fast throughout all Judah. ⁴Judah assembled to seek help from the LORD; from all the towns of Judah they came to seek the LORD.

Jehoshaphat's Prayer and Victory

5 Jehoshaphat stood in the assembly of Judah and Jerusalem, in the house of the LORD, before the new court, ⁶and said, "O LORD, God of our ancestors, are you not God in heaven? Do you not rule over all the kingdoms of the nations? In your hand are power and might, so that no one is able to withstand you. ⁷Did you not, O our God, drive out the inhabitants of this land before your people Israel, and give it forever to the descendants of your friend Abraham? ⁸They have lived in it, and in it have built you a sanctuary for your name, saying, ⁹'If disaster comes upon us, the sword, judgment,ᵈ or pestilence, or famine, we will stand before this house, and before you, for your name is in this house, and cry to you in our distress, and you will hear and save.' ¹⁰See now, the people of Ammon, Moab, and Mount Seir, whom you would not let Israel invade when they came from the land of Egypt, and whom they avoided and did not destroy— ¹¹they reward us by coming to drive us out of your possession that you have given us to inherit. ¹²O our God, will you not execute judgment upon them? For we are powerless against this great multitude that is coming against us. We do not know what to do, but our eyes are on you."

13 Meanwhile all Judah stood before the LORD, with their little ones, their wives, and their children. ¹⁴Then the spirit of the LORD came upon Jahaziel son of Zechariah, son of Benaiah, son of Jeiel, son of Mattaniah, a Levite of the sons of Asaph, in the middle of the assembly. ¹⁵He said, "Listen, all Judah and inhabitants of Jerusalem, and King Jehoshaphat: Thus says the LORD to you: 'Do not fear or be dismayed at this great multitude; for the battle is not yours but God's. ¹⁶Tomorrow go down against them; they will come up by the ascent of Ziz; you will find them at the end of the valley, before the wilderness of Jeruel. ¹⁷This battle is not for you to fight; take your position, stand still, and see the victory of the LORD on your behalf, O Judah and Jerusalem.' Do not fear or be dismayed; tomorrow go out against them, and the LORD will be with you."

18 Then Jehoshaphat bowed down with his face to the ground, and all Judah and the inhabitants of Jerusalem fell down before the LORD, worshiping the LORD. ¹⁹And the Levites, of the Kohathites and the Korahites, stood up to praise the LORD, the God of Israel, with a very loud voice.

20 They rose early in the morning and went out into the wilderness of Tekoa; and as they went out, Jehoshaphat stood and said, "Listen to me, O Judah and inhabitants of Jerusalem! Believe in the LORD your God and you will be established; believe his prophets." ²¹When he had taken counsel with the people, he appointed those who were to sing to the LORD and praise him in holy splendor, as they went before the army, saying,

"Give thanks to the LORD,
    for his steadfast love endures forever."

²²As they began to sing and praise, the LORD set an ambush against the Ammonites, Moab, and Mount Seir, who had come against Judah, so that they were routed. ²³For the Ammonites and Moab attacked the inhabitants of Mount Seir, destroying them utterly; and when they had made an end of the inhabitants of Seir, they all helped to destroy one another.

24 When Judah came to the watchtower of the wilderness, they looked toward the multitude; they were corpses lying on the ground; no one had escaped. ²⁵When Jehoshaphat and his people came to take the booty from them, they found livestockᵉ in great numbers, goods, clothing, and precious things, which they took for themselves until they could carry no more. They spent three days taking the booty, because of its abundance. ²⁶On the fourth day they assembled in the Valley of Beracah, for there they blessed the LORD; therefore that place has been called the Valley of Beracahᶠ to

---

a Compare 26.7: Heb *Ammonites* b Heb *They* c One Ms: MT *Aram* d Or *the sword of judgment* e Gk: Heb *among them* f That is *Blessing*

REALITY ✓

PROJECT RACHEL

All of the talk in **2 Chronicles** about God wanting us to "come home" might be hard to believe—especially if we think that something we've done is unforgivable. Maybe you or someone you know has had an abortion and feels far away from God—maybe grieving, ashamed, or embarrassed. The Church recognizes the enormous destruction caused by abortion—for the unborn child, the mother, the father, family, friends, and medical personnel. That's why the Church speaks in support of life and has established Project Rachel.

Project Rachel's mission is to provide healing and hope for those who have been involved in an abortion. Through spiritual and psychological counseling, support groups, and retreats, the Church offers healing and the invitation to come home again. To find out more, log on to **Learner.CalltoDiscipleship.com**.

this day. ²⁷Then all the people of Judah and Jerusalem, with Jehoshaphat at their head, returned to Jerusalem with joy, for the LORD had enabled them to rejoice over their enemies. ²⁸They came to Jerusalem, with harps and lyres and trumpets, to the house of the LORD. ²⁹The fear of God came on all the kingdoms of the countries when they heard that the LORD had fought against the enemies of Israel. ³⁰And the realm of Jehoshaphat was quiet, for his God gave him rest all around.

The End of Jehoshaphat's Reign

31 So Jehoshaphat reigned over Judah. He was thirty-five years old when he began to reign; he reigned twenty-five years in Jerusalem. His mother's name was Azubah daughter of Shilhi. ³²He walked in the way of his father Asa and did not turn aside from it, doing what was right in the sight of the LORD. ³³Yet the high places were not removed; the people had not yet set their hearts upon the God of their ancestors.

34 Now the rest of the acts of Jehoshaphat, from first to last, are written in the Annals of Jehu son of Hanani, which are recorded in the Book of the Kings of Israel.

35 After this King Jehoshaphat of Judah joined with King Ahaziah of Israel, who did wickedly. ³⁶He joined him in building ships to go to Tarshish; they built the ships in Ezion-geber. ³⁷Then Eliezer son of Dodavahu of Mareshah prophesied against Jehoshaphat, saying, "Because you have joined with Ahaziah, the LORD will destroy what you have made." And the ships were wrecked and were not able to go to Tarshish.

21 Jehoram's Reign

Jehoshaphat slept with his ancestors and was buried with his ancestors in the city of David; his son Jehoram succeeded him. ²He had brothers, the sons of Jehoshaphat: Azariah, Jehiel, Zechariah, Azariah, Michael, and Shephatiah; all these were the sons of King Jehoshaphat of Judah.ᵃ ³Their father gave them many gifts, of silver, gold, and valuable possessions, together with fortified cities in Judah; but he gave the kingdom to Jehoram, because he was the firstborn. ⁴When Jehoram had ascended the throne of his father and was established, he put all his brothers to the sword, and also some of the officials of Israel. ⁵Jehoram was thirty-two years old when he began to reign; he reigned eight years in Jerusalem. ⁶He walked in the way of the kings of Israel, as the house of Ahab had done; for the daughter of Ahab was his wife. He did what was evil in the sight of the LORD. ⁷Yet the LORD would not destroy the house of David because of the covenant that he had made with David, and since he had promised to give a lamp to him and to his descendants forever.

Revolt of Edom

8 In his days Edom revolted against the rule of Judah and set up a king of their own. ⁹Then Jehoram crossed over with his commanders and all his chariots. He set out by night and attacked the Edomites, who had surrounded him and his chariot commanders. ¹⁰So Edom has been in revolt against the rule of Judah to this day. At that time Libnah also revolted against his rule, because he had forsaken the LORD, the God of his ancestors.

Elijah's Letter

11 Moreover he made high places in the hill country of Judah, and led the inhabitants of Jerusalem into unfaithfulness, and made Judah go astray. ¹²A letter came to him from the

a Gk Syr: Heb *Israel*

prophet Elijah, saying: "Thus says the LORD, the God of your father David: Because you have not walked in the ways of your father Jehoshaphat or in the ways of King Asa of Judah, [13]but have walked in the way of the kings of Israel, and have led Judah and the inhabitants of Jerusalem into unfaithfulness, as the house of Ahab led Israel into unfaithfulness, and because you also have killed your brothers, members of your father's house, who were better than yourself, [14]see, the LORD will bring a great plague on your people, your children, your wives, and all your possessions, [15]and you yourself will have a severe sickness with a disease of your bowels, until your bowels come out, day after day, because of the disease."

16 The LORD aroused against Jehoram the anger of the Philistines and of the Arabs who are near the Ethiopians.[a] [17]They came up against Judah, invaded it, and carried away all the possessions they found that belonged to the king's house, along with his sons and his wives, so that no son was left to him except Jehoahaz, his youngest son.

Disease and Death of Jehoram

18 After all this the LORD struck him in his bowels with an incurable disease. [19]In course of time, at the end of two years, his bowels came out because of the disease, and he died in great agony. His people made no fire in his honor, like the fires made for his ancestors. [20]He was thirty-two years old when he began to reign; he reigned eight years in Jerusalem. He departed with no one's regret. They buried him in the city of David, but not in the tombs of the kings.

22 Ahaziah's Reign

The inhabitants of Jerusalem made his youngest son Ahaziah king as his successor; for the troops who came with the Arabs to the camp had killed all the older sons. So Ahaziah son of Jehoram reigned as king of Judah. [2]Ahaziah was forty-two years old when he began to reign; he reigned one year in Jerusalem. His mother's name was Athaliah, a granddaughter of Omri. [3]He also walked in the ways of the house of Ahab, for his mother was his counselor in doing wickedly. [4]He did what was evil in the sight of the LORD, as the house of Ahab had done; for after the death of his father they were his counselors, to his ruin. [5]He even followed their advice, and went with Jehoram son of King Ahab of Israel to make war against King Hazael of Aram at Ramoth-gilead. The Arameans wounded Joram, [6]and he returned to be

healed in Jezreel of the wounds that he had received at Ramah, when he fought King Hazael of Aram. And Ahaziah son of King Jehoram of Judah went down to see Joram son of Ahab in Jezreel, because he was sick.

7 But it was ordained by God that the downfall of Ahaziah should come about through his going to visit Joram. For when he came there he went out with Jehoram to meet Jehu son of Nimshi, whom the LORD had anointed to destroy the house of Ahab. [8]When Jehu was executing judgment on the house of Ahab, he met the officials of Judah and the sons of Ahaziah's brothers, who attended Ahaziah, and he killed them. [9]He searched for Ahaziah, who was captured while hiding in Samaria and was brought to Jehu, and put to death. They buried him, for they said, "He is the grandson of Jehoshaphat, who sought the LORD with all his heart." And the house of Ahaziah had no one able to rule the kingdom.

Athaliah Seizes the Throne

10 Now when Athaliah, Ahaziah's mother, saw that her son was dead, she set about to destroy all the royal family of the house of Judah. [11]But Jehoshabeath, the king's daughter, took Joash son of Ahaziah, and stole him away from among the king's children who were about to be killed; she put him and his nurse in a bedroom. Thus Jehoshabeath, daughter of King Jehoram and wife of the priest Jehoiada—because she was a sister of Ahaziah—hid him from Athaliah, so that she did not kill him; [12]he remained with them six years, hidden in the house of God, while Athaliah reigned over the land.

23 But in the seventh year Jehoiada took courage, and entered into a compact with the commanders of the hundreds, Azariah son of Jeroham, Ishmael son of Jehohanan, Azariah son of Obed, Maaseiah son of Adaiah, and Elishaphat son of Zichri. [2]They went around through Judah and gathered the Levites from all the towns of Judah, and the heads of families of Israel, and they came to Jerusalem. [3]Then the whole assembly made a covenant with the king in the house of God. Jehoiada[b] said to them, "Here is the king's son! Let him reign, as the LORD promised concerning the sons of David. [4]This is what you are to do: one-third of you, priests and Levites, who come on duty on the sabbath, shall be gatekeepers, [5]one-third shall be at the king's house, and one-third at the Gate of the Foundation; and all the people shall be in the courts of the house of the LORD. [6]Do not let anyone enter

a Or Nubians; Heb Cushites b Heb He

the house of the LORD except the priests and ministering Levites; they may enter, for they are holy, but all the other[a] people shall observe the instructions of the LORD. [7]The Levites shall surround the king, each with his weapons in his hand; and whoever enters the house shall be killed. Stay with the king in his comings and goings."

Joash Crowned King

8 The Levites and all Judah did according to all that the priest Jehoiada commanded; each brought his men, who were to come on duty on the sabbath, with those who were to go off duty on the sabbath; for the priest Jehoiada did not dismiss the divisions. [9]The priest Jehoiada delivered to the captains the spears and the large and small shields that had been King David's, which were in the house of God; [10]and he set all the people as a guard for the king, everyone with weapon in hand, from the south side of the house to the north side of the house, around the altar and the house. [11]Then he brought out the king's son, put the crown on him, and gave him the covenant;[b] they proclaimed him king, and Jehoiada and his sons anointed him; and they shouted, "Long live the king!"

Athaliah Murdered

12 When Athaliah heard the noise of the people running and praising the king, she went into the house of the LORD to the people; [13]and when she looked, there was the king standing by his pillar at the entrance, and the captains and the trumpeters beside the king, and all the people of the land rejoicing and blowing trumpets, and the singers with their musical instruments leading in the celebration. Athaliah tore her clothes, and cried, "Treason! Treason!" [14]Then the priest Jehoiada brought out the captains who were set over the army, saying to them, "Bring her out between the ranks; anyone who follows her is to be put to the sword." For the priest said, "Do not put her to death in the house of the LORD." [15]So they laid hands on her; she went into the entrance of the Horse Gate of the king's house, and there they put her to death.

16 Jehoiada made a covenant between himself and all the people and the king that they should be the LORD's people. [17]Then all the people went to the house of Baal, and tore it down; his altars and his images they broke in pieces, and they killed Mattan, the priest of Baal, in front of the altars. [18]Jehoiada assigned the care of the house of the LORD to the leviti-cal priests whom David had organized to be in charge of the house of the LORD, to offer burnt offerings to the LORD, as it is written in the law of Moses, with rejoicing and with singing, according to the order of David. [19]He stationed the gatekeepers at the gates of the house of the LORD so that no one should enter who was in any way unclean. [20]And he took the captains, the nobles, the governors of the people, and all the people of the land, and they brought the king down from the house of the LORD, marching through the upper gate to the king's house. They set the king on the royal throne. [21]So all the people of the land rejoiced, and the city was quiet after Athaliah had been killed with the sword.

24 Joash Repairs the Temple

Joash was seven years old when he began to reign; he reigned forty years in Jerusalem; his mother's name was Zibiah of Beer-sheba. [2]Joash did what was right in the sight of the LORD all the days of the priest Jehoiada. [3]Jehoiada got two wives for him, and he became the father of sons and daughters.

4 Some time afterward Joash decided to restore the house of the LORD. [5]He assembled the priests and the Levites and said to them, "Go out to the cities of Judah and gather money from all Israel to repair the house of your God, year by year; and see that you act quickly." But the Levites did not act quickly. [6]So the king summoned Jehoiada the chief, and said to him, "Why have you not required the Levites to bring in from Judah and Jerusalem the tax levied by Moses, the servant of the LORD, on[c] the congregation of Israel for the tent of the covenant?"[b] [7]For the children of Athaliah, that wicked woman, had broken into the house of God, and had even used all the dedicated things of the house of the LORD for the Baals.

8 So the king gave command, and they made a chest, and set it outside the gate of the house of the LORD. [9]A proclamation was made throughout Judah and Jerusalem to bring in for the LORD the tax that Moses the servant of God laid on Israel in the wilderness. [10]All the leaders and all the people rejoiced and brought their tax and dropped it into the chest until it was full. [11]Whenever the chest was brought to the king's officers by the Levites, when they saw that there was a large amount of money in it, the king's secretary and the officer of the chief priest would come and empty the chest and take it and return it to its place. So they did day after day, and collected money in abundance. [12]The king and Jehoiada gave it to those

---

a Heb lacks *other* b Or *treaty*, or *testimony*; Heb *eduth* c Compare Vg: Heb *and*

who had charge of the work of the house of the Lord, and they hired masons and carpenters to restore the house of the Lord, and also workers in iron and bronze to repair the house of the Lord. [13]So those who were engaged in the work labored, and the repairing went forward at their hands, and they restored the house of God to its proper condition and strengthened it. [14]When they had finished, they brought the rest of the money to the king and Jehoiada, and with it were made utensils for the house of the Lord, utensils for the service and for the burnt offerings, and ladles, and vessels of gold and silver. They offered burnt offerings in the house of the Lord regularly all the days of Jehoiada.

Apostasy of Joash

15 But Jehoiada grew old and full of days, and died; he was one hundred thirty years old at his death. [16]And they buried him in the city of David among the kings, because he had done good in Israel, and for God and his house.

17 Now after the death of Jehoiada the officials of Judah came and did obeisance to the king; then the king listened to them. [18]They abandoned the house of the Lord, the God of their ancestors, and served the sacred poles[a] and the idols. And wrath came upon Judah and Jerusalem for this guilt of theirs. [19]Yet he sent prophets among them to bring them back to the Lord; they testified against them, but they would not listen.

20 Then the spirit of God took possession of[b] Zechariah son of the priest Jehoiada; he stood above the people and said to them, "Thus says God: Why do you transgress the commandments of the Lord, so that you cannot prosper? Because you have forsaken the Lord, he has also forsaken you." [21]But they conspired against him, and by command of the king they stoned him to death in the court of the house of the Lord. [22]King Joash did not remember the kindness that Jehoiada, Zechariah's father, had shown him, but killed his son. As he was dying, he said, "May the Lord see and avenge!"

Death of Joash

23 At the end of the year the army of Aram came up against Joash. They came to Judah and Jerusalem, and destroyed all the officials of the people from among them, and sent all the booty they took to the king of Damascus. [24]Although the army of Aram had come with few men, the Lord delivered into their hand a very great army, because they had abandoned the Lord, the God of their ancestors. Thus they executed judgment on Joash.

25 When they had withdrawn, leaving him severely wounded, his servants conspired against him because of the blood of the son[c] of the priest Jehoiada, and they killed him on his bed. So he died; and they buried him in the city of David, but they did not bury him in the tombs of the kings. [26]Those who conspired against him were Zabad son of Shimeath the Ammonite, and Jehozabad son of Shimrith the Moabite. [27]Accounts of his sons, and of the many oracles against him, and of the rebuilding[d] of the house of God are written in the Commentary on the Book of the Kings. And his son Amaziah succeeded him.

25 Reign of Amaziah

Amaziah was twenty-five years old when he began to reign, and he reigned twenty-nine years in Jerusalem. His mother's name was Jehoaddan of Jerusalem. [2]He did what was right in the sight of the Lord, yet not with a true heart. [3]As soon as the royal power was firmly in his hand he killed his servants who had murdered his father the king. [4]But he did not put their children to death, according to what is written in the law, in the book of Moses, where the Lord commanded, "The parents shall not be put to death for the children, or the children be put to death for the parents; but all shall be put to death for their own sins."

Slaughter of the Edomites

5 Amaziah assembled the people of Judah, and set them by ancestral houses under commanders of the thousands and of the hundreds for all Judah and Benjamin. He mustered

a Heb Asherim b Heb clothed itself with c Gk Vg: Heb sons
d Heb founding

Consuming Fire—© Rachel Ford, 16

those twenty years old and upward, and found that they were three hundred thousand picked troops fit for war, able to handle spear and shield. ⁶He also hired one hundred thousand mighty warriors from Israel for one hundred talents of silver. ⁷But a man of God came to him and said, "O king, do not let the army of Israel go with you, for the LORD is not with Israel—all these Ephraimites. ⁸Rather, go by yourself and act; be strong in battle, or God will fling you down before the enemy; for God has power to help or to overthrow." ⁹Amaziah said to the man of God, "But what shall we do about the hundred talents that I have given to the army of Israel?" The man of God answered, "The LORD is able to give you much more than this." ¹⁰Then Amaziah discharged the army that had come to him from Ephraim, letting them go home again. But they became very angry with Judah, and returned home in fierce anger.

11 Amaziah took courage, and led out his people; he went to the Valley of Salt, and struck down ten thousand men of Seir. ¹²The people of Judah captured another ten thousand alive, took them to the top of Sela, and threw them down from the top of Sela, so that all of them were dashed to pieces. ¹³But the men of the army whom Amaziah sent back, not letting them go with him to battle, fell on the cities of Judah from Samaria to Beth-horon; they killed three thousand people in them, and took much booty.

14 Now after Amaziah came from the slaughter of the Edomites, he brought the gods of the people of Seir, set them up as his gods, and worshiped them, making offerings to them. ¹⁵The LORD was angry with Amaziah and sent to him a prophet, who said to him, "Why have you resorted to a people's gods who could not deliver their own people from your hand?" ¹⁶But as he was speaking the king^a said to him, "Have we made you a royal counselor? Stop! Why should you be put to death?" So the prophet stopped, but said, "I know that God has determined to destroy you, because you have done this and have not listened to my advice."

Israel Defeats Judah

17 Then King Amaziah of Judah took counsel and sent to King Joash son of Jehoahaz son of Jehu of Israel, saying, "Come, let us look one another in the face." ¹⁸King Joash of Israel sent word to King Amaziah of Judah, "A thornbush on Lebanon sent to a cedar on Lebanon, saying, 'Give your daughter to my son for a wife'; but a wild animal of Lebanon passed by and trampled down the thornbush. ¹⁹You say, 'See, I have defeated Edom,' and your heart has lifted you up in boastfulness. Now stay at home; why should you provoke trouble so that you fall, you and Judah with you?"

20 But Amaziah would not listen—it was God's doing, in order to hand them over, be-

a Heb he

cause they had sought the gods of Edom. ²¹So King Joash of Israel went up; he and King Amaziah of Judah faced one another in battle at Beth-shemesh, which belongs to Judah. ²²Judah was defeated by Israel; everyone fled home. ²³King Joash of Israel captured King Amaziah of Judah, son of Joash, son of Ahaziah, at Beth-shemesh; he brought him to Jerusalem, and broke down the wall of Jerusalem from the Ephraim Gate to the Corner Gate, a distance of four hundred cubits. ²⁴He seized all the gold and silver, and all the vessels that were found in the house of God, and Obed-edom with them; he seized also the treasuries of the king's house, also hostages; then he returned to Samaria.

Death of Amaziah

25 King Amaziah son of Joash of Judah, lived fifteen years after the death of King Joash son of Jehoahaz of Israel. ²⁶Now the rest of the deeds of Amaziah, from first to last, are they not written in the Book of the Kings of Judah and Israel? ²⁷From the time that Amaziah turned away from the LORD they made a conspiracy against him in Jerusalem, and he fled to Lachish. But they sent after him to Lachish, and killed him there. ²⁸They brought him back on horses; he was buried with his ancestors in the city of David.

26 Reign of Uzziah

Then all the people of Judah took Uzziah, who was sixteen years old, and made him king to succeed his father Amaziah. ²He rebuilt Eloth and restored it to Judah, after the king slept with his ancestors. ³Uzziah was sixteen years old when he began to reign, and he reigned fifty-two years in Jerusalem. His mother's name was Jecoliah of Jerusalem. ⁴He did what was right in the sight of the LORD, just as his father Amaziah had done. ⁵He set himself to seek God in the days of Zechariah, who instructed him in the fear of God; and as long as he sought the LORD, God made him prosper.

6 He went out and made war against the Philistines, and broke down the wall of Gath and the wall of Jabneh and the wall of Ashdod; he built cities in the territory of Ashdod and elsewhere among the Philistines. ⁷God helped him against the Philistines, against the Arabs who lived in Gur-baal, and against the Meunites. ⁸The Ammonites paid tribute to Uzziah, and his fame spread even to the border of Egypt, for he became very strong. ⁹Moreover Uzziah built towers in Jerusalem at the Corner Gate, at the Valley Gate, and at the Angle, and

fortified them. ¹⁰He built towers in the wilderness and hewed out many cisterns, for he had large herds, both in the Shephelah and in the plain, and he had farmers and vinedressers in the hills and in the fertile lands, for he loved the soil. ¹¹Moreover Uzziah had an army of soldiers, fit for war, in divisions according to the numbers in the muster made by the secretary Jeiel and the officer Maaseiah, under the direction of Hananiah, one of the king's commanders. ¹²The whole number of the heads of ancestral houses of mighty warriors was two thousand six hundred. ¹³Under their command was an army of three hundred seven thousand five hundred, who could make war with mighty power, to help the king against the enemy. ¹⁴Uzziah provided for all the army the shields, spears, helmets, coats of mail, bows, and stones for slinging. ¹⁵In Jerusalem he set up machines, invented by skilled workers, on the towers and the corners for shooting arrows and large stones. And his fame spread far, for he was marvelously helped until he became strong.

Pride and Apostasy

16 But when he had become strong he grew proud, to his destruction. For he was false to the LORD his God, and entered the temple of the LORD to make offering on the altar of incense. ¹⁷But the priest Azariah went in after him, with eighty priests of the LORD who were men of valor; ¹⁸they withstood King Uzziah, and said to him, "It is not for you, Uzziah, to make offering to the LORD, but for the priests the descendants of Aaron, who are consecrated to make offering. Go out of the sanctuary; for you have done wrong, and it will bring you no honor from the LORD God." ¹⁹Then Uzziah was angry. Now he had a censer in his hand to make offering, and when he became angry with the priests a leprous*a* disease broke out on his forehead, in the presence of the priests in the house of the LORD, by the altar of incense. ²⁰When the chief priest Azariah, and all the priests, looked at him, he was leprous*a* in his forehead. They hurried him out, and he himself hurried to get out, because the LORD had struck him. ²¹King Uzziah was leprous*a* to the day of his death, and being leprous*a* lived in a separate house, for he was excluded from the house of the LORD. His son Jotham was in charge of the palace of the king, governing the people of the land.

22 Now the rest of the acts of Uzziah, from first to last, the prophet Isaiah son of Amoz wrote. ²³Uzziah slept with his ancestors; they

---

a A term for several skin diseases; precise meaning uncertain buried him near his ancestors in the burial field that belonged to the kings, for they said, "He is leprous."*a* His son Jotham succeeded him.

27 Reign of Jotham

Jotham was twenty-five years old when he began to reign; he reigned sixteen years in Jerusalem. His mother's name was Jerushah daughter of Zadok. 2He did what was right in the sight of the LORD just as his father Uzziah had done—only he did not invade the temple of the LORD. But the people still followed corrupt practices. 3He built the upper gate of the house of the LORD, and did extensive building on the wall of Ophel. 4Moreover he built cities in the hill country of Judah, and forts and towers on the wooded hills. 5He fought with the king of the Ammonites and prevailed against them. The Ammonites gave him that year one hundred talents of silver, ten thousand cors of wheat and ten thousand of barley. The Ammonites paid him the same amount in the second and the third years. 6So Jotham became strong because he ordered his ways before the LORD his God. 7Now the rest of the acts of Jotham, and all his wars and his ways, are written in the Book of the Kings of Israel and Judah. 8He was twenty-five years old when he began to reign; he reigned sixteen years in Jerusalem. 9Jotham slept with his ancestors, and they buried him in the city of David; and his son Ahaz succeeded him.

28 Reign of Ahaz

Ahaz was twenty years old when he began to reign; he reigned sixteen years in Jerusalem. He did not do what was right in the sight of the LORD, as his ancestor David had done, 2but he walked in the ways of the kings of Israel. He even made cast images for the Baals; 3and he made offerings in the valley of the son of Hinnom, and made his sons pass through fire, according to the abominable practices of the nations whom the LORD drove out before the people of Israel. 4He sacrificed and made offerings on the high places, on the hills, and under every green tree.

Aram and Israel Defeat Judah

5 Therefore the LORD his God gave him into the hand of the king of Aram, who defeated him and took captive a great number of his people and brought them to Damascus. He was also given into the hand of the king of Israel, who defeated him with great slaughter. 6Pekah son of Remaliah killed one hundred twenty

thousand in Judah in one day, all of them valiant warriors, because they had abandoned the LORD, the God of their ancestors. 7And Zichri, a mighty warrior of Ephraim, killed the king's son Maaseiah, Azrikam the commander of the palace, and Elkanah the next in authority to the king.

Intervention of Oded

8 The people of Israel took captive two hundred thousand of their kin, women, sons, and daughters; they also took much booty from them and brought the booty to Samaria. 9But a prophet of the LORD was there, whose name was Oded; he went out to meet the army that came to Samaria, and said to them, "Because the LORD, the God of your ancestors, was angry with Judah, he gave them into your hand, but you have killed them in a rage that has reached up to heaven. 10Now you intend to subjugate the people of Judah and Jerusalem, male and female, as your slaves. But what have you except sins against the LORD your God? 11Now hear me, and send back the captives whom you have taken from your kindred, for the fierce wrath of the LORD is upon you." 12Moreover, certain chiefs of the Ephraimites, Azariah son of Johanan, Berechiah son of Meshillemoth, Jehizkiah son of Shallum, and Amasa son of Hadlai, stood up against those who were coming from the war, 13and said to them, "You shall not bring the captives in here, for you propose to bring on us guilt against the LORD in addition to our present sins and guilt. For our guilt is already great, and there is fierce wrath against Israel." 14So the warriors left the captives and the booty before the officials and all the assembly. 15Then those who were mentioned by name got up and took the captives, and with the booty they clothed all that were naked among them; they clothed them, gave them sandals, provided them with food and drink, and anointed them; and carrying all the feeble among them on donkeys, they brought them to their kindred at Jericho, the city of palm trees. Then they returned to Samaria.

Assyria Refuses to Help Judah

16 At that time King Ahaz sent to the king*b* of Assyria for help. 17For the Edomites had again invaded and defeated Judah, and carried away captives. 18And the Philistines had made raids on the cities in the Shephelah and the Negeb of Judah, and had taken Beth-shemesh, Aijalon, Gederoth, Soco with its villages, Timnah with its villages, and Gimzo with its villages; and they settled there. 19For the LORD brought Ju-

---

a A term for several skin diseases; precise meaning uncertain *b* Gk Syr Vg Compare 2 Kings 16.7: Heb *kings* dah low because of King Ahaz of Israel, for he had behaved without restraint in Judah and had been faithless to the Lord. ²⁰So King Til-gath-pilneser of Assyria came against him, and oppressed him instead of strengthening him. ²¹For Ahaz plundered the house of the Lord and the houses of the king and of the officials, and gave tribute to the king of Assyria; but it did not help him.

Apostasy and Death of Ahaz

22 In the time of his distress he became yet more faithless to the Lord—this same King Ahaz. ²³For he sacrificed to the gods of Damascus, which had defeated him, and said, "Because the gods of the kings of Aram helped them, I will sacrifice to them so that they may help me." But they were the ruin of him, and of all Israel. ²⁴Ahaz gathered together the utensils of the house of God, and cut in pieces the utensils of the house of God. He shut up the doors of the house of the Lord and made himself altars in every corner of Jerusalem. ²⁵In every city of Judah he made high places to make offerings to other gods, provoking to anger the Lord, the God of his ancestors. ²⁶Now the rest of his acts and all his ways, from first to last, are written in the Book of the Kings of Judah and Israel. ²⁷Ahaz slept with his ancestors, and they buried him in the city, in Jerusalem; but they did not bring him into the tombs of the kings of Israel. His son Hezekiah succeeded him.

29 Reign of Hezekiah

Hezekiah began to reign when he was twenty-five years old; he reigned twenty-nine years in Jerusalem. His mother's name was Abijah daughter of Zechariah. ²He did what was right in the sight of the Lord, just as his ancestor David had done.

The Temple Cleansed

3 In the first year of his reign, in the first month, he opened the doors of the house of the Lord and repaired them. ⁴He brought in the priests and the Levites and assembled them in the square on the east. ⁵He said to them, "Listen to me, Levites! Sanctify yourselves, and sanctify the house of the Lord, the God of your ancestors, and carry out the filth from the holy place. ⁶For our ancestors have been unfaithful and have done what was evil in the sight of the Lord our God; they have forsaken him, and have turned away their faces from the dwelling of the Lord, and turned their backs. ⁷They also shut the doors of the vestibule and put out the lamps, and have not offered incense or made burnt offerings in the holy place to the God of Israel. ⁸Therefore the wrath of the

REAL QUESTIONS

I have a lot of major decisions to make about my future. How do I know what God's will is for my life?

Which career path should I pick? Which school should I choose? Or should I even *go* to college? Who should I date? Who should I marry? Or should I even get married at all?

It's easy to get stressed trying to figure out the "right" answers to the many questions and choices you face. Often there is more than one good option and, short of a bolt of lightning or a booming voice from heaven, determining God's plan for you can seem impossible.

But *knowing* God's will may not be as complicated as you think. The hard part is *doing* it. Jesus told us God's will, plain and simple. You are to "love the Lord your God with all your heart, and with all your soul, and with all your mind, and with all your strength" and "love your neighbor as yourself" (Mark 12.30–31).

Following God's will isn't all just about trying to make big decisions. It's in all the little daily decisions too, when you choose to live passionately for God or to pursue another purpose. In every moment of each day, you choose either to serve God and your neighbor or to serve yourself.

Are you willing to seek and do God's will in the "little things"? Is that as high a priority in your life as the big decisions you're facing? You can pray for wisdom. You can ask God for guidance. But when a sign doesn't fall from the sky, God's Word gives you a good place to start. "Teach me to do your will, for you are my God. Let your good spirit lead me on a level path" (Psalm 143.10).

Find some Creative Space in this Bible and write your thoughts about seeking God's will, maybe adding some real questions of your own. Or talk to a trusted friend about your thoughts and questions. Then explore more in the verses below, or talk to someone about your real questions.

(Want to explore more? See how Hezekiah put God's will into action in 2 Chronicles 29; then read Proverbs 3.5–6 and Micah 6.8.)

PROFILE OF FAITH

Thomas Merton, a twentieth-century Trappist monk and writer, didn't have an easy home life. His mom died from stomach cancer when he was six. Then his dad, who hadn't been very involved in his life until then, quickly fell in love with a married woman. Thomas couldn't stand her. So he went to live with his grandparents for a few years.

His dad eventually chose Thomas over the woman and wanted him back in his life—sort of. He was sent to boarding school. Moved again. Sent to another boarding school. His dad died when he was fourteen. This zigzag pattern continued until, at the age of twenty-six, he chose to enter the Trappist monastery of Gethsemani, in Kentucky.

Merton was eventually ordained a priest and lived a life of prayer and study at the abbey. He focused on other faiths and nonviolence. While away from his monastery lecturing in Bangkok, Thai-

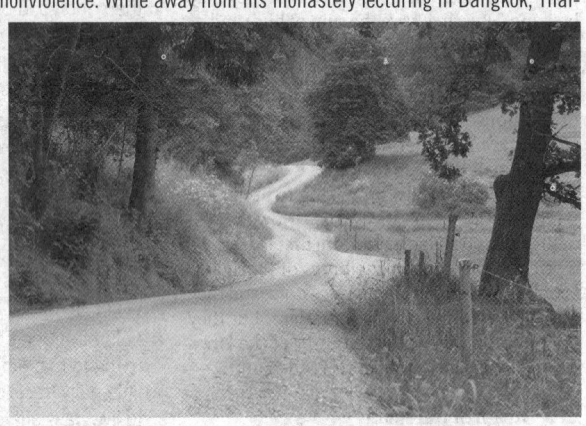

land, he died at the age of forty-six after touching a poorly grounded electrical fan when he stepped out of his bath. In response to his unsettled life, Merton often turned to writing about his faith. His signature prayer is "Thoughts in Solitude," often known as "The Thomas Merton Prayer." In it, he places his faith in God to lead him on "the right road."

LORD came upon Judah and Jerusalem, and he has made them an object of horror, of astonishment, and of hissing, as you see with your own eyes. ⁹Our fathers have fallen by the sword and our sons and our daughters and our wives are in captivity for this. ¹⁰Now it is in my heart to make a covenant with the LORD, the God of Israel, so that his fierce anger may turn away from us. ¹¹My sons, do not now be negligent, for the LORD has chosen you to stand in his presence to minister to him, and to be his ministers and make offerings to him."

12 Then the Levites arose, Mahath son of Amasai, and Joel son of Azariah, of the sons of the Kohathites; and of the sons of Merari, Kish son of Abdi, and Azariah son of Jehallelel; and of the Gershonites, Joah son of Zimmah, and Eden son of Joah; ¹³and of the sons of Elizaphan, Shimri and Jeuel; and of the sons of Asaph, Zechariah and Mattaniah; ¹⁴and of the sons of Heman, Jehuel and Shimei; and of the sons of Jeduthun, Shemaiah and Uzziel. ¹⁵They

gathered their brothers, sanctified themselves, and went in as the king had commanded, by the words of the LORD, to cleanse the house of the LORD. ¹⁶The priests went into the inner part of the house of the LORD to cleanse it, and they brought out all the unclean things that they found in the temple of the LORD into the court of the house of the LORD; and the Levites took them and carried them out to the Wadi Kidron. ¹⁷They began to sanctify on the first day of the first month, and on the eighth day of the month they came to the vestibule of the LORD; then for eight days they sanctified the house of the LORD, and on the sixteenth day of the first month they finished. ¹⁸Then they went inside to King Hezekiah and said, "We have cleansed all the house of the LORD, the altar of burnt offering and all its utensils, and the table for the rows of bread and all its utensils. ¹⁹All the utensils that King Ahaz repudiated during his reign when he was faithless, we have made ready and sanctified; see, they are in front of the altar of the LORD."

Temple Worship Restored

20 Then King Hezekiah rose early, assembled the officials of the city, and went up to the house of the LORD. 21 They brought seven bulls, seven rams, seven lambs, and seven male goats for a sin offering for the kingdom and for the sanctuary and for Judah. He commanded the priests the descendants of Aaron to offer them on the altar of the LORD. 22 So they slaughtered the bulls, and the priests received the blood and dashed it against the altar; they slaughtered the rams and their blood was dashed against the altar; they also slaughtered the lambs and their blood was dashed against the altar. 23 Then the male goats for the sin offering were brought to the king and the assembly; they laid their hands on them, 24 and the priests slaughtered them and made a sin offering with their blood at the altar, to make atonement for all Israel. For the king commanded that the burnt offering and the sin offering should be made for all Israel.

25 He stationed the Levites in the house of the LORD with cymbals, harps, and lyres, according to the commandment of David and of Gad the king's seer and of the prophet Nathan, for the commandment was from the LORD through his prophets. 26 The Levites stood with the instruments of David, and the priests with the trumpets. 27 Then Hezekiah commanded that the burnt offering be offered on the altar. When the burnt offering began, the song to the LORD began also, and the trumpets, accompanied by the instruments of King David of Israel. 28 The whole assembly worshiped, the singers sang, and the trumpeters sounded; all this continued until the burnt offering was finished. 29 When the offering was finished, the king and all who were present with him bowed down and worshiped. 30 King Hezekiah and the officials commanded the Levites to sing praises to the LORD with the words of David and of the seer Asaph. They sang praises with gladness, and they bowed down and worshiped.

31 Then Hezekiah said, "You have now consecrated yourselves to the LORD; come near, bring sacrifices and thank offerings to the house of the LORD." The assembly brought sacrifices and thank offerings; and all who were of a willing heart brought burnt offerings. 32 The number of the burnt offerings that the assembly brought was seventy bulls, one hundred rams, and two hundred lambs; all these were for a burnt offering to the LORD. 33 The conse-

crated offerings were six hundred bulls and three thousand sheep. 34 But the priests were too few and could not skin all the burnt offerings, so, until other priests had sanctified themselves, their kindred, the Levites, helped them until the work was finished—for the Levites were more conscientious*a* than the priests in sanctifying themselves. 35 Besides the great number of burnt offerings there was the fat of the offerings of well-being, and there were the drink offerings for the burnt offerings. Thus the service of the house of the LORD was restored. 36 And Hezekiah and all the people rejoiced because of what God had done for the people; for the thing had come about suddenly.

30 The Great Passover

Hezekiah sent word to all Israel and Judah, and wrote letters also to Ephraim and Manasseh, that they should come to the house of the LORD at Jerusalem, to keep the passover to the LORD the God of Israel. 2 For the king and his officials and all the assembly in Jerusalem had taken counsel to keep the passover in the second month 3 (for they could not keep it at its proper time because the priests had not sanctified themselves in sufficient number, nor had the people assembled in Jerusalem). 4 The plan seemed right to the king and all the assembly. 5 So they decreed to make a proclamation throughout all Israel, from Beer-sheba to Dan, that the people should come and keep the passover to the LORD the God of Israel, at Jerusalem; for they had not kept it in great numbers as prescribed. 6 So couriers went throughout all Israel and Judah with letters from the king and his officials, as the king had commanded, saying, "O people of Israel, return to the LORD, the God of Abraham, Isaac, and Israel, so that he may turn again to the remnant of you who have escaped from the hand of the kings of Assyria. 7 Do not be like your ancestors and your kindred, who were faithless to the LORD God of their ancestors, so that he made them a desolation, as you see. 8 Do not now be stiff-necked as your ancestors were, but yield yourselves to the LORD and come to his sanctuary, which he has sanctified forever, and serve the LORD your God, so that his fierce anger may turn away from you. 9 For as you return to the LORD, your kindred and your children will find compassion with their captors, and return to this land. For the LORD your God is gracious and merciful, and will not turn away his face from you, if you return to him."

10 So the couriers went from city to city

a Heb upright in heart

The Assyrian attack on Lachish (2 Chronicles 32.9) was horrible for its citizens. Archaeologists have found the bones of fifteen hundred bodies in a pit there, a sign of the terrible siege.

Fact

LORD. [16]They took their accustomed posts according to the law of Moses the man of God; the priests dashed the blood that they received[a] from the hands of the Levites. [17]For there were many in the assembly who had not sanctified themselves; therefore the Levites had to slaughter the passover lamb for everyone who was not clean, to make it holy to the LORD. [18]For a multitude of the people, many of them from Ephraim, Manasseh, Issachar, and Zebulun, had not cleansed themselves, yet they ate the passover otherwise than as prescribed. But Hezekiah prayed for them, saying, "The good LORD pardon all [19]who set their hearts to seek God, the LORD the God of their ancestors, even though not in accordance with the sanctuary's rules of cleanness." [20]The LORD heard Hezekiah, and healed the people. [21]The people of Israel who were present at Jerusalem kept the festival of unleavened bread seven days with great gladness; and the Levites and the priests praised the LORD day by day, accompanied by loud instruments for the LORD. [22]Hezekiah spoke encouragingly to all the Levites who showed good skill in the service of the LORD. So the people ate the food of the festival for seven days, sacrificing offerings of well-being and giving thanks to the LORD the God of their ancestors.

23 Then the whole assembly agreed together to keep the festival for another seven days; so they kept it for another seven days with gladness. [24]For King Hezekiah of Judah gave the assembly a thousand bulls and seven thousand sheep for offerings, and the officials gave the assembly a thousand bulls and ten thousand sheep. The priests sanctified themselves in great numbers. [25]The whole assembly of Judah, the priests and the Levites, and the whole assembly that came out of Israel, and the resident aliens who came out of the land of Israel, and the resident aliens who lived in Judah, rejoiced. [26]There was great joy in Jerusalem, for since the time of Solomon son of King David of Israel there had been nothing like this in Jerusalem. [27]Then the priests and the Levites stood up and blessed the people, and their voice was heard; their prayer came to his holy dwelling in heaven.

31 Pagan Shrines Destroyed

Now when all this was finished, all Israel who were present went out to the cities of Judah and broke down the pillars, hewed down the sacred poles,[b] and pulled down the high places and the altars throughout all Judah and Benjamin, and in Ephraim and Manasseh, until they

through the country of Ephraim and Manasseh, and as far as Zebulun; but they laughed them to scorn, and mocked them. [11]Only a few from Asher, Manasseh, and Zebulun humbled themselves and came to Jerusalem. [12]The hand of God was also on Judah to give them one heart to do what the king and the officials commanded by the word of the LORD.

13 Many people came together in Jerusalem to keep the festival of unleavened bread in the second month, a very large assembly. [14]They set to work and removed the altars that were in Jerusalem, and all the altars for offering incense they took away and threw into the Wadi Kidron. [15]They slaughtered the passover lamb on the fourteenth day of the second month. The priests and the Levites were ashamed, and they sanctified themselves and brought burnt offerings into the house of the

a Heb lacks *that they received* *b* Heb *Asherim*

had destroyed them all. Then all the people of Israel returned to their cities, all to their individual properties.

2 Hezekiah appointed the divisions of the priests and of the Levites, division by division, everyone according to his service, the priests and the Levites, for burnt offerings and offerings of well-being, to minister in the gates of the camp of the Lord and to give thanks and praise. ³The contribution of the king from his own possessions was for the burnt offerings: the burnt offerings of morning and evening, and the burnt offerings for the sabbaths, the new moons, and the appointed festivals, as it is written in the law of the Lord. ⁴He commanded the people who lived in Jerusalem to give the portion due to the priests and the Levites, so that they might devote themselves to the law of the Lord. ⁵As soon as the word spread, the people of Israel gave in abundance the first fruits of grain, wine, oil, honey, and of all the produce of the field; and they brought in abundantly the tithe of everything. ⁶The people of Israel and Judah who lived in the cities of Judah also brought in the tithe of cattle and sheep, and the tithe of the dedicated things that had been consecrated to the Lord their God, and laid them in heaps. ⁷In the third month they began to pile up the heaps, and finished them in the seventh month. ⁸When Hezekiah and the officials came and saw the heaps, they blessed the Lord and his people Israel. ⁹Hezekiah questioned the priests and the Levites about the heaps. ¹⁰The chief priest Azariah, who was of the house of Zadok, answered him, "Since they began to bring the contributions into the house of the Lord, we have had enough to eat and have plenty to spare; for the Lord has blessed his people, so that we have this great supply left over."

Reorganization of Priests and Levites

11 Then Hezekiah commanded them to prepare store-chambers in the house of the Lord; and they prepared them. ¹²Faithfully they brought in the contributions, the tithes and the dedicated things. The chief officer in charge of them was Conaniah the Levite, with his brother Shimei as second; ¹³while Jehiel, Azariah, Nahath, Asahel, Jerimoth, Jozabad, Eliel, Ismachiah, Mahath, and Benaiah were overseers assisting Conaniah and his brother Shimei, by the appointment of King Hezekiah and of Azariah the chief officer of the house of God. ¹⁴Kore son of Imnah the Levite, keeper of the east gate, was in charge of the freewill offerings to God, to apportion the contribution

reserved for the Lord and the most holy offerings. ¹⁵Eden, Miniamin, Jeshua, Shemaiah, Amariah, and Shecaniah were faithfully assisting him in the cities of the priests, to distribute the portions to their kindred, old and young alike, by divisions, ¹⁶except those enrolled by genealogy, males from three years old and upwards, all who entered the house of the Lord as the duty of each day required, for their service according to their offices, by their divisions. ¹⁷The enrollment of the priests was according to their ancestral houses; that of the Levites from twenty years old and upwards was according to their offices, by their divisions. ¹⁸The priests were enrolled with all their little children, their wives, their sons, and their daughters, the whole multitude; for they were faithful in keeping themselves holy. ¹⁹And for the descendants of Aaron, the priests, who were in the fields of common land belonging to their towns, town by town, the people designated by name were to distribute portions to every male among the priests and to everyone among the Levites who was enrolled.

20 Hezekiah did this throughout all Judah; he did what was good and right and faithful before the Lord his God. ²¹And every work that he undertook in the service of the house of God, and in accordance with the law and the commandments, to seek his God, he did with all his heart; and he prospered.

32 Sennacherib's Invasion

After these things and these acts of faithfulness, King Sennacherib of Assyria came and invaded Judah and encamped against the fortified cities, thinking to win them for himself. ²When Hezekiah saw that Sennacherib had come and intended to fight against Jerusalem, ³he planned with his officers and his warriors to stop the flow of the springs that were outside the city; and they helped him. ⁴A great many people were gathered, and they stopped all the springs and the wadi that flowed through the land, saying, "Why should the Assyrian kings come and find water in abundance?" ⁵Hezekiah[a] set to work resolutely and built up the entire wall that was broken down, and raised towers on it,[b] and outside it he built another wall; he also strengthened the Millo in the city of David, and made weapons and shields in abundance. ⁶He appointed combat commanders over the people, and gathered them together to him in the square at the gate of the city and spoke encouragingly to them, saying, ⁷"Be strong and of good courage. Do not be afraid or dismayed before the king of Assyria

a Heb He b Vg: Heb and raised on the towers

and all the horde that is with him; for there is one greater with us than with him. ⁸With him is an arm of flesh; but with us is the LORD our God, to help us and to fight our battles." The people were encouraged by the words of King Hezekiah of Judah.

9 After this, while King Sennacherib of Assyria was at Lachish with all his forces, he sent his servants to Jerusalem to King Hezekiah of Judah and to all the people of Judah that were in Jerusalem, saying, ¹⁰"Thus says King Sennacherib of Assyria: On what are you relying, that you undergo the siege of Jerusalem? ¹¹Is not Hezekiah misleading you, handing you over to die by famine and by thirst, when he tells you, 'The LORD our God will save us from the hand of the king of Assyria'? ¹²Was it not this same Hezekiah who took away his high places and his altars and commanded Judah and Jerusalem, saying, 'Before one altar you shall worship, and upon it you shall make your offerings'? ¹³Do you not know what I and my ancestors have done to all the peoples of other lands? Were the gods of the nations of those lands at all able to save their lands out of my hand? ¹⁴Who among all the gods of those nations that my ancestors utterly destroyed was able to save his people from my hand, that your God should be able to save you from my hand? ¹⁵Now therefore do not let Hezekiah deceive you or mislead you in this fashion, and do not believe him, for no god of any nation or kingdom has been able to save his people from my hand or from the hand of my ancestors. How much less will your God save you out of my hand!"

16 His servants said still more against the Lord GOD and against his servant Hezekiah. ¹⁷He also wrote letters to throw contempt on the LORD the God of Israel and to speak against him, saying, "Just as the gods of the nations in other lands did not rescue their people from my hands, so the God of Hezekiah will not rescue his people from my hand." ¹⁸They shouted it with a loud voice in the language of Judah to the people of Jerusalem who were on the wall, to frighten and terrify them, in order that they might take the city. ¹⁹They spoke of the God of Jerusalem as if he were like the gods of the peoples of the earth, which are the work of human hands.

Sennacherib's Defeat and Death

20 Then King Hezekiah and the prophet Isaiah son of Amoz prayed because of this and cried to heaven. ²¹And the LORD sent an angel who cut off all the mighty warriors and commanders and officers in the camp of the king of Assyria. So he returned in disgrace to his own land.

When he came into the house of his god, some of his own sons struck him down there with the sword. ²²So the LORD saved Hezekiah and the inhabitants of Jerusalem from the hand of King Sennacherib of Assyria and from the hand of all his enemies; he gave them rest*ᵃ* on every side. ²³Many brought gifts to the LORD in Jerusalem and precious things to King Hezekiah of Judah, so that he was exalted in the sight of all nations from that time onward.

Hezekiah's Sickness

24 In those days Hezekiah became sick and was at the point of death. He prayed to the LORD, and he answered him and gave him a sign. ²⁵But Hezekiah did not respond according to the benefit done to him, for his heart was proud. Therefore wrath came upon him and upon Judah and Jerusalem. ²⁶Then Hezekiah humbled himself for the pride of his heart, both he and the inhabitants of Jerusalem, so that the wrath of the LORD did not come upon them in the days of Hezekiah.

Hezekiah's Prosperity and Achievements

27 Hezekiah had very great riches and honor; and he made for himself treasuries for silver, for gold, for precious stones, for spices, for shields, and for all kinds of costly objects; ²⁸storehouses also for the yield of grain, wine, and oil; and stalls for all kinds of cattle, and sheepfolds.*ᵇ* ²⁹He likewise provided cities for himself, and flocks and herds in abundance; for God had given him very great possessions. ³⁰This same Hezekiah closed the upper outlet of the waters of Gihon and directed them down to the west side of the city of David. Hezekiah prospered in all his works. ³¹So also in the matter of the envoys of the officials of Babylon, who had been sent to him to inquire about the sign that had been done in the land, God left him to himself, in order to test him and to know all that was in his heart.

32 Now the rest of the acts of Hezekiah, and his good deeds, are written in the vision of the prophet Isaiah son of Amoz in the Book of the Kings of Judah and Israel. ³³Hezekiah slept with his ancestors, and they buried him on the ascent to the tombs of the descendants of David; and all Judah and the inhabitants of Jerusalem did him honor at his death. His son Manasseh succeeded him.

33 Reign of Manasseh

Manasseh was twelve years old when he began to reign; he reigned fifty-five years in Jerusalem. ²He did what was evil in the sight of the

a Gk Vg: Heb *guided them* *b* Gk Vg: Heb *flocks for folds*

Lord, according to the abominable practices of the nations whom the Lord drove out before the people of Israel. ³For he rebuilt the high places that his father Hezekiah had pulled down, and erected altars to the Baals, made sacred poles,ᵃ worshiped all the host of heaven, and served them. ⁴He built altars in the house of the Lord, of which the Lord had said, "In Jerusalem shall my name be forever." ⁵He built altars for all the host of heaven in the two courts of the house of the Lord. ⁶He made his son pass through fire in the valley of the son of Hinnom, practiced soothsaying and augury and sorcery, and dealt with mediums and with wizards. He did much evil in the sight of the Lord, provoking him to anger. ⁷The carved image of the idol that he had made he set in the house of God, of which God said to David and to his son Solomon, "In this house, and in Jerusalem, which I have chosen out of all the tribes of Israel, I will put my name forever; ⁸I will never again remove the feet of Israel from the land that I appointed for your ancestors, if only they will be careful to do all that I have commanded them, all the law, the statutes, and the ordinances given through Moses." ⁹Manasseh misled Judah and the inhabitants of Jerusalem, so that they did more evil than the nations whom the Lord had destroyed before the people of Israel.

Manasseh Restored after Repentance
10 The Lord spoke to Manasseh and to his people, but they gave no heed. ¹¹Therefore the Lord brought against them the commanders of the army of the king of Assyria, who took Manasseh captive in manacles, bound him with fetters, and brought him to Babylon. ¹²While he was in distress he entreated the favor of the Lord his God and humbled himself greatly before the God of his ancestors. ¹³He prayed to him, and God received his entreaty, heard his plea, and restored him again to Jerusalem and to his kingdom. Then Manasseh knew that the Lord indeed was God.

14 Afterward he built an outer wall for the city of David west of Gihon, in the valley, reaching the entrance at the Fish Gate; he carried it around Ophel, and raised it to a very great height. He also put commanders of the army in all the fortified cities in Judah. ¹⁵He took away the foreign gods and the idol from the house of the Lord, and all the altars that he had built on the mountain of the house of the Lord and in Jerusalem, and he threw them out of the city. ¹⁶He also restored the altar of the Lord and offered on it sacrifices of well-being and

Gifts From the Spirit—© Amy Dobbs, 15

of thanksgiving; and he commanded Judah to serve the Lord the God of Israel. ¹⁷The people, however, still sacrificed at the high places, but only to the Lord their God.

Death of Manasseh
18 Now the rest of the acts of Manasseh, his prayer to his God, and the words of the seers who spoke to him in the name of the Lord God of Israel, these are in the Annals of the Kings of Israel. ¹⁹His prayer, and how God received his entreaty, all his sin and his faithlessness, the sites on which he built high places and set up the sacred polesᵇ and the images, before he humbled himself, these are written in the records of the seers.ᶜ ²⁰So Manasseh slept with his ancestors, and they buried him in his house. His son Amon succeeded him.

Amon's Reign and Death
21 Amon was twenty-two years old when he began to reign; he reigned two years in Jerusalem. ²²He did what was evil in the sight of the Lord, as his father Manasseh had done. Amon sacrificed to all the images that his father Manasseh had made, and served them. ²³He did not humble himself before the Lord, as his father Manasseh had humbled himself, but this Amon incurred more and more guilt. ²⁴His servants conspired against him and killed him in his house. ²⁵But the people of the land killed all those who had conspired against King Amon; and the people of the land made his son Josiah king to succeed him.

34 Reign of Josiah
Josiah was eight years old when he began to reign; he reigned thirty-one years in Jerusalem.

a Heb *Asheroth* *b* Heb *Asherim* *c* One Ms Gk: MT *of Hozai*

²He did what was right in the sight of the LORD, and walked in the ways of his ancestor David; he did not turn aside to the right or to the left. ³For in the eighth year of his reign, while he was still a boy, he began to seek the God of his ancestor David, and in the twelfth year he began to purge Judah and Jerusalem of the high places, the sacred poles,ª and the carved and the cast images. ⁴In his presence they pulled down the altars of the Baals; he demolished the incense altars that stood above them. He broke down the sacred polesª and the carved and the cast images; he made dust of them and scattered it over the graves of those who had sacrificed to them. ⁵He also burned the bones of the priests on their altars, and purged Judah and Jerusalem. ⁶In the towns of Manasseh, Ephraim, and Simeon, and as far as Naphtali, in their ruinsᵇ all around, ⁷he broke down the altars, beat the sacred polesª and the images into powder, and demolished all the incense altars throughout all the land of Israel. Then he returned to Jerusalem.

Discovery of the Book of the Law

8 In the eighteenth year of his reign, when he had purged the land and the house, he sent Shaphan son of Azaliah, Maaseiah the governor of the city, and Joah son of Joahaz, the recorder, to repair the house of the LORD his God. ⁹They came to the high priest Hilkiah and delivered the money that had been brought into the house of God, which the Levites, the keepers of the threshold, had collected from Manasseh and Ephraim and from all the remnant of Israel and from all Judah and Benjamin and from the inhabitants of Jerusalem. ¹⁰They delivered it to the workers who had the oversight of the house of the LORD, and the workers who were working in the house of the LORD gave it for repairing and restoring the house. ¹¹They gave it to the carpenters and the builders to buy quarried stone, and timber for binders, and beams for the buildings that the kings of Judah had let go to ruin. ¹²The people did the work faithfully. Over them were appointed the Levites Jahath and Obadiah, of the sons of Merari, along with Zechariah and Meshullam, of the sons of the Kohathites, to have oversight. Other Levites, all skillful with instruments of music, ¹³were over the burden bearers and directed all who did work in every kind of service; and some of the Levites were scribes, and officials, and gatekeepers.

14 While they were bringing out the money that had been brought into the house of the LORD, the priest Hilkiah found the book of the law of the LORD given through Moses. ¹⁵Hilkiah said to the secretary Shaphan, "I have found the book of the law in the house of the LORD"; and Hilkiah gave the book to Shaphan. ¹⁶Shaphan brought the book to the king, and further reported to the king, "All that was committed to your servants they are doing. ¹⁷They have emptied out the money that was found in the house of the LORD and have delivered it into the hand of the overseers and the workers." ¹⁸The secretary Shaphan informed the king, "The priest Hilkiah has given me a book." Shaphan then read it aloud to the king.

19 When the king heard the words of the law he tore his clothes. ²⁰Then the king commanded Hilkiah, Ahikam son of Shaphan, Abdon son of Micah, the secretary Shaphan, and the king's servant Asaiah: ²¹"Go, inquire of the LORD for me and for those who are left in Israel and in Judah, concerning the words of the book that has been found; for the wrath of the LORD that is poured out on us is great, because our ancestors did not keep the word of the LORD, to act in accordance with all that is written in this book."

The Prophet Huldah Consulted

22 So Hilkiah and those whom the king had sent went to the prophet Huldah, the wife of Shallum son of Tokhath son of Hasrah, keeper of the wardrobe (who lived in Jerusalem in the Second Quarter) and spoke to her to that effect. ²³She declared to them, "Thus says the LORD, the God of Israel: Tell the man who sent you to me, ²⁴Thus says the LORD: I will indeed bring disaster upon this place and upon its inhabitants, all the curses that are written in the book that was read before the king of Judah. ²⁵Because they have forsaken me and have made offerings to other gods, so that they have provoked me to anger with all the works of their hands, my wrath will be poured out on this place and will not be quenched. ²⁶But as to the king of Judah, who sent you to inquire of the LORD, thus shall you say to him: Thus says the LORD, the God of Israel: Regarding the words that you have heard, ²⁷because your heart was penitent and you humbled yourself before God when you heard his words against this place and its inhabitants, and you have humbled yourself before me, and have torn your clothes and wept before me, I also have heard you, says the LORD. ²⁸I will gather you to your ancestors and you shall be gathered to your grave in peace; your eyes shall not see all the disaster that I will bring on this place and

ª Heb *Asherim* ᵇ Meaning of Heb uncertain

But God is the Lord of all our life—at least He wants to be, but He is polite and He'll wait for the invite. ... God is a God of the heart, the body, and the soul. Just because the heart tells us that we don't feel God is able to do something doesn't mean anything at all. God doesn't operate according to our feelings—He operates according to His plan, which will give us the very best.

From *Trust In God*—© Randy Reed, 18

Naturally Smooth—© Hannah Miller, 15

its inhabitants." They took the message back to the king.

The Covenant Renewed

29 Then the king sent word and gathered together all the elders of Judah and Jerusalem. ³⁰The king went up to the house of the Lord, with all the people of Judah, the inhabitants of Jerusalem, the priests and the Levites, all the people both great and small; he read in their hearing all the words of the book of the covenant that had been found in the house of the Lord. ³¹The king stood in his place and made a covenant before the Lord, to follow the Lord, keeping his commandments, his decrees, and his statutes, with all his heart and all his soul, to perform the words of the covenant that were written in this book. ³²Then he made all who were present in Jerusalem and in Benjamin pledge themselves to it. And the inhabitants of Jerusalem acted according to the covenant of God, the God of their ancestors. ³³Josiah took away all the abominations from all the territory that belonged to the people of Israel, and made all who were in Israel worship the Lord their God. All his days they did not turn away from following the Lord the God of their ancestors.

35 Celebration of the Passover

Josiah kept a passover to the Lord in Jerusalem; they slaughtered the passover lamb on the fourteenth day of the first month. ²He appointed the priests to their offices and encouraged them in the service of the house of the Lord. ³He said to the Levites who taught all Israel and who were holy to the Lord, "Put the holy ark in the house that Solomon son of David, king of Israel, built; you need no longer carry it on your shoulders. Now serve the Lord your God and his people Israel. ⁴Make preparations by your ancestral houses by your divisions, following the written directions of King David of Israel and the written directions of his son Solomon. ⁵Take position in the holy place according to the groupings of the ancestral houses of your kindred the people, and let there be Levites for each division of an ancestral house.ᵃ ⁶Slaughter the passover lamb, sanctify yourselves, and on behalf of your kindred make preparations, acting according to the word of the Lord by Moses."

7 Then Josiah contributed to the people, as passover offerings for all that were present, lambs and kids from the flock to the number of thirty thousand, and three thousand bulls; these were from the king's possessions. ⁸His officials contributed willingly to the people, to the priests, and to the Levites. Hilkiah, Zechariah, and Jehiel, the chief officers of the house of God, gave to the priests for the passover offerings two thousand six hundred lambs and kids and three hundred bulls. ⁹Conaniah also,

a Meaning of Heb uncertain

and his brothers Shemaiah and Nethanel, and Hashabiah and Jeiel and Jozabad, the chiefs of the Levites, gave to the Levites for the passover offerings five thousand lambs and kids and five hundred bulls.

10 When the service had been prepared for, the priests stood in their place, and the Levites in their divisions according to the king's command. ¹¹They slaughtered the passover lamb, and the priests dashed the blood that they received^a from them, while the Levites did the skinning. ¹²They set aside the burnt offerings so that they might distribute them according to the groupings of the ancestral houses of the people, to offer to the LORD, as it is written in the book of Moses. And they did the same with the bulls. ¹³They roasted the passover lamb with fire according to the ordinance; and they boiled the holy offerings in pots, in caldrons, and in pans, and carried them quickly to all the people. ¹⁴Afterward they made preparations for themselves and for the priests, because the priests the descendants of Aaron were occupied in offering the burnt offerings and the fat parts until night; so the Levites made preparations for themselves and for the priests, the descendants of Aaron. ¹⁵The singers, the descendants of Asaph, were in their place according to the command of David, and Asaph, and Heman, and the king's seer Jeduthun. The gatekeepers were at each gate; they did not need to interrupt their service, for their kindred the Levites made preparations for them.

16 So all the service of the LORD was prepared that day, to keep the passover and to offer burnt offerings on the altar of the LORD, according to the command of King Josiah. ¹⁷The people of Israel who were present kept the passover at that time, and the festival of unleavened bread seven days. ¹⁸No passover like it had been kept in Israel since the days of the prophet Samuel; none of the kings of Israel had kept such a passover as was kept by Josiah, by the priests and the Levites, by all Judah and Israel who were present, and by the inhabitants of Jerusalem. ¹⁹In the eighteenth year of the reign of Josiah this passover was kept.

Defeat by Pharaoh Neco and Death of Josiah

20 After all this, when Josiah had set the temple in order, King Neco of Egypt went up to fight at Carchemish on the Euphrates, and Josiah went out against him. ²¹But Neco^b sent envoys to him, saying, "What have I to do with you, king of Judah? I am not coming against you today, but against the house with which

I am at war; and God has commanded me to hurry. Cease opposing God, who is with me, so that he will not destroy you." ²²But Josiah would not turn away from him, but disguised himself in order to fight with him. He did not listen to the words of Neco from the mouth of God, but joined battle in the plain of Megiddo. ²³The archers shot King Josiah; and the king said to his servants, "Take me away, for I am badly wounded." ²⁴So his servants took him out of the chariot and carried him in his second chariot^c and brought him to Jerusalem. There he died, and was buried in the tombs of his ancestors. All Judah and Jerusalem mourned for Josiah. ²⁵Jeremiah also uttered a lament for Josiah, and all the singing men and singing women have spoken of Josiah in their laments to this day. They made these a custom in Israel; they are recorded in the Laments. ²⁶Now the rest of the acts of Josiah and his faithful deeds in accordance with what is written in the law of the LORD, ²⁷and his acts, first and last, are written in the Book of the Kings of Israel and Judah.

36 Reign of Jehoahaz

The people of the land took Jehoahaz son of Josiah and made him king to succeed his father in Jerusalem. ²Jehoahaz was twenty-three years old when he began to reign; he reigned three months in Jerusalem. ³Then the king of Egypt deposed him in Jerusalem and laid on the land a tribute of one hundred talents of silver and one talent of gold. ⁴The king of Egypt made his brother Eliakim king over Judah and Jerusalem, and changed his name to Jehoiakim; but Neco took his brother Jehoahaz and carried him to Egypt.

Reign and Captivity of Jehoiakim

5 Jehoiakim was twenty-five years old when he began to reign; he reigned eleven years in Jerusalem. He did what was evil in the sight of the LORD his God. ⁶Against him King Nebuchadnezzar of Babylon came up, and bound him with fetters to take him to Babylon. ⁷Nebuchadnezzar also carried some of the vessels of the house of the LORD to Babylon and put them in his palace in Babylon. ⁸Now the rest of the acts of Jehoiakim, and the abominations that he did, and what was found against him, are written in the Book of the Kings of Israel and Judah; and his son Jehoiachin succeeded him.

Reign and Captivity of Jehoiachin

9 Jehoiachin was eight years old when he began to reign; he reigned three months and ten

days in Jerusalem. He did what was evil in the sight of the LORD. [10]In the spring of the year King Nebuchadnezzar sent and brought him to Babylon, along with the precious vessels of the house of the LORD, and made his brother Zedekiah king over Judah and Jerusalem.

Reign of Zedekiah

11 Zedekiah was twenty-one years old when he began to reign; he reigned eleven years in Jerusalem. [12]He did what was evil in the sight of the LORD his God. He did not humble himself before the prophet Jeremiah who spoke from the mouth of the LORD. [13]He also rebelled against King Nebuchadnezzar, who had made him swear by God; he stiffened his neck and hardened his heart against turning to the LORD, the God of Israel. [14]All the leading priests and the people also were exceedingly unfaithful, following all the abominations of the nations; and they polluted the house of the LORD that he had consecrated in Jerusalem.

The Fall of Jerusalem

15 The LORD, the God of their ancestors, sent persistently to them by his messengers, because he had compassion on his people and on his dwelling place; [16]but they kept mocking the messengers of God, despising his words, and scoffing at his prophets, until the wrath of the LORD against his people became so great that there was no remedy.

17 Therefore he brought up against them the king of the Chaldeans, who killed their youths with the sword in the house of their sanctuary, and had no compassion on young man or young woman, the aged or the feeble; he gave them all into his hand. [18]All the vessels of the house of God, large and small, and the treasures of the house of the LORD, and the treasures of the king and of his officials, all these he brought to Babylon. [19]They burned the house of God, broke down the wall of Jerusalem, burned all its palaces with fire, and destroyed all its precious vessels. [20]He took into exile in Babylon those who had escaped from the sword, and they became servants to him and to his sons until the establishment of the kingdom of Persia, [21]to fulfill the word of the LORD by the mouth of Jeremiah, until the land had made up for its sabbaths. All the days that it lay desolate it kept sabbath, to fulfill seventy years.

Cyrus Proclaims Liberty for the Exiles

22 In the first year of King Cyrus of Persia, in fulfillment of the word of the LORD spoken by Jeremiah, the LORD stirred up the spirit of King Cyrus of Persia so that he sent a herald throughout all his kingdom and also declared in a written edict: [23]"Thus says King Cyrus of Persia: The LORD, the God of heaven, has given me all the kingdoms of the earth, and he has charged me to build him a house at Jerusalem, which is in Judah. Whoever is among you of all his people, may the LORD his God be with him! Let him go up."

CREATIVE SPACE

EZRA

THERE'S SOMETHING NEW IN THE AIR

Can One Person Change a Nation?

The book of Ezra picks up the story of God's people right where 2 Kings and 2 Chronicles leave off. The Temple was destroyed, the people had been carted off to a foreign land, and life was looking about as bad as it could get. (For a poetic account of the destruction of Jerusalem, which led to the exile, check out Lamentations.) The book of Ezra tells us what happened on the other side of the exile, when the Jews started to return to their homeland.

The Bible doesn't tell us a lot about the person named Ezra, but what it does say is pretty powerful! Ezra felt the nation's sins deep in his gut, and he couldn't take it anymore. He saw how his people were turning from God and how they weren't honoring him with their lives. In response, Ezra did the most powerful thing he could do: drop to his knees and pray. Ezra, while not personally guilty of the nation's sins, took responsibility for his people and asked God to forgive Israel. How amazing is that? Ezra's love for God was so contagious that soon everyone around him confessed their sins and begged for God's forgiveness.

Can one person change a nation? Ezra did. What about us? How can we start to change our nation? We can take a cue from Ezra and start by praying.

> *"Baptism is the first and chief sacrament of the forgiveness of sins: it unites us to Christ, who died and rose, and gives us the Holy Spirit."*
> —Catechism of the Catholic Church 985

WHO The original author or authors are unknown. The Chronicler likely had a strong influence on the book.

WHAT Contains historical information about the restoration period and rebuilding of the Temple, but was written to reflect the religious meaning of those events

WHEN The return of the exiles and the restoration of the Temple spanned from 539–485 B.C.

WHERE Jerusalem, after God's people returned from exile in Babylon (modern-day Iraq)

PATH OF DISCIPLESHIP

God's love so deeply moved Ezra that to see others falling away from God caused him to take action. He couldn't just sit back and watch things fall apart. Ezra shows the power of one person acting for God.

Just as Ezra's life made a powerful difference for his people, Jesus' life made a difference for all people, across time, all over the globe. Like Ezra, Jesus took action. But he took it farther—way farther—with the ultimate action: his death and Resurrection. He defeated death and sin once and for all, offering all people the opportunity to find forgiveness and live eternally with God in heaven.

How are you inspired to take action? As a disciple and member of the Body of Christ, you are called to make the differences that enable God's Kingdom to come. You can heal a friend's hurt feelings. You can work with others to discourage abuse of drugs and alcohol. You can reach out to the poor, locally and globally. Think about it. Your life can make a powerful difference. You just have to have the courage and energy to act.

1 End of the Babylonian Captivity

In the first year of King Cyrus of Persia, in order that the word of the LORD by the mouth of Jeremiah might be accomplished, the LORD stirred up the spirit of King Cyrus of Persia so that he sent a herald throughout all his kingdom, and also in a written edict declared:

2 "Thus says King Cyrus of Persia: The LORD, the God of heaven, has given me all the kingdoms of the earth, and he has charged me to build him a house at Jerusalem in Judah. ³Any of those among you who are of his people—may their God be with them!—are now permitted to go up to Jerusalem in Judah, and rebuild the house of the LORD, the God of Israel—he is the God who is in Jerusalem; ⁴and let all survivors, in whatever place they reside, be assisted by the people of their place with silver and gold, with goods and with animals, besides freewill offerings for the house of God in Jerusalem."

5 The heads of the families of Judah and Benjamin, and the priests and the Levites—everyone whose spirit God had stirred—got ready to go up and rebuild the house of the LORD in Jerusalem. ⁶All their neighbors aided them with silver vessels, with gold, with goods, with animals, and with valuable gifts, besides all that was freely offered. ⁷King Cyrus himself brought out the vessels of the house of the LORD that Nebuchadnezzar had carried away from Jerusalem and placed in the house of his gods. ⁸King Cyrus of Persia had them released into the charge of Mithredath the treasurer, who counted them out to Sheshbazzar the prince of Judah. ⁹And this was the inventory: gold basins, thirty; silver basins, one thousand; knives,*ᵃ* twenty-nine; ¹⁰gold bowls, thirty; other silver bowls, four hundred ten; other vessels, one thousand; ¹¹the total of the gold and silver vessels was five thousand four hundred. All these Sheshbazzar brought up, when the exiles were brought up from Babylonia to Jerusalem.

2 List of the Returned Exiles

Now these were the people of the province who came from those captive exiles whom King Nebuchadnezzar of Babylon had carried captive to Babylonia; they returned to Jerusalem and Judah, all to their own towns. ²They came with Zerubbabel, Jeshua, Nehemiah, Seraiah, Reelaiah, Mordecai, Bilshan, Mispar, Bigvai, Rehum, and Baanah.

The number of the Israelite people: ³the descendants of Parosh, two thousand one hundred seventy-two. ⁴Of Shephatiah, three hundred seventy-two. ⁵Of Arah, seven hundred seventy-five. ⁶Of Pahath-moab, namely the descendants of Jeshua and Joab, two thousand eight hundred twelve. ⁷Of Elam, one thousand two hundred fifty-four. ⁸Of Zattu, nine hundred forty-five. ⁹Of Zaccai, seven hundred sixty. ¹⁰Of Bani, six hundred forty-two. ¹¹Of Bebai, six hundred twenty-three. ¹²Of Azgad, one thousand two hundred twenty-two. ¹³Of Adonikam, six hundred sixty-six. ¹⁴Of Bigvai, two thousand fifty-six. ¹⁵Of Adin, four hundred fifty-four. ¹⁶Of Ater, namely of Hezekiah, ninety-eight. ¹⁷Of Bezai, three hundred twenty-three. ¹⁸Of Jorah, one hundred twelve. ¹⁹Of Hashum, two hundred twenty-three. ²⁰Of Gibbar, ninety-five. ²¹Of Bethlehem, one hundred twenty-three. ²²The people of Netophah, fifty-six. ²³Of Anathoth, one hundred twenty-eight. ²⁴The descendants of Azmaveth, forty-two. ²⁵Of Kiriatharim, Chephirah, and Beeroth, seven hundred forty-three. ²⁶Of Ramah and Geba, six hundred twenty-one. ²⁷The people of Michmas, one hundred twenty-two. ²⁸Of Bethel and Ai, two hundred twenty-three. ²⁹The descendants of Nebo, fifty-two. ³⁰Of Magbish, one hundred fifty-six. ³¹Of the other Elam, one thousand two hundred fifty-four. ³²Of Harim, three hundred twenty. ³³Of Lod, Hadid, and Ono, seven hundred twenty-five. ³⁴Of Jericho, three hundred forty-five. ³⁵Of Senaah, three thousand six hundred thirty.

36 The priests: the descendants of Jedaiah, of the house of Jeshua, nine hundred seventy-three. ³⁷Of Immer, one thousand fifty-two. ³⁸Of Pashhur, one thousand two hundred forty-seven. ³⁹Of Harim, one thousand seventeen.

40 The Levites: the descendants of Jeshua and Kadmiel, of the descendants of Hodaviah, seventy-four. ⁴¹The singers: the descendants of Asaph, one hundred twenty-eight. ⁴²The descendants of the gatekeepers: of Shallum, of Ater, of Talmon, of Akkub, of Hatita, and of Shobai, in all one hundred thirty-nine.

43 The temple servants: the descendants of Ziha, Hasupha, Tabbaoth, ⁴⁴Keros, Siaha, Padon, ⁴⁵Lebanah, Hagabah, Akkub, ⁴⁶Hagab, Shamlai, Hanan, ⁴⁷Giddel, Gahar, Reaiah, ⁴⁸Rezin, Nekoda, Gazzam, ⁴⁹Uzza, Paseah, Besai, ⁵⁰Asnah, Meunim, Nephisim, ⁵¹Bakbuk, Hakupha, Harhur, ⁵²Bazluth, Mehida, Harsha, ⁵³Barkos, Sisera, Temah, ⁵⁴Neziah, and Hatipha.

55 The descendants of Solomon's servants: Sotai, Hassophereth, Peruda, ⁵⁶Jaalah, Darkon, Giddel, ⁵⁷Shephatiah, Hattil, Pochereth-hazzebaim, and Ami.

ᵃ Vg: Meaning of Heb uncertain

58 All the temple servants and the descendants of Solomon's servants were three hundred ninety-two.

59 The following were those who came up from Tel-melah, Tel-harsha, Cherub, Addan, and Immer, though they could not prove their families or their descent, whether they belonged to Israel: 60 the descendants of Delaiah, Tobiah, and Nekoda, six hundred fifty-two. 61 Also, of the descendants of the priests: the descendants of Habaiah, Hakkoz, and Barzillai (who had married one of the daughters of Barzillai the Gileadite, and was called by their name). 62 These looked for their entries in the genealogical records, but they were not found there, and so they were excluded from the priesthood as unclean; 63 the governor told them that they were not to partake of the most holy food, until there should be a priest to consult Urim and Thummim.

64 The whole assembly together was forty-two thousand three hundred sixty, 65 besides their male and female servants, of whom there were seven thousand three hundred thirty-seven; and they had two hundred male and female singers. 66 They had seven hundred thirty-six horses, two hundred forty-five mules, 67 four hundred thirty-five camels, and six thousand seven hundred twenty donkeys.

68 As soon as they came to the house of the LORD in Jerusalem, some of the heads of families made freewill offerings for the house of God, to erect it on its site. 69 According to their resources they gave to the building fund sixty-one thousand darics of gold, five thousand minas of silver, and one hundred priestly robes.

70 The priests, the Levites, and some of the people lived in Jerusalem and its vicinity;[a] and the singers, the gatekeepers, and the temple servants lived in their towns, and all Israel in their towns.

3 Worship Restored at Jerusalem

When the seventh month came, and the Israelites were in the towns, the people gathered together in Jerusalem. 2 Then Jeshua son of Jozadak, with his fellow priests, and Zerubbabel son of Shealtiel with his kin set out to build the altar of the God of Israel, to offer burnt offerings on it, as prescribed in the law of Moses the man of God. 3 They set up the altar on its foundation, because they were in dread of the neighboring peoples, and they offered burnt offerings upon it to the LORD, morning and evening. 4 And they kept the festival of booths,[b] as prescribed, and offered the daily burnt offerings by number according to the ordinance, as required for each day, 5 and after that the regular burnt offerings, the offerings at the new moon and at all the sacred festivals of the LORD, and the offerings of everyone who made a freewill offering to the LORD. 6 From the first day of the seventh month they began to offer burnt offerings to the LORD. But the foundation of the temple of the LORD was not yet laid. 7 So they gave money to the masons and the carpenters, and food, drink, and oil to the Sidonians and the Tyrians to bring cedar trees from Lebanon to the sea, to Joppa, according to the grant that they had from King Cyrus of Persia.

Foundation Laid for the Temple

8 In the second year after their arrival at the house of God at Jerusalem, in the second month, Zerubbabel son of Shealtiel and Jesh-

TEXT MESSAGE

Not all the Jews returned from exile when the Persians let them leave (Ezra 2.1–2). According to Babylonian records, some Jews had become prominent bankers, businesspeople, and government officials in Babylon.

This information has been scanned and is free of all known viruses. Please forward to all your friends.

a 1 Esdras 5.46: Heb lacks *lived in Jerusalem and its vicinity*
b Or *tabernacles*; Heb *succoth*

REALITY ✓

DESPAIR OR HOPE

What was it like in Ezra's time? The exile had shattered the once tight-knit community. People were gathering with a hope they would once again be united. Ezra was a voice and symbol of hope in the middle of frustration and insecurity, as they began to slowly rebuild their community and land.

There have probably been times in your life when things felt hopeless. Divorce. Depression. Drugs. Life can throw a lot of junk at you, and sometimes you can wonder if things will ever be good again.

When bad things happen, you have a choice: despair or hope. Which path are you going to take?

Here's a way to look at it. Did you know that because of your Baptism you have a power within you to help you not to give up? It is the theological virtue of hope. Hope makes you willing to believe and stay with the belief that, *no matter what*, God is with you even when everything seems like a disaster. Hope makes us willing to begin again or keep on going, because we are sure our God is good, all-powerful, and guiding us even in the most desperate times. We just have to tap into that power.

Think about it. How are you going to tap into that power? Find some Creative Space in this Bible and write down your thoughts. Maybe it's a step-by-step plan to "power up" and feel hopeful, no matter what your situation. Or maybe it's a prayer straight to God asking for hope. Whatever it is, share it at **Learner.CalltoDiscipleship.com**.

LORD. [9]And Jeshua with his sons and his kin, and Kadmiel and his sons, Binnui and Hodaviah[a] along with the sons of Henadad, the Levites, their sons and kin, together took charge of the workers in the house of God.

10 When the builders laid the foundation of the temple of the LORD, the priests in their vestments were stationed to praise the LORD with trumpets, and the Levites, the sons of Asaph, with cymbals, according to the directions of King David of Israel; [11]and they sang responsively, praising and giving thanks to the LORD,

"For he is good,
for his steadfast love endures forever
toward Israel."

And all the people responded with a great shout when they praised the LORD, because the foundation of the house of the LORD was laid. [12]But many of the priests and Levites and heads of families, old people who had seen the first house on its foundations, wept with a loud voice when they saw this house, though many shouted aloud for joy, [13]so that the people could not distinguish the sound of the joyful shout from the sound of the people's weeping, for the people shouted so loudly that the sound was heard far away.

4 **Resistance to Rebuilding the Temple**
When the adversaries of Judah and Benjamin heard that the returned exiles were building a temple to the LORD, the God of Israel, [2]they approached Zerubbabel and the heads of families and said to them, "Let us build with you, for we worship your God as you do, and we have been sacrificing to him ever since the days of King Esar-haddon of Assyria who brought us here." [3]But Zerubbabel, Jeshua, and the rest of the heads of families in Israel said to them, "You shall have no part with us in building a house to our God; but we alone will build to the LORD, the God of Israel, as King Cyrus of Persia has commanded us."

4 Then the people of the land discouraged the people of Judah, and made them afraid to build, [5]and they bribed officials to frustrate their plan throughout the reign of King Cyrus of Persia and until the reign of King Darius of Persia.

Rebuilding of Jerusalem Opposed
6 In the reign of Ahasuerus, in his accession year, they wrote an accusation against the inhabitants of Judah and Jerusalem.

7 And in the days of Artaxerxes, Bishlam and Mithredath and Tabeel and the rest of their

---

ua son of Jozadak made a beginning, together with the rest of their people, the priests and the Levites and all who had come to Jerusalem from the captivity. They appointed the Levites, from twenty years old and upward, to have the oversight of the work on the house of the

a Compare 2.40; Neh 7.43; 1 Esdras 5.58: Heb *sons of Judah* associates wrote to King Artaxerxes of Persia; the letter was written in Aramaic and translated.[a] [8]Rehum the royal deputy and Shimshai the scribe wrote a letter against Jerusalem to King Artaxerxes as follows [9](then Rehum the royal deputy, Shimshai the scribe, and the rest of their associates, the judges, the envoys, the officials, the Persians, the people of Erech, the Babylonians, the people of Susa, that is, the Elamites, [10]and the rest of the nations whom the great and noble Osnappar deported and settled in the cities of Samaria and in the rest of the province Beyond the River wrote—and now [11]this is a copy of the letter that they sent):

"To King Artaxerxes: Your servants, the people of the province Beyond the River, send greeting. And now [12]may it be known to the king that the Jews who came up from you to us have gone to Jerusalem. They are rebuilding that rebellious and wicked city; they are finishing the walls and repairing the foundations. [13]Now may it be known to the king that, if this city is rebuilt and the walls finished, they will not pay tribute, custom, or toll, and the royal revenue will be reduced. [14]Now because we share the salt of the palace and it is not fitting for us to witness the king's dishonor, therefore we send and inform the king, [15]so that a search may be made in the annals of your ancestors. You will discover in the annals that this is a rebellious city, hurtful to kings and provinces, and that sedition was stirred up in it from long ago. On that account this city was laid waste. [16]We make known to the king that, if this city is rebuilt and its walls finished, you will then have no possession in the province Beyond the River."

17 The king sent an answer: "To Rehum the royal deputy and Shimshai the scribe and the rest of their associates who live in Samaria and in the rest of the province Beyond the River, greeting. And now [18]the letter that you sent to us has been read in translation before me. [19]So I made a decree, and someone searched and discovered that this city has risen against kings from long ago, and that rebellion and sedition have been made in it. [20]Jerusalem has had mighty kings who ruled over the whole province Beyond the River, to whom tribute, custom, and toll were paid. [21]Therefore issue an order that these people be made to cease, and that this city not be rebuilt, until I make a decree. [22]Moreover, take care not to be slack in this matter; why should damage grow to the hurt of the king?"

23 Then when the copy of King Artaxerxes'

letter was read before Rehum and the scribe Shimshai and their associates, they hurried to the Jews in Jerusalem and by force and power made them cease. [24]At that time the work on the house of God in Jerusalem stopped and was discontinued until the second year of the reign of King Darius of Persia.

5 Restoration of the Temple Resumed

Now the prophets, Haggai[b] and Zechariah son of Iddo, prophesied to the Jews who were in Judah and Jerusalem, in the name of the God of Israel who was over them. [2]Then Zerubbabel son of Shealtiel and Jeshua son of Jozadak set out to rebuild the house of God in Jerusalem; and with them were the prophets of God, helping them.

3 At the same time Tattenai the governor of the province Beyond the River and Shethar-bozenai and their associates came to them and spoke to them thus, "Who gave you a decree to build this house and to finish this structure?" [4]They[c] also asked them this, "What are the names of the men who are building this building?" [5]But the eye of their God was upon the elders of the Jews, and they did not stop them until a report reached Darius and then answer was returned by letter in reply to it.

6 The copy of the letter that Tattenai the governor of the province Beyond the River and Shethar-bozenai and his associates the envoys who were in the province Beyond the River sent to King Darius; [7]they sent him a report, in which was written as follows: "To Darius the king, all peace! [8]May it be known to the king that we went to the province of Judah, to the house of the great God. It is being built of hewn stone, and timber is laid in the walls; this work is being done diligently and prospers in their hands. [9]Then we spoke to those elders and asked them, 'Who gave you a decree to build this house and to finish this structure?' [10]We also asked them their names, for your information, so that we might write down the names of the men at their head. [11]This was their reply to us: 'We are the servants of the God of heaven and earth, and we are rebuilding the house that

---

a Heb adds *in Aramaic*, indicating that 4.8—6.18 is in Aramaic. Another interpretation is *The letter was written in the Aramaic script and set forth in the Aramaic language* b Aram adds *the prophet* c Gk Syr: Aram *We*

Cross in the Sky—© Charlotte Katheder, 16

was built many years ago, which a great king of Israel built and finished. ¹²But because our ancestors had angered the God of heaven, he gave them into the hand of King Nebuchadnezzar of Babylon, the Chaldean, who destroyed this house and carried away the people to Babylonia. ¹³However, King Cyrus of Babylon, in the first year of his reign, made a decree that this house of God should be rebuilt. ¹⁴Moreover, the gold and silver vessels of the house of God, which Nebuchadnezzar had taken out of the temple in Jerusalem and had brought into the temple of Babylon, these King Cyrus took out of the temple of Babylon, and they were delivered to a man named Sheshbazzar, whom he had made governor. ¹⁵He said to him, "Take these vessels; go and put them in the temple in Jerusalem, and let the house of God be rebuilt on its site." ¹⁶Then this Sheshbazzar came and laid the foundations of the house of God in Jerusalem; and from that time until now it has been under construction, and it is not yet finished.' ¹⁷And now, if it seems good to the king, have a search made in the royal archives there in Babylon, to see whether a decree was issued by King Cyrus for the rebuilding of this house of God in Jerusalem. Let the king send us his pleasure in this matter."

6 The Decree of Darius

Then King Darius made a decree, and they searched the archives where the documents were stored in Babylon. ²But it was in Ecbatana, the capital in the province of Media, that a scroll was found on which this was written: "A record. ³In the first year of his reign, King Cyrus issued a decree: Concerning the house of God at Jerusalem, let the house be rebuilt, the place where sacrifices are offered and burnt offerings are brought;ᵃ its height shall be sixty cubits and its width sixty cubits, ⁴with three courses of hewn stones and one course of timber; let the cost be paid from the royal treasury. ⁵Moreover, let the gold and silver vessels of the house of God, which Nebuchadnezzar took out of the temple in Jerusalem and brought to Babylon, be restored and brought back to the temple in Jerusalem, each to its place; you shall put them in the house of God."

6 "Now you, Tattenai, governor of the province Beyond the River, Shethar-bozenai, and you, their associates, the envoys in the province Beyond the River, keep away; ⁷let the work on this house of God alone; let the governor of the Jews and the elders of the Jews rebuild this house of God on its site. ⁸Moreover I make a decree regarding what you shall do for these elders of the Jews for the rebuilding of this house of God: the cost is to be paid to these people, in full and without delay, from the royal revenue, the tribute of the province Beyond the River. ⁹Whatever is needed—young bulls, rams, or sheep for burnt offerings to the God of heaven, wheat, salt, wine, or oil, as the priests in Jerusalem require—let that be given to them day by day without fail, ¹⁰so that they may offer pleasing sacrifices to the God of heaven, and pray for the life of the king and his children. ¹¹Furthermore I decree that if anyone alters this edict, a beam shall be pulled out of the house of the perpetrator, who then shall be impaled on it. The house shall be made a dunghill. ¹²May the God who has established his name there overthrow any king or people that shall put forth a hand to alter this, or to destroy this house of God in Jerusalem. I, Darius, make a decree; let it be done with all diligence."

Completion and Dedication of the Temple

13 Then, according to the word sent by King Darius, Tattenai, the governor of the province Beyond the River, Shethar-bozenai, and their associates did with all diligence what King Darius had ordered. ¹⁴So the elders of the Jews built and prospered, through the prophesying of the prophet Haggai and Zechariah son of Iddo. They finished their building by command of the God of Israel and by decree of Cyrus, Darius, and King Artaxerxes of Persia;

ᵃ Meaning of Aram uncertain

¹⁵and this house was finished on the third day of the month of Adar, in the sixth year of the reign of King Darius.

16 The people of Israel, the priests and the Levites, and the rest of the returned exiles, celebrated the dedication of this house of God with joy. ¹⁷They offered at the dedication of this house of God one hundred bulls, two hundred rams, four hundred lambs, and as a sin offering for all Israel, twelve male goats, according to the number of the tribes of Israel. ¹⁸Then they set the priests in their divisions and the Levites in their courses for the service of God at Jerusalem, as it is written in the book of Moses.

The Passover Celebrated

19 On the fourteenth day of the first month the returned exiles kept the passover. ²⁰For both the priests and the Levites had purified themselves; all of them were clean. So they killed the passover lamb for all the returned exiles, for their fellow priests, and for themselves. ²¹It was eaten by the people of Israel who had returned from exile, and also by all who had joined them and separated themselves from the pollutions of the nations of the land to worship the LORD, the God of Israel. ²²With joy they celebrated the festival of unleavened bread seven days; for the LORD had made them joyful, and had turned the heart of the king of Assyria to them, so that he aided them in the work on the house of God, the God of Israel.

7 The Coming and Work of Ezra

After this, in the reign of King Artaxerxes of Persia, Ezra son of Seraiah, son of Azariah, son of Hilkiah, ²son of Shallum, son of Zadok, son of Ahitub, ³son of Amariah, son of Azariah, son of Meraioth, ⁴son of Zerahiah, son of Uzzi, son of Bukki, ⁵son of Abishua, son of Phinehas, son of Eleazar, son of the chief priest Aaron— ⁶this Ezra went up from Babylonia. He was a scribe skilled in the law of Moses that the LORD the God of Israel had given; and the king granted him all that he asked, for the hand of the LORD his God was upon him.

7 Some of the people of Israel, and some of the priests and Levites, the singers and gatekeepers, and the temple servants also went up to Jerusalem, in the seventh year of King Artaxerxes. ⁸They came to Jerusalem in the fifth month, which was in the seventh year of the king. ⁹On the first day of the first month the journey up from Babylon was begun, and on the first day of the fifth month he came to Jerusalem, for the gracious hand of his God was upon him. ¹⁰For Ezra had set his heart to study

IT'S TRADITION

PASSOVER

No matter where they were, the Jewish people celebrated Passover—even after escaping slavery from Egypt! Read **Ezra 6.19–22**. Over and over again, year after year for more than five thousand years, the Jewish people faithfully gathered to remember God's saving action in freeing them from their Egyptian oppressors at Passover, the greatest of Jewish festivals.

Are you the oldest in your family? Imagine if your birth order was a death sentence. That was the case in Egypt, until God instructed the Hebrew people to mark the doorposts of their homes with the blood of a lamb. Upon seeing this mark, the spirit of the Lord *passed over* these homes, and all the firstborn children were saved from death. The firstborn Egyptians lost their lives, but the Hebrews had something to celebrate. And that's how the Festival of Passover got its name.

Passover is connected to the Eucharist through the Last Supper. Have you ever been to an Easter Vigil Service? It's longer than a typical Mass, but for good reason: there are more readings to proclaim and it is the time the Church welcomes through Baptism new members of the community. The celebration on that night is our greatest of feasts. Over and over again, year after year, Catholic people gather to remember God's saving action through all of human history. We hear the stories from creation to the Resurrection, the event that saved us from sin and death and gave us life eternal.

the law of the LORD, and to do it, and to teach the statutes and ordinances in Israel.

The Letter of Artaxerxes to Ezra

11 This is a copy of the letter that King Artaxerxes gave to the priest Ezra, the scribe, a scholar of the text of the commandments of the LORD and his statutes for Israel: ¹²"Artaxerxes, king of kings, to the priest Ezra, the scribe of the law of the God of heaven:

Peace.[a] And now [13]I decree that any of the people of Israel or their priests or Levites in my kingdom who freely offers to go to Jerusalem may go with you. [14]For you are sent by the king and his seven counselors to make inquiries about Judah and Jerusalem according to the law of your God, which is in your hand, [15]and also to convey the silver and gold that the king and his counselors have freely offered to the God of Israel, whose dwelling is in Jerusalem, [16]with all the silver and gold that you shall find in the whole province of Babylonia, and with the freewill offerings of the people and the priests, given willingly for the house of their God in Jerusalem. [17]With this money, then, you shall with all diligence buy bulls, rams, and lambs, and their grain offerings and their drink offerings, and you shall offer them on the altar of the house of your God in Jerusalem. [18]Whatever seems good to you and your colleagues to do with the rest of the silver and gold, you may do, according to the will of your God. [19]The vessels that have been given you for the service of the house of your God, you shall deliver before the God of Jerusalem. [20]And whatever else is required for the house of your God, which you are responsible for providing, you may provide out of the king's treasury.

[21] "I, King Artaxerxes, decree to all the treasurers in the province Beyond the River: Whatever the priest Ezra, the scribe of the law of the God of heaven, requires of you, let it be done with all diligence, [22]up to one hundred talents of silver, one hundred cors of wheat, one hundred baths[b] of wine, one hundred baths[b] of oil, and unlimited salt. [23]Whatever is commanded by the God of heaven, let it be done with zeal for the house of the God of heaven, or wrath will come upon the realm of the king and his heirs. [24]We also notify you that it shall not be lawful to impose tribute, custom, or toll on any of the priests, the Levites, the singers, the doorkeepers, the temple servants, or other servants of this house of God.

[25] "And you, Ezra, according to the God-given wisdom you possess, appoint magistrates and judges who may judge all the people in the province Beyond the River who know the laws of your God; and you shall teach those who do not know them. [26]All who will not obey the law of your God and the law of the king, let judgment be strictly executed on them, whether for death or for banishment or for confiscation of their goods or for imprisonment."

[27] Blessed be the Lord, the God of our ancestors, who put such a thing as this into the heart of the king to glorify the house of the Lord in Jerusalem, [28]and who extended to me steadfast love before the king and his counselors, and before all the king's mighty officers. I took courage, for the hand of the Lord my God was upon me, and I gathered leaders from Israel to go up with me.

8 Heads of Families Who Returned with Ezra

These are their family heads, and this is the genealogy of those who went up with me from Babylonia, in the reign of King Artaxerxes: [2]Of the descendants of Phinehas, Gershom. Of Ithamar, Daniel. Of David, Hattush, [3]of the descendants of Shecaniah. Of Parosh, Zechariah, with whom were registered one hundred fifty males. [4]Of the descendants of Pahath-moab, Eliehoenai son of Zerahiah, and with him two hundred males. [5]Of the descendants of Zattu,[c] Shecaniah son of Jahaziel, and with him three hundred males. [6]Of the descendants of Adin, Ebed son of Jonathan, and with him fifty males. [7]Of the descendants of Elam, Jeshaiah son of Athaliah, and with him seventy males. [8]Of the descendants of Shephatiah, Zebadiah son of Michael, and with him eighty males. [9]Of the descendants of Joab, Obadiah son of Jehiel, and with him two hundred eighteen males. [10]Of the descendants of Bani,[d] Shelomith son of Josiphiah, and with him one hundred sixty males. [11]Of the descendants of Bebai, Zechariah son of Bebai, and with him twenty-eight males. [12]Of the descendants of Azgad, Johanan son of Hakkatan, and with him one hundred ten males. [13]Of the descendants of Adonikam, those who came later, their names being Eliphelet, Jeuel, and Shemaiah, and with them sixty males. [14]Of the descendants of Bigvai, Uthai and Zaccur, and with them seventy males.

Servants for the Temple

[15] I gathered them by the river that runs to Ahava, and there we camped three days. As I reviewed the people and the priests, I found there none of the descendants of Levi. [16]Then I sent for Eliezer, Ariel, Shemaiah, Elnathan, Jarib, Elnathan, Nathan, Zechariah, and Meshullam, who were leaders, and for Joiarib and Elnathan, who were wise, [17]and sent them to Iddo, the leader at the place called Casiphia, telling them what to say to Iddo and his colleagues the temple servants at Casiphia, namely, to send us ministers for the house of our God. [18]Since the gracious hand of our God was upon us, they brought us a man of discretion,

---

a Syr Vg 1 Esdras 8.9: Aram *Perfect* b A Heb measure of volume c Gk 1 Esdras 8.32: Heb lacks *of Zattu* d Gk 1 Esdras 8.36: Heb lacks *Bani*

PROFILE OF FAITH

She didn't start out to be famous, but she is. She didn't start out to win any prizes, but she did. She didn't start out to become a saint, but she's on her way.

Born in Macedonia on August 26, 1910, she was named Agnesë Gonxhe Bojaxhiu. The world knows her as Mother Teresa—which sure is a lot easier for most of us to pronounce! Her father died when she was eight years old and by the time she was twelve, she had her mind made up that she would join a religious community. At the age of eighteen, she left home and joined the Sisters of Loreto. Once she left home, she never again set eyes on her mother or sister. In 1937, while working as a teacher in eastern Calcutta, she professed final vows and chose the name "Teresa" after the patron saint of missionaries, St. Thérèse of Lisieux.

In 1946, a "call" came that forever changed her life—and the world. This call was not transmitted by a phone, but through deep listening to God. She obeyed her calling and began to work with the poor and dying in the streets of Calcutta.

The Missionaries of Charity, founded by Mother Teresa in 1950, began as a small group of 13 women. Today, there are more than 4,500 religious sisters, a community of priests, and several lay communities serving in 133 countries. She described the work of her order as caring for "the hungry, the naked, the homeless, the crippled, the blind, the lepers, all the people who feel unwanted, unloved, uncared for throughout society, people who have become a burden to the society and are shunned by everyone."

Mother Teresa received the Nobel Peace Prize in 1979 and the Bharat Ratna—the highest honor for India's citizens—in 1980. When asked how people can promote world peace, she responded, "Go home and love your family."

Mother Teresa died on September 5, 1997, at the age of eighty-seven. Shortly after her death, the Vatican began investigating her cause for sainthood. On October 19, 2003, Pope John Paul II announced her beatification, a step toward canonization. We celebrate the feast day of Bl. Mother Teresa of Calcutta on September 5 and recognize her as one of the patrons of World Youth Day, an outreach started by Pope John Paul II.

> "Everybody today seems to be in such a terrible rush, anxious for greater developments and greater riches and so on, so that children have very little time for their parents. Parents have very little time for each other, and in the home begins the disruption of peace of the world."
>
> —Bl. Mother Teresa of Calcutta

---

of the descendants of Mahli son of Levi son of Israel, namely Sherebiah, with his sons and kin, eighteen; [19]also Hashabiah and with him Jeshaiah of the descendants of Merari, with his kin and their sons, twenty; [20]besides two hundred twenty of the temple servants, whom David and his officials had set apart to attend the Levites. These were all mentioned by name.

a Or might fast

Fasting and Prayer for Protection

21 Then I proclaimed a fast there, at the river Ahava, that we might deny ourselves[a] before our God, to seek from him a safe journey for ourselves, our children, and all our possessions. [22]For I was ashamed to ask the king for a band of soldiers and cavalry to protect us against the enemy on our way, since we had

told the king that the hand of our God is gracious to all who seek him, but his power and his wrath are against all who forsake him. [23]So we fasted and petitioned our God for this, and he listened to our entreaty.

Gifts for the Temple

24 Then I set apart twelve of the leading priests: Sherebiah, Hashabiah, and ten of their kin with them. [25]And I weighed out to them the silver and the gold and the vessels, the offering for the house of our God that the king, his counselors, his lords, and all Israel there present had offered; [26]I weighed out into their hand six hundred fifty talents of silver, and one hundred silver vessels worth . . . talents,[a] and one hundred talents of gold, [27]twenty gold bowls worth a thousand darics, and two vessels of fine polished bronze as precious as gold. [28]And I said to them, "You are holy to the LORD, and the vessels are holy; and the silver and the gold are a freewill offering to the LORD, the God of your ancestors. [29]Guard them and keep them until you weigh them before the chief priests and the Levites and the heads of families in Israel at Jerusalem, within the chambers of the house of the LORD." [30]So the priests and the Levites took over the silver, the gold, and the vessels as they were weighed out, to bring them to Jerusalem, to the house of our God.

The Return to Jerusalem

31 Then we left the river Ahava on the twelfth day of the first month, to go to Jerusalem; the hand of our God was upon us, and he delivered us from the hand of the enemy and from ambushes along the way. [32]We came to Jerusalem and remained there three days. [33]On the fourth day, within the house of our God, the silver, the gold, and the vessels were weighed into the hands of the priest Meremoth son of Uriah, and with him was Eleazar son of Phinehas, and with them were the Levites, Jozabad son of Jeshua and Noadiah son of Binnui. [34]The total

was counted and weighed, and the weight of everything was recorded.

35 At that time those who had come from captivity, the returned exiles, offered burnt offerings to the God of Israel, twelve bulls for all Israel, ninety-six rams, seventy-seven lambs, and as a sin offering twelve male goats; all this was a burnt offering to the LORD. [36]They also delivered the king's commissions to the king's satraps and to the governors of the province Beyond the River; and they supported the people and the house of God.

9 Denunciation of Mixed Marriages

After these things had been done, the officials approached me and said, "The people of Israel, the priests, and the Levites have not separated themselves from the peoples of the lands with their abominations, from the Canaanites, the Hittites, the Perizzites, the Jebusites, the Ammonites, the Moabites, the Egyptians, and the Amorites. [2]For they have taken some of their daughters as wives for themselves and for their sons. Thus the holy seed has mixed itself with the peoples of the lands, and in this faithlessness the officials and leaders have led the way." [3]When I heard this, I tore my garment and my mantle, and pulled hair from my head and beard, and sat appalled. [4]Then all who trembled at the words of the God of Israel, because of the faithlessness of the returned exiles, gathered around me while I sat appalled until the evening sacrifice.

Ezra's Prayer

5 At the evening sacrifice I got up from my fasting, with my garments and my mantle torn, and fell on my knees, spread out my hands to the LORD my God, [6]and said,

"O my God, I am too ashamed and embarrassed to lift my face to you, my God, for our iniquities have risen higher than our heads, and our guilt has mounted up to the heavens. [7]From the days of our ancestors to this day we have been deep in guilt, and for our iniquities we, our kings, and our priests have been handed over to the kings of the lands, to the sword, to captivity, to plundering, and to utter shame, as is now the case. [8]But now for a brief moment favor has been shown by the LORD our God, who has left us a remnant, and given us a stake in his holy place, in order that he[b] may brighten our eyes and grant us a little sustenance in our slavery. [9]For we are slaves; yet our God has not forsaken us in our slavery, but has extended to us his steadfast love before the kings of Persia, to give us new life to set up

Christ be with me, Christ within me,
Christ behind me, Christ before me,
Christ beside me, Christ to win me,
Christ to comfort me and restore me,
Christ beneath me, Christ above me,
Christ in quiet, Christ in danger,
Christ in hearts of all that love me,
Christ in mouth of friend and stranger.

The Breastplate of St. Patrick

a The number of talents is lacking b Heb our God

the house of our God, to repair its ruins, and to give us a wall in Judea and Jerusalem.

10 "And now, our God, what shall we say after this? For we have forsaken your commandments, [11]which you commanded by your servants the prophets, saying, 'The land that you are entering to possess is a land unclean with the pollutions of the peoples of the lands, with their abominations. They have filled it from end to end with their uncleanness. [12]Therefore do not give your daughters to their sons, neither take their daughters for your sons, and never seek their peace or prosperity, so that you may be strong and eat the good of the land and leave it for an inheritance to your children forever.' [13]After all that has come upon us for our evil deeds and for our great guilt, seeing that you, our God, have punished us less than our iniquities deserved and have given us such a remnant as this, [14]shall we break your commandments again and intermarry with the peoples who practice these abominations? Would you not be angry with us until you destroy us without remnant or survivor? [15]O LORD, God of Israel, you are just, but we have escaped as a remnant, as is now the case. Here we are before you in our guilt, though no one can face you because of this."

Nails in Our Hands—© Emily Knollenberg, 17

10 The People's Response

While Ezra prayed and made confession, weeping and throwing himself down before the house of God, a very great assembly of men, women, and children gathered to him out of Israel; the people also wept bitterly. [2]Shecaniah son of Jehiel, of the descendants of Elam, addressed Ezra, saying, "We have broken faith with our God and have married foreign women from the peoples of the land, but even now there is hope for Israel in spite of this. [3]So now let us make a covenant with our God to send away all these wives and their children, according to the counsel of my lord and of those who tremble at the commandment of our God; and let it be done according to the law. [4]Take action, for it is your duty, and we are with you; be strong, and do it." [5]Then Ezra stood up and made the leading priests, the Levites, and all Israel swear that they would do as had been said. So they swore.

Foreign Wives and Their Children Rejected

6 Then Ezra withdrew from before the house of God, and went to the chamber of Jehohanan son of Eliashib, where he spent the night.[a] He did not eat bread or drink water, for he was mourning over the faithlessness of the exiles.

[7]They made a proclamation throughout Judah and Jerusalem to all the returned exiles that they should assemble at Jerusalem, [8]and that if any did not come within three days, by order of the officials and the elders all their property should be forfeited, and they themselves banned from the congregation of the exiles.

9 Then all the people of Judah and Benjamin assembled at Jerusalem within the three days; it was the ninth month, on the twentieth day of the month. All the people sat in the open square before the house of God, trembling because of this matter and because of the heavy rain. [10]Then Ezra the priest stood up and said to them, "You have trespassed and married foreign women, and so increased the guilt of Israel. [11]Now make confession to the LORD God of your ancestors, and do his will; separate yourselves from the peoples of the land and from the foreign wives." [12]Then all the assembly answered with a loud voice, "It is so; we must do as you have said. [13]But the people are many, and it is a time of heavy rain; we cannot stand in the open. Nor is this a task for one day or for two, for many of us have transgressed in this matter. [14]Let our officials represent the whole assembly, and let all in our towns who have taken foreign wives come at appointed times, and with them the elders and judges of every town, until the fierce wrath of our God on this account is averted from us." [15]Only Jonathan son of Asahel and Jahzeiah son of Tikvah opposed this, and Meshullam and Shabbethai the Levites supported them.

16 Then the returned exiles did so. Ezra the priest selected men,[b] heads of families, according to their families, each of them designated by name. On the first day of the tenth month they sat down to examine the matter. [17]By the

a 1 Esdras 9.2: Heb where he went b 1 Esdras 9.16: Syr: Heb And there were selected Ezra, first day of the first month they had come to the end of all the men who had married foreign women.

18 There were found of the descendants of the priests who had married foreign women, of the descendants of Jeshua son of Jozadak and his brothers: Maaseiah, Eliezer, Jarib, and Gedaliah. ¹⁹They pledged themselves to send away their wives, and their guilt offering was a ram of the flock for their guilt. ²⁰Of the descendants of Immer: Hanani and Zebadiah. ²¹Of the descendants of Harim: Maaseiah, Elijah, Shemaiah, Jehiel, and Uzziah. ²²Of the descendants of Pashhur: Elioenai, Maaseiah, Ishmael, Nethanel, Jozabad, and Elasah.

23 Of the Levites: Jozabad, Shimei, Kelaiah (that is, Kelita), Pethahiah, Judah, and Eliezer. ²⁴Of the singers: Eliashib. Of the gatekeepers: Shallum, Telem, and Uri.

25 And of Israel: of the descendants of Parosh: Ramiah, Izziah, Malchijah, Mijamin, Eleazar, Hashabiah,ᵃ and Benaiah. ²⁶Of the descendants of Elam: Mattaniah, Zechariah, Jehiel, Abdi, Jeremoth, and Elijah. ²⁷Of the descendants of Zattu: Elioenai, Eliashib, Mattaniah, Jeremoth, Zabad, and Aziza. ²⁸Of the descendants of Bebai: Jehohanan, Hananiah, Zabbai, and Athlai. ²⁹Of the descendants of Bani: Meshullam, Malluch, Adaiah, Jashub, Sheal, and Jeremoth. ³⁰Of the descendants of Pahath-moab: Adna, Chelal, Benaiah, Maaseiah, Mattaniah, Bezalel, Binnui, and Manasseh. ³¹Of the descendants of Harim: Eliezer, Isshijah, Malchijah, Shemaiah, Shimeon, ³²Benjamin, Malluch, and Shemariah. ³³Of the descendants of Hashum: Mattenai, Mattattah, Zabad, Eliphelet, Jeremai, Manasseh, and Shimei. ³⁴Of the descendants of Bani: Maadai, Amram, Uel, ³⁵Benaiah, Bedeiah, Cheluhi, ³⁶Vaniah, Meremoth, Eliashib, ³⁷Mattaniah, Mattenai, and Jaasu. ³⁸Of the descendants of Binnui:ᵇ Shimei, ³⁹Shelemiah, Nathan, Adaiah, ⁴⁰Machnadebai, Shashai, Sharai, ⁴¹Azarel, Shelemiah, Shemariah, ⁴²Shallum, Amariah, and Joseph. ⁴³Of the descendants of Nebo: Jeiel, Mattithiah, Zabad, Zebina, Jaddai, Joel, and Benaiah. ⁴⁴All these had married foreign women, and they sent them away with their children.ᶜ

a 1 Esdras 9.26 Gk: Heb *Malchijah* *b* Gk: Heb *Bani, Binnui* *c* 1 Esdras 9.36; meaning of Heb uncertain

NEHEMIAH

REBUILDING THE WALL, REBUILDING THE FAITH

The Unforgettable Day

It was like nothing anyone had ever seen. There were so many people that fathers had to put their children on their shoulders, just so they could see what was happening. The whispers in the crowd were about something extraordinary that was going to take place that day at the Water Gate.

Ezra the scribe came forward and stepped up on the platform. He was carrying a book. As he opened the book, people started to stand. Ezra said something, but the words were lost in the noise of the crowd. Some said he was praying to God, so people began to lie prostrate with their faces to the ground in honor of the God who had brought them back to the land.

Then he began.

The words that he spoke from the book poured like honey from his lips. They spoke of God's goodness, his unfailing love for his people, Israel. These were the words of God to God's people! God was calling them back into covenant with him, to be faithful to him and him alone. The people wept with joy and with sorrow for the many wasted years. God still wanted his people, and they still wanted him as their God.

Those words . . . they were unforgettable.

"Must you continue to be your own cross? No matter which way God leads you, you change everything into bitterness by constantly brooding over everything. For the love of God, replace all this self-scrutiny with a pure and simple glance at God's goodness."

—St. Jeanne de Chantal

WHO The original author or authors are unknown. Most likely the Chronicler had a strong influence on the book in this form.

WHAT It contains historical information about the restoration of the wall of Jerusalem and the restoration of the community around the law.

WHEN The events of Nehemiah took place from 465 to 359 B.C.

WHERE Jerusalem, after God's people returned from exile in Babylon (modern-day Iraq)

PATH OF DISCIPLESHIP

Those who came that day to the Water Gate during the Festival of Tabernacles heard the words of the book of the law proclaimed to them (see Nehemiah 8). For some of them, it might have been the first time they had ever heard the words. God was inviting his people to come back home, to live in harmony with him and one another once again. God's Word inspired the nation to rebuild the city.

Some years later, at another Festival of Tabernacles, Jesus stood among the crowd and said, "Let anyone who is thirsty come to me, and let the one who believes in me drink" (John 7.37–38). Being a disciple of Jesus requires you to be at home *with* God and be of service *to* God. Will you accept Jesus' invitation to come and drink?

1 Nehemiah Prays for His People

The words of Nehemiah son of Hacaliah. In the month of Chislev, in the twentieth year, while I was in Susa the capital, ²one of my brothers, Hanani, came with certain men from Judah; and I asked them about the Jews that survived, those who had escaped the captivity, and about Jerusalem. ³They replied, "The survivors there in the province who escaped captivity are in great trouble and shame; the wall of Jerusalem is broken down, and its gates have been destroyed by fire."

4 When I heard these words I sat down and wept, and mourned for days, fasting and praying before the God of heaven. ⁵I said, "O LORD God of heaven, the great and awesome God who keeps covenant and steadfast love with those who love him and keep his commandments; ⁶let your ear be attentive and your eyes open to hear the prayer of your servant that I now pray before you day and night for your servants, the people of Israel, confessing the sins of the people of Israel, which we have sinned against you. Both I and my family have sinned. ⁷We have offended you deeply, failing to keep the commandments, the statutes, and the ordinances that you commanded your servant Moses. ⁸Remember the word that you commanded your servant Moses, 'If you are unfaithful, I will scatter you among the peoples; ⁹but if you return to me and keep my commandments and do them, though your outcasts are under the farthest skies, I will gather them from there and bring them to the place at which I have chosen to establish my name.' ¹⁰They are your servants and your people, whom you redeemed by your great power and your strong hand. ¹¹O Lord, let your ear be attentive to the prayer of your servant, and to the prayer of your servants who delight in revering your name. Give success to your servant today, and grant him mercy in the sight of this man!"

At the time, I was cupbearer to the king.

2 Nehemiah Sent to Judah

In the month of Nisan, in the twentieth year of King Artaxerxes, when wine was served him, I carried the wine and gave it to the king. Now, I had never been sad in his presence before. ²So the king said to me, "Why is your face sad, since you are not sick? This can only be sadness of the heart." Then I was very much afraid. ³I said to the king, "May the king live forever! Why should my face not be sad, when the city, the place of my ancestors' graves, lies waste, and its gates have been destroyed by fire?" ⁴Then the king said to me, "What do you request?" So I prayed to the God of heaven. ⁵Then I said to the king, "If it pleases the king, and if your servant has found favor with you, I ask that you send me to Judah, to the city of my ancestors' graves, so that I may rebuild it." ⁶The king said to me (the queen also was sitting beside him), "How long will you be gone, and when will you return?" So it pleased the king to send me, and I set him a date. ⁷Then I said to the king, "If it pleases the king, let letters be given me to the governors of the province Beyond the River, that they may grant me passage until I arrive in Judah; [8]and a letter to Asaph, the keeper of the king's forest, directing him to give me timber to make beams for the gates of the temple fortress, and for the wall of the city, and for the house that I shall occupy." And the king granted me what I asked, for the gracious hand of my God was upon me.

9 Then I came to the governors of the province Beyond the River, and gave them the king's letters. Now the king had sent officers of the army and cavalry with me. [10]When Sanballat the Horonite and Tobiah the Ammonite official heard this, it displeased them greatly that someone had come to seek the welfare of the people of Israel.

Nehemiah's Inspection of the Walls

11 So I came to Jerusalem and was there for three days. [12]Then I got up during the night, I and a few men with me; I told no one what my God had put into my heart to do for Jerusalem. The only animal I took was the animal I rode. [13]I went out by night by the Valley Gate past the Dragon's Spring and to the Dung Gate, and I inspected the walls of Jerusalem that had been broken down and its gates that had been destroyed by fire. [14]Then I went on to the Fountain Gate and to the King's Pool; but there was no place for the animal I was riding to continue. [15]So I went up by way of the valley by night and inspected the wall. Then I turned back and entered by the Valley Gate, and so returned. [16]The officials did not know where I had gone or what I was doing; I had not yet told the Jews, the priests, the nobles, the officials, and the rest that were to do the work.

Decision to Restore the Walls

17 Then I said to them, "You see the trouble we are in, how Jerusalem lies in ruins with its gates burned. Come, let us rebuild the wall of Jerusalem, so that we may no longer suffer disgrace." [18]I told them that the hand of my God had been gracious upon me, and also the words that the king had spoken to me. Then they said, "Let us start building!" So they committed themselves to the common good. [19]But when Sanballat the Horonite and Tobiah the Ammonite official, and Geshem the Arab heard of it, they mocked and ridiculed us, saying, "What is this that you are doing? Are you rebelling against the king?" [20]Then I replied to them, "The God of heaven is the one who will give us success, and we his servants are going to start building;

but you have no share or claim or historic right in Jerusalem."

3 Organization of the Work

Then the high priest Eliashib set to work with his fellow priests and rebuilt the Sheep Gate. They consecrated it and set up its doors; they consecrated it as far as the Tower of the Hundred and as far as the Tower of Hananel. [2]And the men of Jericho built next to him. And next to them[a] Zaccur son of Imri built.

3 The sons of Hassenaah built the Fish Gate; they laid its beams and set up its doors, its bolts, and its bars. [4]Next to them Meremoth son of Uriah son of Hakkoz made repairs. Next to them Meshullam son of Berechiah son of Meshezabel made repairs. Next to them Zadok son of Baana made repairs. [5]Next to them the Tekoites made repairs; but their nobles would not put their shoulders to the work of their Lord.[b]

6 Joiada son of Paseah and Meshullam son of Besodeiah repaired the Old Gate; they laid its beams and set up its doors, its bolts, and its bars. [7]Next to them repairs were made by Melatiah the Gibeonite and Jadon the Meronothite—the men of Gibeon and of Mizpah—who were under the jurisdiction of[c] the governor of the province Beyond the River. [8]Next to them Uzziel son of Harhaiah, one of the goldsmiths, made repairs. Next to him Hananiah, one of the perfumers, made repairs; and they restored Jerusalem as far as the Broad Wall. [9]Next to them Rephaiah son of Hur, ruler of half the district of[d] Jerusalem, made repairs. [10]Next to them Jedaiah son of Harumaph made repairs opposite his house; and next to him Hattush son of Hashabneiah made repairs. [11]Malchijah son of Harim and Hasshub son of Pahath-moab repaired another section and the Tower of the Ovens. [12]Next to him Shallum son of Hallohesh, ruler of half the district of[d] Jerusalem, made repairs, he and his daughters.

13 Hanun and the inhabitants of Zanoah repaired the Valley Gate; they rebuilt it and set up its doors, its bolts, and its bars, and repaired a thousand cubits of the wall, as far as the Dung Gate.

14 Malchijah son of Rechab, ruler of the district of[e] Beth-haccherem, repaired the Dung Gate; he rebuilt it and set up its doors, its bolts, and its bars.

15 And Shallum son of Col-hozeh, ruler of the district of[e] Mizpah, repaired the Fountain Gate; he rebuilt it and covered it and set up its doors, its bolts, and its bars; and he built the wall of the Pool of Shelah of the king's garden,

---

a Heb *him* b Or *lords* c Meaning of Heb uncertain d Or *supervisor of half the portion assigned to* e Or *supervisor of the portion assigned to*

Put to the Test

Exam week. You haven't slept in days. Your eyes are burning. Your social life is a distant memory. You push your body to the limits to get a certain letter of the alphabet on a piece of recycled paper. When was the last time you offered *God* that kind of dedication?

Nehemiah had a pretty cushy job in Babylon. He brought the king stuff to drink, and he was the official taste tester. This was not exactly a physically grueling job unless someone tried to poison the king and he tasted it first! But this guy had heart. Loyalty. He was important, but never forgot where he came from. When God called him to leave everything behind to head up a dirty, exhausting, controversial reconstruction campaign, he jumped in with determination and efficiency.

Read **Nehemiah 4.1–6.19**. Rebuilding the city wall around disheveled Jerusalem was dangerous. Men held weapons in one hand and worked with the other. While one shift worked, the other stayed awake on guard. The volunteers drained their savings and worked fifty-two days straight without a break or a change of clothes. God asked for exhaustive, overwhelming, unthinkable, total effort. Nehemiah and his team delivered.

Nothing cushy about *that* gig. Could you have handled stepping so far out of your comfort zone? What is your comfort zone? Do you only feel relaxed when you're hanging out with certain people? Are you truly comfortable when you're alone? Do you feel too shy to volunteer for a school project or to participate in a parish event?

How might God be challenging *you* to step out of *your* comfort zone to serve him by serving others? What might God want you to do for his Church—for your local parish or the global Body of Christ? Think of a "God project" that you will undertake, one that does move you out of your comfort zone. If you are shy, doing something from home doesn't count!

Then go outside, pick out several stones, and decorate them with a marker to represent your "God project." Those stones can remind you of the wall Nehemiah helped build and the similar level of dedication God is calling forth from you. Take a picture of the stones—or your project—and upload it to **Learner.CalltoDiscipleship.com**.

---

as far as the stairs that go down from the City of David. [16]After him Nehemiah son of Azbuk, ruler of half the district of[a] Beth-zur, repaired from a point opposite the graves of David, as far as the artificial pool and the house of the warriors. [17]After him the Levites made repairs: Rehum son of Bani; next to him Hashabiah, ruler of half the district of[a] Keilah, made repairs for his district. [18]After him their kin made repairs: Binnui,[b] son of Henadad, ruler of half the district of[a] Keilah; [19]next to him Ezer son of Jeshua, ruler[c] of Mizpah, repaired another section opposite the ascent to the armory at the Angle. [20]After him Baruch son of Zabbai repaired another section from the Angle to the door of the house of the high priest Eliashib. [21]After him Meremoth son of Uriah son of Hakkoz repaired another section from the door of the house of Eliashib to the end of the house of Eliashib. [22]After him the priests, the men of the surrounding area, made repairs. [23]After them Benjamin and Hasshub made repairs opposite their house. After them Azariah son of Maaseiah son of Ananiah made repairs beside his own house. [24]After him Binnui son of Henadad repaired another section, from the house of Azariah to the Angle and to the corner. [25]Palal son of Uzai repaired opposite the Angle and the tower projecting from the upper house of the king at the court of the guard. After him Pedaiah son of Parosh [26]and the temple servants living[d] on Ophel made repairs up to a point opposite the Water Gate on the east and the projecting tower. [27]After him the Tekoites repaired another section opposite the great projecting tower as far as the wall of Ophel.

28 Above the Horse Gate the priests made repairs, each one opposite his own house. [29]After them Zadok son of Immer made repairs opposite his own house. After him Shemaiah son of Shecaniah, the keeper of the East Gate, made repairs. [30]After him Hananiah son of Shelemiah and Hanun sixth son of Zalaph repaired another section. After him Meshullam son of Berechiah made repairs opposite his living quarters. [31]After him Malchijah, one of the goldsmiths, made repairs as far as the house of the temple servants and of the merchants, opposite the Muster Gate,[e] and to the upper room of the corner. [32]And between the upper room of the corner and the Sheep Gate the goldsmiths and the merchants made repairs.

4[f] Hostile Plots Thwarted

Now when Sanballat heard that we were building the wall, he was angry and greatly enraged,

a Or *supervisor of half the portion assigned to* *b* Gk Syr Compare verse 24, 10.9: Heb *Bavvai* *co c* Or *supervisor* *d* Cn: Heb *were living* *e* Or *Hammiphkad Gate* *f* Ch 3.33 in Heb and he mocked the Jews. [2]He said in the presence of his associates and of the army of Samaria, "What are these feeble Jews doing? Will they restore things? Will they sacrifice? Will they finish it in a day? Will they revive the stones out of the heaps of rubbish—and burned ones at that?" [3]Tobiah the Ammonite was beside him, and he said, "That stone wall they are building—any fox going up on it would break it down!" [4]Hear, O our God, for we are despised; turn their taunt back on their own heads, and give them over as plunder in a land of captivity. [5]Do not cover their guilt, and do not let their sin be blotted out from your sight; for they have hurled insults in the face of the builders.

6 So we rebuilt the wall, and all the wall was joined together to half its height; for the people had a mind to work.

[7][a] But when Sanballat and Tobiah and the Arabs and the Ammonites and the Ashdodites heard that the repairing of the walls of Jerusalem was going forward and the gaps were beginning to be closed, they were very angry, [8]and all plotted together to come and fight against Jerusalem and to cause confusion in it. [9]So we prayed to our God, and set a guard as a protection against them day and night.

10 But Judah said, "The strength of the burden bearers is failing, and there is too much rubbish so that we are unable to work on the wall." [11]And our enemies said, "They will not know or see anything before we come upon them and kill them and stop the work." [12]When the Jews who lived near them came, they said to us ten times, "From all the places where they live[b] they will come up against us."[c] [13]So in the lowest parts of the space behind the wall, in open places, I stationed the people according to their families,[d] with their swords, their spears, and their bows. [14]After I looked these things over, I stood up and said to the nobles and the officials and the rest of the people, "Do not be afraid of them. Remember the Lord, who is great and awesome, and fight for your kin, your sons, your daughters, your wives, and your homes."

15 When our enemies heard that their plot was known to us, and that God had frustrated it, we all returned to the wall, each to his work. [16]From that day on, half of my servants worked on construction, and half held the spears, shields, bows, and body-armor; and the leaders posted themselves behind the whole house of Judah, [17]who were building the wall. The burden bearers carried their loads in such a way that each labored on the work with one hand and with the other held a weapon. [18]And each of the builders had his sword strapped at his side while he built. The man who sounded the trumpet was beside me. [19]And I said to the nobles, the officials, and the rest of the people, "The work is great and widely spread out, and we are separated far from one another on the wall. [20]Rally to us wherever you hear the sound of the trumpet. Our God will fight for us."

21 So we labored at the work, and half of them held the spears from break of dawn until the stars came out. [22]I also said to the people at that time, "Let every man and his servant pass the night inside Jerusalem, so that they may be a guard for us by night and may labor by day." [23]So neither I nor my brothers nor my servants nor the men of the guard who followed me ever took off our clothes; each kept his weapon in his right hand.[e]

5 Nehemiah Deals with Oppression

Now there was a great outcry of the people and of their wives against their Jewish kin. [2]For there were those who said, "With our sons and our daughters, we are many; we must get grain, so that we may eat and stay alive." [3]There were also those who said, "We are having to pledge our fields, our vineyards, and our houses in order to get grain during the famine." [4]And there were those who said, "We are having to borrow money on our fields and vineyards to pay the king's tax. [5]Now our flesh is the same as that of our kindred; our children are the same as their children; and yet we are forcing our sons and daughters to be slaves, and some of our daughters have been ravished; we are powerless, and our fields and vineyards now belong to others."

6 I was very angry when I heard their outcry and these complaints. [7]After thinking it over, I brought charges against the nobles and the officials; I said to them, "You are all taking interest from your own people." And I called a great assembly to deal with them, [8]and said to them, "As far as we were able, we have bought back our Jewish kindred who had been sold to other nations; but now you are selling your own kin, who must then be bought back by us!" They were silent, and could not find a word to say. [9]So I said, "The thing that you are doing is not good. Should you not walk in the fear of our God, to prevent the taunts of the nations our enemies? [10]Moreover I and my brothers and my servants are lending them money and grain. Let us stop this taking of interest. [11]Restore to them, this very day, their fields, their

---

a Ch 4.1 in Heb b Cn: Heb you return c Compare Gk Syr: Meaning of Heb uncertain d Meaning of Heb uncertain e Cn: Heb each his weapon the water vineyards, their olive orchards, and their houses, and the interest on money, grain, wine, and oil that you have been exacting from them." ¹²Then they said, "We will restore everything and demand nothing more from them. We will do as you say." And I called the priests, and made them take an oath to do as they had promised. ¹³I also shook out the fold of my garment and said, "So may God shake out everyone from house and from property who does not perform this promise. Thus may they be shaken out and emptied." And all the assembly said, "Amen," and praised the LORD. And the people did as they had promised.

The Generosity of Nehemiah

14 Moreover from the time that I was appointed to be their governor in the land of Judah, from the twentieth year to the thirty-second year of King Artaxerxes, twelve years, neither I nor my brothers ate the food allowance of the governor. ¹⁵The former governors who were before me laid heavy burdens on the people, and took food and wine from them, besides forty shekels of silver. Even their servants lorded it over the people. But I did not do so, because of the fear of God. ¹⁶Indeed, I devoted myself to the work on this wall, and acquired no land; and all my servants were gathered there for the work. ¹⁷Moreover there were at my table one hundred fifty people, Jews and officials, besides those who came to us from the nations around us. ¹⁸Now that which was prepared for one day was one ox and six choice sheep; also fowls were prepared for me, and every ten days skins of wine in abundance; yet with all this I did not demand the food allowance of the governor, because of the heavy burden of labor on the people. ¹⁹Remember for my good, O my God, all that I have done for this people.

6 Intrigues of Enemies Foiled

Now when it was reported to Sanballat and Tobiah and to Geshem the Arab and to the rest of our enemies that I had built the wall and that there was no gap left in it (though up to that time I had not set up the doors in the gates), ²Sanballat and Geshem sent to me, saying, "Come and let us meet together in one of the villages in the plain of Ono." But they intended to do me harm. ³So I sent messengers to them, saying, "I am doing a great work and I cannot come down. Why should the work stop while I leave it to come down to you?" ⁴They sent to me four times in this way, and I answered them in the same manner. ⁵In the same way Sanbal-

lat for the fifth time sent his servant to me with an open letter in his hand. ⁶In it was written, "It is reported among the nations—and Geshem*a* also says it—that you and the Jews intend to rebel; that is why you are building the wall; and according to this report you wish to become their king. ⁷You have also set up prophets to proclaim in Jerusalem concerning you, 'There is a king in Judah!' And now it will be reported to the king according to these words. So come, therefore, and let us confer together." ⁸Then I sent to him, saying, "No such things as you say have been done; you are inventing them out of your own mind" ⁹—for they all wanted to frighten us, thinking, "Their hands will drop from the work, and it will not be done." But now, O God, strengthen my hands.

10 One day when I went into the house of Shemaiah son of Delaiah son of Mehetabel, who was confined to his house, he said, "Let us meet together in the house of God, within the temple, and let us close the doors of the temple, for they are coming to kill you; indeed, tonight they are coming to kill you." ¹¹But I said, "Should a man like me run away? Would a man like me go into the temple to save his life? I will not go in!" ¹²Then I perceived and saw that God had not sent him at all, but he had pronounced the prophecy against me because Tobiah and Sanballat had hired him. ¹³He was hired for this purpose, to intimidate me and make me sin by acting in this way, and so they could give me a bad name, in order to taunt me. ¹⁴Remember Tobiah and Sanballat, O my God, according to these things that they did, and also the prophetess Noadiah and the rest of the prophets who wanted to make me afraid.

The Wall Completed

15 So the wall was finished on the twenty-fifth day of the month Elul, in fifty-two days. ¹⁶And when all our enemies heard of it, all the nations around us were afraid*b* and fell greatly in their own esteem; for they perceived that this work had been accomplished with the help of our God. ¹⁷Moreover in those days the nobles of Judah sent many letters to Tobiah, and Tobiah's letters came to them. ¹⁸For many in Judah were bound by oath to him, because he was the son-in-law of Shecaniah son of Arah; and his son Jehohanan had married the daughter of Meshullam son of Berechiah. ¹⁹Also they spoke of his good deeds in my presence, and reported my words to him. And Tobiah sent letters to intimidate me.

7 Now when the wall had been built and I had set up the doors, and the gatekeepers, the

---

a Heb *Gashmu*   *b* Another reading is *saw*

singers, and the Levites had been appointed, ²I gave my brother Hanani charge over Jerusalem, along with Hananiah the commander of the citadel—for he was a faithful man and feared God more than many. ³And I said to them, "The gates of Jerusalem are not to be opened until the sun is hot; while the gatekeepers*ᵃ* are still standing guard, let them shut and bar the doors. Appoint guards from among the inhabitants of Jerusalem, some at their watch posts, and others before their own houses." ⁴The city was wide and large, but the people within it were few and no houses had been built.

Lists of the Returned Exiles

5 Then my God put it into my mind to assemble the nobles and the officials and the people to be enrolled by genealogy. And I found the book of the genealogy of those who were the first to come back, and I found the following written in it:

6 These are the people of the province who came up out of the captivity of those exiles whom King Nebuchadnezzar of Babylon had carried into exile; they returned to Jerusalem and Judah, each to his town. ⁷They came with Zerubbabel, Jeshua, Nehemiah, Azariah, Raamiah, Nahamani, Mordecai, Bilshan, Mispereth, Bigvai, Nehum, Baanah.

The number of the Israelite people: ⁸the descendants of Parosh, two thousand one hundred seventy-two. ⁹Of Shephatiah, three hundred seventy-two. ¹⁰Of Arah, six hundred fifty-two. ¹¹Of Pahath-moab, namely the descendants of Jeshua and Joab, two thousand eight hundred eighteen. ¹²Of Elam, one thousand two hundred fifty-four. ¹³Of Zattu, eight hundred forty-five. ¹⁴Of Zaccai, seven hundred sixty. ¹⁵Of Binnui, six hundred forty-eight. ¹⁶Of Bebai, six hundred twenty-eight. ¹⁷Of Azgad, two thousand three hundred twenty-two. ¹⁸Of Adonikam, six hundred sixty-seven. ¹⁹Of Bigvai, two thousand sixty-seven. ²⁰Of Adin, six hundred fifty-five. ²¹Of Ater, namely of Hezekiah, ninety-eight. ²²Of Hashum, three hundred twenty-eight. ²³Of Bezai, three hundred twenty-four. ²⁴Of Hariph, one hundred twelve. ²⁵Of Gibeon, ninety-five. ²⁶The people of Bethlehem and Netophah, one hundred eighty-eight. ²⁷Of Anathoth, one hundred twenty-eight. ²⁸Of Beth-azmaveth, forty-two. ²⁹Of Kiriath-jearim, Chephirah, and Beeroth, seven hundred forty-three. ³⁰Of Ramah and Geba, six hundred twenty-one. ³¹Of Michmas, one hundred twenty-two. ³²Of Bethel and Ai, one hundred twenty-three. ³³Of the other Nebo, fifty-two. ³⁴The descendants of the other Elam, one thousand

ᵃ Heb *while they*

PROFILE OF FAITH

PATRON SAINTS OF BUILDERS:
Foundations of Faith

If Judaism had patron saints, Nehemiah and Solomon would probably be patrons of builders and construction. On the Catholic list of patron saints there are several for builders and construction workers. Among them are St. Thomas the Apostle, whose symbol is the builder's square, and St. Barbara.

There are several stories (or they might be legends) that explain why the Church bestowed this patronage on St. Thomas. It is said that he built the first church building in India with his own hands and a palace for King Guduphara. More important than the stories about buildings was his deep faith, which gave all the parishes he began strong foundations.

St. Barbara was a beautiful young woman whose father imprisoned her in a tower because she disobeyed him. While there, she was tutored by several people, came to believe in Jesus, and converted to Christianity. Her father denounced her and had her tortured and killed. Because of her imprisonment in the tower, the Church associated her with the construction and maintenance of bridges and later with their military uses.

two hundred fifty-four. ³⁵Of Harim, three hundred twenty. ³⁶Of Jericho, three hundred forty-five. ³⁷Of Lod, Hadid, and Ono, seven hundred twenty-one. ³⁸Of Senaah, three thousand nine hundred thirty.

39 The priests: the descendants of Jedaiah, namely the house of Jeshua, nine hundred seventy-three. ⁴⁰Of Immer, one thousand fifty-two. ⁴¹Of Pashhur, one thousand two hundred forty-seven. ⁴²Of Harim, one thousand seventeen.

43 The Levites: the descendants of Jeshua, namely of Kadmiel of the descendants of Hodevah, seventy-four. ⁴⁴The singers: the descendants of Asaph, one hundred forty-eight. ⁴⁵The gatekeepers: the descendants of Shal-

The command of love is one not to be taken lightly. Love sounds so simple on the surface, but digging into scripture shows how great a challenge it is to exhibit biblical love.

God's command is to love each other as we love our self (Leviticus 19.18); which is a continuing command. But Christ brought forth a new standard of love: to love one another as Christ has loved us (John 15.12–13). This is not love based on fond acquaintance, but rather a sacrificial love in action. Our attitude toward our abilities, time, and money should focus on what we have to offer someone else. We must forgo the commonly held conception of passive love that our culture condones and begin to love others in the passionate and eager way that Jesus Christ loved us. God has called us, how will you answer the challenge?

Challenge of Love—© Paul Hamilton, 18

Poor—© Lexi Hiland, 16

lum, of Ater, of Talmon, of Akkub, of Hatita, of Shobai, one hundred thirty-eight.

46 The temple servants: the descendants of Ziha, of Hasupha, of Tabbaoth, ⁴⁷of Keros, of Sia, of Padon, ⁴⁸of Lebana, of Hagaba, of Shalmai, ⁴⁹of Hanan, of Giddel, of Gahar, ⁵⁰of Reaiah, of Rezin, of Nekoda, ⁵¹of Gazzam, of Uzza, of Paseah, ⁵²of Besai, of Meunim, of Nephushesim, ⁵³of Bakbuk, of Hakupha, of Harhur, ⁵⁴of Bazlith, of Mehida, of Harsha, ⁵⁵of Barkos, of Sisera, of Temah, ⁵⁶of Neziah, of Hatipha.

57 The descendants of Solomon's servants: of Sotai, of Sophereth, of Perida, ⁵⁸of Jaala, of Darkon, of Giddel, ⁵⁹of Shephatiah, of Hattil, of Pochereth-hazzebaim, of Amon.

60 All the temple servants and the descendants of Solomon's servants were three hundred ninety-two.

61 The following were those who came up from Tel-melah, Tel-harsha, Cherub, Addon, and Immer, but they could not prove their ancestral houses or their descent, whether they belonged to Israel: ⁶²the descendants of Delaiah, of Tobiah, of Nekoda, six hundred forty-two. ⁶³Also, of the priests: the descendants of Hobaiah, of Hakkoz, of Barzillai (who had married one of the daughters of Barzillai the Gileadite and was called by their name). ⁶⁴These sought their registration among those enrolled in the genealogies, but it was not found there, so they were excluded from the priesthood as unclean; ⁶⁵the governor told them that they were not to partake of the most holy food, until a priest with Urim and Thummim should come.

66 The whole assembly together was forty-two thousand three hundred sixty, ⁶⁷besides their male and female slaves, of whom there were seven thousand three hundred thirty-seven; and they had two hundred forty-five singers, male and female. ⁶⁸They had seven hundred thirty-six horses, two hundred forty-five mules,ᵃ ⁶⁹four hundred thirty-five camels, and six thousand seven hundred twenty donkeys.

70 Now some of the heads of ancestral houses contributed to the work. The governor gave to the treasury one thousand darics of gold, fifty basins, and five hundred thirty priestly robes. ⁷¹And some of the heads of ancestral houses gave into the building fund twenty thousand darics of gold and two thousand two hundred minas of silver. ⁷²And what the rest of the people gave was twenty thousand darics of gold, two thousand minas of silver, and sixty-seven priestly robes.

73 So the priests, the Levites, the gatekeepers, the singers, some of the people, the temple servants, and all Israel settled in their towns.

Ezra Summons the People to Obey the Law

8 When the seventh month came—the people of Israel being settled in their towns— ¹all the people gathered together into the square before the Water Gate. They told the scribe Ezra to bring the book of the law of Moses, which the LORD had given to Israel. ²Accordingly, the priest Ezra brought the law before the assembly, both men and women and all who could hear with understanding. This was on the first day of the seventh month. ³He read from it facing the square before the Water Gate from early morning until midday, in the presence of the men and the women and those who could understand; and the ears of all the people were attentive to the book of the law. ⁴The scribe Ezra stood on a wooden platform that had been made for the purpose; and beside him stood Mattithiah, Shema, Anaiah, Uriah, Hilkiah, and Maaseiah on his right hand; and Pedaiah, Mishael, Malchijah, Hashum, Hashbaddanah, Zechariah, and Meshullam on his left hand. ⁵And Ezra opened the book in the sight of all the people, for he was standing above all the people; and when he opened it, all the people stood up. ⁶Then Ezra blessed the LORD, the great God, and all the people answered, "Amen, Amen," lifting up their hands. Then they bowed their heads and worshiped the LORD with their faces to the ground. ⁷Also Jeshua, Bani, Sherebiah, Jamin, Akkub, Shabbethai, Hodiah, Maaseiah, Kelita, Azariah, Jozabad, Hanan, Pelaiah, the Levites,ᵇ helped the people to understand the law, while the people remained in their places. ⁸So they read from the book, from the law of God, with interpretation. They gave the sense, so that the people understood the reading.

9 And Nehemiah, who was the governor, and Ezra the priest and scribe, and the Levites who taught the people said to all the people, "This day is holy to the LORD your God; do not mourn or weep." For all the people wept when they heard the words of the law. ¹⁰Then he said to them, "Go your way, eat the fat and drink sweet wine and send portions of them to those for whom nothing is prepared, for this day is holy to our LORD; and do not be grieved, for the joy of the LORD is your strength." ¹¹So the Levites stilled all the people, saying, "Be quiet, for this day is holy; do not be grieved." ¹²And all the people went their way to eat and drink and to send portions and to make great rejoicing,

---

ᵃ Ezra 2.66 and the margins of some Hebrew Mss: MT lacks *They had . . . forty-five mules* ᵇ 1 Esdras 9.48 Vg: Heb *and the Levites* because they had understood the words that were declared to them.

The Festival of Booths Celebrated

13 On the second day the heads of ancestral houses of all the people, with the priests and the Levites, came together to the scribe Ezra in order to study the words of the law. [14]And they found it written in the law, which the LORD had commanded by Moses, that the people of Israel should live in booths[a] during the festival of the seventh month, [15]and that they should publish and proclaim in all their towns and in Jerusalem as follows, "Go out to the hills and bring branches of olive, wild olive, myrtle, palm, and other leafy trees to make booths,[a] as it is written." [16]So the people went out and brought them, and made booths[a] for themselves, each on the roofs of their houses, and in their courts and in the courts of the house of God, and in the square at the Water Gate and in the square at the Gate of Ephraim. [17]And all the assembly of those who had returned from the captivity made booths[a] and lived in them; for from the days of Jeshua son of Nun to that day the people of Israel had not done so. And there was very great rejoicing. [18]And day by day, from the first day to the last day, he read from the book of the law of God. They kept the festival seven days; and on the eighth day there was a solemn assembly, according to the ordinance.

9 National Confession

Now on the twenty-fourth day of this month the people of Israel were assembled with fasting and in sackcloth, and with earth on their heads.[b] [2]Then those of Israelite descent separated themselves from all foreigners, and stood and confessed their sins and the iniquities of their ancestors. [3]They stood up in their place and read from the book of the law of the LORD their God for a fourth part of the day, and for another fourth they made confession and worshiped the LORD their God. [4]Then Jeshua, Bani, Kadmiel, Shebaniah, Bunni, Sherebiah, Bani, and Chenani stood on the stairs of the Levites and cried out with a loud voice to the LORD their God. [5]Then the Levites, Jeshua, Kadmiel, Bani, Hashabneiah, Sherebiah, Hodiah, Shebaniah, and Pethahiah, said, "Stand up and bless the LORD your God from everlasting to everlasting. Blessed be your glorious name, which is exalted above all blessing and praise."

6 And Ezra said:[c] "You are the LORD, you alone; you have made heaven, the heaven of heavens, with all their host, the earth and all that is on it, the seas and all that is in them. To all of them you give life, and the host of heaven worships you. [7]You are the LORD, the God who chose Abram and brought him out of Ur of the Chaldeans and gave him the name Abraham; [8]and you found his heart faithful before you, and made with him a covenant to give to his descendants the land of the Canaanite, the Hittite, the Amorite, the Perizzite, the Jebusite, and the Girgashite; and you have fulfilled your promise, for you are righteous.

9 "And you saw the distress of our ancestors in Egypt and heard their cry at the Red Sea.[d] [10]You performed signs and wonders against Pharaoh and all his servants and all the people of his land, for you knew that they acted insolently against our ancestors. You made a name for yourself, which remains to this day. [11]And you divided the sea before them, so that they passed through the sea on dry land, but you threw their pursuers into the depths, like a stone into mighty waters. [12]Moreover, you led them by day with a pillar of cloud, and by night with a pillar of fire, to give them light on the way in which they should go. [13]You came down also upon Mount Sinai, and spoke with them from heaven, and gave them right ordinances and true laws, good statutes and commandments, [14]and you made known your holy sabbath to them and gave them commandments and statutes and a law through your servant Moses. [15]For their hunger you gave them bread from heaven, and for their thirst you brought water for them out of the rock, and you told them to go in to possess the land that you swore to give them.

16 "But they and our ancestors acted presumptuously and stiffened their necks and did not obey your commandments; [17]they refused to obey, and were not mindful of the wonders that you performed among them; but they stiffened their necks and determined to return to their slavery in Egypt. But you are a God ready to forgive, gracious and merciful, slow to anger and abounding in steadfast love, and you did not forsake them. [18]Even when they had cast an image of a calf for themselves and said, 'This is your God who brought you up out of Egypt,' and had committed great blasphemies, [19]you in your great mercies did not forsake them in the wilderness; the pillar of cloud that led them in the way did not leave them by day, nor the pillar of fire by night that gave them light on the way by which they should go. [20]You gave your good spirit to instruct them, and did not withhold your manna from their mouths, and gave them water for their thirst. [21]Forty years you sustained them in the wilderness so that they lacked nothing; their clothes did not wear

a Or tabernacles; Heb succoth b Heb on them c Gk: Heb lacks And Ezra said d Or Sea of Reeds out and their feet did not swell. ²²And you gave them kingdoms and peoples, and allotted to them every corner,ᵃ so they took possession of the land of King Sihon of Heshbon and the land of King Og of Bashan. ²³You multiplied their descendants like the stars of heaven, and brought them into the land that you had told their ancestors to enter and possess. ²⁴So the descendants went in and possessed the land, and you subdued before them the inhabitants of the land, the Canaanites, and gave them into their hands, with their kings and the peoples of the land, to do with them as they pleased. ²⁵And they captured fortress cities and a rich land, and took possession of houses filled with all sorts of goods, hewn cisterns, vineyards, olive orchards, and fruit trees in abundance; so they ate, and were filled and became fat, and delighted themselves in your great goodness.

26 "Nevertheless they were disobedient and rebelled against you and cast your law behind their backs and killed your prophets, who had warned them in order to turn them back to you, and they committed great blasphemies. ²⁷Therefore you gave them into the hands of their enemies, who made them suffer. Then in the time of their suffering they cried out to you and you heard them from heaven, and according to your great mercies you gave them saviors who saved them from the hands of their enemies. ²⁸But after they had rest, they again did evil before you, and you abandoned them to the hands of their enemies, so that they had dominion over them; yet when they turned and cried to you, you heard from heaven, and many times you rescued them according to your mercies. ²⁹And you warned them in order to turn them back to your law. Yet they acted presumptuously and did not obey your commandments, but sinned against your ordinances, by the observance of which a person shall live. They turned a stubborn shoulder and stiffened their neck and would not obey. ³⁰Many years you were patient with them, and warned them by your spirit through your prophets; yet they would not listen. Therefore you handed them over to the peoples of the lands. ³¹Nevertheless, in your great mercies you did not make an end of them or forsake them, for you are a gracious and merciful God.

32 "Now therefore, our God—the great and mighty and awesome God, keeping covenant and steadfast love—do not treat lightly all the hardship that has come upon us, upon our kings, our officials, our priests, our prophets, our ancestors, and all your people, since the time of the kings of Assyria until today. ³³You have been just in all that has come upon us, for you have dealt faithfully and we have acted wickedly; ³⁴our kings, our officials, our priests, and our ancestors have not kept your law or heeded the commandments and the warnings that you gave them. ³⁵Even in their own kingdom, and in the great goodness you bestowed on them, and in the large and rich land that you set before them, they did not serve you and did not turn from their wicked works. ³⁶Here we are, slaves to this day—slaves in the land that you gave to our ancestors to enjoy its fruit and its good gifts. ³⁷Its rich yield goes to the kings whom you have set over us because of our sins; they have power also over our bodies and over our livestock at their pleasure, and we are in great distress."

Those Who Signed the Covenant

38ᵇ Because of all this we make a firm agreement in writing, and on that sealed document are inscribed the names of our officials, our Levites, and our priests.

ᵃ Meaning of Heb uncertain ᵇ Ch 10.1 in Heb

Reflection—© Michelle Jozwiak, 18

10[a] Upon the sealed document are the names of Nehemiah the governor, son of Hacaliah, and Zedekiah; [2]Seraiah, Azariah, Jeremiah, [3]Pashhur, Amariah, Malchijah, [4]Hattush, Shebaniah, Malluch, [5]Harim, Meremoth, Obadiah, [6]Daniel, Ginnethon, Baruch, [7]Meshullam, Abijah, Mijamin, [8]Maaziah, Bilgai, Shemaiah; these are the priests. [9]And the Levites: Jeshua son of Azaniah, Binnui of the sons of Henadad, Kadmiel; [10]and their associates, Shebaniah, Hodiah, Kelita, Pelaiah, Hanan, [11]Mica, Rehob, Hashabiah, [12]Zaccur, Sherebiah, Shebaniah, [13]Hodiah, Bani, Beninu. [14]The leaders of the people: Parosh, Pahath-moab, Elam, Zattu, Bani, [15]Bunni, Azgad, Bebai, [16]Adonijah, Bigvai, Adin, [17]Ater, Hezekiah, Azzur, [18]Hodiah, Hashum, Bezai, [19]Hariph, Anathoth, Nebai, [20]Magpiash, Meshullam, Hezir, [21]Meshezabel, Zadok, Jaddua, [22]Pelatiah, Hanan, Anaiah, [23]Hoshea, Hananiah, Hasshub, [24]Hallohesh, Pilha, Shobek, [25]Rehum, Hashabnah, Maaseiah, [26]Ahiah, Hanan, Anan, [27]Malluch, Harim, and Baanah.

Summary of the Covenant

28 The rest of the people, the priests, the Levites, the gatekeepers, the singers, the temple servants, and all who have separated themselves from the peoples of the lands to adhere to the law of God, their wives, their sons, their daughters, all who have knowledge and understanding, [29]join with their kin, their nobles, and enter into a curse and an oath to walk in God's law, which was given by Moses the servant of God, and to observe and do all the commandments of the LORD our Lord and his ordinances and his statutes. [30]We will not give our daughters to the peoples of the land or take their daughters for our sons; [31]and if the peoples of the land bring in merchandise or any grain on the sabbath day to sell, we will not buy it from them on the sabbath or on a holy day; and we will forego the crops of the seventh year and the exaction of every debt.

32 We also lay on ourselves the obligation to charge ourselves yearly one-third of a shekel for the service of the house of our God: [33]for the rows of bread, the regular grain offering, the regular burnt offering, the sabbaths, the new moons, the appointed festivals, the sacred donations, and the sin offerings to make atonement for Israel, and for all the work of the house of our God. [34]We have also cast lots among the priests, the Levites, and the people, for the wood offering, to bring it into the house of our God, by ancestral houses, at appointed times, year by year, to burn on the altar of the LORD our God, as it is written in the law. [35]We obligate ourselves to bring the first fruits of our soil and the first fruits of all fruit of every tree, year by year, to the house of the LORD; [36]also to bring to the house of our God, to the priests who minister in the house of our God, the firstborn of our sons and of our livestock, as it is written in the law, and the firstlings of our herds and of our flocks; [37]and to bring the first of our dough, and our contributions, the fruit of every tree, the wine and the oil, to the priests, to the chambers of the house of our God; and to bring to the Levites the tithes from our soil, for it is the Levites who collect the tithes in all our rural towns. [38]And the priest, the descendant of Aaron, shall be with the Levites when the Levites receive the tithes; and the Levites shall bring up a tithe of the tithes to the house of our God, to the chambers of the storehouse. [39]For the people of Israel and the sons of Levi shall bring the contribution of grain, wine, and oil to the storerooms where the vessels of the sanctuary are, and where the priests that minister, and the gatekeepers and the singers are. We will not neglect the house of our God.

11 **Population of the City Increased**
Now the leaders of the people lived in Jerusalem; and the rest of the people cast lots to bring one out of ten to live in the holy city Jerusalem, while nine-tenths remained in the other towns. [2]And the people blessed all those who willingly offered to live in Jerusalem.

3 These are the leaders of the province who lived in Jerusalem; but in the towns of Judah all lived on their property in their towns: Israel, the priests, the Levites, the temple servants, and the

a Ch 10.2 in Heb

descendants of Solomon's servants. ⁴And in Jerusalem lived some of the Judahites and of the Benjaminites. Of the Judahites: Athaiah son of Uzziah son of Zechariah son of Amariah son of Shephatiah son of Mahalalel, of the descendants of Perez; ⁵and Maaseiah son of Baruch son of Col-hozeh son of Hazaiah son of Adaiah son of Joiarib son of Zechariah son of the Shilonite. ⁶All the descendants of Perez who lived in Jerusalem were four hundred sixty-eight valiant warriors.

7 And these are the Benjaminites: Sallu son of Meshullam son of Joed son of Pedaiah son of Kolaiah son of Maaseiah son of Ithiel son of Jeshaiah. ⁸And his brothers*ᵃ* Gabbai, Sallai: nine hundred twenty-eight. ⁹Joel son of Zichri was their overseer; and Judah son of Hassenuah was second in charge of the city.

10 Of the priests: Jedaiah son of Joiarib, Jachin, ¹¹Seraiah son of Hilkiah son of Meshullam son of Zadok son of Meraioth son of Ahitub, officer of the house of God, ¹²and their associates who did the work of the house, eight hundred twenty-two; and Adaiah son of Jeroham son of Pelaliah son of Amzi son of Zechariah son of Pashhur son of Malchijah, ¹³and his associates, heads of ancestral houses, two hundred forty-two; and Amashsai son of Azarel son of Ahzai son of Meshillemoth son of Immer, ¹⁴and their associates, valiant warriors, one hundred twenty-eight; their overseer was Zabdiel son of Haggedolim.

15 And of the Levites: Shemaiah son of Hasshub son of Azrikam son of Hashabiah son of Bunni; ¹⁶and Shabbethai and Jozabad, of the leaders of the Levites, who were over the outside work of the house of God; ¹⁷and Mattaniah son of Mica son of Zabdi son of Asaph, who was the leader to begin the thanksgiving in prayer, and Bakbukiah, the second among his associates; and Abda son of Shammua son of Galal son of Jeduthun. ¹⁸All the Levites in the holy city were two hundred eighty-four.

19 The gatekeepers, Akkub, Talmon and their associates, who kept watch at the gates, were one hundred seventy-two. ²⁰And the rest of Israel, and of the priests and the Levites, were in all the towns of Judah, all of them in their inheritance. ²¹But the temple servants lived on Ophel; and Ziha and Gishpa were over the temple servants.

22 The overseer of the Levites in Jerusalem was Uzzi son of Bani son of Hashabiah son of Mattaniah son of Mica, of the descendants of Asaph, the singers, in charge of the work of the house of God. ²³For there was a command from the king concerning them, and a settled provision for the singers, as was required every day.

²⁴And Pethahiah son of Meshezabel, of the descendants of Zerah son of Judah, was at the king's hand in all matters concerning the people.

Villages outside Jerusalem

25 And as for the villages, with their fields, some of the people of Judah lived in Kiriath-arba and its villages, and in Dibon and its villages, and in Jekabzeel and its villages, ²⁶and in Jeshua and in Moladah and Beth-pelet, ²⁷in Hazar-shual, in Beer-sheba and its villages, ²⁸in Ziklag, in Meconah and its villages, ²⁹in En-rimmon, in Zorah, in Jarmuth, ³⁰Zanoah, Adullam, and their villages, Lachish and its fields, and Azekah and its villages. So they camped from Beer-sheba to the valley of Hinnom. ³¹The people of Benjamin also lived from Geba onward, at Michmash, Aija, Bethel and its villages, ³²Anathoth, Nob, Ananiah, ³³Hazor, Ramah, Gittaim, ³⁴Hadid, Zeboim, Neballat, ³⁵Lod, and Ono, the valley of artisans. ³⁶And certain divisions of the Levites in Judah were joined to Benjamin.

12 A List of Priests and Levites

These are the priests and the Levites who came up with Zerubbabel son of Shealtiel, and Jeshua: Seraiah, Jeremiah, Ezra, ²Amariah, Malluch, Hattush, ³Shecaniah, Rehum, Meremoth, ⁴Iddo, Ginnethoi, Abijah, ⁵Mijamin, Maadiah, Bilgah, ⁶Shemaiah, Joiarib, Jedaiah, ⁷Sallu, Amok, Hilkiah, Jedaiah. These were the leaders of the priests and of their associates in the days of Jeshua.

8 And the Levites: Jeshua, Binnui, Kadmiel, Sherebiah, Judah, and Mattaniah, who with his associates was in charge of the songs of thanksgiving. ⁹And Bakbukiah and Unno their associates stood opposite them in the service. ¹⁰Jeshua was the father of Joiakim, Joiakim the father of Eliashib, Eliashib the father of Joiada, ¹¹Joiada the father of Jonathan, and Jonathan the father of Jaddua.

12 In the days of Joiakim the priests, heads of ancestral houses, were: of Seraiah, Meraiah; of Jeremiah, Hananiah; ¹³of Ezra, Meshullam; of Amariah, Jehohanan; ¹⁴of Malluchi, Jonathan; of Shebaniah, Joseph; ¹⁵of Harim, Adna; of Meraioth, Helkai; ¹⁶of Iddo, Zechariah; of Ginnethon, Meshullam; ¹⁷of Abijah, Zichri; of Miniamin, of Moadiah, Piltai; ¹⁸of Bilgah, Shammua; of Shemaiah, Jehonathan; ¹⁹of Joiarib, Mattenai; of Jedaiah, Uzzi; ²⁰of Sallai, Kallai; of Amok, Eber; ²¹of Hilkiah, Hashabiah; of Jedaiah, Nethanel.

22 As for the Levites, in the days of Eliashib, Joiada, Johanan, and Jaddua, there were re-

---

a Gk Mss: Heb *And after him*

corded the heads of ancestral houses; also the priests until the reign of Darius the Persian. 23The Levites, heads of ancestral houses, were recorded in the Book of the Annals until the days of Johanan son of Eliashib. 24And the leaders of the Levites: Hashabiah, Sherebiah, and Jeshua son of Kadmiel, with their associates over against them, to praise and to give thanks, according to the commandment of David the man of God, section opposite to section. 25Mattaniah, Bakbukiah, Obadiah, Meshullam, Talmon, and Akkub were gatekeepers standing guard at the storehouses of the gates. 26These were in the days of Joiakim son of Jeshua son of Jozadak, and in the days of the governor Nehemiah and of the priest Ezra, the scribe.

Dedication of the City Wall

27 Now at the dedication of the wall of Jerusalem they sought out the Levites in all their places, to bring them to Jerusalem to celebrate the dedication with rejoicing, with thanksgivings and with singing, with cymbals, harps, and lyres. 28The companies of the singers gathered together from the circuit around Jerusalem and from the villages of the Netophathites; 29also from Beth-gilgal and from the region of Geba and Azmaveth; for the singers had built for themselves villages around Jerusalem. 30And the priests and the Levites purified themselves; and they purified the people and the gates and the wall.

31 Then I brought the leaders of Judah up onto the wall, and appointed two great companies that gave thanks and went in procession. One went to the right on the wall to the Dung Gate; 32and after them went Hoshaiah and half the officials of Judah, 33and Azariah, Ezra, Meshullam, 34Judah, Benjamin, Shemaiah, and Jeremiah, 35and some of the young priests with trumpets: Zechariah son of Jonathan son of Shemaiah son of Mattaniah son of Micaiah son of Zaccur son of Asaph; 36and his kindred, Shemaiah, Azarel, Milalai, Gilalai, Maai, Nethanel, Judah, and Hanani, with the musical instruments of David the man of God; and the scribe Ezra went in front of them. 37At the Fountain Gate, in front of them, they went straight up by the stairs of the city of David, at the ascent of the wall, above the house of David, to the Water Gate on the east.

38 The other company of those who gave thanks went to the left,a and I followed them with half of the people on the wall, above the Tower of the Ovens, to the Broad Wall, 39and above the Gate of Ephraim, and by the Old Gate, and by the Fish Gate and the Tower of Hananel and the Tower of the Hundred, to the Sheep Gate; and they came to a halt at the Gate of the Guard. 40So both companies of those who gave thanks stood in the house of God, and I and half of the officials with me; 41and the priests Eliakim, Maaseiah, Miniamin, Micaiah, Elioenai, Zechariah, and Hananiah, with trumpets; 42and Maaseiah, Shemaiah, Eleazar, Uzzi, Jehohanan, Malchijah, Elam, and Ezer. And the singers sang with Jezrahiah as their leader. 43They offered great sacrifices that day and rejoiced, for God had made them rejoice with great joy; the women and children also rejoiced. The joy of Jerusalem was heard far away.

Temple Responsibilities

44 On that day men were appointed over the chambers for the stores, the contributions, the first fruits, and the tithes, to gather into them the portions required by the law for the priests and for the Levites from the fields belonging to the towns; for Judah rejoiced over the priests and the Levites who ministered. 45They performed the service of their God and the service of purification, as did the singers and the gatekeepers, according to the command of David and his son Solomon. 46For in the days of David and Asaph long ago there was a leader of the singers, and there were songs of praise and thanksgiving to God. 47In the days of Zerubbabel and in the days of Nehemiah all Israel gave the daily portions for the singers and the gatekeepers. They set apart that which was for the Levites; and the Levites set apart that which was for the descendants of Aaron.

13 Foreigners Separated from Israel

On that day they read from the book of Moses in the hearing of the people; and in it was found written that no Ammonite or Moabite should ever enter the assembly of God, 2because they did not meet the Israelites with bread and water, but hired Balaam against them to curse them—yet our God turned the curse into a blessing. 3When the people heard the law, they separated from Israel all those of foreign descent.

The Reforms of Nehemiah

4 Now before this, the priest Eliashib, who was appointed over the chambers of the house of our God, and who was related to Tobiah, 5prepared for Tobiah a large room where they had previously put the grain offering, the frankincense, the vessels, and the tithes of grain, wine, and oil, which were given by

a Cn: Heb opposite

Some of my friends are from different religious backgrounds, but we share many of the same moral values. Aren't we all just worshiping the same God, but in different ways? Is there really just one path to God?

There is a short answer. There is only one God, and that God is God of all. People come to know the one God in many ways. For us, we believe that God came to us in the Person of Jesus Christ and he is the way to God.

Then there is a longer answer. The world is opening up. We're learning more about other religions; we're encountering more people with a wide variety of beliefs. We do have a lot in common with people of other faiths, and we share similar values like charity and peace. And there is some consensus on a sense of morality, which comes from the belief that God's law is written in the hearts and consciences of all human beings (see Romans 2.15). It can be enriching to have friends from other religious traditions; we can, in fact, learn meaningful things from our friends' non-Christian and non-Catholic beliefs. In fact, we can even learn things from the different ways different Catholics express their faith.

Pope Benedict XVI has championed ecumenism (unity between different faiths) and even made it a point to stress its importance at World Youth Day in 2005.

However, there are times (as in Nehemiah 13.23–31) when a community of people has a fractured identity, and in order to rebuild their unique identity they become less willing to include others and more clear and stringent about their beliefs and practices. The main purpose is not to go to extremes to drive away people of other beliefs. It is to renew and rebuild the identity of a fractured community. And that is why Nehemiah was so radical about this issue.

Find some Creative Space in this Bible and write your thoughts about this issue, maybe adding other questions this has brought up for you. Talk to a trusted friend about your thoughts. Then explore more in the verses below, or talk to someone about your real questions. (Want to explore this further? Check out Deuteronomy 6.4; John 14.6–12; Acts 17.16–31; and Hebrews 11.6.)

commandment to the Levites, singers, and gatekeepers, and the contributions for the priests. [6]While this was taking place I was not in Jerusalem, for in the thirty-second year of King Artaxerxes of Babylon I went to the king. After some time I asked leave of the king [7]and returned to Jerusalem. I then discovered the wrong that Eliashib had done on behalf of Tobiah, preparing a room for him in the courts of the house of God. [8]And I was very angry, and I threw all the household furniture of Tobiah out of the room. [9]Then I gave orders and they cleansed the chambers, and I brought back the vessels of the house of God, with the grain offering and the frankincense.

10 I also found out that the portions of the Levites had not been given to them; so that the Levites and the singers, who had conducted the service, had gone back to their fields. [11]So I remonstrated with the officials and said, "Why is the house of God forsaken?" And I gathered them together and set them in their stations. [12]Then all Judah brought the tithe of the grain, wine, and oil into the storehouses. [13]And I appointed as treasurers over the storehouses the priest Shelemiah, the scribe Zadok, and Pedaiah of the Levites, and as their assistant Hanan son of Zaccur son of Mattaniah, for they were considered faithful; and their duty was to distribute to their associates. [14]Remember me, O my God, concerning this, and do not wipe out my good deeds that I have done for the house of my God and for his service.

Sabbath Reforms Begun

15 In those days I saw in Judah people treading wine presses on the sabbath, and bringing in heaps of grain and loading them on donkeys; and also wine, grapes, figs, and all kinds of burdens, which they brought into Jerusalem

CATHOLICS AND THE SABBATH

We live in a world where people work 24/7. Some work hard just to cover very basic needs, while others work hard to afford some extras in life. Nehemiah and his people worked hard, but when some of them tried to work on the Sabbath, as you'll read in **Nehemiah 13.14–22**, he got very upset. You might be thinking, "What's the big deal? What's this Sabbath thing all about anyway? Isn't that a Jewish thing?"

The word "Sabbath" comes from the Hebrew word meaning "to cease" or "to rest." As Catholics, we've learned that the Third Commandment requires us to "keep holy the Sabbath" (see *Catechism of the Catholic Church* 2174–2195). Many of us translate that as just one more rule to follow for some unknown reason. Not so. God had something very awesome in mind when he gave us that commandment. He *knew* we would fill up our calendars and be on the go constantly. He *knew* we might forget that he is the giver of all things in our lives. He didn't want us to have just one more rule— he wanted us to spend time with him and enjoy all that he has given to us.

Sunday is called the "Lord's Day," and we go to Mass to remember Jesus' Resurrection. It's a day of celebration and a day to hang with our families and friends. The Sabbath is supposed to be a day off to rest and gear up for another week. God wants us to take some time out of each week to rest—body, mind, and spirit—so we are ready for the next thing God has planned for us.

on the sabbath day; and I warned them at that time against selling food. [16]Tyrians also, who lived in the city, brought in fish and all kinds of merchandise and sold them on the sabbath to the people of Judah, and in Jerusalem. [17]Then I remonstrated with the nobles of Judah and said to them, "What is this evil thing that you are doing, profaning the sabbath day? [18]Did not your ancestors act in this way, and did not

our God bring all this disaster on us and on this city? Yet you bring more wrath on Israel by profaning the sabbath."

[19] When it began to be dark at the gates of Jerusalem before the sabbath, I commanded that the doors should be shut and gave orders that they should not be opened until after the sabbath. And I set some of my servants over the gates, to prevent any burden from being brought in on the sabbath day. [20]Then the merchants and sellers of all kinds of merchandise spent the night outside Jerusalem once or twice. [21]But I warned them and said to them, "Why do you spend the night in front of the wall? If you do so again, I will lay hands on you." From that time on they did not come on the sabbath. [22]And I commanded the Levites that they should purify themselves and come and guard the gates, to keep the sabbath day holy. Remember this also in my favor, O my God, and spare me according to the greatness of your steadfast love.

Mixed Marriages Condemned

23 In those days also I saw Jews who had married women of Ashdod, Ammon, and Moab; [24]and half of their children spoke the language of Ashdod, and they could not speak the language of Judah, but spoke the language of various peoples. [25]And I contended with them and cursed them and beat some of them and pulled out their hair; and I made them take an oath in the name of God, saying, "You shall not give your daughters to their sons, or take their daughters for your sons or for yourselves. [26]Did not King Solomon of Israel sin on account of such women? Among the many nations there was no king like him, and he was beloved by his God, and God made him king over all Israel; nevertheless, foreign women made even him to sin. [27]Shall we then listen to you and do all this great evil and act treacherously against our God by marrying foreign women?"

28 And one of the sons of Jehoiada, son of the high priest Eliashib, was the son-in-law of Sanballat the Horonite; I chased him away from me. [29]Remember them, O my God, because they have defiled the priesthood, the covenant of the priests and the Levites.

30 Thus I cleansed them from everything foreign, and I established the duties of the priests and Levites, each in his work; [31]and I provided for the wood offering, at appointed times, and for the first fruits. Remember me, O my God, for good.

TOBIT

A FAMILY SAGA

Jewish "Saints"

Have you ever felt hopeless or helpless? Of course! We all have at some point in our lives, which is why it's easy to relate to Tobit. In some ways it's an ordinary story about ordinary people who do and experience some extraordinary things in the midst of feeling hopeless and helpless.

Tobit was successful, and then circumstances beyond his control left him unemployed. Fortunately, his wife still had her job to help keep them afloat. So a two-income family became a one-income family. Still happens today, doesn't it? But unlike today, when we can collect unemployment insurance if we lose a job, Tobit only had his faith to fall back on. He continued his religious practices, but was mocked by other Jews who couldn't see the point in being so strict or righteous.

Then on top of everything, Tobit became blind. The stress and strain of all those trials and tribulations made him want to give up and even die.

At the same time he was praying for his life to end, a young woman miles away, falsely accused of murdering her seven husbands, was praying a similar prayer.

When you have felt hopeless, what have you done? Prayed for relief? Planned an escape?

Maybe you've already learned what Tobit and the young woman did. God intervened in the person of the angel Raphael, and everyone's life changed. So, what's the point of this story? God *does* answer prayer. Not always the way we want him to, but the way he knows is best. And that's a lesson we all can benefit from learning.

> **"Every good Christian ought to be more ready to give a favorable interpretation to another's statement than to condemn it."**
>
> —St. Ignatius of Loyola

WHO The author is unknown.

WHAT A combination of historical romance, genuine Jewish piety, and solid moral instruction, Tobit gives a glimpse into the life of the Jewish people just before New Testament times and emphasizes that God always acts for good, especially in difficult situations.

WHEN Written during the fourth or third century B.C.

WHERE Either in the Diaspora (Jewish communities outside the land of Palestine) or in a setting predominantly inhabited by Gentiles (non-Jews).

PATH OF DISCIPLESHIP

What's your place in the family? Not your birth order, but "your position"? Are you the family hero, the clown, the leader, the easygoing one? Do you appreciate (or at least tolerate) the gifts and quirks of family members?

What's going on in your family life right now? Is your family hurting or is everyone getting along, helping out, having fun? Would you say you are a religious, faithful, or spiritual family because you pray together, talk about God, read Scripture, celebrate the sacraments, work for justice, and reach out to those in need? Or are you all too busy just *surviving* to spend time on your faith?

All of our families are a lot like the family of Tobit—good things happen and tragedies occur. Sometimes we are right there to support one another, and sometimes we fail to do so.

The disciple in us knows how important it is to be consistent about caring and sharing with others—even when we don't feel like it. It flows from our commitment to communicate and work through conflict when bad things happen in our lives. Most of all it flows from a shared faith and a life of prayer together.

1 This book tells the story of Tobit son of Tobiel son of Hananiel son of Aduel son of Gabael son of Raphael son of Raguel of the descendants[a] of Asiel, of the tribe of Naphtali, [2]who in the days of King Shalmaneser[b] of the Assyrians was taken into captivity from Thisbe, which is to the south of Kedesh Naphtali in Upper Galilee, above Asher toward the west, and north of Phogor.

Tobit's Youth and Virtuous Life

3 I, Tobit, walked in the ways of truth and righteousness all the days of my life. I performed many acts of charity for my kindred and my people who had gone with me in exile to Nineveh in the land of the Assyrians. [4]When I was in my own country, in the land of Israel, while I was still a young man, the whole tribe of my ancestor Naphtali deserted the house of David and Jerusalem. This city had been chosen from among all the tribes of Israel, where all the tribes of Israel should offer sacrifice and where the temple, the dwelling of God, had been consecrated and established for all generations forever.

5 All my kindred and our ancestral house of Naphtali sacrificed to the calf[c] that King Jeroboam of Israel had erected in Dan and on all the mountains of Galilee. [6]But I alone went often to Jerusalem for the festivals, as it is prescribed for all Israel by an everlasting decree. I would hurry off to Jerusalem with the first fruits of the crops and the firstlings of the flock, the tithes of the cattle, and the first shearings of the sheep. [7]I would give these to the priests, the sons of Aaron, at the altar; likewise the tenth of the grain, wine, olive oil, pomegranates, figs, and the rest of the fruits to the sons of Levi who ministered at Jerusalem. Also for six years I would save up a second tenth in money and go and distribute it in Jerusalem. [8]A third tenth[d] I would give to the orphans and widows and to the converts who had attached themselves to Israel. I would bring it and give it to them in the third year, and we would eat it according to the ordinance decreed concerning it in the law of Moses and according to the instructions of Deborah, the mother of my father Tobiel,[e] for my father had died and left me an orphan. [9]When I became a man I married a woman,[f] a member of our own family, and by her I became the father of a son whom I named Tobias.

Taken Captive to Nineveh

10 After I was carried away captive to Assyria and came as a captive to Nineveh, everyone of my kindred and my people ate the food of the Gentiles, [11]but I kept myself from eating the food of the Gentiles. [12]Because I was mindful of God with all my heart, [13]the Most High gave me favor and good standing with Shalmaneser,[b] and I used to buy everything he needed. [14]Until his death I used to go into Media, and buy for him there. While in the country of Media I left bags of silver worth ten talents in trust with Gabael, the brother of Gabri. [15]But when Shalmaneser[b] died, and his son Sennacherib reigned in his place, the highways into Media became unsafe and I could no longer go there.

Courage in Burying the Dead

16 In the days of Shalmaneser[b] I performed many acts of charity to my kindred, those of my tribe. [17]I would give my food to the hungry and my clothing to the naked; and if I saw the dead body of any of my people thrown out behind the wall of Nineveh, I would bury it. [18]I also buried any whom King Sennacherib put to death when he came fleeing from Judea in those days of judgment that the king of heaven executed upon him because of his blasphemies. For in his anger he put to death many Israelites; but I would secretly remove the bodies and bury them. So when Sennacherib looked for them he could not find them. [19]Then one of the Ninevites went and informed the king about me, that I was burying them; so I hid myself. But when I realized that the king knew about me and that I was being searched for to be put to death, I was afraid and ran away. [20]Then all my property was confiscated; nothing was left to me that was not taken into the royal treasury except my wife Anna and my son Tobias.

21 But not forty[g] days passed before two of Sennacherib's[h] sons killed him, and they fled to the mountains of Ararat, and his son Esarhaddon[i] reigned after him. He appointed Ahikar, the son of my brother Hanael[j] over all the accounts of his kingdom, and he had author-

---

a Other ancient authorities lack *son of Raphael son of Raguel of the descendants*   b Gk *Enemessaros*   c Other ancient authorities read *heifer*   d A *third tenth* added from other ancient authorities   e Lat: Gk *Hananiel*   f Other ancient authorities add *Anna*   g Other ancient authorities read either *forty-five* or *fifty*   h Gk *his*   i Gk *Sacherdonos*   j Other authorities read *Hananael* ity over the entire administration. ²²Ahikar interceded for me, and I returned to Nineveh. Now Ahikar was chief cupbearer, keeper of the signet, and in charge of administration of the accounts under King Sennacherib of Assyria; so Esar-haddon*^a* reappointed him. He was my nephew and so a close relative.

2 Then during the reign of Esar-haddon*^a* I returned home, and my wife Anna and my son Tobias were restored to me. At our festival of Pentecost, which is the sacred festival of weeks, a good dinner was prepared for me and I reclined to eat. ²When the table was set for me and an abundance of food placed before me, I said to my son Tobias, "Go, my child, and bring whatever poor person you may find of our people among the exiles in Nineveh, who is wholeheartedly mindful of God,*^b* and he shall eat together with me. I will wait for you, until you come back." ³So Tobias went to look for some poor person of our people. When he had returned he said, "Father!" And I replied, "Here I am, my child." Then he went on to say, "Look, father, one of our own people has been murdered and thrown into the market place, and now he lies there strangled." ⁴Then I sprang up, left the dinner before even tasting it, and removed the body*^c* from the square*^d* and laid it*^c* in one of the rooms until sunset when I might bury it.*^c* ⁵When I returned, I washed myself and ate my food in sorrow. ⁶Then I remembered the prophecy of Amos, how he said against Bethel,*^e*

"Your festivals shall be turned into
     mourning,
and all your songs into lamentation."

And I wept.

Tobit Becomes Blind

7 When the sun had set, I went and dug a grave and buried him. ⁸And my neighbors laughed and said, "Is he still not afraid? He has already been hunted down to be put to death for doing this, and he ran away; yet here he is again burying the dead!" ⁹That same night I washed myself and went into my courtyard and slept by the wall of the courtyard; and my face was uncovered because of the heat. ¹⁰I did not know that there were sparrows on the wall; their fresh droppings fell into my eyes and produced white films. I went to physicians to be healed, but the more they treated me with ointments the more my vision was obscured by the white films, until I became completely blind. For four years I remained unable to see. All my kindred

were sorry for me, and Ahikar took care of me for two years before he went to Elymais.

Tobit's Wife Earns Their Livelihood

11 At that time, also, my wife Anna earned money at women's work. ¹²She used to send what she made to the owners and they would pay wages to her. One day, the seventh of Dystrus, when she cut off a piece she had woven and sent it to the owners, they paid her full wages and also gave her a young goat for a meal. ¹³When she returned to me, the goat began to bleat. So I called her and said, "Where did you get this goat? It is surely not stolen, is it? Return it to the owners; for we have no right to eat anything stolen." ¹⁴But she said to me, "It was given to me as a gift in addition to my wages." But I did not believe her, and told her to return it to the owners. I became flushed with anger against her over this. Then she replied to me, "Where are your acts of charity? Where are your righteous deeds? These things are known about you!"*^f*

3 **Tobit's Prayer**

Then with much grief and anguish of heart I wept, and with groaning began to pray:

² "You are righteous, O Lord,
     and all your deeds are just;
all your ways are mercy and truth;
     you judge the world.*^g*
³ And now, O Lord, remember me
     and look favorably upon me.
Do not punish me for my sins
     and for my unwitting offenses
     and those that my ancestors committed
          before you.
They sinned against you,

God's Paintbrush—© Rachel Hostert, 18

---

a Gk *Sacherdonos* *b* Lat: Gk *wholeheartedly mindful* *c* Gk *him*
d Other ancient authorities lack *from the square* *e* Other ancient authorities read *against Bethlehem* *f* Or *to you*; Gk *with you*
g Other ancient authorities read *you render true and righteous judgment forever*

REALITY ✓

LOVE AND FORGIVENESS

Tobit was trying so hard to be good, but he was on edge. Was he angry at God because he was blind? Was he angry at himself for blowing it with Anna? Whatever it was, he totally gave into negative thoughts and thinking the worst of others—even jumping to the conclusion that his wife had received stolen property as payment for her work! And then he wanted to die. It all seems a bit over the top—way too much drama. Read **Tobit 2.11–3.6**.

Ever been there? Have you ever passed judgment on someone without knowing all the facts? Ever said something to harm someone else's reputation?

If so, meditate on these words: "Put away from you all bitterness and wrath and anger and wrangling and slander, together with all malice, and be kind to one another, tenderhearted, forgiving one another, as God in Christ has forgiven you" (Ephesians 4.31–32).

Love one another. Judge not. Engrave these words on your heart.

---

⁴   and disobeyed your commandments.
   So you gave us over to plunder, exile, and death,
     to become the talk, the byword, and an object of reproach
     among all the nations among whom you have dispersed us.
⁵ And now your many judgments are true
   in exacting penalty from me for my sins.
   For we have not kept your commandments
   and have not walked in accordance with truth before you.
⁶ So now deal with me as you will;
   command my spirit to be taken from me,
     so that I may be released from the face of the earth and become dust.
   For it is better for me to die than to live,

because I have had to listen to undeserved insults,
   and great is the sorrow within me.
Command, O Lord, that I be released from this distress;
   release me to go to the eternal home,
   and do not, O Lord, turn your face away from me.
For it is better for me to die
   than to see so much distress in my life and to listen to insults."

Sarah Falsely Accused

7 On the same day, at Ecbatana in Media, it also happened that Sarah, the daughter of Raguel, was reproached by one of her father's maids. ⁸ For she had been married to seven husbands, and the wicked demon Asmodeus had killed each of them before they had been with her as is customary for wives. So the maid said to her, "You are the one who kills*ᵃ* your husbands! See, you have already been married to seven husbands and have not borne the name of*ᵇ* a single one of them. ⁹ Why do you beat us? Because your husbands are dead? Go with them! May we never see a son or daughter of yours!"

Sarah's Prayer for Death

10 On that day she was grieved in spirit and wept. When she had gone up to her father's upper room, she intended to hang herself. But she thought it over and said, "Never shall they reproach my father, saying to him, 'You had only one beloved daughter but she hanged herself because of her distress.' And I shall bring my father in his old age down in sorrow to Hades. It is better for me not to hang myself, but to pray the Lord that I may die and not listen to these reproaches anymore." ¹¹ At that same time, with hands outstretched toward the window, she prayed and said,
   "Blessed are you, merciful God!
     Blessed is your name forever;
     let all your works praise you forever.
¹² And now, Lord,*ᶜ* I turn my face to you,
   and raise my eyes toward you.
¹³ Command that I be released from the earth
   and not listen to such reproaches any more.
¹⁴ You know, O Master, that I am innocent
   of any defilement with a man,
¹⁵ and that I have not disgraced my name
   or the name of my father in the land of my exile.
I am my father's only child;

---

a Other ancient authorities read *strangles* *b* Other ancient authorities read *have had no benefit from* *c* Other ancient authorities lack *Lord*

he has no other child to be his heir;
and he has no close relative or other
        kindred
for whom I should keep myself as wife.
Already seven husbands of mine have died.
    Why should I still live?
But if it is not pleasing to you, O Lord, to
        take my life,
    hear me in my disgrace."

An Answer to Prayer

16 At that very moment, the prayers of both of them were heard in the glorious presence of God. [17]So Raphael was sent to heal both of them: Tobit, by removing the white films from his eyes, so that he might see God's light with his eyes; and Sarah, daughter of Raguel, by giving her in marriage to Tobias son of Tobit, and by setting her free from the wicked demon Asmodeus. For Tobias was entitled to have her before all others who had desired to marry her. At the same time that Tobit returned from the courtyard into his house, Sarah daughter of Raguel came down from her upper room.

4 Tobit Gives Instructions to His Son

That same day Tobit remembered the money that he had left in trust with Gabael at Rages in Media, [2]and he said to himself, "Now I have asked for death. Why do I not call my son Tobias and explain to him about the money before I die?" [3]Then he called his son Tobias, and when he came to him he said, "My son, when I die,[a] give me a proper burial. Honor your mother and do not abandon her all the days of her life. Do whatever pleases her, and do not grieve her in anything. [4]Remember her, my son, because she faced many dangers for you while you were in her womb. And when she dies, bury her beside me in the same grave.

5 "Revere the Lord all your days, my son, and refuse to sin or to transgress his commandments. Live uprightly all the days of your life, and do not walk in the ways of wrongdoing; [6]for those who act in accordance with truth will prosper in all their activities. To all those who practice righteousness[b] [7]give alms from your possessions, and do not let your eye begrudge the gift when you make it. Do not turn your face away from anyone who is poor, and the face of God will not be turned away from you. [8]If you have many possessions, make your gift from them in proportion; if few, do not be afraid to give according to the little you have. [9]So you will be laying up a good treasure for yourself against the day of neces-

sity. [10]For almsgiving delivers from death and keeps you from going into the Darkness. [11]Indeed, almsgiving, for all who practice it, is an

a Lat b The text of codex Sinaiticus goes directly from verse 6 to verse 19, reading *To those who practice righteousness* [19]*the Lord will give good counsel.* In order to fill the lacuna verses 7 to 18 are derived from other ancient authorities excellent offering in the presence of the Most High.

12 "Beware, my son, of every kind of fornication. First of all, marry a woman from among the descendants of your ancestors; do not marry a foreign woman, who is not of your father's tribe; for we are the descendants of the prophets. Remember, my son, that Noah, Abraham, Isaac, and Jacob, our ancestors of old, all took wives from among their kindred. They were blessed in their children, and their posterity will inherit the land. ¹³So now, my son, love your kindred, and in your heart do not disdain your kindred, the sons and daughters of your people, by refusing to take a wife for yourself from among them. For in pride there is ruin and great confusion. And in idleness there is loss and dire poverty, because idleness is the mother of famine.

14 "Do not keep over until the next day the wages of those who work for you, but pay them at once. If you serve God you will receive payment. Watch yourself, my son, in everything you do, and discipline yourself in all your conduct. ¹⁵And what you hate, do not do to anyone. Do not drink wine to excess or let drunkenness go with you on your way. ¹⁶Give some of your food to the hungry, and some of your clothing to the naked. Give all your surplus as alms, and do not let your eye begrudge your giving of alms. ¹⁷Place your bread on the grave of the righteous, but give none to sinners. ¹⁸Seek advice from every wise person and do not despise any useful counsel. ¹⁹At all times bless the Lord God, and ask him that your ways may be made straight and that all your paths and plans may prosper. For none of the nations has understanding, but the Lord himself will give them good counsel; but if he chooses otherwise, he casts down to deepest Hades. So now, my child, remember these commandments, and do not let them be erased from your heart.

Money Left in Trust with Gabael

20 "And now, my son, let me explain to you that I left ten talents of silver in trust with Gabael son of Gabrias, at Rages in Media. ²¹Do not be afraid, my son, because we have become poor. You have great wealth if you fear God and flee from every sin and do what is good in the sight of the Lord your God."

5 The Angel Raphael

Then Tobias answered his father Tobit, "I will do everything that you have commanded me, father; ²but how can I obtain the money*ᵃ* from him, since he does not know me and I do not know him? What evidence*ᵇ* am I to give him so that he will recognize and trust me, and give me the money? Also, I do not know the roads to Media, or how to get there." ³Then Tobit answered his son Tobias, "He gave me his bond and I gave him my bond. I*ᶜ* divided his in two; we each took one part, and I put one with the money. And now twenty years have passed since I left this money in trust. So now, my son, find yourself a trustworthy man to go with you, and we will pay him wages until you return. But get back the money from Gabael."*ᵈ*

4 So Tobias went out to look for a man to go with him to Media, someone who was acquainted with the way. He went out and found the angel Raphael standing in front of him; but he did not perceive that he was an angel of God. ⁵Tobias*ᵉ* said to him, "Where do you come from, young man?" "From your kindred, the Israelites," he replied, "and I have come here to work." Then Tobias*ᶠ* said to him, "Do you know the way to go to Media?" ⁶"Yes," he replied, "I have been there many times; I am acquainted with it and know all the roads. I have often traveled to Media, and would stay with our kinsman Gabael who lives in Rages of Media. It is a journey of two days from Ecbatana to Rages; for it lies in a mountainous area, while Ecbatana is in the middle of the plain." ⁷Then Tobias said to him, "Wait for me, young man, until I go in and tell my father; for I do need you to travel with me, and I will pay you your wages." ⁸He replied, "All right, I will wait; but do not take too long."

9 So Tobias*ᶠ* went in to tell his father Tobit and said to him, "I have just found a man who is one of our own Israelite kindred!" He replied, "Call the man in, my son, so that I may learn about his family and to what tribe he belongs, and whether he is trustworthy enough to go with you."

10 Then Tobias went out and called him, and said, "Young man, my father is calling for you." So he went in to him, and Tobit greeted him first. He replied, "Joyous greetings to you!" But Tobit retorted, "What joy is left for me any more? I am a man without eyesight; I cannot see the light of heaven, but I lie in darkness like the dead who no longer see the light.

a Gk it *b* Gk sign *c* Other authorities read He *d* Gk from him *e* Gk He *f* Gk he

Wondering—© Clay Goswick, 16

Although still alive, I am among the dead. I hear people but I cannot see them." But the young man*a* said, "Take courage; the time is near for God to heal you; take courage." Then Tobit said to him, "My son Tobias wishes to go to Media. Can you accompany him and guide him? I will pay your wages, brother." He answered, "I can go with him and I know all the roads, for I have often gone to Media and have crossed all its plains, and I am familiar with its mountains and all of its roads."

11 Then Tobit*a* said to him, "Brother, of what family are you and from what tribe? Tell me, brother." ¹²He replied, "Why do you need to know my tribe?" But Tobit*a* said, "I want to be sure, brother, whose son you are and what your name is." ¹³He replied, "I am Azariah, the son of the great Hananiah, one of your relatives." ¹⁴Then Tobit said to him, "Welcome! God save you, brother. Do not feel bitter toward me, brother, because I wanted to be sure about your ancestry. It turns out that you are a kinsman, and of good and noble lineage. For I knew Hananiah and Nathan,*b* the two sons of Shemeliah,*c* and they used to go with me to Jerusalem and worshiped with me there, and were not led astray. Your kindred are good people; you come of good stock. Hearty welcome!"

a Gk *he* *b* Other ancient authorities read *Jathan* or *Nathaniah* *c* Other ancient authorities read *Shemaiah*

"

MARY IS MY GUIDE

When I was a child, I always felt a closeness to Mary. I used to have terrible nightmares, and my mother would tell me to pray, asking Mary to help me fall asleep and have no nightmares. So of course I did, and as I lay there, I would close my eyes and pray the Hail Mary to my grandfather and grandmother, praying that they would make it to heaven okay, because they had passed on recently. I always felt as if within minutes Mary was lying next to me praying also. I fell asleep very fast every night after I would do that.

Even now as a teenager I pray the Hail Mary often, and I always feel as if Mary is right beside me, guiding me through the best and tough times of childhood and my teenage years.

Mary Is My Guide—© Delia Blaise Figura, 17

Gentle Strength—© Charlotte Katheder, 16

"

15 Then he added, "I will pay you a drachma a day as wages, as well as expenses for yourself and my son. So go with my son, [16]and[a] I will add something to your wages." Raphael[b] answered, "I will go with him; so do not fear. We shall leave in good health and return to you in good health, because the way is safe." [17]So Tobit[c] said to him, "Blessings be upon you, brother."

Then he called his son and said to him, "Son, prepare supplies for the journey and set out with your brother. May God in heaven bring you safely there and return you in good health to me; and may his angel, my son, accompany you both for your safety."

Before he went out to start his journey, he kissed his father and mother. Tobit then said to him, "Have a safe journey."

18 But his mother[d] began to weep, and said to Tobit, "Why is it that you have sent my child away? Is he not the staff of our hand as he goes in and out before us? [19]Do not heap money upon money, but let it be a ransom for our child. [20]For the life that is given to us by the Lord is enough for us." [21]Tobit[b] said to her, "Do not worry; our child will leave in good health and return to us in good health. Your eyes will see him on the day when he returns to you in good health. Say no more! Do not fear for them, my sister. [22]For a good angel will accompany him; his journey will be successful, and he will come back in good health." [1]So she stopped weeping.

Journey to Rages

The young man went out and the angel went with him; [2]and the dog came out with him and went along with them. So they both journeyed along, and when the first night overtook them they camped by the Tigris river. [3]Then the young man went down to wash his feet in the Tigris river. Suddenly a large fish leaped up from the water and tried to swallow the young man's foot, and he cried out. [4]But the angel said to the young man, "Catch hold of the fish and hang on to it!" So the young man grasped the fish and drew it up on the land. [5]Then the angel said to him, "Cut open the fish and take out its gall, heart, and liver. Keep them with you, but throw away the intestines. For its gall, heart, and liver are useful as medicine." [6]So after cutting open the fish the young man gathered together the gall, heart, and liver; then he roasted and ate some of the fish, and kept some to be salted.

The two continued on their way together until they were near Media.[e] [7]Then the young man

questioned the angel and said to him, "Brother Azariah, what medicinal value is there in the fish's heart and liver, and in the gall?" [8]He replied, "As for the fish's heart and liver, you must burn them to make a smoke in the presence of a man or woman afflicted by a demon or evil spirit, and every affliction will flee away and never remain with that person any longer. [9]And as for the gall, anoint a person's eyes where white films have appeared on them; blow upon them, upon the white films, and the eyes[f] will be healed."

Raphael's Instructions

10 When he entered Media and already was approaching Ecbatana,[g] [11]Raphael said to the young man, "Brother Tobias." "Here I am," he answered. Then Raphael[c] said to him, "We must stay this night in the home of Raguel. He is your relative, and he has a daughter named Sarah. [12]He has no male heir and no daughter except Sarah only, and you, as next of kin to her, have before all other men a hereditary claim on her. Also it is right for you to inherit her father's possessions. Moreover, the girl is sensible, brave, and very beautiful, and her father is a good man." [13]He continued, "You have every right to take her in marriage. So listen to me, brother; tonight I will speak to her father about the girl, so that we may take her to be your bride. When we return from Rages we will celebrate her marriage. For I know that Raguel can by no means keep her from you or promise her to another man without incurring the penalty of death according to the decree of the book of Moses. Indeed he knows that you, rather than any other man, are entitled to marry his daughter. So now listen to me, brother, and tonight we shall speak concerning the girl and arrange her engagement to you. And when we return from Rages we will take her and bring her back with us to your house."

14 Then Tobias said in answer to Raphael, "Brother Azariah, I have heard that she already has been married to seven husbands and that they died in the bridal chamber. On the night when they went in to her, they would die. I have heard people saying that it was a demon

a Other ancient authorities add *when you return safely* b Gk *He* c Gk *he* d Other ancient authorities add *Anna* e Other ancient authorities read *Ecbatana* f Gk *they* g Other ancient authorities read *Rages* that killed them. [15]It does not harm her, but it kills anyone who desires to approach her. So now, since I am the only son my father has, I am afraid that I may die and bring my father's and mother's life down to their grave, grieving for me—and they have no other son to bury them."

16 But Raphael[a] said to him, "Do you not remember your father's orders when he commanded you to take a wife from your father's house? Now listen to me, brother, and say no more about this demon. Take her. I know that this very night she will be given to you in marriage. [17]When you enter the bridal chamber, take some of the fish's liver and heart, and put them on the embers of the incense. An odor will be given off; [18]the demon will smell it and flee, and will never be seen near her any more. Now when you are about to go to bed with her, both of you must first stand up and pray, imploring the Lord of heaven that mercy and safety may be granted to you. Do not be afraid, for she was set apart for you before the world was made. You will save her, and she will go with you. I presume that you will have children by her, and they will be as brothers to you. Now say no more!" When Tobias heard the words of Raphael and learned that she was his kinswoman,[b] related through his father's lineage, he loved her very much, and his heart was drawn to her.

7 Arrival at Home of Raguel

Now when they[c] entered Ecbatana, Tobias[a] said to him, "Brother Azariah, take me straight to our brother Raguel." So he took him to Raguel's house, where they found him sitting beside the courtyard door. They greeted him first, and he replied, "Joyous greetings, brothers; welcome and good health!" Then he brought them into his house. [2]He said to his wife Edna, "How much the young man resembles my kinsman Tobit!" [3]Then Edna questioned them, saying, "Where are you from, brothers?" They answered, "We belong to the descendants of Naphtali who are exiles in Nineveh." [4]She said to them, "Do you know our kinsman Tobit?" And they replied, "Yes, we know him." Then she asked them, "Is he[d] in good health?" [5]They replied, "He is alive and in good health." And Tobias added, "He is my father!" [6]At that Raguel jumped up and kissed him and wept. [7]He also spoke to him as follows, "Blessings on you, my child, son of a good and noble father![e] O most miserable of calamities that such an upright and beneficent man has become blind!" He then embraced his kinsman Tobias and wept. [8]His wife Edna also wept for him, and their daughter Sarah likewise wept. [9]Then Raguel[a] slaughtered a ram from the flock and received them very warmly.

Marriage of Tobias and Sarah

When they had bathed and washed themselves and had reclined to dine, Tobias said to Raphael, "Brother Azariah, ask Raguel to give me my kinswoman[b] Sarah." [10]But Raguel overheard it and said to the lad, "Eat and drink, and be merry tonight. For no one except you, brother, has the right to marry my daughter Sarah. Likewise I am not at liberty to give her to any other man than yourself, because you are my nearest relative. But let me explain to you the true situation more fully, my child. [11]I have given her to seven men of our kinsmen, and all died on the night when they went in to her. But now, my child, eat and drink, and the Lord will act on behalf of you both." But Tobias said, "I will neither eat nor drink anything until you settle the things that pertain to me." So Raguel said, "I will do so. She is given to you in accordance with the decree in the book of Moses, and it has been decreed from heaven that she be given to you. Take your kinswoman;[b] from now on you are

---

a Gk he b Gk sister c Other ancient authorities read he d Other ancient authorities add alive and e Other ancient authorities add When he heard that Tobit had lost his sight, he was stricken with grief and wept. Then he said,

Love in Nature—© Hilary Phillips, 16

her brother and she is your sister. She is given to you from today and forever. May the Lord of heaven, my child, guide and prosper you both this night and grant you mercy and peace." ¹²Then Raguel summoned his daughter Sarah. When she came to him he took her by the hand and gave her to Tobias,^a saying, "Take her to be your wife in accordance with the law and decree written in the book of Moses. Take her and bring her safely to your father. And may the God of heaven prosper your journey with his peace." ¹³Then he called her mother and told her to bring writing material; and he wrote out a copy of a marriage contract, to the effect that he gave her to him as wife according to the decree of the law of Moses. ¹⁴Then they began to eat and drink.

15 Raguel called his wife Edna and said to her, "Sister, get the other room ready, and take her there." ¹⁶So she went and made the bed in the room as he had told her, and brought Sarah^b there. She wept for her daughter.^b Then, wiping away the tears,^c she said to her, "Take courage, my daughter; the Lord of heaven grant you joy^d in place of your sorrow. Take courage, my daughter." Then she went out.

8 Tobias Routs the Demon

When they had finished eating and drinking they wanted to retire; so they took the young man and brought him into the bedroom. ²Then Tobias remembered the words of Raphael, and he took the fish's liver and heart out of the bag where he had them and put them on the embers of the incense. ³The odor of the fish so repelled the demon that he fled to the remotest parts^e of Egypt. But Raphael followed him, and at once bound him there hand and foot.

4 When the parents^f had gone out and shut the door of the room, Tobias got out of bed and said to Sarah,^b "Sister, get up, and let us pray and implore our Lord that he grant us mercy and safety." ⁵So she got up, and they began to pray and implore that they might be kept safe. Tobias^g began by saying,

"Blessed are you, O God of our ancestors,
and blessed is your name in all
generations forever.
Let the heavens and the whole creation
bless you forever.
⁶ You made Adam, and for him you made his
wife Eve
as a helper and support.
From the two of them the human race
has sprung.

---

a Gk *him* *b* Gk *her* *c* Other ancient authorities read *the tears of her daughter* *d* Other ancient authorities read *favor* *e* Or *fled through the air to the parts* *f* Gk *they* *g* Gk *He*

And Only With God's Sunlight Do You Begin to Really Grow—© Eliza German, 20

You said, 'It is not good that the man
    should be alone;
  let us make a helper for him like himself.'
7 I now am taking this kinswoman of mine,
    not because of lust,
      but with sincerity.
  Grant that she and I may find mercy
    and that we may grow old together."
8And they both said, "Amen, Amen." 9Then
they went to sleep for the night.

But Raguel arose and called his servants to
him, and they went and dug a grave, 10for he
said, "It is possible that he will die and we will
become an object of ridicule and derision."
11When they had finished digging the grave,
Raguel went into his house and called his wife,
12saying, "Send one of the maids and have her
go in to see if he is alive. But if he is dead, let
us bury him without anyone knowing it." 13So
they sent the maid, lit a lamp, and opened the
door; and she went in and found them sound
asleep together. 14Then the maid came out
and informed them that he was alive and that
nothing was wrong. 15So they blessed the God
of heaven, and Raguel*a* said,
  "Blessed are you, O God, with every pure
      blessing;
    let all your chosen ones bless you.*b*
    Let them bless you forever.

16 Blessed are you because you have made me
      glad.
    It has not turned out as I expected,
      but you have dealt with us according to
        your great mercy.
17 Blessed are you because you had
      compassion
    on two only children.
  Be merciful to them, O Master, and keep
      them safe;
    bring their lives to fulfillment
    in happiness and mercy."
18Then he ordered his servants to fill in the
grave before daybreak.

Wedding Feast
19 After this he asked his wife to bake many
loaves of bread; and he went out to the herd
and brought two steers and four rams and ordered them to be slaughtered. So they began to
make preparations. 20Then he called for Tobias
and swore on oath to him in these words:*c* "You
shall not leave here for fourteen days, but shall
stay here eating and drinking with me; and you
shall cheer up my daughter, who has been depressed. 21Take at once half of what I own and
return in safety to your father; the other half
will be yours when my wife and I die. Take
courage, my child. I am your father and Edna is

a Gk *they* *b* Other ancient authorities lack this line *c* Other ancient authorities read *Tobias and said to him* your mother, and we belong to you as well as to your wife[a] now and forever. Take courage, my child."

9 The Money Recovered

Then Tobias called Raphael and said to him, [2]"Brother Azariah, take four servants and two camels with you and travel to Rages. Go to the home of Gabael, give him the bond, get the money, and then bring him with you to the wedding celebration. [4]For you know that my father must be counting the days, and if I delay even one day I will upset him very much. [3]You are witness to the oath Raguel has sworn, and I cannot violate his oath."[b] [5]So Raphael with the four servants and two camels went to Rages in Media and stayed with Gabael. Raphael[c] gave him the bond and informed him that Tobit's son Tobias had married and was inviting him to the wedding celebration. So Gabael[d] got up and counted out to him the money bags, with their seals intact; then they loaded them on the camels.[e] [6]In the morning they both got up early and went to the wedding celebration. When they came into Raguel's house they found Tobias reclining at table. He sprang up and greeted Gabael,[f] who wept and blessed him with the words, "Good and noble son of a father good and noble, upright and generous! May the Lord grant the blessing of heaven to you and your wife, and to your wife's father and mother. Blessed be God, for I see in Tobias the very image of my cousin Tobit."

10 Anxiety of the Parents

Now, day by day, Tobit kept counting how many days Tobias[d] would need for going and for returning. And when the days had passed and his son did not appear, [2]he said, "Is it possible that he has been detained? Or that Gabael has died, and there is no one to give him the money?" [3]And he began to worry. [4]His wife Anna said, "My child has perished and is no longer among the living." And she began to weep and mourn for her son, saying, [5]"Woe to me, my child, the light of my eyes, that I let you make the journey." [6]But Tobit kept saying to her, "Be quiet and stop worrying, my dear;[a] he is all right. Probably something unexpected has happened there. The man who went with him is trustworthy and is one of our own kin. Do not grieve for him, my dear;[a] he will soon be here." [7]She answered him, "Be quiet yourself! Stop trying to deceive me! My child has perished." She would rush out every day and watch the road her son had taken, and would

a Gk sister b In other ancient authorities verse 3 precedes verse 4 c Gk He d Gk he e Other ancient authorities lack on the camels f Gk him

JESUS SIGHTING

Apply fish guts directly to your eyes? That's just disgusting, no matter how you look at it! (No pun intended.) But that's what the angel Raphael meant when he told Tobias, "Smear the gall of the fish on his eyes." And it worked. Read **Tobit 11.8**. Tobit could see again after his son followed Raphael's instructions.

Then there was Jesus and the man who was born blind: "When he had said this, he spat on the ground and made mud with the saliva and spread the mud on the man's eyes" (John 9.6).

Here we have two men who could not see. Each had adjusted to his circumstances. If you have good sight, it's hard to imagine what it would be like not to see. If you lost your sight, without a doubt you would hope for a miracle.

What made Tobit and the blind man see? Both of them had natural, earthy substances rubbed on their eyes. Surely there were other ways these miracles could have been accomplished! Don't you think God has a sense of humor?

So, what healed them? Was it the healing action of touch? Regardless of the substances (fish gall or mud made from spit and dirt), in both stories it was the power of God that actually achieved the miracle. In Tobit's healing, that power came through the presence of the angel Raphael. In the healing of the man who was born blind, it came through the power of Jesus, the Son of God. But that's not all. It was also the faith of the two men. In Tobit's story, we get to know him before the healing, and we know his faith. With the blind man, we only see his faith in the moment—the faith of following directions. And when the men are gifted with sight, they both *see* in a whole different way—not just physically, but with the eyes of faith.

JS

heed no one.[a] When the sun had set she would go in and mourn and weep all night long, getting no sleep at all.

Tobias and Sarah Start for Home

Now when the fourteen days of the wedding celebration had ended that Raguel had sworn to observe for his daughter, Tobias came to him and said, "Send me back, for I know that my father and mother do not believe that they will see me again. So I beg of you, father, to let me go so that I may return to my own father. I have already explained to you how I left him." [8]But Raguel said to Tobias, "Stay, my child, stay with me; I will send messengers to your father Tobit and they will inform him about you." [9]But he said, "No! I beg you to send me back to my father." [10]So Raguel promptly gave Tobias his wife Sarah, as well as half of all his property: male and female slaves, oxen and sheep, donkeys and camels, clothing, money, and household goods. [11]Then he saw them safely off; he embraced Tobias[b] and said, "Farewell, my child; have a safe journey. The Lord of heaven prosper you and your wife Sarah, and may I see children of yours before I die." [12]Then he kissed his daughter Sarah and said to her, "My daughter, honor your father-in-law and your mother-in-law,[c] since from now on they are as much your parents as those who gave you birth. Go in peace, daughter, and may I hear a good report about you as long as I live." Then he bade them farewell and let them go. Then Edna said to Tobias, "My child and dear brother, the Lord of heaven bring you back safely, and may I live long enough to see children of you and of my daughter Sarah before I die. In the sight of the Lord I entrust my daughter to you; do nothing to grieve her all the days of your life. Go in peace, my child. From now on I am your mother and Sarah is your beloved wife.[d] May we all prosper together all the days of our lives." Then she kissed them both and saw them safely off. [13]Tobias parted from Raguel with happiness and joy, praising the Lord of heaven and earth, King over all, because he had made his journey a success. Finally, he blessed Raguel and his wife Edna, and said, "I have been commanded by the Lord to honor you all the days of my life."[e]

11 Homeward Journey

When they came near to Kaserin, which is opposite Nineveh, Raphael said, [2]"You are aware of how we left your father. [3]Let us run ahead of your wife and prepare the house while they are still on the way." [4]As they went on together Raphael[f] said to him, "Have the gall ready." And the dog[g] went along behind them.

5 Meanwhile Anna sat looking intently down the road by which her son would come. [6]When she caught sight of him coming, she

---

[a] Other ancient authorities read *and she would eat nothing* b Gk *him* c Other ancient authorities lack parts of *Then . . . mother-in-law*
d Gk *sister* e Lat: Meaning of Gk uncertain f Gk *he* g Codex Sinaiticus reads *And the Lord*

Grandma's Grapes—© Allie Gager, 15

said to his father, "Look, your son is coming, and the man who went with him!"

Tobit's Sight Restored

7 Raphael said to Tobias, before he had approached his father, "I know that his eyes will be opened. 8Smear the gall of the fish on his eyes; the medicine will make the white films shrink and peel off from his eyes, and your father will regain his sight and see the light."

9 Then Anna ran up to her son and threw her arms around him, saying, "Now that I have seen you, my child, I am ready to die." And she wept. 10Then Tobit got up and came stumbling out through the courtyard door. Tobias went up to him, 11with the gall of the fish in his hand, and holding him firmly, he blew into his eyes, saying, "Take courage, father." With this he applied the medicine on his eyes, 12and it made them smart.*a* 13Next, with both his hands he peeled off the white films from the corners of his eyes. Then Tobit*b* saw his son and*c* threw his arms around him, 14and he wept and said to him, "I see you, my son, the light of my eyes!" Then he said,

"Blessed be God,
  and blessed be his great name,
  and blessed be all his holy angels.
May his holy name be blessed*d*
  throughout all the ages.
15 Though he has afflicted me,
  he has had mercy upon me.*e*
  Now I see my son Tobias!"

So Tobit went in rejoicing and praising God at the top of his voice. Tobias reported to his father that his journey had been successful, that he had brought the money, that he had married Raguel's daughter Sarah, and that she was, indeed, on her way there, very near to the gate of Nineveh.

16 Then Tobit, rejoicing and praising God, went out to meet his daughter-in-law at the gate of Nineveh. When the people of Nineveh saw him coming, walking along in full vigor and with no one leading him, they were amazed. 17Before them all, Tobit acknowledged that God had been merciful to him and had restored his sight. When Tobit met Sarah the wife of his son Tobias, he blessed her saying, "Come in, my daughter, and welcome. Blessed be your God who has brought you to us, my daughter. Blessed be your father and your mother, blessed be my son Tobias, and blessed be you, my daughter. Come in now to your home, and welcome, with blessing and joy. Come in, my daughter." So on that day

there was rejoicing among all the Jews who were in Nineveh. 18Ahikar and his nephew Nadab were also present to share Tobit's joy. With merriment they celebrated Tobias's wedding feast for seven days, and many gifts were given to him.*f*

12 Raphael's Wages

When the wedding celebration was ended, Tobit called his son Tobias and said to him, "My child, see to paying the wages of the man who went with you, and give him a bonus as well." 2He replied, "Father, how much shall I pay him? It would do no harm to give him half of the possessions brought back with me. 3For he has led me back to you safely, he cured my wife, he brought the money back with me, and he healed you. How much extra shall I give him as a bonus?" 4Tobit said, "He deserves, my child, to receive half of all that he brought back." 5So Tobias*b* called him and said, "Take for your wages half of all that you brought back, and farewell."

Raphael's Exhortation

6 Then Raphael*b* called the two of them privately and said to them, "Bless God and acknowledge him in the presence of all the living for the good things he has done for you. Bless and sing praise to his name. With fitting honor declare to all people the deeds*g* of God. Do not be slow to acknowledge him. 7It is good to conceal the secret of a king, but to acknowledge and reveal the works of God, and with fitting honor to acknowledge him. Do good and evil will not overtake you. 8Prayer with fasting*h* is good, but better than both is almsgiving with righteousness. A little with righteousness is better than wealth with wrongdoing.*i* It is better to give alms than to lay up gold. 9For almsgiving saves from death and purges away every sin. Those who give alms will enjoy a full life, 10but those who commit sin and do wrong are their own worst enemies.

a Lat: Meaning of Gk uncertain *b* Gk *he* *c* Other ancient authorities lack *saw his son and* *d* Codex Sinaiticus reads *May his great name be upon us and blessed be all the angels* *e* Lat: Gk lacks this line *f* Other ancient authorities lack parts of this sentence *g* Gk *words*; other ancient authorities read *words of the deeds* *h* Codex Sinaiticus *with sincerity* *i* Lat

Raphael Discloses His Identity

11 "I will now declare the whole truth to you and will conceal nothing from you. Already I have declared it to you when I said, 'It is good to conceal the secret of a king, but to reveal with due honor the works of God.' 12So now when you and Sarah prayed, it was I who brought and read*a* the record of your prayer before the glory of the Lord, and likewise whenever you would bury the dead. 13And that time when you did not hesitate to get up and leave your dinner to go and bury the dead, 14I was sent to you to test you. And at the same time God sent me to heal you and Sarah your daughter-in-law. 15I am Raphael, one of the seven angels who stand ready and enter before the glory of the Lord."

16 The two of them were shaken; they fell face down, for they were afraid. 17But he said to them, "Do not be afraid; peace be with you. Bless God forevermore. 18As for me, when I was with you, I was not acting on my own will, but by the will of God. Bless him each and every day; sing his praises. 19Although you were watching me, I really did not eat or drink anything—but what you saw was a vision. 20So now get up from the ground,*b* and acknowledge God. See, I am ascending to him who sent me. Write down all these things that have happened to you." And he ascended. 21Then they stood up, and could see him no more. 22They kept blessing God and singing his praises, and they acknowledged God for these marvelous deeds of his, when an angel of God had appeared to them.

13 Tobit's Thanksgiving to God

Then Tobit*c* said:
"Blessed be God who lives forever,
  because his kingdom*d* lasts throughout all ages.
2 For he afflicts, and he shows mercy;
  he leads down to Hades in the lowest regions of the earth,
  and he brings up from the great abyss,*e*
  and there is nothing that can escape his hand.
3 Acknowledge him before the nations,
  O children of Israel;
  for he has scattered you among them.
4 He has shown you his greatness even there.
Exalt him in the presence of every living being,
  because he is our Lord and he is our God;
  he is our Father and he is God forever.
5 He will afflict*f* you for your iniquities,
  but he will again show mercy on all of you.
He will gather you from all the nations
  among whom you have been scattered.
6 If you turn to him with all your heart and with all your soul,
  to do what is true before him,
then he will turn to you
  and will no longer hide his face from you.
So now see what he has done for you;
  acknowledge him at the top of your voice.
Bless the Lord of righteousness,
  and exalt the King of the ages.*g*
In the land of my exile I acknowledge him,
  and show his power and majesty to a nation of sinners:
'Turn back, you sinners, and do what is right before him;
  perhaps he may look with favor upon you and show you mercy.'
7 As for me, I exalt my God,
  and my soul rejoices in the King of heaven.
8 Let all people speak of his majesty,
  and acknowledge him in Jerusalem.
9 O Jerusalem, the holy city,
  he afflicted*h* you for the deeds of your hands,*i*
  but will again have mercy on the children of the righteous.
10 Acknowledge the Lord, for he is good,*j*
  and bless the King of the ages,
  so that his tent*k* may be rebuilt in you in joy.
May he cheer all those within you who are captives,
  and love all those within you who are distressed,
  to all generations forever.
11 A bright light will shine to all the ends of the earth;
  many nations will come to you from far away,
the inhabitants of the remotest parts of the earth to your holy name,
  bearing gifts in their hands for the King of heaven.
Generation after generation will give joyful praise in you;
  the name of the chosen city will endure forever.

a Lat: Gk lacks *and read* b Other ancient authorities read *now bless the Lord on earth* c Gk he d Other ancient authorities read *forever, and his kingdom* e Gk *from destruction* f Other ancient authorities read *He afflicted* g The lacuna in codex Sinaiticus, verses 6b to 10a, is filled in from other ancient authorities h Other ancient authorities read *will afflict* i Other ancient authorities read *your children* j Other ancient authorities read *Lord worthily* k Or *tabernacle*

¹² Cursed are all who speak a harsh word
        against you;
    cursed are all who conquer you
    and pull down your walls,
all who overthrow your towers
    and set your homes on fire.
    But blessed forever will be all who revere
      you.^a

¹³ Go, then, and rejoice over the children of
      the righteous,
    for they will be gathered together
    and will praise the Lord of the ages.

¹⁴ Happy are those who love you,
    and happy are those who rejoice in your
      prosperity.
    Happy also are all people who grieve with
      you
    because of your afflictions;
    for they will rejoice with you
    and witness all your glory forever.

¹⁵ My soul blesses^b the Lord, the great King!

¹⁶   For Jerusalem will be built^c as his house
      for all ages.
How happy I will be if a remnant of my
      descendants should survive
    to see your glory and acknowledge the
      King of heaven.
The gates of Jerusalem will be built with
      sapphire and emerald,
    and all your walls with precious stones.
The towers of Jerusalem will be built with
      gold,
    and their battlements with pure gold.
The streets of Jerusalem will be paved
      with ruby and with stones of Ophir.

¹⁷ The gates of Jerusalem will sing hymns of
      joy,
    and all her houses will cry, 'Hallelujah!
Blessed be the God of Israel!'
    and the blessed will bless the holy name
      forever and ever."

14 Tobit's Final Counsel

So ended Tobit's words of praise.

2 Tobit^d died in peace when he was one hundred twelve years old, and was buried with great honor in Nineveh. He was sixty-two^e years old when he lost his eyesight, and after regaining it he lived in prosperity, giving alms and continually blessing God and acknowledging God's majesty.

3 When he was about to die, he called his son Tobias and the seven sons of Tobias^f and gave this command: "My son, take your children ⁴and hurry off to Media, for I believe the word of God that Nahum spoke about Nine-

veh, that all these things will take place and overtake Assyria and Nineveh. Indeed, everything that was spoken by the prophets of Israel, whom God sent, will occur. None of all their words will fail, but all will come true at their appointed times. So it will be safer in Media than in Assyria and Babylon. For I know and believe that whatever God has said will be fulfilled and will come true; not a single word of the prophecies will fail. All of our kindred, inhabitants of the land of Israel, will be scattered and taken as captives from the good land; and the whole land of Israel will be desolate, even Samaria and Jerusalem will be desolate. And

---

IT'S TRADITION

HONORING THE DEAD

Burial of the dead is a theme that runs throughout Tobit (see Tobit 2.3–8; 4.3–4; 6.15; 8.12; 14.10–13). The Jewish people had a great respect for the bodies of the dead, and they had certain rituals to care for the dead. (Jesus' followers performed these ancient Jewish rituals when they anointed his body and laid it in a tomb after his crucifixion.)

It was clear that King Sennacherib was not Jewish, because when he killed the Israelites, he left their bodies exposed! This was a sign of his contempt for them.

The Catholic Church has great respect for the dying and for the body after death. When an individual is dying, the priest anoints the body, celebrates the sacrament of Penance, and gives Holy Communion to strengthen the person on the way. Holy Communion at the time of death is called Viaticum (loosely translated, it means "to go with you on the way"). Catholics believe that the body is the temple of the Holy Spirit and it should be honored and reverenced at death.

Catholics also believe in the resurrection of the body. The Church allows organ donation, and cremation is permitted as long as it is not meant as a denial of the resurrection of the body.

_a Other ancient authorities read *who build you up* _b Or *O my soul, bless* _c Other ancient authorities add *for a city* _d Gk *He* _e Other ancient authorities read *fifty-eight* _f Lat: Gk lacks *and the seven sons of Tobias*

the temple of God in it will be burned to the ground, and it will be desolate for a while.[a]

5 "But God will again have mercy on them, and God will bring them back into the land of Israel; and they will rebuild the temple of God, but not like the first one until the period when the times of fulfillment shall come. After this they all will return from their exile and will rebuild Jerusalem in splendor; and in it the temple of God will be rebuilt, just as the prophets of Israel have said concerning it. [6]Then the nations in the whole world will all be converted and worship God in truth. They will all abandon their idols, which deceitfully have led them into their error; [7]and in righteousness they will praise the eternal God. All the Israelites who are saved in those days and are truly mindful of God will be gathered together; they will go to Jerusalem and live in safety forever in the land of Abraham, and it will be given over to them. Those who sincerely love God will rejoice, but those who commit sin and injustice will vanish from all the earth. [8,9]So now, my children, I command you, serve God faithfully and do what is pleasing in his sight. Your children are also to be commanded to do what is right and to give alms, and to be mindful of God and to bless his name at all times with sincerity and with all their strength. So now, my son, leave Nineveh; do not remain here. [10]On whatever day you bury your mother beside me, do not stay overnight within the confines of the city. For I see that there is much wickedness within it, and that much deceit is practiced within it,

while the people are without shame. See, my son, what Nadab did to Ahikar who had reared him. Was he not, while still alive, brought down into the earth? For God repaid him to his face for this shameful treatment. Ahikar came out into the light, but Nadab went into the eternal darkness, because he tried to kill Ahikar. Because he gave alms, Ahikar[b] escaped the fatal trap that Nadab had set for him, but Nadab fell into it himself, and was destroyed. [11]So now, my children, see what almsgiving accomplishes, and what injustice does—it brings death! But now my breath fails me."

Death of Tobit and Anna

Then they laid him on his bed, and he died; and he received an honorable funeral. [12]When Tobias's mother died, he buried her beside his father. Then he and his wife and children[c] returned to Media and settled in Ecbatana with Raguel his father-in-law. [13]He treated his parents-in-law[d] with great respect in their old age, and buried them in Ecbatana of Media. He inherited both the property of Raguel and that of his father Tobit. [14]He died highly respected at the age of one hundred seventeen[e] years. [15]Before he died he heard[f] of the destruction of Nineveh, and he saw its prisoners being led into Media, those whom King Cyaxares[g] of Media had taken captive. Tobias[h] praised God for all he had done to the people of Nineveh and Assyria; before he died he rejoiced over Nineveh, and he blessed the Lord God forever and ever. Amen.[i]

a Lat: Other ancient authorities read *of God will be in distress and will be burned for a while*   b Gk *he*; other ancient authorities read *Manasses*
c Codex Sinaiticus lacks *and children*   d Gk *them*   e Other authorities read other numbers   f Codex Sinaiticus reads *saw and heard*
g Cn: Codex Sinaiticus *Ahikar*; other ancient authorities read *Nebuchadnezzar and Ahasuerus*   h Gk *He*   i Other ancient authorities lack *Amen*

JUDITH

TRUST GOD

Holy Murder

Have you ever found yourself witnessing something that was wrong—really wrong—and all of a sudden you think, "I better do something about this"? It happens to all of us, even in small ways, like when a little brother or sister decides to turn the hose on at an outdoor party and starts to aim at the guests. You see it and you act—*fast*!

Judith, the heroine of this story, is watching something go *really* wrong. Her own leaders and people are going to surrender to the enemy. They had no hope. All the men had fought to defeat the enemy, but even they decided it was no use to fight any longer. In came Judith—the beautiful widow, not the typical heroic warrior. In fact, she was known to be quite religious and devoted to prayer and fasting. She loved her people, and she had a plan for victory. Her plan was outrageous—so outrageous that she wouldn't even reveal it to the elders!

Do you sometimes feel too insignificant to make a difference? Think again! In this story, we learn that God uses the most unlikely people to fulfill God's plan.

"Justice is a certain rectitude of mind whereby a man does what he ought to do in the circumstances confronting him."

—St. Thomas Aquinas

WHO The author is unknown, but was probably a Palestinian Jew.

WHAT A story about God delivering the Jewish people from an oppressor through the actions of a woman

WHEN Written at the end of the second or the beginning of the first century B.C.

WHERE Unknown

PATH OF DISCIPLESHIP

SPOILER ALERT: Judith commits murder to defeat the enemy. A disciple of Jesus will find Judith's actions objectionable. The *Catechism of the Catholic Church* spends quite a few pages explaining the correlation of respect for human life with the taking of the life of another human being (see 2258–2330).

You may wonder where these laws and doctrines come from. Laws and beliefs come out of a community's values. Jesus left us sayings about many of these values in the Sermon on the Mount (see Matthew 5–7). As the Church grew, laws and beliefs were shaped from Jesus' words and example. Why do we fight to preserve life, even that of our enemies? Because we believe in the solidarity of all human beings. All life is important, and important to God.

We hold that we are all one human family, no matter what our national origin, race, or even belief system. Not only do we not kill each other; we actively work to see that others—even our enemies—are treated with reverence and justice. On another level, the same values and actions apply at home and school when we kill another person's spirit through a harsh word, look, or act. Disciples find that objectionable too.

1 Arphaxad Fortifies Ecbatana

It was the twelfth year of the reign of Nebuchadnezzar, who ruled over the Assyrians in the great city of Nineveh. In those days Arphaxad ruled over the Medes in Ecbatana. [2]He built walls around Ecbatana with hewn stones three cubits thick and six cubits long; he made the walls seventy cubits high and fifty cubits wide. [3]At its gates he raised towers one hundred cubits high and sixty cubits wide at the foundations. [4]He made its gates seventy cubits high and forty cubits wide to allow his armies to march out in force and his infantry to form their ranks. [5]Then King Nebuchadnezzar made war against King Arphaxad in the great plain that is on the borders of Ragau. [6]There rallied to him all the people of the hill country and all those who lived along the Euphrates, the Tigris, and the Hydaspes, and, on the plain, Arioch, king of the Elymeans. Thus, many nations joined the forces of the Chaldeans.[a]

Nebuchadnezzar Issues Ultimatum

7 Then Nebuchadnezzar, king of the Assyrians, sent messengers to all who lived in Persia and to all who lived in the west, those who lived in Cilicia and Damascus, Lebanon and Antilebanon, and all who lived along the seacoast, [8]and those among the nations of Carmel and Gilead, and Upper Galilee and the great plain of Esdraelon, [9]and all who were in Samaria and its towns, and beyond the Jordan as far as Jerusalem and Bethany and Chelous and Kadesh and the river of Egypt, and Tahpanhes and Raamses and the whole land of Goshen, [10]even beyond Tanis and Memphis, and all who lived in Egypt as far as the borders of Ethiopia. [11]But all who lived in the whole region disregarded the summons of Nebuchadnezzar, king of the Assyrians, and refused to join him in the war; for they were not afraid of him, but regarded him as only one man.[b] So they sent back his messengers empty-handed and in disgrace.

12 Then Nebuchadnezzar became very angry with this whole region, and swore by his throne and kingdom that he would take revenge on the whole territory of Cilicia and Damascus and Syria, that he would kill with his sword also all the inhabitants of the land of Moab, and the people of Ammon, and all Judea, and every one in Egypt, as far as the coasts of the two seas.

Arphaxad Is Defeated

13 In the seventeenth year he led his forces against King Arphaxad and defeated him in battle, overthrowing the whole army of Arphaxad and all his cavalry and all his chariots. [14]Thus he took possession of his towns and came to Ecbatana, captured its towers, plundered its markets, and turned its glory into disgrace. [15]He captured Arphaxad in the mountains of Ragau and struck him down with his spears, thus destroying him once and for all. [16]Then he returned to Nineveh, he and all his combined forces, a vast body of troops; and there he and his forces rested and feasted for one hundred twenty days.

2 The Expedition against the West

In the eighteenth year, on the twenty-second day of the first month, there was talk in the palace of Nebuchadnezzar, king of the Assyrians, about carrying out his revenge on the whole region, just as he had said. [2]He summoned all his ministers and all his nobles and set be-

---

TEXT MESSAGE

In the first millennium B.C. Assyria was best known as a great military power. It was also a great cultural power. Ashurbanipal, the last great king in Assyria, established the first systematically organized library in the ancient Middle East. Its remains can be seen today at Nineveh.

This information has been scanned and is free of all known viruses. Please forward to all your friends.

---

a Syr: Gk *Cheleoudites*   b Or *a man*

Bus Aisle—© Maggie Hubbard, 15

fore them his secret plan and recounted fully, with his own lips, all the wickedness of the region.[a] 3They decided that every one who had not obeyed his command should be destroyed.

4 When he had completed his plan, Nebuchadnezzar, king of the Assyrians, called Holofernes, the chief general of his army, second only to himself, and said to him, 5"Thus says the Great King, the lord of the whole earth: Leave my presence and take with you men confident in their strength, one hundred twenty thousand foot soldiers and twelve thousand cavalry. 6March out against all the land to the west, because they disobeyed my orders. 7Tell them to prepare earth and water, for I am coming against them in my anger, and will cover the whole face of the earth with the feet of my troops, to whom I will hand them over to be plundered. 8Their wounded shall fill their ravines and gullies, and the swelling river shall be filled with their dead. 9I will lead them away captive to the ends of the whole earth. 10You shall go and seize all their territory for me in advance. They must yield themselves to you, and you shall hold them for me until the day of their punishment. 11But to those who resist show no mercy, but hand them over to slaughter and plunder throughout your whole region. 12For as I live, and by the power of my kingdom, what I have spoken I will accomplish by my own hand. 13And you—take care not to transgress any of your lord's commands, but carry them out exactly as I have ordered you; do it without delay."

Campaign of Holofernes

14 So Holofernes left the presence of his lord, and summoned all the commanders, generals, and officers of the Assyrian army. 15He mustered the picked troops by divisions as his lord had ordered him to do, one hundred twenty

thousand of them, together with twelve thousand archers on horseback, 16and he organized them as a great army is marshaled for a campaign. 17He took along a vast number of camels and donkeys and mules for transport, and innumerable sheep and oxen and goats for food; 18also ample rations for everyone, and a huge amount of gold and silver from the royal palace.

19 Then he set out with his whole army, to go ahead of King Nebuchadnezzar and to cover the whole face of the earth to the west with their chariots and cavalry and picked foot soldiers. 20Along with them went a mixed crowd like a swarm of locusts, like the dust[b] of the earth—a multitude that could not be counted.

21 They marched for three days from Nineveh to the plain of Bectileth, and camped opposite Bectileth near the mountain that is to the north of Upper Cilicia. 22From there Holofernes[c] took his whole army, the infantry, cavalry, and chariots, and went up into the hill country. 23He ravaged Put and Lud, and plundered all the Rassisites and the Ishmaelites on the border of the desert, south of the country of the Chelleans. 24Then he followed[d] the Euphrates and passed through Mesopotamia and destroyed all the fortified towns along the brook Abron, as far as the sea. 25He also seized the territory of Cilicia, and killed everyone who resisted him. Then he came to the southern borders of Japheth, facing Arabia. 26He surrounded all the Midianites, and burned their tents and plundered their sheepfolds. 27Then he went down into the plain of Damascus during the wheat harvest, and burned all their fields and destroyed their flocks and herds and sacked their towns and ravaged their lands and put all their young men to the sword.

28 So fear and dread of him fell upon all the people who lived along the seacoast, at Sidon

a Meaning of Gk uncertain b Gk sand c Gk he d Or crossed

them as you please. ⁴Our towns and their inhabitants are also your slaves; come and deal with them as you see fit."

5 The men came to Holofernes and told him all this. ⁶Then he went down to the seacoast with his army and stationed garrisons in the fortified towns and took picked men from them as auxiliaries. ⁷These people and all in the countryside welcomed him with garlands and dances and tambourines. ⁸Yet he demolished all their shrines[b] and cut down their sacred groves; for he had been commissioned to destroy all the gods of the land, so that all nations should worship Nebuchadnezzar alone, and that all their dialects and tribes should call upon him as a god.

9 Then he came toward Esdraelon, near Dothan, facing the great ridge of Judea; ¹⁰he camped between Geba and Scythopolis, and remained for a whole month in order to collect all the supplies for his army.

4 Judea on the Alert

When the Israelites living in Judea heard of everything that Holofernes, the general of Nebuchadnezzar, the king of the Assyrians, had done to the nations, and how he had plundered and destroyed all their temples, ²they were therefore greatly terrified at his approach; they were alarmed both for Jerusalem and for the temple of the Lord their God. ³For they had only recently returned from exile, and all the people of Judea had just now gathered together, and the sacred vessels and the altar and the temple had been consecrated after their profanation. ⁴So they sent word to every district of Samaria, and to Kona, Beth-horon, Belmain, and Jericho, and to Choba and Aesora, and the valley of Salem. ⁵They immediately seized all the high hilltops and fortified the villages on them and stored up food in preparation for war—since their fields had recently been harvested.

6 The high priest, Joakim, who was in Jerusalem at the time, wrote to the people of Bethulia and Betomesthaim, which faces Esdraelon opposite the plain near Dothan, ⁷ordering them to seize the mountain passes, since by them Judea could be invaded; and it would be easy to stop any who tried to enter, for the approach was narrow, wide enough for only two at a time to pass.

Prayer and Penance

8 So the Israelites did as they had been ordered by the high priest Joakim and the senate of the whole people of Israel, in session at Jerusalem. ⁹And every man of Israel cried out to

and Tyre, and those who lived in Sur and Ocina and all who lived in Jamnia. Those who lived in Azotus and Ascalon feared him greatly.

3 Entreaties for Peace

They therefore sent messengers to him to sue for peace in these words: ²"We, the servants of Nebuchadnezzar, the Great King, lie prostrate before you. Do with us whatever you will. ³See, our buildings and all our land and all our wheat fields and our flocks and herds and all our encampments[a] lie before you; do with

a Gk all the sheepfolds of our tents b Syr: Gk borders

God with great fervor, and they humbled themselves with much fasting. ¹⁰They and their wives and their children and their cattle and every resident alien and hired laborer and purchased slave—they all put sackcloth around their waists. ¹¹And all the Israelite men, women, and children living at Jerusalem prostrated themselves before the temple and put ashes on their heads and spread out their sackcloth before the Lord. ¹²They even draped the altar with sackcloth and cried out in unison, praying fervently to the God of Israel not to allow their infants to be carried off and their wives to be taken as booty, and the towns they had inherited to be destroyed, and the sanctuary to be profaned and desecrated to the malicious joy of the Gentiles.

13 The Lord heard their prayers and had regard for their distress; for the people fasted many days throughout Judea and in Jerusalem before the sanctuary of the Lord Almighty. ¹⁴The high priest Joakim and all the priests who stood before the Lord and ministered to the Lord, with sackcloth around their loins, offered the daily burnt offerings, the votive offerings, and freewill offerings of the people. ¹⁵With ashes on their turbans, they cried out to the Lord with all their might to look with favor on the whole house of Israel.

5 Council against the Israelites
It was reported to Holofernes, the general of the Assyrian army, that the people of Israel had prepared for war and had closed the mountain passes and fortified all the high hilltops and set up barricades in the plains. ²In great anger he called together all the princes of Moab and the commanders of Ammon and all the governors of the coastland, ³and said to them, "Tell me, you Canaanites, what people is this that lives in the hill country? What towns do they inhabit? How large is their army, and in what does their power and strength consist? Who rules over them as king and leads their army? ⁴And why have they alone, of all who live in the west, refused to come out and meet me?"

Achior's Report
5 Then Achior, the leader of all the Ammonites, said to him, "May my lord please listen to a report from the mouth of your servant, and I will tell you the truth about this people that lives in the mountain district near you. No falsehood shall come from your servant's mouth. ⁶These people are descended from the Chaldeans. ⁷At one time they lived in Mesopotamia, because they did not wish to follow the

FASTING

In today's health-conscious, food-mesmerized culture, why would anybody fast? For the most part people refrain from food and drink to lose weight. Some we know go too far and develop the disorders of bulimia or anorexia. Others fast to cleanse the body of toxins. Still others fast to protest war, genocide, oppression, and other causes. In **Judith 4.9** the Israelites fasted as a prayer of petition that God would save them from their enemy.

For Catholics, fasting is an act of penance, like the forty-day fast of Jesus in the desert. When we decide to fast for a specified period, it should be with a desire for spiritual purification and wanting God to fill us up. The fourth Precept of the Church requires us to fast and abstain on the days set aside by the Church.

gods of their ancestors who were in Chaldea. ⁸Since they had abandoned the ways of their ancestors, and worshiped the God of heaven, the God they had come to know, their ancestors*ᵈ* drove them out from the presence of their gods. So they fled to Mesopotamia, and lived there for a long time. ⁹Then their God commanded them to leave the place where they were living and go to the land of Canaan. There they settled, and grew very prosperous in gold and silver and very much livestock. ¹⁰When a famine spread over the land of Canaan they went down to Egypt and lived there as long as they had food. There they became so great a multitude that their race could not be counted. ¹¹So the king of Egypt became hostile to them; he exploited them and forced them to make bricks. ¹²They cried out to their God, and he afflicted the whole land of Egypt with incurable plagues. So the Egyptians drove them out of their sight. ¹³Then God dried up the Red Sea before them, ¹⁴and he led them by the way of Sinai and Kadesh-barnea. They drove out all the people of the desert, ¹⁵and took up residence in the land of the Amorites, and by their might destroyed all the inhabitants of Heshbon; and crossing over the Jordan they took possession

a Gk they

of all the hill country. ¹⁶They drove out before them the Canaanites, the Perizzites, the Jebusites, the Shechemites, and all the Gergesites, and lived there a long time.

17 "As long as they did not sin against their God they prospered, for the God who hates iniquity is with them. ¹⁸But when they departed from the way he had prescribed for them, they were utterly defeated in many battles and were led away captive to a foreign land. The temple of their God was razed to the ground, and their towns were occupied by their enemies. ¹⁹But now they have returned to their God, and have come back from the places where they were scattered, and have occupied Jerusalem, where their sanctuary is, and have settled in the hill country, because it was uninhabited.

20 "So now, my master and lord, if there is any oversight in this people and they sin against their God and we find out their offense, then we can go up and defeat them. ²¹But if they are not a guilty nation, then let my lord pass them by; for their Lord and God will defend them, and we shall become the laughingstock of the whole world."

22 When Achior had finished saying these things, all the people standing around the tent began to complain; Holofernes' officers and all the inhabitants of the seacoast and Moab insisted that he should be cut to pieces. ²³They said, "We are not afraid of the Israelites; they are a people with no strength or power for making war. ²⁴Therefore let us go ahead, Lord Holofernes, and your vast army will swallow them up."

6 Achior Handed over to the Israelites

When the disturbance made by the people outside the council had died down, Holofernes, the commander of the Assyrian army, said to Achior[a] in the presence of all the foreign contingents:

2 "Who are you, Achior and you mercenaries of Ephraim, to prophesy among us as you have done today and tell us not to make war against the people of Israel because their God will defend them? What god is there except Nebuchadnezzar? He will send his forces and destroy them from the face of the earth. Their God will not save them; ³we the king's[b] servants will destroy them as one man. They cannot resist the might of our cavalry. ⁴We will overwhelm them;[c] their mountains will be drunk with their blood, and their fields will be full of their dead. Not even their footprints will survive our attack; they will utterly perish. So says King Nebuchadnezzar, lord of the whole earth. For he has spoken; none of his words shall be in vain.

5 "As for you, Achior, you Ammonite mercenary, you have said these words in a moment of perversity; you shall not see my face again from this day until I take revenge on this race that came out of Egypt. ⁶Then at my return the sword of my army and the spear[d] of my servants shall pierce your sides, and you shall fall among their wounded. ⁷Now my slaves are going to take you back into the hill country and put you in one of the towns beside the passes. ⁸You will not die until you perish along with them. ⁹If you really hope in your heart that they will not be taken, then do not look downcast! I have spoken, and none of my words shall fail to come true."

10 Then Holofernes ordered his slaves, who waited on him in his tent, to seize Achior and take him away to Bethulia and hand him over to the Israelites. ¹¹So the slaves took him and led him out of the camp into the plain, and from the plain they went up into the hill country and came to the springs below Bethulia. ¹²When the men of the town saw them,[e] they seized their weapons and ran out of the town to the top of the hill, and all the slingers kept

---

a Other ancient authorities add *and to all the Moabites* b Gk *his* c Other ancient authorities add *with it* d Lat Syr: Gk *people* e Other ancient authorities add *on the top of the hill*

✒ At The End

At the end what will you choose:

Science or nature?

Smiling or frowning?

What is more important:

Living or dying?

Running in or running out?

Crying or holding everything in?

Jesus or yourself?

Your life or someone else's?

The words or what you choose to make of them?

Today, tomorrow, or yesterday?

What you say or what you mean?

What you see or what you don't?

Doubting or trusting?

At the end what will matter:

What's on TV or what's in your heart?

What's on your mind or what you're told to think?

Finding your place in this world or being told your place?

The things you're told or what you know in your heart that's true?

How you tried or how it didn't work out?

The first day or the last?

Why or how something happened?

What matters:

The way the flower smells or the way it looks?

Going in blind or knowing everything?

Understanding what this means or thinking about it?

Doing what's right or having fun?

Knowing why or just why not?

What we do or why we do it?

Are there answers or just more questions?

At The End—© Katie Duckett, 15

them from coming up by throwing stones at them. [13]So having taken shelter below the hill, they bound Achior and left him lying at the foot of the hill, and returned to their master.

14 Then the Israelites came down from their town and found him; they untied him and brought him into Bethulia and placed him before the magistrates of their town, [15]who in those days were Uzziah son of Micah, of the tribe of Simeon, and Chabris son of Gothoniel, and Charmis son of Melchiel. [16]They called together all the elders of the town, and all their young men and women ran to the assembly. They set Achior in the midst of all their people, and Uzziah questioned him about what had happened. [17]He answered and told them what had taken place at the council of Holofernes, and all that he had said in the presence of the Assyrian leaders, and all that Holofernes had boasted he would do against the house of Israel. [18]Then the people fell down and worshiped God, and cried out:

19 "O Lord God of heaven, see their arrogance, and have pity on our people in their humiliation, and look kindly today on the faces of those who are consecrated to you."

20 Then they reassured Achior, and praised him highly. [21]Uzziah took him from the assembly to his own house and gave a banquet for the elders; and all that night they called on the God of Israel for help.

7 The Campaign against Bethulia

The next day Holofernes ordered his whole army, and all the allies who had joined him, to break camp and move against Bethulia, and to seize the passes up into the hill country and make war on the Israelites. [2]So all their warriors marched off that day; their fighting forces numbered one hundred seventy thousand infantry and twelve thousand cavalry, not counting the baggage and the foot soldiers handling it, a very great multitude. [3]They encamped in the valley near Bethulia, beside the spring, and they spread out in breadth over Dothan as far as Balbaim and in length from Bethulia to Cyamon, which faces Esdraelon.

4 When the Israelites saw their vast numbers, they were greatly terrified and said to one another, "They will now strip clean the whole land; neither the high mountains nor the valleys nor the hills will bear their weight." [5]Yet they all seized their weapons, and when they had kindled fires on their towers, they remained on guard all that night.

6 On the second day Holofernes led out all his cavalry in full view of the Israelites in Bethulia. [7]He reconnoitered the approaches to their town, and visited the springs that supplied their water; he seized them and set guards of soldiers over them, and then returned to his army.

8 Then all the chieftains of the Edomites and all the leaders of the Moabites and the commanders of the coastland came to him and said, [9]"Listen to what we have to say, my lord, and your army will suffer no losses. [10]This people, the Israelites, do not rely on their spears but on the height of the mountains where they live, for it is not easy to reach the tops of their mountains. [11]Therefore, my lord, do not fight against them in regular formation, and not a man of your army will fall. [12]Remain in your camp, and keep all the men in your forces with you; let your servants take possession of the spring of water that flows from the foot of the mountain, [13]for this is where all the people of Bethulia get their water. So thirst will destroy them, and they will surrender their town. Meanwhile, we and our people will go up to the tops of the nearby mountains and camp there to keep watch to see that no one gets out of the town. [14]They and their wives and children will waste away with famine, and before the sword reaches them they will be strewn about in the streets where they live. [15]Thus you will pay them back with evil, because they rebelled and did not receive you peaceably."

16 These words pleased Holofernes and all his attendants, and he gave orders to do as they had said. [17]So the army of the Ammonites moved forward, together with five thousand Assyrians, and they encamped in the valley and seized the water supply and the springs of the Israelites. [18]And the Edomites and Ammonites went up and encamped in the hill country opposite Dothan; and they sent some of their men toward the south and the east, toward Egrebeh, which is near Chusi beside the Wadi Mochmur. The rest of the Assyrian army encamped in the plain, and covered the whole face of the land. Their tents and supply trains spread out in great number, and they formed a vast multitude.

The Distress of the Israelites

19 The Israelites then cried out to the Lord their God, for their courage failed, because all their enemies had surrounded them, and there was no way of escape from them. [20]The whole Assyrian army, their infantry, chariots, and cavalry, surrounded them for thirty-four days, until all the water containers of every inhabitant of Bethulia were empty; [21]their cisterns were going dry, and on no day did they have enough water to drink, for their drinking water was rationed. [22]Their children were listless, and the women and young men fainted from

thirst and were collapsing in the streets of the town and in the gateways; they no longer had any strength.

23 Then all the people, the young men, the women, and the children, gathered around Uzziah and the rulers of the town and cried out with a loud voice, and said before all the elders, [24]"Let God judge between you and us! You have done us a great injury in not making peace with the Assyrians. [25]For now we have no one to help us; God has sold us into their hands, to be strewn before them in thirst and exhaustion. [26]Now summon them and surrender the whole town as booty to the army of Holofernes and to all his forces. [27]For it would be better for us to be captured by them.[a] We shall indeed become slaves, but our lives will be spared, and we shall not witness our little ones dying before our eyes, and our wives and children drawing their last breath. [28]We call to witness against you heaven and earth and our God, the Lord of our ancestors, who punishes us for our sins and the sins of our ancestors; do today the things that we have described!"

29 Then great and general lamentation arose throughout the assembly, and they cried out to the Lord God with a loud voice. [30]But Uzziah said to them, "Courage, my brothers and sisters![b] Let us hold out for five days more; by that time the Lord our God will turn his mercy to us again, for he will not forsake us utterly. [31]But if these days pass by, and no help comes for us, I will do as you say."

32 Then he dismissed the people to their various posts, and they went up on the walls and towers of their town. The women and children he sent home. In the town they were in great misery.

8 The Character of Judith

Now in those days Judith heard about these things: she was the daughter of Merari son of Ox son of Joseph son of Oziel son of Elkiah son of Ananias son of Gideon son of Raphain son of Ahitub son of Elijah son of Hilkiah son of Eliab son of Nathanael son of Salamiel son of Sarasadai son of Israel. [2]Her husband Manasseh, who belonged to her tribe and family, had died during the barley harvest. [3]For as he stood overseeing those who were binding sheaves in the field, he was overcome by the burning heat, and took to his bed and died in his town Bethulia. So they buried him with his ancestors in the field between Dothan and Balamon. [4]Judith remained as a widow for three years and four months [5]at home where she set up a tent for

The Struggle—© Jennifer Lawrence, 19

herself on the roof of her house. She put sackcloth around her waist and dressed in widow's clothing. [6]She fasted all the days of her widowhood, except the day before the sabbath and the sabbath itself, the day before the new moon and the day of the new moon, and the festivals and days of rejoicing of the house of Israel. [7]She was beautiful in appearance, and was very lovely to behold. Her husband Manasseh had left her gold and silver, men and women slaves, livestock, and fields; and she maintained this estate. [8]No one spoke ill of her, for she feared God with great devotion.

Judith and the Elders

9 When Judith heard the harsh words spoken by the people against the ruler, because they were faint for lack of water, and when she heard all that Uzziah said to them, and how he promised them under oath to surrender the town to the Assyrians after five days, [10]she sent her maid, who was in charge of all she possessed, to summon Uzziah and[c] Chabris and Charmis, the elders of her town. [11]They came to her, and she said to them:

"Listen to me, rulers of the people of Bethulia! What you have said to the people today is not right; you have even sworn and pronounced this oath between God and you, promising to surrender the town to our enemies unless the Lord turns and helps us within so many days. [12]Who are you to put God to the test today, and to set yourselves up in the place of[d] God in human affairs? [13]You are put-

---

a Other ancient authorities add *than to die of thirst* b Gk *Courage, brothers* c Other ancient authorities lack *Uzziah and* (see verses 28 and 35) d Or *above*

18 "For never in our generation, nor in these present days, has there been any tribe or family or people or town of ours that worships gods made with hands, as was done in days gone by. ¹⁹That was why our ancestors were handed over to the sword and to pillage, and so they suffered a great catastrophe before our enemies. ²⁰But we know no other god but him, and so we hope that he will not disdain us or any of our nation. ²¹For if we are captured, all Judea will be captured and our sanctuary will be plundered; and he will make us pay for its desecration with our blood. ²²The slaughter of our kindred and the captivity of the land and the desolation of our inheritance—all this he will bring on our heads among the Gentiles, wherever we serve as slaves; and we shall be an offense and a disgrace in the eyes of those who acquire us. ²³For our slavery will not bring us into favor, but the Lord our God will turn it to dishonor.

24 "Therefore, my brothers, let us set an example for our kindred, for their lives depend upon us, and the sanctuary—both the temple and the altar—rests upon us. ²⁵In spite of everything let us give thanks to the Lord our God, who is putting us to the test as he did our ancestors. ²⁶Remember what he did with Abraham, and how he tested Isaac, and what happened to Jacob in Syrian Mesopotamia, while he was tending the sheep of Laban, his mother's brother. ²⁷For he has not tried us with fire, as he did them, to search their hearts, nor has he taken vengeance on us; but the Lord scourges those who are close to him in order to admonish them."

28 Then Uzziah said to her, "All that you have said was spoken out of a true heart, and there is no one who can deny your words. ²⁹Today is not the first time your wisdom has been shown, but from the beginning of your life all the people have recognized your understanding, for your heart's disposition is right. ³⁰But the people were so thirsty that they compelled us to do for them what we have promised, and made us take an oath that we cannot break. ³¹Now since you are a God-fearing woman, pray for us, so that the Lord may send us rain to fill our cisterns. Then we will no longer feel faint from thirst."

32 Then Judith said to them, "Listen to me. I am about to do something that will go down through all generations of our descendants. ³³Stand at the town gate tonight so that I may go out with my maid; and within the days after which you have promised to surrender the town to our enemies, the Lord will deliver Israel by my hand. ³⁴Only, do not try to find out what I am doing; for I will not tell you until I have finished what I am about to do."

ting the Lord Almighty to the test, but you will never learn anything! ¹⁴You cannot plumb the depths of the human heart or understand the workings of the human mind; how do you expect to search out God, who made all these things, and find out his mind or comprehend his thought? No, my brothers, do not anger the Lord our God. ¹⁵For if he does not choose to help us within these five days, he has power to protect us within any time he pleases, or even to destroy us in the presence of our enemies. ¹⁶Do not try to bind the purposes of the Lord our God; for God is not like a human being, to be threatened, or like a mere mortal, to be won over by pleading. ¹⁷Therefore, while we wait for his deliverance, let us call upon him to help us, and he will hear our voice, if it pleases him.

35 Uzziah and the rulers said to her, "Go in peace, and may the Lord God go before you, to take vengeance on our enemies." 36 So they returned from the tent and went to their posts.

9 The Prayer of Judith

Then Judith prostrated herself, put ashes on her head, and uncovered the sackcloth she was wearing. At the very time when the evening incense was being offered in the house of God in Jerusalem, Judith cried out to the Lord with a loud voice, and said,

2 "O Lord God of my ancestor Simeon, to whom you gave a sword to take revenge on those strangers who had torn off a virgin's clothing*a* to defile her, and exposed her thighs to put her to shame, and polluted her womb to disgrace her; for you said, 'It shall not be done'—yet they did it; 3 so you gave up their rulers to be killed, and their bed, which was ashamed of the deceit they had practiced, was stained with blood, and you struck down slaves along with princes, and princes on their thrones. 4 You gave up their wives for booty and their daughters to captivity, and all their booty to be divided among your beloved children who burned with zeal for you and abhorred the pollution of their blood and called on you for help. O God, my God, hear me also, a widow.

5 "For you have done these things and those that went before and those that followed. You have designed the things that are now, and those that are to come. What you had in mind has happened; 6 the things you decided on presented themselves and said, 'Here we are!' For all your ways are prepared in advance, and your judgment is with foreknowledge.

7 "Here now are the Assyrians, a greatly increased force, priding themselves in their horses and riders, boasting in the strength of their foot soldiers, and trusting in shield and spear, in bow and sling. They do not know that you are the Lord who crushes wars; the Lord is your name. 8 Break their strength by your might, and bring down their power in your anger; for they intend to defile your sanctuary, and to pollute the tabernacle where your glorious name resides, and to break off the horns*b* of your altar with the sword. 9 Look at their pride, and send your wrath upon their heads. Give to me, a widow, the strong hand to do what I plan. 10 By the deceit of my lips strike down the slave with the prince and the prince with his servant; crush their arrogance by the hand of a woman.

11 "For your strength does not depend on numbers, nor your might on the powerful. But you are the God of the lowly, helper of the oppressed, upholder of the weak, protector of the forsaken, savior of those without hope. 12 Please, please, God of my father, God of the heritage of Israel, Lord of heaven and earth, Creator of the waters, King of all your creation, hear my prayer! 13 Make my deceitful words bring wound and bruise on those who have planned cruel things against your covenant, and against your sacred house, and against Mount Zion, and against the house your children possess. 14 Let your whole nation and every tribe know and understand that you are God, the God of all power and might, and that there is no other who protects the people of Israel but you alone!"

10 Judith Prepares to Go to Holofernes

When Judith*c* had stopped crying out to the God of Israel, and had ended all these words, 2 she rose from where she lay prostrate. She called her maid and went down into the house where she lived on sabbaths and on her festal days. 3 She removed the sackcloth she had been wearing, took off her widow's garments, bathed her body with water, and anointed herself with precious ointment. She combed her hair, put on a tiara, and dressed herself in the festive attire that she used to wear while her husband Manasseh was living. 4 She put sandals on her feet, and put on her anklets, bracelets, rings, earrings, and all her other jewelry. Thus she made herself very beautiful, to entice the eyes of all the men who might see her. 5 She gave her maid a skin of wine and a flask of oil, and filled a bag with roasted grain, dried fig cakes, and fine bread;*d* then she wrapped up all her dishes and gave them to her to carry.

6 Then they went out to the town gate of Bethulia and found Uzziah standing there with the elders of the town, Chabris and Charmis. 7 When they saw her transformed in appearance and dressed differently, they were very greatly astounded at her beauty and said to her, 8 "May the God of our ancestors grant you favor and fulfill your plans, so that the people of Israel may glory and Jerusalem may be exalted." She bowed down to God.

9 Then she said to them, "Order the gate of the town to be opened for me so that I may go out and accomplish the things you have just said to me." So they ordered the young men to open the gate for her, as she requested. 10 When they had done this, Judith went out, accompanied by her maid. The men of the town watched her until she had gone down the mountain and passed through the valley, where they lost sight of her.

a Cn: Gk *loosed her womb*   *b* Syr: Gk *horn*   *c* Gk *she*   *d* Other ancient authorities add *and cheese*

Star of Wonder—© Charlotte Katheder, 16

Judith Is Captured

11 As the women[a] were going straight on
through the valley, an Assyrian patrol met her
[12]and took her into custody. They asked her,
"To what people do you belong, and where are
you coming from, and where are you going?"
She replied, "I am a daughter of the Hebrews,
but I am fleeing from them, for they are about
to be handed over to you to be devoured. [13]I am
on my way to see Holofernes the commander
of your army, to give him a true report; I will
show him a way by which he can go and capture all the hill country without losing one of
his men, captured or slain."

14 When the men heard her words, and observed her face—she was in their eyes marvelously beautiful—they said to her, [15]"You have
saved your life by hurrying down to see our
lord. Go at once to his tent; some of us will escort you and hand you over to him. [16]When you
stand before him, have no fear in your heart,
but tell him what you have just said, and he will
treat you well."

17 They chose from their number a hundred
men to accompany her and her maid, and they
brought them to the tent of Holofernes. [18]There
was great excitement in the whole camp, for
her arrival was reported from tent to tent. They
came and gathered around her as she stood
outside the tent of Holofernes, waiting until they told him about her. [19]They marveled at
her beauty and admired the Israelites, judging
them by her. They said to one another, "Who
can despise these people, who have women like
this among them? It is not wise to leave one of
their men alive, for if we let them go they will be
able to beguile the whole world!"

Judith Is Brought before Holofernes

20 Then the guards of Holofernes and all his
servants came out and led her into the tent.
[21]Holofernes was resting on his bed under a
canopy that was woven with purple and gold,
emeralds and other precious stones. [22]When
they told him of her, he came to the front of the
tent, with silver lamps carried before him.
[23]When Judith came into the presence of Holofernes[b] and his servants, they all marveled at
the beauty of her face. She prostrated herself
and did obeisance to him, but his slaves raised
her up.

11 Then Holofernes said to her, "Take courage, woman, and do not be afraid in your heart,
for I have never hurt anyone who chose to serve
Nebuchadnezzar, king of all the earth. [2]Even
now, if your people who live in the hill country
had not slighted me, I would never have lifted

a Gk *they* b Gk *him*

my spear against them. They have brought this on themselves. ³But now tell me why you have fled from them and have come over to us. In any event, you have come to safety. Take courage! You will live tonight and ever after. ⁴No one will hurt you. Rather, all will treat you well, as they do the servants of my lord King Nebuchadnezzar."

Judith Explains Her Presence

5 Judith answered him, "Accept the words of your slave, and let your servant speak in your presence. I will say nothing false to my lord this night. ⁶If you follow out the words of your servant, God will accomplish something through you, and my lord will not fail to achieve his purposes. ⁷By the life of Nebuchadnezzar, king of the whole earth, and by the power of him who has sent you to direct every living being! Not only do human beings serve him because of you, but also the animals of the field and the cattle and the birds of the air will live, because of your power, under Nebuchadnezzar and all his house. ⁸For we have heard of your wisdom and skill, and it is reported throughout the whole world that you alone are the best in the whole kingdom, the most informed and the most astounding in military strategy.

9 "Now as for Achior's speech in your council, we have heard his words, for the people of Bethulia spared him and he told them all he had said to you. ¹⁰Therefore, lord and master, do not disregard what he said, but keep it in your mind, for it is true. Indeed our nation cannot be punished, nor can the sword prevail against them, unless they sin against their God.

11 "But now, in order that my lord may not be defeated and his purpose frustrated, death will fall upon them, for a sin has overtaken them by which they are about to provoke their God to anger when they do what is wrong. ¹²Since their food supply is exhausted and their water has almost given out, they have planned to kill their livestock and have determined to use all that God by his laws has forbidden them to eat. ¹³They have decided to consume the first fruits of the grain and the tithes of the wine and oil, which they had consecrated and set aside for the priests who minister in the presence of our God in Jerusalem—things it is not lawful for any of the people even to touch with their hands. ¹⁴Since even the people in Jerusalem have been doing this, they have sent messengers there in order to bring back permission from the council of the elders. ¹⁵When the response reaches them and they act upon it, on that very day they will be handed over to you to be destroyed.

16 "So when I, your slave, learned all this, I fled from them. God has sent me to accomplish with you things that will astonish the whole world wherever people shall hear about them. ¹⁷Your servant is indeed God-fearing and serves the God of heaven night and day. So, my lord, I will remain with you; but every night your servant will go out into the valley and pray to God. He will tell me when they have committed their sins. ¹⁸Then I will come and tell you, so that you may go out with your whole army, and not one of them will be able to withstand you. ¹⁹Then I will lead you through Judea, until you come to Jerusalem; there I will set your throne.ᵃ You will drive them like sheep that have no shepherd, and no dog will so much as growl at you. For this was told me to give me foreknowledge; it was announced to me, and I was sent to tell you."

20 Her words pleased Holofernes and all his servants. They marveled at her wisdom and said, ²¹"No other woman from one end of the earth to the other looks so beautiful or speaks so wisely!" ²²Then Holofernes said to her, "God has done well to send you ahead of the people, to strengthen our hands and bring destruction on those who have despised my lord. ²³You are not only beautiful in appearance, but wise in speech. If you do as you have said, your God shall be my God, and you shall live in the palace of King Nebuchadnezzar and be renowned throughout the whole world."

12 Judith as a Guest of Holofernes

Then he commanded them to bring her in where his silver dinnerware was kept, and ordered them to set a table for her with some of his own delicacies, and with some of his own wine to drink. ²But Judith said, "I cannot partake of them, or it will be an offense; but I will have enough with the things I brought with me." ³Holofernes said to her, "If your supply runs out, where can we get you more of the same? For none of your people are here with us." ⁴Judith replied, "As surely as you live, my lord, your servant will not use up the supplies I have with me before the Lord carries out by my hand what he has determined."

5 Then the servants of Holofernes brought her into the tent, and she slept until midnight. Toward the morning watch she got up ⁶and sent this message to Holofernes: "Let my lord now give orders to allow your servant to go out and pray." ⁷So Holofernes commanded his guards not to hinder her. She remained in the camp three days. She went out each night to the valley of Bethulia, and bathed at the

a Or *chariot*

spring in the camp.[a] 8After bathing, she prayed the Lord God of Israel to direct her way for the triumph of his[b] people. 9Then she returned purified and stayed in the tent until she ate her food toward evening.

Judith Attends Holofernes' Banquet

10 On the fourth day Holofernes held a banquet for his personal attendants only, and did not invite any of his officers. 11He said to Bagoas, the eunuch who had charge of his personal affairs, "Go and persuade the Hebrew woman who is in your care to join us and to eat and drink with us. 12For it would be a disgrace if we let such a woman go without having intercourse with her. If we do not seduce her, she will laugh at us."

13 So Bagoas left the presence of Holofernes, and approached her and said, "Let this pretty girl not hesitate to come to my lord to be honored in his presence, and to enjoy drinking wine with us, and to become today like one of the Assyrian women who serve in the palace of Nebuchadnezzar." 14Judith replied, "Who am I to refuse my lord? Whatever pleases him I will do at once, and it will be a joy to me until the day of my death." 15So she proceeded to dress herself in all her woman's finery. Her maid went ahead and spread for her on the ground before Holofernes the lambskins she had received from Bagoas for her daily use in reclining.

16 Then Judith came in and lay down. Holofernes' heart was ravished with her and his passion was aroused, for he had been waiting for an opportunity to seduce her from the day

he first saw her. 17So Holofernes said to her, "Have a drink and be merry with us!" 18Judith said, "I will gladly drink, my lord, because today is the greatest day in my whole life." 19Then she took what her maid had prepared and ate and drank before him. 20Holofernes was greatly pleased with her, and drank a great quantity of wine, much more than he had ever drunk in any one day since he was born.

13 Judith Beheads Holofernes

When evening came, his slaves quickly withdrew. Bagoas closed the tent from outside and shut out the attendants from his master's presence. They went to bed, for they all were weary because the banquet had lasted so long. 2But Judith was left alone in the tent, with Holofernes stretched out on his bed, for he was dead drunk.

3 Now Judith had told her maid to stand outside the bedchamber and to wait for her to come out, as she did on the other days; for she said she would be going out for her prayers. She had said the same thing to Bagoas. 4So everyone went out, and no one, either small or great, was left in the bedchamber. Then Judith, standing beside his bed, said in her heart, "O Lord God of all might, look in this hour on the work of my hands for the exaltation of Jerusalem. 5Now indeed is the time to help your heritage and to carry out my design to destroy the enemies who have risen up against us."

6 She went up to the bedpost near Holofernes' head, and took down his sword that hung there. 7She came close to his bed, took

a Other ancient authorities lack in the camp   b Other ancient authorities read her

Expressions—© John 3:16 Mission FYC, Cooperative Project, ages 11–14

hold of the hair of his head, and said, "Give me strength today, O Lord God of Israel!" [8]Then she struck his neck twice with all her might, and cut off his head. [9]Next she rolled his body off the bed and pulled down the canopy from the posts. Soon afterward she went out and gave Holofernes' head to her maid, [10]who placed it in her food bag.

Judith Returns to Bethulia
Then the two of them went out together, as they were accustomed to do for prayer. They passed through the camp, circled around the valley, and went up the mountain to Bethulia, and came to its gates. [11]From a distance Judith called out to the sentries at the gates, "Open, open the gate! God, our God, is with us, still showing his power in Israel and his strength against our enemies, as he has done today!"

12 When the people of her town heard her voice, they hurried down to the town gate and summoned the elders of the town. [13]They all ran together, both small and great, for it seemed unbelievable that she had returned. They opened the gate and welcomed them. Then they lit a fire to give light, and gathered around them. [14]Then she said to them with a loud voice, "Praise God, O praise him! Praise God, who has not withdrawn his mercy from the house of Israel, but has destroyed our enemies by my hand this very night!"

15 Then she pulled the head out of the bag and showed it to them, and said, "See here, the head of Holofernes, the commander of the Assyrian army, and here is the canopy beneath which he lay in his drunken stupor. The Lord has struck him down by the hand of a woman. [16]As the Lord lives, who has protected me in the way I went, I swear that it was my face that seduced him to his destruction, and that he committed no sin with me, to defile and shame me."

17 All the people were greatly astonished. They bowed down and worshiped God, and said with one accord, "Blessed are you our God, who have this day humiliated the enemies of your people."

18 Then Uzziah said to her, "O daughter, you are blessed by the Most High God above all other women on earth; and blessed be the Lord God, who created the heavens and the earth, who has guided you to cut off the head of the leader of our enemies. [19]Your praise[a] will never depart from the hearts of those who remember the power of God. [20]May God grant this to be a perpetual honor to you, and may he reward you with blessings, because you risked your own life when our nation was brought

a Other ancient authorities read *hope*

REALITY ✔

MAKE A DIFFERENCE
The call to participate in actions that promote peace and justice is a call for all baptized people. No one is excused.

Most of us want to make a difference, but maybe you aren't sure how or what to do. There are many simple and peaceful ways to advocate for justice and freedom, such as writing letters to elected leaders, making contributions to causes, or serving local projects. What can you do?

One of the first steps is to be *informed*. Go to **Learner.CalltoDiscipleship.com** to find out about the social issues addressed by the U.S. Conference of Catholic Bishops. You'll find suggestions for actions you can take now on issues that are real and important today. You can also identify issues you have an interest in and would be willing to work on for a period of time. When you find something of interest, get one or two family members or friends to act with you.

low, and you averted our ruin, walking in the straight path before our God." And all the people said, "Amen. Amen."

14 Judith's Counsel
Then Judith said to them, "Listen to me, my friends. Take this head and hang it upon the parapet of your wall. [2]As soon as day breaks and the sun rises on the earth, each of you take up your weapons, and let every able-bodied man go out of the town; set a captain over them, as if you were going down to the plain against the Assyrian outpost; only do not go down. [3]Then they will seize their arms and go into the camp and rouse the officers of the Assyrian army. They will rush into the tent of Holofernes and will not find him. Then panic will come over them, and they will flee before you. [4]Then you and all who live within the borders

of Israel will pursue them and cut them down in their tracks. ⁵But before you do all this, bring Achior the Ammonite to me so that he may see and recognize the man who despised the house of Israel and sent him to us as if to his death."

6 So they summoned Achior from the house of Uzziah. When he came and saw the head of Holofernes in the hand of one of the men in the assembly of the people, he fell down on his face in a faint. ⁷When they raised him up he threw himself at Judith's feet, and did obeisance to her, and said, "Blessed are you in every tent of Judah! In every nation those who hear your name will be alarmed. ⁸Now tell me what you have done during these days."

So Judith told him in the presence of the people all that she had done, from the day she left until the moment she began speaking to them. ⁹When she had finished, the people raised a great shout and made a joyful noise in their town. ¹⁰When Achior saw all that the God of Israel had done, he believed firmly in God. So he was circumcised, and joined the house of Israel, remaining so to this day.

Holofernes' Death Is Discovered

11 As soon as it was dawn they hung the head of Holofernes on the wall. Then they all took their weapons, and they went out in companies to the mountain passes. ¹²When the Assyrians saw them they sent word to their commanders, who then went to the generals and the captains and to all their other officers. ¹³They came to Holofernes' tent and said to the steward in charge of all his personal affairs, "Wake up our lord, for the slaves have been so bold as to come down against us to give battle, to their utter destruction."

14 So Bagoas went in and knocked at the entry of the tent, for he supposed that he was sleeping with Judith. ¹⁵But when no one answered, he opened it and went into the bedchamber and found him sprawled on the floor dead, with his head missing. ¹⁶He cried out with a loud voice and wept and groaned and shouted, and tore his clothes. ¹⁷Then he went to the tent where Judith had stayed, and when he did not find her, he rushed out to the people and shouted, ¹⁸"The slaves have tricked us! One He-

brew woman has brought disgrace on the house of King Nebuchadnezzar. Look, Holofernes is lying on the ground, and his head is missing!"

19 When the leaders of the Assyrian army heard this, they tore their tunics and were greatly dismayed, and their loud cries and shouts rose up throughout the camp.

15 The Assyrians Flee in Panic

When the men in the tents heard it, they were amazed at what had happened. ²Overcome with fear and trembling, they did not wait for one another, but with one impulse all rushed out and fled by every path across the plain and through the hill country. ³Those who had camped in the hills around Bethulia also took to flight. Then the Israelites, everyone that was a soldier, rushed out upon them. ⁴Uzziah sent men to Betomasthaimᵃ and Choba and Kola, and to all the frontiers of Israel, to tell what had taken place and to urge all to rush out upon the enemy to destroy them. ⁵When the Israelites heard it, with one accord they fell upon the enemy,ᵇ and cut them down as far as Choba. Those in Jerusalem and all the hill country also came, for they were told what had happened in the camp of the enemy. The men in Gilead and in Galilee outflanked them with great slaughter, even beyond Damascus and its borders. ⁶The rest of the people of Bethulia fell upon the Assyrian camp and plundered it, acquiring great riches. ⁷And the Israelites, when they returned from the slaughter, took possession of what remained. Even the villages and towns in the hill country and in the plain got a great amount of booty, since there was a vast quantity of it.

The Israelites Celebrate Their Victory

8 Then the high priest Joakim and the elders of the Israelites who lived in Jerusalem came to witness the good things that the Lord had done for Israel, and to see Judith and to wish her well. ⁹When they met her, they all blessed her with one accord and said to her, "You are the glory of Jerusalem, you are the great boast of Israel, you are the great pride of our nation! ¹⁰You have done all this with your own hand; you have done great good to Israel, and God is well pleased with it. May the Almighty Lord bless you forever!" And all the people said, "Amen."

11 All the people plundered the camp for thirty days. They gave Judith the tent of Holofernes and all his silver dinnerware, his beds, his bowls, and all his furniture. She took them and loaded her mules and hitched up her carts and piled the things on them.

ᵃ Other ancient authorities add *and Bebai* ᵇ Gk *them*

12 All the women of Israel gathered to see her, and blessed her, and some of them performed a dance in her honor. She took ivy-wreathed wands in her hands and distributed them to the women who were with her; [13]and she and those who were with her crowned themselves with olive wreaths. She went before all the people in the dance, leading all the women, while all the men of Israel followed, bearing their arms and wearing garlands and singing hymns.

Judith Offers Her Hymn of Praise

14 Judith began this thanksgiving before all Israel, and all the people loudly sang this song of praise. [1]And Judith said,

16

Begin a song to my God with tambourines,
    sing to my Lord with cymbals.
Raise to him a new psalm;[a]
    exalt him, and call upon his name.
[2] For the Lord is a God who crushes wars;
    he sets up his camp among his people;
    he delivered me from the hands of my
        pursuers.
[3] The Assyrian came down from the
        mountains of the north;
    he came with myriads of his warriors;
their numbers blocked up the wadis,
    and their cavalry covered the hills.
[4] He boasted that he would burn up my
        territory,
    and kill my young men with the sword,
and dash my infants to the ground,
    and seize my children as booty,
    and take my virgins as spoil.

[5] But the Lord Almighty has foiled them
    by the hand of a woman.[b]
[6] For their mighty one did not fall by the
        hands of the young men,
    nor did the sons of the Titans strike him
        down,
    nor did tall giants set upon him;
but Judith daughter of Merari
    with the beauty of her countenance
        undid him.

[7] For she put away her widow's clothing
    to exalt the oppressed in Israel.
She anointed her face with perfume;
[8]   she fastened her hair with a tiara
    and put on a linen gown to beguile him.
[9] Her sandal ravished his eyes,
    her beauty captivated his mind,
    and the sword severed his neck!
[10] The Persians trembled at her boldness,
    the Medes were daunted at her daring.

[11] Then my oppressed people shouted;
    my weak people cried out,[c] and the
        enemy[d] trembled;
    they lifted up their voices, and the
        enemy[d] were turned back.
[12] Sons of slave-girls pierced them through
    and wounded them like the children of
        fugitives;
    they perished before the army of my
        Lord.
[13] I will sing to my God a new song:
O Lord, you are great and glorious,
    wonderful in strength, invincible.
[14] Let all your creatures serve you,
    for you spoke, and they were made.
You sent forth your spirit,[e] and it formed
        them;[f]

a Other ancient authorities read *a psalm and praise* b Other ancient authorities add *he has confounded them* c Other ancient authorities read *feared* d Gk *they* e Or *breath* f Other ancient authorities read *they were created*

PROFILE OF FAITH

Eunice Kennedy Shriver was a devout Catholic who was committed to public service. At her funeral in August 2009, she was celebrated as "a fearless warrior for the voiceless who changed the world for millions" and "an unconventional woman who smoked Cuban cigars and played tackle football." She worked tirelessly as an advocate for better education for children and for care for teens who were pregnant. She is most known as an advocate for mentally disabled children.

Inspired by the plight of her elder sister Rosemary, who was slightly mentally retarded from birth and later completely incapacitated by an ill-advised brain operation, Shriver wrote a groundbreaking article for the *Saturday Evening Post* in 1962 in which she described Rosemary's condition and her family's attempts to deal with it. She then invited thirty-five mentally disabled boys and girls to a day camp at the Shriver home in Maryland to take part in sports and other physical activities. Inmates from a local prison served as counselors, and teenagers from Catholic high schools volunteered to help run the camp.

Realizing the children were far more capable of sports than experts said, Shriver organized the first Special Olympics in 1968 in Chicago. The two-day event drew more than a thousand participants from twenty-six states and Canada. At the World Games in 2007 in Shanghai, China, there were eighty thousand people in the opening ceremonies, with more than seven thousand mentally disabled athletes from around the world. One of the mothers of a Special Olympian described the impact Shriver had made on their lives: "She helped open doors," she said. "We gained freedom from hiding."

---

there is none that can resist your voice.
¹⁵ For the mountains shall be shaken to their
    foundations with the waters;
    before your glance the rocks shall melt
    like wax.
But to those who fear you
    you show mercy.
¹⁶ For every sacrifice as a fragrant offering is a
    small thing,
    and the fat of all whole burnt offerings to
    you is a very little thing;
but whoever fears the Lord is great forever.
¹⁷ Woe to the nations that rise up against my
    people!
    The Lord Almighty will take vengeance on
    them in the day of judgment;
he will send fire and worms into their flesh;
    they shall weep in pain forever.

18 When they arrived at Jerusalem, they worshiped God. As soon as the people were purified, they offered their burnt offerings, their freewill offerings, and their gifts. ¹⁹Judith also dedicated to God all the possessions of Holofernes, which the people had given her; and the canopy that she had taken for herself from his bedchamber she gave as a votive offering. ²⁰For three months the people continued feasting in Jerusalem before the sanctuary, and Judith remained with them.

The Renown and Death of Judith

21 After this they all returned home to their own inheritances. Judith went to Bethulia, and remained on her estate. For the rest of her life she was honored throughout the whole country. ²²Many desired to marry her, but she gave herself to no man all the days of her life after her husband Manasseh died and was gathered to his people. ²³She became more and more famous, and grew old in her husband's house, reaching the age of one hundred five. She set her maid free. She died in Bethulia, and they buried her in the cave of her husband Manasseh; ²⁴and the house of Israel mourned her for seven days. Before she died she distributed her property to all those who were next of kin to her husband Manasseh, and to her own nearest kindred. ²⁵No one ever again spread terror among the Israelites during the lifetime of Judith, or for a long time after her death.

ESTHER

ONE TOUGH LADY

The Queen Saves the Day

Esther is one of those made-for-TV movies. Some scholars even call it a comedy. There's a king looking for love and a hot young lady who catches his eye. The king digs her so much that he makes her queen. Then a plot is unveiled that will destroy the Jews, and the new queen (who happens to be secretly Jewish) has to decide whether to risk her life to save the lives of many others. She soon learns that God places us right where God wants us when he wants us there. So Esther risks it all and saves the day.

Yup—TV written all over it.

But there's more to the story. Esther isn't a superhero the way we think of superheroes. She was just a regular person who was willing to let God use her in an amazing way. We're a lot like Esther (well, maybe not the *hot queen* thing) in that God places us where he wants us to act in mighty ways. Could we be the generation to stop AIDS? Ethnic cleansing and wars? Homelessness and poverty? The story of Esther reminds us that nothing is impossible with God, especially when we let God work through us!

"Teach us to give and not count the cost."

—St. Ignatius of Loyola

WHO The author is unknown.

WHAT A story of how the Jewish people in Persia averted persecution through the intervention of Esther and Mordecai as well as an explanation of the beginnings of the Jewish Festival of Purim

WHEN The events described in Esther took place between 487 and 465 B.C.

WHERE The Persian Empire; Susa was in the region of modern-day Iran.

PATH OF DISCIPLESHIP

Do you ever play "what if" in your mind? *What if* I was born to different parents? *What if* I were tall and not short? Fat and not skinny? *What if* I never climbed that tree, threw that ball, met that guy? *What if* . . .

Play "what if" with the book of Esther for a minute. What if Mordecai had not adopted Esther? What if Esther had revealed she was Jewish before she became queen? What if Mordecai had stayed at home instead of going to the king's gate and never discovered the conspiracy against the king? What if he had knelt and given Haman some respect? What if the royal officials had not told Haman that Mordecai was Jewish? What if Esther had not invited Haman to dinner or the king fell asleep and never found out that Mordecai saved his life? *What if* . . .

You could play the "what if" game with all of salvation history. What if Mary said no to the angel Gabriel? What if Jesus got scared and decided not to go to Jerusalem? What if the Apostles decided to separate and go home alone and discouraged after Good Friday? *What if* . . .

Get the picture? God has plans for us. God has a plan for the world, for the coming of his Kingdom. Every time we say the Lord's Prayer, we pray, "Thy will be done." That was always Jesus' prayer. We do not have to play a "what if" game with God if we pray the same prayer every day, because no matter where we are or how we got there, God knows we're open to his plan even when we don't know what our role is in it.

ADDITION A

11[a] Mordecai's Dream

²In the second year of the reign of Ahasuerus the Great, on the first day of Nisan, Mordecai son of Jair son of Shimei[b] son of Kish, of the tribe of Benjamin, had a dream. ³He was a Jew living in the city of Susa, a great man, serving in the court of the king. ⁴He was one of the captives whom King Nebuchadnezzar of Babylon had brought from Jerusalem with King Jeconiah of Judah. And this was his dream: ⁵Noises[c] and confusion, thunders and earthquake, tumult on the earth! ⁶Then two great dragons came forward, both ready to fight, and they roared terribly. ⁷At their roaring every nation prepared for war, to fight against the righteous nation. ⁸It was a day of darkness and gloom, of tribulation and distress, affliction and great tumult on the earth! ⁹And the whole righteous nation was troubled; they feared the evils that threatened them,[d] and were ready to perish. ¹⁰Then they cried out to God; and at their outcry, as though from a tiny spring, there came a great river, with abundant water; ¹¹light came, and the sun rose, and the lowly were exalted and devoured those held in honor.

12 Mordecai saw in this dream what God had determined to do, and after he awoke he had it on his mind, seeking all day to understand it in every detail.

12 A Plot against the King

Now Mordecai took his rest in the courtyard with Bigthan and Teresh, the two eunuchs of the king who kept watch in the courtyard. ²He overheard their conversation and inquired into their purposes, and learned that they were preparing to lay hands on King Ahasuerus; and he informed the king concerning them. ³Then the king examined the two eunuchs, and after they had confessed it, they were led away to execution. ⁴The king made a permanent record of these things, and Mordecai wrote an account of them. ⁵And the king ordered Mordecai to serve in the court, and rewarded him for these things. ⁶But Haman son of Hammedatha, the Agagite, who was in great honor with the king, determined to injure Mordecai and his people because of the two eunuchs of the king.

END OF ADDITION A

1 King Ahasuerus Deposes Queen Vashti

This happened in the days of Ahasuerus, the same Ahasuerus who ruled over one hundred twenty-seven provinces from India to Ethiopia.[e] ²In those days when King Ahasuerus sat on his royal throne in the citadel of Susa, ³in the third year of his reign, he gave a banquet for all his officials and ministers. The army of Persia and Media and the nobles and governors of the provinces were present, ⁴while he displayed the great wealth of his kingdom and the splendor and pomp of his majesty for many days, one hundred eighty days in all.

5 When these days were completed, the king gave for all the people present in the citadel of Susa, both great and small, a banquet lasting for seven days, in the court of the garden of the king's palace. ⁶There were white cotton curtains and blue hangings tied with cords of fine linen and purple to silver rings[f] and marble pillars. There were couches of gold and silver on a mosaic pavement of porphyry, marble, mother-of-pearl, and colored stones. ⁷Drinks were served in golden goblets, goblets of different kinds, and the royal wine was lavished according to the bounty of the king. ⁸Drinking was by flagons, without restraint; for the king had given orders to all the officials of his palace to do as each one desired. ⁹Furthermore, Queen Vashti gave a banquet for the women in the palace of King Ahasuerus.

10 On the seventh day, when the king was merry with wine, he commanded Mehuman, Biztha, Harbona, Bigtha and Abagtha, Zethar and Carkas, the seven eunuchs who attended him, ¹¹to bring Queen Vashti before the king, wearing the royal crown, in order to show the

---

a Chapters 11.2—12.6 correspond to chapter A 1–17 in some translations. *b* Gk Semeios *c* Or Voices *d* Gk their own evils *e* Or Nubia; Heb Cush *f* Or rods peoples and the officials her beauty; for she was fair to behold. ¹²But Queen Vashti refused to come at the king's command conveyed by the eunuchs. At this the king was enraged, and his anger burned within him.

13 Then the king consulted the sages who knew the laws*ᵃ* (for this was the king's procedure toward all who were versed in law and custom, ¹⁴and those next to him were Carshena, Shethar, Admatha, Tarshish, Meres, Marsena, and Memucan, the seven officials of Persia and Media, who had access to the king, and sat first in the kingdom): ¹⁵"According to the law, what is to be done to Queen Vashti because she has not performed the command of King Ahasuerus conveyed by the eunuchs?" ¹⁶Then Memucan said in the presence of the king and the officials, "Not only has Queen Vashti done wrong to the king, but also to all the officials and all the peoples who are in all the provinces of King Ahasuerus. ¹⁷For this deed of the queen will be made known to all women, causing them to look with contempt on their husbands, since they will say, 'King Ahasuerus commanded Queen Vashti to be brought before him, and she did not come.' ¹⁸This very day the noble ladies of Persia and Media who have heard of the queen's behavior will rebel against*ᵇ* the king's officials, and there will be no end of contempt and wrath! ¹⁹If it pleases the king, let a royal order go out from him, and let it be written among the laws of the Persians and the Medes so that it may not be altered, that Vashti is never again to come before King Ahasuerus; and let the king give her royal position to another who is better than she. ²⁰So when the decree made by the king is proclaimed throughout all his kingdom, vast as it is, all women will give honor to their husbands, high and low alike."

21 This advice pleased the king and the officials, and the king did as Memucan proposed; ²²he sent letters to all the royal provinces, to every province in its own script and to every people in its own language, declaring that every man should be master in his own house.*ᶜ*

2 Esther Becomes Queen

After these things, when the anger of King Ahasuerus had abated, he remembered Vashti and what she had done and what had been decreed against her. ²Then the king's servants who attended him said, "Let beautiful young virgins be sought out for the king. ³And let the king appoint commissioners in all the provinces of his kingdom to gather all the beautiful young virgins to the harem in the citadel

of Susa under custody of Hegai, the king's eunuch, who is in charge of the women; let their cosmetic treatments be given them. ⁴And let the girl who pleases the king be queen instead of Vashti." This pleased the king, and he did so.

5 Now there was a Jew in the citadel of Susa whose name was Mordecai son of Jair son of Shimei son of Kish, a Benjaminite. ⁶Kish*ᵈ* had been carried away from Jerusalem among the captives carried away with King Jeconiah of Judah, whom King Nebuchadnezzar of Babylon had carried away. ⁷Mordecai*ᵉ* had brought up Hadassah, that is Esther, his cousin, for she had neither father nor mother; the girl was fair and beautiful, and when her father and her mother died, Mordecai adopted her as his own daughter. ⁸So when the king's order and his edict were proclaimed, and when many young women were gathered in the citadel of

a Cn: Heb *times*   *b* Cn: Heb *will tell*   *c* Heb adds *and speak according to the language of his people*   *d* Heb *a Benjaminite* ⁶*who*   *e* Heb *He*

Susa in custody of Hegai, Esther also was taken into the king's palace and put in custody of Hegai, who had charge of the women. ⁹The girl pleased him and won his favor, and he quickly provided her with her cosmetic treatments and her portion of food, and with seven chosen maids from the king's palace, and advanced her and her maids to the best place in the harem. ¹⁰Esther did not reveal her people or kindred, for Mordecai had charged her not to tell. ¹¹Every day Mordecai would walk around in front of the court of the harem, to learn how Esther was and how she fared.

12 The turn came for each girl to go in to King Ahasuerus, after being twelve months under the regulations for the women, since this was the regular period of their cosmetic treatment, six months with oil of myrrh and six months with perfumes and cosmetics for women. ¹³When the girl went in to the king she was given whatever she asked for to take with her from the harem to the king's palace. ¹⁴In the evening she went in; then in the morning she came back to the second harem in custody of Shaashgaz, the king's eunuch, who was in charge of the concubines; she did not go in to the king again, unless the king delighted in her and she was summoned by name.

15 When the turn came for Esther daughter of Abihail the uncle of Mordecai, who had adopted her as his own daughter, to go in to the king, she asked for nothing except what Hegai the king's eunuch, who had charge of the women, advised. Now Esther was admired by all who saw her. ¹⁶When Esther was taken to King Ahasuerus in his royal palace in the tenth month, which is the month of Tebeth, in the seventh year of his reign, ¹⁷the king loved Esther more than all the other women; of all the virgins she won his favor and devotion, so that he set the royal crown on her head and made her queen instead of Vashti. ¹⁸Then the king gave a great banquet to all his officials and ministers—"Esther's banquet." He also granted a holiday*ᵃ* to the provinces, and gave gifts with royal liberality.

Mordecai Discovers a Plot

19 When the virgins were being gathered together,*ᵇ* Mordecai was sitting at the king's gate. ²⁰Now Esther had not revealed her kindred or her people, as Mordecai had charged her; for Esther obeyed Mordecai just as when she was brought up by him. ²¹In those days, while Mordecai was sitting at the king's gate, Bigthan and Teresh, two of the king's eunuchs, who guarded the threshold, became angry and conspired

to assassinate*ᶜ* King Ahasuerus. ²²But the matter came to the knowledge of Mordecai, and he told it to Queen Esther, and Esther told the king in the name of Mordecai. ²³When the affair was investigated and found to be so, both the men were hanged on the gallows. It was recorded in the book of the annals in the presence of the king.

3 Haman Undertakes to Destroy the Jews

After these things King Ahasuerus promoted Haman son of Hammedatha the Agagite, and advanced him and set his seat above all the officials who were with him. ²And all the king's servants who were at the king's gate bowed down and did obeisance to Haman; for the king had so commanded concerning him. But Mordecai did not bow down or do obeisance. ³Then the king's servants who were at the king's gate said to Mordecai, "Why do you disobey the king's command?" ⁴When they spoke to him day after day and he would not listen to them, they told Haman, in order to see whether Mordecai's words would avail; for he had told them that he was a Jew. ⁵When Haman saw that Mordecai did not bow down or do obeisance to him, Haman was infuriated. ⁶But he thought it beneath him to lay hands on Mordecai alone. So, having been told who Mordecai's people were, Haman plotted to destroy all the Jews, the people of Mordecai, throughout the whole kingdom of Ahasuerus.

7 In the first month, which is the month of Nisan, in the twelfth year of King Ahasuerus, they cast Pur—which means "the lot"—before Haman for the day and for the month, and the lot fell on the thirteenth day*ᵈ* of the twelfth month, which is the month of Adar. ⁸Then Haman said to King Ahasuerus, "There is a certain people scattered and separated among the peoples in all the provinces of your kingdom; their laws are different from those of every other people, and they do not keep the king's laws, so that it is not appropriate for the king to tolerate them. ⁹If it pleases the king, let a decree be issued for their destruction, and I will pay ten thousand talents of silver into the hands of those who have charge of the king's business, so that they may put it into the king's treasuries." ¹⁰So the king took his signet ring from his hand and gave it to Haman son of Hammedatha the Agagite, the enemy of the Jews. ¹¹The king said to Haman, "The money is given to you, and the people as well, to do with them as it seems good to you."

12 Then the king's secretaries were summoned on the thirteenth day of the first

---

a Or *an amnesty*   *b* Heb adds *a second time*   *c* Heb *to lay hands on*   *d* Cn Compare Gk and verse 13 below: Heb *the twelfth month*

month, and an edict, according to all that Haman commanded, was written to the king's satraps and to the governors over all the provinces and to the officials of all the peoples, to every province in its own script and every people in its own language; it was written in the name of King Ahasuerus and sealed with the king's ring. ¹³Letters were sent by couriers to all the king's provinces, giving orders to destroy, to kill, and to annihilate all Jews, young and old, women and children, in one day, the thirteenth day of the twelfth month, which is the month of Adar, and to plunder their goods.

ADDITION B

13^a The King's Letter

This is a copy of the letter: "The Great King, Ahasuerus, writes the following to the governors of the hundred twenty-seven provinces from India to Ethiopia and to the officials under them:

2 "Having become ruler of many nations and master of the whole world (not elated with presumption of authority but always acting reasonably and with kindness), I have determined to settle the lives of my subjects in lasting tranquility and, in order to make my kingdom peaceable and open to travel throughout all its extent, to restore the peace desired by all people.

3 "When I asked my counselors how this might be accomplished, Haman—who excels among us in sound judgment, and is distinguished for his unchanging goodwill and steadfast fidelity, and has attained the second place in the kingdom— ⁴pointed out to us that among all the nations in the world there is scattered a certain hostile people, who have laws contrary to those of every nation and continually disregard the ordinances of kings, so that the unifying of the kingdom that we honorably intend cannot be brought about. ⁵We understand that this people, and it alone, stands constantly in opposition to every nation, perversely following a strange manner of life and laws, and is ill-disposed to our government, doing all the harm they can so that our kingdom may not attain stability.

6 "Therefore we have decreed that those indicated to you in the letters written by Haman, who is in charge of affairs and is our second father, shall all—wives and children included—be utterly destroyed by the swords of their enemies, without pity or restraint, on the fourteenth day of the twelfth month, Adar, of this present year, ⁷so that those who have long

been hostile and remain so may in a single day go down in violence to Hades, and leave our government completely secure and untroubled hereafter."

END OF ADDITION B

3 ¹⁴A copy of the document was to be issued as a decree in every province by proclamation, calling on all the peoples to be ready for that day. ¹⁵The couriers went quickly by order of the king, and the decree was issued in the citadel of Susa. The king and Haman sat down to drink; but the city of Susa was thrown into confusion.

4 Esther Agrees to Help the Jews

When Mordecai learned all that had been done, Mordecai tore his clothes and put on sackcloth and ashes, and went through the city, wailing with a loud and bitter cry; ²he went up to the entrance of the king's gate, for no one might enter the king's gate clothed with sackcloth. ³In every province, wherever the king's command and his decree came, there was great mourning among the Jews, with fasting and weeping and lamenting, and most of them lay in sackcloth and ashes.

4 When Esther's maids and her eunuchs came and told her, the queen was deeply distressed; she sent garments to clothe Mordecai, so that he might take off his sackcloth; but he would not accept them. ⁵Then Esther called for Hathach, one of the king's eunuchs, who had been appointed to attend her, and ordered him to go to Mordecai to learn what was happening and why. ⁶Hathach went out to Mordecai in the open square of the city in front of the king's gate, ⁷and Mordecai told him all that had happened to him, and the exact sum of money that Haman had promised to pay into the king's treasuries for the destruction of the Jews. ⁸Mordecai also gave him a copy of the written decree issued in Susa for their destruction, that he might show it to Esther, explain it to her, and charge her to go to the king to make supplication to him and entreat him for her people.

9 Hathach went and told Esther what Mordecai had said. ¹⁰Then Esther spoke to Hathach and gave him a message for Mordecai, saying, ¹¹"All the king's servants and the people of the king's provinces know that if any man or woman goes to the king inside the inner court without being called, there is but one law—all alike are to be put to death. Only if the king holds out the golden scepter to someone, may that person live. I myself have not been called to come in to the king for thirty days."

---

^a Chapter 13.1–7 corresponds to chapter B 1–7 in some translations.

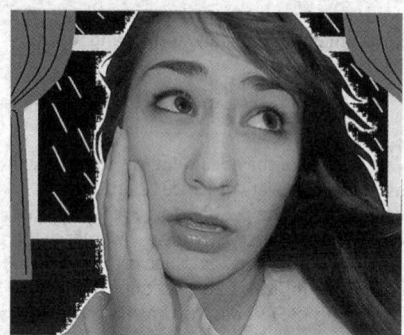

Oh No!—© Rachel Akerley, 16

TRY THIS ◄

STOPPING THE HOLOCAUST

Here's an incident that sounds eerily familiar . . . and chilling.

A government green-lights the systematic extermination of Jews.

The date of the slaughter draws near . . . and a Jewish queen, who's passed as a Persian, faces a no-win decision.

Queen Esther can say nothing and watch her people be destroyed. Or she can reveal her heritage—hoping to stop the killing—and invite execution.

Tough call. Read **Esther 4.14**. It's the question that cemented Esther's resolve.

The question wasn't directed at you, but suppose it was? Would you risk it all for your family—your people?

Mordecai took a risk too when he challenged Esther to take a stand. And that's a risk you can take too. Think of a situation with your friends and family where you can challenge them to take a stand. Maybe a family member who talks about a work environment where racial or gender discrimination is rampant—or maybe there's a friend in your "group" who has a drug problem and the rest of you have been ignoring it.

Who knows? Maybe you were placed in your family or group of friends to challenge them or yourself to take a risk. Are you ready to take that stand?

GOD IS REAL MY FAMILY

12When they told Mordecai what Esther had said, 13Mordecai told them to reply to Esther, "Do not think that in the king's palace you will escape any more than all the other Jews. 14For if you keep silence at such a time as this, relief and deliverance will rise for the Jews from another quarter, but you and your father's family will perish. Who knows? Perhaps you have come to royal dignity for just such a time as this." 15Then Esther said in reply to Mordecai, 16"Go, gather all the Jews to be found in Susa, and hold a fast on my behalf, and neither eat nor drink for three days, night or day. I and my maids will also fast as you do. After that I will go to the king, though it is against the law; and if I perish, I perish." 17Mordecai then went away and did everything as Esther had ordered him.

ADDITION C

13 Mordecai's Prayer

8*a* Then Mordecai*b* prayed to the Lord, calling to remembrance all the works of the Lord.

9 He said, "O Lord, Lord, you rule as King over all things, for the universe is in your power and there is no one who can oppose you when it is your will to save Israel, 10for you have made heaven and earth and every wonderful thing under heaven. 11You are Lord of all, and there is no one who can resist you, the Lord. 12You know all things; you know, O Lord, that it was not in insolence or pride or for any love of glory that I did this, and refused to bow down to this proud Haman; 13for I would have been willing to kiss the soles of his feet to save Israel! 14But I did this so that I might not set human glory above the glory of God, and I will not bow down to anyone but you, who are my Lord; and I will not do these things in pride. 15And now, O Lord God and King, God of Abraham, spare your people; for the eyes of our foes are upon us*c* to annihilate us, and they desire to destroy the inheritance that has been yours from the beginning. 16Do not neglect your portion, which you redeemed for yourself out of the land of Egypt. 17Hear my prayer, and have mercy upon your inheritance; turn our mourning into feasting that we may live and sing praise to your name, O Lord; do not destroy the lips*d* of those who praise you."

18 And all Israel cried out mightily, for their death was before their eyes.

14 Esther's Prayer

Then Queen Esther, seized with deadly anxiety, fled to the Lord. 2She took off her splendid ap-

---

a Chapters 13.8—15.16 correspond to chapters C 1–30 and D 1–16 in some translations. *b* Gk he *c* Gk for they are eying us *d* Gk mouth parel and put on the garments of distress and mourning, and instead of costly perfumes she covered her head with ashes and dung, and she utterly humbled her body; every part that she loved to adorn she covered with her tangled hair. ³She prayed to the Lord God of Israel, and said: "O my Lord, you only are our king; help me, who am alone and have no helper but you, ⁴for my danger is in my hand. ⁵Ever since I was born I have heard in the tribe of my family that you, O Lord, took Israel out of all the nations, and our ancestors from among all their forebears, for an everlasting inheritance, and that you did for them all that you promised. ⁶And now we have sinned before you, and you have handed us over to our enemies ⁷because we glorified their gods. You are righteous, O Lord! ⁸And now they are not satisfied that we are in bitter slavery, but they have covenanted with their idols ⁹to abolish what your mouth has ordained, and to destroy your inheritance, to stop the mouths of those who praise you and to quench your altar and the glory of your house, ¹⁰to open the mouths of the nations for the praise of vain idols, and to magnify forever a mortal king.

11 "O Lord, do not surrender your scepter to what has no being; and do not let them laugh at our downfall; but turn their plan against them, and make an example of him who began this against us. ¹²Remember, O Lord; make yourself known in this time of our affliction, and give me courage, O King of the gods and Master of all dominion! ¹³Put eloquent speech in my mouth before the lion, and turn his heart to hate the man who is fighting against us, so that there may be an end of him and those who agree with him. ¹⁴But save us by your hand, and help me, who am alone and have no helper but you, O Lord. ¹⁵You have knowledge of all things, and you know that I hate the splendor of the wicked and abhor the bed of the uncircumcised and of any alien. ¹⁶You know my necessity—that I abhor the sign of my proud position, which is upon my head on days when I appear in public. I abhor it like a filthy rag, and I do not wear it on the days when I am at leisure. ¹⁷And your servant has not eaten at Haman's table, and I have not honored the king's feast or drunk the wine of libations. ¹⁸Your servant has had no joy since the day that I was brought here until now, except in you, O Lord God of Abraham. ¹⁹O God, whose might is over all, hear the voice of the despairing, and save us from the hands of evildoers. And save me from my fear!"

END OF ADDITION C

15 Esther Is Received by the King

On the third day, when she ended her prayer, she took off the garments in which she had worshiped, and arrayed herself in splendid attire. ²Then, majestically adorned, after invoking the aid of the all-seeing God and Savior, she took two maids with her; ³on one she leaned gently for support, ⁴while the other followed, carrying her train. ⁵She was radiant with perfect beauty, and she looked happy, as if beloved, but her heart was frozen with fear. ⁶When she had gone through all the doors, she stood before the king. He was seated on his royal throne, clothed in the full array of his majesty, all covered with gold and precious stones. He was most terrifying.

7 Lifting his face, flushed with splendor, he looked at her in fierce anger. The queen faltered, and turned pale and faint, and collapsed on the head of the maid who went in front of her. ⁸Then God changed the spirit of the king to gentleness, and in alarm he sprang from his throne and took her in his arms until she came to herself. He comforted her with soothing words, and said to her, ⁹"What is it, Esther? I am your husband.ᵃ Take courage; ¹⁰You shall not die, for our law applies only to our subjects.ᵇ Come near."

11 Then he raised the golden scepter and touched her neck with it; ¹²he embraced her, and said, "Speak to me." ¹³She said to him, "I saw you, my lord, like an angel of God, and my heart was shaken with fear at your glory. ¹⁴For you are wonderful, my lord, and your countenance is full of grace." ¹⁵And while she was speaking, she fainted and fell. ¹⁶Then the king was agitated, and all his servants tried to comfort her.

END OF ADDITION D

5ᶜ Esther's Banquet

³The king said to her, "What is it, Queen Esther? What is your request? It shall be given you, even to the half of my kingdom." ⁴Then Esther said, "If it pleases the king, let the king and Haman come today to a banquet that I have prepared for the king." ⁵Then the king said, "Bring Haman quickly, so that we may do as Esther desires." So the king and Haman came to the banquet that Esther had prepared. ⁶While they were drinking wine, the king said to Esther, "What is your petition? It shall be granted you. And what is your request? Even to

ᵃ Gk brother ᵇ Meaning of Gk uncertain ᶜ In Greek, Chapter D replaces verses 1 and 2 in Hebrew.

the half of my kingdom, it shall be fulfilled." [7]Then Esther said, "This is my petition and request: [8]If I have won the king's favor, and if it pleases the king to grant my petition and fulfill my request, let the king and Haman come tomorrow to the banquet that I will prepare for them, and then I will do as the king has said."

Haman Plans to Have Mordecai Hanged

9 Haman went out that day happy and in good spirits. But when Haman saw Mordecai in the king's gate, and observed that he neither rose nor trembled before him, he was infuriated with Mordecai; [10]nevertheless Haman restrained himself and went home. Then he sent and called for his friends and his wife Zeresh, [11]and Haman recounted to them the splendor of his riches, the number of his sons, all the promotions with which the king had honored him, and how he had advanced him above the officials and the ministers of the king. [12]Haman added, "Even Queen Esther let no one but myself come with the king to the banquet that she prepared. Tomorrow also I am invited by her, together with the king. [13]Yet all this does me no good so long as I see the Jew Mordecai sitting at the king's gate." [14]Then his wife Zeresh and all his friends said to him, "Let a gallows fifty cubits high be made, and in the morning tell the king to have Mordecai hanged on it; then go with the king to the banquet in good spirits." This advice pleased Haman, and he had the gallows made.

6 The King Honors Mordecai

On that night the king could not sleep, and he gave orders to bring the book of records, the annals, and they were read to the king. [2]It was found written how Mordecai had told about Bigthana and Teresh, two of the king's eunuchs, who guarded the threshold, and who had conspired to assassinate[a] King Ahasuerus. [3]Then the king said, "What honor or distinction has been bestowed on Mordecai for this?" The king's servants who attended him said, "Nothing has been done for him." [4]The king said, "Who is in the court?" Now Haman had just entered the outer court of the king's palace to speak to the king about having Mordecai hanged on the gallows that he had prepared for him. [5]So the king's servants told him, "Haman is there, standing in the court." The king said, "Let him come in." [6]So Haman came in, and the king said to him, "What shall be done for the man whom the king wishes to honor?" Haman said to himself, "Whom would the king wish to honor more than me?" [7]So Haman

said to the king, "For the man whom the king wishes to honor, [8]let royal robes be brought, which the king has worn, and a horse that the king has ridden, with a royal crown on its head. [9]Let the robes and the horse be handed over to one of the king's most noble officials; let him[b] robe the man whom the king wishes to honor, and let him[b] conduct the man on horseback through the open square of the city, proclaiming before him: 'Thus shall it be done for the man whom the king wishes to honor.' " [10]Then the king said to Haman, "Quickly, take the robes and the horse, as you have said, and do so to the Jew Mordecai who sits at the king's gate. Leave out nothing that you have mentioned." [11]So Haman took the robes and the horse and robed Mordecai and led him riding through the open square of the city, proclaiming, "Thus shall it be done for the man whom the king wishes to honor."

12 Then Mordecai returned to the king's gate, but Haman hurried to his house, mourning and with his head covered. [13]When Haman told his wife Zeresh and all his friends everything that had happened to him, his advisers and his wife Zeresh said to him, "If Mordecai, before whom your downfall has begun, is of the Jewish people, you will not prevail against him, but will surely fall before him."

Haman's Downfall and Mordecai's Advancement

14 While they were still talking with him, the king's eunuchs arrived and hurried Haman off 7 to the banquet that Esther had prepared. [1]So the king and Haman went in to feast with Queen Esther. [2]On the second day, as they were drinking wine, the king again said to Esther, "What is your petition, Queen Esther? It shall be granted you. And what is your request? Even to the half of my kingdom, it shall be fulfilled." [3]Then Queen Esther answered, "If I have won your favor, O king, and if it pleases the king, let my life be given me—that is my petition—and the lives of my people—that is my request. [4]For we have been sold, I and my people, to be destroyed, to be killed, and to be annihilated. If we had been sold merely as slaves, men and women, I would have held my peace; but no enemy can compensate for this damage to the king."[c] [5]Then King Ahasuerus said to Queen Esther, "Who is he, and where is he, who has presumed to do this?" [6]Esther said, "A foe and enemy, this wicked Haman!" Then Haman was terrified before the king and the queen. [7]The king rose from the feast in wrath and went into the palace garden, but

a Heb to lay hands on b Heb them c Meaning of Heb uncertain

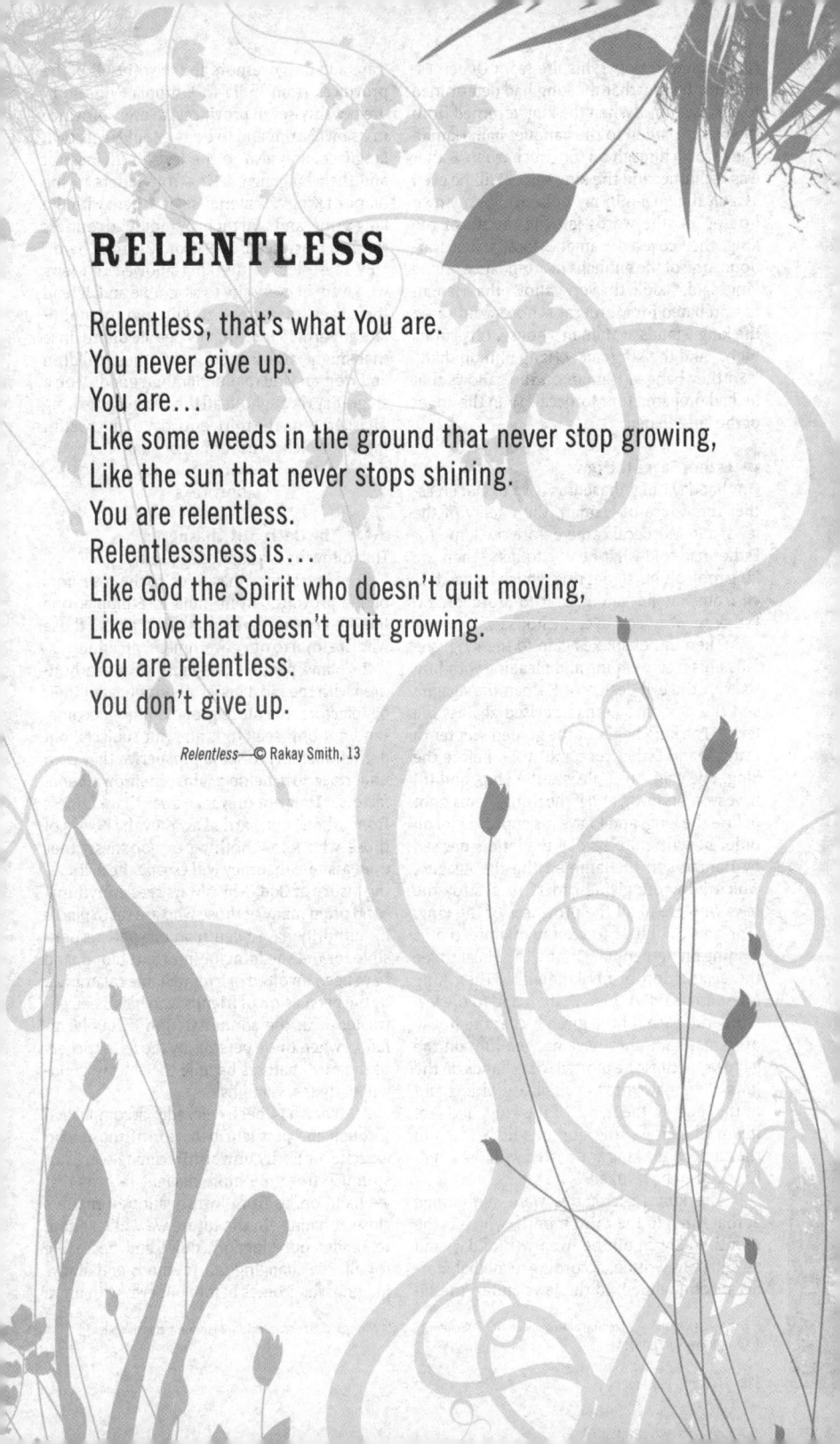

RELENTLESS

Relentless, that's what You are.
You never give up.
You are…
Like some weeds in the ground that never stop growing,
Like the sun that never stops shining.
You are relentless.
Relentlessness is…
Like God the Spirit who doesn't quit moving,
Like love that doesn't quit growing.
You are relentless.
You don't give up.

Relentless—© Rakay Smith, 13

Haman stayed to beg his life from Queen Esther, for he saw that the king had determined to destroy him. [8]When the king returned from the palace garden to the banquet hall, Haman had thrown himself on the couch where Esther was reclining; and the king said, "Will he even assault the queen in my presence, in my own house?" As the words left the mouth of the king, they covered Haman's face. [9]Then Harbona, one of the eunuchs in attendance on the king, said, "Look, the very gallows that Haman has prepared for Mordecai, whose word saved the king, stands at Haman's house, fifty cubits high." And the king said, "Hang him on that." [10]So they hanged Haman on the gallows that he had prepared for Mordecai. Then the anger of the king abated.

8 Esther Saves the Jews

On that day King Ahasuerus gave to Queen Esther the house of Haman, the enemy of the Jews; and Mordecai came before the king, for Esther had told what he was to her. [2]Then the king took off his signet ring, which he had taken from Haman, and gave it to Mordecai. So Esther set Mordecai over the house of Haman.

3 Then Esther spoke again to the king; she fell at his feet, weeping and pleading with him to avert the evil design of Haman the Agagite and the plot that he had devised against the Jews. [4]The king held out the golden scepter to Esther, [5]and Esther rose and stood before the king. She said, "If it pleases the king, and if I have won his favor, and if the thing seems right before the king, and I have his approval, let an order be written to revoke the letters devised by Haman son of Hammedatha the Agagite, which he wrote giving orders to destroy the Jews who are in all the provinces of the king. [6]For how can I bear to see the calamity that is coming on my people? Or how can I bear to see the destruction of my kindred?" [7]Then King Ahasuerus said to Queen Esther and to the Jew Mordecai, "See, I have given Esther the house of Haman, and they have hanged him on the gallows, because he plotted to lay hands on the Jews. [8]You may write as you please with regard to the Jews, in the name of the king, and seal it with the king's ring; for an edict written in the name of the king and sealed with the king's ring cannot be revoked."

9 The king's secretaries were summoned at that time, in the third month, which is the month of Sivan, on the twenty-third day; and an edict was written, according to all that Mordecai commanded, to the Jews and to the sa-traps and the governors and the officials of the provinces from India to Ethiopia,[a] one hundred twenty-seven provinces, to every province in its own script and to every people in its own language, and also to the Jews in their script and their language. [10]He wrote letters in the name of King Ahasuerus, sealed them with the king's ring, and sent them by mounted couriers riding on fast steeds bred from the royal herd.[b] [11]By these letters the king allowed the Jews who were in every city to assemble and defend their lives, to destroy, to kill, and to annihilate any armed force of any people or province that might attack them, with their children and women, and to plunder their goods [12]on a single day throughout all the provinces of King Ahasuerus, on the thirteenth day of the twelfth month, which is the month of Adar.

ADDITION E

16c The Decree of Ahasuerus

The following is a copy of this letter:

"The Great King, Ahasuerus, to the governors of the provinces from India to Ethiopia, one hundred twenty-seven provinces, and to those who are loyal to our government, greetings.

2 "Many people, the more they are honored with the most generous kindness of their benefactors, the more proud do they become, [3]and not only seek to injure our subjects, but in their inability to stand prosperity, they even undertake to scheme against their own benefactors. [4]They not only take away thankfulness from others, but, carried away by the boasts of those who know nothing of goodness, they even assume that they will escape the evil-hating justice of God, who always sees everything. [5]And often many of those who are set in places of authority have been made in part responsible for the shedding of innocent blood, and have been involved in irremediable calamities, by the persuasion of friends who have been entrusted with the administration of public affairs, [6]when these persons by the false trickery of their evil natures beguile the sincere goodwill of their sovereigns.

7 "What has been wickedly accomplished through the pestilent behavior of those who exercise authority unworthily can be seen, not so much from the more ancient records that we hand on, as from investigation of matters close at hand.[d] [8]In the future we will take care to render our kingdom quiet and peaceable for all, [9]by changing our methods and always judging what comes before our eyes with more

---

a Or Nubia; Heb Cush b Meaning of Heb uncertain c Chapter 16.1–24 corresponds to chapter E 1–24 in some translations.
d Gk matters beside (your) feet

equitable consideration. [10]For Haman son of Hammedatha, a Macedonian (really an alien to the Persian blood, and quite devoid of our kindliness), having become our guest, [11]enjoyed so fully the goodwill that we have for every nation that he was called our father and was continually bowed down to by all as the person second to the royal throne. [12]But, unable to restrain his arrogance, he undertook to deprive us of our kingdom and our life,[a] [13]and with intricate craft and deceit asked for the destruction of Mordecai, our savior and perpetual benefactor, and of Esther, the blameless partner of our kingdom, together with their whole nation. [14]He thought that by these methods he would catch us undefended and would transfer the kingdom of the Persians to the Macedonians.

[15] "But we find that the Jews, who were consigned to annihilation by this thrice-accursed man, are not evildoers, but are governed by most righteous laws [16]and are children of the living God, most high, most mighty,[b] who has directed the kingdom both for us and for our ancestors in the most excellent order.

[17] "You will therefore do well not to put in execution the letters sent by Haman son of Hammedatha, [18]since he, the one who did these things, has been hanged at the gate of Susa with all his household—for God, who rules over all things, has speedily inflicted on him the punishment that he deserved.

[19] "Therefore post a copy of this letter publicly in every place, and permit the Jews to live under their own laws. [20]And give them reinforcements, so that on the thirteenth day of the twelfth month, Adar, on that very day, they may defend themselves against those who attack them at the time of oppression. [21]For God, who rules over all things, has made this day to be a joy for his chosen people instead of a day of destruction for them.

[22] "Therefore you shall observe this with all good cheer as a notable day among your commemorative festivals, [23]so that both now and hereafter it may represent deliverance for you[c] and the loyal Persians, but that it may be a reminder of destruction for those who plot against us.

[24] "Every city and country, without exception, that does not act accordingly shall be destroyed in wrath with spear and fire. It shall be made not only impassable for human beings, but also most hateful to wild animals and birds for all time."

END OF ADDITION E

---

a Gk *our spirit* *b* Gk *greatest* *c* Other ancient authorities read *for us*

IT'S TRADITION

LOVE ONE ANOTHER

Don't you think it's sad that people persecute and kill their brothers and sisters because of religion? Dig a little deeper, and it's obvious that most religious wars and persecutions are not about religion, but about political power or money. It's easy to feel superior to those in the book of Esther who intended to persecute and kill the Jews. As Christians taught to "love one another," we'd never participate in religious persecution, right?

Wrong. Jews were persecuted by Christians in Europe throughout the Middle Ages and afterward, especially during the Inquisition. We also participated in the Holocaust, and at times there has been an anti-Semitic (anti-Jewish) bias in our prayers. But since the Second Vatican Council, the Church has urged us to rethink this and to truly embrace Jesus' commandment to "love your neighbor as yourself" (Matthew 22.39). In October 1965, Pope Paul VI issued the Declaration on the Relation of the Church to Non-Christian Religions, which states:

> Likewise, other religions found everywhere try to counter the restlessness of the human heart, each in its own manner, by proposing "ways," comprising teachings, rules of life, and sacred rites. The Catholic Church rejects nothing that is true and holy in these religions. She regards with sincere reverence those ways of conduct and of life, those precepts and teachings which, though differing in many aspects from the ones she holds and sets forth, nonetheless often reflect a ray of that Truth which enlightens all men. Indeed, she proclaims, and ever must proclaim Christ "the way, the truth, and the life" (John 14.6), in whom men may find the fullness of religious life, in whom God has reconciled all things to Himself.

It's really a no-brainer. Love. Everyone. Period.

8 ¹³A copy of the writ was to be issued as a decree in every province and published to all peoples, and the Jews were to be ready on that day to take revenge on their enemies. ¹⁴So the couriers, mounted on their swift royal steeds, hurried out, urged by the king's command. The decree was issued in the citadel of Susa.

15 Then Mordecai went out from the presence of the king, wearing royal robes of blue and white, with a great golden crown and a mantle of fine linen and purple, while the city of Susa shouted and rejoiced. ¹⁶For the Jews there was light and gladness, joy and honor. ¹⁷In every province and in every city, wherever the king's command and his edict came, there was gladness and joy among the Jews, a festival and a holiday. Furthermore, many of the peoples of the country professed to be Jews, because the fear of the Jews had fallen upon them.

9 Destruction of the Enemies of the Jews

Now in the twelfth month, which is the month of Adar, on the thirteenth day, when the king's command and edict were about to be executed, on the very day when the enemies of the Jews hoped to gain power over them, but which had been changed to a day when the Jews would gain power over their foes, ²the Jews gathered in their cities throughout all the provinces of King Ahasuerus to lay hands on those who had sought their ruin; and no one could withstand them, because the fear of them had fallen upon all peoples. ³All the officials of the provinces, the satraps and the governors, and the royal officials were supporting the Jews, because the fear of Mordecai had fallen upon them. ⁴For Mordecai was powerful in the king's house, and his fame spread throughout all the provinces as the man Mordecai grew more and more powerful. ⁵So the Jews struck down all their enemies with the sword, slaughtering, and destroying them, and did as they pleased to those who hated them. ⁶In the citadel of Susa the Jews killed and destroyed five hundred people. ⁷They killed Parshandatha, Dalphon, Aspatha, ⁸Poratha, Adalia, Aridatha, ⁹Parmashta, Arisai, Aridai, Vaizatha, ¹⁰the ten sons of Haman son of Hammedatha, the enemy of the Jews; but they did not touch the plunder.

11 That very day the number of those killed in the citadel of Susa was reported to the king. ¹²The king said to Queen Esther, "In the citadel of Susa the Jews have killed five hundred people and also the ten sons of Haman. What have they done in the rest of the king's provinces? Now what is your petition? It shall be granted you. And what further is your request? It shall

be fulfilled." ¹³Esther said, "If it pleases the king, let the Jews who are in Susa be allowed tomorrow also to do according to this day's edict, and let the ten sons of Haman be hanged on the gallows." ¹⁴So the king commanded this to be done; a decree was issued in Susa, and the ten sons of Haman were hanged. ¹⁵The Jews who were in Susa gathered also on the fourteenth day of the month of Adar and they killed three hundred persons in Susa; but they did not touch the plunder.

16 Now the other Jews who were in the king's provinces also gathered to defend their lives, and gained relief from their enemies, and killed seventy-five thousand of those who hated them; but they laid no hands on the plunder. ¹⁷This was on the thirteenth day of the month of Adar, and on the fourteenth day they rested and made that a day of feasting and gladness.

The Feast of Purim Inaugurated

18 But the Jews who were in Susa gathered on the thirteenth day and on the fourteenth, and rested on the fifteenth day, making that a day of feasting and gladness. ¹⁹Therefore the Jews of the villages, who live in the open towns, hold the fourteenth day of the month of Adar as a day for gladness and feasting, a holiday on which they send gifts of food to one another.

20 Mordecai recorded these things, and sent letters to all the Jews who were in all the provinces of King Ahasuerus, both near and far, ²¹enjoining them that they should keep the fourteenth day of the month Adar and also the fifteenth day of the same month, year by year, ²²as the days on which the Jews gained relief from their enemies, and as the month that had been turned for them from sorrow into gladness and from mourning into a holiday; that they should make them days of feasting and gladness, days for sending gifts of food to one another and presents to the poor. ²³So the Jews adopted as a custom what they had begun to do, as Mordecai had written to them.

24 Haman son of Hammedatha the Agagite, the enemy of all the Jews, had plotted against the Jews to destroy them, and had cast Pur—that is "the lot"—to crush and destroy them; ²⁵but when Esther came before the king, he gave orders in writing that the wicked plot that he had devised against the Jews should come upon his own head, and that he and his sons should be hanged on the gallows. ²⁶Therefore these days are called Purim, from the word Pur. Thus because of all that was written in this letter, and of what they had faced in this matter, and of what had happened to them, ²⁷the Jews established and accepted as a custom for

The Real Worship—© Ezequiel Cuevas, 19

themselves and their descendants and all who joined them, that without fail they would continue to observe these two days every year, as it was written and at the time appointed. [28]These days should be remembered and kept throughout every generation, in every family, province, and city; and these days of Purim should never fall into disuse among the Jews, nor should the commemoration of these days cease among their descendants.

29 Queen Esther daughter of Abihail, along with the Jew Mordecai, gave full written authority, confirming this second letter about Purim. [30]Letters were sent wishing peace and security to all the Jews, to the one hundred twenty-seven provinces of the kingdom of Ahasuerus, [31]and giving orders that these days of Purim should be observed at their appointed seasons, as the Jew Mordecai and Queen Esther enjoined on the Jews, just as they had laid down for themselves and for their descendants regulations concerning their fasts and their lamentations. [32]The command of Queen Esther fixed these practices of Purim, and it was recorded in writing.

10 King Ahasuerus laid tribute on the land and on the islands of the sea. [2]All the acts of his power and might, and the full account of the high honor of Mordecai, to which the king advanced him, are they not written in the annals of the kings of Media and Persia? [3]For Mordecai the Jew was next in rank to King Ahasuerus, and he was powerful among the Jews and popular with his many kindred, for he sought the good of his people and interceded for the welfare of all his descendants.

ADDITION F

Mordecai's Dream Fulfilled

4[a] And Mordecai said, "These things have come from God; [5]for I remember the dream that I had concerning these matters, and none of them has failed to be fulfilled. [6]There was the little spring that became a river, and there was light and sun and abundant water—the river is Esther, whom the king married and made queen. [7]The two dragons are Haman and myself. [8]The nations are those that gathered to destroy the name of the Jews. [9]And my nation, this is Israel, who cried out to God and was saved. The Lord has saved his people; the Lord has rescued us from all these evils; God has done great signs and wonders, wonders that have never

a Chapter 10.4–13 and 11.1 correspond to chapter F 1–11 in some translations.

happened among the nations. [10]For this purpose he made two lots, one for the people of God and one for all the nations, [11]and these two lots came to the hour and moment and day of decision before God and among all the nations. [12]And God remembered his people and vindicated his inheritance. [13]So they will observe these days in the month of Adar, on the fourteenth and fifteenth[a] of that month, with an assembly and joy and gladness before God, from generation to generation forever among his people Israel."

11 Postscript

[1]In the fourth year of the reign of Ptolemy and Cleopatra, Dositheus, who said that he was a priest and a Levite,[b] and his son Ptolemy brought to Egypt[c] the preceding Letter about Purim, which they said was authentic and had been translated by Lysimachus son of Ptolemy, one of the residents of Jerusalem.

END OF ADDITION F

---

a Other ancient authorities lack *and fifteenth* *b* Or *priest, and Levitas* *c* Cn: Gk *brought in*

"ACTION IS THE ANTIDOTE TO DESPAIR."
—Joan Baez

Self Portrait—© Catherine Willms, 15.

1 MACCABEES

FREEDOM FIGHTERS

Give Peace a Chance

Have you noticed the headlines lately? It doesn't seem like a day goes by when we don't see words like "terrorist," "freedom fighter," or "insurgent" in our daily news. Is this a feature only of modern times? Not at all. In light of what's happening in our world today, sometimes it's helpful to view current events against the backdrop of a biblical story and history.

This book describes the Maccabees, the family of Mattathias and five of his sons and a grandson, who became freedom fighters and worked to free their nation from foreign domination. This "independence" was to last approximately a hundred years, until the power of Rome took strict and lasting control.

For other Jewish people, these victories presented a large problem: the bloodline of the Maccabees could not be traced to David or Aaron, and so their leadership was questioned, challenged, and denied by some. In the face of such criticism, the book speaks eloquently of their success, praising Mattathias' son Simon's leadership: "He established peace in the land, and Israel rejoiced with great joy" (1 Maccabees 14.11).

What you'll also find in this book is that there were also tensions within the Jewish community: tensions between the upper classes (who were willing to make compromises with the Greek way of life) and the faithful people of the land (who sought to preserve former traditions, with their emphasis on trust in and fidelity to God).

So, as you read, think about the tension you see in this story, and see if you can find parallels in life today—in your family, group of friends, or even in our world. Do you see tensions between groups who "go with the flow" of popular society and those who try to "keep the faith"?

"If you have men who will exclude any of God's creatures from the shelter of compassion and pity, you will have men who will deal likewise with their fellow men."

—St. Francis of Assisi

WHO Unknown, but probably a nationalist Jew who supported the Hasmoneans, also known as the Maccabees, a priestly family with high standing

WHAT A historical narrative describing the struggle of the Jewish people, led by the Maccabees, for religious and political liberty

WHEN Written between 105 and 63 B.C. The events described took place from 143 B.C. to the end of the second century B.C.

WHERE Palestine, probably Jerusalem

PATH OF DISCIPLESHIP

You hear all kinds of stories of people (like the Maccabees) who dedicate themselves and their whole lives to a cause. And because of their commitment, people's lives are changed and made better. Whether we talk about it in religious terms or not, those people are making God's Kingdom see-able. That's our job too—to commit ourselves to making God's Kingdom visible here on earth.

But how do you decide what you're going to spend time and energy on? Think back on all the service projects you have been involved in. Were there interesting neighborhood or school projects that you enjoyed? Of all those projects, which ones did you willingly spend the most time and energy on? Which of them do you think needed your specific gifts and talents? Think about it: one of those areas could be the one where you will make a difference.

APOCRYPHA

The term "apocrypha" was coined by the fifth-century biblical scholar St. Jerome and refers to the biblical books included as part of the Septuagint (the Greek version of the Old Testament), but not included in the Hebrew Bible.

Several works ranging from the fourth century B.C. to New Testament times are considered apocryphal, including Judith, the Wisdom of Solomon, Tobit, Sirach (or Ecclesiasticus), Baruch, 1 and 2 Maccabees, the two books of Esdras, various additions to the book of Esther (10.4–10), the book of Daniel (3.24–90; 13; 14) and the Prayer of Manasseh.

The apocrypha have been included and omitted from Bibles over the centuries. Protestant churches generally exclude the apocrypha (though the King James Version of 1611 included them). The Roman Catholic and Orthodox churches include all of the apocrypha (except for the books of Esdras and the Prayer of Manasseh), but refer to them as deuterocanonical books, a secondary canon, consisting of books added to the canon later than other Old Testament writings. Generally, the term "apocrypha" refers to writings entirely outside the biblical canon that are not considered inspired (such as the gospel of Thomas).

1 Alexander the Great

After Alexander son of Philip, the Macedonian, who came from the land of Kittim, had defeated[a] King Darius of the Persians and the Medes, he succeeded him as king. (He had previously become king of Greece.) [2]He fought many battles, conquered strongholds, and put to death the kings of the earth. [3]He advanced to the ends of the earth, and plundered many nations. When the earth became quiet before him, he was exalted, and his heart was lifted up. [4]He gathered a very strong army and ruled over countries, nations, and princes, and they became tributary to him.

[5] After this he fell sick and perceived that he was dying. [6]So he summoned his most honored officers, who had been brought up with him from youth, and divided his kingdom among them while he was still alive. [7]And after Alexander had reigned twelve years, he died.

[8] Then his officers began to rule, each in his own place. [9]They all put on crowns after his death, and so did their descendants after them for many years; and they caused many evils on the earth.

Antiochus Epiphanes and Renegade Jews

[10] From them came forth a sinful root, Antiochus Epiphanes, son of King Antiochus; he had been a hostage in Rome. He began to reign in the one hundred thirty-seventh year of the kingdom of the Greeks.[b]

[11] In those days certain renegades came out from Israel and misled many, saying, "Let us go and make a covenant with the Gentiles around us, for since we separated from them many disasters have come upon us." [12]This proposal pleased them, [13]and some of the people eagerly went to the king, who authorized them to observe the ordinances of the Gentiles. [14]So they built a gymnasium in Jerusalem, according to Gentile custom, [15]and removed the marks of circumcision, and abandoned the holy covenant. They joined with the Gentiles and sold themselves to do evil.

Antiochus in Egypt

[16] When Antiochus saw that his kingdom was established, he determined to become king of the land of Egypt, in order that he might reign over both kingdoms. [17]So he invaded Egypt with a strong force, with chariots and elephants and cavalry and with a large fleet. [18]He engaged King Ptolemy of Egypt in battle, and Ptolemy turned and fled before him, and many were wounded and fell. [19]They captured the fortified cities in the land of Egypt, and he plundered the land of Egypt.

Persecution of the Jews

[20] After subduing Egypt, Antiochus returned in the one hundred forty-third year.[c] He went up against Israel and came to Jerusalem with a strong force. [21]He arrogantly entered the sanctuary and took the golden altar, the lampstand for the light, and all its utensils. [22]He took also the table for the bread of the Presence, the cups for drink offerings, the bowls, the golden censers, the curtain, the crowns, and the gold decoration on the front of the temple; he stripped it all off. [23]He took the silver and the

---

a Gk adds *and he defeated* b 175 B.C. c 169 B.C.

gold, and the costly vessels; he took also the hidden treasures that he found. ²⁴Taking them all, he went into his own land.

He shed much blood,
     and spoke with great arrogance.
²⁵ Israel mourned deeply in every community,
²⁶   rulers and elders groaned,
     young women and young men became faint,
     the beauty of the women faded.
²⁷ Every bridegroom took up the lament;
     she who sat in the bridal chamber was mourning.
²⁸ Even the land trembled for its inhabitants,
     and all the house of Jacob was clothed with shame.

The Occupation of Jerusalem

29 Two years later the king sent to the cities of Judah a chief collector of tribute, and he came to Jerusalem with a large force. ³⁰Deceitfully he spoke peaceable words to them, and they believed him; but he suddenly fell upon the city, dealt it a severe blow, and destroyed many people of Israel. ³¹He plundered the city, burned it with fire, and tore down its houses and its surrounding walls. ³²They took captive the women and children, and seized the livestock. ³³Then they fortified the city of David with a great strong wall and strong towers, and it became their citadel. ³⁴They stationed there a sinful people, men who were renegades. These strengthened their position; ³⁵they stored up arms and food, and collecting the spoils of Jerusalem they stored them there, and became a great menace,
³⁶ for the citadel^a became an ambush against the sanctuary,
     an evil adversary of Israel at all times.
³⁷ On every side of the sanctuary they shed innocent blood;
     they even defiled the sanctuary.
³⁸ Because of them the residents of Jerusalem fled;
     she became a dwelling of strangers;
she became strange to her offspring,
     and her children forsook her.
³⁹ Her sanctuary became desolate like a desert;
     her feasts were turned into mourning,
her sabbaths into a reproach,
     her honor into contempt.
⁴⁰ Her dishonor now grew as great as her glory;
     her exaltation was turned into mourning.

Installation of Gentile Cults

41 Then the king wrote to his whole kingdom that all should be one people, ⁴²and that all should give up their particular customs. ⁴³All the Gentiles accepted the command of the king. Many even from Israel gladly adopted his religion; they sacrificed to idols and profaned the sabbath. ⁴⁴And the king sent letters by messengers to Jerusalem and the towns of Judah; he directed them to follow customs strange to the land, ⁴⁵to forbid burnt offerings and sacrifices and drink offerings in the sanctuary, to profane sabbaths and festivals, ⁴⁶to defile the sanctuary and the priests, ⁴⁷to build altars and sacred precincts and shrines for idols, to sacrifice swine and other unclean animals, ⁴⁸and to leave their sons uncircumcised. They were to make themselves abominable by everything unclean and profane, ⁴⁹so that they would forget the law and change all the ordinances. ⁵⁰He added,^b "And whoever does not obey the command of the king shall die."

51 In such words he wrote to his whole kingdom. He appointed inspectors over all the people and commanded the towns of Judah to offer sacrifice, town by town. ⁵²Many of the people, everyone who forsook the law, joined them, and they did evil in the land; ⁵³they drove Israel into hiding in every place of refuge they had.

54 Now on the fifteenth day of Chislev, in the one hundred forty-fifth year,^c they erected a desolating sacrilege on the altar of burnt offering. They also built altars in the surrounding towns of Judah, ⁵⁵and offered incense at the doors of the houses and in the streets. ⁵⁶The books of the law that they found they tore to pieces and burned with fire. ⁵⁷Anyone found possessing the book of the covenant, or anyone who adhered to the law, was condemned to death by decree of the king. ⁵⁸They kept using violence against Israel, against those who were found month after month in the towns. ⁵⁹On the twenty-fifth day of the month they offered sacrifice on the altar that was on top of the altar of burnt offering. ⁶⁰According to the decree, they put to death the women who had their children circumcised, ⁶¹and their families and those who circumcised them; and they hung the infants from their mothers' necks.

62 But many in Israel stood firm and were resolved in their hearts not to eat unclean food. ⁶³They chose to die rather than to be defiled by food or to profane the holy covenant; and they did die. ⁶⁴Very great wrath came upon Israel.

a Gk it *b* Gk lacks *He added* *c* 167 B.C.

2 Mattathias and His Sons

In those days Mattathias son of John son of Simeon, a priest of the family of Joarib, moved from Jerusalem and settled in Modein. ²He had five sons, John surnamed Gaddi, ³Simon called Thassi, ⁴Judas called Maccabeus, ⁵Eleazar called Avaran, and Jonathan called Apphus. ⁶He saw the blasphemies being committed in Judah and Jerusalem, ⁷and said,

"Alas! Why was I born to see this,
the ruin of my people, the ruin of the
holy city,
and to live there when it was given over to
the enemy,
the sanctuary given over to aliens?
⁸ Her temple has become like a person
without honor;ᵃ
⁹ her glorious vessels have been carried
into exile.
Her infants have been killed in her streets,
her youths by the sword of the foe.
¹⁰ What nation has not inherited her palacesᵇ
and has not seized her spoils?
¹¹ All her adornment has been taken away;
no longer free, she has become a slave.
¹² And see, our holy place, our beauty,
and our glory have been laid waste;
the Gentiles have profaned them.
¹³ Why should we live any longer?"

14 Then Mattathias and his sons tore their clothes, put on sackcloth, and mourned greatly.

Pagan Worship Refused

15 The king's officers who were enforcing the apostasy came to the town of Modein to make them offer sacrifice. ¹⁶Many from Israel came to them; and Mattathias and his sons were assembled. ¹⁷Then the king's officers spoke to Mattathias as follows: "You are a leader, honored and great in this town, and supported by sons and brothers. ¹⁸Now be the first to come and do what the king commands, as all the Gentiles and the people of Judah and those that are left in Jerusalem have done. Then you and your sons will be numbered among the Friends of the king, and you and your sons will be honored with silver and gold and many gifts."

19 But Mattathias answered and said in a loud voice: "Even if all the nations that live under the rule of the king obey him, and have chosen to obey his commandments, every one of them abandoning the religion of their ancestors, ²⁰I and my sons and my brothers will continue to live by the covenant of our ancestors. ²¹Far be it from us to desert the law and the ordinances. ²²We will not obey the king's words by turning aside from our religion to the right hand or to the left."

23 When he had finished speaking these words, a Jew came forward in the sight of all to offer sacrifice on the altar in Modein, according to the king's command. ²⁴When Mattathias saw it, he burned with zeal and his heart was stirred. He gave vent to righteous anger; he ran and killed him on the altar. ²⁵At the same time he killed the king's officer who was forcing them to sacrifice, and he tore down the altar. ²⁶Thus he burned with zeal for the law, just as Phinehas did against Zimri son of Salu.

27 Then Mattathias cried out in the town with a loud voice, saying: "Let every one who is zealous for the law and supports the covenant come out with me!" ²⁸Then he and his sons fled to the hills and left all that they had in the town.

29 At that time many who were seeking righteousness and justice went down to the wilderness to live there, ³⁰they, their sons, their wives, and their livestock, because troubles pressed heavily upon them. ³¹And it was reported to the king's officers, and to the troops in Jerusalem the city of David, that those who had rejected the king's command had gone down to the hiding places in the wilderness. ³²Many pursued them, and overtook them; they encamped opposite them and prepared for battle against them on the sabbath day. ³³They said to them, "Enough of this! Come out and do what the king commands, and you will live." ³⁴But they said, "We will not come out, nor will we do what the king commands and so profane the sabbath day." ³⁵Then the enemyᶜ quickly attacked them. ³⁶But they did not answer them or hurl a stone at them or block up their hiding places, ³⁷for they said, "Let us all die in our innocence; heaven and earth testify for us that you are killing us unjustly." ³⁸So they attacked them on the sabbath, and they died, with their wives and children and livestock, to the number of a thousand persons.

39 When Mattathias and his friends learned of it, they mourned for them deeply. ⁴⁰And all said to their neighbors: "If we all do as our kindred have done and refuse to fight with the Gentiles for our lives and for our ordinances, they will quickly destroy us from the earth." ⁴¹So they made this decision that day: "Let us fight against anyone who comes to attack us on the sabbath day; let us not all die as our kindred died in their hiding places."

Counter-Attack

42 Then there united with them a company of Hasideans, mighty warriors of Israel, all

---

ᵃ Meaning of Gk uncertain ᵇ Other ancient authorities read *has not had a part in her kingdom* ᶜ Gk *they* who offered themselves willingly for the law. 43And all who became fugitives to escape their troubles joined them and reinforced them. 44They organized an army, and struck down sinners in their anger and renegades in their wrath; the survivors fled to the Gentiles for safety. 45And Mattathias and his friends went around and tore down the altars; 46they forcibly circumcised all the uncircumcised boys that they found within the borders of Israel. 47They hunted down the arrogant, and the work prospered in their hands. 48They rescued the law out of the hands of the Gentiles and kings, and they never let the sinner gain the upper hand.

The Last Words of Mattathias

49 Now the days drew near for Mattathias to die, and he said to his sons: "Arrogance and scorn have now become strong; it is a time of ruin and furious anger. 50Now, my children, show zeal for the law, and give your lives for the covenant of our ancestors.

51 "Remember the deeds of the ancestors, which they did in their generations; and you will receive great honor and an everlasting name. 52Was not Abraham found faithful when tested, and it was reckoned to him as righteousness? 53Joseph in the time of his distress kept the commandment, and became lord of Egypt. 54Phinehas our ancestor, because he was deeply zealous, received the covenant of everlasting priesthood. 55Joshua, because he fulfilled the command, became a judge in Israel. 56Caleb, because he testified in the assembly, received an inheritance in the land. 57David, because he was merciful, inherited the throne of the kingdom forever. 58Elijah, because of great zeal for the law, was taken up into heaven. 59Hananiah, Azariah, and Mishael believed and were saved from the flame. 60Daniel, because of his innocence, was delivered from the mouth of the lions.

61 "And so observe, from generation to generation, that none of those who put their trust in him will lack strength. 62Do not fear the words of sinners, for their splendor will turn into dung and worms. 63Today they will be exalted, but tomorrow they will not be found, because they will have returned to the dust, and their plans will have perished. 64My children, be courageous and grow strong in the law, for by it you will gain honor.

65 "Here is your brother Simeon who, I know, is wise in counsel; always listen to him; he shall be your father. 66Judas Maccabeus has been a mighty warrior from his youth; he shall command the army for you and fight the battle against the peoples.*a* 67You shall rally around

a Or of the people b 166 B.C.

you all who observe the law, and avenge the wrong done to your people. 68Pay back the Gentiles in full, and obey the commands of the law."

69 Then he blessed them, and was gathered to his ancestors. 70He died in the one hundred forty-sixth year*b* and was buried in the tomb of his ancestors at Modein. And all Israel mourned for him with great lamentation.

3 The Early Victories of Judas

Then his son Judas, who was called Maccabeus, took command in his place. [2]All his brothers and all who had joined his father helped him; they gladly fought for Israel.

[3] He extended the glory of his people.
Like a giant he put on his breastplate;
he bound on his armor of war and waged battles,
protecting the camp by his sword.

[4] He was like a lion in his deeds,
like a lion's cub roaring for prey.

[5] He searched out and pursued those who broke the law;
he burned those who troubled his people.

[6] Lawbreakers shrank back for fear of him;
all the evildoers were confounded;
and deliverance prospered by his hand.

[7] He embittered many kings,
but he made Jacob glad by his deeds,
and his memory is blessed forever.

[8] He went through the cities of Judah;
he destroyed the ungodly out of the land;[a]
thus he turned away wrath from Israel.

[9] He was renowned to the ends of the earth;
he gathered in those who were perishing.

10 Apollonius now gathered together Gentiles and a large force from Samaria to fight against Israel. [11]When Judas learned of it, he went out to meet him, and he defeated and killed him. Many were wounded and fell, and the rest fled. [12]Then they seized their spoils; and Judas took the sword of Apollonius, and used it in battle the rest of his life.

13 When Seron, the commander of the Syrian army, heard that Judas had gathered a large company, including a body of faithful soldiers who stayed with him and went out to battle, [14]he said, "I will make a name for myself and win honor in the kingdom. I will make war on Judas and his companions, who scorn the king's command." [15]Once again a strong army of godless men went up with him to help him, to take vengeance on the Israelites.

16 When he approached the ascent of Bethhoron, Judas went out to meet him with a small company. [17]But when they saw the army coming to meet them, they said to Judas, "How can we, few as we are, fight against so great and so strong a multitude? And we are faint, for we have eaten nothing today." [18]Judas replied, "It is easy for many to be hemmed in by few, for in the sight of Heaven there is no difference between saving by many or by few. [19]It is not on the size of the army that victory in battle depends, but strength comes from Heaven. [20]They come against us in great insolence and lawlessness to destroy us and our wives and our children, and to despoil us; [21]but we fight for our lives and our laws. [22]He himself will crush them before us; as for you, do not be afraid of them."

23 When he finished speaking, he rushed suddenly against Seron and his army, and they were crushed before him. [24]They pursued them[b] down the descent of Beth-horon to the plain; eight hundred of them fell, and the rest fled into the land of the Philistines. [25]Then Judas and his brothers began to be feared, and terror fell on the Gentiles all around them. [26]His fame reached the king, and the Gentiles talked of the battles of Judas.

The Policy of Antiochus

27 When King Antiochus heard these reports, he was greatly angered; and he sent and gathered all the forces of his kingdom, a very strong army. [28]He opened his coffers and gave a year's pay to his forces, and ordered them to be ready for any need. [29]Then he saw that the money in the treasury was exhausted, and that the revenues from the country were small because of the dissension and disaster that he had caused in the land by abolishing the laws that had existed from the earliest days. [30]He feared that he might not have such funds as he had before for his expenses and for the gifts that he used to give more lavishly than preceding kings. [31]He was greatly perplexed in mind; then he determined to go to Persia and collect the revenues from those regions and raise a large fund.

32 He left Lysias, a distinguished man of royal lineage, in charge of the king's affairs from the river Euphrates to the borders of Egypt. [33]Lysias was also to take care of his son Antiochus until he returned. [34]And he turned over to Lysias[c] half of his forces and the elephants, and gave him orders about all that he wanted done. As for the residents of Judea and Jerusalem, [35]Lysias was to send a force against them to wipe out and destroy the strength of Israel and the remnant of Jerusalem; he was to banish the memory of them from the place, [36]settle aliens in all their territory, and distribute their land by lot. [37]Then the king took the remaining half of his forces and left Antioch his capital in the one hundred and forty-seventh year.[d] He crossed the Euphrates river and went through the upper provinces.

Preparations for Battle

38 Lysias chose Ptolemy son of Dorymenes, and Nicanor and Gorgias, able men among the

a Gk it b Other ancient authorities read him c Gk him d 165 B.C.

PROFILE OF FAITH

THE CARROLL FAMILY: Catholics in Politics

In the seventeenth century, life in England was oppressive for Catholics. Many Catholics were looking for a safe place to live where they could exercise their Catholic faith freely. One of these Catholics was Charles Carroll, who sailed to the American colony of Maryland and became the attorney general of the colony.

But it didn't end up being a safe place for Catholics after all. Protestants took over the state government and began passing laws forbidding Catholics to worship in public and soon took the right to vote away from them. Shortly after arriving, Carroll lost his position in the government because of his religion, but he retained the land he was given and began a prosperous farm. He went on to have three grandsons who became very important people in our history.

His grandson Charles signed the Declaration of Independence. All of the signers took the risk of being convicted of treason—a hanging offense. Of all of the signers, Charles Carroll had the most to lose. He was not only a Catholic, but also the wealthiest of all of the men.

When Charles came to sign the document, one man said jokingly, "There are so many Carrolls in Maryland, Charles can feel safe from reprisal!" Charles immediately added "of Carrollton" to his name and said, "Now King George will know with which Carroll he is dealing."

His grandson Daniel was chosen to represent Maryland at the Constitutional Convention. At this convention, he led the fight for the idea that the president of the United States should be elected by the people and not the Congress. He donated some of his family land to the government, which is where the Capitol is located today.

His grandson John became a Jesuit and the first bishop of the United States, continuing Charles Carroll's Catholic legacy in this country despite religious intolerance and persecution.

Friends of the king, ³⁹and sent with them forty thousand infantry and seven thousand cavalry to go into the land of Judah and destroy it, as the king had commanded. ⁴⁰So they set out with their entire force, and when they arrived they encamped near Emmaus in the plain. ⁴¹When the traders of the region heard what was said to them, they took silver and gold in immense amounts, and fetters,ᵃ and went to the camp to get the Israelites for slaves. And forces from Syria and the land of the Philistines joined with them.

42 Now Judas and his brothers saw that misfortunes had increased and that the forces were encamped in their territory. They also learned what the king had commanded to do to the people to cause their final destruction. ⁴³But they said to one another, "Let us restore the ruins of our people, and fight for our people and the sanctuary." ⁴⁴So the congregation assembled to be ready for battle, and to pray and ask for mercy and compassion.

⁴⁵ Jerusalem was uninhabited like a
  wilderness;
    not one of her children went in
      or out.
The sanctuary was trampled down,
  and aliens held the citadel;
    it was a lodging place for the Gentiles.
Joy was taken from Jacob;
    the flute and the harp ceased to play.
46 Then they gathered together and went to Mizpah, opposite Jerusalem, because Israel formerly had a place of prayer in Mizpah. ⁴⁷They fasted that day, put on sackcloth and sprinkled ashes on their heads, and tore their clothes. ⁴⁸And they opened the book of the law to inquire into those matters about which the Gentiles consulted the likenesses of their gods. ⁴⁹They also brought the vestments of the priesthood and the first fruits and the tithes, and they stirred up the naziritesᵇ who had completed their days; ⁵⁰and they cried aloud to Heaven, saying,

a Syr: Gk Mss, Vg slaves b That is those separated or those consecrated

Psychedelic Camel—© Jason Paradis, 14

"What shall we do with these?
  Where shall we take them?
⁵¹ Your sanctuary is trampled down and
    profaned,
  and your priests mourn in
    humiliation.
⁵² Here the Gentiles are assembled against us
    to destroy us;
  you know what they plot against us.
⁵³ How will we be able to withstand them,
    if you do not help us?"

54 Then they sounded the trumpets and gave a loud shout. ⁵⁵After this Judas appointed leaders of the people, in charge of thousands and hundreds and fifties and tens. ⁵⁶Those who were building houses, or were about to be married, or were planting a vineyard, or were fainthearted, he told to go home again, according to the law. ⁵⁷Then the army marched out and encamped to the south of Emmaus.

58 And Judas said, "Arm yourselves and be courageous. Be ready early in the morning to fight with these Gentiles who have assembled against us to destroy us and our sanctuary. ⁵⁹It is better for us to die in battle than to see the misfortunes of our nation and of the sanctuary. ⁶⁰But as his will in heaven may be, so shall he do."

4 The Battle at Emmaus

Now Gorgias took five thousand infantry and one thousand picked cavalry, and this division moved out by night ²to fall upon the camp of the Jews and attack them suddenly. Men from the citadel were his guides. ³But Judas heard of it, and he and his warriors moved out to attack the king's force in Emmaus ⁴while the division was still absent from the camp. ⁵When Gorgias entered the camp of Judas by night, he found no one there, so he looked for them in the hills, because he said, "These men are running away from us."

6 At daybreak Judas appeared in the plain with three thousand men, but they did not have armor and swords such as they desired. ⁷And they saw the camp of the Gentiles, strong and fortified, with cavalry all around it; and these men were trained in war. ⁸But Judas said to those who were with him, "Do not fear their numbers or be afraid when they charge. ⁹Remember how our ancestors were saved at the Red Sea, when Pharaoh with his forces pursued them. ¹⁰And now, let us cry to Heaven, to see whether he will favor us and remember his covenant with our ancestors and crush this army before us today. ¹¹Then all the Gentiles

will know that there is one who redeems and saves Israel."

12 When the foreigners looked up and saw them coming against them, [13]they went out from their camp to battle. Then the men with Judas blew their trumpets [14]and engaged in battle. The Gentiles were crushed, and fled into the plain, [15]and all those in the rear fell by the sword. They pursued them to Gazara, and to the plains of Idumea, and to Azotus and Jamnia; and three thousand of them fell. [16]Then Judas and his force turned back from pursuing them, [17]and he said to the people, "Do not be greedy for plunder, for there is a battle before us; [18]Gorgias and his force are near us in the hills. But stand now against our enemies and fight them, and afterward seize the plunder boldly."

19 Just as Judas was finishing this speech, a detachment appeared, coming out of the hills. [20]They saw that their army[a] had been put to flight, and that the Jews[a] were burning the camp, for the smoke that was seen showed what had happened. [21]When they perceived this, they were greatly frightened, and when they also saw the army of Judas drawn up in the plain for battle, [22]they all fled into the land of the Philistines. [23]Then Judas returned to plunder the camp, and they seized a great amount of gold and silver, and cloth dyed blue and sea purple, and great riches. [24]On their return they sang hymns and praises to Heaven—"For he is good, for his mercy endures forever." [25]Thus Israel had a great deliverance that day.

First Campaign of Lysias

26 Those of the foreigners who escaped went and reported to Lysias all that had happened. [27]When he heard it, he was perplexed and discouraged, for things had not happened to Israel as he had intended, nor had they turned out as the king had ordered. [28]But the next year he mustered sixty thousand picked infantry and five thousand cavalry to subdue them. [29]They came into Idumea and encamped at Beth-zur, and Judas met them with ten thousand men.

30 When he saw that their army was strong, he prayed, saying, "Blessed are you, O Savior of Israel, who crushed the attack of the mighty warrior by the hand of your servant David, and gave the camp of the Philistines into the hands of Jonathan son of Saul, and of the man who carried his armor. [31]Hem in this army by the hand of your people Israel, and let them be ashamed of their troops and their cavalry. [32]Fill them with cowardice; melt the boldness of their strength; let them tremble in their destruction. [33]Strike them down with the sword

of those who love you, and let all who know your name praise you with hymns."

34 Then both sides attacked, and there fell of the army of Lysias five thousand men; they fell in action.[b] [35]When Lysias saw the rout of his troops and observed the boldness that inspired those of Judas, and how ready they were either to live or to die nobly, he withdrew to Antioch and enlisted mercenaries in order to invade Judea again with an even larger army.

Cleansing and Dedication of the Temple

36 Then Judas and his brothers said, "See, our enemies are crushed; let us go up to cleanse the sanctuary and dedicate it." [37]So all the army assembled and went up to Mount Zion. [38]There they saw the sanctuary desolate, the altar profaned, and the gates burned. In the courts they saw bushes sprung up as in a thicket, or as on one of the mountains. They saw also the chambers of the priests in ruins. [39]Then they tore their clothes and mourned with great lamentation; they sprinkled themselves with ashes [40]and fell face down on the ground. And when the signal was given with the trumpets, they cried out to Heaven.

41 Then Judas detailed men to fight against those in the citadel until he had cleansed the sanctuary. [42]He chose blameless priests devoted to the law, [43]and they cleansed the sanctuary and removed the defiled stones to an unclean place. [44]They deliberated what to do about the altar of burnt offering, which had been profaned. [45]And they thought it best to tear it down, so that it would not be a lasting shame to them that the Gentiles had defiled it. So they tore down the altar, [46]and stored the stones in a convenient place on the temple hill until a prophet should come to tell what to do with them. [47]Then they took unhewn[c] stones, as the law directs, and built a new altar like the former one. [48]They also rebuilt the sanctuary and the interior of the temple, and consecrated the courts. [49]They made new holy vessels, and brought the lampstand, the altar of incense, and the table into the temple. [50]Then they offered incense on the altar and lit the lamps on the lampstand, and these gave light in the temple. [51]They placed the bread on the table and hung up the curtains. Thus they finished all the work they had undertaken.

52 Early in the morning on the twenty-fifth day of the ninth month, which is the month of Chislev, in the one hundred forty-eighth year,[d] [53]they rose and offered sacrifice, as the law directs, on the new altar of burnt offering that they had built. [54]At the very season and on the

---

a Gk they *b* Or and some fell on the opposite side *c* Gk whole *d* 164 B.C.

should be observed with joy and gladness for eight days, beginning with the twenty-fifth day of the month of Chislev.

60 At that time they fortified Mount Zion with high walls and strong towers all around, to keep the Gentiles from coming and trampling them down as they had done before. [61]Judas[a] stationed a garrison there to guard it; he also fortified Beth-zur to guard it, so that the people might have a stronghold that faced Idumea.

5 Wars with Neighboring Peoples

When the Gentiles all around heard that the altar had been rebuilt and the sanctuary dedicated as it was before, they became very angry, [2]and they determined to destroy the descendants of Jacob who lived among them. So they began to kill and destroy among the people. [3]But Judas made war on the descendants of Esau in Idumea, at Akrabattene, because they kept lying in wait for Israel. He dealt them a heavy blow and humbled them and despoiled them. [4]He also remembered the wickedness of the sons of Baean, who were a trap and a snare to the people and ambushed them on the highways. [5]They were shut up by him in their[b] towers; and he encamped against them, vowed their complete destruction, and burned with fire their towers and all who were in them. [6]Then he crossed over to attack the Ammonites, where he found a strong band and many people, with Timothy as their leader. [7]He engaged in many battles with them, and they were crushed before him; he struck them down. [8]He also took Jazer and its villages; then he returned to Judea.

Liberation of Galilean Jews

9 Now the Gentiles in Gilead gathered together against the Israelites who lived in their territory, and planned to destroy them. But they fled to the stronghold of Dathema, [10]and sent to Judas and his brothers a letter that said, "The Gentiles around us have gathered together to destroy us. [11]They are preparing to come and capture the stronghold to which we have fled, and Timothy is leading their forces. [12]Now then, come and rescue us from their hands, for many of us have fallen, [13]and all our kindred who were in the land of Tob have been killed; the enemy[c] have captured their wives and children and goods, and have destroyed about a thousand persons there."

14 While the letter was still being read, other messengers, with their garments torn, came from Galilee and made a similar report; [15]they

---

very day that the Gentiles had profaned it, it was dedicated with songs and harps and lutes and cymbals. [55]All the people fell on their faces and worshiped and blessed Heaven, who had prospered them. [56]So they celebrated the dedication of the altar for eight days, and joyfully offered burnt offerings; they offered a sacrifice of well-being and a thanksgiving offering. [57]They decorated the front of the temple with golden crowns and small shields; they restored the gates and the chambers for the priests, and fitted them with doors. [58]There was very great joy among the people, and the disgrace brought by the Gentiles was removed.

59 Then Judas and his brothers and all the assembly of Israel determined that every year at that season the days of dedication of the altar

said that the people of Ptolemais and Tyre and Sidon, and all Galilee of the Gentiles,[a] had gathered together against them "to annihilate us." [16]When Judas and the people heard these messages, a great assembly was called to determine what they should do for their kindred who were in distress and were being attacked by enemies.[b] [17]Then Judas said to his brother Simon, "Choose your men and go and rescue your kindred in Galilee; Jonathan my brother and I will go to Gilead." [18]But he left Joseph, son of Zechariah, and Azariah, a leader of the people, with the rest of the forces, in Judea to guard it; [19]and he gave them this command, "Take charge of this people, but do not engage in battle with the Gentiles until we return." [20]Then three thousand men were assigned to Simon to go to Galilee, and eight thousand to Judas for Gilead.

21 So Simon went to Galilee and fought many battles against the Gentiles, and the Gentiles were crushed before him. [22]He pursued them to the gate of Ptolemais; as many as three thousand of the Gentiles fell, and he despoiled them. [23]Then he took the Jews[c] of Galilee and Arbatta, with their wives and children, and all they possessed, and led them to Judea with great rejoicing.

Judas and Jonathan in Gilead

24 Judas Maccabeus and his brother Jonathan crossed the Jordan and made three days' journey into the wilderness. [25]They encountered the Nabateans, who met them peaceably and told them all that had happened to their kindred in Gilead: [26]"Many of them have been shut up in Bozrah and Bosor, in Alema and Chaspho, Maked and Carnaim"—all these towns were strong and large— [27]"and some have been shut up in the other towns of Gilead; the enemy[d] are getting ready to attack the strongholds tomorrow and capture and destroy all these people in a single day."

28 Then Judas and his army quickly turned back by the wilderness road to Bozrah; and he took the town, and killed every male by the edge of the sword; then he seized all its spoils and burned it with fire. [29]He left the place at night, and they went all the way to the stronghold of Dathema.[e] [30]At dawn they looked out and saw a large company, which could not be counted, carrying ladders and engines of war to capture the stronghold, and attacking the Jews within.[f] [31]So Judas saw that the battle had begun and that the cry of the town went up to Heaven, with trumpets and loud shouts, [32]and he said to the men of his forces, "Fight today for your kindred!" [33]Then he came up behind them in three companies, who sounded their trumpets and cried aloud in prayer. [34]And when the army of Timothy realized that it was Maccabeus, they fled before him, and he dealt them a heavy blow. As many as eight thousand of them fell that day.

35 Next he turned aside to Maapha,[g] and fought against it and took it; and he killed every male in it, plundered it, and burned it with fire. [36]From there he marched on and took Chaspho, Maked, and Bosor, and the other towns of Gilead.

a Gk *aliens* *b* Gk *them* *c* Gk *those* *d* Gk *they* *e* Gk lacks *of Dathema*. See verse 9 *f* Gk *and they were attacking them* *g* Other ancient authorities read *Alema*

37 After these things Timothy gathered another army and encamped opposite Raphon, on the other side of the stream. [38]Judas sent men to spy out the camp, and they reported to him, "All the Gentiles around us have gathered to him; it is a very large force. [39]They also have hired Arabs to help them, and they are encamped across the stream, ready to come and fight against you." And Judas went to meet them.

40 Now as Judas and his army drew near to the stream of water, Timothy said to the officers of his forces, "If he crosses over to us first, we will not be able to resist him, for he will surely defeat us. [41]But if he shows fear and camps on the other side of the river, we will cross over to him and defeat him." [42]When Judas approached the stream of water, he stationed the officers[a] of the army at the stream and gave them this command, "Permit no one to encamp, but make them all enter the battle." [43]Then he crossed over against them first, and the whole army followed him. All the Gentiles were defeated before him, and they threw away their arms and fled into the sacred precincts at Carnaim. [44]But he took the town and burned the sacred precincts with fire, together with all who were in them. Thus Carnaim was conquered; they could stand before Judas no longer.

The Return to Jerusalem

45 Then Judas gathered together all the Israelites in Gilead, the small and the great, with their wives and children and goods, a very large company, to go to the land of Judah. [46]So they came to Ephron. This was a large and very strong town on the road, and they could not go around it to the right or to the left; they had to go through it. [47]But the people of the town shut them out and blocked up the gates with stones. 48 Judas sent them this friendly message, "Let us pass through your land to get to our land. No one will do you harm; we will simply pass by on foot." But they refused to open to him. [49]Then Judas ordered proclamation to be made to the army that all should encamp where they were. [50]So the men of the forces encamped, and he fought against the town all that day and all the night, and the town was delivered into his hands. [51]He destroyed every male by the edge of the sword, and razed and plundered the town. Then he passed through the town over the bodies of the dead. 52 Then they crossed the Jordan into the large plain before Beth-shan. [53]Judas kept rallying the laggards and encouraging the people all the way until he came to the land of Judah. [54]So they went up to Mount Zion with joy and gladness, and offered burnt offerings, because they had returned in safety; not one of them had fallen.

Joseph and Azariah Defeated

55 Now while Judas and Jonathan were in Gilead and their[b] brother Simon was in Galilee before Ptolemais, [56]Joseph son of Zechariah, and Azariah, the commanders of the forces, heard of their brave deeds and of the heroic war they had fought. [57]So they said, "Let us also make a name for ourselves; let us go and make war on the Gentiles around us." [58]So they issued orders to the men of the forces that were with them and marched against Jamnia. [59]Gorgias and his men came out of the town to meet them in battle. [60]Then Joseph and Azariah were routed, and were pursued to the borders of Judea; as many as two thousand of the people of Israel fell that day. [61]Thus the people suffered a great rout because, thinking to do a brave deed, they did not listen to Judas and his brothers. [62]But they did not belong to the family of those men through whom deliverance was given to Israel.

63 The man Judas and his brothers were greatly honored in all Israel and among all the Gentiles, wherever their name was heard. [64]People gathered to them and praised them.

Success at Hebron and Philistia

65 Then Judas and his brothers went out and fought the descendants of Esau in the land to the south. He struck Hebron and its villages and tore down its strongholds and burned its towers on all sides. [66]Then he marched off to go into the land of the Philistines, and passed through Marisa.[c] [67]On that day some priests, who wished to do a brave deed, fell in battle, for they went out to battle unwisely. [68]But Judas turned aside to Azotus in the land of the Philistines; he tore down their altars, and the carved images of their gods he burned with fire; he plundered the towns and returned to the land of Judah.

6 The Last Days of Antiochus Epiphanes

King Antiochus was going through the upper provinces when he heard that Elymais in Persia was a city famed for its wealth in silver and gold. [2]Its temple was very rich, containing golden shields, breastplates, and weapons left there by Alexander son of Philip, the Macedonian king who first reigned over the Greeks. [3]So he came and tried to take the city and plunder it, but he could not because his plan had become known to the citizens [4]and they with-

---

a Or *scribes* b Gk *his* c Other ancient authorities read *Samaria* stood him in battle. So he fled and in great disappointment left there to return to Babylon.

5 Then someone came to him in Persia and reported that the armies that had gone into the land of Judah had been routed; [6]that Lysias had gone first with a strong force, but had turned and fled before the Jews;[a] that the Jews[b] had grown strong from the arms, supplies, and abundant spoils that they had taken from the armies they had cut down; [7]that they had torn down the abomination that he had erected on the altar in Jerusalem; and that they had surrounded the sanctuary with high walls as before, and also Beth-zur, his town.

8 When the king heard this news, he was astounded and badly shaken. He took to his bed and became sick from disappointment, because things had not turned out for him as he had planned. [9]He lay there for many days, because deep disappointment continually gripped him, and he realized that he was dying. [10]So he called all his Friends and said to them, "Sleep has departed from my eyes and I am downhearted with worry. [11]I said to myself, 'To what distress I have come! And into what a great flood I now am plunged! For I was kind and beloved in my power.' [12]But now I remember the wrong I did in Jerusalem. I seized all its vessels of silver and gold, and I sent to destroy the inhabitants of Judah without good reason. [13]I know that it is because of this that these misfortunes have come upon me; here I am, perishing of bitter disappointment in a strange land."

14 Then he called for Philip, one of his Friends, and made him ruler over all his kingdom. [15]He gave him the crown and his robe and the signet, so that he might guide his son Antiochus and bring him up to be king. [16]Thus King Antiochus died there in the one hundred forty-ninth year.[c] [17]When Lysias learned that the king was dead, he set up Antiochus the king's[d] son to reign. Lysias[e] had brought him up from boyhood; he named him Eupator.

Renewed Attacks from Syria

18 Meanwhile the garrison in the citadel kept hemming Israel in around the sanctuary. They were trying in every way to harm them and strengthen the Gentiles. [19]Judas therefore resolved to destroy them, and assembled all the people to besiege them. [20]They gathered together and besieged the citadel[f] in the one hundred fiftieth year;[g] and he built siege towers and other engines of war. [21]But some of the garrison escaped from the siege and some

of the ungodly Israelites joined them. [22]They went to the king and said, "How long will you fail to do justice and to avenge our kindred? [23]We were happy to serve your father, to live by what he said, and to follow his commands. [24]For this reason the sons of our people besieged the citadel[h] and became hostile to us; moreover, they have put to death as many of us as they have caught, and they have seized our inheritances. [25]It is not against us alone that they have stretched out their hands; they have also attacked all the lands on their borders. [26]And see, today they have encamped against the citadel in Jerusalem to take it; they have fortified both the sanctuary and Beth-zur; [27]unless you quickly prevent them, they will do still greater things, and you will not be able to stop them."

28 The king was enraged when he heard this. He assembled all his Friends, the commanders of his forces and those in authority.[i] [29]Mercenary forces also came to him from other kingdoms and from islands of the seas. [30]The number of his forces was one hundred thousand foot soldiers, twenty thousand horsemen, and thirty-two elephants accustomed to war. [31]They came through Idumea and encamped against Beth-zur, and for many days they fought and built engines of war; but the Jews[b] sallied out and burned these with fire, and fought courageously.

The Battle at Beth-zechariah

32 Then Judas marched away from the citadel and encamped at Beth-zechariah, opposite the camp of the king. [33]Early in the morning the king set out and took his army by a forced march along the road to Beth-zechariah, and his troops made ready for battle and sounded their trumpets. [34]They offered the elephants the juice of grapes and mulberries, to arouse them for battle. [35]They distributed the animals among the phalanxes; with each elephant they stationed a thousand men armed with coats of mail, and with brass helmets on their heads; and five hundred picked horsemen were assigned to each beast. [36]These took their position beforehand wherever the animal was; wherever it went, they went with it, and they never left it. [37]On the elephants[g] were wooden towers, strong and covered; they were fastened on each animal by special harness, and on each were four[j] armed men who fought from there, and also its Indian driver. [38]The rest of the cavalry were stationed on either side, on the two flanks of the army, to harass the enemy while

a Gk them b Gk they c 163 B.C. d Gk his e Gk He f Gk it g 162 B.C. h Meaning of Gk uncertain i Gk those over the reins
j Cn: Some authorities read thirty; others thirty-two

being themselves protected by the phalanxes. [39]When the sun shone on the shields of gold and brass, the hills were ablaze with them and gleamed like flaming torches.

40 Now a part of the king's army was spread out on the high hills, and some troops were on the plain, and they advanced steadily and in good order. [41]All who heard the noise made by their multitude, by the marching of the multitude and the clanking of their arms, trembled, for the army was very large and strong. [42]But Judas and his army advanced to the battle, and six hundred of the king's army fell. [43]Now Eleazar, called Avaran, saw that one of the animals was equipped with royal armor. It was taller than all the others, and he supposed that the king was on it. [44]So he gave his life to save his people and to win for himself an everlasting name. [45]He courageously ran into the midst of the phalanx to reach it; he killed men right and left, and they parted before him on both sides. [46]He got under the elephant, stabbed it from beneath, and killed it; but it fell to the ground upon him and he died. [47]When the Jews[a] saw the royal might and the fierce attack of the forces, they turned away in flight.

The Siege of the Temple

48 The soldiers of the king's army went up to Jerusalem against them, and the king encamped in Judea and at Mount Zion. [49]He made peace with the people of Beth-zur, and they evacuated the town because they had no provisions there to withstand a siege, since it was a sabbatical year for the land. [50]So the king took Beth-zur and stationed a guard there to hold it. [51]Then he encamped before the sanctuary for many days. He set up siege towers, engines of war to throw fire and stones, machines to shoot arrows, and catapults. [52]The Jews[a] also made engines of war to match theirs, and fought for many days. [53]But they had no food in storage,[b] because it was the seventh year; those who had found safety in Judea from the Gentiles had consumed the last of the stores. [54]Only a few men were left in the sanctuary; the rest scattered to their own homes, for the famine proved too much for them.

Syria Offers Terms

55 Then Lysias heard that Philip, whom King Antiochus while still living had appointed to bring up his son Antiochus to be king, [56]had returned from Persia and Media with the forces that had gone with the king, and that he was trying to seize control of the government. [57]So he quickly gave orders to withdraw, and said to the king, to the commanders of the forces, and to the troops, "Daily we grow weaker, our food supply is scant, the place against which we are fighting is strong, and the affairs of the kingdom press urgently on us. [58]Now then let us come to terms with these people, and make peace with them and with all their nation. [59]Let us agree to let them live by their laws as they did before; for it was on account of their laws that we abolished that they became angry and did all these things."

60 The speech pleased the king and the commanders, and he sent to the Jews[c] an offer of peace, and they accepted it. [61]So the king and the commanders gave them their oath. On these conditions the Jews[a] evacuated the stronghold. [62]But when the king entered Mount Zion and saw what a strong fortress the place was, he broke the oath he had sworn and gave orders to tear down the wall all around. [63]Then he set off in haste and returned to Antioch. He found Philip in control of the city, but he fought against him, and took the city by force.

7 Expedition of Bacchides and Alcimus

In the one hundred fifty-first year[d] Demetrius son of Seleucus set out from Rome, sailed with a few men to a town by the sea, and there began to reign. [2]As he was entering the royal palace of his ancestors, the army seized Antiochus and Lysias to bring them to him. [3]But when this act became known to him, he said, "Do not let me see their faces!" [4]So the army killed them, and Demetrius took his seat on the throne of his kingdom.

5 Then there came to him all the renegade and godless men of Israel; they were led by Alcimus, who wanted to be high priest. [6]They brought to the king this accusation against the people: "Judas and his brothers have destroyed all your Friends, and have driven us out of our land. [7]Now then send a man whom you trust; let him go and see all the ruin that Judas[e] has brought on us and on the land of the king, and let him punish them and all who help them."

8 So the king chose Bacchides, one of the king's Friends, governor of the province Beyond the River; he was a great man in the kingdom and was faithful to the king. [9]He sent him, and with him he sent the ungodly Alcimus, whom he made high priest; and he commanded him to take vengeance on the Israelites. [10]So they marched away and came with a large force into the land of Judah; and he sent messengers to Judas and his brothers with peaceable but treacherous words. [11]But they paid no

a Gk they   b Other ancient authorities read in the sanctuary   c Gk them   d 161 B.C.   e Gk he attention to their words, for they saw that they had come with a large force.

12 Then a group of scribes appeared in a body before Alcimus and Bacchides to ask for just terms. ¹³The Hasideans were first among the Israelites to seek peace from them, ¹⁴for they said, "A priest of the line of Aaron has come with the army, and he will not harm us." ¹⁵Alcimus*a* spoke peaceable words to them and swore this oath to them, "We will not seek to injure you or your friends." ¹⁶So they trusted him; but he seized sixty of them and killed them in one day, in accordance with the word that was written,

¹⁷ "The flesh of your faithful ones and their
         blood

   they poured out all around Jerusalem,
      and there was no one to bury them."

¹⁸Then the fear and dread of them fell on all the people, for they said, "There is no truth or justice in them, for they have violated the agreement and the oath that they swore."

19 Then Bacchides withdrew from Jerusalem and encamped in Beth-zaith. And he sent and seized many of the men who had deserted to him,*b* and some of the people, and killed them and threw them into a great pit. ²⁰He placed Alcimus in charge of the country and left with him a force to help him; then Bacchides went back to the king.

21 Alcimus struggled to maintain his high priesthood, ²²and all who were troubling their people joined him. They gained control of the land of Judah and did great damage in Israel. ²³And Judas saw all the wrongs that Alcimus and those with him had done among the Israelites; it was more than the Gentiles had done. ²⁴So Judas*c* went out into all the surrounding parts of Judea, taking vengeance on those who had deserted and preventing those in the city*d* from going out into the country. ²⁵When Alcimus saw that Judas and those with him had grown strong, and realized that he could not withstand them, he returned to the king and brought malicious charges against them.

Nicanor in Judea

26 Then the king sent Nicanor, one of his honored princes, who hated and detested Israel, and he commanded him to destroy the people. ²⁷So Nicanor came to Jerusalem with a large force, and treacherously sent to Judas and his brothers this peaceable message, ²⁸"Let there be no fighting between you and me; I shall come with a few men to see you face to face in peace."

29 So he came to Judas, and they greeted

JESUS SIGHTING

Know any arrogant people? You know—the conceited football player who thinks he's more special than anyone else, or the condescending honors student who sighs at your classmates' "stupid" questions, or the girls in the "popular" clique who make sure no one else gets in.

The Jewish people equated salvation with becoming a strong nation. Salvation meant they would be number one. That's one of the reasons the Maccabees reacted against the influence of the Greeks on the traditions of the Jewish people. They wanted a pure Jewish nation—and they believed that purity was the symbol of their salvation, which was only for the Jews. The Messiah who would come was theirs! As you read **1 Maccabees 4.1–6.63**, remind yourself that those ideas were what fueled their actions.

When the Messiah did come in the Person of Jesus, there was no arrogance or exclusivity about salvation or the Kingdom. The Kingdom was for the poor and all those who served them. It was for all those who did the will of the Father. (Want to read more? Check out Matthew 13.36–58 and Matthew 22.1–14 and reflect on Jesus' words.)

one another peaceably; but the enemy were preparing to kidnap Judas. ³⁰It became known to Judas that Nicanor*c* had come to him with treacherous intent, and he was afraid of him and would not meet him again. ³¹When Nicanor learned that his plan had been disclosed, he went out to meet Judas in battle near Caphar-salama. ³²About five hundred of the army of Nicanor fell, and the rest*e* fled into the city of David.

Nicanor Threatens the Temple

33 After these events Nicanor went up to Mount Zion. Some of the priests from the sanctuary and some of the elders of the people

a Gk He *b* Or *many of his men who had deserted* *c* Gk he *d* Gk *and they were prevented* *e* Gk *they* came out to greet him peaceably and to show him the burnt offering that was being offered for the king. [34]But he mocked them and derided them and defiled them and spoke arrogantly, [35]and in anger he swore this oath, "Unless Judas and his army are delivered into my hands this time, then if I return safely I will burn up this house." And he went out in great anger. [36]At this the priests went in and stood before the altar and the temple; they wept and said,

[37] "You chose this house to be called by your
name,
and to be for your people a house of
prayer and supplication.
[38] Take vengeance on this man and on his
army,
and let them fall by the sword;
remember their blasphemies,
and let them live no longer."

The Death of Nicanor

[39] Now Nicanor went out from Jerusalem and encamped in Beth-horon, and the Syrian army joined him. [40]Judas encamped in Adasa with three thousand men. Then Judas prayed and said, [41]"When the messengers from the king spoke blasphemy, your angel went out and struck down one hundred eighty-five thousand of the Assyrians.[a] [42]So also crush this army before us today; let the rest learn that Nicanor[b] has spoken wickedly against the sanctuary, and judge him according to this wickedness."

[43] So the armies met in battle on the thirteenth day of the month of Adar. The army of Nicanor was crushed, and he himself was the first to fall in the battle. [44]When his army saw that Nicanor had fallen, they threw down their arms and fled. [45]The Jews[c] pursued them a day's journey, from Adasa as far as Gazara, and as they followed they kept sounding the battle call on the trumpets. [46]People came out of all the surrounding villages of Judea, and they outflanked the enemy[d] and drove them back to their pursuers,[e] so that they all fell by the sword; not even one of them was left. [47]Then the Jews[c] seized the spoils and the plunder; they cut off Nicanor's head and the right hand that he had so arrogantly stretched out, and brought them and displayed them just outside Jerusalem. [48]The people rejoiced greatly and celebrated that day as a day of great gladness. [49]They decreed that this day should be celebrated each year on the thirteenth day of Adar. [50]So the land of Judah had rest for a few days.

8 A Eulogy of the Romans

Now Judas heard of the fame of the Romans, that they were very strong and were well-disposed toward all who made an alliance with them, that they pledged friendship to those who came to them, [2]and that they were very strong. He had been told of their wars and of the brave deeds that they were doing among the Gauls, how they had defeated them and

a Gk of them b Gk he c Gk they d Gk them e Gk these

forced them to pay tribute, [3]and what they had done in the land of Spain to get control of the silver and gold mines there, [4]and how they had gained control of the whole region by their planning and patience, even though the place was far distant from them. They also subdued the kings who came against them from the ends of the earth, until they crushed them and inflicted great disaster on them; the rest paid them tribute every year. [5]They had crushed in battle and conquered Philip, and King Perseus of the Macedonians,[a] and the others who rose up against them. [6]They also had defeated Antiochus the Great, king of Asia, who went to fight against them with one hundred twenty elephants and with cavalry and chariots and a very large army. He was crushed by them; [7]they took him alive and decreed that he and those who would reign after him should pay a heavy tribute and give hostages and surrender some of their best provinces, [8]the countries of India, Media, and Lydia. These they took from him and gave to King Eumenes. [9]The Greeks planned to come and destroy them, [10]but this became known to them, and they sent a general against the Greeks[b] and attacked them. Many of them were wounded and fell, and the Romans[c] took captive their wives and children; they plundered them, conquered the land, tore down their strongholds, and enslaved them to this day. [11]The remaining kingdoms and islands, as many as ever opposed them, they destroyed and enslaved; [12]but with their friends and those who rely on them they have kept friendship. They have subdued kings far and near, and as many as have heard of their fame have feared them. [13]Those whom they wish to help and to make kings, they make kings, and those whom they wish they depose; and they have been greatly exalted. [14]Yet for all this not one of them has put on a crown or worn purple as a mark of pride, [15]but they have built for themselves a senate chamber, and every day three hundred twenty senators constantly deliberate concerning the people, to govern them well. [16]They trust one man each year to rule over them and to control all their land; they all heed the one man, and there is no envy or jealousy among them.

An Alliance with Rome

17 So Judas chose Eupolemus son of John son of Accos, and Jason son of Eleazar, and sent them to Rome to establish friendship and alliance, [18]and to free themselves from the yoke; for they saw that the kingdom of the Greeks was enslaving Israel completely. [19]They went to Rome, a very long journey; and they entered the senate chamber and spoke as follows: [20]"Judas, who is also called Maccabeus, and his brothers and the people of the Jews have sent us to you to establish alliance and peace with you, so that we may be enrolled as your allies and friends." [21]The proposal pleased them, [22]and this is a copy of the letter that they wrote in reply, on bronze tablets, and sent to Jerusalem to remain with them there as a memorial of peace and alliance:

23 "May all go well with the Romans and with the nation of the Jews at sea and on land forever, and may sword and enemy be far from them. [24]If war comes first to Rome or to any of their allies in all their dominion, [25]the nation of the Jews shall act as their allies wholeheartedly, as the occasion may indicate to them. [26]To the enemy that makes war they shall not give or supply grain, arms, money, or ships, just as Rome has decided; and they shall keep their obligations without receiving any return. [27]In the same way, if war comes first to the nation of the Jews, the Romans shall willingly act as their allies, as the occasion may indicate to them. [28]And to their enemies there shall not be given grain, arms, money, or ships, just as Rome has decided; and they shall keep these obligations and do so without deceit. [29]Thus on these terms the Romans make a treaty with the Jewish people. [30]If after these terms are in effect both parties shall determine to add or delete anything, they shall do so at their discretion, and any addition or deletion that they may make shall be valid.

31 "Concerning the wrongs that King Demetrius is doing to them, we have written to him as follows, 'Why have you made your yoke heavy on our friends and allies the Jews? [32]If now they appeal again for help against you, we will defend their rights and fight you on sea and on land.' "

9 Bacchides Returns to Judea

When Demetrius heard that Nicanor and his army had fallen in battle, he sent Bacchides and Alcimus into the land of Judah a second time, and with them the right wing of the army. [2]They went by the road that leads to Gilgal and encamped against Mesaloth in Arbela, and they took it and killed many people. [3]In the first month of the one hundred fifty-second year[d] they encamped against Jerusalem; [4]then they marched off and went to Berea with twenty thousand foot soldiers and two thousand cavalry.

5 Now Judas was encamped in Elasa, and

a Or Kittim b Gk them c Gk they d 160 b.c.

with him were three thousand picked men. [6]When they saw the huge number of the enemy forces, they were greatly frightened, and many slipped away from the camp, until no more than eight hundred of them were left.

7 When Judas saw that his army had slipped away and the battle was imminent, he was crushed in spirit, for he had no time to assemble them. [8]He became faint, but he said to those who were left, "Let us get up and go against our enemies. We may have the strength to fight them." [9]But they tried to dissuade him, saying, "We do not have the strength. Let us rather save our own lives now, and let us come back with our kindred and fight them; we are too few." [10]But Judas said, "Far be it from us to do such a thing as to flee from them. If our time has come, let us die bravely for our kindred, and leave no cause to question our honor."

The Last Battle of Judas

11 Then the army of Bacchides[a] marched out from the camp and took its stand for the encounter. The cavalry was divided into two companies, and the slingers and the archers went ahead of the army, as did all the chief warriors. [12]Bacchides was on the right wing. Flanked by the two companies, the phalanx advanced to the sound of the trumpets; and the men with Judas also blew their trumpets. [13]The earth was shaken by the noise of the armies, and the battle raged from morning until evening.

14 Judas saw that Bacchides and the strength of his army were on the right; then all the stouthearted men went with him, [15]and they crushed the right wing, and he pursued them as far as Mount Azotus. [16]When those on the left wing saw that the right wing was crushed, they turned and followed close behind Judas and his men. [17]The battle became desperate, and many on both sides were wounded and fell. [18]Judas also fell, and the rest fled.

19 Then Jonathan and Simon took their brother Judas and buried him in the tomb of their ancestors at Modein, [20]and wept for him. All Israel made great lamentation for him; they mourned many days and said,

[21] "How is the mighty fallen,
the savior of Israel!"

[22]Now the rest of the acts of Judas, and his wars and the brave deeds that he did, and his greatness, have not been recorded, but they were very many.

Jonathan Succeeds Judas

23 After the death of Judas, the renegades emerged in all parts of Israel; all the wrong-doers reappeared. [24]In those days a very great famine occurred, and the country went over to their side. [25]Bacchides chose the godless and put them in charge of the country. [26]They made inquiry and searched for the friends of Judas, and brought them to Bacchides, who took vengeance on them and made sport of them. [27]So there was great distress in Israel, such as had not been since the time that prophets ceased to appear among them.

28 Then all the friends of Judas assembled and said to Jonathan, [29]"Since the death of your brother Judas there has been no one like him to go against our enemies and Bacchides, and to deal with those of our nation who hate us. [30]Now therefore we have chosen you today to take his place as our ruler and leader, to fight our battle." [31]So Jonathan accepted the leadership at that time in place of his brother Judas.

The Campaigns of Jonathan

32 When Bacchides learned of this, he tried to kill him. [33]But Jonathan and his brother Simon and all who were with him heard of it, and they fled into the wilderness of Tekoa and camped by the water of the pool of Asphar. [34]Bacchides found this out on the sabbath day, and he with all his army crossed the Jordan.

35 So Jonathan[b] sent his brother as leader of the multitude and begged the Nabateans, who were his friends, for permission to store with them the great amount of baggage that they had. [36]But the family of Jambri from Medeba came out and seized John and all that he had, and left with it.

37 After these things it was reported to Jonathan and his brother Simon, "The family of Jambri are celebrating a great wedding, and are conducting the bride, a daughter of one of the great nobles of Canaan, from Nadabath with a large escort." [38]Remembering how their brother John had been killed, they went up and hid under cover of the mountain. [39]They looked out and saw a tumultuous procession with a great amount of baggage; and the bridegroom came out with his friends and his brothers to meet them with tambourines and musicians and many weapons. [40]Then they rushed on them from the ambush and began killing them. Many were wounded and fell, and the rest fled to the mountain; and the Jews[c] took all their goods. [41]So the wedding was turned into mourning and the voice of their musicians into a funeral dirge. [42]After they had fully avenged the blood of their brother, they returned to the marshes of the Jordan.

43 When Bacchides heard of this, he came

---

a Gk lacks of Bacchides b Gk he c Gk they

PSALM 151 DEDICATING A DAY

My desire is to
See your will done not the
Earth's or the sun's

When I go to school
I want to see your work done
And I want to help

At home I want your
Will done and not Satan's will
I want Satan done

In my life I want
Your will to be my will too
I want you, Jesus

I don't want Earth's will
I don't want popularity no,
I just want you, God.

Psalm 151-Dedicating a Day—© Andrena LeBlanc, 17

with a large force on the sabbath day to the banks of the Jordan. ⁴⁴And Jonathan said to those with him, "Let us get up now and fight for our lives, for today things are not as they were before. ⁴⁵For look! the battle is in front of us and behind us; the water of the Jordan is on this side and on that, with marsh and thicket; there is no place to turn. ⁴⁶Cry out now to Heaven that you may be delivered from the hands of our enemies." ⁴⁷So the battle began, and Jonathan stretched out his hand to strike Bacchides, but he eluded him and went to the rear. ⁴⁸Then Jonathan and the men with him leaped into the Jordan and swam across to the other side, and the enemy*a* did not cross the Jordan to attack them. ⁴⁹And about one thousand of Bacchides' men fell that day.

Bacchides Builds Fortifications

50 Then Bacchides*b* returned to Jerusalem and built strong cities in Judea: the fortress in Jericho, and Emmaus, and Beth-horon, and Bethel, and Timnath, and*c* Pharathon, and Tephon, with high walls and gates and bars. ⁵¹And he placed garrisons in them to harass Israel. ⁵²He also fortified the town of Beth-zur, and Gazara, and the citadel, and in them he put troops and stores of food. ⁵³And he took the sons of the leading men of the land as hostages and put them under guard in the citadel at Jerusalem.

54 In the one hundred and fifty-third year,*d* in the second month, Alcimus gave orders to tear down the wall of the inner court of the sanctuary. He tore down the work of the prophets! ⁵⁵But he only began to tear it down, for at that time Alcimus was stricken and his work was hindered; his mouth was stopped and he was paralyzed, so that he could no longer say a word or give commands concerning his house. ⁵⁶And Alcimus died at that time in great agony. ⁵⁷When Bacchides saw that Alcimus was dead, he returned to the king, and the land of Judah had rest for two years.

The End of the War

58 Then all the lawless plotted and said, "See! Jonathan and his men are living in quiet and confidence. So now let us bring Bacchides back, and he will capture them all in one night." ⁵⁹And they went and consulted with him. ⁶⁰He started to come with a large force, and secretly sent letters to all his allies in Judea, telling them to seize Jonathan and his men; but they were unable to do it, because their plan became known. ⁶¹And Jonathan's men*a* seized about fifty of the men of the country who were leaders in this treachery, and killed them.

62 Then Jonathan with his men, and Simon, withdrew to Bethbasi in the wilderness; he rebuilt the parts of it that had been demolished, and they fortified it. ⁶³When Bacchides learned of this, he assembled all his forces, and sent orders to the men of Judea. ⁶⁴Then he came and encamped against Bethbasi; he fought against it for many days and made machines of war.

65 But Jonathan left his brother Simon in the town, while he went out into the country; and he went with only a few men. ⁶⁶He struck down Odomera and his kindred and the people of Phasiron in their tents. ⁶⁷Then he*e* began to attack and went into battle with his forces; and Simon and his men sallied out from the town and set fire to the machines of war. ⁶⁸They fought with Bacchides, and he was crushed by them. They pressed him very hard, for his plan and his expedition had been in vain. ⁶⁹So he was very angry at the renegades who had counseled him to come into the country, and he killed many of them. Then he decided to go back to his own land.

70 When Jonathan learned of this, he sent ambassadors to him to make peace with him and obtain release of the captives. ⁷¹He agreed, and did as he said; and he swore to Jonathan*f* that he would not try to harm him as long as he lived. ⁷²He restored to him the captives whom he had taken previously from the land of Judah; then he turned and went back to his own land, and did not come again into their territory. ⁷³Thus the sword ceased from Israel. Jonathan settled in Michmash and began to judge the people; and he destroyed the godless out of Israel.

10 Revolt of Alexander Epiphanes

In the one hundred sixtieth year*g* Alexander Epiphanes, son of Antiochus, landed and occupied Ptolemais. They welcomed him, and there he began to reign. ²When King Demetrius heard of it, he assembled a very large army and marched out to meet him in battle. ³Demetrius sent Jonathan a letter in peaceable words to honor him; ⁴for he said to himself, "Let us act first to make peace with him*h* before he makes peace with Alexander against us, ⁵for he will remember all the wrongs that we did to him and to his brothers and his nation." ⁶So Demetrius*b* gave him authority to recruit troops, to equip them with arms, and to become his ally; and he commanded that the hostages in the citadel should be released to him.

7 Then Jonathan came to Jerusalem and read the letter in the hearing of all the people and of those in the citadel. ⁸They were greatly

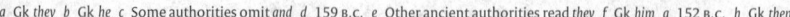

a Gk they *b* Gk he *c* Some authorities omit *and* *d* 159 B.C. *e* Other ancient authorities read *they* *f* Gk *him* *g* 152 B.C. *h* Gk *them*

alarmed when they heard that the king had given him authority to recruit troops. ⁹But those in the citadel released the hostages to Jonathan, and he returned them to their parents.

10 And Jonathan took up residence in Jerusalem and began to rebuild and restore the city. ¹¹He directed those who were doing the work to build the walls and encircle Mount Zion with squared stones, for better fortification; and they did so.

12 Then the foreigners who were in the strongholds that Bacchides had built fled; ¹³all of them left their places and went back to their own lands. ¹⁴Only in Beth-zur did some remain who had forsaken the law and the commandments, for it served as a place of refuge.

15 Now King Alexander heard of all the promises that Demetrius had sent to Jonathan, and he heard of the battles that Jonathanᵍ and his brothers had fought, of the brave deeds that they had done, and of the troubles that they had endured. ¹⁶So he said, "Shall we find another such man? Come now, we will make him our friend and ally." ¹⁷And he wrote a letter and sent it to him, in the following words:

Jonathan Becomes High Priest

18 "King Alexander to his brother Jonathan, greetings. ¹⁹We have heard about you, that you are a mighty warrior and worthy to be our friend. ²⁰And so we have appointed you today to be the high priest of your nation; you are to be called the king's Friend and you are to take our side and keep friendship with us." He also sent him a purple robe and a golden crown.

21 So Jonathan put on the sacred vestments in the seventh month of the one hundred sixtieth year,ᵇ at the festival of booths,ᶜ and he recruited troops and equipped them with arms in abundance. ²²When Demetrius heard of these things he was distressed and said, ²³"What is this that we have done? Alexander has gotten ahead of us in forming a friendship with the Jews to strengthen himself. ²⁴I also will write them words of encouragement and promise them honor and gifts, so that I may have their help." ²⁵So he sent a message to them in the following words:

A Letter from Demetrius to Jonathan

"King Demetrius to the nation of the Jews, greetings. ²⁶Since you have kept your agreement with us and have continued your friendship with us, and have not sided with our enemies, we have heard of it and rejoiced. ²⁷Now continue still to keep faith with us, and we will repay you with good for what you do for us. ²⁸We will grant you many immunities and give you gifts.

29 "I now free you and exempt all the Jews from payment of tribute and salt tax and crown levies, ³⁰and instead of collecting the third of the grain and the half of the fruit of the trees that I should receive, I release them from this day and henceforth. I will not collect them from the land of Judah or from the three districts added to it from Samaria and Galilee, from this day and for all time. ³¹Jerusalem and its environs, its tithes and its revenues, shall be holy and free from tax. ³²I release also my control of the citadel in Jerusalem and give it to the high priest, so that he may station in it men of his own choice to guard it. ³³And everyone of the Jews taken as a captive from the land of Judah into any part of my kingdom, I set free without payment; and let all officials cancel also the taxes on their livestock.

34 "All the festivals and sabbaths and new moons and appointed days, and the three days before a festival and the three after a festival—let them all be days of immunity and release for all the Jews who are in my kingdom. ³⁵No one shall have authority to exact anything from them or annoy any of them about any matter.

36 "Let Jews be enrolled in the king's forces to the number of thirty thousand men, and let the maintenance be given them that is due to all the forces of the king. ³⁷Let some of them be stationed in the great strongholds of the king, and let some of them be put in positions of trust in the kingdom. Let their officers and leaders be of their own number, and let them live by their own laws, just as the king has commanded in the land of Judah.

38 "As for the three districts that have been added to Judea from the country of Samaria, let them be annexed to Judea so that they may be considered to be under one ruler and obey no other authority than the high priest. ³⁹Ptolemais and the land adjoining it I have given as a gift to the sanctuary in Jerusalem, to

> The opposite of love is not hate, it's indifference.
> The opposite of art is not ugliness, it's indifference.
> The opposite of faith is not heresy, it's indifference.
> And the opposite of life is not death, it's indifference.
>
> —**Elie Wiesel, Nobel laureate and Holocaust survivor**

a Gk he b 152 B.C. c Or tabernacles

meet the necessary expenses of the sanctuary. [40]I also grant fifteen thousand shekels of silver yearly out of the king's revenues from appropriate places. [41]And all the additional funds that the government officials have not paid as they did in the first years,[a] they shall give from now on for the service of the temple.[b] [42]Moreover, the five thousand shekels of silver that my officials[c] have received every year from the income of the services of the temple, this too is canceled, because it belongs to the priests who minister there. [43]And all who take refuge at the temple in Jerusalem, or in any of its precincts, because they owe money to the king or are in debt, let them be released and receive back all their property in my kingdom.

[44] "Let the cost of rebuilding and restoring the structures of the sanctuary be paid from the revenues of the king. [45]And let the cost of rebuilding the walls of Jerusalem and fortifying it all around, and the cost of rebuilding the walls in Judea, also be paid from the revenues of the king."

Death of Demetrius

46 When Jonathan and the people heard these words, they did not believe or accept them, because they remembered the great wrongs that Demetrius[d] had done in Israel and how much he had oppressed them. [47]They favored Alexander, because he had been the first to speak peaceable words to them, and they remained his allies all his days.

[48] Now King Alexander assembled large forces and encamped opposite Demetrius. [49]The two kings met in battle, and the army of Demetrius fled, and Alexander[e] pursued him and defeated them. [50]He pressed the battle strongly until the sun set, and on that day Demetrius fell.

Treaty of Ptolemy and Alexander

51 Then Alexander sent ambassadors to Ptolemy king of Egypt with the following message:

a Meaning of Gk uncertain b Gk *house* c Gk *they* d Gk *he* e Other ancient authorities read *Alexander fled, and Demetrius*

52"Since I have returned to my kingdom and have taken my seat on the throne of my ancestors, and established my rule—for I crushed Demetrius and gained control of our country; 53I met him in battle, and he and his army were crushed by us, and we have taken our seat on the throne of his kingdom— 54now therefore let us establish friendship with one another; give me now your daughter as my wife, and I will become your son-in-law, and will make gifts to you and to her in keeping with your position."

55 Ptolemy the king replied and said, "Happy was the day on which you returned to the land of your ancestors and took your seat on the throne of their kingdom. 56And now I will do for you as you wrote, but meet me at Ptolemais, so that we may see one another, and I will become your father-in-law, as you have said."

57 So Ptolemy set out from Egypt, he and his daughter Cleopatra, and came to Ptolemais in the one hundred sixty-second year.[a] 58King Alexander met him, and Ptolemy[b] gave him his daughter Cleopatra in marriage, and celebrated her wedding at Ptolemais with great pomp, as kings do.

59 Then King Alexander wrote to Jonathan to come and meet him. 60So he went with pomp to Ptolemais and met the two kings; he gave them and their Friends silver and gold and many gifts, and found favor with them. 61A group of malcontents from Israel, renegades, gathered together against him to accuse him; but the king paid no attention to them. 62The king gave orders to take off Jonathan's garments and to clothe him in purple, and they did so. 63The king also seated him at his side; and he said to his officers, "Go out with him into the middle of the city and proclaim that no one is to bring charges against him about any matter, and let no one annoy him for any reason." 64When his accusers saw the honor that was paid him, in accord with the proclamation, and saw him clothed in purple, they all fled. 65Thus the king honored him and enrolled him among his chief[c] Friends, and made him general and governor of the province. 66And Jonathan returned to Jerusalem in peace and gladness.

Apollonius Is Defeated by Jonathan

67 In the one hundred sixty-fifth year[d] Demetrius son of Demetrius came from Crete to the land of his ancestors. 68When King Alexander heard of it, he was greatly distressed and returned to Antioch. 69And Demetrius appointed Apollonius the governor of Coelesyria, and he assembled a large force and encamped against Jamnia. Then he sent the following message to the high priest Jonathan:

70 "You are the only one to rise up against us, and I have fallen into ridicule and disgrace because of you. Why do you assume authority against us in the hill country? 71If you now have confidence in your forces, come down to the plain to meet us, and let us match strength with each other there, for I have with me the power of the cities. 72Ask and learn who I am and who the others are that are helping us. People will tell you that you cannot stand before us, for your ancestors were twice put to flight in their own land. 73And now you will not be able to withstand my cavalry and such an army in the plain, where there is no stone or pebble, or place to flee."

74 When Jonathan heard the words of Apollonius, his spirit was aroused. He chose ten thousand men and set out from Jerusalem, and his brother Simon met him to help him. 75He encamped before Joppa, but the people of the city closed its gates, for Apollonius had a garrison in Joppa. 76So they fought against it, and the people of the city became afraid and opened the gates, and Jonathan gained possession of Joppa.

77 When Apollonius heard of it, he mustered three thousand cavalry and a large army, and went to Azotus as though he were going farther. At the same time he advanced into the plain, for he had a large troop of cavalry and put confidence in it. 78Jonathan[b] pursued him to Azotus, and the armies engaged in battle. 79Now Apollonius had secretly left a thousand cavalry behind them. 80Jonathan learned that there was an ambush behind him, for they surrounded his army and shot arrows at his men from early morning until late afternoon. 81But his men stood fast, as Jonathan had commanded, and the enemy's[e] horses grew tired.

82 Then Simon brought forward his force and engaged the phalanx in battle (for the cavalry was exhausted); they were overwhelmed by him and fled, 83and the cavalry was dispersed in the plain. They fled to Azotus and entered Beth-dagon, the temple of their idol, for safety. 84But Jonathan burned Azotus and the surrounding towns and plundered them; and the temple of Dagon, and those who had taken refuge in it, he burned with fire. 85The number of those who fell by the sword, with those burned alive, came to eight thousand.

86 Then Jonathan left there and encamp-

a 150 B.C. b Gk he c Gk first d 147 B.C. e Gk their

ed against Askalon, and the people of the city came out to meet him with great pomp.

87 He and those with him then returned to Jerusalem with a large amount of booty. ⁸⁸When King Alexander heard of these things, he honored Jonathan still more; ⁸⁹and he sent to him a golden buckle, such as it is the custom to give to the King's Kinsmen. He also gave him Ekron and all its environs as his possession.

11 Ptolemy Invades Syria

Then the king of Egypt gathered great forces, like the sand by the seashore, and many ships; and he tried to get possession of Alexander's kingdom by trickery and add it to his own kingdom. ²He set out for Syria with peaceable words, and the people of the towns opened their gates to him and went to meet him, for King Alexander had commanded them to meet him, since he was Alexander's*g* father-in-law. ³But when Ptolemy entered the towns he stationed forces as a garrison in each town.

4 When he*b* approached Azotus, they showed him the burnt-out temple of Dagon, and Azotus and its suburbs destroyed, and the corpses lying about, and the charred bodies of those whom Jonathan*c* had burned in the war, for they had piled them in heaps along his route. ⁵They also told the king what Jonathan had done, to throw blame on him; but the king kept silent. ⁶Jonathan met the king at Joppa with pomp, and they greeted one another and spent the night there. ⁷And Jonathan went with the king as far as the river called Eleutherus; then he returned to Jerusalem.

8 So King Ptolemy gained control of the coastal cities as far as Seleucia by the sea, and he kept devising wicked designs against Alexander. ⁹He sent envoys to King Demetrius, saying, "Come, let us make a covenant with each other, and I will give you in marriage my daughter who was Alexander's wife, and you shall reign over your father's kingdom. ¹⁰I now regret that I gave him my daughter, for he has tried to kill me." ¹¹He threw blame on Alexander*d* because he coveted his kingdom. ¹²So he took his daughter away from him and gave her to Demetrius. He was estranged from Alexander, and their enmity became manifest.

13 Then Ptolemy entered Antioch and put on the crown of Asia. Thus he put two crowns on his head, the crown of Egypt and that of Asia. ¹⁴Now King Alexander was in Cilicia at that time, because the people of that region were in revolt. ¹⁵When Alexander heard of it, he came against him in battle. Ptolemy marched out and met him with a strong force, and put him to flight. ¹⁶So Alexander fled into Arabia to find protection there, and King Ptolemy was triumphant. ¹⁷Zabdiel the Arab cut off the head of Alexander and sent it to Ptolemy. ¹⁸But King Ptolemy died three days later, and his troops in the strongholds were killed by the inhabitants of the strongholds. ¹⁹So Demetrius became king in the one hundred sixty-seventh year.*e*

Jonathan's Diplomacy

20 In those days Jonathan assembled the Judeans to attack the citadel in Jerusalem, and he built many engines of war to use against it. ²¹But certain renegades who hated their nation went to the king and reported to him that Jonathan was besieging the citadel. ²²When he heard this he was angry, and as soon as he heard it he set out and came to Ptolemais; and he wrote Jonathan not to continue the siege, but to meet him for a conference at Ptolemais as quickly as possible.

23 When Jonathan heard this, he gave orders to continue the siege. He chose some of the elders of Israel and some of the priests, and put himself in danger, ²⁴for he went to the king at Ptolemais, taking silver and gold and clothing and numerous other gifts. And he won his favor. ²⁵Although certain renegades of his nation kept making complaints against him, ²⁶the king treated him as his predecessors had treated him; he exalted him in the presence of all his Friends. ²⁷He confirmed him in the high priesthood and in as many other honors as he had formerly had, and caused him to be reckoned among his chief*f* Friends. ²⁸Then Jonathan asked the king to free Judea and the three districts of Samaria*g* from tribute, and promised him three hundred talents. ²⁹The

a Gk *his*   *b* Other ancient authorities read *they*   *c* Gk *he*   *d* Gk *him*   *e* 145 B.C.   *f* Gk *first*   *g* Cn: Gk *the three districts and Samaria* king consented, and wrote a letter to Jonathan about all these things; its contents were as follows:

30 "King Demetrius to his brother Jonathan and to the nation of the Jews, greetings. [31] This copy of the letter that we wrote concerning you to our kinsman Lasthenes we have written to you also, so that you may know what it says. [32] 'King Demetrius to his father Lasthenes, greetings. [33] We have determined to do good to the nation of the Jews, who are our friends and fulfill their obligations to us, because of the goodwill they show toward us. [34] We have confirmed as their possession both the territory of Judea and the three districts of Aphairema and Lydda and Rathamin; the latter, with all the region bordering them, were added to Judea from Samaria. To all those who offer sacrifice in Jerusalem we have granted release from[a] the royal taxes that the king formerly received from them each year, from the crops of the land and the fruit of the trees. [35] And the other payments henceforth due to us of the tithes, and the taxes due to us, and the salt pits and the crown taxes due to us—from all these we shall grant them release. [36] And not one of these grants shall be canceled from this time on forever. [37] Now therefore take care to make a copy of this, and let it be given to Jonathan and put up in a conspicuous place on the holy mountain.' "

The Intrigue of Trypho

38 When King Demetrius saw that the land was quiet before him and that there was no opposition to him, he dismissed all his troops, all of them to their own homes, except the foreign troops that he had recruited from the islands of the nations. So all the troops who had served under his predecessors hated him. [39] A certain Trypho had formerly been one of Alexander's supporters; he saw that all the troops were grumbling against Demetrius. So he went to Imalkue the Arab, who was bringing up Antiochus, the young son of Alexander, [40] and insistently urged him to hand Antiochus[b] over to him, to become king in place of his father. He also reported to Imalkue[b] what Demetrius had done and told of the hatred that the troops of Demetrius[c] had for him; and he stayed there many days.

41 Now Jonathan sent to King Demetrius the request that he remove the troops of the citadel from Jerusalem, and the troops in the strongholds; for they kept fighting against Israel. [42] And Demetrius sent this message back to Jonathan: "Not only will I do these things for you and your nation, but I will confer great honor on you and your nation, if I find an opportunity. [43] Now then you will do well to send me men who will help me, for all my troops have revolted." [44] So Jonathan sent three thousand stalwart men to him at Antioch, and when they came to the king, the king rejoiced at their arrival.

45 Then the people of the city assembled within the city, to the number of a hundred and twenty thousand, and they wanted to kill the king. [46] But the king fled into the palace. Then the people of the city seized the main streets of the city and began to fight. [47] So the king called the Jews to his aid, and they all rallied around him and then spread out through the city; and they killed on that day about one hundred thousand. [48] They set fire to the city and seized a large amount of spoil on that day, and saved the king. [49] When the people of the city saw that the Jews had gained control of the city as they pleased, their courage failed and they cried out to the king with this entreaty: [50] "Grant us peace, and make the Jews stop fighting against us and our city." [51] And they threw down their arms and made peace. So the Jews gained glory in the sight of the king and of all the people in his kingdom, and they returned to Jerusalem with a large amount of spoil.

52 So King Demetrius sat on the throne of his kingdom, and the land was quiet before him. [53] But he broke his word about all that he had promised; he became estranged from Jonathan and did not repay the favors that Jonathan[d] had done him, but treated him very harshly.

Trypho Seizes Power

54 After this Trypho returned, and with him the young boy Antiochus who began to reign and put on the crown. [55] All the troops that Demetrius had discharged gathered around him; they fought against Demetrius,[b] and he fled and was routed. [56] Trypho captured the elephants[e] and gained control of Antioch. [57] Then the young Antiochus wrote to Jonathan, saying, "I confirm you in the high priesthood and set you over the four districts and make you one of the king's Friends." [58] He also sent him gold plates and a table service, and granted him the right to drink from gold cups and dress in purple and wear a gold buckle. [59] He appointed Jonathan's[f] brother Simon governor from the Ladder of Tyre to the borders of Egypt.

a Or Samaria, for all those who offer sacrifice in Jerusalem, in place of b Gk him c Gk his troops d Gk he e Gk animals f Gk his

Campaigns of Jonathan and Simon

60 Then Jonathan set out and traveled beyond the river and among the towns, and all the army of Syria gathered to him as allies. When he came to Askalon, the people of the city met him and paid him honor. [61]From there he went to Gaza, but the people of Gaza shut him out. So he besieged it and burned its suburbs with fire and plundered them. [62]Then the people of Gaza pleaded with Jonathan, and he made peace with them, and took the sons of their rulers as hostages and sent them to Jerusalem. And he passed through the country as far as Damascus.

63 Then Jonathan heard that the officers of Demetrius had come to Kadesh in Galilee with a large army, intending to remove him from office. [64]He went to meet them, but left his brother Simon in the country. [65]Simon encamped before Beth-zur and fought against it for many days and hemmed it in. [66]Then they asked him to grant them terms of peace, and he did so. He removed them from there, took possession of the town, and set a garrison over it.

67 Jonathan and his army encamped by the waters of Gennesaret. Early in the morning they marched to the plain of Hazor, [68]and there in the plain the army of the foreigners met him; they had set an ambush against him in the mountains, but they themselves met him face to face. [69]Then the men in ambush emerged from their places and joined battle. [70]All the men with Jonathan fled; not one of them was left except Mattathias son of Absalom and Judas son of Chalphi, commanders of the forces of the army. [71]Jonathan tore his clothes, put dust on his head, and prayed. [72]Then he turned back to the battle against the enemy[a] and routed them, and they fled. [73]When his men who were fleeing saw this, they returned to him and joined him in the pursuit as far as Kadesh, to their camp, and there they encamped. [74]As many as three thousand of the foreigners fell that day. And Jonathan returned to Jerusalem.

12 Alliances with Rome and Sparta

Now when Jonathan saw that the time was favorable for him, he chose men and sent them to Rome to confirm and renew the friendship with them. [2]He also sent letters to the same effect to the Spartans and to other places. [3]So they went to Rome and entered the senate chamber and said, "The high priest Jonathan and the Jewish nation have sent us to renew the former friendship and alliance with them." [4]And the Romans[b] gave them letters to the people in every place, asking them to provide for the envoys[a] safe conduct to the land of Judah.

5 This is a copy of the letter that Jonathan wrote to the Spartans: [6]"The high priest Jonathan, the senate of the nation, the priests, and the rest of the Jewish people to their brothers the Spartans, greetings. [7]Already in time past a letter was sent to the high priest Onias from Arius,[c] who was king among you, stating that you are our brothers, as the appended copy shows. [8]Onias welcomed the envoy with honor, and received the letter, which contained a clear declaration of alliance and friendship. [9]Therefore, though we have no need of these things, since we have as encouragement the holy books that are in our hands, [10]we have undertaken to send to renew our family ties and friendship with you, so that we may not become estranged from you, for considerable time has passed since you sent your letter to us. [11]We therefore remember you constantly on every occasion, both at our festivals and on other appropriate days, at the sacrifices that we offer and in our prayers, as it is right and proper to remember brothers. [12]And we rejoice in your glory. [13]But as for ourselves, many trials and many wars have encircled us; the kings around us have waged war against us. [14]We were unwilling to annoy you and our other allies and friends with these wars, [15]for we have the help that comes from Heaven for our aid, and so we were delivered from our enemies, and our enemies were humbled. [16]We therefore have chosen Numenius son of Antiochus and Antipater son of Jason, and have sent them to Rome to renew our former friendship and alliance with them. [17]We have commanded

a Gk them b Gk they c Vg Compare verse 20: Gk Darius

them to go also to you and greet you and deliver to you this letter from us concerning the renewal of our family ties. [18]And now please send us a reply to this."

19 This is a copy of the letter that they sent to Onias: [20]"King Arius of the Spartans, to the high priest Onias, greetings. [21]It has been found in writing concerning the Spartans and the Jews that they are brothers and are of the family of Abraham. [22]And now that we have learned this, please write us concerning your welfare; [23]we on our part write to you that your livestock and your property belong to us, and ours belong to you. We therefore command that our envoys[a] report to you accordingly."

Further Campaigns of Jonathan and Simon

24 Now Jonathan heard that the commanders of Demetrius had returned, with a larger force than before, to wage war against him. [25]So he marched away from Jerusalem and met them in the region of Hamath, for he gave them no opportunity to invade his own country. [26]He sent spies to their camp, and they returned and reported to him that the enemy[a] were being drawn up in formation to attack the Jews[b] by night. [27]So when the sun had set, Jonathan commanded his troops to be alert and to keep their arms at hand so as to be ready all night for battle, and he stationed outposts around the camp. [28]When the enemy heard that Jonathan and his troops were prepared for battle, they were afraid and were terrified at heart; so they kindled fires in their camp and withdrew.[c] [29]But Jonathan and his troops did not know it until morning, for they saw the fires burning. [30]Then Jonathan pursued them, but he did not overtake them, for they had crossed the Eleutherus river. [31]So Jonathan turned aside against the Arabs who are called Zabadeans, and he crushed them and plundered them. [32]Then he broke camp and went to Damascus, and marched through all that region.

33 Simon also went out and marched through the country as far as Askalon and the neighboring strongholds. He turned aside to Joppa and took it by surprise, [34]for he had heard that they were ready to hand over the stronghold to those whom Demetrius had sent. And he stationed a garrison there to guard it.

35 When Jonathan returned he convened the elders of the people and planned with them to build strongholds in Judea, [36]to build the walls of Jerusalem still higher, and to erect a high barrier between the citadel and the city to separate it from the city, in order to isolate it so that its garrison[a] could neither buy nor sell. [37]So they gathered together to rebuild the city; part of the wall on the valley to the east had fallen, and he repaired the section called Chaphenatha. [38]Simon also built Adida in the Shephelah; he fortified it and installed gates with bolts.

Trypho Captures Jonathan

39 Then Trypho attempted to become king in Asia and put on the crown, and to raise his hand against King Antiochus. [40]He feared that Jonathan might not permit him to do so, but might make war on him, so he kept seeking to seize and kill him, and he marched out and came to Beth-shan. [41]Jonathan went out to meet him with forty thousand picked warriors, and he came to Beth-shan. [42]When Trypho saw that he had come with a large army, he was afraid to raise his hand against him. [43]So he received him with honor and commended him to all his Friends, and he gave him gifts and commanded his Friends and his troops to obey him as they would himself. [44]Then he said to Jonathan, "Why have you put all these people to so much trouble when we are not at war? [45]Dismiss them now to their homes and choose for yourself a few men to stay with you, and come with me to Ptolemais. I will hand it over to you as well as the other strongholds and the remaining troops and all the officials, and will turn around and go home. For that is why I am here."

46 Jonathan[d] trusted him and did as he said; he sent away the troops, and they returned to the land of Judah. [47]He kept with himself three thousand men, two thousand of whom he left in Galilee, while one thousand accompanied him. [48]But when Jonathan entered Ptolemais, the people of Ptolemais closed the gates and seized him, and they killed with the sword all who had entered with him.

49 Then Trypho sent troops and cavalry into Galilee and the Great Plain to destroy all Jonathan's soldiers. [50]But they realized that Jonathan had been seized and had perished along with his men, and they encouraged one another and kept marching in close formation, ready for battle. [51]When their pursuers saw that they would fight for their lives, they turned back. [52]So they all reached the land of Judah safely, and they mourned for Jonathan and his companions and were in great fear; and all Israel mourned deeply. [53]All the nations around them tried to destroy them, for they said, "They have no leader or helper. Now therefore let us

---

a Gk they   b Gk them   c Other ancient authorities omit *and withdrew*   d Gk he

A Wrong (Right) Turn—Amid the chill and brilliance of a Russian autumn in 1908, Sergius Bulgakov was seeking a change in his young life. Bulgakov, a professor of political economy and a rising star on the Marxist intellectual scene, found himself inexplicably drawn back to the faith of the six generations of Russian Orthodox priests in his family. And yet while on a retreat with a friend at a country hermitage, he was unable to experience anything but deadening formality in the prayers of the religious people around him—a reminder of the grim services that he endured before his doubts drove him from the seminary.

Stumbling out of the church service with his mind in a cloud, Bulgakov thought he was returning to the guesthouse, but instead found himself at the home of the wise and revered elder of the hermitage, a holy man similar to Father Zossima in Dostoevsky's novel *The Brothers Karamazov*. It was in a conversation with this wise man that the avowed atheist's change finally came.

Bulgakov would continue down his new path, even though it drove him from his university post and later into exile in Paris. There he began a school with fellow exiles and was later to become one of the greatest Christian thinkers of the twentieth century. Regarding his conversion, he said:

Water Droplets—© Christy Klink, 18

"I heard from the elder that all human sin was like a drop of water in comparison with the ocean of divine love. I left him, pardoned and reconciled, trembling and in tears, feeling myself returned as on wings within the precincts of the Church."

---

make war on them and blot out the memory of them from humankind."

13 Simon Takes Command

Simon heard that Trypho had assembled a large army to invade the land of Judah and destroy it, ²and he saw that the people were trembling with fear. So he went up to Jerusalem, and gathering the people together ³he encouraged them, saying to them, "You yourselves know what great things my brothers and I and the house of my father have done for the laws and the sanctuary; you know also the wars and the difficulties that my brothers and I have seen. ⁴By reason of this all my brothers have perished for the sake of Israel, and I alone am left. ⁵And now, far be it from me to spare my life in any time of distress, for I am not better than my brothers. ⁶But I will avenge my nation and the sanctuary and your wives and children, for all the nations have gathered together out of hatred to destroy us."

7 The spirit of the people was rekindled when they heard these words, ⁸and they answered in a loud voice, "You are our leader in place of Judas and your brother Jonathan. ⁹Fight our battles, and all that you say to us we will do." ¹⁰So he assembled all the warriors and hurried to complete the walls of Jerusalem, and he fortified it on every side. ¹¹He sent Jonathan son of Absalom to Joppa, and with him a considerable army; he drove out its occupants and remained there.

Deceit and Treachery of Trypho

12 Then Trypho left Ptolemais with a large army to invade the land of Judah, and Jonathan was with him under guard. [13]Simon encamped in Adida, facing the plain. [14]Trypho learned that Simon had risen up in place of his brother Jonathan, and that he was about to join battle with him, so he sent envoys to him and said, [15]"It is for the money that your brother Jonathan owed the royal treasury, in connection with the offices he held, that we are detaining him. [16]Send now one hundred talents of silver and two of his sons as hostages, so that when released he will not revolt against us, and we will release him."

17 Simon knew that they were speaking deceitfully to him, but he sent to get the money and the sons, so that he would not arouse great hostility among the people, who might say, [18]"It was because Simon[a] did not send him the money and the sons, that Jonathan[b] perished." [19]So he sent the sons and the hundred talents, but Trypho[b] broke his word and did not release Jonathan.

20 After this Trypho came to invade the country and destroy it, and he circled around by the way to Adora. But Simon and his army kept marching along opposite him to every place he went. [21]Now the men in the citadel kept sending envoys to Trypho urging him to come to them by way of the wilderness and to send them food. [22]So Trypho got all his cavalry ready to go, but that night a very heavy snow fell, and he did not go because of the snow. He marched off and went into the land of Gilead. [23]When he approached Baskama, he killed Jonathan, and he was buried there. [24]Then Trypho turned and went back to his own land.

Jonathan's Tomb

25 Simon sent and took the bones of his brother Jonathan, and buried him in Modein, the city of his ancestors. [26]All Israel bewailed him with great lamentation, and mourned for him many days. [27]And Simon built a monument over the tomb of his father and his brothers; he made it high so that it might be seen, with polished stone at the front and back. [28]He also erected seven pyramids, opposite one another, for his father and mother and four brothers. [29]For the pyramids[c] he devised an elaborate setting, erecting about them great columns, and on the columns he put suits of armor for a permanent memorial, and beside the suits of armor he carved ships, so that they could be seen by all who sail the sea. [30]This is the tomb that he built in Modein; it remains to this day.

Judea Gains Independence

31 Trypho dealt treacherously with the young King Antiochus; he killed him [32]and became king in his place, putting on the crown of Asia; and he brought great calamity on the land. [33]But Simon built up the strongholds of Judea and walled them all around, with high towers and great walls and gates and bolts, and he stored food in the strongholds. [34]Simon also chose emissaries and sent them to King Demetrius with a request to grant relief to the country, for all that Trypho did was to plunder. [35]King Demetrius sent him a favorable reply to this request, and wrote him a letter as follows, [36]"King Demetrius to Simon, the high priest and friend of kings, and to the elders and nation of the Jews, greetings. [37]We have received the gold crown and the palm branch that you[d] sent, and we are ready to make a general peace with you and to write to our officials to grant you release from tribute. [38]All the grants that we have made to you remain valid, and let the strongholds that you have built be your possession. [39]We pardon any errors and offenses committed to this day, and cancel the crown tax that you owe; and whatever other tax has been collected in Jerusalem shall be collected no longer. [40]And if any of you are qualified to be enrolled in our bodyguard,[e] let them be enrolled, and let there be peace between us."

41 In the one hundred seventieth year[f] the yoke of the Gentiles was removed from Israel, [42]and the people began to write in their documents and contracts, "In the first year of Simon the great high priest and commander and leader of the Jews."

The Capture of Gazara by Simon

43 In those days Simon[b] encamped against Gazara[g] and surrounded it with troops. He made a siege engine, brought it up to the city, and battered and captured one tower. [44]The men in the siege engine leaped out into the city, and a great tumult arose in the city. [45]The men in the city, with their wives and children, went up on the wall with their clothes torn, and they cried out with a loud voice, asking Simon to make peace with them; [46]they said, "Do not treat us according to our wicked acts but according to your mercy." [47]So Simon reached an agreement with them and stopped fighting against them. But he expelled them from the city and cleansed the houses in which the idols were located, and then entered it with hymns

---

a Gk I b Gk he c Gk For these d The word you in verses 37–40 is plural e Or court f 142 B.C. g Cn: Gk Gaza and praise. [48]He removed all uncleanness from it, and settled in it those who observed the law. He also strengthened its fortifications and built in it a house for himself.

Simon Regains the Citadel at Jerusalem

49 Those who were in the citadel at Jerusalem were prevented from going in and out to buy and sell in the country. So they were very hungry, and many of them perished from famine. [50]Then they cried to Simon to make peace with them, and he did so. But he expelled them from there and cleansed the citadel from its pollutions. [51]On the twenty-third day of the second month, in the one hundred seventy-first year,[a] the Jews[b] entered it with praise and palm branches, and with harps and cymbals and stringed instruments, and with hymns and songs, because a great enemy had been crushed and removed from Israel. [52]Simon[c] decreed that every year they should celebrate this day with rejoicing. He strengthened the fortifications of the temple hill alongside the citadel, and he and his men lived there. [53]Simon saw that his son John had reached manhood, and so he made him commander of all the forces; and he lived at Gazara.

14 Capture of Demetrius

In the one hundred seventy-second year[d] King Demetrius assembled his forces and marched into Media to obtain help, so that he could make war against Trypho. [2]When King Arsaces of Persia and Media heard that Demetrius had invaded his territory, he sent one of his generals to take him alive. [3]The general[c] went and defeated the army of Demetrius, and seized him and took him to Arsaces, who put him under guard.

Eulogy of Simon

[4] The land[e] had rest all the days of Simon.
　　He sought the good of his nation;
　　his rule was pleasing to them,
　　　　as was the honor shown him, all his days.
[5] To crown all his honors he took Joppa for a harbor,
　　and opened a way to the isles of the sea.
[6] He extended the borders of his nation,
　　and gained full control of the country.
[7] He gathered a host of captives;
　　he ruled over Gazara and Beth-zur and
　　　　the citadel,
　　and he removed its uncleanness from it;
　　and there was none to oppose him.
[8] They tilled their land in peace;
　　the ground gave its increase,

and the trees of the plains their fruit.
[9] Old men sat in the streets;
　　they all talked together of good things,
　　and the youths put on splendid military attire.
[10] He supplied the towns with food,
　　and furnished them with the means of defense,
　　until his renown spread to the ends of the earth.
[11] He established peace in the land,
　　and Israel rejoiced with great joy.
[12] All the people sat under their own vines and fig trees,
　　and there was none to make them afraid.
[13] No one was left in the land to fight them,
　　and the kings were crushed in those days.
[14] He gave help to all the humble among his people;
　　he sought out the law,
　　and did away with all the renegades and outlaws.
[15] He made the sanctuary glorious,
　　and added to the vessels of the sanctuary.

Diplomacy with Rome and Sparta

16 It was heard in Rome, and as far away as Sparta, that Jonathan had died, and they were deeply grieved. [17]When they heard that his brother Simon had become high priest in his stead, and that he was ruling over the country and the towns in it, [18]they wrote to him on bronze tablets to renew with him the friendship and alliance that they had established with his brothers Judas and Jonathan. [19]And these were read before the assembly in Jerusalem.

20 This is a copy of the letter that the Spartans sent:

"The rulers and the city of the Spartans to the high priest Simon and to the elders and the priests and the rest of the Jewish people, our brothers, greetings. [21]The envoys who were sent to our people have told us about your glory and honor, and we rejoiced at their coming. [22]We have recorded what they said in our public decrees, as follows, 'Numenius son of Antiochus and Antipater son of Jason, envoys of the Jews, have come to us to renew their friendship with us. [23]It has pleased our people to receive these men with honor and to put a copy of their words in the public archives, so that the people of the Spartans may have a record of them. And they have sent a copy of this to the high priest Simon.' "

24 After this Simon sent Numenius to Rome with a large gold shield weighing one

a 141 B.C.　b Gk they　c Gk He　d 140 B.C.　e Other ancient authorities add of Judah thousand minas, to confirm the alliance with the Romans.[a]

Official Honors for Simon

25 When the people heard these things they said, "How shall we thank Simon and his sons? [26]For he and his brothers and the house of his father have stood firm; they have fought and repulsed Israel's enemies and established its freedom." [27]So they made a record on bronze tablets and put it on pillars on Mount Zion.

This is a copy of what they wrote: "On the eighteenth day of Elul, in the one hundred seventy-second year,[b] which is the third year of the great high priest Simon, [28]in Asaramel,[c] in the great assembly of the priests and the people and the rulers of the nation and the elders of the country, the following was proclaimed to us:

29 "Since wars often occurred in the country, Simon son of Mattathias, a priest of the sons[d] of Joarib, and his brothers, exposed themselves to danger and resisted the enemies of their nation, in order that their sanctuary and the law might be preserved; and they brought great glory to their nation. [30]Jonathan rallied the[e] nation, became their high priest, and was gathered to his people. [31]When their enemies decided to invade their country and lay hands on their sanctuary, [32]then Simon rose up and fought for his nation. He spent great sums of his own money; he armed the soldiers of his nation and paid them wages. [33]He fortified the towns of Judea, and Beth-zur on the borders of Judea, where formerly the arms of the enemy had been stored, and he placed there a garrison of Jews. [34]He also fortified Joppa, which is by the sea, and Gazara, which is on the borders of Azotus, where the enemy formerly lived. He settled Jews there, and provided in those towns[a] whatever was necessary for their restoration.

35 "The people saw Simon's faithfulness[f] and the glory that he had resolved to win for his nation, and they made him their leader and high priest, because he had done all these things and because of the justice and loyalty that he had maintained toward his nation. He sought in every way to exalt his people. [36]In his days things prospered in his hands, so that the Gentiles were put out of the[e] country, as were also those in the city of David in Jerusalem, who had built themselves a citadel from which they used to sally forth and defile the environs of the sanctuary, doing great damage to its purity. [37]He settled Jews in it and fortified it

Streets—© Clay Goswick, 16

for the safety of the country and of the city, and built the walls of Jerusalem higher.

38 "In view of these things King Demetrius confirmed him in the high priesthood, [39]made him one of his Friends, and paid him high honors. [40]For he had heard that the Jews were addressed by the Romans as friends and allies and brothers, and that the Romans[g] had received the envoys of Simon with honor.

41 "The Jews and their priests have resolved that Simon should be their leader and high priest forever, until a trustworthy prophet should arise, [42]and that he should be governor over them and that he should take charge of the sanctuary and appoint officials over its tasks and over the country and the weapons and the strongholds, and that he should take charge of the sanctuary, [43]and that he should be obeyed by all, and that all contracts in the country should be written in his name, and that he should be clothed in purple and wear gold.

44 "None of the people or priests shall be permitted to nullify any of these decisions or to oppose what he says, or to convene an assembly in the country without his permission, or to be clothed in purple or put on a gold buckle. [45]Whoever acts contrary to these decisions or rejects any of them shall be liable to punishment."

46 All the people agreed to grant Simon the right to act in accordance with these decisions. [47]So Simon accepted and agreed to be

a Gk them b 140 B.C. c This word resembles the Hebrew words for *the court of the people of God* or *the prince of the people of God* d Meaning of Gk uncertain e Gk *their* f Other ancient authorities read *conduct* g Gk *they* high priest, to be commander and ethnarch of the Jews and priests, and to be protector of them all.[a] [48]And they gave orders to inscribe this decree on bronze tablets, to put them up in a conspicuous place in the precincts of the sanctuary, [49]and to deposit copies of them in the treasury, so that Simon and his sons might have them.

15 Letter of Antiochus VII

Antiochus, son of King Demetrius, sent a letter from the islands of the sea to Simon, the priest and ethnarch of the Jews, and to all the nation; [2]its contents were as follows: "King Antiochus to Simon the high priest and ethnarch and to the nation of the Jews, greetings. [3]Whereas certain scoundrels have gained control of the kingdom of our ancestors, and I intend to lay claim to the kingdom so that I may restore it as it formerly was, and have recruited a host of mercenary troops and have equipped warships, [4]and intend to make a landing in the country so that I may proceed against those who have destroyed our country and those who have devastated many cities in my kingdom, [5]now therefore I confirm to you all the tax remissions that the kings before me have granted you, and a release from all the other payments from which they have released you. [6]I permit you to mint your own coinage as money for your country, [7]and I grant freedom to Jerusalem and the sanctuary. All the weapons that you have prepared and the strongholds that you have built and now hold shall remain yours. [8]Every debt you owe to the royal treasury and any such future debts shall be canceled for you from henceforth and for all time. [9]When we gain control of our kingdom, we will bestow great honor on you and your nation and the temple, so that your glory will become manifest in all the earth."

[10] In the one hundred seventy-fourth year[b] Antiochus set out and invaded the land of his ancestors. All the troops rallied to him, so that there were only a few with Trypho. [11]Antiochus pursued him, and Trypho[c] came in his flight to Dor, which is by the sea; [12]for he knew that troubles had converged on him, and his troops had deserted him. [13]So Antiochus encamped against Dor, and with him were one hundred twenty thousand warriors and eight thousand cavalry. [14]He surrounded the town, and the ships joined battle from the sea; he pressed the town hard from land and sea, and permitted no one to leave or enter it.

Rome Supports the Jews

15 Then Numenius and his companions arrived from Rome, with letters to the kings and countries, in which the following was written: [16]"Lucius, consul of the Romans, to King Ptolemy, greetings. [17]The envoys of the Jews have come to us as our friends and allies to renew our ancient friendship and alliance. They had been sent by the high priest Simon and by the Jewish people [18]and have brought a gold shield weighing one thousand minas. [19]We therefore have decided to write to the kings and countries that they should not seek their harm or make war against them and their cities and their country, or make alliance with those who war against them. [20]And it has seemed good to us to accept the shield from them. [21]Therefore if any scoundrels have fled to you from their country, hand them over to the high priest Simon, so that he may punish them according to their law."

[22] The consul[d] wrote the same thing to King Demetrius and to Attalus and Ariarathes and Arsaces, [23]and to all the countries, and to Sampsames,[e] and to the Spartans, and to Delos, and to Myndos, and to Sicyon, and to Caria, and to Samos, and to Pamphylia, and to Lycia, and to Halicarnassus, and to Rhodes, and to Phaselis, and to Cos, and to Side, and to Aradus and Gortyna and Cnidus and Cyprus and Cyrene. [24]They also sent a copy of these things to the high priest Simon.

Antiochus VII Threatens Simon

25 King Antiochus besieged Dor for the second time, continually throwing his forces against it and making engines of war; and he shut Trypho up and kept him from going out or in. [26]And Simon sent to Antiochus[f] two thousand picked troops, to fight for him, and silver and gold and a large amount of military equipment. [27]But he refused to receive them, and broke all the agreements he formerly had made with Simon, and became estranged from him. [28]He sent to him Athenobius, one of his Friends, to confer with him, saying, "You hold control of Joppa and Gazara and the citadel in Jerusalem; they are cities of my kingdom. [29]You have devastated their territory, you have done great damage in the land, and you have taken possession of many places in my kingdom. [30]Now then, hand over the cities that you have seized and the tribute money of the places that you have conquered outside the borders of Judea; [31]or else pay me five hundred talents of silver for the destruction that you have caused and five hundred talents more for the

---

a Or *to preside over them all* b 138 B.C. c Gk *he* d Gk *He* e The name is uncertain f Gk *him* tribute money of the cities. Otherwise we will come and make war on you."

32 So Athenobius, the king's Friend, came to Jerusalem, and when he saw the splendor of Simon, and the sideboard with its gold and silver plate, and his great magnificence, he was amazed. When he reported to him the king's message, [33]Simon said to him in reply: "We have neither taken foreign land nor seized foreign property, but only the inheritance of our ancestors, which at one time had been unjustly taken by our enemies. [34]Now that we have the opportunity, we are firmly holding the inheritance of our ancestors. [35]As for Joppa and Gazara, which you demand, they were causing great damage among the people and to our land; for them we will give you one hundred talents."

Athenobius[a] did not answer him a word, [36]but returned in wrath to the king and reported to him these words, and also the splendor of Simon and all that he had seen. And the king was very angry.

Victory over Cendebeus

37 Meanwhile Trypho embarked on a ship and escaped to Orthosia. [38]Then the king made Cendebeus commander-in-chief of the coastal country, and gave him troops of infantry and cavalry. [39]He commanded him to encamp against Judea, to build up Kedron and fortify its gates, and to make war on the people; but the king pursued Trypho. [40]So Cendebeus came to Jamnia and began to provoke the people and invade Judea and take the people captive and kill them. [41]He built up Kedron and stationed horsemen and troops there, so that they might go out and make raids along the highways of Judea, as the king had ordered him.

16 John went up from Gazara and reported to his father Simon what Cendebeus had done. [2]And Simon called in his two eldest sons Judas and John, and said to them: "My brothers and I and my father's house have fought the wars of Israel from our youth until this day, and things have prospered in our hands so that we have delivered Israel many times. [3]But now I have grown old, and you by Heaven's[b] mercy are mature in years. Take my place and my brother's, and go out and fight for our nation, and may the help that comes from Heaven be with you."

4 So John[c] chose out of the country twenty thousand warriors and cavalry, and they marched against Cendebeus and camped for the night in Modein. [5]Early in the morning they started out and marched into the plain, where a large force of infantry and cavalry was coming to meet them; and a stream lay between them. [6]Then he and his army lined up against them. He saw that the soldiers were afraid to cross the stream, so he crossed over first; and when his troops saw him, they crossed over af-

a Gk He b Gk his c Other ancient authorities read he

Untitled—© Tony Nappa, 17

ter him. [7]Then he divided the army and placed the cavalry in the center of the infantry, for the cavalry of the enemy were very numerous. [8]They sounded the trumpets, and Cendebeus and his army were put to flight; many of them fell wounded and the rest fled into the stronghold. [9]At that time Judas the brother of John was wounded, but John pursued them until Cendebeus[a] reached Kedron, which he had built. [10]They also fled into the towers that were in the fields of Azotus, and John[a] burned it with fire, and about two thousand of them fell. He then returned to Judea safely.

Murder of Simon and His Sons

11 Now Ptolemy son of Abubus had been appointed governor over the plain of Jericho; he had a large store of silver and gold, [12]for he was son-in-law of the high priest. [13]His heart was lifted up; he determined to get control of the country, and made treacherous plans against Simon and his sons, to do away with them. [14]Now Simon was visiting the towns of the country and attending to their needs, and he went down to Jericho with his sons Mattathias and Judas, in the one hundred seventy-seventh year,[b] in the eleventh month, which is the month of Shebat. [15]The son of Abubus received them treacherously in the little stronghold called Dok, which he had built; he gave them a great banquet, and hid men there. [16]When Simon and his sons were drunk, Ptolemy and his men rose up, took their weapons, rushed in against Simon in the banquet hall and killed him and his two sons, as well as some of his servants. [17]So he committed an act of great treachery and returned evil for good.

John Succeeds Simon

18 Then Ptolemy wrote a report about these things and sent it to the king, asking him to send troops to aid him and to turn over to him the towns and the country. [19]He sent other troops to Gazara to do away with John; he sent letters to the captains asking them to come to him so that he might give them silver and gold and gifts; [20]and he sent other troops to take possession of Jerusalem and the temple hill. [21]But someone ran ahead and reported to John at Gazara that his father and brothers had perished, and that "he has sent men to kill you also." [22]When he heard this, he was greatly shocked; he seized the men who came to destroy him and killed them, for he had found out that they were seeking to destroy him.

23 The rest of the acts of John and his wars and the brave deeds that he did, and the building of the walls that he completed, and his achievements, [24]are written in the annals of his high priesthood, from the time that he became high priest after his father.

a Gk *he* *b* 134 B.C.

2 MACCABEES

GOD'S JUSTICE

Resist or Be Influenced?

Do you remember the last disagreement you had with your parents? What about disagreements with your friends or peers? Have you ever felt like your friends wanted you to do something you really didn't want to do, because you didn't think it was right?

Peer pressure. It's tough to resist sometimes! More often than not, it seems like the dominant leaders in any group do all they can to influence and convince us to do what they want, even if it's not good for us.

There's nothing new about this scenario. A dominant or "conquering" group often attempts to both cajole and impose its ways. This is what was happening during the time of Maccabees. Greek ways and Greek thought were believed by the Greeks, the dominant group of the time, to be the best the world had ever known. Greece expected it would influence the people brought under its control. In Israel, as recorded in both 1 and 2 Maccabees, we hear stories of people who thought otherwise. They saw the Greek influence as a contamination of their faith, their way of life, and their relationship with God.

In Maccabees, the people of faith resisted what they judged as persecution; some acted as witnesses and others were martyrs for their faith—even dying for it. The stories celebrate these witnesses and martyrs, giving hope to those suffering and being persecuted.

Have there been times in your life when you've felt persecuted (or teased or misunderstood) because of your faith? How did you handle it?

"Individual praying is like straw scattered over a field. If you set a straw alight, the flame is small. But if you gather up all the bits of straw, the flame fills out, rising high up in the sky, and it's the same with communal prayer."

—St. John Vianney

WHO Unknown, but sometimes called the "Eupator" (see 2 Maccabees 2.19–32)

WHAT A theological interpretation of the history of the period of Judas Maccabeus with a focus on God's work in the lives of God's people

WHEN Written ca. 100–50 B.C. The events described took place between 180 and 160 B.C.

WHERE Palestine, probably Jerusalem

PATH OF DISCIPLESHIP

There are some amazing stories about people in 2 Maccabees. They would not bend or be influenced. They resisted and were martyred.

Would you die for your beliefs? Seriously—you probably won't have to. But do you feel the constant pull to comply and "go with the flow"? Are you seduced by the culture of consumerism? Think about Catholic social teaching and the preferential option for the poor the next time you want something you don't need. Resist the urge and give the money you would have spent to charity.

What about other influences? Do you have friends who are involved in underage drinking, drugs, gambling, or sexual activity? Are you pressured to join them? Maybe "dying for your beliefs" here means the death of a friendship. Can you do it? Resistance takes faith and courage—a commitment to Jesus and the community of the Church. Praying and participating in the sacraments can help you make that commitment.

1 A Letter to the Jews in Egypt

The Jews in Jerusalem and those in the land of Judea,

To their Jewish kindred in Egypt,

Greetings and true peace.

2 May God do good to you, and may he remember his covenant with Abraham and Isaac and Jacob, his faithful servants. [3]May he give you all a heart to worship him and to do his will with a strong heart and a willing spirit. [4]May he open your heart to his law and his commandments, and may he bring peace. [5]May he hear your prayers and be reconciled to you, and may he not forsake you in time of evil. [6]We are now praying for you here.

7 In the reign of Demetrius, in the one hundred sixty-ninth year,[a] we Jews wrote to you, in the critical distress that came upon us in those years after Jason and his company revolted from the holy land and the kingdom [8]and burned the gate and shed innocent blood. We prayed to the Lord and were heard, and we offered sacrifice and grain offering, and we lit the lamps and set out the loaves. [9]And now see that you keep the festival of booths in the month of Chislev, in the one hundred eighty-eighth year.[b]

A Letter to Aristobulus

10 The people of Jerusalem and of Judea and the senate and Judas,

To Aristobulus, who is of the family of the anointed priests, teacher of King Ptolemy, and to the Jews in Egypt,

Greetings and good health.

11 Having been saved by God out of grave dangers we thank him greatly for taking our side against the king,[c] [12]for he drove out those who fought against the holy city. [13]When the leader reached Persia with a force that seemed irresistible, they were cut to pieces in the temple of Nanea by a deception employed by the priests of the goddess[d] Nanea. [14]On the pretext of intending to marry her, Antiochus came to the place together with his Friends, to secure most of its treasures as a dowry. [15]When the priests of the temple of Nanea had set out the treasures and Antiochus had come with a few men inside the wall of the sacred precinct, they closed the temple as soon as he entered it. [16]Opening a secret door in the ceiling, they threw stones and struck down the leader and his men; they dismembered them and cut off their heads and threw them to the people outside. [17]Blessed in every way be our God, who has brought judgment on those who have behaved impiously.

Fire Consumes Nehemiah's Sacrifice

18 Since on the twenty-fifth day of Chislev we shall celebrate the purification of the temple, we thought it necessary to notify you, in order that you also may celebrate the festival of booths and the festival of the fire given when Nehemiah, who built the temple and the altar, offered sacrifices.

19 For when our ancestors were being led captive to Persia, the pious priests of that time took some of the fire of the altar and secretly hid it in the hollow of a dry cistern, where they took such precautions that the place was unknown to anyone. [20]But after many years had passed, when it pleased God, Nehemiah, having been commissioned by the king of Persia, sent the descendants of the priests who had hidden the fire to get it. And when they reported to us that they had not found fire but only a thick liquid, he ordered them to dip it out and bring it. [21]When the materials for the sacrifices were presented, Nehemiah ordered the priests to sprinkle the liquid on the wood and on the things laid upon it. [22]When this had been done and some time had passed, and when the sun, which had been clouded over, shone out, a great fire blazed up, so that all marveled. [23]And while the sacrifice was being consumed, the priests offered prayer—the priests and everyone. Jonathan led, and the rest responded, as did Nehemiah. [24]The prayer was to this effect:

"O Lord, Lord God, Creator of all things, you are awe-inspiring and strong and just and merciful, you alone are king and are kind, [25]you alone are bountiful, you alone are just and almighty and eternal. You rescue Israel from every evil; you chose the ancestors and consecrated them. [26]Accept this sacrifice on behalf of all your people Israel and preserve your portion and make it holy. [27]Gather together our scattered people, set free those who are slaves among the Gentiles, look on those who are rejected and despised, and let the Gentiles know that you are our God. [28]Punish those who oppress and are insolent with pride. [29]Plant your people in your holy place, as Moses promised."

30 Then the priests sang the hymns. [31]After the materials of the sacrifice had been consumed, Nehemiah ordered that the liquid that was left should be poured on large stones. [32]When this was done, a flame blazed up; but when the light from the altar shone back, it went out. [33]When this matter became known, and it was reported to the king of the Persians that, in the place where the exiled priests had hidden the fire, the liquid had appeared with which Nehemiah and his associates had

---

a 143 B.C. *b* 124 B.C. *c* Cn: Gk *as those who array themselves against a king* *d* Gk lacks *the goddess*

Untitled—© Gabe Anderson, 13

burned the materials of the sacrifice, [34]the king investigated the matter, and enclosed the place and made it sacred. [35]And with those persons whom the king favored he exchanged many excellent gifts. [36]Nehemiah and his associates called this "nephthar," which means purification, but by most people it is called naphtha.[a]

2 Jeremiah Hides the Tent, Ark, and Altar

One finds in the records that the prophet Jeremiah ordered those who were being deported to take some of the fire, as has been mentioned, [2]and that the prophet, after giving them the law, instructed those who were being deported not to forget the commandments of the Lord, or to be led astray in their thoughts on seeing the gold and silver statues and their adornment. [3]And with other similar words he exhorted them that the law should not depart from their hearts.

[4] It was also in the same document that the prophet, having received an oracle, ordered that the tent and the ark should follow with him, and that he went out to the mountain where Moses had gone up and had seen the inheritance of God. [5]Jeremiah came and found a cave-dwelling, and he brought there the tent and the ark and the altar of incense; then he sealed up the entrance. [6]Some of those who followed him came up intending to mark the way, but could not find it. [7]When Jeremiah learned of it, he rebuked them and declared: "The place shall remain unknown until God gathers his people together again and shows his mercy. [8]Then the Lord will disclose these things, and the glory of the Lord and the cloud will appear, as they were shown in the case of Moses, and as Solomon asked that the place should be specially consecrated."

[9] It was also made clear that being possessed of wisdom Solomon[b] offered sacrifice for the dedication and completion of the temple. [10]Just as Moses prayed to the Lord, and fire came down from heaven and consumed the sacrifices, so also Solomon prayed, and the fire came down and consumed the whole burnt offerings. [11]And Moses said, "They were consumed because the sin offering had not been eaten." [12]Likewise Solomon also kept the eight days.

[13] The same things are reported in the records and in the memoirs of Nehemiah, and also that he founded a library and collected the books about the kings and prophets, and the

a Gk nephthai b Gk he

The Compiler's Preface

19 The story of Judas Maccabeus and his brothers, and the purification of the great temple, and the dedication of the altar, 20and further the wars against Antiochus Epiphanes and his son Eupator, 21and the appearances that came from heaven to those who fought bravely for Judaism, so that though few in number they seized the whole land and pursued the barbarian hordes, 22and regained possession of the temple famous throughout the world, and liberated the city, and re-established the laws that were about to be abolished, while the Lord with great kindness became gracious to them— 23all this, which has been set forth by Jason of Cyrene in five volumes, we shall attempt to condense into a single book. 24For considering the flood of statistics involved and the difficulty there is for those who wish to enter upon the narratives of history because of the mass of material, 25we have aimed to please those who wish to read, to make it easy for those who are inclined to memorize, and to profit all readers. 26For us who have undertaken the toil of abbreviating, it is no light matter but calls for sweat and loss of sleep, 27just as it is not easy for one who prepares a banquet and seeks the benefit of others. Nevertheless, to secure the gratitude of many we will gladly endure the uncomfortable toil, 28leaving the responsibility for exact details to the compiler, while devoting our effort to arriving at the outlines of the condensation. 29For as the master builder of a new house must be concerned with the whole construction, while the one who undertakes its painting and decoration has to consider only what is suitable for its adornment, such in my judgment is the case with us. 30It is the duty of the original historian to occupy the ground, to discuss matters from every side, and to take trouble with details, 31but the one who recasts the narrative should be allowed to strive for brevity of expression and to forego exhaustive treatment. 32At this point therefore let us begin our narrative, without adding any more to what has already been said; for it would be foolish to lengthen the preface while cutting short the history itself.

3 Arrival of Heliodorus in Jerusalem

While the holy city was inhabited in unbroken peace and the laws were strictly observed because of the piety of the high priest Onias and his hatred of wickedness, 2it came about that the kings themselves honored the place and glorified the temple with the finest presents, 3even to the extent that King Seleucus of Asia defrayed from his own revenues all the expenses connected with the service of the sacrifices.

writings of David, and letters of kings about votive offerings. 14In the same way Judas also collected all the books that had been lost on account of the war that had come upon us, and they are in our possession. 15So if you have need of them, send people to get them for you.

16 Since, therefore, we are about to celebrate the purification, we write to you. Will you therefore please keep the days? 17It is God who has saved all his people, and has returned the inheritance to all, and the kingship and the priesthood and the consecration, 18as he promised through the law. We have hope in God that he will soon have mercy on us and will gather us from everywhere under heaven into his holy place, for he has rescued us from great evils and has purified the place.

4 But a man named Simon, of the tribe of Benjamin, who had been made captain of the temple, had a disagreement with the high priest about the administration of the city market. 5Since he could not prevail over Onias, he went to Apollonius of Tarsus,*a* who at that time was governor of Coelesyria and Phoenicia, 6and reported to him that the treasury in Jerusalem was full of untold sums of money, so that the amount of the funds could not be reckoned, and that they did not belong to the account of the sacrifices, but that it was possible for them to fall under the control of the king. 7When Apollonius met the king, he told him of the money about which he had been informed. The king*b* chose Heliodorus, who was in charge of his affairs, and sent him with commands to effect the removal of the reported wealth. 8Heliodorus at once set out on his journey, ostensibly to make a tour of inspection of the cities of Coelesyria and Phoenicia, but in fact to carry out the king's purpose.

9 When he had arrived at Jerusalem and had been kindly welcomed by the high priest of*c* the city, he told about the disclosure that had been made and stated why he had come, and he inquired whether this really was the situation. 10The high priest explained that there were some deposits belonging to widows and orphans, 11and also some money of Hyrcanus son of Tobias, a man of very prominent position, and that it totaled in all four hundred talents of silver and two hundred of gold. To such an extent the impious Simon had misrepresented the facts. 12And he said that it was utterly impossible that wrong should be done to those people who had trusted in the holiness of the place and in the sanctity and inviolability of the temple that is honored throughout the whole world.

Heliodorus Plans to Rob the Temple

13 But Heliodorus, because of the orders he had from the king, said that this money must in any case be confiscated for the king's treasury. 14So he set a day and went in to direct the inspection of these funds.

There was no little distress throughout the whole city. 15The priests prostrated themselves before the altar in their priestly vestments and called toward heaven upon him who had given the law about deposits, that he should keep them safe for those who had deposited them. 16To see the appearance of the high priest was to be wounded at heart, for his face and the change in his color disclosed the anguish of his soul. 17For terror and bodily trembling had

come over the man, which plainly showed to those who looked at him the pain lodged in his heart. 18People also hurried out of their houses in crowds to make a general supplication because the holy place was about to be brought into dishonor. 19Women, girded with sackcloth under their breasts, thronged the streets. Some of the young women who were kept indoors ran together to the gates, and some to the walls, while others peered out of the windows. 20And holding up their hands to heaven, they all made supplication. 21There was something pitiable in the prostration of the whole populace and the anxiety of the high priest in his great anguish.

The Lord Protects His Temple

22 While they were calling upon the Almighty Lord that he would keep what had been entrusted safe and secure for those who had entrusted it, 23Heliodorus went on with what had been decided. 24But when he arrived at the treasury with his bodyguard, then and there the Sovereign of spirits and of all authority caused so great a manifestation that all who had been so bold as to accompany him were astounded by the power of God, and became faint with terror. 25For there appeared to them a magnificently caparisoned horse, with a rider of frightening mien; it rushed furiously at Heliodorus and struck at him with its front hoofs. Its rider was seen to have armor and weapons of gold. 26Two young men also appeared to him, remarkably strong, gloriously beautiful and splendidly dressed, who stood on either side of him and flogged him continuously, inflicting many blows on him. 27When he suddenly fell to the ground and deep darkness came over him, his men took him up, put him on a stretcher, 28and carried him away—this man who had just entered the aforesaid treasury with a great retinue and all his bodyguard but was now unable to help himself. They recognized clearly the sovereign power of God.

Onias Prays for Heliodorus

29 While he lay prostrate, speechless because of the divine intervention and deprived of any hope of recovery, 30they praised the Lord who had acted marvelously for his own place. And the temple, which a little while before was full of fear and disturbance, was filled with joy and gladness, now that the Almighty Lord had appeared.

31 Some of Heliodorus's friends quickly begged Onias to call upon the Most High to grant life to one who was lying quite at his last

a Gk *Apollonius son of Tharseas b* Gk *He c* Other ancient authorities read *and*

PROFILE OF FAITH

While other kids played games, little Blaise Pascal figured out complex geometry. By his late teens, this boy genius, who went on to invent the first functional computer, had already earned a place among the intellectuals of Paris. But his life wasn't without problems; Blaise spent much of it in constant physical pain.

Even though he'd been raised a Catholic, Blaise struggled with faith, unable to let it encompass his entire life. But in 1654, when he was thirty years old, he finally discovered in Jesus Christ the love of God who brought "feeling, joy, and peace." During a late-night moment, he had a life-changing encounter with God. He wrote a passionate prayer and personal commitment of faith, then sewed it into the lining of his jacket so that it would always be over his heart.

With a new focus, he began the complex task of helping others understand and embrace faith by writing powerful works that still impact us today. Aware of how short life was, Blaise worked diligently, using his amazing gifts and believing that "the present is the only time that is really ours, and we must use it in accord with God's will."

During the last years of his life, while still in his thirties, disease ravaged his body and pain became a constant presence. Instead of turning inward in despair, Blaise turned outward to help others, visiting the sick in the Paris slums and inviting a homeless family to live with him. Blaise's body was weak, but his heart and mind were united in passion and purpose. He wrote:

"Do small things as if they were great, because of the majesty of Christ, and great things as if they were small and easy, because of his almighty power."

breath. ³²So the high priest, fearing that the king might get the notion that some foul play had been perpetrated by the Jews with regard to Heliodorus, offered sacrifice for the man's recovery. ³³While the high priest was making an atonement, the same young men appeared again to Heliodorus dressed in the same clothing, and they stood and said, "Be very grateful to the high priest Onias, since for his sake the Lord has granted you your life. ³⁴And see that you, who have been flogged by heaven, report to all people the majestic power of God." Having said this they vanished.

The Conversion of Heliodorus

35 Then Heliodorus offered sacrifice to the Lord and made very great vows to the Savior of his life, and having bidden Onias farewell, he marched off with his forces to the king. ³⁶He bore testimony to all concerning the deeds of the supreme God, which he had seen with his own eyes. ³⁷When the king asked Heliodorus what sort of person would be suitable to send on another mission to Jerusalem, he replied, ³⁸"If you have any enemy or plotter against

your government, send him there, for you will get him back thoroughly flogged, if he survives at all; for there is certainly some power of God about the place. ³⁹For he who has his dwelling in heaven watches over that place himself and brings it aid, and he strikes and destroys those who come to do it injury." ⁴⁰This was the outcome of the episode of Heliodorus and the protection of the treasury.

4 Simon Accuses Onias

The previously mentioned Simon, who had informed about the money against[a] his own country, slandered Onias, saying that it was he who had incited Heliodorus and had been the real cause of the misfortune. ²He dared to designate as a plotter against the government the man who was the benefactor of the city, the protector of his compatriots, and a zealot for the laws. ³When his hatred progressed to such a degree that even murders were committed by one of Simon's approved agents, ⁴Onias recognized that the rivalry was serious and that Apollonius son of Menestheus,[b] and governor of Coelesyria and Phoenicia, was intensifying

a Gk and b Vg Compare verse 21: Meaning of Gk uncertain

the malice of Simon. [5]So he appealed to the king, not accusing his compatriots but having in view the welfare, both public and private, of all the people. [6]For he saw that without the king's attention public affairs could not again reach a peaceful settlement, and that Simon would not stop his folly.

Jason's Reforms

7 When Seleucus died and Antiochus, who was called Epiphanes, succeeded to the kingdom, Jason the brother of Onias obtained the high priesthood by corruption, [8]promising the king at an interview[a] three hundred sixty talents of silver, and from another source of revenue eighty talents. [9]In addition to this he promised to pay one hundred fifty more if permission were given to establish by his authority a gymnasium and a body of youth for it, and to enroll the people of Jerusalem as citizens of Antioch. [10]When the king assented and Jason[b] came to office, he at once shifted his compatriots over to the Greek way of life.

11 He set aside the existing royal concessions to the Jews, secured through John the father of Eupolemus, who went on the mission to establish friendship and alliance with the Romans; and he destroyed the lawful ways of living and introduced new customs contrary to the law. [12]He took delight in establishing a gymnasium right under the citadel, and he induced the noblest of the young men to wear the Greek hat. [13]There was such an extreme of Hellenization and increase in the adoption of foreign ways because of the surpassing wickedness of Jason, who was ungodly and no true[c] high priest, [14]that the priests were no longer intent upon their service at the altar. Despising the sanctuary and neglecting the sacrifices, they hurried to take part in the unlawful proceedings in the wrestling arena after the signal for the discus-throwing, [15]disdaining the honors prized by their ancestors and putting the highest value upon Greek forms of prestige. [16]For this reason heavy disaster overtook them, and those whose ways of living they admired and wished to imitate completely became their enemies and punished them. [17]It is no light thing to show irreverence to the divine laws—a fact that later events will make clear.

Jason Introduces Greek Customs

18 When the quadrennial games were being held at Tyre and the king was present, [19]the vile Jason sent envoys, chosen as being Antiochian citizens from Jerusalem, to carry three hundred silver drachmas for the sacrifice to Her-

cules. Those who carried the money, however, thought best not to use it for sacrifice, because that was inappropriate, but to expend it for another purpose. [20]So this money was intended by the sender for the sacrifice to Hercules, but by the decision of its carriers it was applied to the construction of triremes.

21 When Apollonius son of Menestheus was sent to Egypt for the coronation[d] of Philometor as king, Antiochus learned that Philometor[b] had become hostile to his government, and he took measures for his own security. Therefore upon arriving at Joppa he proceeded to Jerusalem. [22]He was welcomed magnificently by Jason and the city, and ushered in with a blaze of torches and with shouts. Then he marched his army into Phoenicia.

Menelaus Becomes High Priest

23 After a period of three years Jason sent Menelaus, the brother of the previously mentioned Simon, to carry the money to the king and to complete the records of essential business. [24]But he, when presented to the king, extolled him with an air of authority, and secured the high priesthood for himself, outbidding Jason by three hundred talents of silver. [25]After receiving the king's orders he returned, possessing no qualification for the high priesthood, but having the hot temper of a cruel tyrant and the rage of a savage wild beast. [26]So Jason, who after supplanting his own brother was supplanted by another man, was driven as a fugitive into the land of Ammon. [27]Although Menelaus continued to hold the office, he did not pay regularly any of the money promised to the king. [28]When Sostratus the captain of the citadel kept requesting payment—for the collection of the revenue was his responsibility—the two of them were summoned by the king on account of this issue. [29]Menelaus left his own brother Lysimachus as deputy in the high priesthood, while Sostratus left Crates, the commander of the Cyprian troops.

> "As a person of faith, of resurrection faith, I see death as a friend, not a foe; and the experience of death is, I am convinced, a transition from life to life, from grace to glory."
>
> —Joseph Cardinal Bernardin, from a speech at Georgetown University, September 9, 1996

a Or by a petition   b Gk he   c Gk lacks true   d Meaning of Gk uncertain

The Murder of Onias

30 While such was the state of affairs, it happened that the people of Tarsus and of Mallus revolted because their cities had been given as a present to Antiochis, the king's concubine. [31] So the king went hurriedly to settle the trouble, leaving Andronicus, a man of high rank, to act as his deputy. [32] But Menelaus, thinking he had obtained a suitable opportunity, stole some of the gold vessels of the temple and gave them to Andronicus; other vessels, as it happened, he had sold to Tyre and the neighboring cities. [33] When Onias became fully aware of these acts, he publicly exposed them, having first withdrawn to a place of sanctuary at Daphne near Antioch. [34] Therefore Menelaus, taking Andronicus aside, urged him to kill Onias. Andronicus[a] came to Onias, and resorting to treachery, offered him sworn pledges and gave him his right hand; he persuaded him, though still suspicious, to come out from the place of sanctuary; then, with no regard for justice, he immediately put him out of the way.

Andronicus Is Punished

35 For this reason not only Jews, but many also of other nations, were grieved and displeased at the unjust murder of the man. [36] When the king returned from the region of Cilicia, the Jews in the city[b] appealed to him with regard to the unreasonable murder of Onias, and the Greeks shared their hatred of the crime. [37] Therefore Antiochus was grieved at heart and filled with pity, and wept because of the moderation and good conduct of the deceased. [38] Inflamed with anger, he immediately stripped off the purple robe from Andronicus, tore off his clothes, and led him around the whole city to that very place where he had committed the outrage against Onias, and there he dispatched the bloodthirsty fellow. The Lord thus repaid him with the punishment he deserved.

Unpopularity of Lysimachus and Menelaus

39 When many acts of sacrilege had been committed in the city by Lysimachus with the connivance of Menelaus, and when report of them had spread abroad, the populace gathered against Lysimachus, because many of the gold vessels had already been stolen. [40] Since the crowds were becoming aroused and filled with anger, Lysimachus armed about three thousand men and launched an unjust attack, under the leadership of a certain Auranus, a man advanced in years and no less advanced

a Gk He b Or in each city

in folly. [41]But when the Jews[a] became aware that Lysimachus was attacking them, some picked up stones, some blocks of wood, and others took handfuls of the ashes that were lying around, and threw them in wild confusion at Lysimachus and his men. [42]As a result, they wounded many of them, and killed some, and put all the rest to flight; the temple robber himself they killed close by the treasury.

43 Charges were brought against Menelaus about this incident. [44]When the king came to Tyre, three men sent by the senate presented the case before him. [45]But Menelaus, already as good as beaten, promised a substantial bribe to Ptolemy son of Dorymenes to win over the king. [46]Therefore Ptolemy, taking the king aside into a colonnade as if for refreshment, induced the king to change his mind. [47]Menelaus, the cause of all the trouble, he acquitted of the charges against him, while he sentenced to death those unfortunate men, who would have been freed uncondemned if they had pleaded even before Scythians. [48]And so those who had spoken for the city and the villages[b] and the holy vessels quickly suffered the unjust penalty. [49]Therefore even the Tyrians, showing their hatred of the crime, provided magnificently for their funeral. [50]But Menelaus, because of the greed of those in power, remained in office, growing in wickedness, having become the chief plotter against his compatriots.

5 Jason Tries to Regain Control

About this time Antiochus made his second invasion of Egypt. [2]And it happened that, for almost forty days, there appeared over all the city golden-clad cavalry charging through the air, in companies fully armed with lances and drawn swords— [3]troops of cavalry drawn up, attacks and counterattacks made on this side and on that, brandishing of shields, massing of spears, hurling of missiles, the flash of golden trappings, and armor of all kinds. [4]Therefore everyone prayed that the apparition might prove to have been a good omen.

5 When a false rumor arose that Antiochus was dead, Jason took no fewer than a thousand men and suddenly made an assault on the city. When the troops on the wall had been forced back and at last the city was being taken, Menelaus took refuge in the citadel. [6]But Jason kept relentlessly slaughtering his compatriots, not realizing that success at the cost of one's kindred is the greatest misfortune, but imagining that he was setting up trophies of victory over enemies and not over compatriots. [7]He did not, however, gain control of the government;

in the end he got only disgrace from his conspiracy, and fled again into the country of the Ammonites. [8]Finally he met a miserable end. Accused[c] before Aretas the ruler of the Arabs, fleeing from city to city, pursued by everyone, hated as a rebel against the laws, and abhorred as the executioner of his country and his compatriots, he was cast ashore in Egypt. [9]There he who had driven many from their own country into exile died in exile, having embarked to go to the Lacedaemonians in hope of finding protection because of their kinship. [10]He who had cast out many to lie unburied had no one to mourn for him; he had no funeral of any sort and no place in the tomb of his ancestors.

11 When news of what had happened reached the king, he took it to mean that Judea was in revolt. So, raging inwardly, he left Egypt and took the city by storm. [12]He commanded his soldiers to cut down relentlessly everyone they met and to kill those who went into their houses. [13]Then there was massacre of young and old, destruction of boys, women, and children, and slaughter of young girls and infants. [14]Within the total of three days eighty thousand were destroyed, forty thousand in hand-to-hand fighting, and as many were sold into slavery as were killed.

Pillage of the Temple

15 Not content with this, Antiochus[d] dared to enter the most holy temple in all the world, guided by Menelaus, who had become a traitor both to the laws and to his country. [16]He took the holy vessels with his polluted hands, and swept away with profane hands the votive offerings that other kings had made to enhance the glory and honor of the place. [17]Antiochus was elated in spirit, and did not perceive that the Lord was angered for a little while because of the sins of those who lived in the city, and that this was the reason he was disregarding the holy place. [18]But if it had not happened that they were involved in many sins, this man would have been flogged and turned back from his rash act as soon as he came forward, just as Heliodorus had been, whom King Seleucus sent to inspect the treasury. [19]But the Lord did not choose the nation for the sake of the holy place, but the place for the sake of the nation. [20]Therefore the place itself shared in the misfortunes that befell the nation and afterward participated in its benefits; and what was forsaken in the wrath of the Almighty was restored again in all its glory when the great Lord became reconciled.

21 So Antiochus carried off eighteen hun-

---

a Gk they   b Other ancient authorities read the people   c Cn: Gk Imprisoned   d Gk he

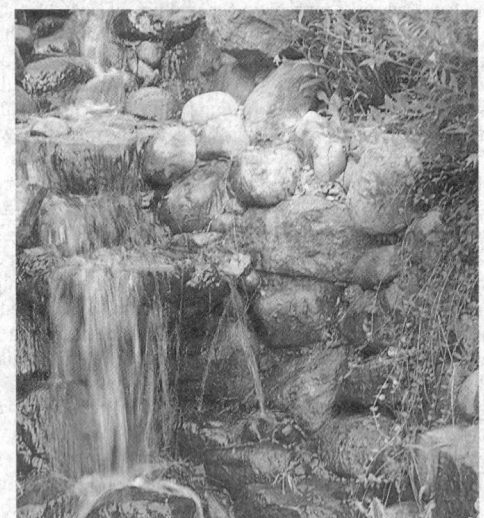

dred talents from the temple, and hurried away to Antioch, thinking in his arrogance that he could sail on the land and walk on the sea, because his mind was elated. [22]He left governors to oppress the people: at Jerusalem, Philip, by birth a Phrygian and in character more barbarous than the man who appointed him; [23]and at Gerizim, Andronicus; and besides these Menelaus, who lorded it over his compatriots worse than the others did. In his malice toward the Jewish citizens,[a] [24]Antiochus[b] sent Apollonius, the captain of the Mysians, with an army of twenty-two thousand, and commanded him to kill all the grown men and to sell the women and boys as slaves. [25]When this man arrived in Jerusalem, he pretended to be peaceably disposed and waited until the holy sabbath day; then, finding the Jews not at work, he ordered his troops to parade under arms. [26]He put to the sword all those who came out to see them, then rushed into the city with his armed warriors and killed great numbers of people.

27 But Judas Maccabeus, with about nine others, got away to the wilderness, and kept himself and his companions alive in the mountains as wild animals do; they continued to live on what grew wild, so that they might not share in the defilement.

6 The Suppression of Judaism

Not long after this, the king sent an Athenian[c] senator[d] to compel the Jews to forsake the laws of their ancestors and no longer to live by the laws of God; [2]also to pollute the temple in Je-

rusalem and to call it the temple of Olympian Zeus, and to call the one in Gerizim the temple of Zeus-the-Friend-of-Strangers, as did the people who lived in that place.

3 Harsh and utterly grievous was the onslaught of evil. [4]For the temple was filled with debauchery and reveling by the Gentiles, who dallied with prostitutes and had intercourse with women within the sacred precincts, and besides brought in things for sacrifice that were unfit. [5]The altar was covered with abominable offerings that were forbidden by the laws. [6]People could neither keep the sabbath, nor observe the festivals of their ancestors, nor so much as confess themselves to be Jews.

7 On the monthly celebration of the king's birthday, the Jews[e] were taken, under bitter constraint, to partake of the sacrifices; and when a festival of Dionysus was celebrated, they were compelled to wear wreaths of ivy and to walk in the procession in honor of Dionysus. [8]At the suggestion of the people of Ptolemais[f] a decree was issued to the neighboring Greek cities that they should adopt the same policy toward the Jews and make them partake of the sacrifices, [9]and should kill those who did not choose to change over to Greek customs. One could see, therefore, the misery that had come upon them. [10]For example, two women were brought in for having circumcised their children. They publicly paraded them around the city, with their babies hanging at their breasts, and then hurled them down headlong from the wall. [11]Others who had assembled in the

caves nearby, in order to observe the seventh day secretly, were betrayed to Philip and were all burned together, because their piety kept them from defending themselves, in view of their regard for that most holy day.

Providential Significance of the Persecution

12 Now I urge those who read this book not to be depressed by such calamities, but to recognize that these punishments were designed not to destroy but to discipline our people. [13]In fact, it is a sign of great kindness not to let the impious alone for long, but to punish them immediately. [14]For in the case of the other nations the Lord waits patiently to punish them until they have reached the full measure of their sins; but he does not deal in this way with us, [15]in order that he may not take vengeance on us afterward when our sins have reached their height. [16]Therefore he never withdraws his mercy from us. Although he disciplines us with calamities, he does not forsake his own people. [17]Let what we have said serve as a reminder; we must go on briefly with the story.

The Martyrdom of Eleazar

18 Eleazar, one of the scribes in high position, a man now advanced in age and of noble presence, was being forced to open his mouth to eat swine's flesh. [19]But he, welcoming death with honor rather than life with pollution, went up to the rack of his own accord, spitting out the flesh, [20]as all ought to go who have the courage to refuse things that it is not right to taste, even for the natural love of life.

21 Those who were in charge of that unlawful sacrifice took the man aside because of their long acquaintance with him, and privately urged him to bring meat of his own providing, proper for him to use, and to pretend that he was eating the flesh of the sacrificial meal that had been commanded by the king, [22]so that by doing this he might be saved from death, and be treated kindly on account of his old friendship with them. [23]But making a high resolve, worthy of his years and the dignity of his old age and the gray hairs that he had reached with distinction and his excellent life even from childhood, and moreover according to the holy God-given law, he declared himself quickly, telling them to send him to Hades. [24]"Such pretense is not worthy of our time of life," he said, "for many of the young might suppose that Eleazar in his ninetieth year had gone over to an alien religion, [25]and through my pretense, for the sake of living a brief moment longer, they would be led astray because of me, while I defile and disgrace my old age. [26]Even if for the present I would avoid the punishment of mortals, yet whether I live or die I will not escape the hands of the Almighty. [27]Therefore, by bravely giving up my life now, I will show myself worthy of my old age [28]and leave to the young a noble example of how to die a good death willingly and nobly for the revered and holy laws."

When he had said this, he went[a] at once to the rack. [29]Those who a little before had acted toward him with goodwill now changed to ill will, because the words he had uttered were in their opinion sheer madness.[b] [30]When he was about to die under the blows, he groaned aloud and said: "It is clear to the Lord in his holy knowledge that, though I might have been saved from death, I am enduring terrible sufferings in my body under this beating, but in my soul I am glad to suffer these things because I fear him."

31 So in this way he died, leaving in his death an example of nobility and a memorial of courage, not only to the young but to the great body of his nation.

7 The Martyrdom of Seven Brothers

It happened also that seven brothers and their mother were arrested and were being compelled by the king, under torture with whips and thongs, to partake of unlawful swine's flesh. [2]One of them, acting as their spokesman, said, "What do you intend to ask and learn from us? For we are ready to die rather than transgress the laws of our ancestors."

3 The king fell into a rage, and gave orders to have pans and caldrons heated. [4]These were heated immediately, and he commanded that the tongue of their spokesman be cut out and that they scalp him and cut off his hands and feet, while the rest of the brothers and the mother looked on. [5]When he was utterly helpless, the king[c] ordered them to take him to the fire, still breathing, and to fry him in a pan. The smoke from the pan spread widely, but the brothers[d] and their mother encouraged one another to die nobly, saying, [6]"The Lord God is watching over us and in truth has compassion on us, as Moses declared in his song that bore witness against the people to their faces, when he said, 'And he will have compassion on his servants.' "[e]

7 After the first brother had died in this way, they brought forward the second for their sport. They tore off the skin of his head with the hair, and asked him, "Will you eat rather

a Other ancient authorities read *was dragged* *b* Meaning of Gk uncertain *c* Gk *he* *d* Gk *they* *e* Gk *slaves*

PROFILE OF FAITH

St. Thomas More was a martyr for his faith. He would not compromise or be influenced by power. Thomas was born in London in 1478, long before King Henry VIII took power and broke away from the Catholic Church.

Thomas studied law at Oxford University, began a legal career, and later was elected to Parliament. A married man with four children, Thomas had a circle of friends that included bishops and scholars and became famous for his book *Utopia*.

Thomas was appointed by King Henry VIII to a succession of high posts and missions, including the position of Lord Chancellor in 1529. However, he resigned in 1532, at the height of his career and reputation, when Henry persisted in holding his own opinions regarding marriage and the supremacy of the pope, which went against Thomas's Roman Catholic beliefs. He spent the rest of his life writing mostly in defense of the Church. In 1534, with his close friend John Fisher, he refused to give allegiance to the king as the head of the Church of England and was confined to the Tower. Fifteen months later he was tried and convicted of treason. He told the judges that he could not go against his conscience. On the scaffold, he told the spectators that he was dying as "the king's good servant, but God's first." He was beheaded on July 6, 1535. St. Thomas More's feast day is June 22.

---

than have your body punished limb by limb?" [8]He replied in the language of his ancestors and said to them, "No." Therefore he in turn underwent tortures as the first brother had done. [9]And when he was at his last breath, he said, "You accursed wretch, you dismiss us from this present life, but the King of the universe will raise us up to an everlasting renewal of life, because we have died for his laws."

10 After him, the third was the victim of their sport. When it was demanded, he quickly put out his tongue and courageously stretched forth his hands, [11]and said nobly, "I got these from Heaven, and because of his laws I disdain them, and from him I hope to get them back again." [12]As a result the king himself and those with him were astonished at the young man's spirit, for he regarded his sufferings as nothing.

13 After he too had died, they maltreated and tortured the fourth in the same way. [14]When he was near death, he said, "One cannot but choose to die at the hands of mortals and to cherish the hope God gives of being raised again by him. But for you there will be no resurrection to life!"

15 Next they brought forward the fifth and maltreated him. [16]But he looked at the king,[a] and said, "Because you have authority among mortals, though you also are mortal, you do

what you please. But do not think that God has forsaken our people. [17]Keep on, and see how his mighty power will torture you and your descendants!"

18 After him they brought forward the sixth. And when he was about to die, he said, "Do not deceive yourself in vain. For we are suffering these things on our own account, because of our sins against our own God. Therefore[b] astounding things have happened. [19]But do not think that you will go unpunished for having tried to fight against God!"

20 The mother was especially admirable and worthy of honorable memory. Although she saw her seven sons perish within a single day, she bore it with good courage because of her hope in the Lord. [21]She encouraged each of them in the language of their ancestors. Filled with a noble spirit, she reinforced her woman's reasoning with a man's courage, and said to them, [22]"I do not know how you came into being in my womb. It was not I who gave you life and breath, nor I who set in order the elements within each of you. [23]Therefore the Creator of the world, who shaped the beginning of humankind and devised the origin of all things, will in his mercy give life and breath back to you again, since you now forget yourselves for the sake of his laws."

24 Antiochus felt that he was being treated

a Gk *at him* *b* Lat: Other ancient authorities lack *Therefore* with contempt, and he was suspicious of her reproachful tone. The youngest brother being still alive, Antiochus[g] not only appealed to him in words, but promised with oaths that he would make him rich and enviable if he would turn from the ways of his ancestors, and that he would take him for his Friend and entrust him with public affairs. [25]Since the young man would not listen to him at all, the king called the mother to him and urged her to advise the youth to save himself. [26]After much urging on his part, she undertook to persuade her son. [27]But, leaning close to him, she spoke in their native language as follows, deriding the cruel tyrant: "My son, have pity on me. I carried you nine months in my womb, and nursed you for three years, and have reared you and brought you up to this point in your life, and have taken care of you.[b] [28]I beg you, my child, to look at the heaven and the earth and see everything that is in them, and recognize that God did not make them out of things that existed.[c] And in the same way the human race came into being. [29]Do not fear this butcher, but prove worthy of your brothers. Accept death, so that in God's mercy I may get you back again along with your brothers."

30 While she was still speaking, the young man said, "What are you[d] waiting for? I will not obey the king's command, but I obey the command of the law that was given to our ancestors through Moses. [31]But you,[e] who have contrived all sorts of evil against the Hebrews, will certainly not escape the hands of God. [32]For we are suffering because of our own sins. [33]And if our living Lord is angry for a little while, to rebuke and discipline us, he will again be reconciled with his own servants.[f] [34]But you, unholy wretch, you most defiled of all mortals, do not be elated in vain and puffed up by uncertain hopes, when you raise your hand against the children of heaven. [35]You have not yet escaped the judgment of the almighty, all-seeing God. [36]For our brothers after enduring a brief suffering have drunk[g] of ever-flowing life, under God's covenant; but you, by the judgment of God, will receive just punishment for your arrogance. [37]I, like my brothers, give up body and life for the laws of our ancestors, appealing to God to show mercy soon to our nation and by trials and plagues to make you confess that he alone is God, [38]and through me and my brothers to bring to an end the wrath of the Almighty that has justly fallen on our whole nation."

39 The king fell into a rage, and handled him worse than the others, being exasperated at his scorn. [40]So he died in his integrity, putting his whole trust in the Lord.

41 Last of all, the mother died, after her sons.

42 Let this be enough, then, about the eating of sacrifices and the extreme tortures.

8 The Revolt of Judas Maccabeus

Meanwhile Judas, who was also called Maccabeus, and his companions secretly entered the villages and summoned their kindred and enlisted those who had continued in the Jewish faith, and so they gathered about six thousand. [2]They implored the Lord to look upon the people who were oppressed by all; and to have pity on the temple that had been profaned by the godless; [3]to have mercy on the city that was being destroyed and about to be leveled to the ground; to hearken to the blood that cried out to him; [4]to remember also the lawless destruction of the innocent babies and the blasphemies committed against his name; and to show his hatred of evil.

5 As soon as Maccabeus got his army organized, the Gentiles could not withstand him, for the wrath of the Lord had turned to mercy. [6]Coming without warning, he would set fire to towns and villages. He captured strategic positions and put to flight not a few of the enemy. [7]He found the nights most advantageous for such attacks. And talk of his valor spread everywhere.

8 When Philip saw that the man was gaining ground little by little, and that he was pushing

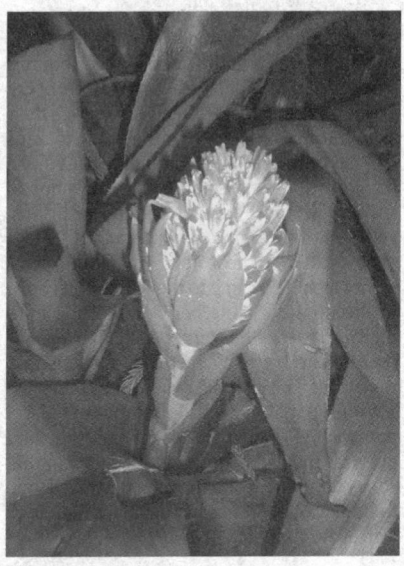

Bloom—© Rose K., 17

a Gk he b Or have borne the burden of your education c Or God made them out of things that did not exist d The Gk here for you is plural e The Gk here for you is singular f Gk slaves g Cn: Gk fallen ahead with more frequent successes, he wrote to Ptolemy, the governor of Coelesyria and Phoenicia, to come to the aid of the king's government. [9]Then Ptolemy[a] promptly appointed Nicanor son of Patroclus, one of the king's chief[b] Friends, and sent him, in command of no fewer than twenty thousand Gentiles of all nations, to wipe out the whole race of Judea. He associated with him Gorgias, a general and a man of experience in military service. [10]Nicanor determined to make up for the king the tribute due to the Romans, two thousand talents, by selling the captured Jews into slavery. [11]So he immediately sent to the towns on the seacoast, inviting them to buy Jewish slaves and promising to hand over ninety slaves for a talent, not expecting the judgment from the Almighty that was about to overtake him.

Preparation for Battle

12 Word came to Judas concerning Nicanor's invasion; and when he told his companions of the arrival of the army, [13]those who were cowardly and distrustful of God's justice ran off and got away. [14]Others sold all their remaining property, and at the same time implored the Lord to rescue those who had been sold by the ungodly Nicanor before he ever met them, [15]if not for their own sake, then for the sake of the covenants made with their ancestors, and because he had called them by his holy and glorious name. [16]But Maccabeus gathered his forces together, to the number six thousand, and exhorted them not to be frightened by the enemy and not to fear the great multitude of Gentiles who were wickedly coming against them, but to fight nobly, [17]keeping before their eyes the lawless outrage that the Gentiles[c] had committed against the holy place, and the torture of the derided city, and besides, the overthrow of their ancestral way of life. [18]"For they trust to arms and acts of daring," he said, "but we trust in the Almighty God, who is able with a single nod to strike down those who are coming against us, and even, if necessary, the whole world."

19 Moreover, he told them of the occasions when help came to their ancestors; how, in the time of Sennacherib, when one hundred eighty-five thousand perished, [20]and the time of the battle against the Galatians that took place in Babylonia, when eight thousand Jews[d] fought along with four thousand Macedonians; yet when the Macedonians were hard pressed, the eight thousand, by the help that came to them from heaven, destroyed one hundred twenty thousand Galatians[e] and took a great amount of booty.

Judas Defeats Nicanor

21 With these words he filled them with courage and made them ready to die for their laws and their country; then he divided his army into four parts. [22]He appointed his brothers also, Simon and Joseph and Jonathan, each to command a division, putting fifteen hundred men under each. [23]Besides, he appointed Eleazar to read aloud[f] from the holy book, and gave the watchword, "The help of God"; then, leading the first division himself, he joined battle with Nicanor.

24 With the Almighty as their ally, they killed more than nine thousand of the enemy, and wounded and disabled most of Nicanor's army, and forced them all to flee. [25]They captured the money of those who had come to buy them as slaves. After pursuing them for some distance, they were obliged to return because the hour was late. [26]It was the day before the sabbath, and for that reason they did not continue their pursuit. [27]When they had collected the arms of the enemy and stripped them of their spoils, they kept the sabbath, giving great praise and thanks to the Lord, who had preserved them for that day and allotted it to them as the beginning of mercy. [28]After the sabbath they gave some of the spoils to those who had been tortured and to the widows and orphans, and distributed the rest among themselves and their children. [29]When they had done this, they made common supplication and implored the merciful Lord to be wholly reconciled with his servants.[g]

Judas Defeats Timothy and Bacchides

30 In encounters with the forces of Timothy and Bacchides they killed more than twenty thousand of them and got possession of some exceedingly high strongholds, and they divided a very large amount of plunder, giving to those who had been tortured and to the orphans and widows, and also to the aged, shares equal to their own. [31]They collected the arms of the enemy,[h] and carefully stored all of them in strategic places; the rest of the spoils they carried to Jerusalem. [32]They killed the commander of Timothy's forces, a most wicked man, and one who had greatly troubled the Jews. [33]While they were celebrating the victory in the city of their ancestors, they burned those who had set fire to the sacred gates, Callisthenes and some others, who had fled into one little house; so these received the proper reward for their impiety.[f]

34 The thrice-accursed Nicanor, who had brought the thousand merchants to buy the

---

a Gk he *b* Gk one of the first *c* Gk they *d* Gk lacks Jews *e* Gk lacks Galatians *f* Meaning of Gk uncertain *g* Gk slaves *h* Gk their arms

"One must not think that a person who is suffering is not praying. He is offering up his sufferings to God, and many a time he is praying much more truly than one who goes away by himself and meditates his head off, and, if he has squeezed out a few tears, thinks that is prayer."

—St. Teresa of Ávila

Crossroads—© Charlotte Katheder, 16

Jews, [35]having been humbled with the help of the Lord by opponents whom he regarded as of the least account, took off his splendid uniform and made his way alone like a runaway slave across the country until he reached Antioch, having succeeded chiefly in the destruction of his own army! [36]So he who had undertaken to secure tribute for the Romans by the capture of the people of Jerusalem proclaimed that the Jews had a Defender, and that therefore the Jews were invulnerable, because they followed the laws ordained by him.

9 The Last Campaign of Antiochus Epiphanes

About that time, as it happened, Antiochus had retreated in disorder from the region of Persia. [2]He had entered the city called Persepolis and attempted to rob the temples and control the city. Therefore the people rushed to the rescue with arms, and Antiochus and his army were defeated,[a] with the result that Antiochus was put to flight by the inhabitants and beat a shameful retreat. [3]While he was in Ecbatana, news came to him of what had happened to Nicanor and the forces of Timothy. [4]Transported with rage, he conceived the idea of turning upon the Jews the injury done by those who had put him to flight; so he ordered his charioteer to drive without stopping until he completed the journey. But the judgment of heaven rode with him! For in his arrogance he said, "When I get there I will make Jerusalem a cemetery of Jews."

[5] But the all-seeing Lord, the God of Israel, struck him with an incurable and invisible blow. As soon as he stopped speaking he was seized with a pain in his bowels, for which there was no relief, and with sharp internal tortures— [6]and that very justly, for he had tortured the bowels of others with many and strange inflictions. [7]Yet he did not in any way stop his insolence, but was even more filled with arrogance, breathing fire in his rage against the Jews, and giving orders to drive even faster. And so it came about that he fell out of his chariot as it was rushing along, and the fall was so hard as to torture every limb of his body. [8]Thus he who only a little while before had thought in his superhuman arrogance that he could command the waves of the sea, and had imagined that he could weigh the high mountains in a balance, was brought down to earth and carried in a litter, making the power of God manifest to all. [9]And so the ungodly man's body swarmed with worms, and while he was still living in anguish and pain, his flesh

rotted away, and because of the stench the whole army felt revulsion at his decay. [10]Because of his intolerable stench no one was able to carry the man who a little while before had thought that he could touch the stars of heaven. [11]Then it was that, broken in spirit, he began to lose much of his arrogance and to come to his senses under the scourge of God, for he was tortured with pain every moment. [12]And when he could not endure his own stench, he uttered these words, "It is right to be subject to God; mortals should not think that they are equal to God."[b]

Antiochus Makes a Promise to God

[13] Then the abominable fellow made a vow to the Lord, who would no longer have mercy on him, stating [14]that the holy city, which he was hurrying to level to the ground and to make a cemetery, he was now declaring to be free; [15]and the Jews, whom he had not considered worth burying but had planned to throw out with their children for the wild animals and for the birds to eat, he would make, all of them, equal to citizens of Athens; [16]and the holy sanctuary, which he had formerly plundered, he would adorn with the finest offerings; and all the holy vessels he would give back, many times over; and the expenses incurred for the sacrifices he would provide from his own revenues; [17]and in addition to all this he also would become a Jew and would visit every inhabited place to proclaim the power of God. [18]But when his sufferings did not in any way abate, for the judgment of God had justly come upon him, he gave up all hope for himself and wrote to the Jews the following letter, in the form of a supplication. This was its content:

Antiochus's Letter and Death

[19] "To his worthy Jewish citizens, Antiochus their king and general sends hearty greetings and good wishes for their health and prosperity. [20]If you and your children are well and your affairs are as you wish, I am glad. As my hope is in heaven, [21]I remember with affection your esteem and goodwill. On my way back from the region of Persia I suffered an annoying illness, and I have deemed it necessary to take thought for the general security of all. [22]I do not despair of my condition, for I have good hope of recovering from my illness, [23]but I observed that my father, on the occasions when he made expeditions into the upper country, appointed his successor, [24]so that, if anything unexpected happened or any unwelcome news came, the people throughout the realm would

---

a Gk *they were defeated*   b Or *not think thoughts proper only to God* not be troubled, for they would know to whom the government was left. 25Moreover, I understand how the princes along the borders and the neighbors of my kingdom keep watching for opportunities and waiting to see what will happen. So I have appointed my son Antiochus to be king, whom I have often entrusted and commended to most of you when I hurried off to the upper provinces; and I have written to him what is written here. 26I therefore urge and beg you to remember the public and private services rendered to you and to maintain your present goodwill, each of you, toward me and my son. 27For I am sure that he will follow my policy and will treat you with moderation and kindness."

28 So the murderer and blasphemer, having endured the more intense suffering, such as he had inflicted on others, came to the end of his life by a most pitiable fate, among the mountains in a strange land. 29And Philip, one of his courtiers, took his body home; then, fearing the son of Antiochus, he withdrew to Ptolemy Philometor in Egypt.

10 Purification of the Temple

Now Maccabeus and his followers, the Lord leading them on, recovered the temple and the city; 2they tore down the altars that had been built in the public square by the foreigners, and also destroyed the sacred precincts. 3They purified the sanctuary, and made another altar of sacrifice; then, striking fire out of flint, they offered sacrifices, after a lapse of two years, and they offered incense and lighted lamps and set out the bread of the Presence. 4When they had done this, they fell prostrate and implored the Lord that they might never again fall into such misfortunes, but that, if they should ever sin, they might be disciplined by him with forbearance and not be handed over to blasphemous and barbarous nations. 5It happened that on the same day on which the sanctuary had been profaned by the foreigners, the purification of the sanctuary took place, that is, on the twenty-fifth day of the same month, which was Chislev. 6They celebrated it for eight days with rejoicing, in the manner of the festival of booths, remembering how not long before, during the festival of booths, they had been wandering in the mountains and caves like wild animals. 7Therefore, carrying ivy-wreathed wands and beautiful branches and also fronds of palm, they offered hymns of thanksgiving to him who had given success to the purifying of his own holy place. 8They decreed by public edict, ratified by vote, that the whole nation of the Jews should observe these days every year.

9 Such then was the end of Antiochus, who was called Epiphanes.

Accession of Antiochus Eupator

10 Now we will tell what took place under Antiochus Eupator, who was the son of that ungodly man, and will give a brief summary of the principal calamities of the wars. 11This man, when he succeeded to the kingdom, appointed one Lysias to have charge of the government and to be chief governor of Coelesyria and Phoenicia. 12Ptolemy, who was called Macron, took the lead in showing justice to the Jews because of the wrong that had been done to them, and attempted to maintain peaceful relations with them. 13As a result he was accused before Eupator by the king's Friends. He heard himself called a traitor at every turn, because he had abandoned Cyprus, which Philometor had entrusted to him, and had gone over to Antiochus Epiphanes. Unable to command the respect due his office,*a* he took poison and ended his life.

Campaign in Idumea

14 When Gorgias became governor of the region, he maintained a force of mercenaries, and at every turn kept attacking the Jews. 15Besides this, the Idumeans, who had control of important strongholds, were harassing the Jews; they received those who were banished from Jerusalem, and endeavored to keep up the war. 16But Maccabeus and his forces, after making solemn supplication and imploring God to fight on their side, rushed to the strongholds of the Idumeans. 17Attacking them vigorously, they gained possession of the places, and beat off all who fought upon the wall, and slaughtered those whom they encountered, killing no fewer than twenty thousand.

18 When at least nine thousand took refuge in two very strong towers well equipped to withstand a siege, 19Maccabeus left Simon and Joseph, and also Zacchaeus and his troops, a force sufficient to besiege them; and he himself set off for places where he was more urgently needed. 20But those with Simon, who were money-hungry, were bribed by some of those who were in the towers, and on receiving seventy thousand drachmas let some of them slip away. 21When word of what had happened came to Maccabeus, he gathered the leaders of the people, and accused these men of having sold their kindred for money by setting their enemies free to fight against them. 22Then he

a Cn: Meaning of Gk uncertain

killed these men who had turned traitor, and immediately captured the two towers. [23]Having success at arms in everything he undertook, he destroyed more than twenty thousand in the two strongholds.

Judas Defeats Timothy

24 Now Timothy, who had been defeated by the Jews before, gathered a tremendous force of mercenaries and collected the cavalry from Asia in no small number. He came on, intending to take Judea by storm. [25]As he drew near, Maccabeus and his men sprinkled dust on their heads and girded their loins with sackcloth, in supplication to God. [26]Falling upon the steps before the altar, they implored him to be gracious to them and to be an enemy to their enemies and an adversary to their adversaries, as the law declares. [27]And rising from their prayer they took up their arms and advanced a considerable distance from the city; and when they came near the enemy they halted. [28]Just as dawn was breaking, the two armies joined battle, the one having as pledge of success and victory not only their valor but also their reliance on the Lord, while the other made rage their leader in the fight.

29 When the battle became fierce, there appeared to the enemy from heaven five resplendent men on horses with golden bridles, and they were leading the Jews. [30]Two of them took Maccabeus between them, and shielding him with their own armor and weapons, they kept him from being wounded. They showered arrows and thunderbolts on the enemy, so that, confused and blinded, they were thrown into disorder and cut to pieces. [31]Twenty thousand five hundred were slaughtered, besides six hundred cavalry.

32 Timothy himself fled to a stronghold called Gazara, especially well garrisoned, where Chaereas was commander. [33]Then Maccabeus and his men were glad, and they besieged the fort for four days. [34]The men within, relying on the strength of the place, kept blaspheming terribly and uttering wicked words. [35]But at dawn of the fifth day, twenty young men in the army of Maccabeus, fired with anger because of the blasphemies, bravely stormed the wall and with savage fury cut down everyone they met. [36]Others who came up in the same way wheeled around against the defenders and set fire to the towers; they kindled fires and burned the blasphemers alive. Others broke open the gates and let in the rest of the force, and they occupied the city. [37]They killed Timothy, who was hiding in a cistern, and his brother Chaereas, and Apollophanes. [38]When they had accomplished these things, with hymns and thanksgivings they blessed the Lord who shows great kindness to Israel and gives them the victory.

11 Lysias Besieges Beth-zur

Very soon after this, Lysias, the king's guardian and kinsman, who was in charge of the government, being vexed at what had happened, [2]gathered about eighty thousand infantry and all his cavalry and came against the Jews. He intended to make the city a home for Greeks, [3]and to levy tribute on the temple as he did on the sacred places of the other nations, and to put up the high priesthood for sale every year. [4]He took no account whatever of the power of God, but was elated with his ten thousands of infantry, and his thousands of cavalry, and his eighty elephants. [5]Invading Judea, he approached Beth-zur, which was a fortified place about five stadia[a] from Jerusalem, and pressed it hard.

6 When Maccabeus and his men got word that Lysias[b] was besieging the strongholds, they and all the people, with lamentations and tears, prayed the Lord to send a good angel to save Israel. [7]Maccabeus himself was the first to take up arms, and he urged the others to risk their lives with him to aid their kindred. Then they eagerly rushed off together. [8]And there, while they were still near Jerusalem, a horseman appeared at their head, clothed in white and brandishing weapons of gold. [9]And together they all praised the merciful God, and were strengthened in heart, ready to assail not only humans but the wildest animals or walls of iron. [10]They advanced in battle order, having their heavenly ally, for the Lord had mercy on them. [11]They hurled themselves like lions against the enemy, and laid low eleven thousand of them and sixteen hundred cavalry, and forced all the rest to flee. [12]Most of them got away stripped and wounded, and Lysias himself escaped by disgraceful flight.

Lysias Makes Peace with the Jews

13 As he was not without intelligence, he pondered over the defeat that had befallen him, and realized that the Hebrews were invincible because the mighty God fought on their side. So he sent to them [14]and persuaded them to settle everything on just terms, promising that he would persuade the king, constraining him to be their friend.[a] [15]Maccabeus, having regard for the common good, agreed to all that Lysias urged. For the king granted every request in be-

a Meaning of Gk uncertain b Gk he

half of the Jews which Maccabeus delivered to Lysias in writing.

16 The letter written to the Jews by Lysias was to this effect:

"Lysias to the people of the Jews, greetings. [17]John and Absalom, who were sent by you, have delivered your signed communication and have asked about the matters indicated in it. [18]I have informed the king of everything that needed to be brought before him, and he has agreed to what was possible. [19]If you will maintain your goodwill toward the government, I will endeavor in the future to help promote your welfare. [20]And concerning such matters and their details, I have ordered these men and my representatives to confer with you. [21]Farewell. The one hundred forty-eighth year,[a] Dioscorinthius twenty-fourth."

22 The king's letter ran thus:

"King Antiochus to his brother Lysias, greetings. [23]Now that our father has gone on to the gods, we desire that the subjects of the kingdom be undisturbed in caring for their own affairs. [24]We have heard that the Jews do not consent to our father's change to Greek customs, but prefer their own way of living and ask that their own customs be allowed them. [25]Accordingly, since we choose that this nation also should be free from disturbance, our decision is that their temple be restored to them and that they shall live according to the customs of their ancestors. [26]You will do well, therefore, to send word to them and give them pledges of friendship, so that they may know our policy and be of good cheer and go on happily in the conduct of their own affairs."

27 To the nation the king's letter was as follows:

"King Antiochus to the senate of the Jews and to the other Jews, greetings. [28]If you are well, it is as we desire. We also are in good health. [29]Menelaus has informed us that you wish to return home and look after your own affairs. [30]Therefore those who go home by the thirtieth of Xanthicus will have our pledge of friendship and full permission [31]for the Jews to enjoy their own food and laws, just as formerly, and none of them shall be molested in any way for what may have been done in ignorance. [32]And I have also sent Menelaus to encourage you. [33]Farewell. The one hundred forty-eighth year,[a] Xanthicus fifteenth."

34 The Romans also sent them a letter, which read thus:

"Quintus Memmius and Titus Manius, envoys of the Romans, to the people of the Jews, greetings. [35]With regard to what Lysias the kinsman of the king has granted you, we also give consent. [36]But as to the matters that he decided are to be referred to the king, as soon as you have considered them, send some one promptly so that we may make proposals appropriate for you. For we are on our way to Antioch. [37]Therefore make haste and send messengers so that we may have your judgment. [38]Farewell. The one hundred forty-eighth year,[a] Xanthicus fifteenth."

12 Incidents at Joppa and Jamnia

When this agreement had been reached, Lysias returned to the king, and the Jews went about their farming.

[a] 164 B.C.

Praise Him—© Orchid Tolentino (youth leader)

RESURRECTION OF THE DEAD

In **2 Maccabees 12.39–45** you'll find a strong influence on Roman Catholic theology. The fact that Judas Maccabee ordered prayers for the dead indicates that he believed in the resurrection of the dead. This passage has been used as support for Roman Catholic belief in the resurrection of the dead, purgatory, and prayers for the dead.

Every time you say the Apostles' or Nicene Creed, you profess "I believe in the resurrection of the body." At the time of the Maccabees, this particular belief was just beginning to come to light. By the time of Jesus there were some who denied it (the Sadducees) and some who believed it (the Pharisees). The Church has always believed in the resurrection of the body—that our body will be reunited with our soul "at the last day." The "how" of that belief can only be understood by faith.

2 But some of the governors in various places, Timothy and Apollonius son of Gennaeus, as well as Hieronymus and Demophon, and in addition to these Nicanor the governor of Cyprus, would not let them live quietly and in peace. ³And the people of Joppa did so ungodly a deed as this: they invited the Jews who lived among them to embark, with their wives and children, on boats that they had provided, as though there were no ill will to the Jews;ᵃ ⁴and this was done by public vote of the city. When they accepted, because they wished to live peaceably and suspected nothing, the people of Joppaᵇ took them out to sea and drowned them, at least two hundred. ⁵When Judas heard of the cruelty visited on his compatriots, he gave orders to his men ⁶and, calling upon God, the righteous judge, attacked the murderers of his kindred. He set fire to the harbor by night, burned the boats, and massacred those who had taken refuge there. ⁷Then, because the city's gates were closed, he withdrew, intending to come again and root out the whole community of Joppa. ⁸But learning that the people

in Jamnia meant in the same way to wipe out the Jews who were living among them, ⁹he attacked the Jamnites by night and set fire to the harbor and the fleet, so that the glow of the light was seen in Jerusalem, thirty milesᶜ distant.

The Campaign in Gilead

10 When they had gone more than a mileᵈ from there, on their march against Timothy, at least five thousand Arabs with five hundred cavalry attacked them. ¹¹After a hard fight, Judas and his companions, with God's help, were victorious. The defeated nomads begged Judas to grant them pledges of friendship, promising to give him livestock and to help his peopleᵉ in all other ways. ¹²Judas, realizing that they might indeed be useful in many ways, agreed to make peace with them; and after receiving his pledges they went back to their tents.

13 He also attacked a certain town that was strongly fortified with earthworksᶠ and walls, and inhabited by all sorts of Gentiles. Its name was Caspin. ¹⁴Those who were within, relying on the strength of the walls and on their supply of provisions, behaved most insolently toward Judas and his men, railing at them and even blaspheming and saying unholy things. ¹⁵But Judas and his men, calling upon the great Sovereign of the world, who without battering rams or engines of war overthrew Jericho in the days of Joshua, rushed furiously upon the walls. ¹⁶They took the town by the will of God, and slaughtered untold numbers, so that the adjoining lake, a quarter of a mileᵍ wide, appeared to be running over with blood.

Judas Defeats Timothy's Army

17 When they had gone ninety-five milesʰ from there, they came to Charax, to the Jews who are called Toubiani. ¹⁸They did not find Timothy in that region, for he had by then left there without accomplishing anything, though in one place he had left a very strong garrison. ¹⁹Dositheus and Sosipater, who were captains under Maccabeus, marched out and destroyed those whom Timothy had left in the stronghold, more than ten thousand men. ²⁰But Maccabeus arranged his army in divisions, set menᵉ in command of the divisions, and hurried after Timothy, who had with him one hundred twenty thousand infantry and two thousand five hundred cavalry. ²¹When Timothy learned of the approach of Judas, he sent off the women and the children and also the baggage to a place called Carnaim; for that

a Gk to them *b* Gk they *c* Gk two hundred forty stadia *d* Gk nine stadia *e* Gk them *f* Meaning of Gk uncertain *g* Gk two stadia *h* Gk seven hundred fifty stadia place was hard to besiege and difficult of access because of the narrowness of all the approaches. [22]But when Judas's first division appeared, terror and fear came over the enemy at the manifestation to them of him who sees all things. In their flight they rushed headlong in every direction, so that often they were injured by their own men and pierced by the points of their own swords. [23]Judas pressed the pursuit with the utmost vigor, putting the sinners to the sword, and destroyed as many as thirty thousand.

24 Timothy himself fell into the hands of Dositheus and Sosipater and their men. With great guile he begged them to let him go in safety, because he held the parents of most of them, and the brothers of some, to whom no consideration would be shown. [25]And when with many words he had confirmed his solemn promise to restore them unharmed, they let him go, for the sake of saving their kindred.

Judas Wins Other Victories

26 Then Judas[a] marched against Carnaim and the temple of Atargatis, and slaughtered twenty-five thousand people. [27]After the rout and destruction of these, he marched also against Ephron, a fortified town where Lysias lived with multitudes of people of all nationalities.[b] Stalwart young men took their stand before the walls and made a vigorous defense; and great stores of war engines and missiles were there. [28]But the Jews[c] called upon the Sovereign who with power shatters the might of his enemies, and they got the town into their hands, and killed as many as twenty-five thousand of those who were in it.

29 Setting out from there, they hastened to Scythopolis, which is seventy-five miles[d] from Jerusalem. [30]But when the Jews who lived there bore witness to the goodwill that the people of Scythopolis had shown them and their kind treatment of them in times of misfortune, [31]they thanked them and exhorted them to be well disposed to their race in the future also. Then they went up to Jerusalem, as the festival of weeks was close at hand.

Judas Defeats Gorgias

32 After the festival called Pentecost, they hurried against Gorgias, the governor of Idumea, [33]who came out with three thousand infantry and four hundred cavalry. [34]When they joined battle, it happened that a few of the Jews fell. [35]But a certain Dositheus, one of Bacenor's men, who was on horseback and was a strong man, caught hold of Gorgias, and grasping his cloak was dragging him off by main strength, wishing to take the accursed man alive, when one of the Thracian cavalry bore down on him and cut off his arm; so Gorgias escaped and reached Marisa.

36 As Esdris and his men had been fighting for a long time and were weary, Judas called upon the Lord to show himself their ally and leader in the battle. [37]In the language of their ancestors he raised the battle cry, with hymns; then he charged against Gorgias's troops when they were not expecting it, and put them to flight.

Prayers for Those Killed in Battle

38 Then Judas assembled his army and went to the city of Adullam. As the seventh day was coming on, they purified themselves according to the custom, and kept the sabbath there.

39 On the next day, as had now become necessary, Judas and his men went to take up the bodies of the fallen and to bring them back to lie with their kindred in the sepulchres of their ancestors. [40]Then under the tunic of each one of the dead they found sacred tokens of the idols of Jamnia, which the law forbids the Jews to wear. And it became clear to all that this was the reason these men had fallen. [41]So they all blessed the ways of the Lord, the righteous judge, who reveals the things that are hidden; [42]and they turned to supplication, praying that the sin that had been committed might be wholly blotted out. The noble Judas exhorted the people to keep themselves free from sin, for they had seen with their own eyes what had happened as the result of the sin of those who had fallen. [43]He also took up a collection, man by man, to the amount of two thousand drachmas of silver, and sent it to Jerusalem to provide for a sin offering. In doing this he acted very well and honorably, taking account of the resurrection. [44]For if he were not expecting that those who had fallen would rise again, it would have been superfluous and foolish to pray for the dead. [45]But if he was looking to the splendid reward that is laid up for those who fall asleep in godliness, it was a holy and pious thought. Therefore he made atonement for the dead, so that they might be delivered from their sin.

13 Menelaus Is Put to Death

In the one hundred forty-ninth year[e] word came to Judas and his men that Antiochus Eupator was coming with a great army against Judea, [2]and with him Lysias, his guardian, who had charge of the government. Each of them

---

a Gk he b Meaning of Gk uncertain c Gk they d Gk six hundred stadia e 163 B.C.

had a Greek force of one hundred ten thousand infantry, five thousand three hundred cavalry, twenty-two elephants, and three hundred chariots armed with scythes.

3 Menelaus also joined them and with utter hypocrisy urged Antiochus on, not for the sake of his country's welfare, but because he thought that he would be established in office. [4]But the King of kings aroused the anger of Antiochus against the scoundrel; and when Lysias informed him that this man was to blame for all the trouble, he ordered them to take him to Beroea and to put him to death by the method that is customary in that place. [5]For there is a tower there, fifty cubits high, full of ashes, and it has a rim running around it that on all sides inclines precipitously into the ashes. [6]There they all push to destruction anyone guilty of sacrilege or notorious for other crimes. [7]By such a fate it came about that Menelaus the lawbreaker died, without even burial in the earth. [8]And this was eminently just; because he had committed many sins against the altar whose fire and ashes were holy, he met his death in ashes.

A Battle Near the City of Modein

9 The king with barbarous arrogance was coming to show the Jews things far worse than those that had been done[a] in his father's time. [10]But when Judas heard of this, he ordered the people to call upon the Lord day and night, now if ever to help those who were on the point of being deprived of the law and their country and the holy temple, [11]and not to let the people who had just begun to revive fall into the hands of the blasphemous Gentiles. [12]When they had all joined in the same petition and had implored the merciful Lord with weeping and fasting and lying prostrate for three days without ceasing, Judas exhorted them and ordered them to stand ready.

13 After consulting privately with the elders, he determined to march out and decide the matter by the help of God before the king's army could enter Judea and get possession of the city. [14]So, committing the decision to the Creator of the world and exhorting his troops to fight bravely to the death for the laws, temple, city, country, and commonwealth, he pitched his camp near Modein. [15]He gave his troops the watchword, "God's victory," and with a picked force of the bravest young men, he attacked the king's pavilion at night and killed as many as two thousand men in the camp. He stabbed[b] the leading elephant and its

rider. [16]In the end they filled the camp with terror and confusion and withdrew in triumph. [17]This happened, just as day was dawning, because the Lord's help protected him.

Antiochus Makes a Treaty with the Jews

18 The king, having had a taste of the daring of the Jews, tried strategy in attacking their positions. [19]He advanced against Beth-zur, a strong fortress of the Jews, was turned back, attacked again,[c] and was defeated. [20]Judas sent in to the garrison whatever was necessary. [21]But Rhodocus, a man from the ranks of the Jews, gave secret information to the enemy; he was sought for, caught, and put in prison. [22]The king negotiated a second time with the people in Beth-zur, gave pledges, received theirs, withdrew, attacked Judas and his men, was defeated; [23]he got word that Philip, who had been left in charge of the government, had revolted in Antioch; he was dismayed, called in the Jews, yielded and swore to observe all their rights, settled with them and offered sacrifice, honored the sanctuary and showed generosity to the holy place. [24]He received Maccabeus, left Hegemonides as governor from Ptolemais to Gerar, [25]and went to Ptolemais. The people of Ptolemais were indignant over the treaty; in fact they were so angry that they wanted to annul its terms.[b] [26]Lysias took the public platform, made the best possible defense, convinced them, appeased them, gained their goodwill, and set out for Antioch. This is how the king's attack and withdrawal turned out.

14 Alcimus Speaks against Judas

Three years later, word came to Judas and his men that Demetrius son of Seleucus had sailed into the harbor of Tripolis with a strong army and a fleet, [2]and had taken possession of the country, having made away with Antiochus and his guardian Lysias.

3 Now a certain Alcimus, who had formerly been high priest but had willfully defiled himself in the times of separation,[d] realized that there was no way for him to be safe or to have access again to the holy altar, [4]and went to King Demetrius in about the one hundred fifty-first year,[e] presenting to him a crown of gold and a palm, and besides these some of the customary olive branches from the temple. During that day he kept quiet. [5]But he found an opportunity that furthered his mad purpose when he was invited by Demetrius to a meeting of the council and was asked about the attitude and intentions of the Jews. He answered:

a Or the worst of the things that had been done *b* Meaning of Gk uncertain *c* Or faltered *d* Other ancient authorities read of mixing *e* 161 B.C.

6 "Those of the Jews who are called Hasideans, whose leader is Judas Maccabeus, are keeping up war and stirring up sedition, and will not let the kingdom attain tranquility. [7]Therefore I have laid aside my ancestral glory—I mean the high priesthood—and have now come here, [8]first because I am genuinely concerned for the interests of the king, and second because I have regard also for my compatriots. For through the folly of those whom I have mentioned our whole nation is now in no small misfortune. [9]Since you are acquainted, O king, with the details of this matter, may it please you to take thought for our country and our hard-pressed nation with the gracious kindness that you show to all. [10]For as long as Judas lives, it is impossible for the government to find peace." [11]When he had said this, the rest of the king's Friends,[a] who were hostile to Judas, quickly inflamed Demetrius still more. [12]He immediately chose Nicanor, who had been in command of the elephants, appointed him governor of Judea, and sent him off [13]with orders to kill Judas and scatter his troops, and to install Alcimus as high priest of the great[b] temple. [14]And the Gentiles throughout Judea, who had fled before[c] Judas, flocked to join Nicanor, thinking that the misfortunes and calamities of the Jews would mean prosperity for themselves.

Nicanor Makes Friends with Judas

15 When the Jews[d] heard of Nicanor's coming and the gathering of the Gentiles, they sprinkled dust on their heads and prayed to him who established his own people forever and always upholds his own heritage by manifesting himself. [16]At the command of the leader, they[e] set out from there immediately and engaged them in battle at a village called Dessau.[c] [17]Simon, the brother of Judas, had encountered Nicanor, but had been temporarily[f] checked because of the sudden consternation created by the enemy.

18 Nevertheless Nicanor, hearing of the valor of Judas and his troops and their courage in battle for their country, shrank from deciding the issue by bloodshed. [19]Therefore he sent Posidonius, Theodotus, and Mattathias to give and receive pledges of friendship. [20]When the terms had been fully considered, and the leader had informed the people, and it had appeared that they were of one mind, they agreed to the covenant. [21]The leaders[g] set a day on

---

a Gk of the Friends b Gk greatest c Meaning of Gk uncertain d Gk they e Gk he f Other ancient authorities read slowly g Gk They

> "The only way to Heaven is prayer; a prayer of the heart, which everyone is capable of, and not of reasonings, which are the fruits of study, or exercise of the imagination, which, in filling the mind with wandering objects, rarely settle it; instead of warming the heart with love to God, they leave it cold and languishing."
> —Jeanne Guyon, seventeenth-century French mystic

which to meet by themselves. A chariot came forward from each army; seats of honor were set in place; 22 Judas posted armed men in readiness at key places to prevent sudden treachery on the part of the enemy; so they duly held the consultation.

23 Nicanor stayed on in Jerusalem and did nothing out of the way, but dismissed the flocks of people that had gathered. 24 And he kept Judas always in his presence; he was warmly attached to the man. 25 He urged him to marry and have children; so Judas*a* married, settled down, and shared the common life.

Nicanor Turns against Judas

26 But when Alcimus noticed their goodwill for one another, he took the covenant that had been made and went to Demetrius. He told him that Nicanor was disloyal to the government, since he had appointed that conspirator against the kingdom, Judas, to be his successor. 27 The king became excited and, provoked by the false accusations of that depraved man, wrote to Nicanor, stating that he was displeased with the covenant and commanding him to send Maccabeus to Antioch as a prisoner without delay.

28 When this message came to Nicanor, he was troubled and grieved that he had to annul their agreement when the man had done no wrong. 29 Since it was not possible to oppose the king, he watched for an opportunity to accomplish this by a stratagem. 30 But Maccabeus, noticing that Nicanor was more austere in his dealings with him and was meeting him more rudely than had been his custom, concluded that this austerity did not spring from the best motives. So he gathered not a few of his men, and went into hiding from Nicanor. 31 When the latter became aware that he had been

cleverly outwitted by the man, he went to the great*b* and holy temple while the priests were offering the customary sacrifices, and commanded them to hand the man over. 32 When they declared on oath that they did not know where the man was whom he wanted, 33 he stretched out his right hand toward the sanctuary, and swore this oath: "If you do not hand Judas over to me as a prisoner, I will level this shrine of God to the ground and tear down the altar, and build here a splendid temple to Dionysus."

34 Having said this, he went away. Then the priests stretched out their hands toward heaven and called upon the constant Defender of our nation, in these words: 35 "O Lord of all, though you have need of nothing, you were pleased that there should be a temple for your habitation among us; 36 so now, O holy One, Lord of all holiness, keep undefiled forever this house that has been so recently purified."

Razis Dies for His Country

37 A certain Razis, one of the elders of Jerusalem, was denounced to Nicanor as a man who loved his compatriots and was very well thought of and for his goodwill was called father of the Jews. 38 In former times, when there was no mingling with the Gentiles, he had been accused of Judaism, and he had most zealously risked body and life for Judaism. 39 Nicanor, wishing to exhibit the enmity that he had for the Jews, sent more than five hundred soldiers to arrest him; 40 for he thought that by arresting*c* him he would do them an injury. 41 When the troops were about to capture the tower and were forcing the door of the courtyard, they ordered that fire be brought and the doors burned. Being surrounded, Razis*a* fell upon his own sword, 42 preferring to die nobly rather than to fall into the hands of sinners and suffer outrages unworthy of his noble birth. 43 But in the heat of the struggle he did not hit exactly, and the crowd was now rushing in through the doors. He courageously ran up on the wall, and bravely threw himself down into the crowd. 44 But as they quickly drew back, a space opened and he fell in the middle of the empty space. 45 Still alive and aflame with anger, he rose, and though his blood gushed forth and his wounds were severe he ran through the crowd; and standing upon a steep rock, 46 with his blood now completely drained from him, he tore out his entrails, took them in both hands and hurled them at the crowd, calling upon the Lord of life and spirit to give them back to him again. This was the manner of his death.

a Gk *he* *b* Gk *greatest* *c* Meaning of Gk uncertain

15 Nicanor's Arrogance

When Nicanor heard that Judas and his troops were in the region of Samaria, he made plans to attack them with complete safety on the day of rest. [2]When the Jews who were compelled to follow him said, "Do not destroy so savagely and barbarously, but show respect for the day that he who sees all things has honored and hallowed above other days," [3]the thrice-accursed wretch asked if there were a sovereign in heaven who had commanded the keeping of the sabbath day. [4]When they declared, "It is the living Lord himself, the Sovereign in heaven, who ordered us to observe the seventh day," [5]he replied, "But I am a sovereign also, on earth, and I command you to take up arms and finish the king's business." Nevertheless, he did not succeed in carrying out his abominable design.

Judas Prepares the Jews for Battle

6 This Nicanor in his utter boastfulness and arrogance had determined to erect a public monument of victory over Judas and his forces. [7]But Maccabeus did not cease to trust with all confidence that he would get help from the Lord. [8]He exhorted his troops not to fear the attack of the Gentiles, but to keep in mind the former times when help had come to them from heaven, and so to look for the victory that the Almighty would give them. [9]Encouraging them from the law and the prophets, and reminding them also of the struggles they had won, he made them the more eager. [10]When he had aroused their courage, he issued his orders, at the same time pointing out the perfidy of the Gentiles and their violation of oaths. [11]He armed each of them not so much with confidence in shields and spears as with the inspiration of brave words, and he cheered them all by relating a dream, a sort of vision,[a] which was worthy of belief.

12 What he saw was this: Onias, who had been high priest, a noble and good man, of modest bearing and gentle manner, one who spoke fittingly and had been trained from childhood in all that belongs to excellence, was praying with outstretched hands for the whole body of the Jews. [13]Then in the same fashion another appeared, distinguished by his gray hair and dignity, and of marvelous majesty and authority. [14]And Onias spoke, saying, "This is a man who loves the family of Israel and prays much for the people and the holy city—Jeremiah, the prophet of God." [15]Jeremiah stretched out his right hand and gave to Judas a golden sword, and as he gave it he addressed him thus: [16]"Take this holy sword, a gift from God, with which you will strike down your adversaries."

17 Encouraged by the words of Judas, so noble and so effective in arousing valor and awaking courage in the souls of the young, they determined not to carry on a campaign[b] but to attack bravely, and to decide the matter by fighting hand to hand with all courage, because the city and the sanctuary and the temple were in danger. [18]Their concern for wives and children, and also for brothers and sisters[c] and relatives, lay upon them less heavily; their greatest and first fear was for the consecrated sanctuary. [19]And those who had to remain in the city were in no little distress, being anxious over the encounter in the open country.

---

a Meaning of Gk uncertain *b* Or *to remain in camp* *c* Gk *for brothers*

INTERCESSORY PRAYER

There are lots of different reasons to pray—like when we want something, when we're grateful, or simply when we want to praise God for being God. In **2 Maccabees 15.12–16**, we hear about the prayers of Onias and Jeremiah and see examples of intercessory prayer. Think of intercessory prayer as an "other-centered" or selfless prayer of petition. It is a prayer that knows no boundaries. (See *Catechism of the Catholic Church* 2636.) Try some of these suggestions for intercessory prayer:

- List the members of your family who have died and pray for each of them by name.
- Choose one of the countries currently being ravaged by war and pray for God's blessings on the young people living there. Name the blessings you want for the young people in that country.
- Pray for the person in your life whom you most dislike. In your prayer, ask God to bless him or her with all the blessings you would like for yourself.

The Defeat and Death of Nicanor

20 When all were now looking forward to the coming issue, and the enemy was already close at hand with their army drawn up for battle, the elephants[a] strategically stationed and the cavalry deployed on the flanks, 21 Maccabeus, observing the masses that were in front of him and the varied supply of arms and the savagery of the elephants, stretched out his hands toward heaven and called upon the Lord who works wonders; for he knew that it is not by arms, but as the Lord[b] decides, that he gains the victory for those who deserve it. 22 He called upon him in these words: "O Lord, you sent your angel in the time of King Hezekiah of Judea, and he killed fully one hundred eighty-five thousand in the camp of Sennacherib. 23 So now, O Sovereign of the heavens, send a good angel to spread terror and trembling before us. 24 By the might of your arm may these blasphemers who come against your holy people be struck down." With these words he ended his prayer.

25 Nicanor and his troops advanced with trumpets and battle songs, 26 but Judas and his troops met the enemy in battle with invocations to God and prayers. 27 So, fighting with their hands and praying to God in their hearts, they laid low at least thirty-five thousand, and were greatly gladdened by God's manifestation.

28 When the action was over and they were returning with joy, they recognized Nicanor, lying dead, in full armor. 29 Then there was shouting and tumult, and they blessed the Sovereign Lord in the language of their ancestors. 30 Then the man who was ever in body and soul the defender of his people, the man who maintained his youthful goodwill toward his compatriots, ordered them to cut off Nicanor's head and arm and carry them to Jerusalem. 31 When he arrived there and had called his compatriots together and stationed the priests before the altar, he sent for those who were in the citadel. 32 He showed them the vile Nicanor's head and that profane man's arm, which had been boastfully stretched out against the holy house of the Almighty. 33 He cut out the tongue of the ungodly Nicanor and said that he would feed it piecemeal to the birds and would hang up these rewards of his folly opposite the sanctuary. 34 And they all, looking to heaven, blessed the Lord who had manifested himself, saying, "Blessed is he who has kept his own place undefiled!" 35 Judas[c] hung Nicanor's head from the citadel, a clear and conspicuous sign to everyone of the help of the Lord. 36 And they all decreed by public vote never to let this day go unobserved, but to celebrate the thirteenth day of the twelfth month—which is called Adar in the Aramaic language—the day before Mordecai's day.

37 This, then, is how matters turned out with Nicanor, and from that time the city has been in the possession of the Hebrews. So I will here end my story.

The Compiler's Epilogue

38 If it is well told and to the point, that is what I myself desired; if it is poorly done and mediocre, that was the best I could do. 39 For just as it is harmful to drink wine alone, or, again, to drink water alone, while wine mixed with water is sweet and delicious and enhances one's enjoyment, so also the style of the story delights the ears of those who read the work. And here will be the end.

---

a Gk animals   b Gk he   c Gk He

JOB

BAD ADVICE IN BAD TIMES

Why Bad Things Happen

When you were a kid, did you ever play hand-slap games or bloody knuckles—contests in which you and a friend tried to see who could endure pain the longest before giving in?

You're about to read a story that's a bit like a bloody-knuckles face-off between Job, Satan, and God. In these pages, Job faces a painful test that's much bigger than any game.

Act One: As the curtain rises, life is moving along swimmingly for the protagonist, Job (pronounced like "globe," not like your career), with a wife, family, home, and herds that made him rich. Little did he know that . . .

Stage Left: A wager placed in heaven will bring it all to an end. Satan bets God that if Job is allowed to suffer terribly, he's certain to abandon his faith and curse God.

Center Stage: To add insult to injury, four "friends" come alongside Job to help him deal with the crises he's facing. They do a great job—until they open their mouths and start blaming him for the disasters that have ruined his life. Their advice is to repent, because obviously God wouldn't have let this happen if Job hadn't done something to deserve it.

Intermission: We're inevitably left to wonder, *Why, God? Why would you let this happen to someone who loved you so much? Why can't you just make Job's life—and our lives—pain-free and happy?*

Act Two: God appears center stage to set things straight. God's answer to Job's (and our) profound questions is a poetic description of his dominance over all of creation. It leaves Job (and us) with a humble sense of awe at God's power.

The curtain closes. **The End**.

But the story of Job doesn't really feel as though it "ends," because it provokes so many big questions about suffering. Not just questions about Job's life, but the looming questions we have when someone we love gets seriously ill, or we read about school shootings, suicide bombings, or natural disasters.

The most challenging theological questions begin here. So start reading and see how the book of Job can speak to you.

WHO Apparently written by several unknown writers

WHAT A folktale written as a poetic story that includes a conversation between Job and God regarding the mysteries of human existence and suffering

WHEN Uncertain, but it appears to have been written sometime between 700 and 400 B.C.

WHERE Job was probably from an area in the ancient Near East located east of Canaan.

"At the beginning of my religious life, suffering and adversities frightened and disheartened me. So I prayed continuously, asking Jesus to strengthen me and to grant me the power of His Holy Spirit."
—St. Faustina

PATH OF DISCIPLESHIP

Whether we like it or not, nobody escapes some kind of suffering in this life. It doesn't matter how good we are. Why? Well, for starters, there's original sin. And sometimes bad things happen to the best people with the best of intentions. Even us. We get sick, people we love die, and then there's the suffering that sometimes comes out of relationships. Job is a good model for us, because through all of his suffering—even when he was most angry with God—Job trusted him.

EXPRESS YOURSELF

Shut Up and Love

How do you respond to your friends when they're totally depressed? Do you try to cheer them up with jokes or movies or sports or small talk? Or do you get too rational with them, trying to explain away all the reasons they feel down? Or maybe you fill the uncomfortable silences with cheesy clichés and slogans like, "God won't ever give you more than you can handle," or "Smile! God loves you!"

Have you ever tried just sitting with them, sharing their grief without saying a word at all?

Job's friends come to see him after he loses everything—his livestock, servants, children, and even his health—only to be left with an angry wife who told him to curse God. If you were Job's friend, how would you show him compassion? Read **Job 2.11–13**.

Are any of your friends or acquaintances hurting? Maybe a loved one has recently died, someone just got dumped, or another's family seems to be facing some big-time challenges. How can you show God's compassion to someone in pain without saying a single word? Express your support and love by creating a meaningful *silent* video clip, slide show, painting, sketch, or photo album to give to your friend. Find silent ways to express your solidarity in this time of need and grief.

(Side note: Unfortunately, after their amazing show of support in 2.11–13, Job's friends start blabbing and go *way* off track, saying things that are hurtful and wrong instead of helpful and true. At some point in the future when you *do* talk with your hurting friend, keep the example of Job's friends in mind—even well-intentioned words can be hurtful. Often prayer and quiet companionship are the best ways to support a person who is hurting.)

1 Job and His Family

There was once a man in the land of Uz whose name was Job. That man was blameless and upright, one who feared God and turned away from evil. [2]There were born to him seven sons and three daughters. [3]He had seven thousand sheep, three thousand camels, five hundred yoke of oxen, five hundred donkeys, and very many servants; so that this man was the greatest of all the people of the east. [4]His sons used to go and hold feasts in one another's houses in turn; and they would send and invite their three sisters to eat and drink with them. [5]And when the feast days had run their course, Job would send and sanctify them, and he would rise early in the morning and offer burnt offerings according to the number of them all; for Job said, "It may be that my children have sinned, and cursed God in their hearts." This is what Job always did.

Attack on Job's Character

6 One day the heavenly beings[a] came to present themselves before the LORD, and Satan[b] also came among them. [7]The LORD said to Satan,[b] "Where have you come from?" Satan[b] answered the LORD, "From going to and fro on the earth, and from walking up and down on it." [8]The LORD said to Satan,[b] "Have you considered my servant Job? There is no one like him on the earth, a blameless and upright man who fears God and turns away from evil." [9]Then Satan[b] answered the LORD, "Does Job fear God for nothing? [10]Have you not put a fence around him and his house and all that he has, on every side? You have blessed the work of his hands, and his possessions have increased in the land. [11]But stretch out your hand now, and touch all that he has, and he will curse you to your face." [12]The LORD said to Satan,[b] "Very well, all that he has is in your power; only do not stretch out your hand against him!" So Satan[b] went out from the presence of the LORD.

Job Loses Property and Children

13 One day when his sons and daughters were eating and drinking wine in the eldest brother's house, [14]a messenger came to Job and said, "The oxen were plowing and the donkeys were feeding beside them, [15]and the Sabeans fell on them and carried them off, and killed the servants with the edge of the sword; I alone have escaped to tell you." [16]While he was still speaking, another came and said, "The fire of God fell from heaven and burned up the sheep and the servants, and consumed them; I alone have escaped to tell you." [17]While he was still speaking, another came and said, "The Chaldeans formed three columns, made a raid on the camels and carried them off, and killed the servants with the edge of the sword; I alone

a Heb *sons of God* *b* Or *the Accuser*; Heb *ha-satan*

have escaped to tell you." ¹⁸While he was still speaking, another came and said, "Your sons and daughters were eating and drinking wine in their eldest brother's house, ¹⁹and suddenly a great wind came across the desert, struck the four corners of the house, and it fell on the young people, and they are dead; I alone have escaped to tell you."

20 Then Job arose, tore his robe, shaved his head, and fell on the ground and worshiped. ²¹He said, "Naked I came from my mother's womb, and naked shall I return there; the LORD gave, and the LORD has taken away; blessed be the name of the LORD."

22 In all this Job did not sin or charge God with wrongdoing.

2 Attack on Job's Health

One day the heavenly beings*ᵃ* came to present themselves before the LORD, and Satan*ᵇ* also came among them to present himself before the LORD. ²The LORD said to Satan,*ᵇ* "Where have you come from?" Satan*ᶜ* answered the LORD, "From going to and fro on the earth, and from walking up and down on it." ³The LORD said to Satan,*ᵇ* "Have you considered my servant Job? There is no one like him on the earth, a blameless and upright man who fears God and turns away from evil. He still persists in his integrity, although you incited me against him, to destroy him for no reason." ⁴Then Satan*ᵇ* answered the LORD, "Skin for skin! All that people have they will give to save their lives.*ᵈ* ⁵But stretch out your hand now and touch his bone and his flesh, and he will curse you to your face." ⁶The LORD said to Satan,*ᵇ* "Very well, he is in your power; only spare his life."

7 So Satan*ᵇ* went out from the presence of the LORD, and inflicted loathsome sores on Job from the sole of his foot to the crown of his head. ⁸Job*ᵉ* took a potsherd with which to scrape himself, and sat among the ashes.

9 Then his wife said to him, "Do you still persist in your integrity? Curse*ᶠ* God, and die." ¹⁰But he said to her, "You speak as any foolish woman would speak. Shall we receive the good at the hand of God, and not receive the bad?" In all this Job did not sin with his lips.

Job's Three Friends

11 Now when Job's three friends heard of all these troubles that had come upon him, each of them set out from his home—Eliphaz the Temanite, Bildad the Shuhite, and Zophar the Naamathite. They met together to go and console and comfort him. ¹²When they saw him

from a distance, they did not recognize him, and they raised their voices and wept aloud; they tore their robes and threw dust in the air upon their heads. ¹³They sat with him on the ground seven days and seven nights, and no one spoke a word to him, for they saw that his suffering was very great.

3 Job Curses the Day He Was Born

After this Job opened his mouth and cursed the day of his birth. ²Job said:

³ "Let the day perish in which I was born,
   and the night that said,
   'A man-child is conceived.'
⁴ Let that day be darkness!
   May God above not seek it,
   or light shine on it.
⁵ Let gloom and deep darkness claim it.
   Let clouds settle upon it;
   let the blackness of the day terrify it.
⁶ That night—let thick darkness seize it!
   let it not rejoice among the days of the
       year;
   let it not come into the number of the
       months.
⁷ Yes, let that night be barren;
   let no joyful cry be heard*ᵍ* in it.
⁸ Let those curse it who curse the Sea,*ʰ*
   those who are skilled to rouse up
       Leviathan.
⁹ Let the stars of its dawn be dark;
   let it hope for light, but have none;
   may it not see the eyelids of the
       morning—
¹⁰ because it did not shut the doors of my
       mother's womb,
   and hide trouble from my eyes.

¹¹ "Why did I not die at birth,
   come forth from the womb and expire?
¹² Why were there knees to receive me,
   or breasts for me to suck?
¹³ Now I would be lying down and quiet;
   I would be asleep; then I would be at rest
¹⁴ with kings and counselors of the earth
   who rebuild ruins for themselves,
¹⁵ or with princes who have gold,
   who fill their houses with silver.
¹⁶ Or why was I not buried like a stillborn
       child,
   like an infant that never sees the light?
¹⁷ There the wicked cease from troubling,
   and there the weary are at rest.
¹⁸ There the prisoners are at ease together;
   they do not hear the voice of the
       taskmaster.
¹⁹ The small and the great are there,

a Heb *sons of God*   *b* Or *the Accuser*; Heb *ha-satan*   *c* Or *The Accuser*; Heb *ha-satan*   *d* Or *All that the man has he will give for his life*   *e* Heb *He*
f Heb *Bless*   *g* Heb *come*   *h* Cn: Heb *day*

and the slaves are free from their
masters.

20 "Why is light given to one in misery,
and life to the bitter in soul,
21 who long for death, but it does not come,
and dig for it more than for hidden
treasures;
22 who rejoice exceedingly,
and are glad when they find the grave?
23 Why is light given to one who cannot see
the way,
whom God has fenced in?
24 For my sighing comes like*a* my bread,
and my groanings are poured out like
water.
25 Truly the thing that I fear comes upon me,
and what I dread befalls me.
26 I am not at ease, nor am I quiet;
I have no rest; but trouble comes."

4 Eliphaz Speaks: Job Has Sinned

Then Eliphaz the Temanite answered:
2 "If one ventures a word with you, will you
be offended?
But who can keep from speaking?
3 See, you have instructed many;
you have strengthened the weak hands.
4 Your words have supported those who were
stumbling,
and you have made firm the feeble knees.
5 But now it has come to you, and you are
impatient;
it touches you, and you are dismayed.
6 Is not your fear of God your confidence,
and the integrity of your ways your hope?

7 "Think now, who that was innocent ever
perished?
Or where were the upright cut off?
8 As I have seen, those who plow iniquity
and sow trouble reap the same.
9 By the breath of God they perish,
and by the blast of his anger they are
consumed.
10 The roar of the lion, the voice of the fierce
lion,
and the teeth of the young lions are
broken.
11 The strong lion perishes for lack of prey,
and the whelps of the lioness are
scattered.

12 "Now a word came stealing to me,
my ear received the whisper of it.
13 Amid thoughts from visions of the night,
when deep sleep falls on mortals,
14 dread came upon me, and trembling,
which made all my bones shake.

15 A spirit glided past my face;
the hair of my flesh bristled.
16 It stood still,
but I could not discern its appearance.
A form was before my eyes;
there was silence, then I heard a voice:
17 'Can mortals be righteous before*b* God?
Can human beings be pure before*b* their
Maker?
18 Even in his servants he puts no trust,
and his angels he charges with error;
19 how much more those who live in houses
of clay,
whose foundation is in the dust,
who are crushed like a moth.
20 Between morning and evening they are
destroyed;
they perish forever without any
regarding it.
21 Their tent-cord is plucked up within them,
and they die devoid of wisdom.'

5 Job Is Corrected by God

"Call now; is there anyone who will answer
you?
To which of the holy ones will you turn?
2 Surely vexation kills the fool,
and jealousy slays the simple.
3 I have seen fools taking root,
but suddenly I cursed their dwelling.
4 Their children are far from safety,
they are crushed in the gate,
and there is no one to deliver them.
5 The hungry eat their harvest,
and they take it even out of the thorns;*c*
and the thirsty*d* pant after their wealth.
6 For misery does not come from the earth,
nor does trouble sprout from the
ground;
7 but human beings are born to trouble
just as sparks*e* fly upward.

8 "As for me, I would seek God,
and to God I would commit my cause.
9 He does great things and unsearchable,
marvelous things without number.
10 He gives rain on the earth
and sends waters on the fields;
11 he sets on high those who are lowly,
and those who mourn are lifted to safety.
12 He frustrates the devices of the crafty,
so that their hands achieve no success.
13 He takes the wise in their own craftiness;
and the schemes of the wily are brought
to a quick end.
14 They meet with darkness in the daytime,
and grope at noonday as in the night.

a Heb before b Or more than c Meaning of Heb uncertain d Aquila Symmachus Syr Vg: Heb snare e Or birds; Heb sons of Resheph

15 But he saves the needy from the sword of
their mouth,
from the hand of the mighty.
16 So the poor have hope,
and injustice shuts its mouth.

17 "How happy is the one whom God reproves;
therefore do not despise the discipline of
the Almighty.*
18 For he wounds, but he binds up;
he strikes, but his hands heal.
19 He will deliver you from six troubles;
in seven no harm shall touch you.
20 In famine he will redeem you from death,
and in war from the power of the sword.
21 You shall be hidden from the scourge of the
tongue,
and shall not fear destruction when it
comes.
22 At destruction and famine you shall laugh,
and shall not fear the wild animals of the
earth.
23 For you shall be in league with the stones of
the field,
and the wild animals shall be at peace
with you.
24 You shall know that your tent is safe,
you shall inspect your fold and miss
nothing.
25 You shall know that your descendants will
be many,
and your offspring like the grass of the
earth.
26 You shall come to your grave in ripe old age,
as a shock of grain comes up to the
threshing floor in its season.
27 See, we have searched this out; it is true.
Hear, and know it for yourself."

6 Job Replies: My Complaint Is Just

Then Job answered:
2 "O that my vexation were weighed,
and all my calamity laid in the balances!
3 For then it would be heavier than the sand
of the sea;
therefore my words have been rash.
4 For the arrows of the Almighty* are in me;
my spirit drinks their poison;
the terrors of God are arrayed against me.
5 Does the wild ass bray over its grass,
or the ox low over its fodder?
6 Can that which is tasteless be eaten without
salt,
or is there any flavor in the juice of
mallows?*
7 My appetite refuses to touch them;
they are like food that is loathsome
to me.*

8 "O that I might have my request,
and that God would grant my desire;
9 that it would please God to crush me,
that he would let loose his hand and cut
me off!
10 This would be my consolation;
I would even exult* in unrelenting pain;

a Traditional rendering of Heb Shaddai b Meaning of Heb uncertain

for I have not denied the words of the
Holy One.

11 What is my strength, that I should wait?
And what is my end, that I should be
patient?

12 Is my strength the strength of stones,
or is my flesh bronze?

13 In truth I have no help in me,
and any resource is driven from me.

14 "Those who withhold[a] kindness from a
friend
forsake the fear of the Almighty.[b]

15 My companions are treacherous like a
torrent-bed,
like freshets that pass away,

16 that run dark with ice,
turbid with melting snow.

17 In time of heat they disappear;
when it is hot, they vanish from their
place.

18 The caravans turn aside from their course;
they go up into the waste, and perish.

19 The caravans of Tema look,
the travelers of Sheba hope.

20 They are disappointed because they were
confident;
they come there and are confounded.

21 Such you have now become to me;[c]
you see my calamity, and are afraid.

22 Have I said, 'Make me a gift'?
Or, 'From your wealth offer a bribe for
me'?

23 Or, 'Save me from an opponent's hand'?
Or, 'Ransom me from the hand of
oppressors'?

24 "Teach me, and I will be silent;
make me understand how I have gone
wrong.

25 How forceful are honest words!
But your reproof, what does it reprove?

26 Do you think that you can reprove words,
as if the speech of the desperate were
wind?

27 You would even cast lots over the orphan,
and bargain over your friend.

28 "But now, be pleased to look at me;
for I will not lie to your face.

29 Turn, I pray, let no wrong be done.
Turn now, my vindication is at stake.

30 Is there any wrong on my tongue?
Cannot my taste discern calamity?

7 Job: My Suffering Is without End

"Do not human beings have a hard service
on earth,

and are not their days like the days of a
laborer?

2 Like a slave who longs for the shadow,
and like laborers who look for their
wages,

3 so I am allotted months of emptiness,
and nights of misery are apportioned
to me.

4 When I lie down I say, 'When shall I rise?'
But the night is long,
and I am full of tossing until dawn.

5 My flesh is clothed with worms and dirt;
my skin hardens, then breaks out again.

6 My days are swifter than a weaver's shuttle,
and come to their end without hope.[d]

7 "Remember that my life is a breath;
my eye will never again see good.

8 The eye that beholds me will see me no
more;
while your eyes are upon me, I shall be
gone.

9 As the cloud fades and vanishes,
so those who go down to Sheol do not
come up;

10 they return no more to their houses,
nor do their places know them any more.

11 "Therefore I will not restrain my mouth;
I will speak in the anguish of my spirit;
I will complain in the bitterness of my
soul.

12 Am I the Sea, or the Dragon,
that you set a guard over me?

13 When I say, 'My bed will comfort me,
my couch will ease my complaint,'

14 then you scare me with dreams
and terrify me with visions,

15 so that I would choose strangling
and death rather than this body.

16 I loathe my life; I would not live forever.
Let me alone, for my days are a breath.

17 What are human beings, that you make so
much of them,
that you set your mind on them,

18 visit them every morning,
test them every moment?

19 Will you not look away from me for a while,
let me alone until I swallow my spittle?

20 If I sin, what do I do to you, you watcher of
humanity?
Why have you made me your target?
Why have I become a burden to you?

21 Why do you not pardon my transgression
and take away my iniquity?
For now I shall lie in the earth;
you will seek me, but I shall not be."

a Syr Vg Compare Tg: Meaning of Heb uncertain   b Traditional rendering of Heb *Shaddai*   c Cn Compare Gk Syr: Meaning of Heb
uncertain   d Or *as the thread runs out*

8 Bildad Speaks: Job Should Repent

Then Bildad the Shuhite answered:

2 "How long will you say these things,
and the words of your mouth be a great
wind?

3 Does God pervert justice?
Or does the Almighty[a] pervert the right?

4 If your children sinned against him,
he delivered them into the power of their
transgression.

5 If you will seek God
and make supplication to the Almighty,[a]

6 if you are pure and upright,
surely then he will rouse himself for you
and restore to you your rightful place.

7 Though your beginning was small,
your latter days will be very great.

8 "For inquire now of bygone generations,
and consider what their ancestors have
found;

9 for we are but of yesterday, and we know
nothing,
for our days on earth are but a shadow.

10 Will they not teach you and tell you
and utter words out of their
understanding?

11 "Can papyrus grow where there is no
marsh?
Can reeds flourish where there is no
water?

12 While yet in flower and not cut down,
they wither before any other plant.

13 Such are the paths of all who forget God;
the hope of the godless shall perish.

14 Their confidence is gossamer,
a spider's house their trust.

15 If one leans against its house, it will not
stand;
if one lays hold of it, it will not endure.

16 The wicked thrive[b] before the sun,
and their shoots spread over the garden.

17 Their roots twine around the stoneheap;
they live among the rocks.[c]

18 If they are destroyed from their place,
then it will deny them, saying, 'I have
never seen you.'

19 See, these are their happy ways,[d]
and out of the earth still others will
spring.

20 "See, God will not reject a blameless
person,
nor take the hand of evildoers.

21 He will yet fill your mouth with laughter,
and your lips with shouts of joy.

Evening Beach—© Justin Dawes, 15

22 Those who hate you will be clothed with
shame,
and the tent of the wicked will be no
more."

9 Job Replies: There Is No Mediator

Then Job answered:

2 "Indeed I know that this is so;
but how can a mortal be just before God?

3 If one wished to contend with him,
one could not answer him once in a
thousand.

4 He is wise in heart, and mighty in strength
—who has resisted him, and succeeded?—

5 he who removes mountains, and they do
not know it,
when he overturns them in his anger;

6 who shakes the earth out of its place,
and its pillars tremble;

7 who commands the sun, and it does not
rise;
who seals up the stars;

8 who alone stretched out the heavens
and trampled the waves of the Sea;[e]

9 who made the Bear and Orion,
the Pleiades and the chambers of the
south;

10 who does great things beyond
understanding,
and marvelous things without number.

11 Look, he passes by me, and I do not see
him;
he moves on, but I do not perceive him.

12 He snatches away; who can stop him?
Who will say to him, 'What are you
doing?'

---

a Traditional rendering of Heb *Shaddai* b Heb *He thrives* c Gk Vg: Meaning of Heb uncertain d Meaning of Heb uncertain
e Or *trampled the back of the sea dragon*

His kids are dead. His belongings are dust and rubble. His friends, if you can still call them that, are bent on blaming him for his fate. His God seems to have either condemned or ignored him. He is a broken man with a broken life. We can understand why Job might have been angry with God—to blame him, to question him, to shout at him, *Why?!*

Yet in his speech in **Job 9.2–35**, Job demonstrates that he has no pride or arrogance about his place in the universe, and he is not up for a fight with God. Here he admits, openly and humbly, that he has no right to take God to court to evaluate whether God has been just. Job knows that God should not be casually approached.

Still, he has one last plea. Job wishes that there might be someone to stand between him and God. **Job 9.33–35** gives voice to the longing that we all have. A longing that somehow, some way, or through *someone* we'd be able to stand in the presence of God.

That someone did eventually come when God became flesh in Jesus. Without him, we are all left to our fates without a plea. But "'In him we live and move and have our being'; as even some of your own poets have said, 'For we too are his offspring'" (Acts 17.28).

(JS)

I must appeal for mercy to my accuser.[a]

16 If I summoned him and he answered me,
   I do not believe that he would listen to
      my voice.

17 For he crushes me with a tempest,
   and multiplies my wounds without
      cause;

18 he will not let me get my breath,
   but fills me with bitterness.

19 If it is a contest of strength, he is the strong
      one!
   If it is a matter of justice, who can
      summon him?[b]

20 Though I am innocent, my own mouth
      would condemn me;
   though I am blameless, he would prove
      me perverse.

21 I am blameless; I do not know myself;
   I loathe my life.

22 It is all one; therefore I say,
   he destroys both the blameless and the
      wicked.

23 When disaster brings sudden death,
   he mocks at the calamity[c] of the
      innocent.

24 The earth is given into the hand of the
      wicked;
   he covers the eyes of its judges—
   if it is not he, who then is it?

25 "My days are swifter than a runner;
   they flee away, they see no good.

26 They go by like skiffs of reed,
   like an eagle swooping on the prey.

27 If I say, 'I will forget my complaint;
   I will put off my sad countenance and be
      of good cheer,'

28 I become afraid of all my suffering,
   for I know you will not hold me
      innocent.

29 I shall be condemned;
   why then do I labor in vain?

30 If I wash myself with soap
   and cleanse my hands with lye,

31 yet you will plunge me into filth,
   and my own clothes will abhor me.

32 For he is not a mortal, as I am, that I might
      answer him,
   that we should come to trial together.

33 There is no umpire[d] between us,
   who might lay his hand on us both.

34 If he would take his rod away from me,
   and not let dread of him terrify me,

35 then I would speak without fear of him,
   for I know I am not what I am thought
      to be.[e]

13 "God will not turn back his anger;
   the helpers of Rahab bowed beneath
      him.

14 How then can I answer him,
   choosing my words with him?

15 Though I am innocent, I cannot answer
      him;

a Or *for my right* b Compare Gk: Heb *me* c Meaning of Heb uncertain d Another reading is *Would that there were an umpire* e Cn: Heb *for I am not so in myself*

10 Job: I Loathe My Life

"I loathe my life;
   I will give free utterance to my complaint;
   I will speak in the bitterness of my soul.
2 I will say to God, Do not condemn me;
   let me know why you contend
      against me.
3 Does it seem good to you to oppress,
   to despise the work of your hands
   and favor the schemes of the wicked?
4 Do you have eyes of flesh?
   Do you see as humans see?
5 Are your days like the days of mortals,
   or your years like human years,
6 that you seek out my iniquity
   and search for my sin,
7 although you know that I am not guilty,
   and there is no one to deliver out of your
      hand?
8 Your hands fashioned and made me;
   and now you turn and destroy me. *a*
9 Remember that you fashioned me like clay;
   and will you turn me to dust again?
10 Did you not pour me out like milk
   and curdle me like cheese?
11 You clothed me with skin and flesh,
   and knit me together with bones and
      sinews.
12 You have granted me life and steadfast love,
   and your care has preserved my spirit.
13 Yet these things you hid in your heart;
   I know that this was your purpose.
14 If I sin, you watch me,
   and do not acquit me of my iniquity.
15 If I am wicked, woe to me!
   If I am righteous, I cannot lift up my
      head,
   for I am filled with disgrace
   and look upon my affliction.
16 Bold as a lion you hunt me;
   you repeat your exploits against me.
17 You renew your witnesses against me,
   and increase your vexation toward me;
   you bring fresh troops against me. *b*
18 "Why did you bring me forth from the
      womb?
   Would that I had died before any eye had
      seen me,
19 and were as though I had not been,
   carried from the womb to the grave.
20 Are not the days of my life few? *c*
   Let me alone, that I may find a little
      comfort *d*
21 before I go, never to return,

to the land of gloom and deep darkness,
22 the land of gloom *e* and chaos,
   where light is like darkness."

11 Zophar Speaks: Job's Guilt Deserves Punishment

Then Zophar the Naamathite answered:
2 "Should a multitude of words go
      unanswered,
   and should one full of talk be vindicated?
3 Should your babble put others to silence,
   and when you mock, shall no one shame
      you?
4 For you say, 'My conduct *f* is pure,
   and I am clean in God's *g* sight.'
5 But O that God would speak,
   and open his lips to you,
6 and that he would tell you the secrets of
      wisdom!
   For wisdom is many-sided. *h*
Know then that God exacts of you less than
      your guilt deserves.

7 "Can you find out the deep things of God?
   Can you find out the limit of the
      Almighty? *i*
8 It is higher than heaven *j*—what can you do?
   Deeper than Sheol—what can you know?
9 Its measure is longer than the earth,
   and broader than the sea.
10 If he passes through, and imprisons,
   and assembles for judgment, who can
      hinder him?
11 For he knows those who are worthless;
   when he sees iniquity, will he not
      consider it?
12 But a stupid person will get understanding,
   when a wild ass is born human. *h*

13 "If you direct your heart rightly,
   you will stretch out your hands toward
      him.
14 If iniquity is in your hand, put it far away,
   and do not let wickedness reside in your
      tents.
15 Surely then you will lift up your face
      without blemish;
   you will be secure, and will not fear.
16 You will forget your misery;
   you will remember it as waters that have
      passed away.
17 And your life will be brighter than the
      noonday;
   its darkness will be like the morning.
18 And you will have confidence, because
      there is hope;

---

a Cn Compare Gk Syr: Heb *made me together all around, and you destroy me* *b* Cn Compare Gk: Heb *toward me; changes and a troop are with me*
c Cn Compare Gk Syr: Heb *Are not my days few? Let him cease!* *d* Heb *that I may brighten up a little* *e* Heb *gloom as darkness, deep darkness*
f Gk: Heb *teaching* *g* Heb *your* *h* Meaning of Heb uncertain *i* Traditional rendering of Heb *Shaddai* *j* Heb *The heights of heaven*

you will be protected[a] and take your rest
in safety.

19 You will lie down, and no one will make you
afraid;
many will entreat your favor.

20 But the eyes of the wicked will fail;
all way of escape will be lost to them,
and their hope is to breathe their last."

12 Job Replies: I Am a Laughingstock

Then Job answered:

2 "No doubt you are the people,
and wisdom will die with you.

3 But I have understanding as well as you;
I am not inferior to you.
Who does not know such things as
these?

4 I am a laughingstock to my friends;
I, who called upon God and he
answered me,
a just and blameless man, I am a
laughingstock.

5 Those at ease have contempt for
misfortune,[b]
but it is ready for those whose feet are
unstable.

6 The tents of robbers are at peace,
and those who provoke God are secure,
who bring their god in their hands.[c]

7 "But ask the animals, and they will teach
you;
the birds of the air, and they will tell you;

8 ask the plants of the earth,[d] and they will
teach you;
and the fish of the sea will declare to you.

9 Who among all these does not know
that the hand of the LORD has done this?

10 In his hand is the life of every living thing
and the breath of every human being.

11 Does not the ear test words
as the palate tastes food?

12 Is wisdom with the aged,
and understanding in length of days?

13 "With God[e] are wisdom and strength;
he has counsel and understanding.

14 If he tears down, no one can rebuild;
if he shuts someone in, no one can
open up.

15 If he withholds the waters, they dry up;
if he sends them out, they overwhelm the
land.

16 With him are strength and wisdom;
the deceived and the deceiver are his.

17 He leads counselors away stripped,
and makes fools of judges.

18 He looses the sash of kings,
and binds a waistcloth on their loins.

19 He leads priests away stripped,
and overthrows the mighty.

20 He deprives of speech those who are
trusted,
and takes away the discernment of the
elders.

21 He pours contempt on princes,
and looses the belt of the strong.

22 He uncovers the deeps out of darkness,
and brings deep darkness to light.

23 He makes nations great, then destroys
them;
he enlarges nations, then leads them
away.

24 He strips understanding from the leaders[f]
of the earth,
and makes them wander in a pathless
waste.

25 They grope in the dark without light;
he makes them stagger like a drunkard.

13 "Look, my eye has seen all this,
my ear has heard and understood it.

2 What you know, I also know;
I am not inferior to you.

3 But I would speak to the Almighty,[g]
and I desire to argue my case with God.

4 As for you, you whitewash with lies;
all of you are worthless physicians.

5 If you would only keep silent,
that would be your wisdom!

6 Hear now my reasoning,
and listen to the pleadings of my lips.

7 Will you speak falsely for God,
and speak deceitfully for him?

8 Will you show partiality toward him,
will you plead the case for God?

9 Will it be well with you when he searches
you out?
Or can you deceive him, as one person
deceives another?

10 He will surely rebuke you
if in secret you show partiality.

11 Will not his majesty terrify you,
and the dread of him fall upon you?

12 Your maxims are proverbs of ashes,
your defenses are defenses of clay.

13 "Let me have silence, and I will speak,
and let come on me what may.

14 I will take my flesh in my teeth,
and put my life in my hand.[h]

15 See, he will kill me; I have no hope;[i]
but I will defend my ways to his face.

16 This will be my salvation,

---

a Or you will look around b Meaning of Heb uncertain c Or whom God brought forth by his hand; Meaning of Heb uncertain d Or speak to
the earth e Heb him f Heb adds of the people g Traditional rendering of Heb Shaddai h Gk: Heb Why should I take . . . in my hand?
i Or Though he kill me, yet I will trust in him

Fallen—© Kristin Sicher, 15

that the godless shall not come before
him.

17 Listen carefully to my words,
and let my declaration be in your ears.

18 I have indeed prepared my case;
I know that I shall be vindicated.

19 Who is there that will contend with me?
For then I would be silent and die.

Job's Despondent Prayer

20 Only grant two things to me,
then I will not hide myself from your
face:

21 withdraw your hand far from me,
and do not let dread of you terrify me.

22 Then call, and I will answer;
or let me speak, and you reply to me.

23 How many are my iniquities and my sins?
Make me know my transgression and my
sin.

24 Why do you hide your face,
and count me as your enemy?

25 Will you frighten a windblown leaf
and pursue dry chaff?

26 For you write bitter things against me,
and make me reap*ᵃ* the iniquities of my
youth.

27 You put my feet in the stocks,
and watch all my paths;
you set a bound to the soles of my feet.

28 One wastes away like a rotten thing,
like a garment that is moth-eaten.

---

14 "A mortal, born of woman, few of days
and full of trouble,

2 comes up like a flower and withers,
flees like a shadow and does not last.

3 Do you fix your eyes on such a one?
Do you bring me into judgment with
you?

4 Who can bring a clean thing out of an
unclean?
No one can.

5 Since their days are determined,
and the number of their months is
known to you,
and you have appointed the bounds that
they cannot pass,

6 look away from them, and desist,*ᵇ*
that they may enjoy, like laborers, their
days.

7 "For there is hope for a tree,
if it is cut down, that it will sprout again,
and that its shoots will not cease.

8 Though its root grows old in the earth,
and its stump dies in the ground,

9 yet at the scent of water it will bud
and put forth branches like a young
plant.

10 But mortals die, and are laid low;
humans expire, and where are they?

11 As waters fail from a lake,
and a river wastes away and dries up,

---

a Heb *inherit* *b* Cn: Heb *that they may desist*

12 so mortals lie down and do not rise again;
     until the heavens are no more, they will
         not awake
     or be roused out of their sleep.
13 O that you would hide me in Sheol,
     that you would conceal me until your
         wrath is past,
     that you would appoint me a set time,
         and remember me!
14 If mortals die, will they live again?
     All the days of my service I would wait
     until my release should come.
15 You would call, and I would answer you;
     you would long for the work of your
         hands.
16 For then you would not*a* number my steps,
     you would not keep watch over my sin;
17 my transgression would be sealed up in a
         bag,
     and you would cover over my iniquity.

18 "But the mountain falls and crumbles away,
     and the rock is removed from its place;
19 the waters wear away the stones;
     the torrents wash away the soil of the
         earth;
     so you destroy the hope of mortals.
20 You prevail forever against them, and they
         pass away;
     you change their countenance, and send
         them away.
21 Their children come to honor, and they do
         not know it;
     they are brought low, and it goes
         unnoticed.
22 They feel only the pain of their own bodies,
     and mourn only for themselves."

15 Eliphaz Speaks: Job Undermines Religion

Then Eliphaz the Temanite answered:
2 "Should the wise answer with windy
         knowledge,
     and fill themselves with the east wind?
3 Should they argue in unprofitable talk,
     or in words with which they can do no
         good?
4 But you are doing away with the fear of God,
     and hindering meditation before God.
5 For your iniquity teaches your mouth,
     and you choose the tongue of the crafty.
6 Your own mouth condemns you, and not I;
     your own lips testify against you.

7 "Are you the firstborn of the human race?
     Were you brought forth before the hills?
8 Have you listened in the council of God?
     And do you limit wisdom to yourself?

9 What do you know that we do not know?
     What do you understand that is not clear
         to us?
10 The gray-haired and the aged are on our
         side,
     those older than your father.
11 Are the consolations of God too small for
         you,
     or the word that deals gently with you?
12 Why does your heart carry you away,
     and why do your eyes flash,*b*
13 so that you turn your spirit against God,
     and let such words go out of your
         mouth?
14 What are mortals, that they can be clean?
     Or those born of woman, that they can
         be righteous?
15 God puts no trust even in his holy ones,
     and the heavens are not clean in his
         sight;
16 how much less one who is abominable and
         corrupt,
     one who drinks iniquity like water!

17 "I will show you; listen to me;
     what I have seen I will declare—
18 what sages have told,
     and their ancestors have not hidden,
19 to whom alone the land was given,
     and no stranger passed among them.
20 The wicked writhe in pain all their days,
     through all the years that are laid up for
         the ruthless.
21 Terrifying sounds are in their ears;
     in prosperity the destroyer will come
         upon them.
22 They despair of returning from darkness,
     and they are destined for the sword.
23 They wander abroad for bread, saying,
         'Where is it?'
     They know that a day of darkness is ready
         at hand;
24 distress and anguish terrify them;
     they prevail against them, like a king
         prepared for battle.
25 Because they stretched out their hands
         against God,
     and bid defiance to the Almighty,*c*
26 running stubbornly against him
     with a thick-bossed shield;
27 because they have covered their faces with
         their fat,
     and gathered fat upon their loins,
28 they will live in desolate cities,
     in houses that no one should inhabit,
     houses destined to become heaps of
         ruins;

a Syr: Heb lacks *not* *b* Meaning of Heb uncertain *c* Traditional rendering of Heb *Shaddai*

29 they will not be rich, and their wealth will
      not endure,
    nor will they strike root in the earth;[a]
30 they will not escape from darkness;
    the flame will dry up their shoots,
    and their blossom[b] will be swept away[c] by
      the wind.
31 Let them not trust in emptiness, deceiving
      themselves;
    for emptiness will be their recompense.
32 It will be paid in full before their time,
    and their branch will not be green.
33 They will shake off their unripe grape, like
      the vine,
    and cast off their blossoms, like the olive
      tree.
34 For the company of the godless is barren,
    and fire consumes the tents of bribery.
35 They conceive mischief and bring forth evil
    and their heart prepares deceit."

16 Job Reaffirms His Innocence

Then Job answered:
2 "I have heard many such things;
    miserable comforters are you all.
3 Have windy words no limit?
    Or what provokes you that you keep on
      talking?
4 I also could talk as you do,
    if you were in my place;
  I could join words together against you,
    and shake my head at you.
5 I could encourage you with my mouth,
    and the solace of my lips would assuage
      your pain.

6 "If I speak, my pain is not assuaged,
    and if I forbear, how much of it leaves
      me?
7 Surely now God has worn me out;
    he has[d] made desolate all my company.
8 And he has[d] shriveled me up,
    which is a witness against me;
  my leanness has risen up against me,
    and it testifies to my face.
9 He has torn me in his wrath, and hated me;
    he has gnashed his teeth at me;
  my adversary sharpens his eyes against me.
10 They have gaped at me with their mouths;
    they have struck me insolently on the
      cheek;
  they mass themselves together against me.
11 God gives me up to the ungodly,
    and casts me into the hands of the
      wicked.
12 I was at ease, and he broke me in two;
    he seized me by the neck and dashed me
      to pieces;

EXPRESS YOURSELF

Blaming God

"Why do bad things happen to good people?"

It's a question as old as time (or at least humanity) itself—and everyone asks it. Unfortunately, there's no quick feel-good answer to this problem. Job, the ancient sufferer, knew this well. Read what he has to say about it in **Job 9.21–24**.

It looks like he's blaming God—and who could fault Job for this, really? In fact, if you read Job 1.12, you'll see that God *did* give his permission for these unfortunate events to take place in Job's life. We don't know if Job *knew* that God gave his permission, but he might have been intuitive enough to figure it out.

(Quick, before this conversation begins to get even darker, grab your camera or a sketch pad. Without going more than a hundred yards from where you are, begin taking pictures of or sketching the bad things that surround you or others. Don't be afraid of them. Name them. Capture them. Try to find at least five images. Once you do, flip your Bible back open to this page and keep reading.)

Sin, sickness, death—it's all tough stuff. It's hard to deal with on both a practical and a philosophical level. But now that you've recognized some of what's around you, take a deep breath and either finish reading Job or (only if you're really pinched for time) skip to the end and read the last chapter. Someone changes . . . is it God or is it Job?

    he set me up as his target;
13   his archers surround me.
  He slashes open my kidneys, and shows no
      mercy;
    he pours out my gall on the ground.
14 He bursts upon me again and again;
    he rushes at me like a warrior.
15 I have sewed sackcloth upon my skin,
    and have laid my strength in the dust.
16 My face is red with weeping,
    and deep darkness is on my eyelids,
17 though there is no violence in my hands,
    and my prayer is pure.

a Vg: Meaning of Heb uncertain   *b* Gk: Heb *mouth*   *c* Cn: Heb *will depart*   *d* Heb *you have*

21 that he would maintain the right of a
mortal with God,
as[a] one does for a neighbor.
22 For when a few years have come,
I shall go the way from which I shall not
return.

17 Job Prays for Relief

My spirit is broken, my days are extinct,
the grave is ready for me.
2 Surely there are mockers around me,
and my eye dwells on their provocation.

3 "Lay down a pledge for me with yourself;
who is there that will give surety for me?
4 Since you have closed their minds to
understanding,
therefore you will not let them triumph.
5 Those who denounce friends for reward—
the eyes of their children will fail.

6 "He has made me a byword of the peoples,
and I am one before whom people spit.
7 My eye has grown dim from grief,
and all my members are like a shadow.
8 The upright are appalled at this,
and the innocent stir themselves up
against the godless.
9 Yet the righteous hold to their way,
and they that have clean hands grow
stronger and stronger.
10 But you, come back now, all of you,
and I shall not find a sensible person
among you.
11 My days are past, my plans are broken off,
the desires of my heart.
12 They make night into day;
'The light,' they say, 'is near to the
darkness.'[b]
13 If I look for Sheol as my house,
if I spread my couch in darkness,
14 if I say to the Pit, 'You are my father,'
and to the worm, 'My mother,' or 'My
sister,'
15 where then is my hope?
Who will see my hope?
16 Will it go down to the bars of Sheol?
Shall we descend together into the
dust?"

18 Bildad Speaks: God Punishes the Wicked

Then Bildad the Shuhite answered:
2 "How long will you hunt for words?
Consider, and then we shall speak.
3 Why are we counted as cattle?
Why are we stupid in your sight?
4 You who tear yourself in your anger—

18 "O earth, do not cover my blood;
let my outcry find no resting place.
19 Even now, in fact, my witness is in heaven,
and he that vouches for me is on high.
20 My friends scorn me;
my eye pours out tears to God,

a Syr Vg Tg: Heb *and* b Meaning of Heb uncertain

shall the earth be forsaken because of
    you,
  or the rock be removed out of its place?

5 "Surely the light of the wicked is put out,
    and the flame of their fire does not
      shine.
6 The light is dark in their tent,
    and the lamp above them is put out.
7 Their strong steps are shortened,
    and their own schemes throw them
      down.
8 For they are thrust into a net by their own
    feet,
    and they walk into a pitfall.
9 A trap seizes them by the heel;
    a snare lays hold of them.
10 A rope is hid for them in the ground,
    a trap for them in the path.
11 Terrors frighten them on every side,
    and chase them at their heels.
12 Their strength is consumed by hunger,[a]
    and calamity is ready for their stumbling.
13 By disease their skin is consumed,[b]
    the firstborn of Death consumes their
      limbs.
14 They are torn from the tent in which they
    trusted,
    and are brought to the king of terrors.
15 In their tents nothing remains;
    sulfur is scattered upon their habitations.
16 Their roots dry up beneath,
    and their branches wither above.
17 Their memory perishes from the earth,
    and they have no name in the street.
18 They are thrust from light into darkness,
    and driven out of the world.
19 They have no offspring or descendant
    among their people,
    and no survivor where they used to live.
20 They of the west are appalled at their fate,
    and horror seizes those of the east.
21 Surely such are the dwellings of the
    ungodly,
    such is the place of those who do not
      know God."

19 Job Replies: I Know That My Redeemer Lives

Then Job answered:
2 "How long will you torment me,
    and break me in pieces with words?
3 These ten times you have cast reproach
    upon me;
    are you not ashamed to wrong me?
4 And even if it is true that I have erred,
    my error remains with me.

5 If indeed you magnify yourselves
    against me,
    and make my humiliation an argument
      against me,
6 know then that God has put me in the
    wrong,
    and closed his net around me.
7 Even when I cry out, 'Violence!' I am not
    answered;
    I call aloud, but there is no justice.
8 He has walled up my way so that I cannot
    pass,
    and he has set darkness upon my paths.
9 He has stripped my glory from me,
    and taken the crown from my head.
10 He breaks me down on every side, and I am
    gone,
    he has uprooted my hope like a tree.
11 He has kindled his wrath against me,
    and counts me as his adversary.
12 His troops come on together;
    they have thrown up siegeworks[c]
      against me,
    and encamp around my tent.

13 "He has put my family far from me,
    and my acquaintances are wholly
      estranged from me.
14 My relatives and my close friends have
    failed me;
15   the guests in my house have
      forgotten me;
  my serving girls count me as a stranger;
    I have become an alien in their eyes.
16 I call to my servant, but he gives me no
    answer;
    I must myself plead with him.
17 My breath is repulsive to my wife;
    I am loathsome to my own family.
18 Even young children despise me;
    when I rise, they talk against me.
19 All my intimate friends abhor me,
    and those whom I loved have turned
      against me.
20 My bones cling to my skin and to my flesh,
    and I have escaped by the skin of my
      teeth.
21 Have pity on me, have pity on me, O you my
    friends,
    for the hand of God has touched me!
22 Why do you, like God, pursue me,
    never satisfied with my flesh?

23 "O that my words were written down!
    O that they were inscribed in a book!
24 O that with an iron pen and with lead
    they were engraved on a rock forever!
25 For I know that my Redeemer[d] lives,

---

a Or *Disaster is hungry for them* b Cn: Heb *It consumes the limbs of his skin* c Cn: Heb *their way* d Or *Vindicator*

TEXT MESSAGE

Snakes were dangerous desert dwellers in biblical times (Job 20.14–16). Numerous varieties of snakes lived in the desert, and about half a dozen species were poisonous. In one instance, snakes invaded an Israelite camp (Numbers 21.6–8), and many of the Israelites died from the bites.

Fact

This information has been scanned and is free of all known viruses. Please forward to all your friends.

and that at the last he*a* will stand upon the earth;*b*

26 and after my skin has been thus destroyed, then in*c* my flesh I shall see God,*d*

27 whom I shall see on my side,*e* and my eyes shall behold, and not another. My heart faints within me!

28 If you say, 'How we will persecute him!' and, 'The root of the matter is found in him';

29 be afraid of the sword, for wrath brings the punishment of the sword, so that you may know there is a judgment."

20 Zophar Speaks: Wickedness Receives Just Retribution

Then Zophar the Naamathite answered:

2 "Pay attention! My thoughts urge me to answer, because of the agitation within me.

3 I hear censure that insults me, and a spirit beyond my understanding answers me.

4 Do you not know this from of old, ever since mortals were placed on earth,

5 that the exulting of the wicked is short, and the joy of the godless is but for a moment?

6 Even though they mount up high as the heavens, and their head reaches to the clouds,

7 they will perish forever like their own dung; those who have seen them will say, 'Where are they?'

8 They will fly away like a dream, and not be found; they will be chased away like a vision of the night.

9 The eye that saw them will see them no more, nor will their place behold them any longer.

10 Their children will seek the favor of the poor, and their hands will give back their wealth.

11 Their bodies, once full of youth, will lie down in the dust with them.

12 "Though wickedness is sweet in their mouth, though they hide it under their tongues,

13 though they are loath to let it go, and hold it in their mouths;

14 yet their food is turned in their stomachs; it is the venom of asps within them.

15 They swallow down riches and vomit them up again; God casts them out of their bellies.

16 They will suck the poison of asps; the tongue of a viper will kill them.

17 They will not look on the rivers, the streams flowing with honey and curds.

18 They will give back the fruit of their toil, and will not swallow it down; from the profit of their trading they will get no enjoyment.

19 For they have crushed and abandoned the poor, they have seized a house that they did not build.

20 "They knew no quiet in their bellies; in their greed they let nothing escape.

a Or *that he the Last* b Heb *dust* c Or *without* d Meaning of Heb of this verse uncertain e Or *for myself*

21 There was nothing left after they had eaten;
   therefore their prosperity will not
   endure.
22 In full sufficiency they will be in distress;
   all the force of misery will come upon
   them.
23 To fill their belly to the full
   God*a* will send his fierce anger into them,
   and rain it upon them as their food.*b*
24 They will flee from an iron weapon;
   a bronze arrow will strike them through.
25 It is drawn forth and comes out of their
   body,
   and the glittering point comes out of
   their gall;
   terrors come upon them.
26 Utter darkness is laid up for their treasures;
   a fire fanned by no one will devour them;
   what is left in their tent will be
   consumed.
27 The heavens will reveal their iniquity,
   and the earth will rise up against them.
28 The possessions of their house will be
   carried away,
   dragged off in the day of God's*c* wrath.
29 This is the portion of the wicked from God,
   the heritage decreed for them by God."

21 Job Replies: The Wicked Often Go Unpunished

Then Job answered:
2 "Listen carefully to my words,
   and let this be your consolation.
3 Bear with me, and I will speak;
   then after I have spoken, mock on.
4 As for me, is my complaint addressed to
   mortals?
   Why should I not be impatient?
5 Look at me, and be appalled,
   and lay your hand upon your mouth.
6 When I think of it I am dismayed,
   and shuddering seizes my flesh.
7 Why do the wicked live on,
   reach old age, and grow mighty in
   power?
8 Their children are established in their
   presence,
   and their offspring before their eyes.
9 Their houses are safe from fear,
   and no rod of God is upon them.
10 Their bull breeds without fail;
   their cow calves and never miscarries.
11 They send out their little ones like a flock,
   and their children dance around.
12 They sing to the tambourine and the lyre,
   and rejoice to the sound of the pipe.
13 They spend their days in prosperity,

and in peace they go down to Sheol.
14 They say to God, 'Leave us alone!
   We do not desire to know your ways.
15 What is the Almighty,*d* that we should serve
   him?
   And what profit do we get if we pray to
   him?'
16 Is not their prosperity indeed their own
   achievement?*e*
   The plans of the wicked are repugnant
   to me.
17 "How often is the lamp of the wicked put
   out?
   How often does calamity come upon
   them?
   How often does God*a* distribute pains in
   his anger?
18 How often are they like straw before the
   wind,
   and like chaff that the storm carries
   away?
19 You say, 'God stores up their iniquity for
   their children.'
   Let it be paid back to them, so that they
   may know it.
20 Let their own eyes see their destruction,
   and let them drink of the wrath of the
   Almighty.*d*
21 For what do they care for their household
   after them,
   when the number of their months is cut
   off?
22 Will any teach God knowledge,
   seeing that he judges those that are on
   high?
23 One dies in full prosperity,
   being wholly at ease and secure,
24 his loins full of milk
   and the marrow of his bones moist.
25 Another dies in bitterness of soul,
   never having tasted of good.
26 They lie down alike in the dust,
   and the worms cover them.
27 "Oh, I know your thoughts,
   and your schemes to wrong me.
28 For you say, 'Where is the house of the
   prince?
   Where is the tent in which the wicked
   lived?'
29 Have you not asked those who travel the
   roads,
   and do you not accept their testimony,
30 that the wicked are spared in the day of
   calamity,
   and are rescued in the day of wrath?
31 Who declares their way to their face,

a Heb *he* *b* Cn: Meaning of Heb uncertain *c* Heb *his* *d* Traditional rendering of Heb *Shaddai* *e* Heb *in their hand*

and who repays them for what they have done?

32 When they are carried to the grave,
a watch is kept over their tomb.

33 The clods of the valley are sweet to them;
everyone will follow after,
and those who went before are innumerable.

34 How then will you comfort me with empty nothings?
There is nothing left of your answers but falsehood."

22 Eliphaz Speaks: Job's Wickedness Is Great

Then Eliphaz the Temanite answered:

2 "Can a mortal be of use to God?
Can even the wisest be of service to him?

3 Is it any pleasure to the Almighty*a* if you are righteous,
or is it gain to him if you make your ways blameless?

4 Is it for your piety that he reproves you,
and enters into judgment with you?

5 Is not your wickedness great?
There is no end to your iniquities.

6 For you have exacted pledges from your family for no reason,
and stripped the naked of their clothing.

7 You have given no water to the weary to drink,
and you have withheld bread from the hungry.

8 The powerful possess the land,
and the favored live in it.

9 You have sent widows away empty-handed,
and the arms of the orphans you have crushed.*b*

10 Therefore snares are around you,
and sudden terror overwhelms you,

11 or darkness so that you cannot see;
a flood of water covers you.

12 "Is not God high in the heavens?
See the highest stars, how lofty they are!

13 Therefore you say, 'What does God know?
Can he judge through the deep darkness?

14 Thick clouds enwrap him, so that he does not see,
and he walks on the dome of heaven.'

15 Will you keep to the old way
that the wicked have trod?

16 They were snatched away before their time;
their foundation was washed away by a flood.

17 They said to God, 'Leave us alone,'
and 'What can the Almighty*a* do to us?'*c*

18 Yet he filled their houses with good things—
but the plans of the wicked are repugnant to me.

19 The righteous see it and are glad;
the innocent laugh them to scorn,

20 saying, 'Surely our adversaries are cut off,
and what they left, the fire has consumed.'

21 "Agree with God,*d* and be at peace;
in this way good will come to you.

22 Receive instruction from his mouth,
and lay up his words in your heart.

23 If you return to the Almighty,*a* you will be restored,
if you remove unrighteousness from your tents,

24 if you treat gold like dust,
and gold of Ophir like the stones of the torrent-bed,

25 and if the Almighty*a* is your gold
and your precious silver,

26 then you will delight yourself in the Almighty,*a*
and lift up your face to God.

27 You will pray to him, and he will hear you,
and you will pay your vows.

28 You will decide on a matter, and it will be established for you,
and light will shine on your ways.

29 When others are humiliated, you say it is pride;
for he saves the humble.

30 He will deliver even those who are guilty;
they will escape because of the cleanness of your hands."*e*

23 Job Replies: My Complaint Is Bitter

Then Job answered:

2 "Today also my complaint is bitter;*f*
his*g* hand is heavy despite my groaning.

3 Oh, that I knew where I might find him,

---

a Traditional rendering of Heb *Shaddai* *b* Gk Syr Tg Vg: Heb *were crushed* *c* Gk Syr: Heb *them* *d* Heb *him* *e* Meaning of Heb uncertain *f* Syr Vg Tg: Heb *rebellious* *g* Gk Syr: Heb *my*

that I might come even to his dwelling!
⁴ I would lay my case before him,
    and fill my mouth with arguments.
⁵ I would learn what he would answer me,
    and understand what he would say to me.
⁶ Would he contend with me in the greatness
        of his power?
    No; but he would give heed to me.
⁷ There an upright person could reason with
        him,
    and I should be acquitted forever by my
        judge.

⁸ "If I go forward, he is not there;
    or backward, I cannot perceive him;
⁹ on the left he hides, and I cannot behold
        him;
    I turn^a to the right, but I cannot see him.
¹⁰ But he knows the way that I take;
    when he has tested me, I shall come out
        like gold.
¹¹ My foot has held fast to his steps;
    I have kept his way and have not turned
        aside.
¹² I have not departed from the
        commandment of his lips;
    I have treasured in^b my bosom the words
        of his mouth.
¹³ But he stands alone and who can dissuade
        him?
    What he desires, that he does.
¹⁴ For he will complete what he appoints
        for me;
    and many such things are in his mind.
¹⁵ Therefore I am terrified at his presence;
    when I consider, I am in dread of him.
¹⁶ God has made my heart faint;
    the Almighty^c has terrified me;
¹⁷ If only I could vanish in darkness,
    and thick darkness would cover my face!^{d}

24 Job Complains of Violence on the Earth

    "Why are times not kept by the Almighty,^{c}
    and why do those who know him never
        see his days?
² The wicked^e remove landmarks;
    they seize flocks and pasture them.
³ They drive away the donkey of the orphan;
    they take the widow's ox for a pledge.
⁴ They thrust the needy off the road;
    the poor of the earth all hide themselves.
⁵ Like wild asses in the desert
    they go out to their toil,
    scavenging in the wasteland
        food for their young.
⁶ They reap in a field not their own

    and they glean in the vineyard of the
        wicked.
⁷ They lie all night naked, without clothing,
    and have no covering in the cold.
⁸ They are wet with the rain of the mountains,
    and cling to the rock for want of shelter.
⁹ "There are those who snatch the orphan
        child from the breast,
    and take as a pledge the infant of the poor.
¹⁰ They go about naked, without clothing;
    though hungry, they carry the sheaves;

---

a Syr Vg: Heb *he turns* *b* Gk Vg: Heb *from* *c* Traditional rendering of Heb *Shaddai* *d* Or *But I am not destroyed by the darkness; he has concealed the thick darkness from me* *e* Gk: Heb *they*

11 between their terraces*a* they press out oil;
    they tread the wine presses, but suffer
       thirst.
12 From the city the dying groan,
    and the throat of the wounded cries for
       help;
    yet God pays no attention to their prayer.

13 "There are those who rebel against the light,
    who are not acquainted with its ways,
    and do not stay in its paths.
14 The murderer rises at dusk
    to kill the poor and needy,
    and in the night is like a thief.
15 The eye of the adulterer also waits for the
       twilight,
    saying, 'No eye will see me';
    and he disguises his face.
16 In the dark they dig through houses;
    by day they shut themselves up;
    they do not know the light.
17 For deep darkness is morning to all of them;
    for they are friends with the terrors of
       deep darkness.

18 "Swift are they on the face of the waters;
    their portion in the land is cursed;
    no treader turns toward their vineyards.
19 Drought and heat snatch away the snow
       waters;
    so does Sheol those who have sinned.
20 The womb forgets them;
    the worm finds them sweet;
    they are no longer remembered;
    so wickedness is broken like a tree.

21 "They harm*b* the childless woman,
    and do no good to the widow.
22 Yet God*c* prolongs the life of the mighty by
       his power;
    they rise up when they despair of life.
23 He gives them security, and they are
       supported;
    his eyes are upon their ways.
24 They are exalted a little while, and then are
       gone;
    they wither and fade like the mallow;*d*
    they are cut off like the heads of grain.
25 If it is not so, who will prove me a liar,
    and show that there is nothing in what I
       say?"

25 Bildad Speaks: How Can a Mortal Be Righteous Before God?

Then Bildad the Shuhite answered:
2 "Dominion and fear are with God;*e*
    he makes peace in his high heaven.
3 Is there any number to his armies?

Upon whom does his light not arise?
4 How then can a mortal be righteous before
       God?
    How can one born of woman be pure?
5 If even the moon is not bright
    and the stars are not pure in his sight,
6 how much less a mortal, who is a maggot,
    and a human being, who is a worm!"

26 Job Replies: God's Majesty Is Unsearchable

Then Job answered:
2 "How you have helped one who has no
       power!
    How you have assisted the arm that has
       no strength!
3 How you have counseled one who has no
       wisdom,
    and given much good advice!
4 With whose help have you uttered words,
    and whose spirit has come forth from
       you?
5 The shades below tremble,
    the waters and their inhabitants.
6 Sheol is naked before God,
    and Abaddon has no covering.
7 He stretches out Zaphon*f* over the void,
    and hangs the earth upon nothing.
8 He binds up the waters in his thick clouds,
    and the cloud is not torn open by them.
9 He covers the face of the full moon,
    and spreads over it his cloud.
10 He has described a circle on the face of the
       waters,
    at the boundary between light and
       darkness.
11 The pillars of heaven tremble,
    and are astounded at his rebuke.
12 By his power he stilled the Sea;
    by his understanding he struck down
       Rahab.
13 By his wind the heavens were made fair;
    his hand pierced the fleeing serpent.
14 These are indeed but the outskirts of his
       ways;
    and how small a whisper do we hear of
       him!
    But the thunder of his power who can
       understand?"

27 Job Maintains His Integrity

Job again took up his discourse and said:
2 "As God lives, who has taken away my right,
    and the Almighty,*g* who has made my
       soul bitter,
3 as long as my breath is in me

---

a Meaning of Heb uncertain   *b* Gk Tg: Heb *feed on* or *associate with*   *c* Heb *he*   *d* Gk: Heb *like all others*   *e* Heb *him*   *f* Or *the North*
g Traditional rendering of Heb *Shaddai*

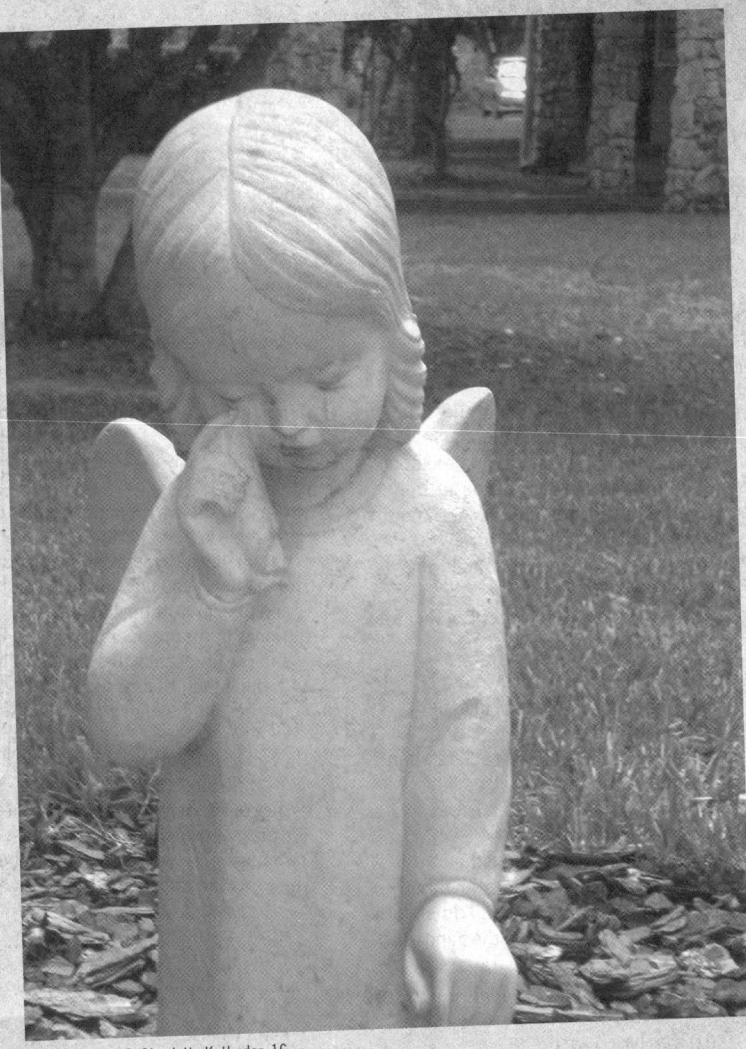

Angel Tears—© Charlotte Katheder, 16

The Path—© Amari Gills, 11

and the spirit of God is in my nostrils,
⁴ my lips will not speak falsehood,
  and my tongue will not utter deceit.
⁵ Far be it from me to say that you are right;
  until I die I will not put away my integrity
    from me.
⁶ I hold fast my righteousness, and will not
    let it go;
  my heart does not reproach me for any of
    my days.

⁷ "May my enemy be like the wicked,
  and may my opponent be like the
    unrighteous.
⁸ For what is the hope of the godless when
    God cuts them off,
  when God takes away their lives?
⁹ Will God hear their cry
  when trouble comes upon them?
¹⁰ Will they take delight in the Almighty?ᵃ
  Will they call upon God at all times?
¹¹ I will teach you concerning the hand of
    God;
  that which is with the Almightyᵃ I will not
    conceal.
¹² All of you have seen it yourselves;
  why then have you become altogether
    vain?

¹³ "This is the portion of the wicked with God,
  and the heritage that oppressors receive
    from the Almighty:ᵃ

¹⁴ If their children are multiplied, it is for the
    sword;
  and their offspring have not enough to
    eat.
¹⁵ Those who survive them the pestilence
    buries,
  and their widows make no lamentation.
¹⁶ Though they heap up silver like dust,
  and pile up clothing like clay—
¹⁷ they may pile it up, but the just will wear it,
  and the innocent will divide the silver.
¹⁸ They build their houses like nests,
  like booths made by sentinels of the
    vineyard.
¹⁹ They go to bed with wealth, but will do so
    no more;
  they open their eyes, and it is gone.
²⁰ Terrors overtake them like a flood;
  in the night a whirlwind carries them off.
²¹ The east wind lifts them up and they are
    gone;
  it sweeps them out of their place.
²² Itᵇ hurls at them without pity;
  they flee from itsᶜ power in headlong
    flight.
²³ Itᵇ claps itsᶜ hands at them,
  and hisses at them from itsᶜ place.

28 Interlude: Where Wisdom Is Found
  "Surely there is a mine for silver,
    and a place for gold to be refined.
² Iron is taken out of the earth,

---

a Traditional rendering of Heb *Shaddai* *b* Or *He* (that is God) *c* Or *his*

and copper is smelted from ore.
3 Miners put[a] an end to darkness,
   and search out to the farthest bound
      the ore in gloom and deep darkness.
4 They open shafts in a valley away from
      human habitation;
   they are forgotten by travelers,
   they sway suspended, remote from
      people.
5 As for the earth, out of it comes bread;
   but underneath it is turned up as by fire.
6 Its stones are the place of sapphires,[b]
   and its dust contains gold.

7 "That path no bird of prey knows,
   and the falcon's eye has not seen it.
8 The proud wild animals have not trodden it;
   the lion has not passed over it.

9 "They put their hand to the flinty rock,
   and overturn mountains by the roots.
10 They cut out channels in the rocks,
   and their eyes see every precious thing.
11 The sources of the rivers they probe;[c]
   hidden things they bring to light.

12 "But where shall wisdom be found?
   And where is the place of understanding?
13 Mortals do not know the way to it,[d]
   and it is not found in the land of the
      living.
14 The deep says, 'It is not in me,'
   and the sea says, 'It is not with me.'
15 It cannot be gotten for gold,
   and silver cannot be weighed out as its
      price.
16 It cannot be valued in the gold of Ophir,
   in precious onyx or sapphire.[b]
17 Gold and glass cannot equal it,
   nor can it be exchanged for jewels of fine
      gold.
18 No mention shall be made of coral or of
      crystal;
   the price of wisdom is above pearls.
19 The chrysolite of Ethiopia[e] cannot compare
      with it,
   nor can it be valued in pure gold.

20 "Where then does wisdom come from?
   And where is the place of understanding?
21 It is hidden from the eyes of all living,
   and concealed from the birds of the air.
22 Abaddon and Death say,
   'We have heard a rumor of it with our
      ears.'

23 "God understands the way to it,
   and he knows its place.
24 For he looks to the ends of the earth,
   and sees everything under the heavens.

25 When he gave to the wind its weight,
   and apportioned out the waters by
      measure;
26 when he made a decree for the rain,
   and a way for the thunderbolt;
27 then he saw it and declared it;
   he established it, and searched it out.
28 And he said to humankind,
   'Truly, the fear of the Lord, that is wisdom;
   and to depart from evil is
      understanding.' "

29 Job Finishes His Defense

Job again took up his discourse and said:
2 "O that I were as in the months of old,
   as in the days when God watched
      over me;
3 when his lamp shone over my head,
   and by his light I walked through
      darkness;
4 when I was in my prime,
   when the friendship of God was upon my
      tent;
5 when the Almighty[f] was still with me,
   when my children were around me;
6 when my steps were washed with milk,
   and the rock poured out for me streams
      of oil!
7 When I went out to the gate of the city,
   when I took my seat in the square,
8 the young men saw me and withdrew,
   and the aged rose up and stood;
9 the nobles refrained from talking,
   and laid their hands on their mouths;
10 the voices of princes were hushed,
   and their tongues stuck to the roof of
      their mouths.
11 When the ear heard, it commended me,
   and when the eye saw, it approved;
12 because I delivered the poor who cried,
   and the orphan who had no helper.
13 The blessing of the wretched came
      upon me,
   and I caused the widow's heart to sing for
      joy.
14 I put on righteousness, and it clothed me;
   my justice was like a robe and a turban.
15 I was eyes to the blind,
   and feet to the lame.
16 I was a father to the needy,
   and I championed the cause of the
      stranger.
17 I broke the fangs of the unrighteous,
   and made them drop their prey from
      their teeth.
18 Then I thought, 'I shall die in my nest,

a Heb He puts b Or lapis lazuli c Gk Vg: Heb bind d Gk: Heb its price e Or Nubia; Heb Cush f Traditional rendering of Heb Shaddai

and I shall multiply my days like the
    phoenix;^a

19 my roots spread out to the waters,
    with the dew all night on my branches;

20 my glory was fresh with me,
    and my bow ever new in my hand.'

21 "They listened to me, and waited,
    and kept silence for my counsel.

22 After I spoke they did not speak again,
    and my word dropped upon them like
    dew.^b

23 They waited for me as for the rain;
    they opened their mouths as for the
    spring rain.

24 I smiled on them when they had no
    confidence;
    and the light of my countenance they did
    not extinguish.^c

25 I chose their way, and sat as chief,
    and I lived like a king among his troops,
    like one who comforts mourners.

30 "But now they make sport of me,
    those who are younger than I,
    whose fathers I would have disdained
    to set with the dogs of my flock.

2 What could I gain from the strength of their
    hands?
    All their vigor is gone.

3 Through want and hard hunger
    they gnaw the dry and desolate ground,

4 they pick mallow and the leaves of bushes,
    and to warm themselves the roots of
    broom.

5 They are driven out from society;
    people shout after them as after a thief.

6 In the gullies of wadis they must live,
    in holes in the ground, and in the rocks.

7 Among the bushes they bray;
    under the nettles they huddle together.

8 A senseless, disreputable brood,
    they have been whipped out of the land.

9 "And now they mock me in song;
    I am a byword to them.

10 They abhor me, they keep aloof from me;
    they do not hesitate to spit at the sight
    of me.

11 Because God has loosed my bowstring and
    humbled me,
    they have cast off restraint in my
    presence.

12 On my right hand the rabble rise up;
    they send me sprawling,
    and build roads for my ruin.

13 They break up my path,
    they promote my calamity;

no one restrains^d them.

14 As through a wide breach they come;
    amid the crash they roll on.

15 Terrors are turned upon me;
    my honor is pursued as by the wind,
    and my prosperity has passed away like a
    cloud.

16 "And now my soul is poured out within me;
    days of affliction have taken hold of me.

17 The night racks my bones,
    and the pain that gnaws me takes no rest.

18 With violence he seizes my garment;^e
    he grasps me by^f the collar of my tunic.

19 He has cast me into the mire,
    and I have become like dust and ashes.

20 I cry to you and you do not answer me;
    I stand, and you merely look at me.

21 You have turned cruel to me;
    with the might of your hand you
    persecute me.

22 You lift me up on the wind, you make me
    ride on it,
    and you toss me about in the roar of the
    storm.

23 I know that you will bring me to death,
    and to the house appointed for all living.

24 "Surely one does not turn against the
    needy,^g
    when in disaster they cry for help.^h

25 Did I not weep for those whose day was
    hard?
    Was not my soul grieved for the poor?

26 But when I looked for good, evil came;
    and when I waited for light, darkness
    came.

27 My inward parts are in turmoil, and are
    never still;
    days of affliction come to meet me.

28 I go about in sunless gloom;
    I stand up in the assembly and cry for
    help.

29 I am a brother of jackals,
    and a companion of ostriches.

30 My skin turns black and falls from me,
    and my bones burn with heat.

31 My lyre is turned to mourning,
    and my pipe to the voice of those who
    weep.

31 "I have made a covenant with my eyes;
    how then could I look upon a virgin?

2 What would be my portion from God above,
    and my heritage from the Almightyⁱ on
    high?

3 Does not calamity befall the unrighteous,
    and disaster the workers of iniquity?

a Or *like sand* *b* Heb lacks *like dew* *c* Meaning of Heb uncertain *d* Cn: Heb *helps* *e* Gk: Heb *my garment is disfigured* *f* Heb *like*
g Heb *ruin* *h* Cn: Meaning of Heb uncertain *i* Traditional rendering of Heb *Shaddai*

⁴ Does he not see my ways,
  and number all my steps?

⁵ "If I have walked with falsehood,
  and my foot has hurried to deceit—
⁶ let me be weighed in a just balance,
  and let God know my integrity!—
⁷ if my step has turned aside from the way,
  and my heart has followed my eyes,
  and if any spot has clung to my hands;
⁸ then let me sow, and another eat;
  and let what grows for me be rooted out.

⁹ "If my heart has been enticed by a woman,
  and I have lain in wait at my neighbor's
    door;
¹⁰ then let my wife grind for another,
  and let other men kneel over her.
¹¹ For that would be a heinous crime;
  that would be a criminal offense;
¹² for that would be a fire consuming down to
    Abaddon,
  and it would burn to the root all my
    harvest.

¹³ "If I have rejected the cause of my male or
    female slaves,
  when they brought a complaint
    against me;
¹⁴ what then shall I do when God rises up?
  When he makes inquiry, what shall I
    answer him?
¹⁵ Did not he who made me in the womb
    make them?
  And did not one fashion us in the womb?

¹⁶ "If I have withheld anything that the poor
    desired,
  or have caused the eyes of the widow to
    fail,
¹⁷ or have eaten my morsel alone,
  and the orphan has not eaten from it—
¹⁸ for from my youth I reared the orphan^a like
    a father,
  and from my mother's womb I guided
    the widow^b—
¹⁹ if I have seen anyone perish for lack of
    clothing,
  or a poor person without covering,
²⁰ whose loins have not blessed me,
  and who was not warmed with the fleece
    of my sheep;
²¹ if I have raised my hand against the orphan,
  because I saw I had supporters at the gate;
²² then let my shoulder blade fall from my
    shoulder,
  and let my arm be broken from its socket.
²³ For I was in terror of calamity from God,
  and I could not have faced his majesty.

Orange Flower—© Rachel Hostert, 18

²⁴ "If I have made gold my trust,
  or called fine gold my confidence;
²⁵ if I have rejoiced because my wealth was
    great,
  or because my hand had gotten much;
²⁶ if I have looked at the sun^c when it shone,
  or the moon moving in splendor,
²⁷ and my heart has been secretly enticed,
  and my mouth has kissed my hand;
²⁸ this also would be an iniquity to be
    punished by the judges,
  for I should have been false to God above.

²⁹ "If I have rejoiced at the ruin of those who
    hated me,
  or exulted when evil overtook them—
³⁰ I have not let my mouth sin
  by asking for their lives with a curse—
³¹ if those of my tent ever said,
  'O that we might be sated with his
    flesh!'^d—
³² the stranger has not lodged in the street;
  I have opened my doors to the traveler—
³³ if I have concealed my transgressions as
    others do,^e
  by hiding my iniquity in my bosom,
³⁴ because I stood in great fear of the
    multitude,
  and the contempt of families terrified me,
  so that I kept silence, and did not go out
    of doors—
³⁵ O that I had one to hear me!
  (Here is my signature! Let the Almighty^f
    answer me!)
  O that I had the indictment written by my
    adversary!

a Heb *him* *b* Heb *her* *c* Heb *the light* *d* Meaning of Heb uncertain *e* Or *as Adam did* *f* Traditional rendering of Heb *Shaddai*

PROFILE OF FAITH

The daughter of a Mohawk warrior and an Algonquin woman, Kateri was born in upstate New York in 1656. When she was four, smallpox swept through her village and took the lives of her mother, father, and brother. Kateri was left with unsightly scars on her face and poor eyesight. She was then adopted by her uncle, who was a chief of the Turtle clan.

When she was ten, her whole village was burned down, and her clan moved to another site. As a teenager Kateri met some Jesuits who were working with Native Americans. She became interested in Catholicism and was baptized at the age of twenty. She took the name Kateri (Catherine) at Baptism.

Kateri suffered great hostility from her tribe because of her conversion. Her new religion angered her relatives and the villagers, who saw her as a traitor for embracing the white man's religion and rejecting tribal customs. She was forbidden food on Sundays and Christian holidays, because she refused to work on those days.

Kateri fled to an established community of Native American Christians in Quebec, where she lived a life dedicated to prayer, penance, and care for the sick and aged. She died at the age of twenty-four; her last words were, "Jesus, I love you!" She was beatified by Pope John Paul II in 1980.

Indian Girl—© Bailey Smith, 17

---

³⁶ Surely I would carry it on my shoulder;
    I would bind it on me like a crown;
³⁷ I would give him an account of all my steps;
    like a prince I would approach him.

³⁸ "If my land has cried out against me,
    and its furrows have wept together;
³⁹ if I have eaten its yield without payment,
    and caused the death of its owners;
⁴⁰ let thorns grow instead of wheat,
    and foul weeds instead of barley."

The words of Job are ended.

32 Elihu Rebukes Job's Friends

So these three men ceased to answer Job, because he was righteous in his own eyes. ²Then Elihu son of Barachel the Buzite, of the family of Ram, became angry. He was angry at Job because he justified himself rather than God; ³he was angry also at Job's three friends because they had found no answer, though they had declared Job to be in the wrong.ᵃ ⁴Now Elihu had waited to speak to Job, because they were older than he. ⁵But when Elihu saw that there was no answer in the mouths of these three men, he became angry.

6 Elihu son of Barachel the Buzite answered:
"I am young in years,
    and you are aged;
therefore I was timid and afraid
    to declare my opinion to you.
⁷ I said, 'Let days speak,
    and many years teach wisdom.'
⁸ But truly it is the spirit in a mortal,
    the breath of the Almighty,ᵇ that makes
      for understanding.
⁹ It is not the oldᶜ that are wise,
    nor the aged that understand what is
      right.
¹⁰ Therefore I say, 'Listen to me;
    let me also declare my opinion.'

¹¹ "See, I waited for your words,
    I listened for your wise sayings,

---

a Another ancient tradition reads *answer, and had put God in the wrong* *b* Traditional rendering of Heb *Shaddai* *c* Gk Syr Vg: Heb *many* while you searched out what to say.

¹² I gave you my attention,
but there was in fact no one that
confuted Job,
no one among you that answered his
words.

¹³ Yet do not say, 'We have found wisdom;
God may vanquish him, not a human.'

¹⁴ He has not directed his words against me,
and I will not answer him with your
speeches.

¹⁵ "They are dismayed, they answer no more;
they have not a word to say.

¹⁶ And am I to wait, because they do not speak,
because they stand there, and answer no
more?

¹⁷ I also will give my answer;
I also will declare my opinion.

¹⁸ For I am full of words;
the spirit within me constrains me.

¹⁹ My heart is indeed like wine that has no
vent;
like new wineskins, it is ready to burst.

²⁰ I must speak, so that I may find relief;
I must open my lips and answer.

²¹ I will not show partiality to any person
or use flattery toward anyone.

²² For I do not know how to flatter—
or my Maker would soon put an end
to me!

33 Elihu Rebukes Job

"But now, hear my speech, O Job,
and listen to all my words.

² See, I open my mouth;
the tongue in my mouth speaks.

³ My words declare the uprightness of my
heart,
and what my lips know they speak
sincerely.

⁴ The spirit of God has made me,
and the breath of the Almighty*a* gives me
life.

⁵ Answer me, if you can;
set your words in order before me; take
your stand.

⁶ See, before God I am as you are;
I too was formed from a piece of clay.

⁷ No fear of me need terrify you;
my pressure will not be heavy on you.

⁸ "Surely, you have spoken in my hearing,
and I have heard the sound of your
words.

⁹ You say, 'I am clean, without transgression;
I am pure, and there is no iniquity in me.

¹⁰ Look, he finds occasions against me,

he counts me as his enemy;

¹¹ he puts my feet in the stocks,
and watches all my paths.'

¹² "But in this you are not right. I will answer
you:
God is greater than any mortal.

¹³ Why do you contend against him,
saying, 'He will answer none of my*b*
words'?

¹⁴ For God speaks in one way,
and in two, though people do not
perceive it.

¹⁵ In a dream, in a vision of the night,
when deep sleep falls on mortals,
while they slumber on their beds,

¹⁶ then he opens their ears,
and terrifies them with warnings,

¹⁷ that he may turn them aside from their
deeds,
and keep them from pride,

¹⁸ to spare their souls from the Pit,
their lives from traversing the River.

¹⁹ They are also chastened with pain upon
their beds,
and with continual strife in their bones,

²⁰ so that their lives loathe bread,
and their appetites dainty food.

²¹ Their flesh is so wasted away that it cannot
be seen;
and their bones, once invisible, now
stick out.

²² Their souls draw near the Pit,
and their lives to those who bring death.

²³ Then, if there should be for one of them an
angel,
a mediator, one of a thousand,
one who declares a person upright,

²⁴ and he is gracious to that person, and says,
'Deliver him from going down into the
Pit;
I have found a ransom;

²⁵ let his flesh become fresh with youth;
let him return to the days of his youthful
vigor';

²⁶ then he prays to God, and is accepted by
him,
he comes into his presence with joy,
and God*c* repays him for his righteousness.

²⁷ That person sings to others and says,
'I sinned, and perverted what was right,
and it was not paid back to me.

²⁸ He has redeemed my soul from going down
to the Pit,
and my life shall see the light.'

²⁹ "God indeed does all these things,
twice, three times, with mortals,

a Traditional rendering of Heb *Shaddai* *b* Compare Gk: Heb *his* *c* Heb *he*

Ancient cultures envisioned the earth resting on everything from pillars to sea turtles (Job 38.4–6). Everyone probably sleeps a little better since Isaac Newton discovered gravity.

30 to bring back their souls from the Pit,
　　so that they may see the light of life. *a*
31 Pay heed, Job, listen to me;
　　be silent, and I will speak.
32 If you have anything to say, answer me;
　　speak, for I desire to justify you.
33 If not, listen to me;
　　be silent, and I will teach you wisdom."

34 Elihu Proclaims God's Justice

Then Elihu continued and said:
2 "Hear my words, you wise men,
　　and give ear to me, you who know;
3 for the ear tests words
　　as the palate tastes food.
4 Let us choose what is right;
　　let us determine among ourselves what is
　　　good.
5 For Job has said, 'I am innocent,
　　and God has taken away my right;

6 in spite of being right I am counted a liar;
　　my wound is incurable, though I am
　　　without transgression.'
7 Who is there like Job,
　　who drinks up scoffing like water,
8 who goes in company with evildoers
　　and walks with the wicked?
9 For he has said, 'It profits one nothing
　　to take delight in God.'

10 "Therefore, hear me, you who have sense,
　　far be it from God that he should do
　　　wickedness,
　　and from the Almighty*b* that he should
　　　do wrong.
11 For according to their deeds he will repay
　　　them,
　　and according to their ways he will make
　　　it befall them.
12 Of a truth, God will not do wickedly,
　　and the Almighty*b* will not pervert
　　　justice.
13 Who gave him charge over the earth
　　and who laid on him*c* the whole world?
14 If he should take back his spirit*d* to himself,
　　and gather to himself his breath,
15 all flesh would perish together,
　　and all mortals return to dust.

16 "If you have understanding, hear this;
　　listen to what I say.
17 Shall one who hates justice govern?
　　Will you condemn one who is righteous
　　　and mighty,
18 who says to a king, 'You scoundrel!'
　　and to princes, 'You wicked men!';
19 who shows no partiality to nobles,
　　nor regards the rich more than the poor,
　　for they are all the work of his hands?
20 In a moment they die;
　　at midnight the people are shaken and
　　　pass away,
　　and the mighty are taken away by no
　　　human hand.

21 "For his eyes are upon the ways of mortals,
　　and he sees all their steps.
22 There is no gloom or deep darkness
　　where evildoers may hide themselves.
23 For he has not appointed a time*e* for anyone
　　to go before God in judgment.
24 He shatters the mighty without
　　　investigation,
　　and sets others in their place.
25 Thus, knowing their works,
　　he overturns them in the night, and they
　　　are crushed.
26 He strikes them for their wickedness

a Syr: Heb *to be lighted with the light of life* *b* Traditional rendering of Heb *Shaddai* *c* Heb lacks *on him* *d* Heb *his heart his spirit*
e Cn: Heb *yet*

while others look on,
27 because they turned aside from following
          him,
    and had no regard for any of his ways,
28 so that they caused the cry of the poor to
          come to him,
    and he heard the cry of the afflicted—
29 When he is quiet, who can condemn?
    When he hides his face, who can behold
          him,
    whether it be a nation or an
          individual?—
30 so that the godless should not reign,
    or those who ensnare the people.

31 "For has anyone said to God,
    'I have endured punishment; I will not
          offend any more;
32 teach me what I do not see;
    if I have done iniquity, I will do it no
          more'?
33 Will he then pay back to suit you,
    because you reject it?
    For you must choose, and not I;
    therefore declare what you know.ᵃ
34 Those who have sense will say to me,
    and the wise who hear me will say,
35 'Job speaks without knowledge,
    his words are without insight.'
36 Would that Job were tried to the limit,
    because his answers are those of the
          wicked.
37 For he adds rebellion to his sin;
    he claps his hands among us,
    and multiplies his words against God."

35 Elihu Condemns Self-Righteousness

Elihu continued and said:
2 "Do you think this to be just?
    You say, 'I am in the right before God.'
3 If you ask, 'What advantage have I?
    How am I better off than if I had sinned?'
4 I will answer you
    and your friends with you.
5 Look at the heavens and see;
    observe the clouds, which are higher
          than you.
6 If you have sinned, what do you accomplish
          against him?
    And if your transgressions are multiplied,
          what do you do to him?
7 If you are righteous, what do you give to
          him;
    or what does he receive from your hand?
8 Your wickedness affects others like you,
    and your righteousness, other human
          beings.

9 "Because of the multitude of oppressions
          people cry out;
    they call for help because of the arm of
          the mighty.
10 But no one says, 'Where is God my Maker,
    who gives strength in the night,
11 who teaches us more than the animals of
          the earth,
    and makes us wiser than the birds of the
          air?'
12 There they cry out, but he does not answer,
    because of the pride of evildoers.
13 Surely God does not hear an empty cry,
    nor does the Almightyᵇ regard it.
14 How much less when you say that you do
          not see him,
    that the case is before him, and you are
          waiting for him!
15 And now, because his anger does not
          punish,
    and he does not greatly heed
          transgression,ᶜ
16 Job opens his mouth in empty talk,
    he multiplies words without
          knowledge."

36 Elihu Exalts God's Goodness

Elihu continued and said:
2 "Bear with me a little, and I will show you,
    for I have yet something to say on God's
          behalf.
3 I will bring my knowledge from far away,
    and ascribe righteousness to my Maker.
4 For truly my words are not false;
    one who is perfect in knowledge is with
          you.

5 "Surely God is mighty and does not despise
          any;
    he is mighty in strength of
          understanding.
6 He does not keep the wicked alive,
    but gives the afflicted their right.
7 He does not withdraw his eyes from the
          righteous,
    but with kings on the throne
    he sets them forever, and they are
          exalted.
8 And if they are bound in fetters
    and caught in the cords of affliction,
9 then he declares to them their work
    and their transgressions, that they are
          behaving arrogantly.
10 He opens their ears to instruction,
    and commands that they return from
          iniquity.
11 If they listen, and serve him,

ᵃ Meaning of Heb of verses 29–33 uncertain   ᵇ Traditional rendering of Heb *Shaddai*   ᶜ Theodotion Symmachus Compare Vg:
Meaning of Heb uncertain

they complete their days in prosperity,
and their years in pleasantness.
¹² But if they do not listen, they shall perish by
the sword,
and die without knowledge.

¹³ "The godless in heart cherish anger;
they do not cry for help when he binds
them.
¹⁴ They die in their youth,
and their life ends in shame.^a
¹⁵ He delivers the afflicted by their affliction,
and opens their ear by adversity.
¹⁶ He also allured you out of distress
into a broad place where there was no
constraint,
and what was set on your table was full of
fatness.

¹⁷ "But you are obsessed with the case of the
wicked;
judgment and justice seize you.
¹⁸ Beware that wrath does not entice you into
scoffing,
and do not let the greatness of the
ransom turn you aside.
¹⁹ Will your cry avail to keep you from distress,
or will all the force of your strength?
²⁰ Do not long for the night,
when peoples are cut off in their place.
²¹ Beware! Do not turn to iniquity;
because of that you have been tried by
affliction.
²² See, God is exalted in his power;
who is a teacher like him?
²³ Who has prescribed for him his way,
or who can say, 'You have done wrong'?

Elihu Proclaims God's Majesty
²⁴ "Remember to extol his work,
of which mortals have sung.
²⁵ All people have looked on it;
everyone watches it from far away.
²⁶ Surely God is great, and we do not know
him;
the number of his years is unsearchable.
²⁷ For he draws up the drops of water;
he distills^b his mist in rain,
²⁸ which the skies pour down
and drop upon mortals abundantly.
²⁹ Can anyone understand the spreading of
the clouds,
the thunderings of his pavilion?
³⁰ See, he scatters his lightning around him
and covers the roots of the sea.
³¹ For by these he governs peoples;
he gives food in abundance.

³² He covers his hands with the lightning,
and commands it to strike the mark.
³³ Its crashing^c tells about him;
he is jealous^c with anger against iniquity.

37 "At this also my heart trembles,
and leaps out of its place.
² Listen, listen to the thunder of his voice
and the rumbling that comes from his
mouth.
³ Under the whole heaven he lets it loose,
and his lightning to the corners of the
earth.
⁴ After it his voice roars;
he thunders with his majestic voice
and he does not restrain the lightnings^d
when his voice is heard.
⁵ God thunders wondrously with his voice;
he does great things that we cannot
comprehend.
⁶ For to the snow he says, 'Fall on the earth';
and the shower of rain, his heavy shower
of rain,
⁷ serves as a sign on everyone's hand,
so that all whom he has made may
know it.^e
⁸ Then the animals go into their lairs
and remain in their dens.
⁹ From its chamber comes the whirlwind,
and cold from the scattering winds.
¹⁰ By the breath of God ice is given,
and the broad waters are frozen fast.
¹¹ He loads the thick cloud with moisture;
the clouds scatter his lightning.
¹² They turn round and round by his guidance,
to accomplish all that he commands
them
on the face of the habitable world.
¹³ Whether for correction, or for his land,
or for love, he causes it to happen.

¹⁴ "Hear this, O Job;
stop and consider the wondrous works of
God.
¹⁵ Do you know how God lays his command
upon them,
and causes the lightning of his cloud to
shine?
¹⁶ Do you know the balancings of the clouds,
the wondrous works of the one whose
knowledge is perfect,
¹⁷ you whose garments are hot
when the earth is still because of the
south wind?
¹⁸ Can you, like him, spread out the skies,
hard as a molten mirror?
¹⁹ Teach us what we shall say to him;

<hr>

^a Heb *ends among the temple prostitutes* ^b Cn: Heb *they distill* ^c Meaning of Heb uncertain ^d Heb *them* ^e Meaning of Heb of verse 7
uncertain

we cannot draw up our case because of
    darkness.
20 Should he be told that I want to speak?
    Did anyone ever wish to be
        swallowed up?
21 Now, no one can look on the light
    when it is bright in the skies,
    when the wind has passed and cleared
        them.
22 Out of the north comes golden splendor;
    around God is awesome majesty.
23 The Almighty*a*—we cannot find him;
    he is great in power and justice,
    and abundant righteousness he will not
        violate.
24 Therefore mortals fear him;
    he does not regard any who are wise in
        their own conceit."

38 The LORD Answers Job

Then the LORD answered Job out of the whirl-wind:
2 "Who is this that darkens counsel by words
    without knowledge?
3 Gird up your loins like a man,
    I will question you, and you shall declare
        to me.

4 "Where were you when I laid the
        foundation of the earth?
    Tell me, if you have understanding.
5 Who determined its measurements—surely
        you know!
    Or who stretched the line upon it?
6 On what were its bases sunk,
    or who laid its cornerstone
7 when the morning stars sang together
    and all the heavenly beings*b* shouted for
        joy?

8 "Or who shut in the sea with doors
    when it burst out from the womb?—
9 when I made the clouds its garment,
    and thick darkness its swaddling band,
10 and prescribed bounds for it,
    and set bars and doors,
11 and said, 'Thus far shall you come, and no
        farther,
    and here shall your proud waves be
        stopped'?

12 "Have you commanded the morning since
        your days began,
    and caused the dawn to know its place,
13 so that it might take hold of the skirts of the
        earth,
    and the wicked be shaken out of it?
14 It is changed like clay under the seal,
    and it is dyed*c* like a garment.

15 Light is withheld from the wicked,
    and their uplifted arm is broken.

16 "Have you entered into the springs of the
        sea,
    or walked in the recesses of the deep?
17 Have the gates of death been revealed to
        you,
    or have you seen the gates of deep
        darkness?
18 Have you comprehended the expanse of the
        earth?
    Declare, if you know all this.

19 "Where is the way to the dwelling of light,
    and where is the place of darkness,
20 that you may take it to its territory
    and that you may discern the paths to its
        home?
21 Surely you know, for you were born then,
    and the number of your days is great!

22 "Have you entered the storehouses of the
        snow,
    or have you seen the storehouses of the
        hail,
23 which I have reserved for the time of
        trouble,
    for the day of battle and war?
24 What is the way to the place where the light
        is distributed,
    or where the east wind is scattered upon
        the earth?
25 "Who has cut a channel for the torrents of
        rain,
    and a way for the thunderbolt,
26 to bring rain on a land where no one lives,
    on the desert, which is empty of human
        life,
27 to satisfy the waste and desolate land,
    and to make the ground put forth grass?

a Traditional rendering of Heb *Shaddai* *b* Heb *sons of God* *c* Cn: Heb *and they stand forth*

28 "Has the rain a father,
      or who has begotten the drops of dew?
29 From whose womb did the ice come forth,
      and who has given birth to the hoarfrost
        of heaven?
30 The waters become hard like stone,
      and the face of the deep is frozen.

31 "Can you bind the chains of the Pleiades,
      or loose the cords of Orion?
32 Can you lead forth the Mazzaroth in their
        season,
      or can you guide the Bear with its
        children?
33 Do you know the ordinances of the
        heavens?
      Can you establish their rule on the earth?

34 "Can you lift up your voice to the clouds,
      so that a flood of waters may cover you?
35 Can you send forth lightnings, so that they
        may go
      and say to you, 'Here we are'?
36 Who has put wisdom in the inward parts,*a*
      or given understanding to the mind?*a*
37 Who has the wisdom to number the
        clouds?
      Or who can tilt the waterskins of the
        heavens,
38 when the dust runs into a mass
      and the clods cling together?

39 "Can you hunt the prey for the lion,
      or satisfy the appetite of the young lions,
40 when they crouch in their dens,
      or lie in wait in their covert?
41 Who provides for the raven its prey,
      when its young ones cry to God,
      and wander about for lack of food?

39 "Do you know when the mountain
        goats give birth?
      Do you observe the calving of the deer?
2 Can you number the months that they
        fulfill,
      and do you know the time when they give
        birth,
3 when they crouch to give birth to their
        offspring,
      and are delivered of their young?
4 Their young ones become strong, they grow
        up in the open;
      they go forth, and do not return to them.

5 "Who has let the wild ass go free?
      Who has loosed the bonds of the swift
        ass,
6 to which I have given the steppe for its
        home,
      the salt land for its dwelling place?

7 It scorns the tumult of the city;
      it does not hear the shouts of the driver.
8 It ranges the mountains as its pasture,
      and it searches after every green thing.

9 "Is the wild ox willing to serve you?
      Will it spend the night at your crib?
10 Can you tie it in the furrow with ropes,
      or will it harrow the valleys after you?
11 Will you depend on it because its strength is
        great,
      and will you hand over your labor to it?
12 Do you have faith in it that it will return,
      and bring your grain to your threshing
        floor?*b*

13 "The ostrich's wings flap wildly,
      though its pinions lack plumage.*a*
14 For it leaves its eggs to the earth,
      and lets them be warmed on the ground,
15 forgetting that a foot may crush them,
      and that a wild animal may trample
        them.
16 It deals cruelly with its young, as if they
        were not its own;
      though its labor should be in vain, yet it
        has no fear;
17 because God has made it forget wisdom,
      and given it no share in understanding.
18 When it spreads its plumes aloft,*a*
      it laughs at the horse and its rider.

19 "Do you give the horse its might?
      Do you clothe its neck with mane?
20 Do you make it leap like the locust?
      Its majestic snorting is terrible.
21 It paws*c* violently, exults mightily;
      it goes out to meet the weapons.
22 It laughs at fear, and is not dismayed;
      it does not turn back from the sword.
23 Upon it rattle the quiver,
      the flashing spear, and the javelin.
24 With fierceness and rage it swallows the
        ground;
      it cannot stand still at the sound of the
        trumpet.
25 When the trumpet sounds, it says 'Aha!'
      From a distance it smells the battle,
      the thunder of the captains, and the
        shouting.

26 "Is it by your wisdom that the hawk soars,
      and spreads its wings toward the south?
27 Is it at your command that the eagle
        mounts up
      and makes its nest on high?
28 It lives on the rock and makes its home
      in the fastness of the rocky crag.
29 From there it spies the prey;

a Meaning of Heb uncertain *b* Heb *your grain and your threshing floor* *c* Gk Syr Vg: Heb *they dig*

its eyes see it from far away.
30 Its young ones suck up blood;
  and where the slain are, there it is."

40 And the LORD said to Job:

2 "Shall a faultfinder contend with the
  Almighty?[a]
  Anyone who argues with God must
  respond."

Job's Response to God

3 Then Job answered the LORD:

4 "See, I am of small account; what shall I
  answer you?
  I lay my hand on my mouth.
5 I have spoken once, and I will not answer;
  twice, but will proceed no further."

God's Challenge to Job

6 Then the LORD answered Job out of the
whirlwind:

7 "Gird up your loins like a man;
  I will question you, and you declare
  to me.
8 Will you even put me in the wrong?
  Will you condemn me that you may be
  justified?
9 Have you an arm like God,
  and can you thunder with a voice like
  his?

10 "Deck yourself with majesty and dignity;
  clothe yourself with glory and splendor.
11 Pour out the overflowings of your anger,
  and look on all who are proud, and abase
  them.
12 Look on all who are proud, and bring them
  low;
  tread down the wicked where they stand.
13 Hide them all in the dust together;
  bind their faces in the world below.[b]
14 Then I will also acknowledge to you
  that your own right hand can give you
  victory.

15 "Look at Behemoth,
  which I made just as I made you;
  it eats grass like an ox.
16 Its strength is in its loins,
  and its power in the muscles of its belly.
17 It makes its tail stiff like a cedar;
  the sinews of its thighs are knit together.
18 Its bones are tubes of bronze,
  its limbs like bars of iron.
19 "It is the first of the great acts of God—
  only its Maker can approach it with the
  sword.

20 For the mountains yield food for it
  where all the wild animals play.
21 Under the lotus plants it lies,
  in the covert of the reeds and in the
  marsh.
22 The lotus trees cover it for shade;
  the willows of the wadi surround it.
23 Even if the river is turbulent, it is not
  frightened;
  it is confident though Jordan rushes
  against its mouth.
24 Can one take it with hooks[c]
  or pierce its nose with a snare?

41[d] "Can you draw out Leviathan[e] with a
  fishhook,
  or press down its tongue with a cord?
2 Can you put a rope in its nose,
  or pierce its jaw with a hook?
3 Will it make many supplications to you?
  Will it speak soft words to you?
4 Will it make a covenant with you
  to be taken as your servant forever?
5 Will you play with it as with a bird,
  or will you put it on leash for your girls?
6 Will traders bargain over it?
  Will they divide it up among the
  merchants?
7 Can you fill its skin with harpoons,
  or its head with fishing spears?
8 Lay hands on it;
  think of the battle; you will not do it
  again!
9[f] Any hope of capturing it[g] will be
  disappointed;
  were not even the gods[h] overwhelmed at
  the sight of it?
10 No one is so fierce as to dare to stir it up.
  Who can stand before it?[i]
11 Who can confront it[i] and be safe?[j]
  —under the whole heaven, who?[k]

12 "I will not keep silence concerning its
  limbs,
  or its mighty strength, or its splendid
  frame.
13 Who can strip off its outer garment?
  Who can penetrate its double coat of
  mail?[l]
14 Who can open the doors of its face?
  There is terror all around its teeth.
15 Its back[m] is made of shields in rows,
  shut up closely as with a seal.
16 One is so near to another
  that no air can come between them.
17 They are joined one to another;

---

a Traditional rendering of Heb *Shaddai* b Heb *the hidden place* c Cn: Heb *in his eyes* d Ch 40.25 in Heb e Or *the crocodile* f Ch 41.1 in
Heb g Heb *of it* h Cn Compare Symmachus Syr: Heb *one is* i Heb *me* j Gk: Heb *that I shall repay* k Heb *to me* l Gk: Heb *bridle*
m Cn Compare Gk Vg: Heb *pride*

they clasp each other and cannot be
separated.
18 Its sneezes flash forth light,
and its eyes are like the eyelids of the
dawn.
19 From its mouth go flaming torches;
sparks of fire leap out.
20 Out of its nostrils comes smoke,
as from a boiling pot and burning
rushes.
21 Its breath kindles coals,
and a flame comes out of its mouth.
22 In its neck abides strength,
and terror dances before it.
23 The folds of its flesh cling together;
it is firmly cast and immovable.
24 Its heart is as hard as stone,
as hard as the lower millstone.
25 When it raises itself up the gods are afraid;
at the crashing they are beside
themselves.
26 Though the sword reaches it, it does not
avail,
nor does the spear, the dart, or the
javelin.
27 It counts iron as straw,
and bronze as rotten wood.
28 The arrow cannot make it flee;
slingstones, for it, are turned to chaff.
29 Clubs are counted as chaff;
it laughs at the rattle of javelins.
30 Its underparts are like sharp potsherds;
it spreads itself like a threshing sledge on
the mire.
31 It makes the deep boil like a pot;
it makes the sea like a pot of ointment.
32 It leaves a shining wake behind it;
one would think the deep to be
white-haired.
33 On earth it has no equal,
a creature without fear.
34 It surveys everything that is lofty;
it is king over all that are proud."

42 Job Is Humbled and Satisfied
Then Job answered the LORD:
2 "I know that you can do all things,
and that no purpose of yours can be
thwarted.
3 'Who is this that hides counsel without
knowledge?'
Therefore I have uttered what I did not
understand,

a Heb a qesitah

things too wonderful for me, which I did
not know.
4 'Hear, and I will speak;
I will question you, and you declare
to me.'
5 I had heard of you by the hearing of the
ear,
but now my eye sees you;
6 therefore I despise myself,
and repent in dust and ashes."

Job's Friends Are Humiliated
7 After the LORD had spoken these words to
Job, the LORD said to Eliphaz the Temanite:
"My wrath is kindled against you and against
your two friends; for you have not spoken of
me what is right, as my servant Job has. 8Now
therefore take seven bulls and seven rams, and
go to my servant Job, and offer up for yourselves a burnt offering; and my servant Job
shall pray for you, for I will accept his prayer
not to deal with you according to your folly;
for you have not spoken of me what is right,
as my servant Job has done." 9So Eliphaz the
Temanite and Bildad the Shuhite and Zophar
the Naamathite went and did what the LORD
had told them; and the LORD accepted Job's
prayer.

Job's Fortunes Are Restored Twofold
10 And the LORD restored the fortunes of Job
when he had prayed for his friends; and the
LORD gave Job twice as much as he had before. 11Then there came to him all his brothers and sisters and all who had known him
before, and they ate bread with him in his
house; they showed him sympathy and comforted him for all the evil that the LORD had
brought upon him; and each of them gave him
a piece of money[a] and a gold ring. 12The LORD
blessed the latter days of Job more than his beginning; and he had fourteen thousand sheep,
six thousand camels, a thousand yoke of oxen,
and a thousand donkeys. 13He also had seven
sons and three daughters. 14He named the first
Jemimah, the second Keziah, and the third
Keren-happuch. 15In all the land there were
no women so beautiful as Job's daughters; and
their father gave them an inheritance along
with their brothers. 16After this Job lived one
hundred and forty years, and saw his children,
and his children's children, four generations.
17And Job died, old and full of days.

PSALMS

KINGDOM POETRY

Real Prayer

Think about your conversations with God and compare them to conversations with family and friends. Who hears the "real you"? In which situation are you more honest, more spontaneous? Are you more comfortable with the people in your life right now, but more reserved and uptight with God?

If you find you're a little shy with God or you just don't know what to say when you pray, the psalms are your answer. The psalms deal with real life, from moments of joy and praise to moments of crushing despair and even violent anger. The psalmists cry, doubt, reject, and dispute. They bring their struggles straight to the gates of heaven and level honest prayers to the Almighty in the form of 150 poems.

There are three psalm categories: lament (sadness), praise (joy), and wisdom (insight). Some of the most famous psalms are Psalm 23 ("The LORD is my shepherd") and Psalms 100 and 150 (short songs of praise). Many of the songs in the book of Psalms have been set to music again and are sung as worship songs today.

Use the psalms to help in your conversations with God. Whether you're happy, depressed, sad, or confused, you can pray their words and make them your own.

"We may always rejoice, if we will only keep our head a little raised above the flood of human things."
—St. John Chrysostom

WHO The psalms were written by a number of authors, though nearly half of them are attributed to King David.

WHAT Psalms are poems that were meant to be sung. They express a range of human emotions in relation to God, including praise, anger, fear, and joy.

WHEN A majority of the psalms were written in the eleventh century B.C.

WHERE The psalms were written in Israel.

PATH OF DISCIPLESHIP

As he was suffering and dying on the cross, Jesus gasped out the words, "My God, my God, why have you forsaken me?" (Mark 15.34). Those nearby would have immediately realized that Jesus wasn't just speaking spontaneously—he was quoting a very familiar psalm, Psalm 22. He was uttering words that most of the people in the crowd would have known by heart. The rest of Psalm 22 goes on to perfectly describe the suffering Jesus endured on the cross. When you think about it, don't you often turn to the prayers you know and love when you are suffering or in a bind? Or maybe you repeat the words of a hymn or psalm refrain you hear often at Mass. Jesus knew his Scripture well. It was a part of him, even—and especially—during the pain of his crucifixion.

JESUS SIGHTING

David sat on his throne, knowing that the former king, Saul, had come to oppose him all the way. The rulers of surrounding nations saw David as a potential threat and competition. One does not take power without provoking others who are hungry for it.

Many of the psalms were written in the heat of battle, as kings of the Gentile lands conspired against the nation of Israel. David, among others, wrote psalms that described God's power over those rebellious outsiders.

Psalm 2 captures the feel of the antagonism and challenges faced by the king God chose to rule his people. Though it seemed as though enemies surrounded him and everyone was against him, the psalmist insists that he is anointed by God. In fact, God even calls him his son! This is someone who has a special calling from God, and the psalm asserts that with God on his side he will triumph over his powerful enemies.

Now read this psalm again, this time with Jesus in mind. Verse 7 seems to anticipate the words of God the Father booming from heaven, saying, "This is my Son, the Beloved," as Jesus was baptized (Matthew 3.17). Verse 2 brings to mind images of the plotting Pharisees, planning how they could kill Jesus, or the angry crowds shouting, "Let him be crucified!" (27.22–23). What other similarities to Jesus' life do you see?

This psalm connects powerfully with what Jesus went through. And is it any wonder that Jesus, heir to the throne of David, would face the same ridicule, conspiracies, and rejection as the psalmist? Jesus became King through a much different road, dying to win the world. But the cry expressed in Psalm 2 is the same. Jesus is the chosen one, loved by God and rejected by humanity.

Ⓙ︎Ⓢ︎

PSALM 1

The Two Ways

¹ Happy are those
  who do not follow the advice of the wicked,
 or take the path that sinners tread,
  or sit in the seat of scoffers;
² but their delight is in the law of the LORD,
  and on his law they meditate day and night.
³ They are like trees
  planted by streams of water,
 which yield their fruit in its season,
  and their leaves do not wither.
 In all that they do, they prosper.

⁴ The wicked are not so,
  but are like chaff that the wind drives away.
⁵ Therefore the wicked will not stand in the judgment,
  nor sinners in the congregation of the righteous;
⁶ for the LORD watches over the way of the righteous,
  but the way of the wicked will perish.

PSALM 2

God's Promise to His Anointed

¹ Why do the nations conspire,
  and the peoples plot in vain?
² The kings of the earth set themselves,
  and the rulers take counsel together,
  against the LORD and his anointed, saying,
³ "Let us burst their bonds asunder,
  and cast their cords from us."

⁴ He who sits in the heavens laughs;
  the LORD has them in derision.
⁵ Then he will speak to them in his wrath,
  and terrify them in his fury, saying,
⁶ "I have set my king on Zion, my holy hill."

⁷ I will tell of the decree of the LORD:
 He said to me, "You are my son;
  today I have begotten you.
⁸ Ask of me, and I will make the nations your heritage,
  and the ends of the earth your possession.
⁹ You shall break them with a rod of iron,
  and dash them in pieces like a potter's vessel."

¹⁰ Now therefore, O kings, be wise;
  be warned, O rulers of the earth.

11 Serve the Lord with fear,
   with trembling 12 kiss his feet,*a*
or he will be angry, and you will perish in
     the way;
   for his wrath is quickly kindled.

   Happy are all who take refuge in him.

PSALM 3

Trust in God under Adversity

A Psalm of David, when he fled from his son Absalom.

1 O Lord, how many are my foes!
   Many are rising against me;
2 many are saying to me,
   "There is no help for you*b* in God."   *Selah*

3 But you, O Lord, are a shield around me,
   my glory, and the one who lifts up my
     head.
4 I cry aloud to the Lord,
   and he answers me from his holy hill.
                                        Selah

5 I lie down and sleep;
   I wake again, for the Lord sustains me.
6 I am not afraid of ten thousands of people
   who have set themselves against me all
     around.

7 Rise up, O Lord!
   Deliver me, O my God!
For you strike all my enemies on the cheek;
   you break the teeth of the wicked.

8 Deliverance belongs to the Lord;
   may your blessing be on your people!
                                        Selah

PSALM 4

Confident Plea for Deliverance from Enemies

To the leader: with stringed instruments. A Psalm of David.

1 Answer me when I call, O God of my right!
   You gave me room when I was in distress.
   Be gracious to me, and hear my prayer.

2 How long, you people, shall my honor
     suffer shame?
   How long will you love vain words, and
     seek after lies?   *Selah*
3 But know that the Lord has set apart the
     faithful for himself;
   the Lord hears when I call to him.

4 When you are disturbed,*c* do not sin;
   ponder it on your beds, and be silent.
                                        Selah
5 Offer right sacrifices,
   and put your trust in the Lord.

6 There are many who say, "O that we might
     see some good!
   Let the light of your face shine on us,
     O Lord!"
7 You have put gladness in my heart
   more than when their grain and wine
     abound.

8 I will both lie down and sleep in peace;
   for you alone, O Lord, make me lie down
     in safety.

PSALM 5

Trust in God for Deliverance from Enemies

To the leader: for the flutes. A Psalm of David.

1 Give ear to my words, O Lord;
   give heed to my sighing.
2 Listen to the sound of my cry,
   my King and my God,
   for to you I pray.
3 O Lord, in the morning you hear my voice;
   in the morning I plead my case to you,
     and watch.

4 For you are not a God who delights in
     wickedness;
   evil will not sojourn with you.
5 The boastful will not stand before your eyes;
   you hate all evildoers.
6 You destroy those who speak lies;
   the Lord abhors the bloodthirsty and
     deceitful.

7 But I, through the abundance of your
     steadfast love,
   will enter your house,
I will bow down toward your holy temple
   in awe of you.
8 Lead me, O Lord, in your righteousness
     because of my enemies;
   make your way straight before me.

9 For there is no truth in their mouths;
   their hearts are destruction;
their throats are open graves;
   they flatter with their tongues.
10 Make them bear their guilt, O God;
   let them fall by their own counsels;
because of their many transgressions cast
     them out,
   for they have rebelled against you.

11 But let all who take refuge in you rejoice;
   let them ever sing for joy.
Spread your protection over them,
   so that those who love your name may
     exult in you.
12 For you bless the righteous, O Lord;
   you cover them with favor as with a shield.

a Cn: Meaning of Heb of verses 11b and 12a is uncertain   *b* Syr: Heb *him*   *c* Or *are angry*

PSALM 6

Prayer for Recovery from Grave Illness

To the leader: with stringed instruments; according to The Sheminith. A Psalm of David.

1 O LORD, do not rebuke me in your anger,
  or discipline me in your wrath.
2 Be gracious to me, O LORD, for I am
    languishing;
  O LORD, heal me, for my bones are
    shaking with terror.
3 My soul also is struck with terror,
  while you, O LORD—how long?

4 Turn, O LORD, save my life;
  deliver me for the sake of your steadfast
    love.
5 For in death there is no remembrance of you;
  in Sheol who can give you praise?

6 I am weary with my moaning;
  every night I flood my bed with tears;
  I drench my couch with my weeping.
7 My eyes waste away because of grief;
  they grow weak because of all my foes.

8 Depart from me, all you workers of evil,
  for the LORD has heard the sound of my
    weeping.
9 The LORD has heard my supplication;
  the LORD accepts my prayer.
10 All my enemies shall be ashamed and struck
    with terror;
  they shall turn back, and in a moment be
    put to shame.

PSALM 7

Plea for Help against Persecutors

A Shiggaion of David, which he sang to the LORD concerning Cush, a Benjaminite.

1 O LORD my God, in you I take refuge;
  save me from all my pursuers, and
    deliver me,
2 or like a lion they will tear me apart;
  they will drag me away, with no one to
    rescue.

3 O LORD my God, if I have done this,
  if there is wrong in my hands,
4 if I have repaid my ally with harm
  or plundered my foe without cause,
5 then let the enemy pursue and overtake me,
  trample my life to the ground,
  and lay my soul in the dust.   *Selah*

6 Rise up, O LORD, in your anger;
  lift yourself up against the fury of my
    enemies;

awake, O my God;[a] you have appointed a
    judgment.
7 Let the assembly of the peoples be gathered
    around you,
  and over it take your seat[b] on high.
8 The LORD judges the peoples;
  judge me, O LORD, according to my
    righteousness
  and according to the integrity that is
    in me.

9 O let the evil of the wicked come to an end,
    but establish the righteous,
  you who test the minds and hearts,
    O righteous God.
10 God is my shield,
  who saves the upright in heart.
11 God is a righteous judge,
  and a God who has indignation every day.

12 If one does not repent, God[c] will whet his
    sword;
  he has bent and strung his bow;
13 he has prepared his deadly weapons,
  making his arrows fiery shafts.
14 See how they conceive evil,
  and are pregnant with mischief,
  and bring forth lies.
15 They make a pit, digging it out,
  and fall into the hole that they have
    made.
16 Their mischief returns upon their own
    heads,
  and on their own heads their violence
    descends.

17 I will give to the LORD the thanks due to his
    righteousness,
  and sing praise to the name of the LORD,
    the Most High.

PSALM 8

Divine Majesty and Human Dignity

To the leader: according to The Gittith. A Psalm of David.

1 O LORD, our Sovereign,
  how majestic is your name in all the
    earth!

You have set your glory above the heavens.
2   Out of the mouths of babes and infants
  you have founded a bulwark because of
    your foes,
  to silence the enemy and the avenger.

3 When I look at your heavens, the work of
    your fingers,
  the moon and the stars that you have
    established;

---

a Or *awake for me* *b* Cn: Heb *return* *c* Heb *he*

4 what are human beings that you are
   mindful of them,
      mortals*a* that you care for them?

5 Yet you have made them a little lower than
   God,*b*
      and crowned them with glory and honor.
6 You have given them dominion over the
   works of your hands;
      you have put all things under their feet,
7 all sheep and oxen,
      and also the beasts of the field,
8 the birds of the air, and the fish of the sea,
      whatever passes along the paths of the
         seas.

9 O LORD, our Sovereign,
      how majestic is your name in all the
         earth!

PSALM 9

God's Power and Justice

To the leader: according to Muth-labben. A Psalm of David.

1 I will give thanks to the LORD with my
   whole heart;
      I will tell of all your wonderful deeds.
2 I will be glad and exult in you;
      I will sing praise to your name, O Most
         High.

3 When my enemies turned back,
      they stumbled and perished before you.
4 For you have maintained my just cause;
      you have sat on the throne giving
         righteous judgment.

5 You have rebuked the nations, you have
   destroyed the wicked;
      you have blotted out their name forever
         and ever.
6 The enemies have vanished in everlasting
   ruins;
      their cities you have rooted out;
      the very memory of them has perished.

7 But the LORD sits enthroned forever,
      he has established his throne for
         judgment.
8 He judges the world with righteousness;
      he judges the peoples with equity.

9 The LORD is a stronghold for the oppressed,
      a stronghold in times of trouble.
10 And those who know your name put their
   trust in you,
      for you, O LORD, have not forsaken those
         who seek you.

11 Sing praises to the LORD, who dwells in
   Zion.

God and the Underdog

You've seen it in movies, on TV, or in school: one kid getting beaten up by another. Maybe she started a Facebook page in someone else's name to slander his reputation. Maybe a student saw something he shouldn't. Maybe she stood up for the slow kid in the front of the bus. Maybe he just told the truth.

David wrote a song about the underdog. It's called **Psalm 12**, and you can read it right now. When someone you love, someone you don't even know, or even you yourself get wrestled to the ground, elbowed in the stomach, and punched in the eye, it's hard to imagine that God cares, that he longs to rescue, and that he will be with the oppressed. But he will. It's not like Spider-Man swinging by to snatch you away from the bad guy (though that would be exciting), but it happens. God is here. You can feel God's presence in the wave of a not-too-close friend, the sound advice of a trusted family member, or the encouraging word of a teammate or coach.

How have you felt God's compassion in your life? In your journal (or in some Creative Space in this Bible), sketch a few cartoons to illustrate specific examples.

Declare his deeds among the peoples.
12 For he who avenges blood is mindful of
      them;
      he does not forget the cry of the afflicted.

13 Be gracious to me, O LORD.
      See what I suffer from those who
         hate me;
      you are the one who lifts me up from the
         gates of death,
14 so that I may recount all your praises,
      and, in the gates of daughter Zion,
      rejoice in your deliverance.

15 The nations have sunk in the pit that they
      made;
      in the net that they hid has their own
         foot been caught.
16 The LORD has made himself known, he has
      executed judgment;

a Heb *ben adam*, lit. *son of man* *b* Or *than the divine beings* or *angels*: Heb *elohim*

20 Put them in fear, O LORD;
    let the nations know that they are only
      human.   *Selah*

PSALM 10

Prayer for Deliverance from Enemies

1 Why, O LORD, do you stand far off?
    Why do you hide yourself in times of
      trouble?
2 In arrogance the wicked persecute the
      poor—
    let them be caught in the schemes they
      have devised.

3 For the wicked boast of the desires of their
      heart,
    those greedy for gain curse and renounce
      the LORD.
4 In the pride of their countenance the
      wicked say, "God will not seek it
      out";
    all their thoughts are, "There is no God."

5 Their ways prosper at all times;
    your judgments are on high, out of their
      sight;
    as for their foes, they scoff at them.
6 They think in their heart, "We shall not be
      moved;
    throughout all generations we shall not
      meet adversity."

7 Their mouths are filled with cursing and
      deceit and oppression;
    under their tongues are mischief and
      iniquity.
8 They sit in ambush in the villages;
    in hiding places they murder the
      innocent.

    Their eyes stealthily watch for the helpless;
9   they lurk in secret like a lion in its covert;
    they lurk that they may seize the poor;
    they seize the poor and drag them off in
      their net.

10 They stoop, they crouch,
    and the helpless fall by their might.
11 They think in their heart, "God has
      forgotten,
    he has hidden his face, he will never
      see it."

    the wicked are snared in the work of their
      own hands.   *Higgaion. Selah*

17 The wicked shall depart to Sheol,
    all the nations that forget God.

18 For the needy shall not always be forgotten,
    nor the hope of the poor perish forever.

19 Rise up, O LORD! Do not let mortals prevail;
    let the nations be judged before you.

12 Rise up, O LORD; O God, lift up your hand;
    do not forget the oppressed.
13 Why do the wicked renounce God,
    and say in their hearts, "You will not call
      us to account"?

14 But you do see! Indeed you note trouble
      and grief,
    that you may take it into your hands;

the helpless commit themselves to you;
you have been the helper of the orphan.

15 Break the arm of the wicked and evildoers;
seek out their wickedness until you find
none.

16 The Lord is king forever and ever;
the nations shall perish from his land.

17 O Lord, you will hear the desire of the meek;
you will strengthen their heart, you will
incline your ear

18 to do justice for the orphan and the
oppressed,
so that those from earth may strike terror
no more. *a*

PSALM 11

Song of Trust in God

To the leader. Of David.

1 In the Lord I take refuge; how can you say
to me,
"Flee like a bird to the mountains;*b*

2 for look, the wicked bend the bow,
they have fitted their arrow to the string,
to shoot in the dark at the upright in
heart.

3 If the foundations are destroyed,
what can the righteous do?"

4 The Lord is in his holy temple;
the Lord's throne is in heaven.
His eyes behold, his gaze examines
humankind.

5 The Lord tests the righteous and the wicked,
and his soul hates the lover of violence.

6 On the wicked he will rain coals of fire and
sulfur;
a scorching wind shall be the portion of
their cup.

7 For the Lord is righteous;
he loves righteous deeds;
the upright shall behold his face.

PSALM 12

Plea for Help in Evil Times

To the leader: according to The Sheminith. A Psalm of David.

1 Help, O Lord, for there is no longer anyone
who is godly;
the faithful have disappeared from
humankind.

2 They utter lies to each other;
with flattering lips and a double heart
they speak.

3 May the Lord cut off all flattering lips,
the tongue that makes great boasts,

4 those who say, "With our tongues we will
prevail;
our lips are our own—who is our
master?"

5 "Because the poor are despoiled, because
the needy groan,
I will now rise up," says the Lord;
"I will place them in the safety for which
they long."

6 The promises of the Lord are promises that
are pure,
silver refined in a furnace on the ground,
purified seven times.

7 You, O Lord, will protect us;
you will guard us from this generation
forever.

8 On every side the wicked prowl,
as vileness is exalted among humankind.

PSALM 13

Prayer for Deliverance from Enemies

To the leader. A Psalm of David.

1 How long, O Lord? Will you forget me
forever?
How long will you hide your face from me?

2 How long must I bear pain*c* in my soul,
and have sorrow in my heart all day long?
How long shall my enemy be exalted
over me?

3 Consider and answer me, O Lord my God!
Give light to my eyes, or I will sleep the
sleep of death,

4 and my enemy will say, "I have prevailed";
my foes will rejoice because I am shaken.

5 But I trusted in your steadfast love;
my heart shall rejoice in your salvation.

6 I will sing to the Lord,
because he has dealt bountifully with me.

PSALM 14

Denunciation of Godlessness

To the leader. Of David.

1 Fools say in their hearts, "There is no God."
They are corrupt, they do abominable
deeds;
there is no one who does good.

2 The Lord looks down from heaven on
humankind
to see if there are any who are wise,
who seek after God.

3 They have all gone astray, they are all alike
perverse;

a Meaning of Heb uncertain *b* Gk Syr Jerome Tg: Heb *flee to your mountain, O bird* *c* Syr: Heb *hold counsels*

> "The Psalms are poems, and poems intended to be sung: not doctrinal treatises, nor even sermons. . . . They must be read as poems if they are to be understood. . . . Otherwise we shall miss what is in them and think we see what is not."
>
> —C. S. Lewis, *Reflections on the Psalms*

there is no one who does good,
no, not one.

4 Have they no knowledge, all the evildoers
who eat up my people as they eat bread,
and do not call upon the LORD?

5 There they shall be in great terror,
for God is with the company of the
righteous.
6 You would confound the plans of the poor,
but the LORD is their refuge.

7 O that deliverance for Israel would come
from Zion!
When the LORD restores the fortunes of
his people,
Jacob will rejoice; Israel will be glad.

PSALM 15

Who Shall Abide in God's Sanctuary?

A Psalm of David.

1 O LORD, who may abide in your tent?
Who may dwell on your holy hill?

2 Those who walk blamelessly, and do what is
right,
and speak the truth from their heart;
3 who do not slander with their tongue,
and do no evil to their friends,
nor take up a reproach against their
neighbors;
4 in whose eyes the wicked are despised,
but who honor those who fear the LORD;
who stand by their oath even to their hurt;
5 who do not lend money at interest,
and do not take a bribe against the
innocent.

Those who do these things shall never be
moved.

PSALM 16

Song of Trust and Security in God

A Miktam of David.

1 Protect me, O God, for in you I take refuge.
2 I say to the LORD, "You are my Lord;
I have no good apart from you."*a*

3 As for the holy ones in the land, they are the
noble,
in whom is all my delight.

4 Those who choose another god multiply
their sorrows;*b*
their drink offerings of blood I will not
pour out
or take their names upon my lips.

5 The LORD is my chosen portion and my cup;
you hold my lot.
6 The boundary lines have fallen for me in
pleasant places;
I have a goodly heritage.

7 I bless the LORD who gives me counsel;
in the night also my heart instructs me.
8 I keep the LORD always before me;
because he is at my right hand, I shall not
be moved.

9 Therefore my heart is glad, and my soul
rejoices;
my body also rests secure.
10 For you do not give me up to Sheol,
or let your faithful one see the Pit.

11 You show me the path of life.
In your presence there is fullness of joy;
in your right hand are pleasures
forevermore.

PSALM 17

Prayer for Deliverance from Persecutors

A Prayer of David.

1 Hear a just cause, O LORD; attend to my cry;
give ear to my prayer from lips free of
deceit.
2 From you let my vindication come;
let your eyes see the right.

3 If you try my heart, if you visit me by night,
if you test me, you will find no
wickedness in me;
my mouth does not transgress.
4 As for what others do, by the word of your
lips
I have avoided the ways of the violent.
5 My steps have held fast to your paths;
my feet have not slipped.

a Jerome Tg: Meaning of Heb uncertain *b* Cn: Meaning of Heb uncertain

⁶ I call upon you, for you will answer me,
 O God;
   incline your ear to me, hear my words.
⁷ Wondrously show your steadfast love,
   O savior of those who seek refuge
     from their adversaries at your right hand.

⁸ Guard me as the apple of the eye;
   hide me in the shadow of your wings,
⁹ from the wicked who despoil me,
   my deadly enemies who surround me.
¹⁰ They close their hearts to pity;
   with their mouths they speak arrogantly.
¹¹ They track me down;ᵃ now they
       surround me;
   they set their eyes to cast me to the
       ground.
¹² They are like a lion eager to tear,
   like a young lion lurking in ambush.

¹³ Rise up, O Lord, confront them, overthrow
     them!
   By your sword deliver my life from the
       wicked,
¹⁴ from mortals—by your hand, O Lord—
   from mortals whose portion in life is in
       this world.
   May their bellies be filled with what you
       have stored up for them;
   may their children have more than
       enough;
   may they leave something over to their
       little ones.

¹⁵ As for me, I shall behold your face in
       righteousness;
   when I awake I shall be satisfied,
       beholding your likeness.

PSALM 18

Royal Thanksgiving for Victory

*To the leader. A Psalm of David the servant of the Lord,
who addressed the words of this song to the Lord on the
day when the Lord delivered him from the hand of all his
enemies, and from the hand of Saul. He said:*

¹ I love you, O Lord, my strength.
² The Lord is my rock, my fortress, and my
     deliverer,
   my God, my rock in whom I take refuge,
   my shield, and the horn of my salvation,
     my stronghold.
³ I call upon the Lord, who is worthy to be
     praised,
   so I shall be saved from my enemies.

⁴ The cords of death encompassed me;
   the torrents of perdition assailed me;
⁵ the cords of Sheol entangled me;
   the snares of death confronted me.

⁶ In my distress I called upon the Lord;
   to my God I cried for help.
 From his temple he heard my voice,
   and my cry to him reached his ears.

⁷ Then the earth reeled and rocked;
   the foundations also of the mountains
       trembled
   and quaked, because he was angry.
⁸ Smoke went up from his nostrils,
   and devouring fire from his mouth;
   glowing coals flamed forth from him.
⁹ He bowed the heavens, and came down;
   thick darkness was under his feet.
¹⁰ He rode on a cherub, and flew;
   he came swiftly upon the wings of the
       wind.
¹¹ He made darkness his covering around him,
   his canopy thick clouds dark with water.
¹² Out of the brightness before him
     there broke through his clouds
     hailstones and coals of fire.
¹³ The Lord also thundered in the heavens,
   and the Most High uttered his voice.ᵇ
¹⁴ And he sent out his arrows, and scattered
       them;
   he flashed forth lightnings, and routed
       them.
¹⁵ Then the channels of the sea were seen,
   and the foundations of the world were
       laid bare
 at your rebuke, O Lord,
   at the blast of the breath of your nostrils.

¹⁶ He reached down from on high, he
       took me;
   he drew me out of mighty waters.
¹⁷ He delivered me from my strong enemy,
   and from those who hated me;
   for they were too mighty for me.
¹⁸ They confronted me in the day of my
       calamity;
   but the Lord was my support.
¹⁹ He brought me out into a broad place;
   he delivered me, because he delighted
       in me.

²⁰ The Lord rewarded me according to my
       righteousness;
   according to the cleanness of my hands
       he recompensed me.
²¹ For I have kept the ways of the Lord,
   and have not wickedly departed from my
       God.
²² For all his ordinances were before me,
   and his statutes I did not put away from
       me.
²³ I was blameless before him,
   and I kept myself from guilt.

---

a One Ms Compare Syr: MT *Our steps* b Gk See 2 Sam 22.14: Heb adds *hailstones and coals of fire*

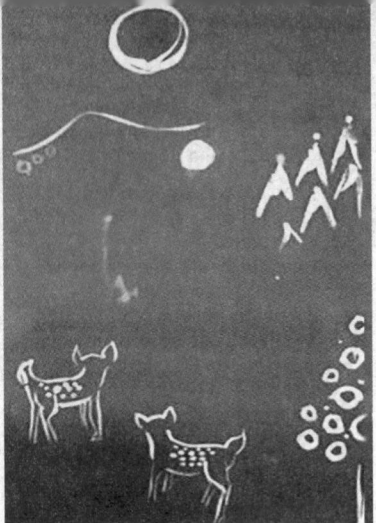

Psalms 19.1–4—© Eliza German, 20

24 Therefore the LORD has recompensed me
    according to my righteousness,
    according to the cleanness of my hands
      in his sight.

25 With the loyal you show yourself loyal;
    with the blameless you show yourself
      blameless;
26 with the pure you show yourself pure;
    and with the crooked you show yourself
      perverse.
27 For you deliver a humble people,
    but the haughty eyes you bring down.
28 It is you who light my lamp;
    the LORD, my God, lights up my darkness.
29 By you I can crush a troop,
    and by my God I can leap over a wall.
30 This God—his way is perfect;
    the promise of the LORD proves true;
    he is a shield for all who take refuge in
      him.

31 For who is God except the LORD?
    And who is a rock besides our God?—
32 the God who girded me with strength,
    and made my way safe.
33 He made my feet like the feet of a deer,
    and set me secure on the heights.
34 He trains my hands for war,
    so that my arms can bend a bow of
      bronze.
35 You have given me the shield of your
      salvation,
    and your right hand has supported me;
    your help[a] has made me great.
36 You gave me a wide place for my steps
    under me,
    and my feet did not slip.
37 I pursued my enemies and overtook them;
    and did not turn back until they were
      consumed.
38 I struck them down, so that they were not
      able to rise;
    they fell under my feet.
39 For you girded me with strength for the
      battle;
    you made my assailants sink under me.
40 You made my enemies turn their backs
    to me,
    and those who hated me I destroyed.
41 They cried for help, but there was no one to
      save them;
    they cried to the LORD, but he did not
      answer them.
42 I beat them fine, like dust before the wind;
    I cast them out like the mire of the
      streets.

43 You delivered me from strife with the
      peoples;[b]
    you made me head of the nations;
    people whom I had not known served me.
44 As soon as they heard of me they
      obeyed me;
    foreigners came cringing to me.
45 Foreigners lost heart,
    and came trembling out of their
      strongholds.

46 The LORD lives! Blessed be my rock,
    and exalted be the God of my salvation,
47 the God who gave me vengeance
    and subdued peoples under me;
48 who delivered me from my enemies;
    indeed, you exalted me above my
      adversaries;
    you delivered me from the violent.

49 For this I will extol you, O LORD, among the
      nations,
    and sing praises to your name.
50 Great triumphs he gives to his king,
    and shows steadfast love to his anointed,
    to David and his descendants forever.

PSALM 19

God's Glory in Creation and the Law

To the leader. A Psalm of David.

1 The heavens are telling the glory of God;
    and the firmament[c] proclaims his
      handiwork.
2 Day to day pours forth speech,
    and night to night declares knowledge.
3 There is no speech, nor are there words;
    their voice is not heard;

a Or *gentleness* b Gk Tg: Heb *people* c Or *dome*

4 yet their voice*a* goes out through all the earth,
and their words to the end of the world.

In the heavens*b* he has set a tent for the sun,
5 which comes out like a bridegroom from his wedding canopy,
and like a strong man runs its course with joy.
6 Its rising is from the end of the heavens,
and its circuit to the end of them;
and nothing is hid from its heat.

7 The law of the LORD is perfect,
reviving the soul;
the decrees of the LORD are sure,
making wise the simple;
8 the precepts of the LORD are right,
rejoicing the heart;
the commandment of the LORD is clear,
enlightening the eyes;
9 the fear of the LORD is pure,
enduring forever;
the ordinances of the LORD are true
and righteous altogether.
10 More to be desired are they than gold,
even much fine gold;
sweeter also than honey,
and drippings of the honeycomb.

11 Moreover by them is your servant warned;
in keeping them there is great reward.
12 But who can detect their errors?
Clear me from hidden faults.
13 Keep back your servant also from the insolent;*c*
do not let them have dominion over me.
Then I shall be blameless,
and innocent of great transgression.

14 Let the words of my mouth and the meditation of my heart
be acceptable to you,
O LORD, my rock and my redeemer.

PSALM 20

Prayer for Victory

To the leader. A Psalm of David.

1 The LORD answer you in the day of trouble!
The name of the God of Jacob protect you!
2 May he send you help from the sanctuary,
and give you support from Zion.
3 May he remember all your offerings,
and regard with favor your burnt sacrifices. *Selah*
4 May he grant you your heart's desire,

and fulfill all your plans.
5 May we shout for joy over your victory,
and in the name of our God set up our banners.
May the LORD fulfill all your petitions.

6 Now I know that the LORD will help his anointed;
he will answer him from his holy heaven
with mighty victories by his right hand.
7 Some take pride in chariots, and some in horses,
but our pride is in the name of the LORD our God.
8 They will collapse and fall,
but we shall rise and stand upright.

9 Give victory to the king, O LORD;
answer us when we call.*d*

PSALM 21

Thanksgiving for Victory

To the leader. A Psalm of David.

1 In your strength the king rejoices, O LORD,
and in your help how greatly he exults!
2 You have given him his heart's desire,
and have not withheld the request of his lips. *Selah*
3 For you meet him with rich blessings;
you set a crown of fine gold on his head.
4 He asked you for life; you gave it to him—
length of days forever and ever.
5 His glory is great through your help;
splendor and majesty you bestow on him.
6 You bestow on him blessings forever;
you make him glad with the joy of your presence.
7 For the king trusts in the LORD,
and through the steadfast love of the Most High he shall not be moved.

8 Your hand will find out all your enemies;
your right hand will find out those who hate you.
9 You will make them like a fiery furnace when you appear.
The LORD will swallow them up in his wrath,
and fire will consume them.
10 You will destroy their offspring from the earth,
and their children from among humankind.
11 If they plan evil against you,
if they devise mischief, they will not succeed.

a Gk Jerome Compare Syr: Heb *line* *b* Heb *In them* *c* Or *from proud thoughts* *d* Gk: Heb *give victory, O LORD; let the King answer us when we call*

JESUS SIGHTING

Imagine David, hidden in a rock cave, alone, chased away from his wealth and home. He wasn't the son of the king, but he was an adopted son of sorts, the beloved hero of Saul's army. Yet Saul's envy and violence drove David away and forced him into isolation and loneliness. Who knows how many of his poems were created during those cold, lonely nights.

David's suffering would find a parallel a thousand years later.

Psalm 22.15–18 captures the gritty details of the crucifixion, recorded a thousand years before it happened: that Jesus was thirsty, that his hands and feet were pierced, that his bones were not broken, and that the onlookers gambled for his clothing. We can't help but see the stunningly obvious prophecy of the cross that is to come. Look back at **22.1**. Clearly Jesus recognized the prophecy and spoke it himself as it was coming to pass (see Matthew 27.46).

On the cross Jesus did not doubt the Father when he said, "Why have you forsaken me?" During Jesus' time, the psalms were titled by their first lines, not by numbers. His cry on the cross draws our attention to the entire psalm—not just the sentiments in the first line. Read **Psalm 22** to the end and see the promise it holds.

David probably didn't know what his own deeply personal cry for help in this psalm was going to become. But it shows us that God not only *hears* our cries for help, but he can also *use* them. Jesus is not offended by our pleas, by our recognition of our weaknesses, or by our raw expression of fear or need. Instead, he takes our cries onto himself and expresses them to his Father.

(JS)

---

12 For you will put them to flight;
  you will aim at their faces with your
    bows.

13 Be exalted, O LORD, in your strength!
  We will sing and praise your power.

PSALM 22

Plea for Deliverance from Suffering and Hostility

To the leader: according to The Deer of the Dawn. A Psalm of David.

1 My God, my God, why have you forsaken me?
  Why are you so far from helping me,
    from the words of my groaning?
2 O my God, I cry by day, but you do not
    answer;
  and by night, but find no rest.

3 Yet you are holy,
  enthroned on the praises of Israel.
4 In you our ancestors trusted;
  they trusted, and you delivered them.
5 To you they cried, and were saved;
  in you they trusted, and were not put to
    shame.

6 But I am a worm, and not human;
  scorned by others, and despised by the
    people.
7 All who see me mock at me;
  they make mouths at me, they shake
    their heads;
8 "Commit your cause to the LORD; let him
    deliver—
  let him rescue the one in whom he
    delights!"

9 Yet it was you who took me from the womb;
  you kept me safe on my mother's breast.
10 On you I was cast from my birth,
  and since my mother bore me you have
    been my God.
11 Do not be far from me,
  for trouble is near
  and there is no one to help.

12 Many bulls encircle me,
  strong bulls of Bashan surround me;
13 they open wide their mouths at me,
  like a ravening and roaring lion.

14 I am poured out like water,
  and all my bones are out of joint;
  my heart is like wax;
    it is melted within my breast;
15 my mouth*a* is dried up like a potsherd,
  and my tongue sticks to my jaws;
  you lay me in the dust of death.

a Cn: Heb *strength*

Bridge—© Rachel Hostert, 18

16 For dogs are all around me;
    a company of evildoers encircles me.
    My hands and feet have shriveled;*a*
17 I can count all my bones.
    They stare and gloat over me;
18 they divide my clothes among themselves,
    and for my clothing they cast lots.

19 But you, O Lord, do not be far away!
    O my help, come quickly to my aid!
20 Deliver my soul from the sword,
    my life*b* from the power of the dog!
21 Save me from the mouth of the lion!

    From the horns of the wild oxen you have
        rescued*c* me.
22 I will tell of your name to my brothers and
        sisters;*d*
    in the midst of the congregation I will
        praise you:
23 You who fear the Lord, praise him!
    All you offspring of Jacob, glorify him;
    stand in awe of him, all you offspring of
        Israel!
24 For he did not despise or abhor
    the affliction of the afflicted;
    he did not hide his face from me,*e*
    but heard when I*f* cried to him.

25 From you comes my praise in the great
        congregation;

    my vows I will pay before those who fear
        him.
26 The poor*g* shall eat and be satisfied;
    those who seek him shall praise the Lord.
    May your hearts live forever!

27 All the ends of the earth shall remember
    and turn to the Lord;
    and all the families of the nations
    shall worship before him.*h*
28 For dominion belongs to the Lord,
    and he rules over the nations.

29 To him,*i* indeed, shall all who sleep in*j* the
        earth bow down;
    before him shall bow all who go down to
        the dust,
    and I shall live for him.*k*
30 Posterity will serve him;
    future generations will be told about the
        Lord,
31 and*l* proclaim his deliverance to a people
        yet unborn,
    saying that he has done it.

PSALM 23

The Divine Shepherd

A Psalm of David.

1 The Lord is my shepherd, I shall not want.
2   He makes me lie down in green pastures;

a Meaning of Heb uncertain *b* Heb *my only one* *c* Heb *answered* *d* Or *kindred* *e* Heb *him* *f* Heb *you* *g* Or *afflicted* *h* Gk Syr Jerome: Heb *you* *i* Cn: Heb *They have eaten* and *j* Cn: Heb *all the fat ones* *k* Compare Gk Syr Vg: Heb *and he who cannot keep himself alive* *l* Compare Gk: Heb *it will be told about the Lord to the generation,* 31 *they will come and*

he leads me beside still waters;[a]
3   he restores my soul.[b]
He leads me in right paths[c]
    for his name's sake.

4 Even though I walk through the darkest
        valley,[d]
    I fear no evil;
for you are with me;
    your rod and your staff—
    they comfort me.

5 You prepare a table before me
    in the presence of my enemies;
you anoint my head with oil;
    my cup overflows.
6 Surely[e] goodness and mercy[f] shall
        follow me
    all the days of my life,
and I shall dwell in the house of the LORD
    my whole life long.[g]

PSALM 24

Entrance into the Temple

Of David. A Psalm.

1 The earth is the LORD's and all that is in it,
    the world, and those who live in it;
2 for he has founded it on the seas,
    and established it on the rivers.

3 Who shall ascend the hill of the LORD?
    And who shall stand in his holy place?
4 Those who have clean hands and pure
        hearts,
    who do not lift up their souls to what is
        false,
    and do not swear deceitfully.
5 They will receive blessing from the LORD,
    and vindication from the God of their
        salvation.
6 Such is the company of those who seek
        him,
    who seek the face of the God of Jacob.[h]
                                            Selah

7 Lift up your heads, O gates!
    and be lifted up, O ancient doors!
    that the King of glory may come in.
8 Who is the King of glory?
    The LORD, strong and mighty,
    the LORD, mighty in battle.
9 Lift up your heads, O gates!
    and be lifted up, O ancient doors!
    that the King of glory may come in.
10 Who is this King of glory?
    The LORD of hosts,
    he is the King of glory.   Selah

PSALM 25

Prayer for Guidance and for Deliverance

Of David.

1 To you, O LORD, I lift up my soul.
2 O my God, in you I trust;
    do not let me be put to shame;
    do not let my enemies exult over me.
3 Do not let those who wait for you be put to
        shame;
    let them be ashamed who are wantonly
        treacherous.

4 Make me to know your ways, O LORD;
    teach me your paths.
5 Lead me in your truth, and teach me,
    for you are the God of my salvation;
    for you I wait all day long.

6 Be mindful of your mercy, O LORD, and of
        your steadfast love,
    for they have been from of old.
7 Do not remember the sins of my youth or
        my transgressions;
    according to your steadfast love
        remember me,
    for your goodness' sake, O LORD!

8 Good and upright is the LORD;
    therefore he instructs sinners in the way.
9 He leads the humble in what is right,
    and teaches the humble his way.
10 All the paths of the LORD are steadfast love
        and faithfulness,
    for those who keep his covenant and his
        decrees.

11 For your name's sake, O LORD,
    pardon my guilt, for it is great.
12 Who are they that fear the LORD?
    He will teach them the way that they
        should choose.
13 They will abide in prosperity,
    and their children shall possess the land.
14 The friendship of the LORD is for those who
        fear him,
    and he makes his covenant known to
        them.
15 My eyes are ever toward the LORD,
    for he will pluck my feet out of the net.

16 Turn to me and be gracious to me,
    for I am lonely and afflicted.
17 Relieve the troubles of my heart,
    and bring me[i] out of my distress.
18 Consider my affliction and my trouble,
    and forgive all my sins.

---

a Heb *waters of rest* b Or *life* c Or *paths of righteousness* d Or *the valley of the shadow of death* e Or *Only* f Or *kindness* g Heb *for length of days* h Gk Syr: Heb *your face, O Jacob* i Or *The troubles of my heart are enlarged; bring me*

19 Consider how many are my foes,
and with what violent hatred they
hate me.
20 O guard my life, and deliver me;
do not let me be put to shame, for I take
refuge in you.
21 May integrity and uprightness preserve me,
for I wait for you.

22 Redeem Israel, O God,
out of all its troubles.

PSALM 26

**Plea for Justice and Declaration
of Righteousness**

Of David.

1 Vindicate me, O Lord,
for I have walked in my integrity,
and I have trusted in the Lord without
wavering.
2 Prove me, O Lord, and try me;
test my heart and mind.
3 For your steadfast love is before my eyes,
and I walk in faithfulness to you.*ᵃ*

4 I do not sit with the worthless,
nor do I consort with hypocrites;
5 I hate the company of evildoers,
and will not sit with the wicked.

6 I wash my hands in innocence,
and go around your altar, O Lord,
7 singing aloud a song of thanksgiving,
and telling all your wondrous deeds.

8 O Lord, I love the house in which you dwell,
and the place where your glory abides.
9 Do not sweep me away with sinners,
nor my life with the bloodthirsty,
10 those in whose hands are evil devices,
and whose right hands are full of bribes.

11 But as for me, I walk in my integrity;
redeem me, and be gracious to me.
12 My foot stands on level ground;
in the great congregation I will bless the
Lord.

PSALM 27

Triumphant Song of Confidence

Of David.

1 The Lord is my light and my salvation;
whom shall I fear?
The Lord is the stronghold*ᵇ* of my life;
of whom shall I be afraid?

2 When evildoers assail me
to devour my flesh—

a Or *in your faithfulness* *b* Or *refuge*

TEXT MESSAGE

**Psalm 23 has always been
one of the favorite, most-
quoted passages in the Old
Testament. The early
Church sang this song when
people were baptized.**

Fact

This information has been scanned and is free of all
known viruses. Please forward to all your friends.

my adversaries and foes—
they shall stumble and fall.

3 Though an army encamp against me,
my heart shall not fear;
though war rise up against me,
yet I will be confident.

4 One thing I asked of the Lord,
that will I seek after:
to live in the house of the Lord
all the days of my life,
to behold the beauty of the Lord,
and to inquire in his temple.

5 For he will hide me in his shelter
in the day of trouble;
he will conceal me under the cover of his tent;
he will set me high on a rock.

6 Now my head is lifted up
above my enemies all around me,

Bad Medicine He said that he was trying to help. Yet it became abundantly clear that the "doctor" who treated the eyes of newborn Fanny J. Crosby had only been after money and had no medical training whatsoever. He was never seen again in the small town of Southeast, New York, but his malpractice would be apparent to Fanny and her family for the next ninety-five years. She had been blinded for life.

Although her blindness held her back from some activities, it allowed her to attend a newly opened school in New York City specifically designed for the blind. It was at this school that Fanny began to discover an uncanny gift for rhyme and meter as well as a warm-hearted faith in Christ. So Fanny began creating.

Rarely did a school assembly go by that did not include one of her poems. As she grew up, Fanny combined her gifts of music and poetry to create hymns. Fanny was eventually hired to write two songs a week, something that was unheard of for either women or blind persons. By the end of her life, Fanny had written more than nine thousand hymns—poems set to music that captured the moving truths of the Christian faith.

Amazingly, Fanny once said that if she had the choice, she still would have chosen to be blind. Why? "Because when I get to

heaven, the first face that shall ever gladden my sight will be that of my Savior!"

What faith! Despite the visual darkness that surrounded her all the days of her life, her songs proclaim the bright light of truth. Fanny's words live on, echoed in churches around the world today:

"To God be the glory, great things He hath done, so loved He the world that He gave us His Son."

---

and I will offer in his tent
   sacrifices with shouts of joy;
I will sing and make melody to the Lord.

7 Hear, O Lord, when I cry aloud,
   be gracious to me and answer me!
8 "Come," my heart says, "seek his face!"
   Your face, Lord, do I seek.
9 Do not hide your face from me.

Do not turn your servant away in anger,
   you who have been my help.
Do not cast me off, do not forsake me,
   O God of my salvation!
10 If my father and mother forsake me,
   the Lord will take me up.

11 Teach me your way, O Lord,
   and lead me on a level path
   because of my enemies.
12 Do not give me up to the will of my
   adversaries,

for false witnesses have risen against me,
   and they are breathing out violence.
13 I believe that I shall see the goodness of the
   Lord
   in the land of the living.
14 Wait for the Lord;
   be strong, and let your heart take
    courage;
   wait for the Lord!

PSALM 28

Prayer for Help and Thanksgiving for It

Of David.

1 To you, O Lord, I call;
   my rock, do not refuse to hear me,
for if you are silent to me,
   I shall be like those who go down to the
    Pit.
2 Hear the voice of my supplication,
   as I cry to you for help,

as I lift up my hands
    toward your most holy sanctuary.[a]

3 Do not drag me away with the wicked,
    with those who are workers of evil,
who speak peace with their neighbors,
    while mischief is in their hearts.
4 Repay them according to their work,
    and according to the evil of their deeds;
repay them according to the work of their
    hands;
    render them their due reward.
5 Because they do not regard the works of the
    Lord,
    or the work of his hands,
he will break them down and build them up
    no more.

6 Blessed be the Lord,
    for he has heard the sound of my
      pleadings.
7 The Lord is my strength and my shield;
    in him my heart trusts;
so I am helped, and my heart exults,
    and with my song I give thanks to him.

8 The Lord is the strength of his people;
    he is the saving refuge of his anointed.
9 O save your people, and bless your heritage;
    be their shepherd, and carry them
      forever.

PSALM 29

The Voice of God in a Great Storm

A Psalm of David.

1 Ascribe to the Lord, O heavenly beings,[b]
    ascribe to the Lord glory and strength.
2 Ascribe to the Lord the glory of his name;
    worship the Lord in holy splendor.

3 The voice of the Lord is over the waters;
    the God of glory thunders,
    the Lord, over mighty waters.
4 The voice of the Lord is powerful;
    the voice of the Lord is full of majesty.

5 The voice of the Lord breaks the cedars;
    the Lord breaks the cedars of Lebanon.
6 He makes Lebanon skip like a calf,
    and Sirion like a young wild ox.

7 The voice of the Lord flashes forth flames
    of fire.
8 The voice of the Lord shakes the wilderness;
    the Lord shakes the wilderness of Kadesh.

9 The voice of the Lord causes the oaks to
    whirl,[c]
    and strips the forest bare;
    and in his temple all say, "Glory!"

10 The Lord sits enthroned over the flood;
    the Lord sits enthroned as king forever.
11 May the Lord give strength to his people!
    May the Lord bless his people with
      peace!

PSALM 30

Thanksgiving for Recovery from Grave Illness

A Psalm. A Song at the dedication of the temple. Of David.

1 I will extol you, O Lord, for you have drawn
    me up,
    and did not let my foes rejoice over me.
2 O Lord my God, I cried to you for help,
    and you have healed me.
3 O Lord, you brought up my soul from Sheol,
    restored me to life from among those
      gone down to the Pit.[d]

4 Sing praises to the Lord, O you his faithful
    ones,
    and give thanks to his holy name.
5 For his anger is but for a moment;
    his favor is for a lifetime.
Weeping may linger for the night,
    but joy comes with the morning.

6 As for me, I said in my prosperity,
    "I shall never be moved."
7 By your favor, O Lord,
    you had established me as a strong
      mountain;
you hid your face;
    I was dismayed.

8 To you, O Lord, I cried,
    and to the Lord I made supplication:
9 "What profit is there in my death,
    if I go down to the Pit?
Will the dust praise you?
    Will it tell of your faithfulness?
10 Hear, O Lord, and be gracious to me!
    O Lord, be my helper!"

11 You have turned my mourning into dancing;
    you have taken off my sackcloth
    and clothed me with joy,
12 so that my soul[e] may praise you and not be
    silent.
    O Lord my God, I will give thanks to you
      forever.

PSALM 31

Prayer and Praise for Deliverance from Enemies

To the leader. A Psalm of David.

1 In you, O Lord, I seek refuge;
    do not let me ever be put to shame;

---

a Heb *your innermost sanctuary* b Heb *sons of gods* c Or *causes the deer to calve* d Or *that I should not go down to the Pit* e Heb *that glory*

in your righteousness deliver me.
2 Incline your ear to me;
    rescue me speedily.
Be a rock of refuge for me,
    a strong fortress to save me.

3 You are indeed my rock and my fortress;
    for your name's sake lead me and
        guide me,
4 take me out of the net that is hidden for me,
    for you are my refuge.
5 Into your hand I commit my spirit;
    you have redeemed me, O LORD, faithful
        God.

6 You hate*a* those who pay regard to
        worthless idols,
    but I trust in the LORD.
7 I will exult and rejoice in your steadfast love,
    because you have seen my affliction;
    you have taken heed of my adversities,
8 and have not delivered me into the hand of
        the enemy;
    you have set my feet in a broad place.

9 Be gracious to me, O LORD, for I am in
        distress;
    my eye wastes away from grief,
    my soul and body also.
10 For my life is spent with sorrow,
    and my years with sighing;
    my strength fails because of my misery,*b*
    and my bones waste away.

11 I am the scorn of all my adversaries,
    a horror*c* to my neighbors,
    an object of dread to my acquaintances;
    those who see me in the street flee
        from me.
12 I have passed out of mind like one who is
        dead;
    I have become like a broken vessel.
13 For I hear the whispering of many—
    terror all around!—
    as they scheme together against me,
    as they plot to take my life.

14 But I trust in you, O LORD;
    I say, "You are my God."
15 My times are in your hand;
    deliver me from the hand of my enemies
        and persecutors.
16 Let your face shine upon your servant;
    save me in your steadfast love.
17 Do not let me be put to shame, O LORD,
    for I call on you;
    let the wicked be put to shame;
    let them go dumbfounded to Sheol.
18 Let the lying lips be stilled

that speak insolently against the righteous
    with pride and contempt.

19 O how abundant is your goodness
    that you have laid up for those who fear
        you,
and accomplished for those who take
        refuge in you,
    in the sight of everyone!
20 In the shelter of your presence you hide them
        from human plots;
    you hold them safe under your shelter
        from contentious tongues.

21 Blessed be the LORD,
    for he has wondrously shown his
        steadfast love to me
    when I was beset as a city under siege.
22 I had said in my alarm,
    "I am driven far*d* from your sight."
But you heard my supplications
    when I cried out to you for help.

23 Love the LORD, all you his saints.
    The LORD preserves the faithful,
    but abundantly repays the one who acts
        haughtily.
24 Be strong, and let your heart take courage,
    all you who wait for the LORD.

PSALM 32

The Joy of Forgiveness

Of David. A Maskil.

1 Happy are those whose transgression is
        forgiven,
    whose sin is covered.
2 Happy are those to whom the LORD
        imputes no iniquity,
    and in whose spirit there is no deceit.

3 While I kept silence, my body wasted away
    through my groaning all day long.
4 For day and night your hand was heavy
        upon me;
    my strength was dried up*e* as by the heat
        of summer.   *Selah*

5 Then I acknowledged my sin to you,
    and I did not hide my iniquity;
I said, "I will confess my transgressions to
        the LORD,"
    and you forgave the guilt of my sin.   *Selah*

6 Therefore let all who are faithful
    offer prayer to you;
at a time of distress,*f* the rush of mighty
        waters
    shall not reach them.
7 You are a hiding place for me;

a One Heb Ms Gk Syr Jerome: MT *I hate* *b* Gk Syr: Heb *my iniquity* *c* Cn: Heb *exceedingly* *d* Another reading is *cut off* *e* Meaning of Heb
uncertain *f* Cn: Heb *at a time of finding only*

you preserve me from trouble;
you surround me with glad cries of
deliverance.   *Selah*

8 I will instruct you and teach you the way you
should go;
I will counsel you with my eye upon you.
9 Do not be like a horse or a mule, without
understanding,
whose temper must be curbed with bit
and bridle,
else it will not stay near you.

10 Many are the torments of the wicked,
but steadfast love surrounds those who
trust in the Lord.
11 Be glad in the Lord and rejoice,
O righteous,
and shout for joy, all you upright in
heart.

PSALM 33

The Greatness and Goodness of God

1 Rejoice in the Lord, O you righteous.
Praise befits the upright.
2 Praise the Lord with the lyre;
make melody to him with the harp of ten
strings.
3 Sing to him a new song;
play skillfully on the strings, with loud
shouts.
4 For the word of the Lord is upright,
and all his work is done in faithfulness.
5 He loves righteousness and justice;
the earth is full of the steadfast love of
the Lord.
6 By the word of the Lord the heavens were
made,
and all their host by the breath of his
mouth.
7 He gathered the waters of the sea as in a
bottle;
he put the deeps in storehouses.

8 Let all the earth fear the Lord;
let all the inhabitants of the world stand
in awe of him.
9 For he spoke, and it came to be;
he commanded, and it stood firm.
10 The Lord brings the counsel of the nations
to nothing;
he frustrates the plans of the peoples.
11 The counsel of the Lord stands forever,
the thoughts of his heart to all
generations.
12 Happy is the nation whose God is the Lord,
the people whom he has chosen as his
heritage.

Playing and Pondering—© Christy Klink, 18

13 The Lord looks down from heaven;
he sees all humankind.
14 From where he sits enthroned he
watches
all the inhabitants of the earth—
15 he who fashions the hearts of them all,
and observes all their deeds.
16 A king is not saved by his great army;
a warrior is not delivered by his great
strength.
17 The war horse is a vain hope for victory,
and by its great might it cannot save.

18 Truly the eye of the Lord is on those who
fear him,
on those who hope in his steadfast love,
19 to deliver their soul from death,
and to keep them alive in famine.

20 Our soul waits for the Lord;
he is our help and shield.
21 Our heart is glad in him,
because we trust in his holy name.
22 Let your steadfast love, O Lord, be upon us,
even as we hope in you.

PSALM 34

Praise for Deliverance from Trouble

*Of David, when he feigned madness before Abimelech,
so that he drove him out, and he went away.*

1 I will bless the Lord at all times;
his praise shall continually be in my
mouth.

² My soul makes its boast in the LORD;
  let the humble hear and be glad.
³ O magnify the LORD with me,
  and let us exalt his name together.

⁴ I sought the LORD, and he answered me,
  and delivered me from all my fears.
⁵ Look to him, and be radiant;
  so your^a faces shall never be
    ashamed.
⁶ This poor soul cried, and was heard by the
    LORD,
  and was saved from every trouble.
⁷ The angel of the LORD encamps
  around those who fear him, and delivers
    them.
⁸ O taste and see that the LORD is good;
  happy are those who take refuge in
    him.
⁹ O fear the LORD, you his holy ones,
  for those who fear him have no want.
¹⁰ The young lions suffer want and hunger,
  but those who seek the LORD lack no
    good thing.

¹¹ Come, O children, listen to me;
  I will teach you the fear of the LORD.
¹² Which of you desires life,
  and covets many days to enjoy good?
¹³ Keep your tongue from evil,
  and your lips from speaking deceit.
¹⁴ Depart from evil, and do good;
  seek peace, and pursue it.

¹⁵ The eyes of the LORD are on the
    righteous,
  and his ears are open to their cry.
¹⁶ The face of the LORD is against evildoers,
  to cut off the remembrance of them
    from the earth.
¹⁷ When the righteous cry for help, the LORD
    hears,
  and rescues them from all their
    troubles.
¹⁸ The LORD is near to the brokenhearted,
  and saves the crushed in spirit.

¹⁹ Many are the afflictions of the righteous,
  but the LORD rescues them from them
    all.
²⁰ He keeps all their bones;
  not one of them will be broken.
²¹ Evil brings death to the wicked,
  and those who hate the righteous will be
    condemned.
²² The LORD redeems the life of his
    servants;
  none of those who take refuge in him
    will be condemned.

PSALM 35

Prayer for Deliverance from Enemies

Of David.

¹ Contend, O LORD, with those who contend
    with me;
  fight against those who fight against me!
² Take hold of shield and buckler,
  and rise up to help me!
³ Draw the spear and javelin
    against my pursuers;
  say to my soul,
  "I am your salvation."

⁴ Let them be put to shame and dishonor
  who seek after my life.
  Let them be turned back and confounded
  who devise evil against me.
⁵ Let them be like chaff before the wind,
  with the angel of the LORD driving
    them on.
⁶ Let their way be dark and slippery,
  with the angel of the LORD pursuing
    them.

⁷ For without cause they hid their net^b for
    me;
  without cause they dug a pit^c for my life.
⁸ Let ruin come on them unawares.
  And let the net that they hid ensnare them;
  let them fall in it—to their ruin.

⁹ Then my soul shall rejoice in the LORD,
  exulting in his deliverance.
¹⁰ All my bones shall say,
  "O LORD, who is like you?
  You deliver the weak
    from those too strong for them,
  the weak and needy from those who
    despoil them."

¹¹ Malicious witnesses rise up;
  they ask me about things I do not know.
¹² They repay me evil for good;
  my soul is forlorn.
¹³ But as for me, when they were sick,
    I wore sackcloth;
  I afflicted myself with fasting.
  I prayed with head bowed^d on my bosom,
¹⁴   as though I grieved for a friend or a
    brother;
  I went about as one who laments for a
    mother,
    bowed down and in mourning.

¹⁵ But at my stumbling they gathered in glee,
  they gathered together against me;
  ruffians whom I did not know
    tore at me without ceasing;

---

a Gk Syr Jerome: Heb *their*   *b* Heb *a pit, their net*   *c* The word *pit* is transposed from the preceding line   *d* Or *My prayer turned back*

16 they impiously mocked more and more,[a]
    gnashing at me with their teeth.

17 How long, O Lord, will you look on?
    Rescue me from their ravages,
    my life from the lions!
18 Then I will thank you in the great
    congregation;
    in the mighty throng I will praise you.

19 Do not let my treacherous enemies rejoice
    over me,
    or those who hate me without cause
    wink the eye.
20 For they do not speak peace,
    but they conceive deceitful words
    against those who are quiet in the land.
21 They open wide their mouths against me;
    they say, "Aha, Aha,
    our eyes have seen it."

22 You have seen, O Lord; do not be silent!
    O Lord, do not be far from me!
23 Wake up! Bestir yourself for my defense,
    for my cause, my God and my Lord!
24 Vindicate me, O Lord, my God,
    according to your righteousness,
    and do not let them rejoice over me.
25 Do not let them say to themselves,
    "Aha, we have our heart's desire."
    Do not let them say, "We have swallowed
    you[b] up."

26 Let all those who rejoice at my calamity
    be put to shame and confusion;
    let those who exalt themselves against me
    be clothed with shame and dishonor.

27 Let those who desire my vindication
    shout for joy and be glad,
    and say evermore,
    "Great is the Lord,
    who delights in the welfare of his
    servant."
28 Then my tongue shall tell of your
    righteousness
    and of your praise all day long.

PSALM 36

Human Wickedness and Divine Goodness

To the leader. Of David, the servant of the Lord.

1 Transgression speaks to the wicked
    deep in their hearts;
    there is no fear of God
    before their eyes.
2 For they flatter themselves in their own eyes
    that their iniquity cannot be found out
    and hated.

> "At the center of every psalm is the presence of Yahweh, the God of Israel, 'the Lord' in Jewish and Christian translations."
>
> —Richard J. Clifford, S.J.

3 The words of their mouths are mischief and
    deceit;
    they have ceased to act wisely and do
    good.
4 They plot mischief while on their beds;
    they are set on a way that is not good;
    they do not reject evil.

5 Your steadfast love, O Lord, extends to the
    heavens,
    your faithfulness to the clouds.
6 Your righteousness is like the mighty
    mountains,
    your judgments are like the great deep;
    you save humans and animals alike,
    O Lord.

7 How precious is your steadfast love, O God!
    All people may take refuge in the shadow
    of your wings.
8 They feast on the abundance of your house,
    and you give them drink from the river of
    your delights.
9 For with you is the fountain of life;
    in your light we see light.

10 O continue your steadfast love to those who
    know you,
    and your salvation to the upright of heart!
11 Do not let the foot of the arrogant tread on
    me,
    or the hand of the wicked drive me away.
12 There the evildoers lie prostrate;
    they are thrust down, unable to rise.

PSALM 37

Exhortation to Patience and Trust

Of David.

1 Do not fret because of the wicked;
    do not be envious of wrongdoers,
2 for they will soon fade like the grass,
    and wither like the green herb.

3 Trust in the Lord, and do good;
    so you will live in the land, and enjoy
    security.
4 Take delight in the Lord,
    and he will give you the desires of your
    heart.

a Cn Compare Gk: Heb *like the profanest of mockers of a cake* b Heb *him*

Amazing—© Aieryon Frazier, 13

5 Commit your way to the LORD;
   trust in him, and he will act.
6 He will make your vindication shine like the
      light,
   and the justice of your cause like the
      noonday.

7 Be still before the LORD, and wait patiently
      for him;
   do not fret over those who prosper in
      their way,
   over those who carry out evil devices.

8 Refrain from anger, and forsake wrath.
   Do not fret—it leads only to evil.
9 For the wicked shall be cut off,
   but those who wait for the LORD shall
      inherit the land.

10 Yet a little while, and the wicked will be no
      more;
   though you look diligently for their
      place, they will not be there.
11 But the meek shall inherit the land,
   and delight themselves in abundant
      prosperity.

12 The wicked plot against the righteous,
   and gnash their teeth at them;
13 but the LORD laughs at the wicked,
   for he sees that their day is coming.

14 The wicked draw the sword and bend their
      bows

to bring down the poor and needy,
   to kill those who walk uprightly;
15 their sword shall enter their own heart,
   and their bows shall be broken.

16 Better is a little that the righteous person
      has
   than the abundance of many wicked.
17 For the arms of the wicked shall be broken,
   but the LORD upholds the righteous.

18 The LORD knows the days of the blameless,
   and their heritage will abide forever;
19 they are not put to shame in evil times,
   in the days of famine they have abundance.

20 But the wicked perish,
   and the enemies of the LORD are like the
      glory of the pastures;
   they vanish—like smoke they vanish
      away.

21 The wicked borrow, and do not pay back,
   but the righteous are generous and keep
      giving;
22 for those blessed by the LORD shall inherit
      the land,
   but those cursed by him shall be cut off.

23 Our steps*a* are made firm by the LORD,
   when he delights in our*b* way;
24 though we stumble,*c* we*d* shall not fall
      headlong,
   for the LORD holds us*e* by the hand.

a Heb *A man's steps* b Heb *his* c Heb *he stumbles* d Heb *he* e Heb *him*

²⁵ I have been young, and now am old,
   yet I have not seen the righteous
      forsaken
   or their children begging bread.
²⁶ They are ever giving liberally and lending,
   and their children become a blessing.

²⁷ Depart from evil, and do good;
   so you shall abide forever.
²⁸ For the LORD loves justice;
   he will not forsake his faithful ones.

   The righteous shall be kept safe forever,
      but the children of the wicked shall be
      cut off.
²⁹ The righteous shall inherit the land,
   and live in it forever.

³⁰ The mouths of the righteous utter wisdom,
   and their tongues speak justice.
³¹ The law of their God is in their hearts;
   their steps do not slip.

³² The wicked watch for the righteous,
   and seek to kill them.
³³ The LORD will not abandon them to their
      power,
   or let them be condemned when they are
      brought to trial.

³⁴ Wait for the LORD, and keep to his way,
   and he will exalt you to inherit the land;
   you will look on the destruction of the
      wicked.

³⁵ I have seen the wicked oppressing,
   and towering like a cedar of Lebanon.^a
³⁶ Again I^b passed by, and they were no more;
   though I sought them, they could not be
      found.

³⁷ Mark the blameless, and behold the upright,
   for there is posterity for the peaceable.
³⁸ But transgressors shall be altogether
      destroyed;
   the posterity of the wicked shall be cut off.

³⁹ The salvation of the righteous is from the
      LORD;
   he is their refuge in the time of trouble.
⁴⁰ The LORD helps them and rescues them;
   he rescues them from the wicked, and
      saves them,
   because they take refuge in him.

PSALM 38

A Penitent Sufferer's Plea for Healing

A Psalm of David, for the memorial offering.

¹ O LORD, do not rebuke me in your anger,
   or discipline me in your wrath.

² For your arrows have sunk into me,
   and your hand has come down on me.

³ There is no soundness in my flesh
   because of your indignation;
   there is no health in my bones
   because of my sin.

⁴ For my iniquities have gone over my head;
   they weigh like a burden too heavy
      for me.

⁵ My wounds grow foul and fester
   because of my foolishness;
⁶ I am utterly bowed down and prostrate;
   all day long I go around mourning.

⁷ For my loins are filled with burning,
   and there is no soundness in my flesh.
⁸ I am utterly spent and crushed;
   I groan because of the tumult of my
      heart.

⁹ O Lord, all my longing is known to you;
   my sighing is not hidden from you.

¹⁰ My heart throbs, my strength fails me;
   as for the light of my eyes—it also has
      gone from me.

¹¹ My friends and companions stand aloof
      from my affliction,
   and my neighbors stand far off.

¹² Those who seek my life lay their snares;
   those who seek to hurt me speak of ruin,
   and meditate treachery all day long.

¹³ But I am like the deaf, I do not hear;
   like the mute, who cannot speak.
¹⁴ Truly, I am like one who does not hear,
   and in whose mouth is no retort.

¹⁵ But it is for you, O LORD, that I wait;
   it is you, O Lord my God, who will
      answer.
¹⁶ For I pray, "Only do not let them rejoice
      over me,
   those who boast against me when my
      foot slips."

¹⁷ For I am ready to fall,
   and my pain is ever with me.
¹⁸ I confess my iniquity;
   I am sorry for my sin.
¹⁹ Those who are my foes without cause^c are
      mighty,
   and many are those who hate me
      wrongfully.
²⁰ Those who render me evil for good
   are my adversaries because I follow after
      good.

²¹ Do not forsake me, O LORD;
   O my God, do not be far from me;

---

a Gk: Meaning of Heb uncertain   *b* Gk Syr Jerome: Heb *he*   *c* Q Ms: MT *my living foes*

make haste to help me,
　　O Lord, my salvation.

PSALM 39
Prayer for Wisdom and Forgiveness

To the leader: to Jeduthun. A Psalm of David.

1 I said, "I will guard my ways
　　that I may not sin with my tongue;
　I will keep a muzzle on my mouth
　　as long as the wicked are in my
　　　　presence."
2 I was silent and still;
　　I held my peace to no avail;
　my distress grew worse,
3 　my heart became hot within me.
　While I mused, the fire burned;
　　then I spoke with my tongue:

4 "Lord, let me know my end,
　　and what is the measure of my days;
　　let me know how fleeting my life is.
5 You have made my days a few
　　　　handbreadths,
　　and my lifetime is as nothing in your
　　　　sight.
　Surely everyone stands as a mere breath.
　　　　　　　　　　　　　　　Selah

6 　Surely everyone goes about like a
　　　　shadow.
　Surely for nothing they are in turmoil;
　　they heap up, and do not know who will
　　　　gather.

7 "And now, O Lord, what do I wait for?
　　My hope is in you.
8 Deliver me from all my transgressions.
　　Do not make me the scorn of the fool.
9 I am silent; I do not open my mouth,
　　for it is you who have done it.
10 Remove your stroke from me;
　　I am worn down by the blows*a* of your
　　　　hand.

11 "You chastise mortals
　　in punishment for sin,
　consuming like a moth what is dear to
　　　　them;
　　surely everyone is a mere breath.　*Selah*

12 "Hear my prayer, O Lord,
　　and give ear to my cry;
　　do not hold your peace at my tears.
　For I am your passing guest,
　　an alien, like all my forebears.
13 Turn your gaze away from me, that I may
　　　　smile again,
　　before I depart and am no
　　　　more."

PSALM 40
Thanksgiving for Deliverance and Prayer for Help

To the leader. Of David. A Psalm.

1 I waited patiently for the Lord;
　　he inclined to me and heard my cry.
2 He drew me up from the desolate pit,*b*
　　out of the miry bog,
　and set my feet upon a rock,
　　making my steps secure.
3 He put a new song in my mouth,
　　a song of praise to our God.
　Many will see and fear,
　　and put their trust in the Lord.

4 Happy are those who make
　　the Lord their trust,
　who do not turn to the proud,
　　to those who go astray after false gods.
5 You have multiplied, O Lord my God,
　　your wondrous deeds and your thoughts
　　　　toward us;
　none can compare with you.
　Were I to proclaim and tell of them,
　　they would be more than can be counted.

6 Sacrifice and offering you do not desire,
　　but you have given me an open ear.*c*
　Burnt offering and sin offering
　　you have not required.
7 Then I said, "Here I am;
　　in the scroll of the book it is written
　　　　of me.*d*
8 I delight to do your will, O my God;
　　your law is within my heart."

9 I have told the glad news of deliverance
　　in the great congregation;
　see, I have not restrained my lips,
　　as you know, O Lord.
10 I have not hidden your saving help within
　　　　my heart,
　　I have spoken of your faithfulness and
　　　　your salvation;
　I have not concealed your steadfast love and
　　　　your faithfulness
　　from the great congregation.

11 Do not, O Lord, withhold
　　your mercy from me;
　let your steadfast love and your faithfulness
　　keep me safe forever.
12 For evils have encompassed me
　　without number;
　my iniquities have overtaken me,
　　until I cannot see;
　they are more than the hairs of my head,
　　and my heart fails me.

---

a Heb *hostility*　*b* Cn: Heb *pit of tumult*　*c* Heb *ears you have dug for me*　*d* Meaning of Heb uncertain

Calling out,
Falling in,
Going right,
Swerving left,
Every which way,
Don't know where to turn.
Life is so confusing—
Without him.

You never know,
He can change your life,
He's surely changed mine:
Blurry to clear,
Sadness to cheer.
Give him a try,
He'll give you a different kind of high.

This isn't a joke,
It's a life or death situation.
You think I'm kidding,
Or there's no way you'd take me seriously.
You're tired and alone,
Nowhere to turn—
What do you have to lose?

You might turn to a beer,
Turn to a knife,
Turn to a drug—
Whatever it is,
Get rid of it.
I'm showing you—
There's another way...

Father to the fatherless,
Friend to the friendless,
Hope to the hopeless,
Happiness to the depressed.
He's God to me,
And he's so much more...

God—© Shelby Steckroth, 15

13 Be pleased, O Lord, to deliver me;
  O Lord, make haste to help me.
14 Let all those be put to shame and confusion
  who seek to snatch away my life;
  let those be turned back and brought to
    dishonor
  who desire my hurt.
15 Let those be appalled because of their
    shame
  who say to me, "Aha, Aha!"

16 But may all who seek you
  rejoice and be glad in you;
  may those who love your salvation
  say continually, "Great is the Lord!"
17 As for me, I am poor and needy,
  but the Lord takes thought for me.
  You are my help and my deliverer;
  do not delay, O my God.

PSALM 41

Assurance of God's Help and a Plea for Healing

To the leader. A Psalm of David.

1 Happy are those who consider the poor;[a]
  the Lord delivers them in the day of
    trouble.
2 The Lord protects them and keeps them
    alive;
  they are called happy in the land.
  You do not give them up to the will of
    their enemies.
3 The Lord sustains them on their sickbed;
  in their illness you heal all their
    infirmities.[b]

4 As for me, I said, "O Lord, be gracious
    to me;
  heal me, for I have sinned against you."
5 My enemies wonder in malice
  when I will die, and my name perish.
6 And when they come to see me, they utter
    empty words,
  while their hearts gather mischief;
  when they go out, they tell it abroad.
7 All who hate me whisper together about
    me;
  they imagine the worst for me.

8 They think that a deadly thing has fastened
    on me,
  that I will not rise again from where I lie.
9 Even my bosom friend in whom I trusted,
  who ate of my bread, has lifted the heel
    against me.
10 But you, O Lord, be gracious to me,
  and raise me up, that I may repay them.

11 By this I know that you are pleased with me;
  because my enemy has not triumphed
    over me.
12 But you have upheld me because of my
    integrity,
  and set me in your presence forever.

13 Blessed be the Lord, the God of Israel,
  from everlasting to everlasting.
      Amen and Amen.

BOOK II (Psalms 42–72)

PSALM 42

Longing for God and His Help in Distress

To the leader. A Maskil of the Korahites.

1 As a deer longs for flowing streams,
  so my soul longs for you, O God.
2 My soul thirsts for God,
  for the living God.
  When shall I come and behold
  the face of God?
3 My tears have been my food
  day and night,
  while people say to me continually,
  "Where is your God?"

4 These things I remember,
  as I pour out my soul:
  how I went with the throng,[c]
    and led them in procession to the house
      of God,
  with glad shouts and songs of thanksgiving,
  a multitude keeping festival.
5 Why are you cast down, O my soul,
  and why are you disquieted within me?
  Hope in God; for I shall again praise him,
  my help 6and my God.

My soul is cast down within me;
  therefore I remember you
  from the land of Jordan and of Hermon,
  from Mount Mizar.
7 Deep calls to deep
  at the thunder of your cataracts;
  all your waves and your billows
  have gone over me.
8 By day the Lord commands his steadfast
    love,
  and at night his song is with me,
  a prayer to the God of my life.
9 I say to God, my rock,
  "Why have you forgotten me?
  Why must I walk about mournfully
  because the enemy oppresses me?"
10 As with a deadly wound in my body,
  my adversaries taunt me,

---

a Or *weak* *b* Heb *you change all his bed* *c* Meaning of Heb uncertain

while they say to me continually,
  "Where is your God?"

[11] Why are you cast down, O my soul,
  and why are you disquieted within me?
Hope in God; for I shall again praise him,
  my help and my God.

PSALM 43

Prayer to God in Time of Trouble

[1] Vindicate me, O God, and defend my cause
  against an ungodly people;
from those who are deceitful and unjust
  deliver me!

[2] For you are the God in whom I take refuge;
  why have you cast me off?
Why must I walk about mournfully
  because of the oppression of the
    enemy?

[3] O send out your light and your truth;
  let them lead me;
let them bring me to your holy hill
  and to your dwelling.

[4] Then I will go to the altar of God,
  to God my exceeding joy;
and I will praise you with the harp,
  O God, my God.

[5] Why are you cast down, O my soul,
  and why are you disquieted within me?
Hope in God; for I shall again praise him,
  my help and my God.

PSALM 44

National Lament and Prayer for Help

To the leader. Of the Korahites. A Maskil.

[1] We have heard with our ears, O God,
  our ancestors have told us,
what deeds you performed in their days,
  in the days of old:

[2] you with your own hand drove out the
    nations,
  but them you planted;
you afflicted the peoples,
  but them you set free;

[3] for not by their own sword did they win the
    land,
  nor did their own arm give them victory;
but your right hand, and your arm,
  and the light of your countenance,
  for you delighted in them.

[4] You are my King and my God;[a]
  you command victories for Jacob.

[5] Through you we push down our foes;
  through your name we tread down our
    assailants.

[6] For not in my bow do I trust,
  nor can my sword save me.

[7] But you have saved us from our foes,
  and have put to confusion those who
    hate us.

[8] In God we have boasted continually,
  and we will give thanks to your name
    forever. *Selah*

[9] Yet you have rejected us and abased us,
  and have not gone out with our armies.

[10] You made us turn back from the foe,
  and our enemies have gotten spoil.

[11] You have made us like sheep for slaughter,
  and have scattered us among the nations.

[12] You have sold your people for a trifle,
  demanding no high price for them.

[13] You have made us the taunt of our
    neighbors,
  the derision and scorn of those
    around us.

[14] You have made us a byword among the
    nations,
  a laughingstock[b] among the peoples.

[15] All day long my disgrace is before me,
  and shame has covered my face

[16] at the words of the taunters and revilers,
  at the sight of the enemy and the
    avenger.

[17] All this has come upon us,
  yet we have not forgotten you,
  or been false to your covenant.

[18] Our heart has not turned back,
  nor have our steps departed from your
    way,

[19] yet you have broken us in the haunt of
    jackals,
  and covered us with deep darkness.

[20] If we had forgotten the name of our God,
  or spread out our hands to a strange god,

[21] would not God discover this?
  For he knows the secrets of the heart.

[22] Because of you we are being killed all day
    long,
  and accounted as sheep for the slaughter.

[23] Rouse yourself! Why do you sleep, O Lord?
  Awake, do not cast us off forever!

[24] Why do you hide your face?
  Why do you forget our affliction and
    oppression?

[25] For we sink down to the dust;
  our bodies cling to the ground.

[26] Rise up, come to our help.
  Redeem us for the sake of your steadfast
    love.

a Gk Syr: Heb *You are my King, O God; command* *b* Heb *a shaking of the head*

PSALM 45

Ode for a Royal Wedding

To the leader: according to Lilies. Of the Korahites. A Maskil. A love song.

1 My heart overflows with a goodly theme;
    I address my verses to the king;
        my tongue is like the pen of a ready
            scribe.

CREATIVE SPACE

2 You are the most handsome of men;
    grace is poured upon your lips;
        therefore God has blessed you forever.
3 Gird your sword on your thigh, O mighty
        one,
    in your glory and majesty.

4 In your majesty ride on victoriously
    for the cause of truth and to defend[a] the
        right;
        let your right hand teach you dread deeds.
5 Your arrows are sharp
    in the heart of the king's enemies;
        the peoples fall under you.

6 Your throne, O God,[b] endures forever and
        ever.
    Your royal scepter is a scepter of equity;
7   you love righteousness and hate
        wickedness.
    Therefore God, your God, has anointed you
        with the oil of gladness beyond your
            companions;
8   your robes are all fragrant with myrrh
        and aloes and cassia.
    From ivory palaces stringed instruments
        make you glad;
9   daughters of kings are among your ladies
        of honor;
        at your right hand stands the queen in
            gold of Ophir.

10 Hear, O daughter, consider and incline your
        ear;
    forget your people and your father's
        house,
11   and the king will desire your beauty.
    Since he is your lord, bow to him;
12   the people[c] of Tyre will seek your favor
        with gifts,
        the richest of the people 13with all kinds
            of wealth.

    The princess is decked in her chamber with
        gold-woven robes;[d]
14   in many-colored robes she is led to the
        king;
        behind her the virgins, her companions,
            follow.
15 With joy and gladness they are led along
    as they enter the palace of the king.

16 In the place of ancestors you, O king,[e] shall
        have sons;
    you will make them princes in all the
        earth.
17 I will cause your name to be celebrated in
        all generations;

a Cn: Heb *and the meekness of* *b* Or *Your throne is a throne of God, it* *c* Heb *daughter* *d* Or *people.* *13All glorious is the princess within, gold embroidery is her clothing* *e* Heb lacks *O king*

therefore the peoples will praise you
    forever and ever.

PSALM 46

God's Defense of His City and People

To the leader. Of the Korahites. According to Alamoth.
A Song.

¹ God is our refuge and strength,
    a very present[a] help in trouble.
² Therefore we will not fear, though the earth
        should change,
    though the mountains shake in the heart
        of the sea;
³ though its waters roar and foam,
    though the mountains tremble with its
        tumult.   *Selah*

⁴ There is a river whose streams make glad
        the city of God,
    the holy habitation of the Most High.
⁵ God is in the midst of the city;[b] it shall not
        be moved;
    God will help it when the morning dawns.
⁶ The nations are in an uproar, the kingdoms
        totter;
    he utters his voice, the earth melts.
⁷ The LORD of hosts is with us;
    the God of Jacob is our refuge.[c]   *Selah*

⁸ Come, behold the works of the LORD;
    see what desolations he has brought on
        the earth.
⁹ He makes wars cease to the end of the earth;
    he breaks the bow, and shatters the spear;
    he burns the shields with fire.
¹⁰ "Be still, and know that I am God!
    I am exalted among the nations,
    I am exalted in the earth."
¹¹ The LORD of hosts is with us;
    the God of Jacob is our refuge.[c]   *Selah*

PSALM 47

God's Rule over the Nations

To the leader. Of the Korahites. A Psalm.

¹ Clap your hands, all you peoples;
    shout to God with loud songs of joy.
² For the LORD, the Most High, is awesome,
    a great king over all the earth.
³ He subdued peoples under us,
    and nations under our feet.
⁴ He chose our heritage for us,
    the pride of Jacob whom he loves.   *Selah*

⁵ God has gone up with a shout,
    the LORD with the sound of a trumpet.
⁶ Sing praises to God, sing praises;
    sing praises to our King, sing praises.

⁷ For God is the king of all the earth;
    sing praises with a psalm.[d]

⁸ God is king over the nations;
    God sits on his holy throne.
⁹ The princes of the peoples gather
    as the people of the God of Abraham.
    For the shields of the earth belong to God;
    he is highly exalted.

PSALM 48

The Glory and Strength of Zion

A Song. A Psalm of the Korahites.

¹ Great is the LORD and greatly to be praised
    in the city of our God.
    His holy mountain, ²beautiful in elevation,
    is the joy of all the earth,
    Mount Zion, in the far north,
    the city of the great King.
³ Within its citadels God
    has shown himself a sure defense.

⁴ Then the kings assembled,
    they came on together.
⁵ As soon as they saw it, they were astounded;
    they were in panic, they took to flight;
⁶ trembling took hold of them there,
    pains as of a woman in labor,
⁷ as when an east wind shatters
    the ships of Tarshish.
⁸ As we have heard, so have we seen
    in the city of the LORD of hosts,
    in the city of our God,
    which God establishes forever.   *Selah*

⁹ We ponder your steadfast love, O God,
    in the midst of your temple.
¹⁰ Your name, O God, like your praise,
    reaches to the ends of the earth.
    Your right hand is filled with victory.
¹¹   Let Mount Zion be glad,
    let the towns[e] of Judah rejoice
    because of your judgments.

¹² Walk about Zion, go all around it,
    count its towers,
¹³ consider well its ramparts;
    go through its citadels,
    that you may tell the next generation
¹⁴   that this is God,
    our God forever and ever.
    He will be our guide forever.

PSALM 49

The Folly of Trust in Riches

To the leader. Of the Korahites. A Psalm.

¹ Hear this, all you peoples;
    give ear, all inhabitants of the world,

---

a Or *well proved* *b* Heb *of it* *c* Or *fortress* *d* Heb *Maskil* *e* Heb *daughters*

² both low and high,
  rich and poor together.
³ My mouth shall speak wisdom;
  the meditation of my heart shall be
    understanding.
⁴ I will incline my ear to a proverb;
  I will solve my riddle to the music of the
    harp.

⁵ Why should I fear in times of trouble,
  when the iniquity of my persecutors
    surrounds me,
⁶ those who trust in their wealth
  and boast of the abundance of their
    riches?
⁷ Truly, no ransom avails for one's life,ᵃ
  there is no price one can give to God for it.
⁸ For the ransom of life is costly,
  and can never suffice,
⁹ that one should live on forever
  and never see the grave.ᵇ

¹⁰ When we look at the wise, they die;
  fool and dolt perish together
  and leave their wealth to others.
¹¹ Their gravesᶜ are their homes forever,
  their dwelling places to all generations,
  though they named lands their own.
¹² Mortals cannot abide in their pomp;
  they are like the animals that perish.

¹³ Such is the fate of the foolhardy,
  the end of thoseᵈ who are pleased with
    their lot.   Selah
¹⁴ Like sheep they are appointed for Sheol;
  Death shall be their shepherd;
  straight to the grave they descend,ᵉ
  and their form shall waste away;
  Sheol shall be their home.ᶠ
¹⁵ But God will ransom my soul from the
    power of Sheol,
  for he will receive me.   Selah

¹⁶ Do not be afraid when some become rich,
  when the wealth of their houses
    increases.
¹⁷ For when they die they will carry nothing
    away;
  their wealth will not go down after them.
¹⁸ Though in their lifetime they count
    themselves happy
  —for you are praised when you do well
    for yourself—
¹⁹ theyᵍ will go to the company of their
    ancestors,
  who will never again see the light.
²⁰ Mortals cannot abide in their pomp;
  they are like the animals that perish.

PSALM 50

The Acceptable Sacrifice

A Psalm of Asaph.

¹ The mighty one, God the LORD,
  speaks and summons the earth
  from the rising of the sun to its setting.
² Out of Zion, the perfection of beauty,
  God shines forth.

³ Our God comes and does not keep silence,
  before him is a devouring fire,
  and a mighty tempest all around him.
⁴ He calls to the heavens above
  and to the earth, that he may judge his
    people:
⁵ "Gather to me my faithful ones,
  who made a covenant with me by
    sacrifice!"
⁶ The heavens declare his righteousness,
  for God himself is judge.   *Selah*

⁷ "Hear, O my people, and I will speak,
  O Israel, I will testify against you.
  I am God, your God.
⁸ Not for your sacrifices do I rebuke you;
  your burnt offerings are continually
    before me.
⁹ I will not accept a bull from your house,
  or goats from your folds.
¹⁰ For every wild animal of the forest is mine,
  the cattle on a thousand hills.
¹¹ I know all the birds of the air,ʰ
  and all that moves in the field is mine.

¹² "If I were hungry, I would not tell you,
  for the world and all that is in it is mine.
¹³ Do I eat the flesh of bulls,
  or drink the blood of goats?
¹⁴ Offer to God a sacrifice of thanksgiving,ⁱ
  and pay your vows to the Most High.
¹⁵ Call on me in the day of trouble;
  I will deliver you, and you shall
    glorify me."

¹⁶ But to the wicked God says:
  "What right have you to recite my
    statutes,
  or take my covenant on your lips?
¹⁷ For you hate discipline,
  and you cast my words behind you.
¹⁸ You make friends with a thief when you see
    one,
  and you keep company with adulterers.

¹⁹ "You give your mouth free rein for evil,
  and your tongue frames deceit.
²⁰ You sit and speak against your kin;

---

a Another reading is *no one can ransom a brother*   *b* Heb *the pit*   *c* Gk Syr Compare Tg: Heb *their inward* (thought)   *d* Tg: Heb *after them*
e Cn: Heb *the upright shall have dominion over them in the morning*   *f* Meaning of Heb uncertain   *g* Cn: Heb *you*   *h* Gk Syr Tg: Heb *mountains*
i Or *make thanksgiving your sacrifice to God*

you slander your own mother's child.

21 These things you have done and I have been silent;
   you thought that I was one just like yourself.
   But now I rebuke you, and lay the charge before you.

22 "Mark this, then, you who forget God,
   or I will tear you apart, and there will be no one to deliver.

23 Those who bring thanksgiving as their sacrifice honor me;
   to those who go the right way[a]
   I will show the salvation of God."

PSALM 51

Prayer for Cleansing and Pardon

To the leader. A Psalm of David, when the prophet Nathan came to him, after he had gone in to Bathsheba.

1 Have mercy on me, O God,
   according to your steadfast love;
   according to your abundant mercy
   blot out my transgressions.

2 Wash me thoroughly from my iniquity,
   and cleanse me from my sin.

3 For I know my transgressions,
   and my sin is ever before me.

4 Against you, you alone, have I sinned,
   and done what is evil in your sight,
   so that you are justified in your sentence
   and blameless when you pass judgment.

5 Indeed, I was born guilty,
   a sinner when my mother conceived me.

6 You desire truth in the inward being;[b]
   therefore teach me wisdom in my secret heart.

7 Purge me with hyssop, and I shall be clean;
   wash me, and I shall be whiter than snow.

8 Let me hear joy and gladness;
   let the bones that you have crushed rejoice.

9 Hide your face from my sins,
   and blot out all my iniquities.

10 Create in me a clean heart, O God,
   and put a new and right[c] spirit within me.

11 Do not cast me away from your presence,
   and do not take your holy spirit from me.

12 Restore to me the joy of your salvation,
   and sustain in me a willing[d] spirit.

13 Then I will teach transgressors your ways,
   and sinners will return to you.

14 Deliver me from bloodshed, O God,
   O God of my salvation,

a Heb *who set away* *b* Meaning of Heb uncertain *c* Or *steadfast*
d Or *generous*

EXPRESS YOURSELF

XXL Mistakes

My dad would swear that the key to a happy marriage is to never buy your wife anything sized XXL. His philosophy has served him well so far.

Mistakes come in all sizes, and typically the large ones are those we try most to avoid. The biggies usually involve something like stealing, lying, cheating, sex, drugs . . . you get the idea.

Psalm 51 is like a page out of the secret journal of someone with an enviable friendship with God. But it isn't what you might expect.

King David messed up, and it was a doozy: adultery with a married woman. She got pregnant, so to gloss over his indiscretion, David had her husband killed in the line of duty. That's right—M-U-R-D-E-R-E-D. Finally, after being confronted head-on with his sin, his conscience caught up with him. He came crawling to God as we all do when we can no longer coexist with our darker side. (You can read about the confrontation in 2 Samuel 12.1–15.)

Read **Psalm 51**. Pause and reflect while you read, allowing the images and emotions of the psalm to speak to you. Whatever your sin problems might be, they cannot come close to matching the hugeness of God's compassion. There is nothing too embarrassing or despicable to keep you from his open arms.

David didn't confront his sin until he was confronted by a prophet. Don't make that same mistake. Take some time to reflect on the issues in your life that are hurting your relationship with God, that make you feel guilty, or that are just plain wrong.

Then confess your sins to God and prepare to celebrate the Sacrament of Reconciliation. Use Psalm 51 as a how-to. Afterward write a poem or song about God's XXL compassion.

and my tongue will sing aloud of your
deliverance.
15 O Lord, open my lips,
and my mouth will declare your praise.
16 For you have no delight in sacrifice;
if I were to give a burnt offering, you
would not be pleased.
17 The sacrifice acceptable to God[a] is a broken
spirit;
a broken and contrite heart, O God, you
will not despise.

18 Do good to Zion in your good pleasure;
rebuild the walls of Jerusalem,
19 then you will delight in right sacrifices,
in burnt offerings and whole burnt
offerings;
then bulls will be offered on your altar.

PSALM 52

Judgment on the Deceitful

*To the leader. A Maskil of David, when Doeg the Edomite
came to Saul and said to him, "David has come to the house
of Ahimelech."*

1 Why do you boast, O mighty one,
of mischief done against the godly?[b]
All day long 2you are plotting
destruction.
Your tongue is like a sharp razor,
you worker of treachery.
3 You love evil more than good,
and lying more than speaking the truth.
Selah

4 You love all words that devour,
O deceitful tongue.

5 But God will break you down forever;
he will snatch and tear you from your
tent;
he will uproot you from the land of the
living. *Selah*
6 The righteous will see, and fear,
and will laugh at the evildoer,[c] saying,
7 "See the one who would not take
refuge in God,
but trusted in abundant riches,
and sought refuge in wealth!"[d]

8 But I am like a green olive tree
in the house of God.
I trust in the steadfast love of God
forever and ever.
9 I will thank you forever,
because of what you have done.
In the presence of the faithful
I will proclaim[e] your name, for it is good.

PSALM 53

Denunciation of Godlessness

To the leader: according to Mahalath. A Maskil of David.

1 Fools say in their hearts, "There is no God."
They are corrupt, they commit
abominable acts;
there is no one who does good.

2 God looks down from heaven on
humankind
to see if there are any who are wise,
who seek after God.

3 They have all fallen away, they are all alike
perverse;
there is no one who does good,
no, not one.

4 Have they no knowledge, those evildoers,
who eat up my people as they eat bread,
and do not call upon God?

5 There they shall be in great terror,
in terror such as has not been.
For God will scatter the bones of the
ungodly;[f]
they will be put to shame,[g] for God has
rejected them.

6 O that deliverance for Israel would come
from Zion!
When God restores the fortunes of his
people,
Jacob will rejoice; Israel will be glad.

PSALM 54

Prayer for Vindication

*To the leader: with stringed instruments. A Maskil of David,
when the Ziphites went and told Saul, "David is in hiding
among us."*

1 Save me, O God, by your name,
and vindicate me by your might.
2 Hear my prayer, O God;
give ear to the words of my mouth.

3 For the insolent have risen against me,
the ruthless seek my life;
they do not set God before them. *Selah*

4 But surely, God is my helper;
the Lord is the upholder of[h] my life.
5 He will repay my enemies for their evil.
In your faithfulness, put an end to them.

6 With a freewill offering I will sacrifice to you;
I will give thanks to your name, O Lord,
for it is good.
7 For he has delivered me from every trouble,

a Or *My sacrifice, O God*, b Cn Compare Syr: Heb *the kindness of God* c Heb *him* d Syr Tg: Heb *in his destruction* e Cn: Heb *wait for*
f Cn Compare Gk Syr: Heb *him who encamps against you* g Gk: Heb *you have put (them) to shame* h Gk Syr Jerome: Heb *is of those who uphold*
or *is with those who uphold*

and my eye has looked in triumph on my
enemies.

PSALM 55

Complaint about a Friend's Treachery

To the leader: with stringed instruments. A Maskil of David.

¹ Give ear to my prayer, O God;
    do not hide yourself from my
        supplication.
² Attend to me, and answer me;
    I am troubled in my complaint.
I am distraught ³by the noise of the enemy,
    because of the clamor of the wicked.
For they bring*ª* trouble upon me,
    and in anger they cherish enmity
        against me.

⁴ My heart is in anguish within me,
    the terrors of death have fallen upon me.
⁵ Fear and trembling come upon me,
    and horror overwhelms me.
⁶ And I say, "O that I had wings like a dove!

I would fly away and be at rest;
⁷ truly, I would flee far away;
    I would lodge in the wilderness;   *Selah*
⁸ I would hurry to find a shelter for myself
    from the raging wind and tempest."

⁹ Confuse, O Lord, confound their speech;
    for I see violence and strife in the city.
¹⁰ Day and night they go around it
    on its walls,
and iniquity and trouble are within it;
¹¹   ruin is in its midst;
oppression and fraud
    do not depart from its marketplace.

¹² It is not enemies who taunt me—
    I could bear that;
it is not adversaries who deal insolently
        with me—
    I could hide from them.
¹³ But it is you, my equal,
    my companion, my familiar friend,
¹⁴ with whom I kept pleasant company;

a Cn Compare Gk: Heb *they cause to totter*

PSALM 55

we walked in the house of God with the
throng.
¹⁵ Let death come upon them;
let them go down alive to Sheol;
for evil is in their homes and in their
hearts.

¹⁶ But I call upon God,
and the LORD will save me.
¹⁷ Evening and morning and at noon
I utter my complaint and moan,
and he will hear my voice.
¹⁸ He will redeem me unharmed
from the battle that I wage,
for many are arrayed against me.
¹⁹ God, who is enthroned from of old,   Selah
will hear, and will humble them—
because they do not change,
and do not fear God.

²⁰ My companion laid hands on a friend
and violated a covenant with me^a
²¹ with speech smoother than butter,
but with a heart set on war;
with words that were softer than oil,
but in fact were drawn swords.

²² Cast your burden^b on the LORD,
and he will sustain you;
he will never permit
the righteous to be moved.

²³ But you, O God, will cast them down
into the lowest pit;
the bloodthirsty and treacherous
shall not live out half their days.
But I will trust in you.

PSALM 56

Trust in God under Persecution

*To the leader: according to The Dove on Far-off Terebinths.
Of David. A Miktam, when the Philistines seized him in Gath.*

¹ Be gracious to me, O God, for people
trample on me;
all day long foes oppress me;
² my enemies trample on me all day long,
for many fight against me.
O Most High, ³when I am afraid,
I put my trust in you.
⁴ In God, whose word I praise,
in God I trust; I am not afraid;
what can flesh do to me?

⁵ All day long they seek to injure my cause;
all their thoughts are against me for evil.
⁶ They stir up strife, they lurk,
they watch my steps.
As they hoped to have my life,
⁷   so repay^c them for their crime;

in wrath cast down the peoples, O God!

⁸ You have kept count of my tossings;
put my tears in your bottle.
Are they not in your record?
⁹ Then my enemies will retreat
in the day when I call.
This I know, that^d God is for me.
¹⁰ In God, whose word I praise,
in the LORD, whose word I praise,
¹¹ in God I trust; I am not afraid.
What can a mere mortal do to me?

¹² My vows to you I must perform, O God;
I will render thank offerings to you.
¹³ For you have delivered my soul from death,
and my feet from falling,
so that I may walk before God
in the light of life.

PSALM 57

Praise and Assurance under Persecution

*To the leader: Do Not Destroy. Of David. A Miktam, when he
fled from Saul, in the cave.*

¹ Be merciful to me, O God, be merciful to me,
for in you my soul takes refuge;
in the shadow of your wings I will take
refuge,
until the destroying storms pass by.
² I cry to God Most High,
to God who fulfills his purpose for me.
³ He will send from heaven and save me,
he will put to shame those who trample
on me.   Selah
God will send forth his steadfast love and
his faithfulness.

⁴ I lie down among lions
that greedily devour^e human prey;
their teeth are spears and arrows,
their tongues sharp swords.

⁵ Be exalted, O God, above the heavens.
Let your glory be over all the earth.

⁶ They set a net for my steps;
my soul was bowed down.
They dug a pit in my path,
but they have fallen into it themselves.
Selah

⁷ My heart is steadfast, O God,
my heart is steadfast.
I will sing and make melody.
⁸   Awake, my soul!
Awake, O harp and lyre!
I will awake the dawn.
⁹ I will give thanks to you, O Lord, among the
peoples;

---

a Heb lacks *with me* *b* Or *Cast what he has given you* *c* Cn: Heb *rescue* *d* Or *because* *e* Cn: Heb *are aflame for*

I will sing praises to you among the
nations.

10 For your steadfast love is as high as the
heavens;
your faithfulness extends to the clouds.

11 Be exalted, O God, above the heavens.
Let your glory be over all the earth.

PSALM 58

Prayer for Vengeance

To the leader: Do Not Destroy. Of David. A Miktam.

1 Do you indeed decree what is right, you
gods?*a*
Do you judge people fairly?

2 No, in your hearts you devise wrongs;
your hands deal out violence on earth.

3 The wicked go astray from the womb;
they err from their birth, speaking lies.

4 They have venom like the venom of a
serpent,
like the deaf adder that stops its ear,

5 so that it does not hear the voice of
charmers
or of the cunning enchanter.

6 O God, break the teeth in their mouths;
tear out the fangs of the young lions,
O LORD!

7 Let them vanish like water that runs away;
like grass let them be trodden down*b* and
wither.

8 Let them be like the snail that dissolves into
slime;
like the untimely birth that never sees
the sun.

9 Sooner than your pots can feel the heat of
thorns,
whether green or ablaze, may he sweep
them away!

10 The righteous will rejoice when they see
vengeance done;
they will bathe their feet in the blood of
the wicked.

11 People will say, "Surely there is a reward for
the righteous;
surely there is a God who judges on earth."

PSALM 59

Prayer for Deliverance from Enemies

*To the leader: Do Not Destroy. Of David. A Miktam, when
Saul ordered his house to be watched in order to kill him.*

1 Deliver me from my enemies, O my God;
protect me from those who rise up
against me.

a Or *mighty lords* *b* Cn: Meaning of Heb uncertain

A Mirror for Your Day

Every day, bad things and good things
happen to everyone. There's an old spiritual
exercise called the *examen*. It's a way of
taking stock of your life in light of your
relationship with God. One way you can try
it looks a bit like this: At the end of a day,
a week, a month, or even a year (the time
frame really doesn't matter here), list two
extremes. One is the most life-giving event
that happened to you—something that filled
you with peace, joy, or sheer gladness to be
alive in God's world. It could be something
as extravagant as finding a twenty-dollar
bill on the street or as simple as seeing your
neighbor's baby take her first steps.

The second extreme to list is the most
"death-dealing" thing that happened to you.
"Death-dealing" things are those bad, dirty,
and disturbing things you see or that happen
to you, and you can't chase them out of your
mental camera. As you list these high and low
points, you can bring them to God. You can
praise and thank God for the blessings you've
thought of. And you can consider how the
difficult things can help you turn to God, grow
closer to him, and choose to live more like Jesus.

In **Psalm 55**, David lists his blow of
death—it's a betrayal by a close friend. Read
55.12–14. David is taking his pain to God.
He's not just nodding and muttering, "Fine,"
when someone asks him how he's doing. He's
not fine. His heart has been broken. And he's
making some pretty powerful statements to
God about it.

What's the most life-giving thing that's
happened to you lately? What's the most death-
dealing? Take Psalm 55 and write your own
version using what's brought you pain. Write
it to God. Tell God how it is. God's here. He's
strong enough to handle what you tell him.

2 Deliver me from those who work evil;
from the bloodthirsty save me.

3 Even now they lie in wait for my life;
the mighty stir up strife against me.

For no transgression or sin of mine,
  O LORD,
4   for no fault of mine, they run and make
  ready.

Rouse yourself, come to my help and see!
5   You, LORD God of hosts, are God of Israel.
Awake to punish all the nations;
  spare none of those who treacherously
    plot evil.   *Selah*

6 Each evening they come back,
  howling like dogs
  and prowling about the city.
7 There they are, bellowing with their
    mouths,
  with sharp words*a* on their lips—
  for "Who," they think,*b* "will hear us?"

8 But you laugh at them, O LORD;
  you hold all the nations in derision.
9 O my strength, I will watch for you;
  for you, O God, are my fortress.
10 My God in his steadfast love will meet me;
  my God will let me look in triumph on
    my enemies.

11 Do not kill them, or my people may forget;
  make them totter by your power, and
    bring them down,
  O Lord, our shield.
12 For the sin of their mouths, the words of
    their lips,
  let them be trapped in their pride.
  For the cursing and lies that they utter,
13   consume them in wrath;
  consume them until they are no more.
  Then it will be known to the ends of the
    earth
  that God rules over Jacob.   *Selah*

14 Each evening they come back,
  howling like dogs
  and prowling about the city.
15 They roam about for food,
  and growl if they do not get their fill.

16 But I will sing of your might;
  I will sing aloud of your steadfast love in
    the morning.
  For you have been a fortress for me
  and a refuge in the day of my distress.
17 O my strength, I will sing praises to you,
  for you, O God, are my fortress,
  the God who shows me steadfast love.

PSALM 60

Prayer for National Victory after Defeat

To the leader: according to the Lily of the Covenant.
A Miktam of David; for instruction; when he struggled with
Aram-naharaim and with Aram-zobah, and when Joab on
his return killed twelve thousand Edomites in the Valley of
Salt.

1 O God, you have rejected us, broken our
    defenses;
  you have been angry; now restore us!
2 You have caused the land to quake; you
    have torn it open;
  repair the cracks in it, for it is tottering.
3 You have made your people suffer hard
    things;

a Heb *with swords* *b* Heb lacks *they think*

you have given us wine to drink that
made us reel.

⁴ You have set up a banner for those who fear
you,
to rally to it out of bowshot.*ᵃ*   *Selah*
⁵ Give victory with your right hand, and
answer us,*ᵇ*
so that those whom you love may be
rescued.

⁶ God has promised in his sanctuary:*ᶜ*
"With exultation I will divide up
Shechem,
and portion out the Vale of Succoth.
⁷ Gilead is mine, and Manasseh is mine;
Ephraim is my helmet;
Judah is my scepter.
⁸ Moab is my washbasin;
on Edom I hurl my shoe;
over Philistia I shout in triumph."

⁹ Who will bring me to the fortified city?
Who will lead me to Edom?
¹⁰ Have you not rejected us, O God?
You do not go out, O God, with our
armies.
¹¹ O grant us help against the foe,
for human help is worthless.
¹² With God we shall do valiantly;
it is he who will tread down our foes.

PSALM 61

Assurance of God's Protection

To the leader: with stringed instruments. Of David.

¹ Hear my cry, O God;
listen to my prayer.
² From the end of the earth I call to you,
when my heart is faint.

Lead me to the rock
that is higher than I;
³ for you are my refuge,
a strong tower against the enemy.

⁴ Let me abide in your tent forever,
find refuge under the shelter of your
wings.   *Selah*
⁵ For you, O God, have heard my vows;
you have given me the heritage of those
who fear your name.

⁶ Prolong the life of the king;
may his years endure to all generations!
⁷ May he be enthroned forever before God;
appoint steadfast love and faithfulness to
watch over him!

⁸ So I will always sing praises to your name,
as I pay my vows day after day.

PSALM 62

Song of Trust in God Alone

To the leader: according to Jeduthun. A Psalm of David.

¹ For God alone my soul waits in silence;
from him comes my salvation.
² He alone is my rock and my salvation,
my fortress; I shall never be shaken.

³ How long will you assail a person,
will you batter your victim, all of you,
as you would a leaning wall, a tottering
fence?
⁴ Their only plan is to bring down a person of
prominence.
They take pleasure in falsehood;
they bless with their mouths,
but inwardly they curse.   *Selah*

⁵ For God alone my soul waits in silence,
for my hope is from him.
⁶ He alone is my rock and my salvation,
my fortress; I shall not be shaken.
⁷ On God rests my deliverance and my honor;
my mighty rock, my refuge is in God.

⁸ Trust in him at all times, O people;
pour out your heart before him;
God is a refuge for us.   *Selah*

⁹ Those of low estate are but a breath,
those of high estate are a delusion;
in the balances they go up;
they are together lighter than a breath.
¹⁰ Put no confidence in extortion,
and set no vain hopes on robbery;
if riches increase, do not set your heart
on them.

¹¹ Once God has spoken;
twice have I heard this:
that power belongs to God,
¹²   and steadfast love belongs to you,
O Lord.
For you repay to all
according to their work.

PSALM 63

Comfort and Assurance in God's Presence

A Psalm of David, when he was in the Wilderness of Judah.

¹ O God, you are my God, I seek you,
my soul thirsts for you;
my flesh faints for you,
as in a dry and weary land where there is
no water.
² So I have looked upon you in the sanctuary,
beholding your power and glory.

---

a Gk Syr Jerome: Heb *because of the truth*   *b* Another reading is *me*   *c* Or *by his holiness*

Untitled—© Rachel Maddox, 14

VAST AND VITAL

The world—it's a beautiful place.

It's easy to get distracted by all the ugliness around us. The garbage. The often heavy human footprint. The environmental scars. But the beauty is still there. The clouds, the trees, the wildlife, the ocean—they're the living brushstrokes of God's creativity.

When you read **Psalm 65**, it's clear that God cares about his creation. He made it beautiful. He made it functional. And, most important, he *made* it. Let's do our part to take care of it.

Grab a friend and a couple of blankets and go outside on a starry night. As you lie on your back staring at the sky, talk about God's creation—the mountains, the moon, the plants, the animals. Remember that among the billions of stars and the vastness of the world, God's creativity—and his creation—touches your life too.

Take some time to draw your own constellation that represents God's creativity, and then share it at **Learner.CalltoDiscipleship.com**.

GOD IS CREATIVE MY WORLD

3 Because your steadfast love is better than
    life,
  my lips will praise you.
4 So I will bless you as long as I live;
    I will lift up my hands and call on your
    name.

5 My soul is satisfied as with a rich feast,[a]
    and my mouth praises you with joyful
    lips
6 when I think of you on my bed,

and meditate on you in the watches of
    the night;
7 for you have been my help,
    and in the shadow of your wings I sing
    for joy.
8 My soul clings to you;
    your right hand upholds me.

9 But those who seek to destroy my life
    shall go down into the depths of the
    earth;
10 they shall be given over to the power of the
    sword,
    they shall be prey for jackals.
11 But the king shall rejoice in God;
    all who swear by him shall exult,
    for the mouths of liars will be stopped.

PSALM 64

Prayer for Protection from Enemies

To the leader. A Psalm of David.

1 Hear my voice, O God, in my complaint;
    preserve my life from the dread enemy.
2 Hide me from the secret plots of the
    wicked,
    from the scheming of evildoers,
3 who whet their tongues like swords,
    who aim bitter words like arrows,
4 shooting from ambush at the blameless;
    they shoot suddenly and without fear.
5 They hold fast to their evil purpose;
    they talk of laying snares secretly,
  thinking, "Who can see us?[b]
6   Who can search out our crimes?[c]
  We have thought out a cunningly conceived
    plot."
  For the human heart and mind are deep.

7 But God will shoot his arrow at them;
    they will be wounded suddenly.
8 Because of their tongue he will bring them
    to ruin;[d]
    all who see them will shake with horror.
9 Then everyone will fear;
    they will tell what God has brought about,
    and ponder what he has done.

10 Let the righteous rejoice in the LORD
    and take refuge in him.
  Let all the upright in heart glory.

PSALM 65

Thanksgiving for Earth's Bounty

To the leader. A Psalm of David. A Song.

1 Praise is due to you,
    O God, in Zion;

a Heb *with fat and fatness* b Syr: Heb *them* c Cn: Heb *They search out crimes* d Cn: Heb *They will bring him to ruin, their tongue being against them*

and to you shall vows be performed,
2   O you who answer prayer!
To you all flesh shall come.
3 When deeds of iniquity overwhelm us,
    you forgive our transgressions.
4 Happy are those whom you choose and
        bring near
    to live in your courts.
We shall be satisfied with the goodness of
        your house,
    your holy temple.

5 By awesome deeds you answer us with
        deliverance,
    O God of our salvation;
you are the hope of all the ends of the earth
    and of the farthest seas.
6 By your*a* strength you established the
        mountains;
    you are girded with might.
7 You silence the roaring of the seas,
    the roaring of their waves,
    the tumult of the peoples.
8 Those who live at earth's farthest bounds
        are awed by your signs;
    you make the gateways of the morning and
        the evening shout for joy.

9 You visit the earth and water it,
    you greatly enrich it;
the river of God is full of water;
    you provide the people with grain,
    for so you have prepared it.
10 You water its furrows abundantly,
    settling its ridges,
    softening it with showers,
    and blessing its growth.
11 You crown the year with your bounty;
    your wagon tracks overflow with
        richness.
12 The pastures of the wilderness overflow,
    the hills gird themselves with joy,
13 the meadows clothe themselves with
        flocks,
    the valleys deck themselves with grain,
    they shout and sing together for joy.

PSALM 66

Praise for God's Goodness to Israel

To the leader. A Song. A Psalm.

1 Make a joyful noise to God, all the earth;
2   sing the glory of his name;
    give to him glorious praise.
3 Say to God, "How awesome are your deeds!
    Because of your great power, your
        enemies cringe before you.
4 All the earth worships you;

they sing praises to you,
    sing praises to your name."   *Selah*

5 Come and see what God has done:
    he is awesome in his deeds among
        mortals.
6 He turned the sea into dry land;
    they passed through the river on foot.
There we rejoiced in him,
7   who rules by his might forever,
whose eyes keep watch on the nations—
    let the rebellious not exalt themselves.
                                          Selah

8 Bless our God, O peoples,
    let the sound of his praise be heard,
9 who has kept us among the living,
    and has not let our feet slip.
10 For you, O God, have tested us;
    you have tried us as silver is tried.
11 You brought us into the net;
    you laid burdens on our backs;
12 you let people ride over our heads;
    we went through fire and through water;
    yet you have brought us out to a spacious
        place.*b*

13 I will come into your house with burnt
        offerings;
    I will pay you my vows,
14 those that my lips uttered
    and my mouth promised when I was in
        trouble.
15 I will offer to you burnt offerings of fatlings,
    with the smoke of the sacrifice of rams;
I will make an offering of bulls and goats.
                                          Selah

16 Come and hear, all you who fear God,
    and I will tell what he has done for me.
17 I cried aloud to him,
    and he was extolled with my tongue.
18 If I had cherished iniquity in my heart,
    the Lord would not have listened.
19 But truly God has listened;
    he has given heed to the words of my
        prayer.

20 Blessed be God,
    because he has not rejected my prayer
    or removed his steadfast love from me.

PSALM 67

The Nations Called to Praise God

To the leader: with stringed instruments. A Psalm. A Song.

1 May God be gracious to us and bless us
    and make his face to shine upon us, *Selah*
2 that your way may be known upon earth,
    your saving power among all nations.

a Gk Jerome: Heb *his* *b* Cn Compare Gk Syr Jerome Tg: Heb *to a saturation*

3 Let the peoples praise you, O God;
  let all the peoples praise you.

4 Let the nations be glad and sing for joy,
  for you judge the peoples with equity
  and guide the nations upon earth.   *Selah*

5 Let the peoples praise you, O God;
  let all the peoples praise you.

6 The earth has yielded its increase;
  God, our God, has blessed us.

7 May God continue to bless us;
  let all the ends of the earth revere him.

PSALM 68

Praise and Thanksgiving

To the leader. Of David. A Psalm. A Song.

1 Let God rise up, let his enemies be
    scattered;
  let those who hate him flee before him.

2 As smoke is driven away, so drive them
    away;
  as wax melts before the fire,
  let the wicked perish before God.

3 But let the righteous be joyful;
  let them exult before God;
  let them be jubilant with joy.

4 Sing to God, sing praises to his name;
  lift up a song to him who rides upon the
    clouds*a*—
  his name is the LORD—
  be exultant before him.

5 Father of orphans and protector of widows
  is God in his holy habitation.

6 God gives the desolate a home to live in;
  he leads out the prisoners to prosperity,
  but the rebellious live in a parched land.

7 O God, when you went out before your
    people,
  when you marched through the
    wilderness,   *Selah*

8 the earth quaked, the heavens poured
    down rain
  at the presence of God, the God of Sinai,
  at the presence of God, the God of Israel.

9 Rain in abundance, O God, you showered
    abroad;
  you restored your heritage when it
    languished;

10 your flock found a dwelling in it;
  in your goodness, O God, you provided
    for the needy.

11 The Lord gives the command;
  great is the company of those*b* who bore
    the tidings:

12 "The kings of the armies, they flee, they
    flee!"
  The women at home divide the spoil,

13 though they stay among the
    sheepfolds—
  the wings of a dove covered with silver,
    its pinions with green gold.

14 When the Almighty*c* scattered kings there,
  snow fell on Zalmon.

15 O mighty mountain, mountain of Bashan;
  O many-peaked mountain, mountain of
    Bashan!

16 Why do you look with envy, O many-peaked
    mountain,
  at the mount that God desired for his
    abode,
  where the LORD will reside forever?

17 With mighty chariotry, twice ten thousand,
    thousands upon thousands,
  the Lord came from Sinai into the holy
    place.*d*

18 You ascended the high mount,
    leading captives in your train
    and receiving gifts from people,
  even from those who rebel against the
    LORD God's abiding there.

19 Blessed be the Lord,
    who daily bears us up;
  God is our salvation.   *Selah*

20 Our God is a God of salvation,
  and to GOD, the Lord, belongs escape
    from death.

21 But God will shatter the heads of his
    enemies,
  the hairy crown of those who walk in
    their guilty ways.

22 The Lord said,
  "I will bring them back from Bashan,
  I will bring them back from the depths of
    the sea,

23 so that you may bathe*e* your feet in blood,
  so that the tongues of your dogs may
    have their share from the foe."

24 Your solemn processions are seen,*f* O God,
    the processions of my God, my King, into
    the sanctuary—

25 the singers in front, the musicians last,
  between them girls playing tambourines:

26 "Bless God in the great congregation,
  the LORD, O you who are of Israel's
    fountain!"

27 There is Benjamin, the least of them, in the
    lead,
  the princes of Judah in a body,

---

a Or *cast up a highway for him who rides through the deserts* *b* Or *company of the women* *c* Traditional rendering of Heb *Shaddai* *d* Cn: Heb
The Lord among them Sinai in the holy (place) *e* Gk Syr Tg: Heb *shatter* *f* Or *have been seen*

the princes of Zebulun, the princes of
Naphtali.

²⁸ Summon your might, O God;
show your strength, O God, as you have
done for us before.
²⁹ Because of your temple at Jerusalem
kings bear gifts to you.
³⁰ Rebuke the wild animals that live among
the reeds,
the herd of bulls with the calves of the
peoples.
Trample*ᵃ* under foot those who lust after
tribute;
scatter the peoples who delight in war.*ᵇ*
³¹ Let bronze be brought from Egypt;
let Ethiopia*ᶜ* hasten to stretch out its
hands to God.

³² Sing to God, O kingdoms of the earth;
sing praises to the Lord,   *Selah*
³³ O rider in the heavens, the ancient heavens;
listen, he sends out his voice, his mighty
voice.
³⁴ Ascribe power to God,
whose majesty is over Israel;
and whose power is in the skies.
³⁵ Awesome is God in his*ᵈ* sanctuary,
the God of Israel;

he gives power and strength to his
people.

Blessed be God!

PSALM 69

Prayer for Deliverance from Persecution

To the leader: according to Lilies. Of David.

¹ Save me, O God,
for the waters have come up to my neck.
² I sink in deep mire,
where there is no foothold;
I have come into deep waters,
and the flood sweeps over me.
³ I am weary with my crying;
my throat is parched.
My eyes grow dim
with waiting for my God.

⁴ More in number than the hairs of my head
are those who hate me without cause;
many are those who would destroy me,
my enemies who accuse me falsely.
What I did not steal
must I now restore?
⁵ O God, you know my folly;
the wrongs I have done are not hidden
from you.

a Cn: Heb *Trampling*   *b* Meaning of Heb of verse 30 is uncertain   *c* Or *Nubia*; Heb *Cush*   *d* Gk: Heb *from your*

6 Do not let those who hope in you be put to
    shame because of me,
  O Lord GOD of hosts;
do not let those who seek you be
    dishonored because of me,
  O God of Israel.
7 It is for your sake that I have borne
    reproach,
  that shame has covered my face.
8 I have become a stranger to my kindred,
  an alien to my mother's children.

9 It is zeal for your house that has consumed
    me;
  the insults of those who insult you have
    fallen on me.
10 When I humbled my soul with fasting,*a*
  they insulted me for doing so.
11 When I made sackcloth my clothing,
  I became a byword to them.
12 I am the subject of gossip for those who sit
    in the gate,
  and the drunkards make songs about me.

13 But as for me, my prayer is to you, O LORD.
  At an acceptable time, O God,
  in the abundance of your steadfast love,
    answer me.
With your faithful help 14rescue me
    from sinking in the mire;
  let me be delivered from my enemies
    and from the deep waters.
15 Do not let the flood sweep over me,
  or the deep swallow me up,
  or the Pit close its mouth over me.

16 Answer me, O LORD, for your steadfast love
    is good;
  according to your abundant mercy, turn
    to me.
17 Do not hide your face from your servant,

for I am in distress—make haste to
    answer me.
18 Draw near to me, redeem me,
  set me free because of my enemies.

19 You know the insults I receive,
  and my shame and dishonor;
  my foes are all known to you.
20 Insults have broken my heart,
  so that I am in despair.
I looked for pity, but there was none;
  and for comforters, but I found none.
21 They gave me poison for food,
  and for my thirst they gave me vinegar to
    drink.

22 Let their table be a trap for them,
  a snare for their allies.
23 Let their eyes be darkened so that they
    cannot see,
  and make their loins tremble continually.
24 Pour out your indignation upon them,
  and let your burning anger overtake them.
25 May their camp be a desolation;
  let no one live in their tents.
26 For they persecute those whom you have
    struck down,
  and those whom you have wounded,
    they attack still more.*b*
27 Add guilt to their guilt;
  may they have no acquittal from you.
28 Let them be blotted out of the book of the
    living;
  let them not be enrolled among the
    righteous.
29 But I am lowly and in pain;
  let your salvation, O God, protect me.

30 I will praise the name of God with a song;
  I will magnify him with thanksgiving.
31 This will please the LORD more than an ox
  or a bull with horns and hoofs.
32 Let the oppressed see it and be glad;
  you who seek God, let your hearts revive.
33 For the LORD hears the needy,
  and does not despise his own that are in
    bonds.

34 Let heaven and earth praise him,
  the seas and everything that moves in
    them.
35 For God will save Zion
  and rebuild the cities of Judah;
and his servants shall live*c* there and
    possess it;
36   the children of his servants shall inherit it,
  and those who love his name shall live
    in it.

Around the Bend—© Taylor-Quinn Yancey, 16

a Gk Syr: Heb *I wept, with fasting my soul*, or *I made my soul mourn with
fasting* b Gk Syr: Heb *recount the pain of* c Syr: Heb *and they shall
live*

Cancer. Car crashes. Earthquakes. AIDS. Everything seems to be broken and falling apart. Why is there pain and suffering in the world if God says he loves us so much?

The reality of pain and brokenness is all around us. We see it every day on the news and in our school hallways. But suffering isn't just "out there." It hits home too. We disciples aren't protected in spiritual Bubble Wrap, kept safe from danger, tragedy, and heartache. Sometimes our suffering is intensely personal. When that happens, it can really rock our faith. It can feel like the pain is destroying us. And we're not alone in that feeling. "I am weary with my crying; my throat is parched. My eyes grow dim with waiting for my God," David wrote in Psalm 69.3. This wasn't just a minor bad day. David, like we often do, was hurting *badly*. And what about Job? His life was completely destroyed and God, it seemed, sat by, watching it all happen. When Job demanded answers from God for his tremendous suffering, God didn't give them. Instead, God answered Job with more questions (see Job 38.1–42.6).

It feels that way for us sometimes when we look at the pain in our lives and in the world around us. Why does God allow little children to die of malnutrition? Why does God let cancer rot out a loved one's bones? Why doesn't God stop suicide bombers or dictators or wars? Simple answers don't work with questions like these.

Sometimes we're left like Job, getting our questions "answered" with more questions: *Who is God—you or me? Will you trust me? Will you serve me? Will you choose to help the hurting, the sick, and the dying in my name? Will you sacrifice your own wants and desires in order to show love and empathy to those who are suffering?*

God doesn't give us an easy answer for why we suffer. Instead, he gave us his Son, who suffers with us (see Isaiah 53.1–12). God's love in Christ goes with us through our deepest pain and our most difficult circumstances.

So, does it mean that God does not love us if we suffer "hardship, or distress, or persecution, or famine, or nakedness, or peril, or sword" (Romans 8.35)? It can *feel* that way sometimes, but the author of Romans answers his own question: "No, in all these things we are more than conquerors through him who loved us" (8.37).

Find some Creative Space in the Bible and write your thoughts and questions about suffering. Consider talking to a trusted friend in faith about your thoughts and questions.

(Want to explore more? Take a closer look at Psalms 42 and 69; Romans 8.18–39; 2 Corinthians 4.16–18; 1 John 3.16.)

PSALM 70

Prayer for Deliverance from Enemies

To the leader. Of David, for the memorial offering.

1 Be pleased, O God, to deliver me.
    O LORD, make haste to help me!
2 Let those be put to shame and confusion
        who seek my life.
    Let those be turned back and brought to
            dishonor
        who desire to hurt me.
3 Let those who say, "Aha, Aha!"
        turn back because of their shame.

4 Let all who seek you
        rejoice and be glad in you.
    Let those who love your salvation
        say evermore, "God is great!"
5 But I am poor and needy;
        hasten to me, O God!
    You are my help and my deliverer;
        O LORD, do not delay!

PSALM 71

Prayer for Lifelong Protection and Help

1 In you, O LORD, I take refuge;
        let me never be put to shame.

The book of Psalms is actually made up of five separate books. Psalms 1–41 are Book One. Psalms 42–72 are Book Two. Psalms 73–89 are Book Three. Psalms 90–106 are Book Four. And Psalms 107–150 are Book Five. Each book may have been put together at a different time.

This information has been scanned and is free of all known viruses. Please forward to all your friends.

2 In your righteousness deliver me and rescue me;
    incline your ear to me and save me.
3 Be to me a rock of refuge,
    a strong fortress,*a* to save me,
    for you are my rock and my fortress.

4 Rescue me, O my God, from the hand of the wicked,
    from the grasp of the unjust and cruel.
5 For you, O Lord, are my hope,
    my trust, O Lord, from my youth.
6 Upon you I have leaned from my birth;
    it was you who took me from my mother's womb.
    My praise is continually of you.

7 I have been like a portent to many,
    but you are my strong refuge.
8 My mouth is filled with your praise,
    and with your glory all day long.
9 Do not cast me off in the time of old age;
    do not forsake me when my strength is spent.
10 For my enemies speak concerning me,
    and those who watch for my life consult together.
11 They say, "Pursue and seize that person whom God has forsaken,
    for there is no one to deliver."

12 O God, do not be far from me;
    O my God, make haste to help me!
13 Let my accusers be put to shame and consumed;
    let those who seek to hurt me
    be covered with scorn and disgrace.
14 But I will hope continually,
    and will praise you yet more and more.
15 My mouth will tell of your righteous acts,
    of your deeds of salvation all day long,
    though their number is past my knowledge.
16 I will come praising the mighty deeds of the Lord God,
    I will praise your righteousness, yours alone.

17 O God, from my youth you have taught me,
    and I still proclaim your wondrous deeds.
18 So even to old age and gray hairs,
    O God, do not forsake me,
    until I proclaim your might
    to all the generations to come.*b*
    Your power 19and your righteousness,
    O God,
    reach the high heavens.

You who have done great things,
    O God, who is like you?
20 You who have made me see many troubles and calamities
    will revive me again;
    from the depths of the earth
    you will bring me up again.
21 You will increase my honor,
    and comfort me once again.

22 I will also praise you with the harp
    for your faithfulness, O my God;
    I will sing praises to you with the lyre,
    O Holy One of Israel.
23 My lips will shout for joy
    when I sing praises to you;
    my soul also, which you have rescued.
24 All day long my tongue will talk of your righteous help,
    for those who tried to do me harm
    have been put to shame, and disgraced.

a Gk Compare 31.3: Heb *to come continually you have commanded*   *b* Gk Compare Syr: Heb *to a generation, to all that come*

PSALM 72

Prayer for Guidance and Support for the King

Of Solomon.

1 Give the king your justice, O God,
    and your righteousness to a king's son.
2 May he judge your people with
        righteousness,
    and your poor with justice.
3 May the mountains yield prosperity for the
        people,
    and the hills, in righteousness.
4 May he defend the cause of the poor of the
        people,
    give deliverance to the needy,
    and crush the oppressor.

5 May he live*a* while the sun endures,
    and as long as the moon, throughout all
        generations.
6 May he be like rain that falls on the mown
        grass,
    like showers that water the earth.
7 In his days may righteousness flourish
    and peace abound, until the moon is no
        more.

8 May he have dominion from sea to sea,
    and from the River to the ends of the
        earth.
9 May his foes*b* bow down before him,
    and his enemies lick the dust.
10 May the kings of Tarshish and of the isles
        render him tribute,
    may the kings of Sheba and Seba
        bring gifts.
11 May all kings fall down before him,
    all nations give him service.

12 For he delivers the needy when they call,
    the poor and those who have no helper.
13 He has pity on the weak and the needy,
    and saves the lives of the needy.
14 From oppression and violence he redeems
        their life;
    and precious is their blood in his sight.

15 Long may he live!
    May gold of Sheba be given to him.
    May prayer be made for him continually,
        and blessings invoked for him all day
            long.
16 May there be abundance of grain in the
        land;
    may it wave on the tops of the
        mountains;
    may its fruit be like Lebanon;
    and may people blossom in the cities
        like the grass of the field.
17 May his name endure forever,
    his fame continue as long as the sun.
    May all nations be blessed in him;*c*
    may they pronounce him happy.

18 Blessed be the LORD, the God of Israel,
    who alone does wondrous things.
19 Blessed be his glorious name forever;
    may his glory fill the whole earth.
        Amen and Amen.

20 The prayers of David son of Jesse are ended.

BOOK III   *(Psalms 73–89)*

PSALM 73

Plea for Relief from Oppressors

A Psalm of Asaph.

1 Truly God is good to the upright,*d*
    to those who are pure in heart.
2 But as for me, my feet had almost
        stumbled;
    my steps had nearly slipped.
3 For I was envious of the arrogant;
    I saw the prosperity of the wicked.

4 For they have no pain;
    their bodies are sound and sleek.
5 They are not in trouble as others are;
    they are not plagued like other people.
6 Therefore pride is their necklace;
    violence covers them like a garment.
7 Their eyes swell out with fatness;
    their hearts overflow with follies.
8 They scoff and speak with malice;
    loftily they threaten oppression.
9 They set their mouths against heaven,
    and their tongues range over the earth.
10 Therefore the people turn and praise
        them,*e*
    and find no fault in them.*f*
11 And they say, "How can God know?
    Is there knowledge in the Most High?"
12 Such are the wicked;
    always at ease, they increase in riches.
13 All in vain I have kept my heart clean
    and washed my hands in innocence.
14 For all day long I have been plagued,
    and am punished every morning.

15 If I had said, "I will talk on in this way,"
    I would have been untrue to the circle of
        your children.
16 But when I thought how to understand this,
    it seemed to me a wearisome task,

---

a Gk: Heb *may they fear you* *b* Cn: Heb *those who live in the wilderness* *c* Or *bless themselves by him* *d* Or *good to Israel* *e* Cn: Heb *his people return here* *f* Cn: Heb *abundant waters are drained by them*

17 until I went into the sanctuary of God;
  then I perceived their end.
18 Truly you set them in slippery places;
  you make them fall to ruin.
19 How they are destroyed in a moment,
  swept away utterly by terrors!
20 They are*a* like a dream when one awakes;
  on awaking you despise their phantoms.

21 When my soul was embittered,
  when I was pricked in heart,
22 I was stupid and ignorant;
  I was like a brute beast toward you.
23 Nevertheless I am continually with you;
  you hold my right hand.
24 You guide me with your counsel,
  and afterward you will receive me with
  honor.*b*
25 Whom have I in heaven but you?
  And there is nothing on earth that I
  desire other than you.
26 My flesh and my heart may fail,
  but God is the strength*c* of my heart and
  my portion forever.

27 Indeed, those who are far from you will
  perish;
  you put an end to those who are false to
  you.
28 But for me it is good to be near God;
  I have made the Lord God my refuge,
  to tell of all your works.

PSALM 74

Plea for Help in Time of National Humiliation

A Maskil of Asaph.

1 O God, why do you cast us off forever?
  Why does your anger smoke against the
  sheep of your pasture?
2 Remember your congregation, which you
  acquired long ago,
  which you redeemed to be the tribe of
  your heritage.
  Remember Mount Zion, where you came
  to dwell.
3 Direct your steps to the perpetual ruins;
  the enemy has destroyed everything in
  the sanctuary.

4 Your foes have roared within your holy
  place;
  they set up their emblems there.
5 At the upper entrance they hacked
  the wooden trellis with axes.*d*
6 And then, with hatchets and hammers,
  they smashed all its carved work.

7 They set your sanctuary on fire;
  they desecrated the dwelling place of
  your name,
  bringing it to the ground.
8 They said to themselves, "We will utterly
  subdue them";
  they burned all the meeting places of
  God in the land.

9 We do not see our emblems;
  there is no longer any prophet,
  and there is no one among us who
  knows how long.
10 How long, O God, is the foe to scoff?
  Is the enemy to revile your name
  forever?
11 Why do you hold back your hand;
  why do you keep your hand in*e* your
  bosom?

12 Yet God my King is from of old,
  working salvation in the earth.
13 You divided the sea by your might;
  you broke the heads of the dragons in
  the waters.
14 You crushed the heads of Leviathan;
  you gave him as food*f* for the creatures of
  the wilderness.
15 You cut openings for springs and torrents;
  you dried up ever-flowing streams.
16 Yours is the day, yours also the night;
  you established the luminaries*g* and the
  sun.
17 You have fixed all the bounds of the
  earth;
  you made summer and winter.

18 Remember this, O Lord, how the enemy
  scoffs,
  and an impious people reviles your
  name.
19 Do not deliver the soul of your dove to the
  wild animals;
  do not forget the life of your poor
  forever.

20 Have regard for your*h* covenant,
  for the dark places of the land are full of
  the haunts of violence.
21 Do not let the downtrodden be put to
  shame;
  let the poor and needy praise your name.
22 Rise up, O God, plead your cause;
  remember how the impious scoff at you
  all day long.
23 Do not forget the clamor of your foes,
  the uproar of your adversaries that goes
  up continually.

---

a Cn: Heb *Lord* *b* Or *to glory* *c* Heb *rock* *d* Cn Compare Gk Syr: Meaning of Heb uncertain *e* Cn: Heb *do you consume your right hand from* *f* Heb *food for the people* *g* Or *moon*; Heb *light* *h* Gk Syr: Heb *the*

PSALM 75

Thanksgiving for God's Wondrous Deeds

To the leader: Do Not Destroy. A Psalm of Asaph. A Song.

1 We give thanks to you, O God;
    we give thanks; your name is near.
    People tell of your wondrous deeds.

2 At the set time that I appoint
    I will judge with equity.
3 When the earth totters, with all its
        inhabitants,
    it is I who keep its pillars steady.   *Selah*
4 I say to the boastful, "Do not boast,"
    and to the wicked, "Do not lift up your
        horn;
5 do not lift up your horn on high,
    or speak with insolent neck."

6 For not from the east or from the west
    and not from the wilderness comes
        lifting up;
7 but it is God who executes judgment,
    putting down one and lifting up another.
8 For in the hand of the Lord there is a cup
    with foaming wine, well mixed;
    he will pour a draught from it,
    and all the wicked of the earth
    shall drain it down to the dregs.
9 But I will rejoice*a* forever;
    I will sing praises to the God of Jacob.

10 All the horns of the wicked I will cut off,
    but the horns of the righteous shall be
        exalted.

PSALM 76

Israel's God—Judge of All the Earth

*To the leader: with stringed instruments. A Psalm of Asaph.
A Song.*

1 In Judah God is known,
    his name is great in Israel.
2 His abode has been established in Salem,
    his dwelling place in Zion.
3 There he broke the flashing arrows,
    the shield, the sword, and the weapons
        of war.   *Selah*

4 Glorious are you, more majestic
    than the everlasting mountains.*b*
5 The stouthearted were stripped of their
        spoil;
    they sank into sleep;
    none of the troops
        was able to lift a hand.
6 At your rebuke, O God of Jacob,
    both rider and horse lay stunned.

7 But you indeed are awesome!
    Who can stand before you
    when once your anger is roused?
8 From the heavens you uttered judgment;
    the earth feared and was still
9 when God rose up to establish judgment,
    to save all the oppressed of the earth.   *Selah*

10 Human wrath serves only to praise you,
    when you bind the last bit of your*c* wrath
        around you.
11 Make vows to the Lord your God, and
        perform them;
    let all who are around him bring gifts
    to the one who is awesome,
12 who cuts off the spirit of princes,
    who inspires fear in the kings of the
        earth.

PSALM 77

God's Mighty Deeds Recalled

To the leader: according to Jeduthun. Of Asaph. A Psalm.

1 I cry aloud to God,
    aloud to God, that he may hear me.
2 In the day of my trouble I seek the Lord;
    in the night my hand is stretched out
        without wearying;
    my soul refuses to be comforted.
3 I think of God, and I moan;
    I meditate, and my spirit faints.   *Selah*

4 You keep my eyelids from closing;
    I am so troubled that I cannot speak.
5 I consider the days of old,
    and remember the years of long ago.
6 I commune*d* with my heart in the night;
    I meditate and search my spirit:*e*
7 "Will the Lord spurn forever,
    and never again be favorable?
8 Has his steadfast love ceased forever?
    Are his promises at an end for all time?
9 Has God forgotten to be gracious?
    Has he in anger shut up his
        compassion?"   *Selah*
10 And I say, "It is my grief
    that the right hand of the Most High has
        changed."

11 I will call to mind the deeds of the Lord;
    I will remember your wonders of old.
12 I will meditate on all your work,
    and muse on your mighty deeds.
13 Your way, O God, is holy.
    What god is so great as our God?
14 You are the God who works wonders;
    you have displayed your might among
        the peoples.

a Gk: Heb declare   b Gk: Heb the mountains of prey   c Heb lacks your   d Gk Syr: Heb My music   e Syr Jerome: Heb my spirit searches

¹⁵ With your strong arm you redeemed your
people,
the descendants of Jacob and Joseph.

Selah

¹⁶ When the waters saw you, O God,
when the waters saw you, they were
afraid;
the very deep trembled.
¹⁷ The clouds poured out water;
the skies thundered;
your arrows flashed on every side.
¹⁸ The crash of your thunder was in the
whirlwind;
your lightnings lit up the world;
the earth trembled and shook.
¹⁹ Your way was through the sea,
your path, through the mighty waters;
yet your footprints were unseen.
²⁰ You led your people like a flock
by the hand of Moses and Aaron.

PSALM 78

God's Goodness and Israel's Ingratitude

A Maskil of Asaph.

¹ Give ear, O my people, to my teaching;
incline your ears to the words of my
mouth.
² I will open my mouth in a parable;
I will utter dark sayings from of old,
³ things that we have heard and known,
that our ancestors have told us.
⁴ We will not hide them from their children;
we will tell to the coming generation
the glorious deeds of the LORD, and his
might,
and the wonders that he has done.

⁵ He established a decree in Jacob,
and appointed a law in Israel,
which he commanded our ancestors
to teach to their children;
⁶ that the next generation might know them,
the children yet unborn,
and rise up and tell them to their children,
⁷ so that they should set their hope in God,
and not forget the works of God,
but keep his commandments;
⁸ and that they should not be like their
ancestors,

a stubborn and rebellious generation,
a generation whose heart was not steadfast,
whose spirit was not faithful to God.
⁹ The Ephraimites, armed with^a the bow,
turned back on the day of battle.
¹⁰ They did not keep God's covenant,
but refused to walk according to his law.
¹¹ They forgot what he had done,
and the miracles that he had shown
them.
¹² In the sight of their ancestors he worked
marvels
in the land of Egypt, in the fields of Zoan.
¹³ He divided the sea and let them pass
through it,
and made the waters stand like a heap.
¹⁴ In the daytime he led them with a cloud,
and all night long with a fiery light.
¹⁵ He split rocks open in the wilderness,
and gave them drink abundantly as from
the deep.
¹⁶ He made streams come out of the rock,
and caused waters to flow down like
rivers.

¹⁷ Yet they sinned still more against him,
rebelling against the Most High in the
desert.
¹⁸ They tested God in their heart
by demanding the food they craved.
¹⁹ They spoke against God, saying,
"Can God spread a table in the
wilderness?
²⁰ Even though he struck the rock so that
water gushed out
and torrents overflowed,
can he also give bread,
or provide meat for his people?"

²¹ Therefore, when the LORD heard, he was
full of rage;
a fire was kindled against Jacob,
his anger mounted against Israel,
²² because they had no faith in God,
and did not trust his saving power.
²³ Yet he commanded the skies above,
and opened the doors of heaven;
²⁴ he rained down on them manna to eat,
and gave them the grain of heaven.
²⁵ Mortals ate of the bread of angels;
he sent them food in abundance.
²⁶ He caused the east wind to blow in the
heavens,
and by his power he led out the south
wind;
²⁷ he rained flesh upon them like dust,
winged birds like the sand of the seas;
²⁸ he let them fall within their camp,

a Heb *armed with shooting*

all around their dwellings.
29 And they ate and were well filled,
for he gave them what they craved.
30 But before they had satisfied their craving,
while the food was still in their mouths,
31 the anger of God rose against them
and he killed the strongest of them,
and laid low the flower of Israel.

32 In spite of all this they still sinned;
they did not believe in his wonders.
33 So he made their days vanish like a breath,
and their years in terror.
34 When he killed them, they sought for him;
they repented and sought God earnestly.
35 They remembered that God was their rock,
the Most High God their redeemer.
36 But they flattered him with their mouths;
they lied to him with their tongues.
37 Their heart was not steadfast toward him;
they were not true to his covenant.
38 Yet he, being compassionate,
forgave their iniquity,
and did not destroy them;
often he restrained his anger,
and did not stir up all his wrath.
39 He remembered that they were but flesh,
a wind that passes and does not come
again.
40 How often they rebelled against him in the
wilderness
and grieved him in the desert!
41 They tested God again and again,
and provoked the Holy One of Israel.
42 They did not keep in mind his power,
or the day when he redeemed them from
the foe;
43 when he displayed his signs in Egypt,
and his miracles in the fields of Zoan.
44 He turned their rivers to blood,
so that they could not drink of their
streams.
45 He sent among them swarms of flies, which
devoured them,
and frogs, which destroyed them.
46 He gave their crops to the caterpillar,
and the fruit of their labor to the locust.
47 He destroyed their vines with hail,
and their sycamores with frost.
48 He gave over their cattle to the hail,
and their flocks to thunderbolts.
49 He let loose on them his fierce anger,
wrath, indignation, and distress,
a company of destroying angels.
50 He made a path for his anger;
he did not spare them from death,
but gave their lives over to the plague.
51 He struck all the firstborn in Egypt,

the first issue of their strength in the
tents of Ham.
52 Then he led out his people like sheep,
and guided them in the wilderness like a
flock.
53 He led them in safety, so that they were not
afraid;
but the sea overwhelmed their enemies.
54 And he brought them to his holy hill,
to the mountain that his right hand had
won.
55 He drove out nations before them;
he apportioned them for a possession
and settled the tribes of Israel in their
tents.

56 Yet they tested the Most High God,
and rebelled against him.
They did not observe his decrees,
57 but turned away and were faithless like
their ancestors;
they twisted like a treacherous bow.
58 For they provoked him to anger with their
high places;
they moved him to jealousy with their
idols.
59 When God heard, he was full of wrath,
and he utterly rejected Israel.
60 He abandoned his dwelling at Shiloh,
the tent where he dwelt among mortals,
61 and delivered his power to captivity,
his glory to the hand of the foe.
62 He gave his people to the sword,
and vented his wrath on his heritage.
63 Fire devoured their young men,
and their girls had no marriage song.
64 Their priests fell by the sword,
and their widows made no lamentation.
65 Then the Lord awoke as from sleep,
like a warrior shouting because of wine.
66 He put his adversaries to rout;
he put them to everlasting disgrace.

67 He rejected the tent of Joseph,
he did not choose the tribe of Ephraim;
68 but he chose the tribe of Judah,
Mount Zion, which he loves.
69 He built his sanctuary like the high heavens,
like the earth, which he has founded
forever.
70 He chose his servant David,
and took him from the sheepfolds;
71 from tending the nursing ewes he brought
him
to be the shepherd of his people Jacob,
of Israel, his inheritance.
72 With upright heart he tended them,
and guided them with skillful hand.

PSALM 79

Plea for Mercy for Jerusalem

A Psalm of Asaph.

1 O God, the nations have come into your
   inheritance;
   they have defiled your holy temple;
   they have laid Jerusalem in ruins.
2 They have given the bodies of your servants
   to the birds of the air for food,
   the flesh of your faithful to the wild
   animals of the earth.
3 They have poured out their blood like water
   all around Jerusalem,
   and there was no one to bury them.
4 We have become a taunt to our neighbors,
   mocked and derided by those around us.

5 How long, O Lord? Will you be angry
   forever?
   Will your jealous wrath burn like fire?
6 Pour out your anger on the nations
   that do not know you,
   and on the kingdoms
   that do not call on your name.
7 For they have devoured Jacob
   and laid waste his habitation.

8 Do not remember against us the iniquities
   of our ancestors;
   let your compassion come speedily to
   meet us,
   for we are brought very low.
9 Help us, O God of our salvation,
   for the glory of your name;
   deliver us, and forgive our sins,
   for your name's sake.
10 Why should the nations say,
   "Where is their God?"
   Let the avenging of the outpoured blood of
   your servants
   be known among the nations before our
   eyes.

11 Let the groans of the prisoners come before
   you;
   according to your great power preserve
   those doomed to die.
12 Return sevenfold into the bosom of our
   neighbors
   the taunts with which they taunted you,
   O Lord!
13 Then we your people, the flock of your
   pasture,
   will give thanks to you forever;
   from generation to generation we will
   recount your praise.

PSALM 80

Prayer for Israel's Restoration

To the leader: on Lilies, a Covenant. Of Asaph. A Psalm.

1 Give ear, O Shepherd of Israel,
   you who lead Joseph like a flock!
   You who are enthroned upon the
   cherubim, shine forth
2   before Ephraim and Benjamin and
   Manasseh.
   Stir up your might,
   and come to save us!

3 Restore us, O God;
   let your face shine, that we may be saved.

4 O Lord God of hosts,
   how long will you be angry with your
   people's prayers?
5 You have fed them with the bread of tears,
   and given them tears to drink in full
   measure.
6 You make us the scorn*a* of our neighbors;
   our enemies laugh among themselves.

7 Restore us, O God of hosts;
   let your face shine, that we may be saved.

8 You brought a vine out of Egypt;
   you drove out the nations and planted it.
9 You cleared the ground for it;
   it took deep root and filled the land.
10 The mountains were covered with its shade,
   the mighty cedars with its branches;
11 it sent out its branches to the sea,
   and its shoots to the River.
12 Why then have you broken down its walls,
   so that all who pass along the way pluck
   its fruit?
13 The boar from the forest ravages it,
   and all that move in the field feed on it.

14 Turn again, O God of hosts;
   look down from heaven, and see;
   have regard for this vine,
15   the stock that your right hand planted.*b*
16 They have burned it with fire, they have cut
   it down;*c*
   may they perish at the rebuke of your
   countenance.
17 But let your hand be upon the one at your
   right hand,
   the one whom you made strong for
   yourself.
18 Then we will never turn back from you;
   give us life, and we will call on your
   name.

19 Restore us, O Lord God of hosts;
   let your face shine, that we may be saved.

a Syr: Heb *strife* *b* Heb adds from verse 17 *and upon the one whom you made strong for yourself* *c* Cn: Heb *it is cut down*

PSALM 81

God's Appeal to Stubborn Israel

To the leader: according to The Gittith. Of Asaph.

1 Sing aloud to God our strength;
   shout for joy to the God of Jacob.
2 Raise a song, sound the tambourine,
   the sweet lyre with the harp.
3 Blow the trumpet at the new moon,
   at the full moon, on our festal day.
4 For it is a statute for Israel,
   an ordinance of the God of Jacob.
5 He made it a decree in Joseph,
   when he went out over*a* the land of Egypt.

I hear a voice I had not known:
6 "I relieved your*b* shoulder of the burden;
   your*b* hands were freed from the basket.
7 In distress you called, and I rescued you;
   I answered you in the secret place of
      thunder;
   I tested you at the waters of Meribah.
                                         Selah
8 Hear, O my people, while I admonish you;
   O Israel, if you would but listen to me!
9 There shall be no strange god among you;
   you shall not bow down to a foreign god.
10 I am the LORD your God,
   who brought you up out of the land of
      Egypt.
   Open your mouth wide and I will fill it.

11 "But my people did not listen to my voice;
   Israel would not submit to me.
12 So I gave them over to their stubborn
      hearts,
   to follow their own counsels.
13 O that my people would listen to me,
   that Israel would walk in my ways!
14 Then I would quickly subdue their enemies,
   and turn my hand against their foes.
15 Those who hate the LORD would cringe
      before him,
   and their doom would last forever.
16 I would feed you*c* with the finest of the
      wheat,
   and with honey from the rock I would
      satisfy you."

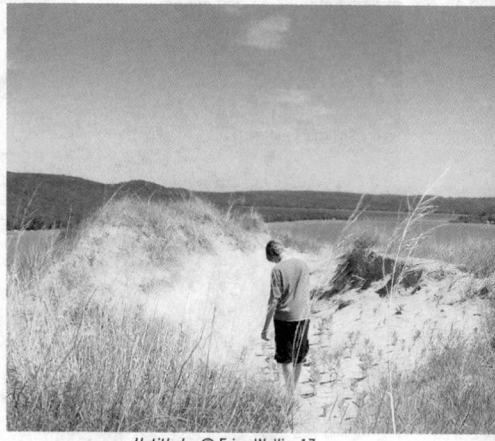
Untitled—© Erica Wallis, 17

PSALM 82

A Plea for Justice

A Psalm of Asaph.

1 God has taken his place in the divine council;
   in the midst of the gods he holds
      judgment:
2 "How long will you judge unjustly
   and show partiality to the wicked? *Selah*
3 Give justice to the weak and the orphan;
   maintain the right of the lowly and the
      destitute.
4 Rescue the weak and the needy;
   deliver them from the hand of the
      wicked."

5 They have neither knowledge nor
      understanding,
   they walk around in darkness;
   all the foundations of the earth are
      shaken.

6 I say, "You are gods,
   children of the Most High, all of you;
7 nevertheless, you shall die like mortals,
   and fall like any prince."*d*

8 Rise up, O God, judge the earth;
   for all the nations belong to you!

PSALM 83

Prayer for Judgment on Israel's Foes

A Song. A Psalm of Asaph.

1 O God, do not keep silence;
   do not hold your peace or be still, O God!
2 Even now your enemies are in tumult;
   those who hate you have raised their
      heads.
3 They lay crafty plans against your people;
   they consult together against those you
      protect.
4 They say, "Come, let us wipe them out as a
      nation;
   let the name of Israel be remembered no
      more."
5 They conspire with one accord;
   against you they make a covenant—

a Or *against* *b* Heb *his* *c* Cn Compare verse 16b: Heb *he would feed him* *d* Or *fall as one man, O princes*

Believe—© Chrissy Riling, 16

6 the tents of Edom and the Ishmaelites,
  Moab and the Hagrites,
7 Gebal and Ammon and Amalek,
  Philistia with the inhabitants of Tyre;
8 Assyria also has joined them;
  they are the strong arm of the children of
  Lot.   *Selah*

9 Do to them as you did to Midian,
  as to Sisera and Jabin at the Wadi Kishon,
10 who were destroyed at En-dor,
  who became dung for the ground.
11 Make their nobles like Oreb and Zeeb,
  all their princes like Zebah and
  Zalmunna,
12 who said, "Let us take the pastures of God
  for our own possession."

13 O my God, make them like whirling dust,*a*
  like chaff before the wind.
14 As fire consumes the forest,
  as the flame sets the mountains ablaze,
15 so pursue them with your tempest
  and terrify them with your hurricane.
16 Fill their faces with shame,
  so that they may seek your name, O LORD.
17 Let them be put to shame and dismayed
  forever;
  let them perish in disgrace.
18 Let them know that you alone,
  whose name is the LORD,
  are the Most High over all the earth.

PSALM 84

The Joy of Worship in the Temple

*To the leader: according to The Gittith. Of the Korahites.
A Psalm.*

1 How lovely is your dwelling place,
  O LORD of hosts!
2 My soul longs, indeed it faints
  for the courts of the LORD;
  my heart and my flesh sing for joy
  to the living God.

3 Even the sparrow finds a home,
  and the swallow a nest for herself,
  where she may lay her young,
  at your altars, O LORD of hosts,
  my King and my God.
4 Happy are those who live in your house,
  ever singing your praise.   *Selah*

5 Happy are those whose strength is in you,
  in whose heart are the highways to Zion.*b*
6 As they go through the valley of Baca
  they make it a place of springs;
  the early rain also covers it with pools.
7 They go from strength to strength;
  the God of gods will be seen in Zion.

8 O LORD God of hosts, hear my prayer;
  give ear, O God of Jacob!   *Selah*
9 Behold our shield, O God;
  look on the face of your anointed.

a Or *a tumbleweed* *b* Heb lacks *to Zion*

¹⁰ For a day in your courts is better
    than a thousand elsewhere.
I would rather be a doorkeeper in the house
    of my God
    than live in the tents of wickedness.
¹¹ For the LORD God is a sun and shield;
    he bestows favor and honor.
No good thing does the LORD withhold
    from those who walk uprightly.
¹² O LORD of hosts,
    happy is everyone who trusts in you.

PSALM 85

Prayer for the Restoration of God's Favor

To the leader. Of the Korahites. A Psalm.

¹ LORD, you were favorable to your land;
    you restored the fortunes of Jacob.
² You forgave the iniquity of your people;
    you pardoned all their sin.   *Selah*
³ You withdrew all your wrath;
    you turned from your hot anger.

⁴ Restore us again, O God of our salvation,
    and put away your indignation toward us.
⁵ Will you be angry with us forever?
    Will you prolong your anger to all
      generations?
⁶ Will you not revive us again,
    so that your people may rejoice in you?
⁷ Show us your steadfast love, O LORD,
    and grant us your salvation.

⁸ Let me hear what God the LORD will speak,
    for he will speak peace to his people,
    to his faithful, to those who turn to him
      in their hearts.^{*a*}
⁹ Surely his salvation is at hand for those who
    fear him,
    that his glory may dwell in our land.

¹⁰ Steadfast love and faithfulness will meet;
    righteousness and peace will kiss each
      other.
¹¹ Faithfulness will spring up from the ground,
    and righteousness will look down from
      the sky.
¹² The LORD will give what is good,
    and our land will yield its increase.
¹³ Righteousness will go before him,
    and will make a path for his steps.

PSALM 86

Supplication for Help against Enemies

A Prayer of David.

¹ Incline your ear, O LORD, and answer me,
    for I am poor and needy.
² Preserve my life, for I am devoted to you;

    save your servant who trusts in you.
You are my God; ³ be gracious to me, O Lord,
    for to you do I cry all day long.
⁴ Gladden the soul of your servant,
    for to you, O Lord, I lift up my soul.
⁵ For you, O Lord, are good and forgiving,
    abounding in steadfast love to all who
      call on you.
⁶ Give ear, O LORD, to my prayer;
    listen to my cry of supplication.
⁷ In the day of my trouble I call on you,
    for you will answer me.

⁸ There is none like you among the gods,
      O Lord,
    nor are there any works like yours.
⁹ All the nations you have made shall come
    and bow down before you, O Lord,
    and shall glorify your name.
¹⁰ For you are great and do wondrous things;
    you alone are God.
¹¹ Teach me your way, O LORD,
    that I may walk in your truth;
    give me an undivided heart to revere your
      name.
¹² I give thanks to you, O Lord my God, with
    my whole heart,
    and I will glorify your name forever.
¹³ For great is your steadfast love toward me;
    you have delivered my soul from the
      depths of Sheol.

¹⁴ O God, the insolent rise up against me;
    a band of ruffians seeks my life,
    and they do not set you before them.
¹⁵ But you, O Lord, are a God merciful and
    gracious,
    slow to anger and abounding in steadfast
      love and faithfulness.
¹⁶ Turn to me and be gracious to me;
    give your strength to your servant;
    save the child of your serving girl.
¹⁷ Show me a sign of your favor,
    so that those who hate me may see it and
      be put to shame,
    because you, LORD, have helped me and
      comforted me.

PSALM 87

The Joy of Living in Zion

Of the Korahites. A Psalm. A Song.

¹ On the holy mount stands the city he
      founded;
²   the LORD loves the gates of Zion
    more than all the dwellings of Jacob.
³ Glorious things are spoken of you,
    O city of God.   *Selah*

---

a Gk: Heb *but let them not turn back to folly*

4 Among those who know me I mention
        Rahab and Babylon;
    Philistia too, and Tyre, with Ethiopia^a—
    "This one was born there," they say.

5 And of Zion it shall be said,
    "This one and that one were born in it";
    for the Most High himself will establish it.
6 The LORD records, as he registers the
        peoples,
    "This one was born there." *Selah*

7 Singers and dancers alike say,
    "All my springs are in you."

PSALM 88

Prayer for Help in Despondency

A Song. A Psalm of the Korahites. To the leader: according to Mahalath Leannoth. A Maskil of Heman the Ezrahite.

1 O LORD, God of my salvation,
    when, at night, I cry out in your presence,
2 let my prayer come before you;
    incline your ear to my cry.

3 For my soul is full of troubles,
    and my life draws near to Sheol.
4 I am counted among those who go down to
        the Pit;
    I am like those who have no help,
5 like those forsaken among the dead,
    like the slain that lie in the grave,
    like those whom you remember no more,
    for they are cut off from your hand.
6 You have put me in the depths of the Pit,
    in the regions dark and deep.
7 Your wrath lies heavy upon me,
    and you overwhelm me with all your
        waves. *Selah*

8 You have caused my companions to shun
        me;
    you have made me a thing of horror to
        them.
    I am shut in so that I cannot escape;
9   my eye grows dim through sorrow.
    Every day I call on you, O LORD;
    I spread out my hands to you.
10 Do you work wonders for the dead?
    Do the shades rise up to praise you? *Selah*
11 Is your steadfast love declared in the grave,
    or your faithfulness in Abaddon?
12 Are your wonders known in the darkness,
    or your saving help in the land of
        forgetfulness?

13 But I, O LORD, cry out to you;
    in the morning my prayer comes before
        you.

14 O LORD, why do you cast me off?
    Why do you hide your face from me?
15 Wretched and close to death from my
        youth up,
    I suffer your terrors; I am desperate.^b
16 Your wrath has swept over me;
    your dread assaults destroy me.
17 They surround me like a flood all day long;
    from all sides they close in on me.
18 You have caused friend and neighbor to
        shun me;
    my companions are in darkness.

PSALM 89

God's Covenant with David

A Maskil of Ethan the Ezrahite.

1 I will sing of your steadfast love, O LORD,^c
        forever;
    with my mouth I will proclaim your
        faithfulness to all generations.
2 I declare that your steadfast love is
        established forever;
    your faithfulness is as firm as the
        heavens.

3 You said, "I have made a covenant with my
        chosen one,
    I have sworn to my servant David:
4 'I will establish your descendants forever,
    and build your throne for all
        generations.' " *Selah*

5 Let the heavens praise your wonders,
        O LORD,
    your faithfulness in the assembly of the
        holy ones.
6 For who in the skies can be compared to the
        LORD?
    Who among the heavenly beings is like
        the LORD,
7 a God feared in the council of the holy ones,
    great and awesome^d above all that are
        around him?
8 O LORD God of hosts,
    who is as mighty as you, O LORD?
    Your faithfulness surrounds you.
9 You rule the raging of the sea;
    when its waves rise, you still them.
10 You crushed Rahab like a carcass;
    you scattered your enemies with your
        mighty arm.
11 The heavens are yours, the earth also is
        yours;
    the world and all that is in it—you have
        founded them.
12 The north and the south^e—you created
        them;

---

a Or *Nubia*; Heb *Cush* b Meaning of Heb uncertain c Gk: Heb *the steadfast love of the LORD* d Gk Syr: Heb *greatly awesome* e Or *Zaphon and Yamin*

PROFILE OF FAITH

ÓSCAR ROMERO: To Give One's Life

At the age of fourteen, Óscar Romero entered the seminary and studied to become a priest. Before he became an archbishop, Romero's service to the Church had been undistinguished. He was a timid and predictable scholar, not an activist, and no one expected him to rock any boats.

That changed within three weeks of his election, when one of his priests, Rutilio Grande, and two parishioners were killed for their support of peasants' rights. At that time, social and political upheaval in El Salvador plunged Romero's Church family into a bloody nightmare. The government, backed by a violent military, was denying its citizens basic human rights, including freedom of religion.

When Romero attended Grande's funeral, he saw the peasants and their lives of desperation and powerlessness. He became their advocate, even as the government continued its reign of terror and oppression.

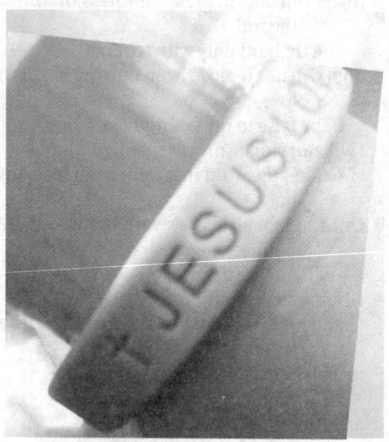

His actions won him the enduring love of the poor, but Romero knew his own life was on the line. Despite the very real danger, he continued to care about the everyday lives of his people, giving them shelter, food, and words of hope. He said, "I do not believe in death without resurrection," he said. "If they kill me, I will be resurrected in the Salvadoran people."

On March 24, 1980, Romero gave his last homily moments before a sharpshooter killed him. Reflecting on Scripture, he said, "One must not love oneself so much as to avoid getting involved in the risks of life that history demands of us, and those who fend off danger will lose their lives."

Jesus on My Wrist—© Mallory Kidwell, 15

    Tabor and Hermon joyously praise your
        name.
13 You have a mighty arm;
    strong is your hand, high your right hand.
14 Righteousness and justice are the
        foundation of your throne;
    steadfast love and faithfulness go before
        you.
15 Happy are the people who know the festal
        shout,
    who walk, O Lord, in the light of your
        countenance;
16 they exult in your name all day long,
    and extol*a* your righteousness.
17 For you are the glory of their strength;
    by your favor our horn is exalted.
18 For our shield belongs to the Lord,
    our king to the Holy One of Israel.

19 Then you spoke in a vision to your faithful
        one, and said:
    "I have set the crown*b* on one who is
        mighty,
    I have exalted one chosen from the
        people.
20 I have found my servant David;
    with my holy oil I have anointed him;
21 my hand shall always remain with him;
    my arm also shall strengthen him.
22 The enemy shall not outwit him,
    the wicked shall not humble him.
23 I will crush his foes before him
    and strike down those who hate him.
24 My faithfulness and steadfast love shall be
        with him;
    and in my name his horn shall be exalted.
25 I will set his hand on the sea

a Cn: Heb *are exalted in* *b* Cn: Heb *help*

and his right hand on the rivers.
26 He shall cry to me, 'You are my Father,
    my God, and the Rock of my salvation!'
27 I will make him the firstborn,
    the highest of the kings of the earth.
28 Forever I will keep my steadfast love for him,
    and my covenant with him will stand
        firm.
29 I will establish his line forever,
    and his throne as long as the heavens
        endure.
30 If his children forsake my law
    and do not walk according to my
        ordinances,
31 if they violate my statutes
    and do not keep my commandments,
32 then I will punish their transgression with
        the rod
    and their iniquity with scourges;
33 but I will not remove from him my steadfast
        love,
    or be false to my faithfulness.
34 I will not violate my covenant,
    or alter the word that went forth from my
        lips.
35 Once and for all I have sworn by my
        holiness;
    I will not lie to David.
36 His line shall continue forever,
    and his throne endure before me like the
        sun.
37 It shall be established forever like the
        moon,
    an enduring witness in the skies."   *Selah*

38 But now you have spurned and rejected
        him;
    you are full of wrath against your
        anointed.
39 You have renounced the covenant with your
        servant;
    you have defiled his crown in the dust.
40 You have broken through all his walls;
    you have laid his strongholds in ruins.
41 All who pass by plunder him;
    he has become the scorn of his neighbors.
42 You have exalted the right hand of his foes;
    you have made all his enemies rejoice.
43 Moreover, you have turned back the edge of
        his sword,
    and you have not supported him in
        battle.
44 You have removed the scepter from his
        hand,*a*
    and hurled his throne to the ground.
45 You have cut short the days of his youth;
    you have covered him with shame.   *Selah*

46 How long, O LORD? Will you hide yourself
        forever?
    How long will your wrath burn like fire?
47 Remember how short my time is—*b*
    for what vanity you have created all
        mortals!
48 Who can live and never see death?
    Who can escape the power of Sheol?   *Selah*

49 Lord, where is your steadfast love of old,
    which by your faithfulness you swore to
        David?
50 Remember, O Lord, how your servant is
        taunted;
    how I bear in my bosom the insults of the
        peoples,*c*
51 with which your enemies taunt, O LORD,
    with which they taunted the footsteps of
        your anointed.

52 Blessed be the LORD forever.
        Amen and Amen.

BOOK IV *(Psalms 90–106)*

PSALM 90

God's Eternity and Human Frailty

A Prayer of Moses, the man of God.

1 Lord, you have been our dwelling place*d*
    in all generations.
2 Before the mountains were brought forth,
    or ever you had formed the earth and the
        world,
    from everlasting to everlasting you are
        God.

3 You turn us*e* back to dust,
    and say, "Turn back, you mortals."
4 For a thousand years in your sight
    are like yesterday when it is past,
    or like a watch in the night.

5 You sweep them away; they are like a
        dream,
    like grass that is renewed in the morning;
6 in the morning it flourishes and is renewed;
    in the evening it fades and withers.

7 For we are consumed by your anger;
    by your wrath we are overwhelmed.
8 You have set our iniquities before you,
    our secret sins in the light of your
        countenance.

9 For all our days pass away under your wrath;
    our years come to an end*f* like a sigh.
10 The days of our life are seventy years,
    or perhaps eighty, if we are strong;

---

a Cn: Heb *removed his cleanness*   *b* Meaning of Heb uncertain   *c* Cn: Heb *bosom all of many peoples*   *d* Another reading is *our refuge*
e Heb *humankind*   *f* Syr: Heb *we bring our years to an end*

even then their span[a] is only toil and
trouble;
they are soon gone, and we fly away.
11 Who considers the power of your anger?
Your wrath is as great as the fear that is
due you.
12 So teach us to count our days
that we may gain a wise heart.

13 Turn, O LORD! How long?
Have compassion on your servants!
14 Satisfy us in the morning with your
steadfast love,
so that we may rejoice and be glad all our
days.
15 Make us glad as many days as you have
afflicted us,
and as many years as we have seen evil.
16 Let your work be manifest to your servants,
and your glorious power to their
children.
17 Let the favor of the Lord our God be
upon us,
and prosper for us the work of our
hands—
O prosper the work of our hands!

PSALM 91

Assurance of God's Protection

1 You who live in the shelter of the Most
High,
who abide in the shadow of the
Almighty,[b]
2 will say to the LORD, "My refuge and my
fortress;
my God, in whom I trust."
3 For he will deliver you from the snare of the
fowler
and from the deadly pestilence;
4 he will cover you with his pinions,
and under his wings you will find refuge;
his faithfulness is a shield and buckler.
5 You will not fear the terror of the night,
or the arrow that flies by day,
6 or the pestilence that stalks in darkness,
or the destruction that wastes at
noonday.

7 A thousand may fall at your side,
ten thousand at your right hand,
but it will not come near you.
8 You will only look with your eyes
and see the punishment of the wicked.

9 Because you have made the LORD your
refuge,[c]
the Most High your dwelling place,

10 no evil shall befall you,
no scourge come near your tent.
11 For he will command his angels concerning
you
to guard you in all your ways.
12 On their hands they will bear you up,
so that you will not dash your foot
against a stone.
13 You will tread on the lion and the adder,
the young lion and the serpent you will
trample under foot.

14 Those who love me, I will deliver;
I will protect those who know my name.
15 When they call to me, I will answer them;
I will be with them in trouble,
I will rescue them and honor them.
16 With long life I will satisfy them,
and show them my salvation.

PSALM 92

Thanksgiving for Vindication

A Psalm. A Song for the Sabbath Day.

1 It is good to give thanks to the LORD,
to sing praises to your name, O Most
High;
2 to declare your steadfast love in the
morning,
and your faithfulness by night,
3 to the music of the lute and the harp,
to the melody of the lyre.
4 For you, O LORD, have made me glad by
your work;
at the works of your hands I sing for joy.

5 How great are your works, O LORD!
Your thoughts are very deep!
6 The dullard cannot know,
the stupid cannot understand this:
7 though the wicked sprout like grass
and all evildoers flourish,
they are doomed to destruction forever,
8 but you, O LORD, are on high forever.

a Cn Compare Gk Syr Jerome Tg: Heb *pride* b Traditional rendering of Heb *Shaddai* c Cn: Heb *Because you, LORD, are my refuge; you have made*

9 For your enemies, O LORD,
　　for your enemies shall perish;
　　all evildoers shall be scattered.

10 But you have exalted my horn like that of
　　the wild ox;
　　you have poured over me*a* fresh oil.
11 My eyes have seen the downfall of my
　　enemies;
　　my ears have heard the doom of my evil
　　assailants.

12 The righteous flourish like the palm tree,
　　and grow like a cedar in Lebanon.
13 They are planted in the house of the LORD;
　　they flourish in the courts of our God.
14 In old age they still produce fruit;
　　they are always green and full of sap,
15 showing that the LORD is upright;
　　he is my rock, and there is no
　　unrighteousness in him.

PSALM 93

The Majesty of God's Rule

1 The LORD is king, he is robed in majesty;
　　the LORD is robed, he is girded with
　　strength.
　　He has established the world; it shall never
　　be moved;
2 your throne is established from of old;
　　you are from everlasting.

3 The floods have lifted up, O LORD,
　　the floods have lifted up their voice;
　　the floods lift up their roaring.
4 More majestic than the thunders of mighty
　　waters,
　　more majestic than the waves*b* of the sea,
　　majestic on high is the LORD!

5 Your decrees are very sure;
　　holiness befits your house,
　　O LORD, forevermore.

PSALM 94

God the Avenger of the Righteous

1 O LORD, you God of vengeance,
　　you God of vengeance, shine forth!
2 Rise up, O judge of the earth;
　　give to the proud what they deserve!
3 O LORD, how long shall the wicked,
　　how long shall the wicked exult?

4 They pour out their arrogant words;
　　all the evildoers boast.
5 They crush your people, O LORD,
　　and afflict your heritage.
6 They kill the widow and the stranger,

they murder the orphan,
7 and they say, "The LORD does not see;
　　the God of Jacob does not perceive."

8 Understand, O dullest of the people;
　　fools, when will you be wise?
9 He who planted the ear, does he not hear?
　　He who formed the eye, does he not see?
10 He who disciplines the nations,
　　he who teaches knowledge to humankind,
　　does he not chastise?
11 The LORD knows our thoughts,*c*
　　that they are but an empty breath.

12 Happy are those whom you discipline,
　　O LORD,
　　and whom you teach out of your law,
13 giving them respite from days of trouble,
　　until a pit is dug for the wicked.
14 For the LORD will not forsake his people;
　　he will not abandon his heritage;
15 for justice will return to the righteous,
　　and all the upright in heart will follow it.

16 Who rises up for me against the wicked?
　　Who stands up for me against evildoers?
17 If the LORD had not been my help,
　　my soul would soon have lived in the
　　land of silence.
18 When I thought, "My foot is slipping,"
　　your steadfast love, O LORD, held me up.
19 When the cares of my heart are many,
　　your consolations cheer my soul.
20 Can wicked rulers be allied with you,
　　those who contrive mischief by statute?
21 They band together against the life of the
　　righteous,
　　and condemn the innocent to death.
22 But the LORD has become my stronghold,
　　and my God the rock of my refuge.
23 He will repay them for their iniquity
　　and wipe them out for their wickedness;
　　the LORD our God will wipe them out.

PSALM 95

A Call to Worship and Obedience

1 O come, let us sing to the LORD;
　　let us make a joyful noise to the rock of
　　our salvation!
2 Let us come into his presence with
　　thanksgiving;
　　let us make a joyful noise to him with
　　songs of praise!
3 For the LORD is a great God,
　　and a great King above all gods.
4 In his hand are the depths of the earth;
　　the heights of the mountains are his
　　also.

a Syr: Meaning of Heb uncertain　*b* Cn: Heb *majestic are the waves*　*c* Heb *the thoughts of humankind*

5 The sea is his, for he made it,
  and the dry land, which his hands have
    formed.

6 O come, let us worship and bow down,
  let us kneel before the LORD, our Maker!
7 For he is our God,
  and we are the people of his pasture,
  and the sheep of his hand.

  O that today you would listen to his voice!
8   Do not harden your hearts, as at
      Meribah,
  as on the day at Massah in the wilderness,
9 when your ancestors tested me,
  and put me to the proof, though they had
    seen my work.
10 For forty years I loathed that generation
  and said, "They are a people whose
    hearts go astray,
  and they do not regard my ways."
11 Therefore in my anger I swore,
  "They shall not enter my rest."

PSALM 96

Praise to God Who Comes in Judgment

1 O sing to the LORD a new song;
  sing to the LORD, all the earth.
2 Sing to the LORD, bless his name;
  tell of his salvation from day to day.
3 Declare his glory among the nations,
  his marvelous works among all the
    peoples.
4 For great is the LORD, and greatly to be
    praised;
  he is to be revered above all gods.
5 For all the gods of the peoples are idols,
  but the LORD made the heavens.
6 Honor and majesty are before him;
  strength and beauty are in his sanctuary.

7 Ascribe to the LORD, O families of the
    peoples,
  ascribe to the LORD glory and strength.
8 Ascribe to the LORD the glory due his name;
  bring an offering, and come into his
    courts.
9 Worship the LORD in holy splendor;
  tremble before him, all the earth.

10 Say among the nations, "The LORD is king!
  The world is firmly established; it shall
    never be moved.
  He will judge the peoples with equity."
11 Let the heavens be glad, and let the earth
    rejoice;
  let the sea roar, and all that fills it;
12 let the field exult, and everything in it.

Then shall all the trees of the forest sing for
    joy
13   before the LORD; for he is coming,
  for he is coming to judge the earth.
  He will judge the world with righteousness,
  and the peoples with his truth.

PSALM 97

The Glory of God's Reign

1 The LORD is king! Let the earth rejoice;
  let the many coastlands be glad!
2 Clouds and thick darkness are all around
    him;
  righteousness and justice are the
    foundation of his throne.
3 Fire goes before him,
  and consumes his adversaries on every
    side.
4 His lightnings light up the world;
  the earth sees and trembles.
5 The mountains melt like wax before the
    LORD,
  before the Lord of all the earth.

6 The heavens proclaim his righteousness;
  and all the peoples behold his glory.
7 All worshipers of images are put to shame,
  those who make their boast in worthless
    idols;
  all gods bow down before him.
8 Zion hears and is glad,
  and the towns[a] of Judah rejoice,
  because of your judgments, O God.
9 For you, O LORD, are most high over all the
    earth;
  you are exalted far above all gods.

10 The LORD loves those who hate[b] evil;
  he guards the lives of his faithful;
  he rescues them from the hand of the
    wicked.
11 Light dawns[c] for the righteous,
  and joy for the upright in heart.
12 Rejoice in the LORD, O you righteous,
  and give thanks to his holy name!

PSALM 98

Praise the Judge of the World

A Psalm.

1 O sing to the LORD a new song,
  for he has done marvelous things.
  His right hand and his holy arm
  have gotten him victory.
2 The LORD has made known his victory;
  he has revealed his vindication in the
    sight of the nations.

---

a Heb *daughters* b Cn: Heb *You who love the LORD hate* c Gk Syr Jerome: Heb *is sown*

³ He has remembered his steadfast love and
faithfulness
  to the house of Israel.
All the ends of the earth have seen
  the victory of our God.

⁴ Make a joyful noise to the LORD, all the
earth;
  break forth into joyous song and sing
  praises.
⁵ Sing praises to the LORD with the lyre,
  with the lyre and the sound of melody.
⁶ With trumpets and the sound of the horn
  make a joyful noise before the King, the
  LORD.

⁷ Let the sea roar, and all that fills it;
  the world and those who live in it.
⁸ Let the floods clap their hands;
  let the hills sing together for joy

⁹ at the presence of the LORD, for he is coming
  to judge the earth.
He will judge the world with righteousness,
  and the peoples with equity.

PSALM 99

Praise to God for His Holiness

¹ The LORD is king; let the peoples tremble!
  He sits enthroned upon the cherubim;
    let the earth quake!
² The LORD is great in Zion;
  he is exalted over all the peoples.
³ Let them praise your great and awesome
  name.
  Holy is he!
⁴ Mighty King,^a lover of justice,
  you have established equity;
you have executed justice
  and righteousness in Jacob.
⁵ Extol the LORD our God;
  worship at his footstool.
  Holy is he!

⁶ Moses and Aaron were among his priests,
  Samuel also was among those who called
    on his name.
  They cried to the LORD, and he answered
    them.
⁷ He spoke to them in the pillar of cloud;
  they kept his decrees,
  and the statutes that he gave them.

⁸ O LORD our God, you answered them;
  you were a forgiving God to them,
  but an avenger of their wrongdoings.
⁹ Extol the LORD our God,
  and worship at his holy mountain;
  for the LORD our God is holy.

PSALM 100

All Lands Summoned to Praise God

A Psalm of thanksgiving.

¹ Make a joyful noise to the LORD, all the earth.
²   Worship the LORD with gladness;
  come into his presence with singing.

³ Know that the LORD is God.
  It is he that made us, and we are his;^b
  we are his people, and the sheep of his
    pasture.

⁴ Enter his gates with thanksgiving,
  and his courts with praise.
  Give thanks to him, bless his name.

⁵ For the LORD is good;
  his steadfast love endures forever,
  and his faithfulness to all generations.

---

a Cn: Heb *And a king's strength* *b* Another reading is *and not we ourselves*

PSALM 101

A Sovereign's Pledge of Integrity and Justice

Of David. A Psalm.

1 I will sing of loyalty and of justice;
to you, O LORD, I will sing.
2 I will study the way that is blameless.
When shall I attain it?

I will walk with integrity of heart
within my house;
3 I will not set before my eyes
anything that is base.

I hate the work of those who fall away;
it shall not cling to me.
4 Perverseness of heart shall be far from me;
I will know nothing of evil.

5 One who secretly slanders a neighbor
I will destroy.
A haughty look and an arrogant heart
I will not tolerate.

6 I will look with favor on the faithful in the
land,
so that they may live with me;
whoever walks in the way that is blameless
shall minister to me.

7 No one who practices deceit
shall remain in my house;
no one who utters lies
shall continue in my presence.

8 Morning by morning I will destroy
all the wicked in the land,
cutting off all evildoers
from the city of the LORD.

PSALM 102

Prayer to the Eternal King for Help

*A prayer of one afflicted, when faint and pleading before the
LORD.*

1 Hear my prayer, O LORD;
let my cry come to you.
2 Do not hide your face from me
in the day of my distress.
Incline your ear to me;
answer me speedily in the day when I call.

3 For my days pass away like smoke,
and my bones burn like a furnace.
4 My heart is stricken and withered like grass;
I am too wasted to eat my bread.
5 Because of my loud groaning
my bones cling to my skin.
6 I am like an owl of the wilderness,
like a little owl of the waste places.
7 I lie awake;
I am like a lonely bird on the housetop.

8 All day long my enemies taunt me;
those who deride me use my name for a
curse.
9 For I eat ashes like bread,
and mingle tears with my drink,
10 because of your indignation and anger;
for you have lifted me up and thrown me
aside.
11 My days are like an evening shadow;
I wither away like grass.

12 But you, O LORD, are enthroned forever;
your name endures to all generations.
13 You will rise up and have compassion on
Zion,
for it is time to favor it;
the appointed time has come.
14 For your servants hold its stones dear,
and have pity on its dust.
15 The nations will fear the name of the LORD,
and all the kings of the earth your glory.
16 For the LORD will build up Zion;
he will appear in his glory.
17 He will regard the prayer of the destitute,
and will not despise their prayer.

18 Let this be recorded for a generation to
come,
so that a people yet unborn may praise
the LORD:
19 that he looked down from his holy height,
from heaven the LORD looked at the earth,
20 to hear the groans of the prisoners,
to set free those who were doomed to die;
21 so that the name of the LORD may be
declared in Zion,
and his praise in Jerusalem,
22 when peoples gather together,
and kingdoms, to worship the LORD.

23 He has broken my strength in midcourse;
he has shortened my days.
24 "O my God," I say, "do not take me away
at the midpoint of my life,
you whose years endure
throughout all generations."

25 Long ago you laid the foundation of the
earth,
and the heavens are the work of your
hands.
26 They will perish, but you endure;
they will all wear out like a garment.
You change them like clothing, and they
pass away;
27 but you are the same, and your years have
no end.
28 The children of your servants shall live
secure;
their offspring shall be established in
your presence.

PSALM 103

Thanksgiving for God's Goodness

Of David.

1 Bless the LORD, O my soul,
   and all that is within me,
   bless his holy name.
2 Bless the LORD, O my soul,
   and do not forget all his benefits—
3 who forgives all your iniquity,
   who heals all your diseases,
4 who redeems your life from the Pit,
   who crowns you with steadfast love and
   mercy,
5 who satisfies you with good as long as you
   live[a]
   so that your youth is renewed like the
   eagle's.

6 The LORD works vindication
   and justice for all who are oppressed.
7 He made known his ways to Moses,
   his acts to the people of Israel.
8 The LORD is merciful and gracious,
   slow to anger and abounding in steadfast
   love.
9 He will not always accuse,
   nor will he keep his anger forever.
10 He does not deal with us according to our
   sins,
   nor repay us according to our iniquities.
11 For as the heavens are high above the earth,
   so great is his steadfast love toward those
   who fear him;
12 as far as the east is from the west,
   so far he removes our transgressions
   from us.
13 As a father has compassion for his children,
   so the LORD has compassion for those
   who fear him.
14 For he knows how we were made;
   he remembers that we are dust.

15 As for mortals, their days are like grass;
   they flourish like a flower of the field;
16 for the wind passes over it, and it is gone,
   and its place knows it no more.
17 But the steadfast love of the LORD is from
   everlasting to everlasting
   on those who fear him,
   and his righteousness to children's
   children,
18 to those who keep his covenant
   and remember to do his
   commandments.

19 The LORD has established his throne in the
   heavens,
and his kingdom rules over all.
20 Bless the LORD, O you his angels,
   you mighty ones who do his bidding,
   obedient to his spoken word.
21 Bless the LORD, all his hosts,
   his ministers that do his will.
22 Bless the LORD, all his works,
   in all places of his dominion.
   Bless the LORD, O my soul.

PSALM 104

God the Creator and Provider

1 Bless the LORD, O my soul.
   O LORD my God, you are very great.
   You are clothed with honor and majesty,
2   wrapped in light as with a garment.
   You stretch out the heavens like a tent,
3   you set the beams of your[b] chambers on
      the waters,
   you make the clouds your[b] chariot,
      you ride on the wings of the wind,
4 you make the winds your[b] messengers,
   fire and flame your[b] ministers.

5 You set the earth on its foundations,
   so that it shall never be shaken.
6 You cover it with the deep as with a
   garment;
   the waters stood above the mountains.
7 At your rebuke they flee;
   at the sound of your thunder they take to
   flight.
8 They rose up to the mountains, ran down to
   the valleys
   to the place that you appointed for them.
9 You set a boundary that they may not pass,
   so that they might not again cover the
   earth.

10 You make springs gush forth in the valleys;
   they flow between the hills,
11 giving drink to every wild animal;
   the wild asses quench their thirst.
12 By the streams[c] the birds of the air have
   their habitation;
   they sing among the branches.
13 From your lofty abode you water the
   mountains;
   the earth is satisfied with the fruit of your
   work.

14 You cause the grass to grow for the cattle,
   and plants for people to use,[d]
   to bring forth food from the earth,
15   and wine to gladden the human heart,
   oil to make the face shine,
   and bread to strengthen the human
   heart.

---

a Meaning of Heb uncertain *b* Heb *his* *c* Heb *By them* *d* Or *to cultivate*

16 The trees of the Lord are watered
        abundantly,
    the cedars of Lebanon that he planted.
17 In them the birds build their nests;
    the stork has its home in the fir trees.
18 The high mountains are for the wild goats;
    the rocks are a refuge for the coneys.
19 You have made the moon to mark the
        seasons;
    the sun knows its time for setting.
20 You make darkness, and it is night,
    when all the animals of the forest come
        creeping out.
21 The young lions roar for their prey,
    seeking their food from God.
22 When the sun rises, they withdraw
    and lie down in their dens.
23 People go out to their work
    and to their labor until the evening.

24 O Lord, how manifold are your works!
    In wisdom you have made them all;
    the earth is full of your creatures.
25 Yonder is the sea, great and wide,
    creeping things innumerable are there,
    living things both small and great.
26 There go the ships,
    and Leviathan that you formed to sport
        in it.

27 These all look to you
    to give them their food in due season;
28 when you give to them, they gather it up;
    when you open your hand, they are filled
        with good things.
29 When you hide your face, they are
        dismayed;
    when you take away their breath, they die
    and return to their dust.
30 When you send forth your spirit,*a* they are
        created;
    and you renew the face of the ground.

31 May the glory of the Lord endure forever;
    may the Lord rejoice in his works—
32 who looks on the earth and it trembles,
    who touches the mountains and they
        smoke.
33 I will sing to the Lord as long as I live;
    I will sing praise to my God while I have
        being.
34 May my meditation be pleasing to him,
    for I rejoice in the Lord.
35 Let sinners be consumed from the earth,
    and let the wicked be no more.
    Bless the Lord, O my soul.
    Praise the Lord!

a Or *your breath*

Criticizing Creation

Awful.

Not exactly how you would describe the perfect sunset, a snow-capped mountain range, or the wonders hidden beneath the coral reefs of the Pacific. But that's really the word for it. Doesn't *awful* mean "full of awe"? Sounds like it should, though somehow it came to mean the opposite. The world around us, when taken as a whole, free from the pollution and noise and busyness of daily living, leaves us full of awe. Maybe we could call it *awe-full*.

Read **Psalm 104**. The psalmist is full of awe as he considers the wonders of creation. There are hints and fingerprints of God visible throughout the world.

Look at the photography of Ansel Adams or the paintings of Georgia O'Keeffe on the Web, then print out a thumbnail of an image that really stands out to you and paste it below. Next, photograph or draw your own picture of creation, one that fills you with awe. Share your creation art at **Learner.CalltoDiscipleship.com**.

CREATIVE SPACE

PSALM 105

God's Faithfulness to Israel

1 O give thanks to the LORD, call on his name,
   make known his deeds among the
   peoples.
2 Sing to him, sing praises to him;
   tell of all his wonderful works.
3 Glory in his holy name;
   let the hearts of those who seek the LORD
   rejoice.
4 Seek the LORD and his strength;
   seek his presence continually.
5 Remember the wonderful works he has
   done,
   his miracles, and the judgments he has
   uttered,
6 O offspring of his servant Abraham,*a*
   children of Jacob, his chosen ones.

7 He is the LORD our God;
   his judgments are in all the earth.
8 He is mindful of his covenant forever,
   of the word that he commanded, for a
   thousand generations,
9 the covenant that he made with Abraham,
   his sworn promise to Isaac,
10 which he confirmed to Jacob as a statute,
   to Israel as an everlasting covenant,
11 saying, "To you I will give the land of
   Canaan
   as your portion for an inheritance."

12 When they were few in number,
   of little account, and strangers in it,
13 wandering from nation to nation,
   from one kingdom to another people,
14 he allowed no one to oppress them;
   he rebuked kings on their account,
15 saying, "Do not touch my anointed ones;
   do my prophets no harm."

16 When he summoned famine against the
   land,
   and broke every staff of bread,
17 he had sent a man ahead of them,
   Joseph, who was sold as a slave.
18 His feet were hurt with fetters,
   his neck was put in a collar of iron;
19 until what he had said came to pass,
   the word of the LORD kept testing him.
20 The king sent and released him;
   the ruler of the peoples set him free.
21 He made him lord of his house,
   and ruler of all his possessions,
22 to instruct*b* his officials at his pleasure,
   and to teach his elders wisdom.

23 Then Israel came to Egypt;
   Jacob lived as an alien in the land of
   Ham.
24 And the LORD made his people very fruitful,
   and made them stronger than their foes,
25 whose hearts he then turned to hate his
   people,
   to deal craftily with his servants.

26 He sent his servant Moses,
   and Aaron whom he had chosen.
27 They performed his signs among them,
   and miracles in the land of Ham.
28 He sent darkness, and made the land dark;
   they rebelled*c* against his words.
29 He turned their waters into blood,
   and caused their fish to die.
30 Their land swarmed with frogs,
   even in the chambers of their kings.
31 He spoke, and there came swarms of flies,
   and gnats throughout their country.
32 He gave them hail for rain,
   and lightning that flashed through their
   land.
33 He struck their vines and fig trees,
   and shattered the trees of their country.
34 He spoke, and the locusts came,
   and young locusts without number;
35 they devoured all the vegetation in their
   land,
   and ate up the fruit of their ground.
36 He struck down all the firstborn in their land,
   the first issue of all their strength.

37 Then he brought Israel*d* out with silver and
   gold,
   and there was no one among their tribes
   who stumbled.
38 Egypt was glad when they departed,
   for dread of them had fallen upon it.
39 He spread a cloud for a covering,
   and fire to give light by night.
40 They asked, and he brought quails,
   and gave them food from heaven in
   abundance.
41 He opened the rock, and water gushed out;
   it flowed through the desert like a river.
42 For he remembered his holy promise,
   and Abraham, his servant.

43 So he brought his people out with joy,
   his chosen ones with singing.
44 He gave them the lands of the nations,
   and they took possession of the wealth
   of the peoples,
45 that they might keep his statutes
   and observe his laws.
   Praise the LORD!

a Another reading is Israel (compare 1 Chr 16.13) b Gk Syr Jerome: Heb *to bind* c Cn Compare Gk Syr: Heb *they did not rebel*
d Heb *them*

PSALM 106

A Confession of Israel's Sins

¹ Praise the LORD!
 O give thanks to the LORD, for he is good;
 for his steadfast love endures forever.
² Who can utter the mighty doings of the
 LORD,
 or declare all his praise?
³ Happy are those who observe justice,
 who do righteousness at all times.

⁴ Remember me, O LORD, when you show
 favor to your people;
 help me when you deliver them;
⁵ that I may see the prosperity of your chosen
 ones,
 that I may rejoice in the gladness of your
 nation,
 that I may glory in your heritage.

⁶ Both we and our ancestors have sinned;
 we have committed iniquity, have done
 wickedly.
⁷ Our ancestors, when they were in Egypt,
 did not consider your wonderful works;
 they did not remember the abundance of
 your steadfast love,
 but rebelled against the Most High[a] at the
 Red Sea.[b]
⁸ Yet he saved them for his name's sake,
 so that he might make known his mighty
 power.
⁹ He rebuked the Red Sea,[b] and it became dry;
 he led them through the deep as through
 a desert.
¹⁰ So he saved them from the hand of the foe,
 and delivered them from the hand of the
 enemy.
¹¹ The waters covered their adversaries;
 not one of them was left.
¹² Then they believed his words;
 they sang his praise.

¹³ But they soon forgot his works;
 they did not wait for his counsel.
¹⁴ But they had a wanton craving in the
 wilderness,
 and put God to the test in the desert;
¹⁵ he gave them what they asked,
 but sent a wasting disease among them.
¹⁶ They were jealous of Moses in the camp,
 and of Aaron, the holy one of the LORD.
¹⁷ The earth opened and swallowed up
 Dathan,
 and covered the faction of Abiram.
¹⁸ Fire also broke out in their company;
 the flame burned up the wicked.

COME TOGETHER

Sin is not just about you or me. Sin has consequences that can affect our friends, family, and even our communities.

And then there are times when we sin and we don't even know it. Let's call it DENIAL: "**D**on't **E**ven k**N**ow **I A**m **L**ying." Like when we gossip or make a racist or sexist comment. Lots of times it's because we live in a sinful society, and we don't recognize that we are participating in social sin. The psalmist in **Psalm 106** names the sins and social sin of the Israelites in verse 6: "Both we and our ancestors have sinned; we have committed iniquity, have done wickedly."

Every Sunday we together confess our sins to our brothers and sisters in Christ. In 1973, the Church presented the faithful with a renewed Rite of Penance, which has three forms. Two of them are celebrations in which the community assembles to confess its sinfulness and to be a sign of a Church in need of confession and purification. As it says in the Rite of Penance, "In fact people frequently join together to commit injustice. But it is also true they help each other in doing penance."

¹⁹ They made a calf at Horeb
 and worshiped a cast image.
²⁰ They exchanged the glory of God[c]
 for the image of an ox that eats grass.
²¹ They forgot God, their Savior,
 who had done great things in Egypt,
²² wondrous works in the land of Ham,
 and awesome deeds by the Red Sea.[b]
²³ Therefore he said he would destroy them—
 had not Moses, his chosen one,
 stood in the breach before him,
 to turn away his wrath from destroying
 them.

²⁴ Then they despised the pleasant land,
 having no faith in his promise.
²⁵ They grumbled in their tents,
 and did not obey the voice of the LORD.
²⁶ Therefore he raised his hand and swore to
 them

---

a Cn Compare 78.17, 56: Heb *rebelled at the sea* b Or *Sea of Reeds* c Compare Gk Mss: Heb *exchanged their glory*

that he would make them fall in the
wilderness,
27 and would disperse*ᵃ* their descendants
among the nations,
scattering them over the lands.

28 Then they attached themselves to the Baal
of Peor,
and ate sacrifices offered to the dead;
29 they provoked the Lord to anger with their
deeds,
and a plague broke out among them.
30 Then Phinehas stood up and interceded,
and the plague was stopped.
31 And that has been reckoned to him as
righteousness
from generation to generation forever.

32 They angered the Lord*ᵇ* at the waters of
Meribah,
and it went ill with Moses on their
account;
33 for they made his spirit bitter,
and he spoke words that were rash.

34 They did not destroy the peoples,
as the Lord commanded them,
35 but they mingled with the nations
and learned to do as they did.
36 They served their idols,
which became a snare to them.
37 They sacrificed their sons
and their daughters to the demons;
38 they poured out innocent blood,
the blood of their sons and daughters,
whom they sacrificed to the idols of
Canaan;

and the land was polluted with blood.
39 Thus they became unclean by their acts,
and prostituted themselves in their
doings.

40 Then the anger of the Lord was kindled
against his people,
and he abhorred his heritage;
41 he gave them into the hand of the nations,
so that those who hated them ruled over
them.
42 Their enemies oppressed them,
and they were brought into subjection
under their power.
43 Many times he delivered them,
but they were rebellious in their
purposes,
and were brought low through their
iniquity.
44 Nevertheless he regarded their distress
when he heard their cry.
45 For their sake he remembered his covenant,
and showed compassion according to
the abundance of his steadfast love.
46 He caused them to be pitied
by all who held them captive.

47 Save us, O Lord our God,
and gather us from among the nations,
that we may give thanks to your holy name
and glory in your praise.

48 Blessed be the Lord, the God of Israel,
from everlasting to everlasting.
And let all the people say, "Amen."
Praise the Lord!

a Syr Compare Ezek 20.23: Heb *cause to fall* *b* Heb *him*

PSALM **107**

Thanksgiving for Deliverance from Many Troubles

1 O give thanks to the LORD, for he is good;
    for his steadfast love endures forever.
2 Let the redeemed of the LORD say so,
    those he redeemed from trouble
3 and gathered in from the lands,
    from the east and from the west,
    from the north and from the south.*a*

4 Some wandered in desert wastes,
    finding no way to an inhabited town;
5 hungry and thirsty,
    their soul fainted within them.
6 Then they cried to the LORD in their trouble,
    and he delivered them from their
        distress;
7 he led them by a straight way,
    until they reached an inhabited town.
8 Let them thank the LORD for his steadfast
        love,
    for his wonderful works to humankind.
9 For he satisfies the thirsty,
    and the hungry he fills with good things.

10 Some sat in darkness and in gloom,
    prisoners in misery and in irons,
11 for they had rebelled against the words of
        God,
    and spurned the counsel of the Most
        High.
12 Their hearts were bowed down with hard
        labor;
    they fell down, with no one to help.
13 Then they cried to the LORD in their trouble,
    and he saved them from their distress;
14 he brought them out of darkness and
        gloom,
    and broke their bonds asunder.
15 Let them thank the LORD for his steadfast
        love,
    for his wonderful works to humankind.
16 For he shatters the doors of bronze,
    and cuts in two the bars of iron.

17 Some were sick*b* through their sinful ways,
    and because of their iniquities endured
        affliction;
18 they loathed any kind of food,
    and they drew near to the gates of death.
19 Then they cried to the LORD in their trouble,
    and he saved them from their distress;
20 he sent out his word and healed them,
    and delivered them from destruction.

21 Let them thank the LORD for his steadfast
        love,
    for his wonderful works to humankind.
22 And let them offer thanksgiving sacrifices,
    and tell of his deeds with songs of joy.

23 Some went down to the sea in ships,
    doing business on the mighty waters;
24 they saw the deeds of the LORD,
    his wondrous works in the deep.
25 For he commanded and raised the stormy
        wind,
    which lifted up the waves of the sea.
26 They mounted up to heaven, they went
        down to the depths;
    their courage melted away in their
        calamity;
27 they reeled and staggered like drunkards,
    and were at their wits' end.
28 Then they cried to the LORD in their trouble,
    and he brought them out from their
        distress;
29 he made the storm be still,
    and the waves of the sea were hushed.
30 Then they were glad because they had quiet,
    and he brought them to their desired
        haven.
31 Let them thank the LORD for his steadfast
        love,
    for his wonderful works to humankind.
32 Let them extol him in the congregation of
        the people,
    and praise him in the assembly of the
        elders.

33 He turns rivers into a desert,
    springs of water into thirsty ground,
34 a fruitful land into a salty waste,
    because of the wickedness of its
        inhabitants.
35 He turns a desert into pools of water,
    a parched land into springs of water.
36 And there he lets the hungry live,
    and they establish a town to live in;
37 they sow fields, and plant vineyards,
    and get a fruitful yield.
38 By his blessing they multiply greatly,
    and he does not let their cattle decrease.

39 When they are diminished and brought low
    through oppression, trouble, and
        sorrow,
40 he pours contempt on princes
    and makes them wander in trackless
        wastes;
41 but he raises up the needy out of distress,
    and makes their families like flocks.
42 The upright see it and are glad;
    and all wickedness stops its mouth.

a Cn: Heb *sea* *b* Cn: Heb *fools*

43 Let those who are wise give heed to these
things,
and consider the steadfast love of the
LORD.

PSALM 108

Praise and Prayer for Victory

A Song. A Psalm of David.

1 My heart is steadfast, O God, my heart is
steadfast;*a*
I will sing and make melody.
Awake, my soul!*b*
2 Awake, O harp and lyre!
I will awake the dawn.
3 I will give thanks to you, O LORD, among
the peoples,
and I will sing praises to you among the
nations.
4 For your steadfast love is higher than the
heavens,
and your faithfulness reaches to the
clouds.

5 Be exalted, O God, above the heavens,
and let your glory be over all the earth.
6 Give victory with your right hand, and
answer me,
so that those whom you love may be
rescued.

7 God has promised in his sanctuary:*c*
"With exultation I will divide up
Shechem,
and portion out the Vale of Succoth.
8 Gilead is mine; Manasseh is mine;
Ephraim is my helmet;
Judah is my scepter.
9 Moab is my washbasin;
on Edom I hurl my shoe;
over Philistia I shout in triumph."

10 Who will bring me to the fortified city?
Who will lead me to Edom?
11 Have you not rejected us, O God?
You do not go out, O God, with our
armies.
12 O grant us help against the foe,
for human help is worthless.
13 With God we shall do valiantly;
it is he who will tread down our foes.

PSALM 109

Prayer for Vindication and Vengeance

To the leader. Of David. A Psalm.

1 Do not be silent, O God of my praise.

2 For wicked and deceitful mouths are
opened against me,
speaking against me with lying tongues.
3 They beset me with words of hate,
and attack me without cause.
4 In return for my love they accuse me,
even while I make prayer for them.*d*
5 So they reward me evil for good,
and hatred for my love.

6 They say,*e* "Appoint a wicked man against
him;
let an accuser stand on his right.
7 When he is tried, let him be found guilty;
let his prayer be counted as sin.
8 May his days be few;
may another seize his position.
9 May his children be orphans,
and his wife a widow.
10 May his children wander about and beg;
may they be driven out of*f* the ruins they
inhabit.
11 May the creditor seize all that he has;
may strangers plunder the fruits of his
toil.
12 May there be no one to do him a kindness,
nor anyone to pity his orphaned
children.
13 May his posterity be cut off;
may his name be blotted out in the
second generation.
14 May the iniquity of his father*g* be
remembered before the LORD,
and do not let the sin of his mother be
blotted out.
15 Let them be before the LORD continually,
and may his*h* memory be cut off from the
earth.
16 For he did not remember to show kindness,
but pursued the poor and needy
and the brokenhearted to their death.
17 He loved to curse; let curses come on him.
He did not like blessing; may it be far
from him.
18 He clothed himself with cursing as his coat,
may it soak into his body like water,
like oil into his bones.
19 May it be like a garment that he wraps
around himself,
like a belt that he wears every day."

20 May that be the reward of my accusers from
the LORD,
of those who speak evil against my life.
21 But you, O LORD my Lord,
act on my behalf for your name's sake;

a Heb Mss Gk Syr: MT lacks *my heart is steadfast* *b* Compare 57.8: Heb *also my soul* *c* Or *by his holiness* *d* Syr: Heb *I prayer* *e* Heb lacks
They say *f* Gk: Heb *and seek* *g* Cn: Heb *fathers* *h* Gk: Heb *their*

because your steadfast love is good,
        deliver me.
22 For I am poor and needy,
        and my heart is pierced within me.
23 I am gone like a shadow at evening;
        I am shaken off like a locust.
24 My knees are weak through fasting;
        my body has become gaunt.
25 I am an object of scorn to my accusers;
        when they see me, they shake their heads.

26 Help me, O LORD my God!
        Save me according to your steadfast love.
27 Let them know that this is your hand;
        you, O LORD, have done it.
28 Let them curse, but you will bless.
        Let my assailants be put to shame;[a] may
            your servant be glad.
29 May my accusers be clothed with dishonor;
        may they be wrapped in their own shame
            as in a mantle.
30 With my mouth I will give great thanks to
            the LORD;
        I will praise him in the midst of the
            throng.
31 For he stands at the right hand of the needy,
        to save them from those who would
            condemn them to death.

PSALM 110

Assurance of Victory for God's Priest-King

Of David. A Psalm.

1 The LORD says to my lord,
    "Sit at my right hand
until I make your enemies your footstool."

2 The LORD sends out from Zion
        your mighty scepter.
        Rule in the midst of your foes.
3 Your people will offer themselves willingly
        on the day you lead your forces
        on the holy mountains.[b]
    From the womb of the morning,
        like dew, your youth[c] will come to you.
4 The LORD has sworn and will not change his
            mind,
        "You are a priest forever according to the
            order of Melchizedek."[d]

5 The Lord is at your right hand;
        he will shatter kings on the day of his
            wrath.
6 He will execute judgment among the
            nations,
        filling them with corpses;
    he will shatter heads
        over the wide earth.

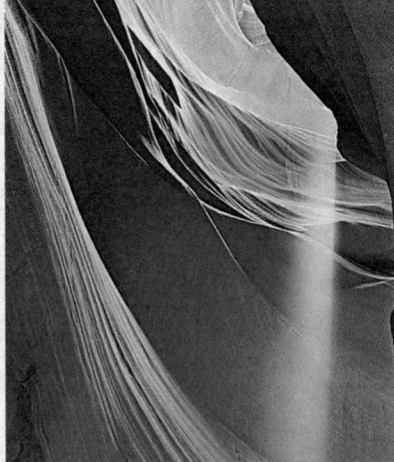

Antelope Canyon—© Vito Paratore, 18

7 He will drink from the stream by the path;
        therefore he will lift up his head.

PSALM 111

Praise for God's Wonderful Works

1 Praise the LORD!
    I will give thanks to the LORD with my
                whole heart,
        in the company of the upright, in the
            congregation.
2 Great are the works of the LORD,
        studied by all who delight in them.
3 Full of honor and majesty is his work,
        and his righteousness endures forever.
4 He has gained renown by his wonderful
            deeds;
        the LORD is gracious and merciful.
5 He provides food for those who fear him;
        he is ever mindful of his covenant.
6 He has shown his people the power of his
            works,
        in giving them the heritage of the
            nations.
7 The works of his hands are faithful and just;
        all his precepts are trustworthy.
8 They are established forever and ever,
        to be performed with faithfulness and
            uprightness.
9 He sent redemption to his people;
        he has commanded his covenant forever.
        Holy and awesome is his name.
10 The fear of the LORD is the beginning of
            wisdom;
        all those who practice it[e] have a good
            understanding.
        His praise endures forever.

---

a Gk: Heb *They have risen up and have been put to shame* b Another reading is *in holy splendor* c Cn: Heb *the dew of your youth* d Or *forever, a rightful king by my edict* e Gk Syr: Heb *them*

Be the One It would have been easy for Pandita Ramabai to give up. The sacred water near Tirupati may have looked like a peaceful escape from the pain of her existence—a place to drown out the hunger and poverty that drained her of hope. Travels across India to religious temples with her devout Hindu family only left all of them exhausted and fatigued. In 1874, when Pandita was sixteen, the family's starvation led her father to commit suicide. By her twenty-second birthday, her mother, brother, and husband were all dead. Pandita had a lot of reasons to be angry with God.

But God's love shocked her. Pandita saw Christians serving outcasts—the type of people devout Hindus shunned. Then she read of Christ's encounter with the Samaritan woman (see John 4). Through God's Word, it was as if she were meeting Jesus herself. Pandita's encounter with this extraordinary man, Jesus, grew into an extraordinary personal faith.

Using her gifts of education and empathy, Pandita became an advocate for women and the poor. Her heart was breaking for her people, and she prayed for missionaries to come to India. But God surprised her with his answer: she felt God challenge *her* to be the one. "How easy it is for anyone to wish that someone else would do a difficult thing, instead of doing it oneself," she reflected.

Child of God—© Morgan Katchuk, 14

Pandita traveled throughout India telling others about Christ. She translated the Bible into the Marathi language, started schools for girls, and created a home for widows. Pandita lived as a tireless servant for Jesus with a contagious love for Christ. She exemplified the words of 1 Corinthians 15.58:

"Be steadfast . . . always excelling in the work of the Lord, because you know that in the Lord your labor is not in vain."

PSALM 112

Blessings of the Righteous

¹ Praise the LORD!
  Happy are those who fear the LORD,
    who greatly delight in his
      commandments.
² Their descendants will be mighty in the
      land;
    the generation of the upright will be
      blessed.
³ Wealth and riches are in their houses,
    and their righteousness endures forever.
⁴ They rise in the darkness as a light for the
      upright;
    they are gracious, merciful, and
      righteous.
⁵ It is well with those who deal generously
      and lend,
    who conduct their affairs with justice.
⁶ For the righteous will never be moved;
    they will be remembered forever.
⁷ They are not afraid of evil tidings;
    their hearts are firm, secure in the LORD.
⁸ Their hearts are steady, they will not be
      afraid;
    in the end they will look in triumph on
      their foes.
⁹ They have distributed freely, they have given
      to the poor;
    their righteousness endures forever;
    their horn is exalted in honor.
¹⁰ The wicked see it and are angry;
    they gnash their teeth and melt away;
    the desire of the wicked comes to
      nothing.

PSALM 113

God the Helper of the Needy

1 Praise the LORD!
  Praise, O servants of the LORD;
    praise the name of the LORD.

2 Blessed be the name of the LORD
    from this time on and forevermore.
3 From the rising of the sun to its setting
    the name of the LORD is to be praised.
4 The LORD is high above all nations,
    and his glory above the heavens.

5 Who is like the LORD our God,
    who is seated on high,
6 who looks far down
    on the heavens and the earth?
7 He raises the poor from the dust,
    and lifts the needy from the ash heap,
8 to make them sit with princes,
    with the princes of his people.
9 He gives the barren woman a home,
    making her the joyous mother of
      children.
  Praise the LORD!

PSALM 114

God's Wonders at the Exodus

1 When Israel went out from Egypt,
    the house of Jacob from a people of
      strange language,
2 Judah became God's*a* sanctuary,
    Israel his dominion.

3 The sea looked and fled;
    Jordan turned back.
4 The mountains skipped like rams,
    the hills like lambs.

5 Why is it, O sea, that you flee?
    O Jordan, that you turn back?
6 O mountains, that you skip like rams?
    O hills, like lambs?

7 Tremble, O earth, at the presence of the
      LORD,
    at the presence of the God of Jacob,
8 who turns the rock into a pool of water,
    the flint into a spring of water.

PSALM 115

The Impotence of Idols and the Greatness of God

1 Not to us, O LORD, not to us, but to your
      name give glory,
    for the sake of your steadfast love and
      your faithfulness.

2 Why should the nations say,
    "Where is their God?"

3 Our God is in the heavens;
    he does whatever he pleases.
4 Their idols are silver and gold,
    the work of human hands.
5 They have mouths, but do not speak;
    eyes, but do not see.
6 They have ears, but do not hear;
    noses, but do not smell.
7 They have hands, but do not feel;
    feet, but do not walk;
    they make no sound in their throats.
8 Those who make them are like them;
    so are all who trust in them.

9 O Israel, trust in the LORD!
    He is their help and their shield.
10 O house of Aaron, trust in the LORD!
    He is their help and their shield.
11 You who fear the LORD, trust in the LORD!
    He is their help and their shield.

12 The LORD has been mindful of us; he will
      bless us;
    he will bless the house of Israel;
    he will bless the house of Aaron;
13 he will bless those who fear the LORD,
    both small and great.

14 May the LORD give you increase,
    both you and your children.
15 May you be blessed by the LORD,
    who made heaven and earth.

16 The heavens are the LORD's heavens,
    but the earth he has given to human
      beings.
17 The dead do not praise the LORD,
    nor do any that go down into silence.
18 But we will bless the LORD
    from this time on and forevermore.
  Praise the LORD!

PSALM 116

Thanksgiving for Recovery from Illness

1 I love the LORD, because he has heard
    my voice and my supplications.
2 Because he inclined his ear to me,
    therefore I will call on him as long as I
      live.
3 The snares of death encompassed me;
    the pangs of Sheol laid hold on me;
    I suffered distress and anguish.
4 Then I called on the name of the LORD:
    "O LORD, I pray, save my life!"

5 Gracious is the LORD, and righteous;
    our God is merciful.

a Heb *his*

⁶ The Lord protects the simple;
when I was brought low, he saved me.
⁷ Return, O my soul, to your rest,
for the Lord has dealt bountifully with
you.

⁸ For you have delivered my soul from death,
my eyes from tears,
my feet from stumbling.
⁹ I walk before the Lord
in the land of the living.
¹⁰ I kept my faith, even when I said,
"I am greatly afflicted";
¹¹ I said in my consternation,
"Everyone is a liar."

¹² What shall I return to the Lord
for all his bounty to me?
¹³ I will lift up the cup of salvation
and call on the name of the Lord,
¹⁴ I will pay my vows to the Lord
in the presence of all his people.
¹⁵ Precious in the sight of the Lord
is the death of his faithful ones.
¹⁶ O Lord, I am your servant;
I am your servant, the child of your
serving girl.
You have loosed my bonds.
¹⁷ I will offer to you a thanksgiving sacrifice
and call on the name of the Lord.
¹⁸ I will pay my vows to the Lord
in the presence of all his people,
¹⁹ in the courts of the house of the Lord,
in your midst, O Jerusalem.
Praise the Lord!

PSALM 117

Universal Call to Worship

¹ Praise the Lord, all you nations!
Extol him, all you peoples!
² For great is his steadfast love toward us,
and the faithfulness of the Lord endures
forever.
Praise the Lord!

PSALM 118

A Song of Victory

¹ O give thanks to the Lord, for he is good;
his steadfast love endures forever!

² Let Israel say,
"His steadfast love endures forever."
³ Let the house of Aaron say,
"His steadfast love endures forever."
⁴ Let those who fear the Lord say,
"His steadfast love endures forever."

⁵ Out of my distress I called on the Lord;
the Lord answered me and set me in a
broad place.
⁶ With the Lord on my side I do not fear.
What can mortals do to me?
⁷ The Lord is on my side to help me;
I shall look in triumph on those who
hate me.
⁸ It is better to take refuge in the Lord
than to put confidence in mortals.
⁹ It is better to take refuge in the Lord
than to put confidence in princes.

¹⁰ All nations surrounded me;
in the name of the Lord I cut them off!
¹¹ They surrounded me, surrounded me on
every side;
in the name of the Lord I cut them off!
¹² They surrounded me like bees;
they blazed^a like a fire of thorns;
in the name of the Lord I cut them off!
¹³ I was pushed hard,^b so that I was falling,
but the Lord helped me.
¹⁴ The Lord is my strength and my might;
he has become my salvation.
¹⁵ There are glad songs of victory in the tents
of the righteous:
"The right hand of the Lord does valiantly;
¹⁶ the right hand of the Lord is exalted;
the right hand of the Lord does
valiantly."
¹⁷ I shall not die, but I shall live,
and recount the deeds of the Lord.
¹⁸ The Lord has punished me severely,
but he did not give me over to death.

¹⁹ Open to me the gates of righteousness,
that I may enter through them
and give thanks to the Lord.

²⁰ This is the gate of the Lord;
the righteous shall enter through it.

²¹ I thank you that you have answered me
and have become my salvation.
²² The stone that the builders rejected
has become the chief cornerstone.
²³ This is the Lord's doing;
it is marvelous in our eyes.
²⁴ This is the day that the Lord has made;
let us rejoice and be glad in it.^c
²⁵ Save us, we beseech you, O Lord!
O Lord, we beseech you, give us success!
²⁶ Blessed is the one who comes in the name
of the Lord.^d
We bless you from the house of the
Lord.

a Gk: Heb were extinguished b Gk Syr Jerome: Heb You pushed me hard c Or in him d Or Blessed in the name of the Lord is the one who comes

How can I know that what I read in the Bible is true?

Some people claim to have the truth. Others claim there is no truth. Some people take every word of the Bible literally. Others say it's just a nice story on par with *Aesop's Fables* or the tooth fairy. But what does the Bible say about itself? It claims to be God's Word. Paul explained it this way: "All scripture is inspired by God and is useful for teaching" (2 Timothy 3.16). The psalmist testified, "For the word of the LORD is upright" (Psalm 33.4). But what evidence do we have outside of the Bible itself that would prove whether it is legitimate? We can turn to archaeological evidence, historical facts, and eyewitness testimony for facts that uphold the Bible's validity. Yet even then, we may be missing out on what makes the Bible different from any other book in history.

Sacred Scripture is more than just words on a page. In Jesus "the Word became flesh and lived among us" (John 1.14). The Word is alive! It is "living and active, sharper than any two-edged sword, piercing until it divides soul from spirit, joints from marrow; it is able to judge the thoughts and intentions of the heart" (Hebrews 4.12). One way to discover that sacred Scripture is true is to live it—to do what God commands; to step inside the powerful stories in Genesis; to pray the prayers in Psalms; to engage with the parables and teachings of Jesus; to explore the stories of changed lives in Acts; to take seriously the challenges in letters like Romans, Galatians, and 1 John.

So what do you think? *Is* the Bible more than just an ancient book, more than just a collection of myths and fables, more than just a historical record? *Is* it God's Word? And what's the difference between looking for proof and looking for truth? What difference has Scripture made in your life? Are you turning to other sources—friends, TV, your own opinions—to guide your life? Or are you finding your compass for life in Scripture? Can you truly say with the psalmist, "Your word is a lamp to my feet and a light to my path" (Psalm 119.105)?

The *Catechism* tells us that, "In Sacred Scripture, God speaks to man in a human way" (CCC 109). For Catholics, both Scripture and Tradition inform our faith, and we rely on Tradition to help us understand the intention of these sacred authors and the times in which they lived: "For the fact is that truth is differently presented and expressed in the various types of historical writing, in prophetical and poetical texts, and in other forms of literary expression" (CCC 110).

Find some Creative Space in the Bible and write your thoughts about what this book—the Bible—means to you. Then jot down specific questions you have about God's Word. Consider talking to a trusted friend in faith about your thoughts and questions.

Then explore more. First read Psalm 119 (yes, all 176 verses) and think about why you love God's Word. Then explore Isaiah 45.19; 55.10–11; Matthew 24.35; John 17.17; and 2 Timothy 3.16–17.

---

27 The LORD is God,
  and he has given us light.
  Bind the festal procession with branches,
  up to the horns of the altar.[a]

28 You are my God, and I will give thanks to you;
  you are my God, I will extol you.

29 O give thanks to the LORD, for he is good,
  for his steadfast love endures forever.

a Meaning of Heb uncertain

PSALM 119

The Glories of God's Law

1 Happy are those whose way is blameless,
  who walk in the law of the LORD.
2 Happy are those who keep his decrees,
  who seek him with their whole heart,
3 who also do no wrong,
  but walk in his ways.

⁴ You have commanded your precepts
   to be kept diligently.
⁵ O that my ways may be steadfast
   in keeping your statutes!
⁶ Then I shall not be put to shame,
   having my eyes fixed on all your
      commandments.
⁷ I will praise you with an upright heart,
   when I learn your righteous ordinances.
⁸ I will observe your statutes;
   do not utterly forsake me.

⁹ How can young people keep their way pure?
   By guarding it according to your word.
¹⁰ With my whole heart I seek you;
   do not let me stray from your
      commandments.
¹¹ I treasure your word in my heart,
   so that I may not sin against you.
¹² Blessed are you, O LORD;
   teach me your statutes.
¹³ With my lips I declare
   all the ordinances of your mouth.
¹⁴ I delight in the way of your decrees
   as much as in all riches.
¹⁵ I will meditate on your precepts,
   and fix my eyes on your ways.
¹⁶ I will delight in your statutes;
   I will not forget your word.

¹⁷ Deal bountifully with your servant,
   so that I may live and observe your word.
¹⁸ Open my eyes, so that I may behold
   wondrous things out of your law.
¹⁹ I live as an alien in the land;
   do not hide your commandments
      from me.
²⁰ My soul is consumed with longing
   for your ordinances at all times.
²¹ You rebuke the insolent, accursed ones,
   who wander from your commandments;
²² take away from me their scorn and
      contempt,
   for I have kept your decrees.
²³ Even though princes sit plotting against
      me,
   your servant will meditate on your
      statutes.
²⁴ Your decrees are my delight,
   they are my counselors.

²⁵ My soul clings to the dust;
   revive me according to your word.
²⁶ When I told of my ways, you answered me;
   teach me your statutes.
²⁷ Make me understand the way of your
      precepts,
   and I will meditate on your wondrous
      works.
²⁸ My soul melts away for sorrow;

strengthen me according to your word.
²⁹ Put false ways far from me;
   and graciously teach me your law.
³⁰ I have chosen the way of faithfulness;
   I set your ordinances before me.
³¹ I cling to your decrees, O LORD;
   let me not be put to shame.
³² I run the way of your commandments,
   for you enlarge my understanding.

³³ Teach me, O LORD, the way of your statutes,
   and I will observe it to the end.
³⁴ Give me understanding, that I may keep
      your law
   and observe it with my whole heart.
³⁵ Lead me in the path of your
      commandments,
   for I delight in it.
³⁶ Turn my heart to your decrees,
   and not to selfish gain.
³⁷ Turn my eyes from looking at vanities;
   give me life in your ways.
³⁸ Confirm to your servant your promise,
   which is for those who fear you.
³⁹ Turn away the disgrace that I dread,
   for your ordinances are good.
⁴⁰ See, I have longed for your precepts;
   in your righteousness give me life.

⁴¹ Let your steadfast love come to me, O LORD,
   your salvation according to your
      promise.
⁴² Then I shall have an answer for those who
      taunt me,
   for I trust in your word.
⁴³ Do not take the word of truth utterly out of
      my mouth,
   for my hope is in your ordinances.
⁴⁴ I will keep your law continually,
   forever and ever.
⁴⁵ I shall walk at liberty,
   for I have sought your precepts.
⁴⁶ I will also speak of your decrees before
      kings,
   and shall not be put to shame;
⁴⁷ I find my delight in your commandments,
   because I love them.
⁴⁸ I revere your commandments, which I love,
   and I will meditate on your statutes.

⁴⁹ Remember your word to your servant,
   in which you have made me hope.
⁵⁰ This is my comfort in my distress,
   that your promise gives me life.
⁵¹ The arrogant utterly deride me,
   but I do not turn away from your law.
⁵² When I think of your ordinances from of
      old,
   I take comfort, O LORD.

53 Hot indignation seizes me because of the
    wicked,
    those who forsake your law.
54 Your statutes have been my songs
    wherever I make my home.
55 I remember your name in the night,
    O Lord,
    and keep your law.
56 This blessing has fallen to me,
    for I have kept your precepts.

57 The Lord is my portion;
    I promise to keep your words.
58 I implore your favor with all my heart;
    be gracious to me according to your
    promise.
59 When I think of your ways,
    I turn my feet to your decrees;
60 I hurry and do not delay
    to keep your commandments.
61 Though the cords of the wicked
    ensnare me,
    I do not forget your law.

62 At midnight I rise to praise you,
    because of your righteous ordinances.
63 I am a companion of all who fear you,
    of those who keep your precepts.
64 The earth, O Lord, is full of your steadfast
    love;
    teach me your statutes.

65 You have dealt well with your servant,
    O Lord, according to your word.
66 Teach me good judgment and knowledge,
    for I believe in your commandments.
67 Before I was humbled I went astray,
    but now I keep your word.
68 You are good and do good;
    teach me your statutes.
69 The arrogant smear me with lies,
    but with my whole heart I keep your
    precepts.
70 Their hearts are fat and gross,
    but I delight in your law.
71 It is good for me that I was humbled,
    so that I might learn your statutes.

72 The law of your mouth is better to me
than thousands of gold and silver pieces.

73 Your hands have made and fashioned me;
give me understanding that I may learn
your commandments.
74 Those who fear you shall see me and
rejoice,
because I have hoped in your word.
75 I know, O LORD, that your judgments are
right,
and that in faithfulness you have
humbled me.
76 Let your steadfast love become my comfort
according to your promise to your
servant.
77 Let your mercy come to me, that I may live;
for your law is my delight.
78 Let the arrogant be put to shame,
because they have subverted me with
guile;
as for me, I will meditate on your
precepts.
79 Let those who fear you turn to me,
so that they may know your decrees.
80 May my heart be blameless in your statutes,
so that I may not be put to shame.

81 My soul languishes for your salvation;
I hope in your word.
82 My eyes fail with watching for your
promise;
I ask, "When will you comfort me?"
83 For I have become like a wineskin in the
smoke,
yet I have not forgotten your statutes.
84 How long must your servant endure?
When will you judge those who
persecute me?
85 The arrogant have dug pitfalls for me;
they flout your law.
86 All your commandments are enduring;
I am persecuted without cause; help me!
87 They have almost made an end of me on
earth;
but I have not forsaken your precepts.
88 In your steadfast love spare my life,
so that I may keep the decrees of your
mouth.

89 The LORD exists forever;
your word is firmly fixed in heaven.
90 Your faithfulness endures to all
generations;
you have established the earth, and it
stands fast.
91 By your appointment they stand today,
for all things are your servants.
92 If your law had not been my delight,
I would have perished in my misery.

93 I will never forget your precepts,
for by them you have given me life.
94 I am yours; save me,
for I have sought your precepts.
95 The wicked lie in wait to destroy me,
but I consider your decrees.
96 I have seen a limit to all perfection,
but your commandment is exceedingly
broad.

97 Oh, how I love your law!
It is my meditation all day long.
98 Your commandment makes me wiser than
my enemies,
for it is always with me.
99 I have more understanding than all my
teachers,
for your decrees are my meditation.
100 I understand more than the aged,
for I keep your precepts.
101 I hold back my feet from every evil way,
in order to keep your word.
102 I do not turn away from your ordinances,
for you have taught me.
103 How sweet are your words to my taste,
sweeter than honey to my mouth!
104 Through your precepts I get understanding;
therefore I hate every false way.

105 Your word is a lamp to my feet
and a light to my path.
106 I have sworn an oath and confirmed it,
to observe your righteous ordinances.
107 I am severely afflicted;
give me life, O LORD, according to your
word.
108 Accept my offerings of praise, O LORD,
and teach me your ordinances.
109 I hold my life in my hand continually,
but I do not forget your law.
110 The wicked have laid a snare for me,
but I do not stray from your precepts.
111 Your decrees are my heritage forever;
they are the joy of my heart.
112 I incline my heart to perform your statutes
forever, to the end.

113 I hate the double-minded,
but I love your law.
114 You are my hiding place and my shield;
I hope in your word.
115 Go away from me, you evildoers,
that I may keep the commandments of
my God.
116 Uphold me according to your promise, that
I may live,
and let me not be put to shame in my
hope.
117 Hold me up, that I may be safe

and have regard for your statutes
continually.
118 You spurn all who go astray from your
statutes;
for their cunning is in vain.
119 All the wicked of the earth you count as
dross;
therefore I love your decrees.
120 My flesh trembles for fear of you,
and I am afraid of your judgments.

121 I have done what is just and right;
do not leave me to my oppressors.
122 Guarantee your servant's well-being;
do not let the godless oppress me.
123 My eyes fail from watching for your
salvation,
and for the fulfillment of your righteous
promise.
124 Deal with your servant according to your
steadfast love,
and teach me your statutes.
125 I am your servant; give me understanding,
so that I may know your decrees.
126 It is time for the Lord to act,
for your law has been broken.
127 Truly I love your commandments
more than gold, more than fine gold.
128 Truly I direct my steps by all your precepts;*a*
I hate every false way.

129 Your decrees are wonderful;
therefore my soul keeps them.
130 The unfolding of your words gives light;
it imparts understanding to the simple.
131 With open mouth I pant,
because I long for your commandments.
132 Turn to me and be gracious to me,
as is your custom toward those who love
your name.
133 Keep my steps steady according to your
promise,
and never let iniquity have dominion
over me.
134 Redeem me from human oppression,
that I may keep your precepts.
135 Make your face shine upon your servant,
and teach me your statutes.
136 My eyes shed streams of tears
because your law is not kept.

137 You are righteous, O Lord,
and your judgments are right.
138 You have appointed your decrees in
righteousness
and in all faithfulness.
139 My zeal consumes me
because my foes forget your words.
140 Your promise is well tried,

and your servant loves it.
141 I am small and despised,
yet I do not forget your precepts.
142 Your righteousness is an everlasting
righteousness,
and your law is the truth.
143 Trouble and anguish have come upon me,
but your commandments are my delight.
144 Your decrees are righteous forever;
give me understanding that I may live.

145 With my whole heart I cry; answer me,
O Lord.
I will keep your statutes.
146 I cry to you; save me,
that I may observe your decrees.
147 I rise before dawn and cry for help;
I put my hope in your words.
148 My eyes are awake before each watch of the
night,
that I may meditate on your promise.
149 In your steadfast love hear my voice;
O Lord, in your justice preserve my life.
150 Those who persecute me with evil purpose
draw near;
they are far from your law.
151 Yet you are near, O Lord,
and all your commandments are true.
152 Long ago I learned from your decrees
that you have established them forever.

153 Look on my misery and rescue me,
for I do not forget your law.
154 Plead my cause and redeem me;
give me life according to your promise.
155 Salvation is far from the wicked,
for they do not seek your statutes.
156 Great is your mercy, O Lord;
give me life according to your justice.
157 Many are my persecutors and my
adversaries,
yet I do not swerve from your decrees.
158 I look at the faithless with disgust,
because they do not keep your
commands.
159 Consider how I love your precepts;
preserve my life according to your
steadfast love.
160 The sum of your word is truth;
and every one of your righteous
ordinances endures forever.

161 Princes persecute me without cause,
but my heart stands in awe of your words.
162 I rejoice at your word
like one who finds great spoil.
163 I hate and abhor falsehood,
but I love your law.
164 Seven times a day I praise you

a Gk Jerome: Meaning of Heb uncertain

for your righteous ordinances.
165 Great peace have those who love your law;
nothing can make them stumble.
166 I hope for your salvation, O LORD,
and I fulfill your commandments.
167 My soul keeps your decrees;
I love them exceedingly.
168 I keep your precepts and decrees,
for all my ways are before you.

169 Let my cry come before you, O LORD;
give me understanding according to your
word.
170 Let my supplication come before you;
deliver me according to your promise.
171 My lips will pour forth praise,
because you teach me your statutes.
172 My tongue will sing of your promise,
for all your commandments are right.
173 Let your hand be ready to help me,
for I have chosen your precepts.
174 I long for your salvation, O LORD,
and your law is my delight.
175 Let me live that I may praise you,
and let your ordinances help me.
176 I have gone astray like a lost sheep; seek out
your servant,
for I do not forget your commandments.

PSALM 120

Prayer for Deliverance from Slanderers

A Song of Ascents.

1 In my distress I cry to the LORD,
that he may answer me:
2 "Deliver me, O LORD,
from lying lips,
from a deceitful tongue."

3 What shall be given to you?
And what more shall be done to you,
you deceitful tongue?
4 A warrior's sharp arrows,
with glowing coals of the broom tree!

5 Woe is me, that I am an alien in Meshech,
that I must live among the tents of Kedar.
6 Too long have I had my dwelling
among those who hate peace.
7 I am for peace;
but when I speak,
they are for war.

PSALM 121

Assurance of God's Protection

A Song of Ascents.

1 I lift up my eyes to the hills—
from where will my help come?
2 My help comes from the LORD,
who made heaven and earth.

3 He will not let your foot be moved;
he who keeps you will not slumber.
4 He who keeps Israel
will neither slumber nor sleep.

5 The LORD is your keeper;
the LORD is your shade at your right
hand.
6 The sun shall not strike you by day,
nor the moon by night.

7 The LORD will keep you from all evil;
he will keep your life.
8 The LORD will keep
your going out and your coming in
from this time on and forevermore.

PSALM 122

Song of Praise and Prayer for Jerusalem

A Song of Ascents. Of David.

1 I was glad when they said to me,
"Let us go to the house of the LORD!"
2 Our feet are standing
within your gates, O Jerusalem.

3 Jerusalem—built as a city
that is bound firmly together.
4 To it the tribes go up,
the tribes of the LORD,
as was decreed for Israel,
to give thanks to the name of the LORD.
5 For there the thrones for judgment were
set up,
the thrones of the house of David.

6 Pray for the peace of Jerusalem:
"May they prosper who love you.
7 Peace be within your walls,
and security within your towers."
8 For the sake of my relatives and friends
I will say, "Peace be within you."
9 For the sake of the house of the LORD our
God,
I will seek your good.

PSALM 123

Supplication for Mercy

A Song of Ascents.

1 To you I lift up my eyes,
O you who are enthroned in the heavens!
2 As the eyes of servants
look to the hand of their master,
as the eyes of a maid
to the hand of her mistress,
so our eyes look to the LORD our God,
until he has mercy upon us.

3 Have mercy upon us, O LORD, have mercy
upon us,

for we have had more than enough of
contempt.
4 Our soul has had more than its fill
of the scorn of those who are at ease,
of the contempt of the proud.

PSALM 124

Thanksgiving for Israel's Deliverance

A Song of Ascents. Of David.

1 If it had not been the LORD who was on our
side
—let Israel now say—
2 if it had not been the LORD who was on our
side,
when our enemies attacked us,
3 then they would have swallowed us up
alive,
when their anger was kindled against us;
4 then the flood would have swept us away,
the torrent would have gone over us;
5 then over us would have gone
the raging waters.

6 Blessed be the LORD,
who has not given us
as prey to their teeth.
7 We have escaped like a bird
from the snare of the fowlers;
the snare is broken,
and we have escaped.

8 Our help is in the name of the LORD,
who made heaven and earth.

PSALM 125

The Security of God's People

A Song of Ascents.

1 Those who trust in the LORD are like Mount
Zion,
which cannot be moved, but abides
forever.
2 As the mountains surround Jerusalem,
so the LORD surrounds his people,
from this time on and forevermore.
3 For the scepter of wickedness shall not rest
on the land allotted to the righteous,
so that the righteous might not stretch out
their hands to do wrong.
4 Do good, O LORD, to those who are good,
and to those who are upright in their
hearts.
5 But those who turn aside to their own
crooked ways
the LORD will lead away with evildoers.
Peace be upon Israel!

"Three things are necessary for the
salvation of man: to know what he
ought to believe; to know what he
ought to desire; and to know what
he ought to do."

—St. Thomas Aquinas

PSALM 126

A Harvest of Joy

A Song of Ascents.

1 When the LORD restored the fortunes of
Zion,*a*
we were like those who dream.
2 Then our mouth was filled with laughter,
and our tongue with shouts of joy;
then it was said among the nations,
"The LORD has done great things for
them."
3 The LORD has done great things for us,
and we rejoiced.

4 Restore our fortunes, O LORD,
like the watercourses in the Negeb.
5 May those who sow in tears
reap with shouts of joy.
6 Those who go out weeping,
bearing the seed for sowing,
shall come home with shouts of joy,
carrying their sheaves.

PSALM 127

God's Blessings in the Home

A Song of Ascents. Of Solomon.

1 Unless the LORD builds the house,
those who build it labor in vain.
Unless the LORD guards the city,
the guard keeps watch in vain.
2 It is in vain that you rise up early
and go late to rest,
eating the bread of anxious toil;
for he gives sleep to his beloved.*b*

3 Sons are indeed a heritage from the LORD,
the fruit of the womb a reward.
4 Like arrows in the hand of a warrior
are the sons of one's youth.
5 Happy is the man who has
his quiver full of them.
He shall not be put to shame
when he speaks with his enemies in the
gate.

a Or *brought back those who returned to Zion* *b* Or *for he provides for his beloved during sleep*

PSALM 128

The Happy Home of the Faithful

A Song of Ascents.

1 Happy is everyone who fears the LORD,
   who walks in his ways.
2 You shall eat the fruit of the labor of your
      hands;
   you shall be happy, and it shall go well
      with you.

3 Your wife will be like a fruitful vine
      within your house;
   your children will be like olive shoots
      around your table.
4 Thus shall the man be blessed
   who fears the LORD.

5 The LORD bless you from Zion.
   May you see the prosperity of Jerusalem
      all the days of your life.
6 May you see your children's children.
   Peace be upon Israel!

PSALM 129

Prayer for the Downfall of Israel's Enemies

A Song of Ascents.

1 "Often have they attacked me from my
      youth"
   —let Israel now say—
2 "often have they attacked me from my
      youth,
   yet they have not prevailed against me.
3 The plowers plowed on my back;
   they made their furrows long."
4 The LORD is righteous;
   he has cut the cords of the wicked.
5 May all who hate Zion
   be put to shame and turned backward.
6 Let them be like the grass on the housetops
   that withers before it grows up,

"I will trust Him. Whatever, wherever
I am, I can never be thrown away. If I
am in sickness, my sickness may serve
Him; in perplexity, my perplexity may
serve Him; if I am in sorrow, my sorrow may serve Him. My sickness, or
perplexity, or sorrow may be necessary
causes of some great end, which is quite
beyond us. He does nothing in vain."

**—Bl. Cardinal John Henry Newman,
nineteenth-century British cardinal-
deacon of the Catholic Church**

7 with which reapers do not fill their hands
   or binders of sheaves their arms,
8 while those who pass by do not say,
   "The blessing of the LORD be upon you!
   We bless you in the name of the LORD!"

PSALM 130

Waiting for Divine Redemption

A Song of Ascents.

1 Out of the depths I cry to you, O LORD.
2   Lord, hear my voice!
   Let your ears be attentive
      to the voice of my supplications!

3 If you, O LORD, should mark iniquities,
   Lord, who could stand?
4 But there is forgiveness with you,
   so that you may be revered.

5 I wait for the LORD, my soul waits,
   and in his word I hope;
6 my soul waits for the Lord
   more than those who watch for the
      morning,
   more than those who watch for the
      morning.

7 O Israel, hope in the LORD!
   For with the LORD there is steadfast love,
   and with him is great power to redeem.
8 It is he who will redeem Israel
   from all its iniquities.

PSALM 131

Song of Quiet Trust

A Song of Ascents. Of David.

1 O LORD, my heart is not lifted up,
   my eyes are not raised too high;
   I do not occupy myself with things
      too great and too marvelous for me.
2 But I have calmed and quieted my soul,
   like a weaned child with its mother;
   my soul is like the weaned child that is
      with me.*a*

3 O Israel, hope in the LORD
   from this time on and forevermore.

PSALM 132

The Eternal Dwelling of God in Zion

A Song of Ascents.

1 O LORD, remember in David's favor
   all the hardships he endured;
2 how he swore to the LORD
   and vowed to the Mighty One of Jacob,
3 "I will not enter my house

a Or *my soul within me is like a weaned child*

or get into my bed;
⁴ I will not give sleep to my eyes
    or slumber to my eyelids,
⁵ until I find a place for the LORD,
    a dwelling place for the Mighty One of
        Jacob."

⁶ We heard of it in Ephrathah;
    we found it in the fields of Jaar.
⁷ "Let us go to his dwelling place;
    let us worship at his footstool."

⁸ Rise up, O LORD, and go to your resting
        place,
    you and the ark of your might.
⁹ Let your priests be clothed with
        righteousness,
    and let your faithful shout for joy.
¹⁰ For your servant David's sake
    do not turn away the face of your
        anointed one.

¹¹ The LORD swore to David a sure oath
    from which he will not turn back:
    "One of the sons of your body
    I will set on your throne.
¹² If your sons keep my covenant
    and my decrees that I shall teach them,
    their sons also, forevermore,
    shall sit on your throne."

¹³ For the LORD has chosen Zion;
    he has desired it for his habitation:
¹⁴ "This is my resting place forever;
    here I will reside, for I have desired it.
¹⁵ I will abundantly bless its provisions;
    I will satisfy its poor with bread.
¹⁶ Its priests I will clothe with salvation,
    and its faithful will shout for joy.
¹⁷ There I will cause a horn to sprout up for
        David;
    I have prepared a lamp for my anointed
        one.
¹⁸ His enemies I will clothe with disgrace,
    but on him, his crown will gleam."

PSALM 133

The Blessedness of Unity

A Song of Ascents.

¹ How very good and pleasant it is
    when kindred live together in unity!
² It is like the precious oil on the head,
    running down upon the beard,
    on the beard of Aaron,
        running down over the collar of his
            robes.
³ It is like the dew of Hermon,
    which falls on the mountains of Zion.
For there the LORD ordained his blessing,
    life forevermore.

PSALM 134

Praise in the Night

A Song of Ascents.

¹ Come, bless the LORD, all you servants of
        the LORD,
    who stand by night in the house of the
        LORD!
² Lift up your hands to the holy place,
    and bless the LORD.

³ May the LORD, maker of heaven and earth,
    bless you from Zion.

PSALM 135

Praise for God's Goodness and Might

¹ Praise the LORD!
    Praise the name of the LORD;
    give praise, O servants of the LORD,
² you that stand in the house of the LORD,
    in the courts of the house of our God.
³ Praise the LORD, for the LORD is good;
    sing to his name, for he is gracious.
⁴ For the LORD has chosen Jacob for himself,
    Israel as his own possession.

⁵ For I know that the LORD is great;
    our Lord is above all gods.
⁶ Whatever the LORD pleases he does,
    in heaven and on earth,
    in the seas and all deeps.
⁷ He it is who makes the clouds rise at the
        end of the earth;
    he makes lightnings for the rain
    and brings out the wind from his
        storehouses.

⁸ He it was who struck down the firstborn of
        Egypt,
    both human beings and animals;
⁹ he sent signs and wonders
    into your midst, O Egypt,
    against Pharaoh and all his servants.
¹⁰ He struck down many nations
    and killed mighty kings—
¹¹ Sihon, king of the Amorites,
    and Og, king of Bashan,
    and all the kingdoms of Canaan—
¹² and gave their land as a heritage,
    a heritage to his people Israel.

¹³ Your name, O LORD, endures forever,
    your renown, O LORD, throughout all
        ages.
¹⁴ For the LORD will vindicate his people,
    and have compassion on his servants.

¹⁵ The idols of the nations are silver and gold,
    the work of human hands.
¹⁶ They have mouths, but they do not speak;

A LABOR OF LOVE

How hard can it be? My great-aunt had glasses as thick as Mr. Magoo's and twisted knuckles that looked like giant grapes. She knitted with ease. If she could do it . . .

My attempt was a tangled, knotted mess. Knitting is a labor of love—slow, meticulous, careful, precise, intentional. Each color and pattern is carefully planned, and every finished product is completely unique. **Psalm 139.13** says that God *knit* us together as we grew in our mom's belly. He knows every inch of us. He spent a great deal of time scrutinizing our every detail. He knows me—and you—through and through.

This is one of my favorite chapters in the Bible. It starts by explaining that God knows every single thing (verses 1–6). And there is nowhere that God isn't (verses 7–12). Weirdly, this greatness doesn't make him standoffish; it translates into a transcendent, enormous love for each one of us in a startling, personal way.

Try this. Make something—a gourmet meal, a painting, a song, a wooden stool. Put a great deal of time and heart into it. When you're done, share it with a friend. Use your creation to start a conversation about the loving care God put into making each one of us.

GOD IS PASSIONATE MY INTERESTS

they have eyes, but they do not see;
¹⁷ they have ears, but they do not hear,
and there is no breath in their mouths.
¹⁸ Those who make them
and all who trust them
shall become like them.

¹⁹ O house of Israel, bless the LORD!
O house of Aaron, bless the LORD!
²⁰ O house of Levi, bless the LORD!
You that fear the LORD, bless the LORD!
²¹ Blessed be the LORD from Zion,
he who resides in Jerusalem.
Praise the LORD!

PSALM 136

God's Work in Creation and in History

¹ O give thanks to the LORD, for he is good,
for his steadfast love endures forever.
² O give thanks to the God of gods,
for his steadfast love endures forever.

³ O give thanks to the Lord of lords,
for his steadfast love endures forever;

⁴ who alone does great wonders,
for his steadfast love endures forever;
⁵ who by understanding made the heavens,
for his steadfast love endures forever;
⁶ who spread out the earth on the waters,
for his steadfast love endures forever;
⁷ who made the great lights,
for his steadfast love endures forever;
⁸ the sun to rule over the day,
for his steadfast love endures forever;
⁹ the moon and stars to rule over the night,
for his steadfast love endures forever;

¹⁰ who struck Egypt through their firstborn,
for his steadfast love endures forever;
¹¹ and brought Israel out from among them,
for his steadfast love endures forever;
¹² with a strong hand and an outstretched arm,
for his steadfast love endures forever;
¹³ who divided the Red Sea[a] in two,
for his steadfast love endures forever;
¹⁴ and made Israel pass through the midst of it,
for his steadfast love endures forever;
¹⁵ but overthrew Pharaoh and his army in the
Red Sea,[a]
for his steadfast love endures forever;
¹⁶ who led his people through the wilderness,
for his steadfast love endures forever;
¹⁷ who struck down great kings,
for his steadfast love endures forever;
¹⁸ and killed famous kings,
for his steadfast love endures forever;
¹⁹ Sihon, king of the Amorites,
for his steadfast love endures forever;
²⁰ and Og, king of Bashan,
for his steadfast love endures forever;
²¹ and gave their land as a heritage,
for his steadfast love endures forever;
²² a heritage to his servant Israel,
for his steadfast love endures forever.

²³ It is he who remembered us in our low
estate,
for his steadfast love endures forever;
²⁴ and rescued us from our foes,
for his steadfast love endures forever;
²⁵ who gives food to all flesh,
for his steadfast love endures forever.

²⁶ O give thanks to the God of heaven,
for his steadfast love endures forever.

PSALM 137

Lament over the Destruction of Jerusalem

¹ By the rivers of Babylon—
there we sat down and there we wept

a Or *Sea of Reeds*

when we remembered Zion.
2 On the willows^a there
we hung up our harps.
3 For there our captors
asked us for songs,
and our tormentors asked for mirth, saying,
"Sing us one of the songs of Zion!"

4 How could we sing the LORD's song
in a foreign land?
5 If I forget you, O Jerusalem,
let my right hand wither!
6 Let my tongue cling to the roof of my
mouth,
if I do not remember you,
if I do not set Jerusalem
above my highest joy.

7 Remember, O LORD, against the Edomites
the day of Jerusalem's fall,
how they said, "Tear it down! Tear it down!
Down to its foundations!"
8 O daughter Babylon, you devastator!^b
Happy shall they be who pay you back
what you have done to us!
9 Happy shall they be who take your little
ones
and dash them against the rock!

PSALM 138

Thanksgiving and Praise

Of David.

1 I give you thanks, O LORD, with my whole
heart;
before the gods I sing your praise;
2 I bow down toward your holy temple
and give thanks to your name for your
steadfast love and your faithfulness;
for you have exalted your name and your
word
above everything.^c
3 On the day I called, you answered me,
you increased my strength of soul.^d

4 All the kings of the earth shall praise you,
O LORD,
for they have heard the words of your
mouth.
5 They shall sing of the ways of the LORD,
for great is the glory of the LORD.
6 For though the LORD is high, he regards the
lowly;
but the haughty he perceives from far
away.

7 Though I walk in the midst of trouble,
you preserve me against the wrath of my
enemies;

you stretch out your hand,
and your right hand delivers me.
8 The LORD will fulfill his purpose for me;
your steadfast love, O LORD, endures
forever.
Do not forsake the work of your hands.

PSALM 139

The Inescapable God

To the leader. Of David. A Psalm.

1 O LORD, you have searched me and
known me.
2 You know when I sit down and when I
rise up;
you discern my thoughts from far away.
3 You search out my path and my lying down,
and are acquainted with all my ways.
4 Even before a word is on my tongue,
O LORD, you know it completely.
5 You hem me in, behind and before,
and lay your hand upon me.
6 Such knowledge is too wonderful for me;
it is so high that I cannot attain it.

7 Where can I go from your spirit?
Or where can I flee from your presence?
8 If I ascend to heaven, you are there;
if I make my bed in Sheol, you are there.
9 If I take the wings of the morning
and settle at the farthest limits of the sea,
10 even there your hand shall lead me,
and your right hand shall hold me fast.
11 If I say, "Surely the darkness shall cover me,
and the light around me become night,"
12 even the darkness is not dark to you;
the night is as bright as the day,
for darkness is as light to you.

13 For it was you who formed my inward parts;
you knit me together in my mother's
womb.
14 I praise you, for I am fearfully and
wonderfully made.
Wonderful are your works;
that I know very well.
15 My frame was not hidden from you,
when I was being made in secret,
intricately woven in the depths of the
earth.
16 Your eyes beheld my unformed substance.
In your book were written
all the days that were formed for me,
when none of them as yet existed.
17 How weighty to me are your thoughts,
O God!
How vast is the sum of them!

---

a Or poplars b Or you who are devastated c Cn: Heb you have exalted your word above all your name d Syr Compare Gk Tg: Heb you made me arrogant in my soul with strength

The Struggle—© Jennifer Lawrence, 19

18 I try to count them—they are more than
the sand;
I come to the end[a]—I am still with you.

19 O that you would kill the wicked, O God,
and that the bloodthirsty would depart
from me—
20 those who speak of you maliciously,
and lift themselves up against you for
evil![b]
21 Do I not hate those who hate you, O LORD?
And do I not loathe those who rise up
against you?
22 I hate them with perfect hatred;
I count them my enemies.
23 Search me, O God, and know my heart;
test me and know my thoughts.
24 See if there is any wicked[c] way in me,
and lead me in the way everlasting.[d]

PSALM 140

Prayer for Deliverance from Enemies

To the leader. A Psalm of David.

1 Deliver me, O LORD, from evildoers;
protect me from those who are violent,
2 who plan evil things in their minds
and stir up wars continually.
3 They make their tongue sharp as a snake's,
and under their lips is the venom of
vipers. *Selah*
4 Guard me, O LORD, from the hands of the
wicked;
protect me from the violent
who have planned my downfall.
5 The arrogant have hidden a trap for me,

and with cords they have spread a net,[e]
along the road they have set snares
for me. *Selah*
6 I say to the LORD, "You are my God;
give ear, O LORD, to the voice of my
supplications."
7 O LORD, my Lord, my strong deliverer,
you have covered my head in the day of
battle.
8 Do not grant, O LORD, the desires of the
wicked;
do not further their evil plot.[f] *Selah*
9 Those who surround me lift up their
heads;[g]
let the mischief of their lips overwhelm
them!
10 Let burning coals fall on them!
Let them be flung into pits, no more to
rise!
11 Do not let the slanderer be established in
the land;
let evil speedily hunt down the violent!
12 I know that the LORD maintains the cause
of the needy,
and executes justice for the poor.
13 Surely the righteous shall give thanks to
your name;
the upright shall live in your presence.

PSALM 141

Prayer for Preservation from Evil

A Psalm of David.

1 I call upon you, O LORD; come quickly
to me;
give ear to my voice when I call to you.
2 Let my prayer be counted as incense before
you,
and the lifting up of my hands as an
evening sacrifice.
3 Set a guard over my mouth, O LORD;
keep watch over the door of my lips.
4 Do not turn my heart to any evil,
to busy myself with wicked deeds
in company with those who work iniquity;
do not let me eat of their delicacies.
5 Let the righteous strike me;
let the faithful correct me.
Never let the oil of the wicked anoint my
head,[h]
for my prayer is continually[i] against their
wicked deeds.

---

a Or I awake b Cn: Meaning of Heb uncertain c Heb hurtful d Or the ancient way. Compare Jer 6.16 e Or they have spread cords as a net
f Heb adds they are exalted g Cn Compare Gk: Heb those who surround me are uplifted in head; Heb divides verses 8 and 9 differently
h Gk: Meaning of Heb uncertain i Cn: Heb for continually and my prayer

6 When they are given over to those who shall condemn them,
then they shall learn that my words were pleasant.
7 Like a rock that one breaks apart and shatters on the land,
so shall their bones be strewn at the mouth of Sheol.[a]

8 But my eyes are turned toward you, O GOD, my Lord;
in you I seek refuge; do not leave me defenseless.
9 Keep me from the trap that they have laid for me,
and from the snares of evildoers.
10 Let the wicked fall into their own nets,
while I alone escape.

PSALM 142

Prayer for Deliverance from Persecutors

A Maskil of David. When he was in the cave. A Prayer.

1 With my voice I cry to the LORD;
with my voice I make supplication to the LORD.
2 I pour out my complaint before him;
I tell my trouble before him.
3 When my spirit is faint,
you know my way.

In the path where I walk
they have hidden a trap for me.
4 Look on my right hand and see—
there is no one who takes notice of me;
no refuge remains to me;
no one cares for me.

5 I cry to you, O LORD;
I say, "You are my refuge,
my portion in the land of the living."
6 Give heed to my cry,
for I am brought very low.

Save me from my persecutors,
for they are too strong for me.
7 Bring me out of prison,
so that I may give thanks to your name.
The righteous will surround me,
for you will deal bountifully with me.

PSALM 143

Prayer for Deliverance from Enemies

A Psalm of David.

1 Hear my prayer, O LORD;
give ear to my supplications in your faithfulness;
answer me in your righteousness.

2 Do not enter into judgment with your servant,
for no one living is righteous before you.
3 For the enemy has pursued me,
crushing my life to the ground,
making me sit in darkness like those long dead.
4 Therefore my spirit faints within me;
my heart within me is appalled.
5 I remember the days of old,
I think about all your deeds,
I meditate on the works of your hands.
6 I stretch out my hands to you;
my soul thirsts for you like a parched land.   *Selah*

7 Answer me quickly, O LORD;
my spirit fails.
Do not hide your face from me,
or I shall be like those who go down to the Pit.
8 Let me hear of your steadfast love in the morning,
for in you I put my trust.
Teach me the way I should go,
for to you I lift up my soul.

9 Save me, O LORD, from my enemies;
I have fled to you for refuge.[b]
10 Teach me to do your will,
for you are my God.
Let your good spirit lead me
on a level path.

11 For your name's sake, O LORD, preserve my life.
In your righteousness bring me out of trouble.
12 In your steadfast love cut off my enemies,
and destroy all my adversaries,
for I am your servant.

PSALM 144

Prayer for National Deliverance and Security

Of David.

1 Blessed be the LORD, my rock,
who trains my hands for war, and my fingers for battle;
2 my rock[c] and my fortress,
my stronghold and my deliverer,
my shield, in whom I take refuge,
who subdues the peoples[d] under me.

3 O LORD, what are human beings that you regard them,
or mortals that you think of them?

---

a Meaning of Heb of verses 5–7 is uncertain b One Heb Ms Gk: MT *to you I have hidden* c With 18.2 and 2 Sam 22.2: Heb *my steadfast love* d Heb Mss Syr Aquila Jerome: MT *my people*

4 They are like a breath;
   their days are like a passing shadow.

5 Bow your heavens, O Lord, and come
      down;
   touch the mountains so that they smoke.
6 Make the lightning flash and scatter them;
   send out your arrows and rout them.
7 Stretch out your hand from on high;
   set me free and rescue me from the
      mighty waters,
   from the hand of aliens,
8 whose mouths speak lies,
   and whose right hands are false.

9 I will sing a new song to you, O God;
   upon a ten-stringed harp I will play to
      you,
10 the one who gives victory to kings,
   who rescues his servant David.
11 Rescue me from the cruel sword,
   and deliver me from the hand of aliens,
   whose mouths speak lies,
   and whose right hands are false.

12 May our sons in their youth
   be like plants full grown,
   our daughters like corner pillars,
   cut for the building of a palace.
13 May our barns be filled,
   with produce of every kind;
   may our sheep increase by thousands,
   by tens of thousands in our fields,
14 and may our cattle be heavy with young.
   May there be no breach in the walls,*a* no
      exile,
   and no cry of distress in our streets.

15 Happy are the people to whom such
      blessings fall;
   happy are the people whose God is the
      Lord.

PSALM 145

The Greatness and the Goodness of God

Praise. Of David.

1 I will extol you, my God and King,
   and bless your name forever and ever.
2 Every day I will bless you,
   and praise your name forever and ever.
3 Great is the Lord, and greatly to be praised;
   his greatness is unsearchable.
4 One generation shall laud your works to
      another,
   and shall declare your mighty acts.
5 On the glorious splendor of your majesty,
   and on your wondrous works, I will
      meditate.

6 The might of your awesome deeds shall be
      proclaimed,
   and I will declare your greatness.
7 They shall celebrate the fame of your
      abundant goodness,
   and shall sing aloud of your
      righteousness.

8 The Lord is gracious and merciful,
   slow to anger and abounding in steadfast
      love.
9 The Lord is good to all,
   and his compassion is over all that he has
      made.

10 All your works shall give thanks to you,
      O Lord,
   and all your faithful shall bless you.
11 They shall speak of the glory of your
      kingdom,
   and tell of your power,
12 to make known to all people your*b* mighty
      deeds,
   and the glorious splendor of your*c*
      kingdom.
13 Your kingdom is an everlasting kingdom,
   and your dominion endures throughout
      all generations.

   The Lord is faithful in all his words,
   and gracious in all his deeds.*d*
14 The Lord upholds all who are falling,
   and raises up all who are bowed down.
15 The eyes of all look to you,
   and you give them their food in due
      season.
16 You open your hand,
   satisfying the desire of every living thing.
17 The Lord is just in all his ways,
   and kind in all his doings.
18 The Lord is near to all who call on him,
   to all who call on him in truth.
19 He fulfills the desire of all who fear him;
   he also hears their cry, and saves them.
20 The Lord watches over all who love him,
   but all the wicked he will destroy.

21 My mouth will speak the praise of the Lord,
   and all flesh will bless his holy name
      forever and ever.

PSALM 146

Praise for God's Help

1 Praise the Lord!
   Praise the Lord, O my soul!
2 I will praise the Lord as long as I live;
   I will sing praises to my God all my life
      long.

---

a Heb lacks *in the walls* *b* Gk Jerome Syr: Heb *his* *c* Heb *his* *d* These two lines supplied by Q Ms Gk Syr

3 Do not put your trust in princes,
   in mortals, in whom there is no help.
4 When their breath departs, they return to
     the earth;
   on that very day their plans perish.

5 Happy are those whose help is the God of
     Jacob,
   whose hope is in the LORD their God,
6   who made heaven and earth,
   the sea, and all that is in them;
   who keeps faith forever;
7   who executes justice for the oppressed;
   who gives food to the hungry.

   The LORD sets the prisoners free;
8   the LORD opens the eyes of the blind.
   The LORD lifts up those who are bowed
     down;
   the LORD loves the righteous.
9 The LORD watches over the strangers;
   he upholds the orphan and the widow,
   but the way of the wicked he brings to
     ruin.

10 The LORD will reign forever,
   your God, O Zion, for all generations.
   Praise the LORD!

PSALM 147

Praise for God's Care for Jerusalem

1 Praise the LORD!
   How good it is to sing praises to our God;
     for he is gracious, and a song of praise is
     fitting.
2 The LORD builds up Jerusalem;
   he gathers the outcasts of Israel.
3 He heals the brokenhearted,
   and binds up their wounds.
4 He determines the number of the stars;
   he gives to all of them their names.
5 Great is our Lord, and abundant in power;
   his understanding is beyond measure.
6 The LORD lifts up the downtrodden;
   he casts the wicked to the ground.

7 Sing to the LORD with thanksgiving;
   make melody to our God on the lyre.
8 He covers the heavens with clouds,
   prepares rain for the earth,
   makes grass grow on the hills.
9 He gives to the animals their food,
   and to the young ravens when they cry.
10 His delight is not in the strength of the
     horse,
   nor his pleasure in the speed of a runner;[a]
11 but the LORD takes pleasure in those who
     fear him,
   in those who hope in his steadfast love.

a Heb legs of a person b Or prosperity

TRY THIS ◀

KIND AND MERCIFUL GOD

Do you know anyone who is truly kind and merciful? Take a moment to picture that person in your mind. What does he or she look like? What expression is on that person's face? What words or actions of kindness or mercy stand out to you?

This kind of person is rare and noticeable in our competitive, self-centered world. That person you pictured in your mind gives you a glimpse of who God is, and how his kindness and mercy stand out far above and beyond the selfish cruelty of this world. Read **Psalm 145**. This psalm of praise written by King David paints a beautiful picture of God's goodness and kindness.

To truly delve into the richness of this song, reread Psalm 145 straight through two or three more times. Try reading it silently, then try reading it aloud. Note all the characteristics that are attributed to God and pay attention to the scope and global feel of this psalm.

Do you get the sense that even though God transcends all his creation, he is still kind and compassionate to all that he made? As you meditate on this psalm, consider how God relates to the world as an integrated whole, not just to individual parts and people. How can this perspective shape how *you* look at the world?

Memorize Psalm 145.8. Not sure how to start? Try reading the verse aloud several times; then write it on an index card and take it with you so you can read it throughout the day. Now you've got meditation "to go"—a piece of God's Word in your heart that you can ponder anytime, anyplace.

GOD IS COMPASSIONATE MY WORLD

12 Praise the LORD, O Jerusalem!
   Praise your God, O Zion!
13 For he strengthens the bars of your gates;
   he blesses your children within you.
14 He grants peace[b] within your borders;
   he fills you with the finest of wheat.
15 He sends out his command to the earth;
   his word runs swiftly.
16 He gives snow like wool;
   he scatters frost like ashes.
17 He hurls down hail like crumbs—

who can stand before his cold?
18 He sends out his word, and melts them;
    he makes his wind blow, and the waters
        flow.
19 He declares his word to Jacob,
    his statutes and ordinances to Israel.
20 He has not dealt thus with any other nation;
    they do not know his ordinances.
    Praise the LORD!

PSALM 148

Praise for God's Universal Glory

1 Praise the LORD!
Praise the LORD from the heavens;
    praise him in the heights!
2 Praise him, all his angels;
    praise him, all his host!

3 Praise him, sun and moon;
    praise him, all you shining stars!
4 Praise him, you highest heavens,
    and you waters above the heavens!

5 Let them praise the name of the LORD,
    for he commanded and they were created.
6 He established them forever and ever;
    he fixed their bounds, which cannot be
        passed. [a]

7 Praise the LORD from the earth,
    you sea monsters and all deeps,
8 fire and hail, snow and frost,
    stormy wind fulfilling his command!

9 Mountains and all hills,
    fruit trees and all cedars!
10 Wild animals and all cattle,
    creeping things and flying birds!

11 Kings of the earth and all peoples,
    princes and all rulers of the earth!
12 Young men and women alike,
    old and young together!

13 Let them praise the name of the LORD,
    for his name alone is exalted;
    his glory is above earth and heaven.
14 He has raised up a horn for his people,
    praise for all his faithful,
        for the people of Israel who are close to
            him.
    Praise the LORD!

PSALM 149

Praise for God's Goodness to Israel

1 Praise the LORD!
Sing to the LORD a new song,
    his praise in the assembly of the faithful.
2 Let Israel be glad in its Maker;
    let the children of Zion rejoice in their
        King.
3 Let them praise his name with dancing,
    making melody to him with tambourine
        and lyre.
4 For the LORD takes pleasure in his people;
    he adorns the humble with victory.

a Or he set a law that cannot pass away

CREATIVE SPACE

5 Let the faithful exult in glory;
    let them sing for joy on their couches.
6 Let the high praises of God be in their
        throats
    and two-edged swords in their hands,
7 to execute vengeance on the nations
    and punishment on the peoples,
8 to bind their kings with fetters
    and their nobles with chains of iron,
9 to execute on them the judgment decreed.
    This is glory for all his faithful ones.
    Praise the LORD!

PSALM 150

Praise for God's Surpassing Greatness

1 Praise the LORD!
    Praise God in his sanctuary;
        praise him in his mighty firmament!*

2 Praise him for his mighty deeds;
        praise him according to his surpassing
        greatness!

3 Praise him with trumpet sound;
        praise him with lute and harp!
4 Praise him with tambourine and dance;
        praise him with strings and pipe!
5 Praise him with clanging cymbals;
        praise him with loud clashing cymbals!
6 Let everything that breathes praise the LORD!
    Praise the LORD!

a Or *dome*

EXPRESS YOURSELF

Deep-Sea Praise

Who should praise God? Well, according to **Psalm 148**, almost everything! Check out verse 7: "Praise the LORD from the earth, you sea monsters and all deeps." What *is* a sea monster? A whale? One of those fish with the lights on it? A marine dinosaur?

Psalm 148, while demonstrating that all creation should praise God, is also a testament to God's creativity. God made all the stuff that is praising him! The angels, the sun, the moon, the stars, the trees, the weather, the animals, and even things we land folks can't see—like the sea monsters—are called to praise God.

God is creative, and so are you. Use some nearby Creative Space to sketch a sea monster praising God. Make it as colorful and loud as you can imagine.

Orca—© Jason Paradis, 14

Together—© Charlotte Katheder, 16

PROVERBS

WORDS OF WISDOM

Live Like a King

Your boss has just fired you, your significant other has broken up with you (by leaving a sticky note on your front door), and your dog is missing. What do you do? Who do you call?

Suddenly, as you sit dejectedly on your bed, your room fills with purple smoke and a kooky soundtrack starts playing. The air sparkles and warps, and you're magically transported in space and time.

To your amazement, you're standing face-to-face with a bona fide king, decked out in a crown and everything. He strolls casually through his gardens with you, a distant look in his eyes. This is your chance—your opportunity to ask a powerful king about what matters most.

How do I get rich? you wonder, eyeing his castle. *How do I become a leader?* you want to ask, noting the legions of soldiers who answer to his call. *How can I conquer the world?* Oh, and how can I find my dog, get my job back, and get my love life back on track?

But the king only wants to talk about one thing: wisdom. As you walk together, he tells you about how to become truly wise and warns you of the things that will distract you from your goal.

Okay, so this wouldn't actually happen. But imagine what it would be like to sit with the wisest ruler in the world and ask his advice. Amazing!

Reading the book of Proverbs is about as close as you'll ever come. Solomon prayed for wisdom at the beginning of his reign and made remarkably wise decisions in tough situations (see 1 Kings 3). In Proverbs, he tells readers not to be drawn in by recklessness, laziness, violence, selfishness, or lust, but instead to live a life guided by clear thinking, delayed gratification, patience, hard work, and common sense.

When life lets us down, we could all use a little wisdom. Try this challenge. For thirty-one days (one month), read one chapter per day, pondering a new bit of wisdom every morning.

> "He is not wise to me who is wise in words only, but he who is wise in deeds."
>
> —Pope St. Gregory the Great

WHO It's not clear who wrote the book, but it bears the influence of both King Solomon, who was king in Israel before the nation split into two kingdoms, and King Hezekiah.

WHAT A collection of wise sayings about life

WHEN Solomon lived in the tenth century B.C. The collection of sayings in Proverbs was likely put together in its final form around 700 B.C.

WHERE Israel, before the nation split into two kingdoms

PATH OF DISCIPLESHIP

We all take our best guesses at life. We often face tough decisions by combining knowledge, advice, and common sense to find the best answers we can. We may turn to wise mentors to get their advice; often that's an invaluable resource. But it's still *human* advice.

The good news is that within us breathes the Holy Spirit as guide and Counselor. Through a personal relationship with the Holy Spirit we can communicate directly with God through prayer. God also can speak to us through people. We can also study and discover God's advice for life in the Scriptures.

In Proverbs we receive wisdom with the authority of God himself. This gives us more than just *advice* about life. It gives us *words* of life! When we face tough decisions, we are not alone. Through prayer and discernment, we discover—and live by—true wisdom.

1

The proverbs of Solomon son of David, king of Israel:

Prologue

2 For learning about wisdom and instruction,
for understanding words of insight,

3 for gaining instruction in wise dealing,
righteousness, justice, and equity;

4 to teach shrewdness to the simple,
knowledge and prudence to the young—

5 let the wise also hear and gain in learning,
and the discerning acquire skill,

6 to understand a proverb and a figure,
the words of the wise and their riddles.

7 The fear of the LORD is the beginning of
knowledge;
fools despise wisdom and instruction.

Warnings against Evil Companions

8 Hear, my child, your father's instruction,
and do not reject your mother's teaching;

9 for they are a fair garland for your head,
and pendants for your neck.

10 My child, if sinners entice you,
do not consent.

11 If they say, "Come with us, let us lie in wait
for blood;
let us wantonly ambush the innocent;

12 like Sheol let us swallow them alive
and whole, like those who go down to
the Pit.

13 We shall find all kinds of costly things;
we shall fill our houses with booty.

14 Throw in your lot among us;
we will all have one purse"—

15 my child, do not walk in their way,
keep your foot from their paths;

16 for their feet run to evil,
and they hurry to shed blood.

17 For in vain is the net baited
while the bird is looking on;

18 yet they lie in wait—to kill themselves!
and set an ambush—for their own lives!

19 Such is the end*a* of all who are greedy for
gain;
it takes away the life of its possessors.

The Call of Wisdom

20 Wisdom cries out in the street;
in the squares she raises her voice.

21 At the busiest corner she cries out;
at the entrance of the city gates she
speaks:

22 "How long, O simple ones, will you love
being simple?

How long will scoffers delight in their
scoffing
and fools hate knowledge?

23 Give heed to my reproof;
I will pour out my thoughts to you;
I will make my words known to you.

24 Because I have called and you refused,
have stretched out my hand and no one
heeded,

25 and because you have ignored all my
counsel
and would have none of my reproof,

26 I also will laugh at your calamity;
I will mock when panic strikes you,

27 when panic strikes you like a storm,
and your calamity comes like a
whirlwind,
when distress and anguish come upon
you.

28 Then they will call upon me, but I will not
answer;
they will seek me diligently, but will not
find me.

29 Because they hated knowledge
and did not choose the fear of the LORD,

30 would have none of my counsel,
and despised all my reproof,

31 therefore they shall eat the fruit of their way
and be sated with their own devices.

32 For waywardness kills the simple,
and the complacency of fools destroys
them;

33 but those who listen to me will be secure
and will live at ease, without dread of
disaster."

2

The Value of Wisdom

My child, if you accept my words
and treasure up my commandments
within you,

2 making your ear attentive to wisdom
and inclining your heart to
understanding;

3 if you indeed cry out for insight,
and raise your voice for understanding;

4 if you seek it like silver,
and search for it as for hidden
treasures—

5 then you will understand the fear of the
LORD
and find the knowledge of God.

6 For the LORD gives wisdom;
from his mouth come knowledge and
understanding;

7 he stores up sound wisdom for the upright;
he is a shield to those who walk
blamelessly,

a Gk: Heb *are the ways*

8 guarding the paths of justice
  and preserving the way of his faithful
    ones.
9 Then you will understand righteousness
    and justice
  and equity, every good path;
10 for wisdom will come into your heart,
  and knowledge will be pleasant to your
    soul;
11 prudence will watch over you;
  and understanding will guard you.
12 It will save you from the way of evil,
  from those who speak perversely,
13 who forsake the paths of uprightness
  to walk in the ways of darkness,
14 who rejoice in doing evil
  and delight in the perverseness of evil;
15 those whose paths are crooked,
  and who are devious in their ways.

16 You will be saved from the loose^a woman,
  from the adulteress with her smooth
    words,
17 who forsakes the partner of her youth
  and forgets her sacred covenant;
18 for her way^b leads down to death,
  and her paths to the shades;
19 those who go to her never come back,
  nor do they regain the paths of life.

20 Therefore walk in the way of the good,
  and keep to the paths of the just.
21 For the upright will abide in the land,
  and the innocent will remain in it;
22 but the wicked will be cut off from the
    land,
  and the treacherous will be rooted out
    of it.

3 Admonition to Trust and Honor God

My child, do not forget my teaching,
  but let your heart keep my
    commandments;
2 for length of days and years of life
  and abundant welfare they will give you.

3 Do not let loyalty and faithfulness forsake
    you;
  bind them around your neck,
  write them on the tablet of your heart.
4 So you will find favor and good repute
  in the sight of God and of people.

5 Trust in the LORD with all your heart,
  and do not rely on your own insight.
6 In all your ways acknowledge him,
  and he will make straight your paths.
7 Do not be wise in your own eyes;
  fear the LORD, and turn away from evil.

a Heb *strange* *b* Cn: Heb *house*

8 It will be a healing for your flesh
  and a refreshment for your body.

9 Honor the LORD with your substance
  and with the first fruits of all your
    produce;
10 then your barns will be filled with plenty,
  and your vats will be bursting with wine.

11 My child, do not despise the LORD's
    discipline
  or be weary of his reproof,
12 for the LORD reproves the one he loves,
  as a father the son in whom he delights.

The True Wealth

13 Happy are those who find wisdom,
  and those who get understanding,
14 for her income is better than silver,
  and her revenue better than gold.
15 She is more precious than jewels,

God's Wisdom in Creation

19 The LORD by wisdom founded the earth;
  by understanding he established the
    heavens;
20 by his knowledge the deeps broke open,
  and the clouds drop down the dew.

The True Security

21 My child, do not let these escape from your
    sight:
  keep sound wisdom and prudence,
22 and they will be life for your soul
  and adornment for your neck.
23 Then you will walk on your way securely
  and your foot will not stumble.
24 If you sit down,*a* you will not be afraid;
  when you lie down, your sleep will be
    sweet.
25 Do not be afraid of sudden panic,
  or of the storm that strikes the wicked;
26 for the LORD will be your confidence
  and will keep your foot from being
    caught.

27 Do not withhold good from those to whom
    it is due,*b*
  when it is in your power to do it.
28 Do not say to your neighbor, "Go, and come
    again,
  tomorrow I will give it"—when you have
    it with you.
29 Do not plan harm against your neighbor
  who lives trustingly beside you.
30 Do not quarrel with anyone without cause,
  when no harm has been done to you.
31 Do not envy the violent
  and do not choose any of their ways;
32 for the perverse are an abomination to the
    LORD,
  but the upright are in his confidence.
33 The LORD's curse is on the house of the
    wicked,
  but he blesses the abode of the
    righteous.
34 Toward the scorners he is scornful,
  but to the humble he shows favor.
35 The wise will inherit honor,
  but stubborn fools, disgrace.

and nothing you desire can compare
    with her.
16 Long life is in her right hand;
  in her left hand are riches and honor.
17 Her ways are ways of pleasantness,
  and all her paths are peace.
18 She is a tree of life to those who lay hold of
    her;
  those who hold her fast are called happy.

4 Parental Advice

Listen, children, to a father's instruction,
  and be attentive, that you may gain*c*
    insight;
2 for I give you good precepts:
  do not forsake my teaching.
3 When I was a son with my father,
  tender, and my mother's favorite,
4 he taught me, and said to me,

a Gk: Heb *lie down* *b* Heb *from its owners* *c* Heb *know*

"Let your heart hold fast my words;
  keep my commandments, and live.
5 Get wisdom; get insight: do not forget, nor
    turn away
  from the words of my mouth.
6 Do not forsake her, and she will keep you;
  love her, and she will guard you.
7 The beginning of wisdom is this: Get
    wisdom,
  and whatever else you get, get insight.
8 Prize her highly, and she will exalt you;
  she will honor you if you embrace her.
9 She will place on your head a fair garland;
  she will bestow on you a beautiful
    crown."

Admonition to Keep to the Right Path

10 Hear, my child, and accept my words,
  that the years of your life may be many.
11 I have taught you the way of wisdom;
  I have led you in the paths of
    uprightness.
12 When you walk, your step will not be
    hampered;
  and if you run, you will not stumble.
13 Keep hold of instruction; do not let go;
  guard her, for she is your life.
14 Do not enter the path of the wicked,
  and do not walk in the way of evildoers.
15 Avoid it; do not go on it;
  turn away from it and pass on.
16 For they cannot sleep unless they have done
    wrong;
  they are robbed of sleep unless they have
    made someone stumble.
17 For they eat the bread of wickedness
  and drink the wine of violence.
18 But the path of the righteous is like the
    light of dawn,
  which shines brighter and brighter until
    full day.
19 The way of the wicked is like deep darkness;
  they do not know what they stumble
    over.

20 My child, be attentive to my words;
  incline your ear to my sayings.
21 Do not let them escape from your sight;
  keep them within your heart.
22 For they are life to those who find them,
  and healing to all their flesh.
23 Keep your heart with all vigilance,
  for from it flow the springs of life.
24 Put away from you crooked speech,
  and put devious talk far from you.
25 Let your eyes look directly forward,
  and your gaze be straight before you.
26 Keep straight the path of your feet,

and all your ways will be sure.
27 Do not swerve to the right or to the left;
  turn your foot away from evil.

5 Warning against Impurity and Infidelity

My child, be attentive to my wisdom;
  incline your ear to my understanding,
2 so that you may hold on to prudence,
  and your lips may guard knowledge.
3 For the lips of a loose*a* woman drip honey,
  and her speech is smoother than oil;
4 but in the end she is bitter as wormwood,
  sharp as a two-edged sword.
5 Her feet go down to death;
  her steps follow the path to Sheol.
6 She does not keep straight to the path of
    life;
  her ways wander, and she does not
    know it.

7 And now, my child,*b* listen to me,
  and do not depart from the words of my
    mouth.
8 Keep your way far from her,
  and do not go near the door of her
    house;
9 or you will give your honor to others,
  and your years to the merciless,
10 and strangers will take their fill of your
    wealth,
  and your labors will go to the house of an
    alien;
11 and at the end of your life you will groan,
  when your flesh and body are consumed,
12 and you say, "Oh, how I hated discipline,
  and my heart despised reproof!
13 I did not listen to the voice of my teachers
  or incline my ear to my instructors.
14 Now I am at the point of utter ruin
  in the public assembly."

15 Drink water from your own cistern,
  flowing water from your own well.
16 Should your springs be scattered abroad,
  streams of water in the streets?
17 Let them be for yourself alone,
  and not for sharing with strangers.
18 Let your fountain be blessed,
  and rejoice in the wife of your youth,
19 a lovely deer, a graceful doe.
  May her breasts satisfy you at all times;
  may you be intoxicated always by her
    love.
20 Why should you be intoxicated, my son, by
    another woman
  and embrace the bosom of an
    adulteress?

a Heb *strange* *b* Gk Vg: Heb *children*

21 For human ways are under the eyes of the
LORD,
and he examines all their paths.
22 The iniquities of the wicked ensnare them,
and they are caught in the toils of their
sin.
23 They die for lack of discipline,
and because of their great folly they are
lost.

6 Practical Admonitions

My child, if you have given your pledge to
your neighbor,
if you have bound yourself to another,[a]
2 you are snared by the utterance of your
lips,[b]
caught by the words of your mouth.
3 So do this, my child, and save yourself,
for you have come into your neighbor's
power:
go, hurry,[c] and plead with your neighbor.
4 Give your eyes no sleep
and your eyelids no slumber;
5 save yourself like a gazelle from the hunter,[d]
like a bird from the hand of the fowler.

6 Go to the ant, you lazybones;
consider its ways, and be wise.
7 Without having any chief
or officer or ruler,
8 it prepares its food in summer,
and gathers its sustenance in harvest.
9 How long will you lie there, O lazybones?
When will you rise from your sleep?
10 A little sleep, a little slumber,
a little folding of the hands to rest,
11 and poverty will come upon you like a
robber,
and want, like an armed warrior.

12 A scoundrel and a villain
goes around with crooked speech,
13 winking the eyes, shuffling the feet,
pointing the fingers,
14 with perverted mind devising evil,
continually sowing discord;
15 on such a one calamity will descend
suddenly;
in a moment, damage beyond repair.

16 There are six things that the LORD hates,
seven that are an abomination to him:
17 haughty eyes, a lying tongue,
and hands that shed innocent blood,
18 a heart that devises wicked plans,
feet that hurry to run to evil,
19 a lying witness who testifies falsely,
and one who sows discord in a family.

20 My child, keep your father's
commandment,
and do not forsake your mother's
teaching.
21 Bind them upon your heart always;
tie them around your neck.
22 When you walk, they[e] will lead you;
when you lie down, they[e] will watch over
you;
and when you awake, they[e] will talk with
you.
23 For the commandment is a lamp and the
teaching a light,
and the reproofs of discipline are the way
of life,
24 to preserve you from the wife of another,[f]
from the smooth tongue of the
adulteress.
25 Do not desire her beauty in your heart,
and do not let her capture you with her
eyelashes;
26 for a prostitute's fee is only a loaf of bread,[g]
but the wife of another stalks a man's
very life.
27 Can fire be carried in the bosom
without burning one's clothes?
28 Or can one walk on hot coals
without scorching the feet?
29 So is he who sleeps with his neighbor's
wife;
no one who touches her will go
unpunished.
30 Thieves are not despised who steal only
to satisfy their appetite when they are
hungry.
31 Yet if they are caught, they will pay
sevenfold;
they will forfeit all the goods of their
house.
32 But he who commits adultery has no sense;
he who does it destroys himself.
33 He will get wounds and dishonor,
and his disgrace will not be wiped away.
34 For jealousy arouses a husband's fury,
and he shows no restraint when he takes
revenge.
35 He will accept no compensation,
and refuses a bribe no matter how great.

7 The False Attractions of Adultery

My child, keep my words
and store up my commandments with
you;
2 keep my commandments and live,
keep my teachings as the apple of your
eye;

---

a Or a stranger b Cn Compare Gk Syr: Heb the words of your mouth c Or humble yourself d Cn: Heb from the hand e Heb it f Gk: MT the
evil woman g Cn Compare Gk Syr Vg Tg: Heb for because of a harlot to a piece of bread

³ bind them on your fingers,
   write them on the tablet of your heart.
⁴ Say to wisdom, "You are my sister,"
   and call insight your intimate friend,
⁵ that they may keep you from the loose*a*
       woman,
   from the adulteress with her smooth
       words.

⁶ For at the window of my house
   I looked out through my lattice,
⁷ and I saw among the simple ones,
   I observed among the youths,
   a young man without sense,
⁸ passing along the street near her corner,
   taking the road to her house
⁹ in the twilight, in the evening,
   at the time of night and darkness.

¹⁰ Then a woman comes toward him,
   decked out like a prostitute, wily of
       heart.*b*
¹¹ She is loud and wayward;
   her feet do not stay at home;
¹² now in the street, now in the squares,
   and at every corner she lies in wait.
¹³ She seizes him and kisses him,
   and with impudent face she says to him:
¹⁴ "I had to offer sacrifices,
   and today I have paid my vows;
¹⁵ so now I have come out to meet you,
   to seek you eagerly, and I have found you!
¹⁶ I have decked my couch with coverings,
   colored spreads of Egyptian linen;
¹⁷ I have perfumed my bed with myrrh,
   aloes, and cinnamon.
¹⁸ Come, let us take our fill of love until
       morning;
   let us delight ourselves with love.
¹⁹ For my husband is not at home;
   he has gone on a long journey.
²⁰ He took a bag of money with him;
   he will not come home until full moon."

²¹ With much seductive speech she persuades
       him;
   with her smooth talk she compels him.
²² Right away he follows her,
   and goes like an ox to the slaughter,
   or bounds like a stag toward the trap*c*
²³   until an arrow pierces its entrails.
   He is like a bird rushing into a snare,
   not knowing that it will cost him his life.

²⁴ And now, my children, listen to me,
   and be attentive to the words of my
       mouth.
²⁵ Do not let your hearts turn aside to her
       ways;

Material Things—© Christy Klink, 18

   do not stray into her paths.
²⁶ For many are those she has laid low,
   and numerous are her victims.
²⁷ Her house is the way to Sheol,
   going down to the chambers of death.

8 The Gifts of Wisdom

Does not wisdom call,
   and does not understanding raise her
       voice?
² On the heights, beside the way,
   at the crossroads she takes her stand;
³ beside the gates in front of the town,
   at the entrance of the portals she cries
       out:
⁴ "To you, O people, I call,
   and my cry is to all that live.
⁵ O simple ones, learn prudence;
   acquire intelligence, you who lack it.
⁶ Hear, for I will speak noble things,
   and from my lips will come what is right;
⁷ for my mouth will utter truth;
   wickedness is an abomination to my lips.
⁸ All the words of my mouth are righteous;
   there is nothing twisted or crooked in
       them.
⁹ They are all straight to one who
       understands
   and right to those who find knowledge.
¹⁰ Take my instruction instead of silver,
   and knowledge rather than choice gold;
¹¹ for wisdom is better than jewels,
   and all that you may desire cannot
       compare with her.
¹² I, wisdom, live with prudence,*b*
   and I attain knowledge and discretion.
¹³ The fear of the LORD is hatred of evil.
   Pride and arrogance and the way of evil
   and perverted speech I hate.

a Heb *strange* *b* Meaning of Heb uncertain *c* Cn Compare Gk: Meaning of Heb uncertain

14 I have good advice and sound wisdom;
    I have insight, I have strength.
15 By me kings reign,
    and rulers decree what is just;
16 by me rulers rule,
    and nobles, all who govern rightly.
17 I love those who love me,
    and those who seek me diligently
        find me.
18 Riches and honor are with me,
    enduring wealth and prosperity.
19 My fruit is better than gold, even fine gold,
    and my yield than choice silver.
20 I walk in the way of righteousness,
    along the paths of justice,
21 endowing with wealth those who love me,
    and filling their treasuries.

Wisdom's Part in Creation

22 The LORD created me at the beginning[a] of
        his work,[b]
    the first of his acts of long ago.
23 Ages ago I was set up,
    at the first, before the beginning of the
        earth.
24 When there were no depths I was brought
        forth,
    when there were no springs abounding
        with water.
25 Before the mountains had been shaped,
    before the hills, I was brought forth—
26 when he had not yet made earth and fields,[c]
    or the world's first bits of soil.
27 When he established the heavens, I was
        there,
    when he drew a circle on the face of the
        deep,
28 when he made firm the skies above,
    when he established the fountains of the
        deep,
29 when he assigned to the sea its limit,
    so that the waters might not transgress
        his command,
    when he marked out the foundations of the
        earth,

30 then I was beside him, like a master
        worker;[d]
    and I was daily his[e] delight,
        rejoicing before him always,
31 rejoicing in his inhabited world
    and delighting in the human race.
32 "And now, my children, listen to me:
    happy are those who keep my ways.
33 Hear instruction and be wise,
    and do not neglect it.
34 Happy is the one who listens to me,
    watching daily at my gates,
        waiting beside my doors.
35 For whoever finds me finds life
    and obtains favor from the LORD;
36 but those who miss me injure themselves;
    all who hate me love death."

9 **Wisdom's Feast**
Wisdom has built her house,
    she has hewn her seven pillars.
2 She has slaughtered her animals, she has
        mixed her wine,
    she has also set her table.
3 She has sent out her servant-girls, she calls
    from the highest places in the town,
4 "You that are simple, turn in here!"
    To those without sense she says,
5 "Come, eat of my bread
    and drink of the wine I have mixed.
6 Lay aside immaturity,[f] and live,
    and walk in the way of insight."

General Maxims

7 Whoever corrects a scoffer wins abuse;
    whoever rebukes the wicked gets hurt.
8 A scoffer who is rebuked will only hate you;
    the wise, when rebuked, will love you.
9 Give instruction[g] to the wise, and they will
        become wiser still;
    teach the righteous and they will gain in
        learning.
10 The fear of the LORD is the beginning of
        wisdom,
    and the knowledge of the Holy One is
        insight.
11 For by me your days will be multiplied,
    and years will be added to your life.
12 If you are wise, you are wise for yourself;
    if you scoff, you alone will bear it.

Folly's Invitation and Promise

13 The foolish woman is loud;
    she is ignorant and knows nothing.
14 She sits at the door of her house,
    on a seat at the high places of the town,

a Or me as the beginning b Heb way c Meaning of Heb uncertain d Another reading is little child e Gk: Heb lacks his f Or simpleness
g Heb lacks instruction

15 calling to those who pass by,
     who are going straight on their way,
16 "You who are simple, turn in here!"
     And to those without sense she says,
17 "Stolen water is sweet,
     and bread eaten in secret is pleasant."
18 But they do not know that the dead[a] are
     there,
     that her guests are in the depths of Sheol.

10 Wise Sayings of Solomon
The proverbs of Solomon.

A wise child makes a glad father,
     but a foolish child is a mother's grief.
2 Treasures gained by wickedness do not
     profit,
     but righteousness delivers from death.
3 The LORD does not let the righteous go
     hungry,
     but he thwarts the craving of the wicked.
4 A slack hand causes poverty,
     but the hand of the diligent makes rich.
5 A child who gathers in summer is prudent,
     but a child who sleeps in harvest brings
     shame.
6 Blessings are on the head of the righteous,
     but the mouth of the wicked conceals
     violence.
7 The memory of the righteous is a blessing,
     but the name of the wicked will rot.
8 The wise of heart will heed
     commandments,
     but a babbling fool will come to ruin.
9 Whoever walks in integrity walks securely,
     but whoever follows perverse ways will
     be found out.
10 Whoever winks the eye causes trouble,
     but the one who rebukes boldly makes
     peace.[b]
11 The mouth of the righteous is a fountain of
     life,
     but the mouth of the wicked conceals
     violence.
12 Hatred stirs up strife,
     but love covers all offenses.
13 On the lips of one who has understanding
     wisdom is found,
     but a rod is for the back of one who lacks
     sense.
14 The wise lay up knowledge,
     but the babbling of a fool brings ruin
     near.
15 The wealth of the rich is their fortress;
     the poverty of the poor is their ruin.
16 The wage of the righteous leads to life,
     the gain of the wicked to sin.

17 Whoever heeds instruction is on the path to
     life,
     but one who rejects a rebuke goes astray.
18 Lying lips conceal hatred,
     and whoever utters slander is a fool.
19 When words are many, transgression is not
     lacking,
     but the prudent are restrained in speech.
20 The tongue of the righteous is choice silver;
     the mind of the wicked is of little worth.
21 The lips of the righteous feed many,
     but fools die for lack of sense.
22 The blessing of the LORD makes rich,
     and he adds no sorrow with it.[c]
23 Doing wrong is like sport to a fool,
     but wise conduct is pleasure to a person
     of understanding.
24 What the wicked dread will come upon
     them,
     but the desire of the righteous will be
     granted.
25 When the tempest passes, the wicked are
     no more,
     but the righteous are established forever.
26 Like vinegar to the teeth, and smoke to the
     eyes,
     so are the lazy to their employers.
27 The fear of the LORD prolongs life,
     but the years of the wicked will be short.
28 The hope of the righteous ends in gladness,
     but the expectation of the wicked comes
     to nothing.
29 The way of the LORD is a stronghold for the
     upright,
     but destruction for evildoers.
30 The righteous will never be removed,
     but the wicked will not remain in the
     land.
31 The mouth of the righteous brings forth
     wisdom,
     but the perverse tongue will be cut off.
32 The lips of the righteous know what is
     acceptable,
     but the mouth of the wicked what is
     perverse.

11 A false balance is an abomination to the
     LORD,
     but an accurate weight is his delight.
2 When pride comes, then comes disgrace;
     but wisdom is with the humble.
3 The integrity of the upright guides them,
     but the crookedness of the treacherous
     destroys them.
4 Riches do not profit in the day of wrath,
     but righteousness delivers from death.
5 The righteousness of the blameless keeps
     their ways straight,

a Heb *shades* b Gk: Heb *but a babbling fool will come to ruin* c Or *and toil adds nothing to it*

but the wicked fall by their own
wickedness.

6 The righteousness of the upright saves
them,
but the treacherous are taken captive by
their schemes.

7 When the wicked die, their hope perishes,
and the expectation of the godless comes
to nothing.

8 The righteous are delivered from trouble,
and the wicked get into it instead.

9 With their mouths the godless would
destroy their neighbors,
but by knowledge the righteous are
delivered.

10 When it goes well with the righteous, the
city rejoices;
and when the wicked perish, there is
jubilation.

11 By the blessing of the upright a city is
exalted,
but it is overthrown by the mouth of the
wicked.

12 Whoever belittles another lacks sense,
but an intelligent person remains silent.

13 A gossip goes about telling secrets,
but one who is trustworthy in spirit
keeps a confidence.

14 Where there is no guidance, a nation*a* falls,
but in an abundance of counselors there
is safety.

15 To guarantee loans for a stranger brings
trouble,
but there is safety in refusing to do so.

16 A gracious woman gets honor,
but she who hates virtue is covered with
shame.*b*
The timid become destitute,*c*
but the aggressive gain riches.

17 Those who are kind reward themselves,
but the cruel do themselves harm.

18 The wicked earn no real gain,
but those who sow righteousness get a
true reward.

19 Whoever is steadfast in righteousness will
live,
but whoever pursues evil will die.

20 Crooked minds are an abomination to the
LORD,
but those of blameless ways are his
delight.

21 Be assured, the wicked will not go
unpunished,
but those who are righteous will escape.

22 Like a gold ring in a pig's snout
is a beautiful woman without good
sense.

23 The desire of the righteous ends only in
good;
the expectation of the wicked in wrath.

24 Some give freely, yet grow all the richer;
others withhold what is due, and only
suffer want.

25 A generous person will be enriched,
and one who gives water will get water.

26 The people curse those who hold back
grain,
but a blessing is on the head of those
who sell it.

27 Whoever diligently seeks good seeks favor,
but evil comes to the one who searches
for it.

28 Those who trust in their riches will wither,*d*
but the righteous will flourish like green
leaves.

29 Those who trouble their households will
inherit wind,
and the fool will be servant to the wise.

30 The fruit of the righteous is a tree of life,
but violence*e* takes lives away.

31 If the righteous are repaid on earth,
how much more the wicked and the
sinner!

12 Whoever loves discipline loves
knowledge,
but those who hate to be rebuked are
stupid.

2 The good obtain favor from the LORD,
but those who devise evil he condemns.

3 No one finds security by wickedness,
but the root of the righteous will never
be moved.

4 A good wife is the crown of her husband,
but she who brings shame is like
rottenness in his bones.

5 The thoughts of the righteous are just;
the advice of the wicked is treacherous.

6 The words of the wicked are a deadly
ambush,
but the speech of the upright delivers
them.

7 The wicked are overthrown and are no
more,
but the house of the righteous will stand.

8 One is commended for good sense,
but a perverse mind is despised.

9 Better to be despised and have a servant,
than to be self-important and lack food.

10 The righteous know the needs of their
animals,
but the mercy of the wicked is cruel.

a Or *an army* b Compare Gk Syr: Heb lacks *but she . . . shame* c Gk: Heb lacks *The timid . . . destitute* d Cn: Heb *fall* e Cn Compare Gk
Syr: Heb *a wise man*

One Way—© Maggie Hubbard, 16

¹¹ Those who till their land will have plenty of
food,
    but those who follow worthless pursuits
        have no sense.
¹² The wicked covet the proceeds of
wickedness,ᵃ
    but the root of the righteous bears fruit.
¹³ The evil are ensnared by the transgression
of their lips,
    but the righteous escape from trouble.
¹⁴ From the fruit of the mouth one is filled
with good things,
    and manual labor has its reward.
¹⁵ Fools think their own way is right,
    but the wise listen to advice.
¹⁶ Fools show their anger at once,
    but the prudent ignore an insult.
¹⁷ Whoever speaks the truth gives honest
evidence,
    but a false witness speaks deceitfully.
¹⁸ Rash words are like sword thrusts,
    but the tongue of the wise brings
        healing.
¹⁹ Truthful lips endure forever,
    but a lying tongue lasts only a moment.
²⁰ Deceit is in the mind of those who plan evil,
    but those who counsel peace have joy.
²¹ No harm happens to the righteous,
    but the wicked are filled with trouble.
²² Lying lips are an abomination to the Lᴏʀᴅ,

but those who act faithfully are his
delight.
²³ One who is clever conceals knowledge,
    but the mind of a foolᵇ broadcasts folly.
²⁴ The hand of the diligent will rule,
    while the lazy will be put to forced labor.
²⁵ Anxiety weighs down the human heart,
    but a good word cheers it up.
²⁶ The righteous gives good advice to friends,ᶜ
    but the way of the wicked leads astray.
²⁷ The lazy do not roastᵈ their game,
    but the diligent obtain precious wealth.ᵈ
²⁸ In the path of righteousness there is life,
    in walking its path there is no death.

13 A wise child loves discipline,ᵉ
    but a scoffer does not listen to rebuke.
² From the fruit of their words good persons
eat good things,
    but the desire of the treacherous is for
        wrongdoing.
³ Those who guard their mouths preserve
their lives;
    those who open wide their lips come to
        ruin.
⁴ The appetite of the lazy craves, and gets
nothing,
    while the appetite of the diligent is richly
        supplied.
⁵ The righteous hate falsehood,

a Or *covet the catch of the wicked* b Heb *the heart of fools* c Syr: Meaning of Heb uncertain d Meaning of Heb uncertain e Cn: Heb *A wise child the discipline of his father*

but the wicked act shamefully and
disgracefully.

6 Righteousness guards one whose way is
upright,
but sin overthrows the wicked.

7 Some pretend to be rich, yet have nothing;
others pretend to be poor, yet have great
wealth.

8 Wealth is a ransom for a person's life,
but the poor get no threats.

9 The light of the righteous rejoices,
but the lamp of the wicked goes out.

10 By insolence the heedless make strife,
but wisdom is with those who take
advice.

11 Wealth hastily gotten*a* will dwindle,
but those who gather little by little will
increase it.

12 Hope deferred makes the heart sick,
but a desire fulfilled is a tree of life.

13 Those who despise the word bring
destruction on themselves,
but those who respect the
commandment will be rewarded.

14 The teaching of the wise is a fountain of
life,
so that one may avoid the snares of
death.

15 Good sense wins favor,
but the way of the faithless is their ruin.*b*

16 The clever do all things intelligently,
but the fool displays folly.

17 A bad messenger brings trouble,
but a faithful envoy, healing.

18 Poverty and disgrace are for the one who
ignores instruction,
but one who heeds reproof is honored.

19 A desire realized is sweet to the soul,
but to turn away from evil is an
abomination to fools.

20 Whoever walks with the wise becomes wise,
but the companion of fools suffers harm.

21 Misfortune pursues sinners,
but prosperity rewards the righteous.

22 The good leave an inheritance to their
children,
but the sinner's wealth is laid up for the
righteous.

23 The field of the poor may yield much food,
but it is swept away through injustice.

24 Those who spare the rod hate their
children,
but those who love them are diligent to
discipline them.

25 The righteous have enough to satisfy their
appetite,
but the belly of the wicked is empty.

14 The wise woman*c* builds her house,
but the foolish tears it down with her
own hands.

2 Those who walk uprightly fear the Lord,
but one who is devious in conduct
despises him.

3 The talk of fools is a rod for their backs,*d*
but the lips of the wise preserve them.

4 Where there are no oxen, there is no grain;
abundant crops come by the strength of
the ox.

5 A faithful witness does not lie,
but a false witness breathes out lies.

6 A scoffer seeks wisdom in vain,
but knowledge is easy for one who
understands.

7 Leave the presence of a fool,
for there you do not find words of
knowledge.

8 It is the wisdom of the clever to understand
where they go,
but the folly of fools misleads.

9 Fools mock at the guilt offering,*e*
but the upright enjoy God's favor.

10 The heart knows its own bitterness,
and no stranger shares its joy.

11 The house of the wicked is destroyed,
but the tent of the upright flourishes.

12 There is a way that seems right to a person,
but its end is the way to death.*f*

13 Even in laughter the heart is sad,
and the end of joy is grief.

14 The perverse get what their ways deserve,
and the good, what their deeds deserve.*g*

15 The simple believe everything,

Narrow Road—© Morgan Katchuk, 14

a Gk Vg: Heb *from vanity* b Cn Compare Gk Syr Vg Tg: Heb *is
enduring* c Heb *Wisdom of women* d Cn: Heb *a rod of pride*
e Meaning of Heb uncertain f Heb *ways of death* g Cn: Heb *from
upon him*

but the clever consider their steps.

16 The wise are cautious and turn away from
evil,
  but the fool throws off restraint and is
  careless.

17 One who is quick-tempered acts foolishly,
  and the schemer is hated.

18 The simple are adorned with*a* folly,
  but the clever are crowned with
  knowledge.

19 The evil bow down before the good,
  the wicked at the gates of the righteous.

20 The poor are disliked even by their
  neighbors,
  but the rich have many friends.

21 Those who despise their neighbors are
  sinners,
  but happy are those who are kind to the
  poor.

22 Do they not err that plan evil?
  Those who plan good find loyalty and
  faithfulness.

23 In all toil there is profit,
  but mere talk leads only to poverty.

24 The crown of the wise is their wisdom,*b*
  but folly is the garland*c* of fools.

25 A truthful witness saves lives,
  but one who utters lies is a betrayer.

26 In the fear of the LORD one has strong
  confidence,
  and one's children will have a refuge.

27 The fear of the LORD is a fountain of life,
  so that one may avoid the snares of
  death.

28 The glory of a king is a multitude of people;
  without people a prince is ruined.

29 Whoever is slow to anger has great
  understanding,
  but one who has a hasty temper exalts
  folly.

30 A tranquil mind gives life to the flesh,
  but passion makes the bones rot.

31 Those who oppress the poor insult their
  Maker,
  but those who are kind to the needy
  honor him.

32 The wicked are overthrown by their
  evildoing,
  but the righteous find a refuge in their
  integrity.*d*

33 Wisdom is at home in the mind of one who
  has understanding,
  but it is not*e* known in the heart of fools.

34 Righteousness exalts a nation,
  but sin is a reproach to any people.

35 A servant who deals wisely has the king's
  favor,
  but his wrath falls on one who acts
  shamefully.

15 A soft answer turns away wrath,
  but a harsh word stirs up anger.

2 The tongue of the wise dispenses
  knowledge,*f*
  but the mouths of fools pour out folly.

3 The eyes of the LORD are in every place,
  keeping watch on the evil and the good.

4 A gentle tongue is a tree of life,
  but perverseness in it breaks the spirit.

5 A fool despises a parent's instruction,
  but the one who heeds admonition is
  prudent.

6 In the house of the righteous there is much
  treasure,
  but trouble befalls the income of the
  wicked.

7 The lips of the wise spread knowledge;
  not so the minds of fools.

8 The sacrifice of the wicked is an
  abomination to the LORD,
  but the prayer of the upright is his
  delight.

9 The way of the wicked is an abomination to
  the LORD,
  but he loves the one who pursues
  righteousness.

10 There is severe discipline for one who
  forsakes the way,
  but one who hates a rebuke will die.

11 Sheol and Abaddon lie open before the
  LORD,
  how much more human hearts!

12 Scoffers do not like to be rebuked;
  they will not go to the wise.

13 A glad heart makes a cheerful countenance,
  but by sorrow of heart the spirit is
  broken.

14 The mind of one who has understanding
  seeks knowledge,
  but the mouths of fools feed on folly.

15 All the days of the poor are hard,
  but a cheerful heart has a continual feast.

16 Better is a little with the fear of the LORD
  than great treasure and trouble with it.

17 Better is a dinner of vegetables where
  love is
  than a fatted ox and hatred with it.

18 Those who are hot-tempered stir up strife,
  but those who are slow to anger calm
  contention.

19 The way of the lazy is overgrown with
  thorns,

a Or *inherit* *b* Cn Compare Gk: Heb *riches* *c* Cn: Heb *is the folly* *d* Gk Syr: Heb *in their death* *e* Gk Syr: Heb lacks *not* *f* Cn: Heb *makes knowledge good*

FOLLOWING GOD'S LEAD

Read **Proverbs 16.3** and **16.9**.

There's a reason Proverbs is called "wisdom literature."

Please get over the notion that just because you dedicate your garage to God, the computer you build there will be bigger than Apple. These verses don't contain a simplistic formula for success. It's a *principle*—a true thread weaving through life. If you value what God wants more than what you want, you'll plan things that line up with his desires and intents. So your plans *will* succeed, because they reflect God's goals. Which means you aren't about manipulating God; you're about obeying him.

Big difference.

Here's your challenge: give your plans and goals over to God instead of pursuing your own agenda for life. Decide to pursue God's agenda—no matter what it is and no matter where it leads you.

Ready for that?

Here's a next step: in the space below write one dream you have for your future—a career, position, or accomplishment.

Now add this: *If it fits your plan, God. If not, tell me what else to do.*

Those words make all the difference.

Make them your prayer.

GOD IS CHALLENGING MY INTERESTS

but the path of the upright is a level
   highway.
20 A wise child makes a glad father,
   but the foolish despise their mothers.
21 Folly is a joy to one who has no sense,
   but a person of understanding walks
      straight ahead.
22 Without counsel, plans go wrong,
   but with many advisers they succeed.
23 To make an apt answer is a joy to anyone,
   and a word in season, how good it is!
24 For the wise the path of life leads upward,
   in order to avoid Sheol below.
25 The LORD tears down the house of the
      proud,
   but maintains the widow's boundaries.
26 Evil plans are an abomination to the LORD,
   but gracious words are pure.
27 Those who are greedy for unjust gain make
      trouble for their households,
   but those who hate bribes will live.
28 The mind of the righteous ponders how to
      answer,
   but the mouth of the wicked pours out
      evil.
29 The LORD is far from the wicked,
   but he hears the prayer of the righteous.
30 The light of the eyes rejoices the heart,
   and good news refreshes the body.
31 The ear that heeds wholesome admonition
   will lodge among the wise.
32 Those who ignore instruction despise
      themselves,
   but those who heed admonition gain
      understanding.
33 The fear of the LORD is instruction in
      wisdom,
   and humility goes before honor.

16 The plans of the mind belong to
      mortals,
   but the answer of the tongue is from the
      LORD.
2 All one's ways may be pure in one's own
      eyes,
   but the LORD weighs the spirit.
3 Commit your work to the LORD,
   and your plans will be established.
4 The LORD has made everything for its
      purpose,
   even the wicked for the day of trouble.
5 All those who are arrogant are an
      abomination to the LORD;
   be assured, they will not go unpunished.
6 By loyalty and faithfulness iniquity is
      atoned for,
   and by the fear of the LORD one avoids
      evil.
7 When the ways of people please the LORD,

he causes even their enemies to be at
peace with them.
8 Better is a little with righteousness
than large income with injustice.
9 The human mind plans the way,
but the LORD directs the steps.
10 Inspired decisions are on the lips of a king;
his mouth does not sin in judgment.
11 Honest balances and scales are the LORD's;
all the weights in the bag are his work.
12 It is an abomination to kings to do evil,
for the throne is established by
righteousness.
13 Righteous lips are the delight of a king,
and he loves those who speak what is
right.
14 A king's wrath is a messenger of death,
and whoever is wise will appease it.
15 In the light of a king's face there is life,
and his favor is like the clouds that bring
the spring rain.
16 How much better to get wisdom than gold!
To get understanding is to be chosen
rather than silver.
17 The highway of the upright avoids evil;
those who guard their way preserve their
lives.
18 Pride goes before destruction,
and a haughty spirit before a fall.
19 It is better to be of a lowly spirit among the
poor
than to divide the spoil with the proud.
20 Those who are attentive to a matter will
prosper,
and happy are those who trust in the
LORD.
21 The wise of heart is called perceptive,
and pleasant speech increases
persuasiveness.
22 Wisdom is a fountain of life to one who
has it,
but folly is the punishment of fools.
23 The mind of the wise makes their speech
judicious,
and adds persuasiveness to their lips.
24 Pleasant words are like a honeycomb,
sweetness to the soul and health to the
body.
25 Sometimes there is a way that seems to be
right,
but in the end it is the way to death.
26 The appetite of workers works for them;
their hunger urges them on.
27 Scoundrels concoct evil,
and their speech is like a scorching fire.
28 A perverse person spreads strife,
and a whisperer separates close friends.

29 The violent entice their neighbors,
and lead them in a way that is not good.
30 One who winks the eyes plans*a* perverse
things;
one who compresses the lips brings evil
to pass.
31 Gray hair is a crown of glory;
it is gained in a righteous life.
32 One who is slow to anger is better than the
mighty,
and one whose temper is controlled than
one who captures a city.
33 The lot is cast into the lap,
but the decision is the LORD's alone.

17 Better is a dry morsel with quiet
than a house full of feasting with strife.
2 A slave who deals wisely will rule over a
child who acts shamefully,
and will share the inheritance as one of
the family.
3 The crucible is for silver, and the furnace is
for gold,
but the LORD tests the heart.
4 An evildoer listens to wicked lips;
and a liar gives heed to a mischievous
tongue.
5 Those who mock the poor insult their
Maker;
those who are glad at calamity will not go
unpunished.
6 Grandchildren are the crown of the aged,
and the glory of children is their parents.
7 Fine speech is not becoming to a fool;
still less is false speech to a ruler.*b*
8 A bribe is like a magic stone in the eyes of
those who give it;
wherever they turn they prosper.
9 One who forgives an affront fosters
friendship,
but one who dwells on disputes will
alienate a friend.
10 A rebuke strikes deeper into a discerning
person
than a hundred blows into a fool.
11 Evil people seek only rebellion,
but a cruel messenger will be sent against
them.
12 Better to meet a she-bear robbed of its cubs
than to confront a fool immersed in
folly.
13 Evil will not depart from the house
of one who returns evil for good.
14 The beginning of strife is like letting out
water;
so stop before the quarrel breaks out.
15 One who justifies the wicked and one who
condemns the righteous

a Gk Syr Vg Tg: Heb *to plan*   *b* Or *a noble person*

are both alike an abomination to the
LORD.

16 Why should fools have a price in hand
to buy wisdom, when they have no mind
to learn?

17 A friend loves at all times,
and kinsfolk are born to share adversity.

18 It is senseless to give a pledge,
to become surety for a neighbor.

19 One who loves transgression loves strife;
one who builds a high threshold invites
broken bones.

20 The crooked of mind do not prosper,
and the perverse of tongue fall into
calamity.

21 The one who begets a fool gets trouble;
the parent of a fool has no joy.

22 A cheerful heart is a good medicine,
but a downcast spirit dries up the bones.

23 The wicked accept a concealed bribe
to pervert the ways of justice.

24 The discerning person looks to wisdom,
but the eyes of a fool to the ends of the
earth.

25 Foolish children are a grief to their father
and bitterness to her who bore them.

26 To impose a fine on the innocent is not
right,
or to flog the noble for their integrity.

27 One who spares words is knowledgeable;
one who is cool in spirit has
understanding.

28 Even fools who keep silent are considered
wise;
when they close their lips, they are
deemed intelligent.

18 The one who lives alone is
self-indulgent,
showing contempt for all who have
sound judgment.*ᵃ*

2 A fool takes no pleasure in understanding,
but only in expressing personal opinion.

3 When wickedness comes, contempt comes
also;
and with dishonor comes disgrace.

4 The words of the mouth are deep waters;
the fountain of wisdom is a gushing
stream.

5 It is not right to be partial to the guilty,
or to subvert the innocent in judgment.

6 A fool's lips bring strife,
and a fool's mouth invites a flogging.

7 The mouths of fools are their ruin,
and their lips a snare to themselves.

8 The words of a whisperer are like delicious
morsels;

they go down into the inner parts of the
body.

9 One who is slack in work
is close kin to a vandal.

10 The name of the LORD is a strong tower;
the righteous run into it and are safe.

11 The wealth of the rich is their strong city;
in their imagination it is like a high wall.

12 Before destruction one's heart is haughty,
but humility goes before honor.

13 If one gives answer before hearing,
it is folly and shame.

14 The human spirit will endure sickness;
but a broken spirit—who can bear?

15 An intelligent mind acquires knowledge,
and the ear of the wise seeks knowledge.

16 A gift opens doors;
it gives access to the great.

17 The one who first states a case seems right,
until the other comes and
cross-examines.

18 Casting the lot puts an end to disputes
and decides between powerful
contenders.

19 An ally offended is stronger than a city;*ᵇ*
such quarreling is like the bars of a castle.

20 From the fruit of the mouth one's stomach
is satisfied;
the yield of the lips brings satisfaction.

21 Death and life are in the power of the
tongue,
and those who love it will eat its fruits.

22 He who finds a wife finds a good thing,
and obtains favor from the LORD.

23 The poor use entreaties,
but the rich answer roughly.

24 Some*ᶜ* friends play at friendship*ᵈ*
but a true friend sticks closer than one's
nearest kin.

19 Better the poor walking in integrity
than one perverse of speech who is a
fool.

2 Desire without knowledge is not good,
and one who moves too hurriedly misses
the way.

3 One's own folly leads to ruin,
yet the heart rages against the LORD.

4 Wealth brings many friends,
but the poor are left friendless.

5 A false witness will not go unpunished,
and a liar will not escape.

6 Many seek the favor of the generous,
and everyone is a friend to a giver of gifts.

7 If the poor are hated even by their kin,
how much more are they shunned by
their friends!

---

a Meaning of Heb uncertain *b* Gk Syr Vg Tg: Meaning of Heb uncertain *c* Syr Tg: Heb *A man of* *d* Cn Compare Syr Vg Tg: Meaning of
Heb uncertain

When they call after them, they are not there.[a]

8 To get wisdom is to love oneself;
   to keep understanding is to prosper.
9 A false witness will not go unpunished,
   and the liar will perish.
10 It is not fitting for a fool to live in luxury,
   much less for a slave to rule over princes.
11 Those with good sense are slow to anger,
   and it is their glory to overlook an
   offense.
12 A king's anger is like the growling of a lion,
   but his favor is like dew on the grass.
13 A stupid child is ruin to a father,
   and a wife's quarreling is a continual
   dripping of rain.
14 House and wealth are inherited from
   parents,
   but a prudent wife is from the LORD.
15 Laziness brings on deep sleep;
   an idle person will suffer hunger.
16 Those who keep the commandment will
   live;
   those who are heedless of their ways will
   die.
17 Whoever is kind to the poor lends to the
   LORD,
   and will be repaid in full.
18 Discipline your children while there is
   hope;
   do not set your heart on their
   destruction.
19 A violent tempered person will pay the
   penalty;
   if you effect a rescue, you will only have
   to do it again.[a]
20 Listen to advice and accept instruction,
   that you may gain wisdom for the future.
21 The human mind may devise many plans,
   but it is the purpose of the LORD that will
   be established.
22 What is desirable in a person is loyalty,
   and it is better to be poor than a liar.
23 The fear of the LORD is life indeed;
   filled with it one rests secure
   and suffers no harm.
24 The lazy person buries a hand in the dish,
   and will not even bring it back to the
   mouth.
25 Strike a scoffer, and the simple will learn
   prudence;
   reprove the intelligent, and they will gain
   knowledge.
26 Those who do violence to their father and
   chase away their mother
   are children who cause shame and bring
   reproach.

a Meaning of Heb uncertain

TEXT MESSAGE

When we think of dripping water, we most often think of a leaking faucet. But the dripping water of Proverbs 19.13 was much more annoying. It probably referred to a leaking roof. In biblical times, homes were made of mud and had flat roofs. With good care, roofs stayed pretty watertight, but leaky roofs were a common problem— and the source of many jokes.

Fact

This information has been scanned and is free of all known viruses. Please forward to all your friends.

27 Cease straying, my child, from the words of
   knowledge,
   in order that you may hear instruction.
28 A worthless witness mocks at justice,
   and the mouth of the wicked devours
   iniquity.
29 Condemnation is ready for scoffers,
   and flogging for the backs of fools.

20 Wine is a mocker, strong drink a
   brawler,
   and whoever is led astray by it is not wise.
2 The dread anger of a king is like the
   growling of a lion;
   anyone who provokes him to anger
   forfeits life itself.
3 It is honorable to refrain from strife,
   but every fool is quick to quarrel.
4 The lazy person does not plow in season;
   harvest comes, and there is nothing to be
   found.

5 The purposes in the human mind are like
    deep water,
    but the intelligent will draw them out.
6 Many proclaim themselves loyal,
    but who can find one worthy of trust?
7 The righteous walk in integrity—
    happy are the children who follow them!
8 A king who sits on the throne of judgment
    winnows all evil with his eyes.
9 Who can say, "I have made my heart clean;
    I am pure from my sin"?
10 Diverse weights and diverse measures
    are both alike an abomination to the
    Lord.
11 Even children make themselves known by
    their acts,
    by whether what they do is pure and
    right.
12 The hearing ear and the seeing eye—
    the Lord has made them both.
13 Do not love sleep, or else you will come to
    poverty;
    open your eyes, and you will have plenty
    of bread.
14 "Bad, bad," says the buyer,
    then goes away and boasts.
15 There is gold, and abundance of costly
    stones;
    but the lips informed by knowledge are a
    precious jewel.
16 Take the garment of one who has given
    surety for a stranger;
    seize the pledge given as surety for
    foreigners.
17 Bread gained by deceit is sweet,
    but afterward the mouth will be full of
    gravel.
18 Plans are established by taking advice;
    wage war by following wise guidance.
19 A gossip reveals secrets;
    therefore do not associate with a
    babbler.
20 If you curse father or mother,
    your lamp will go out in utter darkness.
21 An estate quickly acquired in the beginning
    will not be blessed in the end.
22 Do not say, "I will repay evil";
    wait for the Lord, and he will help you.
23 Differing weights are an abomination to
    the Lord,
    and false scales are not good.
24 All our steps are ordered by the Lord;
    how then can we understand our own
    ways?
25 It is a snare for one to say rashly, "It is holy,"
    and begin to reflect only after making a
    vow.

26 A wise king winnows the wicked,
    and drives the wheel over them.
27 The human spirit is the lamp of the Lord,
    searching every inmost part.
28 Loyalty and faithfulness preserve the king,
    and his throne is upheld by
    righteousness.*a*
29 The glory of youths is their strength,
    but the beauty of the aged is their gray
    hair.
30 Blows that wound cleanse away evil;
    beatings make clean the innermost
    parts.

21 The king's heart is a stream of water in
    the hand of the Lord;
    he turns it wherever he will.
2 All deeds are right in the sight of the doer,
    but the Lord weighs the heart.
3 To do righteousness and justice
    is more acceptable to the Lord than
    sacrifice.
4 Haughty eyes and a proud heart—
    the lamp of the wicked—are sin.
5 The plans of the diligent lead surely to
    abundance,
    but everyone who is hasty comes only to
    want.
6 The getting of treasures by a lying tongue
    is a fleeting vapor and a snare*b* of death.
7 The violence of the wicked will sweep them
    away,
    because they refuse to do what is just.
8 The way of the guilty is crooked,
    but the conduct of the pure is right.
9 It is better to live in a corner of the
    housetop
    than in a house shared with a
    contentious wife.
10 The souls of the wicked desire evil;
    their neighbors find no mercy in their
    eyes.
11 When a scoffer is punished, the simple
    become wiser;
    when the wise are instructed, they
    increase in knowledge.
12 The Righteous One observes the house of
    the wicked;
    he casts the wicked down to ruin.
13 If you close your ear to the cry of the poor,
    you will cry out and not be heard.
14 A gift in secret averts anger;
    and a concealed bribe in the bosom,
    strong wrath.
15 When justice is done, it is a joy to the
    righteous,
    but dismay to evildoers.

a Gk: Heb *loyalty* *b* Gk: Heb *seekers*

¹⁶ Whoever wanders from the way of understanding
will rest in the assembly of the dead.
¹⁷ Whoever loves pleasure will suffer want;
whoever loves wine and oil will not be rich.
¹⁸ The wicked is a ransom for the righteous,
and the faithless for the upright.
¹⁹ It is better to live in a desert land
than with a contentious and fretful wife.
²⁰ Precious treasure remains^a in the house of the wise,
but the fool devours it.
²¹ Whoever pursues righteousness and kindness
will find life^b and honor.
²² One wise person went up against a city of warriors
and brought down the stronghold in which they trusted.
²³ To watch over mouth and tongue
is to keep out of trouble.
²⁴ The proud, haughty person, named "Scoffer,"
acts with arrogant pride.
²⁵ The craving of the lazy person is fatal,
for lazy hands refuse to labor.
²⁶ All day long the wicked covet,^c
but the righteous give and do not hold back.
²⁷ The sacrifice of the wicked is an abomination;
how much more when brought with evil intent.
²⁸ A false witness will perish,
but a good listener will testify successfully.
²⁹ The wicked put on a bold face,
but the upright give thought to^d their ways.
³⁰ No wisdom, no understanding, no counsel,
can avail against the LORD.
³¹ The horse is made ready for the day of battle,
but the victory belongs to the LORD.

22 A good name is to be chosen rather than great riches,
and favor is better than silver or gold.
² The rich and the poor have this in common:
the LORD is the maker of them all.
³ The clever see danger and hide;
but the simple go on, and suffer for it.
⁴ The reward for humility and fear of the LORD
is riches and honor and life.
⁵ Thorns and snares are in the way of the perverse;

IT'S TRADITION

SO, WHERE'S THE GIFT RECEIPT?

Read **Proverbs 10.27** and **22.4**. How can fear of the Lord be a gift? What kind of fear is it, anyway? The kind that makes you afraid to act, or pummels you with guilt, or fills you with dread and anxiety? Doesn't sound like any kind of gift I'd want to open, that's for sure.

Of course, that's not what the gift of fear of the Lord means at all, but somewhere along the way the real meaning got lost in translation. The kind of fear of the Lord that leads to knowledge and wisdom is really a sense of *awe and reverence*. It's what happens when you get in touch with the gracious and transcendent power of the almighty God.

Unwrapping the gift of fear of the Lord and using it happens when you sharpen your awareness to what is happening in God's creation, in your own life, and even in your own body. It happens when you're on a camping trip sitting around the fire and you gaze up at a beautiful starry sky and realize how awesome the God who created it is. It happens when you're involved in a physical activity and you become aware of how easily your body moves and you know something outside yourself made it that way. It happens when you realize you've accomplished something you couldn't have done by yourself, no matter how hard you tried.

This gift of the fear of the Lord leads you to knowing with your heart and mind that God is totally in charge, steering all of creation toward good—and at the same time allowing you the gift of your free will. It's knowing—really knowing and understanding—that God is awesome!

the cautious will keep far from them.
⁶ Train children in the right way,
and when old, they will not stray.
⁷ The rich rule over the poor,

---

a Gk: Heb *and oil* *b* Gk: Heb *life and righteousness* *c* Gk: Heb *all day long one covets covetously* *d* Another reading is *establish*

and the borrower is the slave of the
lender.
8 Whoever sows injustice will reap calamity,
and the rod of anger will fail.
9 Those who are generous are blessed,
for they share their bread with the poor.
10 Drive out a scoffer, and strife goes out;
quarreling and abuse will cease.
11 Those who love a pure heart and are
gracious in speech
will have the king as a friend.
12 The eyes of the LORD keep watch over
knowledge,
but he overthrows the words of the
faithless.
13 The lazy person says, "There is a lion
outside!
I shall be killed in the streets!"
14 The mouth of a loose*a* woman is a deep pit;
he with whom the LORD is angry falls
into it.
15 Folly is bound up in the heart of a boy,
but the rod of discipline drives it far
away.
16 Oppressing the poor in order to enrich
oneself,
and giving to the rich, will lead only to
loss.

Sayings of the Wise

17   The words of the wise:

Incline your ear and hear my words,*b*
and apply your mind to my teaching;
18 for it will be pleasant if you keep them
within you,
if all of them are ready on your lips.
19 So that your trust may be in the LORD,
I have made them known to you today—
yes, to you.
20 Have I not written for you thirty sayings
of admonition and knowledge,
21 to show you what is right and true,
so that you may give a true answer to
those who sent you?

22 Do not rob the poor because they are poor,
or crush the afflicted at the gate;
23 for the LORD pleads their cause
and despoils of life those who despoil
them.
24 Make no friends with those given to anger,
and do not associate with hotheads,
25 or you may learn their ways
and entangle yourself in a snare.
26 Do not be one of those who give pledges,
who become surety for debts.

a Heb *strange*   *b* Cn Compare Gk: Heb *Incline your ear, and hear the
words of the wise*

²⁷ If you have nothing with which to pay,
 why should your bed be taken from
 under you?
²⁸ Do not remove the ancient landmark
 that your ancestors set up.
²⁹ Do you see those who are skillful in their
 work?
 They will serve kings;
 they will not serve common people.

23

When you sit down to eat with a ruler,
 observe carefully what^a is before you,
² and put a knife to your throat
 if you have a big appetite.
³ Do not desire the ruler's^b delicacies,
 for they are deceptive food.
⁴ Do not wear yourself out to get rich;
 be wise enough to desist.
⁵ When your eyes light upon it, it is gone;
 for suddenly it takes wings to itself,
 flying like an eagle toward heaven.
⁶ Do not eat the bread of the stingy;
 do not desire their delicacies;
⁷ for like a hair in the throat, so are they.^c
 "Eat and drink!" they say to you;
 but they do not mean it.
⁸ You will vomit up the little you have eaten,
 and you will waste your pleasant words.
⁹ Do not speak in the hearing of a fool,
 who will only despise the wisdom of your
 words.
¹⁰ Do not remove an ancient landmark
 or encroach on the fields of orphans,
¹¹ for their redeemer is strong;
 he will plead their cause against you.
¹² Apply your mind to instruction
 and your ear to words of knowledge.
¹³ Do not withhold discipline from your
 children;
 if you beat them with a rod, they will not
 die.
¹⁴ If you beat them with the rod,
 you will save their lives from Sheol.
¹⁵ My child, if your heart is wise,
 my heart too will be glad.
¹⁶ My soul will rejoice
 when your lips speak what is right.
¹⁷ Do not let your heart envy sinners,
 but always continue in the fear of the
 LORD.
¹⁸ Surely there is a future,
 and your hope will not be cut off.
¹⁹ Hear, my child, and be wise,
 and direct your mind in the way.
²⁰ Do not be among winebibbers,
 or among gluttonous eaters of meat;

²¹ for the drunkard and the glutton will come
 to poverty,
 and drowsiness will clothe them with
 rags.
²² Listen to your father who begot you,
 and do not despise your mother when
 she is old.
²³ Buy truth, and do not sell it;
 buy wisdom, instruction, and
 understanding.
²⁴ The father of the righteous will greatly
 rejoice;
 he who begets a wise son will be glad in
 him.
²⁵ Let your father and mother be glad;
 let her who bore you rejoice.

²⁶ My child, give me your heart,
 and let your eyes observe^d my ways.
²⁷ For a prostitute is a deep pit;
 an adulteress^e is a narrow well.
²⁸ She lies in wait like a robber
 and increases the number of the
 faithless.

²⁹ Who has woe? Who has sorrow?
 Who has strife? Who has complaining?
 Who has wounds without cause?
 Who has redness of eyes?
³⁰ Those who linger late over wine,
 those who keep trying mixed wines.
³¹ Do not look at wine when it is red,
 when it sparkles in the cup
 and goes down smoothly.
³² At the last it bites like a serpent,
 and stings like an adder.
³³ Your eyes will see strange things,
 and your mind utter perverse things.
³⁴ You will be like one who lies down in the
 midst of the sea,
 like one who lies on the top of a mast.^c
³⁵ "They struck me," you will say,^f "but I was
 not hurt;
 they beat me, but I did not feel it.
 When shall I awake?
 I will seek another drink."

24

Do not envy the wicked,
 nor desire to be with them;
² for their minds devise violence,
 and their lips talk of mischief.

³ By wisdom a house is built,
 and by understanding it is established;
⁴ by knowledge the rooms are filled
 with all precious and pleasant riches.
⁵ Wise warriors are mightier than strong
 ones,^g

---

a Or *who* *b* Heb *his* *c* Meaning of Heb uncertain *d* Another reading is *delight in* *e* Heb *an alien woman* *f* Gk Syr Vg Tg: Heb lacks *you will say* *g* Gk Compare Syr Tg: Heb *A wise man is strength*

House—© Jessica Jones, 18

and those who have knowledge than
  those who have strength;
6 for by wise guidance you can wage your war,
  and in abundance of counselors there is
    victory.

7 Wisdom is too high for fools;
  in the gate they do not open their
    mouths.

8 Whoever plans to do evil
  will be called a mischief-maker.
9 The devising of folly is sin,
  and the scoffer is an abomination to all.

10 If you faint in the day of adversity,
  your strength being small;
11 if you hold back from rescuing those taken
    away to death,
  those who go staggering to the slaughter;
12 if you say, "Look, we did not know this"—
  does not he who weighs the heart
    perceive it?
  Does not he who keeps watch over your
    soul know it?
  And will he not repay all according to
    their deeds?

13 My child, eat honey, for it is good,
  and the drippings of the honeycomb are
    sweet to your taste.
14 Know that wisdom is such to your soul;
  if you find it, you will find a future,
  and your hope will not be cut off.

15 Do not lie in wait like an outlaw against the
    home of the righteous;
  do no violence to the place where the
    righteous live;
16 for though they fall seven times, they will
    rise again;
  but the wicked are overthrown by
    calamity.

17 Do not rejoice when your enemies fall,
  and do not let your heart be glad when
    they stumble,
18 or else the LORD will see it and be
    displeased,
  and turn away his anger from them.

19 Do not fret because of evildoers.
  Do not envy the wicked;
20 for the evil have no future;
  the lamp of the wicked will go out.

21 My child, fear the LORD and the king,
  and do not disobey either of them;*a*
22 for disaster comes from them suddenly,
  and who knows the ruin that both can
    bring?

Further Sayings of the Wise

23   These also are sayings of the wise:

  Partiality in judging is not good.
24 Whoever says to the wicked, "You are
    innocent,"

a Gk: Heb *do not associate with those who change*

will be cursed by peoples, abhorred by
nations;
25 but those who rebuke the wicked will have
delight,
and a good blessing will come upon
them.

26 One who gives an honest answer
gives a kiss on the lips.

27 Prepare your work outside,
get everything ready for you in the field;
and after that build your house.

28 Do not be a witness against your neighbor
without cause,
and do not deceive with your lips.
29 Do not say, "I will do to others as they have
done to me;
I will pay them back for what they have
done."

30 I passed by the field of one who was lazy,
by the vineyard of a stupid person;
31 and see, it was all overgrown with thorns;
the ground was covered with nettles,
and its stone wall was broken down.
32 Then I saw and considered it;
I looked and received instruction.
33 A little sleep, a little slumber,
a little folding of the hands to rest,
34 and poverty will come upon you like a
robber,
and want, like an armed warrior.

25 Further Wise Sayings of Solomon

These are other proverbs of Solomon that the
officials of King Hezekiah of Judah copied.

2 It is the glory of God to conceal things,
but the glory of kings is to search things
out.
3 Like the heavens for height, like the earth
for depth,
so the mind of kings is unsearchable.
4 Take away the dross from the silver,
and the smith has material for a vessel;
5 take away the wicked from the presence of
the king,
and his throne will be established in
righteousness.
6 Do not put yourself forward in the king's
presence
or stand in the place of the great;
7 for it is better to be told, "Come up here,"
than to be put lower in the presence of a
noble.

What your eyes have seen
8 do not hastily bring into court;
for^a what will you do in the end,

when your neighbor puts you to shame?
9 Argue your case with your neighbor directly,
and do not disclose another's secret;
10 or else someone who hears you will bring
shame upon you,
and your ill repute will have no end.

11 A word fitly spoken
is like apples of gold in a setting of silver.
12 Like a gold ring or an ornament of gold
is a wise rebuke to a listening ear.
13 Like the cold of snow in the time of harvest
are faithful messengers to those who
send them;
they refresh the spirit of their masters.
14 Like clouds and wind without rain
is one who boasts of a gift never given.
15 With patience a ruler may be persuaded,
and a soft tongue can break bones.
16 If you have found honey, eat only enough
for you,
or else, having too much, you will
vomit it.
17 Let your foot be seldom in your neighbor's
house,
otherwise the neighbor will become
weary of you and hate you.
18 Like a war club, a sword, or a sharp arrow
is one who bears false witness against a
neighbor.
19 Like a bad tooth or a lame foot
is trust in a faithless person in time of
trouble.
20 Like vinegar on a wound^b
is one who sings songs to a heavy heart.
Like a moth in clothing or a worm in wood,
sorrow gnaws at the human heart.^c
21 If your enemies are hungry, give them bread
to eat;
and if they are thirsty, give them water to
drink;
22 for you will heap coals of fire on their
heads,
and the LORD will reward you.
23 The north wind produces rain,
and a backbiting tongue, angry looks.
24 It is better to live in a corner of the
housetop
than in a house shared with a
contentious wife.
25 Like cold water to a thirsty soul,
so is good news from a far country.
26 Like a muddied spring or a polluted
fountain
are the righteous who give way before
the wicked.
27 It is not good to eat much honey,
or to seek honor on top of honor.

a Cn: Heb or else b Gk: Heb Like one who takes off a garment on a cold day, like vinegar on lye c Gk Syr Tg: Heb lacks Like a moth . . . human heart

28 Like a city breached, without walls,
  is one who lacks self-control.

26

Like snow in summer or rain in harvest,
  so honor is not fitting for a fool.
2 Like a sparrow in its flitting, like a swallow
    in its flying,
  an undeserved curse goes nowhere.
3 A whip for the horse, a bridle for the
    donkey,
  and a rod for the back of fools.
4 Do not answer fools according to their folly,
  or you will be a fool yourself.
5 Answer fools according to their folly,
  or they will be wise in their own eyes.
6 It is like cutting off one's foot and drinking
    down violence,
  to send a message by a fool.
7 The legs of a disabled person hang limp;
  so does a proverb in the mouth of a fool.
8 It is like binding a stone in a sling
  to give honor to a fool.
9 Like a thornbush brandished by the hand of
    a drunkard
  is a proverb in the mouth of a fool.
10 Like an archer who wounds everybody
  is one who hires a passing fool or
    drunkard.[a]
11 Like a dog that returns to its vomit
  is a fool who reverts to his folly.
12 Do you see persons wise in their own eyes?
  There is more hope for fools than for
    them.
13 The lazy person says, "There is a lion in the
    road!
  There is a lion in the streets!"
14 As a door turns on its hinges,
  so does a lazy person in bed.
15 The lazy person buries a hand in the dish,
  and is too tired to bring it back to the
    mouth.
16 The lazy person is wiser in self-esteem
  than seven who can answer discreetly.
17 Like somebody who takes a passing dog by
    the ears
  is one who meddles in the quarrel of
    another.
18 Like a maniac who shoots deadly firebrands
    and arrows,
19 so is one who deceives a neighbor
  and says, "I am only joking!"
20 For lack of wood the fire goes out,
  and where there is no whisperer,
    quarreling ceases.
21 As charcoal is to hot embers and wood to
    fire,

so is a quarrelsome person for kindling
    strife.
22 The words of a whisperer are like delicious
    morsels;
  they go down into the inner parts of the
    body.
23 Like the glaze[b] covering an earthen vessel
  are smooth[c] lips with an evil heart.
24 An enemy dissembles in speaking
  while harboring deceit within;
25 when an enemy speaks graciously, do not
    believe it,
  for there are seven abominations
    concealed within;
26 though hatred is covered with guile,
  the enemy's wickedness will be exposed
    in the assembly.
27 Whoever digs a pit will fall into it,
  and a stone will come back on the one
    who starts it rolling.
28 A lying tongue hates its victims,
  and a flattering mouth works ruin.

27

Do not boast about tomorrow,
  for you do not know what a day may
    bring.
2 Let another praise you, and not your own
    mouth—
  a stranger, and not your own lips.
3 A stone is heavy, and sand is weighty,
  but a fool's provocation is heavier than
    both.
4 Wrath is cruel, anger is overwhelming,
  but who is able to stand before jealousy?
5 Better is open rebuke
  than hidden love.
6 Well meant are the wounds a friend inflicts,
  but profuse are the kisses of an enemy.
7 The sated appetite spurns honey,
  but to a ravenous appetite even the bitter
    is sweet.
8 Like a bird that strays from its nest
  is one who strays from home.
9 Perfume and incense make the heart glad,
  but the soul is torn by trouble.[d]
10 Do not forsake your friend or the friend of
    your parent;
  do not go to the house of your kindred in
    the day of your calamity.
  Better is a neighbor who is nearby
    than kindred who are far away.
11 Be wise, my child, and make my heart glad,
  so that I may answer whoever
    reproaches me.
12 The clever see danger and hide;
  but the simple go on, and suffer for it.

---

a Meaning of Heb uncertain b Cn: Heb *silver of dross* c Gk: Heb *burning* d Gk: Heb *the sweetness of a friend is better than one's own
counsel*

My Great
Commission

Lord, you put this burden on my heart:
To show the world they need to be a part
Of the greatest plan ever made,
Of an idea that will never fade.
But how can I share? Where do I start?
How can I show what you've done with my heart?
They need to know of this love that's so great,
But my words, Lord, I can never get straight.
I know I have no excuse
So, Lord, my life is yours to use.
Be with me as I spread your Word
And never let me be deterred.
I don't know when or where, but I do know
You want me to share.

My Great Commission—© Megan Houtchen, 16

13 Take the garment of one who has given
surety for a stranger;
seize the pledge given as surety for
foreigners.*a*
14 Whoever blesses a neighbor with a loud
voice,
rising early in the morning,
will be counted as cursing.
15 A continual dripping on a rainy day
and a contentious wife are alike;
16 to restrain her is to restrain the wind
or to grasp oil in the right hand.*b*
17 Iron sharpens iron,
and one person sharpens the wits*c* of
another.
18 Anyone who tends a fig tree will eat its fruit,
and anyone who takes care of a master
will be honored.
19 Just as water reflects the face,
so one human heart reflects another.
20 Sheol and Abaddon are never satisfied,
and human eyes are never satisfied.
21 The crucible is for silver, and the furnace is
for gold,
so a person is tested*d* by being praised.
22 Crush a fool in a mortar with a pestle
along with crushed grain,
but the folly will not be driven out.

23 Know well the condition of your flocks,
and give attention to your herds;
24 for riches do not last forever,
nor a crown for all generations.
25 When the grass is gone, and new growth
appears,
and the herbage of the mountains is
gathered,
26 the lambs will provide your clothing,
and the goats the price of a field;
27 there will be enough goats' milk for your
food,
for the food of your household
and nourishment for your servant-girls.

28 The wicked flee when no one pursues,
but the righteous are as bold as a lion.
2 When a land rebels
it has many rulers;
but with an intelligent ruler
there is lasting order.*b*
3 A ruler*e* who oppresses the poor
is a beating rain that leaves no food.
4 Those who forsake the law praise the
wicked,
but those who keep the law struggle
against them.
5 The evil do not understand justice,
but those who seek the Lord understand
it completely.
6 Better to be poor and walk in integrity
than to be crooked in one's ways even
though rich.
7 Those who keep the law are wise children,
but companions of gluttons shame their
parents.
8 One who augments wealth by exorbitant
interest
gathers it for another who is kind to the
poor.
9 When one will not listen to the law,
even one's prayers are an abomination.
10 Those who mislead the upright into evil
ways
will fall into pits of their own making,
but the blameless will have a goodly
inheritance.
11 The rich is wise in self-esteem,
but an intelligent poor person sees
through the pose.
12 When the righteous triumph, there is great
glory,
but when the wicked prevail, people go
into hiding.
13 No one who conceals transgressions will
prosper,
but one who confesses and forsakes
them will obtain mercy.
14 Happy is the one who is never without fear,
but one who is hard-hearted will fall into
calamity.
15 Like a roaring lion or a charging bear
is a wicked ruler over a poor people.
16 A ruler who lacks understanding is a cruel
oppressor;
but one who hates unjust gain will enjoy
a long life.
17 If someone is burdened with the blood of
another,
let that killer be a fugitive until death;
let no one offer assistance.

a Vg and 20.16: Heb *for a foreign woman* *b* Meaning of Heb uncertain *c* Heb *face* *d* Heb lacks *is tested* *e* Cn: Heb *A poor person*

18 One who walks in integrity will be safe,
 but whoever follows crooked ways will
  fall into the Pit.*a*

19 Anyone who tills the land will have plenty
 of bread,
 but one who follows worthless pursuits
  will have plenty of poverty.

20 The faithful will abound with blessings,
 but one who is in a hurry to be rich will
  not go unpunished.

21 To show partiality is not good—
 yet for a piece of bread a person may do
  wrong.

22 The miser is in a hurry to get rich
 and does not know that loss is sure to
  come.

23 Whoever rebukes a person will afterward
 find more favor
 than one who flatters with the tongue.

24 Anyone who robs father or mother
 and says, "That is no crime,"
 is partner to a thug.

25 The greedy person stirs up strife,
 but whoever trusts in the LORD will be
  enriched.

26 Those who trust in their own wits are fools;
 but those who walk in wisdom come
  through safely.

27 Whoever gives to the poor will lack
 nothing,
 but one who turns a blind eye will get
  many a curse.

28 When the wicked prevail, people go into
 hiding;
 but when they perish, the righteous
  increase.

29

One who is often reproved, yet remains
 stubborn,
 will suddenly be broken beyond healing.

2 When the righteous are in authority, the
 people rejoice;
 but when the wicked rule, the people
  groan.

3 A child who loves wisdom makes a parent
 glad,
 but to keep company with prostitutes is
  to squander one's substance.

4 By justice a king gives stability to the land,
 but one who makes heavy exactions
  ruins it.

5 Whoever flatters a neighbor
 is spreading a net for the neighbor's feet.

6 In the transgression of the evil there is a
 snare,
 but the righteous sing and rejoice.

7 The righteous know the rights of the poor;
 the wicked have no such understanding.

8 Scoffers set a city aflame,
 but the wise turn away wrath.

9 If the wise go to law with fools,
 there is ranting and ridicule without
  relief.

10 The bloodthirsty hate the blameless,
 and they seek the life of the upright.

11 A fool gives full vent to anger,
 but the wise quietly holds it back.

12 If a ruler listens to falsehood,
 all his officials will be wicked.

13 The poor and the oppressor have this in
 common:
 the LORD gives light to the eyes of both.

14 If a king judges the poor with equity,
 his throne will be established forever.

15 The rod and reproof give wisdom,
 but a mother is disgraced by a neglected
  child.

16 When the wicked are in authority,
 transgression increases,
 but the righteous will look upon their
  downfall.

17 Discipline your children, and they will give
 you rest;
 they will give delight to your heart.

18 Where there is no prophecy, the people cast
 off restraint,
 but happy are those who keep the law.

19 By mere words servants are not disciplined,
 for though they understand, they will not
  give heed.

20 Do you see someone who is hasty in
 speech?
 There is more hope for a fool than for
  anyone like that.

21 A slave pampered from childhood
 will come to a bad end.*b*

22 One given to anger stirs up strife,
 and the hothead causes much
  transgression.

23 A person's pride will bring humiliation,
 but one who is lowly in spirit will obtain
  honor.

24 To be a partner of a thief is to hate one's
 own life;
 one hears the victim's curse, but
  discloses nothing.*c*

25 The fear of others*d* lays a snare,
 but one who trusts in the LORD is secure.

26 Many seek the favor of a ruler,
 but it is from the LORD that one gets
  justice.

27 The unjust are an abomination to the
 righteous,
 but the upright are an abomination to
  the wicked.

---

a Syr: Heb *fall all at once* *b* Vg: Meaning of Heb uncertain *c* Meaning of Heb uncertain *d* Or *human fear*

30 Sayings of Agur

The words of Agur son of Jakeh. An oracle.

Thus says the man: I am weary, O God,
I am weary, O God. How can I prevail?[a]
2 Surely I am too stupid to be human;
I do not have human understanding.
3 I have not learned wisdom,
nor have I knowledge of the holy ones.[b]
4 Who has ascended to heaven and come
down?
Who has gathered the wind in the hollow
of the hand?
Who has wrapped up the waters in a
garment?
Who has established all the ends of the
earth?
What is the person's name?
And what is the name of the person's
child?
Surely you know!

5 Every word of God proves true;
he is a shield to those who take refuge in
him.
6 Do not add to his words,
or else he will rebuke you, and you will
be found a liar.

7 Two things I ask of you;
do not deny them to me before I die:
8 Remove far from me falsehood and lying;
give me neither poverty nor riches;
feed me with the food that I need,
9 or I shall be full, and deny you,
and say, "Who is the Lord?"
or I shall be poor, and steal,
and profane the name of my God.

10 Do not slander a servant to a master,
or the servant will curse you, and you will
be held guilty.

11 There are those who curse their fathers
and do not bless their mothers.
12 There are those who are pure in their own
eyes
yet are not cleansed of their filthiness.
13 There are those—how lofty are their eyes,
how high their eyelids lift!—
14 there are those whose teeth are swords,
whose teeth are knives,
to devour the poor from off the earth,
the needy from among mortals.

15 The leech[c] has two daughters;
"Give, give," they cry.
Three things are never satisfied;
four never say, "Enough":
16 Sheol, the barren womb,
the earth ever thirsty for water,
and the fire that never says,
"Enough."[c]

17 The eye that mocks a father
and scorns to obey a mother
will be pecked out by the ravens of the
valley
and eaten by the vultures.

18 Three things are too wonderful for me;
four I do not understand:
19 the way of an eagle in the sky,
the way of a snake on a rock,
the way of a ship on the high seas,
and the way of a man with a girl.

20 This is the way of an adulteress:
she eats, and wipes her mouth,
and says, "I have done no wrong."

21 Under three things the earth
trembles;
under four it cannot bear up:
22 a slave when he becomes king,
and a fool when glutted with food;
23 an unloved woman when she gets a
husband,
and a maid when she succeeds her
mistress.

24 Four things on earth are small,
yet they are exceedingly wise:
25 the ants are a people without strength,
yet they provide their food in the
summer;
26 the badgers are a people without
power,
yet they make their homes in the
rocks;
27 the locusts have no king,
yet all of them march in rank;
28 the lizard[d] can be grasped in the hand,
yet it is found in kings' palaces.

29 Three things are stately in their stride;
four are stately in their gait:
30 the lion, which is mightiest among wild
animals
and does not turn back before any;
31 the strutting rooster,[e] the he-goat,
and a king striding before[c] his people.

32 If you have been foolish, exalting yourself,
or if you have been devising evil,
put your hand on your mouth.
33 For as pressing milk produces curds,
and pressing the nose produces blood,
so pressing anger produces strife.

---

a Or *I am spent.* Meaning of Heb uncertain b Or *Holy One* c Meaning of Heb uncertain d Or *spider* e Gk Syr Tg Compare Vg:
Meaning of Heb uncertain

31 The Teaching of King Lemuel's Mother

The words of King Lemuel. An oracle that his mother taught him:

2 No, my son! No, son of my womb!
   No, son of my vows!
3 Do not give your strength to women,
   your ways to those who destroy kings.
4 It is not for kings, O Lemuel,
   it is not for kings to drink wine,
   or for rulers to desire[a] strong drink;
5 or else they will drink and forget what has
         been decreed,
   and will pervert the rights of all the
         afflicted.
6 Give strong drink to one who is perishing,
   and wine to those in bitter distress;
7 let them drink and forget their poverty,
   and remember their misery no more.
8 Speak out for those who cannot speak,
   for the rights of all the destitute.[b]
9 Speak out, judge righteously,
   defend the rights of the poor and needy.

Untitled—© Erica Wallis, 17

Ode to a Capable Wife

10 A capable wife who can find?
   She is far more precious than jewels.
11 The heart of her husband trusts in her,
   and he will have no lack of gain.
12 She does him good, and not harm,
   all the days of her life.
13 She seeks wool and flax,
   and works with willing hands.
14 She is like the ships of the merchant,
   she brings her food from far away.
15 She rises while it is still night
   and provides food for her household
   and tasks for her servant-girls.
16 She considers a field and buys it;
   with the fruit of her hands she plants a
         vineyard.
17 She girds herself with strength,
   and makes her arms strong.
18 She perceives that her merchandise is
         profitable.
   Her lamp does not go out at night.
19 She puts her hands to the distaff,
   and her hands hold the spindle.
20 She opens her hand to the poor,
   and reaches out her hands to the needy.

21 She is not afraid for her household when it
         snows,
   for all her household are clothed in
         crimson.
22 She makes herself coverings;
   her clothing is fine linen and purple.
23 Her husband is known in the city gates,
   taking his seat among the elders of the
         land.
24 She makes linen garments and sells them;
   she supplies the merchant with sashes.
25 Strength and dignity are her clothing,
   and she laughs at the time to come.
26 She opens her mouth with wisdom,
   and the teaching of kindness is on her
         tongue.
27 She looks well to the ways of her
         household,
   and does not eat the bread of idleness.
28 Her children rise up and call her happy;
   her husband too, and he praises her:
29 "Many women have done excellently,
   but you surpass them all."
30 Charm is deceitful, and beauty is vain,
   but a woman who fears the LORD is to be
         praised.
31 Give her a share in the fruit of her hands,
   and let her works praise her in the city
         gates.

a Cn: Heb *where*   b Heb *all children of passing away*

The Show—© Catherine Willms, 15

ECCLESIASTES

A MOMENT OF DOUBT

More!

What do you give to the person who has everything? Someplace to put it, obviously. But what about after that? Something that addresses the still unsatisfied longings of his or her heart. Even the wealthiest people in the world admit to still wanting more—they keep buying, buying, and buying. You know it's true yourself. Even when you've just finished shopping, there's usually still one more thing you wish you had. And once you've bought that extra thing you really wanted, that longing *still* won't go away.

Our society tells us that if we only had . . .

- more money
- a great boyfriend or girlfriend
- a better body
- a smarter brain
- all of the above

. . . then we'd be truly happy.

But the writer of Ecclesiastes just laughs at this idea—it's such a joke. Ask the guy who knows—the guy who had it all. The writer models himself after Solomon, who inherited his dad's kingdom—the Promised Land that Israel had always hoped for—and expanded its territory. He built the Temple, the center of worship for all of Israel. He had seven hundred wives, three hundred girlfriends, gold and silver, the finest Egyptian horses, and peaceful trade with the surrounding empires. He even surpassed all others in wisdom, so that many sought his counsel. Even kings and queens were impressed with his decisions.

So he should be feeling pretty great, right?

The writer has a strong message for us: when it comes down to it, a life built around all this peripheral stuff is just *meaningless.*

Ecclesiastes speaks a truth we don't like to hear. This book zeroes in on the dark and lonely emptiness of human pursuits. It's not until we face this darkness that we are able to recognize the true source of light.

> *"To live without faith, without a patrimony to defend, without a steady struggle for truth, that is not living, but existing."*
> —Bl. Pier Giorgio Frassati

WHO Although Ecclesiastes is traditionally attributed to King Solomon, the author is unknown.

WHAT A poetic book that honestly explores what really matters—and what doesn't—in life

WHEN Written sometime between the third and second century B.C.

WHERE Not known for sure—some scholars say Phoenicia (an ancient middle eastern kingdom); others say Egypt

PATH OF DISCIPLESHIP

Ecclesiastes is full of raw uncertainty. The author wrote down the feelings that many of us deal with, if we're honest. We wonder, *Is there really any meaning in life? What's the point of any of this?* One thing is certain: Jesus wants us to come to him with our doubts (see John 20.24–29).

The *Catechism of the Catholic Church* makes a distinction between voluntary and involuntary doubt: "If deliberately cultivated, doubt can lead to spiritual blindness" (2088). In other words, if a person deliberately looks for reasons to doubt, the ability to see God's action in his or her life and in the world will be reduced. So look for the positive in life, both spiritual and temporal, and leave the deliberate doubting for the things that don't really matter, like "reality TV" and whether your favorite yogurt really is as "low-fat" as the ads claim.

1 Reflections of a Royal Philosopher

The words of the Teacher,[a] the son of David, king in Jerusalem.

² Vanity of vanities, says the Teacher,[a]
vanity of vanities! All is vanity.
³ What do people gain from all the toil
at which they toil under the sun?
⁴ A generation goes, and a generation comes,
but the earth remains forever.
⁵ The sun rises and the sun goes down,
and hurries to the place where it rises.
⁶ The wind blows to the south,
and goes around to the north;
round and round goes the wind,
and on its circuits the wind returns.
⁷ All streams run to the sea,
but the sea is not full;
to the place where the streams flow,
there they continue to flow.
⁸ All things[b] are wearisome;
more than one can express;
the eye is not satisfied with seeing,
or the ear filled with hearing.
⁹ What has been is what will be,
and what has been done is what will be
done;
there is nothing new under the sun.
¹⁰ Is there a thing of which it is said,

"See, this is new"?
It has already been,
in the ages before us.
¹¹ The people of long ago are not
remembered,
nor will there be any remembrance
of people yet to come
by those who come after them.

The Futility of Seeking Wisdom

12 I, the Teacher,[a] when king over Israel in Jerusalem, ¹³applied my mind to seek and to search out by wisdom all that is done under heaven; it is an unhappy business that God has given to human beings to be busy with. ¹⁴I saw all the deeds that are done under the sun; and see, all is vanity and a chasing after wind.[c]

¹⁵ What is crooked cannot be made straight,
and what is lacking cannot be counted.

16 I said to myself, "I have acquired great wisdom, surpassing all who were over Jerusalem before me; and my mind has had great experience of wisdom and knowledge." ¹⁷And I applied my mind to know wisdom and to know madness and folly. I perceived that this also is but a chasing after wind.[c]

¹⁸ For in much wisdom is much vexation,
and those who increase knowledge
increase sorrow.

a Heb *Qoheleth*, traditionally rendered *Preacher* *b* Or *words* *c* Or *a feeding on wind*. See Hos 12.1

Butterfly Beauty—© Lucy Johnson, 15

2 The Futility of Self-Indulgence

I said to myself, "Come now, I will make a test of pleasure; enjoy yourself." But again, this also was vanity. [2]I said of laughter, "It is mad," and of pleasure, "What use is it?" [3]I searched with my mind how to cheer my body with wine—my mind still guiding me with wisdom—and how to lay hold on folly, until I might see what was good for mortals to do under heaven during the few days of their life. [4]I made great works; I built houses and planted vineyards for myself; [5]I made myself gardens and parks, and planted in them all kinds of fruit trees. [6]I made myself pools from which to water the forest of growing trees. [7]I bought male and female slaves, and had slaves who were born in my house; I also had great possessions of herds and flocks, more than any who had been before me in Jerusalem. [8]I also gathered for myself silver and gold and the treasure of kings and of the provinces; I got singers, both men and women, and delights of the flesh, and many concubines.[a]

9 So I became great and surpassed all who were before me in Jerusalem; also my wisdom remained with me. [10]Whatever my eyes desired I did not keep from them; I kept my heart from no pleasure, for my heart found pleasure in all my toil, and this was my reward for all my toil. [11]Then I considered all that my hands had done and the toil I had spent in doing it, and again, all was vanity and a chasing after wind,[b] and there was nothing to be gained under the sun.

Wisdom and Joy Given to One Who Pleases God

12 So I turned to consider wisdom and madness and folly; for what can the one do who comes after the king? Only what has already been done. [13]Then I saw that wisdom excels folly as light excels darkness.

[14] The wise have eyes in their head,
    but fools walk in darkness.

Yet I perceived that the same fate befalls all of them. [15]Then I said to myself, "What happens to the fool will happen to me also; why then have I been so very wise?" And I said to myself that this also is vanity. [16]For there is no enduring remembrance of the wise or of fools, seeing that in the days to come all will have been long forgotten. How can the wise die just like fools? [17]So I hated life, because what is done under the sun was grievous to me; for all is vanity and a chasing after wind.[b]

18 I hated all my toil in which I had toiled under the sun, seeing that I must leave it to those who come after me [19]—and who knows

---

a Meaning of Heb uncertain *b* Or *a feeding on wind*. See Hos 12.1

REALITY

IT'S ABOUT TIME

Here's a reflection on the gift of time itself. Read **Ecclesiastes 3.1–15.**

Time is of the essence today. People are rushed. They're trying to find time, manage time, or buy time. Everyone's busy. *You're* busy. You go to school, spend time with your friends, play sports, read, volunteer, take music lessons, help at home, text, send e-mails, and on and on.

Read and reflect on **Ecclesiastes 3.** It's a reminder that God's time is not always the time of humans. It touches a longing in the human heart. After reflecting on this passage at a retreat, a teen remarked, "If something like this is in the Bible, I'm going to read it all."

After you have read the chapter, find some Creative Space in this Bible and write your thoughts about the following:

- Do I take time to enjoy *time*?
- What season am I in? What about my family members? My best friend?
- What did I learn from reading these verses that I'd like to apply to my life?

Then share your thoughts with us at **Learner.CalltoDiscipleship.com.**

---

whether they will be wise or foolish? Yet they will be master of all for which I toiled and used my wisdom under the sun. This also is vanity. [20]So I turned and gave my heart up to despair concerning all the toil of my labors under the sun, [21]because sometimes one who has toiled with wisdom and knowledge and skill must leave all to be enjoyed by another who did not toil for it. This also is vanity and a great evil. [22]What do mortals get from all the toil and strain with which they toil under the sun? [23]For all their days are full of pain, and their work is a vexation; even at night their minds do not rest. This also is vanity.

24 There is nothing better for mortals than to eat and drink, and find enjoyment in their

Turf Buddies—© Catherine Willms, 15

 THIS

TRUE FRIENDS

Read **Ecclesiastes 4.7–12**.

They're the people who show up even when it was your fault. Who call you again after you forgot to call back. Who have your best interests at heart.

They're friends—*true* friends.

Who are they in your life? Not acquaintances or people who drift in and out, but true friends—the ones who'll help you up when you fall.

Got a name in mind?

Write the name where you can see it, and focus on each letter in turn. Think of an attribute you appreciate in your friend that begins with that first letter . . . then the second . . . and on through the name. Pause often. Picture your friend.

When you've finished your list, ask God to make you the same sort of friend to others. Thank God for bringing a true friendship into your life.

Commit your friend into God's hands, and ask God how you can cooperate with his purposes in your friend's life.

Want to bless your friend even further? Post your friend's name (with attributes) at **Learner.CalltoDiscipleship.com**. Then invite your friend to visit and see how much you value the friendship.

GOD IS REAL MY FRIENDS

toil. This also, I saw, is from the hand of God; [25]for apart from him[a] who can eat or who can have enjoyment? [26]For to the one who pleases him God gives wisdom and knowledge and joy; but to the sinner he gives the work of gathering and heaping, only to give to one who pleas-

es God. This also is vanity and a chasing after wind.[b]

3 Everything Has Its Time

For everything there is a season, and a time for every matter under heaven:

[2] a time to be born, and a time to die;
   a time to plant, and a time to pluck up what is planted;
[3] a time to kill, and a time to heal;
   a time to break down, and a time to build up;
[4] a time to weep, and a time to laugh;
   a time to mourn, and a time to dance;
[5] a time to throw away stones, and a time to gather stones together;
   a time to embrace, and a time to refrain from embracing;
[6] a time to seek, and a time to lose;
   a time to keep, and a time to throw away;
[7] a time to tear, and a time to sew;
   a time to keep silence, and a time to speak;
[8] a time to love, and a time to hate;
   a time for war, and a time for peace.

The God-Given Task

9 What gain have the workers from their toil? [10]I have seen the business that God has given to everyone to be busy with. [11]He has made everything suitable for its time; moreover he has put a sense of past and future into their minds, yet they cannot find out what God has done from the beginning to the end. [12]I know that there is nothing better for them than to be happy and enjoy themselves as long as they live; [13]moreover, it is God's gift that all should eat and drink and take pleasure in all their toil. [14]I know that whatever God does endures forever; nothing can be added to it, nor anything taken from it; God has done this, so that all should stand in awe before him. [15]That which is, already has been; that which is to be, already is; and God seeks out what has gone by.[c]

Judgment and the Future Belong to God

16 Moreover I saw under the sun that in the place of justice, wickedness was there, and in the place of righteousness, wickedness was there as well. [17]I said in my heart, God will judge the righteous and the wicked, for he has appointed a time for every matter, and for every work. [18]I said in my heart with regard to human beings that God is testing them to show that they are but animals. [19]For the fate of humans and the fate of animals is the same; as one dies, so dies the other. They all have the same breath, and humans have no advantage over the animals; for all is vanity. [20]All go to

a Gk Syr: Heb *apart from me* b Or *a feeding on wind.* See Hos 12.1 c Heb *what is pursued* one place; all are from the dust, and all turn to dust again. ²¹Who knows whether the human spirit goes upward and the spirit of animals goes downward to the earth? ²²So I saw that there is nothing better than that all should enjoy their work, for that is their lot; who can bring them to see what will be after them?

4 Again I saw all the oppressions that are practiced under the sun. Look, the tears of the oppressed—with no one to comfort them! On the side of their oppressors there was power— with no one to comfort them. ²And I thought the dead, who have already died, more fortunate than the living, who are still alive; ³but better than both is the one who has not yet been, and has not seen the evil deeds that are done under the sun.

4 Then I saw that all toil and all skill in work come from one person's envy of another. This also is vanity and a chasing after wind.ᵃ

⁵ Fools fold their hands
    and consume their own flesh.
⁶ Better is a handful with quiet
    than two handfuls with toil,
    and a chasing after wind.ᵃ

7 Again, I saw vanity under the sun: ⁸the case of solitary individuals, without sons or brothers; yet there is no end to all their toil, and their eyes are never satisfied with riches. "For whom am I toiling," they ask, "and depriving myself of pleasure?" This also is vanity and an unhappy business.

The Value of a Friend
9 Two are better than one, because they have a good reward for their toil. ¹⁰For if they fall, one will lift up the other; but woe to one who is alone and falls and does not have another to help. ¹¹Again, if two lie together, they keep warm; but how can one keep warm alone? ¹²And though one might prevail against another, two will withstand one. A threefold cord is not quickly broken.

13 Better is a poor but wise youth than an old but foolish king, who will no longer take advice. ¹⁴One can indeed come out of prison to reign, even though born poor in the kingdom. ¹⁵I saw all the living who, moving about under the sun, follow thatᵇ youth who replaced the king;ᶜ ¹⁶there was no end to all those people whom he led. Yet those who come later will not rejoice in him. Surely this also is vanity and a chasing after wind.ᵃ

5ᵈ **Reverence, Humility, and Contentment**
Guard your steps when you go to the house of God; to draw near to listen is better than the sacrifice offered by fools; for they do not know how to keep from doing evil.ᵉ ²ᶠ Never be rash with your mouth, nor let your heart be quick to utter a word before God, for God is in heaven, and you upon earth; therefore let your words be few.

3 For dreams come with many cares, and a fool's voice with many words.

4 When you make a vow to God, do not delay fulfilling it; for he has no pleasure in fools. Fulfill what you vow. ⁵It is better that you should not vow than that you should vow and not fulfill it. ⁶Do not let your mouth lead you into sin, and do not say before the messenger that it was a mistake; why should God be angry at your words, and destroy the work of your hands?

7 With many dreams come vanities and a multitude of words;ᵍ but fear God.

8 If you see in a province the oppression of the poor and the violation of justice and right, do not be amazed at the matter; for the high official is watched by a higher, and there are yet higher ones over them. ⁹But all things considered, this is an advantage for a land: a king for a plowed field.ᵍ

10 The lover of money will not be satisfied with money; nor the lover of wealth, with gain. This also is vanity.

11 When goods increase, those who eat them increase; and what gain has their owner but to see them with his eyes?

12 Sweet is the sleep of laborers, whether they eat little or much; but the surfeit of the rich will not let them sleep.

13 There is a grievous ill that I have seen under the sun: riches were kept by their owners to their hurt, ¹⁴and those riches were lost in a bad venture; though they are parents of children, they have nothing in their hands. ¹⁵As they came from their mother's womb, so they shall go again, naked as they came; they shall take nothing for their toil, which they may carry away with their hands. ¹⁶This also is a grievous ill: just as they came, so shall they go; and what gain do they have from toiling for the wind? ¹⁷Besides, all their days they eat in darkness, in much vexation and sickness and resentment.

18 This is what I have seen to be good: it is fitting to eat and drink and find enjoyment in all the toil with which one toils under the sun the few days of the life God gives us; for this is our lot. ¹⁹Likewise all to whom God gives wealth and possessions and whom he enables to enjoy them, and to accept their lot and find

a Or *a feeding on wind.* See Hos 12.1 *b* Heb *the second* *c* Heb *him* *d* Ch 4.17 in Heb *e* Cn: Heb *they do not know how to do evil* *f* Ch 5.1 in Heb *g* Meaning of Heb uncertain enjoyment in their toil—this is the gift of God. ²⁰For they will scarcely brood over the days of their lives, because God keeps them occupied with the joy of their hearts.

6 The Frustration of Desires

There is an evil that I have seen under the sun, and it lies heavy upon humankind: ²those to whom God gives wealth, possessions, and honor, so that they lack nothing of all that they desire, yet God does not enable them to enjoy these things, but a stranger enjoys them. This is vanity; it is a grievous ill. ³A man may beget a hundred children, and live many years; but however many are the days of his years, if he does not enjoy life's good things, or has no burial, I say that a stillborn child is better off than he. ⁴For it comes into vanity and goes into darkness, and in darkness its name is covered; ⁵moreover it has not seen the sun or known anything; yet it finds rest rather than he. ⁶Even though he should live a thousand years twice over, yet enjoy no good—do not all go to one place?

7 All human toil is for the mouth, yet the appetite is not satisfied. ⁸For what advantage have the wise over fools? And what do the poor have who know how to conduct themselves before the living? ⁹Better is the sight of the eyes than the wandering of desire; this also is vanity and a chasing after wind.^a

10 Whatever has come to be has already been named, and it is known what human beings are, and that they are not able to dispute with those who are stronger. ¹¹The more words, the more vanity, so how is one the better? ¹²For who knows what is good for mortals while they live the few days of their vain life, which they pass like a shadow? For who can tell them what will be after them under the sun?

7 A Disillusioned View of Life

A good name is better than precious ointment,
and the day of death, than the day of birth.
² It is better to go to the house of mourning
than to go to the house of feasting;
for this is the end of everyone,
and the living will lay it to heart.
³ Sorrow is better than laughter,
for by sadness of countenance the heart
is made glad.
⁴ The heart of the wise is in the house of
mourning;
but the heart of fools is in the house of
mirth.
⁵ It is better to hear the rebuke of the wise
than to hear the song of fools.

⁶ For like the crackling of thorns under a pot,
so is the laughter of fools;
this also is vanity.
⁷ Surely oppression makes the wise foolish,
and a bribe corrupts the heart.
⁸ Better is the end of a thing than its
beginning;
the patient in spirit are better than the
proud in spirit.
⁹ Do not be quick to anger,
for anger lodges in the bosom of fools.
¹⁰ Do not say, "Why were the former days
better than these?"
For it is not from wisdom that you ask
this.
¹¹ Wisdom is as good as an inheritance,
an advantage to those who see the sun.
¹² For the protection of wisdom is like the
protection of money,
and the advantage of knowledge is that
wisdom gives life to the one who
possesses it.
¹³ Consider the work of God;
who can make straight what he has made
crooked?

14 In the day of prosperity be joyful, and in the day of adversity consider; God has made the one as well as the other, so that mortals may not find out anything that will come after them.

The Riddles of Life

15 In my vain life I have seen everything; there are righteous people who perish in their righteousness, and there are wicked people who prolong their life in their evildoing. ¹⁶Do not be too righteous, and do not act too wise; why should you destroy yourself? ¹⁷Do not be too wicked, and do not be a fool; why should you die before your time? ¹⁸It is good that you should take hold of the one, without letting go of the other; for the one who fears God shall succeed with both.

19 Wisdom gives strength to the wise more than ten rulers that are in a city.

20 Surely there is no one on earth so righteous as to do good without ever sinning.

21 Do not give heed to everything that people say, or you may hear your servant cursing you; ²²your heart knows that many times you have yourself cursed others.

23 All this I have tested by wisdom; I said, "I will be wise," but it was far from me. ²⁴That which is, is far off, and deep, very deep; who can find it out? ²⁵I turned my mind to know and to search out and to seek wisdom and the sum of things, and to know that wickedness

---

a Or *a feeding on wind*. See Hos 12.1

Living in this twisted world,
I don't know where to turn sometimes.
Seeing the world around me—
The world of drugs, drinking and romance—
I turn away, trying to hide.

I'm not in the "in" crowd and it kills me sometimes.
I don't know where to turn.
I don't do things I know are wrong
In hopes that maybe, maybe someday,
People will look at me and wonder,
"What did she have that gave her so much control?"
And when people ask me I'll say,
"All I did was trust God to show me what was right."
Maybe I'll change someone's life someday.

This twisted world, oh wow,
Sometimes I don't know where to turn.
I've just got to keep my head on my shoulders,
Look up to the sky and say,
"Thank you God, for showing me where I can always turn."

Twisted—© Kim Burton, 18

is folly and that foolishness is madness. 26I found more bitter than death the woman who is a trap, whose heart is snares and nets, whose hands are fetters; one who pleases God escapes her, but the sinner is taken by her. 27See, this is what I found, says the Teacher,*a* adding one thing to another to find the sum, 28which my mind has sought repeatedly, but I have not found. One man among a thousand I found, but a woman among all these I have not found. 29See, this alone I found, that God made human beings straightforward, but they have devised many schemes.

8 Obey the King and Enjoy Yourself

Who is like the wise man?
    And who knows the interpretation of a
        thing?
Wisdom makes one's face shine,
    and the hardness of one's countenance is
        changed.

2 Keep*b* the king's command because of your sacred oath. 3Do not be terrified; go from his presence, do not delay when the matter is unpleasant, for he does whatever he pleases. 4For the word of the king is powerful, and who can say to him, "What are you doing?" 5Whoever obeys a command will meet no harm, and the wise mind will know the time and way. 6For every matter has its time and way, although the troubles of mortals lie heavy upon them. 7Indeed, they do not know what is to be, for who can tell them how it will be? 8No one has power over the wind*c* to restrain the wind,*c* or power over the day of death; there is no discharge from the battle, nor does wickedness deliver those who practice it. 9All this I observed, applying my mind to all that is done under the sun, while one person exercises authority over another to the other's hurt.

God's Ways Are Inscrutable

10 Then I saw the wicked buried; they used to go in and out of the holy place, and were praised in the city where they had done such things.*d* This also is vanity. 11Because sentence against an evil deed is not executed speedily, the human heart is fully set to do evil. 12Though sinners do evil a hundred times and prolong their lives, yet I know that it will be well with those who fear God, because they stand in fear before him, 13but it will not be well with the wicked, neither will they prolong their days like a shadow, because they do not stand in fear before God.

14 There is a vanity that takes place on earth, that there are righteous people who are treated according to the conduct of the wicked, and there are wicked people who are treated according to the conduct of the righteous. I said that this also is vanity. 15So I commend enjoyment, for there is nothing better for people under the sun than to eat, and drink, and enjoy themselves, for this will go with them in their toil through the days of life that God gives them under the sun.

16 When I applied my mind to know wisdom, and to see the business that is done on earth, how one's eyes see sleep neither day nor night, 17then I saw all the work of God, that no one can find out what is happening under the sun. However much they may toil in seeking, they will not find it out; even though those who are wise claim to know, they cannot find it out.

9 Take Life as It Comes

All this I laid to heart, examining it all, how the righteous and the wise and their deeds are in the hand of God; whether it is love or hate one does not know. Everything that confronts them 2is vanity,*e* since the same fate comes to all, to the righteous and the wicked, to the good and the evil,*f* to the clean and the unclean, to those who sacrifice and those who do not sacrifice. As are the good, so are the sinners; those who swear are like those who shun an oath. 3This is an evil in all that happens under the sun, that the same fate comes to everyone. Moreover, the hearts of all are full of evil; madness is in their hearts while they live, and after that they go to the dead. 4But whoever is joined with all the living has hope, for a living dog is better than a dead lion. 5The living know that they will die, but the dead know nothing; they have no more reward, and even the memory of them is lost. 6Their love and their hate

a Qoheleth, traditionally rendered *Preacher   b* Heb *I keep   c* Or *breath   d* Meaning of Heb uncertain   *e* Syr Compare Gk: Heb *Everything that confronts them* 2*is everything   f* Gk Syr Vg: Heb lacks *and the evil* and their envy have already perished; never again will they have any share in all that happens under the sun.

7 Go, eat your bread with enjoyment, and drink your wine with a merry heart; for God has long ago approved what you do. [8]Let your garments always be white; do not let oil be lacking on your head. [9]Enjoy life with the wife whom you love, all the days of your vain life that are given you under the sun, because that is your portion in life and in your toil at which you toil under the sun. [10]Whatever your hand finds to do, do with your might; for there is no work or thought or knowledge or wisdom in Sheol, to which you are going.

11 Again I saw that under the sun the race is not to the swift, nor the battle to the strong, nor bread to the wise, nor riches to the intelligent, nor favor to the skillful; but time and chance happen to them all. [12]For no one can anticipate the time of disaster. Like fish taken in a cruel net, and like birds caught in a snare, so mortals are snared at a time of calamity, when it suddenly falls upon them.

Wisdom Superior to Folly

13 I have also seen this example of wisdom under the sun, and it seemed great to me. [14]There was a little city with few people in it. A great king came against it and besieged it, building great siegeworks against it. [15]Now there was found in it a poor wise man, and he by his wisdom delivered the city. Yet no one remembered that poor man. [16]So I said, "Wisdom is better than might; yet the poor man's wisdom is despised, and his words are not heeded."

[17] The quiet words of the wise are more to be heeded
  than the shouting of a ruler among fools.
[18] Wisdom is better than weapons of war,
  but one bungler destroys much good.

10 Miscellaneous Observations

Dead flies make the perfumer's ointment
    give off a foul odor;
  so a little folly outweighs wisdom and
    honor.
[2] The heart of the wise inclines to the right,
  but the heart of a fool to the left.
[3] Even when fools walk on the road, they lack
    sense,
  and show to everyone that they are fools.
[4] If the anger of the ruler rises against you, do
    not leave your post,
  for calmness will undo great offenses.

5 There is an evil that I have seen under the sun, as great an error as if it proceeded from the ruler: [6]folly is set in many high places, and the rich sit in a low place. [7]I have seen slaves on horseback, and princes walking on foot like slaves.

[8] Whoever digs a pit will fall into it;
  and whoever breaks through a wall will
    be bitten by a snake.
[9] Whoever quarries stones will be hurt by
    them;
  and whoever splits logs will be
    endangered by them.
[10] If the iron is blunt, and one does not whet
    the edge,
  then more strength must be exerted;
  but wisdom helps one to succeed.
[11] If the snake bites before it is charmed,
  there is no advantage in a charmer.

[12] Words spoken by the wise bring them favor,
  but the lips of fools consume them.
[13] The words of their mouths begin in
    foolishness,
  and their talk ends in wicked madness;
[14] yet fools talk on and on.
  No one knows what is to happen,
  and who can tell anyone what the future
    holds?
[15] The toil of fools wears them out,
  for they do not even know the way to
    town.

[16] Alas for you, O land, when your king is a
    servant,[a]
  and your princes feast in the morning!
[17] Happy are you, O land, when your king is a
    nobleman,
  and your princes feast at the proper
    time—
  for strength, and not for drunkenness!
[18] Through sloth the roof sinks in,
  and through indolence the house leaks.
[19] Feasts are made for laughter;
  wine gladdens life,
  and money meets every need.
[20] Do not curse the king, even in your
    thoughts,
  or curse the rich, even in your bedroom;
  for a bird of the air may carry your voice,
  or some winged creature tell the matter.

11 The Value of Diligence

Send out your bread upon the waters,
  for after many days you will get it back.
[2] Divide your means seven ways, or even
    eight,
  for you do not know what disaster may
    happen on earth.
[3] When clouds are full,

_a_ Or _a child_

they empty rain on the earth;
whether a tree falls to the south or to the north,
in the place where the tree falls, there it will lie.
4 Whoever observes the wind will not sow;
and whoever regards the clouds will not reap.

5 Just as you do not know how the breath comes to the bones in the mother's womb, so you do not know the work of God, who makes everything.

6 In the morning sow your seed, and at evening do not let your hands be idle; for you do not know which will prosper, this or that, or whether both alike will be good.

Youth and Old Age

7 Light is sweet, and it is pleasant for the eyes to see the sun.

8 Even those who live many years should rejoice in them all; yet let them remember that the days of darkness will be many. All that comes is vanity.

9 Rejoice, young man, while you are young, and let your heart cheer you in the days of your youth. Follow the inclination of your heart and the desire of your eyes, but know that for all these things God will bring you into judgment.

10 Banish anxiety from your mind, and put away pain from your body; for youth and the dawn of life are vanity.

12 Remember your creator in the days of your youth, before the days of trouble come, and the years draw near when you will say, "I have no pleasure in them"; 2before the sun and the light and the moon and the stars are darkened and the clouds return with*ª* the rain; 3in the day when the guards of the house tremble, and the strong men are bent, and the women who grind cease working because they are few, and those who look through the windows see dimly; 4when the doors on the street are shut, and the sound of the grinding is low, and one rises up at the sound of a bird, and all the daughters of song are brought low; 5when one is afraid of heights, and terrors are in the road; the almond tree blossoms, the grasshopper drags itself along*ᵇ* and desire fails; because all must go to their eternal home, and the mourners will go about the streets; 6before the silver cord is snapped,*ᶜ* and the golden bowl is broken, and the pitcher is broken at the fountain, and the wheel broken at the cistern, 7and the dust returns to the earth as it was, and the breath*ᵈ* returns to God who gave it. 8Vanity of vanities, says the Teacher;*ᵉ* all is vanity.

Epilogue

9 Besides being wise, the Teacher*ᵉ* also taught the people knowledge, weighing and studying and arranging many proverbs. 10The Teacher*ᵉ* sought to find pleasing words, and he wrote words of truth plainly.

11 The sayings of the wise are like goads, and like nails firmly fixed are the collected sayings that are given by one shepherd.*ᶠ* 12Of anything beyond these, my child, beware. Of making many books there is no end, and much study is a weariness of the flesh.

13 The end of the matter; all has been heard. Fear God, and keep his commandments; for that is the whole duty of everyone. 14For God will bring every deed into judgment, including*ᵍ* every secret thing, whether good or evil.

---

a Or *after* ; Heb *'ahar* *b* Or *is a burden* *c* Syr Vg Compare Gk: Heb *is removed* *d* Or *the spirit* *e* Qoheleth, traditionally rendered *Preacher* *f* Meaning of Heb uncertain *g* Or *into the judgment on*

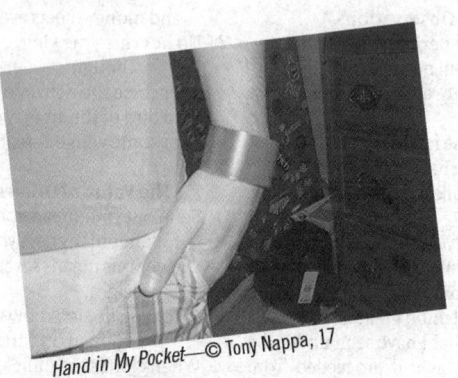

Hand in My Pocket—© Tony Nappa, 17

SONG OF SOLOMON

HOT AND HEAVY

Not Your Typical Bible Study

The texture of your skin is smooth. Your body rolls like hills. Your face is a portrait. Your neck turns at just the right arc to catch my kisses.

Whew! Not your typical Bible study, is it?

Solomon was a man with many wives (see 1 Kings 11), so one could only expect he'd spent some time writing a little love poetry now and then. The Song of Solomon is a scrap he must have left under his pillow, just sexy enough to make you take a second look and wonder how this made it into the Bible. It's not rated G. In fact, it hasn't even been cleaned up for religion class.

The poetry embraces all that is good about *eros* (romantic love): passion, single-minded dedication, and a longing to be with someone. It captures the honesty of the feelings shared between lovers, letting us know that the Bible addresses all of life and has none of the religious pretenses we may have experienced at Mass. The book is meant to be enjoyed the way parents celebrate their kids getting married. It is truly passionate, but there is nothing about it that is out of keeping with God's plans for our lives, love, and sex.

Although different religious traditions have embraced, rejected, debated, and worried about romance and sex, God has never been confused on this issue. This book serves as a reminder that God wants to be a part of all aspects of our lives, including our sexuality.

In search of my Love
I will go over mountains and strands;
I will gather no flowers,
I will fear no wild beasts;
And pass by the mighty and the
frontiers.

—St. John of the Cross, from the *Spiritual Canticle*

WHO Traditionally attributed to King Solomon, it appears, however, to be a collection of different pieces written by several unknown authors.

WHAT Also known as the Song of Songs, a collection of romantic poems between a man and a woman traditionally understood as revealing the mystery of God

WHEN It may have been written between the tenth and the second century B.C.

WHERE Israel

PATH OF DISCIPLESHIP

There are different ways of looking at the Song of Solomon. Some scholars see in it the symbolic union of Yahweh with his people or Christ with his Church. In Roman Catholic liturgy, the girl in the Song of Solomon is sometimes described as the Virgin Mary. And in spiritual writings she often represents the soul's yearning for Christ.

On the surface, the Song of Solomon appears to be about the love between a husband and a wife. And there are some things about love and sexuality that can be learned here. Human sexual love is good. It does not have to be justified or "spiritualized"—it's one of God's gifts to us.

At the same time, without discipline and right thinking and action, sexuality can be overwhelming. It shouldn't be stirred up before it is ready (see Song of Solomon 8.4). Sexuality is meant to be strong and loyal, as strong as death itself (see 8.6).

While it's clear that this book is about the passion between a husband and wife and all that is good about such love, the book also reveals something of God's love for humanity.

1 The Song of Songs, which is Solomon's.

Colloquy of Bride and Friends

2 Let him kiss me with the kisses of his
mouth!
For your love is better than wine,
3 your anointing oils are fragrant,
your name is perfume poured out;
therefore the maidens love you.
4 Draw me after you, let us make haste.
The king has brought me into his
chambers.
We will exult and rejoice in you;
we will extol your love more than wine;
rightly do they love you.

5 I am black and beautiful,
O daughters of Jerusalem,
like the tents of Kedar,
like the curtains of Solomon.
6 Do not gaze at me because I am dark,
because the sun has gazed on me.
My mother's sons were angry with me;
they made me keeper of the vineyards,
but my own vineyard I have not kept!
7 Tell me, you whom my soul loves,
where you pasture your flock,
where you make it lie down at noon;
for why should I be like one who is veiled
beside the flocks of your companions?

8 If you do not know,
O fairest among women,
follow the tracks of the flock,
and pasture your kids
beside the shepherds' tents.

Colloquy of Bridegroom, Friends, and Bride

9 I compare you, my love,
to a mare among Pharaoh's chariots.
10 Your cheeks are comely with ornaments,
your neck with strings of jewels.
11 We will make you ornaments of gold,
studded with silver.

12 While the king was on his couch,
my nard gave forth its fragrance.
13 My beloved is to me a bag of myrrh
that lies between my breasts.
14 My beloved is to me a cluster of henna
blossoms
in the vineyards of En-gedi.

15 Ah, you are beautiful, my love;
ah, you are beautiful;
your eyes are doves.
16 Ah, you are beautiful, my beloved,
truly lovely.
Our couch is green;
17 the beams of our house are cedar,
our rafters*a* are pine.

2 I am a rose*b* of Sharon,
a lily of the valleys.

2 As a lily among brambles,
so is my love among maidens.
3 As an apple tree among the trees of the
wood,
so is my beloved among young men.
With great delight I sat in his shadow,
and his fruit was sweet to my taste.
4 He brought me to the banqueting house,
and his intention toward me was love.
5 Sustain me with raisins,
refresh me with apples;
for I am faint with love.
6 O that his left hand were under my head,
and that his right hand embraced me!
7 I adjure you, O daughters of Jerusalem,
by the gazelles or the wild does:
do not stir up or awaken love
until it is ready!

Springtime Rhapsody

8 The voice of my beloved!
Look, he comes,
leaping upon the mountains,
bounding over the hills.
9 My beloved is like a gazelle
or a young stag.
Look, there he stands
behind our wall,
gazing in at the windows,
looking through the lattice.
10 My beloved speaks and says to me:
"Arise, my love, my fair one,
and come away;
11 for now the winter is past,
the rain is over and gone.
12 The flowers appear on the earth;
the time of singing has come,
and the voice of the turtledove
is heard in our land.
13 The fig tree puts forth its figs,
and the vines are in blossom;

a Meaning of Heb uncertain *b* Heb *crocus*

they give forth fragrance.
Arise, my love, my fair one,
and come away.
[14] O my dove, in the clefts of the rock,
in the covert of the cliff,
let me see your face,
let me hear your voice;
for your voice is sweet,
and your face is lovely.
[15] Catch us the foxes,
the little foxes,
that ruin the vineyards—
for our vineyards are in blossom."

[16] My beloved is mine and I am his;
he pastures his flock among the lilies.
[17] Until the day breathes
and the shadows flee,
turn, my beloved, be like a gazelle
or a young stag on the cleft mountains. [a]

3 Love's Dream
Upon my bed at night
I sought him whom my soul loves;
I sought him, but found him not;
I called him, but he gave no answer. [b]
[2] "I will rise now and go about the city,
in the streets and in the squares;
I will seek him whom my soul loves."
I sought him, but found him not.
[3] The sentinels found me,
as they went about in the city.
"Have you seen him whom my soul loves?"
[4] Scarcely had I passed them,
when I found him whom my soul loves.
I held him, and would not let him go
until I brought him into my mother's
house,
and into the chamber of her that
conceived me.
[5] I adjure you, O daughters of Jerusalem,
by the gazelles or the wild does:
do not stir up or awaken love
until it is ready!

The Groom and His Party Approach
[6] What is that coming up from the
wilderness,
like a column of smoke,
perfumed with myrrh and frankincense,
with all the fragrant powders of the
merchant?
[7] Look, it is the litter of Solomon!
Around it are sixty mighty men
of the mighty men of Israel,
[8] all equipped with swords
and expert in war,

each with his sword at his thigh
because of alarms by night.
[9] King Solomon made himself a palanquin
from the wood of Lebanon.
[10] He made its posts of silver,
its back of gold, its seat of purple;
its interior was inlaid with love. [c]
Daughters of Jerusalem,
[11] come out.
Look, O daughters of Zion,
at King Solomon,
at the crown with which his mother
crowned him
on the day of his wedding,
on the day of the gladness of his heart.

4 The Bride's Beauty Extolled
How beautiful you are, my love,
how very beautiful!
Your eyes are doves
behind your veil.
Your hair is like a flock of goats,
moving down the slopes of Gilead.
[2] Your teeth are like a flock of shorn ewes
that have come up from the washing,
all of which bear twins,
and not one among them is bereaved.
[3] Your lips are like a crimson thread,
and your mouth is lovely.
Your cheeks are like halves of a
pomegranate
behind your veil.
[4] Your neck is like the tower of David,
built in courses;
on it hang a thousand bucklers,
all of them shields of warriors.

Dancing in the Garden—© Rachel Akerley, 17

[a] Or *on the mountains of Bether*; meaning of Heb uncertain
[b] Gk: Heb lacks this line [c] Meaning of Heb uncertain

5 Your two breasts are like two fawns,
    twins of a gazelle,
      that feed among the lilies.
6 Until the day breathes
    and the shadows flee,
  I will hasten to the mountain of myrrh
    and the hill of frankincense.
7 You are altogether beautiful, my love;
    there is no flaw in you.
8 Come with me from Lebanon, my bride;
    come with me from Lebanon.
Depart[a] from the peak of Amana,
    from the peak of Senir and Hermon,
  from the dens of lions,
    from the mountains of leopards.

9 You have ravished my heart, my sister, my
    bride,
you have ravished my heart with a glance
    of your eyes,
  with one jewel of your necklace.
10 How sweet is your love, my sister, my bride!
  how much better is your love than wine,
  and the fragrance of your oils than any
    spice!
11 Your lips distill nectar, my bride;
    honey and milk are under your tongue;
  the scent of your garments is like the
    scent of Lebanon.
12 A garden locked is my sister, my bride,
    a garden locked, a fountain sealed.
13 Your channel[b] is an orchard of
    pomegranates
    with all choicest fruits,
  henna with nard,
14 nard and saffron, calamus and cinnamon,
    with all trees of frankincense,
myrrh and aloes,
    with all chief spices—
15 a garden fountain, a well of living water,
    and flowing streams from Lebanon.

16 Awake, O north wind,
    and come, O south wind!
Blow upon my garden
    that its fragrance may be wafted abroad.
Let my beloved come to his garden,
    and eat its choicest fruits.

5 I come to my garden, my sister, my bride;
  I gather my myrrh with my spice,
  I eat my honeycomb with my honey,
  I drink my wine with my milk.

Eat, friends, drink,
    and be drunk with love.

Another Dream

2 I slept, but my heart was awake.
Listen! my beloved is knocking.
"Open to me, my sister, my love,
    my dove, my perfect one;
for my head is wet with dew,
    my locks with the drops of the night."
3 I had put off my garment;
    how could I put it on again?
I had bathed my feet;
    how could I soil them?
4 My beloved thrust his hand into the
    opening,
    and my inmost being yearned for him.
5 I arose to open to my beloved,
    and my hands dripped with myrrh,
my fingers with liquid myrrh,
    upon the handles of the bolt.
6 I opened to my beloved,
    but my beloved had turned and was gone.

a Or *Look*   b Meaning of Heb uncertain

A Lasting Love

A lasting love…
Will our love last?
Will it be forever?
Is our love strong enough?
A lasting love is
strong and godly—
you and me as one
seeking God.
A lasting love is
kind and not easily angered—
loving, smiling, laughing.
A lasting love is
not easy—it's hard work.
A lasting love is
two people God has placed
together in love.
A lasting love is
not reasonable but crazy,
never knowing what's next.
A lasting love is
forgiveness, for no one can
love without it.
A lasting love is you and me.
A lasting love is forever.

A Lasting Love—© Becca Kenerson, 15

PROFILE OF FAITH

An orphan who was kidnapped, escaped, and became a famous poet—sounds like an unlikely story, right? Not so! Juan de Ypres y Alvarez was born in 1542 and was brought up in an orphanage. He eventually became a Carmelite friar and took the name John of the Cross. Along with St. Teresa of Ávila, he began a reform of the Carmelite order.

His reform was not welcomed by his brother friars, so they had him kidnapped and imprisoned in a monastery for nine months, where he began to write poetry. He escaped to a reformed monastery and continued his writing.

Today St. John of the Cross is considered one of Spain's most important poets. His complete poems only add up to less than twenty-five hundred verses, but two of them—the *Spiritual Canticle* and *Dark Night of the Soul* are considered to be among the best poems ever written in Spanish, because of both their style and their symbolic imagery.

The *Spiritual Canticle* is modeled on the Song of Solomon. In it, the bride (or soul) searches for the bridegroom (Jesus Christ). It was written at a time when translations of the Bible into contemporary languages were forbidden by the Church.

My soul failed me when he spoke.
I sought him, but did not find him;
   I called him, but he gave no answer.
7 Making their rounds in the city
   the sentinels found me;
they beat me, they wounded me,
   they took away my mantle,
those sentinels of the walls.
8 I adjure you, O daughters of Jerusalem,
   if you find my beloved,
tell him this:
   I am faint with love.

Colloquy of Friends and Bride
9 What is your beloved more than another
      beloved,
   O fairest among women?
What is your beloved more than another
      beloved,
   that you thus adjure us?

10 My beloved is all radiant and ruddy,
   distinguished among ten thousand.
11 His head is the finest gold;
   his locks are wavy,
   black as a raven.
12 His eyes are like doves
   beside springs of water,
bathed in milk,
   fitly set. *a*
13 His cheeks are like beds of spices,

yielding fragrance.
His lips are lilies,
   distilling liquid myrrh.
14 His arms are rounded gold,
   set with jewels.
His body is ivory work, *a*
   encrusted with sapphires. *b*
15 His legs are alabaster columns,
   set upon bases of gold.
His appearance is like Lebanon,
   choice as the cedars.
16 His speech is most sweet,
   and he is altogether desirable.
This is my beloved and this is my friend,
   O daughters of Jerusalem.

6 Where has your beloved gone,
   O fairest among women?
Which way has your beloved turned,
   that we may seek him with you?

2 My beloved has gone down to his garden,
   to the beds of spices,
to pasture his flock in the gardens,
   and to gather lilies.
3 I am my beloved's and my beloved is mine;
   he pastures his flock among the lilies.

The Bride's Matchless Beauty
4 You are beautiful as Tirzah, my love,
   comely as Jerusalem,
   terrible as an army with banners.

a Meaning of Heb uncertain *b* Heb *lapis lazuli*

⁵ Turn away your eyes from me,
    for they overwhelm me!
Your hair is like a flock of goats,
    moving down the slopes of Gilead.
⁶ Your teeth are like a flock of ewes,
    that have come up from the washing;
all of them bear twins,
    and not one among them is bereaved.
⁷ Your cheeks are like halves of a
      pomegranate
    behind your veil.
⁸ There are sixty queens and eighty
      concubines,
    and maidens without number.
⁹ My dove, my perfect one, is the only one,
    the darling of her mother,
    flawless to her that bore her.
The maidens saw her and called her happy;
    the queens and concubines also, and
      they praised her.
¹⁰ "Who is this that looks forth like the dawn,
    fair as the moon, bright as the sun,
    terrible as an army with banners?"

¹¹ I went down to the nut orchard,
    to look at the blossoms of the valley,
to see whether the vines had budded,
    whether the pomegranates were in
      bloom.
¹² Before I was aware, my fancy set me
    in a chariot beside my prince.[a]

¹³ [b] Return, return, O Shulammite!
    Return, return, that we may look upon you.

Why should you look upon the
      Shulammite,
    as upon a dance before two armies?[c]

7 Expressions of Praise

How graceful are your feet in sandals,
    O queenly maiden!
Your rounded thighs are like jewels,
    the work of a master hand.
² Your navel is a rounded bowl
    that never lacks mixed wine.
Your belly is a heap of wheat,
    encircled with lilies.
³ Your two breasts are like two fawns,
    twins of a gazelle.
⁴ Your neck is like an ivory tower.
Your eyes are pools in Heshbon,
    by the gate of Bath-rabbim.
Your nose is like a tower of Lebanon,
    overlooking Damascus.
⁵ Your head crowns you like Carmel,
    and your flowing locks are like purple;
    a king is held captive in the tresses.[d]

⁶ How fair and pleasant you are,
    O loved one, delectable maiden![e]
⁷ You are stately[f] as a palm tree,
    and your breasts are like its clusters.
⁸ I say I will climb the palm tree
    and lay hold of its branches.
O may your breasts be like clusters of the
      vine,
    and the scent of your breath like
      apples,
⁹ and your kisses[g] like the best wine
    that goes down[h] smoothly,
    gliding over lips and teeth.[i]

¹⁰ I am my beloved's,
    and his desire is for me.
¹¹ Come, my beloved,
    let us go forth into the fields,
    and lodge in the villages;

EXPRESS YOURSELF

A Raging Flame

Ever been so smitten with someone that you can't think about anything else? That gorgeous face melts you like butter. Eye contact turns you to jelly. And when you're together, your body turns into a boiling pot of noodles—overheated, bubbling, and gushy.

This isn't dinner. It's physical attraction. And God created it, so it's good: "So God created humankind in his image, in the image of God he created them; male and female he created them. God blessed them, and God said to them, 'Be fruitful and multiply, and fill the earth and subdue it'" (Genesis 1.27–28).

Read **Song of Solomon 8.6–7.** The kind of love that is "a raging flame" is real . . . and God-wired. God is the maker of our sexuality, and he designed it to be expressed in a faithful marriage relationship.

Have you ever felt passionate about someone? Write a haiku about him or her. A haiku is a poem with three lines—five syllables in the first line, seven in the second, and five in the third. Share your expression and see others' haikus at **Learner.CalltoDiscipleship.com.**

---

a Cn: Meaning of Heb uncertain   b Ch 7.1 in Heb   c Or *dance of Mahanaim*   d Meaning of Heb uncertain   e Syr: Heb *in delights*
f Heb *This your stature is*   g Heb *palate*   h Heb *down for my lover*   i Gk Syr Vg: Heb *lips of sleepers*

¹² let us go out early to the vineyards,
　　and see whether the vines have budded,
　whether the grape blossoms have opened
　　and the pomegranates are in bloom.
　There I will give you my love.
¹³ The mandrakes give forth fragrance,
　　and over our doors are all choice fruits,
　new as well as old,
　　which I have laid up for you, O my
　　　beloved.

8

O that you were like a brother to me,
　who nursed at my mother's breast!
If I met you outside, I would kiss you,
　and no one would despise me.
² I would lead you and bring you
　into the house of my mother,
　　and into the chamber of the one who
　　　bore me.^a
I would give you spiced wine to drink,
　the juice of my pomegranates.
³ O that his left hand were under my head,
　and that his right hand embraced me!
⁴ I adjure you, O daughters of Jerusalem,
　do not stir up or awaken love
　　until it is ready!

Homecoming

⁵ Who is that coming up from the wilderness,
　leaning upon her beloved?

Under the apple tree I awakened you.
There your mother was in labor with you;
　there she who bore you was in labor.

⁶ Set me as a seal upon your heart,
　as a seal upon your arm;
for love is strong as death,
　passion fierce as the grave.

a Gk Syr: Heb *my mother; she (or you) will teach me* b Or *finds*

Its flashes are flashes of fire,
　a raging flame.
⁷ Many waters cannot quench love,
　neither can floods drown it.
If one offered for love
　all the wealth of one's house,
　　it would be utterly scorned.

⁸ We have a little sister,
　and she has no breasts.
What shall we do for our sister,
　on the day when she is spoken for?
⁹ If she is a wall,
　we will build upon her a battlement of
　　silver;
but if she is a door,
　we will enclose her with boards of cedar.
¹⁰ I was a wall,
　and my breasts were like towers;
then I was in his eyes
　as one who brings^b peace.
¹¹ Solomon had a vineyard at Baal-hamon;
　he entrusted the vineyard to keepers;
　each one was to bring for its fruit a
　　thousand pieces of silver.
¹² My vineyard, my very own, is for myself;
　you, O Solomon, may have the thousand,
　and the keepers of the fruit two
　　hundred!

¹³ O you who dwell in the gardens,
　my companions are listening for your
　　voice;
　let me hear it.

¹⁴ Make haste, my beloved,
　and be like a gazelle
or a young stag
　upon the mountains of spices!

CREATIVE SPACE

THE WISDOM OF SOLOMON

BACK TO BASICS

Got an Identity Problem?

What if you were marooned on an island and the only people you came in contact with were completely different from you? What if they didn't speak English, ate different food, and had totally different religious beliefs and customs? How would you survive? What would you do to try to fit in?

Quite possibly, you would start to adapt to the way they live, yet you'd want to remember the traditions from your past as well as your faith, so you could pass them along to the next generation.

That's what the writer of the book of Wisdom wanted to do—adapt a heritage. His religious heritage came from one cultural context—a strong Jewish one—yet he and others were living in a different culture, a Greek and Egyptian one. His purpose in writing this book was to help the "dispersed" Jews throughout the Greco-Roman world maintain their heritage and remain faithful to their faith and traditions.

> "The patriarchs, prophets, and certain other Old Testament figures have been and always will be honored as saints in all the Church's liturgical traditions."
> —Catechism of the Catholic Church 61

WHO Traditionally described as Solomon, the author is unknown, but is someone with a good historical knowledge of the Exodus, the religious practices of Egypt, and Greek philosophy and science.

WHAT Also called the book of Wisdom, this book is an ode to wisdom, a reinterpretation of Jewish heritage, and a critique of Egyptian and Hellenistic (Greek) culture in which the author's community lived.

WHEN Written during the first century B.C.

WHERE The Jewish community in Alexandria, Egypt

PATH OF DISCIPLESHIP

Faith lived in a new setting always faces some trials and adjustments. The same holds true for us and our families if we experience a change or a new setting. Think about any recent changes in your life. It's probably nothing as dramatic as relocating to a faraway land, but something as simple as changing schools or even migrating to a new group of friends can dramatically affect your environment.

There are many ways that followers of Jesus choose new settings or get into them by happenstance. In those times, it's important to remember your roots, to know and reflect once again on the Scriptures, prayers, and practices of the Church, and to seek *wisdom* as the writer of Wisdom did.

Change the Channel

After the fall of the stock market in 1929, the world sank into the Great Depression. People lost everything—homes, jobs, the ability to provide families with food. "Depression" was a good word for the reality of the day. The Depression was followed by World War II, a time when there was great destruction, loss of life, and inhuman atrocities. Out of that experience came a popular song that encouraged people to focus on the positive things in life instead of allowing negativity to darken their days.

Read Wisdom 1.3–4. The writer of the Wisdom of Solomon goes even further when talking about the dangers of not living a positive life: "For perverse thoughts separate people from God" (1.3).

It doesn't take a rocket scientist to see how focusing on misery, sadness, self-pity, jealousy, envy, and suffering will make you feel farther away from God. If you spend your time moping around and harboring negative thoughts, you block the good gifts God wants to give you.

Happiness truly can be a state of mind— it's how you choose to look at circumstances that determines a positive or negative outlook. For example, if someone suddenly cancels plans with you, you can choose to allow that to ruin your day, or you can decide to view it as an opportunity for doing something else that you enjoy.

Turn to the Holy Spirit to help you make those positive choices. The Spirit of God gives you flexibility and creativity, so you don't have to allow external circumstances to create black holes of despair in your life.

Find a quiet place to do an "accentuate the positive" exercise. Bring your notebook and write down all the things you are grateful for. Recall some of the times you've recently been disappointed or guilty of negative thinking and journal about what positive options or thoughts changed or could have changed the outcome. Then put your ideas to use the next time disappointment or negativity creeps into your life.

1 Exhortation to Uprightness

Love righteousness, you rulers of the earth,
think of the Lord in goodness
and seek him with sincerity of heart;
2 because he is found by those who do not put him to the test,
and manifests himself to those who do not distrust him.
3 For perverse thoughts separate people from God,
and when his power is tested, it exposes the foolish;
4 because wisdom will not enter a deceitful soul,
or dwell in a body enslaved to sin.
5 For a holy and disciplined spirit will flee from deceit,
and will leave foolish thoughts behind,
and will be ashamed at the approach of unrighteousness.

6 For wisdom is a kindly spirit,
but will not free blasphemers from the guilt of their words;
because God is witness of their inmost feelings,
and a true observer of their hearts, and a hearer of their tongues.
7 Because the spirit of the Lord has filled the world,
and that which holds all things together knows what is said,
8 therefore those who utter unrighteous things will not escape notice,
and justice, when it punishes, will not pass them by.
9 For inquiry will be made into the counsels of the ungodly,
and a report of their words will come to the Lord,
to convict them of their lawless deeds;
10 because a jealous ear hears all things,
and the sound of grumbling does not go unheard.
11 Beware then of useless grumbling,
and keep your tongue from slander;
because no secret word is without result,[a]
and a lying mouth destroys the soul.

12 Do not invite death by the error of your life,
or bring on destruction by the works of your hands;
13 because God did not make death,
and he does not delight in the death of the living.
14 For he created all things so that they might exist;

a Or will go unpunished

the generative forces[a] of the world are wholesome,
and there is no destructive poison in them,
and the dominion[b] of Hades is not on earth.
15 For righteousness is immortal.

Life as the Ungodly See It

16 But the ungodly by their words and deeds summoned death;[c]
considering him a friend, they pined away
and made a covenant with him,
because they are fit to belong to his company.

2 For they reasoned unsoundly, saying to themselves,
"Short and sorrowful is our life,
and there is no remedy when a life comes to its end,
and no one has been known to return from Hades.
2 For we were born by mere chance,
and hereafter we shall be as though we had never been,
for the breath in our nostrils is smoke,
and reason is a spark kindled by the beating of our hearts;
3 when it is extinguished, the body will turn to ashes,
and the spirit will dissolve like empty air.
4 Our name will be forgotten in time,
and no one will remember our works;
our life will pass away like the traces of a cloud,
and be scattered like mist
that is chased by the rays of the sun
and overcome by its heat.
5 For our allotted time is the passing of a shadow,
and there is no return from our death,
because it is sealed up and no one turns back.

6 "Come, therefore, let us enjoy the good things that exist,
and make use of the creation to the full as in youth.
7 Let us take our fill of costly wine and perfumes,
and let no flower of spring pass us by.
8 Let us crown ourselves with rosebuds before they wither.
9 Let none of us fail to share in our revelry;
everywhere let us leave signs of enjoyment,
because this is our portion, and this our lot.
10 Let us oppress the righteous poor man;
let us not spare the widow

or regard the gray hairs of the aged.
11 But let our might be our law of right,
for what is weak proves itself to be useless.

12 "Let us lie in wait for the righteous man,
because he is inconvenient to us and opposes our actions;
he reproaches us for sins against the law,
and accuses us of sins against our training.
13 He professes to have knowledge of God,
and calls himself a child[d] of the Lord.
14 He became to us a reproof of our thoughts;
15 the very sight of him is a burden to us,
because his manner of life is unlike that of others,
and his ways are strange.
16 We are considered by him as something base,
and he avoids our ways as unclean;
he calls the last end of the righteous happy,
and boasts that God is his father.
17 Let us see if his words are true,
and let us test what will happen at the end of his life;
18 for if the righteous man is God's child, he will help him,
and will deliver him from the hand of his adversaries.
19 Let us test him with insult and torture,
so that we may find out how gentle he is,
and make trial of his forbearance.
20 Let us condemn him to a shameful death,
for, according to what he says, he will be protected."

Error of the Wicked

21 Thus they reasoned, but they were led astray,
for their wickedness blinded them,
22 and they did not know the secret purposes of God,
nor hoped for the wages of holiness,
nor discerned the prize for blameless souls;
23 for God created us for incorruption,
and made us in the image of his own eternity,[e]

a Or *the creatures* b Or *palace* c Gk *him* d Or *servant* e Other ancient authorities read *nature*

²⁴ but through the devil's envy death entered the world,
and those who belong to his company experience it.

3 The Destiny of the Righteous

But the souls of the righteous are in the hand of God,
and no torment will ever touch them.
² In the eyes of the foolish they seemed to have died,
and their departure was thought to be a disaster,
³ and their going from us to be their destruction;
but they are at peace.
⁴ For though in the sight of others they were punished,
their hope is full of immortality.
⁵ Having been disciplined a little, they will receive great good,
because God tested them and found them worthy of himself;
⁶ like gold in the furnace he tried them,
and like a sacrificial burnt offering he accepted them.
⁷ In the time of their visitation they will shine forth,
and will run like sparks through the stubble.
⁸ They will govern nations and rule over peoples,
and the Lord will reign over them forever.

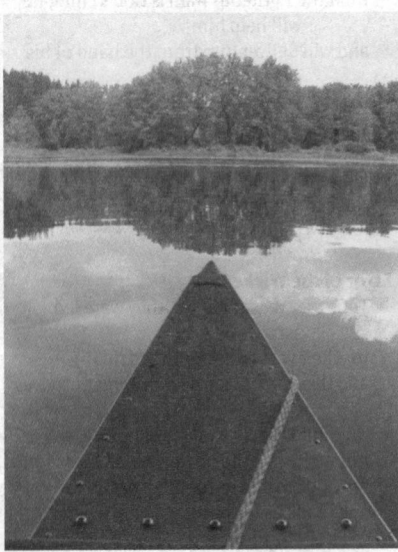

Tranquility of the Spirit—© Megan Schoettler, 17

⁹ Those who trust in him will understand truth,
and the faithful will abide with him in love,
because grace and mercy are upon his holy ones,
and he watches over his elect. ᵃ

The Destiny of the Ungodly

¹⁰ But the ungodly will be punished as their reasoning deserves,
those who disregarded the righteous ᵇ
and rebelled against the Lord;
¹¹ for those who despise wisdom and instruction are miserable.
Their hope is vain, their labors are unprofitable,
and their works are useless.
¹² Their wives are foolish, and their children evil;
¹³ their offspring are accursed.

On Childlessness

For blessed is the barren woman who is undefiled,
who has not entered into a sinful union;
she will have fruit when God examines souls.
¹⁴ Blessed also is the eunuch whose hands have done no lawless deed,
and who has not devised wicked things against the Lord;
for special favor will be shown him for his faithfulness,
and a place of great delight in the temple of the Lord.
¹⁵ For the fruit of good labors is renowned,
and the root of understanding does not fail.
¹⁶ But children of adulterers will not come to maturity,
and the offspring of an unlawful union will perish.
¹⁷ Even if they live long they will be held of no account,
and finally their old age will be without honor.
¹⁸ If they die young, they will have no hope
and no consolation on the day of judgment.
¹⁹ For the end of an unrighteous generation is grievous.

4 Better than this is childlessness with virtue,
for in the memory of virtue ᶜ is immortality,
because it is known both by God and by mortals.
² When it is present, people imitate ᵈ it,

ᵃ Text of this line uncertain; omitted by some ancient authorities. Compare 4.15 ᵇ Or *what is right* ᶜ Gk *it* ᵈ Other ancient authorities read *honor*

and they long for it when it has gone;
    throughout all time it marches, crowned in triumph,
    victor in the contest for prizes that are undefiled.

3 But the prolific brood of the ungodly will be of no use,
    and none of their illegitimate seedlings will strike a deep root
    or take a firm hold.

4 For even if they put forth boughs for a while,
    standing insecurely they will be shaken by the wind,
    and by the violence of the winds they will be uprooted.

5 The branches will be broken off before they come to maturity,
    and their fruit will be useless,
    not ripe enough to eat, and good for nothing.

6 For children born of unlawful unions
    are witnesses of evil against their parents when God examines them.[a]

7 But the righteous, though they die early, will be at rest.

8 For old age is not honored for length of time,
    or measured by number of years;

9 but understanding is gray hair for anyone,
    and a blameless life is ripe old age.

10 There were some who pleased God and were loved by him,
    and while living among sinners were taken up.

11 They were caught up so that evil might not change their understanding
    or guile deceive their souls.

12 For the fascination of wickedness obscures what is good,
    and roving desire perverts the innocent mind.

13 Being perfected in a short time, they fulfilled long years;

14 for their souls were pleasing to the Lord,
    therefore he took them quickly from the midst of wickedness.

15 Yet the peoples saw and did not understand,
    or take such a thing to heart,
    that God's grace and mercy are with his elect,
    and that he watches over his holy ones.

The Triumph of the Righteous

16 The righteous who have died will condemn the ungodly who are living,

JESUS SIGHTING

So who gets to heaven? Read **Wisdom 1.15–26**. According to the writer of Wisdom, it's not those who don't trust God in life, those who break the commandments, or those who judge or put others down. No, only the righteous will live forever.

So, what does "righteous" mean here? In biblical terms, righteousness is synonymous with justice. "To be just" means to live in right relationship. And authentic righteous people are those who live in right relationship with God, themselves, and others.

In the Gospels, we hear Jesus respond twice to the question, "So who gets to heaven?" Once it is asked by a lawyer to whom Jesus tells the story of the good Samaritan in Luke 10.25–37, and then it is asked by a rich ruler in Luke 18.18–23. At the end of the Gospel of Matthew, Jesus describes again who gets to heaven (see Matthew 25.31–46).

Read the three passages and reflect on what those passages challenge you to do today. Identify the positive habits and actions that are a part of your "just" life and those that need some "tweaking."

and youth that is quickly perfected[b] will condemn the prolonged old age of the unrighteous.

17 For they will see the end of the wise,
    and will not understand what the Lord purposed for them,
    and for what he kept them safe.

18 The unrighteous[c] will see, and will have contempt for them,
    but the Lord will laugh them to scorn.
After this they will become dishonored corpses,
    and an outrage among the dead forever;

19 because he will dash them speechless to the ground,
    and shake them from the foundations;
    they will be left utterly dry and barren,

a Gk at their examination b Or ended c Gk They

and they will suffer anguish,
and the memory of them will perish.

The Final Judgment

20 They will come with dread when their sins
are reckoned up,
and their lawless deeds will convict them to
their face.

5 Then the righteous will stand with great
confidence
in the presence of those who have
oppressed them
and those who make light of their labors.

2 When the unrighteous*a* see them, they will
be shaken with dreadful fear,
and they will be amazed at the unexpected
salvation of the righteous.

3 They will speak to one another in
repentance,
and in anguish of spirit they will groan, and
say,

4 "These are persons whom we once held in
derision
and made a byword of reproach—fools that
we were!
We thought that their lives were madness
and that their end was without honor.

5 Why have they been numbered among the
children of God?

And why is their lot among the saints?

6 So it was we who strayed from the way of
truth,
and the light of righteousness did not shine
on us,
and the sun did not rise upon us.

7 We took our fill of the paths of lawlessness
and destruction,
and we journeyed through trackless
deserts,
but the way of the Lord we have not known.

8 What has our arrogance profited us?
And what good has our boasted wealth
brought us?

9 "All those things have vanished like a
shadow,
and like a rumor that passes by;

10 like a ship that sails through the billowy
water,
and when it has passed no trace can be
found,
no track of its keel in the waves;

11 or as, when a bird flies through the air,
no evidence of its passage is found;
the light air, lashed by the beat of its
pinions
and pierced by the force of its rushing
flight,
is traversed by the movement of its wings,

a Gk they

and afterward no sign of its coming is
found there;

12 or as, when an arrow is shot at a target,
the air, thus divided, comes together at
once,
so that no one knows its pathway.

13 So we also, as soon as we were born, ceased
to be,
and we had no sign of virtue to show,
but were consumed in our wickedness."

14 Because the hope of the ungodly is like
thistledown[a] carried by the wind,
and like a light frost[b] driven away by a
storm;
it is dispersed like smoke before the wind,
and it passes like the remembrance of a
guest who stays but a day.

The Reward of the Righteous

15 But the righteous live forever,
and their reward is with the Lord;
the Most High takes care of them.

16 Therefore they will receive a glorious crown
and a beautiful diadem from the hand of
the Lord,
because with his right hand he will cover
them,
and with his arm he will shield them.

17 The Lord[c] will take his zeal as his whole
armor,
and will arm all creation to repel[d] his
enemies;

18 he will put on righteousness as a
breastplate,
and wear impartial justice as a helmet;

19 he will take holiness as an invincible shield,

20 and sharpen stern wrath for a sword,
and creation will join with him to fight
against his frenzied foes.

21 Shafts of lightning will fly with true aim,
and will leap from the clouds to the target,
as from a well-drawn bow,

22 and hailstones full of wrath will be hurled
as from a catapult;
the water of the sea will rage against them,
and rivers will relentlessly overwhelm
them;

23 a mighty wind will rise against them,
and like a tempest it will winnow them
away.
Lawlessness will lay waste the whole earth,
and evildoing will overturn the thrones of
rulers.

6 Kings Should Seek Wisdom

Listen therefore, O kings, and understand;
learn, O judges of the ends of the earth.

"Wisdom is the supreme part of happiness."

—Sophocles

2 Give ear, you that rule over multitudes,
and boast of many nations.

3 For your dominion was given you from the
Lord,
and your sovereignty from the Most High;
he will search out your works and inquire
into your plans.

4 Because as servants of his kingdom you did
not rule rightly,
or keep the law,
or walk according to the purpose of God,

5 he will come upon you terribly and swiftly,
because severe judgment falls on those in
high places.

6 For the lowliest may be pardoned in mercy,
but the mighty will be mightily tested.

7 For the Lord of all will not stand in awe of
anyone,
or show deference to greatness;
because he himself made both small and
great,
and he takes thought for all alike.

8 But a strict inquiry is in store for the mighty.

9 To you then, O monarchs, my words are
directed,
so that you may learn wisdom and not
transgress.

10 For they will be made holy who observe
holy things in holiness,
and those who have been taught them will
find a defense.

11 Therefore set your desire on my words;
long for them, and you will be instructed.

Description of Wisdom

12 Wisdom is radiant and unfading,
and she is easily discerned by those who
love her,
and is found by those who seek her.

13 She hastens to make herself known to
those who desire her.

14 One who rises early to seek her will have no
difficulty,
for she will be found sitting at the gate.

15 To fix one's thought on her is perfect
understanding,
and one who is vigilant on her account will
soon be free from care,

16 because she goes about seeking those
worthy of her,

a Other ancient authorities read *dust*   b Other ancient authorities read *spider's web*   c Gk He   d Or *punish*

THE CHARACTER OF GOD

Look at the world around you. Every creature, from the tiniest insect to the biggest beast, and every thing, from the rocks on the ground to the clouds in the sky, is perfectly formed for its purpose. What does this tell you about the creativity of God? Does it tell you anything about God's character?

The book of Wisdom presents major insights into the character of God and where we can find God. **Wisdom 7.22–8.1** literally piles up for us the creative descriptions of the wisdom that is "a breath of the power of God," that "reaches mightily from one end of the earth to the other." Every title and descriptive phrase here gives us deeper understanding of the mystery of God as well as the mystery of how God is working deep within our human lives.

The *Catechism of the Catholic Church* states: "We really can name God starting from the manifold perfections of his creatures" (48). What have you learned about God's creativity and character? Find some Creative Space in this Bible and write about what new understanding of God you find in reading the book of Wisdom. Then share your thoughts at **Learner.CalltoDiscipleship.com**.

and she graciously appears to them in their paths,
and meets them in every thought.

17 The beginning of wisdom[a] is the most sincere desire for instruction,
and concern for instruction is love of her,
18 and love of her is the keeping of her laws,
and giving heed to her laws is assurance of immortality,
19 and immortality brings one near to God;
20 so the desire for wisdom leads to a kingdom.

21 Therefore if you delight in thrones and scepters, O monarchs over the peoples,
honor wisdom, so that you may reign forever.
22 I will tell you what wisdom is and how she came to be,
and I will hide no secrets from you,
but I will trace her course from the beginning of creation,
and make knowledge of her clear,
and I will not pass by the truth;
23 nor will I travel in the company of sickly envy,
for envy[b] does not associate with wisdom.
24 The multitude of the wise is the salvation of the world,
and a sensible king is the stability of any people.
25 Therefore be instructed by my words, and you will profit.

7 Solomon Like Other Mortals

I also am mortal, like everyone else,
a descendant of the first-formed child of earth;
and in the womb of a mother I was molded into flesh,
2 within the period of ten months, compacted with blood,
from the seed of a man and the pleasure of marriage.
3 And when I was born, I began to breathe the common air,
and fell upon the kindred earth;
my first sound was a cry, as is true of all.
4 I was nursed with care in swaddling cloths.
5 For no king has had a different beginning of existence;
6 there is for all one entrance into life, and one way out.

Solomon's Respect for Wisdom

7 Therefore I prayed, and understanding was given me;
I called on God, and the spirit of wisdom came to me.
8 I preferred her to scepters and thrones, and I accounted wealth as nothing in comparison with her.
9 Neither did I liken to her any priceless gem, because all gold is but a little sand in her sight,
and silver will be accounted as clay before her.
10 I loved her more than health and beauty, and I chose to have her rather than light, because her radiance never ceases.
11 All good things came to me along with her, and in her hands uncounted wealth.

a Gk *Her beginning* b Gk *this*

¹² I rejoiced in them all, because wisdom
leads them;
but I did not know that she was their
mother.
¹³ I learned without guile and I impart
without grudging;
I do not hide her wealth,
¹⁴ for it is an unfailing treasure for mortals;
those who get it obtain friendship with
God,
commended for the gifts that come from
instruction.

Solomon Prays for Wisdom

¹⁵ May God grant me to speak with judgment,
and to have thoughts worthy of what I have
received;
for he is the guide even of wisdom
and the corrector of the wise.
¹⁶ For both we and our words are in his hand,
as are all understanding and skill in crafts.
¹⁷ For it is he who gave me unerring
knowledge of what exists,
to know the structure of the world and the
activity of the elements;
¹⁸ the beginning and end and middle of
times,
the alternations of the solstices and the
changes of the seasons,
¹⁹ the cycles of the year and the constellations
of the stars,
²⁰ the natures of animals and the tempers of
wild animals,
the powers of spirits*a* and the thoughts of
human beings,
the varieties of plants and the virtues of
roots;
²¹ I learned both what is secret and what is
manifest,
²² for wisdom, the fashioner of all things,
taught me.

The Nature of Wisdom

There is in her a spirit that is intelligent,
holy,
unique, manifold, subtle,
mobile, clear, unpolluted,
distinct, invulnerable, loving the good,
keen,
irresistible, ²³beneficent, humane,
steadfast, sure, free from anxiety,
all-powerful, overseeing all,
and penetrating through all spirits
that are intelligent, pure, and altogether
subtle.
²⁴ For wisdom is more mobile than any
motion;

because of her pureness she pervades and
penetrates all things.
²⁵ For she is a breath of the power of God,
and a pure emanation of the glory of the
Almighty;
therefore nothing defiled gains entrance
into her.
²⁶ For she is a reflection of eternal light,
a spotless mirror of the working of God,
and an image of his goodness.
²⁷ Although she is but one, she can do all
things,
and while remaining in herself, she renews
all things;
in every generation she passes into holy
souls
and makes them friends of God, and
prophets;
²⁸ for God loves nothing so much as the
person who lives with wisdom.
²⁹ She is more beautiful than the sun,
and excels every constellation of the stars.
Compared with the light she is found to be
superior,
³⁰ for it is succeeded by the night,
but against wisdom evil does not prevail.

8 She reaches mightily from one end of the
earth to the other,
and she orders all things well.

Solomon's Love for Wisdom

² I loved her and sought her from my youth;
I desired to take her for my bride,
and became enamored of her beauty.
³ She glorifies her noble birth by living with
God,
and the Lord of all loves her.
⁴ For she is an initiate in the knowledge of
God,
and an associate in his works.
⁵ If riches are a desirable possession in life,
what is richer than wisdom, the active cause
of all things?
⁶ And if understanding is effective,
who more than she is fashioner of what
exists?
⁷ And if anyone loves righteousness,
her labors are virtues;
for she teaches self-control and prudence,
justice and courage;
nothing in life is more profitable for
mortals than these.
⁸ And if anyone longs for wide experience,
she knows the things of old, and infers the
things to come;
she understands turns of speech and the
solutions of riddles;

a Or *winds*

Love Rocks—© Charlotte Katheder, 16

she has foreknowledge of signs and
wonders
and of the outcome of seasons and times.

Wisdom Indispensible to Rulers

9 Therefore I determined to take her to live
with me,
knowing that she would give me good
counsel
and encouragement in cares and grief.
10 Because of her I shall have glory among the
multitudes
and honor in the presence of the elders,
though I am young.
11 I shall be found keen in judgment,
and in the sight of rulers I shall be admired.
12 When I am silent they will wait for me,
and when I speak they will give heed;
if I speak at greater length,
they will put their hands on their mouths.
13 Because of her I shall have immortality,
and leave an everlasting remembrance to
those who come after me.
14 I shall govern peoples,
and nations will be subject to me;
15 dread monarchs will be afraid of me when
they hear of me;
among the people I shall show myself
capable, and courageous in war.

16 When I enter my house, I shall find rest
with her;
for companionship with her has no
bitterness,
and life with her has no pain, but gladness
and joy.
17 When I considered these things inwardly,
and pondered in my heart
that in kinship with wisdom there is
immortality,
18 and in friendship with her, pure delight,
and in the labors of her hands, unfailing
wealth,
and in the experience of her company,
understanding,
and renown in sharing her words,
I went about seeking how to get her for
myself.
19 As a child I was naturally gifted,
and a good soul fell to my lot;
20 or rather, being good, I entered an
undefiled body.
21 But I perceived that I would not possess
wisdom unless God gave her to
me—
and it was a mark of insight to know whose
gift she was—
so I appealed to the Lord and implored him,
and with my whole heart I said:

9 Solomon's Prayer for Wisdom

"O God of my ancestors and Lord of mercy,
who have made all things by your word,

2 and by your wisdom have formed
humankind
to have dominion over the creatures you
have made,

3 and rule the world in holiness and
righteousness,
and pronounce judgment in uprightness of
soul,

4 give me the wisdom that sits by your
throne,
and do not reject me from among your
servants.

5 For I am your servant*a* the son of your
serving girl,
a man who is weak and short-lived,
with little understanding of judgment and
laws;

6 for even one who is perfect among human
beings
will be regarded as nothing without the
wisdom that comes from you.

7 You have chosen me to be king of your
people
and to be judge over your sons and
daughters.

8 You have given command to build a temple
on your holy mountain,
and an altar in the city of your habitation,
a copy of the holy tent that you prepared
from the beginning.

9 With you is wisdom, she who knows your
works
and was present when you made the world;
she understands what is pleasing in your
sight
and what is right according to your
commandments.

10 Send her forth from the holy heavens,
and from the throne of your glory send her,
that she may labor at my side,
and that I may learn what is pleasing to you.

11 For she knows and understands all things,
and she will guide me wisely in my actions
and guard me with her glory.

12 Then my works will be acceptable,
and I shall judge your people justly,
and shall be worthy of the throne*b* of my
father.

13 For who can learn the counsel of God?
Or who can discern what the Lord wills?

14 For the reasoning of mortals is worthless,
and our designs are likely to fail;

a Gk slave *b* Gk thrones

¹⁵ for a perishable body weighs down the
soul,
and this earthy tent burdens the
thoughtful^a mind.
¹⁶ We can hardly guess at what is on earth,
and what is at hand we find with labor;
but who has traced out what is in the
heavens?
¹⁷ Who has learned your counsel,
unless you have given wisdom
and sent your holy spirit from on high?
¹⁸ And thus the paths of those on earth were
set right,
and people were taught what pleases you,
and were saved by wisdom."

10 The Work of Wisdom from Adam to Moses

Wisdom^b protected the first-formed father
of the world, when he alone had
been created;
she delivered him from his transgression,
² and gave him strength to rule all things.
³ But when an unrighteous man departed
from her in his anger,
he perished because in rage he killed his
brother.
⁴ When the earth was flooded because of
him, wisdom again saved it,
steering the righteous man by a paltry piece
of wood.

⁵ Wisdom^b also, when the nations in wicked
agreement had been put to
confusion,
recognized the righteous man and
preserved him blameless before
God,
and kept him strong in the face of his
compassion for his child.
⁶ Wisdom^b rescued a righteous man when
the ungodly were perishing;
he escaped the fire that descended on the
Five Cities.^c
⁷ Evidence of their wickedness still remains:
a continually smoking wasteland,
plants bearing fruit that does not ripen,
and a pillar of salt standing as a monument
to an unbelieving soul.
⁸ For because they passed wisdom by,
they not only were hindered from
recognizing the good,
but also left for humankind a reminder of
their folly,
so that their failures could never go
unnoticed.

⁹ Wisdom rescued from troubles those who
served her.
¹⁰ When a righteous man fled from his
brother's wrath,
she guided him on straight paths;
she showed him the kingdom of God,
and gave him knowledge of holy things;
she prospered him in his labors,
and increased the fruit of his toil.
¹¹ When his oppressors were covetous,
she stood by him and made him rich.
¹² She protected him from his enemies,
and kept him safe from those who lay in
wait for him;
in his arduous contest she gave him the
victory,
so that he might learn that godliness is
more powerful than anything else.

¹³ When a righteous man was sold, wisdom^d
did not desert him,
but delivered him from sin.
She descended with him into the dungeon,
¹⁴ and when he was in prison she did not leave
him,
until she brought him the scepter of a
kingdom
and authority over his masters.
Those who accused him she showed to be
false,
and she gave him everlasting honor.

Wisdom Led the Israelites out of Egypt

¹⁵ A holy people and blameless race
wisdom delivered from a nation of
oppressors.
¹⁶ She entered the soul of a servant of the
Lord,
and withstood dread kings with wonders
and signs.
¹⁷ She gave to holy people the reward of their
labors;
she guided them along a marvelous way,
and became a shelter to them by day,
and a starry flame through the night.
¹⁸ She brought them over the Red Sea,
and led them through deep waters;
¹⁹ but she drowned their enemies,
and cast them up from the depth of the sea.
²⁰ Therefore the righteous plundered the
ungodly;
they sang hymns, O Lord, to your holy
name,
and praised with one accord your defending
hand;
²¹ for wisdom opened the mouths of those
who were mute,

---

a Or *anxious* *b* Gk *She* *c* Or *on Pentapolis* *d* Gk *she*

In Stillness God Speaks to Us—© Megan Schoettler, 17

and made the tongues of infants speak clearly.

11 Wisdom Led the Israelites through the Desert

Wisdom*a* prospered their works by the hand of a holy prophet.

2 They journeyed through an uninhabited wilderness,

and pitched their tents in untrodden places.

3 They withstood their enemies and fought off their foes.

4 When they were thirsty, they called upon you,

and water was given them out of flinty rock, and from hard stone a remedy for their thirst.

5 For through the very things by which their enemies were punished,

they themselves received benefit in their need.

6 Instead of the fountain of an ever-flowing river,

stirred up and defiled with blood

7 in rebuke for the decree to kill the infants, you gave them abundant water unexpectedly,

8 showing by their thirst at that time how you punished their enemies.

9 For when they were tried, though they were being disciplined in mercy,

they learned how the ungodly were tormented when judged in wrath.

10 For you tested them as a parent*b* does in warning,

but you examined the ungodly*c* as a stern king does in condemnation.

11 Whether absent or present, they were equally distressed,

12 for a twofold grief possessed them, and a groaning at the memory of what had occurred.

13 For when they heard that through their own punishments

the righteous*d* had received benefit, they perceived it was the Lord's doing.

14 For though they had mockingly rejected him who long before had been cast out and exposed,

at the end of the events they marveled at him,

when they felt thirst in a different way from the righteous.

a Gk *She* *b* Gk *a father* *c* Gk *those* *d* Gk *they*

Unstoppable—© Tasha Price, 16

Punishment of the Wicked

15 In return for their foolish and wicked
thoughts,
which led them astray to worship irrational
serpents and worthless animals,
you sent upon them a multitude of
irrational creatures to punish them,

16 so that they might learn that one is
punished by the very things by
which one sins.

17 For your all-powerful hand,
which created the world out of formless
matter,
did not lack the means to send upon them a
multitude of bears, or bold lions,

18 or newly-created unknown beasts full of
rage,
or such as breathe out fiery breath,
or belch forth a thick pall of smoke,
or flash terrible sparks from their eyes;

19 not only could the harm they did destroy
people,*a*
but the mere sight of them could kill by
fright.

20 Even apart from these, people*b* could fall at
a single breath
when pursued by justice
and scattered by the breath of your power.
But you have arranged all things by measure
and number and weight.

God Is Powerful and Merciful

21 For it is always in your power to show great
strength,
and who can withstand the might of your
arm?

22 Because the whole world before you is like
a speck that tips the scales,
and like a drop of morning dew that falls on
the ground.

23 But you are merciful to all, for you can do
all things,
and you overlook people's sins, so that they
may repent.

24 For you love all things that exist,
and detest none of the things that you have
made,
for you would not have made anything if
you had hated it.

25 How would anything have endured if you
had not willed it?
Or how would anything not called forth by
you have been preserved?

26 You spare all things, for they are yours,
O Lord, you who love the living.

12 For your immortal spirit is in all things.
2 Therefore you correct little by little those
who trespass,
and you remind and warn them of the
things through which they sin,
so that they may be freed from wickedness
and put their trust in you, O Lord.

a Gk *them* *b* Gk *they*

The Sins of the Canaanites

³ Those who lived long ago in your holy land
⁴ you hated for their detestable practices,
   their works of sorcery and unholy rites,
⁵ their merciless slaughter*ᵃ* of children,
   and their sacrificial feasting on human
      flesh and blood.
   These initiates from the midst of a heathen
      cult,*ᵇ*
⁶ these parents who murder helpless lives,
   you willed to destroy by the hands of our
      ancestors,
⁷ so that the land most precious of all to you
   might receive a worthy colony of the
      servants*ᶜ* of God.
⁸ But even these you spared, since they were
      but mortals,
   and sent wasps*ᵈ* as forerunners of your
      army
   to destroy them little by little,
⁹ though you were not unable to give the
      ungodly into the hands of the
      righteous in battle,
   or to destroy them at one blow by dread
      wild animals or your stern word.
¹⁰ But judging them little by little you gave
      them an opportunity to repent,
   though you were not unaware that their
      origin*ᵉ* was evil
   and their wickedness inborn,
   and that their way of thinking would never
      change.
¹¹ For they were an accursed race from the
      beginning,
   and it was not through fear of anyone that
      you left them unpunished for their
      sins.

God Is Sovereign

¹² For who will say, "What have you done?"
   or will resist your judgment?
   Who will accuse you for the destruction of
      nations that you made?
   Or who will come before you to plead as an
      advocate for the unrighteous?
¹³ For neither is there any god besides you,
      whose care is for all people,*ᶠ*
   to whom you should prove that you have
      not judged unjustly;
¹⁴ nor can any king or monarch confront
      you about those whom you have
      punished.
¹⁵ You are righteous and you rule all things
      righteously,
   deeming it alien to your power
   to condemn anyone who does not deserve
      to be punished.

¹⁶ For your strength is the source of
      righteousness,
   and your sovereignty over all causes you to
      spare all.
¹⁷ For you show your strength when people
      doubt the completeness of your
      power,
   and you rebuke any insolence among those
      who know it.*ᵇ*
¹⁸ Although you are sovereign in strength, you
      judge with mildness,
   and with great forbearance you govern us;
   for you have power to act whenever you
      choose.

God's Lessons for Israel

¹⁹ Through such works you have taught your
      people

---

a Gk *slaughterers* *b* Meaning of Gk uncertain *c* Or *children* *d* Or *hornets* *e* Or *nature* *f* Or *all things*

that the righteous must be kind,
and you have filled your children with good hope,
because you give repentance for sins.

20 For if you punished with such great care and indulgence[a]
the enemies of your servants[b] and those deserving of death,
granting them time and opportunity to give up their wickedness,

21 with what strictness you have judged your children,
to whose ancestors you gave oaths and covenants full of good promises!

22 So while chastening us you scourge our enemies ten thousand times more,
so that, when we judge, we may meditate upon your goodness,
and when we are judged, we may expect mercy.

The Punishment of the Egyptians

23 Therefore those who lived unrighteously, in a life of folly,
you tormented through their own abominations.

24 For they went far astray on the paths of error,
accepting as gods those animals that even their enemies[c] despised;
they were deceived like foolish infants.

25 Therefore, as though to children who cannot reason,
you sent your judgment to mock them.

26 But those who have not heeded the warning of mild rebukes
will experience the deserved judgment of God.

27 For when in their suffering they became incensed
at those creatures that they had thought to be gods, being punished by means of them,
they saw and recognized as the true God the one whom they had before refused to know.
Therefore the utmost condemnation came upon them.

13 The Foolishness of Nature Worship

For all people who were ignorant of God were foolish by nature;
and they were unable from the good things that are seen to know the one who exists,
nor did they recognize the artisan while paying heed to his works;

2 but they supposed that either fire or wind or swift air,
or the circle of the stars, or turbulent water,
or the luminaries of heaven were the gods that rule the world.

3 If through delight in the beauty of these things people assumed them to be gods,
let them know how much better than these is their Lord,
for the author of beauty created them.

4 And if people[c] were amazed at their power and working,
let them perceive from them
how much more powerful is the one who formed them.

5 For from the greatness and beauty of created things
comes a corresponding perception of their Creator.

6 Yet these people are little to be blamed,
for perhaps they go astray
while seeking God and desiring to find him.

7 For while they live among his works, they keep searching,
and they trust in what they see, because the things that are seen are beautiful.

8 Yet again, not even they are to be excused;

9 for if they had the power to know so much that they could investigate the world,
how did they fail to find sooner the Lord of these things?

The Foolishness of Idolatry

10 But miserable, with their hopes set on dead things, are those
who give the name "gods" to the works of human hands,
gold and silver fashioned with skill,
and likenesses of animals,
or a useless stone, the work of an ancient hand.

11 A skilled woodcutter may saw down a tree easy to handle
and skillfully strip off all its bark,
and then with pleasing workmanship
make a useful vessel that serves life's needs,

12 and burn the cast-off pieces of his work
to prepare his food, and eat his fill.

---

a Other ancient authorities lack *and indulgence*; others read *and entreaty*   b Or *children*   c Gk *they*

13 But a cast-off piece from among them,
      useful for nothing,
    a stick crooked and full of knots,
    he takes and carves with care in his leisure,
    and shapes it with skill gained in idleness;[a]
    he forms it in the likeness of a human
      being,
14 or makes it like some worthless animal,
    giving it a coat of red paint and coloring its
      surface red
    and covering every blemish in it with paint;
15 then he makes a suitable niche for it,
    and sets it in the wall, and fastens it there
      with iron.
16 He takes thought for it, so that it may not
      fall,
    because he knows that it cannot help itself,
    for it is only an image and has need of help.
17 When he prays about possessions and his
      marriage and children,
    he is not ashamed to address a lifeless
      thing.
18 For health he appeals to a thing that is
      weak;
    for life he prays to a thing that is dead;
    for aid he entreats a thing that is utterly
      inexperienced;
    for a prosperous journey, a thing that
      cannot take a step;
19 for money-making and work and success
      with his hands
    he asks strength of a thing whose hands
      have no strength.

14 Folly of a Navigator Praying to an Idol

    Again, one preparing to sail and about to
      voyage over raging waves
    calls upon a piece of wood more fragile
      than the ship that carries him.
2 For it was desire for gain that planned that
      vessel,
    and wisdom was the artisan who built it;
3 but it is your providence, O Father, that
      steers its course,
    because you have given it a path in the sea,
    and a safe way through the waves,
4 showing that you can save from every
      danger,
    so that even a person who lacks skill may
      put to sea.
5 It is your will that works of your wisdom
      should not be without effect;
    therefore people trust their lives even to
      the smallest piece of wood,
    and passing through the billows on a raft
      they come safely to land.

a Other ancient authorities read *with intelligent skill*

REALITY ✔

IDOLATRY

It may seem strange to you that people would take a golden calf and make it the object of worship. Why would people bow down to worship something they had made?

But think about it. Do you have a special "good luck" token or ritual? Do you carry a rabbit's foot or other superstitious charms in your backpack on test days? Do you wear your "lucky shirt" on game days? Or do you "knock on wood" when you wish for something? Those superstitious practices are just as invalid as worshiping a cow made out of metal.

Then dig a little deeper. Think about the things, people, or activities you put first in your life. Those are the real idols for a contemporary follower of Jesus. What's *your* idol? Money? Designer clothes? A fancy car? What about drugs or sex? Anything that you put between yourself and God—*above* God, even—puts you on even ground with the idol worshipers in Wisdom.

The problem with worshiping false gods is that no one or no thing will ever satisfy the hungry human heart except the *real* God.

Read **Wisdom 14.1–3** to understand the meaning and futility of idolatry. Then think about what your idols might be and how fragile they are in relation to the God who created you, guides your life, provides safety, and in the end is the one true God who will satisfy your deepest longings.

6 For even in the beginning, when arrogant
      giants were perishing,
    the hope of the world took refuge on a raft,
    and guided by your hand left to the world
      the seed of a new generation.
7 For blessed is the wood by which
      righteousness comes.

8 But the idol made with hands is accursed,
    and so is the one who made it—

he for having made it, and the perishable
    thing because it was named a god.

9 For equally hateful to God are the ungodly
    and their ungodliness;
10 for what was done will be punished
    together with the one who did it.
11 Therefore there will be a visitation also
    upon the heathen idols,
because, though part of what God created,
    they became an abomination,
snares for human souls
    and a trap for the feet of the foolish.

The Origin and Evils of Idolatry

12 For the idea of making idols was the
    beginning of fornication,
and the invention of them was the
    corruption of life;
13 for they did not exist from the beginning,
    nor will they last forever.
14 For through human vanity they entered the
    world,
and therefore their speedy end has been
    planned.

15 For a father, consumed with grief at an
    untimely bereavement,
made an image of his child, who had been
    suddenly taken from him;
he now honored as a god what was once a
    dead human being,
and handed on to his dependents secret
    rites and initiations.
16 Then the ungodly custom, grown strong
    with time, was kept as a law,
and at the command of monarchs carved
    images were worshiped.
17 When people could not honor monarchs[a]
    in their presence, since they lived at
    a distance,
they imagined their appearance far away,
and made a visible image of the king whom
    they honored,
so that by their zeal they might flatter the
    absent one as though present.
18 Then the ambition of the artisan impelled
    even those who did not know the king to
    intensify their worship.
19 For he, perhaps wishing to please his ruler,
    skillfully forced the likeness to take more
    beautiful form,
20 and the multitude, attracted by the charm
    of his work,
now regarded as an object of worship the
    one whom shortly before they had
    honored as a human being.

21 And this became a hidden trap for
    humankind,
because people, in bondage to misfortune
    or to royal authority,
bestowed on objects of stone or wood the
    name that ought not to be shared.

22 Then it was not enough for them to err
    about the knowledge of God,
but though living in great strife due to
    ignorance,
they call such great evils peace.
23 For whether they kill children in their
    initiations, or celebrate secret
    mysteries,
or hold frenzied revels with strange
    customs,
24 they no longer keep either their lives or
    their marriages pure,
but they either treacherously kill one
    another, or grieve one another by
    adultery,
25 and all is a raging riot of blood and murder,
    theft and deceit, corruption,
    faithlessness, tumult, perjury,
26 confusion over what is good, forgetfulness
    of favors,
defiling of souls, sexual perversion,
    disorder in marriages, adultery, and
    debauchery.
27 For the worship of idols not to be named
    is the beginning and cause and end of every
    evil.
28 For their worshipers[b] either rave in
    exultation,
or prophesy lies, or live unrighteously, or
    readily commit perjury;
29 for because they trust in lifeless idols
    they swear wicked oaths and expect to
    suffer no harm.
30 But just penalties will overtake them on two
    counts:
because they thought wrongly about God in
    devoting themselves to idols,
and because in deceit they swore
    unrighteously through contempt
    for holiness.
31 For it is not the power of the things by
    which people swear,[c]
but the just penalty for those who sin,
that always pursues the transgression of the
    unrighteous.

15   Benefits of Worshiping the True God

But you, our God, are kind and true,
    patient, and ruling all things[d] in mercy.
2 For even if we sin we are yours, knowing
    your power;

---

a Gk them   b Gk they   c Or of the oaths people swear   d Or ruling the universe

but we will not sin, because we know that
  you acknowledge us as yours.
3 For to know you is complete righteousness,
  and to know your power is the root of
  immortality.
4 For neither has the evil intent of human art
  misled us,
  nor the fruitless toil of painters,
  a figure stained with varied colors,
5 whose appearance arouses yearning in
  fools,
  so that they desire*a* the lifeless form of a
  dead image.
6 Lovers of evil things and fit for such objects
  of hope*b*
  are those who either make or desire or
  worship them.

a Gk *and he desires* *b* Gk *such hopes*

The Foolishness of Worshiping Clay Idols

7 A potter kneads the soft earth
  and laboriously molds each vessel for our
  service,
  fashioning out of the same clay
  both the vessels that serve clean uses
  and those for contrary uses, making all
  alike;
  but which shall be the use of each of them
  the worker in clay decides.
8 With misspent toil, these workers form a
  futile god from the same clay—
  these mortals who were made of earth a
  short time before
  and after a little while go to the earth from
  which all mortals are taken,

Majesty—© Jason Paradis, 14

when the time comes to return the souls
that were borrowed.

9 But the workers are not concerned that
mortals are destined to die
or that their life is brief,
but they compete with workers in gold and
silver,
and imitate workers in copper;
and they count it a glorious thing to mold
counterfeit gods.

10 Their heart is ashes, their hope is cheaper
than dirt,
and their lives are of less worth than clay,

11 because they failed to know the one who
formed them
and inspired them with active souls
and breathed a living spirit into them.

12 But they considered our existence an idle
game,
and life a festival held for profit,
for they say one must get money however
one can, even by base means.

13 For these persons, more than all others,
know that they sin
when they make from earthy matter fragile
vessels and carved images.

14 But most foolish, and more miserable than
an infant,

are all the enemies who oppressed your
people.

15 For they thought that all their heathen idols
were gods,
though these have neither the use of their
eyes to see with,
nor nostrils with which to draw breath,
nor ears with which to hear,
nor fingers to feel with,
and their feet are of no use for walking.

16 For a human being made them,
and one whose spirit is borrowed formed
them;
for none can form gods that are like
themselves.

17 People are mortal, and what they make
with lawless hands is dead;
for they are better than the objects they
worship,
since[a] they have life, but the idols[b] never
had.

Serpents in the Desert

18 Moreover, they worship even the most
hateful animals,
which are worse than all others when
judged by their lack of intelligence;

a Other ancient authorities read *of which* b Gk *but they*

19 and even as animals they are not so
     beautiful in appearance that one
     would desire them,
but they have escaped both the praise of
     God and his blessing.

16 Therefore those people[a] were deservedly
     punished through such creatures,
and were tormented by a multitude of
     animals.
2 Instead of this punishment you showed
     kindness to your people,
and you prepared quails to eat,
a delicacy to satisfy the desire of appetite;
3 in order that those people, when they
     desired food,
might lose the least remnant of appetite[b]
because of the odious creatures sent to
     them,
while your people,[a] after suffering want a
     short time,
might partake of delicacies.
4 For it was necessary that upon those
     oppressors inescapable want
     should come,
while to these others it was merely shown
     how their enemies were being
     tormented.

5 For when the terrible rage of wild animals
     came upon your people[c]
and they were being destroyed by the bites
     of writhing serpents,
your wrath did not continue to the end;
6 they were troubled for a little while as a
     warning,
and received a symbol of deliverance
     to remind them of your law's
     command.
7 For the one who turned toward it was saved,
     not by the thing that was beheld,
but by you, the Savior of all.
8 And by this also you convinced our enemies
that it is you who deliver from every evil.
9 For they were killed by the bites of locusts
     and flies,
and no healing was found for them,
because they deserved to be punished by
     such things.
10 But your children were not conquered even
     by the fangs of venomous serpents,
for your mercy came to their help and
     healed them.
11 To remind them of your oracles they were
     bitten,
and then were quickly delivered,
so that they would not fall into deep
     forgetfulness

> "I hope our wisdom will grow with our
> power, and teach us that the less we
> use our power the greater it will be."
> —**Thomas Jefferson**

and become unresponsive[d] to your
     kindness.
12 For neither herb nor poultice cured them,
but it was your word, O Lord, that heals all
     people.
13 For you have power over life and death;
you lead mortals down to the gates of
     Hades and back again.
14 A person in wickedness kills another,
but cannot bring back the departed spirit,
or set free the imprisoned soul.

Disastrous Storms Strike Egypt
15 To escape from your hand is impossible;
16 for the ungodly, refusing to know you,
     were flogged by the strength of your arm,
pursued by unusual rains and hail and
     relentless storms,
and utterly consumed by fire.
17 For—most incredible of all—in water,
     which quenches all things,
the fire had still greater effect,
for the universe defends the righteous.
18 At one time the flame was restrained,
     so that it might not consume the creatures
     sent against the ungodly,
but that seeing this they might know
that they were being pursued by the
     judgment of God;
19 and at another time even in the midst of
     water it burned more intensely than
     fire,
to destroy the crops of the unrighteous
     land.

The Israelites Receive Manna
20 Instead of these things you gave your
     people food of angels,
and without their toil you supplied them
     from heaven with bread ready to
     eat,
providing every pleasure and suited to every
     taste.
21 For your sustenance manifested your
     sweetness toward your children;
and the bread, ministering[e] to the desire of
     the one who took it,
was changed to suit everyone's liking.

a Gk *they* b Gk *loathed the necessary appetite* c Gk *them* d Meaning of Gk uncertain e Gk *and it, ministering*

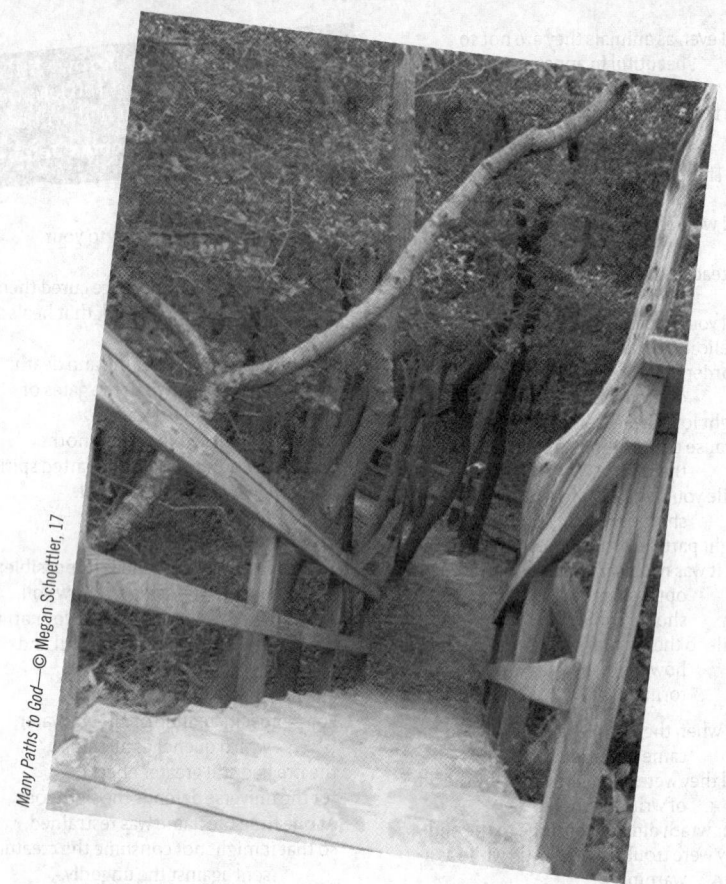

Many Paths to God—© Megan Schoettler, 17

22 Snow and ice withstood fire without
   melting,
   so that they might know that the crops of
   their enemies
   were being destroyed by the fire that blazed
   in the hail
   and flashed in the showers of rain;
23 whereas the fire,ª in order that the
   righteous might be fed,
   even forgot its native power.

24 For creation, serving you who made it,
   exerts itself to punish the unrighteous,
   and in kindness relaxes on behalf of those
   who trust in you.
25 Therefore at that time also, changed into all
   forms,
   it served your all-nourishing bounty,
   according to the desire of those who had
   need,ᵇ
26 so that your children, whom you loved,
   O Lord, might learn

that it is not the production of crops that
   feeds humankind
   but that your word sustains those who trust
   in you.
27 For what was not destroyed by fire
   was melted when simply warmed by a
   fleeting ray of the sun,
28 to make it known that one must rise before
   the sun to give you thanks,
   and must pray to you at the dawning of the
   light;
29 for the hope of an ungrateful person will
   melt like wintry frost,
   and flow away like waste water.

17 Terror Strikes the Egyptians at Night

Great are your judgments and hard to
   describe;
   therefore uninstructed souls have gone
   astray.

a Gk *this* b Or *who made supplication*

2 For when lawless people supposed that
      they held the holy nation in their
      power,
  they themselves lay as captives of darkness
      and prisoners of long night,
  shut in under their roofs, exiles from
      eternal providence.
3 For thinking that in their secret sins they
      were unobserved
  behind a dark curtain of forgetfulness,
  they were scattered, terribly*a* alarmed,
  and appalled by specters.
4 For not even the inner chamber that held
      them protected them from fear,
  but terrifying sounds rang out around
      them,
  and dismal phantoms with gloomy faces
      appeared.
5 And no power of fire was able to give light,
  nor did the brilliant flames of the stars
  avail to illumine that hateful night.
6 Nothing was shining through to them
  except a dreadful, self-kindled fire,
  and in terror they deemed the things that
      they saw
  to be worse than that unseen appearance.
7 The delusions of their magic art lay
      humbled,
  and their boasted wisdom was scornfully
      rebuked.
8 For those who promised to drive off the
      fears and disorders of a sick soul
  were sick themselves with ridiculous fear.
9 For even if nothing disturbing frightened
      them,
  yet, scared by the passing of wild animals
      and the hissing of snakes
10 they perished in trembling fear,
  refusing to look even at the air, though it
      nowhere could be avoided.
11 For wickedness is a cowardly thing,
      condemned by its own testimony;*b*
  distressed by conscience, it has always
      exaggerated*c* the difficulties.
12 For fear is nothing but a giving up of the
      helps that come from reason;
13 and hope, defeated by this inward
      weakness,
  prefers ignorance of what causes the
      torment.
14 But throughout the night, which was really
      powerless
  and which came upon them from the
      recesses of powerless Hades,
  they all slept the same sleep,

15 and now were driven by monstrous
      specters,
  and now were paralyzed by their souls'
      surrender;
  for sudden and unexpected fear
      overwhelmed them.
16 And whoever was there fell down,
  and thus was kept shut up in a prison not
      made of iron;
17 for whether they were farmers or shepherds
  or workers who toiled in the wilderness,
  they were seized, and endured the
      inescapable fate;
  for with one chain of darkness they all were
      bound.
18 Whether there came a whistling wind,
  or a melodious sound of birds in
      wide-spreading branches,

TEXT MESSAGE

Hades means "unseen"
(Wisdom 17.14). It was the
name of the Greek god of
the underworld. It is the
Greek word used to
translate the Hebrew word
Sheol, which for the Jewish
people is the realm of the
dead.

This information has been scanned and is free of all
known viruses. Please forward to all your friends.

a Other ancient authorities read *unobserved, they were darkened
behind a dark curtain of forgetfulness, terribly* *b* Meaning of Gk
uncertain *c* Other ancient authorities read *anticipated*

or the rhythm of violently rushing water,
19 or the harsh crash of rocks hurled down,
or the unseen running of leaping animals,
or the sound of the most savage roaring
beasts,
or an echo thrown back from a hollow of
the mountains,
it paralyzed them with terror.
20 For the whole world was illumined with
brilliant light,
and went about its work unhindered,
21 while over those people alone heavy night
was spread,
an image of the darkness that was destined
to receive them;
but still heavier than darkness were they to
themselves.

18 Light Shines on the Israelites

But for your holy ones there was very great
light.
Their enemies[a] heard their voices but did
not see their forms,
and counted them happy for not having
suffered,
2 and were thankful that your holy ones,[b]
though previously wronged, were
doing them no injury;
and they begged their pardon for having
been at variance with them.[b]
3 Therefore you provided a flaming pillar of
fire
as a guide for your people's[c] unknown
journey,
and a harmless sun for their glorious
wandering.
4 For their enemies[d] deserved to be deprived
of light and imprisoned in
darkness,
those who had kept your children
imprisoned,
through whom the imperishable light
of the law was to be given to the
world.

The Death of the Egyptian Firstborn

5 When they had resolved to kill the infants
of your holy ones,
and one child had been abandoned and
rescued,
you in punishment took away a multitude
of their children;

and you destroyed them all together by a
mighty flood.
6 That night was made known beforehand to
our ancestors,
so that they might rejoice in sure
knowledge of the oaths in which
they trusted.
7 The deliverance of the righteous and the
destruction of their enemies
were expected by your people.
8 For by the same means by which you
punished our enemies
you called us to yourself and glorified us.
9 For in secret the holy children of good
people offered sacrifices,
and with one accord agreed to the divine
law,
so that the saints would share alike the
same things,
both blessings and dangers;
and already they were singing the praises of
the ancestors.[e]
10 But the discordant cry of their enemies
echoed back,
and their piteous lament for their children
was spread abroad.
11 The slave was punished with the same
penalty as the master,
and the commoner suffered the same loss
as the king;
12 and they all together, by the one form[f] of
death,
had corpses too many to count.
For the living were not sufficient even to
bury them,
since in one instant their most valued
children had been destroyed.
13 For though they had disbelieved everything
because of their magic arts,
yet, when their firstborn were destroyed,
they acknowledged your people to
be God's child.
14 For while gentle silence enveloped all
things,
and night in its swift course was now half
gone,
15 your all-powerful word leaped from heaven,
from the royal throne,
into the midst of the land that was doomed,
a stern warrior
16 carrying the sharp sword of your authentic
command,
and stood and filled all things with death,
and touched heaven while standing on the
earth.

a Gk They b Meaning of Gk uncertain c Gk their d Gk those
persons e Other ancient authorities read dangers, the ancestors
already leading the songs of praise f Gk name

¹⁷ Then at once apparitions in dreadful
  dreams greatly troubled them,
and unexpected fears assailed them;
¹⁸ and one here and another there, hurled
  down half dead,
made known why they were dying;
¹⁹ for the dreams that disturbed them
  forewarned them of this,
so that they might not perish without
  knowing why they suffered.

Threat of Annihilation in the Desert

²⁰ The experience of death touched also the
  righteous,
and a plague came upon the multitude in
  the desert,
but the wrath did not long continue.
²¹ For a blameless man was quick to act as
  their champion;
he brought forward the shield of his
  ministry,
prayer and propitiation by incense;
he withstood the anger and put an end to
  the disaster,
showing that he was your servant.
²² He conquered the wrath^a not by strength of
  body,
not by force of arms,
but by his word he subdued the avenger,
appealing to the oaths and covenants given
  to our ancestors.
²³ For when the dead had already fallen on
  one another in heaps,
he intervened and held back the wrath,
and cut off its way to the living.
²⁴ For on his long robe the whole world was
  depicted,
and the glories of the ancestors were
  engraved on the four rows of
  stones,
and your majesty was on the diadem upon
  his head.
²⁵ To these the destroyer yielded, these he^b
  feared;
for merely to test the wrath was enough.

19 The Red Sea

But the ungodly were assailed to the end by
  pitiless anger,
for God^c knew in advance even their future
  actions:
² how, though they themselves had
  permitted^d your people to depart
and hastily sent them out,
they would change their minds and pursue
  them.

REALITY

LIVING OUT WISDOM AND JUSTICE

The book of Wisdom begins with the command
to "Love righteousness" (1.1) and goes on
to praise the work of justice in our lives and
its connection with wise living. What does it
mean to you to live a life of seeking justice?
How often do you think about living justice
as your first response when you are making a
choice?
Think about:

- the choices you make about how you
  spend your money and time.
- the choices you make about who you
  include or exclude in your circle of
  friends or just the people you say "hi" to
  on a daily basis.
- the choices you make when you are
  afraid of how people might judge you.
- the choices you make on a good day and
  on a bad day.

Remember this key lesson of the Wisdom
of Solomon: it is in living justly in all our
relationships that we find our way to the
complete peace that is the fruit of wisdom.

Read **Wisdom 19.22** and reflect on how you
have mirrored God's wisdom and justice with
"your" people—your family and friends.

³ For while they were still engaged in
  mourning,
and were lamenting at the graves of their
  dead,
they reached another foolish decision,
and pursued as fugitives those whom they
  had begged and compelled to leave.
⁴ For the fate they deserved drew them on to
  this end,
and made them forget what had happened,
in order that they might fill up the
  punishment that their torments
  still lacked,
⁵ and that your people might experience^e an
  incredible journey,

^a Cn: Gk *multitude* ^b Other ancient authorities read *they* ^c Gk *he* ^d Other ancient authorities read *had changed their minds to permit*
^e Other ancient authorities read *accomplish*

but they themselves might meet a strange death.

God Guides and Protects His People

6 For the whole creation in its nature was fashioned anew,
complying with your commands,
so that your children[a] might be kept unharmed.

7 The cloud was seen overshadowing the camp,
and dry land emerging where water had stood before,
an unhindered way out of the Red Sea,
and a grassy plain out of the raging waves,

8 where those protected by your hand passed through as one nation,
after gazing on marvelous wonders.

9 For they ranged like horses,
and leaped like lambs,
praising you, O Lord, who delivered them.

10 For they still recalled the events of their sojourn,
how instead of producing animals the earth brought forth gnats,
and instead of fish the river spewed out vast numbers of frogs.

11 Afterward they saw also a new kind[b] of birds,
when desire led them to ask for luxurious food;

12 for, to give them relief, quails came up from the sea.

The Punishment of the Egyptians

13 The punishments did not come upon the sinners
without prior signs in the violence of thunder,
for they justly suffered because of their wicked acts;
for they practiced a more bitter hatred of strangers.

14 Others had refused to receive strangers when they came to them,
but these made slaves of guests who were their benefactors.

15 And not only so—but, while punishment of some sort will come upon the former
for having received strangers with hostility,

16 the latter, having first received them with festal celebrations,
afterward afflicted with terrible sufferings those who had already shared the same rights.

17 They were stricken also with loss of sight—
just as were those at the door of the righteous man—
when, surrounded by yawning darkness,
all of them tried to find the way through their own doors.

A New Harmony in Nature

18 For the elements changed[c] places with one another,
as on a harp the notes vary the nature of the rhythm,
while each note remains the same.[d]
This may be clearly inferred from the sight of what took place.

19 For land animals were transformed into water creatures,
and creatures that swim moved over to the land.

20 Fire even in water retained its normal power,
and water forgot its fire-quenching nature.

21 Flames, on the contrary, failed to consume the flesh of perishable creatures that walked among them,
nor did they melt[e] the crystalline, quick-melting kind of heavenly food.

Conclusion

22 For in everything, O Lord, you have exalted and glorified your people,
and you have not neglected to help them at all times and in all places.

a Or servants   b Or production   c Gk changing   d Meaning of Gk uncertain   e Cn: Gk nor could be melted

SIRACH

WISDOM FOR LIFE

Be Practical

How do you do it? How do you live a good life? You can give me all kinds of reasons and philosophies and theories—but in the end, to be good, wise, or happy, I have to act. So let's be practical. Tell me what to do. Teach me.

If you were a Jewish person living two hundred or so years before Jesus and you were asking these kinds of questions, you would turn to the book of Sirach, because it was a practical guidebook for life.

The "sages," those who wrote wisdom literature, were convinced that to be wise

meant to search for order in this world. It was a very practical affair, based on day-to-day observations of life as it was meant to be lived. And when one found wisdom, one could be assured of living wisely and closely with God. Throughout all the wisdom literature, there's a strong emphasis on practicality.

People who are seeking practical advice for life often turn to the "experts" for help. It's not unlike our culture's fascination with self-help books or TV shows that provide lifestyle advice. In 200 B.C., that expert advice could be found in Sirach.

> *"Of all human activities, man's listening to God is the supreme act of his reasoning and will."*
> —Pope Paul VI

WHO Jesus son of Eleazar son of Sirach (50.27)

WHAT Also known as Ecclesiasticus, Sirach is a combination of instruction and proverbs along with the commandments and laws of Moses found in the Torah

WHEN This book was written ca. 180 B.C.

WHERE The foreword was composed in Egypt, probably Alexandria, and the body of the book was written in Jerusalem.

PATH OF DISCIPLESHIP

Just think for a few minutes. No, really, just *think*. Be quiet, stay still, and think about the author's words. "To fear the Lord is the beginning of wisdom. . . . To fear the Lord is fullness of wisdom" (Sirach 1.14, 16). Is that really all you have to do to be wise?

Fear of the Lord does not mean to be scared of God, but to *stand in awe* of him. To stand in awe of God puts everything in perspective. Consider this: your life is not your own. The God who made and loves you also made and loves your worst enemy and the people you shun or ignore. This is the One who has power over life—all life, yours included.

This is the creator God who created a world out of nothing. This is the artist God whose exquisite handiwork can be seen in every leaf, every flower, every face, *everything*. This is the God the disciple stands in awe of. If you stand in awe of God, and if you keep that perspective and act out of it, you cannot help but make wise and just choices.

Many great teachings have been given to us through the Law and the Prophets and the others[a] that followed them, and for these we should praise Israel for instruction and wisdom. Now, those who read the scriptures must not only themselves understand them, but must also as lovers of learning be able through the spoken and written word to help the outsiders. So my grandfather Jesus, who had devoted himself especially to the reading of the Law and the Prophets and the other books of our ancestors, and had acquired considerable proficiency in them, was himself also led to write something pertaining to instruction and wisdom, so that by becoming familiar also with his book[b] those who love learning might make even greater progress in living according to the law.

You are invited therefore to read it with goodwill and attention, and to be indulgent in cases where, despite our diligent labor in translating, we may seem to have rendered some phrases imperfectly. For what was originally expressed in Hebrew does not have exactly the same sense when translated into another language. Not only this book, but even the Law itself, the Prophecies, and the rest of the books differ not a little when read in the original.

When I came to Egypt in the thirty-eighth year of the reign of Euergetes and stayed for some time, I found opportunity for no little instruction.[c] It seemed highly necessary that I should myself devote some diligence and labor to the translation of this book. During that time I have applied my skill day and night to complete and publish the book for those living abroad who wished to gain learning and are disposed to live according to the law.

1 In Praise of Wisdom

All wisdom is from the Lord,
   and with him it remains forever.
2 The sand of the sea, the drops of rain,
   and the days of eternity—who can count them?
3 The height of heaven, the breadth of the earth,
   the abyss, and wisdom[d]—who can search them out?
4 Wisdom was created before all other things,
   and prudent understanding from eternity.[e]
6 The root of wisdom—to whom has it been revealed?
   Her subtleties—who knows them?[f]
8 There is but one who is wise, greatly to be feared,
   seated upon his throne—the Lord.
9 It is he who created her;

> "Look deep into nature, and then you will understand everything better."
> —Albert Einstein

   he saw her and took her measure;
   he poured her out upon all his works,
10 upon all the living according to his gift;
   he lavished her upon those who love him.[g]

Fear of the Lord Is True Wisdom

11 The fear of the Lord is glory and exultation,
   and gladness and a crown of rejoicing.
12 The fear of the Lord delights the heart,
   and gives gladness and joy and long life.[h]
13 Those who fear the Lord will have a happy end;
   on the day of their death they will be blessed.
14 To fear the Lord is the beginning of wisdom;
   she is created with the faithful in the womb.
15 She made[i] among human beings an eternal foundation,
   and among their descendants she will abide faithfully.
16 To fear the Lord is fullness of wisdom;
   she inebriates mortals with her fruits;
17 she fills their[j] whole house with desirable goods,
   and their[j] storehouses with her produce.
18 The fear of the Lord is the crown of wisdom,
   making peace and perfect health to flourish.[k]
19 She rained down knowledge and discerning comprehension,
   and she heightened the glory of those who held her fast.
20 To fear the Lord is the root of wisdom,
   and her branches are long life.[l]

22 Unjust anger cannot be justified,
   for anger tips the scale to one's ruin.

a Or other books b Gk with these things c Other ancient authorities read I found a copy affording no little instruction d Other ancient authorities read the depth of the abyss e Other ancient authorities add as verse 5, The source of wisdom is God's word in the highest heaven, and her ways are the eternal commandments. f Other ancient authorities add as verse 7, The knowledge of wisdom—to whom was it manifested? And her abundant experience—who has understood it? g Other ancient authorities add Love of the Lord is glorious wisdom; to those to whom he appears he apportions her, that they may see him. h Other ancient authorities add The fear of the Lord is a gift from the Lord; also for love he makes firm paths. i Gk made as a nest j Other ancient authorities read her k Other ancient authorities add Both are gifts of God for peace; glory opens out for those who love him. He saw her and took her measure. l Other ancient authorities add as verse 21, The fear of the Lord drives away sins; and where it abides, it will turn away all anger.

²³ Those who are patient stay calm until the
right moment,
and then cheerfulness comes back to
them.
²⁴ They hold back their words until the right
moment;
then the lips of many tell of their good
sense.

²⁵ In the treasuries of wisdom are wise
sayings,
but godliness is an abomination to a
sinner.
²⁶ If you desire wisdom, keep the
commandments,
and the Lord will lavish her upon you.
²⁷ For the fear of the Lord is wisdom and
discipline,
fidelity and humility are his delight.

²⁸ Do not disobey the fear of the Lord;
do not approach him with a divided
mind.
²⁹ Do not be a hypocrite before others,
and keep watch over your lips.
³⁰ Do not exalt yourself, or you may fall
and bring dishonor upon yourself.
The Lord will reveal your secrets
and overthrow you before the whole
congregation,
because you did not come in the fear of the
Lord,
and your heart was full of deceit.

2 Duties toward God

My child, when you come to serve the Lord,
prepare yourself for testing.^a
² Set your heart right and be steadfast,
and do not be impetuous in time of
calamity.
³ Cling to him and do not depart,
so that your last days may be prosperous.
⁴ Accept whatever befalls you,
and in times of humiliation be patient.
⁵ For gold is tested in the fire,
and those found acceptable, in the
furnace of humiliation.^b
⁶ Trust in him, and he will help you;
make your ways straight, and hope in
him.

⁷ You who fear the Lord, wait for his mercy;
do not stray, or else you may fall.
⁸ You who fear the Lord, trust in him,
and your reward will not be lost.
⁹ You who fear the Lord, hope for good
things,
for lasting joy and mercy.^c

JESUS SIGHTING

If your parents handed
you a sheet of paper and
said, "Here are your duties,"
what would you expect to read
on that paper? Probably a list of well-
defined chores, right?

Read **Sirach 2.1–18**.

Did you find a well-defined list of
things to do? Did you find an expectation
that the items on the list should be done
right and perfectly?

No. What you find there is a consistent
call to fear God, to stand in awe of him.
And if you make a mistake? Your God is
merciful, compassionate, and forgiving.

Think about Jesus and how his
compassion got him in trouble with the
"rules" of the day. Read Luke 15.1–32.
Notice how it begins with the Pharisees
and scribes grumbling, "He's doing it
again!" What was Jesus doing that had
them so annoyed? Healing on the Sabbath,
eating with sinners, respecting the
outcasts. In the eyes of the ever vigilant
Pharisees, Jesus was breaking the laws,
and they planned to put him to death for
it. But Jesus just kept doing it anyway!

Jesus emphasized his message by
telling three stories of God's mercy,
compassion, and forgiveness in the
parables of the lost sheep, the lost coin,
and the prodigal son. What does it all
mean to you? God loves us. God wants
us to make the most of the gift of life he
has given us. And God never, ever gives
up on us.

¹⁰ Consider the generations of old and see:
has anyone trusted in the Lord and been
disappointed?
Or has anyone persevered in the fear of the
Lord^d and been forsaken?
Or has anyone called upon him and been
neglected?
¹¹ For the Lord is compassionate and merciful;

---

a Or trials b Other ancient authorities add in sickness and poverty put your trust in him c Other ancient authorities add For his reward is an
everlasting gift with joy. d Gk of him

he forgives sins and saves in time of
distress.

12 Woe to timid hearts and to slack hands,
and to the sinner who walks a double
path!
13 Woe to the fainthearted who have no trust!
Therefore they will have no shelter.
14 Woe to you who have lost your nerve!
What will you do when the Lord's
reckoning comes?

15 Those who fear the Lord do not disobey his
words,
and those who love him keep his ways.
16 Those who fear the Lord seek to please him,
and those who love him are filled with
his law.
17 Those who fear the Lord prepare their
hearts,
and humble themselves before him.
18 Let us fall into the hands of the Lord,
but not into the hands of mortals;
for equal to his majesty is his mercy,
and equal to his name are his works.[a]

3 Duties toward Parents

Listen to me your father, O children;
act accordingly, that you may be kept in
safety.
2 For the Lord honors a father above his
children,
and he confirms a mother's right over her
children.
3 Those who honor their father atone for
sins,
4 and those who respect their mother are
like those who lay up treasure.
5 Those who honor their father will have joy
in their own children,
and when they pray they will be heard.
6 Those who respect their father will have
long life,
and those who honor[b] their mother obey
the Lord;
7 they will serve their parents as their
masters.[c]
8 Honor your father by word and deed,
that his blessing may come upon you.
9 For a father's blessing strengthens the
houses of the children,
but a mother's curse uproots their
foundations.
10 Do not glorify yourself by dishonoring your
father,
for your father's dishonor is no glory to
you.

11 The glory of one's father is one's own glory,
and it is a disgrace for children not to
respect their mother.
12 My child, help your father in his old age,
and do not grieve him as long as he lives;
13 even if his mind fails, be patient with him;
because you have all your faculties do not
despise him.
14 For kindness to a father will not be
forgotten,
and will be credited to you against your
sins;
15 in the day of your distress it will be
remembered in your favor;
like frost in fair weather, your sins will
melt away.
16 Whoever forsakes a father is like a
blasphemer,
and whoever angers a mother is cursed
by the Lord.

Humility

17 My child, perform your tasks with
humility;[d]
then you will be loved by those whom
God accepts.
18 The greater you are, the more you must
humble yourself;
so you will find favor in the sight of the
Lord.[e]
20 For great is the might of the Lord;
but by the humble he is glorified.
21 Neither seek what is too difficult for you,
nor investigate what is beyond your
power.
22 Reflect upon what you have been
commanded,
for what is hidden is not your concern.
23 Do not meddle in matters that are beyond
you,
for more than you can understand has
been shown you.
24 For their conceit has led many astray,
and wrong opinion has impaired their
judgment.

25 Without eyes there is no light;
without knowledge there is no wisdom.[f]
26 A stubborn mind will fare badly at the end,
and whoever loves danger will perish in it.
27 A stubborn mind will be burdened by
troubles,
and the sinner adds sin to sins.
28 When calamity befalls the proud, there is
no healing,
for an evil plant has taken root in him.

a Syr: Gk lacks this line b Heb: Other ancient authorities read *comfort* c In other ancient authorities this line is preceded by *Those who fear the Lord honor their father* d Heb: Gk *meekness* e Other ancient authorities add as verse 19, *Many are lofty and renowned, but to the humble he reveals his secrets.* f Heb: Other ancient authorities lack verse 25

²⁹ The mind of the intelligent appreciates proverbs,
  and an attentive ear is the desire of the wise.

Alms for the Poor

³⁰ As water extinguishes a blazing fire,
  so almsgiving atones for sin.
³¹ Those who repay favors give thought to the future;
  when they fall they will find support.

4 Duties toward the Poor and the Oppressed

My child, do not cheat the poor of their living,
  and do not keep needy eyes waiting.
² Do not grieve the hungry,
  or anger one in need.
³ Do not add to the troubles of the desperate,
  or delay giving to the needy.
⁴ Do not reject a suppliant in distress,
  or turn your face away from the poor.
⁵ Do not avert your eye from the needy,
  and give no one reason to curse you;
⁶ for if in bitterness of soul some should curse you,
  their Creator will hear their prayer.

⁷ Endear yourself to the congregation;
  bow your head low to the great.
⁸ Give a hearing to the poor,
  and return their greeting politely.
⁹ Rescue the oppressed from the oppressor;
  and do not be hesitant in giving a verdict.
¹⁰ Be a father to orphans,
  and be like a husband to their mother;
you will then be like a son of the Most High,
  and he will love you more than does your mother.

The Rewards of Wisdom

¹¹ Wisdom teaches^a her children
  and gives help to those who seek her.
¹² Whoever loves her loves life,
  and those who seek her from early morning are filled with joy.
¹³ Whoever holds her fast inherits glory,
  and the Lord blesses the place she^b enters.
¹⁴ Those who serve her minister to the Holy One;
  the Lord loves those who love her.
¹⁵ Those who obey her will judge the nations,
  and all who listen to her will live secure.
¹⁶ If they remain faithful, they will inherit her;
  their descendants will also obtain her.

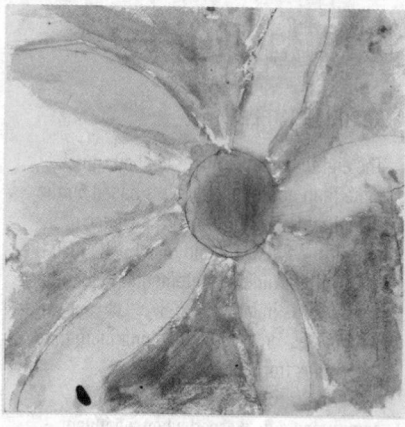

Shine—© John Carter, 14

¹⁷ For at first she will walk with them on tortuous paths;
  she will bring fear and dread upon them,
and will torment them by her discipline
  until she trusts them,^c
and she will test them with her ordinances.
¹⁸ Then she will come straight back to them again and gladden them,
  and will reveal her secrets to them.
¹⁹ If they go astray she will forsake them,
  and hand them over to their ruin.

²⁰ Watch for the opportune time, and beware of evil,
  and do not be ashamed to be yourself.
²¹ For there is a shame that leads to sin,
  and there is a shame that is glory and favor.
²² Do not show partiality, to your own harm,
  or deference, to your downfall.
²³ Do not refrain from speaking at the proper moment,^d
  and do not hide your wisdom.^e
²⁴ For wisdom becomes known through speech,
  and education through the words of the tongue.
²⁵ Never speak against the truth,
  but be ashamed of your ignorance.
²⁶ Do not be ashamed to confess your sins,
  and do not try to stop the current of a river.
²⁷ Do not subject yourself to a fool,
  or show partiality to a ruler.
²⁸ Fight to the death for truth,
  and the Lord God will fight for you.

a Heb Syr: Gk *exalts* *b* Or *he* *c* Or *until they remain faithful in their heart* *d* Heb: Gk *at a time of salvation* *e* So some Gk Mss and Heb Syr Lat: Other Gk Mss lack *and do not hide your wisdom*

IT'S TRADITION

KEEP IT SIMPLE

The eighth commandment is about much more than not telling a lie. It's based on the truth that God is Truth and the source of all truth. We also are told to not embellish the truth with grandiose statements. Remember Jesus' words in Matthew 5:37: "Let your word be 'Yes, Yes' or 'No, No'; anything more than this comes from the evil one."

Read **Sirach 5.9–15**. Truth telling sometimes gets warped when we invent details to justify why we are saying or doing something. When we can't give a simple "yes" or "no," it often means that a little truth leaves and a little dishonesty seeps in. See the *Catechism of the Catholic Church* 2467–2470, which directs us to live our "lives in accordance with the demands of truth."

29 Do not be reckless in your speech,
     or sluggish and remiss in your deeds.
30 Do not be like a lion in your home,
     or suspicious of your servants.
31 Do not let your hand be stretched out to
          receive
     and closed when it is time to give.

5 **Precepts for Everyday Living**
     Do not rely on your wealth,
       or say, "I have enough."
2 Do not follow your inclination and strength
     in pursuing the desires of your heart.
3 Do not say, "Who can have power over me?"
     for the Lord will surely punish you.
4 Do not say, "I sinned, yet what has
          happened to me?"
     for the Lord is slow to anger.
5 Do not be so confident of forgiveness[a]
     that you add sin to sin.
6 Do not say, "His mercy is great,
     he will forgive[b] the multitude of my
          sins,"
   for both mercy and wrath are with him,
     and his anger will rest on sinners.
7 Do not delay to turn back to the Lord,
     and do not postpone it from day to day;

for suddenly the wrath of the Lord will
          come upon you,
     and at the time of punishment you will
          perish.
8 Do not depend on dishonest wealth,
     for it will not benefit you on the day of
          calamity.
9 Do not winnow in every wind,
     or follow every path.[c]
10 Stand firm for what you know,
     and let your speech be consistent.
11 Be quick to hear,
     but deliberate in answering.
12 If you know what to say, answer your
          neighbor;
     but if not, put your hand over your
          mouth.
13 Honor and dishonor come from speaking,
     and the tongue of mortals may be their
          downfall.
14 Do not be called double-tongued[d]
     and do not lay traps with your tongue;
   for shame comes to the thief,
     and severe condemnation to the
          double-tongued.
15 In great and small matters cause no harm,[e]

6 1 and do not become an enemy instead of
          a friend;
     for a bad name incurs shame and reproach;
       so it is with the double-tongued sinner.

2 Do not fall into the grip of passion,[f]
     or you may be torn apart as by a bull.[g]
3 Your leaves will be devoured and your fruit
          destroyed,
     and you will be left like a withered tree.
4 Evil passion destroys those who have it,
     and makes them the laughingstock of
          their enemies.

Friendship, False and True
5 Pleasant speech multiplies friends,
     and a gracious tongue multiplies
          courtesies.
6 Let those who are friendly with you be
          many,
     but let your advisers be one in a
          thousand.
7 When you gain friends, gain them through
          testing,
     and do not trust them hastily.
8 For there are friends who are such when it
          suits them,
     but they will not stand by you in time of
          trouble.

a Heb: Gk *atonement*   b Heb: Gk *he* (or *it*) *will atone for*   c Gk adds *so it is with the double-tongued sinner* (see 6.1)   d Heb: Gk *a slanderer*
e Heb Syr: Gk *be ignorant*   f Heb: Meaning of Gk uncertain   g Meaning of Gk uncertain

9 And there are friends who change into
    enemies,
    and tell of the quarrel to your disgrace.
10 And there are friends who sit at your table,
    but they will not stand by you in time of
    trouble.
11 When you are prosperous, they become
    your second self,
    and lord it over your servants;
12 but if you are brought low, they turn against
    you,
    and hide themselves from you.
13 Keep away from your enemies,
    and be on guard with your friends.

14 Faithful friends are a sturdy shelter:
    whoever finds one has found a treasure.
15 Faithful friends are beyond price;
    no amount can balance their worth.
16 Faithful friends are life-saving medicine;
    and those who fear the Lord will find
    them.
17 Those who fear the Lord direct their
    friendship aright,
    for as they are, so are their neighbors
    also.

Blessings of Wisdom

18 My child, from your youth choose
    discipline,
    and when you have gray hair you will still
    find wisdom.
19 Come to her like one who plows and sows,
    and wait for her good harvest.
    For when you cultivate her you will toil but
    little,
    and soon you will eat of her produce.
20 She seems very harsh to the undisciplined;
    fools cannot remain with her.
21 She will be like a heavy stone to test them,
    and they will not delay in casting her
    aside.
22 For wisdom is like her name;
    she is not readily perceived by many.

23 Listen, my child, and accept my judgment;
    do not reject my counsel.
24 Put your feet into her fetters,
    and your neck into her collar.
25 Bend your shoulders and carry her,
    and do not fret under her bonds.
26 Come to her with all your soul,
    and keep her ways with all your might.
27 Search out and seek, and she will become
    known to you;
    and when you get hold of her, do not let
    her go.
28 For at last you will find the rest she gives,

and she will be changed into joy for you.
29 Then her fetters will become for you a
    strong defense,
    and her collar a glorious robe.
30 Her yoke*a* is a golden ornament,
    and her bonds a purple cord.
31 You will wear her like a glorious robe,
    and put her on like a splendid crown.*b*

32 If you are willing, my child, you can be
    disciplined,
    and if you apply yourself you will become
    clever.
33 If you love to listen you will gain
    knowledge,
    and if you pay attention you will become
    wise.
34 Stand in the company of the elders.
    Who is wise? Attach yourself to such a
    one.
35 Be ready to listen to every godly discourse,
    and let no wise proverbs escape you.
36 If you see an intelligent person, rise early to
    visit him;
    let your foot wear out his doorstep.
37 Reflect on the statutes of the Lord,
    and meditate at all times on his
    commandments.
    It is he who will give insight to*c* your mind,
    and your desire for wisdom will be
    granted.

7 Miscellaneous Advice

Do no evil, and evil will never overtake you.
2 Stay away from wrong, and it will turn away
    from you.
3 Do*d* not sow in the furrows of injustice,
    and you will not reap a sevenfold crop.

4 Do not seek from the Lord high office,
    or the seat of honor from the king.
5 Do not assert your righteousness before the
    Lord,
    or display your wisdom before the king.
6 Do not seek to become a judge,
    or you may be unable to root out
    injustice;
you may be partial to the powerful,
    and so mar your integrity.
7 Commit no offense against the public,
    and do not disgrace yourself among the
    people.

8 Do not commit a sin twice;
    not even for one will you go unpunished.
9 Do not say, "He will consider the great
    number of my gifts,
    and when I make an offering to the Most
    High God, he will accept it."

a Heb: Gk *Upon her* *b* Heb: Gk *crown of gladness* *c* Heb: Gk *will confirm* *d* Gk *My child, do*

15 Do not hate hard labor
or farm work, which was created by the
Most High.
16 Do not enroll in the ranks of sinners;
remember that retribution does not
delay.
17 Humble yourself to the utmost,
for the punishment of the ungodly is fire
and worms.[b]

Relations with Others

18 Do not exchange a friend for money,
or a real brother for the gold of Ophir.
19 Do not dismiss[c] a wise and good wife,
for her charm is worth more than gold.
20 Do not abuse slaves who work faithfully,
or hired laborers who devote themselves
to their task.
21 Let your soul love intelligent slaves;[d]
do not withhold from them their
freedom.

22 Do you have cattle? Look after them;
if they are profitable to you, keep them.
23 Do you have children? Discipline them,
and make them obedient[e] from their
youth.
24 Do you have daughters? Be concerned for
their chastity,[f]
and do not show yourself too indulgent
with them.
25 Give a daughter in marriage, and you
complete a great task;
but give her to a sensible man.
26 Do you have a wife who pleases you?[g] Do
not divorce her;
but do not trust yourself to one whom
you detest.

27 With all your heart honor your father,
and do not forget the birth pangs of your
mother.
28 Remember that it was of your parents[h] you
were born;
how can you repay what they have given
to you?

29 With all your soul fear the Lord,
and revere his priests.
30 With all your might love your Maker,
and do not neglect his ministers.
31 Fear the Lord and honor the priest,
and give him his portion, as you have
been commanded:
the first fruits, the guilt offering, the gift of
the shoulders,
the sacrifice of sanctification, and the
first fruits of the holy things.

10 Do not grow weary when you pray;
do not neglect to give alms.
11 Do not ridicule a person who is embittered
in spirit,
for there is One who humbles and exalts.
12 Do not devise[a] a lie against your brother,
or do the same to a friend.
13 Refuse to utter any lie,
for it is a habit that results in no good.
14 Do not babble in the assembly of the elders,
and do not repeat yourself when you
pray.

a Heb: Gk plow b Heb for the expectation of mortals is worms c Heb: Gk deprive yourself of d Heb Love a wise slave as yourself e Gk bend their necks f Gk body g Heb Syr lack who pleases you h Gk them

32 Stretch out your hand to the poor,
    so that your blessing may be complete.
33 Give graciously to all the living;
    do not withhold kindness even from the dead.
34 Do not avoid those who weep,
    but mourn with those who mourn.
35 Do not hesitate to visit the sick,
    because for such deeds you will be loved.
36 In all you do, remember the end of your life,
    and then you will never sin.

8 Prudence and Common Sense

Do not contend with the powerful,
    or you may fall into their hands.
2 Do not quarrel with the rich,
    in case their resources outweigh yours;
for gold has ruined many,
    and has perverted the minds of kings.
3 Do not argue with the loud of mouth,
    and do not heap wood on their fire.
4 Do not make fun of one who is ill-bred,
    or your ancestors may be insulted.
5 Do not reproach one who is turning away from sin;
    remember that we all deserve punishment.
6 Do not disdain one who is old,
    for some of us are also growing old.
7 Do not rejoice over anyone's death;
    remember that we must all die.

8 Do not slight the discourse of the sages,
    but busy yourself with their maxims;
because from them you will learn discipline
    and how to serve princes.
9 Do not ignore the discourse of the aged,
    for they themselves learned from their parents;[a]
from them you learn how to understand
    and to give an answer when the need arises.

10 Do not kindle the coals of sinners,
    or you may be burned in their flaming fire.
11 Do not let the insolent bring you to your feet,
    or they may lie in ambush against your words.
12 Do not lend to one who is stronger than you;
    but if you do lend anything, count it as a loss.
13 Do not give surety beyond your means;
    but if you give surety, be prepared to pay.

14 Do not go to law against a judge,
    for the decision will favor him because of his standing.
15 Do not go traveling with the reckless,
    or they will be burdensome to you;
for they will act as they please,
    and through their folly you will perish with them.
16 Do not pick a fight with the quick-tempered,
    and do not journey with them through lonely country,
because bloodshed means nothing to them,
    and where no help is at hand, they will strike you down.
17 Do not consult with fools,
    for they cannot keep a secret.
18 In the presence of strangers do nothing that is to be kept secret,
    for you do not know what they will divulge.[b]
19 Do not reveal your thoughts to anyone,
    or you may drive away your happiness.[c]

9 Advice Concerning Women

Do not be jealous of the wife of your bosom,
    or you will teach her an evil lesson to your own hurt.
2 Do not give yourself to a woman
    and let her trample down your strength.
3 Do not go near a loose woman,
    or you will fall into her snares.
4 Do not dally with a singing girl,
    or you will be caught by her tricks.
5 Do not look intently at a virgin,
    or you may stumble and incur penalties for her.
6 Do not give yourself to prostitutes,
    or you may lose your inheritance.
7 Do not look around in the streets of a city,
    or wander about in its deserted sections.
8 Turn away your eyes from a shapely woman,
    and do not gaze at beauty belonging to another;
many have been seduced by a woman's beauty,
    and by it passion is kindled like a fire.

a Or *ancestors* b Or *it will bring forth* c Heb: Gk *and let him not return a favor to you*

You've Got a Friend

Really good friends are keepers. It is a gift to have somebody you really can trust with your secrets, who you can have fun with and be serious with, who will stand by your side, no matter what. **Sirach 9.10** reminds us of the value and joy of longstanding friends. They are the people who have stood with us in the good times and the bad times. They know us well and accept us. They support us and they enjoy our company.

Take some time to reflect on the friendships in your life. Choose the two most important ones.

Pick up your art and supplies and go to a quiet place where you can design a card with a note or a poem expressing your feelings about your friendship with each of them. Send or give your messages to your friends.

9 Never dine with another man's wife,
>   or revel with her at wine;
> or your heart may turn aside to her,
>   and in blood*a* you may be plunged into destruction.

Choice of Friends

10 Do not abandon old friends,
>   for new ones cannot equal them.
> A new friend is like new wine;
>   when it has aged, you can drink it with pleasure.

11 Do not envy the success of sinners,
>   for you do not know what their end will be like.

12 Do not delight in what pleases the ungodly;
>   remember that they will not be held guiltless all their lives.

13 Keep far from those who have power to kill,
>   and you will not be haunted by the fear of death.
> But if you approach them, make no misstep,
>   or they may rob you of your life.
> Know that you are stepping among snares,
>   and that you are walking on the city battlements.

14 As much as you can, aim to know your neighbors,
>   and consult with the wise.

15 Let your conversation be with intelligent people,
>   and let all your discussion be about the law of the Most High.

16 Let the righteous be your dinner companions,
>   and let your glory be in the fear of the Lord.

Concerning Rulers

17 A work is praised for the skill of the artisan;
>   so a people's leader is proved wise by his words.

18 The loud of mouth are feared in their city,
>   and the one who is reckless in speech is hated.

10 A wise magistrate educates his people,
>   and the rule of an intelligent person is well ordered.

2 As the people's judge is, so are his officials;
>   as the ruler of the city is, so are all its inhabitants.

3 An undisciplined king ruins his people,
>   but a city becomes fit to live in through the understanding of its rulers.

4 The government of the earth is in the hand of the Lord,
>   and over it he will raise up the right leader for the time.

5 Human success is in the hand of the Lord,
>   and it is he who confers honor upon the lawgiver.*b*

The Sin of Pride

6 Do not get angry with your neighbor for every injury,
>   and do not resort to acts of insolence.

7 Arrogance is hateful to the Lord and to mortals,
>   and injustice is outrageous to both.

8 Sovereignty passes from nation to nation on account of injustice and insolence and wealth.*c*

9 How can dust and ashes be proud?
>   Even in life the human body decays.*d*

10 A long illness baffles the physician;*e*
>   the king of today will die tomorrow.

11 For when one is dead
>   he inherits maggots and vermin*f* and worms.

12 The beginning of human pride is to forsake the Lord;

a Heb: Gk *by your spirit*   b Heb: Gk *scribe*   c Other ancient authorities add here or after verse 9a, *Nothing is more wicked than one who loves money, for such a person puts his own soul up for sale.*   d Heb: Meaning of Gk uncertain   e Heb Lat: Meaning of Gk uncertain   f Heb: Gk *wild animals*

the heart has withdrawn from its Maker.
13 For the beginning of pride is sin,
and the one who clings to it pours out
abominations.
Therefore the Lord brings upon them
unheard-of calamities,
and destroys them completely.
14 The Lord overthrows the thrones of rulers,
and enthrones the lowly in their place.
15 The Lord plucks up the roots of the
nations,[a]
and plants the humble in their place.
16 The Lord lays waste the lands of the
nations,
and destroys them to the foundations of
the earth.
17 He removes some of them and destroys
them,
and erases the memory of them from the
earth.
18 Pride was not created for human beings,
or violent anger for those born of
women.

Persons Deserving Honor
19 Whose offspring are worthy of honor?
Human offspring.
Whose offspring are worthy of honor?
Those who fear the Lord.
Whose offspring are unworthy of honor?
Human offspring.
Whose offspring are unworthy of honor?
Those who break the commandments.

20 Among family members their leader is
worthy of honor,
but those who fear the Lord are worthy of
honor in his eyes.[b]
22 The rich, and the eminent, and the poor—
their glory is the fear of the Lord.
23 It is not right to despise one who is
intelligent but poor,
and it is not proper to honor one who is
sinful.
24 The prince and the judge and the ruler are
honored,
but none of them is greater than the one
who fears the Lord.
25 Free citizens will serve a wise servant,
and an intelligent person will not
complain.

Concerning Humility
26 Do not make a display of your wisdom
when you do your work,
and do not boast when you are in need.
27 Better is the worker who has goods in
plenty
than the boaster who lacks bread.

28 My child, honor yourself with humility,
and give yourself the esteem you deserve.
29 Who will acquit those who condemn[c]
themselves?
And who will honor those who dishonor
themselves?[d]
30 The poor are honored for their knowledge,

a Other ancient authorities read *proud nations* b Other ancient authorities add as verse 21, *The fear of the Lord is the beginning of acceptance; obduracy and pride are the beginning of rejection.* c Heb: Gk *sin against* d Heb Lat: Gk *their own life*

Bus Aisle—© Maggie Hubbard, 15

while the rich are honored for their
wealth.

³¹ One who is honored in poverty, how much
more in wealth!
And one dishonored in wealth, how
much more in poverty!

11 The Deceptiveness of Appearances

The wisdom of the humble lifts their heads
high,
and seats them among the great.

² Do not praise individuals for their good
looks,
or loathe anyone because of appearance
alone.

³ The bee is small among flying creatures,
but what it produces is the best of sweet
things.

⁴ Do not boast about wearing fine clothes,
and do not exalt yourself when you are
honored;
for the works of the Lord are wonderful,
and his works are concealed from
humankind.

⁵ Many kings have had to sit on the ground,
but one who was never thought of has
worn a crown.

⁶ Many rulers have been utterly disgraced,
and the honored have been handed over
to others.

Deliberation and Caution

⁷ Do not find fault before you investigate;
examine first, and then criticize.

⁸ Do not answer before you listen,
and do not interrupt when another is
speaking.

⁹ Do not argue about a matter that does not
concern you,
and do not sit with sinners when they
judge a case.

¹⁰ My child, do not busy yourself with many
matters;
if you multiply activities, you will not be
held blameless.
If you pursue, you will not overtake,
and by fleeing you will not escape.

¹¹ There are those who work and struggle and
hurry,
but are so much the more in want.

¹² There are others who are slow and need
help,
who lack strength and abound in
poverty;

but the eyes of the Lord look kindly upon
them;
he lifts them out of their lowly condition

¹³ and raises up their heads
to the amazement of the many.

¹⁴ Good things and bad, life and death,
poverty and wealth, come from the Lord.^a

¹⁷ The Lord's gift remains with the devout,
and his favor brings lasting success.

¹⁸ One becomes rich through diligence and
self-denial,
and the reward allotted to him is this:

¹⁹ when he says, "I have found rest,
and now I shall feast on my goods!"
he does not know how long it will be
until he leaves them to others and dies.

²⁰ Stand by your agreement and attend to it,
and grow old in your work.

²¹ Do not wonder at the works of a sinner,
but trust in the Lord and keep at your job;
for it is easy in the sight of the Lord
to make the poor rich suddenly, in an
instant.

²² The blessing of the Lord is^b the reward of
the pious,
and quickly God causes his blessing to
flourish.

²³ Do not say, "What do I need,
and what further benefit can be mine?"

²⁴ Do not say, "I have enough,
and what harm can come to me now?"

²⁵ In the day of prosperity, adversity is
forgotten,
and in the day of adversity, prosperity is
not remembered.

²⁶ For it is easy for the Lord on the day of death
to reward individuals according to their
conduct.

²⁷ An hour's misery makes one forget past
delights,
and at the close of one's life one's deeds
are revealed.

²⁸ Call no one happy before his death;
by how he ends, a person becomes
known.^c

Care in Choosing Friends

²⁹ Do not invite everyone into your home,
for many are the tricks of the crafty.

³⁰ Like a decoy partridge in a cage, so is the
mind of the proud,
and like spies they observe your
weakness;^d

³¹ for they lie in wait, turning good into evil,
and to worthy actions they attach blame.

---

^a Other ancient authorities add as verses 15 and 16, ¹⁵Wisdom, understanding, and knowledge of the law come from the Lord; affection and the ways of good works come from him. ¹⁶Error and darkness were created with sinners; evil grows old with those who take pride in malice. ^b Heb: Gk is in ^c Heb: Gk and through his children a person becomes known ^d Heb: Gk downfall

32 From a spark many coals are kindled,
and a sinner lies in wait to shed blood.
33 Beware of scoundrels, for they devise evil,
and they may ruin your reputation
forever.
34 Receive strangers into your home and they
will stir up trouble for you,
and will make you a stranger to your own
family.

12
If you do good, know to whom you do it,
and you will be thanked for your good
deeds.
2 Do good to the devout, and you will be
repaid—
if not by them, certainly by the Most
High.
3 No good comes to one who persists in evil
or to one who does not give alms.
4 Give to the devout, but do not help the
sinner.
5 Do good to the humble, but do not give
to the ungodly;
hold back their bread, and do not give it to
them,
for by means of it they might subdue you;
then you will receive twice as much evil
for all the good you have done to them.
6 For the Most High also hates sinners
and will inflict punishment on the
ungodly.[a]
7 Give to the one who is good, but do not
help the sinner.
8 A friend is not known[b] in prosperity,
nor is an enemy hidden in adversity.
9 One's enemies are friendly[c] when one
prospers,
but in adversity even one's friend
disappears.
10 Never trust your enemy,
for like corrosion in copper, so is his
wickedness.
11 Even if he humbles himself and walks
bowed down,
take care to be on your guard against
him.
Be to him like one who polishes a mirror,
to be sure it does not become completely
tarnished.
12 Do not put him next to you,
or he may overthrow you and take your
place.
Do not let him sit at your right hand,
or else he may try to take your own seat,
and at last you will realize the truth of my
words,
and be stung by what I have said.

> "It is wonderful how much time good
> people spend fighting the devil. If they
> would only expend the same amount
> of energy loving their fellow men, the
> devil would die in his own tracks of
> ennui."
>
> —Helen Keller

13 Who pities a snake charmer when he is
bitten,
or all those who go near wild animals?
14 So no one pities a person who associates
with a sinner
and becomes involved in the other's sins.
15 He stands by you for a while,
but if you falter, he will not be there.
16 An enemy speaks sweetly with his lips,
but in his heart he plans to throw you
into a pit;
an enemy may have tears in his eyes,
but if he finds an opportunity he will
never have enough of your blood.
17 If evil comes upon you, you will find him
there ahead of you;
pretending to help, he will trip you up.
18 Then he will shake his head, and clap his
hands,
and whisper much, and show his true
face.

13 Caution Regarding Associates
Whoever touches pitch gets dirty,
and whoever associates with a proud
person becomes like him.
2 Do not lift a weight too heavy for you,
or associate with one mightier and richer
than you.
How can the clay pot associate with the iron
kettle?
The pot will strike against it and be
smashed.
3 A rich person does wrong, and even adds
insults;
a poor person suffers wrong, and must
add apologies.
4 A rich person[d] will exploit you if you can be
of use to him,
but if you are in need he will abandon
you.
5 If you own something, he will live with you;
he will drain your resources without a
qualm.
6 When he needs you he will deceive you,

---

a Other ancient authorities add *and he is keeping them for the day of their punishment* b Other ancient authorities read *punished* c Heb: Gk *grieved* d Gk He

and will smile at you and encourage you;
he will speak to you kindly and say, "What
do you need?"

7 He will embarrass you with his delicacies,
until he has drained you two or three
times,
and finally he will laugh at you.
Should he see you afterwards, he will pass
you by
and shake his head at you.

8 Take care not to be led astray
and humiliated when you are enjoying
yourself.[a]

9 When an influential person invites you, be
reserved,
and he will invite you more insistently.

10 Do not be forward, or you may be rebuffed;
do not stand aloof, or you will be
forgotten.

11 Do not try to treat him as an equal,
or trust his lengthy conversations;
for he will test you by prolonged talk,
and while he smiles he will be examining
you.

12 Cruel are those who do not keep your
secrets;
they will not spare you harm or
imprisonment.

13 Be on your guard and very careful,
for you are walking about with your own
downfall.[b]

15 Every creature loves its like,
and every person the neighbor.

16 All living beings associate with their own
kind,
and people stick close to those like
themselves.

17 What does a wolf have in common with a
lamb?
No more has a sinner with the devout.

18 What peace is there between a hyena and a
dog?
And what peace between the rich and the
poor?

19 Wild asses in the wilderness are the prey of
lions;
likewise the poor are feeding grounds for
the rich.

20 Humility is an abomination to the proud;
likewise the poor are an abomination to
the rich.

21 When the rich person totters, he is
supported by friends,

but when the humble[c] falls, he is pushed
away even by friends.

22 If the rich person slips, many come to the
rescue;
he speaks unseemly words, but they
justify him.
If the humble person slips, they even
criticize him;
he talks sense, but is not given a hearing.

23 The rich person speaks and all are silent;
they extol to the clouds what he says.
The poor person speaks and they say, "Who
is this fellow?"
And should he stumble, they even push
him down.

24 Riches are good if they are free from sin;
poverty is evil only in the opinion of the
ungodly.

25 The heart changes the countenance,
either for good or for evil.[d]

26 The sign of a happy heart is a cheerful face,
but to devise proverbs requires painful
thinking.

14 Happy are those who do not blunder
with their lips,
and need not suffer remorse for sin.

2 Happy are those whose hearts do not
condemn them,
and who have not given up their hope.

Responsible Use of Wealth

3 Riches are inappropriate for a
small-minded person;
and of what use is wealth to a miser?

4 What he denies himself he collects for
others;
and others will live in luxury on his
goods.

5 If one is mean to himself, to whom will he
be generous?
He will not enjoy his own riches.

6 No one is worse than one who is grudging
to himself;
this is the punishment for his meanness.

7 If ever he does good, it is by mistake;
and in the end he reveals his meanness.

8 The miser is an evil person;
he turns away and disregards people.

9 The eye of the greedy person is not satisfied
with his share;
greedy injustice withers the soul.

10 A miser begrudges bread,
and it is lacking at his table.

a Other ancient authorities read *in your folly* b Other ancient authorities add as verse 14, *When you hear these things in your sleep, wake up! During all your life love the Lord, and call on him for your salvation.* c Other ancient authorities read *poor* d Other ancient authorities add *and a glad heart makes a cheerful countenance*

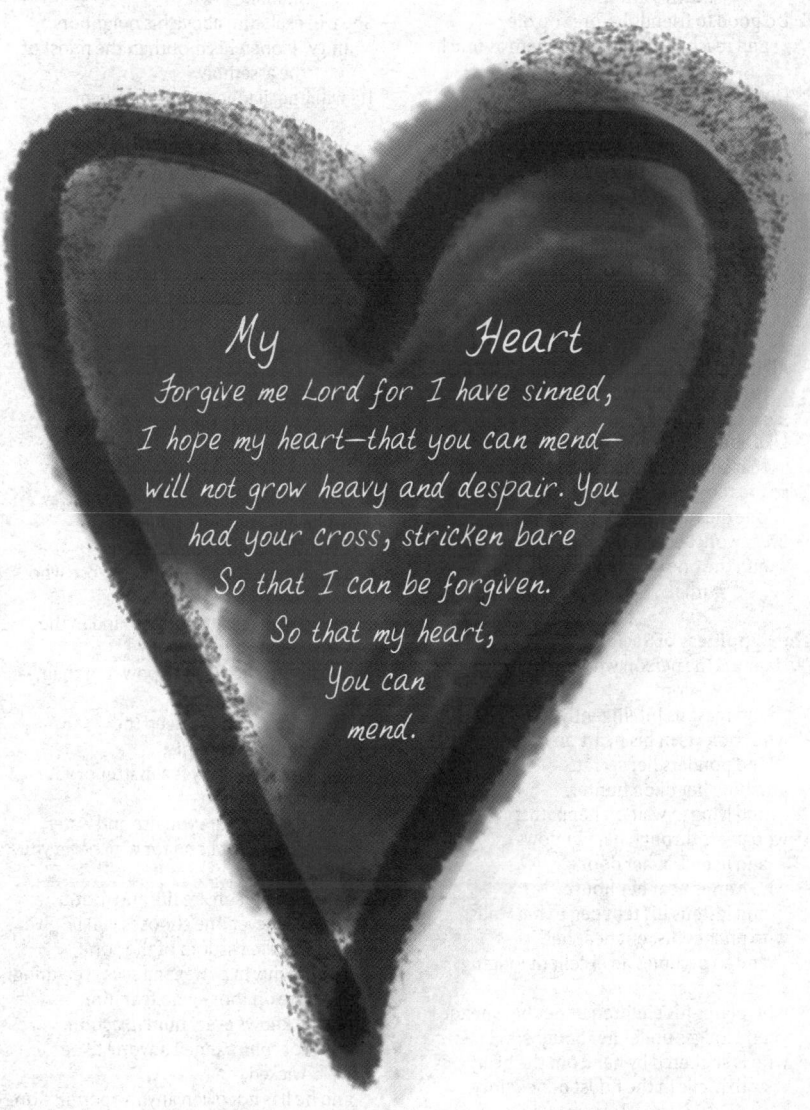

My   Heart

Forgive me Lord for I have sinned,
I hope my heart—that you can mend—
will not grow heavy and despair. You
had your cross, stricken bare
So that I can be forgiven.
So that my heart,
You can
mend.

My Heart—© Marshall Katheder, 19

¹¹ My child, treat yourself well, according to
     your means,
     and present worthy offerings to the Lord.
¹² Remember that death does not tarry,
     and the decree*ᵃ* of Hades has not been
     shown to you.
¹³ Do good to friends before you die,
     and reach out and give to them as much
     as you can.
¹⁴ Do not deprive yourself of a day's
     enjoyment;
     do not let your share of desired good
     pass by you.
¹⁵ Will you not leave the fruit of your labors to
     another,
     and what you acquired by toil to be
     divided by lot?
¹⁶ Give, and take, and indulge yourself,
     because in Hades one cannot look for
     luxury.
¹⁷ All living beings become old like a garment,
     for the decree*ᵇ* from of old is, "You must
     die!"
¹⁸ Like abundant leaves on a spreading tree
     that sheds some and puts forth others,
     so are the generations of flesh and blood:
     one dies and another is born.
¹⁹ Every work decays and ceases to exist,
     and the one who made it will pass away
     with it.

The Happiness of Seeking Wisdom

²⁰ Happy is the person who meditates on*ᶜ*
     wisdom
     and reasons intelligently,
²¹ who*ᵈ* reflects in his heart on her ways
     and ponders her secrets,
²² pursuing her like a hunter,
     and lying in wait on her paths;
²³ who peers through her windows
     and listens at her doors;
²⁴ who camps near her house
     and fastens his tent peg to her walls;
²⁵ who pitches his tent near her,
     and so occupies an excellent lodging
     place;
²⁶ who places his children under her shelter,
     and lodges under her boughs;
²⁷ who is sheltered by her from the heat,
     and dwells in the midst of her glory.

15 Whoever fears the Lord will do this,
     and whoever holds to the law will obtain
     wisdom.*ᵉ*
² She will come to meet him like a mother,
     and like a young bride she will welcome
     him.

³ She will feed him with the bread of learning,
     and give him the water of wisdom to
     drink.
⁴ He will lean on her and not fall,
     and he will rely on her and not be put to
     shame.
⁵ She will exalt him above his neighbors,
     and will open his mouth in the midst of
     the assembly.
⁶ He will find gladness and a crown of
     rejoicing,
     and will inherit an everlasting name.
⁷ The foolish will not obtain her,
     and sinners will not see her.
⁸ She is far from arrogance,
     and liars will never think of her.
⁹ Praise is unseemly on the lips of a sinner,
     for it has not been sent from the Lord.
¹⁰ For in wisdom must praise be uttered,
     and the Lord will make it prosper.

Freedom of Choice

¹¹ Do not say, "It was the Lord's doing that I
     fell away";
     for he does not do*ᶠ* what he hates.
¹² Do not say, "It was he who led me astray";
     for he has no need of the sinful.
¹³ The Lord hates all abominations;
     such things are not loved by those who
     fear him.
¹⁴ It was he who created humankind in the
     beginning,
     and he left them in the power of their
     own free choice.
¹⁵ If you choose, you can keep the
     commandments,
     and to act faithfully is a matter of your
     own choice.
¹⁶ He has placed before you fire and water;
     stretch out your hand for whichever you
     choose.
¹⁷ Before each person are life and death,
     and whichever one chooses will be given.
¹⁸ For great is the wisdom of the Lord;
     he is mighty in power and sees everything;
¹⁹ his eyes are on those who fear him,
     and he knows every human action.
²⁰ He has not commanded anyone to be
     wicked,
     and he has not given anyone permission
     to sin.

16 God's Punishment of Sinners

Do not desire a multitude of worthless*ᵍ*
     children,
     and do not rejoice in ungodly offspring.

a Heb Syr: Gk *covenant* *b* Heb: Gk *covenant* *c* Other ancient authorities read *dies in* *d* The structure adopted in verses 21–27 follows
the Heb *e* Gk *her* *f* Heb: Gk *you ought not to do* *g* Heb: Gk *unprofitable*

² If they multiply, do not rejoice in them,
  unless the fear of the Lord is in them.
³ Do not trust in their survival,
  or rely on their numbers;*a*
  for one can be better than a thousand,
  and to die childless is better than to have
  ungodly children.
⁴ For through one intelligent person a city
  can be filled with people,
  but through a clan of outlaws it becomes
  desolate.
⁵ Many such things my eye has seen,
  and my ear has heard things more
  striking than these.
⁶ In an assembly of sinners a fire is kindled,
  and in a disobedient nation wrath
  blazes up.
⁷ He did not forgive the ancient giants
  who revolted in their might.
⁸ He did not spare the neighbors of Lot,
  whom he loathed on account of their
  arrogance.
⁹ He showed no pity on the doomed nation,
  on those dispossessed because of their
  sins;*b*
¹⁰ or on the six hundred thousand foot
  soldiers

who assembled in their stubbornness.*c*
¹¹ Even if there were only one stiff-necked
  person,
  it would be a wonder if he remained
  unpunished.
For mercy and wrath are with the Lord;*d*
  he is mighty to forgive—but he also
  pours out wrath.
¹² Great as is his mercy, so also is his
  chastisement;
  he judges a person according to his or
  her deeds.
¹³ The sinner will not escape with plunder,
  and the patience of the godly will not be
  frustrated.
¹⁴ He makes room for every act of mercy;
  everyone receives in accordance with his
  or her deeds.*e*

¹⁷ Do not say, "I am hidden from the Lord,
  and who from on high has me in mind?
Among so many people I am unknown,
  for what am I in a boundless creation?
¹⁸ Lo, heaven and the highest heaven,
  the abyss and the earth, tremble at his
  visitation!*f*
¹⁹ The very mountains and the foundations of
  the earth

a Other ancient authorities add *For you will groan in untimely mourning, and will know of their sudden end.*   *b* Other ancient authorities add *All these things he did to the hard-hearted nations, and by the multitude of his holy ones he was not appeased.*   *c* Other ancient authorities add *Chastising, showing mercy, striking, healing, the Lord persisted in mercy and discipline.*   *d* Gk him   *e* Other ancient authorities add *15The Lord hardened Pharaoh so that he did not recognize him, in order that his works might be known under heaven. 16His mercy is manifest to the whole of creation, and he divided his light and darkness with a plumb line.*   *f* Other ancient authorities add *The whole world past and present is in his will.*

Putting on the Mask—© Christy Klink, 18

21 Like a tempest that no one can see,
    so most of his works are concealed.[a]
22 Who is to announce his acts of justice?
    Or who can await them? For his decree[b] is
      far off."[c]
23 Such are the thoughts of one devoid of
    understanding;
    a senseless and misguided person thinks
      foolishly.

God's Wisdom Seen in Creation

24 Listen to me, my child, and acquire
    knowledge,
    and pay close attention to my words.
25 I will impart discipline precisely[d]
    and declare knowledge accurately.

26 When the Lord created[e] his works from the
    beginning,
    and, in making them, determined their
      boundaries,
27 he arranged his works in an eternal order,
    and their dominion[f] for all generations.
They neither hunger nor grow weary,
    and they do not abandon their tasks.
28 They do not crowd one another,
    and they never disobey his word.
29 Then the Lord looked upon the earth,
    and filled it with his good things.
30 With all kinds of living beings he covered its
    surface,
    and into it they must return.

17 The Lord created human beings out of
    earth,
    and makes them return to it again.
2 He gave them a fixed number of days,
    but granted them authority over
      everything on the earth.[g]
3 He endowed them with strength like his
    own,[h]
    and made them in his own image.
4 He put the fear of them[i] in all living beings,
    and gave them dominion over beasts and
      birds.[j]
6 Discretion and tongue and eyes,
    ears and a mind for thinking he gave
      them.
7 He filled them with knowledge and
    understanding,
    and showed them good and evil.
8 He put the fear of him into[k] their hearts
    to show them the majesty of his works.[l]
10 And they will praise his holy name,
9   to proclaim the grandeur of his works.

quiver and quake when he looks upon
    them.
20 But no human mind can grasp this,
    and who can comprehend his ways?

a Meaning of Gk uncertain: Heb Syr *If I sin, no eye can see me, and if I am disloyal all in secret, who is to know?* b Heb *the decree*: Gk *the covenant* c Other ancient authorities add *and a scrutiny for all comes at the end* d Gk *by weight* e Heb: Gk *judged* f Or *elements* g Lat: Gk *it* h Lat: Gk *proper to them* i Syr: Gk *him* j Other ancient authorities add as verse 5, *They obtained the use of the five faculties of the Lord; as sixth he distributed to them the gift of mind, and as seventh, reason, the interpreter of one's faculties.* k Other ancient authorities read *He set his eye upon* l Other ancient authorities add *and he gave them to boast of his marvels forever*

11 He bestowed knowledge upon them,
   and allotted to them the law of life.[a]
12 He established with them an eternal
   covenant,
   and revealed to them his decrees.
13 Their eyes saw his glorious majesty,
   and their ears heard the glory of his
   voice.
14 He said to them, "Beware of all evil."
   And he gave commandment to each of
   them concerning the neighbor.
15 Their ways are always known to him;
   they will not be hid from his eyes.[b]
17 He appointed a ruler for every nation,
   but Israel is the Lord's own portion.[c]
19 All their works are as clear as the sun before
   him,
   and his eyes are ever upon their ways.
20 Their iniquities are not hidden from him,
   and all their sins are before the Lord.[d]
22 One's almsgiving is like a signet ring with
   the Lord,[e]
   and he will keep a person's kindness like
   the apple of his eye.[f]
23 Afterward he will rise up and repay them,
   and he will bring their recompense on
   their heads.
24 Yet to those who repent he grants a return,
   and he encourages those who are losing
   hope.

A Call to Repentance
25 Turn back to the Lord and forsake your sins;
   pray in his presence and lessen your
   offense.
26 Return to the Most High and turn away from
   iniquity,[g]
   and hate intensely what he abhors.
27 Who will sing praises to the Most High in
   Hades
   in place of the living who give thanks?
28 From the dead, as from one who does not
   exist, thanksgiving has ceased;
   those who are alive and well sing the
   Lord's praises.
29 How great is the mercy of the Lord,
   and his forgiveness for those who return
   to him!
30 For not everything is within human
   capability,
   since human beings are not immortal.

> "The function of wisdom is to discriminate between good and evil."
> —Cicero

31 What is brighter than the sun? Yet it can be
   eclipsed.
   So flesh and blood devise evil.
32 He marshals the host of the height of
   heaven;
   but all human beings are dust and ashes.

18 The Majesty of God
He who lives forever created the whole
   universe;
2   the Lord alone is just.[h]
4 To none has he given power to proclaim his
   works;
   and who can search out his mighty
   deeds?
5 Who can measure his majestic power?
   And who can fully recount his mercies?
6 It is not possible to diminish or increase
   them,
   nor is it possible to fathom the wonders
   of the Lord.
7 When human beings have finished, they are
   just beginning,
   and when they stop, they are still
   perplexed.
8 What are human beings, and of what use
   are they?
   What is good in them, and what is evil?
9 The number of days in their life is great if
   they reach one hundred years.[i]
10 Like a drop of water from the sea and a
   grain of sand,
   so are a few years among the days of
   eternity.
11 That is why the Lord is patient with them
   and pours out his mercy upon them.
12 He sees and recognizes that their end is
   miserable;
   therefore he grants them forgiveness all
   the more.
13 The compassion of human beings is for
   their neighbors,
   but the compassion of the Lord is for
   every living thing.
He rebukes and trains and teaches them,

---

a Other ancient authorities add *so that they may know that they who are alive now are mortal* b Other ancient authorities add *16Their ways from youth tend toward evil, and they are unable to make for themselves hearts of flesh in place of their stony hearts. 17For in the division of the nations of the whole earth, he appointed* c Other ancient authorities add as verse 18, *whom, being his firstborn, he brings up with discipline, and allotting to him the light of his love, he does not neglect him.* d Other ancient authorities add as verse 21, *But the Lord, who is gracious and knows how they are formed, has neither left them nor abandoned them, but has spared them.* e Gk *him* f Other ancient authorities add *apportioning repentance to his sons and daughters* g Other ancient authorities add *for he will lead you out of darkness to the light of health.* h Other ancient authorities add *and there is no other beside him; 3he steers the world with the span of his hand, and all things obey his will; for he is king of all things by his power, separating among them the holy things from the profane.* i Other ancient authorities add *but the death of each one is beyond the calculation of all* and turns them back, as a shepherd his flock.

¹⁴ He has compassion on those who accept his discipline
and who are eager for his precepts.

The Right Spirit in Giving Alms

¹⁵ My child, do not mix reproach with your good deeds,
or spoil your gift by harsh words.

¹⁶ Does not the dew give relief from the scorching heat?
So a word is better than a gift.

¹⁷ Indeed, does not a word surpass a good gift?
Both are to be found in a gracious person.

¹⁸ A fool is ungracious and abusive,
and the gift of a grudging giver makes the eyes dim.

The Need of Reflection and Self-control

¹⁹ Before you speak, learn;
and before you fall ill, take care of your health.

²⁰ Before judgment comes, examine yourself;
and at the time of scrutiny you will find forgiveness.

²¹ Before falling ill, humble yourself;
and when you have sinned, repent.

²² Let nothing hinder you from paying a vow promptly,
and do not wait until death to be released from it.

²³ Before making a vow, prepare yourself;
do not be like one who puts the Lord to the test.

²⁴ Think of his wrath on the day of death,
and of the moment of vengeance when he turns away his face.

²⁵ In the time of plenty think of the time of hunger;
in days of wealth think of poverty and need.

²⁶ From morning to evening conditions change;
all things move swiftly before the Lord.

²⁷ One who is wise is cautious in everything;
when sin is all around, one guards against wrongdoing.

²⁸ Every intelligent person knows wisdom,
and praises the one who finds her.

²⁹ Those who are skilled in words become wise themselves,
and pour forth apt proverbs.ᵃ

SELF-CONTROLᵇ

³⁰ Do not follow your base desires,
but restrain your appetites.

³¹ If you allow your soul to take pleasure in base desire,
it will make you the laughingstock of your enemies.

³² Do not revel in great luxury,
or you may become impoverished by its expense.

³³ Do not become a beggar by feasting with borrowed money,
when you have nothing in your purse.ᶜ

19 The one who does thisᵈ will not become rich;
one who despises small things will fail little by little.

ᵃ Other ancient authorities add *Better is confidence in the one Lord than clinging with a dead heart to a dead one.* ᵇ This heading is included in the Gk text. ᶜ Other ancient authorities add *for you will be plotting against your own life* ᵈ Heb: Gk *A worker who is a drunkard*

² Wine and women lead intelligent men
astray,
and the man who consorts with
prostitutes is reckless.
³ Decay and worms will take possession of
him,
and the reckless person will be snatched
away.

Against Loose Talk

⁴ One who trusts others too quickly has a
shallow mind,
and one who sins does wrong to himself.
⁵ One who rejoices in wickedness*ᵃ* will be
condemned,*ᵇ*
⁶ but one who hates gossip has less evil.
⁷ Never repeat a conversation,
and you will lose nothing at all.
⁸ With friend or foe do not report it,
and unless it would be a sin for you, do
not reveal it;
⁹ for someone may have heard you and
watched you,
and in time will hate you.
¹⁰ Have you heard something? Let it die with
you.
Be brave, it will not make you burst!
¹¹ Having heard something, the fool suffers
birth pangs
like a woman in labor with a child.
¹² Like an arrow stuck in a person's thigh,
so is gossip inside a fool.

¹³ Question a friend; perhaps he did not do it;
or if he did, so that he may not do it
again.
¹⁴ Question a neighbor; perhaps he did not
say it;
or if he said it, so that he may not repeat it.
¹⁵ Question a friend, for often it is slander;
so do not believe everything you hear.
¹⁶ A person may make a slip without
intending it.
Who has not sinned with his tongue?
¹⁷ Question your neighbor before you
threaten him;
and let the law of the Most High take its
course.*ᶜ*

True and False Wisdom

²⁰ The whole of wisdom is fear of the Lord,
and in all wisdom there is the fulfillment
of the law.*ᵈ*
²² The knowledge of wickedness is not
wisdom,

Drawing on Faith

You live in a busy time. School, friends, sports, games, hobbies, and on and on. Add to that cell phones, MP3 players, online social networking—it never ends. The author of Sirach instructed the people of his time to pause, reflect, and have self-control. Good advice for us today too.

Read **Sirach 18.19–19.3** and select two or three scenarios. Find some Creative Space in this Bible or grab a piece of paper and either draw a cartoon or write a story about someone you know who practices this wisdom here and now. Share your creation at **Learner.CalltoDiscipleship.com**.

nor is there prudence in the counsel of
sinners.
²³ There is a cleverness that is detestable,
and there is a fool who merely lacks
wisdom.
²⁴ Better are the God-fearing who lack
understanding
than the highly intelligent who
transgress the law.
²⁵ There is a cleverness that is exact but unjust,
and there are people who abuse favors to
gain a verdict.
²⁶ There is the villain bowed down in
mourning,
but inwardly he is full of deceit.
²⁷ He hides his face and pretends not to hear,
but when no one notices, he will take
advantage of you.
²⁸ Even if lack of strength keeps him from
sinning,
he will nevertheless do evil when he finds
the opportunity.
²⁹ A person is known by his appearance,
and a sensible person is known when
first met, face to face.
³⁰ A person's attire and hearty laughter,
and the way he walks, show what he is.

20 Silence and Speech

There is a rebuke that is untimely,
and there is the person who is wise
enough to keep silent.

---

a Other ancient authorities read *heart* *b* Other ancient authorities add *but one who withstands pleasures crowns his life.* ⁶*One who controls the tongue will live without strife,* *c* Other ancient authorities add *and do not be angry.* ¹⁸*The fear of the Lord is the beginning of acceptance, and wisdom obtains his love.* ¹⁹*The knowledge of the Lord's commandments is life-giving discipline; and those who do what is pleasing to him enjoy the fruit of the tree of immortality.* *d* Other ancient authorities add *and the knowledge of his omnipotence.* ²¹*When a slave says to his master, "I will not act as you wish," even if later he does it, he angers the one who supports him.*

² How much better it is to rebuke than to
    fume!
³ And the one who admits his fault will be
    kept from failure.
⁴ Like a eunuch lusting to violate a girl
    is the person who does right under
    compulsion.
⁵ Some people keep silent and are thought to
    be wise,
        while others are detested for being
        talkative.
⁶ Some people keep silent because they have
    nothing to say,
        while others keep silent because they
        know when to speak.
⁷ The wise remain silent until the right
    moment,
        but a boasting fool misses the right
        moment.
⁸ Whoever talks too much is detested,
    and whoever pretends to authority is
    hated.ᵃ

Paradoxes

⁹ There may be good fortune for a person in
    adversity,
    and a windfall may result in a loss.
¹⁰ There is the gift that profits you nothing,
    and the gift to be paid back double.
¹¹ There are losses for the sake of glory,
    and there are some who have raised their
    heads from humble circumstances.
¹² Some buy much for little,
    but pay for it seven times over.
¹³ The wise make themselves beloved by only
    few words,ᵇ
        but the courtesies of fools are wasted.
¹⁴ A fool's gift will profit you nothing,ᶜ
    for he looks for recompense sevenfold.ᵈ
¹⁵ He gives little and upbraids much;
    he opens his mouth like a town crier.
    Today he lends and tomorrow he asks it
        back;
        such a one is hateful to God and
        humans.ᵉ
¹⁶ The fool says, "I have no friends,
    and I get no thanks for my good deeds.
    Those who eat my bread are
        evil-tongued."
¹⁷ How many will ridicule him, and how
    often!ᶠ

Inappropriate Speech

¹⁸ A slip on the pavement is better than a slip
        of the tongue;
    the downfall of the wicked will occur just
        as speedily.
¹⁹ A coarse person is like an inappropriate
        story,
    continually on the lips of the ignorant.
²⁰ A proverb from a fool's lips will be rejected,
    for he does not tell it at the proper time.
²¹ One may be prevented from sinning by
        poverty;
    so when he rests he feels no remorse.

---

a Other ancient authorities add *How good it is to show repentance when you are reproved, for so you will escape deliberate sin!*   b Heb: Gk *by words*
c Other ancient authorities add *so it is with the envious who give under compulsion*   d Syr: Gk *he has many eyes instead of one*   e Other ancient
authorities lack *to God and humans*   f Other ancient authorities add *for he has not honestly received what he has, and what he does not have is
unimportant to him*

22 One may lose his life through shame,
    or lose it because of human respect.*a*
23 Another out of shame makes promises to a
    friend,
    and so makes an enemy for nothing.

Lying

24 A lie is an ugly blot on a person;
    it is continually on the lips of the
    ignorant.
25 A thief is preferable to a habitual liar,
    but the lot of both is ruin.
26 A liar's way leads to disgrace,
    and his shame is ever with him.

Proverbial Sayings*b*

27 The wise person advances himself by his
    words,
    and one who is sensible pleases the
    great.
28 Those who cultivate the soil heap up their
    harvest,
    and those who please the great atone for
    injustice.
29 Favors and gifts blind the eyes of the wise;
    like a muzzle on the mouth they stop
    reproofs.
30 Hidden wisdom and unseen treasure,
    of what value is either?
31 Better are those who hide their folly
    than those who hide their wisdom.*c*

21 Various Sins

Have you sinned, my child? Do so no more,
    but ask forgiveness for your past sins.
2 Flee from sin as from a snake;
    for if you approach sin, it will bite you.
Its teeth are lion's teeth,
    and can destroy human lives.
3 All lawlessness is like a two-edged sword;
    there is no healing for the wound it
    inflicts.
4 Panic and insolence will waste away riches;
    thus the house of the proud will be laid
    waste.*d*
5 The prayer of the poor goes from their lips
    to the ears of God,*e*
    and his judgment comes speedily.
6 Those who hate reproof walk in the sinner's
    steps,
    but those who fear the Lord repent in
    their heart.
7 The mighty in speech are widely known;
    when they slip, the sensible person
    knows it.

8 Whoever builds his house with other
    people's money
    is like one who gathers stones for his
    burial mound.*f*
9 An assembly of the wicked is like a bundle
    of tow,
    and their end is a blazing fire.
10 The way of sinners is paved with smooth
    stones,
    but at its end is the pit of Hades.

Wisdom and Foolishness

11 Whoever keeps the law controls his
    thoughts,
    and the fulfillment of the fear of the Lord
    is wisdom.
12 The one who is not clever cannot be taught,
    but there is a cleverness that increases
    bitterness.
13 The knowledge of the wise will increase like
    a flood,
    and their counsel like a life-giving spring.
14 The mind*g* of a fool is like a broken jar;
    it can hold no knowledge.
15 When an intelligent person hears a wise
    saying,
    he praises it and adds to it;
when a fool*h* hears it, he laughs at*i* it
    and throws it behind his back.
16 A fool's chatter is like a burden on a
    journey,
    but delight is found in the speech of the
    intelligent.
17 The utterance of a sensible person is sought
    in the assembly,
    and they ponder his words in their
    minds.

18 Like a house in ruins is wisdom to a fool,
    and to the ignorant, knowledge is talk
    that has no meaning.
19 To a senseless person education is fetters
    on his feet,
    and like manacles on his right hand.
20 A fool raises his voice when he laughs,
    but the wise*j* smile quietly.
21 To the sensible person education is like a
    golden ornament,
    and like a bracelet on the right arm.

22 The foot of a fool rushes into a house,
    but an experienced person waits
    respectfully outside.
23 A boor peers into the house from the door,
    but a cultivated person remains outside.

a Other ancient authorities read *his foolish look* b This heading is included in the Gk text. c Other ancient authorities add *32Unwearied endurance in seeking the Lord is better than a masterless charioteer of one's own life.* d Other ancient authorities read *uprooted* e Gk *his ears* f Other ancient authorities read *for the winter* g Syr Lat: Gk *entrails* h Syr: Gk *reveler* i Syr: Gk *dislikes* j Syr Lat: Gk *clever*

Daisy Chain—© Rose K., 17

24 It is ill-mannered for a person to listen at a
    door;
        the discreet would be grieved by the
        disgrace.

25 The lips of babblers speak of what is not
        their concern,[a]
        but the words of the prudent are weighed
        in the balance.

26 The mind of fools is in their mouth,
        but the mouth of the wise is in[b] their mind.

27 When an ungodly person curses an
        adversary,[c]
        he curses himself.

28 A whisperer degrades himself
        and is hated in his neighborhood.

22 The Idler

The idler is like a filthy stone,
    and every one hisses at his disgrace.
2 The idler is like the filth of dunghills;
    anyone that picks it up will shake it off
    his hand.

Degenerate Children

3 It is a disgrace to be the father of an
        undisciplined son,
        and the birth of a daughter is a loss.

4 A sensible daughter obtains a husband of
        her own,
        but one who acts shamefully is a grief to
        her father.

5 An impudent daughter disgraces father and
        husband,
        and is despised by both.

6 Like music in time of mourning is ill-timed
        conversation,
        but a thrashing and discipline are at all
        times wisdom.[d]

Wisdom and Folly

9 Whoever teaches a fool is like one who
        glues potsherds together,
        or who rouses a sleeper from deep
        slumber.

10 Whoever tells a story to a fool tells it to a
        drowsy man;
        and at the end he will say, "What is it?"

11 Weep for the dead, for he has left the light
        behind;
        and weep for the fool, for he has left
        intelligence behind.
Weep less bitterly for the dead, for he is at
        rest;
        but the life of the fool is worse than death.

a Other ancient authorities read *of strangers speak of these things* *b* Other ancient authorities omit *in* *c* Or *curses Satan* *d* Other ancient
authorities add *7Children who are brought up in a good life, conceal the lowly birth of their parents.* *8Children who are disdainfully and boorishly haughty
stain the nobility of their kindred.*

12 Mourning for the dead lasts seven days,
    but for the foolish or the ungodly it lasts
        all the days of their lives.

13 Do not talk much with a senseless person
    or visit an unintelligent person.[a]
    Stay clear of him, or you may have trouble,
        and be spattered when he shakes himself
        off.
    Avoid him and you will find rest,
        and you will never be wearied by his lack
        of sense.

14 What is heavier than lead?
    And what is its name except "Fool"?

15 Sand, salt, and a piece of iron
    are easier to bear than a stupid person.

16 A wooden beam firmly bonded into a
        building
    is not loosened by an earthquake;
    so the mind firmly resolved after due
        reflection
    will not be afraid in a crisis.

17 A mind settled on an intelligent thought
    is like stucco decoration that makes a
        wall smooth.

18 Fences[b] set on a high place
    will not stand firm against the wind;
    so a timid mind with a fool's resolve
        will not stand firm against any fear.

The Preservation of Friendship

19 One who pricks the eye brings tears,
    and one who pricks the heart makes clear
        its feelings.

20 One who throws a stone at birds scares
        them away,
    and one who reviles a friend destroys a
        friendship.

21 Even if you draw your sword against a
        friend,
    do not despair, for there is a way back.

22 If you open your mouth against your friend,
    do not worry, for reconciliation is
        possible.
    But as for reviling, arrogance, disclosure of
        secrets, or a treacherous blow—
    in these cases any friend will take to
        flight.

23 Gain the trust of your neighbor in his
        poverty,
    so that you may rejoice with him in his
        prosperity.
    Stand by him in time of distress,
        so that you may share with him in his
        inheritance.[c]

24 The vapor and smoke of the furnace
    precede the fire;
    so insults precede bloodshed.

25 I am not ashamed to shelter a friend,
    and I will not hide from him.

26 But if harm should come to me because of
        him,
    whoever hears of it will beware of him.

A Prayer for Help against Sinning

27 Who will set a guard over my mouth,
    and an effective seal upon my lips,
    so that I may not fall because of them,
    and my tongue may not destroy me?

23 O Lord, Father and Master of my life,
    do not abandon me to their designs,
    and do not let me fall because of them!

2 Who will set whips over my thoughts,
    and the discipline of wisdom over my
        mind,
    so as not to spare me in my errors,
    and not overlook my[d] sins?

3 Otherwise my mistakes may be multiplied,
    and my sins may abound,
    and I may fall before my adversaries,
    and my enemy may rejoice over me.[e]

4 O Lord, Father and God of my life,
    do not give me haughty eyes,

5   and remove evil desire from me.

6 Let neither gluttony nor lust overcome me,
    and do not give me over to shameless
        passion.

DISCIPLINE OF THE TONGUE[f]

7 Listen, my children, to instruction
    concerning the mouth;
    the one who observes it will never be
        caught.

8 Sinners are overtaken through their lips;
    by them the reviler and the arrogant are
        tripped up.

9 Do not accustom your mouth to oaths,
    nor habitually utter the name of the Holy
        One;

10 for as a servant who is constantly under
        scrutiny
    will not lack bruises,
    so also the person who always swears and
        utters the Name
    will never be cleansed[g] from sin.

11 The one who swears many oaths is full of
        iniquity,
    and the scourge will not leave his house.
    If he swears in error, his sin remains on
        him,
    and if he disregards it, he sins doubly;

a Other ancient authorities add For being without sense he will despise everything about you   b Other ancient authorities read Pebbles   c Other ancient authorities add For one should not always despise restricted circumstances, or admire a rich person who is stupid.   d Gk their   e Other ancient authorities add From them the hope of your mercy is remote   f This heading is included in the Gk text.   g Syr be free

if he swears a false oath, he will not be justified,
    for his house will be filled with calamities.

Foul Language

12 There is a manner of speaking comparable to death;*a*
    may it never be found in the inheritance of Jacob!
    Such conduct will be far from the godly,
    and they will not wallow in sins.
13 Do not accustom your mouth to coarse, foul language,
    for it involves sinful speech.
14 Remember your father and mother
    when you sit among the great,
    or you may forget yourself in their presence,
    and behave like a fool through bad habit;
    then you will wish that you had never been born,
    and you will curse the day of your birth.
15 Those who are accustomed to using abusive language
    will never become disciplined as long as they live.

Concerning Sexual Sins

16 Two kinds of individuals multiply sins,
    and a third incurs wrath.
    Hot passion that blazes like a fire
    will not be quenched until it burns itself out;
    one who commits fornication with his near of kin
    will never cease until the fire burns him up.
17 To a fornicator all bread is sweet;
    he will never weary until he dies.
18 The one who sins against his marriage bed
    says to himself, "Who can see me?
    Darkness surrounds me, the walls hide me,
    and no one sees me. Why should I worry?
    The Most High will not remember sins."
19 His fear is confined to human eyes
    and he does not realize that the eyes of the Lord
    are ten thousand times brighter than the sun;
    they look upon every aspect of human behavior
    and see into hidden corners.
20 Before the universe was created, it was known to him,
    and so it is since its completion.

21 This man will be punished in the streets of the city,
    and where he least suspects it, he will be seized.
22 So it is with a woman who leaves her husband
    and presents him with an heir by another man.
23 For first of all, she has disobeyed the law of the Most High;
    second, she has committed an offense against her husband;
    and third, through her fornication she has committed adultery
    and brought forth children by another man.
24 She herself will be brought before the assembly,
    and her punishment will extend to her children.
25 Her children will not take root,
    and her branches will not bear fruit.
26 She will leave behind an accursed memory
    and her disgrace will never be blotted out.
27 Those who survive her will recognize
    that nothing is better than the fear of the Lord,
    and nothing sweeter than to heed the commandments of the Lord.*b*

THE PRAISE OF WISDOM*c*

24 Wisdom praises herself,
    and tells of her glory in the midst of her people.
2 In the assembly of the Most High she opens her mouth,
    and in the presence of his hosts she tells of her glory:
3 "I came forth from the mouth of the Most High,
    and covered the earth like a mist.
4 I dwelt in the highest heavens,
    and my throne was in a pillar of cloud.
5 Alone I compassed the vault of heaven
    and traversed the depths of the abyss.
6 Over waves of the sea, over all the earth,
    and over every people and nation I have held sway.*d*
7 Among all these I sought a resting place;
    in whose territory should I abide?
8 "Then the Creator of all things gave me a command,
    and my Creator chose the place for my tent.

---

a Other ancient authorities read *clothed about with death* *b* Other ancient authorities add as verse 28, *It is a great honor to follow God, and to be received by him is long life.* *c* This heading is included in the Gk text. *d* Other ancient authorities read *I have acquired a possession*

He said, 'Make your dwelling in Jacob,
    and in Israel receive your inheritance.'
9 Before the ages, in the beginning, he
        created me,
    and for all the ages I shall not cease to be.
10 In the holy tent I ministered before him,
    and so I was established in Zion.
11 Thus in the beloved city he gave me a
        resting place,
    and in Jerusalem was my domain.
12 I took root in an honored people,
    in the portion of the Lord, his heritage.

13 "I grew tall like a cedar in Lebanon,
    and like a cypress on the heights of
        Hermon.
14 I grew tall like a palm tree in En-gedi,[a]
    and like rosebushes in Jericho;
    like a fair olive tree in the field,
    and like a plane tree beside water[b] I grew
        tall.
15 Like cassia and camel's thorn I gave forth
        perfume,
    and like choice myrrh I spread my
        fragrance,
    like galbanum, onycha, and stacte,
    and like the odor of incense in the tent.
16 Like a terebinth I spread out my branches,
    and my branches are glorious and
        graceful.
17 Like the vine I bud forth delights,
    and my blossoms become glorious and
        abundant fruit.[c]

19 "Come to me, you who desire me,
    and eat your fill of my fruits.
20 For the memory of me is sweeter than
        honey,
    and the possession of me sweeter than
        the honeycomb.
21 Those who eat of me will hunger for more,
    and those who drink of me will thirst for
        more.
22 Whoever obeys me will not be put to
        shame,
    and those who work with me will not sin."

Wisdom and the Law
23 All this is the book of the covenant of the
        Most High God,
    the law that Moses commanded us
    as an inheritance for the congregations
        of Jacob.[d]
25 It overflows, like the Pishon, with wisdom,
    and like the Tigris at the time of the first
        fruits.

JESUS SIGHTING

You like going to
parties, right? Well, in
Sirach 24.19–22, you're
invited to a feast! The feast
and the banquet are symbols
of God's Kingdom in the New Testament.
Jesus used these symbols often in the
New Testament. He told stories about
banquets and dinners—stories of people
who could not or would not come to a
feast (Matthew 22.1–14; Luke 15.15–24),
and stories of people who would not be
admitted to the banquet of the Kingdom
because they would not feed the hungry
or take care of those in need (Matthew
25.31–46). Finally, there's Jesus'
invitation to his banquet (John 6.35).

The gospel writers make it clear
through the images of the meal, the feast,
and the banquet that Jesus came to feed
us and to nourish our hungry hearts. But
over and over again, Jesus lets us know
this is not an exclusive banquet. All are
invited, even the people we would not
invite or choose to sit next to. (In fact,
they may get there before we do!) And
what if we ignore the hungry and thirsty
here on earth? In the end, that will be the
deciding factor in whether we will be part
of the banquet or not.

26 It runs over, like the Euphrates, with
        understanding,
    and like the Jordan at harvest time.
27 It pours forth instruction like the Nile,[e]
    like the Gihon at the time of vintage.
28 The first man did not know wisdom[f] fully,
    nor will the last one fathom her.
29 For her thoughts are more abundant than
        the sea,
    and her counsel deeper than the great
        abyss.

30 As for me, I was like a canal from a river,
    like a water channel into a garden.

---

a Other ancient authorities read *on the beaches* b Other ancient authorities omit *beside water* c Other ancient authorities add as verse
18, *I am the mother of beautiful love, of fear, of knowledge, and of holy hope; being eternal, I am given to all my children, to those who are named by him.*
d Other ancient authorities add as verse 24, *"Do not cease to be strong in the Lord, cling to him so that he may strengthen you; the Lord Almighty alone
is God, and besides him there is no savior."* e Syr: Gk *It makes instruction shine forth like light* f Gk *her*

31 I said, "I will water my garden
and drench my flower-beds."
And lo, my canal became a river,
and my river a sea.
32 I will again make instruction shine forth
like the dawn,
and I will make it clear from far away.
33 I will again pour out teaching like prophecy,
and leave it to all future generations.
34 Observe that I have not labored for myself
alone,
but for all who seek wisdom.*a*

25 Those Who Are Worthy of Praise

I take pleasure in three things,
and they are beautiful in the sight of God
and of mortals:*b*
agreement among brothers and sisters,
friendship among neighbors,
and a wife and a husband who live in
harmony.
2 I hate three kinds of people,
and I loathe their manner of life:
a pauper who boasts, a rich person who
lies,
and an old fool who commits adultery.
3 If you gathered nothing in your youth,
how can you find anything in your old
age?
4 How attractive is sound judgment in the
gray-haired,
and for the aged to possess good
counsel!
5 How attractive is wisdom in the aged,
and understanding and counsel in the
venerable!
6 Rich experience is the crown of the aged,
and their boast is the fear of the Lord.

7 I can think of nine whom I would call
blessed,
and a tenth my tongue proclaims:
a man who can rejoice in his children;
a man who lives to see the downfall of
his foes.
8 Happy the man who lives with a sensible
wife,
and the one who does not plow with ox
and ass together.*c*
Happy is the one who does not sin with the
tongue,

and the one who has not served an
inferior.
9 Happy is the one who finds a friend,*d*
and the one who speaks to attentive
listeners.
10 How great is the one who finds wisdom!
But none is superior to the one who fears
the Lord.
11 Fear of the Lord surpasses everything;
to whom can we compare the one who
has it?*e*

Some Extreme Forms of Evil

13 Any wound, but not a wound of the heart!
Any wickedness, but not the wickedness
of a woman!
14 Any suffering, but not suffering from those
who hate!
And any vengeance, but not the
vengeance of enemies!
15 There is no venom*f* worse than a snake's
venom,*f*
and no anger worse than a woman's*g*
wrath.

The Evil of a Wicked Woman

16 I would rather live with a lion and a dragon
than live with an evil woman.
17 A woman's wickedness changes her
appearance,
and darkens her face like that of a bear.
18 Her husband sits*h* among the neighbors,
and he cannot help sighing*i* bitterly.
19 Any iniquity is small compared to a
woman's iniquity;
may a sinner's lot befall her!
20 A sandy ascent for the feet of the aged—
such is a garrulous wife to a quiet
husband.
21 Do not be ensnared by a woman's beauty,
and do not desire a woman for her
possessions.*j*
22 There is wrath and impudence and great
disgrace
when a wife supports her husband.
23 Dejected mind, gloomy face,
and wounded heart come from an evil
wife.
Drooping hands and weak knees
come from the wife who does not make
her husband happy.
24 From a woman sin had its beginning,

a Gk *her* *b* Syr Lat: Gk *In three things I was beautiful and I stood in beauty before the Lord and mortals.* *c* Heb Syr: Gk *lacks and the one who does not plow with ox and ass together* *d* Lat Syr: Gk *good sense* *e* Other ancient authorities add as verse 12, *The fear of the Lord is the beginning of love for him, and faith is the beginning of clinging to him.* *f* Syr: Gk *head* *g* Other ancient authorities read *an enemy's* *h* Heb Syr: Gk *loses heart* *i* Other ancient authorities read *and listening he sighs* *j* Heb Syr: Other Gk authorities read *for her beauty*

and because of her we all die.
25 Allow no outlet to water,
    and no boldness of speech to an evil
        wife.
26 If she does not go as you direct,
    separate her from yourself.

26 The Joy of a Good Wife

Happy is the husband of a good wife;
    the number of his days will be doubled.
2 A loyal wife brings joy to her husband,
    and he will complete his years in peace.
3 A good wife is a great blessing;
    she will be granted among the blessings
        of the man who fears the Lord.
4 Whether rich or poor, his heart is content,
    and at all times his face is cheerful.

The Worst of Evils: A Wicked Wife

5 Of three things my heart is frightened,
    and of a fourth I am in great fear:[a]
Slander in the city, the gathering of a mob,
    and false accusation—all these are worse
        than death.
6 But it is heartache and sorrow when a wife
        is jealous of a rival,
    and a tongue-lashing makes it known to
        all.
7 A bad wife is a chafing yoke;
    taking hold of her is like grasping a
        scorpion.
8 A drunken wife arouses great anger;
    she cannot hide her shame.
9 The haughty stare betrays an unchaste wife;
    her eyelids give her away.
10 Keep strict watch over a headstrong
        daughter,
    or else, when she finds liberty, she will
        make use of it.
11 Be on guard against her impudent eye,
    and do not be surprised if she sins
        against you.
12 As a thirsty traveler opens his mouth
    and drinks from any water near him,
so she will sit in front of every tent peg
    and open her quiver to the arrow.

The Blessing of a Good Wife

13 A wife's charm delights her husband,
    and her skill puts flesh on his bones.
14 A silent wife is a gift from the Lord,
    and nothing is so precious as her
        self-discipline.
15 A modest wife adds charm to charm,
    and no scales can weigh the value of her
        chastity.

a Syr: Meaning of Gk uncertain

16 Like the sun rising in the heights of the
        Lord,
    so is the beauty of a good wife in her
        well-ordered home.
17 Like the shining lamp on the holy
        lampstand,
    so is a beautiful face on a stately figure.
18 Like golden pillars on silver bases,
    so are shapely legs and steadfast feet.

_____

Other ancient authorities add verses 19-27:

19 *My child, keep sound the bloom of your youth,*
    and do not give your strength to strangers.
20 *Seek a fertile field within the whole plain,*
    and sow it with your own seed, trusting in your
        fine stock.
21 *So your offspring will prosper,*
    and, having confidence in their good descent, will
        grow great.
22 *A prostitute is regarded as spittle,*
    and a married woman as a tower of death to her
        lovers.
23 *A godless wife is given as a portion to a lawless man,*
    but a pious wife is given to the man who fears the
        Lord.
24 *A shameless woman constantly acts disgracefully,*
    but a modest daughter will even be embarrassed
        before her husband.
25 *A headstrong wife is regarded as a dog,*
    but one who has a sense of shame will fear the
        Lord.
26 *A wife honoring her husband will seem wise to all,*
    but if she dishonors him in her pride she will be
        known to all as ungodly.
    Happy is the husband of a good wife;
    for the number of his years will be doubled.
27 *A loud-voiced and garrulous wife is like a trumpet*
        sounding the charge,
    and every person like this lives in the anarchy of
        war.

_____

Three Depressing Things

28 At two things my heart is grieved,
    and because of a third anger comes
        over me:
a warrior in want through poverty,
    intelligent men who are treated
        contemptuously,
and a man who turns back from
        righteousness to sin—
    the Lord will prepare him for the sword!

The Temptations of Commerce

29 A merchant can hardly keep from
        wrongdoing,
    nor is a tradesman innocent of sin.

27

1 Many have committed sin for gain,[a]
   and those who seek to get rich will avert
      their eyes.
2 As a stake is driven firmly into a fissure
      between stones,
   so sin is wedged in between selling and
      buying.
3 If a person is not steadfast in the fear of the
      Lord,
   his house will be quickly overthrown.

Tests in Life
4 When a sieve is shaken, the refuse appears;
   so do a person's faults when he speaks.
5 The kiln tests the potter's vessels;
   so the test of a person is in his
      conversation.
6 Its fruit discloses the cultivation of a tree;
   so a person's speech discloses the
      cultivation of his mind.
7 Do not praise anyone before he speaks,
   for this is the way people are tested.

Reward and Retribution
8 If you pursue justice, you will attain it
   and wear it like a glorious robe.
9 Birds roost with their own kind,
   so honesty comes home to those who
      practice it.
10 A lion lies in wait for prey;
   so does sin for evildoers.

Varieties of Speech
11 The conversation of the godly is always
      wise,
   but the fool changes like the moon.
12 Among stupid people limit your time,
   but among thoughtful people linger on.
13 The talk of fools is offensive,
   and their laughter is wantonly sinful.
14 Their cursing and swearing make one's hair
      stand on end,
   and their quarrels make others stop their
      ears.
15 The strife of the proud leads to bloodshed,
   and their abuse is grievous to hear.

Betraying Secrets
16 Whoever betrays secrets destroys
      confidence,
   and will never find a congenial friend.
17 Love your friend and keep faith with him;
   but if you betray his secrets, do not
      follow after him.
18 For as a person destroys his enemy,

so you have destroyed the friendship of
   your neighbor.
19 And as you allow a bird to escape from your
      hand,
   so you have let your neighbor go, and
      will not catch him again.
20 Do not go after him, for he is too far off,
   and has escaped like a gazelle from a
      snare.
21 For a wound may be bandaged,
   and there is reconciliation after abuse,
   but whoever has betrayed secrets is
      without hope.

Hypocrisy and Retribution
22 Whoever winks the eye plots mischief,
   and those who know him will keep their
      distance.
23 In your presence his mouth is all sweetness,
   and he admires your words;
   but later he will twist his speech
      and with your own words he will trip
      you up.
24 I have hated many things, but him above
      all;
   even the Lord hates him.
25 Whoever throws a stone straight up throws
      it on his own head,
   and a treacherous blow opens up many
      wounds.
26 Whoever digs a pit will fall into it,
   and whoever sets a snare will be caught
      in it.
27 If a person does evil, it will roll back upon
      him,
   and he will not know where it came
      from.
28 Mockery and abuse issue from the proud,
   but vengeance lies in wait for them like a
      lion.
29 Those who rejoice in the fall of the godly
      will be caught in a snare,
   and pain will consume them before their
      death.

Anger and Vengeance
30 Anger and wrath, these also are
      abominations,
   yet a sinner holds on to them.

28

1 The vengeful will face the Lord's
      vengeance,
   for he keeps a strict account of[b] their
      sins.
2 Forgive your neighbor the wrong he has
      done,
   and then your sins will be pardoned
      when you pray.

---

a Other ancient authorities read *a trifle* b Other ancient authorities read *for he firmly establishes*

Focus on What Is Real in Your Life—© Megan Schoettler, 17

³ Does anyone harbor anger against another,
   and expect healing from the Lord?
⁴ If one has no mercy toward another like
      himself,
   can he then seek pardon for his own
      sins?
⁵ If a mere mortal harbors wrath,
   who will make an atoning sacrifice for
      his sins?
⁶ Remember the end of your life, and set
      enmity aside;
   remember corruption and death, and be
      true to the commandments.
⁷ Remember the commandments, and do
      not be angry with your neighbor;
   remember the covenant of the Most
      High, and overlook faults.

⁸ Refrain from strife, and your sins will be
      fewer;
   for the hot-tempered kindle strife,
⁹ and the sinner disrupts friendships
   and sows discord among those who are
      at peace.
¹⁰ In proportion to the fuel, so will the fire
      burn,
   and in proportion to the obstinacy, so
      will strife increase;ᵃ
   in proportion to a person's strength will be
      his anger,
   and in proportion to his wealth he will
      increase his wrath.

¹¹ A hasty quarrel kindles a fire,
   and a hasty dispute sheds blood.

The Evil Tongue

¹² If you blow on a spark, it will glow;
   if you spit on it, it will be put out;
   yet both come out of your mouth.

¹³ Curse the gossips and the double-tongued,
   for they destroy the peace of many.
¹⁴ Slanderᵇ has shaken many,
   and scattered them from nation to
      nation;
   it has destroyed strong cities,
   and overturned the houses of the great.
¹⁵ Slanderᶜ has driven virtuous women from
      their homes,
   and deprived them of the fruit of their
      toil.
¹⁶ Those who pay heed to slanderᵈ will not
      find rest,
   nor will they settle down in peace.
¹⁷ The blow of a whip raises a welt,
   but a blow of the tongue crushes the
      bones.
¹⁸ Many have fallen by the edge of the sword,
   but not as many as have fallen because of
      the tongue.
¹⁹ Happy is the one who is protected from it,
   who has not been exposed to its anger,
   who has not borne its yoke,
   and has not been bound with its fetters.

---

a Other ancient authorities read *burn*   *b* Gk *A third tongue*   *c* Gk *a third tongue*   *d* Gk *it*

29 On Lending and Borrowing

The merciful lend to their neighbors;
    by holding out a helping hand they keep
      the commandments.
2 Lend to your neighbor in his time of need;
    repay your neighbor when a loan falls
      due.
3 Keep your promise and be honest with him,
    and on every occasion you will find what
      you need.
4 Many regard a loan as a windfall,
    and cause trouble to those who help
      them.
5 One kisses another's hands until he gets a
      loan,
    and is deferential in speaking of his
      neighbor's money;
but at the time for repayment he delays,
    and pays back with empty promises,
    and finds fault with the time.
6 If he can pay, his creditor[b] will hardly get
      back half,
    and will regard that as a windfall.
If he cannot pay, the borrower[b] has robbed
      the other of his money,
    and he has needlessly made him an
      enemy;
he will repay him with curses and
      reproaches,
    and instead of glory will repay him with
      dishonor.
7 Many refuse to lend, not because of
      meanness,
    but from fear[c] of being defrauded
      needlessly.

20 For its yoke is a yoke of iron,
    and its fetters are fetters of bronze;
21 its death is an evil death,
    and Hades is preferable to it.
22 It has no power over the godly;
    they will not be burned in its flame.
23 Those who forsake the Lord will fall into its
      power;
    it will burn among them and will not be
      put out.
It will be sent out against them like a lion;
    like a leopard it will mangle them.
24a As you fence in your property with thorns,
25b   so make a door and a bolt for your
      mouth.
24b As you lock up your silver and gold,
25a   so make balances and scales for your
      words.
26 Take care not to err with your tongue,[a]
    and fall victim to one lying in wait.

8 Nevertheless, be patient with someone in
      humble circumstances,
    and do not keep him waiting for your
      alms.
9 Help the poor for the commandment's
      sake,
    and in their need do not send them away
      empty-handed.
10 Lose your silver for the sake of a brother or
      a friend,
    and do not let it rust under a stone and
      be lost.
11 Lay up your treasure according to the
      commandments of the Most High,
    and it will profit you more than gold.
12 Store up almsgiving in your treasury,
    and it will rescue you from every disaster;
13 better than a stout shield and a sturdy
      spear,
    it will fight for you against the enemy.

a Gk with it b Gk he c Other ancient authorities read *many refuse to lend, therefore, because of such meanness; they are afraid*

On Guaranteeing Debts

14 A good person will be surety for his neighbor,
  but the one who has lost all sense of
    shame will fail him.
15 Do not forget the kindness of your guarantor,
  for he has given his life for you.
16 A sinner wastes the property of his guarantor,
17 and the ungrateful person abandons his
    rescuer.
18 Being surety has ruined many who were
    prosperous,
  and has tossed them about like waves of
    the sea;
  it has driven the influential into exile,
    and they have wandered among foreign
    nations.
19 The sinner comes to grief through surety;
  his pursuit of gain involves him in
    lawsuits.
20 Assist your neighbor to the best of your
    ability,
  but be careful not to fall yourself.

Home and Hospitality

21 The necessities of life are water, bread, and
    clothing,
  and also a house to assure privacy.
22 Better is the life of the poor under their
    own crude roof
  than sumptuous food in the house of
    others.
23 Be content with little or much,
  and you will hear no reproach for being a
    guest.[a]
24 It is a miserable life to go from house to
    house;
  as a guest you should not open your
    mouth;
25 you will play the host and provide drink
    without being thanked,
  and besides this you will hear rude words
    like these:
26 "Come here, stranger, prepare the table;
  let me eat what you have there."
27 "Be off, stranger, for an honored guest is
    here;
  my brother has come for a visit, and I
    need the guest-room."
28 It is hard for a sensible person to bear
  scolding about lodging[b] and the insults
    of the moneylender.

CONCERNING CHILDREN[c]

30 He who loves his son will whip him
    often,

so that he may rejoice at the way he turns
    out.
2 He who disciplines his son will profit by him,
  and will boast of him among
    acquaintances.
3 He who teaches his son will make his
    enemies envious,
  and will glory in him among his friends.
4 When the father dies he will not seem to be
    dead,
  for he has left behind him one like
    himself,
5 whom in his life he looked upon with joy
  and at death, without grief.
6 He has left behind him an avenger against
    his enemies,
  and one to repay the kindness of his
    friends.
7 Whoever spoils his son will bind up his
    wounds,
  and will suffer heartache at every cry.
8 An unbroken horse turns out stubborn,
  and an unchecked son turns out
    headstrong.
9 Pamper a child, and he will terrorize you;
  play with him, and he will grieve you.
10 Do not laugh with him, or you will have
    sorrow with him,
  and in the end you will gnash your teeth.
11 Give him no freedom in his youth,
  and do not ignore his errors.
12 Bow down his neck in his youth,[d]
  and beat his sides while he is young,
  or else he will become stubborn and
    disobey you,
  and you will have sorrow of soul from
    him.[e]
13 Discipline your son and make his yoke
    heavy,[f]
  so that you may not be offended by his
    shamelessness.

14 Better off poor, healthy, and fit
  than rich and afflicted in body.
15 Health and fitness are better than any gold,
  and a robust body than countless riches.
16 There is no wealth better than health of
    body,
  and no gladness above joy of heart.
17 Death is better than a life of misery,
  and eternal sleep[g] than chronic sickness.

CONCERNING FOODS[h]

18 Good things poured out upon a mouth that
    is closed

---

a Lat: Gk *reproach from your family*; other ancient authorities lack this line   b Or *scolding from the household*   c This heading is included in
the Gk text.   d Other ancient authorities lack this line and the preceding line   e Other ancient authorities lack this line   f Heb: Gk
take pains with him   g Other ancient authorities lack *eternal sleep*   h This heading is included in the Gk text; other ancient authorities
place the heading before verse 16

PROFILE OF FAITH

By the age of twenty-four, Joseph Martin was ordained a priest in the archdiocese of Baltimore. A few years later, he was assigned to St. Charles College in Catonsville, Maryland.

But there was a problem. During that time, Fr. Martin began drinking excessively. In 1958, the archdiocese sent Fr. Martin to a treatment facility for the clergy. Once sober, Fr. Martin's life changed dramatically.

He went on to touch the lives of millions of recovering alcoholics and addicts through his unique ability to educate on the disease of alcoholism. Fr. Martin also continued to work within the Church and participated in the International Conference on Drugs and Alcohol sponsored by the Vatican in 1991.

At his funeral in 2009, Fr. Martin was called a "wounded healer," because his addiction enabled him to establish a remarkable ministry to individuals of all faiths, linked by their common struggle with alcoholism and addiction.

are like offerings of food placed upon a grave.

19 Of what use to an idol is a sacrifice?
For it can neither eat nor smell.
So is the one punished by the Lord;
20 he sees with his eyes and groans
as a eunuch groans when embracing a girl.[a]
21 Do not give yourself over to sorrow,
and do not distress yourself deliberately.
22 A joyful heart is life itself,
and rejoicing lengthens one's life span.
23 Indulge yourself[b] and take comfort,
and remove sorrow far from you,
for sorrow has destroyed many,
and no advantage ever comes from it.
24 Jealousy and anger shorten life,
and anxiety brings on premature old age.
25 Those who are cheerful and merry at table
will benefit from their food.

31 Right Attitude toward Riches

Wakefulness over wealth wastes away one's flesh,
and anxiety about it drives away sleep.
2 Wakeful anxiety prevents slumber,

and a severe illness carries off sleep.[c]
3 The rich person toils to amass a fortune,
and when he rests he fills himself with his dainties.
4 The poor person toils to make a meager living,
and if ever he rests he becomes needy.
5 One who loves gold will not be justified;
one who pursues money will be led astray[d] by it.
6 Many have come to ruin because of gold,
and their destruction has met them face to face.
7 It is a stumbling block to those who are avid for it,
and every fool will be taken captive by it.
8 Blessed is the rich person who is found blameless,
and who does not go after gold.
9 Who is he, that we may praise him?
For he has done wonders among his people.
10 Who has been tested by it and been found perfect?
Let it be for him a ground for boasting.

a Other ancient authorities add *So is the person who does right under compulsion* b Other ancient authorities read *Beguile yourself* c Other ancient authorities read *sleep carries off a severe illness* d Heb Syr: Gk *pursues destruction will be filled*

Who has had the power to transgress and
    did not transgress,
    and to do evil and did not do it?
11 His prosperity will be established,^a
    and the assembly will proclaim his acts of
    charity.

Table Etiquette

12 Are you seated at the table of the great?^b
    Do not be greedy at it,
    and do not say, "How much food there is
    here!"
13 Remember that a greedy eye is a bad thing.
    What has been created more greedy than
    the eye?
    Therefore it sheds tears for any reason.
14 Do not reach out your hand for everything
    you see,
    and do not crowd your neighbor^c at the
    dish.
15 Judge your neighbor's feelings by your own,
    and in every matter be thoughtful.
16 Eat what is set before you like a well
    brought-up person,^d
    and do not chew greedily, or you will give
    offense.
17 Be the first to stop, as befits good manners,
    and do not be insatiable, or you will give
    offense.
18 If you are seated among many persons,
    do not help yourself^e before they do.

19 How ample a little is for a well-disciplined
    person!
    He does not breathe heavily when in bed.
20 Healthy sleep depends on moderate eating;
    he rises early, and feels fit.
    The distress of sleeplessness and of nausea
    and colic are with the glutton.
21 If you are overstuffed with food,
    get up to vomit, and you will have relief.
22 Listen to me, my child, and do not
    disregard me,
    and in the end you will appreciate my
    words.
    In everything you do be moderate,^f
    and no sickness will overtake you.
23 People bless the one who is liberal with
    food,
    and their testimony to his generosity is
    trustworthy.
24 The city complains of the one who is stingy
    with food,
    and their testimony to his stinginess is
    accurate.

Temperance in Drinking Wine

25 Do not try to prove your strength by
    wine-drinking,
    for wine has destroyed many.
26 As the furnace tests the work of the smith,^g
    so wine tests hearts when the insolent
    quarrel.
27 Wine is very life to human beings
    if taken in moderation.
    What is life to one who is without wine?
    It has been created to make people
    happy.
28 Wine drunk at the proper time and in
    moderation
    is rejoicing of heart and gladness of soul.
29 Wine drunk to excess leads to bitterness of
    spirit,
    to quarrels and stumbling.
30 Drunkenness increases the anger of a fool
    to his own hurt,
    reducing his strength and adding
    wounds.
31 Do not reprove your neighbor at a banquet
    of wine,
    and do not despise him in his
    merrymaking;
    speak no word of reproach to him,
    and do not distress him by making
    demands of him.

32 Etiquette at a Banquet

If they make you master of the feast, do not
    exalt yourself;
    be among them as one of their number.
    Take care of them first and then sit down;
2   when you have fulfilled all your duties,
    take your place,
    so that you may be merry along with them
    and receive a wreath for your excellent
    leadership.

3 Speak, you who are older, for it is your
    right,
    but with accurate knowledge, and do not
    interrupt the music.
4 Where there is entertainment, do not pour
    out talk;
    do not display your cleverness at the
    wrong time.
5 A ruby seal in a setting of gold
    is a concert of music at a banquet of
    wine.
6 A seal of emerald in a rich setting of gold
    is the melody of music with good wine.
7 Speak, you who are young, if you are
    obliged to,

a Other ancient authorities add because of this   b Heb Syr: Gk at a great table   c Gk him   d Heb: Gk like a human being   e Gk reach out your
hand   f Heb Syr: Gk industrious   g Heb: Gk tests the hardening of steel by dipping

but no more than twice, and only if
asked.
8 Be brief; say much in few words;
be as one who knows and can still hold
his tongue.
9 Among the great do not act as their equal;
and when another is speaking, do not
babble.
10 Lightning travels ahead of the thunder,
and approval goes before one who is
modest.
11 Leave in good time and do not be the last;
go home quickly and do not linger.
12 Amuse yourself there to your heart's
content,
but do not sin through proud speech.
13 But above all bless your Maker,
who fills you with his good gifts.

The Providence of God
14 The one who seeks God[a] will accept his
discipline,
and those who rise early to seek him[b] will
find favor.
15 The one who seeks the law will be filled
with it,
but the hypocrite will stumble at it.
16 Those who fear the Lord will form true
judgments,
and they will kindle righteous deeds like
a light.
17 The sinner will shun reproof,
and will find a decision according to his
liking.

18 A sensible person will not overlook a
thoughtful suggestion;
an insolent[c] and proud person will not
be deterred by fear.[d]
19 Do nothing without deliberation,
but when you have acted, do not regret it.
20 Do not go on a path full of hazards,
and do not stumble at an obstacle twice.[e]
21 Do not be overconfident on a smooth[f]
road,
22 and give good heed to your paths.[g]
23 Guard[h] yourself in every act,
for this is the keeping of the
commandments.
24 The one who keeps the law preserves
himself,[i]
and the one who trusts the Lord will not
suffer loss.

33 No evil will befall the one who fears the
Lord,

but in trials such a one will be rescued
again and again.
2 The wise will not hate the law,
but the one who is hypocritical about it is
like a boat in a storm.
3 The sensible person will trust in the law;
for such a one the law is as dependable as
a divine oracle.

4 Prepare what to say, and then you will be
listened to;
draw upon your training, and give your
answer.
5 The heart of a fool is like a cart wheel,
and his thoughts like a turning axle.
6 A mocking friend is like a stallion
that neighs no matter who the rider is.

Differences in Nature and in Humankind
7 Why is one day more important than
another,
when all the daylight in the year is from
the sun?
8 By the Lord's wisdom they were
distinguished,
and he appointed the different seasons
and festivals.
9 Some days he exalted and hallowed,
and some he made ordinary days.
10 All human beings come from the ground,
and humankind[j] was created out of the
dust.
11 In the fullness of his knowledge the Lord
distinguished them
and appointed their different ways.
12 Some he blessed and exalted,
and some he made holy and brought
near to himself;
but some he cursed and brought low,
and turned them out of their place.
13 Like clay in the hand of the potter,
to be molded as he pleases,
so all are in the hand of their Maker,
to be given whatever he decides.

14 Good is the opposite of evil,
and life the opposite of death;
so the sinner is the opposite of the godly.
15 Look at all the works of the Most High;
they come in pairs, one the opposite of
the other.

16 Now I was the last to keep vigil;
I was like a gleaner following the
grape-pickers;
17 by the blessing of the Lord I arrived first,

---

a Heb: Gk who fears the Lord   b Other ancient authorities lack to seek him   c Heb: Gk alien   d Meaning of Gk uncertain. Other ancient
authorities add and after acting, with him, without deliberation   e Heb: Gk stumble on stony ground   f Or an unexplored   g Heb Syr: Gk and beware
of your children   h Heb Syr: Gk Trust   i Heb: Gk who believes the law heeds the commandments   j Heb: Gk Adam

and like a grape-picker I filled my wine press.

¹⁸ Consider that I have not labored for myself alone,
but for all who seek instruction.

¹⁹ Hear me, you who are great among the people,
and you leaders of the congregation, pay heed!

The Advantage of Independence

²⁰ To son or wife, to brother or friend,
do not give power over yourself, as long as you live;
and do not give your property to another,
in case you change your mind and must ask for it.

²¹ While you are still alive and have breath in you,
do not let anyone take your place.

²² For it is better that your children should ask from you
than that you should look to the hand of your children.

²³ Excel in all that you do;
bring no stain upon your honor.

²⁴ At the time when you end the days of your life,
in the hour of death, distribute your inheritance.

The Treatment of Slaves

²⁵ Fodder and a stick and burdens for a donkey;
bread and discipline and work for a slave.

²⁶ Set your slave to work, and you will find rest;
leave his hands idle, and he will seek liberty.

²⁷ Yoke and thong will bow the neck,
and for a wicked slave there are racks and tortures.

²⁸ Put him to work, in order that he may not be idle,

²⁹ for idleness teaches much evil.

³⁰ Set him to work, as is fitting for him,
and if he does not obey, make his fetters heavy.
Do not be overbearing toward anyone,
and do nothing unjust.

³¹ If you have but one slave, treat him like yourself,
because you have bought him with blood.
If you have but one slave, treat him like a brother,

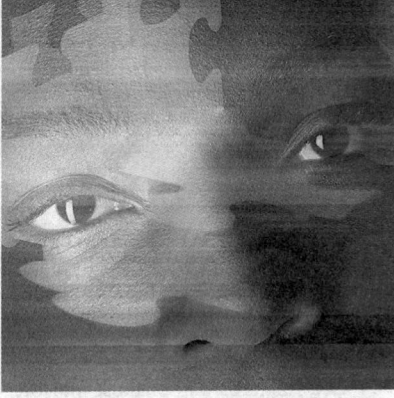

for you will need him as you need your life.

³² If you ill-treat him, and he leaves you and runs away,

³³ which way will you go to seek him?

34 Dreams Mean Nothing

The senseless have vain and false hopes,
and dreams give wings to fools.

² As one who catches at a shadow and pursues the wind,
so is anyone who believes in^a dreams.

³ What is seen in dreams is but a reflection,
the likeness of a face looking at itself.

⁴ From an unclean thing what can be clean?
And from something false what can be true?

⁵ Divinations and omens and dreams are unreal,
and like a woman in labor, the mind has fantasies.

⁶ Unless they are sent by intervention from the Most High,
pay no attention to them.

⁷ For dreams have deceived many,
and those who put their hope in them have perished.

⁸ Without such deceptions the law will be fulfilled,
and wisdom is complete in the mouth of the faithful.

Experience as a Teacher

⁹ An educated^b person knows many things,
and one with much experience knows what he is talking about.

¹⁰ An inexperienced person knows few things,

¹¹ but he that has traveled acquires much cleverness.

¹² I have seen many things in my travels,
and I understand more than I can express.

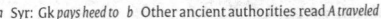

a Syr: Gk *pays heed to* b Other ancient authorities read *A traveled*

¹³ I have often been in danger of death,
   but have escaped because of these
      experiences.

Fear the Lord

¹⁴ The spirit of those who fear the Lord will
      live,
¹⁵   for their hope is in him who saves them.
¹⁶ Those who fear the Lord will not be timid,
   or play the coward, for he is their hope.
¹⁷ Happy is the soul that fears the Lord!
¹⁸   To whom does he look? And who is his
      support?
¹⁹ The eyes of the Lord are on those who love
      him,
   a mighty shield and strong support,
   a shelter from scorching wind and a shade
      from noonday sun,
      a guard against stumbling and a help
         against falling.
²⁰ He lifts up the soul and makes the eyes
      sparkle;
   he gives health and life and blessing.

Offering Sacrifices

²¹ If one sacrifices ill-gotten goods, the
      offering is blemished;^a
²²   the gifts^b of the lawless are not
      acceptable.
²³ The Most High is not pleased with the
      offerings of the ungodly,
   nor for a multitude of sacrifices does he
      forgive sins.
²⁴ Like one who kills a son before his father's
      eyes
   is the person who offers a sacrifice from
      the property of the poor.
²⁵ The bread of the needy is the life of the
      poor;
   whoever deprives them of it is a
      murderer.
²⁶ To take away a neighbor's living is to
      commit murder;
²⁷   to deprive an employee of wages is to
      shed blood.

²⁸ When one builds and another tears down,
   what do they gain but hard work?
²⁹ When one prays and another curses,
   to whose voice will the Lord listen?
³⁰ If one washes after touching a corpse, and
      touches it again,
   what has been gained by washing?
³¹ So if one fasts for his sins,
   and goes again and does the same things,
      who will listen to his prayer?
      And what has he gained by humbling
         himself?

35

The Law and Sacrifices

The one who keeps the law makes many
      offerings;
²   one who heeds the commandments
      makes an offering of well-being.
³ The one who returns a kindness offers
      choice flour,
⁴   and one who gives alms sacrifices a thank
      offering.
⁵ To keep from wickedness is pleasing to the
      Lord,
   and to forsake unrighteousness is an
      atonement.
⁶ Do not appear before the Lord
      empty-handed,
⁷   for all that you offer is in fulfillment of
      the commandment.
⁸ The offering of the righteous enriches the
      altar,
   and its pleasing odor rises before the
      Most High.
⁹ The sacrifice of the righteous is acceptable,
   and it will never be forgotten.
¹⁰ Be generous when you worship the Lord,
   and do not stint the first fruits of your
      hands.
¹¹ With every gift show a cheerful face,
   and dedicate your tithe with gladness.
¹² Give to the Most High as he has given to
      you,
   and as generously as you can afford.
¹³ For the Lord is the one who repays,
   and he will repay you sevenfold.

Divine Justice

¹⁴ Do not offer him a bribe, for he will not
      accept it;
¹⁵   and do not rely on a dishonest sacrifice;
   for the Lord is the judge,
   and with him there is no partiality.
¹⁶ He will not show partiality to the poor;
   but he will listen to the prayer of one
      who is wronged.
¹⁷ He will not ignore the supplication of the
      orphan,
   or the widow when she pours out her
      complaint.
¹⁸ Do not the tears of the widow run down her
      cheek
¹⁹   as she cries out against the one who
      causes them to fall?
²⁰ The one whose service is pleasing to the
      Lord will be accepted,
   and his prayer will reach to the clouds.
²¹ The prayer of the humble pierces the
      clouds,

---

a Other ancient authorities read *is made in mockery*   *b* Other ancient authorities read *mockeries*

and it will not rest until it reaches its goal;
  it will not desist until the Most High
    responds
22 and does justice for the righteous, and
    executes judgment.
Indeed, the Lord will not delay,
  and like a warrior*a* will not be patient
until he crushes the loins of the unmerciful
23 and repays vengeance on the nations;
  until he destroys the multitude of the
    insolent,
  and breaks the scepters of the
    unrighteous;
24 until he repays mortals according to their
    deeds,
  and the works of all according to their
    thoughts;
25 until he judges the case of his people
  and makes them rejoice in his mercy.
26 His mercy is as welcome in time of distress
  as clouds of rain in time of drought.

36 A Prayer for God's People

Have mercy upon us, O God*b* of all,
2 and put all the nations in fear of you.
3 Lift up your hand against foreign nations
  and let them see your might.
4 As you have used us to show your holiness
    to them,
  so use them to show your glory to us.
5 Then they will know,*c* as we have known,
  that there is no God but you, O Lord.
6 Give new signs, and work other wonders;
7 make your hand and right arm glorious.
8 Rouse your anger and pour out your wrath;
9 destroy the adversary and wipe out the
    enemy.
10 Hasten the day, and remember the
    appointed time,*d*
  and let people recount your mighty
    deeds.
11 Let survivors be consumed in the fiery
    wrath,
  and may those who harm your people
    meet destruction.
12 Crush the heads of hostile rulers
  who say, "There is no one but ourselves."
13 Gather all the tribes of Jacob,*e*
16 and give them their inheritance, as at the
    beginning.
17 Have mercy, O Lord, on the people called by
    your name,
  on Israel, whom you have named*f* your
    firstborn,
18 Have pity on the city of your sanctuary,*g*

Jerusalem, the place of your dwelling.*h*
19 Fill Zion with your majesty,*i*
  and your temple*j* with your glory.
20 Bear witness to those whom you created in
    the beginning,
  and fulfill the prophecies spoken in your
    name.
21 Reward those who wait for you
  and let your prophets be found
    trustworthy.
22 Hear, O Lord, the prayer of your servants,
    according to your goodwill toward*k*
    your people,
and all who are on the earth will know
  that you are the Lord, the God of the
    ages.

Concerning Discrimination
23 The stomach will take any food,
  yet one food is better than another.

TEXT MESSAGE

The fact that the author of this book has the same name as Jesus wouldn't have been surprising to early Christian readers of Sirach. "Jesus" was the fifth most common name in the first century A.D.

Fact

This information has been scanned and is free of all known viruses. Please forward to all your friends.

---

a Heb: Gk *and with them*   *b* Heb: Gk *O Master, the God*   *c* Heb: Gk *and let them know you*   *d* Other ancient authorities read *remember your oath*
e Owing to a dislocation in the Greek Mss of Sirach, the verse numbers 14 and 15 are not used in chapter 36, though no text is
missing.   *f* Other ancient authorities read *you have likened to*   *g* Or *on your holy city*   *h* Heb: Gk *your rest*   *i* Heb Syr: Gk *the celebration of your
wondrous deeds*   *j* Heb Syr: Gk Lat *people*   *k* Heb and two Gk witnesses: Lat and most Gk witnesses read *according to the blessing of Aaron for*

but one girl is preferable to another.

27 A woman's beauty lights up a man's face,
and there is nothing he desires more.

28 If kindness and humility mark her speech,
her husband is more fortunate than
other men.

29 He who acquires a wife gets his best
possession,[a]
a helper fit for him and a pillar of
support.[b]

30 Where there is no fence, the property will
be plundered;
and where there is no wife, a man will
become a fugitive and a wanderer.[c]

31 For who will trust a nimble robber
that skips from city to city?
So who will trust a man that has no nest,
but lodges wherever night overtakes
him?

37 False Friends

Every friend says, "I too am a friend";
but some friends are friends only in
name.

2 Is it not a sorrow like that for death itself
when a dear friend turns into an enemy?

3 O inclination to evil, why were you formed
to cover the land with deceit?

4 Some companions rejoice in the happiness
of a friend,
but in time of trouble they are against
him.

5 Some companions help a friend for their
stomachs' sake,
yet in battle they will carry his shield.

6 Do not forget a friend during the battle,[d]
and do not be unmindful of him when
you distribute your spoils.[e]

Caution in Taking Advice

7 All counselors praise the counsel they give,
but some give counsel in their own
interest.

8 Be wary of a counselor,
and learn first what is his interest,
for he will take thought for himself.
He may cast the lot against you

9 and tell you, "Your way is good,"
and then stand aside to see what happens
to you.

10 Do not consult the one who regards you
with suspicion;
hide your intentions from those who are
jealous of you.

11 Do not consult with a woman about her
rival
or with a coward about war,

24 As the palate tastes the kinds of game,
so an intelligent mind detects false
words.

25 A perverse mind will cause grief,
but a person with experience will pay
him back.

26 A woman will accept any man as a husband,

a Heb: Gk enters upon a possession b Heb: Gk rest c Heb: Gk wander about and sigh d Heb: Gk in your heart e Heb: Gk him in your wealth

with a merchant about business
  or with a buyer about selling,
with a miser about generosity[a]
  or with the merciless about kindness,
with an idler about any work
  or with a seasonal laborer about
    completing his work,
with a lazy servant about a big task—
  pay no attention to any advice they give.

12 But associate with a godly person
  whom you know to be a keeper of the
    commandments,
who is like-minded with yourself,
  and who will grieve with you if you fail.

13 And heed[b] the counsel of your own heart,
  for no one is more faithful to you than
    it is.

14 For our own mind sometimes keeps us
    better informed
  than seven sentinels sitting high on a
    watchtower.

15 But above all pray to the Most High
  that he may direct your way in truth.

True and False Wisdom

16 Discussion is the beginning of every work,
  and counsel precedes every undertaking.

17 The mind is the root of all conduct;
18   it sprouts four branches,[c]
good and evil, life and death;
  and it is the tongue that continually rules
    them.

19 Some people may be clever enough to teach
    many,
  and yet be useless to themselves.

20 A skillful speaker may be hated;
  he will be destitute of all food,

21 for the Lord has withheld the gift of charm,
  since he is lacking in all wisdom.

22 If a person is wise to his own advantage,
  the fruits of his good sense will be
    praiseworthy.[d]

23 A wise person instructs his own people,
  and the fruits of his good sense will
    endure.

24 A wise person will have praise heaped upon
    him,
  and all who see him will call him happy.

25 The days of a person's life are numbered,
  but the days of Israel are without
    number.

26 One who is wise among his people will
    inherit honor,[e]
  and his name will live forever.

Concerning Moderation

27 My child, test yourself while you live;
  see what is bad for you and do not give in
    to it.

28 For not everything is good for everyone,
  and no one enjoys everything.

29 Do not be greedy for every delicacy,
  and do not eat without restraint;

30 for overeating brings sickness,
  and gluttony leads to nausea.

31 Many have died of gluttony,
  but the one who guards against it
    prolongs his life.

38 Concerning Physicians and Health

Honor physicians for their services,
  for the Lord created them;

2 for their gift of healing comes from the
    Most High,
  and they are rewarded by the king.

3 The skill of physicians makes them
    distinguished,
  and in the presence of the great they are
    admired.

4 The Lord created medicines out of the
    earth,
  and the sensible will not despise them.

5 Was not water made sweet with a tree
  in order that its[f] power might be known?

6 And he gave skill to human beings
  that he[g] might be glorified in his
    marvelous works.

7 By them the physician[h] heals and takes away
    pain;

8   the pharmacist makes a mixture from
    them.
  God's[i] works will never be finished;
  and from him health[j] spreads over all the
    earth.

9 My child, when you are ill, do not delay,
  but pray to the Lord, and he will heal you.

10 Give up your faults and direct your hands
    rightly,
  and cleanse your heart from all sin.

11 Offer a sweet-smelling sacrifice, and a
    memorial portion of choice flour,
  and pour oil on your offering, as much as
    you can afford.[k]

12 Then give the physician his place, for the
    Lord created him;
  do not let him leave you, for you need him.

13 There may come a time when recovery lies
    in the hands of physicians,[l]

14   for they too pray to the Lord
  that he grant them success in diagnosis[m]

---

a Heb: Gk *gratitude* b Heb: Gk *establish* c Heb: Gk *As a clue to changes of heart four kinds of destiny appear* d Other ancient witnesses read *trustworthy* e Other ancient authorities read *confidence* f Or *his* g Or *they* h Heb: Gk *he* i Gk *His* j Or *peace* k Heb: Lat lacks *as much as you can afford;* Meaning of Gk uncertain l Gk *in their hands* m Heb: Gk *rest*

and in healing, for the sake of preserving
life.

¹⁵ He who sins against his Maker,
will be defiant toward the physician.ᵃ

On Mourning for the Dead

¹⁶ My child, let your tears fall for the dead,
and as one in great pain begin the
lament.
Lay out the body with due ceremony,
and do not neglect the burial.

¹⁷ Let your weeping be bitter and your wailing
fervent;
make your mourning worthy of the
departed,
for one day, or two, to avoid criticism;
then be comforted for your grief.

¹⁸ For grief may result in death,
and a sorrowful heart saps one's
strength.

¹⁹ When a person is taken away, sorrow is
over;
but the life of the poor weighs down the
heart.

²⁰ Do not give your heart to grief;
drive it away, and remember your own
end.

²¹ Do not forget, there is no coming back;
you do the deadᵇ no good, and you injure
yourself.

²² Remember hisᶜ fate, for yours is like it;
yesterday it was his,ᵈ and today it is yours.

²³ When the dead is at rest, let his
remembrance rest too,
and be comforted for him when his spirit
has departed.

Trades and Crafts

²⁴ The wisdom of the scribe depends on the
opportunity of leisure;
only the one who has little business can
become wise.

²⁵ How can one become wise who handles the
plow,
and who glories in the shaft of a goad,
who drives oxen and is occupied with their
work,
and whose talk is about bulls?

²⁶ He sets his heart on plowing furrows,
and he is careful about fodder for the
heifers.

²⁷ So it is with every artisan and master artisan
who labors by night as well as by day;
those who cut the signets of seals,
each is diligent in making a great variety;

they set their heart on painting a lifelike
image,
and they are careful to finish their work.

²⁸ So it is with the smith, sitting by the anvil,
intent on his iron-work;
the breath of the fire melts his flesh,
and he struggles with the heat of the
furnace;
the sound of the hammer deafens his ears,ᵉ
and his eyes are on the pattern of the
object.
He sets his heart on finishing his
handiwork,
and he is careful to complete its
decoration.

²⁹ So it is with the potter sitting at his work
and turning the wheel with his feet;
he is always deeply concerned over his
products,
and he produces them in quantity.

³⁰ He molds the clay with his arm
and makes it pliable with his feet;
he sets his heart to finish the glazing,
and he takes care in firingᶠ the kiln.

³¹ All these rely on their hands,
and all are skillful in their own work.

³² Without them no city can be inhabited,
and wherever they live, they will not go
hungry.ᵍ
Yet they are not sought out for the council
of the people,ʰ

³³ nor do they attain eminence in the public
assembly.
They do not sit in the judge's seat,
nor do they understand the decisions of
the courts;
they cannot expound discipline or
judgment,
and they are not found among the
rulers.ⁱ

³⁴ But they maintain the fabric of the world,
and their concern is forʲ the exercise of
their trade.

The Activity of the Scribe

How different the one who devotes himself
to the study of the law of the Most High!

39 He seeks out the wisdom of all the
ancients,
and is concerned with prophecies;

² he preserves the sayings of the famous
and penetrates the subtleties of parables;

³ he seeks out the hidden meanings of
proverbs

---

a Heb: Gk *may he fall into the hands of the physician* *b* Gk *him* *c* Heb: Gk *my* *d* Heb: Gk *mine* *e* Cn: Gk *renews his ear* *f* Cn: Gk *cleaning*
g Syr: Gk *and people can neither live nor walk there* *h* Most ancient authorities lack this line *i* Cn: Gk *among parables* *j* Syr: Gk *prayer is in*

and is at home with the obscurities of
parables.
4 He serves among the great
and appears before rulers;
he travels in foreign lands
and learns what is good and evil in the
human lot.
5 He sets his heart to rise early
to seek the Lord who made him,
and to petition the Most High;
he opens his mouth in prayer
and asks pardon for his sins.

6 If the great Lord is willing,
he will be filled with the spirit of
understanding;
he will pour forth words of wisdom of his
own
and give thanks to the Lord in prayer.
7 The Lord*a* will direct his counsel and
knowledge,
as he meditates on his mysteries.
8 He will show the wisdom of what he has
learned,
and will glory in the law of the Lord's
covenant.
9 Many will praise his understanding;
it will never be blotted out.
His memory will not disappear,
and his name will live through all
generations.
10 Nations will speak of his wisdom,
and the congregation will proclaim his
praise.
11 If he lives long, he will leave a name greater
than a thousand,
and if he goes to rest, it is enough*b* for
him.

A Hymn of Praise to God

12 I have more on my mind to express;
I am full like the full moon.
13 Listen to me, my faithful children, and
blossom
like a rose growing by a stream of water.
14 Send out fragrance like incense,
and put forth blossoms like a lily.
Scatter the fragrance, and sing a hymn of
praise;
bless the Lord for all his works.
15 Ascribe majesty to his name
and give thanks to him with praise,
with songs on your lips, and with harps;
this is what you shall say in thanksgiving:

16 "All the works of the Lord are very good,
and whatever he commands will be done
at the appointed time.

> "Wise men talk because they have
> something to say; fools, because they
> have to say something."
>
> **—Plato**

17 No one can say, 'What is this?' or 'Why is
that?'—
for at the appointed time all such
questions will be answered.
At his word the waters stood in a heap,
and the reservoirs of water at the word of
his mouth.
18 When he commands, his every purpose is
fulfilled,
and none can limit his saving power.
19 The works of all are before him,
and nothing can be hidden from his eyes.
20 From the beginning to the end of time he
can see everything,
and nothing is too marvelous for him.
21 No one can say, 'What is this?' or 'Why is
that?'—
for everything has been created for its
own purpose.

22 "His blessing covers the dry land like a river,
and drenches it like a flood.
23 But his wrath drives out the nations,
as when he turned a watered land into
salt.
24 To the faithful his ways are straight,
but full of pitfalls for the wicked.
25 From the beginning good things were
created for the good,
but for sinners good things and bad.*c*
26 The basic necessities of human life
are water and fire and iron and salt
and wheat flour and milk and honey,
the blood of the grape and oil and
clothing.
27 All these are good for the godly,
but for sinners they turn into evils.

28 "There are winds created for vengeance,
and in their anger they can dislodge
mountains;*d*
on the day of reckoning they will pour out
their strength
and calm the anger of their Maker.
29 Fire and hail and famine and pestilence,
all these have been created for
vengeance;
30 the fangs of wild animals and scorpions
and vipers,

a Gk *He himself* *b* Cn: Meaning of Gk uncertain *c* Heb Lat: Gk *sinners bad things* *d* Heb Syr: Gk *can scourge mightily*

REALITY ✔

JOYS OF LIFE

What gives you joy? When are you happiest? Is it when you have just completed a beautiful piece of art, run a good race, watched a little child play, laughed with a good friend until your sides hurt, or been complimented on something you have done?

Joy is a fruit of the Holy Spirit. Think about this. Joy happens when we are connected to the presence of God in life. Joy can be quiet, deep, and lasting or it can be noisy and fleeting. How it happens doesn't matter, but experiencing it does.

Think about how you can bring joy to others by doing something as small as giving a smile or a pat on the back or doing something that takes more time and planning. Look into becoming a mentor to a younger child, spending time visiting or volunteering in a nursing home, or working in a food pantry. Then pick a joy-giving task and do it. Make it your mission to bring joy to others and to be aware and grateful for it in your own life.

In the next few days, be mindful of what brings you joy. Find some Creative Space in this Bible and make a list of those things that come to mind, and don't forget to share it on **Learner.CalltoDiscipleship.com.**

---

³⁴ No one can say, "This is not as good as that,"
  for everything proves good in its appointed time.
³⁵ So now sing praise with all your heart and voice,
  and bless the name of the Lord.

40 Human Wretchedness

Hard work was created for everyone,
  and a heavy yoke is laid on the children of Adam,
from the day they come forth from their mother's womb
  until the day they return to*ᵃ* the mother of all the living.*ᵇ*
² Perplexities and fear of heart are theirs,
  and anxious thought of the day of their death.
³ From the one who sits on a splendid throne
  to the one who grovels in dust and ashes,
⁴ from the one who wears purple and a crown
  to the one who is clothed in burlap,
⁵ there is anger and envy and trouble and unrest,
  and fear of death, and fury and strife.
And when one rests upon his bed,
  his sleep at night confuses his mind.
⁶ He gets little or no rest;
  he struggles in his sleep as he did by day.*ᶜ*
He is troubled by the visions of his mind
  like one who has escaped from the battlefield.
⁷ At the moment he reaches safety he wakes up,
  astonished that his fears were groundless.
⁸ To all creatures, human and animal,
  but to sinners seven times more,
⁹ come death and bloodshed and strife and sword,
  calamities and famine and ruin and plague.
¹⁰ All these were created for the wicked,
  and on their account the flood came.
¹¹ All that is of earth returns to earth,
  and what is from above returns above.*ᵈ*

Injustice Will Not Prosper

¹² All bribery and injustice will be blotted out,
  but good faith will last forever.
¹³ The wealth of the unjust will dry up like a river,
  and crash like a loud clap of thunder in a storm.

---

and the sword that punishes the ungodly with destruction.
³¹ They take delight in doing his bidding,
  always ready for his service on earth;
  and when their time comes they never disobey his command."

³² So from the beginning I have been convinced of all this
  and have thought it out and left it in writing:
³³ All the works of the Lord are good,
  and he will supply every need in its time.

---

a Other Gk and Lat authorities read *are buried in* *b* Heb: Gk *of all* *c* Arm: Meaning of Gk uncertain *d* Heb Syr: Gk Lat *from the waters returns to the sea*

14 As a generous person has cause to rejoice,
   so lawbreakers will utterly fail.
15 The children of the ungodly put out few
   branches;
   they are unhealthy roots on sheer rock.
16 The reeds by any water or river bank
   are plucked up before any grass;
17 but kindness is like a garden of blessings,
   and almsgiving endures forever.

The Joys of Life

18 Wealth and wages make life sweet,[a]
   but better than either is finding a
   treasure.
19 Children and the building of a city establish
   one's name,
   but better than either is the one who
   finds wisdom.
   Cattle and orchards make one prosperous;[b]
   but a blameless wife is accounted better
   than either.
20 Wine and music gladden the heart,
   but the love of friends[c] is better than
   either.
21 The flute and the harp make sweet melody,
   but a pleasant voice is better than either.
22 The eye desires grace and beauty,
   but the green shoots of grain more than
   either.
23 A friend or companion is always welcome,
   but a sensible wife[d] is better than either.
24 Kindred and helpers are for a time of
   trouble,
   but almsgiving rescues better than
   either.
25 Gold and silver make one stand firm,
   but good counsel is esteemed more than
   either.
26 Riches and strength build up confidence,
   but the fear of the Lord is better than
   either.
   There is no want in the fear of the Lord,
   and with it there is no need to seek for
   help.
27 The fear of the Lord is like a garden of
   blessing,
   and covers a person better than any
   glory.

The Disgrace of Begging

28 My child, do not lead the life of a beggar;
   it is better to die than to beg.
29 When one looks to the table of another,
   one's way of life cannot be considered a
   life.

One loses self-respect with another
   person's food,
   but one who is intelligent and well
   instructed guards against that.
30 In the mouth of the shameless begging is
   sweet,
   but it kindles a fire inside him.

41 Concerning Death

O death, how bitter is the thought of you
   to the one at peace among possessions,
who has nothing to worry about and is
   prosperous in everything,
   and still is vigorous enough to enjoy
   food!
2 O death, how welcome is your sentence
   to one who is needy and failing in
   strength,
worn down by age and anxious about
   everything;
   to one who is contrary, and has lost all
   patience!
3 Do not fear death's decree for you;
   remember those who went before you
   and those who will come after.
4 This is the Lord's decree for all flesh;
   why then should you reject the will of the
   Most High?
Whether life lasts for ten years or a hundred
   or a thousand,
   there are no questions asked in Hades.

The Fate of the Wicked

5 The children of sinners are abominable
   children,
   and they frequent the haunts of the
   ungodly.
6 The inheritance of the children of sinners
   will perish,
   and on their offspring will be a perpetual
   disgrace.
7 Children will blame an ungodly father,
   for they suffer disgrace because of him.
8 Woe to you, the ungodly,
   who have forsaken the law of the Most
   High God!
9 If you have children, calamity will be theirs;
   you will beget them only for groaning.
When you stumble, there is lasting joy;[e]
   and when you die, a curse is your lot.
10 Whatever comes from earth returns to earth;
   so the ungodly go from curse to
   destruction.
11 The human body is a fleeting thing,
   but a virtuous name will never be blotted
   out.[f]

---

a Heb: Gk Life is sweet for the self-reliant worker   b Heb Syr: Gk lacks but better . . . prosperous   c Heb: Gk wisdom   d Heb Compare Syr: Gk wife
with her husband   e Heb: Meaning of Gk uncertain   f Heb: Gk People grieve over the death of the body, but the bad name of sinners will be blotted out

¹² Have regard for your name, since it will
outlive you
longer than a thousand hoards of gold.
¹³ The days of a good life are numbered,
but a good name lasts forever.

¹⁴ My children, be true to your training and be
at peace;
hidden wisdom and unseen treasure—
of what value is either?

A Series of Contrasts

¹⁵ Better are those who hide their folly
than those who hide their wisdom.
¹⁶ Therefore show respect for my words;
for it is not good to feel shame in every
circumstance,
nor is every kind of abashment to be
approved.ᵃ

¹⁷ Be ashamed of sexual immorality, before
your father or mother;
and of a lie, before a prince or a ruler;
¹⁸ of a crime, before a judge or magistrate;
and of a breach of the law, before the
congregation and the people;
of unjust dealing, before your partner or
your friend;
¹⁹ and of theft, in the place where you live.
Be ashamed of breaking an oath or
agreement,ᵇ
and of leaning on your elbow at meals;
of surliness in receiving or giving,
²⁰ and of silence, before those who greet
you;

of looking at a prostitute,
²¹ and of rejecting the appeal of a relative;
of taking away someone's portion or gift,
and of gazing at another man's wife;
²² of meddling with his servant-girl—
and do not approach her bed;
of abusive words, before friends—
and do not be insulting after making a
gift.

42
Be ashamed of repeating what you hear,
and of betraying secrets.
Then you will show proper shame,
and will find favor with everyone.

Of the following things do not be ashamed,
and do not sin to save face:
² Do not be ashamed of the law of the Most
High and his covenant,
and of rendering judgment to acquit the
ungodly;
³ of keeping accounts with a partner or with
traveling companions,
and of dividing the inheritance of
friends;
⁴ of accuracy with scales and weights,
and of acquiring much or little;
⁵ of profit from dealing with merchants,
and of frequent disciplining of children,
and of drawing blood from the back of a
wicked slave.
⁶ Where there is an untrustworthy wife, a seal
is a good thing;
and where there are many hands, lock
things up.

---

a Heb: Gk *and not everything is confidently esteemed by everyone*   b Heb: Gk *before the truth of God and the covenant*

7 When you make a deposit, be sure it is
counted and weighed,
   and when you give or receive, put it all in
writing.
8 Do not be ashamed to correct the stupid or
foolish
   or the aged who are guilty of sexual
immorality.
Then you will show your sound training,
   and will be approved by all.

Daughters and Fathers

9 A daughter is a secret anxiety to her father,
   and worry over her robs him of sleep;
when she is young, for fear she may not
marry,
   or if married, for fear she may be
disliked;
10 while a virgin, for fear she may be seduced
   and become pregnant in her father's
house;
or having a husband, for fear she may go
astray,
   or, though married, for fear she may be
barren.
11 Keep strict watch over a headstrong
daughter,
   or she may make you a laughingstock to
your enemies,
a byword in the city and the assembly of[a]
the people,
   and put you to shame in public
gatherings.[b]
See that there is no lattice in her room,
   no spot that overlooks the approaches to
the house.[c]
12 Do not let her parade her beauty before any
man,
   or spend her time among married
women;[a]
13 for from garments comes the moth,
   and from a woman comes woman's
wickedness.
14 Better is the wickedness of a man than a
woman who does good;
   it is woman who brings shame and
disgrace.

The Works of God in Nature

15 I will now call to mind the works of the
Lord,
   and will declare what I have seen.
By the word of the Lord his works are made;
   and all his creatures do his will.[d]
16 The sun looks down on everything with its
light,

and the work of the Lord is full of his
glory.
17 The Lord has not empowered even his holy
ones
   to recount all his marvelous works,
which the Lord the Almighty has
established
   so that the universe may stand firm in his
glory.
18 He searches out the abyss and the human
heart;
   he understands their innermost secrets.
For the Most High knows all that may be
known;
   he sees from of old the things that are to
come.[e]
19 He discloses what has been and what is
to be,
   and he reveals the traces of hidden
things.
20 No thought escapes him,
   and nothing is hidden from him.
21 He has set in order the splendors of his
wisdom;
   he is from all eternity one and the same.
Nothing can be added or taken away,
   and he needs no one to be his counselor.
22 How desirable are all his works,
   and how sparkling they are to see![f]
23 All these things live and remain forever;
   each creature is preserved to meet a
particular need.[g]
24 All things come in pairs, one opposite the
other,
   and he has made nothing incomplete.
25 Each supplements the virtues of the other.
   Who could ever tire of seeing his glory?

43 The Splendor of the Sun

The pride of the higher realms is the clear
vault of the sky,
   as glorious to behold as the sight of the
heavens.
2 The sun, when it appears, proclaims as it
rises
   what a marvelous instrument it is, the
work of the Most High.
3 At noon it parches the land,
   and who can withstand its burning heat?

a Heb: Meaning of Gk uncertain   b Heb: Gk to shame before the great multitude   c Heb: Gk lacks See . . . house   d Syr Compare Heb: most
Gk witnesses lack and all . . . will   e Heb: Gk he sees the sign(s) of the age   f Meaning of Gk uncertain   g Heb: Gk forever for every need, and all
are obedient

⁴ A man tending^a a furnace works in burning heat,
　but three times as hot is the sun scorching the mountains;
　it breathes out fiery vapors,
　　and its bright rays blind the eyes.
⁵ Great is the Lord who made it;
　at his orders it hurries on its course.

The Splendor of the Moon

⁶ It is the moon that marks the changing seasons,^b
　governing the times, their everlasting sign.
⁷ From the moon comes the sign for festal days,
　a light that wanes when it completes its course.
⁸ The new moon, as its name suggests, renews itself;^c
　how marvelous it is in this change,
　a beacon to the hosts on high,
　　shining in the vault of the heavens!

The Glory of the Stars and the Rainbow

⁹ The glory of the stars is the beauty of heaven,
　a glittering array in the heights of the Lord.
¹⁰ On the orders of the Holy One they stand in their appointed places;
　they never relax in their watches.
¹¹ Look at the rainbow, and praise him who made it;
　it is exceedingly beautiful in its brightness.
¹² It encircles the sky with its glorious arc;
　the hands of the Most High have stretched it out.

The Marvels of Nature

¹³ By his command he sends the driving snow
　and speeds the lightnings of his judgment.
¹⁴ Therefore the storehouses are opened,
　and the clouds fly out like birds.
¹⁵ In his majesty he gives the clouds their strength,
　and the hailstones are broken in pieces.
^{17a} The voice of his thunder rebukes the earth;
¹⁶　when he appears, the mountains shake.
　At his will the south wind blows,
^{17b}　so do the storm from the north and the whirlwind.
　He scatters the snow like birds flying down,
　and its descent is like locusts alighting.

¹⁸ The eye is dazzled by the beauty of its whiteness,
　and the mind is amazed as it falls.
¹⁹ He pours frost over the earth like salt,
　and icicles form like pointed thorns.
²⁰ The cold north wind blows,
　and ice freezes on the water;
　it settles on every pool of water,
　　and the water puts it on like a breastplate.
²¹ He consumes the mountains and burns up the wilderness,
　and withers the tender grass like fire.
²² A mist quickly heals all things;
　the falling dew gives refreshment from the heat.
²³ By his plan he stilled the deep
　and planted islands in it.
²⁴ Those who sail the sea tell of its dangers,
　and we marvel at what we hear.
²⁵ In it are strange and marvelous creatures,
　all kinds of living things, and huge sea-monsters.
²⁶ Because of him each of his messengers succeeds,
　and by his word all things hold together.
²⁷ We could say more but could never say enough;
　let the final word be: "He is the all."
²⁸ Where can we find the strength to praise him?
　For he is greater than all his works.
²⁹ Awesome is the Lord and very great,
　and marvelous is his power.
³⁰ Glorify the Lord and exalt him as much as you can,
　for he surpasses even that.
　When you exalt him, summon all your strength,
　and do not grow weary, for you cannot praise him enough.
³¹ Who has seen him and can describe him?
　Or who can extol him as he is?
³² Many things greater than these lie hidden,
　for I^d have seen but few of his works.
³³ For the Lord has made all things,
　and to the godly he has given wisdom.

HYMN IN HONOR OF OUR ANCESTORS^e

44 Let us now sing the praises of famous men,
　our ancestors in their generations.
² The Lord apportioned to them^f great glory,
　his majesty from the beginning.

---

a Other ancient authorities read *blowing upon*　*b* Heb: Meaning of Gk uncertain　*c* Heb: Gk *The month is named after the moon*　*d* Heb: Gk *we*　*e* This title is included in the Gk text.　*f* Heb: Gk *created*

³ There were those who ruled in their
       kingdoms,
   and made a name for themselves by their
       valor;
   those who gave counsel because they were
       intelligent;
   those who spoke in prophetic oracles;
⁴ those who led the people by their counsels
   and by their knowledge of the people's
       lore;
   they were wise in their words of
       instruction;
⁵ those who composed musical tunes,
   or put verses in writing;
⁶ rich men endowed with resources,
   living peacefully in their homes—
⁷ all these were honored in their
      generations,
   and were the pride of their times.
⁸ Some of them have left behind a name,
   so that others declare their praise.
⁹ But of others there is no memory;
   they have perished as though they had
      never existed;
   they have become as though they had never
      been born,
   they and their children after them.
¹⁰ But these also were godly men,
   whose righteous deeds have not been
      forgotten;
¹¹ their wealth will remain with their
      descendants,
   and their inheritance with their
      children's children.ᵃ
¹² Their descendants stand by the covenants;
   their children also, for their sake.
¹³ Their offspring will continue forever,
   and their glory will never be blotted out.
¹⁴ Their bodies are buried in peace,
   but their name lives on generation after
      generation.
¹⁵ The assembly declaresᵇ their wisdom,
   and the congregation proclaims their
      praise.

Enoch

¹⁶ Enoch pleased the Lord and was taken up,
   an example of repentance to all
      generations.

Noah

¹⁷ Noah was found perfect and righteous;
   in the time of wrath he kept the race
      alive;ᶜ
   therefore a remnant was left on the earth
   when the flood came.
¹⁸ Everlasting covenants were made with him

IT'S TRADITION

LITANY OF THE SAINTS

On Super Bowl Sunday there's usually a lot of storytelling before the game. Besides the current status of the teams that are playing, you'll hear and see stories of the great games and players of the past.

The same kind of "blast from the past" reminiscing happens in our own families. At family dinners, holidays, and events, you hear stories (often the same ones over and over again!) about family members who have passed on.

It's natural to remember those who have gone before us. The stories of ancestors tell a group something about its own identity. They shine light on the questions "Who are we?" and "What makes us the way we are?"

Read **Sirach 44.1–50.21** with the understanding that the writer is reminding the people who they are, so that even in the midst of their own contemporary thought and non-Jewish influences, they will remember.

As Roman Catholics we invoke our ancestors when we pray the Litany of the Saints. We ask the Blessed Virgin Mary, the angels and all the martyrs and saints, the Patriarchs, and prophets to pray for us and to bring our prayers to God. We pray the Litany of the Saints during the Easter Vigil just before the celebration of the Sacraments of Initiation to remind those who are coming into the Church and those who are celebrating with them of our identity as disciples. We do a shorter remembrance every Sunday during the Liturgy of the Eucharist.

   that all flesh should never again be
      blotted out by a flood.

Abraham

¹⁹ Abraham was the great father of a multitude
   of nations,
   and no one has been found like him in
      glory.

ᵃ Heb Compare Lat Syr: Meaning of Gk uncertain ᵇ Heb: Gk *Peoples declare* ᶜ Heb: Gk *was taken in exchange*

> "It is in deep solitude that I find the gentleness with which I can truly love my brothers."
>
> —Thomas Merton

20 He kept the law of the Most High,
and entered into a covenant with him;
he certified the covenant in his flesh,
and when he was tested he proved
faithful.
21 Therefore the Lord[a] assured him with an
oath
that the nations would be blessed
through his offspring;
that he would make him as numerous as
the dust of the earth,
and exalt his offspring like the stars,
and give them an inheritance from sea to
sea
and from the Euphrates[b] to the ends of
the earth.

Isaac and Jacob

22 To Isaac also he gave the same assurance
for the sake of his father Abraham.
The blessing of all people and the covenant
23   he made to rest on the head of Jacob;
he acknowledged him with his blessings,
and gave him his inheritance;
he divided his portions,
and distributed them among twelve
tribes.

Moses

From his descendants the Lord[a] brought
forth a godly man,
who found favor in the sight of all

45 1 and was beloved by God and people,
Moses, whose memory is blessed.
2 He made him equal in glory to the holy
ones,
and made him great, to the terror of his
enemies.
3 By his words he performed swift miracles;[c]
the Lord[a] glorified him in the presence of
kings.
He gave him commandments for his
people,
and revealed to him his glory.
4 For his faithfulness and meekness he
consecrated him,

choosing him out of all humankind.
5 He allowed him to hear his voice,
and led him into the dark cloud,
and gave him the commandments face to
face,
the law of life and knowledge,
so that he might teach Jacob the covenant,
and Israel his decrees.

Aaron

6 He exalted Aaron, a holy man like Moses[d]
who was his brother, of the tribe of Levi.
7 He made him an everlasting covenant with him,
and gave him the priesthood of the
people.
He blessed him with stateliness,
and put a glorious robe on him.
8 He clothed him in perfect splendor,
and strengthened him with the symbols
of authority,
the linen undergarments, the long robe,
and the ephod.
9 And he encircled him with pomegranates,
with many golden bells all around,
to send forth a sound as he walked,
to make their ringing heard in the
temple
as a reminder to his people;
10 with the sacred vestment, of gold and
violet
and purple, the work of an embroiderer;
with the oracle of judgment, Urim and
Thummim;
11   with twisted crimson, the work of an
artisan;
with precious stones engraved like seals,
in a setting of gold, the work of a jeweler,
to commemorate in engraved letters
each of the tribes of Israel;
12 with a gold crown upon his turban,
inscribed like a seal with "Holiness,"
a distinction to be prized, the work of an
expert,
a delight to the eyes, richly adorned.
13 Before him such beautiful things did not
exist.
No outsider ever put them on,
but only his sons
and his descendants in perpetuity.
14 His sacrifices shall be wholly burned
twice every day continually.
15 Moses ordained him,
and anointed him with holy oil;
it was an everlasting covenant for him
and for his descendants as long as the
heavens endure,
to minister to the Lord[d] and serve as priest

a Gk he b Syr: Heb Gk River c Heb: Gk caused signs to cease d Gk him and bless his people in his name.

16 He chose him out of all the living
    to offer sacrifice to the Lord,
    incense and a pleasing odor as a memorial
        portion,
    to make atonement for the*a* people.
17 In his commandments he gave him
    authority and statutes and*b* judgments,
    to teach Jacob the testimonies,
    and to enlighten Israel with his law.
18 Outsiders conspired against him,
    and envied him in the wilderness,
    Dathan and Abiram and their followers
    and the company of Korah, in wrath and
        anger.
19 The Lord saw it and was not pleased,
    and in the heat of his anger they were
        destroyed;
    he performed wonders against them
    to consume them in flaming fire.
20 He added glory to Aaron
    and gave him a heritage;
    he allotted to him the best of the first fruits,
    and prepared bread of first fruits in
        abundance;
21 for they eat the sacrifices of the Lord,
    which he gave to him and his
        descendants.
22 But in the land of the people he has no
        inheritance,
    and he has no portion among the people;
    for the Lord*c* himself is his*d* portion and
        inheritance.

Phinehas

23 Phinehas son of Eleazar ranks third in glory
    for being zealous in the fear of the Lord,
    and standing firm, when the people turned
        away,
    in the noble courage of his soul;
    and he made atonement for Israel.
24 Therefore a covenant of friendship was
        established with him,
    that he should be leader of the sanctuary
        and of his people,
    that he and his descendants should have
    the dignity of the priesthood forever.
25 Just as a covenant was established with
        David
    son of Jesse of the tribe of Judah,
    that the king's heritage passes only from
        son to son,
    so the heritage of Aaron is for his
        descendants alone.
26 And now bless the Lord
    who has crowned you with glory.*e*

May the Lord*c* grant you wisdom of mind
    to judge his people with justice,
    so that their prosperity may not vanish,
    and that their glory may endure through
        all their generations.

46 Joshua and Caleb

Joshua son of Nun was mighty in war,
    and was the successor of Moses in the
        prophetic office.
He became, as his name implies,
    a great savior of God's*f* elect,
    to take vengeance on the enemies that rose
        against them,
    so that he might give Israel its
        inheritance.
2 How glorious he was when he lifted his
        hands
    and brandished his sword against the
        cities!
3 Who before him ever stood so firm?
    For he waged the wars of the Lord.
4 Was it not through him that the sun stood
        still
    and one day became as long as two?
5 He called upon the Most High, the Mighty
        One,
    when enemies pressed him on every side,
    and the great Lord answered him
    with hailstones of mighty power.
6 He overwhelmed that nation in battle,
    and on the slope he destroyed his
        opponents,
    so that the nations might know his
        armament,
    that he was fighting in the sight of the
        Lord;
    for he was a devoted follower of the
        Mighty One.
7 And in the days of Moses he proved his
        loyalty,
    he and Caleb son of Jephunneh:
    they opposed the congregation,*g*
    restrained the people from sin,
    and stilled their wicked grumbling.
8 And these two alone were spared
    out of six hundred thousand infantry,
    to lead the people*h* into their inheritance,
    the land flowing with milk and honey.
9 The Lord gave Caleb strength,
    which remained with him in his old age,
    so that he went up to the hill country,
    and his children obtained it for an
        inheritance.
10 so that all the Israelites might see
    how good it is to follow the Lord.

a Other ancient authorities read *his* or *your*   *b* Heb: Gk *authority in covenants of*   *c* Gk *he*   *d* Other ancient authorities read *your*   *e* Heb: Gk lacks *And . . . glory*   *f* Gk *his*   *g* Other ancient authorities read *the enemy*   *h* Gk *them*

and may the names of those who have
been honored
live again in their children!

¹³ Samuel was beloved by his Lord;
a prophet of the Lord, he established the
kingdom
and anointed rulers over his people.
¹⁴ By the law of the Lord he judged the
congregation,
and the Lord watched over Jacob.
¹⁵ By his faithfulness he was proved to be a
prophet,
and by his words he became known as a
trustworthy seer.
¹⁶ He called upon the Lord, the Mighty One,
when his enemies pressed him on every
side,
and he offered in sacrifice a suckling
lamb.
¹⁷ Then the Lord thundered from heaven,
and made his voice heard with a mighty
sound;
¹⁸ he subdued the leaders of the enemy*a*
and all the rulers of the Philistines.
¹⁹ Before the time of his eternal sleep,
Samuel*b* bore witness before the Lord
and his anointed:
"No property, not so much as a pair of
shoes,
have I taken from anyone!"
And no one accused him.
²⁰ Even after he had fallen asleep, he
prophesied
and made known to the king his death,
and lifted up his voice from the ground
in prophecy, to blot out the wickedness
of the people.

47 Nathan

After him Nathan rose up
to prophesy in the days of David.

David

² As the fat is set apart from the offering of
well-being,
so David was set apart from the Israelites.
³ He played with lions as though they were
young goats,
and with bears as though they were
lambs of the flock.
⁴ In his youth did he not kill a giant,
and take away the people's disgrace,
when he whirled the stone in the sling
and struck down the boasting Goliath?
⁵ For he called on the Lord, the Most High,
and he gave strength to his right arm
to strike down a mighty warrior,

The Judges

¹¹ The judges also, with their respective
names,
whose hearts did not fall into idolatry
and who did not turn away from the Lord—
may their memory be blessed!
¹² May their bones send forth new life from
where they lie,

a Heb: Gk leaders of the people of Tyre *b* Gk he

and to exalt the power[a] of his people.
6 So they glorified him for the tens of
thousands he conquered,
and praised him for the blessings
bestowed by the Lord,
when the glorious diadem was given to
him.
7 For he wiped out his enemies on every side,
and annihilated his adversaries the
Philistines;
he crushed their power[a] to our own day.
8 In all that he did he gave thanks
to the Holy One, the Most High,
proclaiming his glory;
he sang praise with all his heart,
and he loved his Maker.
9 He placed singers before the altar,
to make sweet melody with their voices.[b]
10 He gave beauty to the festivals,
and arranged their times throughout the
year,[c]
while they praised God's[d] holy name,
and the sanctuary resounded from early
morning.
11 The Lord took away his sins,
and exalted his power[a] forever;
he gave him a covenant of kingship
and a glorious throne in Israel.

Solomon

12 After him a wise son rose up
who because of him lived in security:[e]
13 Solomon reigned in an age of peace,
because God made all his borders
tranquil,
so that he might build a house in his name
and provide a sanctuary to stand forever.
14 How wise you were when you were young!
You overflowed like the Nile[f] with
understanding.
15 Your influence spread throughout the
earth,
and you filled it with proverbs having
deep meaning.
16 Your fame reached to far-off islands,
and you were loved for your peaceful
reign.
17 Your songs, proverbs, and parables,
and the answers you gave astounded the
nations.
18 In the name of the Lord God,
who is called the God of Israel,
you gathered gold like tin
and amassed silver like lead.
19 But you brought in women to lie at your
side,

and through your body you were brought
into subjection.
20 You stained your honor,
and defiled your family line,
so that you brought wrath upon your
children,
and they were grieved[g] at your folly,
21 because the sovereignty was divided
and a rebel kingdom arose out of
Ephraim.
22 But the Lord will never give up his mercy,
or cause any of his works to perish;
he will never blot out the descendants of
his chosen one,
or destroy the family line of him who
loved him.
So he gave a remnant to Jacob,
and to David a root from his own family.

Rehoboam and Jeroboam

23 Solomon rested with his ancestors,
and left behind him one of his sons,
broad in[h] folly and lacking in sense,
Rehoboam, whose policy drove the
people to revolt.
Then Jeroboam son of Nebat led Israel into
sin
and started Ephraim on its sinful ways.
24 Their sins increased more and more,
until they were exiled from their land.
25 For they sought out every kind of
wickedness,
until vengeance came upon them.

48 Elijah

Then Elijah arose, a prophet like fire,
and his word burned like a torch.
2 He brought a famine upon them,
and by his zeal he made them few in
number.
3 By the word of the Lord he shut up the
heavens,
and also three times brought down fire.
4 How glorious you were, Elijah, in your
wondrous deeds!
Whose glory is equal to yours?
5 You raised a corpse from death
and from Hades, by the word of the Most
High.
6 You sent kings down to destruction,
and famous men, from their sickbeds.
7 You heard rebuke at Sinai
and judgments of vengeance at Horeb.
8 You anointed kings to inflict retribution,
and prophets to succeed you.[i]
9 You were taken up by a whirlwind of fire,

a Gk horn b Other ancient authorities add and daily they sing his praises c Gk to completion d Gk his e Heb: Gk in a broad place f Heb: Gk
a river g Other ancient authorities read I was grieved h Heb (with a play on the name Rehoboam) Syr: Gk the people's i Heb: Gk him

in a chariot with horses of fire.

¹⁰ At the appointed time, it is written, you are destined*a*
to calm the wrath of God before it breaks out in fury,
to turn the hearts of parents to their children,
and to restore the tribes of Jacob.

¹¹ Happy are those who saw you
and were adorned*b* with your love!
For we also shall surely live.*c*

Elisha

¹² When Elijah was enveloped in the whirlwind,
Elisha was filled with his spirit.
He performed twice as many signs,
and marvels with every utterance of his mouth.*d*
Never in his lifetime did he tremble before any ruler,
nor could anyone intimidate him at all.

¹³ Nothing was too hard for him,
and when he was dead, his body prophesied.

¹⁴ In his life he did wonders,
and in death his deeds were marvelous.

¹⁵ Despite all this the people did not repent,
nor did they forsake their sins,
until they were carried off as plunder from their land,
and were scattered over all the earth.
The people were left very few in number,
but with a ruler from the house of David.

¹⁶ Some of them did what was right,
but others sinned more and more.

Hezekiah

¹⁷ Hezekiah fortified his city,
and brought water into its midst;
he tunneled the rock with iron tools,
and built cisterns for the water.

¹⁸ In his days Sennacherib invaded the country;
he sent his commander*e* and departed;
he shook his fist against Zion,
and made great boasts in his arrogance.

¹⁹ Then their hearts were shaken and their hands trembled,
and they were in anguish, like women in labor.

²⁰ But they called upon the Lord who is merciful,
spreading out their hands toward him.
The Holy One quickly heard them from heaven,
and delivered them through Isaiah.

²¹ The Lord*f* struck down the camp of the Assyrians,
and his angel wiped them out.

²² For Hezekiah did what was pleasing to the Lord,
and he kept firmly to the ways of his ancestor David,
as he was commanded by the prophet Isaiah,
who was great and trustworthy in his visions.

a Heb: Gk *are for reproofs* *b* Other ancient authorities read *and have died* *c* Text and meaning of Gk uncertain *d* Heb: Gk lacks *He performed . . . mouth* *e* Other ancient authorities add *from Lachish* *f* Gk *He*

Ichthys—© John Carter, 14

Isaiah

23 In Isaiah's[a] days the sun went backward,
  and he prolonged the life of the king.
24 By his dauntless spirit he saw the future,
  and comforted the mourners in Zion.
25 He revealed what was to occur to the end of
    time,
  and the hidden things before they
    happened.

49 Josiah and Other Worthies

The name[b] of Josiah is like blended incense
  prepared by the skill of the perfumer;
his memory[c] is as sweet as honey to every
    mouth,
  and like music at a banquet of wine.
2 He did what was right by reforming the
    people,
  and removing the wicked abominations.
3 He kept his heart fixed on the Lord;
  in lawless times he made godliness
    prevail.

4 Except for David and Hezekiah and Josiah,
  all of them were great sinners,
for they abandoned the law of the Most
    High;
  the kings of Judah came to an end.
5 They[d] gave their power to others,
  and their glory to a foreign nation,
6 who set fire to the chosen city of the
    sanctuary,
  and made its streets desolate,
    as Jeremiah had foretold.[e]
7 For they had mistreated him,
  who even in the womb had been
    consecrated a prophet,
to pluck up and ruin and destroy,
  and likewise to build and to plant.

8 It was Ezekiel who saw the vision of glory,
  which God[f] showed him above the
    chariot of the cherubim.
9 For God[g] also mentioned Job
  who held fast to all the ways of justice.[h]
10 May the bones of the Twelve Prophets
  send forth new life from where they lie,
for they comforted the people of Jacob
  and delivered them with confident hope.

11 How shall we magnify Zerubbabel?
  He was like a signet ring on the right
    hand,
12 and so was Jeshua son of Jozadak;
  in their days they built the house
  and raised a temple[i] holy to the Lord,

destined for everlasting glory.
13 The memory of Nehemiah also is lasting;
  he raised our fallen walls,
and set up gates and bars,
  and rebuilt our ruined houses.

Retrospect

14 Few have[j] ever been created on earth like
    Enoch,
  for he was taken up from the earth.
15 Nor was anyone ever born like Joseph;[k]
  even his bones were cared for.
16 Shem and Seth and Enosh were honored,[l]
  but above every other created living
    being was Adam.

50 Simon Son of Onias

The leader of his brothers and the pride of
    his people[m]
  was the high priest, Simon son of Onias,
who in his life repaired the house,
  and in his time fortified the temple.
2 He laid the foundations for the high double
    walls,
  the high retaining walls for the temple
    enclosure.
3 In his days a water cistern was dug,[n]
  a reservoir like the sea in circumference.
4 He considered how to save his people from
    ruin,
  and fortified the city against siege.
5 How glorious he was, surrounded by the
    people,
  as he came out of the house of the
    curtain.
6 Like the morning star among the clouds,
  like the full moon at the festal season;[n]
7 like the sun shining on the temple of the
    Most High,
  like the rainbow gleaming in splendid
    clouds;
8 like roses in the days of first fruits,
  like lilies by a spring of water,
  like a green shoot on Lebanon on a
    summer day;

---

a Gk *his* *b* Heb: Gk *memory* *c* Heb: Gk *it* *d* Heb *He* *e* Gk *by the hand of Jeremiah* *f* Gk *He* *g* Gk *he* *h* Heb Compare Syr: Meaning of
Gk uncertain *i* Other ancient authorities read *people* *j* Heb Syr: Gk *No one has* *k* Heb Syr: Gk adds *the leader of his brothers, the support of
the people* *l* Heb: Gk *Shem and Seth were honored by people* *m* Heb Syr: Gk lacks this line. Compare 49.15 *n* Heb: Meaning of Gk
uncertain

9 like fire and incense in the censer,
   like a vessel of hammered gold
   studded with all kinds of precious stones;
10 like an olive tree laden with fruit,
   and like a cypress towering in the clouds.
11 When he put on his glorious robe
   and clothed himself in perfect splendor,
   when he went up to the holy altar,
   he made the court of the sanctuary
   glorious.
12 When he received the portions from the
   hands of the priests,
   as he stood by the hearth of the altar
   with a garland of brothers around him,
   he was like a young cedar on Lebanon
   surrounded by the trunks of palm trees.
13 All the sons of Aaron in their splendor
   held the Lord's offering in their hands
   before the whole congregation of Israel.
14 Finishing the service at the altars,[a]
   and arranging the offering to the Most
   High, the Almighty,
15 he held out his hand for the cup
   and poured a drink offering of the blood
   of the grape;
   he poured it out at the foot of the altar,
   a pleasing odor to the Most High, the
   king of all.
16 Then the sons of Aaron shouted;
   they blew their trumpets of hammered
   metal;
   they sounded a mighty fanfare
   as a reminder before the Most High.
17 Then all the people together quickly
   fell to the ground on their faces
to worship their Lord,
   the Almighty, God Most High.
18 Then the singers praised him with their
   voices
   in sweet and full-toned melody.[b]
19 And the people of the Lord Most High
   offered
   their prayers before the Merciful One,
until the order of worship of the Lord was
   ended,
   and they completed his ritual.
20 Then Simon[c] came down and raised his
   hands
   over the whole congregation of
   Israelites,
   to pronounce the blessing of the Lord with
   his lips,
   and to glory in his name;
21 and they bowed down in worship a second
   time,

to receive the blessing from the Most
   High.

A Benediction

22 And now bless the God of all,
   who everywhere works great wonders,
   who fosters our growth from birth,
   and deals with us according to his mercy.
23 May he give us[d] gladness of heart,
   and may there be peace in our[e] days
   in Israel, as in the days of old.
24 May he entrust to us his mercy,
   and may he deliver us in our[f] days!

Epilogue

25 Two nations my soul detests,
   and the third is not even a people:
26 Those who live in Seir,[g] and the Philistines,
   and the foolish people that live in
   Shechem.

27 Instruction in understanding and
   knowledge
   I have written in this book,
Jesus son of Eleazar son of Sirach[h] of
   Jerusalem,
   whose mind poured forth wisdom.
28 Happy are those who concern themselves
   with these things,
   and those who lay them to heart will
   become wise.
29 For if they put them into practice, they will
   be equal to anything,
   for the fear[i] of the Lord is their path.

PRAYER OF JESUS SON OF SIRACH[j]

51 I give you thanks, O Lord and King,
   and praise you, O God my Savior.
I give thanks to your name,
2   for you have been my protector and
   helper
and have delivered me from destruction
   and from the trap laid by a slanderous
   tongue,
   from lips that fabricate lies.
In the face of my adversaries
   you have been my helper ³and
   delivered me,
   in the greatness of your mercy and of
   your name,
from grinding teeth about to devour me,
   from the hand of those seeking my life,
   from the many troubles I endured,
4 from choking fire on every side,
   and from the midst of fire that I had not
   kindled,

a Other ancient authorities read altar b Other ancient authorities read in sweet melody throughout the house c Gk he d Other ancient
authorities read you e Other ancient authorities read your f Other ancient authorities read his g Heb Compare Lat: Gk on the
mountain of Samaria h Heb: Meaning of Gk uncertain i Heb: Other ancient authorities read light j This title is included in the Gk text.

⁵ from the deep belly of Hades,
from an unclean tongue and lying
words—
⁶ the slander of an unrighteous tongue to
the king.
My soul drew near to death,
and my life was on the brink of Hades
below.
⁷ They surrounded me on every side,
and there was no one to help me;
I looked for human assistance,
and there was none.
⁸ Then I remembered your mercy, O Lord,
and your kindness*ᵃ* from of old,
for you rescue those who wait for you
and save them from the hand of their
enemies.
⁹ And I sent up my prayer from the earth,
and begged for rescue from death.
¹⁰ I cried out, "Lord, you are my Father;*ᵇ*
do not forsake me in the days of trouble,
when there is no help against the proud.
¹¹ I will praise your name continually,
and will sing hymns of thanksgiving."
My prayer was heard,
¹² for you saved me from destruction
and rescued me in time of trouble.
For this reason I thank you and praise you,
and I bless the name of the Lord.

———————

Heb adds:
Give thanks to the Lᴏʀᴅ, for he is good,
for his steadfast love endures forever;

Give thanks to the God of praises,
for his steadfast love endures forever;

Give thanks to the guardian of Israel,
for his steadfast love endures forever;

Give thanks to him who formed all things,
for his steadfast love endures forever;

Give thanks to the redeemer of Israel,
for his steadfast love endures forever;

Give thanks to him who gathers the dispersed of
Israel,
for his steadfast love endures forever;

Give thanks to him who rebuilt his city and his
sanctuary,
for his steadfast love endures forever;

Give thanks to him who makes a horn to sprout for
the house of David,
for his steadfast love endures forever;

Give thanks to him who has chosen the sons of Zadok
to be priests,
for his steadfast love endures forever;

Give thanks to the shield of Abraham,
for his steadfast love endures forever;

Give thanks to the rock of Isaac,
for his steadfast love endures forever;

Give thanks to the mighty one of Jacob,
for his steadfast love endures forever;

Give thanks to him who has chosen Zion,
for his steadfast love endures forever;

Give thanks to the King of the kings of kings,
for his steadfast love endures forever;

He has raised up a horn for his people,
praise for all his loyal ones.

For the children of Israel, the people close to him.
Praise the Lᴏʀᴅ!

———————

Autobiographical Poem on Wisdom

¹³ While I was still young, before I went on my
travels,
I sought wisdom openly in my prayer.
¹⁴ Before the temple I asked for her,
and I will search for her until the end.
¹⁵ From the first blossom to the ripening
grape
my heart delighted in her;
my foot walked on the straight path;
from my youth I followed her steps.
¹⁶ I inclined my ear a little and received her,
and I found for myself much instruction.
¹⁷ I made progress in her;
to him who gives wisdom I will give
glory.
¹⁸ For I resolved to live according to wisdom,*ᶜ*
and I was zealous for the good,
and I shall never be disappointed.
¹⁹ My soul grappled with wisdom,*ᶜ*
and in my conduct I was strict;*ᵈ*

I spread out my hands to the heavens,
and lamented my ignorance of her.
²⁰ I directed my soul to her,
and in purity I found her.

With her I gained understanding from the
first;
therefore I will never be forsaken.
²¹ My heart was stirred to seek her;
therefore I have gained a prize
possession.
²² The Lord gave me my tongue as a reward,
and I will praise him with it.
²³ Draw near to me, you who are uneducated,
and lodge in the house of instruction.

———————

a Other ancient authorities read *work* *b* Heb: Gk *the Father of my lord* *c* Gk *her* *d* Meaning of Gk uncertain

24 Why do you say you are lacking in these
    things,[a]
    and why do you endure such great thirst?
25 I opened my mouth and said,
    Acquire wisdom[b] for yourselves without
    money.

26 Put your neck under her[c] yoke,
    and let your souls receive instruction;
    it is to be found close by.

27 See with your own eyes that I have labored
    but little

and found for myself much
    serenity.
28 Hear but a little of my instruction,
    and through me you will acquire silver
    and gold.[d]

29 May your soul rejoice in God's[e] mercy,
    and may you never be ashamed to praise
    him.
30 Do your work in good time,
    and in his own time God[f] will give you
    your reward.

a Cn Compare Heb Syr: Meaning of Gk uncertain b Heb: Gk lacks *wisdom* c Heb: other ancient authorities read *the* d Syr Compare
Heb: Gk *Get instruction with a large sum of silver, and you will gain by it much gold.* e Gk *his* f Gk *he*

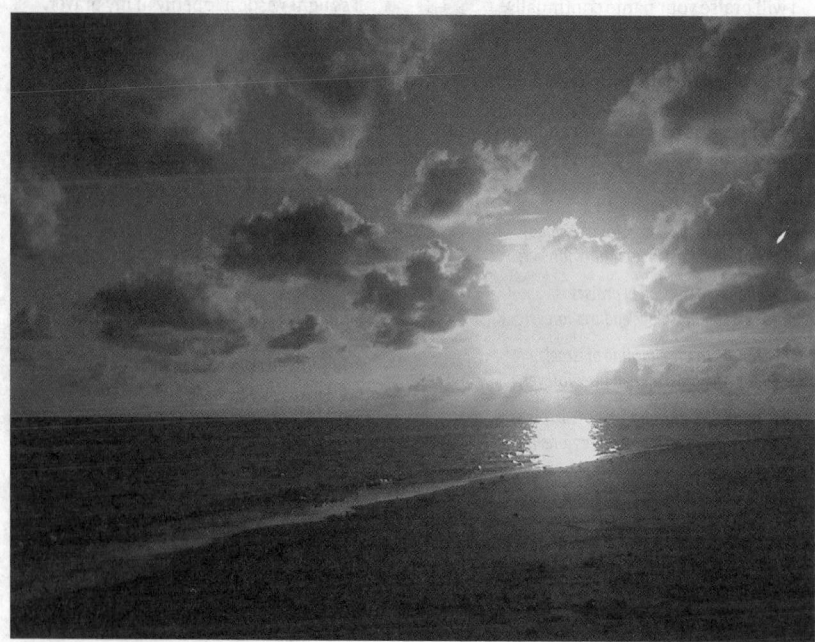

God Is Everywhere—© Charlotte Katheder, 16

ISAIAH

The Cure

Cancer. It can grow unchecked, becoming deadly before you're even aware it's there. It takes over vital organs, preventing their proper function and shutting them down. The strange thing about cancer is that it is our own cells running wild inside us. Nearly one and a half million Americans will be diagnosed with it this year . . . and more than half a million will die of it.

What would it be like if someone discovered the cure? Hospitals would be crammed full of people wanting it. It would be the news of the century.

Now consider this. There's a disease plaguing humanity that's something like cancer. It comes from our own desires and appetites for "more"— more money, more popularity, more sex, more food—running wild inside of us. It is much worse than cancer, because it spreads to other people and structures. It's a disease called *sin,* and it wounds us. Untreated, it rots us and the societies we live in from the inside out and from the outside in! It can leave us and those around us spiritually beaten. But the book of Isaiah reads like a startling breaking-news special report: *There is a cure!* Isaiah 1.18 promises that some way, somehow, God will heal his people from the sickness of sin!

Isaiah prophesied during a time of serious political turmoil. Judah's northern neighbor, Israel, was being ransacked by Assyria, and God's people were on the brink of total destruction. God used Isaiah to challenge his people about their patterns of self-centeredness, self-reliance, and idolatry and to warn them about God's coming judgment. Yet, woven within these prophecies of gloom and doom, God also leaves hints and clues about the cure he speaks of in chapter 1. Through Isaiah, God promises a Messiah and describes him (53.5–6).

Read Isaiah to learn about the One God would send to be the true Cure for all of us.

> **"By following a right conscience you not only do not incur sin, but are also immune from sin, whatever superiors may say to the contrary."**
> —St. Thomas Aquinas

WHO Isaiah, who was a prophet during the reigns of Uzziah through Hezekiah, and other writers

WHAT The book was written during a period of stress and turmoil for God's people. It is a call for faith, trust, and confidence in God.

WHEN The events in the book occurred between 740 and 539 B.C. Isaiah lived in the eighth century B.C.; the book of Isaiah was likely finished around 500 B.C.

WHERE The events took place in Jerusalem (chaps. 1–39, 56–66) and Babylon (chaps. 40–55)

PATH OF DISCIPLESHIP

God raised up prophets like Isaiah when the people were in turmoil. The prophets delivered two main points to the people: (1) you brought it on yourselves, and (2) you're looking in the wrong places to make things better.

Disciples can fall into the same traps. We can blame others or make excuses about why we don't always do the right and just thing. This breaks down our sense of responsibility, and we look for salvation in other places besides our relationship with God and the Church.

It's important to our spiritual health to do periodic checkups. Regularly review your actions and attitudes; make amends quickly when you do wrong; keep up a regular dialogue with Jesus in prayer.

1 The vision of Isaiah son of Amoz, which he saw concerning Judah and Jerusalem in the days of Uzziah, Jotham, Ahaz, and Hezekiah, kings of Judah.

The Wickedness of Judah

2 Hear, O heavens, and listen, O earth;
  for the LORD has spoken:
I reared children and brought them up,
  but they have rebelled against me.
3 The ox knows its owner,
  and the donkey its master's crib;
but Israel does not know,
  my people do not understand.

4 Ah, sinful nation,
  people laden with iniquity,
offspring who do evil,
  children who deal corruptly,
who have forsaken the LORD,
  who have despised the Holy One of Israel,
  who are utterly estranged!

5 Why do you seek further beatings?
  Why do you continue to rebel?
The whole head is sick,
  and the whole heart faint.
6 From the sole of the foot even to the head,
  there is no soundness in it,
but bruises and sores
  and bleeding wounds;
they have not been drained, or bound up,
  or softened with oil.

7 Your country lies desolate,
  your cities are burned with fire;
in your very presence
  aliens devour your land;
  it is desolate, as overthrown by
    foreigners.
8 And daughter Zion is left
  like a booth in a vineyard,
like a shelter in a cucumber field,
  like a besieged city.
9 If the LORD of hosts
  had not left us a few survivors,
we would have been like Sodom,
  and become like Gomorrah.

10 Hear the word of the LORD,
  you rulers of Sodom!
Listen to the teaching of our God,
  you people of Gomorrah!
11 What to me is the multitude of your
    sacrifices?
  says the LORD;
I have had enough of burnt offerings of
    rams

and the fat of fed beasts;
I do not delight in the blood of bulls,
  or of lambs, or of goats.

12 When you come to appear before me,[a]
  who asked this from your hand?
  Trample my courts no more;
13 bringing offerings is futile;
  incense is an abomination to me.
New moon and sabbath and calling of
    convocation—
  I cannot endure solemn assemblies with
    iniquity.
14 Your new moons and your appointed
    festivals
  my soul hates;
they have become a burden to me,
  I am weary of bearing them.
15 When you stretch out your hands,
  I will hide my eyes from you;
even though you make many prayers,
  I will not listen;
  your hands are full of blood.
16 Wash yourselves; make yourselves clean;
  remove the evil of your doings
  from before my eyes;
cease to do evil,
17 learn to do good;
seek justice,
  rescue the oppressed,
defend the orphan,
  plead for the widow.

18 Come now, let us argue it out,
  says the LORD:
though your sins are like scarlet,
  they shall be like snow;
though they are red like crimson,
  they shall become like wool.
19 If you are willing and obedient,
  you shall eat the good of the land;
20 but if you refuse and rebel,
  you shall be devoured by the sword;
  for the mouth of the LORD has spoken.

The Degenerate City

21 How the faithful city
  has become a whore!
  She that was full of justice,
righteousness lodged in her—
  but now murderers!
22 Your silver has become dross,
  your wine is mixed with water.
23 Your princes are rebels
  and companions of thieves.
Everyone loves a bribe
  and runs after gifts.
They do not defend the orphan,

a Or *see my face*

and the widow's cause does not come
before them.

24 Therefore says the Sovereign, the LORD of
hosts, the Mighty One of Israel:
Ah, I will pour out my wrath on my
enemies,
and avenge myself on my foes!
25 I will turn my hand against you;
I will smelt away your dross as with lye
and remove all your alloy.
26 And I will restore your judges as at the first,
and your counselors as at the beginning.
Afterward you shall be called the city of
righteousness,
the faithful city.

27 Zion shall be redeemed by justice,
and those in her who repent, by
righteousness.
28 But rebels and sinners shall be destroyed
together,
and those who forsake the LORD shall be
consumed.
29 For you shall be ashamed of the oaks
in which you delighted;
and you shall blush for the gardens
that you have chosen.
30 For you shall be like an oak
whose leaf withers,
and like a garden without water.
31 The strong shall become like tinder,
and their work[a] like a spark;
they and their work shall burn together,
with no one to quench them.

2 The Future House of God

The word that Isaiah son of Amoz saw concerning Judah and Jerusalem.

2 In days to come
the mountain of the LORD's house
shall be established as the highest of the
mountains,
and shall be raised above the hills;
all the nations shall stream to it.
3 Many peoples shall come and say,
"Come, let us go up to the mountain of the
LORD,
to the house of the God of Jacob;
that he may teach us his ways
and that we may walk in his paths."
For out of Zion shall go forth instruction,
and the word of the LORD from
Jerusalem.
4 He shall judge between the nations,
and shall arbitrate for many peoples;
they shall beat their swords into
plowshares,

a Or its makers

Pleasing God

Have you ever wondered what pleases God?

For some people, it's all about living a certain kind of life free from the influence of the "world." For others it's all about knowing the "truth" and making sure that others know it as well. For some people, it's about being actively involved in the parish. For others, it's about giving off the right image of what it means to be a "good Catholic."

You know what? We can do all the right "religious" stuff and still be _far_ from the way God wants us to live.

In **Isaiah 1.11,** God makes this astounding statement: "What to me is the multitude of your sacrifices? says the LORD; I have had enough . . ." And later he says, "cease to do evil, learn to do good" (1.16–17). Translation: God is more concerned about how we are actually living than how "religious" we appear. So the question is, what is the "good" he wants us to do?

Read all of **Isaiah 1.11–17.** The more we are involved in caring about injustice, defending the defenseless, and helping the overlooked, the more we are in line with living in the way of God.

Take some time to walk around in a public area, like downtown, a city park, a mall, or a town square. Take some photographs of people living in the way of God—the way of hope, generosity, love, forgiveness, redemption, peace, and justice. (This may be hard to find. That should tell you something! But keep looking . . .) Post your pictures at **Learner.CalltoDiscipleship.com** for others to reflect on and enjoy.

and their spears into pruning hooks;
nation shall not lift up sword against
nation,
neither shall they learn war any more.

Judgment Pronounced on Arrogance

5 O house of Jacob,
come, let us walk
in the light of the LORD!

and there is no end to their chariots.
⁸ Their land is filled with idols;
    they bow down to the work of their hands,
    to what their own fingers have made.
⁹ And so people are humbled,
    and everyone is brought low—
    do not forgive them!
¹⁰ Enter into the rock,
    and hide in the dust
from the terror of the LORD,
    and from the glory of his majesty.
¹¹ The haughty eyes of people shall be
    brought low,
    and the pride of everyone shall be
    humbled;
and the LORD alone will be exalted on that
    day.
¹² For the LORD of hosts has a day
    against all that is proud and lofty,
    against all that is lifted up and high;^c
¹³ against all the cedars of Lebanon,
    lofty and lifted up;
    and against all the oaks of Bashan;
¹⁴ against all the high mountains,
    and against all the lofty hills;
¹⁵ against every high tower,
    and against every fortified wall;
¹⁶ against all the ships of Tarshish,
    and against all the beautiful craft.^d
¹⁷ The haughtiness of people shall be
    humbled,
    and the pride of everyone shall be
    brought low;
    and the LORD alone will be exalted on
    that day.
¹⁸ The idols shall utterly pass away.
¹⁹ Enter the caves of the rocks
    and the holes of the ground,
from the terror of the LORD,
    and from the glory of his majesty,
    when he rises to terrify the earth.
²⁰ On that day people will throw away
    to the moles and to the bats
their idols of silver and their idols of gold,
    which they made for themselves to
    worship,
²¹ to enter the caverns of the rocks
    and the clefts in the crags,
from the terror of the LORD,
    and from the glory of his majesty,
    when he rises to terrify the earth.
²² Turn away from mortals,
    who have only breath in their nostrils,
    for of what account are they?

⁶ For you have forsaken the ways of^a your
    people,
    O house of Jacob.
Indeed they are full of diviners^b from the
    east
    and of soothsayers like the Philistines,
    and they clasp hands with foreigners.
⁷ Their land is filled with silver and gold,
    and there is no end to their treasures;
    their land is filled with horses,

3 For now the Sovereign, the LORD of hosts,
    is taking away from Jerusalem and from
    Judah

---

a Heb lacks the ways of b Cn: Heb lacks of diviners c Cn Compare Gk: Heb low d Compare Gk: Meaning of Heb uncertain

support and staff—
    all support of bread,
    and all support of water—
2 warrior and soldier,
    judge and prophet,
    diviner and elder,
3 captain of fifty
    and dignitary,
    counselor and skillful magician
    and expert enchanter.
4 And I will make boys their princes,
    and babes shall rule over them.
5 The people will be oppressed,
    everyone by another
    and everyone by a neighbor;
    the youth will be insolent to the elder,
    and the base to the honorable.

6 Someone will even seize a relative,
    a member of the clan, saying,
"You have a cloak;
    you shall be our leader,
and this heap of ruins
    shall be under your rule."
7 But the other will cry out on that day, saying,
"I will not be a healer;
    in my house there is neither bread nor
        cloak;
you shall not make me
    leader of the people."
8 For Jerusalem has stumbled
    and Judah has fallen,
because their speech and their deeds are
        against the LORD,
    defying his glorious presence.

9 The look on their faces bears witness
        against them;
    they proclaim their sin like Sodom,
    they do not hide it.
Woe to them!
    For they have brought evil on themselves.
10 Tell the innocent how fortunate they are,
    for they shall eat the fruit of their labors.
11 Woe to the guilty! How unfortunate they are,
    for what their hands have done shall be
        done to them.
12 My people—children are their oppressors,
    and women rule over them.
O my people, your leaders mislead you,
    and confuse the course of your paths.

13 The LORD rises to argue his case;
    he stands to judge the peoples.
14 The LORD enters into judgment
    with the elders and princes of his people:
It is you who have devoured the vineyard;
    the spoil of the poor is in your houses.
15 What do you mean by crushing my people,

by grinding the face of the poor? says the
    Lord GOD of hosts.

16 The LORD said:
Because the daughters of Zion are haughty
    and walk with outstretched necks,
    glancing wantonly with their eyes,
mincing along as they go,
    tinkling with their feet;
17 the Lord will afflict with scabs
    the heads of the daughters of Zion,
    and the LORD will lay bare their secret
        parts.

18 In that day the Lord will take away the
finery of the anklets, the headbands, and the
crescents; 19 the pendants, the bracelets, and
the scarfs; 20 the headdresses, the armlets, the
sashes, the perfume boxes, and the amulets;
21 the signet rings and nose rings; 22 the festal
robes, the mantles, the cloaks, and the hand-
bags; 23 the garments of gauze, the linen garments, the turbans, and the veils.
24 Instead of perfume there will be a stench;
    and instead of a sash, a rope;
and instead of well-set hair, baldness;
    and instead of a rich robe, a binding of
        sackcloth;
    instead of beauty, shame. ^a
25 Your men shall fall by the sword
    and your warriors in battle.
26 And her gates shall lament and mourn;
    ravaged, she shall sit upon the ground.

4 Seven women shall take hold of one man
in that day, saying,
"We will eat our own bread and wear our
        own clothes;
just let us be called by your name;
    take away our disgrace."

The Future Glory of the Survivors in Zion

2 On that day the branch of the LORD shall be
beautiful and glorious, and the fruit of the land
shall be the pride and glory of the survivors of
Israel. 3 Whoever is left in Zion and remains in
Jerusalem will be called holy, everyone who has
been recorded for life in Jerusalem, 4 once the
Lord has washed away the filth of the daughters
of Zion and cleansed the bloodstains of Jerusalem from its midst by a spirit of judgment and
by a spirit of burning. 5 Then the LORD will create over the whole site of Mount Zion and over
its places of assembly a cloud by day and smoke
and the shining of a flaming fire by night. Indeed over all the glory there will be a canopy.
6 It will serve as a pavilion, a shade by day from
the heat, and a refuge and a shelter from the
storm and rain.

a Q Ms: MT lacks *shame*

In His Presence

Imagine having dinner with a movie star or the president. Would you be embarrassed or speechless? On a smaller scale, imagine a first date with someone you really like. How would you feel? Talk? Sit?

How would those situations compare to meeting Jesus? Would you feel the same nervousness?

People can naturally expect that God is more loving and personal than some celebrity, but think about what it might mean to stand in the presence of a perfect being. Read the experience of someone who did in **Isaiah 6.1–8**. Being close to God made Isaiah painfully aware of the fact that he didn't belong there because of his sinfulness, a feeling he captured with the description of himself in verse 5. There's nothing to suggest he believed that God didn't love him. He simply realized how messed up the life of a typical human being was in the face of the divine being. For all of his love and goodness, God is still fundamentally challenging. He always makes us aware of what we are meant to be and what we could become.

Take some time to write a journal entry about what it would be like to step into the presence of Jesus. Compare your expectations to the experience of Isaiah and evaluate why he reacted the way he did. Share your responses at **Learner.CalltoDiscipleship.com**.

5 The Song of the Unfruitful Vineyard

Let me sing for my beloved
my love-song concerning his vineyard:
My beloved had a vineyard
on a very fertile hill.
2 He dug it and cleared it of stones,
and planted it with choice vines;
he built a watchtower in the midst of it,
and hewed out a wine vat in it;
he expected it to yield grapes,
but it yielded wild grapes.

3 And now, inhabitants of Jerusalem
and people of Judah,
judge between me

and my vineyard.
4 What more was there to do for my vineyard
that I have not done in it?
When I expected it to yield grapes,
why did it yield wild grapes?

5 And now I will tell you
what I will do to my vineyard.
I will remove its hedge,
and it shall be devoured;
I will break down its wall,
and it shall be trampled down.
6 I will make it a waste;
it shall not be pruned or hoed,
and it shall be overgrown with briers and thorns;
I will also command the clouds
that they rain no rain upon it.

7 For the vineyard of the LORD of hosts
is the house of Israel,
and the people of Judah
are his pleasant planting;
he expected justice,
but saw bloodshed;
righteousness,
but heard a cry!

Social Injustice Denounced

8 Ah, you who join house to house,
who add field to field,
until there is room for no one but you,
and you are left to live alone
in the midst of the land!
9 The LORD of hosts has sworn in my hearing:
Surely many houses shall be desolate,
large and beautiful houses, without inhabitant.
10 For ten acres of vineyard shall yield but one bath,
and a homer of seed shall yield a mere ephah. *a*

11 Ah, you who rise early in the morning
in pursuit of strong drink,
who linger in the evening
to be inflamed by wine,
12 whose feasts consist of lyre and harp,
tambourine and flute and wine,
but who do not regard the deeds of the LORD,
or see the work of his hands!
13 Therefore my people go into exile without knowledge;
their nobles are dying of hunger,
and their multitude is parched with thirst.
14 Therefore Sheol has enlarged its appetite
and opened its mouth beyond measure;

---

a The Heb *bath*, *homer*, and *ephah* are measures of quantity

the nobility of Jerusalem*a* and her
  multitude go down,
  her throng and all who exult in her.
15 People are bowed down, everyone is
    brought low,
  and the eyes of the haughty are humbled.
16 But the LORD of hosts is exalted by justice,
  and the Holy God shows himself holy by
    righteousness.
17 Then the lambs shall graze as in their pasture,
  fatlings and kids*b* shall feed among the
    ruins.

18 Ah, you who drag iniquity along with cords
    of falsehood,
  who drag sin along as with cart ropes,
19 who say, "Let him make haste,
    let him speed his work
    that we may see it;
  let the plan of the Holy One of Israel hasten
    to fulfillment,
    that we may know it!"
20 Ah, you who call evil good
    and good evil,
  who put darkness for light
    and light for darkness,
  who put bitter for sweet
    and sweet for bitter!
21 Ah, you who are wise in your own eyes,
    and shrewd in your own sight!
22 Ah, you who are heroes in drinking wine
    and valiant at mixing drink,
23 who acquit the guilty for a bribe,
    and deprive the innocent of their rights!

Foreign Invasion Predicted

24 Therefore, as the tongue of fire devours the
    stubble,
  and as dry grass sinks down in the flame,
  so their root will become rotten,
    and their blossom go up like dust;
  for they have rejected the instruction of the
    LORD of hosts,
  and have despised the word of the Holy
    One of Israel.

25 Therefore the anger of the LORD was
    kindled against his people,
  and he stretched out his hand against
    them and struck them;
  the mountains quaked,
  and their corpses were like refuse
    in the streets.
  For all this his anger has not turned away,
    and his hand is stretched out still.

26 He will raise a signal for a nation far away,
  and whistle for a people at the ends of
    the earth;

Here they come, swiftly, speedily!
27 None of them is weary, none stumbles,
    none slumbers or sleeps,
  not a loincloth is loose,
    not a sandal-thong broken;
28 their arrows are sharp,
    all their bows bent,
  their horses' hoofs seem like flint,
    and their wheels like the whirlwind.
29 Their roaring is like a lion,
    like young lions they roar;
  they growl and seize their prey,
    they carry it off, and no one can rescue.
30 They will roar over it on that day,
    like the roaring of the sea.
  And if one look to the land—
    only darkness and distress;
  and the light grows dark with clouds.

6 A Vision of God in the Temple

In the year that King Uzziah died, I saw the
Lord sitting on a throne, high and lofty; and
the hem of his robe filled the temple. 2Seraphs
were in attendance above him; each had six
wings: with two they covered their faces, and
with two they covered their feet, and with two
they flew. 3And one called to another and said:
  "Holy, holy, holy is the LORD of hosts;
  the whole earth is full of his glory."
4The pivots*c* on the thresholds shook at the
voices of those who called, and the house filled
with smoke. 5And I said: "Woe is me! I am lost,
for I am a man of unclean lips, and I live among
a people of unclean lips; yet my eyes have seen
the King, the LORD of hosts!"

6 Then one of the seraphs flew to me, holding a live coal that had been taken from the altar with a pair of tongs. 7The seraph*d* touched
my mouth with it and said: "Now that this has
touched your lips, your guilt has departed and
your sin is blotted out." 8Then I heard the voice
of the Lord saying, "Whom shall I send, and
who will go for us?" And I said, "Here am I; send
me!" 9And he said, "Go and say to this people:
  'Keep listening, but do not comprehend;
  keep looking, but do not understand.'
10 Make the mind of this people dull,
    and stop their ears,
    and shut their eyes,
  so that they may not look with their eyes,
    and listen with their ears,
  and comprehend with their minds,
    and turn and be healed."
11 Then I said, "How long, O Lord?" And he
    said:
  "Until cities lie waste
    without inhabitant,

---

a Heb *her nobility* *b* Cn Compare Gk: Heb *aliens* *c* Meaning of Heb uncertain *d* Heb *He*

and houses without people,
and the land is utterly desolate;
12 until the LORD sends everyone far away,
and vast is the emptiness in the midst of
the land.
13 Even if a tenth part remain in it,
it will be burned again,
like a terebinth or an oak
whose stump remains standing
when it is felled."[a]
The holy seed is its stump.

7 Isaiah Reassures King Ahaz

In the days of Ahaz son of Jotham son of Uzziah, king of Judah, King Rezin of Aram and King Pekah son of Remaliah of Israel went up to attack Jerusalem, but could not mount an attack against it. 2When the house of David heard that Aram had allied itself with Ephraim, the heart of Ahaz[b] and the heart of his people shook as the trees of the forest shake before the wind.

3 Then the LORD said to Isaiah, Go out to meet Ahaz, you and your son Shear-jashub,[c] at the end of the conduit of the upper pool on the highway to the Fuller's Field, 4and say to him, Take heed, be quiet, do not fear, and do not let your heart be faint because of these two smoldering stumps of firebrands, because of the fierce anger of Rezin and Aram and the son of Remaliah. 5Because Aram—with Ephraim and the son of Remaliah—has plotted evil against you, saying, 6Let us go up against Judah and cut off Jerusalem[d] and conquer it for ourselves and make the son of Tabeel king in it; 7therefore thus says the Lord GOD:

It shall not stand,
and it shall not come to pass.
8 For the head of Aram is Damascus,
and the head of Damascus is Rezin.
(Within sixty-five years Ephraim will be shattered, no longer a people.)
9 The head of Ephraim is Samaria,
and the head of Samaria is the son of
Remaliah.
If you do not stand firm in faith,
you shall not stand at all.

Isaiah Gives Ahaz the Sign of Immanuel

10 Again the LORD spoke to Ahaz, saying, 11Ask a sign of the LORD your God; let it be deep as Sheol or high as heaven. 12But Ahaz said, I will not ask, and I will not put the LORD to the test. 13Then Isaiah[e] said: "Hear then, O house of David! Is it too little for you to weary mortals, that you weary my God also? 14Therefore the Lord himself will give you a sign. Look, the young woman[f] is with child and shall bear a son, and shall name him Immanuel.[g] 15He shall eat curds and honey by the time he knows how to refuse the evil and choose the good. 16For before the child knows how to refuse the evil and choose the good, the land before whose two kings you are in dread will be deserted. 17The LORD will bring on you and on your people and on your ancestral house such days as have not come since the day that Ephraim departed from Judah—the king of Assyria."

18 On that day the LORD will whistle for the fly that is at the sources of the streams of Egypt, and for the bee that is in the land of Assyria. 19And they will all come and settle in the steep ravines, and in the clefts of the rocks, and on all the thornbushes, and on all the pastures.

20 On that day the Lord will shave with a razor hired beyond the River—with the king of Assyria—the head and the hair of the feet, and it will take off the beard as well.

21 On that day one will keep alive a young cow and two sheep, 22and will eat curds because of the abundance of milk that they give; for everyone that is left in the land shall eat curds and honey.

23 On that day every place where there used to be a thousand vines, worth a thousand shekels of silver, will become briers and thorns. 24With bow and arrows one will go there, for all the land will be briers and thorns; 25and as for all the hills that used to be hoed with a hoe, you will not go there for fear of briers and thorns; but they will become a place where cattle are let loose and where sheep tread.

8 Isaiah's Son a Sign of the Assyrian Invasion

Then the LORD said to me, Take a large tablet and write on it in common characters, "Belonging to Maher-shalal-hash-baz,"[h] 2and have it attested[i] for me by reliable witnesses, the priest Uriah and Zechariah son of Jeberechiah. 3And I went to the prophetess, and she conceived and bore a son. Then the LORD said to me, Name him Maher-shalal-hash-baz; 4for before the child knows how to call "My father" or "My mother," the wealth of Damascus and the spoil of Samaria will be carried away by the king of Assyria.

5 The LORD spoke to me again: 6Because this people has refused the waters of Shiloah that flow gently, and melt in fear before[j] Rezin and the son of Remaliah; 7therefore, the Lord is bringing up against it the mighty flood waters of the River, the king of Assyria and all

---

a Meaning of Heb uncertain b Heb his heart c That is A remnant shall return d Heb cut it off e Heb he f Gk the virgin g That is God is with us h That is The spoil speeds, the prey hastens i Q Ms Gk Syr: MT and I caused to be attested j Cn: Meaning of Heb uncertain his glory; it will rise above all its channels and overflow all its banks; ⁸it will sweep on into Judah as a flood, and, pouring over, it will reach up to the neck; and its outspread wings will fill the breadth of your land, O Immanuel.

⁹ Band together, you peoples, and be
   dismayed;
  listen, all you far countries;
 gird yourselves and be dismayed;
   gird yourselves and be dismayed!
¹⁰ Take counsel together, but it shall be
   brought to naught;
  speak a word, but it will not stand,
   for God is with us.ᵃ

11 For the LORD spoke thus to me while his hand was strong upon me, and warned me not to walk in the way of this people, saying: ¹²Do not call conspiracy all that this people calls conspiracy, and do not fear what it fears, or be in dread. ¹³But the LORD of hosts, him you shall regard as holy; let him be your fear, and let him be your dread. ¹⁴He will become a sanctuary, a stone one strikes against; for both houses of Israel he will become a rock one stumbles over—a trap and a snare for the inhabitants of Jerusalem. ¹⁵And many among them shall stumble; they shall fall and be broken; they shall be snared and taken.

Disciples of Isaiah

16 Bind up the testimony, seal the teaching among my disciples. ¹⁷I will wait for the LORD, who is hiding his face from the house of Jacob, and I will hope in him. ¹⁸See, I and the children whom the LORD has given me are signs and portents in Israel from the LORD of hosts, who dwells on Mount Zion. ¹⁹Now if people say to you, "Consult the ghosts and the familiar spirits that chirp and mutter; should not a people consult their gods, the dead on behalf of the living, ²⁰for teaching and for instruction?" surely, those who speak like this will have no dawn! ²¹They will pass through the land,ᵇ greatly distressed and hungry; when they are hungry, they will be enraged and will curseᶜ their king and their gods. They will turn their faces upward, ²²or they will look to the earth, but will see only distress and darkness, the gloom of anguish; and they will be thrust into thick darkness.ᵈ

9ᵉ The Righteous Reign of the Coming King

But there will be no gloom for those who were in anguish. In the former time he brought into contempt the land of Zebulun and the land of Naphtali, but in the latter time he will make glorious the way of the sea, the land beyond the Jordan, Galilee of the nations.
²ᶠ The people who walked in darkness
   have seen a great light;
  those who lived in a land of deep darkness—
   on them light has shined.
³ You have multiplied the nation,
   you have increased its joy;

ᵃ Heb *immanuel* ᵇ Heb *it* ᶜ Or *curse by* ᵈ Meaning of Heb uncertain ᵉ Ch 8.23 in Heb ᶠ Ch 9.1 in Heb

they rejoice before you
as with joy at the harvest,
as people exult when dividing plunder.
⁴ For the yoke of their burden,
and the bar across their shoulders,
the rod of their oppressor,
you have broken as on the day of Midian.
⁵ For all the boots of the tramping warriors
and all the garments rolled in blood
shall be burned as fuel for the fire.
⁶ For a child has been born for us,
a son given to us;
authority rests upon his shoulders;
and he is named
Wonderful Counselor, Mighty God,
Everlasting Father, Prince of Peace.
⁷ His authority shall grow continually,
and there shall be endless peace
for the throne of David and his kingdom.
He will establish and uphold it
with justice and with righteousness
from this time onward and forevermore.
The zeal of the LORD of hosts will do this.

Judgment on Arrogance and Oppression

⁸ The Lord sent a word against Jacob,
and it fell on Israel;
⁹ and all the people knew it—
Ephraim and the inhabitants of
Samaria—
but in pride and arrogance of heart they
said:
¹⁰ "The bricks have fallen,
but we will build with dressed stones;
the sycamores have been cut down,
but we will put cedars in their place."
¹¹ So the LORD raised adversaries*a* against
them,
and stirred up their enemies,
¹² the Arameans on the east and the
Philistines on the west,
and they devoured Israel with open
mouth.
For all this his anger has not turned away;
his hand is stretched out still.
¹³ The people did not turn to him who struck
them,
or seek the LORD of hosts.
¹⁴ So the LORD cut off from Israel head and
tail,
palm branch and reed in one day—
¹⁵ elders and dignitaries are the head,
and prophets who teach lies are the tail;
¹⁶ for those who led this people led them
astray,
and those who were led by them were left
in confusion.

¹⁷ That is why the Lord did not have pity on*b*
their young people,
or compassion on their orphans and
widows;
for everyone was godless and an evildoer,
and every mouth spoke folly.
For all this his anger has not turned away;
his hand is stretched out still.
¹⁸ For wickedness burned like a fire,
consuming briers and thorns;
it kindled the thickets of the forest,
and they swirled upward in a column of
smoke.
¹⁹ Through the wrath of the LORD of hosts
the land was burned,
and the people became like fuel for the fire;
no one spared another.
²⁰ They gorged on the right, but still were
hungry,
and they devoured on the left, but were
not satisfied;
they devoured the flesh of their own
kindred;*c*
²¹ Manasseh devoured Ephraim, and Ephraim
Manasseh,
and together they were against Judah.
For all this his anger has not turned away;
his hand is stretched out still.

10 Ah, you who make iniquitous decrees,
who write oppressive statutes,
² to turn aside the needy from justice
and to rob the poor of my people of their
right,
that widows may be your spoil,
and that you may make the orphans your
prey!
³ What will you do on the day of punishment,
in the calamity that will come from far
away?
To whom will you flee for help,
and where will you leave your wealth,
⁴ so as not to crouch among the prisoners
or fall among the slain?
For all this his anger has not turned away;
his hand is stretched out still.

Arrogant Assyria Also Judged

⁵ Ah, Assyria, the rod of my anger—
the club in their hands is my fury!
⁶ Against a godless nation I send him,
and against the people of my wrath I
command him,
to take spoil and seize plunder,
and to tread them down like the mire of
the streets.
⁷ But this is not what he intends,

a Cn: Heb *the adversaries of Rezin* b Q Ms: MT *rejoice over* c Or *arm*

Messengers—© Lucy Johnson, 15

nor does he have this in mind;
　but it is in his heart to destroy,
　　and to cut off nations not a few.
⁸ For he says:
　"Are not my commanders all kings?
⁹ Is not Calno like Carchemish?
　　Is not Hamath like Arpad?
　　Is not Samaria like Damascus?
¹⁰ As my hand has reached to the kingdoms of
　　the idols
　　whose images were greater than those of
　　　Jerusalem and Samaria,
¹¹ shall I not do to Jerusalem and her idols
　　what I have done to Samaria and her
　　　images?"

12　When the Lord has finished all his work
on Mount Zion and on Jerusalem, he*ᵃ* will punish the arrogant boasting of the king of Assyria
and his haughty pride. ¹³For he says:
　"By the strength of my hand I have done it,
　　and by my wisdom, for I have
　　　understanding;
　I have removed the boundaries of peoples,
　　and have plundered their treasures;
　　like a bull I have brought down those
　　　who sat on thrones.
¹⁴ My hand has found, like a nest,
　　the wealth of the peoples;
　and as one gathers eggs that have been
　　forsaken,
　　so I have gathered all the earth;

and there was none that moved a wing,
　or opened its mouth, or chirped."

¹⁵ Shall the ax vaunt itself over the one who
　　wields it,
　　or the saw magnify itself against the one
　　　who handles it?
As if a rod should raise the one who lifts it up,
　　or as if a staff should lift the one who is
　　　not wood!
¹⁶ Therefore the Sovereign, the Lᴏʀᴅ of hosts,
　　will send wasting sickness among his
　　　stout warriors,
　and under his glory a burning will be
　　kindled,
　　like the burning of fire.
¹⁷ The light of Israel will become a fire,
　　and his Holy One a flame;
　and it will burn and devour
　　his thorns and briers in one day.
¹⁸ The glory of his forest and his fruitful land
　　the Lᴏʀᴅ will destroy, both soul and body,
　　and it will be as when an invalid wastes
　　　away.
¹⁹ The remnant of the trees of his forest will
　　be so few
　　that a child can write them down.

The Repentant Remnant of Israel

20　On that day the remnant of Israel and the
survivors of the house of Jacob will no more
lean on the one who struck them, but will lean

a Heb *I*

on the LORD, the Holy One of Israel, in truth. [21] A remnant will return, the remnant of Jacob, to the mighty God. [22] For though your people Israel were like the sand of the sea, only a remnant of them will return. Destruction is decreed, overflowing with righteousness. [23] For the Lord GOD of hosts will make a full end, as decreed, in all the earth. [a]

24 Therefore thus says the Lord GOD of hosts: O my people, who live in Zion, do not be afraid of the Assyrians when they beat you with a rod and lift up their staff against you as the Egyptians did. [25] For in a very little while my indignation will come to an end, and my anger will be directed to their destruction. [26] The LORD of hosts will wield a whip against them, as when he struck Midian at the rock of Oreb; his staff will be over the sea, and he will lift it as he did in Egypt. [27] On that day his burden will be removed from your shoulder, and his yoke will be destroyed from your neck.

He has gone up from Rimmon, [b]
[28]　he has come to Aiath;
he has passed through Migron,
　at Michmash he stores his baggage;
[29] they have crossed over the pass,
　at Geba they lodge for the night;
Ramah trembles,
　Gibeah of Saul has fled.
[30] Cry aloud, O daughter Gallim!
　Listen, O Laishah!
　Answer her, O Anathoth!
[31] Madmenah is in flight,
　the inhabitants of Gebim flee for safety.
[32] This very day he will halt at Nob,
　he will shake his fist
　at the mount of daughter Zion,
　the hill of Jerusalem.
[33] Look, the Sovereign, the LORD of hosts,
　will lop the boughs with terrifying power;
　the tallest trees will be cut down,
　and the lofty will be brought low.
[34] He will hack down the thickets of the forest
　　with an ax,
　and Lebanon with its majestic trees [c] will
　　fall.

11 The Peaceful Kingdom

A shoot shall come out from the stump of
　Jesse,
　and a branch shall grow out of his roots.
[2]　The spirit of the LORD shall rest on him,
　the spirit of wisdom and understanding,
　the spirit of counsel and might,
the spirit of knowledge and the fear of
　the LORD.
[3]　His delight shall be in the fear of the LORD.

He shall not judge by what his eyes see,
　or decide by what his ears hear;
[4]　but with righteousness he shall judge the
　　poor,
　and decide with equity for the meek of
　　the earth;
he shall strike the earth with the rod of his
　mouth,
　and with the breath of his lips he shall
　　kill the wicked.
[5]　Righteousness shall be the belt around his
　　waist,
　and faithfulness the belt around his
　　loins.

[6]　The wolf shall live with the lamb,
　the leopard shall lie down with the kid,
the calf and the lion and the fatling together,
　and a little child shall lead them.
[7]　The cow and the bear shall graze,
　their young shall lie down together;
　and the lion shall eat straw like the ox.
[8]　The nursing child shall play over the hole of
　　the asp,
　and the weaned child shall put its hand
　　on the adder's den.
[9]　They will not hurt or destroy
　on all my holy mountain;
for the earth will be full of the knowledge
　　of the LORD
　as the waters cover the sea.

Return of the Remnant of Israel and Judah

10 On that day the root of Jesse shall stand as a signal to the peoples; the nations shall inquire of him, and his dwelling shall be glorious.

11 On that day the Lord will extend his hand yet a second time to recover the remnant that is left of his people, from Assyria, from Egypt, from Pathros, from Ethiopia, [d] from Elam, from Shinar, from Hamath, and from the coastlands of the sea.
[12] He will raise a signal for the nations,
　and will assemble the outcasts of Israel,
　and gather the dispersed of Judah
　from the four corners of the earth.
[13] The jealousy of Ephraim shall depart,
　the hostility of Judah shall be cut off;
Ephraim shall not be jealous of Judah,
　and Judah shall not be hostile towards
　　Ephraim.
[14] But they shall swoop down on the backs of
　　the Philistines in the west,

---

a Or *land* *b* Cn: Heb *and his yoke from your neck, and a yoke will be destroyed because of fatness* *c* Cn Compare Gk Vg: Heb *with a majestic one*
d Or *Nubia*; Heb *Cush*

together they shall plunder the people of
the east.
They shall put forth their hand against
Edom and Moab,
and the Ammonites shall obey them.
15 And the LORD will utterly destroy
the tongue of the sea of Egypt;
and will wave his hand over the River
with his scorching wind;
and will split it into seven channels,
and make a way to cross on foot;
16 so there shall be a highway from Assyria
for the remnant that is left of his people,
as there was for Israel
when they came up from the land of Egypt.

12 Thanksgiving and Praise

You will say in that day:
I will give thanks to you, O LORD,
for though you were angry with me,
your anger turned away,
and you comforted me.

2 Surely God is my salvation;
I will trust, and will not be afraid,
for the LORD GOD[a] is my strength and my
might;
he has become my salvation.

3 With joy you will draw water from the
wells of salvation. 4And you will say in that day:
Give thanks to the LORD,
call on his name;
make known his deeds among the nations;
proclaim that his name is exalted.

5 Sing praises to the LORD, for he has done
gloriously;
let this be known[b] in all the earth.
6 Shout aloud and sing for joy, O royal[c] Zion,
for great in your midst is the Holy One of
Israel.

13 Proclamation against Babylon

The oracle concerning Babylon that Isaiah son
of Amoz saw.

2 On a bare hill raise a signal,
cry aloud to them;
wave the hand for them to enter
the gates of the nobles.
3 I myself have commanded my consecrated
ones,
have summoned my warriors, my
proudly exulting ones,
to execute my anger.

4 Listen, a tumult on the mountains
as of a great multitude!
Listen, an uproar of kingdoms,
of nations gathering together!
The LORD of hosts is mustering
an army for battle.
5 They come from a distant land,
from the end of the heavens,
the LORD and the weapons of his
indignation,
to destroy the whole earth.

6 Wail, for the day of the LORD is near;
it will come like destruction from the
Almighty![d]
7 Therefore all hands will be feeble,
and every human heart will melt,
8 and they will be dismayed.
Pangs and agony will seize them;
they will be in anguish like a woman in
labor.
They will look aghast at one another;
their faces will be aflame.
9 See, the day of the LORD comes,
cruel, with wrath and fierce anger,
to make the earth a desolation,
and to destroy its sinners from it.
10 For the stars of the heavens and their
constellations
will not give their light;
the sun will be dark at its rising,
and the moon will not shed its light.
11 I will punish the world for its evil,
and the wicked for their iniquity;
I will put an end to the pride of the arrogant,
and lay low the insolence of tyrants.
12 I will make mortals more rare than fine
gold,
and humans than the gold of Ophir.
13 Therefore I will make the heavens tremble,
and the earth will be shaken out of its
place,
at the wrath of the LORD of hosts
in the day of his fierce anger.
14 Like a hunted gazelle,
or like sheep with no one to gather them,
all will turn to their own people,
and all will flee to their own lands.
15 Whoever is found will be thrust through,
and whoever is caught will fall by the
sword.
16 Their infants will be dashed to pieces
before their eyes;
their houses will be plundered,
and their wives ravished.
17 See, I am stirring up the Medes against them,
who have no regard for silver
and do not delight in gold.
18 Their bows will slaughter the young men;
they will have no mercy on the fruit of
the womb;

a Heb for Yah, the LORD   b Or this is made known   c Or O inhabitant of   d Traditional rendering of Heb Shaddai

their eyes will not pity children.
¹⁹ And Babylon, the glory of kingdoms,
the splendor and pride of the Chaldeans,
will be like Sodom and Gomorrah
when God overthrew them.
²⁰ It will never be inhabited
or lived in for all generations;
Arabs will not pitch their tents there,
shepherds will not make their flocks lie
down there.
²¹ But wild animals will lie down there,
and its houses will be full of howling
creatures;
there ostriches will live,
and there goat-demons will dance.
²² Hyenas will cry in its towers,
and jackals in the pleasant palaces;
its time is close at hand,
and its days will not be prolonged.

14 Restoration of Judah

But the LORD will have compassion on Jacob and will again choose Israel, and will set them in their own land; and aliens will join them and attach themselves to the house of Jacob. ²And the nations will take them and bring them to their place, and the house of Israel will possess the nations^a as male and female slaves in the LORD's land; they will take captive those who were their captors, and rule over those who oppressed them.

Downfall of the King of Babylon

3 When the LORD has given you rest from your pain and turmoil and the hard service with which you were made to serve, ⁴you will take up this taunt against the king of Babylon:
How the oppressor has ceased!
How his insolence^b has ceased!
⁵ The LORD has broken the staff of the
wicked,
the scepter of rulers,
⁶ that struck down the peoples in wrath
with unceasing blows,
that ruled the nations in anger
with unrelenting persecution.
⁷ The whole earth is at rest and quiet;
they break forth into singing.
⁸ The cypresses exult over you,
the cedars of Lebanon, saying,
"Since you were laid low,
no one comes to cut us down."
⁹ Sheol beneath is stirred up
to meet you when you come;
it rouses the shades to greet you,
all who were leaders of the earth;
it raises from their thrones

a Heb *them* b Q Ms Compare Gk Syr Vg: Meaning of MT uncertain

TEXT MESSAGE

Until God fully sets up the peaceful, new Kingdom, you'll want to steer clear of the snakes mentioned in Isaiah 11.8. Some varieties of snakes (like the cobra) can grow up to six feet long—and spit venom into their victims' eyes.

Fact

This information has been scanned and is free of all known viruses. Please forward to all your friends.

all who were kings of the nations.
¹⁰ All of them will speak
and say to you:
"You too have become as weak as we!
You have become like us!"
¹¹ Your pomp is brought down to Sheol,
and the sound of your harps;
maggots are the bed beneath you,
and worms are your covering.

¹² How you are fallen from heaven,
O Day Star, son of Dawn!
How you are cut down to the ground,
you who laid the nations low!
¹³ You said in your heart,
"I will ascend to heaven;
I will raise my throne
above the stars of God;
I will sit on the mount of assembly

on the heights of Zaphon;[a]

14 I will ascend to the tops of the clouds,
  I will make myself like the Most High."

15 But you are brought down to Sheol,
  to the depths of the Pit.

16 Those who see you will stare at you,
  and ponder over you:
"Is this the man who made the earth tremble,
  who shook kingdoms,

17 who made the world like a desert
  and overthrew its cities,
  who would not let his prisoners go
      home?"

18 All the kings of the nations lie in glory,
  each in his own tomb;

19 but you are cast out, away from your grave,
  like loathsome carrion,[b]
clothed with the dead, those pierced by the
      sword,
  who go down to the stones of the Pit,
  like a corpse trampled underfoot.

20 You will not be joined with them in burial,
  because you have destroyed your land,
  you have killed your people.

May the descendants of evildoers
  nevermore be named!

21 Prepare slaughter for his sons
  because of the guilt of their father.[c]
Let them never rise to possess the earth
  or cover the face of the world with cities.

22 I will rise up against them, says the LORD
of hosts, and will cut off from Babylon name
and remnant, offspring and posterity, says the
LORD. 23And I will make it a possession of the
hedgehog, and pools of water, and I will sweep
it with the broom of destruction, says the LORD
of hosts.

An Oracle concerning Assyria

24 The LORD of hosts has sworn:
As I have designed,
  so shall it be;
and as I have planned,
  so shall it come to pass:

25 I will break the Assyrian in my land,
  and on my mountains trample him
      under foot;

his yoke shall be removed from them,
  and his burden from their shoulders.

26 This is the plan that is planned
  concerning the whole earth;
and this is the hand that is stretched out
  over all the nations.

27 For the LORD of hosts has planned,
  and who will annul it?
His hand is stretched out,
  and who will turn it back?

An Oracle concerning Philistia

28 In the year that King Ahaz died this oracle
came:

29 Do not rejoice, all you Philistines,
  that the rod that struck you is broken,
for from the root of the snake will come
      forth an adder,
  and its fruit will be a flying fiery serpent.

30 The firstborn of the poor will graze,
  and the needy lie down in safety;
but I will make your root die of famine,
  and your remnant I[d] will kill.

31 Wail, O gate; cry, O city;
  melt in fear, O Philistia, all of you!
For smoke comes out of the north,
  and there is no straggler in its ranks.

32 What will one answer the messengers of
      the nation?
"The LORD has founded Zion,
  and the needy among his people
  will find refuge in her."

15 An Oracle concerning Moab

An oracle concerning Moab.

Because Ar is laid waste in a night,
  Moab is undone;
because Kir is laid waste in a night,
  Moab is undone.

2 Dibon[e] has gone up to the temple,
  to the high places to weep;
over Nebo and over Medeba
  Moab wails.
On every head is baldness,
  every beard is shorn;

3 in the streets they bind on sackcloth;
  on the housetops and in the squares
  everyone wails and melts in tears.

4 Heshbon and Elealeh cry out,
  their voices are heard as far as Jahaz;
therefore the loins of Moab quiver;[f]
  his soul trembles.

5 My heart cries out for Moab;
  his fugitives flee to Zoar,
  to Eglath-shelishiyah.

---

a Or *assembly in the far north* *b* Cn Compare Gk: Heb *like a loathed branch* *c* Syr Compare Gk: Heb *fathers* *d* Q Ms Vg: MT *he* *e* Cn: Heb *the house and Dibon* *f* Cn Compare Gk Syr: Heb *the armed men of Moab cry aloud*

For at the ascent of Luhith
    they go up weeping;
on the road to Horonaim
    they raise a cry of destruction;
6 the waters of Nimrim
    are a desolation;
the grass is withered, the new growth fails,
    the verdure is no more.
7 Therefore the abundance they have gained
    and what they have laid up
they carry away
    over the Wadi of the Willows.
8 For a cry has gone
    around the land of Moab;
the wailing reaches to Eglaim,
    the wailing reaches to Beer-elim.
9 For the waters of Dibon*a* are full of blood;
    yet I will bring upon Dibon*a* even more—
a lion for those of Moab who escape,
    for the remnant of the land.

16 Send lambs
    to the ruler of the land,
from Sela, by way of the desert,
    to the mount of daughter Zion.
2 Like fluttering birds,
    like scattered nestlings,
so are the daughters of Moab
    at the fords of the Arnon.
3 "Give counsel,
    grant justice;
make your shade like night
    at the height of noon;
hide the outcasts,
    do not betray the fugitive;
4 let the outcasts of Moab
    settle among you;
be a refuge to them
    from the destroyer."

When the oppressor is no more,
    and destruction has ceased,
and marauders have vanished from the land,
5 then a throne shall be established in
            steadfast love
    in the tent of David,
    and on it shall sit in faithfulness
a ruler who seeks justice
    and is swift to do what is right.

6 We have heard of the pride of Moab
    —how proud he is!—
of his arrogance, his pride, and his
            insolence;
    his boasts are false.
7 Therefore let Moab wail,
    let everyone wail for Moab.
Mourn, utterly stricken,
    for the raisin cakes of Kir-hareseth.

8 For the fields of Heshbon languish,
    and the vines of Sibmah,
whose clusters once made drunk
    the lords of the nations,
reached to Jazer
    and strayed to the desert;
their shoots once spread abroad
    and crossed over the sea.
9 Therefore I weep with the weeping of Jazer
    for the vines of Sibmah;
I drench you with my tears,
    O Heshbon and Elealeh;
for the shout over your fruit harvest
    and your grain harvest has ceased.
10 Joy and gladness are taken away
    from the fruitful field;
and in the vineyards no songs are sung,
    no shouts are raised;
no treader treads out wine in the presses;
    the vintage-shout is hushed.*b*
11 Therefore my heart throbs like a harp for
            Moab,
    and my very soul for Kir-heres.

12 When Moab presents himself, when he
wearies himself upon the high place, when he
comes to his sanctuary to pray, he will not prevail.

13 This was the word that the LORD spoke
concerning Moab in the past. 14But now
the LORD says, In three years, like the years
of a hired worker, the glory of Moab will be
brought into contempt, in spite of all its great
multitude; and those who survive will be very
few and feeble.

17 An Oracle concerning Damascus
An oracle concerning Damascus.

See, Damascus will cease to be a city,
    and will become a heap of ruins.
2 Her towns will be deserted forever;*c*
    they will be places for flocks,
    which will lie down, and no one will
            make them afraid.
3 The fortress will disappear from Ephraim,
    and the kingdom from Damascus;
and the remnant of Aram will be
    like the glory of the children of Israel,
            says the LORD of hosts.

4 On that day
    the glory of Jacob will be brought low,
    and the fat of his flesh will grow lean.
5 And it shall be as when reapers gather
            standing grain
    and their arms harvest the ears,
and as when one gleans the ears of grain
    in the Valley of Rephaim.

a Q Ms Vg Compare Syr: MT *Dimon*   *b* Gk: Heb *I have hushed*   *c* Cn Compare Gk: Heb *the cities of Aroer are deserted*

Fence at the Beach—© Taylor-Quinn Yancey, 16

⁶ Gleanings will be left in it,
    as when an olive tree is beaten—
two or three berries
    in the top of the highest bough,
four or five
    on the branches of a fruit tree,
           says the LORD God of Israel.

7 On that day people will regard their Maker, and their eyes will look to the Holy One of Israel; ⁸they will not have regard for the altars, the work of their hands, and they will not look to what their own fingers have made, either the sacred poles*a* or the altars of incense.

9 On that day their strong cities will be like the deserted places of the Hivites and the Amorites,*b* which they deserted because of the children of Israel, and there will be desolation.

¹⁰ For you have forgotten the God of your
       salvation,
    and have not remembered the Rock of
       your refuge;
    therefore, though you plant pleasant plants
    and set out slips of an alien god,
¹¹ though you make them grow on the day
       that you plant them,
    and make them blossom in the morning
       that you sow;
yet the harvest will flee away
    in a day of grief and incurable pain.

¹² Ah, the thunder of many peoples,
    they thunder like the thundering of the
       sea!
Ah, the roar of nations,
    they roar like the roaring of mighty waters!
¹³ The nations roar like the roaring of many
       waters,

but he will rebuke them, and they will
       flee far away,
chased like chaff on the mountains before
       the wind
    and whirling dust before the storm.
¹⁴ At evening time, lo, terror!
    Before morning, they are no more.
This is the fate of those who despoil us,
    and the lot of those who plunder us.

18 An Oracle concerning Ethiopia

Ah, land of whirring wings
    beyond the rivers of Ethiopia,*c*
² sending ambassadors by the Nile
    in vessels of papyrus on the waters!
Go, you swift messengers,
    to a nation tall and smooth,
to a people feared near and far,
    a nation mighty and conquering,
    whose land the rivers divide.

³ All you inhabitants of the world,
    you who live on the earth,
when a signal is raised on the mountains,
       look!
    When a trumpet is blown, listen!
⁴ For thus the LORD said to me:
I will quietly look from my dwelling
    like clear heat in sunshine,
    like a cloud of dew in the heat of harvest.
⁵ For before the harvest, when the blossom is
       over
    and the flower becomes a ripening
       grape,
he will cut off the shoots with pruning
       hooks,
    and the spreading branches he will hew
       away.
⁶ They shall all be left
    to the birds of prey of the mountains
    and to the animals of the earth.
And the birds of prey will summer on them,
    and all the animals of the earth will
       winter on them.

7 At that time gifts will be brought to the LORD of hosts from*d* a people tall and smooth, from a people feared near and far, a nation mighty and conquering, whose land the rivers divide, to Mount Zion, the place of the name of the LORD of hosts.

19 An Oracle concerning Egypt

An oracle concerning Egypt.

See, the LORD is riding on a swift cloud
    and comes to Egypt;
the idols of Egypt will tremble at his
       presence,

---

a Heb *Asherim* *b* Cn Compare Gk: Heb *places of the wood and the highest bough* *c* Or *Nubia*; Heb *Cush* *d* Q Ms Gk Vg: MT *of*

and the heart of the Egyptians will melt
within them.
2 I will stir up Egyptians against Egyptians,
and they will fight, one against the other,
neighbor against neighbor,
city against city, kingdom against
kingdom;
3 the spirit of the Egyptians within them will
be emptied out,
and I will confound their plans;
they will consult the idols and the spirits of
the dead
and the ghosts and the familiar spirits;
4 I will deliver the Egyptians
into the hand of a hard master;
a fierce king will rule over them,
says the Sovereign, the LORD of hosts.

5 The waters of the Nile will be dried up,
and the river will be parched and dry;
6 its canals will become foul,
and the branches of Egypt's Nile will
diminish and dry up,
reeds and rushes will rot away.
7 There will be bare places by the Nile,
on the brink of the Nile;
and all that is sown by the Nile will dry up,
be driven away, and be no more.
8 Those who fish will mourn;
all who cast hooks in the Nile will
lament,
and those who spread nets on the water
will languish.
9 The workers in flax will be in despair,
and the carders and those at the loom
will grow pale.
10 Its weavers will be dismayed,
and all who work for wages will be
grieved.

11 The princes of Zoan are utterly foolish;
the wise counselors of Pharaoh give
stupid counsel.
How can you say to Pharaoh,
"I am one of the sages,
a descendant of ancient kings"?
12 Where now are your sages?
Let them tell you and make known
what the LORD of hosts has planned
against Egypt.
13 The princes of Zoan have become fools,
and the princes of Memphis are deluded;
those who are the cornerstones of its tribes
have led Egypt astray.
14 The LORD has poured into them[a]
a spirit of confusion;
and they have made Egypt stagger in all its
doings

as a drunkard staggers around in vomit.
15 Neither head nor tail, palm branch or reed,
will be able to do anything for Egypt.

16 On that day the Egyptians will be like
women, and tremble with fear before the hand
that the LORD of hosts raises against them.
17 And the land of Judah will become a terror
to the Egyptians; everyone to whom it is mentioned will fear because of the plan that the
LORD of hosts is planning against them.

Egypt, Assyria, and Israel Blessed

18 On that day there will be five cities in the
land of Egypt that speak the language of Canaan
and swear allegiance to the LORD of hosts. One
of these will be called the City of the Sun.

19 On that day there will be an altar to the
LORD in the center of the land of Egypt, and a
pillar to the LORD at its border. 20 It will be a
sign and a witness to the LORD of hosts in the
land of Egypt; when they cry to the LORD because of oppressors, he will send them a savior, and will defend and deliver them. 21 The
LORD will make himself known to the Egyptians; and the Egyptians will know the LORD
on that day, and will worship with sacrifice and
burnt offering, and they will make vows to the
LORD and perform them. 22 The LORD will strike
Egypt, striking and healing; they will return to
the LORD, and he will listen to their supplications and heal them.

23 On that day there will be a highway from
Egypt to Assyria, and the Assyrian will come
into Egypt, and the Egyptian into Assyria, and
the Egyptians will worship with the Assyrians.

24 On that day Israel will be the third with
Egypt and Assyria, a blessing in the midst of the
earth, 25 whom the LORD of hosts has blessed,
saying, "Blessed be Egypt my people, and Assyria
the work of my hands, and Israel my heritage."

20 Isaiah Dramatizes the Conquest of Egypt and Ethiopia

In the year that the commander-in-chief, who
was sent by King Sargon of Assyria, came to
Ashdod and fought against it and took it— 2 at
that time the LORD had spoken to Isaiah son
of Amoz, saying, "Go, and loose the sackcloth
from your loins and take your sandals off your
feet," and he had done so, walking naked and
barefoot. 3 Then the LORD said, "Just as my servant Isaiah has walked naked and barefoot for
three years as a sign and a portent against Egypt
and Ethiopia,[b] 4 so shall the king of Assyria lead
away the Egyptians as captives and the Ethiopians[c] as exiles, both the young and the old, naked and barefoot, with buttocks uncovered,

a Gk Compare Tg: Heb it b Or Nubia; Heb Cush c Or Nubians; Heb Cushites to the shame of Egypt. ⁵And they shall be dismayed and confounded because of Ethiopia^a their hope and of Egypt their boast. ⁶In that day the inhabitants of this coastland will say, 'See, this is what has happened to those in whom we hoped and to whom we fled for help and deliverance from the king of Assyria! And we, how shall we escape?' "

21 Oracles concerning Babylon, Edom, and Arabia

The oracle concerning the wilderness of the sea.

As whirlwinds in the Negeb sweep on,
   it comes from the desert,
   from a terrible land.
² A stern vision is told to me;
   the betrayer betrays,
   and the destroyer destroys.
Go up, O Elam,
   lay siege, O Media;
all the sighing she has caused
   I bring to an end.
³ Therefore my loins are filled with anguish;
   pangs have seized me,
   like the pangs of a woman in labor;
I am bowed down so that I cannot hear,
   I am dismayed so that I cannot see.
⁴ My mind reels, horror has appalled me;
   the twilight I longed for
   has been turned for me into trembling.
⁵ They prepare the table,
   they spread the rugs,
   they eat, they drink.
Rise up, commanders,
   oil the shield!
⁶ For thus the Lord said to me:
   "Go, post a lookout,
   let him announce what he sees.
⁷ When he sees riders, horsemen in pairs,
   riders on donkeys, riders on camels,
let him listen diligently,
   very diligently."
⁸ Then the watcher^b called out:
   "Upon a watchtower I stand, O Lord,
   continually by day,
and at my post I am stationed
   throughout the night.
⁹ Look, there they come, riders,
   horsemen in pairs!"
Then he responded,
   "Fallen, fallen is Babylon;
   and all the images of her gods
   lie shattered on the ground."
¹⁰ O my threshed and winnowed one,
   what I have heard from the LORD of hosts,
   the God of Israel, I announce to you.

11 The oracle concerning Dumah.

One is calling to me from Seir,
   "Sentinel, what of the night?
   Sentinel, what of the night?"
¹² The sentinel says:
   "Morning comes, and also the night.
   If you will inquire, inquire;
   come back again."

13 The oracle concerning the desert plain.

In the scrub of the desert plain you will lodge,
   O caravans of Dedanites.
¹⁴ Bring water to the thirsty,
   meet the fugitive with bread,
   O inhabitants of the land of Tema.
¹⁵ For they have fled from the swords,
   from the drawn sword,
from the bent bow,
   and from the stress of battle.

16 For thus the Lord said to me: Within a year, according to the years of a hired worker, all the glory of Kedar will come to an end; ¹⁷and the remaining bows of Kedar's warriors will be few; for the LORD, the God of Israel, has spoken.

22 A Warning of Destruction of Jerusalem

The oracle concerning the valley of vision.

What do you mean that you have gone up,
   all of you, to the housetops,
² you that are full of shoutings,
   tumultuous city, exultant town?
Your slain are not slain by the sword,
   nor are they dead in battle.
³ Your rulers have all fled together;
   they were captured without the use of a
      bow.^c
All of you who were found were captured,
   though they had fled far away.^d
⁴ Therefore I said:
Look away from me,
   let me weep bitter tears;
do not try to comfort me
   for the destruction of my beloved people.

⁵ For the Lord GOD of hosts has a day
   of tumult and trampling and confusion
   in the valley of vision,
a battering down of walls
   and a cry for help to the mountains.
⁶ Elam bore the quiver
   with chariots and cavalry,^e
   and Kir uncovered the shield.
⁷ Your choicest valleys were full of chariots,
   and the cavalry took their stand at the
      gates.
⁸ He has taken away the covering of Judah.

On that day you looked to the weapons of the House of the Forest, ⁹and you saw that there were many breaches in the city of David, and you collected the waters of the lower pool. ¹⁰You counted the houses of Jerusalem, and you broke down the houses to fortify the wall. ¹¹You made a reservoir between the two walls for the water of the old pool. But you did not look to him who did it, or have regard for him who planned it long ago.

¹² In that day the Lord GOD of hosts
 called to weeping and mourning,
  to baldness and putting on sackcloth;
¹³ but instead there was joy and festivity,
  killing oxen and slaughtering sheep,
   eating meat and drinking wine.
"Let us eat and drink,
 for tomorrow we die."
¹⁴ The LORD of hosts has revealed himself in
  my ears:
 Surely this iniquity will not be forgiven you
  until you die,
  says the Lord GOD of hosts.

Denunciation of Self-Seeking Officials

15 Thus says the Lord GOD of hosts: Come, go to this steward, to Shebna, who is master of the household, and say to him: ¹⁶What right do you have here? Who are your relatives here, that you have cut out a tomb here for yourself, cutting a tomb on the height, and carving a habitation

for yourself in the rock? ¹⁷The LORD is about to hurl you away violently, my fellow. He will seize firm hold on you, ¹⁸whirl you round and round, and throw you like a ball into a wide land; there you shall die, and there your splendid chariots shall lie, O you disgrace to your master's house! ¹⁹I will thrust you from your office, and you will be pulled down from your post.

20 On that day I will call my servant Eliakim son of Hilkiah, ²¹and will clothe him with your robe and bind your sash on him. I will commit your authority to his hand, and he shall be a father to the inhabitants of Jerusalem and to the house of Judah. ²²I will place on his shoulder the key of the house of David; he shall open, and no one shall shut; he shall shut, and no one shall open. ²³I will fasten him like a peg in a secure place, and he will become a throne of honor to his ancestral house. ²⁴And they will hang on him the whole weight of his ancestral house, the offspring and issue, every small vessel, from the cups to all the flagons. ²⁵On that day, says the LORD of hosts, the peg that was fastened in a secure place will give way; it will be cut down and fall, and the load that was on it will perish, for the LORD has spoken.

23 An Oracle concerning Tyre
The oracle concerning Tyre.

 Wail, O ships of Tarshish,
  for your fortress is destroyed. ᵃ

---

a Cn Compare verse 14: Heb *for it is destroyed, without houses*

When they came in from Cyprus
they learned of it.
2 Be still, O inhabitants of the coast,
O merchants of Sidon,
your messengers crossed over the sea[a]
3 and were on the mighty waters;
your revenue was the grain of Shihor,
the harvest of the Nile;
you were the merchant of the nations.
4 Be ashamed, O Sidon, for the sea has
spoken,
the fortress of the sea, saying:
"I have neither labored nor given birth,
I have neither reared young men
nor brought up young women."
5 When the report comes to Egypt,
they will be in anguish over the report
about Tyre.
6 Cross over to Tarshish—
wail, O inhabitants of the coast!
7 Is this your exultant city
whose origin is from days of old,
whose feet carried her
to settle far away?
8 Who has planned this
against Tyre, the bestower of crowns,
whose merchants were princes,
whose traders were the honored of the
earth?
9 The Lord of hosts has planned it—
to defile the pride of all glory,
to shame all the honored of the earth.
10 Cross over to your own land,
O ships of[b] Tarshish;
this is a harbor[c] no more.
11 He has stretched out his hand over the sea,
he has shaken the kingdoms;
the Lord has given command concerning
Canaan
to destroy its fortresses.
12 He said:
You will exult no longer,
O oppressed virgin daughter Sidon;
rise, cross over to Cyprus—
even there you will have no rest.

13 Look at the land of the Chaldeans! This
is the people; it was not Assyria. They destined
Tyre for wild animals. They erected their siege
towers, they tore down her palaces, they made
her a ruin.[d]
14 Wail, O ships of Tarshish,
for your fortress is destroyed.
15 From that day Tyre will be forgotten for seventy years, the lifetime of one king. At the end
of seventy years, it will happen to Tyre as in the
song about the prostitute:

16 Take a harp,
go about the city,
you forgotten prostitute!
Make sweet melody,
sing many songs,
that you may be remembered.
17 At the end of seventy years, the Lord will visit
Tyre, and she will return to her trade, and will
prostitute herself with all the kingdoms of the
world on the face of the earth. 18 Her merchandise and her wages will be dedicated to the
Lord; her profits[e] will not be stored or hoarded, but her merchandise will supply abundant
food and fine clothing for those who live in the
presence of the Lord.

24 Impending Judgment on the Earth

Now the Lord is about to lay waste the
earth and make it desolate,
and he will twist its surface and scatter its
inhabitants.
2 And it shall be, as with the people, so with
the priest;
as with the slave, so with his master;
as with the maid, so with her mistress;
as with the buyer, so with the seller;
as with the lender, so with the borrower;
as with the creditor, so with the debtor.
3 The earth shall be utterly laid waste and
utterly despoiled;
for the Lord has spoken this word.

4 The earth dries up and withers,
the world languishes and withers;
the heavens languish together with the
earth.
5 The earth lies polluted
under its inhabitants;
for they have transgressed laws,
violated the statutes,
broken the everlasting covenant.
6 Therefore a curse devours the earth,
and its inhabitants suffer for their guilt;
therefore the inhabitants of the earth
dwindled,
and few people are left.
7 The wine dries up,
the vine languishes,
all the merry-hearted sigh.
8 The mirth of the timbrels is stilled,
the noise of the jubilant has ceased,
the mirth of the lyre is stilled.
9 No longer do they drink wine with singing;
strong drink is bitter to those who
drink it.
10 The city of chaos is broken down,

a Q Ms: MT crossing over the sea, they replenished you b Cn Compare Gk: Heb like the Nile, daughter c Cn: Heb restraint d Meaning of Heb
uncertain e Heb it

every house is shut up so that no one can enter.

¹¹ There is an outcry in the streets for lack of wine;
    all joy has reached its eventide;
    the gladness of the earth is banished.

¹² Desolation is left in the city,
    the gates are battered into ruins.

¹³ For thus it shall be on the earth
    and among the nations,
as when an olive tree is beaten,
    as at the gleaning when the grape harvest is ended.

¹⁴ They lift up their voices, they sing for joy;
    they shout from the west over the majesty of the LORD.

¹⁵ Therefore in the east give glory to the LORD;
    in the coastlands of the sea glorify the name of the LORD, the God of Israel.

¹⁶ From the ends of the earth we hear songs of praise,
    of glory to the Righteous One.
But I say, I pine away,
    I pine away. Woe is me!
For the treacherous deal treacherously,
    the treacherous deal very treacherously.

¹⁷ Terror, and the pit, and the snare
    are upon you, O inhabitant of the earth!

¹⁸ Whoever flees at the sound of the terror
    shall fall into the pit;
and whoever climbs out of the pit
    shall be caught in the snare.
For the windows of heaven are opened,
    and the foundations of the earth tremble.

¹⁹ The earth is utterly broken,
    the earth is torn asunder,
    the earth is violently shaken.

²⁰ The earth staggers like a drunkard,
    it sways like a hut;
its transgression lies heavy upon it,
    and it falls, and will not rise again.

²¹ On that day the LORD will punish
    the host of heaven in heaven,
    and on earth the kings of the earth.

²² They will be gathered together
    like prisoners in a pit;
they will be shut up in a prison,
    and after many days they will be punished.

²³ Then the moon will be abashed,
    and the sun ashamed;
for the LORD of hosts will reign
    on Mount Zion and in Jerusalem,
and before his elders he will manifest his glory.

TRY THIS

THE OFTEN OVERLOOKED

If there's one thing that the Scriptures clearly communicate, it's this: God is the God of the poor and the oppressed. Read **Isaiah 25.4**. God always has and always will stand on the side of the poor and the oppressed, the victims and the outcasts, the widowed and the fatherless. To stand up for these people is to stand on the side of God.

In the concordance at the back of this Bible, look up the terms *poor, slave, oppressed, widow,* and *orphan* and see what the Scriptures have to say. (A concordance is a reference tool that shows you where you can find certain words in the Bible. You can also go to **Learner.CalltoDiscipleship.com** and use ours there—just click on the "Reference" button.)

After you've explored how God feels about the poor, the oppressed, and the outcasts, spend some time seeing how people strive to live out God's values. Log on to **Learner.CalltoDiscipleship.com** for a few places to look, such as Catholic Relief Services. After researching, consider these questions: What do you think you need to do with what you've learned? What can your parish do to embrace these kinds of values? What's one step you can take to make a difference?

GOD IS COMPASSIONATE   MY WORLD

25   Praise for Deliverance from Oppression

O LORD, you are my God;
    I will exalt you, I will praise your name;
for you have done wonderful things,
    plans formed of old, faithful and sure.

² For you have made the city a heap,
    the fortified city a ruin;
the palace of aliens is a city no more,
    it will never be rebuilt.

³ Therefore strong peoples will glorify you;
    cities of ruthless nations will fear you.

⁴ For you have been a refuge to the poor,
    a refuge to the needy in their distress,
    a shelter from the rainstorm and a shade from the heat.
When the blast of the ruthless was like a winter rainstorm,

⁵   the noise of aliens like heat in a dry place,
you subdued the heat with the shade of clouds;
    the song of the ruthless was stilled.

REALITY

WHAT DO I REALLY THINK?

Most Catholics remember St. Augustine as the person who coined the term "original sin." What most Catholics are not aware of is how much he preached on social justice and preferential treatment for the poor. Read **Isaiah 25.4**. How have you been a refuge to the poor and needy? Spend some time thinking through each quotation and the questions below:

"God does not demand much of you. He asks back what he gave you, and from him you take what is enough for you. The superfluities of the rich are the necessities of the poor. When you possess superfluities, you possess what belongs to others" (*Exposition on Psalm 147*, 12).

- When you think about your "stuff," is anything superfluous? Do you have more than you need? Does it bother you, if you do? What choices could you make to cut down on extra stuff that would directly help the poor?

"You give bread to a hungry person; but it would be better were no one hungry, and you could give it to no one. You clothe the naked person. Would that all were clothed and this necessity did not exist" (*Tractate 1 John 8*, 8).

- Every day twenty-six thousand children under the age of five die from preventable causes such as undernutrition, diarrhea, unsafe water, or diseases that are easily prevented by vaccines. That's eighteen children every minute. How can you respond? Go to **Learner.CalltoDiscipleship.com** and find opportunities for actions that will make a difference worldwide.

"Christ is at once rich and poor: as God, rich; as a human person, poor. Truly, that Man rose to heaven already rich, and now sits at the right hand of the Father, but here, among us, he still suffers hunger, thirst and nakedness; here he is poor and is in the poor" (*Sermon 123*, 4).

- Read **Matthew 25.31–46**. Ask yourself: When I see someone who is hungry, do I ever think, "God lives there"?

6 On this mountain the LORD of hosts will make for all peoples
a feast of rich food, a feast of well-aged wines,
of rich food filled with marrow, of well-aged wines strained clear.
7 And he will destroy on this mountain
the shroud that is cast over all peoples,
the sheet that is spread over all nations;
8 he will swallow up death forever.
Then the Lord GOD will wipe away the tears from all faces,
and the disgrace of his people he will take away from all the earth,
for the LORD has spoken.
9 It will be said on that day,
Lo, this is our God; we have waited for him, so that he might save us.
This is the LORD for whom we have waited;
let us be glad and rejoice in his salvation.
10 For the hand of the LORD will rest on this mountain.

The Moabites shall be trodden down in their place
as straw is trodden down in a dung-pit.
11 Though they spread out their hands in the midst of it,
as swimmers spread out their hands to swim,
their pride will be laid low despite the struggle*a* of their hands.
12 The high fortifications of his walls will be brought down,
laid low, cast to the ground, even to the dust.

26 Judah's Song of Victory

On that day this song will be sung in the land of Judah:
We have a strong city;
he sets up victory
like walls and bulwarks.
2 Open the gates,
so that the righteous nation that keeps faith
may enter in.
3 Those of steadfast mind you keep in peace—
in peace because they trust in you.
4 Trust in the LORD forever,
for in the LORD GOD*b*
you have an everlasting rock.
5 For he has brought low
the inhabitants of the height;
the lofty city he lays low.
He lays it low to the ground,
casts it to the dust.

---

a Meaning of Heb uncertain *b* Heb *in Yah, the* LORD

⁶ The foot tramples it,
   the feet of the poor,
   the steps of the needy.

⁷ The way of the righteous is level;
   O Just One, you make smooth the path of
      the righteous.
⁸ In the path of your judgments,
   O Lord, we wait for you;
   your name and your renown
      are the soul's desire.
⁹ My soul yearns for you in the night,
   my spirit within me earnestly seeks you.
   For when your judgments are in the earth,
      the inhabitants of the world learn
         righteousness.
¹⁰ If favor is shown to the wicked,
   they do not learn righteousness;
   in the land of uprightness they deal
      perversely
   and do not see the majesty of the Lord.
¹¹ O Lord, your hand is lifted up,
   but they do not see it.
   Let them see your zeal for your people, and
      be ashamed.
   Let the fire for your adversaries consume
      them.
¹² O Lord, you will ordain peace for us,
   for indeed, all that we have done, you
      have done for us.
¹³ O Lord our God,
   other lords besides you have ruled over us,
   but we acknowledge your name alone.
¹⁴ The dead do not live;
   shades do not rise—
   because you have punished and destroyed
      them,
   and wiped out all memory of them.
¹⁵ But you have increased the nation, O Lord,
   you have increased the nation; you are
      glorified;
   you have enlarged all the borders of the
      land.
¹⁶ O Lord, in distress they sought you,
   they poured out a prayer*ᵃ*
   when your chastening was on them.
¹⁷ Like a woman with child,
   who writhes and cries out in her pangs
   when she is near her time,
   so were we because of you, O Lord;
¹⁸ we were with child, we writhed,
   but we gave birth only to wind.
   We have won no victories on earth,
   and no one is born to inhabit the world.
¹⁹ Your dead shall live, their corpses*ᵇ* shall rise.
   O dwellers in the dust, awake and sing for
      joy!

For your dew is a radiant dew,
   and the earth will give birth to those long
      dead.*ᶜ*

²⁰ Come, my people, enter your chambers,
   and shut your doors behind you;
   hide yourselves for a little while
   until the wrath is past.
²¹ For the Lord comes out from his place
   to punish the inhabitants of the earth for
      their iniquity;
   the earth will disclose the blood shed on it,
   and will no longer cover its slain.

27 Israel's Redemption

On that day the Lord with his cruel and great
and strong sword will punish Leviathan the
fleeing serpent, Leviathan the twisting serpent,
and he will kill the dragon that is in the sea.

² On that day:
   A pleasant vineyard, sing about it!
³   I, the Lord, am its keeper;
   every moment I water it.
   I guard it night and day
   so that no one can harm it;
⁴   I have no wrath.
   If it gives me thorns and briers,
   I will march to battle against it.
   I will burn it up.
⁵ Or else let it cling to me for protection,
   let it make peace with me,
   let it make peace with me.

⁶ In days to come*ᵈ* Jacob shall take root,
   Israel shall blossom and put forth shoots,
   and fill the whole world with fruit.

⁷ Has he struck them down as he struck down
      those who struck them?
   Or have they been killed as their killers
      were killed?
⁸ By expulsion,*ᵃ* by exile you struggled
      against them;
   with his fierce blast he removed them in
      the day of the east wind.
⁹ Therefore by this the guilt of Jacob will be
      expiated,
   and this will be the full fruit of the
      removal of his sin:
   when he makes all the stones of the altars
      like chalkstones crushed to pieces,
   no sacred poles *ᵉ* or incense altars will
      remain standing.
¹⁰ For the fortified city is solitary,
   a habitation deserted and forsaken, like
      the wilderness;
   the calves graze there,
   there they lie down, and strip its branches.

---

a Meaning of Heb uncertain *b* Cn Compare Syr Tg: Heb *my corpse* *c* Heb *to the shades* *d* Heb *Those to come* *e* Heb *Asherim*

11 When its boughs are dry, they are broken;
women come and make a fire of them.
For this is a people without understanding;
therefore he that made them will not
have compassion on them,
he that formed them will show them no
favor.

12 On that day the LORD will thresh from the channel of the Euphrates to the Wadi of Egypt, and you will be gathered one by one, O people of Israel. 13 And on that day a great trumpet will be blown, and those who were lost in the land of Assyria and those who were driven out to the land of Egypt will come and worship the LORD on the holy mountain at Jerusalem.

28 Judgment on Corrupt Rulers, Priests, and Prophets

Ah, the proud garland of the drunkards of
Ephraim,
and the fading flower of its glorious
beauty,
which is on the head of those bloated
with rich food, of those overcome
with wine!
2 See, the Lord has one who is mighty and
strong;
like a storm of hail, a destroying tempest,
like a storm of mighty, overflowing waters;
with his hand he will hurl them down to
the earth.
3 Trampled under foot will be
the proud garland of the drunkards of
Ephraim.
4 And the fading flower of its glorious beauty,
which is on the head of those bloated
with rich food,
will be like a first-ripe fig before the
summer;
whoever sees it, eats it up
as soon as it comes to hand.

5 In that day the LORD of hosts will be a
garland of glory,
and a diadem of beauty, to the remnant
of his people;
6 and a spirit of justice to the one who sits in
judgment,
and strength to those who turn back the
battle at the gate.

7 These also reel with wine
and stagger with strong drink;
the priest and the prophet reel with strong
drink,
they are confused with wine,
they stagger with strong drink;
they err in vision,

they stumble in giving judgment.
8 All tables are covered with filthy vomit;
no place is clean.

9 "Whom will he teach knowledge,
and to whom will he explain the
message?
Those who are weaned from milk,
those taken from the breast?
10 For it is precept upon precept, precept
upon precept,
line upon line, line upon line,
here a little, there a little."[a]

11 Truly, with stammering lip
and with alien tongue
he will speak to this people,
12 to whom he has said,
"This is rest;
give rest to the weary;
and this is repose";
yet they would not hear.
13 Therefore the word of the LORD will be to
them,
"Precept upon precept, precept upon
precept,
line upon line, line upon line,
here a little, there a little;"[a]
in order that they may go, and fall
backward,
and be broken, and snared, and taken.

14 Therefore hear the word of the LORD, you
scoffers
who rule this people in Jerusalem.
15 Because you have said, "We have made a
covenant with death,
and with Sheol we have an agreement;
when the overwhelming scourge passes
through
it will not come to us;
for we have made lies our refuge,
and in falsehood we have taken shelter";
16 therefore thus says the Lord GOD,
See, I am laying in Zion a foundation stone,
a tested stone,
a precious cornerstone, a sure foundation:
"One who trusts will not panic."
17 And I will make justice the line,
and righteousness the plummet;
hail will sweep away the refuge of lies,
and waters will overwhelm the shelter.
18 Then your covenant with death will be
annulled,
and your agreement with Sheol will not
stand;
when the overwhelming scourge passes
through
you will be beaten down by it.

a Meaning of Heb of this verse uncertain

19 As often as it passes through, it will take you;
    for morning by morning it will pass
        through,
        by day and by night;
    and it will be sheer terror to understand the
        message.
20 For the bed is too short to stretch oneself
        on it,
    and the covering too narrow to wrap
        oneself in it.
21 For the LORD will rise up as on Mount
        Perazim,
    he will rage as in the valley of Gibeon
to do his deed—strange is his deed!—
    and to work his work—alien is his work!
22 Now therefore do not scoff,
    or your bonds will be made stronger;
for I have heard a decree of destruction
    from the Lord GOD of hosts upon the
        whole land.

23 Listen, and hear my voice;
    Pay attention, and hear my speech.
24 Do those who plow for sowing plow
        continually?
    Do they continually open and harrow
        their ground?
25 When they have leveled its surface,
    do they not scatter dill, sow cummin,
    and plant wheat in rows
    and barley in its proper place,
    and spelt as the border?
26 For they are well instructed;
    their God teaches them.

27 Dill is not threshed with a threshing sledge,
    nor is a cart wheel rolled over cummin;
but dill is beaten out with a stick,
    and cummin with a rod.
28 Grain is crushed for bread,
    but one does not thresh it forever;
one drives the cart wheel and horses over it,
    but does not pulverize it.
29 This also comes from the LORD of hosts;
    he is wonderful in counsel,
    and excellent in wisdom.

29 The Siege of Jerusalem

Ah, Ariel, Ariel,
    the city where David encamped!
Add year to year;
    let the festivals run their round.
2 Yet I will distress Ariel,
    and there shall be moaning and
        lamentation,
    and Jerusalem^a shall be to me like an
        Ariel.^b
3 And like David^c I will encamp against you;

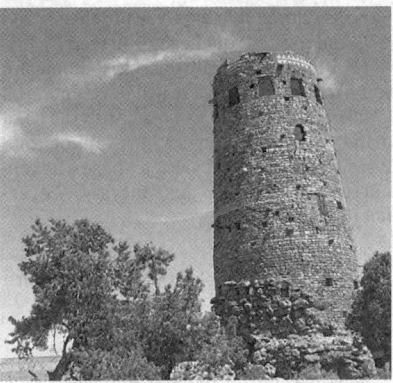

The Watchtower—© Morgan Katchuk, 14

    I will besiege you with towers
    and raise siegeworks against you.
4 Then deep from the earth you shall speak,
    from low in the dust your words shall
        come;
your voice shall come from the ground like
        the voice of a ghost,
    and your speech shall whisper out of the
        dust.

5 But the multitude of your foes^d shall be like
        small dust,
    and the multitude of tyrants like flying
        chaff.
And in an instant, suddenly,
6   you will be visited by the LORD of hosts
with thunder and earthquake and great
        noise,
    with whirlwind and tempest, and the
        flame of a devouring fire.
7 And the multitude of all the nations that
        fight against Ariel,
    all that fight against her and her
        stronghold, and who distress her,
    shall be like a dream, a vision of the
        night.
8 Just as when a hungry person dreams of
        eating
    and wakes up still hungry,
or a thirsty person dreams of drinking
    and wakes up faint, still thirsty,
so shall the multitude of all the nations be
    that fight against Mount Zion.

9 Stupefy yourselves and be in a stupor,
    blind yourselves and be blind!
Be drunk, but not from wine;
    stagger, but not from strong drink!

---

a Heb *she*   *b* Probable meaning, *altar hearth*; compare Ezek 43.15   *c* Gk: Meaning of Heb uncertain   *d* Cn: Heb *strangers*

¹⁰ For the LORD has poured out upon you
a spirit of deep sleep;
he has closed your eyes, you prophets,
and covered your heads, you seers.

11 The vision of all this has become for you like the words of a sealed document. If it is given to those who can read, with the command, "Read this," they say, "We cannot, for it is sealed." ¹²And if it is given to those who cannot read, saying, "Read this," they say, "We cannot read."

¹³ The Lord said:
Because these people draw near with their
mouths
and honor me with their lips,
while their hearts are far from me,
and their worship of me is a human
commandment learned by rote;
¹⁴ so I will again do
amazing things with this people,
shocking and amazing.
The wisdom of their wise shall perish,
and the discernment of the discerning
shall be hidden.

¹⁵ Ha! You who hide a plan too deep for the
LORD,
whose deeds are in the dark,
and who say, "Who sees us? Who knows
us?"
¹⁶ You turn things upside down!
Shall the potter be regarded as the clay?
Shall the thing made say of its maker,
"He did not make me";
or the thing formed say of the one who
formed it,
"He has no understanding"?

Hope for the Future
¹⁷ Shall not Lebanon in a very little while
become a fruitful field,
and the fruitful field be regarded as a
forest?
¹⁸ On that day the deaf shall hear
the words of a scroll,
and out of their gloom and darkness
the eyes of the blind shall see.
¹⁹ The meek shall obtain fresh joy in the LORD,
and the neediest people shall exult in the
Holy One of Israel.
²⁰ For the tyrant shall be no more,
and the scoffer shall cease to be;
all those alert to do evil shall be cut off—
²¹ those who cause a person to lose a lawsuit,
who set a trap for the arbiter in the gate,
and without grounds deny justice to the
one in the right.

²² Therefore thus says the LORD, who redeemed Abraham, concerning the house of Jacob:
No longer shall Jacob be ashamed,
no longer shall his face grow pale.
²³ For when he sees his children,
the work of my hands, in his midst,
they will sanctify my name;
they will sanctify the Holy One of Jacob,
and will stand in awe of the God of Israel.
²⁴ And those who err in spirit will come to
understanding,
and those who grumble will accept
instruction.

30 The Futility of Reliance on Egypt
Oh, rebellious children, says the LORD,
who carry out a plan, but not mine;
who make an alliance, but against my will,
adding sin to sin;
² who set out to go down to Egypt
without asking for my counsel,
to take refuge in the protection of Pharaoh,
and to seek shelter in the shadow of
Egypt;
³ Therefore the protection of Pharaoh shall
become your shame,
and the shelter in the shadow of Egypt
your humiliation.
⁴ For though his officials are at Zoan
and his envoys reach Hanes,
⁵ everyone comes to shame
through a people that cannot profit
them,
that brings neither help nor profit,
but shame and disgrace.

6 An oracle concerning the animals of the Negeb.
Through a land of trouble and distress,
of lioness and roaring^a lion,
of viper and flying serpent,
they carry their riches on the backs of
donkeys,
and their treasures on the humps of
camels,
to a people that cannot profit them.
⁷ For Egypt's help is worthless and empty,
therefore I have called her,
"Rahab who sits still."^b

A Rebellious People
⁸ Go now, write it before them on a tablet,
and inscribe it in a book,
so that it may be for the time to come
as a witness forever.
⁹ For they are a rebellious people,
faithless children,

_a_ Cn: Heb _from them_ _b_ Meaning of Heb uncertain

children who will not hear
    the instruction of the Lord;
10 who say to the seers, "Do not see";
    and to the prophets, "Do not prophesy to
       us what is right;
speak to us smooth things,
    prophesy illusions;
11 leave the way, turn aside from the path,
    let us hear no more about the Holy One
       of Israel."

12 Therefore thus says the Holy One of Israel:
Because you reject this word,
    and put your trust in oppression and
       deceit,
    and rely on them;
13 therefore this iniquity shall become for you
    like a break in a high wall, bulging out,
       and about to collapse,
    whose crash comes suddenly, in an
       instant;
14 its breaking is like that of a potter's vessel
    that is smashed so ruthlessly
that among its fragments not a sherd is
      found
    for taking fire from the hearth,
    or dipping water out of the cistern.

15 For thus said the Lord God, the Holy One of
    Israel:
In returning and rest you shall be saved;
    in quietness and in trust shall be your
      strength.
But you refused 16and said,
"No! We will flee upon horses"—
    therefore you shall flee!
and, "We will ride upon swift steeds"—
    therefore your pursuers shall be swift!
17 A thousand shall flee at the threat of one,
    at the threat of five you shall flee,
until you are left
    like a flagstaff on the top of a mountain,
    like a signal on a hill.

God's Promise to Zion

18 Therefore the Lord waits to be gracious to
    you;
    therefore he will rise up to show mercy to
    you.
For the Lord is a God of justice;
    blessed are all those who wait for him.

19 Truly, O people in Zion, inhabitants of Jerusalem, you shall weep no more. He will surely be gracious to you at the sound of your cry; when he hears it, he will answer you. 20Though the Lord may give you the bread of adversity and the water of affliction, yet your Teacher will not hide himself any more, but your eyes shall see your Teacher. 21And when you turn to the right or when you turn to the left, your ears shall hear a word behind you, saying, "This is the way; walk in it." 22Then you will defile your silver-covered idols and your gold-plated images. You will scatter them like filthy rags; you will say to them, "Away with you!"

23 He will give rain for the seed with which you sow the ground, and grain, the produce of the ground, which will be rich and plenteous. On that day your cattle will graze in broad pastures; 24and the oxen and donkeys that till the ground will eat silage, which has been winnowed with shovel and fork. 25On every lofty mountain and every high hill there will be brooks running with water—on a day of the great slaughter, when the towers fall. 26Moreover the light of the moon will be like the light of the sun, and the light of the sun will be sevenfold, like the light of seven days, on the day when the Lord binds up the injuries of his people, and heals the wounds inflicted by his blow.

Judgment on Assyria

27 See, the name of the Lord comes from far
    away,
    burning with his anger, and in thick
      rising smoke;[a]
his lips are full of indignation,
    and his tongue is like a devouring fire;
28 his breath is like an overflowing stream
    that reaches up to the neck—
to sift the nations with the sieve of
      destruction,
    and to place on the jaws of the peoples a
      bridle that leads them astray.

29 You shall have a song as in the night when a holy festival is kept; and gladness of heart, as when one sets out to the sound of the flute to go to the mountain of the Lord, to the Rock of Israel. 30And the Lord will cause his majestic voice to be heard and the descending blow of his arm to be seen, in furious anger and a flame of devouring fire, with a cloudburst and tempest and hailstones. 31The Assyrian will be terror-stricken at the voice of the Lord, when he strikes with his rod. 32And every stroke of the staff of punishment that the Lord lays upon him will be to the sound of timbrels

> "But there is a Being and He can forgive everything, all and for all, because He gave His innocent blood for all and everything."
>
> **—Alyosha, speaking to his brother Ivan, in Fyodor Dostoevsky's *The Brothers Karamazov***

a Meaning of Heb uncertain

and lyres; battling with brandished arm he will fight with him. [33]For his burning place[a] has long been prepared; truly it is made ready for the king,[b] its pyre made deep and wide, with fire and wood in abundance; the breath of the LORD, like a stream of sulfur, kindles it.

31 Alliance with Egypt Is Futile

Alas for those who go down to Egypt for
    help
  and who rely on horses,
who trust in chariots because they are many
  and in horsemen because they are very
    strong,
but do not look to the Holy One of Israel
  or consult the LORD!
[2] Yet he too is wise and brings disaster;
  he does not call back his words,
but will rise against the house of the
    evildoers,
  and against the helpers of those who
    work iniquity.
[3] The Egyptians are human, and not God;
  their horses are flesh, and not spirit.
When the LORD stretches out his hand,
  the helper will stumble, and the one
    helped will fall,
  and they will all perish together.

[4] For thus the LORD said to me,
As a lion or a young lion growls over its
    prey,

and—when a band of shepherds is called
    out against it—
is not terrified by their shouting
  or daunted at their noise,
so the LORD of hosts will come down
  to fight upon Mount Zion and upon its
    hill.
[5] Like birds hovering overhead, so the LORD
    of hosts
  will protect Jerusalem;
he will protect and deliver it,
  he will spare and rescue it.

6 Turn back to him whom you[c] have deeply betrayed, O people of Israel. [7]For on that day all of you shall throw away your idols of silver and idols of gold, which your hands have sinfully made for you.
[8] "Then the Assyrian shall fall by a sword, not
    of mortals;
  and a sword, not of humans, shall devour
    him;
he shall flee from the sword,
  and his young men shall be put to forced
    labor.
[9] His rock shall pass away in terror,
  and his officers desert the standard in
    panic,"
says the LORD, whose fire is in Zion,
  and whose furnace is in Jerusalem.

---

a Or *Topheth* *b* Or *Molech* *c* Heb *they*

Fire—© Rachel Akerley, 16

32 Government with Justice Predicted

See, a king will reign in righteousness,
and princes will rule with justice.
2 Each will be like a hiding place from the
wind,
a covert from the tempest,
like streams of water in a dry place,
like the shade of a great rock in a weary
land.
3 Then the eyes of those who have sight will
not be closed,
and the ears of those who have hearing
will listen.
4 The minds of the rash will have good
judgment,
and the tongues of stammerers will
speak readily and distinctly.
5 A fool will no longer be called noble,
nor a villain said to be honorable.
6 For fools speak folly,
and their minds plot iniquity:
to practice ungodliness,
to utter error concerning the LORD,
to leave the craving of the hungry
unsatisfied,
and to deprive the thirsty of drink.
7 The villainies of villains are evil;
they devise wicked devices
to ruin the poor with lying words,
even when the plea of the needy is right.
8 But those who are noble plan noble things,
and by noble things they stand.

Complacent Women Warned of Disaster

9 Rise up, you women who are at ease, hear
my voice;
you complacent daughters, listen to my
speech.
10 In little more than a year
you will shudder, you complacent ones;
for the vintage will fail,
the fruit harvest will not come.
11 Tremble, you women who are at ease,
shudder, you complacent ones;
strip, and make yourselves bare,
and put sackcloth on your loins.
12 Beat your breasts for the pleasant fields,
for the fruitful vine,
13 for the soil of my people
growing up in thorns and briers;
yes, for all the joyous houses
in the jubilant city.
14 For the palace will be forsaken,
the populous city deserted;
the hill and the watchtower
will become dens forever,

the joy of wild asses,
a pasture for flocks;
15 until a spirit from on high is poured out
on us,
and the wilderness becomes a fruitful
field,
and the fruitful field is deemed a forest.

The Peace of God's Reign

16 Then justice will dwell in the wilderness,
and righteousness abide in the fruitful
field.
17 The effect of righteousness will be peace,
and the result of righteousness,
quietness and trust forever.
18 My people will abide in a peaceful
habitation,
in secure dwellings, and in quiet resting
places.
19 The forest will disappear completely,[a]
and the city will be utterly laid low.
20 Happy will you be who sow beside every
stream,
who let the ox and the donkey range
freely.

33 A Prophecy of Deliverance from Foes

Ah, you destroyer,
who yourself have not been destroyed;
you treacherous one,
with whom no one has dealt
treacherously!
When you have ceased to destroy,
you will be destroyed;
and when you have stopped dealing
treacherously,
you will be dealt with treacherously.

2 O LORD, be gracious to us; we wait for you.
Be our arm every morning,
our salvation in the time of trouble.
3 At the sound of tumult, peoples fled;
before your majesty, nations scattered.
4 Spoil was gathered as the caterpillar
gathers;
as locusts leap, they leaped[b] upon it.
5 The LORD is exalted, he dwells on high;
he filled Zion with justice and
righteousness;
6 he will be the stability of your times,
abundance of salvation, wisdom, and
knowledge;
the fear of the LORD is Zion's treasure.[c]

7 Listen! the valiant[b] cry in the streets;
the envoys of peace weep bitterly.
8 The highways are deserted,
travelers have quit the road.

---

a Cn: Heb *And it will hail when the forest comes down*   b Meaning of Heb uncertain   c Heb *his treasure*; meaning of Heb uncertain

The treaty is broken,
    its oaths[a] are despised,
    its obligation[b] is disregarded.
9 The land mourns and languishes;
    Lebanon is confounded and withers away;
Sharon is like a desert;
    and Bashan and Carmel shake off their
        leaves.

10 "Now I will arise," says the LORD,
    "now I will lift myself up;
    now I will be exalted.
11 You conceive chaff, you bring forth stubble;
    your breath is a fire that will consume you.
12 And the peoples will be as if burned to lime,
    like thorns cut down, that are burned in
        the fire."

13 Hear, you who are far away, what I have
        done;
    and you who are near, acknowledge my
        might.
14 The sinners in Zion are afraid;
    trembling has seized the godless:
"Who among us can live with the devouring
        fire?
    Who among us can live with everlasting
        flames?"
15 Those who walk righteously and speak
        uprightly,
    who despise the gain of oppression,
who wave away a bribe instead of
        accepting it,
    who stop their ears from hearing of
        bloodshed
    and shut their eyes from looking on evil,
16 they will live on the heights;
    their refuge will be the fortresses of rocks;
    their food will be supplied, their water
        assured.

The Land of the Majestic King

17 Your eyes will see the king in his beauty;
    they will behold a land that stretches far
        away.
18 Your mind will muse on the terror:
    "Where is the one who counted?
    Where is the one who weighed the
        tribute?
    Where is the one who counted the
        towers?"
19 No longer will you see the insolent people,
    the people of an obscure speech that you
        cannot comprehend,
    stammering in a language that you
        cannot understand.
20 Look on Zion, the city of our appointed
        festivals!

Your eyes will see Jerusalem,
    a quiet habitation, an immovable tent,
whose stakes will never be pulled up,
    and none of whose ropes will be broken.
21 But there the LORD in majesty will be for us
    a place of broad rivers and streams,
    where no galley with oars can go,
        nor stately ship can pass.
22 For the LORD is our judge, the LORD is our
        ruler,
    the LORD is our king; he will save us.

23 Your rigging hangs loose;
    it cannot hold the mast firm in its place,
    or keep the sail spread out.

Then prey and spoil in abundance will be
        divided;
    even the lame will fall to plundering.
24 And no inhabitant will say, "I am sick";
    the people who live there will be forgiven
        their iniquity.

34 Judgment on the Nations

Draw near, O nations, to hear;
    O peoples, give heed!
Let the earth hear, and all that fills it;
    the world, and all that comes from it.
2 For the LORD is enraged against all the
        nations,
    and furious against all their hordes;
    he has doomed them, has given them
        over for slaughter.
3 Their slain shall be cast out,
    and the stench of their corpses shall rise;
    the mountains shall flow with their
        blood.
4 All the host of heaven shall rot away,
    and the skies roll up like a scroll.
All their host shall wither
    like a leaf withering on a vine,
    or fruit withering on a fig tree.

5 When my sword has drunk its fill in the
        heavens,
    lo, it will descend upon Edom,
    upon the people I have doomed to
        judgment.
6 The LORD has a sword; it is sated with
        blood,
    it is gorged with fat,
    with the blood of lambs and goats,
    with the fat of the kidneys of rams.
For the LORD has a sacrifice in Bozrah,
    a great slaughter in the land of Edom.
7 Wild oxen shall fall with them,
    and young steers with the mighty bulls.
Their land shall be soaked with blood,
    and their soil made rich with fat.

a Q Ms: MT cities b Or everyone

⁸ For the Lord has a day of vengeance,
   a year of vindication by Zion's cause.^a
⁹ And the streams of Edom^b shall be turned
      into pitch,
   and her soil into sulfur;
   her land shall become burning pitch.
¹⁰ Night and day it shall not be quenched;
   its smoke shall go up forever.
From generation to generation it shall lie
      waste;
   no one shall pass through it forever and
      ever.
¹¹ But the hawk^c and the hedgehog^c shall
      possess it;
   the owl^c and the raven shall live in it.
He shall stretch the line of confusion over it,
   and the plummet of chaos over^d its
      nobles.
¹² They shall name it No Kingdom There,
   and all its princes shall be nothing.
¹³ Thorns shall grow over its strongholds,
   nettles and thistles in its fortresses.
It shall be the haunt of jackals,
   an abode for ostriches.
¹⁴ Wildcats shall meet with hyenas,
   goat-demons shall call to each other;
there too Lilith shall repose,
   and find a place to rest.
¹⁵ There shall the owl nest
   and lay and hatch and brood in its
      shadow;
there too the buzzards shall gather,
   each one with its mate.
¹⁶ Seek and read from the book of the Lord:
   Not one of these shall be missing;
   none shall be without its mate.
For the mouth of the Lord has
      commanded,
   and his spirit has gathered them.
¹⁷ He has cast the lot for them,
   his hand has portioned it out to them
      with the line;
they shall possess it forever,
   from generation to generation they shall
      live in it.

35 The Return of the Redeemed to Zion

The wilderness and the dry land shall be
      glad,
   the desert shall rejoice and blossom;
like the crocus ²it shall blossom
      abundantly,
   and rejoice with joy and singing.
The glory of Lebanon shall be given to it,
   the majesty of Carmel and Sharon.
They shall see the glory of the Lord,
   the majesty of our God.

PROFILE OF FAITH

JAMES CARDINAL GIBBONS: The Boy Bishop

When James Cardinal Gibbons became a bishop at age thirty-four, one of the youngest Catholic bishops in the world at that time, he was often called the "boy bishop."

Cardinal Gibbons advocated for the protection of the laboring class, because of the exploitation of workers by the industrial expansion of America's urban East Coast at the turn of the century. He once said, "It is not only the right of the laboring classes to protect themselves, and the duty of the whole people to aid them in finding a remedy against the dangers with which both civilization and social order are menaced by avarice, oppression, and corruption."

Gibbons had a key role in the granting of papal permission for Catholics to join labor unions. He won a reputation as labor's friend. Although he supported the laboring class, he condemned industrial violence as a form of protest.

In 1917, President Theodore Roosevelt hailed Gibbons as the most venerated, respected, and useful citizen in America. H. L. Mencken, often vocal in his criticism of the clergy, offered rare praise for Cardinal Gibbons, noting that Gibbons' intelligence and political acumen provided solid guidance to the Church, and that even U.S. presidents sought his wise counsel.

³ Strengthen the weak hands,
   and make firm the feeble knees.
⁴ Say to those who are of a fearful heart,
   "Be strong, do not fear!
Here is your God.
   He will come with vengeance,
with terrible recompense.
   He will come and save you."

⁵ Then the eyes of the blind shall be opened,
   and the ears of the deaf unstopped;
⁶ then the lame shall leap like a deer,

---

^a Or *of recompense by Zion's defender* ^b Heb *her streams* ^c Identification uncertain ^d Heb lacks *over*

and the tongue of the speechless sing for
joy.
For waters shall break forth in the
wilderness,
and streams in the desert;
⁷ the burning sand shall become a pool,
and the thirsty ground springs of water;
the haunt of jackals shall become a swamp,ᵃ
the grass shall become reeds and rushes.

⁸ A highway shall be there,
and it shall be called the Holy Way;
the unclean shall not travel on it,ᵇ
but it shall be for God's people;ᶜ
no traveler, not even fools, shall go astray.
⁹ No lion shall be there,
nor shall any ravenous beast come up
on it;
they shall not be found there,
but the redeemed shall walk there.
¹⁰ And the ransomed of the LORD shall return,
and come to Zion with singing;
everlasting joy shall be upon their heads;
they shall obtain joy and gladness,
and sorrow and sighing shall flee away.

36 Sennacherib Threatens Jerusalem

In the fourteenth year of King Hezekiah, King Sennacherib of Assyria came up against all the fortified cities of Judah and captured them. ²The king of Assyria sent the Rabshakeh from Lachish to King Hezekiah at Jerusalem, with a great army. He stood by the conduit of the upper pool on the highway to the Fuller's Field. ³And there came out to him Eliakim son of Hilkiah, who was in charge of the palace, and Shebna the secretary, and Joah son of Asaph, the recorder.

4 The Rabshakeh said to them, "Say to Hezekiah: Thus says the great king, the king of Assyria: On what do you base this confidence of yours? ⁵Do you think that mere words are strategy and power for war? On whom do you now rely, that you have rebelled against me? ⁶See, you are relying on Egypt, that broken reed of a staff, which will pierce the hand of anyone who leans on it. Such is Pharaoh king of Egypt to all who rely on him. ⁷But if you say to me, 'We rely on the LORD our God,' is it not he whose high places and altars Hezekiah has removed, saying to Judah and to Jerusalem, 'You shall worship before this altar'? ⁸Come now, make a wager with my master the king of Assyria: I will give you two thousand horses, if you are able on your part to set riders on them. ⁹How then can you repulse a single captain among the least of my master's servants, when you rely on Egypt for chariots and for horsemen? ¹⁰Moreover, is

it without the LORD that I have come up against this land to destroy it? The LORD said to me, Go up against this land, and destroy it."

11 Then Eliakim, Shebna, and Joah said to the Rabshakeh, "Please speak to your servants in Aramaic, for we understand it; do not speak to us in the language of Judah within the hearing of the people who are on the wall." ¹²But the Rabshakeh said, "Has my master sent me to speak these words to your master and to you, and not to the people sitting on the wall, who are doomed with you to eat their own dung and drink their own urine?"

13 Then the Rabshakeh stood and called out in a loud voice in the language of Judah, "Hear the words of the great king, the king of Assyria! ¹⁴Thus says the king: 'Do not let Hezekiah deceive you, for he will not be able to deliver you. ¹⁵Do not let Hezekiah make you rely on the LORD by saying, The LORD will surely deliver us; this city will not be given into the hand of the king of Assyria.' ¹⁶Do not listen to Hezekiah; for thus says the king of Assyria: 'Make your peace with me and come out to me; then every one of you will eat from your own vine and your own fig tree and drink water from your own cistern, ¹⁷until I come and take you away to a land like your own land, a land of grain and wine, a land of bread and vineyards. ¹⁸Do not let Hezekiah mislead you by saying, The LORD will save us. Has any of the gods of the nations saved their land out of the hand of the king of Assyria? ¹⁹Where are the gods of Hamath and Arpad? Where are the gods of Sepharvaim? Have they delivered Samaria out of my hand? ²⁰Who among all the gods of these countries have saved their countries out of my hand, that the LORD should save Jerusalem out of my hand?' "

21 But they were silent and answered him not a word, for the king's command was, "Do not answer him." ²²Then Eliakim son of Hilkiah, who was in charge of the palace, and Shebna the secretary, and Joah son of Asaph, the recorder, came to Hezekiah with their clothes torn, and told him the words of the Rabshakeh.

37 Hezekiah Consults Isaiah

When King Hezekiah heard it, he tore his clothes, covered himself with sackcloth, and went into the house of the LORD. ²And he sent Eliakim, who was in charge of the palace, and Shebna the secretary, and the senior priests, covered with sackcloth, to the prophet Isaiah son of Amoz. ³They said to him, "Thus says Hezekiah, This day is a day of distress, of rebuke, and of disgrace; children have come

---

a Cn: Heb *in the haunt of jackals is her resting place* b Or *pass it by* c Cn: Heb *for them* to the birth, and there is no strength to bring them forth. [4]It may be that the LORD your God heard the words of the Rabshakeh, whom his master the king of Assyria has sent to mock the living God, and will rebuke the words that the LORD your God has heard; therefore lift up your prayer for the remnant that is left."

5 When the servants of King Hezekiah came to Isaiah, [6]Isaiah said to them, "Say to your master, 'Thus says the LORD: Do not be afraid because of the words that you have heard, with which the servants of the king of Assyria have reviled me. [7]I myself will put a spirit in him, so that he shall hear a rumor, and return to his own land; I will cause him to fall by the sword in his own land.' "

8 The Rabshakeh returned, and found the king of Assyria fighting against Libnah; for he had heard that the king had left Lachish. [9]Now the king[a] heard concerning King Tirhakah of Ethiopia,[b] "He has set out to fight against you." When he heard it, he sent messengers to Hezekiah, saying, [10]"Thus shall you speak to King Hezekiah of Judah: Do not let your God on whom you rely deceive you by promising that Jerusalem will not be given into the hand of the king of Assyria. [11]See, you have heard what the kings of Assyria have done to all lands, destroying them utterly. Shall you be delivered? [12]Have the gods of the nations delivered them, the nations that my predecessors destroyed, Gozan, Haran, Rezeph, and the people of Eden who were in Telassar? [13]Where is the king of Hamath, the king of Arpad, the king of the city of Sepharvaim, the king of Hena, or the king of Ivvah?"

Hezekiah's Prayer

14 Hezekiah received the letter from the hand of the messengers and read it; then Hezekiah went up to the house of the LORD and spread it before the LORD. [15]And Hezekiah prayed to the LORD, saying: [16]"O LORD of hosts, God of Israel, who are enthroned above the cherubim, you are God, you alone, of all the kingdoms of the earth; you have made heaven and earth. [17]Incline your ear, O LORD, and hear; open your eyes, O LORD, and see; hear all the words of Sennacherib, which he has sent to mock the living God. [18]Truly, O LORD, the kings of Assyria have laid waste all the nations and their lands, [19]and have hurled their gods into the fire, though they were no gods, but the work of human hands—wood and stone—and so they were destroyed. [20]So now, O LORD our God, save us from his hand, so that all the kingdoms of the earth may know that you alone are the LORD."

21 Then Isaiah son of Amoz sent to Hezeki-

Read Isaiah 40.12–31.

Now consider. There are 60 seconds in a minute, 60 minutes in an hour, 24 hours in a day, 365 days in a year. That's 31,536,000 seconds per year.

The speed of light is slightly less than 186,000 miles per second. Light travels 5,865,696,000,000 miles per year. Assuming you could coax your car up to light speed, the moon would be 1.28 seconds away. Saturn, 1.18 hours. The next closest galaxy, 2.5 million years. The farthest part of the observable universe, 15 billion years.

With no restrooms along the way.

Consider creation—vast and awesome—all crafted by God. The galaxy, your planet, *you*. Everything you touch, taste, see, feel—all God's handiwork.

So why would you choose to serve anyone else, anything else? Why would you not value God's judgment above the advice of all others?

God is in your world because you live in *his*—the world he shaped. That's reality. There's no turning away, no transferring to a new venue.

But what does that mean to you?

Set aside ten minutes to consider two questions. They're below. And don't rush your answers. Let them bubble up honestly from deep inside you.

- How do I feel about God being my Creator?
- Since God is my Creator, what—if anything—do I owe God?

Post your answers at **Learner.CalltoDiscipleship.com**. Your friends there would love to know what you're thinking.

ah, saying: "Thus says the LORD, the God of Israel: Because you have prayed to me concerning King Sennacherib of Assyria, [22]this is the word that the LORD has spoken concerning him:

She despises you, she scorns you—
    virgin daughter Zion;
she tosses her head—behind your back,
    daughter Jerusalem.

Isaiah's vocal challenges to the different kings of Judah didn't make him popular (see Isaiah 39.1–8, for example). According to tradition, the evil king Manasseh had Isaiah killed by tying him between two planks of wood and sawing him in half.

This information has been scanned and is free of all known viruses. Please forward to all your friends.

23 "Whom have you mocked and reviled?
    Against whom have you raised your voice
    and haughtily lifted your eyes?
    Against the Holy One of Israel!
24 By your servants you have mocked the Lord,
    and you have said, 'With my many chariots
I have gone up the heights of the mountains,
    to the far recesses of Lebanon;
I felled its tallest cedars,
    its choicest cypresses;
I came to its remotest height,
    its densest forest.
25 I dug wells
    and drank waters,
I dried up with the sole of my foot
    all the streams of Egypt.'

26 "Have you not heard
    that I determined it long ago?
I planned from days of old
    what now I bring to pass,
that you should make fortified cities
    crash into heaps of ruins,
27 while their inhabitants, shorn of strength,
    are dismayed and confounded;
they have become like plants of the field
    and like tender grass,
like grass on the housetops,
    blighted*a* before it is grown.

28 "I know your rising up*b* and your sitting
    down,
    your going out and coming in,
    and your raging against me.
29 Because you have raged against me
    and your arrogance has come to my ears,
I will put my hook in your nose
    and my bit in your mouth;
I will turn you back on the way
    by which you came.

30 "And this shall be the sign for you: This year eat what grows of itself, and in the second year what springs from that; then in the third year sow, reap, plant vineyards, and eat their fruit. 31The surviving remnant of the house of Judah shall again take root downward, and bear fruit upward; 32for from Jerusalem a remnant shall go out, and from Mount Zion a band of survivors. The zeal of the LORD of hosts will do this.

33 "Therefore thus says the LORD concerning the king of Assyria: He shall not come into this city, shoot an arrow there, come before it with a shield, or cast up a siege ramp against it. 34By the way that he came, by the same he shall return; he shall not come into this city, says the LORD. 35For I will defend this city to save it, for my own sake and for the sake of my servant David."

Sennacherib's Defeat and Death

36 Then the angel of the LORD set out and struck down one hundred eighty-five thousand in the camp of the Assyrians; when morning dawned, they were all dead bodies. 37Then King Sennacherib of Assyria left, went home, and lived at Nineveh. 38As he was worshiping in the house of his god Nisroch, his sons Adrammelech and Sharezer killed him with the sword, and they escaped into the land of Ararat. His son Esar-haddon succeeded him.

38 Hezekiah's Illness

In those days Hezekiah became sick and was at the point of death. The prophet Isaiah son of Amoz came to him, and said to him, "Thus

a With 2 Kings 19.26: Heb *field*   *b* Q Ms Gk: MT lacks *your rising up* says the LORD: Set your house in order, for you shall die; you shall not recover." ²Then Hezekiah turned his face to the wall, and prayed to the LORD: ³"Remember now, O LORD, I implore you, how I have walked before you in faithfulness with a whole heart, and have done what is good in your sight." And Hezekiah wept bitterly.

4 Then the word of the LORD came to Isaiah: ⁵"Go and say to Hezekiah, Thus says the LORD, the God of your ancestor David: I have heard your prayer, I have seen your tears; I will add fifteen years to your life. ⁶I will deliver you and this city out of the hand of the king of Assyria, and defend this city.

7 "This is the sign to you from the LORD, that the LORD will do this thing that he has promised: ⁸See, I will make the shadow cast by the declining sun on the dial of Ahaz turn back ten steps." So the sun turned back on the dial the ten steps by which it had declined.*a*

9 A writing of King Hezekiah of Judah, after he had been sick and had recovered from his sickness:

¹⁰ I said: In the noontide of my days
        I must depart;
    I am consigned to the gates of Sheol
        for the rest of my years.
¹¹ I said, I shall not see the LORD
        in the land of the living;
    I shall look upon mortals no more
        among the inhabitants of the world.
¹² My dwelling is plucked up and removed
        from me
    like a shepherd's tent;
    like a weaver I have rolled up my life;
        he cuts me off from the loom;
    from day to night you bring me to an end;*a*
¹³   I cry for help*b* until morning;
    like a lion he breaks all my bones;
        from day to night you bring me to an end.*a*

¹⁴ Like a swallow or a crane*a* I clamor,
        I moan like a dove.
    My eyes are weary with looking upward.
        O Lord, I am oppressed; be my security!
¹⁵ But what can I say? For he has spoken to me,
        and he himself has done it.
    All my sleep has fled*c*
        because of the bitterness of my soul.

¹⁶ O Lord, by these things people live,
        and in all these is the life of my spirit.*a*
    Oh, restore me to health and make me
        live!
¹⁷ Surely it was for my welfare
        that I had great bitterness;
    but you have held back*d* my life

from the pit of destruction,
    for you have cast all my sins
        behind your back.
¹⁸ For Sheol cannot thank you,
        death cannot praise you;
    those who go down to the Pit cannot hope
        for your faithfulness.
¹⁹ The living, the living, they thank you,
        as I do this day;
    fathers make known to children
        your faithfulness.

²⁰ The LORD will save me,
        and we will sing to stringed instruments*e*
    all the days of our lives,
        at the house of the LORD.

21 Now Isaiah had said, "Let them take a lump of figs, and apply it to the boil, so that he may recover." ²²Hezekiah also had said, "What is the sign that I shall go up to the house of the LORD?"

39 Envoys from Babylon Welcomed

At that time King Merodach-baladan son of Baladan of Babylon sent envoys with letters and a present to Hezekiah, for he heard that he had been sick and had recovered. ²Hezekiah welcomed them; he showed them his treasure house, the silver, the gold, the spices, the precious oil, his whole armory, all that was found in his storehouses. There was nothing in his house or in all his realm that Hezekiah did not show them. ³Then the prophet Isaiah came to King Hezekiah and said to him, "What did these men say? From where did they come to you?" Hezekiah answered, "They have come to me from a far country, from Babylon." ⁴He said, "What have they seen in your house?" Hezekiah answered, "They have seen all that is in my house; there is nothing in my storehouses that I did not show them."

5 Then Isaiah said to Hezekiah, "Hear the word of the LORD of hosts: ⁶Days are coming when all that is in your house, and that which your ancestors have stored up until this day, shall be carried to Babylon; nothing shall be left, says the LORD. ⁷Some of your own sons who are born to you shall be taken away; they shall be eunuchs in the palace of the king of Babylon." ⁸Then Hezekiah said to Isaiah, "The word of the LORD that you have spoken is good." For he thought, "There will be peace and security in my days."

40 God's People Are Comforted

Comfort, O comfort my people,
    says your God.

---

a Meaning of Heb uncertain   *b* Cn: Meaning of Heb uncertain   *c* Cn Compare Syr: Heb *I will walk slowly all my years*   *d* Cn Compare Gk Vg: Heb *loved*   *e* Heb *my stringed instruments*

² Speak tenderly to Jerusalem,
   and cry to her
that she has served her term,
   that her penalty is paid,
that she has received from the LORD's hand
   double for all her sins.

³ A voice cries out:
"In the wilderness prepare the way of the
   LORD,
   make straight in the desert a highway for
   our God.
⁴ Every valley shall be lifted up,
   and every mountain and hill be made
   low;
the uneven ground shall become level,
   and the rough places a plain.
⁵ Then the glory of the LORD shall be
   revealed,
   and all people shall see it together,
for the mouth of the LORD has spoken."

⁶ A voice says, "Cry out!"
   And I said, "What shall I cry?"
All people are grass,
   their constancy is like the flower of the
   field.
⁷ The grass withers, the flower fades,
   when the breath of the LORD blows
   upon it;
   surely the people are grass.
⁸ The grass withers, the flower fades;
   but the word of our God will stand forever.
⁹ Get you up to a high mountain,
   O Zion, herald of good tidings;^a
lift up your voice with strength,
   O Jerusalem, herald of good tidings,^b
   lift it up, do not fear;
say to the cities of Judah,
   "Here is your God!"
¹⁰ See, the Lord GOD comes with might,
   and his arm rules for him;
his reward is with him,
   and his recompense before him.
¹¹ He will feed his flock like a shepherd;
   he will gather the lambs in his arms,
and carry them in his bosom,
   and gently lead the mother sheep.

¹² Who has measured the waters in the hollow
   of his hand
   and marked off the heavens with a span,
enclosed the dust of the earth in a measure,
   and weighed the mountains in scales
   and the hills in a balance?
¹³ Who has directed the spirit of the LORD,
   or as his counselor has instructed him?
¹⁴ Whom did he consult for his
   enlightenment,

and who taught him the path of justice?
Who taught him knowledge,
   and showed him the way of
   understanding?
¹⁵ Even the nations are like a drop from a
   bucket,
   and are accounted as dust on the scales;
see, he takes up the isles like fine dust.
¹⁶ Lebanon would not provide fuel enough,
   nor are its animals enough for a burnt
   offering.
¹⁷ All the nations are as nothing before him;
   they are accounted by him as less than
   nothing and emptiness.

¹⁸ To whom then will you liken God,
   or what likeness compare with him?
¹⁹ An idol? —A workman casts it,
   and a goldsmith overlays it with gold,
   and casts for it silver chains.
²⁰ As a gift one chooses mulberry wood^c
   —wood that will not rot—
then seeks out a skilled artisan
   to set up an image that will not topple.

²¹ Have you not known? Have you not heard?
   Has it not been told you from the
   beginning?
Have you not understood from the
   foundations of the earth?
²² It is he who sits above the circle of the earth,
   and its inhabitants are like grasshoppers;
who stretches out the heavens like a
   curtain,
   and spreads them like a tent to live in;
²³ who brings princes to naught,
   and makes the rulers of the earth as
   nothing.

²⁴ Scarcely are they planted, scarcely sown,
   scarcely has their stem taken root in the
   earth,
when he blows upon them, and they wither,
   and the tempest carries them off like
   stubble.

²⁵ To whom then will you compare me,
   or who is my equal? says the Holy One.
²⁶ Lift up your eyes on high and see:
   Who created these?
He who brings out their host and numbers
   them,
   calling them all by name;
because he is great in strength,
   mighty in power,
   not one is missing.

²⁷ Why do you say, O Jacob,
   and speak, O Israel,
"My way is hidden from the LORD,

a Or *O herald of good tidings to Zion* *b* Or *O herald of good tidings to Jerusalem* *c* Meaning of Heb uncertain

and my right is disregarded by my God"?
28 Have you not known? Have you not heard?
The LORD is the everlasting God,
 the Creator of the ends of the earth.
He does not faint or grow weary;
 his understanding is unsearchable.
29 He gives power to the faint,
 and strengthens the powerless.
30 Even youths will faint and be weary,
 and the young will fall exhausted;
31 but those who wait for the LORD shall
  renew their strength,
 they shall mount up with wings like
  eagles,
they shall run and not be weary,
 they shall walk and not faint.

41 Israel Assured of God's Help

Listen to me in silence, O coastlands;
 let the peoples renew their strength;
let them approach, then let them speak;
 let us together draw near for judgment.

2 Who has roused a victor from the east,
 summoned him to his service?
He delivers up nations to him,
 and tramples kings under foot;
he makes them like dust with his sword,
 like driven stubble with his bow.
3 He pursues them and passes on safely,
 scarcely touching the path with his feet.
4 Who has performed and done this,
 calling the generations from the
  beginning?
I, the LORD, am first,
 and will be with the last.
5 The coastlands have seen and are afraid,
 the ends of the earth tremble;
they have drawn near and come.
6 Each one helps the other,
 saying to one another, "Take courage!"
7 The artisan encourages the goldsmith,
 and the one who smooths with the
  hammer encourages the one who
  strikes the anvil,
saying of the soldering, "It is good";
 and they fasten it with nails so that it
  cannot be moved.
8 But you, Israel, my servant,
 Jacob, whom I have chosen,
 the offspring of Abraham, my friend;
9 you whom I took from the ends of the earth,
 and called from its farthest corners,
saying to you, "You are my servant,
 I have chosen you and not cast you off";
10 do not fear, for I am with you,
 do not be afraid, for I am your God;
I will strengthen you, I will help you,

Beauty—© Jill Goldstein, 15

I will uphold you with my victorious right
 hand.

11 Yes, all who are incensed against you
 shall be ashamed and disgraced;
those who strive against you
 shall be as nothing and shall perish.
12 You shall seek those who contend with you,
 but you shall not find them;
those who war against you
 shall be as nothing at all.
13 For I, the LORD your God,
 hold your right hand;
it is I who say to you, "Do not fear,
 I will help you."

14 Do not fear, you worm Jacob,
 you insect[a] Israel!
I will help you, says the LORD;
 your Redeemer is the Holy One of Israel.
15 Now, I will make of you a threshing sledge,
 sharp, new, and having teeth;
you shall thresh the mountains and crush
  them,
 and you shall make the hills like chaff.
16 You shall winnow them and the wind shall
  carry them away,
 and the tempest shall scatter them.
Then you shall rejoice in the LORD;
 in the Holy One of Israel you shall glory.

17 When the poor and needy seek water,
 and there is none,
 and their tongue is parched with thirst,
I the LORD will answer them,
 I the God of Israel will not forsake them.
18 I will open rivers on the bare heights,[b]
 and fountains in the midst of the valleys;
I will make the wilderness a pool of water,

a Syr: Heb *men of* *b* Or *trails*

and the dry land springs of water.
¹⁹ I will put in the wilderness the cedar,
   the acacia, the myrtle, and the olive;
 I will set in the desert the cypress,
   the plane and the pine together,
²⁰ so that all may see and know,
   all may consider and understand,
 that the hand of the LORD has done this,
   the Holy One of Israel has created it.

The Futility of Idols

²¹ Set forth your case, says the LORD;
   bring your proofs, says the King of Jacob.
²² Let them bring them, and tell us
   what is to happen.
 Tell us the former things, what they are,
   so that we may consider them,
 and that we may know their outcome;
   or declare to us the things to come.
²³ Tell us what is to come hereafter,
   that we may know that you are gods;
 do good, or do harm,
   that we may be afraid and terrified.
²⁴ You, indeed, are nothing
   and your work is nothing at all;
   whoever chooses you is an abomination.

²⁵ I stirred up one from the north, and he has
     come,
   from the rising of the sun he was
     summoned by name.^a
 He shall trample^b on rulers as on mortar,
   as the potter treads clay.
²⁶ Who declared it from the beginning, so that
     we might know,
   and beforehand, so that we might say,
     "He is right"?
 There was no one who declared it, none
     who proclaimed,
   none who heard your words.
²⁷ I first have declared it to Zion,^c
   and I give to Jerusalem a herald of good
     tidings.
²⁸ But when I look there is no one;
   among these there is no counselor
   who, when I ask, gives an answer.
²⁹ No, they are all a delusion;
   their works are nothing;
   their images are empty wind.

42 The Servant, a Light to the Nations
 Here is my servant, whom I uphold,
   my chosen, in whom my soul delights;
 I have put my spirit upon him;
   he will bring forth justice to the nations.
² He will not cry or lift up his voice,
   or make it heard in the street;

³ a bruised reed he will not break,
   and a dimly burning wick he will not
     quench;
   he will faithfully bring forth justice.
⁴ He will not grow faint or be crushed
   until he has established justice in the
     earth;
   and the coastlands wait for his teaching.

⁵ Thus says God, the LORD,
   who created the heavens and stretched
     them out,
   who spread out the earth and what
     comes from it,
 who gives breath to the people upon it
   and spirit to those who walk in it:
⁶ I am the LORD, I have called you in
     righteousness,
   I have taken you by the hand and kept
     you;
 I have given you as a covenant to the people,^d
   a light to the nations,
⁷   to open the eyes that are blind,
 to bring out the prisoners from the
     dungeon,
   from the prison those who sit in
     darkness.
⁸ I am the LORD, that is my name;
   my glory I give to no other,
   nor my praise to idols.
⁹ See, the former things have come to pass,
   and new things I now declare;
 before they spring forth,
   I tell you of them.

A Hymn of Praise

¹⁰ Sing to the LORD a new song,
   his praise from the end of the earth!
 Let the sea roar^e and all that fills it,
   the coastlands and their inhabitants.
¹¹ Let the desert and its towns lift up their
     voice,
   the villages that Kedar inhabits;
 let the inhabitants of Sela sing for joy,
   let them shout from the tops of the
     mountains.
¹² Let them give glory to the LORD,
   and declare his praise in the coastlands.
¹³ The LORD goes forth like a soldier,
   like a warrior he stirs up his fury;
 he cries out, he shouts aloud,
   he shows himself mighty against his foes.

¹⁴ For a long time I have held my peace,
   I have kept still and restrained myself;
 now I will cry out like a woman in labor,
   I will gasp and pant.

a Cn Compare Q Ms Gk: MT *and he shall call on my name* b Cn: Heb *come* c Cn: Heb *First to Zion—Behold, behold them* d Meaning of Heb uncertain e Cn Compare Ps 96.11; 98.7: Heb *Those who go down to the sea*

Hope—© Rachel Hostert, 18

¹⁵ I will lay waste mountains and hills,
　　and dry up all their herbage;
I will turn the rivers into islands,
　　and dry up the pools.
¹⁶ I will lead the blind
　　by a road they do not know,
by paths they have not known
　　I will guide them.
I will turn the darkness before them into
　　　　light,
　　the rough places into level ground.
These are the things I will do,
　　and I will not forsake them.
¹⁷ They shall be turned back and utterly put to
　　　　shame—
　　those who trust in carved images,
who say to cast images,
　　"You are our gods."

¹⁸ Listen, you that are deaf;
　　and you that are blind, look up and see!
¹⁹ Who is blind but my servant,
　　or deaf like my messenger whom I send?
Who is blind like my dedicated one,
　　or blind like the servant of the LORD?
²⁰ He sees many things, but does^a not observe
　　　　them;
　　his ears are open, but he does not hear.

Israel's Disobedience
²¹ The LORD was pleased, for the sake of his
　　　　righteousness,

to magnify his teaching and make it
　　　　glorious.
²² But this is a people robbed and plundered,
　　all of them are trapped in holes
　　and hidden in prisons;
they have become a prey with no one to
　　　　rescue,
　　a spoil with no one to say, "Restore!"
²³ Who among you will give heed to this,
　　who will attend and listen for the time to
　　　　come?
²⁴ Who gave up Jacob to the spoiler,
　　and Israel to the robbers?
Was it not the LORD, against whom we have
　　　　sinned,
　　in whose ways they would not walk,
　　and whose law they would not obey?
²⁵ So he poured upon him the heat of his
　　　　anger
　　and the fury of war;
it set him on fire all around, but he did not
　　　　understand;
　　it burned him, but he did not take it to
　　　　heart.

43 Restoration and Protection Promised
But now thus says the LORD,
　　he who created you, O Jacob,
　　he who formed you, O Israel:
Do not fear, for I have redeemed you;
　　I have called you by name, you are mine.

a Heb *You see many things but do*

EXPRESS YOURSELF

Feeding on Ashes

When was the last time you carved a little god out of wood and started bowing down to it? Never? Good.

How about the last time you carved out time for your favorite band? Sport? Web site? Video game? Store?

That's okay too. Usually.

Idolatry is alive and well in the twenty-first century. You probably don't know people who literally get on their knees and worship statues. But anyone who gives excessive devotion to something besides God is doing the same thing: worshiping an idol.

Worship involves three things: admiration, public expression, and service. Who or what do you admire? What are you excited to tell other people about? How do you spend the majority of your time?

Read **Isaiah 44.6–20** and decide if there's anything in your life you would consider an idol—something besides God that dominates your admiration, expression, and service. Is God your "one and only"? Or are you "feeding on ashes"?

Go outside and pick up a branch or stick off the ground. Use the branch to draw a simple picture in the dirt of something you might be tempted to idolize in your life. Thank God for allowing you to enjoy that in your life, then commit to worshiping the One who carries you, not what you can carry. (Scan or take a digital picture of your drawing and post it at **Learner.CalltoDiscipleship.com**.)

and honored, and I love you,
I give people in return for you,
    nations in exchange for your life.
5 Do not fear, for I am with you;
    I will bring your offspring from the east,
    and from the west I will gather you;
6 I will say to the north, "Give them up,"
    and to the south, "Do not withhold;
bring my sons from far away
    and my daughters from the end of the
        earth—
7 everyone who is called by my name,
    whom I created for my glory,
    whom I formed and made."

8 Bring forth the people who are blind, yet
      have eyes,
    who are deaf, yet have ears!
9 Let all the nations gather together,
    and let the peoples assemble.
Who among them declared this,
    and foretold to us the former things?
Let them bring their witnesses to justify
      them,
    and let them hear and say, "It is true."
10 You are my witnesses, says the LORD,
    and my servant whom I have chosen,
so that you may know and believe me
    and understand that I am he.
Before me no god was formed,
    nor shall there be any after me.
11 I, I am the LORD,
    and besides me there is no savior.
12 I declared and saved and proclaimed,
    when there was no strange god among
      you;
    and you are my witnesses, says the LORD.
13 I am God, and also henceforth I am He;
    there is no one who can deliver from my
      hand;
    I work and who can hinder it?

14 Thus says the LORD,
    your Redeemer, the Holy One of Israel:
For your sake I will send to Babylon
    and break down all the bars,
    and the shouting of the Chaldeans will be
      turned to lamentation.*b*
15 I am the LORD, your Holy One,
    the Creator of Israel, your King.
16 Thus says the LORD,
    who makes a way in the sea,
    a path in the mighty waters,
17 who brings out chariot and horse,
    army and warrior;
they lie down, they cannot rise,
    they are extinguished, quenched like a
      wick:

2 When you pass through the waters, I will be
    with you;
    and through the rivers, they shall not
      overwhelm you;
    when you walk through fire you shall not be
      burned,
    and the flame shall not consume you.
3 For I am the LORD your God,
    the Holy One of Israel, your Savior.
I give Egypt as your ransom,
    Ethiopia*a* and Seba in exchange for you.
4 Because you are precious in my sight,

a Or *Nubia*; Heb *Cush* *b* Meaning of Heb uncertain

¹⁸ Do not remember the former things,
   or consider the things of old.
¹⁹ I am about to do a new thing;
   now it springs forth, do you not
      perceive it?
   I will make a way in the wilderness
   and rivers in the desert.
²⁰ The wild animals will honor me,
   the jackals and the ostriches;
   for I give water in the wilderness,
   rivers in the desert,
   to give drink to my chosen people,
²¹   the people whom I formed for myself
   so that they might declare my praise.

²² Yet you did not call upon me, O Jacob;
   but you have been weary of me, O Israel!
²³ You have not brought me your sheep for
      burnt offerings,
   or honored me with your sacrifices.
   I have not burdened you with offerings,
   or wearied you with frankincense.
²⁴ You have not bought me sweet cane with
      money,
   or satisfied me with the fat of your
      sacrifices.
   But you have burdened me with your sins;
   you have wearied me with your
      iniquities.

²⁵ I, I am He
   who blots out your transgressions for my
      own sake,
   and I will not remember your sins.
²⁶ Accuse me, let us go to trial;
   set forth your case, so that you may be
      proved right.
²⁷ Your first ancestor sinned,
   and your interpreters transgressed
      against me.
²⁸ Therefore I profaned the princes of the
      sanctuary,
   I delivered Jacob to utter destruction,
   and Israel to reviling.

44 God's Blessing on Israel

   But now hear, O Jacob my servant,
   Israel whom I have chosen!
² Thus says the LORD who made you,
   who formed you in the womb and will
      help you:
   Do not fear, O Jacob my servant,
   Jeshurun whom I have chosen.
³ For I will pour water on the thirsty land,
   and streams on the dry ground;
   I will pour my spirit upon your
      descendants,
   and my blessing on your offspring.

⁴ They shall spring up like a green tamarisk,
   like willows by flowing streams.
⁵ This one will say, "I am the LORD's,"
   another will be called by the name of
      Jacob,
   yet another will write on the hand, "The
      LORD's,"
   and adopt the name of Israel.

⁶ Thus says the LORD, the King of Israel,
   and his Redeemer, the LORD of hosts:
   I am the first and I am the last;
   besides me there is no god.
⁷ Who is like me? Let them proclaim it,
   let them declare and set it forth
      before me.
   Who has announced from of old the things
      to come?^a
   Let them tell us^b what is yet to be.
⁸ Do not fear, or be afraid;
   have I not told you from of old and
      declared it?
   You are my witnesses!
   Is there any god besides me?
   There is no other rock; I know not one.

The Absurdity of Idol Worship

9 All who make idols are nothing, and the things they delight in do not profit; their witnesses neither see nor know. And so they will be put to shame. ¹⁰Who would fashion a god or cast an image that can do no good? ¹¹Look, all its devotees shall be put to shame; the artisans too are merely human. Let them all assemble, let them stand up; they shall be terrified, they shall all be put to shame.

12 The ironsmith fashions it^c and works it over the coals, shaping it with hammers, and forging it with his strong arm; he becomes hungry and his strength fails, he drinks no water and is faint. ¹³The carpenter stretches a line, marks it out with a stylus, fashions it with planes, and marks it with a compass; he makes it in human form, with human beauty, to be set up in a shrine. ¹⁴He cuts down cedars or chooses a holm tree or an oak and lets it grow strong among the trees of the forest. He plants a cedar and the rain nourishes it. ¹⁵Then it can be used as fuel. Part of it he takes and warms himself; he kindles a fire and bakes bread. Then he makes a god and worships it, makes it a carved image and bows down before it. ¹⁶Half of it he burns in the fire; over this half he roasts meat, eats it and is satisfied. He also warms himself and says, "Ah, I am warm, I can feel the fire!" ¹⁷The rest of it he makes into a god, his idol, bows down to it and worships it; he prays to it and says, "Save me, for you are my god!"

---

a Cn: Heb *from my placing an eternal people and things to come*   b Tg: Heb *them*   c Cn: Heb *an ax*

and your sins like mist;
return to me, for I have redeemed you.

23 Sing, O heavens, for the LORD has done it;
shout, O depths of the earth;
break forth into singing, O mountains,
O forest, and every tree in it!
For the LORD has redeemed Jacob,
and will be glorified in Israel.

24 Thus says the LORD, your Redeemer,
who formed you in the womb:
I am the LORD, who made all things,
who alone stretched out the heavens,
who by myself spread out the earth;
25 who frustrates the omens of liars,
and makes fools of diviners;
who turns back the wise,
and makes their knowledge foolish;
26 who confirms the word of his servant,
and fulfills the prediction of his
messengers;
who says of Jerusalem, "It shall be
inhabited,"
and of the cities of Judah, "They shall be
rebuilt,
and I will raise up their ruins";
27 who says to the deep, "Be dry—
I will dry up your rivers";
28 who says of Cyrus, "He is my shepherd,
and he shall carry out all my purpose";
and who says of Jerusalem, "It shall be
rebuilt,"
and of the temple, "Your foundation
shall be laid."

45 Cyrus, God's Instrument

Thus says the LORD to his anointed, to Cyrus,
whose right hand I have grasped
to subdue nations before him
and strip kings of their robes,
to open doors before him—
and the gates shall not be closed:
2 I will go before you
and level the mountains,*a*
I will break in pieces the doors of bronze
and cut through the bars of iron,
3 I will give you the treasures of darkness
and riches hidden in secret places,
so that you may know that it is I, the LORD,
the God of Israel, who call you by your
name.
4 For the sake of my servant Jacob,
and Israel my chosen,
I call you by your name,
I surname you, though you do not
know me.
5 I am the LORD, and there is no other;

18 They do not know, nor do they comprehend; for their eyes are shut, so that they cannot see, and their minds as well, so that they
cannot understand. 19No one considers, nor is
there knowledge or discernment to say, "Half
of it I burned in the fire; I also baked bread on
its coals, I roasted meat and have eaten. Now
shall I make the rest of it an abomination?
Shall I fall down before a block of wood?" 20He
feeds on ashes; a deluded mind has led him
astray, and he cannot save himself or say, "Is
not this thing in my right hand a fraud?"

Israel Is Not Forgotten
21 Remember these things, O Jacob,
and Israel, for you are my servant;
I formed you, you are my servant;
O Israel, you will not be forgotten by me.
22 I have swept away your transgressions like a
cloud,

a Q Ms Gk: MT *the swellings*

besides me there is no god.
I arm you, though you do not know me,
6 so that they may know, from the rising of
the sun
and from the west, that there is no one
besides me;
I am the LORD, and there is no other.
7 I form light and create darkness,
I make weal and create woe;
I the LORD do all these things.

8 Shower, O heavens, from above,
and let the skies rain down
righteousness;
let the earth open, that salvation may
spring up,*a*
and let it cause righteousness to sprout
up also;
I the LORD have created it.

9 Woe to you who strive with your Maker,
earthen vessels with the potter!*b*
Does the clay say to the one who fashions
it, "What are you making"?
or "Your work has no handles"?
10 Woe to anyone who says to a father, "What
are you begetting?"
or to a woman, "With what are you in
labor?"
11 Thus says the LORD,
the Holy One of Israel, and its Maker:
Will you question me*c* about my children,
or command me concerning the work of
my hands?
12 I made the earth,
and created humankind upon it;
it was my hands that stretched out the
heavens,
and I commanded all their host.
13 I have aroused Cyrus*d* in righteousness,
and I will make all his paths straight;
he shall build my city
and set my exiles free,
not for price or reward,
says the LORD of hosts.
14 Thus says the LORD:
The wealth of Egypt and the merchandise of
Ethiopia,*e*
and the Sabeans, tall of stature,
shall come over to you and be yours,
they shall follow you;
they shall come over in chains and bow
down to you.
They will make supplication to you, saying,
"God is with you alone, and there is no
other;
there is no god besides him."

15 Truly, you are a God who hides himself,
O God of Israel, the Savior.
16 All of them are put to shame and
confounded,
the makers of idols go in confusion
together.
17 But Israel is saved by the LORD
with everlasting salvation;
you shall not be put to shame or confounded
to all eternity.

18 For thus says the LORD,
who created the heavens
(he is God!),
who formed the earth and made it
(he established it;
he did not create it a chaos,
he formed it to be inhabited!):
I am the LORD, and there is no other.
19 I did not speak in secret,
in a land of darkness;
I did not say to the offspring of Jacob,
"Seek me in chaos."
I the LORD speak the truth,
I declare what is right.

Idols Cannot Save Babylon

20 Assemble yourselves and come together,
draw near, you survivors of the nations!
They have no knowledge—
those who carry about their wooden idols,
and keep on praying to a god
that cannot save.
21 Declare and present your case;
let them take counsel together!
Who told this long ago?
Who declared it of old?
Was it not I, the LORD?
There is no other god besides me,
a righteous God and a Savior;
there is no one besides me.

22 Turn to me and be saved,
all the ends of the earth!
For I am God, and there is no other.
23 By myself I have sworn,
from my mouth has gone forth in
righteousness
a word that shall not return:
"To me every knee shall bow,
every tongue shall swear."

24 Only in the LORD, it shall be said of me,
are righteousness and strength;
all who were incensed against him
shall come to him and be ashamed.
25 In the LORD all the offspring of Israel
shall triumph and glory.

a Q Ms: MT *that they may bring forth salvation* b Cn: Heb *with the potsherds*, or *with the potters* c Cn: Heb *Ask me of things to come* d Heb *him*
e Or *Nubia*; Heb *Cush*

46 Bel bows down, Nebo stoops,
  their idols are on beasts and cattle;
these things you carry are loaded
  as burdens on weary animals.
2 They stoop, they bow down together;
  they cannot save the burden,
  but themselves go into captivity.

3 Listen to me, O house of Jacob,
  all the remnant of the house of Israel,
who have been borne by me from your birth,
  carried from the womb;
4 even to your old age I am he,
  even when you turn gray I will carry you.
I have made, and I will bear;
  I will carry and will save.

5 To whom will you liken me and make me
    equal,
  and compare me, as though we were
    alike?
6 Those who lavish gold from the purse,
  and weigh out silver in the scales—
they hire a goldsmith, who makes it into a
    god;
  then they fall down and worship!
7 They lift it to their shoulders, they carry it,
  they set it in its place, and it stands there;
  it cannot move from its place.
If one cries out to it, it does not answer
  or save anyone from trouble.

8 Remember this and consider,[a]
  recall it to mind, you transgressors,
9   remember the former things of old;
for I am God, and there is no other;
  I am God, and there is no one like me,
10 declaring the end from the beginning
  and from ancient times things not yet
    done,
saying, "My purpose shall stand,
  and I will fulfill my intention,"
11 calling a bird of prey from the east,
  the man for my purpose from a far
    country.
I have spoken, and I will bring it to pass;
  I have planned, and I will do it.

12 Listen to me, you stubborn of heart,
  you who are far from deliverance:
13 I bring near my deliverance, it is not far off,
  and my salvation will not tarry;
I will put salvation in Zion,
  for Israel my glory.

47 The Humiliation of Babylon
Come down and sit in the dust,
  virgin daughter Babylon!

Sit on the ground without a throne,
  daughter Chaldea!
For you shall no more be called
  tender and delicate.
2 Take the millstones and grind meal,
  remove your veil,
strip off your robe, uncover your legs,
  pass through the rivers.
3 Your nakedness shall be uncovered,
  and your shame shall be seen.
I will take vengeance,
  and I will spare no one.
4 Our Redeemer—the LORD of hosts is his
    name—
  is the Holy One of Israel.

5 Sit in silence, and go into darkness,
  daughter Chaldea!
For you shall no more be called
  the mistress of kingdoms.
6 I was angry with my people,
  I profaned my heritage;
I gave them into your hand,
  you showed them no mercy;
on the aged you made your yoke
  exceedingly heavy.
7 You said, "I shall be mistress forever,"
  so that you did not lay these things to
    heart
  or remember their end.

8 Now therefore hear this, you lover of
    pleasures,
  who sit securely,
who say in your heart,
  "I am, and there is no one besides me;
I shall not sit as a widow
  or know the loss of children"—
9 both these things shall come upon you
  in a moment, in one day:
the loss of children and widowhood
  shall come upon you in full measure,
in spite of your many sorceries
  and the great power of your
    enchantments.

10 You felt secure in your wickedness;
  you said, "No one sees me."
Your wisdom and your knowledge
  led you astray,
and you said in your heart,
  "I am, and there is no one besides me."
11 But evil shall come upon you,
  which you cannot charm away;
disaster shall fall upon you,
  which you will not be able to ward off;
and ruin shall come on you suddenly,
  of which you know nothing.

a Meaning of Heb uncertain

¹² Stand fast in your enchantments
and your many sorceries,
with which you have labored from your
youth;
perhaps you may be able to succeed,
perhaps you may inspire terror.
¹³ You are wearied with your many
consultations;
let those who study*[a]* the heavens
stand up and save you,
those who gaze at the stars,
and at each new moon predict
what*[b]* shall befall you.

¹⁴ See, they are like stubble,
the fire consumes them;
they cannot deliver themselves
from the power of the flame.
No coal for warming oneself is this,
no fire to sit before!
¹⁵ Such to you are those with whom you have
labored,
who have trafficked with you from your
youth;
they all wander about in their own paths;
there is no one to save you.

48 God the Creator and Redeemer

Hear this, O house of Jacob,
who are called by the name of Israel,
and who came forth from the loins*[c]* of
Judah;
who swear by the name of the LORD,
and invoke the God of Israel,
but not in truth or right.
² For they call themselves after the holy city,
and lean on the God of Israel;
the LORD of hosts is his name.

³ The former things I declared long ago,
they went out from my mouth and I
made them known;
then suddenly I did them and they came
to pass.
⁴ Because I know that you are obstinate,
and your neck is an iron sinew
and your forehead brass,
⁵ I declared them to you from long ago,
before they came to pass I announced
them to you,
so that you would not say, "My idol did them,
my carved image and my cast image
commanded them."

⁶ You have heard; now see all this;
and will you not declare it?
From this time forward I make you hear
new things,
hidden things that you have not known.

⁷ They are created now, not long ago;
before today you have never heard of
them,
so that you could not say, "I already knew
them."
⁸ You have never heard, you have never
known,
from of old your ear has not been
opened.
For I knew that you would deal very
treacherously,
and that from birth you were called a
rebel.

⁹ For my name's sake I defer my anger,
for the sake of my praise I restrain it for
you,
so that I may not cut you off.
¹⁰ See, I have refined you, but not like*[d]* silver;
I have tested you in the furnace of
adversity.

a Meaning of Heb uncertain *b* Gk Syr Compare Vg: Heb *from what* *c* Cn: Heb *waters* *d* Cn: Heb *with*

¹¹ For my own sake, for my own sake, I do it,
  for why should my name*ª* be profaned?
  My glory I will not give to another.

¹² Listen to me, O Jacob,
  and Israel, whom I called:
I am He; I am the first,
  and I am the last.
¹³ My hand laid the foundation of the earth,
  and my right hand spread out the heavens;
when I summon them,
  they stand at attention.

¹⁴ Assemble, all of you, and hear!
  Who among them has declared these
    things?
The Lord loves him;
  he shall perform his purpose on Babylon,
  and his arm shall be against the
    Chaldeans.
¹⁵ I, even I, have spoken and called him,
  I have brought him, and he will prosper
    in his way.
¹⁶ Draw near to me, hear this!
  From the beginning I have not spoken in
    secret,
  from the time it came to be I have been
    there.
And now the Lord God has sent me and his
    spirit.

¹⁷ Thus says the Lord,
  your Redeemer, the Holy One of Israel:
I am the Lord your God,
  who teaches you for your own good,
  who leads you in the way you should go.
¹⁸ O that you had paid attention to my
    commandments!
  Then your prosperity would have been
    like a river,
  and your success like the waves of the sea;

Peace— © Rachel Hostert, 18

¹⁹ your offspring would have been like the
    sand,
  and your descendants like its grains;
their name would never be cut off
  or destroyed from before me.

²⁰ Go out from Babylon, flee from Chaldea,
  declare this with a shout of joy,
    proclaim it,
send it forth to the end of the earth;
  say, "The Lord has redeemed his servant
    Jacob!"
²¹ They did not thirst when he led them
    through the deserts;
  he made water flow for them from the
    rock;
  he split open the rock and the water
    gushed out.

²² "There is no peace," says the Lord, "for the
    wicked."

49 The Servant's Mission

Listen to me, O coastlands,
  pay attention, you peoples from far
    away!
The Lord called me before I was born,
  while I was in my mother's womb he
    named me.
² He made my mouth like a sharp sword,
  in the shadow of his hand he hid me;
he made me a polished arrow,
  in his quiver he hid me away.
³ And he said to me, "You are my servant,
  Israel, in whom I will be glorified."
⁴ But I said, "I have labored in vain,
  I have spent my strength for nothing and
    vanity;
yet surely my cause is with the Lord,
  and my reward with my God."

⁵ And now the Lord says,
  who formed me in the womb to be his
    servant,
to bring Jacob back to him,
  and that Israel might be gathered to him,
for I am honored in the sight of the Lord,
  and my God has become my strength—
⁶ he says,
"It is too light a thing that you should be my
    servant
  to raise up the tribes of Jacob
  and to restore the survivors of Israel;
I will give you as a light to the nations,
  that my salvation may reach to the end of
    the earth."

⁷ Thus says the Lord,
  the Redeemer of Israel and his Holy One,

a Gk Old Latin: Heb *for why should it*

to one deeply despised, abhorred by the
nations,
    the slave of rulers,
"Kings shall see and stand up,
    princes, and they shall prostrate
themselves,
because of the LORD, who is faithful,
    the Holy One of Israel, who has chosen
you."

Zion's Children to Be Brought Home

8 Thus says the LORD:
In a time of favor I have answered you,
    on a day of salvation I have helped you;
I have kept you and given you
    as a covenant to the people,[a]
to establish the land,
    to apportion the desolate heritages;
9 saying to the prisoners, "Come out,"
    to those who are in darkness, "Show
yourselves."
They shall feed along the ways,
    on all the bare heights[b] shall be their
pasture;
10 they shall not hunger or thirst,
    neither scorching wind nor sun shall
strike them down,
for he who has pity on them will lead them,
    and by springs of water will guide them.
11 And I will turn all my mountains into a
road,
    and my highways shall be raised up.
12 Lo, these shall come from far away,
    and lo, these from the north and from
the west,
    and these from the land of Syene.[c]

13 Sing for joy, O heavens, and exult, O earth;
    break forth, O mountains, into singing!
For the LORD has comforted his people,
    and will have compassion on his
suffering ones.

14 But Zion said, "The LORD has forsaken me,
    my Lord has forgotten me."
15 Can a woman forget her nursing child,
    or show no compassion for the child of
her womb?
Even these may forget,
    yet I will not forget you.
16 See, I have inscribed you on the palms of
my hands;
    your walls are continually before me.
17 Your builders outdo your destroyers,[d]
    and those who laid you waste go away
from you.
18 Lift up your eyes all around and see;

they all gather, they come to you.
As I live, says the LORD,
    you shall put all of them on like an
ornament,
    and like a bride you shall bind them on.

19 Surely your waste and your desolate places
    and your devastated land—
surely now you will be too crowded for your
inhabitants,
    and those who swallowed you up will be
far away.
20 The children born in the time of your
bereavement
    will yet say in your hearing:
"The place is too crowded for me;
    make room for me to settle."
21 Then you will say in your heart,
    "Who has borne me these?
I was bereaved and barren,
    exiled and put away—
so who has reared these?
I was left all alone—
    where then have these come from?"

22 Thus says the Lord GOD:
I will soon lift up my hand to the nations,
    and raise my signal to the peoples;
and they shall bring your sons in their
bosom,
    and your daughters shall be carried on
their shoulders.
23 Kings shall be your foster fathers,
    and their queens your nursing mothers.
With their faces to the ground they shall
bow down to you,
    and lick the dust of your feet.
Then you will know that I am the LORD;
    those who wait for me shall not be put to
shame.

24 Can the prey be taken from the mighty,
    or the captives of a tyrant[e] be rescued?
25 But thus says the LORD:
Even the captives of the mighty shall be
taken,
    and the prey of the tyrant be rescued;
for I will contend with those who contend
with you,
    and I will save your children.
26 I will make your oppressors eat their own
flesh,
    and they shall be drunk with their own
blood as with wine.
Then all flesh shall know
    that I am the LORD your Savior,
    and your Redeemer, the Mighty One of
Jacob.

a Meaning of Heb uncertain b Or the trails c Q Ms: MT Sinim d Or Your children come swiftly; your destroyers e Q Ms Syr Vg: MT of a
righteous person

50 Thus says the LORD:
Where is your mother's bill of divorce
with which I put her away?
Or which of my creditors is it
to whom I have sold you?
No, because of your sins you were sold,
and for your transgressions your mother
was put away.
[2] Why was no one there when I came?
Why did no one answer when I called?
Is my hand shortened, that it cannot
redeem?
Or have I no power to deliver?
By my rebuke I dry up the sea,
I make the rivers a desert;
their fish stink for lack of water,
and die of thirst.[a]
[3] I clothe the heavens with blackness,
and make sackcloth their covering.

The Servant's Humiliation and Vindication

[4] The Lord GOD has given me
the tongue of a teacher,[b]
that I may know how to sustain
the weary with a word.
Morning by morning he wakens—
wakens my ear
to listen as those who are taught.
[5] The Lord GOD has opened my ear,
and I was not rebellious,
I did not turn backward.
[6] I gave my back to those who struck me,
and my cheeks to those who pulled out
the beard;
I did not hide my face
from insult and spitting.

[7] The Lord GOD helps me;
therefore I have not been disgraced;
therefore I have set my face like flint,
and I know that I shall not be put to
shame;
[8] he who vindicates me is near.
Who will contend with me?
Let us stand up together.
Who are my adversaries?
Let them confront me.
[9] It is the Lord GOD who helps me;
who will declare me guilty?

All of them will wear out like a garment;
the moth will eat them up.
[10] Who among you fears the LORD
and obeys the voice of his servant,
who walks in darkness
and has no light,
yet trusts in the name of the LORD
and relies upon his God?
[11] But all of you are kindlers of fire,
lighters of firebrands.[c]
Walk in the flame of your fire,
and among the brands that you have
kindled!
This is what you shall have from my hand:
you shall lie down in torment.

51 ### Blessings in Store for God's People
Listen to me, you that pursue
righteousness,
you that seek the LORD.
Look to the rock from which you were hewn,
and to the quarry from which you were
dug.
[2] Look to Abraham your father
and to Sarah who bore you;
for he was but one when I called him,
but I blessed him and made him many.
[3] For the LORD will comfort Zion;
he will comfort all her waste places,
and will make her wilderness like Eden,
her desert like the garden of the LORD;
joy and gladness will be found in her,
thanksgiving and the voice of song.

[4] Listen to me, my people,
and give heed to me, my nation;
for a teaching will go out from me,
and my justice for a light to the peoples.
[5] I will bring near my deliverance swiftly,
my salvation has gone out
and my arms will rule the peoples;
the coastlands wait for me,
and for my arm they hope.
[6] Lift up your eyes to the heavens,
and look at the earth beneath;
for the heavens will vanish like smoke,
the earth will wear out like a garment,
and those who live on it will die like
gnats;[d]
but my salvation will be forever,
and my deliverance will never be ended.

[7] Listen to me, you who know righteousness,
you people who have my teaching in your
hearts;
do not fear the reproach of others,
and do not be dismayed when they revile
you.

---

a Or *die on the thirsty ground* *b* Cn: Heb *of those who are taught* *c* Syr: Heb *you gird yourselves with firebrands* *d* Or *in like manner*

8 For the moth will eat them up like a garment,
  and the worm will eat them like wool;
but my deliverance will be forever,
  and my salvation to all generations.

9 Awake, awake, put on strength,
  O arm of the LORD!
Awake, as in days of old,
  the generations of long ago!
Was it not you who cut Rahab in pieces,
  who pierced the dragon?
10 Was it not you who dried up the sea,
  the waters of the great deep;
who made the depths of the sea a way
  for the redeemed to cross over?
11 So the ransomed of the LORD shall return,
  and come to Zion with singing;
everlasting joy shall be upon their heads;
  they shall obtain joy and gladness,
  and sorrow and sighing shall flee away.

12 I, I am he who comforts you;
  why then are you afraid of a mere mortal
    who must die,
  a human being who fades like grass?
13 You have forgotten the LORD, your Maker,
  who stretched out the heavens
  and laid the foundations of the earth.
You fear continually all day long
  because of the fury of the oppressor,
  who is bent on destruction.
  But where is the fury of the oppressor?
14 The oppressed shall speedily be released;
  they shall not die and go down to the Pit,
  nor shall they lack bread.
15 For I am the LORD your God,
  who stirs up the sea so that its waves
    roar—
  the LORD of hosts is his name.
16 I have put my words in your mouth,
  and hidden you in the shadow of my hand,
stretching out[a] the heavens
  and laying the foundations of the earth,
  and saying to Zion, "You are my people."

17 Rouse yourself, rouse yourself!
  Stand up, O Jerusalem,
you who have drunk at the hand of the LORD
  the cup of his wrath,
who have drunk to the dregs
  the bowl of staggering.
18 There is no one to guide her
  among all the children she has borne;
there is no one to take her by the hand
  among all the children she has brought up.
19 These two things have befallen you
  —who will grieve with you?—
  devastation and destruction, famine and
    sword—

who will comfort you?[b]
20 Your children have fainted,
  they lie at the head of every street
  like an antelope in a net;
they are full of the wrath of the LORD,
  the rebuke of your God.

21 Therefore hear this, you who are wounded,[c]
  who are drunk, but not with wine:
22 Thus says your Sovereign, the LORD,
  your God who pleads the cause of his
    people:
See, I have taken from your hand the cup of
    staggering;
you shall drink no more
  from the bowl of my wrath.
23 And I will put it into the hand of your
    tormentors,
  who have said to you,
  "Bow down, that we may walk on you";
and you have made your back like the
    ground
  and like the street for them to walk on.

52 Let Zion Rejoice

Awake, awake,
  put on your strength, O Zion!
Put on your beautiful garments,
  O Jerusalem, the holy city;
for the uncircumcised and the unclean
  shall enter you no more.
2 Shake yourself from the dust, rise up,
  O captive[d] Jerusalem;
loose the bonds from your neck,
  O captive daughter Zion!

3 For thus says the LORD: You were sold for nothing, and you shall be redeemed without money. 4For thus says the Lord GOD: Long ago, my people went down into Egypt to reside there as aliens; the Assyrian, too, has oppressed them without cause. 5Now therefore what am I doing here, says the LORD, seeing that my people are taken away without cause? Their rulers howl, says the LORD, and continually, all day long, my name is despised. 6Therefore my people shall know my name; therefore in that day they shall know that it is I who speak; here am I.

7 How beautiful upon the mountains
  are the feet of the messenger who
    announces peace,
who brings good news,
  who announces salvation,
  who says to Zion, "Your God reigns."
8 Listen! Your sentinels lift up their voices,
  together they sing for joy;
for in plain sight they see

---

a Syr: Heb *planting* b Q Ms Gk Syr Vg: MT *how may I comfort you?* c Or *humbled* d Cn: Heb *rise up, sit* the return of the LORD to Zion.

9 Break forth together into singing,
you ruins of Jerusalem;
for the LORD has comforted his people,
he has redeemed Jerusalem.
10 The LORD has bared his holy arm
before the eyes of all the nations;
and all the ends of the earth shall see
the salvation of our God.

11 Depart, depart, go out from there!
Touch no unclean thing;
go out from the midst of it, purify yourselves,
you who carry the vessels of the LORD.
12 For you shall not go out in haste,
and you shall not go in flight;
for the LORD will go before you,
and the God of Israel will be your rear
guard.

The Suffering Servant

13 See, my servant shall prosper;
he shall be exalted and lifted up,
and shall be very high.
14 Just as there were many who were
astonished at him[a]
—so marred was his appearance, beyond
human semblance,
and his form beyond that of mortals—
15 so he shall startle[b] many nations;
kings shall shut their mouths because of
him;
for that which had not been told them they
shall see,
and that which they had not heard they
shall contemplate.

53 Who has believed what we have heard?
And to whom has the arm of the LORD
been revealed?
2 For he grew up before him like a young
plant,
and like a root out of dry ground;
he had no form or majesty that we should
look at him,
nothing in his appearance that we
should desire him.
3 He was despised and rejected by others;
a man of suffering[c] and acquainted with
infirmity;
and as one from whom others hide their
faces[d]
he was despised, and we held him of no
account.

4 Surely he has borne our infirmities
and carried our diseases;

yet we accounted him stricken,
struck down by God, and afflicted.
5 But he was wounded for our transgressions,
crushed for our iniquities;
upon him was the punishment that made
us whole,
and by his bruises we are healed.
6 All we like sheep have gone astray;
we have all turned to our own way,
and the LORD has laid on him
the iniquity of us all.

7 He was oppressed, and he was afflicted,
yet he did not open his mouth;
like a lamb that is led to the slaughter,
and like a sheep that before its shearers
is silent,
so he did not open his mouth.
8 By a perversion of justice he was taken away.
Who could have imagined his future?
For he was cut off from the land of the
living,
stricken for the transgression of my
people.
9 They made his grave with the wicked
and his tomb[e] with the rich,[f]
although he had done no violence,
and there was no deceit in his mouth.

10 Yet it was the will of the LORD to crush him
with pain.[b]
When you make his life an offering for sin,[g]
he shall see his offspring, and shall
prolong his days;
through him the will of the LORD shall
prosper.
11 Out of his anguish he shall see light;[h]
he shall find satisfaction through his
knowledge.
The righteous one,[i] my servant, shall
make many righteous,
and he shall bear their iniquities.
12 Therefore I will allot him a portion with the
great,
and he shall divide the spoil with the
strong;
because he poured out himself to death,
and was numbered with the
transgressors;
yet he bore the sin of many,
and made intercession for the
transgressors.

54 ## The Eternal Covenant of Peace
Sing, O barren one who did not bear;
burst into song and shout,
you who have not been in labor!

a Syr Tg: Heb *you* b Meaning of Heb uncertain c Or *a man of sorrows* d Or *as one who hides his face from us* e Q Ms: MT *and in his death*
f Cn: Heb *with a rich person* g Or *by disease*; meaning of Heb uncertain h Q Mss: MT lacks *light* i Or *and he shall find satisfaction. Through
his knowledge, the righteous one*

Streets of Ukraine—© Clay Goswick, 16

For the children of the desolate woman will
be more
than the children of her that is married,
says the Lord.
2 Enlarge the site of your tent,
and let the curtains of your habitations
be stretched out;
do not hold back; lengthen your cords
and strengthen your stakes.
3 For you will spread out to the right and to
the left,
and your descendants will possess the
nations
and will settle the desolate towns.

4 Do not fear, for you will not be ashamed;
do not be discouraged, for you will not
suffer disgrace;
for you will forget the shame of your youth,
and the disgrace of your widowhood you
will remember no more.
5 For your Maker is your husband,
the Lord of hosts is his name;
the Holy One of Israel is your Redeemer,
the God of the whole earth he is called.
6 For the Lord has called you
like a wife forsaken and grieved in spirit,
like the wife of a man's youth when she is
cast off,
says your God.
7 For a brief moment I abandoned you,

but with great compassion I will gather
you.
8 In overflowing wrath for a moment
I hid my face from you,
but with everlasting love I will have
compassion on you,
says the Lord, your Redeemer.

9 This is like the days of Noah to me:
Just as I swore that the waters of Noah
would never again go over the earth,
so I have sworn that I will not be angry with
you
and will not rebuke you.
10 For the mountains may depart
and the hills be removed,
but my steadfast love shall not depart from
you,
and my covenant of peace shall not be
removed,
says the Lord, who has compassion on
you.

11 O afflicted one, storm-tossed, and not
comforted,
I am about to set your stones in antimony,
and lay your foundations with sapphires.[a]
12 I will make your pinnacles of rubies,
your gates of jewels,
and all your wall of precious stones.
13 All your children shall be taught by the
Lord,

a Or *lapis lazuli*

and great shall be the prosperity of your
children.
14 In righteousness you shall be established;
you shall be far from oppression, for you
shall not fear;
and from terror, for it shall not come
near you.
15 If anyone stirs up strife,
it is not from me;
whoever stirs up strife with you
shall fall because of you.
16 See it is I who have created the smith
who blows the fire of coals,
and produces a weapon fit for its
purpose;
I have also created the ravager to destroy.
17 No weapon that is fashioned against you
shall prosper,
and you shall confute every tongue that
rises against you in judgment.
This is the heritage of the servants of the
LORD
and their vindication from me, says the
LORD.

55 An Invitation to Abundant Life

Ho, everyone who thirsts,
come to the waters;
and you that have no money,
come, buy and eat!
Come, buy wine and milk
without money and without price.
2 Why do you spend your money for that
which is not bread,
and your labor for that which does not
satisfy?
Listen carefully to me, and eat what is good,
and delight yourselves in rich food.
3 Incline your ear, and come to me;
listen, so that you may live.
I will make with you an everlasting
covenant,
my steadfast, sure love for David.
4 See, I made him a witness to the peoples,
a leader and commander for the peoples.
5 See, you shall call nations that you do not
know,
and nations that do not know you shall
run to you,
because of the LORD your God, the Holy One
of Israel,
for he has glorified you.

6 Seek the LORD while he may be found,
call upon him while he is near;
7 let the wicked forsake their way,
and the unrighteous their thoughts;
let them return to the LORD, that he may
have mercy on them,

and to our God, for he will abundantly
pardon.
8 For my thoughts are not your thoughts,
nor are your ways my ways, says the LORD.
9 For as the heavens are higher than the
earth,
so are my ways higher than your ways
and my thoughts than your thoughts.

10 For as the rain and the snow come down
from heaven,
and do not return there until they have
watered the earth,
making it bring forth and sprout,
giving seed to the sower and bread to the
eater,
11 so shall my word be that goes out from my
mouth;
it shall not return to me empty,
but it shall accomplish that which I purpose,
and succeed in the thing for which I
sent it.

12 For you shall go out in joy,
and be led back in peace;
the mountains and the hills before you
shall burst into song,
and all the trees of the field shall clap
their hands.
13 Instead of the thorn shall come up the
cypress;
instead of the brier shall come up the
myrtle;
and it shall be to the LORD for a memorial,
for an everlasting sign that shall not be
cut off.

56 The Covenant Extended to All Who Obey

Thus says the LORD:
Maintain justice, and do what is right,
for soon my salvation will come,
and my deliverance be revealed.

2 Happy is the mortal who does this,
the one who holds it fast,
who keeps the sabbath, not profaning it,
and refrains from doing any evil.
3 Do not let the foreigner joined to the LORD
say,
"The LORD will surely separate me from
his people";
and do not let the eunuch say,
"I am just a dry tree."
4 For thus says the LORD:
To the eunuchs who keep my sabbaths,
who choose the things that please me
and hold fast my covenant,
5 I will give, in my house and within my walls,
a monument and a name

better than sons and daughters;
   I will give them an everlasting name
      that shall not be cut off.

6 And the foreigners who join themselves to
         the LORD,
      to minister to him, to love the name of
         the LORD,
      and to be his servants,
   all who keep the sabbath, and do not
         profane it,
      and hold fast my covenant—
7 these I will bring to my holy mountain,
      and make them joyful in my house of
         prayer;
   their burnt offerings and their sacrifices
      will be accepted on my altar;
   for my house shall be called a house of
         prayer
      for all peoples.
8 Thus says the Lord GOD,
      who gathers the outcasts of Israel,
   I will gather others to them
      besides those already gathered. *a*

The Corruption of Israel's Rulers
9 All you wild animals,
      all you wild animals in the forest, come
         to devour!
10 Israel's *b* sentinels are blind,
      they are all without knowledge;
   they are all silent dogs
      that cannot bark;
   dreaming, lying down,
      loving to slumber.
11 The dogs have a mighty appetite;
      they never have enough.
   The shepherds also have no understanding;
      they have all turned to their own way,
      to their own gain, one and all.
12 "Come," they say, "let us *c* get wine;
      let us fill ourselves with strong drink.
   And tomorrow will be like today,
      great beyond measure."

57 Israel's Futile Idolatry
The righteous perish,
      and no one takes it to heart;
   the devout are taken away,
      while no one understands.
   For the righteous are taken away from
         calamity,
2   and they enter into peace;
   those who walk uprightly
      will rest on their couches.
3 But as for you, come here,
      you children of a sorceress,

you offspring of an adulterer and a
      whore. *d*
4 Whom are you mocking?
   Against whom do you open your mouth
         wide
      and stick out your tongue?
   Are you not children of transgression,
      the offspring of deceit—
5 you that burn with lust among the oaks,
      under every green tree;
   you that slaughter your children in the
         valleys,
      under the clefts of the rocks?
6 Among the smooth stones of the valley is
         your portion;
      they, they, are your lot;
   to them you have poured out a drink
         offering,
      you have brought a grain offering.
      Shall I be appeased for these things?
7 Upon a high and lofty mountain
      you have set your bed,
   and there you went up to offer sacrifice.
8 Behind the door and the doorpost
      you have set up your symbol;
   for, in deserting me, *e* you have uncovered
         your bed,
      you have gone up to it,
      you have made it wide;
   and you have made a bargain for yourself
         with them,
      you have loved their bed,
      you have gazed on their nakedness. *f*
9 You journeyed to Molech *g* with oil,
      and multiplied your perfumes;
   you sent your envoys far away,
      and sent down even to Sheol.

a Heb *besides his gathered ones* *b* Heb *His* *c* Q Ms Syr Vg Tg: MT *me* *d* Heb *an adulterer and she plays the whore* *e* Meaning of Heb uncertain *f* Or *their phallus;* Heb *the hand* *g* Or *the king*

The promise to Jerusalem that people from Sheba would come to Jerusalem to worship was quite an impressive promise (Isaiah 60.6). Sheba was at least fourteen hundred miles away—across the desert of present-day Saudi Arabia. Years earlier, the queen of Sheba had visited King Solomon and seen all his wealth (1 Kings 10.1–13).

Fact

This information has been scanned and is free of all known viruses. Please forward to all your friends.

¹⁰ You grew weary from your many wanderings,
but you did not say, "It is useless."
You found your desire rekindled,
and so you did not weaken.

¹¹ Whom did you dread and fear
so that you lied,
and did not remember me
or give me a thought?
Have I not kept silent and closed my eyes,*
and so you do not fear me?
¹² I will concede your righteousness and your works,
but they will not help you.
¹³ When you cry out, let your collection of idols deliver you!
The wind will carry them off,
a breath will take them away.

a Gk Vg: Heb *silent even for a long time*

But whoever takes refuge in me shall possess the land
and inherit my holy mountain.

A Promise of Help and Healing
¹⁴ It shall be said,
"Build up, build up, prepare the way,
remove every obstruction from my people's way."
¹⁵ For thus says the high and lofty one
who inhabits eternity, whose name is Holy:
I dwell in the high and holy place,
and also with those who are contrite and humble in spirit,
to revive the spirit of the humble,
and to revive the heart of the contrite.
¹⁶ For I will not continually accuse,
nor will I always be angry;
for then the spirits would grow faint before me,
even the souls that I have made.
¹⁷ Because of their wicked covetousness I was angry;
I struck them, I hid and was angry;
but they kept turning back to their own ways.
¹⁸ I have seen their ways, but I will heal them;
I will lead them and repay them with comfort,
creating for their mourners the fruit of the lips.*
¹⁹ Peace, peace, to the far and the near, says the LORD;
and I will heal them.
²⁰ But the wicked are like the tossing sea
that cannot keep still;
its waters toss up mire and mud.
²¹ There is no peace, says my God, for the wicked.

58 False and True Worship
Shout out, do not hold back!
Lift up your voice like a trumpet!
Announce to my people their rebellion,
to the house of Jacob their sins.
² Yet day after day they seek me
and delight to know my ways,
as if they were a nation that practiced righteousness
and did not forsake the ordinance of their God;
they ask of me righteous judgments,
they delight to draw near to God.
³ "Why do we fast, but you do not see?
Why humble ourselves, but you do not notice?"

Look, you serve your own interest on your
    fast day,
    and oppress all your workers.
4 Look, you fast only to quarrel and to fight
    and to strike with a wicked fist.
Such fasting as you do today
    will not make your voice heard on high.
5 Is such the fast that I choose,
    a day to humble oneself?
Is it to bow down the head like a bulrush,
    and to lie in sackcloth and ashes?
Will you call this a fast,
    a day acceptable to the LORD?

6 Is not this the fast that I choose:
    to loose the bonds of injustice,
    to undo the thongs of the yoke,
to let the oppressed go free,
    and to break every yoke?
7 Is it not to share your bread with the hungry,
    and bring the homeless poor into your
    house;
when you see the naked, to cover them,
    and not to hide yourself from your own
    kin?
8 Then your light shall break forth like the
    dawn,
    and your healing shall spring up quickly;
your vindicator[a] shall go before you,
    the glory of the LORD shall be your rear
    guard.
9 Then you shall call, and the LORD will
    answer;
    you shall cry for help, and he will say,
    Here I am.

If you remove the yoke from among you,
    the pointing of the finger, the speaking
    of evil,
10 if you offer your food to the hungry
    and satisfy the needs of the afflicted,
then your light shall rise in the darkness
    and your gloom be like the noonday.
11 The LORD will guide you continually,
    and satisfy your needs in parched places,
    and make your bones strong;
and you shall be like a watered garden,
    like a spring of water,
    whose waters never fail.
12 Your ancient ruins shall be rebuilt;
    you shall raise up the foundations of
    many generations;
you shall be called the repairer of the breach,
    the restorer of streets to live in.

13 If you refrain from trampling the sabbath,
    from pursuing your own interests on my
    holy day;
if you call the sabbath a delight

and the holy day of the LORD honorable;
if you honor it, not going your own ways,
    serving your own interests, or pursuing
    your own affairs;[b]
14 then you shall take delight in the LORD,
    and I will make you ride upon the heights
    of the earth;
I will feed you with the heritage of your
    ancestor Jacob,
    for the mouth of the LORD has spoken.

59 Injustice and Oppression to Be Punished

See, the LORD's hand is not too short to
    save,
    nor his ear too dull to hear.
2 Rather, your iniquities have been barriers
    between you and your God,
and your sins have hidden his face from you
    so that he does not hear.
3 For your hands are defiled with blood,
    and your fingers with iniquity;
your lips have spoken lies,
    your tongue mutters wickedness.
4 No one brings suit justly,
    no one goes to law honestly;
they rely on empty pleas, they speak lies,
    conceiving mischief and begetting
    iniquity.
5 They hatch adders' eggs,
    and weave the spider's web;
whoever eats their eggs dies,
    and the crushed egg hatches out a viper.
6 Their webs cannot serve as clothing;
    they cannot cover themselves with what
    they make.
Their works are works of iniquity,
    and deeds of violence are in their hands.
7 Their feet run to evil,
    and they rush to shed innocent blood;
their thoughts are thoughts of iniquity,
    desolation and destruction are in their
    highways.
8 The way of peace they do not know,
    and there is no justice in their paths.
Their roads they have made crooked;
    no one who walks in them knows peace.

9 Therefore justice is far from us,
    and righteousness does not reach us;
we wait for light, and lo! there is darkness;
    and for brightness, but we walk in
    gloom.
10 We grope like the blind along a wall,
    groping like those who have no eyes;
we stumble at noon as in the twilight,
    among the vigorous[c] as though we were
    dead.

a Or vindication b Heb or speaking words c Meaning of Heb uncertain

¹¹ We all growl like bears;
    like doves we moan mournfully.
We wait for justice, but there is none;
    for salvation, but it is far from us.
¹² For our transgressions before you are many,
    and our sins testify against us.
Our transgressions indeed are with us,
    and we know our iniquities:
¹³ transgressing, and denying the LORD,
    and turning away from following our God,
talking oppression and revolt,
    conceiving lying words and uttering
      them from the heart.
¹⁴ Justice is turned back,
    and righteousness stands at a distance;
for truth stumbles in the public square,
    and uprightness cannot enter.
¹⁵ Truth is lacking,
    and whoever turns from evil is despoiled.

The LORD saw it, and it displeased him
    that there was no justice.
¹⁶ He saw that there was no one,
    and was appalled that there was no one
      to intervene;
so his own arm brought him victory,
    and his righteousness upheld him.
¹⁷ He put on righteousness like a breastplate,
    and a helmet of salvation on his head;
he put on garments of vengeance for
      clothing,
    and wrapped himself in fury as in a
      mantle.
¹⁸ According to their deeds, so will he repay;
    wrath to his adversaries, requital to his
      enemies;
to the coastlands he will render requital.
¹⁹ So those in the west shall fear the name of
      the LORD,
    and those in the east, his glory;
for he will come like a pent-up stream
    that the wind of the LORD drives on.

²⁰ And he will come to Zion as Redeemer,
    to those in Jacob who turn from
      transgression, says the LORD.
²¹ And as for me, this is my covenant with them,
says the LORD: my spirit that is upon you, and
my words that I have put in your mouth, shall
not depart out of your mouth, or out of the
mouths of your children, or out of the mouths
of your children's children, says the LORD,
from now on and forever.

60 The Ingathering of the Dispersed

Arise, shine; for your light has come,
    and the glory of the LORD has risen upon
      you.

² For darkness shall cover the earth,
    and thick darkness the peoples;
but the LORD will arise upon you,
    and his glory will appear over you.
³ Nations shall come to your light,
    and kings to the brightness of your dawn.

⁴ Lift up your eyes and look around;
    they all gather together, they come to
      you;
your sons shall come from far away,
    and your daughters shall be carried on
      their nurses' arms.
⁵ Then you shall see and be radiant;
    your heart shall thrill and rejoice,^a
because the abundance of the sea shall be
      brought to you,
    the wealth of the nations shall come to
      you.
⁶ A multitude of camels shall cover you,
    the young camels of Midian and Ephah;
    all those from Sheba shall come.
They shall bring gold and frankincense,
    and shall proclaim the praise of the LORD.
⁷ All the flocks of Kedar shall be gathered to
      you,
    the rams of Nebaioth shall minister to
      you;
they shall be acceptable on my altar,
    and I will glorify my glorious house.

⁸ Who are these that fly like a cloud,
    and like doves to their windows?
⁹ For the coastlands shall wait for me,
    the ships of Tarshish first,
to bring your children from far away,
    their silver and gold with them,
for the name of the LORD your God,
    and for the Holy One of Israel,
    because he has glorified you.
¹⁰ Foreigners shall build up your walls,
    and their kings shall minister to you;
for in my wrath I struck you down,
    but in my favor I have had mercy on you.
¹¹ Your gates shall always be open;
    day and night they shall not be shut,
so that nations shall bring you their wealth,
    with their kings led in procession.
¹² For the nation and kingdom
    that will not serve you shall perish;
    those nations shall be utterly laid waste.
¹³ The glory of Lebanon shall come to you,
    the cypress, the plane, and the pine,
to beautify the place of my sanctuary;
    and I will glorify where my feet rest.
¹⁴ The descendants of those who oppressed
      you
    shall come bending low to you,

---

^a Heb *be enlarged*

and all who despised you
    shall bow down at your feet;
they shall call you the City of the Lord,
    the Zion of the Holy One of Israel.
15 Whereas you have been forsaken and hated,
    with no one passing through,
I will make you majestic forever,
    a joy from age to age.
16 You shall suck the milk of nations,
    you shall suck the breasts of kings;
and you shall know that I, the Lord, am
        your Savior
    and your Redeemer, the Mighty One of
        Jacob.

17 Instead of bronze I will bring gold,
    instead of iron I will bring silver;
instead of wood, bronze,
    instead of stones, iron.
I will appoint Peace as your overseer
    and Righteousness as your taskmaster.
18 Violence shall no more be heard in your
        land,
    devastation or destruction within your
        borders;
you shall call your walls Salvation,
    and your gates Praise.

God the Glory of Zion

19 The sun shall no longer be
    your light by day,
nor for brightness shall the moon
    give light to you by night;*a*
but the Lord will be your everlasting light,
    and your God will be your glory.
20 Your sun shall no more go down,
    or your moon withdraw itself;
for the Lord will be your everlasting light,
    and your days of mourning shall be
        ended.
21 Your people shall all be righteous;
    they shall possess the land forever.
They are the shoot that I planted, the work
        of my hands,
    so that I might be glorified.
22 The least of them shall become a clan,
    and the smallest one a mighty nation;
I am the Lord;
    in its time I will accomplish it quickly.

61 The Good News of Deliverance

The spirit of the Lord God is upon me,
    because the Lord has anointed me;
he has sent me to bring good news to the
        oppressed,
    to bind up the brokenhearted,
to proclaim liberty to the captives,
    and release to the prisoners;

a Q Ms Gk Old Latin Tg: MT lacks *by night*

JESUS SIGHTING

The invaders came from the north. They came in the night. They came like a plague of locusts eating everything in its path. One night you were sleeping in your bed, the next morning you were being dragged away in chains. You were separated from your family. You were taken to a place where the language was different, the food was different, and your freedom was gone. Generations would pass as your proud people were broken down in a foreign land.

Roughly the first half of the book of Isaiah speaks from this story, warning a captive people to turn to God. But God's message does not conclude with gloom and doom.

The second half of the book promises a new hope. **Isaiah 61.1–6** and other sections of chapters 40–66 promise that a servant is coming who will bring glory to God, in whose name the blind will see, the captives will be set free, and justice will be brought to the nations. It is no coincidence that when Jesus stood in the synagogue to read from the Scriptures, he read *this* prophetic passage and applied it to himself (see Luke 4.18–19). He was fulfilling the promise—he had come to proclaim good news! Hope!

Read **Isaiah 61.1–6** one more time and pause for a moment to consider what this means in your life. God's people went through difficult times, but God didn't abandon them. And though God also allows you to go through crises that bring you to your knees, Jesus is always there to raise you up again.

2 to proclaim the year of the Lord's favor,
    and the day of vengeance of our God;
    to comfort all who mourn;
3 to provide for those who mourn in Zion—
    to give them a garland instead of ashes,
    the oil of gladness instead of mourning,

Serious About Compassion

It's time to get a little angry.

Even Jesus got mad when he cleared out the Temple. He was ticked off that it had become a hub for cheaters and that the religious leaders allowed it. (Read about it in Mark 11.15–18.)

And that isn't the only time in the Bible that God gives his people a piece of his mind. Read Isaiah 63.5–6. It predicts a grim future for those who don't share God's compassion for the needy.

The image of God portrayed in these verses will probably never be your favorite. It's frightening, but it's meant to wake us up. There's a difference between doing some nice things for poor people (food drives, collecting clothes and toiletries for the homeless), and having a preferential option for the poor.

The prophets remind us that justice is for everyone. A preferential option for the poor means that we make choices that will enable all the poor to have access to the basic necessities for a fully human life. Compassion means to "suffer with," not just to "do for." Social action projects are not just nice things to do. An option for the poor might mean that sometimes you choose to live with less. It may mean you spend time and resources advocating for the poor. It's up to us to make the choices that prefer the poor—even when they're uncomfortable or unpopular.

What might be in store for those who consciously make those choices and live by them? Read Isaiah 65.17–25 for a snapshot!

Now snap a few photos in your town that reveal a lack of compassion. Someone alone. Something in need of God's attention through his people. Paste a shot here in your Bible.

Take a moment to really look at this picture. What could help this person or address this situation? How do you think God wants his Church to respond with compassion? What would compassion look like?

Now consider this: God's admonition is for *you*. How will *you* respond? Will *you* take action? Pray about it, asking God what he wants you to do.

---

the mantle of praise instead of a faint
spirit.
They will be called oaks of righteousness,
the planting of the LORD, to display his
glory.

4 They shall build up the ancient ruins,
they shall raise up the former
devastations;
they shall repair the ruined cities,
the devastations of many generations.

5 Strangers shall stand and feed your flocks,
foreigners shall till your land and dress
your vines;

6 but you shall be called priests of the LORD,
you shall be named ministers of our God;
you shall enjoy the wealth of the nations,
and in their riches you shall glory.

7 Because their[a] shame was double,
and dishonor was proclaimed as their
lot,
therefore they shall possess a double
portion;
everlasting joy shall be theirs.

8 For I the LORD love justice,
I hate robbery and wrongdoing;[b]
I will faithfully give them their recompense,
and I will make an everlasting covenant
with them.

9 Their descendants shall be known among
the nations,
and their offspring among the peoples;
all who see them shall acknowledge
that they are a people whom the LORD
has blessed.

10 I will greatly rejoice in the LORD,
my whole being shall exult in my God;
for he has clothed me with the garments of
salvation,
he has covered me with the robe of
righteousness,
as a bridegroom decks himself with a
garland,
and as a bride adorns herself with her
jewels.

11 For as the earth brings forth its shoots,
and as a garden causes what is sown in it
to spring up,
so the Lord GOD will cause righteousness
and praise
to spring up before all the nations.

62 The Vindication and Salvation of Zion

For Zion's sake I will not keep silent,
and for Jerusalem's sake I will not rest,
until her vindication shines out like the
dawn,

---

a Heb *your* *b* Or *robbery with a burnt offering*

PASTE
PHOTO
HERE

and her salvation like a burning torch.
2 The nations shall see your vindication,
     and all the kings your glory;
  and you shall be called by a new name
     that the mouth of the LORD will give.
3 You shall be a crown of beauty in the hand
       of the LORD,
     and a royal diadem in the hand of your
       God.
4 You shall no more be termed Forsaken,*a*
     and your land shall no more be termed
       Desolate;*b*
  but you shall be called My Delight Is in Her,*c*

and your land Married;*d*
  for the LORD delights in you,
     and your land shall be married.
5 For as a young man marries a young
       woman,
     so shall your builder*e* marry you,
  and as the bridegroom rejoices over the
       bride,
     so shall your God rejoice over you.
6 Upon your walls, O Jerusalem,
     I have posted sentinels;
  all day and all night
     they shall never be silent.

a Heb *Azubah* *b* Heb *Shemamah* *c* Heb *Hephzibah* *d* Heb *Beulah* *e* Cn: Heb *your sons*

ISAIAH 62

Wondering—© Clay Goswick, 16

You who remind the Lᴏʀᴅ,
    take no rest,
⁷ and give him no rest
    until he establishes Jerusalem
    and makes it renowned throughout the
      earth.
⁸ The Lᴏʀᴅ has sworn by his right hand
    and by his mighty arm:
    I will not again give your grain
      to be food for your enemies,
    and foreigners shall not drink the wine
      for which you have labored;
⁹ but those who garner it shall eat it
    and praise the Lᴏʀᴅ,
    and those who gather it shall drink it
    in my holy courts.

¹⁰ Go through, go through the gates,
    prepare the way for the people;
    build up, build up the highway,
      clear it of stones,
    lift up an ensign over the peoples.
¹¹ The Lᴏʀᴅ has proclaimed
    to the end of the earth:
    Say to daughter Zion,
    "See, your salvation comes;
    his reward is with him,
    and his recompense before him."
¹² They shall be called, "The Holy People,
    The Redeemed of the Lᴏʀᴅ";
    and you shall be called, "Sought Out,
    A City Not Forsaken."

63 Vengeance on Edom

"Who is this that comes from Edom,
    from Bozrah in garments stained
      crimson?
Who is this so splendidly robed,
    marching in his great might?"

"It is I, announcing vindication,
    mighty to save."

² "Why are your robes red,
    and your garments like theirs who tread
      the wine press?"

³ "I have trodden the wine press alone,
    and from the peoples no one was
      with me;
I trod them in my anger
    and trampled them in my wrath;
their juice spattered on my garments,
    and stained all my robes.
⁴ For the day of vengeance was in my heart,
    and the year for my redeeming work had
      come.
⁵ I looked, but there was no helper;
    I stared, but there was no one to
      sustain me;
so my own arm brought me victory,
    and my wrath sustained me.
⁶ I trampled down peoples in my anger,
    I crushed them in my wrath,
    and I poured out their lifeblood on the
      earth."

God's Mercy Remembered

⁷ I will recount the gracious deeds of the Lᴏʀᴅ,
  the praiseworthy acts of the Lᴏʀᴅ,
because of all that the Lᴏʀᴅ has done for us,
  and the great favor to the house of Israel
that he has shown them according to his
      mercy,
  according to the abundance of his
    steadfast love.

⁸ For he said, "Surely they are my people,
  children who will not deal falsely";
and he became their savior

⁹   in all their distress.
  It was no messengerᵃ or angel
    but his presence that saved them;ᵇ
  in his love and in his pity he redeemed
      them;
    he lifted them up and carried them all
      the days of old.

¹⁰ But they rebelled
    and grieved his holy spirit;
  therefore he became their enemy;
    he himself fought against them.

¹¹ Then theyᶜ remembered the days of old,
    of Moses his servant.ᵈ
  Where is the one who brought them up out
      of the sea
    with the shepherds of his flock?
  Where is the one who put within them
    his holy spirit,

¹² who caused his glorious arm
    to march at the right hand of Moses,
  who divided the waters before them
    to make for himself an everlasting name,

¹³   who led them through the depths?
  Like a horse in the desert,
    they did not stumble.

¹⁴ Like cattle that go down into the valley,
    the spirit of the Lᴏʀᴅ gave them rest.
  Thus you led your people,
    to make for yourself a glorious name.

A Prayer of Penitence

¹⁵ Look down from heaven and see,
    from your holy and glorious habitation.
  Where are your zeal and your might?
    The yearning of your heart and your
      compassion?
    They are withheld from me.

¹⁶ For you are our father,
    though Abraham does not know us
  and Israel does not acknowledge us;
  you, O Lᴏʀᴅ, are our father;
    our Redeemer from of old is your name.

¹⁷ Why, O Lᴏʀᴅ, do you make us stray from
    your ways

and harden our heart, so that we do not
    fear you?
  Turn back for the sake of your servants,
    for the sake of the tribes that are your
      heritage.

¹⁸ Your holy people took possession for a
      little while;
  but now our adversaries have trampled
    down your sanctuary.

¹⁹ We have long been like those whom you do
    not rule,
  like those not called by your name.

64 O that you would tear open the heavens
      and come down,
    so that the mountains would quake at
      your presence—
²ᵉ as when fire kindles brushwood
    and the fire causes water to boil—
  to make your name known to your
      adversaries,
    so that the nations might tremble at your
      presence!

³ When you did awesome deeds that we did
    not expect,
  you came down, the mountains quaked
    at your presence.

⁴ From ages past no one has heard,
    no ear has perceived,
  no eye has seen any God besides you,
    who works for those who wait for him.

⁵ You meet those who gladly do right,
    those who remember you in your ways.
  But you were angry, and we sinned;
    because you hid yourself we transgressed.ᶠ

⁶ We have all become like one who is unclean,
    and all our righteous deeds are like a
      filthy cloth.
  We all fade like a leaf,
    and our iniquities, like the wind, take us
      away.

⁷ There is no one who calls on your name,
    or attempts to take hold of you;
  for you have hidden your face from us,
    and have deliveredᵍ us into the hand of
      our iniquity.

⁸ Yet, O Lᴏʀᴅ, you are our Father;
  we are the clay, and you are our potter;
    we are all the work of your hand.

⁹ Do not be exceedingly angry, O Lᴏʀᴅ,
    and do not remember iniquity forever.
  Now consider, we are all your people.

¹⁰ Your holy cities have become a wilderness,
    Zion has become a wilderness,
    Jerusalem a desolation.

¹¹ Our holy and beautiful house,
    where our ancestors praised you,

ᵃ Gk: Heb *anguish* ᵇ Or *savior.* ⁹*In all their distress he was distressed; the angel of his presence saved them;* ᶜ Heb *he* ᵈ Cn: Heb *his people* ᵉ Ch 64.1 in Heb ᶠ Meaning of Heb uncertain ᵍ Gk Syr Old Latin Tg: Heb *melted*

has been burned by fire,
>   and all our pleasant places have become
>   ruins.
12 After all this, will you restrain yourself,
>   O Lord?
>   Will you keep silent, and punish us so
>   severely?

65 The Righteousness of God's Judgment

I was ready to be sought out by those who
>   did not ask,
>   to be found by those who did not
>   seek me.
I said, "Here I am, here I am,"
>   to a nation that did not call on my name.
2 I held out my hands all day long
>   to a rebellious people,
who walk in a way that is not good,
>   following their own devices;
3 a people who provoke me
>   to my face continually,
sacrificing in gardens
>   and offering incense on bricks;
4 who sit inside tombs,
>   and spend the night in secret places;
who eat swine's flesh,
>   with broth of abominable things in their
>   vessels;
5 who say, "Keep to yourself,
>   do not come near me, for I am too holy
>   for you."
These are a smoke in my nostrils,
>   a fire that burns all day long.
6 See, it is written before me:
>   I will not keep silent, but I will repay;
I will indeed repay into their laps
7   their*a* iniquities and their*a* ancestors'
>   iniquities together,
>   says the Lord;
because they offered incense on the
>   mountains
>   and reviled me on the hills,
I will measure into their laps
>   full payment for their actions.
8 Thus says the Lord:
As the wine is found in the cluster,
>   and they say, "Do not destroy it,
>   for there is a blessing in it,"
so I will do for my servants' sake,
>   and not destroy them all.
9 I will bring forth descendants*b* from Jacob,
>   and from Judah inheritors*c* of my
>   mountains;
my chosen shall inherit it,
>   and my servants shall settle there.
10 Sharon shall become a pasture for flocks,

and the Valley of Achor a place for herds
>   to lie down,
>   for my people who have sought me.
11 But you who forsake the Lord,
>   who forget my holy mountain,
who set a table for Fortune
>   and fill cups of mixed wine for Destiny;
12 I will destine you to the sword,
>   and all of you shall bow down to the
>   slaughter;
because, when I called, you did not answer,
>   when I spoke, you did not listen,
but you did what was evil in my sight,
>   and chose what I did not delight in.
13 Therefore thus says the Lord God:
My servants shall eat,
>   but you shall be hungry;
my servants shall drink,
>   but you shall be thirsty;
my servants shall rejoice,
>   but you shall be put to shame;
14 my servants shall sing for gladness of heart,
>   but you shall cry out for pain of heart,
>   and shall wail for anguish of spirit.
15 You shall leave your name to my chosen to
>   use as a curse,
>   and the Lord God will put you to death;
but to his servants he will give a different
>   name.
16 Then whoever invokes a blessing in the
>   land
>   shall bless by the God of faithfulness,
and whoever takes an oath in the land
>   shall swear by the God of faithfulness;
because the former troubles are forgotten
>   and are hidden from my sight.

The Glorious New Creation

17 For I am about to create new heavens
>   and a new earth;
the former things shall not be remembered
>   or come to mind.
18 But be glad and rejoice forever
>   in what I am creating;
for I am about to create Jerusalem as a joy,
>   and its people as a delight.
19 I will rejoice in Jerusalem,
>   and delight in my people;
no more shall the sound of weeping be
>   heard in it,
>   or the cry of distress.
20 No more shall there be in it
>   an infant that lives but a few days,
>   or an old person who does not live out a
>   lifetime;
for one who dies at a hundred years will be
>   considered a youth,

a Gk Syr: Heb *your* *b* Or *a descendant* *c* Or *an inheritor*

and one who falls short of a hundred will be considered accursed.
21 They shall build houses and inhabit them;
   they shall plant vineyards and eat their fruit.
22 They shall not build and another inhabit;
   they shall not plant and another eat;
   for like the days of a tree shall the days of my people be,
   and my chosen shall long enjoy the work of their hands.
23 They shall not labor in vain,
   or bear children for calamity;[a]
   for they shall be offspring blessed by the LORD—
   and their descendants as well.
24 Before they call I will answer,
   while they are yet speaking I will hear.
25 The wolf and the lamb shall feed together,
   the lion shall eat straw like the ox;
   but the serpent—its food shall be dust!
   They shall not hurt or destroy
   on all my holy mountain,
                         says the LORD.

66 The Worship God Demands

Thus says the LORD:
Heaven is my throne
   and the earth is my footstool;
what is the house that you would build for me,
   and what is my resting place?
2 All these things my hand has made,
   and so all these things are mine,[b]
                         says the LORD.
But this is the one to whom I will look,
   to the humble and contrite in spirit,
   who trembles at my word.
3 Whoever slaughters an ox is like one who kills a human being;
   whoever sacrifices a lamb, like one who breaks a dog's neck;
   whoever presents a grain offering, like one who offers swine's blood;[c]
   whoever makes a memorial offering of frankincense, like one who blesses an idol.
These have chosen their own ways,
   and in their abominations they take delight;
4 I also will choose to mock[d] them,
   and bring upon them what they fear;
because, when I called, no one answered,
   when I spoke, they did not listen;
but they did what was evil in my sight,
   and chose what did not please me.

Serenity—© Rachel Hostert, 18

The LORD Vindicates Zion

5 Hear the word of the LORD,
   you who tremble at his word:
Your own people who hate you
   and reject you for my name's sake
have said, "Let the LORD be glorified,
   so that we may see your joy";
   but it is they who shall be put to shame.

6 Listen, an uproar from the city!
   A voice from the temple!
The voice of the LORD,
   dealing retribution to his enemies!

7 Before she was in labor
   she gave birth;
before her pain came upon her
   she delivered a son.
8 Who has heard of such a thing?
   Who has seen such things?
Shall a land be born in one day?
   Shall a nation be delivered in one moment?
Yet as soon as Zion was in labor
   she delivered her children.
9 Shall I open the womb and not deliver?
   says the LORD;
shall I, the one who delivers, shut the womb?
   says your God.

10 Rejoice with Jerusalem, and be glad for her,
   all you who love her;
rejoice with her in joy,
   all you who mourn over her—
11 that you may nurse and be satisfied
   from her consoling breast;
that you may drink deeply with delight
   from her glorious bosom.

a Or *sudden terror* b Gk Syr: Heb *these things came to be* c Meaning of Heb uncertain d Or *to punish*

¹² For thus says the LORD:
I will extend prosperity to her like a river,
  and the wealth of the nations like an
    overflowing stream;
and you shall nurse and be carried on her
    arm,
  and dandled on her knees.
¹³ As a mother comforts her child,
  so I will comfort you;
  you shall be comforted in Jerusalem.

The Reign and Indignation of God

¹⁴ You shall see, and your heart shall rejoice;
  your bodies^a shall flourish like the grass;
and it shall be known that the hand of the
    LORD is with his servants,
  and his indignation is against his enemies.
¹⁵ For the LORD will come in fire,
  and his chariots like the whirlwind,
to pay back his anger in fury,
  and his rebuke in flames of fire.
¹⁶ For by fire will the LORD execute judgment,
  and by his sword, on all flesh;
  and those slain by the LORD shall be many.

17 Those who sanctify and purify themselves to go into the gardens, following the one in the center, eating the flesh of pigs, vermin, and rodents, shall come to an end together, says the LORD.

18 For I know^b their works and their thoughts, and I am^c coming to gather all nations and tongues; and they shall come and shall see my glory, ¹⁹and I will set a sign among them. From them I will send survivors to the nations, to Tarshish, Put,^d and Lud—which draw the bow—to Tubal and Javan, to the coastlands far away that have not heard of my fame or seen my glory; and they shall declare my glory among the nations. ²⁰They shall bring all your kindred from all the nations as an offering to the LORD, on horses, and in chariots, and in litters, and on mules, and on dromedaries, to my holy mountain Jerusalem, says the LORD, just as the Israelites bring a grain offering in a clean vessel to the house of the LORD. ²¹And I will also take some of them as priests and as Levites, says the LORD.

²² For as the new heavens and the new earth,
    which I will make,
  shall remain before me, says the LORD;
    so shall your descendants and your name
      remain.
²³ From new moon to new moon,
    and from sabbath to sabbath,
  all flesh shall come to worship before me,
  says the LORD.

24 And they shall go out and look at the dead bodies of the people who have rebelled against me; for their worm shall not die, their fire shall not be quenched, and they shall be an abhorrence to all flesh.

Untitled—© Acacia Martin, 14

JEREMIAH

THE END IS NEAR

The Half-Empty Glass

Everyone loves a "yes man"—someone who'll come alongside you and tell you that all of your decisions are great. The last person *you* want to be is the one who preaches gloom and doom when everyone is already down.

So Jeremiah has a lame job. The high point of Israelite history was when Solomon built the Temple and the walls stood strong. Only a generation later the kingdom was divided by civil war, and the nation was ruled by idol-worshiping kings who forgot about the true God. Now God has Jeremiah utter the unimaginable: the kingdom is going to fall. Jeremiah's reward for speaking God's word? Getting branded as a traitor and thrown into prison.

But Jeremiah's message isn't all bad news.

Despite the fact that they've been carted off to a foreign land, God assures his people that they are still in his hands. God has a plan for them—a plan for a good future, a plan full of hope. (See Jeremiah 29.11.)

God doesn't always give us pats on the back. Sometimes his message to us is, *Shape up, live right, get rid of the "idols" in your life, and worship me alone.* Sometimes God even disciplines us the way he punished his people (see Hebrews 12.6). There's more to living for God than happy moments and feel-good encouragement. Through Scripture, through Jeremiah-like friends, and through tough circumstances, God can push us and stretch us. But it's never random. It's never pointless. God always has a plan—we are always in God's hands.

> *"Truth is so obscure in these times, and falsehood so established, that, unless we love the truth, we cannot know it."*
> —Blaise Pascal

WHO Jeremiah was the original writer of the book; others contributed during his life and later.

WHAT This book describes a loving Creator who wants his people to be faithful and worship him alone. It also warns God's people of a coming punishment they'll face for their unfaithfulness and idolatry. In the book, the predictions come true when the Babylonians attack Judah.

WHEN It was written ca. 640–580 B.C.

WHERE Judah (the southern part of Israel/Palestine). When Jerusalem was destroyed, many of its people were taken as captives to Babylon (in modern-day Iraq).

PATH OF DISCIPLESHIP

Neither Jeremiah nor Jesus escaped being the bearer of bad news. Jesus' message wasn't fluffy good feelings. It was challenging, convicting, and occasionally even harsh. Check out this instance in which Jesus has a Jeremiah-like moment, even quoting Jeremiah word for word. Read Jeremiah 7.1–11 and 8.13 and then Mark 11.12–21. This isn't a meek, serenely glowing Savior with a halo and a peaceful smile. This Jesus is loud and indignant, with muscles flexed. This Jesus isn't safe—in fact, he's so threatening that his enemies move from just disliking him to wanting to *kill* him (Mark 11.18). Like Jeremiah, Jesus plays the role of outspoken prophet.

There is a message here for us as disciples today. Sometimes it's our duty and responsibility to speak the hard word, to confront wrongdoing and evil even when it won't win us any points from friends or family members.

1

The words of Jeremiah son of Hilkiah, of the priests who were in Anathoth in the land of Benjamin, ²to whom the word of the LORD came in the days of King Josiah son of Amon of Judah, in the thirteenth year of his reign. ³It came also in the days of King Jehoiakim son of Josiah of Judah, and until the end of the eleventh year of King Zedekiah son of Josiah of Judah, until the captivity of Jerusalem in the fifth month.

Jeremiah's Call and Commission

4 Now the word of the LORD came to me saying,
5 "Before I formed you in the womb I knew
          you,
     and before you were born I consecrated you;
     I appointed you a prophet to the nations."
⁶Then I said, "Ah, Lord GOD! Truly I do not know how to speak, for I am only a boy." ⁷But the LORD said to me,
     "Do not say, 'I am only a boy';
     for you shall go to all to whom I send you,
     and you shall speak whatever I command
          you.
8 Do not be afraid of them,
     for I am with you to deliver you,
                              says the LORD."
⁹Then the LORD put out his hand and touched my mouth; and the LORD said to me,
     "Now I have put my words in your mouth.
10 See, today I appoint you over nations and
          over kingdoms,
     to pluck up and to pull down,
     to destroy and to overthrow,
     to build and to plant."

11 The word of the LORD came to me, saying, "Jeremiah, what do you see?" And I said, "I see a branch of an almond tree."ᵃ ¹²Then the LORD said to me, "You have seen well, for I am watchingᵇ over my word to perform it." ¹³The word of the LORD came to me a second time, saying, "What do you see?" And I said, "I see a boiling pot, tilted away from the north."

14 Then the LORD said to me: Out of the north disaster shall break out on all the inhabitants of the land. ¹⁵For now I am calling all the tribes of the kingdoms of the north, says the LORD; and they shall come and all of them shall set their thrones at the entrance of the gates of Jerusalem, against all its surrounding walls and against all the cities of Judah. ¹⁶And I will utter my judgments against them, for all their wickedness in forsaking me; they have made offerings to other gods, and worshiped the works of their own hands. ¹⁷But you, gird up your loins; stand up and tell them everything that I command you. Do not break down

before them, or I will break you before them. ¹⁸And I for my part have made you today a fortified city, an iron pillar, and a bronze wall, against the whole land—against the kings of Judah, its princes, its priests, and the people of the land. ¹⁹They will fight against you; but they shall not prevail against you, for I am with you, says the LORD, to deliver you.

2 God Pleads with Israel to Repent

The word of the LORD came to me, saying: ²Go and proclaim in the hearing of Jerusalem, Thus says the LORD:
     I remember the devotion of your youth,
          your love as a bride,
     how you followed me in the wilderness,
          in a land not sown.
3 Israel was holy to the LORD,
          the first fruits of his harvest.
     All who ate of it were held guilty;
          disaster came upon them,
                              says the LORD.

4 Hear the word of the LORD, O house of Jacob, and all the families of the house of Israel. ⁵Thus says the LORD:
     What wrong did your ancestors find in me
          that they went far from me,
     and went after worthless things, and
               became worthless themselves?
6 They did not say, "Where is the LORD
          who brought us up from the land of Egypt,
     who led us in the wilderness,
          in a land of deserts and pits,
     in a land of drought and deep darkness,
     in a land that no one passes through,
          where no one lives?"
7 I brought you into a plentiful land
          to eat its fruits and its good things.
     But when you entered you defiled my land,
          and made my heritage an abomination.
8 The priests did not say, "Where is the LORD?"
          Those who handle the law did not know
               me;
     the rulersᶜ transgressed against me;
          the prophets prophesied by Baal,
          and went after things that do not profit.

9 Therefore once more I accuse you,
                              says the LORD,
          and I accuse your children's children.
10 Cross to the coasts of Cyprus and look,
          send to Kedar and examine with care;
          see if there has ever been such a thing.
11 Has a nation changed its gods,
          even though they are no gods?
     But my people have changed their glory
          for something that does not profit.

ᵃ Heb *shaqed* ᵇ Heb *shoqed* ᶜ Heb *shepherds*

Expressing—© Michelle Graham, 14

¹² Be appalled, O heavens, at this,
  be shocked, be utterly desolate,
            says the Lᴏʀᴅ,
¹³ for my people have committed two evils:
  they have forsaken me,
  the fountain of living water,
    and dug out cisterns for themselves,
  cracked cisterns
    that can hold no water.

¹⁴ Is Israel a slave? Is he a homeborn servant?
  Why then has he become plunder?
¹⁵ The lions have roared against him,
    they have roared loudly.
  They have made his land a waste;
    his cities are in ruins, without
      inhabitant.
¹⁶ Moreover, the people of Memphis and
      Tahpanhes
  have broken the crown of your head.
¹⁷ Have you not brought this upon yourself
    by forsaking the Lᴏʀᴅ your God,
    while he led you in the way?
¹⁸ What then do you gain by going to Egypt,
    to drink the waters of the Nile?
  Or what do you gain by going to Assyria,
    to drink the waters of the Euphrates?
¹⁹ Your wickedness will punish you,
    and your apostasies will convict you.
  Know and see that it is evil and bitter
    for you to forsake the Lᴏʀᴅ your God;
    the fear of me is not in you,
            says the Lord Gᴏᴅ of hosts.

²⁰ For long ago you broke your yoke
    and burst your bonds,
    and you said, "I will not serve!"
  On every high hill
    and under every green tree
    you sprawled and played the whore.
²¹ Yet I planted you as a choice vine,
    from the purest stock.
  How then did you turn degenerate
    and become a wild vine?
²² Though you wash yourself with lye
    and use much soap,
    the stain of your guilt is still before me,
            says the Lord Gᴏᴅ.
²³ How can you say, "I am not defiled,
    I have not gone after the Baals"?
  Look at your way in the valley;
    know what you have done—
  a restive young camel interlacing her tracks,
²⁴   a wild ass at home in the wilderness,
  in her heat sniffing the wind!
    Who can restrain her lust?
  None who seek her need weary themselves;
    in her month they will find her.
²⁵ Keep your feet from going unshod
    and your throat from thirst.
  But you said, "It is hopeless,
    for I have loved strangers,
    and after them I will go."

²⁶ As a thief is shamed when caught,
    so the house of Israel shall be shamed—
    they, their kings, their officials,

If you're planning a barbecue in the Middle East, most of the year you don't have to worry about getting rained out. Almost all the rain falls during spring (May) and fall (October). Since crops depended on this rain, good rains were considered a sign of God's blessing, and a lack of rain was considered a curse (Jeremiah 3.3).

This information has been scanned and is free of all known viruses. Please forward to all your friends.

they accepted no correction.
Your own sword devoured your prophets
like a ravening lion.
31 And you, O generation, behold the word of
the LORD!*
Have I been a wilderness to Israel,
or a land of thick darkness?
Why then do my people say, "We are free,
we will come to you no more"?
32 Can a girl forget her ornaments,
or a bride her attire?
Yet my people have forgotten me,
days without number.

33 How well you direct your course
to seek lovers!
So that even to wicked women
you have taught your ways.
34 Also on your skirts is found
the lifeblood of the innocent poor,
though you did not catch them breaking in.
Yet in spite of all these things*
35 you say, "I am innocent;
surely his anger has turned from me."
Now I am bringing you to judgment
for saying, "I have not sinned."
36 How lightly you gad about,
changing your ways!
You shall be put to shame by Egypt
as you were put to shame by Assyria.
37 From there also you will come away
with your hands on your head;
for the LORD has rejected those in whom
you trust,
and you will not prosper through them.

3 Unfaithful Israel

If *b* a man divorces his wife
and she goes from him
and becomes another man's wife,
will he return to her?
Would not such a land be greatly polluted?
You have played the whore with many
lovers;
and would you return to me?
says the LORD.
2 Look up to the bare heights,* and see!
Where have you not been lain with?
By the waysides you have sat waiting for
lovers,
like a nomad in the wilderness.
You have polluted the land
with your whoring and wickedness.
3 Therefore the showers have been withheld,
and the spring rain has not come;
yet you have the forehead of a whore,
you refuse to be ashamed.
4 Have you not just now called to me,

their priests, and their prophets,
27 who say to a tree, "You are my father,"
and to a stone, "You gave me birth."
For they have turned their backs to me,
and not their faces.
But in the time of their trouble they say,
"Come and save us!"
28 But where are your gods
that you made for yourself?
Let them come, if they can save you,
in your time of trouble;
for you have as many gods
as you have towns, O Judah.

29 Why do you complain against me?
You have all rebelled against me,
says the LORD.
30 In vain I have struck down your children;

a Meaning of Heb uncertain   *b* Q Ms Gk Syr: MT *Saying, If*   *c* Or *the trails*

"My Father, you are the friend of my
          youth—
⁵ will he be angry forever,
     will he be indignant to the end?"
This is how you have spoken,
     but you have done all the evil that you
          could.

A Call to Repentance

6 The LORD said to me in the days of King Josiah: Have you seen what she did, that faithless one, Israel, how she went up on every high
hill and under every green tree, and played the
whore there? ⁷And I thought, "After she has
done all this she will return to me"; but she
did not return, and her false sister Judah saw it.
⁸She*ᵃ* saw that for all the adulteries of that faithless one, Israel, I had sent her away with a decree of divorce; yet her false sister Judah did not
fear, but she too went and played the whore.
⁹Because she took her whoredom so lightly, she
polluted the land, committing adultery with
stone and tree. ¹⁰Yet for all this her false sister Judah did not return to me with her whole
heart, but only in pretense, says the LORD.

11 Then the LORD said to me: Faithless Israel has shown herself less guilty than false Judah. ¹²Go, and proclaim these words toward
the north, and say:
Return, faithless Israel,
                              says the LORD.
     I will not look on you in anger,
          for I am merciful,
                              says the LORD;
     I will not be angry forever.
¹³ Only acknowledge your guilt,
          that you have rebelled against the LORD
               your God,
     and scattered your favors among strangers
          under every green tree,
     and have not obeyed my voice,
                              says the LORD.
¹⁴ Return, O faithless children,
                              says the LORD,
     for I am your master;
     I will take you, one from a city and two from
          a family,
     and I will bring you to Zion.

15 I will give you shepherds after my own
heart, who will feed you with knowledge and
understanding. ¹⁶And when you have multiplied and increased in the land, in those days,
says the LORD, they shall no longer say, "The
ark of the covenant of the LORD." It shall not
come to mind, or be remembered, or missed;
nor shall another one be made. ¹⁷At that time
Jerusalem shall be called the throne of the
LORD, and all nations shall gather to it, to the
presence of the LORD in Jerusalem, and they
shall no longer stubbornly follow their own
evil will. ¹⁸In those days the house of Judah
shall join the house of Israel, and together they
shall come from the land of the north to the
land that I gave your ancestors for a heritage.

¹⁹ I thought
          how I would set you among my children,
     and give you a pleasant land,
          the most beautiful heritage of all the
               nations.
     And I thought you would call me, My Father,
          and would not turn from following me.
²⁰ Instead, as a faithless wife leaves her
               husband,
     so you have been faithless to me,
          O house of Israel,
                              says the LORD.

²¹ A voice on the bare heights*ᵇ* is heard,
          the plaintive weeping of Israel's children,
     because they have perverted their way,
          they have forgotten the LORD their God:
²² Return, O faithless children,
          I will heal your faithlessness.

"Here we come to you;
     for you are the LORD our God.
²³ Truly the hills are*ᶜ* a delusion,
     the orgies on the mountains.
Truly in the LORD our God
     is the salvation of Israel.

24 "But from our youth the shameful thing
has devoured all for which our ancestors had
labored, their flocks and their herds, their
sons and their daughters. ²⁵Let us lie down in
our shame, and let our dishonor cover us; for
we have sinned against the LORD our God, we
and our ancestors, from our youth even to this
day; and we have not obeyed the voice of the
LORD our God."

4 If you return, O Israel,
                              says the LORD,
          if you return to me,
     if you remove your abominations from my
               presence,
          and do not waver,
² and if you swear, "As the LORD lives!"
          in truth, in justice, and in uprightness,
     then nations shall be blessed*ᵈ* by him,
          and by him they shall boast.

3 For thus says the LORD to the people of Judah and to the inhabitants of Jerusalem:
Break up your fallow ground,
     and do not sow among thorns.
⁴ Circumcise yourselves to the LORD,

---

a Q Ms Gk Mss Syr: MT *I*   *b* Or *the trails*   *c* Gk Syr Vg: Heb *Truly from the hills is*   *d* Or *shall bless themselves*

remove the foreskin of your hearts,
O people of Judah and inhabitants of
Jerusalem,
or else my wrath will go forth like fire,
and burn with no one to quench it,
because of the evil of your doings.

Invasion and Desolation of Judah Threatened

5 Declare in Judah, and proclaim in Jerusalem, and say:
Blow the trumpet through the land;
shout aloud[a] and say,
"Gather together, and let us go
into the fortified cities!"
6 Raise a standard toward Zion,
flee for safety, do not delay,
for I am bringing evil from the north,
and a great destruction.
7 A lion has gone up from its thicket,
a destroyer of nations has set out;
he has gone out from his place
to make your land a waste;
your cities will be ruins
without inhabitant.
8 Because of this put on sackcloth,
lament and wail:
"The fierce anger of the LORD
has not turned away from us."

9 On that day, says the LORD, courage shall fail the king and the officials; the priests shall be appalled and the prophets astounded. 10 Then I said, "Ah, Lord GOD, how utterly you have deceived this people and Jerusalem, saying, 'It shall be well with you,' even while the sword is at the throat!"

11 At that time it will be said to this people and to Jerusalem: A hot wind comes from me out of the bare heights[b] in the desert toward my poor people, not to winnow or cleanse— 12 a wind too strong for that. Now it is I who speak in judgment against them.
13 Look! He comes up like clouds,
his chariots like the whirlwind;
his horses are swifter than eagles—
woe to us, for we are ruined!
14 O Jerusalem, wash your heart clean of
wickedness
so that you may be saved.
How long shall your evil schemes
lodge within you?
15 For a voice declares from Dan
and proclaims disaster from Mount
Ephraim.
16 Tell the nations, "Here they are!"
Proclaim against Jerusalem,

"Besiegers come from a distant land;
they shout against the cities of Judah.
17 They have closed in around her like
watchers of a field,
because she has rebelled against me,
says the LORD.
18 Your ways and your doings
have brought this upon you.
This is your doom; how bitter it is!
It has reached your very heart."

Sorrow for a Doomed Nation

19 My anguish, my anguish! I writhe in pain!
Oh, the walls of my heart!
My heart is beating wildly;
I cannot keep silent;
for I[c] hear the sound of the trumpet,
the alarm of war.
20 Disaster overtakes disaster,
the whole land is laid waste.
Suddenly my tents are destroyed,
my curtains in a moment.
21 How long must I see the standard,
and hear the sound of the trumpet?
22 "For my people are foolish,
they do not know me;
they are stupid children,
they have no understanding.
They are skilled in doing evil,
but do not know how to do good."

23 I looked on the earth, and lo, it was waste
and void;
and to the heavens, and they had no
light.
24 I looked on the mountains, and lo, they
were quaking,
and all the hills moved to and fro.
25 I looked, and lo, there was no one at all,
and all the birds of the air had fled.
26 I looked, and lo, the fruitful land was a
desert,
and all its cities were laid in ruins
before the LORD, before his fierce anger.
27 For thus says the LORD: The whole land shall be a desolation; yet I will not make a full end.
28 Because of this the earth shall mourn,
and the heavens above grow black;
for I have spoken, I have purposed;
I have not relented nor will I turn back.

29 At the noise of horseman and archer
every town takes to flight;
they enter thickets; they climb among
rocks;
all the towns are forsaken,
and no one lives in them.

a Or shout, take your weapons: Heb shout, fill (your hand) b Or the trails c Another reading is for you, O my soul,

³⁰ And you, O desolate one,
what do you mean that you dress in
crimson,
that you deck yourself with ornaments of
gold,
that you enlarge your eyes with paint?
In vain you beautify yourself.
Your lovers despise you;
they seek your life.
³¹ For I heard a cry as of a woman in labor,
anguish as of one bringing forth her first
child,
the cry of daughter Zion gasping for breath,
stretching out her hands,
"Woe is me! I am fainting before killers!"

5 The Utter Corruption of God's People

Run to and fro through the streets of
Jerusalem,
look around and take note!
Search its squares and see
if you can find one person
who acts justly
and seeks truth—
so that I may pardon Jerusalem.^a
² Although they say, "As the Lord lives,"
yet they swear falsely.
³ O Lord, do your eyes not look for truth?
You have struck them,
but they felt no anguish;
you have consumed them,
but they refused to take correction.
They have made their faces harder than
rock;
they have refused to turn back.

⁴ Then I said, "These are only the poor,
they have no sense;
for they do not know the way of the Lord,
the law of their God.
⁵ Let me go to the rich^b
and speak to them;
surely they know the way of the Lord,
the law of their God."
But they all alike had broken the yoke,
they had burst the bonds.

⁶ Therefore a lion from the forest shall kill
them,
a wolf from the desert shall destroy them.
A leopard is watching against their cities;
everyone who goes out of them shall be
torn in pieces—
because their transgressions are many,
their apostasies are great.

⁷ How can I pardon you?
Your children have forsaken me,
and have sworn by those who are no gods.

Sunrise Haze—© Lexi Hiland, 16

When I fed them to the full,
they committed adultery
and trooped to the houses of prostitutes.
⁸ They were well-fed lusty stallions,
each neighing for his neighbor's wife.
⁹ Shall I not punish them for these things?
says the Lord;
and shall I not bring retribution
on a nation such as this?

¹⁰ Go up through her vine-rows and destroy,
but do not make a full end;
strip away her branches,
for they are not the Lord's.
¹¹ For the house of Israel and the house of
Judah
have been utterly faithless to me,
says the Lord.
¹² They have spoken falsely of the Lord,
and have said, "He will do nothing.
No evil will come upon us,
and we shall not see sword or famine."
¹³ The prophets are nothing but wind,
for the word is not in them.
Thus shall it be done to them!

¹⁴ Therefore thus says the Lord, the God of
hosts:
Because they^c have spoken this word,
I am now making my words in your mouth
a fire,
and this people wood, and the fire shall
devour them.
¹⁵ I am going to bring upon you
a nation from far away, O house of Israel,
says the Lord.
It is an enduring nation,
it is an ancient nation,

---

a Heb *it* *b* Or *the great* *c* Heb *you*

a nation whose language you do not know,
nor can you understand what they say.

¹⁶ Their quiver is like an open tomb;
all of them are mighty warriors.
¹⁷ They shall eat up your harvest and your food;
they shall eat up your sons and your
daughters;
they shall eat up your flocks and your herds;
they shall eat up your vines and your fig
trees;
they shall destroy with the sword
your fortified cities in which you trust.

18 But even in those days, says the LORD,
I will not make a full end of you. ¹⁹And when
your people say, "Why has the LORD our God
done all these things to us?" you shall say to
them, "As you have forsaken me and served
foreign gods in your land, so you shall serve
strangers in a land that is not yours."

²⁰ Declare this in the house of Jacob,
proclaim it in Judah:
²¹ Hear this, O foolish and senseless people,
who have eyes, but do not see,
who have ears, but do not hear.
²² Do you not fear me? says the LORD;
Do you not tremble before me?
I placed the sand as a boundary for the sea,
a perpetual barrier that it cannot pass;
though the waves toss, they cannot prevail,
though they roar, they cannot pass over it.
²³ But this people has a stubborn and
rebellious heart;
they have turned aside and gone away.
²⁴ They do not say in their hearts,
"Let us fear the LORD our God,
who gives the rain in its season,
the autumn rain and the spring rain,
and keeps for us
the weeks appointed for the harvest."
²⁵ Your iniquities have turned these away,
and your sins have deprived you of good.
²⁶ For scoundrels are found among my people;
they take over the goods of others.
Like fowlers they set a trap;ᵃ
they catch human beings.
²⁷ Like a cage full of birds,
their houses are full of treachery;
therefore they have become great and rich,
²⁸ they have grown fat and sleek.
They know no limits in deeds of
wickedness;
they do not judge with justice
the cause of the orphan, to make it prosper,
and they do not defend the rights of the
needy.
²⁹ Shall I not punish them for these things?
says the LORD,
and shall I not bring retribution
on a nation such as this?

a Meaning of Heb uncertain

Wonder—© Joy Brantl, 17

30 An appalling and horrible thing
    has happened in the land:
31 the prophets prophesy falsely,
    and the priests rule as the prophets
      direct;*a*
my people love to have it so,
    but what will you do when the end
      comes?

6 The Imminence and Horror of the Invasion

Flee for safety, O children of Benjamin,
    from the midst of Jerusalem!
Blow the trumpet in Tekoa,
    and raise a signal on Beth-haccherem;
for evil looms out of the north,
    and great destruction.
2 I have likened daughter Zion
    to the loveliest pasture.*b*
3 Shepherds with their flocks shall come
      against her.
    They shall pitch their tents around her;
    they shall pasture, all in their places.
4 "Prepare war against her;
    up, and let us attack at noon!"
"Woe to us, for the day declines,
    the shadows of evening lengthen!"
5 "Up, and let us attack by night,
    and destroy her palaces!"
6 For thus says the LORD of hosts:
Cut down her trees;
    cast up a siege ramp against Jerusalem.
This is the city that must be punished;*c*
    there is nothing but oppression within
      her.
7 As a well keeps its water fresh,
    so she keeps fresh her wickedness;
violence and destruction are heard within
      her;
    sickness and wounds are ever before me.
8 Take warning, O Jerusalem,
    or I shall turn from you in disgust,
and make you a desolation,
    an uninhabited land.

9 Thus says the LORD of hosts:
Glean*d* thoroughly as a vine
    the remnant of Israel;
like a grape-gatherer, pass your hand again
    over its branches.
10 To whom shall I speak and give warning,
    that they may hear?
See, their ears are closed,*e*
    they cannot listen.
The word of the LORD is to them an object
    of scorn;

they take no pleasure in it.
11 But I am full of the wrath of the LORD;
    I am weary of holding it in.

Pour it out on the children in the street,
    and on the gatherings of young men as
      well;
both husband and wife shall be taken,
    the old folk and the very aged.
12 Their houses shall be turned over to others,
    their fields and wives together;
for I will stretch out my hand
    against the inhabitants of the land,
              says the LORD.
13 For from the least to the greatest of them,
    everyone is greedy for unjust gain;
and from prophet to priest,
    everyone deals falsely.
14 They have treated the wound of my people
      carelessly,
    saying, "Peace, peace,"
    when there is no peace.
15 They acted shamefully, they committed
      abomination;
    yet they were not ashamed,
    they did not know how to blush.
Therefore they shall fall among those who
      fall;
    at the time that I punish them, they shall
      be overthrown,
              says the LORD.
16 Thus says the LORD:
Stand at the crossroads, and look,
    and ask for the ancient paths,
where the good way lies; and walk in it,
    and find rest for your souls.
But they said, "We will not walk in it."
17 Also I raised up sentinels for you:
    "Give heed to the sound of the trumpet!"
But they said, "We will not give heed."
18 Therefore hear, O nations,
    and know, O congregation, what will
      happen to them.
19 Hear, O earth; I am going to bring disaster
      on this people,
    the fruit of their schemes,
because they have not given heed to my
      words;
    and as for my teaching, they have
      rejected it.
20 Of what use to me is frankincense that
      comes from Sheba,
    or sweet cane from a distant land?
Your burnt offerings are not acceptable,
    nor are your sacrifices pleasing to me.
21 Therefore thus says the LORD:

---

a Or *rule by their own authority* *b* Or *I will destroy daughter Zion, the loveliest pasture* *c* Or *the city of license* *d* Cn: Heb *They shall glean* *e* Heb *are uncircumcised*

Role-Playing God's Voice

In Jeremiah 7.16–29, God communicates his passionate anger to Jeremiah. To understand God's fury, read this text aloud. Read it as if you were auditioning for the role of God in a play called *Jeremiah*. Read it several times, several ways. Where would God's voice drop into a whisper of anger? What words would he emphasize? Would he cry? Shout? Would his voice be slow and low? Once you've finished reading the text aloud, think about what you've just read and how you felt as you read it.

Here we see that God is a jealous God. He wants our total attention and obedience. Who or what we worship matters to God. Who receives your worship? What do you spend your time thinking about? What are your deepest passions?

CREATIVE SPACE

See, I am laying before this people
stumbling blocks against which they
shall stumble;
parents and children together,
neighbor and friend shall perish.

22 Thus says the LORD:
See, a people is coming from the land of
the north,
a great nation is stirring from the
farthest parts of the earth.
23 They grasp the bow and the javelin,
they are cruel and have no mercy,
their sound is like the roaring sea;
they ride on horses,
equipped like a warrior for battle,
against you, O daughter Zion!

24 "We have heard news of them,
our hands fall helpless;
anguish has taken hold of us,
pain as of a woman in labor.
25 Do not go out into the field,
or walk on the road;
for the enemy has a sword,
terror is on every side."

26 O my poor people, put on sackcloth,
and roll in ashes;
make mourning as for an only child,
most bitter lamentation:
for suddenly the destroyer
will come upon us.

27 I have made you a tester and a refiner[a]
among my people
so that you may know and test their ways.
28 They are all stubbornly rebellious,
going about with slanders;
they are bronze and iron,
all of them act corruptly.
29 The bellows blow fiercely,
the lead is consumed by the fire;
in vain the refining goes on,
for the wicked are not removed.
30 They are called "rejected silver,"
for the LORD has rejected them.

7 Jeremiah Proclaims God's Judgment on the Nation

The word that came to Jeremiah from the LORD: 2Stand in the gate of the LORD's house, and proclaim there this word, and say, Hear the word of the LORD, all you people of Judah, you that enter these gates to worship the LORD. 3Thus says the LORD of hosts, the God of Israel: Amend your ways and your doings, and let me dwell with you[b] in this place. 4Do not trust in these deceptive words: "This is[c] the temple of

a Or *a fortress* b Or *and I will let you dwell* c Heb *They are* the LORD, the temple of the LORD, the temple of the LORD."

5 For if you truly amend your ways and your doings, if you truly act justly one with another, ⁶if you do not oppress the alien, the orphan, and the widow, or shed innocent blood in this place, and if you do not go after other gods to your own hurt, ⁷then I will dwell with you in this place, in the land that I gave of old to your ancestors forever and ever.

8 Here you are, trusting in deceptive words to no avail. ⁹Will you steal, murder, commit adultery, swear falsely, make offerings to Baal, and go after other gods that you have not known, ¹⁰and then come and stand before me in this house, which is called by my name, and say, "We are safe!"—only to go on doing all these abominations? ¹¹Has this house, which is called by my name, become a den of robbers in your sight? You know, I too am watching, says the LORD. ¹²Go now to my place that was in Shiloh, where I made my name dwell at first, and see what I did to it for the wickedness of my people Israel. ¹³And now, because you have done all these things, says the LORD, and when I spoke to you persistently, you did not listen, and when I called you, you did not answer, ¹⁴therefore I will do to the house that is called by my name, in which you trust, and to the place that I gave to you and to your ancestors, just what I did to Shiloh. ¹⁵And I will cast you out of my sight, just as I cast out all your kinsfolk, all the offspring of Ephraim.

The People's Disobedience

16 As for you, do not pray for this people, do not raise a cry or prayer on their behalf, and do not intercede with me, for I will not hear you. ¹⁷Do you not see what they are doing in the towns of Judah and in the streets of Jerusalem? ¹⁸The children gather wood, the fathers kindle fire, and the women knead dough, to make cakes for the queen of heaven; and they pour out drink offerings to other gods, to provoke me to anger. ¹⁹Is it I whom they provoke? says the LORD. Is it not themselves, to their own hurt? ²⁰Therefore thus says the Lord GOD: My anger and my wrath shall be poured out on this place, on human beings and animals, on the trees of the field and the fruit of the ground; it will burn and not be quenched.

21 Thus says the LORD of hosts, the God of Israel: Add your burnt offerings to your sacrifices, and eat the flesh. ²²For in the day that I brought your ancestors out of the land of Egypt, I did not speak to them or command them concerning burnt offerings and sacri-

fices. ²³But this command I gave them, "Obey my voice, and I will be your God, and you shall be my people; and walk only in the way that I command you, so that it may be well with you." ²⁴Yet they did not obey or incline their ear, but, in the stubbornness of their evil will, they walked in their own counsels, and looked backward rather than forward. ²⁵From the day that your ancestors came out of the land of Egypt until this day, I have persistently sent all my servants the prophets to them, day after day; ²⁶yet they did not listen to me, or pay attention, but they stiffened their necks. They did worse than their ancestors did.

27 So you shall speak all these words to them, but they will not listen to you. You shall call to them, but they will not answer you. ²⁸You shall say to them: This is the nation that did not obey the voice of the LORD their God, and did not accept discipline; truth has perished; it is cut off from their lips.

²⁹ Cut off your hair and throw it away;
  raise a lamentation on the bare heights,ᵃ
for the LORD has rejected and forsaken
  the generation that provoked his wrath.

30 For the people of Judah have done evil in my sight, says the LORD; they have set their abominations in the house that is called by my name, defiling it. ³¹And they go on building the high placeᵇ of Topheth, which is in the valley of the son of Hinnom, to burn their sons and their daughters in the fire—which I did not command, nor did it come into my mind. ³²Therefore, the days are surely coming, says the LORD, when it will no more be called Topheth, or the valley of the son of Hinnom, but the valley of Slaughter: for they will bury in Topheth until there is no more room. ³³The corpses of this people will be food for the birds of the air, and for the animals of the earth; and no one will frighten them away. ³⁴And I will bring to an end the sound of mirth and gladness, the voice of the bride and bridegroom in the cities of Judah and in the streets of Jerusalem; for the land shall become a waste.

8 At that time, says the LORD, the bones of the kings of Judah, the bones of its officials, the bones of the priests, the bones of the prophets, and the bones of the inhabitants of Jerusalem shall be brought out of their tombs; ²and they shall be spread before the sun and the moon and all the host of heaven, which they have loved and served, which they have followed, and which they have inquired of and worshiped; and they shall not be gathered or buried; they shall be like dung on the surface of the ground. ³Death shall be preferred to life by

ᵃ Or the trails ᵇ Gk Tg: Heb high places

all the remnant that remains of this evil family in all the places where I have driven them, says the LORD of hosts.

The Blind Perversity of the Whole Nation

4 You shall say to them, Thus says the LORD:
When people fall, do they not get up again?
    If they go astray, do they not turn back?
5 Why then has this people[a] turned away
    in perpetual backsliding?
They have held fast to deceit,
    they have refused to return.
6 I have given heed and listened,
    but they do not speak honestly;
no one repents of wickedness,
    saying, "What have I done!"
All of them turn to their own course,
    like a horse plunging headlong into battle.
7 Even the stork in the heavens
    knows its times;
and the turtledove, swallow, and crane[b]
    observe the time of their coming;
but my people do not know
    the ordinance of the LORD.

8 How can you say, "We are wise,
    and the law of the LORD is with us,"
when, in fact, the false pen of the scribes
    has made it into a lie?
9 The wise shall be put to shame,
    they shall be dismayed and taken;
since they have rejected the word of the
        LORD,
    what wisdom is in them?
10 Therefore I will give their wives to others
    and their fields to conquerors,
because from the least to the greatest
    everyone is greedy for unjust gain;
from prophet to priest
    everyone deals falsely.
11 They have treated the wound of my people
        carelessly,
    saying, "Peace, peace,"
    when there is no peace.
12 They acted shamefully, they committed
        abomination;
    yet they were not at all ashamed,
    they did not know how to blush.
Therefore they shall fall among those who
        fall;
    at the time when I punish them, they
        shall be overthrown,
                    says the LORD.
13 When I wanted to gather them, says the
        LORD,
    there are[c] no grapes on the vine,
    nor figs on the fig tree;

even the leaves are withered,
    and what I gave them has passed away
        from them.[b]

14 Why do we sit still?
Gather together, let us go into the fortified
        cities
    and perish there;
for the LORD our God has doomed us to
        perish,
    and has given us poisoned water to drink,
    because we have sinned against the
        LORD.
15 We look for peace, but find no good,
    for a time of healing, but there is terror
        instead.

16 The snorting of their horses is heard from
        Dan;
    at the sound of the neighing of their
        stallions
    the whole land quakes.
They come and devour the land and all that
        fills it,
    the city and those who live in it.
17 See, I am letting snakes loose among you,
    adders that cannot be charmed,
    and they shall bite you,
                    says the LORD.

The Prophet Mourns for the People

18 My joy is gone, grief is upon me,
    my heart is sick.
19 Hark, the cry of my poor people
    from far and wide in the land:
"Is the LORD not in Zion?
    Is her King not in her?"
("Why have they provoked me to anger with
        their images,
    with their foreign idols?")
20 "The harvest is past, the summer is ended,
    and we are not saved."
21 For the hurt of my poor people I am hurt,
    I mourn, and dismay has taken hold of me.

22 Is there no balm in Gilead?
    Is there no physician there?
Why then has the health of my poor people
    not been restored?

9[d] O that my head were a spring of water,
    and my eyes a fountain of tears,
so that I might weep day and night
    for the slain of my poor people!
2[e] O that I had in the desert
    a traveler's lodging place,
that I might leave my people
    and go away from them!

a One Ms Gk: MT *this people, Jerusalem*, b Meaning of Heb uncertain c Or *I will make an end of them, says the LORD. There are* d Ch 8.23 in Heb e Ch 9.1 in Heb

For they are all adulterers,
    a band of traitors.
3 They bend their tongues like bows;
    they have grown strong in the land for
        falsehood, and not for truth;
for they proceed from evil to evil,
    and they do not know me, says the LORD.

4 Beware of your neighbors,
    and put no trust in any of your kin;*a*
for all your kin*b* are supplanters,
    and every neighbor goes around like a
        slanderer.
5 They all deceive their neighbors,
    and no one speaks the truth;
they have taught their tongues to speak lies;
    they commit iniquity and are too weary
        to repent.*c*
6 Oppression upon oppression, deceit*d* upon
    deceit!
    They refuse to know me, says the LORD.

7 Therefore thus says the LORD of hosts:
I will now refine and test them,
    for what else can I do with my sinful
        people?*e*
8 Their tongue is a deadly arrow;
    it speaks deceit through the mouth.
They all speak friendly words to their
        neighbors,
    but inwardly are planning to lay an
        ambush.
9 Shall I not punish them for these things?
    says the LORD;
    and shall I not bring retribution
    on a nation such as this?

10 Take up*f* weeping and wailing for the
    mountains,
    and a lamentation for the pastures of the
    wilderness,
because they are laid waste so that no one
    passes through,
    and the lowing of cattle is not heard;
both the birds of the air and the animals
    have fled and are gone.
11 I will make Jerusalem a heap of ruins,
    a lair of jackals;
and I will make the towns of Judah a
    desolation,
    without inhabitant.

12 Who is wise enough to understand this? To whom has the mouth of the LORD spoken, so that they may declare it? Why is the land ruined and laid waste like a wilderness, so that no one passes through? 13And the LORD says: Because they have forsaken my law that I set be-

fore them, and have not obeyed my voice, or walked in accordance with it, 14but have stubbornly followed their own hearts and have gone after the Baals, as their ancestors taught them. 15Therefore thus says the LORD of hosts, the God of Israel: I am feeding this people with wormwood, and giving them poisonous water to drink. 16I will scatter them among nations that neither they nor their ancestors have known; and I will send the sword after them, until I have consumed them.

The People Mourn in Judgment

17 Thus says the LORD of hosts:
    Consider, and call for the mourning women
        to come;
    send for the skilled women to come;

---

a Heb *in a brother*   *b* Heb *for every brother*   *c* Cn Compare Gk: Heb *they weary themselves with iniquity.* *6Your dwelling*   *d* Cn: Heb *Your dwelling in the midst of deceit*   *e* Or *my poor people*   *f* Gk Syr: Heb *I will take up*

¹⁸ let them quickly raise a dirge over us,
so that our eyes may run down with tears,
and our eyelids flow with water.
¹⁹ For a sound of wailing is heard from Zion:
"How we are ruined!
We are utterly shamed,
because we have left the land,
because they have cast down our
dwellings."

²⁰ Hear, O women, the word of the LORD,
and let your ears receive the word of his
mouth;
teach to your daughters a dirge,
and each to her neighbor a lament.
²¹ "Death has come up into our windows,
it has entered our palaces,
to cut off the children from the streets
and the young men from the squares."
²² Speak! Thus says the LORD:
"Human corpses shall fall
like dung upon the open field,
like sheaves behind the reaper,
and no one shall gather them."

23 Thus says the LORD: Do not let the wise boast in their wisdom, do not let the mighty boast in their might, do not let the wealthy boast in their wealth; ²⁴but let those who boast boast in this, that they understand and know me, that I am the LORD; I act with steadfast love, justice, and righteousness in the earth, for in these things I delight, says the LORD.

25 The days are surely coming, says the LORD, when I will attend to all those who are circumcised only in the foreskin: ²⁶Egypt, Judah, Edom, the Ammonites, Moab, and all those with shaven temples who live in the desert. For all these nations are uncircumcised, and all the house of Israel is uncircumcised in heart.

10 Idolatry Has Brought Ruin on Israel

Hear the word that the LORD speaks to you, O house of Israel. ²Thus says the LORD:
Do not learn the way of the nations,
or be dismayed at the signs of the
heavens;
for the nations are dismayed at them.
³ For the customs of the peoples are false:
a tree from the forest is cut down,
and worked with an ax by the hands of an
artisan;
⁴ people deck it with silver and gold;
they fasten it with hammer and nails
so that it cannot move.
⁵ Their idols^a are like scarecrows in a
cucumber field,
and they cannot speak;

they have to be carried,
for they cannot walk.
Do not be afraid of them,
for they cannot do evil,
nor is it in them to do good.
⁶ There is none like you, O LORD;
you are great, and your name is great in
might.
⁷ Who would not fear you, O King of the
nations?
For that is your due;
among all the wise ones of the nations
and in all their kingdoms
there is no one like you.
⁸ They are both stupid and foolish;
the instruction given by idols
is no better than wood!^b
⁹ Beaten silver is brought from Tarshish,
and gold from Uphaz.
They are the work of the artisan and of the
hands of the goldsmith;
their clothing is blue and purple;
they are all the product of skilled workers.
¹⁰ But the LORD is the true God;
he is the living God and the everlasting
King.
At his wrath the earth quakes,
and the nations cannot endure his
indignation.

11 Thus shall you say to them: The gods who did not make the heavens and the earth shall perish from the earth and from under the heavens.^c

¹² It is he who made the earth by his power,
who established the world by his
wisdom,
and by his understanding stretched out
the heavens.
¹³ When he utters his voice, there is a tumult
of waters in the heavens,
and he makes the mist rise from the ends
of the earth.
He makes lightnings for the rain,
and he brings out the wind from his
storehouses.
¹⁴ Everyone is stupid and without knowledge;
goldsmiths are all put to shame by their
idols;
for their images are false,
and there is no breath in them.
¹⁵ They are worthless, a work of delusion;
at the time of their punishment they
shall perish.
¹⁶ Not like these is the LORD,^d the portion of
Jacob,
for he is the one who formed all things,

---

a Heb *They* b Meaning of Heb uncertain c This verse is in Aramaic d Heb lacks *the LORD*

and Israel is the tribe of his inheritance;
    the Lord of hosts is his name.

The Coming Exile

¹⁷ Gather up your bundle from the ground,
    O you who live under siege!
¹⁸ For thus says the Lord:
    I am going to sling out the inhabitants of
        the land
      at this time,
    and I will bring distress on them,
      so that they shall feel it.

¹⁹ Woe is me because of my hurt!
    My wound is severe.
    But I said, "Truly this is my punishment,
      and I must bear it."
²⁰ My tent is destroyed,
    and all my cords are broken;
    my children have gone from me,
      and they are no more;
    there is no one to spread my tent again,
      and to set up my curtains.
²¹ For the shepherds are stupid,
    and do not inquire of the Lord;
    therefore they have not prospered,
    and all their flock is scattered.

²² Hear, a noise! Listen, it is coming—
    a great commotion from the land of the
      north
    to make the cities of Judah a desolation,
      a lair of jackals.

²³ I know, O Lord, that the way of human
      beings is not in their control,
    that mortals as they walk cannot direct
      their steps.
²⁴ Correct me, O Lord, but in just measure;
    not in your anger, or you will bring me to
      nothing.

²⁵ Pour out your wrath on the nations that do
      not know you,
    and on the peoples that do not call on
      your name;
    for they have devoured Jacob;
      they have devoured him and consumed
        him,
    and have laid waste his habitation.

11 Israel and Judah Have Broken the Covenant

The word that came to Jeremiah from the Lord:
²Hear the words of this covenant, and speak
to the people of Judah and the inhabitants of
Jerusalem. ³You shall say to them, Thus says
the Lord, the God of Israel: Cursed be anyone
who does not heed the words of this covenant,

⁴which I commanded your ancestors when I
brought them out of the land of Egypt, from the
iron-smelter, saying, Listen to my voice, and do
all that I command you. So shall you be my people, and I will be your God, ⁵that I may perform
the oath that I swore to your ancestors, to give
them a land flowing with milk and honey, as at
this day. Then I answered, "So be it, Lord."

6 And the Lord said to me: Proclaim all
these words in the cities of Judah, and in the
streets of Jerusalem: Hear the words of this
covenant and do them. ⁷For I solemnly warned
your ancestors when I brought them up out of
the land of Egypt, warning them persistently,
even to this day, saying, Obey my voice. ⁸Yet
they did not obey or incline their ear, but everyone walked in the stubbornness of an evil
will. So I brought upon them all the words of
this covenant, which I commanded them to
do, but they did not.

9 And the Lord said to me: Conspiracy exists among the people of Judah and the inhabitants of Jerusalem. ¹⁰They have turned back to
the iniquities of their ancestors of old, who refused to heed my words; they have gone after
other gods to serve them; the house of Israel
and the house of Judah have broken the cov-
enant that I made with their ancestors. ¹¹There-
fore, thus says the Lord, assuredly I am going
to bring disaster upon them that they cannot
escape; though they cry out to me, I will not listen to them. ¹²Then the cities of Judah and the
inhabitants of Jerusalem will go and cry out to
the gods to whom they make offerings, but they
will never save them in the time of their trouble. ¹³For your gods have become as many as
your towns, O Judah; and as many as the streets
of Jerusalem are the altars to shame you have
set up, altars to make offerings to Baal.

14 As for you, do not pray for this people, or
lift up a cry or prayer on their behalf, for I will
not listen when they call to me in the time of
their trouble. ¹⁵What right has my beloved in
my house, when she has done vile deeds? Can
vows^a and sacrificial flesh avert your doom? Can
you then exult? ¹⁶The Lord once called you, "A
green olive tree, fair with goodly fruit"; but with
the roar of a great tempest he will set fire to it,
and its branches will be consumed. ¹⁷The Lord
of hosts, who planted you, has pronounced evil
against you, because of the evil that the house
of Israel and the house of Judah have done, provoking me to anger by making offerings to Baal.

Jeremiah's Life Threatened

¹⁸ It was the Lord who made it known to me,
    and I knew;

---

a Gk: Heb Can many

God—© Amanda Verburg, 16

then you showed me their evil deeds.
19 But I was like a gentle lamb
    led to the slaughter.
And I did not know it was against me
    that they devised schemes, saying,
"Let us destroy the tree with its fruit,
    let us cut him off from the land of the
        living,
    so that his name will no longer be
        remembered!"
20 But you, O LORD of hosts, who judge
    righteously,
    who try the heart and the mind,
let me see your retribution upon them,
    for to you I have committed my cause.

21 Therefore thus says the LORD concerning the people of Anathoth, who seek your life, and say, "You shall not prophesy in the name of the LORD, or you will die by our hand"— 22therefore thus says the LORD of hosts: I am going to punish them; the young men shall die by the sword; their sons and their daughters shall die by famine; 23and not even a remnant shall be left of them. For I will bring disaster upon the people of Anathoth, the year of their punishment.

12 Jeremiah Complains to God

You will be in the right, O LORD,
    when I lay charges against you;
    but let me put my case to you.
Why does the way of the guilty prosper?
    Why do all who are treacherous thrive?
2 You plant them, and they take root;
    they grow and bring forth fruit;
you are near in their mouths
    yet far from their hearts.

3 But you, O LORD, know me;
    You see me and test me—my heart is
        with you.
Pull them out like sheep for the slaughter,
    and set them apart for the day of slaughter.
4 How long will the land mourn,
    and the grass of every field wither?
For the wickedness of those who live in it
    the animals and the birds are swept away,
    and because people said, "He is blind to
        our ways."[a]

God Replies to Jeremiah

5 If you have raced with foot-runners and
        they have wearied you,
    how will you compete with horses?
And if in a safe land you fall down,
    how will you fare in the thickets of the
        Jordan?
6 For even your kinsfolk and your own family,
    even they have dealt treacherously with
        you;
    they are in full cry after you;
do not believe them,
    though they speak friendly words to you.

7 I have forsaken my house,
    I have abandoned my heritage;
I have given the beloved of my heart
    into the hands of her enemies.
8 My heritage has become to me
    like a lion in the forest;
she has lifted up her voice against me—
    therefore I hate her.
9 Is the hyena greedy[b] for my heritage at my
        command?
    Are the birds of prey all around her?
Go, assemble all the wild animals;
    bring them to devour her.
10 Many shepherds have destroyed my vineyard,
    they have trampled down my portion,
they have made my pleasant portion
    a desolate wilderness.
11 They have made it a desolation;
    desolate, it mourns to me.
The whole land is made desolate,
    but no one lays it to heart.
12 Upon all the bare heights[c] in the desert
        spoilers have come;
for the sword of the LORD devours
    from one end of the land to the other;
    no one shall be safe.
13 They have sown wheat and have reaped
        thorns,
    they have tired themselves out but profit
        nothing.
They shall be ashamed of their[d] harvests
    because of the fierce anger of the LORD.

a Gk: Heb to our future b Cn: Heb Is the hyena, the bird of prey c Or the trails d Heb your

14 Thus says the LORD concerning all my evil neighbors who touch the heritage that I have given my people Israel to inherit: I am about to pluck them up from their land, and I will pluck up the house of Judah from among them. 15And after I have plucked them up, I will again have compassion on them, and I will bring them again to their heritage and to their land, every one of them. 16And then, if they will diligently learn the ways of my people, to swear by my name, "As the LORD lives," as they taught my people to swear by Baal, then they shall be built up in the midst of my people. 17But if any nation will not listen, then I will completely uproot it and destroy it, says the LORD.

13 The Linen Loincloth

Thus said the LORD to me, "Go and buy yourself a linen loincloth, and put it on your loins, but do not dip it in water." 2So I bought a loincloth according to the word of the LORD, and put it on my loins. 3And the word of the LORD came to me a second time, saying, 4"Take the loincloth that you bought and are wearing, and go now to the Euphrates,ᵃ and hide it there in a cleft of the rock." 5So I went, and hid it by the Euphrates,ᵇ as the LORD commanded me. 6And after many days the LORD said to me, "Go now to the Euphrates,ᵃ and take from there the loincloth that I commanded you to hide there." 7Then I went to the Euphrates,ᵃ and dug, and I took the loincloth from the place where I had hidden it. But now the loincloth was ruined; it was good for nothing.

8 Then the word of the LORD came to me: 9Thus says the LORD: Just so I will ruin the pride of Judah and the great pride of Jerusalem. 10This evil people, who refuse to hear my words, who stubbornly follow their own will and have gone after other gods to serve them and worship them, shall be like this loincloth, which is good for nothing. 11For as the loincloth clings to one's loins, so I made the whole house of Israel and the whole house of Judah cling to me, says the LORD, in order that they might be for me a people, a name, a praise, and a glory. But they would not listen.

Symbol of the Wine-Jars

12 You shall speak to them this word: Thus says the LORD, the God of Israel: Every wine-jar should be filled with wine. And they will say to you, "Do you think we do not know that every wine-jar should be filled with wine?" 13Then you shall say to them: Thus says the LORD: I am about to fill all the inhabitants of this land—the kings who sit on David's throne, the priests,

the prophets, and all the inhabitants of Jerusalem—with drunkenness. 14And I will dash them one against another, parents and children together, says the LORD. I will not pity or spare or have compassion when I destroy them.

Exile Threatened

15 Hear and give ear; do not be haughty,
 for the LORD has spoken.
16 Give glory to the LORD your God
 before he brings darkness,
 and before your feet stumble
 on the mountains at twilight;
while you look for light,
 he turns it into gloom
 and makes it deep darkness.
17 But if you will not listen,
 my soul will weep in secret for your pride;
my eyes will weep bitterly and run down
 with tears,
 because the LORD's flock has been taken
 captive.

18 Say to the king and the queen mother:
 "Take a lowly seat,
for your beautiful crown
 has come down from your head."ᶜ
19 The towns of the Negeb are shut up
 with no one to open them;
all Judah is taken into exile,
 wholly taken into exile.

20 Lift up your eyes and see
 those who come from the north.
Where is the flock that was given you,
 your beautiful flock?
21 What will you say when they set as head
 over you
 those whom you have trained
 to be your allies?
Will not pangs take hold of you,
 like those of a woman in labor?
22 And if you say in your heart,
 "Why have these things come upon me?"
it is for the greatness of your iniquity
 that your skirts are lifted up,
 and you are violated.
23 Can Ethiopians ᵈ change their skin
 or leopards their spots?
Then also you can do good
 who are accustomed to do evil.
24 I will scatter youᵉ like chaff
 driven by the wind from the desert.
25 This is your lot,
 the portion I have measured out to you,
 says the LORD,
because you have forgotten me
 and trusted in lies.

ᵃ Or to Parah; Heb perath ᵇ Or by Parah; Heb perath ᶜ Gk Syr Vg: Meaning of Heb uncertain ᵈ Or Nubians; Heb Cushites ᵉ Heb them

26 I myself will lift up your skirts over your face,
   and your shame will be seen.
27 I have seen your abominations,
   your adulteries and neighings, your
      shameless prostitutions
   on the hills of the countryside.
   Woe to you, O Jerusalem!
      How long will it be
   before you are made clean?

14 The Great Drought

The word of the Lord that came to Jeremiah
concerning the drought:
2 Judah mourns
   and her gates languish;
   they lie in gloom on the ground,
      and the cry of Jerusalem goes up.
3 Her nobles send their servants for water;
   they come to the cisterns,
   they find no water,
      they return with their vessels empty.
   They are ashamed and dismayed
   and cover their heads,
4 because the ground is cracked.
   Because there has been no rain on the
      land
   the farmers are dismayed;
      they cover their heads.
5 Even the doe in the field forsakes her
      newborn fawn
   because there is no grass.
6 The wild asses stand on the bare heights,a

they pant for air like jackals;
their eyes fail
   because there is no herbage.

7 Although our iniquities testify against us,
   act, O Lord, for your name's sake;
our apostasies indeed are many,
   and we have sinned against you.
8 O hope of Israel,
   its savior in time of trouble,
why should you be like a stranger in the
      land,
   like a traveler turning aside for the night?
9 Why should you be like someone confused,
   like a mighty warrior who cannot give
      help?
Yet you, O Lord, are in the midst of us,
   and we are called by your name;
   do not forsake us!

10 Thus says the Lord concerning this people:
   Truly they have loved to wander,
      they have not restrained their feet;
   therefore the Lord does not accept them,
      now he will remember their iniquity
   and punish their sins.

11 The Lord said to me: Do not pray for the
welfare of this people. 12Although they fast, I
do not hear their cry, and although they offer
burnt offering and grain offering, I do not accept them; but by the sword, by famine, and by
pestilence I consume them.

a Or the trails

Denunciation of Lying Prophets

13 Then I said: "Ah, Lord GOD! Here are the prophets saying to them, 'You shall not see the sword, nor shall you have famine, but I will give you true peace in this place.' " 14And the LORD said to me: The prophets are prophesying lies in my name; I did not send them, nor did I command them or speak to them. They are prophesying to you a lying vision, worthless divination, and the deceit of their own minds. 15Therefore thus says the LORD concerning the prophets who prophesy in my name though I did not send them, and who say, "Sword and famine shall not come on this land": By sword and famine those prophets shall be consumed. 16And the people to whom they prophesy shall be thrown out into the streets of Jerusalem, victims of famine and sword. There shall be no one to bury them—themselves, their wives, their sons, and their daughters. For I will pour out their wickedness upon them.

17 You shall say to them this word:
Let my eyes run down with tears night and
day,
    and let them not cease,
for the virgin daughter—my people—is
        struck down with a crushing blow,
    with a very grievous wound.
18 If I go out into the field,
    look—those killed by the sword!
And if I enter the city,
    look—those sick with*a* famine!
For both prophet and priest ply their trade
        throughout the land,
    and have no knowledge.

The People Plead for Mercy

19 Have you completely rejected Judah?
    Does your heart loathe Zion?
Why have you struck us down
    so that there is no healing for us?
We look for peace, but find no good;
    for a time of healing, but there is terror
        instead.
20 We acknowledge our wickedness, O LORD,
    the iniquity of our ancestors,
    for we have sinned against you.
21 Do not spurn us, for your name's sake;
    do not dishonor your glorious throne;
    remember and do not break your
        covenant with us.
22 Can any idols of the nations bring rain?
    Or can the heavens give showers?
Is it not you, O LORD our God?
    We set our hope on you,
    for it is you who do all this.

a Heb look—the sicknesses of

15 Punishment Is Inevitable

Then the LORD said to me: Though Moses and Samuel stood before me, yet my heart would not turn toward this people. Send them out of my sight, and let them go! 2And when they say to you, "Where shall we go?" you shall say to them: Thus says the LORD:

Those destined for pestilence, to pestilence,
    and those destined for the sword, to the
        sword;
those destined for famine, to famine,
    and those destined for captivity, to
        captivity.

3And I will appoint over them four kinds of destroyers, says the LORD: the sword to kill, the dogs to drag away, and the birds of the air and the wild animals of the earth to devour and destroy. 4I will make them a horror to all the kingdoms of the earth because of what King Manasseh son of Hezekiah of Judah did in Jerusalem.

5 Who will have pity on you, O Jerusalem,
    or who will bemoan you?
Who will turn aside
    to ask about your welfare?
6 You have rejected me, says the LORD,
    you are going backward;
so I have stretched out my hand against you
        and destroyed you—
    I am weary of relenting.
7 I have winnowed them with a winnowing
        fork
    in the gates of the land;
I have bereaved them, I have destroyed my
        people;
    they did not turn from their ways.
8 Their widows became more numerous
    than the sand of the seas;
I have brought against the mothers of
        youths
    a destroyer at noonday;
I have made anguish and terror
    fall upon her suddenly.
9 She who bore seven has languished;
    she has swooned away;
her sun went down while it was yet day;
    she has been shamed and disgraced.
And the rest of them I will give to the sword
    before their enemies,
                    says the LORD.

Jeremiah Complains Again and Is Reassured

10 Woe is me, my mother, that you ever bore me, a man of strife and contention to the whole land! I have not lent, nor have I borrowed, yet

all of them curse me. ¹¹The Lord said: Surely I have intervened in your life[a] for good, surely I have imposed enemies on you in a time of trouble and in a time of distress.[b] ¹²Can iron and bronze break iron from the north?

13 Your wealth and your treasures I will give as plunder, without price, for all your sins, throughout all your territory. ¹⁴I will make you serve your enemies in a land that you do not know, for in my anger a fire is kindled that shall burn forever.

¹⁵ O Lord, you know;
  remember me and visit me,
  and bring down retribution for me on my
    persecutors.
In your forbearance do not take me away;
  know that on your account I suffer insult.
¹⁶ Your words were found, and I ate them,
  and your words became to me a joy
  and the delight of my heart;
for I am called by your name,
  O Lord, God of hosts.
¹⁷ I did not sit in the company of
    merrymakers,
  nor did I rejoice;
under the weight of your hand I sat alone,
  for you had filled me with indignation.
¹⁸ Why is my pain unceasing,
  my wound incurable,
  refusing to be healed?
Truly, you are to me like a deceitful brook,
  like waters that fail.

¹⁹ Therefore thus says the Lord:
If you turn back, I will take you back,
  and you shall stand before me.
If you utter what is precious, and not what
    is worthless,
  you shall serve as my mouth.
It is they who will turn to you,
  not you who will turn to them.
²⁰ And I will make you to this people
  a fortified wall of bronze;
they will fight against you,
  but they shall not prevail over you,
for I am with you
  to save you and deliver you,
                          says the Lord.
²¹ I will deliver you out of the hand of the
    wicked,
  and redeem you from the grasp of the
    ruthless.

16 Jeremiah's Celibacy and Message

The word of the Lord came to me: ²You shall not take a wife, nor shall you have sons or daughters in this place. ³For thus says the Lord concerning the sons and daughters who are born in this place, and concerning the mothers who bear them and the fathers who beget them in this land: ⁴They shall die of deadly diseases. They shall not be lamented, nor shall they be buried; they shall become like dung on the surface of the ground. They shall perish by the sword and by famine, and their dead bodies shall become food for the birds of the air and for the wild animals of the earth.

5 For thus says the Lord: Do not enter the house of mourning, or go to lament, or bemoan them; for I have taken away my peace from this people, says the Lord, my steadfast love and mercy. ⁶Both great and small shall die in this land; they shall not be buried, and no one shall lament for them; there shall be no gashing, no shaving of the head for them. ⁷No one shall break bread[c] for the mourner, to offer comfort for the dead; nor shall anyone give them the cup of consolation to drink for their fathers or their mothers. ⁸You shall not go into the house of feasting to sit with them, to eat and drink. ⁹For thus says the Lord of hosts, the God of Israel: I am going to banish from this place, in your days and before your eyes, the voice of mirth and the voice of gladness, the voice of the bridegroom and the voice of the bride.

10 And when you tell this people all these words, and they say to you, "Why has the Lord pronounced all this great evil against us? What is our iniquity? What is the sin that we have committed against the Lord our God?" ¹¹then you shall say to them: It is because your ancestors have forsaken me, says the Lord, and have gone after other gods and have served and worshiped them, and have forsaken me and have not kept my law; ¹²and because you have behaved worse than your ancestors, for here you are, every one of you, following your stubborn evil will, refusing to listen to me. ¹³Therefore I will hurl you out of this land into a land that neither you nor your ancestors have known, and there you shall serve other gods day and night, for I will show you no favor.

God Will Restore Israel

14 Therefore, the days are surely coming, says the Lord, when it shall no longer be said, "As the Lord lives who brought the people of Israel up out of the land of Egypt," ¹⁵but "As the Lord lives who brought the people of Israel up out of the land of the north and out of all the lands where he had driven them." For I will bring them back to their own land that I gave to their ancestors.

16 I am now sending for many fishermen, says the Lord, and they shall catch them; and

---

a Heb *intervened with you* b Meaning of Heb uncertain c Two Mss Gk: MT *break for them*

RQ

Is it really fair for people to be sent to hell? The Bible talks about judgment, but also about love. It just doesn't seem fair that some people go to hell.

Jeremiah 15 is just one of many passages in the Bible that describe God's punishment and judgment—and it's pretty ruthless. Things start to seem even worse when you read passages like this: "But I will warn you whom to fear: fear him who, after he has killed, has authority to cast into hell" (Luke 12.5). To put it bluntly, hell is *not* a nice place.

This whole judgment thing is an aspect of God we want to ignore. And it can be really hard to understand why God allows people to go to hell. It can seem uncaring, cruel, or just unfair.

But try looking at it differently for a moment. Does God really send or allow people to go to hell? Or is it a result of their own choice—probably *many* choices throughout their lives? People pave their own road to judgment. There's an old saying: "The road to hell is paved with good intentions." And it's true.

How many empty promises have you made to yourself? You know: *I intend to clean up my act. I intend to quit ruining people's reputations by my gossiping. I intend to respond to the poor. Someday I will think about how my actions affect others.* Good intentions, sure, but without action, they're meaningless.

Jesus tells a lot of stories about this attitude at the same time that he talks about love. (See Matthew 24.45–25.46; Mark 12.1–12; Luke 12.16–21, 35–48; 16.19–31.)

There's good news in the Gospels, and there's hard news in the Gospels. This life is a gift. It's not about fairness or entitlement. It's about being gifted—gifted with a purpose to do God's will.

Find some Creative Space in this Bible and write your thoughts about your own life choices. If God asked you for an accounting of how you've spent the gift of your life so far and how you've done his will, what would you say?

Share your thoughts and see what others have posted at **Learner.CalltoDiscipleship.com**.

---

afterward I will send for many hunters, and they shall hunt them from every mountain and every hill, and out of the clefts of the rocks. ¹⁷ For my eyes are on all their ways; they are not hidden from my presence, nor is their iniquity concealed from my sight. ¹⁸ And^a I will doubly repay their iniquity and their sin, because they have polluted my land with the carcasses of their detestable idols, and have filled my inheritance with their abominations.

¹⁹ O LORD, my strength and my stronghold,
   my refuge in the day of trouble,
to you shall the nations come
   from the ends of the earth and say:
Our ancestors have inherited nothing but
     lies,
   worthless things in which there is no
     profit.
²⁰ Can mortals make for themselves gods?
   Such are no gods!

   21 "Therefore I am surely going to teach them, this time I am going to teach them my power and my might, and they shall know that my name is the LORD."

17 Judah's Sin and Punishment

The sin of Judah is written with an iron pen; with a diamond point it is engraved on the tablet of their hearts, and on the horns of their altars, ² while their children remember their altars and their sacred poles,^b beside every green tree, and on the high hills, ³ on the mountains in the open country. Your wealth and all your treasures I will give for spoil as the price of your sin^c throughout all your territory. ⁴ By your own act you shall lose the heritage that I gave you, and I will make you serve your enemies in a land that you do not know, for in my anger a fire is kindled^d that shall burn forever.

  ⁵ Thus says the LORD:
   Cursed are those who trust in mere mortals
     and make mere flesh their strength,

---

a Gk: Heb *And first* *b* Heb *Asherim* *c* Cn: Heb *spoil your high places for sin* *d* Two Mss Theodotion: *you kindled*

whose hearts turn away from the LORD.
6 They shall be like a shrub in the desert,
    and shall not see when relief comes.
They shall live in the parched places of the
        wilderness,
    in an uninhabited salt land.

7 Blessed are those who trust in the LORD,
    whose trust is the LORD.
8 They shall be like a tree planted by water,
    sending out its roots by the stream.
It shall not fear when heat comes,
    and its leaves shall stay green;
in the year of drought it is not anxious,
    and it does not cease to bear fruit.

9 The heart is devious above all else;
    it is perverse—
    who can understand it?
10 I the LORD test the mind
    and search the heart,
to give to all according to their ways,
    according to the fruit of their doings.

11 Like the partridge hatching what it did not
        lay,
    so are all who amass wealth unjustly;
in mid-life it will leave them,
    and at their end they will prove to be
        fools.

12 O glorious throne, exalted from the
        beginning,
    shrine of our sanctuary!
13 O hope of Israel! O LORD!
    All who forsake you shall be put to
        shame;
those who turn away from you*a* shall be
        recorded in the underworld,*b*
    for they have forsaken the fountain of
        living water, the LORD.

Jeremiah Prays for Vindication

14 Heal me, O LORD, and I shall be healed;
    save me, and I shall be saved;
    for you are my praise.
15 See how they say to me,
    "Where is the word of the LORD?
    Let it come!"
16 But I have not run away from being a
        shepherd*c* in your service,
    nor have I desired the fatal day.
You know what came from my lips;
    it was before your face.
17 Do not become a terror to me;
    you are my refuge in the day of disaster;
18 Let my persecutors be shamed,
    but do not let me be shamed;
let them be dismayed,

a Heb *me* *b* Or *in the earth* *c* Meaning of Heb uncertain

but do not let me be dismayed;
    bring on them the day of disaster;
        destroy them with double destruction!

Hallow the Sabbath Day

19 Thus said the Lord to me: Go and stand in the People's Gate, by which the kings of Judah enter and by which they go out, and in all the gates of Jerusalem, 20and say to them: Hear the word of the Lord, you kings of Judah, and all Judah, and all the inhabitants of Jerusalem, who enter by these gates. 21Thus says the Lord: For the sake of your lives, take care that you do not bear a burden on the sabbath day or bring it in by the gates of Jerusalem. 22And do not carry a burden out of your houses on the sabbath or do any work, but keep the sabbath day holy, as I commanded your ancestors. 23Yet they did not listen or incline their ear; they stiffened their necks and would not hear or receive instruction.

24 But if you listen to me, says the Lord, and bring in no burden by the gates of this city on the sabbath day, but keep the sabbath day holy and do no work on it, 25then there shall enter by the gates of this city kings*a* who sit on the throne of David, riding in chariots and on horses, they and their officials, the people of Judah and the inhabitants of Jerusalem; and this city shall be inhabited forever. 26And people shall come from the towns of Judah and the places around Jerusalem, from the land of Benjamin, from the Shephelah, from the hill country, and from the Negeb, bringing burnt offerings and sacrifices, grain offerings and frankincense, and bringing thank offerings to the house of the Lord. 27But if you do not listen to me, to keep the sabbath day holy, and to carry in no burden through the gates of Jerusalem on the sabbath day, then I will kindle a fire in its gates; it shall devour the palaces of Jerusalem and shall not be quenched.

18 The Potter and the Clay

The word that came to Jeremiah from the Lord: 2"Come, go down to the potter's house, and there I will let you hear my words." 3So I went down to the potter's house, and there he was working at his wheel. 4The vessel he was making of clay was spoiled in the potter's hand, and he reworked it into another vessel, as seemed good to him.

5 Then the word of the Lord came to me: 6Can I not do with you, O house of Israel, just as this potter has done? says the Lord. Just like the clay in the potter's hand, so are you in my hand, O house of Israel. 7At one moment I may declare concerning a nation or a kingdom, that I will pluck up and break down and destroy it, 8but if that nation, concerning which I have spoken, turns from its evil, I will change my mind about the disaster that I intended to bring on it. 9And at another moment I may declare concerning a nation or a kingdom that I will build and plant it, 10but if it does evil in my sight, not listening to my voice, then I will change my mind about the good that I had intended to do to it. 11Now, therefore, say to the people of Judah and the inhabitants of Jerusalem: Thus says the Lord: Look, I am a potter shaping evil against you and devising a plan against you. Turn now, all of you from your evil way, and amend your ways and your doings.

Israel's Stubborn Idolatry

12 But they say, "It is no use! We will follow our own plans, and each of us will act according to the stubbornness of our evil will."

13 Therefore thus says the Lord:
    Ask among the nations:
        Who has heard the like of this?
    The virgin Israel has done
        a most horrible thing.
14 Does the snow of Lebanon leave
        the crags of Sirion?*b*
    Do the mountain*c* waters run dry,*d*
        the cold flowing streams?
15 But my people have forgotten me,
        they burn offerings to a delusion;
    they have stumbled*e* in their ways,
        in the ancient roads,
    and have gone into bypaths,
        not the highway,
16 making their land a horror,
        a thing to be hissed at forever.
    All who pass by it are horrified
        and shake their heads.
17 Like the wind from the east,
        I will scatter them before the enemy.
    I will show them my back, not my face,
        in the day of their calamity.

A Plot against Jeremiah

18 Then they said, "Come, let us make plots against Jeremiah—for instruction shall not perish from the priest, nor counsel from the wise, nor the word from the prophet. Come, let us bring charges against him,*f* and let us not heed any of his words."

19 Give heed to me, O Lord,
        and listen to what my adversaries say!

---

a Cn: Heb *kings and officials* *b* Cn: Heb *of the field* *c* Cn: Heb *foreign* *d* Cn: Heb *Are . . . plucked up?* *e* Gk Syr Vg: Heb *they made them stumble* *f* Heb *strike him with the tongue*

20 Is evil a recompense for good?
  Yet they have dug a pit for my life.
Remember how I stood before you
  to speak good for them,
  to turn away your wrath from them.
21 Therefore give their children over to
      famine;
  hurl them out to the power of the sword,
let their wives become childless and
      widowed.
  May their men meet death by pestilence,
    their youths be slain by the sword in
      battle.
22 May a cry be heard from their houses,
  when you bring the marauder suddenly
      upon them!
For they have dug a pit to catch me,
  and laid snares for my feet.
23 Yet you, O LORD, know
  all their plotting to kill me.
Do not forgive their iniquity,
  do not blot out their sin from your sight.
Let them be tripped up before you;
  deal with them while you are angry.

19 The Broken Earthenware Jug

Thus said the LORD: Go and buy a potter's
earthenware jug. Take with you[a] some of the
elders of the people and some of the senior
priests, 2and go out to the valley of the son of
Hinnom at the entry of the Potsherd Gate, and
proclaim there the words that I tell you. 3You
shall say: Hear the word of the LORD, O kings of
Judah and inhabitants of Jerusalem. Thus says
the LORD of hosts, the God of Israel: I am going to bring such disaster upon this place that
the ears of everyone who hears of it will tingle.

---

a Syr Tg Compare Gk: Heb lacks take with you

4Because the people have forsaken me, and
have profaned this place by making offerings
in it to other gods whom neither they nor their
ancestors nor the kings of Judah have known,
and because they have filled this place with the
blood of the innocent, 5and gone on building
the high places of Baal to burn their children in
the fire as burnt offerings to Baal, which I did
not command or decree, nor did it enter my
mind; 6therefore the days are surely coming,
says the LORD, when this place shall no more
be called Topheth, or the valley of the son of
Hinnom, but the valley of Slaughter. 7And in
this place I will make void the plans of Judah
and Jerusalem, and will make them fall by the
sword before their enemies, and by the hand of
those who seek their life. I will give their dead
bodies for food to the birds of the air and to the
wild animals of the earth. 8And I will make this
city a horror, a thing to be hissed at; everyone
who passes by it will be horrified and will hiss
because of all its disasters. 9And I will make
them eat the flesh of their sons and the flesh
of their daughters, and all shall eat the flesh of
their neighbors in the siege, and in the distress
with which their enemies and those who seek
their life afflict them.

10 Then you shall break the jug in the sight
of those who go with you, 11and shall say to
them: Thus says the LORD of hosts: So will I
break this people and this city, as one breaks
a potter's vessel, so that it can never be mended. In Topheth they shall bury until there is
no more room to bury. 12Thus will I do to this
place, says the LORD, and to its inhabitants,
making this city like Topheth. 13And the houses
of Jerusalem and the houses of the kings of Judah shall be defiled like the place of Topheth—
all the houses upon whose roofs offerings have
been made to the whole host of heaven, and
libations have been poured out to other gods.

14 When Jeremiah came from Topheth,
where the LORD had sent him to prophesy, he
stood in the court of the LORD's house and said
to all the people: 15Thus says the LORD of hosts,
the God of Israel: I am now bringing upon this
city and upon all its towns all the disaster that I
have pronounced against it, because they have
stiffened their necks, refusing to hear my words.

20 Jeremiah Persecuted by Pashhur

Now the priest Pashhur son of Immer, who was
chief officer in the house of the LORD, heard Jeremiah prophesying these things. 2Then Pashhur struck the prophet Jeremiah, and put him
in the stocks that were in the upper Benjamin
Gate of the house of the LORD. 3The next morn-

ing when Pashhur released Jeremiah from the stocks, Jeremiah said to him, The Lord has named you not Pashhur but "Terror-all-around." ⁴For thus says the Lord: I am making you a terror to yourself and to all your friends; and they shall fall by the sword of their enemies while you look on. And I will give all Judah into the hand of the king of Babylon; he shall carry them captive to Babylon, and shall kill them with the sword. ⁵I will give all the wealth of this city, all its gains, all its prized belongings, and all the treasures of the kings of Judah into the hand of their enemies, who shall plunder them, and seize them, and carry them to Babylon. ⁶And you, Pashhur, and all who live in your house, shall go into captivity, and to Babylon you shall go; there you shall die, and there you shall be buried, you and all your friends, to whom you have prophesied falsely.

Jeremiah Denounces His Persecutors

⁷ O Lord, you have enticed me,
    and I was enticed;
you have overpowered me,
    and you have prevailed.
I have become a laughingstock all day long;
    everyone mocks me.
⁸ For whenever I speak, I must cry out,
    I must shout, "Violence and
        destruction!"
For the word of the Lord has become for me
    a reproach and derision all day long.
⁹ If I say, "I will not mention him,
    or speak any more in his name,"
then within me there is something like a
        burning fire
    shut up in my bones;
I am weary with holding it in,
    and I cannot.
¹⁰ For I hear many whispering:
    "Terror is all around!
Denounce him! Let us denounce him!"
    All my close friends
    are watching for me to stumble.
"Perhaps he can be enticed,
    and we can prevail against him,
    and take our revenge on him."
¹¹ But the Lord is with me like a dread
        warrior;
    therefore my persecutors will stumble,
    and they will not prevail.
They will be greatly shamed,
    for they will not succeed.
Their eternal dishonor
    will never be forgotten.
¹² O Lord of hosts, you test the righteous,
    you see the heart and the mind;
let me see your retribution upon them,
    for to you I have committed my cause.

¹³ Sing to the Lord;
    praise the Lord!
For he has delivered the life of the needy
    from the hands of evildoers.

¹⁴ Cursed be the day
    on which I was born!
The day when my mother bore me,
    let it not be blessed!
¹⁵ Cursed be the man
    who brought the news to my father,
        saying,
"A child is born to you, a son,"
    making him very glad.
¹⁶ Let that man be like the cities
    that the Lord overthrew without pity;
let him hear a cry in the morning
    and an alarm at noon,
¹⁷ because he did not kill me in the womb;
    so my mother would have been my grave,
    and her womb forever great.
¹⁸ Why did I come forth from the womb
    to see toil and sorrow,
    and spend my days in shame?

21 Jerusalem Will Fall to Nebuchadrezzar

This is the word that came to Jeremiah from the Lord, when King Zedekiah sent to him Pashhur son of Malchiah and the priest Zephaniah son of Maaseiah, saying, ²"Please inquire of the Lord on our behalf, for King Nebuchadrezzar of Babylon is making war against us; perhaps the Lord will perform a wonderful deed for us, as he has often done, and will make him withdraw from us."

3 Then Jeremiah said to them: ⁴Thus you shall say to Zedekiah: Thus says the Lord, the God of Israel: I am going to turn back the weapons of war that are in your hands and with which you are fighting against the king of Babylon and against the Chaldeans who are besieging you outside the walls; and I will bring them together into the center of this city. ⁵I myself will fight against you with outstretched hand and mighty arm, in anger, in fury, and in great wrath. ⁶And I will strike down the inhabitants of this city, both human beings and animals; they shall die of a great pestilence. ⁷Afterward, says the Lord, I will give King Zedekiah of Judah, and his servants, and the people in this city—those who survive the pestilence, sword, and famine—into the hands of King Nebuchadrezzar of Babylon, into the hands of their enemies, into the hands of those who seek their lives. He shall strike them down with the edge of the sword; he shall not pity them, or spare them, or have compassion.

8 And to this people you shall say: Thus says the Lord: See, I am setting before you the way

of life and the way of death. ⁹Those who stay in this city shall die by the sword, by famine, and by pestilence; but those who go out and surrender to the Chaldeans who are besieging you shall live and shall have their lives as a prize of war. ¹⁰For I have set my face against this city for evil and not for good, says the LORD: it shall be given into the hands of the king of Babylon, and he shall burn it with fire.

Message to the House of David

11 To the house of the king of Judah say: Hear the word of the LORD, ¹²O house of David! Thus says the LORD:

> Execute justice in the morning,
> and deliver from the hand of the
> oppressor
> anyone who has been robbed,
> or else my wrath will go forth like fire,
> and burn, with no one to quench it,
> because of your evil doings.

¹³ See, I am against you, O inhabitant of the
valley,
O rock of the plain,
says the LORD;
you who say, "Who can come down
against us,
or who can enter our places of refuge?"
¹⁴ I will punish you according to the fruit of
your doings,
says the LORD;
I will kindle a fire in its forest,
and it shall devour all that is around it.

22 Exhortation to Repent

Thus says the LORD: Go down to the house of the king of Judah, and speak there this word, ²and say: Hear the word of the LORD, O King of Judah sitting on the throne of David—you, and your servants, and your people who enter these gates. ³Thus says the LORD: Act with justice and righteousness, and deliver from the hand of the oppressor anyone who has been robbed. And do no wrong or violence to the alien, the orphan, and the widow, or shed innocent blood in this place. ⁴For if you will indeed obey this word, then through the gates of this house shall enter kings who sit on the throne of David, riding in chariots and on horses, they, and their servants, and their people. ⁵But if you will not heed these words, I swear by myself, says the LORD, that this house shall become a desolation. ⁶For thus says the LORD concerning the house of the king of Judah:

> You are like Gilead to me,
> like the summit of Lebanon;
> but I swear that I will make you a desert,

an uninhabited city.^a

⁷ I will prepare destroyers against you,
all with their weapons;
they shall cut down your choicest cedars
and cast them into the fire.

8 And many nations will pass by this city, and all of them will say one to another, "Why has the LORD dealt in this way with that great city?" ⁹And they will answer, "Because they abandoned the covenant of the LORD their God, and worshiped other gods and served them."

¹⁰ Do not weep for him who is dead,
nor bemoan him;
weep rather for him who goes away,
for he shall return no more
to see his native land.

Message to the Sons of Josiah

11 For thus says the LORD concerning Shallum son of King Josiah of Judah, who succeeded his father Josiah, and who went away from this place: He shall return here no more, ¹²but in the place where they have carried him captive he shall die, and he shall never see this land again.

¹³ Woe to him who builds his house by
unrighteousness,
and his upper rooms by injustice;
who makes his neighbors work for
nothing,
and does not give them their wages;
¹⁴ who says, "I will build myself a spacious
house
with large upper rooms,"
and who cuts out windows for it,
paneling it with cedar,
and painting it with vermilion.
¹⁵ Are you a king
because you compete in cedar?
Did not your father eat and drink
and do justice and righteousness?
Then it was well with him.
¹⁶ He judged the cause of the poor and needy;
then it was well.
Is not this to know me?
says the LORD.
¹⁷ But your eyes and heart
are only on your dishonest gain,
for shedding innocent blood,
and for practicing oppression and
violence.

18 Therefore thus says the LORD concerning King Jehoiakim son of Josiah of Judah:

> They shall not lament for him, saying,
> "Alas, my brother!" or "Alas, sister!"
> They shall not lament for him, saying,
> "Alas, lord!" or "Alas, his majesty!"

---

^a Cn: Heb *uninhabited cities*

¹⁹ With the burial of a donkey he shall be
buried—
dragged off and thrown out beyond the
gates of Jerusalem.

²⁰ Go up to Lebanon, and cry out,
and lift up your voice in Bashan;
cry out from Abarim,
for all your lovers are crushed.
²¹ I spoke to you in your prosperity,
but you said, "I will not listen."
This has been your way from your youth,
for you have not obeyed my voice.
²² The wind shall shepherd all your shepherds,
and your lovers shall go into captivity;
then you will be ashamed and dismayed
because of all your wickedness.
²³ O inhabitant of Lebanon,
nested among the cedars,
how you will groan^a when pangs come
upon you,
pain as of a woman in labor!

Judgment on Coniah (Jehoiachin)

24 As I live, says the LORD, even if King Coniah
son of Jehoiakim of Judah were the signet ring
on my right hand, even from there I would tear
you off ²⁵and give you into the hands of those
who seek your life, into the hands of those of
whom you are afraid, even into the hands of
King Nebuchadrezzar of Babylon and into the
hands of the Chaldeans. ²⁶I will hurl you and
the mother who bore you into another coun-
try, where you were not born, and there you
shall die. ²⁷But they shall not return to the land
to which they long to return.
²⁸ Is this man Coniah a despised broken pot,
a vessel no one wants?
Why are he and his offspring hurled out
and cast away in a land that they do not
know?
²⁹ O land, land, land,
hear the word of the LORD!
³⁰ Thus says the LORD:
Record this man as childless,
a man who shall not succeed in his days;
for none of his offspring shall succeed
in sitting on the throne of David,
and ruling again in Judah.

23 Restoration after Exile

Woe to the shepherds who destroy and scatter
the sheep of my pasture! says the LORD. ²There-
fore thus says the LORD, the God of Israel, concerning the shepherds who shepherd my
people: It is you who have scattered my flock,
and have driven them away, and you have not
attended to them. So I will attend to you for

a Gk Vg Syr: Heb *will be pitied*

your evil doings, says the LORD. ³Then I myself
will gather the remnant of my flock out of all
the lands where I have driven them, and I will
bring them back to their fold, and they shall be
fruitful and multiply. ⁴I will raise up shepherds
over them who will shepherd them, and they
shall not fear any longer, or be dismayed, nor
shall any be missing, says the LORD.

The Righteous Branch of David

5 The days are surely coming, says the LORD,
when I will raise up for David a righteous
Branch, and he shall reign as king and deal
wisely, and shall execute justice and righteousness in the land. ⁶In his days Judah will be saved
and Israel will live in safety. And this is the
name by which he will be called: "The LORD is
our righteousness."

7 Therefore, the days are surely coming,
says the LORD, when it shall no longer be said,
"As the LORD lives who brought the people of

TEXT MESSAGE

If you have trouble figuring
out all the oracles, history,
and stories in the book of
Jeremiah, read a summary
of his ministry in Jeremiah
25. This may be the first
Reader's Digest Condensed
Book.

This information has been scanned and is free of all
known viruses. Please forward to all your friends.

JESUS SIGHTING

Imagine the devastation.

One year you're in Jerusalem, ruled by David's descendants. You're in a fourth generation of kings, but Solomon's poor choices finally bear the fruit of the bad seeds he's sown. Civil war divides the nation, and a divided kingdom will fall. Jesus would later use this same image (see Luke 11.17).

In slavery, the Israelites had nothing but memories and a text. They read, discussed, and reviewed it. This was the way they kept their identity in a foreign land.

And the text contained a secret promise, something that would be a threat to any king who ruled over the Israelites. The word was that a king in the line of David would one day sit again on the throne of Israel. The bloodline would be continued, and the line would be remade. The days of David would one day be resurrected, as **Jeremiah 23.1–6** guaranteed.

When Jesus came on the scene, that guarantee proved true. Jesus was a descendant of King David. But he didn't come as a political ruler—he came to sow the seeds of God's Kingdom. He taught about true freedom and peace—through his death and Resurrection, all people can be saved.

Israel up out of the land of Egypt," ⁸but "As the Lord lives who brought out and led the offspring of the house of Israel out of the land of the north and out of all the lands where he*a* had driven them." Then they shall live in their own land.

False Prophets of Hope Denounced

9 Concerning the prophets:
My heart is crushed within me,

all my bones shake;
I have become like a drunkard,
like one overcome by wine,
because of the Lord
and because of his holy words.
¹⁰ For the land is full of adulterers;
because of the curse the land mourns,
and the pastures of the wilderness are
dried up.
Their course has been evil,
and their might is not right.
¹¹ Both prophet and priest are ungodly;
even in my house I have found their
wickedness,
says the Lord.
¹² Therefore their way shall be to them
like slippery paths in the darkness,
into which they shall be driven and fall;
for I will bring disaster upon them
in the year of their punishment,
says the Lord.
¹³ In the prophets of Samaria
I saw a disgusting thing:
they prophesied by Baal
and led my people Israel astray.
¹⁴ But in the prophets of Jerusalem
I have seen a more shocking thing:
they commit adultery and walk in lies;
they strengthen the hands of evildoers,
so that no one turns from wickedness;
all of them have become like Sodom to me,
and its inhabitants like Gomorrah.
¹⁵ Therefore thus says the Lord of hosts
concerning the prophets:
"I am going to make them eat wormwood,
and give them poisoned water to drink;
for from the prophets of Jerusalem
ungodliness has spread throughout the
land."

16 Thus says the Lord of hosts: Do not listen to the words of the prophets who prophesy to you; they are deluding you. They speak visions of their own minds, not from the mouth of the Lord. ¹⁷They keep saying to those who despise the word of the Lord, "It shall be well with you"; and to all who stubbornly follow their own stubborn hearts, they say, "No calamity shall come upon you."

¹⁸ For who has stood in the council of the Lord
so as to see and to hear his word?
Who has given heed to his word so as to
proclaim it?
¹⁹ Look, the storm of the Lord!
Wrath has gone forth,
a whirling tempest;

a Gk: Heb *I*

it will burst upon the head of the wicked. ²⁰ The anger of the Lord will not turn back
until he has executed and accomplished
the intents of his mind.
In the latter days you will understand it
clearly.

²¹ I did not send the prophets,
yet they ran;
I did not speak to them,
yet they prophesied.
²² But if they had stood in my council,
then they would have proclaimed my
words to my people,
and they would have turned them from
their evil way,
and from the evil of their doings.

23 Am I a God near by, says the Lord, and
not a God far off? ²⁴Who can hide in secret places so that I cannot see them? says the Lord. Do
I not fill heaven and earth? says the Lord. ²⁵I
have heard what the prophets have said who
prophesy lies in my name, saying, "I have
dreamed, I have dreamed!" ²⁶How long? Will
the hearts of the prophets ever turn back—
those who prophesy lies, and who prophe-
sy the deceit of their own heart? ²⁷They plan
to make my people forget my name by their
dreams that they tell one another, just as their
ancestors forgot my name for Baal. ²⁸Let the
prophet who has a dream tell the dream, but
let the one who has my word speak my word
faithfully. What has straw in common with
wheat? says the Lord. ²⁹Is not my word like
fire, says the Lord, and like a hammer that
breaks a rock in pieces? ³⁰See, therefore, I
am against the prophets, says the Lord, who
steal my words from one another. ³¹See, I am
against the prophets, says the Lord, who use
their own tongues and say, "Says the Lord."
³²See, I am against those who prophesy lying
dreams, says the Lord, and who tell them, and
who lead my people astray by their lies and
their recklessness, when I did not send them or
appoint them; so they do not profit this people
at all, says the Lord.

33 When this people, or a prophet, or a
priest asks you, "What is the burden of the
Lord?" you shall say to them, "You are the burden,ᵃ and I will cast you off, says the Lord."
³⁴And as for the prophet, priest, or the people
who say, "The burden of the Lord," I will punish them and their households. ³⁵Thus shall
you say to one another, among yourselves,
"What has the Lord answered?" or "What has
the Lord spoken?" ³⁶But "the burden of the
Lord" you shall mention no more, for the bur-

den is everyone's own word, and so you pervert
the words of the living God, the Lord of hosts,
our God. ³⁷Thus you shall ask the prophet,
"What has the Lord answered you?" or "What
has the Lord spoken?" ³⁸But if you say, "the
burden of the Lord," thus says the Lord: Because you have said these words, "the burden of
the Lord," when I sent to you, saying, You shall
not say, "the burden of the Lord," ³⁹therefore,
I will surely lift you upᵇ and cast you away from
my presence, you and the city that I gave to you
and your ancestors. ⁴⁰And I will bring upon
you everlasting disgrace and perpetual shame,
which shall not be forgotten.

24 The Good and the Bad Figs

The Lord showed me two baskets of figs placed
before the temple of the Lord. This was after
King Nebuchadrezzar of Babylon had taken
into exile from Jerusalem King Jeconiah son
of Jehoiakim of Judah, together with the officials of Judah, the artisans, and the smiths, and
had brought them to Babylon. ²One basket had
very good figs, like first-ripe figs, but the other
basket had very bad figs, so bad that they could
not be eaten. ³And the Lord said to me, "What
do you see, Jeremiah?" I said, "Figs, the good
figs very good, and the bad figs very bad, so bad
that they cannot be eaten."

4 Then the word of the Lord came to me:
⁵Thus says the Lord, the God of Israel: Like
these good figs, so I will regard as good the exiles from Judah, whom I have sent away from
this place to the land of the Chaldeans. ⁶I will
set my eyes upon them for good, and I will
bring them back to this land. I will build them
up, and not tear them down; I will plant them,
and not pluck them up. ⁷I will give them a heart
to know that I am the Lord; and they shall be
my people and I will be their God, for they shall
return to me with their whole heart.

8 But thus says the Lord: Like the bad figs
that are so bad they cannot be eaten, so will I
treat King Zedekiah of Judah, his officials, the
remnant of Jerusalem who remain in this land,
and those who live in the land of Egypt. ⁹I will
make them a horror, an evil thing, to all the
kingdoms of the earth—a disgrace, a byword,
a taunt, and a curse in all the places where I
shall drive them. ¹⁰And I will send sword, famine, and pestilence upon them, until they are
utterly destroyed from the land that I gave to
them and their ancestors.

25 The Babylonian Captivity Foretold

The word that came to Jeremiah concerning all
the people of Judah, in the fourth year of King

ᵃ Gk Vg: Heb *What burden*   ᵇ Heb Mss Gk Vg: MT *forget you*

Putting on the Mask—© Christy Klink, 18

Jehoiakim son of Josiah of Judah (that was the first year of King Nebuchadrezzar of Babylon), ²which the prophet Jeremiah spoke to all the people of Judah and all the inhabitants of Jerusalem: ³For twenty-three years, from the thirteenth year of King Josiah son of Amon of Judah, to this day, the word of the LORD has come to me, and I have spoken persistently to you, but you have not listened. ⁴And though the LORD persistently sent you all his servants the prophets, you have neither listened nor inclined your ears to hear ⁵when they said, "Turn now, every one of you, from your evil way and wicked doings, and you will remain upon the land that the LORD has given to you and your ancestors from of old and forever; ⁶do not go after other gods to serve and worship them, and do not provoke me to anger with the work of your hands. Then I will do you no harm." ⁷Yet you did not listen to me, says the LORD, and so you have provoked me to anger with the work of your hands to your own harm.

8 Therefore thus says the LORD of hosts: Because you have not obeyed my words, ⁹I am going to send for all the tribes of the north, says the LORD, even for King Nebuchadrezzar of Babylon, my servant, and I will bring them against this land and its inhabitants, and against all these nations around; I will utterly destroy them, and make them an object of horror and of hissing, and an everlasting disgrace.ᵃ ¹⁰And I will banish from them the sound of mirth and the sound of gladness, the voice of the bridegroom and the voice of the bride, the sound of the millstones and the light of the lamp. ¹¹This whole land shall become a ruin and a waste, and these nations shall serve the king of Babylon seventy years. ¹²Then after seventy years are completed, I will punish the king of Babylon and that nation, the land of the Chaldeans, for their iniquity, says the LORD, making the land an everlasting waste. ¹³I will bring upon that land all the words that I have uttered against it, everything written in this book, which Jeremiah prophesied against all the nations. ¹⁴For many nations and great kings shall make slaves of them also; and I will repay them according to their deeds and the work of their hands.

The Cup of God's Wrath

15 For thus the LORD, the God of Israel, said to me: Take from my hand this cup of the wine of wrath, and make all the nations to whom I send you drink it. ¹⁶They shall drink and stagger and go out of their minds because of the sword that I am sending among them.

17 So I took the cup from the LORD's hand, and made all the nations to whom the LORD sent me drink it: ¹⁸Jerusalem and the towns of Judah, its kings and officials, to make them

ᵃ Gk Compare Syr: Heb *and everlasting desolations*

PROFILE OF FAITH

Can you imagine having the guts to tell popes, queens, and kings how to behave? That's exactly what St. Catherine of Siena did. As a prophet in her day, Catherine was spontaneous, unafraid of authority, and fearless in speaking the truth to popes and peasants alike. Born in 1347, she lived through the Black Death, famine, and numerous civil wars. During her lifetime the papal residence moved from Rome to Avignon and back again, and the Great Western Schism pitted a pope against an antipope.

Even at a young age, Catherine sensed the trouble in society around her and wanted to help. She wrote bold letters that were meant to shock the reader into reality. In one letter, she rebuked three Italian cardinals who were supporting the antipope, writing to them, "What made you do this? You are flowers who shed no perfume, but stench that makes the whole world reek." Catherine risked death by sending such direct letters to Church and civil authorities. But she was fearless. "I trust in the Lord Jesus Christ, not in myself" was one of her favorite prayers.

St. Catherine's impact on her times was so great that she was canonized only eighty-one years after her death.

---

a desolation and a waste, an object of hissing and of cursing, as they are today; ¹⁹Pharaoh king of Egypt, his servants, his officials, and all his people; ²⁰all the mixed people;ᵃ all the kings of the land of Uz; all the kings of the land of the Philistines—Ashkelon, Gaza, Ekron, and the remnant of Ashdod; ²¹Edom, Moab, and the Ammonites; ²²all the kings of Tyre, all the kings of Sidon, and the kings of the coastland across the sea; ²³Dedan, Tema, Buz, and all who have shaven temples; ²⁴all the kings of Arabia and all the kings of the mixed peoplesᵃ that live in the desert; ²⁵all the kings of Zimri, all the kings of Elam, and all the kings of Media; ²⁶all the kings of the north, far and near, one after another, and all the kingdoms of the world that are on the face of the earth. And after them the king of Sheshachᵇ shall drink.

27 Then you shall say to them, Thus says the LORD of hosts, the God of Israel: Drink, get drunk and vomit, fall and rise no more, because of the sword that I am sending among you.

28 And if they refuse to accept the cup from your hand to drink, then you shall say to them: Thus says the LORD of hosts: You must drink! ²⁹See, I am beginning to bring disaster on the city that is called by my name, and how can you possibly avoid punishment? You shall not go unpunished, for I am summoning a sword against all the inhabitants of the earth, says the LORD of hosts.

30 You, therefore, shall prophesy against them all these words, and say to them:

The LORD will roar from on high,
  and from his holy habitation utter his
    voice;
he will roar mightily against his fold,
  and shout, like those who tread grapes,
  against all the inhabitants of the earth.
31 The clamor will resound to the ends of the
    earth,
  for the LORD has an indictment against
    the nations;
he is entering into judgment with all flesh,
  and the guilty he will put to the sword,
                    says the LORD.

32 Thus says the LORD of hosts:
  See, disaster is spreading
    from nation to nation,
  and a great tempest is stirring
    from the farthest parts of the earth!

33 Those slain by the LORD on that day shall extend from one end of the earth to the other. They shall not be lamented, or gathered, or buried; they shall become dung on the surface of the ground.

34 Wail, you shepherds, and cry out;
  roll in ashes, you lords of the flock,
  for the days of your slaughter have come—
    and your dispersions,ᵃ
  and you shall fall like a choice vessel.
35 Flight shall fail the shepherds,
  and there shall be no escape for the lords
    of the flock.
36 Hark! the cry of the shepherds,

---

a Meaning of Heb uncertain b Sheshach is a cryptogram for Babel, Babylon

and the wail of the lords of the flock!
For the Lord is despoiling their pasture,

37   and the peaceful folds are devastated,
        because of the fierce anger of the Lord.

38 Like a lion he has left his covert;
        for their land has become a waste
    because of the cruel sword,
        and because of his fierce anger.

26 Jeremiah's Prophecies in the Temple

At the beginning of the reign of King Jehoiakim son of Josiah of Judah, this word came from the Lord: [2]Thus says the Lord: Stand in the court of the Lord's house, and speak to all the cities of Judah that come to worship in the house of the Lord; speak to them all the words that I command you; do not hold back a word. [3]It may be that they will listen, all of them, and will turn from their evil way, that I may change my mind about the disaster that I intend to bring on them because of their evil doings. [4]You shall say to them: Thus says the Lord: If you will not listen to me, to walk in my law that I have set before you, [5]and to heed the words of my servants the prophets whom I send to you urgently—though you have not heeded— [6]then I will make this house like Shiloh, and I will make this city a curse for all the nations of the earth.

7 The priests and the prophets and all the people heard Jeremiah speaking these words in the house of the Lord. [8]And when Jeremiah had finished speaking all that the Lord had commanded him to speak to all the people, then the priests and the prophets and all the people laid hold of him, saying, "You shall die! [9]Why have you prophesied in the name of the Lord, saying, 'This house shall be like Shiloh, and this city shall be desolate, without inhabitant'?" And all the people gathered around Jeremiah in the house of the Lord.

10 When the officials of Judah heard these things, they came up from the king's house to the house of the Lord and took their seat in the entry of the New Gate of the house of the Lord. [11]Then the priests and the prophets said to the officials and to all the people, "This man deserves the sentence of death because he has prophesied against this city, as you have heard with your own ears."

12 Then Jeremiah spoke to all the officials and all the people, saying, "It is the Lord who sent me to prophesy against this house and this city all the words you have heard. [13]Now therefore amend your ways and your doings, and obey the voice of the Lord your God, and the Lord will change his mind about the disaster that he has pronounced against you. [14]But

as for me, here I am in your hands. Do with me as seems good and right to you. [15]Only know for certain that if you put me to death, you will be bringing innocent blood upon yourselves and upon this city and its inhabitants, for in truth the Lord sent me to you to speak all these words in your ears."

16 Then the officials and all the people said to the priests and the prophets, "This man does not deserve the sentence of death, for he has spoken to us in the name of the Lord our God." [17]And some of the elders of the land arose and said to all the assembled people, [18]"Micah of Moresheth, who prophesied during the days of King Hezekiah of Judah, said to all the people of Judah: 'Thus says the Lord of hosts,

Zion shall be plowed as a field;
    Jerusalem shall become a heap of ruins,
        and the mountain of the house a wooded
            height.'

[19]Did King Hezekiah of Judah and all Judah actually put him to death? Did he not fear the Lord and entreat the favor of the Lord, and did not the Lord change his mind about the disaster that he had pronounced against them? But we are about to bring great disaster on ourselves!"

20 There was another man prophesying in the name of the Lord, Uriah son of Shemaiah from Kiriath-jearim. He prophesied against this city and against this land in words exactly like those of Jeremiah. [21]And when King Jehoiakim, with all his warriors and all the officials, heard his words, the king sought to put him to death; but when Uriah heard of it, he was afraid and fled and escaped to Egypt. [22]Then King Jehoiakim sent[a] Elnathan son of Achbor and men with him to Egypt, [23]and they took Uriah from Egypt and brought him to King Jehoiakim, who struck him down with the sword and threw his dead body into the burial place of the common people.

24 But the hand of Ahikam son of Shaphan was with Jeremiah so that he was not given over into the hands of the people to be put to death.

27 The Sign of the Yoke

In the beginning of the reign of King Zedekiah[b] son of Josiah of Judah, this word came to Jeremiah from the Lord. [2]Thus the Lord said to me: Make yourself a yoke of straps and bars, and put them on your neck. [3]Send word[c] to the king of Edom, the king of Moab, the king of the Ammonites, the king of Tyre, and the king of Sidon by the hand of the envoys who have come to Jerusalem to King Zedekiah of Judah. [4]Give them this charge for their masters:

---

a Heb adds *men to Egypt*   b Another reading is *Jehoiakim*   c Cn: Heb *send them*

Thus says the Lord of hosts, the God of Israel: This is what you shall say to your masters: [5]It is I who by my great power and my outstretched arm have made the earth, with the people and animals that are on the earth, and I give it to whomever I please. [6]Now I have given all these lands into the hand of King Nebuchadnezzar of Babylon, my servant, and I have given him even the wild animals of the field to serve him. [7]All the nations shall serve him and his son and his grandson, until the time of his own land comes; then many nations and great kings shall make him their slave.

8 But if any nation or kingdom will not serve this king, Nebuchadnezzar of Babylon, and put its neck under the yoke of the king of Babylon, then I will punish that nation with the sword, with famine, and with pestilence, says the Lord, until I have completed its[a] destruction by his hand. [9]You, therefore, must not listen to your prophets, your diviners, your dreamers,[b] your soothsayers, or your sorcerers, who are saying to you, "You shall not serve the king of Babylon." [10]For they are prophesying a lie to you, with the result that you will be removed far from your land; I will drive you out, and you will perish. [11]But any nation that will bring its neck under the yoke of the king of Babylon and serve him, I will leave on its own land, says the Lord, to till it and live there.

12 I spoke to King Zedekiah of Judah in the same way: Bring your necks under the yoke of the king of Babylon, and serve him and his people, and live. [13]Why should you and your people die by the sword, by famine, and by pestilence, as the Lord has spoken concerning any nation that will not serve the king of Babylon? [14]Do not listen to the words of the prophets who are telling you not to serve the king of Babylon, for they are prophesying a lie to you. [15]I have not sent them, says the Lord, but they are prophesying falsely in my name, with the result that I will drive you out and you will perish, you and the prophets who are prophesying to you.

16 Then I spoke to the priests and to all this people, saying, Thus says the Lord: Do not listen to the words of your prophets who are prophesying to you, saying, "The vessels of the Lord's house will soon be brought back from Babylon," for they are prophesying a lie to you. [17]Do not listen to them; serve the king of Babylon and live. Why should this city become a desolation? [18]If indeed they are prophets, and if the word of the Lord is with them, then let them intercede with the Lord of hosts, that the vessels left in the house of the Lord, in

Birds of the Air—© Ricky Williamson, 18

the house of the king of Judah, and in Jerusalem may not go to Babylon. [19]For thus says the Lord of hosts concerning the pillars, the sea, the stands, and the rest of the vessels that are left in this city, [20]which King Nebuchadnezzar of Babylon did not take away when he took into exile from Jerusalem to Babylon King Jeconiah son of Jehoiakim of Judah, and all the nobles of Judah and Jerusalem— [21]thus says the Lord of hosts, the God of Israel, concerning the vessels left in the house of the Lord, in the house of the king of Judah, and in Jerusalem: [22]They shall be carried to Babylon, and there they shall stay, until the day when I give attention to them, says the Lord. Then I will bring them up and restore them to this place.

28 Hananiah Opposes Jeremiah and Dies

In that same year, at the beginning of the reign of King Zedekiah of Judah, in the fifth month of the fourth year, the prophet Hananiah son of Azzur, from Gibeon, spoke to me in the house of the Lord, in the presence of the priests and all the people, saying, [2]"Thus says the Lord of hosts, the God of Israel: I have broken the yoke of the king of Babylon. [3]Within two years I will bring back to this place all the vessels of the Lord's house, which King Nebuchadnezzar of Babylon took away from this place and carried to Babylon. [4]I will also bring back to this place King Jeconiah son of Jehoiakim of Judah, and all the exiles from Judah who went to Babylon, says the Lord, for I will break the yoke of the king of Babylon."

5 Then the prophet Jeremiah spoke to the prophet Hananiah in the presence of the priests and all the people who were standing

---

a Heb *their* *b* Gk Syr Vg: Heb *dreams*

Though most of Jeremiah is bad news, chapters 30–33 are good news. These chapters have been called the "Book of Consolation" or the "Little Book of Comfort," because of their message of hope.

Fact

This information has been scanned and is free of all known viruses. Please forward to all your friends.

Nebuchadnezzar of Babylon from the neck of all the nations within two years." At this, the prophet Jeremiah went his way.

12 Sometime after the prophet Hananiah had broken the yoke from the neck of the prophet Jeremiah, the word of the LORD came to Jeremiah: ¹³Go, tell Hananiah, Thus says the LORD: You have broken wooden bars only to forge iron bars in place of them! ¹⁴For thus says the LORD of hosts, the God of Israel: I have put an iron yoke on the neck of all these nations so that they may serve King Nebuchadnezzar of Babylon, and they shall indeed serve him; I have even given him the wild animals. ¹⁵And the prophet Jeremiah said to the prophet Hananiah, "Listen, Hananiah, the LORD has not sent you, and you made this people trust in a lie. ¹⁶Therefore thus says the LORD: I am going to send you off the face of the earth. Within this year you will be dead, because you have spoken rebellion against the LORD."

17 In that same year, in the seventh month, the prophet Hananiah died.

29 Jeremiah's Letter to the Exiles in Babylon

These are the words of the letter that the prophet Jeremiah sent from Jerusalem to the remaining elders among the exiles, and to the priests, the prophets, and all the people, whom Nebuchadnezzar had taken into exile from Jerusalem to Babylon. ²This was after King Jeconiah, and the queen mother, the court officials, the leaders of Judah and Jerusalem, the artisans, and the smiths had departed from Jerusalem. ³The letter was sent by the hand of Elasah son of Shaphan and Gemariah son of Hilkiah, whom King Zedekiah of Judah sent to Babylon to King Nebuchadnezzar of Babylon. It said: ⁴Thus says the LORD of hosts, the God of Israel, to all the exiles whom I have sent into exile from Jerusalem to Babylon: ⁵Build houses and live in them; plant gardens and eat what they produce. ⁶Take wives and have sons and daughters; take wives for your sons, and give your daughters in marriage, that they may bear sons and daughters; multiply there, and do not decrease. ⁷But seek the welfare of the city where I have sent you into exile, and pray to the LORD on its behalf, for in its welfare you will find your welfare. ⁸For thus says the LORD of hosts, the God of Israel: Do not let the prophets and the diviners who are among you deceive you, and do not listen to the dreams that they dream,ᵃ ⁹for it is a lie that they are prophesying to you in my name; I did not send them, says the LORD.

in the house of the LORD; ⁶and the prophet Jeremiah said, "Amen! May the LORD do so; may the LORD fulfill the words that you have prophesied, and bring back to this place from Babylon the vessels of the house of the LORD, and all the exiles. ⁷But listen now to this word that I speak in your hearing and in the hearing of all the people. ⁸The prophets who preceded you and me from ancient times prophesied war, famine, and pestilence against many countries and great kingdoms. ⁹As for the prophet who prophesies peace, when the word of that prophet comes true, then it will be known that the LORD has truly sent the prophet."

10 Then the prophet Hananiah took the yoke from the neck of the prophet Jeremiah, and broke it. ¹¹And Hananiah spoke in the presence of all the people, saying, "Thus says the LORD: This is how I will break the yoke of King

a Cn: Heb your dreams that you cause to dream

10 For thus says the Lord: Only when Babylon's seventy years are completed will I visit you, and I will fulfill to you my promise and bring you back to this place. [11] For surely I know the plans I have for you, says the Lord, plans for your welfare and not for harm, to give you a future with hope. [12] Then when you call upon me and come and pray to me, I will hear you. [13] When you search for me, you will find me; if you seek me with all your heart, [14] I will let you find me, says the Lord, and I will restore your fortunes and gather you from all the nations and all the places where I have driven you, says the Lord, and I will bring you back to the place from which I sent you into exile.

15 Because you have said, "The Lord has raised up prophets for us in Babylon,"— [16] Thus says the Lord concerning the king who sits on the throne of David, and concerning all the people who live in this city, your kinsfolk who did not go out with you into exile: [17] Thus says the Lord of hosts, I am going to let loose on them sword, famine, and pestilence, and I will make them like rotten figs that are so bad they cannot be eaten. [18] I will pursue them with the sword, with famine, and with pestilence, and will make them a horror to all the kingdoms of the earth, to be an object of cursing, and horror, and hissing, and a derision among all the nations where I have driven them, [19] because they did not heed my words, says the Lord, when I persistently sent to you my servants the prophets, but they[a] would not listen, says the Lord. [20] But now, all you exiles whom I sent away from Jerusalem to Babylon, hear the word of the Lord: [21] Thus says the Lord of hosts, the God of Israel, concerning Ahab son of Kolaiah and Zedekiah son of Maaseiah, who are prophesying a lie to you in my name: I am going to deliver them into the hand of King Nebuchadrezzar of Babylon, and he shall kill them before your eyes. [22] And on account of them this curse shall be used by all the exiles from Judah in Babylon: "The Lord make you like Zedekiah and Ahab, whom the king of Babylon roasted in the fire," [23] because they have perpetrated outrage in Israel and have committed adultery with their neighbors' wives, and have spoken in my name lying words that I did not command them; I am the one who knows and bears witness, says the Lord.

The Letter of Shemaiah

24 To Shemaiah of Nehelam you shall say: [25] Thus says the Lord of hosts, the God of Israel: In your own name you sent a letter to all the people who are in Jerusalem, and to the

TRY THIS

ASSISTANCE ON AISLE THREE

Yesterday I saw something new—a huge seeing-eye dog right in the middle of Wal-Mart, leading his master through the perilous twists and turns of the personal hygiene department. The man still had a mind of his own and a general idea of the direction to head toward the things wanted. But he needed a good set of eyes to guide him.

That's a pretty clear picture of the content in **Jeremiah 29.4–14**. God creatively weaves the Israelites through the hidden roadblocks they are oblivious to. He knows where to take them and how to make it safely through.

We can fully expect God to do the same for us. God has a good set of eyes. God can easily create a path for us, even when we can't see the way.

Try closing your eyes tight and feeling your way around the house in the dark. As you do, imagine the things in your future you feel uncertain about: college, relationships, career path. Then pray. Thank God for his creative plans for you and for his gentle leadership guiding you safely through.

GOD IS CREATIVE   MY WORLD

priest Zephaniah son of Maaseiah, and to all the priests, saying, [26] The Lord himself has made you priest instead of the priest Jehoiada, so that there may be officers in the house of the Lord to control any madman who plays the prophet, to put him in the stocks and the collar. [27] So now why have you not rebuked Jeremiah of Anathoth who plays the prophet for you? [28] For he has actually sent to us in Babylon, saying, "It will be a long time; build houses and live in them, and plant gardens and eat what they produce."

29 The priest Zephaniah read this letter in the hearing of the prophet Jeremiah: [30] Then the word of the Lord came to Jeremiah: [31] Send to all the exiles, saying, Thus says the Lord concerning Shemaiah of Nehelam: Because Shemaiah has prophesied to you, though I did not send him, and has led you to trust in a lie, [32] therefore thus says the Lord: I am going to punish Shemaiah of Nehelam and his descendants; he shall not have anyone living among this people to see[b] the good that I am going to

a Syr: Heb *you* b Gk: Heb *and he shall not see*

do to my people, says the LORD, for he has spoken rebellion against the LORD.

30 Restoration Promised for Israel and Judah

The word that came to Jeremiah from the LORD: ²Thus says the LORD, the God of Israel: Write in a book all the words that I have spoken to you. ³For the days are surely coming, says the LORD, when I will restore the fortunes of my people, Israel and Judah, says the LORD, and I will bring them back to the land that I gave to their ancestors and they shall take possession of it.

4 These are the words that the LORD spoke concerning Israel and Judah:

⁵ Thus says the LORD:
We have heard a cry of panic,
    of terror, and no peace.
⁶ Ask now, and see,
    can a man bear a child?
Why then do I see every man
    with his hands on his loins like a woman
        in labor?
    Why has every face turned pale?
⁷ Alas! that day is so great
    there is none like it;
it is a time of distress for Jacob;
    yet he shall be rescued from it.

8 On that day, says the LORD of hosts, I will break the yoke from off his*ᵃ* neck, and I will burst his*ᵃ* bonds, and strangers shall no more make a servant of him. ⁹But they shall serve the LORD their God and David their king, whom I will raise up for them.

¹⁰ But as for you, have no fear, my servant
        Jacob, says the LORD,
    and do not be dismayed, O Israel;
for I am going to save you from far away,
    and your offspring from the land of their
        captivity.
Jacob shall return and have quiet and ease,
    and no one shall make him afraid.
¹¹ For I am with you, says the LORD, to save you;
    I will make an end of all the nations
        among which I scattered you,
        but of you I will not make an end.
    I will chastise you in just measure,
        and I will by no means leave you
            unpunished.

¹² For thus says the LORD:
    Your hurt is incurable,
        your wound is grievous.
¹³ There is no one to uphold your cause,
    no medicine for your wound,
    no healing for you.
¹⁴ All your lovers have forgotten you;

they care nothing for you;
for I have dealt you the blow of an enemy,
    the punishment of a merciless foe,
because your guilt is great,
    because your sins are so numerous.
¹⁵ Why do you cry out over your hurt?
    Your pain is incurable.
Because your guilt is great,
    because your sins are so numerous,
    I have done these things to you.
¹⁶ Therefore all who devour you shall be
        devoured,
    and all your foes, every one of them,
        shall go into captivity;
those who plunder you shall be plundered,
    and all who prey on you I will make a
        prey.
¹⁷ For I will restore health to you,
    and your wounds I will heal,
                            says the LORD,
because they have called you an outcast:
    "It is Zion; no one cares for her!"

¹⁸ Thus says the LORD:
I am going to restore the fortunes of the
        tents of Jacob,
    and have compassion on his dwellings;
the city shall be rebuilt upon its mound,
    and the citadel set on its rightful site.
¹⁹ Out of them shall come thanksgiving,
    and the sound of merrymakers.
I will make them many, and they shall not
        be few;
    I will make them honored, and they shall
        not be disdained.
²⁰ Their children shall be as of old,
    their congregation shall be established
        before me;
    and I will punish all who oppress them.
²¹ Their prince shall be one of their own,
    their ruler shall come from their midst;
I will bring him near, and he shall approach
        me,
    for who would otherwise dare to
        approach me?
                            says the LORD.
²² And you shall be my people,
    and I will be your God.

²³ Look, the storm of the LORD!
    Wrath has gone forth,
a whirling*ᵇ* tempest;
    it will burst upon the head of the wicked.
²⁴ The fierce anger of the LORD will not turn
        back
    until he has executed and accomplished
        the intents of his mind.
In the latter days you will understand this.

a Cn: Heb *your* *b* One Ms: Meaning of MT uncertain

31 The Joyful Return of the Exiles

At that time, says the LORD, I will be the God of all the families of Israel, and they shall be my people.

2 Thus says the LORD:
The people who survived the sword
   found grace in the wilderness;
when Israel sought for rest,
3   the LORD appeared to him[a] from far
      away.[b]
I have loved you with an everlasting love;
   therefore I have continued my
      faithfulness to you.
4 Again I will build you, and you shall be
      built,
   O virgin Israel!
Again you shall take[c] your tambourines,
   and go forth in the dance of the
      merrymakers.
5 Again you shall plant vineyards
   on the mountains of Samaria;
the planters shall plant,
   and shall enjoy the fruit.
6 For there shall be a day when sentinels will
      call
   in the hill country of Ephraim:
"Come, let us go up to Zion,
   to the LORD our God."

7 For thus says the LORD:
Sing aloud with gladness for Jacob,
   and raise shouts for the chief of the
      nations;
proclaim, give praise, and say,
   "Save, O LORD, your people,
   the remnant of Israel."
8 See, I am going to bring them from the land
      of the north,
   and gather them from the farthest parts
      of the earth,
among them the blind and the lame,
   those with child and those in labor,
      together;
a great company, they shall return here.
9 With weeping they shall come,
   and with consolations[d] I will lead them
      back,
I will let them walk by brooks of water,
   in a straight path in which they shall not
      stumble;
for I have become a father to Israel,
   and Ephraim is my firstborn.

10 Hear the word of the LORD, O nations,
   and declare it in the coastlands far away;
say, "He who scattered Israel will gather him,
   and will keep him as a shepherd a flock."

A NEW COVENANT

Read **Jeremiah 31.31–40**.

One of the most fascinating and hopeful things about God's interaction with his people is that he keeps his promises. No matter what.

He promised Abraham that he would be the "ancestor of a multitude of nations" (Genesis 17.4). He promised Moses he would do "an awesome thing" (Exodus 34.10). And in Jesus—in his death on the cross—God made his covenant promise forever (see *Catechism of the Catholic Church* 73).

A covenant is a mutual promise between two parties. It's like the promise of two people when they enter into a marriage, but it's even more than that. It's a pledge of faithfulness till death and beyond.

Today you live in the New Covenant, the new promise. Every time you celebrate the Eucharist and receive Communion, you renew your part of the pledge; you're strengthened to keep up your part of the covenant to "bring good news to the oppressed, to bind up the brokenhearted, to proclaim liberty to the captives, and release to the prisoners" (Isaiah 61.1). Don't forget: this covenant is a two-way street.

11 For the LORD has ransomed Jacob,
   and has redeemed him from hands too
      strong for him.
12 They shall come and sing aloud on the
      height of Zion,
   and they shall be radiant over the
      goodness of the LORD,
over the grain, the wine, and the oil,
   and over the young of the flock and the
      herd;
their life shall become like a watered
      garden,
   and they shall never languish again.
13 Then shall the young women rejoice in the
      dance,
   and the young men and the old shall be
      merry.
I will turn their mourning into joy,

---

a Gk: Heb *me* *b* Or *to him long ago* *c* Or *adorn yourself with* *d* Gk Compare Vg Tg: Heb *supplications*

I will comfort them, and give them
gladness for sorrow.
14 I will give the priests their fill of fatness,
and my people shall be satisfied with my
bounty,
says the LORD.

15 Thus says the LORD:
A voice is heard in Ramah,
lamentation and bitter weeping.
Rachel is weeping for her children;
she refuses to be comforted for her
children,
because they are no more.
16 Thus says the LORD:
Keep your voice from weeping,
and your eyes from tears;
for there is a reward for your work,
says the LORD:
they shall come back from the land of the
enemy;
17 there is hope for your future,
says the LORD:
your children shall come back to their
own country.

18 Indeed I heard Ephraim pleading:
"You disciplined me, and I took the
discipline;
I was like a calf untrained.
Bring me back, let me come back,
for you are the LORD my God.
19 For after I had turned away I repented;
and after I was discovered, I struck my
thigh;
I was ashamed, and I was dismayed
because I bore the disgrace of my youth."
20 Is Ephraim my dear son?
Is he the child I delight in?
As often as I speak against him,
I still remember him.
Therefore I am deeply moved for him;
I will surely have mercy on him,
says the LORD.

21 Set up road markers for yourself,
make yourself signposts;
consider well the highway,
the road by which you went.
Return, O virgin Israel,
return to these your cities.
22 How long will you waver,
O faithless daughter?
For the LORD has created a new thing on the
earth:
a woman encompasses*a* a man.

23 Thus says the LORD of hosts, the God of
Israel: Once more they shall use these words

in the land of Judah and in its towns when I restore their fortunes:
"The LORD bless you, O abode of
righteousness,
O holy hill!"
24 And Judah and all its towns shall live there
together, and the farmers and those who wander*b* with their flocks.
25 I will satisfy the weary,
and all who are faint I will replenish.
26 Thereupon I awoke and looked, and my
sleep was pleasant to me.

Individual Retribution

27 The days are surely coming, says the LORD,
when I will sow the house of Israel and the
house of Judah with the seed of humans and
the seed of animals. 28 And just as I have watched
over them to pluck up and break down, to overthrow, destroy, and bring evil, so I will watch
over them to build and to plant, says the LORD.
29 In those days they shall no longer say:
"The parents have eaten sour grapes,
and the children's teeth are set on edge."
30 But all shall die for their own sins; the teeth
of everyone who eats sour grapes shall be set
on edge.

A New Covenant

31 The days are surely coming, says the LORD,
when I will make a new covenant with the
house of Israel and the house of Judah. 32 It
will not be like the covenant that I made with
their ancestors when I took them by the hand
to bring them out of the land of Egypt—a covenant that they broke, though I was their husband,*c* says the LORD. 33 But this is the covenant
that I will make with the house of Israel after
those days, says the LORD: I will put my law
within them, and I will write it on their hearts;
and I will be their God, and they shall be my
people. 34 No longer shall they teach one another, or say to each other, "Know the LORD,"
for they shall all know me, from the least of
them to the greatest, says the LORD; for I will
forgive their iniquity, and remember their sin
no more.

35 Thus says the LORD,
who gives the sun for light by day
and the fixed order of the moon and the
stars for light by night,
who stirs up the sea so that its waves roar—
the LORD of hosts is his name:
36 If this fixed order were ever to cease
from my presence, says the LORD,
then also the offspring of Israel would cease
to be a nation before me forever.

---

a Meaning of Heb uncertain   b Cn Compare Syr Vg Tg: Heb *and they shall wander*   c Or *master*

Winding Path—© Christy Klink, 17

³⁷ Thus says the LORD:
  If the heavens above can be measured,
    and the foundations of the earth below
      can be explored,
  then I will reject all the offspring of Israel
    because of all they have done,
                                    says the LORD.

Jerusalem to Be Enlarged
38 The days are surely coming, says the LORD, when the city shall be rebuilt for the LORD from the tower of Hananel to the Corner Gate. ³⁹And the measuring line shall go out farther, straight to the hill Gareb, and shall then turn to Goah. ⁴⁰The whole valley of the dead bodies and the ashes, and all the fields as far as the Wadi Kidron, to the corner of the Horse Gate toward the east, shall be sacred to the LORD. It shall never again be uprooted or overthrown.

32 Jeremiah Buys a Field During the Siege
The word that came to Jeremiah from the LORD in the tenth year of King Zedekiah of Judah, which was the eighteenth year of Nebuchadrezzar. ²At that time the army of the king of Babylon was besieging Jerusalem, and the prophet Jeremiah was confined in the court of the guard that was in the palace of the king of Judah, ³where King Zedekiah of Judah had confined him. Zedekiah had said, "Why do you prophesy and say: Thus says the LORD: I am going to give this city into the hand of the king of Babylon, and he shall take it; ⁴King Zedekiah of Judah shall not escape out of the hands of the Chaldeans, but shall surely be given into the hands of the king of Babylon, and shall speak with him face to face and see him eye to eye; ⁵and he shall take Zedekiah to Babylon, and there he shall remain until I attend to him, says the LORD; though you fight against the Chaldeans, you shall not succeed?"

6 Jeremiah said, The word of the LORD came to me: ⁷Hanamel son of your uncle Shallum is going to come to you and say, "Buy my field that is at Anathoth, for the right of redemption by purchase is yours." ⁸Then my cousin Hanamel came to me in the court of the guard, in accordance with the word of the LORD, and said to me, "Buy my field that is at Anathoth in the land of Benjamin, for the right of possession and redemption is yours; buy it for yourself." Then I knew that this was the word of the LORD.

9 And I bought the field at Anathoth from my cousin Hanamel, and weighed out the money to him, seventeen shekels of silver. ¹⁰I signed the deed, sealed it, got witnesses, and weighed the money on scales. ¹¹Then I took the sealed deed of purchase, containing the terms and conditions, and the open copy; ¹²and I gave the deed of purchase to Baruch son of Neriah son of Mahseiah, in the presence of my cousin Hanamel, in the presence of the witnesses who signed the deed of purchase, and in the presence of all the Judeans who were sit-

ting in the court of the guard. ¹³In their presence I charged Baruch, saying, ¹⁴Thus says the LORD of hosts, the God of Israel: Take these deeds, both this sealed deed of purchase and this open deed, and put them in an earthenware jar, in order that they may last for a long time. ¹⁵For thus says the LORD of hosts, the God of Israel: Houses and fields and vineyards shall again be bought in this land.

Jeremiah Prays for Understanding

16 After I had given the deed of purchase to Baruch son of Neriah, I prayed to the LORD, saying: ¹⁷Ah Lord GOD! It is you who made the heavens and the earth by your great power and by your outstretched arm! Nothing is too hard for you. ¹⁸You show steadfast love to the thousandth generation,ᵃ but repay the guilt of parents into the laps of their children after them, O great and mighty God whose name is the LORD of hosts, ¹⁹great in counsel and mighty in deed; whose eyes are open to all the ways of mortals, rewarding all according to their ways and according to the fruit of their doings. ²⁰You showed signs and wonders in the land of Egypt, and to this day in Israel and among all humankind, and have made yourself a name that continues to this very day. ²¹You brought your people Israel out of the land of Egypt with signs and wonders, with a strong hand and outstretched arm, and with great terror; ²²and you gave them this land, which you swore to their ancestors to give them, a land flowing with milk and honey; ²³and they entered and took possession of it. But they did not obey your voice or follow your law; of all you commanded them to do, they did nothing. Therefore you have made all these disasters come upon them. ²⁴See, the siege ramps have been cast up against the city to take it, and the city, faced with sword, famine, and pestilence, has been given into the hands of the Chaldeans who are fighting against it. What you spoke has happened, as you yourself can see. ²⁵Yet you, O Lord GOD, have said to me, "Buy the field for money and get witnesses"—though the city has been given into the hands of the Chaldeans.

God's Assurance of the People's Return

26 The word of the LORD came to Jeremiah: ²⁷See, I am the LORD, the God of all flesh; is anything too hard for me? ²⁸Therefore, thus says the LORD: I am going to give this city into the hands of the Chaldeans and into the hand of King Nebuchadrezzar of Babylon, and he shall take it. ²⁹The Chaldeans who are fighting against this city shall come, set it on fire, and burn it, with the houses on whose roofs offerings have been made to Baal and libations have been poured out to other gods, to provoke me to anger. ³⁰For the people of Israel and the people of Judah have done nothing but evil in my sight from their youth; the people of Israel have done nothing but provoke me to anger by the work of their hands, says the LORD. ³¹This city has aroused my anger and wrath, from the day it was built until this day, so that I will remove it from my sight ³²because of all the evil of the people of Israel and the people of Judah that they did to provoke me to anger—they, their kings and their officials, their priests and their prophets, the citizens of Judah and the inhabitants of Jerusalem. ³³They have turned their backs to me, not their faces; though I have taught them persistently, they would not listen and accept correction. ³⁴They set up their abominations in the house that bears my name, and defiled it. ³⁵They built the high places of Baal in the valley of the son of Hinnom, to offer up their sons and daughters to Molech, though I did not command them, nor did it enter my mind that they should do this abomination, causing Judah to sin.

36 Now therefore thus says the LORD, the God of Israel, concerning this city of which you say, "It is being given into the hand of the king of Babylon by the sword, by famine, and by pestilence": ³⁷See, I am going to gather them from all the lands to which I drove them in my anger and my wrath and in great indignation; I will bring them back to this place, and I will settle them in safety. ³⁸They shall be my people, and I will be their God. ³⁹I will give them one heart and one way, that they may fear me for all time, for their own good and the good of their children after them. ⁴⁰I will make an everlasting covenant with them, never to draw back from doing good to them; and I will put the fear of me in their hearts, so that they may not turn from me. ⁴¹I will rejoice in doing good to them, and I will plant them in this land in faithfulness, with all my heart and all my soul.

42 For thus says the LORD: Just as I have brought all this great disaster upon this people, so I will bring upon them all the good fortune that I now promise them. ⁴³Fields shall be bought in this land of which you are saying, It is a desolation, without human beings or animals; it has been given into the hands of the Chaldeans. ⁴⁴Fields shall be bought for money, and deeds shall be signed and sealed and witnessed, in the land of Benjamin, in the places around Jerusalem, and in the cities of Judah, of the hill country, of the Shephelah, and of

a Or to thousands

the Negeb; for I will restore their fortunes, says the LORD.

33 Healing after Punishment

The word of the LORD came to Jeremiah a second time, while he was still confined in the court of the guard: [2]Thus says the LORD who made the earth,[a] the LORD who formed it to establish it—the LORD is his name: [3]Call to me and I will answer you, and will tell you great and hidden things that you have not known. [4]For thus says the LORD, the God of Israel, concerning the houses of this city and the houses of the kings of Judah that were torn down to make a defense against the siege ramps and before the sword:[b] [5]The Chaldeans are coming in to fight[c] and to fill them with the dead bodies of those whom I shall strike down in my anger and my wrath, for I have hidden my face from this city because of all their wickedness. [6]I am going to bring it recovery and healing; I will heal them and reveal to them abundance[b] of prosperity and security. [7]I will restore the fortunes of Judah and the fortunes of Israel, and rebuild them as they were at first. [8]I will cleanse them from all the guilt of their sin against me, and I will forgive all the guilt of their sin and rebellion against me. [9]And this city[d] shall be to me a name of joy, a praise and a glory before all the nations of the earth who shall hear of all the good that I do for them; they shall fear and tremble because of all the good and all the prosperity I provide for it.

[10] Thus says the LORD: In this place of which you say, "It is a waste without human beings or animals," in the towns of Judah and the streets of Jerusalem that are desolate, without inhabitants, human or animal, there shall once more be heard [11]the voice of mirth and the voice of gladness, the voice of the bridegroom and the voice of the bride, the voices of those who sing, as they bring thank offerings to the house of the LORD:

"Give thanks to the LORD of hosts,
      for the LORD is good,
      for his steadfast love endures forever!"

For I will restore the fortunes of the land as at first, says the LORD.

[12] Thus says the LORD of hosts: In this place that is waste, without human beings or animals, and in all its towns there shall again be pasture for shepherds resting their flocks. [13]In the towns of the hill country, of the Shephelah, and of the Negeb, in the land of Benjamin, the places around Jerusalem, and in the towns of Judah, flocks shall again pass under the hands of the one who counts them, says the LORD.

a Gk: Heb it b Meaning of Heb uncertain c Cn: Heb They are coming in to fight against the Chaldeans d Heb And it

CREATIVE SPACE

THE BIGGEST LOSER

Dear God, I am such a mess. Somehow I find myself wanting to just hand all of this to you and say, "Voilà! Work your magic." But how can you when I have no willpower? I'm addicted to leisure, comfort, material things. Sometimes I watch TV marathon-style. What a waste. I justify my bad behavior by comparing myself to those in my parish—good people, all struggling. **Jeremiah 31** *marks out plans you had for another band of self-admitted mess-ups. You showed constant mercy and patience.*

Once I saw a show where a four-hundred-pound man transformed himself into a serious athlete. The change was slow and hard and almost imperceptible for weeks and even months. But he did it.

God, give me that kind of tenacity. Help me stick with you the way you stick with me.

How can you still stomach me? You keep pursuing me and loving me despite all my failures. I want to get serious about holiness. I want to tune out all the voices and temptations that are making me more and more self-centered. I want my heart to focus on you—to hear your words for me and to take them seriously. Please help me, God. Fill me with your power. Help me adjust my focus. Change me bit by bit until real transformation becomes visible. In Jesus' name. Amen.

Try this. Make a deliberate choice to tune out the persuasive and powerful (and too often negative) messages of the world and zero in on God's presence. How? Try a media fast. How long can you go without TV? Surfing the Internet? Your MP3 player? Can you go a day or even a week? Instead of wasting that time, spend it with God, listening to his voice and worshiping him as you ask him to help you change and grow.

GOD IS RELENTLESS MY SELF

The Righteous Branch and the Covenant with David

14 The days are surely coming, says the LORD, when I will fulfill the promise I made to the house of Israel and the house of Judah. 15In those days and at that time I will cause a righteous Branch to spring up for David; and he shall execute justice and righteousness in the

land. 16In those days Judah will be saved and Jerusalem will live in safety. And this is the name by which it will be called: "The LORD is our righteousness."

17 For thus says the LORD: David shall never lack a man to sit on the throne of the house of Israel, 18and the levitical priests shall never lack a man in my presence to offer burnt offerings, to make grain offerings, and to make sacrifices for all time.

19 The word of the LORD came to Jeremiah: 20Thus says the LORD: If any of you could break my covenant with the day and my covenant with the night, so that day and night would not come at their appointed time, 21only then could my covenant with my servant David be broken, so that he would not have a son to reign on his throne, and my covenant with my ministers the Levites. 22Just as the host of heaven cannot be numbered and the sands of the sea cannot be measured, so I will increase the offspring of my servant David, and the Levites who minister to me.

23 The word of the LORD came to Jeremiah: 24Have you not observed how these people say, "The two families that the LORD chose have been rejected by him," and how they hold my people in such contempt that they no longer regard them as a nation? 25Thus says the LORD: Only if I had not established my covenant with day and night and the ordinances of heaven and earth, 26would I reject the offspring of Jacob and of my servant David and not choose any of his descendants as rulers over the offspring of Abraham, Isaac, and Jacob. For I will restore their fortunes, and will have mercy upon them.

34 Death in Captivity Predicted for Zedekiah

The word that came to Jeremiah from the LORD, when King Nebuchadrezzar of Babylon and all his army and all the kingdoms of the earth and all the peoples under his dominion were fighting against Jerusalem and all its cities: 2Thus says the LORD, the God of Israel: Go and speak to King Zedekiah of Judah and say to him: Thus says the LORD: I am going to give this city into the hand of the king of Babylon, and he shall burn it with fire. 3And you yourself shall not escape from his hand, but shall surely be captured and handed over to him; you shall see the king of Babylon eye to eye and speak with him face to face; and you shall go to Babylon. 4Yet hear the word of the LORD, O King Zedekiah of Judah! Thus says the LORD concerning you: You shall not die by the sword; 5you shall die in peace. And as spices were burned[a] for

a Heb *as there was burning*

your ancestors, the earlier kings who preceded you, so they shall burn spices[a] for you and lament for you, saying, "Alas, lord!" For I have spoken the word, says the Lord.

6 Then the prophet Jeremiah spoke all these words to Zedekiah king of Judah, in Jerusalem, [7] when the army of the king of Babylon was fighting against Jerusalem and against all the cities of Judah that were left, Lachish and Azekah; for these were the only fortified cities of Judah that remained.

Treacherous Treatment of Slaves

8 The word that came to Jeremiah from the Lord, after King Zedekiah had made a covenant with all the people in Jerusalem to make a proclamation of liberty to them— [9] that all should set free their Hebrew slaves, male and female, so that no one should hold another Judean in slavery. [10] And they obeyed, all the officials and all the people who had entered into the covenant that all would set free their slaves, male or female, so that they would not be enslaved again; they obeyed and set them free. [11] But afterward they turned around and took back the male and female slaves they had set free, and brought them again into subjection as slaves. [12] The word of the Lord came to Jeremiah from the Lord: [13] Thus says the Lord, the God of Israel: I myself made a covenant with your ancestors when I brought them out of the land of Egypt, out of the house of slavery, saying, [14] "Every seventh year each of you must set free any Hebrews who have been sold to you and have served you six years; you must set them free from your service." But your ancestors did not listen to me or incline their ears to me. [15] You yourselves recently repented and did what was right in my sight by proclaiming liberty to one another, and you made a covenant before me in the house that is called by my name; [16] but then you turned around and profaned my name when each of you took back your male and female slaves, whom you had set free according to their desire, and you brought them again into subjection to be your slaves. [17] Therefore, thus says the Lord: You have not obeyed me by granting a release to your neighbors and friends; I am going to grant a release to you, says the Lord—a release to the sword, to pestilence, and to famine. I will make you a horror to all the kingdoms of the earth. [18] And those who transgressed my covenant and did not keep the terms of the covenant that they made before me, I will make like[b] the calf when they cut it in two and passed between its parts: [19] the officials of Judah, the officials of Jerusa-

lem, the eunuchs, the priests, and all the people of the land who passed between the parts of the calf [20] shall be handed over to their enemies and to those who seek their lives. Their corpses shall become food for the birds of the air and the wild animals of the earth. [21] And as for King Zedekiah of Judah and his officials, I will hand them over to their enemies and to those who seek their lives, to the army of the king of Babylon, which has withdrawn from you. [22] I am going to command, says the Lord, and will bring them back to this city; and they will fight against it, and take it, and burn it with fire. The towns of Judah I will make a desolation without inhabitant.

35 The Rechabites Commended

The word that came to Jeremiah from the Lord in the days of King Jehoiakim son of Josiah of Judah: [2] Go to the house of the Rechabites, and speak with them, and bring them to the house of the Lord, into one of the chambers; then offer them wine to drink. [3] So I took Jaazaniah son of Jeremiah son of Habazziniah, and his brothers, and all his sons, and the whole house of the Rechabites. [4] I brought them to the house of the Lord into the chamber of the sons of Hanan son of Igdaliah, the man of God, which was near the chamber of the officials, above the chamber of Maaseiah son of Shallum, keeper of the threshold. [5] Then I set before the Rechabites pitchers full of wine, and cups; and I said to them, "Have some wine." [6] But they answered, "We will drink no wine, for our ancestor Jonadab son of Rechab commanded us, 'You shall never drink wine, neither you nor your children; [7] nor shall you ever build a house, or sow seed; nor shall you plant a vineyard, or even own one; but you shall live in tents all your days, that you may live many days in the land where you reside.' [8] We have obeyed the charge of our ancestor Jonadab son of Rechab in all that he commanded us, to drink no wine all our days, ourselves, our wives, our sons, or our daughters, [9] and not to build houses to live in. We have no vineyard or field or seed; [10] but we have lived in tents, and have obeyed and done all that our ancestor Jonadab commanded us. [11] But when King Nebuchadrezzar of Babylon came up against the land, we said, 'Come, and let us go to Jerusalem for fear of the army of the Chaldeans and the army of the Arameans.' That is why we are living in Jerusalem."

12 Then the word of the Lord came to Jeremiah: [13] Thus says the Lord of hosts, the God of Israel: Go and say to the people of Judah

---

a Heb *shall burn* b Cn: Heb lacks *like*

and the inhabitants of Jerusalem, Can you not learn a lesson and obey my words? says the LORD. 14The command has been carried out that Jonadab son of Rechab gave to his descendants to drink no wine; and they drink none to this day, for they have obeyed their ancestor's command. But I myself have spoken to you persistently, and you have not obeyed me. 15I have sent to you all my servants the prophets, sending them persistently, saying, "Turn now every one of you from your evil way, and amend your doings, and do not go after other gods to serve them, and then you shall live in the land that I gave to you and your ancestors." But you did not incline your ear or obey me. 16The descendants of Jonadab son of Rechab have carried out the command that their ancestor gave them, but this people has not obeyed me. 17Therefore, thus says the LORD, the God of hosts, the God of Israel: I am going to bring on Judah and on all the inhabitants of Jerusalem every disaster that I have pronounced against them; because I have spoken to them and they have not listened, I have called to them and they have not answered.

18 But to the house of the Rechabites Jeremiah said: Thus says the LORD of hosts, the God of Israel: Because you have obeyed the command of your ancestor Jonadab, and kept all his precepts, and done all that he commanded you, 19therefore thus says the LORD of hosts, the God of Israel: Jonadab son of Rechab shall not lack a descendant to stand before me for all time.

36 The Scroll Read in the Temple

In the fourth year of King Jehoiakim son of Josiah of Judah, this word came to Jeremiah from the LORD: 2Take a scroll and write on it all the words that I have spoken to you against Israel and Judah and all the nations, from the day I spoke to you, from the days of Josiah until today. 3It may be that when the house of Judah hears of all the disasters that I intend to do to them, all of them may turn from their evil ways, so that I may forgive their iniquity and their sin.

4 Then Jeremiah called Baruch son of Neriah, and Baruch wrote on a scroll at Jeremiah's dictation all the words of the LORD that he had spoken to him. 5And Jeremiah ordered Baruch, saying, "I am prevented from entering the house of the LORD; 6so you go yourself, and on a fast day in the hearing of the people in the LORD's house you shall read the words of the LORD from the scroll that you have written at my dictation. You shall read them also in the hearing of all the people of Judah who come up from their towns. 7It may be that their plea will come before the LORD, and that all of them will turn from their evil ways, for great is the anger and wrath that the LORD has pronounced against this people." 8And Baruch son of Neriah did all that the prophet Jeremiah ordered him about reading from the scroll the words of the LORD in the LORD's house.

9 In the fifth year of King Jehoiakim son of Josiah of Judah, in the ninth month, all the people in Jerusalem and all the people who came from the towns of Judah to Jerusalem proclaimed a fast before the LORD. 10Then, in the hearing of all the people, Baruch read the words of Jeremiah from the scroll, in the house of the LORD, in the chamber of Gemariah son of Shaphan the secretary, which was in the upper court, at the entry of the New Gate of the LORD's house.

The Scroll Read in the Palace

11 When Micaiah son of Gemariah son of Shaphan heard all the words of the LORD from the scroll, 12he went down to the king's house, into the secretary's chamber; and all the officials were sitting there: Elishama the secretary, Delaiah son of Shemaiah, Elnathan son of Achbor, Gemariah son of Shaphan, Zedekiah son of Hananiah, and all the officials. 13And Micaiah told them all the words that he had heard, when Baruch read the scroll in the hearing of the people. 14Then all the officials sent Jehudi son of Nethaniah son of Shelemiah son of Cushi to say to Baruch, "Bring the scroll that you read in the hearing of the people, and come." So Baruch son of Neriah took the scroll in his hand and came to them. 15And they said to him, "Sit down and read it to us." So Baruch read it to them. 16When they heard all the words, they turned to one another in alarm, and said to Baruch, "We certainly must report all these words to the king." 17Then they questioned Baruch, "Tell us now, how did you write all these words? Was it at his dictation?" 18Baruch answered them, "He dictated all these words to me, and I wrote them with ink on the scroll." 19Then the officials said to Baruch, "Go and hide, you and Jeremiah, and let no one know where you are."

Jehoiakim Burns the Scroll

20 Leaving the scroll in the chamber of Elishama the secretary, they went to the court of the king; and they reported all the words to the king. 21Then the king sent Jehudi to get the scroll, and he took it from the chamber of Elishama the secretary; and Jehudi read it to the king and all the officials who stood beside the king. 22Now the king was sitting in his winter apartment (it was the ninth month), and there was a fire burning in the brazier before him. 23As Jehudi read three or four columns,

the king^a would cut them off with a penknife and throw them into the fire in the brazier, until the entire scroll was consumed in the fire that was in the brazier. ²⁴Yet neither the king, nor any of his servants who heard all these words, was alarmed, nor did they tear their garments. ²⁵Even when Elnathan and Delaiah and Gemariah urged the king not to burn the scroll, he would not listen to them. ²⁶And the king commanded Jerahmeel the king's son and Seraiah son of Azriel and Shelemiah son of Abdeel to arrest the secretary Baruch and the prophet Jeremiah. But the Lord hid them.

Jeremiah Dictates Another

27 Now, after the king had burned the scroll with the words that Baruch wrote at Jeremiah's dictation, the word of the Lord came to Jeremiah: ²⁸Take another scroll and write on it all the former words that were in the first scroll, which King Jehoiakim of Judah has burned. ²⁹And concerning King Jehoiakim of Judah you shall say: Thus says the Lord, You have dared to burn this scroll, saying, Why have you written in it that the king of Babylon will certainly come and destroy this land, and will cut off from it human beings and animals? ³⁰Therefore thus says the Lord concerning King Jehoiakim of Judah: He shall have no one to sit upon the throne of David, and his dead body shall be cast out to the heat by day and the frost by night. ³¹And I will punish him and his offspring and his servants for their iniquity; I will bring on them, and on the inhabitants of Jerusalem, and on the people of Judah, all the disasters with which I have threatened them— but they would not listen.

32 Then Jeremiah took another scroll and gave it to the secretary Baruch son of Neriah, who wrote on it at Jeremiah's dictation all the words of the scroll that King Jehoiakim of Judah had burned in the fire; and many similar words were added to them.

37 Zedekiah's Vain Hope

Zedekiah son of Josiah, whom King Nebuchadrezzar of Babylon made king in the land of Judah, succeeded Coniah son of Jehoiakim. ²But neither he nor his servants nor the people of the land listened to the words of the Lord that he spoke through the prophet Jeremiah.

3 King Zedekiah sent Jehucal son of Shelemiah and the priest Zephaniah son of Maaseiah to the prophet Jeremiah saying, "Please pray for us to the Lord our God." ⁴Now Jeremiah was still going in and out among the people, for he had not yet been put in prison.

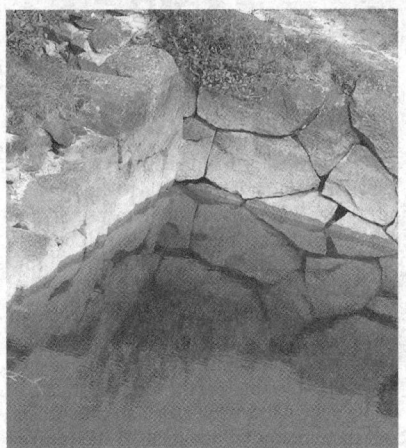

⁵Meanwhile, the army of Pharaoh had come out of Egypt; and when the Chaldeans who were besieging Jerusalem heard news of them, they withdrew from Jerusalem.

6 Then the word of the Lord came to the prophet Jeremiah: ⁷Thus says the Lord, God of Israel: This is what the two of you shall say to the king of Judah, who sent you to me to inquire of me: Pharaoh's army, which set out to help you, is going to return to its own land, to Egypt. ⁸And the Chaldeans shall return and fight against this city; they shall take it and burn it with fire. ⁹Thus says the Lord: Do not deceive yourselves, saying, "The Chaldeans will surely go away from us," for they will not go away. ¹⁰Even if you defeated the whole army of Chaldeans who are fighting against you, and there remained of them only wounded men in their tents, they would rise up and burn this city with fire.

Jeremiah Is Imprisoned

11 Now when the Chaldean army had withdrawn from Jerusalem at the approach of Pharaoh's army, ¹²Jeremiah set out from Jerusalem to go to the land of Benjamin to receive his share of property^b among the people there. ¹³When he reached the Benjamin Gate, a sentinel there named Irijah son of Shelemiah son of Hananiah arrested the prophet Jeremiah saying, "You are deserting to the Chaldeans." ¹⁴And Jeremiah said, "That is a lie; I am not deserting to the Chaldeans." But Irijah would not listen to him, and arrested Jeremiah and brought him to the officials. ¹⁵The officials were enraged at Jeremiah, and they beat him and imprisoned him in the house of the secretary Jonathan, for it had been made a prison.

a Heb *he* *b* Meaning of Heb uncertain

[16]Thus Jeremiah was put in the cistern house, in the cells, and remained there many days.

17 Then King Zedekiah sent for him, and received him. The king questioned him secretly in his house, and said, "Is there any word from the LORD?" Jeremiah said, "There is!" Then he said, "You shall be handed over to the king of Babylon." [18]Jeremiah also said to King Zedekiah, "What wrong have I done to you or your servants or this people, that you have put me in prison? [19]Where are your prophets who prophesied to you, saying, 'The king of Babylon will not come against you and against this land'? [20]Now please hear me, my lord king: be good enough to listen to my plea, and do not send me back to the house of the secretary Jonathan to die there." [21]So King Zedekiah gave orders, and they committed Jeremiah to the court of the guard; and a loaf of bread was given him daily from the bakers' street, until all the bread of the city was gone. So Jeremiah remained in the court of the guard.

38 Jeremiah in the Cistern

Now Shephatiah son of Mattan, Gedaliah son of Pashhur, Jucal son of Shelemiah, and Pashhur son of Malchiah heard the words that Jeremiah was saying to all the people, [2]Thus says the LORD, Those who stay in this city shall die by the sword, by famine, and by pestilence; but those who go out to the Chaldeans shall live; they shall have their lives as a prize of war, and live. [3]Thus says the LORD, This city shall surely be handed over to the army of the king of Babylon and be taken. [4]Then the officials said to the king, "This man ought to be put to death, because he is discouraging the soldiers who are left in this city, and all the people, by speaking such words to them. For this man is not seeking the welfare of this people, but their harm." [5]King Zedekiah said, "Here he is; he is in your hands; for the king is powerless against you." [6]So they took Jeremiah and threw him into the cistern of Malchiah, the king's son, which was in the court of the guard, letting Jeremiah down by ropes. Now there was no water in the cistern, but only mud, and Jeremiah sank in the mud.

Jeremiah Is Rescued by Ebed-melech

7 Ebed-melech the Ethiopian,[a] a eunuch in the king's house, heard that they had put Jeremiah into the cistern. The king happened to be sitting at the Benjamin Gate, [8]So Ebed-melech left the king's house and spoke to the king, [9]"My lord king, these men have acted wickedly in all they did to the prophet Jeremiah by throwing him into the cistern to die there of hunger, for there is no bread left in the city." [10]Then the king commanded Ebed-melech the Ethiopian,[a] "Take three men with you from here, and pull the prophet Jeremiah up from the cistern before he dies." [11]So Ebed-melech took the men with him and went to the house of the king, to a wardrobe of[b] the storehouse, and took from there old rags and worn-out clothes, which he let down to Jeremiah in the cistern by ropes. [12]Then Ebed-melech the Ethiopian[a] said to Jeremiah, "Just put the rags and clothes between your armpits and the ropes." Jeremiah did so. [13]Then they drew Jeremiah up by the ropes and pulled him out of the cistern. And Jeremiah remained in the court of the guard.

Zedekiah Consults Jeremiah Again

14 King Zedekiah sent for the prophet Jeremiah and received him at the third entrance of the temple of the LORD. The king said to Jeremiah, "I have something to ask you; do not hide anything from me." [15]Jeremiah said to Zedekiah, "If I tell you, you will put me to death, will you not? And if I give you advice, you will not listen to me." [16]So King Zedekiah swore an oath in secret to Jeremiah, "As the LORD lives, who gave us our lives, I will not put you to death or hand you over to these men who seek your life."

17 Then Jeremiah said to Zedekiah, "Thus says the LORD, the God of hosts, the God of Israel, If you will only surrender to the officials of the king of Babylon, then your life shall be spared, and this city shall not be burned with fire, and you and your house shall live. [18]But if you do not surrender to the officials of the king of Babylon, then this city shall be handed over to the Chaldeans, and they shall burn it with fire, and you yourself shall not escape from their hand." [19]King Zedekiah said to Jeremiah, "I am afraid of the Judeans who have deserted to the Chaldeans, for I might be handed over to them and they would abuse me." [20]Jeremiah said, "That will not happen. Just obey the voice of the LORD in what I say to you, and it shall go well with you, and your life shall be spared. [21]But if you are determined not to surrender, this is what the LORD has shown me— [22]a vision of all the women remaining in the house of the king of Judah being led out to the officials of the king of Babylon and saying,

'Your trusted friends have seduced you
      and have overcome you;
Now that your feet are stuck in the mud,
      they desert you.'
[23]All your wives and your children shall be led out to the Chaldeans, and you yourself shall not escape from their hand, but shall be seized

a Or Nubian; Heb Cushite b Cn: Heb to under

by the king of Babylon; and this city shall be burned with fire."

24 Then Zedekiah said to Jeremiah, "Do not let anyone else know of this conversation, or you will die. ²⁵If the officials should hear that I have spoken with you, and they should come and say to you, 'Just tell us what you said to the king; do not conceal it from us, or we will put you to death. What did the king say to you?' ²⁶then you shall say to them, 'I was presenting my plea to the king not to send me back to the house of Jonathan to die there.' " ²⁷All the officials did come to Jeremiah and questioned him; and he answered them in the very words the king had commanded. So they stopped questioning him, for the conversation had not been overheard. ²⁸And Jeremiah remained in the court of the guard until the day that Jerusalem was taken.

39 The Fall of Jerusalem

In the ninth year of King Zedekiah of Judah, in the tenth month, King Nebuchadrezzar of Babylon and all his army came against Jerusalem and besieged it; ²in the eleventh year of Zedekiah, in the fourth month, on the ninth day of the month, a breach was made in the city. ³When Jerusalem was taken,ᵃ all the officials of the king of Babylon came and sat in the middle gate: Nergal-sharezer, Samgar-nebo, Sarsechim the Rabsaris, Nergal-sharezer the

---

a This clause has been transposed from 38.28

Rabmag, with all the rest of the officials of the king of Babylon. ⁴When King Zedekiah of Judah and all the soldiers saw them, they fled, going out of the city at night by way of the king's garden through the gate between the two walls; and they went toward the Arabah. ⁵But the army of the Chaldeans pursued them, and overtook Zedekiah in the plains of Jericho; and when they had taken him, they brought him up to King Nebuchadrezzar of Babylon, at Riblah, in the land of Hamath; and he passed sentence on him. ⁶The king of Babylon slaughtered the sons of Zedekiah at Riblah before his eyes; also the king of Babylon slaughtered all the nobles of Judah. ⁷He put out the eyes of Zedekiah, and bound him in fetters to take him to Babylon. ⁸The Chaldeans burned the king's house and the houses of the people, and broke down the walls of Jerusalem. ⁹Then Nebuzaradan the captain of the guard exiled to Babylon the rest of the people who were left in the city, those who had deserted to him, and the people who remained. ¹⁰Nebuzaradan the captain of the guard left in the land of Judah some of the poor people who owned nothing, and gave them vineyards and fields at the same time.

Jeremiah, Set Free, Remembers Ebed-melech

11 King Nebuchadrezzar of Babylon gave command concerning Jeremiah through Nebuzaradan, the captain of the guard, saying,

Freedom—© Jesse Bernard, 17

¹²"Take him, look after him well and do him no harm, but deal with him as he may ask you." ¹³So Nebuzaradan the captain of the guard, Nebushazban the Rabsaris, Nergal-sharezer the Rabmag, and all the chief officers of the king of Babylon sent ¹⁴and took Jeremiah from the court of the guard. They entrusted him to Gedaliah son of Ahikam son of Shaphan to be brought home. So he stayed with his own people.

15 The word of the LORD came to Jeremiah while he was confined in the court of the guard: ¹⁶Go and say to Ebed-melech the Ethiopian:ᵃ Thus says the LORD of hosts, the God of Israel: I am going to fulfill my words against this city for evil and not for good, and they shall be accomplished in your presence on that day. ¹⁷But I will save you on that day, says the LORD, and you shall not be handed over to those whom you dread. ¹⁸For I will surely save you, and you shall not fall by the sword; but you shall have your life as a prize of war, because you have trusted in me, says the LORD.

40 Jeremiah with Gedaliah the Governor

The word that came to Jeremiah from the LORD after Nebuzaradan the captain of the guard had let him go from Ramah, when he took him bound in fetters along with all the captives of Jerusalem and Judah who were being exiled to Babylon. ²The captain of the guard took Jeremiah and said to him, "The LORD your God threatened this place with this disaster; ³and now the LORD has brought it about, and has done as he said, because all of you sinned against the LORD and did not obey his voice. Therefore this thing has come upon you. ⁴Now look, I have just released you today from the fetters on your hands. If you wish to come with me to Babylon, come, and I will take good care of you; but if you do not wish to come with me to Babylon, you need not come. See, the whole land is before you; go wherever you think it good and right to go. ⁵If you remain,ᵇ

then return to Gedaliah son of Ahikam son of Shaphan, whom the king of Babylon appointed governor of the towns of Judah, and stay with him among the people; or go wherever you think it right to go." So the captain of the guard gave him an allowance of food and a present, and let him go. ⁶Then Jeremiah went to Gedaliah son of Ahikam at Mizpah, and stayed with him among the people who were left in the land.

7 When all the leaders of the forces in the open country and their troops heard that the king of Babylon had appointed Gedaliah son of Ahikam governor in the land, and had committed to him men, women, and children, those of the poorest of the land who had not been taken into exile to Babylon, ⁸they went to Gedaliah at Mizpah—Ishmael son of Nethaniah, Johanan son of Kareah, Seraiah son of Tanhumeth, the sons of Ephai the Netophathite, Jezaniah son of the Maacathite, they and their troops. ⁹Gedaliah son of Ahikam son of Shaphan swore to them and their troops, saying, "Do not be afraid to serve the Chaldeans. Stay in the land and serve the king of Babylon, and it shall go well with you. ¹⁰As for me, I am staying at Mizpah to represent you before the Chaldeans who come to us; but as for you, gather wine and summer fruits and oil, and store them in your vessels, and live in the towns that you have taken over." ¹¹Likewise, when all the Judeans who were in Moab and among the Ammonites and in Edom and in other lands heard that the king of Babylon had left a remnant in Judah and had appointed Gedaliah son of Ahikam son of Shaphan as governor over them, ¹²then all the Judeans returned from all the places to which they had been scattered and came to the land of Judah, to Gedaliah at Mizpah; and they gathered wine and summer fruits in great abundance.

13 Now Johanan son of Kareah and all the leaders of the forces in the open country came to Gedaliah at Mizpah ¹⁴and said to him, "Are you at all aware that Baalis king of the Ammonites has sent Ishmael son of Nethaniah to take your life?" But Gedaliah son of Ahikam would not believe them. ¹⁵Then Johanan son of Kareah spoke secretly to Gedaliah at Mizpah, "Please let me go and kill Ishmael son of Nethaniah, and no one else will know. Why should he take your life, so that all the Judeans who are gathered around you would be scattered, and the remnant of Judah would perish?" ¹⁶But Gedaliah son of Ahikam said to Johanan son of Kareah, "Do not do such a thing, for you are telling a lie about Ishmael."

ᵃ Or *Nubian*; Heb *Cushite* ᵇ Syr: Meaning of Heb uncertain

41 Insurrection against Gedaliah

In the seventh month, Ishmael son of Nethaniah son of Elishama, of the royal family, one of the chief officers of the king, came with ten men to Gedaliah son of Ahikam, at Mizpah. As they ate bread together there at Mizpah, ²Ishmael son of Nethaniah and the ten men with him got up and struck down Gedaliah son of Ahikam son of Shaphan with the sword and killed him, because the king of Babylon had appointed him governor in the land. ³Ishmael also killed all the Judeans who were with Gedaliah at Mizpah, and the Chaldean soldiers who happened to be there.

4 On the day after the murder of Gedaliah, before anyone knew of it, ⁵eighty men arrived from Shechem and Shiloh and Samaria, with their beards shaved and their clothes torn, and their bodies gashed, bringing grain offerings and incense to present at the temple of the LORD. ⁶And Ishmael son of Nethaniah came out from Mizpah to meet them, weeping as he came. As he met them, he said to them, "Come to Gedaliah son of Ahikam." ⁷When they reached the middle of the city, Ishmael son of Nethaniah and the men with him slaughtered them, and threw them*a* into a cistern. ⁸But there were ten men among them who said to Ishmael, "Do not kill us, for we have stores of wheat, barley, oil, and honey hidden in the fields." So he refrained, and did not kill them along with their companions.

9 Now the cistern into which Ishmael had thrown all the bodies of the men whom he had struck down was the large cistern*b* that King Asa had made for defense against King Baasha of Israel; Ishmael son of Nethaniah filled that cistern with those whom he had killed. ¹⁰Then Ishmael took captive all the rest of the people who were in Mizpah, the king's daughters and all the people who were left at Mizpah, whom Nebuzaradan, the captain of the guard, had committed to Gedaliah son of Ahikam. Ishmael son of Nethaniah took them captive and set out to cross over to the Ammonites.

11 But when Johanan son of Kareah and all the leaders of the forces with him heard of all the crimes that Ishmael son of Nethaniah had done, ¹²they took all their men and went to fight against Ishmael son of Nethaniah. They came upon him at the great pool that is in Gibeon. ¹³And when all the people who were with Ishmael saw Johanan son of Kareah and all the leaders of the forces with him, they were glad. ¹⁴So all the people whom Ishmael had carried away captive from Mizpah turned around and came back, and went to Johanan son of Kareah. ¹⁵But Ishmael son of Nethaniah escaped from Johanan with eight men, and went to the Ammonites. ¹⁶Then Johanan son of Kareah and all the leaders of the forces with him took all the rest of the people whom Ishmael son of Nethaniah had carried away captive*c* from Mizpah after he had slain Gedaliah son of Ahikam—soldiers, women, children, and eunuchs, whom Johanan brought back from Gibeon.*d* ¹⁷And they set out, and stopped at Geruth Chimham near Bethlehem, intending to go to Egypt ¹⁸because of the Chaldeans; for they were afraid of them, because Ishmael son of Nethaniah had killed Gedaliah son of Ahikam, whom the king of Babylon had made governor over the land.

42 Jeremiah Advises Survivors Not to Migrate

Then all the commanders of the forces, and Johanan son of Kareah and Azariah*e* son of Hoshaiah, and all the people from the least to the greatest, approached ²the prophet Jeremiah and said, "Be good enough to listen to our plea, and pray to the LORD your God for us— for all this remnant. For there are only a few of us left out of many, as your eyes can see. ³Let the LORD your God show us where we should go and what we should do." ⁴The prophet Jeremiah said to them, "Very well: I am going to pray to the LORD your God as you request, and whatever the LORD answers you I will tell you; I will keep nothing back from you." ⁵They in their turn said to Jeremiah, "May the LORD be a true and faithful witness against us if we do not act according to everything that the LORD your God sends us through you. ⁶Whether it is good or bad, we will obey the voice of the LORD our God to whom we are sending you, in order that it may go well with us when we obey the voice of the LORD our God."

7 At the end of ten days the word of the LORD came to Jeremiah. ⁸Then he summoned Johanan son of Kareah and all the commanders of the forces who were with him, and all the people from the least to the greatest, ⁹and said to them, "Thus says the LORD, the God of Israel, to whom you sent me to present your plea before him: ¹⁰If you will only remain in this land, then I will build you up and not pull you down; I will plant you, and not pluck you up; for I am sorry for the disaster that I have brought upon you. ¹¹Do not be afraid of the king of Babylon, as you have been; do not be afraid of him, says the LORD, for I am with you, to save you and to res-

a Syr: Heb lacks *and threw them*; compare verse 9 *b* Gk: Heb *whom he had killed by the hand of Gedaliah* *c* Cn: Heb *whom he recovered from Ishmael son of Nethaniah* *d* Meaning of Heb uncertain *e* Gk: Heb *Jezaniah* cue you from his hand. ¹²I will grant you mercy, and he will have mercy on you and restore you to your native soil. ¹³But if you continue to say, 'We will not stay in this land,' thus disobeying the voice of the LORD your God ¹⁴and saying, 'No, we will go to the land of Egypt, where we shall not see war, or hear the sound of the trumpet, or be hungry for bread, and there we will stay,' ¹⁵then hear the word of the LORD, O remnant of Judah. Thus says the LORD of hosts, the God of Israel: If you are determined to enter Egypt and go to settle there, ¹⁶then the sword that you fear shall overtake you there, in the land of Egypt; and the famine that you dread shall follow close after you into Egypt; and there you shall die. ¹⁷All the people who have determined to go to Egypt to settle there shall die by the sword, by famine, and by pestilence; they shall have no remnant or survivor from the disaster that I am bringing upon them.

18 "For thus says the LORD of hosts, the God of Israel: Just as my anger and my wrath were poured out on the inhabitants of Jerusalem, so my wrath will be poured out on you when you go to Egypt. You shall become an object of execration and horror, of cursing and ridicule. You shall see this place no more. ¹⁹The LORD has said to you, O remnant of Judah, Do not go to Egypt. Be well aware that I have warned you today ²⁰that you have made a fatal mistake. For you yourselves sent me to the LORD your God, saying, 'Pray for us to the LORD our God, and whatever the LORD our God says, tell us and we will do it.' ²¹So I have told you today, but you have not obeyed the voice of the LORD your God in anything that he sent me to tell you. ²²Be well aware, then, that you shall die by the sword, by famine, and by pestilence in the place where you desire to go and settle."

43 Taken to Egypt, Jeremiah Warns of Judgment

When Jeremiah finished speaking to all the people all these words of the LORD their God, with which the LORD their God had sent him to them, ²Azariah son of Hoshaiah and Johanan son of Kareah and all the other insolent men said to Jeremiah, "You are telling a lie. The LORD our God did not send you to say, 'Do not go to Egypt to settle there'; ³but Baruch son of Neriah is inciting you against us, to hand us over to the Chaldeans, in order that they may kill us or take us into exile in Babylon." ⁴So Johanan son of Kareah and all the commanders of the forces and all the people did not obey the voice of the LORD, to stay in the land of Judah. ⁵But Johanan son of Kareah and all the com-

manders of the forces took all the remnant of Judah who had returned to settle in the land of Judah from all the nations to which they had been driven— ⁶the men, the women, the children, the princesses, and everyone whom Nebuzaradan the captain of the guard had left with Gedaliah son of Ahikam son of Shaphan; also the prophet Jeremiah and Baruch son of Neriah. ⁷And they came into the land of Egypt, for they did not obey the voice of the LORD. And they arrived at Tahpanhes.

8 Then the word of the LORD came to Jeremiah in Tahpanhes: ⁹Take some large stones in your hands, and bury them in the clay pavement*a* that is at the entrance to Pharaoh's palace in Tahpanhes. Let the Judeans see you do it, ¹⁰and say to them, Thus says the LORD of hosts, the God of Israel: I am going to send and take my servant King Nebuchadrezzar of Babylon, and he*b* will set his throne above these stones that I have buried, and he will spread his royal canopy over them. ¹¹He shall come and ravage the land of Egypt, giving

those who are destined for pestilence, to
    pestilence,
and those who are destined for captivity,
    to captivity,
and those who are destined for the
    sword, to the sword.

¹²He*c* shall kindle a fire in the temples of the gods of Egypt; and he shall burn them and carry them away captive; and he shall pick clean the land of Egypt, as a shepherd picks his cloak clean of vermin; and he shall depart from there safely. ¹³He shall break the obelisks of Heliopolis, which is in the land of Egypt; and the temples of the gods of Egypt he shall burn with fire.

44 Denunciation of Persistent Idolatry

The word that came to Jeremiah for all the Judeans living in the land of Egypt, at Migdol, at Tahpanhes, at Memphis, and in the land of Pathros, ²Thus says the LORD of hosts, the God of Israel: You yourselves have seen all the disaster that I have brought on Jerusalem and on all the towns of Judah. Look at them; today they are a desolation, without an inhabitant in them, ³because of the wickedness that they committed, provoking me to anger, in that they went to make offerings and serve other gods that they had not known, neither they, nor you, nor your ancestors. ⁴Yet I persistently sent to you all my servants the prophets, saying, "I beg you not to do this abominable thing that I hate!" ⁵But they did not listen or incline their ear, to turn from their wickedness and make no offerings to other gods. ⁶So my wrath

a Meaning of Heb uncertain   *b* Gk Syr: Heb *I*   *c* Gk Syr Vg: Heb *I* and my anger were poured out and kindled in the towns of Judah and in the streets of Jerusalem; and they became a waste and a desolation, as they still are today. ⁷And now thus says the LORD God of hosts, the God of Israel: Why are you doing such great harm to yourselves, to cut off man and woman, child and infant, from the midst of Judah, leaving yourselves without a remnant? ⁸Why do you provoke me to anger with the works of your hands, making offerings to other gods in the land of Egypt where you have come to settle? Will you be cut off and become an object of cursing and ridicule among all the nations of the earth? ⁹Have you forgotten the crimes of your ancestors, of the kings of Judah, of their*ᵈ* wives, your own crimes and those of your wives, which they committed in the land of Judah and in the streets of Jerusalem? ¹⁰They have shown no contrition or fear to this day, nor have they walked in my law and my statutes that I set before you and before your ancestors.

11 Therefore thus says the LORD of hosts, the God of Israel: I am determined to bring disaster on you, to bring all Judah to an end. ¹²I will take the remnant of Judah who are determined to come to the land of Egypt to settle, and they shall perish, everyone; in the land of Egypt they shall fall; by the sword and by famine they shall perish; from the least to the greatest, they shall die by the sword and by famine; and they shall become an object of execration and horror, of cursing and ridicule. ¹³I will punish those who live in the land of Egypt, as I have punished Jerusalem, with the sword, with famine, and with pestilence, ¹⁴so that none of the remnant of Judah who have come to settle in the land of Egypt shall escape or survive or return to the land of Judah. Although they long to go back to live there, they shall not go back, except some fugitives.

15 Then all the men who were aware that their wives had been making offerings to other gods, and all the women who stood by, a great assembly, all the people who lived in Pathros in the land of Egypt, answered Jeremiah: ¹⁶"As for the word that you have spoken to us in the name of the LORD, we are not going to listen to you. ¹⁷Instead, we will do everything that we have vowed, make offerings to the queen of heaven and pour out libations to her, just as we and our ancestors, our kings and our officials, used to do in the towns of Judah and in the streets of Jerusalem. We used to have plenty of food, and prospered, and saw no misfortune. ¹⁸But from the time we stopped making offerings to the queen of heaven and pouring out li-

bations to her, we have lacked everything and have perished by the sword and by famine." ¹⁹And the women said,ᵇ "Indeed we will go on making offerings to the queen of heaven and pouring out libations to her; do you think that we made cakes for her, marked with her image, and poured out libations to her without our husbands' being involved?"

20 Then Jeremiah said to all the people, men and women, all the people who were giving him this answer: ²¹"As for the offerings that you made in the towns of Judah and in the streets of Jerusalem, you and your ancestors, your kings and your officials, and the people of the land, did not the LORD remember them? Did it not come into his mind? ²²The LORD could no longer bear the sight of your evil doings, the abominations that you committed; therefore your land became a desolation and

Slum Lord Most people wouldn't choose to live in a smelly shack in the slums. And when Toyohiko Kagawa turned from his Buddhist upbringing and prayed, "Make me like Christ!" he had no idea where it would lead. Toyohiko was baptized as a fifteen-year-old, then decided to begin theological training so he could preach in the slums of Kobe, Japan. In 1909, when he was only twenty-one years old, Toyohiko moved into the poorest part of the city. Then he took it one step further: he invited the poor, including a murderer and a severely physically deformed outcast, to live *with him*.

Toyohiko eventually chose to leave the slums to go to America to study economics at Princeton. But when he went back to Japan, Toyohiko didn't forget his old neighbors. He returned to the slums, eager to help those in need. Toyohiko challenged other Christians to "take [the gospel] seriously and live it adventurously." Following his own advice, he took on the injustice that surrounded him. He fought for workers' rights and lived out a peaceful response to oppression. Toyohiko paid a high price for his efforts—at one point his home was raided and he was imprisoned for leading a labor strike.

Though a lot of people didn't understand his decision to care for outcasts and live among the lower class, Toyohiko won many people's respect because of his character. He lived simply and gave generously.

Though he could have afforded much

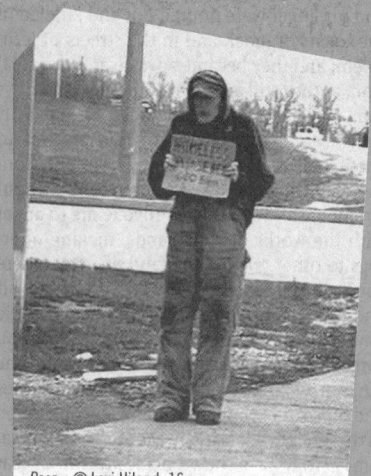

Poor—© Lexi Hiland, 16

better, Toyohiko chose to wear the same $1.85 outfit as the workers. Instead of spending his money on himself, he used it to start schools and medical clinics for the poor and uneducated.

As the years went on, even his own sickness, imprisonment, and partial blindness didn't stop him. Toyohiko was determined to follow Jesus' example and bring the message of salvation to people at every level of society. He didn't just *say* these words—he *lived* them:

"It is through love manifest in the lives of His followers that Christ may conquer the world."

---

a waste and a curse, without inhabitant, as it is to this day. 23It is because you burned offerings, and because you sinned against the LORD and did not obey the voice of the LORD or walk in his law and in his statutes and in his decrees, that this disaster has befallen you, as is still evident today."

24 Jeremiah said to all the people and all the women, "Hear the word of the LORD, all you Judeans who are in the land of Egypt, 25Thus says the LORD of hosts, the God of Israel: You and your wives have accomplished in deeds what you declared in words, saying, 'We are determined to perform the vows that we have made, to make offerings to the queen of heaven and to pour out libations to her.' By all means, keep your vows and make your liba-

tions! 26Therefore hear the word of the LORD, all you Judeans who live in the land of Egypt: Lo, I swear by my great name, says the LORD, that my name shall no longer be pronounced on the lips of any of the people of Judah in all the land of Egypt, saying, 'As the Lord GOD lives.' 27I am going to watch over them for harm and not for good; all the people of Judah who are in the land of Egypt shall perish by the sword and by famine, until not one is left. 28And those who escape the sword shall return from the land of Egypt to the land of Judah, few in number; and all the remnant of Judah, who have come to the land of Egypt to settle, shall know whose words will stand, mine or theirs! 29This shall be the sign to you, says the LORD, that I am going to punish you in this place, in order that you may know that my words against you will surely be carried out: ³⁰Thus says the LORD, I am going to give Pharaoh Hophra, king of Egypt, into the hands of his enemies, those who seek his life, just as I gave King Zedekiah of Judah into the hand of King Nebuchadrezzar of Babylon, his enemy who sought his life."

45 A Word of Comfort to Baruch

The word that the prophet Jeremiah spoke to Baruch son of Neriah, when he wrote these words in a scroll at the dictation of Jeremiah, in the fourth year of King Jehoiakim son of Josiah of Judah: ²Thus says the LORD, the God of Israel, to you, O Baruch: ³You said, "Woe is me! The LORD has added sorrow to my pain; I am weary with my groaning, and I find no rest." ⁴Thus you shall say to him, "Thus says the LORD: I am going to break down what I have built, and pluck up what I have planted—that is, the whole land. ⁵And you, do you seek great things for yourself? Do not seek them; for I am going to bring disaster upon all flesh, says the LORD; but I will give you your life as a prize of war in every place to which you may go."

46 Judgment on Egypt

The word of the LORD that came to the prophet Jeremiah concerning the nations.

2 Concerning Egypt, about the army of Pharaoh Neco, king of Egypt, which was by the river Euphrates at Carchemish and which King Nebuchadrezzar of Babylon defeated in the fourth year of King Jehoiakim son of Josiah of Judah:

³ Prepare buckler and shield,
and advance for battle!
⁴ Harness the horses;
mount the steeds!
Take your stations with your helmets,
whet your lances,
put on your coats of mail!
⁵ Why do I see them terrified?
They have fallen back;
their warriors are beaten down,
and have fled in haste.
They do not look back—
terror is all around!
says the LORD.
⁶ The swift cannot flee away,
nor can the warrior escape;
in the north by the river Euphrates
they have stumbled and fallen.

⁷ Who is this, rising like the Nile,
like rivers whose waters surge?
⁸ Egypt rises like the Nile,
like rivers whose waters surge.

It said, Let me rise, let me cover the earth,
let me destroy cities and their inhabitants.
⁹ Advance, O horses,
and dash madly, O chariots!
Let the warriors go forth:
Ethiopia*ᵃ* and Put who carry the shield,
the Ludim, who draw*ᵇ* the bow.
¹⁰ That day is the day of the Lord GOD of hosts,
a day of retribution,
to gain vindication from his foes.
The sword shall devour and be sated,
and drink its fill of their blood.
For the Lord GOD of hosts holds a sacrifice
in the land of the north by the river
Euphrates.
¹¹ Go up to Gilead, and take balm,
O virgin daughter Egypt!
In vain you have used many medicines;
there is no healing for you.
¹² The nations have heard of your shame,
and the earth is full of your cry;
for warrior has stumbled against warrior;
both have fallen together.

Babylonia Will Strike Egypt

13 The word that the LORD spoke to the prophet Jeremiah about the coming of King Nebuchadrezzar of Babylon to attack the land of Egypt:

¹⁴ Declare in Egypt, and proclaim in Migdol;
proclaim in Memphis and Tahpanhes;
Say, "Take your stations and be ready,
for the sword shall devour those around
you."
¹⁵ Why has Apis fled?*ᶜ*
Why did your bull not stand?
—because the LORD thrust him down.
¹⁶ Your multitude stumbled*ᵈ* and fell,
and one said to another,*ᵉ*
"Come, let us go back to our own people
and to the land of our birth,
because of the destroying sword."
¹⁷ Give Pharaoh, king of Egypt, the name
"Braggart who missed his chance."

¹⁸ As I live, says the King,
whose name is the LORD of hosts,
one is coming
like Tabor among the mountains,
and like Carmel by the sea.
¹⁹ Pack your bags for exile,
sheltered daughter Egypt!
For Memphis shall become a waste,
a ruin, without inhabitant.

²⁰ A beautiful heifer is Egypt—
a gadfly from the north lights upon her.

---

a Or Nubia; Heb Cush *b* Cn: Heb who grasp, who draw *c* Gk: Heb Why was it swept away *d* Gk: Meaning of Heb uncertain *e* Gk: Heb and fell one to another and they said

²¹ Even her mercenaries in her midst
    are like fatted calves;
they too have turned and fled together,
    they did not stand;
for the day of their calamity has come upon
    them,
    the time of their punishment.

²² She makes a sound like a snake gliding away;
    for her enemies march in force,
and come against her with axes,
    like those who fell trees.
²³ They shall cut down her forest,
              says the Lord,
    though it is impenetrable,
because they are more numerous
    than locusts;
    they are without number.
²⁴ Daughter Egypt shall be put to shame;
    she shall be handed over to a people
      from the north.

25 The Lord of hosts, the God of Israel, said: See, I am bringing punishment upon Amon of Thebes, and Pharaoh, and Egypt and her gods and her kings, upon Pharaoh and those who trust in him. ²⁶I will hand them over to those who seek their life, to King Nebuchadrezzar of Babylon and his officers. Afterward Egypt shall be inhabited as in the days of old, says the Lord.

God Will Save Israel

²⁷ But as for you, have no fear, my servant
    Jacob,
    and do not be dismayed, O Israel;
for I am going to save you from far away,
    and your offspring from the land of their
      captivity.
Jacob shall return and have quiet and ease,
    and no one shall make him afraid.
²⁸ As for you, have no fear, my servant Jacob,
              says the Lord,
    for I am with you.
I will make an end of all the nations
    among which I have banished you,
    but I will not make an end of you!
I will chastise you in just measure,
    and I will by no means leave you
      unpunished.

47 Judgment on the Philistines

The word of the Lord that came to the prophet Jeremiah concerning the Philistines, before Pharaoh attacked Gaza:

 ² Thus says the Lord:
    See, waters are rising out of the north
      and shall become an overflowing torrent;

they shall overflow the land and all that
    fills it,
    the city and those who live in it.
People shall cry out,
    and all the inhabitants of the land shall
      wail.
³ At the noise of the stamping of the hoofs of
    his stallions,
    at the clatter of his chariots, at the
      rumbling of their wheels,
parents do not turn back for children,
    so feeble are their hands,
⁴ because of the day that is coming
    to destroy all the Philistines,
to cut off from Tyre and Sidon
    every helper that remains.
For the Lord is destroying the Philistines,
    the remnant of the coastland of
      Caphtor.
⁵ Baldness has come upon Gaza,
    Ashkelon is silenced.
O remnant of their power!^a
    How long will you gash yourselves?
⁶ Ah, sword of the Lord!
    How long until you are quiet?
Put yourself into your scabbard,
    rest and be still!
⁷ How can it^b be quiet,
    when the Lord has given it an order?
Against Ashkelon and against the
      seashore—
    there he has appointed it.

48 Judgment on Moab

Concerning Moab.

Thus says the Lord of hosts, the God of Israel:
    Alas for Nebo, it is laid waste!
    Kiriathaim is put to shame, it is taken;
    the fortress is put to shame and broken
      down;
²   the renown of Moab is no more.
In Heshbon they planned evil against her:
    "Come, let us cut her off from being a
      nation!"
You also, O Madmen, shall be brought to
      silence;^c
    the sword shall pursue you.

³ Hark! a cry from Horonaim,
    "Desolation and great destruction!"
⁴ "Moab is destroyed!"
    her little ones cry out.
⁵ For at the ascent of Luhith
    they go^d up weeping bitterly;
for at the descent of Horonaim
    they have heard the distressing cry of
      anguish.

a Gk: Heb *their valley*   *b* Gk Vg: Heb *you*   *c* The place-name *Madmen* sounds like the Hebrew verb *to be silent*   *d* Cn: Heb *he goes*

6 Flee! Save yourselves!
    Be like a wild ass^a in the desert!

7 Surely, because you trusted in your
      strongholds^b and your treasures,
    you also shall be taken;
    Chemosh shall go out into exile,
      with his priests and his attendants.

8 The destroyer shall come upon every town,
    and no town shall escape;
    the valley shall perish,
      and the plain shall be destroyed,
      as the Lord has spoken.

9 Set aside salt for Moab,
    for she will surely fall;
    her towns shall become a desolation,
      with no inhabitant in them.

10 Accursed is the one who is slack in doing the work of the Lord; and accursed is the one who keeps back the sword from bloodshed.

11 Moab has been at ease from his youth,
    settled like wine^c on its dregs;
    he has not been emptied from vessel to
      vessel,
    nor has he gone into exile;
    therefore his flavor has remained
      and his aroma is unspoiled.

12 Therefore, the time is surely coming, says the Lord, when I shall send to him decanters to decant him, and empty his vessels, and break his^d jars in pieces. 13Then Moab shall be ashamed of Chemosh, as the house of Israel was ashamed of Bethel, their confidence.

14 How can you say, "We are heroes
    and mighty warriors"?

15 The destroyer of Moab and his towns has
      come up,
    and the choicest of his young men have
      gone down to slaughter,
    says the King, whose name is the Lord of
      hosts.

16 The calamity of Moab is near at hand
    and his doom approaches swiftly.

17 Mourn over him, all you his neighbors,
    and all who know his name;
    say, "How the mighty scepter is broken,
      the glorious staff!"

18 Come down from glory,
    and sit on the parched ground,
    enthroned daughter Dibon!
    For the destroyer of Moab has come up
      against you;
    he has destroyed your strongholds.

19 Stand by the road and watch,
    you inhabitant of Aroer!
    Ask the man fleeing and the woman
      escaping;
    say, "What has happened?"

20 Moab is put to shame, for it is broken down;
    wail and cry!

---

a Gk Aquila: Heb *like Aroer* *b* Gk: Heb *works* *c* Heb lacks *like wine* *d* Gk Aquila: Heb *their*

Tell it by the Arnon,
　　that Moab is laid waste.

21　Judgment has come upon the tableland, upon Holon, and Jahzah, and Mephaath, ²²and Dibon, and Nebo, and Beth-diblathaim, ²³and Kiriathaim, and Beth-gamul, and Beth-meon, ²⁴and Kerioth, and Bozrah, and all the towns of the land of Moab, far and near. ²⁵The horn of Moab is cut off, and his arm is broken, says the LORD.

26　Make him drunk, because he magnified himself against the LORD; let Moab wallow in his vomit; he too shall become a laughingstock. ²⁷Israel was a laughingstock for you, though he was not caught among thieves; but whenever you spoke of him you shook your head!

28　Leave the towns, and live on the rock,
　　O inhabitants of Moab!
Be like the dove that nests
　　on the sides of the mouth of a gorge.
29　We have heard of the pride of Moab—
　　he is very proud—
of his loftiness, his pride, and his arrogance,
　　and the haughtiness of his heart.
30　I myself know his insolence, says the LORD;
　　his boasts are false,
　　his deeds are false.
31　Therefore I wail for Moab;
　　I cry out for all Moab;
　　for the people of Kir-heres I mourn.
32　More than for Jazer I weep for you,
　　O vine of Sibmah!
Your branches crossed over the sea,
　　reached as far as Jazer;ᵃ
upon your summer fruits and your vintage
　　the destroyer has fallen.

33　Gladness and joy have been taken away
　　from the fruitful land of Moab;
I have stopped the wine from the wine
　　presses;
　　no one treads them with shouts of joy;
　　the shouting is not the shout of joy.

34　Heshbon and Elealeh cry out;ᵇ as far as Jahaz they utter their voice, from Zoar to Horonaim and Eglath-shelishiyah. For even the waters of Nimrim have become desolate. ³⁵And I will bring to an end in Moab, says the LORD, those who offer sacrifice at a high place and make offerings to their gods. ³⁶Therefore my heart moans for Moab like a flute, and my heart moans like a flute for the people of Kir-heres; for the riches they gained have perished.

37　For every head is shaved and every beard cut off; on all the hands there are gashes, and on the loins sackcloth. ³⁸On all the housetops of Moab and in the squares there is nothing but lamentation; for I have broken Moab like a vessel that no one wants, says the LORD. ³⁹How it is broken! How they wail! How Moab has turned his back in shame! So Moab has become a derision and a horror to all his neighbors.
40　For thus says the LORD:
　　Look, he shall swoop down like an eagle,
　　and spread his wings against Moab;
41　the townsᶜ shall be taken
　　and the strongholds seized.
The hearts of the warriors of Moab, on that
　　day,
　　shall be like the heart of a woman in
　　labor.
42　Moab shall be destroyed as a people,
　　because he magnified himself against
　　the LORD.
43　Terror, pit, and trap
　　are before you, O inhabitants of Moab!
　　　　　　　　　　　　says the LORD.
44　Everyone who flees from the terror
　　shall fall into the pit,
and everyone who climbs out of the pit
　　shall be caught in the trap.
For I will bring these thingsᵈ upon Moab
　　in the year of their punishment,
　　　　　　　　　　　　says the LORD.

45　In the shadow of Heshbon
　　fugitives stop exhausted;
for a fire has gone out from Heshbon,
　　a flame from the house of Sihon;
it has destroyed the forehead of Moab,
　　the scalp of the people of tumult.ᵉ
46　Woe to you, O Moab!
　　The people of Chemosh have perished,

ᵃ Two Mss and Isa 16.8: MT *the sea of Jazer*　b Cn: Heb *From the cry of Heshbon to Elealeh*　c Or *Kerioth*　d Gk Syr: Heb *bring upon it*　e Or *of Shaon*

for your sons have been taken captive,
and your daughters into captivity.
47 Yet I will restore the fortunes of Moab
in the latter days, says the LORD.
Thus far is the judgment on Moab.

49 Judgment on the Ammonites

Concerning the Ammonites.

Thus says the LORD:
Has Israel no sons?
Has he no heir?
Why then has Milcom dispossessed Gad,
and his people settled in its towns?
2 Therefore, the time is surely coming,
says the LORD,
when I will sound the battle alarm
against Rabbah of the Ammonites;
it shall become a desolate mound,
and its villages shall be burned with fire;
then Israel shall dispossess those who
dispossessed him,
says the LORD.

3 Wail, O Heshbon, for Ai is laid waste!
Cry out, O daughters*a* of Rabbah!
Put on sackcloth,
lament, and slash yourselves with
whips!*b*
For Milcom shall go into exile,
with his priests and his attendants.
4 Why do you boast in your strength?
Your strength is ebbing,
O faithless daughter.
You trusted in your treasures, saying,
"Who will attack me?"
5 I am going to bring terror upon you,
says the Lord GOD of hosts,
from all your neighbors,
and you will be scattered, each headlong,
with no one to gather the fugitives.
6 But afterward I will restore the fortunes of
the Ammonites, says the LORD.

Judgment on Edom

7 Concerning Edom.

Thus says the LORD of hosts:
Is there no longer wisdom in Teman?
Has counsel perished from the prudent?
Has their wisdom vanished?
8 Flee, turn back, get down low,
inhabitants of Dedan!
For I will bring the calamity of Esau upon
him,
the time when I punish him.
9 If grape-gatherers came to you,
would they not leave gleanings?

If thieves came by night,
even they would pillage only what they
wanted.
10 But as for me, I have stripped Esau bare,
I have uncovered his hiding places,
and he is not able to conceal himself.
His offspring are destroyed, his kinsfolk
and his neighbors; and he is no more.
11 Leave your orphans, I will keep them alive;
and let your widows trust in me.

12 For thus says the LORD: If those who do
not deserve to drink the cup still have to drink
it, shall you be the one to go unpunished? You
shall not go unpunished; you must drink it.
13 For by myself I have sworn, says the LORD,
that Bozrah shall become an object of horror
and ridicule, a waste, and an object of cursing;
and all her towns shall be perpetual wastes.
14 I have heard tidings from the LORD,
and a messenger has been sent among
the nations:
"Gather yourselves together and come
against her,
and rise up for battle!"
15 For I will make you least among the
nations,
despised by humankind.
16 The terror you inspire
and the pride of your heart have deceived
you,
you who live in the clefts of the rock,*c*
who hold the height of the hill.
Although you make your nest as high as the
eagle's,
from there I will bring you down,
says the LORD.

17 Edom shall become an object of horror;
everyone who passes by it will be horrified and
will hiss because of all its disasters. 18As when
Sodom and Gomorrah and their neighbors
were overthrown, says the LORD, no one shall
live there, nor shall anyone settle in it. 19Like
a lion coming up from the thickets of the Jordan against a perennial pasture, I will suddenly
chase Edom*d* away from it; and I will appoint
over it whomever I choose.*e* For who is like me?
Who can summon me? Who is the shepherd
who can stand before me? 20Therefore hear the
plan that the LORD has made against Edom and
the purposes that he has formed against the inhabitants of Teman: Surely the little ones of the
flock shall be dragged away; surely their fold
shall be appalled at their fate. 21At the sound of
their fall the earth shall tremble; the sound of
their cry shall be heard at the Red Sea.*f* 22Look,
he shall mount up and swoop down like an ea-

---

a Or *villages* *b* Cn: Meaning of Heb uncertain *c* Or *of Sela* *d* Heb *him* *e* Or *and I will single out the choicest of his rams:* Meaning of Heb
uncertain *f* Or *Sea of Reeds*

gle, and spread his wings against Bozrah, and the heart of the warriors of Edom in that day shall be like the heart of a woman in labor.

Judgment on Damascus

23 Concerning Damascus.

Hamath and Arpad are confounded,
for they have heard bad news;
they melt in fear, they are troubled like the sea*a*
that cannot be quiet.
24 Damascus has become feeble, she turned to flee,
and panic seized her;
anguish and sorrows have taken hold of her,
as of a woman in labor.
25 How the famous city is forsaken,*b*
the joyful town!*c*
26 Therefore her young men shall fall in her squares,
and all her soldiers shall be destroyed in that day,
says the Lord of hosts.
27 And I will kindle a fire at the wall of Damascus,
and it shall devour the strongholds of Ben-hadad.

Judgment on Kedar and Hazor

28 Concerning Kedar and the kingdoms of Hazor that King Nebuchadrezzar of Babylon defeated.

Thus says the Lord:
Rise up, advance against Kedar!
Destroy the people of the east!
29 Take their tents and their flocks,
their curtains and all their goods;
carry off their camels for yourselves,
and a cry shall go up: "Terror is all around!"
30 Flee, wander far away, hide in deep places,
O inhabitants of Hazor!
says the Lord.
For King Nebuchadrezzar of Babylon
has made a plan against you
and formed a purpose against you.

31 Rise up, advance against a nation at ease,
that lives secure,
says the Lord,
that has no gates or bars,
that lives alone.
32 Their camels shall become booty,
their herds of cattle a spoil.
I will scatter to every wind
those who have shaven temples,

and I will bring calamity
against them from every side,
says the Lord.
33 Hazor shall become a lair of jackals,
an everlasting waste;
no one shall live there,
nor shall anyone settle in it.

Judgment on Elam

34 The word of the Lord that came to the prophet Jeremiah concerning Elam, at the beginning of the reign of King Zedekiah of Judah.

35 Thus says the Lord of hosts: I am going to break the bow of Elam, the mainstay of their might; 36and I will bring upon Elam the four winds from the four quarters of heaven; and I will scatter them to all these winds, and there shall be no nation to which the exiles from Elam shall not come. 37I will terrify Elam before their enemies, and before those who seek their life; I will bring disaster upon them, my fierce anger, says the Lord. I will send the sword after them, until I have consumed them; 38and I will set my throne in Elam, and destroy their king and officials, says the Lord.

39 But in the latter days I will restore the fortunes of Elam, says the Lord.

50 Judgment on Babylon

The word that the Lord spoke concerning Babylon, concerning the land of the Chaldeans, by the prophet Jeremiah:
2 Declare among the nations and proclaim,
set up a banner and proclaim,
do not conceal it, say:
Babylon is taken,
Bel is put to shame,
Merodach is dismayed.
Her images are put to shame,
her idols are dismayed.

3 For out of the north a nation has come up against her; it shall make her land a desolation, and no one shall live in it; both human beings and animals shall flee away.

4 In those days and in that time, says the Lord, the people of Israel shall come, they and the people of Judah together; they shall come weeping as they seek the Lord their God. 5They shall ask the way to Zion, with faces turned toward it, and they shall come and join*d* themselves to the Lord by an everlasting covenant that will never be forgotten.

6 My people have been lost sheep; their shepherds have led them astray, turning them away on the mountains; from mountain to hill they have gone, they have forgotten their fold.

a Cn: Heb *there is trouble in the sea*   *b* Vg: Heb *is not forsaken*   *c* Syr Vg Tg: Heb *the town of my joy*   *d* Gk: Heb *toward it. Come! They shall join*

[7] All who found them have devoured them, and their enemies have said, "We are not guilty, because they have sinned against the LORD, the true pasture, the LORD, the hope of their ancestors."

8 Flee from Babylon, and go out of the land of the Chaldeans, and be like male goats leading the flock. [9] For I am going to stir up and bring against Babylon a company of great nations from the land of the north; and they shall array themselves against her; from there she shall be taken. Their arrows are like the arrows of a skilled warrior who does not return empty-handed. [10] Chaldea shall be plundered; all who plunder her shall be sated, says the LORD.

[11] Though you rejoice, though you exult,
    O plunderers of my heritage,
though you frisk about like a heifer on the
      grass,
    and neigh like stallions,
[12] your mother shall be utterly shamed,
    and she who bore you shall be disgraced.
Lo, she shall be the last of the nations,
    a wilderness, dry land, and a desert.
[13] Because of the wrath of the LORD she shall
    not be inhabited,
    but shall be an utter desolation;
everyone who passes by Babylon shall be
    appalled
    and hiss because of all her wounds.
[14] Take up your positions around Babylon,
    all you that bend the bow;
shoot at her, spare no arrows,
    for she has sinned against the LORD.
[15] Raise a shout against her from all sides,
    "She has surrendered;
her bulwarks have fallen,
    her walls are thrown down."
For this is the vengeance of the LORD:
    take vengeance on her,
    do to her as she has done.
[16] Cut off from Babylon the sower,
    and the wielder of the sickle in time of
      harvest;
because of the destroying sword
    all of them shall return to their own
      people,
    and all of them shall flee to their own
      land.

17 Israel is a hunted sheep driven away by lions. First the king of Assyria devoured it, and now at the end King Nebuchadrezzar of Babylon has gnawed its bones. [18] Therefore, thus says the LORD of hosts, the God of Israel: I am going to punish the king of Babylon and his land, as I punished the king of Assyria. [19] I will restore Israel to its pasture, and it shall feed on Carmel and in Bashan, and on the hills of Ephraim and in Gilead its hunger shall be satisfied. [20] In those days and at that time, says the LORD, the iniquity of Israel shall be sought, and there shall be none; and the sins of Judah, and none shall be found; for I will pardon the remnant that I have spared.

[21] Go up to the land of Merathaim;[a]
    go up against her,
and attack the inhabitants of Pekod[b]
    and utterly destroy the last of them,[c]
                  says the LORD;
    do all that I have commanded you.
[22] The noise of battle is in the land,
    and great destruction!
[23] How the hammer of the whole earth
    is cut down and broken!
How Babylon has become
    a horror among the nations!
[24] You set a snare for yourself and you were
      caught, O Babylon,
    but you did not know it;
you were discovered and seized,
    because you challenged the LORD.
[25] The LORD has opened his armory,
    and brought out the weapons of his
      wrath,
for the Lord GOD of hosts has a task to do
    in the land of the Chaldeans.
[26] Come against her from every quarter;
    open her granaries;
pile her up like heaps of grain, and destroy
      her utterly;
    let nothing be left of her.
[27] Kill all her bulls,
    let them go down to the slaughter.
Alas for them, their day has come,
    the time of their punishment!

28 Listen! Fugitives and refugees from the land of Babylon are coming to declare in Zion the vengeance of the LORD our God, vengeance for his temple.

29 Summon archers against Babylon, all who bend the bow. Encamp all around her; let no one escape. Repay her according to her deeds; just as she has done, do to her—for she has arrogantly defied the LORD, the Holy One

"Come, take a closer walk with me."
—God speaking to Bruce,
in the movie
Bruce Almighty

a Or of Double Rebellion b Or of Punishment c Tg: Heb destroy after them

that they may be dried up!
For it is a land of images,
and they go mad over idols.

39 Therefore wild animals shall live with hyenas in Babylon,ᶜ and ostriches shall inhabit her; she shall never again be peopled, or inhabited for all generations. ⁴⁰As when God overthrew Sodom and Gomorrah and their neighbors, says the Lord, so no one shall live there, nor shall anyone settle in her.

⁴¹ Look, a people is coming from the north;
a mighty nation and many kings
are stirring from the farthest parts of the earth.
⁴² They wield bow and spear,
they are cruel and have no mercy.
The sound of them is like the roaring sea;
they ride upon horses,
set in array as a warrior for battle,
against you, O daughter Babylon!

⁴³ The king of Babylon heard news of them,
and his hands fell helpless;
anguish seized him,
pain like that of a woman in labor.

44 Like a lion coming up from the thickets of the Jordan against a perennial pasture, I will suddenly chase them away from her; and I will appoint over her whomever I choose.ᵈ For who is like me? Who can summon me? Who is the shepherd who can stand before me? ⁴⁵Therefore hear the plan that the Lord has made against Babylon, and the purposes that he has formed against the land of the Chaldeans: Surely the little ones of the flock shall be dragged away; surely theirᵉ fold shall be appalled at their fate. ⁴⁶At the sound of the capture of Babylon the earth shall tremble, and her cry shall be heard among the nations.

51 Thus says the Lord:
I am going to stir up a destructive windᶠ
against Babylon
and against the inhabitants of
Leb-qamai;ᵍ
² and I will send winnowers to Babylon,
and they shall winnow her.
They shall empty her land
when they come against her from every side
on the day of trouble.
³ Let not the archer bend his bow,
and let him not array himself in his coat
of mail.
Do not spare her young men;
utterly destroy her entire army.

of Israel. ³⁰Therefore her young men shall fall in her squares, and all her soldiers shall be destroyed on that day, says the Lord.

³¹ I am against you, O arrogant one,
says the Lord God of hosts;
for your day has come,
the time when I will punish you.
³² The arrogant one shall stumble and fall,
with no one to raise him up,
and I will kindle a fire in his cities,
and it will devour everything around
him.

33 Thus says the Lord of hosts: The people of Israel are oppressed, and so too are the people of Judah; all their captors have held them fast and refuse to let them go. ³⁴Their Redeemer is strong; the Lord of hosts is his name. He will surely plead their cause, that he may give rest to the earth, but unrest to the inhabitants of Babylon.

³⁵ A sword against the Chaldeans, says the
Lord,
and against the inhabitants of Babylon,
and against her officials and her sages!
³⁶ A sword against the diviners,
so that they may become fools!
A sword against her warriors,
so that they may be destroyed!
³⁷ A sword against herᵃ horses and against
herᵃ chariots,
and against all the foreign troops in her
midst,
so that they may become women!
A sword against all her treasures,
that they may be plundered!
³⁸ A droughtᵇ against her waters,

a Cn: Heb his b Another reading is A sword c Heb lacks in Babylon d Or and I will single out the choicest of her rams: Meaning of Heb uncertain e Syr Gk Tg Compare 49.20: Heb lacks their f Or stir up the spirit of a destroyer g Leb-qamai is a cryptogram for Kasdim, Chaldea

4 They shall fall down slain in the land of the
Chaldeans,
and wounded in her streets.
5 Israel and Judah have not been forsaken
by their God, the LORD of hosts,
though their land is full of guilt
before the Holy One of Israel.

6 Flee from the midst of Babylon,
save your lives, each of you!
Do not perish because of her guilt,
for this is the time of the LORD's
vengeance;
he is repaying her what is due.
7 Babylon was a golden cup in the LORD's
hand,
making all the earth drunken;
the nations drank of her wine,
and so the nations went mad.
8 Suddenly Babylon has fallen and is shattered;
wail for her!
Bring balm for her wound;
perhaps she may be healed.
9 We tried to heal Babylon,
but she could not be healed.
Forsake her, and let each of us go
to our own country;
for her judgment has reached up to heaven
and has been lifted up even to the skies.
10 The LORD has brought forth our vindication;
come, let us declare in Zion
the work of the LORD our God.

11 Sharpen the arrows!
Fill the quivers!
The LORD has stirred up the spirit of the kings
of the Medes, because his purpose concerning Babylon is to destroy it, for that is the vengeance of the LORD, vengeance for his temple.
12 Raise a standard against the walls of
Babylon;
make the watch strong;
post sentinels;
prepare the ambushes;
for the LORD has both planned and done
what he spoke concerning the
inhabitants of Babylon.
13 You who live by mighty waters,
rich in treasures,
your end has come,
the thread of your life is cut.
14 The LORD of hosts has sworn by himself:
Surely I will fill you with troops like a swarm
of locusts,
and they shall raise a shout of victory
over you.

15 It is he who made the earth by his power,
who established the world by his wisdom,
and by his understanding stretched out the
heavens.
16 When he utters his voice there is a tumult of
waters in the heavens,
and he makes the mist rise from the ends
of the earth.
He makes lightnings for the rain,
and he brings out the wind from his
storehouses.
17 Everyone is stupid and without knowledge;
goldsmiths are all put to shame by their
idols;
for their images are false,
and there is no breath in them.
18 They are worthless, a work of delusion;
at the time of their punishment they
shall perish.
19 Not like these is the LORD,[a] the portion of
Jacob,
for he is the one who formed all things,
and Israel is the tribe of his inheritance;
the LORD of hosts is his name.

Israel the Creator's Instrument
20 You are my war club, my weapon of battle:
with you I smash nations;
with you I destroy kingdoms;
21 with you I smash the horse and its rider;
with you I smash the chariot and the
charioteer;
22 with you I smash man and woman;
with you I smash the old man and the
boy;
with you I smash the young man and the
girl;
23 with you I smash shepherds and their
flocks;
with you I smash farmers and their teams;
with you I smash governors and deputies.

The Doom of Babylon
24 I will repay Babylon and all the inhabitants of Chaldea before your very eyes for all
the wrong that they have done in Zion, says the
LORD.

25 I am against you, O destroying mountain,
says the LORD,
that destroys the whole earth;
I will stretch out my hand against you,
and roll you down from the crags,
and make you a burned-out mountain.
26 No stone shall be taken from you for a
corner
and no stone for a foundation,
but you shall be a perpetual waste,
says the LORD.

a Heb lacks the LORD

²⁷ Raise a standard in the land,
  blow the trumpet among the nations;
prepare the nations for war against her,
  summon against her the kingdoms,
  Ararat, Minni, and Ashkenaz;
appoint a marshal against her,
  bring up horses like bristling locusts.
²⁸ Prepare the nations for war against her,
  the kings of the Medes, with their
    governors and deputies,
  and every land under their dominion.
²⁹ The land trembles and writhes,
  for the LORD's purposes against Babylon
    stand,
to make the land of Babylon a desolation,
  without inhabitant.
³⁰ The warriors of Babylon have given up
    fighting,
  they remain in their strongholds;
their strength has failed,
  they have become women;
her buildings are set on fire,
  her bars are broken.
³¹ One runner runs to meet another,
  and one messenger to meet another,
to tell the king of Babylon
  that his city is taken from end to end:
³² the fords have been seized,
  the marshes have been burned with fire,
  and the soldiers are in panic.
³³ For thus says the LORD of hosts, the God of
    Israel:
Daughter Babylon is like a threshing floor
  at the time when it is trodden;
yet a little while
  and the time of her harvest will come.

³⁴ "King Nebuchadrezzar of Babylon has
    devoured me,
  he has crushed me;
he has made me an empty vessel,
  he has swallowed me like a monster;
he has filled his belly with my delicacies,
  he has spewed me out.
³⁵ May my torn flesh be avenged on Babylon,"
  the inhabitants of Zion shall say.
"May my blood be avenged on the
    inhabitants of Chaldea,"
  Jerusalem shall say.
³⁶ Therefore thus says the LORD:
I am going to defend your cause
  and take vengeance for you.
I will dry up her sea
  and make her fountain dry;
³⁷ and Babylon shall become a heap of ruins,
  a den of jackals,
an object of horror and of hissing,
  without inhabitant.

³⁸ Like lions they shall roar together;
  they shall growl like lions' whelps.
³⁹ When they are inflamed, I will set out their
    drink
  and make them drunk, until they
    become merry
and then sleep a perpetual sleep
  and never wake, says the LORD.
⁴⁰ I will bring them down like lambs to the
    slaughter,
  like rams and goats.

⁴¹ How Sheshach^a is taken,
  the pride of the whole earth seized!
How Babylon has become
  an object of horror among the nations!
⁴² The sea has risen over Babylon;
  she has been covered by its tumultuous
    waves.
⁴³ Her cities have become an object of horror,
  a land of drought and a desert,
a land in which no one lives,
  and through which no mortal passes.
⁴⁴ I will punish Bel in Babylon,
  and make him disgorge what he has
    swallowed.
The nations shall no longer stream to him;
  the wall of Babylon has fallen.

⁴⁵ Come out of her, my people!
  Save your lives, each of you,
  from the fierce anger of the LORD!
⁴⁶ Do not be fainthearted or fearful
  at the rumors heard in the land—
one year one rumor comes,
  the next year another,
rumors of violence in the land
  and of ruler against ruler.

⁴⁷ Assuredly, the days are coming
  when I will punish the images of
    Babylon;
her whole land shall be put to shame,
  and all her slain shall fall in her midst.
⁴⁸ Then the heavens and the earth,
  and all that is in them,
shall shout for joy over Babylon;
  for the destroyers shall come against
    them out of the north,
        says the LORD.
⁴⁹ Babylon must fall for the slain of Israel,
  as the slain of all the earth have fallen
    because of Babylon.

⁵⁰ You survivors of the sword,
  go, do not linger!
Remember the LORD in a distant land,
  and let Jerusalem come into your mind:

---

a Sheshach is a cryptogram for *Babel,* Babylon

⁵¹ We are put to shame, for we have heard
insults;
dishonor has covered our face,
for aliens have come
into the holy places of the LORD's house.

⁵² Therefore the time is surely coming, says
the LORD,
when I will punish her idols,
and through all her land
the wounded shall groan.

⁵³ Though Babylon should mount up to heaven,
and though she should fortify her strong
height,
from me destroyers would come upon her,
says the LORD.

⁵⁴ Listen!—a cry from Babylon!
A great crashing from the land of the
Chaldeans!

⁵⁵ For the LORD is laying Babylon waste,
and stilling her loud clamor.
Their waves roar like mighty waters,
the sound of their clamor resounds;

⁵⁶ for a destroyer has come against her,
against Babylon;
her warriors are taken,
their bows are broken;
for the LORD is a God of recompense,
he will repay in full.

⁵⁷ I will make her officials and her sages drunk,
also her governors, her deputies, and her
warriors;
they shall sleep a perpetual sleep and never
wake,
says the King, whose name is the LORD of
hosts.

⁵⁸ Thus says the LORD of hosts:
The broad wall of Babylon

shall be leveled to the ground,
and her high gates
shall be burned with fire.
The peoples exhaust themselves for nothing,
and the nations weary themselves only
for fire.ᵃ

Jeremiah's Command to Seraiah

59 The word that the prophet Jeremiah commanded Seraiah son of Neriah son of Mahseiah, when he went with King Zedekiah of Judah
to Babylon, in the fourth year of his reign. Seraiah was the quartermaster. ⁶⁰Jeremiah wrote
in aᵇ scroll all the disasters that would come on
Babylon, all these words that are written concerning Babylon. ⁶¹And Jeremiah said to Seraiah: "When you come to Babylon, see that
you read all these words, ⁶²and say, 'O LORD,
you yourself threatened to destroy this place
so that neither human beings nor animals
shall live in it, and it shall be desolate forever.' ⁶³When you finish reading this scroll, tie a
stone to it, and throw it into the middle of the
Euphrates, ⁶⁴and say, 'Thus shall Babylon sink,
to rise no more, because of the disasters that I
am bringing on her.' "ᶜ
Thus far are the words of Jeremiah.

52 The Destruction of Jerusalem Reviewed

Zedekiah was twenty-one years old when he
began to reign; he reigned eleven years in Jerusalem. His mother's name was Hamutal daughter of Jeremiah of Libnah. ²He did what was evil
in the sight of the LORD, just as Jehoiakim had
done. ³Indeed, Jerusalem and Judah so angered the LORD that he expelled them from his
presence.
Zedekiah rebelled against the king of Bab-

ᵃ Gk Syr Compare Hab 2.13: Heb *and the nations for fire, and they are weary* ᵇ Or *one* ᶜ Gk: Heb *on her. And they shall weary themselves* ylon. ⁴And in the ninth year of his reign, in the tenth month, on the tenth day of the month, King Nebuchadrezzar of Babylon came with all his army against Jerusalem, and they laid siege to it; they built siegeworks against it all around. ⁵So the city was besieged until the eleventh year of King Zedekiah. ⁶On the ninth day of the fourth month the famine became so severe in the city that there was no food for the people of the land. ⁷Then a breach was made in the city wall;ᵃ and all the soldiers fled and went out from the city by night by the way of the gate between the two walls, by the king's garden, though the Chaldeans were all around the city. They went in the direction of the Arabah. ⁸But the army of the Chaldeans pursued the king, and overtook Zedekiah in the plains of Jericho; and all his army was scattered, deserting him. ⁹Then they captured the king, and brought him up to the king of Babylon at Riblah in the land of Hamath, and he passed sentence on him. ¹⁰The king of Babylon killed the sons of Zedekiah before his eyes, and also killed all the officers of Judah at Riblah. ¹¹He put out the eyes of Zedekiah, and bound him in fetters, and the king of Babylon took him to Babylon, and put him in prison until the day of his death.

12 In the fifth month, on the tenth day of the month—which was the nineteenth year of King Nebuchadrezzar, king of Babylon—Nebuzaradan the captain of the bodyguard who served the king of Babylon, entered Jerusalem. ¹³He burned the house of the Lᴏʀᴅ, the king's house, and all the houses of Jerusalem; every great house he burned down. ¹⁴All the army of the Chaldeans, who were with the captain of the guard, broke down all the walls around Jerusalem. ¹⁵Nebuzaradan the captain of the guard carried into exile some of the poorest of the people and the rest of the people who were left in the city and the deserters who had defected to the king of Babylon, together with the rest of the artisans. ¹⁶But Nebuzaradan the captain of the guard left some of the poorest people of the land to be vinedressers and tillers of the soil.

17 The pillars of bronze that were in the house of the Lᴏʀᴅ, and the stands and the bronze sea that were in the house of the Lᴏʀᴅ, the Chaldeans broke in pieces, and carried all the bronze to Babylon. ¹⁸They took away the pots, the shovels, the snuffers, the basins, the ladles, and all the vessels of bronze used in the temple service. ¹⁹The captain of the guard took away the small bowls also, the firepans, the basins, the pots, the lampstands, the ladles, and the bowls for libation, both those of gold and those of silver. ²⁰As for the two pillars, the one sea, the twelve bronze bulls that were under the sea, and the stands,ᵇ which King Solomon had made for the house of the Lᴏʀᴅ, the bronze of all these vessels was beyond weighing. ²¹As for the pillars, the height of the one pillar was eighteen cubits, its circumference was twelve cubits; it was hollow and its thickness was four fingers. ²²Upon it was a capital of bronze; the height of the capital was five cubits; latticework and pomegranates, all of bronze, encircled the top of the capital. And the second pillar had the same, with pomegranates. ²³There were ninety-six pomegranates on the sides; all the pomegranates encircling the latticework numbered one hundred.

24 The captain of the guard took the chief priest Seraiah, the second priest Zephaniah, and the three guardians of the threshold; ²⁵and from the city he took an officer who had been in command of the soldiers, and seven men of the king's council who were found in the city; the secretary of the commander of the army who mustered the people of the land; and sixty men of the people of the land who were found inside the city. ²⁶Then Nebuzaradan the captain of the guard took them, and brought them to the king of Babylon at Riblah. ²⁷And the king of Babylon struck them down, and put them to death at Riblah in the land of Hamath. So Judah went into exile out of its land.

28 This is the number of the people whom Nebuchadrezzar took into exile: in the seventh year, three thousand twenty-three Judeans; ²⁹in the eighteenth year of Nebuchadrezzar he took into exile from Jerusalem eight hundred thirty-two persons; ³⁰in the twenty-third year of Nebuchadrezzar, Nebuzaradan the captain of the guard took into exile of the Judeans seven hundred forty-five persons; all the persons were four thousand six hundred.

Jehoiachin Favored in Captivity

31 In the thirty-seventh year of the exile of King Jehoiachin of Judah, in the twelfth month, on the twenty-fifth day of the month, King Evil-merodach of Babylon, in the year he began to reign, showed favor to King Jehoiachin of Judah and brought him out of prison; ³²he spoke kindly to him, and gave him a seat above the seats of the other kings who were with him in Babylon. ³³So Jehoiachin put aside his prison clothes, and every day of his life he dined regularly at the king's table. ³⁴For his allowance, a regular daily allowance was given him by the king of Babylon, as long as he lived, up to the day of his death.

---

a Heb lacks *wall* *b* Cn: Heb *that were under the stands*

LAMENTATIONS

THE WEEPING CITY

A Time to Mourn

The news breaks that someone at school has committed suicide. A few seconds later you hear that it was one of your friends.

What would you say? Would there even be *words* for that?

We may cry when a friend moves away or when a family member dies. We may feel torn up inside when something tragic like suicide, a school shooting, or a terrorist act happens. But imagine the agony you'd feel if your *nation* was destroyed. Imagine mourning the loss of an entire nation of people. Imagine that you are the lookout who is the first to see invaders pouring across your borders, knowing that soon your homeland will be totally demolished. Now imagine that you try your hardest to warn the people around you, but no one listens. They dismiss you as a traitor, a naysayer, a cynic.

In other words, imagine you're in Jeremiah's shoes.

Jeremiah saw the coming power of the Chaldeans, the growing Babylonian Empire that would envelop the Middle East like the dark cloud of Mordor in *The Lord of the Rings*. What was left of the once great kingdom of David and Solomon was about to be destroyed. The great story of God's people being freed from slavery and oppression to receive a land of their own was coming to ruin. All Jeremiah could do was weep.

This book is his poem. These words are his tears. These stanzas are the sorrow of his heart. It's a poem of confession and repentance, a declaration of submission to God's will, a desperate prayer for God to intercede and restore his people.

> **"If I am in sorrow, my sorrow may serve Him. . . . He does nothing in vain."**
> —Bl. Cardinal John Henry Newman

WHO Traditionally attributed to the prophet Jeremiah

WHAT The word *lamentation* means "an expression of tremendous grief and deep sadness." The book of Lamentations fits this definition perfectly. It's a sorrow-filled poem describing the tragedy of Jerusalem's fall to Babylon.

WHEN It was likely written shortly after the destruction of Jerusalem in 586 B.C.

WHERE Jeremiah prophesied in Judah (located in the southern part of modern-day Israel/Palestine).

 ## PATH OF DISCIPLESHIP

In Lamentations Jeremiah weeps and prays for Jerusalem—the sins of its inhabitants and the resulting horror that had come at the hands of the Babylonians (see 1.1–5). Jesus, soon before he's crucified, also weeps for Jerusalem as he prays. In his prayer he scolds Israel for killing its prophets (Luke 19.41–44).

Whether Jesus was referring to the coming Roman conquest or a spiritual ruin, he joins Jeremiah in mourning the sins of his people.

1 The Deserted City

How lonely sits the city
    that once was full of people!
How like a widow she has become,
    she that was great among the nations!
She that was a princess among the
            provinces
    has become a vassal.

2 She weeps bitterly in the night,
    with tears on her cheeks;
among all her lovers
    she has no one to comfort her;
all her friends have dealt treacherously with
            her,
    they have become her enemies.

3 Judah has gone into exile with suffering
    and hard servitude;
she lives now among the nations,
    and finds no resting place;
her pursuers have all overtaken her
    in the midst of her distress.

4 The roads to Zion mourn,
    for no one comes to the festivals;
all her gates are desolate,
    her priests groan;
her young girls grieve, *a*
    and her lot is bitter.

5 Her foes have become the masters,
    her enemies prosper,
because the LORD has made her suffer
    for the multitude of her transgressions;
her children have gone away,
    captives before the foe.

6 From daughter Zion has departed
    all her majesty.
Her princes have become like stags
    that find no pasture;
they fled without strength
    before the pursuer.

7 Jerusalem remembers,
    in the days of her affliction and
            wandering,
all the precious things
    that were hers in days of old.
When her people fell into the hand of the
            foe,

a Meaning of Heb uncertain

and there was no one to help her,
    the foe looked on mocking
        over her downfall.

8 Jerusalem sinned grievously,
    so she has become a mockery;
all who honored her despise her,
    for they have seen her nakedness;
she herself groans,
    and turns her face away.

9 Her uncleanness was in her skirts;
    she took no thought of her future;
her downfall was appalling,
    with none to comfort her.
"O LORD, look at my affliction,
    for the enemy has triumphed!"

10 Enemies have stretched out their hands
    over all her precious things;
she has even seen the nations
    invade her sanctuary,
those whom you forbade
    to enter your congregation.

11 All her people groan
    as they search for bread;
they trade their treasures for food
    to revive their strength.
Look, O LORD, and see
    how worthless I have become.

12 Is it nothing to you, *a* all you who pass by?
    Look and see
if there is any sorrow like my sorrow,
    which was brought upon me,
which the LORD inflicted
    on the day of his fierce anger.

13 From on high he sent fire;
    it went deep into my bones;
he spread a net for my feet;
    he turned me back;
he has left me stunned,
    faint all day long.

14 My transgressions were bound *a* into a yoke;
    by his hand they were fastened together;
they weigh on my neck,
    sapping my strength;
the Lord handed me over
    to those whom I cannot withstand.

15 The LORD has rejected
    all my warriors in the midst of me;
he proclaimed a time against me
    to crush my young men;
the Lord has trodden as in a wine press
    the virgin daughter Judah.

16 For these things I weep;
    my eyes flow with tears;

for a comforter is far from me,
  one to revive my courage;
my children are desolate,
  for the enemy has prevailed.

17 Zion stretches out her hands,
    but there is no one to comfort her;
the LORD has commanded against Jacob
    that his neighbors should become his
      foes;
Jerusalem has become
    a filthy thing among them.

18 The LORD is in the right,
    for I have rebelled against his word;
but hear, all you peoples,
    and behold my suffering;
my young women and young men
    have gone into captivity.

19 I called to my lovers
    but they deceived me;
my priests and elders
    perished in the city
while seeking food
    to revive their strength.

20 See, O LORD, how distressed I am;
    my stomach churns,
my heart is wrung within me,
    because I have been very rebellious.
In the street the sword bereaves;
    in the house it is like death.

21 They heard how I was groaning,
    with no one to comfort me.
All my enemies heard of my trouble;
    they are glad that you have done it.
Bring on the day you have announced,
    and let them be as I am.

22 Let all their evil doing come before you;
    and deal with them
as you have dealt with me
    because of all my transgressions;
for my groans are many
    and my heart is faint.

2 God's Warnings Fulfilled

How the Lord in his anger
  has humiliated[a] daughter Zion!
He has thrown down from heaven to earth
  the splendor of Israel;
he has not remembered his footstool
  in the day of his anger.

2 The Lord has destroyed without mercy
    all the dwellings of Jacob;
in his wrath he has broken down
    the strongholds of daughter Judah;

---

a Meaning of Heb uncertain

---

he has brought down to the ground in
    dishonor
  the kingdom and its rulers.

3 He has cut down in fierce anger
    all the might of Israel;
he has withdrawn his right hand from them
    in the face of the enemy;
he has burned like a flaming fire in Jacob,
    consuming all around.

4 He has bent his bow like an enemy,
    with his right hand set like a foe;
he has killed all in whom we took pride
    in the tent of daughter Zion;
he has poured out his fury like fire.

5 The Lord has become like an enemy;
    he has destroyed Israel.
He has destroyed all its palaces,
    laid in ruins its strongholds,
and multiplied in daughter Judah
    mourning and lamentation.

6 He has broken down his booth like a garden,
    he has destroyed his tabernacle;
the LORD has abolished in Zion
    festival and sabbath,
and in his fierce indignation has spurned
    king and priest.

7 The Lord has scorned his altar,
    disowned his sanctuary;
he has delivered into the hand of the enemy
    the walls of her palaces;
a clamor was raised in the house of the LORD
    as on a day of festival.

8 The LORD determined to lay in ruins
    the wall of daughter Zion;
he stretched the line;
    he did not withhold his hand from
      destroying;
he caused rampart and wall to lament;
    they languish together.

9 Her gates have sunk into the ground;
    he has ruined and broken her bars;
her king and princes are among the nations;
    guidance is no more,
and her prophets obtain
    no vision from the LORD.

10 The elders of daughter Zion
    sit on the ground in silence;
they have thrown dust on their heads
    and put on sackcloth;
the young girls of Jerusalem
    have bowed their heads to the ground.

11 My eyes are spent with weeping;
    my stomach churns;

my bile is poured out on the ground
because of the destruction of my people,
because infants and babes faint
in the streets of the city.

12 They cry to their mothers,
"Where is bread and wine?"
as they faint like the wounded
in the streets of the city,
as their life is poured out
on their mothers' bosom.

13 What can I say for you, to what compare you,
O daughter Jerusalem?
To what can I liken you, that I may comfort
you,
O virgin daughter Zion?
For vast as the sea is your ruin;
who can heal you?

14 Your prophets have seen for you
false and deceptive visions;
they have not exposed your iniquity
to restore your fortunes,
but have seen oracles for you
that are false and misleading.

15 All who pass along the way
clap their hands at you;
they hiss and wag their heads
at daughter Jerusalem;
"Is this the city that was called
the perfection of beauty,
the joy of all the earth?"

16 All your enemies
open their mouths against you;
they hiss, they gnash their teeth,
they cry: "We have devoured her!
Ah, this is the day we longed for;
at last we have seen it!"

17 The LORD has done what he purposed,
he has carried out his threat;
as he ordained long ago,
he has demolished without pity;
he has made the enemy rejoice over you,
and exalted the might of your foes.

18 Cry aloud*a* to the Lord!
O wall of daughter Zion!
Let tears stream down like a torrent
day and night!
Give yourself no rest,
your eyes no respite!

19 Arise, cry out in the night,
at the beginning of the watches!
Pour out your heart like water
before the presence of the Lord!
Lift your hands to him

for the lives of your children,
who faint for hunger
at the head of every street.

20 Look, O LORD, and consider!
To whom have you done this?
Should women eat their offspring,
the children they have borne?
Should priest and prophet be killed
in the sanctuary of the Lord?

21 The young and the old are lying
on the ground in the streets;
my young women and my young men
have fallen by the sword;
in the day of your anger you have killed
them,
slaughtering without mercy.

22 You invited my enemies from all around
as if for a day of festival;
and on the day of the anger of the LORD
no one escaped or survived;
those whom I bore and reared
my enemy has destroyed.

3 **God's Steadfast Love Endures**
I am one who has seen affliction
under the rod of God's*b* wrath;
2 he has driven and brought me
into darkness without any light;
3 against me alone he turns his hand,
again and again, all day long.

4 He has made my flesh and my skin waste
away,
and broken my bones;
5 he has besieged and enveloped me
with bitterness and tribulation;
6 he has made me sit in darkness
like the dead of long ago.

7 He has walled me about so that I cannot
escape;
he has put heavy chains on me;
8 though I call and cry for help,
he shuts out my prayer;
9 he has blocked my ways with hewn stones,
he has made my paths crooked.

10 He is a bear lying in wait for me,
a lion in hiding;
11 he led me off my way and tore me to pieces;
he has made me desolate;
12 he bent his bow and set me
as a mark for his arrow.

13 He shot into my vitals
the arrows of his quiver;
14 I have become the laughingstock of all my
people,

a Cn: Heb *Their heart cried*   b Heb *his*

the object of their taunt-songs all day
long.
¹⁵ He has filled me with bitterness,
he has sated me with wormwood.

¹⁶ He has made my teeth grind on gravel,
and made me cower in ashes;
¹⁷ my soul is bereft of peace;
I have forgotten what happiness is;
¹⁸ so I say, "Gone is my glory,
and all that I had hoped for from the
LORD."

¹⁹ The thought of my affliction and my
homelessness
is wormwood and gall!
²⁰ My soul continually thinks of it
and is bowed down within me.
²¹ But this I call to mind,
and therefore I have hope:

²² The steadfast love of the LORD never ceases,ᵃ
his mercies never come to an end;
²³ they are new every morning;
great is your faithfulness.
²⁴ "The LORD is my portion," says my soul,
"therefore I will hope in him."

²⁵ The LORD is good to those who wait for him,
to the soul that seeks him.
²⁶ It is good that one should wait quietly
for the salvation of the LORD.
²⁷ It is good for one to bear
the yoke in youth,
²⁸ to sit alone in silence
when the Lord has imposed it,
²⁹ to put one's mouth to the dust
(there may yet be hope),
³⁰ to give one's cheek to the smiter,
and be filled with insults.

³¹ For the Lord will not
reject forever.
³² Although he causes grief, he will have
compassion
according to the abundance of his
steadfast love;
³³ for he does not willingly afflict
or grieve anyone.

³⁴ When all the prisoners of the land
are crushed under foot,
³⁵ when human rights are perverted
in the presence of the Most High,
³⁶ when one's case is subverted
—does the Lord not see it?

³⁷ Who can command and have it done,
if the Lord has not ordained it?
³⁸ Is it not from the mouth of the Most High
that good and bad come?

ᵃ Syr Tg: Heb LORD, we are not cut off

TRY THIS ◄

NOT EXACTLY A HAND-CLAPPER

What's your favorite worship song? Take a
moment to think about it or listen to it on your
MP3 player; then write some of your favorite
lyrics from it here:

Many of the songs we sing at Mass today focus
on the uplifting aspects of faith like God's
awesome power, holiness, faithfulness, or love.

Now imagine for a moment a worship song
about these themes: death, depression,
loneliness, heartbreak, sorrow, slavery,
emptiness, violence, anger, bitterness,
devastation. Imagine it set to a popular tune.
Try to picture the parish singing and clapping
along.

Pretty tough.

Read **Lamentations 3**. This isn't a happy song
of praise. Behind it are raw, brutal emotions.
Jeremiah feels as though God has shot him in
the heart. He's dying inside.

Though you'll never be in the same situation
as Jeremiah, you *will* have moments in your
faith journey when your feelings about God are
anything but upbeat and cheery. You may feel
confused, furious, or abandoned. You may look
at the circumstances of your life and feel like
you just want to scream at God.

Lamentations is more than just a depressing
book—it shows us an important truth: we can
come to God with our honest feelings. We don't
have to sanitize our emotions or put on a fake
smile for God. And likewise we don't have to turn
away from God when we're angry or upset. We
can—and should—be real with him. God can
take it.

Find some Creative Space in your Bible and
write your own lament—a poem or song
exploring negative feelings or inner hurts and
how they relate to your faith in God.

GOD IS COMPASSIONATE   MY SELF

39 Why should any who draw breath complain
about the punishment of their sins?

40 Let us test and examine our ways,
and return to the LORD.
41 Let us lift up our hearts as well as our hands
to God in heaven.
42 We have transgressed and rebelled,
and you have not forgiven.

43 You have wrapped yourself with anger and
pursued us,
killing without pity;
44 you have wrapped yourself with a cloud
so that no prayer can pass through.
45 You have made us filth and rubbish
among the peoples.

46 All our enemies
have opened their mouths against us;
47 panic and pitfall have come upon us,
devastation and destruction.
48 My eyes flow with rivers of tears
because of the destruction of my people.

49 My eyes will flow without ceasing,
without respite,
50 until the LORD from heaven
looks down and sees.
51 My eyes cause me grief
at the fate of all the young women in my
city.

52 Those who were my enemies without cause
have hunted me like a bird;
53 they flung me alive into a pit
and hurled stones on me;
54 water closed over my head;
I said, "I am lost."

55 I called on your name, O LORD,
from the depths of the pit;
56 you heard my plea, "Do not close your ear
to my cry for help, but give me relief!"
57 You came near when I called on you;
you said, "Do not fear!"

58 You have taken up my cause, O Lord,
you have redeemed my life.
59 You have seen the wrong done to me,
O LORD;
judge my cause.
60 You have seen all their malice,
all their plots against me.

61 You have heard their taunts, O LORD,
all their plots against me.
62 The whispers and murmurs of my assailants
are against me all day long.
63 Whether they sit or rise—see,
I am the object of their taunt-songs.

64 Pay them back for their deeds, O LORD,
according to the work of their hands!
65 Give them anguish of heart;
your curse be on them!
66 Pursue them in anger and destroy them
from under the LORD's heavens.

4 The Punishment of Zion

How the gold has grown dim,
how the pure gold is changed!
The sacred stones lie scattered
at the head of every street.

2 The precious children of Zion,
worth their weight in fine gold—
how they are reckoned as earthen pots,
the work of a potter's hands!

3 Even the jackals offer the breast
and nurse their young,
but my people has become cruel,
like the ostriches in the wilderness.

4 The tongue of the infant sticks
to the roof of its mouth for thirst;
the children beg for food,
but no one gives them anything.

5 Those who feasted on delicacies
perish in the streets;
those who were brought up in purple
cling to ash heaps.

6 For the chastisement*a* of my people has
been greater
than the punishment*b* of Sodom,
which was overthrown in a moment,
though no hand was laid on it.*c*

7 Her princes were purer than snow,
whiter than milk;
their bodies were more ruddy than coral,
their hair*c* like sapphire.*d*

8 Now their visage is blacker than soot;
they are not recognized in the streets.
Their skin has shriveled on their bones;
it has become as dry as wood.

9 Happier were those pierced by the
sword
than those pierced by hunger,
whose life drains away, deprived
of the produce of the field.

10 The hands of compassionate women
have boiled their own children;
they became their food
in the destruction of my people.

11 The LORD gave full vent to his wrath;
he poured out his hot anger,

---

a Or *iniquity* *b* Or *sin* *c* Meaning of Heb uncertain *d* Or *lapis lazuli*

Presence

As time flies
There have been many tries
To be Here.
Some have failed,
Most succeed.
You dazzle and amaze
Like sparks through a haze
Or lights at the ends of a maze.
Your soft touch,
My leap, you a crutch.
The love pours out.
Some will scream,
Others shout,
The greatness Here,
Works from inside out.
Better Here for now
Than there for who knows how,
Long. A moment in time
More precious than a shiny dime.
You are Here.

REALITY

CRY OUT TO GOD

The book of Lamentations is a collection of heartfelt and heart-wrenching prayers to God. It expresses the grief of the writer and mirrors the grief of the Israelites as they realized the heart of their faith was now destroyed.

Jesus cried heart-wrenching prayers to God as well. When Lazarus died, Jesus wept and prayed (John 11.33).

Do you ever pray with your feelings? Even when you are angry or sad? For some reason, lots of people don't connect their "hard" feelings with praying. It's easy to just turn God off when we're mad or sad. Why do we do this? Do we think that God will be disappointed in us? Or do we blame God somehow for our sorrow or anger?

Consider how you communicate with your best friends. Aren't they the first people you text or call when you are mad or sad? And aren't they the first people who know you are mad or sad even when you haven't said a word? It's the same with God. So pray your feelings. No matter what they are. It will only bring you closer to God.

Prayer involves the totality of our lives— our loves *and* our hates, our successes *and* our failures, our sorrows *and* our joys. It demands an openness of life before God, and trust in an open God before us.

Go to a quiet place. Think about the difficult things in your life or the devastating things that are happening in the world today. Bring to mind some of the images you have seen on TV or the Internet. Jot down some of the phrases you could bring to a prayer of lament and write your own prayer of lament for our world today. Post your prayer at **Learner.CalltoDiscipleship.com**.

and kindled a fire in Zion
  that consumed its foundations.

12 The kings of the earth did not believe,
  nor did any of the inhabitants of the
    world,
that foe or enemy could enter
  the gates of Jerusalem.

13 It was for the sins of her prophets
  and the iniquities of her priests,
who shed the blood of the righteous
  in the midst of her.

14 Blindly they wandered through the streets,
  so defiled with blood
that no one was able
  to touch their garments.

15 "Away! Unclean!" people shouted at them;
  "Away! Away! Do not touch!"
So they became fugitives and wanderers;
  it was said among the nations,
  "They shall stay here no longer."

16 The LORD himself has scattered them,
  he will regard them no more;
no honor was shown to the priests,
  no favor to the elders.

17 Our eyes failed, ever watching
  vainly for help;
we were watching eagerly
  for a nation that could not save.

18 They dogged our steps
  so that we could not walk in our streets;
our end drew near; our days were
    numbered;
  for our end had come.

19 Our pursuers were swifter
  than the eagles in the heavens;
they chased us on the mountains,
  they lay in wait for us in the wilderness.

20 The LORD's anointed, the breath of our life,
  was taken in their pits—
the one of whom we said, "Under his
    shadow
  we shall live among the nations."

21 Rejoice and be glad, O daughter Edom,
  you that live in the land of Uz;
but to you also the cup shall pass;
  you shall become drunk and strip
    yourself bare.

22 The punishment of your iniquity,
    O daughter Zion, is accomplished,
  he will keep you in exile no longer;
but your iniquity, O daughter Edom, he will
    punish,
  he will uncover your sins.

5 A Plea for Mercy

Remember, O LORD, what has befallen us;
  look, and see our disgrace!
2 Our inheritance has been turned over to
    strangers,
  our homes to aliens.
3 We have become orphans, fatherless;
  our mothers are like widows.
4 We must pay for the water we drink;
  the wood we get must be bought.
5 With a yoke*a* on our necks we are hard
    driven;
  we are weary, we are given no rest.
6 We have made a pact with*b* Egypt and
    Assyria,
  to get enough bread.
7 Our ancestors sinned; they are no more,
  and we bear their iniquities.
8 Slaves rule over us;
  there is no one to deliver us from their
    hand.
9 We get our bread at the peril of our lives,
  because of the sword in the wilderness.
10 Our skin is black as an oven
  from the scorching heat of famine.
11 Women are raped in Zion,
  virgins in the towns of Judah.
12 Princes are hung up by their hands;
  no respect is shown to the elders.
13 Young men are compelled to grind,
  and boys stagger under loads of wood.
14 The old men have left the city gate,
  the young men their music.
15 The joy of our hearts has ceased;
  our dancing has been turned to
    mourning.
16 The crown has fallen from our head;
  woe to us, for we have sinned!
17 Because of this our hearts are sick,
  because of these things our eyes have
    grown dim:
18 because of Mount Zion, which lies
    desolate;
  jackals prowl over it.

19 But you, O LORD, reign forever;
  your throne endures to all generations.
20 Why have you forgotten us completely?
  Why have you forsaken us these many
    days?
21 Restore us to yourself, O LORD, that we may
    be restored;
  renew our days as of old—
22 unless you have utterly rejected us,
  and are angry with us beyond measure.

a Symmachus: Heb lacks *With a yoke*   *b* Heb *have given the hand to*

CREATIVE SPACE

BARUCH

A PEOPLE IN EXILE

No Matter What, God Is with You

Have you ever felt like things were falling apart around you? Maybe you had to move, leave all of your friends, and be that new kid in school. Or maybe you had a falling out with your best friend, or you broke your leg or got cut from the team. Our country experienced things falling apart when the World Trade Towers were destroyed by terrorists and when the economy tanked. In those kinds of situations we experience great loss. We grieve. We don't feel like doing what we usually enjoy. We try to move on, but it's not easy.

The same was true for the Israelites in the book of Baruch. Things had fallen apart. They were exiled. They could not return home. They had to rebuild. Often when things fall apart we can only make sense of it in bits and pieces. There are lessons to be learned in it and from it, and those lessons can't be hurried. It takes time and effort, patience, repentance, and change. All these subjects are covered in various ways by Baruch.

What Baruch did was give exiles the sense that no matter what, no matter how bad things had gotten, they could turn to God, admit any mistakes they may have made, and start over. If you feel like your world is falling apart, hold on. God will not let you go.

> **"Despair is contrary to God's goodness, to his justice—for the Lord is faithful to his promises—and to his mercy."**
> —Catechism of the Catholic Church 2091

WHO Baruch, the scribe of Jeremiah

WHAT A short collection of prayers and poems meant as a guide for those in exile

WHEN Written in the early second century B.C.; the events took place ca. 587–538 B.C.

WHERE Babylon (in the area now known as Iraq)

 ## PATH OF DISCIPLESHIP

Whether or not you're feeling that things are, will be, or have been falling apart, Baruch gives us a very practical way to grow in faith. You can see it in the way he put his book together for the exiled people. At first the book appears to be a collection of several different, independent writings, yet the writings are well chosen for the homeless exiles who were living in a foreign land. He went back to the stories and prayers of the Hebrew Scriptures that the people were familiar with and put them in context of what the people were experiencing at the time.

There is no "story progression" here, but several different themes emerge from the writings to encourage those in exile. Baruch urged the people to learn from life itself: "Learn where there is wisdom, where there is strength, where there is understanding, so that you may at the same time discern where there is length of days, and life, where there is light for the eyes, and peace" (3.14). That's what we need to do when times are tough. Go back and forth, from Scripture to life and back to Scripture again. Scripture informs life, and life brings Scripture alive.

1 Baruch and the Jews in Babylon

These are the words of the book that Baruch son of Neriah son of Mahseiah son of Zedekiah son of Hasadiah son of Hilkiah wrote in Babylon, ²in the fifth year, on the seventh day of the month, at the time when the Chaldeans took Jerusalem and burned it with fire.

3 Baruch read the words of this book to Jeconiah son of Jehoiakim, king of Judah, and to all the people who came to hear the book, ⁴and to the nobles and the princes, and to the elders, and to all the people, small and great, all who lived in Babylon by the river Sud.

5 Then they wept, and fasted, and prayed before the Lord; ⁶they collected as much money as each could give, ⁷and sent it to Jerusalem to the high priest*a* Jehoiakim son of Hilkiah son of Shallum, and to the priests, and to all the people who were present with him in Jerusalem. ⁸At the same time, on the tenth day of Sivan, Baruch*b* took the vessels of the house of the Lord, which had been carried away from the temple, to return them to the land of Judah—the silver vessels that Zedekiah son of Josiah, king of Judah, had made, ⁹after King Nebuchadnezzar of Babylon had carried away from Jerusalem Jeconiah and the princes and the prisoners and the nobles and the people of the land, and brought them to Babylon.

A Letter to Jerusalem

10 They said: Here we send you money; so buy with the money burnt offerings and sin offerings and incense, and prepare a grain offering, and offer them on the altar of the Lord our God; ¹¹and pray for the life of King Nebuchadnezzar of Babylon, and for the life of his son Belshazzar, so that their days on earth may be like the days of heaven. ¹²The Lord will give us strength, and light to our eyes; we shall live under the protection*c* of King Nebuchadnezzar of Babylon, and under the protection of his son Belshazzar, and we shall serve them many days and find favor in their sight. ¹³Pray also for us to the Lord our God, for we have sinned against the Lord our God, and to this day the anger of the Lord and his wrath have not turned away from us. ¹⁴And you shall read aloud this scroll that we are sending you, to make your confession in the house of the Lord on the days of the festivals and at appointed seasons.

Confession of Sins

15 And you shall say: The Lord our God is in the right, but there is open shame on us today, on the people of Judah, on the inhabitants of Jerusalem, ¹⁶and on our kings, our rulers, our priests, our prophets, and our ancestors, ¹⁷because we have sinned before the Lord. ¹⁸We have disobeyed him, and have not heeded the voice of the Lord our God, to walk in the statutes of the Lord that he set before us. ¹⁹From the time when the Lord brought our ancestors out of the land of Egypt until today, we have been disobedient to the Lord our God, and we have been negligent, in not heeding his voice. ²⁰So to this day there have clung to us the calamities and the curse that the Lord declared through his servant Moses at the time when he brought our ancestors out of the land of Egypt to give to us a land flowing with milk and honey. ²¹We did not listen to the voice of the Lord our God in all the words of the prophets whom he sent to us, ²²but all of us followed the intent of our own wicked hearts by serving other gods and doing what is evil in the sight of the Lord our God.

2

So the Lord carried out the threat he spoke against us: against our judges who ruled Israel, and against our kings and our rulers and the people of Israel and Judah. ²Under the whole heaven there has not been done the like of what he has done in Jerusalem, in accordance with the threats that were*d* written in the law of Moses. ³Some of us ate the flesh of their sons and others the flesh of their daughters. ⁴He made them subject to all the kingdoms around us, to be an object of scorn and a desolation among all the surrounding peoples, where the Lord has scattered them. ⁵They were brought down and not raised up, because our nation*e* sinned against the Lord our God, in not heeding his voice.

6 The Lord our God is in the right, but there is open shame on us and our ancestors this very day. ⁷All those calamities with which the Lord threatened us have come upon us. ⁸Yet we have not entreated the favor of the Lord by turning away, each of us, from the thoughts of our wicked hearts. ⁹And the Lord has kept the calamities ready, and the Lord has brought them upon us, for the Lord is just in all the works that he has commanded us to do. ¹⁰Yet we have not obeyed his voice, to walk in the statutes of the Lord that he set before us.

Prayer for Deliverance

11 And now, O Lord God of Israel, who brought your people out of the land of Egypt with a mighty hand and with signs and wonders and with great power and outstretched arm, and made yourself a name that continues to this day, ¹²we have sinned, we have been ungodly, we have done wrong, O Lord our God, against all your ordinances. ¹³Let your anger turn away from us, for we are left, few in number,

---

a Gk the priest   b Gk he   c Gk in the shadow   d Gk in accordance with what is   e Gk because we among the nations where you have scattered us. [14]Hear, O Lord, our prayer and our supplication, and for your own sake deliver us, and grant us favor in the sight of those who have carried us into exile; [15]so that all the earth may know that you are the Lord our God, for Israel and his descendants are called by your name.

16 O Lord, look down from your holy dwelling, and consider us. Incline your ear, O Lord, and hear; [17]open your eyes, O Lord, and see, for the dead who are in Hades, whose spirit has been taken from their bodies, will not ascribe glory or justice to the Lord; [18]but the person who is deeply grieved, who walks bowed and feeble, with failing eyes and famished soul, will declare your glory and righteousness, O Lord.

19 For it is not because of any righteous deeds of our ancestors or our kings that we bring before you our prayer for mercy, O Lord our God. [20]For you have sent your anger and your wrath upon us, as you declared by your servants the prophets, saying: [21]Thus says the Lord: Bend your shoulders and serve the king of Babylon, and you will remain in the land that I gave to your ancestors. [22]But if you will not obey the voice of the Lord and will not serve the king of Babylon, [23]I will make to cease from the towns of Judah and from the region around Jerusalem the voice of mirth and the voice of gladness, the voice of the bridegroom and the voice of the bride, and the whole land will be a desolation without inhabitants.

24 But we did not obey your voice, to serve the king of Babylon; and you have carried out your threats, which you spoke by your servants the prophets, that the bones of our kings and the bones of our ancestors would be brought out of their resting place; [25]and indeed they have been thrown out to the heat of day and the frost of night. They perished in great misery, by famine and sword and pestilence. [26]And the house that is called by your name you have made as it is today, because of the wickedness of the house of Israel and the house of Judah.

God's Promise Recalled

27 Yet you have dealt with us, O Lord our God, in all your kindness and in all your great compassion, [28]as you spoke by your servant Moses on the day when you commanded him to write your law in the presence of the people of Israel, saying, [29]"If you will not obey my voice, this very great multitude will surely turn into a small number among the nations, where I will scatter them. [30]For I know that they will not obey me, for they are a stiff-necked people. But in the land of their exile they will come to themselves [31]and know that I am the Lord their God. I will give them a heart that obeys and ears

that hear; [32]they will praise me in the land of their exile, and will remember my name [33]and turn from their stubbornness and their wicked deeds; for they will remember the ways of their ancestors, who sinned before the Lord. [34]I will bring them again into the land that I swore to give to their ancestors, to Abraham, Isaac, and Jacob, and they will rule over it; and I will increase them, and they will not be diminished. [35]I will make an everlasting covenant with them to be their God and they shall be my people; and I will never again remove my people Israel from the land that I have given them."

3 O Lord Almighty, God of Israel, the soul in anguish and the wearied spirit cry out to you. [2]Hear, O Lord, and have mercy, for we have sinned before you. [3]For you are enthroned forever, and we are perishing forever. [4]O Lord Almighty, God of Israel, hear now the prayer of

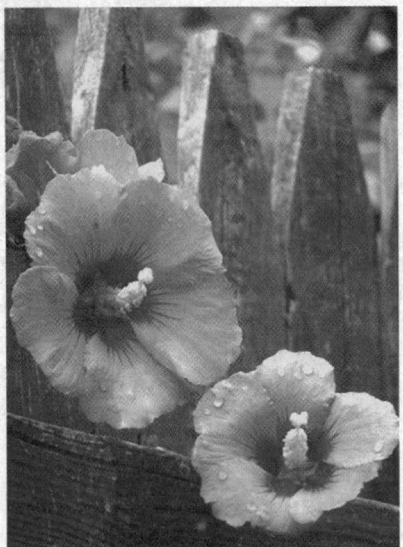

God's Handiwork—© Megan Schoettler, 17

the people[a] of Israel, the children of those who sinned before you, who did not heed the voice of the Lord their God, so that calamities have clung to us. 5 Do not remember the iniquities of our ancestors, but in this crisis remember your power and your name. 6 For you are the Lord our God, and it is you, O Lord, whom we will praise. 7 For you have put the fear of you in our hearts so that we would call upon your name; and we will praise you in our exile, for we have put away from our hearts all the iniquity of our ancestors who sinned against you. 8 See, we are today in our exile where you have scattered us, to be reproached and cursed and punished for all the iniquities of our ancestors, who forsook the Lord our God.

In Praise of Wisdom

9 Hear the commandments of life, O Israel;
  give ear, and learn wisdom!
10 Why is it, O Israel, why is it that you are in
    the land of your enemies,
  that you are growing old in a foreign
    country,
  that you are defiled with the dead,
11 that you are counted among those in
    Hades?
12 You have forsaken the fountain of wisdom.
13 If you had walked in the way of God,
  you would be living in peace forever.
14 Learn where there is wisdom,
  where there is strength,
  where there is understanding,
so that you may at the same time discern
  where there is length of days, and life,
  where there is light for the eyes, and
    peace.
15 Who has found her place?
  And who has entered her storehouses?
16 Where are the rulers of the nations,
  and those who lorded it over the animals
    on earth;
17 those who made sport of the birds of the
    air,
  and who hoarded up silver and gold
in which people trust,
  and there is no end to their getting;
18 those who schemed to get silver, and were
    anxious,
  but there is no trace of their works?
19 They have vanished and gone down to
    Hades,
  and others have arisen in their place.
20 Later generations have seen the light of day,
  and have lived upon the earth;
but they have not learned the way to
    knowledge,
  nor understood her paths,
  nor laid hold of her.
21 Their descendants have strayed far from
    her[b] way.
22 She has not been heard of in Canaan,
  or seen in Teman;
23 the descendants of Hagar, who seek for
    understanding on the earth,
  the merchants of Merran and Teman,
  the story-tellers and the seekers for
    understanding,
have not learned the way to wisdom,
  or given thought to her paths.
24 O Israel, how great is the house of God,
  how vast the territory that he possesses!
25 It is great and has no bounds;
  it is high and immeasurable.
26 The giants were born there, who were
    famous of old,
  great in stature, expert in war.

"We know certainly that our God calls us to a holy life. We know that he gives us every grace, every abundant grace; and though we are so weak of ourselves, this grace is able to carry us through every obstacle and difficulty."

—St. Elizabeth Ann Seton

a Gk *dead* *b* Other ancient authorities read *their*

PROFILE OF FAITH

ST. FRANCES XAVIER CABRINI:
The Immigrant Saint

Plans change, and life can give us some detours. These detours were not an uncommon experience for St. Frances. But no matter what detour she experienced, she persevered to pursue God's best for her life story.

Born in Lombardi, Italy, in 1850, to a large family of thirteen children, St. Frances dreamed of becoming a nun when she was in her teens. Enter detour #1: poor health. Because of her health, she instead got a teaching certificate. After a few years of teaching, her bishop asked her to start a new religious community of women whose mission was to care for poor children in schools and hospitals. Her goal was to become a missionary in China. Enter detour #2: Pope Leo XIII urged her to serve in Chinatown and "Little Italy" on New York's East Side instead. With a willing heart, she went to New York with six other sisters, arriving on March 23, 1889. Enter detour #3: her first meeting with Archbishop Corrigan was unsuccessful, and he told her that her projected orphanage was out of the question. Rather than just packing up and going home, she waited out the archbishop's dismissal and in the end won him over. Displaying his Irish wit, he made peace not with an olive branch, but by personally delivering to her the palm frond he had carried in the Palm Sunday procession.

With the archbishop's blessing St. Frances raised money to buy a house for a convent and orphanage. Soon afterward she began the small hospital that was to become Columbus Hospital and later Cabrini Health Care Center. She was a great influence in helping Italian immigrants adjust to life in a new country and keep their faith.

St. Frances' story inspired others to build hospitals, orphanages, convents, and schools in Italy, France, Spain, Panama, Chile, Argentina, and Brazil as well as throughout the United States. She became an American citizen in Seattle in 1909 and in 1910 was named General Superior of her community for life. Frances was beatified by Pope Pius XI in 1938 and canonized by Pope Pius XII in 1946—the first American citizen to be named a saint. She is the patron saint of immigrants. At the time of her death in 1917, a longtime friend, Cardinal Mundelein of Chicago, recalled the paradox of her dynamic power in so frail a frame and asked: "Does not all this fulfill the concept of a noble woman?"

---

²⁷ God did not choose them,
    or give them the way to knowledge;
²⁸ so they perished because they had no
    wisdom,
    they perished through their folly.

²⁹ Who has gone up into heaven, and taken
    her,
    and brought her down from the clouds?
³⁰ Who has gone over the sea, and found her,
    and will buy her for pure gold?
³¹ No one knows the way to her,
    or is concerned about the path to her.
³² But the one who knows all things knows
    her,
    he found her by his understanding.
    The one who prepared the earth for all time
    filled it with four-footed creatures;

³³ the one who sends forth the light, and it
    goes;
    he called it, and it obeyed him,
    trembling;
³⁴ the stars shone in their watches, and were
    glad;
    he called them, and they said, "Here we
    are!"
    They shone with gladness for him who
    made them.
³⁵ This is our God;
    no other can be compared to him.
³⁶ He found the whole way to knowledge,
    and gave her to his servant Jacob
    and to Israel, whom he loved.
³⁷ Afterward she appeared on earth
    and lived with humankind.

REALITY ✓

GIVE ME SHELTER

How can you understand the feelings of the homeless or exiled if you have never been homeless or exiled? What's the point of reading Baruch? This book was a guide for the Jewish exiles, but it can also be a guide for you today, especially in times when you feel lost or separated from people you love and who love you.

Read **Baruch 4.5**. Think of Baruch as a coach or mentor. If he were sitting with you with his life playbook in hand, he would tell you to pray, because God is always waiting to hear from you, willing to listen, and ready to act. He would point out your favorite Scripture passages and tell you to use them to pray and reflect on what is happening in your life. He would keep saying, "It's going to be okay." He would ask you to take a look at yourself and think about any things that you may have to change to get yourself out of the situation. He would tell you not to give in to loneliness or depression, but to look at all your options and take the next right step.

4 She is the book of the commandments of God,
the law that endures forever.
All who hold her fast will live,
and those who forsake her will die.
2 Turn, O Jacob, and take her;
walk toward the shining of her light.
3 Do not give your glory to another,
or your advantages to an alien people.
4 Happy are we, O Israel,
for we know what is pleasing to God.

Encouragement for Israel
5 Take courage, my people,
who perpetuate Israel's name!
6 It was not for destruction
that you were sold to the nations,
but you were handed over to your enemies
because you angered God.
7 For you provoked the one who made you

by sacrificing to demons and not to God.
8 You forgot the everlasting God, who
brought you up,
and you grieved Jerusalem, who reared
you.
9 For she saw the wrath that came upon you
from God,
and she said:
Listen, you neighbors of Zion,
God has brought great sorrow upon me;
10 for I have seen the exile of my sons and
daughters,
which the Everlasting brought upon
them.
11 With joy I nurtured them,
but I sent them away with weeping and
sorrow.
12 Let no one rejoice over me, a widow
and bereaved of many;
I was left desolate because of the sins of my
children,
because they turned away from the law of
God.
13 They had no regard for his statutes;
they did not walk in the ways of God's
commandments,
or tread the paths his righteousness
showed them.
14 Let the neighbors of Zion come;
remember the capture of my sons and
daughters,
which the Everlasting brought upon
them.
15 For he brought a distant nation against
them,
a nation ruthless and of a strange
language,
which had no respect for the aged
and no pity for a child.
16 They led away the widow's beloved sons,
and bereaved the lonely woman of her
daughters.

17 But I, how can I help you?
18 For he who brought these calamities upon
you
will deliver you from the hand of your
enemies.
19 Go, my children, go;
for I have been left desolate.
20 I have taken off the robe of peace
and put on sackcloth for my
supplication;
I will cry to the Everlasting all my days.

21 Take courage, my children, cry to God,
and he will deliver you from the power
and hand of the enemy.
22 For I have put my hope in the Everlasting to
save you,

and joy has come to me from the Holy
One,
because of the mercy that will soon come to
you
from your everlasting savior.[a]

23 For I sent you out with sorrow and weeping,
but God will give you back to me with joy
and gladness forever.

24 For as the neighbors of Zion have now seen
your capture,
so they soon will see your salvation by
God,
which will come to you with great glory
and with the splendor of the Everlasting.

25 My children, endure with patience the wrath
that has come upon you from God.
Your enemy has overtaken you,
but you will soon see their destruction
and will tread upon their necks.

26 My pampered children have traveled rough
roads;
they were taken away like a flock carried
off by the enemy.

27 Take courage, my children, and cry to God,
for you will be remembered by the one
who brought this upon you.

28 For just as you were disposed to go astray
from God,
return with tenfold zeal to seek him.

a Or *from the Everlasting, your savior*

29 For the one who brought these calamities
upon you
will bring you everlasting joy with your
salvation.

Jerusalem Is Assured of Help

30 Take courage, O Jerusalem,
for the one who named you will comfort
you.

31 Wretched will be those who mistreated you
and who rejoiced at your fall.

32 Wretched will be the cities that your
children served as slaves;
wretched will be the city that received
your offspring.

33 For just as she rejoiced at your fall
and was glad for your ruin,
so she will be grieved at her own
desolation.

34 I will take away her pride in her great
population,
and her insolence will be turned to grief.

35 For fire will come upon her from the
Everlasting for many days,
and for a long time she will be inhabited
by demons.

36 Look toward the east, O Jerusalem,
and see the joy that is coming to you
from God.

And Only with God's Sunlight Do You Begin to Really Grow—© Eliza German, 20

NO OTHER GODS

In **Baruch 6** the Israelites were warned of the dangers and uselessness (and downright foolishness) of worshiping false gods. Today, idolatry happens when we make a god of some person, place, or thing that is less than God.

Most of the time, we may not even be aware that we're worshiping a false god. We most likely won't be making statues of gold or bowing down in front of certain animals anytime soon. Our idols can be subtle. Maybe we think money is what will satisfy us, so we do everything we can to get it and hoard it for ourselves. Maybe it's our reputation that we worship, so much so that we neglect relationships with people whom God puts in front of us. Maybe we idolize our body, physical perfection, or our sports ability. In themselves, not one of these things is bad. What makes them First Commandment—breakers is when they become the thing we believe in and hope in above everything else.

The Church teaches us to love and respect our bodies—not worship them. Worried about crossing the line? Here's what the *Catechism of the Catholic Church* has to say on the danger of idolizing our bodies: "If morality requires respect for the life of the body, it does not make it an absolute value. It rejects a neo-pagan notion that tends to promote the *cult of the body*, to sacrifice everything for its sake, to idolize physical perfection and success at sports. By its selective preference of the strong over the weak, such a conception can lead to the perversion of human relationships" (2289). When you are tempted to worship false idols, ask God to give you the strength to worship him, and him alone.

37 Look, your children are coming, whom you
　　sent away;
　　　they are coming, gathered from east and
　　　　west,
　　at the word of the Holy One,
　　　rejoicing in the glory of God.

5 Take off the garment of your sorrow and
　　affliction, O Jerusalem,
　　　and put on forever the beauty of the glory
　　　　from God.
2 Put on the robe of the righteousness that
　　comes from God;
　　　put on your head the diadem of the glory
　　　　of the Everlasting;
3 for God will show your splendor everywhere
　　under heaven.
4 For God will give you evermore the name,
　　"Righteous Peace, Godly Glory."

5 Arise, O Jerusalem, stand upon the height;
　　look toward the east,
　　and see your children gathered from west
　　　and east
　　　at the word of the Holy One,
　　　rejoicing that God has remembered them.
6 For they went out from you on foot,
　　led away by their enemies;
　　but God will bring them back to you,
　　　carried in glory, as on a royal throne.
7 For God has ordered that every high
　　　　mountain and the everlasting hills
　　　　be made low
　　and the valleys filled up, to make level
　　　ground,
　　　so that Israel may walk safely in the glory
　　　　of God.
8 The woods and every fragrant tree
　　have shaded Israel at God's command.
9 For God will lead Israel with joy,
　　in the light of his glory,
　　　with the mercy and righteousness that
　　　　come from him.

6ᵃ The Letter of Jeremiah

A copy of a letter that Jeremiah sent to those who were to be taken to Babylon as exiles by the king of the Babylonians, to give them the message that God had commanded him.

The People Face a Long Captivity

2 Because of the sins that you have committed before God, you will be taken to Babylon as exiles by Nebuchadnezzar, king of the Babylonians. 3 Therefore when you have come to

---

a The King James Version (like the Latin Vulgate) prints The Letter of Jeremiah as Chapter 6 of the Book of Baruch, and the chapter and verse numbers are here retained. In the Greek Septuagint, the Letter is separated from Baruch by the Book of Lamentations.

Babylon you will remain there for many years, for a long time, up to seven generations; after that I will bring you away from there in peace. [4]Now in Babylon you will see gods made of silver and gold and wood, which people carry on their shoulders, and which cause the heathen to fear. [5]So beware of becoming at all like the foreigners or of letting fear for these gods[a] possess you [6]when you see the multitude before and behind them worshiping them. But say in your heart, "It is you, O Lord, whom we must worship." [7]For my angel is with you, and he is watching over your lives.

The Helplessness of Idols

8 Their tongues are smoothed by the carpenter, and they themselves are overlaid with gold and silver; but they are false and cannot speak. [9]People[b] take gold and make crowns for the heads of their gods, as they might for a girl who loves ornaments. [10]Sometimes the priests secretly take gold and silver from their gods and spend it on themselves, [11]or even give some of it to the prostitutes on the terrace. They deck their gods[c] out with garments like human beings—these gods of silver and gold and wood [12]that cannot save themselves from rust and corrosion. When they have been dressed in purple robes, [13]their faces are wiped because of the dust from the temple, which is thick upon them. [14]One of them holds a scepter, like a district judge, but is unable to destroy anyone who offends it. [15]Another has a dagger in its right hand, and an ax, but cannot defend itself from war and robbers. [16]From this it is evident that they are not gods; so do not fear them.

17 For just as someone's dish is useless when it is broken, [18]so are their gods when they have been set up in the temples. Their eyes are full of the dust raised by the feet of those who enter. And just as the gates are shut on every side against anyone who has offended a king, as though under sentence of death, so the priests make their temples secure with doors and locks and bars, in order that they may not be plundered by robbers. [19]They light more lamps for them than they light for themselves, though their gods[d] can see none of them. [20]They are[e] just like a beam of the temple, but their hearts, it is said, are eaten away when crawling creatures from the earth devour them and their robes. They do not notice [21]when their faces have been blackened by the smoke of the temple. [22]Bats, swallows, and birds alight on their bodies and heads; and so

do cats. [23]From this you will know that they are not gods; so do not fear them.

24 As for the gold that they wear for beauty—it[f] will not shine unless someone wipes off the tarnish; for even when they were being cast, they did not feel it. [25]They are bought without regard to cost, but there is no breath in them. [26]Having no feet, they are carried on the shoulders of others, revealing to humankind their worthlessness. And those who serve them are put to shame [27]because, if any of these gods falls[g] to the ground, they themselves must pick it up. If anyone sets it upright, it cannot move itself; and if it is tipped over, it cannot straighten itself. Gifts are placed before them just as before the dead. [28]The priests sell the sacrifices that are offered to these gods[h] and use the money themselves. Likewise their wives preserve some of the meat[i] with salt, but give none to the poor or helpless. [29]Sacrifices to them may even be touched by women in their periods or at childbirth. Since you know by these things that they are not gods, do not fear them.

30 For how can they be called gods? Women serve meals for gods of silver and gold and wood; [31]and in their temples the priests sit with their clothes torn, their heads and beards shaved, and their heads uncovered. [32]They howl and shout before their gods as some do at a funeral banquet. [33]The priests take some of the clothing of their gods[j] to clothe their wives and children. [34]Whether one does evil to them or good, they will not be able to repay it. They cannot set up a king or depose one. [35]Likewise they are not able to give either wealth or money; if one makes a vow to them and does not keep it, they will not require it. [36]They cannot save anyone from death or rescue the weak from the strong. [37]They cannot restore sight to the blind; they cannot rescue one who is in distress. [38]They cannot take pity on a widow or do good to an orphan. [39]These things that are made of wood and overlaid with gold and silver are like stones from the mountain, and those who serve them will be put to shame. [40]Why then must anyone think that they are gods, or call them gods?

The Foolishness of Worshiping Idols

Besides, even the Chaldeans themselves dishonor them; for when they see someone who cannot speak, they bring Bel and pray that the mute may speak, as though Bel[k] were able to understand! [41]Yet they themselves cannot perceive this and abandon them, for they have no

---

a Gk for them *b* Gk They *c* Gk them *d* Gk they *e* Gk It is *f* Lat Syr: Gk they *g* Gk if they fall *h* Gk to them *i* Gk of them *j* Gk some of their clothing *k* Gk he

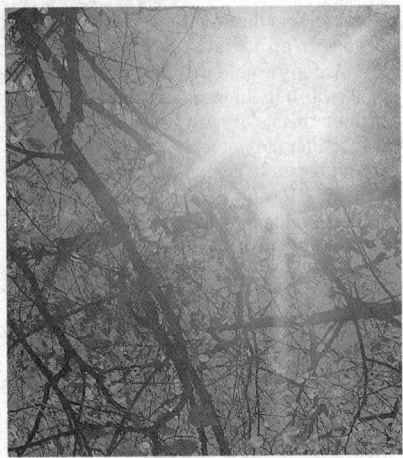
Leaves and Sunshine—© Taylor-Quinn Yancey, 16

sense. ⁴²And the women, with cords around them, sit along the passageways, burning bran for incense. ⁴³When one of them is led off by one of the passers-by and is taken to bed by him, she derides the woman next to her, because she was not as attractive as herself and her cord was not broken. ⁴⁴Whatever is done for these idols*ᵃ* is false. Why then must anyone think that they are gods, or call them gods?

45 They are made by carpenters and goldsmiths; they can be nothing but what the artisans wish them to be. ⁴⁶Those who make them will certainly not live very long themselves; ⁴⁷how then can the things that are made by them be gods? They have left only lies and reproach for those who come after. ⁴⁸For when war or calamity comes upon them, the priests consult together as to where they can hide themselves and their gods.*ᵃ* ⁴⁹How then can one fail to see that these are not gods, for they cannot save themselves from war or calamity? ⁵⁰Since they are made of wood and overlaid with gold and silver, it will afterward be known that they are false. ⁵¹It will be manifest to all the nations and kings that they are not gods but the work of human hands, and that there is no work of God in them. ⁵²Who then can fail to know that they are not gods?*ᵇ*

53 For they cannot set up a king over a country or give rain to people. ⁵⁴They cannot judge their own cause or deliver one who is wronged, for they have no power; ⁵⁵they are like crows between heaven and earth. When fire breaks out in a temple of wooden gods overlaid with gold or silver, their priests will flee and escape, but the gods*ᶜ* will be burned up like timbers. ⁵⁶Besides, they can offer no resistance to king or enemy. Why then must anyone admit or think that they are gods?

57 Gods made of wood and overlaid with silver and gold are unable to save themselves from thieves or robbers. ⁵⁸Anyone who can will strip them of their gold and silver and of the robes they wear, and go off with this booty, and they will not be able to help themselves. ⁵⁹So it is better to be a king who shows his courage, or a household utensil that serves its owner's need, than to be these false gods; better even the door of a house that protects its contents, than these false gods; better also a wooden pillar in a palace, than these false gods.

60 For sun and moon and stars are bright, and when sent to do a service, they are obedient. ⁶¹So also the lightning, when it flashes, is widely seen; and the wind likewise blows in every land. ⁶²When God commands the clouds to go over the whole world, they carry out his command. ⁶³And the fire sent from above to consume mountains and woods does what it is ordered. But these idols*ᵈ* are not to be compared with them in appearance or power. ⁶⁴Therefore one must not think that they are gods, nor call them gods, for they are not able either to decide a case or to do good to anyone. ⁶⁵Since you know then that they are not gods, do not fear them.

66 They can neither curse nor bless kings; ⁶⁷they cannot show signs in the heavens for the nations, or shine like the sun or give light like the moon. ⁶⁸The wild animals are better than they are, for they can flee to shelter and help themselves. ⁶⁹So we have no evidence whatever that they are gods; therefore do not fear them.

70 Like a scarecrow in a cucumber bed, which guards nothing, so are their gods of wood, overlaid with gold and silver. ⁷¹In the same way, their gods of wood, overlaid with gold and silver, are like a thornbush in a garden on which every bird perches; or like a corpse thrown out in the darkness. ⁷²From the purple and linen*ᵉ* that rot upon them you will know that they are not gods; and they will finally be consumed themselves, and be a reproach in the land. ⁷³Better, therefore, is someone upright who has no idols; such a person will be far above reproach.

a Gk them *b* Meaning of Gk uncertain *c* Gk they *d* Gk these things *e* Cn: Gk marble, Syr silk

EZEKIEL
AN ARTIST SHOWS THE WAY BACK TO GOD

Acting Out Truth

Imagine you're out shopping when you come across a man lying on his side on the sidewalk with a clay model in front of him. You're not sure what to make of it, but he's there when you go back the next week. And the next. And the next—for over a year. Wouldn't you take notice, ask him what he's doing, talk about it with your friends?

With dramatic methods like this, Ezekiel, the prophetic performance artist, communicates just where Judah is going wrong. He eats a scroll, shaves his hair and beard and burns the hair, digs through a wall, tells stories, and packs his belongings and acts out going into exile. What did the Hebrews think of him? Eccentric? Maybe. Crazy? Possibly. But his passion and creativity meant they couldn't ignore the words of God or the consequences of their actions. Israel's rebellion was as offensive to God as cooking a meal over human excrement would be to us. Yes, he was *that* graphic!

But again, there is hope in the strong words—stories of breath breathed into dry bones and people coming to life again, images of the Temple being rebuilt so that God could be at the heart of his people again. Make no mistake—God *never* gives up. He never gives up.

"Go ahead! Courage! In the spiritual life he who does not go forward goes backward."

—St. Padre Pio

WHO The author, Ezekiel, was a priest and a prophet.

WHAT Using dramatic actions, words, and symbols, Ezekiel warned the people of Judah about their rebellion and called them back to God.

WHEN The prophet was active for about twenty years, beginning in 593 B.C.

WHERE Ezekiel was in captivity in Babylon along with the people of Judah he was writing to. (Babylon was in the area now known as Iraq.)

PATH OF DISCIPLESHIP

For Ezekiel, words weren't as important as symbolic actions and demonstrations of faith. Ezekiel seemed to know that the mystery of God's presence with people demanded expression. That's what liturgy is. When we gather as a community, it is to give public, dramatic, and physical expression of the assembly's faith and interaction with the presence of God in history—past, present, and future.

Do you see going to Mass as being part of a drama that is being enacted throughout the world? Do you play your part well—sing, move your body, say the prayers with expression, and really participate? Liturgy isn't a passive experience for God's people; at least it's not supposed to be. Don't be a spectator at Mass—actively celebrate the sacred mystery of God's presence.

1 The Vision of the Chariot

In the thirtieth year, in the fourth month, on the fifth day of the month, as I was among the exiles by the river Chebar, the heavens were opened, and I saw visions of God. 2 On the fifth day of the month (it was the fifth year of the exile of King Jehoiachin), 3 the word of the Lord came to the priest Ezekiel son of Buzi, in the land of the Chaldeans by the river Chebar; and the hand of the Lord was on him there.

4 As I looked, a stormy wind came out of the north: a great cloud with brightness around it and fire flashing forth continually, and in the middle of the fire, something like gleaming amber. 5 In the middle of it was something like four living creatures. This was their appearance: they were of human form. 6 Each had four faces, and each of them had four wings. 7 Their legs were straight, and the soles of their feet were like the sole of a calf's foot; and they sparkled like burnished bronze. 8 Under their wings on their four sides they had human hands. And the four had their faces and their wings thus: 9 their wings touched one another; each of them moved straight ahead, without turning as they moved. 10 As for the appearance of their faces: the four had the face of a human being, the face of a lion on the right side, the face of an ox on the left side, and the face of an eagle; 11 such were their faces. Their wings were spread out above; each creature had two wings, each of which touched the wing of another, while two covered their bodies. 12 Each moved straight ahead; wherever the spirit would go, they went, without turning as they went. 13 In the middle of*a* the living creatures there was something that looked like burning coals of fire, like torches moving to and fro among the living creatures; the fire was bright, and lightning issued from the fire. 14 The living creatures darted to and fro, like a flash of lightning.

15 As I looked at the living creatures, I saw a wheel on the earth beside the living creatures, one for each of the four of them.*b* 16 As for the appearance of the wheels and their construction: their appearance was like the gleaming of beryl; and the four had the same form, their construction being something like a wheel within a wheel. 17 When they moved, they moved in any of the four directions without veering as they moved. 18 Their rims were tall and awesome, for the rims of all four were full of eyes all around. 19 When the living creatures moved, the wheels moved beside them; and when the living creatures rose from the earth, the wheels rose. 20 Wherever the spirit would

go, they went, and the wheels rose along with them; for the spirit of the living creatures was in the wheels. 21 When they moved, the others moved; when they stopped, the others stopped; and when they rose from the earth, the wheels rose along with them; for the spirit of the living creatures was in the wheels.

22 Over the heads of the living creatures there was something like a dome, shining like crystal,*c* spread out above their heads. 23 Under the dome their wings were stretched out straight, one toward another; and each of the creatures had two wings covering its body. 24 When they moved, I heard the sound of their wings like the sound of mighty waters, like the thunder of the Almighty,*d* a sound of tumult like the sound of an army; when they stopped, they let down their wings. 25 And there came a voice from above the dome over their heads; when they stopped, they let down their wings.

26 And above the dome over their heads there was something like a throne, in appearance like sapphire;*e* and seated above the likeness of a throne was something that seemed like a human form. 27 Upward from what appeared like the loins I saw something like gleaming amber, something that looked like fire enclosed all around; and downward from what looked like the loins I saw something that looked like fire, and there was a splendor all around. 28 Like the bow in a cloud on a rainy day, such was the appearance of the splendor all around. This was the appearance of the likeness of the glory of the Lord.

When I saw it, I fell on my face, and I heard the voice of someone speaking.

2 The Vision of the Scroll

He said to me: O mortal,*f* stand up on your feet, and I will speak with you. 2 And when he spoke to me, a spirit entered into me and set me on my feet; and I heard him speaking to me. 3 He said to me, Mortal, I am sending you to the people of Israel, to a nation*g* of rebels who have rebelled against me; they and their ancestors have transgressed against me to this very day. 4 The descendants are impudent and stubborn. I am sending you to them, and you shall say to them, "Thus says the Lord God." 5 Whether they hear or refuse to hear (for they are a rebellious house), they shall know that there has been a prophet among them. 6 And you, O mortal, do not be afraid of them, and do not be afraid of their words, though briers and thorns surround you and you live among scorpions; do not be afraid of their words, and

---

a Gk OL: Heb *And the appearance of* *b* Heb *of their faces* *c* Gk: Heb *like the awesome crystal* *d* Traditional rendering of Heb *Shaddai*
e Or *lapis lazuli* *f* Or *son of man*; Heb *ben adam* (and so throughout the book when Ezekiel is addressed) *g* Syr: Heb *to nations*

do not be dismayed at their looks, for they are a rebellious house. [7]You shall speak my words to them, whether they hear or refuse to hear; for they are a rebellious house.

8 But you, mortal, hear what I say to you; do not be rebellious like that rebellious house; open your mouth and eat what I give you. [9]I looked, and a hand was stretched out to me, and a written scroll was in it. [10]He spread it before me; it had writing on the front and on the back, and written on it were words of lamentation and mourning and woe.

3 He said to me, O mortal, eat what is offered to you; eat this scroll, and go, speak to the house of Israel. [2]So I opened my mouth, and he gave me the scroll to eat. [3]He said to me, Mortal, eat this scroll that I give you and fill your stomach with it. Then I ate it; and in my mouth it was as sweet as honey.

4 He said to me: Mortal, go to the house of Israel and speak my very words to them. [5]For you are not sent to a people of obscure speech and difficult language, but to the house of Israel— [6]not to many peoples of obscure speech and difficult language, whose words you cannot understand. Surely, if I sent you to them, they would listen to you. [7]But the house of Israel will not listen to you, for they are not willing to listen to me; because all the house of Israel have a hard forehead and a stubborn heart. [8]See, I have made your face hard against their faces, and your forehead hard against their foreheads. [9]Like the hardest stone, harder than flint, I have made your forehead; do not fear them or be dismayed at their looks, for they are a rebellious house. [10]He said to me: Mortal, all my words that I shall speak to you receive in your heart and hear with your ears; [11]then go to the exiles, to your people, and speak to them. Say to them, "Thus says the Lord GOD"; whether they hear or refuse to hear.

Ezekiel at the River Chebar

12 Then the spirit lifted me up, and as the glory of the LORD rose[a] from its place, I heard behind me the sound of loud rumbling; [13]it was the sound of the wings of the living creatures brushing against one another, and the sound of the wheels beside them, that sounded like a loud rumbling. [14]The spirit lifted me up and bore me away; I went in bitterness in the heat of my spirit, the hand of the LORD being strong upon me. [15]I came to the exiles at Tel-abib, who lived by the river Chebar.[b] And I sat there among them, stunned, for seven days.

16 At the end of seven days, the word of the LORD came to me: [17]Mortal, I have made

you a sentinel for the house of Israel; whenever you hear a word from my mouth, you shall give them warning from me. [18]If I say to the wicked, "You shall surely die," and you give them no warning, or speak to warn the wicked from their wicked way, in order to save their life, those wicked persons shall die for their iniquity; but their blood I will require at your hand. [19]But if you warn the wicked, and they do not turn from their wickedness, or from their wicked way, they shall die for their iniquity; but you will have saved your life. [20]Again, if the righteous turn from their righteousness and commit iniquity, and I lay a stumbling block before them, they shall die; because you have not warned them, they shall die for their sin, and their righteous deeds that they have done shall not be remembered; but their blood I will require at your hand. [21]If, however, you warn the righteous not to sin, and they do not sin,

a Cn: Heb *and blessed be the glory of the LORD* b Two Mss Syr: Heb *Chebar, and to where they lived.* Another reading is *Chebar, and I sat where they sat*

Odd God

Creativity's a wild and crazy thing. Though it sparks incredible works of art, music, and books, it also inspires some people to get a little wacky. (Ever visited an inventors' convention?) When you describe something that's especially creative, you might use words like *bizarre, freaky,* and *odd.*

Sometimes God, who's something of an old pro at creativity, might seem a bit bizarre, freaky, and odd too. Just read **Ezekiel 4–5**. This is some weird stuff. Not creepy, exactly. But definitely weird. It's another vivid example of God's unbridled creativity. Sometimes he works through people in strange, unusual, and unexpected ways.

And sometimes *you* can work in strange, unusual, and unexpected ways too.

How might God's creativity impact *your* life? Let **Ezekiel 4.1** provide some inspiration. Draw a simple map of your community. Add four or five key landmarks or places you like to hang out. Then use your creative brain to think of a way you could honor God in each of those places. Be sure to share your ideas with others at **Learner.CalltoDiscipleship.com**.

they shall surely live, because they took warning; and you will have saved your life.

Ezekiel Isolated and Silenced

22 Then the hand of the LORD was upon me there; and he said to me, Rise up, go out into the valley, and there I will speak with you. 23 So I rose up and went out into the valley; and the glory of the LORD stood there, like the glory that I had seen by the river Chebar; and I fell on my face. 24 The spirit entered into me, and set me on my feet; and he spoke with me and said to me: Go, shut yourself inside your house. 25 As for you, mortal, cords shall be placed on you, and you shall be bound with them, so that you cannot go out among the people; 26 and I will make your tongue cling to the roof of your mouth, so that you shall be speechless and unable to reprove them; for they are a rebellious house. 27 But when I speak with you, I will open your mouth, and you shall say to them, "Thus says the Lord GOD"; let those who will hear, hear; and let those who refuse to hear, refuse; for they are a rebellious house.

4 The Siege of Jerusalem Portrayed

And you, O mortal, take a brick and set it before you. On it portray a city, Jerusalem; 2 and put siegeworks against it, and build a siege wall against it, and cast up a ramp against it; set camps also against it, and plant battering rams against it all around. 3 Then take an iron plate and place it as an iron wall between you and the city; set your face toward it, and let it be in a state of siege, and press the siege against it. This is a sign for the house of Israel.

4 Then lie on your left side, and place the punishment of the house of Israel upon it; you shall bear their punishment for the number of the days that you lie there. 5 For I assign to you a number of days, three hundred ninety days, equal to the number of the years of their punishment; and so you shall bear the punishment of the house of Israel. 6 When you have completed these, you shall lie down a second time, but on your right side, and bear the punishment of the house of Judah; forty days I assign you, one day for each year. 7 You shall set your face toward the siege of Jerusalem, and with your arm bared you shall prophesy against it. 8 See, I am putting cords on you so that you cannot turn from one side to the other until you have completed the days of your siege.

9 And you, take wheat and barley, beans and lentils, millet and spelt; put them into one vessel, and make bread for yourself. During the number of days that you lie on your side, three hundred ninety days, you shall eat it. 10 The food that you eat shall be twenty shekels a day by weight; at fixed times you shall eat it. 11 And you shall drink water by measure, one-sixth of a hin; at fixed times you shall drink. 12 You shall eat it as a barley-cake, baking it in their sight on human dung. 13 The LORD said, "Thus shall the people of Israel eat their bread, unclean, among the nations to which I will drive them." 14 Then I said, "Ah Lord GOD! I have never defiled myself; from my youth up until now I have never eaten what died of itself or was torn by animals, nor has carrion flesh come into my mouth." 15 Then he said to me, "See, I will let you have cow's dung instead of human dung, on which you may prepare your bread."

16 Then he said to me, Mortal, I am going to break the staff of bread in Jerusalem; they shall eat bread by weight and with fearfulness; and they shall drink water by measure and in dismay. 17 Lacking bread and water, they will look at one another in dismay, and waste away under their punishment.

5 A Sword against Jerusalem

And you, O mortal, take a sharp sword; use it as a barber's razor and run it over your head and your beard; then take balances for weighing, and divide the hair. [2]One third of the hair you shall burn in the fire inside the city, when the days of the siege are completed; one third you shall take and strike with the sword all around the city;[a] and one third you shall scatter to the wind, and I will unsheathe the sword after them. [3]Then you shall take from these a small number, and bind them in the skirts of your robe. [4]From these, again, you shall take some, throw them into the fire and burn them up; from there a fire will come out against all the house of Israel.

5 Thus says the Lord God: This is Jerusalem; I have set her in the center of the nations, with countries all around her. [6]But she has rebelled against my ordinances and my statutes, becoming more wicked than the nations and the countries all around her, rejecting my ordinances and not following my statutes. [7]Therefore thus says the Lord God: Because you are more turbulent than the nations that are all around you, and have not followed my statutes or kept my ordinances, but have acted according to the ordinances of the nations that are all around you; [8]therefore thus says the Lord God: I, I myself, am coming against you; I will execute judgments among you in the sight of the nations. [9]And because of all your abominations, I will do to you what I have never yet done, and the like of which I will never do again. [10]Surely, parents shall eat their children in your midst, and children shall eat their parents; I will execute judgments on you, and any of you who survive I will scatter to every wind. [11]Therefore, as I live, says the Lord God, surely, because you have defiled my sanctuary with all your detestable things and with all your abominations—therefore I will cut you down;[b] my eye will not spare, and I will have no pity. [12]One third of you shall die of pestilence or be consumed by famine among you; one third shall fall by the sword around you; and one third I will scatter to every wind and will unsheathe the sword after them.

13 My anger shall spend itself, and I will vent my fury on them and satisfy myself; and they shall know that I, the Lord, have spoken in my jealousy, when I spend my fury on them. [14]Moreover I will make you a desolation and an object of mocking among the nations around you, in the sight of all that pass by. [15]You shall be[c] a mockery and a taunt, a warning and a horror, to the nations around you, when I execute judgments on you in anger and fury, and with furious punishments—I, the Lord, have spoken— [16]when I loose against you[d] my deadly arrows of famine, arrows for destruction, which I will let loose to destroy you, and when I bring more and more famine upon you, and break your staff of bread. [17]I will send famine and wild animals against you, and they will rob you of your children; pestilence and bloodshed shall pass through you; and I will bring the sword upon you. I, the Lord, have spoken.

6 Judgment on Idolatrous Israel

The word of the Lord came to me: [2]O mortal, set your face toward the mountains of Israel, and prophesy against them, [3]and say, You mountains of Israel, hear the word of the Lord God! Thus says the Lord God to the mountains and the hills, to the ravines and the valleys: I, I myself, will bring a sword upon you, and I will destroy your high places. [4]Your altars shall become desolate, and your incense stands shall be broken; and I will throw down your slain in front of your idols. [5]I will lay the corpses of the people of Israel in front of their idols; and I will scatter your bones around your altars. [6]Wherever you live, your towns shall be waste and your high places ruined, so that your altars will be waste and ruined,[e] your idols broken and destroyed, your incense stands cut down, and your works wiped out. [7]The slain shall fall in your midst; then you shall know that I am the Lord.

8 But I will spare some. Some of you shall escape the sword among the nations and be scattered through the countries. [9]Those of you who escape shall remember me among the nations where they are carried captive, how I was crushed by their wanton heart that turned away from me, and their wanton eyes that turned after their idols. Then they will be loathsome in their own sight for the evils that they have committed, for all their abominations. [10]And they shall know that I am the Lord; I did not threaten in vain to bring this disaster upon them.

11 Thus says the Lord God: Clap your hands and stamp your foot, and say, Alas for all the vile abominations of the house of Israel! For they shall fall by the sword, by famine, and by pestilence. [12]Those far off shall die of pestilence; those nearby shall fall by the sword; and any who are left and are spared shall die of famine. Thus I will spend my fury upon them. [13]And you shall know that I am the Lord, when their slain lie among their idols around their altars, on every high hill, on all the mountain tops, under every green tree, and under every leafy oak, wherever they offered pleasing odor to all their idols. [14]I will stretch out my hand against them, and make the land desolate and waste, throughout all their settlements,

---

a Heb it b Another reading is I will withdraw c Gk Syr Vg Tg: Heb It shall be d Heb them e Syr Vg Tg: Heb and be made guilty

from the wilderness to Riblah.[a] Then they shall
know that I am the LORD.

7 Impending Disaster

The word of the LORD came to me: [2]You, O mortal, thus says the Lord GOD to the land of Israel:
>   An end! The end has come
>   upon the four corners of the land.
> [3] Now the end is upon you,
>   I will let loose my anger upon you;
>   I will judge you according to your ways,
>   I will punish you for all your
>   abominations.
> [4] My eye will not spare you, I will have no
>   pity.
>   I will punish you for your ways,
>   while your abominations are among you.

Then you shall know that I am the LORD.

>   5 Thus says the Lord GOD:
>   Disaster after disaster! See, it comes.
> [6]   An end has come, the end has come.
>   It has awakened against you; see, it comes!
> [7] Your doom[b] has come to you,
>   O inhabitant of the land.
>   The time has come, the day is near—
>   of tumult, not of reveling on the
>   mountains.
> [8] Soon now I will pour out my wrath upon
>   you;
>   I will spend my anger against you.
>   I will judge you according to your ways,
>   and punish you for all your
>   abominations.
> [9] My eye will not spare; I will have no pity.
>   I will punish you according to your ways,
>   while your abominations are among you.

Then you shall know that it is I the LORD who
strike.

> [10] See, the day! See, it comes!
>   Your doom[b] has gone out.
>   The rod has blossomed, pride has budded.
> [11]   Violence has grown into a rod of
>   wickedness.
>   None of them shall remain,
>   not their abundance, not their wealth;
>   no pre-eminence among them.[b]
> [12] The time has come, the day draws near;
>   let not the buyer rejoice, nor the seller
>   mourn,
>   for wrath is upon all their multitude.

[13]For the sellers shall not return to what has
been sold as long as they remain alive. For the
vision concerns all their multitude; it shall not
be revoked. Because of their iniquity, they cannot maintain their lives.[b]

> [14] They have blown the horn and made
>   everything ready;

---

a Another reading is *Diblah*   *b* Meaning of Heb uncertain

but no one goes to battle,
for my wrath is upon all their multitude.

15 The sword is outside, pestilence and famine
are inside;
those in the field die by the sword;
those in the city—famine and pestilence
devour them.

16 If any survivors escape,
they shall be found on the mountains
like doves of the valleys,
all of them moaning over their iniquity.

17 All hands shall grow feeble,
all knees turn to water.

18 They shall put on sackcloth,
horror shall cover them.
Shame shall be on all faces,
baldness on all their heads.

19 They shall fling their silver into the streets,
their gold shall be treated as unclean.
Their silver and gold cannot save them on the
day of the wrath of the Lord. They shall not satisfy their hunger or fill their stomachs with it.
For it was the stumbling block of their iniquity. 20 From their*a* beautiful ornament, in which
they took pride, they made their abominable
images, their detestable things; therefore I will
make of it an unclean thing to them.

21 I will hand it over to strangers as booty,
to the wicked of the earth as plunder;
they shall profane it.

22 I will avert my face from them,
so that they may profane my treasured*b*
place;
the violent shall enter it,
they shall profane it.

23 Make a chain!*c*
For the land is full of bloody crimes;
the city is full of violence.

24 I will bring the worst of the nations
to take possession of their houses.
I will put an end to the arrogance of the
strong,
and their holy places shall be profaned.

25 When anguish comes, they will seek peace,
but there shall be none.

26 Disaster comes upon disaster,
rumor follows rumor;
they shall keep seeking a vision from the
prophet;
instruction shall perish from the priest,
and counsel from the elders.

27 The king shall mourn,
the prince shall be wrapped in despair,
and the hands of the people of the land
shall tremble.
According to their way I will deal with them;

according to their own judgments I will
judge them.
And they shall know that I am the Lord.

8 Abominations in the Temple

In the sixth year, in the sixth month, on the
fifth day of the month, as I sat in my house,
with the elders of Judah sitting before me, the
hand of the Lord God fell upon me there. 2 I
looked, and there was a figure that looked like
a human being;*d* below what appeared to be
its loins it was fire, and above the loins it was
like the appearance of brightness, like gleaming amber. 3 It stretched out the form of a hand,
and took me by a lock of my head; and the spirit lifted me up between earth and heaven, and
brought me in visions of God to Jerusalem, to
the entrance of the gateway of the inner court
that faces north, to the seat of the image of
jealousy, which provokes to jealousy. 4 And the
glory of the God of Israel was there, like the vision that I had seen in the valley.

5 Then God*e* said to me, "O mortal, lift up
your eyes now in the direction of the north." So
I lifted up my eyes toward the north, and there,
north of the altar gate, in the entrance, was this
image of jealousy. 6 He said to me, "Mortal, do
you see what they are doing, the great abominations that the house of Israel are committing here, to drive me far from my sanctuary?
Yet you will see still greater abominations."

7 And he brought me to the entrance of the
court; I looked, and there was a hole in the wall.
8 Then he said to me, "Mortal, dig through the
wall"; and when I dug through the wall, there
was an entrance. 9 He said to me, "Go in, and
see the vile abominations that they are committing here." 10 So I went in and looked; there,
portrayed on the wall all around, were all kinds
of creeping things, and loathsome animals,
and all the idols of the house of Israel. 11 Before them stood seventy of the elders of the
house of Israel, with Jaazaniah son of Shaphan
standing among them. Each had his censer in
his hand, and the fragrant cloud of incense was
ascending. 12 Then he said to me, "Mortal, have
you seen what the elders of the house of Israel
are doing in the dark, each in his room of images? For they say, 'The Lord does not see us,
the Lord has forsaken the land.' " 13 He said
also to me, "You will see still greater abominations that they are committing."

14 Then he brought me to the entrance of
the north gate of the house of the Lord; wom-
en were sitting there weeping for Tammuz.
15 Then he said to me, "Have you seen this,

---

a Syr Symmachus: Heb *its* *b* Or *secret* *c* Meaning of Heb uncertain *d* Gk: Heb *like fire* *e* Heb *he*

O mortal? You will see still greater abominations than these."

16 And he brought me into the inner court of the house of the LORD; there, at the entrance of the temple of the LORD, between the porch and the altar, were about twenty-five men, with their backs to the temple of the LORD, and their faces toward the east, prostrating themselves to the sun toward the east. 17Then he said to me, "Have you seen this, O mortal? Is it not bad enough that the house of Judah commits the abominations done here? Must they fill the land with violence, and provoke my anger still further? See, they are putting the branch to their nose! 18Therefore I will act in wrath; my eye will not spare, nor will I have pity; and though they cry in my hearing with a loud voice, I will not listen to them."

9 The Slaughter of the Idolaters

Then he cried in my hearing with a loud voice, saying, "Draw near, you executioners of the city, each with his destroying weapon in his hand." 2And six men came from the direction of the upper gate, which faces north, each with his weapon for slaughter in his hand; among them was a man clothed in linen, with a writing case at his side. They went in and stood beside the bronze altar.

3 Now the glory of the God of Israel had gone up from the cherub on which it rested to the threshold of the house. The LORD called to the man clothed in linen, who had the writing case at his side; 4and said to him, "Go through the city, through Jerusalem, and put a mark on the foreheads of those who sigh and groan over all the abominations that are committed in it." 5To the others he said in my hearing, "Pass through the city after him, and kill; your eye shall not spare, and you shall show no pity. 6Cut down old men, young men and young women, little children and women, but touch no one who has the mark. And begin at my sanctuary." So they began with the elders who were in front of the house. 7Then he said to them, "Defile the house, and fill the courts with the slain. Go!" So they went out and killed in the city. 8While they were killing, and I was left alone, I fell prostrate on my face and cried out, "Ah Lord GOD! will you destroy all who remain of Israel as you pour out your wrath upon Jerusalem?" 9He said to me, "The guilt of the house of Israel and Judah is exceedingly great; the land is full of bloodshed and the city full of perversity; for they say, 'The LORD has forsaken the land, and the LORD does not see.' 10As for me, my eye will not spare, nor will I have pity,

but I will bring down their deeds upon their heads."

11 Then the man clothed in linen, with the writing case at his side, brought back word, saying, "I have done as you commanded me."

10 God's Glory Leaves Jerusalem

Then I looked, and above the dome that was over the heads of the cherubim there appeared above them something like a sapphire,[a] in form resembling a throne. 2He said to the man clothed in linen, "Go within the wheelwork underneath the cherubim; fill your hands with burning coals from among the cherubim, and scatter them over the city." He went in as I looked on. 3Now the cherubim were standing on the south side of the house when the man went in; and a cloud filled the inner court. 4Then the glory of the LORD rose up from the cherub to the threshold of the house; the house was filled with the cloud, and the court was full of the brightness of the glory of the LORD. 5The sound of the wings of the cherubim was heard as far as the outer court, like the voice of God Almighty[b] when he speaks.

6 When he commanded the man clothed in linen, "Take fire from within the wheelwork, from among the cherubim," he went in and stood beside a wheel. 7And a cherub stretched out his hand from among the cherubim to the fire that was among the cherubim, took some of it and put it into the hands of the man clothed in linen, who took it and went out. 8The cherubim appeared to have the form of a human hand under their wings.

9 I looked, and there were four wheels beside the cherubim, one beside each cherub; and the appearance of the wheels was like gleaming beryl. 10And as for their appearance, the four looked alike, something like a wheel within a wheel. 11When they moved, they moved in any of the four directions without veering as they moved; but in whatever direction the front wheel faced, the others followed without veering as they moved. 12Their entire body, their rims, their spokes, their wings, and the wheels—the wheels of the four of them— were full of eyes all around. 13As for the wheels, they were called in my hearing "the wheelwork." 14Each one had four faces: the first face was that of the cherub, the second face was that of a human being, the third that of a lion, and the fourth that of an eagle.

15 The cherubim rose up. These were the living creatures that I saw by the river Chebar. 16When the cherubim moved, the wheels moved beside them; and when the cherubim

a Or lapis lazuli b Traditional rendering of Heb El Shaddai

lifted up their wings to rise up from the earth, the wheels at their side did not veer. ¹⁷When they stopped, the others stopped, and when they rose up, the others rose up with them; for the spirit of the living creatures was in them.

18 Then the glory of the Lᴏʀᴅ went out from the threshold of the house and stopped above the cherubim. ¹⁹The cherubim lifted up their wings and rose up from the earth in my sight as they went out with the wheels beside them. They stopped at the entrance of the east gate of the house of the Lᴏʀᴅ; and the glory of the God of Israel was above them.

20 These were the living creatures that I saw underneath the God of Israel by the river Chebar; and I knew that they were cherubim. ²¹Each had four faces, each four wings, and underneath their wings something like human hands. ²²As for what their faces were like, they were the same faces whose appearance I had seen by the river Chebar. Each one moved straight ahead.

11 Judgment on Wicked Counselors

The spirit lifted me up and brought me to the east gate of the house of the Lᴏʀᴅ, which faces east. There, at the entrance of the gateway, were twenty-five men; among them I saw Jaazaniah son of Azzur, and Pelatiah son of Benaiah, officials of the people. ²He said to me, "Mortal, these are the men who devise iniquity and who give wicked counsel in this city; ³they say, 'The time is not near to build houses; this city is the pot, and we are the meat.' ⁴Therefore prophesy against them; prophesy, O mortal."

5 Then the spirit of the Lᴏʀᴅ fell upon me, and he said to me, "Say, Thus says the Lᴏʀᴅ: This is what you think, O house of Israel; I know the things that come into your mind. ⁶You have killed many in this city, and have filled its streets with the slain. ⁷Therefore thus says the Lord Gᴏᴅ: The slain whom you have placed within it are the meat, and this city is the pot; but you shall be taken out of it. ⁸You have feared the sword; and I will bring the sword upon you, says the Lord Gᴏᴅ. ⁹I will take you out of it and give you over to the hands of foreigners, and execute judgments upon you. ¹⁰You shall fall by the sword; I will judge you at the border of Israel. And you shall know that I am the Lᴏʀᴅ. ¹¹This city shall not be your pot, and you shall not be the meat inside it; I will judge you at the border of Israel. ¹²Then you shall know that I am the Lᴏʀᴅ, whose statutes you have not followed, and whose ordinances you have not kept, but you have acted according to the ordinances of the nations that are around you."

13 Now, while I was prophesying, Pelatiah son of Benaiah died. Then I fell down on my face, cried with a loud voice, and said, "Ah Lord Gᴏᴅ! will you make a full end of the remnant of Israel?"

God Will Restore Israel

14 Then the word of the Lᴏʀᴅ came to me: ¹⁵Mortal, your kinsfolk, your own kin, your fellow exiles,ᵃ the whole house of Israel, all of them, are those of whom the inhabitants of Jerusalem have said, "They have gone far from the Lᴏʀᴅ; to us this land is given for a possession." ¹⁶Therefore say: Thus says the Lord Gᴏᴅ: Though I removed them far away among the nations, and though I scattered them among the countries, yet I have been a sanctuary to them for a little whileᵇ in the countries where they have gone. ¹⁷Therefore say: Thus says the Lord Gᴏᴅ: I will gather you from the peoples, and assemble you out of the countries where you have been scattered, and I will give you the land of Israel. ¹⁸When they come there, they will remove from it all its detestable things and all its abominations. ¹⁹I will give them oneᶜ heart, and put a new spirit within them; I will remove the heart of stone from their flesh and give them a heart of flesh, ²⁰so that they may follow my statutes and keep my ordinances and obey them. Then they shall be my people, and I will be their God. ²¹But as for those whose heart goes after their detestable things and their abominations,ᵈ I will bring their deeds upon their own heads, says the Lord Gᴏᴅ.

22 Then the cherubim lifted up their wings, with the wheels beside them; and the glory of the God of Israel was above them. ²³And the

---

a Gk Syr: Heb *people of your kindred* b Or *to some extent* c Another reading is *a new* d Cn: Heb *And to the heart of their detestable things and their abominations their heart goes* glory of the LORD ascended from the middle of the city, and stopped on the mountain east of the city. [24]The spirit lifted me up and brought me in a vision by the spirit of God into Chaldea, to the exiles. Then the vision that I had seen left me. [25]And I told the exiles all the things that the LORD had shown me.

12 Judah's Captivity Portrayed

The word of the LORD came to me: [2]Mortal, you are living in the midst of a rebellious house, who have eyes to see but do not see, who have ears to hear but do not hear; [3]for they are a rebellious house. Therefore, mortal, prepare for yourself an exile's baggage, and go into exile by day in their sight; you shall go like an exile from your place to another place in their sight. Perhaps they will understand, though they are a rebellious house. [4]You shall bring out your baggage by day in their sight, as baggage for exile; and you shall go out yourself at evening in their sight, as those do who go into exile. [5]Dig through the wall in their sight, and carry the baggage through it. [6]In their sight you shall lift the baggage on your shoulder, and carry it out in the dark; you shall cover your face, so that you may not see the land; for I have made you a sign for the house of Israel.

[7] I did just as I was commanded. I brought out my baggage by day, as baggage for exile, and in the evening I dug through the wall with my own hands; I brought it out in the dark, carrying it on my shoulder in their sight.

[8] In the morning the word of the LORD came to me: [9]Mortal, has not the house of Israel, the rebellious house, said to you, "What are you doing?" [10]Say to them, "Thus says the Lord GOD: This oracle concerns the prince in Jerusalem and all the house of Israel in it." [11]Say, "I am a sign for you: as I have done, so shall it be done to them; they shall go into exile, into captivity." [12]And the prince who is among them shall lift his baggage on his shoulder in the dark, and shall go out; he[a] shall dig through the wall and carry it through; he shall cover his face, so that he may not see the land with his eyes. [13]I will spread my net over him, and he shall be caught in my snare; and I will bring him to Babylon, the land of the Chaldeans, yet he shall not see it; and he shall die there. [14]I will scatter to every wind all who are around him, his helpers and all his troops; and I will unsheathe the sword behind them. [15]And they shall know that I am the LORD, when I disperse them among the nations and scatter them through the countries. [16]But I will let a few of them escape from the sword, from famine

and pestilence, so that they may tell of all their abominations among the nations where they go; then they shall know that I am the LORD.

Judgment Not Postponed

[17] The word of the LORD came to me: [18]Mortal, eat your bread with quaking, and drink your water with trembling and with fearfulness; [19]and say to the people of the land, Thus says the Lord GOD concerning the inhabitants of Jerusalem in the land of Israel: They shall eat their bread with fearfulness, and drink their water in dismay, because their land shall be stripped of all it contains, on account of the violence of all those who live in it. [20]The inhabited cities shall be laid waste, and the land shall become a desolation; and you shall know that I am the LORD.

[21] The word of the LORD came to me: [22]Mortal, what is this proverb of yours about the land of Israel, which says, "The days are prolonged, and every vision comes to nothing"? [23]Tell them therefore, "Thus says the Lord GOD: I will put an end to this proverb, and they shall use it no more as a proverb in Israel." But say to them, The days are near, and the fulfillment of every vision. [24]For there shall no longer be any false vision or flattering divination within the house of Israel. [25]But I the LORD will speak the word that I speak, and it will be fulfilled. It will no longer be delayed; but in your days, O rebellious house, I will speak the word and fulfill it, says the Lord GOD.

[26] The word of the LORD came to me: [27]Mortal, the house of Israel is saying, "The vision that he sees is for many years ahead; he prophesies for distant times." [28]Therefore say to them, Thus says the Lord GOD: None of my words will be delayed any longer, but the word that I speak will be fulfilled, says the Lord GOD.

13 False Prophets Condemned

The word of the LORD came to me: [2]Mortal, prophesy against the prophets of Israel who are prophesying; say to those who prophesy out of their own imagination: "Hear the word of the LORD!" [3]Thus says the Lord GOD, Alas for the senseless prophets who follow their own spirit, and have seen nothing! [4]Your prophets have been like jackals among ruins, O Israel. [5]You have not gone up into the breaches, or repaired a wall for the house of Israel, so that it might stand in battle on the day of the LORD. [6]They have envisioned falsehood and lying divination; they say, "Says the LORD," when the LORD has not sent them, and yet they wait for the fulfillment of their word! [7]Have you not

a Gk Syr: Heb *they*

seen a false vision or uttered a lying divination, when you have said, "Says the LORD," even though I did not speak?

8 Therefore thus says the Lord GOD: Because you have uttered falsehood and envisioned lies, I am against you, says the Lord GOD. ⁹My hand will be against the prophets who see false visions and utter lying divinations; they shall not be in the council of my people, nor be enrolled in the register of the house of Israel, nor shall they enter the land of Israel; and you shall know that I am the Lord GOD. ¹⁰Because, in truth, because they have misled my people, saying, "Peace," when there is no peace; and because, when the people build a wall, these prophetsᵃ smear whitewash on it. ¹¹Say to those who smear whitewash on it that it shall fall. There will be a deluge of rain,ᵇ great hailstones will fall, and a stormy wind will break out. ¹²When the wall falls, will it not be said to you, "Where is the whitewash you smeared on it?" ¹³Therefore thus says the Lord GOD: In my wrath I will make a stormy wind break out, and in my anger there shall be a deluge of rain, and hailstones in wrath to destroy it. ¹⁴I will break down the wall that you have smeared with whitewash, and bring it to the ground, so that its foundation will be laid bare; when it falls, you shall perish within it; and you shall know that I am the LORD. ¹⁵Thus I will spend my wrath upon the wall, and upon those who have smeared it with whitewash; and I will say to you, The wall is no more, nor those who smeared it— ¹⁶the prophets of Israel who prophesied concerning Jerusalem and saw visions of peace for it, when there was no peace, says the Lord GOD.

17 As for you, mortal, set your face against the daughters of your people, who prophesy out of their own imagination; prophesy against them ¹⁸and say, Thus says the Lord GOD: Woe to the women who sew bands on all wrists, and make veils for the heads of persons of every height, in the hunt for human lives! Will you hunt down lives among my people, and maintain your own lives? ¹⁹You have profaned me among my people for handfuls of barley and for pieces of bread, putting to death persons who should not die and keeping alive persons who should not live, by your lies to my people, who listen to lies.

20 Therefore thus says the Lord GOD: I am against your bands with which you hunt lives;ᶜ I will tear them from your arms, and let the lives go free, the lives that you hunt down like birds. ²¹I will tear off your veils, and save my people from your hands; they shall no longer be prey

a Heb *they*   b Heb *rain and you*   c Gk Syr: Heb *lives for birds*

A Weird Question

One of the weirdest questions I've ever been asked by someone who was challenging my belief in Jesus was, "So if God is so forgiving—if God will forgive *any* sin if someone accepts Jesus—then would God forgive Hitler? Are you really claiming that if Hitler asked for forgiveness, God would forgive *him*?!"

It was an extremely uncomfortable moment. I agreed with my friend's point: Could somebody who'd done so much evil be forgiven?

But I knew the right answer. The answer was *yes*—God forgives. Isn't that what Jesus preached?

I had plenty of evidence. "Love your enemies" (Matthew 5.44). Forgive over and over (see Matthew 18.22). Don't judge or condemn; forgive and you will be forgiven (see Luke 6.37). Jesus even forgave those who nailed him to a cross (see Luke 23.43).

God's like that. And this isn't a concept that just showed up when Jesus came on the scene and taught about God's love. God has been a forgiving God since the start of time. Read **Ezekiel 11.16–20**.

Yes, God judges the sins of his people. And yes, God punishes them. But God also offers forgiveness, hope, and a new start. God *wants* to renew his people, to give them a new start, to give them a new heart!

And this passionate love of God isn't just for a select group of people. It's available to the whole world. To every culture. To every economic class. And even to people in the world who've done terrible, horrible, awful things. Even to terrorist masterminds and evil dictators. God's love and forgiveness are that big.

Go outside and find a stone. Hold it in your hand and think about how humanity tends to have a stubborn, stony heart toward God. Then think about how you feel when you consider the powerful forgiveness of God and God's willingness to give you and all people a new, tender, responsive heart. Grab some paints and give that stone a new look to represent how you feel. Make it festive, beautiful, or funky. (Upload a photo of it onto **Learner.CalltoDiscipleship.com**.) And next time you talk about God to a friend who doesn't believe in Jesus, use that rock to talk about God's power to forgive us and change our lives.

N

Gettin' Ready—© Catherine Willms, 15

in your hands; and you shall know that I am the LORD. 22 Because you have disheartened the righteous falsely, although I have not disheartened them, and you have encouraged the wicked not to turn from their wicked way and save their lives; 23 therefore you shall no longer see false visions or practice divination; I will save my people from your hand. Then you will know that I am the LORD.

14 God's Judgments Justified

Certain elders of Israel came to me and sat down before me. 2 And the word of the LORD came to me: 3 Mortal, these men have taken their idols into their hearts, and placed their iniquity as a stumbling block before them; shall I let myself be consulted by them? 4 Therefore speak to them, and say to them, Thus says the Lord GOD: Any of those of the house of Israel who take their idols into their hearts and place their iniquity as a stumbling block before them, and yet come to the prophet—I the LORD will answer those who come with the multitude of their idols, 5 in order that I may take hold of the hearts of the house of Israel, all of whom are estranged from me through their idols.

6 Therefore say to the house of Israel, Thus says the Lord GOD: Repent and turn away from your idols; and turn away your faces from all your abominations. 7 For any of those of the

house of Israel, or of the aliens who reside in Israel, who separate themselves from me, taking their idols into their hearts and placing their iniquity as a stumbling block before them, and yet come to a prophet to inquire of me by him, I the LORD will answer them myself. 8 I will set my face against them; I will make them a sign and a byword and cut them off from the midst of my people; and you shall know that I am the LORD.

9 If a prophet is deceived and speaks a word, I, the LORD, have deceived that prophet, and I will stretch out my hand against him, and will destroy him from the midst of my people Israel. 10 And they shall bear their punishment—the punishment of the inquirer and the punishment of the prophet shall be the same— 11 so that the house of Israel may no longer go astray from me, nor defile themselves any more with all their transgressions. Then they shall be my people, and I will be their God, says the Lord GOD.

12 The word of the LORD came to me: 13 Mortal, when a land sins against me by acting faithlessly, and I stretch out my hand against it, and break its staff of bread and send famine upon it, and cut off from it human beings and animals, 14 even if Noah, Daniel,ᵃ and Job, these three, were in it, they would save only their own lives by their righteousness, says the

a Or, as otherwise read, Danel

Lord God. [15]If I send wild animals through the land to ravage it, so that it is made desolate, and no one may pass through because of the animals; [16]even if these three men were in it, as I live, says the Lord God, they would save neither sons nor daughters; they alone would be saved, but the land would be desolate. [17]Or if I bring a sword upon that land and say, "Let a sword pass through the land," and I cut off human beings and animals from it; [18]though these three men were in it, as I live, says the Lord God, they would save neither sons nor daughters, but they alone would be saved. [19]Or if I send a pestilence into that land, and pour out my wrath upon it with blood, to cut off humans and animals from it; [20]even if Noah, Daniel,[a] and Job were in it, as I live, says the Lord God, they would save neither son nor daughter; they would save only their own lives by their righteousness.

21 For thus says the Lord God: How much more when I send upon Jerusalem my four deadly acts of judgment, sword, famine, wild animals, and pestilence, to cut off humans and animals from it! [22]Yet, survivors shall be left in it, sons and daughters who will be brought out; they will come out to you. When you see their ways and their deeds, you will be consoled for the evil that I have brought upon Jerusalem, for all that I have brought upon it. [23]They shall console you, when you see their ways and their deeds; and you shall know that it was not without cause that I did all that I have done in it, says the Lord God.

15 The Useless Vine

The word of the Lord came to me:
2 O mortal, how does the wood of the vine
    surpass all other wood—
  the vine branch that is among the trees
    of the forest?
3 Is wood taken from it to make anything?
  Does one take a peg from it on which to
    hang any object?
4 It is put in the fire for fuel;
  when the fire has consumed both ends
    of it
  and the middle of it is charred,
  is it useful for anything?
5 When it was whole it was used for nothing;
  how much less—when the fire has
    consumed it,
  and it is charred—
  can it ever be used for anything!

6 Therefore thus says the Lord God: Like the wood of the vine among the trees of the forest, which I have given to the fire for fuel, so I will give up the inhabitants of Jerusalem. [7]I will set my face against them; although they escape from the fire, the fire shall still consume them; and you shall know that I am the Lord, when I set my face against them. [8]And I will make the land desolate, because they have acted faithlessly, says the Lord God.

16 God's Faithless Bride

The word of the Lord came to me: [2]Mortal, make known to Jerusalem her abominations, [3]and say, Thus says the Lord God to Jerusalem: Your origin and your birth were in the land of the Canaanites; your father was an Amorite, and your mother a Hittite. [4]As for your birth, on the day you were born your navel cord was not cut, nor were you washed with water to cleanse you, nor rubbed with salt, nor wrapped in cloths. [5]No eye pitied you, to do any of these things for you out of compassion for you; but you were thrown out in the open field, for you were abhorred on the day you were born.

6 I passed by you, and saw you flailing about in your blood. As you lay in your blood, I said to you, "Live! [7]and grow up[b] like a plant of the field." You grew up and became tall and arrived at full womanhood;[c] your breasts were formed, and your hair had grown; yet you were naked and bare.

8 I passed by you again and looked on you; you were at the age for love. I spread the edge of my cloak over you, and covered your nakedness: I pledged myself to you and entered into a covenant with you, says the Lord God, and you became mine. [9]Then I bathed you with water and washed off the blood from you, and anointed you with oil. [10]I clothed you with embroidered cloth and with sandals of fine leather; I bound you in fine linen and covered you with rich fabric.[d] [11]I adorned you with ornaments: I put bracelets on your arms, a chain on your neck, [12]a ring on your nose, earrings in your ears, and a beautiful crown upon your head. [13]You were adorned with gold and silver, while your clothing was of fine linen, rich fabric,[d] and embroidered cloth. You had choice flour and honey and oil for food. You grew exceedingly beautiful, fit to be a queen. [14]Your fame spread among the nations on account of your beauty, for it was perfect because of my splendor that I had bestowed on you, says the Lord God.

15 But you trusted in your beauty, and played the whore because of your fame, and lavished your whorings on any passer-by.[e] [16]You

---

a Or, as otherwise read, *Danel* b Gk Syr: Heb *Live! I made you a myriad* c Cn: Heb *ornament of ornaments* d Meaning of Heb uncertain
e Heb adds *let it be his*

took some of your garments, and made for yourself colorful shrines, and on them played the whore; nothing like this has ever been or ever shall be.[a] 17You also took your beautiful jewels of my gold and my silver that I had given you, and made for yourself male images, and with them played the whore; 18and you took your embroidered garments to cover them, and set my oil and my incense before them. 19Also my bread that I gave you—I fed you with choice flour and oil and honey—you set it before them as a pleasing odor; and so it was, says the Lord God. 20You took your sons and your daughters, whom you had borne to me, and these you sacrificed to them to be devoured. As if your whorings were not enough! 21You slaughtered my children and delivered them up as an offering to them. 22And in all your abominations and your whorings you did not remember the days of your youth, when you were naked and bare, flailing about in your blood.

23 After all your wickedness (woe, woe to you! says the Lord God), 24you built yourself a platform and made yourself a lofty place in every square; 25at the head of every street you built your lofty place and prostituted your beauty, offering yourself to every passer-by, and multiplying your whoring. 26You played the whore with the Egyptians, your lustful neighbors, multiplying your whoring, to provoke me to anger. 27Therefore I stretched out my hand against you, reduced your rations, and gave you up to the will of your enemies, the daughters of the Philistines, who were ashamed of your lewd behavior. 28You played the whore with the Assyrians, because you were insatiable; you played the whore with them, and still you were not satisfied. 29You multiplied your whoring with Chaldea, the land of merchants; and even with this you were not satisfied.

30 How sick is your heart, says the Lord God, that you did all these things, the deeds of a brazen whore; 31building your platform at the head of every street, and making your lofty place in every square! Yet you were not like a whore, because you scorned payment. 32Adulterous wife, who receives strangers instead of her husband! 33Gifts are given to all whores; but you gave your gifts to all your lovers, bribing them to come to you from all around for your whorings. 34So you were different from other women in your whorings: no one solicited you to play the whore; and you gave payment, while no payment was given to you; you were different.

35 Therefore, O whore, hear the word of the Lord: 36Thus says the Lord God, Because your lust was poured out and your nakedness uncovered in your whoring with your lovers, and because of all your abominable idols, and because of the blood of your children that you gave to them, 37therefore, I will gather all your lovers, with whom you took pleasure, all those you loved and all those you hated; I will gather them against you from all around, and will uncover your nakedness to them, so that they may see all your nakedness. 38I will judge you as women who commit adultery and shed blood are judged, and bring blood upon you in wrath and jealousy. 39I will deliver you into their hands, and they shall throw down your platform and break down your lofty places; they shall strip you of your clothes and take your beautiful objects and leave you naked and bare. 40They shall bring up a mob against you, and they shall stone you and cut you to pieces with their swords. 41They shall burn your houses and execute judgments on you in the sight of many women; I will stop you from playing the whore, and you shall also make no more payments. 42So I will satisfy my fury on you, and my jealousy shall turn away from you; I will be calm, and will be angry no longer. 43Because you have not remembered the days of your youth, but have enraged me with all these things; therefore, I have returned your deeds upon your head, says the Lord God.

Have you not committed lewdness beyond all your abominations? 44See, everyone who uses proverbs will use this proverb about you, "Like mother, like daughter." 45You are the daughter of your mother, who loathed her husband and her children; and you are the sister of your sisters, who loathed their husbands and their children. Your mother was a Hittite and your father an Amorite. 46Your elder sister is Samaria, who lived with her daughters to the north of you; and your younger sister, who lived to the south of you, is Sodom with her daughters. 47You not only followed their ways, and acted according to their abominations; within a very little time you were more corrupt than they in all your ways. 48As I live, says the Lord God, your sister Sodom and her daughters have not done as you and your daughters have done. 49This was the guilt of your sister Sodom: she and her daughters had pride, excess of food, and prosperous ease, but did not aid the poor and needy. 50They were haughty, and did abominable things before me; therefore I removed them when I saw it. 51Samaria has not committed half your sins; you have committed more abominations than they, and have made your sisters appear righteous by all

a Meaning of Heb uncertain

the abominations that you have committed. [52]Bear your disgrace, you also, for you have brought about for your sisters a more favorable judgment; because of your sins in which you acted more abominably than they, they are more in the right than you. So be ashamed, you also, and bear your disgrace, for you have made your sisters appear righteous.

53 I will restore their fortunes, the fortunes of Sodom and her daughters and the fortunes of Samaria and her daughters, and I will restore your own fortunes along with theirs, [54]in order that you may bear your disgrace and be ashamed of all that you have done, becoming a consolation to them. [55]As for your sisters, Sodom and her daughters shall return to their former state, Samaria and her daughters shall return to their former state, and you and your daughters shall return to your former state. [56]Was not your sister Sodom a byword in your mouth in the day of your pride, [57]before your wickedness was uncovered? Now you are a mockery to the daughters of Aram[a] and all her neighbors, and to the daughters of the Philistines, those all around who despise you. [58]You must bear the penalty of your lewdness and your abominations, says the LORD.

An Everlasting Covenant

59 Yes, thus says the Lord GOD: I will deal with you as you have done, you who have despised the oath, breaking the covenant; [60]yet I will remember my covenant with you in the days of your youth, and I will establish with you an everlasting covenant. [61]Then you will remember your ways, and be ashamed when I[b] take your sisters, both your elder and your younger, and give them to you as daughters, but not on account of my[c] covenant with you. [62]I will establish my covenant with you, and you shall know that I am the LORD, [63]in order that you may remember and be confounded, and never open your mouth again because of your shame, when I forgive you all that you have done, says the Lord GOD.

17 The Two Eagles and the Vine

The word of the LORD came to me: [2]O mortal, propound a riddle, and speak an allegory to the house of Israel. [3]Say: Thus says the Lord GOD:

A great eagle, with great wings and long
    pinions,
  rich in plumage of many colors,
  came to the Lebanon.
He took the top of the cedar,
4 broke off its topmost shoot;
  he carried it to a land of trade,

REALITY ✔

THE CHURCH: HERE COMES THE BRIDE

Ezekiel 16 is one of the most heartbreaking chapters of the Bible. Here, the prophet Ezekiel describes Jerusalem (God's people) as a young girl who was rejected at birth. God took her in, binding his life to hers with a covenant. He bathed her, clothed her, and treated her with honor. He hung jewelry around her neck, and her fame and beauty spread far and wide. And then she repaid his love by becoming a prostitute, squandering his gifts, and forgetting him. The New Testament describes the Church as Jesus' bride, whom he loves and made sacrifices for (see Ephesians 5.25).

Besides being called the "bride," the Church has been given many other descriptive names throughout history. In the New Testament we have images of the Church as a community of believers, the Body of Christ. After the Reformation, Robert Bellarmine described the Church as a "perfect society." Pope Pius XII described the Church as the Mystical Body of Christ. At the Second Vatican Council, the bishops of the world gave us many images of Church, including the image of a sacrament, the people of God, a mother, a pilgrim people, a sheepfold, and a piece of land to be tilled by God.

Think about your experience of Church, your parish, your diocese, the worldwide Church. What do you see? How would you describe it in images that people could understand without much explanation? Put your description in art or word form. Share it on **Learner.CalltoDiscipleship.com**.

    set it in a city of merchants.
5 Then he took a seed from the land,
    placed it in fertile soil;
a plant[d] by abundant waters,
    he set it like a willow twig.
6 It sprouted and became a vine
    spreading out, but low;

---

a Another reading is *Edom* *b* Syr: Heb *you* *c* Heb lacks *my* *d* Meaning of Heb uncertain

its branches turned toward him,
    its roots remained where it stood.
So it became a vine;
    it brought forth branches,
    put forth foliage.

7 There was another great eagle,
    with great wings and much plumage.
And see! This vine stretched out
    its roots toward him;
it shot out its branches toward him,
    so that he might water it.
From the bed where it was planted
8   it was transplanted
to good soil by abundant waters,
    so that it might produce branches
    and bear fruit
    and become a noble vine.

9 Say: Thus says the Lord God:
    Will it prosper?
Will he not pull up its roots,
    cause its fruit to rot[a] and wither,
    its fresh sprouting leaves to fade?
No strong arm or mighty army will be
    needed
    to pull it from its roots.
10 When it is transplanted, will it thrive?
When the east wind strikes it,
    will it not utterly wither,
    wither on the bed where it grew?

11 Then the word of the Lord came to me:
12 Say now to the rebellious house: Do you not know what these things mean? Tell them: The king of Babylon came to Jerusalem, took its king and its officials, and brought them back with him to Babylon. 13 He took one of the royal offspring and made a covenant with him, putting him under oath (he had taken away the chief men of the land), 14 so that the kingdom might be humble and not lift itself up, and that by keeping his covenant it might stand. 15 But he rebelled against him by sending ambassadors to Egypt, in order that they might give him horses and a large army. Will he succeed? Can one escape who does such things? Can he break the covenant and yet escape? 16 As I live, says the Lord God, surely in the place where the king resides who made him king, whose oath he despised, and whose covenant with him he broke—in Babylon he shall die. 17 Pharaoh with his mighty army and great company will not help him in war, when ramps are cast up and siege walls built to cut off many lives. 18 Because he despised the oath and broke the covenant, because he gave his hand and yet did all these things, he shall not escape. 19 Therefore thus says the Lord God: As I live, I will surely return upon his head my oath that he despised, and my covenant that he broke. 20 I will spread my net over him, and he shall be caught in my snare; I will bring him to Babylon and enter into judgment with him there for the treason he has committed against me. 21 All the pick[b] of his troops shall fall by the sword, and the survivors shall be scattered to every wind; and you shall know that I, the Lord, have spoken.

Israel Exalted at Last

22 Thus says the Lord God:
    I myself will take a sprig
      from the lofty top of a cedar;
    I will set it out.
I will break off a tender one
    from the topmost of its young twigs;
I myself will plant it
    on a high and lofty mountain.
23 On the mountain height of Israel
    I will plant it,
in order that it may produce boughs and
      bear fruit,
    and become a noble cedar.
Under it every kind of bird will live;
    in the shade of its branches will nest
    winged creatures of every kind.
24 All the trees of the field shall know
    that I am the Lord.
I bring low the high tree,
    I make high the low tree;
I dry up the green tree
    and make the dry tree flourish.
I the Lord have spoken;
    I will accomplish it.

18 Individual Retribution

The word of the Lord came to me: 2 What do you mean by repeating this proverb concerning the land of Israel, "The parents have eaten sour grapes, and the children's teeth are set on edge"? 3 As I live, says the Lord God, this proverb shall no more be used by you in Israel. 4 Know that all lives are mine; the life of the parent as well as the life of the child is mine: it is only the person who sins that shall die.

5 If a man is righteous and does what is lawful and right— 6 if he does not eat upon the mountains or lift up his eyes to the idols of the house of Israel, does not defile his neighbor's wife or approach a woman during her menstrual period, 7 does not oppress anyone, but restores to the debtor his pledge, commits no robbery, gives his bread to the hungry and covers the naked with a garment, 8 does not take advance or accrued interest, withholds his hand from iniquity, executes true justice between contending parties, 9 follows my stat-

---

a Meaning of Heb uncertain b Another reading is *fugitives* utes, and is careful to observe my ordinances, acting faithfully—such a one is righteous; he shall surely live, says the Lord God.

10 If he has a son who is violent, a shedder of blood, ¹¹who does any of these things (though his father^a does none of them), who eats upon the mountains, defiles his neighbor's wife, ¹²oppresses the poor and needy, commits robbery, does not restore the pledge, lifts up his eyes to the idols, commits abomination, ¹³takes advance or accrued interest; shall he then live? He shall not. He has done all these abominable things; he shall surely die; his blood shall be upon himself.

14 But if this man has a son who sees all the sins that his father has done, considers, and does not do likewise, ¹⁵who does not eat upon the mountains or lift up his eyes to the idols of the house of Israel, does not defile his neighbor's wife, ¹⁶does not wrong anyone, exacts no pledge, commits no robbery, but gives his bread to the hungry and covers the naked with a garment, ¹⁷withholds his hand from iniquity,^b takes no advance or accrued interest, observes my ordinances, and follows my statutes; he shall not die for his father's iniquity; he shall surely live. ¹⁸As for his father, because he practiced extortion, robbed his brother, and did what is not good among his people, he dies for his iniquity.

19 Yet you say, "Why should not the son suffer for the iniquity of the father?" When the son has done what is lawful and right, and has been careful to observe all my statutes, he shall surely live. ²⁰The person who sins shall die. A child shall not suffer for the iniquity of a parent, nor a parent suffer for the iniquity of a child; the righteousness of the righteous shall be his own, and the wickedness of the wicked shall be his own.

21 But if the wicked turn away from all their sins that they have committed and keep all my statutes and do what is lawful and right, they shall surely live; they shall not die. ²²None of the transgressions that they have committed shall be remembered against them; for the righteousness that they have done they shall live. ²³Have I any pleasure in the death of the wicked, says the Lord God, and not rather that they should turn from their ways and live? ²⁴But when the righteous turn away from their righteousness and commit iniquity and do the same abominable things that the wicked do, shall they live? None of the righteous deeds that they have done shall be remembered; for the treachery of which they are guilty and the sin they have committed, they shall die.

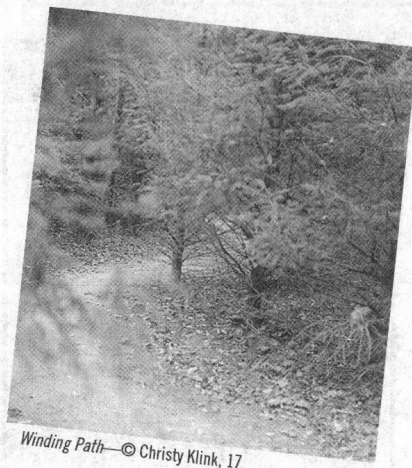

Winding Path—© Christy Klink, 17

25 Yet you say, "The way of the Lord is unfair." Hear now, O house of Israel: Is my way unfair? Is it not your ways that are unfair? ²⁶When the righteous turn away from their righteousness and commit iniquity, they shall die for it; for the iniquity that they have committed they shall die. ²⁷Again, when the wicked turn away from the wickedness they have committed and do what is lawful and right, they shall save their life. ²⁸Because they considered and turned away from all the transgressions that they had committed, they shall surely live; they shall not die. ²⁹Yet the house of Israel says, "The way of the Lord is unfair." O house of Israel, are my ways unfair? Is it not your ways that are unfair?

30 Therefore I will judge you, O house of Israel, all of you according to your ways, says the Lord God. Repent and turn from all your transgressions; otherwise iniquity will be your ruin.^c ³¹Cast away from you all the transgressions that you have committed against me, and get yourselves a new heart and a new spirit! Why will you die, O house of Israel? ³²For I have no pleasure in the death of anyone, says the Lord God. Turn, then, and live.

19 Israel Degraded

As for you, raise up a lamentation for the princes of Israel, ²and say:
> What a lioness was your mother
> among lions!
> She lay down among young lions,
> rearing her cubs.
> ³ She raised up one of her cubs;
> he became a young lion,
> and he learned to catch prey;
> he devoured humans.

---

^a Heb *he* ^b Gk: Heb *the poor* ^c Or *so that they shall not be a stumbling block of iniquity to you*

they spread their net over him;
he was caught in their pit.
9 With hooks they put him in a cage,
and brought him to the king of Babylon;
they brought him into custody,
so that his voice should be heard no more
on the mountains of Israel.
10 Your mother was like a vine in a vineyard[b]
transplanted by the water,
fruitful and full of branches
from abundant water.
11 Its strongest stem became
a ruler's scepter;[c]
it towered aloft
among the thick boughs;
it stood out in its height
with its mass of branches.
12 But it was plucked up in fury,
cast down to the ground;
the east wind dried it up;
its fruit was stripped off,
its strong stem was withered;
the fire consumed it.
13 Now it is transplanted into the wilderness,
into a dry and thirsty land.
14 And fire has gone out from its stem,
has consumed its branches and fruit,
so that there remains in it no strong stem,
no scepter for ruling.

This is a lamentation, and it is used as a lamentation.

20 Israel's Continuing Rebellion

In the seventh year, in the fifth month, on the tenth day of the month, certain elders of Israel came to consult the LORD, and sat down before me. 2And the word of the LORD came to me: 3Mortal, speak to the elders of Israel, and say to them: Thus says the Lord GOD: Why are you coming? To consult me? As I live, says the Lord GOD, I will not be consulted by you. 4Will you judge them, mortal, will you judge them? Then let them know the abominations of their ancestors, 5and say to them: Thus says the Lord GOD: On the day when I chose Israel, I swore to the offspring of the house of Jacob—making myself known to them in the land of Egypt—I swore to them, saying, I am the LORD your God. 6On that day I swore to them that I would bring them out of the land of Egypt into a land that I had searched out for them, a land flowing with milk and honey, the most glorious of all lands. 7And I said to them, Cast away the detestable things your eyes feast on, every one of you, and do not defile yourselves with the idols of Egypt; I am the LORD your God. 8But they rebelled against me and would not listen to me; not

4 The nations sounded an alarm against him;
he was caught in their pit;
and they brought him with hooks
to the land of Egypt.
5 When she saw that she was thwarted,
that her hope was lost,
she took another of her cubs
and made him a young lion.
6 He prowled among the lions;
he became a young lion,
and he learned to catch prey;
he devoured people.
7 And he ravaged their strongholds,[a]
and laid waste their towns;
the land was appalled, and all in it,
at the sound of his roaring.
8 The nations set upon him
from the provinces all around;

a Heb *his widows* b Cn: Heb *in your blood* c Heb *Its strongest stems became rulers' scepters* one of them cast away the detestable things their eyes feasted on, nor did they forsake the idols of Egypt.

Then I thought I would pour out my wrath upon them and spend my anger against them in the midst of the land of Egypt. ⁹But I acted for the sake of my name, that it should not be profaned in the sight of the nations among whom they lived, in whose sight I made myself known to them in bringing them out of the land of Egypt. ¹⁰So I led them out of the land of Egypt and brought them into the wilderness. ¹¹I gave them my statutes and showed them my ordinances, by whose observance everyone shall live. ¹²Moreover I gave them my sabbaths, as a sign between me and them, so that they might know that I the LORD sanctify them. ¹³But the house of Israel rebelled against me in the wilderness; they did not observe my statutes but rejected my ordinances, by whose observance everyone shall live; and my sabbaths they greatly profaned.

Then I thought I would pour out my wrath upon them in the wilderness, to make an end of them. ¹⁴But I acted for the sake of my name, so that it should not be profaned in the sight of the nations, in whose sight I had brought them out. ¹⁵Moreover I swore to them in the wilderness that I would not bring them into the land that I had given them, a land flowing with milk and honey, the most glorious of all lands, ¹⁶because they rejected my ordinances and did not observe my statutes, and profaned my sabbaths; for their heart went after their idols. ¹⁷Nevertheless my eye spared them, and I did not destroy them or make an end of them in the wilderness.

18 I said to their children in the wilderness, Do not follow the statutes of your parents, nor observe their ordinances, nor defile yourselves with their idols. ¹⁹I the LORD am your God; follow my statutes, and be careful to observe my ordinances, ²⁰and hallow my sabbaths that they may be a sign between me and you, so that you may know that I the LORD am your God. ²¹But the children rebelled against me; they did not follow my statutes, and were not careful to observe my ordinances, by whose observance everyone shall live; they profaned my sabbaths.

Then I thought I would pour out my wrath upon them and spend my anger against them in the wilderness. ²²But I withheld my hand, and acted for the sake of my name, so that it should not be profaned in the sight of the nations, in whose sight I had brought them out. ²³Moreover I swore to them in the wilderness that I would scatter them among the nations and disperse them through the countries, ²⁴because they had not executed my ordinances, but had rejected my statutes and profaned my sabbaths, and their eyes were set on their ancestors' idols. ²⁵Moreover I gave them statutes that were not good and ordinances by which they could not live. ²⁶I defiled them through their very gifts, in their offering up all their firstborn, in order that I might horrify them, so that they might know that I am the LORD.

27 Therefore, mortal, speak to the house of Israel and say to them, Thus says the Lord GOD: In this again your ancestors blasphemed me, by dealing treacherously with me. ²⁸For when I had brought them into the land that I swore to give them, then wherever they saw any high hill or any leafy tree, there they offered their sacrifices and presented the provocation of their offering; there they sent up their pleasing odors, and there they poured out their drink offerings. ²⁹(I said to them, What is the high place to which you go? So it is called Bamah*ᵃ* to this day.) ³⁰Therefore say to the house of Israel, Thus says the Lord GOD: Will you defile yourselves after the manner of your ancestors and go astray after their detestable things? ³¹When you offer your gifts and make your children pass through the fire, you defile yourselves with all your idols to this day. And shall I be consulted by you, O house of Israel? As I live, says the Lord GOD, I will not be consulted by you.

32 What is in your mind shall never happen—the thought, "Let us be like the nations, like the tribes of the countries, and worship wood and stone."

God Will Restore Israel

33 As I live, says the Lord GOD, surely with a mighty hand and an outstretched arm, and with wrath poured out, I will be king over you. ³⁴I will bring you out from the peoples and gather you out of the countries where you are scattered, with a mighty hand and an outstretched arm, and with wrath poured out; ³⁵and I will bring you into the wilderness of the peoples, and there I will enter into judgment with you face to face. ³⁶As I entered into judgment with your ancestors in the wilderness of the land of Egypt, so I will enter into judgment with you, says the Lord GOD. ³⁷I will make you pass under the staff, and will bring you within the bond of the covenant. ³⁸I will purge out the rebels among you, and those who transgress against me; I will bring them out of the land where they reside as aliens, but they shall not enter the land of Israel. Then you shall know that I am the LORD.

a That is *High Place*

Imagine what it would be like to belong to a prestigious, important family and then to be kidnapped and sold into slavery—not once, but several times! That was the fate of St. Josephine Bakhita in the late nineteenth century. She was born in a village in the western region of Darfur, Sudan, where her uncle was the tribal chief.

When she was nine, she was kidnapped by Arab slave traders. Over the next eight years, she was sold and resold five times in slave markets. Her final owner was an Italian diplomat who brought her to Italy as a nanny. It was there that St. Josephine and her charge were left in the custody of the Canossian Sisters in Venice, where St. Josephine became a Catholic.

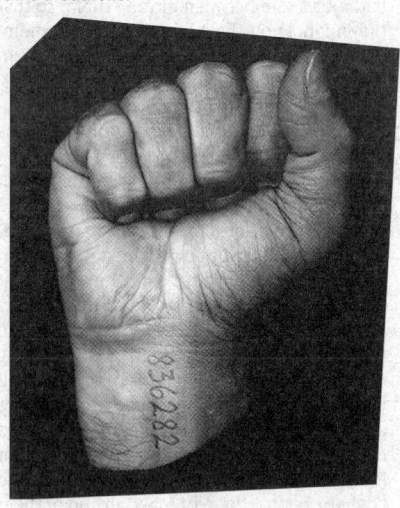

When her owner returned, St. Josephine did not want to leave the convent. An Italian court ruled that since Sudan had outlawed slavery before her birth and Italian law did not recognize slavery, St. Josephine had never in fact been a slave. St. Josephine chose to remain with the sisters as a free woman.

St. Josephine spent most of the rest of her life in northern Italy. Her special charisma and reputation for holiness were noticed by the sisters, and they encouraged her to publish her memoirs and give talks about her experiences, which made her famous throughout Italy.

St. Josephine is venerated as a modern African saint and as a saint with a special relevance for slavery and oppression. She has been adopted as the patron saint of Sudan. Her feast day is February 8.

---

39 As for you, O house of Israel, thus says the Lord GOD: Go serve your idols, every one of you now and hereafter, if you will not listen to me; but my holy name you shall no more profane with your gifts and your idols.

40 For on my holy mountain, the mountain height of Israel, says the Lord GOD, there all the house of Israel, all of them, shall serve me in the land; there I will accept them, and there I will require your contributions and the choicest of your gifts, with all your sacred things. [41] As a pleasing odor I will accept you, when I bring you out from the peoples, and gather you out of the countries where you have been scattered; and I will manifest my holiness among you in the sight of the nations. [42] You shall know that I am the LORD, when I bring you into the land of Israel, the country that I swore to give to your ancestors. [43] There you shall remember your ways and all the deeds by which you have polluted yourselves; and you shall loathe yourselves for all the evils that you have committed. [44] And you shall know that I am the LORD, when I deal with you for my name's sake, not according to your evil ways, or corrupt deeds, O house of Israel, says the Lord GOD.

A Prophecy against the Negeb

45[a] The word of the LORD came to me: [46] Mortal, set your face toward the south, preach against the south, and prophesy against the forest land in the Negeb; [47] say to the forest of the Negeb, Hear the word of the LORD: Thus says the Lord GOD, I will kindle a fire in you, and it shall devour every green tree in you and every dry tree; the blazing flame shall not be quenched, and

a Ch 21.1 in Heb

all faces from south to north shall be scorched by it. ⁴⁸All flesh shall see that I the LORD have kindled it; it shall not be quenched. ⁴⁹Then I said, "Ah Lord GOD! they are saying of me, 'Is he not a maker of allegories?' "

21 *ᵃ* The Drawn Sword of God

The word of the LORD came to me: ²Mortal, set your face toward Jerusalem and preach against the sanctuaries; prophesy against the land of Israel ³and say to the land of Israel, Thus says the LORD: I am coming against you, and will draw my sword out of its sheath, and will cut off from you both righteous and wicked. ⁴Because I will cut off from you both righteous and wicked, therefore my sword shall go out of its sheath against all flesh from south to north; ⁵and all flesh shall know that I the LORD have drawn my sword out of its sheath; it shall not be sheathed again. ⁶Moan therefore, mortal; moan with breaking heart and bitter grief before their eyes. ⁷And when they say to you, "Why do you moan?" you shall say, "Because of the news that has come. Every heart will melt and all hands will be feeble, every spirit will faint and all knees will turn to water. See, it comes and it will be fulfilled," says the Lord GOD.

8 And the word of the LORD came to me: ⁹Mortal, prophesy and say: Thus says the Lord; Say:

A sword, a sword is sharpened,
  it is also polished;
¹⁰ it is sharpened for slaughter,
  honed to flash like lightning!
How can we make merry?
  You have despised the rod,
  and all discipline.*ᵇ*
¹¹ The sword*ᶜ* is given to be polished,
  to be grasped in the hand;
it is sharpened, the sword is polished,
  to be placed in the slayer's hand.
¹² Cry and wail, O mortal,
  for it is against my people;
it is against all Israel's princes;
  they are thrown to the sword,
  together with my people.
  Ah! Strike the thigh!
¹³For consider: What! If you despise the rod, will it not happen?*ᵇ* says the Lord GOD.
¹⁴ And you, mortal, prophesy;
  strike hand to hand.
Let the sword fall twice, thrice;
  it is a sword for killing.
A sword for great slaughter—
  it surrounds them;
¹⁵ therefore hearts melt

and many stumble.
At all their gates I have set
  the point*ᵇ* of the sword.
Ah! It is made for flashing,
  it is polished*ᵈ* for slaughter.
¹⁶ Attack to the right!
  Engage to the left!
  —wherever your edge is directed.
¹⁷ I too will strike hand to hand,
  I will satisfy my fury;
  I the LORD have spoken.

18 The word of the LORD came to me: ¹⁹Mortal, mark out two roads for the sword of the king of Babylon to come; both of them shall issue from the same land. And make a signpost, make it for a fork in the road leading to a city; ²⁰mark out the road for the sword to come to Rabbah of the Ammonites or to Judah and to*ᵉ* Jerusalem the fortified. ²¹For the king of Babylon stands at the parting of the way, at the fork in the two roads, to use divination; he shakes the arrows, he consults the teraphim,*ᶠ* he inspects the liver. ²²Into his right hand comes the lot for Jerusalem, to set battering rams, to call out for slaughter, for raising the battle cry, to set battering rams against the gates, to cast up ramps, to build siege towers. ²³But to them it will seem like a false divination; they have sworn solemn oaths; but he brings their guilt to remembrance, bringing about their capture.

24 Therefore thus says the Lord GOD: Because you have brought your guilt to remembrance, in that your transgressions are uncovered, so that in all your deeds your sins appear—because you have come to remembrance, you shall be taken in hand.*ᵍ*
²⁵ As for you, vile, wicked prince of Israel,
  you whose day has come,
  the time of final punishment,
²⁶ thus says the Lord GOD:
Remove the turban, take off the crown;
  things shall not remain as they are.
Exalt that which is low,
  abase that which is high.
²⁷ A ruin, a ruin, a ruin—
  I will make it!
  (Such has never occurred.)
Until he comes whose right it is;
  to him I will give it.
28 As for you, mortal, prophesy, and say, Thus says the Lord GOD concerning the Ammonites, and concerning their reproach; say:
A sword, a sword! Drawn for slaughter,
  polished to consume,*ʰ* to flash like
  lightning.

---

a Ch 21.6 in Heb *b* Meaning of Heb uncertain *c* Heb lt *d* Tg: Heb *wrapped up* *e* Gk Syr: Heb *Judah in* *f* Or *the household gods* *g* Or *be taken captive* *h* Cn: Heb *to contain*

²⁹ Offering false visions for you,
  divining lies for you,
they place you over the necks
  of the vile, wicked ones—
those whose day has come,
  the time of final punishment.
³⁰ Return it to its sheath!
In the place where you were created,
  in the land of your origin,
  I will judge you.
³¹ I will pour out my indignation upon you,
  with the fire of my wrath
  I will blow upon you.
I will deliver you into brutish hands,
  those skillful to destroy.
³² You shall be fuel for the fire,
  your blood shall enter the earth;
you shall be remembered no more,
  for I the LORD have spoken.

22 The Bloody City

The word of the LORD came to me: ²You, mortal, will you judge, will you judge the bloody city? Then declare to it all its abominable deeds. ³You shall say, Thus says the Lord GOD: A city! Shedding blood within itself; its time has come; making its idols, defiling itself. ⁴You have become guilty by the blood that you have shed, and defiled by the idols that you have made; you have brought your day near, the appointed time of your years has come. Therefore I have made you a disgrace before the nations, and a mockery to all the countries. ⁵Those who are near and those who are far from you will mock you, you infamous one, full of tumult.

6 The princes of Israel in you, everyone according to his power, have been bent on shedding blood. ⁷Father and mother are treated with contempt in you; the alien residing within you suffers extortion; the orphan and the widow are wronged in you. ⁸You have despised my holy things, and profaned my sabbaths. ⁹In you are those who slander to shed blood, those in you who eat upon the mountains, who commit lewdness in your midst. ¹⁰In you they uncover their fathers' nakedness; in you they violate women in their menstrual periods. ¹¹One commits abomination with his neighbor's wife; another lewdly defiles his daughter-in-law; another in you defiles his sister, his father's daughter. ¹²In you, they take bribes to shed blood; you take both advance interest and accrued interest, and make gain of your neighbors by extortion; and you have forgotten me, says the Lord GOD.

13 See, I strike my hands together at the dishonest gain you have made, and at the blood that has been shed within you. ¹⁴Can your courage endure, or can your hands remain strong in the days when I shall deal with you? I the LORD have spoken, and I will do it. ¹⁵I will scatter you among the nations and disperse you through the countries, and I will purge your filthiness out of you. ¹⁶And I^a shall be profaned through you in the sight of the nations; and you shall know that I am the LORD.

17 The word of the LORD came to me: ¹⁸Mortal, the house of Israel has become dross to me; all of them, silver,^b bronze, tin, iron, and lead. In the smelter they have become dross. ¹⁹Therefore thus says the Lord GOD: Because you have all become dross, I will gather you into the midst of Jerusalem. ²⁰As one gathers silver, bronze, iron, lead, and tin into a smelter, to blow the fire upon them in order to melt them; so I will gather you in my anger and in my wrath, and I will put you in and melt you. ²¹I will gather you and blow upon you with the fire of my wrath, and you shall be melted within it. ²²As silver is melted in a smelter, so you shall be melted in it; and you shall know that I the LORD have poured out my wrath upon you.

23 The word of the LORD came to me: ²⁴Mortal, say to it: You are a land that is not cleansed, not rained upon in the day of indignation. ²⁵Its princes^c within it are like a roaring lion tearing the prey; they have devoured human lives; they have taken treasure and precious things; they have made many widows within it. ²⁶Its priests have done violence to my teaching and have profaned my holy things; they have made no distinction between the holy and the common, neither have they taught the difference between the unclean and the clean, and they have disregarded my sabbaths, so that I am profaned among them. ²⁷Its officials within it are like wolves tearing the prey, shedding blood, destroying lives to get dishonest gain. ²⁸Its prophets have smeared whitewash on their behalf, seeing false visions and divining lies for them, saying, "Thus says the Lord GOD," when the LORD has not spoken. ²⁹The people of the land have practiced extortion and committed robbery; they have oppressed the poor and needy, and have extorted from the alien without redress. ³⁰And I sought for anyone among them who would repair the wall and stand in the breach before me on behalf of the land, so that I would not destroy it; but I found no one. ³¹Therefore I have poured out my indignation upon them; I have consumed them with the fire of my wrath; I have returned their conduct upon their heads, says the Lord GOD.

---

a Gk Syr Vg: Heb *you* *b* Transposed from the end of the verse; compare verse 20 *c* Gk: Heb *indignation*. 25A conspiracy of its prophets

23 Oholah and Oholibah

The word of the LORD came to me: ²Mortal, there were two women, the daughters of one mother; ³they played the whore in Egypt; they played the whore in their youth; their breasts were caressed there, and their virgin bosoms were fondled. ⁴Oholah was the name of the elder and Oholibah the name of her sister. They became mine, and they bore sons and daughters. As for their names, Oholah is Samaria, and Oholibah is Jerusalem.

5 Oholah played the whore while she was mine; she lusted after her lovers the Assyrians, warriors⁹ ⁶clothed in blue, governors and commanders, all of them handsome young men, mounted horsemen. ⁷She bestowed her favors upon them, the choicest men of Assyria all of them; and she defiled herself with all the idols of everyone for whom she lusted. ⁸She did not give up her whorings that she had practiced since Egypt; for in her youth men had lain with her and fondled her virgin bosom and poured out their lust upon her. ⁹Therefore I delivered her into the hands of her lovers, into the hands of the Assyrians, for whom she lusted. ¹⁰These uncovered her nakedness; they seized her sons and her daughters; and they killed her with the sword. Judgment was executed upon her, and she became a byword among women.

11 Her sister Oholibah saw this, yet she was more corrupt than she in her lusting and in her whorings, which were worse than those of her sister. ¹²She lusted after the Assyrians, governors and commanders, warriors⁹ clothed in full armor, mounted horsemen, all of them handsome young men. ¹³And I saw that she was defiled; they both took the same way. ¹⁴But she carried her whorings further; she saw male figures carved on the wall, images of the Chaldeans portrayed in vermilion, ¹⁵with belts around their waists, with flowing turbans on their heads, all of them looking like officers— a picture of Babylonians whose native land was Chaldea. ¹⁶When she saw them she lusted after them, and sent messengers to them in Chaldea. ¹⁷And the Babylonians came to her into the bed of love, and they defiled her with their lust; and after she defiled herself with them, she turned from them in disgust. ¹⁸When she carried on her whorings so openly and flaunted her nakedness, I turned in disgust from her, as I had turned from her sister. ¹⁹Yet she increased her whorings, remembering the days of her youth, when she played the whore in the land of Egypt ²⁰and lusted after her paramours there, whose members were like those of donkeys, and whose emission was like that of stallions. ²¹Thus you longed for the lewdness of your youth, when the Egyptians⁹ fondled your bosom and caressed⁶ your young breasts.

22 Therefore, O Oholibah, thus says the Lord GOD: I will rouse against you your lovers from whom you turned in disgust, and I will bring them against you from every side: ²³the Babylonians and all the Chaldeans, Pekod and Shoa and Koa, and all the Assyrians with them, handsome young men, governors and commanders all of them, officers and warriors,⁹ all of them riding on horses. ²⁴They shall come against you from the north⁶ with chariots and wagons and a host of peoples; they shall set themselves against you on every side with buckler, shield, and helmet, and I will commit the judgment to them, and they shall judge you according to their ordinances. ²⁵I will direct my indignation against you, in order that they may deal with you in fury. They shall cut off your nose and your ears, and your survivors shall fall by the sword. They shall seize your sons and your daughters, and your survivors shall be devoured by fire. ²⁶They shall also strip you of your clothes and take away your fine jewels. ²⁷So I will put an end to your lewdness and your whoring brought from the land of Egypt; you shall not long for them, or remember Egypt any more. ²⁸For thus says the Lord GOD: I will deliver you into the hands of those whom you hate, into the hands of those from whom you turned in disgust; ²⁹and they shall deal with you in hatred, and take away all the fruit of your labor, and leave you naked and bare, and the nakedness of your whorings shall be exposed. Your lewdness and your whorings

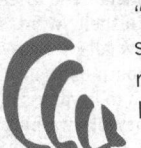

"Even when times are rough and my faith is shaky, I am grateful that I have been able to recover my trust in God, because I know that I would be nothing without him."
—Melissa Smith, 14,
Catholic high school student

Untitled—© Chris Modlin, 17

30 have brought this upon you, because you played the whore with the nations, and polluted yourself with their idols. 31 You have gone the way of your sister; therefore I will give her cup into your hand. 32 Thus says the Lord GOD:

You shall drink your sister's cup,
    deep and wide;
you shall be scorned and derided,
    it holds so much.
33 You shall be filled with drunkenness and
      sorrow.

A cup of horror and desolation
    is the cup of your sister Samaria;
34 you shall drink it and drain it out,
    and gnaw its sherds,
    and tear out your breasts;

for I have spoken, says the Lord GOD. 35 Therefore thus says the Lord GOD: Because you have forgotten me and cast me behind your back, therefore bear the consequences of your lewdness and whorings.

36 The LORD said to me: Mortal, will you judge Oholah and Oholibah? Then declare to them their abominable deeds. 37 For they have committed adultery, and blood is on their hands; with their idols they have committed adultery; and they have even offered up to them for food the children whom they had borne to me. 38 Moreover this they have done to me: they have defiled my sanctuary on the same day and profaned my sabbaths. 39 For

when they had slaughtered their children for their idols, on the same day they came into my sanctuary to profane it. This is what they did in my house.

40 They even sent for men to come from far away, to whom a messenger was sent, and they came. For them you bathed yourself, painted your eyes, and decked yourself with ornaments; 41 you sat on a stately couch, with a table spread before it on which you had placed my incense and my oil. 42 The sound of a raucous multitude was around her, with many of the rabble brought in drunken from the wilderness; and they put bracelets on the arms*a* of the women, and beautiful crowns upon their heads.

43 Then I said, Ah, she is worn out with adulteries, but they carry on their sexual acts with her. 44 For they have gone in to her, as one goes in to a whore. Thus they went in to Oholah and to Oholibah, wanton women. 45 But righteous judges shall declare them guilty of adultery and of bloodshed; because they are adulteresses and blood is on their hands.

46 For thus says the Lord GOD: Bring up an assembly against them, and make them an object of terror and of plunder. 47 The assembly shall stone them and with their swords they shall cut them down; they shall kill their sons and their daughters, and burn up their houses. 48 Thus will I put an end to lewdness in the land, so that all women may take warning and

a Heb *hands*

not commit lewdness as you have done. ⁴⁹They shall repay you for your lewdness, and you shall bear the penalty for your sinful idolatry; and you shall know that I am the Lord GOD.

24 The Boiling Pot

In the ninth year, in the tenth month, on the tenth day of the month, the word of the LORD came to me: ²Mortal, write down the name of this day, this very day. The king of Babylon has laid siege to Jerusalem this very day. ³And utter an allegory to the rebellious house and say to them, Thus says the Lord GOD:

Set on the pot, set it on,
  pour in water also;
⁴ put in it the pieces,
  all the good pieces, the thigh and the
    shoulder;
  fill it with choice bones.
⁵ Take the choicest one of the flock,
  pile the logs^a under it;
  boil its pieces,^b
  seethe^c also its bones in it.

⁶ Therefore thus says the Lord GOD:
Woe to the bloody city,
  the pot whose rust is in it,
  whose rust has not gone out of it!
Empty it piece by piece,
  making no choice at all.^d
⁷ For the blood she shed is inside it;
  she placed it on a bare rock;
  she did not pour it out on the ground,
    to cover it with earth.
⁸ To rouse my wrath, to take vengeance,
  I have placed the blood she shed
    on a bare rock,
  so that it may not be covered.
⁹Therefore thus says the Lord GOD:
Woe to the bloody city!
  I will even make the pile great.
¹⁰ Heap up the logs, kindle the fire;
  boil the meat well, mix in the spices,
  let the bones be burned.
¹¹ Stand it empty upon the coals,
  so that it may become hot, its copper
    glow,
  its filth melt in it, its rust be consumed.
¹² In vain I have wearied myself;^e
  its thick rust does not depart.
  To the fire with its rust!^f
¹³ Yet, when I cleansed you in your filthy
    lewdness,
  you did not become clean from your filth;
  you shall not again be cleansed
    until I have satisfied my fury upon you.
¹⁴I the LORD have spoken; the time is coming, I will act. I will not refrain, I will not spare, I will not relent. According to your ways and your doings I will judge you, says the Lord GOD.

Ezekiel's Bereavement

15 The word of the LORD came to me: ¹⁶Mortal, with one blow I am about to take away from you the delight of your eyes; yet you shall not mourn or weep, nor shall your tears run down. ¹⁷Sigh, but not aloud; make no mourning for the dead. Bind on your turban, and put your sandals on your feet; do not cover your upper lip or eat the bread of mourners.^g ¹⁸So I spoke to the people in the morning, and at evening my wife died. And on the next morning I did as I was commanded.

19 Then the people said to me, "Will you not tell us what these things mean for us, that you are acting this way?" ²⁰Then I said to them: The word of the LORD came to me: ²¹Say to the house of Israel, Thus says the Lord GOD: I will profane my sanctuary, the pride of your power, the delight of your eyes, and your heart's desire; and your sons and your daughters whom you left behind shall fall by the sword. ²²And you shall do as I have done; you shall not cover your upper lip or eat the bread of mourners.^g ²³Your turbans shall be on your heads and your sandals on your feet; you shall not mourn or weep, but you shall pine away in your iniquities and groan to one another. ²⁴Thus Ezekiel shall be a sign to you; you shall do just as he has done. When this comes, then you shall know that I am the Lord GOD.

25 And you, mortal, on the day when I take from them their stronghold, their joy and glory, the delight of their eyes and their heart's affection, and also^h their sons and their daughters, ²⁶on that day, one who has escaped will come to you to report to you the news. ²⁷On that day your mouth shall be opened to the one who has escaped, and you shall speak and no longer be silent. So you shall be a sign to them; and they shall know that I am the LORD.

25 Proclamation against Ammon

The word of the LORD came to me: ²Mortal, set your face toward the Ammonites and prophesy against them. ³Say to the Ammonites, Hear the word of the Lord GOD: Thus says the Lord GOD, Because you said, "Aha!" over my sanctuary when it was profaned, and over the land of Israel when it was made desolate, and over the house of Judah when it went into exile; ⁴therefore I am handing you over to the people of the east for a possession. They shall set their en-

---

a Compare verse 10: Heb *the bones* b Two Mss: Heb *its boilings* c Cn: Heb *its bones seethe* d Heb *piece, no lot has fallen on it*
e Cn: Meaning of Heb uncertain f Meaning of Heb uncertain g Vg Tg: Heb *of men* h Heb lacks *and also*

campments among you and pitch their tents in your midst; they shall eat your fruit, and they shall drink your milk. [5] I will make Rabbah a pasture for camels and Ammon a fold for flocks. Then you shall know that I am the Lord. [6] For thus says the Lord God: Because you have clapped your hands and stamped your feet and rejoiced with all the malice within you against the land of Israel, [7] therefore I have stretched out my hand against you, and will hand you over as plunder to the nations. I will cut you off from the peoples and will make you perish out of the countries; I will destroy you. Then you shall know that I am the Lord.

Proclamation against Moab

8 Thus says the Lord God: Because Moab[a] said, The house of Judah is like all the other nations, [9] therefore I will lay open the flank of Moab from the towns[b] on its frontier, the glory of the country, Beth-jeshimoth, Baal-meon, and Kiriathaim. [10] I will give it along with Ammon to the people of the east as a possession. Thus Ammon shall be remembered no more among the nations, [11] and I will execute judgments upon Moab. Then they shall know that I am the Lord.

Proclamation against Edom

12 Thus says the Lord God: Because Edom acted revengefully against the house of Judah and has grievously offended in taking vengeance upon them, [13] therefore thus says the Lord God, I will stretch out my hand against Edom, and cut off from it humans and animals, and I will make it desolate; from Teman even to Dedan they shall fall by the sword. [14] I will lay my vengeance upon Edom by the hand of my people Israel; and they shall act in Edom according to my anger and according to my wrath; and they shall know my vengeance, says the Lord God.

Proclamation against Philistia

15 Thus says the Lord God: Because with unending hostilities the Philistines acted in vengeance, and with malice of heart took revenge in destruction; [16] therefore thus says the Lord God, I will stretch out my hand against the Philistines, cut off the Cherethites, and destroy the rest of the seacoast. [17] I will execute great vengeance on them with wrathful punishments. Then they shall know that I am the Lord, when I lay my vengeance on them.

26 Proclamation against Tyre

In the eleventh year, on the first day of the month, the word of the Lord came to me:

[2] Mortal, because Tyre said concerning Jerusalem,
"Aha, broken is the gateway of the peoples;
    it has swung open to me;
I shall be replenished,
    now that it is wasted,"
[3] therefore, thus says the Lord God:
See, I am against you, O Tyre!
    I will hurl many nations against you,
    as the sea hurls its waves.
[4] They shall destroy the walls of Tyre
    and break down its towers.
I will scrape its soil from it
    and make it a bare rock.
[5] It shall become, in the midst of the sea,
    a place for spreading nets.
I have spoken, says the Lord God.
    It shall become plunder for the nations,
[6] and its daughter-towns in the country
    shall be killed by the sword.
Then they shall know that I am the Lord.

7 For thus says the Lord God: I will bring against Tyre from the north King Nebuchadrezzar of Babylon, king of kings, together with horses, chariots, cavalry, and a great and powerful army.

[8] Your daughter-towns in the country
    he shall put to the sword.
He shall set up a siege wall against you,
    cast up a ramp against you,
    and raise a roof of shields against you.
[9] He shall direct the shock of his battering
    rams against your walls
    and break down your towers with his
        axes.
[10] His horses shall be so many
    that their dust shall cover you.
At the noise of cavalry, wheels, and chariots
    your very walls shall shake,
when he enters your gates
    like those entering a breached city.
[11] With the hoofs of his horses
    he shall trample all your streets.
He shall put your people to the sword,
    and your strong pillars shall fall to the
        ground.
[12] They will plunder your riches
    and loot your merchandise;
they shall break down your walls
    and destroy your fine houses.
Your stones and timber and soil
    they shall cast into the water.
[13] I will silence the music of your songs;
    the sound of your lyres shall be heard no
        more.
[14] I will make you a bare rock;
    you shall be a place for spreading nets.

---

a Gk Old Latin: Heb *Moab and Seir* b Heb *towns from its towns*

You shall never again be rebuilt,
for I the LORD have spoken,
says the Lord GOD.

15 Thus says the Lord GOD to Tyre: Shall not the coastlands shake at the sound of your fall, when the wounded groan, when slaughter goes on within you? [16]Then all the princes of the sea shall step down from their thrones; they shall remove their robes and strip off their embroidered garments. They shall clothe themselves with trembling, and shall sit on the ground; they shall tremble every moment, and be appalled at you. [17]And they shall raise a lamentation over you, and say to you:

How you have vanished[a] from the seas,
  O city renowned,
once mighty on the sea,
  you and your inhabitants,[b]
who imposed your[c] terror
  on all the mainland![d]
[18] Now the coastlands tremble
  on the day of your fall;
the coastlands by the sea
  are dismayed at your passing.

19 For thus says the Lord GOD: When I make you a city laid waste, like cities that are not inhabited, when I bring up the deep over you, and the great waters cover you, [20]then I will thrust you down with those who descend into the Pit, to the people of long ago, and I will make you live in the world below, among primeval ruins, with those who go down to the Pit, so that you will not be inhabited or have a place[e] in the land of the living. [21]I will bring you to a dreadful end, and you shall be no more; though sought for, you will never be found again, says the Lord GOD.

27 Lamentation over Tyre

The word of the LORD came to me: [2]Now you, mortal, raise a lamentation over Tyre, [3]and say to Tyre, which sits at the entrance to the sea, merchant of the peoples on many coastlands, Thus says the Lord GOD:

O Tyre, you have said,
  "I am perfect in beauty."
[4] Your borders are in the heart of the seas;
  your builders made perfect your beauty.
[5] They made all your planks
  of fir trees from Senir;
they took a cedar from Lebanon
  to make a mast for you.
[6] From oaks of Bashan
  they made your oars;
they made your deck of pines[f]
  from the coasts of Cyprus,

inlaid with ivory.
[7] Of fine embroidered linen from Egypt
  was your sail,
  serving as your ensign;
blue and purple from the coasts of Elishah
  was your awning.
[8] The inhabitants of Sidon and Arvad
  were your rowers;
skilled men of Zemer[g] were within you,
  they were your pilots.
[9] The elders of Gebal and its artisans were
  within you,
  caulking your seams;
all the ships of the sea with their mariners
  were within you,
  to barter for your wares.
[10] Paras[h] and Lud and Put
  were in your army,
  your mighty warriors;
they hung shield and helmet in you;
  they gave you splendor.
[11] Men of Arvad and Helech[i]
  were on your walls all around;
  men of Gamad were at your towers.
They hung their quivers all around your
  walls;
  they made perfect your beauty.

12 Tarshish did business with you out of the abundance of your great wealth; silver, iron, tin, and lead they exchanged for your wares. [13]Javan, Tubal, and Meshech traded with you; they exchanged human beings and vessels of bronze for your merchandise. [14]Beth-togarmah exchanged for your wares horses, war horses, and mules. [15]The Rhodians[j] traded with you; many coastlands were your own special markets; they brought you in payment ivory tusks and ebony. [16]Edom[k] did business with you because of your abundant goods; they exchanged for your wares turquoise, purple, embroidered work, fine linen, coral, and rubies. [17]Judah and the land of Israel traded with you; they exchanged for your merchandise wheat from Minnith, millet,[l] honey, oil, and balm. [18]Damascus traded with you for your abundant goods—because of your great wealth of every

a Gk OL Aquila: Heb have vanished, O inhabited one, b Heb it and its inhabitants c Heb their d Cn: Heb its inhabitants e Gk: Heb I will give beauty f Or boxwood g Cn Compare Gen 10.18: Heb your skilled men, O Tyre h Or Persia i Or and your army j Gk: Heb The Dedanites k Another reading is Aram l Meaning of Heb uncertain kind—wine of Helbon, and white wool. [19]Vedan and Javan from Uzal[a] entered into trade for your wares; wrought iron, cassia, and sweet cane were bartered for your merchandise. [20]Dedan traded with you in saddlecloths for riding. [21]Arabia and all the princes of Kedar were your favored dealers in lambs, rams, and goats; in these they did business with you. [22]The merchants of Sheba and Raamah traded with you; they exchanged for your wares the best of all kinds of spices, and all precious stones, and gold. [23]Haran, Canneh, Eden, the merchants of Sheba, Asshur, and Chilmad traded with you. [24]These traded with you in choice garments, in clothes of blue and embroidered work, and in carpets of colored material, bound with cords and made secure; in these they traded with you.[b] [25]The ships of Tarshish traveled for you in your trade.

So you were filled and heavily laden
in the heart of the seas.
[26] Your rowers have brought you
into the high seas.
The east wind has wrecked you
in the heart of the seas.
[27] Your riches, your wares, your merchandise,
your mariners and your pilots,
your caulkers, your dealers in merchandise,
and all your warriors within you,
with all the company
that is with you,
sink into the heart of the seas
on the day of your ruin.
[28] At the sound of the cry of your pilots
the countryside shakes,
[29] and down from their ships
come all that handle the oar.
The mariners and all the pilots of the sea
stand on the shore
[30] and wail aloud over you,
and cry bitterly.
They throw dust on their heads
and wallow in ashes;
[31] they make themselves bald for you,
and put on sackcloth,
and they weep over you in bitterness of soul,
with bitter mourning.
[32] In their wailing they raise a lamentation for
you,
and lament over you:
"Who was ever destroyed[c] like Tyre
in the midst of the sea?
[33] When your wares came from the seas,
you satisfied many peoples;
with your abundant wealth and
merchandise
you enriched the kings of the earth.
[34] Now you are wrecked by the seas,
in the depths of the waters;
your merchandise and all your crew
have sunk with you.
[35] All the inhabitants of the coastlands
are appalled at you;
and their kings are horribly afraid,
their faces are convulsed.
[36] The merchants among the peoples hiss at
you;
you have come to a dreadful end
and shall be no more forever."

28 Proclamation against the King of Tyre

The word of the LORD came to me: [2]Mortal, say to the prince of Tyre, Thus says the Lord GOD:
Because your heart is proud
and you have said, "I am a god;
I sit in the seat of the gods,
in the heart of the seas,"
yet you are but a mortal, and no god,
though you compare your mind
with the mind of a god.
[3] You are indeed wiser than Daniel;[d]
no secret is hidden from you;
[4] by your wisdom and your understanding
you have amassed wealth for yourself,
and have gathered gold and silver
into your treasuries.
[5] By your great wisdom in trade
you have increased your wealth,
and your heart has become proud in your
wealth.
[6] Therefore thus says the Lord GOD:
Because you compare your mind
with the mind of a god,
[7] therefore, I will bring strangers against you,
the most terrible of the nations;
they shall draw their swords against the
beauty of your wisdom
and defile your splendor.
[8] They shall thrust you down to the Pit,
and you shall die a violent death
in the heart of the seas.
[9] Will you still say, "I am a god,"
in the presence of those who kill you,
though you are but a mortal, and no god,
in the hands of those who wound you?
[10] You shall die the death of the
uncircumcised
by the hand of foreigners;
for I have spoken, says the Lord GOD.

Lamentation over the King of Tyre

11 Moreover the word of the LORD came to me: [12]Mortal, raise a lamentation over the king of Tyre, and say to him, Thus says the Lord GOD:

---

a Meaning of Heb uncertain *b* Cn: Heb *in your market* *c* Tg Vg: Heb *like silence* *d* Or, as otherwise read, *Danel*

You were the signet of perfection,[a]
full of wisdom and perfect in beauty.
13 You were in Eden, the garden of God;
every precious stone was your covering,
carnelian, chrysolite, and moonstone,
beryl, onyx, and jasper,
sapphire,[b] turquoise, and emerald;
and worked in gold were your settings
and your engravings.[a]
On the day that you were created
they were prepared.
14 With an anointed cherub as guardian I
placed you;[a]
you were on the holy mountain of God;
you walked among the stones of fire.
15 You were blameless in your ways
from the day that you were created,
until iniquity was found in you.
16 In the abundance of your trade
you were filled with violence, and you
sinned;
so I cast you as a profane thing from the
mountain of God,
and the guardian cherub drove you out
from among the stones of fire.
17 Your heart was proud because of your beauty;
you corrupted your wisdom for the sake
of your splendor.
I cast you to the ground;
I exposed you before kings,
to feast their eyes on you.
18 By the multitude of your iniquities,
in the unrighteousness of your trade,
you profaned your sanctuaries.
So I brought out fire from within you;
it consumed you,
and I turned you to ashes on the earth
in the sight of all who saw you.
19 All who know you among the peoples
are appalled at you;
you have come to a dreadful end
and shall be no more forever.

Proclamation against Sidon

20 The word of the Lord came to me: 21 Mortal, set your face toward Sidon, and prophesy against it, 22 and say, Thus says the Lord God:
I am against you, O Sidon,
and I will gain glory in your midst.
They shall know that I am the Lord
when I execute judgments in it,
and manifest my holiness in it;
23 for I will send pestilence into it,
and bloodshed into its streets;
and the dead shall fall in its midst,
by the sword that is against it on every
side.

And they shall know that I am the Lord.
24 The house of Israel shall no longer find a pricking brier or a piercing thorn among all their neighbors who have treated them with contempt. And they shall know that I am the Lord God.

Future Blessing for Israel

25 Thus says the Lord God: When I gather the house of Israel from the peoples among whom they are scattered, and manifest my holiness in them in the sight of the nations, then they shall settle on their own soil that I gave to my servant Jacob. 26 They shall live in safety in it, and shall build houses and plant vineyards. They shall live in safety, when I execute judgments upon all their neighbors who have treated them with contempt. And they shall know that I am the Lord their God.

a Meaning of Heb uncertain   b Or lapis lazuli

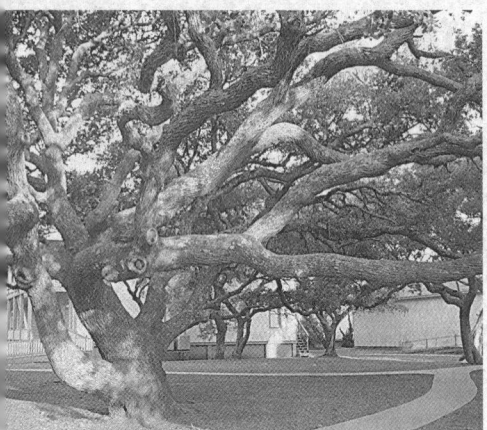

Tree at Fort Caswell—© Taylor-Quinn Yancey, 16

29 Proclamation against Egypt

In the tenth year, in the tenth month, on the twelfth day of the month, the word of the LORD came to me: [2]Mortal, set your face against Pharaoh king of Egypt, and prophesy against him and against all Egypt; [3]speak, and say, Thus says the Lord GOD:

I am against you,
   Pharaoh king of Egypt,
the great dragon sprawling
   in the midst of its channels,
saying, "My Nile is my own;
   I made it for myself."
[4] I will put hooks in your jaws,
   and make the fish of your channels stick
      to your scales.
I will draw you up from your channels,
   with all the fish of your channels
      sticking to your scales.
[5] I will fling you into the wilderness,
   you and all the fish of your channels;
you shall fall in the open field,
   and not be gathered and buried.
To the animals of the earth and to the birds
      of the air
   I have given you as food.
[6] Then all the inhabitants of Egypt shall know
      that I am the LORD
because you[a] were a staff of reed
   to the house of Israel;
[7] when they grasped you with the hand, you
      broke,
   and tore all their shoulders;
and when they leaned on you, you broke,
   and made all their legs unsteady.[b]
[8] Therefore, thus says the Lord GOD: I will bring a sword upon you, and will cut off from

you human being and animal; [9]and the land of Egypt shall be a desolation and a waste. Then they shall know that I am the LORD.

Because you[c] said, "The Nile is mine, and I made it," [10]therefore, I am against you, and against your channels, and I will make the land of Egypt an utter waste and desolation, from Migdol to Syene, as far as the border of Ethiopia.[d] [11]No human foot shall pass through it, and no animal foot shall pass through it; it shall be uninhabited forty years. [12]I will make the land of Egypt a desolation among desolated countries; and her cities shall be a desolation forty years among cities that are laid waste. I will scatter the Egyptians among the nations, and disperse them among the countries.

13 Further, thus says the Lord GOD: At the end of forty years I will gather the Egyptians from the peoples among whom they were scattered; [14]and I will restore the fortunes of Egypt, and bring them back to the land of Pathros, the land of their origin; and there they shall be a lowly kingdom. [15]It shall be the most lowly of the kingdoms, and never again exalt itself above the nations; and I will make them so small that they will never again rule over the nations. [16]The Egyptians[e] shall never again be the reliance of the house of Israel; they will recall their iniquity, when they turned to them for aid. Then they shall know that I am the Lord GOD.

Babylonia Will Plunder Egypt

17 In the twenty-seventh year, in the first month, on the first day of the month, the word of the LORD came to me: [18]Mortal, King Nebuchadrezzar of Babylon made his army labor hard against Tyre; every head was made bald and every shoulder was rubbed bare; yet neither he nor his army got anything from Tyre to pay for the labor that he had expended against it. [19]Therefore thus says the Lord GOD: I will give the land of Egypt to King Nebuchadrezzar of Babylon; and he shall carry off its wealth and despoil it and plunder it; and it shall be the wages for his army. [20]I have given him the land of Egypt as his payment for which he labored, because they worked for me, says the Lord GOD.

21 On that day I will cause a horn to sprout up for the house of Israel, and I will open your lips among them. Then they shall know that I am the LORD.

30 Lamentation for Egypt

The word of the LORD came to me: [2]Mortal, prophesy, and say, Thus says the Lord GOD:

a Gk Syr Vg: Heb *they*   *b* Syr: Heb *stand*   *c* Gk Syr Vg: Heb *he*   *d* Or *Nubia*; Heb *Cush*   *e* Heb *It*

Wail, "Alas for the day!"

3 For a day is near,
   the day of the LORD is near;
it will be a day of clouds,
   a time of doom*a* for the nations.
4 A sword shall come upon Egypt,
   and anguish shall be in Ethiopia,*b*
when the slain fall in Egypt,
   and its wealth is carried away,
   and its foundations are torn down.
5 Ethiopia,*b* and Put, and Lud, and all Arabia, and Libya,*c* and the people of the allied land*d* shall fall with them by the sword.

6 Thus says the LORD:
   Those who support Egypt shall fall,
      and its proud might shall come down;
   from Migdol to Syene
      they shall fall within it by the sword,
   says the Lord GOD.
7 They shall be desolated among other
         desolated countries,
      and their cities shall lie among cities laid
         waste.
8 Then they shall know that I am the LORD,
      when I have set fire to Egypt,
      and all who help it are broken.
9 On that day, messengers shall go out from me in ships to terrify the unsuspecting Ethiopians;*e* and anguish shall come upon them on the day of Egypt's doom;*f* for it is coming!

10 Thus says the Lord GOD:
   I will put an end to the hordes of Egypt,
      by the hand of King Nebuchadrezzar of
         Babylon.
11 He and his people with him, the most
         terrible of the nations,
      shall be brought in to destroy the land;
   and they shall draw their swords against
         Egypt,
      and fill the land with the slain.
12 I will dry up the channels,
      and will sell the land into the hand of
         evildoers;
   I will bring desolation upon the land and
         everything in it
      by the hand of foreigners;
   I the LORD have spoken.

13 Thus says the Lord GOD:
   I will destroy the idols
      and put an end to the images in
         Memphis;
   there shall no longer be a prince in the land
         of Egypt;
      so I will put fear in the land of Egypt.
14 I will make Pathros a desolation,

and will set fire to Zoan,
   and will execute acts of judgment on
      Thebes.
15 I will pour my wrath upon Pelusium,
   the stronghold of Egypt,
   and cut off the hordes of Thebes.
16 I will set fire to Egypt;
   Pelusium shall be in great agony;
Thebes shall be breached,
   and Memphis face adversaries by day.
17 The young men of On and of Pi-beseth shall
      fall by the sword;
   and the cities themselves*g* shall go into
      captivity.
18 At Tehaphnehes the day shall be dark,
   when I break there the dominion of
      Egypt,
and its proud might shall come to an end;
   the city*h* shall be covered by a cloud,
   and its daughter-towns shall go into
      captivity.
19 Thus I will execute acts of judgment on
      Egypt.
   Then they shall know that I am the LORD.

Proclamation against Pharaoh

20 In the eleventh year, in the first month, on the seventh day of the month, the word of the LORD came to me: 21 Mortal, I have broken the arm of Pharaoh king of Egypt; it has not been bound up for healing or wrapped with a bandage, so that it may become strong to wield the sword. 22 Therefore thus says the Lord GOD: I am against Pharaoh king of Egypt, and will break his arms, both the strong arm and the one that was broken; and I will make the sword fall from his hand. 23 I will scatter the Egyptians among the nations, and disperse them throughout the lands. 24 I will strengthen the arms of the king of Babylon, and put my sword in his hand; but I will break the arms of Pharaoh, and he will groan before him with the groans of one mortally wounded. 25 I will strengthen the arms of the king of Babylon, but the arms of Pharaoh shall fall. And they shall know that I am the LORD, when I put my sword into the hand of the king of Babylon. He shall stretch it out against the land of Egypt, 26 and I will scatter the Egyptians among the nations and disperse them throughout the countries. Then they shall know that I am the LORD.

31 The Lofty Cedar

In the eleventh year, in the third month, on the first day of the month, the word of the LORD

---

a Heb lacks *of doom* *b* Or *Nubia*; Heb *Cush* *c* Compare Gk Syr Vg: Heb *Cub* *d* Meaning of Heb uncertain *e* Or *Nubians*; Heb *Cush*
f Heb *the day of Egypt* *g* Heb *and they* *h* Heb *she*

came to me: ²Mortal, say to Pharaoh king of Egypt and to his hordes:

Whom are you like in your greatness?
³ Consider Assyria, a cedar of Lebanon,
with fair branches and forest shade,
   and of great height,
   its top among the clouds.ᵃ
⁴ The waters nourished it,
   the deep made it grow tall,
making its rivers flowᵇ
   around the place it was planted,
sending forth its streams
   to all the trees of the field.
⁵ So it towered high
   above all the trees of the field;
its boughs grew large
   and its branches long,
   from abundant water in its shoots.
⁶ All the birds of the air
   made their nests in its boughs;
under its branches all the animals of the
      field
   gave birth to their young;
and in its shade
   all great nations lived.
⁷ It was beautiful in its greatness,
   in the length of its branches;
for its roots went down
   to abundant water.
⁸ The cedars in the garden of God could not
      rival it,
   nor the fir trees equal its boughs;
the plane trees were as nothing
   compared with its branches;
no tree in the garden of God
   was like it in beauty.
⁹ I made it beautiful
   with its mass of branches,
the envy of all the trees of Eden
   that were in the garden of God.

10 Therefore thus says the Lord GOD: Because itᶜ towered high and set its top among the clouds,ᵃ and its heart was proud of its height, ¹¹I gave it into the hand of the prince of the nations; he has dealt with it as its wickedness deserves. I have cast it out. ¹²Foreigners from the most terrible of the nations have cut it down and left it. On the mountains and in all the valleys its branches have fallen, and its boughs lie broken in all the watercourses of the land; and all the peoples of the earth went away from its shade and left it. ¹³ On its fallen trunk settle
   all the birds of the air,
and among its boughs lodge
   all the wild animals.

¹⁴All this is in order that no trees by the waters may grow to lofty height or set their tops among the clouds,ᵃ and that no trees that drink water may reach up to them in height.

For all of them are handed over to death,
   to the world below;
along with all mortals,
   with those who go down to the Pit.

15 Thus says the Lord GOD: On the day it went down to Sheol I closed the deep over it and covered it; I restrained its rivers, and its mighty waters were checked. I clothed Lebanon in gloom for it, and all the trees of the field fainted because of it. ¹⁶I made the nations quake at the sound of its fall, when I cast it down to Sheol with those who go down to the Pit; and all the trees of Eden, the choice and best of Lebanon, all that were well watered, were consoled in the world below. ¹⁷They also went down to Sheol with it, to those killed by the sword, along with its allies,ᵈ those who lived in its shade among the nations.

18 Which among the trees of Eden was like you in glory and in greatness? Now you shall be brought down with the trees of Eden to the world below; you shall lie among the uncircumcised, with those who are killed by the sword. This is Pharaoh and all his horde, says the Lord GOD.

32 Lamentation over Pharaoh and Egypt

In the twelfth year, in the twelfth month, on the first day of the month, the word of the LORD came to me: ²Mortal, raise a lamentation over Pharaoh king of Egypt, and say to him:

You consider yourself a lion among the
      nations,
   but you are like a dragon in the seas;
you thrash about in your streams,
   trouble the water with your feet,
   and foul yourᵉ streams.
³ Thus says the Lord GOD:
   In an assembly of many peoples
   I will throw my net over you;
   and Iᶠ will haul you up in my dragnet.
⁴ I will throw you on the ground,
   on the open field I will fling you,
and will cause all the birds of the air to
      settle on you,
   and I will let the wild animals of the
      whole earth gorge themselves with
      you.
⁵ I will strew your flesh on the mountains,
   and fill the valleys with your carcass.ᵍ
⁶ I will drench the land with your flowing
      blood

ᵃ Gk: Heb thick boughs ᵇ Gk: Heb rivers going ᶜ Syr Vg: Heb you ᵈ Heb its arms ᵉ Heb their ᶠ Gk Vg: Heb they ᵍ Symmachus Syr Vg: Heb your height

Untitled—© Chris Modlin, 17

up to the mountains,
and the watercourses will be filled with
you.
⁷ When I blot you out, I will cover the heavens,
and make their stars dark;
I will cover the sun with a cloud,
and the moon shall not give its light.
⁸ All the shining lights of the heavens
I will darken above you,
and put darkness on your land,
says the Lord GOD.
⁹ I will trouble the hearts of many peoples,
as I carry you captive*ᵃ* among the nations,
into countries you have not known.
¹⁰ I will make many peoples appalled at you;
their kings shall shudder because of you.
When I brandish my sword before them,
they shall tremble every moment
for their lives, each one of them,
on the day of your downfall.
¹¹ For thus says the Lord GOD:
The sword of the king of Babylon shall
come against you.
¹² I will cause your hordes to fall
by the swords of mighty ones,
all of them most terrible among the
nations.
They shall bring to ruin the pride of Egypt,
and all its hordes shall perish.
¹³ I will destroy all its livestock

from beside abundant waters;
and no human foot shall trouble them any
more,
nor shall the hoofs of cattle trouble them.
¹⁴ Then I will make their waters clear,
and cause their streams to run like oil,
says the Lord GOD.
¹⁵ When I make the land of Egypt desolate
and when the land is stripped of all that
fills it,
when I strike down all who live in it,
then they shall know that I am the LORD.
¹⁶ This is a lamentation; it shall be chanted.
The women of the nations shall chant it.
Over Egypt and all its hordes they shall
chant it,
says the Lord GOD.

Dirge over Egypt

17 In the twelfth year, in the first month,*ᵇ* on
the fifteenth day of the month, the word of the
LORD came to me:
¹⁸ Mortal, wail over the hordes of Egypt,
and send them down,
with Egypt*ᶜ* and the daughters of majestic
nations,
to the world below,
with those who go down to the Pit.
¹⁹ "Whom do you surpass in beauty?

a Gk: Heb *bring your destruction*   *b* Gk: Heb lacks *in the first month*   *c* Heb *it*

A well-dressed and well-fed priest strides to the front of the Temple. He scans the offerings for the pieces of meat that would best serve the Lord—and his own stomach. There is not enough to satisfy him, so he warns the gathering that the Lord will punish those who keep back offerings.

This is three thousand years ago.

A preacher steps up to the pulpit. He scans the offering plates. They look light. He launches into his best hellfire-and-brimstone warning about the dangers of failed generosity in God's house. He tells the story of Ananias and Sapphira (Acts 5.1–11) and points a sturdy index finger at a few congregants he thinks might be responsible for holding back.

This is today.

Read **Ezekiel 34.1–10**. Whether it's ancient or modern-day priests, God sees "shepherds" who prey on the sheep and are not patient with them. In Ezekiel, he doesn't let them carry on; God warns that they will be brought low. Instead, he will replace them with a shepherd of his own—a shepherd who will truly care for and about his people. Read **Ezekiel 34.11–31**. Here the text calls the shepherd David (v. 23), but strangely, King David had already lived and died by the time this text was written. So if it wasn't David, who was God talking about?

Here's a clue: Do these words sound familiar? "I am the good shepherd. The good shepherd lays down his life for the sheep. . . . I am the good shepherd. I know my own and my own know me" (John 10.11, 14). These are Jesus' words, echoing back to this ancient promise. Jesus, a direct descendant of David, is the one true Shepherd. Earthly leaders—even wonderful, Christlike pastors—will let us down at times. They're only human. But Jesus will *not* let his Church down. Jesus is the Shepherd who will go to great lengths—even death—to love, protect, and care for his sheep. If you want to get a sense of how much this Shepherd loves *you*, read Matthew 18.12–14.

Go down! Be laid to rest with the uncircumcised!"

[20] They shall fall among those who are killed by the sword. Egypt[a] has been handed over to the sword; carry away both it and its hordes. [21] The mighty chiefs shall speak of them, with their helpers, out of the midst of Sheol: "They have come down, they lie still, the uncircumcised, killed by the sword."

22 Assyria is there, and all its company, their graves all around it, all of them killed, fallen by the sword. [23] Their graves are set in the uttermost parts of the Pit. Its company is all around its grave, all of them killed, fallen by the sword, who spread terror in the land of the living.

24 Elam is there, and all its hordes around its grave; all of them killed, fallen by the sword, who went down uncircumcised into the world below, who spread terror in the land of the living. They bear their shame with those who go down to the Pit. [25] They have made Elam[b] a bed among the slain with all its hordes, their graves all around it, all of them uncircumcised, killed by the sword; for terror of them was spread in the land of the living, and they bear their shame with those who go down to the Pit; they are placed among the slain.

26 Meshech and Tubal are there, and all their multitude, their graves all around them, all of them uncircumcised, killed by the sword; for they spread terror in the land of the living. [27] And they do not lie with the fallen warriors of long ago[c] who went down to Sheol with their weapons of war, whose swords were laid under their heads, and whose shields[d] are upon their bones; for the terror of the warriors was in the land of the living. [28] So you shall be broken and lie among the uncircumcised, with those who are killed by the sword.

29 Edom is there, its kings and all its princes, who for all their might are laid with those who are killed by the sword; they lie with the uncircumcised, with those who go down to the Pit.

30 The princes of the north are there, all of them, and all the Sidonians, who have gone down in shame with the slain, for all the terror that they caused by their might; they lie uncircumcised with those who are killed by the sword, and bear their shame with those who go down to the Pit.

31 When Pharaoh sees them, he will be consoled for all his hordes—Pharaoh and all his army, killed by the sword, says the Lord God. [32] For he[e] spread terror in the land of the living; therefore he shall be laid to rest among the uncircumcised, with those who are slain

a Heb It b Heb it c Gk Old Latin: Heb of the uncircumcised
d Cn: Heb iniquities e Cn: Heb I

by the sword—Pharaoh and all his multitude, says the Lord God.

33 Ezekiel Israel's Sentry

The word of the Lord came to me: [2]O Mortal, speak to your people and say to them, If I bring the sword upon a land, and the people of the land take one of their number as their sentinel; [3]and if the sentinel sees the sword coming upon the land and blows the trumpet and warns the people; [4]then if any who hear the sound of the trumpet do not take warning, and the sword comes and takes them away, their blood shall be upon their own heads. [5]They heard the sound of the trumpet and did not take warning; their blood shall be upon themselves. But if they had taken warning, they would have saved their lives. [6]But if the sentinel sees the sword coming and does not blow the trumpet, so that the people are not warned, and the sword comes and takes any of them, they are taken away in their iniquity, but their blood I will require at the sentinel's hand.

7 So you, mortal, I have made a sentinel for the house of Israel; whenever you hear a word from my mouth, you shall give them warning from me. [8]If I say to the wicked, "O wicked ones, you shall surely die," and you do not speak to warn the wicked to turn from their ways, the wicked shall die in their iniquity, but their blood I will require at your hand. [9]But if you warn the wicked to turn from their ways, and they do not turn from their ways, the wicked shall die in their iniquity, but you will have saved your life.

God's Justice and Mercy

10 Now you, mortal, say to the house of Israel, Thus you have said: "Our transgressions and our sins weigh upon us, and we waste away because of them; how then can we live?" [11]Say to them, As I live, says the Lord God, I have no pleasure in the death of the wicked, but that the wicked turn from their ways and live; turn back, turn back from your evil ways; for why will you die, O house of Israel? [12]And you, mortal, say to your people, The righteousness of the righteous shall not save them when they transgress; and as for the wickedness of the wicked, it shall not make them stumble when they turn from their wickedness; and the righteous shall not be able to live by their righteousness[a] when they sin. [13]Though I say to the righteous that they shall surely live, yet if they trust in their righteousness and commit iniquity, none of their righteous deeds shall be remembered; but in the iniquity that they have committed they shall die. [14]Again, though I say to the wicked, "You shall surely die," yet if they turn from their sin and do what is lawful and right— [15]if the wicked restore the pledge, give back what they have taken by robbery, and walk in the statutes of life, committing no iniquity—they shall surely live, they shall not die. [16]None of the sins that they have committed shall be remembered against them; they have done what is lawful and right, they shall surely live.

17 Yet your people say, "The way of the Lord is not just," when it is their own way that is not just. [18]When the righteous turn from their righteousness, and commit iniquity, they shall die for it.[b] [19]And when the wicked turn from their wickedness, and do what is lawful and right, they shall live by it.[b] [20]Yet you say, "The way of the Lord is not just." O house of Israel, I will judge all of you according to your ways!

The Fall of Jerusalem

21 In the twelfth year of our exile, in the tenth month, on the fifth day of the month, someone who had escaped from Jerusalem came to me and said, "The city has fallen." [22]Now the hand of the Lord had been upon me the evening before the fugitive came; but he had opened my mouth by the time the fugitive came to me in the morning; so my mouth was opened, and I was no longer unable to speak.

The Survivors in Judah

23 The word of the Lord came to me: [24]Mortal, the inhabitants of these waste places in the land of Israel keep saying, "Abraham was only one man, yet he got possession of the land; but we are many; the land is surely given us to possess." [25]Therefore say to them, Thus says the Lord God: You eat flesh with the blood, and lift up your eyes to your idols, and shed blood; shall you then possess the land? [26]You depend on your swords, you commit abominations, and each of you defiles his neighbor's wife; shall you then possess the land? [27]Say this to them, Thus says the Lord God: As I live, surely those who are in the waste places shall fall by the sword; and those who are in the open field I will give to the wild animals to be devoured; and those who are in strongholds and in caves shall die by pestilence. [28]I will make the land a desolation and a waste, and its proud might shall come to an end; and the mountains of Israel shall be so desolate that no one will pass through. [29]Then they shall know that I am the Lord, when I have made the land a desolation and a waste because of all their abominations that they have committed.

30 As for you, mortal, your people who talk

a Heb *by it* *b* Heb *them*

together about you by the walls, and at the doors of the houses, say to one another, each to a neighbor, "Come and hear what the word is that comes from the LORD." ³¹They come to you as people come, and they sit before you as my people, and they hear your words, but they will not obey them. For flattery is on their lips, but their heart is set on their gain. ³²To them you are like a singer of love songs,ᵃ one who has a beautiful voice and plays well on an instrument; they hear what you say, but they will not do it. ³³When this comes—and come it will!—then they shall know that a prophet has been among them.

34 Israel's False Shepherds

The word of the LORD came to me: ²Mortal, prophesy against the shepherds of Israel: prophesy, and say to them—to the shepherds: Thus says the Lord GOD: Ah, you shepherds of Israel who have been feeding yourselves! Should not shepherds feed the sheep? ³You eat the fat, you clothe yourselves with the wool, you slaughter the fatlings; but you do not feed the sheep. ⁴You have not strengthened the weak, you have not healed the sick, you have not bound up the injured, you have not brought back the strayed, you have not sought the lost, but with force and harshness you have ruled them. ⁵So they were scattered, because there was no shepherd; and scattered, they became food for all the wild animals. ⁶My sheep were scattered, they wandered over all the mountains and on every high hill; my sheep were scattered over all the face of the earth, with no one to search or seek for them.

7 Therefore, you shepherds, hear the word of the LORD: ⁸As I live, says the Lord GOD, because my sheep have become a prey, and my sheep have become food for all the wild animals, since there was no shepherd; and because my shepherds have not searched for my sheep, but the shepherds have fed themselves, and have not fed my sheep; ⁹therefore, you shepherds, hear the word of the LORD: ¹⁰Thus says the Lord GOD, I am against the shepherds; and I will demand my sheep at their hand, and put a stop to their feeding the sheep; no longer shall the shepherds feed themselves. I will rescue my sheep from their mouths, so that they may not be food for them.

God, the True Shepherd

11 For thus says the Lord GOD: I myself will search for my sheep, and will seek them out. ¹²As shepherds seek out their flocks when they are among their scattered sheep, so I will seek out my sheep. I will rescue them from all the places to which they have been scattered on a day of clouds and thick darkness. ¹³I will bring them out from the peoples and gather them from the countries, and will bring them into their own land; and I will feed them on the mountains of Israel, by the watercourses, and in all the inhabited parts of the land. ¹⁴I will feed them with good pasture, and the mountain heights of Israel shall be their pasture; there they shall lie down in good grazing land, and they shall feed on rich pasture on the mountains of Israel. ¹⁵I myself will be the shepherd of my sheep, and I will make them lie down, says the Lord GOD. ¹⁶I will seek the lost, and I will bring back the strayed, and I will bind up the injured, and I will strengthen the weak, but the fat and the strong I will destroy. I will feed them with justice.

17 As for you, my flock, thus says the Lord GOD: I shall judge between sheep and sheep, between rams and goats: ¹⁸Is it not enough for you to feed on the good pasture, but you must tread down with your feet the rest of your pasture? When you drink of clear water, must you foul the rest with your feet? ¹⁹And must my sheep eat what you have trodden with your feet, and drink what you have fouled with your feet?

20 Therefore, thus says the Lord GOD to them: I myself will judge between the fat sheep and the lean sheep. ²¹Because you pushed with flank and shoulder, and butted at all the weak animals with your horns until you scattered them far and wide, ²²I will save my flock, and they shall no longer be ravaged; and I will judge between sheep and sheep.

23 I will set up over them one shepherd, my servant David, and he shall feed them: he shall feed them and be their shepherd. ²⁴And I, the LORD, will be their God, and my servant David shall be prince among them; I, the LORD, have spoken.

25 I will make with them a covenant of peace and banish wild animals from the land, so that they may live in the wild and sleep in the woods securely. ²⁶I will make them and the region around my hill a blessing; and I will send down the showers in their season; they shall be showers of blessing. ²⁷The trees of the field shall yield their fruit, and the earth shall yield its increase. They shall be secure on their soil; and they shall know that I am the LORD, when I break the bars of their yoke, and save them from the hands of those who enslaved them. ²⁸They shall no more be plunder for the nations, nor shall the animals of the land devour them; they shall live in safety, and no one shall

---

ᵃ Cn: Heb *like a love song*

make them afraid. 29I will provide for them a splendid vegetation so that they shall no more be consumed with hunger in the land, and no longer suffer the insults of the nations. 30They shall know that I, the LORD their God, am with them, and that they, the house of Israel, are my people, says the Lord GOD. 31You are my sheep, the sheep of my pasture*a* and I am your God, says the Lord GOD.

> "I have been all things unholy. If God can work through me, he can work through anyone."
>
> —St. Francis of Assisi

35 Judgment on Mount Seir

The word of the LORD came to me: 2Mortal, set your face against Mount Seir, and prophesy against it, 3and say to it, Thus says the Lord GOD:

I am against you, Mount Seir;
  I stretch out my hand against you
  to make you a desolation and a waste.
4 I lay your towns in ruins;
  you shall become a desolation,
  and you shall know that I am the LORD.

5Because you cherished an ancient enmity, and gave over the people of Israel to the power of the sword at the time of their calamity, at the time of their final punishment; 6therefore, as I live, says the Lord GOD, I will prepare you for blood, and blood shall pursue you; since you did not hate bloodshed, bloodshed shall pursue you. 7I will make Mount Seir a waste and a desolation; and I will cut off from it all who come and go. 8I will fill its mountains with the slain; on your hills and in your valleys and in all your watercourses those killed with the sword shall fall. 9I will make you a perpetual desolation, and your cities shall never be inhabited. Then you shall know that I am the LORD.

10 Because you said, "These two nations and these two countries shall be mine, and we will take possession of them,"—although the LORD was there— 11therefore, as I live, says the Lord GOD, I will deal with you according to the anger and envy that you showed because of your hatred against them; and I will make myself known among you,*b* when I judge you. 12You shall know that I, the LORD, have heard all the abusive speech that you uttered against the mountains of Israel, saying, "They are laid desolate, they are given us to devour." 13And you magnified yourselves against me with your mouth, and multiplied your words against me; I heard it. 14Thus says the Lord GOD: As the whole earth rejoices, I will make you desolate. 15As you rejoiced over the inheritance of the house of Israel, because it was desolate, so I will deal with you; you shall be desolate, Mount Seir, and all Edom, all of it. Then they shall know that I am the LORD.

36 Blessing on Israel

And you, mortal, prophesy to the mountains of Israel, and say: O mountains of Israel, hear the word of the LORD. 2Thus says the Lord GOD: Because the enemy said of you, "Aha!" and, "The ancient heights have become our possession," 3therefore prophesy, and say: Thus says the Lord GOD: Because they made you desolate indeed, and crushed you from all sides, so that you became the possession of the rest of the nations, and you became an object of gossip and slander among the people; 4therefore, O mountains of Israel, hear the word of the Lord GOD: Thus says the Lord GOD to the mountains and the hills, the watercourses and the valleys, the desolate wastes and the deserted towns, which have become a source of plunder and an object of derision to the rest of the nations all around; 5therefore thus says the Lord GOD: I am speaking in my hot jealousy against the rest of the nations, and against all Edom, who, with wholehearted joy and utter contempt, took my land as their possession, because of its pasture, to plunder it. 6Therefore prophesy concerning the land of Israel, and say to the mountains and hills, to the watercourses and valleys, Thus says the Lord GOD: I am speaking in my jealous wrath, because you have suffered the insults of the nations; 7therefore thus says the Lord GOD: I swear that the nations that are all around you shall themselves suffer insults.

8 But you, O mountains of Israel, shall shoot out your branches, and yield your fruit to my people Israel; for they shall soon come home. 9See now, I am for you; I will turn to you, and you shall be tilled and sown; 10and I will multiply your population, the whole house of Israel, all of it; the towns shall be inhabited and the waste places rebuilt; 11and I will multiply human beings and animals upon you. They shall increase and be fruitful; and I will cause you to be inhabited as in your former times, and will do more good to you than ever before. Then you shall know that I am the LORD. 12I will lead people upon you—my people Israel—and they shall possess you, and you shall be their inheritance. No longer shall you bereave them of children.

---

a Gk OL: Heb *pasture, you are people* *b* Gk: Heb *them*

13 Thus says the Lord God: Because they say to you, "You devour people, and you bereave your nation of children," ¹⁴therefore you shall no longer devour people and no longer bereave your nation of children, says the Lord God; ¹⁵and no longer will I let you hear the insults of the nations, no longer shall you bear the disgrace of the peoples; and no longer shall you cause your nation to stumble, says the Lord God.

The Renewal of Israel

16 The word of the Lord came to me: ¹⁷Mortal, when the house of Israel lived on their own soil, they defiled it with their ways and their deeds; their conduct in my sight was like the uncleanness of a woman in her menstrual period. ¹⁸So I poured out my wrath upon them for the blood that they had shed upon the land, and for the idols with which they had defiled it. ¹⁹I scattered them among the nations, and they were dispersed through the countries; in accordance with their conduct and their deeds I judged them. ²⁰But when they came to the nations, wherever they came, they profaned my holy name, in that it was said of them, "These are the people of the Lord, and yet they had to go out of his land." ²¹But I had concern for my holy name, which the house of Israel had profaned among the nations to which they came.

22 Therefore say to the house of Israel, Thus says the Lord God: It is not for your sake, O house of Israel, that I am about to act, but for the sake of my holy name, which you have profaned among the nations to which you came. ²³I will sanctify my great name, which has been profaned among the nations, and which you have profaned among them; and the nations shall know that I am the Lord, says the Lord God, when through you I display my holiness before their eyes. ²⁴I will take you from the nations, and gather you from all the countries, and bring you into your own land. ²⁵I will sprinkle clean water upon you, and you shall be clean from all your uncleannesses, and from all your idols I will cleanse you. ²⁶A new heart I will give you, and a new spirit I will put within you; and I will remove from your body the heart of stone and give you a heart of flesh. ²⁷I will put my spirit within you, and make you follow my statutes and be careful to observe my ordinances. ²⁸Then you shall live in the land that I gave to your ancestors; and you shall be my people, and I will be your God. ²⁹I will save you from all your uncleannesses, and I will summon the grain and make it abundant and lay no famine upon you. ³⁰I will make the fruit of the tree and the produce of the field abundant, so that you may never again suffer the disgrace of famine among the nations. ³¹Then you shall remember your evil ways, and your dealings that were not good; and you shall loathe yourselves for your iniquities and your abominable deeds. ³²It is not for your sake that I will act, says the Lord God; let that be known to you. Be ashamed and dismayed for your ways, O house of Israel.

33 Thus says the Lord God: On the day that I cleanse you from all your iniquities, I will cause the towns to be inhabited, and the waste places shall be rebuilt. ³⁴The land that was desolate shall be tilled, instead of being the desolation that it was in the sight of all who passed by. ³⁵And they will say, "This land that was desolate has become like the garden of Eden; and the waste and desolate and ruined towns are now inhabited and fortified." ³⁶Then the nations that are left all around you shall know that I, the Lord, have rebuilt the ruined places, and replanted that which was desolate; I, the Lord, have spoken, and I will do it.

37 Thus says the Lord God: I will also let the house of Israel ask me to do this for them: to increase their population like a flock. ³⁸Like the flock for sacrifices,ᵃ like the flock at Jerusalem during her appointed festivals, so shall the ruined towns be filled with flocks of people. Then they shall know that I am the Lord.

37 The Valley of Dry Bones

The hand of the Lord came upon me, and he brought me out by the spirit of the Lord and set me down in the middle of a valley; it was full of bones. ²He led me all around them; there were very many lying in the valley, and they were very dry. ³He said to me, "Mortal, can these bones live?" I answered, "O Lord God, you know." ⁴Then he said to me, "Prophesy to these bones, and say to them: O dry bones, hear the word of the Lord. ⁵Thus says the Lord God to these bones: I will cause breathᵇ to enter you, and you shall live. ⁶I will lay sinews on you, and will cause flesh to come upon you, and cover you with skin, and put breathᵇ in you, and you shall live; and you shall know that I am the Lord."

7 So I prophesied as I had been commanded; and as I prophesied, suddenly there was a noise, a rattling, and the bones came together, bone to its bone. ⁸I looked, and there were sinews on them, and flesh had come upon them, and skin had covered them; but there was no breath in them. ⁹Then he said to me, "Prophesy to the breath, prophesy, mortal, and say to the breath:ᶜ Thus says the Lord God: Come from the four winds, O breath,ᶜ and breathe

---

ᵃ Heb *flock of holy things*   ᵇ Or *spirit*   ᶜ Or *wind* or *spirit* upon these slain, that they may live." [10]I prophesied as he commanded me, and the breath came into them, and they lived, and stood on their feet, a vast multitude.

11 Then he said to me, "Mortal, these bones are the whole house of Israel. They say, 'Our bones are dried up, and our hope is lost; we are cut off completely.' [12]Therefore prophesy, and say to them, Thus says the Lord GOD: I am going to open your graves, and bring you up from your graves, O my people; and I will bring you back to the land of Israel. [13]And you shall know that I am the LORD, when I open your graves, and bring you up from your graves, O my people. [14]I will put my spirit within you, and you shall live, and I will place you on your own soil; then you shall know that I, the LORD, have spoken and will act, says the LORD."

The Two Sticks

15 The word of the LORD came to me: [16]Mortal, take a stick and write on it, "For Judah, and the Israelites associated with it"; then take another stick and write on it, "For Joseph (the stick of Ephraim) and all the house of Israel associated with it"; [17]and join them together into one stick, so that they may become one in your hand. [18]And when your people say to you, "Will you not show us what you mean by these?" [19]say to them, Thus says the Lord GOD: I am about to take the stick of Joseph (which is in the hand of Ephraim) and the tribes of Israel associated with it; and I will put the stick of Judah upon it,[a] and make them one stick, in order that they may be one in my hand. [20]When the sticks on which you write are in your hand before their eyes, [21]then say to them, Thus says the Lord GOD: I will take the people of Israel from the nations among which they have gone, and will gather them from every quarter, and bring them to their own land. [22]I will make them one nation in the land, on the mountains of Israel; and one king shall be king over them all. Never again shall they be two nations, and never again shall they be divided into two kingdoms. [23]They shall never again defile themselves with their idols and their detestable things, or with any of their transgressions. I will save them from all the apostasies into which they have fallen,[b] and will cleanse them. Then they shall be my people, and I will be their God.

24 My servant David shall be king over them; and they shall all have one shepherd. They shall follow my ordinances and be careful to observe my statutes. [25]They shall live in the land that I gave to my servant Jacob, in which your ancestors lived; they and their children and their children's children shall live there forever; and my servant David shall be their prince forever. [26]I will make a covenant of peace with them; it shall be an everlasting covenant with them; and I will bless[c] them and multiply them, and will set my sanctuary among them forevermore. [27]My dwelling place shall be with them; and I will be their God, and they shall be my people. [28]Then the nations shall know that I the LORD sanctify Israel, when my sanctuary is among them forevermore.

38 Invasion by Gog

The word of the LORD came to me: [2]Mortal, set your face toward Gog, of the land of Magog, the chief prince of Meshech and Tubal. Prophesy against him [3]and say: Thus says the Lord GOD: I am against you, O Gog, chief prince of Meshech and Tubal; [4]I will turn you around

---

TEXT MESSAGE

Ezekiel's final vision is packed with measurements for a restored Temple in Jerusalem (Ezekiel 40–48). Its total floor space was about 861 square feet, which is about the size of three large bedrooms today.

This information has been scanned and is free of all known viruses. Please forward to all your friends.

---

a Heb I will put them upon it   b Another reading is from all the settlements in which they have sinned   c Tg: Heb give and put hooks into your jaws, and I will lead you out with all your army, horses and horsemen, all of them clothed in full armor, a great company, all of them with shield and buckler, wielding swords. 5Persia, Ethiopia,a and Put are with them, all of them with buckler and helmet; 6Gomer and all its troops; Beth-togarmah from the remotest parts of the north with all its troops—many peoples are with you.

7 Be ready and keep ready, you and all the companies that are assembled around you, and hold yourselves in reserve for them. 8After many days you shall be mustered; in the latter years you shall go against a land restored from war, a land where people were gathered from many nations on the mountains of Israel, which had long lain waste; its people were brought out from the nations and now are living in safety, all of them. 9You shall advance, coming on like a storm; you shall be like a cloud covering the land, you and all your troops, and many peoples with you.

10 Thus says the Lord GOD: On that day thoughts will come into your mind, and you will devise an evil scheme. 11You will say, "I will go up against the land of unwalled villages; I will fall upon the quiet people who live in safety, all of them living without walls, and having no bars or gates"; 12to seize spoil and carry off plunder; to assail the waste places that are now inhabited, and the people who were gathered from the nations, who are acquiring cattle and goods, who live at the centerb of the earth. 13Sheba and Dedan and the merchants of Tarshish and all its young warriorsc will say to you, "Have you come to seize spoil? Have you assembled your horde to carry off plunder, to carry away silver and gold, to take away cattle and goods, to seize a great amount of booty?"

14 Therefore, mortal, prophesy, and say to Gog: Thus says the Lord GOD: On that day when my people Israel are living securely, you will rouse yourselfd 15and come from your place out of the remotest parts of the north, you and many peoples with you, all of them riding on horses, a great horde, a mighty army; 16you will come up against my people Israel, like a cloud covering the earth. In the latter days I will bring you against my land, so that the nations may know me, when through you, O Gog, I display my holiness before their eyes.

Judgment on Gog

17 Thus says the Lord GOD: Are you he of whom I spoke in former days by my servants the prophets of Israel, who in those days prophesied for years that I would bring you against

them? 18On that day, when Gog comes against the land of Israel, says the Lord GOD, my wrath shall be aroused. 19For in my jealousy and in my blazing wrath I declare: On that day there shall be a great shaking in the land of Israel; 20the fish of the sea, and the birds of the air, and the animals of the field, and all creeping things that creep on the ground, and all human beings that are on the face of the earth, shall quake at my presence, and the mountains shall be thrown down, and the cliffs shall fall, and every wall shall tumble to the ground. 21I will summon the sword against Goge inf all my mountains, says the Lord GOD; the swords of all will be against their comrades. 22With pestilence and bloodshed I will enter into judgment with him; and I will pour down torrential rains and hailstones, fire and sulfur, upon him and his troops and the many peoples that are with him. 23So I will display my greatness and my holiness and make myself known in the eyes of many nations. Then they shall know that I am the LORD.

39 Gog's Armies Destroyed

And you, mortal, prophesy against Gog, and say: Thus says the Lord GOD: I am against you, O Gog, chief prince of Meshech and Tubal! 2I will turn you around and drive you forward, and bring you up from the remotest parts of the north, and lead you against the mountains of Israel. 3I will strike your bow from your left hand, and will make your arrows drop out of your right hand. 4You shall fall on the mountains of Israel, you and all your troops and the peoples that are with you; I will give you to birds of prey of every kind and to the wild animals to be devoured. 5You shall fall in the open field; for I have spoken, says the Lord GOD. 6I will send fire on Magog and on those who live securely in the coastlands; and they shall know that I am the LORD.

7 My holy name I will make known among my people Israel; and I will not let my holy name be profaned any more; and the nations shall know that I am the LORD, the Holy One in Israel. 8It has come! It has happened, says the Lord GOD. This is the day of which I have spoken.

9 Then those who live in the towns of Israel will go out and make fires of the weapons and burn them—bucklers and shields, bows and arrows, handpikes and spears—and they will make fires of them for seven years. 10They will not need to take wood out of the field or cut down any trees in the forests, for they will make their fires of the weapons; they will despoil those who despoiled them, and plunder those who plundered them, says the Lord GOD.

a Or Nubia; Heb Cush b Heb navel c Heb young lions d Gk: Heb will you not know? e Heb him f Heb to or for

The Burial of Gog

11 On that day I will give to Gog a place for burial in Israel, the Valley of the Travelers[a] east of the sea; it shall block the path of the travelers, for there Gog and all his horde will be buried; it shall be called the Valley of Hamon-gog.[b] 12Seven months the house of Israel shall spend burying them, in order to cleanse the land. 13All the people of the land shall bury them; and it will bring them honor on the day that I show my glory, says the Lord God. 14They will set apart men to pass through the land regularly and bury any invaders[c] who remain on the face of the land, so as to cleanse it; for seven months they shall make their search. 15As the searchers[c] pass through the land, anyone who sees a human bone shall set up a sign by it, until the buriers have buried it in the Valley of Hamon-gog.[b] 16(A city Hamonah[d] is there also.) Thus they shall cleanse the land.

17 As for you, mortal, thus says the Lord God: Speak to the birds of every kind and to all the wild animals: Assemble and come, gather from all around to the sacrificial feast that I am preparing for you, a great sacrificial feast on the mountains of Israel, and you shall eat flesh and drink blood. 18You shall eat the flesh of the mighty, and drink the blood of the princes of the earth—of rams, of lambs, and of goats, of bulls, all of them fatlings of Bashan. 19You shall eat fat until you are filled, and drink blood until you are drunk, at the sacrificial feast that I am preparing for you. 20And you shall be filled at my table with horses and charioteers,[e] with warriors and all kinds of soldiers, says the Lord God.

Israel Restored to the Land

21 I will display my glory among the nations; and all the nations shall see my judgment that I have executed, and my hand that I have laid on them. 22The house of Israel shall know that I am the Lord their God, from that day forward. 23And the nations shall know that the house of Israel went into captivity for their iniquity, because they dealt treacherously with me. So I hid my face from them and gave them into the hand of their adversaries, and they all fell by the sword. 24I dealt with them according to their uncleanness and their transgressions, and hid my face from them.

25 Therefore thus says the Lord God: Now I will restore the fortunes of Jacob, and have mercy on the whole house of Israel; and I will be jealous for my holy name. 26They shall forget[f] their shame, and all the treachery they have practiced against me, when they live se-

curely in their land with no one to make them afraid, 27when I have brought them back from the peoples and gathered them from their enemies' lands, and through them have displayed my holiness in the sight of many nations. 28Then they shall know that I am the Lord their God because I sent them into exile among the nations, and then gathered them into their own land. I will leave none of them behind; 29and I will never again hide my face from them, when I pour out my spirit upon the house of Israel, says the Lord God.

40 The Vision of the New Temple

In the twenty-fifth year of our exile, at the beginning of the year, on the tenth day of the month, in the fourteenth year after the city was

---

a Or of the Abarim b That is, the Horde of Gog c Heb travelers d That is The Horde e Heb chariots f Another reading is They shall bear struck down, on that very day, the hand of the LORD was upon me, and he brought me there. [2]He brought me, in visions of God, to the land of Israel, and set me down upon a very high mountain, on which was a structure like a city to the south. [3]When he brought me there, a man was there, whose appearance shone like bronze, with a linen cord and a measuring reed in his hand; and he was standing in the gateway. [4]The man said to me, "Mortal, look closely and listen attentively, and set your mind upon all that I shall show you, for you were brought here in order that I might show it to you; declare all that you see to the house of Israel."

5 Now there was a wall all around the outside of the temple area. The length of the measuring reed in the man's hand was six long cubits, each being a cubit and a handbreadth in length; so he measured the thickness of the wall, one reed; and the height, one reed. [6]Then he went into the gateway facing east, going up its steps, and measured the threshold of the gate, one reed deep.[a] There were [7]recesses, and each recess was one reed wide and one reed deep; and the space between the recesses, five cubits; and the threshold of the gate by the vestibule of the gate at the inner end was one reed deep. [8]Then he measured the inner vestibule of the gateway, one cubit. [9]Then he measured the vestibule of the gateway, eight cubits; and its pilasters, two cubits; and the vestibule of the gate was at the inner end. [10]There were three recesses on either side of the east gate; the three were of the same size; and the pilasters on either side were of the same size. [11]Then he measured the width of the opening of the gateway, ten cubits; and the width of the gateway, thirteen cubits. [12]There was a barrier before the recesses, one cubit on either side; and the recesses were six cubits on either side. [13]Then he measured the gate from the back[b] of the one recess to the back[b] of the other, a width of twenty-five cubits, from wall to wall.[c] [14]He measured[d] also the vestibule, twenty cubits; and the gate next to the pilaster on every side of the court.[e] [15]From the front of the gate at the entrance to the end of the inner vestibule of the gate was fifty cubits. [16]The recesses and their pilasters had windows, with shutters[f] on the inside of the gateway all around, and the vestibules also had windows on the inside all around; and on the pilasters were palm trees.

17 Then he brought me into the outer court; there were chambers there, and a pavement, all around the court; thirty chambers fronted on the pavement. [18]The pavement ran along the side of the gates, corresponding to the length of the gates; this was the lower pavement. [19]Then he measured the distance from the inner front of[f] the lower gate to the outer front of the inner court, one hundred cubits.[g]

20 Then he measured the gate of the outer court that faced north—its depth and width. [21]Its recesses, three on either side, and its pilasters and its vestibule were of the same size as those of the first gate; its depth was fifty cubits, and its width twenty-five cubits. [22]Its windows, its vestibule, and its palm trees were of the same size as those of the gate that faced toward the east. Seven steps led up to it; and its vestibule was on the inside.[h] [23]Opposite the gate on the north, as on the east, was a gate to the inner court; he measured from gate to gate, one hundred cubits.

24 Then he led me toward the south, and there was a gate on the south; and he measured its pilasters and its vestibule; they had the same dimensions as the others. [25]There were windows all around in it and in its vestibule, like the windows of the others; its depth was fifty cubits, and its width twenty-five cubits. [26]There were seven steps leading up to it; its vestibule was on the inside.[h] It had palm trees on its pilasters, one on either side. [27]There was a gate on the south of the inner court; and he measured from gate to gate toward the south, one hundred cubits.

28 Then he brought me to the inner court by the south gate, and he measured the south gate; it was of the same dimensions as the others. [29]Its recesses, its pilasters, and its vestibule were of the same size as the others; and there were windows all around in it and in its vestibule; its depth was fifty cubits, and its width twenty-five cubits. [30]There were vestibules all around, twenty-five cubits deep and five cubits wide. [31]Its vestibule faced the outer court, and palm trees were on its pilasters, and its stairway had eight steps.

32 Then he brought me to the inner court on the east side, and he measured the gate; it was of the same size as the others. [33]Its recesses, its pilasters, and its vestibule were of the same dimensions as the others; and there were windows all around in it and in its vestibule; its depth was fifty cubits, and its width twenty-five cubits. [34]Its vestibule faced the outer court, and it had palm trees on its pilasters, on either side; and its stairway had eight steps.

35 Then he brought me to the north gate, and he measured it; it had the same dimensions as the others. [36]Its recesses, its pilas-

a Heb deep, and one threshold, one reed deep b Gk: Heb roof c Heb opening facing opening d Heb made e Meaning of Heb uncertain f Compare Gk: Heb from before g Heb adds the east and the north h Gk: Heb before them

UNTITLED

My feet tread upon this crooked glass
Waiting for this pain to pass.
The heart I hold is slowly bleeding
And yet it's still faintly beating.
I try to cry, but all I see is blood,
Coming from my eyelids as a rushing flood.
Loneliness is all I have left…
My wishing star has been long gone,
I saw it faintly disappear with the dawn.
Will you someday come back to me?
Can you bring back an answer to let me see?
Dreams mutilated, my mind growing dark,
Still trying to hold on, you have made a mark
On my sensitive eyes…
I have told you before I deserve nothing,
And yet you still believe I am worth something.
Why do you still have faith in this pathetic state?
Perhaps this is supposed to be my fate.
You are so far away; I miss your voice.
Whether you miss me back, it's your choice.
I just want you to hold me…

Untitled—© Jessica Jones, 17

ters, and its vestibule were of the same size as the others;[a] and it had windows all around. Its depth was fifty cubits, and its width twenty-five cubits. [37] Its vestibule[b] faced the outer court, and it had palm trees on its pilasters, on either side; and its stairway had eight steps.

38 There was a chamber with its door in the vestibule of the gate,[c] where the burnt offering was to be washed. [39] And in the vestibule of the gate were two tables on either side, on which the burnt offering and the sin offering and the guilt offering were to be slaughtered. [40] On the outside of the vestibule[d] at the entrance of the north gate were two tables; and on the other side of the vestibule of the gate were two tables. [41] Four tables were on the inside, and four tables on the outside of the side of the gate, eight tables, on which the sacrifices were to be slaughtered. [42] There were also four tables of hewn stone for the burnt offering, a cubit and a half long, and one cubit and a half wide, and one cubit high, on which the instruments were to be laid with which the burnt offerings and the sacrifices were slaughtered. [43] There were pegs, one handbreadth long, fastened all around the inside. And on the tables the flesh of the offering was to be laid.

44 On the outside of the inner gateway there were chambers for the singers in the inner court, one[e] at the side of the north gate facing south, the other at the side of the east gate facing north. [45] He said to me, "This chamber that faces south is for the priests who have charge of the temple, [46] and the chamber that faces north is for the priests who have charge of the altar; these are the descendants of Zadok, who alone among the descendants of Levi may come near to the LORD to minister to him." [47] He measured the court, one hundred cubits deep, and one hundred cubits wide, a square; and the altar was in front of the temple.

The Temple

48 Then he brought me to the vestibule of the temple and measured the pilasters of the vestibule, five cubits on either side; and the width of the gate was fourteen cubits; and the sidewalls of the gate were three cubits[f] on either side. [49] The depth of the vestibule was twenty cubits, and the width twelve[g] cubits; ten steps led up[h] to it; and there were pillars beside the pilasters on either side.

41 Then he brought me to the nave, and measured the pilasters; on each side six cubits was the width of the pilasters.[i] [2] The width of the entrance was ten cubits; and the sidewalls of the entrance were five cubits on either side. He measured the length of the nave, forty cubits, and its width, twenty cubits. [3] Then he went into the inner room and measured the

a One Ms: Compare verses 29 and 33: MT lacks *were of the same size as the others*   b Gk Vg Compare verses 26, 31, 34: Heb *pilasters*
c Cn: Heb *at the pilasters of the gates*   d Cn: Heb *to him who goes up*   e Heb lacks *one*   f Gk: Heb *and the width of the gate was three cubits*
g Gk: Heb *eleven*   h Gk: Heb *and by steps that went up*   i Compare Gk: Heb *tent*

pilasters of the entrance, two cubits; and the width of the entrance, six cubits; and the side-walls*g* of the entrance, seven cubits. 4He measured the depth of the room, twenty cubits, and its width, twenty cubits, beyond the nave. And he said to me, This is the most holy place.

5 Then he measured the wall of the temple, six cubits thick; and the width of the side chambers, four cubits, all around the temple. 6The side chambers were in three stories, one over another, thirty in each story. There were offsets*b* all around the wall of the temple to serve as supports for the side chambers, so that they should not be supported by the wall of the temple. 7The passageway*c* of the side chambers widened from story to story; for the structure was supplied with a stairway all around the temple. For this reason the structure became wider from story to story. One ascended from the bottom story to the uppermost story by way of the middle one. 8I saw also that the temple had a raised platform all around; the foundations of the side chambers measured a full reed of six long cubits. 9The thickness of the outer wall of the side chambers was five cubits; and the free space between the side chambers of the temple 10and the chambers of the court was a width of twenty cubits all around the temple on every side. 11The side chambers opened onto the area left free, one door toward the north, and another door toward the south; and the width of the part that was left free was five cubits all around.

12 The building that was facing the temple yard on the west side was seventy cubits wide; and the wall of the building was five cubits thick all around, and its depth ninety cubits.

13 Then he measured the temple, one hundred cubits deep; and the yard and the building with its walls, one hundred cubits deep; 14also the width of the east front of the temple and the yard, one hundred cubits.

15 Then he measured the depth of the building facing the yard at the west, together with its galleries*d* on either side, one hundred cubits.

The nave of the temple and the inner room and the outer*e* vestibule 16were paneled,*f* and, all around, all three had windows with recessed*g* frames. Facing the threshold the temple was paneled with wood all around, from the floor up to the windows (now the windows were covered), 17to the space above the door, even to the inner room, and on the outside. And on all the walls all around in the in-

ner room and the nave there was a pattern.*h* 18It was formed of cherubim and palm trees, a palm tree between cherub and cherub. Each cherub had two faces: 19a human face turned toward the palm tree on the one side, and the face of a young lion turned toward the palm tree on the other side. They were carved on the whole temple all around; 20from the floor to the area above the door, cherubim and palm trees were carved on the wall.*i*

21 The doorposts of the nave were square. In front of the holy place was something resembling 22an altar of wood, three cubits high, two cubits long, and two cubits wide;*j* its corners, its base,*k* and its walls were of wood. He said to me, "This is the table that stands before the LORD." 23The nave and the holy place had each a double door. 24The doors had two leaves apiece, two swinging leaves for each door. 25On the doors of the nave were carved cherubim and palm trees, such as were carved on the walls; and there was a canopy of wood in front of the vestibule outside. 26And there were recessed windows and palm trees on either side, on the sidewalls of the vestibule.*l*

42 The Holy Chambers and the Outer Wall

Then he led me out into the outer court, toward the north, and he brought me to the chambers that were opposite the temple yard and opposite the building on the north. 2The length of the building that was on the north side*m* was*n* one hundred cubits, and the width fifty cubits. 3Across the twenty cubits that belonged to the inner court, and facing the pavement that belonged to the outer court, the chambers rose*o* gallery*p* by gallery*p* in three stories. 4In front of the chambers was a passage on the inner side, ten cubits wide and one hundred cubits deep,*q* and its*r* entrances were on the north. 5Now the upper chambers were narrower, for the galleries*p* took more away from them than from the lower and middle chambers in the building. 6For they were in three stories, and they had no pillars like the pillars of the outer*s* court; for this reason the upper chambers were set back from the ground more than the lower and the middle ones. 7There was a wall outside parallel to the chambers, toward the outer court, opposite the chambers, fifty cubits long. 8For the chambers on the outer court were fifty cubits long, while those opposite the temple were one hundred cubits long. 9At the foot of these chambers ran a passage that one entered from

a Gk: Heb *width* *b* Gk Compare 1 Kings 6.6: Heb *they entered* *c* Cn: Heb *it was surrounded* *d* Cn: Meaning of Heb uncertain *e* Gk: Heb *of the court* *f* Gk: Heb *the thresholds* *g* Cn Compare Gk 1 Kings 6.4: Meaning of Heb uncertain *h* Heb *measures* *i* Cn Compare verse 25: Heb *and the wall* *j* Gk: Heb lacks *two cubits wide* *k* Gk: Heb *length* *l* Cn: Heb *vestibule. And the side chambers of the temple and the canopies* *m* Gk: Heb *door* *n* Gk: Heb *before the length* *o* Heb lacks *the chambers rose* *p* Meaning of Heb uncertain *q* Gk Syr: Heb *a way of one cubit* *r* Heb *their* *s* Gk: Heb lacks *outer* the east in order to enter them from the outer court. [10]The width of the passage[a] was fixed by the wall of the court.

On the south[b] also, opposite the vacant area and opposite the building, there were chambers [11]with a passage in front of them; they were similar to the chambers on the north, of the same length and width, with the same exits[c] and arrangements and doors. [12]So the entrances of the chambers to the south were entered through the entrance at the head of the corresponding passage, from the east, along the matching wall.[d]

13 Then he said to me, "The north chambers and the south chambers opposite the vacant area are the holy chambers, where the priests who approach the Lord shall eat the most holy offerings; there they shall deposit the most holy offerings—the grain offering, the sin offering, and the guilt offering—for the place is holy. [14]When the priests enter the holy place, they shall not go out of it into the outer court without laying there the vestments in which they minister, for these are holy; they shall put on other garments before they go near to the area open to the people."

15 When he had finished measuring the interior of the temple area, he led me out by the gate that faces east, and measured the temple area all around. [16]He measured the east side with the measuring reed, five hundred cubits by the measuring reed. [17]Then he turned and measured[e] the north side, five hundred cubits by the measuring reed. [18]Then he turned and measured[e] the south side, five hundred cubits by the measuring reed. [19]Then he turned to the west side and measured, five hundred cubits by the measuring reed. [20]He measured it on the four sides. It had a wall around it, five hundred cubits long and five hundred cubits wide, to make a separation between the holy and the common.

43 The Divine Glory Returns to the Temple

Then he brought me to the gate, the gate facing east. [2]And there, the glory of the God of Israel was coming from the east; the sound was like the sound of mighty waters; and the earth shone with his glory. [3]The[f] vision I saw was like the vision that I had seen when he came to destroy the city, and[g] like the vision that I had seen by the river Chebar; and I fell upon my face. [4]As the glory of the Lord entered the temple by the gate facing east, [5]the spirit lifted me up, and brought me into the inner court; and the glory of the Lord filled the temple.

6 While the man was standing beside me, I heard someone speaking to me out of the temple. [7]He said to me: Mortal, this is the place of my throne and the place for the soles of my feet, where I will reside among the people of Israel forever. The house of Israel shall no more defile my holy name, neither they nor their kings, by their whoring, and by the corpses of their kings at their death.[h] [8]When they placed their threshold by my threshold and their doorposts beside my doorposts, with only a wall between me and them, they were defiling my holy name by their abominations that they committed; therefore I have consumed them in my anger. [9]Now let them put away their idolatry and the corpses of their kings far from me, and I will reside among them forever.

10 As for you, mortal, describe the temple to the house of Israel, and let them measure the pattern; and let them be ashamed of their iniquities. [11]When they are ashamed of all that they have done, make known to them the plan of the temple, its arrangement, its exits and its entrances, and its whole form—all its ordinances and its entire plan and all its laws; and write it down in their sight, so that they may observe and follow the entire plan and all its ordinances. [12]This is the law of the temple: the whole territory on the top of the mountain all around shall be most holy. This is the law of the temple.

The Altar

13 These are the dimensions of the altar by cubits (the cubit being one cubit and a handbreadth): its base shall be one cubit high,[i] and one cubit wide, with a rim of one span around its edge. This shall be the height of the altar: [14]From the base on the ground to the lower ledge, two cubits, with a width of one cubit; and from the smaller ledge to the larger ledge, four cubits, with a width of one cubit; [15]and the altar hearth, four cubits; and from the altar hearth projecting upward, four horns. [16]The altar hearth shall be square, twelve cubits long by twelve wide. [17]The ledge also shall be square, fourteen cubits long by fourteen wide, with a rim around it half a cubit wide, and its surrounding base, one cubit. Its steps shall face east.

18 Then he said to me: Mortal, thus says the Lord God: These are the ordinances for the altar: On the day when it is erected for offering burnt offerings upon it and for dashing blood against it, [19]you shall give to the levitical priests of the family of Zadok, who draw near to me to minister to me, says the Lord God, a bull for a sin offering. [20]And you shall take some of its

a Heb lacks of the passage   b Gk: Heb east   c Heb and all their exits   d Meaning of Heb uncertain   e Gk: Heb measuring reed all around. He measured   f Gk: Heb Like the vision   g Syr: Heb and the visions   h Or on their high places   i Gk: Heb lacks high blood, and put it on the four horns of the altar, and on the four corners of the ledge, and upon the rim all around; thus you shall purify it and make atonement for it. ²¹You shall also take the bull of the sin offering, and it shall be burnt in the appointed place belonging to the temple, outside the sacred area.

22 On the second day you shall offer a male goat without blemish for a sin offering; and the altar shall be purified, as it was purified with the bull. ²³When you have finished purifying it, you shall offer a bull without blemish and a ram from the flock without blemish. ²⁴You shall present them before the Lord, and the priests shall throw salt on them and offer them up as a burnt offering to the Lord. ²⁵For seven days you shall provide daily a goat for a sin offering; also a bull and a ram from the flock, without blemish, shall be provided. ²⁶Seven days shall they make atonement for the altar and cleanse it, and so consecrate it. ²⁷When these days are over, then from the eighth day onward the priests shall offer upon the altar your burnt offerings and your offerings of well-being; and I will accept you, says the Lord God.

44 The Closed Gate

Then he brought me back to the outer gate of the sanctuary, which faces east; and it was shut. ²The Lord said to me: This gate shall remain shut; it shall not be opened, and no one shall enter by it; for the Lord, the God of Israel, has entered by it; therefore it shall remain shut. ³Only the prince, because he is a prince, may sit in it to eat food before the Lord; he shall enter by way of the vestibule of the gate, and shall go out by the same way.

Admission to the Temple

4 Then he brought me by way of the north gate to the front of the temple; and I looked, and lo! the glory of the Lord filled the temple of the Lord; and I fell upon my face. ⁵The Lord said to me: Mortal, mark well, look closely, and listen attentively to all that I shall tell you concerning all the ordinances of the temple of the Lord and all its laws; and mark well those who may be admitted to^a the temple and all those who are to be excluded from the sanctuary. ⁶Say to the rebellious house,^b to the house of Israel, Thus says the Lord God: O house of Israel, let there be an end to all your abominations ⁷in admitting foreigners, uncircumcised in heart and flesh, to be in my sanctuary, profaning my temple when you offer to me my food, the fat and the blood. You^c have broken

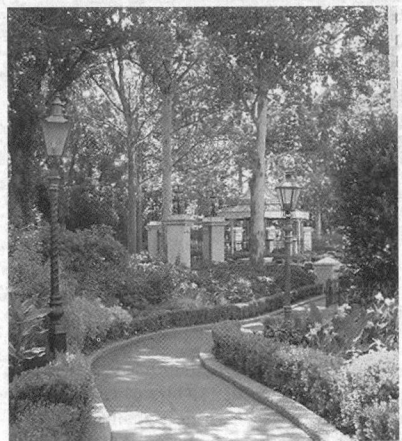

God's Handiwork—© Kate Douglas, 17

my covenant with all your abominations. ⁸And you have not kept charge of my sacred offerings; but you have appointed foreigners^d to act for you in keeping my charge in my sanctuary.

9 Thus says the Lord God: No foreigner, uncircumcised in heart and flesh, of all the foreigners who are among the people of Israel, shall enter my sanctuary. ¹⁰But the Levites who went far from me, going astray from me after their idols when Israel went astray, shall bear their punishment. ¹¹They shall be ministers in my sanctuary, having oversight at the gates of the temple, and serving in the temple; they shall slaughter the burnt offering and the sacrifice for the people, and they shall attend on them and serve them. ¹²Because they ministered to them before their idols and made the house of Israel stumble into iniquity, therefore I have sworn concerning them, says the Lord God, that they shall bear their punishment. ¹³They shall not come near to me, to serve me as priest, nor come near any of my sacred offerings, the things that are most sacred; but they shall bear their shame, and the consequences of the abominations that they have committed. ¹⁴Yet I will appoint them to keep charge of the temple, to do all its chores, all that is to be done in it.

The Levitical Priests

15 But the levitical priests, the descendants of Zadok, who kept the charge of my sanctuary when the people of Israel went astray from me, shall come near to me to minister to me; and they shall attend me to offer me the fat and the blood, says the Lord God. ¹⁶It is they who shall enter my sanctuary, it is they who shall approach my table, to minister to me, and they

___

a Cn: Heb the entrance of   b Gk: Heb lacks house   c Gk Syr Vg: Heb They   d Heb lacks foreigners shall keep my charge. ¹⁷When they enter the gates of the inner court, they shall wear linen vestments; they shall have nothing of wool on them, while they minister at the gates of the inner court, and within. ¹⁸They shall have linen turbans on their heads, and linen undergarments on their loins; they shall not bind themselves with anything that causes sweat. ¹⁹When they go out into the outer court to the people, they shall remove the vestments in which they have been ministering, and lay them in the holy chambers; and they shall put on other garments, so that they may not communicate holiness to the people with their vestments. ²⁰They shall not shave their heads or let their locks grow long; they shall only trim the hair of their heads. ²¹No priest shall drink wine when he enters the inner court. ²²They shall not marry a widow, or a divorced woman, but only a virgin of the stock of the house of Israel, or a widow who is the widow of a priest. ²³They shall teach my people the difference between the holy and the common, and show them how to distinguish between the unclean and the clean. ²⁴In a controversy they shall act as judges, and they shall decide it according to my judgments. They shall keep my laws and my statutes regarding all my appointed festivals, and they shall keep my sabbaths holy. ²⁵They shall not defile themselves by going near to a dead person; for father or mother, however, and for son or daughter, and for brother or unmarried sister they may defile themselves. ²⁶After he has become clean, they shall count seven days for him. ²⁷On the day that he goes into the holy place, into the inner court, to minister in the holy place, he shall offer his sin offering, says the Lord God.

28 This shall be their inheritance: I am their inheritance; and you shall give them no holding in Israel; I am their holding. ²⁹They shall eat the grain offering, the sin offering, and the guilt offering; and every devoted thing in Israel shall be theirs. ³⁰The first of all the first fruits of all kinds, and every offering of all kinds from all your offerings, shall belong to the priests; you shall also give to the priests the first of your dough, in order that a blessing may rest on your house. ³¹The priests shall not eat of anything, whether bird or animal, that died of itself or was torn by animals.

45 The Holy District

When you allot the land as an inheritance, you shall set aside for the Lord a portion of the land as a holy district, twenty-five thousand cubits long and twenty^a thousand cubits wide; it

shall be holy throughout its entire extent. ²Of this, a square plot of five hundred by five hundred cubits shall be for the sanctuary, with fifty cubits for an open space around it. ³In the holy district you shall measure off a section twenty-five thousand cubits long and ten thousand wide, in which shall be the sanctuary, the most holy place. ⁴It shall be a holy portion of the land; it shall be for the priests, who minister in the sanctuary and approach the Lord to minister to him; and it shall be both a place for their houses and a holy place for the sanctuary. ⁵Another section, twenty-five thousand cubits long and ten thousand cubits wide, shall be for the Levites who minister at the temple, as their holding for cities to live in.^b

6 Alongside the portion set apart as the holy district you shall assign as a holding for the city an area five thousand cubits wide, and twenty-five thousand cubits long; it shall belong to the whole house of Israel.

7 And to the prince shall belong the land on both sides of the holy district and the holding of the city, alongside the holy district and the holding of the city, on the west and on the east, corresponding in length to one of the tribal portions, and extending from the western to the eastern boundary ⁸of the land. It is to be his property in Israel. And my princes shall no longer oppress my people; but they shall let the house of Israel have the land according to their tribes.

9 Thus says the Lord God: Enough, O princes of Israel! Put away violence and oppression, and do what is just and right. Cease your evictions of my people, says the Lord God.

Weights and Measures

10 You shall have honest balances, an honest ephah, and an honest bath.^c ¹¹The ephah and the bath shall be of the same measure, the bath containing one-tenth of a homer, and the ephah one-tenth of a homer; the homer shall be the standard measure. ¹²The shekel shall be twenty gerahs. Twenty shekels, twenty-five shekels, and fifteen shekels shall make a mina for you.

Offerings

13 This is the offering that you shall make: one-sixth of an ephah from each homer of wheat, and one-sixth of an ephah from each homer of barley, ¹⁴and as the fixed portion of oil,^d one-tenth of a bath from each cor (the cor,^e like the homer, contains ten baths); ¹⁵and one sheep from every flock of two hundred, from the pastures of Israel. This is the offer-

---

a Gk: Heb *ten* *b* Gk: Heb *as their holding, twenty chambers* *c* A Heb measure of volume *d* Cn: Heb *oil, the bath the oil* *e* Vg: Heb *homer* ing for grain offerings, burnt offerings, and offerings of well-being, to make atonement for them, says the Lord God. ¹⁶All the people of the land shall join with the prince in Israel in making this offering. ¹⁷But this shall be the obligation of the prince regarding the burnt offerings, grain offerings, and drink offerings, at the festivals, the new moons, and the sabbaths, all the appointed festivals of the house of Israel: he shall provide the sin offerings, grain offerings, the burnt offerings, and the offerings of well-being, to make atonement for the house of Israel.

Festivals

18 Thus says the Lord God: In the first month, on the first day of the month, you shall take a young bull without blemish, and purify the sanctuary. ¹⁹The priest shall take some of the blood of the sin offering and put it on the doorposts of the temple, the four corners of the ledge of the altar, and the posts of the gate of the inner court. ²⁰You shall do the same on the seventh day of the month for anyone who has sinned through error or ignorance; so you shall make atonement for the temple.

21 In the first month, on the fourteenth day of the month, you shall celebrate the festival of the passover, and for seven days unleavened bread shall be eaten. ²²On that day the prince shall provide for himself and all the people of the land a young bull for a sin offering. ²³And during the seven days of the festival he shall provide as a burnt offering to the Lord seven young bulls and seven rams without blemish, on each of the seven days; and a male goat daily for a sin offering. ²⁴He shall provide as a grain offering an ephah for each bull, an ephah for each ram, and a hin of oil to each ephah. ²⁵In the seventh month, on the fifteenth day of the month and for the seven days of the festival, he shall make the same provision for sin offerings, burnt offerings, and grain offerings, and for the oil.

46 Miscellaneous Regulations

Thus says the Lord God: The gate of the inner court that faces east shall remain closed on the six working days; but on the sabbath day it shall be opened and on the day of the new moon it shall be opened. ²The prince shall enter by the vestibule of the gate from outside, and shall take his stand by the post of the gate. The priests shall offer his burnt offering and his offerings of well-being, and he shall bow down at the threshold of the gate. Then he shall go out, but the gate shall not be closed until evening.

³The people of the land shall bow down at the entrance of that gate before the Lord on the sabbaths and on the new moons. ⁴The burnt offering that the prince offers to the Lord on the sabbath day shall be six lambs without blemish and a ram without blemish; ⁵and the grain offering with the ram shall be an ephah, and the grain offering with the lambs shall be as much as he wishes to give, together with a hin of oil to each ephah. ⁶On the day of the new moon he shall offer a young bull without blemish, and six lambs and a ram, which shall be without blemish; ⁷as a grain offering he shall provide an ephah with the bull and an ephah with the ram, and with the lambs as much as he wishes, together with a hin of oil to each ephah. ⁸When the prince enters, he shall come in by the vestibule of the gate, and he shall go out by the same way.

9 When the people of the land come before the Lord at the appointed festivals, whoever enters by the north gate to worship shall go out by the south gate; and whoever enters by the south gate shall go out by the north gate: they shall not return by way of the gate by which they entered, but shall go out straight ahead. ¹⁰When they come in, the prince shall come in with them; and when they go out, he shall go out.

11 At the festivals and the appointed seasons the grain offering with a young bull shall be an ephah, and with a ram an ephah, and with the lambs as much as one wishes to give, together with a hin of oil to an ephah. ¹²When the prince provides a freewill offering, either a burnt offering or offerings of well-being as a freewill offering to the Lord, the gate facing east shall be opened for him; and he shall offer his burnt offering or his offerings of well-being as he does on the sabbath day. Then he shall go out, and after he has gone out the gate shall be closed.

13 He shall provide a lamb, a yearling, without blemish, for a burnt offering to the Lord daily; morning by morning he shall provide it. ¹⁴And he shall provide a grain offering with it morning by morning regularly, one-sixth of an ephah, and one-third of a hin of oil to moisten the choice flour, as a grain offering to the Lord; this is the ordinance for all time. ¹⁵Thus the lamb and the grain offering and the oil shall be provided, morning by morning, as a regular burnt offering.

16 Thus says the Lord God: If the prince makes a gift to any of his sons out of his inheritance,ᵃ it shall belong to his sons, it is their holding by inheritance. ¹⁷But if he makes a gift

_a_ Gk: Heb _it is his inheritance_

out of his inheritance to one of his servants, it shall be his to the year of liberty; then it shall revert to the prince; only his sons may keep a gift from his inheritance. ¹⁸The prince shall not take any of the inheritance of the people, thrusting them out of their holding; he shall give his sons their inheritance out of his own holding, so that none of my people shall be dispossessed of their holding.

19 Then he brought me through the entrance, which was at the side of the gate, to the north row of the holy chambers for the priests; and there I saw a place at the extreme western end of them. ²⁰He said to me, "This is the place where the priests shall boil the guilt offering and the sin offering, and where they shall bake

the grain offering, in order not to bring them out into the outer court and so communicate holiness to the people."

21 Then he brought me out to the outer court, and led me past the four corners of the court; and in each corner of the court there was a court— ²²in the four corners of the court were small*a* courts, forty cubits long and thirty wide; the four were of the same size. ²³On the inside, around each of the four courts*b* was a row of masonry, with hearths made at the bottom of the rows all around. ²⁴Then he said to me, "These are the kitchens where those who serve at the temple shall boil the sacrifices of the people."

47 Water Flowing from the Temple

Then he brought me back to the entrance of the temple; there, water was flowing from below the threshold of the temple toward the east (for the temple faced east); and the water was flowing down from below the south end of the threshold of the temple, south of the altar. ²Then he brought me out by way of the north gate, and led me around on the outside to the outer gate that faces toward the east;*c* and the water was coming out on the south side.

3 Going on eastward with a cord in his hand, the man measured one thousand cubits, and then led me through the water; and it was ankle-deep. ⁴Again he measured one thousand, and led me through the water; and it was knee-deep. Again he measured one thousand, and led me through the water; and it was up to the waist. ⁵Again he measured one thousand, and it was a river that I could not cross, for the water had risen; it was deep enough to swim in, a river that could not be crossed. ⁶He said to me, "Mortal, have you seen this?"

Then he led me back along the bank of the river. ⁷As I came back, I saw on the bank of the river a great many trees on the one side and on the other. ⁸He said to me, "This water flows toward the eastern region and goes down into the Arabah; and when it enters the sea, the sea of stagnant waters, the water will become fresh. ⁹Wherever the river goes,*d* every living creature that swarms will live, and there will be very many fish, once these waters reach there. It will become fresh; and everything will live where the river goes. ¹⁰People will stand fishing beside the sea*e* from En-gedi to En-eglaim; it will be a place for the spreading of nets; its fish will be of a great many kinds, like the fish of the Great Sea. ¹¹But its swamps and marshes will not become fresh; they are to be left for salt. ¹²On the banks, on both sides of the river, there

a Gk Syr Vg: Meaning of Heb uncertain   *b* Heb *the four of them*   *c* Meaning of Heb uncertain   *d* Gk Syr Vg Tg: Heb *the two rivers go*
e Heb *it*

will grow all kinds of trees for food. Their leaves will not wither nor their fruit fail, but they will bear fresh fruit every month, because the water for them flows from the sanctuary. Their fruit will be for food, and their leaves for healing."

The New Boundaries of the Land

13 Thus says the Lord GOD: These are the boundaries by which you shall divide the land for inheritance among the twelve tribes of Israel. Joseph shall have two portions. ¹⁴You shall divide it equally; I swore to give it to your ancestors, and this land shall fall to you as your inheritance.

15 This shall be the boundary of the land: On the north side, from the Great Sea by way of Hethlon to Lebo-hamath, and on to Zedad,ᵃ ¹⁶Berothah, Sibraim (which lies between the border of Damascus and the border of Hamath), as far as Hazer-hatticon, which is on the border of Hauran. ¹⁷So the boundary shall run from the sea to Hazar-enon, which is north of the border of Damascus, with the border of Hamath to the north.ᵇ This shall be the north side.

18 On the east side, between Hauran and Damascus; along the Jordan between Gilead and the land of Israel; to the eastern sea and as far as Tamar.ᶜ This shall be the east side.

19 On the south side, it shall run from Tamar as far as the waters of Meribath-kadesh, from there along the Wadi of Egyptᵈ to the Great Sea. This shall be the south side.

20 On the west side, the Great Sea shall be the boundary to a point opposite Lebo-hamath. This shall be the west side.

21 So you shall divide this land among you according to the tribes of Israel. ²²You shall allot it as an inheritance for yourselves and for the aliens who reside among you and have begotten children among you. They shall be to you as citizens of Israel; with you they shall be allotted an inheritance among the tribes of Israel. ²³In whatever tribe aliens reside, there you shall assign them their inheritance, says the Lord GOD.

48 The Tribal Portions

These are the names of the tribes: Beginning at the northern border, on the Hethlon road,ᵉ from Lebo-hamath, as far as Hazar-enon (which is on the border of Damascus, with Hamath to the north), andᶠ extending from the east side to the west,ᵍ Dan, one portion. ²Adjoining the territory of Dan, from the east side to the west, Asher, one portion. ³Adjoining the territory of Asher, from the east side to the west, Naphtali, one portion. ⁴Adjoining the territory of Naphtali, from the east side to the west, Manasseh, one portion. ⁵Adjoining the territory of Manasseh, from the east side to the west, Ephraim, one portion. ⁶Adjoining the territory of Ephraim, from the east side to the west, Reuben, one portion. ⁷Adjoining the territory of Reuben, from the east side to the west, Judah, one portion.

8 Adjoining the territory of Judah, from the east side to the west, shall be the portion that you shall set apart, twenty-five thousand cubits in width, and in length equal to one of the tribal portions, from the east side to the west, with the sanctuary in the middle of it. ⁹The portion that you shall set apart for the LORD shall be twenty-five thousand cubits in length, and twentyʰ thousand in width. ¹⁰These shall be the allotments of the holy portion: the priests shall have an allotment measuring twenty-five thousand cubits on the northern side, ten thousand cubits in width on the western side, ten thousand in width on the eastern side, and twenty-five thousand in length on the southern side, with the sanctuary of the LORD in the middle of it. ¹¹This shall be for the consecrated priests, the descendantsⁱ of Zadok, who kept my charge, who did not go astray when the people of Israel went astray, as the Levites did. ¹²It shall belong to them as a special portion from the holy portion of the land, a most holy place, adjoining the territory of the Levites. ¹³Alongside the territory of the priests, the Levites shall have an allotment twenty-five thousand cubits in length and ten thousand in width. The whole length shall be twenty-five thousand cubits and the width twentyʲ thousand. ¹⁴They shall not sell or exchange any of it; they shall not transfer this choice portion of the land, for it is holy to the LORD.

15 The remainder, five thousand cubits in width and twenty-five thousand in length, shall be for ordinary use for the city, for dwellings and for open country. In the middle of it shall be the city; ¹⁶and these shall be its dimensions: the north side four thousand five hundred cubits, the south side four thousand five hundred, the east side four thousand five hundred, and the west side four thousand five hundred. ¹⁷The city shall have open land: on the north two hundred fifty cubits, on the south two hundred fifty, on the east two hundred fifty, on the west two hundred fifty. ¹⁸The remainder of the length alongside the holy portion shall be ten thousand cubits to the east, and ten thousand to the west, and it shall be alongside the holy portion. Its produce shall

---

a Gk: Heb *Lebo-zedad,* ¹⁶*Hamath* *b* Meaning of Heb uncertain *c* Compare Syr: Heb *you shall measure* *d* Heb lacks *of Egypt* *e* Compare 47.15: Heb *by the side of the way* *f* Cn: Heb *and they shall be his* *g* Gk Compare verses 2–8: Heb *the east side the west* *h* Compare 45.1: Heb *ten* *i* One Ms Gk: Heb *of the descendants* *j* Gk: Heb *ten* be food for the workers of the city. ¹⁹The workers of the city, from all the tribes of Israel, shall cultivate it. ²⁰The whole portion that you shall set apart shall be twenty-five thousand cubits square, that is, the holy portion together with the property of the city.

21 What remains on both sides of the holy portion and of the property of the city shall belong to the prince. Extending from the twenty-five thousand cubits of the holy portion to the east border, and westward from the twenty-five thousand cubits to the west border, parallel to the tribal portions, it shall belong to the prince. The holy portion with the sanctuary of the temple in the middle of it, ²²and the property of the Levites and of the city, shall be in the middle of that which belongs to the prince. The portion of the prince shall lie between the territory of Judah and the territory of Benjamin.

23 As for the rest of the tribes: from the east side to the west, Benjamin, one portion. ²⁴Adjoining the territory of Benjamin, from the east side to the west, Simeon, one portion. ²⁵Adjoining the territory of Simeon, from the east side to the west, Issachar, one portion. ²⁶Adjoining the territory of Issachar, from the east side to the west, Zebulun, one portion.

²⁷Adjoining the territory of Zebulun, from the east side to the west, Gad, one portion. ²⁸And adjoining the territory of Gad to the south, the boundary shall run from Tamar to the waters of Meribath-kadesh, from there along the Wadi of Egypt*ᵃ* to the Great Sea. ²⁹This is the land that you shall allot as an inheritance among the tribes of Israel, and these are their portions, says the Lord God.

30 These shall be the exits of the city: On the north side, which is to be four thousand five hundred cubits by measure, ³¹three gates, the gate of Reuben, the gate of Judah, and the gate of Levi, the gates of the city being named after the tribes of Israel. ³²On the east side, which is to be four thousand five hundred cubits, three gates, the gate of Joseph, the gate of Benjamin, and the gate of Dan. ³³On the south side, which is to be four thousand five hundred cubits by measure, three gates, the gate of Simeon, the gate of Issachar, and the gate of Zebulun. ³⁴On the west side, which is to be four thousand five hundred cubits, three gates,*ᵇ* the gate of Gad, the gate of Asher, and the gate of Naphtali. ³⁵The circumference of the city shall be eighteen thousand cubits. And the name of the city from that time on shall be, The Lord is There.

a Heb lacks *of Egypt*   *b* One Ms Gk Syr: MT *their gates three*

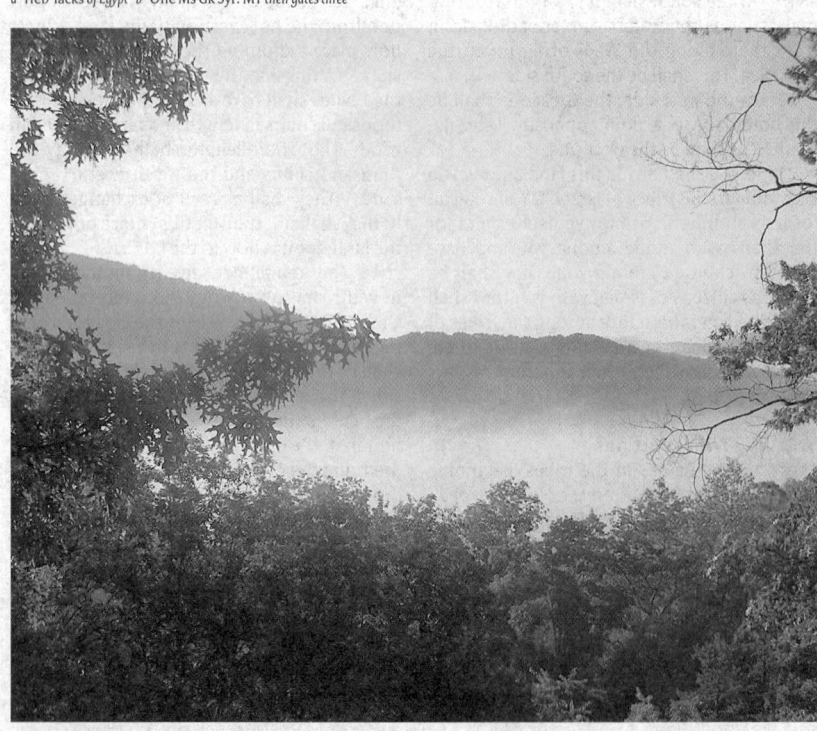

Masterpiece—© Lucy Johnson, 15

DANIEL

GOD AMONG US

Shadrach's Plea

Baruch atah Adonai, Elohenu melech ha'olam . . .

Blessed are you, Lord, King of all creation . . . We acknowledge that you are our creator and sustainer, the One who gives breath to every living thing. Our life, our every breath, comes from you. You have heard the cry of your people from the days of Moses when we were slaves in Egypt. You heard and you acted. You brought your people out of Egypt with mighty deeds, and brought us into a great land flowing with milk and honey.

Yet here we are, O God, living in Babylon, a foreign land. We look to you, our strength and our sustainer. Come once again and rescue your people, so that all the nations will know that you are the Lord Almighty.

And to your servant, Shadrach, may you give strength, for I know not what awaits me as I go before King Nebuchadnezzar this very day and take my stand. Yet I know that I have never seen the righteous forsaken. You have been with us in the past. Be present with your trusting servant this day. Great is the Lord, and worthy of praise. He has been faithful to a thousand generations. Be faithful today.

> **"Be faithful in small things, because it is in them that your strength lies."**
> —Bl. Mother Teresa of Calcutta

WHO Daniel, a Jew exiled to Babylon

WHAT This book describes real historical events involving the lives of Daniel and his friends (Daniel 1–6) and visions of the future (Daniel 7–12).

WHEN Daniel was exiled from 605 to 536 B.C. Many believe the book was written between 536 and 530 B.C.

WHERE The book of Daniel was most likely written in Judah. Many of the events in this book took place in Babylon (modern-day Iraq).

PATH OF DISCIPLESHIP

Some people's image of God is that of a God who is up in the clouds, detached from this world. This picture of God couldn't be further from the truth. God has always been a God among us.

As Shadrach and the others were tossed into a furnace to assuredly face their death, those standing there saw this truth, for in the midst of the fire was a fourth person: an angel sent by God (Daniel 3.25).

And when Daniel was sealed into a den filled with ferocious and hungry lions, God was with him, sending an angel to protect him from certain death (Daniel 6.22).

It's unlikely you'll ever be in a furnace or a lions' den, but there will be times in your life when you'll be afraid or confused—and you'll wonder where God is. The stories of Shadrach and the others and Daniel are ones to hold on to. It will help you remember that God is always there for you; you just have to pay attention.

DON'T BE A SELLOUT!

When people try to tell you what to do or who to be, are you confident enough *not* to give in when you know it's not for you? When you become a sellout just to fit in, it can feel cheap, like you're cheating yourself out of what you know is best.

Read **Daniel 1.1–20**. This story is about four young men who refused to just do what they were told. They stayed true to themselves and God. And in the end, God gave them great success in the face of their captors as they boldly, yet humbly, stood up for what was right. They demonstrated that God was their One and Only simply by eating a diet that did not defile them.

How do you respond in high-stress situations?

If you are going to stand up for your faith, there are two extreme ways *not* to respond. First, it's not appropriate to degrade those with whom you disagree. (Look at how Daniel treated Nebuchadnezzar in chapter 2—always showing humility, kindness, and respect.) And second, it's also wrong to do nothing and just go with the flow.

Grab your journal or use some Creative Space in this Bible to write a short personal plan for handling the social pressures you face—a plan that doesn't take either of these extremes. Pray and ask God to help you stick to your plan in any situation. Come back to it in a year. Did God answer your prayer? How? Tell us about it at **Learner.CalltoDiscipleship.com**.

GOD IS ONE AND ONLY   MY WORLD

Wondering Alone—© Clay Goswick, 16

1 Four Young Israelites at the Babylonian Court

In the third year of the reign of King Jehoiakim of Judah, King Nebuchadnezzar of Babylon came to Jerusalem and besieged it. ²The Lord let King Jehoiakim of Judah fall into his power, as well as some of the vessels of the house of God. These he brought to the land of Shinar,ᵃ and placed the vessels in the treasury of his gods.

3 Then the king commanded his palace master Ashpenaz to bring some of the Israelites of the royal family and of the nobility, ⁴young men without physical defect and handsome, versed in every branch of wisdom, endowed with knowledge and insight, and competent to serve in the king's palace; they were to be taught the literature and language of the Chaldeans. ⁵The king assigned them a daily portion of the royal rations of food and wine. They were to be educated for three years, so that at the end of that time they could be stationed in the king's court. ⁶Among them were Daniel, Hananiah, Mishael, and Azariah, from the tribe of Judah. ⁷The palace master gave them other names: Daniel he called Belteshazzar, Hananiah he called Shadrach, Mishael he called Meshach, and Azariah he called Abednego.

8 But Daniel resolved that he would not defile himself with the royal rations of food and wine; so he asked the palace master to allow him not to defile himself. ⁹Now God allowed Daniel to receive favor and compassion from the palace master. ¹⁰The palace master said to Daniel, "I am afraid of my lord the king; he has appointed your food and your drink. If he should see you in poorer condition than the other young men of your own age, you would endanger my head with the king." ¹¹Then Daniel asked the guard whom the palace master had appointed over Daniel, Hananiah, Mishael, and Azariah; ¹²"Please test your servants for ten days. Let us be given vegetables to eat and water to drink. ¹³You can then compare our appearance with the appearance of the young men who eat the royal rations, and deal with your servants according to what you observe." ¹⁴So he agreed to this proposal and tested them for ten days. ¹⁵At the end of ten days it was observed that they appeared better and fatter than all the young men who had been eating the royal rations. ¹⁶So the guard continued to withdraw their royal rations and the wine they were to drink, and gave them vegetables. ¹⁷To these four young men God gave knowledge and skill in every aspect of literature and wisdom; Daniel also had insight into all visions and dreams.

a Gk Theodotion: Heb adds *to the house of his own gods*

18 At the end of the time that the king had set for them to be brought in, the palace master brought them into the presence of Nebuchadnezzar, ¹⁹and the king spoke with them. And among them all, no one was found to compare with Daniel, Hananiah, Mishael, and Azariah; therefore they were stationed in the king's court. ²⁰In every matter of wisdom and understanding concerning which the king inquired of them, he found them ten times better than all the magicians and enchanters in his whole kingdom. ²¹And Daniel continued there until the first year of King Cyrus.

2 Nebuchadnezzar's Dream

In the second year of Nebuchadnezzar's reign, Nebuchadnezzar dreamed such dreams that his spirit was troubled and his sleep left him. ²So the king commanded that the magicians, the enchanters, the sorcerers, and the Chaldeans be summoned to tell the king his dreams. When they came in and stood before the king, ³he said to them, "I have had such a dream that my spirit is troubled by the desire to understand it." ⁴The Chaldeans said to the king (in Aramaic),ᵃ "O king, live forever! Tell your servants the dream, and we will reveal the interpretation." ⁵The king answered the Chaldeans, "This is a public decree: if you do not tell me both the dream and its interpretation, you shall be torn limb from limb, and your houses shall be laid in ruins. ⁶But if you do tell me the dream and its interpretation, you shall receive from me gifts and rewards and great honor. Therefore tell me the dream and its interpretation." ⁷They answered a second time, "Let the king first tell his servants the dream, then we can give its interpretation." ⁸The king answered, "I know with certainty that you are trying to gain time, because you see I have firmly decreed: ⁹if you do not tell me the dream, there is but one verdict for you. You have agreed to speak lying and misleading words to me until things take a turn. Therefore, tell me the dream, and I shall know that you can give me its interpretation." ¹⁰The Chaldeans answered the king, "There is no one on earth who can reveal what the king demands! In fact no king, however great and powerful, has ever asked such a thing of any magician or enchanter or Chaldean. ¹¹The thing that the king is asking is too difficult, and no one can reveal it to the king except the gods, whose dwelling is not with mortals."

12 Because of this the king flew into a violent rage and commanded that all the wise men of Babylon be destroyed. ¹³The decree was issued, and the wise men were about to be executed; and they looked for Daniel and his companions, to execute them. ¹⁴Then Daniel responded with prudence and discretion to Arioch, the king's chief executioner, who had gone out to execute the wise men of Babylon; ¹⁵he asked Arioch, the royal official, "Why is the decree of the king so urgent?" Arioch then explained the matter to Daniel. ¹⁶So Daniel went in and requested that the king give him time and he would tell the king the interpretation.

God Reveals Nebuchadnezzar's Dream

17 Then Daniel went to his home and informed his companions, Hananiah, Mishael, and Azariah, ¹⁸and told them to seek mercy from the God of heaven concerning this mystery, so that Daniel and his companions with the rest of the wise men of Babylon might not perish. ¹⁹Then the mystery was revealed to Daniel in a vision of the night, and Daniel blessed the God of heaven.

²⁰ Daniel said:

"Blessed be the name of God from age to
        age,
    for wisdom and power are his.
²¹ He changes times and seasons,
        deposes kings and sets up kings;
    he gives wisdom to the wise
        and knowledge to those who have
            understanding.
²² He reveals deep and hidden things;
    he knows what is in the darkness,
        and light dwells with him.
²³ To you, O God of my ancestors,
    I give thanks and praise,
for you have given me wisdom and power,
    and have now revealed to me what we
            asked of you,
        for you have revealed to us what the king
            ordered."

Daniel Interprets the Dream

24 Therefore Daniel went to Arioch, whom the king had appointed to destroy the wise men of Babylon, and said to him, "Do not destroy the wise men of Babylon; bring me in before the king, and I will give the king the interpretation."

25 Then Arioch quickly brought Daniel before the king and said to him: "I have found among the exiles from Judah a man who can tell the king the interpretation." ²⁶The king said to Daniel, whose name was Belteshazzar, "Are you able to tell me the dream that I have seen and its interpretation?" ²⁷Daniel answered the king, "No wise men, enchanters,

ᵃ The text from this point to the end of chapter 7 is in Aramaic, except for 3.24–91a, the text of which is in Greek magicians, or diviners can show to the king the mystery that the king is asking, [28] but there is a God in heaven who reveals mysteries, and he has disclosed to King Nebuchadnezzar what will happen at the end of days. Your dream and the visions of your head as you lay in bed were these: [29] To you, O king, as you lay in bed, came thoughts of what would be hereafter, and the revealer of mysteries disclosed to you what is to be. [30] But as for me, this mystery has not been revealed to me because of any wisdom that I have more than any other living being, but in order that the interpretation may be known to the king and that you may understand the thoughts of your mind.

[31] "You were looking, O king, and lo! there was a great statue. This statue was huge, its brilliance extraordinary; it was standing before you, and its appearance was frightening. [32] The head of that statue was of fine gold, its chest and arms of silver, its middle and thighs of bronze, [33] its legs of iron, its feet partly of iron and partly of clay. [34] As you looked on, a stone was cut out, not by human hands, and it struck the statue on its feet of iron and clay and broke them in pieces. [35] Then the iron, the clay, the bronze, the silver, and the gold, were all broken in pieces and became like the chaff of the summer threshing floors; and the wind carried them away, so that not a trace of them could be found. But the stone that struck the statue became a great mountain and filled the whole earth.

[36] "This was the dream; now we will tell the king its interpretation. [37] You, O king, the king of kings—to whom the God of heaven has given the kingdom, the power, the might, and the glory, [38] into whose hand he has given human beings, wherever they live, the wild animals of the field, and the birds of the air, and whom he has established as ruler over them all—you are the head of gold. [39] After you shall arise another kingdom inferior to yours, and yet a third kingdom of bronze, which shall rule over the whole earth. [40] And there shall be a fourth kingdom, strong as iron; just as iron crushes and smashes everything,[a] it shall crush and shatter all these. [41] As you saw the feet and toes partly of potter's clay and partly of iron, it shall be a divided kingdom; but some of the strength of iron shall be in it, as you saw the iron mixed with the clay. [42] As the toes of the feet were part iron and part clay, so the kingdom shall be partly strong and partly brittle. [43] As you saw the iron mixed with clay, so will they mix with one another in marriage,[b] but they will not hold together, just as iron does not mix with clay. [44] And in the days of those kings the God

of heaven will set up a kingdom that shall never be destroyed, nor shall this kingdom be left to another people. It shall crush all these kingdoms and bring them to an end, and it shall stand forever; [45] just as you saw that a stone was cut from the mountain not by hands, and that it crushed the iron, the bronze, the clay, the silver, and the gold. The great God has informed the king what shall be hereafter. The dream is certain, and its interpretation trustworthy."

Daniel and His Friends Promoted

[46] Then King Nebuchadnezzar fell on his face, worshiped Daniel, and commanded that a grain offering and incense be offered to him. [47] The king said to Daniel, "Truly, your God is God of gods and Lord of kings and a revealer of mysteries, for you have been able to reveal this mystery!" [48] Then the king promoted Daniel, gave him many great gifts, and made him ruler over the whole province of Babylon and chief prefect over all the wise men of Babylon. [49] Daniel made a request of the king, and he appointed Shadrach, Meshach, and Abednego over the affairs of the province of Babylon. But Daniel remained at the king's court.

3 The Golden Image

King Nebuchadnezzar made a golden statue whose height was sixty cubits and whose width was six cubits; he set it up on the plain of Dura in the province of Babylon. [2] Then King Nebuchadnezzar sent for the satraps, the prefects, and the governors, the counselors, the treasurers, the justices, the magistrates, and all the officials of the provinces, to assemble and come to the dedication of the statue that King Nebuchadnezzar had set up. [3] So the satraps, the prefects, and the governors, the counselors, the treasurers, the justices, the magistrates, and all the officials of the provinces, assembled for the dedication of the statue that King Nebuchadnezzar had set up. When they were standing before the statue that Nebuchadnezzar had set up, [4] the herald proclaimed aloud, "You are commanded, O peoples, nations, and languages, [5] that when you hear the sound of the horn, pipe, lyre, trigon, harp, drum, and entire musical ensemble, you are to fall down and worship the golden statue that King Nebuchadnezzar has set up. [6] Whoever does not fall down and worship shall immediately be thrown into a furnace of blazing fire." [7] Therefore, as soon as all the peoples heard the sound of the horn, pipe, lyre, trigon, harp, drum, and entire musical ensemble, all the peoples, nations, and

a Gk Theodotion Syr Vg: Aram adds and like iron that crushes   b Aram by human seed languages fell down and worshiped the golden statue that King Nebuchadnezzar had set up.

8 Accordingly, at this time certain Chaldeans came forward and denounced the Jews. 9They said to King Nebuchadnezzar, "O king, live forever! 10You, O king, have made a decree, that everyone who hears the sound of the horn, pipe, lyre, trigon, harp, drum, and entire musical ensemble, shall fall down and worship the golden statue, 11and whoever does not fall down and worship shall be thrown into a furnace of blazing fire. 12There are certain Jews whom you have appointed over the affairs of the province of Babylon: Shadrach, Meshach, and Abednego. These pay no heed to you, O king. They do not serve your gods and they do not worship the golden statue that you have set up."

13 Then Nebuchadnezzar in furious rage commanded that Shadrach, Meshach, and Abednego be brought in; so they brought those men before the king. 14Nebuchadnezzar said to them, "Is it true, O Shadrach, Meshach, and Abednego, that you do not serve my gods and you do not worship the golden statue that I have set up? 15Now if you are ready when you hear the sound of the horn, pipe, lyre, trigon, harp, drum, and entire musical ensemble to fall down and worship the statue that I have made, well and good.*a* But if you do not worship, you shall immediately be thrown into a furnace of blazing fire, and who is the god that will deliver you out of my hands?"

16 Shadrach, Meshach, and Abednego answered the king, "O Nebuchadnezzar, we have no need to present a defense to you in this matter. 17If our God whom we serve is able to deliver us from the furnace of blazing fire and out of your hand, O king, let him deliver us.*b* 18But if not, be it known to you, O king, that we will not serve your gods and we will not worship the golden statue that you have set up."

The Fiery Furnace
19 Then Nebuchadnezzar was so filled with rage against Shadrach, Meshach, and Abednego that his face was distorted. He ordered the furnace heated up seven times more than was customary, 20and ordered some of the strongest guards in his army to bind Shadrach, Meshach, and Abednego and to throw them into the furnace of blazing fire. 21So the men were bound, still wearing their tunics,*c* their trousers,*c* their hats, and their other garments, and they were thrown into the furnace of blazing fire. 22Because the king's command was urgent and the furnace was so overheated, the raging

IT'S TRADITION

APOCALYPTIC LITERATURE

The books of Daniel and Revelation are examples of apocalyptic literature found in the Bible. This form of writing takes its name from the Greek word *apokalypsis*, which means "revelation."

Using very symbolic language, the apocalyptic books describe mysterious revelations given by angels or in visions or dreams. Although they focus on the end times, apocalyptic books were written for a contemporary audience that was facing persecution, disaster, or distress—to offer hope when all seemed hopeless. The unique vision of this type of literature often proclaims that God is the Lord of creation and history. It brings attention to some type of new world order. It rejects the power of evil and affirms life after death and the judgment of the dead. This type of literature helped form the early Christians' belief in the Resurrection and the Second Coming of Christ.

flames killed the men who lifted Shadrach, Meshach, and Abednego. 23But the three men, Shadrach, Meshach, and Abednego, fell down, bound, into the furnace of blazing fire.

The Prayer of Azariah in the Furnace
24 They walked around in the midst of the flames, singing hymns to God and blessing the Lord. 25Then Azariah stood still in the fire and prayed aloud:
26 "Blessed are you, O Lord, God of our
  ancestors, and worthy of praise;
  and glorious is your name forever!
27 For you are just in all you have done;
  all your works are true and your ways
   right,
  and all your judgments are true.
28 You have executed true judgments in all you
   have brought upon us
  and upon Jerusalem, the holy city of our
   ancestors;
  by a true judgment you have brought all
   this upon us because of our sins.

a Aram lacks *well and good* *b* Or *If our God whom we serve is able to deliver us, he will deliver us from the furnace of blazing fire and out of your hand, O king.* *c* Meaning of Aram word uncertain

²⁹ For we have sinned and broken your law in
turning away from you;
in all matters we have sinned grievously.
³⁰ We have not obeyed your commandments,
we have not kept them or done what you
have commanded us for our own
good.
³¹ So all that you have brought upon us,
and all that you have done to us,
you have done by a true judgment.
³² You have handed us over to our enemies,
lawless and hateful rebels,
and to an unjust king, the most wicked in
all the world.
³³ And now we cannot open our mouths;
we, your servants who worship you, have
become a shame and a reproach.
³⁴ For your name's sake do not give us up
forever,
and do not annul your covenant.
³⁵   Do not withdraw your mercy from us,
for the sake of Abraham your beloved
and for the sake of your servant Isaac
and Israel your holy one,
³⁶ to whom you promised
to multiply their descendants like the
stars of heaven
and like the sand on the shore of the sea.
³⁷ For we, O Lord, have become fewer than any
other nation,
and are brought low this day in all the
world because of our sins.
³⁸ In our day we have no ruler, or prophet, or
leader,
no burnt offering, or sacrifice, or
oblation, or incense,
no place to make an offering before you
and to find mercy.
³⁹ Yet with a contrite heart and a humble spirit
may we be accepted,
⁴⁰   as though it were with burnt offerings of
rams and bulls,
or with tens of thousands of fat lambs;
such may our sacrifice be in your sight
today,
and may we unreservedly follow you,^a
for no shame will come to those who
trust in you.
⁴¹ And now with all our heart we follow you;
we fear you and seek your presence.
⁴² Do not put us to shame,
but deal with us in your patience
and in your abundant mercy.
⁴³ Deliver us in accordance with your
marvelous works,
and bring glory to your name, O Lord.

^a Meaning of Gk uncertain

⁴⁴ Let all who do harm to your servants be put
to shame;
let them be disgraced and deprived of all
power,
and let their strength be broken.
⁴⁵ Let them know that you alone are the Lord
God,
glorious over the whole world."

The Song of the Three Jews

46 Now the king's servants who threw them in
kept stoking the furnace with naphtha, pitch,
tow, and brushwood. ⁴⁷ And the flames poured
out above the furnace forty-nine cubits, ⁴⁸ and
spread out and burned those Chaldeans who
were caught near the furnace. ⁴⁹ But the angel
of the Lord came down into the furnace to be
with Azariah and his companions, and drove
the fiery flame out of the furnace, ⁵⁰ and made
the inside of the furnace as though a moist
wind were whistling through it. The fire did
not touch them at all and caused them no pain
or distress.

51 Then the three with one voice praised
and glorified and blessed God in the furnace:
⁵² "Blessed are you, O Lord, God of our
ancestors,
and to be praised and highly exalted
forever;
And blessed is your glorious, holy name,
and to be highly praised and highly
exalted forever.
⁵³ Blessed are you in the temple of your holy
glory,
and to be extolled and highly glorified
forever.
⁵⁴ Blessed are you who look into the depths
from your throne on the cherubim,
and to be praised and highly exalted
forever.
⁵⁵ Blessed are you on the throne of your
kingdom,
and to be extolled and highly exalted
forever.
⁵⁶ Blessed are you in the firmament of heaven,
and to be sung and glorified forever.

⁵⁷ "Bless the Lord, all you works of the Lord;
sing praise to him and highly exalt him
forever.
⁵⁸ Bless the Lord, you heavens;
sing praise to him and highly exalt him
forever.
⁵⁹ Bless the Lord, you angels of the Lord;
sing praise to him and highly exalt him
forever.
⁶⁰ Bless the Lord, all you waters above the
heavens;

sing praise to him and highly exalt him
forever.
61 Bless the Lord, all you powers of the Lord;
sing praise to him and highly exalt him
forever.
62 Bless the Lord, sun and moon;
sing praise to him and highly exalt him
forever.
63 Bless the Lord, stars of heaven;
sing praise to him and highly exalt him
forever.
64 "Bless the Lord, all rain and dew;
sing praise to him and highly exalt him
forever.
65 Bless the Lord, all you winds;
sing praise to him and highly exalt him
forever.
66 Bless the Lord, fire and heat;
sing praise to him and highly exalt him
forever.
67 Bless the Lord, winter cold and summer
heat;
sing praise to him and highly exalt him
forever.
68 Bless the Lord, dews and falling snow;
sing praise to him and highly exalt him
forever.
69 Bless the Lord, ice and cold;
sing praise to him and highly exalt him
forever.
70 Bless the Lord, frosts and snows;
sing praise to him and highly exalt him
forever.
71 Bless the Lord, nights and days;
sing praise to him and highly exalt him
forever.
72 Bless the Lord, light and darkness;
sing praise to him and highly exalt him
forever.
73 Bless the Lord, lightnings and clouds;
sing praise to him and highly exalt him
forever.
74 "Let the earth bless the Lord;
let it sing praise to him and highly exalt
him forever.
75 Bless the Lord, mountains and hills;
sing praise to him and highly exalt him
forever.
76 Bless the Lord, all that grows in the ground;
sing praise to him and highly exalt him
forever.
77 Bless the Lord, you springs;
sing praise to him and highly exalt him
forever.
78 Bless the Lord, seas and rivers;

sing praise to him and highly exalt him
forever.
79 Bless the Lord, you whales and all that swim
in the waters;
sing praise to him and highly exalt him
forever.
80 Bless the Lord, all birds of the air;
sing praise to him and highly exalt him
forever.
81 Bless the Lord, all wild animals and cattle;
sing praise to him and highly exalt him
forever.
82 "Bless the Lord, all people on earth;
sing praise to him and highly exalt him
forever.
83 Bless the Lord, O Israel;
sing praise to him and highly exalt him
forever.
84 Bless the Lord, you priests of the Lord;
sing praise to him and highly exalt him
forever.
85 Bless the Lord, you servants of the Lord;
sing praise to him and highly exalt him
forever.
86 Bless the Lord, spirits and souls of the
righteous;
sing praise to him and highly exalt him
forever.
87 Bless the Lord, you who are holy and
humble in heart;
sing praise to him and highly exalt him
forever.
88 "Bless the Lord, Hananiah, Azariah, and
Mishael;
sing praise to him and highly exalt him
forever.
For he has rescued us from Hades and saved
us from the power[a] of death,
and delivered us from the midst of the
burning fiery furnace;
from the midst of the fire he has
delivered us.
89 Give thanks to the Lord, for he is good,
for his mercy endures forever.
90 All who worship the Lord, bless the God of
gods,
sing praise to him and give thanks to him,
for his mercy endures forever."

91 Hearing them sing, and amazed at seeing them alive, King Nebuchadnezzar rose up
quickly. He said to his counselors, "Was it not
three men that we threw bound into the fire?"
They answered the king, "True, O king." 92 He
replied, "But I see four men unbound, walking in the middle of the fire, and they are not
hurt; and the fourth has the appearance of a

a Gk hand

REALITY ✔

STUFF HAPPENS

Nebuchadnezzar was the king of Babylonia from 605 to 562 B.C. He was a great military leader and a very powerful man, known for conquering Judah and destroying its Temple. He extravagantly rebuilt Babylon with beautiful palaces and temples. The "Hanging Gardens of Babylon," one of the seven wonders of the ancient world, are also attributed to him. **Daniel 4.34–37** describes Nebuchadnezzar as a person who had a conversion experience. He had observed his three Jewish officials stand fast in their faith and come through fire unharmed, and he seemed to have suffered a bout of insanity caused by the loss of his kingdom. He was humbled. The person who offered praise and thanks to God in these verses was a different person from the conquering hero.

No doubt, you've often heard that faith is a journey. It is. It's a journey of growth and change, which is another way of saying it is a conversion journey. Life happens. You have successes and failures. Friends love you, and they leave you. You may suffer a serious illness or handicap along the way. Some times are real highs when you feel like life is so awesome, and other times you feel like you're in the pits. People of faith grow from these experiences.

Recall some of the high and low points of your life in the last few years and examine how those events have changed you for the better. Find some Creative Space in this Bible and draw your path of conversion so far.

god."[a] [93]Nebuchadnezzar then approached the door of the furnace of blazing fire and said, "Shadrach, Meshach, and Abednego, servants of the Most High God, come out! Come here!" So Shadrach, Meshach, and Abednego came

out from the fire. [94]And the satraps, the prefects, the governors, and the king's counselors gathered together and saw that the fire had not had any power over the bodies of those men; the hair of their heads was not singed, their tunics[b] were not harmed, and not even the smell of fire came from them. [95]Nebuchadnezzar said, "Blessed be the God of Shadrach, Meshach, and Abednego, who has sent his angel and delivered his servants who trusted in him. They disobeyed the king's command and yielded up their bodies rather than serve and worship any god except their own God. [96]Therefore I make a decree: Any people, nation, or language that utters blasphemy against the God of Shadrach, Meshach, and Abednego shall be torn limb from limb, and their houses laid in ruins; for there is no other god who is able to deliver in this way." [97]Then the king promoted Shadrach, Meshach, and Abednego in the province of Babylon.

4[c] Nebuchadnezzar's Second Dream

King Nebuchadnezzar to all peoples, nations, and languages that live throughout the earth: May you have abundant prosperity! [2]The signs and wonders that the Most High God has worked for me I am pleased to recount.

[3] How great are his signs,
   how mighty his wonders!
His kingdom is an everlasting kingdom,
   and his sovereignty is from generation to
      generation.

4[d] I, Nebuchadnezzar, was living at ease in my home and prospering in my palace. [5]I saw a dream that frightened me; my fantasies in bed and the visions of my head terrified me. [6]So I made a decree that all the wise men of Babylon should be brought before me, in order that they might tell me the interpretation of the dream. [7]Then the magicians, the enchanters, the Chaldeans, and the diviners came in, and I told them the dream, but they could not tell me its interpretation. [8]At last Daniel came in before me—he who was named Belteshazzar after the name of my god, and who is endowed with a spirit of the holy gods[e]—and I told him the dream: [9]"O Belteshazzar, chief of the magicians, I know that you are endowed with a spirit of the holy gods[e] and that no mystery is too difficult for you. Hear[f] the dream that I saw; tell me its interpretation.
[10][g] Upon my bed this is what I saw;
   there was a tree at the center of the earth,
      and its height was great.
[11] The tree grew great and strong,

---

[a] Aram *a son of the gods* [b] Meaning of Aram word uncertain [c] Ch 3.31 in Aram [d] Ch 4.1 in Aram [e] Or *a holy, divine spirit*
[f] Theodotion: Aram *The visions of* [g] Theodotion Syr Compare Gk: Aram adds *The visions of my head*

its top reached to heaven,
    and it was visible to the ends of the
        whole earth.
12 Its foliage was beautiful,
    its fruit abundant,
    and it provided food for all.
The animals of the field found shade
    under it,
    the birds of the air nested in its branches,
and from it all living beings were fed.

13 "I continued looking, in the visions of my head as I lay in bed, and there was a holy watcher, coming down from heaven. ¹⁴He cried aloud and said:

'Cut down the tree and chop off its branches,
    strip off its foliage and scatter its fruit.
Let the animals flee from beneath it
    and the birds from its branches.
¹⁵ But leave its stump and roots in the ground,
    with a band of iron and bronze,
    in the tender grass of the field.
Let him be bathed with the dew of heaven,
    and let his lot be with the animals of the
        field
    in the grass of the earth.
¹⁶ Let his mind be changed from that of a
    human,
    and let the mind of an animal be given to
        him.
    And let seven times pass over him.
¹⁷ The sentence is rendered by decree of the
    watchers,
    the decision is given by order of the holy
        ones,
in order that all who live may know
    that the Most High is sovereign over the
        kingdom of mortals;
he gives it to whom he will
    and sets over it the lowliest of human
        beings.'

18 "This is the dream that I, King Nebuchadnezzar, saw. Now you, Belteshazzar, declare the interpretation, since all the wise men of my kingdom are unable to tell me the interpretation. You are able, however, for you are endowed with a spirit of the holy gods."ᵃ

Daniel Interprets the Second Dream

19 Then Daniel, who was called Belteshazzar, was severely distressed for a while. His thoughts terrified him. The king said, "Belteshazzar, do not let the dream or the interpretation terrify you." Belteshazzar answered, "My lord, may the dream be for those who hate you, and its interpretation for your enemies! ²⁰The tree that you saw, which grew great and strong, so that its top reached to heaven and was visible to the end of the whole earth, ²¹whose foliage was beautiful and its fruit abundant, and which provided food for all, under which animals of the field lived, and in whose branches the birds of the air had nests— ²²it is you, O king! You have grown great and strong. Your greatness has increased and reaches to heaven, and your sovereignty to the ends of the earth. ²³And whereas the king saw a holy watcher coming down from heaven and saying, 'Cut down the tree and destroy it, but leave its stump and roots in the ground, with a band of iron and bronze, in the grass of the field; and let him be bathed with the dew of heaven, and let his lot be with the animals of the field, until seven times pass over him'— ²⁴this is the interpretation, O king, and it is a decree of the Most High that has come upon my lord the king: ²⁵You shall be driven away from human society, and your dwelling shall be with the wild animals. You shall be made to eat grass like oxen, you shall be bathed with the dew of heaven, and seven times shall pass over you, until you have learned that the Most High has sovereignty over the kingdom of mortals, and gives it to whom he will. ²⁶As it was commanded to leave the stump and roots of the tree, your kingdom shall be re-established for you from the time that you learn that Heaven is sovereign. ²⁷Therefore, O king, may my counsel be acceptable to you: atone forᵇ your sins with righteousness, and your iniquities with mercy to the oppressed, so that your prosperity may be prolonged."

Nebuchadnezzar's Humiliation

28 All this came upon King Nebuchadnezzar. ²⁹At the end of twelve months he was walking on the roof of the royal palace of Babylon, ³⁰and the king said, "Is this not magnificent Babylon, which I have built as a royal capital by my mighty power and for my glorious majesty?" ³¹While the words were still in the king's mouth, a voice came from heaven: "O King Nebuchadnezzar, to you it is declared: The kingdom has departed from you! ³²You shall be driven away from human society, and your dwelling shall be with the animals of the field. You shall be made to eat grass like oxen, and seven times shall pass over you, until you have learned that the Most High has sovereignty over the kingdom of mortals and gives it to whom he will." ³³Immediately the sentence was fulfilled against Nebuchadnezzar. He was driven away from human society, ate grass like oxen, and his body was bathed with the dew of

---

a Or *a holy, divine spirit* b Aram *break off*

THE WALL

SP   IP

FR-ISuper   TYPE 1 (NORMAL) POSITION   90

The wall in front of me—
I've tried to act godly.
But I grew farther from him,
And life became so grim.
It seemed like the easy way out...
Now I'm so worn-out,
Working every day,
Trying to keep it my way.
Can't see beyond this dark wall,
I became my own rival.
Wait—there's a door in the middle,
Yet I pass it feeling fretful.
I look up trying to see the end,
Trying to pretend
That everything's okay.
I climb halfway
And give up...
I fall on my knees and worship.
I open the door to places unknown,
Am I not alone?

The Wall—© Shelby Steckroth, 15

heaven, until his hair grew as long as eagles' feathers and his nails became like birds' claws.

Nebuchadnezzar Praises God

34 When that period was over, I, Nebuchadnezzar, lifted my eyes to heaven, and my reason returned to me.

I blessed the Most High,
and praised and honored the one who
lives forever.

For his sovereignty is an everlasting
sovereignty,
and his kingdom endures from
generation to generation.

35 All the inhabitants of the earth are
accounted as nothing,
and he does what he wills with the host
of heaven
and the inhabitants of the earth.

There is no one who can stay his hand
or say to him, "What are you doing?"

36At that time my reason returned to me; and my majesty and splendor were restored to me for the glory of my kingdom. My counselors and my lords sought me out, I was reestablished over my kingdom, and still more greatness was added to me. 37Now I, Nebuchadnezzar, praise and extol and honor the King of heaven,

for all his works are truth,
and his ways are justice;
and he is able to bring low
those who walk in pride.

5 Belshazzar's Feast

King Belshazzar made a great festival for a thousand of his lords, and he was drinking wine in the presence of the thousand.

2 Under the influence of the wine, Belshazzar commanded that they bring in the vessels of gold and silver that his father Nebuchadnezzar had taken out of the temple in Jerusalem, so that the king and his lords, his wives, and his concubines might drink from them. 3So they brought in the vessels of gold and silver*a* that had been taken out of the temple, the house of God in Jerusalem, and the king and his lords, his wives, and his concubines drank from them. 4They drank the wine and praised the gods of gold and silver, bronze, iron, wood, and stone.

The Writing on the Wall

5 Immediately the fingers of a human hand appeared and began writing on the plaster of the wall of the royal palace, next to the lampstand. The king was watching the hand as it wrote. 6Then the king's face turned pale, and his thoughts terrified him. His limbs gave way, and his knees knocked together. 7The king cried aloud to bring in the enchanters, the Chaldeans, and the diviners; and the king said to the wise men of Babylon, "Whoever can read this writing and tell me its interpretation shall be clothed in purple, have a chain of gold around his neck, and rank third in the kingdom." 8Then all the king's wise men came in, but they could not read the writing or tell the king the interpretation. 9Then King Belshazzar became greatly terrified and his face turned pale, and his lords were perplexed.

10 The queen, when she heard the discussion of the king and his lords, came into the banqueting hall. The queen said, "O king, live forever! Do not let your thoughts terrify you or your face grow pale. 11There is a man in your kingdom who is endowed with a spirit of the holy gods.*b* In the days of your father he was found to have enlightenment, understanding, and wisdom like the wisdom of the gods. Your father, King Nebuchadnezzar, made him chief of the magicians, enchanters, Chaldeans, and diviners,*c* 12because an excellent spirit, knowledge, and understanding to interpret dreams, explain riddles, and solve problems were found in this Daniel, whom the king named Belteshazzar. Now let Daniel be called, and he will give the interpretation."

The Writing on the Wall Interpreted

13 Then Daniel was brought in before the king. The king said to Daniel, "So you are Daniel, one of the exiles of Judah, whom my father the king brought from Judah? 14I have heard of you that a spirit of the gods*d* is in you, and that enlightenment, understanding, and excellent wisdom are found in you. 15Now the wise men, the enchanters, have been brought in before me to read this writing and tell me its interpretation, but they were not able to give the interpretation of the matter. 16But I have heard that you can give interpretations and solve problems. Now if you are able to read the writing and tell me its interpretation, you shall be clothed in purple, have a chain of gold around your neck, and rank third in the kingdom."

17 Then Daniel answered in the presence of the king, "Let your gifts be for yourself, or give your rewards to someone else! Nevertheless I will read the writing to the king and let him know the interpretation. 18O king, the Most High God gave your father Nebuchadnezzar kingship, greatness, glory, and majesty. 19And because of the greatness that he gave him, all

a Theodotion Vg: Aram lacks *and silver* *b* Or *a holy, divine spirit* *c* Aram adds *the king your father* *d* Or *a divine spirit* peoples, nations, and languages trembled and feared before him. He killed those he wanted to kill, kept alive those he wanted to keep alive, honored those he wanted to honor, and degraded those he wanted to degrade. [20]But when his heart was lifted up and his spirit was hardened so that he acted proudly, he was deposed from his kingly throne, and his glory was stripped from him. [21]He was driven from human society, and his mind was made like that of an animal. His dwelling was with the wild asses, he was fed grass like oxen, and his body was bathed with the dew of heaven, until he learned that the Most High God has sovereignty over the kingdom of mortals, and sets over it whomever he will. [22]And you, Belshazzar his son, have not humbled your heart, even though you knew all this! [23]You have exalted yourself against the Lord of heaven! The vessels of his temple have been brought in before you, and you and your lords, your wives and your concubines have been drinking wine from them. You have praised the gods of silver and gold, of bronze, iron, wood, and stone, which do not see or hear or know; but the God in whose power is your very breath, and to whom belong all your ways, you have not honored.

[24] "So from his presence the hand was sent and this writing was inscribed. [25]And this is the writing that was inscribed: MENE, MENE, TEKEL, and PARSIN. [26]This is the interpretation of the matter: MENE, God has numbered the days of[a] your kingdom and brought it to an end; [27]TEKEL, you have been weighed on the scales and found wanting; [28]PERES,[b] your kingdom is divided and given to the Medes and Persians."

[29] Then Belshazzar gave the command, and Daniel was clothed in purple, a chain of gold was put around his neck, and a proclamation was made concerning him that he should rank third in the kingdom.

[30] That very night Belshazzar, the Chaldean king, was killed. [31][c] And Darius the Mede received the kingdom, being about sixty-two years old.

6 The Plot against Daniel

It pleased Darius to set over the kingdom one hundred twenty satraps, stationed throughout the whole kingdom, [2]and over them three presidents, including Daniel; to these the satraps gave account, so that the king might suffer no loss. [3]Soon Daniel distinguished himself above all the other presidents and satraps because an excellent spirit was in him, and the king planned to appoint him over the whole kingdom. [4]So the presidents and the satraps tried to find grounds for complaint against Daniel in connection with the kingdom. But they could find no grounds for complaint or any corruption, because he was faithful, and no negligence or corruption could be found in him. [5]The men said, "We shall not find any ground for complaint against this Daniel unless we find it in connection with the law of his God."

6 So the presidents and satraps conspired and came to the king and said to him, "O King Darius, live forever! [7]All the presidents of the kingdom, the prefects and the satraps, the counselors and the governors are agreed that the king should establish an ordinance and enforce an interdict, that whoever prays to anyone, divine or human, for thirty days, except to you, O king, shall be thrown into a den of lions. [8]Now, O king, establish the interdict and sign the document, so that it cannot be changed, according to the law of the Medes and the Persians, which cannot be revoked." [9]Therefore King Darius signed the document and interdict.

Daniel in the Lions' Den

10 Although Daniel knew that the document had been signed, he continued to go to his house, which had windows in its upper room open toward Jerusalem, and to get down on his knees three times a day to pray to his God and praise him, just as he had done previously. [11]The conspirators came and found Daniel praying and seeking mercy before his God. [12]Then they approached the king and said concerning the interdict, "O king! Did you not sign an interdict, that anyone who prays to anyone, divine or human, within thirty days except to you, O king, shall be thrown into a den of lions?" The king answered, "The thing stands fast, according to the law of the Medes and Persians, which cannot be revoked." [13]Then they responded to the king, "Daniel, one of the exiles from Judah, pays no attention to you, O king, or to the interdict you have signed, but he is saying his prayers three times a day."

14 When the king heard the charge, he was very much distressed. He was determined to save Daniel, and until the sun went down he made every effort to rescue him. [15]Then the conspirators came to the king and said to him, "Know, O king, that it is a law of the Medes and Persians that no interdict or ordinance that the king establishes can be changed."

16 Then the king gave the command, and Daniel was brought and thrown into the den of lions. The king said to Daniel, "May your God, whom you faithfully serve, deliver you!"

a Aram lacks the days of b The singular of Parsin c Ch 6.1 in Aram

¹⁷A stone was brought and laid on the mouth of the den, and the king sealed it with his own signet and with the signet of his lords, so that nothing might be changed concerning Daniel. ¹⁸Then the king went to his palace and spent the night fasting; no food was brought to him, and sleep fled from him.

Daniel Saved from the Lions

19 Then, at break of day, the king got up and hurried to the den of lions. ²⁰When he came near the den where Daniel was, he cried out anxiously to Daniel, "O Daniel, servant of the living God, has your God whom you faithfully serve been able to deliver you from the lions?" ²¹Daniel then said to the king, "O king, live forever! ²²My God sent his angel and shut the lions' mouths so that they would not hurt me, because I was found blameless before him; and also before you, O king, I have done no wrong." ²³Then the king was exceedingly glad and commanded that Daniel be taken up out of the den. So Daniel was taken up out of the den, and no kind of harm was found on him, because he had trusted in his God. ²⁴The king gave a command, and those who had accused Daniel were brought and thrown into the den of lions—they, their children, and their wives. Before they reached the bottom of the den the lions overpowered them and broke all their bones in pieces.

25 Then King Darius wrote to all peoples and nations of every language throughout the whole world: "May you have abundant prosperity! ²⁶I make a decree, that in all my royal dominion people should tremble and fear before the God of Daniel:

For he is the living God,
  enduring forever.
His kingdom shall never be destroyed,
  and his dominion has no end.
²⁷ He delivers and rescues,
  he works signs and wonders in heaven
    and on earth;
for he has saved Daniel
  from the power of the lions."

²⁸So this Daniel prospered during the reign of Darius and the reign of Cyrus the Persian.

7 Visions of the Four Beasts

In the first year of King Belshazzar of Babylon, Daniel had a dream and visions of his head as he lay in bed. Then he wrote down the dream:^a ²I,^b Daniel, saw in my vision by night the four winds of heaven stirring up the great sea, ³and four great beasts came up out of the sea, dif-

Reverence—© Kate Douglas, 17

ferent from one another. ⁴The first was like a lion and had eagles' wings. Then, as I watched, its wings were plucked off, and it was lifted up from the ground and made to stand on two feet like a human being; and a human mind was given to it. ⁵Another beast appeared, a second one, that looked like a bear. It was raised up on one side, had three tusks^c in its mouth among its teeth and was told, "Arise, devour many bodies!" ⁶After this, as I watched, another appeared, like a leopard. The beast had four wings of a bird on its back and four heads; and dominion was given to it. ⁷After this I saw in the visions by night a fourth beast, terrifying and dreadful and exceedingly strong. It had great iron teeth and was devouring, breaking in pieces, and stamping what was left with its feet. It was different from all the beasts that preceded it, and it had ten horns. ⁸I was considering the horns, when another horn appeared, a little one coming up among them; to make room for it, three of the earlier horns were plucked up by the roots. There were eyes like human eyes in this horn, and a mouth speaking arrogantly.

Judgment before the Ancient One

⁹ As I watched,
  thrones were set in place,
    and an Ancient One^d took his throne,
  his clothing was white as snow,
    and the hair of his head like pure wool;
  his throne was fiery flames,
    and its wheels were burning fire.
¹⁰ A stream of fire issued
    and flowed out from his presence.
  A thousand thousands served him,

<hr>

a Q Ms Theodotion: MT adds *the beginning of the words; he said* b Theodotion: Aram *Daniel answered and said,* I c Or *ribs* d Aram *an Ancient of Days*

and ten thousand times ten thousand
    stood attending him.
The court sat in judgment,
    and the books were opened.
[11]I watched then because of the noise of the arrogant words that the horn was speaking. And as I watched, the beast was put to death, and its body destroyed and given over to be burned with fire. [12]As for the rest of the beasts, their dominion was taken away, but their lives were prolonged for a season and a time. [13]As I watched in the night visions,
    I saw one like a human being[a]
        coming with the clouds of heaven.
    And he came to the Ancient One[b]
        and was presented before him.
[14] To him was given dominion
    and glory and kingship,
    that all peoples, nations, and languages
        should serve him.
His dominion is an everlasting dominion
    that shall not pass away,
    and his kingship is one
        that shall never be destroyed.

Daniel's Visions Interpreted

15 As for me, Daniel, my spirit was troubled within me,[c] and the visions of my head terrified me. [16]I approached one of the attendants to ask him the truth concerning all this. So he said that he would disclose to me the interpretation of the matter: [17]"As for these four great beasts, four kings shall arise out of the earth. [18]But the holy ones of the Most High shall receive the kingdom and possess the kingdom forever—forever and ever."

19 Then I desired to know the truth concerning the fourth beast, which was different from all the rest, exceedingly terrifying, with its teeth of iron and claws of bronze, and which devoured and broke in pieces, and stamped what was left with its feet; [20]and concerning the ten horns that were on its head, and concerning the other horn, which came up and to make room for which three of them fell out— the horn that had eyes and a mouth that spoke arrogantly, and that seemed greater than the others. [21]As I looked, this horn made war with the holy ones and was prevailing over them, [22]until the Ancient One[b] came; then judgment was given for the holy ones of the Most High, and the time arrived when the holy ones gained possession of the kingdom.

23 This is what he said: "As for the fourth beast,
    there shall be a fourth kingdom on earth

    that shall be different from all the other
        kingdoms;
it shall devour the whole earth,
    and trample it down, and break it to
        pieces.
[24] As for the ten horns,
    out of this kingdom ten kings shall arise,
    and another shall arise after them.
This one shall be different from the former
        ones,
    and shall put down three kings.
[25] He shall speak words against the Most High,
    shall wear out the holy ones of the Most
        High,
    and shall attempt to change the sacred
        seasons and the law;
and they shall be given into his power
    for a time, two times,[d] and half a time.
[26] Then the court shall sit in judgment,
    and his dominion shall be taken away,
    to be consumed and totally destroyed.
[27] The kingship and dominion
    and the greatness of the kingdoms under
        the whole heaven
    shall be given to the people of the holy
        ones of the Most High;
their kingdom shall be an everlasting
        kingdom,
    and all dominions shall serve and obey
        them."

28 Here the account ends. As for me, Daniel, my thoughts greatly terrified me, and my face turned pale; but I kept the matter in my mind.

8 Vision of a Ram and a Goat

In the third year of the reign of King Belshazzar a vision appeared to me, Daniel, after the one that had appeared to me at first. [2]In the vision I was looking and saw myself in Susa the capital, in the province of Elam,[e] and I was by the river Ulai.[f] [3]I looked up and saw a ram standing beside the river.[g] It had two horns. Both horns were long, but one was longer than the other, and the longer one came up second. [4]I saw the ram charging westward and northward and southward. All beasts were powerless to withstand it, and no one could rescue from its power; it did as it pleased and became strong.

5 As I was watching, a male goat appeared from the west, coming across the face of the whole earth without touching the ground. The goat had a horn[h] between its eyes. [6]It came toward the ram with the two horns that I had seen standing beside the river,[g] and it ran at it with savage force. [7]I saw it approaching the ram. It was enraged against it and struck the

---

a Aram *one like a son of man* b Aram *the Ancient of Days* c Aram *troubled in its sheath* d Aram *a time, times* e Gk Theodotion: MT Q Ms
repeat *in the vision I was looking* f Or *the Ulai Gate* g Or *gate* h Theodotion: Gk *one horn*; Heb *a horn of vision*

ram, breaking its two horns. The ram did not have power to withstand it; it threw the ram down to the ground and trampled upon it, and there was no one who could rescue the ram from its power. [8]Then the male goat grew exceedingly great; but at the height of its power, the great horn was broken, and in its place there came up four prominent horns toward the four winds of heaven.

9 Out of one of them came another[a] horn, a little one, which grew exceedingly great toward the south, toward the east, and toward the beautiful land. [10]It grew as high as the host of heaven. It threw down to the earth some of the host and some of the stars, and trampled on them. [11]Even against the prince of the host it acted arrogantly; it took the regular burnt offering away from him and overthrew the place of his sanctuary. [12]Because of wickedness, the host was given over to it together with the regular burnt offering;[b] it cast truth to the ground, and kept prospering in what it did. [13]Then I heard a holy one speaking, and another holy one said to the one that spoke, "For how long is this vision concerning the regular burnt offering, the transgression that makes desolate, and the giving over of the sanctuary and host to be trampled?"[b] [14]And he answered him,[c] "For two thousand three hundred evenings and mornings; then the sanctuary shall be restored to its rightful state."

Gabriel Interprets the Vision

15 When I, Daniel, had seen the vision, I tried to understand it. Then someone appeared standing before me, having the appearance of a man, [16]and I heard a human voice by the Ulai, calling, "Gabriel, help this man understand the vision." [17]So he came near where I stood; and when he came, I became frightened and fell prostrate. But he said to me, "Understand, O mortal,[d] that the vision is for the time of the end."

18 As he was speaking to me, I fell into a trance, face to the ground; then he touched me and set me on my feet. [19]He said, "Listen, and I will tell you what will take place later in the period of wrath; for it refers to the appointed time of the end. [20]As for the ram that you saw with the two horns, these are the kings of Media and Persia. [21]The male goat[e] is the king of Greece, and the great horn between its eyes is the first king. [22]As for the horn that was broken, in place of which four others arose, four kingdoms shall arise from his[f] nation, but not with his power.

23 At the end of their rule,

when the transgressions have reached
    their full measure,
a king of bold countenance shall arise,
    skilled in intrigue.
[24] He shall grow strong in power,[g]
    shall cause fearful destruction,
    and shall succeed in what he does.
He shall destroy the powerful
    and the people of the holy ones.
[25] By his cunning

---

a Cn Compare 7.8: Heb *one* *b* Meaning of Heb uncertain *c* Gk Theodotion Syr Vg: Heb *me* *d* Heb *son of man* *e* Or *shaggy male goat* *f* Gk Theodotion Vg: Heb *the* *g* Theodotion and one Gk Ms: Heb repeats (from 8.22) *but not with his power*

he shall make deceit prosper under his
hand,
and in his own mind he shall be great.
Without warning he shall destroy many
and shall even rise up against the Prince
of princes.
But he shall be broken, and not by human
hands.

²⁶The vision of the evenings and the mornings that has been told is true. As for you, seal up the vision, for it refers to many days from now."

27 So I, Daniel, was overcome and lay sick for some days; then I arose and went about the king's business. But I was dismayed by the vision and did not understand it.

9 Daniel's Prayer for the People

In the first year of Darius son of Ahasuerus, by birth a Mede, who became king over the realm of the Chaldeans— ²in the first year of his reign, I, Daniel, perceived in the books the number of years that, according to the word of the LORD to the prophet Jeremiah, must be fulfilled for the devastation of Jerusalem, namely, seventy years.

3 Then I turned to the Lord God, to seek an answer by prayer and supplication with fasting and sackcloth and ashes. ⁴I prayed to the LORD my God and made confession, saying,

"Ah, Lord, great and awesome God, keeping covenant and steadfast love with those who love you and keep your commandments, ⁵we have sinned and done wrong, acted wickedly and rebelled, turning aside from your commandments and ordinances. ⁶We have not listened to your servants the prophets, who spoke in your name to our kings, our princes, and our ancestors, and to all the people of the land.

7 "Righteousness is on your side, O Lord, but open shame, as at this day, falls on us, the people of Judah, the inhabitants of Jerusalem, and all Israel, those who are near and those who are far away, in all the lands to which you have driven them, because of the treachery that they have committed against you. ⁸Open shame, O LORD, falls on us, our kings, our officials, and our ancestors, because we have sinned against you. ⁹To the Lord our God belong mercy and forgiveness, for we have rebelled against him, ¹⁰and have not obeyed the voice of the LORD our God by following his laws, which he set before us by his servants the prophets.

11 "All Israel has transgressed your law and turned aside, refusing to obey your voice. So the curse and the oath written in the law of Moses, the servant of God, have been poured out upon us, because we have sinned against you.

¹²He has confirmed his words, which he spoke against us and against our rulers, by bringing upon us a calamity so great that what has been done against Jerusalem has never before been done under the whole heaven. ¹³Just as it is written in the law of Moses, all this calamity has come upon us. We did not entreat the favor of the LORD our God, turning from our iniquities and reflecting on hisᵃ fidelity. ¹⁴So the LORD kept watch over this calamity until he brought it upon us. Indeed, the LORD our God is right in all that he has done; for we have disobeyed his voice.

15 "And now, O Lord our God, who brought your people out of the land of Egypt with a mighty hand and made your name renowned even to this day—we have sinned, we have done wickedly. ¹⁶O Lord, in view of all your righteous acts, let your anger and wrath, we pray, turn away from your city Jerusalem, your holy mountain; because of our sins and the iniquities of our ancestors, Jerusalem and your people have become a disgrace among all our neighbors. ¹⁷Now therefore, O our God, listen to the prayer of your servant and to his supplication, and for your own sake, Lord,ᵇ let your face shine upon your desolated sanctuary. ¹⁸Incline your ear, O my God, and hear. Open your eyes and look at our desolation and the city that bears your name. We do not present our supplication before you on the ground of our righteousness, but on the ground of your great mercies. ¹⁹O Lord, hear; O Lord, forgive; O Lord, listen and act and do not delay! For your own sake, O my God, because your city and your people bear your name!"

The Seventy Weeks

20 While I was speaking, and was praying and confessing my sin and the sin of my people Israel, and presenting my supplication before the LORD my God on behalf of the holy mountain of my God— ²¹while I was speaking in prayer, the man Gabriel, whom I had seen before in a vision, came to me in swift flight at the time of the evening sacrifice. ²²He cameᶜ and said to me, "Daniel, I have now come out to give you wisdom and understanding. ²³At the beginning of your supplications a word went out, and I have come to declare it, for you are greatly beloved. So consider the word and understand the vision:

24 "Seventy weeks are decreed for your people and your holy city: to finish the transgression, to put an end to sin, and to atone for iniquity, to bring in everlasting righteousness, to seal both vision and prophet, and to anoint a

ᵃ Heb your b Theodotion Vg Compare Syr: Heb for the Lord's sake c Gk Syr: Heb He made to understand most holy place.*a* 25Know therefore and understand: from the time that the word went out to restore and rebuild Jerusalem until the time of an anointed prince, there shall be seven weeks; and for sixty-two weeks it shall be built again with streets and moat, but in a troubled time. 26After the sixty-two weeks, an anointed one shall be cut off and shall have nothing, and the troops of the prince who is to come shall destroy the city and the sanctuary. Its*b* end shall come with a flood, and to the end there shall be war. Desolations are decreed. 27He shall make a strong covenant with many for one week, and for half of the week he shall make sacrifice and offering cease; and in their place*c* shall be an abomination that desolates, until the decreed end is poured out upon the desolator."

10 Conflict of Nations and Heavenly Powers

In the third year of King Cyrus of Persia a word was revealed to Daniel, who was named Belteshazzar. The word was true, and it concerned a great conflict. He understood the word, having received understanding in the vision.

2 At that time I, Daniel, had been mourning for three weeks. 3I had eaten no rich food, no meat or wine had entered my mouth, and I had not anointed myself at all, for the full three weeks. 4On the twenty-fourth day of the first month, as I was standing on the bank of the great river (that is, the Tigris), 5I looked up and saw a man clothed in linen, with a belt of gold from Uphaz around his waist. 6His body was like beryl, his face like lightning, his eyes like flaming torches, his arms and legs like the gleam of burnished bronze, and the sound of his words like the roar of a multitude. 7I, Daniel, alone saw the vision; the people who were with me did not see the vision, though a great trembling fell upon them, and they fled and hid themselves. 8So I was left alone to see this great vision. My strength left me, and my complexion grew deathly pale, and I retained no strength. 9Then I heard the sound of his words; and when I heard the sound of his words, I fell into a trance, face to the ground.

10 But then a hand touched me and roused me to my hands and knees. 11He said to me, "Daniel, greatly beloved, pay attention to the words that I am going to speak to you. Stand on your feet, for I have now been sent to you." So while he was speaking this word to me, I stood up trembling. 12He said to me, "Do not fear, Daniel, for from the first day that you set your mind to gain understanding and to humble yourself before your God, your words have been heard, and I have come because of your words. 13But the prince of the kingdom of Persia opposed me twenty-one days. So Michael, one of the chief princes, came to help me, and I left him there with the prince of the kingdom of Persia,*d* 14and have come to help you understand what is to happen to your people at the end of days. For there is a further vision for those days."

15 While he was speaking these words to me, I turned my face toward the ground and was speechless. 16Then one in human form touched my lips, and I opened my mouth to speak, and said to the one who stood before me, "My lord, because of the vision such pains have come upon me that I retain no strength.

a Or *thing* or *one* *b* Or *His* *c* Cn: Meaning of Heb uncertain *d* Gk Theodotion: Heb *I was left there with the kings of Persia*

17 How can my lord's servant talk with my lord? For I am shaking,[a] no strength remains in me, and no breath is left in me."

18 Again one in human form touched me and strengthened me. [19]He said, "Do not fear, greatly beloved, you are safe. Be strong and courageous!" When he spoke to me, I was strengthened and said, "Let my lord speak, for you have strengthened me." [20]Then he said, "Do you know why I have come to you? Now I must return to fight against the prince of Persia, and when I am through with him, the prince of Greece will come. [21]But I am to tell you what is inscribed in the book of truth. There is no one with me who contends against these princes except Michael, your prince.

11

[1]As for me, in the first year of Darius the Mede, I stood up to support and strengthen him.

2 "Now I will announce the truth to you. Three more kings shall arise in Persia. The fourth shall be far richer than all of them, and when he has become strong through his riches, he shall stir up all against the kingdom of Greece. [3]Then a warrior king shall arise, who shall rule with great dominion and take action as he pleases. [4]And while still rising in power, his kingdom shall be broken and divided toward the four winds of heaven, but not to his posterity, nor according to the dominion with which he ruled; for his kingdom shall be uprooted and go to others besides these.

5 "Then the king of the south shall grow strong, but one of his officers shall grow stronger than he and shall rule a realm greater than his own realm. [6]After some years they shall make an alliance, and the daughter of the king of the south shall come to the king of the north to ratify the agreement. But she shall not retain her power, and his offspring shall not endure. She shall be given up, she and her attendants and her child and the one who supported her.

"In those times [7]a branch from her roots shall rise up in his place. He shall come against the army and enter the fortress of the king of the north, and he shall take action against them and prevail. [8]Even their gods, with their idols and with their precious vessels of silver and gold, he shall carry off to Egypt as spoils of war. For some years he shall refrain from attacking the king of the north; [9]then the latter shall invade the realm of the king of the south, but will return to his own land.

10 "His sons shall wage war and assemble a multitude of great forces, which shall advance like a flood and pass through, and again shall carry the war as far as his fortress. [11]Moved with rage, the king of the south shall go out and do battle against the king of the north, who shall muster a great multitude, which shall, however, be defeated by his enemy. [12]When the multitude has been carried off, his heart shall be exalted, and he shall overthrow tens of thousands, but he shall not prevail. [13]For the king of the north shall again raise a multitude, larger than the former, and after some years[b] he shall advance with a great army and abundant supplies.

14 "In those times many shall rise against the king of the south. The lawless among your own people shall lift themselves up in order to fulfill the vision, but they shall fail. [15]Then the king of the north shall come and throw up siegeworks, and take a well-fortified city. And the forces of the south shall not stand, not even his picked troops, for there shall be no strength to resist. [16]But he who comes against him shall take the actions he pleases, and no one shall withstand him. He shall take a position in the beautiful land, and all of it shall be in his power. [17]He shall set his mind to come with the strength of his whole kingdom, and he shall bring terms of peace[c] and perform them. In order to destroy the kingdom,[d] he shall give him a woman in marriage; but it shall not succeed or be to his advantage. [18]Afterward he shall turn to the coastlands, and shall capture many. But a commander shall put an end to his insolence; indeed,[e] he shall turn his insolence back upon him. [19]Then he shall turn back toward the fortresses of his own land, but he shall stumble and fall, and shall not be found.

20 "Then shall arise in his place one who shall send an official for the glory of the kingdom; but within a few days he shall be broken, though not in anger or in battle. [21]In his place shall arise a contemptible person on whom royal majesty had not been conferred; he shall come in without warning and obtain the kingdom through intrigue. [22]Armies shall be utterly swept away and broken before him, and the prince of the covenant as well. [23]And after an alliance is made with him, he shall act deceitfully and become strong with a small party. [24]Without warning he shall come into the richest parts[f] of the province and do what none of his predecessors had ever done, lavishing plunder, spoil, and wealth on them. He shall devise plans against strongholds, but only for a time. [25]He shall stir up his power and determination against the king of the south with a great army, and the king of the south shall wage war with a much greater and stron-

---

a Gk: Heb *from now* *b* Heb *and at the end of the times years* *c* Gk: Heb *kingdom, and upright ones with him* *d* Heb *it* *e* Meaning of Heb uncertain *f* Or *among the richest men* ger army. But he shall not succeed, for plots shall be devised against him ²⁶by those who eat of the royal rations. They shall break him, his army shall be swept away, and many shall fall slain. ²⁷The two kings, their minds bent on evil, shall sit at one table and exchange lies. But it shall not succeed, for there remains an end at the time appointed. ²⁸He shall return to his land with great wealth, but his heart shall be set against the holy covenant. He shall work his will, and return to his own land.

29 "At the time appointed he shall return and come into the south, but this time it shall not be as it was before. ³⁰For ships of Kittim shall come against him, and he shall lose heart and withdraw. He shall be enraged and take action against the holy covenant. He shall turn back and pay heed to those who forsake the holy covenant. ³¹Forces sent by him shall occupy and profane the temple and fortress. They shall abolish the regular burnt offering and set up the abomination that makes desolate. ³²He shall seduce with intrigue those who violate the covenant; but the people who are loyal to their God shall stand firm and take action. ³³The wise among the people shall give understanding to many; for some days, however, they shall fall by sword and flame, and suffer captivity and plunder. ³⁴When they fall victim, they shall receive a little help, and many shall join them insincerely. ³⁵Some of the wise shall fall, so that they may be refined, purified, and cleansed,ᵃ until the time of the end, for there is still an interval until the time appointed.

36 "The king shall act as he pleases. He shall exalt himself and consider himself greater than any god, and shall speak horrendous things against the God of gods. He shall prosper until the period of wrath is completed, for what is determined shall be done. ³⁷He shall pay no respect to the gods of his ancestors, or to the one beloved by women; he shall pay no respect to any other god, for he shall consider himself greater than all. ³⁸He shall honor the god of fortresses instead of these; a god whom his ancestors did not know he shall honor with gold and silver, with precious stones and costly gifts. ³⁹He shall deal with the strongest fortresses by the help of a foreign god. Those who acknowledge him he shall make more wealthy, and shall appoint them as rulers over many, and shall distribute the land for a price.

The Time of the End

40 "At the time of the end the king of the south shall attack him. But the king of the north shall rush upon him like a whirlwind, with chariots and horsemen, and with many ships. He shall advance against countries and pass through like a flood. ⁴¹He shall come into the beautiful land, and tens of thousands shall fall victim, but Edom and Moab and the main part of the Ammonites shall escape from his power. ⁴²He shall stretch out his hand against the countries, and the land of Egypt shall not escape. ⁴³He shall become ruler of the treasures of gold and of silver, and all the riches of Egypt; and the Libyans and the Ethiopiansᵇ shall follow in his train. ⁴⁴But reports from the east and the north shall alarm him, and he shall go out with great fury to bring ruin and complete destruction to many. ⁴⁵He shall pitch his palatial tents between the sea and the beautiful holy mountain. Yet he shall come to his end, with no one to help him.

12 The Resurrection of the Dead

"At that time Michael, the great prince, the protector of your people, shall arise. There shall be a time of anguish, such as has never occurred since nations first came into existence. But at that time your people shall be delivered, everyone who is found written in the book. ²Many of those who sleep in the dust of the earthᶜ shall awake, some to everlasting life, and some to shame and everlasting contempt. ³Those who are wise shall shine like the brightness of the sky,ᵈ and those who lead many to righteousness, like the stars forever and ever. ⁴But you, Daniel, keep the words secret and the book sealed until the time of the end. Many shall be running back and forth, and evilᵉ shall increase."

5 Then I, Daniel, looked, and two others appeared, one standing on this bank of the stream and one on the other. ⁶One of them said to the man clothed in linen, who was upstream, "How long shall it be until the end of these wonders?" ⁷The man clothed in linen, who was upstream, raised his right hand and his left hand toward heaven. And I heard him swear by the one who lives forever that it would be for a time, two times, and half a time,ᶠ and that when the shattering of the power of the holy people comes to an end, all these things would be accomplished. ⁸I heard but could not understand; so I said, "My lord, what shall be the outcome of these things?" ⁹He said, "Go your way, Daniel, for the words are to remain secret and sealed until the time of the end. ¹⁰Many shall be purified, cleansed, and refined, but the wicked shall continue to act wickedly. None of the wicked shall understand, but those who are wise shall

---

a Heb *made them white* b Or *Nubians*; Heb *Cushites* c Or *the land of dust* d Or *dome* e Cn Compare Gk: Heb *knowledge* f Heb *a time, times, and a half* understand. ¹¹From the time that the regular burnt offering is taken away and the abomination that desolates is set up, there shall be one thousand two hundred ninety days. ¹²Happy are those who persevere and attain the thousand three hundred thirty-five days. ¹³But you, go your way,ᵃ and rest; you shall rise for your reward at the end of the days."

13 Susanna's Beauty Attracts Two Elders

There was a man living in Babylon whose name was Joakim. ²He married the daughter of Hilkiah, named Susanna, a very beautiful woman and one who feared the Lord. ³Her parents were righteous, and had trained their daughter according to the law of Moses. ⁴Joakim was very rich, and had a fine garden adjoining his house; the Jews used to come to him because he was the most honored of them all.

5 That year two elders from the people were appointed as judges. Concerning them the Lord had said: "Wickedness came forth from Babylon, from elders who were judges, who were supposed to govern the people." ⁶These men were frequently at Joakim's house, and all who had a case to be tried came to them there.

7 When the people left at noon, Susanna would go into her husband's garden to walk. ⁸Every day the two elders used to see her, going in and walking about, and they began to lust for her. ⁹They suppressed their consciences and turned away their eyes from looking to Heaven or remembering their duty to administer justice. ¹⁰Both were overwhelmed with passion for her, but they did not tell each other of their distress, ¹¹for they were ashamed to disclose their lustful desire to seduce her. ¹²Day after day they watched eagerly to see her.

13 One day they said to each other, "Let us go home, for it is time for lunch." So they both left and parted from each other. ¹⁴But turning back, they met again; and when each pressed the other for the reason, they confessed their lust. Then together they arranged for a time when they could find her alone.

The Elders Attempt to Seduce Susanna

15 Once, while they were watching for an opportune day, she went in as before with only two maids, and wished to bathe in the garden, for it was a hot day. ¹⁶No one was there except the two elders, who had hidden themselves and were watching her. ¹⁷She said to her maids, "Bring me olive oil and ointments, and shut the garden doors so that I can bathe." ¹⁸They did as she told them: they shut the doors of the garden and went out by the side doors to bring what they had been commanded; they did not see the elders, because they were hiding.

19 When the maids had gone out, the two elders got up and ran to her. ²⁰They said, "Look, the garden doors are shut, and no one can see us. We are burning with desire for you; so give your consent, and lie with us. ²¹If you refuse, we will testify against you that a young man was with you, and this was why you sent your maids away."

22 Susanna groaned and said, "I am completely trapped. For if I do this, it will mean death for me; if I do not, I cannot escape your hands. ²³I choose not to do it; I will fall into your hands, rather than sin in the sight of the Lord."

24 Then Susanna cried out with a loud voice, and the two elders shouted against her. ²⁵And one of them ran and opened the garden doors. ²⁶When the people in the house heard the shouting in the garden, they rushed in at the side door to see what had happened to her. ²⁷And when the elders told their story, the servants felt very much ashamed, for nothing like this had ever been said about Susanna.

The Elders Testify against Susanna

28 The next day, when the people gathered at the house of her husband Joakim, the two elders came, full of their wicked plot to have Susanna put to death. In the presence of the people they said, ²⁹"Send for Susanna daughter of Hilkiah, the wife of Joakim." ³⁰So they sent for her. And she came with her parents, her children, and all her relatives.

31 Now Susanna was a woman of great refinement and beautiful in appearance. ³²As she was veiled, the scoundrels ordered her to be unveiled, so that they might feast their eyes on her beauty. ³³Those who were with her and all who saw her were weeping. ³⁴Then the two elders stood up before the people and laid their hands on her head. ³⁵Through her tears she looked up toward Heaven, for her heart trusted in the Lord. ³⁶The elders said, "While we were walking in the garden alone, this woman came in with two maids, shut the garden doors, and dismissed the maids. ³⁷Then a young man, who was hiding there, came to her and lay with her. ³⁸We were in a corner of the garden, and when we saw this wickedness we ran to them. ³⁹Although we saw them embracing, we could not hold the man, because he was stronger than we, and he opened the doors and got away. ⁴⁰We did, however, seize this woman and asked who the young man was, ⁴¹but she would not tell us. These things we testify."

ᵃ Gk Theodotion: Heb adds *to the end*

Because they were elders of the people and judges, the assembly believed them and condemned her to death.

42 Then Susanna cried out with a loud voice, and said, "O eternal God, you know what is secret and are aware of all things before they come to be; 43you know that these men have given false evidence against me. And now I am to die, though I have done none of the wicked things that they have charged against me!"

44 The Lord heard her cry. 45Just as she was being led off to execution, God stirred up the holy spirit of a young lad named Daniel, 46and he shouted with a loud voice, "I want no part in shedding this woman's blood!"

Daniel Rescues Susanna

47 All the people turned to him and asked, "What is this you are saying?" 48Taking his stand among them he said, "Are you such fools, O Israelites, as to condemn a daughter of Israel without examination and without learning the facts? 49Return to court, for these men have given false evidence against her."

50 So all the people hurried back. And the rest of the*a* elders said to him, "Come, sit among us and inform us, for God has given you the standing of an elder." 51Daniel said to them, "Separate them far from each other, and I will examine them."

52 When they were separated from each other, he summoned one of them and said to him, "You old relic of wicked days, your sins have now come home, which you have committed in the past, 53pronouncing unjust judgments, condemning the innocent and acquitting the guilty, though the Lord said, 'You shall not put an innocent and righteous person to death.' 54Now then, if you really saw this woman, tell me this: Under what tree did you see them being intimate with each other?" He answered, "Under a mastic tree."*b* 55And Daniel said, "Very well! This lie has cost you your head, for the angel of God has received the sentence from God and will immediately cut*b* you in two."

56 Then, putting him to one side, he ordered them to bring the other. And he said to him, "You offspring of Canaan and not of Judah, beauty has beguiled you and lust has perverted your heart. 57This is how you have been treating the daughters of Israel, and they were intimate with you through fear; but a daughter of Judah would not tolerate your wickedness. 58Now then, tell me: Under what tree did you catch them being intimate with each oth-

er?" He answered, "Under an evergreen oak."*c* 59Daniel said to him, "Very well! This lie has cost you also your head, for the angel of God is waiting with his sword to split*c* you in two, so as to destroy you both."

60 Then the whole assembly raised a great shout and blessed God, who saves those who hope in him. 61And they took action against the two elders, because out of their own mouths Daniel had convicted them of bearing false witness; they did to them as they had wickedly planned to do to their neighbor. 62Acting in accordance with the law of Moses, they put them to death. Thus innocent blood was spared that day.

63 Hilkiah and his wife praised God for their daughter Susanna, and so did her husband Joakim and all her relatives, because she was found innocent of a shameful deed. 64And from that day onward Daniel had a great reputation among the people.

14 Daniel and the Priests of Bel

When King Astyages was laid to rest with his ancestors, Cyrus the Persian succeeded to his kingdom. 2Daniel was a companion of the king, and was the most honored of all his Friends.

3 Now the Babylonians had an idol called Bel, and every day they provided for it twelve bushels of choice flour and forty sheep and six measures*d* of wine. 4The king revered it and went every day to worship it. But Daniel worshiped his own God.

So the king said to him, "Why do you not worship Bel?" 5He answered, "Because I do not revere idols made with hands, but the living God, who created heaven and earth and has dominion over all living creatures."

6 The king said to him, "Do you not think that Bel is a living god? Do you not see how much he eats and drinks every day?" 7And Daniel laughed, and said, "Do not be deceived, O king, for this thing is only clay inside and bronze outside, and it never ate or drank anything."

8 Then the king was angry and called the priests of Bel*e* and said to them, "If you do not tell me who is eating these provisions, you shall die. 9But if you prove that Bel is eating them, Daniel shall die, because he has spoken blasphemy against Bel." Daniel said to the king, "Let it be done as you have said."

10 Now there were seventy priests of Bel, besides their wives and children. So the king went with Daniel into the temple of Bel. 11The priests of Bel said, "See, we are now going outside; you yourself, O king, set out the food and

---

a Gk lacks *rest of the*   *b* The Greek words for *mastic tree* and *cut* are similar, thus forming an ironic wordplay   *c* The Greek words for *evergreen oak* and *split* are similar, thus forming an ironic wordplay   *d* A little more than fifty gallons   *e* Gk *his priests* prepare the wine, and shut the door and seal it with your signet. [12]When you return in the morning, if you do not find that Bel has eaten it all, we will die; otherwise Daniel will, who is telling lies about us." [13]They were unconcerned, for beneath the table they had made a hidden entrance, through which they used to go in regularly and consume the provisions. [14]After they had gone out, the king set out the food for Bel. Then Daniel ordered his servants to bring ashes, and they scattered them throughout the whole temple in the presence of the king alone. Then they went out, shut the door and sealed it with the king's signet, and departed. [15]During the night the priests came as usual, with their wives and children, and they ate and drank everything.

16 Early in the morning the king rose and came, and Daniel with him. [17]The king said, "Are the seals unbroken, Daniel?" He answered, "They are unbroken, O king." [18]As soon as the doors were opened, the king looked at the table, and shouted in a loud voice, "You are great, O Bel, and in you there is no deceit at all!"

19 But Daniel laughed and restrained the king from going in. "Look at the floor," he said, "and notice whose footprints these are." [20]The king said, "I see the footprints of men and women and children."

21 Then the king was enraged, and he arrested the priests and their wives and children. They showed him the secret doors through which they used to enter to consume what was on the table. [22]Therefore the king put them to death, and gave Bel over to Daniel, who destroyed it and its temple.

Daniel Kills the Dragon

23 Now in that place[a] there was a great dragon, which the Babylonians revered. [24]The king said to Daniel, "You cannot deny that this is a living god; so worship him." [25]Daniel said, "I worship the Lord my God, for he is the living God. [26]But give me permission, O king, and I will kill the dragon without sword or club." The king said, "I give you permission."

27 Then Daniel took pitch, fat, and hair, and boiled them together and made cakes, which he fed to the dragon. The dragon ate them, and burst open. Then Daniel said, "See what you have been worshiping!"

28 When the Babylonians heard about it, they were very indignant and conspired against the king, saying, "The king has become a Jew; he has destroyed Bel, and killed the dragon, and slaughtered the priests." [29]Going to the king, they said, "Hand Daniel over to us, or else we will kill you and your household." [30]The king saw that they were pressing him hard, and under compulsion he handed Daniel over to them.

Daniel in the Lions' Den

31 They threw Daniel into the lions' den, and he was there for six days. [32]There were seven lions in the den, and every day they had been given two human bodies and two sheep; but now they were given nothing, so that they would devour Daniel.

33 Now the prophet Habakkuk was in Judea; he had made a stew and had broken bread into a bowl, and was going into the field to take it to the reapers. [34]But the angel of the Lord said to Habakkuk, "Take the food that you have to Babylon, to Daniel, in the lions' den." [35]Habakkuk said, "Sir, I have never seen Babylon, and I know nothing about the den." [36]Then the angel of the Lord took him by the crown of his head and carried him by his hair; with the speed of the wind[b] he set him down in Babylon, right over the den.

37 Then Habakkuk shouted, "Daniel, Daniel! Take the food that God has sent you." [38]Daniel said, "You have remembered me, O God, and have not forsaken those who love you." [39]So Daniel got up and ate. And the angel of God immediately returned Habakkuk to his own place.

40 On the seventh day the king came to mourn for Daniel. When he came to the den he looked in, and there sat Daniel! [41]The king shouted with a loud voice, "You are great, O Lord, the God of Daniel, and there is no other besides you!" [42]Then he pulled Daniel[c] out, and drew into the den those who had attempted his destruction, and they were instantly eaten before his eyes.

a Other ancient authorities lack *in that place* b Or *by the power of his spirit* c Gk *him*

"Prayer consists as much of praise for the past, as of supplication for the future."

—John Donne,
English poet and preacher

HOSEA

WHAT GOD CAN TEACH A GUY WHOSE WIFE KEEPS CHEATING ON HIM

We ♥ Cheaters

Have you ever worked with analogies? They're often in tests and go something like this: "*House* is to *yard* as *egg yolk* is to *egg white*" or "*Bat* is to *ball* as *stick* is to *puck*." In this book, God makes a living analogy by commanding Hosea, his prophet, to marry a prostitute named Gomer. God's analogy is this: Israel is to me as Gomer is to Hosea.

Cheating happens all the time. You know how it is. Once you've finally had the "DTR" (Define the Relationship) talk and buy your prom dress or rent that tux, you see him leaning on that new girl's locker or you see her smile at that guy in chemistry class. Sure, it's not the same thing as "marital unfaithfulness," but it still hurts. You're still jealous. "What does that other person have that I don't?" you may wonder. God's analogy is one that everyone who's ever felt a tiny pang of jealousy can understand.

And God's analogy in the book of Hosea grows as the family gets larger. Each time Gomer had a baby, God commanded Hosea to give that child a symbolic name. Imagine being named "Lo-ruhamah," which means "not loved," or "Lo-ammi," which means "not my people"! After leaving Hosea for other lovers, Gomer is eventually reconciled to Hosea. Then the rest of the book is prophetic (truth-telling) poetry about God's relationship with Israel, the "wife" who continually leaves him to pursue other gods, other loves, and other desires.

It's a sad but true fact. We all live lives that are unfaithful to God. We love our *stuff* more. We love our *selves* more. We care more about what others think of us than what God thinks of us. We're wooed by the promises of advertising, promises of popularity, and promises of "success." How are you unfaithful to God? How has God lovingly pursued you despite that unfaithfulness?

WHO Hosea, whose name means "salvation," was a Hebrew prophet and preacher.

WHAT Prophecies and stories about God and his people told through the story of Hosea and his unfaithful wife, Gomer

WHEN The events in this book probably took place around the fall of Samaria, which was in 722 B.C. The book of Hosea was likely written around 715 B.C.

WHERE The northern kingdom (Israel), perhaps in or near Samaria

> *"What could make me love my fellow Christian better than to see that God loves us all as we were all one soul?"*
> —Julian of Norwich, medieval mystic

PATH OF DISCIPLESHIP

When we encounter the Hosea-Gomer marriage analogy for the first time, we may struggle with God's command to Hosea to "take for yourself a wife of whoredom" (Hosea 1.2). The use of this image of marriage is symbolic for the covenant between God and God's people, who had turned away from him. This marriage analogy illustrates that God in the Old Testament is not merely a God of law, but is also a God of love—a forgiving love.

What experiences in your life have given you a deeper realization of God's passion for you? What difference does God's love for you and others make in your life? How do you cultivate and respond to God's passion and forgiveness in your life?

1 The word of the LORD that came to Hosea son of Beeri, in the days of Kings Uzziah, Jotham, Ahaz, and Hezekiah of Judah, and in the days of King Jeroboam son of Joash of Israel.

The Family of Hosea

2 When the LORD first spoke through Hosea, the LORD said to Hosea, "Go, take for yourself a wife of whoredom and have children of whoredom, for the land commits great whoredom by forsaking the LORD." ³So he went and took Gomer daughter of Diblaim, and she conceived and bore him a son.

4 And the LORD said to him, "Name him Jezreel;ᵃ for in a little while I will punish the house of Jehu for the blood of Jezreel, and I will put an end to the kingdom of the house of Israel. ⁵On that day I will break the bow of Israel in the valley of Jezreel."

6 She conceived again and bore a daughter. Then the LORD said to him, "Name her Lo-ruhamah,ᵇ for I will no longer have pity on the house of Israel or forgive them. ⁷But I will have pity on the house of Judah, and I will save them by the LORD their God; I will not save them by bow, or by sword, or by war, or by horses, or by horsemen."

8 When she had weaned Lo-ruhamah, she conceived and bore a son. ⁹Then the LORD said, "Name him Lo-ammi,ᶜ for you are not my people and I am not your God."ᵈ

The Restoration of Israel

10 ᵉ Yet the number of the people of Israel shall be like the sand of the sea, which can be neither measured nor numbered; and in the place where it was said to them, "You are not my people," it shall be said to them, "Children of the living God." ¹¹The people of Judah and the people of Israel shall be gathered together, and they shall appoint for themselves one head; and they shall take possession ofᶠ the land, for great shall be the day of Jezreel.

2ᵍ Say to your brother,ʰ Ammi,ⁱ and to your sister,ʲ Ruhamah.ᵏ

Israel's Infidelity, Punishment, and Redemption

2 Plead with your mother, plead—
   for she is not my wife,
   and I am not her husband—
that she put away her whoring from her
      face,
   and her adultery from between her
      breasts,

3 or I will strip her naked
   and expose her as in the day she was
      born,
and make her like a wilderness,
   and turn her into a parched land,
   and kill her with thirst.
4 Upon her children also I will have no pity,
   because they are children of whoredom.
5 For their mother has played the whore;
   she who conceived them has acted
      shamefully.
For she said, "I will go after my lovers;
   they give me my bread and my water,
   my wool and my flax, my oil and my
      drink."
6 Therefore I will hedge up herˡ way with
      thorns;
   and I will build a wall against her,
   so that she cannot find her paths.
7 She shall pursue her lovers,
   but not overtake them;
and she shall seek them,
   but shall not find them.
Then she shall say, "I will go
   and return to my first husband,
   for it was better with me then than
      now."
8 She did not know
   that it was I who gave her
   the grain, the wine, and the oil,
and who lavished upon her silver
   and gold that they used for Baal.
9 Therefore I will take back
   my grain in its time,
   and my wine in its season;
and I will take away my wool and my flax,
   which were to cover her nakedness.
10 Now I will uncover her shame
   in the sight of her lovers,
   and no one shall rescue her out of my
      hand.
11 I will put an end to all her mirth,
   her festivals, her new moons, her
      sabbaths,
   and all her appointed festivals.
12 I will lay waste her vines and her fig trees,
   of which she said,
"These are my pay,
   which my lovers have given me."
I will make them a forest,
   and the wild animals shall devour them.
13 I will punish her for the festival days of the
      Baals,
   when she offered incense to them
and decked herself with her ring and
      jewelry,

ᵃ That is God sows ᵇ That is Not pitied ᶜ That is Not my people ᵈ Heb I am not yours ᵉ Ch 2.1 in Heb ᶠ Heb rise up from ᵍ Ch 2.3 in Heb
ʰ Gk: Heb brothers ⁱ That is My people ʲ Gk Vg: Heb sisters ᵏ That is Pitied ˡ Gk Syr: Heb your

and went after her lovers,
and forgot me, says the LORD.

¹⁴ Therefore, I will now allure her,
and bring her into the wilderness,
and speak tenderly to her.

¹⁵ From there I will give her her vineyards,
and make the Valley of Achor a door of
hope.
There she shall respond as in the days of her
youth,
as at the time when she came out of the
land of Egypt.

¹⁶On that day, says the LORD, you will call me,
"My husband," and no longer will you call me,
"My Baal."*a* ¹⁷ For I will remove the names of the
Baals from her mouth, and they shall be mentioned by name no more. ¹⁸I will make for you*b*
a covenant on that day with the wild animals,
the birds of the air, and the creeping things of
the ground; and I will abolish*c* the bow, the
sword, and war from the land; and I will make
you lie down in safety. ¹⁹And I will take you for
my wife forever; I will take you for my wife in
righteousness and in justice, in steadfast love,
and in mercy. ²⁰I will take you for my wife in
faithfulness; and you shall know the LORD.

²¹ On that day I will answer, says the LORD,
I will answer the heavens
and they shall answer the earth;

²² and the earth shall answer the grain, the
wine, and the oil,
and they shall answer Jezreel;*d*

²³ and I will sow him*e* for myself in the land.
And I will have pity on Lo-ruhamah,*f*
and I will say to Lo-ammi,*g* "You are my
people";
and he shall say, "You are my God."

3 Further Assurances of God's Redeeming Love

The LORD said to me again, "Go, love a woman who has a lover and is an adulteress, just
as the LORD loves the people of Israel, though
they turn to other gods and love raisin cakes."
²So I bought her for fifteen shekels of silver
and a homer of barley and a measure of wine.*h*
³And I said to her, "You must remain as mine
for many days; you shall not play the whore,
you shall not have intercourse with a man, nor
I with you." ⁴For the Israelites shall remain
many days without king or prince, without
sacrifice or pillar, without ephod or teraphim.
⁵Afterward the Israelites shall return and seek
the LORD their God, and David their king; they

a That is, *"My master"* *b* Heb *them* *c* Heb *break* *d* That is *God
sows* *e* Cn: Heb *her* *f* That is *Not pitied* *g* That is *Not my people*
h Gk: Heb *a homer of barley and a lethech of barley*

Love Talk

Take a moment to think about your most
recent crush—or your feelings for the person
you're dating. On a scale of 1 to 10, how
passionate would you say your feelings are
for that person?

1	2	3	4	5	6	7	8	9	10

ABOUT AS   PRETTY   I CAN'T GET
PASSIONATE   PASSIONATE   HIM/HER
AS A COLD   OFF OF MY
FISH   MIND

The story of the Scriptures is the story of
a God who is in pursuit of his creation just
as a lover passionately pursues the beloved.
Though this kind of thinking can seem really
strange to us, keep in mind that it's an
analogy. There aren't any weirdly romantic
feelings involved here. But passionate,
romantic human love is powerful stuff—
Scripture even describes it as "strong as
death" (Song of Solomon 8.6)! And so it's
the best symbol there is to describe the
most *powerful* love of all—the love of God
for humanity. Just as a lover pursues his or
her beloved, so God pursues us. Just as a
lover and a beloved live in faithfulness to
one another, so we are to live faithfully to our
decision to follow the way of God. On and on,
the connections are profound.

In **Hosea 1.2**, God tells the prophet to
marry a prostitute, knowing all along that
she will be unfaithful to him, big-time. Like
a mirror, the pain of unfaithfulness—of an
unkept promise—which is so tangibly visible
in the life of Hosea, exposes something deeper
about how *our* unfaithfulness affects God.

Take a few minutes to write a short
fictional dialogue between a guy and a girl
who are in love (or maybe between a husband
and a wife). You could write it like a poem, a
screenplay, or just a plain old conversation.
Use it to explore the ideas of faithfulness,
passion, or jealousy. Consider what it means
to be truly loved and sought after. When you're
done, read what you've created and consider
how it is similar to (or different from) God's
love for you. (And if you're up for it, post your
dialogue on **Learner.CalltoDiscipleship.com**.)

HOSEA 3

shall come in awe to the LORD and to his goodness in the latter days.

4 God Accuses Israel

Hear the word of the LORD, O people of
Israel;
    for the LORD has an indictment against
        the inhabitants of the land.
There is no faithfulness or loyalty,
    and no knowledge of God in the land.
[2] Swearing, lying, and murder,
    and stealing and adultery break out;
        bloodshed follows bloodshed.
[3] Therefore the land mourns,
    and all who live in it languish;
together with the wild animals
    and the birds of the air,
        even the fish of the sea are perishing.

[4] Yet let no one contend,
    and let none accuse,
        for with you is my contention, O priest. [a]
[5] You shall stumble by day;
    the prophet also shall stumble with you
        by night,
    and I will destroy your mother.
[6] My people are destroyed for lack of
        knowledge;
    because you have rejected knowledge,
    I reject you from being a priest to me.
And since you have forgotten the law of
        your God,
    I also will forget your children.

[7] The more they increased,
    the more they sinned against me;
        they changed [b] their glory into shame.
[8] They feed on the sin of my people;
    they are greedy for their iniquity.
[9] And it shall be like people, like priest;
    I will punish them for their ways,
    and repay them for their deeds.
[10] They shall eat, but not be satisfied;
    they shall play the whore, but not
        multiply;
because they have forsaken the LORD
    to devote themselves to [11]whoredom.

The Idolatry of Israel

Wine and new wine
    take away the understanding.
[12] My people consult a piece of wood,
    and their divining rod gives them
        oracles.
For a spirit of whoredom has led them
    astray,

and they have played the whore,
    forsaking their God.
[13] They sacrifice on the tops of the mountains,
    and make offerings upon the hills,
under oak, poplar, and terebinth,
    because their shade is good.

Therefore your daughters play the whore,
    and your daughters-in-law commit
        adultery.
[14] I will not punish your daughters when they
        play the whore,
    nor your daughters-in-law when they
        commit adultery;
for the men themselves go aside with
        whores,
    and sacrifice with temple prostitutes;
thus a people without understanding
    comes to ruin.

[15] Though you play the whore, O Israel,
    do not let Judah become guilty.
Do not enter into Gilgal,
    or go up to Beth-aven,
    and do not swear, "As the LORD lives."
[16] Like a stubborn heifer,
    Israel is stubborn;
can the LORD now feed them
    like a lamb in a broad pasture?

[17] Ephraim is joined to idols—
    let him alone.
[18] When their drinking is ended, they indulge
        in sexual orgies;
    they love lewdness more than their
        glory. [c]
[19] A wind has wrapped them [d] in its wings,
    and they shall be ashamed because of
        their altars. [e]

5 Impending Judgment on Israel and Judah

Hear this, O priests!
    Give heed, O house of Israel!
Listen, O house of the king!
    For the judgment pertains to you;
for you have been a snare at Mizpah,
    and a net spread upon Tabor,
[2] and a pit dug deep in Shittim; [a]
    but I will punish all of them.

[3] I know Ephraim,
    and Israel is not hidden from me;
for now, O Ephraim, you have played the
        whore;
    Israel is defiled.
[4] Their deeds do not permit them
    to return to their God.

a Cn: Meaning of Heb uncertain *b* Ancient Heb tradition: MT *I will change* *c* Cn Compare Gk: Meaning of Heb uncertain *d* Heb *her*
e Gk Syr: Heb *sacrifices*

For the spirit of whoredom is within them,
and they do not know the Lord.

5 Israel's pride testifies against him;
Ephraim[a] stumbles in his guilt;
Judah also stumbles with them.
6 With their flocks and herds they shall go
to seek the Lord,
but they will not find him;
he has withdrawn from them.
7 They have dealt faithlessly with the Lord;
for they have borne illegitimate children.
Now the new moon shall devour them
along with their fields.

8 Blow the horn in Gibeah,
the trumpet in Ramah.
Sound the alarm at Beth-aven;
look behind you, Benjamin!
9 Ephraim shall become a desolation
in the day of punishment;
among the tribes of Israel
I declare what is sure.
10 The princes of Judah have become
like those who remove the landmark;
on them I will pour out
my wrath like water.
11 Ephraim is oppressed, crushed in
judgment,
because he was determined to go after
vanity.[b]
12 Therefore I am like maggots to Ephraim,
and like rottenness to the house of
Judah.
13 When Ephraim saw his sickness,
and Judah his wound,
then Ephraim went to Assyria,
and sent to the great king.[c]
But he is not able to cure you
or heal your wound.
14 For I will be like a lion to Ephraim,
and like a young lion to the house of
Judah.
I myself will tear and go away;
I will carry off, and no one shall rescue.
15 I will return again to my place
until they acknowledge their guilt and
seek my face.
In their distress they will beg my favor:

6 A Call to Repentance

"Come, let us return to the Lord;
for it is he who has torn, and he will
heal us;
he has struck down, and he will bind
us up.
2 After two days he will revive us;
on the third day he will raise us up,

that we may live before him.
3 Let us know, let us press on to know the
Lord;
his appearing is as sure as the dawn;
he will come to us like the showers,
like the spring rains that water the
earth."

IT'S TRADITION

BODY TALK

It's just about impossible to reflect on the book of Hosea without having some thoughts or feelings about sex and sexuality. It's a good opportunity to take a look at some of the Church's basic beliefs about sexuality.

As Catholics, we believe we were created sexual beings, male and female, in God's own image. Sexuality is who you are. It generates your capacity to love and procreate. It's important to remember that sexuality is much broader and more encompassing than any sexual act, no matter what contemporary culture tells you.

Today's permissive lifestyles, advertising, media, and music can lead you to believe that sex is an end in itself; that it's okay to "hook up" just for the experience, as long as no one gets hurt; that "friends with benefits" or sex without "strings attached" is okay.

Those attitudes are far from the Church's teaching on sexuality and farther still from the values in the Creation story. The Creation story says that since we are created in God's image we are wired to love and be loved. Our sexuality is a basic force in how we relate to others; it fuels our desire to move from isolation to being with others as a first step toward true love. As the United States Conference of Catholic Bishops defines it, "*Sexuality* is a fundamental component of personality in and through which we, as male or female, experience our relatedness to self, others, the world and even God" (*Human Sexuality*, 9).

a Heb *Israel and Ephraim*   b Gk: Meaning of Heb uncertain   c Cn: Heb *to a king who will contend*

HOSEA 6

Painted Love—© Mallory Kidwell, 15

and the bandits raid outside.
2 But they do not consider
  that I remember all their wickedness.
Now their deeds surround them,
  they are before my face.
3 By their wickedness they make the king glad,
  and the officials by their treachery.
4 They are all adulterers;
  they are like a heated oven,
whose baker does not need to stir the fire,
  from the kneading of the dough until it is leavened.
5 On the day of our king the officials
  became sick with the heat of wine;
  he stretched out his hand with mockers.
6 For they are kindled[e] like an oven, their
    heart burns within them;
  all night their anger smolders;
  in the morning it blazes like a flaming fire.
7 All of them are hot as an oven,
  and they devour their rulers.
All their kings have fallen;
  none of them calls upon me.

8 Ephraim mixes himself with the peoples;
  Ephraim is a cake not turned.
9 Foreigners devour his strength,
  but he does not know it;
gray hairs are sprinkled upon him,
  but he does not know it.
10 Israel's pride testifies against[f] him;
  yet they do not return to the LORD their God,
  or seek him, for all this.

Futile Reliance on the Nations
11 Ephraim has become like a dove,
    silly and without sense;
  they call upon Egypt, they go to Assyria.
12 As they go, I will cast my net over them;
  I will bring them down like birds of the air;
  I will discipline them according to the
    report made to their assembly.[g]
13 Woe to them, for they have strayed from me!
  Destruction to them, for they have
    rebelled against me!
I would redeem them,
  but they speak lies against me.

14 They do not cry to me from the heart,
  but they wail upon their beds;
they gash themselves for grain and wine;
  they rebel against me.

Impenitence of Israel and Judah
4 What shall I do with you, O Ephraim?
    What shall I do with you, O Judah?
  Your love is like a morning cloud,
    like the dew that goes away early.
5 Therefore I have hewn them by the prophets,
    I have killed them by the words of my mouth,
  and my[a] judgment goes forth as the light.
6 For I desire steadfast love and not sacrifice,
    the knowledge of God rather than burnt offerings.

7 But at[b] Adam they transgressed the covenant;
    there they dealt faithlessly with me.
8 Gilead is a city of evildoers,
    tracked with blood.
9 As robbers lie in wait[c] for someone,
    so the priests are banded together;[d]
  they murder on the road to Shechem,
    they commit a monstrous crime.
10 In the house of Israel I have seen a horrible thing;
    Ephraim's whoredom is there, Israel is defiled.

11 For you also, O Judah, a harvest is appointed.

  When I would restore the fortunes of my people,

7 ¹when I would heal Israel,
    the corruption of Ephraim is revealed,
    and the wicked deeds of Samaria;
  for they deal falsely,
    the thief breaks in,

a Gk Syr: Heb *your* *b* Cn: Heb *like* *c* Cn: Meaning of Heb uncertain *d* Syr: Heb *are a company* *e* Gk Syr: Heb *brought near* *f* Or *humbles* *g* Meaning of Heb uncertain

15 It was I who trained and strengthened their
    arms,
    yet they plot evil against me.
16 They turn to that which does not profit;[a]
    they have become like a defective bow;
  their officials shall fall by the sword
    because of the rage of their tongue.
  So much for their babbling in the land of
    Egypt.

8 Israel's Apostasy

Set the trumpet to your lips!
    One like a vulture[b] is over the house of
    the LORD,
because they have broken my covenant,
    and transgressed my law.
2 Israel cries to me,
    "My God, we—Israel—know you!"
3 Israel has spurned the good;
    the enemy shall pursue him.

4 They made kings, but not through me;
    they set up princes, but without my
    knowledge.
With their silver and gold they made idols
    for their own destruction.
5 Your calf is rejected, O Samaria.
    My anger burns against them.
How long will they be incapable of
    innocence?
6   For it is from Israel,
an artisan made it;
    it is not God.
The calf of Samaria
    shall be broken to pieces.[c]

7 For they sow the wind,
    and they shall reap the whirlwind.
The standing grain has no heads,
    it shall yield no meal;
if it were to yield,
    foreigners would devour it.
8 Israel is swallowed up;
    now they are among the nations
    as a useless vessel.
9 For they have gone up to Assyria,
    a wild ass wandering alone;
    Ephraim has bargained for lovers.
10 Though they bargain with the nations,
    I will now gather them up.
They shall soon writhe
    under the burden of kings and princes.

11 When Ephraim multiplied altars to expiate
    sin,
    they became to him altars for sinning.
12 Though I write for him the multitude of my
    instructions,

they are regarded as a strange thing.
13 Though they offer choice sacrifices,[a]
    though they eat flesh,
    the LORD does not accept them.
Now he will remember their iniquity,
    and punish their sins;
    they shall return to Egypt.
14 Israel has forgotten his Maker,
    and built palaces;
and Judah has multiplied fortified cities;
    but I will send a fire upon his cities,
    and it shall devour his strongholds.

9 Punishment for Israel's Sin

Do not rejoice, O Israel!
  Do not exult[d] as other nations do;
for you have played the whore, departing
    from your God.
    You have loved a prostitute's pay
    on all threshing floors.
2 Threshing floor and wine vat shall not feed
    them,
    and the new wine shall fail them.
3 They shall not remain in the land of the
    LORD;
    but Ephraim shall return to Egypt,
    and in Assyria they shall eat unclean
    food.

4 They shall not pour drink offerings of wine
    to the LORD,
    and their sacrifices shall not please him.
Such sacrifices shall be like mourners'
    bread;
    all who eat of it shall be defiled;
for their bread shall be for their hunger
    only;
    it shall not come to the house of the
    LORD.

5 What will you do on the day of appointed
    festival,
    and on the day of the festival of the
    LORD?
6 For even if they escape destruction,
    Egypt shall gather them,
    Memphis shall bury them.
Nettles shall possess their precious things
    of silver;[b]
    thorns shall be in their tents.

7 The days of punishment have come,
    the days of recompense have come;
    Israel cries,[e]
"The prophet is a fool,
    the man of the spirit is mad!"
Because of your great iniquity,
    your hostility is great.

---

a Cn: Meaning of Heb uncertain   b Meaning of Heb uncertain   c Or *shall go up in flames*   d Gk: Heb *To exultation*   e Cn Compare Gk:
Heb *shall know*

⁸ The prophet is a sentinel for my God over
     Ephraim,
 yet a fowler's snare is on all his ways,
     and hostility in the house of his God.
⁹ They have deeply corrupted themselves
     as in the days of Gibeah;
 he will remember their iniquity,
 he will punish their sins.

¹⁰ Like grapes in the wilderness,
     I found Israel.
 Like the first fruit on the fig tree,
     in its first season,
     I saw your ancestors.
 But they came to Baal-peor,
     and consecrated themselves to a thing of
     shame,
     and became detestable like the thing
     they loved.
¹¹ Ephraim's glory shall fly away like a bird—
     no birth, no pregnancy, no conception!
¹² Even if they bring up children,
     I will bereave them until no one is left.
 Woe to them indeed
     when I depart from them!
¹³ Once I saw Ephraim as a young palm
     planted in a lovely meadow,ᵃ
     but now Ephraim must lead out his
     children for slaughter.
¹⁴ Give them, O LORD—
     what will you give?
 Give them a miscarrying womb
     and dry breasts.

¹⁵ Every evil of theirs began at Gilgal;
     there I came to hate them.
 Because of the wickedness of their deeds
     I will drive them out of my house.
 I will love them no more;
     all their officials are rebels.

¹⁶ Ephraim is stricken,
     their root is dried up,
     they shall bear no fruit.
 Even though they give birth,
     I will kill the cherished offspring of their
     womb.
¹⁷ Because they have not listened to him,
     my God will reject them;
     they shall become wanderers among the
     nations.

10 Israel's Sin and Captivity

 Israel is a luxuriant vine
     that yields its fruit.
 The more his fruit increased
     the more altars he built;
 as his country improved,

he improved his pillars.
² Their heart is false;
     now they must bear their guilt.
 The LORDᵇ will break down their altars,
     and destroy their pillars.

³ For now they will say:
     "We have no king,
 for we do not fear the LORD,
     and a king—what could he do for us?"
⁴ They utter mere words;
     with empty oaths they make covenants;
 so litigation springs up like poisonous
     weeds
     in the furrows of the field.
⁵ The inhabitants of Samaria tremble
     for the calfᶜ of Beth-aven.
 Its people shall mourn for it,
     and its idolatrous priests shall wailᵈ
     over it,
     over its glory that has departed from it.
⁶ The thing itself shall be carried to Assyria
     as tribute to the great king.ᵉ
 Ephraim shall be put to shame,
     and Israel shall be ashamed of his idol.ᶠ

⁷ Samaria's king shall perish
     like a chip on the face of the waters.
⁸ The high places of Aven, the sin of Israel,
     shall be destroyed.
 Thorn and thistle shall grow up
     on their altars.
 They shall say to the mountains, Cover us,
     and to the hills, Fall on us.

⁹ Since the days of Gibeah you have sinned,
     O Israel;
     there they have continued.
     Shall not war overtake them in Gibeah?
¹⁰ I will comeᵍ against the wayward people to
     punish them;
     and nations shall be gathered against
     them
     when they are punishedʰ for their double
     iniquity.

¹¹ Ephraim was a trained heifer
     that loved to thresh,
     and I spared her fair neck;
 but I will make Ephraim break the ground;
     Judah must plow;
     Jacob must harrow for himself.
¹² Sow for yourselves righteousness;
     reap steadfast love;
     break up your fallow ground;
 for it is time to seek the LORD,
     that he may come and rain righteousness
     upon you.

ᵃ Meaning of Heb uncertain ᵇ Heb *he* ᶜ Gk Syr: Heb *calves* ᵈ Cn: Heb *exult* ᵉ Cn: Heb *to a king who will contend* ᶠ Cn: Heb *counsel*
ᵍ Cn Compare Gk: Heb *In my desire* ʰ Gk: Heb *bound*

"Most people think that Christianity is all about us seeking God when the truth is that it's more about God seeking us. He works through events in our lives in order to put Himself in position for us to seek Him, reach out for Him, and find Him. He is in white-hot, zealous, passionate pursuit of a relationship with each one of us."

—Chris Seidman, *Little Buddy*

WHAT'S THAT SMELL COMING FROM THE LAUNDRY ROOM?

My family's history with pets isn't so good. We once had a hamster that ended up lost *inside* the walls of the house. Once my pet crawfish from fourth-grade science class got loose, and we all had to walk around on tiptoes, scared we'd get pinched. (We eventually found him—fried—under the dryer.) The snails in our family fish tank multiplied exponentially, till there were hundreds (maybe even thousands) of them. And our dog! Not only did he consistently TP our house by strewing about roll after roll of toilet paper; he was so prissy that he had to eat hypoallergenic, organic dog food or else he'd break out in a rash. His food was more expensive than mine!

Caring for pets is fun, but also a lot of work. So imagine, for a moment, what it's like to actually be a parent, to be responsible for the life of a helpless human being. To feed her. To clothe him. To teach her to walk. To teach him to talk. It's a 24/7 commitment that lasts at least eighteen years!

Read **Hosea 11.1–4**. The married-to-a-cheating-wife concept isn't the only analogy God uses in Hosea. Here's a different and very powerful image: God as a patient parent, tenderly loving and caring for Israel.

Did you know God loves his Church that way too? Meditate on this truth, but do it in an active way. How? Arrange to babysit a child who is one year old or younger, or help out in the cry room next Sunday. Feed the child, play with him, feed him his snacks, care for him. And as you do, prayerfully think about what this experience shows you about God's patient, passionate, parental love for you and for the rest of his Church.

GOD IS PASSIONATE MY CHURCH

---

13 You have plowed wickedness,
    you have reaped injustice,
      you have eaten the fruit of lies.
    Because you have trusted in your power
      and in the multitude of your warriors,
14 therefore the tumult of war shall rise
      against your people,
    and all your fortresses shall be destroyed,
    as Shalman destroyed Beth-arbel on the day
      of battle

---

when mothers were dashed in pieces
    with their children.
15 Thus it shall be done to you, O Bethel,
    because of your great wickedness.
At dawn the king of Israel
    shall be utterly cut off.

11 God's Compassion Despite Israel's Ingratitude

When Israel was a child, I loved him,
    and out of Egypt I called my son.
2 The more I[a] called them,
    the more they went from me;[b]
they kept sacrificing to the Baals,
    and offering incense to idols.

3 Yet it was I who taught Ephraim to walk,
    I took them up in my[c] arms;
    but they did not know that I healed them.
4 I led them with cords of human kindness,
    with bands of love.
I was to them like those
    who lift infants to their cheeks.[d]
    I bent down to them and fed them.

5 They shall return to the land of Egypt,
    and Assyria shall be their king,
    because they have refused to return
      to me.
6 The sword rages in their cities,
    it consumes their oracle-priests,
    and devours because of their schemes.
7 My people are bent on turning away
      from me.
    To the Most High they call,
    but he does not raise them up at all.[e]

8 How can I give you up, Ephraim?
    How can I hand you over, O Israel?
How can I make you like Admah?
    How can I treat you like Zeboiim?
My heart recoils within me;
    my compassion grows warm and tender.
9 I will not execute my fierce anger;
    I will not again destroy Ephraim;
for I am God and no mortal,
    the Holy One in your midst,
    and I will not come in wrath.[e]

10 They shall go after the LORD,
    who roars like a lion;
when he roars,
    his children shall come trembling from
      the west.
11 They shall come trembling like birds from
      Egypt,
    and like doves from the land of Assyria;
    and I will return them to their homes,
      says the LORD.

---

a Gk: Heb *they* b Gk: Heb *them* c Gk Syr Vg: Heb *his* d Or *who ease the yoke on their jaws* e Meaning of Heb uncertain

^{12a} Ephraim has surrounded me with lies,
  and the house of Israel with deceit;
but Judah still walks^b with God,
  and is faithful to the Holy One.

12 Ephraim herds the wind,
  and pursues the east wind all day long;
they multiply falsehood and violence;
  they make a treaty with Assyria,
  and oil is carried to Egypt.

The Long History of Rebellion

² The Lord has an indictment against Judah,
  and will punish Jacob according to his
    ways,
  and repay him according to his deeds.
³ In the womb he tried to supplant his
    brother,
  and in his manhood he strove with God.
⁴ He strove with the angel and prevailed,
  he wept and sought his favor;
he met him at Bethel,
  and there he spoke with him.^c
⁵ The Lord the God of hosts,
  the Lord is his name!
⁶ But as for you, return to your God,
  hold fast to love and justice,
  and wait continually for your God.

⁷ A trader, in whose hands are false balances,
  he loves to oppress.
⁸ Ephraim has said, "Ah, I am rich,
  I have gained wealth for myself;
in all of my gain
  no offense has been found in me
  that would be sin."^d
⁹ I am the Lord your God
  from the land of Egypt;
I will make you live in tents again,
  as in the days of the appointed festival.

¹⁰ I spoke to the prophets;
  it was I who multiplied visions,
  and through the prophets I will bring
    destruction.
¹¹ In Gilead^e there is iniquity,
  they shall surely come to nothing.
In Gilgal they sacrifice bulls,
  so their altars shall be like stone heaps
  on the furrows of the field.
¹² Jacob fled to the land of Aram,
  there Israel served for a wife,
  and for a wife he guarded sheep.^f
¹³ By a prophet the Lord brought Israel up
    from Egypt,
  and by a prophet he was guarded.
¹⁴ Ephraim has given bitter offense,

so his Lord will bring his crimes down on
    him
  and pay him back for his insults.

13 Relentless Judgment on Israel

When Ephraim spoke, there was trembling;
  he was exalted in Israel;
  but he incurred guilt through Baal and
    died.
² And now they keep on sinning
  and make a cast image for themselves,
idols of silver made according to their
    understanding,
  all of them the work of artisans.
"Sacrifice to these," they say.^g
  People are kissing calves!
³ Therefore they shall be like the morning
    mist
  or like the dew that goes away early,
like chaff that swirls from the threshing
    floor
  or like smoke from a window.

⁴ Yet I have been the Lord your God
  ever since the land of Egypt;
you know no God but me,
  and besides me there is no savior.
⁵ It was I who fed^h you in the wilderness,
  in the land of drought.
⁶ When I fedⁱ them, they were satisfied;
  they were satisfied, and their heart was
    proud;
  therefore they forgot me.
⁷ So I will become like a lion to them,
  like a leopard I will lurk beside the way.
⁸ I will fall upon them like a bear robbed of
    her cubs,
  and will tear open the covering of their
    heart;
there I will devour them like a lion,
  as a wild animal would mangle them.

⁹ I will destroy you, O Israel;
  who can help you?^j
¹⁰ Where now is^k your king, that he may save
    you?
  Where in all your cities are your rulers,
of whom you said,
  "Give me a king and rulers"?
¹¹ I gave you a king in my anger,
  and I took him away in my wrath.

¹² Ephraim's iniquity is bound up;
  his sin is kept in store.
¹³ The pangs of childbirth come for him,
  but he is an unwise son;

^a Ch 12.1 in Heb ^b Heb *roams* or *rules* ^c Gk Syr: Heb *us* ^d Meaning of Heb uncertain ^e Compare Syr: Heb *Gilead* ^f Heb lacks *sheep*
^g Cn Compare Gk: Heb *To these they say sacrifices of people* ^h Gk Syr: Heb *knew* ⁱ Cn: Heb *according to their pasture* ^j Gk Syr: Heb *for in me is your help* ^k Gk Syr Vg: Heb *I will be*

for at the proper time he does not present
himself
at the mouth of the womb.

14 Shall I ransom them from the power of
Sheol?
Shall I redeem them from Death?
O Death, where are[a] your plagues?
O Sheol, where is[a] your destruction?
Compassion is hidden from my eyes.

15 Although he may flourish among rushes,[b]
the east wind shall come, a blast from
the LORD,
rising from the wilderness;
and his fountain shall dry up,
his spring shall be parched.
It shall strip his treasury
of every precious thing.

16[c] Samaria shall bear her guilt,
because she has rebelled against her God;
they shall fall by the sword,
their little ones shall be dashed in pieces,
and their pregnant women ripped open.

14 A Plea for Repentance

Return, O Israel, to the LORD your God,
for you have stumbled because of your
iniquity.
2 Take words with you
and return to the LORD;
say to him,
"Take away all guilt;
accept that which is good,
and we will offer

the fruit[d] of our lips.
3 Assyria shall not save us;
we will not ride upon horses;
we will say no more, 'Our God,'
to the work of our hands.
In you the orphan finds mercy."

Assurance of Forgiveness

4 I will heal their disloyalty;
I will love them freely,
for my anger has turned from them.
5 I will be like the dew to Israel;
he shall blossom like the lily,
he shall strike root like the forests of
Lebanon.[e]
6 His shoots shall spread out;
his beauty shall be like the olive tree,
and his fragrance like that of Lebanon.
7 They shall again live beneath my[f] shadow,
they shall flourish as a garden;[g]
they shall blossom like the vine,
their fragrance shall be like the wine of
Lebanon.

8 O Ephraim, what have I[h] to do with idols?
It is I who answer and look after you.[i]
I am like an evergreen cypress;
your faithfulness[j] comes from me.
9 Those who are wise understand these
things;
those who are discerning know them.
For the ways of the LORD are right,
and the upright walk in them,
but transgressors stumble in them.

a Gk Syr: Heb I will be b Or among brothers c Ch 14.1 in Heb d Gk Syr: Heb bulls e Cn: Heb like Lebanon f Heb his g Cn: Heb they shall
grow grain h Or What more has Ephraim i Heb him j Heb your fruit

CREATIVE SPACE

JOEL

DESOLATION OR DELIVERANCE?

Time to Choose

When earthquakes crumble houses, when tsunamis overwhelm cities, when drought sucks life from the land, we usually ask, *Why?!* It's a desperate cry to make sense of such terrible destruction. And it's hard to find answers. Maybe there are no answers to be found. But when a plague of locusts marches over his country, eating everything in their path, Joel senses that something else is going on. He gazes out over the barren fields, aware of the suffering of those who have nothing left, and he catches a glimpse of the heart of God. If people don't turn back to God, then there's worse destruction ahead. Not because God is a mad tyrant who likes to make people suffer, but because God is just and holy and can't stand sin.

Joel paints rich, dramatic pictures of the choice facing God's people. They can have more death and devastation, or they can have plenty, peace, and prosperity. They can continue in their ways, or they can be drenched with the Spirit of God and overflow with dreams and visions. Repentance is the key that turns one into the other, a deep heartfelt turning back to God.

Joel's two alternative futures still stand. When you're faced with a choice as simple and stark as that, you'd be crazy to reject the life that God offers. Wouldn't you?

> *"Those who are led by the Holy Spirit have true ideas; that is why so many ignorant people are wiser than the learned. The Holy Spirit is light and strength."*
>
> —St. John Vianney

WHO Joel, a prophet who lived in Judah

WHAT A plague of locusts has eaten everything in sight. Joel says this is nothing compared to what God could do as judgment on the people's sin. But there's a chance to repent and receive a blessing instead.

WHEN Because Joel doesn't mention specific events or kings, we don't know for certain when it was written. Some scholars believe Joel served as a prophet from 835 to ca. 800 B.C.

WHERE Judah, the southern kingdom—today this is the southern region of Israel/Palestine.

PATH OF DISCIPLESHIP

When Peter stood up to explain why his friends were suddenly able to speak languages they had never learned, he quoted from the book of Joel (Acts 2.17–21). Their transformation from scared disciples to bold ambassadors was the fulfillment of this ancient promise that God would pour out his Spirit (Joel 2.28–32). Having been taught and inspired by Jesus, the disciples needed the power of his Spirit to make them active, effective agents of his Kingdom.

Joel saw ahead to a new reality. Hundreds of years later Jesus created that reality around him: a place where young, old, men, women—*all* are included in the purposes of God. However you describe yourself, that includes *you*, if you want to be part of it.

1

The word of the LORD that came to Joel son of Pethuel:

Lament over the Ruin of the Country

2 Hear this, O elders,
   give ear, all inhabitants of the land!
Has such a thing happened in your days,
   or in the days of your ancestors?
3 Tell your children of it,
   and let your children tell their children,
   and their children another generation.

4 What the cutting locust left,
   the swarming locust has eaten.
What the swarming locust left,
   the hopping locust has eaten,
and what the hopping locust left,
   the destroying locust has eaten.

5 Wake up, you drunkards, and weep;
   and wail, all you wine-drinkers,
over the sweet wine,
   for it is cut off from your mouth.
6 For a nation has invaded my land,
   powerful and innumerable;
its teeth are lions' teeth,
   and it has the fangs of a lioness.
7 It has laid waste my vines,
   and splintered my fig trees;
it has stripped off their bark and thrown it
      down;
   their branches have turned white.

8 Lament like a virgin dressed in sackcloth
   for the husband of her youth.
9 The grain offering and the drink offering
      are cut off
   from the house of the LORD.
The priests mourn,
   the ministers of the LORD.
10 The fields are devastated,
   the ground mourns;
for the grain is destroyed,
   the wine dries up,
   the oil fails.

11 Be dismayed, you farmers,
   wail, you vinedressers,
over the wheat and the barley;
   for the crops of the field are ruined.
12 The vine withers,
   the fig tree droops.
Pomegranate, palm, and apple—
   all the trees of the field are dried up;
surely, joy withers away
   among the people.

A Call to Repentance and Prayer

13 Put on sackcloth and lament, you priests;
   wail, you ministers of the altar.
Come, pass the night in sackcloth,
   you ministers of my God!
Grain offering and drink offering
   are withheld from the house of your God.

14 Sanctify a fast,
   call a solemn assembly.
Gather the elders
   and all the inhabitants of the land
to the house of the LORD your God,
   and cry out to the LORD.

15 Alas for the day!
For the day of the LORD is near,
   and as destruction from the Almighty[a] it
      comes.
16 Is not the food cut off
   before our eyes,
joy and gladness
   from the house of our God?

17 The seed shrivels under the clods,[b]
   the storehouses are desolate;
the granaries are ruined
   because the grain has failed.
18 How the animals groan!
   The herds of cattle wander about
because there is no pasture for them;
   even the flocks of sheep are dazed.[c]

19 To you, O LORD, I cry.
For fire has devoured
   the pastures of the wilderness,
and flames have burned
   all the trees of the field.
20 Even the wild animals cry to you
   because the watercourses are dried up,
and fire has devoured
   the pastures of the wilderness.

2

Blow the trumpet in Zion;
   sound the alarm on my holy mountain!
Let all the inhabitants of the land tremble,
   for the day of the LORD is coming, it is
      near—
2 a day of darkness and gloom,
   a day of clouds and thick darkness!
Like blackness spread upon the mountains
   a great and powerful army comes;
their like has never been from of old,
   nor will be again after them
   in ages to come.

3 Fire devours in front of them,
   and behind them a flame burns.
Before them the land is like the garden of
      Eden,

---

a Traditional rendering of Heb Shaddai   b Meaning of Heb uncertain   c Compare Gk Syr Vg: Meaning of Heb uncertain

but after them a desolate wilderness,
and nothing escapes them.

4 They have the appearance of horses,
and like war-horses they charge.
5 As with the rumbling of chariots,
they leap on the tops of the mountains,
like the crackling of a flame of fire
devouring the stubble,
like a powerful army
drawn up for battle.

6 Before them peoples are in anguish,
all faces grow pale. [a]
7 Like warriors they charge,
like soldiers they scale the wall.
Each keeps to its own course,
they do not swerve from [b] their paths.
8 They do not jostle one another,
each keeps to its own track;
they burst through the weapons
and are not halted.
9 They leap upon the city,
they run upon the walls;
they climb up into the houses,
they enter through the windows like a
thief.

10 The earth quakes before them,
the heavens tremble.
The sun and the moon are darkened,
and the stars withdraw their shining.
11 The Lord utters his voice
at the head of his army;
how vast is his host!
Numberless are those who obey his
command.
Truly the day of the Lord is great;
terrible indeed—who can endure it?

12 Yet even now, says the Lord,
return to me with all your heart,
with fasting, with weeping, and with
mourning;
13 rend your hearts and not your clothing.
Return to the Lord, your God,
for he is gracious and merciful,
slow to anger, and abounding in steadfast
love,
and relents from punishing.
14 Who knows whether he will not turn and
relent,
and leave a blessing behind him,
a grain offering and a drink offering
for the Lord, your God?

15 Blow the trumpet in Zion;
sanctify a fast;
call a solemn assembly;
16 gather the people.

Having a Bad Day?

So you got in a fight with your boyfriend or girlfriend. Or maybe a close friend or trusted teacher misunderstood you, and you feel rejected. Or perhaps you felt the consequence of a poor decision. It's been a bad day, and the result is often a broken relationship or a situation that needs restoration.

In the midst of a locust plague, God called his people to repentance. If they repented, God promised he would show mercy. In his compassion, God promised he'd restore them, and their shame would be taken away. Read **Joel 2.18–27** for more details on this story.

Did you recently have one of those bad days, and now you have a situation in your life that needs restoration by God? In his compassion, God can redeem any bad situation you may find yourself in. Draw a picture in a Creative Space in this Bible that portrays either a time when God restored you or a way that God could bring healing to something that's currently happening in your life. (Scan or take a digital photo of your drawing and share it with others at **Learner.CalltoDiscipleship.com**.)

Sanctify the congregation;
assemble the aged;
gather the children,
even infants at the breast.
Let the bridegroom leave his room,
and the bride her canopy.

17 Between the vestibule and the altar
let the priests, the ministers of the Lord,
weep.
Let them say, "Spare your people, O Lord,
and do not make your heritage a mockery,
a byword among the nations.
Why should it be said among the peoples,
'Where is their God?' "

God's Response and Promise

18 Then the Lord became jealous for his land,
and had pity on his people.
19 In response to his people the Lord said:
I am sending you
grain, wine, and oil,
and you will be satisfied;

a Meaning of Heb uncertain b Gk Syr Vg: Heb they do not take a pledge along

Beautiful

17 years have gone by. The color of your skin is as BLACK as dye. You made so many MIS-TAKES you want to take them back. You are not PRETTY, or skinny—don't even think of that. In fact, you may as well be a rat. No one talks to you, cares for you or shares with you. You are PROUD to cover up your insecurities. We walk all over you, because you let us. Just because you are DIFFERENT, we feel we should HURT you to make us feel better than you. You mean nothing. No one loves you. Except—me, God—I do. I made you in *MY* image. I have a plan for you, a house for you. I care for you. Your skin is beautiful. You made mistakes...and I *FORGIVE* you. You are pretty; and who cares if you aren't skinny. I am here for you; I will share with you. Don't let them walk all over you. They don't love you like *I* do. And of course you are different—that is how *I MADE YOU*. You mean *EVERYTHING* to me! Look what I have given you! The grass is green, and the sky is blue. What else do I have to give you to show you that I love you? Don't be rude, mean, and cruel like the others do. Just be beautiful the way *I* made you!

Beautiful—© Allie Gager, 15

and I will no more make you
    a mockery among the nations.

20 I will remove the northern army far from
        you,
    and drive it into a parched and desolate
        land,
    its front into the eastern sea,
    and its rear into the western sea;
    its stench and foul smell will rise up.
    Surely he has done great things!

21 Do not fear, O soil;
    be glad and rejoice,
    for the LORD has done great things!
22 Do not fear, you animals of the field,
    for the pastures of the wilderness are
        green;
    the tree bears its fruit,
    the fig tree and vine give their full yield.

23 O children of Zion, be glad
    and rejoice in the LORD your God;
    for he has given the early rain*a* for your
        vindication,
    he has poured down for you abundant
        rain,
    the early and the later rain, as before.
24 The threshing floors shall be full of grain,
    the vats shall overflow with wine and oil.

25 I will repay you for the years
    that the swarming locust has eaten,
    the hopper, the destroyer, and the cutter,
    my great army, which I sent against you.

26 You shall eat in plenty and be satisfied,
    and praise the name of the LORD your
        God,
    who has dealt wondrously with you.
    And my people shall never again be put to
        shame.
27 You shall know that I am in the midst of
        Israel,
    and that I, the LORD, am your God and
        there is no other.
    And my people shall never again be put to
        shame.

God's Spirit Poured Out

28*b* Then afterward
    I will pour out my spirit on all flesh;
    your sons and your daughters shall
        prophesy,
    your old men shall dream dreams,
    and your young men shall see visions.
29 Even on the male and female slaves,
    in those days, I will pour out my spirit.

30 I will show portents in the heavens and

IT'S TRADITION

NOT JUST YOUR IMAGINATION

Your imagination is one of the places in your being where the Holy Spirit lives—the same Holy Spirit who prompted Joel, Peter, and the disciples to speak, to have a vision, and to work for that vision. Read **Joel 3.18**. When you look at almost any of the prophets' writings, you see that many of their prophetic "God-given" messages are poetry.

    To understand these messages and how the Holy Spirit may be moving you into a new reality requires you to pay attention to your imagination, to use it in guided mediation, and to pay attention to what it tells you about God (see *Catechism of the Catholic Church* 2705).

on the earth, blood and fire and columns of smoke. 31 The sun shall be turned to darkness, and the moon to blood, before the great and terrible day of the LORD comes. 32 Then everyone who calls on the name of the LORD shall be saved; for in Mount Zion and in Jerusalem there shall be those who escape, as the LORD has said, and among the survivors shall be those whom the LORD calls.

3*c* For then, in those days and at that time, when I restore the fortunes of Judah and Jerusalem, 2 I will gather all the nations and bring them down to the valley of Jehoshaphat, and I will enter into judgment with them there, on account of my people and my heritage Israel, because they have scattered them among the nations. They have divided my land, 3 and cast lots for my people, and traded boys for prostitutes, and sold girls for wine, and drunk it down.

4 What are you to me, O Tyre and Sidon, and all the regions of Philistia? Are you paying me back for something? If you are paying me back, I will turn your deeds back upon your own heads swiftly and speedily. 5 For you have taken my silver and my gold, and have carried my rich treasures into your temples.*d* 6 You have sold the people of Judah and Jerusalem to the Greeks, removing them far from their own border. 7 But now I will rouse them to leave the places to which you have sold them, and I will

a Meaning of Heb uncertain *b* Ch 3.1 in Heb *c* Ch 4.1 in Heb *d* Or *palaces*

REALITY ✔

STEWARDSHIP AND ECOLOGY

It doesn't take a lot of imagination to see the parallels between what's happening to the earth today and the plagues described in Joel. Technology, waste, and improper use of resources have outstripped and brought devastation to the gifts of creation now in our hands. Read **Joel 3.17–21**. Joel's overriding word is one of grace to a people who have heard, imagined, and responded to God's call to "return to me with all your heart" (2.12). His call for repentance should move us as faithful disciples to take some responsibility for the stewardship of our earth today.

In the 2009 encyclical *Caritas in Veritate* ("Charity in Truth"), Pope Benedict XVI gave the Church some things to think about when making decisions about the environment: "The environment is God's gift to everyone, and in our use of it we have a responsibility towards the poor, towards future generations and towards humanity as a whole" (48).

How will you answer Catholic social teaching's call to care for all creation? Share your ideas at **Learner.CalltoDiscipleship.com**.

turn your deeds back upon your own heads. ⁸I will sell your sons and your daughters into the hand of the people of Judah, and they will sell them to the Sabeans, to a nation far away; for the LORD has spoken.

Judgment in the Valley of Jehoshaphat

⁹ Proclaim this among the nations:
  Prepare war,*
   stir up the warriors.
 Let all the soldiers draw near,
   let them come up.
¹⁰ Beat your plowshares into swords,
   and your pruning hooks into spears;
   let the weakling say, "I am a warrior."
¹¹ Come quickly,*
   all you nations all around,

gather yourselves there.
  Bring down your warriors, O LORD.
¹² Let the nations rouse themselves,
   and come up to the valley of
     Jehoshaphat;
 for there I will sit to judge
   all the neighboring nations.

¹³ Put in the sickle,
   for the harvest is ripe.
 Go in, tread,
   for the wine press is full.
 The vats overflow,
   for their wickedness is great.

¹⁴ Multitudes, multitudes,
   in the valley of decision!
 For the day of the LORD is near
   in the valley of decision.
¹⁵ The sun and the moon are darkened,
   and the stars withdraw their shining.

¹⁶ The LORD roars from Zion,
   and utters his voice from Jerusalem,
   and the heavens and the earth shake.
 But the LORD is a refuge for his people,
   a stronghold for the people of Israel.

The Glorious Future of Judah

¹⁷ So you shall know that I, the LORD your
     God,
   dwell in Zion, my holy mountain.
 And Jerusalem shall be holy,
   and strangers shall never again pass
     through it.

¹⁸ In that day
 the mountains shall drip sweet wine,
   the hills shall flow with milk,
 and all the stream beds of Judah
   shall flow with water;
 a fountain shall come forth from the house
     of the LORD
   and water the Wadi Shittim.

¹⁹ Egypt shall become a desolation
   and Edom a desolate wilderness,
 because of the violence done to the people
     of Judah,
   in whose land they have shed innocent
     blood.
²⁰ But Judah shall be inhabited forever,
   and Jerusalem to all generations.
²¹ I will avenge their blood, and I will not clear
     the guilty,*
   for the LORD dwells in Zion.

a Heb *sanctify war*   *b* Meaning of Heb uncertain   *c* Gk Syr: Heb *I will hold innocent their blood that I have not held innocent*

AMOS

GOD'S FAVORITE WORSHIP STYLE

The Song of Your Life

Worship can seem like a real refuge at times. Having struggled to follow God during the week, having been distracted and made mistakes, we find it comforting to meet with friends on a Sunday and get lost in familiar songs of worship and praise. But Amos shatters that comfort with God's view: "Get lost! I can't stand the noise of your songs. I'm not going to listen!"

Wow! What's going on? Like us, the Jews thought worship was what God wanted. They made all the right sacrifices and played all the right songs, but in the rest of their lives they were no different from anyone else. They oppressed the poor, deprived them of justice, and ignored the prophets who called them back to God. Their acts of worship had become a superficial, smiley-faced indulgence done out of habit in an effort to fool themselves into thinking that everything was all right.

But God wanted more from them, and God wants more from us. He wants integrity in our lives. He wants us to *act* with justice, not just sing about it. It matters to God how we treat the poor, how we spend our money, how we do our work. So ask yourself: What kind of worship song am I singing through the way I live every day? Is it a discordant racket that God doesn't want to hear or a song of beauty and harmony?

> "We ought to speak, shout out against injustices, with confidence and without fear. We proclaim the principles of the Church, the reign of love, without forgetting that it is also a reign of justice."
>
> —Bl. Miguel Pro

WHO Amos, a shepherd from Judah

WHAT Amos had a powerful message from God: worship from people who oppress the poor is just a horrible noise in God's ears; treating others with justice is far more important.

WHEN This book was likely written around 760 B.C., when King Uzziah ruled Judah and King Jeroboam ruled Israel.

WHERE Amos lived in Tekoa, a village near Jerusalem. His prophecies, though, were directed mainly at the people of Israel (the northern kingdom).

PATH OF DISCIPLESHIP

As you read Amos' prophecies against the nations surrounding Israel, including Judah, you can almost see heads nodding in righteous indignation at the prophetic pronouncements against all these "others" and the wrongs they had committed. But then Amos plays the "gotcha" game: he turns to the Israelites with pronouncements against their wrongdoings as well (Amos 1.1–6.14).

There's a lot here to apply to life today. It's easy to be judgmental, to point the finger at individuals, groups, and even nations who don't measure up to our ideals. We're all too ready to offer to remove the speck from a friend's eye without ever seeing the "log" in our own (see Luke 6.42). We can become just as complacent as the Israelites were. They were doing the "right" things, worshiping God, following the rules, *and* at the same time not living in right relationships with the people around them. They confused following the rituals of their faith with actually *living* their faith. The path of discipleship calls us to keep both practicing and living our faith in balance. One without the other won't cut it with God.

1 The words of Amos, who was among the shepherds of Tekoa, which he saw concerning Israel in the days of King Uzziah of Judah and in the days of King Jeroboam son of Joash of Israel, two years*ᵃ* before the earthquake.

Judgment on Israel's Neighbors

²And he said:

The LORD roars from Zion,
and utters his voice from Jerusalem;
the pastures of the shepherds wither,
and the top of Carmel dries up.

³ Thus says the LORD:
For three transgressions of Damascus,
and for four, I will not revoke the
punishment;*ᵇ*
because they have threshed Gilead
with threshing sledges of iron.
⁴ So I will send a fire on the house of Hazael,
and it shall devour the strongholds of
Ben-hadad.
⁵ I will break the gate bars of Damascus,
and cut off the inhabitants from the
Valley of Aven,
and the one who holds the scepter from
Beth-eden;
and the people of Aram shall go into
exile to Kir,
says the LORD.

⁶ Thus says the LORD:
For three transgressions of Gaza,
and for four, I will not revoke the
punishment;*ᵇ*
because they carried into exile entire
communities,
to hand them over to Edom.
⁷ So I will send a fire on the wall of Gaza,
fire that shall devour its strongholds.
⁸ I will cut off the inhabitants from Ashdod,
and the one who holds the scepter from
Ashkelon;
I will turn my hand against Ekron,
and the remnant of the Philistines shall
perish,
says the Lord GOD.

⁹ Thus says the LORD:
For three transgressions of Tyre,
and for four, I will not revoke the
punishment;*ᵇ*
because they delivered entire communities
over to Edom,
and did not remember the covenant of
kinship.
¹⁰ So I will send a fire on the wall of Tyre,
fire that shall devour its strongholds.

¹¹ Thus says the LORD:
For three transgressions of Edom,
and for four, I will not revoke the
punishment;*ᵇ*
because he pursued his brother with the
sword
and cast off all pity;
he maintained his anger perpetually,*ᶜ*
and kept his wrath*ᵈ* forever.
¹² So I will send a fire on Teman,
and it shall devour the strongholds of
Bozrah.

¹³ Thus says the LORD:
For three transgressions of the Ammonites,
and for four, I will not revoke the
punishment;*ᵇ*
because they have ripped open pregnant
women in Gilead
in order to enlarge their territory.
¹⁴ So I will kindle a fire against the wall of
Rabbah,
fire that shall devour its strongholds,
with shouting on the day of battle,
with a storm on the day of the whirlwind;
¹⁵ then their king shall go into exile,
he and his officials together,
says the LORD.

2 Thus says the LORD:
For three transgressions of Moab,
and for four, I will not revoke the
punishment;*ᵇ*
because he burned to lime
the bones of the king of Edom.
² So I will send a fire on Moab,
and it shall devour the strongholds of
Kerioth,
and Moab shall die amid uproar,
amid shouting and the sound of the
trumpet;
³ I will cut off the ruler from its midst,
and will kill all its officials with him,
says the LORD.

Judgment on Judah

⁴ Thus says the LORD:
For three transgressions of Judah,
and for four, I will not revoke the
punishment;*ᵇ*
because they have rejected the law of the
LORD,
and have not kept his statutes,
but they have been led astray by the same
lies
after which their ancestors walked.
⁵ So I will send a fire on Judah,

---

a Or *during two years* *b* Heb *cause it to return* *c* Syr Vg: Heb *and his anger tore perpetually* *d* Gk Syr Vg: Heb *and his wrath kept*

All Along

You were there for me
all along.
Through the pain and suffering,
through the voices and the torment,
you were there...
all along.
How can that be?
All I've been through...
you were there...
all along.

All along you've been here?
Why did you send me through
the torture and torment?
All along it was you who made me miserable...

Or was it?

No, you protected me
all along.
You were testing me for something more,
something big.

All along, I treated you so badly.
I condemned you,
sent you away from my sight
and took in the darkness...

But you were there...
all along.

and it shall devour the strongholds of
Jerusalem.

Judgment on Israel

6 Thus says the LORD:

For three transgressions of Israel,
and for four, I will not revoke the
punishment;[a]
because they sell the righteous for silver,
and the needy for a pair of sandals—
7 they who trample the head of the poor into
the dust of the earth,
and push the afflicted out of the way;
father and son go in to the same girl,
so that my holy name is profaned;
8 they lay themselves down beside every altar
on garments taken in pledge;
and in the house of their God they drink
wine bought with fines they imposed.

9 Yet I destroyed the Amorite before them,
whose height was like the height of cedars,
and who was as strong as oaks;
I destroyed his fruit above,
and his roots beneath.
10 Also I brought you up out of the land of
Egypt,
and led you forty years in the wilderness,
to possess the land of the Amorite.
11 And I raised up some of your children to be
prophets
and some of your youths to be nazirites.[b]
Is it not indeed so, O people of Israel?
says the LORD.

12 But you made the nazirites[b] drink wine,
and commanded the prophets,
saying, "You shall not prophesy."

13 So, I will press you down in your place,
just as a cart presses down
when it is full of sheaves.[c]
14 Flight shall perish from the swift,
and the strong shall not retain their
strength,
nor shall the mighty save their lives;
15 those who handle the bow shall not stand,
and those who are swift of foot shall not
save themselves,
nor shall those who ride horses save
their lives;
16 and those who are stout of heart among the
mighty
shall flee away naked in that day,
says the LORD.

3 Israel's Guilt and Punishment

Hear this word that the LORD has spoken
against you, O people of Israel, against the
whole family that I brought up out of the land
of Egypt:

2 You only have I known
of all the families of the earth;
therefore I will punish you
for all your iniquities.

3 Do two walk together
unless they have made an appointment?
4 Does a lion roar in the forest,
when it has no prey?
Does a young lion cry out from its den,
if it has caught nothing?
5 Does a bird fall into a snare on the earth,
when there is no trap for it?
Does a snare spring up from the ground,
when it has taken nothing?
6 Is a trumpet blown in a city,
and the people are not afraid?
Does disaster befall a city,
unless the LORD has done it?
7 Surely the Lord GOD does nothing,
without revealing his secret
to his servants the prophets.
8 The lion has roared;
who will not fear?
The Lord GOD has spoken;
who can but prophesy?

9 Proclaim to the strongholds in Ashdod,
and to the strongholds in the land of
Egypt,
and say, "Assemble yourselves on Mount[d]
Samaria,
and see what great tumults are within it,
and what oppressions are in its midst."
10 They do not know how to do right, says the
LORD,
those who store up violence and robbery
in their strongholds.
11 Therefore thus says the Lord GOD:
An adversary shall surround the land,
and strip you of your defense;
and your strongholds shall be plundered.

12 Thus says the LORD: As the shepherd rescues from the mouth of the lion two legs, or
a piece of an ear, so shall the people of Israel
who live in Samaria be rescued, with the corner
of a couch and part[c] of a bed.

13 Hear, and testify against the house of Jacob,
says the Lord GOD, the God of hosts:
14 On the day I punish Israel for its
transgressions,
I will punish the altars of Bethel,
and the horns of the altar shall be cut off
and fall to the ground.

a Heb *cause it to return* b That is, *those separated* or *those consecrated* c Meaning of Heb uncertain d Gk Syr: Heb *the mountains of*

¹⁵ I will tear down the winter house as well as
     the summer house;
  and the houses of ivory shall perish,
  and the great houses*a* shall come to an end,
                           says the LORD.

4 Hear this word, you cows of Bashan
     who are on Mount Samaria,
  who oppress the poor, who crush the needy,
     who say to their husbands, "Bring
       something to drink!"
² The Lord GOD has sworn by his holiness:
     The time is surely coming upon you,
  when they shall take you away with hooks,
     even the last of you with fishhooks.
³ Through breaches in the wall you shall
     leave,
  each one straight ahead;
  and you shall be flung out into Harmon,*b*
                           says the LORD.
⁴ Come to Bethel—and transgress;
     to Gilgal—and multiply transgression;
  bring your sacrifices every morning,
     your tithes every three days;
⁵ bring a thank offering of leavened bread,
     and proclaim freewill offerings, publish
       them;
  for so you love to do, O people of Israel!
                       says the Lord GOD.

Israel Rejects Correction

⁶ I gave you cleanness of teeth in all your
     cities,
  and lack of bread in all your places,
  yet you did not return to me,
                           says the LORD.

⁷ And I also withheld the rain from you
     when there were still three months to
       the harvest;
  I would send rain on one city,
     and send no rain on another city;
  one field would be rained upon,
     and the field on which it did not rain
       withered;
⁸ so two or three towns wandered to one
     town
  to drink water, and were not satisfied;
  yet you did not return to me,
                           says the LORD.

⁹ I struck you with blight and mildew;
  I laid waste*c* your gardens and your
     vineyards;
  the locust devoured your fig trees and
     your olive trees;
  yet you did not return to me,
                           says the LORD.

a Or *many houses* *b* Meaning of Heb uncertain *c* Cn: Heb *the
multitude of*

Nothing but Noise . . .
It can be extremely painful to watch a movie
filled with horrible acting. The actors struggle
to keep your attention with lame attempts
to convince you they are someone else. But
they are not believable, and they just end up
looking pathetic.

So imagine a liturgy or prayer service about
caring for creation or ending neighborhood
violence. Perhaps all the motions and words
are right—there's been lots of planning and
practice—but it's done in the midst of a
group of people who are nasty to each other
and to outsiders. The result is a shallow and
meaningless "show" of faith that's just not
convincing. That's a bit like how God felt when
his people performed acts of worship without
an authentic lifestyle to back it up.

Read **Amos 5.21–24**. Have you ever
entertained the thought that God may
consider the songs you sing to him just *noise*?
The source of God's contention with his people
was that they ignored justice and right living.
They were guilty of buying into lies (Amos 2.4),
not helping the poor (2.6), and being self-
centered (5.11–12). Could you, your family, or
your parish be guilty of injustice? The words
of Dorothy Day, the founder of the Catholic
Worker movement, have something to say
about this: "I have long since come to believe
that people never mean half of what they say,
and that it is best to disregard their talk and
judge only their actions."

Talking a good game, using the right
words, spending energy being "politically
correct," singing hymns, or praying Prayers
of the Faithful about justice does not equate
to *doing* justice. The challenge is for you not
to join in on the flood of noise that reaches
the ears of God every day, but instead
give God something to smile about. Think
about some of the injustice in this world:
slavery, sweatshops, disease, poverty, racial
discrimination, and so much more. Look
through a magazine or find a picture online
that represents someone who needs justice;
tear it out or print it and tape it somewhere
in this Bible. Then think about how God may
want you to fight this injustice. Log on to
Learner.CalltoDiscipleship.com for ideas.

REALITY ✔

AS AMOS SEES HIM

There's a lot you can apply to life today from a reading of the words and woes of judgment. Amos focuses all of his utterances on injustice. Read **Amos 5.14–15**. The God he describes is the God of justice and judgment. Amos does not hold out a lot of hope for the masses. If Israel repents there will be forgiveness (Amos 7.2–6), but this will be for a few—a remnant. He doesn't bother with any of Israel's other infidelities. Rather, he lays bare the oppression of the poor, unethical business practices, bribery, and using money for privilege and power.

How does Amos' description of God challenge or comfort you? If Amos were preaching in your parish this week, what would you be called to change in your life, or at least think about? What about your parish community?

---

¹⁰ I sent among you a pestilence after the
        manner of Egypt;
    I killed your young men with the sword;
    I carried away your horses;ᵃ
        and I made the stench of your camp go up
            into your nostrils;
    yet you did not return to me,
                                says the LORD.

¹¹ I overthrew some of you,
        as when God overthrew Sodom and
            Gomorrah,
    and you were like a brand snatched from
        the fire;
    yet you did not return to me,
                                says the LORD.

¹² Therefore thus I will do to you, O Israel;
        because I will do this to you,
    prepare to meet your God, O Israel!

¹³ For lo, the one who forms the mountains,
        creates the wind,
    reveals his thoughts to mortals,
    makes the morning darkness,

and treads on the heights of the earth—
    the LORD, the God of hosts, is his name!

5 A Lament for Israel's Sin

Hear this word that I take up over you in lamentation, O house of Israel:
² Fallen, no more to rise,
        is maiden Israel;
    forsaken on her land,
        with no one to raise her up.

³ For thus says the Lord GOD:
    The city that marched out a thousand
        shall have a hundred left,
    and that which marched out a hundred
        shall have ten left.ᵇ

⁴ For thus says the LORD to the house of
        Israel:
    Seek me and live;
⁵   but do not seek Bethel,
    and do not enter into Gilgal
        or cross over to Beer-sheba;
    for Gilgal shall surely go into exile,
        and Bethel shall come to nothing.

⁶ Seek the LORD and live,
        or he will break out against the house of
            Joseph like fire,
    and it will devour Bethel, with no one to
        quench it.

⁷ Ah, you that turn justice to wormwood,
        and bring righteousness to the ground!

⁸ The one who made the Pleiades and Orion,
        and turns deep darkness into the
            morning,
    and darkens the day into night,
    who calls for the waters of the sea,
        and pours them out on the surface of the
            earth,
    the LORD is his name;
⁹ who makes destruction flash out against
        the strong,
    so that destruction comes upon the
        fortress.

¹⁰ They hate the one who reproves in the gate,
        and they abhor the one who speaks the
            truth.

¹¹ Therefore because you trample on the poor
        and take from them levies of grain,
    you have built houses of hewn stone,
        but you shall not live in them;
    you have planted pleasant vineyards,
        but you shall not drink their wine.

¹² For I know how many are your
        transgressions,
    and how great are your sins—

---

a Heb *with the captivity of your horses* *b* Heb adds *to the house of Israel*

you who afflict the righteous, who take a
bribe,
and push aside the needy in the gate.
13 Therefore the prudent will keep silent in
such a time;
for it is an evil time.

14 Seek good and not evil,
that you may live;
and so the LORD, the God of hosts, will be
with you,
just as you have said.
15 Hate evil and love good,
and establish justice in the gate;
it may be that the LORD, the God of hosts,
will be gracious to the remnant of Joseph.

16 Therefore thus says the LORD, the God of
hosts, the Lord:
In all the squares there shall be wailing;
and in all the streets they shall say, "Alas!
alas!"
They shall call the farmers to mourning,
and those skilled in lamentation, to
wailing;
17 in all the vineyards there shall be wailing,
for I will pass through the midst of you,
says the LORD.

The Day of the LORD a Dark Day

18 Alas for you who desire the day of the LORD!
Why do you want the day of the LORD?
It is darkness, not light;
19 as if someone fled from a lion,
and was met by a bear;
or went into the house and rested a hand
against the wall,
and was bitten by a snake.
20 Is not the day of the LORD darkness, not
light,
and gloom with no brightness in it?

21 I hate, I despise your festivals,
and I take no delight in your solemn
assemblies.
22 Even though you offer me your burnt
offerings and grain offerings,
I will not accept them;
and the offerings of well-being of your
fatted animals
I will not look upon.
23 Take away from me the noise of your songs;
I will not listen to the melody of your
harps.
24 But let justice roll down like waters,
and righteousness like an ever-flowing
stream.

25 Did you bring to me sacrifices and offerings the forty years in the wilderness, O house
of Israel? 26You shall take up Sakkuth your
king, and Kaiwan your star-god, your images,*a*
which you made for yourselves; 27therefore I
will take you into exile beyond Damascus, says
the LORD, whose name is the God of hosts.

6 Complacent Self-Indulgence Will Be Punished

Alas for those who are at ease in Zion,
and for those who feel secure on Mount
Samaria,
the notables of the first of the nations,
to whom the house of Israel resorts!
2 Cross over to Calneh, and see;
from there go to Hamath the great;
then go down to Gath of the Philistines.
Are you better*b* than these kingdoms?
Or is your*c* territory greater than their*d*
territory,
3 O you that put far away the evil day,
and bring near a reign of violence?

4 Alas for those who lie on beds of ivory,
and lounge on their couches,
and eat lambs from the flock,
and calves from the stall;
5 who sing idle songs to the sound of the harp,
and like David improvise on instruments
of music;
6 who drink wine from bowls,
and anoint themselves with the finest
oils,
but are not grieved over the ruin of
Joseph!
7 Therefore they shall now be the first to go
into exile,
and the revelry of the loungers shall pass
away.

8 The Lord GOD has sworn by himself
(says the LORD, the God of hosts):
I abhor the pride of Jacob
and hate his strongholds;
and I will deliver up the city and all that is
in it.

9 If ten people remain in one house, they
shall die. 10And if a relative, one who burns the
dead,*e* shall take up the body to bring it out of
the house, and shall say to someone in the innermost parts of the house, "Is anyone else
with you?" the answer will come, "No." Then
the relative*f* shall say, "Hush! We must not
mention the name of the LORD."

11 See, the LORD commands,
and the great house shall be shattered to
bits,

---

a Heb *your images, your star-god* *b* Or *Are they better* *c* Heb *their* *d* Heb *your* *e* Or *who makes a burning for him* *f* Heb *he*

and the little house to pieces.
12 Do horses run on rocks?
  Does one plow the sea with oxen?^{a}
  But you have turned justice into poison
  and the fruit of righteousness into
    wormwood—
13 you who rejoice in Lo-debar,^{b}
  who say, "Have we not by our own
    strength
  taken Karnaim^c for ourselves?"
14 Indeed, I am raising up against you a nation,
  O house of Israel, says the LORD, the God
    of hosts,
  and they shall oppress you from
    Lebo-hamath
  to the Wadi Arabah.

7 Locusts, Fire, and a Plumb Line

This is what the Lord GOD showed me: he was forming locusts at the time the latter growth began to sprout (it was the latter growth after the king's mowings). ²When they had finished eating the grass of the land, I said,
  "O Lord GOD, forgive, I beg you!
  How can Jacob stand?
  He is so small!"
3 The LORD relented concerning this;
  "It shall not be," said the LORD.

4 This is what the Lord GOD showed me: the Lord GOD was calling for a shower of fire,^{d} and it devoured the great deep and was eating up the land. ⁵Then I said,
  "O Lord GOD, cease, I beg you!
  How can Jacob stand?
  He is so small!"
6 The LORD relented concerning this;
  "This also shall not be," said the Lord
    GOD.

7 This is what he showed me: the Lord was standing beside a wall built with a plumb line, with a plumb line in his hand. ⁸And the LORD said to me, "Amos, what do you see?" And I said, "A plumb line." Then the Lord said,
  "See, I am setting a plumb line
  in the midst of my people Israel;
  I will never again pass them by;
9 the high places of Isaac shall be made
    desolate,
  and the sanctuaries of Israel shall be laid
    waste,
  and I will rise against the house of
    Jeroboam with the sword."

Amaziah Complains to the King

10 Then Amaziah, the priest of Bethel, sent to King Jeroboam of Israel, saying, "Amos has conspired against you in the very center of the house of Israel; the land is not able to bear all his words. ¹¹For thus Amos has said,
  'Jeroboam shall die by the sword,
  and Israel must go into exile
  away from his land.' "

¹²And Amaziah said to Amos, "O seer, go, flee away to the land of Judah, earn your bread there, and prophesy there; ¹³but never again prophesy at Bethel, for it is the king's sanctuary, and it is a temple of the kingdom."

14 Then Amos answered Amaziah, "I am^e no prophet, nor a prophet's son; but I am^e a herdsman, and a dresser of sycamore trees, ¹⁵and the LORD took me from following the flock, and the LORD said to me, 'Go, prophesy to my people Israel.'
16 "Now therefore hear the word of the LORD.
  You say, 'Do not prophesy against Israel,
  and do not preach against the house of
    Isaac.'
17 Therefore thus says the LORD:
  'Your wife shall become a prostitute in the
    city,
  and your sons and your daughters shall
    fall by the sword,
  and your land shall be parceled out by line;
  you yourself shall die in an unclean land,
  and Israel shall surely go into exile away
    from its land.' "

8 The Basket of Fruit

This is what the Lord GOD showed me—a basket of summer fruit.^{f} ²He said, "Amos, what do you see?" And I said, "A basket of summer fruit."^{f} Then the LORD said to me,
  "The end^g has come upon my people Israel;
  I will never again pass them by.
3 The songs of the temple^h shall become
    wailings in that day,"

                  says the Lord GOD;

a Or *Does one plow them with oxen* b Or *in a thing of nothingness* c Or *horns* d Or *for a judgment by fire* e Or *was* f Heb *qayits* g Heb *qets*
h Or *palace*

"the dead bodies shall be many,
    cast out in every place. Be silent!"

4 Hear this, you that trample on the needy,
    and bring to ruin the poor of the land,
5 saying, "When will the new moon be over
    so that we may sell grain;
and the sabbath,
    so that we may offer wheat for sale?
We will make the ephah small and the
    shekel great,
    and practice deceit with false balances,
6 buying the poor for silver
    and the needy for a pair of sandals,
    and selling the sweepings of the wheat."

7 The LORD has sworn by the pride of Jacob:
    Surely I will never forget any of their deeds.
8 Shall not the land tremble on this account,
    and everyone mourn who lives in it,
and all of it rise like the Nile,
    and be tossed about and sink again, like
        the Nile of Egypt?

9 On that day, says the Lord GOD,
    I will make the sun go down at noon,
    and darken the earth in broad daylight.
10 I will turn your feasts into mourning,
    and all your songs into lamentation;
I will bring sackcloth on all loins,
    and baldness on every head;
I will make it like the mourning for an only
    son,
    and the end of it like a bitter day.

11 The time is surely coming, says the Lord
        GOD,
    when I will send a famine on the land;
not a famine of bread, or a thirst for water,
    but of hearing the words of the LORD.
12 They shall wander from sea to sea,
    and from north to east;
they shall run to and fro, seeking the word
        of the LORD,
    but they shall not find it.
13 In that day the beautiful young women and
        the young men
    shall faint for thirst.
14 Those who swear by Ashimah of Samaria,
    and say, "As your god lives, O Dan,"
and, "As the way of Beer-sheba lives"—
    they shall fall, and never rise again.

9 The Destruction of Israel

I saw the LORD standing beside*a* the altar, and
he said:
    Strike the capitals until the thresholds
        shake,

and shatter them on the heads of all the
    people;*b*
and those who are left I will kill with the
    sword;
    not one of them shall flee away,
    not one of them shall escape.

2 Though they dig into Sheol,
    from there shall my hand take them;
though they climb up to heaven,
    from there I will bring them down.
3 Though they hide themselves on the top of
        Carmel,
    from there I will search out and take
        them;
and though they hide from my sight at the
        bottom of the sea,
    there I will command the sea-serpent,
    and it shall bite them.
4 And though they go into captivity in front
        of their enemies,
    there I will command the sword, and it
        shall kill them;
and I will fix my eyes on them
    for harm and not for good.

5 The Lord, GOD of hosts,
he who touches the earth and it melts,
    and all who live in it mourn,
and all of it rises like the Nile,
    and sinks again, like the Nile of Egypt;
6 who builds his upper chambers in the
        heavens,
    and founds his vault upon the earth;
who calls for the waters of the sea,
    and pours them out upon the surface of
        the earth—
the LORD is his name.

7 Are you not like the Ethiopians*c* to me,
    O people of Israel? says the LORD.
Did I not bring Israel up from the land of
        Egypt,
    and the Philistines from Caphtor and the
        Arameans from Kir?
8 The eyes of the Lord GOD are upon the
        sinful kingdom,
    and I will destroy it from the face of the
        earth
    —except that I will not utterly destroy
        the house of Jacob,
                        says the LORD.

9 For lo, I will command,
    and shake the house of Israel among all
        the nations
as one shakes with a sieve,
    but no pebble shall fall to the ground.

a Or on b Heb all of them c Or Nubians; Heb Cushites

Have you ever received a special card or letter from a friend or relative that you've saved? Handwritten letters have a way of encouraging, inspiring, and connecting us in ways that a quick e-mail or text can never match. Through the power of one letter, Sr. Helen Prejean embarked in a powerful ministry with death-row inmates. This ministry began for her in 1981 while she was working in a housing project in New Orleans.

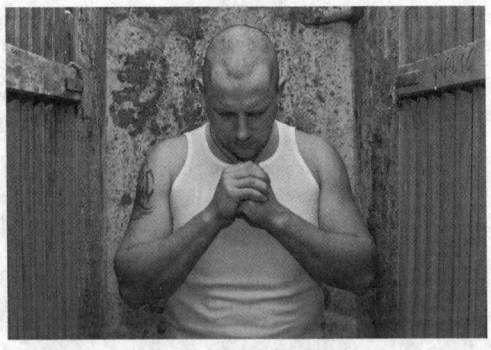

During that time she began writing letters to Patrick Sonnier, the convicted killer of two teenagers, who had been sentenced to execution by electric chair. At his request, she began to visit him and serve as his spiritual director. It was her experience with Patrick and her disgust with the American execution process that prompted her to write her famous book *Dead Man Walking*, which later became an award-winning film.

Both of these works affected thousands of people, sensitizing them to the issue of capital punishment in the United States. In 1999, she formed Moratorium 2000, a petition that collected 2.5 million signatures calling for a worldwide moratorium on the death penalty and was presented to the U.N. Secretary-General. Today, she continues to serve death-row inmates, reach out to murder victims, educate the public about the death penalty, and advocate against its practice. And it all started with one letter.

---

¹⁰ All the sinners of my people shall die by the
  sword,
  who say, "Evil shall not overtake or
   meet us."

The Restoration of David's Kingdom

¹¹ On that day I will raise up
  the booth of David that is fallen,
 and repair its^a breaches,
  and raise up its^b ruins,
  and rebuild it as in the days of old;
¹² in order that they may possess the remnant
  of Edom
  and all the nations who are called by my
   name,
  says the LORD who does this.

¹³ The time is surely coming, says the LORD,

when the one who plows shall overtake
  the one who reaps,
 and the treader of grapes the one who
  sows the seed;
the mountains shall drip sweet wine,
 and all the hills shall flow with it.
¹⁴ I will restore the fortunes of my people
  Israel,
 and they shall rebuild the ruined cities
  and inhabit them;
they shall plant vineyards and drink their
  wine,
 and they shall make gardens and eat their
  fruit.
¹⁵ I will plant them upon their land,
 and they shall never again be plucked up
  out of the land that I have given them,
   says the LORD your God.

a Gk: Heb *their*   *b* Gk: Heb *his*

OBADIAH

PRIDE...AND THEN THE FALL

The Worst Sin of All?

Pride. It's that burning sensation in the back of your mind that doesn't want you to ask that question in math class, because you're afraid you'll look stupid. It's that lump in your throat that won't allow you to talk to that less-than-popular kid in the hall. It's that persistent idea that you can do things on your own—you don't need anyone's help, even God's.

Pride. It's something God has no part in.

Pride can be a horrible sin, and it's what led to the nation of Edom's downfall. The Edomites had built a perfect fortress in the mountains and felt protected from all their enemies and invaders. But when their neighbor Israel was attacked, in their pride they only laughed. The people of Edom only cared about their own safety, not the safety of others. Because of this, God sent judgment on Edom.

The problem with pride is that it makes us think we're better than we really are. And that's why the Edomites fell. Their pride had grown so bad that they didn't give a rip about Israel in their time of need.

So what about pride in our lives? Do we make ourselves out to be more than we are? Do we boast in our gifts and abilities, or do we look for ways to help others with our gifts? Do we try to live by relying on our own strengths and talents, or are we constantly aware of the truth that we *need* God? The Apostle Paul reminded us that our model is Jesus Christ. We are to be like Christ—humbly offering ourselves, even to the point of death (Philippians 2.2–11).

"A man who governs his passions is master of the world. We must either command them, or be enslaved by them. It is better to be a hammer than an anvil."

—St. Dominic

WHO The prophet Obadiah, but very little is known of him

WHAT When the people of Judah had been taken captive by the Babylonians, the Edomites looted Judah. This is a vision given to the prophet Obadiah foretelling God's judgment against the nation of Edom.

WHEN Scholars are not certain when Obadiah was written, though some believe it was written around the fall of Jerusalem, ca. 586 B.C.

WHERE Obadiah prophesies against Edom, the nation neighboring Judah. Edom was located on the southeastern edge of the Dead Sea. Today that region is in the country of Jordan.

PATH OF DISCIPLESHIP

There's no room for arrogance or false pride in the life of a disciple. If anyone had cause to be prideful, it was Jesus Christ. He is, after all, the Son of God. But Jesus' actions tell a different story. In John's gospel (John 13.1–17), Jesus taught his disciples with a shocking demonstration of how they were to treat one another—he washed their feet. He got down on his hands and knees and scrubbed dirty, stinky feet. He then instructed all who followed him to do the same. This is our calling, and it starts and ends with humility and service.

REALITY ✔

A HISTORY OF HATE

A central theme of this book is God's judgment against Edom, one of Israel's neighbors. Read **Obadiah 17–18**. The hateful relationship between Edom and Israel was longstanding and complex. It had its roots in the enmity between Esau and Jacob (see Genesis 33–35). The Edomites were descendants of Esau, and the Israelites descendants of Jacob. The Edomites refused to let Israel pass through their land on their way to the Promised Land (see Numbers 20.14–21).

Herod the Great, a descendant of the Edomites, continued to foster this resentment and animosity, which we read about in the Gospels (see Matthew 2.1–16). Obadiah, a son of Judah, had great trust in God that a better day was coming. The Edomites would be crushed.

The *Catechism of the Catholic Church* tells us that forgiving others is a necessary part of loving God and receiving God's grace (see 2840). Think about the story in this book and how long the effects of anger and resentment can last. Then reflect on these questions:

- What do you do when animosity or hate toward others wells up in you?
- What can you learn about hate and reconciliation for yourself from this book and the story behind it?

Proud Edom Will Be Brought Low

1 The vision of Obadiah.

Thus says the Lord GOD concerning Edom:
We have heard a report from the LORD,
and a messenger has been sent among
the nations:
"Rise up! Let us rise against it for battle!"
2 I will surely make you least among the
nations;
you shall be utterly despised.
3 Your proud heart has deceived you,
you that live in the clefts of the rock,[a]
whose dwelling is in the heights.
You say in your heart,
"Who will bring me down to the ground?"
4 Though you soar aloft like the eagle,
though your nest is set among the stars,
from there I will bring you down,
says the LORD.

Pillage and Slaughter Will Repay Edom's Cruelty

5 If thieves came to you,
if plunderers by night
—how you have been destroyed!—
would they not steal only what they
wanted?
If grape-gatherers came to you,
would they not leave gleanings?
6 How Esau has been pillaged,
his treasures searched out!
7 All your allies have deceived you,
they have driven you to the border;
your confederates have prevailed against
you;
those who ate[b] your bread have set a trap
for you—
there is no understanding of it.
8 On that day, says the LORD,
I will destroy the wise out of Edom,
and understanding out of Mount Esau.
9 Your warriors shall be shattered, O Teman,
so that everyone from Mount Esau will be
cut off.

Edom Mistreated His Brother

10 For the slaughter and violence done to your
brother Jacob,
shame shall cover you,
and you shall be cut off forever.
11 On the day that you stood aside,
on the day that strangers carried off his
wealth,
and foreigners entered his gates
and cast lots for Jerusalem,
you too were like one of them.
12 But you should not have gloated[c] over[d] your
brother
on the day of his misfortune;
you should not have rejoiced over the
people of Judah
on the day of their ruin;
you should not have boasted
on the day of distress.
13 You should not have entered the gate of my
people
on the day of their calamity;

---

a Or *clefts of Sela* b Cn: Heb lacks *those who ate* c Heb *But do not gloat* (and similarly through verse 14) d Heb *on the day of*

OBADIAH

From a Small Farm to the Whole World

Albert Simpson had a problem. He had his heart set on going to college, but his family only had enough money to send his older brother. The family's plan was for Albert to stay behind and tend the farm on the western Ontario frontier in Canada, a bitter final destiny for a fourteen-year-old with big dreams. He just couldn't see himself on the same plot of land for the rest of his life; Albert wanted to see the world.

But Albert had an idea that he thought might work. When his family had a discussion, Albert laid out his plan. He would teach school and make enough to put himself through college in Toronto. Since he wasn't interested in being a farmer, the responsibilities of the family farm could pass instead to another of his younger siblings. As he shared his ideas, Albert was afraid. Though his father was a kind man, he was also very stern and not used to being contradicted. Still, as young Albert finished laying out his plan, his heart beating anxiously in his chest, he was surprised to hear from his father, "God bless you, my boy." Albert was overjoyed and began at once to put his plan into action.

Albert soon went on to get an education in theology and pastoral ministry. While he was in rapidly growing Toronto, he became aware of

Chicago 2—© Rachel Hostert, 18

the enormous task of bringing the truth about Jesus to the world. He passionately wanted to see the news of Jesus' love spread far and wide. Albert pastored churches in Ontario and Kentucky, but then made a strategic move to New York City, so that he could minister close to the shipping lines that crisscrossed the world. In New York in 1882, this small-town farm boy's huge vision became a reality when Albert began a mission organization called the Christian Missionary Alliance, which today has over two million members in more than fifty countries around the world.

---

you should not have joined in the gloating
  over Judah's[a] disaster
 on the day of his calamity;
you should not have looted his goods
 on the day of his calamity.
¹⁴ You should not have stood at the crossings
  to cut off his fugitives;
you should not have handed over his
  survivors
 on the day of distress.

¹⁵ For the day of the LORD is near against all
  the nations.
As you have done, it shall be done to you;
 your deeds shall return on your own
  head.
¹⁶ For as you have drunk on my holy
  mountain,
 all the nations around you shall drink;
they shall drink and gulp down,[b]

and shall be as though they had never
  been.

Israel's Final Triumph
¹⁷ But on Mount Zion there shall be those that
  escape,
 and it shall be holy;
and the house of Jacob shall take
  possession of those who
  dispossessed them.
¹⁸ The house of Jacob shall be a fire,
 the house of Joseph a flame,
 and the house of Esau stubble;
they shall burn them and consume them,
 and there shall be no survivor of the
  house of Esau;
   for the LORD has spoken.
¹⁹ Those of the Negeb shall possess Mount
  Esau,

a Heb *his* b Meaning of Heb uncertain

and those of the Shephelah the land of
the Philistines;
they shall possess the land of Ephraim and
the land of Samaria,
and Benjamin shall possess Gilead.
20 The exiles of the Israelites who are in Halah[a]
shall possess[b] Phoenicia as far as
Zarephath;
and the exiles of Jerusalem who are in
Sepharad
shall possess the towns of the
Negeb.
21 Those who have been saved[c] shall go up to
Mount Zion
to rule Mount Esau;
and the kingdom shall be the LORD's.

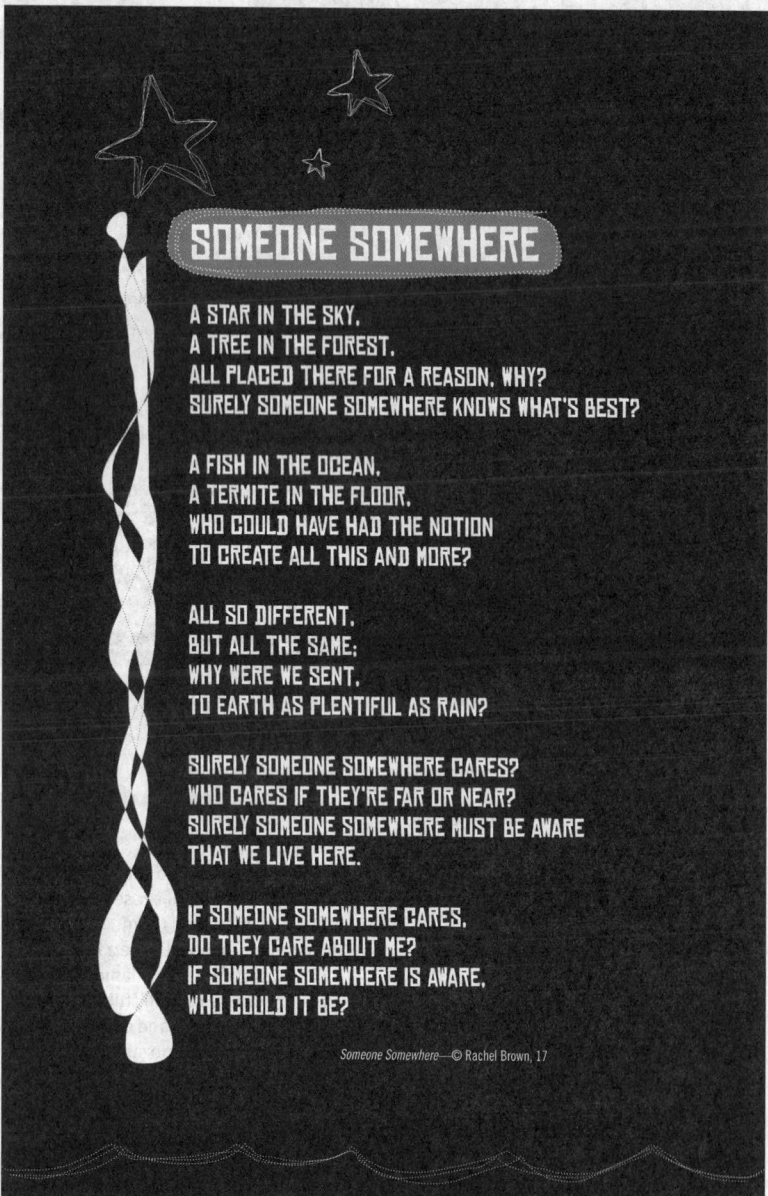

SOMEONE SOMEWHERE

A STAR IN THE SKY,
A TREE IN THE FOREST,
ALL PLACED THERE FOR A REASON, WHY?
SURELY SOMEONE SOMEWHERE KNOWS WHAT'S BEST?

A FISH IN THE OCEAN,
A TERMITE IN THE FLOOR,
WHO COULD HAVE HAD THE NOTION
TO CREATE ALL THIS AND MORE?

ALL SO DIFFERENT,
BUT ALL THE SAME;
WHY WERE WE SENT,
TO EARTH AS PLENTIFUL AS RAIN?

SURELY SOMEONE SOMEWHERE CARES?
WHO CARES IF THEY'RE FAR OR NEAR?
SURELY SOMEONE SOMEWHERE MUST BE AWARE
THAT WE LIVE HERE.

IF SOMEONE SOMEWHERE CARES,
DO THEY CARE ABOUT ME?
IF SOMEONE SOMEWHERE IS AWARE,
WHO COULD IT BE?

Someone Somewhere—© Rachel Brown, 17

JONAH

TICKED-OFF BITTERNESS VS. GOD-SIZE GRACE

Jonah: Hero or Loser?

At first Jonah looks like a certifiable hero—he's practically wearing a red cape and tights. After running from God and living in a fish's gut for three days, he changes his mind and takes God's message of repentance to the Ninevites. Success! He's a prophetic superstar. The entire city repents and turns to God.

But that's not the end of the story. It turns out that Jonah is so hateful toward the Ninevites that he's ticked off at God for forgiving them! The book of Jonah ends by painting a picture of Jonah the loser and God the *true* hero. Jonah can't get out of his tiny, limited human perspective and see the big picture of God's love. He wants to feel the satisfaction of holding tight to old hatreds and prejudices. He'd rather see his enemies demolished than forgiven.

What about us? The book of Jonah is like a big mirror right in front of our face. If we're honest, we all see a bit of ourselves in Jonah's small-minded bitterness. Do we relish the thought of our enemies suffering? Would we rather hold on to self-righteous anger than forgive? Or do we celebrate God's mercy, even when he lavishes it on those who've hurt us, on those who are difficult to forgive?

"Whoever entertains in his heart any trace of hatred for anyone, regardless of what the offense may have been, is a stranger to the love of God."

—St. Maximus the Confessor

WHO The author of Jonah isn't known for certain, though it's possible Jonah wrote it himself.

WHAT An account of the prophet Jonah's encounter with the people of Nineveh

WHEN Written sometime between 800 and 600 B.C.

WHERE Begins in Israel and ends in Nineveh, a large city in the Assyrian Empire (now northern Iraq)

PATH OF DISCIPLESHIP

Have you ever struggled to get along with others at your school who have something against your friends? You know, the ones who compete with them or bully or tease them or whatever. Your feelings about them might be like Jonah's for the Ninevites. They were the enemies of God and God's people, the Jews. They were so wicked and did such atrocious things that God was ready to totally destroy them. Yet when God (through Jonah) called them to repent and change their ways, they *did*! But Jonah couldn't forgive them—he couldn't get over his own hatred and disgust.

But God could. And that is the model for a disciple—a forgiver.

But that's a tough act to follow. When you think about how many people hold on to hurts and resentments instead of letting go and forgiving, Jonah's behavior isn't surprising. True disciples cultivate an attitude of forgiveness by practicing it daily. Practice may not make perfect, but it makes permanent. That's the goal: to be a permanent forgiver in the image of God, who made you.

A Great Escape

Trying to run away from God is a fruitless venture. He may let you off the hook for a short while, but in the end his purposes will be realized. You can choose to live outside his best for you, or you can participate with him in the big picture he has designed for your life, your circle of friends, your community, and the world. When we try to run away from God, we miss out on the joy of obedience.

The prophet Jonah is quite a complex (and sometimes humorous) character, as we watch his attempt to do the exact opposite of what God asked him to do: go to Nineveh. We're a lot like Jonah—complex and sometimes humorous in how we respond to God. It's such a short book, so go ahead and read **Jonah 1–4**. You might see yourself in Jonah's story.

Jonah prayed to God in the great fish and repented of his wily ways. In creative response to this action-filled and insightful story, write a song to God about your desire to turn back to him and obey him in an area of your life in which you're running away from him. If you're not skilled musically or lyrically, feel free to write a prayer or poem with the same idea. Post your song, poem, or prayer on **Learner.CalltoDiscipleship.com**.

1 Jonah Tries to Run Away from God

Now the word of the LORD came to Jonah son of Amittai, saying, ²"Go at once to Nineveh, that great city, and cry out against it; for their wickedness has come up before me." ³But Jonah set out to flee to Tarshish from the presence of the LORD. He went down to Joppa and found a ship going to Tarshish; so he paid his fare and went on board, to go with them to Tarshish, away from the presence of the LORD.

4 But the LORD hurled a great wind upon the sea, and such a mighty storm came upon the sea that the ship threatened to break up. ⁵Then the mariners were afraid, and each cried to his god. They threw the cargo that was in the ship into the sea, to lighten it for them. Jonah, meanwhile, had gone down into the hold of the ship and had lain down, and was

fast asleep. ⁶The captain came and said to him, "What are you doing sound asleep? Get up, call on your god! Perhaps the god will spare us a thought so that we do not perish."

7 The sailors[a] said to one another, "Come, let us cast lots, so that we may know on whose account this calamity has come upon us." So they cast lots, and the lot fell on Jonah. ⁸Then they said to him, "Tell us why this calamity has come upon us. What is your occupation? Where do you come from? What is your country? And of what people are you?" ⁹"I am a Hebrew," he replied. "I worship the LORD, the God of heaven, who made the sea and the dry land." ¹⁰Then the men were even more afraid, and said to him, "What is this that you have done!" For the men knew that he was fleeing from the presence of the LORD, because he had told them so.

11 Then they said to him, "What shall we do to you, that the sea may quiet down for us?" For the sea was growing more and more tempestuous. ¹²He said to them, "Pick me up and throw me into the sea; then the sea will quiet down for you; for I know it is because of me that this great storm has come upon you." ¹³Nevertheless the men rowed hard to bring the ship back to land, but they could not, for the sea grew more and more stormy against them. ¹⁴Then they cried out to the LORD, "Please, O LORD, we pray, do not let us perish on account of this man's life. Do not make us guilty of innocent blood; for you, O LORD, have done as it pleased you." ¹⁵So they picked Jonah up and threw him into the sea; and the sea ceased from its raging. ¹⁶Then the men feared the LORD even more, and they offered a sacrifice to the LORD and made vows.

17[b] But the LORD provided a large fish to swallow up Jonah; and Jonah was in the belly of the fish three days and three nights.

2 A Psalm of Thanksgiving

Then Jonah prayed to the LORD his God from the belly of the fish, ²saying,

"I called to the LORD out of my distress,
    and he answered me;
out of the belly of Sheol I cried,
    and you heard my voice.
³ You cast me into the deep,
    into the heart of the seas,
      and the flood surrounded me;
all your waves and your billows
    passed over me.
⁴ Then I said, 'I am driven away
    from your sight;
how[c] shall I look again

---

a Heb *They* b Ch 2.1 in Heb c Theodotion: Heb *surely*

upon your holy temple?'

5 The waters closed in over me;
   the deep surrounded me;
weeds were wrapped around my head
6   at the roots of the mountains.
I went down to the land
   whose bars closed upon me forever;
yet you brought up my life from the Pit,
   O LORD my God.
7 As my life was ebbing away,
   I remembered the LORD;
and my prayer came to you,
   into your holy temple.
8 Those who worship vain idols
   forsake their true loyalty.
9 But I with the voice of thanksgiving
   will sacrifice to you;
what I have vowed I will pay.
   Deliverance belongs to the LORD!"

10Then the LORD spoke to the fish, and it spewed Jonah out upon the dry land.

3 Conversion of Nineveh

The word of the LORD came to Jonah a second time, saying, 2"Get up, go to Nineveh, that great city, and proclaim to it the message that I tell you." 3So Jonah set out and went to Nineveh, according to the word of the LORD. Now Nineveh was an exceedingly large city, a three days' walk across. 4Jonah began to go into the city, going a day's walk. And he cried out, "Forty days more, and Nineveh shall be overthrown!" 5And the people of Nineveh believed God; they proclaimed a fast, and everyone, great and small, put on sackcloth.

6 When the news reached the king of Nineveh, he rose from his throne, removed his robe, covered himself with sackcloth, and sat in ashes. 7Then he had a proclamation made in Nineveh: "By the decree of the king and his nobles: No human being or animal, no herd or flock, shall taste anything. They shall not feed, nor shall they drink water. 8Human beings and animals shall be covered with sackcloth, and they shall cry mightily to God. All shall turn from their evil ways and from the violence that is in their hands. 9Who knows? God may relent and change his mind; he may turn from his fierce anger, so that we do not perish."

10 When God saw what they did, how they turned from their evil ways, God changed his mind about the calamity that he had said he would bring upon them; and he did not do it.

4 Jonah's Anger

But this was very displeasing to Jonah, and he became angry. 2He prayed to the LORD and said, "O LORD! Is not this what I said while I was still in my own country? That is why I fled to

TRY THIS ◄

THE HEART OF OUR CREATOR

Sometimes it's all too easy for us to become prejudiced. *That kid in my history class is so annoying. Why doesn't he know when to shut up? That girl in study hall is so mean. Why does she always have to put people down? They would never come to Mass—they're too far gone. I'm not even sure if I would want them to come. Why would God even give them a chance after all that they've done?* There are times when our hearts are less than compassionate. We become judges with impure motives. So consider this question honestly: What would be your reaction if God specifically led you to share his love with the one person who annoys you the most at your school?

Read **Jonah 3.10—4.4**. Jonah apparently couldn't get very excited about the fact that God had shown mercy on the people of Nineveh. From Jonah's self-righteous perspective, these people deserved to be destroyed for all of their wickedness! Jonah's heart was filled with hate and spite, the opposite of the compassion that filled the heart of God. Ezekiel 18.23 says, "Have I any pleasure in the death of the wicked, says the Lord GOD, and not rather that they should turn from their ways and live?" Of course God prefers that we reject sin and death and instead choose eternal life.

The news from our heavenly Father is this. You *are* called to share his love with the people who annoy you. How will you make it happen today or tomorrow when you wake up? Think of three people you know who are challenging for you to reach out to. Take three days over the next three weeks to pray for them, and then look for opportunities to share God's love with them.

GOD IS RELENTLESS MY SCHOOL

"Man can certainly flee from God... but he cannot escape him. He can certainly hate God and be hateful to God, but he cannot change into its opposite the eternal love of God which triumphs even in his hate."

—Karl Barth,
Swiss theologian

REALITY

FORGIVE WHO?

In four little chapters, intended almost as a spoof of Jonah himself, we hear a very serious question: Can we actually handle God's mercy?

Humor and pouting are the strong threads in this folk story. It begins right away. God orders the prophet to go preach repentance in Nineveh, the capital of Assyria, an empire known for its cruelty and abuse of its conquests. Instead, the prophet immediately jumps aboard a ship and heads in the opposite direction. Throughout the story, even after his success in Nineveh, Jonah remains a reluctant and angry prophet.

It's easier to want mercy for ourselves than justice for our enemies. It's easier to pray for those we love and respect than for those we just can't stand, even when they may be in greater need.

Think about the times in your life when you have rejected God's mercy and forgiveness—either for yourself or for others. Have you held a grudge or given someone the silent treatment, or have you kept beating yourself up about something you wish you had done differently? Find some Creative Space in this Bible and write about it.

Tarshish at the beginning; for I knew that you are a gracious God and merciful, slow to anger, and abounding in steadfast love, and ready to relent from punishing. ³And now, O Lord, please take my life from me, for it is better for me to die than to live." ⁴And the Lord said, "Is it right for you to be angry?" ⁵Then Jonah went out of the city and sat down east of the city, and made a booth for himself there. He sat under it in the shade, waiting to see what would become of the city.

6 The Lord God appointed a bush,ᵃ and made it come up over Jonah, to give shade over his head, to save him from his discomfort; so Jonah was very happy about the bush. ⁷But when dawn came up the next day, God appointed a worm that attacked the bush, so that it withered. ⁸When the sun rose, God prepared a sultry east wind, and the sun beat down on the head of Jonah so that he was faint and asked that he might die. He said, "It is better for me to die than to live."

Jonah Is Reproved

9 But God said to Jonah, "Is it right for you to be angry about the bush?" And he said, "Yes, angry enough to die." ¹⁰Then the Lord said, "You are concerned about the bush, for which you did not labor and which you did not grow; it came into being in a night and perished in a night. ¹¹And should I not be concerned about Nineveh, that great city, in which there are more than a hundred and twenty thousand persons who do not know their right hand from their left, and also many animals?"

a Heb qiqayon, possibly the castor bean plant

CREATIVE SPACE

MICAH

CARROTS AND STICKS

Jewels of Hope

Imagine you've been given what seems like an impossible task. No, you haven't been asked to save the world—you've simply been asked to get a donkey to walk about a half mile up a dirt road. The problem is this donkey is *really* stubborn. No matter how hard you tug or push, that donkey is not going to move unless it is of its own free will. You have to get that donkey to *want* to move. So you're faced with the dilemma farmers and horsemen throughout the centuries have pondered: Do you use a reward like carrots or hay to lure the donkey forward? Or do you use punishment—swats with a stick—to get it moving down the path?

Okay, now consider this. When you're finding it hard to focus on your homework, take out the trash, clean up your room, or obey your parents' rules, which is most likely to motivate you: the promise of a reward or the threat of a punishment? Do you respond better to carrots or to sticks?

Like most of the prophets, Micah has lots of details on both approaches. He describes the judgment Israel and Judah will face if they continue with their current behavior. But in among the descriptions of punishment are amazing jewels of hope. It's like God can't stop himself from describing just how great life could be, if only his people would walk in his ways. God's enthusiasm for a future of peace bubbles over in images of weapons being transformed into tools, of people sitting under their own fig trees, of gathering together those who thought they were rejected and left out.

Sometimes the Old Testament seems full of war and judgment. But Micah reminds us of the other side of the story, of the rich, abundant life that God offers. This is what God wants you to experience, and Micah lets you in on the secret of how to get it: do justice, love kindness, and walk humbly with your God.

"May he support us all the day long, till the shades lengthen, and the evening comes, and the busy world is hushed, and the fever of life is over, and our work is done! Then in his mercy may he give us a safe lodging and a holy rest, and peace at last."
—Bl. Cardinal John Henry Newman

WHO The prophet Micah

WHAT Micah focused on social justice and honesty in relationships.

WHEN Written between 750 and 686 B.C., during the reigns of the kings who are mentioned in Micah

WHERE Micah lived in Judah and addressed the people of Jerusalem and Samaria.

PATH OF DISCIPLESHIP

Feeling busy? Do you feel like you're constantly on the run—racing to school, then practice or an after-school job, and, to top it off, you have a bunch of homework to do before you crash? Feeling busy and overwhelmed happens to all of us. But when we're too busy, we forget to pause, reflect, and remember how God desires for us to live.

One of the things reading and reflecting on Scripture offers the disciple is the time and place to "reflect" on the deeper questions and meaning of life. Micah is just one voice in Scripture who gives us time to take seriously the meaning of life. One thing is clear: it's essential for disciples to take time, be quiet, and let the Scriptures speak to our hearts.

1 The word of the LORD that came to Micah of Moresheth in the days of Kings Jotham, Ahaz, and Hezekiah of Judah, which he saw concerning Samaria and Jerusalem.

Judgment Pronounced against Samaria

2 Hear, you peoples, all of you;
    listen, O earth, and all that is in it;
    and let the Lord GOD be a witness against you,
        the Lord from his holy temple.
3 For lo, the LORD is coming out of his place,
    and will come down and tread upon the
        high places of the earth.
4 Then the mountains will melt under him
    and the valleys will burst open,
    like wax near the fire,
        like waters poured down a steep place.
5 All this is for the transgression of Jacob
    and for the sins of the house of Israel.
    What is the transgression of Jacob?
        Is it not Samaria?
    And what is the high place*a* of Judah?
        Is it not Jerusalem?
6 Therefore I will make Samaria a heap in the
        open country,
    a place for planting vineyards.
    I will pour down her stones into the valley,
        and uncover her foundations.
7 All her images shall be beaten to pieces,
    all her wages shall be burned with fire,
    and all her idols I will lay waste;
    for as the wages of a prostitute she gathered
        them,
        and as the wages of a prostitute they shall
            again be used.

The Doom of the Cities of Judah

8 For this I will lament and wail;
    I will go barefoot and naked;
    I will make lamentation like the jackals,
        and mourning like the ostriches.
9 For her wound*b* is incurable.
    It has come to Judah;
    it has reached to the gate of my people,
        to Jerusalem.

10 Tell it not in Gath,
        weep not at all;
    in Beth-leaphrah
        roll yourselves in the dust.
11 Pass on your way,
        inhabitants of Shaphir,
        in nakedness and shame;
    the inhabitants of Zaanan
        do not come forth;
    Beth-ezel is wailing

and shall remove its support from you.
12 For the inhabitants of Maroth
        wait anxiously for good,
    yet disaster has come down from the LORD
        to the gate of Jerusalem.
13 Harness the steeds to the chariots,
        inhabitants of Lachish;
    it was the beginning of sin
        to daughter Zion,
    for in you were found
        the transgressions of Israel.
14 Therefore you shall give parting gifts
        to Moresheth-gath;
    the houses of Achzib shall be a deception
        to the kings of Israel.
15 I will again bring a conqueror upon you,
        inhabitants of Mareshah;
    the glory of Israel
        shall come to Adullam.
16 Make yourselves bald and cut off your hair
        for your pampered children;
    make yourselves as bald as the eagle,
        for they have gone from you into exile.

2 Social Evils Denounced

Alas for those who devise wickedness
        and evil deeds*c* on their beds!
    When the morning dawns, they perform it,
        because it is in their power.
2 They covet fields, and seize them;
        houses, and take them away;
    they oppress householder and house,
        people and their inheritance.
3 Therefore thus says the LORD:
    Now, I am devising against this family an
        evil
    from which you cannot remove your
            necks;
    and you shall not walk haughtily,
        for it will be an evil time.
4 On that day they shall take up a taunt song
        against you,
    and wail with bitter lamentation,
    and say, "We are utterly ruined;
        the LORD*d* alters the inheritance of my
            people;
    how he removes it from me!
        Among our captors*e* he parcels out our
            fields."
5 Therefore you will have no one to cast the
        line by lot
    in the assembly of the LORD.

6 "Do not preach"—thus they preach—
    "one should not preach of such things;
        disgrace will not overtake us."
7 Should this be said, O house of Jacob?
    Is the LORD's patience exhausted?

---

a Heb *what are the high places* *b* Gk Syr Vg: Heb *wounds* *c* Cn: Heb *work evil* *d* Heb *he* *e* Cn: Heb *the rebellious*

Worry

"So don't worry about these things, saying, 'What will we eat? What will we drink? What will we wear?' **These things dominate the thoughts of unbelievers,** but your heavenly Father already knows all your needs. Seek the Kingdom of God above all else, and live righteously, and he will give you **everything you need.** So don't worry about tomorrow, for tomorrow will bring its own worries. Today's troubles are enough for today." **Matthew 6:31-34**

Each day at school **I worry about everything!** I worry about each test, every project, and everything else I face as a senior. These verses teach me to rely on the Lord and He will help me through each day!

God is always here for us. I want you to know that. We don't need to waste our lives away by worrying about the next day. **Take each day one at a time** and focus on the present day. Remember that God always provides us with what we need.

This is my prayer for today:

Dear Lord, I pray for help during the stressful times. Help me while I wait on important decisions and future opportunities. Also, help me deal with the everyday stress of work and school; remind me daily that everything will work out just fine because of You. Amen.

Worry—© Bailey Lyons, 18

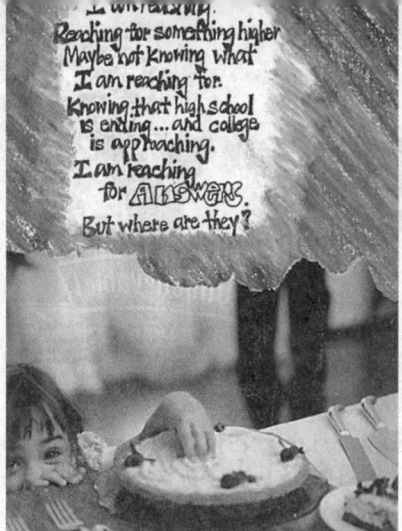

I am reaching...

Reaching for something higher
Maybe not knowing what
I am reaching for.
Knowing that high school
is ending... and college
is approaching.
I am reaching
for ANSWERS.
But where are they?

Are these his doings?
Do not my words do good
   to one who walks uprightly?

8 But you rise up against my people[a] as an
      enemy;
   you strip the robe from the peaceful,[b]
from those who pass by trustingly
   with no thought of war.
9 The women of my people you drive out
   from their pleasant houses;
from their young children you take away
   my glory forever.
10 Arise and go;
   for this is no place to rest,
because of uncleanness that destroys
   with a grievous destruction.[c]
11 If someone were to go about uttering
      empty falsehoods,
   saying, "I will preach to you of wine and
      strong drink,"
   such a one would be the preacher for this
      people!

A Promise for the Remnant of Israel

12 I will surely gather all of you, O Jacob,
   I will gather the survivors of Israel;
I will set them together
   like sheep in a fold,
like a flock in its pasture;
   it will resound with people.
13 The one who breaks out will go up before
      them;
   they will break through and pass the
      gate,
   going out by it.
Their king will pass on before them,
   the LORD at their head.

3 Wicked Rulers and Prophets

And I said:
Listen, you heads of Jacob
   and rulers of the house of Israel!
Should you not know justice?—
2   you who hate the good and love the evil,
who tear the skin off my people,[d]
   and the flesh off their bones;
3 who eat the flesh of my people,
   flay their skin off them,
break their bones in pieces,
   and chop them up like meat[e] in a kettle,
   like flesh in a caldron.

4 Then they will cry to the LORD,
   but he will not answer them;
he will hide his face from them at that time,
   because they have acted wickedly.

5 Thus says the LORD concerning the
      prophets
who lead my people astray,
who cry "Peace"
   when they have something to eat,
but declare war against those
   who put nothing into their mouths.
6 Therefore it shall be night to you, without
      vision,
   and darkness to you, without revelation.
The sun shall go down upon the prophets,
   and the day shall be black over them;
7 the seers shall be disgraced,
   and the diviners put to shame;
they shall all cover their lips,
   for there is no answer from God.
8 But as for me, I am filled with power,
   with the spirit of the LORD,
   and with justice and might,
to declare to Jacob his transgression
   and to Israel his sin.

9 Hear this, you rulers of the house of Jacob
   and chiefs of the house of Israel,
who abhor justice
   and pervert all equity,
10 who build Zion with blood
   and Jerusalem with wrong!
11 Its rulers give judgment for a bribe,
   its priests teach for a price,
   its prophets give oracles for money;
yet they lean upon the LORD and say,
   "Surely the LORD is with us!
   No harm shall come upon us."
12 Therefore because of you
   Zion shall be plowed as a field;
Jerusalem shall become a heap of ruins,
   and the mountain of the house a wooded
      height.

---

a Cn: Heb *But yesterday my people rose* b Cn: Heb *from before a garment* c Meaning of Heb uncertain d Heb *from them* e Gk: Heb *as*

4 Peace and Security through Obedience

In days to come
   the mountain of the LORD's house
shall be established as the highest of the
   mountains,
   and shall be raised up above the hills.
Peoples shall stream to it,
2   and many nations shall come and say:
"Come, let us go up to the mountain of the
   LORD,
   to the house of the God of Jacob;
that he may teach us his ways
   and that we may walk in his paths."
For out of Zion shall go forth instruction,
   and the word of the LORD from
      Jerusalem.
3 He shall judge between many peoples,
   and shall arbitrate between strong
      nations far away;
they shall beat their swords into
   plowshares,
   and their spears into pruning hooks;
nation shall not lift up sword against
   nation,
   neither shall they learn war any more;
4 but they shall all sit under their own vines
   and under their own fig trees,
   and no one shall make them afraid;
   for the mouth of the LORD of hosts has
      spoken.

5 For all the peoples walk,
   each in the name of its god,
but we will walk in the name of the LORD
   our God
   forever and ever.

Restoration Promised after Exile

6 In that day, says the LORD,
   I will assemble the lame
and gather those who have been driven
   away,
   and those whom I have afflicted.
7 The lame I will make the remnant,
   and those who were cast off, a strong
      nation;
and the LORD will reign over them in Mount
   Zion
   now and forevermore.

8 And you, O tower of the flock,
   hill of daughter Zion,
to you it shall come,
   the former dominion shall come,
   the sovereignty of daughter Jerusalem.

9 Now why do you cry aloud?

Is there no king in you?
Has your counselor perished,
   that pangs have seized you like a woman
      in labor?
10 Writhe and groan,ᵃ O daughter Zion,
   like a woman in labor;
for now you shall go forth from the city
   and camp in the open country;
   you shall go to Babylon.
There you shall be rescued,
   there the LORD will redeem you
   from the hands of your enemies.

11 Now many nations
   are assembled against you,
saying, "Let her be profaned,
   and let our eyes gaze upon Zion."
12 But they do not know
   the thoughts of the LORD;
they do not understand his plan,
   that he has gathered them as sheaves to
      the threshing floor.
13 Arise and thresh,
   O daughter Zion,
for I will make your horn iron
   and your hoofs bronze;
you shall beat in pieces many peoples,
   and shallᵇ devote their gain to the LORD,
   their wealth to the Lord of the whole
      earth.

5ᶜ Now you are walled around with a wall;ᵈ
   siege is laid against us;
with a rod they strike the ruler of Israel
   upon the cheek.

The Ruler from Bethlehem

2ᵉ But you, O Bethlehem of Ephrathah,
   who are one of the little clans of Judah,
from you shall come forth for me
   one who is to rule in Israel,
whose origin is from of old,
   from ancient days.
3 Therefore he shall give them up until the
      time
   when she who is in labor has brought
      forth;
then the rest of his kindred shall return
   to the people of Israel.
4 And he shall stand and feed his flock in the
      strength of the LORD,
   in the majesty of the name of the LORD
      his God.
And they shall live secure, for now he shall
      be great
   to the ends of the earth;
5 and he shall be the one of peace.

---

a Meaning of Heb uncertain   *b* Gk Syr Tg: Heb *and I will*   *c* Ch 4.14 in Heb   *d* Cn Compare Gk: Meaning of Heb uncertain   *e* Ch 5.1
in Heb

THE LEAST OF THESE

Contrary to popular opinion at times, God *is* a compassionate, loving, kind, and merciful God! And from the people of ancient Israel to today's followers of Jesus, God calls his children to be the same. Read **Micah 6.8**. Israel was judged harshly for not taking care of aliens, orphans, and widows. Who are the aliens, orphans, and widows in our culture? Immigrants or illegal aliens? Foster children? Single parents or teen moms? Families stuck in a cycle of poverty? Illiterate high-school dropouts? The homeless or those who live in shelters? Victims of domestic abuse? God calls us to live out 6.8 with some strong words: we will be judged by how we've cared for "the least of these." (See Matthew 25.31–46 to read Jesus' words.)

How are you doing in the mercy department? Are you using your interests, passions, and hobbies in a compassionate way? First, memorize **Micah 6.8** and allow it to sink into your soul. Next, ask God how he may want you to be more merciful and serve those around you with your talents. There are countless ways you can show God's compassion in your community, like playing your musical instrument every week in a nursing home or kicking around the soccer ball with a child down the street whose single mom is so exhausted from work that she needs a break.

List three interests or talents you have here:

-
-
-

Then brainstorm and list ways these interests can match up with God's compassion—ways you can use your abilities to minister to others in justice, mercy, and humility. You can use some Creative Space in this Bible to write them down. Share your great ideas at **Learner.CalltoDiscipleship.com**.

GOD IS COMPASSIONATE MY INTERESTS

If the Assyrians come into our land
and tread upon our soil,[a]
we will raise against them seven shepherds
and eight installed as rulers.
6 They shall rule the land of Assyria with the
sword,

and the land of Nimrod with the drawn
sword;[b]
they[c] shall rescue us from the Assyrians
if they come into our land
or tread within our border.

The Future Role of the Remnant

7 Then the remnant of Jacob,
surrounded by many peoples,
shall be like dew from the LORD,
like showers on the grass,
which do not depend upon people
or wait for any mortal.
8 And among the nations the remnant of
Jacob,
surrounded by many peoples,
shall be like a lion among the animals of
the forest,
like a young lion among the flocks of
sheep,
which, when it goes through, treads down
and tears in pieces, with no one to
deliver.
9 Your hand shall be lifted up over your
adversaries,
and all your enemies shall be cut off.

10 In that day, says the LORD,
I will cut off your horses from among you
and will destroy your chariots;
11 and I will cut off the cities of your land
and throw down all your strongholds;
12 and I will cut off sorceries from your hand,
and you shall have no more soothsayers;
13 and I will cut off your images
and your pillars from among you,
and you shall bow down no more
to the work of your hands;
14 and I will uproot your sacred poles[d] from
among you
and destroy your towns.
15 And in anger and wrath I will execute
vengeance
on the nations that did not obey.

6 God Challenges Israel

Hear what the LORD says:
Rise, plead your case before the
mountains,
and let the hills hear your voice.
2 Hear, you mountains, the controversy of
the LORD,
and you enduring foundations of the
earth;
for the LORD has a controversy with his
people,
and he will contend with Israel.

a Gk: Heb *in our palaces* *b* Cn: Heb *in its entrances* *c* Heb *he* *d* Heb *Asherim*

3 "O my people, what have I done to you?
In what have I wearied you? Answer me!
4 For I brought you up from the land of Egypt,
and redeemed you from the house of
slavery;
and I sent before you Moses,
Aaron, and Miriam.
5 O my people, remember now what King
Balak of Moab devised,
what Balaam son of Beor answered him,
and what happened from Shittim to Gilgal,
that you may know the saving acts of the
LORD."

What God Requires

6 "With what shall I come before the LORD,
and bow myself before God on high?
Shall I come before him with burnt
offerings,
with calves a year old?
7 Will the LORD be pleased with thousands of
rams,
with ten thousands of rivers of oil?
Shall I give my firstborn for my
transgression,
the fruit of my body for the sin of my
soul?"
8 He has told you, O mortal, what is good;
and what does the LORD require of you
but to do justice, and to love kindness,
and to walk humbly with your God?

Cheating and Violence to Be Punished

9 The voice of the LORD cries to the city
(it is sound wisdom to fear your name):
Hear, O tribe and assembly of the city!ᵃ
10 Can I forgetᵇ the treasures of wickedness
in the house of the wicked,
and the scant measure that is accursed?
11 Can I tolerate wicked scales
and a bag of dishonest weights?
12 Yourᶜ wealthy are full of violence;
yourᵈ inhabitants speak lies,
with tongues of deceit in their mouths.
13 Therefore I have begunᵉ to strike you down,
making you desolate because of your
sins.
14 You shall eat, but not be satisfied,
and there shall be a gnawing hunger
within you;
you shall put away, but not save,
and what you save, I will hand over to the
sword.
15 You shall sow, but not reap;
you shall tread olives, but not anoint
yourselves with oil;

you shall tread grapes, but not drink
wine.
16 For you have kept the statutes of Omriᶠ
and all the works of the house of Ahab,
and you have followed their counsels.
Therefore I will make you a desolation,
and yourᵍ inhabitants an object of
hissing;
so you shall bear the scorn of my people.

7 The Total Corruption of the People

Woe is me! For I have become like one who,
after the summer fruit has been
gathered,
after the vintage has been gleaned,
finds no cluster to eat;
there is no first-ripe fig for which I
hunger.
2 The faithful have disappeared from the
land,
and there is no one left who is upright;
they all lie in wait for blood,
and they hunt each other with nets.
3 Their hands are skilled to do evil;
the official and the judge ask for a bribe,
and the powerful dictate what they desire;
thus they pervert justice.ʰ
4 The best of them is like a brier,
the most upright of them a thorn hedge.
The day of theirⁱ sentinels, of theirⁱ
punishment, has come;
now their confusion is at hand.
5 Put no trust in a friend,
have no confidence in a loved one;
guard the doors of your mouth
from her who lies in your embrace;
6 for the son treats the father with contempt,
the daughter rises up against her mother,
the daughter-in-law against her
mother-in-law;
your enemies are members of your own
household.
7 But as for me, I will look to the LORD,
I will wait for the God of my salvation;
my God will hear me.

Penitence and Trust in God

8 Do not rejoice over me, O my enemy;
when I fall, I shall rise;
when I sit in darkness,
the LORD will be a light to me.
9 I must bear the indignation of the LORD,
because I have sinned against him,
until he takes my side
and executes judgment for me.
He will bring me out to the light;

---

a Cn Compare Gk: Heb tribe, and who has appointed it yet? b Cn: Meaning of Heb uncertain c Heb Whose d Heb whose e Gk Syr Vg:
Heb have made sick f Gk Syr Vg Tg: Heb the statutes of Omri are kept g Heb its h Cn: Heb they weave it i Heb your

HOPE

What is hope? Hope is the virtue of trust, and a virtue is a habit. Read **Micah 7.8–10**. We become and stay hopeful that God's Kingdom will come when we hold fast to Christ's promises. We practice hope when we rely on the power of the Holy Spirit instead of ourselves or any other human thing. When we practice hope, our hope grows.

There are two sins against hope: despair and presumption. Despair happens when we stop hoping in God's faithfulness to us, his goodness, and his forgiveness. Presumption happens when we think we can save ourselves without God's help or when we think we will be forgiven without being sorry and changing our lives. For more, see the *Catechism of the Catholic Church* 1817, 2090.

CREATIVE SPACE

I shall see his vindication.
¹⁰ Then my enemy will see,
   and shame will cover her who said to me,
   "Where is the LORD your God?"
My eyes will see her downfall;*ᵃ*
   now she will be trodden down
   like the mire of the streets.

A Prophecy of Restoration
¹¹ A day for the building of your walls!
   In that day the boundary shall be far
      extended.
¹² In that day they will come to you
      from Assyria to*ᵇ* Egypt,
   and from Egypt to the River,
      from sea to sea and from mountain to
         mountain.
¹³ But the earth will be desolate
      because of its inhabitants,
   for the fruit of their doings.

¹⁴ Shepherd your people with your staff,
      the flock that belongs to you,
   which lives alone in a forest
      in the midst of a garden land;
   let them feed in Bashan and Gilead
      as in the days of old.
¹⁵ As in the days when you came out of the
         land of Egypt,
      show us*ᶜ* marvelous things.
¹⁶ The nations shall see and be ashamed
      of all their might;
   they shall lay their hands on their mouths;
      their ears shall be deaf;
¹⁷ they shall lick dust like a snake,
      like the crawling things of the earth;
   they shall come trembling out of their
         fortresses;
      they shall turn in dread to the LORD our
         God,
   and they shall stand in fear of you.

God's Compassion and Steadfast Love
¹⁸ Who is a God like you, pardoning iniquity
      and passing over the transgression
      of the remnant of your*ᵈ* possession?
   He does not retain his anger forever,
      because he delights in showing
         clemency.
¹⁹ He will again have compassion upon us;
      he will tread our iniquities under foot.
   You will cast all our*ᵉ* sins
      into the depths of the sea.
²⁰ You will show faithfulness to Jacob
      and unswerving loyalty to Abraham,
   as you have sworn to our ancestors
      from the days of old.

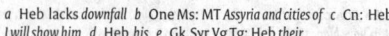

a Heb lacks *downfall* *b* One Ms: MT *Assyria and cities of* *c* Cn: Heb *I will show him* *d* Heb *his* *e* Gk Syr Vg Tg: Heb *their*

NAHUM

AN ODE TO IMMINENT DESTRUCTION

Verbal Harassment

After reading the book of Nahum, it may strike you as unkind, perhaps, or downright mean. Who says things like: "I will burn your chariots" (Nahum 2.13) or "piles of dead, heaps of corpses" (3.3)?

God does.

Why? The Assyrians won a lot of wars. And when they won, they would celebrate their victories in horrific ways. King Ashurbanipal, for instance, would cut off the hands, feet, noses, and ears of his captives and gouge out their eyes. Other times, the victors would make giant piles of their enemies' heads in celebration. It was not a good time. It was a time of judgment, and God's judgment on Nineveh, one of Assyria's chief cities, was severe.

Here's how it happened. About 612 or 606 B.C., nomadic people from northeastern lands made an alliance with the independent governor of Babylon, and they captured and destroyed Nineveh. At the same time, the Tigris River rose and destroyed a huge portion of the city wall, which would have been Nineveh's primary defense.

The book of Nahum reminds us that God judges—and sometimes the verdict is "not guilty." But in the case of Nineveh, it's "guilty as charged," with a penalty of full destruction and death. God sees how we treat others, who are created in his image, how we treat our enemies, and how we treat the competition. God sees, and sometimes he does not like what he sees.

"The religions should not be used as a tragic excuse for enmities which have their origins elsewhere. No one has the right to call upon God to satisfy their own selfish interests."
—Pope John Paul II

WHO A prophet named Nahum wrote this book.

WHAT A prophetic declaration of the forthcoming destruction of Nineveh because of its oppression of the people

WHEN This book was written between 663 and 612 B.C.

WHERE The southern kingdom of Judah; Nineveh was a city in ancient Assyria and would now be in modern-day Iraq.

PATH OF DISCIPLESHIP

The name Nahum means "comfort." How can the news of future destruction bring comfort? Well, sadly, it did—just not to the folks who were destined to be destroyed! People in Judah, who had just suffered the ravages of Assyria, would have found comfort in this message. *Finally,* they may have thought, *those little* (insert insult of your choice) *will get what they deserve!*

It's only human to want revenge. You've probably had a few revenge-filled thoughts in your life as well. But, as disciples, we know not to act on those thoughts. It's unacceptable to talk about one's hopes for violent justice, especially the sort of violence seen in the prophecy of Nahum. When injustice or suffering in this world tears us up, we don't have to take the route of revenge or violence. We can turn to the Holy Spirit, the Comforter, who is with us now— and ask that he guide that energy to work for peaceful and just solutions.

YOUR IMAGE OF GOD

Read **Nahum 1.2–3** and think about how the prophet describes God. God is bigger than we are. There is no way we, with our finite human limitations, can understand or get our minds around the mystery of God.

When you think of God, what images or words come to mind? Depending on where you are in life and what's happening in your life right now, you'll find that you have different ways to imagine and describe God. God may be comforter or healer to you. God may be a quiet breeze or the roar of thunder and lightning. God may be your patron and defender or God may be a relentless teacher.

You might also be making requests from God. If you are going through a difficult time, you might be asking that God be kind and merciful. In some Creative Space in this Bible, divide your life into three-year periods and write your thoughts about the images and requests you have had about God during those years. Then concentrate on your images and wishes about God today. Share your thoughts at **Learner.CalltoDiscipleship.com**.

1 An oracle concerning Nineveh. The book of the vision of Nahum of Elkosh.

The Consuming Wrath of God

2 A jealous and avenging God is the LORD,
   the LORD is avenging and wrathful;
the LORD takes vengeance on his adversaries
   and rages against his enemies.
3 The LORD is slow to anger but great in power,
   and the LORD will by no means clear the guilty.

His way is in whirlwind and storm,
   and the clouds are the dust of his feet.
4 He rebukes the sea and makes it dry,
   and he dries up all the rivers;

Bashan and Carmel wither,
   and the bloom of Lebanon fades.
5 The mountains quake before him,
   and the hills melt;
the earth heaves before him,
   the world and all who live in it.

6 Who can stand before his indignation?
   Who can endure the heat of his anger?
His wrath is poured out like fire,
   and by him the rocks are broken in pieces.
7 The LORD is good,
   a stronghold in a day of trouble;
he protects those who take refuge in him,
8   even in a rushing flood.
He will make a full end of his adversaries,[a]
   and will pursue his enemies into darkness.
9 Why do you plot against the LORD?
   He will make an end;
   no adversary will rise up twice.
10 Like thorns they are entangled,
   like drunkards they are drunk;
   they are consumed like dry straw.
11 From you one has gone out
   who plots evil against the LORD,
   one who counsels wickedness.

Good News for Judah

12 Thus says the LORD,
   "Though they are at full strength and many,[b]
   they will be cut off and pass away.
Though I have afflicted you,
   I will afflict you no more.
13 And now I will break off his yoke from you
   and snap the bonds that bind you."

14 The LORD has commanded concerning you:
   "Your name shall be perpetuated no longer;
from the house of your gods I will cut off
   the carved image and the cast image.
I will make your grave, for you are worthless."

15c Look! On the mountains the feet of one
   who brings good tidings,
   who proclaims peace!
Celebrate your festivals, O Judah,
   fulfill your vows,
for never again shall the wicked invade you;
   they are utterly cut off.

2 The Destruction of the Wicked City

A shatterer[d] has come up against you.
   Guard the ramparts;
   watch the road;

a Gk: Heb *of her place* *b* Meaning of Heb uncertain *c* Ch 2.1 in Heb *d* Cn: Heb *scatterer*

gird your loins;
    collect all your strength.
2 (For the LORD is restoring the majesty of
        Jacob,
    as well as the majesty of Israel,
    though ravagers have ravaged them
        and ruined their branches.)

3 The shields of his warriors are red;
    his soldiers are clothed in crimson.
The metal on the chariots flashes
    on the day when he musters them;
    the chargers*a* prance.
4 The chariots race madly through the streets,
    they rush to and fro through the squares;
their appearance is like torches,
    they dart like lightning.
5 He calls his officers;
    they stumble as they come forward;
they hasten to the wall,
    and the mantelet*b* is set up.
6 The river gates are opened,
    the palace trembles.
7 It is decreed*b* that the city*c* be exiled,
    its slave women led away,
moaning like doves
    and beating their breasts.
8 Nineveh is like a pool
    whose waters*d* run away.
"Halt! Halt!"—
    but no one turns back.
9 "Plunder the silver,
    plunder the gold!
There is no end of treasure!
    An abundance of every precious thing!"

10 Devastation, desolation, and destruction!
    Hearts faint and knees tremble,
all loins quake,
    all faces grow pale!
11 What became of the lions' den,
    the cave*e* of the young lions,
where the lion goes,
    and the lion's cubs, with no one to
        disturb them?
12 The lion has torn enough for his whelps
    and strangled prey for his lionesses;
he has filled his caves with prey
    and his dens with torn flesh.

13 See, I am against you, says the LORD of
hosts, and I will burn your*f* chariots in smoke,
and the sword shall devour your young lions;
I will cut off your prey from the earth, and the
voice of your messengers shall be heard no
more.

3 Ruin Imminent and Inevitable
Ah! City of bloodshed,
    utterly deceitful, full of booty—
    no end to the plunder!
2 The crack of whip and rumble of wheel,
    galloping horse and bounding chariot!
3 Horsemen charging,
    flashing sword and glittering spear,
piles of dead,
    heaps of corpses,
dead bodies without end—
    they stumble over the bodies!
4 Because of the countless debaucheries of
        the prostitute,
    gracefully alluring, mistress of sorcery,
who enslaves*g* nations through her
        debaucheries,
    and peoples through her sorcery,
5 I am against you,
    says the LORD of hosts,
    and will lift up your skirts over your
        face;
and I will let nations look on your
        nakedness
    and kingdoms on your shame.
6 I will throw filth at you
    and treat you with contempt,
    and make you a spectacle.
7 Then all who see you will shrink from you
        and say,
"Nineveh is devastated; who will bemoan
        her?"
    Where shall I seek comforters for you?

8 Are you better than Thebes*h*
    that sat by the Nile,
with water around her,
    her rampart a sea,
    water her wall?
9 Ethiopia*i* was her strength,
    Egypt too, and that without limit;
    Put and the Libyans were her*j* helpers.

> "If there's anyone who can appear
> before Aslan without their knees
> knocking, they're either braver than
> most or else just silly."
> "Then he isn't safe?" said Lucy.
> "Safe?" said Mr. Beaver. . . . "Who
> said anything about safe? 'Course he
> isn't safe. But he's good. He's the King,
> I tell you."
> —C. S. Lewis, *The Lion, the Witch
> and the Wardrobe*

a Cn Compare Gk Syr: Heb *cypresses* b Meaning of Heb
uncertain c Heb *it* d Cn Compare Gk: Heb *a pool, from the days
that she has become, and they* e Cn: Heb *pasture* f Heb *her*
g Heb *sells* h Heb *No-amon* i Or *Nubia*; Heb *Cush* j Gk: Heb *your*

¹⁰ Yet she became an exile,
    she went into captivity;
even her infants were dashed in pieces
    at the head of every street;
lots were cast for her nobles,
    all her dignitaries were bound in fetters.
¹¹ You also will be drunken,
    you will go into hiding;ᵃ
you will seek
    a refuge from the enemy.
¹² All your fortresses are like fig trees
    with first-ripe figs—
if shaken they fall
    into the mouth of the eater.
¹³ Look at your troops:
    they are women in your midst.
The gates of your land
    are wide open to your foes;
    fire has devoured the bars of your gates.

¹⁴ Draw water for the siege,
    strengthen your forts;
trample the clay,
    tread the mortar,
    take hold of the brick mold!
¹⁵ There the fire will devour you,

a Meaning of Heb uncertain

the sword will cut you off.
    It will devour you like the locust.

Multiply yourselves like the locust,
    multiply like the grasshopper!
¹⁶ You increased your merchants
    more than the stars of the heavens.
    The locust sheds its skin and flies away.
¹⁷ Your guards are like grasshoppers,
    your scribes like swarmsᵃ of locusts
settling on the fences
    on a cold day—
when the sun rises, they fly away;
    no one knows where they have gone.

¹⁸ Your shepherds are asleep,
    O king of Assyria;
    your nobles slumber.
Your people are scattered on the mountains
    with no one to gather them.
¹⁹ There is no assuaging your hurt,
    your wound is mortal.
All who hear the news about you
    clap their hands over you.
For who has ever escaped
    your endless cruelty?

HABAKKUK

THIS IS NOT THE END OF THE STORY

Just Around the Corner

Have you ever met those people whose entire lives are defined by something that happened in the past? It's as if whatever took place in the past, whatever pain might have happened there, is now a lens through which they see everything. Their entire identity, the way they look at life, is defined by that moment. It is as if the story stopped right then and there. Perhaps you've met someone like that.

Perhaps that person is you.

And now everything you see is somehow seen through the lens of that moment, those words that were said or what was done to you.

The book of Habakkuk was written in one of those kinds of moments. The kingdom of Judah was about to fall to the invading Babylonian army; the countryside was laid waste, along with the hope of the people of God. Where was God? Why was this happening? Couldn't God see what was going on? In the midst of the destruction and pain, the prophet Habakkuk was given a vision, a glimpse of the bigger picture. This was not the end of the story.

What if that moment in time, the one that enslaves you to pain and doubt, was not the end of the story? What if there could be hope in the midst of the rubble?

The hope Habakkuk saw is the same hope that God offers to each of us. The hope of faith is that this is not all there is; there is something more. This is not the end of the story. Your life is being beautifully written chapter by chapter, and wherever you are today—whatever you are going through— know that hope is just around the corner.

"If you do not hope, you will not find what is beyond your hope."
—St. Clement of Alexandria

WHO The prophet Habakkuk

WHAT Habakkuk expressed faith in God's justice during a terrible time of loss.

WHEN This book was written between 610 and 597 B.C.

WHERE Judah

PATH OF DISCIPLESHIP

Jesus made this fascinating statement once. He said, "I came that they may have life, and have it abundantly" (John 10.10). When Jesus invites us to follow him, he is inviting us into something so much larger than just getting into heaven when we die. Jesus is inviting us into the Kingdom kind of life now—a life that is forgiven and redeemed, restored, and renewed. Jesus came not to give us a religion or a set of beliefs—he came to set us free, not only *from* something, but also *to* something. We've been set free so we can really live in the here and now, not just someday, somewhere else.

Just as Habakkuk clung to hope despite the terrible destruction surrounding him, the hope we find in Jesus is that what we are experiencing in this tiny moment is not the end of the story. Our lives are a grand story with many chapters. Whatever you are going through in life right now, know that the message of Jesus is that *this*—whatever "this" is—is not the end of the story. God has the final word.

1

The oracle that the prophet Habakkuk saw.

The Prophet's Complaint

2 O Lord, how long shall I cry for help,
    and you will not listen?
Or cry to you "Violence!"
    and you will not save?
3 Why do you make me see wrongdoing
    and look at trouble?
Destruction and violence are before me;
    strife and contention arise.
4 So the law becomes slack
    and justice never prevails.
The wicked surround the righteous—
    therefore judgment comes forth
        perverted.

5 Look at the nations, and see!
    Be astonished! Be astounded!
For a work is being done in your days
    that you would not believe if you were
        told.
6 For I am rousing the Chaldeans,
    that fierce and impetuous nation,
who march through the breadth of the earth
    to seize dwellings not their own.
7 Dread and fearsome are they;
    their justice and dignity proceed from
        themselves.
8 Their horses are swifter than leopards,
    more menacing than wolves at dusk;
    their horses charge.
Their horsemen come from far away;
    they fly like an eagle swift to devour.
9 They all come for violence,
    with faces pressing[a] forward;
    they gather captives like sand.
10 At kings they scoff,
    and of rulers they make sport.
They laugh at every fortress,
    and heap up earth to take it.
11 Then they sweep by like the wind;
    they transgress and become guilty;
    their own might is their god!

12 Are you not from of old,
    O Lord my God, my Holy One?
You[b] shall not die.
O Lord, you have marked them for
        judgment;
    and you, O Rock, have established them
        for punishment.
13 Your eyes are too pure to behold evil,
    and you cannot look on wrongdoing;
why do you look on the treacherous,
    and are silent when the wicked swallow
        those more righteous than they?

14 You have made people like the fish of the
        sea,
    like crawling things that have no ruler.
15 The enemy[c] brings all of them up with a
        hook;
    he drags them out with his net,
he gathers them in his seine;
    so he rejoices and exults.
16 Therefore he sacrifices to his net
    and makes offerings to his seine;
for by them his portion is lavish,
    and his food is rich.
17 Is he then to keep on emptying his net,
    and destroying nations without mercy?

2

God's Reply to the Prophet's Complaint

I will stand at my watchpost,
    and station myself on the rampart;
I will keep watch to see what he will say to me,
    and what he[d] will answer concerning my
        complaint.
2 Then the Lord answered me and said:
Write the vision;
    make it plain on tablets,
    so that a runner may read it.
3 For there is still a vision for the appointed
        time;
    it speaks of the end, and does not lie.
If it seems to tarry, wait for it;
    it will surely come, it will not delay.
4 Look at the proud!
    Their spirit is not right in them,
    but the righteous live by their faith.[e]
5 Moreover, wealth[f] is treacherous;
    the arrogant do not endure.
They open their throats wide as Sheol;
    like Death they never have enough.
They gather all nations for themselves,
    and collect all peoples as their own.

The Woes of the Wicked

6 Shall not everyone taunt such people and,
with mocking riddles, say about them,
    "Alas for you who heap up what is not your
        own!"
        How long will you load yourselves with
            goods taken in pledge?
7 Will not your own creditors suddenly rise,
    and those who make you tremble
        wake up?
    Then you will be booty for them.
8 Because you have plundered many nations,
    all that survive of the peoples shall
        plunder you—
because of human bloodshed, and violence
        to the earth,
    to cities and all who live in them.

---

a Meaning of Heb uncertain b Ancient Heb tradition: MT We c Heb He d Syr: Heb I e Or faithfulness f Other Heb Mss read wine

9 "Alas for you who get evil gain for your house,
     setting your nest on high
     to be safe from the reach of harm!"
10 You have devised shame for your house
     by cutting off many peoples;
     you have forfeited your life.
11 The very stones will cry out from the wall,
     and the plaster[a] will respond from the
          woodwork.

12 "Alas for you who build a town by bloodshed,
     and found a city on iniquity!"
13 Is it not from the LORD of hosts
     that peoples labor only to feed the flames,
     and nations weary themselves for nothing?
14 But the earth will be filled
     with the knowledge of the glory of the
          LORD,
     as the waters cover the sea.

15 "Alas for you who make your neighbors drink,
     pouring out your wrath[b] until they are
          drunk,
     in order to gaze on their nakedness!"
16 You will be sated with contempt instead of
          glory.
     Drink, you yourself, and stagger![c]
     The cup in the LORD's right hand
     will come around to you,
     and shame will come upon your glory!
17 For the violence done to Lebanon will
          overwhelm you;
     the destruction of the animals will terrify
          you—[d]
     because of human bloodshed and violence
          to the earth,
     to cities and all who live in them.

18 What use is an idol
     once its maker has shaped it—
     a cast image, a teacher of lies?
     For its maker trusts in what has been made,
     though the product is only an idol that
          cannot speak!
19 Alas for you who say to the wood, "Wake up!"
     to silent stone, "Rouse yourself!"
     Can it teach?
     See, it is gold and silver plated,
     and there is no breath in it at all.

20 But the LORD is in his holy temple;
     let all the earth keep silence before him!

3 A prayer of the prophet Habakkuk according to Shigionoth.

The Prophet's Prayer

2 O LORD, I have heard of your renown,
     and I stand in awe, O LORD, of your work.
     In our own time revive it;

Ego

I'm not a cat person. I know, because we
have a cat.

Cats live twenty years, maybe. Lucky me.

More than anything, cats like to race you
wherever you are going, bobbing between
your legs and tripping you up. They make
simple things like opening the refrigerator or
answering the phone riddled with complexity.

The cat completely misunderstands the
master-pet relationship. Since I feed, water,
and clean disgusting things out of her litter
box, she supposes I'm subservient. She
doesn't get that I'm her provider.

Isn't it uncanny how people resemble their
pets?

Forgive me, God, when I get in your way,
trip up the plans you have for me, and
(*shudder*) make you my personal servant.
This life is *so* about you. **Habakkuk 3.19**
makes things clear—you are the provider,
the giver of even those things that feel so
intrinsically *mine*.

Let's make this easy. Put me in my place.
Use me up for your purposes. Wherever.
Whenever. However. You have given me all
things—health, strength, abilities. But I've
exploited them to serve myself. Here—they
are yours.

Now, what are we going to do about this
ego? Write:

     in our own time make it known;
     in wrath may you remember mercy.
3 God came from Teman,
     the Holy One from Mount Paran.   *Selah*
His glory covered the heavens,
     and the earth was full of his praise.

a Or beam b Or poison c Q Ms Gk: MT *be uncircumcised* d Gk Syr: Meaning of Heb uncertain

REALITY ✓

THE WAITING GAME

Habakkuk opens boldly with the haunting plea: "O LORD, how long shall I cry for help, and you will not listen?" (1.2).

It's the kind of plea that most people will make at some time in their lives. Habakkuk isn't afraid to question God regarding the invasion of Babylonian armies, violence, and injustice. Habakkuk asks the timeless question: "If God is a God of justice, then why is the world so peppered with injustice?" For some of us the persistence of injustice raises the question of God's justice. Is that fair?

Unlike us, Habakkuk didn't know Jesus. He didn't know that Jesus would tell his followers that unjust action toward even the lowliest of society was unacceptable (see Matthew 25.34–40). He hadn't heard over and over again that he was part of the Body of Christ or that the coming of the Kingdom meant his involvement.

The question for today is not, "How does one maintain a belief in God's just rule of the world in spite of an unjust world?" But that's the question driving Habakkuk's world and the questions in this book. He wants answers from God. Think about the difference for us today—God wants answers from *us*. List the ways you participate in building a just world and how you avoid adding to evil in your own world. Could God be asking you, "O (*your name here*), how long shall I cry for help, and you will not listen?"

4 The brightness was like the sun;
    rays came forth from his hand,
        where his power lay hidden.
5 Before him went pestilence,
    and plague followed close behind.
6 He stopped and shook the earth;
    he looked and made the nations tremble.
The eternal mountains were shattered;

along his ancient pathways
    the everlasting hills sank low.
7 I saw the tents of Cushan under affliction;
    the tent-curtains of the land of Midian
        trembled.
8 Was your wrath against the rivers,[a] O LORD?
    Or your anger against the rivers,[a]
    or your rage against the sea,[b]
when you drove your horses,
    your chariots to victory?
9 You brandished your naked bow,
    sated[c] were the arrows at your
        command.[d]   *Selah*
You split the earth with rivers.
10 The mountains saw you, and writhed;
    a torrent of water swept by;
the deep gave forth its voice.
    The sun[e] raised high its hands;
11 the moon[f] stood still in its exalted place,
    at the light of your arrows speeding by,
    at the gleam of your flashing spear.
12 In fury you trod the earth,
    in anger you trampled nations.
13 You came forth to save your people,
    to save your anointed.
You crushed the head of the wicked house,
    laying it bare from foundation to roof.[d]
                                                        Selah
14 You pierced with their[g] own arrows the
        head[h] of his warriors,[i]
    who came like a whirlwind to scatter us,[j]
    gloating as if ready to devour the poor
        who were in hiding.
15 You trampled the sea with your horses,
    churning the mighty waters.

16 I hear, and I tremble within;
    my lips quiver at the sound.
Rottenness enters into my bones,
    and my steps tremble[k] beneath me.
I wait quietly for the day of calamity
    to come upon the people who attack us.

Trust and Joy in the Midst of Trouble
17 Though the fig tree does not blossom,
    and no fruit is on the vines;
though the produce of the olive fails,
    and the fields yield no food;
though the flock is cut off from the fold,
    and there is no herd in the stalls,
18 yet I will rejoice in the LORD;
    I will exult in the God of my salvation.
19 GOD, the Lord, is my strength;
    he makes my feet like the feet of a deer,
    and makes me tread upon the heights.[l]

To the leader: with stringed[m] instruments.

a Or *against River* b Or *against Sea* c Cn: Heb *oaths* d Meaning of Heb uncertain e Heb *It* f Heb *sun, moon* g Heb *his* h Or *leader*
i Vg Compare Gk Syr: Meaning of Heb uncertain j Heb *me* k Cn Compare Gk: Meaning of Heb uncertain l Heb *my heights*
m Heb *my stringed*

ZEPHANIAH

A LIGHT AT THE END OF THE TUNNEL

"I've Got Some Good News . . . and I've Got Some Bad News"

"First, the bad news. Since you and your ancestors have been particularly sinful the last few decades, God's decided that your country is going to be destroyed. Crushed. Reduced to heaps of rubble. Swept away. And not just you, but all your neighbors too. Sorry about that.

"But, hey, I've got some good news too! After all this doom and mayhem is over, God's going to come live with you! There are gonna be happy days again, and you won't have anything to be afraid of anymore. It'll be good times. Good times."

Prophets weren't always the most popular guys back in the biblical days. As God's spokespeople, they had pretty tough jobs. They had to deliver a lot of *very* bad news. "Sorry, but you're all pretty much going to die."

Zephaniah lived during the aftermath of Israel's worst years ever. His king, Josiah, had to pick up the pieces of his father's and grandfather's evil reigns. Things had been so awful that God had to clean things up. Things would get ugly. And Zephaniah had to let everyone know.

But Zephaniah also got to deliver some very good news. He prophesied that soon those who were humble and trusted in God would get to see the most wonderful event in history: the coming of the Messiah!

> *"Everything comes from love, all is ordained for the salvation of man. God does nothing without this goal in mind."*
>
> —St. Catherine of Siena

WHO The prophet Zephaniah, the only prophet descended from royalty (the great-great-grandson of King Hezekiah)

WHAT A prophecy about the coming judgment of God on his people for their sin as well as the promise of hope and joy when God will come to live among them

WHEN Zephaniah began his ministry in 640 B.C. This book was likely written sometime between 640 and 609 B.C.

WHERE Judah (the southern kingdom)

PATH OF DISCIPLESHIP

As is so often the case, the light at the end of the tunnel for Israel points to one thing: Jesus. Even though they faced some very dark days ahead, the Israelites could count on God to restore them again.

It's clear at the end of the book of Zephaniah that the promise of restoration is Jesus. Once God is finished with his judgment on Israel, we are told that we "shall fear disaster no more" (Zephaniah 3.15). The book refers to him as a "warrior," who "will rejoice over you with gladness" (3.17). With this promise, we can live each day as hopeful disciples with Jesus as our guide!

1

The word of the LORD that came to Zephaniah son of Cushi son of Gedaliah son of Amariah son of Hezekiah, in the days of King Josiah son of Amon of Judah.

The Coming Judgment on Judah

2 I will utterly sweep away everything
   from the face of the earth, says the LORD.
3 I will sweep away humans and animals;
   I will sweep away the birds of the air
   and the fish of the sea.
   I will make the wicked stumble.*a*
   I will cut off humanity
   from the face of the earth, says the LORD.
4 I will stretch out my hand against Judah,
   and against all the inhabitants of
      Jerusalem;
   and I will cut off from this place every
      remnant of Baal
   and the name of the idolatrous priests;*b*
5 those who bow down on the roofs
   to the host of the heavens;
   those who bow down and swear to the
      LORD,
   but also swear by Milcom;*c*
6 those who have turned back from following
      the LORD,
   who have not sought the LORD or
      inquired of him.

7 Be silent before the Lord GOD!
   For the day of the LORD is at hand;
   the LORD has prepared a sacrifice,
   he has consecrated his guests.
8 And on the day of the LORD's sacrifice
   I will punish the officials and the king's sons
   and all who dress themselves in foreign
      attire.
9 On that day I will punish
   all who leap over the threshold,
   who fill their master's house
   with violence and fraud.

10 On that day, says the LORD,
   a cry will be heard from the Fish Gate,
   a wail from the Second Quarter,
   a loud crash from the hills.
11 The inhabitants of the Mortar wail,
   for all the traders have perished;
   all who weigh out silver are cut off.
12 At that time I will search Jerusalem with
      lamps,
   and I will punish the people
   who rest complacently*d* on their dregs,
   those who say in their hearts,
   "The LORD will not do good,
      nor will he do harm."

13 Their wealth shall be plundered,
   and their houses laid waste.
   Though they build houses,
   they shall not inhabit them;
   though they plant vineyards,
   they shall not drink wine from them.

The Great Day of the LORD

14 The great day of the LORD is near,
   near and hastening fast;
   the sound of the day of the LORD is bitter,
   the warrior cries aloud there.
15 That day will be a day of wrath,
   a day of distress and anguish,
   a day of ruin and devastation,
   a day of darkness and gloom,
   a day of clouds and thick darkness,
16   a day of trumpet blast and battle cry
   against the fortified cities
   and against the lofty battlements.

17 I will bring such distress upon people
   that they shall walk like the blind;
   because they have sinned against the
      LORD,
   their blood shall be poured out like dust,
   and their flesh like dung.
18 Neither their silver nor their gold
   will be able to save them
   on the day of the LORD's wrath;
   in the fire of his passion
   the whole earth shall be consumed;
   for a full, a terrible end
   he will make of all the inhabitants of the
      earth.

2 Judgment on Israel's Enemies

Gather together, gather,
   O shameless nation,
2 before you are driven away
   like the drifting chaff,*e*
   before there comes upon you
   the fierce anger of the LORD,
   before there comes upon you
   the day of the LORD's wrath.
3 Seek the LORD, all you humble of the land,
   who do his commands;
   seek righteousness, seek humility;
   perhaps you may be hidden
   on the day of the LORD's wrath.
4 For Gaza shall be deserted,
   and Ashkelon shall become a desolation;
   Ashdod's people shall be driven out at noon,
   and Ekron shall be uprooted.

5 Ah, inhabitants of the seacoast,
   you nation of the Cherethites!

a Cn: Heb sea, and those who cause the wicked to stumble b Compare Gk: Heb the idolatrous priests with the priests c Gk Mss Syr Vg: Heb Malcam (or, their king) d Heb who thicken e Cn Compare Gk Syr: Heb before a decree is born; like chaff a day has passed away

The word of the Lord is against you,
O Canaan, land of the Philistines;
and I will destroy you until no inhabitant
is left.
6 And you, O seacoast, shall be pastures,
meadows for shepherds
and folds for flocks.
7 The seacoast shall become the possession
of the remnant of the house of Judah,
on which they shall pasture,
and in the houses of Ashkelon
they shall lie down at evening.
For the Lord their God will be mindful of
them
and restore their fortunes.

8 I have heard the taunts of Moab
and the revilings of the Ammonites,
how they have taunted my people
and made boasts against their territory.
9 Therefore, as I live, says the Lord of hosts,
the God of Israel,
Moab shall become like Sodom
and the Ammonites like Gomorrah,
a land possessed by nettles and salt pits,
and a waste forever.
The remnant of my people shall plunder
them,
and the survivors of my nation shall
possess them.
10 This shall be their lot in return for their pride,
because they scoffed and boasted
against the people of the Lord of hosts.
11 The Lord will be terrible against them;
he will shrivel all the gods of the earth,
and to him shall bow down,
each in its place,
all the coasts and islands of the nations.

12 You also, O Ethiopians,ᵃ
shall be killed by my sword.

13 And he will stretch out his hand against the
north,
and destroy Assyria;
and he will make Nineveh a desolation,
a dry waste like the desert.
14 Herds shall lie down in it,
every wild animal;ᵇ
the desert owlᶜ and the screech owlᶜ
shall lodge on its capitals;
the owlᵈ shall hoot at the window,
the ravenᵉ croak on the threshold;
for its cedar work will be laid bare.
15 Is this the exultant city
that lived secure,
that said to itself,
"I am, and there is no one else"?
What a desolation it has become,

REALITY ✓

BROKEN PROMISES

Read **Zephaniah 1.1–18**. Zephaniah took
great pains to point out that God's people had
broken their original covenant with God. We
have also broken our covenant by choosing to
live for ourselves, rather than for God alone.
We too must seek God's healing, no matter
how painful. Only then can hope and salvation
be restored.

Take some time to think about your
responses to the following: What are some of
the things in our world today that appear to
be the result of broken promises between God
and his creation? What needs to be healed?
How might that happen? Envision the "great
day of the Lord" (v. 14) as it might look today.

Write your own two-part poem. In part
one, warn the people and list who and
how they will be "punished." In part two,
describe the "great day." Post your poem
at **Learner.CalltoDiscipleship.com**.

a lair for wild animals!
Everyone who passes by it
hisses and shakes the fist.

3 The Wickedness of Jerusalem
Ah, soiled, defiled,
oppressing city!
2 It has listened to no voice;
it has accepted no correction.
It has not trusted in the Lord;
it has not drawn near to its God.

3 The officials within it
are roaring lions;
its judges are evening wolves
that leave nothing until the morning.
4 Its prophets are reckless,
faithless persons;
its priests have profaned what is sacred,
they have done violence to the law.
5 The Lord within it is righteous;
he does no wrong.
Every morning he renders his judgment,

a Or *Nubians*; Heb *Cushites* b Tg Compare Gk: Heb *nation* c Meaning of Heb uncertain d Cn: Heb *a voice* e Gk Vg: Heb *desolation*

each dawn without fail;
  but the unjust knows no shame.

6 I have cut off nations;
    their battlements are in ruins;
  I have laid waste their streets
    so that no one walks in them;
  their cities have been made desolate,
    without people, without inhabitants.
7 I said, "Surely the city*a* will fear me,
    it will accept correction;
  it will not lose sight*b*
    of all that I have brought upon it."
  But they were the more eager
    to make all their deeds corrupt.

Punishment and Conversion of the Nations

8 Therefore wait for me, says the LORD,
    for the day when I arise as a witness.
  For my decision is to gather nations,
    to assemble kingdoms,
  to pour out upon them my indignation,
    all the heat of my anger;
  for in the fire of my passion
    all the earth shall be consumed.

9 At that time I will change the speech of the
      peoples
    to a pure speech,
  that all of them may call on the name of the
      LORD
    and serve him with one accord.
10 From beyond the rivers of Ethiopia*c*
    my suppliants, my scattered ones,
    shall bring my offering.
11 On that day you shall not be put to shame
    because of all the deeds by which you
      have rebelled against me;
  for then I will remove from your midst
    your proudly exultant ones,
  and you shall no longer be haughty
    in my holy mountain.
12 For I will leave in the midst of you
    a people humble and lowly.

They shall seek refuge in the name of the
    LORD—
13   the remnant of Israel;
  they shall do no wrong
    and utter no lies,
  nor shall a deceitful tongue
    be found in their mouths.
  Then they will pasture and lie down,
    and no one shall make them afraid.

A Song of Joy

14 Sing aloud, O daughter Zion;
    shout, O Israel!
  Rejoice and exult with all your heart,
    O daughter Jerusalem!
15 The LORD has taken away the judgments
      against you,
    he has turned away your enemies.
  The king of Israel, the LORD, is in your midst;
    you shall fear disaster no more.
16 On that day it shall be said to Jerusalem:
  Do not fear, O Zion;
    do not let your hands grow weak.
17 The LORD, your God, is in your midst,
    a warrior who gives victory;
  he will rejoice over you with gladness,
    he will renew you*d* in his love;
  he will exult over you with loud singing
18   as on a day of festival.*e*
  I will remove disaster from you,*f*
    so that you will not bear reproach for it.
19 I will deal with all your oppressors
    at that time.
  And I will save the lame
    and gather the outcast,
  and I will change their shame into praise
    and renown in all the earth.
20 At that time I will bring you home,
    at the time when I gather you;
  for I will make you renowned and praised
    among all the peoples of the earth,
  when I restore your fortunes
    before your eyes, says the LORD.

a Heb *it* *b* Gk Syr: Heb *its dwelling will not be cut off* *c* Or *Nubia*; Heb *Cush* *d* Gk Syr: Heb *he will be silent* *e* Gk Syr: Meaning of Heb
uncertain *f* Cn: Heb *I will remove from you; they were*

HAGGAI

GET YOUR PRIORITIES RIGHT!

Back on Track

Step back in time for a moment. After approximately seventy years in exile, imagine how the Jews feel when they finally get home—a mixture of relief, excitement, and a determination to put right all the damage those Babylonians had done to their beloved city. So they throw themselves into rebuilding the Temple . . . and then they run out of steam. Reality hits hard, and the renovations grind to a halt. Life seems oh-so-difficult, and all the energy they are putting into trying to better themselves just isn't getting them anywhere. The outline of the ruined Temple reminds them what they should be doing, but how can they rebuild a Temple when they can barely look after themselves?

Fast forward to now, to today. To you—right now—reading these words in your Bible. Does this scenario sound familiar? Deep down, aren't we just the same as the people of Judah? We want a good life—enough to eat, a place to live, trendy clothes—and friends and family to share it with. Trouble is, we can put all our energy into getting those things and still end up disappointed.

Haggai came up with the answer, straight from God's mouth: "Get your priorities right!" He challenged the people along these lines: "Why are you living in nice houses when God's Temple is a mess?" (see Haggai 1.4). The reason life was so hard was that they weren't putting God first. Get that right and God's blessing will follow. Will you give it a try?

"Whatsoever good work you undertake, pray earnestly to God that He will enable you to bring it to a successful conclusion."

—St. Benedict

WHO Haggai, a prophet, wrote this book.

WHAT When the Jews first got back home, their efforts to rebuild the Temple stalled. Haggai told them to get their priorities right and start building again.

WHEN Haggai prophesied in 520 B.C., during the second year of King Darius' reign in Persia.

WHERE God's people are now back home in Jerusalem, some fifty years after the destruction of the Temple and the final deportation to Babylon.

 ## PATH OF DISCIPLESHIP

Many people say that if you want to be successful and happy and have a comfortable life, you need to work for it—study hard, get a good job, buy a house, keep working hard. (It's a bit like the scenario the people of Judah were buying into during Haggai's time—putting their focus and energy into trying to better their lives.)

But Jesus had different priorities. Why worry about food, drink, and clothes? he asked. You'll never be better off or more beautiful than the birds and flowers that God looks after, and you're much more valuable than them. Put God's Kingdom first and you'll have all you need. (Read Matthew 6.25–34 for more on this.)

Jesus' and Haggai's message is an important one for disciples today, and one we need to hear often: set your priorities! What are your priorities? Do they fit the lifestyle of a follower of Jesus? Are you afraid to live like that? But who knows best what life is about and how to live as a disciple? I think I'll take it from Jesus.

1 The Command to Rebuild the Temple

In the second year of King Darius, in the sixth month, on the first day of the month, the word of the LORD came by the prophet Haggai to Zerubbabel son of Shealtiel, governor of Judah, and to Joshua son of Jehozadak, the high priest: ²Thus says the LORD of hosts: These people say the time has not yet come to rebuild the LORD's house. ³Then the word of the LORD came by the prophet Haggai, saying: ⁴Is it a time for you yourselves to live in your paneled houses, while this house lies in ruins? ⁵Now therefore thus says the LORD of hosts: Consider how you have fared. ⁶You have sown much, and harvested little; you eat, but you never have enough; you drink, but you never have your fill; you clothe yourselves, but no one is warm; and you that earn wages earn wages to put them into a bag with holes.

7 Thus says the LORD of hosts: Consider how you have fared. ⁸Go up to the hills and bring wood and build the house, so that I may take pleasure in it and be honored, says the LORD. ⁹You have looked for much, and, lo, it came to little; and when you brought it home, I blew it away. Why? says the LORD of hosts. Because my house lies in ruins, while all of you hurry off to your own houses. ¹⁰Therefore the heavens above you have withheld the dew, and the earth has withheld its produce. ¹¹And I have called for a drought on the land and the hills, on the grain, the new wine, the oil, on what the soil produces, on human beings and animals, and on all their labors.

12 Then Zerubbabel son of Shealtiel, and Joshua son of Jehozadak, the high priest, with all the remnant of the people, obeyed the voice of the LORD their God, and the words of the prophet Haggai, as the LORD their God had sent him; and the people feared the LORD. ¹³Then Haggai, the messenger of the LORD, spoke to the people with the LORD's message, saying, I am with you, says the LORD. ¹⁴And the LORD stirred up the spirit of Zerubbabel son of Sheal-tiel, governor of Judah, and the spirit of Joshua son of Jehozadak, the high priest, and the spirit of all the remnant of the people; and they came and worked on the house of the LORD of hosts, their God, ¹⁵on the twenty-fourth day of the month, in the sixth month.

2 The Future Glory of the Temple

In the second year of King Darius, ¹in the seventh month, on the twenty-first day of the month, the word of the LORD came by the prophet Haggai, saying: ²Speak now to Zerubbabel son of Shealtiel, governor of Judah, and to Joshua son of Jehozadak, the high priest, and to the remnant of the people, and say, ³Who is left among you that saw this house in its former glory? How does it look to you now? Is it not in your sight as nothing? ⁴Yet now take courage, O Zerubbabel, says the LORD; take courage, O Joshua, son of Jehozadak, the high priest; take courage, all you people of the land, says the LORD; work, for I am with you, says the LORD of hosts, ⁵according to the promise that I made you when you came out of Egypt. My spirit abides among you; do not fear. ⁶For thus says the LORD of hosts: Once again, in a little while, I will shake the heavens and the earth and the sea and the dry land; ⁷and I will shake all the nations, so that the treasure of all nations shall come, and I will fill this house with splendor, says the LORD of hosts. ⁸The silver is mine, and the gold is mine, says the LORD of hosts. ⁹The latter splendor of this house shall be greater than the former, says the LORD of hosts; and in this place I will give prosperity, says the LORD of hosts.

A Rebuke and a Promise

10 On the twenty-fourth day of the ninth month, in the second year of Darius, the word of the LORD came by the prophet Haggai, saying: ¹¹Thus says the LORD of hosts: Ask the priests for a ruling: ¹²If one carries consecrated meat in the fold of one's garment, and with the fold touches bread, or stew, or wine, or oil, or any kind of food, does it become holy? The priests answered, "No." ¹³Then Haggai said, "If one who is unclean by contact with a dead body touches any of these, does it become unclean?" The priests answered, "Yes, it becomes unclean." ¹⁴Haggai then said, So is it with this people, and with this nation before me, says the LORD; and so with every work of their hands; and what they offer there is unclean. ¹⁵But now, consider what will come to pass from this day on. Before a stone was placed upon a stone in the LORD's temple, ¹⁶how did you fare?ᵃ When

> "[God] loves us when we don't want him to love us. . . . He loves us when our lives are a mess. His love is sticky, resistant to rejection, aggressive, and persistent. The challenge is on, so go ahead—resist his love, run from it, hide from it. Go ahead and try."
>
> —Mike Yaconelli,
> *Messy Spirituality*

---

a Gk: Heb *since they were*

one came to a heap of twenty measures, there were but ten; when one came to the wine vat to draw fifty measures, there were but twenty. ¹⁷I struck you and all the products of your toil with blight and mildew and hail; yet you did not return to me, says the LORD. ¹⁸Consider from this day on, from the twenty-fourth day of the ninth month. Since the day that the foundation of the LORD's temple was laid, consider: ¹⁹Is there any seed left in the barn? Do the vine, the fig tree, the pomegranate, and the olive tree still yield nothing? From this day on I will bless you.

God's Promise to Zerubbabel

20 The word of the LORD came a second time to Haggai on the twenty-fourth day of the month: ²¹Speak to Zerubbabel, governor of Judah, saying, I am about to shake the heavens and the earth, ²²and to overthrow the throne of kingdoms; I am about to destroy the strength of the kingdoms of the nations, and overthrow the chariots and their riders; and the horses and their riders shall fall, every one by the sword of a comrade. ²³On that day, says the LORD of hosts, I will take you, O Zerubbabel my servant, son of Shealtiel, says the LORD, and make you like a signet ring; for I have chosen you, says the LORD of hosts.

IT'S TRADITION

FRUITFUL WORK

In this very short book, Haggai is called "the prophet" five times. He uses the prophetic messenger formula, "Thus says the LORD," several times.

A prophet isn't someone who foresees or foretells the future, but one who delivers a message from God to the people. Haggai's task was to speak hope, not false optimism, to the people who after the exile had returned to a destroyed land. His "word of the LORD" was about the very hard reality of rebuilding. His words called the people to do the "grunt work" of rebuilding the center of their own religious lives: the Temple in Jerusalem. The *Catechism of the Catholic Church* reminds us that the prophets' proclamations are the fruit of prayer and attentiveness to the "Word of God" (2584).

CREATIVE SPACE

Sacrifice at the Temple—© Mateusz Bukowiecki, 16

ZECHARIAH

BUILDING THE FUTURE

Time to Get Back to Work

The book of Zechariah isn't read very often. It sits here in the far back of the Old Testament, usually flipped over on the way to more popular books like Psalms or Romans. That's too bad, because this book is full of fascinating information about . . . the future.

February 15, 519 B.C., was a very restless night for Zechariah. As he tossed and turned in his bed, God gave him eight visions. These visions were kind of strange—a flying scroll, a gold lampstand, and a woman in a basket, just for starters—and they were a bit hard to interpret. But Zechariah passed along these and other oracles to the people of Israel as an encouragement . . . and a warning.

The people in Israel were rebuilding the Temple in Jerusalem, but it was taking a long time. Zechariah shared his visions with them as an encouragement to complete their work. He told them that the Messiah (Jesus) would soon be coming, and they needed to be humble, work hard, and be ready for his arrival.

Zechariah also had a message about the Second Coming of Jesus. This book contains some details about what will happen when Jesus returns. His message to us is the same as it was to the Israelites: be humble, work hard, and be ready!

> *"We must wait for God long, meekly, in the wind and wet, in the thunder and lightning, in the cold and the dark. Wait, and he will come."*
>
> —F. W. Faber, oratorian and devotional writer

WHO Zechariah was born in Babylon when God's people were exiles there and then returned to Jerusalem, where he was a prophet and a priest.

WHAT God tells Zechariah to encourage the returned Israelites to keep working hard on rebuilding the Temple, because the Messiah will soon be coming.

WHEN The first eight chapters of this book take place from 520 to 518 B.C., the same time as the book of Haggai. The last six chapters were likely written much later, probably between 480 and 470 B.C.

WHERE Judah, modern-day southern Israel

PATH OF DISCIPLESHIP

Reformation is always the work of God. We can try as hard as possible, but in the end it is God who is the master reformer. First we read in Zechariah, "Not by might, nor by power, but by my spirit, says the LORD of hosts" (4.6), and then we are reminded later in the book that reformation comes by God's hand and God's work: "I will signal for them . . . though I scattered them. . . . I will bring them home. . . . I will make them strong in the LORD, and they shall walk in his name" (10.8–12). The words of Zechariah emphasize a cooperative effort between God and his people—the type of effort in which disciples find restoration and renewal.

1 Israel Urged to Repent

In the eighth month, in the second year of Darius, the word of the LORD came to the prophet Zechariah son of Berechiah son of Iddo, saying: [2]The LORD was very angry with your ancestors. [3]Therefore say to them, Thus says the LORD of hosts: Return to me, says the LORD of hosts, and I will return to you, says the LORD of hosts. [4]Do not be like your ancestors, to whom the former prophets proclaimed, "Thus says the LORD of hosts, Return from your evil ways and from your evil deeds." But they did not hear or heed me, says the LORD. [5]Your ancestors, where are they? And the prophets, do they live forever? [6]But my words and my statutes, which I commanded my servants the prophets, did they not overtake your ancestors? So they repented and said, "The LORD of hosts has dealt with us according to our ways and deeds, just as he planned to do."

First Vision: The Horsemen

7 On the twenty-fourth day of the eleventh month, the month of Shebat, in the second year of Darius, the word of the LORD came to the prophet Zechariah son of Berechiah son of Iddo; and Zechariah*a* said, [8]In the night I saw a man riding on a red horse! He was standing among the myrtle trees in the glen; and behind him were red, sorrel, and white horses. [9]Then I said, "What are these, my lord?" The angel who talked with me said to me, "I will show you what they are." [10]So the man who was standing among the myrtle trees answered, "They are those whom the LORD has sent to patrol the earth." [11]Then they spoke to the angel of the LORD who was standing among the myrtle trees, "We have patrolled the earth, and lo, the whole earth remains at peace." [12]Then the angel of the LORD said, "O LORD of hosts, how long will you withhold mercy from Jerusalem and the cities of Judah, with which you have been angry these seventy years?" [13]Then the LORD replied with gracious and comforting words to the angel who talked with me. [14]So the angel who talked with me said to me, Proclaim this message: Thus says the LORD of hosts; I am very jealous for Jerusalem and for Zion. [15]And I am extremely angry with the nations that are at ease; for while I was only a little angry, they made the disaster worse. [16]Therefore, thus says the LORD, I have returned to Jerusalem with compassion; my house shall be built in it, says the LORD of hosts, and the measuring line shall be stretched out over Jerusalem. [17]Proclaim further: Thus says the LORD of hosts: My cities shall again overflow with prosperity; the LORD will again comfort Zion and again choose Jerusalem.

Second Vision: The Horns and the Smiths

18 *b* And I looked up and saw four horns. [19]I asked the angel who talked with me, "What are these?" And he answered me, "These are the horns that have scattered Judah, Israel, and Jerusalem." [20]Then the LORD showed me four blacksmiths. [21]And I asked, "What are they coming to do?" He answered, "These are the horns that scattered Judah, so that no head could be raised; but these have come to terrify them, to strike down the horns of the nations that lifted up their horns against the land of Judah to scatter its people."*c*

2*d* Third Vision: The Man with a Measuring Line

I looked up and saw a man with a measuring line in his hand. [2]Then I asked, "Where are you going?" He answered me, "To measure Jerusalem, to see what is its width and what is its length." [3]Then the angel who talked with me came forward, and another angel came forward to meet him, [4]and said to him, "Run, say to that young man: Jerusalem shall be inhabited like villages without walls, because of the multitude of people and animals in it. [5]For I will be a wall of fire all around it, says the LORD, and I will be the glory within it."

Interlude: An Appeal to the Exiles

6 Up, up! Flee from the land of the north, says the LORD; for I have spread you abroad like the four winds of heaven, says the LORD. [7]Up! Escape to Zion, you that live with daughter Babylon. [8]For thus said the LORD of hosts (after his glory*e* sent me) regarding the nations that plundered you: Truly, one who touches you touches the apple of my eye.*f* [9]See now, I am going to raise*g* my hand against them, and they shall become plunder for their own slaves. Then you will know that the LORD of hosts has sent me. [10]Sing and rejoice, O daughter Zion! For lo, I will come and dwell in your midst, says the LORD. [11]Many nations shall join themselves to the LORD on that day, and shall be my people; and I will dwell in your midst. And you shall know that the LORD of hosts has sent me to you. [12]The LORD will inherit Judah as his portion in the holy land, and will again choose Jerusalem.

13 Be silent, all people, before the LORD; for he has roused himself from his holy dwelling.

---

a Heb *and he*   *b* Ch 2.1 in Heb   *c* Heb *it*   *d* Ch 2.5 in Heb   *e* Cn: Heb *after glory he*   *f* Heb *his eye*   *g* Or *wave*

Impossible Forgiveness The delicious smell of baking bread. The beautiful sounds of a Bach prelude. The reassuring sight of her father's head bowed in prayer. These comforts were far away as Corrie ten Boom sat in the stench of a crowded train car bound for Ravensbrück concentration camp, where nearly a hundred thousand people were exterminated by the Nazi regime.

As she grew up in a welcoming and faith-filled home in Holland at the turn of the twentieth century, Corrie was taught that all people had worth in God's eyes. Her family put that belief into action years later, harboring Jews who were fleeing the Nazis. Yet even when she and some of her family members were arrested by the Germans, Corrie's faith remained intact. As she described, "There are years of preparation, years of experience, which God uses in ways we may never know until we meet Him face to face."

Unlike the eleven million people put to death by the Nazis, Corrie miraculously survived the concentration camp. Years later, as Europe was recovering from Nazism and the impact of the war, Corrie traveled around Europe and America speaking about her experience and her faith. But there was a nagging feeling in her heart: God was calling her to go back to Germany. She overcame obstacles of nervousness, heartache, and self-doubt. Her "I can't" quickly became "I can" through prayer and the Holy Spirit's prompting. So she did it— Corrie courageously went back to Germany

to speak about God's love and forgiveness. At one point, she stood face-to-face with one of the concentration camp guards from Ravensbrück—the place where Corrie saw others beaten, starved, and worked to death. The place where guards tortured and murdered innocent people. The place of terror and fear. And Corrie shook that man's hand. Through God's power, she forgave him.

Corrie made the rest of her life's work sharing Christ. Even in her eighties, she traveled around the world, telling others of God's remarkable grace, still challenging herself and others along the way with this powerful, convicting question:

"What have I done today that only a Christian would do?"

3 Fourth Vision: Joshua and Satan

Then he showed me the high priest Joshua standing before the angel of the Lord, and Satan[a] standing at his right hand to accuse him. [2]And the Lord said to Satan,[a] "The Lord rebuke you, O Satan![a] The Lord who has chosen Jerusalem rebuke you! Is not this man a brand plucked from the fire?" [3]Now Joshua was dressed with filthy clothes as he stood before the angel. [4]The angel said to those who were standing before him, "Take off his filthy clothes." And to him he said, "See, I have taken your guilt away from you, and I will clothe you

with festal apparel." [5]And I said, "Let them put a clean turban on his head." So they put a clean turban on his head and clothed him with the apparel; and the angel of the Lord was standing by.

6 Then the angel of the Lord assured Joshua, saying [7]"Thus says the Lord of hosts: If you will walk in my ways and keep my requirements, then you shall rule my house and have charge of my courts, and I will give you the right of access among those who are standing here. [8]Now listen, Joshua, high priest, you and your colleagues who sit before you! For they are an omen of things to come: I am going to bring

a Or the Accuser; Heb the Adversary

UNHIDDEN PAIN

The signs are there
You see them but you look away
Can you not see my cries for help?
I am practically screaming at you
Yet you do not hear me
The signs are so clear and crimson
How can I get you to open your eyes?
How much pain must I endure?
I bet if I took my life you would see
But I can't do that
I am not that weak, I will not give in
My soul is weak, my heart broken but I won't quit
You might not see my pain
But I know someone who does
He will always be there for me
Even when you are not
And He will forever love me
Even when you do not
I don't need you to see my pain
Not anymore, not with Him
Forever by my side
Always will He love me
He knows my pain and my suffering
When I was dead He brought me back
Now, my signs are gone

Unhidden Pain—© Alicia Glenn, 16

my servant the Branch. ⁹For on the stone that I have set before Joshua, on a single stone with seven facets, I will engrave its inscription, says the LORD of hosts, and I will remove the guilt of this land in a single day. ¹⁰On that day, says the LORD of hosts, you shall invite each other to come under your vine and fig tree."

4 Fifth Vision: The Lampstand and Olive Trees

The angel who talked with me came again, and wakened me, as one is wakened from sleep. ²He said to me, "What do you see?" And I said, "I see a lampstand all of gold, with a bowl on the top of it; there are seven lamps on it, with seven lips on each of the lamps that are on top of it. ³And by it there are two olive trees, one on the right of the bowl and the other on its left." ⁴I said to the angel who talked with me, "What are these, my lord?" ⁵Then the angel who talked with me answered me, "Do you not know what these are?" I said, "No, my lord." ⁶He said to me, "This is the word of the LORD to Zerubbabel: Not by might, nor by power, but by my spirit, says the LORD of hosts. ⁷What are you, O great mountain? Before Zerubbabel you shall become a plain; and he shall bring out the top stone amid shouts of 'Grace, grace to it!' "

8 Moreover the word of the LORD came to me, saying, ⁹"The hands of Zerubbabel have laid the foundation of this house; his hands shall also complete it. Then you will know that the LORD of hosts has sent me to you. ¹⁰For whoever has despised the day of small things shall rejoice, and shall see the plummet in the hand of Zerubbabel.

"These seven are the eyes of the LORD, which range through the whole earth." ¹¹Then I said to him, "What are these two olive trees on the right and the left of the lampstand?" ¹²And a second time I said to him, "What are these two branches of the olive trees, which pour out the oil*ᵃ* through the two golden pipes?" ¹³He said to me, "Do you not know what these are?" I said, "No, my lord." ¹⁴Then he said, "These are the two anointed ones who stand by the Lord of the whole earth."

5 Sixth Vision: The Flying Scroll

Again I looked up and saw a flying scroll. ²And he said to me, "What do you see?" I answered, "I see a flying scroll; its length is twenty cubits, and its width ten cubits." ³Then he said to me, "This is the curse that goes out over the face of the whole land; for everyone who steals shall

be cut off according to the writing on one side, and everyone who swears falsely*ᵇ* shall be cut off according to the writing on the other side. ⁴I have sent it out, says the LORD of hosts, and it shall enter the house of the thief, and the house of anyone who swears falsely by my name; and it shall abide in that house and consume it, both timber and stones."

Seventh Vision: The Woman in a Basket

5 Then the angel who talked with me came forward and said to me, "Look up and see what this is that is coming out." ⁶I said, "What is it?" He said, "This is a basket*ᶜ* coming out." And he said, "This is their iniquity*ᵈ* in all the land." ⁷Then a leaden cover was lifted, and there was a woman sitting in the basket!*ᶜ* ⁸And he said, "This is Wickedness." So he thrust her back into the basket,*ᶜ* and pressed the leaden weight down on its mouth. ⁹Then I looked up and saw two women coming forward. The wind was in their wings; they had wings like the wings of a stork, and they lifted up the basket*ᶜ* between earth and sky. ¹⁰Then I said to the angel who talked with me, "Where are they taking the basket?"*ᶜ* ¹¹He said to me, "To the land of Shinar, to build a house for it; and when this is prepared, they will set the basket*ᶜ* down there on its base."

6 Eighth Vision: Four Chariots

And again I looked up and saw four chariots coming out from between two mountains—mountains of bronze. ²The first chariot had red horses, the second chariot black horses, ³the third chariot white horses, and the fourth chariot dappled gray*ᵉ* horses. ⁴Then I said to the angel who talked with me, "What are these, my lord?" ⁵The angel answered me, "These are the four winds*ᶠ* of heaven going out, after presenting themselves before the Lord of all the earth. ⁶The chariot with the black horses goes toward the north country, the white ones go toward the west country,*ᵍ* and the dappled ones go toward the south country." ⁷When the steeds came out, they were impatient to get off and patrol the earth. And he said, "Go, patrol the earth." So they patrolled the earth. ⁸Then he cried out to me, "Lo, those who go toward the north country have set my spirit at rest in the north country."

The Coronation of the Branch

9 The word of the LORD came to me: ¹⁰Collect silver and gold*ʰ* from the exiles—from Heldai, Tobijah, and Jedaiah—who have arrived from

---

a Cn: Heb *gold* *b* The word *falsely* added from verse 4 *c* Heb *ephah* *d* Gk Compare Syr: Heb *their eye* *e* Compare Gk: Meaning of Heb uncertain *f* Or *spirits* *g* Cn: Heb *go after them* *h* Cn Compare verse 11: Heb lacks *silver and gold*

REALITY

7 Hypocritical Fasting Condemned

In the fourth year of King Darius, the word of the LORD came to Zechariah on the fourth day of the ninth month, which is Chislev. ²Now the people of Bethel had sent Sharezer and Regem-melech and their men, to entreat the favor of the LORD, ³and to ask the priests of the house of the LORD of hosts and the prophets, "Should I mourn and practice abstinence in the fifth month, as I have done for so many years?" ⁴Then the word of the LORD of hosts came to me: ⁵Say to all the people of the land and the priests: When you fasted and lamented in the fifth month and in the seventh, for these seventy years, was it for me that you fasted? ⁶And when you eat and when you drink, do you not eat and drink only for yourselves? ⁷Were not these the words that the LORD proclaimed by the former prophets, when Jerusalem was inhabited and in prosperity, along with the towns around it, and when the Negeb and the Shephelah were inhabited?

Punishment for Rejecting God's Demands

8 The word of the LORD came to Zechariah, saying: ⁹Thus says the LORD of hosts: Render true judgments, show kindness and mercy to one another; ¹⁰do not oppress the widow, the orphan, the alien, or the poor; and do not devise evil in your hearts against one another. ¹¹But they refused to listen, and turned a stubborn shoulder, and stopped their ears in order not to hear. ¹²They made their hearts adamant in order not to hear the law and the words that the LORD of hosts had sent by his spirit through the former prophets. Therefore great wrath came from the LORD of hosts. ¹³Just as, when I*ᵉ* called, they would not hear, so, when they called, I would not hear, says the LORD of hosts, ¹⁴and I scattered them with a whirlwind among all the nations that they had not known. Thus the land they left was desolate, so that no one went to and fro, and a pleasant land was made desolate.

8 God's Promises to Zion

The word of the LORD of hosts came to me, saying: ²Thus says the LORD of hosts: I am jealous for Zion with great jealousy, and I am jealous for her with great wrath. ³Thus says the LORD: I will return to Zion, and will dwell in the midst of Jerusalem; Jerusalem shall be called the faithful city, and the mountain of the LORD of hosts shall be called the holy mountain. ⁴Thus says the LORD of hosts: Old men and old women shall again sit in the streets of Jerusalem,

Babylon; and go the same day to the house of Josiah son of Zephaniah. ¹¹Take the silver and gold and make a crown,*ᵃ* and set it on the head of the high priest Joshua son of Jehozadak; ¹²say to him: Thus says the LORD of hosts: Here is a man whose name is Branch: for he shall branch out in his place, and he shall build the temple of the LORD. ¹³It is he that shall build the temple of the LORD; he shall bear royal honor, and shall sit upon his throne and rule. There shall be a priest by his throne, with peaceful understanding between the two of them. ¹⁴And the crown*ᵇ* shall be in the care of Heldai,*ᶜ* Tobijah, Jedaiah, and Josiah*ᵈ* son of Zephaniah, as a memorial in the temple of the LORD.

15 Those who are far off shall come and help to build the temple of the LORD; and you shall know that the LORD of hosts has sent me to you. This will happen if you diligently obey the voice of the LORD your God.

a Gk Mss Syr Tg: Heb *crowns*   *b* Gk Syr: Heb *crowns*   *c* Syr Compare verse 10: Heb *Helem*   *d* Syr Compare verse 10: Heb *Hen*   *e* Heb *he* each with staff in hand because of their great age. [5]And the streets of the city shall be full of boys and girls playing in its streets. [6]Thus says the LORD of hosts: Even though it seems impossible to the remnant of this people in these days, should it also seem impossible to me, says the LORD of hosts? [7]Thus says the LORD of hosts: I will save my people from the east country and from the west country; [8]and I will bring them to live in Jerusalem. They shall be my people and I will be their God, in faithfulness and in righteousness.

9 Thus says the LORD of hosts: Let your hands be strong—you that have recently been hearing these words from the mouths of the prophets who were present when the foundation was laid for the rebuilding of the temple, the house of the LORD of hosts. [10]For before those days there were no wages for people or for animals, nor was there any safety from the foe for those who went out or came in, and I set them all against one another. [11]But now I will not deal with the remnant of this people as in the former days, says the LORD of hosts. [12]For there shall be a sowing of peace; the vine shall yield its fruit, the ground shall give its produce, and the skies shall give their dew; and I will cause the remnant of this people to possess all these things. [13]Just as you have been a cursing among the nations, O house of Judah and house of Israel, so I will save you and you shall be a blessing. Do not be afraid, but let your hands be strong.

14 For thus says the LORD of hosts: Just as I purposed to bring disaster upon you, when your ancestors provoked me to wrath, and I did not relent, says the LORD of hosts, [15]so again I have purposed in these days to do good to Jerusalem and to the house of Judah; do not be afraid. [16]These are the things that you shall do: Speak the truth to one another, render in your gates judgments that are true and make for peace, [17]do not devise evil in your hearts against one another, and love no false oath; for all these are things that I hate, says the LORD.

Joyful Fasting

18 The word of the LORD of hosts came to me, saying: [19]Thus says the LORD of hosts: The fast of the fourth month, and the fast of the fifth, and the fast of the seventh, and the fast of the tenth, shall be seasons of joy and gladness, and cheerful festivals for the house of Judah: therefore love truth and peace.

Many Peoples Drawn to Jerusalem

20 Thus says the LORD of hosts: Peoples shall yet come, the inhabitants of many cities; [21]the inhabitants of one city shall go to another, say-

ing, "Come, let us go to entreat the favor of the LORD, and to seek the LORD of hosts; I myself am going." [22]Many peoples and strong nations shall come to seek the LORD of hosts in Jerusalem, and to entreat the favor of the LORD. [23]Thus says the LORD of hosts: In those days ten men from nations of every language shall take hold of a Jew, grasping his garment and saying, "Let us go with you, for we have heard that God is with you."

9 Judgment on Israel's Enemies

An Oracle.

The word of the LORD is against the land of Hadrach
and will rest upon Damascus.

John 10.29—© Jesse Bernard, 17

For to the Lord belongs the capital^a of
    Aram,^b
    as do all the tribes of Israel;
2 Hamath also, which borders on it,
    Tyre and Sidon, though they are very
      wise.
3 Tyre has built itself a rampart,
    and heaped up silver like dust,
    and gold like the dirt of the streets.
4 But now, the Lord will strip it of its
      possessions
    and hurl its wealth into the sea,
    and it shall be devoured by fire.

5 Ashkelon shall see it and be afraid;
    Gaza too, and shall writhe in anguish;
    Ekron also, because its hopes are
      withered.
The king shall perish from Gaza;
    Ashkelon shall be uninhabited;
6 a mongrel people shall settle in Ashdod,
    and I will make an end of the pride of
      Philistia.
7 I will take away its blood from its mouth,
    and its abominations from between its
      teeth;
it too shall be a remnant for our God;
    it shall be like a clan in Judah,
    and Ekron shall be like the Jebusites.
8 Then I will encamp at my house as a guard,
    so that no one shall march to and fro;

no oppressor shall again overrun them,
    for now I have seen with my own eyes.

The Coming Ruler of God's People
9 Rejoice greatly, O daughter Zion!
    Shout aloud, O daughter Jerusalem!
Lo, your king comes to you;
    triumphant and victorious is he,
humble and riding on a donkey,
    on a colt, the foal of a donkey.
10 He^c will cut off the chariot from
      Ephraim
    and the war-horse from Jerusalem;
and the battle bow shall be cut off,
    and he shall command peace to the
      nations;
his dominion shall be from sea to sea,
    and from the River to the ends of the
      earth.

11 As for you also, because of the blood of my
      covenant with you,
    I will set your prisoners free from the
      waterless pit.
12 Return to your stronghold, O prisoners of
      hope;
    today I declare that I will restore to you
      double.
13 For I have bent Judah as my bow;
    I have made Ephraim its arrow.
I will arouse your sons, O Zion,

---

a Heb *eye*   *b* Cn: Heb *of Adam* (or *of humankind*)   *c* Gk: Heb I

against your sons, O Greece,
and wield you like a warrior's sword.
14 Then the LORD will appear over them,
and his arrow go forth like lightning;
the Lord GOD will sound the trumpet
and march forth in the whirlwinds of the
south.
15 The LORD of hosts will protect them,
and they shall devour and tread down the
slingers;[a]
they shall drink their blood[b] like wine,
and be full like a bowl,
drenched like the corners of the altar.
16 On that day the LORD their God will save
them
for they are the flock of his people;
for like the jewels of a crown
they shall shine on his land.
17 For what goodness and beauty are his!
Grain shall make the young men
flourish,
and new wine the young women.

10 Restoration of Judah and Israel

Ask rain from the LORD
in the season of the spring rain,
from the LORD who makes the storm
clouds,
who gives showers of rain to you,[c]
the vegetation in the field to everyone.
2 For the teraphim[d] utter nonsense,
and the diviners see lies;
the dreamers tell false dreams,
and give empty consolation.
Therefore the people wander like sheep;
they suffer for lack of a shepherd.

3 My anger is hot against the shepherds,
and I will punish the leaders;[e]
for the LORD of hosts cares for his flock, the
house of Judah,
and will make them like his proud
war-horse.
4 Out of them shall come the cornerstone,
out of them the tent peg,
out of them the battle bow,
out of them every commander.
5 Together they shall be like warriors in
battle,
trampling the foe in the mud of the
streets;
they shall fight, for the LORD is with them,
and they shall put to shame the riders on
horses.

6 I will strengthen the house of Judah,
and I will save the house of Joseph.

I will bring them back because I have
compassion on them,
and they shall be as though I had not
rejected them;
for I am the LORD their God and I will
answer them.
7 Then the people of Ephraim shall become
like warriors,
and their hearts shall be glad as with
wine.
Their children shall see it and rejoice,
their hearts shall exult in the LORD.
8 I will signal for them and gather them in,
for I have redeemed them,
and they shall be as numerous as they
were before.
9 Though I scattered them among the
nations,
yet in far countries they shall
remember me,
and they shall rear their children and
return.
10 I will bring them home from the land of
Egypt,
and gather them from Assyria;
I will bring them to the land of Gilead and
to Lebanon,
until there is no room for them.
11 They[f] shall pass through the sea of distress,
and the waves of the sea shall be struck
down,
and all the depths of the Nile dried up.
The pride of Assyria shall be laid low,
and the scepter of Egypt shall depart.
12 I will make them strong in the LORD,
and they shall walk in his name,
says the LORD.

11 Open your doors, O Lebanon,
so that fire may devour your cedars!
2 Wail, O cypress, for the cedar has fallen,
for the glorious trees are ruined!
Wail, oaks of Bashan,
for the thick forest has been felled!
3 Listen, the wail of the shepherds,
for their glory is despoiled!
Listen, the roar of the lions,
for the thickets of the Jordan are
destroyed!

Two Kinds of Shepherds

4 Thus said the LORD my God: Be a shepherd
of the flock doomed to slaughter. 5Those who
buy them kill them and go unpunished; and
those who sell them say, "Blessed be the LORD,
for I have become rich"; and their own shepherds have no pity on them. 6For I will no lon-

ger have pity on the inhabitants of the earth, says the LORD. I will cause them, every one, to fall each into the hand of a neighbor, and each into the hand of the king; and they shall devastate the earth, and I will deliver no one from their hand.

7 So, on behalf of the sheep merchants, I became the shepherd of the flock doomed to slaughter. I took two staffs; one I named Favor, the other I named Unity, and I tended the sheep. 8In one month I disposed of the three shepherds, for I had become impatient with them, and they also detested me. 9So I said, "I will not be your shepherd. What is to die, let it die; what is to be destroyed, let it be destroyed; and let those that are left devour the flesh of one another!" 10I took my staff Favor and broke it, annulling the covenant that I had made with all the peoples. 11So it was annulled on that day, and the sheep merchants, who were watching me, knew that it was the word of the LORD. 12I then said to them, "If it seems right to you, give me my wages; but if not, keep them." So they weighed out as my wages thirty shekels of silver. 13Then the LORD said to me, "Throw it into the treasury"[a]—this lordly price at which I was valued by them. So I took the thirty shekels of silver and threw them into the treasury[a] in the house of the LORD. 14Then I broke my second staff Unity, annulling the family ties between Judah and Israel.

15 Then the LORD said to me: Take once more the implements of a worthless shepherd. 16For I am now raising up in the land a shepherd who does not care for the perishing, or seek the wandering,[b] or heal the maimed, or nourish the healthy,[c] but devours the flesh of the fat ones, tearing off even their hoofs.

17 Oh, my worthless shepherd,
  who deserts the flock!
May the sword strike his arm
  and his right eye!
Let his arm be completely withered,
  his right eye utterly blinded!

12 Jerusalem's Victory

An Oracle.

The word of the LORD concerning Israel: Thus says the LORD, who stretched out the heavens and founded the earth and formed the human spirit within: 2See, I am about to make Jerusalem a cup of reeling for all the surrounding peoples; it will be against Judah also in the siege against Jerusalem. 3On that day I will make Jerusalem a heavy stone for all the peoples; all who lift it shall grievously hurt themselves. And all the nations of the earth shall come together against it. 4On that day, says the LORD, I will strike every horse with panic, and its rider with madness. But on the house of Judah I will keep a watchful eye, when I strike every horse of the peoples with blindness. 5Then the clans of Judah shall say to themselves, "The inhabitants of Jerusalem have strength through the LORD of hosts, their God."

6 On that day I will make the clans of Judah like a blazing pot on a pile of wood, like a flaming torch among sheaves; and they shall devour to the right and to the left all the surrounding peoples, while Jerusalem shall again be inhabited in its place, in Jerusalem.

7 And the LORD will give victory to the tents of Judah first, that the glory of the house of David and the glory of the inhabitants of Jerusalem may not be exalted over that of Judah. 8On that day the LORD will shield the inhabitants of Jerusalem so that the feeblest among them on that day shall be like David, and the house of David shall be like God, like the angel of the LORD, at their head. 9And on that day I will seek to destroy all the nations that come against Jerusalem.

Mourning for the Pierced One

10 And I will pour out a spirit of compassion and supplication on the house of David and the inhabitants of Jerusalem, so that, when they look on the one[d] whom they have pierced, they shall mourn for him, as one mourns for an only child, and weep bitterly over him, as one weeps over a firstborn. 11On that day the mourning in Jerusalem will be as great as the mourning for Hadad-rimmon in the plain of Megiddo. 12The land shall mourn, each family by itself; the family of the house of David by itself, and their wives by themselves; the family of the house of Nathan by itself, and their wives by themselves; 13the family of the house of Levi by itself, and their wives by themselves; the family of the Shimeites by itself, and their wives by themselves; 14and all the families that are left, each by itself, and their wives by themselves.

13 On that day a fountain shall be opened for the house of David and the inhabitants of Jerusalem, to cleanse them from sin and impurity.

Idolatry Cut Off

2 On that day, says the LORD of hosts, I will cut off the names of the idols from the land, so that they shall be remembered no more; and also I will remove from the land the prophets

---

a Syr: Heb it to the potter b Syr Compare Gk Vg: Heb the youth c Meaning of Heb uncertain d Heb on me and the unclean spirit. ³And if any prophets appear again, their fathers and mothers who bore them will say to them, "You shall not live, for you speak lies in the name of the LORD"; and their fathers and their mothers who bore them shall pierce them through when they prophesy. ⁴On that day the prophets will be ashamed, every one, of their visions when they prophesy; they will not put on a hairy mantle in order to deceive, ⁵but each of them will say, "I am no prophet, I am a tiller of the soil; for the land has been my possession*a* since my youth." ⁶And if anyone asks them, "What are these wounds on your chest?"*b* the answer will be "The wounds I received in the house of my friends."

The Shepherd Struck, the Flock Scattered

⁷ "Awake, O sword, against my shepherd,
  against the man who is my associate,"
    says the LORD of hosts.
  Strike the shepherd, that the sheep may be
      scattered;
    I will turn my hand against the little
      ones.
⁸ In the whole land, says the LORD,
    two-thirds shall be cut off and perish,
    and one-third shall be left alive.
⁹ And I will put this third into the fire,
    refine them as one refines silver,
    and test them as gold is tested.
  They will call on my name,
    and I will answer them.
  I will say, "They are my people";
    and they will say, "The LORD is our God."

14 Future Warfare and Final Victory

See, a day is coming for the LORD, when the plunder taken from you will be divided in your midst. ²For I will gather all the nations against Jerusalem to battle, and the city shall be taken and the houses looted and the women raped; half the city shall go into exile, but the rest of the people shall not be cut off from the city. ³Then the LORD will go forth and fight against those nations as when he fights on a day of battle. ⁴On that day his feet shall stand on the Mount of Olives, which lies before Jerusalem on the east; and the Mount of Olives shall be split in two from east to west by a very wide valley; so that one half of the Mount shall withdraw northward, and the other half southward. ⁵And you shall flee by the valley of the LORD's mountain,*c* for the valley between the mountains shall reach to Azal;*d* and you shall flee as you fled from the earthquake in the days of

King Uzziah of Judah. Then the LORD my God will come, and all the holy ones with him.

6 On that day there shall not be*e* either cold or frost.*f* ⁷And there shall be continuous day (it is known to the LORD), not day and not night, for at evening time there shall be light.

8 On that day living waters shall flow out from Jerusalem, half of them to the eastern sea and half of them to the western sea; it shall continue in summer as in winter.

9 And the LORD will become king over all the earth; on that day the LORD will be one and his name one.

10 The whole land shall be turned into a plain from Geba to Rimmon south of Jerusalem. But Jerusalem shall remain aloft on its site from the Gate of Benjamin to the place of

a Cn: Heb *for humankind has caused me to possess*   *b* Heb *wounds between your hands*   *c* Heb *my mountains*   *d* Meaning of Heb uncertain
e Cn: Heb *there shall not be light*   *f* Compare Gk Syr Vg Tg: Meaning of Heb uncertain

the former gate, to the Corner Gate, and from the Tower of Hananel to the king's wine presses. ¹¹And it shall be inhabited, for never again shall it be doomed to destruction; Jerusalem shall abide in security.

12 This shall be the plague with which the LORD will strike all the peoples that wage war against Jerusalem: their flesh shall rot while they are still on their feet; their eyes shall rot in their sockets, and their tongues shall rot in their mouths. ¹³On that day a great panic from the LORD shall fall on them, so that each will seize the hand of a neighbor, and the hand of the one will be raised against the hand of the other; ¹⁴even Judah will fight at Jerusalem. And the wealth of all the surrounding nations shall be collected—gold, silver, and garments in great abundance. ¹⁵And a plague like this plague shall fall on the horses, the mules, the camels, the donkeys, and whatever animals may be in those camps.

16 Then all who survive of the nations that have come against Jerusalem shall go up year after year to worship the King, the LORD of hosts, and to keep the festival of booths.ᵃ ¹⁷If any of the families of the earth do not go up to Jerusalem to worship the King, the LORD of hosts, there will be no rain upon them. ¹⁸And if the family of Egypt do not go up and present themselves, then on them shallᵇ come the plague that the LORD inflicts on the nations that do not go up to keep the festival of booths.ᵃ ¹⁹Such shall be the punishment of Egypt and the punishment of all the nations that do not go up to keep the festival of booths.ᵃ

20 On that day there shall be inscribed on the bells of the horses, "Holy to the LORD." And the cooking pots in the house of the LORD shall be as holy asᶜ the bowls in front of the altar; ²¹and every cooking pot in Jerusalem and Judah shall be sacred to the LORD of hosts, so that all who sacrifice may come and use them to boil the flesh of the sacrifice. And there shall no longer be tradersᵈ in the house of the LORD of hosts on that day.

a Or tabernacles; Heb succoth b Gk Syr: Heb shall not c Heb shall be like d Or Canaanites

Cross on the Top of the Fort—© Taylor-Quinn Yancey, 16

MALACHI

LOVE AND FAITHFULNESS

A Plea from the Heart

Surely they should have gotten the message by now. God had sent prophet after prophet to his people, pointing out where they were going wrong and calling them back to himself. Sometimes there was change, but it only lasted for a while and was never very deeply rooted.

So this book, Malachi, is the last-ditch attempt before four hundred years of silence from God. No prophets. No big miracles. Nothing.

Malachi's message is similar to that of other prophets: don't just go through the motions; don't try to cheat God; have some integrity. But look how this prophetic book begins. Instead of starting with declarations of judgment, there's a statement of love at the beginning and a promise of redemption at the end.

This, at heart, is the message of all the prophets. Look past the evidence of Israel's disobedience, the threat of punishment, the signs of where it's all gone wrong, and see the generosity of God. God's love and faithfulness never run out. When you let God down, when you go your own way, when you take God for granted, when you try so hard and yet still mess up, it's God's love that greets you, not his wrath. His promises of fruitfulness and forgiveness, of welcome and restoration are there for you just like they were for the people who first heard from Malachi. God's love and faithfulness *never* run out.

> **"Love God, serve God: everything is in that."**
>
> —St. Clare of Assisi

WHO The author is unknown. The name Malachi means "my messenger."

WHAT The Israelites' worship had become shallow and corrupt. Malachi urged them to get it right and to expect God's blessing in return.

WHEN Written ca. 430 B.C.

WHERE Judah, present-day southern Israel

PATH OF DISCIPLESHIP

Malachi spoke to God's people at a time when their country no longer enjoyed prominence as a world power. Those days were in the past. They had no king and no political independence; they were now just a small part of the vast Persian Empire. Malachi's words spoke to the "everyday" concerns of God's people and to faith in a new time. Many of the same messages from previous prophets were reused, but now they were placed in the new context of the everyday; there was still need for passionate justice, concern for those most in need, and for true and honest worship. There was also hope of a new day.

Like the people to whom this book was addressed, we live our lives in the everyday of routine and "small stuff." It is in the everydayness of life that we find our faith tested and brought to life. It is in the everyday life of school and interacting with friends and family that God calls us to love and serve him. It is in the everydayness of life we must seek God, hear what God says, and respond. The depth of everyday life and faith depend on our ability to ask and listen.

1

An oracle. The word of the Lord to Israel by Malachi.[a]

Israel Preferred to Edom

2 I have loved you, says the Lord. But you say, "How have you loved us?" Is not Esau Jacob's brother? says the Lord. Yet I have loved Jacob 3 but I have hated Esau; I have made his hill country a desolation and his heritage a desert for jackals. 4 If Edom says, "We are shattered but we will rebuild the ruins," the Lord of hosts says: They may build, but I will tear down, until they are called the wicked country, the people with whom the Lord is angry forever. 5 Your own eyes shall see this, and you shall say, "Great is the Lord beyond the borders of Israel!"

Corruption of the Priesthood

6 A son honors his father, and servants their master. If then I am a father, where is the honor due me? And if I am a master, where is the respect due me? says the Lord of hosts to you, O priests, who despise my name. You say, "How have we despised your name?" 7 By offering polluted food on my altar. And you say, "How have we polluted it?"[b] By thinking that the Lord's table may be despised. 8 When you offer blind animals in sacrifice, is that not wrong? And when you offer those that are lame or sick, is that not wrong? Try presenting that to your governor; will he be pleased with you or show you favor? says the Lord of hosts. 9 And now implore the favor of God, that he may be gracious to us. The fault is yours. Will he show favor to any of you? says the Lord of hosts. 10 Oh, that someone among you would shut the temple[c] doors, so that you would not kindle fire on my altar in vain! I have no pleasure in you, says the Lord of hosts, and I will not accept an offering from your hands. 11 For

from the rising of the sun to its setting my name is great among the nations, and in every place incense is offered to my name, and a pure offering; for my name is great among the nations, says the Lord of hosts. 12 But you profane it when you say that the Lord's table is polluted, and the food for it[d] may be despised. 13 "What a weariness this is," you say, and you sniff at me,[e] says the Lord of hosts. You bring what has been taken by violence or is lame or sick, and this you bring as your offering! Shall I accept that from your hand? says the Lord. 14 Cursed be the cheat who has a male in the flock and vows to give it, and yet sacrifices to the Lord what is blemished; for I am a great King, says the Lord of hosts, and my name is reverenced among the nations.

2

And now, O priests, this command is for you. 2 If you will not listen, if you will not lay it to heart to give glory to my name, says the Lord of hosts, then I will send the curse on you and I will curse your blessings; indeed I have already cursed them,[f] because you do not lay it to heart. 3 I will rebuke your offspring, and spread dung on your faces, the dung of your offerings, and I will put you out of my presence.[g]

4 Know, then, that I have sent this command to you, that my covenant with Levi may hold, says the Lord of hosts. 5 My covenant with him was a covenant of life and well-being, which I gave him; this called for reverence, and he revered me and stood in awe of my name. 6 True instruction was in his mouth, and no wrong was found on his lips. He walked with me in integrity and uprightness, and he turned many from iniquity. 7 For the lips of a priest should guard knowledge, and people should seek instruction from his mouth, for he is the messenger of the Lord of hosts. 8 But you have turned aside from the way; you have caused many to stumble by your instruction; you have corrupted the covenant of Levi, says the Lord of hosts, 9 and so I make you despised and abased before all the people, inasmuch as you have not kept my ways but have shown partiality in your instruction.

The Covenant Profaned by Judah

10 Have we not all one father? Has not one God created us? Why then are we faithless to one another, profaning the covenant of our ancestors? 11 Judah has been faithless, and abomination has been committed in Israel and in Jerusalem; for Judah has profaned the sanctuary of the Lord, which he loves, and has

> I asked for wisdom and God gave me problems to solve.
> I asked for prosperity and God gave me brain and brawn to work.
> I asked for courage and God gave me danger to overcome.
> I asked for love and God gave me troubled people to help.
> I asked for favors and God gave me opportunities.
> I received nothing I wanted.
>
> —St. Gregory Nazianzen

---

a Or by my messenger b Gk: Heb you c Heb lacks temple
d Compare Syr Tg: Heb its fruit, its food e Another reading is at it
f Heb it g Cn Compare Gk Syr: Heb and he shall bear you to it

married the daughter of a foreign god. ¹²May the Lord cut off from the tents of Jacob anyone who does this—any to witness[a] or answer, or to bring an offering to the Lord of hosts.

13 And this you do as well: You cover the Lord's altar with tears, with weeping and groaning because he no longer regards the offering or accepts it with favor at your hand. ¹⁴You ask, "Why does he not?" Because the Lord was a witness between you and the wife of your youth, to whom you have been faithless, though she is your companion and your wife by covenant. ¹⁵Did not one God make her?[b] Both flesh and spirit are his.[c] And what does the one God[d] desire? Godly offspring. So look to yourselves, and do not let anyone be faithless to the wife of his youth. ¹⁶For I hate[e] divorce, says the Lord, the God of Israel, and covering one's garment with violence, says the Lord of hosts. So take heed to yourselves and do not be faithless.

17 You have wearied the Lord with your words. Yet you say, "How have we wearied him?" By saying, "All who do evil are good in the sight of the Lord, and he delights in them." Or by asking, "Where is the God of justice?"

3 The Coming Messenger

See, I am sending my messenger to prepare the way before me, and the Lord whom you seek will suddenly come to his temple. The messenger of the covenant in whom you delight—indeed, he is coming, says the Lord of hosts. ²But who can endure the day of his coming, and who can stand when he appears?

For he is like a refiner's fire and like fullers' soap; ³he will sit as a refiner and purifier of silver, and he will purify the descendants of Levi and refine them like gold and silver, until they present offerings to the Lord in righteousness.[f] ⁴Then the offering of Judah and Jerusalem will be pleasing to the Lord as in the days of old and as in former years.

5 Then I will draw near to you for judgment; I will be swift to bear witness against the sorcerers, against the adulterers, against those who swear falsely, against those who oppress the hired workers in their wages, the widow and the orphan, against those who thrust aside the alien, and do not fear me, says the Lord of hosts.

6 For I the Lord do not change; therefore you, O children of Jacob, have not perished. ⁷Ever since the days of your ancestors you have turned aside from my statutes and have not kept them. Return to me, and I will return to

LITURGY FORMS US

Malachi emphasized the renewal of worship in **Malachi 1.6–2.9**. Worship had fallen flat. Did you know that at the time of the Second Vatican Council, the renewal of worship was also an issue? It wasn't one of the aims of the council; the bishops didn't go to Rome to change the liturgy. The goals of the council were to look at ways to adapt to the needs of the day and to promote union among all believers in Christ (see *Constitution on the Sacred Liturgy*, 1; go to **Learner.CalltoDiscipleship.com** for a link).

But the bishops knew, as Malachi did, that liturgical worship, rituals, and prayers shape people and transform them as a community of faith. A renewal of worship was essential, so that all disciples could witness to that faith by living faithfully in the world today.

And the renewal continues: A new English translation of the Roman Missal was approved in 2009. It includes updated translations of the prayers in the sacred liturgy.

you, says the Lord of hosts. But you say, "How shall we return?"

Do Not Rob God

8 Will anyone rob God? Yet you are robbing me! But you say, "How are we robbing you?" In your tithes and offerings! ⁹You are cursed with a curse, for you are robbing me—the whole nation of you! ¹⁰Bring the full tithe into the storehouse, so that there may be food in my house, and thus put me to the test, says the Lord of hosts; see if I will not open the windows of heaven for you and pour down for you an overflowing blessing. ¹¹I will rebuke the locust[g] for you, so that it will not destroy the produce of your soil; and your vine in the field shall not be barren, says the Lord of hosts. ¹²Then all nations will count you happy, for you will be a land of delight, says the Lord of hosts.

13 You have spoken harsh words against me, says the Lord. Yet you say, "How have we spoken against you?" ¹⁴You have said, "It is vain to serve God. What do we profit by keeping

a Cn Compare Gk: Heb *arouse* b Or *Has he not made one?* c Cn: Heb *and a remnant of spirit was his* d Heb *he* e Cn: Heb *he hates* f Or *right offerings to the Lord* g Heb *devourer*

JESUS SIGHTING

his command or by going about as mourners before the LORD of hosts? [15]Now we count the arrogant happy; evildoers not only prosper, but when they put God to the test they escape."

The Reward of the Faithful

16 Then those who revered the LORD spoke with one another. The LORD took note and listened, and a book of remembrance was written before him of those who revered the LORD and thought on his name. [17]They shall be mine, says the LORD of hosts, my special possession on the day when I act, and I will spare them as parents spare their children who serve them. [18]Then once more you shall see the difference between the righteous and the wicked, between one who serves God and one who does not serve him.

4[a] The Great Day of the LORD

See, the day is coming, burning like an oven, when all the arrogant and all evildoers will be stubble; the day that comes shall burn them up, says the LORD of hosts, so that it will leave them neither root nor branch. [2]But for you who revere my name the sun of righteousness shall rise, with healing in its wings. You shall go out leaping like calves from the stall. [3]And you shall tread down the wicked, for they will be ashes under the soles of your feet, on the day when I act, says the LORD of hosts.

4 Remember the teaching of my servant Moses, the statutes and ordinances that I commanded him at Horeb for all Israel.

5 Lo, I will send you the prophet Elijah before the great and terrible day of the LORD comes. [6]He will turn the hearts of parents to their children and the hearts of children to their parents, so that I will not come and strike the land with a curse.[b]

a Ch 4.1–6 are Ch 3.19–24 in Heb b Or a ban of utter destruction

NEW
testament

A LOVE STORY

	Name		Time
1	Jesus Christ	●	5:18
2	Only Jesus	●	3:49
3	L' Enfance du Christ Op. 25, P...	●	2:02
4	I Told Jesus Christ How Much I...	●	3:54
5	The Lord's Prayer: Vater unser ...	●	2:22
6	Christmas Jesus	●	3:49
7	It's Jesus	●	3:22
8	Jesus Jesus Christ the King	●	4:11
9	"Herr Jesu Christ, Du Höchstes...	●	4:23
10	The Seven Last Words Of Jesus...	●	5:43
11	The Seven Last Words of Chris...	●	9:51
12	Jesus Is the Best Thing That Ev...	●	6:07
13	I Don't Know How to Love Him...	●	3:57
14	Messe des Jésuites de Pékin: P...	●	2:37
15	Jesus (Is the Savior)	●	5:00
16	Thank You Jesus	●	5:12
17	Give Me Jesus	●	5:37
18	Jesus the Christ	●	4:20
19	Chorale Preludes BWV 1090 – ...	●	2:00
20	Sund@y7	●	
21	I Don't Know How to Love Him...	●	3:29
22	Jesus, meine Zuversicht, BWV ...	●	2:11

LIVE

Jesus

JESUS
THERE IS POWER
IN THE NAME

37	The Eyes of Jesus Christ	●	5:46
38	Jesus Christ	●	2:39
39	Jesus Christ Pose	●	5:50
40	Jesus Christ Was Born	●	2:18
41	Chorale, Op. 28 No. 32. Lord J...	●	0:34
42	Jesus Christ Is the Way	●	5:07
43	Jesus Christ	●	2:39
44	The Church of Jesus Christ	●	0:47
45	Jesus Christ Is the Way (I`ll Fo...	●	4:01
46	Jesus Christ, the Apple Tree	●	3:13
47	Jesus Christ Is the Light	●	4:21

MATTHEW

THE NEW WORD ON THE OLD LAW

"Come Follow Me"

You sit on the side of the road at the tax table, collecting from those who pass by you on the way into Jerusalem for the Passover.

"Due to Caesar!" you call out. "Hail Caesar!"

You have long since tuned out the taunts of the passersby, who roll past you like waves.

"Sellout," they mutter. "Traitor."

You will pass the garnishings on to those in Herod's court, who will take what they want and then pass the rest on to Caesar's men. Out of spite for their greed and resentment of your own people's mockery, you pocket a little yourself. This is how the world works, and if the whole world is on its way to Hades, you might as well take what you can along the way.

You've never hoped for anything more in life, like being tapped by a rabbi for a ministry opportunity. So when one of them comes walking by, you drop your head. "Due to Caesar!" you call out.

There is silence. No coins fall on your table. You look up to see the man you've heard of.

"Come follow me," he tells you. In an instant, you rise from your place.

You are Matthew. One of those called.

The gospel of Matthew seems to have relied on Mark's gospel account, which was most likely written first. The author adds to Mark's gospel with descriptions of Jesus' birth, his post-Resurrection appearances, and additional material on his teachings. But Matthew is placed first in the order of the New Testament books because of its Jewish flavor and its strong emphasis on Jesus as the fulfillment of the expectations of God's people.

This gospel also focuses on Jesus' ministry and words being the "new law" for the Jewish people—a new way of living, worshiping, and pleasing God. Some scholars think that the five major groupings of Jesus' teachings in Matthew—chapters 5–7, 10, 13, 18, and 24–25—are meant to parallel the first five books of the Bible (the Pentateuch). In the Sermon on the Mount, instead of focusing on rule keeping, Jesus challenged his listeners to take their obedience to the commandments a step further by striving to act in the spirit of and beyond the letter of those commandments (chapters 5–7).

> *"If anyone comes to me, I want to lead them to Him."*
>
> —St. Edith Stein

WHO It is uncertain if Matthew wrote this gospel. The author was probably a Greek-speaking, second-generation Jewish Christian.

WHAT Firsthand accounts of Jesus' life, ministry, and teachings on the "new law"

WHEN Written between A.D. 70 and 90

WHERE Antioch in Syria

PATH OF DISCIPLESHIP

Who's been your favorite teacher? Was it your third-grade teacher who always told great jokes? Was it a history teacher who brought boring dates and facts to life? Here in Matthew's gospel, you'll see a portrait of Jesus as the greatest of all teachers. Crowds mob around him to hear him speak; his words and stories are unusual, amazing, and challenging. They're the kind of things you'd never forget. As you dive into Matthew, imagine you're there, in the crowd, listening to Jesus' life-changing words. As a disciple, what is he teaching you? How will you respond?

1 The Genealogy of Jesus the Messiah

An account of the genealogy[a] of Jesus the Messiah,[b] the son of David, the son of Abraham.

2 Abraham was the father of Isaac, and Isaac the father of Jacob, and Jacob the father of Judah and his brothers, 3and Judah the father of Perez and Zerah by Tamar, and Perez the father of Hezron, and Hezron the father of Aram, 4and Aram the father of Aminadab, and Aminadab the father of Nahshon, and Nahshon the father of Salmon, 5and Salmon the father of Boaz by Rahab, and Boaz the father of Obed by Ruth, and Obed the father of Jesse, 6and Jesse the father of King David.

And David was the father of Solomon by the wife of Uriah, 7and Solomon the father of Rehoboam, and Rehoboam the father of Abijah, and Abijah the father of Asaph,[c] 8and Asaph[c] the father of Jehoshaphat, and Jehoshaphat the father of Joram, and Joram the father of Uzziah, 9and Uzziah the father of Jotham, and Jotham the father of Ahaz, and Ahaz the father of Hezekiah, 10and Hezekiah the father of Manasseh, and Manasseh the father of Amos,[d] and Amos[d] the father of Josiah, 11and Josiah the father of Jechoniah and his brothers, at the time of the deportation to Babylon.

12 And after the deportation to Babylon: Jechoniah was the father of Salathiel, and Salathiel the father of Zerubbabel, 13and Zerubbabel the father of Abiud, and Abiud the father of Eliakim, and Eliakim the father of Azor, 14and Azor the father of Zadok, and Zadok the father of Achim, and Achim the father of Eliud, 15and Eliud the father of Eleazar, and Eleazar the father of Matthan, and Matthan the father of Jacob, 16and Jacob the father of Joseph the husband of Mary, of whom Jesus was born, who is called the Messiah.[e]

17 So all the generations from Abraham to David are fourteen generations; and from David to the deportation to Babylon, fourteen generations; and from the deportation to Babylon to the Messiah,[e] fourteen generations.

The Birth of Jesus the Messiah

18 Now the birth of Jesus the Messiah[b] took place in this way. When his mother Mary had been engaged to Joseph, but before they lived together, she was found to be with child from the Holy Spirit. 19Her husband Joseph, being a righteous man and unwilling to expose her to public disgrace, planned to dismiss her quietly. 20But just when he had resolved to do this, an angel of the Lord appeared to him in a dream and said, "Joseph, son of David, do not be afraid to take Mary as your wife, for the child conceived in her is from the Holy Spirit. 21She will bear a son, and you are to name him Jesus, for he will save his people from their sins." 22All this took place to fulfill what had been spoken by the Lord through the prophet:

23 "Look, the virgin shall conceive and bear a
    son,
    and they shall name him Emmanuel,"

which means, "God is with us." 24When Joseph awoke from sleep, he did as the angel of the Lord commanded him; he took her as his wife, 25but had no marital relations with her until she had borne a son;[f] and he named him Jesus.

2 The Visit of the Wise Men

In the time of King Herod, after Jesus was born in Bethlehem of Judea, wise men[g] from the East came to Jerusalem, 2asking, "Where is the child who has been born king of the Jews? For we observed his star at its rising,[h] and have come to pay him homage." 3When King Herod heard this, he was frightened, and all Jerusalem with him; 4and calling together all the chief priests and scribes of the people, he inquired of them where the Messiah[e] was to be born. 5They told him, "In Bethlehem of Judea; for so it has been written by the prophet:

6 'And you, Bethlehem, in the land of Judah,
    are by no means least among the rulers
        of Judah;
    for from you shall come a ruler
        who is to shepherd[i] my people Israel.' "

7 Then Herod secretly called for the wise men[g] and learned from them the exact time when the star had appeared. 8Then he sent them to Bethlehem, saying, "Go and search diligently for the child; and when you have found him, bring me word so that I may also go and pay him homage." 9When they had heard the king, they set out; and there, ahead of them, went the star that they had seen at its rising,[h] until it stopped over the place where the child was. 10When they saw that the star had stopped,[j] they were overwhelmed with joy. 11On entering the house, they saw the child with Mary his mother; and they knelt down and paid him homage. Then, opening their treasure chests, they offered him gifts of gold, frankincense, and myrrh. 12And having been warned in a dream not to return to Herod, they left for their own country by another road.

The Escape to Egypt

13 Now after they had left, an angel of the Lord appeared to Joseph in a dream and said,

---

a Or birth b Or Jesus Christ c Other ancient authorities read Asa d Other ancient authorities read Amon e Or the Christ f Other ancient authorities read her firstborn son g Or astrologers; Gk magi h Or in the East i Or rule j Gk saw the star

"Get up, take the child and his mother, and flee to Egypt, and remain there until I tell you; for Herod is about to search for the child, to destroy him." [14]Then Joseph[a] got up, took the child and his mother by night, and went to Egypt, [15]and remained there until the death of Herod. This was to fulfill what had been spoken by the Lord through the prophet, "Out of Egypt I have called my son."

The Massacre of the Infants

16 When Herod saw that he had been tricked by the wise men,[b] he was infuriated, and he sent and killed all the children in and around Bethlehem who were two years old or under, according to the time that he had learned from the wise men.[b] [17]Then was fulfilled what had been spoken through the prophet Jeremiah:
[18] "A voice was heard in Ramah,
    wailing and loud lamentation,
Rachel weeping for her children;
    she refused to be consoled, because they
        are no more."

The Return from Egypt

19 When Herod died, an angel of the Lord suddenly appeared in a dream to Joseph in Egypt and said, [20]"Get up, take the child and his mother, and go to the land of Israel, for those who were seeking the child's life are dead." [21]Then Joseph[a] got up, took the child and his mother, and went to the land of Israel. [22]But when he heard that Archelaus was ruling over Judea in place of his father Herod, he was afraid to go there. And after being warned in a dream, he went away to the district of Galilee. [23]There he made his home in a town called Nazareth, so that what had been spoken through the prophets might be fulfilled, "He will be called a Nazorean."

3   The Proclamation of John the Baptist

In those days John the Baptist appeared in the wilderness of Judea, proclaiming, [2]"Repent, for the kingdom of heaven has come near."[c] [3]This is the one of whom the prophet Isaiah spoke when he said,
    "The voice of one crying out in the
        wilderness:
    'Prepare the way of the Lord,
      make his paths straight.' "
[4]Now John wore clothing of camel's hair with a leather belt around his waist, and his food was locusts and wild honey. [5]Then the people of Jerusalem and all Judea were going out to him, and all the region along the Jordan, [6]and they

Hope—© Jesse Bernard, 17

FAMILY TREES AND MOSAICS

Some of my relatives are obsessed with dead people. They're really into researching our family tree, which doesn't excite me much.

Typically when I'm reading my Bible, I skip right over the genealogies and get on to the good stuff (like Jesus wiping spit in somebody's eye; see Mark 8.22–26). But instead of skipping over it, read **Matthew 1.1–17**. These verses remind me of the pictures and stories of my family tree. There are some wild stories—the good, the bad, and the ugly. But as my grandmother says, "They make you *you*!" And when I think about it, I know she's right.

Isn't that what DNA is? Together we make a DNA mosaic. Each of us is a piece of what God is making into a beautiful picture of his Kingdom. Throughout time, God was endlessly piecing together the lives mentioned in this genealogy in unexpected ways to bring his Son into the world at just the right time and place.

Try this. Use colorful art materials to make a mosaic of people who have brought you this far on your faith journey. Give it a three-word title. Then scan or take a digital picture of your mosaic and upload it to **Learner.CalltoDiscipleship.com**.

GOD IS RELENTLESS   MY FAMILY

were baptized by him in the river Jordan, confessing their sins.

7 But when he saw many Pharisees and Sadducees coming for baptism, he said to them, "You brood of vipers! Who warned you to flee from the wrath to come? [8]Bear fruit worthy of repentance. [9]Do not presume to say to yourselves, 'We have Abraham as our ancestor'; for

a Gk he b Or astrologers; Gk magi c Or is at hand

I tell you, God is able from these stones to raise up children to Abraham. [10]Even now the ax is lying at the root of the trees; every tree therefore that does not bear good fruit is cut down and thrown into the fire.

11 "I baptize you with[a] water for repentance, but one who is more powerful than I is coming after me; I am not worthy to carry his sandals. He will baptize you with[a] the Holy Spirit and fire. [12]His winnowing fork is in his hand, and he will clear his threshing floor and will gather his wheat into the granary; but the chaff he will burn with unquenchable fire."

The Baptism of Jesus

13 Then Jesus came from Galilee to John at the Jordan, to be baptized by him. [14]John would have prevented him, saying, "I need to be baptized by you, and do you come to me?" [15]But Jesus answered him, "Let it be so now; for it is proper for us in this way to fulfill all righteousness." Then he consented. [16]And when Jesus had been baptized, just as he came up from the water, suddenly the heavens were opened to him and he saw the Spirit of God descending like a dove and alighting on him. [17]And a voice from heaven said, "This is my Son, the Beloved,[b] with whom I am well pleased."

4 The Temptation of Jesus

Then Jesus was led up by the Spirit into the wilderness to be tempted by the devil. [2]He fasted forty days and forty nights, and afterwards he was famished. [3]The tempter came and said to him, "If you are the Son of God, command these stones to become loaves of bread." [4]But he answered, "It is written,

> 'One does not live by bread alone,
>> but by every word that comes from the
>> mouth of God.' "

5 Then the devil took him to the holy city and placed him on the pinnacle of the temple, [6]saying to him, "If you are the Son of God, throw yourself down; for it is written,

> 'He will command his angels concerning
>> you,'
>> and 'On their hands they will bear you
>> up,
> so that you will not dash your foot against a
>> stone.' "

[7]Jesus said to him, "Again it is written, 'Do not put the Lord your God to the test.' "

8 Again, the devil took him to a very high mountain and showed him all the kingdoms of the world and their splendor; [9]and he said to him, "All these I will give you, if you will fall

down and worship me." [10]Jesus said to him, "Away with you, Satan! for it is written,

> 'Worship the Lord your God,
>> and serve only him.' "

[11]Then the devil left him, and suddenly angels came and waited on him.

Jesus Begins His Ministry in Galilee

12 Now when Jesus[c] heard that John had been arrested, he withdrew to Galilee. [13]He left Nazareth and made his home in Capernaum by the sea, in the territory of Zebulun and Naphtali, [14]so that what had been spoken through the prophet Isaiah might be fulfilled:

15 "Land of Zebulun, land of Naphtali,
>> on the road by the sea, across the Jordan,
>>> Galilee of the Gentiles—
16 the people who sat in darkness
>> have seen a great light,
> and for those who sat in the region and
>>> shadow of death
>> light has dawned."

[17]From that time Jesus began to proclaim, "Repent, for the kingdom of heaven has come near."[d]

Jesus Calls the First Disciples

18 As he walked by the Sea of Galilee, he saw two brothers, Simon, who is called Peter, and Andrew his brother, casting a net into the sea—for they were fishermen. [19]And he said to them, "Follow me, and I will make you fish for people." [20]Immediately they left their nets and followed him. [21]As he went from there, he saw two other brothers, James son of Zebedee and his brother John, in the boat with their father Zebedee, mending their nets, and he called them. [22]Immediately they left the boat and their father, and followed him.

Jesus Ministers to Crowds of People

23 Jesus[e] went throughout Galilee, teaching in their synagogues and proclaiming the good news[f] of the kingdom and curing every disease and every sickness among the people. [24]So his fame spread throughout all Syria, and they brought to him all the sick, those who were afflicted with various diseases and pains, demoniacs, epileptics, and paralytics, and he cured them. [25]And great crowds followed him from Galilee, the Decapolis, Jerusalem, Judea, and from beyond the Jordan.

5 The Beatitudes

When Jesus[c] saw the crowds, he went up the mountain; and after he sat down, his disciples

---

a Or in b Or my beloved Son c Gk he d Or is at hand e Gk He f Gk gospel

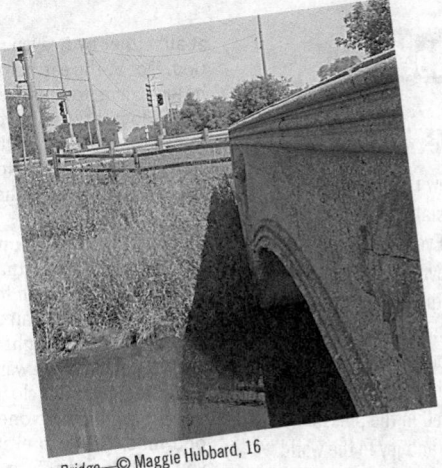

Bridge—© Maggie Hubbard, 16

came to him. ²Then he began to speak, and taught them, saying:

3 "Blessed are the poor in spirit, for theirs is the kingdom of heaven.

4 "Blessed are those who mourn, for they will be comforted.

5 "Blessed are the meek, for they will inherit the earth.

6 "Blessed are those who hunger and thirst for righteousness, for they will be filled.

7 "Blessed are the merciful, for they will receive mercy.

8 "Blessed are the pure in heart, for they will see God.

9 "Blessed are the peacemakers, for they will be called children of God.

10 "Blessed are those who are persecuted for righteousness' sake, for theirs is the kingdom of heaven.

11 "Blessed are you when people revile you and persecute you and utter all kinds of evil against you falsely*a* on my account. ¹²Rejoice and be glad, for your reward is great in heaven, for in the same way they persecuted the prophets who were before you.

Salt and Light

13 "You are the salt of the earth; but if salt has lost its taste, how can its saltiness be restored? It is no longer good for anything, but is thrown out and trampled under foot.

14 "You are the light of the world. A city built on a hill cannot be hid. ¹⁵No one after lighting a lamp puts it under the bushel basket, but on the lampstand, and it gives light to all in the house. ¹⁶In the same way, let your light shine before others, so that they may see your good works and give glory to your Father in heaven.

The Law and the Prophets

17 "Do not think that I have come to abolish the law or the prophets; I have come not to abolish but to fulfill. ¹⁸For truly I tell you, until heaven and earth pass away, not one letter,*b* not one stroke of a letter, will pass from the law until all is accomplished. ¹⁹Therefore, whoever breaks*c* one of the least of these commandments, and teaches others to do the same, will be called least in the kingdom of heaven; but whoever does them and teaches them will be called great in the kingdom of heaven. ²⁰For I tell you, unless your righteousness exceeds that of the scribes and Pharisees, you will never enter the kingdom of heaven.

Concerning Anger

21 "You have heard that it was said to those of ancient times, 'You shall not murder'; and 'whoever murders shall be liable to judgment.' ²²But I say to you that if you are angry with a brother or sister,*d* you will be liable to judgment; and if you insult*e* a brother or sister,*f* you will be liable to the council; and if you say, 'You fool,' you will be liable to the hell*g* of fire. ²³So when you are offering your gift at the altar, if you remember that your brother or sister*h* has something against you, ²⁴leave your gift there before the altar and go; first be reconciled to your brother or sister,*h* and then come and offer your gift. ²⁵Come to terms quickly with your accuser while you are on the way to court*i* with him, or your accuser may hand you over to the judge, and the judge to the guard, and you will

---

a Other ancient authorities lack *falsely* *b* Gk *one iota* *c* Or *annuls* *d* Gk *a brother*; other ancient authorities add *without cause* *e* Gk *say Raca to* (an obscure term of abuse) *f* Gk *a brother* *g* Gk *Gehenna* *h* Gk *your brother* *i* Gk lacks *to court*

THY KINGDOM COME

The gospel of Matthew talks a lot about Jesus being the Messiah and preaching about the Kingdom. Every time you pray the Lord's Prayer, you pray, "Thy Kingdom come." The Church teaches that even though this phrase refers to the final coming or return of Jesus, it should not sidetrack us from our responsibility in the here and now. We are called to be committed in the present—to bring justice, peace, and joy to the world. It is our baptismal calling to work for the type of justice and peace that causes people and nations to repent and change their lifestyles. Saying the words of the prayer without doing the actions our prayer implies is fruitless—we need to walk the walk too.

be thrown into prison. 26Truly I tell you, you will never get out until you have paid the last penny.

Concerning Adultery

27 "You have heard that it was said, 'You shall not commit adultery.' 28But I say to you that everyone who looks at a woman with lust has already committed adultery with her in his heart. 29If your right eye causes you to sin, tear it out and throw it away; it is better for you to lose one of your members than for your whole body to be thrown into hell.*a* 30And if your right hand causes you to sin, cut it off and throw it away; it is better for you to lose one of your members than for your whole body to go into hell.*a*

Concerning Divorce

31 "It was also said, 'Whoever divorces his wife, let him give her a certificate of divorce.' 32But I say to you that anyone who divorces his wife, except on the ground of unchastity, causes her to commit adultery; and whoever marries a divorced woman commits adultery.

Concerning Oaths

33 "Again, you have heard that it was said to those of ancient times, 'You shall not swear falsely, but carry out the vows you have made to the Lord.' 34But I say to you, Do not swear

at all, either by heaven, for it is the throne of God, 35or by the earth, for it is his footstool, or by Jerusalem, for it is the city of the great King. 36And do not swear by your head, for you cannot make one hair white or black. 37Let your word be 'Yes, Yes' or 'No, No'; anything more than this comes from the evil one.*b*

Concerning Retaliation

38 "You have heard that it was said, 'An eye for an eye and a tooth for a tooth.' 39But I say to you, Do not resist an evildoer. But if anyone strikes you on the right cheek, turn the other also; 40and if anyone wants to sue you and take your coat, give your cloak as well; 41and if anyone forces you to go one mile, go also the second mile. 42Give to everyone who begs from you, and do not refuse anyone who wants to borrow from you.

Love for Enemies

43 "You have heard that it was said, 'You shall love your neighbor and hate your enemy.' 44But I say to you, Love your enemies and pray for those who persecute you, 45so that you may be children of your Father in heaven; for he makes his sun rise on the evil and on the good, and sends rain on the righteous and on the unrighteous. 46For if you love those who love you, what reward do you have? Do not even the tax collectors do the same? 47And if you greet only your brothers and sisters,*c* what more are you doing than others? Do not even the Gentiles do the same? 48Be perfect, therefore, as your heavenly Father is perfect.

6 Concerning Almsgiving

"Beware of practicing your piety before others in order to be seen by them; for then you have no reward from your Father in heaven.

2 "So whenever you give alms, do not sound a trumpet before you, as the hypocrites do in the synagogues and in the streets, so that they may be praised by others. Truly I tell you, they have received their reward. 3But when you give alms, do not let your left hand know what your right hand is doing, 4so that your alms may be done in secret; and your Father who sees in secret will reward you.*d*

Concerning Prayer

5 "And whenever you pray, do not be like the hypocrites; for they love to stand and pray in the synagogues and at the street corners, so that they may be seen by others. Truly I tell you, they have received their reward. 6But whenever you pray, go into your room and shut the door

---

a Gk Gehenna *b* Or evil *c* Gk your brothers *d* Other ancient authorities add openly and pray to your Father who is in secret; and your Father who sees in secret will reward you.[a]

7 "When you are praying, do not heap up empty phrases as the Gentiles do; for they think that they will be heard because of their many words. [8]Do not be like them, for your Father knows what you need before you ask him.

9 "Pray then in this way:

Our Father in heaven,
    hallowed be your name.
[10]   Your kingdom come.
    Your will be done,
        on earth as it is in heaven.
[11]   Give us this day our daily bread.[b]
[12]   And forgive us our debts,
        as we also have forgiven our debtors.
[13]   And do not bring us to the time of trial,[c]
        but rescue us from the evil one.[d]

[14]For if you forgive others their trespasses, your heavenly Father will also forgive you; [15]but if you do not forgive others, neither will your Father forgive your trespasses.

Concerning Fasting

16 "And whenever you fast, do not look dismal, like the hypocrites, for they disfigure their faces so as to show others that they are fasting. Truly I tell you, they have received their reward. [17]But when you fast, put oil on your head and wash your face, [18]so that your fasting may be seen not by others but by your Father who is in secret; and your Father who sees in secret will reward you.[a]

Concerning Treasures

19 "Do not store up for yourselves treasures on earth, where moth and rust[e] consume and where thieves break in and steal; [20]but store up for yourselves treasures in heaven, where neither moth nor rust[e] consumes and where thieves do not break in and steal. [21]For where your treasure is, there your heart will be also.

The Sound Eye

22 "The eye is the lamp of the body. So, if your eye is healthy, your whole body will be full of light; [23]but if your eye is unhealthy, your whole body will be full of darkness. If then the light in you is darkness, how great is the darkness!

Serving Two Masters

24 "No one can serve two masters; for a slave will either hate the one and love the other, or be devoted to the one and despise the other. You cannot serve God and wealth.[f]

REAL QUESTIONS

RQ

Some people do horrendous things— child molesters, suicide bombers, school shooters, rapists, or serial killers. Does God really want us to love them and forgive them for what they've done? It just doesn't seem right.

Do you think it's possible to "Hate the sin, love the sinner"? Jesus said "Love your enemies" (Matthew 5.44), and we can safely assume that "enemies" includes pretty much *everyone* we feel hatred for. But what does loving sinners actually look and feel like? How can you zero in on God's all-powerful mercy instead of focusing on the cruel and evil stuff someone does?

Colossians 3.13 challenges us, "Just as the Lord has forgiven you, so you also must forgive." When someone's terrible evil is all you can see, turn your eyes in another direction— to the cross. What did Jesus' death accomplish in *your* life? What sins, lies, betrayals, and hurts has God forgiven *you* for? Do you have the courage to offer this same Jesus-sized forgiveness to others? You can't do it on your own, but the Holy Spirit will help you choose love and forgiveness even if you don't feel them at all.

Find some Creative Space in this Bible and write your thoughts about forgiveness and love even for those who deserve to be hated. You might want to add some real questions of your own. Talk to a trusted friend about your thoughts and questions.

(Want to explore more? Read the book of Hosea and consider God's amazingly forgiving love. Then take a closer look at Matthew 6.12–15; Romans 5.6–10; 12.17–21; Colossians 3.12–15; and read the story of Corrie ten Boom on p. 1143.)

Do Not Worry

25 "Therefore I tell you, do not worry about your life, what you will eat or what you will drink,[g] or about your body, what you will wear. Is not life more than food, and the body

---

a Other ancient authorities add *openly* b Or *our bread for tomorrow* c Or *us into temptation* d Or *from evil*. Other ancient authorities add, in some form, *For the kingdom and the power and the glory are yours forever. Amen.* e Gk *eating* f Gk *mammon* g Other ancient authorities lack *or what you will drink*

PROFILE OF FAITH

There's probably no saint better known than Nicholas of Myra—but you may not know him by that name. He's the model for jolly St. Nicholas, or Santa Claus.

Legend holds that St. Nicholas was born into a very wealthy family and orphaned at a young age. When he grew older, St. Nicholas decided to give all of his possessions to the poor and dedicate himself to serving Christ. He would toss little pouches of coins through the windows of the homes of the poor, and sometimes the pouches would land in freshly washed stockings that had been hung on the windowsill to dry. Once, finding all the windows in a house firmly shut, St. Nicholas tossed the pouch up to the roof, where it went down the chimney. These stories became the basis for some of our most treasured holiday traditions.

Even after he became the bishop of Myra, St. Nicholas had a special place in his heart for orphans and poor children. He continued to give them small gifts and money.

St. Nicholas was one of the first people to be venerated as a saint who had not been a martyr. During his lifetime in the fourth century, Christian persecutions had stopped and Christians began to look for other models of holiness. St. Nicholas lived his life according to Jesus' words: "In everything do to others as you would have them do to you" (Matthew 7.12).

---

more than clothing? [26]Look at the birds of the air; they neither sow nor reap nor gather into barns, and yet your heavenly Father feeds them. Are you not of more value than they? [27]And can any of you by worrying add a single hour to your span of life?[a] [28]And why do you worry about clothing? Consider the lilies of the field, how they grow; they neither toil nor spin, [29]yet I tell you, even Solomon in all his glory was not clothed like one of these. [30]But if God so clothes the grass of the field, which is alive today and tomorrow is thrown into the oven, will he not much more clothe you—you of little faith? [31]Therefore do not worry, saying, 'What will we eat?' or 'What will we drink?' or 'What will we wear?' [32]For it is the Gentiles who strive for all these things; and indeed your heavenly Father knows that you need all these things. [33]But strive first for the kingdom of God[b] and his[c] righteousness, and all these things will be given to you as well.

[34] "So do not worry about tomorrow, for tomorrow will bring worries of its own. Today's trouble is enough for today.

7 Judging Others

"Do not judge, so that you may not be judged. [2]For with the judgment you make you will be judged, and the measure you give will be the measure you get. [3]Why do you see the speck in your neighbor's[d] eye, but do not notice the log in your own eye? [4]Or how can you say to your neighbor,[e] 'Let me take the speck out of your eye,' while the log is in your own eye? [5]You hypocrite, first take the log out of your own eye, and then you will see clearly to take the speck out of your neighbor's[d] eye.

Profaning the Holy

6 "Do not give what is holy to dogs; and do not throw your pearls before swine, or they will trample them under foot and turn and maul you.

Ask, Search, Knock

7 "Ask, and it will be given you; search, and you will find; knock, and the door will be opened for you. [8]For everyone who asks receives, and everyone who searches finds, and for everyone who knocks, the door will be opened. [9]Is there anyone among you who, if your child asks for bread, will give a stone? [10]Or if the child asks for a fish, will give a snake? [11]If you then, who are evil, know how to give good gifts to your children, how much more will your Father in heaven give good things to those who ask him!

The Golden Rule

12 "In everything do to others as you would have them do to you; for this is the law and the prophets.

---

a Or *add one cubit to your height* b Other ancient authorities lack *of God* c Or *its* d Gk *brother's* e Gk *brother*

The Narrow Gate

13 "Enter through the narrow gate; for the gate is wide and the road is easy[a] that leads to destruction, and there are many who take it. 14For the gate is narrow and the road is hard that leads to life, and there are few who find it.

A Tree and Its Fruit

15 "Beware of false prophets, who come to you in sheep's clothing but inwardly are ravenous wolves. 16You will know them by their fruits. Are grapes gathered from thorns, or figs from thistles? 17In the same way, every good tree bears good fruit, but the bad tree bears bad fruit. 18A good tree cannot bear bad fruit, nor can a bad tree bear good fruit. 19Every tree that does not bear good fruit is cut down and thrown into the fire. 20Thus you will know them by their fruits.

Concerning Self-Deception

21 "Not everyone who says to me, 'Lord, Lord,' will enter the kingdom of heaven, but only the one who does the will of my Father in heaven. 22On that day many will say to me, 'Lord, Lord, did we not prophesy in your name, and cast out demons in your name, and do many deeds of power in your name?' 23Then I will declare to them, 'I never knew you; go away from me, you evildoers.'

Hearers and Doers

24 "Everyone then who hears these words of mine and acts on them will be like a wise man who built his house on rock. 25The rain fell, the floods came, and the winds blew and beat on that house, but it did not fall, because it had been founded on rock. 26And everyone who hears these words of mine and does not act on them will be like a foolish man who built his house on sand. 27The rain fell, and the floods came, and the winds blew and beat against that house, and it fell—and great was its fall!"

28 Now when Jesus had finished saying these things, the crowds were astounded at his teaching, 29for he taught them as one having authority, and not as their scribes.

8 Jesus Cleanses a Leper

When Jesus[b] had come down from the mountain, great crowds followed him; 2and there was a leper[c] who came to him and knelt before him, saying, "Lord, if you choose, you can make me clean." 3He stretched out his hand and touched him, saying, "I do choose. Be made clean!" Immediately his leprosy[c] was cleansed. 4Then Jesus said to him, "See that you say nothing to anyone; but go, show yourself to the priest, and offer the gift that Moses commanded, as a testimony to them."

Jesus Heals a Centurion's Servant

5 When he entered Capernaum, a centurion came to him, appealing to him 6and saying, "Lord, my servant is lying at home paralyzed, in terrible distress." 7And he said to him, "I will come and cure him." 8The centurion answered, "Lord, I am not worthy to have you come under my roof; but only speak the word, and my servant will be healed. 9For I also am a man under authority, with soldiers under me; and I say to one, 'Go,' and he goes, and to another, 'Come,' and he comes, and to my slave, 'Do this,' and the slave does it." 10When Jesus heard him, he was amazed and said to those who followed him, "Truly I tell you, in no one[d] in Israel have I found such faith. 11I tell you, many will come from east and west and will eat with Abraham and Isaac and Jacob in the kingdom of heaven, 12while the heirs of the kingdom will be thrown into the outer darkness, where there will be weeping and gnashing of teeth." 13And to the centurion Jesus said, "Go; let it be done for you according to your faith." And the servant was healed in that hour.

Jesus Heals Many at Peter's House

14 When Jesus entered Peter's house, he saw his mother-in-law lying in bed with a fever; 15he touched her hand, and the fever left her, and she got up and began to serve him. 16That evening they brought to him many who were possessed with demons; and he cast out the spirits with a word, and cured all who were sick. 17This was to fulfill what had been spoken through the prophet Isaiah, "He took our infirmities and bore our diseases."

Would-Be Followers of Jesus

18 Now when Jesus saw great crowds around him, he gave orders to go over to the other side. 19A scribe then approached and said, "Teacher, I will follow you wherever you go." 20And Jesus said to him, "Foxes have holes, and birds of the air have nests; but the Son of Man has nowhere to lay his head." 21Another of his disciples said to him, "Lord, first let me go and bury my father." 22But Jesus said to him, "Follow me, and let the dead bury their own dead."

Jesus Stills the Storm

23 And when he got into the boat, his disciples followed him. 24A windstorm arose on the

---

a Other ancient authorities read *for the road is wide and easy* b Gk *he* c The terms *leper* and *leprosy* can refer to several diseases d Other ancient authorities read *Truly I tell you, not even*

TEXT MESSAGE

As a tax collector, Matthew was hardly Mr. Popularity (Matthew 9.9–13). He could tax you for crossing a bridge. He could also tax your cart, its axle, and the engine (or donkey). And you thought toll roads were bad!

Fact

This information has been scanned and is free of all known viruses. Please forward to all your friends.

ment us before the time?" ³⁰Now a large herd of swine was feeding at some distance from them. ³¹The demons begged him, "If you cast us out, send us into the herd of swine." ³²And he said to them, "Go!" So they came out and entered the swine; and suddenly, the whole herd rushed down the steep bank into the sea and perished in the water. ³³The swineherds ran off, and on going into the town, they told the whole story about what had happened to the demoniacs. ³⁴Then the whole town came out to meet Jesus; and when they saw him, they begged him to leave their neighborhood.

9 ¹And after getting into a boat he crossed the sea and came to his own town.

Jesus Heals a Paralytic

2 And just then some people were carrying a paralyzed man lying on a bed. When Jesus saw their faith, he said to the paralytic, "Take heart, son; your sins are forgiven." ³Then some of the scribes said to themselves, "This man is blaspheming." ⁴But Jesus, perceiving their thoughts, said, "Why do you think evil in your hearts? ⁵For which is easier, to say, 'Your sins are forgiven,' or to say, 'Stand up and walk'? ⁶But so that you may know that the Son of Man has authority on earth to forgive sins"— he then said to the paralytic—"Stand up, take your bed and go to your home." ⁷And he stood up and went to his home. ⁸When the crowds saw it, they were filled with awe, and they glorified God, who had given such authority to human beings.

The Call of Matthew

9 As Jesus was walking along, he saw a man called Matthew sitting at the tax booth; and he said to him, "Follow me." And he got up and followed him.

10 And as he sat at dinner*b* in the house, many tax collectors and sinners came and were sitting*c* with him and his disciples. ¹¹When the Pharisees saw this, they said to his disciples, "Why does your teacher eat with tax collectors and sinners?" ¹²But when he heard this, he said, "Those who are well have no need of a physician, but those who are sick. ¹³Go and learn what this means, 'I desire mercy, not sacrifice.' For I have come to call not the righteous but sinners."

The Question about Fasting

14 Then the disciples of John came to him, saying, "Why do we and the Pharisees fast often,*d* but your disciples do not fast?" ¹⁵And Jesus said to them, "The wedding guests can-

sea, so great that the boat was being swamped by the waves; but he was asleep. ²⁵And they went and woke him up, saying, "Lord, save us! We are perishing!" ²⁶And he said to them, "Why are you afraid, you of little faith?" Then he got up and rebuked the winds and the sea; and there was a dead calm. ²⁷They were amazed, saying, "What sort of man is this, that even the winds and the sea obey him?"

Jesus Heals the Gadarene Demoniacs

28 When he came to the other side, to the country of the Gadarenes,*a* two demoniacs coming out of the tombs met him. They were so fierce that no one could pass that way. ²⁹Suddenly they shouted, "What have you to do with us, Son of God? Have you come here to tor-

a Other ancient authorities read Gergesenes ; others, Gerasenes b Gk reclined c Gk were reclining d Other ancient authorities lack often not mourn as long as the bridegroom is with them, can they? The days will come when the bridegroom is taken away from them, and then they will fast. [16]No one sews a piece of unshrunk cloth on an old cloak, for the patch pulls away from the cloak, and a worse tear is made. [17]Neither is new wine put into old wineskins; otherwise, the skins burst, and the wine is spilled, and the skins are destroyed; but new wine is put into fresh wineskins, and so both are preserved."

A Girl Restored to Life and a Woman Healed

18 While he was saying these things to them, suddenly a leader of the synagogue[a] came in and knelt before him, saying, "My daughter has just died; but come and lay your hand on her, and she will live." [19]And Jesus got up and followed him, with his disciples. [20]Then suddenly a woman who had been suffering from hemorrhages for twelve years came up behind him and touched the fringe of his cloak, [21]for she said to herself, "If I only touch his cloak, I will be made well." [22]Jesus turned, and seeing her he said, "Take heart, daughter; your faith has made you well." And instantly the woman was made well. [23]When Jesus came to the leader's house and saw the flute players and the crowd making a commotion, [24]he said, "Go away; for the girl is not dead but sleeping." And they laughed at him. [25]But when the crowd had been put outside, he went in and took her by the hand, and the girl got up. [26]And the report of this spread throughout that district.

Jesus Heals Two Blind Men

27 As Jesus went on from there, two blind men followed him, crying loudly, "Have mercy on us, Son of David!" [28]When he entered the house, the blind men came to him; and Jesus said to them, "Do you believe that I am able to do this?" They said to him, "Yes, Lord." [29]Then he touched their eyes and said, "According to your faith let it be done to you." [30]And their eyes were opened. Then Jesus sternly ordered them, "See that no one knows of this." [31]But they went away and spread the news about him throughout that district.

Jesus Heals One Who Was Mute

32 After they had gone away, a demoniac who was mute was brought to him. [33]And when the demon had been cast out, the one who had been mute spoke; and the crowds were amazed and said, "Never has anything like this been seen in Israel." [34]But the Pharisees said, "By the ruler of the demons he casts out the demons."[b]

The Harvest Is Great, the Laborers Few

35 Then Jesus went about all the cities and villages, teaching in their synagogues, and proclaiming the good news of the kingdom, and curing every disease and every sickness. [36]When he saw the crowds, he had compassion for them, because they were harassed and helpless, like sheep without a shepherd. [37]Then he said to his disciples, "The harvest is plentiful, but the laborers are few; [38]therefore ask the Lord of the harvest to send out laborers into his harvest."

10   The Twelve Apostles

Then Jesus[c] summoned his twelve disciples and gave them authority over unclean spirits, to cast them out, and to cure every disease and every sickness. [2]These are the names of the twelve apostles: first, Simon, also known as Peter, and his brother Andrew; James son of Zebedee, and his brother John; [3]Philip and Bartholomew; Thomas and Matthew the tax collector; James son of Alphaeus, and Thaddaeus;[d] [4]Simon the Cananaean, and Judas Iscariot, the one who betrayed him.

The Mission of the Twelve

5 These twelve Jesus sent out with the following instructions: "Go nowhere among the Gentiles, and enter no town of the Samaritans, [6]but go rather to the lost sheep of the house of Israel. [7]As you go, proclaim the good news, 'The kingdom of heaven has come near.'[e] [8]Cure the sick, raise the dead, cleanse the lepers,[f] cast out demons. You received without payment; give without payment. [9]Take no gold, or silver, or copper in your belts, [10]no bag for your journey, or two tunics, or sandals, or a staff; for laborers deserve their food. [11]Whatever town or village you enter, find out who in it is worthy, and stay there until you leave. [12]As you enter the house, greet it. [13]If the house is worthy, let your peace come upon it; but if it is not worthy, let your peace return to you. [14]If anyone will not welcome you or listen to your words, shake off the dust from your feet as you leave that house or town. [15]Truly I tell you, it will be more tolerable for the land of Sodom and Gomorrah on the day of judgment than for that town.

Coming Persecutions

16 "See, I am sending you out like sheep into the midst of wolves; so be wise as serpents and

---

a Gk lacks *of the synagogue* b Other ancient authorities lack this verse c Gk *he* d Other ancient authorities read *Lebbaeus*, or *Lebbaeus called Thaddaeus* e Or *is at hand* f The terms *leper* and *leprosy* can refer to several diseases innocent as doves. ¹⁷Beware of them, for they will hand you over to councils and flog you in their synagogues; ¹⁸and you will be dragged before governors and kings because of me, as a testimony to them and the Gentiles. ¹⁹When they hand you over, do not worry about how you are to speak or what you are to say; for what you are to say will be given to you at that time; ²⁰for it is not you who speak, but the Spirit of your Father speaking through you. ²¹Brother will betray brother to death, and a father his child, and children will rise against parents and have them put to death; ²²and you will be hated by all because of my name. But the one who endures to the end will be saved. ²³When they persecute you in one town, flee to the next; for truly I tell you, you will not have gone through all the towns of Israel before the Son of Man comes.

24 "A disciple is not above the teacher, nor a slave above the master; ²⁵it is enough for the disciple to be like the teacher, and the slave like the master. If they have called the master of the house Beelzebul, how much more will they malign those of his household!

Whom to Fear

26 "So have no fear of them; for nothing is covered up that will not be uncovered, and nothing secret that will not become known. ²⁷What I say to you in the dark, tell in the light; and what you hear whispered, proclaim from the housetops. ²⁸Do not fear those who kill the body but cannot kill the soul; rather fear him who can destroy both soul and body in hell.ᵃ ²⁹Are not two sparrows sold for a penny? Yet not one of them will fall to the ground apart from your Father. ³⁰And even the hairs of your head are all counted. ³¹So do not be afraid; you are of more value than many sparrows.

32 "Everyone therefore who acknowledges me before others, I also will acknowledge before my Father in heaven; ³³but whoever denies me before others, I also will deny before my Father in heaven.

Not Peace, but a Sword

34 "Do not think that I have come to bring peace to the earth; I have not come to bring peace, but a sword.
35 For I have come to set a man against his
            father,
        and a daughter against her mother,
        and a daughter-in-law against her
            mother-in-law;

³⁶ and one's foes will be members of one's
            own household.
³⁷Whoever loves father or mother more than me is not worthy of me; and whoever loves son or daughter more than me is not worthy of me; ³⁸and whoever does not take up the cross and follow me is not worthy of me. ³⁹Those who find their life will lose it, and those who lose their life for my sake will find it.

Rewards

40 "Whoever welcomes you welcomes me, and whoever welcomes me welcomes the one who sent me. ⁴¹Whoever welcomes a prophet in the name of a prophet will receive a prophet's reward; and whoever welcomes a righteous person in the name of a righteous person will receive the reward of the righteous; ⁴²and whoever gives even a cup of cold water to one of these little ones in the name of a disciple— truly I tell you, none of these will lose their reward."

11 Now when Jesus had finished instructing his twelve disciples, he went on from there to teach and proclaim his message in their cities.

Messengers from John the Baptist

2 When John heard in prison what the Messiahᵇ was doing, he sent word by hisᶜ disciples ³and said to him, "Are you the one who is to come, or are we to wait for another?" ⁴Jesus answered them, "Go and tell John what you hear and see: ⁵the blind receive their sight, the lame walk, the lepersᵈ are cleansed, the deaf hear, the dead are raised, and the poor have good news brought to them. ⁶And blessed is anyone who takes no offense at me."

Jesus Praises John the Baptist

7 As they went away, Jesus began to speak to the crowds about John: "What did you go out into the wilderness to look at? A reed shaken by the wind? ⁸What then did you go out to see? Someoneᵉ dressed in soft robes? Look, those who wear soft robes are in royal palaces. ⁹What then did you go out to see? A prophet?ᶠ Yes, I tell you, and more than a prophet. ¹⁰This is the one about whom it is written,
    'See, I am sending my messenger ahead of
            you,
        who will prepare your way before you.'
¹¹Truly I tell you, among those born of women no one has arisen greater than John the Baptist; yet the least in the kingdom of heaven is greater than he. ¹²From the days of John the Baptist until now the kingdom of heaven has

---

a Gk Gehenna b Or the Christ c Other ancient authorities read two of his d The terms leper and leprosy can refer to several diseases
e Or Why then did you go out? To see someone f Other ancient authorities read Why then did you go out? To see a prophet?

Friends—© Catherine Willms, 15

suffered violence,[a] and the violent take it by force. [13]For all the prophets and the law prophesied until John came; [14]and if you are willing to accept it, he is Elijah who is to come. [15]Let anyone with ears[b] listen!

[16] "But to what will I compare this generation? It is like children sitting in the marketplaces and calling to one another,

[17] 'We played the flute for you, and you did not dance;

we wailed, and you did not mourn.'

[18]For John came neither eating nor drinking, and they say, 'He has a demon'; [19]the Son of Man came eating and drinking, and they say, 'Look, a glutton and a drunkard, a friend of tax collectors and sinners!' Yet wisdom is vindicated by her deeds."[c]

Woes to Unrepentant Cities

[20] Then he began to reproach the cities in which most of his deeds of power had been done, because they did not repent. [21]"Woe to you, Chorazin! Woe to you, Bethsaida! For if the deeds of power done in you had been done in Tyre and Sidon, they would have repented long ago in sackcloth and ashes. [22]But I tell you, on the day of judgment it will be more tol-

erable for Tyre and Sidon than for you. [23]And you, Capernaum,

will you be exalted to heaven?

No, you will be brought down to Hades. For if the deeds of power done in you had been done in Sodom, it would have remained until this day. [24]But I tell you that on the day of judgment it will be more tolerable for the land of Sodom than for you."

Jesus Thanks His Father

[25] At that time Jesus said, "I thank[d] you, Father, Lord of heaven and earth, because you have hidden these things from the wise and the intelligent and have revealed them to infants; [26]yes, Father, for such was your gracious will.[e] [27]All things have been handed over to me by my Father; and no one knows the Son except the Father, and no one knows the Father except the Son and anyone to whom the Son chooses to reveal him.

[28] "Come to me, all you that are weary and are carrying heavy burdens, and I will give you rest. [29]Take my yoke upon you, and learn from me; for I am gentle and humble in heart, and you will find rest for your souls. [30]For my yoke is easy, and my burden is light."

a Or has been coming violently b Other ancient authorities add to hear c Other ancient authorities read children d Or praise e Or for so it was well-pleasing in your sight

12 Plucking Grain on the Sabbath

At that time Jesus went through the grainfields on the sabbath; his disciples were hungry, and they began to pluck heads of grain and to eat. [2]When the Pharisees saw it, they said to him, "Look, your disciples are doing what is not lawful to do on the sabbath." [3]He said to them, "Have you not read what David did when he and his companions were hungry? [4]He entered the house of God and ate the bread of the Presence, which it was not lawful for him or his companions to eat, but only for the priests. [5]Or have you not read in the law that on the sabbath the priests in the temple break the sabbath and yet are guiltless? [6]I tell you, something greater than the temple is here. [7]But if you had known what this means, 'I desire mercy and not sacrifice,' you would not have condemned the guiltless. [8]For the Son of Man is lord of the sabbath."

The Man with a Withered Hand

9 He left that place and entered their synagogue; [10]a man was there with a withered hand, and they asked him, "Is it lawful to cure on the sabbath?" so that they might accuse him. [11]He said to them, "Suppose one of you has only one sheep and it falls into a pit on the sabbath; will you not lay hold of it and lift it out? [12]How much more valuable is a human being than a sheep! So it is lawful to do good on the sabbath." [13]Then he said to the man, "Stretch out your hand." He stretched it out, and it was restored, as sound as the other. [14]But the Pharisees went out and conspired against him, how to destroy him.

God's Chosen Servant

15 When Jesus became aware of this, he departed. Many crowds[a] followed him, and he cured all of them, [16]and he ordered them not to make him known. [17]This was to fulfill what had been spoken through the prophet Isaiah:
[18] "Here is my servant, whom I have chosen,
   my beloved, with whom my soul is well pleased.
   I will put my Spirit upon him,
      and he will proclaim justice to the Gentiles.
[19] He will not wrangle or cry aloud,
      nor will anyone hear his voice in the streets.
[20] He will not break a bruised reed
      or quench a smoldering wick
   until he brings justice to victory.
[21]   And in his name the Gentiles will hope."

Jesus and Beelzebul

22 Then they brought to him a demoniac who was blind and mute; and he cured him, so that the one who had been mute could speak and see. [23]All the crowds were amazed and said, "Can this be the Son of David?" [24]But when the Pharisees heard it, they said, "It is only by Beelzebul, the ruler of the demons, that this fellow casts out the demons." [25]He knew what they were thinking and said to them, "Every kingdom divided against itself is laid waste, and no city or house divided against itself will stand. [26]If Satan casts out Satan, he is divided against himself; how then will his kingdom stand? [27]If I cast out demons by Beelzebul, by whom do your own exorcists[b] cast them out? Therefore they will be your judges. [28]But if it is by the Spirit of God that I cast out demons, then the kingdom of God has come to you. [29]Or how can one enter a strong man's house and plunder his property, without first tying up the strong man? Then indeed the house can be plundered. [30]Whoever is not with me is against me, and whoever does not gather with me scatters. [31]Therefore I tell you, people will be forgiven for every sin and blasphemy, but blasphemy against the Spirit will not be forgiven. [32]Whoever speaks a word against the Son of Man will be forgiven, but whoever speaks against the Holy Spirit will not be forgiven, either in this age or in the age to come.

A Tree and Its Fruit

33 "Either make the tree good, and its fruit good; or make the tree bad, and its fruit bad; for the tree is known by its fruit. [34]You brood of vipers! How can you speak good things, when you are evil? For out of the abundance of the heart the mouth speaks. [35]The good person brings good things out of a good treasure, and the evil person brings evil things out of an evil treasure. [36]I tell you, on the day of judgment you will have to give an account for every careless word you utter; [37]for by your words you will be justified, and by your words you will be condemned."

The Sign of Jonah

38 Then some of the scribes and Pharisees said to him, "Teacher, we wish to see a sign from you." [39]But he answered them, "An evil and adulterous generation asks for a sign, but no sign will be given to it except the sign of the prophet Jonah. [40]For just as Jonah was three days and three nights in the belly of the sea monster, so for three days and three nights the Son of Man will be in the heart of the earth.

---

a Other ancient authorities lack *crowds* b Gk *sons*

⁴¹The people of Nineveh will rise up at the judgment with this generation and condemn it, because they repented at the proclamation of Jonah, and see, something greater than Jonah is here! ⁴²The queen of the South will rise up at the judgment with this generation and condemn it, because she came from the ends of the earth to listen to the wisdom of Solomon, and see, something greater than Solomon is here!

The Return of the Unclean Spirit

43 "When the unclean spirit has gone out of a person, it wanders through waterless regions looking for a resting place, but it finds none. ⁴⁴Then it says, 'I will return to my house from which I came.' When it comes, it finds it empty, swept, and put in order. ⁴⁵Then it goes and brings along seven other spirits more evil than itself, and they enter and live there; and the last state of that person is worse than the first. So will it be also with this evil generation."

The True Kindred of Jesus

46 While he was still speaking to the crowds, his mother and his brothers were standing outside, wanting to speak to him. ⁴⁷Someone told him, "Look, your mother and your brothers are standing outside, wanting to speak to you."ᵃ ⁴⁸But to the one who had told him this, Jesusᵇ replied, "Who is my mother, and who are my brothers?" ⁴⁹And pointing to his disciples, he said, "Here are my mother and my brothers! ⁵⁰For whoever does the will of my Father in heaven is my brother and sister and mother."

13 The Parable of the Sower

That same day Jesus went out of the house and sat beside the sea. ²Such great crowds gathered around him that he got into a boat and sat there, while the whole crowd stood on the beach. ³And he told them many things in parables, saying: "Listen! A sower went out to sow. ⁴And as he sowed, some seeds fell on the path, and the birds came and ate them up. ⁵Other seeds fell on rocky ground, where they did not have much soil, and they sprang up quickly, since they had no depth of soil. ⁶But when the sun rose, they were scorched; and since they had no root, they withered away. ⁷Other seeds fell among thorns, and the thorns grew up and choked them. ⁸Other seeds fell on good soil and brought forth grain, some a hundredfold, some sixty, some thirty. ⁹Let anyone with earsᶜ listen!"

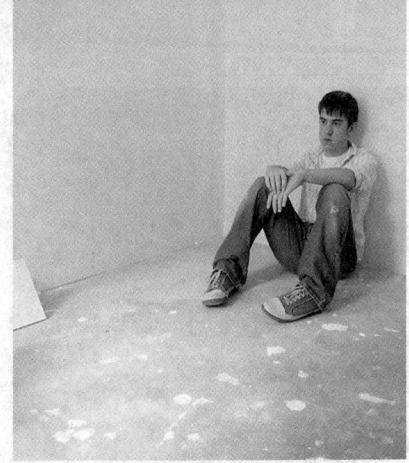
Wondering—© Clay Goswick, 16

The Purpose of the Parables

10 Then the disciples came and asked him, "Why do you speak to them in parables?" ¹¹He answered, "To you it has been given to know the secretsᵈ of the kingdom of heaven, but to them it has not been given. ¹²For to those who have, more will be given, and they will have an abundance; but from those who have nothing, even what they have will be taken away. ¹³The reason I speak to them in parables is that 'seeing they do not perceive, and hearing they do not listen, nor do they understand.' ¹⁴With them indeed is fulfilled the prophecy of Isaiah that says:

'You will indeed listen, but never
        understand,
    and you will indeed look, but never
        perceive.
¹⁵ For this people's heart has grown dull,
    and their ears are hard of hearing,
        and they have shut their eyes;
        so that they might not look with their
            eyes,
    and listen with their ears,
and understand with their heart and turn—
    and I would heal them.'

¹⁶But blessed are your eyes, for they see, and your ears, for they hear. ¹⁷Truly I tell you, many prophets and righteous people longed to see what you see, but did not see it, and to hear what you hear, but did not hear it.

The Parable of the Sower Explained

18 "Hear then the parable of the sower. ¹⁹When anyone hears the word of the kingdom and does not understand it, the evil one comes and snatches away what is sown in the heart; this is what was sown on the path. ²⁰As for

---

a Other ancient authorities lack verse 47 *b* Gk *he* *c* Other ancient authorities add *to hear* *d* Or *mysteries*

Field of Dreams
Read **Matthew 13.44–45**.

Slick, huh?

If you were certain a treasure was hidden in a tumble-down house, wouldn't you cash out your savings and run up a couple of credit cards in a scramble to buy the property?

What looked like an idiotic move to the neighborhood ("Did you hear what he *paid* for that shack?") would prove shrewd the moment you hauled out a box of gold or stuck a pipe in the ground and hit the oil field you knew was there.

Nailing down a sure thing—every investor's dream.

So why don't you do it?

Either you believe that Jesus was serious about this whole heaven and eternal life thing, or you don't. And if you *do,* then there's simply no way to hang on to your current life and also live the one he has in mind for you. Sorry—you can't serve two masters. That's not how it works.

If Jesus is right about that treasure, then trading in what you can't keep for what you can't lose is the best deal in town. It *will* look stupid to some of the people surrounding you, but that's part of the price to be paid.

So . . . which is it? Are you in or out?

Go to an empty field (or a nearby park or patch of grass). Walk around. As you walk, pray. Ask God: *What's the treasure? And what's the price?*

Tell us what you decide at **Learner.CalltoDiscipleship.com**.

And if you happen to stumble across heaven while you're out there, buy the field.

and the lure of wealth choke the word, and it yields nothing. [23]But as for what was sown on good soil, this is the one who hears the word and understands it, who indeed bears fruit and yields, in one case a hundredfold, in another sixty, and in another thirty."

The Parable of Weeds among the Wheat
24 He put before them another parable: "The kingdom of heaven may be compared to someone who sowed good seed in his field; [25]but while everybody was asleep, an enemy came and sowed weeds among the wheat, and then went away. [26]So when the plants came up and bore grain, then the weeds appeared as well. [27]And the slaves of the householder came and said to him, 'Master, did you not sow good seed in your field? Where, then, did these weeds come from?' [28]He answered, 'An enemy has done this.' The slaves said to him, 'Then do you want us to go and gather them?' [29]But he replied, 'No; for in gathering the weeds you would uproot the wheat along with them. [30]Let both of them grow together until the harvest; and at harvest time I will tell the reapers, Collect the weeds first and bind them in bundles to be burned, but gather the wheat into my barn.' "

The Parable of the Mustard Seed
31 He put before them another parable: "The kingdom of heaven is like a mustard seed that someone took and sowed in his field; [32]it is the smallest of all the seeds, but when it has grown it is the greatest of shrubs and becomes a tree, so that the birds of the air come and make nests in its branches."

The Parable of the Yeast
33 He told them another parable: "The kingdom of heaven is like yeast that a woman took and mixed in with[b] three measures of flour until all of it was leavened."

The Use of Parables
34 Jesus told the crowds all these things in parables; without a parable he told them nothing. [35]This was to fulfill what had been spoken through the prophet:[c]

"I will open my mouth to speak in parables;
I will proclaim what has been hidden
from the foundation of the world."[d]

Jesus Explains the Parable of the Weeds
36 Then he left the crowds and went into the house. And his disciples approached him, saying, "Explain to us the parable of the weeds

what was sown on rocky ground, this is the one who hears the word and immediately receives it with joy; [21]yet such a person has no root, but endures only for a while, and when trouble or persecution arises on account of the word, that person immediately falls away.[a] [22]As for what was sown among thorns, this is the one who hears the word, but the cares of the world

a Gk *stumbles* *b* Gk *hid in* *c* Other ancient authorities read *the prophet Isaiah* *d* Other ancient authorities lack *of the world* of the field." [37]He answered, "The one who sows the good seed is the Son of Man; [38]the field is the world, and the good seed are the children of the kingdom; the weeds are the children of the evil one, [39]and the enemy who sowed them is the devil; the harvest is the end of the age, and the reapers are angels. [40]Just as the weeds are collected and burned up with fire, so will it be at the end of the age. [41]The Son of Man will send his angels, and they will collect out of his kingdom all causes of sin and all evildoers, [42]and they will throw them into the furnace of fire, where there will be weeping and gnashing of teeth. [43]Then the righteous will shine like the sun in the kingdom of their Father. Let anyone with ears[a] listen!

Three Parables

44 "The kingdom of heaven is like treasure hidden in a field, which someone found and hid; then in his joy he goes and sells all that he has and buys that field.

45 "Again, the kingdom of heaven is like a merchant in search of fine pearls; [46]on finding one pearl of great value, he went and sold all that he had and bought it.

47 "Again, the kingdom of heaven is like a net that was thrown into the sea and caught fish of every kind; [48]when it was full, they drew it ashore, sat down, and put the good into baskets but threw out the bad. [49]So it will be at the end of the age. The angels will come out and separate the evil from the righteous [50]and throw them into the furnace of fire, where there will be weeping and gnashing of teeth.

Treasures New and Old

51 "Have you understood all this?" They answered, "Yes." [52]And he said to them, "Therefore every scribe who has been trained for the kingdom of heaven is like the master of a household who brings out of his treasure what is new and what is old." [53]When Jesus had finished these parables, he left that place.

The Rejection of Jesus at Nazareth

54 He came to his hometown and began to teach the people[b] in their synagogue, so that they were astounded and said, "Where did this man get this wisdom and these deeds of power? [55]Is not this the carpenter's son? Is not his mother called Mary? And are not his brothers James and Joseph and Simon and Judas? [56]And are not all his sisters with us? Where then did this man get all this?" [57]And they took offense at him. But Jesus said to them, "Prophets are not without honor except in their own country

and in their own house." [58]And he did not do many deeds of power there, because of their unbelief.

14 The Death of John the Baptist

At that time Herod the ruler[c] heard reports about Jesus; [2]and he said to his servants, "This is John the Baptist; he has been raised from the dead, and for this reason these powers are at work in him." [3]For Herod had arrested John, bound him, and put him in prison on account of Herodias, his brother Philip's wife,[d] [4]because John had been telling him, "It is not lawful for you to have her." [5]Though Herod[e] wanted to put him to death, he feared the crowd, because they regarded him as a prophet. [6]But when Herod's birthday came, the daughter of Herodias danced before the company, and she pleased Herod [7]so much that he promised on oath to grant her whatever she might ask. [8]Prompted by her mother, she said, "Give me the head of John the Baptist here on a platter." [9]The king was grieved, yet out of regard for his oaths and for the guests, he commanded it to be given; [10]he sent and had John beheaded in the prison. [11]The head was brought on a platter and given to the girl, who brought it to her mother. [12]His disciples came and took the body and buried it; then they went and told Jesus.

Feeding the Five Thousand

13 Now when Jesus heard this, he withdrew from there in a boat to a deserted place by himself. But when the crowds heard it, they followed him on foot from the towns. [14]When he went ashore, he saw a great crowd; and he had compassion for them and cured their sick. [15]When it was evening, the disciples came to him and said, "This is a deserted place, and the hour is now late; send the crowds away so that they may go into the villages and buy food for themselves." [16]Jesus said to them, "They need not go away; you give them something to eat." [17]They replied, "We have nothing here but five loaves and two fish." [18]And he said, "Bring them here to me." [19]Then he ordered the crowds to sit down on the grass. Taking the five loaves and the two fish, he looked up to heaven, and blessed and broke the loaves, and gave them to the disciples, and the disciples gave them to the crowds. [20]And all ate and were filled; and they took up what was left over of the broken pieces, twelve baskets full. [21]And those who ate were about five thousand men, besides women and children.

---

a Other ancient authorities add to hear b Gk them c Gk tetrarch d Other ancient authorities read his brother's wife e Gk he

Jesus Walks on the Water

22 Immediately he made the disciples get into the boat and go on ahead to the other side, while he dismissed the crowds. 23 And after he had dismissed the crowds, he went up the mountain by himself to pray. When evening came, he was there alone, 24 but by this time the boat, battered by the waves, was far from the land,a for the wind was against them. 25 And early in the morning he came walking toward them on the sea. 26 But when the disciples saw him walking on the sea, they were terrified, saying, "It is a ghost!" And they cried out in fear. 27 But immediately Jesus spoke to them and said, "Take heart, it is I; do not be afraid."

28 Peter answered him, "Lord, if it is you, command me to come to you on the water." 29 He said, "Come." So Peter got out of the boat, started walking on the water, and came toward Jesus. 30 But when he noticed the strong wind,b he became frightened, and beginning to sink, he cried out, "Lord, save me!" 31 Jesus immediately reached out his hand and caught him, saying to him, "You of little faith, why did you doubt?" 32 When they got into the boat, the wind ceased. 33 And those in the boat worshiped him, saying, "Truly you are the Son of God."

Jesus Heals the Sick in Gennesaret

34 When they had crossed over, they came to land at Gennesaret. 35 After the people of that place recognized him, they sent word throughout the region and brought all who were sick to him, 36 and begged him that they might touch even the fringe of his cloak; and all who touched it were healed.

15 The Tradition of the Elders

Then Pharisees and scribes came to Jesus from Jerusalem and said, 2 "Why do your disciples break the tradition of the elders? For they do not wash their hands before they eat." 3 He answered them, "And why do you break the commandment of God for the sake of your tradition? 4 For God said,c 'Honor your father and your mother,' and, 'Whoever speaks evil of father or mother must surely die.' 5 But you say that whoever tells father or mother, 'Whatever support you might have had from me is given to God,'d then that person need not honor the father.e 6 So, for the sake of your tradition, you make void the wordf of God. 7 You hypocrites! Isaiah prophesied rightly about you when he said:

8 'This people honors me with their lips,

but their hearts are far from me;
9 in vain do they worship me,
teaching human precepts as doctrines.' "

Things That Defile

10 Then he called the crowd to him and said to them, "Listen and understand: 11 it is not what goes into the mouth that defiles a person, but it is what comes out of the mouth that defiles." 12 Then the disciples approached and said to him, "Do you know that the Pharisees took offense when they heard what you said?" 13 He answered, "Every plant that my heavenly Father has not planted will be uprooted. 14 Let them alone; they are blind guides of the blind.g And if one blind person guides another, both will fall into a pit." 15 But Peter said to him, "Explain this parable to us." 16 Then he said, "Are you also still without understanding? 17 Do you not see that whatever goes into the mouth enters the stomach, and goes out into the sewer? 18 But what comes out of the mouth proceeds from the heart, and this is what defiles. 19 For out of the heart come evil intentions, murder, adultery, fornication, theft, false witness, slander. 20 These are what defile a person, but to eat with unwashed hands does not defile."

The Canaanite Woman's Faith

21 Jesus left that place and went away to the district of Tyre and Sidon. 22 Just then a Canaanite woman from that region came out and started shouting, "Have mercy on me, Lord, Son of David; my daughter is tormented by a demon." 23 But he did not answer her at all. And his disciples came and urged him, saying, "Send her away, for she keeps shouting after us." 24 He answered, "I was sent only to the lost sheep of the house of Israel." 25 But she came and knelt before him, saying, "Lord, help me." 26 He answered, "It is not fair to take the children's food and throw it to the dogs." 27 She said, "Yes, Lord, yet even the dogs eat the crumbs that fall from their masters' table." 28 Then Jesus answered her, "Woman, great is your faith! Let it be done for you as you wish." And her daughter was healed instantly.

Jesus Cures Many People

29 After Jesus had left that place, he passed along the Sea of Galilee, and he went up the mountain, where he sat down. 30 Great crowds came to him, bringing with them the lame, the maimed, the blind, the mute, and many others. They put them at his feet, and he cured them, 31 so that the crowd was amazed when

a Other ancient authorities read was out on the sea b Other ancient authorities read the wind c Other ancient authorities read commanded, saying d Or is an offering e Other ancient authorities add or the mother f Other ancient authorities read law; others, commandment g Other ancient authorities lack of the blind they saw the mute speaking, the maimed whole, the lame walking, and the blind seeing. And they praised the God of Israel.

Feeding the Four Thousand

32 Then Jesus called his disciples to him and said, "I have compassion for the crowd, because they have been with me now for three days and have nothing to eat; and I do not want to send them away hungry, for they might faint on the way." 33The disciples said to him, "Where are we to get enough bread in the desert to feed so great a crowd?" 34Jesus asked them, "How many loaves have you?" They said, "Seven, and a few small fish." 35Then ordering the crowd to sit down on the ground, 36he took the seven loaves and the fish; and after giving thanks he broke them and gave them to the disciples, and the disciples gave them to the crowds. 37And all of them ate and were filled; and they took up the broken pieces left over, seven baskets full. 38Those who had eaten were four thousand men, besides women and children. 39After sending away the crowds, he got into the boat and went to the region of Magadan.*a*

16 The Demand for a Sign

The Pharisees and Sadducees came, and to test Jesus*b* they asked him to show them a sign from heaven. 2He answered them, "When it is evening, you say, 'It will be fair weather, for the sky is red.' 3And in the morning, 'It will be stormy today, for the sky is red and threatening.' You know how to interpret the appearance of the sky, but you cannot interpret the signs of the times.*c* 4An evil and adulterous generation asks for a sign, but no sign will be given to it except the sign of Jonah." Then he left them and went away.

The Yeast of the Pharisees and Sadducees

5 When the disciples reached the other side, they had forgotten to bring any bread. 6Jesus said to them, "Watch out, and beware of the yeast of the Pharisees and Sadducees." 7They said to one another, "It is because we have brought no bread." 8And becoming aware of it, Jesus said, "You of little faith, why are you talking about having no bread? 9Do you still not perceive? Do you not remember the five loaves for the five thousand, and how many

a Other ancient authorities read *Magdala* or *Magdalan* *b* Gk *him* *c* Other ancient authorities lack *²When it is . . . of the times*

REALITY ✓

LIGHTEN UP

Read **Matthew 16.18**. The author of Matthew is the only gospel writer who reports that Jesus used the term "church," or *ekklesia,* which refers to those assembled or gathered—not a church building. Jesus also alluded to leadership and authority in the Church (Matthew 16.19–20) and how the Church should discipline conflicting members (18.15–18). But overall, Jesus taught that this community of believers must be as humble as children and temper judgment with mercy (18.1–14, 21–35).

Think of this community as a household in which every member is part of the family. This household is to go forth to spread good news, teach others about Christ, and baptize them into the new life offered by the suffering, death, and Resurrection of the Lord.

In other words, the Church has a mission. In the *Catechism of the Catholic Church,* the Church is described as the "soul of human society" and the "leaven" (854). Just as yeast leavens bread and makes it rise, we are to "raise up" others in our human family.

Find some Creative Space in this Bible and jot down your responses to the following:

- I see my parish as a household because . . .

- My place in the household is . . .

- The three ways my parish acts as leaven in the local community are . . .

baskets you gathered? ¹⁰Or the seven loaves for the four thousand, and how many baskets you gathered? ¹¹How could you fail to perceive that I was not speaking about bread? Beware of the yeast of the Pharisees and Sadducees!" ¹²Then they understood that he had not told them to beware of the yeast of bread, but of the teaching of the Pharisees and Sadducees.

Peter's Declaration about Jesus

13 Now when Jesus came into the district of Caesarea Philippi, he asked his disciples, "Who do people say that the Son of Man is?" ¹⁴And they said, "Some say John the Baptist, but others Elijah, and still others Jeremiah or one of the prophets." ¹⁵He said to them, "But who do you say that I am?" ¹⁶Simon Peter answered, "You are the Messiah,ᵃ the Son of the living God." ¹⁷And Jesus answered him, "Blessed are you, Simon son of Jonah! For flesh and blood has not revealed this to you, but my Father in heaven. ¹⁸And I tell you, you are Peter,ᵇ and on this rockᶜ I will build my church, and the gates of Hades will not prevail against it. ¹⁹I will give you the keys of the kingdom of heaven, and whatever you bind on earth will be bound in heaven, and whatever you loose on earth will be loosed in heaven." ²⁰Then he sternly ordered the disciples not to tell anyone that he wasᵈ the Messiah.ᵃ

Jesus Foretells His Death and Resurrection

21 From that time on, Jesus began to show his disciples that he must go to Jerusalem and undergo great suffering at the hands of the elders and chief priests and scribes, and be killed, and on the third day be raised. ²²And Peter took him aside and began to rebuke him, saying, "God forbid it, Lord! This must never happen to you." ²³But he turned and said to Peter, "Get behind me, Satan! You are a stumbling block to me; for you are setting your mind not on divine things but on human things."

The Cross and Self-Denial

24 Then Jesus told his disciples, "If any want to become my followers, let them deny themselves and take up their cross and follow me. ²⁵For those who want to save their life will lose it, and those who lose their life for my sake will find it. ²⁶For what will it profit them if they gain the whole world but forfeit their life? Or what will they give in return for their life?

27 "For the Son of Man is to come with his angels in the glory of his Father, and then he will repay everyone for what has been done. ²⁸Truly I tell you, there are some standing here who will not taste death before they see the Son of Man coming in his kingdom."

17 The Transfiguration

Six days later, Jesus took with him Peter and James and his brother John and led them up a high mountain, by themselves. ²And he was

---

a Or *the Christ* *b* Gk *Petros* *c* Gk *petra* *d* Other ancient authorities add *Jesus* transfigured before them, and his face shone like the sun, and his clothes became dazzling white. 3Suddenly there appeared to them Moses and Elijah, talking with him. 4Then Peter said to Jesus, "Lord, it is good for us to be here; if you wish, I*a* will make three dwellings*b* here, one for you, one for Moses, and one for Elijah." 5While he was still speaking, suddenly a bright cloud overshadowed them, and from the cloud a voice said, "This is my Son, the Beloved;*c* with him I am well pleased; listen to him!" 6When the disciples heard this, they fell to the ground and were overcome by fear. 7But Jesus came and touched them, saying, "Get up and do not be afraid." 8And when they looked up, they saw no one except Jesus himself alone.

9 As they were coming down the mountain, Jesus ordered them, "Tell no one about the vision until after the Son of Man has been raised from the dead." 10And the disciples asked him, "Why, then, do the scribes say that Elijah must come first?" 11He replied, "Elijah is indeed coming and will restore all things; 12but I tell you that Elijah has already come, and they did not recognize him, but they did to him whatever they pleased. So also the Son of Man is about to suffer at their hands." 13Then the disciples understood that he was speaking to them about John the Baptist.

Jesus Cures a Boy with a Demon

14 When they came to the crowd, a man came to him, knelt before him, 15and said, "Lord, have mercy on my son, for he is an epileptic and he suffers terribly; he often falls into the fire and often into the water. 16And I brought him to your disciples, but they could not cure him." 17Jesus answered, "You faithless and perverse generation, how much longer must I be with you? How much longer must I put up with you? Bring him here to me." 18And Jesus rebuked the demon,*d* and it*e* came out of him, and the boy was cured instantly. 19Then the disciples came to Jesus privately and said, "Why could we not cast it out?" 20He said to them, "Because of your little faith. For truly I tell you, if you have faith the size of a*f* mustard seed, you will say to this mountain, 'Move from here to there,' and it will move; and nothing will be impossible for you."*g*

Jesus Again Foretells His Death and Resurrection

22 As they were gathering*h* in Galilee, Jesus said to them, "The Son of Man is going to be betrayed into human hands, 23and they will kill him, and on the third day he will be raised." And they were greatly distressed.

Jesus and the Temple Tax

24 When they reached Capernaum, the collectors of the temple tax*i* came to Peter and said, "Does your teacher not pay the temple tax?"*i* 25He said, "Yes, he does." And when he came home, Jesus spoke of it first, asking, "What do you think, Simon? From whom do kings of the earth take toll or tribute? From their children or from others?" 26When Peter*j* said, "From others," Jesus said to him, "Then the children are free. 27However, so that we do not give offense to them, go to the sea and cast a hook; take the first fish that comes up; and when you open its mouth, you will find a coin;*k* take that and give it to them for you and me."

18 True Greatness

At that time the disciples came to Jesus and asked, "Who is the greatest in the kingdom of heaven?" 2He called a child, whom he put among them, 3and said, "Truly I tell you, unless you change and become like children, you will never enter the kingdom of heaven. 4Whoever becomes humble like this child is the greatest in the kingdom of heaven. 5Whoever welcomes one such child in my name welcomes me.

Temptations to Sin

6 "If any of you put a stumbling block before one of these little ones who believe in me, it would be better for you if a great millstone were fastened around your neck and you were drowned in the depth of the sea. 7Woe to the world because of stumbling blocks! Occasions for stumbling are bound to come, but woe to the one by whom the stumbling block comes!

8 "If your hand or your foot causes you to stumble, cut it off and throw it away; it is better for you to enter life maimed or lame than to have two hands or two feet and to be thrown into the eternal fire. 9And if your eye causes you to stumble, tear it out and throw it away; it is better for you to enter life with one eye than to have two eyes and to be thrown into the hell*l* of fire.

The Parable of the Lost Sheep

10 "Take care that you do not despise one of these little ones; for, I tell you, in heaven their angels continually see the face of my Father in heaven.*m* 12What do you think? If a shep-

---

a Other ancient authorities read *we* *b* Or *tents* *c* Or *my beloved Son* *d* Gk *it* or *him* *e* Gk *the demon* *f* Gk *faith as a grain of* *g* Other ancient authorities add verse 21, *But this kind does not come out except by prayer and fasting* *h* Other ancient authorities read *living* *i* Gk *didrachma* *j* Gk *he* *k* Gk *stater* ; the stater was worth two didrachmas *l* Gk *Gehenna* *m* Other ancient authorities add verse 11, *For the Son of Man came to save the lost*

Untitled—© Erica Wallis, 17

herd has a hundred sheep, and one of them has gone astray, does he not leave the ninety-nine on the mountains and go in search of the one that went astray? [13]And if he finds it, truly I tell you, he rejoices over it more than over the ninety-nine that never went astray. [14]So it is not the will of your[a] Father in heaven that one of these little ones should be lost.

Reproving Another Who Sins

15 "If another member of the church[b] sins against you,[c] go and point out the fault when the two of you are alone. If the member listens to you, you have regained that one.[d] [16]But if you are not listened to, take one or two others along with you, so that every word may be confirmed by the evidence of two or three witnesses. [17]If the member refuses to listen to them, tell it to the church; and if the offender refuses to listen even to the church, let such a one be to you as a Gentile and a tax collector. [18]Truly I tell you, whatever you bind on earth will be bound in heaven, and whatever you loose on earth will be loosed in heaven. [19]Again, truly I tell you, if two of you agree on earth about anything you ask, it will be done for you by my Father in heaven. [20]For where two or three are gathered in my name, I am there among them."

Forgiveness

21 Then Peter came and said to him, "Lord, if another member of the church[e] sins against me, how often should I forgive? As many as seven times?" [22]Jesus said to him, "Not seven times, but, I tell you, seventy-seven[f] times.

The Parable of the Unforgiving Servant

23 "For this reason the kingdom of heaven may be compared to a king who wished to settle accounts with his slaves. [24]When he began the reckoning, one who owed him ten thousand talents[g] was brought to him; [25]and, as he could not pay, his lord ordered him to be sold, together with his wife and children and all his possessions, and payment to be made. [26]So the slave fell on his knees before him, saying, 'Have patience with me, and I will pay you everything.' [27]And out of pity for him, the lord of that slave released him and forgave him the debt. [28]But that same slave, as he went out, came upon one of his fellow slaves who owed him a hundred denarii;[h] and seizing him by the throat, he said, 'Pay what you owe.' [29]Then his fellow slave fell down and pleaded with him, 'Have patience with me, and I will pay you.' [30]But he refused; then he went and threw him into prison until he would pay the debt. [31]When his fellow slaves saw what had

a Other ancient authorities read my b Gk *If your brother* c Other ancient authorities lack *against you* d Gk *the brother* e Gk *if my brother*
f Or *seventy times seven* g A talent was worth more than fifteen years' wages of a laborer h The denarius was the usual day's wage for a laborer

happened, they were greatly distressed, and they went and reported to their lord all that had taken place. ³²Then his lord summoned him and said to him, 'You wicked slave! I forgave you all that debt because you pleaded with me. ³³Should you not have had mercy on your fellow slave, as I had mercy on you?' ³⁴And in anger his lord handed him over to be tortured until he would pay his entire debt. ³⁵So my heavenly Father will also do to every one of you, if you do not forgive your brother or sister^a from your heart."

19 Teaching about Divorce

When Jesus had finished saying these things, he left Galilee and went to the region of Judea beyond the Jordan. ²Large crowds followed him, and he cured them there.

3 Some Pharisees came to him, and to test him they asked, "Is it lawful for a man to divorce his wife for any cause?" ⁴He answered, "Have you not read that the one who made them at the beginning 'made them male and female,' ⁵and said, 'For this reason a man shall leave his father and mother and be joined to his wife, and the two shall become one flesh'? ⁶So they are no longer two, but one flesh. Therefore what God has joined together, let no one separate." ⁷They said to him, "Why then did Moses command us to give a certificate of dismissal and to divorce her?" ⁸He said to them, "It was because you were so hard-hearted that Moses allowed you to divorce your wives, but from the beginning it was not so. ⁹And I say to you, whoever divorces his wife, except for unchastity, and marries another commits adultery."^b

10 His disciples said to him, "If such is the case of a man with his wife, it is better not to marry." ¹¹But he said to them, "Not everyone can accept this teaching, but only those to whom it is given. ¹²For there are eunuchs who have been so from birth, and there are eunuchs who have been made eunuchs by others, and there are eunuchs who have made themselves eunuchs for the sake of the kingdom of heaven. Let anyone accept this who can."

Jesus Blesses Little Children

13 Then little children were being brought to him in order that he might lay his hands on them and pray. The disciples spoke sternly to those who brought them; ¹⁴but Jesus said, "Let the little children come to me, and do not stop them; for it is to such as these that the kingdom of heaven belongs." ¹⁵And he laid his hands on them and went on his way.

The Rich Young Man

16 Then someone came to him and said, "Teacher, what good deed must I do to have eternal life?" ¹⁷And he said to him, "Why do you ask me about what is good? There is only one who is good. If you wish to enter into life, keep the commandments." ¹⁸He said to him, "Which ones?" And Jesus said, "You shall not murder; You shall not commit adultery; You shall not steal; You shall not bear false witness; ¹⁹Honor your father and mother; also, You shall love your neighbor as yourself." ²⁰The young man said to him, "I have kept all these;^c what do I still lack?" ²¹Jesus said to him, "If you wish to be perfect, go, sell your possessions, and give the money^d to the poor, and you will have treasure in heaven; then come, follow me." ²²When the young man heard this word, he went away grieving, for he had many possessions.

23 Then Jesus said to his disciples, "Truly I tell you, it will be hard for a rich person to enter the kingdom of heaven. ²⁴Again I tell you, it is easier for a camel to go through the eye of a needle than for someone who is rich to enter the kingdom of God." ²⁵When the disciples heard this, they were greatly astounded and said, "Then who can be saved?" ²⁶But Jesus looked at them and said, "For mortals it is impossible, but for God all things are possible."

27 Then Peter said in reply, "Look, we have left everything and followed you. What then will we have?" ²⁸Jesus said to them, "Truly I tell you, at the renewal of all things, when the Son of Man is seated on the throne of his glory, you who have followed me will also sit on twelve thrones, judging the twelve tribes of Israel. ²⁹And everyone who has left houses or brothers or sisters or father or mother or children or fields, for my name's sake, will receive a hundredfold,^e and will inherit eternal life. ³⁰But many who are first will be last, and the last will be first.

> "If we don't carry our cross, we are going to be crushed under the weight of it. So let's go and do it."
>
> —Jim Caviezel in the role of Jesus in *The Passion of the Christ*

---

a Gk *brother* b Other ancient authorities read *except on the ground of unchastity, causes her to commit adultery*; others add at the end of the verse *and he who marries a divorced woman commits adultery*
c Other ancient authorities add *from my youth* d Gk lacks *the money* e Other ancient authorities read *manifold*

vineyard.' ⁸When evening came, the owner of the vineyard said to his manager, 'Call the laborers and give them their pay, beginning with the last and then going to the first.' ⁹When those hired about five o'clock came, each of them received the usual daily wage.ᵃ ¹⁰Now when the first came, they thought they would receive more; but each of them also received the usual daily wage.ᵃ ¹¹And when they received it, they grumbled against the landowner, ¹²saying, 'These last worked only one hour, and you have made them equal to us who have borne the burden of the day and the scorching heat.' ¹³But he replied to one of them, 'Friend, I am doing you no wrong; did you not agree with me for the usual daily wage?ᵃ ¹⁴Take what belongs to you and go; I choose to give to this last the same as I give to you. ¹⁵Am I not allowed to do what I choose with what belongs to me? Or are you envious because I am generous?'ᵇ ¹⁶So the last will be first, and the first will be last."ᶜ

A Third Time Jesus Foretells His Death and Resurrection

17 While Jesus was going up to Jerusalem, he took the twelve disciples aside by themselves, and said to them on the way, ¹⁸"See, we are going up to Jerusalem, and the Son of Man will be handed over to the chief priests and scribes, and they will condemn him to death; ¹⁹then they will hand him over to the Gentiles to be mocked and flogged and crucified; and on the third day he will be raised."

The Request of the Mother of James and John

20 Then the mother of the sons of Zebedee came to him with her sons, and kneeling before him, she asked a favor of him. ²¹And he said to her, "What do you want?" She said to him, "Declare that these two sons of mine will sit, one at your right hand and one at your left, in your kingdom." ²²But Jesus answered, "You do not know what you are asking. Are you able to drink the cup that I am about to drink?"ᵈ They said to him, "We are able." ²³He said to them, "You will indeed drink my cup, but to sit at my right hand and at my left, this is not mine to grant, but it is for those for whom it has been prepared by my Father."

24 When the ten heard it, they were angry with the two brothers. ²⁵But Jesus called them to him and said, "You know that the rulers of the Gentiles lord it over them, and their great ones are tyrants over them. ²⁶It will not be so among you; but whoever wishes to be great

20 The Laborers in the Vineyard

"For the kingdom of heaven is like a landowner who went out early in the morning to hire laborers for his vineyard. ²After agreeing with the laborers for the usual daily wage,ᵃ he sent them into his vineyard. ³When he went out about nine o'clock, he saw others standing idle in the marketplace; ⁴and he said to them, 'You also go into the vineyard, and I will pay you whatever is right.' So they went. ⁵When he went out again about noon and about three o'clock, he did the same. ⁶And about five o'clock he went out and found others standing around; and he said to them, 'Why are you standing here idle all day?' ⁷They said to him, 'Because no one has hired us.' He said to them, 'You also go into the

ᵃ Gk a denarius ᵇ Gk is your eye evil because I am good? ᶜ Other ancient authorities add for many are called but few are chosen ᵈ Other ancient authorities add or to be baptized with the baptism that I am baptized with?

among you must be your servant, 27and whoever wishes to be first among you must be your slave; 28just as the Son of Man came not to be served but to serve, and to give his life a ransom for many."

Jesus Heals Two Blind Men

29 As they were leaving Jericho, a large crowd followed him. 30There were two blind men sitting by the roadside. When they heard that Jesus was passing by, they shouted, "Lord,a have mercy on us, Son of David!" 31The crowd sternly ordered them to be quiet; but they shouted even more loudly, "Have mercy on us, Lord, Son of David!" 32Jesus stood still and called them, saying, "What do you want me to do for you?" 33They said to him, "Lord, let our eyes be opened." 34Moved with compassion, Jesus touched their eyes. Immediately they regained their sight and followed him.

21 Jesus' Triumphal Entry into Jerusalem

When they had come near Jerusalem and had reached Bethphage, at the Mount of Olives, Jesus sent two disciples, 2saying to them, "Go into the village ahead of you, and immediately you will find a donkey tied, and a colt with her; untie them and bring them to me. 3If anyone says anything to you, just say this, 'The Lord needs them.' And he will send them immediately.b" 4This took place to fulfill what had been spoken through the prophet, saying,

5 "Tell the daughter of Zion,
   Look, your king is coming to you,
      humble, and mounted on a donkey,
         and on a colt, the foal of a donkey."

6The disciples went and did as Jesus had directed them; 7they brought the donkey and the colt, and put their cloaks on them, and he sat on them. 8A very large crowdc spread their cloaks on the road, and others cut branches from the trees and spread them on the road. 9The crowds that went ahead of him and that followed were shouting,

   "Hosanna to the Son of David!
      Blessed is the one who comes in the
         name of the Lord!
      Hosanna in the highest heaven!"

10When he entered Jerusalem, the whole city was in turmoil, asking, "Who is this?" 11The crowds were saying, "This is the prophet Jesus from Nazareth in Galilee."

Jesus Cleanses the Temple

12 Then Jesus entered the templed and drove out all who were selling and buying in the temple, and he overturned the tables of the money changers and the seats of those who sold doves. 13He said to them, "It is written,

   'My house shall be called a house of prayer';
      but you are making it a den of robbers."

14 The blind and the lame came to him in the temple, and he cured them. 15But when the chief priests and the scribes saw the amazing things that he did, and hearde the children crying out in the temple, "Hosanna to the Son of David," they became angry 16and said to him, "Do you hear what these are saying?" Jesus said to them, "Yes; have you never read,

   'Out of the mouths of infants and nursing
      babies
   you have prepared praise for yourself'?"

17He left them, went out of the city to Bethany, and spent the night there.

Jesus Curses the Fig Tree

18 In the morning, when he returned to the city, he was hungry. 19And seeing a fig tree by the side of the road, he went to it and found nothing at all on it but leaves. Then he said to it, "May no fruit ever come from you again!" And the fig tree withered at once. 20When the disciples saw it, they were amazed, saying, "How did the fig tree wither at once?" 21Jesus answered them, "Truly I tell you, if you have faith and do not doubt, not only will you do what has been done to the fig tree, but even if you say to this mountain, 'Be lifted up and thrown into the sea,' it will be done. 22Whatever you ask for in prayer with faith, you will receive."

a Other ancient authorities lack *Lord* b Or *'The Lord needs them and will send them back immediately.'* c Or *Most of the crowd* d Other ancient authorities add *of God* e Gk lacks *heard*

The Authority of Jesus Questioned

23 When he entered the temple, the chief priests and the elders of the people came to him as he was teaching, and said, "By what authority are you doing these things, and who gave you this authority?" 24 Jesus said to them, "I will also ask you one question; if you tell me the answer, then I will also tell you by what authority I do these things. 25 Did the baptism of John come from heaven, or was it of human origin?" And they argued with one another, "If we say, 'From heaven,' he will say to us, 'Why then did you not believe him?' 26 But if we say, 'Of human origin,' we are afraid of the crowd; for all regard John as a prophet." 27 So they answered Jesus, "We do not know." And he said to them, "Neither will I tell you by what authority I am doing these things.

The Parable of the Two Sons

28 "What do you think? A man had two sons; he went to the first and said, 'Son, go and work in the vineyard today.' 29 He answered, 'I will not'; but later he changed his mind and went. 30 The father*a* went to the second and said the same; and he answered, 'I go, sir'; but he did not go. 31 Which of the two did the will of his father?" They said, "The first." Jesus said to them, "Truly I tell you, the tax collectors and the prostitutes are going into the kingdom of God ahead of you. 32 For John came to you in the way of righteousness and you did not believe him, but the tax collectors and the prostitutes believed him; and even after you saw it, you did not change your minds and believe him.

The Parable of the Wicked Tenants

33 "Listen to another parable. There was a landowner who planted a vineyard, put a fence around it, dug a wine press in it, and built a watchtower. Then he leased it to tenants and went to another country. 34 When the harvest time had come, he sent his slaves to the tenants to collect his produce. 35 But the tenants seized his slaves and beat one, killed another, and stoned another. 36 Again he sent other slaves, more than the first; and they treated them in the same way. 37 Finally he sent his son to them, saying, 'They will respect my son.' 38 But when the tenants saw the son, they said to themselves, 'This is the heir; come, let us kill him and get his inheritance.' 39 So they seized him, threw him out of the vineyard, and killed him. 40 Now when the owner of the vineyard comes, what will he do to those tenants?" 41 They said to him, "He will put those wretches to a miserable death, and lease the vineyard to other tenants who will give him the produce at the harvest time."

42 Jesus said to them, "Have you never read in the scriptures:

'The stone that the builders rejected
has become the cornerstone;*b*
this was the Lord's doing,
and it is amazing in our eyes'?

43 Therefore I tell you, the kingdom of God will be taken away from you and given to a people that produces the fruits of the kingdom.*c* 44 The one who falls on this stone will be broken to pieces; and it will crush anyone on whom it falls."*d*

45 When the chief priests and the Pharisees heard his parables, they realized that he was speaking about them. 46 They wanted to arrest him, but they feared the crowds, because they regarded him as a prophet.

22 The Parable of the Wedding Banquet

Once more Jesus spoke to them in parables, saying: 2 "The kingdom of heaven may be compared to a king who gave a wedding banquet for his son. 3 He sent his slaves to call those who had been invited to the wedding banquet, but they would not come. 4 Again he sent other slaves, saying, 'Tell those who have been invited: Look, I have prepared my dinner, my oxen and my fat calves have been slaughtered, and everything is ready; come to the wedding banquet.' 5 But they made light of it and went away, one to his farm, another to his business, 6 while the rest seized his slaves, mistreated them, and killed them. 7 The king was enraged. He sent his troops, destroyed those murderers, and burned their city. 8 Then he said to his slaves, 'The wedding is ready, but those invited were not worthy. 9 Go therefore into the main streets, and invite everyone you find to the wedding banquet.' 10 Those slaves went out into the streets and gathered all whom they found, both good and bad; so the wedding hall was filled with guests.

11 "But when the king came in to see the guests, he noticed a man there who was not wearing a wedding robe, 12 and he said to him, 'Friend, how did you get in here without a wedding robe?' And he was speechless. 13 Then the king said to the attendants, 'Bind him hand and foot, and throw him into the outer darkness, where there will be weeping and gnashing of teeth.' 14 For many are called, but few are chosen."

The Question about Paying Taxes

15 Then the Pharisees went and plotted to entrap him in what he said. 16 So they sent their

---

a Gk He *b* Or *keystone* *c* Gk *the fruits of it* *d* Other ancient authorities lack verse 44 disciples to him, along with the Herodians, saying, "Teacher, we know that you are sincere, and teach the way of God in accordance with truth, and show deference to no one; for you do not regard people with partiality. [17]Tell us, then, what you think. Is it lawful to pay taxes to the emperor, or not?" [18]But Jesus, aware of their malice, said, "Why are you putting me to the test, you hypocrites? [19]Show me the coin used for the tax." And they brought him a denarius. [20]Then he said to them, "Whose head is this, and whose title?" [21]They answered, "The emperor's." Then he said to them, "Give therefore to the emperor the things that are the emperor's, and to God the things that are God's." [22]When they heard this, they were amazed; and they left him and went away.

The Question about the Resurrection

23 The same day some Sadducees came to him, saying there is no resurrection;[a] and they asked him a question, saying, [24]"Teacher, Moses said, 'If a man dies childless, his brother shall marry the widow, and raise up children for his brother.' [25]Now there were seven brothers among us; the first married, and died childless, leaving the widow to his brother. [26]The second did the same, so also the third, down to the seventh. [27]Last of all, the woman herself died. [28]In the resurrection, then, whose wife of the seven will she be? For all of them had married her."

29 Jesus answered them, "You are wrong, because you know neither the scriptures nor the power of God. [30]For in the resurrection they neither marry nor are given in marriage, but are like angels[b] in heaven. [31]And as for the resurrection of the dead, have you not read what was said to you by God, [32]'I am the God of Abraham, the God of Isaac, and the God of Jacob'? He is God not of the dead, but of the living." [33]And when the crowd heard it, they were astounded at his teaching.

The Greatest Commandment

34 When the Pharisees heard that he had silenced the Sadducees, they gathered together, [35]and one of them, a lawyer, asked him a question to test him. [36]"Teacher, which commandment in the law is the greatest?" [37]He said to him, " 'You shall love the Lord your God with all your heart, and with all your soul, and with all your mind.' [38]This is the greatest and first commandment. [39]And a second is like it: 'You shall love your neighbor as yourself.' [40]On

these two commandments hang all the law and the prophets."

The Question about David's Son

41 Now while the Pharisees were gathered together, Jesus asked them this question: [42]"What do you think of the Messiah?[c] Whose son is he?" They said to him, "The son of David." [43]He said to them, "How is it then that David by the Spirit[d] calls him Lord, saying,

[44] 'The Lord said to my Lord,
"Sit at my right hand,
until I put your enemies under your
feet" '?

[45]If David thus calls him Lord, how can he be his son?" [46]No one was able to give him an answer, nor from that day did anyone dare to ask him any more questions.

23 Jesus Denounces Scribes and Pharisees

Then Jesus said to the crowds and to his disciples, [2]"The scribes and the Pharisees sit on Moses' seat; [3]therefore, do whatever they teach you and follow it; but do not do as they do, for they do not practice what they teach. [4]They tie up heavy burdens, hard to bear,[e] and lay them on the shoulders of others; but they themselves are unwilling to lift a finger to move them. [5]They do all their deeds to be seen by others; for they make their phylacteries broad and their fringes long. [6]They love to have the place of honor at banquets and the best seats in the synagogues, [7]and to be greeted with respect in the marketplaces, and to have people call them rabbi. [8]But you are not to be called rabbi, for you have one teacher, and you are all students.[f] [9]And call no one your father on earth, for you have one Father—the one in heaven. [10]Nor are you to be called instructors, for you have one instructor, the Messiah.[g] [11]The greatest among you will be your servant. [12]All who exalt themselves will be humbled, and all who humble themselves will be exalted.

13 "But woe to you, scribes and Pharisees, hypocrites! For you lock people out of the kingdom of heaven. For you do not go in yourselves, and when others are going in, you stop them.[h] [15]Woe to you, scribes and Pharisees, hypocrites! For you cross sea and land to make a single convert, and you make the new convert twice as much a child of hell[i] as yourselves.

16 "Woe to you, blind guides, who say, 'Whoever swears by the sanctuary is bound by nothing, but whoever swears by the gold

---

a Other ancient authorities read *who say that there is no resurrection* b Other ancient authorities add *of God* c Or *Christ* d Gk *in spirit*
e Other ancient authorities lack *hard to bear* f Gk *brothers* g Or *the Christ* h Other authorities add here (or after verse 12) verse 14, *Woe to you, scribes and Pharisees, hypocrites! For you devour widows' houses and for the sake of appearance you make long prayers; therefore you will receive the greater condemnation* i Gk *Gehenna*

of the sanctuary is bound by the oath.' [17]You blind fools! For which is greater, the gold or the sanctuary that has made the gold sacred? [18]And you say, 'Whoever swears by the altar is bound by nothing, but whoever swears by the gift that is on the altar is bound by the oath.' [19]How blind you are! For which is greater, the gift or the altar that makes the gift sacred? [20]So whoever swears by the altar, swears by it and by everything on it; [21]and whoever swears by the sanctuary, swears by it and by the one who dwells in it; [22]and whoever swears by heaven, swears by the throne of God and by the one who is seated upon it.

23 "Woe to you, scribes and Pharisees, hypocrites! For you tithe mint, dill, and cummin, and have neglected the weightier matters of the law: justice and mercy and faith. It is these you ought to have practiced without neglecting the others. [24]You blind guides! You strain out a gnat but swallow a camel!

25 "Woe to you, scribes and Pharisees, hypocrites! For you clean the outside of the cup and of the plate, but inside they are full of greed and self-indulgence. [26]You blind Pharisee! First clean the inside of the cup,[a] so that the outside also may become clean.

27 "Woe to you, scribes and Pharisees, hypocrites! For you are like whitewashed tombs, which on the outside look beautiful, but inside they are full of the bones of the dead and of all kinds of filth. [28]So you also on the outside look righteous to others, but inside you are full of hypocrisy and lawlessness.

29 "Woe to you, scribes and Pharisees, hypocrites! For you build the tombs of the prophets and decorate the graves of the righteous, [30]and you say, 'If we had lived in the days of our ancestors, we would not have taken part with them in shedding the blood of the prophets.' [31]Thus you testify against yourselves that you are descendants of those who murdered the prophets. [32]Fill up, then, the measure of your ancestors! [33]You snakes, you brood of vipers! How can you escape being sentenced to hell?[b] [34]Therefore I send you prophets, sages, and scribes, some of whom you will kill and crucify, and some you will flog in your synagogues and pursue from town to town, [35]so that upon you may come all the righteous blood shed on earth, from the blood of righteous Abel to the blood of Zechariah son of Barachiah, whom you murdered between the sanctuary and the altar. [36]Truly I tell you, all this will come upon this generation.

The Lament over Jerusalem

37 "Jerusalem, Jerusalem, the city that kills the prophets and stones those who are sent to it! How often have I desired to gather your children together as a hen gathers her brood under her wings, and you were not willing! [38]See, your house is left to you, desolate.[c] [39]For I tell you, you will not see me again until you say, 'Blessed is the one who comes in the name of the Lord.' "

24 The Destruction of the Temple Foretold

As Jesus came out of the temple and was going away, his disciples came to point out to him the buildings of the temple. [2]Then he asked them, "You see all these, do you not? Truly I tell you, not one stone will be left here upon another; all will be thrown down."

Signs of the End of the Age

3 When he was sitting on the Mount of Olives, the disciples came to him privately, saying, "Tell us, when will this be, and what will be the sign of your coming and of the end of the age?" [4]Jesus answered them, "Beware that no one leads you astray. [5]For many will come in my name, saying, 'I am the Messiah!'[d] and they will lead many astray. [6]And you will hear of wars and rumors of wars; see that you are not alarmed; for this must take place, but the end is not yet. [7]For nation will rise against nation, and kingdom against kingdom, and there will be famines[e] and earthquakes in various places: [8]all this is but the beginning of the birth pangs.

Persecutions Foretold

9 "Then they will hand you over to be tortured and will put you to death, and you will be hated by all nations because of my name. [10]Then many will fall away,[f] and they will betray one another and hate one another. [11]And many false prophets will arise and lead many astray. [12]And because of the increase of lawlessness, the love of many will grow cold. [13]But the one who endures to the end will be saved. [14]And this good news[g] of the kingdom will be proclaimed throughout the world, as a testimony to all the nations; and then the end will come.

The Desolating Sacrilege

15 "So when you see the desolating sacrilege standing in the holy place, as was spoken of by the prophet Daniel (let the reader understand), [16]then those in Judea must flee to the mountains; [17]the one on the housetop must

---

a Other ancient authorities add *and of the plate* *b* Gk *Gehenna* *c* Other ancient authorities lack *desolate* *d* Or *the Christ* *e* Other ancient authorities add *and pestilences* *f* Or *stumble* *g* Or *gospel* not go down to take what is in the house; [18]the one in the field must not turn back to get a coat. [19]Woe to those who are pregnant and to those who are nursing infants in those days! [20]Pray that your flight may not be in winter or on a sabbath. [21]For at that time there will be great suffering, such as has not been from the beginning of the world until now, no, and never will be. [22]And if those days had not been cut short, no one would be saved; but for the sake of the elect those days will be cut short. [23]Then if anyone says to you, 'Look! Here is the Messiah!'[a] or 'There he is!'—do not believe it. [24]For false messiahs[b] and false prophets will appear and produce great signs and omens, to lead astray, if possible, even the elect. [25]Take note, I have told you beforehand. [26]So, if they say to you, 'Look! He is in the wilderness,' do not go out. If they say, 'Look! He is in the inner rooms,' do not believe it. [27]For as the lightning comes from the east and flashes as far as the west, so will be the coming of the Son of Man. [28]Wherever the corpse is, there the vultures will gather.

Descent—© Catherine Willms, 15

The Coming of the Son of Man

29 "Immediately after the suffering of those days

the sun will be darkened,
and the moon will not give its light;
the stars will fall from heaven,
and the powers of heaven will be shaken.

[30]Then the sign of the Son of Man will appear in heaven, and then all the tribes of the earth will mourn, and they will see 'the Son of Man coming on the clouds of heaven' with power and great glory. [31]And he will send out his angels with a loud trumpet call, and they will gather his elect from the four winds, from one end of heaven to the other.

The Lesson of the Fig Tree

32 "From the fig tree learn its lesson: as soon as its branch becomes tender and puts forth its leaves, you know that summer is near. [33]So also, when you see all these things, you know that he[c] is near, at the very gates. [34]Truly I tell you, this generation will not pass away until all these things have taken place. [35]Heaven and earth will pass away, but my words will not pass away.

The Necessity for Watchfulness

36 "But about that day and hour no one knows, neither the angels of heaven, nor the Son,[d] but only the Father. [37]For as the days of Noah were, so will be the coming of the Son of Man. [38]For as in those days before the flood they were eating and drinking, marrying and giving in marriage, until the day Noah entered the ark, [39]and they knew nothing until the flood came and swept them all away, so too will be the coming of the Son of Man. [40]Then two will be in the field; one will be taken and one will be left. [41]Two women will be grinding meal together; one will be taken and one will be left. [42]Keep awake therefore, for you do not know on what day[e] your Lord is coming. [43]But understand this: if the owner of the house had known in what part of the night the thief was coming, he would have stayed awake and would not have let his house be broken into. [44]Therefore you also must be ready, for the Son of Man is coming at an unexpected hour.

The Faithful or the Unfaithful Slave

45 "Who then is the faithful and wise slave, whom his master has put in charge of his household, to give the other slaves[f] their allowance of food at the proper time? [46]Blessed is that slave whom his master will find at work when he arrives. [47]Truly I tell you, he will put that one in charge of all his possessions. [48]But if that wicked slave says to himself, 'My master is delayed,' [49]and he begins to beat his fellow slaves, and eats and drinks with drunkards, [50]the master of that slave will come on a day when he does not expect him and at an hour that he does not know. [51]He will cut him in pieces[g] and put him with the hypocrites, where there will be weeping and gnashing of teeth.

a Or the Christ b Or christs c Or it d Other ancient authorities lack nor the Son e Other ancient authorities read at what hour f Gk to give them g Or cut him off

25 The Parable of the Ten Bridesmaids

"Then the kingdom of heaven will be like this. Ten bridesmaids[a] took their lamps and went to meet the bridegroom.[b] [2]Five of them were foolish, and five were wise. [3]When the foolish took their lamps, they took no oil with them; [4]but the wise took flasks of oil with their lamps. [5]As the bridegroom was delayed, all of them became drowsy and slept. [6]But at midnight there was a shout, 'Look! Here is the bridegroom! Come out to meet him.' [7]Then all those bridesmaids[a] got up and trimmed their lamps. [8]The foolish said to the wise, 'Give us some of your oil, for our lamps are going out.' [9]But the wise replied, 'No! there will not be enough for you and for us; you had better go to the dealers and buy some for yourselves.' [10]And while they went to buy it, the bridegroom came, and those who were ready went with him into the wedding banquet; and the door was shut. [11]Later the other bridesmaids[a] came also, saying, 'Lord, lord, open to us.' [12]But he replied, 'Truly I tell you, I do not know you.' [13]Keep awake therefore, for you know neither the day nor the hour.[c]

The Parable of the Talents

14 "For it is as if a man, going on a journey, summoned his slaves and entrusted his property to them; [15]to one he gave five talents,[d] to another two, to another one, to each according to his ability. Then he went away. [16]The one who had received the five talents went off at once and traded with them, and made five more talents. [17]In the same way, the one who had the two talents made two more talents. [18]But the one who had received the one talent went off and dug a hole in the ground and hid his master's money. [19]After a long time the master of those slaves came and settled accounts with them. [20]Then the one who had received the five talents came forward, bringing five more talents, saying, 'Master, you handed over to me five talents; see, I have made five more talents.' [21]His master said to him, 'Well done, good and trustworthy slave; you have been trustworthy in a few things, I will put you in charge of many things; enter into the joy of your master.' [22]And the one with the two talents also came forward, saying, 'Master, you handed over to me two talents; see, I have made two more talents.' [23]His master said to him, 'Well done, good and trustworthy slave; you have been trustworthy in a few things, I will put you in charge of many things; enter into the joy of your master.' [24]Then the one who had received the one talent also came forward, saying, 'Master, I knew that you were a harsh man, reaping where you did not sow, and gathering where you did not scatter seed; [25]so I was afraid, and I went and hid your talent in the ground. Here you have what is yours.' [26]But his master replied, 'You wicked and lazy slave! You knew, did you, that I reap where I did not sow, and gather where I did not scatter? [27]Then you ought to have invested my money with the bankers, and on my return I would have received what was my own with interest. [28]So take the talent from him, and give it to the one with the ten talents. [29]For to all those who have, more will be given, and they will have an abundance; but from those who have nothing, even what they have will be taken away. [30]As for this worthless slave, throw him into the outer darkness, where there will be weeping and gnashing of teeth.'

The Judgment of the Nations

31 "When the Son of Man comes in his glory, and all the angels with him, then he will sit on the throne of his glory. [32]All the nations will be gathered before him, and he will separate people one from another as a shepherd separates the sheep from the goats, [33]and he will put the sheep at his right hand and the goats at the left. [34]Then the king will say to those at his right hand, 'Come, you that are blessed by my Father, inherit the kingdom prepared for you from the foundation of the world; [35]for I was hungry and you gave me food, I was thirsty and you gave me something to drink, I was a stranger and you welcomed me, [36]I was naked and you gave me clothing, I was sick and you took care of me, I was in prison and you visited me.' [37]Then the righteous will answer him, 'Lord, when was it that we saw you hungry and gave you food, or thirsty and gave you something to drink? [38]And when was it that we saw you a stranger and welcomed you, or naked and gave you clothing? [39]And when was it that we saw you sick or in prison and visited you?' [40]And the king will answer them, 'Truly I tell you, just as you did it to one of the least of these who are members of my family,[e] you did it to me.' [41]Then he will say to those at his left hand, 'You that are accursed, depart from me into the eternal fire prepared for the devil and his angels; [42]for I was hungry and you gave me no food, I was thirsty and you gave me nothing to drink, [43]I was a stranger and you did not welcome me, naked and you did not give me clothing, sick and in prison and you did not

---

a Gk virgins b Other ancient authorities add *and the bride* c Other ancient authorities add *in which the Son of Man is coming* d A talent was worth more than fifteen years' wages of a laborer e Gk *these my brothers*

Untitled—© Tony Nappa, 17

visit me.' ⁴⁴Then they also will answer, 'Lord, when was it that we saw you hungry or thirsty or a stranger or naked or sick or in prison, and did not take care of you?' ⁴⁵Then he will answer them, 'Truly I tell you, just as you did not do it to one of the least of these, you did not do it to me.' ⁴⁶And these will go away into eternal punishment, but the righteous into eternal life."

26 The Plot to Kill Jesus

When Jesus had finished saying all these things, he said to his disciples, ²"You know that after two days the Passover is coming, and the Son of Man will be handed over to be crucified."

3 Then the chief priests and the elders of the people gathered in the palace of the high priest, who was called Caiaphas, ⁴and they conspired to arrest Jesus by stealth and kill him. ⁵But they said, "Not during the festival, or there may be a riot among the people."

The Anointing at Bethany

6 Now while Jesus was at Bethany in the house of Simon the leper,ᵃ ⁷a woman came to him with an alabaster jar of very costly ointment, and she poured it on his head as he sat at the table. ⁸But when the disciples saw it, they were angry and said, "Why this waste? ⁹For this ointment could have been sold for a large sum,

and the money given to the poor." ¹⁰But Jesus, aware of this, said to them, "Why do you trouble the woman? She has performed a good service for me. ¹¹For you always have the poor with you, but you will not always have me. ¹²By pouring this ointment on my body she has prepared me for burial. ¹³Truly I tell you, wherever this good newsᵇ is proclaimed in the whole world, what she has done will be told in remembrance of her."

Judas Agrees to Betray Jesus

14 Then one of the twelve, who was called Judas Iscariot, went to the chief priests ¹⁵and said, "What will you give me if I betray him to you?" They paid him thirty pieces of silver. ¹⁶And from that moment he began to look for an opportunity to betray him.

The Passover with the Disciples

17 On the first day of Unleavened Bread the disciples came to Jesus, saying, "Where do you want us to make the preparations for you to eat the Passover?" ¹⁸He said, "Go into the city to a certain man, and say to him, 'The Teacher says, My time is near; I will keep the Passover at your house with my disciples.' " ¹⁹So the disciples did as Jesus had directed them, and they prepared the Passover meal.

20 When it was evening, he took his place

ᵃ The terms *leper* and *leprosy* can refer to several diseases ᵇ Or *gospel* with the twelve;[a] [21]and while they were eating, he said, "Truly I tell you, one of you will betray me." [22]And they became greatly distressed and began to say to him one after another, "Surely not I, Lord?" [23]He answered, "The one who has dipped his hand into the bowl with me will betray me. [24]The Son of Man goes as it is written of him, but woe to that one by whom the Son of Man is betrayed! It would have been better for that one not to have been born." [25]Judas, who betrayed him, said, "Surely not I, Rabbi?" He replied, "You have said so."

The Institution of the Lord's Supper

26 While they were eating, Jesus took a loaf of bread, and after blessing it he broke it, gave it to the disciples, and said, "Take, eat; this is my body." [27]Then he took a cup, and after giving thanks he gave it to them, saying, "Drink from it, all of you; [28]for this is my blood of the[b] covenant, which is poured out for many for the forgiveness of sins. [29]I tell you, I will never again drink of this fruit of the vine until that day when I drink it new with you in my Father's kingdom."

30 When they had sung the hymn, they went out to the Mount of Olives.

Peter's Denial Foretold

31 Then Jesus said to them, "You will all become deserters because of me this night; for it is written,

'I will strike the shepherd,
    and the sheep of the flock will be
        scattered.'

[32]But after I am raised up, I will go ahead of you to Galilee." [33]Peter said to him, "Though all become deserters because of you, I will never desert you." [34]Jesus said to him, "Truly I tell you, this very night, before the cock crows, you will deny me three times." [35]Peter said to him, "Even though I must die with you, I will not deny you." And so said all the disciples.

Jesus Prays in Gethsemane

36 Then Jesus went with them to a place called Gethsemane; and he said to his disciples, "Sit here while I go over there and pray." [37]He took with him Peter and the two sons of Zebedee, and began to be grieved and agitated. [38]Then he said to them, "I am deeply grieved, even to death; remain here, and stay awake with me." [39]And going a little farther, he threw himself on the ground and prayed, "My Father, if it is possible, let this cup pass from me; yet not what I want but what you want." [40]Then he came to the disciples and found them sleeping; and he said to Peter, "So, could you not stay awake with me one hour? [41]Stay awake and pray that you may not come into the time of trial;[c] the spirit indeed is willing, but the flesh is weak." [42]Again he went away for the second time and prayed, "My Father, if this cannot pass unless I drink it, your will be done." [43]Again he came and found them sleeping, for their eyes were heavy. [44]So leaving them again, he went away and prayed for the third time, saying the same words. [45]Then he came to the disciples and said to them, "Are you still sleeping and taking your rest? See, the hour is at hand, and the Son of Man is betrayed into the hands of sinners. [46]Get up, let us be going. See, my betrayer is at hand."

The Betrayal and Arrest of Jesus

47 While he was still speaking, Judas, one of the twelve, arrived; with him was a large crowd with swords and clubs, from the chief priests and the elders of the people. [48]Now the betrayer had given them a sign, saying, "The one I will kiss is the man; arrest him." [49]At once he came up to Jesus and said, "Greetings, Rabbi!" and kissed him. [50]Jesus said to him, "Friend, do what you are here to do." Then they came and laid hands on Jesus and arrested him. [51]Suddenly, one of those with Jesus put his hand on his sword, drew it, and struck the slave of the high priest, cutting off his ear. [52]Then Jesus said to him, "Put your sword back into its place; for all who take the sword will perish by the sword. [53]Do you think that I cannot appeal to my Father, and he will at once send me more than twelve legions of angels? [54]But how then would the scriptures be fulfilled, which say it must happen in this way?" [55]At that hour Jesus said to the crowds, "Have you come out with swords and clubs to arrest me as though I were a bandit? Day after day I sat in the temple teaching, and you did not arrest me. [56]But all this has taken place, so that the scriptures of the prophets may be fulfilled." Then all the disciples deserted him and fled.

Jesus before the High Priest

57 Those who had arrested Jesus took him to Caiaphas the high priest, in whose house the scribes and the elders had gathered. [58]But Peter was following him at a distance, as far as the courtyard of the high priest; and going inside, he sat with the guards in order to see how this would end. [59]Now the chief priests and the whole council were looking for false testimony against Jesus so that they might put him to death, [60]but they found none, though many

---

a Other ancient authorities add *disciples* b Other ancient authorities add *new* c Or *into temptation* false witnesses came forward. At last two came forward ⁶¹and said, "This fellow said, 'I am able to destroy the temple of God and to build it in three days.' " ⁶²The high priest stood up and said, "Have you no answer? What is it that they testify against you?" ⁶³But Jesus was silent. Then the high priest said to him, "I put you under oath before the living God, tell us if you are the Messiah,ᵃ the Son of God." ⁶⁴Jesus said to him, "You have said so. But I tell you,

> From now on you will see the Son of Man
>> seated at the right hand of Power
>> and coming on the clouds of heaven."

⁶⁵Then the high priest tore his clothes and said, "He has blasphemed! Why do we still need witnesses? You have now heard his blasphemy. ⁶⁶What is your verdict?" They answered, "He deserves death." ⁶⁷Then they spat in his face and struck him; and some slapped him, ⁶⁸saying, "Prophesy to us, you Messiah!ᵃ Who is it that struck you?"

Peter's Denial of Jesus

69 Now Peter was sitting outside in the courtyard. A servant-girl came to him and said, "You also were with Jesus the Galilean." ⁷⁰But he denied it before all of them, saying, "I do not know what you are talking about." ⁷¹When he went out to the porch, another servant-girl saw him, and she said to the bystanders, "This man was with Jesus of Nazareth."ᵇ ⁷²Again he denied it with an oath, "I do not know the man." ⁷³After a little while the bystanders came up and said to Peter, "Certainly you are also one of them, for your accent betrays you." ⁷⁴Then he began to curse, and he swore an oath, "I do not know the man!" At that moment the cock crowed. ⁷⁵Then Peter remembered what Jesus had said: "Before the cock crows, you will deny me three times." And he went out and wept bitterly.

27 Jesus Brought before Pilate

When morning came, all the chief priests and the elders of the people conferred together against Jesus in order to bring about his death. ²They bound him, led him away, and handed him over to Pilate the governor.

The Suicide of Judas

3 When Judas, his betrayer, saw that Jesusᶜ was condemned he repented and brought back the thirty pieces of silver to the chief priests and the elders. ⁴He said, "I have sinned by betraying innocentᵈ blood." But they said, "What is that to us? See to it yourself." ⁵Throwing down

a Or *Christ* *b* Gk *the Nazorean* *c* Gk *he* *d* Other ancient authorities read *righteous*

Dive In—The Water's Fine

There's a good reason the great cities of the ancient world perched on riverbanks. Rivers provided food, water, transportation—everything that made life possible.

The Egyptians conquered a harsh land precisely because they wanted to spread out along the Nile. Every year, the Nile overflowed its banks and swept new soil onto tired fields. It watered thirsty crops. The water washed away what was no longer needed. The river never stopped flowing, never paused, never disappointed.

God's relentless love is like that river: beautiful, powerful, pure, relentless, and life-giving.

There's no turning away the flow of God's love. It flows over our protests, pushes past our excuses. And with it comes life.

Read **Matthew 28.16–20**. When Jesus called his followers to go and make disciples, he was telling them to invite people to step into the river of his love, to wade deep into something beautiful, powerful, pure, relentless.

And life-giving.

The next time you're in the shower, take a moment to really *feel* the water pouring over your shoulders and rushing around your ankles. Stand and thank God for his love that washes over you—and invites you to bring others to life with you.

Write about God's pure, cleaning love and post your thoughts at **Learner.CalltoDiscipleship.com**.

the pieces of silver in the temple, he departed; and he went and hanged himself. [6]But the chief priests, taking the pieces of silver, said, "It is not lawful to put them into the treasury, since they are blood money." [7]After conferring together, they used them to buy the potter's field as a place to bury foreigners. [8]For this reason that field has been called the Field of Blood to this day. [9]Then was fulfilled what had been spoken through the prophet Jeremiah,[a] "And they

took[b] the thirty pieces of silver, the price of the one on whom a price had been set,[c] on whom some of the people of Israel had set a price, [10]and they gave[d] them for the potter's field, as the Lord commanded me."

Pilate Questions Jesus

11 Now Jesus stood before the governor; and the governor asked him, "Are you the King of the Jews?" Jesus said, "You say so." [12]But when he was accused by the chief priests and elders, he did not answer. [13]Then Pilate said to him, "Do you not hear how many accusations they make against you?" [14]But he gave him no answer, not even to a single charge, so that the governor was greatly amazed.

Barabbas or Jesus?

15 Now at the festival the governor was accustomed to release a prisoner for the crowd, anyone whom they wanted. [16]At that time they had a notorious prisoner, called Jesus[e] Barabbas. [17]So after they had gathered, Pilate said to them, "Whom do you want me to release for you, Jesus[e] Barabbas or Jesus who is called the Messiah?"[f] [18]For he realized that it was out of jealousy that they had handed him over. [19]While he was sitting on the judgment seat, his wife sent word to him, "Have nothing to do with that innocent man, for today I have suffered a great deal because of a dream about him." [20]Now the chief priests and the elders persuaded the crowds to ask for Barabbas and to have Jesus killed. [21]The governor again said to them, "Which of the two do you want me to release for you?" And they said, "Barabbas." [22]Pilate said to them, "Then what should I do with Jesus who is called the Messiah?"[f] All of them said, "Let him be crucified!" [23]Then he asked, "Why, what evil has he done?" But they shouted all the more, "Let him be crucified!"

Pilate Hands Jesus over to Be Crucified

24 So when Pilate saw that he could do nothing, but rather that a riot was beginning, he took some water and washed his hands before the crowd, saying, "I am innocent of this man's blood;[g] see to it yourselves." [25]Then the people as a whole answered, "His blood be on us and on our children!" [26]So he released Barabbas for them; and after flogging Jesus, he handed him over to be crucified.

The Soldiers Mock Jesus

27 Then the soldiers of the governor took Jesus into the governor's headquarters,[h] and

a Other ancient authorities read *Zechariah* or *Isaiah* *b* Or *I took* *c* Or *the price of the precious One* *d* Other ancient authorities read *I gave* *e* Other ancient authorities lack *Jesus* *f* Or *the Christ* *g* Other ancient authorities read *this righteous blood*, or *this righteous man's blood* *h* Gk *the praetorium* they gathered the whole cohort around him. [28]They stripped him and put a scarlet robe on him, [29]and after twisting some thorns into a crown, they put it on his head. They put a reed in his right hand and knelt before him and mocked him, saying, "Hail, King of the Jews!" [30]They spat on him, and took the reed and struck him on the head. [31]After mocking him, they stripped him of the robe and put his own clothes on him. Then they led him away to crucify him.

The Crucifixion of Jesus

32 As they went out, they came upon a man from Cyrene named Simon; they compelled this man to carry his cross. [33]And when they came to a place called Golgotha (which means Place of a Skull), [34]they offered him wine to drink, mixed with gall; but when he tasted it, he would not drink it. [35]And when they had crucified him, they divided his clothes among themselves by casting lots;[a] [36]then they sat down there and kept watch over him. [37]Over his head they put the charge against him, which read, "This is Jesus, the King of the Jews."

38 Then two bandits were crucified with him, one on his right and one on his left. [39]Those who passed by derided[b] him, shaking their heads [40]and saying, "You who would destroy the temple and build it in three days, save yourself! If you are the Son of God, come down from the cross." [41]In the same way the chief priests also, along with the scribes and elders, were mocking him, saying, [42]"He saved others; he cannot save himself.[c] He is the King of Israel; let him come down from the cross now, and we will believe in him. [43]He trusts in God; let God deliver him now, if he wants to; for he said, 'I am God's Son.'" [44]The bandits who were crucified with him also taunted him in the same way.

The Death of Jesus

45 From noon on, darkness came over the whole land[d] until three in the afternoon. [46]And about three o'clock Jesus cried with a loud voice, "Eli, Eli, lema sabachthani?" that is, "My God, my God, why have you forsaken me?" [47]When some of the bystanders heard it, they said, "This man is calling for Elijah." [48]At once one of them ran and got a sponge, filled it with sour wine, put it on a stick, and gave it to him to drink. [49]But the others said, "Wait, let us see whether Elijah will come to save him."[e] [50]Then Jesus cried again with a loud voice and breathed his last.[f] [51]At that moment the cur-

tain of the temple was torn in two, from top to bottom. The earth shook, and the rocks were split. [52]The tombs also were opened, and many bodies of the saints who had fallen asleep were raised. [53]After his resurrection they came out of the tombs and entered the holy city and appeared to many. [54]Now when the centurion and those with him, who were keeping watch over Jesus, saw the earthquake and what took place, they were terrified and said, "Truly this man was God's Son!"[g]

55 Many women were also there, looking on from a distance; they had followed Jesus from Galilee and had provided for him. [56]Among them were Mary Magdalene, and Mary the mother of James and Joseph, and the mother of the sons of Zebedee.

The Burial of Jesus

57 When it was evening, there came a rich man from Arimathea, named Joseph, who was also a disciple of Jesus. [58]He went to Pilate and asked for the body of Jesus; then Pilate ordered it to be given to him. [59]So Joseph took the body and wrapped it in a clean linen cloth [60]and laid it in his own new tomb, which he had hewn in the rock. He then rolled a great stone to the door of the tomb and went away. [61]Mary Magdalene and the other Mary were there, sitting opposite the tomb.

The Guard at the Tomb

62 The next day, that is, after the day of Preparation, the chief priests and the Pharisees gathered before Pilate [63]and said, "Sir, we remember what that impostor said while he was still alive, 'After three days I will rise again.' [64]Therefore command the tomb to be made secure until the third day; otherwise his disciples may go and steal him away, and tell the people, 'He has been raised from the dead,' and the last deception would be worse than the first." [65]Pilate said to them, "You have a guard[h] of soldiers; go, make it as secure as you can."[i] [66]So they went with the guard and made the tomb secure by sealing the stone.

28 The Resurrection of Jesus

After the sabbath, as the first day of the week was dawning, Mary Magdalene and the other Mary went to see the tomb. [2]And suddenly there was a great earthquake; for an angel of the Lord, descending from heaven, came and rolled back the stone and sat on it. [3]His appearance was like lightning, and his clothing white as snow. [4]For fear of him the guards shook and

---

a Other ancient authorities add in order that what had been spoken through the prophet might be fulfilled, "They divided my clothes among themselves, and for my clothing they cast lots." b Or blasphemed c Or is he unable to save himself? d Or earth e Other ancient authorities add And another took a spear and pierced his side, and out came water and blood f Or gave up his spirit g Or a son of God h Or Take a guard i Gk you know how became like dead men. [5]But the angel said to the women, "Do not be afraid; I know that you are looking for Jesus who was crucified. [6]He is not here; for he has been raised, as he said. Come, see the place where he[a] lay. [7]Then go quickly and tell his disciples, 'He has been raised from the dead,[b] and indeed he is going ahead of you to Galilee; there you will see him.' This is my message for you." [8]So they left the tomb quickly with fear and great joy, and ran to tell his disciples. [9]Suddenly Jesus met them and said, "Greetings!" And they came to him, took hold of his feet, and worshiped him. [10]Then Jesus said to them, "Do not be afraid; go and tell my brothers to go to Galilee; there they will see me."

The Report of the Guard

11 While they were going, some of the guard went into the city and told the chief priests everything that had happened. [12]After the priests[c] had assembled with the elders, they devised a plan to give a large sum of money to the soldiers, [13]telling them, "You must say, 'His disciples came by night and stole him away while we were asleep.' [14]If this comes to the governor's ears, we will satisfy him and keep you out of trouble." [15]So they took the money and did as they were directed. And this story is still told among the Jews to this day.

The Commissioning of the Disciples

16 Now the eleven disciples went to Galilee, to the mountain to which Jesus had directed them. [17]When they saw him, they worshiped him; but some doubted. [18]And Jesus came and said to them, "All authority in heaven and on earth has been given to me. [19]Go therefore and make disciples of all nations, baptizing them in the name of the Father and of the Son and of the Holy Spirit, [20]and teaching them to obey everything that I have commanded you. And remember, I am with you always, to the end of the age."[d]

---

a Other ancient authorities read *the Lord* *b* Other ancient authorities lack *from the dead* *c* Gk *they* *d* Other ancient authorities add *Amen*

CREATIVE SPACE

MARK

THE KINGDOM OF GOD

The Call

How does a person become a disciple of Jesus? The first step is hearing and responding to God's call. In the Old Testament, people experienced God's call through dreams, voices in the night, and prophetic visions. In the Gospel According to Mark, Jesus called people directly. He first summoned four ordinary people to join the Kingdom of God. He asked them to drop everything—yes, *everything*—and follow him.

Jesus kept on calling until he had gathered a very diverse group—his twelve Apostles. They listened to Jesus preach about the Kingdom in words and actions. They heard the demands of discipleship—a way of life that was very different from the way most people lived during that time—a way of life that would further God's Kingdom.

In a world ruled by the most powerful empire around, the most dangerous thing you could do was proclaim that a new kingdom was being birthed right in the midst of the Roman Empire. Hearing about a new king and kingdom made the Roman rulers feel threatened and wary. What they didn't understand was that Jesus came to inaugurate God's Kingdom—one not built through oppression and domination, but one propelled by love and compassion.

A Kingdom of hope over a kingdom of despair.

A Kingdom of freedom over a kingdom of bondage.

A Kingdom of liberation over a kingdom of oppression.

A Kingdom of generosity over a kingdom of greed.

A Kingdom of love over a kingdom of power.

A Kingdom of light over a kingdom of darkness.

> *"Christ acts like a loving mother. To induce us to follow him, he gives us himself as an example and promises us a reward in his kingdom."*
>
> —St. Anthony of Padua

WHO The author of this gospel account is not known for certain. Some think it was John Mark.

WHAT This gospel stresses the suffering and death of Jesus.

WHEN This may be the first of the four gospels to have been written down. It was probably written in the early to mid-60s A.D.

WHERE This gospel was probably written for Christians living in Rome.

PATH OF DISCIPLESHIP

In the Gospel According to Mark, one of the ways Jesus invites us to be his disciples is through *parables*, or teachings. When you think of parables, think of "stories with a double meaning." Check out what the *Catechism of the Catholic Church* tells us about Jesus' parables:

"Through his parables he invites people to the feast of the kingdom, but he also asks for a radical choice: to gain the kingdom, one must give everything. Words are not enough; deeds are required" (CCC 546). Only those who listen well and commit to discipleship will truly understand the secrets of the Kingdom contained in the parables.

As you read Mark's gospel, remember the challenge for discipleship: "Words are not enough; deeds are required." How will you respond?

Going to the Mat for Jesus

Read **Mark 2.1–12.** The scene is crazy. Jesus is rock-star popular, and everyone in town is coming to see and hear him. The house where he's speaking is jam-packed, and people are lining up just to get a glimpse of him. That's when a group of friends do something crazy. They tear open a roof just so their paralyzed friend can get an audience with Jesus. And when their friend does come in contact with Jesus, he is healed! The Church continues that practice today in the sacrament of the Anointing of the Sick. You don't have to be at death's door to celebrate this sacrament—just in need of God's healing.

Find a mat, rug, or towel and sit on it. In the Creative Space provided below, list some of your friends who need Jesus. Next, list some of the creative ways you could get them to meet with Jesus. You could write a song or poem about what Jesus means to you and give it to them. You could draw a cartoon about your faith and see what they think. You could invite them to read through this gospel—Mark—with you. You could invite them to come to Mass with you. Anything—just think outside the box! Then drop in at **Learner.CalltoDiscipleship.com** and tell us what happens when your friends encounter Jesus.

CREATIVE SPACE

1 The Proclamation of John the Baptist

The beginning of the good news[a] of Jesus Christ, the Son of God.[b]

2 As it is written in the prophet Isaiah,[c]

"See, I am sending my messenger ahead of you,[d]

who will prepare your way;

3 the voice of one crying out in the wilderness:

'Prepare the way of the Lord,

make his paths straight,' "

[4]John the baptizer appeared[e] in the wilderness, proclaiming a baptism of repentance for the forgiveness of sins. [5]And people from the whole Judean countryside and all the people of Jerusalem were going out to him, and were baptized by him in the river Jordan, confessing their sins. [6]Now John was clothed with camel's hair, with a leather belt around his waist, and he ate locusts and wild honey. [7]He proclaimed, "The one who is more powerful than I is coming after me; I am not worthy to stoop down and untie the thong of his sandals. [8]I have baptized you with[f] water; but he will baptize you with[f] the Holy Spirit."

The Baptism of Jesus

9 In those days Jesus came from Nazareth of Galilee and was baptized by John in the Jordan. [10]And just as he was coming up out of the water, he saw the heavens torn apart and the Spirit descending like a dove on him. [11]And a voice came from heaven, "You are my Son, the Beloved;[g] with you I am well pleased."

The Temptation of Jesus

12 And the Spirit immediately drove him out into the wilderness. [13]He was in the wilderness forty days, tempted by Satan; and he was with the wild beasts; and the angels waited on him.

The Beginning of the Galilean Ministry

14 Now after John was arrested, Jesus came to Galilee, proclaiming the good news[g] of God,[h] [15]and saying, "The time is fulfilled, and the kingdom of God has come near;[i] repent, and believe in the good news."[h]

Jesus Calls the First Disciples

16 As Jesus passed along the Sea of Galilee, he saw Simon and his brother Andrew casting a net into the sea—for they were fishermen. [17]And Jesus said to them, "Follow me and I will make you fish for people." [18]And immediately they

a Or *gospel* b Other ancient authorities lack *the Son of God* c Other ancient authorities read *in the prophets* d Gk *before your face* e Other ancient authorities read *John was baptizing* f Or *in* g Or *my beloved Son* h Other ancient authorities read *of the kingdom* i Or *is at hand* left their nets and followed him. [19]As he went a little farther, he saw James son of Zebedee and his brother John, who were in their boat mending the nets. [20]Immediately he called them; and they left their father Zebedee in the boat with the hired men, and followed him.

The Man with an Unclean Spirit

21 They went to Capernaum; and when the sabbath came, he entered the synagogue and taught. [22]They were astounded at his teaching, for he taught them as one having authority, and not as the scribes. [23]Just then there was in their synagogue a man with an unclean spirit, [24]and he cried out, "What have you to do with us, Jesus of Nazareth? Have you come to destroy us? I know who you are, the Holy One of God." [25]But Jesus rebuked him, saying, "Be silent, and come out of him!" [26]And the unclean spirit, convulsing him and crying with a loud voice, came out of him. [27]They were all amazed, and they kept on asking one another, "What is this? A new teaching—with authority! He[a] commands even the unclean spirits, and they obey him." [28]At once his fame began to spread throughout the surrounding region of Galilee.

Jesus Heals Many at Simon's House

29 As soon as they[b] left the synagogue, they entered the house of Simon and Andrew, with James and John. [30]Now Simon's mother-in-law was in bed with a fever, and they told him about her at once. [31]He came and took her by the hand and lifted her up. Then the fever left her, and she began to serve them.

32 That evening, at sunset, they brought to him all who were sick or possessed with demons. [33]And the whole city was gathered around the door. [34]And he cured many who were sick with various diseases, and cast out many demons; and he would not permit the demons to speak, because they knew him.

A Preaching Tour in Galilee

35 In the morning, while it was still very dark, he got up and went out to a deserted place, and there he prayed. [36]And Simon and his companions hunted for him. [37]When they found him, they said to him, "Everyone is searching for you." [38]He answered, "Let us go on to the neighboring towns, so that I may proclaim the message there also; for that is what I came out to do." [39]And he went throughout Galilee, proclaiming the message in their synagogues and casting out demons.

Jesus Cleanses a Leper

40 A leper[c] came to him begging him, and kneeling[d] he said to him, "If you choose, you can make me clean." [41]Moved with pity,[e] Jesus[f] stretched out his hand and touched him, and said to him, "I do choose. Be made clean!" [42]Immediately the leprosy[c] left him, and he was made clean. [43]After sternly warning him he sent him away at once, [44]saying to him, "See that you say nothing to anyone; but go, show yourself to the priest, and offer for your cleansing what Moses commanded, as a testimony to them." [45]But he went out and began to proclaim it freely, and to spread the word, so that Jesus[f] could no longer go into a town openly, but stayed out in the country; and people came to him from every quarter.

2 Jesus Heals a Paralytic

When he returned to Capernaum after some days, it was reported that he was at home. [2]So many gathered around that there was no longer room for them, not even in front of the door; and he was speaking the word to them. [3]Then some people[g] came, bringing to him a paralyzed man, carried by four of them. [4]And when they could not bring him to Jesus because of the crowd, they removed the roof above him; and after having dug through it, they let down the mat on which the paralytic lay. [5]When Jesus saw their faith, he said to the paralytic, "Son, your sins are forgiven." [6]Now some of the scribes were sitting there, questioning in their hearts, [7]"Why does this fellow speak in this way? It is blasphemy! Who can forgive sins but God alone?" [8]At once Jesus perceived in his spirit that they were discussing these questions among themselves; and he said to them, "Why do you raise such questions in your hearts? [9]Which is easier, to say to the paralytic, 'Your sins are forgiven,' or to say, 'Stand up and take your mat and walk'? [10]But so that you may know that the Son of Man has authority on earth to forgive sins"—he said to the paralytic— [11]"I say to you, stand up, take your mat and go to your home." [12]And he stood up, and immediately took the mat and went out before all of them; so that they were all amazed and glorified God, saying, "We have never seen anything like this!"

Jesus Calls Levi

13 Jesus[h] went out again beside the sea; the whole crowd gathered around him, and he taught them. [14]As he was walking along, he saw Levi son of Alphaeus sitting at the tax

---

a Or A new teaching! With authority he   b Other ancient authorities read he   c The terms leper and leprosy can refer to several diseases   d Other ancient authorities lack kneeling   e Other ancient authorities read anger   f Gk he   g Gk they   h Gk He booth, and he said to him, "Follow me." And he got up and followed him.

15 And as he sat at dinner*ᵃ* in Levi's*ᵇ* house, many tax collectors and sinners were also sitting*ᶜ* with Jesus and his disciples—for there were many who followed him. ¹⁶When the scribes of*ᵈ* the Pharisees saw that he was eating with sinners and tax collectors, they said to his disciples, "Why does he eat*ᵉ* with tax collectors and sinners?" ¹⁷When Jesus heard this, he said to them, "Those who are well have no need of a physician, but those who are sick; I have come to call not the righteous but sinners."

The Question about Fasting

18 Now John's disciples and the Pharisees were fasting; and people*ᶠ* came and said to him, "Why do John's disciples and the disciples of the Pharisees fast, but your disciples do not fast?" ¹⁹Jesus said to them, "The wedding guests cannot fast while the bridegroom is with them, can they? As long as they have the bridegroom with them, they cannot fast. ²⁰The days will come when the bridegroom is taken away from them, and then they will fast on that day.

21 "No one sews a piece of unshrunk cloth on an old cloak; otherwise, the patch pulls away from it, the new from the old, and a worse tear is made. ²²And no one puts new wine into old wineskins; otherwise, the wine will burst the skins, and the wine is lost, and so are the skins; but one puts new wine into fresh wineskins."*ᵍ*

Pronouncement about the Sabbath

23 One sabbath he was going through the grainfields; and as they made their way his disciples began to pluck heads of grain. ²⁴The Pharisees said to him, "Look, why are they doing what is not lawful on the sabbath?" ²⁵And he said to them, "Have you never read what David did when he and his companions were hungry and in need of food? ²⁶He entered the house of God, when Abiathar was high priest, and ate the bread of the Presence, which it is not lawful for any but the priests to eat, and he gave some to his companions." ²⁷Then he said to them, "The sabbath was made for humankind, and not humankind for the sabbath; ²⁸so the Son of Man is lord even of the sabbath."

3 The Man with a Withered Hand

Again he entered the synagogue, and a man was there who had a withered hand. ²They watched him to see whether he would cure him on the sabbath, so that they might accuse him. ³And he said to the man who had the withered hand, "Come forward." ⁴Then he said to them, "Is it lawful to do good or to do harm on the sabbath, to save life or to kill?" But they were silent. ⁵He looked around at them with anger; he was grieved at their hardness of heart and said to the man, "Stretch out your hand." He stretched it out, and his hand was restored. ⁶The Pharisees went out and immediately conspired with the Herodians against him, how to destroy him.

A Multitude at the Seaside

7 Jesus departed with his disciples to the sea, and a great multitude from Galilee followed him; ⁸hearing all that he was doing, they came to him in great numbers from Judea, Jerusalem, Idumea, beyond the Jordan, and the region around Tyre and Sidon. ⁹He told his disciples to have a boat ready for him because of the crowd, so that they would not crush him; ¹⁰for he had cured many, so that all who had diseases pressed upon him to touch him. ¹¹Whenever the unclean spirits saw him, they fell down before him and shouted, "You are the Son of God!" ¹²But he sternly ordered them not to make him known.

Jesus Appoints the Twelve

13 He went up the mountain and called to him those whom he wanted, and they came to him. ¹⁴And he appointed twelve, whom he also named apostles,*ʰ* to be with him, and to be sent out to proclaim the message, ¹⁵and to

a Gk reclined b Gk his c Gk reclining d Other ancient authorities read and e Other ancient authorities add and drink f Gk they
g Other ancient authorities lack but one puts new wine into fresh wineskins h Other ancient authorities lack whom he also named apostles

have authority to cast out demons. ¹⁶So he appointed the twelve:ᵃ Simon (to whom he gave the name Peter); ¹⁷James son of Zebedee and John the brother of James (to whom he gave the name Boanerges, that is, Sons of Thunder); ¹⁸and Andrew, and Philip, and Bartholomew, and Matthew, and Thomas, and James son of Alphaeus, and Thaddaeus, and Simon the Cananaean, ¹⁹and Judas Iscariot, who betrayed him.

Jesus and Beelzebul

Then he went home; ²⁰and the crowd came together again, so that they could not even eat. ²¹When his family heard it, they went out to restrain him, for people were saying, "He has gone out of his mind." ²²And the scribes who came down from Jerusalem said, "He has Beelzebul, and by the ruler of the demons he casts out demons." ²³And he called them to him, and spoke to them in parables, "How can Satan cast out Satan? ²⁴If a kingdom is divided against itself, that kingdom cannot stand. ²⁵And if a house is divided against itself, that house will not be able to stand. ²⁶And if Satan has risen up against himself and is divided, he cannot stand, but his end has come. ²⁷But no one can enter a strong man's house and plunder his property without first tying up the strong man; then indeed the house can be plundered.

28 "Truly I tell you, people will be forgiven for their sins and whatever blasphemies they utter; ²⁹but whoever blasphemes against the Holy Spirit can never have forgiveness, but is guilty of an eternal sin"— ³⁰for they had said, "He has an unclean spirit."

The True Kindred of Jesus

31 Then his mother and his brothers came; and standing outside, they sent to him and called him. ³²A crowd was sitting around him; and they said to him, "Your mother and your brothers and sistersᵇ are outside, asking for you." ³³And he replied, "Who are my mother and my brothers?" ³⁴And looking at those who sat around him, he said, "Here are my mother and my brothers! ³⁵Whoever does the will of God is my brother and sister and mother."

4 The Parable of the Sower

Again he began to teach beside the sea. Such a very large crowd gathered around him that he got into a boat on the sea and sat there, while the whole crowd was beside the sea on the land. ²He began to teach them many things in parables, and in his teaching he said to them: ³"Listen! A sower went out to sow. ⁴And as he sowed, some seed fell on the path, and the birds came and ate it up. ⁵Other seed fell on rocky ground, where it did not have much soil, and it sprang up quickly, since it had no depth of soil. ⁶And when the sun rose, it was scorched; and since it had no root, it withered away. ⁷Other seed fell among thorns, and the thorns grew up and choked it, and it yielded no grain. ⁸Other seed fell into good soil and brought forth grain, growing up and increasing and yielding thirty and sixty and a hundredfold." ⁹And he said, "Let anyone with ears to hear listen!"

The Purpose of the Parables

10 When he was alone, those who were around him along with the twelve asked him about the parables. ¹¹And he said to them, "To you has been given the secretᶜ of the kingdom of God, but for those outside, everything comes in parables; ¹²in order that

'they may indeed look, but not perceive,
    and may indeed listen, but not
        understand;
so that they may not turn again and be
        forgiven.' "

13 And he said to them, "Do you not understand this parable? Then how will you understand all the parables? ¹⁴The sower sows the word. ¹⁵These are the ones on the path where the word is sown: when they hear, Satan immediately comes and takes away the word that is sown in them. ¹⁶And these are the ones sown on rocky ground: when they hear the word, they immediately receive it with joy. ¹⁷But they have no root, and endure only for a while; then, when trouble or persecution arises on account of the word, immediately they fall away.ᵈ ¹⁸And others are those sown among the thorns: these are the ones who hear the word, ¹⁹but the cares of the world, and the lure of wealth, and the desire for other things come in and choke the word, and it yields nothing. ²⁰And these are the ones sown on the good soil: they hear the word and accept it and bear fruit, thirty and sixty and a hundredfold."

A Lamp under a Bushel Basket

21 He said to them, "Is a lamp brought in to be put under the bushel basket, or under the bed, and not on the lampstand? ²²For there is nothing hidden, except to be disclosed; nor is anything secret, except to come to light. ²³Let anyone with ears to hear listen!" ²⁴And he said to them, "Pay attention to what you hear; the measure you give will be the measure you get, and still more will be given you. ²⁵For to those

---

ᵃ Other ancient authorities lack *So he appointed the twelve* ᵇ Other ancient authorities lack *and sisters* ᶜ Or *mystery* ᵈ Or *stumble* who have, more will be given; and from those who have nothing, even what they have will be taken away."

The Parable of the Growing Seed

26 He also said, "The kingdom of God is as if someone would scatter seed on the ground, 27and would sleep and rise night and day, and the seed would sprout and grow, he does not know how. 28The earth produces of itself, first the stalk, then the head, then the full grain in the head. 29But when the grain is ripe, at once he goes in with his sickle, because the harvest has come."

The Parable of the Mustard Seed

30 He also said, "With what can we compare the kingdom of God, or what parable will we use for it? 31It is like a mustard seed, which, when sown upon the ground, is the smallest of all the seeds on earth; 32yet when it is sown it grows up and becomes the greatest of all shrubs, and puts forth large branches, so that the birds of the air can make nests in its shade."

The Use of Parables

33 With many such parables he spoke the word to them, as they were able to hear it; 34he did not speak to them except in parables, but he explained everything in private to his disciples.

Jesus Stills a Storm

35 On that day, when evening had come, he said to them, "Let us go across to the other side." 36And leaving the crowd behind, they took him with them in the boat, just as he was. Other boats were with him. 37A great windstorm arose, and the waves beat into the boat, so that the boat was already being swamped. 38But he was in the stern, asleep on the cushion; and they woke him up and said to him, "Teacher, do you not care that we are perishing?" 39He woke up and rebuked the wind, and said to the sea, "Peace! Be still!" Then the wind ceased, and there was a dead calm. 40He said to them, "Why are you afraid? Have you still no faith?" 41And they were filled with great awe and said to one another, "Who then is this, that even the wind and the sea obey him?"

5 Jesus Heals the Gerasene Demoniac

They came to the other side of the sea, to the country of the Gerasenes.*a* 2And when he had stepped out of the boat, immediately a man out of the tombs with an unclean spirit met him. 3He lived among the tombs; and no one could restrain him any more, even with a chain; 4for he had often been restrained with shackles and chains, but the chains he wrenched apart, and the shackles he broke in pieces; and no one had the strength to subdue him. 5Night and day among the tombs and on the mountains he was always howling and bruising himself with stones. 6When he saw Jesus from a distance, he ran and bowed down before him; 7and he shouted at the top of his voice, "What have you to do with me, Jesus, Son of the Most High God? I adjure you by God, do not torment me." 8For he had said to him, "Come out of the man, you unclean spirit!" 9Then Jesus*b* asked him, "What is your name?" He replied, "My name is Legion; for we are many." 10He begged him earnestly not to send them out of the country. 11Now there on the hillside a great herd of swine was feeding; 12and the unclean spirits*c* begged him, "Send us into the swine; let us enter them." 13So he gave them permission. And the unclean spirits came out and entered the swine; and the herd, numbering about two thousand, rushed down the steep bank into the sea, and were drowned in the sea.

14 The swineherds ran off and told it in the city and in the country. Then people came to see what it was that had happened. 15They came to Jesus and saw the demoniac sitting there, clothed and in his right mind, the very man who had had the legion; and they were afraid. 16Those who had seen what had happened to the demoniac and to the swine reported it. 17Then they began to beg Jesus*d* to leave their neighborhood. 18As he was getting into the boat, the man who had been possessed by demons begged him that he might be with him. 19But Jesus*b* refused, and said to him, "Go home to your friends, and tell them how much the Lord has done for you, and what mercy he has shown you." 20And he went away and began to proclaim in the Decapolis how much Jesus had done for him; and everyone was amazed.

A Girl Restored to Life and a Woman Healed

21 When Jesus had crossed again in the boat*e* to the other side, a great crowd gathered around him; and he was by the sea. 22Then one of the leaders of the synagogue named Jairus came and, when he saw him, fell at his feet 23and begged him repeatedly, "My little daughter is at the point of death. Come and lay your

---

a Other ancient authorities read *Gergesenes*; others, *Gadarenes* *b* Gk *he* *c* Gk *they* *d* Gk *him* *e* Other ancient authorities lack *in the boat* hands on her, so that she may be made well, and live." 24 So he went with him.

And a large crowd followed him and pressed in on him. 25 Now there was a woman who had been suffering from hemorrhages for twelve years. 26 She had endured much under many physicians, and had spent all that she had; and she was no better, but rather grew worse. 27 She had heard about Jesus, and came up behind him in the crowd and touched his cloak, 28 for she said, "If I but touch his clothes, I will be made well." 29 Immediately her hemorrhage stopped; and she felt in her body that she was healed of her disease. 30 Immediately aware that power had gone forth from him, Jesus turned about in the crowd and said, "Who touched my clothes?" 31 And his disciples said to him, "You see the crowd pressing in on you; how can you say, 'Who touched me?' " 32 He looked all around to see who had done it. 33 But the woman, knowing what had happened to her, came in fear and trembling, fell down before him, and told him the whole truth. 34 He said to her, "Daughter, your faith has made you well; go in peace, and be healed of your disease."

35 While he was still speaking, some people came from the leader's house to say, "Your daughter is dead. Why trouble the teacher any further?" 36 But overhearing[a] what they said, Jesus said to the leader of the synagogue, "Do not fear, only believe." 37 He allowed no one to follow him except Peter, James, and John, the brother of James. 38 When they came to the house of the leader of the synagogue, he saw a commotion, people weeping and wailing loudly. 39 When he had entered, he said to them, "Why do you make a commotion and weep? The child is not dead but sleeping." 40 And they laughed at him. Then he put them all outside, and took the child's father and mother and those who were with him, and went in where the child was. 41 He took her by the hand and said to her, "Talitha cum," which means, "Little girl, get up!" 42 And immediately the girl got up and began to walk about (she was twelve years of age). At this they were overcome with amazement. 43 He strictly ordered them that no one should know this, and told them to give her something to eat.

6 The Rejection of Jesus at Nazareth

He left that place and came to his hometown, and his disciples followed him. 2 On the sabbath he began to teach in the synagogue, and many who heard him were astounded. They said, "Where did this man get all this? What is this wisdom that has been given to him? What

Joining the Rejects

Read **Mark 2.13–17.** Here, Jesus called Levi (Matthew) to follow him and be his friend. Jesus challenged the social norms of his time by befriending the "scum"—tax collectors, prostitutes, foreigners, and worse. What kinds of people do you and your social circle reject? Most likely it's the socially awkward, the unconfident, the shy, the obnoxious, the geeks, the nerds, the idiots, and the "Losers" with a capital "L."

Who have you rejected? At least one person probably comes to mind. It doesn't do much good to spend time feeling guilty about how you rejected someone in the past. Instead, ask God for forgiveness, apologize where needed, and resolve to begin the process of becoming who God wants you to be. If you want to be like Christ, you are called to befriend those whom the world judges. Can you see beyond outer appearances, reputations, stereotypes, and cliques to instead see the heart of a person Jesus loves?

Use the Creative Space on the next page to draw a picture of a person you've rejected. As you draw him or her, reflect on the way Jesus would see that person and forget the way you've seen him or her in the past.

deeds of power are being done by his hands! 3 Is not this the carpenter, the son of Mary[b] and brother of James and Joses and Judas and Simon, and are not his sisters here with us?" And they took offense[c] at him. 4 Then Jesus said to them, "Prophets are not without honor, except in their hometown, and among their own kin, and in their own house." 5 And he could do no deed of power there, except that he laid his hands on a few sick people and cured them. 6 And he was amazed at their unbelief.

The Mission of the Twelve

Then he went about among the villages teaching. 7 He called the twelve and began to send them out two by two, and gave them author-

a Or *ignoring*; other ancient authorities read *hearing*   b Other ancient authorities read *son of the carpenter and of Mary*   c Or *stumbled* ity over the unclean spirits. [8]He ordered them to take nothing for their journey except a staff; no bread, no bag, no money in their belts; [9]but to wear sandals and not to put on two tunics. [10]He said to them, "Wherever you enter a house, stay there until you leave the place. [11]If any place will not welcome you and they refuse to hear you, as you leave, shake off the dust that is on your feet as a testimony against them." [12]So they went out and proclaimed that all should repent. [13]They cast out many demons, and anointed with oil many who were sick and cured them.

The Death of John the Baptist

14 King Herod heard of it, for Jesus'[a] name had become known. Some were[b] saying, "John the baptizer has been raised from the dead; and for this reason these powers are at work in him." [15]But others said, "It is Elijah." And others said, "It is a prophet, like one of the prophets of old." [16]But when Herod heard of it, he said, "John, whom I beheaded, has been raised."

17 For Herod himself had sent men who arrested John, bound him, and put him in prison on account of Herodias, his brother Philip's wife, because Herod[c] had married her. [18]For John had been telling Herod, "It is not lawful for you to have your brother's wife." [19]And Herodias had a grudge against him, and wanted to kill him. But she could not, [20]for Herod feared John, knowing that he was a righteous and holy man, and he protected him. When he heard him, he was greatly perplexed;[d] and yet he liked to listen to him. [21]But an opportunity came when Herod on his birthday gave a banquet for his courtiers and officers and for the leaders of Galilee. [22]When his daughter Herodias[e] came in and danced, she pleased Herod and his guests; and the king said to the girl, "Ask me for whatever you wish, and I will give it." [23]And he solemnly swore to her, "Whatever you ask me, I will give you, even half of my kingdom." [24]She went out and said to her mother, "What should I ask for?" She replied, "The head of John the baptizer." [25]Immediately she rushed back to the king and requested, "I want you to give me at once the head of John the Baptist on a platter." [26]The king was deeply grieved; yet out of regard for his oaths and for the guests, he did not want to refuse her. [27]Immediately the king sent a soldier of the guard with orders to bring John's[d] head. He went and

a Gk his b Other ancient authorities read He was c Gk he d Other ancient authorities read he did many things e Other ancient authorities read the daughter of Herodias herself beheaded him in the prison, 28brought his head on a platter, and gave it to the girl. Then the girl gave it to her mother. 29When his disciples heard about it, they came and took his body, and laid it in a tomb.

Feeding the Five Thousand

30 The apostles gathered around Jesus, and told him all that they had done and taught. 31He said to them, "Come away to a deserted place all by yourselves and rest a while." For many were coming and going, and they had no leisure even to eat. 32And they went away in the boat to a deserted place by themselves. 33Now many saw them going and recognized them, and they hurried there on foot from all the towns and arrived ahead of them. 34As he went ashore, he saw a great crowd; and he had compassion for them, because they were like sheep without a shepherd; and he began to teach them many things. 35When it grew late, his disciples came to him and said, "This is a deserted place, and the hour is now very late; 36send them away so that they may go into the surrounding country and villages and buy something for themselves to eat." 37But he answered them, "You give them something to eat." They said to him, "Are we to go and buy two hundred denarii*a* worth of bread, and give it to them to eat?" 38And he said to them, "How many loaves have you? Go and see." When they had found out, they said, "Five, and two fish." 39Then he ordered them to get all the people to sit down in groups on the green grass. 40So they sat down in groups of hundreds and of fifties. 41Taking the five loaves and the two fish, he looked up to heaven, and blessed and broke the loaves, and gave them to his disciples to set before the people; and he divided the two fish among them all. 42And all ate and were filled; 43and they took up twelve baskets full of broken pieces and of the fish. 44Those who had eaten the loaves numbered five thousand men.

Jesus Walks on the Water

45 Immediately he made his disciples get into the boat and go on ahead to the other side, to Bethsaida, while he dismissed the crowd. 46After saying farewell to them, he went up on the mountain to pray.

47 When evening came, the boat was out on the sea, and he was alone on the land. 48When he saw that they were straining at the oars against an adverse wind, he came towards them early in the morning, walking on the sea. He intended to pass them by. 49But when they

saw him walking on the sea, they thought it was a ghost and cried out; 50for they all saw him and were terrified. But immediately he spoke to them and said, "Take heart, it is I; do not be afraid." 51Then he got into the boat with them and the wind ceased. And they were utterly astounded, 52for they did not understand about the loaves, but their hearts were hardened.

Healing the Sick in Gennesaret

53 When they had crossed over, they came to land at Gennesaret and moored the boat. 54When they got out of the boat, people at once recognized him, 55and rushed about that whole region and began to bring the sick on mats to wherever they heard he was. 56And wherever he went, into villages or cities or farms, they laid the sick in the marketplaces, and begged him that they might touch even the fringe of his cloak; and all who touched it were healed.

7 The Tradition of the Elders

Now when the Pharisees and some of the scribes who had come from Jerusalem gathered around him, 2they noticed that some of his disciples were eating with defiled hands, that is, without washing them. 3(For the Pharisees, and all the Jews, do not eat unless they thoroughly wash their hands,*b* thus observing the tradition of the elders; 4and they do not eat anything from the market unless they wash it;*c* and there are also many other traditions that they observe, the washing of cups, pots, and bronze kettles.*d*) 5So the Pharisees and the scribes asked him, "Why do your disciples not live*e* according to the tradition of the elders, but eat with defiled hands?" 6He said to them, "Isaiah prophesied rightly about you hypocrites, as it is written,

'This people honors me with their lips,
   but their hearts are far from me;
7 in vain do they worship me,
   teaching human precepts as doctrines.'
8You abandon the commandment of God and hold to human tradition."

9 Then he said to them, "You have a fine way of rejecting the commandment of God in order to keep your tradition! 10For Moses said, 'Honor your father and your mother'; and, 'Whoever speaks evil of father or mother must surely die.' 11But you say that if anyone tells father or mother, 'Whatever support you might have had from me is Corban' (that is, an offering to God*f*)— 12then you no longer permit doing anything for a father or mother, 13thus making

---

a The denarius was the usual day's wage for a laborer *b* Meaning of Gk uncertain *c* Other ancient authorities read *and when they come from the marketplace, they do not eat unless they purify themselves* *d* Other ancient authorities add *and beds* *e* Gk *walk* *f* Gk lacks *to God*

TEXT MESSAGE

Just as Jesus healed the deaf man and the blind man (see Mark 7.31–37; 8.22–26), he continues to heal in today's world. Today we are invited to celebrate the Sacrament of Reconciliation and experience God's healing, pardon, and peace. It's free, it's available, and it feels great! Contact your local parish for details.

This information has been scanned and is free of all known viruses. Please forward to all your friends.

void the word of God through your tradition that you have handed on. And you do many things like this."

14 Then he called the crowd again and said to them, "Listen to me, all of you, and understand: ¹⁵there is nothing outside a person that by going in can defile, but the things that come out are what defile."ᵃ

17 When he had left the crowd and entered the house, his disciples asked him about the parable. ¹⁸He said to them, "Then do you also fail to understand? Do you not see that whatever goes into a person from outside cannot defile, ¹⁹since it enters, not the heart but the stomach, and goes out into the sewer?" (Thus he declared all foods clean.) ²⁰And he said, "It is what comes out of a person that defiles.

²¹For it is from within, from the human heart, that evil intentions come: fornication, theft, murder, ²²adultery, avarice, wickedness, deceit, licentiousness, envy, slander, pride, folly. ²³All these evil things come from within, and they defile a person."

The Syrophoenician Woman's Faith
24 From there he set out and went away to the region of Tyre.ᵇ He entered a house and did not want anyone to know he was there. Yet he could not escape notice, ²⁵but a woman whose little daughter had an unclean spirit immediately heard about him, and she came and bowed down at his feet. ²⁶Now the woman was a Gentile, of Syrophoenician origin. She begged him to cast the demon out of her daughter. ²⁷He said to her, "Let the children be fed first, for it is not fair to take the children's food and throw it to the dogs." ²⁸But she answered him, "Sir,ᶜ even the dogs under the table eat the children's crumbs." ²⁹Then he said to her, "For saying that, you may go—the demon has left your daughter." ³⁰So she went home, found the child lying on the bed, and the demon gone.

Jesus Cures a Deaf Man
31 Then he returned from the region of Tyre, and went by way of Sidon towards the Sea of Galilee, in the region of the Decapolis. ³²They brought to him a deaf man who had an impediment in his speech; and they begged him to lay his hand on him. ³³He took him aside in private, away from the crowd, and put his fingers into his ears, and he spat and touched his tongue. ³⁴Then looking up to heaven, he sighed and said to him, "Ephphatha," that is, "Be opened." ³⁵And immediately his ears were opened, his tongue was released, and he spoke plainly. ³⁶Then Jesusᵈ ordered them to tell no one; but the more he ordered them, the more zealously they proclaimed it. ³⁷They were astounded beyond measure, saying, "He has done everything well; he even makes the deaf to hear and the mute to speak."

8 Feeding the Four Thousand
In those days when there was again a great crowd without anything to eat, he called his disciples and said to them, ²"I have compassion for the crowd, because they have been with me now for three days and have nothing to eat. ³If I send them away hungry to their homes, they will faint on the way—and some of them have come from a great distance." ⁴His

a Other ancient authorities add verse 16, "Let anyone with ears to hear listen" b Other ancient authorities add and Sidon c Or Lord; other ancient authorities prefix Yes d Gk he disciples replied, "How can one feed these people with bread here in the desert?" [5]He asked them, "How many loaves do you have?" They said, "Seven." [6]Then he ordered the crowd to sit down on the ground; and he took the seven loaves, and after giving thanks he broke them and gave them to his disciples to distribute; and they distributed them to the crowd. [7]They had also a few small fish; and after blessing them, he ordered that these too should be distributed. [8]They ate and were filled; and they took up the broken pieces left over, seven baskets full. [9]Now there were about four thousand people. And he sent them away. [10]And immediately he got into the boat with his disciples and went to the district of Dalmanutha.[a]

The Demand for a Sign
11 The Pharisees came and began to argue with him, asking him for a sign from heaven, to test him. [12]And he sighed deeply in his spirit and said, "Why does this generation ask for a sign? Truly I tell you, no sign will be given to this generation." [13]And he left them, and getting into the boat again, he went across to the other side.

The Yeast of the Pharisees and of Herod
14 Now the disciples[b] had forgotten to bring any bread; and they had only one loaf with them in the boat. [15]And he cautioned them, saying, "Watch out—beware of the yeast of the Pharisees and the yeast of Herod."[c] [16]They said to one another, "It is because we have no bread." [17]And becoming aware of it, Jesus said to them, "Why are you talking about having no bread? Do you still not perceive or understand? Are your hearts hardened? [18]Do you have eyes, and fail to see? Do you have ears, and fail to hear? And do you not remember? [19]When I broke the five loaves for the five thousand, how many baskets full of broken pieces did you collect?" They said to him, "Twelve." [20]"And the seven for the four thousand, how many baskets full of broken pieces did you collect?" And they said to him, "Seven." [21]Then he said to them, "Do you not yet understand?"

Jesus Cures a Blind Man at Bethsaida
22 They came to Bethsaida. Some people[d] brought a blind man to him and begged him to touch him. [23]He took the blind man by the hand and led him out of the village; and when he had put saliva on his eyes and laid his hands on him, he asked him, "Can you see anything?" [24]And the man[e] looked up and said, "I can see people, but they look like trees, walking." [25]Then Jesus[e] laid his hands on his eyes again; and he looked intently and his sight was restored, and he saw everything clearly. [26]Then he sent him away to his home, saying, "Do not even go into the village."[f]

Peter's Declaration about Jesus
27 Jesus went on with his disciples to the villages of Caesarea Philippi; and on the way he asked his disciples, "Who do people say that I am?" [28]And they answered him, "John the Baptist; and others, Elijah; and still others, one of the prophets." [29]He asked them, "But who do you say that I am?" Peter answered him, "You are the Messiah."[g] [30]And he sternly ordered them not to tell anyone about him.

Jesus Foretells His Death and Resurrection
31 Then he began to teach them that the Son of Man must undergo great suffering, and be rejected by the elders, the chief priests, and the scribes, and be killed, and after three days rise again. [32]He said all this quite openly. And Peter took him aside and began to rebuke him. [33]But turning and looking at his disciples, he rebuked Peter and said, "Get behind me, Satan! For you are setting your mind not on divine things but on human things."

34 He called the crowd with his disciples, and said to them, "If any want to become my followers, let them deny themselves and take up their cross and follow me. [35]For those who want to save their life will lose it, and those who lose their life for my sake, and for the sake of the gospel,[h] will save it. [36]For what will it profit them to gain the whole world and forfeit their life? [37]Indeed, what can they give in return for their life? [38]Those who are ashamed of me and of my words[i] in this adulterous and sinful generation, of them the Son of Man will also be ashamed when he comes in the glory of his Father with **9** the holy angels." [1]And he said to them, "Truly I tell you, there are some standing here who will not taste death until they see that the kingdom of God has come with[j] power."

The Transfiguration
2 Six days later, Jesus took with him Peter and James and John, and led them up a high mountain apart, by themselves. And he was transfigured before them, [3]and his clothes became dazzling white, such as no one[k] on earth could bleach them. [4]And there appeared to them Elijah with Moses, who were talking with Jesus.

---

a Other ancient authorities read *Mageda* or *Magdala* b Gk *they* c Other ancient authorities read *the Herodians* d Gk *They* e Gk *he* f Other ancient authorities add *or tell anyone in the village* g Or *the Christ* h Other ancient authorities read *lose their life for the sake of the gospel* i Other ancient authorities read *and of mine* j Or *in* k Gk *no fuller*

⁵Then Peter said to Jesus, "Rabbi, it is good for us to be here; let us make three dwellings,ᵃ one for you, one for Moses, and one for Elijah." ⁶He did not know what to say, for they were terrified. ⁷Then a cloud overshadowed them, and from the cloud there came a voice, "This is my Son, the Beloved;ᵇ listen to him!" ⁸Suddenly when they looked around, they saw no one with them any more, but only Jesus.

The Coming of Elijah

9 As they were coming down the mountain, he ordered them to tell no one about what they had seen, until after the Son of Man had risen from the dead. ¹⁰So they kept the matter to themselves, questioning what this rising from the dead could mean. ¹¹Then they asked him, "Why do the scribes say that Elijah must come first?" ¹²He said to them, "Elijah is indeed coming first to restore all things. How then is it written about the Son of Man, that he is to go through many sufferings and be treated with contempt? ¹³But I tell you that Elijah has come, and they did to him whatever they pleased, as it is written about him."

The Healing of a Boy with a Spirit

14 When they came to the disciples, they saw a great crowd around them, and some scribes arguing with them. ¹⁵When the whole crowd saw him, they were immediately overcome with awe, and they ran forward to greet him. ¹⁶He asked them, "What are you arguing about with them?" ¹⁷Someone from the crowd answered him, "Teacher, I brought you my son; he has a spirit that makes him unable to speak; ¹⁸and whenever it seizes him, it dashes him down; and he foams and grinds his teeth and becomes rigid; and I asked your disciples to cast it out, but they could not do so." ¹⁹He answered them, "You faithless generation, how much longer must I be among you? How much longer must I put up with you? Bring him to me." ²⁰And they brought the boyᶜ to him. When the spirit saw him, immediately it convulsed the boy,ᶜ and he fell on the ground and rolled about, foaming at the mouth. ²¹Jesusᵈ asked the father, "How long has this been happening to him?" And he said, "From childhood. ²²It has often cast him into the fire and into the water, to destroy him; but if you are able to do anything, have pity on us and help us." ²³Jesus said to him, "If you are able!—All things can be done for the one who believes." ²⁴Immediately the father of the child cried out,ᵉ "I believe; help my unbelief!" ²⁵When Jesus saw that a crowd came running together, he rebuked the unclean spirit, saying to it, "You spirit that keeps this boy from speaking and hearing, I command you, come out of him, and never enter him again!" ²⁶After crying out and convulsing him terribly, it came out, and the boy was like a corpse, so that most of them said, "He is dead." ²⁷But Jesus took him by the hand and lifted him up, and he was able to stand. ²⁸When he had entered the house, his disciples asked him privately, "Why could we not cast it out?" ²⁹He said to them, "This kind can come out only through prayer."ᶠ

Jesus Again Foretells His Death and Resurrection

30 They went on from there and passed through Galilee. He did not want anyone to know it; ³¹for he was teaching his disciples, saying to them, "The Son of Man is to be betrayed into human hands, and they will kill him, and three days after being killed, he will rise again." ³²But they did not understand what he was saying and were afraid to ask him.

Who Is the Greatest?

33 Then they came to Capernaum; and when he was in the house he asked them, "What were you arguing about on the way?" ³⁴But they were silent, for on the way they had argued with one another who was the greatest. ³⁵He sat down, called the twelve, and said to them, "Whoever wants to be first must be last of all and servant of all." ³⁶Then he took a little child and put it among them; and taking it in his arms, he said to them, ³⁷"Whoever welcomes one such child in my name welcomes me, and whoever welcomes me welcomes not me but the one who sent me."

Another Exorcist

38 John said to him, "Teacher, we saw someoneᵍ casting out demons in your name, and we tried to stop him, because he was not following us." ³⁹But Jesus said, "Do not stop him; for no one who does a deed of power in my name will be able soon afterward to speak evil of me. ⁴⁰Whoever is not against us is for us. ⁴¹For truly I tell you, whoever gives you a cup of water to drink because you bear the name of Christ will by no means lose the reward.

Temptations to Sin

42 "If any of you put a stumbling block before one of these little ones who believe in me,ʰ it would be better for you if a great millstone

---

a Or tents b Or my beloved Son c Gk him d Gk He e Other ancient authorities add with tears f Other ancient authorities add and fasting g Other ancient authorities add who does not follow us h Other ancient authorities lack in me

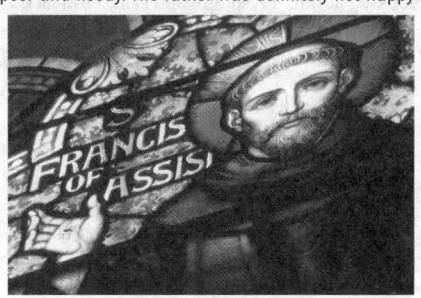
were hung around your neck and you were thrown into the sea. ⁴³If your hand causes you to stumble, cut it off; it is better for you to enter life maimed than to have two hands and to go to hell,^a to the unquenchable fire.^b ⁴⁵And if your foot causes you to stumble, cut it off; it is better for you to enter life lame than to have two feet and to be thrown into hell.^{a,b} ⁴⁷And if your eye causes you to stumble, tear it out; it is better for you to enter the kingdom of God with one eye than to have two eyes and to be thrown into hell,^a ⁴⁸where their worm never dies, and the fire is never quenched.

49 "For everyone will be salted with fire.^c ⁵⁰Salt is good; but if salt has lost its saltiness, how can you season it?^d Have salt in yourselves, and be at peace with one another."

10 Teaching about Divorce

He left that place and went to the region of Judea and^e beyond the Jordan. And crowds again gathered around him; and, as was his custom, he again taught them.

2 Some Pharisees came, and to test him they asked, "Is it lawful for a man to divorce his wife?" ³He answered them, "What did Moses command you?" ⁴They said, "Moses allowed a man to write a certificate of dismissal and to divorce her." ⁵But Jesus said to them, "Because of your hardness of heart he wrote this commandment for you. ⁶But from the beginning of creation, 'God made them male and female.' ⁷'For this reason a man shall leave his father and mother and be joined to his wife,^f ⁸and the two shall become one flesh.' So they are no longer two, but one flesh. ⁹Therefore what God has joined together, let no one separate."

10 Then in the house the disciples asked him again about this matter. ¹¹He said to them, "Whoever divorces his wife and marries another commits adultery against her; ¹²and if she divorces her husband and marries another, she commits adultery."

Jesus Blesses Little Children

13 People were bringing little children to him in order that he might touch them; and the disciples spoke sternly to them. ¹⁴But when Jesus saw this, he was indignant and said to them, "Let the little children come to me; do not stop them; for it is to such as these that the kingdom of God belongs. ¹⁵Truly I tell you, whoever does not receive the kingdom of God as a little child will never enter it." ¹⁶And he took them up in his arms, laid his hands on them, and blessed them.

---

a Gk *Gehenna* *b* Verses 44 and 46 (which are identical with verse 48) are lacking in the best ancient authorities *c* Other ancient authorities either add or substitute *and every sacrifice will be salted with salt* *d* Or *how can you restore its saltiness?* *e* Other ancient authorities lack *and* *f* Other ancient authorities lack *and be joined to his wife*

The Rich Man

17 As he was setting out on a journey, a man ran up and knelt before him, and asked him, "Good Teacher, what must I do to inherit eternal life?" 18Jesus said to him, "Why do you call me good? No one is good but God alone. 19You know the commandments: 'You shall not murder; You shall not commit adultery; You shall not steal; You shall not bear false witness; You shall not defraud; Honor your father and mother.' " 20He said to him, "Teacher, I have kept all these since my youth." 21Jesus, looking at him, loved him and said, "You lack one thing; go, sell what you own, and give the money*a* to the poor, and you will have treasure in heaven; then come, follow me." 22When he heard this, he was shocked and went away grieving, for he had many possessions.

23 Then Jesus looked around and said to his disciples, "How hard it will be for those who have wealth to enter the kingdom of God!" 24And the disciples were perplexed at these words. But Jesus said to them again, "Children, how hard it is*b* to enter the kingdom of God! 25It is easier for a camel to go through the eye of a needle than for someone who is rich to enter the kingdom of God." 26They were greatly astounded and said to one another,*c* "Then who can be saved?" 27Jesus looked at them and said, "For mortals it is impossible, but not for God; for God all things are possible."

28 Peter began to say to him, "Look, we have left everything and followed you." 29Jesus said, "Truly I tell you, there is no one who has left house or brothers or sisters or mother or father or children or fields, for my sake and for the sake of the good news,*d* 30who will not receive a hundredfold now in this age—houses, brothers and sisters, mothers and children, and fields, with persecutions—and in the age to come eternal life. 31But many who are first will be last, and the last will be first."

A Third Time Jesus Foretells His Death and Resurrection

32 They were on the road, going up to Jerusalem, and Jesus was walking ahead of them; they were amazed, and those who followed were afraid. He took the twelve aside again and began to tell them what was to happen to him, 33saying, "See, we are going up to Jerusalem, and the Son of Man will be handed over to the chief priests and the scribes, and they will condemn him to death; then they will hand him over to the Gentiles; 34they will mock him, and

spit upon him, and flog him, and kill him; and after three days he will rise again."

The Request of James and John

35 James and John, the sons of Zebedee, came forward to him and said to him, "Teacher, we want you to do for us whatever we ask of you." 36And he said to them, "What is it you want me to do for you?" 37And they said to him, "Grant us to sit, one at your right hand and one at your left, in your glory." 38But Jesus said to them, "You do not know what you are asking. Are you able to drink the cup that I drink, or be baptized with the baptism that I am baptized with?" 39They replied, "We are able." Then Jesus said to them, "The cup that I drink you will drink; and with the baptism with which I am baptized, you will be baptized; 40but to sit at my right hand or at my left is not mine to grant, but it is for those for whom it has been prepared."

41 When the ten heard this, they began to be angry with James and John. 42So Jesus called them and said to them, "You know that among the Gentiles those whom they recognize as their rulers lord it over them, and their great ones are tyrants over them. 43But it is not so among you; but whoever wishes to become great among you must be your servant, 44and whoever wishes to be first among you must be slave of all. 45For the Son of Man came not to be served but to serve, and to give his life a ransom for many."

The Healing of Blind Bartimaeus

46 They came to Jericho. As he and his disciples and a large crowd were leaving Jericho, Bartimaeus son of Timaeus, a blind beggar, was sitting by the roadside. 47When he heard that it was Jesus of Nazareth, he began to shout out and say, "Jesus, Son of David, have mercy on me!" 48Many sternly ordered him to be quiet, but he cried out even more loudly, "Son of David, have mercy on me!" 49Jesus stood still and said, "Call him here." And they called the blind man, saying to him, "Take heart; get up, he is calling you." 50So throwing off his cloak, he sprang up and came to Jesus. 51Then Jesus said to him, "What do you want me to do for you?" The blind man said to him, "My teacher,*e* let me see again." 52Jesus said to him, "Go; your faith has made you well." Immediately he regained his sight and followed him on the way.

11 Jesus' Triumphal Entry into Jerusalem

When they were approaching Jerusalem, at

---

a Gk lacks *the money* *b* Other ancient authorities add *for those who trust in riches* *c* Other ancient authorities read *to him* *d* Or *gospel* *e* Aramaic *Rabbouni*

Bethphage and Bethany, near the Mount of Olives, he sent two of his disciples ²and said to them, "Go into the village ahead of you, and immediately as you enter it, you will find tied there a colt that has never been ridden; untie it and bring it. ³If anyone says to you, 'Why are you doing this?' just say this, 'The Lord needs it and will send it back here immediately.' " ⁴They went away and found a colt tied near a door, outside in the street. As they were untying it, ⁵some of the bystanders said to them, "What are you doing, untying the colt?" ⁶They told them what Jesus had said; and they allowed them to take it. ⁷Then they brought the colt to Jesus and threw their cloaks on it; and he sat on it. ⁸Many people spread their cloaks on the road, and others spread leafy branches that they had cut in the fields. ⁹Then those who went ahead and those who followed were shouting,

"Hosanna!
    Blessed is the one who comes in the
        name of the Lord!
¹⁰   Blessed is the coming kingdom of our
        ancestor David!
    Hosanna in the highest heaven!"

11 Then he entered Jerusalem and went into the temple; and when he had looked around at everything, as it was already late, he went out to Bethany with the twelve.

Jesus Curses the Fig Tree
12 On the following day, when they came from Bethany, he was hungry. ¹³Seeing in the distance a fig tree in leaf, he went to see whether perhaps he would find anything on it. When he came to it, he found nothing but leaves, for it was not the season for figs. ¹⁴He said to it, "May no one ever eat fruit from you again." And his disciples heard it.

Jesus Cleanses the Temple
15 Then they came to Jerusalem. And he entered the temple and began to drive out those who were selling and those who were buying in the temple, and he overturned the tables of the money changers and the seats of those who sold doves; ¹⁶and he would not allow anyone to carry anything through the temple. ¹⁷He was teaching and saying, "Is it not written,

'My house shall be called a house of prayer
        for all the nations'?
But you have made it a den of robbers."

¹⁸And when the chief priests and the scribes heard it, they kept looking for a way to kill him; for they were afraid of him, because the whole crowd was spellbound by his teaching. ¹⁹And

TRY THIS ◄

WHAT'S YOUR TEMPTATION?
After his baptism, Jesus removed himself from worldly distractions and went into the desert, where he prayed and fasted from food for forty days (see Mark 1.12–13). Despite being tempted by Satan, Jesus remained faithful to God. Consider the worldly distractions and temptations that you face in your life. What material things can you do without in order to strengthen your relationship with God?

Each year during the season of Lent, we dedicate forty days to praying, fasting, and giving alms. Translation: talk to God, stay away from things that tempt you, and give some of what you have to help others. Just as Jesus strengthened his relationship with God in the desert, you can also strengthen your commitment to live as a faithful disciple. Whether you are reading this during Lent or at another time of the year, try taking a week to do three things each day: set aside fifteen minutes for prayer; abstain from something— texting, your favorite food, watching TV; and give something to help another person, like your time, money, or a listening ear.

These things should be done in your own "desert"—in other words, in private, just between you and God. Use the Lord's Prayer as part of your conversation (see CCC 1969). And though you don't need to brag, complain about, or announce your experience to your friends and family, you can share it with us. Post your thoughts about your experience on **Learner.CalltoDiscipleship.com.**

GOD IS CHALLENGING MY SELF

when evening came, Jesus and his disciples*a* went out of the city.

The Lesson from the Withered Fig Tree
20 In the morning as they passed by, they saw the fig tree withered away to its roots. ²¹Then Peter remembered and said to him, "Rabbi, look! The fig tree that you cursed has withered." ²²Jesus answered them, "Have*b* faith in God. ²³Truly I tell you, if you say to this mountain, 'Be taken up and thrown into the sea,' and if you do not doubt in your heart, but believe that what you say will come to pass, it will be

a Gk *they*: other ancient authorities read *he* *b* Other ancient authorities read *"If you have* done for you. ²⁴So I tell you, whatever you ask for in prayer, believe that you have receivedᵃ it, and it will be yours.

25 "Whenever you stand praying, forgive, if you have anything against anyone; so that your Father in heaven may also forgive you your trespasses."ᵇ

Jesus' Authority Is Questioned

27 Again they came to Jerusalem. As he was walking in the temple, the chief priests, the scribes, and the elders came to him ²⁸and said, "By what authority are you doing these things? Who gave you this authority to do them?" ²⁹Jesus said to them, "I will ask you one question; answer me, and I will tell you by what authority I do these things. ³⁰Did the baptism of John come from heaven, or was it of human origin? Answer me." ³¹They argued with one another, "If we say, 'From heaven,' he will say, 'Why then did you not believe him?' ³²But shall we say, 'Of human origin'?"—they were afraid of the crowd, for all regarded John as truly a prophet. ³³So they answered Jesus, "We do not know." And Jesus said to them, "Neither will I tell you by what authority I am doing these things."

12 The Parable of the Wicked Tenants

Then he began to speak to them in parables. "A man planted a vineyard, put a fence around it, dug a pit for the wine press, and built a watchtower; then he leased it to tenants and went to another country. ²When the season came, he sent a slave to the tenants to collect from them his share of the produce of the vineyard. ³But they seized him, and beat him, and sent him away empty-handed. ⁴And again he sent another slave to them; this one they beat over the head and insulted. ⁵Then he sent another, and that one they killed. And so it was with many others; some they beat, and others they killed. ⁶He had still one other, a beloved son. Finally he sent him to them, saying, 'They will respect my son.' ⁷But those tenants said to one another, 'This is the heir; come, let us kill him, and the inheritance will be ours.' ⁸So they seized him, killed him, and threw him out of the vineyard. ⁹What then will the owner of the vineyard do? He will come and destroy the tenants and give the vineyard to others. ¹⁰Have you not read this scripture:

'The stone that the builders rejected
    has become the cornerstone;ᶜ
¹¹ this was the Lord's doing,
    and it is amazing in our eyes'?"

12 When they realized that he had told this parable against them, they wanted to arrest him, but they feared the crowd. So they left him and went away.

The Question about Paying Taxes

13 Then they sent to him some Pharisees and some Herodians to trap him in what he said. ¹⁴And they came and said to him, "Teacher, we know that you are sincere, and show deference to no one; for you do not regard people with partiality, but teach the way of God in accordance with truth. Is it lawful to pay taxes to the emperor, or not? ¹⁵Should we pay them, or should we not?" But knowing their hypocrisy, he said to them, "Why are you putting me to the test? Bring me a denarius and let me see it." ¹⁶And they brought one. Then he said to them, "Whose head is this, and whose title?" They answered, "The emperor's." ¹⁷Jesus said to them, "Give to the emperor the things that are the emperor's, and to God the things that are God's." And they were utterly amazed at him.

The Question about the Resurrection

18 Some Sadducees, who say there is no resurrection, came to him and asked him a question, saying, ¹⁹"Teacher, Moses wrote for us that if a man's brother dies, leaving a wife but no child, the manᵈ shall marry the widow and raise up children for his brother. ²⁰There were seven brothers; the first married and, when he died, left no children; ²¹and the second married the widowᵉ and died, leaving no children; and the third likewise; ²²none of the seven left children. Last of all the woman herself died. ²³In the resurrectionᶠ whose wife will she be? For the seven had married her."

ᵃ Other ancient authorities read *are receiving* ᵇ Other ancient authorities add verse 26, *"But if you do not forgive, neither will your Father in heaven forgive your trespasses."* ᶜ Or *keystone* ᵈ Gk *his brother* ᵉ Gk *her* ᶠ Other ancient authorities add *when they rise*

24 Jesus said to them, "Is not this the reason you are wrong, that you know neither the scriptures nor the power of God? 25For when they rise from the dead, they neither marry nor are given in marriage, but are like angels in heaven. 26And as for the dead being raised, have you not read in the book of Moses, in the story about the bush, how God said to him, 'I am the God of Abraham, the God of Isaac, and the God of Jacob'? 27He is God not of the dead, but of the living; you are quite wrong."

The First Commandment

28 One of the scribes came near and heard them disputing with one another, and seeing that he answered them well, he asked him, "Which commandment is the first of all?" 29Jesus answered, "The first is, 'Hear, O Israel: the Lord our God, the Lord is one; 30you shall love the Lord your God with all your heart, and with all your soul, and with all your mind, and with all your strength.' 31The second is this, 'You shall love your neighbor as yourself.' There is no other commandment greater than these." 32Then the scribe said to him, "You are right, Teacher; you have truly said that 'he is one, and besides him there is no other'; 33and 'to love him with all the heart, and with all the understanding, and with all the strength,' and 'to love one's neighbor as oneself,'—this is much more important than all whole burnt offerings and sacrifices." 34When Jesus saw that he answered wisely, he said to him, "You are not far from the kingdom of God." After that no one dared to ask him any question.

The Question about David's Son

35 While Jesus was teaching in the temple, he said, "How can the scribes say that the Messiah*a* is the son of David? 36David himself, by the Holy Spirit, declared,

'The Lord said to my Lord,
  "Sit at my right hand,
    until I put your enemies under your
        feet." '

37David himself calls him Lord; so how can he be his son?" And the large crowd was listening to him with delight.

Jesus Denounces the Scribes

38 As he taught, he said, "Beware of the scribes, who like to walk around in long robes, and to be greeted with respect in the marketplaces, 39and to have the best seats in the synagogues and places of honor at banquets! 40They devour widows' houses and for the sake of appearance say long prayers. They will receive the greater condemnation."

The Widow's Offering

41 He sat down opposite the treasury, and watched the crowd putting money into the treasury. Many rich people put in large sums. 42A poor widow came and put in two small copper coins, which are worth a penny. 43Then he called his disciples and said to them, "Truly I tell you, this poor widow has put in more than all those who are contributing to the treasury. 44For all of them have contributed out of their abundance; but she out of her poverty has put in everything she had, all she had to live on."

13 The Destruction of the Temple Foretold

As he came out of the temple, one of his disciples said to him, "Look, Teacher, what large stones and what large buildings!" 2Then Jesus asked him, "Do you see these great buildings? Not one stone will be left here upon another; all will be thrown down."

3 When he was sitting on the Mount of Olives opposite the temple, Peter, James, John, and Andrew asked him privately, 4"Tell us, when will this be, and what will be the sign that all these things are about to be accomplished?" 5Then Jesus began to say to them, "Beware that no one leads you astray. 6Many will come in my name and say, 'I am he!'*b* and they will lead many astray. 7When you hear of wars and rumors of wars, do not be alarmed; this must take place, but the end is still to come. 8For nation will rise against nation, and kingdom against kingdom; there will be earthquakes in various places; there will be famines. This is but the beginning of the birth pangs.

Persecution Foretold

9 "As for yourselves, beware; for they will hand you over to councils; and you will be beaten in synagogues; and you will stand before governors and kings because of me, as a testimony to them. 10And the good news*c* must first be proclaimed to all nations. 11When they bring you to trial and hand you over, do not worry beforehand about what you are to say; but say whatever is given you at that time, for it is not you who speak, but the Holy Spirit. 12Brother will betray brother to death, and a father his child, and children will rise against parents and have them put to death; 13and you will be hated by all because of my name. But the one who endures to the end will be saved.

a Or *the Christ* *b* Gk *I am* *c* Gk *gospel*

The Desolating Sacrilege

14 "But when you see the desolating sacrilege set up where it ought not to be (let the reader understand), then those in Judea must flee to the mountains; ¹⁵the one on the housetop must not go down or enter the house to take anything away; ¹⁶the one in the field must not turn back to get a coat. ¹⁷Woe to those who are pregnant and to those who are nursing infants in those days! ¹⁸Pray that it may not be in winter. ¹⁹For in those days there will be suffering, such as has not been from the beginning of the creation that God created until now, no, and never will be. ²⁰And if the Lord had not cut short those days, no one would be saved; but for the sake of the elect, whom he chose, he has cut short those days. ²¹And if anyone says to you at that time, 'Look! Here is the Messiah!'ᵃ or 'Look! There he is!'—do not believe it. ²²False messiahsᵇ and false prophets will appear and produce signs and omens, to lead astray, if possible, the elect. ²³But be alert; I have already told you everything.

The Coming of the Son of Man

24 "But in those days, after that suffering,
the sun will be darkened,
and the moon will not give its light,
²⁵ and the stars will be falling from heaven,
and the powers in the heavens will be shaken.

²⁶Then they will see 'the Son of Man coming in clouds' with great power and glory. ²⁷Then he will send out the angels, and gather his elect from the four winds, from the ends of the earth to the ends of heaven.

The Lesson of the Fig Tree

28 "From the fig tree learn its lesson: as soon as its branch becomes tender and puts forth its leaves, you know that summer is near. ²⁹So also, when you see these things taking place, you know that heᶜ is near, at the very gates. ³⁰Truly I tell you, this generation will not pass away until all these things have taken place. ³¹Heaven and earth will pass away, but my words will not pass away.

The Necessity for Watchfulness

32 "But about that day or hour no one knows, neither the angels in heaven, nor the Son, but only the Father. ³³Beware, keep alert;ᵈ for you do not know when the time will come. ³⁴It is like a man going on a journey, when he leaves home and puts his slaves in charge, each with his work, and commands the doorkeeper to be on the watch. ³⁵Therefore, keep awake—for you do not know when the master of the house will come, in the evening, or at midnight, or at cockcrow, or at dawn, ³⁶or else he may find you asleep when he comes suddenly. ³⁷And what I say to you I say to all: Keep awake."

14 The Plot to Kill Jesus

It was two days before the Passover and the festival of Unleavened Bread. The chief priests and the scribes were looking for a way to arrest Jesusᵉ by stealth and kill him; ²for they said, "Not during the festival, or there may be a riot among the people."

The Anointing at Bethany

3 While he was at Bethany in the house of Simon the leper,ᶠ as he sat at the table, a woman came with an alabaster jar of very costly ointment of nard, and she broke open the jar and poured the ointment on his head. ⁴But some were there who said to one another in anger, "Why was the ointment wasted in this way? ⁵For this ointment could have been sold for more than three hundred denarii,ᵍ and the money given to the poor." And they scolded her. ⁶But Jesus said, "Let her alone; why do you trouble her? She has performed a good service for me. ⁷For you always have the poor with you, and you can show kindness to them whenever you wish; but you will not always have me. ⁸She has done what she could; she has anointed my body beforehand for its burial. ⁹Truly I tell you, wherever the good newsʰ is proclaimed in the whole world, what she has done will be told in remembrance of her."

Judas Agrees to Betray Jesus

10 Then Judas Iscariot, who was one of the twelve, went to the chief priests in order to betray him to them. ¹¹When they heard it, they were greatly pleased, and promised to give him money. So he began to look for an opportunity to betray him.

The Passover with the Disciples

12 On the first day of Unleavened Bread, when the Passover lamb is sacrificed, his disciples said to him, "Where do you want us to go and make the preparations for you to eat the Passover?" ¹³So he sent two of his disciples, saying to them, "Go into the city, and a man carrying a jar of water will meet you; follow him, ¹⁴and wherever he enters, say to the owner of the house, 'The Teacher asks, Where is my guest room where I may eat the Passover with my

---

a Or the Christ b Or christs c Or it d Other ancient authorities add and pray e Gk him f The terms leper and leprosy can refer to several diseases g The denarius was the usual day's wage for a laborer h Or gospel

I KNOW

I know I'm to serve you Lord,
There is so much to look forward
To (heaven)
I know I'm to serve you again
And I know that you'll call me when

With every stumble on my way
I know to just drop to my knees
And (pray)
And I know that you'll bring the light
Even in the darkest of night

I want to know how to grow
I want to spread my arms wide
And flap (and fly)
I know that you'll be by my side
So I'll serve you until I die.

"I Know"—© Marshall Katheder, 19

Bench—© Jessica Jones, 18

disciples?' [15]He will show you a large room upstairs, furnished and ready. Make preparations for us there." [16]So the disciples set out and went to the city, and found everything as he had told them; and they prepared the Passover meal.

[17] When it was evening, he came with the twelve. [18]And when they had taken their places and were eating, Jesus said, "Truly I tell you, one of you will betray me, one who is eating with me." [19]They began to be distressed and to say to him one after another, "Surely, not I?" [20]He said to them, "It is one of the twelve, one who is dipping bread[a] into the bowl[b] with me. [21]For the Son of Man goes as it is written of him, but woe to that one by whom the Son of Man is betrayed! It would have been better for that one not to have been born."

The Institution of the Lord's Supper
[22] While they were eating, he took a loaf of bread, and after blessing it he broke it, gave it to them, and said, "Take; this is my body." [23]Then he took a cup, and after giving thanks he gave it to them, and all of them drank from it. [24]He said to them, "This is my blood of the[c] covenant, which is poured out for many. [25]Truly I tell you, I will never again drink of the fruit of the vine until that day when I drink it new in the kingdom of God."

Peter's Denial Foretold
[26] When they had sung the hymn, they went out to the Mount of Olives. [27]And Jesus said to them, "You will all become deserters; for it is written,

'I will strike the shepherd,
and the sheep will be scattered.'

[28]But after I am raised up, I will go before you to Galilee." [29]Peter said to him, "Even though all become deserters, I will not." [30]Jesus said to him, "Truly I tell you, this day, this very night, before the cock crows twice, you will deny me three times." [31]But he said vehemently, "Even though I must die with you, I will not deny you." And all of them said the same.

Jesus Prays in Gethsemane
[32] They went to a place called Gethsemane; and he said to his disciples, "Sit here while I pray." [33]He took with him Peter and James and John, and began to be distressed and agitated. [34]And he said to them, "I am deeply grieved, even to death; remain here, and keep awake." [35]And going a little farther, he threw himself on the ground and prayed that, if it were possible, the hour might pass from him. [36]He said, "Abba,[d] Father, for you all things are possible; remove this cup from me; yet, not what I want, but what you want." [37]He came and found them sleeping; and he said to Peter, "Simon,

a Gk lacks *bread* b Other ancient authorities read *same bowl* c Other ancient authorities add *new* d Aramaic for *Father* are you asleep? Could you not keep awake one hour? [38]Keep awake and pray that you may not come into the time of trial;[a] the spirit indeed is willing, but the flesh is weak." [39]And again he went away and prayed, saying the same words. [40]And once more he came and found them sleeping, for their eyes were very heavy; and they did not know what to say to him. [41]He came a third time and said to them, "Are you still sleeping and taking your rest? Enough! The hour has come; the Son of Man is betrayed into the hands of sinners. [42]Get up, let us be going. See, my betrayer is at hand."

The Betrayal and Arrest of Jesus

43 Immediately, while he was still speaking, Judas, one of the twelve, arrived; and with him there was a crowd with swords and clubs, from the chief priests, the scribes, and the elders. [44]Now the betrayer had given them a sign, saying, "The one I will kiss is the man; arrest him and lead him away under guard." [45]So when he came, he went up to him at once and said, "Rabbi!" and kissed him. [46]Then they laid hands on him and arrested him. [47]But one of those who stood near drew his sword and struck the slave of the high priest, cutting off his ear. [48]Then Jesus said to them, "Have you come out with swords and clubs to arrest me as though I were a bandit? [49]Day after day I was with you in the temple teaching, and you did not arrest me. But let the scriptures be fulfilled." [50]All of them deserted him and fled.

51 A certain young man was following him, wearing nothing but a linen cloth. They caught hold of him, [52]but he left the linen cloth and ran off naked.

Jesus before the Council

53 They took Jesus to the high priest; and all the chief priests, the elders, and the scribes were assembled. [54]Peter had followed him at a distance, right into the courtyard of the high priest; and he was sitting with the guards, warming himself at the fire. [55]Now the chief priests and the whole council were looking for testimony against Jesus to put him to death; but they found none. [56]For many gave false testimony against him, and their testimony did not agree. [57]Some stood up and gave false testimony against him, saying, [58]"We heard him say, 'I will destroy this temple that is made with hands, and in three days I will build another, not made with hands.' " [59]But even on this point their testimony did not agree. [60]Then the high priest stood up before them and asked Jesus, "Have you no answer? What is it that they testify against you?" [61]But he was silent and did not answer. Again the high priest asked him, "Are you the Messiah,[b] the Son of the Blessed One?" [62]Jesus said, "I am; and

'you will see the Son of Man
seated at the right hand of the Power,'
and 'coming with the clouds of heaven.' "

[63]Then the high priest tore his clothes and said, "Why do we still need witnesses? [64]You have heard his blasphemy! What is your decision?" All of them condemned him as deserving death. [65]Some began to spit on him, to blindfold him, and to strike him, saying to him, "Prophesy!" The guards also took him over and beat him.

Peter Denies Jesus

66 While Peter was below in the courtyard, one of the servant-girls of the high priest came by. [67]When she saw Peter warming himself, she stared at him and said, "You also were with Jesus, the man from Nazareth." [68]But he denied it, saying, "I do not know or understand what you are talking about." And he went out into the forecourt.[c] Then the cock crowed.[d] [69]And the servant-girl, on seeing him, began again to say to the bystanders, "This man is one of them." [70]But again he denied it. Then after a little while the bystanders again said to Peter, "Certainly you are one of them; for you are a Galilean." [71]But he began to curse, and he swore an oath, "I do not know this man you are talking about." [72]At that moment the cock crowed for the second time. Then Peter remembered that Jesus had said to him, "Before the cock crows twice, you will deny me three times." And he broke down and wept.

15 Jesus before Pilate

As soon as it was morning, the chief priests held a consultation with the elders and scribes and the whole council. They bound Jesus, led him away, and handed him over to Pilate. [2]Pilate asked him, "Are you the King of the Jews?" He answered him, "You say so." [3]Then the chief priests accused him of many things. [4]Pilate asked him again, "Have you no answer? See how many charges they bring against you." [5]But Jesus made no further reply, so that Pilate was amazed.

Pilate Hands Jesus over to Be Crucified

6 Now at the festival he used to release a prisoner for them, anyone for whom they asked. [7]Now a man called Barabbas was in prison with the rebels who had committed murder during the insurrection. [8]So the crowd came

---

a Or into temptation b Or the Christ c Or gateway d Other ancient authorities lack Then the cock crowed and began to ask Pilate to do for them according to his custom. [9]Then he answered them, "Do you want me to release for you the King of the Jews?" [10]For he realized that it was out of jealousy that the chief priests had handed him over. [11]But the chief priests stirred up the crowd to have him release Barabbas for them instead. [12]Pilate spoke to them again, "Then what do you wish me to do[a] with the man you call[b] the King of the Jews?" [13]They shouted back, "Crucify him!" [14]Pilate asked them, "Why, what evil has he done?" But they shouted all the more, "Crucify him!" [15]So Pilate, wishing to satisfy the crowd, released Barabbas for them; and after flogging Jesus, he handed him over to be crucified.

The Soldiers Mock Jesus

16 Then the soldiers led him into the courtyard of the palace (that is, the governor's headquarters[c]); and they called together the whole cohort. [17]And they clothed him in a purple cloak; and after twisting some thorns into a crown, they put it on him. [18]And they began saluting him, "Hail, King of the Jews!" [19]They struck his head with a reed, spat upon him, and knelt down in homage to him. [20]After mocking him, they stripped him of the purple cloak and put his own clothes on him. Then they led him out to crucify him.

The Crucifixion of Jesus

21 They compelled a passer-by, who was coming in from the country, to carry his cross; it was Simon of Cyrene, the father of Alexander and Rufus. [22]Then they brought Jesus[d] to the place called Golgotha (which means the place of a skull). [23]And they offered him wine mixed with myrrh; but he did not take it. [24]And they crucified him, and divided his clothes among them, casting lots to decide what each should take.

25 It was nine o'clock in the morning when they crucified him. [26]The inscription of the charge against him read, "The King of the Jews." [27]And with him they crucified two bandits, one on his right and one on his left.[e] [29]Those who passed by derided[f] him, shaking their heads and saying, "Aha! You who would destroy the temple and build it in three days, [30]save yourself, and come down from the cross!" [31]In the same way the chief priests, along with the scribes, were also mocking him among themselves and saying, "He saved others; he cannot save himself. [32]Let the Messiah,[g] the King of Israel, come down from the cross now, so that we may see and believe." Those who were crucified with him also taunted him.

The Death of Jesus

33 When it was noon, darkness came over the whole land[h] until three in the afternoon. [34]At three o'clock Jesus cried out with a loud voice, "Eloi, Eloi, lema sabachthani?" which means, "My God, my God, why have you forsaken me?"[i] [35]When some of the bystanders heard it, they said, "Listen, he is calling for Elijah." [36]And someone ran, filled a sponge with sour wine, put it on a stick, and gave it to him to drink, saying, "Wait, let us see whether Elijah will come to take him down." [37]Then Jesus gave a loud cry and breathed his last. [38]And the curtain of the temple was torn in two, from top to bottom. [39]Now when the centurion, who stood facing him, saw that in this way he[j] breathed his last, he said, "Truly this man was God's Son!"[k]

40 There were also women looking on from a distance; among them were Mary Magdalene, and Mary the mother of James the younger and of Joses, and Salome. [41]These used to follow him and provided for him when he was in Galilee; and there were many other women who had come up with him to Jerusalem.

The Burial of Jesus

42 When evening had come, and since it was the day of Preparation, that is, the day before the sabbath, [43]Joseph of Arimathea, a respected member of the council, who was also himself waiting expectantly for the kingdom of God, went boldly to Pilate and asked for the body of Jesus. [44]Then Pilate wondered if he were already dead; and summoning the centurion, he asked him whether he had been dead for some time. [45]When he learned from the centurion that he was dead, he granted the body to Joseph. [46]Then Joseph[l] bought a linen cloth, and taking down the body,[m] wrapped it in the linen cloth, and laid it in a tomb that

---

a Other ancient authorities read *what should I do* b Other ancient authorities lack *the man you call* c Gk *the praetorium* d Gk *him*
e Other ancient authorities add verse 28, *And the scripture was fulfilled that says, "And he was counted among the lawless."* f Or *blasphemed*
g Or *the Christ* h Or *earth* i Other ancient authorities read *made me a reproach* j Other ancient authorities add *cried out and* k Or *a son of God* l Gk *he* m Gk *it*

had been hewn out of the rock. He then rolled a stone against the door of the tomb. [47] Mary Magdalene and Mary the mother of Joses saw where the body[a] was laid.

16 The Resurrection of Jesus

When the sabbath was over, Mary Magdalene, and Mary the mother of James, and Salome bought spices, so that they might go and anoint him. [2] And very early on the first day of the week, when the sun had risen, they went to the tomb. [3] They had been saying to one another, "Who will roll away the stone for us from the entrance to the tomb?" [4] When they looked up, they saw that the stone, which was very large, had already been rolled back. [5] As they entered the tomb, they saw a young man, dressed in a white robe, sitting on the right side; and they were alarmed. [6] But he said to them, "Do not be alarmed; you are looking for Jesus of Nazareth, who was crucified. He has been raised; he is not here. Look, there is the place they laid him. [7] But go, tell his disciples and Peter that he is going ahead of you to Galilee; there you will see him, just as he told you." [8] So they went out and fled from the tomb, for terror and amazement had seized them; and they said nothing to anyone, for they were afraid.[b]

THE SHORTER ENDING OF MARK

⟦And all that had been commanded them they told briefly to those around Peter. And afterward Jesus himself sent out through them, from east to west, the sacred and imperishable proclamation of eternal salvation.[c] ⟧

THE LONGER ENDING OF MARK

Jesus Appears to Mary Magdalene

9 ⟦Now after he rose early on the first day of the week, he appeared first to Mary Magda-lene, from whom he had cast out seven demons. [10] She went out and told those who had been with him, while they were mourning and weeping. [11] But when they heard that he was alive and had been seen by her, they would not believe it.

Jesus Appears to Two Disciples

12 After this he appeared in another form to two of them, as they were walking into the country. [13] And they went back and told the rest, but they did not believe them.

Jesus Commissions the Disciples

14 Later he appeared to the eleven themselves as they were sitting at the table; and he upbraided them for their lack of faith and stubbornness, because they had not believed those who saw him after he had risen.[d] [15] And he said to them, "Go into all the world and proclaim the good news[e] to the whole creation. [16] The one who believes and is baptized will be saved; but the one who does not believe will be condemned. [17] And these signs will accompany those who believe: by using my name they will cast out demons; they will speak in new tongues; [18] they will pick up snakes in their hands,[f] and if they drink any deadly thing, it will not hurt them; they will lay their hands on the sick, and they will recover."

The Ascension of Jesus

19 So then the Lord Jesus, after he had spoken to them, was taken up into heaven and sat down at the right hand of God. [20] And they went out and proclaimed the good news everywhere, while the Lord worked with them and confirmed the message by the signs that accompanied it.[c] ⟧

a Gk *it* *b* Some of the most ancient authorities bring the book to a close at the end of verse 8. One authority concludes the book with the shorter ending; others include the shorter ending and then continue with verses 9–20. In most authorities verses 9–20 follow immediately after verse 8, though in some of these authorities the passage is marked as being doubtful. *c* Other ancient authorities add *Amen* *d* Other ancient authorities add, in whole or in part, *And they excused themselves, saying, "This age of lawlessness and unbelief is under Satan, who does not allow the truth and power of God to prevail over the unclean things of the spirits. Therefore reveal your righteousness now"—thus they spoke to Christ. And Christ replied to them, "The term of years of Satan's power has been fulfilled, but other terrible things draw near. And for those who have sinned I was handed over to death, that they may return to the truth and sin no more, that they may inherit the spiritual and imperishable glory of righteousness that is in heaven.* *e* Or *gospel* *f* Other ancient authorities lack *in their hands*

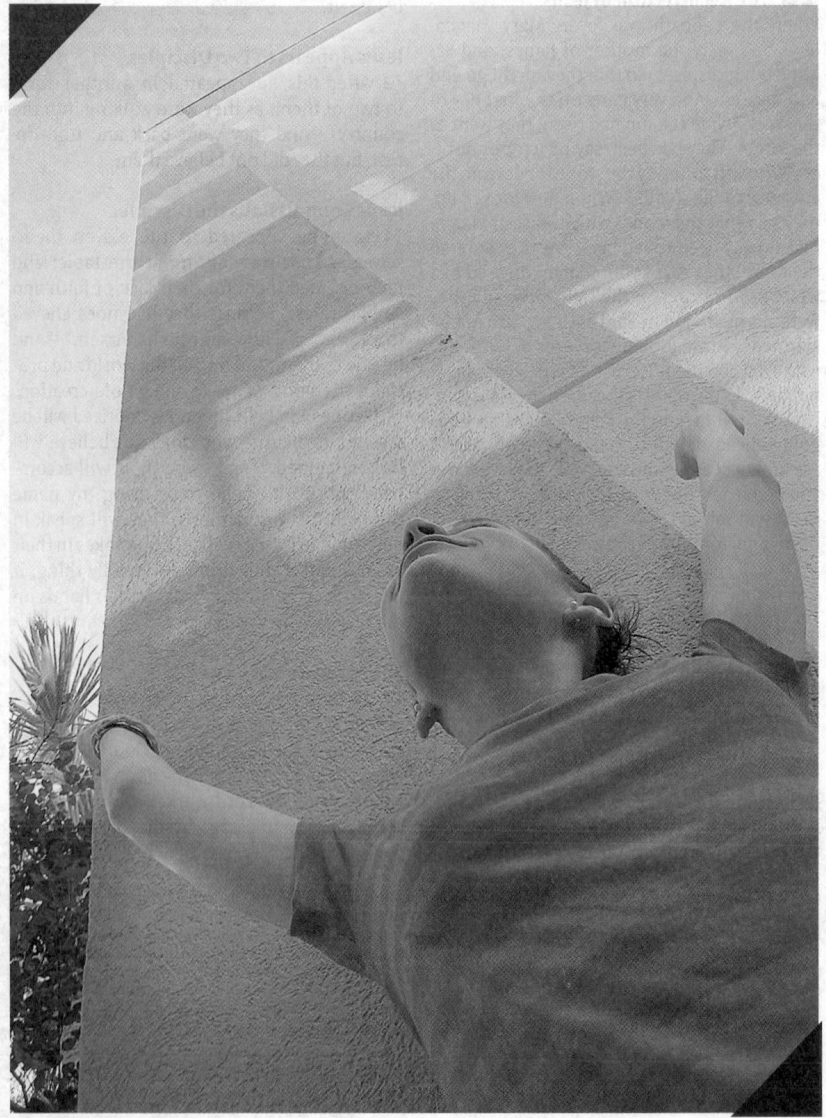

Big—© Kristin Sicher, 15

LUKE
GOOD NEWS FOR EVERYONE

She's Got It

Jesus reclines at Simon's table, aware that he's not really welcome, aware that there's a hidden agenda. Then suddenly the atmosphere changes. A woman walks in uninvited. With her scandalous reputation, she'd never get on the guest list for this kind of dinner party. The tension and embarrassment grow as she stands by Jesus— weeping, kissing his feet, anointing them with perfume, wiping them with her hair.

What made her do it? What gave her the courage to walk into a room where she had no place and no power? What made her able to face the condemnation and looks of disgust from those men? Because, out of all the "religious" people around that table, she got it. She understood what the Kingdom of God is all about. And Simon, in spite of all his years of theological study, in spite of his responsibility to draw people closer to God, completely missed the point.

All Simon saw was the external. He judged her by what she'd done. This woman knew that what mattered to Jesus was who she *was*. She knew how much she needed forgiveness. She gave Jesus the most costly, tender, heartfelt expression of love that she could, and she knew that it was nothing compared to how God felt about her. And she was the one who went away in peace, forgiven. (See Luke 7.36–50.)

Roll the credits for the gospel of Luke and you'll see some surprising cast members alongside the woman who anointed Jesus' feet. Shepherds, who were outcasts in their own culture and yet were the first to welcome the newborn Messiah; tax collectors and sinners, who ate with Jesus; a thief on the cross, who was promised entry into God's Kingdom; prostitutes, Gentiles, swindlers, and beggars, who all had life-changing encounters. As a Gentile (non-Jew) himself, Luke wrote as an "outsider" and was able to see the truth that God's redemption extends to everyone, regardless of background, status, wealth, or power.

"Love for others, and in the first place love for the poor, in whom the Church sees Christ himself, is made concrete in the promotion of justice."

—Pope John Paul II

WHO Luke, the doctor mentioned in Colossians 4.14, who also wrote Acts of the Apostles

WHAT A clear presentation of Jesus' words, life, and deeds, showing an interest in those who were not usually included in the community

WHEN Written sometime between A.D. 60 and 90

WHERE Antioch in Syria

PATH OF DISCIPLESHIP

The Jesus described in the gospel of Luke shows great compassion for those who are considered outcasts by the religious leaders. He eats with sinners and offers them forgiveness. He is a man of prayer. Jesus is a human being who enjoys life and at the same time is the Son of God.

Jesus teaches that life isn't all-pray and no-play—there needs to be a balance between being human and being spiritual. One doesn't cancel—or rule out—the other. And part of being human is being part of the human family; an important part of your life of discipleship is to be an advocate for social justice, just as Jesus was.

1 Dedication to Theophilus

Since many have undertaken to set down an orderly account of the events that have been fulfilled among us, [2]just as they were handed on to us by those who from the beginning were eyewitnesses and servants of the word, [3]I too decided, after investigating everything carefully from the very first,[a] to write an orderly account for you, most excellent Theophilus, [4]so that you may know the truth concerning the things about which you have been instructed.

The Birth of John the Baptist Foretold

5 In the days of King Herod of Judea, there was a priest named Zechariah, who belonged to the priestly order of Abijah. His wife was a descendant of Aaron, and her name was Elizabeth. [6]Both of them were righteous before God, living blamelessly according to all the commandments and regulations of the Lord. [7]But they had no children, because Elizabeth was barren, and both were getting on in years.

8 Once when he was serving as priest before God and his section was on duty, [9]he was chosen by lot, according to the custom of the priesthood, to enter the sanctuary of the Lord and offer incense. [10]Now at the time of the incense offering, the whole assembly of the people was praying outside. [11]Then there appeared to him an angel of the Lord, standing at the right side of the altar of incense. [12]When Zechariah saw him, he was terrified; and fear overwhelmed him. [13]But the angel said to him, "Do not be afraid, Zechariah, for your prayer has been heard. Your wife Elizabeth will bear you a son, and you will name him John. [14]You will have joy and gladness, and many will rejoice at his birth, [15]for he will be great in the sight of the Lord. He must never drink wine or strong drink; even before his birth he will be filled with the Holy Spirit. [16]He will turn many of the people of Israel to the Lord their God. [17]With the spirit and power of Elijah he will go before him, to turn the hearts of parents to their children, and the disobedient to the wisdom of the righteous, to make ready a people prepared for the Lord." [18]Zechariah said to the angel, "How will I know that this is so? For I am an old man, and my wife is getting on in years." [19]The angel replied, "I am Gabriel. I stand in the presence of God, and I have been sent to speak to you and to bring you this good news. [20]But now, because you did not believe my words, which will be fulfilled in their time, you will become mute, unable to speak, until the day these things occur."

21 Meanwhile the people were waiting for Zechariah, and wondered at his delay in the sanctuary. [22]When he did come out, he could not speak to them, and they realized that he had seen a vision in the sanctuary. He kept motioning to them and remained unable to speak. [23]When his time of service was ended, he went to his home.

24 After those days his wife Elizabeth conceived, and for five months she remained in seclusion. She said, [25]"This is what the Lord has done for me when he looked favorably on me and took away the disgrace I have endured among my people."

The Birth of Jesus Foretold

26 In the sixth month the angel Gabriel was sent by God to a town in Galilee called Nazareth, [27]to a virgin engaged to a man whose name was Joseph, of the house of David. The virgin's name was Mary. [28]And he came to her and said, "Greetings, favored one! The Lord is with you."[b] [29]But she was much perplexed by his words and pondered what sort of greeting this might be. [30]The angel said to her, "Do not be afraid, Mary, for you have found favor with God. [31]And now, you will conceive in your womb and bear a son, and you will name him Jesus. [32]He will be great, and will be called the Son of the Most High, and the Lord God will give to him the throne of his ancestor David. [33]He will reign over the house of Jacob forever, and of his kingdom there will be no end." [34]Mary said to the angel, "How can this be, since I am a virgin?"[c] [35]The angel said to her, "The Holy Spirit will come upon you, and the power of the Most High will overshadow you; therefore the child to be born[d] will be holy; he will be called Son of God. [36]And now, your relative Elizabeth in her old age has also conceived a son; and this is the sixth month for her who was said to be barren. [37]For nothing will be impossible with God." [38]Then Mary said, "Here am I, the servant of the Lord; let it be with me according to your word." Then the angel departed from her.

Mary Visits Elizabeth

39 In those days Mary set out and went with haste to a Judean town in the hill country, [40]where she entered the house of Zechariah and greeted Elizabeth. [41]When Elizabeth heard Mary's greeting, the child leaped in her womb. And Elizabeth was filled with the Holy Spirit [42]and exclaimed with a loud cry, "Blessed are you among women, and blessed is the fruit of your womb. [43]And why has this happened to me, that the mother of my Lord comes to

---

a Or *for a long time* b Other ancient authorities add *Blessed are you among women* c Gk *I do not know a man* d Other ancient authorities add *of you* me? ⁴⁴For as soon as I heard the sound of your greeting, the child in my womb leaped for joy. ⁴⁵And blessed is she who believed that there would be^a a fulfillment of what was spoken to her by the Lord."

Mary's Song of Praise

46 And Mary^b said,
"My soul magnifies the Lord,
⁴⁷   and my spirit rejoices in God my Savior,
⁴⁸ for he has looked with favor on the
         lowliness of his servant.
    Surely, from now on all generations will
         call me blessed;
⁴⁹ for the Mighty One has done great things
         for me,
    and holy is his name.
⁵⁰ His mercy is for those who fear him
    from generation to generation.
⁵¹ He has shown strength with his arm;
    he has scattered the proud in the
         thoughts of their hearts.
⁵² He has brought down the powerful from
         their thrones,
    and lifted up the lowly;
⁵³ he has filled the hungry with good things,
    and sent the rich away empty.
⁵⁴ He has helped his servant Israel,
    in remembrance of his mercy,
⁵⁵ according to the promise he made to our
         ancestors,
    to Abraham and to his descendants
         forever."

56 And Mary remained with her about three months and then returned to her home.

The Birth of John the Baptist

57 Now the time came for Elizabeth to give birth, and she bore a son. ⁵⁸Her neighbors and relatives heard that the Lord had shown his great mercy to her, and they rejoiced with her.

59 On the eighth day they came to circumcise the child, and they were going to name him Zechariah after his father. ⁶⁰But his mother said, "No; he is to be called John." ⁶¹They said to her, "None of your relatives has this name." ⁶²Then they began motioning to his father to find out what name he wanted to give him. ⁶³He asked for a writing tablet and wrote, "His name is John." And all of them were amazed. ⁶⁴Immediately his mouth was opened and his tongue freed, and he began to speak, praising God. ⁶⁵Fear came over all their neighbors, and all these things were talked about throughout the entire hill country of Judea. ⁶⁶All who heard them pondered them and said, "What

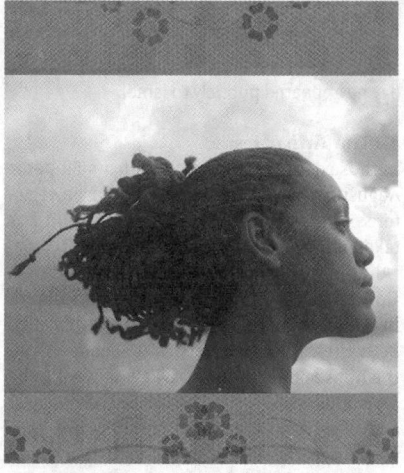

then will this child become?" For, indeed, the hand of the Lord was with him.

Zechariah's Prophecy

67 Then his father Zechariah was filled with the Holy Spirit and spoke this prophecy:
⁶⁸ "Blessed be the Lord God of Israel,
    for he has looked favorably on his people
         and redeemed them.
⁶⁹ He has raised up a mighty savior^c for us
    in the house of his servant David,
⁷⁰ as he spoke through the mouth of his holy
         prophets from of old,
⁷¹   that we would be saved from our enemies
         and from the hand of all who
         hate us.
⁷² Thus he has shown the mercy promised to
         our ancestors,
    and has remembered his holy covenant,
⁷³ the oath that he swore to our ancestor
         Abraham,
    to grant us ⁷⁴that we, being rescued from
         the hands of our enemies,
    might serve him without fear, ⁷⁵in holiness
         and righteousness
    before him all our days.
⁷⁶ And you, child, will be called the prophet of
         the Most High;
    for you will go before the Lord to prepare
         his ways,
⁷⁷ to give knowledge of salvation to his people
    by the forgiveness of their sins.
⁷⁸ By the tender mercy of our God,
    the dawn from on high will break
         upon^d us,
⁷⁹ to give light to those who sit in darkness
         and in the shadow of death,
    to guide our feet into the way of peace."

a Or believed, for there will be   b Other ancient authorities read Elizabeth   c Gk a horn of salvation   d Other ancient authorities read has broken upon

LUKE 1

80 The child grew and became strong in spirit, and he was in the wilderness until the day he appeared publicly to Israel.

2 The Birth of Jesus

In those days a decree went out from Emperor Augustus that all the world should be registered. ²This was the first registration and was taken while Quirinius was governor of Syria. ³All went to their own towns to be registered. ⁴Joseph also went from the town of Nazareth in Galilee to Judea, to the city of David called Bethlehem, because he was descended from the house and family of David. ⁵He went to be registered with Mary, to whom he was engaged and who was expecting a child. ⁶While they were there, the time came for her to deliver her child. ⁷And she gave birth to her firstborn son and wrapped him in bands of cloth, and laid him in a manger, because there was no place for them in the inn.

The Shepherds and the Angels

8 In that region there were shepherds living in the fields, keeping watch over their flock by night. ⁹Then an angel of the Lord stood before them, and the glory of the Lord shone around them, and they were terrified. ¹⁰But the angel said to them, "Do not be afraid; for see—I am bringing you good news of great joy for all the people: ¹¹to you is born this day in the city of David a Savior, who is the Messiah,ᵃ the Lord. ¹²This will be a sign for you: you will find a child wrapped in bands of cloth and lying in a manger." ¹³And suddenly there was with the angel a multitude of the heavenly host,ᵇ praising God and saying,

¹⁴ "Glory to God in the highest heaven,
    and on earth peace among those whom
        he favors!"ᶜ

15 When the angels had left them and gone into heaven, the shepherds said to one another, "Let us go now to Bethlehem and see this thing that has taken place, which the Lord has made known to us." ¹⁶So they went with haste and found Mary and Joseph, and the child lying in the manger. ¹⁷When they saw this, they made known what had been told them about this child; ¹⁸and all who heard it were amazed at what the shepherds told them. ¹⁹But Mary treasured all these words and pondered them in her heart. ²⁰The shepherds returned, glorifying and praising God for all they had heard and seen, as it had been told them.

Jesus Is Named

21 After eight days had passed, it was time to circumcise the child; and he was called Jesus, the name given by the angel before he was conceived in the womb.

Jesus Is Presented in the Temple

22 When the time came for their purification according to the law of Moses, they brought him up to Jerusalem to present him to the Lord ²³(as it is written in the law of the Lord, "Every firstborn male shall be designated as holy to the Lord"), ²⁴and they offered a sacrifice according to what is stated in the law of the Lord, "a pair of turtledoves or two young pigeons."

25 Now there was a man in Jerusalem whose name was Simeon;ᵈ this man was righteous and devout, looking forward to the consolation of Israel, and the Holy Spirit rested on him. ²⁶It had been revealed to him by the Holy Spirit that he would not see death before he had seen the Lord's Messiah.ᵉ ²⁷Guided by the Spirit, Simeonᶠ came into the temple; and when the parents brought in the child Jesus, to do for him what was customary under the law, ²⁸Simeonᵍ took him in his arms and praised God, saying,

²⁹ "Master, now you are dismissing your
        servantʰ in peace,
    according to your word;
³⁰ for my eyes have seen your salvation,
³¹   which you have prepared in the presence
            of all peoples,
³² a light for revelation to the Gentiles
        and for glory to your people Israel."

33 And the child's father and mother were amazed at what was being said about him. ³⁴Then Simeonᵈ blessed them and said to his mother Mary, "This child is destined for the falling and the rising of many in Israel, and to be a sign that will be opposed ³⁵so that the inner thoughts of many will be revealed—and a sword will pierce your own soul too."

36 There was also a prophet, Annaⁱ the daughter of Phanuel, of the tribe of Asher. She was of a great age, having lived with her husband seven years after her marriage, ³⁷then as a widow to the age of eighty-four. She never left the temple but worshiped there with fasting and prayer night and day. ³⁸At that moment she came, and began to praise God and to speak about the childʲ to all who were looking for the redemption of Jerusalem.

The Return to Nazareth

39 When they had finished everything required by the law of the Lord, they returned to

---

a Or the Christ b Gk army c Other ancient authorities read peace, goodwill among people d Gk Symeon e Or the Lord's Christ f Gk In the Spirit, he g Gk he h Gk slave i Gk Hanna j Gk him

Lakeside View—© Katie Stein, 15

Galilee, to their own town of Nazareth. 40 The child grew and became strong, filled with wisdom; and the favor of God was upon him.

The Boy Jesus in the Temple

41 Now every year his parents went to Jerusalem for the festival of the Passover. 42 And when he was twelve years old, they went up as usual for the festival. 43 When the festival was ended and they started to return, the boy Jesus stayed behind in Jerusalem, but his parents did not know it. 44 Assuming that he was in the group of travelers, they went a day's journey. Then they started to look for him among their relatives and friends. 45 When they did not find him, they returned to Jerusalem to search for him. 46 After three days they found him in the temple, sitting among the teachers, listening to them and asking them questions. 47 And all who heard him were amazed at his understanding and his answers. 48 When his parents*a* saw him they were astonished; and his mother said to him, "Child, why have you treated us like this? Look, your father and I have been searching for you in great anxiety." 49 He said to them, "Why were you searching for me? Did you not know that I must be in my Father's house?"*b* 50 But they did not understand what he said to them. 51 Then he went down with them and came to Nazareth, and was obedient to them. His mother treasured all these things in her heart.

52 And Jesus increased in wisdom and in years,*c* and in divine and human favor.

3 The Proclamation of John the Baptist

In the fifteenth year of the reign of Emperor Tiberius, when Pontius Pilate was governor of Judea, and Herod was ruler*d* of Galilee, and his brother Philip ruler*d* of the region of Ituraea and Trachonitis, and Lysanias ruler*d* of Abilene, 2 during the high priesthood of Annas and Caiaphas, the word of God came to John son of Zechariah in the wilderness. 3 He went into all the region around the Jordan, proclaiming a baptism of repentance for the forgiveness of sins, 4 as it is written in the book of the words of the prophet Isaiah,
"The voice of one crying out in the
        wilderness:
    'Prepare the way of the Lord,
        make his paths straight.
5 Every valley shall be filled,
        and every mountain and hill shall be
            made low,
    and the crooked shall be made straight,
        and the rough ways made smooth;
6 and all flesh shall see the salvation of God.' "

7 John said to the crowds that came out to be baptized by him, "You brood of vipers! Who warned you to flee from the wrath to come? 8 Bear fruits worthy of repentance. Do not begin to say to yourselves, 'We have Abraham as our

a Gk *they* b Or *be about my Father's interests?* c Or *in stature* d Gk *tetrarch* ancestor'; for I tell you, God is able from these stones to raise up children to Abraham. ⁹Even now the ax is lying at the root of the trees; every tree therefore that does not bear good fruit is cut down and thrown into the fire."

10 And the crowds asked him, "What then should we do?" ¹¹In reply he said to them, "Whoever has two coats must share with anyone who has none; and whoever has food must do likewise." ¹²Even tax collectors came to be baptized, and they asked him, "Teacher, what should we do?" ¹³He said to them, "Collect no more than the amount prescribed for you." ¹⁴Soldiers also asked him, "And we, what should we do?" He said to them, "Do not extort money from anyone by threats or false accusation, and be satisfied with your wages."

15 As the people were filled with expectation, and all were questioning in their hearts concerning John, whether he might be the Messiah,ᵃ ¹⁶John answered all of them by saying, "I baptize you with water; but one who is more powerful than I is coming; I am not worthy to untie the thong of his sandals. He will baptize you withᵇ the Holy Spirit and fire. ¹⁷His winnowing fork is in his hand, to clear his threshing floor and to gather the wheat into his granary; but the chaff he will burn with unquenchable fire."

18 So, with many other exhortations, he proclaimed the good news to the people. ¹⁹But Herod the ruler,ᶜ who had been rebuked by him because of Herodias, his brother's wife, and because of all the evil things that Herod had done, ²⁰added to them all by shutting up John in prison.

The Baptism of Jesus

21 Now when all the people were baptized, and when Jesus also had been baptized and was praying, the heaven was opened, ²²and the Holy Spirit descended upon him in bodily form like a dove. And a voice came from heaven, "You are my Son, the Beloved;ᵈ with you I am well pleased."ᵉ

The Ancestors of Jesus

23 Jesus was about thirty years old when he began his work. He was the son (as was thought) of Joseph son of Heli, ²⁴son of Matthat, son of Levi, son of Melchi, son of Jannai, son of Joseph, ²⁵son of Mattathias, son of Amos, son of Nahum, son of Esli, son of Naggai, ²⁶son of Maath, son of Mattathias, son of Semein, son of Josech, son of Joda, ²⁷son of Joanan, son of Rhesa, son of Zerubbabel, son

of Shealtiel,ᶠ son of Neri, ²⁸son of Melchi, son of Addi, son of Cosam, son of Elmadam, son of Er, ²⁹son of Joshua, son of Eliezer, son of Jorim, son of Matthat, son of Levi, ³⁰son of Simeon, son of Judah, son of Joseph, son of Jonam, son of Eliakim, ³¹son of Melea, son of Menna, son of Mattatha, son of Nathan, son of David, ³²son of Jesse, son of Obed, son of Boaz, son of Sala,ᵍ son of Nahshon, ³³son of Amminadab, son of Admin, son of Arni,ʰ son of Hezron, son of Perez, son of Judah, ³⁴son of Jacob, son of Isaac, son of Abraham, son of Terah, son of Nahor, ³⁵son of Serug, son of Reu, son of Peleg, son of Eber, son of Shelah, ³⁶son of Cainan, son of Arphaxad, son of Shem, son of Noah, son of Lamech, ³⁷son of Methuselah, son of Enoch, son of Jared, son of Mahalaleel, son of Cainan, ³⁸son of Enos, son of Seth, son of Adam, son of God.

4 The Temptation of Jesus

Jesus, full of the Holy Spirit, returned from the Jordan and was led by the Spirit in the wilderness, ²where for forty days he was tempted by the devil. He ate nothing at all during those days, and when they were over, he was famished. ³The devil said to him, "If you are the Son of God, command this stone to become a loaf of bread." ⁴Jesus answered him, "It is written, 'One does not live by bread alone.' "

5 Then the devilⁱ led him up and showed him in an instant all the kingdoms of the world. ⁶And the devilⁱ said to him, "To you I will give their glory and all this authority; for it has been given over to me, and I give it to anyone I please. ⁷If you, then, will worship me, it will all be yours." ⁸Jesus answered him, "It is written,

'Worship the Lord your God,
    and serve only him.' "

9 Then the devilⁱ took him to Jerusalem, and placed him on the pinnacle of the temple, saying to him, "If you are the Son of God, throw yourself down from here, ¹⁰for it is written,

'He will command his angels concerning
        you,
    to protect you,'

¹¹and

'On their hands they will bear you up,
    so that you will not dash your foot
            against a stone.' "

¹²Jesus answered him, "It is said, 'Do not put the Lord your God to the test.' " ¹³When the devil had finished every test, he departed from him until an opportune time.

a Or the Christ b Or in c Gk tetrarch d Or my beloved Son e Other ancient authorities read You are my Son, today I have begotten you f Gk Salathiel g Other ancient authorities read Salmon h Other ancient authorities read Amminadab, son of Aram; others vary widely i Gk he

The Beginning of the Galilean Ministry

14 Then Jesus, filled with the power of the Spirit, returned to Galilee, and a report about him spread through all the surrounding country. ¹⁵He began to teach in their synagogues and was praised by everyone.

The Rejection of Jesus at Nazareth

16 When he came to Nazareth, where he had been brought up, he went to the synagogue on the sabbath day, as was his custom. He stood up to read, ¹⁷and the scroll of the prophet Isaiah was given to him. He unrolled the scroll and found the place where it was written:
¹⁸ "The Spirit of the Lord is upon me,
    because he has anointed me
        to bring good news to the poor.
He has sent me to proclaim release to the captives
    and recovery of sight to the blind,
        to let the oppressed go free,
¹⁹ to proclaim the year of the Lord's favor."
²⁰And he rolled up the scroll, gave it back to the attendant, and sat down. The eyes of all in the synagogue were fixed on him. ²¹Then he began to say to them, "Today this scripture has been fulfilled in your hearing." ²²All spoke well of him and were amazed at the gracious words that came from his mouth. They said, "Is not this Joseph's son?" ²³He said to them, "Doubtless you will quote to me this proverb, 'Doctor, cure yourself!' And you will say, 'Do here also in your hometown the things that we have heard you did at Capernaum.' " ²⁴And he said, "Truly I tell you, no prophet is accepted in the prophet's hometown. ²⁵But the truth is, there were many widows in Israel in the time of Elijah, when the heaven was shut up three years and six months, and there was a severe famine over all the land; ²⁶yet Elijah was sent to none of them except to a widow at Zarephath in Sidon. ²⁷There were also many lepers*a* in Israel in the time of the prophet Elisha, and none of them was cleansed except Naaman the Syrian." ²⁸When they heard this, all in the synagogue were filled with rage. ²⁹They got up, drove him out of the town, and led him to the brow of the hill on which their town was built, so that they might hurl him off the cliff. ³⁰But he passed through the midst of them and went on his way.

The Man with an Unclean Spirit

31 He went down to Capernaum, a city in Galilee, and was teaching them on the sabbath. ³²They were astounded at his teaching, because he spoke with authority. ³³In the syna-

---

a The terms leper and leprosy can refer to several diseases

 TRY THIS

REJECT

Ever been labeled? Ever been misunderstood? Read **Luke 4.14–30**.

Here in his hometown, Jesus wore some labels. He was Joseph's son. He was the kid from down the block. His old neighbors thought they knew him. So when he challenged them with this amazing claim—that *he* was the one Isaiah had promised as the Messiah for God's people—they were aghast and filled with rage (see Luke 4.28–29).

You? You've got to be kidding!

They rejected him. Their labels and assumptions only saw the human aspect of Jesus—the guy they'd known for years. But here Jesus revealed another side of who he is: more than just human, he's also God! Jesus made this astounding claim once: "Whoever has seen me has seen the Father" (John 14.9).

If you want to know what God is like, watch Jesus. Rip off any of the labels religion or culture has stuck on him and see Jesus for who he really is. Do you want to see how God would love or show compassion? Who he would include? Then look at how Jesus did it. To see Jesus is to see God in action. In Jesus the invisible God is made visible.

This has profound ramifications for us. If Jesus was the human face of God and we are called to live as Jesus did, then in a truly mysterious way we also show the face of God to this world. Ask yourself: *When people watch me, do they gain a better sense of who God is?*

Use some masking tape or other adhesive tape to make a label that says something you want to be known for, like "Kind and honest," "Jesus follower," or "Trusts God no matter what." Then stick your label in the Creative Space on the next page.

GOD IS REAL MY FRIENDS

gogue there was a man who had the spirit of an unclean demon, and he cried out with a loud voice, ³⁴"Let us alone! What have you to do with us, Jesus of Nazareth? Have you come to destroy us? I know who you are, the Holy One of God." ³⁵But Jesus rebuked him, saying, "Be silent, and come out of him!" When the demon had thrown him down before them, he came out of him without having done him any harm. ³⁶They were all amazed and kept saying to one another, "What kind of utterance is this? For with authority and power he commands the unclean spirits, and out they come!" [37] And a report about him began to reach every place in the region.

Healings at Simon's House

38 After leaving the synagogue he entered Simon's house. Now Simon's mother-in-law was suffering from a high fever, and they asked him about her. [39] Then he stood over her and rebuked the fever, and it left her. Immediately she got up and began to serve them.

40 As the sun was setting, all those who had any who were sick with various kinds of diseases brought them to him; and he laid his hands on each of them and cured them. [41] Demons also came out of many, shouting, "You are the Son of God!" But he rebuked them and would not allow them to speak, because they knew that he was the Messiah.[a]

Jesus Preaches in the Synagogues

42 At daybreak he departed and went into a deserted place. And the crowds were looking for him; and when they reached him, they wanted to prevent him from leaving them. [43] But he said to them, "I must proclaim the good news of the kingdom of God to the other cities also; for I was sent for this purpose." [44] So he continued proclaiming the message in the synagogues of Judea.[b]

5 Jesus Calls the First Disciples

Once while Jesus[c] was standing beside the lake of Gennesaret, and the crowd was pressing in on him to hear the word of God, [2] he saw two boats there at the shore of the lake; the fishermen had gone out of them and were washing their nets. [3] He got into one of the boats, the one belonging to Simon, and asked him to put out a little way from the shore. Then he sat down and taught the crowds from the boat. [4] When he had finished speaking, he said to Simon, "Put out into the deep water and let down your nets for a catch." [5] Simon answered, "Master, we have worked all night long but have caught nothing. Yet if you say so, I will let down the nets." [6] When they had done this, they caught so many fish that their nets were beginning to break. [7] So they signaled their partners in the other boat to come and help them. And they came and filled both boats, so that they began to sink. [8] But when Simon Peter saw it, he fell down at Jesus' knees, saying, "Go away from me, Lord, for I am a sinful man!" [9] For he and all who were with him were amazed at the catch of fish that they had taken; [10] and so also were James and John, sons of Zebedee, who were partners with Simon. Then Jesus said to Simon, "Do not be afraid; from now on you will be catching people." [11] When they had brought their boats to shore, they left everything and followed him.

Jesus Cleanses a Leper

12 Once, when he was in one of the cities, there was a man covered with leprosy.[d] When he saw Jesus, he bowed with his face to the ground and begged him, "Lord, if you choose, you can make me clean." [13] Then Jesus[c] stretched out his hand, touched him, and said,

---

a Or the Christ b Other ancient authorities read Galilee c Gk he d The terms leper and leprosy can refer to several diseases

"I do choose. Be made clean." Immediately the leprosy[a] left him. [14]And he ordered him to tell no one. "Go," he said, "and show yourself to the priest, and, as Moses commanded, make an offering for your cleansing, for a testimony to them." [15]But now more than ever the word about Jesus[b] spread abroad; many crowds would gather to hear him and to be cured of their diseases. [16]But he would withdraw to deserted places and pray.

Jesus Heals a Paralytic

17 One day, while he was teaching, Pharisees and teachers of the law were sitting near by (they had come from every village of Galilee and Judea and from Jerusalem); and the power of the Lord was with him to heal.[c] [18]Just then some men came, carrying a paralyzed man on a bed. They were trying to bring him in and lay him before Jesus;[b] [19]but finding no way to bring him in because of the crowd, they went up on the roof and let him down with his bed through the tiles into the middle of the crowd[d] in front of Jesus. [20]When he saw their faith, he said, "Friend,[e] your sins are forgiven you." [21]Then the scribes and the Pharisees began to question, "Who is this who is speaking blasphemies? Who can forgive sins but God alone?" [22]When Jesus perceived their questionings, he answered them, "Why do you raise such questions in your hearts? [23]Which is easier, to say, 'Your sins are forgiven you,' or to say, 'Stand up and walk'? [24]But so that you may know that the Son of Man has authority on earth to forgive sins"—he said to the one who was paralyzed—"I say to you, stand up and take your bed and go to your home." [25]Immediately he stood up before them, took what he had been lying on, and went to his home, glorifying God. [26]Amazement seized all of them, and they glorified God and were filled with awe, saying, "We have seen strange things today."

Jesus Calls Levi

27 After this he went out and saw a tax collector named Levi, sitting at the tax booth; and he said to him, "Follow me." [28]And he got up, left everything, and followed him.

29 Then Levi gave a great banquet for him in his house; and there was a large crowd of tax collectors and others sitting at the table[f] with them. [30]The Pharisees and their scribes were complaining to his disciples, saying, "Why do you eat and drink with tax collectors and sinners?" [31]Jesus answered, "Those who are well have no need of a physician, but those who are sick; [32]I have come to call not the righteous but sinners to repentance."

The Question about Fasting

33 Then they said to him, "John's disciples, like the disciples of the Pharisees, frequently fast and pray, but your disciples eat and drink." [34]Jesus said to them, "You cannot make wedding guests fast while the bridegroom is with them, can you? [35]The days will come when the bridegroom will be taken away from them, and then they will fast in those days." [36]He also told them a parable: "No one tears a piece from a new garment and sews it on an old garment; otherwise the new will be torn, and the piece from the new will not match the old. [37]And no one puts new wine into old wineskins; otherwise the new wine will burst the skins and will be spilled, and the skins will be destroyed. [38]But new wine must be put into fresh wineskins. [39]And no one after drinking old wine desires new wine, but says, 'The old is good.' "[g]

6 The Question about the Sabbath

One sabbath[h] while Jesus[i] was going through the grainfields, his disciples plucked some heads of grain, rubbed them in their hands, and ate them. [2]But some of the Pharisees said, "Why are you doing what is not lawful[j] on the sabbath?" [3]Jesus answered, "Have you not read what David did when he and his companions were hungry? [4]He entered the house of God and took and ate the bread of the Presence, which it is not lawful for any but the priests to eat, and gave some to his companions?" [5]Then he said to them, "The Son of Man is lord of the sabbath."

The Man with a Withered Hand

6 On another sabbath he entered the synagogue and taught, and there was a man there whose right hand was withered. [7]The scribes and the Pharisees watched him to see whether he would cure on the sabbath, so that they might find an accusation against him. [8]Even though he knew what they were thinking, he said to the man who had the withered hand, "Come and stand here." He got up and stood there. [9]Then Jesus said to them, "I ask you, is it lawful to do good or to do harm on the sabbath, to save life or to destroy it?" [10]After looking around at all of them, he said to him, "Stretch out your hand." He did so, and his hand was restored. [11]But they were filled with fury and discussed with one another what they might do to Jesus.

a The terms *leper* and *leprosy* can refer to several diseases *b* Gk *him* *c* Other ancient authorities read *was present to heal them* *d* Gk *into the midst* *e* Gk *Man* *f* Gk *reclining* *g* Other ancient authorities read *better*; others lack verse 39 *h* Other ancient authorities read *On the second first sabbath* *i* Gk *he* *j* Other ancient authorities add *to do*

The coffin where the boy lay when Jesus brought him back to life (Luke 7.11–15) wasn't like coffins today. In fact, it was probably just a board on which they laid the body. Just like today, wealthier people sometimes had more elaborate "funeral biers," as they were called.

Fact

This information has been scanned and is free of all known viruses. Please forward to all your friends.

Jerusalem, and the coast of Tyre and Sidon. [18]They had come to hear him and to be healed of their diseases; and those who were troubled with unclean spirits were cured. [19]And all in the crowd were trying to touch him, for power came out from him and healed all of them.

Blessings and Woes

20 Then he looked up at his disciples and said:
    "Blessed are you who are poor,
        for yours is the kingdom of God.
[21] "Blessed are you who are hungry now,
        for you will be filled.
    "Blessed are you who weep now,
        for you will laugh.
    22 "Blessed are you when people hate you, and when they exclude you, revile you, and defame you[a] on account of the Son of Man. [23]Rejoice in that day and leap for joy, for surely your reward is great in heaven; for that is what their ancestors did to the prophets.
[24] "But woe to you who are rich,
        for you have received your consolation.
[25] "Woe to you who are full now,
        for you will be hungry.
    "Woe to you who are laughing now,
        for you will mourn and weep.
    26 "Woe to you when all speak well of you, for that is what their ancestors did to the false prophets.

Love for Enemies

27 "But I say to you that listen, Love your enemies, do good to those who hate you, [28]bless those who curse you, pray for those who abuse you. [29]If anyone strikes you on the cheek, offer the other also; and from anyone who takes away your coat do not withhold even your shirt. [30]Give to everyone who begs from you; and if anyone takes away your goods, do not ask for them again. [31]Do to others as you would have them do to you.

32 "If you love those who love you, what credit is that to you? For even sinners love those who love them. [33]If you do good to those who do good to you, what credit is that to you? For even sinners do the same. [34]If you lend to those from whom you hope to receive, what credit is that to you? Even sinners lend to sinners, to receive as much again. [35]But love your enemies, do good, and lend, expecting nothing in return.[b] Your reward will be great, and you will be children of the Most High; for he is kind to the ungrateful and the wicked. [36]Be merciful, just as your Father is merciful.

Jesus Chooses the Twelve Apostles

12 Now during those days he went out to the mountain to pray; and he spent the night in prayer to God. [13]And when day came, he called his disciples and chose twelve of them, whom he also named apostles: [14]Simon, whom he named Peter, and his brother Andrew, and James, and John, and Philip, and Bartholomew, [15]and Matthew, and Thomas, and James son of Alphaeus, and Simon, who was called the Zealot, [16]and Judas son of James, and Judas Iscariot, who became a traitor.

Jesus Teaches and Heals

17 He came down with them and stood on a level place, with a great crowd of his disciples and a great multitude of people from all Judea,

a Gk *cast out your name as evil* *b* Other ancient authorities read *despairing of no one*

Judging Others

37 "Do not judge, and you will not be judged; do not condemn, and you will not be condemned. Forgive, and you will be forgiven; [38]give, and it will be given to you. A good measure, pressed down, shaken together, running over, will be put into your lap; for the measure you give will be the measure you get back."

39 He also told them a parable: "Can a blind person guide a blind person? Will not both fall into a pit? [40]A disciple is not above the teacher, but everyone who is fully qualified will be like the teacher. [41]Why do you see the speck in your neighbor's[a] eye, but do not notice the log in your own eye? [42]Or how can you say to your neighbor,[b] 'Friend,[b] let me take out the speck in your eye,' when you yourself do not see the log in your own eye? You hypocrite, first take the log out of your own eye, and then you will see clearly to take the speck out of your neighbor's[a] eye.

A Tree and Its Fruit

43 "No good tree bears bad fruit, nor again does a bad tree bear good fruit; [44]for each tree is known by its own fruit. Figs are not gathered from thorns, nor are grapes picked from a bramble bush. [45]The good person out of the good treasure of the heart produces good, and the evil person out of evil treasure produces evil; for it is out of the abundance of the heart that the mouth speaks.

The Two Foundations

46 "Why do you call me 'Lord, Lord,' and do not do what I tell you? [47]I will show you what someone is like who comes to me, hears my words, and acts on them. [48]That one is like a man building a house, who dug deeply and laid the foundation on rock; when a flood arose, the river burst against that house but could not shake it, because it had been well built.[c] [49]But the one who hears and does not act is like a man who built a house on the ground without a foundation. When the river burst against it, immediately it fell, and great was the ruin of that house."

7 Jesus Heals a Centurion's Servant

After Jesus[d] had finished all his sayings in the hearing of the people, he entered Capernaum. [2]A centurion there had a slave whom he valued highly, and who was ill and close to death. [3]When he heard about Jesus, he sent some Jewish elders to him, asking him to come and heal his slave. [4]When they came to Jesus, they appealed to him earnestly, saying, "He is worthy of having you do this for him, [5]for he loves our people, and it is he who built our synagogue for us." [6]And Jesus went with them, but when he was not far from the house, the centurion sent friends to say to him, "Lord, do not trouble yourself, for I am not worthy to have you come under my roof; [7]therefore I did not presume to come to you. But only speak the word, and let my servant be healed. [8]For I also am a man set under authority, with soldiers under me; and I say to one, 'Go,' and he goes, and to another, 'Come,' and he comes, and to my slave, 'Do this,' and the slave does it." [9]When Jesus heard this he was amazed at him, and turning to the crowd that followed him, he said, "I tell you, not even in Israel have I found such faith." [10]When those who had been sent returned to the house, they found the slave in good health.

Jesus Raises the Widow's Son at Nain

11 Soon afterwards[e] he went to a town called Nain, and his disciples and a large crowd went with him. [12]As he approached the gate of the town, a man who had died was being carried out. He was his mother's only son, and she was a widow; and with her was a large crowd from the town. [13]When the Lord saw her, he had compassion for her and said to her, "Do not weep." [14]Then he came forward and touched the bier, and the bearers stood still. And he said, "Young man, I say to you, rise!" [15]The dead man sat up and began to speak, and Jesus[d] gave him to his mother. [16]Fear seized all of them; and they glorified God, saying, "A great prophet has risen among us!" and "God has looked favorably on his people!" [17]This word about him spread throughout Judea and all the surrounding country.

Messengers from John the Baptist

18 The disciples of John reported all these things to him. So John summoned two of his disciples [19]and sent them to the Lord to ask, "Are you the one who is to come, or are we to wait for another?" [20]When the men had come to him, they said, "John the Baptist has sent us to you to ask, 'Are you the one who is to come, or are we to wait for another?'" [21]Jesus[f] had just then cured many people of diseases, plagues, and evil spirits, and had given sight to many who were blind. [22]And he answered them, "Go and tell John what you have seen and heard: the blind receive their sight, the lame walk, the lepers[g] are cleansed, the deaf

a Gk brother's b Gk brother c Other ancient authorities read founded upon the rock d Gk he e Other ancient authorities read Next day f Gk He g The terms leper and leprosy can refer to several diseases hear, the dead are raised, the poor have good news brought to them. [23]And blessed is anyone who takes no offense at me."

24 When John's messengers had gone, Jesus[a] began to speak to the crowds about John:[b] "What did you go out into the wilderness to look at? A reed shaken by the wind? [25]What then did you go out to see? Someone[c] dressed in soft robes? Look, those who put on fine clothing and live in luxury are in royal palaces. [26]What then did you go out to see? A prophet? Yes, I tell you, and more than a prophet. [27]This is the one about whom it is written,

'See, I am sending my messenger ahead of you,
who will prepare your way before you.'

[28]I tell you, among those born of women no one is greater than John; yet the least in the kingdom of God is greater than he." [29](And all the people who heard this, including the tax collectors, acknowledged the justice of God,[d] because they had been baptized with John's baptism. [30]But by refusing to be baptized by him, the Pharisees and the lawyers rejected God's purpose for themselves.)

31 "To what then will I compare the people of this generation, and what are they like? [32]They are like children sitting in the marketplace and calling to one another,

'We played the flute for you, and you did not dance;
we wailed, and you did not weep.'

[33]For John the Baptist has come eating no bread and drinking no wine, and you say, 'He has a demon'; [34]the Son of Man has come eating and drinking, and you say, 'Look, a glutton and a drunkard, a friend of tax collectors and sinners!' [35]Nevertheless, wisdom is vindicated by all her children."

A Sinful Woman Forgiven

36 One of the Pharisees asked Jesus[b] to eat with him, and he went into the Pharisee's house and took his place at the table. [37]And a woman in the city, who was a sinner, having learned that he was eating in the Pharisee's house, brought an alabaster jar of ointment. [38]She stood behind him at his feet, weeping, and began to bathe his feet with her tears and to dry them with her hair. Then she continued kissing his feet and anointing them with the ointment. [39]Now when the Pharisee who had invited him saw it, he said to himself, "If this man were a prophet, he would have known who and what kind of woman this is who is touching him—that she is a sinner." [40]Jesus

spoke up and said to him, "Simon, I have something to say to you." "Teacher," he replied, "speak." [41]"A certain creditor had two debtors; one owed five hundred denarii,[e] and the other fifty. [42]When they could not pay, he canceled the debts for both of them. Now which of them will love him more?" [43]Simon answered, "I suppose the one for whom he canceled the greater debt." And Jesus[g] said to him, "You have judged rightly." [44]Then turning toward the woman, he said to Simon, "Do you see this woman? I entered your house; you gave me no water for my feet, but she has bathed my feet with her tears and dried them with her hair. [45]You gave me no kiss, but from the time I came in she has not stopped kissing my feet. [46]You did not anoint my head with oil, but she has anointed my feet with ointment. [47]Therefore, I tell you, her sins, which were many, have been forgiven; hence she has shown great love. But the one to whom little is forgiven, loves little." [48]Then he said to her, "Your sins are forgiven." [49]But those who were at the table with him began to say among themselves, "Who is this who even forgives sins?" [50]And he said to the woman, "Your faith has saved you; go in peace."

8   Some Women Accompany Jesus

Soon afterwards he went on through cities and villages, proclaiming and bringing the good news of the kingdom of God. The twelve were with him, [2]as well as some women who had been cured of evil spirits and infirmities: Mary, called Magdalene, from whom seven demons had gone out, [3]and Joanna, the wife of Herod's steward Chuza, and Susanna, and many others, who provided for them[f] out of their resources.

The Parable of the Sower

4 When a great crowd gathered and people from town after town came to him, he said in a parable: [5]"A sower went out to sow his seed; and as he sowed, some fell on the path and was trampled on, and the birds of the air ate it up. [6]Some fell on the rock; and as it grew up, it withered for lack of moisture. [7]Some fell among thorns, and the thorns grew with it and choked it. [8]Some fell into good soil, and when it grew, it produced a hundredfold." As he said this, he called out, "Let anyone with ears to hear listen!"

The Purpose of the Parables

9 Then his disciples asked him what this parable meant. [10]He said, "To you it has been given to know the secrets[g] of the kingdom of God; but to others I speak[h] in parables, so that

---

a Gk he b Gk him c Or Why then did you go out? To see someone d Or praised God e The denarius was the usual day's wage for a laborer
f Other ancient authorities read him g Or mysteries h Gk lacks I speak

'looking they may not perceive,
and listening they may not understand.'

The Parable of the Sower Explained

11 "Now the parable is this: The seed is the word of God. [12]The ones on the path are those who have heard; then the devil comes and takes away the word from their hearts, so that they may not believe and be saved. [13]The ones on the rock are those who, when they hear the word, receive it with joy. But these have no root; they believe only for a while and in a time of testing fall away. [14]As for what fell among the thorns, these are the ones who hear; but as they go on their way, they are choked by the cares and riches and pleasures of life, and their fruit does not mature. [15]But as for that in the good soil, these are the ones who, when they hear the word, hold it fast in an honest and good heart, and bear fruit with patient endurance.

A Lamp under a Jar

16 "No one after lighting a lamp hides it under a jar, or puts it under a bed, but puts it on a lampstand, so that those who enter may see the light. [17]For nothing is hidden that will not be disclosed, nor is anything secret that will not become known and come to light. [18]Then pay attention to how you listen; for to those who have, more will be given; and from those who do not have, even what they seem to have will be taken away."

The True Kindred of Jesus

19 Then his mother and his brothers came to him, but they could not reach him because of the crowd. [20]And he was told, "Your mother and your brothers are standing outside, wanting to see you." [21]But he said to them, "My mother and my brothers are those who hear the word of God and do it."

Jesus Calms a Storm

22 One day he got into a boat with his disciples, and he said to them, "Let us go across to the other side of the lake." So they put out, [23]and while they were sailing he fell asleep. A windstorm swept down on the lake, and the boat was filling with water, and they were in danger. [24]They went to him and woke him up, shouting, "Master, Master, we are perishing!" And he woke up and rebuked the wind and the raging waves; they ceased, and there was a calm. [25]He said to them, "Where is your faith?" They were afraid and amazed, and said to one another, "Who then is this, that he commands even the winds and the water, and they obey him?"

Jesus Heals the Gerasene Demoniac

26 Then they arrived at the country of the Gerasenes,[a] which is opposite Galilee. [27]As he stepped out on land, a man of the city who had demons met him. For a long time he had worn[b] no clothes, and he did not live in a house but in the tombs. [28]When he saw Jesus, he fell down before him and shouted at the top of his voice, "What have you to do with me, Jesus, Son of the Most High God? I beg you, do not torment me"— [29]for Jesus[c] had commanded the unclean spirit to come out of the man. (For many times it had seized him; he was kept under guard and bound with chains and shackles, but he would break the bonds and be driven by the demon into the wilds.) [30]Jesus then asked him, "What is your name?" He said, "Legion"; for many demons had entered him. [31]They begged him not to order them to go back into the abyss.

32 Now there on the hillside a large herd of swine was feeding; and the demons[d] begged Jesus[e] to let them enter these. So he gave them permission. [33]Then the demons came out of the man and entered the swine, and the herd rushed down the steep bank into the lake and was drowned.

34 When the swineherds saw what had happened, they ran off and told it in the city and in the country. [35]Then people came out to see what had happened, and when they came to Jesus, they found the man from whom the demons had gone sitting at the feet of Jesus, clothed and in his right mind. And they were afraid. [36]Those who had seen it told them how the one who had been possessed by demons had been healed. [37]Then all the people of the

Untitled—© Kate Douglas, 17

---

a Other ancient authorities read *Gadarenes*; others, *Gergesenes*
b Other ancient authorities read *a man of the city who had had demons for a long time met him. He wore* c Gk *he* d Gk *they* e Gk *him*

At Sea—© Kate Douglas, 17

surrounding country of the Gerasenes*ᵃ* asked Jesus*ᵇ* to leave them; for they were seized with great fear. So he got into the boat and returned. ³⁸The man from whom the demons had gone begged that he might be with him; but Jesus*ᶜ* sent him away, saying, ³⁹"Return to your home, and declare how much God has done for you." So he went away, proclaiming throughout the city how much Jesus had done for him.

A Girl Restored to Life and a Woman Healed

40 Now when Jesus returned, the crowd welcomed him, for they were all waiting for him. ⁴¹Just then there came a man named Jairus, a leader of the synagogue. He fell at Jesus' feet and begged him to come to his house, ⁴²for he had an only daughter, about twelve years old, who was dying.

As he went, the crowds pressed in on him. ⁴³Now there was a woman who had been suffering from hemorrhages for twelve years; and though she had spent all she had on physicians,*ᵈ* no one could cure her. ⁴⁴She came up behind him and touched the fringe of his clothes, and immediately her hemorrhage stopped. ⁴⁵Then Jesus asked, "Who touched me?" When all denied it, Peter*ᵉ* said, "Master, the crowds surround you and press in on you." ⁴⁶But Jesus said, "Someone touched me; for I noticed that power had gone out from me." ⁴⁷When the woman saw that she could not remain hidden, she came trembling; and falling down before him, she declared in the presence of all the people why she

had touched him, and how she had been immediately healed. ⁴⁸He said to her, "Daughter, your faith has made you well; go in peace."

49 While he was still speaking, someone came from the leader's house to say, "Your daughter is dead; do not trouble the teacher any longer." ⁵⁰When Jesus heard this, he replied, "Do not fear. Only believe, and she will be saved." ⁵¹When he came to the house, he did not allow anyone to enter with him, except Peter, John, and James, and the child's father and mother. ⁵²They were all weeping and wailing for her; but he said, "Do not weep; for she is not dead but sleeping." ⁵³And they laughed at him, knowing that she was dead. ⁵⁴But he took her by the hand and called out, "Child, get up!" ⁵⁵Her spirit returned, and she got up at once. Then he directed them to give her something to eat. ⁵⁶Her parents were astounded; but he ordered them to tell no one what had happened.

9   The Mission of the Twelve

Then Jesus*ᶜ* called the twelve together and gave them power and authority over all demons and to cure diseases, ²and he sent them out to proclaim the kingdom of God and to heal. ³He said to them, "Take nothing for your journey, no staff, nor bag, nor bread, nor money—not even an extra tunic. ⁴Whatever house you enter, stay there, and leave from there. ⁵Wherever they do not welcome you, as you are leaving that town shake the dust off your feet as a testimony against them." ⁶They departed and went

a Other ancient authorities read *Gadarenes*; others, *Gergesenes*   *b* Gk *him*   *c* Gk *he*   *d* Other ancient authorities lack *and though she had spent all she had on physicians*   *e* Other ancient authorities add *and those who were with him* through the villages, bringing the good news and curing diseases everywhere.

Herod's Perplexity

7 Now Herod the ruler[a] heard about all that had taken place, and he was perplexed, because it was said by some that John had been raised from the dead, [8]by some that Elijah had appeared, and by others that one of the ancient prophets had arisen. [9]Herod said, "John I beheaded; but who is this about whom I hear such things?" And he tried to see him.

Feeding the Five Thousand

10 On their return the apostles told Jesus[b] all they had done. He took them with him and withdrew privately to a city called Bethsaida. [11]When the crowds found out about it, they followed him; and he welcomed them, and spoke to them about the kingdom of God, and healed those who needed to be cured.

12 The day was drawing to a close, and the twelve came to him and said, "Send the crowd away, so that they may go into the surrounding villages and countryside, to lodge and get provisions; for we are here in a deserted place." [13]But he said to them, "You give them something to eat." They said, "We have no more than five loaves and two fish—unless we are to go and buy food for all these people." [14]For there were about five thousand men. And he said to his disciples, "Make them sit down in groups of about fifty each." [15]They did so and made them all sit down. [16]And taking the five loaves and the two fish, he looked up to heaven, and blessed and broke them, and gave them to the disciples to set before the crowd. [17]And all ate and were filled. What was left over was gathered up, twelve baskets of broken pieces.

Peter's Declaration about Jesus

18 Once when Jesus[c] was praying alone, with only the disciples near him, he asked them, "Who do the crowds say that I am?" [19]They answered, "John the Baptist; but others, Elijah; and still others, that one of the ancient prophets has arisen." [20]He said to them, "But who do you say that I am?" Peter answered, "The Messiah[d] of God."

Jesus Foretells His Death and Resurrection

21 He sternly ordered and commanded them not to tell anyone, [22]saying, "The Son of Man must undergo great suffering, and be rejected by the elders, chief priests, and scribes, and be killed, and on the third day be raised."

23 Then he said to them all, "If any want to become my followers, let them deny themselves and take up their cross daily and follow me. [24]For those who want to save their life will lose it, and those who lose their life for my sake will save it. [25]What does it profit them if they gain the whole world, but lose or forfeit themselves? [26]Those who are ashamed of me and of my words, of them the Son of Man will be ashamed when he comes in his glory and the glory of the Father and of the holy angels. [27]But truly I tell you, there are some standing here who will not taste death before they see the kingdom of God."

The Transfiguration

28 Now about eight days after these sayings Jesus[c] took with him Peter and John and James, and went up on the mountain to pray. [29]And while he was praying, the appearance of his face changed, and his clothes became dazzling white. [30]Suddenly they saw two men, Moses and Elijah, talking to him. [31]They appeared in glory and were speaking of his departure, which he was about to accomplish at Jerusalem. [32]Now Peter and his companions were weighed down with sleep; but since they had stayed awake,[e] they saw his glory and the two men who stood with him. [33]Just as they were leaving him, Peter said to Jesus, "Master, it is good for us to be here; let us make three dwellings,[f] one for you, one for Moses, and one for Elijah"—not knowing what he said. [34]While he was saying this, a cloud came and overshadowed them; and they were terrified as they entered the cloud. [35]Then from the cloud came a voice that said, "This is my Son, my Chosen;[g] listen to him!" [36]When the voice had spoken, Jesus was found alone. And they kept silent and in those days told no one any of the things they had seen.

Jesus Heals a Boy with a Demon

37 On the next day, when they had come down from the mountain, a great crowd met him. [38]Just then a man from the crowd shouted, "Teacher, I beg you to look at my son; he is my only child. [39]Suddenly a spirit seizes him, and all at once he[h] shrieks. It convulses him until he foams at the mouth; it mauls him and will scarcely leave him. [40]I begged your disciples to cast it out, but they could not." [41]Jesus answered, "You faithless and perverse generation, how much longer must I be with you and bear with you? Bring your son here." [42]While he was coming, the demon dashed him to the ground in convulsions. But Jesus rebuked the

a Gk tetrarch b Gk him c Gk he d Or The Christ e Or but when they were fully awake f Or tents g Other ancient authorities read my Beloved h Or it

<TRY THIS ←

DON'T PASS ME BY

Jesus' parable in **Luke 10.30–37** makes us uncomfortable. It's *supposed* to. As much as we hate to admit it, we're not always the Good Samaritan. We usually pass right by the hurting, the outcast, and the different—like the priest and the Levite, we go out of our way to avoid them.

We've become experts at avoiding their eye contact, at evading unwanted conversations, at keeping to ourselves. We *should* care. We *want* to. But we just don't have the time . . . or the guts.

Tomorrow at school, look around with new eyes. Turn each period change into a prayer walk. Think about these questions as you make your way to your next class: Who do *I* pass by without noticing? Whose needs are hidden from my eyes by my busyness, by my stereotypes, by the limits of my comfort zone, by fear? Who does God want me to notice? How can I be the "neighbor" Jesus challenges me to be?

GOD IS CHALLENGING MY SCHOOL

unclean spirit, healed the boy, and gave him back to his father. [43]And all were astounded at the greatness of God.

Jesus Again Foretells His Death

While everyone was amazed at all that he was doing, he said to his disciples, [44]"Let these words sink into your ears: The Son of Man is going to be betrayed into human hands." [45]But they did not understand this saying; its meaning was concealed from them, so that they could not perceive it. And they were afraid to ask him about this saying.

True Greatness

46 An argument arose among them as to which one of them was the greatest. [47]But Jesus, aware of their inner thoughts, took a little child and put it by his side, [48]and said to them, "Whoever welcomes this child in my name welcomes me, and whoever welcomes me welcomes the one who sent me; for the least among all of you is the greatest."

Another Exorcist

49 John answered, "Master, we saw someone casting out demons in your name, and we tried to stop him, because he does not follow with us." [50]But Jesus said to him, "Do not stop him; for whoever is not against you is for you."

A Samaritan Village Refuses to Receive Jesus

51 When the days drew near for him to be taken up, he set his face to go to Jerusalem. [52]And he sent messengers ahead of him. On their way they entered a village of the Samaritans to make ready for him; [53]but they did not receive him, because his face was set toward Jerusalem. [54]When his disciples James and John saw it, they said, "Lord, do you want us to command fire to come down from heaven and consume them?"[a] [55]But he turned and rebuked them. [56]Then[b] they went on to another village.

Would-Be Followers of Jesus

57 As they were going along the road, someone said to him, "I will follow you wherever you go." [58]And Jesus said to him, "Foxes have holes, and birds of the air have nests; but the Son of Man has nowhere to lay his head." [59]To another he said, "Follow me." But he said, "Lord, first let me go and bury my father." [60]But Jesus[c] said to him, "Let the dead bury their own dead; but as for you, go and proclaim the kingdom of God." [61]Another said, "I will follow you, Lord; but let me first say farewell to those at my home." [62]Jesus said to him, "No one who puts a hand to the plow and looks back is fit for the kingdom of God."

10 The Mission of the Seventy

After this the Lord appointed seventy[d] others and sent them on ahead of him in pairs to every town and place where he himself intended to go. [2]He said to them, "The harvest is plentiful, but the laborers are few; therefore ask the Lord of the harvest to send out laborers into his harvest. [3]Go on your way. See, I am sending you out like lambs into the midst of wolves. [4]Carry no purse, no bag, no sandals; and greet no one on the road. [5]Whatever house you enter, first say, 'Peace to this house!' [6]And if anyone is there who shares in peace, your peace will rest on that person; but if not, it will return to you. [7]Remain in the same house, eating and drinking whatever they provide, for the laborer deserves to be paid. Do not move about from house to house. [8]Whenever you enter a town and its people welcome you, eat what is set before you; [9]cure the sick who are there, and say to them, 'The kingdom of God has come near

a Other ancient authorities add *as Elijah did* b Other ancient authorities read *rebuked them, and said, "You do not know what spirit you are of,* [56]*for the Son of Man has not come to destroy the lives of human beings but to save them." Then* c Gk *he* d Other ancient authorities read *seventy-two*

1234 LIVE new testament

LUKE 10

to you.'[a] 10But whenever you enter a town and they do not welcome you, go out into its streets and say, 11'Even the dust of your town that clings to our feet, we wipe off in protest against you. Yet know this: the kingdom of God has come near.'[b] 12I tell you, on that day it will be more tolerable for Sodom than for that town.

Woes to Unrepentant Cities

13 "Woe to you, Chorazin! Woe to you, Bethsaida! For if the deeds of power done in you had been done in Tyre and Sidon, they would have repented long ago, sitting in sackcloth and ashes. 14But at the judgment it will be more tolerable for Tyre and Sidon than for you. 15And you, Capernaum,

will you be exalted to heaven?

No, you will be brought down to Hades.

16 "Whoever listens to you listens to me, and whoever rejects you rejects me, and whoever rejects me rejects the one who sent me."

The Return of the Seventy

17 The seventy[c] returned with joy, saying, "Lord, in your name even the demons submit to us!" 18He said to them, "I watched Satan fall from heaven like a flash of lightning. 19See, I have given you authority to tread on snakes and scorpions, and over all the power of the enemy; and nothing will hurt you. 20Nevertheless, do not rejoice at this, that the spirits submit to you, but rejoice that your names are written in heaven."

Jesus Rejoices

21 At that same hour Jesus[d] rejoiced in the Holy Spirit[e] and said, "I thank[f] you, Father, Lord of heaven and earth, because you have hidden these things from the wise and the intelligent and have revealed them to infants; yes, Father, for such was your gracious will.[g] 22All things have been handed over to me by my Father; and no one knows who the Son is except the Father, or who the Father is except the Son and anyone to whom the Son chooses to reveal him."

23 Then turning to the disciples, Jesus[d] said to them privately, "Blessed are the eyes that see what you see! 24For I tell you that many prophets and kings desired to see what you see, but did not see it, and to hear what you hear, but did not hear it."

The Parable of the Good Samaritan

25 Just then a lawyer stood up to test Jesus.[h] "Teacher," he said, "what must I do to inherit eternal life?" 26He said to him, "What is written in the law? What do you read there?" 27He answered, "You shall love the Lord your God with all your heart, and with all your soul, and with all your strength, and with all your mind; and your neighbor as yourself." 28And he said to him, "You have given the right answer; do this, and you will live."

29 But wanting to justify himself, he asked Jesus, "And who is my neighbor?" 30Jesus replied, "A man was going down from Jerusalem to Jericho, and fell into the hands of robbers, who stripped him, beat him, and went away, leaving him half dead. 31Now by chance a priest was going down that road; and when he saw him, he passed by on the other side. 32So likewise a Levite, when he came to the place and saw him, passed by on the other side. 33But a Samaritan while traveling came near him; and when he saw him, he was moved with pity. 34He went to him and bandaged his wounds, having poured oil and wine on them. Then he put him on his own animal, brought him to an inn, and took care of him. 35The next day he took out two denarii,[i] gave them to the innkeeper, and said, 'Take care of him; and when I come back, I will repay you whatever more you spend.' 36Which of these three, do you think, was a neighbor to the man who fell into the hands of the robbers?" 37He said, "The one who showed him mercy." Jesus said to him, "Go and do likewise."

Jesus Visits Martha and Mary

38 Now as they went on their way, he entered a certain village, where a woman named Martha welcomed him into her home. 39She had a sister named Mary, who sat at the Lord's feet and listened to what he was saying. 40But Martha was distracted by her many tasks; so she came to him and asked, "Lord, do you not care that my sister has left me to do all the work by myself? Tell her then to help me." 41But the Lord answered her, "Martha, Martha, you are worried and distracted by many things; 42there is need of only one thing.[j] Mary has chosen the better part, which will not be taken away from her."

11 The Lord's Prayer

He was praying in a certain place, and after he had finished, one of his disciples said to him, "Lord, teach us to pray, as John taught his disciples." 2He said to them, "When you pray, say:

Father,[k] hallowed be your name.

Your kingdom come.[l]

a Or is at hand for you b Or is at hand c Other ancient authorities read seventy-two d Gk he e Other authorities read in the spirit
f Or praise g Or for so it was well-pleasing in your sight h Gk him i The denarius was the usual day's wage for a laborer j Other ancient
authorities read few things are necessary, or only one k Other ancient authorities read Our Father in heaven l A few ancient authorities read
Your Holy Spirit come upon us and cleanse us. Other ancient authorities add Your will be done, on earth as in heaven

³ Give us each day our daily bread.^a
⁴ And forgive us our sins,
   for we ourselves forgive everyone
       indebted to us.
   And do not bring us to the time of trial."^b

Perseverance in Prayer

5 And he said to them, "Suppose one of you has a friend, and you go to him at midnight and say to him, 'Friend, lend me three loaves of bread; ⁶for a friend of mine has arrived, and I have nothing to set before him.' ⁷And he answers from within, 'Do not bother me; the door has already been locked, and my children are with me in bed; I cannot get up and give you anything.' ⁸I tell you, even though he will not get up and give him anything because he is his friend, at least because of his persistence he will get up and give him whatever he needs.

9 "So I say to you, Ask, and it will be given you; search, and you will find; knock, and the door will be opened for you. ¹⁰For everyone who asks receives, and everyone who searches finds, and for everyone who knocks, the door will be opened. ¹¹Is there anyone among you who, if your child asks for^c a fish, will give a snake instead of a fish? ¹²Or if the child asks for an egg, will give a scorpion? ¹³If you then, who are evil, know how to give good gifts to your children, how much more will the heavenly Father give the Holy Spirit^d to those who ask him!"

Jesus and Beelzebul

14 Now he was casting out a demon that was mute; when the demon had gone out, the one who had been mute spoke, and the crowds were amazed. ¹⁵But some of them said, "He casts out demons by Beelzebul, the ruler of the demons." ¹⁶Others, to test him, kept demanding from him a sign from heaven. ¹⁷But he knew what they were thinking and said to them, "Every kingdom divided against itself becomes a desert, and house falls on house. ¹⁸If Satan also is divided against himself, how will his kingdom stand?—for you say that I cast out the demons by Beelzebul. ¹⁹Now if I cast out the demons by Beelzebul, by whom do your exorcists^e cast them out? Therefore they will be your judges. ²⁰But if it is by the finger of God that I cast out the demons, then the kingdom of God has come to you. ²¹When a strong man, fully armed, guards his castle, his property is safe. ²²But when one stronger than he attacks him and overpowers him, he takes away his armor in which he trusted and divides his plunder.

²³Whoever is not with me is against me, and whoever does not gather with me scatters.

The Return of the Unclean Spirit

24 "When the unclean spirit has gone out of a person, it wanders through waterless regions looking for a resting place, but not finding any, it says, 'I will return to my house from which I came.' ²⁵When it comes, it finds it swept and put in order. ²⁶Then it goes and brings seven other spirits more evil than itself, and they enter and live there; and the last state of that person is worse than the first."

True Blessedness

27 While he was saying this, a woman in the crowd raised her voice and said to him, "Blessed is the womb that bore you and the breasts that nursed you!" ²⁸But he said, "Blessed rather are those who hear the word of God and obey it!"

The Sign of Jonah

29 When the crowds were increasing, he began to say, "This generation is an evil generation; it asks for a sign, but no sign will be given to it except the sign of Jonah. ³⁰For just as Jonah became a sign to the people of Nineveh, so the Son of Man will be to this generation. ³¹The queen of the South will rise at the judgment with the people of this generation and condemn them, because she came from the ends of the earth to listen to the wisdom of Solomon, and see, something greater than Solomon is here! ³²The people of Nineveh will rise up at the judgment with this generation and condemn it, because they repented at the proclamation of Jonah, and see, something greater than Jonah is here!

The Light of the Body

33 "No one after lighting a lamp puts it in a cellar,^f but on the lampstand so that those who enter may see the light. ³⁴Your eye is the lamp of your body. If your eye is healthy, your whole body is full of light; but if it is not healthy, your body is full of darkness. ³⁵Therefore consider whether the light in you is not darkness. ³⁶If then your whole body is full of light, with no part of it in darkness, it will be as full of light as when a lamp gives you light with its rays."

Jesus Denounces Pharisees and Lawyers

37 While he was speaking, a Pharisee invited him to dine with him; so he went in and took his place at the table. ³⁸The Pharisee was

amazed to see that he did not first wash before dinner. 39Then the Lord said to him, "Now you Pharisees clean the outside of the cup and of the dish, but inside you are full of greed and wickedness. 40You fools! Did not the one who made the outside make the inside also? 41So give for alms those things that are within; and see, everything will be clean for you.

42 "But woe to you Pharisees! For you tithe mint and rue and herbs of all kinds, and neglect justice and the love of God; it is these you ought to have practiced, without neglecting the others. 43Woe to you Pharisees! For you love to have the seat of honor in the synagogues and to be greeted with respect in the marketplaces. 44Woe to you! For you are like unmarked graves, and people walk over them without realizing it."

45 One of the lawyers answered him, "Teacher, when you say these things, you insult us too." 46And he said, "Woe also to you lawyers! For you load people with burdens hard to bear, and you yourselves do not lift a finger to ease them. 47Woe to you! For you build the tombs of the prophets whom your ancestors killed. 48So you are witnesses and approve of the deeds of your ancestors; for they killed them, and you build their tombs. 49Therefore also the Wisdom of God said, 'I will send them prophets and apostles, some of whom they will kill and persecute,' 50so that this generation may be charged with the blood of all the prophets shed since the foundation of the world, 51from the blood of Abel to the blood of Zechariah, who perished between the altar and the sanctuary. Yes, I tell you, it will be charged against this generation. 52Woe to you lawyers! For you have taken away the key of knowledge; you did not enter yourselves, and you hindered those who were entering."

53 When he went outside, the scribes and the Pharisees began to be very hostile toward him and to cross-examine him about many things, 54lying in wait for him, to catch him in something he might say.

12 A Warning against Hypocrisy

Meanwhile, when the crowd gathered by the thousands, so that they trampled on one another, he began to speak first to his disciples, "Beware of the yeast of the Pharisees, that is, their hypocrisy. 2Nothing is covered up that will not be uncovered, and nothing secret that will not become known. 3Therefore whatever you have said in the dark will be heard in the light, and what you have whispered behind closed doors will be proclaimed from the housetops.

a Or *power* *b* Gk *Gehenna*

Exhortation to Fearless Confession

4 "I tell you, my friends, do not fear those who kill the body, and after that can do nothing more. 5But I will warn you whom to fear: fear him who, after he has killed, has authority*a* to cast into hell.*b* Yes, I tell you, fear him! 6Are not five sparrows sold for two pennies? Yet not one of them is forgotten in God's sight. 7But even the hairs of your head are all counted. Do not be afraid; you are of more value than many sparrows.

8 "And I tell you, everyone who acknowledges me before others, the Son of Man also will acknowledge before the angels of God; 9but whoever denies me before others will be denied before the angels of God. 10And everyone who speaks a word against the Son of Man will be forgiven; but whoever blasphemes against the Holy Spirit will not be forgiven. 11When

TEXT MESSAGE

The Jerusalem-to-Jericho road where the man was robbed in Jesus' story (Luke 10.30) was notoriously dangerous. With a 3,600-foot drop in only seventeen miles, this narrow, steep, twisting path—nicknamed "The Bloody Way"—was an infamous robbers' hangout.

This information has been scanned and is free of all known viruses. Please forward to all your friends.

they bring you before the synagogues, the rulers, and the authorities, do not worry about how*a* you are to defend yourselves or what you are to say; 12for the Holy Spirit will teach you at that very hour what you ought to say."

The Parable of the Rich Fool

13 Someone in the crowd said to him, "Teacher, tell my brother to divide the family inheritance with me." 14But he said to him, "Friend, who set me to be a judge or arbitrator over you?" 15And he said to them, "Take care! Be on your guard against all kinds of greed; for one's life does not consist in the abundance of possessions." 16Then he told them a parable: "The land of a rich man produced abundantly. 17And he thought to himself, 'What should I do, for I have no place to store my crops?' 18Then he said, 'I will do this: I will pull down my barns and build larger ones, and there I will store all my grain and my goods. 19And I will say to my soul, Soul, you have ample goods laid up for many years; relax, eat, drink, be merry.' 20But God said to him, 'You fool! This very night your life is being demanded of you. And the things you have prepared, whose will they be?' 21So it is with those who store up treasures for themselves but are not rich toward God."

Do Not Worry

22 He said to his disciples, "Therefore I tell you, do not worry about your life, what you will eat, or about your body, what you will wear. 23For life is more than food, and the body more than clothing. 24Consider the ravens: they neither sow nor reap, they have neither storehouse nor barn, and yet God feeds them. Of how much more value are you than the birds! 25And can any of you by worrying add a single hour to your span of life?*b* 26If then you are not able to do so small a thing as that, why do you worry about the rest? 27Consider the lilies, how they grow: they neither toil nor spin;*c* yet I tell you, even Solomon in all his glory was not clothed like one of these. 28But if God so clothes the grass of the field, which is alive today and tomorrow is thrown into the oven, how much more will he clothe you—you of little faith! 29And do not keep striving for what you are to eat and what you are to drink, and do not keep worrying. 30For it is the nations of the world that strive after all these things, and your Father knows that you need them. 31Instead, strive for his*d* kingdom, and these things will be given to you as well.

32 "Do not be afraid, little flock, for it is your Father's good pleasure to give you the kingdom. 33Sell your possessions, and give alms. Make purses for yourselves that do not wear out, an unfailing treasure in heaven, where no thief comes near and no moth destroys. 34For where your treasure is, there your heart will be also.

Watchful Slaves

35 "Be dressed for action and have your lamps lit; 36be like those who are waiting for their master to return from the wedding banquet, so that they may open the door for him as soon as he comes and knocks. 37Blessed are those slaves whom the master finds alert when he comes; truly I tell you, he will fasten his belt and have them sit down to eat, and he will come and serve them. 38If he comes during the middle of the night, or near dawn, and finds them so, blessed are those slaves.

39 "But know this: if the owner of the house had known at what hour the thief was coming, he*e* would not have let his house be broken into. 40You also must be ready, for the Son of Man is coming at an unexpected hour."

The Faithful or the Unfaithful Slave

41 Peter said, "Lord, are you telling this parable for us or for everyone?" 42And the Lord said, "Who then is the faithful and prudent manager whom his master will put in charge of his slaves, to give them their allowance of food at the proper time? 43Blessed is that slave whom his master will find at work when he arrives. 44Truly I tell you, he will put that one in charge of all his possessions. 45But if that slave says to himself, 'My master is delayed in coming,' and if he begins to beat the other slaves, men and women, and to eat and drink and get drunk, 46the master of that slave will come on a day when he does not expect him and at an hour that he does not know, and will cut him in pieces,*f* and put him with the unfaithful. 47That slave who knew what his master wanted, but did not prepare himself or do what was wanted, will receive a severe beating. 48But the one who did not know and did what deserved a beating will receive a light beating. From everyone to whom much has been given, much will be required; and from the one to whom much has been entrusted, even more will be demanded.

Jesus the Cause of Division

49 "I came to bring fire to the earth, and how I wish it were already kindled! 50I have a baptism with which to be baptized, and what stress I am under until it is completed! 51Do you think

---

a Other ancient authorities add *or what* *b* Or *add a cubit to your stature* *c* Other ancient authorities read *Consider the lilies; they neither spin nor weave* *d* Other ancient authorities read *God's* *e* Other ancient authorities add *would have watched and* *f* Or *cut him off*

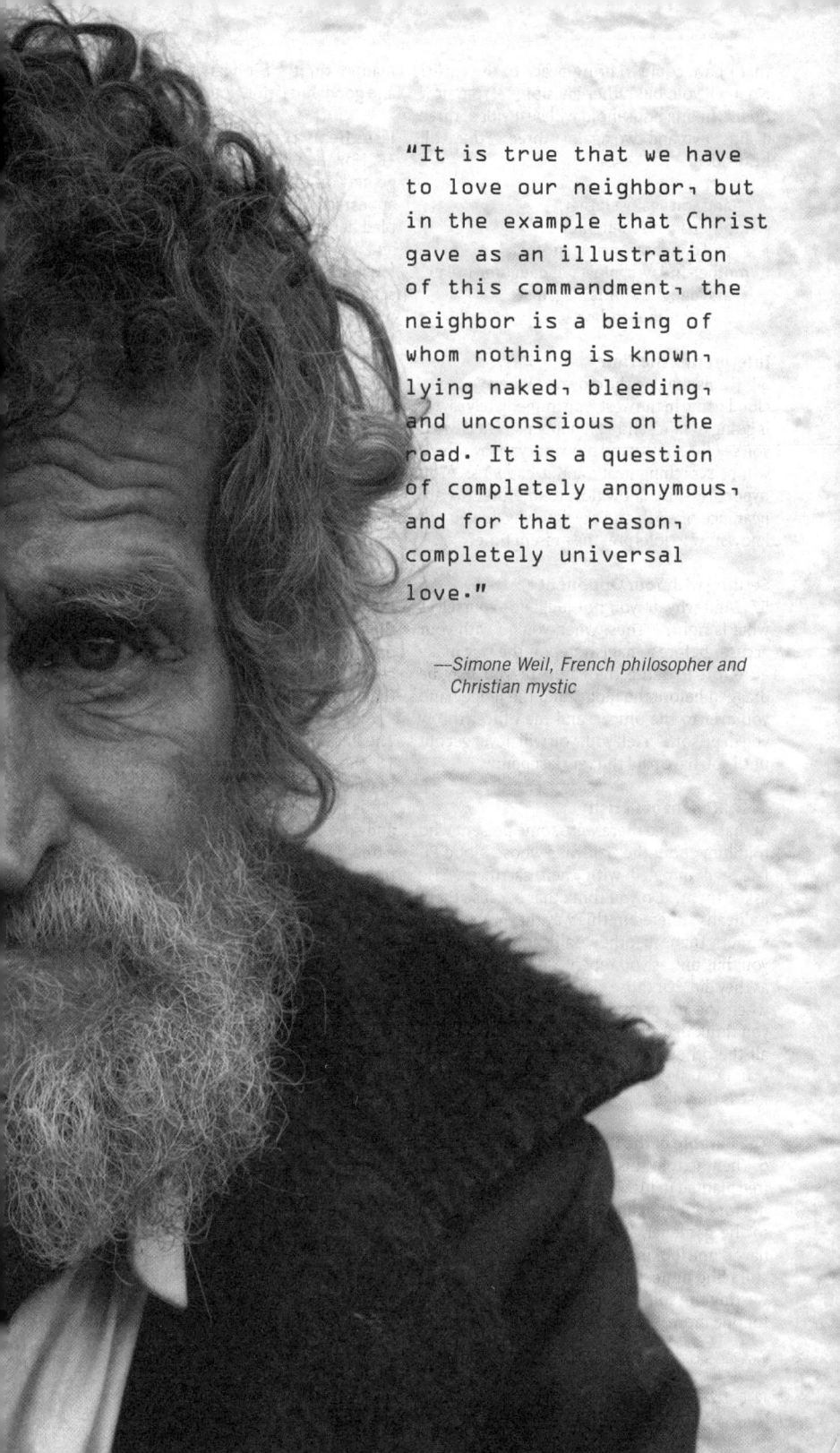

"It is true that we have to love our neighbor, but in the example that Christ gave as an illustration of this commandment, the neighbor is a being of whom nothing is known, lying naked, bleeding, and unconscious on the road. It is a question of completely anonymous, and for that reason, completely universal love."

—Simone Weil, French philosopher and Christian mystic

that I have come to bring peace to the earth? No, I tell you, but rather division! ⁵²From now on five in one household will be divided, three against two and two against three; ⁵³they will be divided:

father against son
 and son against father,
mother against daughter
 and daughter against mother,
mother-in-law against her daughter-in-law
 and daughter-in-law against
  mother-in-law."

Interpreting the Time

54 He also said to the crowds, "When you see a cloud rising in the west, you immediately say, 'It is going to rain'; and so it happens. ⁵⁵And when you see the south wind blowing, you say, 'There will be scorching heat'; and it happens. ⁵⁶You hypocrites! You know how to interpret the appearance of earth and sky, but why do you not know how to interpret the present time?

Settling with Your Opponent

57 "And why do you not judge for yourselves what is right? ⁵⁸Thus, when you go with your accuser before a magistrate, on the way make an effort to settle the case,ᵃ or you may be dragged before the judge, and the judge hand you over to the officer, and the officer throw you in prison. ⁵⁹I tell you, you will never get out until you have paid the very last penny."

13 Repent or Perish

At that very time there were some present who told him about the Galileans whose blood Pilate had mingled with their sacrifices. ²He asked them, "Do you think that because these Galileans suffered in this way they were worse sinners than all other Galileans? ³No, I tell you; but unless you repent, you will all perish as they did. ⁴Or those eighteen who were killed when the tower of Siloam fell on them—do you think that they were worse offenders than all the others living in Jerusalem? ⁵No, I tell you; but unless you repent, you will all perish just as they did."

The Parable of the Barren Fig Tree

6 Then he told this parable: "A man had a fig tree planted in his vineyard; and he came looking for fruit on it and found none. ⁷So he said to the gardener, 'See here! For three years I have come looking for fruit on this fig tree, and still I find none. Cut it down! Why should it be wasting the soil?' ⁸He replied, 'Sir, let it alone for one more year, until I dig around it and put

manure on it. ⁹If it bears fruit next year, well and good; but if not, you can cut it down.' "

Jesus Heals a Crippled Woman

10 Now he was teaching in one of the synagogues on the sabbath. ¹¹And just then there appeared a woman with a spirit that had crippled her for eighteen years. She was bent over and was quite unable to stand up straight. ¹²When Jesus saw her, he called her over and said, "Woman, you are set free from your ailment." ¹³When he laid his hands on her, immediately she stood up straight and began praising God. ¹⁴But the leader of the synagogue, indignant because Jesus had cured on the sabbath, kept saying to the crowd, "There are six days on which work ought to be done; come on those days and be cured, and not on the sabbath day." ¹⁵But the Lord answered him and said, "You hypocrites! Does not each of you on the sabbath untie his ox or his donkey from the manger, and lead it away to give it water? ¹⁶And ought not this woman, a daughter of Abraham whom Satan bound for eighteen long years, be set free from this bondage on the sabbath day?" ¹⁷When he said this, all his opponents were put to shame; and the entire crowd was rejoicing at all the wonderful things that he was doing.

The Parable of the Mustard Seed

18 He said therefore, "What is the kingdom of God like? And to what should I compare it? ¹⁹It is like a mustard seed that someone took and sowed in the garden; it grew and became a tree, and the birds of the air made nests in its branches."

The Parable of the Yeast

20 And again he said, "To what should I compare the kingdom of God? ²¹It is like yeast that a woman took and mixed in withᵇ three measures of flour until all of it was leavened."

The Narrow Door

22 Jesusᶜ went through one town and village after another, teaching as he made his way to Jerusalem. ²³Someone asked him, "Lord, will only a few be saved?" He said to them, ²⁴"Strive to enter through the narrow door; for many, I tell you, will try to enter and will not be able. ²⁵When once the owner of the house has got up and shut the door, and you begin to stand outside and to knock at the door, saying, 'Lord, open to us,' then in reply he will say to you, 'I do not know where you come from.' ²⁶Then you will begin to say, 'We ate and drank with

ᵃ Gk *settle with him* ᵇ Gk *hid in* ᶜ Gk *He*

you, and you taught in our streets.' 27But he will say, 'I do not know where you come from; go away from me, all you evildoers!' 28There will be weeping and gnashing of teeth when you see Abraham and Isaac and Jacob and all the prophets in the kingdom of God, and you yourselves thrown out. 29Then people will come from east and west, from north and south, and will eat in the kingdom of God. 30Indeed, some are last who will be first, and some are first who will be last."

The Lament over Jerusalem

31 At that very hour some Pharisees came and said to him, "Get away from here, for Herod wants to kill you." 32He said to them, "Go and tell that fox for me,[a] 'Listen, I am casting out demons and performing cures today and tomorrow, and on the third day I finish my work. 33Yet today, tomorrow, and the next day I must be on my way, because it is impossible for a prophet to be killed outside of Jerusalem.' 34Jerusalem, Jerusalem, the city that kills the prophets and stones those who are sent to it! How often have I desired to gather your children together as a hen gathers her brood under her wings, and you were not willing! 35See, your house is left to you. And I tell you, you will not see me until the time comes when[b] you say, 'Blessed is the one who comes in the name of the Lord.' "

14 Jesus Heals the Man with Dropsy

On one occasion when Jesus[c] was going to the house of a leader of the Pharisees to eat a meal on the sabbath, they were watching him closely. 2Just then, in front of him, there was a man who had dropsy. 3And Jesus asked the lawyers and Pharisees, "Is it lawful to cure people on the sabbath, or not?" 4But they were silent. So Jesus[c] took him and healed him, and sent him away. 5Then he said to them, "If one of you has a child[d] or an ox that has fallen into a well, will you not immediately pull it out on a sabbath day?" 6And they could not reply to this.

Humility and Hospitality

7 When he noticed how the guests chose the places of honor, he told them a parable. 8"When you are invited by someone to a wedding banquet, do not sit down at the place of honor, in case someone more distinguished than you has been invited by your host; 9and the host who invited both of you may come and say to you, 'Give this person your place,' and then in disgrace you would start to take the lowest place. 10But when you are invited, go and sit down at the lowest place, so that when your host comes, he may say to you, 'Friend, move up higher'; then you will be honored in the presence of all who sit at the table with you. 11For all who exalt themselves will be humbled, and those who humble themselves will be exalted."

12 He said also to the one who had invited him, "When you give a luncheon or a dinner, do not invite your friends or your brothers or your relatives or rich neighbors, in case they may invite you in return, and you would be repaid. 13But when you give a banquet, invite the poor, the crippled, the lame, and the blind. 14And you will be blessed, because they cannot repay you, for you will be repaid at the resurrection of the righteous."

---

a Gk lacks *for me* *b* Other ancient authorities lack *the time comes when* *c* Gk *he* *d* Other ancient authorities read *a donkey*

The Speech

Want to make a large crowd of admirers nervous? Deliver a speech like the one Jesus pitched to his followers in **Luke 14.25–35**.

It's a no-nonsense proclamation. It's a "this is the deal" announcement. It's a "fork in the road" warning. Otherwise, why does Jesus emphasize planning ahead? "Do you want to follow me? It's not going to be a picnic and you can't bring all your stuff."

Can't you just hear the crowd groan? Luke doesn't say what happened, but use your imagination. The crowds soon thinned out. No wonder.

Like those crowds, we like thinking of Jesus as our *Savior*. He loves us. He died for us. He is coming back for us. We're less eager to put ourselves in his sandals.

Read this passage again. Is Jesus demanding that you walk away from your life to follow him? Not necessarily. But he is asking you to be at his disposal . . . to make him your top priority.

So if you're an artist, create art that reflects Jesus' values. If you play basketball, play to honor him. Whatever your enthusiasms or passions, they can't be your top priority . . . but they *can* become prayer.

If they can't—and you know which ones those are in your life—leave them behind. They're dust—dead already.

Jesus doesn't ask you to join a herd of mindless zombie followers. He asks— *commands*—you to join him in an adventure that transforms your passions . . . enthusiasms . . . hobbies.

How can your life reflect his values? Jot a note at **Learner.CalltoDiscipleship.com** to tell the rest of us. We'll pray for you.

The Parable of the Great Dinner

15 One of the dinner guests, on hearing this, said to him, "Blessed is anyone who will eat bread in the kingdom of God!" 16Then Jesus[a] said to him, "Someone gave a great dinner and invited many. 17At the time for the dinner he sent his slave to say to those who had been invited, 'Come; for everything is ready now.' 18But they all alike began to make excuses. The first said to him, 'I have bought a piece of land, and I must go out and see it; please accept my regrets.' 19Another said, 'I have bought five yoke of oxen, and I am going to try them out; please accept my regrets.' 20Another said, 'I have just been married, and therefore I cannot come.' 21So the slave returned and reported this to his master. Then the owner of the house became angry and said to his slave, 'Go out at once into the streets and lanes of the town and bring in the poor, the crippled, the blind, and the lame.' 22And the slave said, 'Sir, what you ordered has been done, and there is still room.' 23Then the master said to the slave, 'Go out into the roads and lanes, and compel people to come in, so that my house may be filled. 24For I tell you,[b] none of those who were invited will taste my dinner.' "

The Cost of Discipleship

25 Now large crowds were traveling with him; and he turned and said to them, 26"Whoever comes to me and does not hate father and mother, wife and children, brothers and sisters, yes, and even life itself, cannot be my disciple. 27Whoever does not carry the cross and follow me cannot be my disciple. 28For which of you, intending to build a tower, does not first sit down and estimate the cost, to see whether he has enough to complete it? 29Otherwise, when he has laid a foundation and is not able to finish, all who see it will begin to ridicule him, 30saying, 'This fellow began to build and was not able to finish.' 31Or what king, going out to wage war against another king, will not sit down first and consider whether he is able with ten thousand to oppose the one who comes against him with twenty thousand? 32If he cannot, then, while the other is still far away, he sends a delegation and asks for the terms of peace. 33So therefore, none of you can become my disciple if you do not give up all your possessions.

About Salt

34 "Salt is good; but if salt has lost its taste, how can its saltiness be restored?[c] 35It is fit neither for the soil nor for the manure pile; they throw it away. Let anyone with ears to hear listen!"

15 The Parable of the Lost Sheep

Now all the tax collectors and sinners were coming near to listen to him. 2And the Pharisees and the scribes were grumbling and saying, "This fellow welcomes sinners and eats with them."

---

a Gk he b The Greek word for *you* here is plural c Or *how can it be used for seasoning?*

3 So he told them this parable: [4]"Which one of you, having a hundred sheep and losing one of them, does not leave the ninety-nine in the wilderness and go after the one that is lost until he finds it? [5]When he has found it, he lays it on his shoulders and rejoices. [6]And when he comes home, he calls together his friends and neighbors, saying to them, 'Rejoice with me, for I have found my sheep that was lost.' [7]Just so, I tell you, there will be more joy in heaven over one sinner who repents than over ninety-nine righteous persons who need no repentance.

The Parable of the Lost Coin

8 "Or what woman having ten silver coins,[a] if she loses one of them, does not light a lamp, sweep the house, and search carefully until she finds it? [9]When she has found it, she calls together her friends and neighbors, saying, 'Rejoice with me, for I have found the coin that I had lost.' [10]Just so, I tell you, there is joy in the presence of the angels of God over one sinner who repents."

The Parable of the Prodigal and His Brother

11 Then Jesus[b] said, "There was a man who had two sons. [12]The younger of them said to his father, 'Father, give me the share of the property that will belong to me.' So he divided his property between them. [13]A few days later the younger son gathered all he had and traveled to a distant country, and there he squandered his property in dissolute living. [14]When he had spent everything, a severe famine took place throughout that country, and he began to be in need. [15]So he went and hired himself out to one of the citizens of that country, who sent him to his fields to feed the pigs. [16]He would gladly have filled himself with[c] the pods that the pigs were eating; and no one gave him anything. [17]But when he came to himself he said, 'How many of my father's hired hands have bread enough and to spare, but here I am dying of hunger! [18]I will get up and go to my father, and I will say to him, "Father, I have sinned against heaven and before you; [19]I am no longer worthy to be called your son; treat me like one of your hired hands." ' [20]So he set off and went to his father. But while he was still far off, his father saw him and was filled with compassion; he ran and put his arms around him and kissed him. [21]Then the son said to him, 'Father, I have sinned against heaven and before you; I am no longer worthy to be called your son.'[d] [22]But the father said to his slaves, 'Quickly, bring out a robe—the best one—and

put it on him; put a ring on his finger and sandals on his feet. [23]And get the fatted calf and kill it, and let us eat and celebrate; [24]for this son of mine was dead and is alive again; he was lost and is found!' And they began to celebrate.

25 "Now his elder son was in the field; and when he came and approached the house, he heard music and dancing. [26]He called one of the slaves and asked what was going on. [27]He replied, 'Your brother has come, and your father has killed the fatted calf, because he has got him back safe and sound.' [28]Then he became angry and refused to go in. His father came out and began to plead with him. [29]But he answered his father, 'Listen! For all these years I have been working like a slave for you, and I have never disobeyed your command; yet

a Gk drachmas, each worth about a day's wage for a laborer b Gk he c Other ancient authorities read filled his stomach with d Other ancient authorities add Treat me like one of your hired servants

REALITY

FORGIVE OR RESENT?

Luke gives three parables in a row about God's forgiveness. Read **Luke 15.1–32**. The first two parables, the lost sheep and the lost coin, are pretty similar. They move from losing to finding to rejoicing, while drawing a picture of a God who goes out to find us when we are lost.

The third parable, of the lost son, adds another dimension: *resenting*. It's a jibe at the Pharisees and scribes, who refused to open themselves to the mercy and extravagant generosity of God. They were like the older son who couldn't bring himself to rejoice with the father or the rest of the household over the return of the younger son.

The Pharisees saw things in black and white. Keeping the law at all costs had become so important to them, that they put the law above the needs of people. They were enraged by Jesus' message that God is kind and merciful and actively reaches out to sinners.

What about you? Is resentment a familiar feeling for you? Do you sometimes feel like God gives others more than you, even people you think don't deserve it and who don't play by the rules? Is there a Pharisee in you?

---

you have never given me even a young goat so that I might celebrate with my friends. 30But when this son of yours came back, who has devoured your property with prostitutes, you killed the fatted calf for him!' 31Then the father*a* said to him, 'Son, you are always with me, and all that is mine is yours. 32But we had to celebrate and rejoice, because this brother of yours was dead and has come to life; he was lost and has been found.' "

16 **The Parable of the Dishonest Manager**
Then Jesus*a* said to the disciples, "There was a rich man who had a manager, and charges were

---

brought to him that this man was squandering his property. 2So he summoned him and said to him, 'What is this that I hear about you? Give me an accounting of your management, because you cannot be my manager any longer.' 3Then the manager said to himself, 'What will I do, now that my master is taking the position away from me? I am not strong enough to dig, and I am ashamed to beg. 4I have decided what to do so that, when I am dismissed as manager, people may welcome me into their homes.' 5So, summoning his master's debtors one by one, he asked the first, 'How much do you owe my master?' 6He answered, 'A hundred jugs of olive oil.' He said to him, 'Take your bill, sit down quickly, and make it fifty.' 7Then he asked another, 'And how much do you owe?' He replied, 'A hundred containers of wheat.' He said to him, 'Take your bill and make it eighty.' 8And his master commended the dishonest manager because he had acted shrewdly; for the children of this age are more shrewd in dealing with their own generation than are the children of light. 9And I tell you, make friends for yourselves by means of dishonest wealth*b* so that when it is gone, they may welcome you into the eternal homes.*c*

10 "Whoever is faithful in a very little is faithful also in much; and whoever is dishonest in a very little is dishonest also in much. 11If then you have not been faithful with the dishonest wealth,*b* who will entrust to you the true riches? 12And if you have not been faithful with what belongs to another, who will give you what is your own? 13No slave can serve two masters; for a slave will either hate the one and love the other, or be devoted to the one and despise the other. You cannot serve God and wealth."*b*

The Law and the Kingdom of God
14 The Pharisees, who were lovers of money, heard all this, and they ridiculed him. 15So he said to them, "You are those who justify yourselves in the sight of others; but God knows your hearts; for what is prized by human beings is an abomination in the sight of God.

16 "The law and the prophets were in effect until John came; since then the good news of the kingdom of God is proclaimed, and everyone tries to enter it by force.*d* 17But it is easier for heaven and earth to pass away, than for one stroke of a letter in the law to be dropped.

18 "Anyone who divorces his wife and marries another commits adultery, and whoever marries a woman divorced from her husband commits adultery.

---

a Gk *he* *b* Gk *mammon* *c* Gk *tents* *d* Or *everyone is strongly urged to enter it*

The Rich Man and Lazarus

19 "There was a rich man who was dressed in purple and fine linen and who feasted sumptuously every day. 20And at his gate lay a poor man named Lazarus, covered with sores, 21who longed to satisfy his hunger with what fell from the rich man's table; even the dogs would come and lick his sores. 22The poor man died and was carried away by the angels to be with Abraham.ᵃ The rich man also died and was buried. 23In Hades, where he was being tormented, he looked up and saw Abraham far away with Lazarus by his side.ᵇ 24He called out, 'Father Abraham, have mercy on me, and send Lazarus to dip the tip of his finger in water and cool my tongue; for I am in agony in these flames.' 25But Abraham said, 'Child, remember that during your lifetime you received your good things, and Lazarus in like manner evil things; but now he is comforted here, and you are in agony. 26Besides all this, between you and us a great chasm has been fixed, so that those who might want to pass from here to you cannot do so, and no one can cross from there to us.' 27He said, 'Then, father, I beg you to send him to my father's house— 28for I have five brothers—that he may warn them, so that they will not also come into this place of torment.' 29Abraham replied, 'They have Moses and the prophets; they should listen to them.' 30He said, 'No, father Abraham; but if someone goes to them from the dead, they will repent.' 31He said to him, 'If they do not listen to Moses and the prophets, neither will they be convinced even if someone rises from the dead.' "

17 Some Sayings of Jesus

Jesusᶜ said to his disciples, "Occasions for stumbling are bound to come, but woe to anyone by whom they come! 2It would be better for you if a millstone were hung around your neck and you were thrown into the sea than for you to cause one of these little ones to stumble. 3Be on your guard! If another discipleᵈ sins, you must rebuke the offender, and if there is repentance, you must forgive. 4And if the same person sins against you seven times a day, and turns back to you seven times and says, 'I repent,' you must forgive."

5 The apostles said to the Lord, "Increase our faith!" 6The Lord replied, "If you had faith the size of aᵉ mustard seed, you could say to this mulberry tree, 'Be uprooted and planted in the sea,' and it would obey you.

7 "Who among you would say to your slave who has just come in from plowing or tending sheep in the field, 'Come here at once and take your place at the table'? 8Would you not rather say to him, 'Prepare supper for me, put on your apron and serve me while I eat and drink; later you may eat and drink'? 9Do you thank the slave for doing what was commanded? 10So you also, when you have done all that you were ordered to do, say, 'We are worthless slaves; we have done only what we ought to have done!' "

Jesus Cleanses Ten Lepers

11 On the way to Jerusalem Jesusᶠ was going through the region between Samaria and Galilee. 12As he entered a village, ten lepersᵍ approached him. Keeping their distance, 13they called out, saying, "Jesus, Master, have mercy on us!" 14When he saw them, he said to them,

a Gk to Abraham's bosom b Gk in his bosom c Gk He d Gk your brother e Gk faith as a grain of f Gk he g The terms leper and leprosy can refer to several diseases they say, 'Look, here it is!' or 'There it is!' For, in fact, the kingdom of God is among^c you."

22 Then he said to the disciples, "The days are coming when you will long to see one of the days of the Son of Man, and you will not see it. ²³They will say to you, 'Look there!' or 'Look here!' Do not go, do not set off in pursuit. ²⁴For as the lightning flashes and lights up the sky from one side to the other, so will the Son of Man be in his day.^d ²⁵But first he must endure much suffering and be rejected by this generation. ²⁶Just as it was in the days of Noah, so too it will be in the days of the Son of Man. ²⁷They were eating and drinking, and marrying and being given in marriage, until the day Noah entered the ark, and the flood came and destroyed all of them. ²⁸Likewise, just as it was in the days of Lot: they were eating and drinking, buying and selling, planting and building, ²⁹but on the day that Lot left Sodom, it rained fire and sulfur from heaven and destroyed all of them ³⁰—it will be like that on the day that the Son of Man is revealed. ³¹On that day, anyone on the housetop who has belongings in the house must not come down to take them away; and likewise anyone in the field must not turn back. ³²Remember Lot's wife. ³³Those who try to make their life secure will lose it, but those who lose their life will keep it. ³⁴I tell you, on that night there will be two in one bed; one will be taken and the other left. ³⁵There will be two women grinding meal together; one will be taken and the other left."^e ³⁷Then they asked him, "Where, Lord?" He said to them, "Where the corpse is, there the vultures will gather."

18 The Parable of the Widow and the Unjust Judge

Then Jesus^b told them a parable about their need to pray always and not to lose heart. ²He said, "In a certain city there was a judge who neither feared God nor had respect for people. ³In that city there was a widow who kept coming to him and saying, 'Grant me justice against my opponent.' ⁴For a while he refused; but later he said to himself, 'Though I have no fear of God and no respect for anyone, ⁵yet because this widow keeps bothering me, I will grant her justice, so that she may not wear me out by continually coming.' "^f ⁶And the Lord said, "Listen to what the unjust judge says. ⁷And will not God grant justice to his chosen ones who cry to him day and night? Will he delay long in helping them? ⁸I tell you, he will quickly grant justice to them. And yet, when the Son of Man comes, will he find faith on earth?"

"Go and show yourselves to the priests." And as they went, they were made clean. ¹⁵Then one of them, when he saw that he was healed, turned back, praising God with a loud voice. ¹⁶He prostrated himself at Jesus'^a feet and thanked him. And he was a Samaritan. ¹⁷Then Jesus asked, "Were not ten made clean? But the other nine, where are they? ¹⁸Was none of them found to return and give praise to God except this foreigner?" ¹⁹Then he said to him, "Get up and go on your way; your faith has made you well."

The Coming of the Kingdom

20 Once Jesus^b was asked by the Pharisees when the kingdom of God was coming, and he answered, "The kingdom of God is not coming with things that can be observed; ²¹nor will

a Gk his *b* Gk he *c* Or within *d* Other ancient authorities lack *in his day* *e* Other ancient authorities add verse 36, "Two will be in the field; one will be taken and the other left." *f* Or *so that she may not finally come and slap me in the face*

1246 LIVE new testament

LUKE 18

The Parable of the Pharisee and the Tax Collector

9 He also told this parable to some who trusted in themselves that they were righteous and regarded others with contempt: ¹⁰"Two men went up to the temple to pray, one a Pharisee and the other a tax collector. ¹¹The Pharisee, standing by himself, was praying thus, 'God, I thank you that I am not like other people: thieves, rogues, adulterers, or even like this tax collector. ¹²I fast twice a week; I give a tenth of all my income.' ¹³But the tax collector, standing far off, would not even look up to heaven, but was beating his breast and saying, 'God, be merciful to me, a sinner!' ¹⁴I tell you, this man went down to his home justified rather than the other; for all who exalt themselves will be humbled, but all who humble themselves will be exalted."

Jesus Blesses Little Children

15 People were bringing even infants to him that he might touch them; and when the disciples saw it, they sternly ordered them not to do it. ¹⁶But Jesus called for them and said, "Let the little children come to me, and do not stop them; for it is to such as these that the kingdom of God belongs. ¹⁷Truly I tell you, whoever does not receive the kingdom of God as a little child will never enter it."

The Rich Ruler

18 A certain ruler asked him, "Good Teacher, what must I do to inherit eternal life?" ¹⁹Jesus said to him, "Why do you call me good? No one is good but God alone. ²⁰You know the commandments: 'You shall not commit adultery; You shall not murder; You shall not steal; You shall not bear false witness; Honor your father and mother.' " ²¹He replied, "I have kept all these since my youth." ²²When Jesus heard this, he said to him, "There is still one thing lacking. Sell all that you own and distribute the money*ᵃ* to the poor, and you will have treasure in heaven; then come, follow me." ²³But when he heard this, he became sad; for he was very rich. ²⁴Jesus looked at him and said, "How hard it is for those who have wealth to enter the kingdom of God! ²⁵Indeed, it is easier for a camel to go through the eye of a needle than for someone who is rich to enter the kingdom of God."

26 Those who heard it said, "Then who can be saved?" ²⁷He replied, "What is impossible for mortals is possible for God."

28 Then Peter said, "Look, we have left our homes and followed you." ²⁹And he said to them, "Truly I tell you, there is no one who has left house or wife or brothers or parents or children, for the sake of the kingdom of God, ³⁰who will not get back very much more in this age, and in the age to come eternal life."

A Third Time Jesus Foretells His Death and Resurrection

31 Then he took the twelve aside and said to them, "See, we are going up to Jerusalem, and everything that is written about the Son of Man by the prophets will be accomplished. ³²For he will be handed over to the Gentiles; and he will be mocked and insulted and spat upon. ³³After they have flogged him, they will kill him, and on the third day he will rise again." ³⁴But they understood nothing about all these things; in fact, what he said was hidden from them, and they did not grasp what was said.

Jesus Heals a Blind Beggar Near Jericho

35 As he approached Jericho, a blind man was sitting by the roadside begging. ³⁶When he heard a crowd going by, he asked what was happening. ³⁷They told him, "Jesus of Nazareth*ᵇ* is passing by." ³⁸Then he shouted, "Jesus, Son of David, have mercy on me!" ³⁹Those who were in front sternly ordered him to be quiet; but he shouted even more loudly, "Son of David, have mercy on me!" ⁴⁰Jesus stood still and ordered the man to be brought to him; and when he came near, he asked him, ⁴¹"What do you want me to do for you?" He said, "Lord, let me see again." ⁴²Jesus said to him, "Receive your sight; your faith has saved you." ⁴³Immediately he regained his sight and followed him, glorifying God; and all the people, when they saw it, praised God.

19 Jesus and Zacchaeus

He entered Jericho and was passing through it. ²A man was there named Zacchaeus; he was a chief tax collector and was rich. ³He was trying to see who Jesus was, but on account of the crowd he could not, because he was short in stature. ⁴So he ran ahead and climbed a sycamore tree to see him, because he was going to pass that way. ⁵When Jesus came to the place, he looked up and said to him, "Zacchaeus, hurry and come down; for I must stay at your house today." ⁶So he hurried down and was happy to welcome him. ⁷All who saw it began to grumble and said, "He has gone to be the guest of one who is a sinner." ⁸Zacchaeus stood there and said to the Lord, "Look, half of my possessions, Lord, I will give to the poor; and if I have defrauded anyone of anything, I will pay back

a Gk lacks *the money* *b* Gk *the Nazorean*

having received royal power, he ordered these slaves, to whom he had given the money, to be summoned so that he might find out what they had gained by trading. ¹⁶The first came forward and said, 'Lord, your pound has made ten more pounds.' ¹⁷He said to him, 'Well done, good slave! Because you have been trustworthy in a very small thing, take charge of ten cities.' ¹⁸Then the second came, saying, 'Lord, your pound has made five pounds.' ¹⁹He said to him, 'And you, rule over five cities.' ²⁰Then the other came, saying, 'Lord, here is your pound. I wrapped it up in a piece of cloth, ²¹for I was afraid of you, because you are a harsh man; you take what you did not deposit, and reap what you did not sow.' ²²He said to him, 'I will judge you by your own words, you wicked slave! You knew, did you, that I was a harsh man, taking what I did not deposit and reaping what I did not sow? ²³Why then did you not put my money into the bank? Then when I returned, I could have collected it with interest.' ²⁴He said to the bystanders, 'Take the pound from him and give it to the one who has ten pounds.' ²⁵(And they said to him, 'Lord, he has ten pounds!') ²⁶'I tell you, to all those who have, more will be given; but from those who have nothing, even what they have will be taken away. ²⁷But as for these enemies of mine who did not want me to be king over them—bring them here and slaughter them in my presence.' "

Jesus' Triumphal Entry into Jerusalem

28 After he had said this, he went on ahead, going up to Jerusalem.

29 When he had come near Bethphage and Bethany, at the place called the Mount of Olives, he sent two of the disciples, ³⁰saying, "Go into the village ahead of you, and as you enter it you will find tied there a colt that has never been ridden. Untie it and bring it here. ³¹If anyone asks you, 'Why are you untying it?' just say this, 'The Lord needs it.' " ³²So those who were sent departed and found it as he had told them. ³³As they were untying the colt, its owners asked them, "Why are you untying the colt?" ³⁴They said, "The Lord needs it." ³⁵Then they brought it to Jesus; and after throwing their cloaks on the colt, they set Jesus on it. ³⁶As he rode along, people kept spreading their cloaks on the road. ³⁷As he was now approaching the path down from the Mount of Olives, the whole multitude of the disciples began to praise God joyfully with a loud voice for all the deeds of power that they had seen, ³⁸saying,

"Blessed is the king
who comes in the name of the Lord!

four times as much." ⁹Then Jesus said to him, "Today salvation has come to this house, because he too is a son of Abraham. ¹⁰For the Son of Man came to seek out and to save the lost."

The Parable of the Ten Pounds

11 As they were listening to this, he went on to tell a parable, because he was near Jerusalem, and because they supposed that the kingdom of God was to appear immediately. ¹²So he said, "A nobleman went to a distant country to get royal power for himself and then return. ¹³He summoned ten of his slaves, and gave them ten pounds,ᵃ and said to them, 'Do business with these until I come back.' ¹⁴But the citizens of his country hated him and sent a delegation after him, saying, 'We do not want this man to rule over us.' ¹⁵When he returned,

ᵃ The mina, rendered here by _pound_, was about three months' wages for a laborer

Peace in heaven,
    and glory in the highest heaven!"
³⁹Some of the Pharisees in the crowd said to him, "Teacher, order your disciples to stop." ⁴⁰He answered, "I tell you, if these were silent, the stones would shout out."

Jesus Weeps over Jerusalem

41 As he came near and saw the city, he wept over it, ⁴²saying, "If you, even you, had only recognized on this day the things that make for peace! But now they are hidden from your eyes. ⁴³Indeed, the days will come upon you, when your enemies will set up ramparts around you and surround you, and hem you in on every side. ⁴⁴They will crush you to the ground, you and your children within you, and they will not leave within you one stone upon another; because you did not recognize the time of your visitation from God."ᵃ

Jesus Cleanses the Temple

45 Then he entered the temple and began to drive out those who were selling things there; ⁴⁶and he said, "It is written,
'My house shall be a house of prayer';
    but you have made it a den of robbers."
47 Every day he was teaching in the temple. The chief priests, the scribes, and the leaders of the people kept looking for a way to kill him; ⁴⁸but they did not find anything they could do, for all the people were spellbound by what they heard.

20 The Authority of Jesus Questioned

One day, as he was teaching the people in the temple and telling the good news, the chief priests and the scribes came with the elders ²and said to him, "Tell us, by what authority are you doing these things? Who is it who gave you this authority?" ³He answered them, "I will also ask you a question, and you tell me: ⁴Did the baptism of John come from heaven, or was it of human origin?" ⁵They discussed it with one another, saying, "If we say, 'From heaven,' he will say, 'Why did you not believe him?' ⁶But if we say, 'Of human origin,' all the people will stone us; for they are convinced that John was a prophet." ⁷So they answered that they did not know where it came from. ⁸Then Jesus said to them, "Neither will I tell you by what authority I am doing these things."

The Parable of the Wicked Tenants

9 He began to tell the people this parable: "A man planted a vineyard, and leased it to tenants, and went to another country for a long time. ¹⁰When the season came, he sent a slave to the tenants in order that they might give him his share of the produce of the vineyard; but the tenants beat him and sent him away empty-handed. ¹¹Next he sent another slave; that one also they beat and insulted and sent away empty-handed. ¹²And he sent still a third; this one also they wounded and threw out. ¹³Then the owner of the vineyard said, 'What shall I do? I will send my beloved son; perhaps they will respect him.' ¹⁴But when the tenants saw him, they discussed it among themselves and said, 'This is the heir; let us kill him so that the inheritance may be ours.' ¹⁵So they threw him out of the vineyard and killed him. What then will the owner of the vineyard do to them? ¹⁶He will come and destroy those tenants and give the vineyard to others." When they heard this, they said, "Heaven forbid!" ¹⁷But he looked at them and said, "What then does this text mean:
'The stone that the builders rejected
    has become the cornerstone'?ᵇ
¹⁸Everyone who falls on that stone will be broken to pieces; and it will crush anyone on whom it falls." ¹⁹When the scribes and chief priests realized that he had told this parable against them, they wanted to lay hands on him at that very hour, but they feared the people.

The Question about Paying Taxes

20 So they watched him and sent spies who pretended to be honest, in order to trap him by what he said, so as to hand him over to the jurisdiction and authority of the governor. ²¹So they asked him, "Teacher, we know that you are right in what you say and teach, and you show deference to no one, but teach the way of God in accordance with truth. ²²Is it lawful for us to pay taxes to the emperor, or not?" ²³But he perceived their craftiness and said to them, ²⁴"Show me a denarius. Whose head and whose title does it bear?" They said, "The emperor's." ²⁵He said to them, "Then give to the emperor the things that are the emperor's, and to God the things that are God's." ²⁶And they were not able in the presence of the people to trap him by what he said; and being amazed by his answer, they became silent.

The Question about the Resurrection

27 Some Sadducees, those who say there is no resurrection, came to him ²⁸and asked him a question, "Teacher, Moses wrote for us that if a man's brother dies, leaving a wife but no children, the manᶜ shall marry the widow and raise up children for his brother. ²⁹Now there were seven brothers; the first married, and died

---

a Gk lacks *from God* b Or *keystone* c Gk *his brother*

childless; ³⁰then the second ³¹and the third married her, and so in the same way all seven died childless. ³²Finally the woman also died. ³³In the resurrection, therefore, whose wife will the woman be? For the seven had married her."

34 Jesus said to them, "Those who belong to this age marry and are given in marriage; ³⁵but those who are considered worthy of a place in that age and in the resurrection from the dead neither marry nor are given in marriage. ³⁶Indeed they cannot die anymore, because they are like angels and are children of God, being children of the resurrection. ³⁷And the fact that the dead are raised Moses himself showed, in the story about the bush, where he speaks of the Lord as the God of Abraham, the God of Isaac, and the God of Jacob. ³⁸Now he is God not of the dead, but of the living; for to him all of them are alive." ³⁹Then some of the scribes answered, "Teacher, you have spoken well." ⁴⁰For they no longer dared to ask him another question.

The Question about David's Son

41 Then he said to them, "How can they say that the Messiah*a* is David's son? ⁴²For David himself says in the book of Psalms,

'The Lord said to my Lord,
  "Sit at my right hand,
⁴³   until I make your enemies your
         footstool." '
⁴⁴David thus calls him Lord; so how can he be his son?"

Jesus Denounces the Scribes

45 In the hearing of all the people he said to the*b* disciples, ⁴⁶"Beware of the scribes, who like to walk around in long robes, and love to be greeted with respect in the marketplaces, and to have the best seats in the synagogues and places of honor at banquets. ⁴⁷They devour widows' houses and for the sake of appearance say long prayers. They will receive the greater condemnation."

21 The Widow's Offering

He looked up and saw rich people putting their gifts into the treasury; ²he also saw a poor widow put in two small copper coins. ³He said, "Truly I tell you, this poor widow has put in more than all of them; ⁴for all of them have contributed out of their abundance, but she out of her poverty has put in all she had to live on."

The Destruction of the Temple Foretold

5 When some were speaking about the temple, how it was adorned with beautiful stones and gifts dedicated to God, he said, ⁶"As for these things that you see, the days will come when not one stone will be left upon another; all will be thrown down."

Signs and Persecutions

7 They asked him, "Teacher, when will this be, and what will be the sign that this is about to take place?" ⁸And he said, "Beware that you are not led astray; for many will come in my name and say, 'I am he!'*c* and, 'The time is near!'*d* Do not go after them.

9 "When you hear of wars and insurrections, do not be terrified; for these things must take place first, but the end will not follow immediately." ¹⁰Then he said to them, "Nation will rise against nation, and kingdom against kingdom; ¹¹there will be great earthquakes, and in various places famines and plagues; and there will be dreadful portents and great signs from heaven.

12 "But before all this occurs, they will arrest you and persecute you; they will hand you over to synagogues and prisons, and you will be brought before kings and governors because of my name. ¹³This will give you an opportunity to testify. ¹⁴So make up your minds not to prepare your defense in advance; ¹⁵for I will give you words*e* and a wisdom that none of your opponents will be able to withstand or contradict. ¹⁶You will be betrayed even by parents and brothers, by relatives and friends; and they will put some of you to death. ¹⁷You will be hated by all because of my name. ¹⁸But not a hair of your head will perish. ¹⁹By your endurance you will gain your souls.

The Destruction of Jerusalem Foretold

20 "When you see Jerusalem surrounded by armies, then know that its desolation has come near.*f* ²¹Then those in Judea must flee to the mountains, and those inside the city must leave it, and those out in the country must not enter it; ²²for these are days of vengeance, as a fulfillment of all that is written. ²³Woe to those who are pregnant and to those who are nursing infants in those days! For there will be great distress on the earth and wrath against this people; ²⁴they will fall by the edge of the sword and be taken away as captives among all nations; and Jerusalem will be trampled on by the Gentiles, until the times of the Gentiles are fulfilled.

The Coming of the Son of Man

25 "There will be signs in the sun, the moon, and the stars, and on the earth distress among nations confused by the roaring of the sea and

---

a Or *the Christ* *b* Other ancient authorities read *his* *c* Gk *I am* *d* Or *at hand* *e* Gk *a mouth* *f* Or *is at hand*

His Glory—© Kate Douglas, 17

the waves. ²⁶People will faint from fear and foreboding of what is coming upon the world, for the powers of the heavens will be shaken. ²⁷Then they will see 'the Son of Man coming in a cloud' with power and great glory. ²⁸Now when these things begin to take place, stand up and raise your heads, because your redemption is drawing near."

The Lesson of the Fig Tree

29 Then he told them a parable: "Look at the fig tree and all the trees; ³⁰as soon as they sprout leaves you can see for yourselves and know that summer is already near. ³¹So also, when you see these things taking place, you know that the kingdom of God is near. ³²Truly I tell you, this generation will not pass away until all things have taken place. ³³Heaven and earth will pass away, but my words will not pass away.

Exhortation to Watch

34 "Be on guard so that your hearts are not weighed down with dissipation and drunkenness and the worries of this life, and that day does not catch you unexpectedly, ³⁵like a trap. For it will come upon all who live on the face of the whole earth. ³⁶Be alert at all times, praying that you may have the strength to escape all these things that will take place, and to stand before the Son of Man."

a Gk *him* *b* Gk *he*

37 Every day he was teaching in the temple, and at night he would go out and spend the night on the Mount of Olives, as it was called. ³⁸And all the people would get up early in the morning to listen to him in the temple.

22 The Plot to Kill Jesus

Now the festival of Unleavened Bread, which is called the Passover, was near. ²The chief priests and the scribes were looking for a way to put Jesus*ᵃ* to death, for they were afraid of the people.

3 Then Satan entered into Judas called Iscariot, who was one of the twelve; ⁴he went away and conferred with the chief priests and officers of the temple police about how he might betray him to them. ⁵They were greatly pleased and agreed to give him money. ⁶So he consented and began to look for an opportunity to betray him to them when no crowd was present.

The Preparation of the Passover

7 Then came the day of Unleavened Bread, on which the Passover lamb had to be sacrificed. ⁸So Jesus*ᵇ* sent Peter and John, saying, "Go and prepare the Passover meal for us that we may eat it." ⁹They asked him, "Where do you want us to make preparations for it?" ¹⁰"Listen," he said to them, "when you have entered the city,

Angelo Roncalli is a good example of someone who lived the message of Luke's gospel. He approached prayer and faith more like the tax collector in Luke than the Pharisee. He managed his high office in the Church with humility and humor, and worked to bring the Church closer to the people—and the people closer to the Church.

He became a priest in 1904 and was consecrated as an archbishop in 1925. He spent most of his life as a papal diplomat. In that role he created goodwill everywhere he went.

In 1944 he was chosen by Pius XII for the difficult post of nuncio to Paris, where he worked to heal the divisions caused by World War II. In 1958, at nearly seventy-seven years old, he was elected pope. No one expected him to make any waves, but he astonished the Church and the world with his energy and reforming spirit.

Before Pope John XXIII, when the official Vatican newspaper, the *Osservatore Romano*, quoted any statement by the pope, it had a standard introduction: "These are the words of the Holy Father, as we were able to gather them from his august lips." Under Pope John, this was changed to, "The Pope said." Little changes like this helped to set the tone for the new pontificate. He convened the Second Vatican Council in 1962 to renew the life of the Church.

---

a man carrying a jar of water will meet you; follow him into the house he enters [11]and say to the owner of the house, 'The teacher asks you, "Where is the guest room, where I may eat the Passover with my disciples?" ' [12]He will show you a large room upstairs, already furnished. Make preparations for us there." [13]So they went and found everything as he had told them; and they prepared the Passover meal.

The Institution of the Lord's Supper

14 When the hour came, he took his place at the table, and the apostles with him. [15]He said to them, "I have eagerly desired to eat this Passover with you before I suffer; [16]for I tell you, I will not eat it[a] until it is fulfilled in the kingdom of God." [17]Then he took a cup, and after giving thanks he said, "Take this and divide it among yourselves; [18]for I tell you that from

now on I will not drink of the fruit of the vine until the kingdom of God comes." [19]Then he took a loaf of bread, and when he had given thanks, he broke it and gave it to them, saying, "This is my body, which is given for you. Do this in remembrance of me." [20]And he did the same with the cup after supper, saying, "This cup that is poured out for you is the new covenant in my blood.[b] [21]But see, the one who betrays me is with me, and his hand is on the table. [22]For the Son of Man is going as it has been determined, but woe to that one by whom he is betrayed!" [23]Then they began to ask one another which one of them it could be who would do this.

The Dispute about Greatness

24 A dispute also arose among them as to which one of them was to be regarded as the greatest. [25]But he said to them, "The kings of

---

a Other ancient authorities read *never eat it again*   b Other ancient authorities lack, in whole or in part, verses 19b-20 (*which is given . . . in my blood*) the Gentiles lord it over them; and those in authority over them are called benefactors. 26But not so with you; rather the greatest among you must become like the youngest, and the leader like one who serves. 27For who is greater, the one who is at the table or the one who serves? Is it not the one at the table? But I am among you as one who serves.

28 "You are those who have stood by me in my trials; 29and I confer on you, just as my Father has conferred on me, a kingdom, 30so that you may eat and drink at my table in my kingdom, and you will sit on thrones judging the twelve tribes of Israel.

Jesus Predicts Peter's Denial

31 "Simon, Simon, listen! Satan has demanded*a* to sift all of you like wheat, 32but I have prayed for you that your own faith may not fail; and you, when once you have turned back, strengthen your brothers." 33And he said to him, "Lord, I am ready to go with you to prison and to death!" 34Jesus*b* said, "I tell you, Peter, the cock will not crow this day, until you have denied three times that you know me."

Purse, Bag, and Sword

35 He said to them, "When I sent you out without a purse, bag, or sandals, did you lack anything?" They said, "No, not a thing." 36He said to them, "But now, the one who has a purse must take it, and likewise a bag. And the one who has no sword must sell his cloak and buy one. 37For I tell you, this scripture must be fulfilled in me, 'And he was counted among the lawless'; and indeed what is written about me is being fulfilled." 38They said, "Lord, look, here are two swords." He replied, "It is enough."

Jesus Prays on the Mount of Olives

39 He came out and went, as was his custom, to the Mount of Olives; and the disciples followed him. 40When he reached the place, he said to them, "Pray that you may not come into the time of trial."*c* 41Then he withdrew from them about a stone's throw, knelt down, and prayed, 42"Father, if you are willing, remove this cup from me; yet, not my will but yours be done." ⟦43Then an angel from heaven appeared to him and gave him strength. 44In his anguish he prayed more earnestly, and his sweat became like great drops of blood falling down on the ground.⟧*d* 45When he got up from prayer, he came to the disciples and found them sleeping because of grief, 46and he said to them, "Why are you sleeping? Get up and pray that you may not come into the time of trial."*c*

The Betrayal and Arrest of Jesus

47 While he was still speaking, suddenly a crowd came, and the one called Judas, one of the twelve, was leading them. He approached Jesus to kiss him; 48but Jesus said to him, "Judas, is it with a kiss that you are betraying the Son of Man?" 49When those who were around him saw what was coming, they asked, "Lord, should we strike with the sword?" 50Then one of them struck the slave of the high priest and cut off his right ear. 51But Jesus said, "No more of this!" And he touched his ear and healed him. 52Then Jesus said to the chief priests, the officers of the temple police, and the elders who had come for him, "Have you come out with swords and clubs as if I were a bandit? 53When I was with you day after day in the temple, you did not lay hands on me. But this is your hour, and the power of darkness!"

Peter Denies Jesus

54 Then they seized him and led him away, bringing him into the high priest's house. But Peter was following at a distance. 55When they had kindled a fire in the middle of the courtyard and sat down together, Peter sat among them. 56Then a servant-girl, seeing him in the firelight, stared at him and said, "This man also was with him." 57But he denied it, saying, "Woman, I do not know him." 58A little later someone else, on seeing him, said, "You also are one of them." But Peter said, "Man, I am not!" 59Then about an hour later still another kept insisting, "Surely this man also was with him; for he is a Galilean." 60But Peter said, "Man, I do not know what you are talking about!" At that moment, while he was still speaking, the cock crowed. 61The Lord turned and looked at Peter. Then Peter remembered the word of the Lord, how he had said to him, "Before the cock crows today, you will deny me three times." 62And he went out and wept bitterly.

The Mocking and Beating of Jesus

63 Now the men who were holding Jesus began to mock him and beat him; 64they also blindfolded him and kept asking him, "Prophesy! Who is it that struck you?" 65They kept heaping many other insults on him.

Jesus before the Council

66 When day came, the assembly of the elders of the people, both chief priests and scribes, gathered together, and they brought him to their council. 67They said, "If you are the Messiah,*e* tell us." He replied, "If I tell you, you will not believe; 68and if I question you, you will

---

a Or *has obtained permission* *b* Gk *He* *c* Or *into temptation* *d* Other ancient authorities lack verses 43 and 44 *e* Or *the Christ* not answer. [69]But from now on the Son of Man will be seated at the right hand of the power of God." [70]All of them asked, "Are you, then, the Son of God?" He said to them, "You say that I am." [71]Then they said, "What further testimony do we need? We have heard it ourselves from his own lips!"

23 Jesus before Pilate

Then the assembly rose as a body and brought Jesus[a] before Pilate. [2]They began to accuse him, saying, "We found this man perverting our nation, forbidding us to pay taxes to the emperor, and saying that he himself is the Messiah, a king."[b] [3]Then Pilate asked him, "Are you the king of the Jews?" He answered, "You say so." [4]Then Pilate said to the chief priests and the crowds, "I find no basis for an accusation against this man." [5]But they were insistent and said, "He stirs up the people by teaching throughout all Judea, from Galilee where he began even to this place."

Jesus before Herod

6 When Pilate heard this, he asked whether the man was a Galilean. [7]And when he learned that he was under Herod's jurisdiction, he sent him off to Herod, who was himself in Jerusalem at that time. [8]When Herod saw Jesus, he was very glad, for he had been wanting to see him for a long time, because he had heard about him and was hoping to see him perform some sign. [9]He questioned him at some length, but Jesus[c] gave him no answer. [10]The chief priests and the scribes stood by, vehemently accusing him. [11]Even Herod with his soldiers treated him with contempt and mocked him; then he put an elegant robe on him, and sent him back to Pilate. [12]That same day Herod and Pilate became friends with each other; before this they had been enemies.

Jesus Sentenced to Death

13 Pilate then called together the chief priests, the leaders, and the people, [14]and said to them, "You brought me this man as one who was perverting the people; and here I have examined him in your presence and have not found this man guilty of any of your charges against him. [15]Neither has Herod, for he sent him back to us. Indeed, he has done nothing to deserve death. [16]I will therefore have him flogged and release him."[d]

18 Then they all shouted out together, "Away with this fellow! Release Barabbas for us!" [19](This was a man who had been put in prison for an insurrection that had taken place in the city, and for murder.) [20]Pilate, wanting to release Jesus, addressed them again; [21]but they kept shouting, "Crucify, crucify him!" [22]A third time he said to them, "Why, what evil has he done? I have found in him no ground for the sentence of death; I will therefore have him flogged and then release him." [23]But they kept urgently demanding with loud shouts that he should be crucified; and their voices prevailed. [24]So Pilate gave his verdict that their demand should be granted. [25]He released the man they asked for, the one who had been put in prison for insurrection and murder, and he handed Jesus over as they wished.

The Crucifixion of Jesus

26 As they led him away, they seized a man, Simon of Cyrene, who was coming from the country, and they laid the cross on him, and made him carry it behind Jesus. [27]A great number of the people followed him, and among them were women who were beating their breasts and wailing for him. [28]But Jesus turned to them and said, "Daughters of Jerusalem, do not weep for me, but weep for yourselves and for your children. [29]For the days are surely coming when they will say, 'Blessed are the barren, and the wombs that never bore, and the breasts that never nursed.' [30]Then they will begin to say to the mountains, 'Fall on us'; and to the hills, 'Cover us.' [31]For if they do this when the wood is green, what will happen when it is dry?"

32 Two others also, who were criminals, were led away to be put to death with him. [33]When they came to the place that is called The Skull, they crucified Jesus[g] there with the criminals, one on his right and one on his left. 〚[34]Then Jesus said, "Father, forgive them; for they do not know what they are doing."〛[e] And they cast lots to divide his clothing. [35]And the people stood by, watching; but the leaders scoffed at him, saying, "He saved others; let him save himself if he is the Messiah[f] of God,

> "From the ashes, a fire shall be woken. A light from the shadow shall spring. Renewed shall be blade that was broken. The crownless again shall be king."
>
> —Arwen, in J. R. R. Tolkien, *The Lord of the Rings: The Return of the King*

a Gk him b Or is an anointed king c Gk he d Here, or after verse 19, other ancient authorities add verse 17, Now he was obliged to release someone for them at the festival e Other ancient authorities lack the sentence Then Jesus . . . what they are doing f Or the Christ his chosen one!" ³⁶The soldiers also mocked him, coming up and offering him sour wine, ³⁷and saying, "If you are the King of the Jews, save yourself!" ³⁸There was also an inscription over him,*a* "This is the King of the Jews."

39 One of the criminals who were hanged there kept deriding*b* him and saying, "Are you not the Messiah?*c* Save yourself and us!" ⁴⁰But the other rebuked him, saying, "Do you not fear God, since you are under the same sentence of condemnation? ⁴¹And we indeed have been condemned justly, for we are getting what we deserve for our deeds, but this man has done nothing wrong." ⁴²Then he said, "Jesus, remember me when you come into*d* your kingdom." ⁴³He replied, "Truly I tell you, today you will be with me in Paradise."

The Death of Jesus

44 It was now about noon, and darkness came over the whole land*e* until three in the afternoon, ⁴⁵while the sun's light failed;*f* and the curtain of the temple was torn in two. ⁴⁶Then Jesus, crying with a loud voice, said, "Father, into your hands I commend my spirit." Having said this, he breathed his last. ⁴⁷When the centurion saw what had taken place, he praised God and said, "Certainly this man was innocent."*g* ⁴⁸And when all the crowds who had gathered there for this spectacle saw what had taken place, they returned home, beating their breasts. ⁴⁹But all his acquaintances, including the women who had followed him from Galilee, stood at a distance, watching these things.

The Burial of Jesus

50 Now there was a good and righteous man named Joseph, who, though a member of the council, ⁵¹had not agreed to their plan and action. He came from the Jewish town of Arimathea, and he was waiting expectantly for the kingdom of God. ⁵²This man went to Pilate and asked for the body of Jesus. ⁵³Then he took it down, wrapped it in a linen cloth, and laid it in a rock-hewn tomb where no one had ever been laid. ⁵⁴It was the day of Preparation, and the sabbath was beginning.*h* ⁵⁵The women who had come with him from Galilee followed, and they saw the tomb and how his body was laid. ⁵⁶Then they returned, and prepared spices and ointments.

On the sabbath they rested according to the commandment.

24 The Resurrection of Jesus

But on the first day of the week, at early dawn, they came to the tomb, taking the spices that they had prepared. ²They found the stone rolled away from the tomb, ³but when they went in, they did not find the body.*i* ⁴While they were perplexed about this, suddenly two men in dazzling clothes stood beside them. ⁵The women*j* were terrified and bowed their faces to the ground, but the men*k* said to them, "Why do you look for the living among the dead? He is not here, but has risen.*l* ⁶Remember how he told you, while he was still in Galilee, ⁷that the Son of Man must be handed over to sinners, and be crucified, and on the third day rise again." ⁸Then they remembered his words, ⁹and returning from the tomb, they told all this to the eleven and to all the rest. ¹⁰Now it was Mary Magdalene, Joanna, Mary the mother of James, and the other women with them who told this to the apostles. ¹¹But these words seemed to them an idle tale, and they did not believe them. ¹²But Peter got up and ran to the tomb; stooping and looking in, he saw the linen cloths by themselves; then he went home, amazed at what had happened.*m*

The Walk to Emmaus

13 Now on that same day two of them were going to a village called Emmaus, about seven miles*n* from Jerusalem, ¹⁴and talking with each other about all these things that had happened. ¹⁵While they were talking and discussing, Jesus himself came near and went with them, ¹⁶but their eyes were kept from recognizing him. ¹⁷And he said to them, "What are you discussing with each other while you walk along?" They stood still, looking sad.*o* ¹⁸Then one of them, whose name was Cleopas, answered him, "Are you the only stranger in Jerusalem who does not know the things that have taken place there in these days?" ¹⁹He asked them, "What things?" They replied, "The things about Jesus of Nazareth,*p* who was a prophet mighty in deed and word before God and all the people, ²⁰and how our chief priests and leaders handed him over to be condemned to death and crucified him. ²¹But we had hoped that he was the one to redeem Israel.*q* Yes, and besides all this, it is now the third day since these things took place. ²²Moreover, some women of our group astounded us. They were at the tomb early this morning, ²³and when

a Other ancient authorities add *written in Greek and Latin and Hebrew* (that is, *Aramaic*) *b* Or *blaspheming* *c* Or *the Christ* *d* Other ancient authorities read *in* *e* Or *earth* *f* Or *the sun was eclipsed.* Other ancient authorities read *the sun was darkened* *g* Or *righteous* *h* Gk *was dawning* *i* Other ancient authorities add *of the Lord Jesus* *j* Gk *They* *k* Gk *but they* *l* Other ancient authorities lack *He is not here, but has risen* *m* Other ancient authorities lack verse 12 *n* Gk *sixty stadia*; other ancient authorities read *a hundred sixty stadia* *o* Other ancient authorities read *walk along, looking sad?"* *p* Other ancient authorities read *Jesus the Nazorean* *q* Or *to set Israel free* they did not find his body there, they came back and told us that they had indeed seen a vision of angels who said that he was alive. ²⁴Some of those who were with us went to the tomb and found it just as the women had said; but they did not see him." ²⁵Then he said to them, "Oh, how foolish you are, and how slow of heart to believe all that the prophets have declared! ²⁶Was it not necessary that the Messiah*ᵃ should suffer these things and then enter into his glory?" ²⁷Then beginning with Moses and all the prophets, he interpreted to them the things about himself in all the scriptures.

28 As they came near the village to which they were going, he walked ahead as if he were going on. ²⁹But they urged him strongly, saying, "Stay with us, because it is almost evening and the day is now nearly over." So he went in to stay with them. ³⁰When he was at the table with them, he took bread, blessed and broke it, and gave it to them. ³¹Then their eyes were opened, and they recognized him; and he vanished from their sight. ³²They said to each other, "Were not our hearts burning within us*ᵇ while he was talking to us on the road, while he was opening the scriptures to us?" ³³That same hour they got up and returned to Jerusalem; and they found the eleven and their companions gathered together. ³⁴They were saying, "The Lord has risen indeed, and he has appeared to Simon!" ³⁵Then they told what had happened on the road, and how he had been made known to them in the breaking of the bread.

Jesus Appears to His Disciples

36 While they were talking about this, Jesus himself stood among them and said to them, "Peace be with you."*ᶜ ³⁷They were startled and terrified, and thought that they were seeing a ghost. ³⁸He said to them, "Why are you frightened, and why do doubts arise in your hearts? ³⁹Look at my hands and my feet; see that it is I myself. Touch me and see; for a ghost does not have flesh and bones as you see that I have." ⁴⁰And when he had said this, he showed them his hands and his feet.*ᵈ ⁴¹While in their joy

they were disbelieving and still wondering, he said to them, "Have you anything here to eat?" ⁴²They gave him a piece of broiled fish, ⁴³and he took it and ate in their presence.

44 Then he said to them, "These are my words that I spoke to you while I was still with you—that everything written about me in the law of Moses, the prophets, and the psalms must be fulfilled." ⁴⁵Then he opened their minds to understand the scriptures, ⁴⁶and he said to them, "Thus it is written, that the Messiah*ᵃ is to suffer and to rise from the dead on the third day, ⁴⁷and that repentance and forgiveness of sins is to be proclaimed in his name to all nations, beginning from Jerusalem. ⁴⁸You are witnesses*ᵉ of these things. ⁴⁹And see, I am sending upon you what my Father promised; so stay here in the city until you have been clothed with power from on high."

The Ascension of Jesus

50 Then he led them out as far as Bethany, and, lifting up his hands, he blessed them. ⁵¹While he was blessing them, he withdrew from them and was carried up into heaven.*ᶠ ⁵²And they worshiped him, and*ᵍ returned to Jerusalem with great joy; ⁵³and they were continually in the temple blessing God.*ʰ

Untitled—© Justin Celedonia, 18

a Or *the Christ* b Other ancient authorities lack *within us*
c Other ancient authorities lack *and said to them, "Peace be with you."* d Other ancient authorities lack verse 40 e Or *nations. Beginning from Jerusalem* ⁴⁸*you are witnesses* f Other ancient authorities lack *and was carried up into heaven* g Other ancient authorities lack *worshiped him, and* h Other ancient authorities add *Amen*

JOHN

GOD'S PERSISTENT LOVE FOR THE WORLD

Reimagining Jesus

From the first few words, John stands apart from the other three gospels. The author skips the birth story—the manger, the shepherds, the star. John doesn't start with pregnant women or wise men. Instead, he takes us even further back, to the creation of the world, and artistically describes how it all came to be through the power of God: "In the beginning was the Word, and the Word was with God, and the Word was God. . . . In him was life, and the life was the light of all people" (John 1.1, 4). But the picture painted by the author of this gospel is not what we might expect God to look or act like. Turning water into wine at a party, talking with women who sleep around, and saying things that might sound crazy like, "I am the bread of life" (6.35), aren't what many of us imagine when we think of someone who has the banner "Creator of the Universe" on his Web page.

But *should* it be?

Stereotypes or religious ideas about Jesus are broken into bits and pieces when we read John. Jesus isn't a boring guy. His teachings are mysterious, compelling, and sometimes uncomfortable and challenging. He's shocking and scandalous, always willing to stand up for those without a voice. But Jesus isn't just a social critic; he came to give us a rich and satisfying life (see 10.10) by giving up *his* life for us. We live this satisfying new life as baptized followers of Jesus when we live as he did and believe Jesus is who he said he is—God's own Son.

"The more rain falls on the earth, the softer it makes it; similarly, Christ's holy name gladdens the earth of our heart the more we call upon it."

—St. Hesychois the Priest

WHO There was more than one writer of this gospel, and they were probably followers of John, the Beloved Apostle.

WHAT This book presents Jesus differently than the other gospels do: he is divine, the Son of God, peaceful and powerful.

WHEN Written sometime between A.D. 90 and 100

WHERE A non-Palestinian setting, perhaps Ephesus (modern-day Turkey) or Alexandria

PATH OF DISCIPLESHIP

Have you ever gone camping at a big campground with tons of other campers? You instantly become one of them—no matter who you are. When you pitch your tent, you are a camper just like everyone else.

The beautiful hymn of praise that opens this gospel tells us that God pitches his tent among his people in a new and totally unique way in Jesus. That says something marvelous about being a human being. In Christ we see our God made visible in the man from Bethlehem and Nazareth. It is important to hang on to the reality that Jesus was God among us. What Jesus did and said were God's words and deeds—and he said them and did them as a total human being . . . just like us . . . except that he was without sin!

We have a choice. We can choose not to recognize or receive God among us. But if we do make that choice, then we lose the promise of John's gospel: "But to all who received him, who believed in his name, he gave power to become children of God" (John 1.12). It is that power that makes us disciples.

1 The Word Became Flesh

In the beginning was the Word, and the Word was with God, and the Word was God. [2]He was in the beginning with God. [3]All things came into being through him, and without him not one thing came into being. What has come into being [4]in him was life,[a] and the life was the light of all people. [5]The light shines in the darkness, and the darkness did not overcome it.

6 There was a man sent from God, whose name was John. [7]He came as a witness to testify to the light, so that all might believe through him. [8]He himself was not the light, but he came to testify to the light. [9]The true light, which enlightens everyone, was coming into the world.[b]

10 He was in the world, and the world came into being through him; yet the world did not know him. [11]He came to what was his own,[c] and his own people did not accept him. [12]But to all who received him, who believed in his name, he gave power to become children of God, [13]who were born, not of blood or of the will of the flesh or of the will of man, but of God.

14 And the Word became flesh and lived among us, and we have seen his glory, the glory as of a father's only son,[d] full of grace and truth. [15](John testified to him and cried out, "This was he of whom I said, 'He who comes after me ranks ahead of me because he was before me.' ") [16]From his fullness we have all received, grace upon grace. [17]The law indeed was given through Moses; grace and truth came through Jesus Christ. [18]No one has ever seen God. It is God the only Son,[e] who is close to the Father's heart,[f] who has made him known.

The Testimony of John the Baptist

19 This is the testimony given by John when the Jews sent priests and Levites from Jerusalem to ask him, "Who are you?" [20]He confessed and did not deny it, but confessed, "I am not the Messiah."[g] [21]And they asked him, "What then? Are you Elijah?" He said, "I am not." "Are you the prophet?" He answered, "No." [22]Then they said to him, "Who are you? Let us have an answer for those who sent us. What do you say about yourself?" [23]He said,

"I am the voice of one crying out in the
    wilderness,
'Make straight the way of the Lord,' "
as the prophet Isaiah said.

24 Now they had been sent from the Pharisees. [25]They asked him, "Why then are you baptizing if you are neither the Messiah,[g] nor Elijah, nor the prophet?" [26]John answered them, "I baptize with water. Among you stands one whom you do not know, [27]the one who is coming after me; I am not worthy to untie the thong of his sandal." [28]This took place in Bethany across the Jordan where John was baptizing.

The Lamb of God

29 The next day he saw Jesus coming toward him and declared, "Here is the Lamb of God who takes away the sin of the world! [30]This is he of whom I said, 'After me comes a man who ranks ahead of me because he was before me.' [31]I myself did not know him; but I came baptizing with water for this reason, that he might be revealed to Israel." [32]And John testified, "I saw the Spirit descending from heaven like a dove, and it remained on him. [33]I myself did not know him, but the one who sent me to baptize with water said to me, 'He on whom you see the Spirit descend and remain is the one who baptizes with the Holy Spirit.' [34]And I myself have seen and have testified that this is the Son of God."[h]

The First Disciples of Jesus

35 The next day John again was standing with two of his disciples, [36]and as he watched Jesus walk by, he exclaimed, "Look, here is the Lamb of God!" [37]The two disciples heard him say this, and they followed Jesus. [38]When Jesus turned and saw them following, he said to them, "What are you looking for?" They said to him, "Rabbi" (which translated means Teacher), "where are you staying?" [39]He said to them, "Come and see." They came and saw where he was staying, and they remained with him that day. It was about four o'clock in the afternoon. [40]One of the two who heard John speak and followed him was Andrew, Simon Peter's brother. [41]He first found his brother Simon and said to him, "We have found the Messiah" (which is translated Anointed[i]). [42]He brought Simon[j] to Jesus, who looked at him and said, "You are Simon son of John. You are to be called Cephas" (which is translated Peter[k]).

Jesus Calls Philip and Nathanael

43 The next day Jesus decided to go to Galilee. He found Philip and said to him, "Follow me." [44]Now Philip was from Bethsaida,

a Or [3]through him. And without him not one thing came into being that has come into being. [4]In him was life b Or He was the true light that enlightens everyone coming into the world c Or to his own home d Or the Father's only Son e Other ancient authorities read It is an only Son, God, or It is the only Son f Gk bosom g Or the Christ h Other ancient authorities read is God's chosen one i Or Christ j Gk him k From the word for rock in Aramaic (kepha) and Greek (petra), respectively

Believe—© Chrissy Riling, 16

the city of Andrew and Peter. [45]Philip found Nathanael and said to him, "We have found him about whom Moses in the law and also the prophets wrote, Jesus son of Joseph from Nazareth." [46]Nathanael said to him, "Can anything good come out of Nazareth?" Philip said to him, "Come and see." [47]When Jesus saw Nathanael coming toward him, he said of him, "Here is truly an Israelite in whom there is no deceit!" [48]Nathanael asked him, "Where did you get to know me?" Jesus answered, "I saw you under the fig tree before Philip called you." [49]Nathanael replied, "Rabbi, you are the Son of God! You are the King of Israel!" [50]Jesus answered, "Do you believe because I told you that I saw you under the fig tree? You will see greater things than these." [51]And he said to him, "Very truly, I tell you,*a* you will see heaven opened and the angels of God ascending and descending upon the Son of Man."

2 The Wedding at Cana

On the third day there was a wedding in Cana of Galilee, and the mother of Jesus was there. [2]Jesus and his disciples had also been invited to the wedding. [3]When the wine gave out, the mother of Jesus said to him, "They have no wine." [4]And Jesus said to her, "Woman, what concern is that to you and to me? My hour has not yet come." [5]His mother said to the servants, "Do whatever he tells you." [6]Now standing there were six stone water jars for the Jewish rites of purification, each holding twenty or thirty gallons. [7]Jesus said to them, "Fill the jars with water." And they filled them up to the brim. [8]He said to them, "Now draw some out, and take it to the chief steward." So they took it. [9]When the steward tasted the water that had become wine, and did not know where it came from (though the servants who had drawn the water knew), the steward called the bridegroom [10]and said to him, "Everyone serves the good wine first, and then the inferior wine after the guests have become drunk. But you have kept the good wine until now." [11]Jesus did this, the first of his signs, in Cana of Galilee, and revealed his glory; and his disciples believed in him.

12 After this he went down to Capernaum with his mother, his brothers, and his disciples; and they remained there a few days.

Jesus Cleanses the Temple

13 The Passover of the Jews was near, and Jesus went up to Jerusalem. [14]In the temple he found people selling cattle, sheep, and doves, and the money changers seated at their tables. [15]Making a whip of cords, he drove all of them out of the temple, both the sheep and the cattle. He also poured out the coins of the money

a Both instances of the Greek word for *you* in this verse are plural

The Banner Guy

If you're watching sports on TV, every so often you'll notice some slightly embarrassing Christian in the stands. He or she is holding up some sort of enormous banner, totally blocking the view of the people nearby. Spray-painted on the banner in huge neon letters is the reference **John 3.16**.

It's the same verse that appears on bumper stickers, T-shirts, and greeting cards. It's the verse Jesus followers often point to in order to sum up the Bible's message. In a way, it's become a "banner."

When Jesus spoke the words we now know as **John 3.16**, he was having a late-night conversation with a religious leader named Nicodemus. Nicodemus had lots of questions about who Jesus really was, but instead of answering them directly, Jesus summed up the most important truth of the universe in a single sentence. Read **John 3.16**.

According to Jesus, God isn't a distant cosmic presence, a cruel force of nature, or a cold impersonal deity. *God loves this world so much . . .*

When we let this reality seep into our hearts, it changes everything. It gives us a purpose for waking up each morning. It gives us a sense of who we are and why we matter. It gives us a perspective on how God feels about all the other people on this planet.

Imagine you had a banner, a sign on your life that you held up for all to see. What would it say? What would you want to tell others about God's love? Jot down your thoughts here:

changers and overturned their tables. [16]He told those who were selling the doves, "Take these things out of here! Stop making my Father's house a marketplace!" [17]His disciples remembered that it was written, "Zeal for your house will consume me." [18]The Jews then said to him, "What sign can you show us for doing this?" [19]Jesus answered them, "Destroy this temple, and in three days I will raise it up." [20]The Jews then said, "This temple has been under construction for forty-six years, and will you raise it up in three days?" [21]But he was speaking of the temple of his body. [22]After he was raised from the dead, his disciples remembered that he had said this; and they believed the scripture and the word that Jesus had spoken.

23 When he was in Jerusalem during the Passover festival, many believed in his name because they saw the signs that he was doing. [24]But Jesus on his part would not entrust himself to them, because he knew all people [25]and needed no one to testify about anyone; for he himself knew what was in everyone.

3 Nicodemus Visits Jesus

Now there was a Pharisee named Nicodemus, a leader of the Jews. [2]He came to Jesus[a] by night and said to him, "Rabbi, we know that you are a teacher who has come from God; for no one can do these signs that you do apart from the presence of God." [3]Jesus answered him, "Very truly, I tell you, no one can see the kingdom of God without being born from above."[b] [4]Nicodemus said to him, "How can anyone be born after having grown old? Can one enter a second time into the mother's womb and be born?" [5]Jesus answered, "Very truly, I tell you, no one can enter the kingdom of God without being born of water and Spirit. [6]What is born of the flesh is flesh, and what is born of the Spirit is spirit.[c] [7]Do not be astonished that I said to you, 'You[d] must be born from above.'[e] [8]The wind[c] blows where it chooses, and you hear the sound of it, but you do not know where it comes from or where it goes. So it is with everyone who is born of the Spirit." [9]Nicodemus said to him, "How can these things be?" [10]Jesus answered him, "Are you a teacher of Israel, and yet you do not understand these things?

11 "Very truly, I tell you, we speak of what we know and testify to what we have seen; yet you[f] do not receive our testimony. [12]If I have told you about earthly things and you do not believe, how can you believe if I tell you about heavenly things? [13]No one has ascended into

---

a Gk *him* b Or *born anew* c The same Greek word means both *wind* and *spirit* d The Greek word for *you* here is plural e Or *anew* f The Greek word for *you* here and in verse 12 is plural heaven except the one who descended from heaven, the Son of Man.[a] [14]And just as Moses lifted up the serpent in the wilderness, so must the Son of Man be lifted up, [15]that whoever believes in him may have eternal life.[b]

[16] "For God so loved the world that he gave his only Son, so that everyone who believes in him may not perish but may have eternal life.

[17] "Indeed, God did not send the Son into the world to condemn the world, but in order that the world might be saved through him. [18]Those who believe in him are not condemned; but those who do not believe are condemned already, because they have not believed in the name of the only Son of God. [19]And this is the judgment, that the light has come into the world, and people loved darkness rather than light because their deeds were evil. [20]For all who do evil hate the light and do not come to the light, so that their deeds may not be exposed. [21]But those who do what is true come to the light, so that it may be clearly seen that their deeds have been done in God."[b]

Jesus and John the Baptist

[22] After this Jesus and his disciples went into the Judean countryside, and he spent some time there with them and baptized. [23]John also was baptizing at Aenon near Salim because water was abundant there; and people kept coming and were being baptized [24]—John, of course, had not yet been thrown into prison.

[25] Now a discussion about purification arose between John's disciples and a Jew.[c] [26]They came to John and said to him, "Rabbi, the one who was with you across the Jordan, to whom you testified, here he is baptizing, and all are going to him." [27]John answered, "No one can receive anything except what has been given from heaven. [28]You yourselves are my witnesses that I said, 'I am not the Messiah,[d] but I have been sent ahead of him.' [29]He who has the bride is the bridegroom. The friend of the bridegroom, who stands and hears him, rejoices greatly at the bridegroom's voice. For this reason my joy has been fulfilled. [30]He must increase, but I must decrease."[e]

The One Who Comes from Heaven

[31] The one who comes from above is above all; the one who is of the earth belongs to the earth and speaks about earthly things. The one who comes from heaven is above all. [32]He testifies to what he has seen and heard, yet no one accepts his testimony. [33]Whoever has accept-

ed his testimony has certified[f] this, that God is true. [34]He whom God has sent speaks the words of God, for he gives the Spirit without measure. [35]The Father loves the Son and has placed all things in his hands. [36]Whoever believes in the Son has eternal life; whoever disobeys the Son will not see life, but must endure God's wrath.

4 Jesus and the Woman of Samaria

Now when Jesus[g] learned that the Pharisees had heard, "Jesus is making and baptizing more disciples than John" [2]—although it was not Jesus himself but his disciples who baptized— [3]he left Judea and started back to Galilee. [4]But he had to go through Samaria. [5]So he came to a Samaritan city called Sychar, near the plot of ground that Jacob had given to his son Joseph. [6]Jacob's well was there, and Jesus, tired out by his journey, was sitting by the well. It was about noon.

[7] A Samaritan woman came to draw water, and Jesus said to her, "Give me a drink." [8](His disciples had gone to the city to buy food.) [9]The Samaritan woman said to him, "How is it that you, a Jew, ask a drink of me, a woman of Samaria?" (Jews do not share things in common with Samaritans.)[h] [10]Jesus answered her, "If you knew the gift of God, and who it is that is saying to you, 'Give me a drink,' you would have asked him, and he would have given you living water." [11]The woman said to him, "Sir, you have no bucket, and the well is deep. Where do you get that living water? [12]Are you greater than our ancestor Jacob, who gave us the well, and with his sons and his flocks drank from it?" [13]Jesus said to her, "Everyone who drinks of this water will be thirsty again, [14]but those who drink of the water that I will give them will never be thirsty. The water that I will give will become in them a spring of water gushing up to eternal life." [15]The woman said to him, "Sir, give me this water, so that I may never be thirsty or have to keep coming here to draw water."

[16] Jesus said to her, "Go, call your husband, and come back." [17]The woman answered him, "I have no husband." Jesus said to her, "You are right in saying, 'I have no husband'; [18]for you have had five husbands, and the one you have now is not your husband. What you have said is true!" [19]The woman said to him, "Sir, I see that you are a prophet. [20]Our ancestors worshiped on this mountain, but you[i] say that the place where people must worship is in Jerusa-

---

a Other ancient authorities add *who is in heaven* b Some interpreters hold that the quotation concludes with verse 15 c Other ancient authorities read *the Jews* d Or *the Christ* e Some interpreters hold that the quotation continues through verse 36 f Gk *set a seal to* g Other ancient authorities read *the Lord* h Other ancient authorities lack this sentence i The Greek word for *you* here and in verses 21 and 22 is plural

REALITY ✔

PERSIST IN THE DIALOGUE

Read **John 4.1–30**. The unnamed Samaritan woman at the well did what Jesus' own disciples were reluctant or afraid to do: she boldly held up her end of the conversation with Jesus. They had an extended discussion—and it got pretty personal!

When the disciples returned to the well after buying provisions in the village, they noticed that their master was speaking to this Samaritan woman. Alone. And unescorted. This violated the social norms of the day, especially since she wasn't even Jewish. She was a "heretical" Samaritan in the disciples' eyes!

Yet do any of the disciples engage Jesus in discussion? Nope. They didn't have the nerve to ask Jesus why he was talking to this woman. Yet the Samaritan woman was *not* silent. She did what a good disciple should do—she asked questions and engaged Jesus in conversation to further her understanding of his teaching. It's not surprising that when the woman hurried back to the village, the other Samaritans began to believe in Jesus because of her testimony.

How often do *you* engage in dialogue with Jesus?

What are the *real* issues in your life? Find some Creative Space in this Bible and list them there. Then go off to a quiet place and engage in a dialogue with Jesus about one of them. Listen. Talk. Listen. And be open to how Jesus speaks to you in your heart.

lem." ²¹Jesus said to her, "Woman, believe me, the hour is coming when you will worship the Father neither on this mountain nor in Jerusalem. ²²You worship what you do not know; we worship what we know, for salvation is from the Jews. ²³But the hour is coming, and is now here, when the true worshipers will worship the Father in spirit and truth, for the Father seeks such as these to worship him. ²⁴God is spirit, and those who worship him must worship in spirit and truth." ²⁵The woman said to him, "I know that Messiah is coming" (who is called Christ). "When he comes, he will proclaim all things to us." ²⁶Jesus said to her, "I am he,ᵃ the one who is speaking to you."

27 Just then his disciples came. They were astonished that he was speaking with a woman, but no one said, "What do you want?" or, "Why are you speaking with her?" ²⁸Then the woman left her water jar and went back to the city. She said to the people, ²⁹"Come and see a man who told me everything I have ever done! He cannot be the Messiah,ᵇ can he?" ³⁰They left the city and were on their way to him.

31 Meanwhile the disciples were urging him, "Rabbi, eat something." ³²But he said to them, "I have food to eat that you do not know about." ³³So the disciples said to one another, "Surely no one has brought him something to eat?" ³⁴Jesus said to them, "My food is to do the will of him who sent me and to complete his work. ³⁵Do you not say, 'Four months more, then comes the harvest'? But I tell you, look around you, and see how the fields are ripe for harvesting. ³⁶The reaper is already receivingᶜ wages and is gathering fruit for eternal life, so that sower and reaper may rejoice together. ³⁷For here the saying holds true, 'One sows and another reaps.' ³⁸I sent you to reap that for which you did not labor. Others have labored, and you have entered into their labor."

39 Many Samaritans from that city believed in him because of the woman's testimony, "He told me everything I have ever done." ⁴⁰So when the Samaritans came to him, they asked him to stay with them; and he stayed there two days. ⁴¹And many more believed because of his word. ⁴²They said to the woman, "It is no longer because of what you said that we believe, for we have heard for ourselves, and we know that this is truly the Savior of the world."

Jesus Returns to Galilee

43 When the two days were over, he went from that place to Galilee ⁴⁴(for Jesus himself had testified that a prophet has no honor in the prophet's own country). ⁴⁵When he came to Galilee, the Galileans welcomed him, since they had seen all that he had done in Jerusalem at the festival; for they too had gone to the festival.

Jesus Heals an Official's Son

46 Then he came again to Cana in Galilee where he had changed the water into wine.

ᵃ Gk I am ᵇ Or the Christ ᶜ Or ³⁵. . . the fields are already ripe for harvesting. ³⁶The reaper is receiving

Now there was a royal official whose son lay ill in Capernaum. [47]When he heard that Jesus had come from Judea to Galilee, he went and begged him to come down and heal his son, for he was at the point of death. [48]Then Jesus said to him, "Unless you[a] see signs and wonders you will not believe." [49]The official said to him, "Sir, come down before my little boy dies." [50]Jesus said to him, "Go; your son will live." The man believed the word that Jesus spoke to him and started on his way. [51]As he was going down, his slaves met him and told him that his child was alive. [52]So he asked them the hour when he began to recover, and they said to him, "Yesterday at one in the afternoon the fever left him." [53]The father realized that this was the hour when Jesus had said to him, "Your son will live." So he himself believed, along with his whole household. [54]Now this was the second sign that Jesus did after coming from Judea to Galilee.

5 Jesus Heals on the Sabbath

After this there was a festival of the Jews, and Jesus went up to Jerusalem.

[2] Now in Jerusalem by the Sheep Gate there is a pool, called in Hebrew[b] Beth-zatha,[c] which has five porticoes. [3]In these lay many invalids—blind, lame, and paralyzed.[d] [5]One man was there who had been ill for thirty-eight years. [6]When Jesus saw him lying there and knew that he had been there a long time, he said to him, "Do you want to be made well?" [7]The sick man answered him, "Sir, I have no one to put me into the pool when the water is stirred up; and while I am making my way, someone else steps down ahead of me." [8]Jesus said to him, "Stand up, take your mat and walk." [9]At once the man was made well, and he took up his mat and began to walk.

Now that day was a sabbath. [10]So the Jews said to the man who had been cured, "It is the sabbath; it is not lawful for you to carry your mat." [11]But he answered them, "The man who made me well said to me, 'Take up your mat and walk.' " [12]They asked him, "Who is the man who said to you, 'Take it up and walk'?" [13]Now the man who had been healed did not know who it was, for Jesus had disappeared in[e] the crowd that was there. [14]Later Jesus found him in the temple and said to him, "See, you have been made well! Do not sin any more, so that nothing worse happens to you." [15]The man went away and told the Jews that it was Jesus who had made him well. [16]Therefore the

> "If only we could be a bit more like Him, the world would be transformed."
>
> —Bono, of the band U2

Jews started persecuting Jesus, because he was doing such things on the sabbath. [17]But Jesus answered them, "My Father is still working, and I also am working." [18]For this reason the Jews were seeking all the more to kill him, because he was not only breaking the sabbath, but was also calling God his own Father, thereby making himself equal to God.

The Authority of the Son

[19] Jesus said to them, "Very truly, I tell you, the Son can do nothing on his own, but only what he sees the Father doing; for whatever the Father[f] does, the Son does likewise. [20]The Father loves the Son and shows him all that he himself is doing; and he will show him greater works than these, so that you will be astonished. [21]Indeed, just as the Father raises the dead and gives them life, so also the Son gives life to whomever he wishes. [22]The Father judges no one but has given all judgment to the Son, [23]so that all may honor the Son just as they honor the Father. Anyone who does not honor the Son does not honor the Father who sent him. [24]Very truly, I tell you, anyone who hears my word and believes him who sent me has eternal life, and does not come under judgment, but has passed from death to life.

[25] "Very truly, I tell you, the hour is coming, and is now here, when the dead will hear the voice of the Son of God, and those who hear will live. [26]For just as the Father has life in himself, so he has granted the Son also to have life in himself; [27]and he has given him authority to execute judgment, because he is the Son of Man. [28]Do not be astonished at this; for the hour is coming when all who are in their graves will hear his voice [29]and will come out—those who have done good, to the resurrection of life, and those who have done evil, to the resurrection of condemnation.

Witnesses to Jesus

[30] "I can do nothing on my own. As I hear, I judge; and my judgment is just, because I seek to do not my own will but the will of him who sent me.

a Both instances of the Greek word for *you* in this verse are plural b That is, *Aramaic* c Other ancient authorities read *Bethesda*, others *Bethsaida* d Other ancient authorities add, wholly or in part, *waiting for the stirring of the water;* [4]*for an angel of the Lord went down at certain seasons into the pool, and stirred up the water; whoever stepped in first after the stirring of the water was made well from whatever disease that person had.* e Or *had left because of* f Gk *that one*

There were three types of bread in Jesus' day: small loaves (sort of like our biscuits), round loaves (about the size of basketballs), and flat loaves (large, breadlike pancakes). The boy who gave loaves to Jesus gave the first type (John 6.9). His were made from barley, indicating he was probably poor.

Fact

This information has been scanned and is free of all known viruses. Please forward to all your friends.

31 "If I testify about myself, my testimony is not true. ³²There is another who testifies on my behalf, and I know that his testimony to me is true. ³³You sent messengers to John, and he testified to the truth. ³⁴Not that I accept such human testimony, but I say these things so that you may be saved. ³⁵He was a burning and shining lamp, and you were willing to rejoice for a while in his light. ³⁶But I have a testimony greater than John's. The works that the Father has given me to complete, the very works that I am doing, testify on my behalf that the Father has sent me. ³⁷And the Father who sent me has himself testified on my behalf. You have never heard his voice or seen his form, ³⁸and you do not have his word abiding in you, because you do not believe him whom he has sent.

39 "You search the scriptures because you think that in them you have eternal life; and it is they that testify on my behalf. ⁴⁰Yet you refuse to come to me to have life. ⁴¹I do not accept glory from human beings. ⁴²But I know that you do not have the love of God in*a* you. ⁴³I have come in my Father's name, and you do not accept me; if another comes in his own name, you will accept him. ⁴⁴How can you believe when you accept glory from one another and do not seek the glory that comes from the one who alone is God? ⁴⁵Do not think that I will accuse you before the Father; your accuser is Moses, on whom you have set your hope. ⁴⁶If you believed Moses, you would believe me, for he wrote about me. ⁴⁷But if you do not believe what he wrote, how will you believe what I say?"

6 Feeding the Five Thousand

After this Jesus went to the other side of the Sea of Galilee, also called the Sea of Tiberias.*b* ²A large crowd kept following him, because they saw the signs that he was doing for the sick. ³Jesus went up the mountain and sat down there with his disciples. ⁴Now the Passover, the festival of the Jews, was near. ⁵When he looked up and saw a large crowd coming toward him, Jesus said to Philip, "Where are we to buy bread for these people to eat?" ⁶He said this to test him, for he himself knew what he was going to do. ⁷Philip answered him, "Six months' wages*c* would not buy enough bread for each of them to get a little." ⁸One of his disciples, Andrew, Simon Peter's brother, said to him, ⁹"There is a boy here who has five barley loaves and two fish. But what are they among so many people?" ¹⁰Jesus said, "Make the people sit down." Now there was a great deal of grass in the place; so they*d* sat down, about five thousand in all. ¹¹Then Jesus took the loaves, and when he had given thanks, he distributed them to those who were seated; so also the fish, as much as they wanted. ¹²When they were satisfied, he told his disciples, "Gather up the fragments left over, so that nothing may be lost." ¹³So they gathered them up, and from the fragments of the five barley loaves, left by those who had eaten, they filled twelve baskets. ¹⁴When the people saw the sign that he had done, they began to say, "This is indeed the prophet who is to come into the world."

15 When Jesus realized that they were about to come and take him by force to make him king, he withdrew again to the mountain by himself.

a Or *among* *b* Gk *of Galilee of Tiberias* *c* Gk *Two hundred denarii;* the denarius was the usual day's wage for a laborer *d* Gk *the men*

Jesus Walks on the Water

16 When evening came, his disciples went down to the sea, [17]got into a boat, and started across the sea to Capernaum. It was now dark, and Jesus had not yet come to them. [18]The sea became rough because a strong wind was blowing. [19]When they had rowed about three or four miles,[a] they saw Jesus walking on the sea and coming near the boat, and they were terrified. [20]But he said to them, "It is I;[b] do not be afraid." [21]Then they wanted to take him into the boat, and immediately the boat reached the land toward which they were going.

The Bread from Heaven

22 The next day the crowd that had stayed on the other side of the sea saw that there had been only one boat there. They also saw that Jesus had not got into the boat with his disciples, but that his disciples had gone away alone. [23]Then some boats from Tiberias came near the place where they had eaten the bread after the Lord had given thanks.[c] [24]So when the crowd saw that neither Jesus nor his disciples were there, they themselves got into the boats and went to Capernaum looking for Jesus.

25 When they found him on the other side of the sea, they said to him, "Rabbi, when did you come here?" [26]Jesus answered them, "Very truly, I tell you, you are looking for me, not because you saw signs, but because you ate your fill of the loaves. [27]Do not work for the food that perishes, but for the food that endures for eternal life, which the Son of Man will give you. For it is on him that God the Father has set his seal." [28]Then they said to him, "What must we do to perform the works of God?" [29]Jesus answered them, "This is the work of God, that you believe in him whom he has sent." [30]So they said to him, "What sign are you going to give us then, so that we may see it and believe you? What work are you performing? [31]Our ancestors ate the manna in the wilderness; as it is written, 'He gave them bread from heaven to eat.' " [32]Then Jesus said to them, "Very truly, I tell you, it was not Moses who gave you the bread from heaven, but it is my Father who gives you the true bread from heaven. [33]For the bread of God is that which[d] comes down from heaven and gives life to the world." [34]They said to him, "Sir, give us this bread always."

35 Jesus said to them, "I am the bread of life. Whoever comes to me will never be hungry, and whoever believes in me will never be thirsty. [36]But I said to you that you have seen me and yet do not believe. [37]Everything that the Father gives me will come to me, and any-

one who comes to me I will never drive away; [38]for I have come down from heaven, not to do my own will, but the will of him who sent me. [39]And this is the will of him who sent me, that I should lose nothing of all that he has given me, but raise it up on the last day. [40]This is indeed the will of my Father, that all who see the Son and believe in him may have eternal life; and I will raise them up on the last day."

41 Then the Jews began to complain about him because he said, "I am the bread that came down from heaven." [42]They were saying, "Is not this Jesus, the son of Joseph, whose father and mother we know? How can he now say, 'I have come down from heaven'?" [43]Jesus answered them, "Do not complain among yourselves. [44]No one can come to me unless drawn by the Father who sent me; and I will raise that person up on the last day. [45]It is written in the prophets, 'And they shall all be taught by God.' Everyone who has heard and learned from the Father comes to me. [46]Not that anyone has seen the Father except the one who is from God; he has seen the Father. [47]Very truly, I tell you, whoever believes has eternal life. [48]I am the bread of life. [49]Your ancestors ate the manna in the wilderness, and they died. [50]This is the bread that comes down from heaven, so that one may eat of it and not die. [51]I am the living bread that came down from heaven. Whoever eats of this bread will live forever; and the

---

a Gk *about twenty-five or thirty stadia*   *b* Gk *I am*   *c* Other ancient authorities lack *after the Lord had given thanks*   *d* Or *he who*

PROFILE OF FAITH

It seems Nicodemus didn't want to jeopardize his membership in the ruling council, so he went to Jesus under cover of night. It might seem a little cowardly, but he did what few others in the gospel did: he actively sought out Jesus to explore with him the rationale for his ministry. Jesus responded, evoking powerful images of being born again by water and the Spirit.

Over time, Nicodemus' caution gave way to a greater boldness. Read **John 7.50**. He appeared again at a meeting of the ruling council, where he supported a fair hearing for Jesus against other members who proposed otherwise. These members lashed out at Nicodemus. Finally, in a very public show of support, Nicodemus assisted in the burial of Jesus' body.

Nicodemus grew into faith slowly. How about *you*? Has your faith journey been fast, or slow and steady like Nicodemus'?

---

bread that I will give for the life of the world is my flesh."

52 The Jews then disputed among themselves, saying, "How can this man give us his flesh to eat?" ⁵³So Jesus said to them, "Very truly, I tell you, unless you eat the flesh of the Son of Man and drink his blood, you have no life in you. ⁵⁴Those who eat my flesh and drink my blood have eternal life, and I will raise them up on the last day; ⁵⁵for my flesh is true food and my blood is true drink. ⁵⁶Those who eat my flesh and drink my blood abide in me, and I in them. ⁵⁷Just as the living Father sent me, and I live because of the Father, so whoever eats me will live because of me. ⁵⁸This is the bread that came down from heaven, not like that which your ancestors ate, and they died. But the one who eats this bread will live forever." ⁵⁹He said these things while he was teaching in the synagogue at Capernaum.

The Words of Eternal Life

60 When many of his disciples heard it, they said, "This teaching is difficult; who can accept it?" ⁶¹But Jesus, being aware that his disciples were complaining about it, said to them, "Does this offend you? ⁶²Then what if you were to see the Son of Man ascending to where he was before? ⁶³It is the spirit that gives life; the flesh is useless. The words that I have spoken to you are spirit and life. ⁶⁴But among you there are some who do not believe." For Jesus knew from the first who were the ones that did not believe, and who was the one that would betray him. ⁶⁵And he said, "For this reason I have told you that no one can come to me unless it is granted by the Father."

66 Because of this many of his disciples turned back and no longer went about with him. ⁶⁷So Jesus asked the twelve, "Do you also wish to go away?" ⁶⁸Simon Peter answered him, "Lord, to whom can we go? You have the words of eternal life. ⁶⁹We have come to believe and know that you are the Holy One of God."ᵃ ⁷⁰Jesus answered them, "Did I not choose you, the twelve? Yet one of you is a devil." ⁷¹He was speaking of Judas son of Simon Iscariot,ᵇ for he, though one of the twelve, was going to betray him.

7 The Unbelief of Jesus' Brothers

After this Jesus went about in Galilee. He did not wishᶜ to go about in Judea because the Jews were looking for an opportunity to kill him. ²Now the Jewish festival of Boothsᵈ was near. ³So his brothers said to him, "Leave here and go to Judea so that your disciples also may see the works you are doing; ⁴for no one who

---

a Other ancient authorities read *the Christ, the Son of the living God* b Other ancient authorities read *Judas Iscariot son of Simon*; others, *Judas son of Simon from Karyot* (Kerioth) c Other ancient authorities read *was not at liberty* d Or *Tabernacles* wants[a] to be widely known acts in secret. If you do these things, show yourself to the world." [5](For not even his brothers believed in him.) [6]Jesus said to them, "My time has not yet come, but your time is always here. [7]The world cannot hate you, but it hates me because I testify against it that its works are evil. [8]Go to the festival yourselves. I am not[b] going to this festival, for my time has not yet fully come." [9]After saying this, he remained in Galilee.

Jesus at the Festival of Booths

[10] But after his brothers had gone to the festival, then he also went, not publicly but as it were[c] in secret. [11]The Jews were looking for him at the festival and saying, "Where is he?" [12]And there was considerable complaining about him among the crowds. While some were saying, "He is a good man," others were saying, "No, he is deceiving the crowd." [13]Yet no one would speak openly about him for fear of the Jews.

[14] About the middle of the festival Jesus went up into the temple and began to teach. [15]The Jews were astonished at it, saying, "How does this man have such learning,[d] when he has never been taught?" [16]Then Jesus answered them, "My teaching is not mine but his who sent me. [17]Anyone who resolves to do the will of God will know whether the teaching is from God or whether I am speaking on my own. [18]Those who speak on their own seek their own glory; but the one who seeks the glory of him who sent him is true, and there is nothing false in him. [19] "Did not Moses give you the law? Yet none of you keeps the law. Why are you looking for an opportunity to kill me?" [20]The crowd answered, "You have a demon! Who is trying to kill you?" [21]Jesus answered them, "I performed one work, and all of you are astonished. [22]Moses gave you circumcision (it is, of course, not from Moses, but from the patriarchs), and you circumcise a man on the sabbath. [23]If a man receives circumcision on the sabbath in order that the law of Moses may not be broken, are you angry with me because I healed a man's whole body on the sabbath? [24]Do not judge by appearances, but judge with right judgment."

Is This the Christ?

[25] Now some of the people of Jerusalem were saying, "Is not this the man whom they are trying to kill? [26]And here he is, speaking openly, but they say nothing to him! Can it be that the authorities really know that this is the Messi-

ah?[e] [27]Yet we know where this man is from; but when the Messiah[e] comes, no one will know where he is from." [28]Then Jesus cried out as he was teaching in the temple, "You know me, and you know where I am from. I have not come on my own. But the one who sent me is true, and you do not know him. [29]I know him, because I am from him, and he sent me." [30]Then they tried to arrest him, but no one laid hands on him, because his hour had not yet come. [31]Yet many in the crowd believed in him and were saying, "When the Messiah[e] comes, will he do more signs than this man has done?"[f]

Officers Are Sent to Arrest Jesus

[32] The Pharisees heard the crowd muttering such things about him, and the chief priests and Pharisees sent temple police to arrest him. [33]Jesus then said, "I will be with you a little while longer, and then I am going to him who sent me. [34]You will search for me, but you will not find me; and where I am, you cannot come." [35]The Jews said to one another, "Where does this man intend to go that we will not find him? Does he intend to go to the Dispersion among the Greeks and teach the Greeks? [36]What does he mean by saying, 'You will search for me and you will not find me' and 'Where I am, you cannot come'?"

Rivers of Living Water

[37] On the last day of the festival, the great day, while Jesus was standing there, he cried out, "Let anyone who is thirsty come to me, [38]and let the one who believes in me drink. As[g] the scripture has said, 'Out of the believer's heart[h] shall flow rivers of living water.' " [39]Now he said this about the Spirit, which believers in him were to receive; for as yet there was no Spirit,[i] because Jesus was not yet glorified.

Division among the People

[40] When they heard these words, some in the crowd said, "This is really the prophet." [41]Others said, "This is the Messiah."[e] But some asked, "Surely the Messiah[e] does not come from Galilee, does he? [42]Has not the scripture said that the Messiah[e] is descended from David and comes from Bethlehem, the village where David lived?" [43]So there was a division in the crowd because of him. [44]Some of them wanted to arrest him, but no one laid hands on him.

The Unbelief of Those in Authority

[45] Then the temple police went back to the chief priests and Pharisees, who asked them,

---

a Other ancient authorities read *wants it* b Other ancient authorities add *yet* c Other ancient authorities lack *as it were* d Or *this man know his letters* e Or *the Christ* f Other ancient authorities read *is doing* g Or *come to me and drink.* [38]*The one who believes in me, as* h Gk *out of his belly* i Other ancient authorities read *for as yet the Spirit* (others, *Holy Spirit*) *had not been given*

QUICK TO THE GAVEL?

School can be brutal. Every day you hear nasty name-calling—vicious, horrible words—used to label, hurt, and destroy. Read **John 8.1–11.**

Adulterer. Sinner. Doesn't deserve to live. These were the labels thrown at the woman John describes. She wasn't just stripped of her self-respect—she was about to be tortured to death.

But in one courageous act, Jesus gave her back her dignity. He wasn't afraid to be kind to an outcast. He saw right through the Pharisees' manipulative words and went straight to the heart of the issue: judging others' sin. (Read Matthew 7.1–5 to get an even deeper understanding of what Jesus thinks about judging others.)

Think through a typical day at school. Who are the people *you* judge? Girls who are pregnant or who've had abortions? Homosexuals? Drug users and partyers? Kids of other faiths or denominations? Ask God to help you get rid of your judgmental attitude and see those people with his loving perspective. Then go one step further. Take a risk. Be courageous. Say something sincere and kind to someone you might judge. Let Jesus speak through *you*!

GOD IS COMPASSIONATE MY SCHOOL

"Why did you not arrest him?" ⁴⁶The police answered, "Never has anyone spoken like this!" ⁴⁷Then the Pharisees replied, "Surely you have not been deceived too, have you? ⁴⁸Has any one of the authorities or of the Pharisees believed in him? ⁴⁹But this crowd, which does not know the law—they are accursed." ⁵⁰Nicodemus, who had gone to Jesus*ᵃ* before, and who was one of them, asked, ⁵¹"Our law does not judge people without first giving them a hearing to find out what they are doing, does it?" ⁵²They replied, "Surely you are not also from Galilee, are you? Search and you will see that no prophet is to arise from Galilee."

8 The Woman Caught in Adultery

⟦ ⁵³Then each of them went home, ¹while Jesus went to the Mount of Olives. ²Early in the morning he came again to the temple. All the people came to him and he sat down and began to teach them. ³The scribes and the Phar-

isees brought a woman who had been caught in adultery; and making her stand before all of them, ⁴they said to him, "Teacher, this woman was caught in the very act of committing adultery. ⁵Now in the law Moses commanded us to stone such women. Now what do you say?" ⁶They said this to test him, so that they might have some charge to bring against him. Jesus bent down and wrote with his finger on the ground. ⁷When they kept on questioning him, he straightened up and said to them, "Let anyone among you who is without sin be the first to throw a stone at her." ⁸And once again he bent down and wrote on the ground.*ᵇ* ⁹When they heard it, they went away, one by one, beginning with the elders; and Jesus was left alone with the woman standing before him. ¹⁰Jesus straightened up and said to her, "Woman, where are they? Has no one condemned you?" ¹¹She said, "No one, sir."*ᶜ* And Jesus said, "Neither do I condemn you. Go your way, and from now on do not sin again."⟧*ᵈ*

Jesus the Light of the World

12 Again Jesus spoke to them, saying, "I am the light of the world. Whoever follows me will never walk in darkness but will have the light of life." ¹³Then the Pharisees said to him, "You are testifying on your own behalf; your testimony is not valid." ¹⁴Jesus answered, "Even if I testify on my own behalf, my testimony is valid because I know where I have come from and where I am going, but you do not know where I come from or where I am going. ¹⁵You judge by human standards;*ᵉ* I judge no one. ¹⁶Yet even if I do judge, my judgment is valid; for it is not I alone who judge, but I and the Father*ᶠ* who sent me. ¹⁷In your law it is written that the testimony of two witnesses is valid. ¹⁸I testify on my own behalf, and the Father who sent me testifies on my behalf." ¹⁹Then they said to him, "Where is your Father?" Jesus answered, "You know neither me nor my Father. If you knew me, you would know my Father also." ²⁰He spoke these words while he was teaching in the treasury of the temple, but no one arrested him, because his hour had not yet come.

Jesus Foretells His Death

21 Again he said to them, "I am going away, and you will search for me, but you will die in your sin. Where I am going, you cannot come." ²²Then the Jews said, "Is he going to kill himself? Is that what he means by saying, 'Where I am going, you cannot come'?" ²³He said to them, "You are from below, I am from above;

---

a Gk *him* *b* Other ancient authorities add *the sins of each of them* *c* Or *Lord* *d* The most ancient authorities lack 7.53—8.11; other authorities add the passage here or after 7.36 or after 21.25 or after Luke 21.38, with variations of text; some mark the passage as doubtful. *e* Gk *according to the flesh* *f* Other ancient authorities read *he*

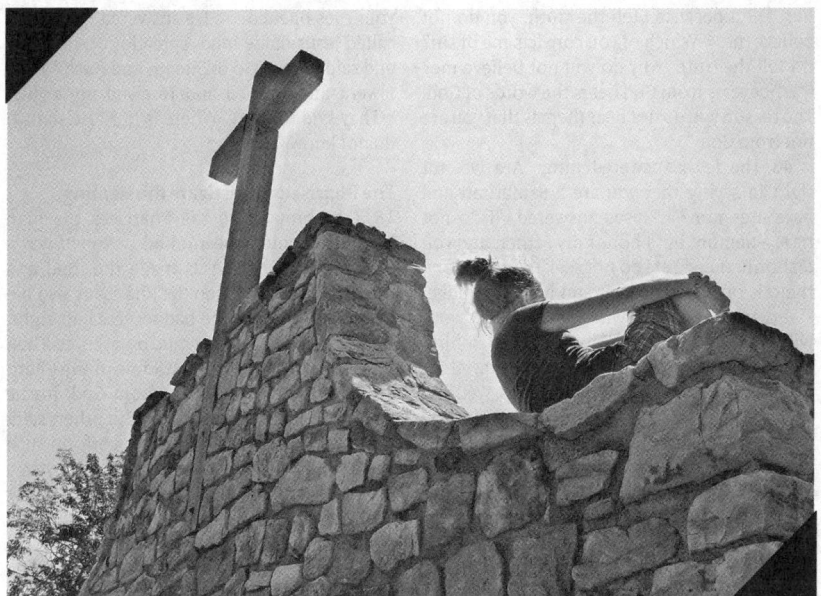

Wondering—© Rachel Akerley, 16

you are of this world, I am not of this world. [24]I told you that you would die in your sins, for you will die in your sins unless you believe that I am he."[a] [25]They said to him, "Who are you?" Jesus said to them, "Why do I speak to you at all?[b] [26]I have much to say about you and much to condemn; but the one who sent me is true, and I declare to the world what I have heard from him." [27]They did not understand that he was speaking to them about the Father. [28]So Jesus said, "When you have lifted up the Son of Man, then you will realize that I am he,[a] and that I do nothing on my own, but I speak these things as the Father instructed me. [29]And the one who sent me is with me; he has not left me alone, for I always do what is pleasing to him." [30]As he was saying these things, many believed in him.

True Disciples

31 Then Jesus said to the Jews who had believed in him, "If you continue in my word, you are truly my disciples; [32]and you will know the truth, and the truth will make you free." [33]They answered him, "We are descendants of Abraham and have never been slaves to anyone. What do you mean by saying, 'You will be made free'?"

34 Jesus answered them, "Very truly, I tell you, everyone who commits sin is a slave to sin. [35]The slave does not have a permanent place in the household; the son has a place there forever. [36]So if the Son makes you free, you will be free indeed. [37]I know that you are descendants of Abraham; yet you look for an opportunity to kill me, because there is no place in you for my word. [38]I declare what I have seen in the Father's presence; as for you, you should do what you have heard from the Father."[c]

Jesus and Abraham

39 They answered him, "Abraham is our father." Jesus said to them, "If you were Abraham's children, you would be doing[d] what Abraham did, [40]but now you are trying to kill me, a man who has told you the truth that I heard from God. This is not what Abraham did. [41]You are indeed doing what your father does." They said to him, "We are not illegitimate children; we have one father, God himself." [42]Jesus said to them, "If God were your Father, you would love me, for I came from God and now I am here. I did not come on my own, but he sent me. [43]Why do you not understand what I say? It is because you cannot accept my word. [44]You are from your father the devil, and you choose to do your father's desires. He was a murderer from the beginning and does not stand in the truth, because there is no truth in him. When he lies, he speaks according to his own nature, for he is a liar and the father of

a Gk I am b Or What I have told you from the beginning c Other ancient authorities read you do what you have heard from your father d Other ancient authorities read If you are Abraham's children, then do lies. ⁴⁵But because I tell the truth, you do not believe me. ⁴⁶Which of you convicts me of sin? If I tell the truth, why do you not believe me? ⁴⁷Whoever is from God hears the words of God. The reason you do not hear them is that you are not from God."

48 The Jews answered him, "Are we not right in saying that you are a Samaritan and have a demon?" ⁴⁹Jesus answered, "I do not have a demon; but I honor my Father, and you dishonor me. ⁵⁰Yet I do not seek my own glory; there is one who seeks it and he is the judge. ⁵¹Very truly, I tell you, whoever keeps my word will never see death." ⁵²The Jews said to him, "Now we know that you have a demon. Abraham died, and so did the prophets; yet you say, 'Whoever keeps my word will never taste death.' ⁵³Are you greater than our father Abraham, who died? The prophets also died. Who do you claim to be?" ⁵⁴Jesus answered, "If I glorify myself, my glory is nothing. It is my Father who glorifies me, he of whom you say, 'He is our God,' ⁵⁵though you do not know him. But I know him; if I would say that I do not know him, I would be a liar like you. But I do know him and I keep his word. ⁵⁶Your ancestor Abraham rejoiced that he would see my day; he saw it and was glad." ⁵⁷Then the Jews said to him, "You are not yet fifty years old, and have you seen Abraham?"ᵃ ⁵⁸Jesus said to them, "Very truly, I tell you, before Abraham was, I am." ⁵⁹So they picked up stones to throw at him, but Jesus hid himself and went out of the temple.

9 A Man Born Blind Receives Sight

As he walked along, he saw a man blind from birth. ²His disciples asked him, "Rabbi, who sinned, this man or his parents, that he was born blind?" ³Jesus answered, "Neither this man nor his parents sinned; he was born blind so that God's works might be revealed in him. ⁴Weᵇ must work the works of him who sent meᶜ while it is day; night is coming when no one can work. ⁵As long as I am in the world, I am the light of the world." ⁶When he had said this, he spat on the ground and made mud with the saliva and spread the mud on the man's eyes, ⁷saying to him, "Go, wash in the pool of Siloam" (which means Sent). Then he went and washed and came back able to see. ⁸The neighbors and those who had seen him before as a beggar began to ask, "Is this not the man who used to sit and beg?" ⁹Some were saying, "It is he." Others were saying, "No, but it is someone like him." He kept saying, "I am the man." ¹⁰But they kept asking him, "Then how were your eyes opened?" ¹¹He answered, "The man called Jesus made mud, spread it on my eyes, and said to me, 'Go to Siloam and wash.' Then I went and washed and received my sight." ¹²They said to him, "Where is he?" He said, "I do not know."

The Pharisees Investigate the Healing

13 They brought to the Pharisees the man who had formerly been blind. ¹⁴Now it was a sabbath day when Jesus made the mud and opened his eyes. ¹⁵Then the Pharisees also began to ask him how he had received his sight. He said to them, "He put mud on my eyes. Then I washed, and now I see." ¹⁶Some of the Pharisees said, "This man is not from God, for he does not observe the sabbath." But others said, "How can a man who is a sinner perform such signs?" And they were divided. ¹⁷So they said again to the blind man, "What do you say about him? It was your eyes he opened." He said, "He is a prophet."

18 The Jews did not believe that he had been blind and had received his sight until they called the parents of the man who had received his sight ¹⁹and asked them, "Is this your son, who you say was born blind? How then does he now see?" ²⁰His parents answered, "We know that this is our son, and that he was born blind; ²¹but we do not know how it is that now he sees, nor do we know who opened his eyes. Ask him; he is of age. He will speak for himself." ²²His parents said this because they were afraid of the Jews; for the Jews had already agreed that anyone who confessed Jesusᵈ to be the Messiahᵉ would be put out of the synagogue. ²³Therefore his parents said, "He is of age; ask him."

24 So for the second time they called the man who had been blind, and they said to him, "Give glory to God! We know that this man is a sinner." ²⁵He answered, "I do not know whether he is a sinner. One thing I do know, that though I was blind, now I see." ²⁶They said to him, "What did he do to you? How did he open your eyes?" ²⁷He answered them, "I have told you already, and you would not listen. Why do you want to hear it again? Do you also want to become his disciples?" ²⁸Then they reviled him, saying, "You are his disciple, but we are disciples of Moses. ²⁹We know that God has spoken to Moses, but as for this man, we do not know where he comes from." ³⁰The man answered, "Here is an astonishing thing! You do not know where he comes from, and yet he opened my eyes. ³¹We know that God does not

---

a Other ancient authorities read *has Abraham seen you?* *b* Other ancient authorities read *I* *c* Other ancient authorities read *us*
d Gk *him* *e* Or *the Christ*

listen to sinners, but he does listen to one who worships him and obeys his will. ³²Never since the world began has it been heard that anyone opened the eyes of a person born blind. ³³If this man were not from God, he could do nothing." ³⁴They answered him, "You were born entirely in sins, and are you trying to teach us?" And they drove him out.

Spiritual Blindness

35 Jesus heard that they had driven him out, and when he found him, he said, "Do you believe in the Son of Man?"ᵃ ³⁶He answered, "And who is he, sir?ᵇ Tell me, so that I may believe in him." ³⁷Jesus said to him, "You have seen him, and the one speaking with you is he." ³⁸He said, "Lord,ᵇ I believe." And he worshiped him. ³⁹Jesus said, "I came into this world for judgment so that those who do not see may see, and those who do see may become blind." ⁴⁰Some of the Pharisees near him heard this and said to him, "Surely we are not blind, are we?" ⁴¹Jesus said to them, "If you were blind, you would not have sin. But now that you say, 'We see,' your sin remains.

10 Jesus the Good Shepherd

"Very truly, I tell you, anyone who does not enter the sheepfold by the gate but climbs in by another way is a thief and a bandit. ²The one who enters by the gate is the shepherd of the sheep. ³The gatekeeper opens the gate for him, and the sheep hear his voice. He calls his own sheep by name and leads them out. ⁴When he has brought out all his own, he goes ahead of them, and the sheep follow him because they know his voice. ⁵They will not follow a stranger, but they will run from him because they do not know the voice of strangers." ⁶Jesus used this figure of speech with them, but they did not understand what he was saying to them.

7 So again Jesus said to them, "Very truly, I tell you, I am the gate for the sheep. ⁸All who came before me are thieves and bandits; but the sheep did not listen to them. ⁹I am the gate. Whoever enters by me will be saved, and will come in and go out and find pasture. ¹⁰The thief comes only to steal and kill and destroy. I came that they may have life, and have it abundantly.

11 "I am the good shepherd. The good shepherd lays down his life for the sheep. ¹²The hired hand, who is not the shepherd and does not own the sheep, sees the wolf coming and leaves the sheep and runs away—and the wolf snatches them and scatters them. ¹³The hired

Lock—© Lexi Hiland, 16

hand runs away because a hired hand does not care for the sheep. ¹⁴I am the good shepherd. I know my own and my own know me, ¹⁵just as the Father knows me and I know the Father. And I lay down my life for the sheep. ¹⁶I have other sheep that do not belong to this fold. I must bring them also, and they will listen to my voice. So there will be one flock, one shepherd. ¹⁷For this reason the Father loves me, because I lay down my life in order to take it up again. ¹⁸No one takesᶜ it from me, but I lay it down of my own accord. I have power to lay it down, and I have power to take it up again. I have received this command from my Father."

19 Again the Jews were divided because of these words. ²⁰Many of them were saying, "He has a demon and is out of his mind. Why listen to him?" ²¹Others were saying, "These are not the words of one who has a demon. Can a demon open the eyes of the blind?"

Jesus Is Rejected by the Jews

22 At that time the festival of the Dedication took place in Jerusalem. It was winter, ²³and Jesus was walking in the temple, in the portico of Solomon. ²⁴So the Jews gathered around him and said to him, "How long will you keep us in suspense? If you are the Messiah,ᵈ tell us plainly." ²⁵Jesus answered, "I have told you, and you do not believe. The works that I do in my Father's name testify to me; ²⁶but you do not believe, because you do not belong to my sheep. ²⁷My sheep hear my voice. I know them, and they follow me. ²⁸I give them eternal life, and they will never perish. No one will snatch them out of my hand. ²⁹What my Father has

---

a Other ancient authorities read *the Son of God* b *Sir* and *Lord* translate the same Greek word c Other ancient authorities read *has taken*
d Or *the Christ*

given me is greater than all else, and no one can snatch it out of the Father's hand.[a] [30]The Father and I are one."

[31] The Jews took up stones again to stone him. [32]Jesus replied, "I have shown you many good works from the Father. For which of these are you going to stone me?" [33]The Jews answered, "It is not for a good work that we are going to stone you, but for blasphemy, because you, though only a human being, are making yourself God." [34]Jesus answered, "Is it not written in your law,[b] 'I said, you are gods'? [35]If those to whom the word of God came were called 'gods'—and the scripture cannot be annulled— [36]can you say that the one whom the Father has sanctified and sent into the world is blaspheming because I said, 'I am God's Son'? [37]If I am not doing the works of my Father, then do not believe me. [38]But if I do them, even though you do not believe me, believe the works, so that you may know and understand[c] that the Father is in me and I am in the Father." [39]Then they tried to arrest him again, but he escaped from their hands.

[40] He went away again across the Jordan to the place where John had been baptizing earlier, and he remained there. [41]Many came to him, and they were saying, "John performed no sign, but everything that John said about this man was true." [42]And many believed in him there.

11 The Death of Lazarus

Now a certain man was ill, Lazarus of Bethany, the village of Mary and her sister Martha. [2]Mary was the one who anointed the Lord with perfume and wiped his feet with her hair; her brother Lazarus was ill. [3]So the sisters sent a message to Jesus,[d] "Lord, he whom you love is ill." [4]But when Jesus heard it, he said, "This illness does not lead to death; rather it is for God's glory, so that the Son of God may be glorified through it." [5]Accordingly, though Jesus loved Martha and her sister and Lazarus, [6]after having heard that Lazarus[e] was ill, he stayed two days longer in the place where he was.

[7] Then after this he said to the disciples, "Let us go to Judea again." [8]The disciples said to him, "Rabbi, the Jews were just now trying to stone you, and are you going there again?" [9]Jesus answered, "Are there not twelve hours of daylight? Those who walk during the day do not stumble, because they see the light of this world. [10]But those who walk at night stumble, because the light is not in them." [11]After saying this, he told them, "Our friend Lazarus has

fallen asleep, but I am going there to awaken him." [12]The disciples said to him, "Lord, if he has fallen asleep, he will be all right." [13]Jesus, however, had been speaking about his death, but they thought that he was referring merely to sleep. [14]Then Jesus told them plainly, "Lazarus is dead. [15]For your sake I am glad I was not there, so that you may believe. But let us go to him." [16]Thomas, who was called the Twin,[f] said to his fellow disciples, "Let us also go, that we may die with him."

Jesus the Resurrection and the Life

[17] When Jesus arrived, he found that Lazarus[e] had already been in the tomb four days. [18]Now Bethany was near Jerusalem, some two miles[g] away, [19]and many of the Jews had come to Martha and Mary to console them about their brother. [20]When Martha heard that Jesus was coming, she went and met him, while Mary stayed at home. [21]Martha said to Jesus, "Lord, if you had been here, my brother would not have died. [22]But even now I know that God will give you whatever you ask of him." [23]Jesus said to her, "Your brother will rise again." [24]Martha said to him, "I know that he will rise again in the resurrection on the last day." [25]Jesus said to her, "I am the resurrection and the life.[h] Those who believe in me, even though they die, will live, [26]and everyone who lives and believes in me will never die. Do you believe this?" [27]She said to him, "Yes, Lord, I believe that you are the Messiah,[i] the Son of God, the one coming into the world."

Jesus Weeps

[28] When she had said this, she went back and called her sister Mary, and told her privately, "The Teacher is here and is calling for you." [29]And when she heard it, she got up quickly and went to him. [30]Now Jesus had not yet come to the village, but was still at the place where Martha had met him. [31]The Jews who were with her in the house, consoling her, saw Mary get up quickly and go out. They followed her because they thought that she was going to the tomb to weep there. [32]When Mary came where Jesus was and saw him, she knelt at his feet and said to him, "Lord, if you had been here, my brother would not have died." [33]When Jesus saw her weeping, and the Jews who came with her also weeping, he was greatly disturbed in spirit and deeply moved. [34]He said, "Where have you laid him?" They said to him, "Lord, come and see." [35]Jesus began to weep. [36]So the Jews said, "See how he loved him!" [37]But some of them said,

a Other ancient authorities read My Father who has given them to me is greater than all, and no one can snatch them out of the Father's hand   b Other ancient authorities read in the law   c Other ancient authorities lack and understand; others read and believe   d Gk him   e Gk he   f Gk Didymus   g Gk fifteen stadia   h Other ancient authorities lack and the life   i Or the Christ

"Could not he who opened the eyes of the blind man have kept this man from dying?"

Jesus Raises Lazarus to Life

38 Then Jesus, again greatly disturbed, came to the tomb. It was a cave, and a stone was lying against it. ³⁹Jesus said, "Take away the stone." Martha, the sister of the dead man, said to him, "Lord, already there is a stench because he has been dead four days." ⁴⁰Jesus said to her, "Did I not tell you that if you believed, you would see the glory of God?" ⁴¹So they took away the stone. And Jesus looked upward and said, "Father, I thank you for having heard me. ⁴²I knew that you always hear me, but I have said this for the sake of the crowd standing here, so that they may believe that you sent me." ⁴³When he had said this, he cried with a loud voice, "Lazarus, come out!" ⁴⁴The dead man came out, his hands and feet bound with strips of cloth, and his face wrapped in a cloth. Jesus said to them, "Unbind him, and let him go."

The Plot to Kill Jesus

45 Many of the Jews therefore, who had come with Mary and had seen what Jesus did, believed in him. ⁴⁶But some of them went to the Pharisees and told them what he had done. ⁴⁷So the chief priests and the Pharisees called a meeting of the council, and said, "What are we to do? This man is performing many signs. ⁴⁸If we let him go on like this, everyone will believe in him, and the Romans will come and destroy both our holy place*ᵃ* and our nation." ⁴⁹But one of them, Caiaphas, who was high priest that year, said to them, "You know nothing at all! ⁵⁰You do not understand that it is better for you to have one man die for the people than to have the whole nation destroyed." ⁵¹He did not say this on his own, but being high priest that year he prophesied that Jesus was about to die for the nation, ⁵²and not for the nation only, but to gather into one the dispersed children of God. ⁵³So from that day on they planned to put him to death.

54 Jesus therefore no longer walked about openly among the Jews, but went from there to a town called Ephraim in the region near the wilderness; and he remained there with the disciples.

55 Now the Passover of the Jews was near, and many went up from the country to Jerusalem before the Passover to purify themselves. ⁵⁶They were looking for Jesus and were asking one another as they stood in the temple, "What do you think? Surely he will not come to the festival, will he?" ⁵⁷Now the chief priests

and the Pharisees had given orders that anyone who knew where Jesus*ᵇ* was should let them know, so that they might arrest him.

12   Mary Anoints Jesus

Six days before the Passover Jesus came to Bethany, the home of Lazarus, whom he had raised from the dead. ²There they gave a dinner for him. Martha served, and Lazarus was one of those at the table with him. ³Mary took a pound of costly perfume made of pure nard, anointed Jesus' feet, and wiped them*ᶜ* with her hair. The house was filled with the fragrance of the perfume. ⁴But Judas Iscariot, one of his disciples (the one who was about to betray him), said, ⁵"Why was this perfume not sold for three hundred denarii*ᵈ* and the money given to the poor?" ⁶(He said this not because he cared

ᵃ Or *our temple*; Greek *our place* *ᵇ* Gk *he* *ᶜ* Gk *his feet* *ᵈ* Three hundred denarii would be nearly a year's wages for a laborer about the poor, but because he was a thief; he kept the common purse and used to steal what was put into it.) [7]Jesus said, "Leave her alone. She bought it[a] so that she might keep it for the day of my burial. [8]You always have the poor with you, but you do not always have me."

The Plot to Kill Lazarus

9 When the great crowd of the Jews learned that he was there, they came not only because of Jesus but also to see Lazarus, whom he had raised from the dead. [10]So the chief priests planned to put Lazarus to death as well, [11]since it was on account of him that many of the Jews were deserting and were believing in Jesus.

Jesus' Triumphal Entry into Jerusalem

12 The next day the great crowd that had come to the festival heard that Jesus was coming to Jerusalem. [13]So they took branches of palm trees and went out to meet him, shouting,

"Hosanna!
Blessed is the one who comes in the name
of the Lord—
the King of Israel!"

[14]Jesus found a young donkey and sat on it; as it is written:

[15] "Do not be afraid, daughter of Zion.
Look, your king is coming,
sitting on a donkey's colt!"

[16]His disciples did not understand these things at first; but when Jesus was glorified, then they remembered that these things had been written of him and had been done to him. [17]So the crowd that had been with him when he called Lazarus out of the tomb and raised him from the dead continued to testify.[b] [18]It was also because they heard that he had performed this sign that the crowd went to meet him. [19]The Pharisees then said to one another, "You see, you can do nothing. Look, the world has gone after him!"

Some Greeks Wish to See Jesus

20 Now among those who went up to worship at the festival were some Greeks. [21]They came to Philip, who was from Bethsaida in Galilee, and said to him, "Sir, we wish to see Jesus." [22]Philip went and told Andrew; then Andrew and Philip went and told Jesus. [23]Jesus answered them, "The hour has come for the Son of Man to be glorified. [24]Very truly, I tell you, unless a grain of wheat falls into the earth and dies, it remains just a single grain; but if it dies, it bears much fruit. [25]Those who love their life lose it, and those who hate their life in this world will keep it for eternal life. [26]Whoever serves me must follow me, and where I am, there will my servant be also. Whoever serves me, the Father will honor.

Jesus Speaks about His Death

27 "Now my soul is troubled. And what should I say—'Father, save me from this hour'? No, it is for this reason that I have come to this hour. [28]Father, glorify your name." Then a voice came from heaven, "I have glorified it, and I will glorify it again." [29]The crowd standing there heard it and said that it was thunder. Others said, "An angel has spoken to him." [30]Jesus answered, "This voice has come for your sake, not for mine. [31]Now is the judgment of this world; now the ruler of this world will be driven out. [32]And I, when I am lifted up from the earth, will draw all people[c] to myself." [33]He said this to indicate the kind of death he was to die. [34]The crowd answered him, "We have heard from the law that the Messiah[d] remains forever. How can you say that the Son of Man must be lifted up? Who is this Son of Man?" [35]Jesus said to them, "The light is with you for a little longer. Walk while you have the light, so that the darkness may not overtake you. If you walk in the darkness, you do not know where you are going. [36]While you have the light, believe in the light, so that you may become children of light."

The Unbelief of the People

After Jesus had said this, he departed and hid from them. [37]Although he had performed so many signs in their presence, they did not believe in him. [38]This was to fulfill the word spoken by the prophet Isaiah:

"Lord, who has believed our message,
and to whom has the arm of the Lord
been revealed?"

[39]And so they could not believe, because Isaiah also said,

[40] "He has blinded their eyes
and hardened their heart,
so that they might not look with their eyes,
and understand with their heart and
turn—
and I would heal them."

[41]Isaiah said this because[e] he saw his glory and spoke about him. [42]Nevertheless many, even of the authorities, believed in him. But because of the Pharisees they did not confess it, for fear that they would be put out of the synagogue; [43]for they loved human glory more than the glory that comes from God.

a Gk lacks She bought it b Other ancient authorities read with him began to testify that he had called . . . from the dead c Other ancient authorities read all things d Or the Christ e Other ancient witnesses read when

Summary of Jesus' Teaching

44 Then Jesus cried aloud: "Whoever believes in me believes not in me but in him who sent me. 45And whoever sees me sees him who sent me. 46I have come as light into the world, so that everyone who believes in me should not remain in the darkness. 47I do not judge anyone who hears my words and does not keep them, for I came not to judge the world, but to save the world. 48The one who rejects me and does not receive my word has a judge; on the last day the word that I have spoken will serve as judge, 49for I have not spoken on my own, but the Father who sent me has himself given me a commandment about what to say and what to speak. 50And I know that his commandment is eternal life. What I speak, therefore, I speak just as the Father has told me."

13 Jesus Washes the Disciples' Feet

Now before the festival of the Passover, Jesus knew that his hour had come to depart from this world and go to the Father. Having loved his own who were in the world, he loved them to the end. 2The devil had already put it into the heart of Judas son of Simon Iscariot to betray him. And during supper 3Jesus, knowing that the Father had given all things into his hands, and that he had come from God and was going to God, 4got up from the table,*a* took off his outer robe, and tied a towel around himself. 5Then he poured water into a basin and began to wash the disciples' feet and to wipe them with the towel that was tied around him. 6He came to Simon Peter, who said to him, "Lord, are you going to wash my feet?" 7Jesus answered, "You do not know now what I am doing, but later you will understand." 8Peter said to him, "You will never wash my feet." Jesus answered, "Unless I wash you, you have no share with me." 9Simon Peter said to him, "Lord, not my feet only but also my hands and my head!" 10Jesus said to him, "One who has bathed does not need to wash, except for the feet,*b* but is entirely clean. And you*c* are clean, though not all of you." 11For he knew who was to betray him; for this reason he said, "Not all of you are clean."

12 After he had washed their feet, had put on his robe, and had returned to the table, he said to them, "Do you know what I have done to you? 13You call me Teacher and Lord—and you are right, for that is what I am. 14So if I, your Lord and Teacher, have washed your feet, you also ought to wash one another's feet. 15For I have set you an example, that you also should

do as I have done to you. 16Very truly, I tell you, servants*d* are not greater than their master, nor are messengers greater than the one who sent them. 17If you know these things, you are blessed if you do them. 18I am not speaking of all of you; I know whom I have chosen. But it is to fulfill the scripture, 'The one who ate my bread*e* has lifted his heel against me.' 19I tell you this now, before it occurs, so that when it does occur, you may believe that I am he.*f* 20Very truly, I tell you, whoever receives one whom I send receives me; and whoever receives me receives him who sent me."

Jesus Foretells His Betrayal

21 After saying this Jesus was troubled in spirit, and declared, "Very truly, I tell you, one of you will betray me." 22The disciples looked at one another, uncertain of whom he was speaking. 23One of his disciples—the one whom Jesus loved—was reclining next to him; 24Simon Peter therefore motioned to him to ask Jesus of whom he was speaking. 25So while reclining next to Jesus, he asked him, "Lord, who is it?" 26Jesus answered, "It is the one to whom I give this piece of bread when I have dipped it in the dish."*g* So when he had dipped the piece of bread, he gave it to Judas son of

a Gk *from supper* *b* Other ancient authorities lack *except for the feet* *c* The Greek word for *you* here is plural *d* Gk *slaves* *e* Other ancient authorities read *ate bread with me* *f* Gk *I am* *g* Gk *dipped it*

All my life, the time I have spent in the adoration chapel has been very meaningful. Members of our parish sign up for set times so that Jesus is never alone in the adoration chapel. My father has had an hour in the middle of the night for as long as I can remember.

During the summer, he would wake my brother and me up, and if we felt up to it we would grab a pillow and blanket and head to chapel with him. When he sat down in the pew, we would each lay our head on one of his knees. As I lay there, I always felt as if I was laying my head on Jesus' knee and I could tell him anything. I would often pray to him till I fell asleep.

Nowadays I go to the chapel every Sunday with my mom. She often has trouble concentrating so she brings prayer books with her, but I have always felt content with just sitting there and speaking to Jesus about what has happened throughout the past week. I often stop by the chapel on the way home from work, because being in adoration and speaking to Jesus have always helped me put what is most important into view—which is, of course, him.

The Adoration Chapel—© Delia Blaise Figura, 17

Simon Iscariot.[a] [27]After he received the piece of bread,[b] Satan entered into him. Jesus said to him, "Do quickly what you are going to do." [28]Now no one at the table knew why he said this to him. [29]Some thought that, because Judas had the common purse, Jesus was telling him, "Buy what we need for the festival"; or, that he should give something to the poor. [30]So, after receiving the piece of bread, he immediately went out. And it was night.

The New Commandment

[31] When he had gone out, Jesus said, "Now the Son of Man has been glorified, and God has been glorified in him. [32]If God has been glorified in him,[c] God will also glorify him in himself and will glorify him at once. [33]Little children, I am with you only a little longer. You will look for me; and as I said to the Jews so now I say to you, 'Where I am going, you cannot come.' [34]I give you a new commandment, that you love one another. Just as I have loved you, you also should love one another. [35]By this everyone will know that you are my disciples, if you have love for one another."

Jesus Foretells Peter's Denial

[36] Simon Peter said to him, "Lord, where are you going?" Jesus answered, "Where I am going, you cannot follow me now; but you will follow afterward." [37]Peter said to him, "Lord, why can I not follow you now? I will lay down my life for you." [38]Jesus answered, "Will you lay down your life for me? Very truly, I tell you, before the cock crows, you will have denied me three times.

14 Jesus the Way to the Father

"Do not let your hearts be troubled. Believe[d] in God, believe also in me. [2]In my Father's house there are many dwelling places. If it were not so, would I have told you that I go to prepare a place for you?[e] [3]And if I go and prepare a place for you, I will come again and will take you to myself, so that where I am, there you may be also. [4]And you know the way to the place where I am going."[f] [5]Thomas said to him, "Lord, we do not know where you are going. How can we know the way?" [6]Jesus said to him, "I am the way, and the truth, and the life. No one comes to the Father except through me. [7]If you know me, you will know[g] my Father also. From now on you do know him and have seen him."

[8] Philip said to him, "Lord, show us the Father, and we will be satisfied." [9]Jesus said to

him, "Have I been with you all this time, Philip, and you still do not know me? Whoever has seen me has seen the Father. How can you say, 'Show us the Father'? [10]Do you not believe that I am in the Father and the Father is in me? The words that I say to you I do not speak on my own; but the Father who dwells in me does his works. [11]Believe me that I am in the Father and the Father is in me; but if you do not, then believe me because of the works themselves. [12]Very truly, I tell you, the one who believes in me will also do the works that I do and, in fact, will do greater works than these, because I am going to the Father. [13]I will do whatever you ask in my name, so that the Father may be glorified in the Son. [14]If in my name you ask me[h] for anything, I will do it.

The Promise of the Holy Spirit

[15] "If you love me, you will keep[i] my commandments. [16]And I will ask the Father, and he will give you another Advocate,[j] to be with you forever. [17]This is the Spirit of truth, whom the world cannot receive, because it neither sees him nor knows him. You know him, because he abides with you, and he will be in[k] you.

[18] "I will not leave you orphaned; I am coming to you. [19]In a little while the world will no longer see me, but you will see me; because I live, you also will live. [20]On that day you will know that I am in my Father, and you in me, and I in you. [21]They who have my commandments and keep them are those who love me; and those who love me will be loved by my Father, and I will love them and reveal myself to them." [22]Judas (not Iscariot) said to him, "Lord, how is it that you will reveal yourself to us, and not to the world?" [23]Jesus answered him, "Those who love me will keep my word, and my Father will love them, and we will come to them and make our home with them. [24]Whoever does not love me does not keep my words; and the word that you hear is not mine, but is from the Father who sent me.

[25] "I have said these things to you while I am still with you. [26]But the Advocate,[j] the Holy Spirit, whom the Father will send in my name, will teach you everything, and remind you of all that I have said to you. [27]Peace I leave with you; my peace I give to you. I do not give to you as the world gives. Do not let your hearts be troubled, and do not let them be afraid. [28]You heard me say to you, 'I am going away, and I am coming to you.' If you loved me, you would rejoice that I am going to the Father, because the

a Other ancient authorities read *Judas Iscariot son of Simon*; others, *Judas son of Simon from Karyot* (Kerioth) b Gk *After the piece of bread*
c Other ancient authorities lack *If God has been glorified in him* d Or *You believe* e Or *If it were not so, I would have told you; for I go to prepare a place for you* f Other ancient authorities read *Where I am going you know, and the way you know* g Other ancient authorities read *If you had known me, you would have known* h Other ancient authorities lack *me* i Other ancient authorities read *me, keep* j Or *Helper* k Or *among*

Father is greater than I. ²⁹And now I have told you this before it occurs, so that when it does occur, you may believe. ³⁰I will no longer talk much with you, for the ruler of this world is coming. He has no power over me; ³¹but I do as the Father has commanded me, so that the world may know that I love the Father. Rise, let us be on our way.

15 Jesus the True Vine

"I am the true vine, and my Father is the vine-grower. ²He removes every branch in me that bears no fruit. Every branch that bears fruit he prunes*a* to make it bear more fruit. ³You have already been cleansed*a* by the word that I have spoken to you. ⁴Abide in me as I abide in you. Just as the branch cannot bear fruit by itself unless it abides in the vine, neither can you unless you abide in me. ⁵I am the vine, you are the branches. Those who abide in me and I in them bear much fruit, because apart from me you can do nothing. ⁶Whoever does not abide in me is thrown away like a branch and withers; such branches are gathered, thrown into the fire, and burned. ⁷If you abide in me, and my words abide in you, ask for whatever you wish, and it will be done for you. ⁸My Father is glorified by this, that you bear much fruit and become*b* my disciples. ⁹As the Father has loved me, so I have loved you; abide in my love. ¹⁰If you keep my commandments, you will abide in my love, just as I have kept my Father's commandments and abide in his love. ¹¹I have said these things to you so that my joy may be in you, and that your joy may be complete.

12 "This is my commandment, that you love one another as I have loved you. ¹³No one has greater love than this, to lay down one's life for one's friends. ¹⁴You are my friends if you do what I command you. ¹⁵I do not call you servants*c* any longer, because the servant*d* does not know what the master is doing; but I have called you friends, because I have made known to you everything that I have heard from my Father. ¹⁶You did not choose me but I chose you. And I appointed you to go and bear fruit, fruit that will last, so that the Father will give you whatever you ask him in my name. ¹⁷I am giving you these commands so that you may love one another.

The World's Hatred

18 "If the world hates you, be aware that it hated me before it hated you. ¹⁹If you belonged to the world,*e* the world would love you as its own. Because you do not belong to the world,

but I have chosen you out of the world—therefore the world hates you. ²⁰Remember the word that I said to you, 'Servants*f* are not greater than their master.' If they persecuted me, they will persecute you; if they kept my word, they will keep yours also. ²¹But they will do all these things to you on account of my name, because they do not know him who sent me. ²²If I had not come and spoken to them, they would not have sin; but now they have no excuse for their sin. ²³Whoever hates me hates my Father also. ²⁴If I had not done among them the works that no one else did, they would not have sin. But now they have seen and hated both me and my Father. ²⁵It was to fulfill the word that is written in their law, 'They hated me without a cause.'

26 "When the Advocate*g* comes, whom I will send to you from the Father, the Spirit of truth who comes from the Father, he will testify on my behalf. ²⁷You also are to testify because you have been with me from the beginning.

16 "I have said these things to you to keep you from stumbling. ²They will put you out of the synagogues. Indeed, an hour is coming when those who kill you will think that by doing so they are offering worship to God. ³And they will do this because they have not known the Father or me. ⁴But I have said these things to you so that when their hour comes you may remember that I told you about them.

The Work of the Spirit

"I did not say these things to you from the beginning, because I was with you. ⁵But now I am going to him who sent me; yet none of you asks me, 'Where are you going?' ⁶But because I have said these things to you, sorrow has filled your hearts. ⁷Nevertheless I tell you the truth: it is to your advantage that I go away, for if I do not go away, the Advocate*g* will not come to you; but if I go, I will send him to you. ⁸And when he comes, he will prove the world wrong about*h* sin and righteousness and judgment: ⁹about sin, because they do not believe in me; ¹⁰about righteousness, because I am going to the Father and you will see me no longer; ¹¹about judgment, because the ruler of this world has been condemned.

12 "I still have many things to say to you, but you cannot bear them now. ¹³When the Spirit of truth comes, he will guide you into all the truth; for he will not speak on his own, but will speak whatever he hears, and he will declare to you the things that are to come. ¹⁴He will glorify me, because he will take what is

---

a The same Greek root refers to pruning and cleansing *b* Or *be* *c* Gk *slaves* *d* Gk *slave* *e* Gk *were of the world* *f* Gk *Slaves* *g* Or *Helper* *h* Or *convict the world of* mine and declare it to you. ¹⁵All that the Father has is mine. For this reason I said that he will take what is mine and declare it to you.

Sorrow Will Turn into Joy

16 "A little while, and you will no longer see me, and again a little while, and you will see me." ¹⁷Then some of his disciples said to one another, "What does he mean by saying to us, 'A little while, and you will no longer see me, and again a little while, and you will see me'; and 'Because I am going to the Father'?" ¹⁸They said, "What does he mean by this 'a little while'? We do not know what he is talking about." ¹⁹Jesus knew that they wanted to ask him, so he said to them, "Are you discussing among yourselves what I meant when I said, 'A little while, and you will no longer see me, and again a little while, and you will see me'? ²⁰Very truly, I tell you, you will weep and mourn, but the world will rejoice; you will have pain, but your pain will turn into joy. ²¹When a woman is in labor, she has pain, because her hour has come. But when her child is born, she no longer remembers the anguish because of the joy of having brought a human being into the world. ²²So you have pain now; but I will see you again, and your hearts will rejoice, and no one will take your joy from you. ²³On that day you will ask nothing of me.ᵃ Very truly, I tell you, if you ask anything of the Father in my name, he will give it to you.ᵇ ²⁴Until now you have not asked for anything in my name. Ask and you will receive, so that your joy may be complete.

Peace for the Disciples

25 "I have said these things to you in figures of speech. The hour is coming when I will no longer speak to you in figures, but will tell you plainly of the Father. ²⁶On that day you will ask in my name. I do not say to you that I will ask the Father on your behalf; ²⁷for the Father himself loves you, because you have loved me and have believed that I came from God.ᶜ ²⁸I came from the Father and have come into the world; again, I am leaving the world and am going to the Father."

29 His disciples said, "Yes, now you are speaking plainly, not in any figure of speech! ³⁰Now we know that you know all things, and do not need to have anyone question you; by this we believe that you came from God." ³¹Jesus answered them, "Do you now believe? ³²The hour is coming, indeed it has come, when you will be scattered, each one to his

---

ᵃ Or will ask me no question ᵇ Other ancient authorities read Father, he will give it to you in my name ᶜ Other ancient authorities read the Father

---

REAL QUESTIONS

RQ

Does God really answer our prayers? Jesus said, "Ask and you will receive" (John 16.24). But I asked God for something and it didn't happen. Why?

"Ask and you will receive." Sounds simple enough. But what does asking in Jesus' name really mean? Even Jesus asked for something he didn't get, praying, "Remove this cup [of suffering] from me." But then he said to his Father in heaven, "Yet, not what I want, but what you want" (Mark 14.36). Think about it for a minute. If the *first* part of his prayer had been answered with a yes, then all of our prayers would be meaningless. Why? Because there'd be no cross. There'd be no Resurrection. There'd be no hope—no forgiveness, no grace, no eternal life, no friendship with God—for any of us.

Is a yes to our prayers *really* always the best answer?

God wants us to pray; the Bible urges us to pray "at all times" (Ephesians 6.18). But think about this. How often are your prayers merely a personal wish list? Does your attitude in prayer mirror Christ's humility—his willingness to put his wants and desires aside in order to obey God? Are *you* willing to honestly pray along with Christ those gutsy words, "Your will be done" (Matthew 6.10), even if God's response is the opposite of what *you* want? Prayer is more than just getting what we want from God; it's a relationship.

Find some Creative Space in this Bible and write your thoughts on these issues, maybe adding some real questions of your own. Then explore more in the verses below, or talk to someone about your real questions.

(Want to explore more? Check out 2 Chronicles 7.14; Matthew 6.1–15; and Philippians 4.6–7.)

home, and you will leave me alone. Yet I am not alone because the Father is with me. ³³I have said this to you, so that in me you may have peace. In the world you face persecution. But take courage; I have conquered the world!"

17 Jesus Prays for His Disciples

After Jesus had spoken these words, he looked up to heaven and said, "Father, the hour has come; glorify your Son so that the Son may glorify you, ²since you have given him authority over all people,ᵃ to give eternal life to all whom you have given him. ³And this is eternal life, that they may know you, the only true God, and Jesus Christ whom you have sent. ⁴I glorified you on earth by finishing the work that you gave me to do. ⁵So now, Father, glorify me in your own presence with the glory that I had in your presence before the world existed.

6 "I have made your name known to those whom you gave me from the world. They were yours, and you gave them to me, and they have kept your word. ⁷Now they know that everything you have given me is from you; ⁸for the words that you gave to me I have given to them, and they have received them and know in truth that I came from you; and they have believed that you sent me. ⁹I am asking on their behalf; I am not asking on behalf of the world, but on behalf of those whom you gave me, because they are yours. ¹⁰All mine are yours, and yours are mine; and I have been glorified in them. ¹¹And now I am no longer in the world, but they are in the world, and I am coming to you. Holy Father, protect them in your name that

a Gk flesh

you have given me, so that they may be one, as we are one. [12]While I was with them, I protected them in your name that[a] you have given me. I guarded them, and not one of them was lost except the one destined to be lost,[b] so that the scripture might be fulfilled. [13]But now I am coming to you, and I speak these things in the world so that they may have my joy made complete in themselves.[c] [14]I have given them your word, and the world has hated them because they do not belong to the world, just as I do not belong to the world. [15]I am not asking you to take them out of the world, but I ask you to protect them from the evil one.[d] [16]They do not belong to the world, just as I do not belong to the world. [17]Sanctify them in the truth; your word is truth. [18]As you have sent me into the world, so I have sent them into the world. [19]And for their sakes I sanctify myself, so that they also may be sanctified in truth.

20 "I ask not only on behalf of these, but also on behalf of those who will believe in me through their word, [21]that they may all be one. As you, Father, are in me and I am in you, may they also be in us,[e] so that the world may believe that you have sent me. [22]The glory that you have given me I have given them, so that they may be one, as we are one, [23]I in them and you in me, that they may become completely one, so that the world may know that you have sent me and have loved them even as you have loved me. [24]Father, I desire that those also, whom you have given me, may be with me where I am, to see my glory, which you have given me because you loved me before the foundation of the world.

25 "Righteous Father, the world does not know you, but I know you; and these know that you have sent me. [26]I made your name known to them, and I will make it known, so that the love with which you have loved me may be in them, and I in them."

18 The Betrayal and Arrest of Jesus

After Jesus had spoken these words, he went out with his disciples across the Kidron valley to a place where there was a garden, which he and his disciples entered. [2]Now Judas, who betrayed him, also knew the place, because Jesus often met there with his disciples. [3]So Judas brought a detachment of soldiers together with police from the chief priests and the Pharisees, and they came there with lanterns and torches and weapons. [4]Then Jesus, knowing all that was to happen to him, came forward and asked them, "Whom are you looking for?"

[5]They answered, "Jesus of Nazareth."[f] Jesus replied, "I am he."[g] Judas, who betrayed him, was standing with them. [6]When Jesus[h] said to them, "I am he,"[g] they stepped back and fell to the ground. [7]Again he asked them, "Whom are you looking for?" And they said, "Jesus of Nazareth."[f] [8]Jesus answered, "I told you that I am he.[g] So if you are looking for me, let these men go." [9]This was to fulfill the word that he had spoken, "I did not lose a single one of those whom you gave me." [10]Then Simon Peter, who had a sword, drew it, struck the high priest's slave, and cut off his right ear. The slave's name was Malchus. [11]Jesus said to Peter, "Put your sword back into its sheath. Am I not to drink the cup that the Father has given me?"

Jesus before the High Priest

12 So the soldiers, their officer, and the Jewish police arrested Jesus and bound him. [13]First they took him to Annas, who was the father-in-law of Caiaphas, the high priest that year. [14]Caiaphas was the one who had advised the Jews that it was better to have one person die for the people.

Peter Denies Jesus

15 Simon Peter and another disciple followed Jesus. Since that disciple was known to the high priest, he went with Jesus into the courtyard of the high priest, [16]but Peter was standing outside at the gate. So the other disciple, who was known to the high priest, went out, spoke to the woman who guarded the gate, and brought Peter in. [17]The woman said to Peter, "You are not also one of this man's disciples, are you?" He said, "I am not." [18]Now the slaves and the police had made a charcoal fire because it was cold, and they were standing around it and warming themselves. Peter also was standing with them and warming himself.

The High Priest Questions Jesus

19 Then the high priest questioned Jesus about his disciples and about his teaching. [20]Jesus answered, "I have spoken openly to the world; I have always taught in synagogues and in the temple, where all the Jews come together. I have said nothing in secret. [21]Why do you ask me? Ask those who heard what I said to them; they know what I said." [22]When he had said this, one of the police standing nearby struck Jesus on the face, saying, "Is that how you answer the high priest?" [23]Jesus answered, "If I have spoken wrongly, testify to the wrong. But if I have spoken rightly, why do you strike

a Other ancient authorities read protected in your name those whom b Gk except the son of destruction c Or among themselves d Or from evil
e Other ancient authorities read be one in us f Gk the Nazorean g Gk I am h Gk he

me?" ²⁴Then Annas sent him bound to Caiaphas the high priest.

Peter Denies Jesus Again

25 Now Simon Peter was standing and warming himself. They asked him, "You are not also one of his disciples, are you?" He denied it and said, "I am not." ²⁶One of the slaves of the high priest, a relative of the man whose ear Peter had cut off, asked, "Did I not see you in the garden with him?" ²⁷Again Peter denied it, and at that moment the cock crowed.

Jesus before Pilate

28 Then they took Jesus from Caiaphas to Pilate's headquarters.^a It was early in the morning. They themselves did not enter the headquarters,^a so as to avoid ritual defilement and to be able to eat the Passover. ²⁹So Pilate went out to them and said, "What accusation do you bring against this man?" ³⁰They answered, "If this man were not a criminal, we would not have handed him over to you." ³¹Pilate said to them, "Take him yourselves and judge him according to your law." The Jews replied, "We are not permitted to put anyone to death." ³²(This was to fulfill what Jesus had said when he indicated the kind of death he was to die.)

33 Then Pilate entered the headquarters^a again, summoned Jesus, and asked him, "Are you the King of the Jews?" ³⁴Jesus answered, "Do you ask this on your own, or did others tell you about me?" ³⁵Pilate replied, "I am not a Jew, am I? Your own nation and the chief priests have handed you over to me. What have you done?" ³⁶Jesus answered, "My kingdom is not from this world. If my kingdom were from this world, my followers would be fighting to keep me from being handed over to the Jews. But as it is, my kingdom is not from here." ³⁷Pilate asked him, "So you are a king?" Jesus answered, "You say that I am a king. For this I was born, and for this I came into the world, to testify to the truth. Everyone who belongs to the truth listens to my voice." ³⁸Pilate asked him, "What is truth?"

Jesus Sentenced to Death

After he had said this, he went out to the Jews again and told them, "I find no case against him. ³⁹But you have a custom that I release someone for you at the Passover. Do you want me to release for you the King of the Jews?" ⁴⁰They shouted in reply, "Not this man, but Barabbas!" Now Barabbas was a bandit.

19 Then Pilate took Jesus and had him flogged. ²And the soldiers wove a crown of thorns and put it on his head, and they dressed him in a purple robe. ³They kept coming up to him, saying, "Hail, King of the Jews!" and striking him on the face. ⁴Pilate went out again and said to them, "Look, I am bringing him out to you to let you know that I find no case against him." ⁵So Jesus came out, wearing the crown of thorns and the purple robe. Pilate said to them, "Here is the man!" ⁶When the chief priests and the police saw him, they shouted, "Crucify him! Crucify him!" Pilate said to them, "Take him yourselves and crucify him; I find no case against him." ⁷The Jews answered him, "We have a law, and according to that law he ought to die because he has claimed to be the Son of God."

8 Now when Pilate heard this, he was more afraid than ever. ⁹He entered his headquarters^a again and asked Jesus, "Where are you from?" But Jesus gave him no answer. ¹⁰Pilate therefore said to him, "Do you refuse to speak to me? Do you not know that I have power to release you, and power to crucify you?" ¹¹Jesus answered him, "You would have no power over me unless it had been given you from above; therefore the one who handed me over to you is guilty of a greater sin." ¹²From then on Pilate tried to release him, but the Jews cried out, "If you release this man, you are no friend of the emperor. Everyone who claims to be a king sets himself against the emperor."

13 When Pilate heard these words, he brought Jesus outside and sat^b on the judge's bench at a place called The Stone Pavement, or in Hebrew^c Gabbatha. ¹⁴Now it was the day of Preparation for the Passover; and it was about noon. He said to the Jews, "Here is your King!" ¹⁵They cried out, "Away with him! Away with him! Crucify him!" Pilate asked them, "Shall I crucify your King?" The chief priests answered, "We have no king but the emperor." ¹⁶Then he handed him over to them to be crucified.

The Crucifixion of Jesus

So they took Jesus; ¹⁷and carrying the cross by himself, he went out to what is called The Place of the Skull, which in Hebrew^c is called Golgotha. ¹⁸There they crucified him, and with him two others, one on either side, with Jesus between them. ¹⁹Pilate also had an inscription written and put on the cross. It read, "Jesus of Nazareth,^d the King of the Jews." ²⁰Many of the Jews read this inscription, because the place where Jesus was crucified was near the city; and it was written in Hebrew,^c in Latin, and in Greek. ²¹Then the chief priests of the Jews said to Pilate, "Do not write, 'The King of the Jews,'

---

a Gk the praetorium b Or seated him c That is, Aramaic d Gk the Nazorean but, 'This man said, I am King of the Jews.' " ²²Pilate answered, "What I have written I have written." ²³When the soldiers had crucified Jesus, they took his clothes and divided them into four parts, one for each soldier. They also took his tunic; now the tunic was seamless, woven in one piece from the top. ²⁴So they said to one another, "Let us not tear it, but cast lots for it to see who will get it." This was to fulfill what the scripture says,

"They divided my clothes among
        themselves,
    and for my clothing they cast lots."

²⁵And that is what the soldiers did.

Meanwhile, standing near the cross of Jesus were his mother, and his mother's sister, Mary the wife of Clopas, and Mary Magdalene. ²⁶When Jesus saw his mother and the disciple whom he loved standing beside her, he said to his mother, "Woman, here is your son." ²⁷Then he said to the disciple, "Here is your mother." And from that hour the disciple took her into his own home.

28 After this, when Jesus knew that all was now finished, he said (in order to fulfill the scripture), "I am thirsty." ²⁹A jar full of sour wine was standing there. So they put a sponge full of the wine on a branch of hyssop and held it to his mouth. ³⁰When Jesus had received the wine, he said, "It is finished." Then he bowed his head and gave up his spirit.

Jesus' Side Is Pierced

31 Since it was the day of Preparation, the Jews did not want the bodies left on the cross during the sabbath, especially because that sabbath was a day of great solemnity. So they asked Pilate to have the legs of the crucified men broken and the bodies removed. ³²Then the soldiers came and broke the legs of the first and of the other who had been crucified with him. ³³But when they came to Jesus and saw that he was already dead, they did not break his legs. ³⁴Instead, one of the soldiers pierced his side with a spear, and at once blood and water came out. ³⁵(He who saw this has testified so that you also may believe. His testimony is true, and he knows*a* that he tells the truth.) ³⁶These things occurred so that the scripture might be fulfilled, "None of his bones shall be broken." ³⁷And again another passage of scripture says, "They will look on the one whom they have pierced."

The Burial of Jesus

38 After these things, Joseph of Arimathea, who was a disciple of Jesus, though a secret one because of his fear of the Jews, asked Pilate to let him take away the body of Jesus. Pilate gave him permission; so he came and removed his body. ³⁹Nicodemus, who had at first come to Jesus by night, also came, bringing a mixture of myrrh and aloes, weighing about a hundred pounds. ⁴⁰They took the body of Jesus and wrapped it with the spices in linen cloths, according to the burial custom of the Jews. ⁴¹Now there was a garden in the place where he was crucified, and in the garden there was a new tomb in which no one had ever been laid. ⁴²And so, because it was the Jewish day of Preparation, and the tomb was nearby, they laid Jesus there.

20 The Resurrection of Jesus

Early on the first day of the week, while it was still dark, Mary Magdalene came to the tomb and saw that the stone had been removed from the tomb. ²So she ran and went to Simon Peter and the other disciple, the one whom Jesus loved, and said to them, "They have taken the Lord out of the tomb, and we do not know where they have laid him." ³Then Peter and the other disciple set out and went toward the tomb. ⁴The two were running together, but the other disciple outran Peter and reached the tomb first. ⁵He bent down to look in and saw the linen wrappings lying there, but he did not go in. ⁶Then Simon Peter came, following him, and went into the tomb. He saw the linen wrappings lying there, ⁷and the cloth that had been on Jesus' head, not lying with the linen wrappings but rolled up in a place by itself. ⁸Then the other disciple, who reached the tomb first, also went in, and he saw and believed; ⁹for as yet they did not understand the scripture, that he must rise from the dead. ¹⁰Then the disciples returned to their homes.

Jesus Appears to Mary Magdalene

11 But Mary stood weeping outside the tomb. As she wept, she bent over to look*b* into the tomb; ¹²and she saw two angels in white, sitting where the body of Jesus had been lying, one at the head and the other at the feet. ¹³They said to her, "Woman, why are you weeping?" She said to them, "They have taken away my Lord, and I do not know where they have laid him." ¹⁴When she had said this, she turned around and saw Jesus standing there, but she did not know that it was Jesus. ¹⁵Jesus said to her, "Woman, why are you weeping? Whom are you looking for?" Supposing him to be the gardener, she said to him, "Sir, if you have carried him away, tell me where you have laid

a Or *there is one who knows* *b* Gk lacks *to look*

PROFILE OF FAITH

Poor Thomas. He sure gets a bad rap. Was he a cynic or what? Read John 20.24–29.

Actually, most of the followers of Jesus had to see before they believed. But you can learn a lot about believing from Thomas. Yes, doubt can lead to faith. If you think about it, you've probably had moments of doubt more than once in your life.

Thomas shows that there are two important aspects of believing. There is a believing *in* Jesus and a believing *because* of the community. The personal part of faith relies on each one of us, individually. We each personally choose to believe in Jesus. The personal part of our faith continues, because there is a community that nurtures and supports our faith and accepts our doubt.

At first, when Jesus appeared to his followers, Thomas was absent. When Thomas heard about it, he just couldn't believe it. For him, seeing was believing. Later, when the Risen Jesus appeared again, Thomas was present in the group of disciples. He believed. Thomas' faith teaches us that we come to believe even more fully when we are part of a believing community.

---

him, and I will take him away." [16]Jesus said to her, "Mary!" She turned and said to him in Hebrew,[a] "Rabbouni!" (which means Teacher). [17]Jesus said to her, "Do not hold on to me, because I have not yet ascended to the Father. But go to my brothers and say to them, 'I am ascending to my Father and your Father, to my God and your God.' " [18]Mary Magdalene went and announced to the disciples, "I have seen the Lord"; and she told them that he had said these things to her.

Jesus Appears to the Disciples

19 When it was evening on that day, the first day of the week, and the doors of the house where the disciples had met were locked for fear of the Jews, Jesus came and stood among them and said, "Peace be with you." [20]After he said this, he showed them his hands and his side. Then the disciples rejoiced when they saw the Lord. [21]Jesus said to them again, "Peace be with you. As the Father has sent me, so I send you." [22]When he had said this, he breathed on them and said to them, "Receive the Holy Spirit. [23]If you forgive the sins of any, they are forgiven them; if you retain the sins of any, they are retained."

Jesus and Thomas

24 But Thomas (who was called the Twin[b]), one of the twelve, was not with them when Jesus came. [25]So the other disciples told him, "We have seen the Lord." But he said to them,

"Unless I see the mark of the nails in his hands, and put my finger in the mark of the nails and my hand in his side, I will not believe."

26 A week later his disciples were again in the house, and Thomas was with them. Although the doors were shut, Jesus came and stood among them and said, "Peace be with you." [27]Then he said to Thomas, "Put your finger here and see my hands. Reach out your hand and put it in my side. Do not doubt but believe." [28]Thomas answered him, "My Lord and my God!" [29]Jesus said to him, "Have you believed because you have seen me? Blessed are those who have not seen and yet have come to believe."

The Purpose of This Book

30 Now Jesus did many other signs in the presence of his disciples, which are not written in this book. [31]But these are written so that you may come to believe[c] that Jesus is the Messiah,[d] the Son of God, and that through believing you may have life in his name.

21 Jesus Appears to Seven Disciples

After these things Jesus showed himself again to the disciples by the Sea of Tiberias; and he showed himself in this way. [2]Gathered there together were Simon Peter, Thomas called the Twin,[b] Nathanael of Cana in Galilee, the sons of Zebedee, and two others of his disciples. [3]Simon Peter said to them, "I am going fishing." They said to him, "We will go with you." They

---

a That is, Aramaic b Gk Didymus c Other ancient authorities read *may continue to believe* d Or *the Christ* went out and got into the boat, but that night they caught nothing.

4 Just after daybreak, Jesus stood on the beach; but the disciples did not know that it was Jesus. [5]Jesus said to them, "Children, you have no fish, have you?" They answered him, "No." [6]He said to them, "Cast the net to the right side of the boat, and you will find some." So they cast it, and now they were not able to haul it in because there were so many fish. [7]That disciple whom Jesus loved said to Peter, "It is the Lord!" When Simon Peter heard that it was the Lord, he put on some clothes, for he was naked, and jumped into the sea. [8]But the other disciples came in the boat, dragging the net full of fish, for they were not far from the land, only about a hundred yards[a] off.

9 When they had gone ashore, they saw a charcoal fire there, with fish on it, and bread. [10]Jesus said to them, "Bring some of the fish that you have just caught." [11]So Simon Peter went aboard and hauled the net ashore, full of large fish, a hundred fifty-three of them; and though there were so many, the net was not torn. [12]Jesus said to them, "Come and have breakfast." Now none of the disciples dared to ask him, "Who are you?" because they knew it was the Lord. [13]Jesus came and took the bread and gave it to them, and did the same with the fish. [14]This was now the third time that Jesus appeared to the disciples after he was raised from the dead.

Jesus and Peter

15 When they had finished breakfast, Jesus said to Simon Peter, "Simon son of John, do you love me more than these?" He said to him, "Yes, Lord; you know that I love you." Jesus said to him, "Feed my lambs." [16]A second time he said to him, "Simon son of John, do you love me?" He said to him, "Yes, Lord; you know that I love you." Jesus said to him, "Tend my sheep." [17]He said to him the third time, "Simon son of John, do you love me?" Peter hurt because he said to him the third time, "Do you love me?" And he said to him, "Lord, you know everything; you know that I love you." Jesus said to him, "Feed my sheep. [18]Very truly, I tell you, when you were younger, you used to fasten your own belt and to go wherever you wished. But when you grow old, you will stretch out your hands, and someone else will fasten a belt around you and take you where you do not wish to go." [19](He said this to indicate the kind of death by which he would glorify God.) After this he said to him, "Follow me."

a Gk two hundred cubits

Pippin: I didn't think it would end this way.

Gandalf: End? No, the journey doesn't end here. Death is just another path...One that we all must take. The grey rain-curtain of this world rolls back and all turns to silver glass...And then you see it.

Pippin: What? Gandalf? See what?

Gandalf: White shores...and beyond, a far green country under a swift sunrise.

Pippin: (smiling) Well, that isn't so bad.

Gandalf: (softly) No...No it isn't.

—Dialogue from the movie
The Lord of the Rings: The Return of the King

Jesus and the Beloved Disciple

20 Peter turned and saw the disciple whom Jesus loved following them; he was the one who had reclined next to Jesus at the supper and had said, "Lord, who is it that is going to betray you?" 21When Peter saw him, he said to Jesus, "Lord, what about him?" 22Jesus said to him, "If it is my will that he remain until I come, what is that to you? Follow me!" 23So the rumor spread in the community*a* that this disciple would not die. Yet Jesus did not say to him that he would not die, but, "If it is my will that he remain until I come, what is that to you?"*b*

24 This is the disciple who is testifying to these things and has written them, and we know that his testimony is true. 25But there are also many other things that Jesus did; if every one of them were written down, I suppose that the world itself could not contain the books that would be written.

a Gk *among the brothers* *b* Other ancient authorities lack *what is that to you*

CREATIVE SPACE

ACTS
THE START OF SOMETHING BIG

Complete Turnaround

First, you have small groups of new disciples of Christ living together, sharing all things, and being a sign of love to those around them. And then you have Paul.

Paul, passionate and committed, won't let anything stop him from achieving his goal of wiping out these new Christians who are an insult to his Jewish faith. He's prepared to travel, use his influence, and do whatever it takes to make that happen.

Fast-forward a few months, and there's Paul again, passionate and committed, determined to do what it takes to achieve his goal. Only this time he's on the other side. This time he's spreading the gospel—preaching, traveling, and getting arrested and imprisoned for his Christian faith.

This tells you a lot about Paul (who earlier was called Saul). He's the type of person who throws himself wholeheartedly into whatever he does. But it tells you even more about Jesus and his power to transform people's lives. Paul hated Christians so much that he participated in killing them. One encounter with Jesus, and Paul's life was turned around. It's a compelling story that's repeated again and again through Acts. And it keeps on being repeated throughout history. The power of the Risen Jesus can revolutionize people's lives. Just think what he might do for you.

> *"I am a man of hope, not for human reasons, nor from any natural optimism, but because I believe the Holy Spirit is at work in the Church and in the world, even when his name remains unheard."*
> —Cardinal Leo Suenens

WHO Acts was written by Luke, the same person who wrote the gospel of Luke.

WHAT Acts reports the growth of the early Church and the power and work of the Holy Spirit.

WHEN Probably written between A.D. 80 and 90

WHERE The action starts in Jerusalem and then spreads to surrounding countries, including modern-day Turkey, Italy, Syria, and Greece.

PATH OF DISCIPLESHIP

As Acts begins, the early Church starts small, with 120 believers wondering what they should do now that Jesus has gone back to be with his Father in heaven. It ends with Paul preaching in Rome, the capital of the empire and a place of power and influence. In between, *thousands* come to believe in Jesus, house churches start from scratch, people get healed, others endure imprisonment for their faith, and the gospel spreads out from the epicenter of Jerusalem.

While all this was going on, the Church faced difficulty, confusion, and conflicts as it grew and expanded. Yet under the influence of the Holy Spirit, Church leaders were able to listen to each other and to the people and come to good resolutions. For us today, as the Church continues to deal with ever changing global issues, the same Spirit that led the early followers is still with us. And how does it happen? God's Spirit fills ordinary people like you who are called by Jesus and gives them the power to put their faith into action, to listen, and to work for the common good. It's that simple. The mission of God is not the exclusive domain of clergy, experts, and professionals. It depends on people like *you*.

GUIDANCE OF THE HOLY SPIRIT

For Jewish people, casting lots was a method used to discern God's will. In **Acts 1.26** the disciples used this method to decide who would replace Judas as a member of the Twelve. That all changed after the coming of the Holy Spirit at Pentecost. After all, why take a chance with the roll of the dice when the Holy Spirit is there for guidance? The disciples waited for the Holy Spirit before continuing their mission (Acts 1.13–14). The Holy Spirit descended on each new group of believers: Jews (4.31), Samaritans (8.17), Gentiles (10.44–45), and followers of John the Baptist (19.6).

In Acts, Luke describes the Holy Spirit as actively guiding the expansion of the early Church. How is the Holy Spirit guiding you?

(Want to explore more? Check out the accounts of Philip and the Ethiopian in 8.29, Barnabas and Saul in 13.2, Paul's travels in 13.4, and the Council of Jerusalem in 15.28.)

1 The Promise of the Holy Spirit

In the first book, Theophilus, I wrote about all that Jesus did and taught from the beginning [2]until the day when he was taken up to heaven, after giving instructions through the Holy Spirit to the apostles whom he had chosen. [3]After his suffering he presented himself alive to them by many convincing proofs, appearing to them during forty days and speaking about the kingdom of God. [4]While staying[a] with them, he ordered them not to leave Jerusalem, but to wait there for the promise of the Father. "This," he said, "is what you have heard from me; [5]for John baptized with water, but you will be baptized with[b] the Holy Spirit not many days from now."

The Ascension of Jesus

[6] So when they had come together, they asked him, "Lord, is this the time when you will restore the kingdom to Israel?" [7]He replied, "It is not for you to know the times or periods that the Father has set by his own authority. [8]But you will receive power when the Holy Spirit has come upon you; and you will be my witnesses in Jerusalem, in all Judea and Samaria, and to the ends of the earth." [9]When he had said this, as they were watching, he was lifted up, and a cloud took him out of their sight. [10]While he was going and they were gazing up toward heaven, suddenly two men in white robes stood by them. [11]They said, "Men of Galilee, why do you stand looking up toward heaven? This Jesus, who has been taken up from you into heaven, will come in the same way as you saw him go into heaven."

Matthias Chosen to Replace Judas

[12] Then they returned to Jerusalem from the mount called Olivet, which is near Jerusalem, a sabbath day's journey away. [13]When they had entered the city, they went to the room upstairs where they were staying, Peter, and John, and James, and Andrew, Philip and Thomas, Bartholomew and Matthew, James son of Alphaeus, and Simon the Zealot, and Judas son of[c] James. [14]All these were constantly devoting themselves to prayer, together with certain women, including Mary the mother of Jesus, as well as his brothers.

[15] In those days Peter stood up among the believers[d] (together the crowd numbered about one hundred twenty persons) and said, [16]"Friends,[e] the scripture had to be fulfilled, which the Holy Spirit through David foretold concerning Judas, who became a guide for those who arrested Jesus— [17]for he was numbered among us and was allotted his share in this ministry." [18](Now this man acquired a field with the reward of his wickedness; and falling headlong,[f] he burst open in the middle and all his bowels gushed out. [19]This became known to all the residents of Jerusalem, so that the field was called in their language Hakeldama, that is, Field of Blood.) [20]"For it is written in the book of Psalms,

'Let his homestead become desolate,
    and let there be no one to live in it';

and

'Let another take his position of overseer.'

[21]So one of the men who have accompanied us during all the time that the Lord Jesus went in and out among us, [22]beginning from the baptism of John until the day when he was taken up from us—one of these must become a witness with us to his resurrection." [23]So they proposed two, Joseph called Barsabbas, who was also known as Justus, and Matthias. [24]Then they prayed and said, "Lord, you know every-

a Or eating b Or by c Or the brother of d Gk brothers e Gk Men, brothers f Or swelling up one's heart. Show us which one of these two you have chosen ²⁵to take the place[a] in this ministry and apostleship from which Judas turned aside to go to his own place." ²⁶And they cast lots for them, and the lot fell on Matthias; and he was added to the eleven apostles.

2 The Coming of the Holy Spirit

When the day of Pentecost had come, they were all together in one place. ²And suddenly from heaven there came a sound like the rush of a violent wind, and it filled the entire house where they were sitting. ³Divided tongues, as of fire, appeared among them, and a tongue rested on each of them. ⁴All of them were filled with the Holy Spirit and began to speak in other languages, as the Spirit gave them ability.

5 Now there were devout Jews from every nation under heaven living in Jerusalem. ⁶And at this sound the crowd gathered and was bewildered, because each one heard them speaking in the native language of each. ⁷Amazed and astonished, they asked, "Are not all these who are speaking Galileans? ⁸And how is it that we hear, each of us, in our own native language? ⁹Parthians, Medes, Elamites, and residents of Mesopotamia, Judea and Cappadocia, Pontus and Asia, ¹⁰Phrygia and Pamphylia, Egypt and the parts of Libya belonging to Cyrene, and visitors from Rome, both Jews and proselytes, ¹¹Cretans and Arabs—in our own languages we hear them speaking about God's deeds of power." ¹²All were amazed and perplexed, saying to one another, "What does this mean?" ¹³But others sneered and said, "They are filled with new wine."

Peter Addresses the Crowd

14 But Peter, standing with the eleven, raised his voice and addressed them, "Men of Judea and all who live in Jerusalem, let this be known to you, and listen to what I say. ¹⁵Indeed, these are not drunk, as you suppose, for it is only nine o'clock in the morning. ¹⁶No, this is what was spoken through the prophet Joel:

¹⁷ 'In the last days it will be, God declares,
   that I will pour out my Spirit upon all flesh,
      and your sons and your daughters shall prophesy,
   and your young men shall see visions,
      and your old men shall dream dreams.
¹⁸ Even upon my slaves, both men and women,
      in those days I will pour out my Spirit;
         and they shall prophesy.
¹⁹ And I will show portents in the heaven above
      and signs on the earth below,
         blood, and fire, and smoky mist.

Sunday

Sunday morning. There's the early morning race to get ready. The hunt for the missing shoe. Bathroom feuds. The harried drive. Then the standing, the sitting, the kneeling, the singing, the listening. The mind wanders. The comfort of routine. On occasion, a shakeup—a visiting priest. A message from the bishop. A parishioner speaking about a recent mission trip. A Baptism.

And somehow people aren't lined up at the door to get in. And we feel awkward, even uncomfortable, inviting someone to come with us. Maybe we aren't all that excited about what we are inviting them to.

How did Jesus capture the hearts and imaginations of multitudes—of tens of thousands of enthusiastic followers? What made the first Church so over-the-top, in-your-face that governments felt threatened enough to try to kill it? What are we missing?

Read **Acts 2.42–47**.

Dirt. Sweat. Raw emotion. Passion. Acceptance. Some had witnessed God in the flesh walking the Judean countryside. Talk about an attraction! But Jesus is long gone to heaven, isn't he? How can we recapture that magic?

Find some Creative Space and write a vision of what you want your parish to be like. Share your thoughts at **Learner.CalltoDiscipleship .com**. Through the power of the Holy Spirit, God can make it happen.

²⁰ The sun shall be turned to darkness
      and the moon to blood,
         before the coming of the Lord's great
            and glorious day.
²¹ Then everyone who calls on the name of the
            Lord shall be saved.'

22 "You that are Israelites,[b] listen to what I have to say: Jesus of Nazareth,[c] a man attested to you by God with deeds of power, wonders, and signs that God did through him among you, as you yourselves know— ²³this man, handed over to you according to the definite plan and foreknowledge of God, you crucified and killed by the hands of those outside the law. ²⁴But God raised him up, having freed him

a Other ancient authorities read the *share* b Gk *Men, Israelites* c Gk *the Nazorean*

27 For you will not abandon my soul to Hades,
   or let your Holy One experience
      corruption.
28 You have made known to me the ways of
      life;
      you will make me full of gladness with
         your presence.'

29 "Fellow Israelites,[b] I may say to you confidently of our ancestor David that he both died and was buried, and his tomb is with us to this day. 30Since he was a prophet, he knew that God had sworn with an oath to him that he would put one of his descendants on his throne. 31Foreseeing this, David[c] spoke of the resurrection of the Messiah,[d] saying,

'He was not abandoned to Hades,
   nor did his flesh experience corruption.'

32This Jesus God raised up, and of that all of us are witnesses. 33Being therefore exalted at[e] the right hand of God, and having received from the Father the promise of the Holy Spirit, he has poured out this that you both see and hear. 34For David did not ascend into the heavens, but he himself says,

'The Lord said to my Lord,
   "Sit at my right hand,
35   until I make your enemies your
         footstool." '

36Therefore let the entire house of Israel know with certainty that God has made him both Lord and Messiah,[f] this Jesus whom you crucified."

The First Converts

37 Now when they heard this, they were cut to the heart and said to Peter and to the other apostles, "Brothers,[b] what should we do?" 38Peter said to them, "Repent, and be baptized every one of you in the name of Jesus Christ so that your sins may be forgiven; and you will receive the gift of the Holy Spirit. 39For the promise is for you, for your children, and for all who are far away, everyone whom the Lord our God calls to him." 40And he testified with many other arguments and exhorted them, saying, "Save yourselves from this corrupt generation." 41So those who welcomed his message were baptized, and that day about three thousand persons were added. 42They devoted themselves to the apostles' teaching and fellowship, to the breaking of bread and the prayers.

Life among the Believers

43 Awe came upon everyone, because many wonders and signs were being done by the apostles. 44All who believed were together and had all things in common; 45they would sell

from death,[a] because it was impossible for him to be held in its power. 25For David says concerning him,

'I saw the Lord always before me,
   for he is at my right hand so that I will
      not be shaken;
26 therefore my heart was glad, and my tongue
      rejoiced;
   moreover my flesh will live in hope.

a Gk the pains of death b Gk Men, brothers c Gk he d Or the Christ e Or by f Or Christ their possessions and goods and distribute the proceeds[a] to all, as any had need. [46]Day by day, as they spent much time together in the temple, they broke bread at home[b] and ate their food with glad and generous[c] hearts, [47]praising God and having the goodwill of all the people. And day by day the Lord added to their number those who were being saved.

3 Peter Heals a Crippled Beggar

One day Peter and John were going up to the temple at the hour of prayer, at three o'clock in the afternoon. [2]And a man lame from birth was being carried in. People would lay him daily at the gate of the temple called the Beautiful Gate so that he could ask for alms from those entering the temple. [3]When he saw Peter and John about to go into the temple, he asked them for alms. [4]Peter looked intently at him, as did John, and said, "Look at us." [5]And he fixed his attention on them, expecting to receive something from them. [6]But Peter said, "I have no silver or gold, but what I have I give you; in the name of Jesus Christ of Nazareth,[d] stand up and walk." [7]And he took him by the right hand and raised him up; and immediately his feet and ankles were made strong. [8]Jumping up, he stood and began to walk, and he entered the temple with them, walking and leaping and praising God. [9]All the people saw him walking and praising God, [10]and they recognized him as the one who used to sit and ask for alms at the Beautiful Gate of the temple; and they were filled with wonder and amazement at what had happened to him.

Peter Speaks in Solomon's Portico

[11] While he clung to Peter and John, all the people ran together to them in the portico called Solomon's Portico, utterly astonished. [12]When Peter saw it, he addressed the people, "You Israelites,[e] why do you wonder at this, or why do you stare at us, as though by our own power or piety we had made him walk? [13]The God of Abraham, the God of Isaac, and the God of Jacob, the God of our ancestors has glorified his servant[f] Jesus, whom you handed over and rejected in the presence of Pilate, though he had decided to release him. [14]But you rejected the Holy and Righteous One and asked to have a murderer given to you, [15]and you killed the Author of life, whom God raised from the dead. To this we are witnesses. [16]And by faith in his name, his name itself has made this man strong, whom you see and know; and the faith

that is through Jesus[g] has given him this perfect health in the presence of all of you.

[17] "And now, friends,[h] I know that you acted in ignorance, as did also your rulers. [18]In this way God fulfilled what he had foretold through all the prophets, that his Messiah[i] would suffer. [19]Repent therefore, and turn to God so that your sins may be wiped out, [20]so that times of refreshing may come from the presence of the Lord, and that he may send the Messiah[j] appointed for you, that is, Jesus, [21]who must remain in heaven until the time of universal restoration that God announced long ago through his holy prophets. [22]Moses said, 'The Lord your God will raise up for you from your own people[h] a prophet like me. You must listen to whatever he tells you. [23]And it will be that everyone who does not listen to that prophet will be utterly rooted out of the people.' [24]And all the prophets, as many as have spoken, from Samuel and those after him, also predicted these days. [25]You are the descendants of the prophets and of the covenant that God gave to your ancestors, saying to Abraham, 'And in your descendants all the families of the earth shall be blessed.' [26]When God raised up his servant,[f] he sent him first to you, to bless you by turning each of you from your wicked ways."

4 Peter and John before the Council

While Peter and John[k] were speaking to the people, the priests, the captain of the temple, and the Sadducees came to them, [2]much annoyed because they were teaching the people and proclaiming that in Jesus there is the resurrection of the dead. [3]So they arrested them and put them in custody until the next day, for it was already evening. [4]But many of those who heard the word believed; and they numbered about five thousand.

[5] The next day their rulers, elders, and scribes assembled in Jerusalem, [6]with Annas the high priest, Caiaphas, John,[l] and Alexander, and all who were of the high-priestly family. [7]When they had made the prisoners[a] stand in their midst, they inquired, "By what power or by what name did you do this?" [8]Then Peter, filled with the Holy Spirit, said to them, "Rulers of the people and elders, [9]if we are questioned today because of a good deed done to someone who was sick and are asked how this man has been healed, [10]let it be known to all of you, and to all the people of Israel, that this man is standing before you in good health by the name of Jesus Christ of Nazareth,[d] whom

---

a Gk them b Or from house to house c Or sincere d Gk the Nazorean e Gk Men, Israelites f Or child g Gk him h Gk brothers i Or his Christ
j Or the Christ k Gk While they l Other ancient authorities read Jonathan

you crucified, whom God raised from the dead. [11]This Jesus[a] is

'the stone that was rejected by you, the builders;

it has become the cornerstone.'[b]

[12]There is salvation in no one else, for there is no other name under heaven given among mortals by which we must be saved."

13 Now when they saw the boldness of Peter and John and realized that they were uneducated and ordinary men, they were amazed and recognized them as companions of Jesus. [14]When they saw the man who had been cured standing beside them, they had nothing to say in opposition. [15]So they ordered them to leave the council while they discussed the matter with one another. [16]They said, "What will we do with them? For it is obvious to all who live in Jerusalem that a notable sign has been done through them; we cannot deny it. [17]But to keep it from spreading further among the people, let us warn them to speak no more to anyone in this name." [18]So they called them and ordered them not to speak or teach at all in the name of Jesus. [19]But Peter and John answered them, "Whether it is right in God's sight to listen to you rather than to God, you must judge; [20]for we cannot keep from speaking about what we have seen and heard." [21]After threatening them again, they let them go, finding no way to punish them because of the people, for all of them praised God for what had happened. [22]For the man on whom this sign of healing had been performed was more than forty years old.

The Believers Pray for Boldness

23 After they were released, they went to their friends[c] and reported what the chief priests and the elders had said to them. [24]When they heard it, they raised their voices together to God and said, "Sovereign Lord, who made the heaven and the earth, the sea, and everything in them, [25]it is you who said by the Holy Spirit through our ancestor David, your servant:[d]

'Why did the Gentiles rage,

and the peoples imagine vain things?

[26] The kings of the earth took their stand,

and the rulers have gathered together

against the Lord and against his

Messiah.'[e]

[27]For in this city, in fact, both Herod and Pontius Pilate, with the Gentiles and the peoples of Israel, gathered together against your holy servant[d] Jesus, whom you anointed, [28]to do whatever your hand and your plan had predestined to take place. [29]And now, Lord, look

at their threats, and grant to your servants[f] to speak your word with all boldness, [30]while you stretch out your hand to heal, and signs and wonders are performed through the name of your holy servant[d] Jesus." [31]When they had prayed, the place in which they were gathered together was shaken; and they were all filled with the Holy Spirit and spoke the word of God with boldness.

The Believers Share Their Possessions

32 Now the whole group of those who believed were of one heart and soul, and no one claimed private ownership of any possessions, but everything they owned was held in common. [33]With great power the apostles gave their testimony to the resurrection of the Lord Jesus, and great grace was upon them all. [34]There was not a needy person among them, for as many as owned lands or houses sold them and brought the proceeds of what was sold. [35]They laid it at the apostles' feet, and it was distributed to each as any had need. [36]There was a Levite, a native of Cyprus, Joseph, to whom the apostles gave the name Barnabas (which means "son of encouragement"). [37]He sold a field that belonged to him, then brought the money, and laid it at the apostles' feet.

5 Ananias and Sapphira

But a man named Ananias, with the consent of his wife Sapphira, sold a piece of property; [2]with his wife's knowledge, he kept back some of the proceeds, and brought only a part and laid it at the apostles' feet. [3]"Ananias," Peter asked, "why has Satan filled your heart to lie to the Holy Spirit and to keep back part of the proceeds of the land? [4]While it remained unsold, did it not remain your own? And after it was sold, were not the proceeds at your disposal? How is it that you have contrived this deed in your heart? You did not lie to us[g] but to God!" [5]Now when Ananias heard these words, he fell down and died. And great fear seized all who heard of it. [6]The young men came and wrapped up his body,[h] then carried him out and buried him.

7 After an interval of about three hours his wife came in, not knowing what had happened. [8]Peter said to her, "Tell me whether you and your husband sold the land for such and such a price." And she said, "Yes, that was the price." [9]Then Peter said to her, "How is it that you have agreed together to put the Spirit of the Lord to the test? Look, the feet of those who have buried your husband are at the door, and they will carry you out." [10]Immediately she fell down at his feet and died. When the young

---

a Gk This *b* Or keystone *c* Gk their own *d* Or child *e* Or his Christ *f* Gk slaves *g* Gk to men *h* Meaning of Gk uncertain men came in they found her dead, so they carried her out and buried her beside her husband. ¹¹And great fear seized the whole church and all who heard of these things.

The Apostles Heal Many

12 Now many signs and wonders were done among the people through the apostles. And they were all together in Solomon's Portico. ¹³None of the rest dared to join them, but the people held them in high esteem. ¹⁴Yet more than ever believers were added to the Lord, great numbers of both men and women, ¹⁵so that they even carried out the sick into the streets, and laid them on cots and mats, in order that Peter's shadow might fall on some of them as he came by. ¹⁶A great number of people would also gather from the towns around Jerusalem, bringing the sick and those tormented by unclean spirits, and they were all cured.

The Apostles Are Persecuted

17 Then the high priest took action; he and all who were with him (that is, the sect of the Sadducees), being filled with jealousy, ¹⁸arrested the apostles and put them in the public prison. ¹⁹But during the night an angel of the Lord opened the prison doors, brought them out, and said, ²⁰"Go, stand in the temple and tell the people the whole message about this life."

²¹When they heard this, they entered the temple at daybreak and went on with their teaching.

When the high priest and those with him arrived, they called together the council and the whole body of the elders of Israel, and sent to the prison to have them brought. ²²But when the temple police went there, they did not find them in the prison; so they returned and reported, ²³"We found the prison securely locked and the guards standing at the doors, but when we opened them, we found no one inside." ²⁴Now when the captain of the temple and the chief priests heard these words, they were perplexed about them, wondering what might be going on. ²⁵Then someone arrived and announced, "Look, the men whom you put in prison are standing in the temple and teaching the people!" ²⁶Then the captain went with the temple police and brought them, but without violence, for they were afraid of being stoned by the people.

27 When they had brought them, they had them stand before the council. The high priest questioned them, ²⁸saying, "We gave you strict orders not to teach in this name,ᵃ yet here you have filled Jerusalem with your teaching and you are determined to bring this man's blood on us." ²⁹But Peter and the apostles answered, "We must obey God rather than any human authority.ᵇ ³⁰The God of our ancestors raised up Jesus, whom you had killed by hanging him

---

a Other ancient authorities read *Did we not give you strict orders not to teach in this name?* *b* Gk *than men* on a tree. [31]God exalted him at his right hand as Leader and Savior that he might give repentance to Israel and forgiveness of sins. [32]And we are witnesses to these things, and so is the Holy Spirit whom God has given to those who obey him."

33 When they heard this, they were enraged and wanted to kill them. [34]But a Pharisee in the council named Gamaliel, a teacher of the law, respected by all the people, stood up and ordered the men to be put outside for a short time. [35]Then he said to them, "Fellow Israelites,[a] consider carefully what you propose to do to these men. [36]For some time ago Theudas rose up, claiming to be somebody, and a number of men, about four hundred, joined him; but he was killed, and all who followed him were dispersed and disappeared. [37]After him Judas the Galilean rose up at the time of the census and got people to follow him; he also perished, and all who followed him were scattered. [38]So in the present case, I tell you, keep away from these men and let them alone; because if this plan or this undertaking is of human origin, it will fail; [39]but if it is of God, you will not be able to overthrow them—in that case you may even be found fighting against God!"

They were convinced by him, [40]and when they had called in the apostles, they had them flogged. Then they ordered them not to speak in the name of Jesus, and let them go. [41]As they left the council, they rejoiced that they were considered worthy to suffer dishonor for the sake of the name. [42]And every day in the temple and at home[b] they did not cease to teach and proclaim Jesus as the Messiah.[c]

6 Seven Chosen to Serve

Now during those days, when the disciples were increasing in number, the Hellenists complained against the Hebrews because their widows were being neglected in the daily distribution of food. [2]And the twelve called together the whole community of the disciples and said, "It is not right that we should neglect the word of God in order to wait on tables.[d] [3]Therefore, friends,[e] select from among yourselves seven men of good standing, full of the Spirit and of wisdom, whom we may appoint to this task, [4]while we, for our part, will devote ourselves to prayer and to serving the word." [5]What they said pleased the whole community, and they chose Stephen, a man full of faith and the Holy Spirit, together with Philip, Prochorus, Nicanor, Timon, Parmenas, and Nicolaus, a proselyte of Antioch. [6]They had these men stand before the apostles, who prayed and laid their hands on them.

7 The word of God continued to spread; the number of the disciples increased greatly in Jerusalem, and a great many of the priests became obedient to the faith.

The Arrest of Stephen

8 Stephen, full of grace and power, did great wonders and signs among the people. [9]Then some of those who belonged to the synagogue of the Freedmen (as it was called), Cyrenians, Alexandrians, and others of those from Cilicia and Asia, stood up and argued with Stephen. [10]But they could not withstand the wisdom and the Spirit[f] with which he spoke. [11]Then they secretly instigated some men to say, "We have heard him speak blasphemous words against Moses and God." [12]They stirred up the people as well as the elders and the scribes; then they suddenly confronted him, seized him, and brought him before the council. [13]They set up false witnesses who said, "This man never stops saying things against this holy place and the law; [14]for we have heard him say that this Jesus of Nazareth[g] will destroy this place and will change the customs that Moses handed on to us." [15]And all who sat in the council looked intently at him, and they saw that his face was like the face of an angel.

7 Stephen's Speech to the Council

Then the high priest asked him, "Are these things so?" [2]And Stephen replied:

"Brothers[h] and fathers, listen to me. The God of glory appeared to our ancestor Abraham when he was in Mesopotamia, before he lived in Haran, [3]and said to him, 'Leave your country and your relatives and go to the land that I will show you.' [4]Then he left the country of the Chaldeans and settled in Haran. After his father died, God had him move from there to this

---

a Gk Men, Israelites b Or from house to house c Or the Christ d Or keep accounts e Gk brothers f Or spirit g Gk the Nazorean h Gk Men, brothers country in which you are now living. [5]He did not give him any of it as a heritage, not even a foot's length, but promised to give it to him as his possession and to his descendants after him, even though he had no child. [6]And God spoke in these terms, that his descendants would be resident aliens in a country belonging to others, who would enslave them and mistreat them during four hundred years. [7]'But I will judge the nation that they serve,' said God, 'and after that they shall come out and worship me in this place.' [8]Then he gave him the covenant of circumcision. And so Abraham[a] became the father of Isaac and circumcised him on the eighth day; and Isaac became the father of Jacob, and Jacob of the twelve patriarchs.

9 "The patriarchs, jealous of Joseph, sold him into Egypt; but God was with him, [10]and rescued him from all his afflictions, and enabled him to win favor and to show wisdom when he stood before Pharaoh, king of Egypt, who appointed him ruler over Egypt and over all his household. [11]Now there came a famine throughout Egypt and Canaan, and great suffering, and our ancestors could find no food. [12]But when Jacob heard that there was grain in Egypt, he sent our ancestors there on their first visit. [13]On the second visit Joseph made himself known to his brothers, and Joseph's family became known to Pharaoh. [14]Then Joseph sent and invited his father Jacob and all his relatives to come to him, seventy-five in all; [15]so Jacob went down to Egypt. He himself died there as well as our ancestors, [16]and their bodies[b] were brought back to Shechem and laid in the tomb that Abraham had bought for a sum of silver from the sons of Hamor in Shechem.

17 "But as the time drew near for the fulfillment of the promise that God had made to Abraham, our people in Egypt increased and multiplied [18]until another king who had not known Joseph ruled over Egypt. [19]He dealt craftily with our race and forced our ancestors to abandon their infants so that they would die. [20]At this time Moses was born, and he was beautiful before God. For three months he was brought up in his father's house; [21]and when he was abandoned, Pharaoh's daughter adopted him and brought him up as her own son. [22]So Moses was instructed in all the wisdom of the Egyptians and was powerful in his words and deeds.

23 "When he was forty years old, it came into his heart to visit his relatives, the Israelites.[c] [24]When he saw one of them being wronged, he defended the oppressed man and avenged him by striking down the Egyp-

tian. [25]He supposed that his kinsfolk would understand that God through him was rescuing them, but they did not understand. [26]The next day he came to some of them as they were quarreling and tried to reconcile them, saying, 'Men, you are brothers; why do you wrong each other?' [27]But the man who was wronging his neighbor pushed Moses[d] aside, saying, 'Who made you a ruler and a judge over us? [28]Do you want to kill me as you killed the Egyptian yesterday?' [29]When he heard this, Moses fled and became a resident alien in the land of Midian. There he became the father of two sons.

30 "Now when forty years had passed, an angel appeared to him in the wilderness of Mount Sinai, in the flame of a burning bush. [31]When Moses saw it, he was amazed at the sight; and as he approached to look, there came the voice of the Lord: [32]'I am the God of your ancestors, the God of Abraham, Isaac, and Jacob.' Moses began to tremble and did not dare to look. [33]Then the Lord said to him, 'Take off the sandals from your feet, for the place where you are standing is holy ground. [34]I have surely seen the mistreatment of my people who are in Egypt and have heard their groaning, and I have come down to rescue them. Come now, I will send you to Egypt.'

35 "It was this Moses whom they rejected when they said, 'Who made you a ruler and a judge?' and whom God now sent as both ruler and liberator through the angel who appeared to him in the bush. [36]He led them out, having performed wonders and signs in Egypt, at the Red Sea, and in the wilderness for forty years. [37]This is the Moses who said to the Israelites, 'God will raise up a prophet for you from your own people[e] as he raised me up.' [38]He is the one who was in the congregation in the wilderness with the angel who spoke to him at Mount Sinai, and with our ancestors; and he received living oracles to give to us. [39]Our ancestors were unwilling to obey him; instead, they pushed him aside, and in their hearts they turned back to Egypt, [40]saying to Aaron, 'Make gods for us who will lead the way for us; as for this Moses who led us out from the land of Egypt, we do not know what has happened to him.' [41]At that time they made a calf, offered a sacrifice to the idol, and reveled in the works of their hands. [42]But God turned away from them and handed them over to worship the host of heaven, as it is written in the book of the prophets:

'Did you offer to me slain victims and
        sacrifices
    forty years in the wilderness, O house of
        Israel?

---

a Gk he b Gk they c Gk his brothers, the sons of Israel d Gk him e Gk your brothers

Scaly Eyes

Think of the person you'd be least likely to have a conversation with at school. This person may have a different circle of friends and different values. This person may have different taste in music or clothes. This person may have a different cultural background, a different religion, a different perspective of the world. This person is the least likely candidate to ever know Jesus or, conversely, may hypocritically call himself or herself a Christian. You may not like this person very much, if at all.

Read **Acts 9.1–26**. Now imagine the situation for some of the early Christians in Jerusalem. One of their worst enemies—Saul, a religious leader who had been eager to kill Jesus followers—had now *supposedly* become a Christian. Put yourself in their shoes (or sandals). Would *you* believe it? Would *you* welcome this creep, this enemy, this murderer with open arms? Would you be able to overlook your past differences and embrace him as part of your Church family?

Read the rest of the story in **Acts 9.27–31**. Now, if you have a computer and enjoy graphic design, create a 3-D model of what it looks like to be separated from someone. Then design another model of what it would look like to reach out to others and bridge the gap of separation. (If you don't have access to a computer or know how to do graphic design, you can also draw these contrasting pictures by hand.) As you make your designs, think about these questions. How might God be challenging you to extend kindness to those you don't like? (After all, God loves those people just as much as he loves you!)

Imagine overcoming the separations between you and others. How could that be done? How might that feel? What difference could you make in your school if you lived as a bridge builder instead of just sticking with your own group of friends?

Share your creation on **Learner.CalltoDiscipleship.com** and see what kinds of comments come your way.

---

⁴³ No; you took along the tent of Moloch,
    and the star of your god Rephan,
        the images that you made to worship;
    so I will remove you beyond Babylon.'

44 "Our ancestors had the tent of testimony in the wilderness, as God[a] directed when he spoke to Moses, ordering him to make it according to the pattern he had seen. ⁴⁵Our ancestors in turn brought it in with Joshua when they dispossessed the nations that God drove out before our ancestors. And it was there until the time of David, ⁴⁶who found favor with God and asked that he might find a dwelling place for the house of Jacob.[b] ⁴⁷But it was Solomon who built a house for him. ⁴⁸Yet the Most High does not dwell in houses made with human hands;[c] as the prophet says,

⁴⁹ 'Heaven is my throne,
    and the earth is my footstool.
  What kind of house will you build for me,
        says the Lord,
    or what is the place of my rest?
⁵⁰ Did not my hand make all these things?'

51 "You stiff-necked people, uncircumcised in heart and ears, you are forever opposing the Holy Spirit, just as your ancestors used to do. ⁵²Which of the prophets did your ancestors not persecute? They killed those who foretold the coming of the Righteous One, and now you have become his betrayers and murderers. ⁵³You are the ones that received the law as ordained by angels, and yet you have not kept it."

The Stoning of Stephen

54 When they heard these things, they became enraged and ground their teeth at Stephen.[d] ⁵⁵But filled with the Holy Spirit, he gazed into heaven and saw the glory of God and Jesus standing at the right hand of God. ⁵⁶"Look," he said, "I see the heavens opened and the Son of Man standing at the right hand of God!" ⁵⁷But they covered their ears, and with a loud shout all rushed together against him. ⁵⁸Then they dragged him out of the city and began to stone him; and the witnesses laid their coats at the feet of a young man named Saul. ⁵⁹While they were stoning Stephen, he prayed, "Lord Jesus, receive my spirit." ⁶⁰Then he knelt down and cried out in a loud voice, "Lord, do not hold this sin against them." When he had

8 said this, he died.[e] ¹And Saul approved of their killing him.

Saul Persecutes the Church

That day a severe persecution began against the church in Jerusalem, and all except the apos-

a Gk he b Other ancient authorities read *for the God of Jacob*
c Gk *with hands* d Gk *him* e Gk *fell asleep*

tles were scattered throughout the countryside of Judea and Samaria. [2]Devout men buried Stephen and made loud lamentation over him. [3]But Saul was ravaging the church by entering house after house; dragging off both men and women, he committed them to prison.

Philip Preaches in Samaria

4 Now those who were scattered went from place to place, proclaiming the word. [5]Philip went down to the city[a] of Samaria and proclaimed the Messiah[b] to them. [6]The crowds with one accord listened eagerly to what was said by Philip, hearing and seeing the signs that he did, [7]for unclean spirits, crying with loud shrieks, came out of many who were possessed; and many others who were paralyzed or lame were cured. [8]So there was great joy in that city.

9 Now a certain man named Simon had previously practiced magic in the city and amazed the people of Samaria, saying that he was someone great. [10]All of them, from the least to the greatest, listened to him eagerly, saying, "This man is the power of God that is called Great." [11]And they listened eagerly to him because for a long time he had amazed them with his magic. [12]But when they believed Philip, who was proclaiming the good news about the kingdom of God and the name of Jesus Christ, they were baptized, both men and women. [13]Even Simon himself believed. After being baptized, he stayed constantly with Philip and was amazed when he saw the signs and great miracles that took place.

14 Now when the apostles at Jerusalem heard that Samaria had accepted the word of God, they sent Peter and John to them. [15]The two went down and prayed for them that they might receive the Holy Spirit [16](for as yet the Spirit had not come[c] upon any of them; they had only been baptized in the name of the Lord Jesus). [17]Then Peter and John[d] laid their hands on them, and they received the Holy Spirit. [18]Now when Simon saw that the Spirit was given through the laying on of the apostles' hands, he offered them money, [19]saying, "Give me also this power so that anyone on whom I lay my hands may receive the Holy Spirit." [20]But Peter said to him, "May your silver perish with you, because you thought you could obtain God's gift with money! [21]You have no part or share in this, for your heart is not right before God. [22]Repent therefore of this wickedness of yours, and pray to the Lord that, if possible, the intent of your heart may be forgiven you. [23]For I see that you are in the gall of bitterness and the chains of wickedness." [24]Simon answered, "Pray for me to the Lord, that nothing of what you[e] have said may happen to me."

25 Now after Peter and John[f] had testified and spoken the word of the Lord, they returned to Jerusalem, proclaiming the good news to many villages of the Samaritans.

Philip and the Ethiopian Eunuch

26 Then an angel of the Lord said to Philip, "Get up and go toward the south[g] to the road that goes down from Jerusalem to Gaza." (This is a wilderness road.) [27]So he got up and went. Now there was an Ethiopian eunuch, a court official of the Candace, queen of the Ethiopians, in charge of her entire treasury. He had come to Jerusalem to worship [28]and was returning home; seated in his chariot, he was reading the prophet Isaiah. [29]Then the Spirit said to Philip, "Go over to this chariot and join it." [30]So Philip ran up to it and heard him reading the prophet Isaiah. He asked, "Do you understand what you are reading?" [31]He replied, "How can I, unless someone guides me?" And he invited Philip to get in and sit beside him. [32]Now the passage of the scripture that he was reading was this:

"Like a sheep he was led to the slaughter,
  and like a lamb silent before its shearer,
    so he does not open his mouth.
[33] In his humiliation justice was denied him.
  Who can describe his generation?
    For his life is taken away from the earth."

[34]The eunuch asked Philip, "About whom, may I ask you, does the prophet say this, about himself or about someone else?" [35]Then Philip began to speak, and starting with this scripture, he proclaimed to him the good news about Jesus. [36]As they were going along the road, they came to some water; and the eunuch said, "Look, here is water! What is to prevent me from being baptized?"[h] [38]He commanded the chariot to stop, and both of them, Philip and the eunuch, went down into the water, and Philip[i] baptized him. [39]When they came up out of the water, the Spirit of the Lord snatched Philip away; the eunuch saw him no more, and went on his way rejoicing. [40]But Philip found himself at Azotus, and as he was passing through the region, he proclaimed the good news to all the towns until he came to Caesarea.

9 The Conversion of Saul

Meanwhile Saul, still breathing threats and murder against the disciples of the Lord, went to the high priest [2]and asked him for letters

---

a Other ancient authorities read a city b Or the Christ c Gk fallen d Gk they e The Greek word for you and the verb pray are plural f Gk after they g Or go at noon h Other ancient authorities add all or most of verse 37, And Philip said, "If you believe with all your heart, you may." And he replied, "I believe that Jesus Christ is the Son of God." i Gk he to the synagogues at Damascus, so that if he found any who belonged to the Way, men or women, he might bring them bound to Jerusalem. ³Now as he was going along and approaching Damascus, suddenly a light from heaven flashed around him. ⁴He fell to the ground and heard a voice saying to him, "Saul, Saul, why do you persecute me?" ⁵He asked, "Who are you, Lord?" The reply came, "I am Jesus, whom you are persecuting. ⁶But get up and enter the city, and you will be told what you are to do." ⁷The men who were traveling with him stood speechless because they heard the voice but saw no one. ⁸Saul got up from the ground, and though his eyes were open, he could see nothing; so they led him by the hand and brought him into Damascus. ⁹For three days he was without sight, and neither ate nor drank.

10 Now there was a disciple in Damascus named Ananias. The Lord said to him in a vision, "Ananias." He answered, "Here I am, Lord." ¹¹The Lord said to him, "Get up and go to the street called Straight, and at the house of Judas look for a man of Tarsus named Saul. At this moment he is praying, ¹²and he has seen in a vision[a] a man named Ananias come in and lay his hands on him so that he might regain his sight." ¹³But Ananias answered, "Lord, I have heard from many about this man, how much evil he has done to your saints in Jerusalem; ¹⁴and here he has authority from the chief priests to bind all who invoke your name." ¹⁵But the Lord said to him, "Go, for he is an instrument whom I have chosen to bring my name before Gentiles and kings and before the people of Israel; ¹⁶I myself will show him how much he must suffer for the sake of my name." ¹⁷So Ananias went and entered the house. He laid his hands on Saul[b] and said, "Brother Saul, the Lord Jesus, who appeared to you on your way here, has sent me so that you may regain your sight and be filled with the Holy Spirit." ¹⁸And immediately something like scales fell from his eyes, and his sight was restored. Then he got up and was baptized, ¹⁹and after taking some food, he regained his strength.

Saul Preaches in Damascus

For several days he was with the disciples in Damascus, ²⁰and immediately he began to proclaim Jesus in the synagogues, saying, "He is the Son of God." ²¹All who heard him were amazed and said, "Is not this the man who made havoc in Jerusalem among those who invoked this name? And has he not come here for the purpose of bringing them bound be-fore the chief priests?" ²²Saul became increasingly more powerful and confounded the Jews who lived in Damascus by proving that Jesus[c] was the Messiah.[d]

Saul Escapes from the Jews

23 After some time had passed, the Jews plotted to kill him, ²⁴but their plot became known to Saul. They were watching the gates day and night so that they might kill him; ²⁵but his disciples took him by night and let him down through an opening in the wall,[e] lowering him in a basket.

Saul in Jerusalem

26 When he had come to Jerusalem, he attempted to join the disciples; and they were all afraid of him, for they did not believe that he was a disciple. ²⁷But Barnabas took him, brought him to the apostles, and described for them how on the road he had seen the Lord, who had spoken to him, and how in Damascus he had spoken boldly in the name of Jesus. ²⁸So he went in and out among them in Jerusalem, speaking boldly in the name of the Lord. ²⁹He spoke and argued with the Hellenists; but they were attempting to kill him. ³⁰When the believers[f] learned of it, they brought him down to Caesarea and sent him off to Tarsus.

31 Meanwhile the church throughout Judea, Galilee, and Samaria had peace and was built up. Living in the fear of the Lord and in the comfort of the Holy Spirit, it increased in numbers.

The Healing of Aeneas

32 Now as Peter went here and there among all the believers,[g] he came down also to the saints living in Lydda. ³³There he found a man named Aeneas, who had been bedridden for eight years, for he was paralyzed. ³⁴Peter said to him, "Aeneas, Jesus Christ heals you; get up and make your bed!" And immediately he got up. ³⁵And all the residents of Lydda and Sharon saw him and turned to the Lord.

Peter in Lydda and Joppa

36 Now in Joppa there was a disciple whose name was Tabitha, which in Greek is Dorcas.[h] She was devoted to good works and acts of charity. ³⁷At that time she became ill and died. When they had washed her, they laid her in a room upstairs. ³⁸Since Lydda was near Joppa, the disciples, who heard that Peter was there, sent two men to him with the request, "Please come to us without delay." ³⁹So Peter got up and went with them; and when he arrived, they

a Other ancient authorities lack in a vision b Gk him c Gk that this d Or the Christ e Gk through the wall f Gk brothers g Gk all of them h The name Tabitha in Aramaic and the name Dorcas in Greek mean a gazelle took him to the room upstairs. All the widows stood beside him, weeping and showing tunics and other clothing that Dorcas had made while she was with them. ⁴⁰Peter put all of them outside, and then he knelt down and prayed. He turned to the body and said, "Tabitha, get up." Then she opened her eyes, and seeing Peter, she sat up. ⁴¹He gave her his hand and helped her up. Then calling the saints and widows, he showed her to be alive. ⁴²This became known throughout Joppa, and many believed in the Lord. ⁴³Meanwhile he stayed in Joppa for some time with a certain Simon, a tanner.

10 Peter and Cornelius

In Caesarea there was a man named Cornelius, a centurion of the Italian Cohort, as it was called. ²He was a devout man who feared God with all his household; he gave alms generously to the people and prayed constantly to God. ³One afternoon at about three o'clock he had a vision in which he clearly saw an angel of God coming in and saying to him, "Cornelius." ⁴He stared at him in terror and said, "What is it, Lord?" He answered, "Your prayers and your alms have ascended as a memorial before God. ⁵Now send men to Joppa for a certain Simon who is called Peter; ⁶he is lodging with Simon, a tanner, whose house is by the seaside." ⁷When the angel who spoke to him had left, he called two of his slaves and a devout soldier from the ranks of those who served him, ⁸and after telling them everything, he sent them to Joppa.

9 About noon the next day, as they were on their journey and approaching the city, Peter went up on the roof to pray. ¹⁰He became hungry and wanted something to eat; and while it was being prepared, he fell into a trance. ¹¹He saw the heaven opened and something like a large sheet coming down, being lowered to the ground by its four corners. ¹²In it were all kinds of four-footed creatures and reptiles and birds of the air. ¹³Then he heard a voice saying, "Get up, Peter; kill and eat." ¹⁴But Peter said, "By no means, Lord; for I have never eaten anything that is profane or unclean." ¹⁵The voice said to him again, a second time, "What God has made clean, you must not call profane." ¹⁶This happened three times, and the thing was suddenly taken up to heaven.

17 Now while Peter was greatly puzzled about what to make of the vision that he had seen, suddenly the men sent by Cornelius appeared. They were asking for Simon's house and were standing by the gate. ¹⁸They called out to ask whether Simon, who was called Pe-

ter, was staying there. ¹⁹While Peter was still thinking about the vision, the Spirit said to him, "Look, three*ᵃ* men are searching for you. ²⁰Now get up, go down, and go with them without hesitation; for I have sent them." ²¹So Peter went down to the men and said, "I am the one you are looking for; what is the reason for your coming?" ²²They answered, "Cornelius, a centurion, an upright and God-fearing man, who is well spoken of by the whole Jewish nation, was directed by a holy angel to send for you to come to his house and to hear what you have to say." ²³So Peter*ᵇ* invited them in and gave them lodging.

The next day he got up and went with them, and some of the believers*ᶜ* from Joppa accompanied him. ²⁴The following day they came to Caesarea. Cornelius was expecting them and had called together his relatives and close friends. ²⁵On Peter's arrival Cornelius met him,

TEXT MESSAGE

There were a variety of names used to describe the group of early followers of Jesus: the Way (Acts 9.2), the brothers (9.30), the sect of the Nazarenes (24.5), Christian (26.28). Back then, the word "Christian" was sometimes used scornfully by those who were antagonistic toward the early Church.

This information has been scanned and is free of all known viruses. Please forward to all your friends.

a One ancient authority reads *two*; others lack the word
b Gk *he* *c* Gk *brothers*

and falling at his feet, worshiped him. 26But Peter made him get up, saying, "Stand up; I am only a mortal." 27And as he talked with him, he went in and found that many had assembled; 28and he said to them, "You yourselves know that it is unlawful for a Jew to associate with or to visit a Gentile; but God has shown me that I should not call anyone profane or unclean. 29So when I was sent for, I came without objection. Now may I ask why you sent for me?"

30 Cornelius replied, "Four days ago at this very hour, at three o'clock, I was praying in my house when suddenly a man in dazzling clothes stood before me. 31He said, 'Cornelius, your prayer has been heard and your alms have been remembered before God. 32Send therefore to Joppa and ask for Simon, who is called Peter; he is staying in the home of Simon, a tanner, by the sea.' 33Therefore I sent for you immediately, and you have been kind enough to come. So now all of us are here in the presence of God to listen to all that the Lord has commanded you to say."

Gentiles Hear the Good News

34 Then Peter began to speak to them: "I truly understand that God shows no partiality, 35but in every nation anyone who fears him and does what is right is acceptable to him. 36You know the message he sent to the people of Israel, preaching peace by Jesus Christ—he is Lord of all. 37That message spread throughout Judea, beginning in Galilee after the baptism that John announced: 38how God anointed Jesus of Nazareth with the Holy Spirit and with power; how he went about doing good and healing all who were oppressed by the devil, for God was with him. 39We are witnesses to all that he did both in Judea and in Jerusalem. They put him to death by hanging him on a tree; 40but God raised him on the third day and allowed him to appear, 41not to all the people but to us who were chosen by God as witnesses, and who ate and drank with him after he rose from the dead. 42He commanded us to preach to the people and to testify that he is the one ordained by God as judge of the living and the dead. 43All the prophets testify about him that everyone who believes in him receives forgiveness of sins through his name."

Gentiles Receive the Holy Spirit

44 While Peter was still speaking, the Holy Spirit fell upon all who heard the word. 45The circumcised believers who had come with Peter were astounded that the gift of the Holy Spirit had been poured out even on the Gentiles, 46for they heard them speaking in tongues and extolling God. Then Peter said, 47"Can anyone withhold the water for baptizing these people who have received the Holy Spirit just as we have?" 48So he ordered them to be baptized in the name of Jesus Christ. Then they invited him to stay for several days.

11 Peter's Report to the Church at Jerusalem

Now the apostles and the believers*a* who were in Judea heard that the Gentiles had also accepted the word of God. 2So when Peter went up to Jerusalem, the circumcised believers*b* criticized him, 3saying, "Why did you go to uncircumcised men and eat with them?" 4Then Peter began to explain it to them, step by step, saying, 5"I was in the city of Joppa praying, and in a trance I saw a vision. There was something like a large sheet coming down from heaven, being lowered by its four corners; and it came close to me. 6As I looked at it closely I saw four-footed animals, beasts of prey, reptiles, and birds of the air. 7I also heard a voice saying to me, 'Get up, Peter; kill and eat.' 8But I replied, 'By no means, Lord; for nothing profane or unclean has ever entered my mouth.' 9But a second time the voice answered from heaven, 'What God has made clean, you must not call profane.' 10This happened three times; then everything was pulled up again to heaven. 11At that very moment three men, sent to me from Caesarea, arrived at the house where we were. 12The Spirit told me to go with them and not to make a distinction between them and us.*c* These six brothers also accompanied me, and we entered the man's house. 13He told us how he had seen the angel standing in his house and saying, 'Send to Joppa and bring Simon, who is called Peter; 14he will give you a message by which you and your entire household will be saved.' 15And as I began to speak, the Holy Spirit fell upon them just as it had upon us at the beginning. 16And I remembered the word of the Lord, how he had said, 'John baptized with water, but you will be baptized with the Holy Spirit.' 17If then God gave them the same gift that he gave us when we believed in the Lord Jesus Christ, who was I that I could hinder God?" 18When they heard this, they were silenced. And they praised God, saying, "Then God has given even to the Gentiles the repentance that leads to life."

The Church in Antioch

19 Now those who were scattered because of the persecution that took place over Stephen

a Gk brothers *b* Gk lacks believers *c* Or not to hesitate traveled as far as Phoenicia, Cyprus, and Antioch, and they spoke the word to no one except Jews. [20]But among them were some men of Cyprus and Cyrene who, on coming to Antioch, spoke to the Hellenists[a] also, proclaiming the Lord Jesus. [21]The hand of the Lord was with them, and a great number became believers and turned to the Lord. [22]News of this came to the ears of the church in Jerusalem, and they sent Barnabas to Antioch. [23]When he came and saw the grace of God, he rejoiced, and he exhorted them all to remain faithful to the Lord with steadfast devotion; [24]for he was a good man, full of the Holy Spirit and of faith. And a great many people were brought to the Lord. [25]Then Barnabas went to Tarsus to look for Saul, [26]and when he had found him, he brought him to Antioch. So it was that for an entire year they met with[b] the church and taught a great many people, and it was in Antioch that the disciples were first called "Christians."

27 At that time prophets came down from Jerusalem to Antioch. [28]One of them named Agabus stood up and predicted by the Spirit that there would be a severe famine over all the world; and this took place during the reign of Claudius. [29]The disciples determined that according to their ability, each would send relief to the believers[c] living in Judea; [30]this they did, sending it to the elders by Barnabas and Saul.

12 James Killed and Peter Imprisoned

About that time King Herod laid violent hands upon some who belonged to the church. [2]He had James, the brother of John, killed with the sword. [3]After he saw that it pleased the Jews, he proceeded to arrest Peter also. (This was during the festival of Unleavened Bread.) [4]When he had seized him, he put him in prison and handed him over to four squads of soldiers to guard him, intending to bring him out to the people after the Passover. [5]While Peter was kept in prison, the church prayed fervently to God for him.

Peter Delivered from Prison

6 The very night before Herod was going to bring him out, Peter, bound with two chains, was sleeping between two soldiers, while guards in front of the door were keeping watch over the prison. [7]Suddenly an angel of the Lord appeared and a light shone in the cell. He tapped Peter on the side and woke him, saying, "Get up quickly." And the chains fell off his wrists. [8]The angel said to him, "Fasten your belt and put on your sandals." He did so. Then he said to him, "Wrap your cloak around

Angel on Earth—© Mallory Kidwell, 15

you and follow me." [9]Peter[d] went out and followed him; he did not realize that what was happening with the angel's help was real; he thought he was seeing a vision. [10]After they had passed the first and the second guard, they came before the iron gate leading into the city. It opened for them of its own accord, and they went outside and walked along a lane, when suddenly the angel left him. [11]Then Peter came to himself and said, "Now I am sure that the Lord has sent his angel and rescued me from the hands of Herod and from all that the Jewish people were expecting."

12 As soon as he realized this, he went to the house of Mary, the mother of John whose other name was Mark, where many had gathered and were praying. [13]When he knocked at the outer gate, a maid named Rhoda came to answer. [14]On recognizing Peter's voice, she was so overjoyed that, instead of opening the gate, she ran in and announced that Peter was standing at the gate. [15]They said to her, "You are out of your mind!" But she insisted that it was so. They said, "It is his angel." [16]Meanwhile Peter continued knocking; and when they opened the gate, they saw him and were amazed. [17]He motioned to them with his hand to be silent, and described for them how the Lord had brought him out of the prison. And he added, "Tell this to James and to the believers."[c] Then he left and went to another place.

18 When morning came, there was no small commotion among the soldiers over what had become of Peter. [19]When Herod had searched for him and could not find him, he examined the guards and ordered them to be

a Other ancient authorities read *Greeks* b Or *were guests of* c Gk *brothers* d Gk *He* put to death. Then he went down from Judea to Caesarea and stayed there.

The Death of Herod

20 Now Herod[a] was angry with the people of Tyre and Sidon. So they came to him in a body; and after winning over Blastus, the king's chamberlain, they asked for a reconciliation, because their country depended on the king's country for food. 21 On an appointed day Herod put on his royal robes, took his seat on the platform, and delivered a public address to them. 22 The people kept shouting, "The voice of a god, and not of a mortal!" 23 And immediately, because he had not given the glory to God, an angel of the Lord struck him down, and he was eaten by worms and died.

24 But the word of God continued to advance and gain adherents. 25 Then after completing their mission Barnabas and Saul returned to[b] Jerusalem and brought with them John, whose other name was Mark.

13 Barnabas and Saul Commissioned

Now in the church at Antioch there were prophets and teachers: Barnabas, Simeon who was called Niger, Lucius of Cyrene, Manaen a member of the court of Herod the ruler,[c] and Saul. 2 While they were worshiping the Lord and fasting, the Holy Spirit said, "Set apart for me Barnabas and Saul for the work to which I have called them." 3 Then after fasting and praying they laid their hands on them and sent them off.

The Apostles Preach in Cyprus

4 So, being sent out by the Holy Spirit, they went down to Seleucia; and from there they sailed to Cyprus. 5 When they arrived at Salamis, they proclaimed the word of God in the synagogues of the Jews. And they had John also to assist them. 6 When they had gone through the whole island as far as Paphos, they met a certain magician, a Jewish false prophet, named Bar-Jesus. 7 He was with the proconsul, Sergius Paulus, an intelligent man, who summoned Barnabas and Saul and wanted to hear the word of God. 8 But the magician Elymas (for that is the translation of his name) opposed them and tried to turn the proconsul away from the faith. 9 But Saul, also known as Paul, filled with the Holy Spirit, looked intently at him 10 and said, "You son of the devil, you enemy of all righteousness, full of all deceit and villainy, will you not stop making crooked the straight paths of the Lord? 11 And now listen—the hand of the Lord is against you, and you will be blind for a while, unable to see the sun." Immediately mist and darkness came over him, and he went about groping for someone to lead him by the hand. 12 When the proconsul saw what had happened, he believed, for he was astonished at the teaching about the Lord.

Paul and Barnabas in Antioch of Pisidia

13 Then Paul and his companions set sail from Paphos and came to Perga in Pamphylia. John, however, left them and returned to Jerusalem; 14 but they went on from Perga and came to Antioch in Pisidia. And on the sabbath day they went into the synagogue and sat down. 15 After the reading of the law and the prophets, the officials of the synagogue sent them a message, saying, "Brothers, if you have any word of exhortation for the people, give it." 16 So Paul stood up and with a gesture began to speak:

TEXT MESSAGE

Paul and Barnabas faced a real case of mistaken identity when they visited Lystra, a town in the center of modern-day Turkey (Acts 14.8–18). The people in the region believed a myth that the Greek gods Zeus and Hermes had previously visited the area. When Paul and Barnabas healed a cripple, the people thought the gods had returned, putting the Christian missionaries in an awkward situation.

Fact

This information has been scanned and is free of all known viruses. Please forward to all your friends.

---

a Gk he b Other ancient authorities read from c Gk tetrarch

"You Israelites,[a] and others who fear God, listen. [17]The God of this people Israel chose our ancestors and made the people great during their stay in the land of Egypt, and with uplifted arm he led them out of it. [18]For about forty years he put up with[b] them in the wilderness. [19]After he had destroyed seven nations in the land of Canaan, he gave them their land as an inheritance [20]for about four hundred fifty years. After that he gave them judges until the time of the prophet Samuel. [21]Then they asked for a king; and God gave them Saul son of Kish, a man of the tribe of Benjamin, who reigned for forty years. [22]When he had removed him, he made David their king. In his testimony about him he said, 'I have found David, son of Jesse, to be a man after my heart, who will carry out all my wishes.' [23]Of this man's posterity God has brought to Israel a Savior, Jesus, as he promised; [24]before his coming John had already proclaimed a baptism of repentance to all the people of Israel. [25]And as John was finishing his work, he said, 'What do you suppose that I am? I am not he. No, but one is coming after me; I am not worthy to untie the thong of the sandals[c] on his feet.'

26 "My brothers, you descendants of Abraham's family, and others who fear God, to us[d] the message of this salvation has been sent. [27]Because the residents of Jerusalem and their leaders did not recognize him or understand the words of the prophets that are read every sabbath, they fulfilled those words by condemning him. [28]Even though they found no cause for a sentence of death, they asked Pilate to have him killed. [29]When they had carried out everything that was written about him, they took him down from the tree and laid him in a tomb. [30]But God raised him from the dead; [31]and for many days he appeared to those who came up with him from Galilee to Jerusalem, and they are now his witnesses to the people. [32]And we bring you the good news that what God promised to our ancestors [33]he has fulfilled for us, their children, by raising Jesus; as also it is written in the second psalm,

'You are my Son;
today I have begotten you.'

[34]As to his raising him from the dead, no more to return to corruption, he has spoken in this way,

'I will give you the holy promises made to David.'

[35]Therefore he has also said in another psalm,

'You will not let your Holy One experience corruption.'

[36]For David, after he had served the purpose of God in his own generation, died,[e] was laid beside his ancestors, and experienced corruption; [37]but he whom God raised up experienced no corruption. [38]Let it be known to you therefore, my brothers, that through this man forgiveness of sins is proclaimed to you; [39]by this Jesus[f] everyone who believes is set free from all those sins[g] from which you could not be freed by the law of Moses. [40]Beware, therefore, that what the prophets said does not happen to you:

[41] 'Look, you scoffers!
Be amazed and perish,
for in your days I am doing a work,
a work that you will never believe, even if someone tells you.' "

42 As Paul and Barnabas[h] were going out, the people urged them to speak about these things again the next sabbath. [43]When the meeting of the synagogue broke up, many Jews and devout converts to Judaism followed Paul and Barnabas, who spoke to them and urged them to continue in the grace of God.

44 The next sabbath almost the whole city gathered to hear the word of the Lord.[i] [45]But when the Jews saw the crowds, they were filled with jealousy; and blaspheming, they contradicted what was spoken by Paul. [46]Then both Paul and Barnabas spoke out boldly, saying, "It was necessary that the word of God should be spoken first to you. Since you reject it and judge yourselves to be unworthy of eternal life, we are now turning to the Gentiles. [47]For so the Lord has commanded us, saying,

'I have set you to be a light for the Gentiles,
so that you may bring salvation to the ends of the earth.' "

48 When the Gentiles heard this, they were glad and praised the word of the Lord; and as many as had been destined for eternal life became believers. [49]Thus the word of the Lord spread throughout the region. [50]But the Jews incited the devout women of high standing and the leading men of the city, and stirred up persecution against Paul and Barnabas, and drove them out of their region. [51]So they shook the dust off their feet in protest against them, and went to Iconium. [52]And the disciples were filled with joy and with the Holy Spirit.

14 Paul and Barnabas in Iconium

The same thing occurred in Iconium, where Paul and Barnabas[h] went into the Jewish synagogue and spoke in such a way that a great number of both Jews and Greeks became be-

---

a Gk Men, Israelites b Other ancient authorities read cared for c Gk untie the sandals d Other ancient authorities read you e Gk fell asleep f Gk this g Gk all h Gk they i Other ancient authorities read God

JESUS SIGHTING

The start of the Church seems so inspiring, so revolutionary—a small group of passionate Jesus followers, ready to take on the world. But just about twenty years after Jesus' Resurrection, this ragtag bunch called followers of "the Way" had by then become a bona fide institution. There was structure, there was leadership, there were rules, and there was some serious conflict.

In **Acts 15.1–35** we see that a council of Church leaders had been convened. These Christians gathered in the Holy City, where just fifteen or twenty years before they had been betrayed and beaten and some had died outside the walls. Now the Church was growing and spreading. There were guests from Asia, Antioch, and regions to the south. A huge conflict was looming in front of them. Some difficult issues needed to be sorted through, important decisions needed to be made, and everyone wanted a say. An influential group of Jewish believers was insisting that Gentile converts be forced to adopt Jewish customs in order to be accepted. The Gentiles didn't think they should have to do that, but confronting such a powerful group was no small challenge. Fortunately, one member of the meeting, Paul of Tarsus, was not one to turn away from challenges.

At the heart of the issue was this question: Was the faith of God's people—stretching way back to the time of Abraham—now open to outsiders, to non-Jews? It was one thing for Jesus to be *kind* to them, but quite another thing to call them *family*!

It would have been so much easier if Jesus had just been there to answer the questions and settle the issues.

But it turns out he *was* there. You won't find Jesus there "in person," but verse 28 gives us an important clue. The leaders, faced with a difficult decision, spent serious time listening to the Holy Spirit and seeking Jesus' guidance. Jesus' promise to send his Spirit was fulfilled on Pentecost (Acts 1.8; 2.1–4). Jesus hadn't left them alone to try to solve the world's problems on their own! Through the power of the Holy Spirit and a willingness to obey the Spirit's direction, the Church leaders were able to navigate this issue, which threatened to split the Church. God's presence lived in them and worked through them; the Holy Spirit gave them gifts and abilities, empowered them, and led them.

If you have a friendship with Jesus, God's Spirit does the same for you! When you face seemingly unanswerable questions or tangled-up conflicts, you can rely on the Holy Spirit to show you the way.

(JS)

---

lievers. [2] But the unbelieving Jews stirred up the Gentiles and poisoned their minds against the brothers. [3] So they remained for a long time, speaking boldly for the Lord, who testified to the word of his grace by granting signs and wonders to be done through them. [4] But the residents of the city were divided; some sided with the Jews, and some with the apostles. [5] And when an attempt was made by both Gentiles and Jews, with their rulers, to mistreat them and to stone them, [6] the apostles[a] learned of it and fled to Lystra and Derbe, cit-ies of Lycaonia, and to the surrounding country; [7] and there they continued proclaiming the good news.

Paul and Barnabas in Lystra and Derbe

8 In Lystra there was a man sitting who could not use his feet and had never walked, for he had been crippled from birth. [9] He listened to Paul as he was speaking. And Paul, looking at him intently and seeing that he had faith to be healed, [10] said in a loud voice, "Stand upright on your feet." And the man[b] sprang up and

a Gk they *b* Gk he

began to walk. ¹¹When the crowds saw what Paul had done, they shouted in the Lycaonian language, "The gods have come down to us in human form!" ¹²Barnabas they called Zeus, and Paul they called Hermes, because he was the chief speaker. ¹³The priest of Zeus, whose temple was just outside the city,ᵃ brought oxen and garlands to the gates; he and the crowds wanted to offer sacrifice. ¹⁴When the apostles Barnabas and Paul heard of it, they tore their clothes and rushed out into the crowd, shouting, ¹⁵"Friends,ᵇ why are you doing this? We are mortals just like you, and we bring you good news, that you should turn from these worthless things to the living God, who made the heaven and the earth and the sea and all that is in them. ¹⁶In past generations he allowed all the nations to follow their own ways; ¹⁷yet he has not left himself without a witness in doing good—giving you rains from heaven and fruitful seasons, and filling you with food and your hearts with joy." ¹⁸Even with these words, they scarcely restrained the crowds from offering sacrifice to them.

19 But Jews came there from Antioch and Iconium and won over the crowds. Then they stoned Paul and dragged him out of the city, supposing that he was dead. ²⁰But when the disciples surrounded him, he got up and went into the city. The next day he went on with Barnabas to Derbe.

The Return to Antioch in Syria

21 After they had proclaimed the good news to that city and had made many disciples, they returned to Lystra, then on to Iconium and Antioch. ²²There they strengthened the souls of the disciples and encouraged them to continue in the faith, saying, "It is through many persecutions that we must enter the kingdom of God." ²³And after they had appointed elders for them in each church, with prayer and fasting they entrusted them to the Lord in whom they had come to believe.

24 Then they passed through Pisidia and came to Pamphylia. ²⁵When they had spoken the word in Perga, they went down to Attalia. ²⁶From there they sailed back to Antioch, where they had been commended to the grace of God for the workᶜ that they had completed. ²⁷When they arrived, they called the church together and related all that God had done with them, and how he had opened a door of faith for the Gentiles. ²⁸And they stayed there with the disciples for some time.

15 The Council at Jerusalem

Then certain individuals came down from Judea and were teaching the brothers, "Unless you are circumcised according to the custom of Moses, you cannot be saved." ²And after Paul and Barnabas had no small dissension and debate with them, Paul and Barnabas and some of the others were appointed to go up to Jerusalem to discuss this question with the apostles and the elders. ³So they were sent on their way by the church, and as they passed through both Phoenicia and Samaria, they reported the conversion of the Gentiles, and brought great joy to all the believers.ᵈ ⁴When they came to Jerusalem, they were welcomed by the church and the apostles and the elders, and they reported all that God had done with them. ⁵But some believers who belonged to the sect of the Pharisees stood up and said, "It is necessary for them to be circumcised and ordered to keep the law of Moses."

6 The apostles and the elders met together to consider this matter. ⁷After there had been much debate, Peter stood up and said to them, "My brothers,ᵉ you know that in the early days God made a choice among you, that I should be the one through whom the Gentiles would hear the message of the good news and become believers. ⁸And God, who knows the human heart, testified to them by giving them the Holy Spirit, just as he did to us; ⁹and in cleansing their hearts by faith he has made no distinction between them and us. ¹⁰Now therefore why are you putting God to the test by placing on the neck of the disciples a yoke that neither our ancestors nor we have been able to bear? ¹¹On the contrary, we believe that we will be saved through the grace of the Lord Jesus, just as they will."

12 The whole assembly kept silence, and listened to Barnabas and Paul as they told of all the signs and wonders that God had done through them among the Gentiles. ¹³After they finished speaking, James replied, "My brothers,ᵉ listen to me. ¹⁴Simeon has related how God first looked favorably on the Gentiles, to take from among them a people for his name. ¹⁵This agrees with the words of the prophets, as it is written,

¹⁶ 'After this I will return,
  and I will rebuild the dwelling of David,
    which has fallen;
    from its ruins I will rebuild it,
      and I will set it up,
¹⁷ so that all other peoples may seek the Lord—
    even all the Gentiles over whom my
      name has been called.

a Or *The priest of Zeus-Outside-the-City* b Gk Men c Or *committed in the grace of God to the work* d Gk *brothers* e Gk *Men, brothers*

LIVE new testament 1305

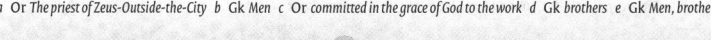

Thus says the Lord, who has been making these things [18]known from long ago.'[a]

[19]Therefore I have reached the decision that we should not trouble those Gentiles who are turning to God, [20]but we should write to them to abstain only from things polluted by idols and from fornication and from whatever has been strangled[b] and from blood. [21]For in every city, for generations past, Moses has had those who proclaim him, for he has been read aloud every sabbath in the synagogues."

The Council's Letter to Gentile Believers

22 Then the apostles and the elders, with the consent of the whole church, decided to choose men from among their members[c] and to send them to Antioch with Paul and Barnabas. They sent Judas called Barsabbas, and Silas, leaders among the brothers, [23]with the following letter: "The brothers, both the apostles and the elders, to the believers[d] of Gentile origin in Antioch and Syria and Cilicia, greetings. [24]Since we have heard that certain persons who have gone out from us, though with no instructions from us, have said things to disturb you and have unsettled your minds,[e] [25]we have decided unanimously to choose representatives[f] and send them to you, along with our beloved Barnabas and Paul, [26]who have risked their lives for the sake of our Lord Jesus Christ. [27]We have therefore sent Judas and Silas, who themselves will tell you the same things by word of mouth. [28]For it has seemed good to the Holy Spirit and to us to impose on you no further burden than these essentials: [29]that you abstain from what has been sacrificed to idols and from blood and from what is strangled[g] and from fornication. If you keep yourselves from these, you will do well. Farewell."

30 So they were sent off and went down to Antioch. When they gathered the congregation together, they delivered the letter. [31]When its members[h] read it, they rejoiced at the exhortation. [32]Judas and Silas, who were themselves prophets, said much to encourage and strengthen the believers.[d] [33]After they had been there for some time, they were sent off in peace by the believers[d] to those who had sent them.[i] [35]But Paul and Barnabas remained in Antioch, and there, with many others, they taught and proclaimed the word of the Lord.

Paul and Barnabas Separate

36 After some days Paul said to Barnabas, "Come, let us return and visit the believers[d] in every city where we proclaimed the word of the Lord and see how they are doing." [37]Barnabas wanted to take with them John called Mark. [38]But Paul decided not to take with them one who had deserted them in Pamphylia and had not accompanied them in the work. [39]The disagreement became so sharp that they parted company; Barnabas took Mark with him and sailed away to Cyprus. [40]But Paul chose Silas and set out, the believers[d] commending him to the grace of the Lord. [41]He went through Syria and Cilicia, strengthening the churches.

16 Timothy Joins Paul and Silas

Paul[j] went on also to Derbe and to Lystra, where there was a disciple named Timothy, the son of a Jewish woman who was a believer; but his father was a Greek. [2]He was well spoken of by the believers[d] in Lystra and Iconium. [3]Paul wanted Timothy to accompany him; and he took him and had him circumcised because of the Jews who were in those places, for they all knew that his father was a Greek. [4]As they went from town to town, they delivered to them for observance the decisions that had been reached by the apostles and elders who were in Jerusalem. [5]So the churches were strengthened in the faith and increased in numbers daily.

Paul's Vision of the Man of Macedonia

6 They went through the region of Phrygia and Galatia, having been forbidden by the Holy Spirit to speak the word in Asia. [7]When they had come opposite Mysia, they attempted to go into Bithynia, but the Spirit of Jesus did not allow them; [8]so, passing by Mysia, they went down to Troas. [9]During the night Paul had a vision: there stood a man of Macedonia pleading with him and saying, "Come over to Macedonia and help us." [10]When he had seen the vision, we immediately tried to cross over to Macedonia, being convinced that God had called us to proclaim the good news to them.

The Conversion of Lydia

11 We set sail from Troas and took a straight course to Samothrace, the following day to Neapolis, [12]and from there to Philippi, which is a leading city of the district[k] of Macedonia and a Roman colony. We remained in this city for some days. [13]On the sabbath day we went outside the gate by the river, where we supposed there was a place of prayer; and we sat down and spoke to the women who had gathered there. [14]A certain woman named Lydia, a

---

a Other ancient authorities read *things.* *[18]Known to God from of old are all his works.'* b Other ancient authorities lack *and from whatever has been strangled* c Gk *from among them* d Gk *brothers* e Other ancient authorities add *saying, 'You must be circumcised and keep the law,'* f Gk *men* g Other ancient authorities lack *and from what is strangled* h Gk *When they* i Other ancient authorities add verse 34, *But it seemed good to Silas to remain there* j Gk *He* k Other authorities read *a city of the first district* worshiper of God, was listening to us; she was from the city of Thyatira and a dealer in purple cloth. The Lord opened her heart to listen eagerly to what was said by Paul. [15]When she and her household were baptized, she urged us, saying, "If you have judged me to be faithful to the Lord, come and stay at my home." And she prevailed upon us.

Paul and Silas in Prison

16 One day, as we were going to the place of prayer, we met a slave-girl who had a spirit of divination and brought her owners a great deal of money by fortune-telling. [17]While she followed Paul and us, she would cry out, "These men are slaves of the Most High God, who proclaim to you[a] a way of salvation." [18]She kept doing this for many days. But Paul, very much annoyed, turned and said to the spirit, "I order you in the name of Jesus Christ to come out of her." And it came out that very hour.

19 But when her owners saw that their hope of making money was gone, they seized Paul and Silas and dragged them into the marketplace before the authorities. [20]When they had brought them before the magistrates, they said, "These men are disturbing our city; they are Jews [21]and are advocating customs that are not lawful for us as Romans to adopt or observe." [22]The crowd joined in attacking them, and the magistrates had them stripped of their clothing and ordered them to be beaten with rods. [23]After they had given them a severe flogging, they threw them into prison and ordered the jailer to keep them securely. [24]Following these instructions, he put them in the innermost cell and fastened their feet in the stocks.

25 About midnight Paul and Silas were praying and singing hymns to God, and the prisoners were listening to them. [26]Suddenly there was an earthquake, so violent that the foundations of the prison were shaken; and immediately all the doors were opened and everyone's chains were unfastened. [27]When the jailer woke up and saw the prison doors wide open, he drew his sword and was about to kill himself, since he supposed that the prisoners had escaped. [28]But Paul shouted in a loud voice, "Do not harm yourself, for we are all here." [29]The jailer[b] called for lights, and rushing in, he fell down trembling before Paul and Silas. [30]Then he brought them outside and said, "Sirs, what must I do to be saved?" [31]They answered, "Believe on the Lord Jesus, and you will be saved, you and your household." [32]They spoke the word of the Lord[c] to him and to all who were in his house. [33]At the same hour

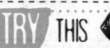

THE HOLY SPIRIT IN YOUR HOUSE

Do you ever feel like you have nothing in common with your family besides your last name (and in some cases, not even that)? Or maybe your family appears perfect, but you know your bond doesn't run as deep as it could?

Read **Acts 16.16–34**. A jailer comes to believe in Jesus, and his whole family is baptized into faith! God isn't just passionate about individuals—he's passionate about families. God wants us to grow in faith with our parents, brothers, and sisters—to have trusting, meaningful relationships with them. You can show God's love to your family whether they're religious or not. And let's face it—even if they are totally weirded out by your faith, they can't stop being your family!

Don't see each other much? Don't feel as connected as you could be? Get your family to share an experience beyond the norm. Make your family dinner. Watch a movie together that can open up a discussion about an important issue like love and marriage, fear, faith, death, friendship, dreams and goals, or forgiveness. If you already attend Mass with your family, get them to have a meaningful discussion about last Sunday's homily. Show that you care about what goes on in their lives and in their brains. And most important, ask God to help you have the same passion for your family that he does!

GOD IS PASSIONATE   MY FAMILY

of the night he took them and washed their wounds; then he and his entire family were baptized without delay. [34]He brought them up into the house and set food before them; and he and his entire household rejoiced that he had become a believer in God.

35 When morning came, the magistrates sent the police, saying, "Let those men go." [36]And the jailer reported the message to Paul, saying, "The magistrates sent word to let you go; therefore come out now and go in peace." [37]But Paul replied, "They have beaten us in public, uncondemned, men who are Roman citizens, and have thrown us into prison; and now are they going to discharge us in secret? Certainly not! Let them come and take us out themselves." [38]The police reported these words to the magistrates, and they were afraid

a Other ancient authorities read *to us* b Gk *He* c Other ancient authorities read *word of God*

Doubting Thomas? Yep, that's Me!

Lately I've been having trouble with doubting God's existence. I mean, I'm pretty sure that I can feel His presence in my heart, guiding my thoughts, but that doesn't erase the fact that for once, just once, I would like to see some actual proof.

It scares me to think about that, because, in the Bible you read about how God talked to people, I mean verbally conversed with them. He also gave them all those awesome visions and dreams. Or all those incredible miracles and signs, like people rising from the dead right before the eyes of the crowds, like Lazarus, or the handwriting on the wall with Daniel. But what do we get? A bunch of weird feelings and an appropriate verse or two at the right time?

It makes me jealous sometimes that God made it so easy for those people in the Bible to believe in Him. How when they asked for proof, He would give them something miraculous! Sometimes He'd even do it twice, like with Gideon and his wool! You try to do that now a days and all you get is a soggy sweater! Instead of signs or miracles, it feels as if all I get are a lot of technical thoughts that I'm constantly second-guessing.

I'm not saying I don't believe in God. I DEFINITELY do, and I suppose that I somehow know He's always around, listening to my thoughts, but it would be really great to get some REAL proof! To have a vision or dream when I doubt, or to witness a miracle, or experience a visitation from an angel!

I know God isn't like a vending machine where you ask and receive anything you order, but you'd think that He could give a struggling Christian girl some proof...or at least let her see the proof He's already granted her.

when they heard that they were Roman citizens; [39]so they came and apologized to them. And they took them out and asked them to leave the city. [40]After leaving the prison they went to Lydia's home; and when they had seen and encouraged the brothers and sisters[a] there, they departed.

17 The Uproar in Thessalonica

After Paul and Silas[b] had passed through Amphipolis and Apollonia, they came to Thessalonica, where there was a synagogue of the Jews. [2]And Paul went in, as was his custom, and on three sabbath days argued with them from the scriptures, [3]explaining and proving that it was necessary for the Messiah[c] to suffer and to rise from the dead, and saying, "This is the Messiah,[c] Jesus whom I am proclaiming to you." [4]Some of them were persuaded and joined Paul and Silas, as did a great many of the devout Greeks and not a few of the leading women. [5]But the Jews became jealous, and with the help of some ruffians in the marketplaces they formed a mob and set the city in an uproar. While they were searching for Paul and Silas to bring them out to the assembly, they attacked Jason's house. [6]When they could not find them, they dragged Jason and some believers[a] before the city authorities,[d] shouting, "These people who have been turning the world upside down have come here also, [7]and Jason has entertained them as guests. They are all acting contrary to the decrees of the emperor, saying that there is another king named Jesus." [8]The people and the city officials were disturbed when they heard this, [9]and after they had taken bail from Jason and the others, they let them go.

Paul and Silas in Beroea

[10] That very night the believers[a] sent Paul and Silas off to Beroea; and when they arrived, they went to the Jewish synagogue. [11]These Jews were more receptive than those in Thessalonica, for they welcomed the message very eagerly and examined the scriptures every day to see whether these things were so. [12]Many of them therefore believed, including not a few Greek women and men of high standing. [13]But when the Jews of Thessalonica learned that the word of God had been proclaimed by Paul in Beroea as well, they came there too, to stir up and incite the crowds. [14]Then the believers[a] immediately sent Paul away to the coast, but Silas and Timothy remained behind. [15]Those who conducted Paul brought him as far as Athens; and after receiving instructions to have Silas and Timothy join him as soon as possible, they left him.

Paul in Athens

[16] While Paul was waiting for them in Athens, he was deeply distressed to see that the city was full of idols. [17]So he argued in the synagogue with the Jews and the devout persons, and also in the marketplace[e] every day with those who happened to be there. [18]Also some Epicurean and Stoic philosophers debated with him. Some said, "What does this babbler want to say?" Others said, "He seems to be a proclaimer of foreign divinities." (This was because he was telling the good news about Jesus and the resurrection.) [19]So they took him and brought him to the Areopagus and asked him, "May we know what this new teaching is that you are presenting? [20]It sounds rather strange to us, so we would like to know what it means." [21]Now all the Athenians and the foreigners living there would spend their time in nothing but telling or hearing something new.

[22] Then Paul stood in front of the Areopagus and said, "Athenians, I see how extremely religious you are in every way. [23]For as I went through the city and looked carefully at the objects of your worship, I found among them an altar with the inscription, 'To an unknown god.' What therefore you worship as unknown, this I proclaim to you. [24]The God who made the world and everything in it, he who is Lord of heaven and earth, does not live in shrines made by human hands, [25]nor is he served by human hands, as though he needed anything, since he himself gives to all mortals life and breath and all things. [26]From one ancestor[f] he made all nations to inhabit the whole earth, and he allotted the times of their existence and the boundaries of the places where they would live, [27]so that they would search for God[g] and perhaps grope for him and find him—though indeed he is not far from each one of us. [28]For 'In him we live and move and have our being'; as even some of your own poets have said,

'For we too are his offspring.'

[29]Since we are God's offspring, we ought not to think that the deity is like gold, or silver, or stone, an image formed by the art and imagination of mortals. [30]While God has overlooked the times of human ignorance, now he commands all people everywhere to repent, [31]because he has fixed a day on which he will have the world judged in righteousness by a man whom he has appointed, and of this he has given assurance to all by raising him from the dead."

---

a Gk brothers b Gk they c Or the Christ d Gk politarchs e Or civic center; Gk agora f Gk From one; other ancient authorities read From one blood g Other ancient authorities read the Lord

32 When they heard of the resurrection of the dead, some scoffed; but others said, "We will hear you again about this." ³³At that point Paul left them. ³⁴But some of them joined him and became believers, including Dionysius the Areopagite and a woman named Damaris, and others with them.

18 Paul in Corinth

After this Paul^a left Athens and went to Corinth. ²There he found a Jew named Aquila, a native of Pontus, who had recently come from Italy with his wife Priscilla, because Claudius had ordered all Jews to leave Rome. Paul^b went to see them, ³and, because he was of the same trade, he stayed with them, and they worked together—by trade they were tentmakers. ⁴Every sabbath he would argue in the synagogue and would try to convince Jews and Greeks.

5 When Silas and Timothy arrived from Macedonia, Paul was occupied with proclaiming the word,^c testifying to the Jews that the Messiah^d was Jesus. ⁶When they opposed and reviled him, in protest he shook the dust from his clothes^e and said to them, "Your blood be on your own heads! I am innocent. From now on I will go to the Gentiles." ⁷Then he left the synagogue^f and went to the house of a man named Titius^g Justus, a worshiper of God; his house was next door to the synagogue. ⁸Crispus, the official of the synagogue, became a believer in the Lord, together with all his household; and many of the Corinthians who heard Paul became believers and were baptized. ⁹One night the Lord said to Paul in a vision, "Do not be afraid, but speak and do not be silent; ¹⁰for I am with you, and no one will lay a hand on you to harm you, for there are many in this city who are my people." ¹¹He stayed there a year and six months, teaching the word of God among them.

12 But when Gallio was proconsul of Achaia, the Jews made a united attack on Paul and brought him before the tribunal. ¹³They said, "This man is persuading people to worship God in ways that are contrary to the law." ¹⁴Just as Paul was about to speak, Gallio said to the Jews, "If it were a matter of crime or serious villainy, I would be justified in accepting the complaint of you Jews; ¹⁵but since it is a matter of questions about words and names and your own law, see to it yourselves; I do not wish to be a judge of these matters." ¹⁶And he dismissed them from the tribunal. ¹⁷Then all of them^h seized Sosthenes, the official of the synagogue, and beat him in front of the tribu-

nal. But Gallio paid no attention to any of these things.

Paul's Return to Antioch

18 After staying there for a considerable time, Paul said farewell to the believers^i and sailed for Syria, accompanied by Priscilla and Aquila. At Cenchreae he had his hair cut, for he was under a vow. ¹⁹When they reached Ephesus, he left them there, but first he himself went into the synagogue and had a discussion with the Jews. ²⁰When they asked him to stay longer, he declined; ²¹but on taking leave of them, he said, "I^j will return to you, if God wills." Then he set sail from Ephesus.

22 When he had landed at Caesarea, he went up to Jerusalem^k and greeted the church, and then went down to Antioch. ²³After spending some time there he departed and went from place to place through the region of Galatia^l and Phrygia, strengthening all the disciples.

Ministry of Apollos

24 Now there came to Ephesus a Jew named Apollos, a native of Alexandria. He was an eloquent man, well-versed in the scriptures. ²⁵He had been instructed in the Way of the Lord; and he spoke with burning enthusiasm and taught accurately the things concerning Jesus, though he knew only the baptism of John. ²⁶He began to speak boldly in the synagogue; but when Priscilla and Aquila heard him, they took him aside and explained the Way of God to him more accurately. ²⁷And when he wished to cross over to Achaia, the believers^i encouraged him and wrote to the disciples to welcome him. On his arrival he greatly helped those who through grace had become believers, ²⁸for he powerfully refuted the Jews in public, showing by the scriptures that the Messiah^d is Jesus.

19 Paul in Ephesus

While Apollos was in Corinth, Paul passed through the interior regions and came to Ephesus, where he found some disciples. ²He said to them, "Did you receive the Holy Spirit when you became believers?" They replied, "No, we have not even heard that there is a Holy Spirit." ³Then he said, "Into what then were you baptized?" They answered, "Into John's baptism." ⁴Paul said, "John baptized with the baptism of repentance, telling the people to believe in the one who was to come after him, that is, in Jesus." ⁵On hearing this, they were baptized in the name of the Lord Jesus. ⁶When Paul had laid his hands on them, the Holy Spir-

---

a Gk he b Gk He c Gk with the word d Or the Christ e Gk reviled him, he shook out his clothes f Gk left there g Other ancient authorities read Titus h Other ancient authorities read all the Greeks i Gk brothers j Other ancient authorities read I must at all costs keep the approaching festival in Jerusalem, but I k Gk went up l Gk the Galatian region it came upon them, and they spoke in tongues and prophesied— [7]altogether there were about twelve of them.

8 He entered the synagogue and for three months spoke out boldly, and argued persuasively about the kingdom of God. [9]When some stubbornly refused to believe and spoke evil of the Way before the congregation, he left them, taking the disciples with him, and argued daily in the lecture hall of Tyrannus.[a] [10]This continued for two years, so that all the residents of Asia, both Jews and Greeks, heard the word of the Lord.

The Sons of Sceva

11 God did extraordinary miracles through Paul, [12]so that when the handkerchiefs or aprons that had touched his skin were brought to the sick, their diseases left them, and the evil spirits came out of them. [13]Then some itinerant Jewish exorcists tried to use the name of the Lord Jesus over those who had evil spirits, saying, "I adjure you by the Jesus whom Paul proclaims." [14]Seven sons of a Jewish high priest named Sceva were doing this. [15]But the evil spirit said to them in reply, "Jesus I know, and Paul I know; but who are you?" [16]Then the man with the evil spirit leaped on them, mastered them all, and so overpowered them that they fled out of the house naked and wounded. [17]When this became known to all residents of Ephesus, both Jews and Greeks, everyone was awestruck; and the name of the Lord Jesus was praised. [18]Also many of those who became believers confessed and disclosed their practices. [19]A number of those who practiced magic collected their books and burned them publicly; when the value of these books[b] was calculated, it was found to come to fifty thousand silver coins. [20]So the word of the Lord grew mightily and prevailed.

The Riot in Ephesus

21 Now after these things had been accomplished, Paul resolved in the Spirit to go through Macedonia and Achaia, and then to go on to Jerusalem. He said, "After I have gone there, I must also see Rome." [22]So he sent two of his helpers, Timothy and Erastus, to Macedonia, while he himself stayed for some time longer in Asia.

23 About that time no little disturbance broke out concerning the Way. [24]A man named Demetrius, a silversmith who made silver shrines of Artemis, brought no little business to the artisans. [25]These he gathered together, with the workers of the same trade, and said,

a Other ancient authorities read of a certain Tyrannus, from eleven o'clock in the morning to four in the afternoon b Gk them

TRY THIS ◄

MAKING SENSE

"I like to pick and choose from all kinds of religions."

"Organized religion isn't for me, but I'm a spiritual person."

"It's arrogant to think there's only one true religion—every religion has some truth in it."

"I believe in God and try to be a good person, so why are you making this a big deal?"

"I'm glad you like your religion. I'm just not into that stuff."

You may have heard these comments from friends, if you've ever tried to discuss your faith with them. What other responses to your faith have you gotten from your friends? Write a few of them here:

Now take a look at **Acts 17.16–34** and note how Paul crafted his message to communicate effectively with the Athenians. These weren't just average Joes—these were philosophers, deep thinkers, devotees of ancient Greek ideas taught by Epicurus and the Stoics. (Learn more about Stoicism and Epicureanism at **Learner.CalltoDiscipleship.com**.) Paul understood their beliefs and tailored what he said to them about Jesus. He put things in a way that would make sense to them. He emphasized the uniqueness of the one true God by telling the story of God's relationship with humankind.

Think about your friends and how they view the world. How could you share the gospel effectively? How can you be creative in the way you talk about God in order to understand and speak to their mind-set, needs, and concerns? What specific roadblocks stand in the way of those friends coming to know Jesus—and how can you address those roadblocks? Like Paul you could just tell the story. You could create a video or write a letter. You could ask meaningful or tough questions. Pray, and ask God to help you share with your friends in a way they'll understand. Then share your experience on **Learner.CalltoDiscipleship.com**.

GOD IS ONE AND ONLY MY FRIENDS

"Men, you know that we get our wealth from this business. ²⁶You also see and hear that not only in Ephesus but in almost the whole of Asia this Paul has persuaded and drawn away a considerable number of people by saying that gods made with hands are not gods. ²⁷And there is danger not only that this trade of ours may come into disrepute but also that the temple of the great goddess Artemis will be scorned, and she will be deprived of her majesty that brought all Asia and the world to worship her."

28 When they heard this, they were enraged and shouted, "Great is Artemis of the Ephesians!" ²⁹The city was filled with the confusion; and people*ᵃ* rushed together to the theater, dragging with them Gaius and Aristarchus, Macedonians who were Paul's travel companions. ³⁰Paul wished to go into the crowd, but the disciples would not let him; ³¹even some officials of the province of Asia,*ᵇ* who were friendly to him, sent him a message urging him not to venture into the theater. ³²Meanwhile, some were shouting one thing, some another; for the assembly was in confusion, and most of them did not know why they had come together. ³³Some of the crowd gave instructions to Alexander, whom the Jews had pushed forward. And Alexander motioned for silence and tried to make a defense before the people. ³⁴But when they recognized that he was a Jew, for about two hours all of them shouted in unison, "Great is Artemis of the Ephesians!" ³⁵But when the town clerk had quieted the crowd, he said, "Citizens of Ephesus, who is there that does not know that the city of the Ephesians is the temple keeper of the great Artemis and of the statue that fell from heaven?*ᶜ* ³⁶Since these things cannot be denied, you ought to be quiet and do nothing rash. ³⁷You have brought these men here who are neither temple robbers nor blasphemers of our*ᵈ* goddess. ³⁸If therefore Demetrius and the artisans with him have a complaint against anyone, the courts are open, and there are proconsuls; let them bring charges there against one another. ³⁹If there is anything further*ᵉ* you want to know, it must be settled in the regular assembly. ⁴⁰For we are in danger of being charged with rioting today, since there is no cause that we can give to justify this commotion." ⁴¹When he had said this, he dismissed the assembly.

20 Paul Goes to Macedonia and Greece

After the uproar had ceased, Paul sent for the disciples; and after encouraging them and saying farewell, he left for Macedonia. ²When he

had gone through those regions and had given the believers*ᶠ* much encouragement, he came to Greece, ³where he stayed for three months. He was about to set sail for Syria when a plot was made against him by the Jews, and so he decided to return through Macedonia. ⁴He was accompanied by Sopater son of Pyrrhus from Beroea, by Aristarchus and Secundus from Thessalonica, by Gaius from Derbe, and by Timothy, as well as by Tychicus and Trophimus from Asia. ⁵They went ahead and were waiting for us in Troas; ⁶but we sailed from Philippi after the days of Unleavened Bread, and in five days we joined them in Troas, where we stayed for seven days.

Paul's Farewell Visit to Troas

7 On the first day of the week, when we met to break bread, Paul was holding a discussion with them; since he intended to leave the next day, he continued speaking until midnight. ⁸There were many lamps in the room upstairs where we were meeting. ⁹A young man named Eutychus, who was sitting in the window, began to sink off into a deep sleep while Paul talked still longer. Overcome by sleep, he fell to the ground three floors below and was picked up dead. ¹⁰But Paul went down, and bending over him took him in his arms, and said, "Do not be alarmed, for his life is in him." ¹¹Then Paul went upstairs, and after he had broken bread and eaten, he continued to converse with them until dawn; then he left. ¹²Meanwhile they had taken the boy away alive and were not a little comforted.

The Voyage from Troas to Miletus

13 We went ahead to the ship and set sail for Assos, intending to take Paul on board there; for he had made this arrangement, intending to go by land himself. ¹⁴When he met us in Assos, we took him on board and went to Mitylene. ¹⁵We sailed from there, and on the following day we arrived opposite Chios. The next day we touched at Samos, and*ᵍ* the day after that we came to Miletus. ¹⁶For Paul had decided to sail past Ephesus, so that he might not have to spend time in Asia; he was eager to be in Jerusalem, if possible, on the day of Pentecost.

Paul Speaks to the Ephesian Elders

17 From Miletus he sent a message to Ephesus, asking the elders of the church to meet him. ¹⁸When they came to him, he said to them:

"You yourselves know how I lived among you the entire time from the first day that I set foot

---

a Gk *they*   *b* Gk *some of the Asiarchs*   *c* Meaning of Gk uncertain   *d* Other ancient authorities read *your*   *e* Other ancient authorities read *about other matters*   *f* Gk *given them*   *g* Other ancient authorities add *after remaining at Trogyllium* in Asia, ¹⁹serving the Lord with all humility and with tears, enduring the trials that came to me through the plots of the Jews. ²⁰I did not shrink from doing anything helpful, proclaiming the message to you and teaching you publicly and from house to house, ²¹as I testified to both Jews and Greeks about repentance toward God and faith toward our Lord Jesus. ²²And now, as a captive to the Spirit,ᵃ I am on my way to Jerusalem, not knowing what will happen to me there, ²³except that the Holy Spirit testifies to me in every city that imprisonment and persecutions are waiting for me. ²⁴But I do not count my life of any value to myself, if only I may finish my course and the ministry that I received from the Lord Jesus, to testify to the good news of God's grace.

25 "And now I know that none of you, among whom I have gone about proclaiming the kingdom, will ever see my face again. ²⁶Therefore I declare to you this day that I am not responsible for the blood of any of you, ²⁷for I did not shrink from declaring to you the whole purpose of God. ²⁸Keep watch over yourselves and over all the flock, of which the Holy Spirit has made you overseers, to shepherd the church of Godᵇ that he obtained with the blood of his own Son.ᶜ ²⁹I know that after I have gone, savage wolves will come in among you, not sparing the flock. ³⁰Some even from your own group will come distorting the truth in order to entice the disciples to follow them. ³¹Therefore be alert, remembering that for three years I did not cease night or day to warn everyone with tears. ³²And now I commend you to God and to the message of his grace, a message that is able to build you up and to give you the inheritance among all who are sanctified. ³³I coveted no one's silver or gold or clothing. ³⁴You know for yourselves that I worked with my own hands to support myself and my companions. ³⁵In all this I have given you an example that by such work we must support the weak, remembering the words of the Lord Jesus, for he himself said, 'It is more blessed to give than to receive.' "

36 When he had finished speaking, he knelt down with them all and prayed. ³⁷There was much weeping among them all; they embraced Paul and kissed him, ³⁸grieving especially because of what he had said, that they would not see him again. Then they brought him to the ship.

21 Paul's Journey to Jerusalem

When we had parted from them and set sail, we came by a straight course to Cos, and the

REALITY

ENERGIZED BY THE SPIRIT

Read **Acts 20.1–36**. All of Paul's travels have to make us wonder. Where in the world did he get all his energy? I think it's safe to say that there weren't any sports or power drinks in those days. All of the early Christians were so energetic and enthused. What was it? What revved them up? The power of the Holy Spirit.

Through the guidance of the same Spirit who directed and empowered Jesus, the disciples were transformed from timid and fearful people into articulate and zealous proclaimers of salvation. The Spirit gave them direction and energy to follow a path that led a small sect of Judaism to grow into a movement that would be known as Christianity.

What about you? That same Spirit is yours. It lives in you. Draw on the power of the Spirit through prayer, meditation, and acts of service. If you can't find a faith-sharing group in your school or parish, follow Paul's lead and start one.

next day to Rhodes, and from there to Patara.ᵈ ²When we found a ship bound for Phoenicia, we went on board and set sail. ³We came in sight of Cyprus; and leaving it on our left, we sailed to Syria and landed at Tyre, because the ship was to unload its cargo there. ⁴We looked up the disciples and stayed there for seven days. Through the Spirit they told Paul not to go on to Jerusalem. ⁵When our days there were ended, we left and proceeded on our journey; and all of them, with wives and children, escorted us outside the city. There we knelt down on the beach and prayed ⁶and said farewell to one another. Then we went on board the ship, and they returned home.

7 When we had finishedᵉ the voyage from Tyre, we arrived at Ptolemais; and we greeted the believersᶠ and stayed with them for one day. ⁸The next day we left and came to Caesarea; and we went into the house of Philip the evange-

---

ᵃ Or *And now, bound in the spirit*   ᵇ Other ancient authorities read *of the Lord*   ᶜ Or *with his own blood*; Gk *with the blood of his Own*   ᵈ Other ancient authorities add *and Myra*   ᵉ Or *continued*   ᶠ Gk *brothers*

15 After these days we got ready and started to go up to Jerusalem. ¹⁶Some of the disciples from Caesarea also came along and brought us to the house of Mnason of Cyprus, an early disciple, with whom we were to stay.

Paul Visits James at Jerusalem

17 When we arrived in Jerusalem, the brothers welcomed us warmly. ¹⁸The next day Paul went with us to visit James; and all the elders were present. ¹⁹After greeting them, he related one by one the things that God had done among the Gentiles through his ministry. ²⁰When they heard it, they praised God. Then they said to him, "You see, brother, how many thousands of believers there are among the Jews, and they are all zealous for the law. ²¹They have been told about you that you teach all the Jews living among the Gentiles to forsake Moses, and that you tell them not to circumcise their children or observe the customs. ²²What then is to be done? They will certainly hear that you have come. ²³So do what we tell you. We have four men who are under a vow. ²⁴Join these men, go through the rite of purification with them, and pay for the shaving of their heads. Thus all will know that there is nothing in what they have been told about you, but that you yourself observe and guard the law. ²⁵But as for the Gentiles who have become believers, we have sent a letter with our judgment that they should abstain from what has been sacrificed to idols and from blood and from what is strangled*ᵇ* and from fornication." ²⁶Then Paul took the men, and the next day, having purified himself, he entered the temple with them, making public the completion of the days of purification when the sacrifice would be made for each of them.

Paul Arrested in the Temple

27 When the seven days were almost completed, the Jews from Asia, who had seen him in the temple, stirred up the whole crowd. They seized him, ²⁸shouting, "Fellow Israelites, help! This is the man who is teaching everyone everywhere against our people, our law, and this place; more than that, he has actually brought Greeks into the temple and has defiled this holy place." ²⁹For they had previously seen Trophimus the Ephesian with him in the city, and they supposed that Paul had brought him into the temple. ³⁰Then all the city was aroused, and the people rushed together. They seized Paul and dragged him out of the temple, and immediately the doors were shut. ³¹While they were trying to kill him, word came to the

list, one of the seven, and stayed with him. ⁹He had four unmarried daughters*ᵃ* who had the gift of prophecy. ¹⁰While we were staying there for several days, a prophet named Agabus came down from Judea. ¹¹He came to us and took Paul's belt, bound his own feet and hands with it, and said, "Thus says the Holy Spirit, 'This is the way the Jews in Jerusalem will bind the man who owns this belt and will hand him over to the Gentiles.' " ¹²When we heard this, we and the people there urged him not to go up to Jerusalem. ¹³Then Paul answered, "What are you doing, weeping and breaking my heart? For I am ready not only to be bound but even to die in Jerusalem for the name of the Lord Jesus." ¹⁴Since he would not be persuaded, we remained silent except to say, "The Lord's will be done."

a Gk *four daughters, virgins,* *b* Other ancient authorities lack *and from what is strangled* tribune of the cohort that all Jerusalem was in an uproar. ³²Immediately he took soldiers and centurions and ran down to them. When they saw the tribune and the soldiers, they stopped beating Paul. ³³Then the tribune came, arrested him, and ordered him to be bound with two chains; he inquired who he was and what he had done. ³⁴Some in the crowd shouted one thing, some another; and as he could not learn the facts because of the uproar, he ordered him to be brought into the barracks. ³⁵When Paul*ᵃ* came to the steps, the violence of the mob was so great that he had to be carried by the soldiers. ³⁶The crowd that followed kept shouting, "Away with him!"

Paul Defends Himself

37 Just as Paul was about to be brought into the barracks, he said to the tribune, "May I say something to you?" The tribune*ᵇ* replied, "Do you know Greek? ³⁸Then you are not the Egyptian who recently stirred up a revolt and led the four thousand assassins out into the wilderness?" ³⁹Paul replied, "I am a Jew, from Tarsus in Cilicia, a citizen of an important city; I beg you, let me speak to the people." ⁴⁰When he had given him permission, Paul stood on the steps and motioned to the people for silence; and when there was a great hush, he addressed them in the Hebrew*ᶜ* language, saying:

22 "Brothers and fathers, listen to the defense that I now make before you."

2 When they heard him addressing them in Hebrew,*ᶜ* they became even more quiet. Then he said:

3 "I am a Jew, born in Tarsus in Cilicia, but brought up in this city at the feet of Gamaliel, educated strictly according to our ancestral law, being zealous for God, just as all of you are today. ⁴I persecuted this Way up to the point of death by binding both men and women and putting them in prison, ⁵as the high priest and the whole council of elders can testify about me. From them I also received letters to the brothers in Damascus, and I went there in order to bind those who were there and to bring them back to Jerusalem for punishment.

Paul Tells of His Conversion

6 "While I was on my way and approaching Damascus, about noon a great light from heaven suddenly shone about me. ⁷I fell to the ground and heard a voice saying to me, 'Saul, Saul, why are you persecuting me?' ⁸I answered, 'Who are you, Lord?' Then he said to me, 'I am Jesus of Nazareth*ᵈ* whom you are persecuting.' ⁹Now those who were with me saw the light but did not hear the voice of the one who was speaking to me. ¹⁰I asked, 'What am I to do, Lord?' The Lord said to me, 'Get up and go to Damascus; there you will be told everything that has been assigned to you to do.' ¹¹Since I could not see because of the brightness of that light, those who were with me took my hand and led me to Damascus.

12 "A certain Ananias, who was a devout man according to the law and well spoken of by all the Jews living there, ¹³came to me; and standing beside me, he said, 'Brother Saul, regain your sight!' In that very hour I regained my sight and saw him. ¹⁴Then he said, 'The God of our ancestors has chosen you to know his will, to see the Righteous One and to hear his own voice; ¹⁵for you will be his witness to all the world of what you have seen and heard. ¹⁶And now why do you delay? Get up, be baptized, and have your sins washed away, calling on his name.'

Paul Sent to the Gentiles

17 "After I had returned to Jerusalem and while I was praying in the temple, I fell into a trance ¹⁸and saw Jesus*ᵉ* saying to me, 'Hurry and get out of Jerusalem quickly, because they will not accept your testimony about me.' ¹⁹And I said, 'Lord, they themselves know that in every synagogue I imprisoned and beat those who believed in you. ²⁰And while the blood of your witness Stephen was shed, I myself was standing by, approving and keeping the coats of those who killed him.' ²¹Then he said to me, 'Go, for I will send you far away to the Gentiles.' "

Paul and the Roman Tribune

22 Up to this point they listened to him, but then they shouted, "Away with such a fellow from the earth! For he should not be allowed to live." ²³And while they were shouting, throwing off their cloaks, and tossing dust into the air, ²⁴the tribune directed that he was to be brought into the barracks, and ordered him to be examined by flogging, to find out the reason for this outcry against him. ²⁵But when they had tied him up with thongs,*ᶠ* Paul said to the centurion who was standing by, "Is it legal for you to flog a Roman citizen who is uncondemned?" ²⁶When the centurion heard that, he went to the tribune and said to him, "What are you about to do? This man is a Roman citizen." ²⁷The tribune came and asked Paul,*ᵉ* "Tell me, are you a Roman citizen?" And he said, "Yes." ²⁸The tribune answered, "It cost me a large sum of money to get my citizenship."

a Gk he *b* Gk He *c* That is, *Aramaic* *d* Gk *the Nazorean* *e* Gk *him* *f* Or *up for the lashes*

REALITY

STORIES OF CONVERSION

Have you ever shared your faith journey? There are three accounts of Paul sharing his conversion story in Acts. Read **Acts 22.6–11**. Here, Paul shares his conversion story in self-defense before a Jewish crowd ready to kill him. (The other two accounts are in Acts 9.1–19 and 26.1–23.) Each of the accounts varies in details. Read each of the stories and discover what the differences are.

Find some Creative Space in this Bible and write the story of your faith journey up to this point. Mention important events and people. Include good times and bad times.

Paul said, "But I was born a citizen." [29]Immediately those who were about to examine him drew back from him; and the tribune also was afraid, for he realized that Paul was a Roman citizen and that he had bound him.

Paul before the Council

30 Since he wanted to find out what Paul[a] was being accused of by the Jews, the next day he released him and ordered the chief priests and the entire council to meet. He brought Paul down and had him stand before them.

23 While Paul was looking intently at the council he said, "Brothers,[b] up to this day I have lived my life with a clear conscience before God." [2]Then the high priest Ananias ordered those standing near him to strike him on the mouth. [3]At this Paul said to him, "God will strike you, you whitewashed wall! Are you sitting there to judge me according to the law, and yet in violation of the law you order me to be struck?" [4]Those standing nearby said, "Do you dare to insult God's high priest?" [5]And Paul said, "I did not realize, brothers, that he was high priest; for it is written, 'You shall not speak evil of a leader of your people.' "

6 When Paul noticed that some were Sadducees and others were Pharisees, he called out in the council, "Brothers, I am a Pharisee, a son of Pharisees. I am on trial concerning the hope of the resurrection[c] of the dead." [7]When he said this, a dissension began between the Pharisees and the Sadducees, and the assembly was divided. [8](The Sadducees say that there is no resurrection, or angel, or spirit; but the Pharisees acknowledge all three.) [9]Then a great clamor arose, and certain scribes of the Pharisees' group stood up and contended, "We find nothing wrong with this man. What if a spirit or an angel has spoken to him?" [10]When the dissension became violent, the tribune, fearing that they would tear Paul to pieces, ordered the soldiers to go down, take him by force, and bring him into the barracks.

11 That night the Lord stood near him and said, "Keep up your courage! For just as you have testified for me in Jerusalem, so you must bear witness also in Rome."

The Plot to Kill Paul

12 In the morning the Jews joined in a conspiracy and bound themselves by an oath neither to eat nor drink until they had killed Paul. [13]There were more than forty who joined in this conspiracy. [14]They went to the chief priests and elders and said, "We have strictly bound ourselves by an oath to taste no food until we have killed Paul. [15]Now then, you and the council must notify the tribune to bring him down to you, on the pretext that you want to make a more thorough examination of his case. And we are ready to do away with him before he arrives."

16 Now the son of Paul's sister heard about the ambush; so he went and gained entrance to the barracks and told Paul. [17]Paul called one of the centurions and said, "Take this young man to the tribune, for he has something to report to him." [18]So he took him, brought him to the tribune, and said, "The prisoner Paul called me and asked me to bring this young man to you; he has something to tell you." [19]The tribune took him by the hand, drew him aside privately, and asked, "What is it that you have to report to me?" [20]He answered, "The Jews have agreed to ask you to bring Paul down to the council tomorrow, as though they were going to inquire more thoroughly into his case. [21]But do not be persuaded by them, for more than forty of their men are lying in ambush for him. They have bound themselves by an oath neither to eat nor drink until they kill him. They are ready now and are waiting for your consent." [22]So the tribune dismissed the young man, ordering him, "Tell no one that you have informed me of this."

a Gk he b Gk Men, brothers c Gk concerning hope and resurrection

Paul Sent to Felix the Governor

23 Then he summoned two of the centurions and said, "Get ready to leave by nine o'clock tonight for Caesarea with two hundred soldiers, seventy horsemen, and two hundred spearmen. [24]Also provide mounts for Paul to ride, and take him safely to Felix the governor." [25]He wrote a letter to this effect:

26 "Claudius Lysias to his Excellency the governor Felix, greetings. [27]This man was seized by the Jews and was about to be killed by them, but when I had learned that he was a Roman citizen, I came with the guard and rescued him. [28]Since I wanted to know the charge for which they accused him, I had him brought to their council. [29]I found that he was accused concerning questions of their law, but was charged with nothing deserving death or imprisonment. [30]When I was informed that there would be a plot against the man, I sent him to you at once, ordering his accusers also to state before you what they have against him.[a]"

31 So the soldiers, according to their instructions, took Paul and brought him during the night to Antipatris. [32]The next day they let the horsemen go on with him, while they returned to the barracks. [33]When they came to Caesarea and delivered the letter to the governor, they presented Paul also before him. [34]On reading the letter, he asked what province he belonged to, and when he learned that he was from Cilicia, [35]he said, "I will give you a hearing when your accusers arrive." Then he ordered that he be kept under guard in Herod's headquarters.[b]

24 Paul before Felix at Caesarea

Five days later the high priest Ananias came down with some elders and an attorney, a certain Tertullus, and they reported their case against Paul to the governor. [2]When Paul[c] had been summoned, Tertullus began to accuse him, saying:

"Your Excellency,[d] because of you we have long enjoyed peace, and reforms have been made for this people because of your foresight. [3]We welcome this in every way and everywhere with utmost gratitude. [4]But, to detain you no further, I beg you to hear us briefly with your customary graciousness. [5]We have, in fact, found this man a pestilent fellow, an agitator among all the Jews throughout the world, and a ringleader of the sect of the Nazarenes.[e] [6]He even tried to profane the temple, and so we seized him.[f] [8]By examining him yourself you

will be able to learn from him concerning everything of which we accuse him."

9 The Jews also joined in the charge by asserting that all this was true.

Paul's Defense before Felix

10 When the governor motioned to him to speak, Paul replied:

"I cheerfully make my defense, knowing that for many years you have been a judge over this nation. [11]As you can find out, it is not more than twelve days since I went up to worship in Jerusalem. [12]They did not find me disputing with anyone in the temple or stirring up a crowd either in the synagogues or throughout the city. [13]Neither can they prove to you the charge that they now bring against me. [14]But this I admit to you, that according to the Way, which they call a sect, I worship the God of our ancestors, believing everything laid down according to the law or written in the prophets. [15]I have a hope in God—a hope that they themselves also accept—that there will be a resurrection of both[g] the righteous and the unrighteous. [16]Therefore I do my best always to have a clear conscience toward God and all people. [17]Now after some years I came to bring alms to my nation and to offer sacrifices. [18]While I was doing this, they found me in the temple, completing the rite of purification, without any crowd or disturbance. [19]But there were some Jews from Asia—they ought to be here before you to make an accusation, if they have anything against me. [20]Or let these men here tell what crime they had found when I stood before the council, [21]unless it was this one sentence that I called out while standing before them, 'It is about the resurrection of the dead that I am on trial before you today.' "

22 But Felix, who was rather well informed about the Way, adjourned the hearing with the comment, "When Lysias the tribune comes down, I will decide your case." [23]Then he ordered the centurion to keep him in custody, but to let him have some liberty and not to prevent any of his friends from taking care of his needs.

Paul Held in Custody

24 Some days later when Felix came with his wife Drusilla, who was Jewish, he sent for Paul and heard him speak concerning faith in Christ Jesus. [25]And as he discussed justice, self-control, and the coming judgment, Felix became frightened and said, "Go away for the present; when I have an opportunity, I will send for

---

a Other ancient authorities add *Farewell* b Gk *praetorium* c Gk *he* d Gk lacks *Your Excellency* e Gk *Nazoreans* f Other ancient authorities add *and we would have judged him according to our law.* [7]*But the chief captain Lysias came and with great violence took him out of our hands,* [8]*commanding his accusers to come before you.* g Other ancient authorities read *of the dead, both of* you." ²⁶At the same time he hoped that money would be given him by Paul, and for that reason he used to send for him very often and converse with him.

27 After two years had passed, Felix was succeeded by Porcius Festus; and since he wanted to grant the Jews a favor, Felix left Paul in prison.

25 Paul Appeals to the Emperor

Three days after Festus had arrived in the province, he went up from Caesarea to Jerusalem ²where the chief priests and the leaders of the Jews gave him a report against Paul. They appealed to him ³and requested, as a favor to them against Paul,ᵃ to have him transferred to Jerusalem. They were, in fact, planning an ambush to kill him along the way. ⁴Festus replied that Paul was being kept at Caesarea, and that he himself intended to go there shortly. ⁵"So," he said, "let those of you who have the authority come down with me, and if there is anything wrong about the man, let them accuse him."

6 After he had stayed among them not more than eight or ten days, he went down to Caesarea; the next day he took his seat on the tribunal and ordered Paul to be brought. ⁷When he arrived, the Jews who had gone down from Jerusalem surrounded him, bringing many serious charges against him, which they could not prove. ⁸Paul said in his defense, "I have in no way committed an offense against the law of the Jews, or against the temple, or against the emperor." ⁹But Festus, wishing to do the Jews a favor, asked Paul, "Do you wish to go up to Jerusalem and be tried there before me on these charges?" ¹⁰Paul said, "I am appealing to the emperor's tribunal; this is where I should be tried. I have done no wrong to the Jews, as you very well know. ¹¹Now if I am in the wrong and have committed something for which I deserve to die, I am not trying to escape death; but if

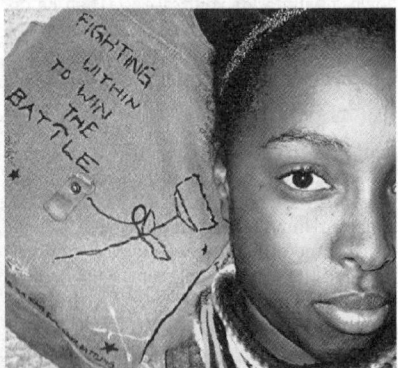

Fighting Within to Win the Battle—© Jennifer Lawrence, 19

there is nothing to their charges against me, no one can turn me over to them. I appeal to the emperor." ¹²Then Festus, after he had conferred with his council, replied, "You have appealed to the emperor; to the emperor you will go."

Festus Consults King Agrippa

13 After several days had passed, King Agrippa and Bernice arrived at Caesarea to welcome Festus. ¹⁴Since they were staying there several days, Festus laid Paul's case before the king, saying, "There is a man here who was left in prison by Felix. ¹⁵When I was in Jerusalem, the chief priests and the elders of the Jews informed me about him and asked for a sentence against him. ¹⁶I told them that it was not the custom of the Romans to hand over anyone before the accused had met the accusers face to face and had been given an opportunity to make a defense against the charge. ¹⁷So when they met here, I lost no time, but on the next day took my seat on the tribunal and ordered the man to be brought. ¹⁸When the accusers stood up, they did not charge him with any of the crimesᵇ that I was expecting. ¹⁹Instead they had certain points of disagreement with him about their own religion and about a certain Jesus, who had died, but whom Paul asserted to be alive. ²⁰Since I was at a loss how to investigate these questions, I asked whether he wished to go to Jerusalem and be tried there on these charges.ᶜ ²¹But when Paul had appealed to be kept in custody for the decision of his Imperial Majesty, I ordered him to be held until I could send him to the emperor." ²²Agrippa said to Festus, "I would like to hear the man myself." "Tomorrow," he said, "you will hear him."

Paul Brought before Agrippa

23 So on the next day Agrippa and Bernice came with great pomp, and they entered the audience hall with the military tribunes and the prominent men of the city. Then Festus gave the order and Paul was brought in. ²⁴And Festus said, "King Agrippa and all here present with us, you see this man about whom the whole Jewish community petitioned me, both in Jerusalem and here, shouting that he ought not to live any longer. ²⁵But I found that he had done nothing deserving death; and when he appealed to his Imperial Majesty, I decided to send him. ²⁶But I have nothing definite to write to our sovereign about him. Therefore I have brought him before all of you, and especially before you, King Agrippa, so that, after we have examined him, I may have something to

a Gk *him*   *b* Other ancient authorities read *with anything*
c Gk *on them*

write— [27]for it seems to me unreasonable to send a prisoner without indicating the charges against him."

26 Paul Defends Himself before Agrippa

Agrippa said to Paul, "You have permission to speak for yourself." Then Paul stretched out his hand and began to defend himself:

2 "I consider myself fortunate that it is before you, King Agrippa, I am to make my defense today against all the accusations of the Jews, [3]because you are especially familiar with all the customs and controversies of the Jews; therefore I beg of you to listen to me patiently.

4 "All the Jews know my way of life from my youth, a life spent from the beginning among my own people and in Jerusalem. [5]They have known for a long time, if they are willing to testify, that I have belonged to the strictest sect of our religion and lived as a Pharisee. [6]And now I stand here on trial on account of my hope in the promise made by God to our ancestors, [7]a promise that our twelve tribes hope to attain, as they earnestly worship day and night. It is for this hope, your Excellency,[a] that I am accused by Jews! [8]Why is it thought incredible by any of you that God raises the dead?

9 "Indeed, I myself was convinced that I ought to do many things against the name of Jesus of Nazareth.[b] [10]And that is what I did in Jerusalem; with authority received from the chief priests, I not only locked up many of the saints in prison, but I also cast my vote against them when they were being condemned to death. [11]By punishing them often in all the synagogues I tried to force them to blaspheme; and since I was so furiously enraged at them, I pursued them even to foreign cities.

Paul Tells of His Conversion

12 "With this in mind, I was traveling to Damascus with the authority and commission of the chief priests, [13]when at midday along the road, your Excellency,[a] I saw a light from heaven, brighter than the sun, shining around me and my companions. [14]When we had all fallen to the ground, I heard a voice saying to me in the Hebrew[c] language, 'Saul, Saul, why are you persecuting me? It hurts you to kick against the goads.' [15]I asked, 'Who are you, Lord?' The Lord answered, 'I am Jesus whom you are persecuting. [16]But get up and stand on your feet; for I have appeared to you for this purpose, to appoint you to serve and testify to the things in which you have seen me[d] and to those in which I will appear to you. [17]I will rescue you from

your people and from the Gentiles—to whom I am sending you [18]to open their eyes so that they may turn from darkness to light and from the power of Satan to God, so that they may receive forgiveness of sins and a place among those who are sanctified by faith in me.'

Paul Tells of His Preaching

19 "After that, King Agrippa, I was not disobedient to the heavenly vision, [20]but declared first to those in Damascus, then in Jerusalem and throughout the countryside of Judea, and also to the Gentiles, that they should repent and turn to God and do deeds consistent with repentance. [21]For this reason the Jews seized me in the temple and tried to kill me. [22]To this day I have had help from God, and so I stand here, testifying to both small and great, saying nothing but what the prophets and Moses said would take place: [23]that the Messiah[e] must suffer, and that, by being the first to rise from the dead, he would proclaim light both to our people and to the Gentiles."

Paul Appeals to Agrippa to Believe

24 While he was making this defense, Festus exclaimed, "You are out of your mind, Paul! Too much learning is driving you insane!" [25]But Paul said, "I am not out of my mind, most excellent Festus, but I am speaking the sober truth. [26]Indeed the king knows about these things, and to him I speak freely; for I am certain that none of these things has escaped his notice, for this was not done in a corner. [27]King Agrippa, do you believe the prophets? I know that you believe." [28]Agrippa said to Paul, "Are you so quickly persuading me to become a Christian?"[f] [29]Paul replied, "Whether quickly or not, I pray to God that not only you but also all who are listening to me today might become such as I am—except for these chains."

30 Then the king got up, and with him the governor and Bernice and those who had been seated with them; [31]and as they were leaving, they said to one another, "This man is doing nothing to deserve death or imprisonment." [32]Agrippa said to Festus, "This man could have been set free if he had not appealed to the emperor."

27 Paul Sails for Rome

When it was decided that we were to sail for Italy, they transferred Paul and some other prisoners to a centurion of the Augustan Cohort, named Julius. [2]Embarking on a ship of Adramyttium that was about to set sail to the

---

a Gk O king b Gk the Nazorean c That is, Aramaic d Other ancient authorities read the things that you have seen e Or the Christ
f Or Quickly you will persuade me to play the Christian

9 Since much time had been lost and sailing was now dangerous, because even the Fast had already gone by, Paul advised them, ¹⁰saying, "Sirs, I can see that the voyage will be with danger and much heavy loss, not only of the cargo and the ship, but also of our lives." ¹¹But the centurion paid more attention to the pilot and to the owner of the ship than to what Paul said. ¹²Since the harbor was not suitable for spending the winter, the majority was in favor of putting to sea from there, on the chance that somehow they could reach Phoenix, where they could spend the winter. It was a harbor of Crete, facing southwest and northwest.

The Storm at Sea

13 When a moderate south wind began to blow, they thought they could achieve their purpose; so they weighed anchor and began to sail past Crete, close to the shore. ¹⁴But soon a violent wind, called the northeaster, rushed down from Crete.*ᵃ* ¹⁵Since the ship was caught and could not be turned head-on into the wind, we gave way to it and were driven. ¹⁶By running under the lee of a small island called Cauda*ᵇ* we were scarcely able to get the ship's boat under control. ¹⁷After hoisting it up they took measures*ᶜ* to undergird the ship; then, fearing that they would run on the Syrtis, they lowered the sea anchor and so were driven. ¹⁸We were being pounded by the storm so violently that on the next day they began to throw the cargo overboard, ¹⁹and on the third day with their own hands they threw the ship's tackle overboard. ²⁰When neither sun nor stars appeared for many days, and no small tempest raged, all hope of our being saved was at last abandoned.

21 Since they had been without food for a long time, Paul then stood up among them and said, "Men, you should have listened to me and not have set sail from Crete and thereby avoided this damage and loss. ²²I urge you now to keep up your courage, for there will be no loss of life among you, but only of the ship. ²³For last night there stood by me an angel of the God to whom I belong and whom I worship, ²⁴and he said, 'Do not be afraid, Paul; you must stand before the emperor; and indeed, God has granted safety to all those who are sailing with you.' ²⁵So keep up your courage, men, for I have faith in God that it will be exactly as I have been told. ²⁶But we will have to run aground on some island."

27 When the fourteenth night had come, as we were drifting across the sea of Adria, about midnight the sailors suspected that they were nearing land. ²⁸So they took soundings and

ports along the coast of Asia, we put to sea, accompanied by Aristarchus, a Macedonian from Thessalonica. ³The next day we put in at Sidon; and Julius treated Paul kindly, and allowed him to go to his friends to be cared for. ⁴Putting out to sea from there, we sailed under the lee of Cyprus, because the winds were against us. ⁵After we had sailed across the sea that is off Cilicia and Pamphylia, we came to Myra in Lycia. ⁶There the centurion found an Alexandrian ship bound for Italy and put us on board. ⁷We sailed slowly for a number of days and arrived with difficulty off Cnidus, and as the wind was against us, we sailed under the lee of Crete off Salmone. ⁸Sailing past it with difficulty, we came to a place called Fair Havens, near the city of Lasea.

a Gk *it* *b* Other ancient authorities read *Clauda* *c* Gk *helps* found twenty fathoms; a little farther on they took soundings again and found fifteen fathoms. [29] Fearing that we might run on the rocks, they let down four anchors from the stern and prayed for day to come. [30] But when the sailors tried to escape from the ship and had lowered the boat into the sea, on the pretext of putting out anchors from the bow, [31] Paul said to the centurion and the soldiers, "Unless these men stay in the ship, you cannot be saved." [32] Then the soldiers cut away the ropes of the boat and set it adrift.

[33] Just before daybreak, Paul urged all of them to take some food, saying, "Today is the fourteenth day that you have been in suspense and remaining without food, having eaten nothing. [34] Therefore I urge you to take some food, for it will help you survive; for none of you will lose a hair from your heads." [35] After he had said this, he took bread; and giving thanks to God in the presence of all, he broke it and began to eat. [36] Then all of them were encouraged and took food for themselves. [37] (We were in all two hundred seventy-six[a] persons in the ship.) [38] After they had satisfied their hunger, they lightened the ship by throwing the wheat into the sea.

The Shipwreck

[39] In the morning they did not recognize the land, but they noticed a bay with a beach, on which they planned to run the ship ashore, if they could. [40] So they cast off the anchors and left them in the sea. At the same time they loosened the ropes that tied the steering-oars; then hoisting the foresail to the wind, they made for the beach. [41] But striking a reef,[b] they ran the ship aground; the bow stuck and remained immovable, but the stern was being broken up by the force of the waves. [42] The soldiers' plan was to kill the prisoners, so that none might swim away and escape; [43] but the centurion, wishing to save Paul, kept them from carrying out their plan. He ordered those who could swim to jump overboard first and make for the land, [44] and the rest to follow, some on planks and others on pieces of the ship. And so it was that all were brought safely to land.

28 Paul on the Island of Malta

After we had reached safety, we then learned that the island was called Malta. [2] The natives showed us unusual kindness. Since it had begun to rain and was cold, they kindled a fire and welcomed all of us around it. [3] Paul had gathered a bundle of brushwood and was putting it on the fire, when a viper, driven out by the heat, fastened itself on his hand. [4] When the natives saw the creature hanging from his hand, they said to one another, "This man must be a murderer; though he has escaped from the sea, justice has not allowed him to

a Other ancient authorities read *seventy-six*; others, *about seventy-six* *b* Gk *place of two seas*

Omega—© Maggie Hubbard, 16

live." [5]He, however, shook off the creature into the fire and suffered no harm. [6]They were expecting him to swell up or drop dead, but after they had waited a long time and saw that nothing unusual had happened to him, they changed their minds and began to say that he was a god.

[7] Now in the neighborhood of that place were lands belonging to the leading man of the island, named Publius, who received us and entertained us hospitably for three days. [8]It so happened that the father of Publius lay sick in bed with fever and dysentery. Paul visited him and cured him by praying and putting his hands on him. [9]After this happened, the rest of the people on the island who had diseases also came and were cured. [10]They bestowed many honors on us, and when we were about to sail, they put on board all the provisions we needed.

Paul Arrives at Rome

[11] Three months later we set sail on a ship that had wintered at the island, an Alexandrian ship with the Twin Brothers as its figurehead. [12]We put in at Syracuse and stayed there for three days; [13]then we weighed anchor and came to Rhegium. After one day there a south wind sprang up, and on the second day we came to Puteoli. [14]There we found believers[a] and were invited to stay with them for seven days. And so we came to Rome. [15]The believers[a] from there, when they heard of us, came as far as the Forum of Appius and Three Taverns to meet us. On seeing them, Paul thanked God and took courage.

[16] When we came into Rome, Paul was allowed to live by himself, with the soldier who was guarding him.

Paul and Jewish Leaders in Rome

[17] Three days later he called together the local leaders of the Jews. When they had assembled, he said to them, "Brothers, though I had done nothing against our people or the customs of our ancestors, yet I was arrested in Jerusalem and handed over to the Romans. [18]When they had examined me, the Romans[b] wanted to release me, because there was no reason for the death penalty in my case. [19]But when the Jews objected, I was compelled to appeal to the emperor—even though I had no charge to bring against my nation. [20]For this reason therefore I have asked to see you and speak with you,[c] since it is for the sake of the hope of Israel that I am bound with this chain." [21]They replied, "We have received no letters from Judea about you, and none of the brothers coming here has reported or spoken anything evil about you. [22]But we would like to hear from you what you think, for with regard to this sect we know that everywhere it is spoken against."

Paul Preaches in Rome

[23] After they had set a day to meet with him, they came to him at his lodgings in great numbers. From morning until evening he explained the matter to them, testifying to the kingdom of God and trying to convince them about Jesus both from the law of Moses and from the prophets. [24]Some were convinced by what he had said, while others refused to believe. [25]So they disagreed with each other; and as they were leaving, Paul made one further statement: "The Holy Spirit was right in saying to your ancestors through the prophet Isaiah,

[26] 'Go to this people and say,
You will indeed listen, but never understand,
   and you will indeed look, but never
      perceive.
[27] For this people's heart has grown dull,
   and their ears are hard of hearing,
      and they have shut their eyes;
         so that they might not look with their
            eyes,
   and listen with their ears,
and understand with their heart and turn—
   and I would heal them.'

[28]Let it be known to you then that this salvation of God has been sent to the Gentiles; they will listen."[d]

[30] He lived there two whole years at his own expense[e] and welcomed all who came to him, [31]proclaiming the kingdom of God and teaching about the Lord Jesus Christ with all boldness and without hindrance.

---

a Gk brothers b Gk they c Or I have asked you to see me and speak with me d Other ancient authorities add verse 29, And when he had said these words, the Jews departed, arguing vigorously among themselves e Or in his own hired dwelling

ROMANS

MAKING THE WORLD RIGHT

This World Is Falling Apart

There is no way anyone can look at the world and say this is how it's supposed to be. Horrible wars, terrorism, rampant poverty, government corruption—it seems things just keep getting worse. It can all make us wonder if God is in control of this mess.

The letter to the Romans is the explanation of God's answer to this mess. Sin has completely soaked through every aspect of life, corrupting our relationships—the way we treat others and, most important, how we relate to God.

But through Jesus, this all changes.

The remedy to the world's sin that unfolds in the letter of Romans is God's faithfulness. The Creator of everything sent his only Son to rescue this lost and dying world. And through Jesus, our relationships with God and others can be restored. Paul calls this *faith*. We place our belief in what Jesus has done to defeat the power of sin in this world and in our own lives (see Romans 3.21–26).

We follow the way of Jesus, not the way of the world. We treat our friends and enemies the way we would want to be treated. We look out for those who are hurting. And because of our new relationship with God through Jesus, we *can* act differently. We care for those who are poor and hurting because that is what God does. We call out against injustices and acts of violence as God begins to make the world right.

"And to be like Our Lord perfectly is our very salvation and our full bliss. And if we do not know how we shall do all this, ask Our Lord and he will teach us."

—Julian of Norwich, medieval mystic

WHO Paul wrote this letter to the Christians in Rome.

WHAT This letter stresses that salvation and the grace of God free people from sin when they choose to believe in Jesus.

WHEN It was written at the end of Paul's third missionary journey, around A.D. 57.

WHERE Paul most likely wrote this during his stay in Corinth while on his way to Rome.

 PATH OF DISCIPLESHIP

In Romans, Paul's message is loud and clear: Jesus is the *only* way. Through his death and Resurrection, he is the source of reconciliation with the Father, with one another, and with ourselves.

Some of us try to impress God by acting moral or religious, and some of us shy away from him, because we're afraid that we're not good enough for God to love us. But in the end there's only one thing God really wants for us. He wants us to live in an awareness that we have been baptized into the death and Resurrection of Jesus and we have been made new people through our Baptism. True disciples bask in the awareness of new life and act accordingly to bring it to others. How do your actions bring an awareness of new life through Christ to others?

1 Salutation

Paul, a servant[a] of Jesus Christ, called to be an apostle, set apart for the gospel of God, ²which he promised beforehand through his prophets in the holy scriptures, ³the gospel concerning his Son, who was descended from David according to the flesh ⁴and was declared to be Son of God with power according to the spirit[b] of holiness by resurrection from the dead, Jesus Christ our Lord, ⁵through whom we have received grace and apostleship to bring about the obedience of faith among all the Gentiles for the sake of his name, ⁶including yourselves who are called to belong to Jesus Christ,

7 To all God's beloved in Rome, who are called to be saints:

Grace to you and peace from God our Father and the Lord Jesus Christ.

Prayer of Thanksgiving

8 First, I thank my God through Jesus Christ for all of you, because your faith is proclaimed throughout the world. ⁹For God, whom I serve with my spirit by announcing the gospel[c] of his Son, is my witness that without ceasing I remember you always in my prayers, ¹⁰asking that by God's will I may somehow at last succeed in coming to you. ¹¹For I am longing to see you so that I may share with you some spiritual gift to strengthen you— ¹²or rather so that we may be mutually encouraged by each other's faith, both yours and mine. ¹³I want you to know, brothers and sisters,[d] that I have often intended to come to you (but thus far have been prevented), in order that I may reap some harvest among you as I have among the rest of the Gentiles. ¹⁴I am a debtor both to Greeks and to barbarians, both to the wise and to the foolish ¹⁵—hence my eagerness to proclaim the gospel to you also who are in Rome.

The Power of the Gospel

16 For I am not ashamed of the gospel; it is the power of God for salvation to everyone who has faith, to the Jew first and also to the Greek. ¹⁷For in it the righteousness of God is revealed through faith for faith; as it is written, "The one who is righteous will live by faith."[e]

The Guilt of Humankind

18 For the wrath of God is revealed from heaven against all ungodliness and wickedness of those who by their wickedness suppress the truth. ¹⁹For what can be known about God is plain to them, because God has shown it to them. ²⁰Ever since the creation of the world

his eternal power and divine nature, invisible though they are, have been understood and seen through the things he has made. So they are without excuse; ²¹for though they knew God, they did not honor him as God or give thanks to him, but they became futile in their thinking, and their senseless minds were darkened. ²²Claiming to be wise, they became fools; ²³and they exchanged the glory of the immortal God for images resembling a mortal human being or birds or four-footed animals or reptiles.

24 Therefore God gave them up in the lusts of their hearts to impurity, to the degrading of their bodies among themselves, ²⁵because they exchanged the truth about God for a lie and worshiped and served the creature rather than the Creator, who is blessed forever! Amen.

26 For this reason God gave them up to degrading passions. Their women exchanged natural intercourse for unnatural, ²⁷and in the same way also the men, giving up natural intercourse with women, were consumed with passion for one another. Men committed shameless acts with men and received in their own persons the due penalty for their error.

28 And since they did not see fit to acknowledge God, God gave them up to a debased mind and to things that should not be done. ²⁹They were filled with every kind of wickedness, evil, covetousness, malice. Full of envy, murder, strife, deceit, craftiness, they are gossips, ³⁰slanderers, God-haters,[f] insolent, haughty, boastful, inventors of evil, rebellious toward parents, ³¹foolish, faithless, heartless, ruthless. ³²They know God's decree, that those who practice such things deserve to die—yet they not only do them but even applaud others who practice them.

2 The Righteous Judgment of God

Therefore you have no excuse, whoever you are, when you judge others; for in passing judgment on another you condemn yourself, because you, the judge, are doing the very same things. ²You say,[g] "We know that God's judgment on those who do such things is in accordance with truth." ³Do you imagine, whoever you are, that when you judge those who do such things and yet do them yourself, you will escape the judgment of God? ⁴Or do you despise the riches of his kindness and forbearance and patience? Do you not realize that God's kindness is meant to lead you to repentance? ⁵But by your hard and impenitent heart

---

a Gk slave b Or Spirit c Gk my spirit in the gospel d Gk brothers e Or The one who is righteous through faith will live f Or God-hated
g Gk lacks You say

you are storing up wrath for yourself on the day of wrath, when God's righteous judgment will be revealed. 6For he will repay according to each one's deeds: 7to those who by patiently doing good seek for glory and honor and immortality, he will give eternal life; 8while for those who are self-seeking and who obey not the truth but wickedness, there will be wrath and fury. 9There will be anguish and distress for everyone who does evil, the Jew first and also the Greek, 10but glory and honor and peace for everyone who does good, the Jew first and also the Greek. 11For God shows no partiality.

12 All who have sinned apart from the law will also perish apart from the law, and all who have sinned under the law will be judged by the law. 13For it is not the hearers of the law who are righteous in God's sight, but the doers of the law who will be justified. 14When Gentiles, who do not possess the law, do instinctively what the law requires, these, though not having the law, are a law to themselves. 15They show that what the law requires is written on their hearts, to which their own conscience also bears witness; and their conflicting thoughts will accuse or perhaps excuse them 16on the day when, according to my gospel, God, through Jesus Christ, will judge the secret thoughts of all.

The Jews and the Law

17 But if you call yourself a Jew and rely on the law and boast of your relation to God 18and know his will and determine what is best because you are instructed in the law, 19and if you are sure that you are a guide to the blind, a light to those who are in darkness, 20a corrector of the foolish, a teacher of children, having in the law the embodiment of knowledge and truth, 21you, then, that teach others, will you not teach yourself? While you preach against stealing, do you steal? 22You that forbid adultery, do you commit adultery? You that abhor idols, do you rob temples? 23You that boast in the law, do you dishonor God by breaking the law? 24For, as it is written, "The name of God is blasphemed among the Gentiles because of you."

25 Circumcision indeed is of value if you obey the law; but if you break the law, your circumcision has become uncircumcision. 26So, if those who are uncircumcised keep the requirements of the law, will not their uncircumcision be regarded as circumcision? 27Then those who are physically uncircumcised but keep the law will condemn you that have the written code and circumcision but break the law. 28For a person is not a Jew who is one out-

a Gk they

It Doesn't Take a Genius . . .

Is God really out there? We all wonder at times, looking at the big, gaping universe, walking through the hallway during a mundane day at school, staring eyeball to eyeball at ourselves in the mirror. *Are we alone in this universe? Is there* really *more to this world than what I can see and feel?*

Albert Einstein wondered about these things too. He once wrote about a childhood memory, saying, "A wonder of this kind I experienced as a child of four or five years when my father showed me a compass." As he watched the needle move, persistently veering north whichever way the compass was tipped or turned, young Albert was deeply perplexed. "This experience made a deep and lasting impression on me. Something deeply hidden had to be behind things."

Something (or maybe Someone?) . . . hidden from our sight, behind everything . . .

Read **Romans 1.20**. What answers *your* wonderings? What is it that assures (or reassures) you of God's very real presence? The giant oak tree out back, your kid sister's smile, the amoeba under the microscope, the melody of your favorite song—so many things can be that needle pointing north for us, that evidence that Someone *is* there, deeply hidden behind everything.

Grab a camera or a sketch pad and visually capture an image of that simple "compass" that points you to profound truth. Share your expression and see others' pics at **Learner.CalltoDiscipleship.com**.

wardly, nor is true circumcision something external and physical. 29Rather, a person is a Jew who is one inwardly, and real circumcision is a matter of the heart—it is spiritual and not literal. Such a person receives praise not from others but from God.

3 Then what advantage has the Jew? Or what is the value of circumcision? 2Much, in every way. For in the first place the Jews*a* were entrusted with the oracles of God. 3What if some

were unfaithful? Will their faithlessness nullify the faithfulness of God? ⁴By no means! Although everyone is a liar, let God be proved true, as it is written,

> "So that you may be justified in your words,
> and prevail in your judging."ᵃ

⁵But if our injustice serves to confirm the justice of God, what should we say? That God is unjust to inflict wrath on us? (I speak in a human way.) ⁶By no means! For then how could God judge the world? ⁷But if through my falsehood God's truthfulness abounds to his glory, why am I still being condemned as a sinner? ⁸And why not say (as some people slander us by saying that we say), "Let us do evil so that good may come"? Their condemnation is deserved!

None Is Righteous

9 What then? Are we any better off?ᵇ No, not at all; for we have already charged that all, both Jews and Greeks, are under the power of sin, ¹⁰as it is written:

> "There is no one who is righteous, not even one;
> ¹¹   there is no one who has understanding,
>   there is no one who seeks God.
> ¹² All have turned aside, together they have
>   become worthless;
>   there is no one who shows kindness,
>   there is not even one."
> ¹³ "Their throats are opened graves;
>   they use their tongues to deceive."
>   "The venom of vipers is under their lips."
> ¹⁴   "Their mouths are full of cursing and
>   bitterness."
> ¹⁵ "Their feet are swift to shed blood;
> ¹⁶   ruin and misery are in their paths,
> ¹⁷ and the way of peace they have not known."
> ¹⁸   "There is no fear of God before their
>   eyes."

19 Now we know that whatever the law says, it speaks to those who are under the law, so that every mouth may be silenced, and the whole world may be held accountable to God. ²⁰For "no human being will be justified in his sight" by deeds prescribed by the law, for through the law comes the knowledge of sin.

Righteousness through Faith

21 But now, apart from law, the righteousness of God has been disclosed, and is attested by the law and the prophets, ²²the righteousness of God through faith in Jesus Christᶜ for all who believe. For there is no distinction, ²³since all have sinned and fall short of the glory of God; ²⁴they are now justified by his grace as a gift,

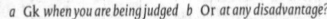

a Gk *when you are being judged*   b Or *at any disadvantage?*
c Or *through the faith of Jesus Christ*

through the redemption that is in Christ Jesus, [25]whom God put forward as a sacrifice of atonement[a] by his blood, effective through faith. He did this to show his righteousness, because in his divine forbearance he had passed over the sins previously committed; [26]it was to prove at the present time that he himself is righteous and that he justifies the one who has faith in Jesus.[b]

27 Then what becomes of boasting? It is excluded. By what law? By that of works? No, but by the law of faith. [28]For we hold that a person is justified by faith apart from works prescribed by the law. [29]Or is God the God of Jews only? Is he not the God of Gentiles also? Yes, of Gentiles also, [30]since God is one; and he will justify the circumcised on the ground of faith and the uncircumcised through that same faith. [31]Do we then overthrow the law by this faith? By no means! On the contrary, we uphold the law.

4 The Example of Abraham

What then are we to say was gained by[c] Abraham, our ancestor according to the flesh? [2]For if Abraham was justified by works, he has something to boast about, but not before God. [3]For what does the scripture say? "Abraham believed God, and it was reckoned to him as righteousness." [4]Now to one who works, wages are not reckoned as a gift but as something due. [5]But to one who without works trusts him who justifies the ungodly, such faith is reckoned as righteousness. [6]So also David speaks of the blessedness of those to whom God reckons righteousness apart from works:

7 "Blessed are those whose iniquities are forgiven,
  and whose sins are covered;
8 blessed is the one against whom the Lord will not reckon sin."

9 Is this blessedness, then, pronounced only on the circumcised, or also on the uncircumcised? We say, "Faith was reckoned to Abraham as righteousness." [10]How then was it reckoned to him? Was it before or after he had been circumcised? It was not after, but before he was circumcised. [11]He received the sign of circumcision as a seal of the righteousness that he had by faith while he was still uncircumcised. The purpose was to make him the ancestor of all who believe without being circumcised and who thus have righteousness reckoned to them, [12]and likewise the ancestor of the circumcised who are not only circumcised but who also follow the example of the faith that our ancestor Abraham had before he was circumcised.

God's Promise Realized through Faith

13 For the promise that he would inherit the world did not come to Abraham or to his descendants through the law but through the righteousness of faith. [14]If it is the adherents of the law who are to be the heirs, faith is null and the promise is void. [15]For the law brings wrath; but where there is no law, neither is there violation.

16 For this reason it depends on faith, in order that the promise may rest on grace and be guaranteed to all his descendants, not only to the adherents of the law but also to those who share the faith of Abraham (for he is the father of all of us, [17]as it is written, "I have made you the father of many nations")—in the presence of the God in whom he believed, who gives life to the dead and calls into existence the things that do not exist. [18]Hoping against hope, he believed that he would become "the father of many nations," according to what was said, "So numerous shall your descendants be." [19]He did not weaken in faith when he considered his own body, which was already[d] as good as dead (for he was about a hundred years old), or when he considered the barrenness of Sarah's womb. [20]No distrust made him waver concerning the promise of God, but he grew strong in his faith as he gave glory to God, [21]being fully convinced that God was able to do what he had promised. [22]Therefore his faith[e] "was reckoned to him as righteousness." [23]Now the words, "it was reckoned to him," were written not for his sake alone, [24]but for ours also. It will be reckoned to us who believe in him who raised Jesus our Lord from the dead, [25]who was handed over to death for our trespasses and was raised for our justification.

5 Results of Justification

Therefore, since we are justified by faith, we[h] have peace with God through our Lord Jesus Christ, [2]through whom we have obtained access[g] to this grace in which we stand; and we[h] boast in our hope of sharing the glory of God. [3]And not only that, but we[f] also boast in our sufferings, knowing that suffering produces endurance, [4]and endurance produces character, and character produces hope, [5]and hope does not disappoint us, because God's love has been poured into our hearts through the Holy Spirit that has been given to us.

6 For while we were still weak, at the right time Christ died for the ungodly. [7]Indeed, rare-

---

a Or a place of atonement b Or who has the faith of Jesus c Other ancient authorities read say about d Other ancient authorities lack already e Gk Therefore it f Other ancient authorities read let us g Other ancient authorities add by faith h Or let us

Eden—© Rebecca Novak, 15

ly will anyone die for a righteous person—though perhaps for a good person someone might actually dare to die. [8]But God proves his love for us in that while we still were sinners Christ died for us. [9]Much more surely then, now that we have been justified by his blood, will we be saved through him from the wrath of God.[a] [10]For if while we were enemies, we were reconciled to God through the death of his Son, much more surely, having been reconciled, will we be saved by his life. [11]But more than that, we even boast in God through our Lord Jesus Christ, through whom we have now received reconciliation.

Adam and Christ

12 Therefore, just as sin came into the world through one man, and death came through sin, and so death spread to all because all have sinned— [13]sin was indeed in the world before the law, but sin is not reckoned when there is no law. [14]Yet death exercised dominion from Adam to Moses, even over those whose sins were not like the transgression of Adam, who is a type of the one who was to come.

15 But the free gift is not like the trespass. For if the many died through the one man's trespass, much more surely have the grace of God and the free gift in the grace of the one man, Jesus Christ, abounded for the many. [16]And the free gift is not like the effect of the one man's sin. For the judgment following one trespass brought condemnation, but the free gift following many trespasses brings justification. [17]If, because of the one man's trespass, death exercised dominion through that one, much more surely will those who receive the abundance of grace and the free gift of righteousness exercise dominion in life through the one man, Jesus Christ.

18 Therefore just as one man's trespass led to condemnation for all, so one man's act of righteousness leads to justification and life for all. [19]For just as by the one man's disobedience the many were made sinners, so by the one man's obedience the many will be made righteous. [20]But law came in, with the result that the trespass multiplied; but where sin increased, grace abounded all the more, [21]so that, just as sin exercised dominion in death, so grace might also exercise dominion through justification[b] leading to eternal life through Jesus Christ our Lord.

6 Dying and Rising with Christ

What then are we to say? Should we continue in sin in order that grace may abound? [2]By no

a Gk *the wrath*   b Or *righteousness*

means! How can we who died to sin go on living in it? ³Do you not know that all of us who have been baptized into Christ Jesus were baptized into his death? ⁴Therefore we have been buried with him by baptism into death, so that, just as Christ was raised from the dead by the glory of the Father, so we too might walk in newness of life.

5 For if we have been united with him in a death like his, we will certainly be united with him in a resurrection like his. ⁶We know that our old self was crucified with him so that the body of sin might be destroyed, and we might no longer be enslaved to sin. ⁷For whoever has died is freed from sin. ⁸But if we have died with Christ, we believe that we will also live with him. ⁹We know that Christ, being raised from the dead, will never die again; death no longer has dominion over him. ¹⁰The death he died, he died to sin, once for all; but the life he lives, he lives to God. ¹¹So you also must consider yourselves dead to sin and alive to God in Christ Jesus.

12 Therefore, do not let sin exercise dominion in your mortal bodies, to make you obey their passions. ¹³No longer present your members to sin as instruments^a of wickedness, but present yourselves to God as those who have been brought from death to life, and present your members to God as instruments^a of righteousness. ¹⁴For sin will have no dominion over you, since you are not under law but under grace.

Slaves of Righteousness

15 What then? Should we sin because we are not under law but under grace? By no means! ¹⁶Do you not know that if you present yourselves to anyone as obedient slaves, you are slaves of the one whom you obey, either of sin, which leads to death, or of obedience, which leads to righteousness? ¹⁷But thanks be to God that you, having once been slaves of sin, have become obedient from the heart to the form of teaching to which you were entrusted, ¹⁸and that you, having been set free from sin, have become slaves of righteousness. ¹⁹I am speaking in human terms because of your natural limitations.^{b} For just as you once presented your members as slaves to impurity and to greater and greater iniquity, so now present your members as slaves to righteousness for sanctification.

20 When you were slaves of sin, you were free in regard to righteousness. ²¹So what advantage did you then get from the things of which you now are ashamed? The end of those things is death. ²²But now that you have been freed from sin and enslaved to God, the advantage you get is sanctification. The end is eternal life. ²³For the wages of sin is death, but the free gift of God is eternal life in Christ Jesus our Lord.

7 An Analogy from Marriage

Do you not know, brothers and sisters^c—for I am speaking to those who know the law—that the law is binding on a person only during that person's lifetime? ²Thus a married woman is bound by the law to her husband as long as he lives; but if her husband dies, she is discharged from the law concerning the husband. ³Accordingly, she will be called an adulteress if she lives with another man while her husband is alive. But if her husband dies, she is free from that law, and if she marries another man, she is not an adulteress.

4 In the same way, my friends,^{c} you have died to the law through the body of Christ, so that you may belong to another, to him who has been raised from the dead in order that we may bear fruit for God. ⁵While we were living in the flesh, our sinful passions, aroused by the law, were at work in our members to bear fruit for death. ⁶But now we are discharged from the law, dead to that which held us captive, so that we are slaves not under the old written code but in the new life of the Spirit.

The Law and Sin

7 What then should we say? That the law is sin? By no means! Yet, if it had not been for the law, I would not have known sin. I would not have known what it is to covet if the law had not said, "You shall not covet." ⁸But sin, seizing an opportunity in the commandment, produced in me all kinds of covetousness. Apart from the law sin lies dead. ⁹I was once alive apart from the law, but when the commandment came, sin revived ¹⁰and I died, and the very commandment that promised life proved to be death to me. ¹¹For sin, seizing an opportunity in the commandment, deceived me and through it killed me. ¹²So the law is holy, and the commandment is holy and just and good.

13 Did what is good, then, bring death to me? By no means! It was sin, working death in me through what is good, in order that sin might be shown to be sin, and through the commandment might become sinful beyond measure.

The Inner Conflict

14 For we know that the law is spiritual; but I am of the flesh, sold into slavery under sin.^{d} ¹⁵I

a Or weapons b Gk the weakness of your flesh c Gk brothers d Gk sold under sin do not understand my own actions. For I do not do what I want, but I do the very thing I hate. [16]Now if I do what I do not want, I agree that the law is good. [17]But in fact it is no longer I that do it, but sin that dwells within me. [18]For I know that nothing good dwells within me, that is, in my flesh. I can will what is right, but I cannot do it. [19]For I do not do the good I want, but the evil I do not want is what I do. [20]Now if I do what I do not want, it is no longer I that do it, but sin that dwells within me.

[21] So I find it to be a law that when I want to do what is good, evil lies close at hand. [22]For I delight in the law of God in my inmost self, [23]but I see in my members another law at war with the law of my mind, making me captive to the law of sin that dwells in my members. [24]Wretched man that I am! Who will rescue me from this body of death? [25]Thanks be to God through Jesus Christ our Lord!

So then, with my mind I am a slave to the law of God, but with my flesh I am a slave to the law of sin.

8 Life in the Spirit

There is therefore now no condemnation for those who are in Christ Jesus. [2]For the law of the Spirit[a] of life in Christ Jesus has set you[b] free from the law of sin and of death. [3]For God has done what the law, weakened by the flesh, could not do: by sending his own Son in the likeness of sinful flesh, and to deal with sin,[c] he condemned sin in the flesh, [4]so that the just requirement of the law might be fulfilled in us, who walk not according to the flesh but according to the Spirit.[a] [5]For those who live according to the flesh set their minds on the things of the flesh, but those who live according to the Spirit[a] set their minds on the things of the Spirit.[a] [6]To set the mind on the flesh is death, but to set the mind on the Spirit[a] is life and peace. [7]For this reason the mind that is set on the flesh is hostile to God; it does not submit to God's law—indeed it cannot, [8]and those who are in the flesh cannot please God.

[9] But you are not in the flesh; you are in the Spirit,[a] since the Spirit of God dwells in you. Anyone who does not have the Spirit of Christ does not belong to him. [10]But if Christ is in you, though the body is dead because of sin, the Spirit[a] is life because of righteousness. [11]If the Spirit of him who raised Jesus from the dead dwells in you, he who raised Christ[d] from the dead will give life to your mortal bodies also through[e] his Spirit that dwells in you.

[12] So then, brothers and sisters,[f] we are debtors, not to the flesh, to live according to the flesh— [13]for if you live according to the flesh, you will die; but if by the Spirit you put to death the deeds of the body, you will live. [14]For all who are led by the Spirit of God are children of God. [15]For you did not receive a spirit of slavery to fall back into fear, but you have received a spirit of adoption. When we cry, "Abba![g] Father!" [16]it is that very Spirit bearing witness[h] with our spirit that we are children of God, [17]and if children, then heirs, heirs of God and joint heirs with Christ—if, in fact, we suffer with him so that we may also be glorified with him.

Future Glory

[18] I consider that the sufferings of this present time are not worth comparing with the glory about to be revealed to us. [19]For the creation waits with eager longing for the revealing of the children of God; [20]for the creation was subjected to futility, not of its own will but by the will of the one who subjected it, in hope [21]that the creation itself will be set free from its bondage to decay and will obtain the freedom of the glory of the children of God. [22]We know that the whole creation has been groaning in labor pains until now; [23]and not only the creation, but we ourselves, who have the first fruits of the Spirit, groan inwardly while we wait for adoption, the redemption of our bodies. [24]For in[i] hope we were saved. Now hope that is seen is not hope. For who hopes[j] for what is seen? [25]But if we hope for what we do not see, we wait for it with patience.

[26] Likewise the Spirit helps us in our weakness; for we do not know how to pray as we ought, but that very Spirit intercedes[k] with sighs too deep for words. [27]And God,[l] who searches the heart, knows what is the mind of the Spirit, because the Spirit[m] intercedes for the saints according to the will of God.[n]

[28] We know that all things work together for good[o] for those who love God, who are called according to his purpose. [29]For those whom he foreknew he also predestined to be conformed to the image of his Son, in order that he might be the firstborn within a large family.[p] [30]And those whom he predestined he also called; and those whom he called he also

a Or spirit b Here the Greek word you is singular number; other ancient authorities read me or us c Or and as a sin offering d Other ancient authorities read the Christ or Christ Jesus or Jesus Christ e Other ancient authorities read on account of f Gk brothers g Aramaic for Father h Or 15a spirit of adoption, by which we cry, "Abba! Father!" 16The Spirit itself bears witness i Or by j Other ancient authorities read awaits k Other ancient authorities add for us l Gk the one m Gk he or it n Gk according to God o Other ancient authorities read God makes all things work together for good, or in all things God works for good p Gk among many brothers justified; and those whom he justified he also glorified.

God's Love in Christ Jesus

31 What then are we to say about these things? If God is for us, who is against us? [32]He who did not withhold his own Son, but gave him up for all of us, will he not with him also give us everything else? [33]Who will bring any charge against God's elect? It is God who justifies. [34]Who is to condemn? It is Christ Jesus, who died, yes, who was raised, who is at the right hand of God, who indeed intercedes for us.[a] [35]Who will separate us from the love of Christ? Will hardship, or distress, or persecution, or famine, or nakedness, or peril, or sword? [36]As it is written,

"For your sake we are being killed all day
   long;
   we are accounted as sheep to be
      slaughtered."

[37]No, in all these things we are more than conquerors through him who loved us. [38]For I am convinced that neither death, nor life, nor angels, nor rulers, nor things present, nor things to come, nor powers, [39]nor height, nor depth, nor anything else in all creation, will be able to separate us from the love of God in Christ Jesus our Lord.

9 God's Election of Israel

I am speaking the truth in Christ—I am not lying; my conscience confirms it by the Holy Spirit— [2]I have great sorrow and unceasing anguish in my heart. [3]For I could wish that I myself were accursed and cut off from Christ for the sake of my own people,[b] my kindred according to the flesh. [4]They are Israelites, and to them belong the adoption, the glory, the covenants, the giving of the law, the worship, and the promises; [5]to them belong the patriarchs, and from them, according to the flesh, comes the Messiah,[c] who is over all, God blessed forever.[d] Amen.

6 It is not as though the word of God had failed. For not all Israelites truly belong to Israel, [7]and not all of Abraham's children are his true descendants; but "It is through Isaac that descendants shall be named for you." [8]This means that it is not the children of the flesh who are the children of God, but the children of the promise are counted as descendants. [9]For this is what the promise said, "About this time I will return and Sarah shall have a son." [10]Nor is that all; something similar happened to Rebecca when she had conceived children by one husband, our ancestor Isaac. [11]Even before

REALITY ✔

SAVING GRACE

Read **Romans 8.28**. All things work together for good? Really?

Some days you can read this passage and say, "I don't think so." On other days you might smile and say, "I wish." And then there are the days when you read it and say, "Oh, I hope so!"

This is the kind of statement that becomes real when it becomes an attitude. That's when you adopt a confident way of thinking and an approach to life that says, "Yes, all things do work together for good—or they will, even though I can't see it right now."

How do people develop that kind of attitude? It's a faith thing.

Now, read Hebrews 11.1–6. The faith that gives you that kind of attitude is always strengthened by evidence. Take a few minutes to think about the times in your life when you thought things wouldn't work out, but they did. Then think about the times when things didn't work out they way you wanted them to, but something better happened or some unexpected good came out of it. There's your evidence that this faith thing *works*!

Write a poem or a letter to God about evidence of his care for you. Post it at **Learner.CalltoDiscipleship.com**.

they had been born or had done anything good or bad (so that God's purpose of election might continue, [12]not by works but by his call) she was told, "The elder shall serve the younger." [13]As it is written,

"I have loved Jacob,
   but I have hated Esau."

14 What then are we to say? Is there injustice on God's part? By no means! [15]For he says to Moses,

"I will have mercy on whom I have mercy,
   and I will have compassion on whom I
      have compassion."

---

a Or Is it Christ Jesus . . . for us? b Gk my brothers c Or the Christ d Or Messiah, who is God over all, blessed forever; or Messiah. May he who is God over all be blessed forever

I Want to Go Up!

I want to go up-up-up in the sky, Lord
I want to go up-up-up in the sky

I want to fly-fly-fly into those Holy Clouds
I want to meet up with the Angels
I want to feel their joy spreading over me—
I want to see Christ in His Glory.
I want to see him waiting there for me.

I want to go up-up-up in the sky, Lord
I want to go up-up-up in the sky

I know you'll be there with me, Lord
You will show your love and mercy, too
'Cause you know how much I love you
I just can't wait until that day

When I go up-up-up in the sky, Lord
When I go up-up-up in the sky

I will fly-fly-fly into those Holy Clouds
I will meet up with the Angels
And feel their joy spreading over me
I will see Christ in His Glory
He will be there waiting just for me
Just for me! Just for me!

I Want to Go Up!—© Cady Carlson, 15

[16]So it depends not on human will or exertion, but on God who shows mercy. [17]For the scripture says to Pharaoh, "I have raised you up for the very purpose of showing my power in you, so that my name may be proclaimed in all the earth." [18]So then he has mercy on whomever he chooses, and he hardens the heart of whomever he chooses.

God's Wrath and Mercy

19 You will say to me then, "Why then does he still find fault? For who can resist his will?" [20]But who indeed are you, a human being, to argue with God? Will what is molded say to the one who molds it, "Why have you made me like this?" [21]Has the potter no right over the clay, to make out of the same lump one object for special use and another for ordinary use? [22]What if God, desiring to show his wrath and to make known his power, has endured with much patience the objects of wrath that are made for destruction; [23]and what if he has done so in order to make known the riches of his glory for the objects of mercy, which he has prepared beforehand for glory— [24]including us whom he has called, not from the Jews only but also from the Gentiles? [25]As indeed he says in Hosea,

"Those who were not my people I will call
   'my people,'
   and her who was not beloved I will call
   'beloved.' "

[26] "And in the very place where it was said to
      them, 'You are not my people,'
   there they shall be called children of the
      living God."

27 And Isaiah cries out concerning Israel, "Though the number of the children of Israel were like the sand of the sea, only a remnant of them will be saved; [28]for the Lord will execute his sentence on the earth quickly and decisively."[a] [29]And as Isaiah predicted,

"If the Lord of hosts had not left survivors[b]
      to us,
   we would have fared like Sodom
      and been made like Gomorrah."

Israel's Unbelief

30 What then are we to say? Gentiles, who did not strive for righteousness, have attained it, that is, righteousness through faith; [31]but Israel, who did strive for the righteousness that is based on the law, did not succeed in fulfilling that law. [32]Why not? Because they did not strive for it on the basis of faith, but as if it were based on works. They have stumbled over the stumbling stone, [33]as it is written,

"See, I am laying in Zion a stone that will
      make people stumble, a rock that
      will make them fall,
   and whoever believes in him[c] will not be
      put to shame."

10 Brothers and sisters,[d] my heart's desire and prayer to God for them is that they may be saved. [2]I can testify that they have a zeal for God, but it is not enlightened. [3]For, being ignorant of the righteousness that comes from God, and seeking to establish their own, they have not submitted to God's righteousness. [4]For Christ is the end of the law so that there may be righteousness for everyone who believes.

Salvation Is for All

5 Moses writes concerning the righteousness that comes from the law, that "the person who does these things will live by them." [6]But the righteousness that comes from faith says, "Do not say in your heart, 'Who will ascend into heaven?' " (that is, to bring Christ down) [7]"or 'Who will descend into the abyss?' " (that is, to bring Christ up from the dead). [8]But what does it say?

"The word is near you,
   on your lips and in your heart"
(that is, the word of faith that we proclaim); [9]because[e] if you confess with your lips that Jesus is Lord and believe in your heart that God raised him from the dead, you will be saved. [10]For one believes with the heart and so is justified, and one confesses with the mouth and so is saved. [11]The scripture says, "No one who believes in him will be put to shame." [12]For there is no distinction between Jew and Greek; the same Lord is Lord of all and is generous to all who call on him. [13]For, "Everyone who calls on the name of the Lord shall be saved."

14 But how are they to call on one in whom they have not believed? And how are they to believe in one of whom they have never heard? And how are they to hear without someone to proclaim him? [15]And how are they to proclaim him unless they are sent? As it is written, "How beautiful are the feet of those who bring good news!" [16]But not all have obeyed the good news;[f] for Isaiah says, "Lord, who has believed our message?" [17]So faith comes from what is heard, and what is heard comes through the word of Christ.[g]

---

a Other ancient authorities read for he will finish his work and cut it short in righteousness, because the Lord will make the sentence shortened on the earth b Or descendants; Gk seed c Or trusts in it d Gk Brothers e Or namely, that f Or gospel g Or about Christ; other ancient authorities read of God

18 But I ask, have they not heard? Indeed they have; for

"Their voice has gone out to all the earth,
    and their words to the ends of the
        world."

[19]Again I ask, did Israel not understand? First Moses says,

"I will make you jealous of those who are
    not a nation;
with a foolish nation I will make you
    angry."

[20]Then Isaiah is so bold as to say,

"I have been found by those who did not
    seek me;
I have shown myself to those who did not
    ask for me."

[21]But of Israel he says, "All day long I have held out my hands to a disobedient and contrary people."

11 Israel's Rejection Is Not Final

I ask, then, has God rejected his people? By no means! I myself am an Israelite, a descendant of Abraham, a member of the tribe of Benjamin. [2]God has not rejected his people whom he foreknew. Do you not know what the scripture says of Elijah, how he pleads with God against Israel? [3]"Lord, they have killed your prophets, they have demolished your altars; I alone am left, and they are seeking my life." [4]But what is the divine reply to him? "I have kept for myself seven thousand who have not bowed the knee to Baal." [5]So too at the present time there is a remnant, chosen by grace. [6]But if it is by grace, it is no longer on the basis of works, otherwise grace would no longer be grace.[a]

7 What then? Israel failed to obtain what it was seeking. The elect obtained it, but the rest were hardened, [8]as it is written,

"God gave them a sluggish spirit,
    eyes that would not see
    and ears that would not hear,
    down to this very day."

[9]And David says,

"Let their table become a snare and a trap,
    a stumbling block and a retribution for
        them;
[10] let their eyes be darkened so that they
        cannot see,
    and keep their backs forever bent."

The Salvation of the Gentiles

11 So I ask, have they stumbled so as to fall? By no means! But through their stumbling[b] salvation has come to the Gentiles, so as to make Israel[c] jealous. [12]Now if their stumbling[b] means riches for the world, and if their defeat means riches for Gentiles, how much more will their full inclusion mean!

13 Now I am speaking to you Gentiles. Inasmuch then as I am an apostle to the Gentiles, I glorify my ministry [14]in order to make my own people[d] jealous, and thus save some of them. [15]For if their rejection is the reconciliation of the world, what will their acceptance be but life from the dead! [16]If the part of the dough offered as first fruits is holy, then the whole batch is holy; and if the root is holy, then the branches also are holy.

17 But if some of the branches were broken off, and you, a wild olive shoot, were grafted in their place to share the rich root[e] of the olive tree, [18]do not boast over the branches. If you do boast, remember that it is not you that support the root, but the root that supports you. [19]You will say, "Branches were broken off so that I might be grafted in." [20]That is true. They were broken off because of their unbelief, but you stand only through faith. So do not become proud, but stand in awe. [21]For if God did not spare the natural branches, perhaps he will not spare you.[f] [22]Note then the kindness and the severity of God: severity toward those who have fallen, but God's kindness toward you, provided you continue in his kindness; otherwise you also will be cut off. [23]And even those of Israel,[g] if they do not persist in unbelief, will be grafted in, for God has the power to graft them in again. [24]For if you have been cut from what is by nature a wild olive tree and grafted, contrary to nature, into a cultivated olive tree, how much more will these natural branches be grafted back into their own olive tree.

All Israel Will Be Saved

25 So that you may not claim to be wiser than you are, brothers and sisters,[h] I want you to understand this mystery: a hardening has come upon part of Israel, until the full number of the

---

a Other ancient authorities add But if it is by works, it is no longer on the basis of grace, otherwise work would no longer be work   b Gk transgression
c Gk them   d Gk my flesh   e Other ancient authorities read the richness   f Other ancient authorities read neither will he spare you
g Gk lacks of Israel   h Gk brothers

Gentiles has come in. ²⁶And so all Israel will be saved; as it is written,

"Out of Zion will come the Deliverer;
he will banish ungodliness from Jacob."

²⁷ "And this is my covenant with them,
when I take away their sins."

²⁸As regards the gospel they are enemies of God[a] for your sake; but as regards election they are beloved, for the sake of their ancestors; ²⁹for the gifts and the calling of God are irrevocable. ³⁰Just as you were once disobedient to God but have now received mercy because of their disobedience, ³¹so they have now been disobedient in order that, by the mercy shown to you, they too may now[b] receive mercy. ³²For God has imprisoned all in disobedience so that he may be merciful to all.

33 O the depth of the riches and wisdom and knowledge of God! How unsearchable are his judgments and how inscrutable his ways!

³⁴ "For who has known the mind of the Lord?
Or who has been his counselor?"

³⁵ "Or who has given a gift to him,
to receive a gift in return?"

³⁶For from him and through him and to him are all things. To him be the glory forever. Amen.

12 The New Life in Christ

I appeal to you therefore, brothers and sisters,[c] by the mercies of God, to present your bodies as a living sacrifice, holy and acceptable to God, which is your spiritual[d] worship. ²Do not be conformed to this world,[e] but be transformed by the renewing of your minds, so that you may discern what is the will of God—what is good and acceptable and perfect.[f]

3 For by the grace given to me I say to everyone among you not to think of yourself more highly than you ought to think, but to think with sober judgment, each according to the measure of faith that God has assigned. ⁴For as in one body we have many members, and not all the members have the same function, ⁵so we, who are many, are one body in Christ, and individually we are members one of another. ⁶We have gifts that differ according to the grace given to us: prophecy, in proportion to faith; ⁷ministry, in ministering; the teacher, in teaching; ⁸the exhorter, in exhortation; the giver, in generosity; the leader, in diligence; the compassionate, in cheerfulness.

Marks of the True Christian

9 Let love be genuine; hate what is evil, hold fast to what is good; ¹⁰love one another with mutual affection; outdo one another in showing honor. ¹¹Do not lag in zeal, be ardent in spirit, serve the Lord.[g] ¹²Rejoice in hope, be patient in suffering, persevere in prayer. ¹³Contribute to the needs of the saints; extend hospitality to strangers.

14 Bless those who persecute you; bless and do not curse them. ¹⁵Rejoice with those who rejoice, weep with those who weep. ¹⁶Live in harmony with one another; do not be haughty, but associate with the lowly;[h] do not claim to be wiser than you are. ¹⁷Do not repay anyone evil for evil, but take thought for what is noble in the sight of all. ¹⁸If it is possible, so far as it depends on you, live peaceably with all. ¹⁹Beloved, never avenge yourselves, but leave room for the wrath of God;[i] for it is written, "Vengeance is mine, I will repay, says the Lord." ²⁰No, "if your enemies are hungry, feed them; if they are thirsty, give them something to drink; for by doing this you will heap burning coals on their heads." ²¹Do not be overcome by evil, but overcome evil with good.

13 Being Subject to Authorities

Let every person be subject to the governing authorities; for there is no authority except from God, and those authorities that exist have been instituted by God. ²Therefore whoever resists authority resists what God has appointed, and those who resist will incur judgment. ³For rulers are not a terror to good conduct, but to bad. Do you wish to have no fear of the authority? Then do what is good, and you will receive its approval; ⁴for it is God's servant for your good. But if you do what is wrong, you should be afraid, for the authority[j] does not bear the sword in vain! It is the servant of God to execute wrath on the wrongdoer. ⁵Therefore one must be subject, not only because of wrath but also because of conscience. ⁶For the same reason you also pay taxes, for the authorities are God's servants, busy with this very thing. ⁷Pay to all what is due them—taxes to whom taxes are due, revenue to whom revenue is due, respect to whom respect is due, honor to whom honor is due.

Love for One Another

8 Owe no one anything, except to love one another; for the one who loves another has fulfilled the law. ⁹The commandments, "You shall not commit adultery; You shall not murder; You shall not steal; You shall not covet"; and any other commandment, are summed up in this word, "Love your neighbor as yourself."

---

a Gk lacks of God   b Other ancient authorities lack now   c Gk brothers   d Or reasonable   e Gk age   f Or what is the good and acceptable and perfect will of God   g Other ancient authorities read serve the opportune time   h Or give yourselves to humble tasks   i Gk the wrath   j Gk it

¹⁰Love does no wrong to a neighbor; therefore, love is the fulfilling of the law.

An Urgent Appeal

11 Besides this, you know what time it is, how it is now the moment for you to wake from sleep. For salvation is nearer to us now than when we became believers; ¹²the night is far gone, the day is near. Let us then lay aside the works of darkness and put on the armor of light; ¹³let us live honorably as in the day, not in reveling and drunkenness, not in debauchery and licentiousness, not in quarreling and jealousy. ¹⁴Instead, put on the Lord Jesus Christ, and make no provision for the flesh, to gratify its desires.

14 Do Not Judge Another

Welcome those who are weak in faith,ᵃ but not for the purpose of quarreling over opinions. ²Some believe in eating anything, while the weak eat only vegetables. ³Those who eat must not despise those who abstain, and those who abstain must not pass judgment on those who eat; for God has welcomed them. ⁴Who are you to pass judgment on servants of another? It is

before their own lord that they stand or fall. And they will be upheld, for the Lordᵇ is able to make them stand.

5 Some judge one day to be better than another, while others judge all days to be alike. Let all be fully convinced in their own minds. ⁶Those who observe the day, observe it in honor of the Lord. Also those who eat, eat in honor of the Lord, since they give thanks to God; while those who abstain, abstain in honor of the Lord and give thanks to God.

7 We do not live to ourselves, and we do not die to ourselves. ⁸If we live, we live to the Lord, and if we die, we die to the Lord; so then, whether we live or whether we die, we are the Lord's. ⁹For to this end Christ died and lived again, so that he might be Lord of both the dead and the living.

10 Why do you pass judgment on your brother or sister?ᶜ Or you, why do you despise your brother or sister?ᶜ For we will all stand before the judgment seat of God.ᵈ ¹¹For it is written,

"As I live, says the Lord, every knee shall
    bow to me,

---

a Or *conviction* b Other ancient authorities read *for God* c Gk *brother* d Other ancient authorities read *of Christ* and every tongue shall give praise to[a] God."

[12]So then, each of us will be accountable to God.[b]

Do Not Make Another Stumble

13 Let us therefore no longer pass judgment on one another, but resolve instead never to put a stumbling block or hindrance in the way of another.[c] [14]I know and am persuaded in the Lord Jesus that nothing is unclean in itself; but it is unclean for anyone who thinks it unclean. [15]If your brother or sister[d] is being injured by what you eat, you are no longer walking in love. Do not let what you eat cause the ruin of one for whom Christ died. [16]So do not let your good be spoken of as evil. [17]For the kingdom of God is not food and drink but righteousness and peace and joy in the Holy Spirit. [18]The one who thus serves Christ is acceptable to God and has human approval. [19]Let us then pursue what makes for peace and for mutual upbuilding. [20]Do not, for the sake of food, destroy the work of God. Everything is indeed clean, but it is wrong for you to make others fall by what you eat; [21]it is good not to eat meat or drink wine or do anything that makes your brother or sister[d] stumble.[e] [22]The faith that you have, have as your own conviction before God. Blessed are those who have no reason to condemn themselves because of what they approve. [23]But those who have doubts are condemned if they eat, because they do not act from faith;[f] for whatever does not proceed from faith[f] is sin.[g]

15 Please Others, Not Yourselves

We who are strong ought to put up with the failings of the weak, and not to please ourselves. [2]Each of us must please our neighbor for the good purpose of building up the neighbor. [3]For Christ did not please himself; but, as it is written, "The insults of those who insult you have fallen on me." [4]For whatever was written in former days was written for our instruction, so that by steadfastness and by the encouragement of the scriptures we might have hope. [5]May the God of steadfastness and encouragement grant you to live in harmony with one another, in accordance with Christ Jesus, [6]so that together you may with one voice glorify the God and Father of our Lord Jesus Christ.

The Gospel for Jews and Gentiles Alike

7 Welcome one another, therefore, just as Christ has welcomed you, for the glory of God. [8]For I tell you that Christ has become a servant

TRY THIS

THAT OTHER ARMS RACE
Read **Romans 15.20–21**.

You drift through the Louvre in Paris, soaking in gallery after gallery of priceless paintings, pottery, and sculpture. It's overwhelming. And then you see . . . her.

The Venus de Milo—the Greek masterpiece that, even armless, has captivated millions since being unearthed in 1820.

You think, *I'll just finish this up*. So you pull out some modeling clay and start adding arms.

Bad idea.

No one needs to "complete" the Venus de Milo (or do a knockoff version).

But even in a crowded world, there's plenty of room for someone—you, perhaps—to do what's never been done. Which is exactly what Paul's example challenges us to do—to take truth where it's not been heard before. Maybe that's around the block. Or around the world.

Find an old-fashioned globe. Spin it and lightly place a finger on it. When the spinning stops, pray for whatever group of people lives closest to where your finger is. (Or if you're interested in praying more specifically, go to **Learner.CalltoDiscipleship.com** for information about an unreached group and pray for their needs.) How will you share truth with those people? With the people in your neighborhood who've never seen truth in action?

GOD IS RELENTLESS   MY WORLD

of the circumcised on behalf of the truth of God in order that he might confirm the promises given to the patriarchs, [9]and in order that the Gentiles might glorify God for his mercy. As it is written,

"Therefore I will confess[h] you among the
        Gentiles,
    and sing praises to your name";
[10]and again he says,
    "Rejoice, O Gentiles, with his people";
[11]and again,
    "Praise the Lord, all you Gentiles,
        and let all the peoples praise him";
[12]and again Isaiah says,
    "The root of Jesse shall come,

a Or confess b Other ancient authorities lack to God c Gk of a brother d Gk brother e Other ancient authorities add or be upset or be weakened f Or conviction g Other authorities, some ancient, add here 16.25–27 h Or thank

the one who rises to rule the Gentiles;
in him the Gentiles shall hope."

[13] May the God of hope fill you with all joy and peace in believing, so that you may abound in hope by the power of the Holy Spirit.

Paul's Reason for Writing So Boldly

14 I myself feel confident about you, my brothers and sisters,[a] that you yourselves are full of goodness, filled with all knowledge, and able to instruct one another. [15] Nevertheless on some points I have written to you rather boldly by way of reminder, because of the grace given me by God [16] to be a minister of Christ Jesus to the Gentiles in the priestly service of the gospel of God, so that the offering of the Gentiles may be acceptable, sanctified by the Holy Spirit. [17] In Christ Jesus, then, I have reason to boast of my work for God. [18] For I will not venture to speak of anything except what Christ has accomplished[b] through me to win obedience from the Gentiles, by word and deed, [19] by the power of signs and wonders, by the power of the Spirit of God,[c] so that from Jerusalem and as far around as Illyricum I have fully proclaimed the good news[d] of Christ. [20] Thus I make it my ambition to proclaim the good news,[d] not where Christ has already been named, so that I do not build on someone else's foundation, [21] but as it is written,

"Those who have never been told of him
shall see,
and those who have never heard of him
shall understand."

Paul's Plan to Visit Rome

22 This is the reason that I have so often been hindered from coming to you. [23] But now, with no further place for me in these regions, I desire, as I have for many years, to come to you [24] when I go to Spain. For I do hope to see you on my journey and to be sent on by you, once I have enjoyed your company for a little while. [25] At present, however, I am going to Jerusalem in a ministry to the saints; [26] for Macedonia and Achaia have been pleased to share their resources with the poor among the saints at Jerusalem. [27] They were pleased to do this, and indeed they owe it to them; for if the Gentiles have come to share in their spiritual blessings, they ought also to be of service to them in material things. [28] So, when I have completed this, and have delivered to them what has been collected,[e] I will set out by way of you to Spain;

[29] and I know that when I come to you, I will come in the fullness of the blessing[f] of Christ.

30 I appeal to you, brothers and sisters,[g] by our Lord Jesus Christ and by the love of the Spirit, to join me in earnest prayer to God on my behalf, [31] that I may be rescued from the unbelievers in Judea, and that my ministry[g] to Jerusalem may be acceptable to the saints, [32] so that by God's will I may come to you with joy and be refreshed in your company. [33] The God of peace be with all of you.[h] Amen.

16 Personal Greetings

I commend to you our sister Phoebe, a deacon[i] of the church at Cenchreae, [2] so that you may welcome her in the Lord as is fitting for the saints, and help her in whatever she may require from you, for she has been a benefactor of many and of myself as well.

3 Greet Prisca and Aquila, who work with me in Christ Jesus, [4] and who risked their necks for my life, to whom not only I give thanks, but also all the churches of the Gentiles. [5] Greet also the church in their house. Greet my beloved Epaenetus, who was the first convert[j] in Asia for Christ. [6] Greet Mary, who has worked very hard among you. [7] Greet Andronicus and Junia,[k] my relatives[l] who were in prison with me; they are prominent among the apostles, and they were in Christ before I was. [8] Greet Ampliatus, my beloved in the Lord. [9] Greet Urbanus, our co-worker in Christ, and my beloved Stachys. [10] Greet Apelles, who is approved in Christ. Greet those who belong to the family of Aristobulus. [11] Greet my relative[m] Herodion. Greet those in the Lord who belong to the family of Narcissus. [12] Greet those workers in the Lord, Tryphaena and Tryphosa. Greet the beloved Persis, who has worked hard in the Lord. [13] Greet Rufus, chosen in the Lord; and greet his mother—a mother to me also. [14] Greet Asyncritus, Phlegon, Hermes, Patrobas, Hermas, and the brothers and sisters[g] who are with them. [15] Greet Philologus, Julia, Nereus and his sister, and Olympas, and all the saints who are with them. [16] Greet one another with a holy kiss. All the churches of Christ greet you.

Final Instructions

17 I urge you, brothers and sisters,[g] to keep an eye on those who cause dissensions and offenses, in opposition to the teaching that you have learned; avoid them. [18] For such people do not serve our Lord Christ, but their own appetites,[n] and by smooth talk and flattery they

---

a Gk brothers   b Gk speak of those things that Christ has not accomplished   c Other ancient authorities read of the Spirit or of the Holy Spirit
d Or gospel   e Gk have sealed to them this fruit   f Other ancient authorities add of the gospel   g Other ancient authorities read my bringing of
a gift   h One ancient authority adds 16.25–27 here   i Or minister   j Gk first fruits   k Or Junias; other ancient authorities read Julia
l Or compatriots   m Or compatriot   n Gk their own belly

deceive the hearts of the simple-minded. [19]For while your obedience is known to all, so that I rejoice over you, I want you to be wise in what is good and guileless in what is evil. [20]The God of peace will shortly crush Satan under your feet. The grace of our Lord Jesus Christ be with you.[a]

21 Timothy, my co-worker, greets you; so do Lucius and Jason and Sosipater, my relatives.[b]

22 I Tertius, the writer of this letter, greet you in the Lord.[c]

23 Gaius, who is host to me and to the whole church, greets you. Erastus, the city treasurer, and our brother Quartus, greet you.[d]

Final Doxology

25 Now to God[e] who is able to strengthen you according to my gospel and the proclamation of Jesus Christ, according to the revelation of the mystery that was kept secret for long ages [26]but is now disclosed, and through the prophetic writings is made known to all the Gentiles, according to the command of the eternal God, to bring about the obedience of faith— [27]to the only wise God, through Jesus Christ, to whom[f] be the glory forever! Amen.[g]

a Other ancient authorities lack this sentence b Or compatriots
c Or I Tertius, writing this letter in the Lord, greet you d Other ancient
authorities add verse 24, The grace of our Lord Jesus Christ be with all of
you. Amen. e Gk the one f Other ancient authorities lack to whom.
The verse then reads, to the only wise God be the glory through Jesus
Christ forever. Amen. g Other ancient authorities lack 16.25–27 or
include it after 14.23 or 15.33; others put verse 24 after verse 27

TEXT MESSAGE

Since the early Christians didn't have church buildings to go to, they usually met in homes (Romans 16.3–5). Priscilla and Aquila might have been wealthy and had a large house where Christians could gather for worship. You would probably have to clean your room more often if this were still standard practice.

This information has been scanned and is free of all known viruses. Please forward to all your friends.

CREATIVE SPACE

The Final Walk—© Daniel Jauch, 14

1 CORINTHIANS

ADVICE FOR LIFE

Let Love Transform You

Money. Sex. Power.

These three words perfectly describe Corinth, the wild city in Greece featured in the title of this letter. The immoral attitudes of Corinth's citizens were seeping into the Corinthian Church like smoke. Confused about how to live, Christians were putting their energy into arguments about which leader was best rather than addressing their problems. No wonder Paul wades into the muck with this letter. He gives instructions on a whole host of issues, from incest to food sacrificed to idols, from marriage to the right way to conduct worship.

And then toward the end of the letter comes one of the best-known passages from the Bible. It's a beautiful, poetic piece about love that seems almost out of place alongside Paul's earthy, practical advice. But in fact it's deeply relevant. Because if you truly love someone, how can you bring a lawsuit against that person? If you truly love others in the holy way that God loves us, how can you exploit them sexually? Or look down on the way they worship? Or discriminate against them?

But you can't manufacture that kind of love; you can only receive it. The challenge for us is to open ourselves up to the love of God, to drink it in, to let it transform us and take root in our hearts and then see it overflow to the people around us.

"Peace begins with a smile—smile five times a day at someone you really don't want to smile at. . . . Do it for peace."

—Bl. Mother Teresa of Calcutta

WHO Paul wrote this letter to the Church community he had established in Corinth.

WHAT Here Paul gives sound advice to people who are struggling to live as Christians in a very pagan culture. He tells them to sort out the divisions in their Church family and gives them ethical guidelines on topics like sex, marriage, and expressions of worship.

WHEN Written around A.D. 55

WHERE Corinth was an important trading city in Greece. Paul was likely in Ephesus (a city in modern-day Turkey) when he wrote this letter.

PATH OF DISCIPLESHIP

Someone once asked Jesus what the greatest commandment is (see Matthew 22.36–40). Jesus answered by talking about love. "You shall love the Lord your God with all your heart, and with all your soul, and with all your mind," he said. And he added that it was equally important to "love your neighbor as yourself."

Love is the heart of Jesus' message. Love is what motivated Jesus to live on earth and journey to the cross. Love is how we cope with disagreements and divisions. Love is how we decide the right way to behave. It sounds simple, doesn't it? It's a lifetime's work to receive God's love and to pass it on to others.

1 Salutation

Paul, called to be an apostle of Christ Jesus by the will of God, and our brother Sosthenes,

2 To the church of God that is in Corinth, to those who are sanctified in Christ Jesus, called to be saints, together with all those who in every place call on the name of our Lord Jesus Christ, both their Lord[a] and ours:

3 Grace to you and peace from God our Father and the Lord Jesus Christ.

4 I give thanks to my[b] God always for you because of the grace of God that has been given you in Christ Jesus, [5]for in every way you have been enriched in him, in speech and knowledge of every kind— [6]just as the testimony of[c] Christ has been strengthened among you— [7]so that you are not lacking in any spiritual gift as you wait for the revealing of our Lord Jesus Christ. [8]He will also strengthen you to the end, so that you may be blameless on the day of our Lord Jesus Christ. [9]God is faithful; by him you were called into the fellowship of his Son, Jesus Christ our Lord.

Divisions in the Church

10 Now I appeal to you, brothers and sisters,[d] by the name of our Lord Jesus Christ, that all of you be in agreement and that there be no divisions among you, but that you be united in the same mind and the same purpose. [11]For it has been reported to me by Chloe's people that there are quarrels among you, my brothers and sisters.[e] [12]What I mean is that each of you says, "I belong to Paul," or "I belong to Apollos," or "I belong to Cephas," or "I belong to Christ." [13]Has Christ been divided? Was Paul crucified for you? Or were you baptized in the name of Paul? [14]I thank God[f] that I baptized none of you except Crispus and Gaius, [15]so that no one can say that you were baptized in my name. [16](I did baptize also the household of Stephanas; beyond that, I do not know whether I baptized anyone else.) [17]For Christ did not send me to baptize but to proclaim the gospel, and not with eloquent wisdom, so that the cross of Christ might not be emptied of its power.

Christ the Power and Wisdom of God

18 For the message about the cross is foolishness to those who are perishing, but to us who are being saved it is the power of God. [19]For it is written,

"I will destroy the wisdom of the wise,

and the discernment of the discerning I will thwart."

[20]Where is the one who is wise? Where is the scribe? Where is the debater of this age? Has not God made foolish the wisdom of the world? [21]For since, in the wisdom of God, the world did not know God through wisdom, God decided, through the foolishness of our proclamation, to save those who believe. [22]For Jews demand signs and Greeks desire wisdom, [23]but we proclaim Christ crucified, a stumbling block to Jews and foolishness to Gentiles, [24]but to those who are the called, both Jews and Greeks, Christ the power of God and the wisdom of God. [25]For God's foolishness is wiser than human wisdom, and God's weakness is stronger than human strength.

26 Consider your own call, brothers and sisters:[d] not many of you were wise by human standards,[g] not many were powerful, not many were of noble birth. [27]But God chose what is foolish in the world to shame the wise; God chose what is weak in the world to shame the strong; [28]God chose what is low and despised in the world, things that are not, to reduce to nothing things that are, [29]so that no one[h] might boast in the presence of God. [30]He is the source of your life in Christ Jesus, who became for us wisdom from God, and righteousness and sanctification and redemption, [31]in order that, as it is written, "Let the one who boasts, boast in[i] the Lord."

2 Proclaiming Christ Crucified

When I came to you, brothers and sisters,[d] I did not come proclaiming the mystery[j] of God to you in lofty words or wisdom. [2]For I decided to know nothing among you except Jesus Christ, and him crucified. [3]And I came to you in weakness and in fear and in much trembling. [4]My speech and my proclamation were not with plausible words of wisdom,[k] but with a demonstration of the Spirit and of power, [5]so that your faith might rest not on human wisdom but on the power of God.

The True Wisdom of God

6 Yet among the mature we do speak wisdom, though it is not a wisdom of this age or of the rulers of this age, who are doomed to perish. [7]But we speak God's wisdom, secret and hidden, which God decreed before the ages for our glory. [8]None of the rulers of this age understood this; for if they had, they would not have crucified the Lord of glory. [9]But, as it is written,

"What no eye has seen, nor ear heard,

---

a Gk theirs b Other ancient authorities lack my c Or to d Gk brothers e Gk my brothers f Other ancient authorities read I am thankful g Gk according to the flesh h Gk no flesh i Or of j Other ancient authorities read testimony k Other ancient authorities read the persuasiveness of wisdom

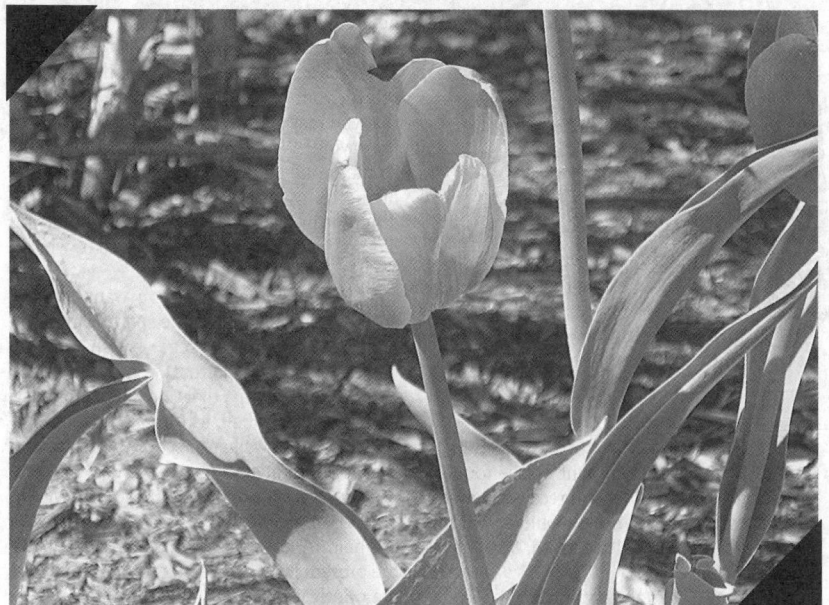

Small Wonder—© Rachel Hostert, 18

nor the human heart conceived,
what God has prepared for those who love
him"—
[10] these things God has revealed to us through the Spirit; for the Spirit searches everything, even the depths of God. [11] For what human being knows what is truly human except the human spirit that is within? So also no one comprehends what is truly God's except the Spirit of God. [12] Now we have received not the spirit of the world, but the Spirit that is from God, so that we may understand the gifts bestowed on us by God. [13] And we speak of these things in words not taught by human wisdom but taught by the Spirit, interpreting spiritual things to those who are spiritual.[a]

14 Those who are unspiritual[b] do not receive the gifts of God's Spirit, for they are foolishness to them, and they are unable to understand them because they are spiritually discerned. [15] Those who are spiritual discern all things, and they are themselves subject to no one else's scrutiny.
[16] "For who has known the mind of the Lord
so as to instruct him?"
But we have the mind of Christ.

3 On Divisions in the Corinthian Church

And so, brothers and sisters,[c] I could not speak to you as spiritual people, but rather as people of the flesh, as infants in Christ. [2] I fed you with milk, not solid food, for you were not ready for solid food. Even now you are still not ready, [3] for you are still of the flesh. For as long as there is jealousy and quarreling among you, are you not of the flesh, and behaving according to human inclinations? [4] For when one says, "I belong to Paul," and another, "I belong to Apollos," are you not merely human?

5 What then is Apollos? What is Paul? Servants through whom you came to believe, as the Lord assigned to each. [6] I planted, Apollos watered, but God gave the growth. [7] So neither the one who plants nor the one who waters is anything, but only God who gives the growth. [8] The one who plants and the one who waters have a common purpose, and each will receive wages according to the labor of each. [9] For we are God's servants, working together; you are God's field, God's building.

10 According to the grace of God given to me, like a skilled master builder I laid a foundation, and someone else is building on it. Each builder must choose with care how to build on it. [11] For no one can lay any foundation other than the one that has been laid; that foundation is Jesus Christ. [12] Now if anyone builds on the foundation with gold, silver, precious stones, wood, hay, straw— [13] the work of each builder will become visible, for the Day will disclose it, because it will be revealed with fire, and the fire will test what sort of work each has

---

a Or *interpreting spiritual things in spiritual language*, or *comparing spiritual things with spiritual* *b* Or *natural* *c* Gk *brothers* done. [14]If what has been built on the foundation survives, the builder will receive a reward. [15]If the work is burned up, the builder will suffer loss; but the builder will be saved, but only as through fire.

16 Do you not know that you are God's temple and that God's Spirit dwells in you?[a] [17]If anyone destroys God's temple, God will destroy that person. For God's temple is holy, and you are that temple.

18 Do not deceive yourselves. If you think that you are wise in this age, you should become fools so that you may become wise. [19]For the wisdom of this world is foolishness with God. For it is written,

"He catches the wise in their craftiness,"

[20]and again,

"The Lord knows the thoughts of the wise,
    that they are futile."

[21]So let no one boast about human leaders. For all things are yours, [22]whether Paul or Apollos or Cephas or the world or life or death or the present or the future—all belong to you, [23]and you belong to Christ, and Christ belongs to God.

4 The Ministry of the Apostles

Think of us in this way, as servants of Christ and stewards of God's mysteries. [2]Moreover, it is required of stewards that they be found trustworthy. [3]But with me it is a very small thing that I should be judged by you or by any human court. I do not even judge myself. [4]I am not aware of anything against myself, but I am not thereby acquitted. It is the Lord who judges me. [5]Therefore do not pronounce judgment before the time, before the Lord comes, who will bring to light the things now hidden in darkness and will disclose the purposes of the heart. Then each one will receive commendation from God.

6 I have applied all this to Apollos and myself for your benefit, brothers and sisters,[b] so that you may learn through us the meaning of the saying, "Nothing beyond what is written," so that none of you will be puffed up in favor of one against another. [7]For who sees anything different in you?[c] What do you have that you did not receive? And if you received it, why do you boast as if it were not a gift?

8 Already you have all you want! Already you have become rich! Quite apart from us you have become kings! Indeed, I wish that you had become kings, so that we might be kings with you! [9]For I think that God has exhibited us apostles as last of all, as though sentenced to death, because we have become a spectacle to the world, to angels and to mortals. [10]We are fools for the sake of Christ, but you are wise in Christ. We are weak, but you are strong. You are held in honor, but we in disrepute. [11]To the present hour we are hungry and thirsty, we are poorly clothed and beaten and homeless, [12]and we grow weary from the work of our own hands. When reviled, we bless; when persecuted, we endure; [13]when slandered, we speak kindly. We have become like the rubbish of the world, the dregs of all things, to this very day.

Fatherly Admonition

14 I am not writing this to make you ashamed, but to admonish you as my beloved children. [15]For though you might have ten thousand guardians in Christ, you do not have many fathers. Indeed, in Christ Jesus I became your father through the gospel. [16]I appeal to you, then, be imitators of me. [17]For this reason I sent[d] you Timothy, who is my beloved and faithful child in the Lord, to remind you of my ways in Christ Jesus, as I teach them everywhere in every church. [18]But some of you, thinking that I am not coming to you, have become arrogant. [19]But I will come to you soon, if the Lord wills, and I will find out not the talk of these arrogant people but their power. [20]For the kingdom of God depends not on talk but on power. [21]What would you prefer? Am I to come to you with a stick, or with love in a spirit of gentleness?

5 Sexual Immorality Defiles the Church

It is actually reported that there is sexual immorality among you, and of a kind that is not found even among pagans; for a man is living with his father's wife. [2]And you are arrogant! Should you not rather have mourned, so that

a In verses 16 and 17 the Greek word for you is plural   b Gk brothers   c Or Who makes you different from another?   d Or am sending he who has done this would have been removed from among you?

3 For though absent in body, I am present in spirit; and as if present I have already pronounced judgment [4]in the name of the Lord Jesus on the man who has done such a thing.[a] When you are assembled, and my spirit is present with the power of our Lord Jesus, [5]you are to hand this man over to Satan for the destruction of the flesh, so that his spirit may be saved in the day of the Lord.[b]

6 Your boasting is not a good thing. Do you not know that a little yeast leavens the whole batch of dough? [7]Clean out the old yeast so that you may be a new batch, as you really are unleavened. For our paschal lamb, Christ, has been sacrificed. [8]Therefore, let us celebrate the festival, not with the old yeast, the yeast of malice and evil, but with the unleavened bread of sincerity and truth.

Sexual Immorality Must Be Judged

9 I wrote to you in my letter not to associate with sexually immoral persons— [10]not at all meaning the immoral of this world, or the greedy and robbers, or idolaters, since you would then need to go out of the world. [11]But now I am writing to you not to associate with anyone who bears the name of brother or sister[c] who is sexually immoral or greedy, or is an idolater, reviler, drunkard, or robber. Do not even eat with such a one. [12]For what have I to do with judging those outside? Is it not those who are inside that you are to judge? [13]God will judge those outside. "Drive out the wicked person from among you."

6 Lawsuits among Believers

When any of you has a grievance against another, do you dare to take it to court before the unrighteous, instead of taking it before the saints? [2]Do you not know that the saints will judge the world? And if the world is to be judged by you, are you incompetent to try trivial cases? [3]Do you not know that we are to judge angels—to say nothing of ordinary matters? [4]If you have ordinary cases, then, do you appoint as judges those who have no standing in the church? [5]I say this to your shame. Can it be that there is no one among you wise enough to decide between one believer[c] and another, [6]but a believer[c] goes to court against a believer[c]—and before unbelievers at that?

7 In fact, to have lawsuits at all with one another is already a defeat for you. Why not rather be wronged? Why not rather be defrauded?

[8]But you yourselves wrong and defraud—and believers[d] at that.

9 Do you not know that wrongdoers will not inherit the kingdom of God? Do not be deceived! Fornicators, idolaters, adulterers, male prostitutes, sodomites, [10]thieves, the greedy, drunkards, revilers, robbers—none of these will inherit the kingdom of God. [11]And this is what some of you used to be. But you were washed, you were sanctified, you were justified in the name of the Lord Jesus Christ and in the Spirit of our God.

Glorify God in Body and Spirit

12 "All things are lawful for me," but not all things are beneficial. "All things are lawful for me," but I will not be dominated by anything. [13]"Food is meant for the stomach and the stomach for food,"[e] and God will destroy both one and the other. The body is meant not for fornication but for the Lord, and the Lord for the body. [14]And God raised the Lord and will also raise us by his power. [15]Do you not know that your bodies are members of Christ? Should I therefore take the members of Christ and make them members of a prostitute? Never! [16]Do you not know that whoever is united to a prostitute becomes one body with her? For it is said, "The two shall be one flesh." [17]But anyone united to the Lord becomes one spirit with him. [18]Shun fornication! Every sin that a person commits is outside the body; but the fornicator sins against the body itself. [19]Or do you not know that your body is a temple[f] of the Holy Spirit within you, which you have from God, and that you are not your own? [20]For you were bought with a price; therefore glorify God in your body.

7 Directions concerning Marriage

Now concerning the matters about which you wrote: "It is well for a man not to touch a woman." [2]But because of cases of sexual immorality, each man should have his own wife and each woman her own husband. [3]The husband should give to his wife her conjugal rights, and likewise the wife to her husband. [4]For the wife does not have authority over her own body, but the husband does; likewise the husband does not have authority over his own body, but the wife does. [5]Do not deprive one another except perhaps by agreement for a set time, to devote yourselves to prayer, and then come together again, so that Satan may not tempt you because of your lack of self-control. [6]This I say by way of concession, not of command. [7]I wish

---

a Or on the man who has done such a thing in the name of the Lord Jesus b Other ancient authorities add Jesus c Gk brother d Gk brothers
e The quotation may extend to the word other f Or sanctuary

that all were as I myself am. But each has a particular gift from God, one having one kind and another a different kind.

8 To the unmarried and the widows I say that it is well for them to remain unmarried as I am. ⁹But if they are not practicing self-control, they should marry. For it is better to marry than to be aflame with passion.

10 To the married I give this command—not I but the Lord—that the wife should not separate from her husband ¹¹(but if she does separate, let her remain unmarried or else be reconciled to her husband), and that the husband should not divorce his wife.

12 To the rest I say—I and not the Lord—that if any believer⁴ has a wife who is an unbeliever, and she consents to live with him, he should not divorce her. ¹³And if any woman has a husband who is an unbeliever, and he consents to live with her, she should not divorce him. ¹⁴For the unbelieving husband is made holy through his wife, and the unbelieving wife is made holy through her husband. Otherwise, your children would be unclean, but as it is, they are holy. ¹⁵But if the unbelieving partner separates, let it be so; in such a case the brother or sister is not bound. It is to peace that God has called you.ᵇ ¹⁶Wife, for all you know, you might save your husband. Husband, for all you know, you might save your wife.

The Life That the Lord Has Assigned

17 However that may be, let each of you lead the life that the Lord has assigned, to which God called you. This is my rule in all the churches. ¹⁸Was anyone at the time of his call already circumcised? Let him not seek to remove the marks of circumcision. Was anyone at the time of his call uncircumcised? Let him not seek circumcision. ¹⁹Circumcision is nothing, and uncircumcision is nothing; but obeying the commandments of God is everything. ²⁰Let each of you remain in the condition in which you were called.

21 Were you a slave when called? Do not be concerned about it. Even if you can gain your freedom, make use of your present condition now more than ever.ᶜ ²²For whoever was called in the Lord as a slave is a freed person belonging to the Lord, just as whoever was free when called is a slave of Christ. ²³You were bought with a price; do not become slaves of human masters. ²⁴In whatever condition you were called, brothers and sisters,ᵈ there remain with God.

The Unmarried and the Widows

25 Now concerning virgins, I have no command of the Lord, but I give my opinion as one who by the Lord's mercy is trustworthy. ²⁶I think that, in view of the impendingᵉ crisis, it is well for you to remain as you are. ²⁷Are you bound to a wife? Do not seek to be free. Are you free from a wife? Do not seek a wife. ²⁸But if you marry, you do not sin, and if a virgin marries, she does not sin. Yet those who marry will experience distress in this life,ᶠ and I would spare you that. ²⁹I mean, brothers and sisters,ᵈ the appointed time has grown short; from now on, let even those who have wives be as though they had none, ³⁰and those who mourn as though they were not mourning, and those who rejoice as though they were not rejoicing, and those who buy as though they had no possessions, ³¹and those who deal with the world as though they had no dealings with it. For the present form of this world is passing away.

32 I want you to be free from anxieties. The unmarried man is anxious about the affairs of the Lord, how to please the Lord; ³³but the married man is anxious about the affairs of the world, how to please his wife, ³⁴and his interests are divided. And the unmarried woman and the virgin are anxious about the affairs of the Lord, so that they may be holy in body and spirit; but the married woman is anxious about the affairs of the world, how to please her husband. ³⁵I say this for your own benefit, not to put any restraint upon you, but to promote good order and unhindered devotion to the Lord.

36 If anyone thinks that he is not behaving properly toward his fiancée,ᵍ if his passions are strong, and so it has to be, let him marry as he wishes; it is no sin. Let them marry. ³⁷But if someone stands firm in his resolve, being under no necessity but having his own desire under control, and has determined in his own mind to keep her as his fiancée,ᵍ he will do well. ³⁸So then, he who marries his fiancéeᵍ does well; and he who refrains from marriage will do better.

39 A wife is bound as long as her husband lives. But if the husband dies,ʰ she is free to marry anyone she wishes, only in the Lord. ⁴⁰But in my judgment she is more blessed if she remains as she is. And I think that I too have the Spirit of God.

8 Food Offered to Idols

Now concerning food sacrificed to idols: we know that "all of us possess knowledge."

---

a Gk brother b Other ancient authorities read us c Or avail yourself of the opportunity d Gk brothers e Or present f Gk in the flesh g Gk virgin h Gk falls asleep

I'M A LESSER BEING.

STILL YOU WASH MY FEET.

AND YOUR BODY'S BROKEN.

BLOOD WAS SPILT FOR ME.

WE WALK TOGETHER.

BY WATERS CALM.

THANK YOU JESUS.

YOU KNOW I'VE DONE WRONG.

Escape—© Tyler Ramsey, 16

Knowledge puffs up, but love builds up. ²Anyone who claims to know something does not yet have the necessary knowledge; ³but anyone who loves God is known by him.

4 Hence, as to the eating of food offered to idols, we know that "no idol in the world really exists," and that "there is no God but one." ⁵Indeed, even though there may be so-called gods in heaven or on earth—as in fact there are many gods and many lords— ⁶yet for us there is one God, the Father, from whom are all things and for whom we exist, and one Lord, Jesus Christ, through whom are all things and through whom we exist.

7 It is not everyone, however, who has this knowledge. Since some have become so accustomed to idols until now, they still think of the food they eat as food offered to an idol; and their conscience, being weak, is defiled. ⁸"Food will not bring us close to God."ᵃ We are no worse off if we do not eat, and no better off if we do. ⁹But take care that this liberty of yours does not somehow become a stumbling block to the weak. ¹⁰For if others see you, who possess knowledge, eating in the temple of an idol, might they not, since their conscience is weak, be encouraged to the point of eating food sacrificed to idols? ¹¹So by your knowledge those weak believers for whom Christ died are destroyed.ᵇ ¹²But when you thus sin against members of your family,ᶜ and wound their conscience when it is weak, you sin against Christ. ¹³Therefore, if food is a cause of their falling,ᵈ I will never eat meat, so that I may not cause one of themᵉ to fall.

9 The Rights of an Apostle

Am I not free? Am I not an apostle? Have I not seen Jesus our Lord? Are you not my work in the Lord? ²If I am not an apostle to others, at least I am to you; for you are the seal of my apostleship in the Lord.

3 This is my defense to those who would examine me. ⁴Do we not have the right to our food and drink? ⁵Do we not have the right to be accompanied by a believing wife,ᶠ as do the other apostles and the brothers of the Lord and Cephas? ⁶Or is it only Barnabas and I who have no right to refrain from working for a living? ⁷Who at any time pays the expenses for doing military service? Who plants a vineyard and does not eat any of its fruit? Or who tends a flock and does not get any of its milk?

8 Do I say this on human authority? Does not the law also say the same? ⁹For it is written in the law of Moses, "You shall not muzzle an ox while it is treading out the grain." Is it for oxen that God is concerned? ¹⁰Or does he not speak entirely for our sake? It was indeed written for our sake, for whoever plows should plow in hope and whoever threshes should thresh in hope of a share in the crop. ¹¹If we have sown spiritual good among you, is it too much if we reap your material benefits? ¹²If others share this rightful claim on you, do not we still more?

Nevertheless, we have not made use of this right, but we endure anything rather than put an obstacle in the way of the gospel of Christ. ¹³Do you not know that those who are employed in the temple service get their food from the temple, and those who serve at the altar share in what is sacrificed on the altar? ¹⁴In the same way, the Lord commanded that those who proclaim the gospel should get their living by the gospel.

15 But I have made no use of any of these rights, nor am I writing this so that they may be applied in my case. Indeed, I would rather die than that—no one will deprive me of my ground for boasting! ¹⁶If I proclaim the gospel, this gives me no ground for boasting, for an obligation is laid on me, and woe to me if I do not proclaim the gospel! ¹⁷For if I do this of my own will, I have a reward; but if not of my own will, I am entrusted with a commission. ¹⁸What then is my reward? Just this: that in my proclamation I may make the gospel free of charge, so as not to make full use of my rights in the gospel.

19 For though I am free with respect to all, I have made myself a slave to all, so that I might win more of them. ²⁰To the Jews I became as a Jew, in order to win Jews. To those under the law I became as one under the law (though I myself am not under the law) so that I might win those under the law. ²¹To those outside the law I became as one outside the law (though I am not free from God's law but am under Christ's law) so that I might win those outside the law. ²²To the weak I became weak, so that I might win the weak. I have become all things to all people, that I might by all means save some. ²³I do it all for the sake of the gospel, so that I may share in its blessings.

24 Do you not know that in a race the runners all compete, but only one receives the prize? Run in such a way that you may win it. ²⁵Athletes exercise self-control in all things; they do it to receive a perishable wreath, but we an imperishable one. ²⁶So I do not run aimlessly, nor do I box as though beating the air;

ᵃ The quotation may extend to the end of the verse ᵇ Gk *the weak brother . . . is destroyed* ᶜ Gk *against the brothers* ᵈ Gk *my brother's falling* ᵉ Gk *cause my brother* ᶠ Gk *a sister as wife*

27but I punish my body and enslave it, so that after proclaiming to others I myself should not be disqualified.

10 Warnings from Israel's History

I do not want you to be unaware, brothers and sisters,*a* that our ancestors were all under the cloud, and all passed through the sea, 2and all were baptized into Moses in the cloud and in the sea, 3and all ate the same spiritual food, 4and all drank the same spiritual drink. For they drank from the spiritual rock that followed them, and the rock was Christ. 5Nevertheless, God was not pleased with most of them, and they were struck down in the wilderness.

6 Now these things occurred as examples for us, so that we might not desire evil as they did. 7Do not become idolaters as some of them did; as it is written, "The people sat down to eat and drink, and they rose up to play." 8We must not indulge in sexual immorality as some of them did, and twenty-three thousand fell in a single day. 9We must not put Christ*b* to the test, as some of them did, and were destroyed by serpents. 10And do not complain as some of them did, and were destroyed by the destroyer. 11These things happened to them to serve as an example, and they were written down to instruct us, on whom the ends of the ages have come. 12So if you think you are standing, watch out that you do not fall. 13No testing has overtaken you that is not common to everyone. God is faithful, and he will not let you be tested beyond your strength, but with the testing he will also provide the way out so that you may be able to endure it.

14 Therefore, my dear friends,*c* flee from the worship of idols. 15I speak as to sensible people; judge for yourselves what I say. 16The cup of blessing that we bless, is it not a sharing in the blood of Christ? The bread that we break, is it not a sharing in the body of Christ? 17Because there is one bread, we who are many are one body, for we all partake of the one bread. 18Consider the people of Israel;*d* are not those who eat the sacrifices partners in the altar? 19What do I imply then? That food sacrificed to idols is anything, or that an idol is anything? 20No, I imply that what pagans sacrifice, they sacrifice to demons and not to God. I do not want you to be partners with demons. 21You cannot drink the cup of the Lord and the cup of demons. You cannot partake of the table of the Lord and the table of demons. 22Or are we provoking the Lord to jealousy? Are we stronger than he?

 TRY THIS

SLOW LEARNERS

Read **1 Corinthians 10.1–11.1**. Pay careful attention to 10.6–13.

If ever there was a time to learn from the example of others—*here it is*. Paul reminds the Corinthians that the Israelites lost their focus and paid for it. They forgot they were on a journey to follow God and instead got busy seeking security and creature comforts.

Big mistake.

Paul's caution applies to us too. We're inclined to make the same mistake. We easily shift our focus off of worshiping and obeying God. Instead, we spend our energy and our efforts on making our camp more comfortable—on meeting our own needs, setting our own goals, satisfying our own desires, looking out for number one.

Still a big mistake.

So how can you get off the "me" track and get back to following and serving God? Here's an idea. Look for a place where you see your parish in single-minded pursuit of God-following—where parishioners are focused on the needs of others. (Hint: It's probably a messy corner of your parish's programming, like a food pantry for the homeless or an outreach program.)

Then ask yourself how you can you join the adventure. Speak with those who are already on the journey and offer to join them.

GOD IS ONE AND ONLY   MY CHURCH

Do All to the Glory of God

23 "All things are lawful," but not all things are beneficial. "All things are lawful," but not all things build up. 24Do not seek your own advantage, but that of the other. 25Eat whatever is sold in the meat market without raising any question on the ground of conscience, 26for "the earth and its fullness are the Lord's." 27If an unbeliever invites you to a meal and you are disposed to go, eat whatever is set before you without raising any question on the ground of conscience. 28But if someone says to you, "This has been offered in sacrifice," then do not eat it, out of consideration for the one who informed you, and for the sake of conscience— 29I mean the other's conscience, not your own. For why should my liberty be subject to the judgment of

a Gk brothers *b* Other ancient authorities read the Lord *c* Gk my beloved *d* Gk Israel according to the flesh

1 CORINTHIANS 10

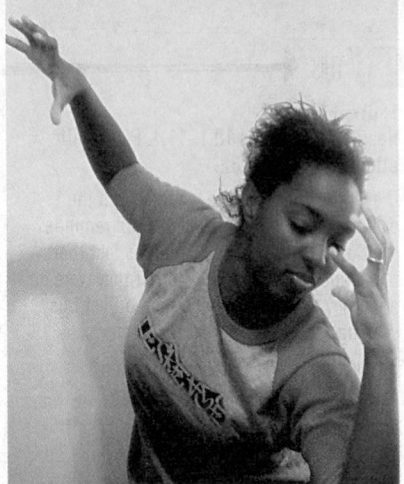

I Can Do All Things—© Jennifer Lawrence, 20

someone else's conscience? ³⁰If I partake with thankfulness, why should I be denounced because of that for which I give thanks?

31 So, whether you eat or drink, or whatever you do, do everything for the glory of God. ³²Give no offense to Jews or to Greeks or to the church of God, ³³just as I try to please everyone in everything I do, not seeking my own advantage, but that of many, so that they may **11** be saved. ¹Be imitators of me, as I am of Christ.

Head Coverings

2 I commend you because you remember me in everything and maintain the traditions just as I handed them on to you. ³But I want you to understand that Christ is the head of every man, and the husband*ᵃ* is the head of his wife,*ᵇ* and God is the head of Christ. ⁴Any man who prays or prophesies with something on his head disgraces his head, ⁵but any woman who prays or prophesies with her head unveiled disgraces her head—it is one and the same thing as having her head shaved. ⁶For if a woman will not veil herself, then she should cut off her hair; but if it is disgraceful for a woman to have her hair cut off or to be shaved, she should wear a veil. ⁷For a man ought not to have his head veiled, since he is the image and reflection*ᶜ* of God; but woman is the reflection*ᶜ* of man. ⁸Indeed, man was not made from woman, but woman from man. ⁹Neither was man created for the sake of woman, but woman for the sake of man. ¹⁰For this reason a woman ought to have a symbol of*ᵈ* authority on her head,*ᵉ* because of the angels. ¹¹Nevertheless, in the Lord

woman is not independent of man or man independent of woman. ¹²For just as woman came from man, so man comes through woman; but all things come from God. ¹³Judge for yourselves: is it proper for a woman to pray to God with her head unveiled? ¹⁴Does not nature itself teach you that if a man wears long hair, it is degrading to him, ¹⁵but if a woman has long hair, it is her glory? For her hair is given to her for a covering. ¹⁶But if anyone is disposed to be contentious—we have no such custom, nor do the churches of God.

Abuses at the Lord's Supper

17 Now in the following instructions I do not commend you, because when you come together it is not for the better but for the worse. ¹⁸For, to begin with, when you come together as a church, I hear that there are divisions among you; and to some extent I believe it. ¹⁹Indeed, there have to be factions among you, for only so will it become clear who among you are genuine. ²⁰When you come together, it is not really to eat the Lord's supper. ²¹For when the time comes to eat, each of you goes ahead with your own supper, and one goes hungry and another becomes drunk. ²²What! Do you not have homes to eat and drink in? Or do you show contempt for the church of God and humiliate those who have nothing? What should I say to you? Should I commend you? In this matter I do not commend you!

The Institution of the Lord's Supper

23 For I received from the Lord what I also handed on to you, that the Lord Jesus on the night when he was betrayed took a loaf of bread, ²⁴and when he had given thanks, he broke it and said, "This is my body that is for*ᶠ* you. Do this in remembrance of me." ²⁵In the same way he took the cup also, after supper, saying, "This cup is the new covenant in my blood. Do this, as often as you drink it, in remembrance of me." ²⁶For as often as you eat this bread and drink the cup, you proclaim the Lord's death until he comes.

Partaking of the Supper Unworthily

27 Whoever, therefore, eats the bread or drinks the cup of the Lord in an unworthy manner will be answerable for the body and blood of the Lord. ²⁸Examine yourselves, and only then eat of the bread and drink of the cup. ²⁹For all who eat and drink*ᵍ* without discerning the body,*ʰ* eat and drink judgment against themselves. ³⁰For this reason many of you are weak

---

a The same Greek word means *man* or *husband* *b* Or *head of the woman* *c* Or *glory* *d* Gk lacks *a symbol of* *e* Or *have freedom of choice regarding her head* *f* Other ancient authorities read *is broken for* *g* Other ancient authorities add *in an unworthy manner,* *h* Other ancient authorities read *the Lord's body* and ill, and some have died.*ª* *³¹*But if we judged ourselves, we would not be judged. *³²*But when we are judged by the Lord, we are disciplined*ᵇ* so that we may not be condemned along with the world.

33 So then, my brothers and sisters,*ᶜ* when you come together to eat, wait for one another. *³⁴*If you are hungry, eat at home, so that when you come together, it will not be for your condemnation. About the other things I will give instructions when I come.

12 Spiritual Gifts

Now concerning spiritual gifts,*ᵈ* brothers and sisters,*ᶜ* I do not want you to be uninformed. *²*You know that when you were pagans, you were enticed and led astray to idols that could not speak. *³*Therefore I want you to understand that no one speaking by the Spirit of God ever says "Let Jesus be cursed!" and no one can say "Jesus is Lord" except by the Holy Spirit.

4 Now there are varieties of gifts, but the same Spirit; *⁵*and there are varieties of services, but the same Lord; *⁶*and there are varieties of activities, but it is the same God who activates all of them in everyone. *⁷*To each is given the manifestation of the Spirit for the common good. *⁸*To one is given through the Spirit the utterance of wisdom, and to another the utterance of knowledge according to the same Spirit, *⁹*to another faith by the same Spirit, to another gifts of healing by the one Spirit, *¹⁰*to another the working of miracles, to another prophecy, to another the discernment of spirits, to another various kinds of tongues, to another the interpretation of tongues. *¹¹*All these are activated by one and the same Spirit, who allots to each one individually just as the Spirit chooses.

One Body with Many Members

12 For just as the body is one and has many members, and all the members of the body, though many, are one body, so it is with Christ. *¹³*For in the one Spirit we were all baptized into one body—Jews or Greeks, slaves or free—and we were all made to drink of one Spirit.

14 Indeed, the body does not consist of one member but of many. *¹⁵*If the foot would say, "Because I am not a hand, I do not belong to the body," that would not make it any less a part of the body. *¹⁶*And if the ear would say, "Because I am not an eye, I do not belong to the body," that would not make it any less a part of the body. *¹⁷*If the whole body were an eye, where would the hearing be? If the whole body

were hearing, where would the sense of smell be? *¹⁸*But as it is, God arranged the members in the body, each one of them, as he chose. *¹⁹*If all were a single member, where would the body be? *²⁰*As it is, there are many members, yet one body. *²¹*The eye cannot say to the hand, "I have no need of you," nor again the head to the feet, "I have no need of you." *²²*On the contrary, the members of the body that seem to be weaker are indispensable, *²³*and those members of the body that we think less honorable we clothe with greater honor, and our less respectable members are treated with greater respect; *²⁴*whereas our more respectable members do not need this. But God has so arranged the body, giving the greater honor to the inferior member, *²⁵*that there may be no dissension within the body, but the members may have the same care for one another. *²⁶*If one member suffers, all suffer together with it; if one member is honored, all rejoice together with it.

27 Now you are the body of Christ and individually members of it. *²⁸*And God has appointed in the church first apostles, second prophets, third teachers; then deeds of power, then gifts of healing, forms of assistance, forms of leadership, various kinds of tongues. *²⁹*Are all apostles? Are all prophets? Are all teachers? Do all work miracles? *³⁰*Do all possess gifts of healing? Do all speak in tongues? Do all interpret? *³¹*But strive for the greater gifts. And I will show you a still more excellent way.

13 The Gift of Love

If I speak in the tongues of mortals and of angels, but do not have love, I am a noisy gong or a clanging cymbal. *²*And if I have prophetic powers, and understand all mysteries and all knowledge, and if I have all faith, so as to remove mountains, but do not have love, I am nothing. *³*If I give away all my possessions, and if I hand over my body so that I may boast,*ᵉ* but do not have love, I gain nothing.

4 Love is patient; love is kind; love is not envious or boastful or arrogant *⁵*or rude. It does not insist on its own way; it is not irritable or resentful; *⁶*it does not rejoice in wrongdoing, but rejoices in the truth. *⁷*It bears all things, believes all things, hopes all things, endures all things.

8 Love never ends. But as for prophecies, they will come to an end; as for tongues, they will cease; as for knowledge, it will come to an end. *⁹*For we know only in part, and we proph-

---

a Gk *fallen asleep* *b* Or *When we are judged, we are being disciplined by the Lord* *c* Gk *brothers* *d* Or *spiritual persons* *e* Other ancient authorities read *body to be burned*

PLAYING THE PART

Think about your favorite band. They're up on stage, the lights are flashing, the crowd is bouncing, your ears are thumping. Good times. Now imagine the drummer. What if the band were playing without him? How would the music sound without his or her creative banging?

Or what about the person controlling the volume on the microphones or the guy in the gray jumpsuit who made sure the arena's air-conditioning was working?

Not everyone gets to be the lead singer. But God has plenty of other creative talents to go around. God wired that drummer to keep rhythm so the band stays on track. God gave the volume guy great ears. And Mr. Jumpsuit has a God-given knack for pipes and wires.

Read **1 Corinthians 12.27.** You have a part to play in Christ's Body. Our creative God gave you something special, something *only you* can do. It might be something creative. It might be something you do behind the scenes that no one ever notices. No matter what it is, it's important. Whether you become a research scientist, a songwriter, or a janitor, you're part of Christ's Body.

Next time you're at school or work, find the janitors. Thank them for all their hard work that often goes unnoticed. Consider how important "behind the scenes" jobs really are. Think about how the place would be without them, then thank them again!

GOD IS CREATIVE MY INTERESTS

esy only in part; ¹⁰but when the complete comes, the partial will come to an end. ¹¹When I was a child, I spoke like a child, I thought like a child, I reasoned like a child; when I became an adult, I put an end to childish ways. ¹²For now we see in a mirror, dimly,ᵃ but then we will see face to face. Now I know only in part; then I will know fully, even as I have been fully known. ¹³And now faith, hope, and love abide, these three; and the greatest of these is love.

14 Gifts of Prophecy and Tongues

Pursue love and strive for the spiritual gifts, and especially that you may prophesy. ²For those who speak in a tongue do not speak to other people but to God; for nobody under-

stands them, since they are speaking mysteries in the Spirit. ³On the other hand, those who prophesy speak to other people for their upbuilding and encouragement and consolation. ⁴Those who speak in a tongue build up themselves, but those who prophesy build up the church. ⁵Now I would like all of you to speak in tongues, but even more to prophesy. One who prophesies is greater than one who speaks in tongues, unless someone interprets, so that the church may be built up.

6 Now, brothers and sisters,ᵇ if I come to you speaking in tongues, how will I benefit you unless I speak to you in some revelation or knowledge or prophecy or teaching? ⁷It is the same way with lifeless instruments that produce sound, such as the flute or the harp. If they do not give distinct notes, how will anyone know what is being played? ⁸And if the bugle gives an indistinct sound, who will get ready for battle? ⁹So with yourselves; if in a tongue you utter speech that is not intelligible, how will anyone know what is being said? For you will be speaking into the air. ¹⁰There are doubtless many different kinds of sounds in the world, and nothing is without sound. ¹¹If then I do not know the meaning of a sound, I will be a foreigner to the speaker and the speaker a foreigner to me. ¹²So with yourselves; since you are eager for spiritual gifts, strive to excel in them for building up the church.

13 Therefore, one who speaks in a tongue should pray for the power to interpret. ¹⁴For if I pray in a tongue, my spirit prays but my mind is unproductive. ¹⁵What should I do then? I will pray with the spirit, but I will pray with the mind also; I will sing praise with the spirit, but I will sing praise with the mind also. ¹⁶Otherwise, if you say a blessing with the spirit, how can anyone in the position of an outsider say the "Amen" to your thanksgiving, since the outsider does not know what you are saying? ¹⁷For you may give thanks well enough, but the other person is not built up. ¹⁸I thank God that I speak in tongues more than all of you; ¹⁹nevertheless, in church I would rather speak five words with my mind, in order to instruct others also, than ten thousand words in a tongue.

20 Brothers and sisters,ᵇ do not be children in your thinking; rather, be infants in evil, but in thinking be adults. ²¹In the law it is written,

"By people of strange tongues
    and by the lips of foreigners
I will speak to this people;
    yet even then they will not listen to me,"
says the Lord. ²²Tongues, then, are a sign not for believers but for unbelievers, while proph-

ᵃ Gk *in a riddle* ᵇ Gk *brothers*

ecy is not for unbelievers but for believers. ²³If, therefore, the whole church comes together and all speak in tongues, and outsiders or unbelievers enter, will they not say that you are out of your mind? ²⁴But if all prophesy, an unbeliever or outsider who enters is reproved by all and called to account by all. ²⁵After the secrets of the unbeliever's heart are disclosed, that person will bow down before God and worship him, declaring, "God is really among you."

Orderly Worship

26 What should be done then, my friends?ᵃ When you come together, each one has a hymn, a lesson, a revelation, a tongue, or an interpretation. Let all things be done for building up. ²⁷If anyone speaks in a tongue, let there be only two or at most three, and each in turn; and let one interpret. ²⁸But if there is no one to interpret, let them be silent in church and speak to themselves and to God. ²⁹Let two or three prophets speak, and let the others weigh what is said. ³⁰If a revelation is made to someone else sitting nearby, let the first person be silent. ³¹For you can all prophesy one by one, so that all may learn and all be encouraged. ³²And the spirits of prophets are subject to the prophets, ³³for God is a God not of disorder but of peace.

(As in all the churches of the saints, ³⁴women should be silent in the churches. For they are not permitted to speak, but should be subordinate, as the law also says. ³⁵If there is anything they desire to know, let them ask their husbands at home. For it is shameful for a woman to speak in church.ᵇ ³⁶Or did the word of God originate with you? Or are you the only ones it has reached?)

37 Anyone who claims to be a prophet, or to have spiritual powers, must acknowledge that what I am writing to you is a command of the Lord. ³⁸Anyone who does not recognize this is not to be recognized. ³⁹So, my friends,ᶜ be eager to prophesy, and do not forbid speaking in tongues; ⁴⁰but all things should be done decently and in order.

15 The Resurrection of Christ

Now I would remind you, brothers and sisters,ᵃ of the good newsᵈ that I proclaimed to you, which you in turn received, in which also you stand, ²through which also you are being saved, if you hold firmly to the message that I proclaimed to you—unless you have come to believe in vain.

3 For I handed on to you as of first impor-

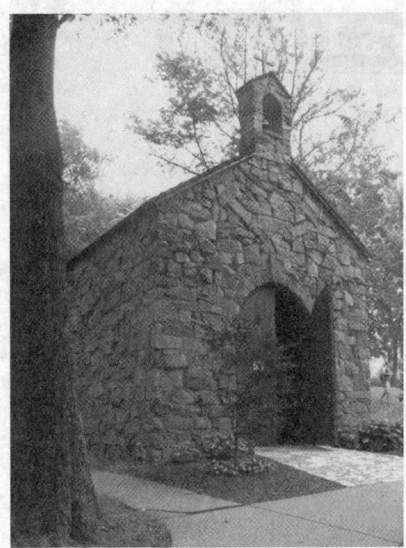

God Is Always Available—© Megan Schoettler, 17

tance what I in turn had received: that Christ died for our sins in accordance with the scriptures, ⁴and that he was buried, and that he was raised on the third day in accordance with the scriptures, ⁵and that he appeared to Cephas, then to the twelve. ⁶Then he appeared to more than five hundred brothers and sistersᵃ at one time, most of whom are still alive, though some have died.ᵉ ⁷Then he appeared to James, then to all the apostles. ⁸Last of all, as to one untimely born, he appeared also to me. ⁹For I am the least of the apostles, unfit to be called an apostle, because I persecuted the church of God. ¹⁰But by the grace of God I am what I am, and his grace toward me has not been in vain. On the contrary, I worked harder than any of them—though it was not I, but the grace of God that is with me. ¹¹Whether then it was I or they, so we proclaim and so you have come to believe.

The Resurrection of the Dead

12 Now if Christ is proclaimed as raised from the dead, how can some of you say there is no resurrection of the dead? ¹³If there is no resurrection of the dead, then Christ has not been raised; ¹⁴and if Christ has not been raised, then our proclamation has been in vain and your faith has been in vain. ¹⁵We are even found to be misrepresenting God, because we testified of God that he raised Christ—whom he did not raise if it is true that the dead are not raised.

ᵃ Gk brothers ᵇ Other ancient authorities put verses 34–35 after verse 40 ᶜ Gk my brothers ᵈ Or gospel ᵉ Gk fallen asleep

MORE TO LIFE

The center of Paul's belief in Jesus was in the fact that Jesus died and rose to new life. Read **1 Corinthians 15.3–8**. In this letter he urges the Corinthians to reexamine their lives in light of that belief. In other words, if they truly believed in the Resurrection, they would be motivated to avoid sinful actions and relationships.

When we believe in the Resurrection, we hold on to the hope that there is more to this life—that we too will rise again. Sin and death do not have power over us.

But it's easy to lose sight of the meaning and power of the Resurrection. Sometimes that belief is a challenge to our human minds. Did Jesus *really* rise from the grave? We believe the empty tomb points to the fact that, yes, the Resurrection really happened. But even more convincing than the empty tomb are the appearances of the Risen Christ to his disciples.

When it all comes down to it, we're really not all that different from the Corinthians—we often need to be reminded of the meaning of the Resurrection as well. And, like Paul, the Church urges us to hold fast to our belief in the Resurrection.

(Want to learn more about it? Read Matthew 28.1–15; Mark 16.1–20; Luke 24.1–49; and John 20.1–23.)

[16] For if the dead are not raised, then Christ has not been raised. [17] If Christ has not been raised, your faith is futile and you are still in your sins. [18] Then those also who have died[a] in Christ have perished. [19] If for this life only we have hoped in Christ, we are of all people most to be pitied.

[20] But in fact Christ has been raised from the dead, the first fruits of those who have died.[a] [21] For since death came through a human being, the resurrection of the dead has also come through a human being; [22] for as all die in Adam, so all will be made alive in Christ. [23] But each in his own order: Christ the first fruits, then at his coming those who belong to

Christ. [24] Then comes the end,[b] when he hands over the kingdom to God the Father, after he has destroyed every ruler and every authority and power. [25] For he must reign until he has put all his enemies under his feet. [26] The last enemy to be destroyed is death. [27] For "God[c] has put all things in subjection under his feet." But when it says, "All things are put in subjection," it is plain that this does not include the one who put all things in subjection under him. [28] When all things are subjected to him, then the Son himself will also be subjected to the one who put all things in subjection under him, so that God may be all in all.

29 Otherwise, what will those people do who receive baptism on behalf of the dead? If the dead are not raised at all, why are people baptized on their behalf?

30 And why are we putting ourselves in danger every hour? [31] I die every day! That is as certain, brothers and sisters,[d] as my boasting of you—a boast that I make in Christ Jesus our Lord. [32] If with merely human hopes I fought with wild animals at Ephesus, what would I have gained by it? If the dead are not raised,

"Let us eat and drink,
    for tomorrow we die."
[33] Do not be deceived:

"Bad company ruins good morals."
[34] Come to a sober and right mind, and sin no more; for some people have no knowledge of God. I say this to your shame.

The Resurrection Body

35 But someone will ask, "How are the dead raised? With what kind of body do they come?" [36] Fool! What you sow does not come to life unless it dies. [37] And as for what you sow, you do not sow the body that is to be, but a bare seed, perhaps of wheat or of some other grain. [38] But God gives it a body as he has chosen, and to each kind of seed its own body. [39] Not all flesh is alike, but there is one flesh for human beings, another for animals, another for birds, and another for fish. [40] There are both heavenly bodies and earthly bodies, but the glory of the heavenly is one thing, and that of the earthly is another. [41] There is one glory of the sun, and another glory of the moon, and another glory of the stars; indeed, star differs from star in glory.

42 So it is with the resurrection of the dead. What is sown is perishable, what is raised is imperishable. [43] It is sown in dishonor, it is raised in glory. It is sown in weakness, it is raised in power. [44] It is sown a physical body, it is raised a spiritual body. If there is a physical body, there is also a spiritual body. [45] Thus it is writ-

a Gk *fallen asleep* *b* Or *Then come the rest* *c* Gk *he* *d* Gk *brothers* ten, "The first man, Adam, became a living being"; the last Adam became a life-giving spirit. ⁴⁶But it is not the spiritual that is first, but the physical, and then the spiritual. ⁴⁷The first man was from the earth, a man of dust; the second man is*ᵃ* from heaven. ⁴⁸As was the man of dust, so are those who are of the dust; and as is the man of heaven, so are those who are of heaven. ⁴⁹Just as we have borne the image of the man of dust, we will*ᵇ* also bear the image of the man of heaven.

50 What I am saying, brothers and sisters,*ᶜ* is this: flesh and blood cannot inherit the kingdom of God, nor does the perishable inherit the imperishable. ⁵¹Listen, I will tell you a mystery! We will not all die,*ᵈ* but we will all be changed, ⁵²in a moment, in the twinkling of an eye, at the last trumpet. For the trumpet will sound, and the dead will be raised imperishable, and we will be changed. ⁵³For this perishable body must put on imperishability, and this mortal body must put on immortality. ⁵⁴When this perishable body puts on imperishability, and this mortal body puts on immortality, then the saying that is written will be fulfilled:
"Death has been swallowed up in victory."
⁵⁵ "Where, O death, is your victory?
  Where, O death, is your sting?"
⁵⁶The sting of death is sin, and the power of sin is the law. ⁵⁷But thanks be to God, who gives us the victory through our Lord Jesus Christ.

58 Therefore, my beloved,*ᵉ* be steadfast, immovable, always excelling in the work of the Lord, because you know that in the Lord your labor is not in vain.

16 The Collection for the Saints

Now concerning the collection for the saints: you should follow the directions I gave to the churches of Galatia. ²On the first day of every week, each of you is to put aside and save whatever extra you earn, so that collections need not be taken when I come. ³And when I arrive, I will send any whom you approve with letters to take your gift to Jerusalem. ⁴If it seems advisable that I should go also, they will accompany me.

Plans for Travel

5 I will visit you after passing through Macedonia—for I intend to pass through Macedonia— ⁶and perhaps I will stay with you or even spend the winter, so that you may send me on my way, wherever I go. ⁷I do not want to see you now just in passing, for I hope to spend some time with you, if the Lord permits. ⁸But I will stay in Ephesus until Pentecost, ⁹for a wide door for effective work has opened to me, and there are many adversaries.

10 If Timothy comes, see that he has nothing to fear among you, for he is doing the work of the Lord just as I am; ¹¹therefore let no one despise him. Send him on his way in peace, so that he may come to me; for I am expecting him with the brothers.

12 Now concerning our brother Apollos, I strongly urged him to visit you with the other brothers, but he was not at all willing*ᶠ* to come now. He will come when he has the opportunity.

Final Messages and Greetings

13 Keep alert, stand firm in your faith, be courageous, be strong. ¹⁴Let all that you do be done in love.

TEXT MESSAGE

Though Paul probably didn't fight wild animals himself (1 Corinthians 15.32), it's likely he's referring to the Roman "sport" of putting prisoners in an arena and then releasing wild animals to maul them while huge crowds watched. Animals used included lions, bears, rhinoceroses, crocodiles, and elephants. A decade after Paul wrote this letter, Christians faced this kind of persecution.

Fact

This information has been scanned and is free of all known viruses. Please forward to all your friends.

15 Now, brothers and sisters,^a you know that members of the household of Stephanas were the first converts in Achaia, and they have devoted themselves to the service of the saints; ¹⁶I urge you to put yourselves at the service of such people, and of everyone who works and toils with them. ¹⁷I rejoice at the coming of Stephanas and Fortunatus and Achaicus, because they have made up for your absence; ¹⁸for they refreshed my spirit as well as yours. So give recognition to such persons.

19 The churches of Asia send greetings. Aquila and Prisca, together with the church in their house, greet you warmly in the Lord. ²⁰All the brothers and sisters^a send greetings. Greet one another with a holy kiss.

21 I, Paul, write this greeting with my own hand. ²²Let anyone be accursed who has no love for the Lord. Our Lord, come!^b ²³The grace of the Lord Jesus be with you. ²⁴My love be with all of you in Christ Jesus.^c

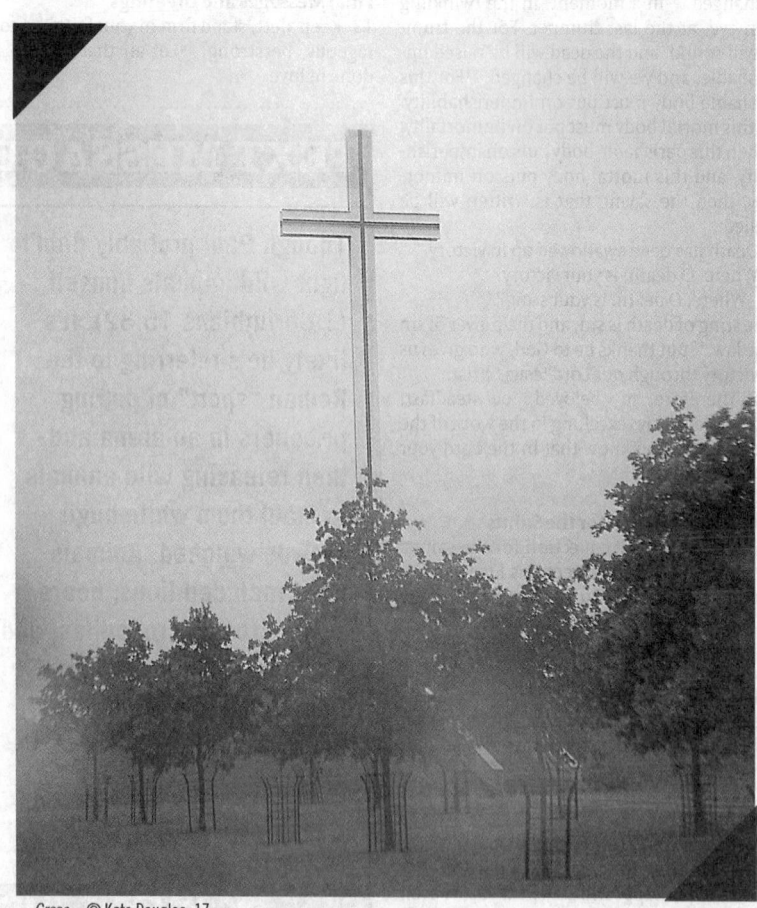

Cross—© Kate Douglas, 17

2 CORINTHIANS

A LETTER TO LAS VEGAS?

Discipleship on the Strip

Glitzy new houses. A stunningly beautiful setting. People from all over the world. All this in a city that had been built the day before yesterday. Corinth at the time that Paul wrote this letter was a lot like the flashy city of Las Vegas: well known, fast growing, and infamous.

Despite the differences between the city's style and his, Paul had a special bond with the Corinthians. But a bunch of newcomers to the Church sought to impress Paul's friends with more "successful" preaching—they challenged Paul's authority. They grabbed people's attention with polished speaking, they performed signs and wonders, and they were even paid for their preaching (something that would certainly have turned heads in style-conscious Corinth).

So often we too are looking for the next new thing. Even if we don't have money to buy the latest electronic gadget, we look for newer and more exciting spiritual experiences. Yet Paul in 2 Corinthians calls us to a more centered understanding of how to follow Jesus. These lounge-act leaders might have turned the heads of the Corinthian Christians at first, but Paul was the real deal. He was the steady friend who quietly went about his craft, whether tent making or disciple making. In the same way, the artificial lights of Vegas might be impressive in the dark night, but they're nothing compared to the daylight of the Creator.

"This is the mission entrusted to the Church, a hard mission: To uproot sins from history; to uproot sins from the political order; to uproot sins from the economy; to uproot sins wherever they are."
—Archbishop Óscar Romero

WHO Paul wrote this letter to the Christians in Corinth.

WHAT In this emotional letter, Paul makes a case for his own authenticity as an Apostle while also defending his ministry.

WHEN Paul wrote this letter sometime between A.D. 55 and 57.

WHERE The recipients of this letter lived in Corinth, a major trading city in ancient Greece. Paul likely wrote this letter from Macedonia, in northern Greece.

PATH OF DISCIPLESHIP

"I'd like an order of faith, please, with an extra serving of God and good feelings on the side. But no Jesus, please. Yes, hold the Jesus."

It's popular in our culture to approach religion as if we were in a restaurant— get the parts you like, but not the parts you don't. And for many people, Jesus' claims and teachings aren't appetizing. He's not the soup du jour.

But in 2 Corinthians, Paul emphasizes over and over again that Jesus isn't optional—Jesus is *indispensable* to true faith. Jesus "is the image of God" (2 Corinthians 4.4). The "glory of God" is seen on Jesus' face (4.6). We can't know God any other way. For the disciple, Jesus is central. It's important to meditate on the Gospels and develop an authentic personal relationship with him.

1 Salutation

Paul, an apostle of Christ Jesus by the will of God, and Timothy our brother,

To the church of God that is in Corinth, including all the saints throughout Achaia:

2 Grace to you and peace from God our Father and the Lord Jesus Christ.

Paul's Thanksgiving after Affliction

3 Blessed be the God and Father of our Lord Jesus Christ, the Father of mercies and the God of all consolation, 4who consoles us in all our affliction, so that we may be able to console those who are in any affliction with the consolation with which we ourselves are consoled by God. 5For just as the sufferings of Christ are abundant for us, so also our consolation is abundant through Christ. 6If we are being afflicted, it is for your consolation and salvation; if we are being consoled, it is for your consolation, which you experience when you patiently endure the same sufferings that we are also suffering. 7Our hope for you is unshaken; for we know that as you share in our sufferings, so also you share in our consolation.

8 We do not want you to be unaware, brothers and sisters,a of the affliction we experienced in Asia; for we were so utterly, unbearably crushed that we despaired of life itself. 9Indeed, we felt that we had received the sentence of death so that we would rely not on ourselves but on God who raises the dead. 10He who rescued us from so deadly a peril will continue to rescue us; on him we have set our hope that he will rescue us again, 11as you also join in helping us by your prayers, so that many will give thanks on ourb behalf for the blessing granted us through the prayers of many.

The Postponement of Paul's Visit

12 Indeed, this is our boast, the testimony of our conscience: we have behaved in the world with franknessc and godly sincerity, not by earthly wisdom but by the grace of God—and all the more toward you. 13For we write you nothing other than what you can read and also understand; I hope you will understand until the end— 14as you have already understood us in part—that on the day of the Lord Jesus we are your boast even as you are our boast.

15 Since I was sure of this, I wanted to come to you first, so that you might have a double favor;d 16I wanted to visit you on my way to Macedonia, and to come back to you from Macedonia and have you send me on to Judea. 17Was I vacillating when I wanted to do this? Do I make my plans according to ordinary human standards,e ready to say "Yes, yes" and "No, no" at the same time? 18As surely as God is faithful, our word to you has not been "Yes and No." 19For the Son of God, Jesus Christ, whom we proclaimed among you, Silvanus and Timothy and I, was not "Yes and No"; but in him it is always "Yes." 20For in him every one of God's promises is a "Yes." For this reason it is through him that we say the "Amen," to the glory of God. 21But it is God who establishes us with you in Christ and has anointed us, 22by putting his seal on us and giving us his Spirit in our hearts as a first installment.

23 But I call on God as witness against me: it was to spare you that I did not come again to Corinth. 24I do not mean to imply that we lord it over your faith; rather, we are workers with you for your joy, because you stand firm in the faith. 1So I made up my mind not to make you another painful visit. 2For if I cause you pain, who is there to make me glad but the one whom I have pained? 3And I wrote as I did, so that when I came, I might not suffer pain from those who should have made me rejoice; for I am confident about all of you, that my joy would be the joy of all of you. 4For I wrote you out of much distress and anguish of heart and with many tears, not to cause you pain, but to let you know the abundant love that I have for you.

Forgiveness for the Offender

5 But if anyone has caused pain, he has caused it not to me, but to some extent—not to exaggerate it—to all of you. 6This punishment by the majority is enough for such a person; 7so now instead you should forgive and console him, so that he may not be overwhelmed by excessive sorrow. 8So I urge you to reaffirm your love for him. 9I wrote for this reason: to test you and to know whether you are obedient in everything. 10Anyone whom you forgive, I also forgive. What I have forgiven, if I have forgiven anything, has been for your sake in the presence of Christ. 11And we do this so that we may not be outwitted by Satan; for we are not ignorant of his designs.

Paul's Anxiety in Troas

12 When I came to Troas to proclaim the good news of Christ, a door was opened for me in the Lord; 13but my mind could not rest because I did not find my brother Titus there. So I said farewell to them and went on to Macedonia.

14 But thanks be to God, who in Christ al-

a Gk brothers b Other ancient authorities read your c Other ancient authorities read holiness d Other ancient authorities read pleasure e Gk according to the flesh ways leads us in triumphal procession, and through us spreads in every place the fragrance that comes from knowing him. ¹⁵For we are the aroma of Christ to God among those who are being saved and among those who are perishing; ¹⁶to the one a fragrance from death to death, to the other a fragrance from life to life. Who is sufficient for these things? ¹⁷For we are not peddlers of God's word like so many;*a* but in Christ we speak as persons of sincerity, as persons sent from God and standing in his presence.

3 Ministers of the New Covenant

Are we beginning to commend ourselves again? Surely we do not need, as some do, letters of recommendation to you or from you, do we? ²You yourselves are our letter, written on our*b* hearts, to be known and read by all; ³and you show that you are a letter of Christ, prepared by us, written not with ink but with the Spirit of the living God, not on tablets of stone but on tablets of human hearts.

4 Such is the confidence that we have through Christ toward God. ⁵Not that we are competent of ourselves to claim anything as coming from us; our competence is from God, ⁶who has made us competent to be ministers of a new covenant, not of letter but of spirit; for the letter kills, but the Spirit gives life.

7 Now if the ministry of death, chiseled in letters on stone tablets,*c* came in glory so that the people of Israel could not gaze at Moses' face because of the glory of his face, a glory now set aside, ⁸how much more will the ministry of the Spirit come in glory? ⁹For if there was glory in the ministry of condemnation, much more does the ministry of justification abound in glory! ¹⁰Indeed, what once had glory has lost its glory because of the greater glory; ¹¹for if what was set aside came through glory, much more has the permanent come in glory!

12 Since, then, we have such a hope, we act with great boldness, ¹³not like Moses, who put a veil over his face to keep the people of Israel from gazing at the end of the glory that*d* was being set aside. ¹⁴But their minds were hardened. Indeed, to this very day, when they hear the reading of the old covenant, that same veil is still there, since only in Christ is it set aside. ¹⁵Indeed, to this very day whenever Moses is read, a veil lies over their minds; ¹⁶but when one turns to the Lord, the veil is removed. ¹⁷Now the Lord is the Spirit, and where the Spirit of the Lord is, there is freedom. ¹⁸And all of us, with unveiled faces, seeing the glory of the Lord as though reflected in a mirror, are be-

ing transformed into the same image from one degree of glory to another; for this comes from the Lord, the Spirit.

4 Treasure in Clay Jars

Therefore, since it is by God's mercy that we are engaged in this ministry, we do not lose heart. ²We have renounced the shameful things that one hides; we refuse to practice cunning or to

a Other ancient authorities read *like the others* b Other ancient authorities read *your* c Gk *on stones* d Gk *of what*

Gritty Faith

A missionary came to our parish. It wasn't your typical presentation with a polished PowerPoint or even a cheesy slide show. He just talked. No background music to get us all choked up. No visual aids to inspire us. He must have spoken for over an hour. His English was poor.

We were all spellbound.

He had spent years in a Chinese prison. Charges were trumped up, but everyone knew he was really there for ministering to a fledgling parish. He lived in miserable conditions. His health deteriorated. He was malnourished, with no food or water for long periods of time. He drank his urine to stay alive.

It's really hard for me to imagine what some missionaries around the world endure. I've never really suffered because I love God. But for many, many Christians in the world today, danger and suffering are a daily reality.

In **2 Corinthians 4.8–10** God promises that he will never abandon his people, no matter what. We can hang on, knowing that he is there with us. Go to **Learner.CalltoDiscipleship.com** for a link to information about people who are unjustly imprisoned for their faith. Spend some time reading the profiles there. These are *real people,* today, suffering for Christ. These are your brothers and sisters. Pick a profile, pray for him or her, then go a step further and write a letter to that person. Put it in an envelope, seal it, stamp it, and mail it.

of God. ⁵For we do not proclaim ourselves; we proclaim Jesus Christ as Lord and ourselves as your slaves for Jesus' sake. ⁶For it is the God who said, "Let light shine out of darkness," who has shone in our hearts to give the light of the knowledge of the glory of God in the face of Jesus Christ.

7 But we have this treasure in clay jars, so that it may be made clear that this extraordinary power belongs to God and does not come from us. ⁸We are afflicted in every way, but not crushed; perplexed, but not driven to despair; ⁹persecuted, but not forsaken; struck down, but not destroyed; ¹⁰always carrying in the body the death of Jesus, so that the life of Jesus may also be made visible in our bodies. ¹¹For while we live, we are always being given up to death for Jesus' sake, so that the life of Jesus may be made visible in our mortal flesh. ¹²So death is at work in us, but life in you.

13 But just as we have the same spirit of faith that is in accordance with scripture—"I believed, and so I spoke"—we also believe, and so we speak, ¹⁴because we know that the one who raised the Lord Jesus will raise us also with Jesus, and will bring us with you into his presence. ¹⁵Yes, everything is for your sake, so that grace, as it extends to more and more people, may increase thanksgiving, to the glory of God.

Living by Faith

16 So we do not lose heart. Even though our outer nature is wasting away, our inner nature is being renewed day by day. ¹⁷For this slight momentary affliction is preparing us for an eternal weight of glory beyond all measure, ¹⁸because we look not at what can be seen but at what cannot be seen; for what can be seen is temporary, but what cannot be seen is eternal.

5 For we know that if the earthly tent we live in is destroyed, we have a building from God, a house not made with hands, eternal in the heavens. ²For in this tent we groan, longing to be clothed with our heavenly dwelling— ³if indeed, when we have taken it off*ᵃ* we will not be found naked. ⁴For while we are still in this tent, we groan under our burden, because we wish not to be unclothed but to be further clothed, so that what is mortal may be swallowed up by life. ⁵He who has prepared us for this very thing is God, who has given us the Spirit as a guarantee.

6 So we are always confident; even though we know that while we are at home in the body we are away from the Lord— ⁷for we walk by faith, not by sight. ⁸Yes, we do have confi-

falsify God's word; but by the open statement of the truth we commend ourselves to the conscience of everyone in the sight of God. ³And even if our gospel is veiled, it is veiled to those who are perishing. ⁴In their case the god of this world has blinded the minds of the unbelievers, to keep them from seeing the light of the gospel of the glory of Christ, who is the image

a Other ancient authorities read *put it on*

dence, and we would rather be away from the body and at home with the Lord. [9]So whether we are at home or away, we make it our aim to please him. [10]For all of us must appear before the judgment seat of Christ, so that each may receive recompense for what has been done in the body, whether good or evil.

The Ministry of Reconciliation

11 Therefore, knowing the fear of the Lord, we try to persuade others; but we ourselves are well known to God, and I hope that we are also well known to your consciences. [12]We are not commending ourselves to you again, but giving you an opportunity to boast about us, so that you may be able to answer those who boast in outward appearance and not in the heart. [13]For if we are beside ourselves, it is for God; if we are in our right mind, it is for you. [14]For the love of Christ urges us on, because we are convinced that one has died for all; therefore all have died. [15]And he died for all, so that those who live might live no longer for themselves, but for him who died and was raised for them.

16 From now on, therefore, we regard no one from a human point of view;[a] even though we once knew Christ from a human point of view,[a] we know him no longer in that way. [17]So if anyone is in Christ, there is a new creation: everything old has passed away; see, everything has become new! [18]All this is from God, who reconciled us to himself through Christ, and has given us the ministry of reconciliation; [19]that is, in Christ God was reconciling the world to himself,[b] not counting their trespasses against them, and entrusting the message of reconciliation to us. [20]So we are ambassadors for Christ, since God is making his appeal through us; we entreat you on behalf of Christ, be reconciled to God. [21]For our sake he made him to be sin who knew no sin, so that in him we might become the righteousness of God.

6 As we work together with him,[c] we urge you also not to accept the grace of God in vain. [2]For he says,

> "At an acceptable time I have listened to you,
> and on a day of salvation I have helped you."

See, now is the acceptable time; see, now is the day of salvation! [3]We are putting no obstacle in anyone's way, so that no fault may be found with our ministry, [4]but as servants of God we have commended ourselves in every way: through great endurance, in afflictions, hardships, calamities, [5]beatings, imprisonments,

REUNITED—AND IT FEELS SO GOOD

Sin hurts our relationships with God, the Church, others, and even ourselves. One of the effects of the Sacrament of Penance is to restore these relationships. It brings us back to an intimate relationship with God.

Read **2 Corinthians 5.11–21**. Then think about the last time you participated in this sacrament. Did you do it with a real, sincere sense of repentance and responsibility for your actions? When celebrated sincerely, the sacrament can give us a sense of peace and serenity about our relationship with God and the Church. There's nothing like the feeling of a clean conscience, is there?

Healing relationships with friends and family can be a little trickier. Reconciliation is a two-way street and sometimes, no matter how sorry and honest we are about our sins, others are not as willing as God and the Church to forgive us.

Even if some are unwilling to forgive and restore their relationship with us, the Sacrament of Penance can still help us heal. What it can restore in us is a firm commitment not to engage in the same behaviors with others and a resolution to make some kind of amends.

riots, labors, sleepless nights, hunger; [6]by purity, knowledge, patience, kindness, holiness of spirit, genuine love, [7]truthful speech, and the power of God; with the weapons of righteousness for the right hand and for the left; [8]in honor and dishonor, in ill repute and good repute. We are treated as impostors, and yet are true; [9]as unknown, and yet are well known; as dying, and see—we are alive; as punished, and yet not killed; [10]as sorrowful, yet always rejoicing; as poor, yet making many rich; as having nothing, and yet possessing everything.

11 We have spoken frankly to you Corinthians; our heart is wide open to you. [12]There is no restriction in our affections, but only in yours. [13]In return—I speak as to children—open wide your hearts also.

a Gk according to the flesh b Or God was in Christ reconciling the world to himself c Gk As we work together

Reflection—© Morgan Katchuk, 14

Who Is She?

Who is this woman?
What is her name?

She is so different than the other ladies these days!
What could it be, that makes her so strong?

How could she be so confident and happy in her life's song?

What is it we don't know? What could it be?
Her smile says it all, but we still can't see!

What they couldn't find, nor understand
Was that this woman knows God has a plan.

She knows God loves her and sent His only Son
To pay the price for all the wrong she has done.

Her smile mirrors the hope inside,
That confidence of salvation is what they see in her eyes.

A woman of God is sometimes hard to find.
But when one comes around, it blows people's minds.

Who Is She?—© Megan Houtchen, 16

The Temple of the Living God

14 Do not be mismatched with unbelievers. For what partnership is there between righteousness and lawlessness? Or what fellowship is there between light and darkness? 15What agreement does Christ have with Beliar? Or what does a believer share with an unbeliever? 16What agreement has the temple of God with idols? For we*a* are the temple of the living God; as God said,

"I will live in them and walk among them,
    and I will be their God,
    and they shall be my people.
17 Therefore come out from them,
    and be separate from them, says the
        Lord,
and touch nothing unclean;
    then I will welcome you,
18 and I will be your father,
    and you shall be my sons and daughters,
    says the Lord Almighty."

7 Since we have these promises, beloved, let us cleanse ourselves from every defilement of body and of spirit, making holiness perfect in the fear of God.

Paul's Joy at the Church's Repentance

2 Make room in your hearts*b* for us; we have wronged no one, we have corrupted no one, we have taken advantage of no one. 3I do not say this to condemn you, for I said before that you are in our hearts, to die together and to live together. 4I often boast about you; I have great pride in you; I am filled with consolation; I am overjoyed in all our affliction.

5 For even when we came into Macedonia, our bodies had no rest, but we were afflicted in every way—disputes without and fears within. 6But God, who consoles the downcast, consoled us by the arrival of Titus, 7and not only by his coming, but also by the consolation with which he was consoled about you, as he told us of your longing, your mourning, your zeal for me, so that I rejoiced still more. 8For even if I made you sorry with my letter, I do not regret it (though I did regret it, for I see that I grieved you with that letter, though only briefly). 9Now I rejoice, not because you were grieved, but because your grief led to repentance; for you felt a godly grief, so that you were not harmed in any way by us. 10For godly grief produces a repentance that leads to salvation and brings no regret, but worldly grief produces death. 11For see what earnestness this godly grief has produced in you, what eagerness to clear yourselves, what indignation, what alarm, what

longing, what zeal, what punishment! At every point you have proved yourselves guiltless in the matter. 12So although I wrote to you, it was not on account of the one who did the wrong, nor on account of the one who was wronged, but in order that your zeal for us might be made known to you before God. 13In this we find comfort.

In addition to our own consolation, we rejoiced still more at the joy of Titus, because his mind has been set at rest by all of you. 14For if I have been somewhat boastful about you to him, I was not disgraced; but just as everything we said to you was true, so our boasting to Titus has proved true as well. 15And his heart goes out all the more to you, as he remembers the obedience of all of you, and how you welcomed him with fear and trembling. 16I rejoice, because I have complete confidence in you.

8 Encouragement to Be Generous

We want you to know, brothers and sisters,*c* about the grace of God that has been granted to the churches of Macedonia; 2for during a severe ordeal of affliction, their abundant joy and their extreme poverty have overflowed in a wealth of generosity on their part. 3For, as I can testify, they voluntarily gave according to their means, and even beyond their means, 4begging us earnestly for the privilege*d* of sharing in this ministry to the saints— 5and this, not merely as we expected; they gave themselves first to the Lord and, by the will of God, to us, 6so that we might urge Titus that, as he had already made a beginning, so he should also complete this generous undertaking*e* among you. 7Now as you excel in everything—in faith, in speech, in knowledge, in utmost eagerness, and in our love for you*f*—so we want you to excel also in this generous undertaking.*e*

8 I do not say this as a command, but I am testing the genuineness of your love against the earnestness of others. 9For you know the generous act*g* of our Lord Jesus Christ, that though he was rich, yet for your sakes he became poor, so that by his poverty you might become rich. 10And in this matter I am giving my advice: it is appropriate for you who began last year not only to do something but even to desire to do something— 11now finish doing it, so that your eagerness may be matched by completing it according to your means. 12For if the eagerness is there, the gift is acceptable according to what one has—not according to what one does not have. 13I do not mean that

a Other ancient authorities read *you* *b* Gk lacks *in your hearts* *c* Gk *brothers* *d* Gk *grace* *e* Gk *this grace* *f* Other ancient authorities read *your love for us* *g* Gk *the grace* there should be relief for others and pressure on you, but it is a question of a fair balance between [14]your present abundance and their need, so that their abundance may be for your need, in order that there may be a fair balance. [15]As it is written,

"The one who had much did not have too
       much,
  and the one who had little did not have
       too little."

Commendation of Titus

16 But thanks be to God who put in the heart of Titus the same eagerness for you that I myself have. [17]For he not only accepted our appeal, but since he is more eager than ever, he is going to you of his own accord. [18]With him we are sending the brother who is famous among all the churches for his proclaiming the good news;[a] [19]and not only that, but he has also been appointed by the churches to travel with us while we are administering this generous undertaking[b] for the glory of the Lord himself[c] and to show our goodwill. [20]We intend that no one should blame us about this generous gift that we are administering, [21]for we intend to do what is right not only in the Lord's sight but also in the sight of others. [22]And with them we are sending our brother whom we have often tested and found eager in many matters, but who is now more eager than ever because of his great confidence in you. [23]As for Titus, he is my partner and co-worker in your service; as for our brothers, they are messengers[d] of the churches, the glory of Christ. [24]Therefore openly before the churches, show them the proof of your love and of our reason for boasting about you.

9 The Collection for Christians at Jerusalem

Now it is not necessary for me to write you about the ministry to the saints, [2]for I know your eagerness, which is the subject of my boasting about you to the people of Macedonia, saying that Achaia has been ready since last year; and your zeal has stirred up most of them. [3]But I am sending the brothers in order that our boasting about you may not prove to have been empty in this case, so that you may be ready, as I said you would be; [4]otherwise, if some Macedonians come with me and find that you are not ready, we would be humiliated—to say nothing of you—in this undertaking.[e] [5]So I thought it necessary to urge the brothers to go on ahead to you, and arrange in advance for this bountiful gift that you have promised, so that it may be ready as a voluntary gift and not as an extortion.

6 The point is this: the one who sows sparingly will also reap sparingly, and the one who sows bountifully will also reap bountifully. [7]Each of you must give as you have made up your mind, not reluctantly or under compulsion, for God loves a cheerful giver. [8]And God is able to provide you with every blessing in abundance, so that by always having enough of everything, you may share abundantly in every good work. [9]As it is written,

"He scatters abroad, he gives to the poor;
  his righteousness[f] endures forever."

[10]He who supplies seed to the sower and bread for food will supply and multiply your seed for sowing and increase the harvest of your righteousness.[f] [11]You will be enriched in every way for your great generosity, which will produce thanksgiving to God through us; [12]for the rendering of this ministry not only supplies the needs of the saints but also overflows with many thanksgivings to God. [13]Through the testing of this ministry you glorify God by your obedience to the confession of the gospel of Christ and by the generosity of your sharing with them and with all others, [14]while they long for you and pray for you because of the surpassing grace of God that he has given you. [15]Thanks be to God for his indescribable gift!

10 Paul Defends His Ministry

I myself, Paul, appeal to you by the meekness and gentleness of Christ—I who am humble when face to face with you, but bold toward you when I am away!— [2]I ask that when I am present I need not show boldness by daring to oppose those who think we are acting according to human standards.[g] [3]Indeed, we live as human beings,[h] but we do not wage war according to human standards;[g] [4]for the weapons of our warfare are not merely human,[i]

"I never liked it when the preachers . . . would make [Jesus] sound angry. But I liked the story the folksinger told. I liked the idea of Jesus becoming man, so that we would be able to trust Him, and I like that He healed people and loved them and cared deeply about how people were feeling."

—Donald Miller, Blue Like Jazz

a Or the gospel b Gk this grace c Other ancient authorities lack himself d Gk apostles e Other ancient authorities add of boasting f Or benevolence g Gk according to the flesh h Gk in the flesh i Gk fleshly but they have divine power to destroy strongholds. We destroy arguments [5]and every proud obstacle raised up against the knowledge of God, and we take every thought captive to obey Christ. [6]We are ready to punish every disobedience when your obedience is complete.

[7] Look at what is before your eyes. If you are confident that you belong to Christ, remind yourself of this, that just as you belong to Christ, so also do we. [8]Now, even if I boast a little too much of our authority, which the Lord gave for building you up and not for tearing you down, I will not be ashamed of it. [9]I do not want to seem as though I am trying to frighten you with my letters. [10]For they say, "His letters are weighty and strong, but his bodily presence is weak, and his speech contemptible." [11]Let such people understand that what we say by letter when absent, we will also do when present.

[12] We do not dare to classify or compare ourselves with some of those who commend themselves. But when they measure themselves by one another, and compare themselves with one another, they do not show good sense. [13]We, however, will not boast beyond limits, but will keep within the field that God has assigned to us, to reach out even as far as you. [14]For we were not overstepping our limits when we reached you; we were the first to come all the way to you with the good news[a] of Christ. [15]We do not boast beyond limits, that is, in the labors of others; but our hope is that, as your faith increases, our sphere of action among you may be greatly enlarged, [16]so that we may proclaim the good news[a] in lands beyond you, without boasting of work already done in someone else's sphere of action. [17]"Let the one who boasts, boast in the Lord." [18]For it is not those who commend themselves that are approved, but those whom the Lord commends.

11 Paul and the False Apostles

I wish you would bear with me in a little foolishness. Do bear with me! [2]I feel a divine jealousy for you, for I promised you in marriage to one husband, to present you as a chaste virgin to Christ. [3]But I am afraid that as the serpent deceived Eve by its cunning, your thoughts will be led astray from a sincere and pure[b] devotion to Christ. [4]For if someone comes and proclaims another Jesus than the one we proclaimed, or if you receive a different spirit from the one you received, or a different gospel from the one you accepted, you submit to it readily enough. [5]I think that I am not in the least inferior to these super-apostles. [6]I may be untrained in speech, but not in knowledge; certainly in every way and in all things we have made this evident to you.

[7] Did I commit a sin by humbling myself so that you might be exalted, because I proclaimed God's good news[c] to you free of charge? [8]I robbed other churches by accepting support from them in order to serve you. [9]And when I was with you and was in need, I did not burden anyone, for my needs were supplied by the friends[d] who came from Macedonia. So I refrained and will continue to refrain from burdening you in any way. [10]As the truth of Christ is in me, this boast of mine will not be silenced in the regions of Achaia. [11]And why? Because I do not love you? God knows I do!

[12] And what I do I will also continue to do, in order to deny an opportunity to those who want an opportunity to be recognized as our equals in what they boast about. [13]For such boasters are false apostles, deceitful workers, disguising themselves as apostles of Christ. [14]And no wonder! Even Satan disguises himself as an angel of light. [15]So it is not strange if his ministers also disguise themselves as ministers of righteousness. Their end will match their deeds.

Paul's Sufferings as an Apostle

[16] I repeat, let no one think that I am a fool; but if you do, then accept me as a fool, so that I too may boast a little. [17]What I am saying in regard to this boastful confidence, I am saying not with the Lord's authority, but as a fool; [18]since many boast according to human standards,[e] I will also boast. [19]For you gladly put up with fools, being wise yourselves! [20]For you put up with it when someone makes slaves of you, or preys upon you, or takes advantage of you, or puts on airs, or gives you a slap in the face. [21]To my shame, I must say, we were too weak for that!

But whatever anyone dares to boast of—I am speaking as a fool—I also dare to boast of that. [22]Are they Hebrews? So am I. Are they Israelites? So am I. Are they descendants of Abraham? So am I. [23]Are they ministers of Christ? I am talking like a madman—I am a better one: with far greater labors, far more imprisonments, with countless floggings, and often near death. [24]Five times I have received from the Jews the forty lashes minus one. [25]Three times I was beaten with rods. Once I received a stoning. Three times I was shipwrecked; for a night and a day I was adrift at sea; [26]on frequent journeys, in danger from rivers, danger from bandits, dan-

---

a Or *the gospel* *b* Other ancient authorities lack *and pure* *c* Gk *the gospel of God* *d* Gk *brothers* *e* Gk *according to the flesh* ger from my own people, danger from Gentiles, danger in the city, danger in the wilderness, danger at sea, danger from false brothers and sisters;[a] 27 in toil and hardship, through many a sleepless night, hungry and thirsty, often without food, cold and naked. 28 And, besides other things, I am under daily pressure because of my anxiety for all the churches. 29 Who is weak, and I am not weak? Who is made to stumble, and I am not indignant?

30 If I must boast, I will boast of the things that show my weakness. 31 The God and Father of the Lord Jesus (blessed be he forever!) knows that I do not lie. 32 In Damascus, the governor[b] under King Aretas guarded the city of Damascus in order to[c] seize me, 33 but I was let down in a basket through a window in the wall,[d] and escaped from his hands.

12 Paul's Visions and Revelations

It is necessary to boast; nothing is to be gained by it, but I will go on to visions and revelations of the Lord. 2 I know a person in Christ who fourteen years ago was caught up to the third heaven—whether in the body or out of the body I do not know; God knows. 3 And I know that such a person—whether in the body or out of the body I do not know; God knows— 4 was caught up into Paradise and heard things that are not to be told, that no mortal is permitted to repeat. 5 On behalf of such a one I will boast, but on my own behalf I will not boast, except of my weaknesses. 6 But if I wish to boast, I will not be a fool, for I will be speaking the truth. But I refrain from it, so that no one may think better of me than what is seen in me or heard from me, 7 even considering the exceptional character of the revelations. Therefore, to keep[e] me from being too elated, a thorn was given me in the flesh, a messenger of Satan to torment me, to keep me from being too elated.[f] 8 Three times I appealed to the Lord about this, that it would leave me, 9 but he said to me, "My grace is sufficient for you, for power[g] is made perfect in weakness." So, I will boast all the more gladly of my weaknesses, so that the power of Christ may dwell in me. 10 Therefore I am content with weaknesses, insults, hardships, persecutions, and calamities for the sake of Christ; for whenever I am weak, then I am strong.

Paul's Concern for the Corinthian Church

11 I have been a fool! You forced me to it. Indeed you should have been the ones commending me, for I am not at all inferior to these super-apostles, even though I am nothing. 12 The signs of a true apostle were performed among you with utmost patience, signs and wonders and mighty works. 13 How have you been worse off than the other churches, except that I myself did not burden you? Forgive me this wrong!

14 Here I am, ready to come to you this third time. And I will not be a burden, because I do not want what is yours but you; for children ought not to lay up for their parents, but parents for their children. 15 I will most gladly spend and be spent for you. If I love you more, am I to be loved less? 16 Let it be assumed that I did not burden you. Nevertheless (you say) since I was crafty, I took you in by deceit. 17 Did I take advantage of you through any of those whom I sent to you? 18 I urged Titus to go, and sent the brother with him. Titus did not take advantage of you, did he? Did we not conduct ourselves with the same spirit? Did we not take the same steps?

19 Have you been thinking all along that we have been defending ourselves before you? We are speaking in Christ before God. Everything we do, beloved, is for the sake of building you up. 20 For I fear that when I come, I may find you not as I wish, and that you may find me not as you wish; I fear that there may perhaps be quarreling, jealousy, anger, selfishness, slander, gossip, conceit, and disorder. 21 I fear that when I come again, my God may humble me before you, and that I may have to mourn over many who previously sinned and have not repented of the impurity, sexual immorality, and licentiousness that they have practiced.

13 Further Warning

This is the third time I am coming to you. "Any charge must be sustained by the evidence of two or three witnesses." 2 I warned those who sinned previously and all the others, and I warn them now while absent, as I did when present on my second visit, that if I come again, I will not be lenient— 3 since you desire proof that Christ is speaking in me. He is not weak in dealing with you, but is powerful in you. 4 For he was crucified in weakness, but lives by the power of God. For we are weak in him,[h] but in dealing with you we will live with him by the power of God.

5 Examine yourselves to see whether you are living in the faith. Test yourselves. Do you not realize that Jesus Christ is in you?—unless, indeed, you fail to meet the test! 6 I hope you will find out that we have not failed. 7 But

a Gk brothers b Gk ethnarch c Other ancient authorities read and wanted to d Gk through the wall e Other ancient authorities read To keep f Other ancient authorities lack to keep me from being too elated g Other ancient authorities read my power h Other ancient authorities read with him

Why is there so much division among Christians, like competition between denominations and fighting within denominations? If we're supposed to be the family of God, why can't we all just get along?

"Quarreling, jealousy, anger, selfishness, slander, gossip, conceit, and disorder"—this is what Paul expected to find when he visited the Corinthian Church community (2 Corinthians 12.20). This depressing description sounds more like a really dysfunctional family than a group of Christian brothers and sisters! It's true that the Church should be a place where people get along, but it isn't always that way. Our selfishness and stubbornness get in the way. And this isn't anything new. Throughout history, the Church has splintered over issues of substance and style, and other Christian denominations have sprung up as a result of some of those conflicts. We've come to define ourselves and our faith in contrast to others instead of as who we are together in Christ.

Feuds and fragmentation don't show up in the refreshing picture of Christian unity we see described in the book of Revelation: "A great multitude that no one could count, from every nation, from all tribes and peoples and languages," all standing together, worshiping God (Revelation 7.9). Church unity like this may seem as impossible to accomplish as world peace, but we have a God who doesn't mind difficult odds. And we can't let ourselves off with the excuse that we're all sinners and conflict is inevitable. Through Paul, God calls us to an amazingly high standard: "making every effort to maintain the unity of the Spirit in the bond of peace" (Ephesians 4.3).

You read about ecumenism—unity between faiths—earlier in this Bible (see "Real Questions" in Nehemiah 10). It's something that's important to our Church. And it's something we need to strive for. Every day.

So instead of pointing the finger at others who cause disunity, like arrogant leaders, gossiping busybodies, or "our faith is better than yours" braggers, you must face this question yourself. Are *you* making every effort to build unity and peace within the Body of Christ? Notice this verse doesn't say "some effort" or "occasional effort"—it says *every effort*. Are you passionately, devotedly seeking to build connections and overcome differences? And are you honestly seeking to change behaviors in your life that reinforce those divisions, like promoting stereotypes of other Christians or making fun of people in your parish or youth group?

Are you willing to step outside of your comfort zone and get to know someone from another parish or denomination, honestly discussing your differences but focusing on your similar faith in Jesus? Do you have the same passion for unity among Christians that Jesus expressed to God the Father, saying, "I ask not only on behalf of these, but also on behalf of those who will believe in me through their word, that they may all be one" (John 17.20–21)?

Find some Creative Space in this Bible and write your thoughts about the things that divide Christians and what can be done to build unity. You might also want to add some real questions of your own. Talk to a trusted Christian friend about your thoughts and questions.

(Want to explore more? Read John 17; Romans 15.5–13; 2 Corinthians 13.11–12; Galatians 3.26–28; and Colossians 3.12–17.)

---

we pray to God that you may not do anything wrong—not that we may appear to have met the test, but that you may do what is right, though we may seem to have failed. [8] For we cannot do anything against the truth, but only for the truth. [9] For we rejoice when we are weak and you are strong. This is what we pray for, that you may become perfect. [10] So I write these things while I am away from you, so that when I come, I may not have to be severe in using the authority that the Lord has given me for building up and not for tearing down.

Final Greetings and Benediction

11 Finally, brothers and sisters,[a] farewell.[b] Put things in order, listen to my appeal,[c] agree with one another, live in peace; and the God of love and peace will be with you. 12 Greet one another with a holy kiss. All the saints greet you.

13 The grace of the Lord Jesus Christ, the love of God, and the communion of[d] the Holy Spirit be with all of you.

a Gk brothers *b* Or rejoice *c* Or encourage one another *d* Or and the sharing in

CREATIVE SPACE

Crossing Over—© Hilary Phillips, 16

GALATIANS

AMAZING GRACE

Freedom Is Free

A lot of people have a hard time believing that something can actually be "free." They suspect that strings are attached. Or they feel that somehow they have to earn it or pay it back.

That's what was happening in the early Church in Galatia. Some leaders were teaching that in order to be true Christians people still had to follow the old Mosaic laws—circumcision, rules about food, keeping the Sabbath, and so on. Some people had a very difficult time accepting that God's grace was truly a free gift.

If you try to get right with God by following all the rules and doing all the right things, you'll never get there. You're a slave to those rules, and they'll never make you free, no matter how good you are.

But friendship with Jesus really *is* free. It isn't about being good or doing certain things the right way. It's all about grace—freedom from having to try to earn God's approval. Jesus already paid the price through his death and Resurrection. When you live your life by following Jesus, no amount of money, time, or possessions can take the place of the freedom you get from faith.

"The Jews are our elder brothers in faith."

—Pope John Paul II

WHO This book is a letter Paul wrote to the Church communities of Galatia.

WHAT Paul found out that Jewish Christians were telling Gentile converts that all new Christians had to obey the Jewish laws and rituals. He wrote this letter to tell them that this was not true.

WHEN Galatians was written between A.D. 49 and 55.

WHERE Galatia was a Roman province in the central part of Asia Minor. Today this area is in Turkey.

PATH OF DISCIPLESHIP

In this letter, Paul gives us the first complete statement of Christian theology—something he says he learned from the Big Guy himself—Jesus. That's right. Jesus spoke to Paul during Paul's powerful conversion experience.

Paul shows us that Christian life is not just a new way of thinking; it's a new way of *living*. Jesus' death and Resurrection totally reshaped and reformed human life.

Loving service and good works flow from a relationship with Christ and through the fruit of the Holy Spirit living in us. The Holy Spirit leads us to act generously and courageously. Ask yourself: In what ways do my daily activities and choices exhibit the fruits of the Spirit?

CHOSEN BEFORE BIRTH

"I have no idea what I am going to do with my life!"

How many times have you made a statement like this? Does God want you to be confused about what you're supposed to be doing for the rest of your life?

In the late 1700s, God called a poor shoemaker from England named William Carey to be a missionary to India. Carey endured extreme poverty, an unsupportive family (his father labeled him crazy), and seven years of preaching without one person coming to faith in Christ. He continued to press on and proceeded to reach hundreds of people in India with the gospel. Today he is called the "Father of Modern Missions." Do you think God can make clear to you what he wants you to do for his Kingdom, just as he did for William Carey? Do you think God has plans for you—plans he's had in mind for you from before you were even born?

Read **Galatians 1.11–24**, focusing especially on verse 15. God *does not* want you to be confused and distraught about the purpose he has for your life. He wants to do the same for you as he did for the Apostle Paul and William Carey. It may be a distinct realization or a moment of clear direction. Or, little by little, God may nudge you this way and that as you make choices about your career path, your dating life, and your friendships. God *will* lead you. You just need to be on the lookout for his leading.

Take the next seven days to explore these seven Scripture passages. As you read each of them, really think about the words and ask God what purpose he had in mind for you since before you were born.

Day 1: Jeremiah 1.4–10.
Day 2: Amos 7.14–15.
Day 3: Isaiah 6.1–8.
Day 4: Exodus 3.1–4.17.
Day 5: Matthew 28.18–20.
Day 6: Jeremiah 29.11–13.
Day 7: Acts 9.1–19.

GOD IS REAL MY INTERESTS

1 Salutation

Paul an apostle—sent neither by human commission nor from human authorities, but through Jesus Christ and God the Father, who raised him from the dead— [2]and all the members of God's family[a] who are with me,

To the churches of Galatia:

3 Grace to you and peace from God our Father and the Lord Jesus Christ, [4]who gave himself for our sins to set us free from the present evil age, according to the will of our God and Father, [5]to whom be the glory forever and ever. Amen.

There Is No Other Gospel

6 I am astonished that you are so quickly deserting the one who called you in the grace of Christ and are turning to a different gospel— [7]not that there is another gospel, but there are some who are confusing you and want to pervert the gospel of Christ. [8]But even if we or an angel[b] from heaven should proclaim to you a gospel contrary to what we proclaimed to you, let that one be accursed! [9]As we have said before, so now I repeat, if anyone proclaims to you a gospel contrary to what you received, let that one be accursed!

10 Am I now seeking human approval, or God's approval? Or am I trying to please people? If I were still pleasing people, I would not be a servant[c] of Christ.

Paul's Vindication of His Apostleship

11 For I want you to know, brothers and sisters,[d] that the gospel that was proclaimed by me is not of human origin; [12]for I did not receive it from a human source, nor was I taught it, but I received it through a revelation of Jesus Christ.

13 You have heard, no doubt, of my earlier life in Judaism. I was violently persecuting the church of God and was trying to destroy it. [14]I advanced in Judaism beyond many among my people of the same age, for I was far more zealous for the traditions of my ancestors. [15]But when God, who had set me apart before I was born and called me through his grace, was pleased [16]to reveal his Son to me,[e] so that I might proclaim him among the Gentiles, I did not confer with any human being, [17]nor did I go up to Jerusalem to those who were already apostles before me, but I went away at once into Arabia, and afterwards I returned to Damascus.

18 Then after three years I did go up to Jerusalem to visit Cephas and stayed with him

a Gk all the brothers *b* Or a messenger *c* Gk slave *d* Gk brothers
e Gk in me

fifteen days; [19]but I did not see any other apostle except James the Lord's brother. [20]In what I am writing to you, before God, I do not lie! [21]Then I went into the regions of Syria and Cilicia, [22]and I was still unknown by sight to the churches of Judea that are in Christ; [23]they only heard it said, "The one who formerly was persecuting us is now proclaiming the faith he once tried to destroy." [24]And they glorified God because of me.

2 Paul and the Other Apostles

Then after fourteen years I went up again to Jerusalem with Barnabas, taking Titus along with me. [2]I went up in response to a revelation. Then I laid before them (though only in a private meeting with the acknowledged leaders) the gospel that I proclaim among the Gentiles, in order to make sure that I was not running, or had not run, in vain. [3]But even Titus, who was with me, was not compelled to be circumcised, though he was a Greek. [4]But because of false believers[a] secretly brought in, who slipped in to spy on the freedom we have in Christ Jesus, so that they might enslave us— [5]we did not submit to them even for a moment, so that the truth of the gospel might always remain with you. [6]And from those who were supposed to be acknowledged leaders (what they actually were makes no difference to me; God shows no partiality)—those leaders contributed nothing to me. [7]On the contrary, when they saw that I had been entrusted with the gospel for the uncircumcised, just as Peter had been entrusted with the gospel for the circumcised [8](for he who worked through Peter making him an apostle to the circumcised also worked through me in sending me to the Gentiles), [9]and when James and Cephas and John, who were acknowledged pillars, recognized the grace that had been given to me, they gave to Barnabas and me the right hand of fellowship, agreeing that we should go to the Gentiles and they to the circumcised. [10]They asked only one thing, that we remember the poor, which was actually what I was[b] eager to do.

Paul Rebukes Peter at Antioch

11 But when Cephas came to Antioch, I opposed him to his face, because he stood self-condemned; [12]for until certain people came from James, he used to eat with the Gentiles. But after they came, he drew back and kept himself separate for fear of the circumcision faction. [13]And the other Jews joined him in this hypocrisy, so that even Barnabas was led astray by their hypocrisy. [14]But when I saw that they were not acting consistently with the truth of the gospel, I said to Cephas before them all, "If you, though a Jew, live like a Gentile and not like a Jew, how can you compel the Gentiles to live like Jews?"[c]

Jews and Gentiles Are Saved by Faith

15 We ourselves are Jews by birth and not Gentile sinners; [16]yet we know that a person is justified[d] not by the works of the law but through faith in Jesus Christ.[e] And we have come to believe in Christ Jesus, so that we might be justified by faith in Christ,[f] and not by doing the works of the law, because no one will be justified by the works of the law. [17]But if, in our effort to be justified in Christ, we ourselves have been found to be sinners, is Christ then a servant of sin? Certainly not! [18]But if I build up again the very things that I once tore down, then I demonstrate that I am a transgressor. [19]For through the law I died to the law, so that I might live to God. I have been crucified with Christ; [20]and it is no longer I who live, but it is Christ who lives in me. And the life I now live in the flesh I live by faith in the Son of God,[g] who loved me and gave himself for me. [21]I do not nullify the grace of God; for if justification[h] comes through the law, then Christ died for nothing.

3 Law or Faith

You foolish Galatians! Who has bewitched you? It was before your eyes that Jesus Christ was publicly exhibited as crucified! [2]The only thing I want to learn from you is this: Did you receive the Spirit by doing the works of the law or by believing what you heard? [3]Are you so foolish? Having started with the Spirit, are you now ending with the flesh? [4]Did you experience so much for nothing?—if it really was for nothing. [5]Well then, does God[i] supply you with the Spirit and work miracles among you by your doing the works of the law, or by your believing what you heard?

6 Just as Abraham "believed God, and it was reckoned to him as righteousness," [7]so, you see, those who believe are the descendants of Abraham. [8]And the scripture, foreseeing that God would justify the Gentiles by faith, declared the gospel beforehand to Abraham, saying, "All the Gentiles shall be blessed in you." [9]For this reason, those who believe are blessed with Abraham who believed.

10 For all who rely on the works of the law are under a curse; for it is written, "Cursed

---

a Gk false brothers b Or had been c Some interpreters hold that the quotation extends into the following paragraph d Or reckoned as righteous; and so elsewhere e Or the faith of Jesus Christ f Or the faith of Christ g Or by the faith of the Son of God h Or righteousness i Gk he

EXPRESS YOURSELF

Space to Breathe

One of the most passionate forms of love in this world is the love of a parent for a child. Go to your local forest or zoo and try snuggling with a bear cub. You'll quickly learn how much his mother loves him! (Just kidding! Don't try it!)

God has this same fierce love for us. Read **Galatians 3.26**. We are God's children, who are called to be part of God's family. Maybe you don't want to associate God with family, because your family has hurt you in some way. God, however, is the perfect Father, who watches over us and wants to spend time with us.

Set up an area that can be just for you and God. It might be in your bedroom or closet—wherever you have personal space. Decorate that small space to honor God and help you reflect on him. Make it a special place you *want* to be to spend time with God. You might want to put a pillow in front of a milk crate or a short table where you can set your Bible. If you have wall space in front of you, hang up an image that reminds you of God—it could be a cross or a photo torn from *National Geographic*. Maybe you want to keep it private, but if you'd like to inspire others, post a photo of your God space on **Learner.CalltoDiscipleship.com**.

The Promise to Abraham

15 Brothers and sisters,[c] I give an example from daily life: once a person's will[d] has been ratified, no one adds to it or annuls it. [16]Now the promises were made to Abraham and to his offspring;[e] it does not say, "And to offsprings,"[f] as of many; but it says, "And to your offspring,"[e] that is, to one person, who is Christ. [17]My point is this: the law, which came four hundred thirty years later, does not annul a covenant previously ratified by God, so as to nullify the promise. [18]For if the inheritance comes from the law, it no longer comes from the promise; but God granted it to Abraham through the promise.

The Purpose of the Law

19 Why then the law? It was added because of transgressions, until the offspring[e] would come to whom the promise had been made; and it was ordained through angels by a mediator. [20]Now a mediator involves more than one party; but God is one.

21 Is the law then opposed to the promises of God? Certainly not! For if a law had been given that could make alive, then righteousness would indeed come through the law. [22]But the scripture has imprisoned all things under the power of sin, so that what was promised through faith in Jesus Christ[g] might be given to those who believe.

23 Now before faith came, we were imprisoned and guarded under the law until faith would be revealed. [24]Therefore the law was our disciplinarian until Christ came, so that we might be justified by faith. [25]But now that faith has come, we are no longer subject to a disciplinarian, [26]for in Christ Jesus you are all children of God through faith. [27]As many of you as were baptized into Christ have clothed yourselves with Christ. [28]There is no longer Jew or Greek, there is no longer slave or free, there is no longer male and female; for all of you are one in Christ Jesus. [29]And if you belong to Christ, then you are Abraham's offspring,[e] heirs according to the promise.

4 My point is this: heirs, as long as they are minors, are no better than slaves, though they are the owners of all the property; [2]but they remain under guardians and trustees until the date set by the father. [3]So with us; while we were minors, we were enslaved to the elemental spirits[h] of the world. [4]But when the fullness of time had come, God sent his Son, born of a woman, born under the law, [5]in order to redeem those who were under the law, so that we

is everyone who does not observe and obey all the things written in the book of the law." [11]Now it is evident that no one is justified before God by the law; for "The one who is righteous will live by faith."[a] [12]But the law does not rest on faith; on the contrary, "Whoever does the works of the law[b] will live by them." [13]Christ redeemed us from the curse of the law by becoming a curse for us—for it is written, "Cursed is everyone who hangs on a tree"— [14]in order that in Christ Jesus the blessing of Abraham might come to the Gentiles, so that we might receive the promise of the Spirit through faith.

a Or *The one who is righteous through faith will live* *b* Gk *does them* *c* Gk *Brothers* *d* Or *covenant* (as in verse 17) *e* Gk *seed* *f* Gk *seeds* *g* Or *through the faith of Jesus Christ* *h* Or *the rudiments* might receive adoption as children. ⁶And because you are children, God has sent the Spirit of his Son into our^a hearts, crying, "Abba!^b Father!" ⁷So you are no longer a slave but a child, and if a child then also an heir, through God.^c

Paul Reproves the Galatians

8 Formerly, when you did not know God, you were enslaved to beings that by nature are not gods. ⁹Now, however, that you have come to know God, or rather to be known by God, how can you turn back again to the weak and beggarly elemental spirits?^d How can you want to be enslaved to them again? ¹⁰You are observing special days, and months, and seasons, and years. ¹¹I am afraid that my work for you may have been wasted.

12 Friends,^e I beg you, become as I am, for I also have become as you are. You have done me no wrong. ¹³You know that it was because of a physical infirmity that I first announced the gospel to you; ¹⁴though my condition put you to the test, you did not scorn or despise me, but welcomed me as an angel of God, as Christ Jesus. ¹⁵What has become of the goodwill you felt? For I testify that, had it been possible, you would have torn out your eyes and given them to me. ¹⁶Have I now become your enemy by telling you the truth? ¹⁷They make much of you, but for no good purpose; they want to exclude you, so that you may make much of them. ¹⁸It is good to be made much of for a good purpose at all times, and not only when I am present with you. ¹⁹My little children, for whom I am again in the pain of childbirth until Christ is formed in you, ²⁰I wish I were present with you now and could change my tone, for I am perplexed about you.

The Allegory of Hagar and Sarah

21 Tell me, you who desire to be subject to the law, will you not listen to the law? ²²For it is written that Abraham had two sons, one by a slave woman and the other by a free woman. ²³One, the child of the slave, was born according to the flesh; the other, the child of the free woman, was born through the promise. ²⁴Now this is an allegory: these women are two covenants. One woman, in fact, is Hagar, from Mount Sinai, bearing children for slavery. ²⁵Now Hagar is Mount Sinai in Arabia^f and corresponds to the present Jerusalem, for she is in slavery with her children. ²⁶But the other woman corresponds to the Jerusalem above; she is free, and she is our mother. ²⁷For it is written,

"Rejoice, you childless one, you who bear
no children,
burst into song and shout, you who
endure no birth pangs;
for the children of the desolate woman are
more numerous
than the children of the one who is
married."

²⁸Now you,^g my friends,^h are children of the promise, like Isaac. ²⁹But just as at that time the child who was born according to the flesh persecuted the child who was born according to the Spirit, so it is now also. ³⁰But what does the scripture say? "Drive out the slave and her child; for the child of the slave will not share the inheritance with the child of the free woman." ³¹So then, friends,^h we are children, not of the slave but of the free woman. ¹For freedom Christ has set us free. Stand firm, therefore, and do not submit again to a yoke of slavery.

The Nature of Christian Freedom

2 Listen! I, Paul, am telling you that if you let yourselves be circumcised, Christ will be of no benefit to you. ³Once again I testify to every man who lets himself be circumcised that he is obliged to obey the entire law. ⁴You who want to be justified by the law have cut yourselves off from Christ; you have fallen away from grace. ⁵For through the Spirit, by faith, we eagerly wait for the hope of righteousness. ⁶For in Christ Jesus neither circumcision nor uncircumcision counts for anything; the only thing that counts is faith workingⁱ through love.

7 You were running well; who prevented you from obeying the truth? ⁸Such persuasion does not come from the one who calls you. ⁹A little yeast leavens the whole batch of dough. ¹⁰I am confident about you in the Lord that you will not think otherwise. But whoever it is that is confusing you will pay the penalty. ¹¹But my friends,^h why am I still being persecuted if I am still preaching circumcision? In that case the offense of the cross has been removed. ¹²I wish those who unsettle you would castrate themselves!

13 For you were called to freedom, brothers and sisters;^h only do not use your freedom as an opportunity for self-indulgence,^j but through love become slaves to one another. ¹⁴For the whole law is summed up in a single commandment, "You shall love your neighbor as yourself." ¹⁵If, however, you bite and devour one another, take care that you are not consumed by one another.

a Other ancient authorities read *your* b Aramaic for *Father* c Other ancient authorities read *an heir of God through Christ* d Or *beggarly rudiments* e Gk *Brothers* f Other ancient authorities read *For Sinai is a mountain in Arabia* g Other ancient authorities read *we* h Gk *brothers* i Or *made effective* j Gk *the flesh*

REALITY

FREE WILL HUNTING

Read **Galatians 5.1**. Freedom gives us the ability to act—or not to act—responsibly. The free will to make choices can be a blessing or a curse, depending on the choices we make.

Think about the choices you make every day:

- to study or to play computer games
- to work out or to veg out
- to reach out to change a wrong or to keep quiet
- to be kind or to make an insulting remark

Consider this. If you choose a positive action, like studying, your good grades will open up more college choices. If you choose to work out instead of vegging out, you'll feel better and be more fit to play different types of sports. The more you choose the good, the freer you become. But the more you choose to go the other direction, like being passive, the more likely you'll lose your freedom entirely.

It's your choice.

We're given the amazing freedom to choose, even to choose evil. God does not force himself upon us. It's up to us to choose to follow Jesus and to believe that the death of Jesus on the cross has freed us from sin. Paul's vision of freedom for believers is founded on the principle that in Baptism, we are rooted in the death of Christ (see Romans 6).

Need help making tough choices? Open yourself to a relationship with Christ and the Holy Spirit for loving guidance.

(Want to learn more? Read these passages about freedom: Sirach 15.4 and Romans 6.17 and 8.21.)

The Works of the Flesh

16 Live by the Spirit, I say, and do not gratify the desires of the flesh. [17]For what the flesh desires is opposed to the Spirit, and what the Spirit desires is opposed to the flesh; for these are opposed to each other, to prevent you from doing what you want. [18]But if you are led by the Spirit, you are not subject to the law. [19]Now the works of the flesh are obvious: fornication, impurity, licentiousness, [20]idolatry, sorcery, enmities, strife, jealousy, anger, quarrels, dissensions, factions, [21]envy,[a] drunkenness, carousing, and things like these. I am warning you, as I warned you before: those who do such things will not inherit the kingdom of God.

The Fruit of the Spirit

22 By contrast, the fruit of the Spirit is love, joy, peace, patience, kindness, generosity, faithfulness, [23]gentleness, and self-control. There is no law against such things. [24]And those who belong to Christ Jesus have crucified the flesh with its passions and desires. [25]If we live by the Spirit, let us also be guided by the Spirit. [26]Let us not become conceited, competing against one another, envying one another.

6 Bear One Another's Burdens

My friends,[b] if anyone is detected in a transgression, you who have received the Spirit should restore such a one in a spirit of gentleness. Take care that you yourselves are not tempted. [2]Bear one another's burdens, and in this way you will fulfill[c] the law of Christ. [3]For if those who are nothing think they are something, they deceive themselves. [4]All must test their own work; then that work, rather than their neighbor's work, will become a cause for pride. [5]For all must carry their own loads.

6 Those who are taught the word must share in all good things with their teacher.

7 Do not be deceived; God is not mocked, for you reap whatever you sow. [8]If you sow to your own flesh, you will reap corruption from the flesh; but if you sow to the Spirit, you will reap eternal life from the Spirit. [9]So let us not grow weary in doing what is right, for we will reap at harvest time, if we do not give up. [10]So then, whenever we have an opportunity, let us work for the good of all, and especially for those of the family of faith.

Final Admonitions and Benediction

11 See what large letters I make when I am writing in my own hand! [12]It is those who want to make a good showing in the flesh that try to

---

a Other ancient authorities add *murder* *b* Gk *Brothers* *c* Other ancient authorities read *in this way fulfill*

THINK FAST

Quick. If you were to describe the essence of who you are in a few words, what would they be?

Okay, try this. Imagine you are being typecast in movies. What roles are you playing?

Need more room? Use the Creative Space below.

Galatians 5.22–26 tells us who God is and what God is like.

A person's spirit is what breathes life, personality, and imagination into an otherwise motionless body, right? We believe God's own Spirit lives inside of us. Imagine that! God's own Spirit in me! When we are Spirit-filled, we are consumed by God's goodness, expressing God's qualities, possessed by God's presence, and capable of doing the works of God every day no matter where we are or who we are with. We are free to always choose the good.

Dig up a picture of your family and tape it on your bathroom mirror. Write one fruit of the Spirit on the picture or below it. Every time you see it, think of a way to show this quality to your family.

GOD IS CREATIVE MY FAMILY

CREATIVE SPACE

compel you to be circumcised—only that they may not be persecuted for the cross of Christ. [13]Even the circumcised do not themselves obey the law, but they want you to be circumcised so that they may boast about your flesh. [14]May I never boast of anything except the cross of our Lord Jesus Christ, by which[a] the world has been crucified to me, and I to the world. [15]For[b] neither circumcision nor uncircumcision is anything; but a new creation is everything! [16]As for those who will follow this rule—peace be upon them, and mercy, and upon the Israel of God.

17 From now on, let no one make trouble for me; for I carry the marks of Jesus branded on my body.

18 May the grace of our Lord Jesus Christ be with your spirit, brothers and sisters.[c] Amen.

a Or through whom b Other ancient authorities add in Christ Jesus
c Gk brothers

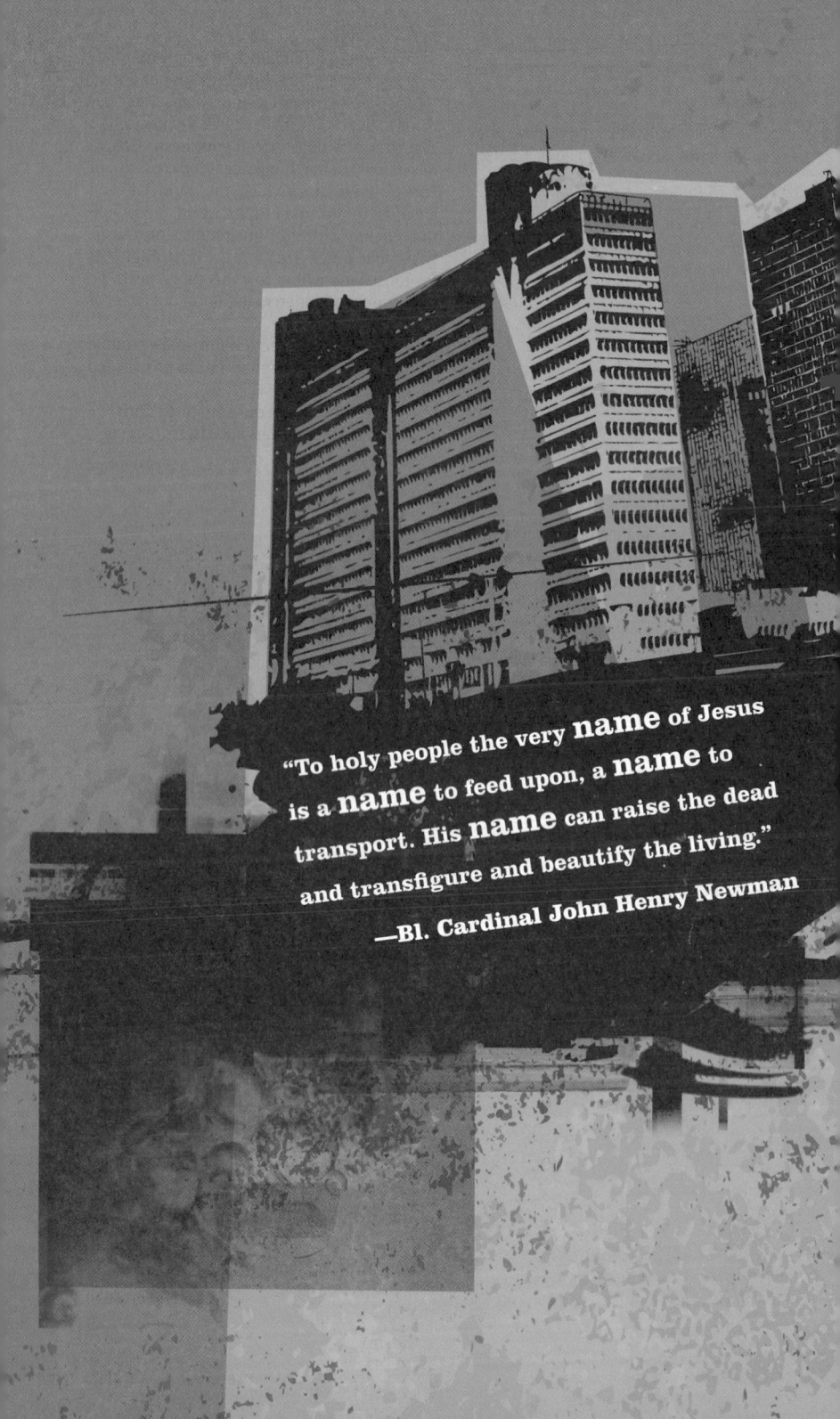

"To holy people the very **name** of Jesus is a **name** to feed upon, a **name** to transport. His **name** can raise the dead and transfigure and beautify the living."

—Bl. Cardinal John Henry Newman

EPHESIANS

THE *MITZVOT* OF GOD

Here . . . Now

I was talking with a friend of mine a few weeks ago when she said this: "You know, the idea of heaven and hell or where I was going to spend eternity didn't really factor in my decision to follow Jesus at all. I figured that the goal of being a follower of Jesus was to live in harmony with the way of God in the here and now. And the future would just take care of itself. I figured following Jesus was the best way to live in the here and now."

People in the days of Jesus would have understood a faith like this. They believed the commandments—the *mitzvot*—of God were given to them in order to have a way of living in harmony with God. By doing these *mitzvot*—often translated "good deeds"—they were in essence living the way of God. Even more, they saw themselves participating with God in his plan for restoring all things to the way they should be.

Paul picks up on this when he states God has "made us, created in Christ Jesus for good works, which God prepared beforehand to be our way of life" (Ephesians 2.10). *Mitzvot* may have been what Paul had in mind when he wrote about the "good things" God has planned for us. For Paul, getting into heaven is not the ultimate goal of our faith. We, as the people of Jesus' day, have been created anew for a reason: to do good deeds. Our faith isn't just about a heavenly future. It's a faith meant to be lived out now—a faith that makes a difference for God in our world.

As a disciple of Christ you have a challenge to *do* something—here . . . now.

> **"Religious ideas have no value at all if they are not practical and positive. Religion is meant for acting more than thinking."**
> —Bl. Frederic Ozanam

WHO Many Scripture scholars believe this letter may have been written by one of Paul's earliest followers who understood him. It represents a development of Paul's later thought.

WHAT This letter emphasizes the importance of unity among Christians. It gives practical advice about how to live out that unity in everyday ways. It also addresses issues like ethnic and cultural differences, family relationships, and spiritual warfare.

WHEN Written around A.D. 60

WHERE This letter was written for the Church community in Ephesus (a city in modern-day Turkey).

PATH OF DISCIPLESHIP

Jesus was eating with his disciples one night when he said: "Very truly, I tell you, the one who believes in me will also do the works that I do and, in fact, will do greater works than these, because I am going to the Father" (John 14.12).

Imagine what may have been going through the disciples' minds. *Us? Doing greater things than you? We've seen you heal the sick, cast out demons, even raise the dead! Are you serious?*

Apparently so.

The Kingdom of God was breaking into the disciples' midst, and its influence was going to expand beyond one person. It was going to be carried to the ends of the earth . . . through them! They were being invited into nothing less than a movement.

And so are we. The invitation was not merely for then; it is for today. Live the way of this new Kingdom, and you'll be involved in something greater than you ever imagined.

1 Salutation

Paul, an apostle of Christ Jesus by the will of God,

To the saints who are in Ephesus and are faithful*a* in Christ Jesus:

2 Grace to you and peace from God our Father and the Lord Jesus Christ.

Spiritual Blessings in Christ

3 Blessed be the God and Father of our Lord Jesus Christ, who has blessed us in Christ with every spiritual blessing in the heavenly places, ⁴just as he chose us in Christ*b* before the foundation of the world to be holy and blameless before him in love. ⁵He destined us for adoption as his children through Jesus Christ, according to the good pleasure of his will, ⁶to the praise of his glorious grace that he freely bestowed on us in the Beloved. ⁷In him we have redemption through his blood, the forgiveness of our trespasses, according to the riches of his grace ⁸that he lavished on us. With all wisdom and insight ⁹he has made known to us the mystery of his will, according to his good pleasure that he set forth in Christ, ¹⁰as a plan for the fullness of time, to gather up all things in him, things in heaven and things on earth. ¹¹In Christ we have also obtained an inheritance,*c* having been destined according to the purpose of him who accomplishes all things according to his counsel and will, ¹²so that we, who were the first to set our hope on Christ, might live for the praise of his glory. ¹³In him you also, when you had heard the word of truth, the gospel of your salvation, and had believed in him, were marked with the seal of the promised Holy Spirit; ¹⁴this*d* is the pledge of our inheritance toward redemption as God's own people, to the praise of his glory.

Paul's Prayer

15 I have heard of your faith in the Lord Jesus and your love*e* toward all the saints, and for this reason ¹⁶I do not cease to give thanks for you as I remember you in my prayers. ¹⁷I pray that the God of our Lord Jesus Christ, the Father of glory, may give you a spirit of wisdom and revelation as you come to know him, ¹⁸so that, with the eyes of your heart enlightened, you may know what is the hope to which he has called you, what are the riches of his glorious inheritance among the saints, ¹⁹and what is the immeasurable greatness of his power for us who believe, according to the working of his great power. ²⁰God*f* put this power to work in Christ when he raised him from the dead and seated him at his right hand in the heavenly places, ²¹far above all rule and authority and power and dominion, and above every name that is named, not only in this age but also in the age to come. ²²And he has put all things under his feet and has made him the head over all things for the church, ²³which is his body, the fullness of him who fills all in all.

2 From Death to Life

You were dead through the trespasses and sins ²in which you once lived, following the course of this world, following the ruler of the power of the air, the spirit that is now at work among those who are disobedient. ³All of us once lived among them in the passions of our flesh, following the desires of flesh and senses, and we were by nature children of wrath, like everyone else. ⁴But God, who is rich in mercy, out of the great love with which he loved us ⁵even when we were dead through our trespasses, made us alive together with Christ*g*— by grace you have been saved— ⁶and raised us up with him and seated us with him in the heavenly places in Christ Jesus, ⁷so that in the ages to come he might show the immeasurable riches of his grace in kindness toward us in Christ Jesus. ⁸For by grace you have been saved through faith, and this is not your own doing; it is the gift of God— ⁹not the result of works, so that no one may boast. ¹⁰For we are what he has made us, created in Christ Jesus for good works, which God prepared beforehand to be our way of life.

One in Christ

11 So then, remember that at one time you Gentiles by birth,*h* called "the uncircumcision" by those who are called "the circumcision"— a physical circumcision made in the flesh by human hands— ¹²remember that you were at that time without Christ, being aliens from the commonwealth of Israel, and strangers to the covenants of promise, having no hope and without God in the world. ¹³But now in Christ Jesus you who once were far off have been brought near by the blood of Christ. ¹⁴For he is our peace; in his flesh he has made both groups into one and has broken down the dividing wall, that is, the hostility between us. ¹⁵He has abolished the law with its commandments and ordinances, that he might create in himself one new humanity in place of the two, thus making peace, ¹⁶and might reconcile both groups to God in one body*i* through the cross,

---

a Other ancient authorities lack *in Ephesus*, reading *saints who are also faithful* *b* Gk *in him* *c* Or *been made a heritage* *d* Other ancient authorities read *who* *e* Other ancient authorities lack *and your love* *f* Gk *He* *g* Other ancient authorities read *in Christ* *h* Gk *in the flesh* *i* Or *reconcile both of us in one body for God* thus putting to death that hostility through it.*a* [17]So he came and proclaimed peace to you who were far off and peace to those who were near; [18]for through him both of us have access in one Spirit to the Father. [19]So then you are no longer strangers and aliens, but you are citizens with the saints and also members of the household of God, [20]built upon the foundation of the apostles and prophets, with Christ Jesus himself as the cornerstone.*b* [21]In him the whole structure is joined together and grows into a holy temple in the Lord; [22]in whom you also are built together spiritually*c* into a dwelling place for God.

3 Paul's Ministry to the Gentiles

This is the reason that I Paul am a prisoner for*d* Christ Jesus for the sake of you Gentiles— [2]for surely you have already heard of the commission of God's grace that was given me for you, [3]and how the mystery was made known to me by revelation, as I wrote above in a few words, [4]a reading of which will enable you to perceive my understanding of the mystery of Christ. [5]In former generations this mystery*e* was not made known to humankind, as it has now been revealed to his holy apostles and prophets by the Spirit: [6]that is, the Gentiles have become fellow heirs, members of the same body, and sharers in the promise in Christ Jesus through the gospel.

[7] Of this gospel I have become a servant according to the gift of God's grace that was given me by the working of his power. [8]Although I am the very least of all the saints, this grace was given to me to bring to the Gentiles the news of the boundless riches of Christ, [9]and to make everyone see*f* what is the plan of the mystery hidden for ages in*g* God who created all things; [10]so that through the church the wisdom of God in its rich variety might now be made known to the rulers and authorities in the heavenly places. [11]This was in accordance with the eternal purpose that he has carried out in Christ Jesus our Lord, [12]in whom we have access to God in boldness and confidence through faith in him.*h* [13]I pray therefore that you*i* may not lose heart over my sufferings for you; they are your glory.

Prayer for the Readers

[14] For this reason I bow my knees before the Father,*j* [15]from whom every family*k* in heaven and on earth takes its name. [16]I pray that, according to the riches of his glory, he may grant that you may be strengthened in your inner

being with power through his Spirit, [17]and that Christ may dwell in your hearts through faith, as you are being rooted and grounded in love. [18]I pray that you may have the power to comprehend, with all the saints, what is the breadth and length and height and depth, [19]and to know the love of Christ that surpasses knowledge, so that you may be filled with all the fullness of God.

[20] Now to him who by the power at work within us is able to accomplish abundantly far more than all we can ask or imagine, [21]to him be glory in the church and in Christ Jesus to all generations, forever and ever. Amen.

4 Unity in the Body of Christ

I therefore, the prisoner in the Lord, beg you to lead a life worthy of the calling to which you

a Or *in him,* or *in himself* *b* Or *keystone* *c* Gk *in the Spirit* *d* Or *of* *e* Gk it *f* Other ancient authorities read *to bring to light* *g* Or *by* *h* Or *the faith of him* *i* Or *I* *j* Other ancient authorities add *of our Lord Jesus Christ* *k* Gk *fatherhood*

"

To be a believer in Christ, we do not need to have reached a certain level of righteousness. God wants us to come to Him just as we are, knowing we could never do enough in our strength to be righteous. The only thing God requires is that we accept Christ as our Lord and Savior. This is awesome, because when I dedicated my life to God, *He* made the changes in me that brought me closer to Him.

Religion article for newspaper—© Randy Reed, 18

"

have been called, ²with all humility and gentleness, with patience, bearing with one another in love, ³making every effort to maintain the unity of the Spirit in the bond of peace. ⁴There is one body and one Spirit, just as you were called to the one hope of your calling, ⁵one Lord, one faith, one baptism, ⁶one God and Father of all, who is above all and through all and in all.

7 But each of us was given grace according to the measure of Christ's gift. ⁸Therefore it is said,

"When he ascended on high he made
    captivity itself a captive;
he gave gifts to his people."

⁹(When it says, "He ascended," what does it mean but that he had also descended*a* into the lower parts of the earth? ¹⁰He who descended is the same one who ascended far above all the heavens, so that he might fill all things.) ¹¹The gifts he gave were that some would be apostles, some prophets, some evangelists, some pastors and teachers, ¹²to equip the saints for the work of ministry, for building up the body of Christ, ¹³until all of us come to the unity of the faith and of the knowledge of the Son of God, to maturity, to the measure of the full stature of Christ. ¹⁴We must no longer be children, tossed to and fro and blown about by every wind of doctrine, by people's trickery, by their craftiness in deceitful scheming. ¹⁵But speaking the truth in love, we must grow up in every way into him who is the head, into Christ, ¹⁶from whom the whole body, joined and knit together by every ligament with which it is equipped, as each part is working properly, promotes the body's growth in building itself up in love.

The Old Life and the New

17 Now this I affirm and insist on in the Lord: you must no longer live as the Gentiles live, in the futility of their minds. ¹⁸They are darkened in their understanding, alienated from the life of God because of their ignorance and hardness of heart. ¹⁹They have lost all sensitivity and have abandoned themselves to licentiousness, greedy to practice every kind of impurity. ²⁰That is not the way you learned Christ! ²¹For surely you have heard about him and were taught in him, as truth is in Jesus. ²²You were taught to put away your former way of life, your old self, corrupt and deluded by its lusts, ²³and to be renewed in the spirit of your minds, ²⁴and to clothe yourselves with the new self, created according to the likeness of God in true righteousness and holiness.

Glowing

"God's not real. Well, *maybe* he's real. I'm not sure if he's part of the earth or something that lives far away. Either way, I can't see God, so why bother trying to figure him out?"

Many of your peers at school or work aren't sure God is real. For some of them, the idea of a God out there may hardly ever cross their mind. Even people in your parish can be a bit detached from the reality of God's existence. They forget to trust in his promises and take his commands seriously.

Read **Ephesians 4.17–24** and **5.8**. If we live in the light, the way it's described in these passages, we are *revealing* the real God to them. God is very real in this world, and we point others to this real God by allowing his light to fill us until it shines out. It shines out in joy, in hope, in acts of kindness, in words of grace. And when you glow with God's light, not only will you be showing others truth, but your thoughts and attitudes will be renewed as well.

Flyers are usually ads. Make a flyer that's not an ad. Make it an image that expresses that God is light or write a few words about who God is. Post the flyers where they'll be visible, like on community bulletin boards at coffee shops and grocery stores or on the outside of your school locker. If you want to do it on the sly, get up early! Scan it or take a photo so you can post it to **Learner.CalltoDiscipleship.com**.

Rules for the New Life

25 So then, putting away falsehood, let all of us speak the truth to our neighbors, for we are members of one another. ²⁶Be angry but do not sin; do not let the sun go down on your anger, ²⁷and do not make room for the devil. ²⁸Thieves must give up stealing; rather let them labor and work honestly with their own hands, so as to have something to share with the needy. ²⁹Let no evil talk come out of your mouths, but only what is useful for building up,*b* as there is need, so that your words may give grace to those who hear. ³⁰And do not

a Other ancient authorities add *first* *b* Other ancient authorities read *building up faith*

LIKE IT OR NOT

Read **Ephesians 6.1–4** and try not to immediately look for loopholes.

Maybe you're a teenager or adult. Is it even *appropriate* to obey parents as you did when you were six? Isn't that codependency?

Or maybe your parents don't seem worthy of obedience. Why follow someone who's heading over a cliff?

Because this isn't really about your parents. It's about you . . . and your relationship with God.

Though God loves you deeply, your heavenly Father also expects obedience. Practicing with earthly parents is a good idea. So good, in fact, that it's not optional.

Clearly, a healthy parent-child relationship doesn't include a 7:00 P.M. weekend curfew for eighteen-year-olds. There's negotiation and communication.

But there's also obedience.

Do this. Think of one specific way you find it challenging to honor your parents. Keeping curfew? Calling home regularly to stay in touch? Write it here:

And now—do it. Don't think about it, make excuses, or delay.

Do it, "so that it may be well with you and you may live long on the earth" (6.3).

GOD IS CHALLENGING MY FAMILY

Renounce Pagan Ways

3 But fornication and impurity of any kind, or greed, must not even be mentioned among you, as is proper among saints. [4]Entirely out of place is obscene, silly, and vulgar talk; but instead, let there be thanksgiving. [5]Be sure of this, that no fornicator or impure person, or one who is greedy (that is, an idolater), has any inheritance in the kingdom of Christ and of God.

6 Let no one deceive you with empty words, for because of these things the wrath of God comes on those who are disobedient. [7]Therefore do not be associated with them. [8]For once you were darkness, but now in the Lord you are light. Live as children of light— [9]for the fruit of the light is found in all that is good and right and true. [10]Try to find out what is pleasing to the Lord. [11]Take no part in the unfruitful works of darkness, but instead expose them. [12]For it is shameful even to mention what such people do secretly; [13]but everything exposed by the light becomes visible, [14]for everything that becomes visible is light. Therefore it says,
"Sleeper, awake!
Rise from the dead,
and Christ will shine on you."

15 Be careful then how you live, not as unwise people but as wise, [16]making the most of the time, because the days are evil. [17]So do not be foolish, but understand what the will of the Lord is. [18]Do not get drunk with wine, for that is debauchery; but be filled with the Spirit, [19]as you sing psalms and hymns and spiritual songs among yourselves, singing and making melody to the Lord in your hearts, [20]giving thanks to God the Father at all times and for everything in the name of our Lord Jesus Christ.

The Christian Household

21 Be subject to one another out of reverence for Christ.

22 Wives, be subject to your husbands as you are to the Lord. [23]For the husband is the head of the wife just as Christ is the head of the church, the body of which he is the Savior. [24]Just as the church is subject to Christ, so also wives ought to be, in everything, to their husbands.

25 Husbands, love your wives, just as Christ loved the church and gave himself up for her, [26]in order to make her holy by cleansing her with the washing of water by the word, [27]so as to present the church to himself in splendor, without a spot or wrinkle or anything of the kind—yes, so that she may be holy and without blemish. [28]In the same way, husbands should love their wives as they do their own bodies.

grieve the Holy Spirit of God, with which you were marked with a seal for the day of redemption. [31]Put away from you all bitterness and wrath and anger and wrangling and slander, together with all malice, [32]and be kind to one another, tenderhearted, forgiving one another, as God in Christ has forgiven you.[a] [1]Therefore be imitators of God, as beloved children, [2]and live in love, as Christ loved us[b] and gave himself up for us, a fragrant offering and sacrifice to God.

5

a Other ancient authorities read *us* *b* Other ancient authorities read *you*

He who loves his wife loves himself. [29]For no one ever hates his own body, but he nourishes and tenderly cares for it, just as Christ does for the church, [30]because we are members of his body.[a] [31]"For this reason a man will leave his father and mother and be joined to his wife, and the two will become one flesh." [32]This is a great mystery, and I am applying it to Christ and the church. [33]Each of you, however, should love his wife as himself, and a wife should respect her husband.

6 Children and Parents

Children, obey your parents in the Lord,[b] for this is right. [2]"Honor your father and mother"—this is the first commandment with a promise: [3]"so that it may be well with you and you may live long on the earth."

4 And, fathers, do not provoke your children to anger, but bring them up in the discipline and instruction of the Lord.

Slaves and Masters

5 Slaves, obey your earthly masters with fear and trembling, in singleness of heart, as you obey Christ; [6]not only while being watched, and in order to please them, but as slaves of Christ, doing the will of God from the heart. [7]Render service with enthusiasm, as to the Lord and not to men and women, [8]knowing that whatever good we do, we will receive the same again from the Lord, whether we are slaves or free.

9 And, masters, do the same to them. Stop threatening them, for you know that both of you have the same Master in heaven, and with him there is no partiality.

The Whole Armor of God

10 Finally, be strong in the Lord and in the strength of his power. [11]Put on the whole ar-mor of God, so that you may be able to stand against the wiles of the devil. [12]For our[c] struggle is not against enemies of blood and flesh, but against the rulers, against the authorities, against the cosmic powers of this present darkness, against the spiritual forces of evil in the heavenly places. [13]Therefore take up the whole armor of God, so that you may be able to withstand on that evil day, and having done everything, to stand firm. [14]Stand therefore, and fasten the belt of truth around your waist, and put on the breastplate of righteousness. [15]As shoes for your feet put on whatever will make you ready to proclaim the gospel of peace. [16]With all of these,[d] take the shield of faith, with which you will be able to quench all the flaming arrows of the evil one. [17]Take the helmet of salvation, and the sword of the Spirit, which is the word of God.

18 Pray in the Spirit at all times in every prayer and supplication. To that end keep alert and always persevere in supplication for all the saints. [19]Pray also for me, so that when I speak, a message may be given to me to make known with boldness the mystery of the gospel,[e] [20]for which I am an ambassador in chains. Pray that I may declare it boldly, as I must speak.

Personal Matters and Benediction

21 So that you also may know how I am and what I am doing, Tychicus will tell you everything. He is a dear brother and a faithful minister in the Lord. [22]I am sending him to you for this very purpose, to let you know how we are, and to encourage your hearts.

23 Peace be to the whole community,[f] and love with faith, from God the Father and the Lord Jesus Christ. [24]Grace be with all who have an undying love for our Lord Jesus Christ.[g]

---

a Other ancient authorities add *of his flesh and of his bones* b Other ancient authorities lack *in the Lord* c Other ancient authorities read *your* d Or *In all circumstances* e Other ancient authorities lack *of the gospel* f Gk *to the brothers* g Other ancient authorities add *Amen*

CREATIVE SPACE

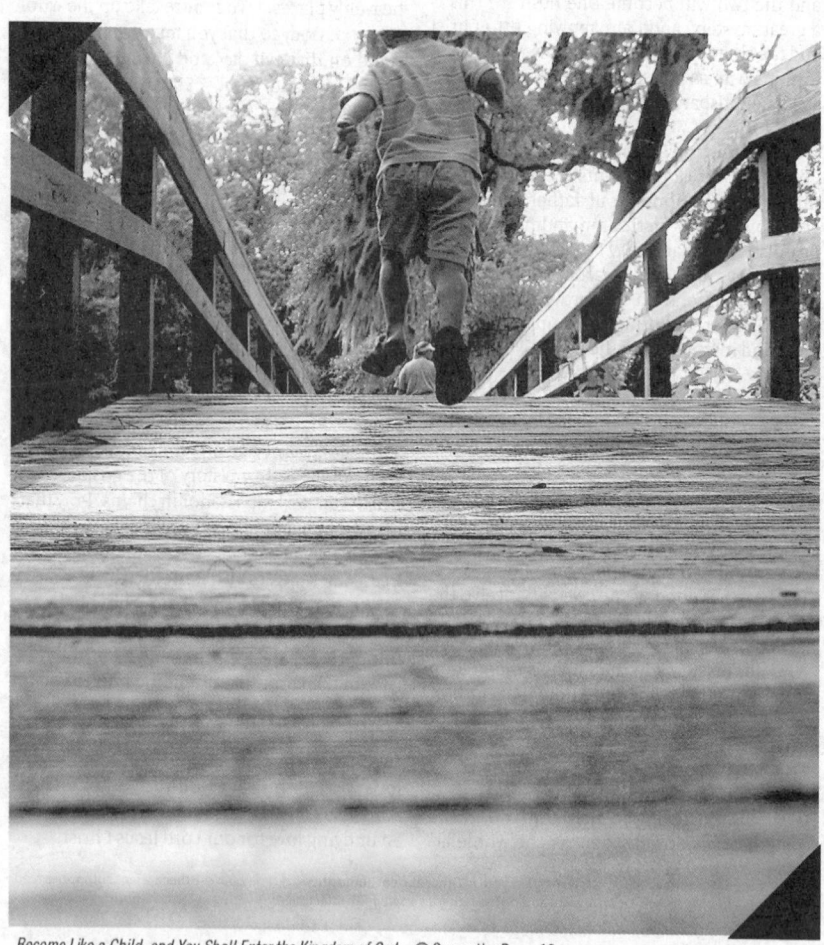

Become Like a Child, and You Shall Enter the Kingdom of God—© Samantha Perry, 18

PHILIPPIANS

JOY IN SUFFERING

Jesus at the Center

How does this work? Here's Paul, in prison, writing a letter to the Church community in Philippi—and over and over again his letter tells them to *rejoice*! There's no hint of frustration, anger, bitterness, or self-pity. Is he ill? Is he in denial? Is he mental?

No, he's just discovered the secret of a full and deep life, and that's to have Jesus at the heart of it. That's why he can say that life is all about Jesus and death will be even better. Paul is genuinely not bothered about his outward circumstances as long as he has his relationship with Jesus and he knows that he's being faithful to what God has called him to. Nor is he content to sit back and be complacent. He wants to keep going, to know Jesus better, to suffer more if necessary, to grab hold of all that God has for him.

I can't honestly say that I'm in the same place. But Paul inspires me to join him in that race, to persevere, to expect great things from God, and to attempt great things for God. Are you up for it?

> *"The whole sanctity and perfection of a person consists in loving Jesus Christ."*
>
> —St. Alphonsus Liguori

WHO Paul wrote this letter (with greetings from Timothy) to the Christians in Philippi.

WHAT Paul encouraged the Christians in Philippi to persevere in their mission of proclaiming the gospel joyfully. There is evidence that Philippians was once three letters before being edited into one.

WHEN Probably around A.D. 55, while Paul was in prison in Ephesus

WHERE Philippi was a city in Macedonia. Today the region is part of Greece.

PATH OF DISCIPLESHIP

Jesus promised lots of amazing things to his followers: the presence of his Spirit within them (John 14.17), the certainty of a future with God (14.2), life in all its fullness (10.10). But he also said that we would face persecution and trouble (Matthew 5.11–12; John 16.33). We don't tend to shout quite so loudly about that teaching, do we?

As disciples, that's the reality of the life he calls us to. And that's why it's a life worth living. Because Jesus is with us through everything that we experience—through suffering, persecution, disappointment, and grief as well as times of joy, victory, excitement, and growth.

1 Salutation

Paul and Timothy, servants[a] of Christ Jesus,

To all the saints in Christ Jesus who are in Philippi, with the bishops[b] and deacons:[c]

2 Grace to you and peace from God our Father and the Lord Jesus Christ.

Paul's Prayer for the Philippians

3 I thank my God every time I remember you, [4]constantly praying with joy in every one of my prayers for all of you, [5]because of your sharing in the gospel from the first day until now. [6]I am confident of this, that the one who began a good work among you will bring it to completion by the day of Jesus Christ. [7]It is right for me to think this way about all of you, because you hold me in your heart,[d] for all of you share in God's grace[e] with me, both in my imprisonment and in the defense and confirmation of the gospel. [8]For God is my witness, how I long for all of you with the compassion of Christ Jesus. [9]And this is my prayer, that your love may overflow more and more with knowledge and full insight [10]to help you to determine what is best, so that in the day of Christ you may be pure and blameless, [11]having produced the harvest of righteousness that comes through Jesus Christ for the glory and praise of God.

Paul's Present Circumstances

12 I want you to know, beloved,[f] that what has happened to me has actually helped to spread the gospel, [13]so that it has become known throughout the whole imperial guard[g] and to everyone else that my imprisonment is for Christ; [14]and most of the brothers and sisters,[f] having been made confident in the Lord by my imprisonment, dare to speak the word[h] with greater boldness and without fear.

15 Some proclaim Christ from envy and rivalry, but others from goodwill. [16]These proclaim Christ out of love, knowing that I have

---

a Gk slaves b Or overseers c Or overseers and helpers d Or because I hold you in my heart e Gk in grace f Gk brothers g Gk whole praetorium
h Other ancient authorities read word of God

PROFILE OF FAITH

ST. MAXIMILIAN KOLBE: Attitude in Action

Do you sometimes need an attitude check? Paul urged the Philippians to have the attitude of Christ—an attitude toward suffering and emptying of self. Read **Philippians 1.27–2.18**. St. Maximilian Kolbe is an example of this attitude in action.

While he was a student in Rome, after being ordained as a Franciscan priest in 1918, he witnessed violent demonstrations against popes St. Pius X and Benedict XV and was inspired to establish the Army of Mary. The mission of this army was to work toward the conversion of sinners and enemies of the Catholic Church.

In 1919 he returned to Poland, where he founded and supervised a monastery near Warsaw as well as a seminary, a radio station, and several other organizations and publications. In the 1930s, he was a missionary to Japan, where he founded yet another monastery before again returning to Poland.

Then came the Nazis. He was imprisoned, released, arrested again, and finally was sent to the notorious concentration camp at Auschwitz. There, on July 31, 1941, as punishment for one prisoner's escape, ten men were chosen to die. St. Maximilian Kolbe offered himself in place of a young husband and father. Like Christ, he was willing to suffer and empty himself for others. He was the last of the ten to die, enduring two weeks of starvation, thirst, and neglect. He was canonized by Pope John Paul II in 1982. His feast day is August 14.

I Ask Why

I pray too much but yet not enough.
I tell you I will then I don't.
You know it all,
But yet you love me.
I use the ultimate copout—"I am only human"—way too much.
I strive for perfection,
But I always fail.
If you heal broken hearts, why does mine still feel broken?
I run from you,
But you wait with open arms to welcome me back every time.
Who am I to judge
When you're the only one who really can?
I love you,
But I can never love you enough.
You don't know how much that hurts me.
Why do I try when I know I'll fail?
Why do I worry
Why do I know you protect?
When I know you protect?
Why is it so hard to do what you want?
Am I just afraid that I'll screw everything up again?
I need to reach people for you.
So why don't I do it more?
You know what I do.
So why do I run and hide?
And why do you still love me?
I want things to happen in my time,
But you're not imprisoned in our time.
You have your own.
My words,
They are pathetic,
My life, it's pathetic.
I'm a sorry human,
Trying to do what you want,
Trying to tell myself the world is just fine,
But still knowing it's not and it needs you.
Trying to be more like you,
When I can't.
Crying just because I can't stand it anymore.
Keeping the joy and love for myself
When that's the meanest thing I can do.
Praying my problems just go away,
And knowing that's not the way it works.
You give but yet you take away.
I'm filled with what seems to be endless doubt.
I'm filled with what seems to be endless doubt.
But I just don't know why.
But I just don't know why.
I'm trying too much to fit in with this world,
I'm just passing by.
But I'm just passing by.
I know what you want,
But I pretend I don't.
I'm a human trying to be perfect,
Trying to be more than I can be,
Trying to tell myself everything's okay.
Drowning in sin,
But yet you love me,
So the only thing I can ask is why?

I Ask Why—© Katie Duckett, 15

DRIVEN

Imagine you're driving a car. The road stretches straight as an arrow for miles and miles. The sky is clear. Everything seems perfect. Even your sunglasses are cool.

Your hands turn the steering wheel just a hair—a barely noticeable hair. Now, if you made no adjustments, where would your car be in another mile? In ten miles? How good is your insurance?

Every choice you make in life is just like that. Every decision at school—even the smallest one—leads you in a certain direction. That's why it takes concentration and dedication to keep heading the right way.

Thankfully, God is passionate about helping you reach your destination. Read **Philippians 3.12–21** to see what happens when you commit your life to faith.

Now go sit in a car and grip the steering wheel. Think about ten "minor" choices you make in a day at school—what you say, what you look at, what you listen to. Are your small decisions taking you in the right direction? Share your thoughts at **Learner.CalltoDiscipleship.com**.

GOD IS PASSIONATE MY SCHOOL

been put here for the defense of the gospel; [17]the others proclaim Christ out of selfish ambition, not sincerely but intending to increase my suffering in my imprisonment. [18]What does it matter? Just this, that Christ is proclaimed in every way, whether out of false motives or true; and in that I rejoice.

Yes, and I will continue to rejoice, [19]for I know that through your prayers and the help of the Spirit of Jesus Christ this will turn out for my deliverance. [20]It is my eager expectation and hope that I will not be put to shame in any way, but that by my speaking with all boldness, Christ will be exalted now as always in my body, whether by life or by death. [21]For to me, living is Christ and dying is gain. [22]If I am to live in the flesh, that means fruitful labor for me; and I do not know which I prefer. [23]I am hard pressed between the two: my desire is to depart and be with Christ, for that is far better; [24]but to remain in the flesh is more necessary for you. [25]Since I am convinced of this, I know that I will remain and continue with all of you for

your progress and joy in faith, [26]so that I may share abundantly in your boasting in Christ Jesus when I come to you again.

27 Only, live your life in a manner worthy of the gospel of Christ, so that, whether I come and see you or am absent and hear about you, I will know that you are standing firm in one spirit, striving side by side with one mind for the faith of the gospel, [28]and are in no way intimidated by your opponents. For them this is evidence of their destruction, but of your salvation. And this is God's doing. [29]For he has graciously granted you the privilege not only of believing in Christ, but of suffering for him as well— [30]since you are having the same struggle that you saw I had and now hear that I still have.

2 Imitating Christ's Humility

If then there is any encouragement in Christ, any consolation from love, any sharing in the Spirit, any compassion and sympathy, [2]make my joy complete: be of the same mind, having the same love, being in full accord and of one mind. [3]Do nothing from selfish ambition or conceit, but in humility regard others as better than yourselves. [4]Let each of you look not to your own interests, but to the interests of others. [5]Let the same mind be in you that was*a* in Christ Jesus,

6 who, though he was in the form of God,
      did not regard equality with God
         as something to be exploited,
7 but emptied himself,
      taking the form of a slave,
      being born in human likeness.
   And being found in human form,
8   he humbled himself
      and became obedient to the point of
         death—
      even death on a cross.
9 Therefore God also highly exalted him
      and gave him the name
      that is above every name,
10 so that at the name of Jesus
      every knee should bend,
      in heaven and on earth and under the
         earth,
11 and every tongue should confess
      that Jesus Christ is Lord,
      to the glory of God the Father.

Shining as Lights in the World

12 Therefore, my beloved, just as you have always obeyed me, not only in my presence, but much more now in my absence, work out your own salvation with fear and trembling; [13]for it

a Or *that you have*

is God who is at work in you, enabling you both to will and to work for his good pleasure.

14 Do all things without murmuring and arguing, [15]so that you may be blameless and innocent, children of God without blemish in the midst of a crooked and perverse generation, in which you shine like stars in the world. [16]It is by your holding fast to the word of life that I can boast on the day of Christ that I did not run in vain or labor in vain. [17]But even if I am being poured out as a libation over the sacrifice and the offering of your faith, I am glad and rejoice with all of you— [18]and in the same way you also must be glad and rejoice with me.

Timothy and Epaphroditus

19 I hope in the Lord Jesus to send Timothy to you soon, so that I may be cheered by news of you. [20]I have no one like him who will be genuinely concerned for your welfare. [21]All of them are seeking their own interests, not those of Jesus Christ. [22]But Timothy's[a] worth you know, how like a son with a father he has served with me in the work of the gospel. [23]I hope therefore to send him as soon as I see how things go with me; [24]and I trust in the Lord that I will also come soon.

25 Still, I think it necessary to send to you Epaphroditus—my brother and co-worker and fellow soldier, your messenger[b] and minister to my need; [26]for he has been longing for[c] all of you, and has been distressed because you heard that he was ill. [27]He was indeed so ill that he nearly died. But God had mercy on him, and not only on him but on me also, so that I would not have one sorrow after another. [28]I am the more eager to send him, therefore, in order that you may rejoice at seeing him again, and that I may be less anxious. [29]Welcome him then in the Lord with all joy, and honor such people, [30]because he came close to death for the work of Christ,[d] risking his life to make up for those services that you could not give me.

3 Finally, my brothers and sisters,[e] rejoice[f] in the Lord.

Breaking with the Past

To write the same things to you is not troublesome to me, and for you it is a safeguard. 2 Beware of the dogs, beware of the evil workers, beware of those who mutilate the flesh![g] [3]For it is we who are the circumcision, who worship in the Spirit of God[h] and boast in Christ Jesus and have no confidence in the flesh— [4]even though I, too, have reason for confidence in the flesh.

If anyone else has reason to be confident in the flesh, I have more: [5]circumcised on the eighth day, a member of the people of Israel, of the tribe of Benjamin, a Hebrew born of Hebrews; as to the law, a Pharisee; [6]as to zeal, a persecutor of the church; as to righteousness under the law, blameless.

7 Yet whatever gains I had, these I have come to regard as loss because of Christ. [8]More than that, I regard everything as loss because of the surpassing value of knowing Christ Jesus

a Gk his b Gk apostle c Other ancient authorities read longing to see d Other ancient authorities read of the Lord e Gk my brothers f Or farewell g Gk the mutilation h Other ancient authorities read worship God in spirit

EXPRESS YOURSELF

Consumption

What separates human beings from the animal kingdom?

Wii. PlayStation. Computer games.

Pocket Tetris changed my life. I took it everywhere. I even knew a guy who had been separated from his friends for months. He ran into them by chance at a restaurant, but opted to stay in the car to finish up a match on his Game Boy.

These little games are powerful and addictive. Most of our hobbies are—sports, instruments, art. Excellence always demands commitment. Commitment demands time and effort.

Sometimes I feel a little guilty that I don't approach my faith life the way I do Pocket Tetris—trying, practicing, improving. **Philippians 4.8–9** encourages us to get passionate about the things God cares about. Purity. Goodness. Spiritual excellence demands commitment, time, and effort.

Find a dictionary and look up the word consumption. It was once used to describe tuberculosis, a vicious lung disease that can claim and overtake an otherwise healthy person. Today we use it to describe something that is completely used up by something else.

Could a person ever be consumed by good things? By God things? In some Creative Space in this Bible, write your own definition for consumption, for what it really means to be consumed by the things of God.

What are you consumed by? Upload your thoughts to **Learner.CalltoDiscipleship.com.**

PHILIPPIANS 3

my Lord. For his sake I have suffered the loss of all things, and I regard them as rubbish, in order that I may gain Christ [9]and be found in him, not having a righteousness of my own that comes from the law, but one that comes through faith in Christ,[a] the righteousness from God based on faith. [10]I want to know Christ[b] and the power of his resurrection and the sharing of his sufferings by becoming like him in his death, [11]if somehow I may attain the resurrection from the dead.

Pressing toward the Goal

12 Not that I have already obtained this or have already reached the goal;[c] but I press on to make it my own, because Christ Jesus has made me his own. [13]Beloved,[d] I do not consider that I have made it my own;[e] but this one thing I do: forgetting what lies behind and straining forward to what lies ahead, [14]I press on toward the goal for the prize of the heavenly[f] call of God in Christ Jesus. [15]Let those of us who are mature be of the same mind; and if you think differently about anything, this too God will reveal to you. [16]Only let us hold fast to what we have attained.

17 Brothers and sisters,[d] join in imitating me, and observe those who live according to the example you have in us. [18]For many live as enemies of the cross of Christ; I have often told you of them, and now I tell you even with tears. [19]Their end is destruction; their god is the belly; and their glory is in their shame; their minds are set on earthly things. [20]But our citizenship[g] is in heaven, and it is from there that we are expecting a Savior, the Lord Jesus Christ. [21]He will transform the body of our humiliation[h] that it may be conformed to the body of his glory,[i] by the power that also enables him to make all things subject to himself. [1]Therefore, my brothers and sisters,[j] whom I love and long for, my joy and crown, stand firm in the Lord in this way, my beloved.

Exhortations

2 I urge Euodia and I urge Syntyche to be of the same mind in the Lord. [3]Yes, and I ask you also, my loyal companion,[k] help these women, for they have struggled beside me in the work of the gospel, together with Clement and the rest of my co-workers, whose names are in the book of life.

4 Rejoice[l] in the Lord always; again I will say, Rejoice.[l] [5]Let your gentleness be known to everyone. The Lord is near. [6]Do not worry about anything, but in everything by prayer and supplication with thanksgiving let your requests be made known to God. [7]And the peace of God, which surpasses all understanding, will guard your hearts and your minds in Christ Jesus.

8 Finally, beloved,[m] whatever is true, whatever is honorable, whatever is just, whatever is pure, whatever is pleasing, whatever is commendable, if there is any excellence and if there is anything worthy of praise, think about[n] these things. [9]Keep on doing the things that you have learned and received and heard and seen in me, and the God of peace will be with you.

Acknowledgment of the Philippians' Gift

10 I rejoice[o] in the Lord greatly that now at last you have revived your concern for me; indeed, you were concerned for me, but had no opportunity to show it.[p] [11]Not that I am referring to being in need; for I have learned to be content with whatever I have. [12]I know what it is to have little, and I know what it is to have plenty. In any and all circumstances I have learned the secret of being well-fed and of going hungry, of having plenty and of being in need. [13]I can do all things through him who strengthens me. [14]In any case, it was kind of you to share my distress.

15 You Philippians indeed know that in the early days of the gospel, when I left Macedonia, no church shared with me in the matter of giving and receiving, except you alone. [16]For even when I was in Thessalonica, you sent me help for my needs more than once. [17]Not that I seek the gift, but I seek the profit that accumulates to your account. [18]I have been paid in full and have more than enough; I am fully satisfied, now that I have received from Epaphroditus the gifts you sent, a fragrant offering, a sacrifice acceptable and pleasing to God. [19]And my God will fully satisfy every need of yours according to his riches in glory in Christ Jesus. [20]To our God and Father be glory forever and ever. Amen.

Final Greetings and Benediction

21 Greet every saint in Christ Jesus. The friends[m] who are with me greet you. [22]All the saints greet you, especially those of the emperor's household.

23 The grace of the Lord Jesus Christ be with your spirit.[q]

COLOSSIANS

THE ONE AND ONLY JESUS

Simply Christ

When the letter came in, the Colossians were all pretty excited. When the Apostle Paul wrote one of the early Church groups a letter, it was a big deal. But often the reason he wrote was because something was screwed up and needed to be fixed.

At first the young believers in Colossae were told they were forgiven by believing in Jesus. But then a group of people visited them and said that believing wasn't enough. They told the Colossians that Christ is just another god and that angels need to be worshiped and different philosophies followed. Needless to say, the Colossians were confused.

It was up to Paul to clear things up. His letter was like a breath of fresh air for these early followers of Christ. He told them that they didn't need to worship rulers or angels or sacrifice to unknown gods. Jesus is enough! Those who told the Colossians that they needed to follow rules and regulations were trashing God's great gift in Jesus.

What about us living in the twenty-first century? What does society tell us we must have or do to make us complete? What additions are tacked on to faith in Jesus? Colossians still speaks to us: Jesus is all we need.

"Truth may be stretched, but it cannot be broken, and always gets above falsehood, as oil does above water."

—Miguel de Cervantes, seventeenth-century Spanish author

WHO Many Scripture scholars are uncertain who wrote Colossians, but it was written in Paul's name.

WHAT This letter was written to combat wrong ideas that were infiltrating the Church community in Colossae. These false teachings twisted the truth about Christ's nature and identity.

WHEN Written between A.D. 63 and 90

WHERE Colossae was a small city in an area that is now part of Turkey.

PATH OF DISCIPLESHIP

Colossians paints a huge picture of Jesus: Jesus is the fullness of God. All of creation was made through him, and Jesus has authority to rule over all— every nation, every ruler, every president. But the beauty of Jesus that really comes out in Colossians is his nearness. Paul says we are *united* to God through Jesus (see Colossians 2.9–10). Through Jesus, God is as close to you as the air you breathe—and even closer! God, the Holy Spirit, lives within you. And God calls you his own. But just like the Colossians were, it's easy to be seduced by false teachers and prophets, ones who tell you that finite and self-centered attitudes and actions will make you happy and successful. If you stay close and in touch with the Holy Spirit within you, you will see through the seductions and see Jesus more clearly.

Is Somebody There?

Is it a sin to say that I don't believe?
Well, it's true...
But if you're God, you already knew.

All my life they said "God is love"
But they didn't know love
Was something I ran away from.

Well now is the time
I'm listening.
Are you there?
Is anybody there?

I have to admit before I go any further
That I have trouble calling anyone "Father."
All my life, they said he
Was love.

So now is the time
I'm listening.
Are you there?
Is anybody there?

Is Somebody There?

Is it a sin to say that I don't believe?
Well, it's true...
But if you're God, you already knew.

All my life they said "God is love"
But they didn't know love
Was something I ran away from.

Well now is the time
I'm listening.
Are you there?
Is anybody there?

Is Somebody There?

Is it a sin to say that I don't believe?
Well, it's
But if you're God, you already
So now is the time
All my life they said "God is
Are you But they didn't know
Is anybody Was something I ran away

Well now is the
I'm list
Are you t
Is anybody t

I have to admit before I go any f
That I have trouble calling anyone "Fo
All my life, they s
Wa

So now is the
I'm list
Are you
Is anybody

1 Salutation

Paul, an apostle of Christ Jesus by the will of God, and Timothy our brother,

2 To the saints and faithful brothers and sisters[a] in Christ in Colossae:

Grace to you and peace from God our Father.

Paul Thanks God for the Colossians

3 In our prayers for you we always thank God, the Father of our Lord Jesus Christ, [4]for we have heard of your faith in Christ Jesus and of the love that you have for all the saints, [5]because of the hope laid up for you in heaven. You have heard of this hope before in the word of the truth, the gospel [6]that has come to you. Just as it is bearing fruit and growing in the whole world, so it has been bearing fruit among yourselves from the day you heard it and truly comprehended the grace of God. [7]This you learned from Epaphras, our beloved fellow servant.[b] He is a faithful minister of Christ on your[c] behalf, [8]and he has made known to us your love in the Spirit.

9 For this reason, since the day we heard it, we have not ceased praying for you and asking that you may be filled with the knowledge of God's[d] will in all spiritual wisdom and understanding, [10]so that you may lead lives worthy of the Lord, fully pleasing to him, as you bear fruit in every good work and as you grow in the knowledge of God. [11]May you be made strong with all the strength that comes from his glorious power, and may you be prepared to endure everything with patience, while joyfully [12]giving thanks to the Father, who has enabled[e] you[f] to share in the inheritance of the saints in the light. [13]He has rescued us from the power of darkness and transferred us into the kingdom of his beloved Son, [14]in whom we have redemption, the forgiveness of sins.[g]

The Supremacy of Christ

15 He is the image of the invisible God, the firstborn of all creation; [16]for in[h] him all things in heaven and on earth were created, things visible and invisible, whether thrones or dominions or rulers or powers—all things have been created through him and for him. [17]He himself is before all things, and in[h] him all things hold together. [18]He is the head of the body, the church; he is the beginning, the firstborn from the dead, so that he might come to have first place in everything. [19]For in him all

the fullness of God was pleased to dwell, [20]and through him God was pleased to reconcile to himself all things, whether on earth or in heaven, by making peace through the blood of his cross.

21 And you who were once estranged and hostile in mind, doing evil deeds, [22]he has now reconciled[i] in his fleshly body[j] through death, so as to present you holy and blameless and irreproachable before him— [23]provided that you continue securely established and steadfast in the faith, without shifting from the hope promised by the gospel that you heard, which has been proclaimed to every creature under heaven. I, Paul, became a servant of this gospel.

Paul's Interest in the Colossians

24 I am now rejoicing in my sufferings for your sake, and in my flesh I am completing what is lacking in Christ's afflictions for the sake of his body, that is, the church. [25]I became its servant according to God's commission that was given to me for you, to make the word of God fully known, [26]the mystery that has been hidden throughout the ages and generations but has now been revealed to his saints. [27]To them God chose to make known how great among the Gentiles are the riches of the glory of this mystery, which is Christ in you, the hope of glory. [28]It is he whom we proclaim, warning everyone and teaching everyone in all wisdom, so that we may present everyone mature in Christ. [29]For this I toil and struggle with all the energy that he powerfully inspires within me.

2

For I want you to know how much I am struggling for you, and for those in Laodicea, and for all who have not seen me face to face. [2]I want their hearts to be encouraged and united in love, so that they may have all the riches of assured understanding and have the knowledge of God's mystery, that is, Christ himself,[k] [3]in whom are hidden all the treasures of wisdom and knowledge. [4]I am saying this so that no one may deceive you with plausible arguments. [5]For though I am absent in body, yet I am with you in spirit, and I rejoice to see your morale and the firmness of your faith in Christ.

> "Most people are bothered by those passages of Scripture they do not understand, but the passages that bother me are those I do understand."
>
> —Mark Twain

---

a Gk brothers b Gk slave c Other ancient authorities read our d Gk his e Other ancient authorities read called f Other ancient authorities read us g Other ancient authorities add through his blood h Or by i Other ancient authorities read you have now been reconciled j Gk in the body of his flesh k Other ancient authorities read of the mystery of God, both of the Father and of Christ

REALITY

DOS AND DON'TS

In this part of Colossians, Paul wrote a set of dos and don'ts for the early Christian community. They were based on the image of the Church as the Body of Christ and the command to love God, neighbor, and self.

Read **Colossians 3.1–4.6** and then write your own set of dos and don'ts that address contemporary life and issues. Base them on the same Church teachings that Paul did. Post your list at **Learner.CalltoDiscipleship.com.**

Fullness of Life in Christ

6 As you therefore have received Christ Jesus the Lord, continue to live your lives*a* in him, [7]rooted and built up in him and established in the faith, just as you were taught, abounding in thanksgiving.

8 See to it that no one takes you captive through philosophy and empty deceit, according to human tradition, according to the elemental spirits of the universe,*b* and not according to Christ. [9]For in him the whole fullness of deity dwells bodily, [10]and you have come to fullness in him, who is the head of every ruler and authority. [11]In him also you were circumcised with a spiritual circumcision,*c* by putting off the body of the flesh in the circumcision of Christ; [12]when you were buried with him in baptism, you were also raised with him through faith in the power of God, who raised him from the dead. [13]And when you were dead in trespasses and the uncircumcision of your flesh, God*d* made you*e* alive together with him, when he forgave us all our trespasses, [14]erasing the record that stood against us with its legal demands. He set this aside, nailing it to the cross. [15]He disarmed*f* the rulers and authorities and made a public example of them, triumphing over them in it.

16 Therefore do not let anyone condemn you in matters of food and drink or of observing festivals, new moons, or sabbaths. [17]These are only a shadow of what is to come, but the substance belongs to Christ. [18]Do not let anyone disqualify you, insisting on self-abasement and worship of angels, dwelling*g* on visions,*h* puffed up without cause by a human way of thinking,*i* [19]and not holding fast to the head, from whom the whole body, nourished and held together by its ligaments and sinews, grows with a growth that is from God.

Warnings against False Teachers

20 If with Christ you died to the elemental spirits of the universe,*b* why do you live as if you still belonged to the world? Why do you submit to regulations, [21]"Do not handle, Do not taste, Do not touch"? [22]All these regulations refer to things that perish with use; they are simply human commands and teachings. [23]These have indeed an appearance of wisdom in promoting self-imposed piety, humility, and severe treatment of the body, but they are of no value in checking self-indulgence.*j*

3 The New Life in Christ

So if you have been raised with Christ, seek the things that are above, where Christ is, seated at the right hand of God. [2]Set your minds on things that are above, not on things that are on earth, [3]for you have died, and your life is hidden with Christ in God. [4]When Christ who is your*k* life is revealed, then you also will be revealed with him in glory.

5 Put to death, therefore, whatever in you is earthly: fornication, impurity, passion, evil desire, and greed (which is idolatry). [6]On account of these the wrath of God is coming on those who are disobedient.*l* [7]These are the ways you also once followed, when you were living that life.*m* [8]But now you must get rid of all such things—anger, wrath, malice, slander, and abusive*n* language from your mouth. [9]Do not lie to one another, seeing that you have stripped off the old self with its practices [10]and have clothed yourselves with the new self, which is being renewed in knowledge according to the image of its creator. [11]In that renewal*o* there is no longer Greek and Jew, circumcised and uncircumcised, barbarian, Scythian, slave and free; but Christ is all and in all!

12 As God's chosen ones, holy and beloved, clothe yourselves with compassion, kindness, humility, meekness, and patience. [13]Bear with one another and, if anyone has a complaint against another, forgive each other; just as the

---

a Gk to walk *b* Or the rudiments of the world *c* Gk a circumcision made without hands *d* Gk he *e* Other ancient authorities read made us; others, made *f* Or divested himself of *g* Other ancient authorities read not dwelling *h* Meaning of Gk uncertain *i* Gk by the mind of his flesh *j* Or are of no value, serving only to indulge the flesh *k* Other authorities read our *l* Other ancient authorities lack on those who are disobedient (Gk the children of disobedience) *m* Or living among such people *n* Or filthy *o* Gk its creator, [11]where

Lord*a* has forgiven you, so you also must forgive. ¹⁴Above all, clothe yourselves with love, which binds everything together in perfect harmony. ¹⁵And let the peace of Christ rule in your hearts, to which indeed you were called in the one body. And be thankful. ¹⁶Let the word of Christ*b* dwell in you richly; teach and admonish one another in all wisdom; and with gratitude in your hearts sing psalms, hymns, and spiritual songs to God.*c* ¹⁷And whatever you do, in word or deed, do everything in the name of the Lord Jesus, giving thanks to God the Father through him.

Rules for Christian Households

18 Wives, be subject to your husbands, as is fitting in the Lord. ¹⁹Husbands, love your wives and never treat them harshly.

20 Children, obey your parents in everything, for this is your acceptable duty in the Lord. ²¹Fathers, do not provoke your children, or they may lose heart. ²²Slaves, obey your earthly masters*d* in everything, not only while being watched and in order to please them, but wholeheartedly, fearing the Lord.*d* ²³Whatever your task, put yourselves into it, as done for the Lord and not for your masters,*e* ²⁴since you know that from the Lord you will receive the inheritance as your reward; you serve*f* the Lord Christ. ²⁵For the wrongdoer will be paid back for whatever wrong has been done, and there is no partiality. 4 ¹Masters, treat your slaves justly and fairly, for you know that you also have a Master in heaven.

Further Instructions

2 Devote yourselves to prayer, keeping alert in it with thanksgiving. ³At the same time pray for us as well that God will open to us a door for the word, that we may declare the mystery of Christ, for which I am in prison, ⁴so that I may reveal it clearly, as I should.

5 Conduct yourselves wisely toward outsiders, making the most of the time.*g* ⁶Let your speech always be gracious, seasoned with salt, so that you may know how you ought to answer everyone.

Final Greetings and Benediction

7 Tychicus will tell you all the news about me; he is a beloved brother, a faithful minister, and a fellow servant*h* in the Lord. ⁸I have sent him to you for this very purpose, so that you may know how we are*i* and that he may encourage

a Other ancient authorities read *just as Christ* *b* Other ancient authorities read *of God,* or *of the Lord* *c* Other ancient authorities read *to the Lord* *d* In Greek the same word is used for *master* and *Lord* *e* Gk *not for men* *f* Or *you are slaves of,* or *be slaves of* *g* Or *opportunity* *h* Gk *slave* *i* Other authorities read *that I may know how you are*

What's on Your Inside?

Earrings. Tattoos. Jerseys. Letter jackets. Band T-shirts. Ripped jeans. Low-rider jeans. Skinny jeans. Sunglasses. Ball caps. Highlights. Sideburns.

We tend to present ourselves to the world in a way that expresses who we are on the inside. Some try very hard to identify with a certain subculture or group, while others see clothing and accessories only as a functional part of life.

Even though God cares more about the inside, he does care about our clothes on the outside. He has pursued us, and now it's time for us to clothe ourselves *spiritually* and pursue him in return. The spiritual clothes listed in **Colossians 3.1–17** are important, and so are other "accessories," like our interests, hobbies, dreams, and passions.

Think through all the spiritual accessories you present in your life. How can you show your faith—your passionate love for God—in what you do?

Here's a challenge. Write a few haiku poems expressing your thoughts on this question. There are lots of ways to go about writing haiku, but here's the easiest. Simply write three short lines, with five syllables in the first line, seven in the next line, and five again in the last line. Your haiku can be serious, simple, or just plain funny. (Go to **Learner.CalltoDiscipleship.com** for a link to a haiku how-to site.) Once you've jotted out a few poems, write your favorite haiku in the Creative Space below.

CREATIVE SPACE

your hearts; ⁹he is coming with Onesimus, the faithful and beloved brother, who is one of you. They will tell you about everything here.

10 Aristarchus my fellow prisoner greets you, as does Mark the cousin of Barnabas, concerning whom you have received instructions—if he comes to you, welcome him. ¹¹And Jesus who is called Justus greets you. These are the only ones of the circumcision among my co-workers for the kingdom of God, and they have been a comfort to me. ¹²Epaphras, who is one of you, a servant*ᵃ* of Christ Jesus, greets you. He is always wrestling in his prayers on your behalf, so that you may stand mature and fully assured in everything that God wills. ¹³For

I testify for him that he has worked hard for you and for those in Laodicea and in Hierapolis. ¹⁴Luke, the beloved physician, and Demas greet you. ¹⁵Give my greetings to the brothers and sisters*ᵇ* in Laodicea, and to Nympha and the church in her house. ¹⁶And when this letter has been read among you, have it read also in the church of the Laodiceans; and see that you read also the letter from Laodicea. ¹⁷And say to Archippus, "See that you complete the task that you have received in the Lord."

18 I, Paul, write this greeting with my own hand. Remember my chains. Grace be with you.*ᶜ*

a Gk slave *b* Gk brothers *c* Other ancient authorities add *Amen*

Tranquility of the Spirit—© Megan Schoettler, 17

1 THESSALONIANS

ROCK STEADY

Rubberneckers and Tailgaters

Learning to drive can be quite a challenge. It doesn't matter what vehicle you're driving—Beetle, Hummer, Mustang, or John Deere—it takes a while to get it right. Even though driving can be very exciting, we all still need some coaching.

The Apostle Paul was kind of like a driving coach for the Church in Thessalonica. When he wrote this letter to them, they were just baby Christians. They were learning the ropes about what it means to follow Jesus. And so far, their grip on the steering wheel had been just about perfect.

Paul spends the first three chapters rubber-necking—taking a good, long look back at all the Thessalonians were doing right. They were loving, faithful, and steadfast. Paul was excited to hear about their progress.

But Paul also wanted to make sure they understood that the Christian life is more like a cross-country road trip than a drive around the block. In the final two chapters, Paul encourages his readers to take their eyes off the rearview mirror and focus on the road ahead, which they can't quite see. And he tells them the only way to get there is to tailgate Jesus as close as they can. It doesn't matter where you are in your Christian road trip. Read 1 Thessalonians to see where you should rubberneck and tailgate in your faith.

> *"You were rubbed with oil like an athlete, Christ's athlete, as though in preparation for an earthly wrestling match, and you agreed to take on your opponent."*
>
> —St. Ambrose

WHO This is the Apostle Paul's first letter to the Thessalonian Church community.

WHAT Paul encourages the members of this faithful Church community to remain steady in their faith because Jesus could return at any time.

WHEN Paul wrote this letter from Corinth around A.D. 51.

WHERE Thessalonica was a popular seaport and served as the capital of Macedonia (part of present-day Greece).

PATH OF DISCIPLESHIP

First Thessalonians portrays Jesus as the Savior of the past, present, and future. Paul talks about Christ's role in the Thessalonians' early Christian walk—how they left their pagan lives behind to embrace a new life in Jesus. He also encourages them to keep steady in their present lives and continue all the faithful things they've been doing already. Paul also writes a lot about the future Jesus—the One who'll someday raise all the Christians who've died and reunite with all his followers. When that day comes, he'll reward, resurrect, and perfect us.

Do you ever think about what it will be like when Jesus returns or when you meet him at death? It's something to think about, but it's more important to focus on how you are living as a disciple today. Just as Paul told the Thessalonians, living right—right now—ensures you'll be ready to meet Jesus.

1

Salutation

Paul, Silvanus, and Timothy,

To the church of the Thessalonians in God the Father and the Lord Jesus Christ:

Grace to you and peace.

The Thessalonians' Faith and Example

2 We always give thanks to God for all of you and mention you in our prayers, constantly [3] remembering before our God and Father your work of faith and labor of love and steadfastness of hope in our Lord Jesus Christ. [4] For we know, brothers and sisters[a] beloved by God, that he has chosen you, [5] because our message of the gospel came to you not in word only, but also in power and in the Holy Spirit and with full conviction; just as you know what kind of persons we proved to be among you for your sake. [6] And you became imitators of us and of the Lord, for in spite of persecution you received the word with joy inspired by the Holy Spirit, [7] so that you became an example to all the believers in Macedonia and in Achaia. [8] For the word of the Lord has sounded forth from you not only in Macedonia and Achaia, but in every place your faith in God has become known, so that we have no need to speak about it. [9] For the people of those regions[b] report about us what kind of welcome we had among you, and how you turned to God from idols, to serve a living and true God, [10] and to wait for his Son from heaven, whom he raised from the dead—Jesus, who rescues us from the wrath that is coming.

2

Paul's Ministry in Thessalonica

You yourselves know, brothers and sisters,[a] that our coming to you was not in vain, [2] but though we had already suffered and been shamefully mistreated at Philippi, as you know, we had courage in our God to declare to you the gospel of God in spite of great opposition. [3] For our appeal does not spring from deceit or impure motives or trickery, [4] but just as we have been approved by God to be entrusted with the message of the gospel, even so we speak, not to please mortals, but to please God who tests our hearts. [5] As you know and as God is our witness, we never came with words of flattery or with a pretext for greed; [6] nor did we seek praise from mortals, whether from you or from others, [7] though we might have made demands as apostles of Christ. But we were gentle[c] among you, like a nurse tenderly caring for her own children. [8] So deeply do we care for you that we are determined to share with you not only the gospel of God but also our own selves, because you have become very dear to us.

9 You remember our labor and toil, brothers and sisters;[a] we worked night and day, so that we might not burden any of you while we proclaimed to you the gospel of God. [10] You are witnesses, and God also, how pure, upright, and blameless our conduct was toward you believers. [11] As you know, we dealt with each one of you like a father with his children, [12] urging and encouraging you and pleading that you lead a life worthy of God, who calls you into his own kingdom and glory.

13 We also constantly give thanks to God for this, that when you received the word of God that you heard from us, you accepted it not as a human word but as what it really is, God's word, which is also at work in you believers. [14] For you, brothers and sisters,[a] became imitators of the churches of God in Christ Jesus that are in Judea, for you suffered the same things from your own compatriots as they did from the Jews, [15] who killed both the Lord Jesus and the prophets,[d] and drove us out; they displease God and oppose everyone [16] by hindering us from speaking to the Gentiles so that they may be saved. Thus they have constantly been filling up the measure of their sins; but God's wrath has overtaken them at last.[e]

Paul's Desire to Visit the Thessalonians Again

17 As for us, brothers and sisters,[a] when, for a short time, we were made orphans by being separated from you—in person, not in heart—we longed with great eagerness to see you face to face. [18] For we wanted to come to you—certainly I, Paul, wanted to again and again—but Satan blocked our way. [19] For what is our hope or joy or crown of boasting before our Lord Jesus at his coming? Is it not you? [20] Yes, you are our glory and joy!

a Gk brothers b Gk For they c Other ancient authorities read infants d Other ancient authorities read their own prophets e Or completely or forever

Saying Goodbye

Dear Sarah,

Hmm...clean my room, unload the dishwasher, or write another letter to you? Um, I think I'll take the last one on that!

Hey, I just heard that we're going to have one last sleepover tomorrow before you move to Texas. How does that make me feel, you may ask? Depressed. I've had this sort of dull, numbness in the pit of my stomach, and it's only gotten worse since the countdown started for your move.

But I've been thinking about it, and well, I've noticed something. Throughout all of my letters to you, there has been one main subject: me. I've talked about how terrible it will be for me when you're gone.

So I figure it's about time I try and give you some advice, from one best friend to another. So here goes:

Whenever you start to feel lonely, unpopular, or under-loved in your new home, you need to know that God is always there for you. I know that a lot of people just say that, but this year I've gone through a lot of "personal phases" where I honestly did not know where else to turn—times I was in tears, begging God to help me, and He did.

In all my life, He has never, EVER let me down, even though it may have seemed like it at the time.

Psalm 66:10-12 says, "You have tested us, O God; you have purified us like silver...you have laid a burden" (like troubles and pain) "...on our backs...but you brought us to a place of great abundance."

It's not like you're never going to be mad at God for certain situations or about people that He sometimes throws into your life. But when those things do happen (and they will), cling somehow to the hope that this is all a part of the refining process. God is polishing your life so that it can come from being a dirty piece of rock to a priceless ring of sparkling silver. One that shimmers with His brilliance, and demonstrates His beautiful handiwork.

Be yourself, be who God refines you to be, and I think that you'll do okay, wherever He sends you.

Love, Adelee

REALITY ✓

IT'S HARD TO BE HUMBLE . . .

Read **1 Thessalonians 2.13.** Paul realizes the effect of his preaching in Thessalonica is God's gift. Instead of thinking that *he's* God's gift and bragging about the Thessalonian success story, Paul gives credit where credit is due and gives thanks unceasingly to God.

An attitude of gratitude is the mark of a humble believer who realizes that God is the source of *all* good.

Find some Creative Space in this Bible and write your response to this question: How has God used my gifts for the good of others? Then say a prayer of thanksgiving to God and look for ways to use your gifts for others. Share your ideas at **Learner.CalltoDiscipleship.com.**

---

3 Therefore when we could bear it no longer, we decided to be left alone in Athens; ²and we sent Timothy, our brother and co-worker for God in proclaiming*a* the gospel of Christ, to strengthen and encourage you for the sake of your faith, ³so that no one would be shaken by these persecutions. Indeed, you yourselves know that this is what we are destined for. ⁴In fact, when we were with you, we told you beforehand that we were to suffer persecution; so it turned out, as you know. ⁵For this reason, when I could bear it no longer, I sent to find out about your faith; I was afraid that somehow the tempter had tempted you and that our labor had been in vain.

Timothy's Encouraging Report

6 But Timothy has just now come to us from you, and has brought us the good news of your faith and love. He has told us also that you always remember us kindly and long to see us—just as we long to see you. ⁷For this reason, brothers and sisters,*b* during all our distress and persecution we have been encouraged about you through your faith. ⁸For we now live, if you continue to stand firm in the Lord. ⁹How can we thank God enough for you in return for all the joy that we feel before our God because of you? ¹⁰Night and day we pray most earnestly that we may see you face to face and restore whatever is lacking in your faith.

11 Now may our God and Father himself and our Lord Jesus direct our way to you. ¹²And may the Lord make you increase and abound in love for one another and for all, just as we abound in love for you. ¹³And may he so strengthen your hearts in holiness that you may be blameless before our God and Father at the coming of our Lord Jesus with all his saints.

4 ### A Life Pleasing to God

Finally, brothers and sisters,*a* we ask and urge you in the Lord Jesus that, as you learned from us how you ought to live and to please God (as, in fact, you are doing), you should do so more and more. ²For you know what instructions we gave you through the Lord Jesus. ³For this is the will of God, your sanctification: that you abstain from fornication; ⁴that each one of you know how to control your own body*c* in holiness and honor, ⁵not with lustful passion, like the Gentiles who do not know God; ⁶that no one wrong or exploit a brother or sister*d* in this matter, because the Lord is an avenger in all these things, just as we have already told you beforehand and solemnly warned you. ⁷For God did not call us to impurity but in holiness. ⁸Therefore whoever rejects this rejects not human authority but God, who also gives his Holy Spirit to you.

9 Now concerning love of the brothers and sisters,*a* you do not need to have anyone write to you, for you yourselves have been taught by God to love one another; ¹⁰and indeed you do love all the brothers and sisters*a* throughout Macedonia. But we urge you, beloved,*a* to do so more and more, ¹¹to aspire to live quietly, to mind your own affairs, and to work with your hands, as we directed you, ¹²so that you may behave properly toward outsiders and be dependent on no one.

The Coming of the Lord

13 But we do not want you to be uninformed, brothers and sisters,*a* about those who have died,*e* so that you may not grieve as others do who have no hope. ¹⁴For since we believe that Jesus died and rose again, even so, through Jesus, God will bring with him those who have died.*e* ¹⁵For this we declare to you by the word of the Lord, that we who are alive, who are left until the coming of the Lord, will by no means precede those who have died.*e* ¹⁶For the Lord himself, with a cry of command, with the arch-

---

a Gk lacks *proclaiming* *b* Gk *brothers* *c* Or *how to take a wife for himself* *d* Gk *brother* *e* Gk *fallen asleep* angel's call and with the sound of God's trumpet, will descend from heaven, and the dead in Christ will rise first. [17]Then we who are alive, who are left, will be caught up in the clouds together with them to meet the Lord in the air; and so we will be with the Lord forever. [18]Therefore encourage one another with these words.

5 Now concerning the times and the seasons, brothers and sisters,[a] you do not need to have anything written to you. [2]For you yourselves know very well that the day of the Lord will come like a thief in the night. [3]When they say, "There is peace and security," then sudden destruction will come upon them, as labor pains come upon a pregnant woman, and there will be no escape! [4]But you, beloved,[a] are not in darkness, for that day to surprise you like a thief; [5]for you are all children of light and children of the day; we are not of the night or of darkness. [6]So then let us not fall asleep as others do, but let us keep awake and be sober; [7]for those who sleep sleep at night, and those who are drunk get drunk at night. [8]But since we belong to the day, let us be sober, and put on the breastplate of faith and love, and for a helmet the hope of salvation. [9]For God has destined us not for wrath but for obtaining salvation through our Lord Jesus Christ, [10]who died for us, so that whether we are awake or asleep we may live with him. [11]Therefore encourage one another and build up each other, as indeed you are doing.

a Gk brothers

TRY THIS

THE WORST OF TIMES

Comfort zones are for sissies.

The Apostle Paul and other first-century Christians didn't have comfort zones. They had a hard time being Jesus' followers in those early years. When times were bad, they were *really* bad. They underwent ridicule, imprisonment, beatings, suffering, torturous execution—the complete opposite of comfort.

But the early Christians loved God anyway. And through the worst of times they loved each other.

Read **1 Thessalonians 4.9**. God showed his compassion for his Church, and believers mirrored it to each other. That's exactly what God wants from his Church—from *you*—today, especially during tough circumstances.

Do you know someone who's going through a hard time? How does God want you to step out of your comfort zone and reflect his compassion to that person?

Ask your pastor, deacon, or another parish leader to point you in the right direction. Join a group or individual on a visit to the sick or another ministry outreach. If it's appropriate, take some photos and then write about your experience at **Learner.CalltoDiscipleship.com**.

GOD IS COMPASSIONATE MY CHURCH

Three Candles Burning—© Catherine Willms, 15

Final Exhortations, Greetings, and Benediction

12 But we appeal to you, brothers and sisters,[a] to respect those who labor among you, and have charge of you in the Lord and admonish you; [13]esteem them very highly in love because of their work. Be at peace among yourselves. [14]And we urge you, beloved,[a] to admonish the idlers, encourage the fainthearted, help the weak, be patient with all of them. [15]See that none of you repays evil for evil, but always seek to do good to one another and to all. [16]Rejoice always, [17]pray without ceasing, [18]give thanks in all circumstances; for this is the will of God in Christ Jesus for you. [19]Do not quench the Spirit. [20]Do not despise the words of prophets,[b] [21]but test everything; hold fast to what is good; [22]abstain from every form of evil.

23 May the God of peace himself sanctify you entirely; and may your spirit and soul and body be kept sound[c] and blameless at the coming of our Lord Jesus Christ. [24]The one who calls you is faithful, and he will do this.

25 Beloved,[d] pray for us.

26 Greet all the brothers and sisters[a] with a holy kiss. [27]I solemnly command you by the Lord that this letter be read to all of them.[e]

28 The grace of our Lord Jesus Christ be with you.[f]

a Gk brothers b Gk despise prophecies c Or complete d Gk Brothers
e Gk to all the brothers f Other ancient authorities add Amen

2 THESSALONIANS

JESUS IS COMING!

You Better Believe It

You can't believe everything you read these days. Hoaxes and misquotes spread like wildfire on the Internet, and before you blink everyone believes something that's entirely untrue. And no one's immune. It bleeds through the established news sources almost as much as the racy tabloids.

It's nothing new. In fact, not much has changed in the last two thousand years. It had only been a few months since the young Church at Thessalonica had received its first letter. The letter went on and on about how well the Thessalonians were doing in their faith.

But the writer soon got wind of some disturbing news. Someone had been telling the Church that the "day of the Lord" had already begun (2 Thessalonians 2.2). This caused some of them to stop working because they thought Jesus was just about to return. The writer quashed this "hoax" by clarifying some of the details about Christ's return. And he encouraged them not to be lazy in their faith and work.

You may not be able to believe everything you read on the Internet or hear on television. But take this author's word for it: You *can* believe the inherent truth you read in the Bible. Check out what the *Catechism of the Catholic Church* says about truth in Scripture in 81, 82, 107, and 136.

"Wait upon the Lord; be faithful to His commandments; He will elevate your hope, and put you in possession of His Kingdom."
—St. Bernard of Clairvaux

WHO Many Scripture scholars believe that this was probably written by a second-generation follower of Paul.

WHAT A message of hope to a Church community suffering persecution and confusion

WHEN Uncertain, but could have been written as late as A.D. 70.

WHERE Thessalonica was a popular seaport and served as the capital of Macedonia (part of present-day Greece).

PATH OF DISCIPLESHIP

In this letter, the writer urges the Thessalonians to be hopeful and to live lives of holiness. But, since attacks were coming from people outside the Church, some in the community were misinterpreting Paul's teaching on the Second Coming of Christ and using it as an excuse not to work.

Instead, the people were becoming busybodies, poking their noses into other people's business and causing hard feelings. This kind of behavior doesn't bring hope or build up the community—not in Thessalonica, and not anywhere else.

As disciples, it's our task to build up our community and to give hope to others. We can do this by using our gifts and talents. Or we can do it by sharing our experiences with others who are going through a difficult time. How do you bring hope and faith to your community? How can you do an even better job of it and inspire others to do the same?

1 Salutation

Paul, Silvanus, and Timothy,

To the church of the Thessalonians in God our Father and the Lord Jesus Christ:

2 Grace to you and peace from God our*a* Father and the Lord Jesus Christ.

Thanksgiving

3 We must always give thanks to God for you, brothers and sisters,*b* as is right, because your faith is growing abundantly, and the love of every one of you for one another is increasing. ⁴Therefore we ourselves boast of you among the churches of God for your steadfastness and faith during all your persecutions and the afflictions that you are enduring.

The Judgment at Christ's Coming

5 This is evidence of the righteous judgment of God, and is intended to make you worthy of the kingdom of God, for which you are also suffering. ⁶For it is indeed just of God to repay with affliction those who afflict you, ⁷and to give relief to the afflicted as well as to us, when the Lord Jesus is revealed from heaven with his mighty angels ⁸in flaming fire, inflicting vengeance on those who do not know God and on those who do not obey the gospel of our Lord Jesus. ⁹These will suffer the punishment of eternal destruction, separated from the presence of the Lord and from the glory of his might, ¹⁰when he comes to be glorified by his saints and to be marveled at on that day among all who have believed, because our testimony to you was believed. ¹¹To this end we always pray for you, asking that our God will make you worthy of his call and will fulfill by his power every good resolve and work of faith, ¹²so that the name of our Lord Jesus may be glorified in you, and you in him, according to the grace of our God and the Lord Jesus Christ.

2 The Man of Lawlessness

As to the coming of our Lord Jesus Christ and our being gathered together to him, we beg you, brothers and sisters,*b* ²not to be quickly shaken in mind or alarmed, either by spirit or by word or by letter, as though from us, to the effect that the day of the Lord is already here. ³Let no one deceive you in any way; for that day will not come unless the rebellion comes first and the lawless one*c* is revealed, the one destined for destruction.*d* ⁴He opposes and exalts himself above every so-called god or object of worship, so that he takes his seat in the temple of God, declaring himself to be God. ⁵Do you not remember that I told you these things when I was still with you? ⁶And you know what is now restraining him, so that he may be revealed when his time comes. ⁷For the mystery of lawlessness is already at work, but only until the one who now restrains it is removed. ⁸And then the lawless one will be revealed, whom the Lord Jesus*e* will destroy*f* with the breath of his mouth, annihilating him by the manifestation of his coming. ⁹The coming of the lawless one is apparent in the working of Satan, who uses all power, signs, lying wonders, ¹⁰and every kind of wicked deception for those who are perishing, because they refused to love the truth and so be saved. ¹¹For this reason God sends them a powerful delusion, leading them to believe what is false, ¹²so that all who have

a Other ancient authorities read *the* *b* Gk *brothers* *c* Gk *the man of lawlessness;* other ancient authorities read *the man of sin* *d* Gk *the son of destruction* *e* Other ancient authorities lack *Jesus* *f* Other ancient authorities read *consume* not believed the truth but took pleasure in un-righteousness will be condemned.

Chosen for Salvation

13 But we must always give thanks to God for you, brothers and sisters[a] beloved by the Lord, because God chose you as the first fruits[b] for salvation through sanctification by the Spirit and through belief in the truth. [14]For this purpose he called you through our proclamation of the good news,[c] so that you may obtain the glory of our Lord Jesus Christ. [15]So then, brothers and sisters,[a] stand firm and hold fast to the traditions that you were taught by us, either by word of mouth or by our letter.

16 Now may our Lord Jesus Christ himself and God our Father, who loved us and through grace gave us eternal comfort and good hope, [17]comfort your hearts and strengthen them in every good work and word.

3 Request for Prayer

Finally, brothers and sisters,[a] pray for us, so that the word of the Lord may spread rapidly and be glorified everywhere, just as it is among you, [2]and that we may be rescued from wicked and evil people; for not all have faith. [3]But the Lord is faithful; he will strengthen you and guard you from the evil one.[d] [4]And we have confidence in the Lord concerning you, that you are doing and will go on doing the things that we command. [5]May the Lord direct your hearts to the love of God and to the steadfastness of Christ.

a Gk *brothers* *b* Other ancient authorities read *from the beginning* *c* Or *through our gospel* *d* Or *from evil*

CREATIVE SPACE

EXPRESS YOURSELF

Hands That Hang on Tight

Have you ever had a day when you felt backed into a corner as soon as you woke up? Maybe you had a day at school that was so terrible you felt like giving up on your Christian faith and God was the one to blame for what had happened. Days like this will raise their ugly heads more than you'd like. Is it worth it to continue to trust God?

Read **2 Thessalonians 2.13–17**. The Christians in Thessalonica were obviously very discouraged and ready to call it quits. Paul presents them with a solution in verse 15: "Stand firm and hold fast" to everything he'd taught them. Paul inspires them to stay committed to what they *know* to be true and not to be swayed by their emotions. They are to "stand firm," as though their feet were in cement, and "hold fast," even if their hands begin to bleed.

God's desire is for you to stand firm and to hold on to your faith, no matter what the cost. To allow this image to be impressed upon your heart, take a creative photo of your feet and hands. Tape it to the inside back cover of this Bible and then share your photo at **Learner.CalltoDiscipleship.com**.

This World, You, and Me...Him

We live in a world of possibilities—
A world of *ifs*.
But what will you do with them?
Because you're only happy if you want to be.
I want you to see
Everything happens for a reason.
Reasons aren't always understood—
But are we always meant to understand?
Understanding is a gift
That we're not always given.
Everything is bigger than you think.
Love isn't just a feeling,
It's a way of life.
There's more to life than complacency.
This world is full of hate,
Full of sin,
But will you join in?
Or do something to change it?
Because if you won't, who will?
If you think there's no hope,
Believe me there isn't.
But if you believe with all your heart,
Anything can happen.
Your life will fall apart from time to time,
But things will get better.
You can only dig yourself so far into a hole
Before you realize you need to climb out.
Have a little faith,
Dry up your tears,
Because it's not all your fault.
You didn't choose,
You were chosen.
Life will go on,
And it's not really fair
That your world is a mess
And others keep on turning.
But life isn't fair—
Do you really want it to be?
When you can't change anything,
Look at your life,
Change it.
What will I do with the possibilities?
When will I learn to listen?
I don't know who I want to be,
I'll worry and I'll cry,
But I'll get better.
Decide what's important,
Then act.
Don't settle for less than your best—
Only accept your very best.
Because it's not all about you,
And it's not all about me.
Who are we living for?
In this world full of hate, sin, ifs and possibilities?

This World, You, and Me...Him—© Katie Duckett, 15

Warning against Idleness

6 Now we command you, beloved,[a] in the name of our Lord Jesus Christ, to keep away from believers who are[b] living in idleness and not according to the tradition that they[c] received from us. [7]For you yourselves know how you ought to imitate us; we were not idle when we were with you, [8]and we did not eat anyone's bread without paying for it; but with toil and labor we worked night and day, so that we might not burden any of you. [9]This was not because we do not have that right, but in order to give you an example to imitate. [10]For even when we were with you, we gave you this command: Anyone unwilling to work should not eat. [11]For we hear that some of you are living in idleness, mere busybodies, not doing any work. [12]Now such persons we command and exhort in the Lord Jesus Christ to do their work quietly and to earn their own living. [13]Brothers and sisters,[d] do not be weary in doing what is right.

14 Take note of those who do not obey what we say in this letter; have nothing to do with them, so that they may be ashamed. [15]Do not regard them as enemies, but warn them as believers.[e]

Final Greetings and Benediction

16 Now may the Lord of peace himself give you peace at all times in all ways. The Lord be with all of you.

17 I, Paul, write this greeting with my own hand. This is the mark in every letter of mine; it is the way I write. [18]The grace of our Lord Jesus Christ be with all of you.[f]

IT'S TRADITION

PLEASE COME AGAIN!

Have you ever seen "Please come again!" at the bottom of a bill at a restaurant? Or maybe you've heard a shopkeeper say it as you're leaving a store. These places of businesses would love for you to come again to spend money and keep their doors open.

So who do you say "Please come again" to? How about Jesus? That's what we're waiting for. As Catholics, we believe that Jesus will return in glory as judge of the living and the dead at the end of time.

Sometimes this is called the *parousia*, the Greek word meaning "presence." Though Jesus is always present in the Eucharist and in our hearts, parousia refers to Jesus' presence at the Second Coming, when history and all creation will achieve fulfillment.

---

a Gk brothers *b* Gk from every brother who is *c* Other ancient authorities read you *d* Gk Brothers *e* Gk a brother *f* Other ancient authorities add Amen

CREATIVE SPACE

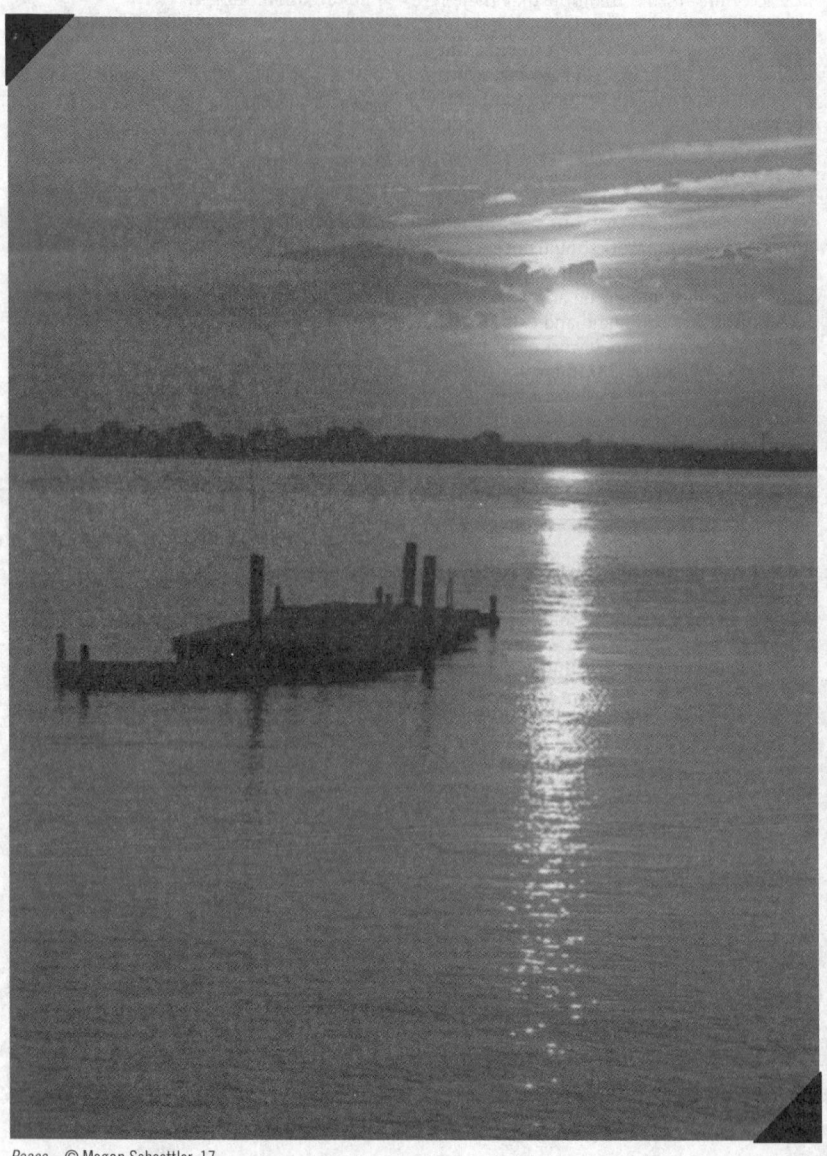

Peace—© Megan Schoettler, 17

Record Company Executive: Your fans are church folk, Johnny. Christians. They don't wanna hear you singing to a bunch of murderers and rapists, tryin' to cheer 'em up.

Johnny Cash: Well, they're not Christians then.

—Dialogue from the film *Walk the Line*

WALK THE TALK

WALK TALK

WALK

in godliness combined with contentment; [7]for we brought nothing into the world, so that[b] we can take nothing out of it; [8]but if we have food and clothing, we will be content with these. [9]But those who want to be rich fall into temptation and are trapped by many senseless and harmful desires that plunge people into ruin and destruction. [10]For the love of money is a root of all kinds of evil, and in their eagerness to be rich some have wandered away from the faith and pierced themselves with many pains.

The Good Fight of Faith

11 But as for you, man of God, shun all this; pursue righteousness, godliness, faith, love, endurance, gentleness. [12]Fight the good fight of the faith; take hold of the eternal life, to which you were called and for which you made[c] the good confession in the presence of many witnesses. [13]In the presence of God, who gives life to all things, and of Christ Jesus, who in his testimony before Pontius Pilate made the good confession, I charge you [14]to keep the commandment without spot or blame until the manifestation of our Lord Jesus Christ, [15]which he will bring about at the right time—he who is the blessed and only Sovereign, the King of kings and Lord of lords. [16]It is he alone who has immortality and dwells in unapproachable light, whom no one has ever seen or can see; to him be honor and eternal dominion. Amen.

17 As for those who in the present age are rich, command them not to be haughty, or to set their hopes on the uncertainty of riches, but rather on God who richly provides us with everything for our enjoyment. [18]They are to do good, to be rich in good works, generous, and ready to share, [19]thus storing up for themselves the treasure of a good foundation for the future, so that they may take hold of the life that really is life.

Personal Instructions and Benediction

20 Timothy, guard what has been entrusted to you. Avoid the profane chatter and contradictions of what is falsely called knowledge; [21]by professing it some have missed the mark as regards the faith.

Grace be with you.[d]

False Teaching and True Riches

Teach and urge these duties. [3]Whoever teaches otherwise and does not agree with the sound words of our Lord Jesus Christ and the teaching that is in accordance with godliness, [4]is conceited, understanding nothing, and has a morbid craving for controversy and for disputes about words. From these come envy, dissension, slander, base suspicions, [5]and wrangling among those who are depraved in mind and bereft of the truth, imagining that godliness is a means of gain.[a] [6]Of course, there is great gain

a Other ancient authorities add *Withdraw yourself from such people* b Other ancient authorities read *world—it is certain that* c Gk *confessed*
d The Greek word for *you* here is plural; in other ancient authorities it is singular. Other ancient authorities add *Amen*

2 TIMOTHY

LOVE GOD'S WORD

Dive In

How do you know who the false teachers are? I mean, people aren't going to stand up and introduce themselves as someone who distorts the truth and shouldn't be trusted. And we can't judge teaching purely by whether it sounds good to us. As Paul points out, it's very tempting to listen only to people who say what we want to hear. So how do we decide who to listen to and who to ignore?

The secret is to have something solid to measure teaching against. Timothy grew up with the Scriptures, and it shows. Rather than dry, dusty words, he knew that they were infused with the breath of God—a powerful tool to equip God's people.

Maybe you didn't grow up with the Bible, but you have a choice about how you treat it now. So dive into it. Immerse yourself in these stories and words. Wrestle with the bits you don't understand. Ask God to make it come alive for you. Talk with friends about how the Bible all hangs together and what difference it makes to your life. Ask questions. Find someone who loves God's Word and spend time with that person, so you catch his or her enthusiasm. And expect to hear God, because he has plenty to say to you through these pages.

> *"Don't lose your inner peace for anything whatsoever, even if your whole world seems upset."*
> —St. Francis de Sales

WHO The Apostle Paul wrote this to his young friend Timothy.

WHAT Paul had more advice on how to stay strong and how to deal with false teaching. He ended this letter on a personal note. Aware that his life was drawing to an end, Paul asked his friend Timothy to come and see him.

WHEN Written around A.D. 66

WHERE Paul wrote this letter from prison in Rome. Timothy was still leading the Church in Ephesus (a city in modern-day Turkey).

PATH OF DISCIPLESHIP

When Satan tempted Jesus to turn stones into bread, to try BASE jumping without a parachute, and to worship him instead of God, Jesus coolly disarmed him with a powerful weapon: the Word of God (Matthew 4.1–11). When the people got excited about the new teaching they heard from Jesus, he pointed out that he hadn't come to get rid of the old Scriptures—he'd come to show they were right (5.17–20). If Jesus put such a high value on the Bible, shouldn't we do the same? As you hear the Scriptures preached and as you read them and pray with them, consider how to make them the force that energizes and nourishes your life.

Courage

I'm having one of those days—a double-chin, weird-hair, big-nose day. Maybe with the touch of a magic wand and a few plastic surgeries, I'd feel good in my skin. Maybe not. Sometimes I try hard to imagine how God sees me . . . and how he sees everyone around me. The Bible says God is enamored. Whether or not my hairdo is cooperating, he sees me with an artist's eye—"Ah, potential!"

This changes things. For one, I feel more courageous. In **2 Timothy 1.6–7** we find a reminder that we don't need to be shy about who we are. I'm an eternal somebody with some special bonus features—I'm not an eight-time gold-medal Olympian, mind you, but I have gifts.

Each of us is like stock God has heavily invested in, and he's hoping for a great return. He wants us to make a serious impact in our world. It just isn't possible to chase the dreams he put in us if we're stuck wondering if we are good for anything.

I guess what I'm trying to say here is this. God made you awesome, and he thinks you're great. So go do something incredible. What God-given gifts are inside of you? Tape a photo of yourself to a piece of copy paper. Under your picture, list five gifts God has given you. Hang your list somewhere in your room to remind yourself of your gifts—and think about how you can use those gifts to positively impact your school.

1 Salutation

Paul, an apostle of Christ Jesus by the will of God, for the sake of the promise of life that is in Christ Jesus,

2 To Timothy, my beloved child:

Grace, mercy, and peace from God the Father and Christ Jesus our Lord.

Thanksgiving and Encouragement

3 I am grateful to God—whom I worship with a clear conscience, as my ancestors did—when I remember you constantly in my prayers night and day. 4Recalling your tears, I long to see you so that I may be filled with joy. 5I am reminded of your sincere faith, a faith that lived first in your grandmother Lois and your mother Eunice and now, I am sure, lives in you. 6For this reason I remind you to rekindle the gift of God that is within you through the laying on of my hands; 7for God did not give us a spirit of cowardice, but rather a spirit of power and of love and of self-discipline.

8 Do not be ashamed, then, of the testimony about our Lord or of me his prisoner, but join with me in suffering for the gospel, relying on the power of God, 9who saved us and called us with a holy calling, not according to our works but according to his own purpose and grace. This grace was given to us in Christ Jesus before the ages began, 10but it has now been revealed through the appearing of our Savior Christ Jesus, who abolished death and brought life and immortality to light through the gospel. 11For this gospel I was appointed a herald and an apostle and a teacher,*a* 12and for this reason I suffer as I do. But I am not ashamed, for I know the one in whom I have put my trust, and I am sure that he is able to guard until that day what I have entrusted to him.*b* 13Hold to the standard of sound teaching that you have heard from me, in the faith and love that are in Christ Jesus. 14Guard the good treasure entrusted to you, with the help of the Holy Spirit living in us.

15 You are aware that all who are in Asia have turned away from me, including Phygelus and Hermogenes. 16May the Lord grant mercy to the household of Onesiphorus, because he often refreshed me and was not ashamed of my chain; 17when he arrived in Rome, he eagerly*c* searched for me and found me 18—may the Lord grant that he will find mercy from the Lord on that day! And you know very well how much service he rendered in Ephesus.

2 A Good Soldier of Christ Jesus

You then, my child, be strong in the grace that is in Christ Jesus; 2and what you have heard from me through many witnesses entrust to faithful people who will be able to teach others as well. 3Share in suffering like a good soldier of Christ Jesus. 4No one serving in the army gets entangled in everyday affairs; the soldier's aim is to please the enlisting officer. 5And in the case of an athlete, no one is crowned without competing according to the rules. 6It is the farmer who does the work who ought to have the first share of the crops. 7Think over what I say, for the Lord will give you understanding in all things.

a Other ancient authorities add *of the Gentiles*   *b* Or *what has been entrusted to me*   *c* Or *promptly*

8 Remember Jesus Christ, raised from the dead, a descendant of David—that is my gospel, ⁹for which I suffer hardship, even to the point of being chained like a criminal. But the word of God is not chained. ¹⁰Therefore I endure everything for the sake of the elect, so that they may also obtain the salvation that is in Christ Jesus, with eternal glory. ¹¹The saying is sure:

If we have died with him, we will also live
    with him;
¹² if we endure, we will also reign with him;
    if we deny him, he will also deny us;
¹³ if we are faithless, he remains faithful—
    for he cannot deny himself.

A Worker Approved by God

14 Remind them of this, and warn them before God[a] that they are to avoid wrangling over words, which does no good but only ruins those who are listening. ¹⁵Do your best to present yourself to God as one approved by him, a worker who has no need to be ashamed, rightly explaining the word of truth. ¹⁶Avoid profane chatter, for it will lead people into more and more impiety, ¹⁷and their talk will spread like gangrene. Among them are Hymenaeus and Philetus, ¹⁸who have swerved from the truth by claiming that the resurrection has already taken place. They are upsetting the faith of some. ¹⁹But God's firm foundation stands, bearing this inscription: "The Lord knows those who are his," and, "Let everyone who calls on the name of the Lord turn away from wickedness."

20 In a large house there are utensils not only of gold and silver but also of wood and clay, some for special use, some for ordinary. ²¹All who cleanse themselves of the things I have mentioned[b] will become special utensils, dedicated and useful to the owner of the house, ready for every good work. ²²Shun youthful passions and pursue righteousness, faith, love, and peace, along with those who call on the Lord from a pure heart. ²³Have nothing to do with stupid and senseless controversies; you know that they breed quarrels. ²⁴And the Lord's servant[c] must not be quarrelsome but kindly to everyone, an apt teacher, patient, ²⁵correcting opponents with gentleness. God may perhaps grant that they will repent and come to know the truth, ²⁶and that they may escape from the snare of the devil, having been held captive by him to do his will.[d]

3 Godlessness in the Last Days

You must understand this, that in the last days distressing times will come. ²For people

will be lovers of themselves, lovers of money, boasters, arrogant, abusive, disobedient to their parents, ungrateful, unholy, ³inhuman, implacable, slanderers, profligates, brutes, haters of good, ⁴treacherous, reckless, swollen with conceit, lovers of pleasure rather than lovers of God, ⁵holding to the outward form of godliness but denying its power. Avoid them! ⁶For among them are those who make their way into households and captivate silly women, overwhelmed by their sins and swayed by all kinds of desires, ⁷who are always being instructed and can never arrive at a knowledge of the truth. ⁸As Jannes and Jambres opposed Moses, so these people, of corrupt mind and counterfeit faith, also oppose the truth. ⁹But they will not make much progress, because, as in the case of those two men,[e] their folly will become plain to everyone.

Paul's Charge to Timothy

10 Now you have observed my teaching, my conduct, my aim in life, my faith, my patience,

a Other ancient authorities read *the Lord* b Gk *of these things* c Gk *slave* d Or *by him, to do his* (that is, God's) *will* e Gk lacks *two men*

WHAT GOD GAVE ME

God gave me hands;

I use them to create a masterpiece.

God gave me feet;

I use them to run toward Him.

God gave me ears;

I use them to hear the Truth.

God gave me eyes;

I use them to truly see.

God gave me a tongue;

I use it to spread the Word.

God gave me a mind;

I use it to choose between good and evil.

God gave me an angel;

I use him to guide me.

God gave me a heart;

I use it for love.

What God Gave Me—© Jessica Jones, 17

my love, my steadfastness, 11my persecutions, and my suffering the things that happened to me in Antioch, Iconium, and Lystra. What persecutions I endured! Yet the Lord rescued me from all of them. 12Indeed, all who want to live a godly life in Christ Jesus will be persecuted. 13But wicked people and impostors will go from bad to worse, deceiving others and being deceived. 14But as for you, continue in what you have learned and firmly believed, knowing from whom you learned it, 15and how from childhood you have known the sacred writings that are able to instruct you for salvation through faith in Christ Jesus. 16All scripture is inspired by God and is*a* useful for teaching, for reproof, for correction, and for training in righteousness, 17so that everyone who belongs to God may be proficient, equipped for every good work.

4 In the presence of God and of Christ Jesus, who is to judge the living and the dead, and in view of his appearing and his kingdom, I solemnly urge you: 2proclaim the message; be persistent whether the time is favorable or unfavorable; convince, rebuke, and encourage, with the utmost patience in teaching. 3For the time is coming when people will not put up with sound doctrine, but having itching ears, they will accumulate for themselves teachers to suit their own desires, 4and will turn away from listening to the truth and wander away to myths. 5As for you, always be sober, endure suffering, do the work of an evangelist, carry out your ministry fully.

6 As for me, I am already being poured out as a libation, and the time of my departure has come. 7I have fought the good fight, I have finished the race, I have kept the faith. 8From now on there is reserved for me the crown of righteousness, which the Lord, the righteous judge, will give me on that day, and not only to me but also to all who have longed for his appearing.

Personal Instructions
9 Do your best to come to me soon, 10for Demas, in love with this present world, has deserted me and gone to Thessalonica; Crescens has gone to Galatia,*b* Titus to Dalmatia. 11Only Luke is with me. Get Mark and bring him with you, for he is useful in my ministry. 12I have sent Tychicus to Ephesus. 13When you come, bring the cloak that I left with Carpus at Troas, also the books, and above all the parchments. 14Alexander the coppersmith did me great harm; the Lord will pay him back for his deeds. 15You also must beware of him, for he strongly opposed our message.

a Or *Every scripture inspired by God is also* *b* Other ancient authorities read *Gaul*

If Only the Bible Said…
"You shall go to the state university and major in sports medicine" (4 John 321.10).

"And the Lord said, 'Yes, you should ask Kaitlyn to the prom'" (2 Queens 900.2).

"The Lord appeared in a vision, and a voice boomed from the clouds saying, 'Excellent goal in the game last night!'" (3 Crudinthians 2.1)

Okay, so these aren't exact quotes from the Bible. But have you ever wished the Bible *did* say stuff like this? Wouldn't it be amazing to find real, black-and-white answers to your questions? Wouldn't it be great if you could find practical guidance from God about the specific issues in your life?

Read **2 Timothy 3.16–17.**

So *no,* you're not going to find a passage in the Bible telling you what to major in, who to date, which sport to focus on, how often to practice an instrument, which friends to hang out with, or what to name your pet. But the truth of the matter is that with a little effort on your part, you *can* find relevant truth here in God's Word to apply to every area of your life. God isn't distant—he's here and he's real. He walks with you through every moment of your life, and he cares about the things that are important to you—your relationships, choices, hobbies, interests, and decisions. And God wants to speak to you about your life through his Word.

In this book you'll find trustworthy guidance on important topics like friendship, romance and sex, family relationships, discovering your gifts and talents, making wise choices, and so much more. And when you can't find specifics (like a verse on how to tactfully break up with someone or a passage detailing a training plan for your next cross-country meet), you *will* find principles and important teachings that can shape the person you are, equipping you to make God-honoring decisions on your own.

Grab a favorite magazine or two and tear out a few pictures that represent the important things in your life. Then glue them like a collage onto a small strip of cardboard or thick paper. Keep this bookmark in your Bible to remind you that God is present in your life, that he speaks to you through his Word, and that he cares about the things that are important to you.

N

16 At my first defense no one came to my support, but all deserted me. May it not be counted against them! [17]But the Lord stood by me and gave me strength, so that through me the message might be fully proclaimed and all the Gentiles might hear it. So I was rescued from the lion's mouth. [18]The Lord will rescue me from every evil attack and save me for his heavenly kingdom. To him be the glory forever and ever. Amen.

Final Greetings and Benediction

19 Greet Prisca and Aquila, and the household of Onesiphorus. [20]Erastus remained in Corinth; Trophimus I left ill in Miletus. [21]Do your best to come before winter. Eubulus sends greetings to you, as do Pudens and Linus and Claudia and all the brothers and sisters.[a]

22 The Lord be with your spirit. Grace be with you.[b]

a Gk *all the brothers*   b The Greek word for *you* here is plural. Other ancient authorities add *Amen*

CREATIVE SPACE

TITUS

RIGHT LIVING IN A MESSED-UP WORLD

Living Like Christ on Sunday, but Come Monday . . .

Imagine the worst things that go on in your high-school hallways—selfishness, intolerance, cruelty. Got them in your mind? Now picture a city full of that. It's a bit like the island of Crete when Titus lived there. It was definitely not the place to go against the crowd and follow Christ.

As in Crete, being a follower of Christ at school can be hard. The pressure to act a certain way can weigh down on us and make us lose our focus on Jesus. It's all too easy to set aside how Jesus wants us to act in the face of peer pressure.

The letter to Titus is a giant reminder that what we believe will affect how we live. If we truly believe that God showed us the ultimate kindness and love, we will, in turn, show that love to others. If we believe that God saved us, not because of something *we* did, but because of something *he* did, then we'll stop trying to impress God with how holy or moral we are. God already knows the grimy, raw insides of our lives. But that doesn't mean we can live any way we want. Titus teaches us that Christians should live like Christ—with absolute love for others.

Even *if* we live in a place like Crete.

"A tree is known by its fruit; a man by his deeds. A good deed is never lost; he who sows courtesy reaps friendship, and he who plants kindness gathers love."

—St. Basil

WHO Many Scripture scholars believe that this letter was probably written by a disciple of Paul.

WHAT This letter contains practical advice to Titus, an early Church leader, about how to live right and how to lead a healthy Church community.

WHEN Written about A.D. 100

WHERE Titus was leading an early Church community in Crete, a large Greek island in the Mediterranean Sea.

PATH OF DISCIPLESHIP

During this period in history, the people of Crete had a reputation for being lazy, mean liars (see Titus 1.12). Their lives were so bad, in fact, that the people of Crete had become famous—or infamous—for their behavior. But the grace of God touched that island. Jesus can reach and change *anyone*—no matter what their well-deserved reputation is. This letter emphasizes that God's kindness through Christ is for "all people" (2.11).

Crete's reputation back then isn't too far off from some situations or people in our world today. What about you? Do you think that Christ can't reach you because of something you've done? There is no one that Jesus cannot reach. There is no place that his grace cannot touch.

THE F WORD

I was just making casual conversation with a girl I know. Or knew. Or *thought* I knew. This is how it went down.

"So, I'm applying for jobs, but I'm not sure what's gonna happen. I have faith that God will work it out, though," I said.

"Why are you shoving God and *faith* down my throat? You're such a freak!" And with that she flicked her head around so fast that her hair whipped my face, causing severe corneal damage. She stormed off and never spoke to me again.

Okay. Reality check. Do you really think this is what will happen if you bring up your faith?

Read **Titus 3.4–8**. This moving passage challenges us to live out our faith and share it with others. We should respond to Christ's salvation and the gift of the Holy Spirit with devotion. If we lived with outrageous devotion and appreciation for God's grace, how would it impact our friends who don't believe or don't live out their faith? In powerful ways, for sure! Help your friends, classmates, or co-workers see that God is challenging them to live out their faith and be powerful examples of godliness.

We speak to our friends about things that are important to us in casual conversation. Your *faith* is important to you, but you may be reluctant to bring it up. It's not as though you have to pull out your rosary beads, quote Scripture, or draw a diagram every time it comes up! It's just part of who you are. So let your faith seep into your conversations with friends.

Try it out tomorrow. Then write in your journal or share on **Learner.CalltoDiscipleship.com** about how it went.

GOD IS CHALLENGING MY FRIENDS

---

1 Salutation

Paul, a servant[a] of God and an apostle of Jesus Christ, for the sake of the faith of God's elect and the knowledge of the truth that is in accordance with godliness, [2]in the hope of eternal life that God, who never lies, promised before the ages began— [3]in due time he revealed his word through the proclamation with which I have been entrusted by the command of God our Savior,

[4] To Titus, my loyal child in the faith we share:

Grace[b] and peace from God the Father and Christ Jesus our Savior.

Titus in Crete

[5] I left you behind in Crete for this reason, so that you should put in order what remained to be done, and should appoint elders in every town, as I directed you: [6]someone who is blameless, married only once,[c] whose children are believers, not accused of debauchery and not rebellious. [7]For a bishop,[d] as God's steward, must be blameless; he must not be arrogant or quick-tempered or addicted to wine or violent or greedy for gain; [8]but he must be hospitable, a lover of goodness, prudent, upright, devout, and self-controlled. [9]He must have a firm grasp of the word that is trustworthy in accordance with the teaching, so that he may be able both to preach with sound doctrine and to refute those who contradict it.

[10] There are also many rebellious people, idle talkers and deceivers, especially those of the circumcision; [11]they must be silenced, since they are upsetting whole families by teaching for sordid gain what it is not right to teach. [12]It was one of them, their very own prophet, who said,

"Cretans are always liars, vicious brutes, lazy
    gluttons."

[13]That testimony is true. For this reason rebuke them sharply, so that they may become sound in the faith, [14]not paying attention to Jewish myths or to commandments of those who reject the truth. [15]To the pure all things are pure, but to the corrupt and unbelieving nothing is pure. Their very minds and consciences are corrupted. [16]They profess to know God, but they deny him by their actions. They are detestable, disobedient, unfit for any good work.

2 Teach Sound Doctrine

But as for you, teach what is consistent with sound doctrine. [2]Tell the older men to be temperate, serious, prudent, and sound in faith, in love, and in endurance.

[3] Likewise, tell the older women to be reverent in behavior, not to be slanderers or slaves to drink; they are to teach what is good, [4]so that they may encourage the young women to love their husbands, to love their children, [5]to be self-controlled, chaste, good managers of

---

a Gk *slave* b Other ancient authorities read *Grace, mercy,* c Gk *husband of one wife* d Or *an overseer* the household, kind, being submissive to their husbands, so that the word of God may not be discredited.

6 Likewise, urge the younger men to be self-controlled. [7]Show yourself in all respects a model of good works, and in your teaching show integrity, gravity, [8]and sound speech that cannot be censured; then any opponent will be put to shame, having nothing evil to say of us.

9 Tell slaves to be submissive to their masters and to give satisfaction in every respect; they are not to talk back, [10]not to pilfer, but to show complete and perfect fidelity, so that in everything they may be an ornament to the doctrine of God our Savior.

11 For the grace of God has appeared, bringing salvation to all,[a] [12]training us to renounce impiety and worldly passions, and in the present age to live lives that are self-controlled, upright, and godly, [13]while we wait for the blessed hope and the manifestation of the glory of our great God and Savior,[b] Jesus Christ. [14]He it is who gave himself for us that he might redeem us from all iniquity and purify for himself a people of his own who are zealous for good deeds.

15 Declare these things; exhort and reprove with all authority.[c] Let no one look down on you.

3 Maintain Good Deeds

Remind them to be subject to rulers and authorities, to be obedient, to be ready for every good work, [2]to speak evil of no one, to avoid quarreling, to be gentle, and to show every courtesy to everyone. [3]For we ourselves were once foolish, disobedient, led astray, slaves to various passions and pleasures, passing our days in malice and envy, despicable, hating one another. [4]But when the goodness and loving kindness of God our Savior appeared, [5]he saved us, not because of any works of righteousness that we had done, but according to his mercy, through the water[d] of rebirth and renewal by the Holy Spirit. [6]This Spirit he poured out on us richly through Jesus Christ our Savior, [7]so that, having been justified by his grace, we might become heirs according to the hope of eternal life. [8]The saying is sure.

I desire that you insist on these things, so that those who have come to believe in God may be careful to devote themselves to good works; these things are excellent and profitable to everyone. [9]But avoid stupid controversies, genealogies, dissensions, and quarrels about the law, for they are unprofitable and

REALITY ✔

A LIGHT FOR THE WORLD

This letter to Titus points to the fact that the community of believers is to become leaven for the world. Just as leaven makes bread rise, we are what makes things rise . . . lighten . . . brighten. Through our good works, the evidence of faith, we can meet the needs of all and shine a light in the darkest of places—a kind word to a friend who is suffering, a shared meal with someone who is lonely or hungry, an act of service for a family who has lost their home. This letter offers us a glimpse of what is means to live in society and be transformed by God's grace so that the Church—and we as her disciples—can be a light for the world. Think about it:

- What living persons do you look to as models for your own Christian behavior?
- In what areas of life do you experience tensions between being a Christian and being part of "the world"?

Then share your thoughts about being a light in the world at **Learner.CalltoDiscipleship.com**.

worthless. [10]After a first and second admonition, have nothing more to do with anyone who causes divisions, [11]since you know that such a person is perverted and sinful, being self-condemned.

Final Messages and Benediction

12 When I send Artemas to you, or Tychicus, do your best to come to me at Nicopolis, for I have decided to spend the winter there. [13]Make every effort to send Zenas the lawyer and Apollos on their way, and see that they lack nothing. [14]And let people learn to devote themselves to good works in order to meet urgent needs, so that they may not be unproductive.

15 All who are with me send greetings to you. Greet those who love us in the faith. Grace be with all of you.[e]

STUMBLING BLOCKS

Lost, scared, confused.
I'm lost in classes,
I'm scared about the future,
I'm confused about activities.
My confidence is shattered,
My heart is broken.
I want to give up...
But there are so many people looking.
I'm scared of failing.
All those things I've worked for—
They don't seem worth it.
Being lost, scared, confused...
They're stumbling blocks for me,
Stumbling blocks for many.

Today is a new day.
I broke down,
I prayed,
I'm still struggling
But today is a new day.
Each day brings new hope,
New opportunities to grow.
The day brings back loving smiles.
The struggles don't disappear,
You just think of them differently.
You can't hide from them,
You just have to reflect,
Learn how to grow,
TRUST in the Lord,
TRUST those around you,
Listen to them.
LET them HELP you.

Everyone is lost, scared, confused at times.
Keep your hopes up.
Remember that it is OK to break down,
As long as you work through it.
DON'T ever give up!
There's ALWAYS someone, somewhere who BELIEVES in you,
COUNTS on you,
And LOVES you.

Work past the stumbling blocks,
They aren't YOU.
YOU are the believer—
YOU and GOD work together,
That is something that can never be taken away from you.

Stumbling Blocks—© Kim Burton, 18

PHILEMON
THAT TINY, HIDDEN LETTER

It's Not Just About Saying "Please"

How have you tried to get what you want? In this brief, personal letter, we get a glimpse of how Paul requested something he wanted. Onesimus, whose name means "useful" in Greek, came to Paul while Paul was imprisoned. (Usually Onesimus is thought to be a *runaway* slave, but there is nothing in the text that clearly states this. Perhaps Philemon sent Onesimus to visit Paul, and Onesimus stayed longer than his owner had intended.) What we do know is this: While with Paul, Onesimus became a believer in Christ and demonstrated that he was *useful* (see why the Greek is significant?) to Paul in his work. Rather than sending Onesimus back to Philemon to face potential punishment, Paul writes a diplomatic letter to Philemon, requesting that his perspective and treatment of Onesimus change, since he is "no longer as a slave" to him (Philemon 1.16).

Paul didn't resort to demanding that Philemon do what he wanted him to do (even though Paul had the authority to do so). Instead, Paul acknowledged Philemon's noble character and tactfully requested forgiveness for Onesimus.

The letter to Philemon is a real-life illustration of something Paul once wrote to the Colossian Church. In this new life, "there is no longer Greek and Jew, circumcised and uncircumcised, barbarian, Scythian, slave and free; but Christ is all and in all!" (Colossians 3.11).

"Why don't you give yourself to God once and for all . . . really . . . now!"
—St. Josemaría Escrivá

WHO A personal letter from Paul to Philemon, his wealthy Christian friend, about Onesimus, a new believer in Jesus

WHAT Philemon is one of the shortest and most personal books in the Bible. In it, Paul requests that Philemon accept Onesimus (a returned and converted slave) as a Christian brother.

WHEN Written around A.D. 60, while Paul was in prison

WHERE Colossae was a city in Asia Minor that is now in modern-day Turkey.

PATH OF DISCIPLESHIP

Isaiah 58.6 says, "Is not this the fast that I choose: to loose the bonds of injustice, to undo the thongs of the yoke, to let the oppressed go free, and to break every yoke?" The story of Philemon and Onesimus shows us how this command and prophecy was coming true in the early Church due to the work of Christ and the teachings of the Apostles. Onesimus, who was once a slave to Philemon, became a brother in Christ. What a transformation!

As disciples of Jesus, we are transformed by him, and our relationships are transformed too. We stop viewing others by our culture's labels—*loner, all-star, loser, popular, geek, smart, stupid*. We step over the fences set up by cliques and social groups. We stop caring about superficial differences and start concentrating on what's truly important. All the divisions fall away. We form unusual and surprising friendships. We learn to get to know and care for people we may never have befriended before.

Does this describe your friendships? Have you allowed Jesus to transform your relationships? How can your actions lead others to the path of discipleship?

ONLY YOU

Music beats through
Letting me feel you
Missed you for so long
Know you were never gone
With the sound, all around
Know I was always loved
Know I will forever be
You will always dance next to me
Forever I will sing
Forever you will live as King!
Will praise your name
Heart will shine without shame
I will beat, pound, drum out loud
Scream, shout, cry without any doubt
Music lives deep through you
Where my home calls
Where my soul holds my all
Sound thumping, pulsing
Making my feet come alive, tapping out of control
Tempo knocking my body afloat
Drumming my heartbeat away
Soul can no longer run astray
Blaring the soul above
Dancing out my love
Letting you work your passion within every chord
You're my Savior, my Lord
You reign above all, like no other love
Warmth oozing through the deepest of cracks
Flames roar to call you God
You're my only dream, you're my only wish
My only song, my only hope
You are my one and only
My one desire
My heart lives for you
You and only…
YOU!!!

Only You— © Katelyn Kwiatkowski, 17

Salutation

1 Paul, a prisoner of Christ Jesus, and Timothy our brother,[a]

To Philemon our dear friend and co-worker, [2]to Apphia our sister,[b] to Archippus our fellow soldier, and to the church in your house:

3 Grace to you and peace from God our Father and the Lord Jesus Christ.

Philemon's Love and Faith

4 When I remember you[c] in my prayers, I always thank my God [5]because I hear of your love for all the saints and your faith toward the Lord Jesus. [6]I pray that the sharing of your faith may become effective when you perceive all the good that we[d] may do for Christ. [7]I have indeed received much joy and encouragement from your love, because the hearts of the saints have been refreshed through you, my brother.

Paul's Plea for Onesimus

8 For this reason, though I am bold enough in Christ to command you to do your duty, [9]yet I would rather appeal to you on the basis of love—and I, Paul, do this as an old man, and now also as a prisoner of Christ Jesus.[e] [10]I am appealing to you for my child, Onesimus, whose father I have become during my imprisonment. [11]Formerly he was useless to you, but now he is indeed useful[f] both to you and to me. [12]I am sending him, that is, my own heart, back to you. [13]I wanted to keep him with me, so that he might be of service to me in your place during my imprisonment for the gospel; [14]but I preferred to do nothing without your consent, in order that your good deed might be voluntary and not something forced. [15]Perhaps this is the reason he was separated from you for a while, so that you might have him back forever, [16]no longer as a slave but more than a slave, a beloved brother—especially to me but how much more to you, both in the flesh and in the Lord.

17 So if you consider me your partner, welcome him as you would welcome me. [18]If he has wronged you in any way, or owes you anything, charge that to my account. [19]I, Paul, am writing this with my own hand: I will repay it. I say nothing about your owing me even your own self. [20]Yes, brother, let me have this benefit from you in the Lord! Refresh my heart in

Christ. [21]Confident of your obedience, I am writing to you, knowing that you will do even more than I say.

22 One thing more—prepare a guest room for me, for I am hoping through your prayers to be restored to you.

Final Greetings and Benediction

23 Epaphras, my fellow prisoner in Christ Jesus, sends greetings to you,[g] [24]and so do Mark, Aristarchus, Demas, and Luke, my fellow workers.

25 The grace of the Lord Jesus Christ be with your spirit.[h]

---

a Gk the brother b Gk the sister c From verse 4 through verse 21, you is singular d Other ancient authorities read you (plural) e Or as an ambassador of Christ Jesus, and now also his prisoner f The name Onesimus means useful or (compare verse 20) beneficial g Here you is singular h Other ancient authorities add Amen

---

REALITY ✔

FREE TO LOVE

In this letter, Paul appeals to Philemon, a fellow believer, on behalf of Onesimus, a new convert and slave of Philemon. In fact, both men owe their conversion to Paul's efforts.

So Paul uses this fact to influence Philemon to accept Onesimus—not as his slave, but as a brother in Christ. By pleading with Philemon to accept Onesimus as a brother, Paul seeks to change their relationship from one of legality to one of love. Paul points to a new relationship that is deeper and more binding than any slave contract, that of communion in the Body of Christ.

Could Paul be talking to you and to the Church today? The letter has implications far beyond this private matter. What is our obligation to the immigrant? To the refugee? To Native Americans? To the homeless? To those outside your "in" crowd? How might Paul's appeal for partnership in the Lord influence your own prejudices?

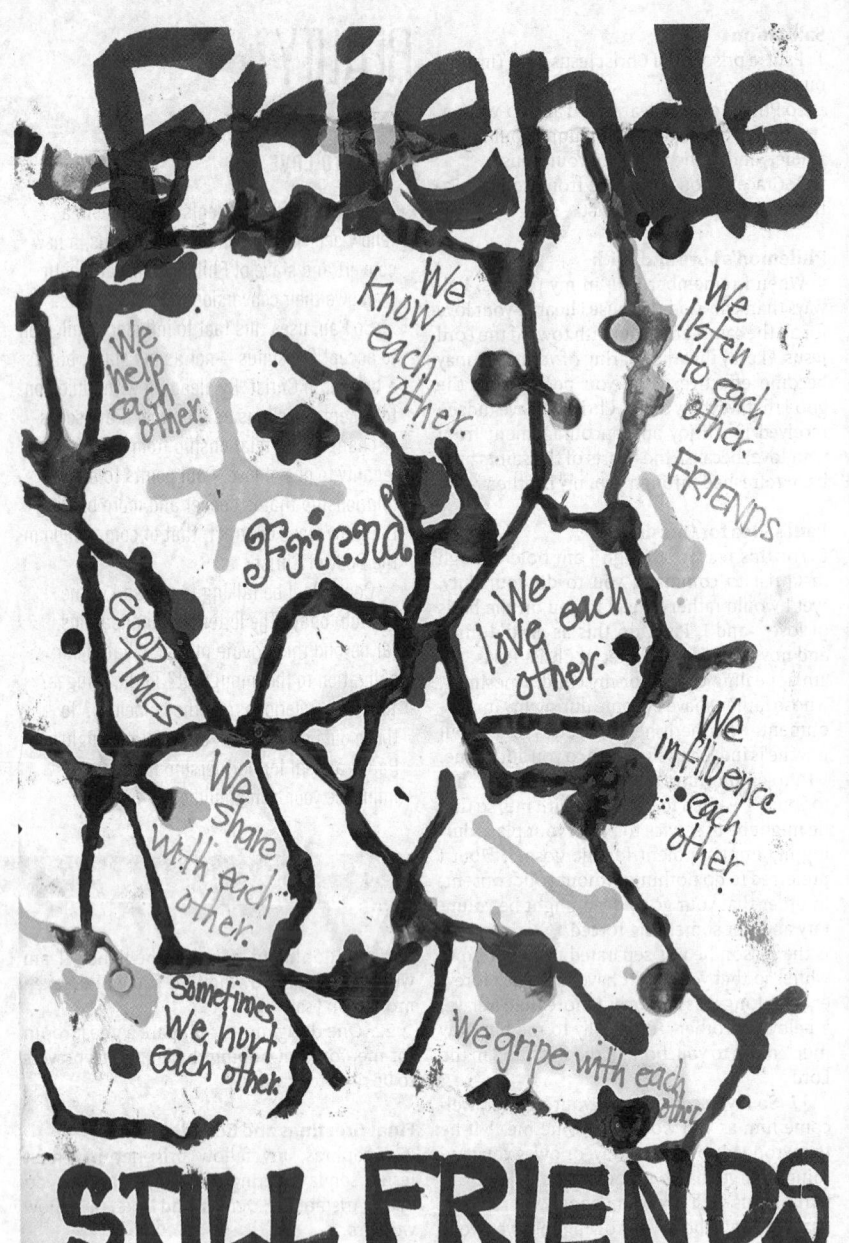

HEBREWS

ONE LIKE US

Me Too

Have you ever been in the middle of a crowd of people, but felt completely alone? Have you ever hungered just to know that someone knows you, knows what you're going through, and somehow cares? Yeah, we've all been there.

Perhaps the most powerful words in the English language are the words *me too*. Can anything be more comforting than knowing that someone understands and is standing with you?

The message of Hebrews is simply "You are not alone." This letter paints an amazing picture of a God who knows and understands what it's like to be us, because he became *one of us*. In Jesus, God wasn't just put on display for us to see. God stepped into the world and experienced what it's like to be you and me.

Can anything be more beautiful? Can anything be more loving?

No matter where you are, no matter what you've done, no matter what is happening in your life right now—God not only knows about it, but in a very real way he has experienced it too. Feeling alone? Misunderstood? Fragile? Unsure? Betrayed? Hurting? Humiliated? Jesus knows. He's been there before.

You see, the message of Hebrews is that God knows; he's been there before. And because of that, we can trust him: trust that he understands, trust that he's tasted it all before, and that when we are in those places of hurt and despair, we have someone who can step in and bring wholeness and healing exactly where we need it the most.

You are not alone.

"Faith is the firm foundation of all the virtues."

—St. Ambrose

WHO The author is anonymous.

WHAT Hebrews is more like a sermon than a letter, written to encourage the early Jewish Christian community to continue in faith and hope as they dealt with intense persecution.

WHEN Probably written between A.D. 60 and 70

WHERE No one knows for certain where this letter was written. The recipients of this letter may have lived in Alexandria (Egypt), Jerusalem, or possibly Rome.

PATH OF DISCIPLESHIP

When was the last time you cried? I mean *really* cried?

In John 11, Jesus is face-to-face with his friends Mary and Martha. This isn't another happy dinner at their house. This is a very different scene. They're devastated, exhausted, and heartbroken. Their beloved brother—and Jesus' close friend—Lazarus, has died.

Jesus doesn't preach a sermon or tell them to cheer up because a miracle's on the way. Instead, Jesus begins to weep (John 11.35). He cries . . . hard.

Jesus was *there* with Mary and Martha—not just physically, but emotionally too. He joined them in their sorrow. He deeply felt their loss. He cared about their fear, sorrow, and confusion. *He hurt too.* This scene, like many others in the Gospels, reveals the truth that Hebrews 4.15 emphasizes: Jesus truly understands our weaknesses . . . and he cares. As disciples, we are called to do the same with those around us.

1 God Has Spoken by His Son

Long ago God spoke to our ancestors in many and various ways by the prophets, [2] but in these last days he has spoken to us by a Son,[a] whom he appointed heir of all things, through whom he also created the worlds. [3] He is the reflection of God's glory and the exact imprint of God's very being, and he sustains[b] all things by his powerful word. When he had made purification for sins, he sat down at the right hand of the Majesty on high, [4] having become as much superior to angels as the name he has inherited is more excellent than theirs.

The Son Is Superior to Angels

5 For to which of the angels did God ever say,

"You are my Son;
today I have begotten you"?

Or again,

"I will be his Father,
and he will be my Son"?

[6] And again, when he brings the firstborn into the world, he says,

"Let all God's angels worship him."

[7] Of the angels he says,

"He makes his angels winds,
and his servants flames of fire."

[8] But of the Son he says,

"Your throne, O God, is[c] forever and ever,
and the righteous scepter is the scepter
of your[d] kingdom.
9 You have loved righteousness and hated
wickedness;
therefore God, your God, has anointed you
with the oil of gladness beyond your
companions."

[10] And,

"In the beginning, Lord, you founded the
earth,
and the heavens are the work of your
hands;
11 they will perish, but you remain;
they will all wear out like clothing;
12 like a cloak you will roll them up,
and like clothing[e] they will be changed.
But you are the same,
and your years will never end."

[13] But to which of the angels has he ever said,

"Sit at my right hand
until I make your enemies a footstool for
your feet"?

[14] Are not all angels[f] spirits in the divine service, sent to serve for the sake of those who are to inherit salvation?

2 Warning to Pay Attention

Therefore we must pay greater attention to what we have heard, so that we do not drift away from it. [2] For if the message declared through angels was valid, and every transgression or disobedience received a just penalty, [3] how can we escape if we neglect so great a salvation? It was declared at first through the Lord, and it was attested to us by those who heard him, [4] while God added his testimony by signs and wonders and various miracles, and by gifts of the Holy Spirit, distributed according to his will.

Exaltation through Abasement

5 Now God[g] did not subject the coming world, about which we are speaking, to angels. [6] But someone has testified somewhere,

"What are human beings that you are
mindful of them,[h]
or mortals, that you care for them?[i]
7 You have made them for a little while lower[j]
than the angels;
you have crowned them with glory and
honor,[k]
8 subjecting all things under their feet."

Now in subjecting all things to them, God[g] left nothing outside their control. As it is, we do not yet see everything in subjection to them, [9] but we do see Jesus, who for a little while was made lower[l] than the angels, now crowned with glory and honor because of the suffering of death, so that by the grace of God[m] he might taste death for everyone.

10 It was fitting that God,[g] for whom and through whom all things exist, in bringing many children to glory, should make the pioneer of their salvation perfect through sufferings. [11] For the one who sanctifies and those who are sanctified all have one Father.[n] For this reason Jesus[g] is not ashamed to call them brothers and sisters,[o] [12] saying,

"I will proclaim your name to my brothers
and sisters,[o]
in the midst of the congregation I will
praise you."

[13] And again,

"I will put my trust in him."

And again,

"Here am I and the children whom God has
given me."

14 Since, therefore, the children share flesh and blood, he himself likewise shared the same things, so that through death he

---

a Or *the Son* b Or *bears along* c Or *God is your throne* d Other ancient authorities read *his* e Other ancient authorities lack *like clothing* f Gk *all of them* g Gk *he* h Gk *What is man that you are mindful of him?* i Gk *or the son of man that you care for him?* In the Hebrew of Psalm 8.4–6 both *man* and *son of man* refer to all humankind j Or *them only a little lower* k Other ancient authorities add *and set them over the works of your hands* l Or *who was made a little lower* m Other ancient authorities read *apart from God* n Gk *are all of one* o Gk *brothers* might destroy the one who has the power of death, that is, the devil, [15]and free those who all their lives were held in slavery by the fear of death. [16]For it is clear that he did not come to help angels, but the descendants of Abraham. [17]Therefore he had to become like his brothers and sisters*ᵃ* in every respect, so that he might be a merciful and faithful high priest in the service of God, to make a sacrifice of atonement for the sins of the people. [18]Because he himself was tested by what he suffered, he is able to help those who are being tested.

3 Moses a Servant, Christ a Son

Therefore, brothers and sisters,*ᵃ* holy partners in a heavenly calling, consider that Jesus, the apostle and high priest of our confession, [2]was faithful to the one who appointed him, just as Moses also "was faithful in all*ᵇ* God's*ᶜ* house." [3]Yet Jesus*ᵈ* is worthy of more glory than Moses, just as the builder of a house has more honor than the house itself. [4](For every house is built by someone, but the builder of all things is God.) [5]Now Moses was faithful in all God's*ᶜ* house as a servant, to testify to the things that would be spoken later. [6]Christ, however, was faithful over God's*ᶜ* house as a son, and we are his house if we hold firm*ᵉ* the confidence and the pride that belong to hope.

Warning against Unbelief

7 Therefore, as the Holy Spirit says,
  "Today, if you hear his voice,
8 do not harden your hearts as in the rebellion,
   as on the day of testing in the wilderness,
9 where your ancestors put me to the test,
   though they had seen my works [10]for forty years.
  Therefore I was angry with that generation,
   and I said, 'They always go astray in their hearts,
   and they have not known my ways.'
11 As in my anger I swore,
   'They will not enter my rest.' "

[12]Take care, brothers and sisters,*ᵃ* that none of you may have an evil, unbelieving heart that turns away from the living God. [13]But exhort one another every day, as long as it is called "today," so that none of you may be hardened by the deceitfulness of sin. [14]For we have become partners of Christ, if only we hold our first confidence firm to the end. [15]As it is said,
  "Today, if you hear his voice,
  do not harden your hearts as in the rebellion."

a Gk *brothers* *b* Other ancient authorities lack *all* *c* Gk *his*
d Gk *this one* *e* Other ancient authorities add *to the end*

 TRY THIS

BEEN THERE, DONE THAT

Do you want to know one of the most important truths in the Bible? Jesus was 100 percent God . . . and he was also 100 percent human. Jesus experienced the things we all experience, except sin. He was flesh and blood and bone and he also experienced stress and pain; he felt joy and love. Jesus wasn't an ethereal being floating about with a halo over his head. He had muscle; he had sweat. He ate, bathed, and got dressed. He hammered nails. He hiked up hills. He laughed out loud.

He was *real*.

And grabbing hold of this truth that Jesus was a real human can make your faith strong, powerful, and steady. How? Read **Hebrews 2.14–18** and **4.14–16**.

When you face heartache, physical pain, or serious temptation, you can know Jesus has been there. Jesus faced hurt and temptation too. He knows what they're like. Not only can he relate to what you're going through, but he can help you face it with courage.

Close your eyes for a moment and imagine what Jesus might have been like when he was your age. Think creatively—what issues, challenges, or temptations do you think he may have faced? Consider some of the stuff you're facing right now; then imagine how Jesus might have dealt with similar situations.

And next time you feel hurt, tempted, or unsure of yourself, pray to Jesus—the Jesus who is real, who is present, and who knows what it's like.

GOD IS REAL   MY SELF

CREATIVE SPACE

¹⁶Now who were they who heard and yet were rebellious? Was it not all those who left Egypt under the leadership of Moses? ¹⁷But with whom was he angry forty years? Was it not those who sinned, whose bodies fell in the wilderness? ¹⁸And to whom did he swear that they would not enter his rest, if not to those who were disobedient? ¹⁹So we see that they were unable to enter because of unbelief.

4 The Rest That God Promised

Therefore, while the promise of entering his rest is still open, let us take care that none of you should seem to have failed to reach it. ²For indeed the good news came to us just as to them; but the message they heard did not benefit them, because they were not united by faith with those who listened.ᵃ ³For we who have believed enter that rest, just as Godᵇ has said,

"As in my anger I swore,
'They shall not enter my rest,' "

though his works were finished at the foundation of the world. ⁴For in one place it speaks about the seventh day as follows, "And God rested on the seventh day from all his works." ⁵And again in this place it says, "They shall not enter my rest." ⁶Since therefore it remains open for some to enter it, and those who formerly received the good news failed to enter because of disobedience, ⁷again he sets a certain day—"today"—saying through David much later, in the words already quoted,

"Today, if you hear his voice,
do not harden your hearts."

⁸For if Joshua had given them rest, Godᵇ would not speak later about another day. ⁹So then, a sabbath rest still remains for the people of God; ¹⁰for those who enter God's rest also cease from their labors as God did from his. ¹¹Let us therefore make every effort to enter that rest, so that no one may fall through such disobedience as theirs.

12 Indeed, the word of God is living and active, sharper than any two-edged sword, piercing until it divides soul from spirit, joints from marrow; it is able to judge the thoughts and intentions of the heart. ¹³And before him no creature is hidden, but all are naked and laid bare to the eyes of the one to whom we must render an account.

Jesus the Great High Priest

14 Since, then, we have a great high priest who has passed through the heavens, Jesus, the Son of God, let us hold fast to our confession. ¹⁵For we do not have a high priest who is unable to sympathize with our weaknesses, but we have one who in every respect has been testedᶜ as we are, yet without sin. ¹⁶Let us therefore approach the throne of grace with boldness, so that we may receive mercy and find grace to help in time of need.

5

Every high priest chosen from among mortals is put in charge of things pertaining to God on their behalf, to offer gifts and sacrifices for sins. ²He is able to deal gently with the ignorant and wayward, since he himself is subject to weakness; ³and because of this he must offer sacrifice for his own sins as well as for those of the people. ⁴And one does not presume to take this honor, but takes it only when called by God, just as Aaron was.

5 So also Christ did not glorify himself in becoming a high priest, but was appointed by the one who said to him,

"You are my Son,
today I have begotten you";
⁶as he says also in another place,
"You are a priest forever,
according to the order of Melchizedek."

7 In the days of his flesh, Jesusᵇ offered up prayers and supplications, with loud cries and tears, to the one who was able to save him from death, and he was heard because of his reverent submission. ⁸Although he was a Son, he learned obedience through what he suffered; ⁹and having been made perfect, he became the source of eternal salvation for all who obey him, ¹⁰having been designated by God a high priest according to the order of Melchizedek.

Warning against Falling Away

11 About thisᵈ we have much to say that is hard to explain, since you have become dull in understanding. ¹²For though by this time you ought to be teachers, you need someone to teach you again the basic elements of the oracles of God. You need milk, not solid food; ¹³for everyone who lives on milk, being still an infant, is unskilled in the word of righteousness. ¹⁴But solid food is for the mature, for those whose faculties have been trained by practice to distinguish good from evil.

6 The Peril of Falling Away

Therefore let us go on toward perfection,ᵉ leaving behind the basic teaching about Christ, and not laying again the foundation: repentance from dead works and faith toward God, ²instruction about baptisms, laying on of hands, resurrection of the dead, and eternal judgment. ³And we will doᶠ this, if God permits.

a Other ancient authorities read it did not meet with faith in those who listened b Gk he c Or tempted d Or him e Or toward maturity
f Other ancient authorities read let us do

⁴For it is impossible to restore again to repentance those who have once been enlightened, and have tasted the heavenly gift, and have shared in the Holy Spirit, ⁵and have tasted the goodness of the word of God and the powers of the age to come, ⁶and then have fallen away, since on their own they are crucifying again the Son of God and are holding him up to contempt. ⁷Ground that drinks up the rain falling on it repeatedly, and that produces a crop useful to those for whom it is cultivated, receives a blessing from God. ⁸But if it produces thorns and thistles, it is worthless and on the verge of being cursed; its end is to be burned over.

9 Even though we speak in this way, beloved, we are confident of better things in your case, things that belong to salvation. ¹⁰For God is not unjust; he will not overlook your work and the love that you showed for his sake*a* in serving the saints, as you still do. ¹¹And we want each one of you to show the same diligence so as to realize the full assurance of hope to the very end, ¹²so that you may not become sluggish, but imitators of those who through faith and patience inherit the promises.

The Certainty of God's Promise

13 When God made a promise to Abraham, because he had no one greater by whom to swear, he swore by himself, ¹⁴saying, "I will surely bless you and multiply you." ¹⁵And thus Abraham,*b* having patiently endured, obtained the promise. ¹⁶Human beings, of course, swear by someone greater than themselves, and an oath given as confirmation puts an end to all dispute. ¹⁷In the same way, when God desired to show even more clearly to the heirs of the promise the unchangeable character of his purpose, he guaranteed it by an oath, ¹⁸so that through two unchangeable things, in which it is impossible that God would prove false, we who have taken refuge might be strongly encouraged to seize the hope set before us. ¹⁹We have this hope, a sure and steadfast anchor of the soul, a hope that enters the inner shrine behind the curtain, ²⁰where Jesus, a forerunner on our behalf, has entered, having become a high priest forever according to the order of Melchizedek.

7 The Priestly Order of Melchizedek

This "King Melchizedek of Salem, priest of the Most High God, met Abraham as he was returning from defeating the kings and blessed him"; ²and to him Abraham apportioned "one-tenth of everything." His name, in the first place, means "king of righteousness"; next he is also

king of Salem, that is, "king of peace." ³Without father, without mother, without genealogy, having neither beginning of days nor end of life, but resembling the Son of God, he remains a priest forever.

4 See how great he is! Even*c* Abraham the patriarch gave him a tenth of the spoils. ⁵And those descendants of Levi who receive the priestly office have a commandment in the law to collect tithes*d* from the people, that is, from their kindred,*e* though these also are descended from Abraham. ⁶But this man, who does not belong to their ancestry, collected tithes*d* from Abraham and blessed him who had received the promises. ⁷It is beyond dispute that the inferior is blessed by the superior. ⁸In the one case, tithes are received by those who are mortal; in the other, by one of whom it is tes-

a Gk for his name b Gk he c Other ancient authorities lack Even d Or a tenth e Gk brothers tified that he lives. [9]One might even say that Levi himself, who receives tithes, paid tithes through Abraham, [10]for he was still in the loins of his ancestor when Melchizedek met him.

Another Priest, Like Melchizedek

[11] Now if perfection had been attainable through the levitical priesthood—for the people received the law under this priesthood—what further need would there have been to speak of another priest arising according to the order of Melchizedek, rather than one according to the order of Aaron? [12]For when there is a change in the priesthood, there is necessarily a change in the law as well. [13]Now the one of whom these things are spoken belonged to another tribe, from which no one has ever served at the altar. [14]For it is evident that our Lord was descended from Judah, and in connection with that tribe Moses said nothing about priests.

[15] It is even more obvious when another priest arises, resembling Melchizedek, [16]one who has become a priest, not through a legal requirement concerning physical descent, but through the power of an indestructible life. [17]For it is attested of him,

"You are a priest forever,
    according to the order of Melchizedek."
[18]There is, on the one hand, the abrogation of an earlier commandment because it was weak and ineffectual [19](for the law made nothing perfect); there is, on the other hand, the introduction of a better hope, through which we approach God.

[20] This was confirmed with an oath; for others who became priests took their office without an oath, [21]but this one became a priest with an oath, because of the one who said to him,

"The Lord has sworn
    and will not change his mind,
'You are a priest forever' "—
[22]accordingly Jesus has also become the guarantee of a better covenant.

[23] Furthermore, the former priests were many in number, because they were prevented by death from continuing in office; [24]but he holds his priesthood permanently, because he continues forever. [25]Consequently he is able for all time to save[a] those who approach God through him, since he always lives to make intercession for them.

[26] For it was fitting that we should have such a high priest, holy, blameless, undefiled, separated from sinners, and exalted above the heavens. [27]Unlike the other[b] high priests, he has no need to offer sacrifices day after day, first for his own sins, and then for those of the people; this he did once for all when he offered himself. [28]For the law appoints as high priests those who are subject to weakness, but the word of the oath, which came later than the law, appoints a Son who has been made perfect forever.

8 Mediator of a Better Covenant

Now the main point in what we are saying is this: we have such a high priest, one who is seated at the right hand of the throne of the Majesty in the heavens, [2]a minister in the sanctuary and the true tent[c] that the Lord, and not any mortal, has set up. [3]For every high priest is appointed to offer gifts and sacrifices; hence it is necessary for this priest also to have something to offer. [4]Now if he were on earth, he would not be a priest at all, since there are priests who offer gifts according to the law. [5]They offer worship in a sanctuary that is a sketch and shadow of the heavenly one; for Moses, when he was about to erect the tent,[c] was warned, "See that you make everything according to the pattern that was shown you on the mountain." [6]But Jesus[d] has now obtained a more excellent ministry, and to that degree he is the mediator of a better covenant, which has been enacted through better promises. [7]For if that first covenant had been faultless, there would have been no need to look for a second one.

[8] God[e] finds fault with them when he says:
"The days are surely coming, says the Lord,
    when I will establish a new covenant with
        the house of Israel
    and with the house of Judah;
[9] not like the covenant that I made with their
        ancestors,
    on the day when I took them by the hand
        to lead them out of the land of
        Egypt;
for they did not continue in my covenant,
    and so I had no concern for them, says
        the Lord.
[10] This is the covenant that I will make with
        the house of Israel
    after those days, says the Lord:
I will put my laws in their minds,
    and write them on their hearts,
and I will be their God,
    and they shall be my people.
[11] And they shall not teach one another
    or say to each other, 'Know the Lord,'
for they shall all know me,
    from the least of them to the greatest.

¹² For I will be merciful toward their
iniquities,
and I will remember their sins no more."
¹³In speaking of "a new covenant," he has
made the first one obsolete. And what is obsolete and growing old will soon disappear.

9 The Earthly and the Heavenly Sanctuaries

Now even the first covenant had regulations
for worship and an earthly sanctuary. ²For a
tent*a* was constructed, the first one, in which
were the lampstand, the table, and the bread of
the Presence;*b* this is called the Holy Place. ³Behind the second curtain was a tent*a* called the
Holy of Holies. ⁴In it stood the golden altar of
incense and the ark of the covenant overlaid on
all sides with gold, in which there were a golden urn holding the manna, and Aaron's rod
that budded, and the tablets of the covenant;
⁵above it were the cherubim of glory overshadowing the mercy seat.*c* Of these things we cannot speak now in detail.

6 Such preparations having been made,
the priests go continually into the first tent*a* to
carry out their ritual duties; ⁷but only the high
priest goes into the second, and he but once
a year, and not without taking the blood that
he offers for himself and for the sins committed unintentionally by the people. ⁸By this the
Holy Spirit indicates that the way into the sanctuary has not yet been disclosed as long as the
first tent*a* is still standing. ⁹This is a symbol*d* of
the present time, during which gifts and sacrifices are offered that cannot perfect the conscience of the worshiper, ¹⁰but deal only with
food and drink and various baptisms, regulations for the body imposed until the time
comes to set things right.

11 But when Christ came as a high priest of
the good things that have come,*e* then through
the greater and perfect*f* tent*a* (not made with
hands, that is, not of this creation), ¹²he entered once for all into the Holy Place, not with
the blood of goats and calves, but with his own
blood, thus obtaining eternal redemption. ¹³For
if the blood of goats and bulls, with the sprinkling of the ashes of a heifer, sanctifies those
who have been defiled so that their flesh is purified, ¹⁴how much more will the blood of Christ,
who through the eternal Spirit*g* offered himself
without blemish to God, purify our*h* conscience
from dead works to worship the living God!

15 For this reason he is the mediator of a
new covenant, so that those who are called
may receive the promised eternal inheritance,
because a death has occurred that redeems

JESUS SIGHTING

Imagine what it must
have been like for Jews
during ancient times. What
was it like to have to make
sacrifices—actual blood-and-
guts animal sacrifices—to "pay for" their
sins?

Each year they made the long trek
to Jerusalem. Their destination: the
Temple. The building was immense and
awe-inspiring. The air was filled with the
bleating of sheep, the smell of burning
flesh, and a rising plume of smoke, an
aroma for God's nose.

They changed the coins, paid the fees,
bought the animals, and offered the
sacrifices. This wasn't done to placate
God, but instead was the offering up of
the best they had out of love and loyalty
to God—a God who wished to be in union
with his people and whom they believed
was present among them.

What would bring an end to the need
for these blood sacrifices?

Hebrews 9.11–28 points to Jesus'
death on the cross as fulfillment of the
requirements of the Levitical sacrifices
and says that they're done—"once for
all." Jesus' death is the *final one*. No
more Temple or sacrifices; God has been
satisfied. Sin has been answered once
and for all in the blood of a more perfect
sacrifice than any that had ever come
before.

them from the transgressions under the first
covenant.*i* ¹⁶Where a will*i* is involved, the death
of the one who made it must be established.
¹⁷For a will*i* takes effect only at death, since it
is not in force as long as the one who made it
is alive. ¹⁸Hence not even the first covenant
was inaugurated without blood. ¹⁹For when
every commandment had been told to all the
people by Moses in accordance with the law,
he took the blood of calves and goats,*j* with wa-

a Or tabernacle *b* Gk *the presentation of the loaves* *c* Or *the place of atonement* *d* Gk *parable* *e* Other ancient authorities read *good things to*
come *f* Gk *more perfect* *g* Other ancient authorities read *Holy Spirit* *h* Other ancient authorities read *your* *i* The Greek word used here
means both *covenant* and *will* *j* Other ancient authorities lack *and goats*

"Greater love has no one than this, than to lay down one's life for his friends."
John 15:13

"I Love You"—© Katie Blum, 17

ter and scarlet wool and hyssop, and sprinkled both the scroll itself and all the people, ²⁰saying, "This is the blood of the covenant that God has ordained for you." ²¹And in the same way he sprinkled with the blood both the tent*ᵃ* and all the vessels used in worship. ²²Indeed, under the law almost everything is purified with blood, and without the shedding of blood there is no forgiveness of sins.

Christ's Sacrifice Takes Away Sin

23 Thus it was necessary for the sketches of the heavenly things to be purified with these rites, but the heavenly things themselves need better sacrifices than these. ²⁴For Christ did not enter a sanctuary made by human hands, a mere copy of the true one, but he entered into heaven itself, now to appear in the presence of God on our behalf. ²⁵Nor was it to offer himself again and again, as the high priest enters the Holy Place year after year with blood that is not his own; ²⁶for then he would have had to suffer again and again since the foundation of the world. But as it is, he has appeared once for all at the end of the age to remove sin by the sacrifice of himself. ²⁷And just as it is appointed for mortals to die once, and after that the judgment, ²⁸so Christ, having been offered once to bear the sins of many, will appear a second time, not to deal with sin, but to save those who are eagerly waiting for him.

10 Christ's Sacrifice Once for All

Since the law has only a shadow of the good things to come and not the true form of these realities, it*ᵇ* can never, by the same sacrifices that are continually offered year after year, make perfect those who approach. ²Otherwise, would they not have ceased being offered, since the worshipers, cleansed once for all, would no longer have any consciousness of sin? ³But in these sacrifices there is a reminder of sin year after year. ⁴For it is impossible for the blood of bulls and goats to take away sins. ⁵Consequently, when Christ*ᶜ* came into the world, he said,

"Sacrifices and offerings you have not desired,
    but a body you have prepared for me;
⁶ in burnt offerings and sin offerings
    you have taken no pleasure.
⁷ Then I said, 'See, God, I have come to do your will, O God'
    (in the scroll of the book*ᵈ* it is written of me)."

⁸When he said above, "You have neither desired nor taken pleasure in sacrifices and offerings and burnt offerings and sin offerings"

a Or tabernacle *b* Other ancient authorities read they *c* Gk he *d* Meaning of Gk uncertain (these are offered according to the law), ⁹then he added, "See, I have come to do your will." He abolishes the first in order to establish the second. ¹⁰And it is by God's will*ᵃ* that we have been sanctified through the offering of the body of Jesus Christ once for all.

11 And every priest stands day after day at his service, offering again and again the same sacrifices that can never take away sins. ¹²But when Christ*ᵇ* had offered for all time a single sacrifice for sins, "he sat down at the right hand of God," ¹³and since then has been waiting "until his enemies would be made a footstool for his feet." ¹⁴For by a single offering he has perfected for all time those who are sanctified. ¹⁵And the Holy Spirit also testifies to us, for after saying,

¹⁶ "This is the covenant that I will make with
     them
  after those days, says the Lord:
  I will put my laws in their hearts,
     and I will write them on their minds,"
¹⁷he also adds,
  "I will remember*ᶜ* their sins and their
     lawless deeds no more."
¹⁸Where there is forgiveness of these, there is no longer any offering for sin.

A Call to Persevere

19 Therefore, my friends,*ᵈ* since we have confidence to enter the sanctuary by the blood of Jesus, ²⁰by the new and living way that he opened for us through the curtain (that is, through his flesh), ²¹and since we have a great priest over the house of God, ²²let us approach with a true heart in full assurance of faith, with our hearts sprinkled clean from an evil conscience and our bodies washed with pure water. ²³Let us hold fast to the confession of our hope without wavering, for he who has promised is faithful. ²⁴And let us consider how to provoke one another to love and good deeds, ²⁵not neglecting to meet together, as is the habit of some, but encouraging one another, and all the more as you see the Day approaching.

26 For if we willfully persist in sin after having received the knowledge of the truth, there no longer remains a sacrifice for sins, ²⁷but a fearful prospect of judgment, and a fury of fire that will consume the adversaries. ²⁸Anyone who has violated the law of Moses dies without mercy "on the testimony of two or three witnesses." ²⁹How much worse punishment do you think will be deserved by those who have spurned the Son of God, profaned the blood

of the covenant by which they were sanctified, and outraged the Spirit of grace? ³⁰For we know the one who said, "Vengeance is mine, I will repay." And again, "The Lord will judge his people." ³¹It is a fearful thing to fall into the hands of the living God.

32 But recall those earlier days when, after you had been enlightened, you endured a hard struggle with sufferings, ³³sometimes being publicly exposed to abuse and persecution, and sometimes being partners with those so treated. ³⁴For you had compassion for those who were in prison, and you cheerfully accepted the plundering of your possessions, knowing that you yourselves possessed something better and more lasting. ³⁵Do not, therefore, abandon that confidence of yours; it brings a great reward. ³⁶For you need endurance, so that when you have done the will of God, you may receive what was promised. ³⁷For yet

  "in a very little while,
     the one who is coming will come and will
       not delay;
³⁸ but my righteous one will live by faith.
     My soul takes no pleasure in anyone who
       shrinks back."
³⁹But we are not among those who shrink back and so are lost, but among those who have faith and so are saved.

11   The Meaning of Faith

Now faith is the assurance of things hoped for, the conviction of things not seen. ²Indeed, by faith*ᵉ* our ancestors received approval. ³By faith we understand that the worlds were prepared by the word of God, so that what is seen was made from things that are not visible.*ᶠ*

The Examples of Abel, Enoch, and Noah

4 By faith Abel offered to God a more acceptable*ᵍ* sacrifice than Cain's. Through this he received approval as righteous, God himself giving approval to his gifts; he died, but through his faith*ʰ* he still speaks. ⁵By faith Enoch was taken so that he did not experience death; and "he was not found, because God had taken him." For it was attested before he was taken away that "he had pleased God." ⁶And without faith it is impossible to please God, for whoever would approach him must believe that he exists and that he rewards those who seek him. ⁷By faith Noah, warned by God about events as yet unseen, respected the warning and built an ark to save his household; by this he condemned the world and became

---

ᵃ Gk *by that will* ᵇ Gk *this one* ᶜ Gk *on their minds and I will remember* ᵈ Gk *Therefore, brothers* ᵉ Gk *by this* ᶠ Or *was not made out of visible things* ᵍ Gk *greater* ʰ Gk *through it*

A Triumphant Hope

Woe to the darkness who says to light,
"Your ways will not overcome me."
And woe to Death who says to Life,
"You shall surely know the taste of defeat!"

For even the bare and still trees of
winter shake with delight towards the
warm winds of spring;
and the dancing stars anticipate the glorious song
the dawn never ceases to sing.

I know the battles may seem never ending
and tears are always waiting to fall,
but the blessed soul rejoices with recognition
that the war is won after all.

So take care
tender spirit
when the night beckons and its sympathies
are none.
Take care,
and listen to the comforting whispers of the morn,
and turn to the victorious radiance of the sun.

A Triumphant Hope—© Ashly Stage, 18

an heir to the righteousness that is in accordance with faith.

The Faith of Abraham

8 By faith Abraham obeyed when he was called to set out for a place that he was to receive as an inheritance; and he set out, not knowing where he was going. ⁹By faith he stayed for a time in the land he had been promised, as in a foreign land, living in tents, as did Isaac and Jacob, who were heirs with him of the same promise. ¹⁰For he looked forward to the city that has foundations, whose architect and builder is God. ¹¹By faith he received power of procreation, even though he was too old—and Sarah herself was barren—because he considered him faithful who had promised.ᵃ ¹²Therefore from one person, and this one as good as dead, descendants were born, "as many as the stars of heaven and as the innumerable grains of sand by the seashore."

13 All of these died in faith without having received the promises, but from a distance they saw and greeted them. They confessed that they were strangers and foreigners on the earth, ¹⁴for people who speak in this way make it clear that they are seeking a homeland. ¹⁵If they had been thinking of the land that they had left behind, they would have had opportunity to return. ¹⁶But as it is, they desire a better country, that is, a heavenly one. Therefore God is not ashamed to be called their God; indeed, he has prepared a city for them.

17 By faith Abraham, when put to the test, offered up Isaac. He who had received the promises was ready to offer up his only son, ¹⁸of whom he had been told, "It is through Isaac that descendants shall be named for you." ¹⁹He considered the fact that God is able even to raise someone from the dead—and figuratively speaking, he did receive him back. ²⁰By faith Isaac invoked blessings for the future on Jacob and Esau. ²¹By faith Jacob, when dying, blessed each of the sons of Joseph, "bowing in worship over the top of his staff." ²²By faith Joseph, at the end of his life, made mention of the exodus of the Israelites and gave instructions about his burial.ᵇ

The Faith of Moses

23 By faith Moses was hidden by his parents for three months after his birth, because they saw that the child was beautiful; and they were not afraid of the king's edict.ᶜ ²⁴By faith Moses, when he was grown up, refused to be called a

son of Pharaoh's daughter, ²⁵choosing rather to share ill-treatment with the people of God than to enjoy the fleeting pleasures of sin. ²⁶He considered abuse suffered for the Christᵈ to be greater wealth than the treasures of Egypt, for he was looking ahead to the reward. ²⁷By faith he left Egypt, unafraid of the king's anger; for he persevered as thoughᵉ he saw him who is invisible. ²⁸By faith he kept the Passover and the sprinkling of blood, so that the destroyer of the firstborn would not touch the firstborn of Israel.ᶠ

The Faith of Other Israelite Heroes

29 By faith the people passed through the Red Sea as if it were dry land, but when the Egyptians attempted to do so they were drowned. ³⁰By faith the walls of Jericho fell after they had been encircled for seven days. ³¹By faith Rahab the prostitute did not perish with those who were disobedient,ᵍ because she had received the spies in peace.

32 And what more should I say? For time would fail me to tell of Gideon, Barak, Samson, Jephthah, of David and Samuel and the prophets— ³³who through faith conquered kingdoms, administered justice, obtained promises, shut the mouths of lions, ³⁴quenched raging fire, escaped the edge of the sword, won strength out of weakness, became mighty in war, put foreign armies to flight. ³⁵Women received their dead by resurrection. Others were tortured, refusing to accept release, in order to obtain a better resurrection. ³⁶Others suffered mocking and flogging, and even chains and imprisonment. ³⁷They were stoned to death, they were sawn in two,ʰ they were killed by the sword; they went about in skins of sheep and goats, destitute, persecuted, tormented— ³⁸of whom the world was not worthy. They wandered in deserts and mountains, and in caves and holes in the ground.

39 Yet all these, though they were commended for their faith, did not receive what was promised, ⁴⁰since God had provided something better so that they would not, apart from us, be made perfect.

12 The Example of Jesus

Therefore, since we are surrounded by so great a cloud of witnesses, let us also lay aside every weight and the sin that clings so closely,ⁱ and let us run with perseverance the race that is set before us, ²looking to Jesus the pioneer and perfecter of our faith, who for the sake ofʲ the

---

a Or By faith Sarah herself, though barren, received power to conceive, even when she was too old, because she considered him faithful who had promised.
b Gk his bones c Other ancient authorities add By faith Moses, when he was grown up, killed the Egyptian, because he observed the humiliation of his people (Gk brothers) d Or the Messiah e Or because f Gk would not touch them g Or unbelieving h Other ancient authorities add they were tempted i Other ancient authorities read sin that easily distracts j Or who instead of

joy that was set before him endured the cross, disregarding its shame, and has taken his seat at the right hand of the throne of God.

3 Consider him who endured such hostility against himself from sinners,[a] so that you may not grow weary or lose heart. 4In your struggle against sin you have not yet resisted to the point of shedding your blood. 5And you have forgotten the exhortation that addresses you as children—

"My child, do not regard lightly the
discipline of the Lord,
or lose heart when you are punished by
him;
6 for the Lord disciplines those whom he
loves,
and chastises every child whom he
accepts."

7Endure trials for the sake of discipline. God is treating you as children; for what child is there whom a parent does not discipline? 8If you do not have that discipline in which all children share, then you are illegitimate and not his children. 9Moreover, we had human parents to discipline us, and we respected them. Should we not be even more willing to be subject to the Father of spirits and live? 10For they disciplined us for a short time as seemed best to them, but he disciplines us for our good, in order that we may share his holiness. 11Now, discipline always seems painful rather than pleasant at the time, but later it yields the peaceful fruit of righteousness to those who have been trained by it.

12 Therefore lift your drooping hands and strengthen your weak knees, 13and make straight paths for your feet, so that what is lame may not be put out of joint, but rather be healed.

Warnings against Rejecting God's Grace

14 Pursue peace with everyone, and the holiness without which no one will see the Lord. 15See to it that no one fails to obtain the grace of God; that no root of bitterness springs up and causes trouble, and through it many become defiled. 16See to it that no one becomes like Esau, an immoral and godless person, who sold his birthright for a single meal. 17You know that later, when he wanted to inherit the blessing, he was rejected, for he found no chance to repent,[b] even though he sought the blessing[c] with tears.

18 You have not come to something[d] that can be touched, a blazing fire, and darkness, and gloom, and a tempest, 19and the sound of a trumpet, and a voice whose words made the hearers beg that not another word be spoken to them. 20(For they could not endure the order that was given, "If even an animal touches the mountain, it shall be stoned to death." 21Indeed, so terrifying was the sight that Moses said, "I tremble with fear.") 22But you have come to Mount Zion and to the city of the living God, the heavenly Jerusalem, and to innumerable angels in festal gathering, 23and to the assembly[e] of the firstborn who are enrolled in heaven, and to God the judge of all, and to the spirits of the righteous made perfect, 24and to Jesus, the mediator of a new covenant, and to the sprinkled blood that speaks a better word than the blood of Abel.

25 See that you do not refuse the one who is speaking; for if they did not escape when they refused the one who warned them on earth, how much less will we escape if we reject the one who warns from heaven! 26At that time his voice shook the earth; but now he has promised, "Yet once more I will shake not only the earth but also the heaven." 27This phrase, "Yet once more," indicates the removal of what is shaken—that is, created things—so that what cannot be shaken may remain. 28Therefore, since we are receiving a kingdom that cannot be shaken, let us give thanks, by which we offer to God an acceptable worship with reverence and awe; 29for indeed our God is a consuming fire.

13 Service Well-Pleasing to God

Let mutual love continue. 2Do not neglect to show hospitality to strangers, for by doing that some have entertained angels without knowing it. 3Remember those who are in prison, as though you were in prison with them; those who are being tortured, as though you yourselves were being tortured.[f] 4Let marriage be held in honor by all, and let the marriage bed be kept undefiled; for God will judge fornicators and adulterers. 5Keep your lives free from the love of money, and be content with what you have; for he has said, "I will never leave you or forsake you." 6So we can say with confidence,

---

a Other ancient authorities read such hostility from sinners against themselves b Or no chance to change his father's mind c Gk it d Other ancient authorities read a mountain e Or angels, and to the festal gathering 23and assembly f Gk were in the body

"The Lord is my helper;
   I will not be afraid.
What can anyone do to me?"

7 Remember your leaders, those who spoke the word of God to you; consider the outcome of their way of life, and imitate their faith. [8]Jesus Christ is the same yesterday and today and forever. [9]Do not be carried away by all kinds of strange teachings; for it is well for the heart to be strengthened by grace, not by regulations about food,[a] which have not benefited those who observe them. [10]We have an altar from which those who officiate in the tent[b] have no right to eat. [11]For the bodies of those animals whose blood is brought into the sanctuary by the high priest as a sacrifice for sin are burned outside the camp. [12]Therefore Jesus also suffered outside the city gate in order to sanctify the people by his own blood. [13]Let us then go to him outside the camp and bear the abuse he endured. [14]For here we have no lasting city, but we are looking for the city that is to come. [15]Through him, then, let us continually offer a sacrifice of praise to God, that is, the fruit of lips that confess his name. [16]Do not neglect to do good and to share what you have, for such sacrifices are pleasing to God.

17 Obey your leaders and submit to them, for they are keeping watch over your souls and will give an account. Let them do this with joy and not with sighing—for that would be harmful to you.

18 Pray for us; we are sure that we have a clear conscience, desiring to act honorably in all things. [19]I urge you all the more to do this, so that I may be restored to you very soon.

Benediction

20 Now may the God of peace, who brought back from the dead our Lord Jesus, the great shepherd of the sheep, by the blood of the eternal covenant, [21]make you complete in everything good so that you may do his will, working among us[c] that which is pleasing in his sight, through Jesus Christ, to whom be the glory forever and ever. Amen.

Final Exhortation and Greetings

22 I appeal to you, brothers and sisters,[d] bear with my word of exhortation, for I have written to you briefly. [23]I want you to know that our brother Timothy has been set free; and if he comes in time, he will be with me when I see you. [24]Greet all your leaders and all the saints. Those from Italy send you greetings. [25]Grace be with all of you.[e]

a Gk not by foods b Or tabernacle c Other ancient authorities read you d Gk brothers e Other ancient authorities add Amen

REALITY ✔

WITNESS PROTECTION PROGRAM

How many times have you heard the stories of your ancestors? You know—Great-Uncle Joe, the war hero. Grandma Mary, the amazing cook. Great-Grandpa Bob, who signed something important. Blah, blah, blah.
And how many times have they been retold as inspirational tales, with the purpose of inspiring *you* to imitate their good deeds and works?

Hebrews does that too. It tells us to persevere in the faith like our spiritual ancestors did. Read **Hebrews 11.1** and **12.1**. Who are the "witnesses" who have influenced you and increased your faith? Write their names here:

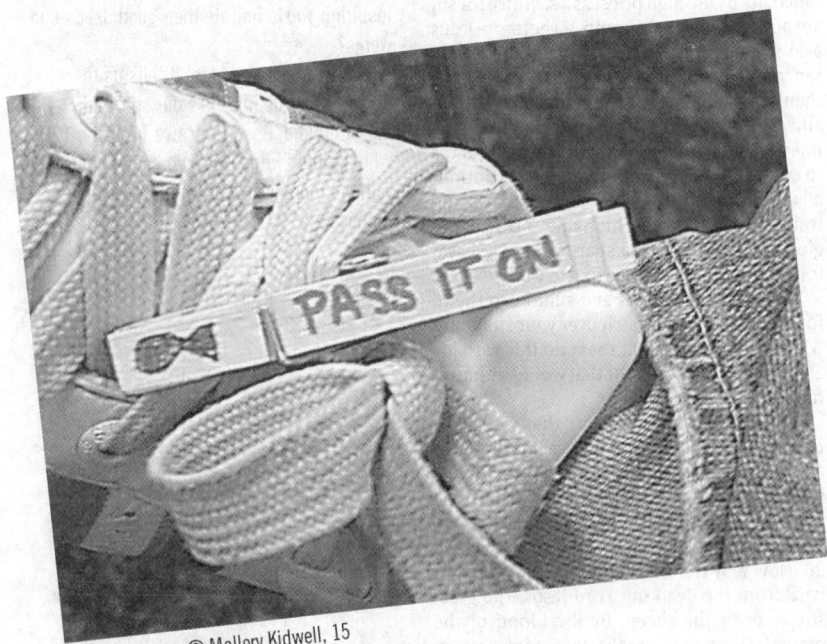

Pass It On—© Mallory Kidwell, 15

JAMES

ACTION, NOT WORDS!

The Right Balance

Does it matter how you act as a Christian?

Some people have the impression that James and Paul offer opposing answers to this question. They think Paul says no, our actions don't matter, and that James says yes, they do. After all, James is famous for pointing out that faith without actions is dead (James 2.26). Paul, on the other hand, is well known for stressing that we're saved by grace, not by our own actions (Ephesians 2.8–9). Hey, sounds like they're gearing up for a fight! In the red corner, we have James. In the blue corner, we have Paul, missionary extraordinaire. Who will win? Who's right?

In fact, they both are. They're just outlining the traps that we so easily fall into. James makes the point that real faith will be expressed in acts of love, courage, and mercy. If those actions aren't there, you have to question whether the faith is. If you read Paul's letters, you'll soon discover that he and James really do agree on this point. But Paul goes to great lengths to stress that there is nothing we can do to make God love us more. We can't buy our salvation by impressing him with our good deeds.

Which of these views do you tend to distort? Do you think that you have to earn God's approval by doing good things? Or do you live like everyone else because you know God will forgive anything you do wrong? It's important to know, to be able to hold one truth in each hand, and to live a life of vibrant balance.

> *"Faith is a habit of mind, which begins eternal life in us, and induces a reasonable assent to things unseen."*
>
> —St. Thomas Aquinas

WHO James, the leader of the Church in Jerusalem, or another writer who used his name

WHAT James' message is clear and to the point: if your faith doesn't affect what you do and the way you live, then you might as well not bother.

WHEN It is unknown when this book was written.

WHERE Written to Christians all over the Mediterranean world

PATH OF DISCIPLESHIP

In Matthew 7.24–27, Jesus told a story about two men building houses—one on rock and one on sand. When the storm came, you know which one stayed standing. It's no good just listening to what Jesus said. We need to put it into practice.

Having a relationship with Jesus is not an accessory we wear like a badge. It needs to permeate every part of who we are: to affect our attitude toward money, our decisions about careers, the way we relate to others, our plans for the future. We need to let it get way under our skin, to the heart of who we are. It needs to be the foundation we build every aspect of our lives upon. That may not be very comfortable at times, but it's the only way to live a life that counts.

How do you live your life as a disciple? Is your faith built on rock or sand?

The Rose—© Catherine Willms, 15

1 Salutation

James, a servant[a] of God and of the Lord Jesus Christ,

To the twelve tribes in the Dispersion:
Greetings.

Faith and Wisdom

2 My brothers and sisters,[b] whenever you face trials of any kind, consider it nothing but joy, [3]because you know that the testing of your faith produces endurance; [4]and let endurance have its full effect, so that you may be mature and complete, lacking in nothing.

5 If any of you is lacking in wisdom, ask God, who gives to all generously and ungrudgingly, and it will be given you. [6]But ask in faith, never doubting, for the one who doubts is like a wave of the sea, driven and tossed by the wind; [7, 8]for the doubter, being double-minded and unstable in every way, must not expect to receive anything from the Lord.

Poverty and Riches

9 Let the believer[c] who is lowly boast in being raised up, [10]and the rich in being brought low, because the rich will disappear like a flower in the field. [11]For the sun rises with its scorching heat and withers the field; its flower falls, and its beauty perishes. It is the same way with the rich; in the midst of a busy life, they will wither away.

Trial and Temptation

12 Blessed is anyone who endures temptation. Such a one has stood the test and will receive the crown of life that the Lord[d] has promised to those who love him. [13]No one,

when tempted, should say, "I am being tempted by God"; for God cannot be tempted by evil and he himself tempts no one. [14]But one is tempted by one's own desire, being lured and enticed by it; [15]then, when that desire has conceived, it gives birth to sin, and that sin, when it is fully grown, gives birth to death. [16]Do not be deceived, my beloved.[e]

17 Every generous act of giving, with every perfect gift, is from above, coming down from the Father of lights, with whom there is no variation or shadow due to change.[f] [18]In fulfillment of his own purpose he gave us birth by the word of truth, so that we would become a kind of first fruits of his creatures.

Hearing and Doing the Word

19 You must understand this, my beloved:[e] let everyone be quick to listen, slow to speak, slow to anger; [20]for your anger does not produce God's righteousness. [21]Therefore rid yourselves of all sordidness and rank growth of wickedness, and welcome with meekness the implanted word that has the power to save your souls.

22 But be doers of the word, and not merely hearers who deceive themselves. [23]For if any are hearers of the word and not doers, they are like those who look at themselves[g] in a mirror; [24]for they look at themselves and, on going away, immediately forget what they were like. [25]But those who look into the perfect law, the law of liberty, and persevere, being not hearers who forget but doers who act—they will be blessed in their doing.

26 If any think they are religious, and do not bridle their tongues but deceive their hearts, their religion is worthless. [27]Religion that is pure and undefiled before God, the Father, is this: to care for orphans and widows in their distress, and to keep oneself unstained by the world.

2 Warning against Partiality

My brothers and sisters,[h] do you with your acts of favoritism really believe in our glorious Lord Jesus Christ?[i] [2]For if a person with gold rings and in fine clothes comes into your assembly, and if a poor person in dirty clothes also comes in, [3]and if you take notice of the one wearing the fine clothes and say, "Have a seat here, please," while to the one who is poor you say, "Stand there," or, "Sit at my feet,"[j] [4]have you not made distinctions among yourselves, and become judges with evil thoughts? [5]Listen, my beloved brothers and sisters.[b] Has not

God chosen the poor in the world to be rich in faith and to be heirs of the kingdom that he has promised to those who love him? [6]But you have dishonored the poor. Is it not the rich who oppress you? Is it not they who drag you into court? [7]Is it not they who blaspheme the excellent name that was invoked over you?

[8] You do well if you really fulfill the royal law according to the scripture, "You shall love your neighbor as yourself." [9]But if you show partiality, you commit sin and are convicted by the law as transgressors. [10]For whoever keeps the whole law but fails in one point has become accountable for all of it. [11]For the one who said, "You shall not commit adultery," also said, "You shall not murder." Now if you do not commit adultery but if you murder, you have become a transgressor of the law. [12]So speak and so act as those who are to be judged by the law of liberty. [13]For judgment will be without mercy to anyone who has shown no mercy; mercy triumphs over judgment.

Faith without Works Is Dead

[14] What good is it, my brothers and sisters,[a] if you say you have faith but do not have works? Can faith save you? [15]If a brother or sister is naked and lacks daily food, [16]and one of you says to them, "Go in peace; keep warm and eat your fill," and yet you do not supply their bodily needs, what is the good of that? [17]So faith by itself, if it has no works, is dead.

[18] But someone will say, "You have faith and I have works." Show me your faith apart from your works, and I by my works will show you my faith. [19]You believe that God is one; you do well. Even the demons believe—and shudder. [20]Do you want to be shown, you senseless person, that faith apart from works is barren? [21]Was not our ancestor Abraham justified by works when he offered his son Isaac on the altar? [22]You see that faith was active along with his works, and faith was brought to completion by the works. [23]Thus the scripture was fulfilled that says, "Abraham believed God, and it was reckoned to him as righteousness," and he was called the friend of God. [24]You see that a person is justified by works and not by faith alone. [25]Likewise, was not Rahab the prostitute also justified by works when she welcomed the messengers and sent them out by another road? [26]For just as the body without the spirit is dead, so faith without works is also dead.

3 Taming the Tongue

Not many of you should become teachers, my brothers and sisters,[a] for you know that we who teach will be judged with greater strictness. [2]For all of us make many mistakes. Anyone who makes no mistakes in speaking is perfect, able to keep the whole body in check with a bridle. [3]If we put bits into the mouths of horses to make them obey us, we guide their whole bodies. [4]Or look at ships: though they are so large that it takes strong winds to drive them, yet they are guided by a very small rudder wherever the will of the pilot directs. [5]So also the tongue is a small member, yet it boasts of great exploits.

How great a forest is set ablaze by a small fire! [6]And the tongue is a fire. The tongue is placed among our members as a world of iniquity; it stains the whole body, sets on fire the cycle of nature,[b] and is itself set on fire by hell.[c] [7]For every species of beast and bird, of reptile

a Gk brothers b Or wheel of birth c Gk Gehenna

JAMES 3

My God

I have a feeling that He is all around me.
It is not just a feeling; it is the truth.
My God is always with me.
My God is my strength.
When he provides me strength,
   I provide my *self*...
I am willing to give all of myself
   as He gave himself for us all.

My God—© Amanda Eatman, 16

and sea creature, can be tamed and has been tamed by the human species, [8]but no one can tame the tongue—a restless evil, full of deadly poison. [9]With it we bless the Lord and Father, and with it we curse those who are made in the likeness of God. [10]From the same mouth come blessing and cursing. My brothers and sisters,[a] this ought not to be so. [11]Does a spring pour forth from the same opening both fresh and brackish water? [12]Can a fig tree, my brothers and sisters,[b] yield olives, or a grapevine figs? No more can salt water yield fresh.

Two Kinds of Wisdom

13 Who is wise and understanding among you? Show by your good life that your works are done with gentleness born of wisdom. [14]But if you have bitter envy and selfish ambition in your hearts, do not be boastful and false to the truth. [15]Such wisdom does not come down from above, but is earthly, unspiritual, devilish. [16]For where there is envy and selfish ambition, there will also be disorder and wickedness of every kind. [17]But the wisdom from above is first pure, then peaceable, gentle, willing to yield, full of mercy and good fruits, without a trace of partiality or hypocrisy. [18]And a harvest of righteousness is sown in peace for[c] those who make peace.

4 Friendship with the World

Those conflicts and disputes among you, where do they come from? Do they not come from your cravings that are at war within you? [2]You want something and do not have it; so you commit murder. And you covet[d] something and cannot obtain it; so you engage in disputes and conflicts. You do not have, because you do not ask. [3]You ask and do not receive, because you ask wrongly, in order to spend what you get on your pleasures. [4]Adulterers! Do you not know that friendship with the world is enmity with God? Therefore whoever wishes to be a friend of the world becomes an enemy of God. [5]Or do you suppose that it is for nothing that the scripture says, "God[e] yearns jealously for the spirit that he has made to dwell in us"? [6]But he gives all the more grace; therefore it says,

"God opposes the proud,
    but gives grace to the humble."

[7]Submit yourselves therefore to God. Resist the devil, and he will flee from you. [8]Draw near to God, and he will draw near to you. Cleanse your hands, you sinners, and purify your hearts, you double-minded. [9]Lament and mourn and weep. Let your laughter be turned into mourn-

ing and your joy into dejection. [10]Humble yourselves before the Lord, and he will exalt you.

Warning against Judging Another

11 Do not speak evil against one another, brothers and sisters.[f] Whoever speaks evil against another or judges another, speaks evil against the law and judges the law; but if you judge the law, you are not a doer of the law but a judge. [12]There is one lawgiver and judge who is able to save and to destroy. So who, then, are you to judge your neighbor?

Boasting about Tomorrow

13 Come now, you who say, "Today or tomorrow we will go to such and such a town and spend a year there, doing business and making money." [14]Yet you do not even know what tomorrow will bring. What is your life? For you are a mist that appears for a little while and then vanishes. [15]Instead you ought to say, "If the Lord wishes, we will live and do this or that." [16]As it is, you boast in your arrogance; all such boasting is evil. [17]Anyone, then, who knows the right thing to do and fails to do it, commits sin.

5 Warning to Rich Oppressors

Come now, you rich people, weep and wail for the miseries that are coming to you. [2]Your riches have rotted, and your clothes are motheaten. [3]Your gold and silver have rusted, and their rust will be evidence against you, and it will eat your flesh like fire. You have laid up treasure[g] for the last days. [4]Listen! The wages of the laborers who mowed your fields, which you kept back by fraud, cry out, and the cries of the harvesters have reached the ears of the Lord of hosts. [5]You have lived on the earth in luxury and in pleasure; you have fattened your hearts in a day of slaughter. [6]You have condemned and murdered the righteous one, who does not resist you.

Patience in Suffering

7 Be patient, therefore, beloved,[f] until the coming of the Lord. The farmer waits for the precious crop from the earth, being patient with it until it receives the early and the late

---

a Gk *My brothers* *b* Gk *my brothers* *c* Or *by* *d* Or *you murder and you covet* *e* Gk *He* *f* Gk *brothers* *g* Or *will eat your flesh, since you have stored up fire*

> "Action speaks louder than words but not nearly as often."
>
> —Mark Twain

SACRAMENTS OF HEALING

Read **James 5.13**. Here James tells his community to call the elders to pray and anoint the sick with oil, and if they have sinned their sins will be forgiven. Then he encourages them to tell their sins to one another and pray for each other.

Forgiveness of sins and healing the sick were a significant part of Jesus' mission. He wanted the communities that grew up around him and formed the Church to continue that mission as individuals and as a community. Today the Church gives the Sacraments of Penance and the Anointing of the Sick the title Sacraments of Healing.

One of the elements of healing and forgiveness in James' letter is the role of the community. With the revision of the rites of all the sacraments after the Second Vatican Council, an emphasis was placed once again on the role of the community in the celebration of these sacraments. This renewed emphasis is why parishes offer communal celebrations of Penance, especially during the seasons of Advent and Lent. It's also why the Sacrament of the Sick is often celebrated with the community during a celebration of the Eucharist.

rains. ⁸You also must be patient. Strengthen your hearts, for the coming of the Lord is near.ᵃ ⁹Beloved,ᵇ do not grumble against one another, so that you may not be judged. See, the Judge is standing at the doors! ¹⁰As an example of suffering and patience, beloved,ᶜ take the prophets who spoke in the name of the Lord. ¹¹Indeed we call blessed those who showed endurance. You have heard of the endurance of Job, and you have seen the purpose of the Lord, how the Lord is compassionate and merciful.

12 Above all, my beloved,ᶜ do not swear, either by heaven or by earth or by any other oath, but let your "Yes" be yes and your "No" be no, so that you may not fall under condemnation.

The Prayer of Faith

13 Are any among you suffering? They should pray. Are any cheerful? They should sing songs of praise. ¹⁴Are any among you sick? They should call for the elders of the church and have them pray over them, anointing them with oil in the name of the Lord. ¹⁵The prayer of faith will save the sick, and the Lord will raise them up; and anyone who has committed sins will be forgiven. ¹⁶Therefore confess your sins to one another, and pray for one another, so that you may be healed. The prayer of the righteous is powerful and effective. ¹⁷Elijah was a human being like us, and he prayed fervently that it might not rain, and for three years and six months it did not rain on the earth. ¹⁸Then he prayed again, and the heaven gave rain and the earth yielded its harvest.

19 My brothers and sisters,ᵈ if anyone among you wanders from the truth and is brought back by another, ²⁰you should know that whoever brings back a sinner from wandering will save the sinner'sᵉ soul from death and will cover a multitude of sins.

ᵃ Or is at hand ᵇ Gk Brothers ᶜ Gk brothers ᵈ Gk My brothers
ᵉ Gk his

Follow—© Maggie Hubbard, 16

1 PETER

WHO CARES?

This Might Hurt a Little . . .

Ever been in a place where you felt like you just didn't belong? Like you're the outsider who just couldn't fit in? Like everyone seemed to be picking on you?

The earliest Christians felt exactly like that. And they weren't just being paranoid. Jesus' followers faced hostility and violence on a regular basis. They suffered in every way imaginable—they were publicly scorned, beaten, thrown in prison, even killed, all for their faith in Christ.

But Peter had good news for these downtrodden Christians. He reminded them, in the middle of all their trials and tribulations, that God cared about them. He even went so far as to tell them to welcome their hardships with open arms, because it would make their faith stronger.

That sounds a bit like your mom telling you to eat your slimy Brussels sprouts because they're good for you. No one actually enjoys going through hard times. But Jesus never promised the easy life for those who believe in him. In fact, when we choose sides with Jesus, sometimes the world becomes our antagonist.

If you're experiencing a difficult time in your life, read 1 Peter. Then *pray* through 1 Peter. You'll feel a lot better. Promise.

> *"Do not be held back by doubts or fears. . . . Say 'yes' with courage and without reserve."*
>
> —Pope John Paul II

WHO Some Scripture scholars say Peter wrote this letter. Other scholars think someone else wrote the letter and attributed it to Peter.

WHAT Since Christians were starting to experience a dangerous increase in persecution, Peter encouraged them to be courageous and stay faithful.

WHEN Likely written sometime between A.D. 70 and 90

WHERE The letter was written for Christians dispersed throughout Asia Minor (modern-day Turkey).

PATH OF DISCIPLESHIP

What is the meaning behind Christian Baptism? 1 Peter expresses some of the clearest teachings on Baptism in the New Testament. Baptism is a birth into the life of Christ and assumes that you'll face moments of change and conversion throughout your lifetime. This means that there will be times when you'll choose to separate yourself from people, places, and things to grow more Christlike—that may mean keeping your distance from peers who are making negative choices, turning down an invitation to a party where you know alcohol will be served, or tossing your death-metal CDs.

Sometimes, these choices may cause suffering—ridicule, rejection, or even being put down in front of your friends by peers who don't understand your choices. But as disciples we are called to rejoice in that suffering, for in our suffering, we come to understand the fullness of God's love.

First You Must Give Your Insecurities to Him —
© Eliza German, 20

TRY THIS

SET APART

The Bible says some scary things. Like this: "Be holy yourselves in all your conduct; for it is written, 'You shall be holy, for I am holy'" (1 Peter 1.15).

It seems as if the Bible is asking us to be Superman (or Wonder Woman, whichever you prefer). After all, God is totally, absolutely, 100 percent *perfect*. And if we're supposed to be just like him . . . well, that sounds impossible! Does God really expect us never to screw up again? Does he require perfection?

Not even. To be holy means to be "set apart." Not perfect. *Set apart*. Being holy isn't just some long list of dos and don'ts. It means being specially selected for a specific purpose.

Read the big picture in **1 Peter 1.13–25**. Jesus paid a high price—his very life—to make it possible for you to be set apart from the world's traps and garbage. You could read verse 16 this way: "You must be *set apart*, because I am *set apart*."

Find your parents' fine china and hold one of the plates in your hands. (*Carefully!*) Then think about how this plate is "set apart" from the other dishes. What makes it special? Unique? Now think about your life. How are you set apart from the rest of the world?

GOD IS ONE AND ONLY   MY SELF

1 Salutation

Peter, an apostle of Jesus Christ,

To the exiles of the Dispersion in Pontus, Galatia, Cappadocia, Asia, and Bithynia, [2]who have been chosen and destined by God the Father and sanctified by the Spirit to be obedi-ent to Jesus Christ and to be sprinkled with his blood:

May grace and peace be yours in abundance.

A Living Hope

3 Blessed be the God and Father of our Lord Jesus Christ! By his great mercy he has given us a new birth into a living hope through the res-urrection of Jesus Christ from the dead, [4]and into an inheritance that is imperishable, un-defiled, and unfading, kept in heaven for you, [5]who are being protected by the power of God through faith for a salvation ready to be re-vealed in the last time. [6]In this you rejoice,[a] even if now for a little while you have had to suffer various trials, [7]so that the genuineness of your faith—being more precious than gold that, though perishable, is tested by fire—may be found to result in praise and glory and hon-or when Jesus Christ is revealed. [8]Although you have not seen[b] him, you love him; and even though you do not see him now, you believe in him and rejoice with an indescribable and glo-rious joy, [9]for you are receiving the outcome of your faith, the salvation of your souls.

10 Concerning this salvation, the proph-ets who prophesied of the grace that was to be yours made careful search and inquiry, [11]inquiring about the person or time that the Spirit of Christ within them indicated when it testified in advance to the sufferings destined for Christ and the subsequent glory. [12]It was revealed to them that they were serving not themselves but you, in regard to the things that have now been announced to you through those who brought you good news by the Holy Spirit sent from heaven—things into which angels long to look!

A Call to Holy Living

13 Therefore prepare your minds for action;[c] discipline yourselves; set all your hope on the grace that Jesus Christ will bring you when he is revealed. [14]Like obedient children, do not be conformed to the desires that you formerly had in ignorance. [15]Instead, as he who called you is holy, be holy yourselves in all your con-duct; [16]for it is written, "You shall be holy, for I am holy."

17 If you invoke as Father the one who judges all people impartially according to their deeds, live in reverent fear during the time of your exile. [18]You know that you were ransomed from the futile ways inherited from your ances-tors, not with perishable things like silver or gold, [19]but with the precious blood of Christ, like that of a lamb without defect or blemish.

a Or *Rejoice in this* *b* Other ancient authorities read *known* *c* Gk *gird up the loins of your mind*

²⁰He was destined before the foundation of the world, but was revealed at the end of the ages for your sake. ²¹Through him you have come to trust in God, who raised him from the dead and gave him glory, so that your faith and hope are set on God.

22 Now that you have purified your souls by your obedience to the truth[a] so that you have genuine mutual love, love one another deeply[b] from the heart.[c] ²³You have been born anew, not of perishable but of imperishable seed, through the living and enduring word of God.[d] ²⁴For

"All flesh is like grass
    and all its glory like the flower of grass.
The grass withers,
    and the flower falls,
²⁵ but the word of the Lord endures forever."

That word is the good news that was announced to you.

2 The Living Stone and a Chosen People

Rid yourselves, therefore, of all malice, and all guile, insincerity, envy, and all slander. ²Like newborn infants, long for the pure, spiritual milk, so that by it you may grow into salvation— ³if indeed you have tasted that the Lord is good.

4 Come to him, a living stone, though rejected by mortals yet chosen and precious in God's sight, and ⁵like living stones, let yourselves be built[e] into a spiritual house, to be a holy priesthood, to offer spiritual sacrifices acceptable to God through Jesus Christ. ⁶For it stands in scripture:

"See, I am laying in Zion a stone,
    a cornerstone chosen and precious;
and whoever believes in him[f] will not be
        put to shame."

⁷To you then who believe, he is precious; but for those who do not believe,

"The stone that the builders rejected
    has become the very head of the corner,"

⁸and

"A stone that makes them stumble,
    and a rock that makes them fall."

They stumble because they disobey the word, as they were destined to do.

9 But you are a chosen race, a royal priesthood, a holy nation, God's own people,[g] in order that you may proclaim the mighty acts of him who called you out of darkness into his marvelous light.

¹⁰ Once you were not a people,
    but now you are God's people;
once you had not received mercy,
    but now you have received mercy.

Live as Servants of God

11 Beloved, I urge you as aliens and exiles to abstain from the desires of the flesh that wage war against the soul. ¹²Conduct yourselves honorably among the Gentiles, so that, though they malign you as evildoers, they may see your honorable deeds and glorify God when he comes to judge.[h]

13 For the Lord's sake accept the authority of every human institution,[i] whether of the emperor as supreme, ¹⁴or of governors, as sent

---

a Other ancient authorities add *through the Spirit* b Or *constantly* c Other ancient authorities read *a pure heart* d Or *through the word of the living and enduring God* e Or *you yourselves are being built* f Or *it* g Gk *a people for his possession* h Gk *God on the day of visitation* i Or *every institution ordained for human beings* by him to punish those who do wrong and to praise those who do right. ¹⁵For it is God's will that by doing right you should silence the ignorance of the foolish. ¹⁶As servants*a* of God, live as free people, yet do not use your freedom as a pretext for evil. ¹⁷Honor everyone. Love the family of believers.*b* Fear God. Honor the emperor.

The Example of Christ's Suffering

18 Slaves, accept the authority of your masters with all deference, not only those who are kind and gentle but also those who are harsh. ¹⁹For it is a credit to you if, being aware of God, you endure pain while suffering unjustly. ²⁰If you endure when you are beaten for doing wrong, what credit is that? But if you endure when you do right and suffer for it, you have God's approval. ²¹For to this you have been called, because Christ also suffered for you, leaving you an example, so that you should follow in his steps.

²² "He committed no sin,
and no deceit was found in his mouth."

²³When he was abused, he did not return abuse; when he suffered, he did not threaten; but he entrusted himself to the one who judges justly. ²⁴He himself bore our sins in his body on the cross,*c* so that, free from sins, we might live for righteousness; by his wounds*d* you have been healed. ²⁵For you were going astray like sheep, but now you have returned to the shepherd and guardian of your souls.

3 Wives and Husbands

Wives, in the same way, accept the authority of your husbands, so that, even if some of them do not obey the word, they may be won over without a word by their wives' conduct, ²when they see the purity and reverence of your lives. ³Do not adorn yourselves outwardly by braiding your hair, and by wearing gold ornaments or fine clothing; ⁴rather, let your adornment be the inner self with the lasting beauty of a gentle and quiet spirit, which is very precious in God's sight. ⁵It was in this way long ago that the holy women who hoped in God used to adorn themselves by accepting the authority of their husbands. ⁶Thus Sarah obeyed Abraham and called him lord. You have become her daughters as long as you do what is good and never let fears alarm you.

7 Husbands, in the same way, show consideration for your wives in your life together, paying honor to the woman as the weaker sex,*e* since they too are also heirs of the gracious gift of life—so that nothing may hinder your prayers.

Suffering for Doing Right

8 Finally, all of you, have unity of spirit, sympathy, love for one another, a tender heart, and a humble mind. ⁹Do not repay evil for evil or abuse for abuse; but, on the contrary, repay with a blessing. It is for this that you were called—that you might inherit a blessing. ¹⁰For

"Those who desire life
and desire to see good days,
let them keep their tongues from evil
and their lips from speaking deceit;
¹¹ let them turn away from evil and do good;
let them seek peace and pursue it.
¹² For the eyes of the Lord are on the
righteous,
and his ears are open to their prayer.
But the face of the Lord is against those
who do evil."

13 Now who will harm you if you are eager to do what is good? ¹⁴But even if you do suffer for doing what is right, you are blessed. Do not fear what they fear,*f* and do not be intimidated; ¹⁵but in your hearts sanctify Christ as Lord. Always be ready to make your defense to anyone who demands from you an accounting for the hope that is in you; ¹⁶yet do it with gentleness and reverence.*g* Keep your conscience clear, so that, when you are maligned, those who abuse you for your good conduct in Christ may be put to shame. ¹⁷For it is better to suffer for doing good, if suffering should be God's will, than to suffer for doing evil. ¹⁸For Christ also suffered*h* for sins once for all, the righteous for the unrighteous, in order to bring you*i* to God. He was put to death in the flesh, but made alive in the spirit, ¹⁹in which also he went and made a proclamation to the spirits in prison, ²⁰who in former times did not obey, when God waited patiently in the days of Noah, during the building of the ark, in which a few, that is, eight persons, were saved through water. ²¹And baptism, which this prefigured, now saves you—not as a removal of dirt from the body, but as an appeal to God for*j* a good conscience, through the resurrection of Jesus Christ, ²²who has gone into heaven and is at the right hand of God, with angels, authorities, and powers made subject to him.

4 Good Stewards of God's Grace

Since therefore Christ suffered in the flesh,*k* arm yourselves also with the same intention (for whoever has suffered in the flesh has fin-

---

a Gk *slaves* b Gk *Love the brotherhood* c Or *carried up our sins in his body to the tree* d Gk *bruise* e Gk *vessel* f Gk *their fear* g Or *respect* h Other ancient authorities read *died* i Other ancient authorities read *us* j Or *a pledge to God from* k Other ancient authorities add *for us*; others, *for you*

SLOW

"CONVERSION FOR ME WAS NOT A DAMASCUS ROAD EXPERIENCE. I SLOWLY MOVED INTO AN INTELLECTUAL ACCEPTANCE OF WHAT MY INTUITION HAD ALWAYS KNOWN."

—Madeleine L'Engle, author of *A Wrinkle in Time*

God is Father, Son, and Spirit? I'm confused. Why does God make it so complicated? I'm trying to wrap my head around the idea of a three-in-one God, but it just doesn't make sense.

"Trinity" means three in one. It's a word that doesn't ever actually appear in the Bible, but it's a big part of what we believe as Christians. Let's get one thing straight. Christians *don't* worship three different "Gods." We believe in only one God. Isaiah 44.6 makes this clear: "I am the first and I am the last; besides me there is no god."

But here's the mysterious part: God is fully expressed in relationship to us as three. Peter emphasizes the different "Persons" of God several times in this letter. One example that points out some of the unique roles of each part of the Trinity is when he describes the Christians addressed in this letter as "chosen and destined by God the Father and sanctified by the Spirit to be obedient to Jesus Christ" (1 Peter 1.2). You'll find more references to the three aspects of God in 1 Peter 3.18 and 4.14.

Peter didn't come up with this idea himself—it's woven throughout the Bible. In fact, Jesus himself pointed to the truth of the Trinity when he commanded his followers to make disciples, "baptizing them in the name of the Father and of the Son and of the Holy Spirit" (Matthew 28.19).

Let's just be honest. God *is* mysterious. And the Trinity is mysterious. And it's okay to live with mystery. We don't have to fear the mysterious parts of faith or explain them away (see 1 Corinthians 13.12). So what are your questions about the Trinity? Does it seem to defy logic to you? If so, is that okay? Is there a metaphor or image that helps you understand the Trinity? Why is the Trinity an important distinction of the Christian faith? Does your faith encompass the whole Trinity, or do you usually just focus on one or two aspects of who God is? How has God the Father played a role in your life? How about Jesus, the Son? In what ways have you experienced the presence of the Holy Spirit? How do you feel about living with mystery as part of your faith?

Find some Creative Space in this Bible and write your thoughts about the Trinity. Be sure to jot down your own questions about the Trinity. Then talk to a trusted friend who shares your faith about your thoughts and questions.

(Want to explore more? Read Luke 1.35; John 14.7, 9–10, 26; 2 Corinthians 13.14; 1 Peter 1.2; 3.18; 4.14; and 1 John 5.6–7.)

---

ished with sin), [2] so as to live for the rest of your earthly life[a] no longer by human desires but by the will of God. [3] You have already spent enough time in doing what the Gentiles like to do, living in licentiousness, passions, drunkenness, revels, carousing, and lawless idolatry. [4] They are surprised that you no longer join them in the same excesses of dissipation, and so they blaspheme.[b] [5] But they will have to give an accounting to him who stands ready to judge the living and the dead. [6] For this is the reason the gospel was proclaimed even to the dead, so that, though they had been judged in the flesh as everyone is judged, they might live in the spirit as God does.

[7] The end of all things is near;[c] therefore be serious and discipline yourselves for the sake of your prayers. [8] Above all, maintain constant love for one another, for love covers a multitude of sins. [9] Be hospitable to one another without complaining. [10] Like good stewards of the manifold grace of God, serve one another with whatever gift each of you has received. [11] Whoever speaks must do so as one speaking the very words of God; whoever serves must do so with the strength that God supplies, so that God may be glorified in all things through Jesus Christ. To him belong the glory and the power forever and ever. Amen.

a Gk *rest of the time in the flesh* *b* Or *they malign you* *c* Or *is at hand*

Suffering as a Christian

12 Beloved, do not be surprised at the fiery ordeal that is taking place among you to test you, as though something strange were happening to you. [13]But rejoice insofar as you are sharing Christ's sufferings, so that you may also be glad and shout for joy when his glory is revealed. [14]If you are reviled for the name of Christ, you are blessed, because the spirit of glory,[a] which is the Spirit of God, is resting on you.[b] [15]But let none of you suffer as a murderer, a thief, a criminal, or even as a mischief maker. [16]Yet if any of you suffers as a Christian, do not consider it a disgrace, but glorify God because you bear this name. [17]For the time has come for judgment to begin with the household of God; if it begins with us, what will be the end for those who do not obey the gospel of God? [18]And

"If it is hard for the righteous to be saved,
what will become of the ungodly and the sinners?"

[19]Therefore, let those suffering in accordance with God's will entrust themselves to a faithful Creator, while continuing to do good.

5 Tending the Flock of God

Now as an elder myself and a witness of the sufferings of Christ, as well as one who shares in the glory to be revealed, I exhort the elders among you [2]to tend the flock of God that is in your charge, exercising the oversight,[c] not under compulsion but willingly, as God would have you do it[d]—not for sordid gain but eager-ly. [3]Do not lord it over those in your charge, but be examples to the flock. [4]And when the chief shepherd appears, you will win the crown of glory that never fades away. [5]In the same way, you who are younger must accept the authority of the elders.[e] And all of you must clothe yourselves with humility in your dealings with one another, for

"God opposes the proud,
but gives grace to the humble."

6 Humble yourselves therefore under the mighty hand of God, so that he may exalt you in due time. [7]Cast all your anxiety on him, because he cares for you. [8]Discipline yourselves, keep alert.[f] Like a roaring lion your adversary the devil prowls around, looking for someone to devour. [9]Resist him, steadfast in your faith, for you know that your brothers and sisters[g] in all the world are undergoing the same kinds of suffering. [10]And after you have suffered for a little while, the God of all grace, who has called you to his eternal glory in Christ, will himself restore, support, strengthen, and establish you. [11]To him be the power forever and ever. Amen.

Final Greetings and Benediction

12 Through Silvanus, whom I consider a faithful brother, I have written this short letter to encourage you and to testify that this is the true grace of God. Stand fast in it. [13]Your sister church[h] in Babylon, chosen together with you, sends you greetings; and so does my son Mark. [14]Greet one another with a kiss of love.

Peace to all of you who are in Christ.[i]

---

a Other ancient authorities add *and of power* *b* Other ancient authorities add *On their part he is blasphemed, but on your part he is glorified* *c* Other ancient authorities lack *exercising the oversight* *d* Other ancient authorities lack *as God would have you do it* *e* Or *of those who are older* *f* Or *be vigilant* *g* Gk *your brotherhood* *h* Gk *She who is* *i* Other ancient authorities add *Amen*

Storm of Birds—© Justin Dawes, 15

2 PETER

Dodgeball

Life is like a never-ending game of dodgeball. No matter where you go, you're bombarded with messages about what to do with your life. Buy this product. Go to that movie. Eat this food. Look like that person. Do this activity. Question that authority. It's constant. And it's confusing.

You can duck and dodge and run all you want, but a lot of those messages are going to hit you square in the face. Or worse, square in the heart.

It wasn't much different two thousand years ago. Even though the early Christians worked hard to do and believe the right things, they too were blitzed with one harmful message after another. It was the same kind of stuff—subtle but dangerous suggestions for focusing on themselves rather than Jesus. Many early Christians were attracted—and distracted—by these wayward notions.

But Peter saw right through these "false teachers" and their foolish beliefs. He even called them "irrational animals" and "waterless springs and mists driven by a storm" (2 Peter 2.12, 17). He had very strong words for people who teach and promote beliefs that contradict the Bible. Peter wasn't a big fan of theological dodgeball.

If you're ever uncertain about whether something is in line with your Christian beliefs, read 2 Peter. You'll be on your way to avoiding the world's barrage of lies.

"God's precepts are light to the loving, heavy to the fearful."
—St. Thomas Aquinas

WHO Some Scripture scholars say Peter wrote this letter. Other scholars think someone else wrote the letter and attributed it to Peter.

WHAT While 1 Peter focuses on external dangers to Christians, 2 Peter centers on the internal dangers of buying into twisted teachings and false ideas about God and Christianity.

WHEN Written around A.D. 80–90

WHERE Unknown

PATH OF DISCIPLESHIP

Almost every time Peter refers to Jesus in this letter, he calls him "Lord." Most people don't use "lord" much in their everyday conversations, but here it has a lot of meaning. The word "lord" means "master" or "a person of power." The fact that Peter calls Jesus "Lord" so much in this book is significant because of the subject he's talking about: Christian beliefs. Being confident and steadfast in your beliefs comes down to one thing: Who's going to be the person of power in your life? Who's in charge of you? Is it a human leader who merely claims to know everything, or the Lord Jesus, who actually does?

I ♥ the Ocean—© Charlotte Katheder, 16

"Dear God, Thank you
for the ocean. Whenever
I go to the beach, I have
fun in the ocean. When I
watch the sunset on the
horizon, it always reminds
me of how much you love
me. It is a great symbol
of your love for the world.
Whenever I see it, I think
of you and how much I
appreciate everything
you do."

—Melissa Smith, 14,
Catholic high school student

1

Salutation

Simeon[a] Peter, a servant[b] and apostle of Jesus Christ,

To those who have received a faith as precious as ours through the righteousness of our God and Savior Jesus Christ:[c]

2 May grace and peace be yours in abundance in the knowledge of God and of Jesus our Lord.

The Christian's Call and Election

3 His divine power has given us everything needed for life and godliness, through the knowledge of him who called us by[d] his own glory and goodness. 4Thus he has given us, through these things, his precious and very great promises, so that through them you may escape from the corruption that is in the world because of lust, and may become participants of the divine nature. 5For this very reason, you must make every effort to support your faith with goodness, and goodness with knowledge, 6and knowledge with self-control, and self-control with endurance, and endurance with godliness, 7and godliness with mutual[e] affection, and mutual[e] affection with love. 8For if these things are yours and are increasing among you, they keep you from being ineffective and unfruitful in the knowledge of our Lord Jesus Christ. 9For anyone who lacks these things is short-sighted and blind, and is forgetful of the cleansing of past sins. 10Therefore, brothers and sisters,[f] be all the more eager to confirm your call and election, for if you do this, you will never stumble. 11For in this way, entry into the eternal kingdom of our Lord and Savior Jesus Christ will be richly provided for you.

12 Therefore I intend to keep on reminding you of these things, though you know them already and are established in the truth that has come to you. 13I think it right, as long as I am in this body,[g] to refresh your memory, 14since I know that my death[h] will come soon, as indeed our Lord Jesus Christ has made clear to me. 15And I will make every effort so that after my departure you may be able at any time to recall these things.

Eyewitnesses of Christ's Glory

16 For we did not follow cleverly devised myths when we made known to you the power and coming of our Lord Jesus Christ, but we had been eyewitnesses of his majesty. 17For he received honor and glory from God the Father when that voice was conveyed to him by the Majestic Glory, saying, "This is my Son, my Beloved,[i] with whom I am well pleased." 18We ourselves heard this voice come from heaven, while we were with him on the holy mountain.

19 So we have the prophetic message more fully confirmed. You will do well to be attentive to this as to a lamp shining in a dark place, until the day dawns and the morning star rises in your hearts. 20First of all you must understand this, that no prophecy of scripture is a matter of one's own interpretation, 21because no prophecy ever came by human will, but men and women moved by the Holy Spirit spoke from God.[j]

2

False Prophets and Their Punishment

But false prophets also arose among the people, just as there will be false teachers among you, who will secretly bring in destructive opinions. They will even deny the Master who bought them—bringing swift destruction on themselves. 2Even so, many will follow their licentious ways, and because of these teachers[k] the way of truth will be maligned. 3And in their greed they will exploit you with deceptive words. Their condemnation, pronounced against them long ago, has not been idle, and their destruction is not asleep.

4 For if God did not spare the angels when they sinned, but cast them into hell[l] and committed them to chains[m] of deepest darkness to be kept until the judgment; 5and if he did not spare the ancient world, even though he saved Noah, a herald of righteousness, with seven others, when he brought a flood on a world of the ungodly; 6and if by turning the cities of Sodom and Gomorrah to ashes he condemned them to extinction[n] and made them an example of what is coming to the ungodly;[o] 7and if he rescued Lot, a righteous man greatly distressed by the licentiousness of the lawless 8(for that righteous man, living among them day after day, was tormented in his righteous soul by their lawless deeds that he saw and heard), 9then the Lord knows how to rescue the godly from trial, and to keep the unrighteous under punishment until the day of judgment 10—especially those who indulge their flesh in depraved lust, and who despise authority.

Bold and willful, they are not afraid to slander the glorious ones,[p] 11whereas angels, though

a Other ancient authorities read *Simon* b Gk *slave* c Or *of our God and the Savior Jesus Christ* d Other ancient authorities read *through* e Gk *brotherly* f Gk *brothers* g Gk *tent* h Gk *the putting off of my tent* i Other ancient authorities read *my beloved Son* j Other ancient authorities read *but moved by the Holy Spirit saints of God spoke* k Gk *because of them* l Gk *Tartaros* m Other ancient authorities read *pits* n Other ancient authorities lack *to extinction* o Other ancient authorities read *an example to those who were to be ungodly* p Or *angels*; Gk *glories*

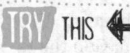
PATIENCE, PLEASE

When someone promises to meet you at a specific time, you expect that person to do it. Anything less leaves you feeling offended or hurt. Sitting in a café watching the door, hoping your date shows, is exactly zero fun.

Read **2 Peter 3.9**. So what does this verse say about God showing up as promised?

He's not taking his sweet time for the sake of watching us wait. Rather, he delays his return so that we can *benefit* from the delay. So the entire *world* can benefit from hearing about his Son.

God's not really keeping us waiting. Quite the opposite. *He's* waiting for *us* to finish the job we accepted when we became believers. He called us to change the world for him and with his help (see Matthew 28.18–20).

Fortunately, God doesn't get offended and impatient as easily as we do.

Using a bar of soap or tube of lipstick, write "Use the time" on your bathroom mirror where you'll see it first thing tomorrow morning. Then live the day as if you believe it.

GOD IS PASSIONATE MY WORLD

greater in might and power, do not bring against them a slanderous judgment from the Lord.[a] [12]These people, however, are like irrational animals, mere creatures of instinct, born to be caught and killed. They slander what they do not understand, and when those creatures are destroyed,[b] they also will be destroyed, [13]suffering[c] the penalty for doing wrong. They count it a pleasure to revel in the daytime. They are blots and blemishes, reveling in their dissipation[d] while they feast with you. [14]They have eyes full of adultery, insatiable for sin. They entice unsteady souls. They have hearts trained in greed. Accursed children! [15]They have left the straight road and have gone astray, following the road of Balaam son of Bosor,[e] who loved the wages of doing wrong, [16]but was rebuked for his own transgression; a speechless donkey spoke with a human voice and restrained the prophet's madness.

17 These are waterless springs and mists driven by a storm; for them the deepest darkness has been reserved. [18]For they speak bombastic nonsense, and with licentious desires of the flesh they entice people who have just[f] escaped from those who live in error. [19]They promise them freedom, but they themselves are slaves of corruption; for people are slaves to whatever masters them. [20]For if, after they have escaped the defilements of the world through the knowledge of our Lord and Savior Jesus Christ, they are again entangled in them and overpowered, the last state has become worse for them than the first. [21]For it would have been better for them never to have known the way of righteousness than, after knowing it, to turn back from the holy commandment that was passed on to them. [22]It has happened to them according to the true proverb,

"The dog turns back to its own vomit," and,

"The sow is washed only to wallow in the mud."

3 The Promise of the Lord's Coming

This is now, beloved, the second letter I am writing to you; in them I am trying to arouse your sincere intention by reminding you [2]that you should remember the words spoken in the past by the holy prophets, and the commandment of the Lord and Savior spoken through your apostles. [3]First of all you must understand this, that in the last days scoffers will come, scoffing and indulging their own lusts [4]and saying, "Where is the promise of his coming? For ever since our ancestors died,[g] all things continue as they were from the beginning of creation!" [5]They deliberately ignore this fact, that by the word of God heavens existed long ago and an earth was formed out of water and by means of water, [6]through which the world of that time was deluged with water and perished. [7]But by the same word the present heavens and earth have been reserved for fire, being kept until the day of judgment and destruction of the godless.

8 But do not ignore this one fact, beloved, that with the Lord one day is like a thousand years, and a thousand years are like one day. [9]The Lord is not slow about his promise, as some think of slowness, but is patient with you,[h] not wanting any to perish, but all to come to repentance. [10]But the day of the Lord will come like a thief, and then the heavens will pass away with a loud noise, and the elements will be dissolved with fire, and the earth and everything that is done on it will be disclosed.[i]

11 Since all these things are to be dissolved

---

a Other ancient authorities read *before the Lord*; others lack the phrase b Gk *in their destruction* c Other ancient authorities read *receiving* d Other ancient authorities read *love-feasts* e Other ancient authorities read *Beor* f Other ancient authorities read *actually* g Gk *our fathers fell asleep* h Other ancient authorities read *on your account* i Other ancient authorities read *will be burned up* in this way, what sort of persons ought you to be in leading lives of holiness and godliness, [12]waiting for and hastening[a] the coming of the day of God, because of which the heavens will be set ablaze and dissolved, and the elements will melt with fire? [13]But, in accordance with his promise, we wait for new heavens and a new earth, where righteousness is at home.

Final Exhortation and Doxology

14 Therefore, beloved, while you are waiting for these things, strive to be found by him at peace, without spot or blemish; [15]and regard the patience of our Lord as salvation. So also our beloved brother Paul wrote to you according to the wisdom given him, [16]speaking of this as he does in all his letters. There are some things in them hard to understand, which the ignorant and unstable twist to their own destruction, as they do the other scriptures. [17]You therefore, beloved, since you are forewarned, beware that you are not carried away with the error of the lawless and lose your own stability. [18]But grow in the grace and knowledge of our Lord and Savior Jesus Christ. To him be the glory both now and to the day of eternity. Amen.[b]

a Or *earnestly desiring* *b* Other ancient authorities lack *Amen*

REALITY ✔

STRENGTH FOR THE JOURNEY

This letter seeks to strengthen readers in faith and hope for the future. Read it and see. It calls on you to maintain faith and hope in the promised Second Coming. It reassures you that the Word of God is to be trusted by recalling the promises of God from the beginning of creation.

Read **2 Peter 3.17–18**. Those verses are timeless. They're speaking to *you:* "You therefore, beloved, since you are forewarned, beware that you are not carried away with the error of the lawless and lose your own stability. But grow in the grace and knowledge of our Lord and Savior Jesus Christ."

Who or what encourages you when your faith is shaken? In what ways can you encourage others to trust in God's promises? Journal about it, and share your thoughts at **Learner.CalltoDiscipleship.com**.

CREATIVE SPACE

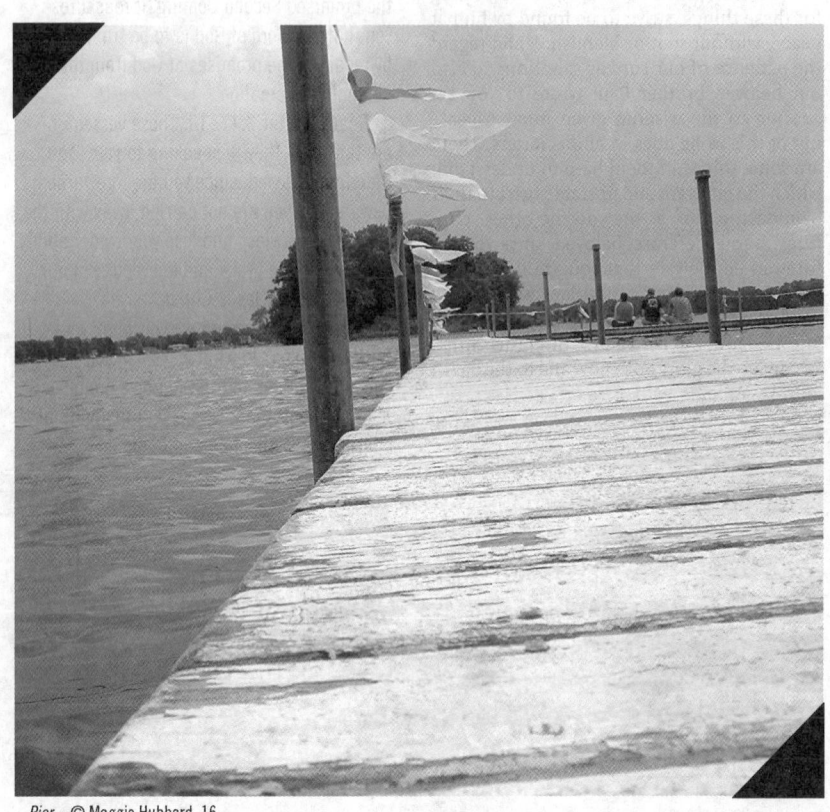

Pier—© Maggie Hubbard, 16

1 JOHN

A DIFFERENT KIND OF LOVE LETTER

Words to Savor

Does anyone even send letters anymore (a.k.a. snail mail)? The mail still comes every day, but so often it's filled with catalogs and pizza coupons—nothing from anyone you know. Text messages and e-mails abound, but when a real letter does arrive, it's an event. You may rip it open or wait to savor it, but you will read it from beginning to end. Now imagine receiving a letter from a best friend on your worst day ever. This begins to describe how eager the recipients of 1 John were to hear from John.

Yet the letter, however eagerly awaited, is only part of the story. What makes letters such a joy are the *words* of someone from far away, giving news and encouragement. John gave news about his situation and encouraged his friends and fellow Christians to turn away from false teaching. John speaks kindly and hopefully to his friends in Asia Minor, reminding them of their unique relationship with Jesus, the Son of God, and encouraging them to live out this knowledge in the way they treat one another.

In the same way, this letter is to you. Though your geographical and chronological situation is wildly different, John's encouragement to love in spite of tough circumstances can still make a difference. So whether you read frantically or leisurely, here's a letter for you.

"The most beautiful act of faith is the one made in darkness, in sacrifice, and with extreme effort."
—St. Padre Pio

WHO Anonymous, but probably written by someone from the same "school" as the author of the gospel of John

WHAT A letter to encourage several groups of Christians to take heart, be strong, and show courageous love and faith in Jesus as the divine Son of God

WHEN Written around A.D. 100

WHERE Ephesus, a city in what is now modern-day Turkey

PATH OF DISCIPLESHIP

Think about the people you really love. Who are they? Why do you love them? Then think about the people who sometimes annoy you, the ones you're able to love only some of the time. Who are they? What makes your love sporadic?

Now think about the people you definitely do *not* love—the ones you cannot forgive, the ones who drive you crazy, or the ones you can't stand to be in the same room with.

Now say, "Those who say, 'I love God,' and hate their brothers or sisters, are liars; for those who do not love a brother or sister whom they have seen, cannot love God whom they have not seen" (1 John 4.20). Think about what you need to change in yourself to love God by loving others—*all* others—more.

1 The Word of Life

We declare to you what was from the beginning, what we have heard, what we have seen with our eyes, what we have looked at and touched with our hands, concerning the word of life— ²this life was revealed, and we have seen it and testify to it, and declare to you the eternal life that was with the Father and was revealed to us— ³we declare to you what we have seen and heard so that you also may have fellowship with us; and truly our fellowship is with the Father and with his Son Jesus Christ. ⁴We are writing these things so that our*a* joy may be complete.

God Is Light

5 This is the message we have heard from him and proclaim to you, that God is light and in him there is no darkness at all. ⁶If we say that we have fellowship with him while we are walking in darkness, we lie and do not do what is true; ⁷but if we walk in the light as he himself is in the light, we have fellowship with one another, and the blood of Jesus his Son cleanses us from all sin. ⁸If we say that we have no sin, we deceive ourselves, and the truth is not in us. ⁹If we confess our sins, he who is faithful and just will forgive us our sins and cleanse us from all unrighteousness. ¹⁰If we say that we have not sinned, we make him a liar, and his word is not in us.

2 Christ Our Advocate

My little children, I am writing these things to you so that you may not sin. But if anyone does sin, we have an advocate with the Father, Jesus Christ the righteous; ²and he is the atoning sacrifice for our sins, and not for ours only but also for the sins of the whole world.

3 Now by this we may be sure that we know him, if we obey his commandments. ⁴Whoever says, "I have come to know him," but does not obey his commandments, is a liar, and in such a person the truth does not exist; ⁵but whoever obeys his word, truly in this person the love of God has reached perfection. By this we may be sure that we are in him: ⁶whoever says, "I abide in him," ought to walk just as he walked.

A New Commandment

7 Beloved, I am writing you no new commandment, but an old commandment that you have had from the beginning; the old commandment is the word that you have heard. ⁸Yet I am writing you a new commandment that is true in him and in you, because*b* the darkness is passing away and the true light is already shining. ⁹Whoever says, "I am in the light," while hating a brother or sister,*c* is still in the darkness. ¹⁰Whoever loves a brother or sister*d* lives in the light, and in such a person*e* there is no cause for stumbling. ¹¹But whoever hates another believer*f* is in the darkness, walks in the darkness, and does not know the way to go, because the darkness has brought on blindness.

¹² I am writing to you, little children,
    because your sins are forgiven on
        account of his name.
¹³ I am writing to you, fathers,
    because you know him who is from the
        beginning.
I am writing to you, young people,
    because you have conquered the evil one.
¹⁴ I write to you, children,
    because you know the Father.
I write to you, fathers,
    because you know him who is from the
        beginning.
I write to you, young people,
    because you are strong
    and the word of God abides in you,
        and you have overcome the evil one.

15 Do not love the world or the things in the world. The love of the Father is not in those who love the world; ¹⁶for all that is in the world—the desire of the flesh, the desire of the eyes, the pride in riches—comes not from the Father but from the world. ¹⁷And the world and its desire*g* are passing away, but those who do the will of God live forever.

Warning against Antichrists

18 Children, it is the last hour! As you have heard that antichrist is coming, so now many antichrists have come. From this we know that it is the last hour. ¹⁹They went out from us, but they did not belong to us; for if they had belonged to us, they would have remained with us. But by going out they made it plain that none of them belongs to us. ²⁰But you have been anointed by the Holy One, and all of you have knowledge.*h* ²¹I write to you, not because you do not know the truth, but because you know it, and you know that no lie comes from the truth. ²²Who is the liar but the one who denies that Jesus is the Christ?*i* This is the antichrist, the one who denies the Father and the Son. ²³No one who denies the Son has the Father; everyone who confesses the Son has the Father also. ²⁴Let what you heard from the beginning abide in you. If what you heard from the beginning abides in you, then you will

---

a Other ancient authorities read *your* *b* Or *that* *c* Gk *hating a brother* *d* Gk *loves a brother* *e* Or *in it* *f* Gk *hates a brother* *g* Or *the desire for it* *h* Other ancient authorities read *you know all things* *i* Or *the Messiah* abide in the Son and in the Father. ²⁵And this is what he has promised us,^a eternal life.

26 I write these things to you concerning those who would deceive you. ²⁷As for you, the anointing that you received from him abides in you, and so you do not need anyone to teach you. But as his anointing teaches you about all things, and is true and is not a lie, and just as it has taught you, abide in him.^b

28 And now, little children, abide in him, so that when he is revealed we may have confidence and not be put to shame before him at his coming.

Children of God

29 If you know that he is righteous, you may be sure that everyone who does right has been born of him. ¹See what love the Father has given us, that we should be called children of God; and that is what we are. The reason the world does not know us is that it did not know him. ²Beloved, we are God's children now; what we will be has not yet been revealed. What we do know is this: when he^b is revealed, we will be like him, for we will see him as he is. ³And all who have this hope in him purify themselves, just as he is pure.

4 Everyone who commits sin is guilty of lawlessness; sin is lawlessness. ⁵You know that he was revealed to take away sins, and in him there is no sin. ⁶No one who abides in him sins; no one who sins has either seen him or known him. ⁷Little children, let no one deceive you. Everyone who does what is right is righteous, just as he is righteous. ⁸Everyone who commits sin is a child of the devil; for the devil has been sinning from the beginning. The Son of God was revealed for this purpose, to destroy the works of the devil. ⁹Those who have been born of God do not sin, because God's seed abides in them;^c they cannot sin, because they have been born of God. ¹⁰The children of God and the children of the devil are revealed in this way: all who do not do what is right are not from God, nor are those who do not love their brothers and sisters.^d

Love One Another

11 For this is the message you have heard from the beginning, that we should love one another. ¹²We must not be like Cain who was from the evil one and murdered his brother. And why did he murder him? Because his own deeds were evil and his brother's righteous. ¹³Do not be astonished, brothers and sisters,^e that the world hates you. ¹⁴We know that we have passed from death to life because we love

one another. Whoever does not love abides in death. ¹⁵All who hate a brother or sister^d are murderers, and you know that murderers do not have eternal life abiding in them. ¹⁶We know love by this, that he laid down his life for us—and we ought to lay down our lives for one another. ¹⁷How does God's love abide in anyone who has the world's goods and sees a brother or sister^f in need and yet refuses help?

18 Little children, let us love, not in word or speech, but in truth and action. ¹⁹And by this we will know that we are from the truth and

The Other Passionate Love

Read **1 John 2.28–3.3**.

Basic biology: everyone is someone's child. Everyone has a parent. Some parents are abusive, some too demanding, some dismissive. All are wrong on occasion.

But as our Father, God is unique. He never tears us down, never asks more of us than we can give. He's bigger than our disappointments.

God's love for you is a passionate love, the sort every father should have for his children.

But why, exactly, should you believe that?

Because God doesn't lie. When God says you're his child, he means it. When he says he loves you with a passionate, never-ending love, he doesn't just say it—he demonstrates it. In creation. Through forgiveness. In the gift of Jesus.

You simply can't find a way to keep God from loving you. He's promised that love, and God keeps his promises.

And not just love, mind you, but *passionate* love. Love that goes the distance, that pays the price.

God's love for you will last as long as he does.

So it's there—a constant as reliable as the sun rising in the east—more reliable, actually.

What will you do with that love? How will you respond?

Visit **Learner.CalltoDiscipleship.com** and journal your response. We'd love to know.

---

a Other ancient authorities read *you* *b* Or *it* *c* Or *because the children of God abide in him* *d* Gk *his brother* *e* Gk *brothers* *f* Gk *brother*

BEGIN HERE >>>

PRAYER FOR YOU

I said a prayer for you last night—
It went a little something like this:

∨
∨ STEP 1
∨

Hey God, it's me.
I want to pray for someone,
It doesn't even matter who it is because you already know.
I don't know exactly what they're going through,
I only know part of the story.
I just want to pray for their safety and comfort,
I hope that they find the strength to carry on.
Lord just help them, please…
You know the right way—
I hope they can find it.
Thank you Lord,
You do great things for us.
Amen.

Prayer for You—© Kim Burton, 18

∧
∧
∧

∨
∨ STEP 2

ANSWER	DATE

∨
∨

DAILY...REPEAT STEP 1

will reassure our hearts before him [20]whenever our hearts condemn us; for God is greater than our hearts, and he knows everything. [21]Beloved, if our hearts do not condemn us, we have boldness before God; [22]and we receive from him whatever we ask, because we obey his commandments and do what pleases him.

[23] And this is his commandment, that we should believe in the name of his Son Jesus Christ and love one another, just as he has commanded us. [24]All who obey his commandments abide in him, and he abides in them. And by this we know that he abides in us, by the Spirit that he has given us.

4 Testing the Spirits

Beloved, do not believe every spirit, but test the spirits to see whether they are from God; for many false prophets have gone out into the world. [2]By this you know the Spirit of God: every spirit that confesses that Jesus Christ has come in the flesh is from God, [3]and every spirit that does not confess Jesus[a] is not from God. And this is the spirit of the antichrist, of which you have heard that it is coming; and now it is already in the world. [4]Little children, you are from God, and have conquered them; for the one who is in you is greater than the one who is in the world. [5]They are from the world; therefore what they say is from the world, and the world listens to them. [6]We are from God. Whoever knows God listens to us, and whoever is not from God does not listen to us. From this we know the spirit of truth and the spirit of error.

God Is Love

[7] Beloved, let us love one another, because love is from God; everyone who loves is born of God and knows God. [8]Whoever does not love does not know God, for God is love. [9]God's love was revealed among us in this way: God sent his only Son into the world so that we might live through him. [10]In this is love, not that we loved God but that he loved us and sent his Son to be the atoning sacrifice for our sins. [11]Beloved, since God loved us so much, we also ought to love one another. [12]No one has ever seen God; if we love one another, God lives in us, and his love is perfected in us.

[13] By this we know that we abide in him and he in us, because he has given us of his Spirit. [14]And we have seen and do testify that the Father has sent his Son as the Savior of the world. [15]God abides in those who confess that Jesus is the Son of God, and they abide in God. [16]So we

REALITY

ALL YOU NEED IS LOVE

Let's face it—we're all sinners. We all need the cleansing that flows from Christ, who sacrificed his life to save us. Real Christian love is possible because of the Incarnation and sacrifice of Jesus.

Read **1 John 4.7**. When we follow Jesus, we can be confident that we are indeed children of God. As God's own children, we are to live in love, "not in word or speech, but in truth and action" (1 John 3.18). The fullness of the Christian faith is based on true belief and results in charitable living. We can come to know God by our love for one another.

How has your relationship with Jesus helped you to love others with a sincere heart?

have known and believe the love that God has for us.

God is love, and those who abide in love abide in God, and God abides in them. [17]Love has been perfected among us in this: that we may have boldness on the day of judgment, because as he is, so are we in this world. [18]There is no fear in love, but perfect love casts out fear; for fear has to do with punishment, and whoever fears has not reached perfection in love. [19]We love[b] because he first loved us. [20]Those who say, "I love God," and hate their brothers or sisters,[c] are liars; for those who do not love a brother or sister[d] whom they have seen, cannot love God whom they have not seen. [21]The commandment we have from him is this: those who love God must love their brothers and sisters[c] also.

5 Faith Conquers the World

Everyone who believes that Jesus is the Christ[e] has been born of God, and everyone who loves the parent loves the child. [2]By this we know that we love the children of God, when we love God and obey his commandments. [3]For the love of God is this, that we obey his commandments. And his commandments are not burdensome, [4]for whatever is born of God con-

---

a Other ancient authorities read *does away with Jesus* (Gk *dissolves Jesus*) *b* Other ancient authorities add *him*; others add *God*
c Gk *brothers* *d* Gk *brother* *e* Or *the Messiah*

quers the world. And this is the victory that conquers the world, our faith. ⁵Who is it that conquers the world but the one who believes that Jesus is the Son of God?

Testimony concerning the Son of God

6 This is the one who came by water and blood, Jesus Christ, not with the water only but with the water and the blood. And the Spirit is the one that testifies, for the Spirit is the truth. ⁷There are three that testify:ᵃ ⁸the Spirit and the water and the blood, and these three agree. ⁹If we receive human testimony, the testimony of God is greater; for this is the testimony of God that he has testified to his Son. ¹⁰Those who believe in the Son of God have the testimony in their hearts. Those who do not believe in Godᵇ have made him a liar by not believing in the testimony that God has given concerning his Son. ¹¹And this is the testimony: God gave us eternal life, and this life is in his Son. ¹²Whoever has the Son has life; whoever does not have the Son of God does not have life.

Epilogue

13 I write these things to you who believe in the name of the Son of God, so that you may know that you have eternal life.

14 And this is the boldness we have in him, that if we ask anything according to his will, he hears us. ¹⁵And if we know that he hears us in whatever we ask, we know that we have obtained the requests made of him. ¹⁶If you see your brother or sisterᶜ committing what is not a mortal sin, you will ask, and Godᵈ will give life to such a one—to those whose sin is not mortal. There is sin that is mortal; I do not say that you should pray about that. ¹⁷All wrongdoing is sin, but there is sin that is not mortal.

18 We know that those who are born of God do not sin, but the one who was born of God protects them, and the evil one does not touch them. ¹⁹We know that we are God's children, and that the whole world lies under the power of the evil one. ²⁰And we know that the Son of God has come and has given us understanding so that we may know him who is true;ᵉ and we are in him who is true, in his Son Jesus Christ. He is the true God and eternal life.

21 Little children, keep yourselves from idols.ᶠ

ᵃ A few other authorities read (with variations) ⁷There are three that testify in heaven, the Father, the Word, and the Holy Spirit, and these three are one. ⁸And there are three that testify on earth: b Other ancient authorities read in the Son c Gk your brother d Gk he e Other ancient authorities read know the true God f Other ancient authorities add Amen

2 JOHN

JUST LOVE

God Is . . .

There's this *Far Side* comic that I find fascinating. It's a picture of God with a full, gray beard sitting on a high-tech throne, gazing intently into a computer screen in front of him. As he observes the world below, the screen focuses on a single person, and God's finger hovers over a button with a single word etched onto it: *smite*.

Sadly, this is exactly how many people in our world picture God—safely tucked away far from the tough realities of life on planet Earth, peering down and looking for someone doing something wrong.

The Bible doesn't say "God is judgment" or "God is wrath." It says "God is *love*" (1 John 4.8), and this truth is a common theme in all of John's writings. It's easy to forget the revolutionary nature of that statement, God is love. This tells us God's essential character, who and what God is at his core. Everything God does he does through the lens of love.

And if we are to believe what John wrote, those who know God cannot help but do and be the same. If we want to follow God, there is only one way.

Love.

> *"To fall in love with God is the greatest of all romances; to seek Him, the greatest adventure; to find Him, the greatest human achievement."*
>
> —St. Augustine

WHO John the elder (not John the Apostle)

WHAT This letter was sent to encourage readers to continue in love, all the while being aware of deceptive teachers. The recipients were encouraged to steer clear of such teachers and not help them in their work.

WHEN Written around A.D. 100

WHERE Ephesus, a city in what is now modern-day Turkey

PATH OF DISCIPLESHIP

It might have been a typical day in Jerusalem. Jesus was walking with his disciples when someone asked him, "Teacher, which commandment in the law is the greatest?" (Matthew 22.36). The question, a common one posed to teachers in the first century, in essence is asking this: If you could boil the entire law of Moses down to one thought, what would it be? Of all the laws and commandments, what central idea holds them all together?

Can you guess Jesus' answer? Yup, you got it: *love*. We're to love God with all of our being *and* we're to love others as ourselves. (See Matthew 22.36–40 for the full story. And check out what the *Catechism of the Catholic Church* 1823 says.) Think about it. Everything in the Scriptures can be summed up in a single thought: love. Yet even more profound is this. By linking these two commandments together, Jesus declares something radical: *The way in which you love those around you is a reflection of how you love God.* The two are not just inseparable; they are the same.

Love. Just love.

THE BIG FAKEOUT

Have you ever believed something a friend has told you, and then found out later it wasn't true? Read **2 John 1.7**. The false teachings addressed in 2 John were serious business. These false teachers denied the teachings about the Incarnation, humanity, and death of Jesus. For them, Jesus wasn't really human. The purpose of 2 John was to set these misguided souls straight.

Catholics believe that Jesus Christ was fully human and fully divine. This is the doctrine of the Incarnation. God became a human being.

That's a brain-twisting concept, but it's a fundamental part of our faith. Jesus was a human person in addition to being one of the three Persons of the Trinity. Consider this: How would you explain the Incarnation to someone who isn't familiar with it?

Salutation

1 The elder to the elect lady and her children, whom I love in the truth, and not only I but also all who know the truth, [2] because of the truth that abides in us and will be with us forever:

3 Grace, mercy, and peace will be with us from God the Father and from[a] Jesus Christ, the Father's Son, in truth and love.

Truth and Love

4 I was overjoyed to find some of your children walking in the truth, just as we have been commanded by the Father. [5] But now, dear lady, I ask you, not as though I were writing you a new commandment, but one we have had from the beginning, let us love one another. [6] And this is love, that we walk according to his commandments; this is the commandment just as you have heard it from the beginning—you must walk in it.

7 Many deceivers have gone out into the world, those who do not confess that Jesus Christ has come in the flesh; any such person is the deceiver and the antichrist! [8] Be on your guard, so that you do not lose what we[b] have worked for, but may receive a full reward. [9] Ev-

a Other ancient authorities add *the Lord* b Other ancient authorities read *you*

Joseph and Jesus—© Charlotte Katheder, 16

eryone who does not abide in the teaching of Christ, but goes beyond it, does not have God; whoever abides in the teaching has both the Father and the Son. ¹⁰Do not receive into the house or welcome anyone who comes to you and does not bring this teaching; ¹¹for to welcome is to participate in the evil deeds of such a person.

Final Greetings

12 Although I have much to write to you, I would rather not use paper and ink; instead I hope to come to you and talk with you face to face, so that our joy may be complete.

13 The children of your elect sister send you their greetings.*

a Other ancient authorities add *Amen*

> "God breaks open ground in our hearts like a pickax going into rock. He transfigured Christ on a mountaintop, and made radiant all that humble flesh. . . . This power transfigures us. . . . This is where the world begins, and where it begins to make sense. This is a love that will rend you and compel you to love in turn."
>
> —**Frederica Mathewes-Green,**
> writer

CREATIVE SPACE

Happiness—© Jesse Bernard, 17

3 JOHN

TOUGH LOVE, TENDER LOVE

Love in Action

Over and over we hear that being a Christian is about having a personal relationship with Jesus. Well, yes, of course . . . but also a big, fat *no*. Because it's not just about "me and Jesus." It's also about me and a worldwide community of believers that I'm called to engage with. John knows from experience that it's a huge blessing, but sometimes an even bigger challenge.

John's letter shows what real love looks like. It's welcoming fellow Christians even when you don't know them, like Gaius (his friend) is doing. But it's also confronting people like Diotrephes (a false teacher) who have gotten things badly wrong and being persistent when they don't pay any attention. This kind of love is not fluffy, touchy-feely stuff—it's gritty, real, and determined. And it's hard, isn't it? We all want to be liked; we don't want to make people angry at us or distrustful of us or uncomfortable around us. But like John we need to be able to show tough love as well as tender love, to challenge as well as affirm.

> *"Your intention should be to defend the faith, not prove it up to the hilt."*
> —St. Thomas Aquinas

WHO John the elder (not John the Apostle)

WHAT In this letter of encouragement and love to a dear friend, John warns against a false teacher named Diotrephes.

WHEN Written around A.D. 100

WHERE Ephesus, a city in what is now modern-day Turkey

PATH OF DISCIPLESHIP

Jesus said there would be an easy way to spot his followers. The Christian bumper stickers on their cars? The fish badge on their T-shirts? The cross around their necks? No.

By how they treat each other. (Check out John 13.35.)

God's Kingdom is not made up of go-it-alone heroes, but of a family that cares, supports, encourages, confronts, challenges, and motivates each other. That's easy when you're relating to people who think the same way as you. It's more difficult with those cranky old Christians who don't like your music, or don't think the same way, or try to tell you what to do. But, like it or not, they're your brothers and sisters. And you have as much to learn from them as they do from you.

Part of being a disciple is serving others, including those unlovable types. After all, they're family.

REALITY

FIGHT CLUB

This short letter points to the fact that there were differences and disagreements in the early Church. We're not clear on the specifics, but we do know that there were differing opinions on faith and how to live as disciples. This letter was written to help maintain unity amid the divisions in the early Church.

The writer also expresses his support for the growing number of missionaries who were helping to spread the good news and hold up the values of truth.

The kinds of conflicts addressed in this letter are still alive and well; as long as humans are involved, there will be differences of opinion! What about in your own faith community? Are there disagreements? How do you help spread the good news today?

Salutation
1 The elder to the beloved Gaius, whom I love in truth.

Gaius Commended for His Hospitality
2 Beloved, I pray that all may go well with you and that you may be in good health, just as it is well with your soul. ³I was overjoyed when some of the friends[a] arrived and testified to your faithfulness to the truth, namely how you walk in the truth. ⁴I have no greater joy than this, to hear that my children are walking in the truth.

5 Beloved, you do faithfully whatever you do for the friends,[a] even though they are strangers to you; ⁶they have testified to your love before the church. You will do well to send them on in a manner worthy of God; ⁷for they began their journey for the sake of Christ,[b] accepting no support from non-believers.[c] ⁸Therefore we ought to support such people, so that we may become co-workers with the truth.

Diotrephes and Demetrius
9 I have written something to the church; but Diotrephes, who likes to put himself first, does not acknowledge our authority. ¹⁰So if I come, I will call attention to what he is doing in spreading false charges against us. And not content with those charges, he refuses to welcome the friends,[a] and even prevents those who want to do so and expels them from the church.

11 Beloved, do not imitate what is evil but imitate what is good. Whoever does good is from God; whoever does evil has not seen God. ¹²Everyone has testified favorably about Demetrius, and so has the truth itself. We also testify for him,[d] and you know that our testimony is true.

Final Greetings
13 I have much to write to you, but I would rather not write with pen and ink; ¹⁴instead I hope to see you soon, and we will talk together face to face.

15 Peace to you. The friends send you their greetings. Greet the friends there, each by name.

a Gk brothers b Gk for the sake of the name c Gk the Gentiles d Gk lacks for him

CREATIVE SPACE

JUDE

DON'T GET DISTRACTED—STAY TRUE

No Shortcuts

The snake starts it. God, generous and loving, gives Adam and Eve a whole world to explore with just one restriction. The snake zeroes in on it, twisting God's words to make God sound unreasonable, suggesting that the snake knows best and God is out to deceive. And people have been doing it ever since—trying to find ways around the truth, to suggest that God didn't really mean what he said, to make God serve *their* agenda.

Passionate and poetic, Jude gets straight to the point. He's outraged that these false teachers are getting airtime. He quotes from writings that his first readers would have recognized immediately, although they're lost to us. But you can tell how strongly he feels about this. He lists the most evil people he can think of to compare them to and paints rich metaphors of what these false teachers are like.

And we need to listen, because we're suckers for a shortcut. Like with those diets that claim you can stuff your face with burgers and *still* lose weight, we like the idea of gain with no pain. Of love without cost. Of eternal life without sacrifice. But it just doesn't work, and we know it deep down. Hold fast, says Jude, to God's love. Don't get distracted—stay true.

> *"Human reason is weak and may be deceived; but true faith cannot be deceived."*
>
> —Thomas à Kempis, medieval monk and author of *The Imitation of Christ*

WHO Jude, the brother of James

WHAT Jude warns against false teachers and encourages people to hold on to the Apostles' teaching.

WHEN Written around A.D. 65

WHERE We don't know where it was written or who exactly it was written for.

PATH OF DISCIPLESHIP

"You snakes, you brood of vipers! How can you escape being sentenced to hell?" Someone cursing the guy who stole his 4x4? A drunk yelling at the cops who picked him up?

No, it's Jesus talking to the Pharisees—the respectable religious leaders of his day (Matthew 23.33). We're so used to images of a nice, kind, freshly shampooed Jesus that we forget he showed anger too. But he did, about issues similar to the ones Jude was upset about. Instead of showing people the way to God, the Pharisees ended up driving people away, and that made Jesus mad. You see, everyone is invited to the party in God's Kingdom. Not just the good and the nice. Everyone—the sad, the mad, people like me, and definitely, definitely people like you.

It's okay for disciples to follow Jesus' example and get angry—for the right reasons. If you see someone suffering, go ahead and get mad. And then get busy finding a solution to that suffering.

Salutation

1 Jude,[a] a servant[b] of Jesus Christ and brother of James,

To those who are called, who are beloved[c] in[d] God the Father and kept safe for[d] Jesus Christ:

2 May mercy, peace, and love be yours in abundance.

Occasion of the Letter

3 Beloved, while eagerly preparing to write to you about the salvation we share, I find it necessary to write and appeal to you to contend for the faith that was once for all entrusted to the saints. 4 For certain intruders have stolen in among you, people who long ago were designated for this condemnation as ungodly, who pervert the grace of our God into licentiousness and deny our only Master and Lord, Jesus Christ.[e]

Judgment on False Teachers

5 Now I desire to remind you, though you are fully informed, that the Lord, who once for all saved[f] a people out of the land of Egypt, afterward destroyed those who did not believe. 6 And the angels who did not keep their own position, but left their proper dwelling, he has kept in eternal chains in deepest darkness for the judgment of the great day. 7 Likewise, Sodom and Gomorrah and the surrounding cities, which, in the same manner as they, indulged in sexual immorality and pursued unnatural lust,[g] serve as an example by undergoing a punishment of eternal fire.

8 Yet in the same way these dreamers also defile the flesh, reject authority, and slander the glorious ones.[h] 9 But when the archangel Michael contended with the devil and disputed about the body of Moses, he did not dare to bring a condemnation of slander[i] against him, but said, "The Lord rebuke you!" 10 But these people slander whatever they do not understand, and they are destroyed by those things that, like irrational animals, they know by instinct. 11 Woe to them! For they go the way of Cain, and abandon themselves to Balaam's error for the sake of gain, and perish in Korah's rebellion. 12 These are blemishes[j] on your love-feasts, while they feast with you without fear, feeding themselves.[k] They are waterless clouds carried along by the winds; autumn trees without fruit, twice dead, uprooted; 13 wild waves of the sea, casting up the foam of their own shame; wandering stars, for whom the deepest darkness has been reserved forever.

14 It was also about these that Enoch, in the seventh generation from Adam, prophesied, saying, "See, the Lord is coming[l] with ten thousands of his holy ones, 15 to execute judgment on all, and to convict everyone of all the deeds of ungodliness that they have committed in such an ungodly way, and of all the harsh things that ungodly sinners have spoken

a Gk Judas b Gk slave c Other ancient authorities read *sanctified* d Or *by* e Or *the only Master and our Lord Jesus Christ* f Other ancient authorities read *though you were once for all fully informed, that Jesus* (or *Joshua*) *who saved* g Gk *went after other flesh* h Or *angels*; Gk *glories* i Or *condemnation for blasphemy* j Or *reefs* k Or *without fear. They are shepherds who care only for themselves* l Gk *came*

CREATIVE SPACE

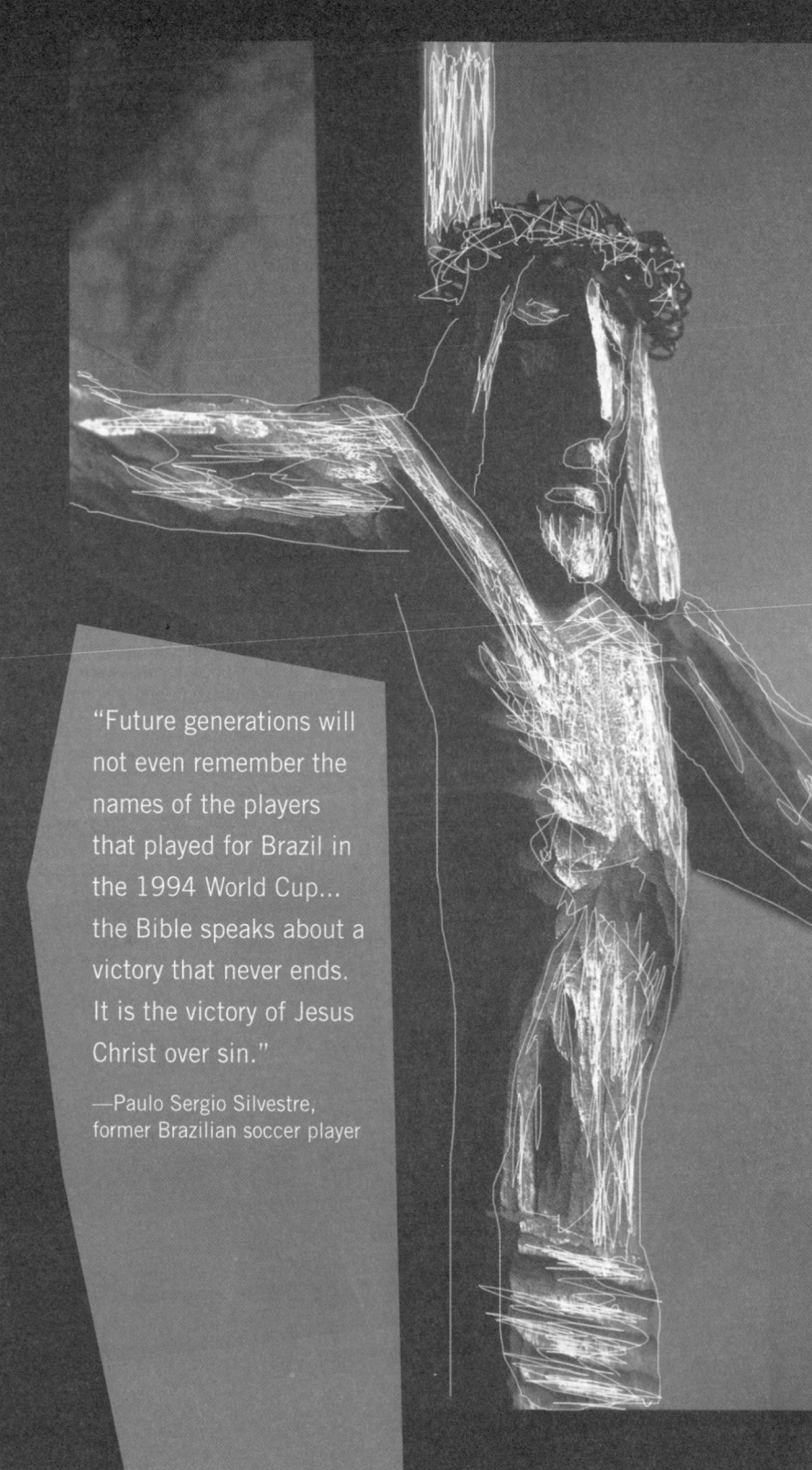

"Future generations will not even remember the names of the players that played for Brazil in the 1994 World Cup... the Bible speaks about a victory that never ends. It is the victory of Jesus Christ over sin."

—Paulo Sergio Silvestre, former Brazilian soccer player

REALITY

FAITH BUILDING

In this short letter, the writer has some choice words for the charismatic leaders of the time who were leading their flocks astray. These were the ones promoting an "anything goes" lifestyle. If they had bumper stickers back then, this one would have said, "If it feels good, do it; you'll be saved no matter what." Not exactly what Christ or his Apostles had in mind.

The letter urges the early Christians to build themselves up in faith and to stay in God's love. The letters speaks to us too and is an important reminder to have a strong prayer life and to remain open to God's forgiveness when we fail.

So how does this letter speak to you? Find some Creative Space in this Bible and answer these questions from your heart:

- What are some things (people, attitudes, behaviors) that tempt you to move away from living a Christian life?
- Do you think you make conscious choices to build up your faith? If so, what are they?

against him." ¹⁶These are grumblers and malcontents; they indulge their own lusts; they are bombastic in speech, flattering people to their own advantage.

Warnings and Exhortations

17 But you, beloved, must remember the predictions of the apostles of our Lord Jesus Christ; ¹⁸for they said to you, "In the last time there will be scoffers, indulging their own ungodly lusts." ¹⁹It is these worldly people, devoid of the Spirit, who are causing divisions. ²⁰But you, beloved, build yourselves up on your most holy faith; pray in the Holy Spirit; ²¹keep yourselves in the love of God; look forward to the mercy of our Lord Jesus Christ that leads to*a* eternal life. ²²And have mercy on some who are wavering; ²³save others by snatching them out of the fire; and have mercy on still others with fear, hating even the tunic defiled by their bodies.*b*

Benediction

24 Now to him who is able to keep you from falling, and to make you stand without blemish in the presence of his glory with rejoicing, ²⁵to the only God our Savior, through Jesus Christ our Lord, be glory, majesty, power, and authority, before all time and now and forever. Amen.

a Gk *Christ* to *b* Gk *by the flesh.* The Greek text of verses 22–23 is uncertain at several points

Tunnel—© Kate Douglas, 17

JUDE

REVELATION

THE ULTIMATE PARTY

It's the End of the World . . . and I Feel Fine?

Our world seems fascinated with the future. Aside from those who flat-out predict the future, we have organizations helping us secure our future—bankers, investors, insurance specialists. (Does our future need "securing"?) Looking ahead can be a good thing, but what about life in the now?

Written during a time of horrible persecution, Revelation was a word of hope to the first-century Church. Revelation definitely talks about the future, but it also has lots to say about the present. Those being slaughtered for their faith in Jesus needed to know that Christianity offered hope not only in the far-off future, but in the midst of their present persecution by Rome.

Revelation still speaks to the current situation in our world. Christians are still being tortured and murdered all over the globe for their faith. Men, women, and children are still being sold into slavery. The poor and disenfranchised are still being oppressed. John's book teaches us that Jesus is near to those who are hurting and dying. He is the Lamb that was slain for us and for our salvation. As followers of Jesus, we must also be near to those in the darkest of situations.

Revelation is our reminder that there is hope . . . even when it looks as if no hope can be found.

"Who except God can give you peace? Has the world ever been able to satisfy the heart?"

—St. Gerard Majella

WHO Another John, not John the Apostle

WHAT This letter addresses how Christians are to live and hold on to their faith, even in the midst of persecution.

WHEN Written around A.D. 95

WHERE John wrote this from the island of Patmos on the Aegean Sea. He wrote it to seven different church communities spread throughout Asia Minor (modern-day Turkey).

PATH OF DISCIPLESHIP

The aim of Revelation was—and is—to warn against compromise with the cultural values of a world heading for self-destruction because of beliefs in false gods. As disciples, we need to take time out once in a while to think about what values in today's culture are contrary to the Christian life.

Revelation is also an encouragement to change our life where it needs changing and to hold fast to the belief that the Risen Lord will triumph over evil. Disciples act in the faith that they are part of the Body of the Christ. We have a responsibility to work for the coming of the Kingdom by living out the values of the gospel. Even when those values contradict the values of society—even when they mark you, the disciple, as *different*.

1 Introduction and Salutation

The revelation of Jesus Christ, which God gave him to show his servants[a] what must soon take place; he made[b] it known by sending his angel to his servant[c] John, [2]who testified to the word of God and to the testimony of Jesus Christ, even to all that he saw.

TRY THIS ←

FAMOUS LAST WORDS

Okay, name the book that begins: "It was the best of times, it was the worst of times, it was the age of wisdom, it was the age of foolishness, it was the epoch of belief, it was the epoch of incredulity . . ."

If you guessed *A Tale of Two Cities* by Charles Dickens, then congrats for paying attention in English class. This is one of the most famous opening lines in literature. But it doesn't quite rival the opening lines on the first page of the Bible: "In the beginning when God created the heavens and the earth" (Genesis 1.1).

The beginning of the Bible focuses on, well, the beginning. So you may be surprised by what you find emphasized here at the *end* of the Bible. Read **Revelation 1.8**.

Jesus' words here in John's vision echo back to the start of Scripture—God was not only *there* at the beginning, he *is* the beginning. He's the letter *A* and the letter *Z*. He's the one and only true God—he has always been, is now, and always will be. God was present in prehistory (before the creation of the world) and throughout all the events of human history.

How can you see God's enduring presence in the world? Grab your history textbook or log on to **Learner.CalltoDiscipleship.com** for links to history sites, and look at events throughout human history with a new perspective in mind— with an eye to God's presence. What examples can you find of God's sovereign control over human events? Where can you see examples of God performing miracles? What evidence do you see of God's power? How do you observe God at work in and through his Church? Take note of what you discover and observe. Then underline **Revelation 1.8** in your Bible and pray, praising God for being the one and only true God who is, who always was, and who is still to come.

GOD IS ONE AND ONLY MY WORLD

[3] Blessed is the one who reads aloud the words of the prophecy, and blessed are those who hear and who keep what is written in it; for the time is near.

[4] John to the seven churches that are in Asia:

Grace to you and peace from him who is and who was and who is to come, and from the seven spirits who are before his throne, [5]and from Jesus Christ, the faithful witness, the firstborn of the dead, and the ruler of the kings of the earth.

To him who loves us and freed[d] us from our sins by his blood, [6]and made[b] us to be a kingdom, priests serving[e] his God and Father, to him be glory and dominion forever and ever. Amen.

[7] Look! He is coming with the clouds;
    every eye will see him,
  even those who pierced him;
    and on his account all the tribes of the
      earth will wail.
So it is to be. Amen.

[8] "I am the Alpha and the Omega," says the Lord God, who is and who was and who is to come, the Almighty.

A Vision of Christ

[9] I, John, your brother who share with you in Jesus the persecution and the kingdom and the patient endurance, was on the island called Patmos because of the word of God and the testimony of Jesus.[f] [10]I was in the spirit[g] on the Lord's day, and I heard behind me a loud voice like a trumpet [11]saying, "Write in a book what you see and send it to the seven churches, to Ephesus, to Smyrna, to Pergamum, to Thyatira, to Sardis, to Philadelphia, and to Laodicea."

[12] Then I turned to see whose voice it was that spoke to me, and on turning I saw seven golden lampstands, [13]and in the midst of the lampstands I saw one like the Son of Man, clothed with a long robe and with a golden sash across his chest. [14]His head and his hair were white as white wool, white as snow; his eyes were like a flame of fire, [15]his feet were like burnished bronze, refined as in a furnace, and his voice was like the sound of many waters. [16]In his right hand he held seven stars, and from his mouth came a sharp, two-edged sword, and his face was like the sun shining with full force.

[17] When I saw him, I fell at his feet as though dead. But he placed his right hand on me, saying, "Do not be afraid; I am the first and

a Gk slaves *b* Gk and he made *c* Gk slave *d* Other ancient authorities read *washed* *e* Gk *priests to* *f* Or *testimony to Jesus* *g* Or *in the Spirit* the last, [18]and the living one. I was dead, and see, I am alive forever and ever; and I have the keys of Death and of Hades. [19]Now write what you have seen, what is, and what is to take place after this. [20]As for the mystery of the seven stars that you saw in my right hand, and the seven golden lampstands: the seven stars are the angels of the seven churches, and the seven lampstands are the seven churches.

2 The Message to Ephesus

"To the angel of the church in Ephesus write: These are the words of him who holds the seven stars in his right hand, who walks among the seven golden lampstands:

[2] "I know your works, your toil and your patient endurance. I know that you cannot tolerate evildoers; you have tested those who claim to be apostles but are not, and have found them to be false. [3]I also know that you are enduring patiently and bearing up for the sake of my name, and that you have not grown weary. [4]But I have this against you, that you have abandoned the love you had at first. [5]Remember then from what you have fallen; repent, and do the works you did at first. If not, I will come to you and remove your lampstand from its place, unless you repent. [6]Yet this is to your credit: you hate the works of the Nicolaitans, which I also hate. [7]Let anyone who has an ear listen to what the Spirit is saying to the churches. To everyone who conquers, I will give permission to eat from the tree of life that is in the paradise of God.

The Message to Smyrna

8 "And to the angel of the church in Smyrna write: These are the words of the first and the last, who was dead and came to life:

[9] "I know your affliction and your poverty, even though you are rich. I know the slander on the part of those who say that they are Jews and are not, but are a synagogue of Satan. [10]Do not fear what you are about to suffer. Beware, the devil is about to throw some of you into prison so that you may be tested, and for ten days you will have affliction. Be faithful until death, and I will give you the crown of life. [11]Let anyone who has an ear listen to what the Spirit is saying to the churches. Whoever conquers will not be harmed by the second death.

The Message to Pergamum

12 "And to the angel of the church in Pergamum write: These are the words of him who has the sharp two-edged sword:

[13] "I know where you are living, where Sa-

a Or deny my faith

REALITY ✔

THE ALPHA AND OMEGA

The book of Revelation portrays a vision of Jesus that's very different from the Jesus of the Gospels or the letters. In Revelation, Jesus is described in an exalted state as a mighty ruler in control of the cosmic forces and with power over all evil. The promise of this book is that Jesus will triumph over all evil.

Quietly read **Revelation 1.8–20**. Imagine Jesus as Lord in all his glory as described here. Think about the evils in society, particularly the ones that cause you the most concern. Name them and tell them to the Lord. Hear him say the words: "Do not be afraid; I am the first and the last, and the living one. I was dead, and see, I am alive forever and ever; and I have the keys of Death and of Hades" (1.17–18). Remain with those words and allow the Lord to relieve your fears.

During the next few days, recall your meditation and pray the words, "Do not be afraid; I am the first and the last, and the living one. I was dead, and see, I am alive forever and ever" as a mantra when you are confronted with concern about evil.

tan's throne is. Yet you are holding fast to my name, and you did not deny your faith in me[a] even in the days of Antipas my witness, my faithful one, who was killed among you, where Satan lives. [14]But I have a few things against you: you have some there who hold to the teaching of Balaam, who taught Balak to put a stumbling block before the people of Israel, so that they would eat food sacrificed to idols and practice fornication. [15]So you also have some who hold to the teaching of the Nicolaitans. [16]Repent then. If not, I will come to you soon and make war against them with the sword of my mouth. [17]Let anyone who has an ear listen to what the Spirit is saying to the churches. To everyone who conquers I will give some of the hidden manna, and I will give a white stone, and on the white stone is written a new name that no one knows except the one who receives it.

The Message to Thyatira

18 "And to the angel of the church in Thyatira write: These are the words of the Son of God, who has eyes like a flame of fire, and whose feet are like burnished bronze:

19 "I know your works—your love, faith, service, and patient endurance. I know that your last works are greater than the first. 20But I have this against you: you tolerate that woman Jezebel, who calls herself a prophet and is teaching and beguiling my servants*a* to practice fornication and to eat food sacrificed to idols. 21I gave her time to repent, but she refuses to repent of her fornication. 22Beware, I am throwing her on a bed, and those who commit adultery with her I am throwing into great distress, unless they repent of her doings; 23and I will strike her children dead. And all the churches will know that I am the one who searches minds and hearts, and I will give to each of you as your works deserve. 24But to the rest of you in Thyatira, who do not hold this teaching, who have not learned what some call 'the deep things of Satan,' to you I say, I do not lay on you any other burden; 25only hold fast to what you have until I come. 26To everyone who conquers and continues to do my works to the end,

I will give authority over the nations;
27 to rule*b* them with an iron rod,
as when clay pots are shattered—
28even as I also received authority from my Father. To the one who conquers I will also give the morning star. 29Let anyone who has an ear listen to what the Spirit is saying to the churches.

3 The Message to Sardis

"And to the angel of the church in Sardis write: These are the words of him who has the seven spirits of God and the seven stars:

"I know your works; you have a name of being alive, but you are dead. 2Wake up, and strengthen what remains and is on the point of death, for I have not found your works perfect in the sight of my God. 3Remember then what you received and heard; obey it, and repent. If you do not wake up, I will come like a thief, and you will not know at what hour I will come to you. 4Yet you have still a few persons in Sardis who have not soiled their clothes; they will walk with me, dressed in white, for they are worthy. 5If you conquer, you will be clothed like them in white robes, and I will not blot your name out of the book of life; I will confess your name before my Father and be-

fore his angels. 6Let anyone who has an ear listen to what the Spirit is saying to the churches.

The Message to Philadelphia

7 "And to the angel of the church in Philadelphia write:

These are the words of the holy one, the true one,
who has the key of David,
who opens and no one will shut,
who shuts and no one opens:

8 "I know your works. Look, I have set before you an open door, which no one is able to shut. I know that you have but little power, and yet you have kept my word and have not denied my name. 9I will make those of the synagogue of Satan who say that they are Jews and are not, but are lying—I will make them come and bow down before your feet, and they will learn that I have loved you. 10Because you have kept my word of patient endurance, I will keep you from the hour of trial that is coming on the whole world to test the inhabitants of the earth. 11I am coming soon; hold fast to what you have, so that no one may seize your crown. 12If you conquer, I will make you a pillar in the temple of my God; you will never go out of it. I will write on you the name of my God, and the name of the city of my God, the new Jerusalem that comes down from my God out of heaven, and my own new name. 13Let anyone who has an ear listen to what the Spirit is saying to the churches.

The Message to Laodicea

14 "And to the angel of the church in Laodicea write: The words of the Amen, the faithful and true witness, the origin*c* of God's creation:

15 "I know your works; you are neither cold nor hot. I wish that you were either cold or hot. 16So, because you are lukewarm, and neither cold nor hot, I am about to spit you out of my mouth. 17For you say, 'I am rich, I have prospered, and I need nothing.' You do not realize that you are wretched, pitiable, poor, blind, and naked. 18Therefore I counsel you to buy from me gold refined by fire so that you may be rich; and white robes to clothe you and to keep the shame of your nakedness from being seen; and salve to anoint your eyes so that you may see. 19I reprove and discipline those whom I love. Be earnest, therefore, and repent. 20Listen! I am standing at the door, knocking; if you hear my voice and open the door, I will come in to you and eat with you, and you with me. 21To the one who conquers I will give a place with me on my throne, just as I myself conquered

a Gk slaves *b* Or to shepherd *c* Or beginning

and sat down with my Father on his throne. [22]Let anyone who has an ear listen to what the Spirit is saying to the churches."

4 The Heavenly Worship

After this I looked, and there in heaven a door stood open! And the first voice, which I had heard speaking to me like a trumpet, said, "Come up here, and I will show you what must take place after this." [2]At once I was in the spirit,[a] and there in heaven stood a throne, with one seated on the throne! [3]And the one seated there looks like jasper and carnelian, and around the throne is a rainbow that looks like an emerald. [4]Around the throne are twenty-four thrones, and seated on the thrones are twenty-four elders, dressed in white robes, with golden crowns on their heads. [5]Coming from the throne are flashes of lightning, and rumblings and peals of thunder, and in front of the throne burn seven flaming torches, which are the seven spirits of God; [6]and in front of the throne there is something like a sea of glass, like crystal.

Around the throne, and on each side of the throne, are four living creatures, full of eyes in front and behind: [7]the first living creature like a lion, the second living creature like an ox, the third living creature with a face like a human face, and the fourth living creature like a flying eagle. [8]And the four living creatures, each of them with six wings, are full of eyes all around and inside. Day and night without ceasing they sing,

"Holy, holy, holy,
the Lord God the Almighty,
who was and is and is to come."

[9]And whenever the living creatures give glory and honor and thanks to the one who is seated on the throne, who lives forever and ever, [10]the twenty-four elders fall before the one who is seated on the throne and worship the one who lives forever and ever; they cast their crowns before the throne, singing,

[11] "You are worthy, our Lord and God,
to receive glory and honor and power,
for you created all things,
and by your will they existed and were
created."

5 The Scroll and the Lamb

Then I saw in the right hand of the one seated on the throne a scroll written on the inside and on the back, sealed[b] with seven seals; [2]and I saw a mighty angel proclaiming with a loud voice, "Who is worthy to open the scroll and break its seals?" [3]And no one in heaven or on

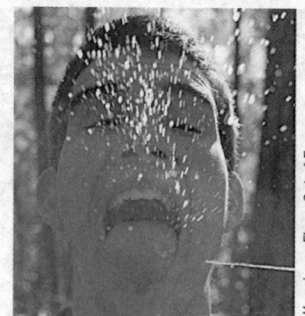

TRY THIS

NO ROOM FOR ROOM TEMPERATURE

Imagine for a moment that you wake up one morning with a serious craving for a cool, refreshing glass of chocolate milk. You don't have time to make yourself a glass before school, but it is first on your list to do when you get home. After school, you burst through the front door and find that the milk is already on the kitchen counter. You grab a cup and pour yourself a generous amount of milk and mix in the chocolate syrup. As the milk touches your lips, slides past your tongue, and passes to the back of your throat, you realize that someone had left it out of the fridge from earlier that morning. How do you think you would react? *Blech!* Room temperature chocolate milk would be everywhere.

Read **Revelation 3.14–21**. It's scary to think about Jesus spitting anyone out of his mouth, but this is the reality of the passage. Those in the Church in Laodicea had become complacent in their relationship with Christ. It led them to become "wretched, pitiable, poor, blind, and naked" (v. 17), and the worst part was that they didn't have a clue about the state they were actually in.

Revelation 3.20 shows us that God's great desire is for us to hear his knock and open the door, so that he can come in and share a meal with us. So take steps in the direction of becoming *hot*, not room temperature, by putting aside your Bible right now and making yourself a mug of hot coffee, cocoa, or tea. As you sip it and hold it in your hands, think about different ways you can become spiritually hot. After this time of meditation, share your experience with others at **Learner.CalltoDiscipleship.com**.

GOD IS CHALLENGING MY WORLD

---

a Or *in the Spirit* b Or *written on the inside, and sealed on the back*

REVELATION 5

Harp & Music—© Eric Engle, 16

earth or under the earth was able to open the scroll or to look into it. ⁴And I began to weep bitterly because no one was found worthy to open the scroll or to look into it. ⁵Then one of the elders said to me, "Do not weep. See, the Lion of the tribe of Judah, the Root of David, has conquered, so that he can open the scroll and its seven seals."

6 Then I saw between the throne and the four living creatures and among the elders a Lamb standing as if it had been slaughtered, having seven horns and seven eyes, which are the seven spirits of God sent out into all the earth. ⁷He went and took the scroll from the right hand of the one who was seated on the throne. ⁸When he had taken the scroll, the four living creatures and the twenty-four elders fell before the Lamb, each holding a harp and golden bowls full of incense, which are the prayers of the saints. ⁹They sing a new song:

"You are worthy to take the scroll
    and to open its seals,
for you were slaughtered and by your blood
        you ransomed for God
    saints from*ᵈ* every tribe and language and
        people and nation;
¹⁰ you have made them to be a kingdom and
        priests serving*ᵇ* our God,
    and they will reign on earth."

11 Then I looked, and I heard the voice of many angels surrounding the throne and the living creatures and the elders; they numbered myriads of myriads and thousands of thousands, ¹²singing with full voice,

"Worthy is the Lamb that was slaughtered
    to receive power and wealth and wisdom
        and might
    and honor and glory and blessing!"

¹³Then I heard every creature in heaven and on earth and under the earth and in the sea, and all that is in them, singing,

"To the one seated on the throne and to the
        Lamb
    be blessing and honor and glory and might
        forever and ever!"

¹⁴And the four living creatures said, "Amen!" And the elders fell down and worshiped.

6 The Seven Seals

Then I saw the Lamb open one of the seven seals, and I heard one of the four living creatures call out, as with a voice of thunder, "Come!"*ᶜ* ²I looked, and there was a white horse! Its rider had a bow; a crown was given to him, and he came out conquering and to conquer.

3 When he opened the second seal, I heard the second living creature call out, "Come!"*ᶜ* ⁴And out came*ᵈ* another horse, bright red; its rider was permitted to take peace from the earth, so that people would slaughter one another; and he was given a great sword.

5 When he opened the third seal, I heard the third living creature call out, "Come!"*ᶜ* I looked, and there was a black horse! Its rider held a pair of scales in his hand, ⁶and I heard what seemed to be a voice in the midst of the four living creatures saying, "A quart of wheat for a day's pay,*ᵉ* and three quarts of barley for a day's pay,*ᵉ* but do not damage the olive oil and the wine!"

7 When he opened the fourth seal, I heard the voice of the fourth living creature call out, "Come!"*ᶜ* ⁸I looked and there was a pale green horse! Its rider's name was Death, and Hades followed with him; they were given authority over a fourth of the earth, to kill with sword, famine, and pestilence, and by the wild animals of the earth.

9 When he opened the fifth seal, I saw under the altar the souls of those who had been slaughtered for the word of God and for the testimony they had given; ¹⁰they cried out with a loud voice, "Sovereign Lord, holy and true, how long will it be before you judge and avenge our blood on the inhabitants of the earth?" ¹¹They were each given a white robe and told to rest a little longer, until the number would be complete both of their fellow servants*ᶠ* and of their brothers and sisters,*ᵍ* who were soon to be killed as they themselves had been killed.

12 When he opened the sixth seal, I looked, and there came a great earthquake; the sun became black as sackcloth, the full moon became like blood, ¹³and the stars of the sky fell to the earth as the fig tree drops its winter fruit when shaken by a gale. ¹⁴The sky vanished like a scroll rolling itself up, and every mountain and island was removed from its place. ¹⁵Then

a Gk *ransomed for God from* *b* Gk *priests to* *c* Or *"Go!"* *d* Or *went* *e* Gk *a denarius* *f* Gk *slaves* *g* Gk *brothers* the kings of the earth and the magnates and the generals and the rich and the powerful, and everyone, slave and free, hid in the caves and among the rocks of the mountains, [16]calling to the mountains and rocks, "Fall on us and hide us from the face of the one seated on the throne and from the wrath of the Lamb; [17]for the great day of their wrath has come, and who is able to stand?"

7 The 144,000 of Israel Sealed

After this I saw four angels standing at the four corners of the earth, holding back the four winds of the earth so that no wind could blow on earth or sea or against any tree. [2]I saw another angel ascending from the rising of the sun, having the seal of the living God, and he called with a loud voice to the four angels who had been given power to damage earth and sea, [3]saying, "Do not damage the earth or the sea or the trees, until we have marked the servants[a] of our God with a seal on their foreheads."

4 And I heard the number of those who were sealed, one hundred forty-four thousand, sealed out of every tribe of the people of Israel:

5 From the tribe of Judah twelve thousand sealed,
from the tribe of Reuben twelve thousand,
from the tribe of Gad twelve thousand,
6 from the tribe of Asher twelve thousand,
from the tribe of Naphtali twelve thousand,
from the tribe of Manasseh twelve thousand,
7 from the tribe of Simeon twelve thousand,
from the tribe of Levi twelve thousand,
from the tribe of Issachar twelve thousand,
8 from the tribe of Zebulun twelve thousand,
from the tribe of Joseph twelve thousand,
from the tribe of Benjamin twelve thousand sealed.

The Multitude from Every Nation

9 After this I looked, and there was a great multitude that no one could count, from every nation, from all tribes and peoples and languages, standing before the throne and before the Lamb, robed in white, with palm branches in their hands. [10]They cried out in a loud voice, saying,

"Salvation belongs to our God who is seated on the throne, and to the Lamb!"

[11]And all the angels stood around the throne and around the elders and the four living creatures, and they fell on their faces before the throne and worshiped God, [12]singing,

"Amen! Blessing and glory and wisdom
and thanksgiving and honor
and power and might
be to our God forever and ever! Amen."

13 Then one of the elders addressed me, saying, "Who are these, robed in white, and where have they come from?" [14]I said to him, "Sir, you are the one that knows." Then he said to me, "These are they who have come out of the great ordeal; they have washed their robes and made them white in the blood of the Lamb.

[15] For this reason they are before the throne of God,
and worship him day and night within his temple,
and the one who is seated on the throne will shelter them.
[16] They will hunger no more, and thirst no more;
the sun will not strike them,
nor any scorching heat;
[17] for the Lamb at the center of the throne will be their shepherd,
and he will guide them to springs of the water of life,
and God will wipe away every tear from their eyes."

8 The Seventh Seal and the Golden Censer

When the Lamb opened the seventh seal, there was silence in heaven for about half an hour. [2]And I saw the seven angels who stand before God, and seven trumpets were given to them.

3 Another angel with a golden censer came and stood at the altar; he was given a great quantity of incense to offer with the prayers of all the saints on the golden altar that is before the throne. [4]And the smoke of the incense, with the prayers of the saints, rose before God from the hand of the angel. [5]Then the angel took the censer and filled it with fire from the altar and threw it on the earth; and there were peals of thunder, rumblings, flashes of lightning, and an earthquake.

The Seven Trumpets

6 Now the seven angels who had the seven trumpets made ready to blow them.

7 The first angel blew his trumpet, and there came hail and fire, mixed with blood, and they were hurled to the earth; and a third of the earth was burned up, and a third of the trees were burned up, and all green grass was burned up.

a Gk slaves

8 The second angel blew his trumpet, and something like a great mountain, burning with fire, was thrown into the sea. ⁹A third of the sea became blood, a third of the living creatures in the sea died, and a third of the ships were destroyed.

10 The third angel blew his trumpet, and a great star fell from heaven, blazing like a torch, and it fell on a third of the rivers and on the springs of water. ¹¹The name of the star is Wormwood. A third of the waters became wormwood, and many died from the water, because it was made bitter.

12 The fourth angel blew his trumpet, and a third of the sun was struck, and a third of the moon, and a third of the stars, so that a third of their light was darkened; a third of the day was kept from shining, and likewise the night.

13 Then I looked, and I heard an eagle crying with a loud voice as it flew in midheaven, "Woe, woe, woe to the inhabitants of the earth, at the blasts of the other trumpets that the three angels are about to blow!"

9 And the fifth angel blew his trumpet, and I saw a star that had fallen from heaven to earth, and he was given the key to the shaft of the bottomless pit; ²he opened the shaft of the bottomless pit, and from the shaft rose smoke like the smoke of a great furnace, and the sun and the air were darkened with the smoke from the shaft. ³Then from the smoke came locusts on the earth, and they were given authority like the authority of scorpions of the earth. ⁴They were told not to damage the grass of the earth or any green growth or any tree, but only those people who do not have the seal of God on their foreheads. ⁵They were allowed to torture them for five months, but not to kill them, and their torture was like the torture of a scorpion when it stings someone. ⁶And in those days people will seek death but will not find it; they will long to die, but death will flee from them.

7 In appearance the locusts were like horses equipped for battle. On their heads were what looked like crowns of gold; their faces were like human faces, ⁸their hair like women's hair, and their teeth like lions' teeth; ⁹they had scales like iron breastplates, and the noise of their wings was like the noise of many chariots with horses rushing into battle. ¹⁰They have tails like scorpions, with stingers, and in their tails is their power to harm people for five months. ¹¹They have as king over them the angel of the bottomless pit; his name in Hebrew is Abaddon,ᵈ and in Greek he is called Apollyon.ᵇ

12 The first woe has passed. There are still two woes to come.

13 Then the sixth angel blew his trumpet, and I heard a voice from the fourᶜ horns of the golden altar before God, ¹⁴saying to the sixth angel who had the trumpet, "Release the four angels who are bound at the great river Euphrates." ¹⁵So the four angels were released, who had been held ready for the hour, the day, the month, and the year, to kill a third of humankind. ¹⁶The number of the troops of cavalry was two hundred million; I heard their number. ¹⁷And this was how I saw the horses in my vision: the riders wore breastplates the color of fire and of sapphireᵈ and of sulfur; the heads of the horses were like lions' heads, and fire and smoke and sulfur came out of their mouths. ¹⁸By these three plagues a third of humankind was killed, by the fire and smoke and sulfur coming out of their mouths. ¹⁹For the power of the horses is in their mouths and in their tails; their tails are like serpents, having heads; and with them they inflict harm.

20 The rest of humankind, who were not killed by these plagues, did not repent of the works of their hands or give up worshiping demons and idols of gold and silver and bronze and stone and wood, which cannot see or hear or walk. ²¹And they did not repent of their murders or their sorceries or their fornication or their thefts.

10 The Angel with the Little Scroll

And I saw another mighty angel coming down from heaven, wrapped in a cloud, with a rainbow over his head; his face was like the sun, and his legs like pillars of fire. ²He held a little scroll open in his hand. Setting his right foot on the sea and his left foot on the land, ³he gave a great shout, like a lion roaring. And when he shouted, the seven thunders sounded. ⁴And when the seven thunders had sounded, I was about to write, but I heard a voice from heaven saying, "Seal up what the seven thunders have said, and do not write it down." ⁵Then the angel whom I saw standing on the sea and the land

raised his right hand to heaven

6 and swore by him who lives forever and ever,

who created heaven and what is in it, the earth and what is in it, and the sea and what is in it: "There will be no more delay, ⁷but in the days when the seventh angel is to blow his trumpet, the mystery of God will be fulfilled, as he announced to his servantsᵉ the prophets."

8 Then the voice that I had heard from heaven spoke to me again, saying, "Go, take the scroll that is open in the hand of the angel who

---

a That is, *Destruction* b That is, *Destroyer* c Other ancient authorities lack *four* d Gk *hyacinth* e Gk *slaves*

Naturally Smooth—© Hannah Miller, 15

Strength

In Luke 22:42, Jesus says, "Father, if you are willing, please take this cup of suffering from me. Yet I want your will to be done, not mine." I find myself being able to relate to the way Jesus was feeling in this passage. Obviously, dying on the cross was going to be a very painful and excruciating experience. Would you want to endure it? I know I sure wouldn't! But Jesus recognized God's challenge to die so that we could be with God in heaven forever. He was willing to go through dying on the cross to prove that he loved God, and he loved us.

But God didn't just challenge people in the Bible. God still challenges people today, in modern times! I went through one of God's challenges in October of 2006. Although I didn't realize it at the time, God was challenging me to make my faith in Him stronger. It was the beginning of the school year, and I was starting to make friends with my new lab partner, a boy who I found was very sweet and kind and funny. He was just what you'd want in a friend. But one day his life was taken in a skateboarding accident, after he chose not to wear a helmet. I was devastated, and so was everyone else in my school. I started to question God and my beliefs. Was God really there? Did He care at all about me? But I continued reading my Bible and praying, which was my way of accepting and later overcoming this challenge.

Now my faith is stronger than ever before, and my friend's death (he was a Christian) gave me the opportunity to share Christ with a lot more kids than I ever had before. And just think, all this good came out of something I thought at first was very bad: God's challenge!

Strength—© Krista Hoxie, 13

TEXT MESSAGE

Since no one had invented lick-and-seal envelopes in biblical times, people would fold or roll up documents, tie string around them, and press a lump of clay over the knot (Revelation 8.1). Then the sender would stamp the hardening clay with a special ring or seal, which was intended to be broken only by the recipient.

Fact

This information has been scanned and is free of all known viruses. Please forward to all your friends.

is standing on the sea and on the land." ⁹So I went to the angel and told him to give me the little scroll; and he said to me, "Take it, and eat; it will be bitter to your stomach, but sweet as honey in your mouth." ¹⁰So I took the little scroll from the hand of the angel and ate it; it was sweet as honey in my mouth, but when I had eaten it, my stomach was made bitter.

11 Then they said to me, "You must prophesy again about many peoples and nations and languages and kings."

11 The Two Witnesses

Then I was given a measuring rod like a staff, and I was told, "Come and measure the temple of God and the altar and those who worship there, ²but do not measure the court outside the temple; leave that out, for it is given over to the nations, and they will trample over the holy city for forty-two months. ³And I will grant my two witnesses authority to prophesy for one thousand two hundred sixty days, wearing sackcloth."

4 These are the two olive trees and the two lampstands that stand before the Lord of the earth. ⁵And if anyone wants to harm them, fire pours from their mouth and consumes their foes; anyone who wants to harm them must be killed in this manner. ⁶They have authority to shut the sky, so that no rain may fall during the days of their prophesying, and they have authority over the waters to turn them into blood, and to strike the earth with every kind of plague, as often as they desire.

7 When they have finished their testimony, the beast that comes up from the bottomless pit will make war on them and conquer them and kill them, ⁸and their dead bodies will lie in the street of the great city that is prophetically*ᵃ* called Sodom and Egypt, where also their Lord was crucified. ⁹For three and a half days members of the peoples and tribes and languages and nations will gaze at their dead bodies and refuse to let them be placed in a tomb; ¹⁰and the inhabitants of the earth will gloat over them and celebrate and exchange presents, because these two prophets had been a torment to the inhabitants of the earth.

11 But after the three and a half days, the breath*ᵇ* of life from God entered them, and they stood on their feet, and those who saw them were terrified. ¹²Then they*ᶜ* heard a loud voice from heaven saying to them, "Come up here!" And they went up to heaven in a cloud while their enemies watched them. ¹³At that moment there was a great earthquake, and a tenth of the city fell; seven thousand people were killed in the earthquake, and the rest were terrified and gave glory to the God of heaven.

14 The second woe has passed. The third woe is coming very soon.

The Seventh Trumpet

15 Then the seventh angel blew his trumpet, and there were loud voices in heaven, saying,

"The kingdom of the world has become the
    kingdom of our Lord
    and of his Messiah,*ᵈ*
and he will reign forever and ever."

16 Then the twenty-four elders who sit on their thrones before God fell on their faces and worshiped God, ¹⁷singing,

"We give you thanks, Lord God Almighty,
    who are and who were,
for you have taken your great power
    and begun to reign.

a Or *allegorically;* Gk *spiritually* *b* Or *the spirit* *c* Other ancient authorities read *I* *d* Gk *Christ*

¹⁸ The nations raged,
>but your wrath has come,
>and the time for judging the dead,
>for rewarding your servants,^a the prophets
>and saints and all who fear your name,
>both small and great,
>and for destroying those who destroy the
>earth."

19 Then God's temple in heaven was opened, and the ark of his covenant was seen within his temple; and there were flashes of lightning, rumblings, peals of thunder, an earthquake, and heavy hail.

12 The Woman and the Dragon

A great portent appeared in heaven: a woman clothed with the sun, with the moon under her feet, and on her head a crown of twelve stars. ²She was pregnant and was crying out in birth pangs, in the agony of giving birth. ³Then another portent appeared in heaven: a great red dragon, with seven heads and ten horns, and seven diadems on his heads. ⁴His tail swept down a third of the stars of heaven and threw them to the earth. Then the dragon stood before the woman who was about to bear a child, so that he might devour her child as soon as it was born. ⁵And she gave birth to a son, a male child, who is to rule^b all the nations with a rod of iron. But her child was snatched away and taken to God and to his throne; ⁶and the woman fled into the wilderness, where she has a place prepared by God, so that there she can be nourished for one thousand two hundred sixty days.

Michael Defeats the Dragon

7 And war broke out in heaven; Michael and his angels fought against the dragon. The dragon and his angels fought back, ⁸but they were defeated, and there was no longer any place for them in heaven. ⁹The great dragon was thrown down, that ancient serpent, who is called the Devil and Satan, the deceiver of the whole world—he was thrown down to the earth, and his angels were thrown down with him.

10 Then I heard a loud voice in heaven, proclaiming,

>"Now have come the salvation and the
>power
>and the kingdom of our God
>and the authority of his Messiah,^c
>for the accuser of our comrades^d has been
>thrown down,
>who accuses them day and night before
>our God.

¹¹ But they have conquered him by the blood
>of the Lamb
>and by the word of their testimony,
>for they did not cling to life even in the face
>of death.
¹² Rejoice then, you heavens
>and those who dwell in them!
>But woe to the earth and the sea,
>for the devil has come down to you
>with great wrath,
>because he knows that his time is short!"

The Dragon Fights Again on Earth

13 So when the dragon saw that he had been thrown down to the earth, he pursued^e the woman who had given birth to the male child. ¹⁴But the woman was given the two wings of the great eagle, so that she could fly from the serpent into the wilderness, to her place where she is nourished for a time, and times, and half a time. ¹⁵Then from his mouth the serpent poured water like a river after the woman, to sweep her away with the flood. ¹⁶But the earth came to the help of the woman; it opened its mouth and swallowed the river that the dragon had poured from his mouth. ¹⁷Then the dragon was angry with the woman, and went off to make war on the rest of her children, those who keep the commandments of God and hold the testimony of Jesus.

The First Beast

18 Then the dragon^f took his stand on the
13 sand of the seashore. ¹And I saw a beast rising out of the sea, having ten horns and seven heads; and on its horns were ten diadems, and on its heads were blasphemous names. ²And the beast that I saw was like a leopard, its feet were like a bear's, and its mouth was like a lion's mouth. And the dragon gave it his power and his throne and great authority. ³One of its heads seemed to have received a death-blow, but its mortal wound^g had been healed. In amazement the whole earth followed the beast. ⁴They worshiped the dragon, for he had given his authority to the beast, and they worshiped the beast, saying, "Who is like the beast, and who can fight against it?"

5 The beast was given a mouth uttering haughty and blasphemous words, and it was allowed to exercise authority for forty-two months. ⁶It opened its mouth to utter blasphemies against God, blaspheming his name and his dwelling, that is, those who dwell in heaven. ⁷Also it was allowed to make war on the saints and to conquer them.^h It was given

a Gk *slaves* *b* Or *to shepherd* *c* Gk *Christ* *d* Gk *brothers* *e* Or *persecuted* *f* Gk *Then he*; other ancient authorities read *Then I stood*
g Gk *the plague of its death* *h* Other ancient authorities lack this sentence

Dragons. Beasts. Human-faced locusts? Why does the book of Revelation read like a science-fiction novel? How do I make sense of all the popular end-times predictions and ideas?

Reality is often stranger than fiction. God wants to get our attention, and John's vivid depictions in this letter to the churches are a beautifully bizarre and sometimes scary wake-up call (see Revelation 3.2). Scripture warns us to be ready for Christ's return (see Luke 12.40; Revelation 22.7), but we can't just sit around with "The End Is Near" signs. Revelation challenges us to put our faith into action in the here and now (see also Revelation 2.5).

We can get fixated on diagrams, charts, and theories based on the book of Revelation. It can be sort of fun to try to figure things out or read best-sellers describing a fictionalized version of end-time events. But we need to keep in mind the warning at the end of Revelation, telling us not to add to or remove any of what's written in this book (see 22.18–19). As we try to make sense of Revelation's teachings, we should make sure not to hold others' interpretations and ideas in such high regard that we're "adding" them to Scripture.

We can understand Scripture best when we look at the *whole* instead of fixating on just one aspect of it. The Bible's focus isn't all about how and when Jesus will return—it's about who God is and how we should live in response.

So how can we go about eagerly waiting for Jesus' return without having our thoughts so wrapped up in end-time issues that we lose focus on living our faith in the present? And what does it really mean to eagerly wait for Jesus? What emotions do the powerful images in Revelation stir up in you? What effect do you think this book might have had on its first readers—early Christians being persecuted for their faith? What characteristics of God jump out at you most from Revelation? How do you feel about Jesus' return? Excited? Afraid? Challenged?

Find some Creative Space in this Bible and write your thoughts and questions about the end times. Talk about your thoughts on Revelation with a trusted friend in faith.

(Want to explore more? Read Matthew 24; Acts 1.7; 1 Thessalonians 4.13–5.11; and 2 Peter 3.8–14.)

---

authority over every tribe and people and language and nation, [8]and all the inhabitants of the earth will worship it, everyone whose name has not been written from the foundation of the world in the book of life of the Lamb that was slaughtered.[a]

9 Let anyone who has an ear listen:
[10] If you are to be taken captive,
   into captivity you go;
if you kill with the sword,
   with the sword you must be killed.
Here is a call for the endurance and faith of the saints.

The Second Beast

11 Then I saw another beast that rose out of the earth; it had two horns like a lamb and it spoke like a dragon. [12]It exercises all the au-

thority of the first beast on its behalf, and it makes the earth and its inhabitants worship the first beast, whose mortal wound[b] had been healed. [13]It performs great signs, even making fire come down from heaven to earth in the sight of all; [14]and by the signs that it is allowed to perform on behalf of the beast, it deceives the inhabitants of earth, telling them to make an image for the beast that had been wounded by the sword[c] and yet lived; [15]and it was allowed to give breath[d] to the image of the beast so that the image of the beast could even speak and cause those who would not worship the image of the beast to be killed. [16]Also it causes all, both small and great, both rich and poor, both free and slave, to be marked on the right hand or the forehead, [17]so that no one can buy or sell who does not have the mark, that is, the

---

a Or written in the book of life of the Lamb that was slaughtered from the foundation of the world   b Gk whose plague of its death   c Or that had received the plague of the sword   d Or spirit name of the beast or the number of its name. [18]This calls for wisdom: let anyone with understanding calculate the number of the beast, for it is the number of a person. Its number is six hundred sixty-six.[a]

14 The Lamb and the 144,000

Then I looked, and there was the Lamb, standing on Mount Zion! And with him were one hundred forty-four thousand who had his name and his Father's name written on their foreheads. [2]And I heard a voice from heaven like the sound of many waters and like the sound of loud thunder; the voice I heard was like the sound of harpists playing on their harps, [3]and they sing a new song before the throne and before the four living creatures and before the elders. No one could learn that song except the one hundred forty-four thousand who have been redeemed from the earth. [4]It is these who have not defiled themselves with women, for they are virgins; these follow the Lamb wherever he goes. They have been redeemed from humankind as first fruits for God and the Lamb, [5]and in their mouth no lie was found; they are blameless.

The Messages of the Three Angels

6 Then I saw another angel flying in midheaven, with an eternal gospel to proclaim to those who live[b] on the earth—to every nation and tribe and language and people. [7]He said in a loud voice, "Fear God and give him glory, for the hour of his judgment has come; and worship him who made heaven and earth, the sea and the springs of water."

8 Then another angel, a second, followed, saying, "Fallen, fallen is Babylon the great! She has made all nations drink of the wine of the wrath of her fornication."

9 Then another angel, a third, followed them, crying with a loud voice, "Those who worship the beast and its image, and receive a mark on their foreheads or on their hands, [10]they will also drink the wine of God's wrath, poured unmixed into the cup of his anger, and they will be tormented with fire and sulfur in the presence of the holy angels and in the presence of the Lamb. [11]And the smoke of their torment goes up forever and ever. There is no rest day or night for those who worship the beast and its image and for anyone who receives the mark of its name."

12 Here is a call for the endurance of the saints, those who keep the commandments of God and hold fast to the faith of[c] Jesus.

13 And I heard a voice from heaven saying, "Write this: Blessed are the dead who from now on die in the Lord." "Yes," says the Spirit, "they will rest from their labors, for their deeds follow them."

Reaping the Earth's Harvest

14 Then I looked, and there was a white cloud, and seated on the cloud was one like the Son of Man, with a golden crown on his head, and a sharp sickle in his hand! [15]Another angel came out of the temple, calling with a loud voice to the one who sat on the cloud, "Use your sickle and reap, for the hour to reap has come, because the harvest of the earth is fully ripe." [16]So the one who sat on the cloud swung his sickle over the earth, and the earth was reaped.

17 Then another angel came out of the temple in heaven, and he too had a sharp sickle. [18]Then another angel came out from the altar, the angel who has authority over fire, and he called with a loud voice to him who had the sharp sickle, "Use your sharp sickle and gather the clusters of the vine of the earth, for its grapes are ripe." [19]So the angel swung his sickle over the earth and gathered the vintage of the earth, and he threw it into the great wine press of the wrath of God. [20]And the wine press was trodden outside the city, and blood flowed from the wine press, as high as a horse's bridle, for a distance of about two hundred miles.[d]

15 The Angels with the Seven Last Plagues

Then I saw another portent in heaven, great and amazing: seven angels with seven plagues, which are the last, for with them the wrath of God is ended.

2 And I saw what appeared to be a sea of glass mixed with fire, and those who had conquered the beast and its image and the number of its name, standing beside the sea of glass with harps of God in their hands. [3]And they sing the song of Moses, the servant[e] of God, and the song of the Lamb:

"Great and amazing are your deeds,
    Lord God the Almighty!
Just and true are your ways,
    King of the nations![f]
[4] Lord, who will not fear
    and glorify your name?
For you alone are holy.
    All nations will come
    and worship before you,
for your judgments have been revealed."

5 After this I looked, and the temple of the tent[g] of witness in heaven was opened, [6]and

---

a Other ancient authorities read *six hundred sixteen* b Gk *sit* c Or *to their faith in* d Gk *one thousand six hundred stadia* e Gk *slave* f Other ancient authorities read *the ages* g Or *tabernacle* out of the temple came the seven angels with the seven plagues, robed in pure bright linen,[a] with golden sashes across their chests. [7]Then one of the four living creatures gave the seven angels seven golden bowls full of the wrath of God, who lives forever and ever; [8]and the temple was filled with smoke from the glory of God and from his power, and no one could enter the temple until the seven plagues of the seven angels were ended.

16 The Bowls of God's Wrath

Then I heard a loud voice from the temple telling the seven angels, "Go and pour out on the earth the seven bowls of the wrath of God."

2 So the first angel went and poured his bowl on the earth, and a foul and painful sore came on those who had the mark of the beast and who worshiped its image.

3 The second angel poured his bowl into the sea, and it became like the blood of a corpse, and every living thing in the sea died.

4 The third angel poured his bowl into the rivers and the springs of water, and they became blood. [5]And I heard the angel of the waters say,

"You are just, O Holy One, who are and were,
    for you have judged these things;
[6] because they shed the blood of saints and prophets,
    you have given them blood to drink.
It is what they deserve!"
[7]And I heard the altar respond,
"Yes, O Lord God, the Almighty,
    your judgments are true and just!"

8 The fourth angel poured his bowl on the sun, and it was allowed to scorch people with fire; [9]they were scorched by the fierce heat, but they cursed the name of God, who had authority over these plagues, and they did not repent and give him glory.

10 The fifth angel poured his bowl on the throne of the beast, and its kingdom was plunged into darkness; people gnawed their tongues in agony, [11]and cursed the God of heaven because of their pains and sores, and they did not repent of their deeds.

12 The sixth angel poured his bowl on the great river Euphrates, and its water was dried up in order to prepare the way for the kings from the east. [13]And I saw three foul spirits like frogs coming from the mouth of the dragon, from the mouth of the beast, and from the mouth of the false prophet. [14]These are demonic spirits, performing signs, who go abroad to the kings of the whole world, to assemble them

for battle on the great day of God the Almighty. [15]("See, I am coming like a thief! Blessed is the one who stays awake and is clothed,[b] not going about naked and exposed to shame.") [16]And they assembled them at the place that in Hebrew is called Harmagedon.

17 The seventh angel poured his bowl into the air, and a loud voice came out of the temple, from the throne, saying, "It is done!" [18]And there came flashes of lightning, rumblings, peals of thunder, and a violent earthquake, such as had not occurred since people were upon the earth, so violent was that earthquake. [19]The great city was split into three parts, and the cities of the nations fell. God remembered great Babylon and gave her the wine-cup of the fury of his wrath. [20]And every island fled away, and no mountains were to be found; [21]and huge hailstones, each weighing about a hundred pounds,[c] dropped from heaven on people, until they cursed God for the plague of the hail, so fearful was that plague.

17 The Great Whore and the Beast

Then one of the seven angels who had the seven bowls came and said to me, "Come, I will show you the judgment of the great whore who is seated on many waters, [2]with whom the kings of the earth have committed fornication, and with the wine of whose fornication the inhabitants of the earth have become drunk." [3]So he carried me away in the spirit[d] into a wilderness, and I saw a woman sitting on a scarlet beast that was full of blasphemous names, and it had seven heads and ten horns. [4]The woman was clothed in purple and scarlet, and adorned with gold and jewels and pearls, holding in her hand a golden cup full of abominations and the impurities of her fornication; [5]and on her forehead was written a name, a mystery: "Babylon the great, mother of whores and of earth's abominations." [6]And I saw that the woman was drunk with the blood of the saints and the blood of the witnesses to Jesus.

When I saw her, I was greatly amazed. [7]But the angel said to me, "Why are you so amazed? I will tell you the mystery of the woman, and of the beast with seven heads and ten horns that carries her. [8]The beast that you saw was, and is not, and is about to ascend from the bottomless pit and go to destruction. And the inhabitants of the earth, whose names have not been written in the book of life from the foundation of the world, will be amazed when they see the beast, because it was and is not and is to come.

9 "This calls for a mind that has wisdom: the seven heads are seven mountains on which

---

a Other ancient authorities read stone b Gk and keeps his robes c Gk weighing about a talent d Or in the Spirit

Arms for Hugging—© Amy Bardenhagen, 18

the woman is seated; also, they are seven kings, ¹⁰of whom five have fallen, one is living, and the other has not yet come; and when he comes, he must remain only a little while. ¹¹As for the beast that was and is not, it is an eighth but it belongs to the seven, and it goes to destruction. ¹²And the ten horns that you saw are ten kings who have not yet received a kingdom, but they are to receive authority as kings for one hour, together with the beast. ¹³These are united in yielding their power and authority to the beast; ¹⁴they will make war on the Lamb, and the Lamb will conquer them, for he is Lord of lords and King of kings, and those with him are called and chosen and faithful."

15 And he said to me, "The waters that you saw, where the whore is seated, are peoples and multitudes and nations and languages. ¹⁶And the ten horns that you saw, they and the beast will hate the whore; they will make her desolate and naked; they will devour her flesh and burn her up with fire. ¹⁷For God has put it into their hearts to carry out his purpose by agreeing to give their kingdom to the beast, until the words of God will be fulfilled. ¹⁸The woman you saw is the great city that rules over the kings of the earth."

18 The Fall of Babylon

After this I saw another angel coming down from heaven, having great authority; and the earth was made bright with his splendor. ²He called out with a mighty voice,

"Fallen, fallen is Babylon the great!
    It has become a dwelling place of
        demons,
a haunt of every foul spirit,
    a haunt of every foul bird,
    a haunt of every foul and hateful beast.*ᵃ*
³ For all the nations have drunkᵇ
    of the wine of the wrath of her
        fornication,
and the kings of the earth have committed
        fornication with her,
    and the merchants of the earth have
        grown rich from the powerᶜ of her
        luxury."

4 Then I heard another voice from heaven saying,

"Come out of her, my people,
    so that you do not take part in her sins,
and so that you do not share in her plagues;
⁵ for her sins are heaped high as heaven,
    and God has remembered her iniquities.
⁶ Render to her as she herself has rendered,
    and repay her double for her deeds;
    mix a double draught for her in the cup
        she mixed.
⁷ As she glorified herself and lived
        luxuriously,
    so give her a like measure of torment and
        grief.

---

a Other ancient authorities lack the words *a haunt of every foul beast* and attach the words *and hateful* to the previous line so as to read *a haunt of every foul and hateful bird*   *b* Other ancient authorities read *She has made all nations drink*   *c* Or *resources*

Since in her heart she says,
 'I rule as a queen;
I am no widow,
 and I will never see grief,'
8 therefore her plagues will come in a single
     day—
     pestilence and mourning and famine—
 and she will be burned with fire;
     for mighty is the Lord God who judges
        her."

9 And the kings of the earth, who committed fornication and lived in luxury with her, will weep and wail over her when they see the smoke of her burning; 10they will stand far off, in fear of her torment, and say,
 "Alas, alas, the great city,
     Babylon, the mighty city!
 For in one hour your judgment has come."

11 And the merchants of the earth weep and mourn for her, since no one buys their cargo anymore, 12cargo of gold, silver, jewels and pearls, fine linen, purple, silk and scarlet, all kinds of scented wood, all articles of ivory, all articles of costly wood, bronze, iron, and marble, 13cinnamon, spice, incense, myrrh, frankincense, wine, olive oil, choice flour and wheat, cattle and sheep, horses and chariots, slaves—and human lives.a
14 "The fruit for which your soul longed
     has gone from you,
 and all your dainties and your splendor
     are lost to you,
     never to be found again!"
15The merchants of these wares, who gained wealth from her, will stand far off, in fear of her torment, weeping and mourning aloud,
16 "Alas, alas, the great city,
     clothed in fine linen,
        in purple and scarlet,
     adorned with gold,
        with jewels, and with pearls!
17 For in one hour all this wealth has been laid
     waste!"

And all shipmasters and seafarers, sailors and all whose trade is on the sea, stood far off 18and cried out as they saw the smoke of her burning,
 "What city was like the great city?"
19And they threw dust on their heads, as they wept and mourned, crying out,
 "Alas, alas, the great city,
     where all who had ships at sea
     grew rich by her wealth!
 For in one hour she has been laid waste."
20 Rejoice over her, O heaven, you saints and apostles and prophets! For God has given judgment for you against her.

21 Then a mighty angel took up a stone like a great millstone and threw it into the sea, saying,
 "With such violence Babylon the great city
     will be thrown down,
     and will be found no more;
22 and the sound of harpists and minstrels
        and of flutists and trumpeters
     will be heard in you no more;
 and an artisan of any trade
     will be found in you no more;
 and the sound of the millstone
     will be heard in you no more;
23 and the light of a lamp
     will shine in you no more;
 and the voice of bridegroom and bride
     will be heard in you no more;
 for your merchants were the magnates of
        the earth,
     and all nations were deceived by your
        sorcery.
24 And in youb was found the blood of
        prophets and of saints,
     and of all who have been slaughtered on
        earth."

19 The Rejoicing in Heaven

After this I heard what seemed to be the loud voice of a great multitude in heaven, saying,
 "Hallelujah!
 Salvation and glory and power to our God,
2   for his judgments are true and just;
 he has judged the great whore
     who corrupted the earth with her
        fornication,
 and he has avenged on her the blood of his
        servants."c
3Once more they said,
 "Hallelujah!
 The smoke goes up from her forever and
        ever."
4And the twenty-four elders and the four living creatures fell down and worshiped God who is seated on the throne, saying,
 "Amen. Hallelujah!"
5 And from the throne came a voice saying,
 "Praise our God,
     all you his servants,c
 and all who fear him,
     small and great."
6Then I heard what seemed to be the voice of a great multitude, like the sound of many waters and like the sound of mighty thunderpeals, crying out,
 "Hallelujah!
 For the Lord our God
     the Almighty reigns.

a Or chariots, and human bodies and souls b Gk her c Gk slaves

⁷ Let us rejoice and exult
    and give him the glory,
  for the marriage of the Lamb has come,
    and his bride has made herself ready;
⁸ to her it has been granted to be clothed
    with fine linen, bright and pure"—
for the fine linen is the righteous deeds of the saints.

9 And the angel said*ᵃ* to me, "Write this: Blessed are those who are invited to the marriage supper of the Lamb." And he said to me, "These are true words of God." ¹⁰Then I fell down at his feet to worship him, but he said to me, "You must not do that! I am a fellow servant*ᵇ* with you and your comrades*ᶜ* who hold the testimony of Jesus.*ᵈ* Worship God! For the testimony of Jesus*ᵈ* is the spirit of prophecy."

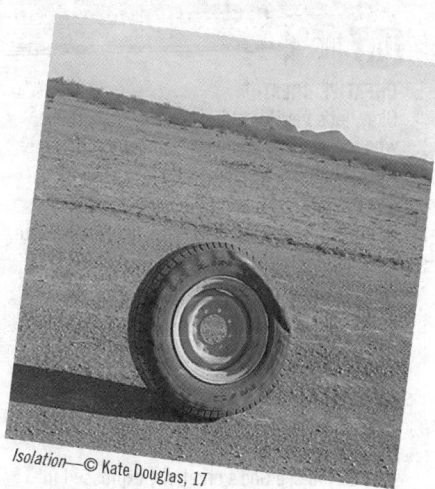

Isolation—© Kate Douglas, 17

The Rider on the White Horse

11 Then I saw heaven opened, and there was a white horse! Its rider is called Faithful and True, and in righteousness he judges and makes war. ¹²His eyes are like a flame of fire, and on his head are many diadems; and he has a name inscribed that no one knows but himself. ¹³He is clothed in a robe dipped in*ᵉ* blood, and his name is called The Word of God. ¹⁴And the armies of heaven, wearing fine linen, white and pure, were following him on white horses. ¹⁵From his mouth comes a sharp sword with which to strike down the nations, and he will rule*ᶠ* them with a rod of iron; he will tread the wine press of the fury of the wrath of God the Almighty. ¹⁶On his robe and on his thigh he has a name inscribed, "King of kings and Lord of lords."

The Beast and Its Armies Defeated

17 Then I saw an angel standing in the sun, and with a loud voice he called to all the birds that fly in midheaven, "Come, gather for the great supper of God, ¹⁸to eat the flesh of kings, the flesh of captains, the flesh of the mighty, the flesh of horses and their riders—flesh of all, both free and slave, both small and great." ¹⁹Then I saw the beast and the kings of the earth with their armies gathered to make war against the rider on the horse and against his army. ²⁰And the beast was captured, and with it the false prophet who had performed in its presence the signs by which he deceived those who had received the mark of the beast and those who worshiped its image. These two were thrown alive into the lake of fire that burns with sulfur. ²¹And the rest were killed by the sword of the rider on the horse, the sword that came from his mouth; and all the birds were gorged with their flesh.

20 The Thousand Years

Then I saw an angel coming down from heaven, holding in his hand the key to the bottomless pit and a great chain. ²He seized the dragon, that ancient serpent, who is the Devil and Satan, and bound him for a thousand years, ³and threw him into the pit, and locked and sealed it over him, so that he would deceive the nations no more, until the thousand years were ended. After that he must be let out for a little while.

4 Then I saw thrones, and those seated on them were given authority to judge. I also saw the souls of those who had been beheaded for their testimony to Jesus*ᵍ* and for the word of God. They had not worshiped the beast or its image and had not received its mark on their foreheads or their hands. They came to life and reigned with Christ a thousand years. ⁵(The rest of the dead did not come to life until the thousand years were ended.) This is the first resurrection. ⁶Blessed and holy are those who share in the first resurrection. Over these the second death has no power, but they will be priests of God and of Christ, and they will reign with him a thousand years.

Satan's Doom

7 When the thousand years are ended, Satan will be released from his prison ⁸and will come out to deceive the nations at the four corners of the earth, Gog and Magog, in order to gather them for battle; they are as numerous as the sands of the sea. ⁹They marched up over

a Gk *he said* *b* Gk *slave* *c* Gk *brothers* *d* Or *to Jesus* *e* Other ancient authorities read *sprinkled with* *f* Or *will shepherd* *g* Or *for the testimony of Jesus*

CREATIVE CREATOR

Okay, let's get this out of the way first. Those who tell you they completely understand **Revelation 21** are kidding themselves.

It's a glimpse of something completely new, totally transcendent. New Jerusalem. New Earth. New Creation.

Which means at least two things even nontheologians can grasp:

1. We're in for a surprise, and

2. God didn't run out of creativity back in the beginning while filling a garden with aardvarks and zebras; he's still at it—right now.

How do you see God's creativity expressed in your parish (not the building, the *people*)? In their lives? Their skills and gifts, like the cantor at Mass? How about the kids who perform the Passion every Easter?

And what about the creative diversity you see in the faces at Mass? "Catholic" means "universal," and we come in every color, shape, and size. God didn't make "one face fits all" humans—we're all beautifully, creatively *different*.

Do this. When Mass ends this week, stay in your seat for a while and open your Bible to this page. Take five minutes to jot notes about God's creativity in the space below. Include specific, praiseworthy stuff that comes to mind as you look around at his Church.

the breadth of the earth and surrounded the camp of the saints and the beloved city. And fire came down from heaven*a* and consumed them. ¹⁰And the devil who had deceived them was thrown into the lake of fire and sulfur, where the beast and the false prophet were, and they will be tormented day and night forever and ever.

The Dead Are Judged

11 Then I saw a great white throne and the one who sat on it; the earth and the heaven fled from his presence, and no place was found for them. ¹²And I saw the dead, great and small, standing before the throne, and books were opened. Also another book was opened, the book of life. And the dead were judged according to their works, as recorded in the books. ¹³And the sea gave up the dead that were in it, Death and Hades gave up the dead that were in them, and all were judged according to what they had done. ¹⁴Then Death and Hades were thrown into the lake of fire. This is the second death, the lake of fire; ¹⁵and anyone whose name was not found written in the book of life was thrown into the lake of fire.

21 The New Heaven and the New Earth

Then I saw a new heaven and a new earth; for the first heaven and the first earth had passed away, and the sea was no more. ²And I saw the holy city, the new Jerusalem, coming down out of heaven from God, prepared as a bride adorned for her husband. ³And I heard a loud voice from the throne saying,

"See, the home*b* of God is among mortals.
He will dwell*c* with them;
they will be his peoples,*d*
and God himself will be with them;*e*
⁴ he will wipe every tear from their eyes.
Death will be no more;
mourning and crying and pain will be no more,
for the first things have passed away."

5 And the one who was seated on the throne said, "See, I am making all things new." Also he said, "Write this, for these words are trustworthy and true." ⁶Then he said to me, "It is done! I am the Alpha and the Omega, the beginning and the end. To the thirsty I will give water as a gift from the spring of the water of life. ⁷Those who conquer will inherit these things, and I will be their God and they will be my children. ⁸But as for the cowardly, the faithless,*f* the polluted, the murderers, the fornicators, the sor-

a Other ancient authorities read *from God, out of heaven*, or *out of heaven from God* *b* Gk *the tabernacle* *c* Gk *will tabernacle* *d* Other ancient authorities read *people* *e* Other ancient authorities add *and be their God* *f* Or *the unbelieving* cerers, the idolaters, and all liars, their place will be in the lake that burns with fire and sulfur, which is the second death."

Vision of the New Jerusalem

9 Then one of the seven angels who had the seven bowls full of the seven last plagues came and said to me, "Come, I will show you the bride, the wife of the Lamb." [10]And in the spirit[a] he carried me away to a great, high mountain and showed me the holy city Jerusalem coming down out of heaven from God. [11]It has the glory of God and a radiance like a very rare jewel, like jasper, clear as crystal. [12]It has a great, high wall with twelve gates, and at the gates twelve angels, and on the gates are inscribed the names of the twelve tribes of the Israelites; [13]on the east three gates, on the north three gates, on the south three gates, and on the west three gates. [14]And the wall of the city has twelve foundations, and on them are the twelve names of the twelve apostles of the Lamb.

15 The angel[b] who talked to me had a measuring rod of gold to measure the city and its gates and walls. [16]The city lies foursquare, its length the same as its width; and he measured the city with his rod, fifteen hundred miles;[c] its length and width and height are equal. [17]He also measured its wall, one hundred forty-four cubits[d] by human measurement, which the angel was using. [18]The wall is built of jasper, while the city is pure gold, clear as glass. [19]The foundations of the wall of the city are adorned with every jewel; the first was jasper, the second sapphire, the third agate, the fourth emerald, [20]the fifth onyx, the sixth carnelian, the seventh chrysolite, the eighth beryl, the ninth topaz, the tenth chrysoprase, the eleventh jacinth, the twelfth amethyst. [21]And the twelve gates are twelve pearls, each of the gates is a single pearl, and the street of the city is pure gold, transparent as glass.

22 I saw no temple in the city, for its temple is the Lord God the Almighty and the Lamb. [23]And the city has no need of sun or moon to shine on it, for the glory of God is its light, and its lamp is the Lamb. [24]The nations will walk by its light, and the kings of the earth will bring their glory into it. [25]Its gates will never be shut by day—and there will be no night there. [26]People will bring into it the glory and the honor of the nations. [27]But nothing unclean will enter it, nor anyone who practices abomination or falsehood, but only those who are written in the Lamb's book of life.

22 The River of Life

Then the angel[e] showed me the river of the water of life, bright as crystal, flowing from the throne of God and of the Lamb [2]through the middle of the street of the city. On either side of the river is the tree of life[f] with its twelve kinds of fruit, producing its fruit each month; and the leaves of the tree are for the healing of the nations. [3]Nothing accursed will be found there any more. But the throne of God and of the Lamb will be in it, and his servants[g] will worship him; [4]they will see his face, and his name will be on their foreheads. [5]And there will be no more night; they need no light of lamp or sun, for the Lord God will be their light, and they will reign forever and ever.

6 And he said to me, "These words are trustworthy and true, for the Lord, the God of the spirits of the prophets, has sent his angel to show his servants[g] what must soon take place."

7 "See, I am coming soon! Blessed is the one who keeps the words of the prophecy of this book."

Epilogue and Benediction

8 I, John, am the one who heard and saw these things. And when I heard and saw them, I fell down to worship at the feet of the angel who showed them to me; [9]but he said to me, "You must not do that! I am a fellow servant[h] with you and your comrades[i] the prophets, and with those who keep the words of this book. Worship God!"

10 And he said to me, "Do not seal up the words of the prophecy of this book, for the time is near. [11]Let the evildoer still do evil, and the filthy still be filthy, and the righteous still do right, and the holy still be holy."

12 "See, I am coming soon; my reward is with me, to repay according to everyone's work. [13]I am the Alpha and the Omega, the first and the last, the beginning and the end."

14 Blessed are those who wash their robes,[j] so that they will have the right to the tree of life and may enter the city by the gates. [15]Outside are the dogs and sorcerers and fornicators and murderers and idolaters, and everyone who loves and practices falsehood.

16 "It is I, Jesus, who sent my angel to you with this testimony for the churches. I am the root and the descendant of David, the bright morning star."

17 The Spirit and the bride say, "Come."
And let everyone who hears say, "Come."

a Or in the Spirit b Gk He c Gk twelve thousand stadia d That is, almost seventy-five yards e Gk he f Or the Lamb. [2]In the middle of the street of the city, and on either side of the river, is the tree of life g Gk slaves h Gk slave i Gk brothers j Other ancient authorities read do his commandments

And let everyone who is thirsty come.
Let anyone who wishes take the water of life as a gift.

18 I warn everyone who hears the words of the prophecy of this book: if anyone adds to them, God will add to that person the plagues described in this book; [19]if anyone takes away from the words of the book of this prophecy, God will take away that person's share in the tree of life and in the holy city, which are described in this book.

20 The one who testifies to these things says, "Surely I am coming soon."

Amen. Come, Lord Jesus!

21 The grace of the Lord Jesus be with all the saints. Amen.[a]

---

a Other ancient authorities lack *all*; others lack *the saints*; others lack *Amen*

Looking Back—© Kate Douglas, 17

WHERE TO TURN

Sometimes life can get confusing . . . discouraging . . . depressing . . . stressful. Sometimes the questions in life seem overwhelming . . . and the answers are hard to find. God's Word in Scripture is a good place to look for answers. But reading Scripture alone just doesn't cut it! It's also important to consult God's Word in the teachings of Church Tradition in order to get a fuller understanding of Scripture. So reflect on it, pray about it, and ask the Holy Spirit to shed some light on what you're reading. Talk to your trusted friends of faith and members of your parish community who might have had some of the same questions you do. God speaks to you through all those things. Here's a place to start. Discover what God has to say!

Where to Turn in the Bible When I'm . . .

Afraid

Joshua 1.9 "I hereby command you . . ."
Psalm 46.10 "Be still, and know . . ."
   91.11 "For he will command his angels . . ."
   118.6 "With the Lord on my side . . ."
Isaiah 41.10 "Do not fear, for . . ."
Romans 8.28 "We know that all things . . ."
Ephesians 6.11–12 "Put on all the whole armor of God . . ."
James 1.2–3 "My brothers and sisters, whenever you face trials . . ."

Alone

Joshua 1.9 "I hereby command you . . ."
Psalm 139.1–6 "O Lord, you have searched me . . ."
Isaiah 41.10 "Do not fear, for . . ."
Matthew 28.20b "And remember, I am with you . . ."
Philippians 4.13 "I can do all things through him . . ."

Angry

Proverbs 15.1 "A soft answer . . ."
   19.11 "Those with good sense . . ."
Luke 6.27–30 "But I say to you that listen . . ."
   6.31 "Do to others . . ."
John 13.34–35 "I give you . . ."
Ephesians 4.26–27 "Be angry but do not sin . . ."
   4.31–32 "Put away from you all bitterness . . ."
Colossians 3.8–10 "But now you must get rid . . ."

Anxious

Psalm 46.10 "Be still, and know . . ."
Isaiah 40.31 "But those who wait for the Lord . . ."

Matthew 6.25–26 "Therefore I tell you . . ."
    6.33–34 "But strive first for the kingdom of God . . ."
    11.28 "Come to me . . ."
Romans 8.28 "We know that all things . . ."
Philippians 4.6–7 "Do not worry about anything . . ."
1 Peter 5.7 "Cast all your anxiety on him . . ."

Ashamed

Luke 15.10 "Just so, I tell you, there is joy . . ."
John 1.12 "But to all who received him . . ."
    3.17–18 "Indeed, God did not send . . ."
2 Corinthians 5.17 "So if anyone is in Christ . . ."
1 John 1.9 "If we confess our sins . . ."

Depressed

Nehemiah 9.17b "But you are a God ready to forgive . . ."
Psalm 46.10 "Be still, and know . . ."
2 Corinthians 5.17 "So if anyone is in Christ . . ."
Philippians 4.4 "Rejoice in the Lord always . . ."
    4.6–7 "Do not worry about anything . . ."

Untitled—© Erica Wallis, 17

Doubtful

Psalm 121 "I lift up my eyes . . ."
    139 "O Lord, you have searched me . . ."
Isaiah 43.1b–5 "Do not fear . . ."
Mark 4.31–45 "It is like a mustard seed . . ."
Luke 11.3–4 "Give us each day our daily bread . . ."

Enjoying life

Exodus 15.1b–2 "I will sing to the Lord . . ."
Psalm 98 "O sing to the Lord . . ."
    136 "O give thanks to the Lord . . ."
John 15.12–17 "This is my commandment . . ."
Romans 8.31–39 "What then are we to say . . ."

Jealous

Psalm 37.8 "Refrain from anger . . ."
Proverbs 23.17–18 "Do not let your heart envy sinners . . ."
Matthew 6.19–21 "Do not store up for yourselves treasures . . ."
Ephesians 4.29 "Let no evil talk come out of your mouths . . ."
Colossians 3.13 "Bear with one another . . ."
1 Thessalonians 5.11 "Therefore encourage one another . . ."

Tempted

Matthew 26.41 "Stay awake and pray . . ."
1 Corinthians 10.13 "No testing has overtaken you . . ."
Galatians 6.1 "My friends, if anyone . . ."
Ephesians 6.11–12 "Put on the whole armor of God . . ."
Hebrews 2.18 "Because he himself was tested . . ."

Confidence

Psalm 139.14 "I praise you . . ."
Matthew 5.16 "In the same way, let your light . . ."
John 15.5 "I am the vine . . ."
2 Corinthians 5.17 "So if anyone is in Christ . . ."
Ephesians 6.11–12 "Put on the whole armor of God . . ."
Philippians 4.13 "I can do all things through him . . ."
Hebrews 4.16 "Let us therefore approach . . ."

Encouragement

Matthew 6.33–34 "But strive first for the kingdom of God . . ."
  11.28 "Come to me . . ."
Luke 11.9 "So I say to you, Ask . . ."
John 1.12 "But to all who received him . . ."
Romans 8.28 "We know that all things . . ."
Philippians 4.6–7 "Do not worry about anything . . ."
  4.13 "I can do all things through him . . ."

Forgiveness

2 Chronicles 7.14 "If my people who are called by my name . . ."
Nehemiah 9.17b "But you are a God ready to forgive . . ."
Luke 6.27–30 "But I say to you that listen . . ."
  6.31 "Do to others . . ."
  15.10 "Just so, I tell you, there is joy . . ."
John 3.17–18 "Indeed, God did not send . . ."
1 John 1.9 "If we confess our sins . . ."

To forgive someone else

Luke 6.27–30 "But I say to you that listen . . ."
  6.31 "Do to others . . ."
Romans 3.10 "As it is written . . ."
1 Corinthians 13.4–10 "Love is patient; love is kind . . ."
Ephesians 4.32 "And be kind to each other . . ."
Colossians 3.13 "Bear with one another . . ."

Bench—© Jessica Jones, 18

Help

Psalm 23 "The Lord is my shepherd . . ."
  121.1–2 "I lift up my eyes . . ."
Isaiah 40.31 "But those who wait for the Lord . . ."
  41.10 "Do not fear, for . . ."
Luke 11.9 "So I say to you, Ask . . ."
John 15.5 "I am the vine . . ."
Ephesians 6.11–12 "Put on the whole armor of God . . ."
Revelation 3.20 "Listen! I am standing at the door . . ."

Obedience

Deuteronomy 6.5–6 "You shall love the Lord your God . . ."
Matthew 5.16 "In the same way, let your light . . ."
Mark 16.15 "And he said to them, 'Go into all the world . . .'"

Luke 6.31 "Do to others . . ."
John 13.34 "I give you . . ."
    14.15 "If you love me, you will keep . . ."
Romans 12.1–2 "I appeal to you therefore, brothers and sisters . . ."
    12.13 "Contribute to the needs . . ."
1 Peter 5.7 "Cast all your anxiety on him . . ."

Patience

Psalm 23 "The LORD is my shepherd . . ."
    37.7 "Be still before the LORD . . ."
    46.10 "Be still, and know . . ."
Matthew 6.33–34 "But strive first for the kingdom of God . . ."
Romans 8.38–39 "For I am convinced that neither . . ."
Galatians 5.22 "By contrast, the fruit of the Spirit is . . ."
2 Peter 1.5–7 "For this very reason . . ."

Wisdom

Proverbs 1.7 "The fear of the LORD is the beginning . . ."
    10.14 "The wise lay up knowledge . . ."
Jeremiah 33.3 "Call to me and I will answer you . . ."
Matthew 6.19–21 "Do not store up for yourselves treasures . . ."
John 14.26 "But the Advocate, the Holy Spirit . . ."
Ephesians 6.11–12 "Put on the whole armor of God . . ."
James 1.5 "If any of you is lacking in wisdom . . ."

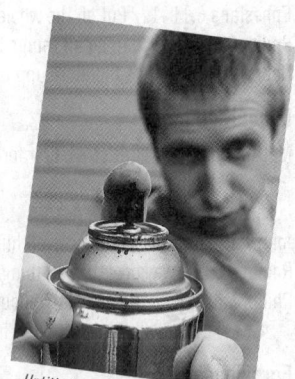

Untitled—© Gabe Anderson, 13

Where to Turn in the Bible When . . .

I have doubts about God

Psalm 19.1 "The heavens are telling the glory . . ."
    46.10 "Be still, and know . . ."
Luke 21.33 "Heaven and earth will pass away . . ."
John 1.1 "In the beginning was the Word . . ."
    1.14 "And the Word became flesh . . ."
    3.16 "For God so loved the world . . ."
    14.6 "Jesus said to him, 'I am the way . . .'"
    20.31 "But these are written so that you may come to believe . . ."
Hebrews 4.16 "Let us therefore approach . . ."
    11.1 "Now faith is the assurance of things hoped for . . ."
1 John 4.10 "In this is love . . ."

I don't know what decision to make

Deuteronomy 6.5–6 "You shall love the LORD your God . . ."
Isaiah 40.8 "The grass withers, the flower fades . . ."
Matthew 19.19 "Honor your father and mother . . ."
Luke 6.31 "Do to others . . ."
John 14.26 "But the Advocate, the Holy Spirit . . ."
Romans 12.1–2 "I appeal to you therefore, brothers and sisters . . ."
Galatians 6.7 "Do not be deceived . . ."
Ephesians 6.11–12 "Put on the whole armor of God . . ."

Philippians 4.8 "Finally, beloved, whatever is true . . ."
James 1.5 "If any of you is lacking in wisdom . . ."

I need to act with justice

Exodus 22.21–27 "You shall not wrong or oppress . . ."
Deuteronomy 24.10–21 "When you make your neighbor a loan . . ."
Isaiah 58.7–12 "Is it not to share your bread . . ."
Matthew 25.31–46 "When the Son of Man comes . . ."
Acts 3.1–10 "One day Peter and John . . ."

I want to do God's will

Joshua 1.5–9 "No one shall be able to stand . . ."
Psalm 16 "Protect me, O God . . ."
   27 "The Lord is my light . . ."
Luke 1.38 "Then Mary said, 'Here am I . . .'"
2 Timothy 3.14–15 "But as for you, continue in what you have learned . . ."

I'm experiencing new beginnings

Ruth 1.6–18 "Then she started to return . . ."
Psalm 131 "O Lord, my heart is not lifted up . . ."
Sirach 6.14–17 "Faithful friends are a sturdy shelter . . ."
Luke 12.22b–32 "Do not worry about your life . . ."
Revelation 21.1–7 "Then I saw a new heaven and a new earth . . ."

I don't know how to pray

Psalm 100.4 "Enter his gates with thanksgiving . . ."
   118.1 "O give thanks to the Lord, for . . ."
Luke 6.27–30 "But I say to you that listen . . ."
   11.9 "So I say to you, Ask . . ."
1 Thessalonians 5.16–18 "Rejoice always . . ."

I'm worried about going to heaven

John 3.16 "For God so loved the world . . ."
   3.17–18 "Indeed, God did not send . . ."
Romans 6.23 "For the wages of sin is death . . ."
   10.9 "Because if you confess with your lips . . ."
Ephesians 2.8–9 "For by grace you have been saved . . ."
1 John 4.10 "In this is love . . ."
   5.12 "Whoever has the Son has life . . ."

My friends talk behind my back

Luke 6.31 "Do to others . . ."
Romans 3.23 "Since all have sinned . . ."
Ephesians 4.32 "And be kind to one another . . ."
Philippians 4.6–7 "Do not worry about anything . . ."
Colossians 3.13 "Bear with one another . . ."
1 Peter 3.9 "Do not repay evil for evil . . ."

I'm afraid to share my faith

Matthew 5.15–16 "No one after lighting a lamp . . ."
   28.19–20 "Go therefore and make disciples . . ."

WHERE TO TURN

Romans 1.16 "For I am not ashamed of the gospel . . ."
Hebrews 11.6 "And without faith it is impossible . . ."
James 1.2–3 "My brothers and sisters, whenever you face trials . . ."
1 Peter 3.15 "But in your hearts sanctify Christ . . ."
1 John 3.18 "Little children, let us love . . ."

My parents fight

Psalm 23 "The Lord is my shepherd . . ."
    46.1 "God is our refuge and strength . . ."
Matthew 6.33–34 "But strive first for the kingdom of God . . ."
    11.28 "Come to me . . ."
Philippians 4.6–7 "Do not worry about anything . . ."
Hebrews 4.16 "Let us therefore approach . . ."

I want to praise God

Psalm 92 "It is good to give thanks . . ."
    150 "Praise the Lord! . . ."
Luke 1.46b–56 "My soul magnifies the Lord . . . "
Colossians 3.15–17 "And let the peace of Christ . . ."
1 Thessalonians 5.16–18 "Rejoice always . . ."

I'm stressed

Deuteronomy 30.15–20 "See, I have set before you today . . ."
Matthew 6.28–30 "And why do you worry . . ."
Luke 15.11–24 "Then Jesus said, 'There was a man . . .'"
John 10.10b "I came that they may have life . . ."
    14.18–21 "I will not leave you orphaned . . ."

Find It on Your Own

If you want to dig deeper into any of these topics, or if there are other issues you want to explore, just flip a few more pages to the concordance. It's a Bible-study tool you can use to look up a specific word and find where it occurs in Scripture. Want to know more about angels? Prayer? David? Love? Jealousy? Esther? Just look up the word or name in the concordance.

Then, keep digging! Delve even deeper into the topic by researching the word or name in the *Catechism of the Catholic Church* or the Catholic Encyclopedia online (go to **Learner.CalltoDiscipleship.com** for a link), and don't forget your faithful friends and members of your parish community—God also speaks through them!

Reflection—© Michelle Jozwiak, 18

REAL-LIFE INSPIRATION

Profile of Faith

Have you ever felt inspired by someone who truly lived by faith? If you only know certain saints by name and not by their lives and works, here's a chance to learn more about them as well as others who chose to follow God and made a difference in their relationships and communities. Allow their stories to inspire you with their courage, their faithfulness to the Church, and their steadfast love for the triune God. You'll read about people like:

St. Moses the Black (p. 65)
Slavery . . . freedom . . . faith

César E. Chávez (p. 134)
Life and dignity of the human person . . . option for the poor and vulnerable . . . dignity of work . . . the rights of workers

St. Augustine (p. 195)
Wasted youth and misery . . . happiness found in Scripture . . . shaper of Church Tradition

Bl. Miguel Pro (p. 238)
Faced anti-Catholic laws . . . forced to celebrate Mass in secret . . . martyred for his beliefs

PROFILE OF FAITH

TIMOTHY: A Brother and Co-worker

Timothy is an important figure in the establishment of the early Church. Paul referred to him as his "brother and co-worker" (see Romans 16.21; 2 Corinthians 1.1; 1 Thessalonians 3.2).

Because Timothy's mother, Eunice, and his grandmother, Lois, were Jewish believers in Christ, Timothy was probably raised in a Christian household. Timothy became Paul's emissary to the Christian communities in Greece, helping to spread the Word of God. At the time of the writing of this letter, Timothy was leading the community in Ephesus.

Dorothy Day (p. 311)
Writer and activist . . . voice for the poor . . . helped start the Catholic Worker movement

Fr. Mychal Judge (p. 391)
Struggled with alcoholism . . . ministered to the needy . . . killed while ministering to World Trade Center victims on September 11, 2001

Sr. Thea Bowman (p. 416)
African American nun . . . teacher and catechist . . . worked for black Catholic evangelization efforts

Thomas Merton (p. 452)
Unruly youth . . . religious conversion . . . advocate for peace

Bl. Mother Teresa of Calcutta (p. 471)
Ministered to the poor and dying in Calcutta, India . . . founded the Missionaries of Charity . . . received the Nobel Peace Prize

Patron Saints of Builders (p. 481)
Helped construct churches . . . laid the foundations for many parishes

Eunice Kennedy Shriver (p. 526)
Committed to public service . . . advocate for mentally disabled children . . . organized the first Special Olympics

The Carroll Family (p. 547)
Religious persecution . . . bravery and rebellion . . . keeping the faith

Blaise Pascal (p. 580)
Mathematical genius . . . suffered from lifelong physical pain . . . wrote powerful works about embracing faith

St. Thomas More (p. 586)
"The king's good servant, but God's first" . . . chose execution over compromising his faith

Bl. Kateri Tekakwitha (p. 626)
Illness, tragedy, and loss . . . conversion . . . happiness with God

Óscar Romero (p. 689)

Fighter for justice for the poor . . . champion of the oppressed . . . bravery

St. John of the Cross (p. 770)

Reformer . . . poet . . . passion for the faith

Fr. Joseph Martin (p. 832)

Alcoholism . . . the fight for sobriety . . . helping others battle addiction

James Cardinal Gibbons (p. 889)

Advocate for the laboring class . . . condemned industrial violence . . . gained papal approval for labor unions

St. Catherine of Siena (p. 953)

A mighty pen . . . brave words . . . speaker of truth

St. Frances Xavier Cabrini (p. 1001)

Accepted life's detours . . . didn't take "no" for an answer . . . opened hospitals, orphanages, convents, and schools

St. Josephine Bakhita (p. 1026)

Slavery and oppression . . . conversion . . . freedom

Sr. Helen Prejean (p. 1108)

Death penalty opponent . . . prisoner advocate . . . fighter for justice

St. Nicholas (p. 1166)

Orphaned at a young age . . . gave to the poor and orphans . . . a model of holiness

St. Francis of Assisi (p. 1207)

Rich boy . . . poor man . . . a life of love and service

Pope John XXIII (p. 1252)

Humility and humor . . . unexpected reformer . . . renewed the life of the Church

Nicodemus (p. 1266)

Caution . . . boldness . . . bravery

Doubting Thomas (p. 1284)

Seeing is believing . . . walked in faith . . . spread the Word of God

St. Maximilian Kolbe (p. 1386)

Worked for conversion . . . tireless defender of the faith . . . the ultimate sacrifice

Timothy (p. 1410)

Helped establish the early Church . . . emissary to Christian communities in Greece . . . "brother and co-worker" to Paul

Just Like You

People from different faith traditions can also serve as a source of inspiration. The **Just Like You** stories tell of people who applied Christ's lessons to their own lives. These stories provide insights that will help you think about and act upon ways you can live your life as a disciple. Check out the stories of people like:

Hannah More (p. 257)

A bad breakup . . . singleness . . . limited opportunities . . . slavery

Sergius Bulgakov (p. 568)

Atheism . . . doubts . . . a changed life

Fanny J. Crosby (p. 650)

Physical challenges (blindness) . . . hope . . . music and poetry

Pandita Ramabai (p. 704)

Hinduism . . . death and loss . . . reaching out to those in need

Toyohiko Kagawa (p. 974)

Buddhism . . . intellectual achievement . . . taking a stand . . . giving up privileges . . . caring for the poor

Albert Simpson (p. 1111)

Having big dreams . . . following God's call . . . leadership

Corrie ten Boom (p. 1143)

Nazi concentration camp . . . courage . . . forgiveness

JUST LIKE YOU

From a Small Farm to the Whole World

Albert Simpson had a problem. He had his heart set on going to college, but his family only had enough money to send his older brother. The family's plan was for Albert to stay behind and tend the farm on the western Ontario frontier in Canada, a bitter final destiny for a fourteen-year-old with big dreams. He just couldn't see himself on the same plot of land for the rest of his life; Albert wanted to see the world.

But Albert had an idea that he thought might work. When his family had a discussion, Albert laid out his plan. He would teach school and make enough to put himself through the college in Toronto. Since he wasn't interested in being a farmer, the responsibilities of the family farm could pass instead to another of his younger siblings. As he shared his ideas, Albert was afraid. Though his father was a kind [man] he was also very stern and not used [to being] contradicted. Still, as young Albert [laid out] his plan, his heart be[gan . . .]

Chicago 2—© Rachel [. . .]

the enormous t[. . .] Jesus to the [. . .] to see th[. . .] wide[. . .]

> REAL-LIFE INSPIRATION

FEATURES INDEX

The LIVE Bible is more than just a compilation of Scripture—it's a living, breathing, interactive way to make Scripture a part of your life. Throughout this Bible, you'll find features that will make you think, take action, and increase your awareness of the Word of God in every aspect of your life.

Reality Check

It's Tradition

Both Scripture and Tradition inform our Catholic faith, and **It's Tradition** spotlights key aspects of our faith, including the sacraments, the liturgy, and Church teachings.

and wisdom is really a sense of awe and
reverence.

The Character of God (p. 780)

The book of Wisdom presents major insights
into the character of God and where we can
find God.

Keep It Simple (p. 804)

God is Truth and the source of all truth;
do not embellish the truth with grandiose
statements.

Litany of the Saints (p. 847)

In the Litany of the Saints we ask the Blessed
Virgin Mary, the angels and all the martyrs
and saints, the Patriarchs, and prophets to
pray for us and to bring our prayers to God.

A New Covenant (p. 959)

Every time we celebrate the Eucharist and
receive Communion, we renew our part of the
New Covenant.

No Other Gods (p. 1004)

Idolatry happens when we make a god of
some person, place, or thing that is less than
God.

Blessing and Consecration (p. 1047)

The Roman Catholic Church consecrates and
blesses both people and things.

Apocalyptic Literature (p. 1063)

Using very symbolic language, the apocalyptic
books of the Bible describe mysterious
revelations given by angels or in visions or
dreams.

Body Talk (p. 1085)

The United States Conference of Catholic
Bishops defines sexuality as a fundamental
part of the human person.

Not Just Your Imagination (p. 1097)

Your imagination is one of the places in your
being where the Holy Spirit lives.

Hope (p. 1124)

When we practice hope, our hope grows.

Fruitful Work (p. 1139)

The prophets' proclamations are the fruit of
prayer and attentiveness to God's Word.

Liturgy Forms Us (p. 1155)

Renewal of worship is essential, so that all
disciples can live faithfully in the world today.

Thy Kingdom Come (p. 1164)

We are called to be committed in the present
to bring justice, peace, and joy to the world.

Nourished in Word and Sacrament (p. 1265)

Holy Communion nourishes, strengthens, and
gives energy to our spiritual life.

Guidance of the Holy Spirit (p. 1288)

The Holy Spirit continues to guide us, just as
it guided the early Church.

More to Life (p. 1354)

The Resurrection gives us hope that there
is more than this life—that we too will rise
again.

Reunited—and It Feels So Good (p. 1361)

The Sacrament of Penance can help heal us
of our sins.

Please Come Again! (p. 1407)

Catholics believe that Jesus will return in
glory at the end of time.

Hope Springs Eternal (p. 1417)

Christian hope is based upon faith in God's
promises that he will never abandon us.

Sacraments of Healing (p. 1448)

The Sacraments of Penance and the Anointing
of the Sick are known as the Sacraments of
Healing.

Priestly People (p. 1451)

The universal priesthood refers to all those
who have been baptized.

The Big Fakeout (p. 1470)

The doctrine of Incarnation teaches us that
Jesus was fully human and fully divine.

Express Yourself

Shout it loud and proud, write it secretly to
yourself, create a piece of art to show your
faith—there are countless ways to express it,
and **Express Yourself** gives you some creative
ideas for inspiration.

Imagination (p. 10)

We are all part of the human family.

Addiction? (p. 14)

God will never give up his relationship with us.

**And You Thought Your Family Was
Dysfunctional . . .** (p. 46)

Good can come out of family chaos and pain.

Higher-ups (p. 57)

Dealing with bullies

The Next Time You're in Rome . . . (p. 83)

God appreciates our creativity.

Accept No Substitutes (p. 87)

No idol is a substitute for the living God.

Try This

Living as a disciple is what God calls all of us to do, but it isn't easy. **Try This** takes scenarios right out of Scripture and puts them into a right-now perspective—and then challenges *you* to apply the lessons within.

Jesus Sighting

The prophets knew—and they shared that knowledge with those who dared to believe. The Messiah was coming, and the path for his arrival was laid in the Old Testament. Each **Jesus Sighting** will show you how the Old Testament connects to the New Testament.

Real Questions

God gave you a brain, so it's only natural that you'll have questions about faith. Flip to the pages indicated to get the answers to those questions, plain and simple.

SCRIPTURE:
SO WHAT'S IT TO YOU?

"According to the hopes of the Second Vatican Council, Sacred Scripture will then be a perpetual source of spiritual life, the chief instrument for handing down Christian doctrine, and the center of all theological study."
— **Pope Paul VI, Apostolic Constitution**
Missale Romanum **(April 3, 1969)**

What Pope Paul VI means here is that Scripture is important in all of Catholic life. Church teachings and Tradition help to clarify its meaning and put it into a context we can understand and apply.

The Second Vatican Council also created the Lectionary, a series of readings that are proclaimed on Sunday. Each Sunday, a selection from the Old Testament is read (except during the Easter season, when the Acts of the Apostles is used), a psalm is sung after the first reading, and then there's a second reading from one of the New Testament books, always followed by the gospel text.

The Lectionary is set up like this for each three-year period:

- Cycle A features the gospel of Matthew.
- Cycle B features the gospel of Mark.
- Cycle C features the gospel of Luke.

Texts from John's gospel are interspersed at various other times in all three years. The complete Lectionary also includes weekday readings (on a two-year cycle) and readings for feasts, seasons, and other ritual celebrations.

Take note of the readings for each daily, Sunday, and special-feast Mass (they're listed in the Missalette and may also appear in your parish bulletin or on its Web site) and use sticky notes to flag them in this Bible. Use a pen or highlighter to mark words or passages that are especially meaningful to you, so you can go back and reflect on them later (remember that there are different translations of Scripture, so the readings may not match the Missalette word for word).

Scripture Study: You Don't Really Have to Pluck Your Eye Out

You've probably met people who quote passages from the Bible—and take each word literally. That's not the Catholic understanding of Scripture. Catholic Scripture study involves the explanation, or **critical interpretation,** of a biblical passage. This first involves looking for the **literal sense** of Scripture—the actual words and their meaning as they appear on the page. But don't stop there! We believe the purpose of the Bible is to communicate religious truths, not to present historical or scientific facts.

As Catholics, we understand that different forms of literature were used in the Bible (fables, poetry, narrative, etc.), and we know that not everything in the Bible is factually true, but we also believe the fundamental beliefs and teachings of the Bible are without error. The Scriptures faithfully teach the saving truths of faith that God wishes us to know and live by. Considering the literal sense means that we study the culture in which the words were written—the meaning of those words in the time they were written. This prepares us for considering the **spiritual sense** of Scripture.

When you're looking to uncover the meaning of a biblical text, discovering the author's intention is important. This involves understanding the historical setting in which the author wrote, knowing the meaning of key concepts (such as sin or redemption) as the author uses them and not as defined in modern terms, and appreciating the literary form (style of writing) chosen by the author.

The *way* a biblical text expresses the truth must first be understood in order to comprehend the truth being expressed. Remember, the literal sense as explained here is the basis for how Catholic scholars and laypeople study the Scriptures. The guidance of the Holy Spirit, who first inspired the authors, and the Church—through its creeds, sacraments, prayers, and teachings—can help us understand the truth God wishes to convey.

Scripture & Tradition: Together Forever

Scripture and Tradition together make up the one source of God's Revelation. Scripture is central to Tradition, and Tradition helps the Church correctly interpret and apply the message of Scripture to our lives. Some examples of Tradition are the creeds, the liturgy and prayers of the Church, and the authentic teachings of the popes and bishops.

There's no way to separate the written Scripture from the living Tradition of the Church—they're like two halves that together form the whole of our understanding. The Church helps us understand and connect God's Word as revealed in the Scripture to our lives. For example, bishops write pastoral letters guiding and instructing Catholics in their dioceses, and in papal encyclicals the pope teaches Catholics everywhere about important issues of faith and morals.

Church council documents are also part of the Tradition of the Church. These documents are the records of the conversations and decisions made during ecumenical councils—gatherings of the bishops of the world called together by the pope for the purpose of teaching and guiding the Church.

How Scripture Can Work for You

Reading, reflecting on, and studying Scripture bring richness and hope to our personal lives and to our spirituality. Scripture study can also challenge us to do more for others, to step out of our comfort zone, and to bravely stand up for our beliefs. Here are some ways to invite Scripture into your life:

- **Small-group Bible study.** Small-group Bible-study gatherings are a great way to experience the Scriptures in a new way. Sharing your thoughts and questions with a group will give you new insights about God and his message for your life.

- **Personal Scripture reading and reflection.** Reflecting on God's Word in the Bible isn't just for Scripture scholars and priests. When you prayerfully read a passage of Scripture and quietly think about it, you'll often be led to some positive action for yourself or toward others. This way of using Scripture will help you answer the question, "What is God calling me to do or be?" Be sure to begin with a prayer to the Holy Spirit to open your heart to God's Word.

- **Christian meditation.** Meditation is a form of quiet contemplation often associated with Scripture. To practice this form of meditation, find a quiet place where you will not be distracted. Quiet yourself by breathing deeply. Choose a Scripture passage and read it slowly. Focus your attention on a word or phrase. Think about it for a time. Read the passage again and ask yourself the question, "How does this apply to my life today?"

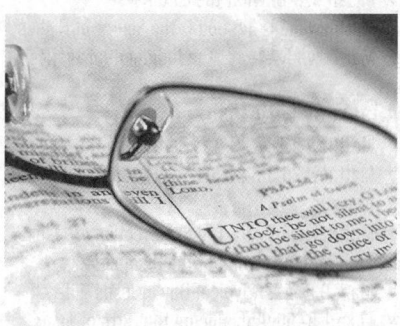

Psalm 28—© Christy Klink, 18

BIBLE READING PLANS

Here are some reading plans to help you reflect on and pray with the Bible.

Biblical Prayers
- 1 Samuel 2.1–10: Hannah's Prayer
- 2 Samuel 1.17–27: David's Lament
- 2 Samuel 7.18–29: David's Prayer of Thanks
- Ezra 9.5–15: Ezra's Prayer
- Job 3.1–26: Job Complains to God
- Psalm 57: Prayer for Help
- Psalm 80: Prayer for a Nation
- Sirach 39.116–35: Sirach's Prayer of Praise
- Matthew 6.9–13: The Lord's Prayer
- Luke 1.46–55: Mary's Prayer
- Luke 2.28–32: Canticle of Simeon
- Luke 17.5: Prayer of the Apostles
- John 17.1–26: Jesus' Prayer for His Disciples
- Ephesians 3.14: Paul's Prayer of Thanks

Meditations on Social Justice
- Exodus 3.7–10: God Hears the Cry of the Poor
- Leviticus 25.1–53: A Jubilee Year of Rest, Forgiveness, and Generosity
- 1 Kings 21.1–29: Elijah Speaks Out Against Economic Oppression
- Psalm 82–83: Prayers for the Justice of God
- Micah 6.1–8: What the Lord Asks
- Matthew 6.24–34: God Is the Source of Riches
- Matthew 25.14–45: The Judgment of Justice

A Journey with Jesus
- Matthew 5.1–7.29: The Sermon on the Mount
- Matthew 26.36–27.66: The Passion and Death of Jesus
- Matthew 28.1–20: The Resurrection of Jesus and Commissioning of the Disciples
- Mark 9.2–49: A Typical Day in Jesus' Life
- Luke 1.5–56: Announcing the Birth of Jesus
- Luke 1.57; Matthew 3.4–7; Luke 3.21–22; Luke 9.7–9: John the Baptizer

- Luke 2.1–52: Birth and Childhood of Jesus
- Luke 3.21–4.12: Beginning of Jesus' Public Life; Baptism and Temptation of Jesus
- Luke 4.16–30: Jesus' Rejection at Nazareth
- Luke 5.2–11; Mark 1.16–20: Call of the Disciples
- Luke 14.1–24; 15:1–32: Parables of Jesus
- Luke 22.14–38; John 13.1–17.26: The Last Supper
- Luke 24.13–35; John 21.15–19: The Risen Christ

Advent Meditations
- Genesis 2.7–9, 18–24: Adam and Eve
- Genesis 3.1–7, 23–24: The Fall of Humans
- Genesis 6.5–8, 13–22; 7.17, 23, 24; 8.1, 6–22: Noah
- Genesis 12.1–3: Abraham
- Genesis 22.1–14: Isaac
- Genesis 25.1–34; 28.10–15: Jacob
- Genesis 37.23–28; 45.3–15: Joseph
- Exodus 2.1–10: Moses
- 1 Samuel 3.1–18: Samuel
- 1 Samuel 16.1–13: Jesse
- 1 Samuel 17.12–51: David
- 1 Kings 3.5–14, 16–28: Solomon
- Matthew 1.18–25: Joseph
- Matthew 1.18–25; Luke 1.26–38: Mary

Lenten Reflections on Sin and Conversion
- Genesis 3: The First Sin and the Promise of Salvation
- Genesis 6: Evil
- Genesis 12.1–9: The Beginning of the Covenant

- Exodus 6.1–9: God Rescues the People
- Psalm 44: A Prayer of Lament
- Psalm 51: A Prayer for Cleansing and Pardon
- Matthew 9.2–8: Authority to Forgive Sins
- Luke 18.18–23: The Rich Ruler
- Luke 19.1–10: Zacchaeus
- John 3.1–21: God Sends the Promised Savior
- John 3.1–21: Nicodemus
- John 4.1–42: The Woman at the Well
- John 9.1–41: The Man Born Blind
- John 21.15–19: Jesus and Peter

Eastertime Readings

- John 14.1–14: The Holy Spirit as Advocate
- John 16.4–15: The Holy Spirit as Guide
- Acts 2.1–41: The Coming of the Holy Spirit at Pentecost
- Acts 8.4–21: The Power of the Holy Spirit
- 1 Corinthians 12.1–27: The Gifts of the Spirit
- Galatians 5.1–26: Living by the Spirit
- Ephesians 4.25–32: Do Not Grieve the Holy Spirit
- 1 John 4.1–21: Discerning the Holy Spirit

ABBREVIATIONS

The following abbreviations are used for the books of the Bible:

1Ch	1 Chronicles	Ecc	Ecclesiastes	Lk	Luke
1Co	1 Corinthians	Eph	Ephesians	Mal	Malachi
1Jn	1 John	Est	Esther	Mic	Micah
1Ki	1 Kings	Ex	Exodus	Mk	Mark
1Mc	1 Maccabees	Eze	Ezekiel	Mt	Matthew
1Pe	1 Peter	Ezr	Ezra	Na	Nahum
1Sa	1 Samuel	Gal	Galatians	Ne	Nehemiah
1Th	1 Thessalonians	Ge	Genesis	Nu	Numbers
1Ti	1 Timothy	Hab	Habakkuk	Ob	Obadiah
2Ch	2 Chronicles	Hag	Haggai	Phm	Philemon
2Co	2 Corinthians	Heb	Hebrews	Php	Philippians
2Jn	2 John	Hos	Hosea	Pr	Proverbs
2Ki	2 Kings	Isa	Isaiah	Ps	Psalms
2Mc	2 Maccabees	Jas	James	Rev	Revelation
2Pe	2 Peter	Jdg	Judges	Ro	Romans
2Sa	2 Samuel	Jdt	Judith	Ru	Ruth
2Th	2 Thessalonians	Jer	Jeremiah	Sir	Sirach (Ecclesiasticus)
2Ti	2 Timothy	Jn	John	SS	Song of Solomon
3Jn	3 John	Jnh	Jonah	Tit	Titus
Ac	Acts	Job	Job	Tob	Tobit
Am	Amos	Joel	Joel	Wis	Wisdom of Solomon
Bar	Baruch	Jos	Joshua	Zec	Zechariah
Col	Colossians	Jude	Jude	Zep	Zephaniah
Da	Daniel	La	Lamentations		
Dt	Deuteronomy	Lev	Leviticus		

Other abbreviations and special symbols used:

S	Shorter ending of Mark
T	Psalm titles
Pr.	Sirach Prologue
†	A Dagger distinguishes "Lord" and "God" from "Lord" and "God" in Hebrew Bible references
→	An arrow following an entry heading points to related words for additional study
⟦ ⟧	Contexts in double brackets are from passages that are similarly bracketed in the NRSV (e.g., John 7:53—8:11)

For further study consult *The Concise Concordance to the New Revised Standard Version* (Oxford University Press, 1993) and *The NRSV Concordance Unabridged* (Zondervan, 1991).

—John R. Kohlenberger III

NRSV CONCORDANCE

A

ABANDON → ABANDONED
Dt   4.31   will neither **a** you nor destroy you;
2Ch 15. 2   but if you **a** him, he will **a** you.
Ac   2.27   For you will not **a** my soul to Hades

ABANDONED → ABANDON
Dt 29.25   they **a** the covenant of the Lᴏʀᴅ,
Sir 49. 4   for they **a** the law of the Most High;
Isa 54. 7   For a brief moment I **a** you,

ABBA
Mk 14.36   **"A,** Father, for you all things are possible;
Ro   8.15   When we cry, **"A!** Father!"
Gal   4. 6   into our hearts, crying, **"A!** Father!"

ABIDE → ABLE
Ge   6. 3   My spirit shall not **a** in mortals forever,
Ps 91. 1   **a** in the shadow of the Almighty,
Wis   3. 9   the faithful will **a** with him in love,
Jn 15. 4   **A** in me as I **a** in you.
1Co 13.13   faith, hope, and love **a,** these three;
1Jn   2.28   And now, little children, **a** in him,

ABILITY → ABLE
Mt 25.15   to each according to his **a.**
Ac   2. 4   as the Spirit gave them **a.**

ABLE → ABILITY
Jdt 11.18   of them will be **a** to withstand you.
Da   3.17   God whom we serve is **a** to deliver
Mk 10.38   you **a** to drink the cup that I drink,
Ro 14. 4   the Lord is **a** to make them stand.
2Co 9. 8   God is **a** to provide you with every
Eph 6.11   **a** to stand against the wiles of the devil.
Heb 2.18   **a** to help those who are being tested.
      7.25   he is **a** for all time to save

ABOLISH → ABOLISHED
Da 11.31   shall **a** the regular burnt offering
Mt   5.17   I have come not to **a** but to fulfill.

ABOLISHED → ABOLISH
Eph 2.15   **a** the law with its commandments
2Ti   1.10   who **a** death and brought life

ABOMINABLE → ABOMINATION
2Ch 28. 3   the **a** practices of the nations
1Mc 1.48   to make themselves **a** by everything
Eze   7.20   they made their **a** images,

ABOMINATION → ABOMINABLE
1Mc 6. 7   that they had torn down the **a** that
Pr   6.16   seven that are an **a** to him:
Sir   1.25   but godliness is an **a** to a sinner.
Da   9.27   shall be an **a** that desolates,

ABOUND → ABOUNDED, ABOUNDING
Dt 28.11   Lᴏʀᴅ will make you **a** in prosperity,
Ro   6. 1   in sin in order that grace may **a?**

ABOUNDED → ABOUND
Ro   5.20   sin increased, grace **a** all the more,

ABOUNDING → ABOUND
Ex 34. 6   **a** in steadfast love and faithfulness,
Ps 86. 5   **a** in steadfast love to all who call
Joel 2.13   to anger, and **a** in steadfast love,
Jnh   4. 2   to anger, and **a** in steadfast love,

ABUNDANCE → ABUNDANTLY
Lk 12.15   one's life does not consist in the **a**
2Co 9. 8   provide you with every blessing in **a**

ABUNDANTLY → ABUNDANCE
Jn 10.10   that they may have life, and have it **a.**

ACCEPT → ACCEPTABLE
Jn   1.11   his own people did not **a** him.

ACCEPTABLE → ACCEPT
Ps 19.14   meditation of my heart be **a** to you,
    51.17   sacrifice **a** to God is a broken spirit;
Ro 12. 1   a living sacrifice, holy and **a** to God,

ACCOUNT → ACCOUNTABLE
Mt 12.36   judgment you will have to give an **a**
Heb 4.13   to whom we must render an **a.**

ACCOUNTABLE → ACCOUNT
Ro 14.12   each of us will be **a** to God.

ACCURSED → CURSE
Ro   9. 3   I could wish that I myself were **a**
Rev 22. 3   Nothing **a** will be found there any

ACCUSATION → ACCUSE
Lk 23. 4   no basis for an **a** against this man."

ACCUSE → ACCUSATION, ACCUSER
Ps 103. 9   He will not always **a,**
Zec   3. 1   Satan standing at his right hand to **a**
Mt 12.10   so that they might **a** him.

ACCUSER → ACCUSE
Rev 12.10   the **a** of our comrades has been thrown

ACKNOWLEDGE
Dt   4.35   would **a** that the Lᴏʀᴅ is God;
Pr   3. 6   In all your ways **a** him,
Mt 10.32   I also will **a** before my Father in

ACTIVE
Heb 4.12   the word of God is living and **a,**

ADD → ADDED
Dt 4. 2 You must neither **a** anything
Pr 30. 6 Do not **a** to his words, or else
Lk 12.25 by worrying **a** a single hour to your

ADDED → ADD
Ecc 3.14 nothing can be **a** to it, nor anything
Sir 42.21 Nothing can be **a** or taken away,

ADOPTION
Ro 8.23 groan inwardly while we wait for **a,**
Gal 4. 5 that we might receive **a** as children.

ADORNMENT
Pr 3.22 for your soul and **a** for your neck.
1Pe 3. 4 let your **a** be the inner self with the

ADULTERERS → ADULTERY
Jer 23.10 For the land is full of **a;**
1Co 6. 9 idolaters, **a,** male prostitutes,

ADULTERESS → ADULTERY
Lev 20.10 the **a** shall be put to death.
Pr 2.16 from the **a** with her smooth words,

ADULTERY → ADULTERERS, ADULTERESS
Ex 20.14 You shall not commit **a.**
Jer 3. 9 committing **a** with stone and tree.
Mt 5.28 committed **a** with her in his heart.
Lk 16.18 and marries another commits **a,**
Jn 8. 3 ⟦a woman who had been caught in **a;**⟧

ADVANTAGE
Ecc 7.12 **a** of knowledge is that wisdom gives
1Co 10.24 Do not seek your own **a,** but that of

ADVERSARY
1Pe 5. 8 roaring lion your **a** the devil prowls

ADVICE
Tob 4.18 Seek **a** from every wise person
Ps 1. 1 do not follow the **a** of the wicked,
Pr 8.14 I have good **a** and sound wisdom;
Sir 37.11 pay no attention to any **a** they give.

ADVOCATE
Jn 14.26 But the **A,** the Holy Spirit,
15.26 the **A** comes, whom I will send
1Jn 2. 1 we have an **a** with the Father,

AFFLICT → AFFLICTED, AFFLICTION, AFFLICTIONS, AFFLICTS
2Sa 7.10 evildoers shall **a** them no more,
La 3.33 for he does not willingly **a**
2Th 1. 6 repay with affliction those who **a**

AFFLICTED → AFFLICT
Na 1.12 Though I have **a** you, I will afflict
2Co 4. 8 are **a** in every way, but not crushed;

AFFLICTION → AFFLICT
Ps 25.18 Consider my **a** and my trouble,
La 1. 9 "O Lord, look at my **a,**
2Co 4.17 this slight momentary **a** is preparing

AFFLICTIONS → AFFLICT
Ps 34.19 Many are the **a** of the righteous,

AFFLICTS → AFFLICT
Tob 13. 2 For he **a,** and he shows mercy;

AFRAID → FEAR
Ex 3. 6 for he was **a** to look at God.

Lev 26. 6 and no one shall make you **a;**
Dt 20. 3 Do not lose heart, or be **a,**
Ps 3. 6 I am not **a** of ten thousands
27. 1 of whom shall I be **a?**
Isa 12. 2 I will trust, and will not be **a,**
Mt 28.10 Jesus said to them, "Do not be **a;**
Lk 12.32 "Do not be **a,** little flock,
Heb 13. 6 Lord is my helper; I will not be **a.**

AGE → AGES
Mt 28.20 with you always, to the end of the **a."**
Gal 1. 4 to set us free from the present evil **a,**

AGES → AGE
Col 1.26 has been hidden throughout the **a**
1Ti 1.17 To the King of the **a,** immortal,

AGREE
Mt 18.19 if two of you **a** on earth about
Mk 14.56 and their testimony did not **a.**

AIR
Eph 2. 2 the ruler of the power of the **a,**
1Th 4.17 to meet the Lord in the **a;**

ALERT
Lk 12.37 slaves whom the master finds **a**
1Co 16.13 Keep **a,** stand firm in your faith,
Eph 6.18 keep **a** and always persevere
1Pe 5. 8 Discipline yourselves, keep **a.**

ALIEN → ALIENS
Ex 2.22 an **a** residing in a foreign land."
Lev 19.34 you shall love the **a** as yourself,
Dt 24.17 You shall not deprive a resident **a**

ALIENS → ALIEN
1Mc 2. 7 the sanctuary given over to **a?**
Eph 2.19 you are no longer strangers and **a,**
1Pe 2.11 I urge you as **a** and exiles to abstain

ALIVE → LIVE
Ac 1. 3 suffering he presented himself **a**
Ro 6.11 dead to sin and **a** to God
Eph 2. 5 made us **a** together with Christ—
1Th 4.17 Then we who are **a,** who are left,
Rev 1.18 I am **a** forever and ever;
19.20 were thrown **a** into the lake of fire

ALMIGHTY → MIGHT
Ge 17. 1 "I am God **A;** walk before me,
Ps 91. 1 who abide in the shadow of the **A,**
Bar 3. 1 O Lord **A,** God of Israel,
Rev 1. 8 who was and who is to come, the **A.**
21.22 its temple is the Lord God the **A**

ALMS
Tob 12. 8 better to give **a** than to lay up gold.
Sir 7.10 do not neglect to give **a.**
Mt 6. 2 "So whenever you give **a,**

ALONE
Ge 2.18 not good that the man should be **a;**
Dt 6. 4 The Lord is our God, the Lord **a.**
Mk 2. 7 Who can forgive sins but God **a?"**
10.18 No one is good but God **a.**

ALPHA
Rev 1. 8 "I am the **A** and the Omega,"
22.13 I am the **A** and the Omega,

ALTAR

Ex	27. 1	shall make the **a** of acacia wood,
	30. 1	an **a** on which to offer incense;
1Mc	1.54	a desolating sacrilege on the **a** of
	4.47	built a new **a** like the former one.
Heb	13.10	We have an **a** from which those
Rev	6. 9	I saw under the **a** the souls of those

ALWAYS

Mt	28.20	And remember, I am with you **a,**
Php	4. 4	Rejoice in the Lord **a;** again I will

AMAZED → AMAZING

Mt	8.27	**a,** saying, "What sort of man is this,
Mk	6. 6	And he was **a** at their unbelief.
Ac	2. 7	**A** and astonished, they asked,

AMAZING → AMAZED

Mk	12.11	and it is **a** in our eyes'?"
Rev	15. 3	"Great and **a** are your deeds,

AMBASSADORS

2Co	5.20	So we are **a** for Christ,

AMBITION

Php	2. 3	Do nothing from selfish **a** or conceit
Jas	3.14	envy and selfish **a** in your hearts,

AMEN

Dt	27.15	people shall respond, saying, **"A!"**
2Co	1.20	through him that we say the **"A,"**
Rev	3.14	The words of the **A,** the faithful and

ANCESTORS

Ex	3.13	'The God of your **a** has sent me to
Dt	4.31	not forget the covenant with your **a**
La	5. 7	Our **a** sinned; they are no more,
Ac	5.30	The God of our **a** raised up Jesus,
Heb	1. 1	Long ago God spoke to our **a** in

ANCHOR

Heb	6.19	a sure and steadfast **a** of the soul,

ANCIENT

Da	7. 9	and an **A** One took his throne,
Mic	5. 2	origin is from of old, from **a** days.
Rev	20. 2	He seized the dragon, that **a** serpent,

ANGEL → ANGELS, ARCHANGEL, ARCHANGEL'S

Ex	3. 2	the **a** of the LORD appeared to him
	23.20	going to send an **a** in front of you,
Tob	5. 4	the **a** Raphael standing in front of
1Mc	7.41	your **a** went out and struck
Ps	34. 7	The **a** of the LORD encamps
Sir	48.21	and his **a** wiped them out.
Isa	37.36	the **a** of the LORD set out and
Bar	6. 7	For my **a** is with you,
Da	3.28	who has sent his **a** and delivered
	6.22	God sent his **a** and shut the lions'
	13.59	of God is waiting with his sword
	14.34	the **a** of the Lord said to Habakkuk,
Mt	1.20	an **a** of the Lord appeared to him in
Lk	1.26	In the sixth month the **a** Gabriel
Ac	5.19	during the night an **a** of the Lord
	23. 8	say that there is no resurrection, or **a,**
2Co	11.14	Satan disguises himself as an **a** of light.

ANGELS → ANGEL

Ge	28.12	**a** of God were ascending and
Tob	11.14	and blessed be all his holy **a.**
Ps	103.20	Bless the LORD, O you his **a,**

Mk	12.25	but are like **a** in heaven.
Jn	1.51	and the **a** of God ascending and
Ro	8.38	that neither death, nor life, nor **a,**
1Co	6. 3	not know that we are to judge **a—**
Heb	2. 7	for a little while lower than the **a;**
2Pe	2. 4	not spare the **a** when they sinned,
Rev	1.20	stars are the **a** of the seven churches,
	21.12	and at the gates twelve **a,**

ANGER → ANGRY

Ex	34. 6	merciful and gracious, slow to **a,**
Jdg	2.12	they provoked the LORD to **a.**
1Ki	16.13	God of Israel to **a** with their idols.
Ps	30. 5	For his **a** is but for a moment;
Pr	12.16	Fools show their **a** at once,
Sir	5. 4	for the Lord is slow to **a.**
Joel	2.13	slow to **a,** and abounding in
Jnh	4. 2	slow to **a,** and abounding in
Mk	3. 5	He looked around at them with **a;**
Eph	4.26	not let the sun go down on your **a,**
Jas	1.19	slow to speak, slow to **a;**

ANGRY → ANGER

Jer	3.12	I will not be **a** forever.
Mt	5.22	that if you are **a** with a brother

ANGUISH

Isa	53.11	Out of his **a** he shall see light;
Da	12. 1	There shall be a time of **a,**
Zep	1.15	a day of distress and **a,**

ANIMAL → ANIMALS

Ge	2.19	God formed every **a** of the field

ANIMALS → ANIMAL

Ge	3.14	cursed are you among all **a**
Ps	36. 6	save humans and **a** alike, O LORD.

ANOINT → ANOINTED, ANOINTING

Ex	30.30	You shall **a** Aaron and his sons,
1Sa	15. 1	"The LORD sent me to **a** you king
Ps	23. 5	you **a** my head with oil; my cup
Da	9.24	and to **a** a most holy place.

ANOINTED → ANOINT

1Ch	16.22	"Do not touch my **a** ones;
Ps	2. 2	against the LORD and his **a,**
Isa	61. 1	because the LORD has **a** me;
Da	9.26	an **a** one shall be cut off and
Lk	4.18	he has **a** me to bring good news to
Jn	1.41	Messiah" (which is translated **A**).

ANOINTING → ANOINT

Ex	30.25	it shall be a holy **a** oil.
Jas	5.14	**a** them with oil in the name of the Lord
1Jn	2.27	as his **a** teaches you about all things,

ANOTHER

Isa	48.11	My glory I will not give to **a.**
Jn	14.16	and he will give you **a** Advocate,
Gal	1. 7	not that there is **a** gospel,

ANSWER

Pr	15. 1	A soft **a** turns away wrath,
Isa	65.24	Before they call I will **a,**
Lk	23. 9	but Jesus gave him no **a.**

ANT

Pr	6. 6	Go to the **a,** you lazybones;

ANTICHRIST

1Jn	2.18	As you have heard that **a** is coming,
	2.22	the **a**, the one who denies the Father
	4. 3	And this is the spirit of the **a**,
2Jn	1. 7	person is the deceiver and the **a**!

ANXIETIES → ANXIETY

1Co	7.32	I want you to be free from **a**.

ANXIETY → ANXIETIES

Ecc	11.10	Banish **a** from your mind,
1Pe	5. 7	Cast all your **a** on him, because he

ANYTHING

Ge	18.14	Is **a** too wonderful for the LORD?
Jer	32.27	is **a** too hard for me?
Mt	18.19	if two of you agree on earth about **a**
Jn	16.23	if you ask **a** of the Father in my name,

APART

Jn	15. 5	**a** from me you can do nothing.
Jas	2.20	that faith **a** from works is barren?

APOSTASIES → APOSTASY

Jer	2.19	and your **a** will convict you.
Eze	37.23	I will save them from all the **a**

APOSTASY → APOSTASIES

1Mc	2.15	officers who were enforcing the **a**

APOSTLE → APOSTLES

Ro	11.13	as I am an **a** to the Gentiles,
1Co	9. 1	Am I not an **a**?
2Co	12.12	signs of a true **a** were performed
Heb	3. 1	**a** and high priest of our confession,

APOSTLES → APOSTLE

Mt	10. 2	the names of the twelve **a**:
Ac	2.43	and signs were being done by the **a**.
1Co	12.28	has appointed in the church first **a**,
Eph	2.20	foundation of the **a** and prophets,
	4.11	he gave were that some would be **a**,
Rev	21.14	are the twelve names of the twelve **a**

APPEAR → APPEARANCE, APPEARANCES, APPEARED, APPEARING

Mt	24.30	the sign of the Son of Man will **a** in
Mk	13.22	messiahs and false prophets will **a**

APPEARANCE → APPEAR

1Sa	16. 7	not look on his **a** or on the height
Jdt	11.23	You are not only beautiful in **a**,
2Co	5.12	those who boast in outward **a**

APPEARANCES → APPEAR

Jn	7.24	not judge by **a**, but judge with right

APPEARED → APPEAR

Jn	21.14	that Jesus **a** to the disciples after he
1Co	15. 5	he **a** to Cephas, then to the twelve.
Heb	9.26	**a** once for all at the end of the age

APPEARING → APPEAR

Ac	1. 3	**a** to them during forty days and
2Ti	4. 8	to all who have longed for his **a**.

APPETITES

Sir	18.30	base desires, but restrain your **a**.
Ro	16.18	our Lord Christ, but their own **a**,

APPOINTED → APPOINT

Mk	3.16	So he **a** the twelve: Simon (to whom
Ac	3.20	that he may send the Messiah **a** for
Heb	1. 2	whom he **a** heir of all things,
	9.27	as it is **a** for mortals to die once,

APPROACH

Heb	4.16	**a** the throne of grace with boldness,
	11. 6	whoever would **a** him must believe

APPROVAL → APPROVED

Gal	1.10	I now seeking human **a**, or God's **a**?
Heb	11. 2	by faith our ancestors received **a**.

APPROVED → APPROVAL

1Th	2. 4	but just as we have been **a** by God
2Ti	2.15	to present yourself to God as one **a**

ARARAT

Ge	8. 4	ark came to rest on the mountains of **A**.

ARCHANGEL → ANGEL

Jude	1. 9	**a** Michael contended with the devil

ARCHANGEL'S → ANGEL

1Th	4.16	**a** call and with the sound of God's

ARCHITECT

Heb	11.10	whose **a** and builder is God.

AREOPAGUS

Ac	17.22	Then Paul stood in front of the **A**

ARGUE → ARGUMENTS

Isa	1.18	let us **a** it out, says the LORD:
Ac	18. 4	Every sabbath he would **a** in the
Ro	9.20	a human being, to **a** with God?

ARGUMENTS → ARGUE

2Co	10. 4	destroy strongholds. We destroy **a**
Col	2. 4	may deceive you with plausible **a**.

ARISE → RISE

1Mc	14.41	until a trustworthy prophet should **a**,
Isa	60. 1	**A**, shine; for your light has come,
Mt	24.11	false prophets will **a** and lead many

ARK

Ge	6.14	Make yourself an **a** of cypress wood
Ex	25.10	shall make an **a** of acacia wood;
1Sa	4.11	The **a** of God was captured;
2Mc	2. 4	that the tent and the **a** should follow
Rev	11.19	the **a** of his covenant was seen

ARM → ARMOR, ARMS, ARMY

Ex	6. 6	redeem you with an outstretched **a**
Dt	7.19	mighty hand and the outstretched **a**
2Ch	32. 8	With him is an **a** of flesh;
Ps	98. 1	his holy **a** have gotten him victory.
Isa	53. 1	the **a** of the LORD been revealed?
Jn	12.38	the **a** of the Lord been revealed?"

ARMOR → ARM

Wis	5.17	will take his zeal as his whole **a**,
Ro	13.12	and put on the **a** of light;
Eph	6.11	Put on the whole **a** of God,

ARMS → ARM

Hos	11. 3	I took them up in my **a**;
Mk	10.16	And he took them up in his **a**,

ARMY → ARM

Jos   5.14   as commander of the **a** of the L<small>ORD</small>
Ps   27. 3   Though an **a** encamp against me,
     33.16   A king is not saved by his great **a**;
Rev 19.19   rider on the horse and against his **a**.

AROMA

2Co   2.15   For we are the **a** of Christ to God

ARRESTED

Mt   26.50   and laid hands on Jesus and **a** him.
Ac   5.18   **a** the apostles and put them in the

ARROGANCE → ARROGANT

Jdt   9.10   their **a** by the hand of a woman.
1Mc 1.24   much blood, and spoke with great **a**.
Pr   8.13   Pride and **a** and the way of evil
Sir   10. 7   **A** is hateful to the Lord and to
Eze   7.24   put an end to the **a** of the strong,

ARROGANT → ARROGANCE

Ps   73. 3   For I was envious of the **a**;
1Co 13. 4   love is not envious or boastful or **a**

ARROW

Ps   64. 7   But God will shoot his **a** at them;
Isa   49. 2   he made me a polished **a**,

ASCEND → ASCENDED

Ps 139. 8   If I **a** to heaven, you are there;
Isa 14.13   in your heart, "I will **a** to heaven;
Ro   10. 6   'Who will **a** into heaven?'"

ASCENDED → ASCEND

2Ki 2.11   Elijah **a** in a whirlwind into heaven.
Jn   3.13   No one has **a** into heaven except

ASHAMED → SHAME

Ge   2.25   were both naked, and were not **a**.
Mk   8.38   who are **a** of me and of my words
Ro   1.16   For I am not **a** of the gospel;
2Ti   2.15   a worker who has no need to be **a**,
Heb 2.11   Jesus is not **a** to call them brothers
     11.16   God is not **a** to be called their God;

ASHES

Ge   18.27   I who am but dust and **a**.
Jdt   4.11   the temple and put **a** on their heads
Est   4. 1   and put on sackcloth and **a**,
Job 42. 6   and repent in dust and **a**."
Sir 17.32   but all human beings are dust and **a**.
Jnh   3. 6   himself with sackcloth, and sat in **a**.
Mt   11.21   long ago in sackcloth and **a**.

ASK

Isa   65. 1   sought out by those who did not **a**,
Mt   6. 8   knows what you need before you **a**
     7. 7   "**A**, and it will be given you;
Jn   16.24   **A** and you will receive,
Jas   4. 3   You **a** and do not receive, because
1Jn   5.14   we **a** anything according to his will,

ASLEEP → SLEEP

Jnh   1. 5   had lain down, and was fast **a**.
Mt   8.24   by the waves; but he was **a**.
1Th   5. 6   So then let us not fall **a** as others do,

ASSIGNED

Ro   12. 3   the measure of faith that God has **a**.
1Co   3. 5   as the Lord **a** to each.
     7.17   lead the life that the Lord has **a**,

ASSURANCE

Dt   28.66   in dread, with no **a** of your life.
Heb   6.11   so as to realize the full **a** of hope
    11. 1   faith is the **a** of things hoped for,

ASTONISHED

Isa   52.14   there were many who were **a** at him
Lk   2.48   his parents saw him they were **a**;

ASTRAY → STRAY

Dt   30.17   are led **a** to bow down to other gods
Isa   53. 6   All we like sheep have gone **a**;
Jer   50. 6   their shepherds have led them **a**,
Mt   18.12   go in search of the one that went **a**?
1Pe   2.25   For you were going **a** like sheep,

ATE → EAT

Ge   3. 6   she took of its fruit and **a**;
Ex   16.35   The Israelites **a** manna forty years,
Ps   78.25   Mortals **a** of the bread of angels;
Mt   14.20   And all **a** and were filled;
     15.37   And all of them **a** and were filled;

ATHLETE → ATHLETES

2Ti   2. 5   And in the case of an **a**,

ATHLETES → ATHLETE

1Co   9.25   **A** exercise self-control in all

ATONE → ATONEMENT

Sir   3. 3   who honor their father **a** for sins,
Da   9.24   an end to sin, and to **a** for iniquity,

ATONED → ATONEMENT

Pr   16. 6   and faithfulness iniquity is **a** for,

ATONEMENT → ATONE, ATONED, ATONING

Ex   29.36   a bull as a sin offering for **a**.
     30.10   Aaron shall perform the rite of **a**
     32.30   perhaps I can make **a** for your sin."
Lev   23.28   for it is a day of **a**,
Ro   3.25   God put forward as a sacrifice of **a**
Heb   2.17   to make a sacrifice of **a** for the sins

ATONING → ATONEMENT

Sir   28. 5   will make an **a** sacrifice for his sins?
1Jn   2. 2   and he is the **a** sacrifice for our sins,
     4.10   sent his Son to be the **a** sacrifice for

ATTENTION

Heb   2. 1   greater **a** to what we have heard,

AUTHOR

Wis 13. 3   for the **a** of beauty created them.
Ac   3.15   and you killed the **A** of life,

AUTHORITIES → AUTHORITY

Ro   13. 1   be subject to the governing **a**;
Col   2.15   He disarmed the rulers and **a** and

AUTHORITY → AUTHORITIES

Pr   29. 2   When the righteous are in **a**,
Mk   1.27   A new teaching—with **a**!
Lk   5.24   Son of Man has **a** on earth to forgive
Ac   5.29   obey God rather than any human **a**.
Ro   13. 1   for there is no **a** except from God,
1Co 11.10   woman ought to have a symbol of **a**
Col   2.10   who is the head of every ruler and **a**.
1Ti   2.12   no woman to teach or to have **a** over
Rev 12.10   and the **a** of his Messiah,
     20. 4   on them were given **a** to judge.

AVENGE → VENGEANCE

Dt 32.43 he will **a** the blood of his children,
1Mc 2.67 **a** the wrong done to your people.
Ro 12.19 Beloved, never **a** yourselves,
Rev 6.10 and **a** our blood on the inhabitants

AVENGER → VENGEANCE

Nu 35.12 shall be for you a refuge from the **a,**
Ps 8. 2 to silence the enemy and the **a.**
1Th 4. 6 the Lord is an **a** in all these things,

AVENGING → VENGEANCE

Na 1. 2 A jealous and **a** God is the Lord,

AWAKE

Da 12. 2 in the dust of the earth shall **a,**
Mk 14.37 Could you not keep **a** one hour?
Eph 5.14 "Sleeper, **a!** Rise from the dead,
1Th 5. 6 but let us keep **a** and be sober;
Rev 16.15 Blessed is the one who stays **a** and

AWE → AWESOME

Ps 119.161 my heart stands in **a** of your words.
Isa 29.23 will stand in **a** of the God of Israel.
Mt 9. 8 saw it, they were filled with **a,**
Ac 2.43 **A** came upon everyone, because
Ro 11.20 do not become proud, but stand in **a.**

AWESOME → AWE

Ex 15.11 majestic in holiness, **a** in splendor,
Dt 10.17 the great God, mighty and **a,**
Ne 1. 5 and **a** God who keeps covenant
Ps 47. 2 For the Lord, the Most High, is **a,**
Sir 43.29 **A** is the Lord and very great,
Da 9. 4 saying, "Ah, Lord, great and **a** God,

B

BAAL

Jdg 2.13 and worshiped **B** and the Astartes.
1Ki 18.25 Elijah said to the prophets of **B,**
Jer 2. 8 the prophets prophesied by **B,**
Ro 11. 4 not bowed the knee to **B."**

BABEL → BABYLON

Ge 11. 9 Therefore it was called **B,**

BABES

Ps 8. 2 Out of the mouths of **b** and infants
Isa 3. 4 and **b** shall rule over them.

BABYLON → BABEL

2Ki 24.15 into captivity from Jerusalem to **B.**
Ps 137. 1 By the rivers of **B**—there we sat
Isa 14. 4 this taunt against the king of **B:**
  21. 9 he responded, "Fallen, fallen is **B;**
Jer 25.11 serve the king of **B** seventy years.
Da 14.36 he set him down in **B,**
1Pe 5.13 Your sister church in **B,** chosen
Rev 14. 8 "Fallen, fallen is **B** the great!

BACKSLIDING

Jer 8. 5 people turned away in perpetual **b?**

BAD

Mt 7.17 but the **b** tree bears **b** fruit.
1Co 15.33 "**B** company ruins good morals."

BALM

Jer 8.22 Is there no **b** in Gilead?

BANISH

Ecc 11.10 **B** anxiety from your mind,
Ro 11.26 he will **b** ungodliness from Jacob."

BANNER

Ex 17.15 and called it, The Lord is my **b.**

BAPTISM → BAPTIZE

Mk 1. 4 proclaiming a **b** of repentance for
  10.38 be baptized with the **b** that I am
Lk 20. 4 the **b** of John come from heaven,
Ac 18.25 though he knew only the **b** of John.
  19. 3 They answered, "Into John's **b."**
Ro 6. 4 buried with him by **b** into death,
1Co 15.29 receive **b** on behalf of the dead?
Eph 4. 5 one Lord, one faith, one **b,**
Col 2.12 when you were buried with him in **b,**
1Pe 3.21 **b,** which this prefigured, now saves

BAPTISMS → BAPTIZE

Heb 6. 2 about **b,** laying on of hands,

BAPTIST → BAPTIZE

Mt 3. 1 In those days John the **B** appeared
  11.11 has arisen greater than John the **B;**
  14. 8 the head of John the **B** here on a

BAPTIZE → BAPTISM, BAPTISMS, BAPTIST, BAPTIZED, BAPTIZING

Mt 3.11 "I **b** you with water for repentance.
Lk 3.16 He will **b** you with the Holy Spirit
1Co 1.17 For Christ did not send me to **b** but

BAPTIZED → BAPTIZE

Mt 3.13 to John at the Jordan, to be **b**
Ac 1. 5 John **b** with water, but you will be **b** with the Holy
  2.38 "Repent, and be **b** every one of you
Ro 6. 3 **b** into Christ Jesus were **b** into his
1Co 10. 2 all were **b** into Moses in the cloud
  12.13 one Spirit we were all **b** into one

BAPTIZING → BAPTIZE

Mt 28.19 **b** them in the name of the Father
Jn 4. 1 "Jesus is making and **b** more

BARN → BARNS

Lk 12.24 they have neither storehouse nor **b,**

BARNS → BARN

Dt 28. 8 the blessing upon you in your **b,**
Ps 144.13 May our **b** be filled, with produce
Lk 12.18 pull down my **b** and build larger

BARREN

Ge 11.30 Now Sarai was **b;** she had no child.
Ex 23.26 No one shall miscarry or be **b** in
1Sa 2. 5 The **b** has borne seven, but she who
Ps 113. 9 He gives the **b** woman a home,
Isa 54. 1 Sing, O one who did not bear;
Lk 1. 7 because Elizabeth was **b,**
Heb 11.11 too old—and Sarah herself was **b**—

BASIN

Ex 30.18 You shall make a bronze **b** with a
1Ki 7.30 four corners were supports for a **b.**
Jn 13. 5 **b** and began to wash the disciples'

BASKET

Mt 5.15 a lamp puts it under the bushel **b,**
Ac 9.25 in the wall, lowering him in a **b.**

∧ ∨ CONCORDANCE

BATTLE

1Mc	3. 19	the army that victory in **b** depends,
Ps	24. 8	and mighty, the LORD, mighty in **b.**
Ecc	9. 11	nor the **b** to the strong, nor bread to
Rev	16. 14	them for **b** on the great day of God
	20. 8	Magog, in order to gather them for **b;**

BEAR → BEARS, BIRTH, BIRTHRIGHT, BORE, BORN, CHILDBEARING, FIRSTBORN

Ge	4. 13	punishment is greater than I can **b!**
Isa	7. 14	is with child and shall **b** a son,
Mt	1. 23	virgin shall conceive and **b** a son,
	7. 18	A good tree cannot **b** bad fruit,
Lk	11. 46	load people with burdens hard to **b,**
Jn	15. 2	he prunes to make it **b** more fruit.
Gal	6. 2	**B** one another's burdens,
Col	3. 13	**B** with one another and,
Heb	9. 28	offered once to **b** the sins of many,
Rev	12. 4	woman who was about to **b** a child,

BEARS → BEAR

Ps	68. 19	Blessed be the Lord, who daily **b** us
1Co	13. 7	It **b** all things, believes all things,

BEAST → BEASTS

Rev	11. 7	**b** that comes up from the bottomless pit
	13. 18	calculate the number of the **b,**
	16. 2	who had the mark of the **b**
	19. 20	who had received the mark of the **b**

BEASTS → BEAST

Da	7. 3	four great **b** came up out of the sea,

BEAT → BEATEN

Isa	2. 4	shall **b** their swords into plowshares,
Joel	3. 10	**B** your plowshares into swords,
Lk	22. 63	began to mock him and **b** him;

BEATEN → BEAT

2Co	11. 25	Three times I was **b** with rods.
1Pe	2. 20	If you endure when you are **b** for

BEAUTIFUL → BEAUTY

Ge	12. 11	you are a woman **b** in appearance;
1Sa	25. 3	The woman was clever and **b,**
Tob	6. 12	girl is sensible, brave, and very **b,**
Jdt	8. 7	She was **b** in appearance,
Est	2. 7	the girl was fair and **b,**
Job	42. 15	no women so **b** as Job's daughters;
SS	1. 5	I am black and **b,** O daughters of
Wis	7. 29	She is more **b** than the sun,
Sir	25. 1	and they are **b** in the sight of God
Isa	4. 2	the branch of the LORD shall be **b**
	52. 7	How **b** upon the mountains are the
Da	13. 2	very **b** woman and one who feared
Ac	3. 2	the temple called the **B** Gate so that
Ro	10. 15	**b** are the feet of those who bring

BEAUTY → BEAUTIFUL

Jdt	16. 9	her **b** captivated his mind,
1Mc	2. 12	And see, our holy place, our **b,**
Ps	27. 4	to behold the **b** of the LORD,
Pr	31. 30	Charm is deceitful, and **b** is vain,
Wis	13. 3	for the author of **b** created them.
Sir	9. 8	not gaze at **b** belonging to another;
Da	13. 56	**b** has beguiled you and lust has
1Pe	3. 4	with the lasting **b** of a gentle

BEGGAR → BEGS

Mk	10. 46	son of Timaeus, a blind **b,**
Jn	9. 8	who had seen him before as a **b**

BEGINNING

Ge	1. 1	In the **b** when God created the
Ps	111. 10	fear of the LORD is the **b** of wisdom;
Pr	1. 7	The fear of the LORD is the **b** of
	8. 22	The LORD created me at the **b** of his
Sir	1. 14	To fear the Lord is the **b** of wisdom;
Isa	40. 21	Has it not been told you from the **b?**
Mt	24. 8	this is but the **b** of the birth pangs.
Jn	1. 1	In the **b** was the Word,
1Jn	1. 1	declare to you what was from the **b,**
2Jn	1. 6	as you have heard it from the **b**—
Rev	21. 6	and the Omega, the **b** and the end.

BEGOTTEN

Ps	2. 7	You are my son; today I have **b** you.
Ac	13. 33	are my Son; today I have **b** you.'
Heb	1. 5	are my Son; today I have **b** you"?

BEGS → BEG

Lk	6. 30	Give to everyone who **b** from you;

BEHEADED → HEAD

Lk	9. 9	Herod said, "John I **b;**
Rev	20. 4	the souls of those who had been **b**

BEHEMOTH

Job	40. 15	"Look at **B,** which I made just as I

BELIEF → BELIEVE

2Th	2. 13	the Spirit and through **b** in the truth.

BELIEVE → BELIEF, BELIEVED, BELIEVER, BELIEVERS, BELIEVES

Nu	14. 11	long will they refuse to **b** in me,
2Ki	17. 14	not **b** in the LORD their God.
Ps	119. 66	for I **b** in your commandments.
Sir	19. 15	so do not **b** everything you hear.
Mt	18. 6	one of these little ones who **b** in me,
	24. 23	or 'There he is!'—do not **b** it.
Mk	1. 15	repent, and **b** in the good news."
	9. 24	"I **b;** help my unbelief!"
Lk	24. 25	how slow of heart to **b** all that the
Jn	1. 7	so that all might **b** through him.
	3. 18	who **b** in him are not condemned;
	5. 46	believed Moses, you would **b** me,
	6. 29	you **b** in him whom he has sent."
	14. 1	**B** in God, **b** also in me.
	17. 20	will **b** in me through their word,
	20. 29	not seen and yet have come to **b."**
Ac	16. 31	answered, **"B** on the Lord Jesus,
	28. 24	while others refused to **b.**
Ro	3. 22	faith in Jesus Christ for all who **b.**
	10. 9	**b** in your heart that God raised him
Gal	3. 9	this reason, those who **b** are blessed
1Th	4. 14	For since we **b** that Jesus died and
Heb	11. 6	would approach him must **b**
Jas	2. 19	Even the demons **b**—and shudder.
1Pe	1. 8	you do not see him now, you **b**
1Jn	4. 1	Beloved, do not **b** every spirit,
Jude	1. 5	destroyed those who did not **b.**

BELIEVED → BELIEVE

Ge	15. 6	And he **b** the LORD;
Ex	14. 31	**b** in the LORD and in his
Jdt	14. 10	had done, he **b** firmly in God.
1Mc	2. 59	**b** and were saved from the flame.
Isa	53. 1	Who has **b** what we have heard?
Jn	1. 12	received him, who **b** in his name,
	12. 38	"Lord, who has **b** our message,
Ac	2. 44	All who **b** were together and had
Ro	4. 3	"Abraham **b** God, and it was

2Co	4.13	"I **b**, and so I spoke"—
Gal	3. 6	Just as Abraham "**b** God,
1Ti	3.16	**b** in throughout the world, taken up
Heb	4. 3	For we who have **b** enter that rest,
Jas	2.23	that says, "Abraham **b** God,

BELIEVER → BELIEVE

1Co	7.12	**b** has a wife who is an unbeliever,
2Co	6.15	Or what does a **b** share with an

BELIEVERS → BELIEVE

Gal	2. 4	because of false **b** secretly brought
2Th	3. 6	keep away from **b** who are living in
1Pe	2.17	Love the family of **b.**

BELIEVES → BELIEVE

Jn	3.15	whoever **b** in him may have eternal
	11.26	everyone who lives and **b** in me
Ro	10.10	**b** with the heart and so is justified,
1Co	13. 7	It bears all things, **b** all things,

BELLY

Ge	3.14	upon your **b** you shall go,
Jnh	1.17	and Jonah was in the **b** of the fish
Mt	12.40	three days and three nights in the **b**

BELOVED → LOVE

SS	2.16	My **b** is mine and I am his;
Mt	3.17	heaven said, "This is my Son, the **B,**
	12.18	my **b**, with whom my soul is well
	17. 5	"This is my Son, the **B;**
Col	3.12	As God's chosen ones, holy and **b,**
Rev	20. 9	camp of the saints and the **b** city.

BEND → BENT

Php	2.10	name of Jesus every knee should **b,**

BENEFICIAL → BENEFIT

1Co	6.12	but not all things are **b.**
	10.23	lawful," but not all things are **b.**

BENEFIT → BENEFICIAL, BENEFITS

Gal	5. 2	Christ will be of no **b** to you.
Phm	1.20	have this **b** from you in the Lord!
Heb	4. 2	message they heard did not **b** them,

BENEFITS → BENEFIT

Ps	103. 2	and do not forget all his **b**—
1Co	9.11	if we reap your material **b?**

BENT → BEND

Hos	11. 4	I **b** down to them and fed them.
Jn	8. 6	⟦Jesus **b** down and wrote with his⟧

BEST → GOOD

Dt	33.21	He chose the **b** for himself,
Mk	12.39	the **b** seats in the synagogues and
2Ti	2.15	your **b** to present yourself to God

BETHANY

Mt	26. 6	Jesus was at **B** in the house of
Jn	11. 1	a certain man was ill, Lazarus of **B,**

BETHLEHEM

1Sa	17.12	David was the son of an Ephrathite of **B**
Mic	5. 2	But you, O **B** of Ephrathah,
Mt	2. 1	after Jesus was born in **B** of Judea,
Lk	2.15	"Let us go now to **B** and see this

BETRAY → BETRAYED

Mt	10.21	Brother will **b** brother to death,
Mk	14.11	to look for an opportunity to **b** him.
Jn	13.11	For he knew who was to **b** him;

BETRAYED → BETRAY

Lk	21.16	You will be **b** even by parents and
1Co	11.23	Jesus on the night when he was **b**

BETTER → GOOD

1Sa	15.22	Surely, to obey is **b** than sacrifice,
Tob	12. 8	A little with righteousness is **b** than
Ps	63. 3	your steadfast love is **b** than life,
Pr	15.16	**B** is a little with the fear of
Ecc	2.24	There is nothing **b** for mortals than
SS	1. 2	For your love is **b** than wine,
Sir	40.26	the fear of the Lord is **b** than either.
Mt	5.29	it is **b** for you to lose one of your
Mk	14.21	It would have been **b** for that one
Jn	11.50	**b** for you to have one man die for
Php	1.23	be with Christ, for that is far **b;**
	2. 3	in humility regard others as **b** than
Heb	7.22	the guarantee of a **b** covenant.
	9.23	need **b** sacrifices than these.

BIND → BINDS

Dt	6. 8	**B** them as a sign on your hand,
Pr	6.21	**B** them upon your heart always;
Isa	61. 1	to **b** up the brokenhearted,
Mt	16.19	whatever you **b** on earth will be

BINDS → BIND

Job	5.18	For he wounds, but he **b** up;
Col	3.14	**b** everything together in perfect

BIRD → BIRDS

Ge	1.21	and every winged **b** of every kind.
Lev	20.25	the unclean **b** and the clean;

BIRDS → BIRD

Ge	7. 3	and seven pairs of the **b** of the air
Ps	50.11	I know all the **b** of the air,
Mt	6.26	Look at the **b** of the air;

BIRTH → BEAR

Dt	32.18	you forgot the God who gave you **b.**
Ps	22.10	On you I was cast from my **b,**
Mt	24. 8	is but the beginning of the **b** pangs.
Jas	1.18	he gave us **b** by the word of truth,
1Pe	1. 3	given us a new **b** into a living hope

BIRTHRIGHT → BEAR, RIGHT

Ge	25.34	Thus Esau despised his **b.**
Heb	12.16	who sold his **b** for a single meal.

BISHOP

1Ti	3. 1	whoever aspires to the office of **b**
Tit	1. 7	For a **b**, as God's steward, must be

BITE

Sir	21. 2	if you approach sin, it will **b** you.
Gal	5.15	If, however, you **b** and devour one

BITTER → BITTERNESS

Ex	1.14	made their lives **b** with hard service
	12. 8	with unleavened bread and **b** herbs.
Rev	8.11	the water, because it was made **b.**

BITTERNESS → BITTER

Pr	14.10	The heart knows its own **b,**
Ro	3.14	mouths are full of cursing and **b.**"
Eph	4.31	Put away from you all **b** and wrath

BLACK

SS	1. 5	I am **b** and beautiful, O daughters
Zec	6. 2	the second chariot **b** horses,
Mt	5.36	cannot make one hair white or **b**.
Rev	6. 5	I looked, and there was a **b** horse!

BLAMELESS

2Sa	22.26	with the **b** you show yourself **b;**
1Mc	4.42	chose **b** priests devoted to the law,
Ps	37.18	The Lord knows the days of the **b,**
Pr	11.20	but those of **b** ways are his delight.
Eph	1. 4	holy and **b** before him in love.
Php	2.15	so that you may be **b** and innocent,
1Th	5.23	and **b** at the coming of our Lord
Tit	1. 7	bishop, as God's steward, must be **b**
Heb	7.26	**b**, undefiled, separated from sinners,
Rev	14. 5	mouth no lie was found; they are **b**.

BLASPHEME → BLASPHEMED, BLASPHEMER, BLASPHEMES, BLASPHEMIES, BLASPHEMOUS

Ac	26.11	I tried to force them to **b;**
1Ti	1.20	so that they may learn not to **b**.

BLASPHEMED → BLASPHEME

Eze	20.27	In this again your ancestors **b** me,
Mt	26.65	tore his clothes and said, "He has **b!**

BLASPHEMER → BLASPHEME

Sir	3.16	forsakes a father is like a **b,**
1Ti	1.13	even though I was formerly a **b,**

BLASPHEMES → BLASPHEME

Lev	24.16	One who **b** the name of the Lord
Lk	12.10	whoever **b** against the Holy Spirit

BLASPHEMIES → BLASPHEME

1Mc	2. 6	He saw the **b** being committed in
Mk	3.28	their sins and whatever **b** they utter;
Rev	13. 6	its mouth to utter **b** against God,

BLASPHEMOUS → BLASPHEME

Ac	6.11	"We have heard him speak **b** words
Rev	13. 1	and on its heads were **b** names.

BLEMISH

Ex	12. 5	Your lamb shall be without **b,**
Lev	22.20	not offer anything that has a **b,**
Eph	5.27	that she may be holy and without **b**
Heb	9.14	offered himself without **b** to God,
1Pe	1.19	that of a lamb without defect or **b**.
Jude	1.24	to make you stand without **b** in the

BLESS → BLESSED, BLESSING, BLESSINGS

Ge	12. 2	I will **b** you, and make your name
	22.17	I will indeed **b** you, and I will make
	26. 3	I will be with you, and will **b** you;
Ex	20.24	I will come to you and **b** you.
Nu	6.24	The Lord **b** you and keep you;
	23.20	See, I received a command to **b;**
Dt	7.13	he will love you, **b** you, and
	30.16	the Lord your God will **b** you
1Ch	29.20	"**B** the Lord your God."
Tob	4.19	At all times **b** the Lord God,
Ps	5.12	For you **b** the righteous, O Lord;
	34. 1	I will **b** the Lord at all times;
	103. 1	**B** the Lord, O my soul,
Sir	32.13	But above all **b** your Maker,
Hag	2.19	From this day on I will **b** you.
Lk	6.28	**b** those who curse you, pray
Ro	12.14	**B** those who persecute you;
1Co	4.12	When reviled, we **b;**

Jas	3. 9	With it we **b** the Lord and Father,

BLESSED → BLESS

Ge	1.22	God **b** them, saying, "Be fruitful
	2. 3	So God **b** the seventh day and
	14.19	He **b** him and said, "**B** be Abram
Nu	24. 9	**B** is everyone who blesses you,
Tob	3.11	she prayed and said, "**B** are you,
Jdt	13.17	one accord, "**B** are you our God,
Job	1.21	**b** be the name of the Lord."
Ps	118.26	**B** is the one who comes in the name
Isa	30.18	**b** are all those who wait for him.
Jer	17. 7	**B** are those who trust in the Lord,
Da	13.60	raised a great shout and **b** God,
Mt	5. 3	"**B** are the poor in spirit,
Mk	10.16	laid his hands on them, and **b** them.
Lk	1.42	"**B** are you among women,
	6.20	"**B** are you who are poor,
Jn	12.13	**B** is the one who comes in the name
	20.29	**B** are those who have not seen and
Ac	20.35	It is more **b** to give than to receive.
Gal	3. 8	"All the Gentiles shall be **b** in you."
Eph	1. 3	who has **b** us in Christ
1Pe	3.14	for doing what is right, you are **b**.
Rev	22. 7	**B** is the one who keeps the words of

BLESSING → BLESS

Ge	12. 2	so that you will be a **b**.
	22.18	the nations of the earth gain **b** for
Dt	11.26	before you today a **b** and a curse:
	23. 5	your God turned the curse into a **b**.
Ne	13. 2	our God turned the curse into a **b**.
Tob	8.15	you, O God, with every pure **b;**
Sir	34.20	he gives health and life and **b**.
Eze	34.26	they shall be showers of **b**.
Mk	14.22	bread, and after **b** it he broke it,
Lk	24.51	While he was **b** them, he withdrew
1Co	10.16	The cup of **b** that we bless,
Gal	3.14	in Christ Jesus the **b** of Abraham
Eph	1. 3	every spiritual **b** in the heavenly
Rev	5.12	might and honor and glory and **b!**"
	7.12	"**B** and glory and wisdom and

BLESSINGS → BLESS

Dt	28. 2	all these **b** shall come upon you
Jos	8.34	the words of the law, **b** and curses,
Mal	2. 2	and I will curse your **b;**
Ro	15.27	come to share in their spiritual **b,**

BLIND → BLINDED, BLINDNESS

Ex	4.11	mute or deaf, seeing or **b?**
Tob	2.10	until I became completely **b**.
Ps	146. 8	the Lord opens the eyes of the **b**.
Isa	35. 5	the eyes of the **b** shall be opened,
Bar	6.37	They cannot restore sight to the **b;**
Mt	11. 5	**b** receive their sight, the lame walk,
Lk	6.39	"Can a **b** person guide a **b** person?
Jn	9.25	though I was **b**, now I see."
Ro	2.19	sure that you are a guide to the **b,**

BLINDED → BLIND

Jn	12.40	"He has **b** their eyes and hardened
2Co	4. 4	has **b** the minds of the unbelievers,

BLINDNESS → BLIND

Dt	28.28	will afflict you with madness, **b,**
1Jn	2.11	the darkness has brought on **b**.

BLOCK → BLOCKS

Sir	31. 7	It is a stumbling **b** to those who are
Eze	14. 7	their iniquity as a stumbling **b**

Mt   16.23   You are a stumbling **b** to me;
Ro   11. 9   a stumbling **b** and a retribution for
1Co   1.23   stumbling **b** to Jews and foolishness

Jer   6.21   before this people stumbling **b**
Mt   18. 7   the world because of stumbling **b**!

Ge   9. 6   sheds the **b** of a human, by a human shall that
             person's **b** be shed;
Ex   7.17   and it shall be turned to **b.**
     12.13   when I see the **b,** I will pass over
     24. 8   the **b** of the covenant that the LORD
Lev   17.11   it is the **b** that makes atonement.
Nu   35.33   for **b** pollutes the land,
Ps   72.14   and precious is their **b** in his sight.
Isa   1.11   I do not delight in the **b** of bulls,
Eze   33. 4   **b** shall be upon their own heads.
Joel   2.30   **b** and fire and columns of smoke.
Mt   27. 8   field has been called the Field of **B**
Mk   14.24   "This is my **b** of the covenant,
Lk   22.44   ⟦sweat became like great drops of **b**⟧
Jn   1.13   who were born, not of **b**
     6.53   of the Son of Man and drink his **b,**
     19.34   and at once **b** and water came out.
Ac   2.20   to darkness and the moon to **b,**
Ro   5. 9   that we have been justified by his **b,**
1Co   11.25   cup is the new covenant in my **b.**
Eph   1. 7   we have redemption through his **b,**
Heb   9.12   the **b** of goats and calves, but with his own **b,**
     9.22   without the shedding of **b** there is no
1Jn   5. 6   the one who came by water and **b,**
Rev   6.12   the full moon became like **b,**
     8. 9   A third of the sea became **b,**
     12.11   conquered him by the **b** of the Lamb

Isa   5. 7   he expected justice, but saw **b;**
Eze   35. 6   you did not hate **b, b** shall pursue
Hab   2. 8   because of human **b,** and violence

Ge   6. 7   "I will **b** out from the earth
Ex   32.32   **b** me out of the book that you have
Ps   51. 1   mercy **b** out my transgressions.
Rev   3. 5   not **b** your name out of the book of

Ps   34. 2   My soul makes its **b** in the LORD;
Pr   27. 1   Do not **b** about tomorrow,
Sir   25. 6   and their **b** is the fear of the Lord.
Jer   9.24   but let those who **b b** in this,
Ro   2.23   You that **b** in the law,
1Co   1.31   the one who boasts, **b** in the Lord."
2Co   11.30   If I must **b,** I will **b** of the things that
Gal   6.14   never **b** of anything except the cross
Eph   2. 9   of works, so that no one may **b.**

2Co   11.13   For such **b** are false apostles,
2Ti   3. 2   **b,** arrogant, abusive, disobedient to

1Co   5. 6   Your **b** is not a good thing.
1Th   2.19   or crown of **b** before our Lord Jesus

Ro   12. 1   present your **b** as a living sacrifice,
1Co   6.15   that your **b** are members of Christ?
Heb   10.22   and our **b** washed with pure water.

Lk   3.22   upon him in **b** form like a dove.
Col   2. 9   the whole fullness of deity dwells **b,**

Mic   6. 7   fruit of my **b** for the sin of my soul?
Mt   6.22   "The eye is the lamp of the **b.**
Mk   14.22   and said, "Take; this is my **b."**
Lk   12. 4   do not fear those who kill the **b,**
Jn   2.21   speaking of the temple of his **b.**
1Co   15.44   It is sown a physical **b,** it is raised a
             spiritual **b.**
2Co   5. 8   from the **b** and at home with the Lord.
Eph   4. 4   There is one **b** and one Spirit,

Dt   31. 6   Be strong and **b;** have no fear
Pr   28. 1   the righteous are as **b** as a lion.

Eph   3.12   whom we have access to God in **b**
Heb   4.16   approach the throne of grace with **b,**
1Jn   4.17   may have **b** on the day of judgment,

Ge   2.23   "This at last is **b** of my bones and
Eze   37. 7   came together, **b** to its **b.**

Ex   12.46   you shall not break any of its **b.**
Ps   34.20   He keeps all their **b;** not one of
Jn   19.36   "None of his **b** shall be broken."

Ex   17.14   "Write this as a reminder in a **b** and
Dt   31.24   writing down in a **b** the words of
Jos   1. 8   This **b** of the law shall not depart
1Mc   1.57   possessing the **b** of the covenant,
Ps   69.28   be blotted out of the **b** of the living;
Rev   1.11   "Write in a **b** what you see and
     21.27   who are written in the Lamb's **b**

1Mc   1.56   The **b** of the law that they found
Ecc   12.12   Of making many **b** there is no end,
Da   7.10   in judgment, and the **b** were opened.
Jn   21.25   world itself could not contain the **b**

Lev   23.34   the festival of **b** to the LORD.
Ezr   3. 4   kept the festival of **b,** as prescribed,
Zec   14.16   and to keep the festival of **b.**

Isa   53.12   yet he **b** the sin of many,
Mt   8.17   our infirmities and **b** our diseases."
1Pe   2.24   He himself **b** our sins in his body

Ecc   3. 2   a time to be **b,** and a time to die;
Isa   9. 6   For a child has been **b** for us,
     66. 8   Shall a land be **b** in one day?
Lk   2.11   is **b** this day in the city of David
Jn   3. 7   'You must be **b** from above.'
1Pe   1.23   You have been **b** anew,
1Jn   4. 7   everyone who loves is **b** of God

Dt   28.12   to many nations, but you will not **b.**
Ps   37.21   The wicked **b,** and do not pay back,
Mt   5.42   anyone who wants to **b** from you.

BORROWER → BORROW
Pr   22. 7 the **b** is the slave of the lender.

BOUGHT → BUY
1Co   6.20 For you were **b** with a price;
2Pe   2. 1 even deny the Master who **b** them—

BOW → RAINBOW
Ge   9.13 I have set my **b** in the clouds,
Ex   20. 5 You shall not **b** down to them or
Ps   95. 6 O come, let us worship and **b** down,
Isa 45.23 "To me every knee shall **b,**
Ro   14.11 every knee shall **b** to me,

BOWLS
Rev 16. 1 the seven **b** of the wrath of God."

BRANCH → BRANCHES
Isa   4. 2 On that day the **b** of the LORD shall
     11. 1 and a **b** shall grow out of his roots.
Jer 23. 5 raise up for David a righteous **B,**
Zec   3. 8 going to bring my servant the **B.**
Jn   15. 2 every **b** in me that bears no fruit.

BRANCHES → BRANCH
Ro   11.21 if God did not spare the natural **b,**

BREAD
Ge   3.19 sweat of your face you shall eat **b**
Ex   12. 8 with unleavened **b** and bitter herbs.
     25.30 set the **b** of the Presence on the table
Dt   8. 3 that one does not live by **b** alone,
Ecc 11. 1 Send out your **b** upon the waters,
Wis 16.20 from heaven with **b** ready to eat,
Sir 15. 3 will feed him with the **b** of learning,
Mt   6.11 Give us this day our daily **b.**
Lk   4. 4 'One does not live by **b** alone.'"
Jn   6.35 said to them, "I am the **b** of life.
1Co 11.26 For as often as you eat this **b** and

BREAK → BREAKING, BROKEN, BROKENHEARTED
Mt   6.19 where thieves **b** in and steal;
Jn   19.33 they did not **b** his legs.

BREASTPIECE → BREASTPLATE
Ex   28.15 You shall make a **b** of judgment,

BREASTPLATE → BREASTPIECE
Wis   5.18 he will put on righteousness as a **b,**
Isa 59.17 He put on righteousness like a **b,**
Eph   6.14 and put on the **b** of righteousness.

BREATH
Ge   2. 7 into his nostrils the **b** of life;
      6.17 all flesh in which is the **b** of life;
Job   7. 7 "Remember that my life is a **b;**
Ecc 12. 7 the **b** returns to God who gave it.
2Th   2. 8 will destroy with the **b** of his mouth,

BRIBE
Dt   16.19 for a **b** blinds the eyes of the wise
Pr   6.35 and refuses a **b** no matter how great.

BRIDE → BRIDEGROOM
Isa 62. 5 the bridegroom rejoices over the **b,**
Rev 21. 9 the **b,** the wife of the Lamb."

BRIDEGROOM → BRIDE
Mt   9.15 as long as the **b** is with them,
Jn   3.29 He who has the bride is the **b.**

BRIGHT
Mt   17. 5 suddenly a **b** cloud overshadowed
Rev 15. 6 robed in pure **b** linen,
     22.16 of David, the **b** morning star."

BROKE → BREAK
Ex   32.19 tablets from his hands and **b** them
2Ch 36.19 **b** down the wall of Jerusalem,
1Mc   3. 5 and pursued those who **b** the law;
Jer 31.32 a covenant that they **b,**
Mt   14.19 and blessed and **b** the loaves,
1Co 11.24 he **b** it and said, "This is my body

BROKEN → BREAK
Ne   1. 3 the wall of Jerusalem is **b** down,
Ps   51.17 acceptable to God is a **b** spirit;
Mt   15.37 they took up the **b** pieces left over,
Lk   20.18 who falls on that stone will be **b**
Ro   11.20 were **b** off because of their unbelief,

BROKENHEARTED → BREAK, HEART
Ps 147. 3 He heals the **b,** and binds up their
Isa 61. 1 the oppressed, to bind up the **b,**

BRONZE
Nu   21. 9 look at the serpent of **b** and live.
Dt   28.23 The sky over your head shall be **b,**
Da   10. 6 legs like the gleam of burnished **b,**
Rev   1.15 his feet were like burnished **b,**

BROTHER → BROTHER'S, BROTHERS
Ge   4. 8 Cain rose up against his **b** Abel.
Mt   5.24 first be reconciled to your **b** or
     10.21 **B** will betray **b** to death,

BROTHER'S → BROTHER
Dt   25. 7 has no desire to marry his **b** widow,
Mk   6.18 lawful for you to have your **b** wife."

BROTHERS → BROTHER
Ge   9.25 lowest of slaves shall he be to his **b.**
     37.11 So his **b** were jealous of him,
Mk   3.33 "Who are my mother and my **b?"**
Lk   22.32 turned back, strengthen your **b."**
Heb   2.11 not ashamed to call them **b** and

BUILD → BUILDER, BUILDERS, BUILDING, BUILDS, BUILT, REBUILD
Ge   11. 4 "Come, let us **b** ourselves a city,
Ps 127. 1 those who **b** it labor in vain.
Mt   16.18 and on this rock I will **b** my church,
     27.40 destroy the temple and **b** it in three
1Co   3.10 must choose with care how to **b**
     10.23 are lawful," but not all things **b** up.

BUILDER → BUILD
Heb   3. 4 but the **b** of all things is God.)
     11.10 whose architect and **b** is God.

BUILDERS → BUILD
Ps 118.22 The stone that the **b** rejected has
Mk   12.10 'The stone that the **b** rejected has
1Pe   2. 7 "The stone that the **b** rejected has

BUILDING → BUILD
1Co   3. 9 you are God's field, God's **b.**
2Co   5. 1 we have a **b** from God,
Eph   4.12 for **b** up the body of Christ,

BUILDS → BUILD
Ps 127. 1 Unless the LORD **b** the house,

Pr   14. 1   The wise woman **b** her house,
1Co   8. 1   Knowledge puffs up, but love **b** up.

BUILT → BUILD
1Ki   6.14   Solomon **b** the house, and finished
Ne   7. 1   the wall had been **b** and I had set up
Tob 13.16   Jerusalem will be **b** as his house for
1Mc   4.47   **b** a new altar like the former one.
Pr   9. 1   Wisdom has **b** her house,
Da   9.25   sixty-two weeks it shall be **b** again
Eph   2.20   **b** upon the foundation of the

BULL → BULLS
Ps   50. 9   will not accept a **b** from your house,

BULLS → BULL
Ps   22.12   **b** encircle me, strong **b** of Bashan
Isa   1.11   I do not delight in the blood of **b,**
Heb 10. 4   it is impossible for the blood of **b**

BURDEN → BURDENS, BURDENSOME
Ps   55.22   Cast your **b** on the LORD,
Mt   11.30   my yoke is easy, and my **b** is light."

BURDENS → BURDEN
Ex   6. 6   free you from the **b** of the Egyptians
Lk   11.46   you load people with **b** hard to bear,
Gal   6. 2   Bear one another's **b,** and

BURDENSOME → BURDEN
1Jn   5. 3   And his commandments are not **b,**

BURIED → BURY
Ro   6. 4   have been **b** with him by baptism
1Co   15. 4   he was **b,** and that he was raised on

BURN → BURNED, BURNT
Ex   21.25   **b** for **b,** wound for wound,
Mal   4. 1   the day that comes shall **b** them up,
Lk   3.17   but the chaff he will **b** with

BURNED → BURN
Ex   3. 3   and see why the bush is not **b** up."
Jn   15. 6   thrown into the fire, and **b.**
1Co   3.15   If the work is **b** up, the builder

BURNT → BURN
Ex   40. 6   You shall set the altar of **b** offering
Lev   1. 3   If the offering is a **b** offering from
1Sa   15.22   LORD as great delight in **b** offerings
1Mc   1.45   to forbid **b** offerings and sacrifices
   4.56   and joyfully offered **b** offerings;
Ps   51.16   if I were to give a **b** offering,
Da   8.11   it took the regular **b** offering away
Hos   6. 6   the knowledge of God rather than **b**
Mic   6. 6   Shall I come before him with **b**
Mk   12.33   more important than all whole **b**

BURY → BURIED
Lk   9.60   "Let the dead **b** their own dead;

BUSH
Ex   3. 2   he looked, and the **b** was blazing,
Jnh   4. 6   The LORD God appointed a **b,**

C

CALAMITIES → CALAMITY
1Sa   10.19   who saves you from all your **c** and
2Co   6. 4   in afflictions, hardships, **c,**
   12.10   and **c** for the sake of Christ;

CALAMITY → CALAMITIES
Da   9.13   all this **c** has come upon us.
Hab   3.16   wait quietly for the day of **c** to come

CALF
Ex   32. 4   and cast an image of a **c;**
Lk   15.23   And get the fatted **c** and kill it,

CALL → CALLED, CALLING
1Ch   16. 8   to the LORD, **c** on his name,
Ps   61. 2   From the end of the earth I **c** to you,
Pr   8. 1   Does not wisdom **c,** and does
Isa   65.24   Before they **c** I will answer,
Mt   9.13   to **c** not the righteous but sinners."
Lk   6.46   "Why do you **c** me 'Lord, Lord,'
Jn   15.15   I do not **c** you servants any longer,
Php   3.14   goal for the prize of the heavenly **c**

CALLED → CALL
2Sa   22. 7   In my distress I **c** upon the LORD;
Isa   43. 1   I have **c** you by name, you are mine.
1Co   7.15   It is to peace that God has **c** you.
Eph   1.18   the hope to which he has **c** you,
1Jn   3. 1   that we should be **c** children of God;

CALLING → CALL
Ro   11.29   and the **c** of God are irrevocable.
Eph   4. 1   lead a life worthy of the **c** to which

CAMEL
Mt   23.24   strain out a gnat but swallow a **c!**
Mk   10.25   **c** to go through the eye of a needle

CANAAN
Ge   9.25   "Cursed be **C;** lowest of slaves
Nu   13. 2   "Send men to spy out the land of **C,**
1Ch   16.18   "To you I will give the land of **C**

CAPTIVE → CAPTIVITY
2Ki   15.29   he carried the people **c** to Assyria.
   24.16   king of Babylon brought **c** to
Ro   7.23   making me **c** to the law of sin
Eph   4. 8   he made captivity itself a **c;**

CAPTIVITY → CAPTIVE
Dt   28.41   for they shall go into **c.**
Ezr   8.35   those who had come from **c,**

CARE → CAREFUL, CARES, CARING
Ps   8. 4   mortals that you **c** for them?
Heb   2. 6   or mortals, that you **c** for them?
Jas   1.27   to **c** for orphans and widows in

CAREFUL → CARE
Dt   4.23   So be **c** not to forget the covenant
Jos   1. 8   you may be **c** to act in accordance
Eph   5.15   Be **c** then how you live,

CARES → CARE
1Pe   5. 7   on him, because he **c** for you.

CARPENTER'S
Mt   13.55   Is not this the **c** son?

CASE
Isa   41.21   Set forth your **c,** says the LORD;
Lk   12.58   make an effort to settle the **c,**
Jn   18.38   "I find no **c** against him.

CAST
Ex   34.17   You shall not make **c** idols.

Ps	22.18	and for my clothing they **c** lots.
	55.22	**C** your burden on the LORD,
Mk	3.23	"How can Satan **c** out Satan?
Jn	19.24	and for my clothing they **c** lots."
1Pe	5. 7	**C** all your anxiety on him,

CATTLE
Ge	1.25	and the **c** of every kind,
Ps	50.10	the **c** on a thousand hills.

CELEBRATE
Lev	23.37	shall **c** as times of holy convocation,
1Co	5. 8	Therefore, let us **c** the festival,

CENSER
Lev	10. 1	Nadab and Abihu, each took his **c**,
Eze	8.11	Each had his **c** in his hand,
Rev	8. 3	Another angel with a golden **c** came

CENTURION
Mt	8. 5	he entered Capernaum, a **c** came to
Lk	23.47	the **c** saw what had taken place,
Ac	10. 1	a man named Cornelius, a **c**

CERTIFICATE
Dt	24. 1	so he writes her a **c** of divorce,
Mt	5.31	let him give her a **c** of divorce.'
Mk	10. 4	a man to write a **c** of dismissal

CHAFF
Ps	1. 4	like **c** that the wind drives away.
Lk	3.17	**c** he will burn with unquenchable

CHAINS
Eph	6.20	for which I am an ambassador in **c.**
Heb	11.36	and even **c** and imprisonment.
2Pe	2. 4	them to **c** of deepest darkness

CHANGE → CHANGERS
Ex	32.12	**c** your mind and do not bring
Nu	23.19	a mortal, that he should **c** his mind.
1Sa	15.29	will not recant or **c** his mind;
Jer	18. 8	I will **c** my mind about the disaster
Jas	1.17	is no variation or shadow due to **c.**

CHANGERS → CHANGE
Mk	11.15	overturned the tables of the money **c**
Jn	2.15	poured out the coins of the money **c**

CHARGE
Mt	25.21	I will put you in **c** of many things;
Mk	15.26	The inscription of the **c** against him
Ro	8.33	will bring any **c** against God's elect?
1Co	9.18	I may make the gospel free of **c,**

CHARM
Pr	31.30	**C** is deceitful, and beauty is vain,
Sir	7.19	for her **c** is worth more than gold.
	26.15	A modest wife adds **c** to **c,**

CHASTISEMENT → CHASTISES
Sir	16.12	Great as his mercy, so also is his **c;**
La	4. 6	the **c** of my people has been greater

CHASTISES → CHASTISEMENT
Heb	12. 6	and **c** every child whom he accepts.

CHEEK
Ps	3. 7	you strike all my enemies on the **c;**
Mt	5.39	if anyone strikes you on the right **c,**

CHEERFUL
Pr	15.13	A glad heart makes a **c** countenance,
	17.22	A **c** heart is a good medicine,
2Co	9. 7	for God loves a **c** giver.
Jas	5.13	Are any **c?** They should sing songs

CHERUB → CHERUBIM
2Ch	3.11	touched the wing of the other **c;**
Ps	18.10	He rode on a **c,** and flew;
Eze	10.14	the first face was that of the **c,**
	28.14	an anointed **c** as guardian I placed

CHERUBIM → CHERUB
Ge	3.24	the garden of Eden he placed the **c,**
Ex	25.18	You shall make two **c** of gold;
Ps	80. 1	You who are enthroned upon the **c,**
Heb	9. 5	the **c** of glory overshadowing the

CHIEF
Ps	118.22	has become the **c** cornerstone.
Mk	15. 3	the **c** priests accused him of many
1Pe	5. 4	And when the **c** shepherd appears,

CHILD → CHILDBEARING, CHILDREN
Isa	11. 6	and a little **c** shall lead them.
	49.15	Can a woman forget her nursing **c,**
Hos	11. 1	When Israel was a **c,** I loved him,
Mt	1.18	with **c** from the Holy Spirit.
Mk	10.15	the kingdom of God as a little **c**
Lk	2.12	you will find a **c** wrapped in bands
1Co	13.11	When I was a **c,** I spoke like a **c,**
Rev	12. 4	that he might devour her **c** as soon

CHILDBEARING → CHILD, BEAR
Ge	3.16	greatly increase your pangs in **c;**
1Ti	2.15	Yet she will be saved through **c,**

CHILDREN → CHILD
Pr	22. 6	Train **c** in the right way, and when
Mt	3. 9	stones to raise up **c** to Abraham.
Lk	18.16	"Let the little **c** come to me,
Jn	1.12	he gave power to become **c** of God,
Ro	8.14	by the Spirit of God are **c** of God.
Eph	6. 4	do not provoke your **c** to anger,
Heb	12. 7	God is treating you as **c;**
1Jn	3.10	The **c** of God and the **c** of the devil

CHOOSE → CHOOSES, CHOSE, CHOSEN
Dt	30.19	**C** life so that you and your
Jos	24.15	**c** this day whom you will serve,
Jn	15.16	You did not **c** me but I chose you.

CHOOSES → CHOOSE
Ro	9.18	he has mercy on whomever he **c,**

CHOSE → CHOOSE
Mk	13.20	for the sake of the elect, whom he **c,**
1Co	1.27	God **c** what is foolish in the world

CHOSEN → CHOOSE
Isa	42. 1	my servant, whom I uphold, my **c,**
Mt	22.14	For many are called, but few are **c."**
Ro	11. 5	there is a remnant, **c** by grace.
1Pe	2. 6	a cornerstone **c** and precious;
	2. 9	are a **c** race, a royal priesthood,

CHRIST → CHRISTIAN, CHRISTIANS, JESUS, MESSIAH
Jn	4.25	Messiah is coming" (who is called **C).**
Ro	5. 6	right time **C** died for the ungodly,
	8.35	will separate us from the love of **C?**
1Co	1.23	but we proclaim **C** crucified,

> CONCORDANCE

3.11 that foundation is Jesus **C.**
11. 1 Be imitators of me, as I am of **C.**
Gal 5. 1 For freedom **C** has set us free.
Eph 4.15 into him who is the head, into **C,**
Php 1.21 to me, living is **C** and dying is gain.
2.11 should confess that Jesus **C** is Lord,
Col 1.27 **C** in you, the hope of glory.
Rev 20. 4 reigned with **C** a thousand years.

CHRISTIAN → CHRIST
Ac 26.28 persuading me to become a **C?"**
1Pe 4.16 Yet if any of you suffers as a **C,**

CHRISTIANS → CHRIST
Ac 11.26 the disciples were first called **"C."**

CHURCH
Mt 16.18 on this rock I will build my **c,**
Ac 8. 1 persecution began against the **c**
1Co 12.28 appointed in the **c** first apostles,
14. 4 those who prophesy build up the **c.**
Col 1.18 He is the head of the body, the **c;**

CIRCUMCISE → CIRCUMCISED, CIRCUMCISION
Ge 17.11 shall **c** the flesh of your foreskins,
Dt 10.16 **C,** then, the foreskin of your heart,
Lk 1.59 the eighth day they came to **c** the
Jn 7.22 and you **c** a man on the sabbath.

CIRCUMCISED → CIRCUMCISE
Ge 17.10 Every male among you shall be **c.**
1Mc 1.60 the women who had their children **c,**
Gal 6.13 **c** do not themselves obey the law,
Col 2.11 also you were **c** with a spiritual

CIRCUMCISION → CIRCUMCISE
Ro 2.29 real **c** is a matter of the heart—
Gal 5. 6 For in Christ Jesus neither **c**

CITIES → CITY
Jos 20. 2 'Appoint the **c** of refuge,
Rev 16.19 and the **c** of the nations fell.

CITIZENSHIP
Php 3.20 But our **c** is in heaven,

CITY → CITIES
1Ch 11. 7 it was called the **c** of David.
Ps 127. 1 Unless the LORD guards the **c,**
Mt 5.14 A **c** built on a hill cannot be hid.
Heb 12.22 Zion and to the **c** of the living God,
Rev 21. 2 I saw the holy **c,** the new Jerusalem,

CLAY
Isa 45. 9 Does the **c** say to the one who
Jer 18. 6 Just like the **c** in the potter's hand,
Ro 9.21 Has the potter no right over the **c,**
2Co 4. 7 But we have this treasure in **c** jars,

CLEAN → CLEANSE, CLEANSING
Ge 7. 2 seven pairs of all **c** animals,
Lev 10.10 and between the unclean and the **c;**
Ps 51. 7 with hyssop, and I shall be **c;**
Mk 7.19 (Thus he declared all foods **c.**)
Heb 10.22 with our hearts sprinkled **c** from

CLEANSE → CLEAN
Ps 51. 2 and **c** me from my sin.
Sir 38.10 and **c** your heart from all sin.
1Jn 1. 9 **c** us from all unrighteousness.

CLEANSING → CLEAN
Eph 5.26 by **c** her with the washing of water
2Pe 1. 9 is forgetful of the **c** of past sins.

CLOTH
Isa 64. 6 righteous deeds are like a filthy **c.**
Lk 2. 7 and wrapped him in bands of **c,**

CLOTHE → CLOTHED, CLOTHING
Col 3.14 Above all, **c** yourselves with love,
1Pe 5. 5 you must **c** yourselves with humility

CLOTHED → CLOTHE
2Co 5. 2 longing to be **c** with our heavenly
Gal 3.27 have **c** yourselves with Christ.
Rev 12. 1 a woman **c** with the sun,

CLOTHING → CLOTHE
Ps 22.18 and for my **c** they cast lots.
Mt 25.36 I was naked and you gave me **c,**
Jn 19.24 and for my **c** they cast lots."

CLOUD → CLOUDS
Ex 13.21 went in front of them in a pillar of **c**
Mk 9. 7 Then a **c** overshadowed them,
Lk 21.27 'the Son of Man coming in a **c'**
Heb 12. 1 by so great a **c** of witnesses,
Rev 14.14 on the **c** was one like the Son of Man,

CLOUDS → CLOUD
Ge 9.13 I have set my bow in the **c,**
Da 7.13 being coming with the **c** of heaven.
Mt 24.30 'the Son of Man coming on the **c** of
1Th 4.17 be caught up in the **c** together with
Rev 1. 7 He is coming with the **c;**

COIN
Mt 17.27 open its mouth, you will find a **c;**
22.19 Show me the **c** used for the tax."
Lk 15. 9 I have found the **c** that I had lost.'

COLLECTOR → COLLECTORS
Mt 10. 3 Thomas and Matthew the tax **c;**
Lk 18.10 one a Pharisee and the other a tax **c.**
19. 2 he was a chief tax **c** and was rich.

COLLECTORS → COLLECTOR
Mt 5.46 Do not even the tax **c** do the same?
11.19 a friend of tax **c** and sinners!'

COLT
Ge 49.11 his donkey's **c** to the choice vine,
Zec 9. 9 and riding on a donkey, on a **c,**
Jn 12.15 coming, sitting on a donkey's **c!"**

COME → COMES, COMING
Mt 6.10 Your kingdom **c.** Your will be done,
Lk 7.20 'Are you the one who is to **c,**
1Co 16.22 Our Lord, **c!**
Rev 1. 4 who is and who was and who is to **c,**
22.20 Amen. **C,** Lord Jesus!

COMES → COME
Ps 118.26 who **c** in the name of the LORD.
Lk 19.38 "Blessed is the king who **c** in the
Jn 14. 6 No one **c** to the Father except through

COMFORT → COMFORTED, COMFORTS
Ps 23. 4 your rod and your staff—they **c** me.
Isa 40. 1 **C,** O **c** my people, says your God.

COMFORTED → COMFORT
Ps   86.17 Lord, have helped me and **c** me.
Isa 49.13 For the Lord has **c** his people,
Mt   5. 4 those who mourn, for they will be **c.**

COMFORTS → COMFORT
Isa 66.13 As a mother **c** her child, so I will

COMING → COME
Mal   3. 2 But who can endure the day of his **c,**
Heb 10.37 is **c** will come and will not delay;
2Pe   3. 4 "Where is the promise of his **c?**
Rev 22.20 "Surely I am **c** soon."

COMMAND → COMMANDED, COMMANDING, COMMANDMENT, COMMANDMENTS
Ex 34.11 Observe what I **c** you today.
Jdg   2. 2 But you have not obeyed my **c.**

COMMANDED → COMMAND
Mt 28.20 to obey everything that I have **c** you.
Jn 14.31 but I do as the Father has **c** me,

COMMANDING → COMMAND
Dt   4.40 **c** you today for your own well-being
   30.11 **c** you today is not too hard for you,

COMMANDMENT → COMMAND
Dt   6. 1 Now this is the **c**—the statutes
Ps 19. 8 **c** of the Lord is clear,
Mt 22.38 This is the greatest and first **c.**
Ro   7.12 and the **c** is holy and just and good.
Gal   5.14 law is summed up in a single **c,**
1Jn 3.23 this is his **c,** that we should believe

COMMANDMENTS → COMMAND
Ex 20. 6 those who love me and keep my **c.**
Dt   4.13 to observe, that is, the ten **c;**
1Mc 2.19 and have chosen to obey his **c,**
Ps 119.66 for I believe in your **c.**
Pr 10. 8 The wise of heart will heed **c,**
Ecc 12.13 Fear God, and keep his **c;**
Sir 1.26 If you desire wisdom, keep the **c,**
Mt 22.40 On these two **c** hang all the law and
Jn 14.15 If you love me, you will keep my **c.**
1Co 7.19 obeying the **c** of God is everything.
1Jn 5. 3 And his **c** are not burdensome,
Rev 14.12 those who keep the **c** of God and

COMMON
Lev 10.10 between the holy and the **c,**
Eze 22.26 between the holy and the **c,**
Ac   2.44 and had all things in **c;**

COMMUNION
2Co 13.13 the **c** of the Holy Spirit be with

COMPANY
1Co 15.33 "Bad **c** ruins good morals."

COMPASSION → COMPASSIONATE
Dt 32.36 will vindicate his people, have **c**
Ps 103.13 As a father has **c** for his children,
Sir 18.13 the **c** of the Lord is for every living
Hos 11. 8 my **c** grows warm and tender.
Mt 14.14 had **c** for them and cured their sick.
Ro   9.15 I will have **c** on whom I have **c."**
Col   3.12 clothe yourselves with **c,** kindness,

COMPASSIONATE → COMPASSION
Ex 22.27 I will listen, for I am **c.**

Sir   2.11 For the Lord is **c** and merciful;
Jas   5.11 how the Lord is **c** and merciful.

COMPLAIN → COMPLAINING, COMPLAINT
Nu 14.27 shall this wicked congregation **c**
Jer   2.29 Why do you **c** against me?
1Co 10.10 And do not **c** as some of them did,

COMPLAINING → COMPLAIN
Ex 16. 7 heard your **c** against the Lord.
1Pe 4. 9 hospitable to one another without **c.**

COMPLAINT → COMPLAIN
Ps 142. 2 I pour out my **c** before him;
Hab 2. 1 he will answer concerning my **c.**
Col   3.13 if anyone has a **c** against another,

COMPLETE → COMPLETED
Jn   4.34 him who sent me and to **c** his work.
Rev 6.11 until the number would be **c**

COMPLETED → COMPLETE
Jer 25.12 Then after seventy years are **c,**
Da 11.36 until the period of wrath is **c,**

CONCEIT → CONCEITED
Sir   3.24 For their **c** has led many astray,
Php 2. 3 nothing from selfish ambition or **c,**
1Ti   3. 6 he may be puffed up with **c** and fall

CONCEITED → CONCEIT
Gal 5.26 Let us not become **c,** competing
1Ti   6. 4 is **c,** understanding nothing,

CONCEIVE
Mt   1.23 the virgin shall **c** and bear a son,
Lk   1.31 you will **c** in your womb and bear

CONDEMN → CONDEMNATION, CONDEMNED
Lk 11.31 of this generation and **c** them,
Jn   3.17 not send the Son into the world to **c**
Ro   8.34 Who is to **c?**
1Jn 3.21 Beloved, if our hearts do not **c** us,

CONDEMNATION → CONDEMN
Mk 12.40 They will receive the greater **c."**
Ro   5.18 one man's trespass led to **c** for all,
1Ti   3. 6 fall into the **c** of the devil.
Jas   5.12 so that you may not fall under **c.**

CONDEMNED → CONDEMN
Mt 12.37 and by your words you will be **c."**
Lk 24.20 handed him over to be **c** to death
Jn   3.18 Those who believe in him are not **c;**
   16.11 the ruler of this world has been **c.**
1Co 11.32 disciplined so that we may not be **c**

CONDUCT
Tob 4.14 and discipline yourself in all your **c.**
Sir 37.17 The mind is the root of all **c;**
1Pe 1.15 be holy yourselves in all your **c;**

CONFESS → CONFESSES, CONFESSION
Lev 5. 5 you shall **c** the sin that you have
Ps 38.18 **c** my iniquity; I am sorry for my sin.
Sir 4.26 Do not be ashamed to **c** your sins,
Php 2.11 should **c** that Jesus Christ is Lord,
1Jn 1. 9 If we **c** our sins, he who is faithful
Rev 3. 5 will **c** your name before my Father

∧ CONCORDANCE ∧

CONFESSES → CONFESS
Ro 10.10 **c** with the mouth and so is saved.
1Jn 2.23 who **c** the Son has the Father also.

CONFESSION → CONFESS
Da 9. 4 to the LORD my God and made **c,**
1Ti 6.12 for which you made the good **c** in
Heb 4.14 let us hold fast to our **c.**

CONFIDENCE
Ps 118. 8 LORD than to put **c** in mortals.
Php 3. 3 and have no **c** in the flesh—
Heb 10.19 we have **c** to enter the sanctuary

CONFORMED
Ro 8.29 predestined to be **c** to the image of
12. 2 Do not be **c** to this world,
Php 3.21 may be **c** to the body of his glory,
1Pe 1.14 do not be **c** to the desires that you

CONFUSE
Ge 11. 7 go down, and **c** their language there,

CONGREGATION
Ps 1. 5 nor sinners in the **c** of the righteous;
Heb 2.12 the midst of the **c** I will praise you."

CONQUER → CONQUERED, CONQUERORS, CONQUERS
Rev 17.14 and the Lamb will **c** them,
21. 7 who **c** will inherit these things,

CONQUERED → CONQUER
Jn 16.33 take courage; I have **c** the world!"
Heb 11.33 who through faith **c** kingdoms,
1Jn 2.13 because you have **c** the evil one.
Rev 15. 2 who had **c** the beast and its image

CONQUERORS → CONQUER
Ro 8.37 all these things we are more than **c**

CONQUERS → CONQUER
1Jn 5. 4 victory that **c** the world, our faith.
Rev 2. 7 To everyone who **c,** I will give

CONSCIENCE
Ro 2.15 their own **c** also bears witness;
1Co 8. 7 and their **c,** being weak, is defiled.
1Ti 1. 5 a good **c,** and sincere faith.
Heb 9.14 purify our **c** from dead works to
1Pe 3.21 as an appeal to God for a good **c,**

CONSIDER
1Sa 12.24 for **c** what great things he has done
Ps 107.43 and **c** the steadfast love of the LORD.
Lk 12.27 **C** the lilies, how they grow:

CONSOLATION
Lk 2.25 looking forward to the **c** of Israel,
2Co 1. 3 of mercies and the God of all **c,**

CONSPIRED
Da 6. 6 So the presidents and satraps **c**
Mt 26. 4 they **c** to arrest Jesus by stealth

CONSUME → CONSUMED, CONSUMING
Ex 32.12 **c** them from the face of the earth'?
Nu 16.21 so that I may **c** them in a moment.
Mt 6.19 where moth and rust **c** and where
Jn 2.17 "Zeal for your house will **c** me."

CONSUMED → CONSUME
Ex 3. 2 bush was blazing, yet it was not **c.**
Ps 69. 9 zeal for your house that has **c** me;
Zep 3. 8 all the earth shall be **c.**
Gal 5.15 that you are not **c** by one another.

CONSUMING → CONSUME
Heb 12.29 for indeed our God is a **c** fire.

CONTEMPT
Da 12. 2 some to shame and everlasting **c.**
Mk 9.12 sufferings and be treated with **c?**
Heb 6. 6 and are holding him up to **c.**

CONTENT → CONTENTMENT
Sir 29.23 Be **c** with little or much,
2Co 12.10 Therefore I am **c** with weaknesses,
Php 4.11 learned to be **c** with whatever I have
Heb 13. 5 and be **c** with what you have;

CONTENTMENT → CONTENT
1Ti 6. 6 gain in godliness combined with **c;**

CONTRITE
Ps 51.17 broken and **c** heart, O God, you
Isa 57.15 who are **c** and humble in spirit,

CONVERT
Mt 23.15 sea and land to make a single **c,**
1Ti 3. 6 He must not be a recent **c,**

CONVICT → CONVICTION
Dt 19.15 to **c** a person of any crime
Jude 1.15 to **c** everyone of all the deeds of

CONVICTION → CONVICT
Heb 11. 1 the **c** of things not seen.

CONVINCE → CONVINCED, CONVINCING
Ac 28.23 and trying to **c** them about Jesus
2Ti 4. 2 **c,** rebuke, and encourage,

CONVINCED → CONVINCE
Lk 16.31 neither will they be **c** even if
Ro 8.38 For I am **c** that neither death, nor
2Co 5.14 we are **c** that one has died for all;

CONVINCING → CONVINCE
Ac 1. 3 to them by many **c** proofs,

COPPER
Mk 12.42 and put in two small **c** coins,

CORNERSTONE → STONE
Ps 118.22 rejected has become the chief **c.**
Isa 28.16 a tested stone, a precious **c,** a sure
Zec 10. 4 Out of them shall come the **c,**
Lk 20.17 builders rejected has become the **c'?**
Eph 2.20 with Christ Jesus himself as the **c.**
1Pe 2. 6 laying in Zion a stone, a **c** chosen

CORRECT → CORRECTING, CORRECTION
Ps 141. 5 let the faithful **c** me.
Sir 42. 8 Do not be ashamed to **c** the stupid

CORRECTING → CORRECT
2Ti 2.25 **c** opponents with gentleness.

CORRECTION → CORRECT
Jer 5. 3 but they refused to take **c.**
2Ti 3.16 **c,** and for training in righteousness,

CORRUPT → CORRUPTION
Ge 6.11 Now the earth was **c** in God's sight,
Ac 2.40 yourselves from this **c** generation."
Eph 4.22 your old self, **c** and deluded

CORRUPTION → CORRUPT
Ac 2.31 nor did his flesh experience **c.'**
2Pe 1. 4 you may escape from the **c**

COST
1Ch 21.24 burnt offerings that **c** me nothing."
Lk 14.28 not first sit down and estimate the **c,**

COUNCIL → COUNCILS
Jer 23.18 who has stood in the **c** of the Lord
Mt 26.59 the whole **c** were looking for false

COUNCILS → COUNCIL
Mk 13. 9 for they will hand you over to **c;**

COUNSEL → COUNSELOR, COUNSELORS
Ps 2. 2 and the rulers take **c** together,
  33.11 The **c** of the Lord stands forever,
Isa 28.29 he is wonderful in **c,** and excellent

COUNSELOR → COUNSEL
Sir 42.21 and he needs no one to be his **c.**
Isa 9. 6 and he is named Wonderful **C,**
Ro 11.34 Or who has been his **c?"**

COUNSELORS → COUNSEL
Pr 11.14 in an abundance of **c** there is safety.
  24. 6 in abundance of **c** there is victory.

COUNTENANCE
Nu 6.26 the Lord lift up his **c** upon you,
Ps 89.15 O Lord, in the light of your **c;**
Pr 15.13 A glad heart makes a cheerful **c,**

COURAGE → COURAGEOUS
1Ch 22.13 Be strong and of good **c.**
Jn 16.33 But take **c;** I have conquered

COURAGEOUS → COURAGE
Jos 1. 6 Be strong and **c;** for you shall put
1Mc 2.64 be **c** and grow strong in the law,
Da 10.19 Be strong and **c!"**
1Co 16.13 stand firm in your faith, be **c,**

COURT → COURTS
Ex 27. 9 shall make the **c** of the tabernacle.
Pr 25. 8 do not hastily bring into **c;**
Mt 5.25 while you are on the way to **c**
1Co 6. 6 believer goes to **c** against a believer

COURTS → COURT
Ps 84.10 in your **c** is better than a thousand
  96. 8 an offering, and come into his **c.**

COVENANT → COVENANTS
Ge 6.18 But I will establish my **c** with you;
  9. 9 I am establishing my **c** with you
  15.18 the Lord made a **c** with Abram,
Ex 19. 5 you obey my voice and keep my **c,**
  24. 7 Then he took the book of the **c,**
  40. 3 put in it the ark of the **c,**
Jdg 2. 1 'I will never break my **c** with you.
1Ki 8.23 keeping **c** and steadfast love
Jdt 9.13 planned cruel things against your **c,**
1Mc 1.15 and abandoned the holy **c.**
Ps 105. 8 He is mindful of his **c** forever,

Sir 28. 7 remember the **c** of the Most High,
Isa 61. 8 I will make an everlasting **c** with
Jer 31.31 when I will make a new **c** with
Eze 16.60 establish with you an everlasting **c.**
Mal 3. 1 The messenger of the **c** in whom
Lk 22.20 is the new **c** in my blood.
1Co 11.25 "This cup is the new **c** in my blood.
2Co 3. 6 be ministers of a new **c,** not of letter
Heb 7.22 become the guarantee of a better **c.**
  12.24 the mediator of a new **c,**
Rev 11.19 the ark of his **c** was seen within his

COVENANTS → COVENANT
Ro 9. 4 the adoption, the glory, the **c,**
Gal 4.24 an allegory: these women are two **c.**

COVET
Ex 20.17 shall not **c** your neighbor's house;
Ro 7. 7 had not said, "You shall not **c."**
Jas 4. 2 you **c** something and cannot obtain

CRAFTINESS → CRAFTY
Ro 1.29 of envy, murder, strife, deceit, **c,**
1Co 3.19 "He catches the wise in their **c,"**

CRAFTY → CRAFTINESS
Ge 3. 1 serpent was more **c** than any other

CRAVING
Nu 11. 4 rabble among them had a strong **c;**
Ps 78.30 But before they had satisfied their **c,**

CREATE → CREATED, CREATION, CREATOR
Ps 51.10 **C** in me a clean heart, O God,
Isa 65.17 to **c** new heavens and a new earth;
Eph 2.15 **c** in himself one new humanity

CREATED → CREATE
Ge 1. 1 In the beginning when God **c** the
  1.27 So God **c** humankind in his image,
Dt 32. 6 Is not he your father, who **c** you,
Jdt 13.18 who **c** the heavens and the earth,
Pr 8.22 The Lord **c** me at the beginning
Wis 2.23 for God **c** us for incorruption,
Sir 1. 4 Wisdom was **c** before all other
Mal 2.10 Has not one God **c** us?
1Co 11. 9 Neither was man **c** for the sake of
Eph 2.10 **c** in Christ Jesus for good works,
Col 1.16 all things have been **c** through him
1Ti 4. 4 For everything **c** by God is good,
Rev 4.11 you **c** all things, and by your will

CREATION → CREATE
Ge 2. 3 all the work that he had done in **c.**
Mk 10. 6 But from the beginning of **c,**
Ro 8.19 the **c** waits with eager longing for
2Co 5.17 anyone is in Christ, there is a new **c:**
Col 1.15 invisible God, the firstborn of all **c;**

CREATOR → CREATE
Ecc 12. 1 Remember your **c** in the days of
Ro 1.25 served the creature rather than the **C**
1Pe 4.19 to a faithful **C,**

CREATURE → CREATURES
Ge 2.19 the man called every living **c,**

CREATURES → CREATURE
Lev 11. 2 these are the **c** that you may eat.
Ps 104.24 the earth is full of your **c.**

CRIED → CRY
Ps 22. 5 To you they **c**, and were saved;
Mt 27.46 Jesus **c** with a loud voice,

CRIMINAL → CRIMINALS
Jn 18.30 "If this man were not a **c**,
2Ti 2. 9 the point of being chained like a **c**.
1Pe 4.15 suffer as a murderer, a thief, a **c**,

CRIMINALS → CRIMINAL
Lk 23.32 Two others also, who were **c**,

CROOKED
Dt 32. 5 a perverse and **c** generation.
Ps 18.26 the **c** you show yourself perverse.
Ecc 1.15 What is **c** cannot be made straight,
Lk 3. 5 and the **c** shall be made straight,

CROSS
Dt 31. 3 your God himself will **c** over before
Mk 15.30 and come down from the **c**!"
Lk 14.27 the **c** and follow me cannot be my
1Co 1.18 the **c** is foolishness to those who are
Gal 6.14 never boast of anything except the **c**
Php 2. 8 of death—even death on a **c**.
Col 1.20 peace through the blood of his **c**.
Heb 12. 2 was set before him endured the **c**,

CROW
Lk 22.34 the cock will not **c** this day,

CROWD → CROWDS
Mk 8. 2 "I have compassion for the **c**,
14.43 a **c** with swords and clubs,

CROWDS → CROWD
Mt 7.28 **c** were astounded at his teaching,

CROWN → CROWNED, CROWNS
Lev 8. 9 the golden ornament, the holy **c**,
Jn 19. 2 soldiers wove a **c** of thorns and put
Php 4. 1 my joy and **c**, stand firm in the Lord
2Ti 4. 8 there is reserved for me the **c**
1Pe 5. 4 the **c** of glory that never fades away.
Rev 6. 2 Its rider had a bow; a **c** was given
14.14 with a golden **c** on his head,

CROWNED → CROWN
Ps 8. 5 and **c** them with glory and honor.
2Ti 2. 5 no one is **c** without competing
Heb 2. 9 now **c** with glory and honor

CROWNS → CROWN
Rev 4.10 they cast their **c** before the throne,

CRUCIFIED → CRUCIFY
Mt 27.22 All of them said, "Let him be **c**!"
Lk 24. 7 **c**, and on the third day rise again."
Ac 4.10 whom you **c**, whom God raised
Ro 6. 6 We know that our old self was **c**
1Co 1.23 but we proclaim Christ **c**,
Gal 2.19 I have been **c** with Christ;

CRUCIFY → CRUCIFIED, CRUCIFYING
Lk 23.21 they kept shouting, "**C**, **c** him!"
Jn 19.15 asked them, "Shall I **c** your King?"

CRUCIFYING → CRUCIFY
Heb 6. 6 they are **c** again the Son of God

CRUSH
Mt 21.44 it will **c** anyone on whom it falls."
Ro 16.20 will shortly **c** Satan under your feet.

CRY → CRIED, CRYING
Pr 130. 1 Out of the depths I **c** to you,
Hab 1. 2 how long shall I **c** for help,
Mk 15.37 Then Jesus gave a loud **c**

CRYING → CRY
Mk 1. 3 the voice of one **c** out in the
Rev 21. 4 **c** and pain will be no more,

CUP
Ps 23. 5 my head with oil; my **c** overflows.
Mt 26.39 if it is possible, let this **c** pass
Mk 10.38 you able to drink the **c** that I drink,
Lk 22.17 he took a **c**, and after giving thanks
1Co 11.25 **c** is the new covenant in my blood.
Rev 14.10 unmixed into the **c** of his anger,

CURED
Mt 8.16 and **c** all who were sick.
Ac 5.16 and they were all **c**.

CURSE → ACCURSED, CURSED, CURSES
Ge 8.21 "I will never again **c** the ground
12. 3 the one who curses you I will **c**;
Job 2. 9 **C** God, and die."
Ps 109.28 Let them **c**, but you will bless.
Sir 4. 5 and give no one reason to **c** you;
Mal 4. 6 come and strike the land with a **c**.
Mk 14.71 he began to **c**, and he swore an oath,
Lk 6.28 bless those who **c** you, pray
Ro 12.14 bless and do not **c** them.
Gal 3.13 redeemed us from the **c** of the law by
becoming a **c** for us—

CURSED → CURSE
Ge 3.17 **c** is the ground because of you;
27.29 **C** be everyone who curses you,
Nu 23. 8 can I curse whom God has not **c**?
Mk 11.21 fig tree that you **c** has withered."
Gal 3.10 "**C** is everyone who does not
Rev 16. 9 but they **c** the name of God,

CURSES → CURSE
Lev 24.15 who **c** God shall bear the sin.

CURTAIN
Ex 26.31 You shall make a **c** of blue, purple,
2Ch 3.14 And Solomon made the **c** of blue
Lk 23.45 the **c** of the temple was torn in two.
Heb 10.20 that he opened for us through the **c**

CUT
Ge 9.11 never again shall all flesh be **c** off
Ps 37. 9 For the wicked shall be **c** off,
Isa 53. 8 **c** off from the land of the living,
Mt 3.10 does not bear good fruit is **c** down
Mk 9.43 hand causes you to stumble, **c** it off;
Ro 11.22 otherwise you also will be **c** off.

D

DAILY → DAY
Mt 6.11 Give us this day our **d** bread.
Lk 9.23 take up their cross **d** and follow me.

DANCE → DANCED
Ps 150. 4 Praise him with tambourine and **d**;

Ecc   3. 4   a time to mourn, and a time to **d;**
Lk   7.32   the flute for you, and you did not **d;**

DANCED → DANCE
2Sa   6.14   David **d** before the Lᴏʀᴅ with all
Mt   14. 6   the daughter of Herodias **d** before

DARK → DARKEST, DARKNESS
Ps   139.12   even the darkness is not **d** to you;
Lk   12. 3   whatever you have said in the **d** will
2Pe   1.19   as to a lamp shining in a **d** place,

DARKEST → DARK
Ps   23. 4   though I walk through the **d** valley,

DARKNESS → DARK
Ge   1. 2   the earth was a formless void and **d**
Ex   10.22   was dense **d** in all the land of Egypt
Isa   9. 2   walked in **d** have seen a great light;
Joel   2.31   The sun shall be turned to **d,**
Mt   4.16   who sat in **d** have seen a great light,
Jn   1. 5   light shines in the **d,** and the **d** did not
Col   1.13   from the power of **d** and transferred
1Jn   1. 5   God is light and in him there is no **d**

DAUGHTER → DAUGHTERS
Mic   7. 6   the **d** rises up against her mother,
Lk   12.53   against **d** and **d** against mother,

DAUGHTERS → DAUGHTER
Ge   6. 4   of God went in to the **d** of humans,
Joel   2.28   sons and your **d** shall prophesy,
Ac   2.17   sons and your **d** shall prophesy,
2Co   6.18   and you shall be my sons and **d,**

DAWN → DAWNS
Isa   14.12   from heaven, O Day Star, son of **D!**
Hos   6. 3   his appearing is as sure as the **d;**

DAWNS → DAWN
Ps   97.11   Light **d** for the righteous,
2Pe   1.19   until the day **d** and the morning star

DAY → DAILY, DAYS
Ge   1. 5   God called the light **D,** and
Ex   13.21   of them in a pillar of cloud by **d,**
      20. 8   Remember the sabbath **d,** and keep
Ps   1. 2   his law they meditate **d** and night.
     118.24   is the **d** that the Lᴏʀᴅ has made;
Joel   1.15   For the **d** of the Lᴏʀᴅ is near,
Zec   14. 1   See, a **d** is coming for the Lᴏʀᴅ,
Mal   3. 2   who can endure the **d** of his coming,
Mt   25.13   you know neither the **d** nor the hour.
Lk   11. 3   Give us each **d** our daily bread.
      24.46   to rise from the dead on the third **d,**
Jn   6.40   I will raise them up on the last **d."**
Ro   14. 5   Some judge one **d** to be better than
1Th   5. 2   very well that the **d** of the Lord
2Pe   3. 8   one **d** is like a thousand years,
       3.10   **d** of the Lord will come like a thief,
1Jn   4.17   have boldness on the **d** of judgment,
Rev   16.14   for battle on the great **d** of God

DAYS → DAY
Ge   1.14   and for seasons and for **d** and years,
Ex   24.18   on the mountain for forty **d** and
1Ki   19. 8   that food forty **d** and forty nights
1Mc   4.56   dedication of the altar for eight **d,**
Ps   90.10   The **d** of our life are seventy years,
Eph   5.16   of the time, because the **d** are evil.
2Ti   3. 1   in the last **d** distressing times will

DEACON → DEACONS
Ro   16. 1   a **d** of the church at Cenchreae,

DEACONS → DEACON
1Ti   3. 8   **D** likewise must be serious, not

DEAD → DEATH, DIE, DIED, DYING
Mt   8.22   and let the **d** bury their own **d."**
Mk   12.27   God not of the **d,** but of the living;
Lk   24. 5   look for the living among the **d?**
Ro   6.11   must consider yourselves **d** to sin
Eph   2. 1   You were **d** through the trespasses
Rev   1. 5   witness, the firstborn of the **d,**
      20.12   And the **d** were judged according to

DEAF
Ex   4.11   Who makes them mute or **d,**
Isa   29.18   On that day the **d** shall hear the
Lk   7.22   the lepers are cleansed, the **d** hear,

DEATH → DEAD
Dt   30.19   that I have set before you life and **d,**
Sir   15.17   Before each person are life and **d,**
Isa   25. 7   he will swallow up **d** forever.
Hos   13.14   O **D,** where are your plagues?
Lk   1.79   in darkness and in the shadow of **d,**
Jn   5.24   but has passed from **d** to life.
Ro   6.23   For the wages of sin is **d,**
1Co   15.55   "Where, O **d,** is your victory?
Heb   2.14   through **d** he might destroy the one who has
                the power of **d,**
1Jn   3.14   that we have passed from **d** to life
Rev   1.18   I have the keys of **D** and of Hades.
      20.14   **D** and Hades were thrown into the lake
      21. 4   **D** will be no more;

DEBTS
Mt   6.12   And forgive us our **d,** as we

DECEIT → DECEITFUL, DECEIVE
Dt   32. 4   A faithful God, without **d,**
Isa   53. 9   and there was no **d** in his mouth.
Ro   1.29   Full of envy, murder, strife, **d,**
1Pe   2.22   and no **d** was found in his mouth."

DECEITFUL → DECEIT
1Ti   4. 1   by paying attention to **d** spirits

DECEIVE → DECEIT
Eph   5. 6   Let no one **d** you with empty words,
1Jn   1. 8   that we have no sin, we **d** ourselves,
Rev   20. 8   to **d** the nations at the four corners

DECREES
Dt   6. 2   and keep all his **d** and his
Ps   19. 7   the **d** of the Lᴏʀᴅ are sure,
     119. 2   Happy are those who keep his **d,**

DEDICATION
1Mc   4.56   the **d** of the altar for eight days,
2Ch   7. 9   the **d** of the altar seven days and
Ezr   6.16   the **d** of this house of God with joy.

DEED → DEEDS
Ecc   12.14   will bring every **d** into judgment,
Mt   19.16   good **d** must I do to have eternal life
Col   3.17   And whatever you do, in word or **d,**

DEEDS → DEED
Jer   50.29   Repay her according to her **d;**
Lk   23.41   getting what we deserve for our **d,**

Ro	2. 6	repay according to each one's **d:**
Rev	15. 3	"Great and amazing are your **d,**
	19. 8	the righteous **d** of the saints.

DEEP → DEPTH, DEPTHS
Ge	1. 2	darkness covered the face of the **d,**
	7.11	the fountains of the great **d** burst
Ro	8.26	with sighs too **d** for words.

DEFEND
Jdt	5.21	for their Lord and God will **d** them,
Ps	72. 4	May he **d** the cause of the poor of
Pr	31. 9	**d** the rights of the poor and needy.

DEFILE
Lev	11.43	you shall not **d** yourselves
Nu	35.34	You shall not **d** the land
Mk	7.15	things that come out are what **d."**

DEITY
| Col | 2. 9 | whole fullness of **d** dwells bodily, |

DELAY
Dt	7.10	He does not **d** but repays
Ps	70. 5	my deliverer; O LORD, do not **d!**
Heb	10.37	will come and will not **d;**

DELIGHT
1Sa	15.22	"Has the LORD as great **d** in burnt
Ps	1. 2	their **d** is in the law of the LORD,
	40. 8	I **d** to do your will, O my God;
Pr	8.30	I was daily his **d,** rejoicing before
Sir	1.27	fidelity and humility are his **d.**
Ro	7.22	For I **d** in the law of God in my

DELIVER → DELIVERANCE, DELIVERER, DELIVERS
Ex	3. 8	to **d** them from the Egyptians,
Da	3.17	able to **d** us from the furnace
	6.20	able to **d** you from the lions?"
Mt	27.43	let God **d** him now,

DELIVERANCE → DELIVER
Ex	14.13	and see the **d** that the LORD will
Jdt	8.17	while we wait for his **d,**
Ps	3. 8	**D** belongs to the LORD;
Php	1.19	this will turn out for my **d.**

DELIVERER → DELIVER
| Ps | 140. 7 | O LORD, my Lord, my strong **d,** |
| Ro | 11.26 | "Out of Zion will come the **D;** |

DEMON → DEMONIACS, DEMONIC, DEMONS
Tob	3. 8	the wicked **d** Asmodeus had killed
	6. 8	of a man or woman afflicted by a **d**
Mt	11.18	and they say, 'He has a **d';**
	17.18	Jesus rebuked the **d,** and it came out
Jn	8.48	you are a Samaritan and have a **d?"**
	10.21	not the words of one who has a **d.**

DEMONIACS → DEMON
| Mt | 4.24 | **d,** epileptics, and paralytics, and he |
| | 8.28 | two **d** coming out of the tombs met |

DEMONIC → DEMON
| Rev | 16.14 | These are **d** spirits, performing signs |

DEMONS → DEMON
Dt	32.17	They sacrificed to **d,** not God,
Bar	4. 7	by sacrificing to **d** and not
Lk	11.18	that I cast out the **d** by Beelzebul.
1Co	10.20	not want you to be partners with **d.**

1Ti	4. 1	deceitful spirits and teachings of **d,**
Jas	2.19	Even the **d** believe—and shudder.
Rev	9.20	their hands or give up worshiping **d**

DEN
Jer	7.11	a **d** of robbers in your sight?
Da	6. 7	shall be thrown into a **d** of lions.
Mk	11.17	you have made it a **d** of robbers."

DENARIUS
| Mk | 12.15 | Bring me a **d** and let me see it." |

DENIED → DENY
Mt	26.70	But he **d** it before all of them,
1Ti	5. 8	has **d** the faith and is worse than
Rev	3. 8	my word and have not **d** my name.

DENIES → DENY
| Lk | 12. 9 | but whoever **d** me before others |
| 1Jn | 2.22 | liar but the one who **d** that Jesus |

DENY → DENIED, DENIES
Mt	16.24	let them **d** themselves and take up
2Ti	2.12	if we **d** him, he will also **d** us;
2Pe	2. 1	**d** the Master who bought them—

DEPRAVED → DEPRAVITY
| 1Ti | 6. 5 | among those who are **d** in mind |
| 2Pe | 2.10 | who indulge their flesh in **d** lust, |

DEPRAVITY → DEPRAVED
| Lev | 20.14 | that there may be no **d** among you. |

DEPTH → DEEP
Mt	13. 5	since they had no **d** of soil.
Ro	11.33	O the **d** of the riches and wisdom
Eph	3.18	and length and height and **d,**

DEPTHS → DEEP
| Ps | 130. 1 | Out of the **d** I cry to you, |
| 1Co | 2.10 | even the **d** of God. |

DESCENDANTS
Ge	15.18	saying, "To your **d** I give this land,
Dt	4.37	he chose their **d** after them.
Isa	44. 3	I will pour my spirit upon your **d,**
Ro	9. 7	Abraham's children are his true **d;**
Gal	3. 7	who believe are the **d** of Abraham.

DESERT
Ps	106.14	and put God to the test in the **d;**
Isa	40. 3	make straight in the **d** a highway
Mk	8. 4	with bread here in the **d?"**

DESERVE
Pr	14.14	and the good, what their deeds **d.**
Lk	23.15	he has done nothing to **d** death.
Ac	26.31	man is doing nothing to **d** death
Rev	2.23	give to each of you as your works **d.**

DESIRE → DESIRES
Ge	3.16	your **d** shall be for your husband,
Ps	20. 4	May he grant you your heart's **d,**
Hos	6. 6	I **d** steadfast love and not sacrifice,
Mt	9.13	learn what this means, 'I **d** mercy,
1Jn	2.16	the **d** of the flesh, the **d** of the eyes,

DESIRES → DESIRE
Sir	18.30	Do not follow your base **d,**
1Ti	2. 4	who **d** everyone to be saved
2Ti	4. 3	teachers to suit their own **d,**

DESOLATE → DESOLATES
1Mc 1.39 sanctuary became **d** like a desert;
Da   11.31 the abomination that makes **d.**

DESOLATES → DESOLATE
Da   9.27 shall be an abomination that **d,**

DESPISE → DESPISED
Job 5.17 not **d** the discipline of the Almighty.
Pr   1. 7 fools **d** wisdom and instruction.
Lk   16.13 devoted to the one and **d** the other.

DESPISED → DESPISE
Isa 53. 3 He was **d** and rejected by others;
1Co 1.28 God chose what is low and **d** in the

DESTINED
Eph 1. 5 He **d** us for adoption as his children
1Th 5. 9 For God has **d** us not for wrath but
1Pe 1.11 to the sufferings **d** for Christ

DESTROY → DESTROYED, DESTRUCTION
Ge   6.13 to **d** them along with the earth.
Mt   10.28 rather fear him who can **d** both soul
Jn   10.10 comes only to steal and kill and **d.**
Jas 4.12 who is able to save and to **d.**
1Jn 3. 8 to **d** the works of the devil.

DESTROYED → DESTROY
Da   6.26 His kingdom shall never be **d,**
1Co 15.26 The last enemy to be **d** is death.

DESTRUCTION → DESTROY
Pr   16.18 Pride goes before **d,** and a haughty
Mt   7.13 and the road is easy that leads to **d,**

DEVIL
Mt   4. 1 wilderness to be tempted by the **d.**
Lk   8.12 **d** comes and takes away the word
Jn   8.44 You are from your father the **d,**
Eph 4.27 and do not make room for the **d.**
     6.11 to stand against the wiles of the **d.**
1Ti 3. 6 fall into the condemnation of the **d.**
Heb 2.14 the power of death, that is, the **d,**
Jas 4. 7 Resist the **d,** and he will flee from
1Pe 5. 8 lion your adversary the **d** prowls
1Jn 3. 8 to destroy the works of the **d.**
Jude 1. 9 Michael contended with the **d**
Rev 12. 9 who is called the **D** and Satan,
     20. 2 that ancient serpent, who is the **D**

DIE → DEAD
Ge   2.17 eat of it you shall **d."**
     3. 4 to the woman, "You will not **d;**
Ru   1.17 Where you **d,** I will **d—**
Ecc 3. 2 a time to be born, and a time to **d;**
Isa 22.13 eat and drink, for tomorrow we **d."**
Jer 31.30 But all shall **d** for their own sins;
Mt   26.35 "Even though I must **d** with you,
Jn   11.26 and believes in me will never **d.**
Ro   14. 8 if we **d,** we **d** to the Lord;
1Co 15.32 eat and drink, for tomorrow we **d."**
Heb 9.27 appointed for mortals to **d** once,

DIED → DEAD
Ro   5. 6 right time Christ **d** for the ungodly.
1Co 15. 3 Christ **d** for our sins in accordance
Gal 2.19 the law I **d** to the law,

DIFFERENT
2Co 11. 4 or a **d** gospel from the one you

Gal 1. 6 and are turning to a **d** gospel—

DISAPPOINT
Ro   5. 5 and hope does not **d** us,

DISCIPLE → DISCIPLES
Mt   10.24 "A **d** is not above the teacher,
Lk   14.26 even life itself, cannot be my **d.**

DISCIPLES → DISCIPLE
Mt   26.56 all the **d** deserted him and fled.
     28.19 therefore and make **d** of all nations,
Lk   6.13 he called his **d** and chose twelve of
Jn   8.31 in my word, you are truly my **d;**
Ac   11.26 the **d** were first called "Christians."

DISCIPLINE → DISCIPLINED
Job 5.17 not despise the **d** of the Almighty.
Ps   94.12 Happy are those whom you **d,**
Sir 1.27 fear of the Lord is wisdom and **d,**
Eph 6. 4 in the **d** and instruction of the Lord.
Heb 12. 5 not regard lightly the **d** of the Lord,

DISCIPLINED → DISCIPLINE
Wis 3. 5 Having been **d** a little, they will
1Co 11.32 **d** so that we may not be condemned

DISEASE → DISEASES
Mt   4.23 of the kingdom and curing every **d**
     9.35 curing every **d** and every sickness.

DISEASES → DISEASE
Ex   15.26 **d** that I brought upon the Egyptians;
Ps   103. 3 your iniquity, who heals all your **d,**
Isa 53. 4 our infirmities and carried our **d;**
Mt   8.17 took our infirmities and bore our **d."**

DISMAYED
Dt   1.21 do not fear or be **d."**
Jos 1. 9 do not be frightened or **d,**

DISOBEDIENT → DISOBEY
Ne   9.26 they were **d** and rebelled
Ro   10.21 I have held out my hands to a **d**
Tit 3. 3 ourselves were once foolish, **d,**

DISOBEY → DISOBEDIENT
Lev 26.27 But if, despite this, you **d** me,
Sir 1.28 Do not **d** the fear of the Lord;
1Pe 2. 8 stumble because they **d** the word,

DISTINCTION → DISTINCTIONS
Ex   8.23 I will make a **d** between my people
Lev 11.47 make a **d** between the unclean and
Eze 22.26 have made no **d** between the holy

DISTINCTIONS → DISTINCTION
Jas 2. 4 you not made **d** among yourselves,

DISTRESS → DISTRESSED
2Sa 22. 7 In my **d** I called upon the Lord;
Ps   81. 7 In **d** you called, and I rescued you;
Sir 2.11 and saves in time of **d.**
Lk   21.23 For there will be great **d** on the earth
Ro   8.35 Will hardship, or **d,** or persecution,

DISTRESSED → DISTRESS
La   1.20 See, O Lord, how **d** I am;

DISTRIBUTED
Ac   4.35 it was **d** to each as any had need.

Heb   2. 4   gifts of the Holy Spirit, **d** according

DIVIDED
Lev   11. 3   Any animal that has **d** hoofs
Ps   136.13   who **d** the Red Sea in two,
Lk   11.18   If Satan also is **d** against himself,

DIVINE
Ro   1.20   his eternal power and **d** nature,
2Pe   1. 4   become participants of the **d** nature.

DIVORCE → DIVORCED
Dt   24. 1   so he writes her a certificate of **d,**
Sir   7.26   Do not **d** her;
Isa   50. 1   Where is your mother's bill of **d**
Jer   3. 8   sent her away with a decree of **d;**
Mal   2.16   For I hate **d,** says the LORD,
Mt   5.31   let him give her a certificate of **d.'**
     19. 3   a man to **d** his wife for any cause?"
1Co   7.11   the husband should not **d** his wife.

DIVORCED → DIVORCE
Lev   21. 7   neither shall they marry a woman **d**
Mt   5.32   whoever marries a **d** woman

DOCTOR
Lk   4.23   this proverb, '**D,** cure yourself!'

DOCTRINE → DOCTRINES
Eph   4.14   blown about by every wind of **d,**
1Ti   1. 3   not to teach any different **d,**
2Ti   4. 3   people will not put up with sound **d,**
Tit   1. 9   able both to preach with sound **d**

DOCTRINES → DOCTRINE
Mk   7. 7   teaching human precepts as **d.'**

DOERS
Jas   1.22   But be **d** of the word,

DOGS
Mt   7. 6   "Do not give what is holy to **d;**

DOMINION
Ge   1.26   and let them have **d** over
Ps   22.28   For **d** belongs to the LORD,
Da   7.14   His **d** is an everlasting **d**
Rev   1. 6   to him be glory and **d** forever

DONKEY
Zec   9. 9   humble and riding on a **d,**
Mt   21. 5   humble, and mounted on a **d,**

DOOR → DOORPOSTS
Mt   7. 7   knock, and the **d** will be opened
Lk   13.24   Strive to enter through the narrow **d**
Rev   3.20   I am standing at the **d,** knocking;

DOORPOSTS → DOOR
Ex   12. 7   the blood and put it on the two **d**

DOUBT → DOUBTED, DOUBTING
Mt   14.31   of little faith, why did you **d?"**
Jn   20.27   Do not **d** but believe."

DOUBTED → DOUBT
Mt   28.17   they worshiped him; but some **d.**

DOUBTING → DOUBT
Jas   1. 6   But ask in faith, never **d,**

DOVE
Ge   8. 8   Then he sent out the **d** from him,
Mk   1.10   Spirit descending like a **d** on him.

DRAGON
Isa   27. 1   and he will kill the **d** that
Da   14.23   in that place there was a great **d,**
Rev   12. 3   a great red **d,** with seven heads and
     20. 2   seized the **d,** that ancient serpent,

DRANK → DRINK
Ex   24.11   beheld God, and they ate and **d.**
Mk   14.23   and all of them **d** from it.
1Co   10. 4   all **d** the same spiritual drink.

DRAW
Jas   4. 8   **D** near to God, and he will **d** near

DREAM → DREAMS
Joel   2.28   your old men shall **d** dreams,
Ac   2.17   and your old men shall **d** dreams.

DREAMS → DREAM
Nu   12. 6   I speak to them in **d.**
Sir   34. 7   For **d** have deceived many,

DRIED → DRY
Ge   8.13   the waters were **d** up from the earth;
Jos   5. 1   had **d** up the waters of the Jordan
Isa   51.10   Was it not you who **d** up the sea,

DRINK → DRANK, DRUNK, DRUNKARD, DRUNKENNESS
Ex   32. 6   the people sat down to eat and **d,**
Ecc   9. 7   and **d** your wine with a merry heart;
Isa   22.13   eat and **d,** for tomorrow we die."
Mt   20.22   to **d** the cup that I am about to **d?"**
Jn   18.11   not to **d** the cup that the Father has
Ro   14.17   kingdom of God is not food and **d**
1Co   12.13   we were all made to **d** of one Spirit.
Rev   14.10   also **d** the wine of God's wrath,

DRUNK → DRINK
Jdt   13. 2   on his bed, for he was dead **d.**
Jn   2.10   after the guests have become **d.**
Ac   2.15   these are not **d,** as you suppose,
Eph   5.18   Do not get **d** with wine,

DRUNKARD → DRINK
Mt   11.19   they say, 'Look, a glutton and a **d,**
1Co   5.11   is an idolater, reviler, **d,** or robber.
1Ti   3. 3   not a **d,** not violent but gentle,

DRUNKENNESS → DRINK
Tob   4.15   to excess or let **d** go with you
Gal   5.21   **d,** carousing, and things like these.

DRY → DRIED
Ge   1. 9   and let the **d** land appear."
Ex   14.16   may go into the sea on **d** ground;
Eze   37. 4   **d** bones, hear the word of the LORD.

DUST
Ge   2. 7   LORD God formed man from the **d**
1Sa   2. 8   He raises up the poor from the **d;**
Ps   103.14   he remembers that we are **d.**
Ecc   3.20   from the **d,** and all turn to **d** again.
Mt   10.14   shake off the **d** from your feet
1Co   15.47   man was from the earth, a man of **d;**

DWELL → DWELLING, DWELLS
Ex   25. 8   so that I may **d** among them.

1Ki	8.27	But will God indeed **d** on the earth?
Ps	23.6	and I shall **d** in the house of
Eph	3.17	that Christ may **d** in your hearts
Col	1.19	fullness of God was pleased to **d,**
Rev	21.3	He will **d** with them as their God;

DWELLING → DWELL

Ps	90.1	our **d** place in all generations.
Jn	14.2	my Father's house there are many **d**
2Co	5.2	to be clothed with our heavenly **d**—
Eph	2.22	spiritually into a **d** place for God.

DWELLS → DWELL

Jn	14.10	but the Father who **d** in me
Ro	7.17	but sin that **d** within me.
1Co	3.16	and that God's Spirit **d** in you?
Col	2.9	whole fullness of deity **d** bodily,

E

EAGLES

Isa	40.31	shall mount up with wings like **e,**

EAR

Isa	64.4	has heard, no **e** has perceived,
Lk	22.51	he touched his **e** and healed him.
1Co	2.9	"What no eye has seen, nor **e** heard,

EARTH

Ge	1.1	God created the heavens and the **e,**
	6.11	the **e** was corrupt in God's sight,
Sir	40.11	All that is of **e** returns to **e,**
Isa	6.3	the whole **e** is full of his glory."
	65.17	to create new heavens and a new **e;**
Mt	5.5	meek, for they will inherit the **e.**
	24.35	Heaven and **e** will pass away,
2Pe	3.13	wait for new heavens and a new **e,**
Rev	21.1	I saw a new heaven and a new **e;**

EAST

Ge	2.8	planted a garden in Eden, in the **e;**
Ps	103.12	as far as the **e** is from the west,
Mt	2.1	wise men from the **E** came to

EASY

Mt	11.30	For my yoke is **e,** and my burden is

EAT → ATE, EATS

Ge	2.16	freely **e** of every tree of the garden;
Lev	11.4	you shall not **e** the following:
Mt	26.26	to the disciples, and said, "Take, **e;**
Ac	10.13	"Get up, Peter; kill and **e."**
1Co	10.31	whether you **e** or drink, or whatever
Rev	3.20	I will come in to you and **e** with you

EATS → EAT

Jn	6.51	**e** of this bread will live forever;
1Co	11.27	**e** the bread or drinks the cup of the

EDEN

Ge	2.8	a garden in **E,** in the east;

EGYPT

Ge	47.27	Israel settled in the land of **E,**
Hos	11.1	and out of **E** I called my son.
Mt	2.15	"Out of **E** I have called my son."
Rev	11.8	prophetically called Sodom and **E,**

ELDER → ELDERS

1Ti	5.19	any accusation against an **e** except
1Pe	5.1	as an **e** myself and a witness of the

ELDERS → ELDER

Ex	24.1	and seventy of the **e** of Israel,
Da	13.61	they took action against the two **e,**
Mt	27.12	accused by the chief priests and **e,**
Mk	7.3	thus observing the tradition of the **e;**
1Ti	5.17	the **e** who rule well be considered
Jas	5.14	**e** of the church and have them pray
1Pe	5.5	must accept the authority of the **e.**
Rev	4.4	on the thrones are twenty-four **e,**

ELECT → ELECTION

Wis	4.15	grace and mercy are with his **e,**
Mt	24.22	sake of the **e** those days will be cut
Mk	13.22	to lead astray, if possible, the **e.**

ELECTION → ELECT

Ro	9.11	God's purpose of **e** might continue,
2Pe	1.10	eager to confirm your call and **e,**

ELEVEN

Mt	28.16	Now the **e** disciples went to Galilee,
Ac	1.26	and he was added to the **e** apostles.

EMMANUEL → IMMANUEL

Mt	1.23	and they shall name him **E,"**

ENCOURAGE → ENCOURAGEMENT

1Th	4.18	**e** one another with these words.
1Pe	5.12	written this short letter to **e** you

ENCOURAGEMENT → ENCOURAGE

Ro	15.5	God of steadfastness and **e** grant
Php	2.1	If then there is any **e** in Christ,

END

Ge	6.13	determined to make an **e** of all flesh,
Pr	14.12	but its **e** is the way to death.
Ecc	12.12	making many books there is no **e,**
Mt	24.13	But the one who endures to the **e**
	28.20	always, to the **e** of the age."
Ro	10.4	For Christ is the **e** of the law so
Rev	22.13	the beginning and the **e."**

ENDURANCE → ENDURE

Ro	5.3	knowing that suffering produces **e,**
1Ti	6.11	godliness, faith, love, **e,**
Heb	10.36	For you need **e,** so that when you
Jas	1.3	the testing of your faith produces **e;**
2Pe	1.6	and self-control with **e,**

ENDURE → ENDURANCE, ENDURED, ENDURES

Mal	3.2	who can **e** the day of his coming,
1Co	10.13	so that you may be able to **e** it.
2Ti	2.12	if we **e,** we will also reign with him;

ENDURED → ENDURE

Heb	12.2	that was set before him **e** the cross,

ENDURES → ENDURE

Sir	40.17	and almsgiving **e** forever.
Bar	4.1	the law that **e** forever.
1Co	13.7	hopes all things, **e** all things.
1Pe	1.25	but the word of the Lord **e** forever."

ENEMIES → ENEMY

Mt	5.44	But I say to you, Love your **e** and
Ro	5.10	For if while we were **e,**

ENEMY → ENEMIES, ENMITY

Mt	13.39	the **e** who sowed them is the devil;
1Co	15.26	The last **e** to be destroyed is death.

ENGAGED
Mt   1.18   mother Mary had been **e** to Joseph,

ENJOYMENT
Ecc   8.15   So I commend **e,** for there is nothing
1Ti   6.17   with everything for our **e.**

ENLIGHTENED → LIGHT
Ro   10. 2   a zeal for God, but it is not **e.**
Eph   1.18   with the eyes of your heart **e,**
Heb   6. 4   those who have once been **e,**

ENLIGHTENS → LIGHT
Jn   1. 9   The true light, which **e** everyone,

ENMITY → ENEMY
Ge   3.15   put **e** between you and the woman,
Jas   4. 4   with the world is **e** with God?

ENTER → ENTRY
Mt   7.13   "**E** through the narrow gate;
Mk   10.15   as a little child will never **e** it."
Jn   3. 5   no one can **e** the kingdom of God
Rev   21.27   But nothing unclean will **e** it,

ENTRUSTED → TRUST
Lk   12.48   the one to whom much has been **e,**
2Ti   1.12   guard until that day what I have **e**
Jude   1. 3   the faith that was once for all **e**

ENVY
Pr   23.17   Do not let your heart **e** sinners,
Mk   7.22   deceit, licentiousness, **e,** slander,
Ro   1.29   Full of **e,** murder, strife, deceit,

EPHOD
Ex   28. 6   They shall make the **e** of gold,

EQUAL → EQUALITY
Isa   40.25   you compare me, or who is my **e?**
      46. 5   will you liken me and make me **e,**
Jn   5.18   thereby making himself **e** to God.

EQUALITY → EQUAL
Php   2. 6   not regard **e** with God as something

ERROR
Lev   5.18   for the **e** that you committed
Ro   1.27   the due penalty for their **e.**
1Jn   4. 6   of truth and the spirit of **e.**

ESTABLISH → ESTABLISHED
Eze   16.60   **e** with you an everlasting covenant.
Heb   8. 8   when I will **e** a new covenant with

ESTABLISHED → ESTABLISH
2Sa   7.16   your throne shall be **e** forever.
Ps   89. 2   your steadfast love is **e** forever;
    103.19   The LORD has **e** his throne in the

ETERNAL → ETERNITY
Mt   25.46   but the righteous into **e** life."
Mk   10.17   what must I do to inherit **e** life?"
Jn   3.16   may not perish but may have **e** life.
Ro   5.21   **e** life through Jesus Christ our Lord.
2Co   4.17   an **e** weight of glory beyond all
Heb   5. 9   the source of **e** salvation for all who
1Jn   5.13   may know that you have **e** life.

ETERNITY → ETERNAL
Wis   2.23   made us in the image of his own **e,**

EUNUCH
Ac   8.27   Now there was an Ethiopian **e,**

Sir   42.21   he is from all **e** one and the same.
Isa   57.15   high and lofty one who inhabits **e,**
2Pe   3.18   glory both now and to the day of **e.**

EVANGELIST → EVANGELISTS
2Ti   4. 5   do the work of an **e,** carry out your

EVANGELISTS → EVANGELIST
Eph   4.11   some **e,** some pastors and teachers,

EVERLASTING → LAST
Ge   9.16   remember the **e** covenant between
Ps   90. 2   from **e** to **e** you are God.
Isa   9. 6   **E** Father, Prince of Peace.
Jer   31. 3   I have loved you with an **e** love;
Da   4. 3   His kingdom is an **e** kingdom,

EVIL
Ge   2. 9   tree of the knowledge of good and **e.**
Jdg   2.11   Then the Israelites did what was **e**
Tob   12. 7   Do good and **e** will not overtake
Ps   23. 4   the darkest valley, I fear no **e;**
Pr   8.13   fear of the LORD is hatred of **e.**
Mt   6.13   but rescue us from the **e** one.
    12.35   **e** person brings **e** things out of an **e**
Lk   11.13   who are **e,** know how to give good
Jn   17.15   to protect them from the **e** one.
Ro   12.17   Do not repay anyone **e** for **e,**
Eph   5.16   of the time, because the days are **e.**
1Ti   6.10   of money is a root of all kinds of **e,**
1Jn   5.18   and the **e** one does not touch them.
2Jn   1.11   to welcome is to participate in the **e**
3Jn   1.11   do not imitate what is **e** but imitate

EXALT → EXALTED
Lk   14.11   who **e** themselves will be humbled,
Jas   4.10   before the Lord, and he will **e** you.

EXALTED → EXALT
Ps   57. 5   Be **e,** O God, above the heavens.
Php   2. 9   highly **e** him and gave him the name

EXAMPLES
1Co   10. 6   these things occurred as **e** for us,
1Pe   5. 3   but be **e** to the flock.

EXCELLENCE → EXCELLENT
Php   4. 8   if there is any **e** and if there is

EXCELLENT → EXCELLENCE
Isa   28.29   in counsel, and **e** in wisdom.
1Co   12.31   I will show you a still more **e** way.
Heb   1. 4   the name he has inherited is more **e**

EXCUSE
Jn   15.22   they have no **e** for their sin.
Ro   1.20   So they are without **e;**

EXHORT
Tit   2.15   **e** and reprove with all authority.
Heb   3.13   But **e** one another every day,

EXILE
2Ki   25.11   carried into **e** the rest of the people
Ezr   6.21   of Israel who had returned from **e,**

EYE → EYES, EYEWITNESSES
Ex   21.24   **e** for **e,** tooth for tooth,

> CONCORDANCE

Ps	17. 8	Guard me as the apple of the **e**;
Mt	5.29	If your right **e** causes you to sin,
	5.38	An **e** for an **e** and a tooth for
	7. 3	see the speck in your neighbor's **e**,
Mk	10.25	to go through the **e** of a needle
1Co	15.52	in the twinkling of an **e**, at the last
Rev	1. 7	the clouds; every **e** will see him,

EYES → EYE

Ge	3. 7	Then the **e** of both were opened,
Ps	121. 1	I lift up my **e** to the hills—
Pr	3. 7	Do not be wise in your own **e**;
Mt	9.30	And their **e** were opened.
Eph	1.18	with the **e** of your heart enlightened,
1Pe	3.12	of the Lord are on the righteous,
1Jn	2.16	of the flesh, the desire of the **e**,
Rev	21. 4	he will wipe every tear from their **e**.

EYEWITNESSES → EYE, WITNESS

Lk	1. 2	who from the beginning were **e**
2Pe	1.16	but we had been **e** of his majesty.

F

FACE

Ge	32.30	"For I have seen God **f** to **f**,
Nu	6.25	LORD make his **f** to shine upon
	12. 8	With him I speak **f** to **f**—
Ps	4. 6	Let the light of your **f** shine on us,
Isa	54. 8	wrath for a moment I hid my **f**
Eze	39.29	I will never again hide my **f** from
Lk	9.29	the appearance of his **f** changed,

FADE → FADES

Ps	37. 2	for they will soon **f** like the grass,
Isa	64. 6	We all **f** like a leaf,

FADES → FADE

Isa	40. 7	The grass withers, the flower **f**,
1Pe	5. 4	crown of glory that never **f** away.

FAINT

Ps	142. 3	When my spirit is **f**, you know
Isa	40.31	they shall walk and not **f**.

FAITH → FAITHFUL, FAITHFULNESS

Isa	7. 9	If you do not stand firm in **f**,
Hab	2. 4	but the righteous live by their **f**.
Mt	17.20	have **f** the size of a mustard seed,
Ac	3.16	and the **f** that is through Jesus
Ro	3.28	that a person is justified by **f** apart
1Co	13.13	And now **f**, hope, and love abide,
Eph	4. 5	one Lord, one **f**, one baptism,
Heb	11. 1	**f** is the assurance of things hoped
Jas	2.17	**f** by itself, if it has no works,
1Jn	5. 4	that conquers the world, our **f**.
Rev	2.13	and you did not deny your **f** in me

FAITHFUL → FAITH

Dt	32. 4	A **f** God, without deceit, just and
Ps	4. 3	LORD has set apart the **f** for
Wis	3. 9	the **f** will abide with him in love,
Sir	4.16	If they remain **f**, they will inherit
Mt	24.45	"Who then is the **f** and wise slave,
1Th	5.24	The one who calls you is **f**,
Heb	10.23	for he who has promised is **f**.
1Jn	1. 9	**f** and just will forgive us our sins
Rev	19.11	Its rider is called **F** and True,

FAITHFULNESS → FAITH

Ex	34. 6	abounding in steadfast love and **f**,

Jos	24.14	and serve him in sincerity and in **f**;
Isa	11. 5	and **f** the belt around his loins.
La	3.23	new every morning; great is your **f**.
Gal	5.22	patience, kindness, generosity, **f**,

FALL → FELL

Pr	16.18	and a haughty spirit before a **f**.
Sir	28.23	Those who forsake the Lord will **f**
Ro	9.33	a rock that will make them **f**,
1Co	10.12	watch out that you do not **f**.

FALSE

Dt	5.20	Neither shall you bear **f** witness
Bar	6. 8	but they are **f** and cannot speak.
Mk	13.22	**F** messiahs and **f** prophets will
Heb	6.18	impossible that God would prove **f**
2Pe	2. 1	there will be **f** teachers among you,
Rev	20.10	where the beast and the **f** prophet

FAMILY

Pr	6.19	and one who sows discord in a **f**.
Gal	6.10	especially for those of the **f** of faith.
Eph	3.15	from whom every **f** in heaven and
1Pe	2.17	Love the **f** of believers.

FAST

Isa	58. 5	Is such the **f** that I choose,
Mt	6.16	"And whenever you **f**,

FATHER → FATHER'S

Ge	2.24	a man leaves his **f** and his mother
Ex	20.12	Honor your **f** and your mother,
Ps	89.26	cry to me, 'You are my **F**, my God,
Wis	2.16	and boasts that God is his **f**.
Sir	3. 3	who honor their **f** atone for sins,
Isa	9. 6	Mighty God, Everlasting **F**, Prince
Mt	6. 9	Our **F** in heaven, hallowed be your
	28.19	the name of the **F** and of the Son and
Jn	5.18	but was also calling God his own **F**,
	14. 6	comes to the **F** except through me.
Gal	4. 6	into our hearts, crying, "Abba! **F**!"
Rev	3. 5	confess your name before my **F**

FATHER'S → FATHER

Lk	2.49	that I must be in my **F** house?"
Jn	1.14	the glory as of a **f** only son,
	14. 2	**F** house there are many dwelling

FAVOR

Ps	30. 5	his **f** is for a lifetime.
Isa	49. 8	In a time of **f** I have answered you,
Lk	4.19	proclaim the year of the Lord's **f**."

FEAR → AFRAID

Dt	6.13	The LORD your God you shall **f**;
Ps	19. 9	the **f** of the LORD is pure,
	23. 4	the darkest valley, I **f** no evil;
Pr	1. 7	**f** of the LORD is the beginning
Ecc	12.13	**F** God, and keep his commandments
Sir	1.11	The **f** of the Lord is glory
Mt	10.28	rather **f** him who can destroy both
Mk	5.36	"Do not **f**, only believe."
1Pe	3.14	Do not **f** what they **f**,
1Jn	4.18	but perfect love casts out **f**;
Rev	14. 7	"**F** God and give him glory,

FEET

Ps	119.105	Your word is a lamp to my **f**
Lk	24.39	Look at my hands and my **f**;
Jn	13. 5	and began to wash the disciples' **f**
1Co	15.25	put all his enemies under his **f**.

> CONCORDANCE

FELLOWSHIP

Ac	2.42	to the apostles' teaching and **f**,
2Co	6.14	Or what **f** is there between light and
1Jn	1. 3	and truly our **f** is with the Father

FEMALE

Ge	1.27	male and **f** he created them.
Mk	10. 6	'God made them male and **f**.'
Gal	3.28	there is no longer male and **f**;

FESTIVAL → FESTIVALS

Ex	23.14	in the year you shall hold a **f** for me.
1Co	5. 8	Therefore, let us celebrate the **f**,

FESTIVALS → FESTIVAL

Lev	23. 2	the appointed **f** of the LORD
Ne	10.33	the new moons, the appointed **f**,
Col	2.16	of food and drink or of observing **f**,

FEW

Mt	22.14	many are called, but **f** are chosen."
Lk	13.23	"Lord, will only a **f** be saved?"

FIG

Ge	3. 7	and they sewed **f** leaves together
Hab	3.17	Though the **f** tree does not blossom,
Mt	24.32	"From the **f** tree learn its lesson:

FILL → FILLED, FULL, FULLNESS

Ge	1.28	and **f** the earth and subdue it;
Jer	23.24	Do I not **f** heaven and earth?
Eph	4.10	so that he might **f** all things.)

FILLED → FILL

Lk	1.15	will be **f** with the Holy Spirit.
Ac	2. 4	were **f** with the Holy Spirit and
Eph	5.18	but be **f** with the Spirit,

FIND

Dt	4.29	you will **f** him if you search after
Jer	29.13	you search for me, you will **f** me;
Mt	16.25	lose their life for my sake will **f** it.

FINISHED

Ge	2. 2	on the seventh day God **f** the work
Sir	38. 8	God's works will never be **f**;
Jn	19.30	the wine, he said, "It is **f**."

FIRE → FIERY

Ex	13.21	and in a pillar of **f** by night,
Sir	7.17	punishment of the ungodly is **f**
Da	3.25	walking in the middle of the **f**,
Mal	3. 2	For he is like a refiner's **f** and like
Mt	3.11	baptize you with the Holy Spirit and **f**.
Mk	9.43	to go to hell, to the unquenchable **f**.
Ac	2. 3	Divided tongues, as of **f**, appeared
Heb	12.29	indeed our God is a consuming **f**.
Rev	20.14	the second death, the lake of **f**;

FIRST → FIRSTBORN

Ge	1. 5	and there was morning, the **f** day.
Pr	8.22	the **f** of his acts of long ago.
Isa	41. 4	I, the LORD, am **f**,
Mt	6.33	But strive **f** for the kingdom of God
Mk	10.31	But many who are **f** will be last, and the last will be **f**."
1Th	4.16	the dead in Christ will rise **f**.
1Jn	4.19	We love because he **f** loved us.
Rev	1.17	I am the **f** and the last,
	20. 5	This is the **f** resurrection.
	21. 1	the **f** heaven and the **f** earth

FIRSTBORN → BEAR, FIRST

Ex	4.22	'Thus says the LORD: Israel is my **f**
Ps	78.51	He struck all the **f** in Egypt,
Sir	36.17	whom you have named your **f**,
Zec	12.10	as one weeps over a **f**.
Lk	2. 7	And she gave birth to her **f** son and
Col	1.15	invisible God, the **f** of all creation;
Rev	1. 5	faithful witness, the **f** of the dead,

FISH

Jnh	2. 1	his God from the belly of the **f**,
Jn	6. 9	has five barley loaves and two **f**.

FLESH

Ge	2.23	of my bones and **f** of my **f**;
	2.24	and they become one **f**.
Eze	36.26	of stone and give you a heart of **f**.
Mt	16.17	For **f** and blood has not revealed this
	26.41	but the **f** is weak."
Jn	1.14	the Word became **f** and lived among
	3. 6	What is born of the **f** is **f**,
Ro	8. 4	to the **f** but according to the Spirit.
2Co	12. 7	a thorn was given me in the **f**,
Gal	5.19	Now the works of the **f** are obvious:
1Pe	1.24	"All **f** is like grass and all its glory
1Jn	4. 2	that Jesus Christ has come in the **f**

FLOOD

Ge	7. 7	the ark to escape the waters of the **f**.
Sir	40.10	and on their account the **f** came.
2Pe	2. 5	a **f** on a world of the ungodly;

FLOWING

Ex	3. 8	a land **f** with milk and honey,
Jos	5. 6	a land **f** with milk and honey.

FOLLOW → FOLLOWED

1Ki	18.21	If the LORD is God, **f** him;
Lk	9.23	take up their cross daily and **f** me.

FOLLOWED → FOLLOW

Mk	1.18	they left their nets and **f** him.
Rev	13. 3	the whole earth **f** the beast.

FOOD

Ge	1.30	I have given every green plant for **f**.
1Mc	1.63	to die rather than to be defiled by **f**
Ps	136.25	who gives **f** to all flesh,
Jn	6.55	for my flesh is true **f** and my blood
1Co	8. 8	"**F** will not bring us close to God."

FOOL → FOOLISH, FOOLISHNESS, FOOLS

Pr	15. 5	A **f** despises a parent's instruction,

FOOLISH → FOOL

Mt	7.26	like a **f** man who built his house
1Co	1.20	Has not God made **f** the wisdom of
Tit	3. 3	For we ourselves were once **f**,

FOOLISHNESS → FOOL

1Co	1.18	cross is **f** to those who are perishing,
	3.19	wisdom of this world is **f** with God.

FOOLS → FOOL

Ps	14. 1	**F** say in their hearts, "There is no God."
Pr	1. 7	**f** despise wisdom and instruction.
Ro	1.22	Claiming to be wise, they became **f**;
1Co	4.10	We are **f** for the sake of Christ,

FOREHEADS

Eze	9. 4	and put a mark on the **f** of those

Rev 7. 3 of our God with a seal on their **f**."
20. 4 not received its mark on their **f**

FOREKNEW → KNOW
Ro 8.29 whom he **f** he also predestined to
11. 2 not rejected his people whom he **f**.

FOREVER
Ge 3.22 the tree of life, and eat, and live **f**"
6. 3 spirit shall not abide in mortals **f**,
Ex 3.15 This is my name **f**, and this my title
Ps 110. 4 "You are a priest **f** according to the
Ecc 3.14 that whatever God does endures **f**;
Wis 5.15 But the righteous live **f**,
Isa 40. 8 the word of our God will stand **f**.
Jn 6.51 eats of this bread will live **f**;
14.16 another Advocate, to be with you **f**.
Heb 13. 8 the same yesterday and today and **f**.
Rev 11.15 and he will reign **f** and ever."

FORGET
Dt 4.23 So be careful not to **f** the covenant
Isa 49.15 these may **f**, yet I will not **f** you.

FORGIVE → FORGAVE, FORGIVEN, FORGIVENESS, FORGIVING
Ne 9.17 But you are a God ready to **f**,
Sir 5. 6 he will **f** the multitude of my sins,"
Mt 6.12 And **f** us our debts, as we
Lk 5.24 has authority on earth to **f** sins"—
1Jn 1. 9 is faithful and just will **f** us our sins

FORGIVEN → FORGIVE
Ps 32. 1 are those whose transgression is **f**,
Mt 6.12 as we also have **f** our debtors.
12.31 against the Spirit will not be **f**.
Ro 4. 7 are those whose iniquities are **f**,
Eph 4.32 as God in Christ has **f** you.

FORGIVENESS → FORGIVE
Mk 1. 4 a baptism of repentance for the **f**
Col 1.14 we have redemption, the **f** of sins.

FORGIVING → FORGIVE
Ex 34. 7 **f** iniquity and transgression and sin,
Eph 4.32 **f** one another, as God in Christ has

FORMED → FORMLESS
Ge 2. 7 Lord God **f** man from the dust
Ps 139.13 you who **f** my inward parts;

FORMLESS → FORMED
Ge 1. 2 the earth was a **f** void and darkness
Wis 11.17 created the world out of **f** matter,

FORSAKE → FORSAKEN
Dt 31. 6 he will not fail you or **f** you."
Jos 1. 5 I will not fail you or **f** you.
Heb 13. 5 "I will never leave you or **f** you."

FORSAKEN → FORSAKE
Ps 22. 1 my God, why have you **f** me?
Mt 27.46 my God, why have you **f** me?"
2Co 4. 9 persecuted, but not **f**;

FORTRESS
2Sa 22. 2 The Lord is my rock, my **f**,
Ps 71. 3 for you are my rock and my **f**.

FORTY
Ge 7. 4 rain on the earth for **f** days and **f**
Nu 14.34 **f** days, for every day a year,

1Ki 19. 8 days and **f** nights to Horeb
Jnh 3. 4 And he cried out, "**F** days more,
Mt 4. 2 He fasted **f** days and **f** nights,
Heb 3.17 with whom was he angry **f** years?

FOUNDATION → FOUNDATIONS
Isa 28.16 See, I am laying in Zion a **f** stone,
1Co 3.11 that **f** is Jesus Christ.
Eph 2.20 built upon the **f** of the apostles

FOUNDATIONS → FOUNDATION
Heb 11.10 looked forward to the city that has **f**,
Rev 21.14 the wall of the city has twelve **f**,

FRANKINCENSE → INCENSE
Isa 60. 6 They shall bring gold and **f**,
Mt 2.11 gifts of gold, **f**, and myrrh.

FREE
Jn 8.32 and the truth will make you **f**."
Ro 6.23 the **f** gift of God is eternal life
Gal 3.28 there is no longer slave or **f**,

FRIEND → FRIENDS
Pr 18.24 but a true **f** sticks closer than
Sir 7.18 Do not exchange a **f** for money,
Mt 11.19 a **f** of tax collectors and sinners!'
Jas 2.23 and he was called the **f** of God.

FRIENDS → FRIEND
Jn 15.13 to lay down one's life for one's **f**.

FRUIT → FRUITFUL, FRUITLESS, FRUITS
Ge 3. 6 she took of its **f** and ate;
Lk 6.44 each tree is known by its own **f**.
Jn 15. 2 branch that bears **f** he prunes to make it bear
more **f**.
Rev 22. 2 tree of life with its twelve kinds of **f**,

FRUITFUL → FRUIT
Ge 9. 1 said to them, "Be **f** and multiply,

FRUITS → FRUIT
Ro 8.23 who have the first **f** of the Spirit,
1Co 15.23 in his own order: Christ the first **f**,
Rev 14. 4 as first **f** for God and the Lamb,

FULFILL → FULFILLED, FULFILLING
Mt 5.17 I have come not to abolish but to **f**.

FULFILLED → FULFILL
Mk 1.15 "The time is **f**, and the kingdom
Lk 24.44 prophets, and the psalms must be **f**."
Ro 8. 4 requirement of the law might be **f**

FULFILLING → FULFILL
Ro 13.10 love is the **f** of the law.

FULL → FILL
Sir 42.16 work of the Lord is **f** of his glory.
Isa 6. 3 the whole earth is **f** of his glory."
Jn 1.14 **f** of grace and truth.

FULLNESS → FILL
Jn 1.16 From his **f** we have all received,
1Co 10.26 "the earth and its **f** are the Lord's."
Gal 4. 4 But when the **f** of time had come,
Eph 3.19 may be filled with all the **f** of God.
Col 1.19 in him all the **f** of God was pleased

FURNACE
Da   3. 6 be thrown into a **f** of blazing fire."

FUTURE
Pr   24.20 for the evil have no **f;**
Jer 31.17 hope for your **f,** says the LORD:
1Co 3.22 or death or the present or the **f—**

G

GAIN
Lk   9.25 if they **g** the whole world,
Php 1.21 living is Christ and dying is **g.**

GALILEE
Isa   9. 1 beyond the Jordan, **G** of the nations.
Mt   4.15 across the Jordan, **G** of the Gentiles
Jn   7.41 the Messiah does not come from **G,**

GARDEN
Ge   2. 8 LORD God planted a **g** in Eden,
Jn 19.41 and in the **g** there was a new tomb

GATE → GATES
Mt   7.13 "Enter through the narrow **g;**
Jn 10. 7 I am the **g** for the sheep.

GATES → GATE
Mt 16.18 and the **g** of Hades will not prevail
Rev 21.21 And the twelve **g** are twelve pearls,

GATHERED
Mt 18.20 two or three are **g** in my name,

GENERATION
Ex 20. 6 steadfast love to the thousandth **g**
Da   4.34 his kingdom endures from **g** to **g.**
Mt 12.39 evil and adulterous **g** asks for a sign,
Lk 21.32 this **g** will not pass away

GENEROSITY
Gal   5.22 joy, peace, patience, kindness, **g,**

GENTILE → GENTILES
1Mc 1.14 according to **G** custom,
Mt 18.17 as a **G** and a tax collector.
Gal   2.14 live like a **G** and not like a Jew,

GENTILES → GENTILE
Tob 1.11 from eating the food of the **G.**
1Mc 1.11 and make a covenant with the **G**
Ro   3.29 Is he not the God of **G** also?

GENTLENESS
Gal   5.23 **g,** and self-control.
Php 4. 5 Let your **g** be known to everyone.
1Ti 6.11 godliness, faith, love, endurance, **g.**

GETHSEMANE
Mk 14.32 They went to a place called **G;**

GHOST
Mt 14.26 were terrified, saying, "It is a **g!**"
Lk 24.39 for a **g** does not have flesh and

GIFT → GIFTS
Ecc 5.19 this is the **g** of God.
Jn   4.10 "If you knew the **g** of God,
Ac   2.38 will receive the **g** of the Holy Spirit.
Ro   6.23 but the free **g** of God is eternal life
1Co 7. 7 each has a particular **g** from God,
Jas 1.17 with every perfect **g,** is from above,

Rev 21. 6 the thirsty I will give water as a **g**

GIFTS → GIFT
Mt   2.11 offered him **g** of gold, frankincense,
1Co 12. 1 Now concerning spiritual **g,**

GIVE → GIVEN, GIVER
Mt   6.11 **G** us this day our daily bread.
Mk 10.45 to **g** his life a ransom for many."
Jn 10.28 I **g** them eternal life, and they will
Ac 20.35 more blessed to **g** than to receive.'"

GIVEN → GIVE
Sir 35.12 Give to the Most High as he has **g**
Mt   7. 7 "Ask, and it will be **g** you;
Lk 22.19 "This is my body, which is **g** for
Ro   5. 5 Holy Spirit that has been **g** to us.

GIVER → GIVE
2Co 9. 7 for God loves a cheerful **g.**

GLADNESS
Ps 100. 2 Worship the LORD with **g;**
Pr 10.28 The hope of the righteous ends in **g,**
Isa 16.10 Joy and **g** are taken away from the
Zep 3.17 he will rejoice over you with **g,**
Heb 1. 9 has anointed you with the oil of **g**

GLORIFIED → GLORY
Jn 13.31 "Now the Son of Man has been **g,**
Ac   3.13 has **g** his servant Jesus,
Ro   8.30 those whom he justified he also **g.**

GLORIFY → GLORY
Ps 86.12 and I will **g** your name forever.
Sir 43.30 **G** the Lord and exalt him as much
Jn 17. 1 **g** your Son so that the Son may **g** you,
1Co 6.20 therefore **g** God in your body.

GLORY → GLORIFIED, GLORIFY
Ex 33.18 Moses said, "Show me your **g,**
1Sa 4.21 "The **g** has departed from Israel,"
1Mc 1.40 dishonor now grew as great as her **g**
Ps 8. 5 crowned them with **g** and honor.
Sir 1.11 The fear of the Lord is **g** and
Isa 6. 3 the whole earth is full of his **g.**"
Bar 5. 4 "Righteous Peace, Godly **G.**"
Mt 25.31 the Son of Man comes in his **g,**
Lk 2.14 "**G** to God in the highest heaven,
Jn 1.14 and we have seen his **g,**
Ro   3.23 sinned and fall short of the **g** of God;
1Co 10.31 do everything for the **g** of God.
2Co 4.17 for an eternal weight of **g** beyond
Heb 1. 3 reflection of God's **g** and the exact
Rev 4.11 to receive **g** and honor and power,
     21.23 for the **g** of God is its light,

GNASHING
Mt   8.12 will be weeping and **g** of teeth."
    25.30 will be weeping and **g** of teeth.'

GOAT → GOATS
Lev 16. 9 Aaron shall present the **g** on which

GOATS → GOAT
Mt 25.32 separates the sheep from the **g,**

GOD → GOD'S, GODLINESS, GODLY, GODS
Ge   1. 1 In the beginning when **G** created
     1.27 So **G** created humankind in his image,
     6. 2 sons of **G** saw that they were fair;

Ex	34. 6	a **G** merciful and gracious, slow to
Nu	23.19	**G** is not a human being,
Dt	6. 5	love the Lᴏʀᴅ your **G** with all
1Ki	8.27	will **G** indeed dwell on the earth?
2Ch	2. 5	for our **G** is greater than other gods.
Tob	4.19	At all times bless the Lord **G,**
Ps	19. 1	heavens are telling the glory of **G;**
	22. 1	My **G,** my **G,** why have you forsaken
	46.10	"Be still, and know that I am **G!**
	53. 1	Fools say in their hearts, "There is no **G."**
Ecc	12.13	Fear **G,** and keep his
Sir	32.14	seeks **G** will accept his discipline,
Isa	9. 6	Wonderful Counselor, Mighty **G,**
	44. 6	besides me there is no **g.**
Jer	10.10	But the Lᴏʀᴅ is the true **G;**
Bar	4. 8	You forgot the everlasting **G,**
Da	14. 4	But Daniel worshiped his own **G.**
Mt	1.23	which means, **"G** is with us."
	6.24	You cannot serve **G** and wealth.
Mk	1. 1	news of Jesus Christ, the Son of **G.**
	2. 7	Who can forgive sins but **G** alone?"
Lk	2.14	"Glory to **G** in the highest heaven,
	18.19	No one is good but **G** alone.
	22.70	"Are you, then, the Son of **G?"**
Jn	1. 1	was with **G,** and the Word was **G.**
	1.18	It is **G** the only Son,
	3.16	**G** so loved the world that he gave his
	5.18	calling **G** his own Father, thereby making
		himself equal to **G.**
Ac	5.29	"We must obey **G** rather than any
Ro	6.23	gift of **G** is eternal life in Christ
2Co	4. 4	Christ, who is the image of **G.**
Eph	4. 6	one **G** and Father of all,
Php	2. 6	though he was in the form of **G,**
Col	1.19	fullness of **G** was pleased to dwell,
1Jn	4.16	**G** is love, and those who abide
Rev	4. 8	"Holy, holy, holy, the Lord **G**

GOD'S → GOD

Mt	27.43	for he said, 'I am **G** Son.'"
	27.54	"Truly this man was **G** Son!"

GODLINESS → GOD

Wis	10.12	**g** is more powerful than anything
1Ti	4. 7	Train yourself in **g,**
2Pe	1. 3	everything needed for life and **g,**

GODLY → GOD

Sir	37.12	But associate with a **g** person
Bar	5. 4	"Righteous Peace, **G** Glory."
2Co	7.10	For **g** grief produces a repentance
2Pe	2. 9	how to rescue the **g** from trial,

GODS → GOD

Ex	20. 3	you shall have no other **g** before me.
1Co	8. 5	so-called **g** in heaven or on earth—

GOLD

Tob	12. 8	better to give alms than to lay up **g.**
Ps	119.127	love your commandments more than **g,**
Sir	31. 5	who loves **g** will not be justified;
1Pe	1. 7	being more precious than **g** that,
Rev	21.21	and the street of the city is pure **g,**

GOLGOTHA

Mt	27.33	**G** (which means Place of a Skull),

GOMORRAH

Ge	19.24	Lᴏʀᴅ rained on Sodom and **G** sulfur
Jude	1. 7	Sodom and **G** and the surrounding

GOOD → BEST, BETTER, GOODNESS

Ge	1.31	and indeed, it was very **g.**
	2. 9	tree of the knowledge of **g** and evil.
2Ch	7. 3	"For he is **g,** for his steadfast love
Tob	4. 9	laying up a **g** treasure for yourself
Ps	34. 8	taste and see that the Lᴏʀᴅ is **g;**
Isa	52. 7	who brings **g** news, who announces
Mt	5.45	his sun rise on the evil and on the **g,**
Mk	10.18	No one is **g** but God alone.
Jn	10.11	"I am the **g** shepherd.
Ro	12.21	but overcome evil with **g.**
Eph	2.10	created in Christ Jesus for **g** works,

GOODNESS → GOOD

Ps	23. 6	Surely **g** and mercy shall follow me
Heb	6. 5	tasted the **g** of the word of God and
2Pe	1. 5	support your faith with **g,**

GOSPEL

Mk	8.35	and for the sake of the **g,**
Ro	1.16	For I am not ashamed of the **g;**
Gal	1. 6	and are turning to a different **g—**
Php	1.27	life in a manner worthy of the **g**
Rev	14. 6	an eternal **g** to proclaim to those

GRACE → GRACIOUS

Wis	3. 9	**g** and mercy are upon his holy ones,
Jn	1.14	father's only son, full of **g** and truth.
	1.16	we have all received, **g** upon **g.**
Ac	15.11	that we will be saved through the **g**
Ro	3.24	are now justified by his **g** as a gift,
	11. 6	otherwise **g** would no longer be **g.**
2Co	12. 9	"My **g** is sufficient for you,
Eph	2. 5	by **g** you have been saved—
Heb	4.16	approach the throne of **g** with
Jas	4. 6	But he gives all the more **g;**

GRACIOUS → GRACE

Ex	34. 6	the Lᴏʀᴅ, a God merciful and **g,**
Nu	6.25	to shine upon you, and be **g** to you;
Ps	116. 5	**G** is the Lᴏʀᴅ, and righteous;

GREAT → GREATER, GREATEST

Ge	1.16	God made the two **g** lights—
	12. 2	I will make of you a **g** nation,
Dt	10.17	the **g** God, mighty and awesome,
Jdt	16.13	O Lord, you are **g** and glorious,
Sir	17.29	How **g** is the mercy of the Lord,
La	3.23	**g** is your faithfulness.
Mt	4.16	sat in darkness have seen a **g** light,
	20.26	whoever wishes to be **g** among you
Heb	2. 3	if we neglect so **g** a salvation?
	13.20	the **g** shepherd of the sheep,
Rev	12. 9	The **g** dragon was thrown down,
	20.11	I saw a **g** white throne and the one

GREATER → GREAT

Ex	18.11	that the Lᴏʀᴅ is **g** than all gods,
Mk	12.31	no other commandment **g** than these
Jn	14.12	in fact, will do **g** works than these,
	15.13	No one has **g** love than this,

GREATEST → GREAT

Mt	22.38	the **g** and first commandment.
Lk	9.48	the least among all of you is the **g."**
1Co	13.13	and the **g** of these is love.

GREEK

Jn	19.20	in Hebrew, in Latin, and in **G.**
Ro	1.16	to the Jew first and also to the **G.**
Gal	3.28	There is no longer Jew or **G,**

GRIEF → GRIEVE, GRIEVED
2Co 7. 9 your **g** led to repentance;

GRIEVE → GRIEF
Eph 4.30 do not **g** the Holy Spirit of God,
1Th 4.13 not **g** as others do who have no hope

GRIEVED → GRIEF
Isa 63.10 they rebelled and **g** his holy spirit;

GROUND
Ge   2. 7 formed man from the dust of the **g,**
Sir 33.10 All human beings come from the **g,**
Isa 53. 2 and like a root out of dry **g;**
Mt   13. 5 Other seeds fell on rocky **g,**

GROW
Col 1.10 as you **g** in the knowledge of God.
2Pe 3.18 But **g** in the grace and knowledge of

GUARANTEE → GUARANTEED
2Co 5. 5 who has given us the Spirit as a **g.**
Heb 7.22 Jesus has also become the **g** of a

GUARANTEED → GUARANTEE
Ro   4.16 promise may rest on grace and be **g**
Heb 6.17 he **g** it by an oath,

GUIDE
Ps   48.14 He will be our **g** forever.
Isa 58.11 The Lᴏʀᴅ will **g** you continually,
Lk   6.39 Can a blind person **g** a blind person?
Jn   16.13 he will **g** you into all the truth;

GUILT → GUILTY
Ps   32. 5 and you forgave the **g** of my sin.
Hos 14. 2 say to him, "Take away all **g;**
Zec 3. 9 I will remove the **g** of this land

GUILTY → GUILT
Ex   23. 7 for I will not acquit the **g.**
Nu   14.18 but by no means clearing the **g,**
Da   13.53 the innocent and acquitting the **g,**
Mk   3.29 but is **g** of an eternal sin"—

H

HADES
Sir 21.10 but at its end is the pit of **H.**
Mt   16.18 and the gates of **H** will not prevail
Ac   2.27 not abandon my soul to **H,**
Rev 1.18 I have the keys of Death and of **H.**
     20.14 **H** were thrown into the lake of fire.

HALLOWED
Ge   2. 3 blessed the seventh day and **h** it,
Mt   6. 9 Father in heaven, **h** be your name.

HAND → HANDS
Ex   15. 6 Your right **h,** O Lᴏʀᴅ, glorious
Dt   19.21 tooth for tooth, **h** for **h,**
Ps   110. 1 says to my lord, "Sit at my right **h**
Mk   9.43 If your **h** causes you to stumble, cut
Lk   20.42 said to my Lord, "Sit at my right **h,**
Heb 10.12 "he sat down at the right **h** of God,"
Rev 5. 1 saw in the right **h** of the one seated

HANDS → HAND
Ps   24. 4 who have clean **h** and pure hearts,
Lk   23.46 into your **h** I commend my spirit."
     24.40 he showed them his **h** and his feet.

Jn   3.35 has placed all things in his **h.**
Ac   8.18 the laying on of the apostles' **h,**
Heb 6. 2 laying on of **h,** resurrection of the

HARD → HARDENED
Jer 32.17 Nothing is too **h** for you.
Mt   7.14 the road is **h** that leads to life,
     19.23 **h** for a rich person to enter the

HARDENED → HARD
Ex   10.20 But the Lᴏʀᴅ **h** Pharaoh's heart,
Mk   8.17 Are your hearts **h?**
2Co 3.14 But their minds were **h.**

HARVEST → HARVESTING
Ge   8.22 the earth endures, seedtime and **h,**
Mt   13.39 **h** is the end of the age, and the
Rev 14.15 the **h** of the earth is fully ripe."

HARVESTING → HARVEST
Jn   4.35 see how the fields are ripe for **h.**

HATE → HATES, HATING
Ps   97.10 The Lᴏʀᴅ loves those who **h** evil;
Ecc 3. 8 a time to love, and a time to **h;**
Am   5.15 **H** evil and love good, and establish
Mt   5.43 your neighbor and **h** your enemy.'
Lk   6.27 do good to those who **h** you,

HATES → HATE
Pr   6.16 six things that the Lᴏʀᴅ **h,**
Sir 15.13 The Lord **h** all abominations;

HEAD
Mt   8.20 of Man has nowhere to lay his **h."**
Mk   6.28 brought his **h** on a platter,
Eph 1.22 has made him the **h** over all things

HEAL → HEALED, HEALING, HEALS, HEALTH
Dt   32.39 and I make alive; I wound and I **h;**
Ecc 3. 3 a time to kill, and a time to **h;**
Jn   12.40 and turn—and I would **h** them."

HEALED → HEAL
Isa 53. 5 and by his bruises we are **h.**
Jas 5.16 one another, so that you may be **h.**
1Pe 2.24 by his wounds you have been **h.**

HEALING → HEAL
Eze 47.12 for food, and their leaves for **h."**
Mal 4. 2 shall rise, with **h** in its wings.
1Co 12. 9 another gifts of **h** by the one Spirit,
Rev 22. 2 leaves of the tree are for the **h** of

HEALS → HEAL
Ex   15.26 for I am the Lᴏʀᴅ who **h** you."
Ps   103. 3 iniquity, who **h** all your diseases,
Wis 16.12 your word, O Lord, that **h** all people

HEALTH → HEAL
3Jn 1. 2 and that you may be in good **h,**

HEAR → HEARERS, HEARS
Dt   6. 4 **H,** O Israel: The Lᴏʀᴅ is our God,
Sir 5.11 Be quick to **h,** but deliberate in
Mk   12.29 answered, "The first is, '**H,** O Israel:
Lk   7.22 the lepers are cleansed, the deaf **h,**
Heb 3. 7 says, "Today, if you **h** his voice,

HEARERS → HEAR
Ro   2.13 For it is not the **h** of the law who

Jas 1.22 merely **h** who deceive themselves.

HEARS → HEAR
Ps 69.33 For the Lᴏʀᴅ **h** the needy,
Pr 15.29 but he **h** the prayer of the righteous.
Mt 7.24 then who **h** these words of mine
1Jn 5.14 according to his will, he **h** us.

HEART → BROKENHEARTED, HEARTS
Dt 6. 5 the Lᴏʀᴅ your God with all your **h**,
30.14 in your mouth and in your **h** for you
Jos 22. 5 all your **h** and with all your soul."
1Sa 16. 7 but the Lᴏʀᴅ looks on the **h**."
Ps 51.10 Create in me a clean **h**, O God,
Pr 3. 5 Trust in the Lᴏʀᴅ with all your **h**,
Sir 1.12 The fear of the Lord delights the **h**,
Jer 9.26 of Israel is uncircumcised in **h**.
Eze 36.26 A new **h** I will give you,
Mt 5. 8 "Blessed are the pure in **h**, for they
Mk 12.30 the Lord your God with all your **h**,
Ro 2.29 circumcision is a matter of the **h**—

HEARTS → HEART
Jer 31.33 and I will write it on their **h**;
Jn 14. 1 "Do not let your **h** be troubled.
Ro 2.15 law requires is written on their **h**,
Eph 3.17 Christ may dwell in your **h** through
Col 3.15 the peace of Christ rule in your **h**,
Heb 10.16 I will put my laws in their **h**,
1Jn 3.20 for God is greater than our **h**,
Rev 2.23 the one who searches minds and **h**,

HEAVEN → HEAVENLY, HEAVENS
Dt 30.12 "Who will go up to **h** for us,
Ecc 3. 1 and a time for every matter under **h**:
Mt 6. 9 Father in **h**, hallowed be your name.
24.35 **H** and earth will pass away,
26.64 and coming on the clouds of **h**."
Mk 10.21 and you will have treasure in **h**;
Lk 24.51 and was carried up into **h**.
Ro 10. 6 'Who will ascend into **h**?'"
Php 3.20 But our citizenship is in **h**,
1Th 1.10 to wait for his Son from **h**,
Heb 9.24 but he entered into **h** itself,
Rev 21. 1 I saw a new **h** and a new earth;

HEAVENLY → HEAVEN
Mt 5.48 as your **h** Father is perfect.
Eph 1. 3 spiritual blessing in the **h** places,
Heb 3. 1 holy partners in a **h** calling,

HEAVENS → HEAVEN
Ge 1. 1 when God created the **h** and
Isa 65.17 to create new **h** and a new earth;
Heb 4.14 priest who has passed through the **h**,
2Pe 3.10 the **h** will pass away with a loud

HEIR → HEIRS
Gal 4. 7 then also an **h**, through God.
Heb 1. 2 whom he appointed **h** of all things,

HEIRS → HEIR
Ro 8.17 **h** of God and joint **h** with Christ—
Eph 3. 6 the Gentiles have become fellow **h**,
1Pe 3. 7 also **h** of the gracious gift of life—

HELL
Mt 10.28 both soul and body in **h**.
Mk 9.43 to have two hands and to go to **h**,
2Pe 2. 4 cast them into **h** and committed

HELP → HELPER, HELPS
Ps 46. 1 a very present **h** in trouble.
Sir 2. 6 Trust in him, and he will **h** you;
Mk 9.24 "I believe; **h** my unbelief!"
Heb 2.18 able to **h** those who are being tested.

HELPER → HELP
Ge 2.18 will make him a **h** as his partner."
Tob 8. 6 Eve as a **h** and support.
Ps 30.10 O Lᴏʀᴅ, be my **h**!"
Heb 13. 6 Lord is my **h**; I will not be afraid.

HELPS → HELP
Ps 37.40 The Lᴏʀᴅ **h** them and rescues
Ro 8.26 the Spirit **h** us in our weakness;

HIDDEN → HIDE
Mt 13.44 is like treasure **h** in a field,
Mk 4.22 nothing **h**, except to be disclosed;
Col 3. 3 your life is **h** with Christ in God.
Rev 2.17 the **h** manna, and I will give a white

HIDE → HIDDEN
Dt 31.17 I will forsake them and **h** my face
Ps 13. 1 How long will you **h** your face
17. 8 **h** me in the shadow of your wings,

HIGH → HIGHEST
Ps 91. 1 live in the shelter of the Most **H**,
Mk 5. 7 Jesus, Son of the Most **H** God?
Eph 4. 8 "When he ascended on **h** he made
Heb 2.17 a merciful and faithful **h** priest
7.26 that we should have such a **h** priest,

HIGHEST → HIGH
1Ki 8.27 the **h** heaven cannot contain you,
Mt 21. 9 Hosanna in the **h** heaven!"
Lk 2.14 "Glory to God in the **h** heaven,

HOLINESS → HOLY
Ro 1. 4 according to the spirit of **h** by
2Co 6. 6 **h** of spirit, genuine love,
1Ti 2.15 continue in faith and love and **h**,
Heb 12.14 **h** without which no one will see

HOLY → HOLINESS
Ex 20. 8 the sabbath day, and keep it **h**.
26.33 the **h** place from the most **h**.
Lev 11.44 and be **h**, for I am **h**.
1Sa 2. 2 "There is no **H** One like the Lᴏʀᴅ,
1Mc 1.15 and abandoned the **h** covenant.
Wis 4.15 he watches over his **h** ones.
Isa 6. 3 "**H, h, h** is the Lᴏʀᴅ of hosts;
Mt 1.18 to be with child from the **H** Spirit.
3.11 baptize you with the **H** Spirit and
Mk 1.24 who you are, the **H** One of God."
3.29 against the **H** Spirit can never have
Lk 3.22 the **H** Spirit descended upon him in
Jn 14.26 But the Advocate, the **H** Spirit,
Ac 2. 4 were filled with the **H** Spirit and
Ro 12. 1 living sacrifice, **h** and acceptable
Eph 4.30 do not grieve the **H** Spirit of God,
Heb 6. 4 and have shared in the **H** Spirit,
1Pe 1.16 "You shall be **h**, for I am **h**."
1Jn 2.20 have been anointed by the **H** One,
Jude 1.14 with ten thousands of his **h** ones,
Rev 4. 8 **H, h, h**, the Lord God the Almighty
21. 2 I saw the **h** city, the new Jerusalem,

HOMETOWN
Mk 6. 4 not without honor, except in their **h**,

∧ CONCORDANCE ∧

HONEY

Ex 3. 8 a land flowing with milk and **h,**
Mt 3. 4 and his food was locusts and wild **h.**

HONOR

Dt 5.16 **H** your father and your mother,
Ps 8. 5 and crowned them with glory and **h.**
Mt 15. 4 For God said, '**H** your father and
Ro 13. 7 **h** to whom **h** is due.
Eph 6. 2 "**H** your father and mother"—
Rev 4.11 to receive glory and **h** and power,

HOPE → HOPES

Sir 34.15 their **h** is in him who saves them.
La 3.21 and therefore I have **h:**
Da 13.60 who saves those who **h** in him.
1Co 13.13 And now faith, **h,** and love abide,
Col 1.27 Christ in you, the **h** of glory.
1Jn 3. 3 all who have this **h** in him purify

HOPES → HOPE

1Co 13. 7 believes all things, **h** all things,

HOSANNA

Mk 11.10 **H** in the highest heaven!"
Jn 12.13 went out to meet him, shouting, "**H!**

HOSPITABLE → HOSPITALITY

1Ti 3. 2 temperate, sensible, respectable, **h,**
Tit 1. 8 but he must be **h,** a lover
1Pe 4. 9 Be **h** to one another without

HOSPITALITY → HOSPITABLE

Ro 12.13 of the saints; extend **h** to strangers,
1Ti 5.10 has brought up children, shown **h,**
Heb 13. 2 not neglect to show **h** to strangers,

HOSTS

Ps 46. 7 The LORD of **h** is with us;
Isa 48. 2 the LORD of **h** is his name.

HOUR

Mt 24.36 about that day and **h** no one knows,
Jn 2. 4 My **h** has not yet come."
17. 1 "Father, the **h** has come;
Rev 3.10 I will keep you from the **h** of trial
14. 7 for the **h** of his judgment has come;

HOUSE → HOUSEHOLD, STOREHOUSE

Ex 20.17 shall not covet your neighbor's **h;**
1Ch 22. 1 "Here shall be the **h** of the LORD
Ezr 1. 5 rebuild the **h** of the LORD in
Ps 69. 9 zeal for your **h** that has consumed
Mt 7.24 like a wise man who built his **h**
Jn 2.17 "Zeal for your **h** will consume me."
14. 2 In my Father's **h** there are many
1Pe 2. 5 be built into a spiritual **h,**

HOUSEHOLD → HOUSE

Jos 24.15 my **h,** we will serve the LORD."

HUMAN → HUMANKIND

Jdt 8.16 for God is not like a **h** being,
Ps 8. 4 are **h** beings that you are mindful
Mt 15. 9 teaching **h** precepts as doctrines.'"
Ac 5.29 obey God rather than any **h**
Php 2. 7 being born in **h** likeness.

HUMANKIND → HUMAN

Ge 1.26 "Let us make **h** in our image,
1Ti 2. 5 one mediator between God and **h,**

HUMBLE → HUMBLED, HUMBLY, HUMILITY

Ps 25. 9 He leads the **h** in what is right,
Sir 3.20 but by the **h** he is glorified.
Isa 57.15 to revive the spirit of the **h,**
Mt 11.29 for I am gentle and **h** in heart,
Jas 4.10 **H** yourselves before the Lord,

HUMBLED → HUMBLE

Lk 14.11 all who exalt themselves will be **h,**
Php 2. 8 he **h** himself and became obedient

HUMBLY → HUMBLE

Mic 6. 8 and to walk **h** with your God?

HUMILITY → HUMBLE

Pr 15.33 and **h** goes before honor.
Sir 1.27 fidelity and **h** are his delight.
Zep 2. 3 seek righteousness, seek **h;**
Php 2. 3 in **h** regard others as better than

HUNGER → HUNGRY

Mt 5. 6 "Blessed are those who **h** and thirst
Rev 7.16 will **h** no more, and thirst no more;

HUNGRY → HUNGER

Ps 146. 7 who gives food to the **h.**
Jn 6.35 comes to me will never be **h,**
Ro 12.20 "if your enemies are **h,** feed them;

HUSBAND → HUSBANDS

Sir 26. 1 Happy is the **h** of a good wife;
Isa 54. 5 For your Maker is your **h,**
Eph 5.23 **h** is the head of the wife just as
Rev 21. 2 as a bride adorned for her **h.**

HUSBANDS → HUSBAND

Eph 5.25 **H,** love your wives, just as Christ
Col 3.18 Wives, be subject to your **h,**
1Pe 3. 7 **H,** in the same way, show

I

IDOL → IDOLS

Ex 20. 4 shall not make for yourself an **i,**
Isa 40.19 An **i**?—A workman casts it,
1Co 10.19 or that an **i** is anything?

IDOLS → IDOL

Ex 34.17 You shall not make cast **i.**
1Mc 1.43 they sacrificed to **i** and profaned the
1Co 8. 1 concerning food sacrificed to **i:**

IMAGE

Ge 1.26 "Let us make humankind in our **i,**
Sir 17. 3 and made them in his own **i.**
1Co 15.49 the **i** of the man of heaven.
Col 1.15 He is the **i** of the invisible God,
Rev 20. 4 not worshiped the beast or its **i**

IMMANUEL → EMMANUEL

Isa 7.14 bear a son, and shall name him **I.**

IMMORAL → IMMORALITY

1Co 5. 9 not to associate with sexually **i**
Heb 12.16 an **i** and godless person,

IMMORALITY → IMMORAL

Sir 41.17 Be ashamed of sexual **i,**
2Co 12.21 sexual **i,** and licentiousness
Jude 1. 7 indulged in sexual **i** and pursued

IMMORTAL → IMMORTALITY
Ro   1.23   the glory of the **i** God for images
1Ti 1.17   the King of the ages, **i**, invisible,

IMMORTALITY → IMMORTAL
1Co 15.53 and this mortal body must put on **i**.
1Ti 6.16   It is he alone who has **i** and dwells

IMPOSSIBLE
Mt   17.20 and nothing will be **i** for you."
Mk   10.27 "For mortals it is **i**, but not for God;
Heb 11.6   without faith it is **i** to please God,

INCENSE → FRANKINCENSE
Ex   25.6   anointing oil and for the fragrant **i**,

INFANTS
Ps   8.2   Out of the mouths of babes and **i**
Mt   21.16 'Out of the mouths of **i** and nursing
1Co 14.20 **i** in evil, but in thinking be adults.

INHERIT → INHERITANCE
Ps   37.11 But the meek shall **i** the land,
Lk   10.25 "what must I do to **i** eternal life?"
1Co 6.9   wrongdoers will not **i** the kingdom
Heb 1.14   sake of those who are to **i** salvation?

INHERITANCE → INHERIT
Eph 1.11   In Christ we have also obtained an **i**,
Heb 9.15   the promised eternal **i**,

INIQUITY
Ex   34.7   forgiving **i** and transgression and
Ps   103.3 who forgives all your **i**,
Isa 53.6   has laid on him the **i** of us all.
Tit 2.14   that he might redeem us from all **i**

INN
Lk   2.7   no place for them in the **i**.

INNOCENT
Pr   6.17   and hands that shed **i** blood,
Mt   27.24 "I am **i** of this man's blood;

INSPIRED
Ex   35.34 And he has **i** him to teach,
2Ti 3.16   All scripture is **i** by God and is

INSTRUCT → INSTRUCTED, INSTRUCTION, INSTRUCTOR
Dt   17.10 observing everything they **i** you.
Ne   9.20   You gave your good spirit to **i** them,

INSTRUCTED → INSTRUCT
Isa 40.13 or as his counselor has **i** him?
Jn   8.28   these things as the Father **i** me.

INSTRUCTION → INSTRUCT
Pr   8.10   Take my **i** instead of silver,
Sir 51.26 and let your souls receive **i**;
Ro   15.4   in former days was written for our **i**,
1Ti 1.5   But the aim of such **i** is love

INSTRUCTOR → INSTRUCT
Mt   23.10 for you have one **i**, the Messiah.

INTERCEDES → INTERCESSION
Ro   8.26   Spirit **i** with sighs too deep for

INTERCESSION → INTERCEDES
1Sa 2.25   against the LORD, who can make **i**?"
Isa 53.12 and made **i** for the transgressors.
Heb 7.25   he always lives to make **i** for them.

INTERPRET → INTERPRETATION, INTERPRETATIONS
Mt   16.3   cannot **i** the signs of the times.
1Co 12.30 Do all speak in tongues? Do all **i**?

INTERPRETATION → INTERPRET
1Co 12.10 to another the **i** of tongues.

INTERPRETATIONS → INTERPRET
Ge   40.8   to them, "Do not **i** belong to God?

INVISIBLE
Col 1.15   He is the image of the **i** God,
1Ti 1.17   To the King of the ages, immortal, **i**,

ISRAEL → JACOB
Ge   49.28 All these are the twelve tribes of **I**,
Ex   28.11 with the names of the sons of **I**;
Nu   24.17 and a scepter shall rise out of **I**;
Dt   6.4   Hear, O **I**: The LORD is our God,
Sir 17.17 but **I** is the Lord's own portion.
Jer 31.31 a new covenant with the house of **I**
Mt   2.6   who is to shepherd my people **I**.'"
Mk   12.29 answered, "The first is, 'Hear, O **I**:
Ac   1.6   you will restore the kingdom to **I**?"
Heb 8.8   a new covenant with the house of **I**
Rev 7.4   out of every tribe of the people of **I**:

J

JACOB → ISRAEL
1Mc 1.28   house of **J** was clothed with shame.
Ps   135.4 the LORD has chosen **J** for himself,
Mic 7.20   You will show faithfulness to **J**
Ro   9.13   "I have loved **J**,

JARS
2Co 4.7   But we have this treasure in clay **j**,

JEALOUS
Ex   34.14 whose name is **J**, is a **j** God).
Dt   4.24   God is a devouring fire, a **j** God.
Ro   10.19 "I will make you **j** of those

JERUSALEM
2Sa 5.5   and at **J** he reigned over all Israel
2Ki 25.10 broke down the walls around **J**.
1Mc 1.29   and he came to **J** with a large force.
Ezr 2.1   they returned to **J** and Judah,
Ne   2.17   Come, let us rebuild the wall of **J**,
Isa 40.2   Speak tenderly to **J**,
La   1.8   **J** sinned grievously, so she has
Da   9.25   went out to restore and rebuild **J**
Mt   23.37 "**J, J**, the city that kills the prophets
Gal 4.25   corresponds to the present **J**,
Heb 12.22 of the living God, the heavenly **J**,
Rev 21.2   And I saw the holy city, the new **J**,

JESUS → CHRIST
LIFE: Genealogy (Mt 1.1–17; Lk 3.21–37). Birth announced (Mt 1.18–25; Lk 1.26–45). Birth (Mt 2.1–12; Lk 2.1–40). Escape to Egypt (Mt 2.13–23). As a boy in the temple (Lk 2.41–52). Baptism (Mt 3.13–17; Mk 1.9–11; Lk 3.21–22; Jn 1.32–34). Temptation (Mt 4.1–11; Mk 1.12–13; Lk 4.1–13). Ministry in Galilee (Mt 4.12–18.35; Mk 1.14–9.50; Lk 4.14–13.9; Jn 1.35–2.11; 4; 6), Transfiguration (Mt 17.1–8; Mk 9.2–8; Lk 9.28–36), on the way to Jerusalem (Mt 19–20; Mk 10; Lk 13.10–19.27), in Jerusalem (Mt 21–25; Mk 11–13; Lk 19.28–21.38; Jn 2.12–3.36; 5; 7–12). Last supper (Mt 26.17–35; Mk 14.12–31; Lk 22.1–38; Jn 13–17). Arrest and trial (Mt 26.36–27.31; Mk 14.43–15.20; Lk 22.39–23.25; Jn 18.1–19.16). Crucifixion (Mt 27.32–66; Mk 15.21–47; Lk 23.26–55;

Jn 19.28–42). Resurrection and appearances (Mt 28; Mk 16; Lk 24; Jn 20–21; Ac 1.1–11; 7.56; 9.3–6; 1Co 15.1–8; Rev 1.1–20).

MIRACLES. *Healings:* official's son (Jn 4.43–54), demoniac in Capernaum (Mk 1.23–26; Lk 4.33–35), Peter's mother-in-law (Mt 8.14–17; Mk 1.29–31; Lk 4.38–39), leper (Mt 8.2–4; Mk 1.40–45; Lk 5.12–16), paralytic (Mt 9.1–8; Mk 2.1–12; Lk 5.17–26), cripple (Jn 5.1–9), shriveled hand (Mt 12.10–13; Mk 3.1–5; Lk 6.6–11), centurion's servant (Mt 8.5–13; Lk 7.1–10), widow's son raised (Lk 7.11–17), demoniac (Mt 12.22–23; Lk 11.14), Gadarene demoniacs (Mt 8.28–34; Mk 5.1–20; Lk 8.26–39), woman's bleeding and Jairus' daughter (Mt 9.18–26; Mk 5.21–43; Lk 8.40–56), blind man (Mt 9.27–31), mute man (Mt 9.32–33), Canaanite woman's daughter (Mt 15.21–28; Mk 7.24–30), deaf man (Mk 7.31–37), blind man (Mk 8.22–26), demoniac boy (Mt 17.14–18; Mk 9.14–29; Lk 9.37–43), ten lepers (Lk 17.11–19), man born blind (Jn 9.1–7), crippled woman (Lk 13.11–17), man with dropsy (Lk 14.1–6), two blind men (Mt 20.29–34; Mk 10.46–52; Lk 18.35–43), Malchus' ear (Lk 22.50–51). *Other Miracles:* water to wine (Jn 2.1–11), catch of fish (Lk 5.1–11), storm stilled (Mt 8.23–27; Mk 4.37–41; Lk 8.22–25), 5,000 fed (Mt 14.15–21; Mk 6.35–44; Lk 9.10–17; Jn 6.1–14), walking on water (Mt 14.25–33; Mk 6.48–52; Jn 6.15–21), 4,000 fed (Mt 15.32–39; Mk 8.1–9), money from fish (Mt 17.24–27), fig tree cursed (Mt 21.18–22; Mk 11.12–14), catch of fish (Jn 21.1–14).

MAJOR TEACHING: Sermon on the Mount (Mt 5–7; Lk 6.17–49), to Nicodemus (Jn 3), to Samaritan woman (Jn 4), Bread of Life (Jn 6.22–59), at Feast of Tabernacles (Jn 7–8), woes to Pharisees (Mt 23; Lk 11.37–54), Good Shepherd (Jn 10.1–18), Olivet Discourse (Mt 24–25; Mk 13; Lk 21.5–36), Upper Room Discourse (Jn 13–16).

PARABLES: Sower (Mt 13.3–23; Mk 4.3–25; Lk 8.5–18), seed's growth (Mk 4.26–29), wheat and weeds (Mt 13.24–30, 36–43), mustard seed (Mt 13.31–32; Mk 4.30–32), yeast (Mt 13.33; Lk 13.20–21), hidden treasure (Mt 13.44), valuable pearl (Mt 13.45–46), net (Mt 13.47–51), house owner (Mt 13.52), good Samaritan (Lk 10.25–37), unmerciful servant (Mt 18.15–35), lost sheep (Mt 18.10–14; Lk 15.4–7), lost coin (Lk 15.8–10), prodigal son (Lk 15.11–32), dishonest manager (Lk 16.1–13), rich man and Lazarus (Lk 16.19–31), persistent widow (Lk 18.1–8), Pharisee and tax collector (Lk 18.9–14), payment of workers (Mt 20.1–16), tenants and the vineyard (Mt 21.28–46; Mt 12.1–12; Lk 20.9–19), wedding banquet (Mt 22.1–14), faithful servant (Mt 24.45–51), ten virgins (Mt 25.1–13), talents (Mt 25.1–30; Lk 19.12–27).

DISCIPLES see APOSTLES. Call (Jn 1.35–51; Mt 4.18–22; 9.9; Mk 1.16–20; 2.13–14; Lk 5.1–11, 27–28). Named Apostles (Mk 3.13–19; Lk 6.12–16). Twelve sent out (Mt 10; Mk 6.7–11; Lk 9.1–5). Seventy sent out (Lk 10.1–24). Defection of (Jn 6.60–71; Mt 26.56; Mk 14.50–52). Final commission (Mt 28.16–20; Jn 21.15–23; Ac 1.3–8).

Ac	9.5	"I am **J,** whom you are persecuting.
1Co	8.6	and one Lord, **J** Christ,
Php	2.10	name of **J** every knee should bend,
2Th	2.1	the coming of our Lord **J** Christ
1Ti	1.15	**J** came into the world to save
Heb	12.2	to **J** the pioneer and perfecter of our
	13.8	**J** Christ is the same yesterday and
1Jn	1.7	the blood of **J** his Son cleanses us
Rev	1.1	The revelation of **J** Christ,
	22.20	Amen. Come, Lord **J!**

JEW → JEWS

Ro	1.16	to the **J** first and also to the Greek.
	2.29	a person is a **J** who is one inwardly,
Col	3.11	there is no longer Greek and **J,**

JEWEL → JEWELS

| Rev | 21.19 | of the city are adorned with every **j;** |

JEWELS → JEWEL

Pr	3.15	She is more precious than **j,**
Isa	54.12	your gates of **j,** and all your wall
Rev	17.4	adorned with gold and **j** and pearls,

JEWS → JEW

Est	3.13	to kill, and to annihilate all **J,**
Mt	2.2	who has been born king of the **J?**
	27.11	"Are you the King of the **J?"**
Ro	3.29	Or is God the God of **J** only?

JOINED

| Mt | 19.6 | what God has **j** together, let no one |
| Eph | 2.21 | the whole structure is **j** together |

JORDAN

Ge	13.10	the plain of the **J** was well watered
Nu	34.12	the boundary shall go down to the **J,**
Mt	3.6	were baptized by him in the river **J,**

JOY

Ne	8.10	the **j** of the LORD is your strength."
Tob	13.17	Jerusalem will sing hymns of **j,**
Job	20.5	**j** of the godless is but for a moment?
Ps	51.12	Restore to me the **j** of your salvation
Pr	21.15	When justice is done, it is a **j** to the
Isa	35.10	everlasting **j** shall be upon their
Bar	5.9	For God will lead Israel with **j,**
La	2.15	of beauty, the **j** of all the earth?"
Lk	1.44	the child in my womb leaped for **j.**
	2.10	bringing you good news of great **j**
Ro	14.17	but righteousness and peace and **j** in
Gal	5.22	the fruit of the Spirit is love, **j,**
Heb	12.2	**j** that was set before him endured
Jas	1.2	consider it nothing but **j,**

JUBILEE

| Lev | 25.10 | It shall be a **j** for you: |
| Nu | 36.4 | when the **j** of the Israelites comes, |

JUDEA

Mt	2.1	Jesus was born in Bethlehem of **J,**
Lk	3.1	Pontius Pilate was governor of **J,**
Ac	1.8	my witnesses in Jerusalem, in all **J**

JUDGE → JUDGED, JUDGES, JUDGMENT, JUDGMENTS

1Sa	2.10	LORD will **j** the ends of the earth;
Ps	96.13	for he is coming to **j** the earth.
Sir	35.15	for the Lord is the **j,**
Eze	34.17	I shall **j** between sheep and sheep,
Lk	6.37	not **j,** and you will not be judged;
Jn	7.24	Do not **j** by appearances,
Ro	3.6	then how could God **j** the world?
1Co	6.2	that the saints will **j** the world?
2Ti	4.1	who is to **j** the living and the dead,
Rev	20.4	on them were given authority to **j.**

JUDGED → JUDGE

| 1Co | 11.31 | if we **j** ourselves, we would not be **j.** |
| Rev | 20.12 | dead were **j** according to their works |

JUDGES → JUDGE

Jdg	2.16	Then the LORD raised up **j,**
Sir	16.12	**j** a person according to one's deeds.
Lk	11.19	Therefore they will be your **j.**

JUDGMENT → JUDGE

| Ex | 6.6 | arm and with mighty acts of **j.** |

Ps	1. 5	wicked will not stand in the **j,**
Ecc	12.14	God will bring every deed into **j,**
Wis	12.12	Or will resist your **j?**
Sir	18.20	Before **j** comes, examine yourself;
Jer	25.31	he is entering into **j** with all flesh,
Da	7.22	**j** was given for the holy ones of the
Ro	14.10	we will all stand before the **j** seat of
2Co	5.10	all of us must appear before the **j**
Heb	9.27	to die once, and after that the **j,**
Jas	2.13	mercy triumphs over **j.**
1Jn	4.17	may have boldness on the day of **j,**
Rev	18.10	For in one hour your **j** has come."

JUDGMENTS → JUDGE

Ps	119.75	LORD, that your **j** are right,
Ro	11.33	How unsearchable are his **j** and
Rev	19. 2	for his **j** are true and just;

JUST → JUSTICE, JUSTIFICATION, JUSTIFIED, JUSTIFY

Ge	18.25	Judge of all the earth do what is **j?"**
Tob	3. 2	O Lord, and all your deeds are **j;**
Sir	18. 2	the Lord alone is **j.**
1Jn	1. 9	he who is faithful and **j** will forgive
Rev	15. 3	**J** and true are your ways, King of

JUSTICE → JUST

Ex	23. 6	not pervert the **j** due to your poor
Ps	33. 5	He loves righteousness and **j;**
Isa	30.18	For the LORD is a God of **j;**
Jer	9.24	I act with steadfast love, **j,**
Hos	12. 6	to your God, hold fast to love and **j,**
Am	5.24	But let **j** roll down like waters,
Lk	11.42	and neglect **j** and the love of God;

JUSTIFICATION → JUST

Ro	4.25	trespasses and was raised for our **j.**
2Co	3. 9	more does the ministry of **j** abound
Gal	2.21	for if **j** comes through the law,

JUSTIFIED → JUST

Mt	12.37	for by your words you will be **j,**
Ro	5. 1	Therefore, since we are **j** by faith,
	10.10	believes with the heart and so is **j,**
Gal	2.16	that we might be **j** by faith in Christ,
Jas	2.24	is **j** by works and not by faith alone.

K

KEEP → KEEPER

Ge	17. 9	for you, you shall **k** my covenant,
Ex	19. 5	obey my voice and **k** my covenant,
Nu	6.24	The LORD bless you and **k** you;
Dt	5.10	love me and **k** my commandments.
Ne	1. 5	love him and **k** his commandments;
Pr	7. 2	**k** my commandments and live,
Ecc	3. 6	time to **k,** and a time to throw away;
	12.13	Fear God, and **k** his commandments
Lk	17.33	those who lose their life will **k** it.

KEEPER → KEEP

Ge	4. 9	am I my brother's **k?"**
Ps	121. 5	The LORD is your **k;**

KEY → KEYS

Rev	3. 7	true one, who has the **k** of David,

KEYS → KEY

Mt	16.19	you the **k** of the kingdom of heaven,
Rev	1.18	I have the **k** of Death and of Hades.

KILL → KILLED, KILLS

Ecc	3. 3	a time to **k,** and a time to heal;
Mt	10.28	not fear those who **k** the body but cannot **k** the soul;
Mk	14. 1	to arrest Jesus by stealth and **k** him;

KILLED → KILL

Mk	9.31	after being **k,** he will rise again."
Ac	3.15	and you **k** the Author of life,

KILLS → KILL

2Co	3. 6	the letter **k,** but the Spirit gives life.

KIND → KINDNESS

1Co	13. 4	Love is patient; love is **k;**
Eph	4.32	and be **k** to one another,

KINDNESS → KIND

Pr	31.26	teaching of **k** is on her tongue.
Ro	2. 4	**k** is meant to lead you to repentance
Gal	5.22	joy, peace, patience, **k,** generosity,

KING → KINGDOM, KINGS

2Sa	2. 4	there they anointed David **k** over
Tob	10.13	Lord of heaven and earth, **K** over all
Jdt	9.12	**K** of all your creation,
Ps	2. 6	set my **k** on Zion, my holy hill."
	10.16	The LORD is **k** forever and ever;
Isa	6. 5	have seen the **K,** the LORD of hosts!
Mt	2. 2	who has been born **k** of the Jews?
	27.37	"This is Jesus, the **K** of the Jews."
1Ti	1.17	To the **K** of the ages, immortal,
Rev	19.16	**"K** of kings and Lord of lords."

KINGDOM → KING

Ex	19. 6	you shall be for me a priestly **k** and
2Sa	7.12	and I will establish his **k.**
Ps	145.13	Your **k** is an everlasting **k,**
Wis	10.10	she showed him the **k** of God,
Mt	4.17	"Repent, for the **k** of heaven has
	5. 3	for theirs is the **k** of heaven.
	6.10	Your **k** come. Your will be done,
Mk	10.24	how hard it is to enter the **k** of God!
Lk	17.21	in fact, the **k** of God is among you."
Jn	18.36	"My **k** is not from this world.
Ro	14.17	the **k** of God is not food and drink
1Co	6. 9	wrongdoers will not inherit the **k**
1Th	2.12	calls you into his own **k** and glory.
Heb	12.28	receiving a **k** that cannot be shaken,
Rev	11.15	world has become the **k** of our Lord

KINGS → KING

Ps	2. 2	The **k** of the earth set themselves,
Isa	52.15	**k** shall shut their mouths because of
Ac	4.26	The **k** of the earth took their stand,
1Ti	6.15	the King of **k** and Lord of lords.
Rev	19.16	"King of **k** and Lord of lords."

KISS

Ps	2.12	**k** his feet, or he will be angry,
SS	1. 2	Let him **k** me with the kisses of his
Mt	26.48	"The one I will **k** is the man; arrest
2Co	13.12	Greet one another with a holy **k.**

KNEE → KNEES

Isa	45.23	"To me every **k** shall bow,
Ro	14.11	says the Lord, every **k** shall bow to
Php	2.10	at the name of Jesus every **k** should

KNEES → KNEE

1Ki	19.18	the **k** that have not bowed to Baal,

˄ CONCORDANCE

˄

Eph 3.14 I bow my **k** before the Father,

KNOCK → KNOCKING
Lk 11. 9 **k,** and the door will be opened for

KNOCKING → KNOCK
Rev 3.20 I am standing at the door, **k;**

KNOW → FOREKNEW, KNOWLEDGE, KNOWN, KNOWS
Job 19.25 For I **k** that my Redeemer lives,
Ps 46.10 "Be still, and **k** that I am God!
Jer 31.34 "**K** the LORD," for they shall all **k**
Mt 6. 3 left hand **k** what your right hand is
22.34 denied three times that you **k** me."
Jn 10.14 I **k** my own and my own **k** me,
1Co 13.12 I **k** only in part; then I will **k** fully,
Heb 8.11 '**K** the Lord,' for they shall all **k** me,
1Jn 2. 4 Whoever says, "I have come to **k**
Rev 3. 3 not **k** at what hour I will come to

KNOWLEDGE → KNOW
Ge 2. 9 the tree of the **k** of good and evil.
Pr 1. 7 of the LORD is the beginning of **k;**
Sir 3.25 without **k** there is no wisdom.
1Co 8. 1 **K** puffs up, but love builds up.
Eph 3.19 the love of Christ that surpasses **k,**
Col 2. 3 the treasures of wisdom and **k.**
1Jn 2.20 and all of you have **k.**

KNOWN → KNOW
Ps 139. 1 you have searched me and **k** me.
Lk 6.44 for each tree is **k** by its own fruit.

KNOWS → KNOW
Ps 94.11 The LORD **k** our thoughts,
Sir 42.18 Most High **k** all that may be known;
Mt 6. 8 your Father **k** what you need before
24.36 about that day and hour no one **k,**

L

LABOR
Ex 20. 9 Six days you shall **l** and do all your

LADDER
Ge 28.12 there was a **l** set up on the earth,

LAID → LAY
Isa 53. 6 the LORD has **l** on him the iniquity
Mk 16. 6 Look, there is the place they **l** him.
1Jn 3.16 that he **l** down his life for us—

LAKE
Rev 19.20 were thrown alive into the **l** of fire
20.14 This is the second death, the **l** of fire

LAMB
Ge 22. 8 "God himself will provide the **l** for
Ex 12.21 and slaughter the passover **l.**
Isa 53. 7 like a **l** that is led to the slaughter,
Mk 14.12 when the Passover **l** is sacrificed,
Jn 1.29 **L** of God who takes away the sin of
1Co 5. 7 For our paschal **l,** Christ, has been
1Pe 1.19 like that of a **l** without defect or
Rev 5.12 the **L** that was slaughtered to
21.23 and its lamp is the **L.**

LAME
Isa 35. 6 then the **l** shall leap like a deer,
Zep 3.19 And I will save the **l** and gather the
Mt 11. 5 the **l** walk, the lepers are cleansed,

LAMP → LAMPS, LAMPSTAND, LAMPSTANDS
Ps 119.105 Your word is a **l** to my feet and a
Mt 5.15 lighting a **l** puts it under the bushel

LAMPS → LAMP
Ex 25.37 You shall make the seven **l** for it;

LAMPSTAND → LAMP
Ex 25.31 You shall make a **l** of pure gold.
1Mc 4.50 and lit the lamps on the **l,**

LAMPSTANDS → LAMP
Rev 1.20 the seven **l** are the seven churches.

LAND
Ge 1.10 God called the dry **l** Earth,
Ex 3. 8 a **l** flowing with milk and honey,
Nu 13. 2 to spy out the **l** of Canaan,
Jos 11.23 So Joshua took the whole **l,**
2Ki 17. 5 the king of Assyria invaded all the **l**
25.21 So Judah went into exile out of its **l.**
2Ch 7.14 will forgive their sin and heal their **l.**
Ps 37.11 But the meek shall inherit the **l,**

LANGUAGE
Ge 11. 9 LORD confused the **l** of all the earth;

LAST → EVERLASTING
Isa 44. 6 I am the first and I am the **l;**
Mt 19.30 first will be **l,** and the **l** will be first.
Heb 1. 2 **l** days he has spoken to us by a Son,
Rev 1.17 I am the first and the **l,**

LAUGH
Ecc 3. 4 a time to weep, and a time to **l;**
Lk 6.21 you who weep now, for you will **l.**

LAW → LAWFUL
Dt 1. 5 Moses undertook to expound this **l**
31. 9 Then Moses wrote down this **l,**
Jos 1. 8 book of the **l** shall not depart out of
1Mc 2.48 They rescued the **l** out of the hands
Ps 1. 2 their delight is in the **l** of the LORD,
119.97 Oh, how I love your **l!**
Jer 31.33 I will put my **l** within them,
Mt 5.17 come to abolish the **l** or the prophets
Lk 24.44 written about me in the **l** of Moses,
Ro 6.14 you are not under **l** but under grace.
10. 4 For Christ is the end of the **l** so that
Heb 10. 1 Since the **l** has only a shadow of the
Jas 2.10 For whoever keeps the whole **l** but

LAWFUL → LAW
1Co 6.12 "All things are **l** for me,"
10.23 "All things are **l,**" but

LAY → LAID
Mt 28. 6 Come, see the place where he **l.**
Jn 10.15 I **l** down my life for the sheep.

LEAD → LEADS
Isa 11. 6 and a little child shall **l** them.

LEADS → LEAD
Ps 23. 2 he **l** me beside still waters;

LEAST
Mt 2. 6 are by no means **l** among the rulers
5.19 called **l** in the kingdom of heaven;
Lk 9.48 **l** among all of you is the greatest."

LEAVE → LEFT

Mk 10. 7 this reason a man shall **l** his father
Heb 13. 5 said, "I will never **l** you or forsake

LEAVEN

Ex 12.15 on the first day you shall remove **l**

LEAVES

Ge 3. 7 and they sewed fig **l** together
Eze 47.12 and their **l** for healing."
Rev 22. 2 **l** of the tree are for the healing of

LEFT → LEAVE

Mt 6. 3 your **l** hand know what your right
Lk 17.34 one will be taken and the other **l**.

LEGS

Jn 19.33 they did not break his **l**.

LEPER → LEPROUS

Mt 8. 2 and there was a **l** who came to him
26. 6 in the house of Simon the **l**,

LEPERS → LEPROUS

Lk 7.22 the lame walk, the **l** are cleansed,

LEPROUS → LEPER, LEPERS

Ex 4. 6 he took it out, his hand was **l**,
Nu 12.10 Miriam had become **l**,

LETTER

Mt 5.18 not one **l**, not one stroke of a **l**,
2Co 3. 6 the **l** kills, but the Spirit gives life.

LEVIATHAN

Job 41. 1 you draw out **l** with a fishhook,
Ps 74.14 You crushed the heads of **l**;

LEVITES → LEVITICAL

Nu 1.53 **L** shall camp around the tabernacle
Jos 14. 4 no portion was given to the **L** in the
Ne 8. 9 **L** who taught the people said to all

LEVITICAL → LEVITES

Heb 7.11 attainable through the **l** priesthood

LIAR → LIE

Pr 19.22 and it is better to be poor than a **l**.
Jn 8.44 for he is a **l** and the father of lies.

LIE → LIAR, LYING

Nu 23.19 that he should **l**, or a mortal,
Ps 23. 2 makes me **l** down in green pastures;
1Jn 2.21 know that no **l** comes from the truth.

LIFE → LIVE

Ge 2. 7 into his nostrils the breath of **l**;
2. 9 the tree of **l** also in the midst of the
9. 5 require a reckoning for human **l**.
Ex 21.23 then you shall give **l** for **l**,
Dt 30.19 Choose **l** so that you and your
Sir 4.12 Whoever loves her loves **l**,
Isa 53.10 you make his **l** an offering for sin,
Da 12. 2 shall awake, some to everlasting **l**,
Mt 7.14 and the road is hard that leads to **l**,
10.39 Those who find their **l** will lose it,
20.28 to give his **l** a ransom for many."
Jn 1. 4 in him was **l**, and the **l** was the light
3.15 believes in him may have eternal **l**.
6.35 said to them, "I am the bread of **l**.
11.25 "I am the resurrection and the **l**.

14. 6 "I am the way, and the truth, and the **l**.
Ac 3.15 and you killed the Author of **l**,
Ro 5.21 eternal **l** through Jesus Christ our
2Co 3. 6 the letter kills, but the Spirit gives **l**.
Php 4. 3 whose names are in the book of **l**.
1Jn 5.20 He is the true God and eternal **l**.
Rev 2. 8 who was dead and came to **l**:
20. 4 came to **l** and reigned with Christ
20.12 book was opened, the book of **l**.
22. 2 the tree of **l** with its twelve kinds

LIGHT → ENLIGHTENED, ENLIGHTENS, LIGHTS

Ge 1. 3 "Let there be **l**"; and there was **l**.
Isa 9. 2 in darkness have seen a great **l**;
60. 1 Arise, shine; for your **l** has come,
Mt 4.16 in darkness have seen a great **l**,
5.14 "You are the **l** of the world.
Jn 1. 9 true **l**, which enlightens everyone,
8.12 saying, "I am the **l** of the world.
Ro 13.12 and put on the armor of **l**;
2Co 11.14 Satan disguises himself as an angel of **l**.
Rev 22. 5 for the Lord God will be their **l**,

LIGHTS → LIGHT

Ge 1.16 God made the two great **l**—
Jas 1.17 coming down from the Father of **l**,

LIKENESS

Ge 1.26 in our image, according to our **l**;
Ro 8. 3 his own Son in the **l** of sinful flesh,
Php 2. 7 of a slave, being born in human **l**.

LION → LIONS

Isa 11. 7 the **l** shall eat straw like the ox.
Rev 5. 5 See, the **L** of the tribe of Judah,

LIONS → LION

Da 6.20 able to deliver you from the **l**?"

LISTEN

Ex 23.22 But if you **l** attentively to his voice
2Ki 17.40 They would not **l**, however,
Sir 11. 8 Do not answer before you **l**,
Mk 9. 7 my Son, the Beloved; **l** to him!"
Lk 16.31 'If they do not **l** to Moses and the
Jas 1.19 be quick to **l**, slow to speak,

LIVE → ALIVE, LIFE, LIVES, LIVING

Ge 3.22 and eat, and **l** forever"—
Ex 33.20 for no one shall see me and **l**."
Lev 18. 5 by doing so one shall **l**:
Dt 8. 3 one does not **l** by bread alone,
Wis 5.15 But the righteous **l** forever,
Sir 34.14 those who fear the Lord will **l**,
Hab 2. 4 but the righteous **l** by their faith.
Mt 4. 4 'One does not **l** by bread alone,
Jn 11.25 even though they die, will **l**,
Ro 14. 8 If we **l**, we **l** to the Lord,
2Co 5.15 those who **l** might **l** no longer for

LIVES → LIVE

Tob 13. 1 "Blessed be God who **l** forever,
Job 19.25 For I know that my Redeemer **l**,
Ro 6.10 but the life he **l**, he **l** to God.
Rev 15. 7 of God, who **l** forever and ever;

LIVING → LIVE

Ge 2. 7 and the man became a **l** being.
Dt 5.26 the voice of the **l** God speaking out
Jer 2.13 forsaken me, the fountain of **l** water,
Zec 14. 8 that day **l** waters shall flow out from

> CONCORDANCE

Mt	16.16	the Messiah, the Son of the **l** God."
Jn	4.10	he would have given you **l** water."
	6.51	I am the **l** bread that came down
Ro	12.1	present your bodies as a **l** sacrifice,
Heb	4.12	the word of God is **l** and active,

LOAVES

Mk	6.41	Taking the five **l** and the two fish,
	8.6	and he took the seven **l,**

LOCUSTS

Ex	10.4	I will bring **l** into your country.
Mt	3.4	and his food was **l** and wild honey.
Rev	9.3	from the smoke came **l** on the earth,

LONG

Ex	20.12	that your days may be **l** in the land
Ps	13.1	How **l,** O Lord?
Rev	6.10	how **l** will it be before you judge

LORD → LORD'S, LORDS

Dt	10.17	God is God of gods and **L** of lords,
Jdt	6.19	**L** God of heaven, see their
Ps	110.1	The Lord says to my **l,**
Wis	8.3	and the **L** of all loves her.
Sir	1.1	All wisdom is from the **L,**
Da	13.2	and one who feared the **L.**
Mt	7.22	many will say to me, '**L, L,**
Mk	1.3	'Prepare the way of the **L,**
	12.29	the **L** our God, the **L** is one;
Lk	2.11	who is the Messiah, the **L.**
Jn	13.13	You call me Teacher and **L**—
	20.28	"My **L** and my God!"
Ac	2.34	'The **L** said to my **L,** "Sit at my
Ro	4.24	in him who raised Jesus our **L**
	10.12	the same **L** is **L** of all and
1Co	8.6	and one **L,** Jesus Christ,
2Co	3.17	Now the **L** is the Spirit,
Eph	4.5	one **L,** one faith, one baptism,
Php	2.11	that Jesus Christ is **L,** to the glory
1Pe	3.15	in your hearts sanctify Christ as **L.**
Rev	4.8	"Holy, holy, holy, the **L** God
	19.16	"King of kings and **L** of lords."
	22.20	Amen. Come, **L** Jesus!

†LORD → †LORD'S

Ge	2.7	**L** God formed man from the dust of
	13.4	Abram called on the name of the **L.**
	18.14	Is anything too wonderful for the **L?**
Ex	15.3	The **L** is a warrior; the **L** is his name.
	34.6	and proclaimed, "The **L,** the **L,**
Lev	19.2	for I the **L** your God am holy.
Nu	6.24	The **L** bless you and keep you;
Dt	6.4	The **L** is our God, the **L** alone.
Jos	24.15	my household, we will serve the **L.**"
1Sa	2.2	"There is no Holy One like the **L,**
Ne	8.10	the joy of the **L** is your strength."
Job	1.21	the **L** gave, and the **L** has taken
Ps	1.2	their delight is in the law of the **L,**
	10.16	The **L** is king forever and ever;
	23.1	The **L** is my shepherd, I shall not
	33.12	Happy is the nation whose God is the **L**
	110.1	The **L** says to my lord,
	150.6	that breathes praise the **L!**
Pr	1.7	fear of the **L** is the beginning of
	3.5	Trust in the **L** with all your heart,
Isa	6.3	"Holy, holy, holy is the **L** of hosts;
	53.6	the **L** has laid on him the iniquity
Jer	31.34	"Know the **L,**" for they shall all
La	3.25	The **L** is good to those who wait for

Eze	37.4	O dry bones, hear the word of the **L.**
	48.35	time on shall be, The **L** is There.
Hos	14.1	Return, O Israel, to the **L** your God,
Joel	1.15	For the day of the **L** is near,
Am	5.6	Seek the **L** and live,
Ob	1.15	the day of the **L** is near against all
Na	1.3	The **L** is slow to anger but great in
Zep	1.14	The great day of the **L** is near,
Zec	14.9	the **L** will be one and his name one.
Mal	4.5	and terrible day of the **L** comes.

LORD'S → LORD

Mk	12.11	was the **L** doing, and it is amazing
Lk	4.19	to proclaim the year of the **L** favor."
Ro	14.8	or whether we die, we are the **L.**
1Co	10.26	the earth and its fullness are the **L.**"

†LORD'S → †LORD

Dt	32.9	the **L** own portion was his people,
Isa	59.1	the **L** hand is not too short to save,
Ob	1.21	and the kingdom shall be the **L.**

LORDS → LORD

Dt	10.17	God is God of gods and Lord of **l,**
Rev	19.16	"King of kings and Lord of **l.**"

LOSS → LOST

Sir	32.24	who trusts the Lord will not suffer **l.**
Php	3.8	I regard everything as **l** because of

LOST → LOSS

Ps	119.176	I have gone astray like a **l** sheep;
Lk	15.6	I have found my sheep that was **l.**'
	19.10	came to seek out and to save the **l.**"

LOTS → LOT

Ps	22.18	and for my clothing they cast **l.**
Mt	27.35	among themselves by casting **l;**

LOVE → BELOVED, LOVED, LOVES

Ex	20.6	but showing steadfast **l** to the
	34.6	and abounding in steadfast **l** and
Lev	19.18	shall **l** your neighbor as yourself:
Dt	6.5	You shall **l** the Lord your God
2Ch	6.42	Remember your steadfast **l**
Ne	1.5	steadfast **l** with those who **l** him
1Mc	4.33	with the sword of those who **l** you,
Ps	18.1	I **l** you, O Lord, my strength.
	86.5	abounding in steadfast **l** to all who
	119.97	Oh, how I **l** your law!
	136.1	for his steadfast **l** endures forever.
Pr	8.17	I **l** those who **l** me,
Ecc	3.8	a time to **l,** and a time to hate;
SS	1.2	For your **l** is better than wine,
Sir	2.15	and those who **l** him keep his ways.
	7.30	With all your might **l** your Maker,
Isa	54.8	but with everlasting **l** I will have
La	3.22	steadfast **l** of the Lord never ceases,
Da	14.38	have not forsaken those who **l** you."
Hos	11.4	of human kindness, with bands of **l.**
Joel	2.13	and abounding in steadfast **l,**
Jnh	4.2	and abounding in steadfast **l,**
Mt	5.44	**L** your enemies and pray
	6.24	either hate the one and **l** the other,
Mk	12.31	shall **l** your neighbor as yourself.'
Lk	6.32	For even sinners **l** those who **l** them.
	10.27	"You shall **l** the Lord your God
Jn	12.25	Those who **l** their life lose it,
	13.34	new commandment, that you **l** one
	14.15	"If you **l** me, you will keep my
	15.13	No one has greater **l** than this,

Ro	5. 8	But God proves his **l** for us in that
	12. 9	Let **l** be genuine; hate what is evil,
1Co	8. 1	Knowledge puffs up, but **l** builds up.
	13. 4	**L** is patient; **l** is kind;
	13.13	and the greatest of these is **l**.
Gal	5.22	the fruit of the Spirit is **l**, joy,
Eph	3.19	**l** of Christ that surpasses knowledge
	5.25	Husbands, **l** your wives,
1Ti	6.10	For the **l** of money is a root of all
Heb	10.24	provoke one another to **l** and good
	13. 5	your lives free from the **l** of money,
2Pe	1. 7	and mutual affection with **l**.
1Jn	2.15	not **l** the world or the things in the
	3. 1	See what **l** the Father has given us,
	5. 3	For the **l** of God is this,
2Jn	1. 6	And this is **l**, that we walk according
Jude	1.21	keep yourselves in the **l** of God;
Rev	2. 4	abandoned the **l** you had at first.

LOVED → LOVE

Jer	31. 3	have **l** you with an everlasting love;
Jn	3.16	God so **l** the world that he gave his
	15. 9	the Father has **l** me, so I have **l** you;
	15.12	love one another as I have **l** you.
1Jn	4.19	We love because he first **l** us.

LOVES → LOVE

Pr	3.12	the Lᴏʀᴅ reproves the one he **l**,
	17.17	A friend **l** at all times,
Wis	8. 3	and the Lord of all **l** her.
Sir	4.12	Whoever **l** her **l** life,
Lk	7.47	to whom little is forgiven, **l** little."
Ro	13. 8	who **l** another has fulfilled the law.
Eph	5.28	He who **l** his wife **l** himself.
Heb	12. 6	Lord disciplines those whom he **l**,
Rev	1. 5	who **l** us and freed us from our sins

LOWER → LOWLY

| Ps | 8. 5 | have made them a little **l** than God, |
| Heb | 2. 7 | made them for a little while **l** than |

LOWLY → LOWER

Jdt	9.11	But you are the God of the **l**,
Pr	16.19	It is better to be of a **l** spirit
Ro	12.16	but associate with the **l**;

LOYALTY

Dt	7. 9	God who maintains covenant **l**
Ru	3.10	this last instance of your **l**
Ps	101. 1	I will sing of **l** and of justice;
Hos	4. 1	There is no faithfulness or **l**,

LUKEWARM

| Rev | 3.16 | because you are **l**, and neither cold |

LUST → LUSTS

| Mt | 5.28 | looks at a woman with **l** has already |
| 2Pe | 1. 4 | that is in the world because of **l**, |

LUSTS → LUST

| Ro | 1.24 | gave them up in the **l** of their hearts |

LYING → LIE

| Pr | 6.17 | a **l** tongue, and hands that shed |
| Wis | 1.11 | and a **l** mouth destroys the soul. |

M

MADE → MAKE

| Ge | 1.31 | God saw everything that he had **m**, |
| | 2.22 | he **m** into a woman and brought her |

	6. 6	was sorry that he had **m** humankind
	15.18	the Lᴏʀᴅ **m** a covenant with Abram,
Ex	20.11	For in six days the Lᴏʀᴅ **m** heaven
Ps	8. 5	have **m** them a little lower than God
	118.24	This is the day that the Lᴏʀᴅ has **m**;
	139.14	I am fearfully and wonderfully **m**.
Sir	43.33	For the Lord has **m** all things,
Ac	2.36	that God has **m** him both Lord and
Eph	2. 5	**m** us alive together with Christ—

MAGDALENE

| Mt | 27.56 | Among them were Mary **M**, |

MAJESTIC → MAJESTY

| Ex | 15.11 | Who is like you, **m** in holiness, |
| Ps | 8. 1 | how **m** is your name in all the earth! |

MAJESTY → MAJESTIC

1Ch	29.11	the glory, the victory, and the **m**;
Ps	93. 1	The Lᴏʀᴅ is king, he is robed in **m**;
2Pe	1.16	we had been eyewitnesses of his **m**.

MAKE → MADE, MAKER

Ge	1.26	"Let us **m** humankind in our image,
	2.18	will **m** him a helper as his partner."
Ex	20. 4	You shall not **m** for yourself an idol,
Nu	6.25	Lᴏʀᴅ **m** his face to shine upon you,
Mt	28.19	and **m** disciples of all nations,

MAKER → MAKE

Ge	14.19	God Most High, **m** of heaven and
Ps	95. 6	kneel before the Lᴏʀᴅ, our **M**!
Sir	7.30	With all your might love your **M**,
Isa	54. 5	For your **M** is your husband,

MALE

Ge	1.27	**m** and female he created them.
Lev	20.13	If a man lies with a **m** as with a
Rev	12. 5	she gave birth to a son, a **m** child,

MAN

Ge	2. 7	Lᴏʀᴅ God formed **m** from the dust
	2.18	not good that the **m** should be alone;
Mt	9. 6	Son of **M** has authority on earth to
Lk	6. 5	The Son of **M** is lord of the sabbath.
Jn	9.35	"Do you believe in the Son of **M**?"
1Co	11. 3	that Christ is the head of every **m**,
Rev	1.13	I saw one like the Son of **M**,

MANGER

| Lk | 2.12 | in bands of cloth and lying in a **m**." |

MANNA

Ex	16.31	The house of Israel called it **m**;
Jn	6.49	ate the **m** in the wilderness,
Rev	2.17	I will give some of the hidden **m**,

MANY

Mt	22.14	**m** are called, but few are chosen."
Mk	10.45	and to give his life a ransom for **m**."
Ro	12. 5	who are **m**, are one body in Christ,

MARK

Ge	4.15	And the Lᴏʀᴅ put a **m** on Cain,
Eze	9. 6	but touch no one who has the **m**.
Rev	19.20	who had received the **m** of the beast

MARRIAGE → MARRIED, MARRIES

Mt	22.30	are given in **m**, but are like angels
Heb	13. 4	Let **m** be held in honor by all,
Rev	19. 7	for the **m** of the Lamb has come,

MARRIED → MARRIAGE
1Ti	3. 2	be above reproach, **m** only once,
Tit	1. 6	**m** only once, whose children are

MARRIES → MARRIAGE
Mk	10.11	and **m** another commits adultery
Ro	7. 3	if she **m** another man, she is not an
1Co	7.28	and if a virgin **m**, she does not sin.

MASTER → MASTERS, TASKMASTERS
Mal	1. 6	if I am a **m**, where is the respect due
Jn	15.20	Servants are not greater than their **m**
2Pe	2. 1	deny the **M** who bought them—

MASTERS → MASTER
Mt	6.24	"No one can serve two **m;**

MEDIATOR
Gal	3.19	ordained through angels by a **m.**
1Ti	2. 5	**m** between God and humankind,
Heb	8. 6	he is the **m** of a better covenant,

MEDITATE → MEDITATION
Jos	1. 8	you shall **m** on it day and night,
Ps	1. 2	on his law they **m** day and night.
Wis	12.22	we may **m** upon your goodness,
Sir	6.37	and **m** at all times on his

MEDITATION → MEDITATE
Ps	19.14	of my mouth and the **m** of my heart
	119.97	It is my **m** all day long.

MEEK → MEEKNESS
Ps	37.11	But the **m** shall inherit the land,
Mt	5. 5	"Blessed are the **m**, for they will

MEEKNESS → MEEK
Col	3.12	kindness, humility, **m**, and patience.
Jas	1.21	with **m** the implanted word

MEETING
Ex	27.21	In the tent of **m**, outside the curtain
	40.34	the cloud covered the tent of **m,**

MELCHIZEDEK
Ge	14.18	King **M** of Salem brought out bread
Ps	110. 4	forever according to the order of **M.**"
Heb	7. 1	This "King **M** of Salem, priest of

MEMBERS
Ro	7.23	I see in my **m** another law at war
1Co	6.15	that your bodies are **m** of Christ?
	12.18	God arranged the **m** in the body,

MERCIES → MERCY
La	3.22	his **m** never come to an end;
2Co	1. 3	the Father of **m** and the God of all

MERCIFUL → MERCY
Dt	4.31	the LORD your God is a **m** God,
Ps	111. 4	the LORD is gracious and **m.**
Sir	2.11	the Lord is compassionate and **m;**
Jer	3.12	not look on you in anger, for I am **m**
Mt	5. 7	"Blessed are the **m**, for they will
Lk	6.36	Be **m**, just as your Father is **m.**

MERCY → MERCIES, MERCIFUL
Ex	25.17	make a **m** seat of pure gold;
1Ch	21.13	of the LORD, for his **m** is very great;
Sir	2.17	for equal to his majesty is his **m,**
Hab	3. 2	in wrath may you remember **m.**

Mt	9.13	learn what this means, 'I desire **m,**
	23.23	of the law: justice and **m** and faith.
Ro	9.15	"I will have **m** on whom I have **m,**
Eph	2. 4	But God, who is rich in **m,**
Jas	2.13	**m** triumphs over judgment.

MESSENGER → MESSAGE
Mt	11.10	I am sending my **m** ahead of you,
2Co	12. 7	a **m** of Satan to torment me,

MESSIAH → CHRIST, MESSIAHS
Mt	16.16	Peter answered, "You are the **M,**
Lk	2.11	a Savior, who is the **M**, the Lord.
Ac	2.36	God has made him both Lord and **M**
Ro	9. 5	according to the flesh, comes the **M,**
Rev	11.15	kingdom of our Lord and of his **M,**

MESSIAHS → MESSIAH
Mk	13.22	False **m** and false prophets will

MIDWIVES
Ex	1.17	But the **m** feared God; they did not

MIGHT → ALMIGHTY, MIGHTY
2Ch	20. 6	In your hand are power and **m,**
Sir	7.30	With all your **m** love your Maker,
Zec	4. 6	**m**, nor by power, but by my spirit,

MIGHTY → MIGHT
Ge	49.24	by the hands of the **M** One of Jacob,
Ex	6. 1	by a **m** hand he will let them go;
Ps	99. 4	**M** King, lover of justice, you have
Isa	9. 6	Wonderful Counselor, **M** God,
Rev	18. 8	for **m** is the Lord God who judges

MILE
Mt	5.41	one **m**, go also the second **m.**

MILK
Ex	3. 8	a land flowing with **m** and honey,
Heb	5.12	You need **m**, not solid food;

MILLSTONE → STONE
Lk	17. 2	better for you if a **m** were hung

MIND → MINDFUL
Nu	23.19	mortal, that he should change his **m.**
Sir	37.17	The **m** is the root of all conduct;
Jnh	3. 9	God may relent and change his **m;**
Mt	22.37	all your soul, and with all your **m.'**
1Co	2.16	who has known the **m** of the Lord
Php	2. 5	same **m** be in you that was in Christ
Heb	7.21	sworn and will not change his **m,**

MINDFUL → MIND
Ps	8. 4	beings that you are **m** of them,
Heb	2. 6	beings that you are **m** of them,

MINISTERS → MINISTRY
2Co	3. 6	to be **m** of a new covenant,
	11.15	if his **m** also disguise themselves as **m**

MINISTRY → MINISTERS
2Co	5.18	has given us the **m** of reconciliation;
Eph	4.12	equip the saints for the work of **m,**
Heb	8. 6	now obtained a more excellent **m,**

MIRACLES → See also JESUS: MIRACLES
Ps	78.11	and the **m** that he had shown them.
Ac	19.11	did extraordinary **m** through Paul,
1Co	12.29	Are all teachers? Do all work **m?**

Heb 2. 4 signs and wonders and various **m,**

MOCKED → MOCK
Gal 6. 7 God is not **m,** for you reap

MOMENT → MOMENTARY
Ps 30. 5 For his anger is but for a **m;**
Isa 54. 7 For a brief **m** I abandoned you,
1Co 15.52 in a **m,** in the twinkling of an eye,

MOMENTARY → MOMENT
2Co 4.17 this slight **m** affliction is preparing

MONEY
Mk 11.15 the tables of the **m** changers
1Ti 6.10 love of **m** is a root of all kinds
Heb 13. 5 your lives free from the love of **m,**

MOON → MOONS
Joel 2.31 to darkness, and the **m** to blood,
Ac 2.20 to darkness and the **m** to blood,
Rev 6.12 the full **m** became like blood,
  21.23 no need of sun or **m** to shine on it,

MOONS → MOON
2Ch 8.13 the new **m,** and the three annual
Col 2.16 or of observing festivals, new **m,**

MORALS
1Co 15.33 "Bad company ruins good **m."**

MORNING
Ge 1. 5 and there was **m,** the first day.
Ps 30. 5 but joy comes with the **m.**
La 3.23 every **m;** great is your faithfulness.
Lk 24.22 They were at the tomb early this **m,**
2Pe 1.19 the day dawns and the **m** star rises
Rev 22.16 of David, the bright **m** star."

MOST
Ge 14.18 he was priest of God **M** High.
Ex 26.33 the holy place from the **m** holy.
Ps 91. 1 live in the shelter of the **M** High,
Mk 5. 7 Jesus, Son of the **M** High God?

MOTH
Ps 39.11 consuming like a **m** what is dear to
Mt 6.19 where **m** and rust consume and

MOTHER
Ge 2.24 a man leaves his father and his **m**
  3.20 because she was the **m** of all living.
Ex 20.12 Honor your father and your **m,**
Tob 4. 3 Honor your **m** and do not abandon
Sir 3. 6 who honor their **m** obey the Lord;
Isa 66.13 As a **m** comforts her child, so I will
Mt 10.37 loves father or **m** more than me is
Jn 19.27 to the disciple, "Here is your **m."**
Eph 5.31 a man will leave his father and **m**
Rev 17. 5 **m** of whores and of earth's

MOUNT → MOUNTAIN, MOUNTAINS
Ex 19.20 the Lord descended upon **M** Sinai,
Ps 78.68 **M** Zion, which he loves.
Mk 13. 3 he was sitting on the **M** of Olives
Rev 14. 1 the Lamb, standing on **M** Zion!

MOUNTAIN → MOUNT
Isa 2. 2 the **m** of the Lord's house shall
Mt 4. 8 a very high **m** and showed him all
  17.20 you will say to this **m,** 'Move from

MOUNTAINS → MOUNT
1Co 13. 2 have all faith, so as to remove **m,**

MOURN → MOURNFUL, MOURNING
Ecc 3. 4 a time to **m,** and a time to dance;
Sir 7.34 but **m** with those who **m.**
Mt 5. 4 "Blessed are those who **m,**

MOURNING → MOURN
Rev 21. 4 **m** and crying and pain will be no

MOUTH
Dt 8. 3 that comes from the **m** of the Lord.
Ps 19.14 Let the words of my **m** and
Sir 28.25 and a bolt for your **m.**
Mt 4. 4 every word that comes from the **m**
Rev 19.15 From his **m** comes a sharp sword

MULTIPLY
Ge 1.28 to them, "Be fruitful and **m,**
  9. 7 And you, be fruitful and **m,**
Dt 6. 3 that you may **m** greatly in a land

MULTITUDE
Jas 5.20 and will cover a **m** of sins.
1Pe 4. 8 for love covers a **m** of sins.

MURDER → MURDERER
Ex 20.13 You shall not **m.**
Hos 4. 2 lying, and **m,** and stealing and
Mt 5.21 of ancient times, 'You shall not **m';**

MURDERER → MURDER
Nu 35.16 the **m** shall be put to death.
Jn 8.44 He was a **m** from the beginning

MUSTARD
Mt 17.20 have faith the size of a **m** seed,
Mk 4.31 It is like a **m** seed, which,

MYRRH
Mt 2.11 gifts of gold, frankincense, and **m.**
Mk 15.23 offered him wine mixed with **m;**

MYSTERY
Da 2.19 **m** was revealed to Daniel in a vision
Ro 11.25 I want you to understand this **m:**
1Co 15.51 Listen, I will tell you a **m!**
Eph 3. 4 my understanding of the **m** of Christ
1Ti 3. 9 must hold fast to the **m** of the faith
Rev 17. 5 a name, a **m:** "Babylon the great,

N

NAILING → NAILS
Col 2.14 He set this aside, **n** it to the cross.

NAILS → NAILING
Jn 20.25 put my finger in the mark of the **n**

NAKED
Ge 2.25 the man and his wife were both **n,**
Job 1.21 **"N** I came from my mother's womb, and **n** shall

NAME → NAMES
Ge 2.19 every living creature, that was its **n.**
  4.26 people began to invoke the **n** of
Ex 3.15 my **n** forever, and this my title
  20. 7 wrongful use of the **n** of the Lord
Ps 9.10 know your **n** put their trust in you,
Pr 18.10 The **n** of the Lord is a strong tower;

Sir   2.17   and equal to his **n** are his works.
Isa   42. 8   I am the LORD, that is my **n;**
Eze   20. 9   But I acted for the sake of my **n,**
Joel   2.32   on the **n** of the LORD shall be saved;
Mt   1.21   a son, and you are to **n** him Jesus,
     6. 9   Father in heaven, hallowed be your **n.**
   28.19   baptizing them in the **n** of the Father
Jn   1.12   received him, who believed in his **n,**
   20.31   believing you may have life in his **n.**
Ac   4.12   for there is no other **n** under heaven
Php   2. 9   gave him the **n** that is above every **n**
Rev   13.17   **n** of the beast or the number of its **n.**
   19.13   his **n** is called The Word of God.

NAMES → NAME
Mt   10. 2   are the **n** of the twelve apostles:
Rev   21.14   the twelve **n** of the twelve apostles

NARROW
Lk   13.24   "Strive to enter through the **n** door;

NATION → NATIONS
Ge   12. 2   I will make of you a great **n,** and
Ex   32.10   and of you I will make a great **n.**"
Isa   66. 8   a **n** be delivered in one moment?
1Pe   2. 9   a holy **n,** God's own people,

NATIONS → NATION
Ge   18.18   the **n** of the earth shall be blessed in
Am   9.12   and all the **n** who are called
Mt   28.19   and make disciples of all **n,**
Mk   11.17   a house of prayer for all the **n'?**
Ro   4.18   become "the father of many **n,**"
Rev   22. 2   the tree are for the healing of the **n.**

NAZARETH
Mt   2.23   made his home in a town called **N,**
Jn   1.46   Can anything good come out of **N?**
   19.19   "Jesus of **N,** the King of the Jews."

NAZIRITE
Nu   6. 2   make a special vow, the vow of a **n,**
Jdg   13. 5   boy shall be a **n** to God from birth.

NEAR
Dt   30.14   No, the word is very **n** to you;
Isa   55. 6   call upon him while he is **n;**
Lk   10. 9   'The kingdom of God has come **n**
Jas   4. 8   Draw **n** to God, and he will draw **n** to

NEED → NEEDY
Mt   6. 8   for your Father knows what you **n**
Heb   4.16   and find grace to help in time of **n.**

NEEDLE
Lk   18.25   a camel to go through the eye of a **n**

NEEDY → NEED
1Sa   2. 8   he lifts the **n** from the ash heap,
Ps   113. 7   and lifts the **n** from the ash heap,

NEIGHBOR
Lev   19.18   shall love your **n** as yourself:
Dt   5.20   bear false witness against your **n.**
Mt   19.19   You shall love your **n** as yourself."

NEVER
La   3.22   steadfast love of the LORD **n** ceases,
1Co   13. 8   Love **n** ends. But as for prophecies,
Heb   13. 5   he has said, "I will **n** leave you or

NEW
Ecc   1. 9   there is nothing **n** under the sun.
Isa   65.17   create **n** heavens and a **n** earth,
Jer   31.31   I will make a **n** covenant with the
La   3.23   they are **n** every morning;
Eze   36.26   A **n** heart I will give you,
Mt   9.17   is **n** wine put into old wineskins;
Lk   22.20   is the **n** covenant in my blood.
Jn   13.34   I give you a **n** commandment,
2Co   3. 6   to be ministers of a **n** covenant,
Heb   8. 8   when I will establish a **n** covenant
2Pe   3.13   we wait for **n** heavens and a **n** earth,
Rev   21. 1   I saw a **n** heaven and a **n** earth;
   21. 5   "See, I am making all things **n.**"

NEWS
Isa   52. 7   who brings good **n,** who announces
Mt   11. 5   the poor have good **n** brought to
Mk   1.15   repent, and believe in the good **n.**"

NIGHT → NIGHTS
Ge   1. 5   and the darkness he called **N.**
1Th   5. 2   Lord will come like a thief in the **n.**
Rev   22. 5   And there will be no more **n;**

NIGHTS → NIGHT
Ge   7.12   on the earth forty days and forty **n.**
Jnh   1.17   of the fish three days and three **n.**
Mt   4. 2   He fasted forty days and forty **n,**
   12.40   for three days and three **n** the Son

NOISE
Ps   66. 1   Make a joyful **n** to God, all the earth
2Pe   3.10   will pass away with a loud **n,**

NOTHING
Ecc   1. 9   there is **n** new under the sun.
Jer   32.17   **N** is too hard for you.
Mt   17.20   and **n** will be impossible for you."
Jn   15. 5   apart from me you can do **n.**

NUMBER
Rev   13.18   Its **n** is six hundred sixty-six.

O

OATH
Dt   7. 8   and kept the **o** that he swore to your
Heb   7.20   This was confirmed with an **o;**

OBEDIENCE → OBEY
Ro   5.19   so by the one man's **o** the many will
Heb   5. 8   learned **o** through what he suffered;

OBEDIENT → OBEY
Php   2. 8   and became **o** to the point of death

OBEY → OBEDIENCE, OBEDIENT
Ex   19. 5   if you **o** my voice and keep my
Dt   12.28   Be careful to **o** all these words that
Mt   28.20   **o** everything that I have commanded
Ac   5.29   "We must **o** God rather than any
Eph   6. 1   Children, **o** your parents in the Lord,
1Jn   5. 3   love of God is this, that we **o** his

OFFENSE
Mk   6. 3   And they took **o** at him.
Gal   5.11   **o** of the cross has been removed.

OFFERING → OFFERINGS
Ge   4. 4   LORD had regard for Abel and his **o,**

1Mc 4.44 what to do about the altar of burnt **o,**
Ps 40. 6 Sacrifice and **o** you do not desire,
Da 11.31 shall abolish the regular burnt **o**
Eph 5. 2 a fragrant **o** and sacrifice to God.
Heb 10.14 For by a single **o** he has perfected

OFFERINGS → OFFERING
1Mc 1.45 to forbid burnt **o** and sacrifices
Hos 6. 6 of God rather than burnt **o.**
Mk 12.33 important than all whole burnt **o**

OIL
Ex 25. 6 **o** for the lamps, spices for the anointing **o**
Ps 23. 5 you anoint my head with **o;**
Jas 5.14 anointing them with **o** in the name

OLD
Mk 2.22 puts new wine into **o** wineskins;
Eph 4.22 your **o** self, corrupt and deluded by

OLIVE → OLIVES
Zec 4. 3 And by it there are two **o** trees,
Ro 11.17 and you, a wild **o** shoot,
Rev 11. 4 two **o** trees and the two lampstands

OLIVES → OLIVE
Zec 14. 4 Mount of **O** shall be split in two
Mt 24. 3 he was sitting on the Mount of **O,**

OMEGA
Rev 1. 8 "I am the Alpha and the **O,**"

ONCE → ONE
Ro 6.10 he died, he died to sin, **o** for all;
Heb 7.27 this he did **o** for all when he offered
      9.27 it is appointed for mortals to die **o,**

ONE → FIRST, ONCE
Ge 2.24 and they become **o** flesh.
Zec 14. 9 the LORD will be **o** and his name **o.**
Mk 12.29 the Lord our God, the Lord is **o;**
Jn 10.30 The Father and I are **o."**
1Co 12.13 For in the **o** Spirit we were all baptized
Eph 4. 5 **o** Lord, **o** faith, **o** baptism,

ONLY
Jn 1.14 the glory as of a father's **o** son,
      3.16 that he gave his **o** Son,
1Ti 1.17 the **o** God, be honor and glory
1Jn 4. 9 God sent his **o** Son into the world so

OPPRESSED
Jdt 9.11 God of the lowly, helper of the **o,**
Ps 146. 7 who executes justice for the **o;**
Isa 53. 7 He was **o,** and he was afflicted,

ORACLES
Ro 3. 2 entrusted with the **o** of God.

ORDAIN
Ex 29. 9 shall then **o** Aaron and his sons.
1Ti 5.22 Do not **o** anyone hastily,

ORPHAN → ORPHANED, ORPHANS
Ex 22.22 You shall not abuse any widow or **o.**
Hos 14. 3 In you the **o** finds mercy."

ORPHANED → ORPHAN
Jn 14.18 will not leave you **o;** I am coming

ORPHANS → ORPHAN
Sir 4.10 Be a father to **o,** and be like a
Jas 1.27 to care for **o** and widows in their

OUTSTRETCHED
Ex 6. 6 I will redeem you with an **o** arm
Ps 136.12 an **o** arm, for his steadfast love
Jer 27. 5 by my great power and my **o** arm

OVERCOME
Jn 1. 5 and the darkness did not **o** it.
Ro 12.21 Do not be **o** by evil, but **o** evil with
1Jn 2.14 and you have **o** the evil one.

OVERSHADOW → OVERSHADOWED
Lk 1.35 power of the Most High will **o** you;

OVERSHADOWED → OVERSHADOW
Lk 9.34 a cloud came and **o** them;

OWE
Mt 18.28 he said, 'Pay what you **o.'**
Ro 13. 8 **O** no one anything, except to love

P

PAIN
Ge 3.16 in **p** you shall bring forth children,
Rev 21. 4 and crying and **p** will be no more,

PALM
Jn 12.13 So they took branches of **p** trees
Rev 7. 9 robed in white, with **p** branches in

PARABLE → PARABLES
Ps 78. 2 I will open my mouth in a **p;**

PARABLES → PARABLE; See also JESUS: PARABLES
Sir 39. 2 penetrates the subtleties of **p;**
Mt 13.35 I will open my mouth to speak in **p;**

PARADISE
Lk 23.43 today you will be with me in **P."**
2Co 12. 4 was caught up into **P** and heard
Rev 2. 7 tree of life that is in the **p** of God.

PARALYTIC → PARALYZED
Mt 9. 2 saw their faith, he said to the **p,**

PARALYZED → PARALYTIC
Jn 5. 3 many invalids—blind, lame, and **p.**
Ac 8. 7 who were **p** or lame were cured.

PARCHMENTS
2Ti 4.13 also the books, and above all the **p.**

PARDON
Ex 34. 9 **p** our iniquity and our sin,
Isa 55. 7 our God, for he will abundantly **p.**

PARENTS
Eph 6. 1 Children, obey your **p** in the Lord,

PARTIALITY
Dt 16.19 distort justice; you must not show **p;**
Pr 24.23 **P** in judging is not good.
Sir 35.15 and with him there is no **p.**
Ro 2.11 For God shows no **p.**
Jas 3.17 without a trace of **p** or hypocrisy.

PARTNERS
1Co 10.20 not want you to be **p** with demons.

Heb 3. 1 holy **p** in a heavenly calling,

PASS → PASSED, PASSING
Ex 12.13 when I see the blood, I will **p** over
     33.19 make all my goodness **p** before you,
Am 5.17 I will **p** through the midst of you,
Mt 24.35 Heaven and earth will **p** away, but my words
            will not **p**
2Pe 3.10 then the heavens will **p** away

PASSED → PASS
Ex 12.27 he **p** over the houses of the Israelites
2Co 5.17 everything old has **p** away;
Rev 21.4 for the first things have **p** away."

PASSING → PASS
1Co 7.31 present form of this world is **p** away
1Jn 2.17 the world and its desire are **p** away,

PASSIONS
Gal 5.24 have crucified the flesh with its **p**
2Ti 2.22 Shun youthful **p** and pursue

PASSOVER
Ex 12.11 It is the **p** of the LORD.
Dt 16.1 the month of Abib by keeping the **p**
Mk 14.12 when the **P** lamb is sacrificed,

PASTORS
Eph 4.11 evangelists, some **p** and teachers,

PASTURES
Ps 23.2 He makes me lie down in green **p**;

PATH → PATHS
Ps 119.105 lamp to my feet and a light to my **p**.

PATHS → PATH
Mt 3.3 of the Lord, make his **p** straight.'"
Heb 12.13 and make straight **p** for your feet,

PATIENCE → PATIENT
Mic 2.7 Is the LORD's **p** exhausted?
Ro 2.4 his kindness and forbearance and **p**?
Gal 5.22 fruit of the Spirit is love, joy, peace, **p**,
2Pe 3.15 regard the **p** of our Lord as salvation

PATIENT → PATIENCE
1Co 13.4 Love is **p**; love is kind;

PEACE → PEACEMAKERS
Ps 122.6 Pray for the **p** of Jerusalem:
Isa 57.19 **P, p**, to the far and the near,
Jer 6.14 saying, **"P, p,"** when there is no **p**.
Mic 5.5 and he shall be the one of **p**.
Lk 2.14 on earth **p** among those whom he
Jn 14.27 **P** I leave with you; my **p** I give
1Co 14.33 is a God not of disorder but of **p**.
Gal 5.22 the fruit of the Spirit is love, joy, **p**,
Php 4.7 the **p** of God, which surpasses all

PEACEMAKERS → PEACE
Mt 5.9 "Blessed are the **p**, for they will be

PEARLS
Mt 7.6 do not throw your **p** before swine,

PENTECOST
Ac 2.1 When the day of **P** had come,

PEOPLE
Ex 5.1 the God of Israel, 'Let my **p** go,

Dt 4.20 a **p** of his very own possession,
Ru 1.16 your **p** shall be my **p**,
Ps 29.11 the LORD bless his **p** with peace!
Isa 40.1 Comfort, O comfort my **p**, says
Mt 1.21 he will save his **p** from their sins."
Heb 8.10 their God, and they shall be my **p**.
1Pe 2.9 a holy nation, God's own **p**,

PERFECT → PERFECTER, PERFECTION
2Sa 22.31 This God—his way is **p**;
Ps 19.7 The law of the LORD is **p**, reviving
Mt 5.48 Be **p**, therefore, as your heavenly Father is **p**.
Ro 12.2 what is good and acceptable and **p**.
Heb 7.19 (for the law made nothing **p**);
1Jn 4.18 in love, but **p** love casts out fear;

PERFECTER → PERFECT
Heb 12.2 Jesus the pioneer and **p** of our faith,

PERFECTION → PERFECT
Heb 6.1 Therefore let us go on toward **p**,
1Jn 2.5 the love of God has reached **p**.

PERISH → PERISHABLE
Est 4.16 and if I **p**, I **p**."
Ps 1.6 but the way of the wicked will **p**.
Jn 3.16 who believes in him may not **p**
2Pe 3.9 with you, not wanting any to **p**,

PERISHABLE → PERISH
1Co 9.25 they do it to receive a **p** wreath,
     15.42 What is sown is **p**, what is raised is
1Pe 1.23 not of **p** but of imperishable seed,

PERSECUTE → PERSECUTED, PERSECUTION
Mt 5.44 and pray for those who **p** you,
Ac 9.4 "Saul, Saul, why do you **p** me?"
Ro 12.14 Bless those who **p** you; bless

PERSECUTED → PERSECUTE
2Co 4.9 **p**, but not forsaken; struck down,
2Ti 3.12 godly life in Christ Jesus will be **p**.

PERSECUTION → PERSECUTE
Mt 13.21 or **p** arises on account of the word,
Ro 8.35 Will hardship, or distress, or **p**, or
Heb 10.33 publicly exposed to abuse and **p**,

PERSEVERANCE → PERSEVERE
Heb 12.1 let us run with **p** the race that is set

PERSEVERE → PERSEVERANCE
Da 12.12 Happy are those who **p**
Ro 12.12 be patient in suffering, **p** in prayer.

PHARAOH → PHARAOH'S
Ex 14.17 I will gain glory for myself over **P**

PHARAOH'S → PHARAOH
Ex 7.3 But I will harden **P** heart,
Heb 11.24 refused to be called a son of **P**

PHARISEE → PHARISEES
Lk 11.37 a **P** invited him to dine with him;
Jn 3.1 a **P** named Nicodemus,
Ac 5.34 a **P** in the council named Gamaliel,
Php 3.5 as to the law, a **P**;

PHARISEES → PHARISEE
Mt 5.20 that of the scribes and **P**,
    16.6 beware of the yeast of the **P** and

23.13 "But woe to you, scribes and **P,**

PHILISTINE → PHILISTINES
1Sa 17.37 save me from the hand of this **P."**

PHILISTINES → PHILISTINE
1Sa 5. 1 the **P** captured the ark of God,
Am 1. 8 the remnant of the **P** shall perish,

PIERCED
Zec 12.10 look on the one whom they have **p,**
Jn 19.37 look on the one whom they have **p."**
Rev 1. 7 even those who **p** him;

PIG
Dt 14. 8 the **p,** because it divides the hoof

PILLAR
Ge 19.26 and she became a **p** of salt.
Ex 13.21 and in a **p** of fire by night,

PIONEER
Heb 2.10 make the **p** of their salvation perfect
12. 2 Jesus the **p** and perfecter of our faith

PIT
Sir 21.10 but at its end is the **p** of Hades.
Rev 20. 3 into the **p,** and locked and sealed it

PLACE
Jn 14. 3 And if I go and prepare a **p** for you,

PLAGUE → PLAGUES
Zec 14.12 the **p** with which the Lord will
Rev 11. 6 strike the earth with every kind of **p,**

PLAGUES → PLAGUE
Hos 13.14 O Death, where are your **p?**
Rev 15. 1 seven angels with seven **p,** which

PLANT
Ge 1.29 I have given you every **p** yielding
Ecc 3. 2 time to **p,** and a time to pluck up

PLEASE → PLEASED, PLEASES, PLEASING
Sir 2.16 Those who fear the Lord seek to **p**
Ro 8. 8 who are in the flesh cannot **p** God.
15. 3 For Christ did not **p** himself;
Heb 11. 6 without faith it is impossible to **p** God,

PLEASED → PLEASE
Mic 6. 7 Will the Lord be **p** with thousands
Mt 3.17 Beloved, with whom I am well **p."**
Col 1.19 the fullness of God was **p** to dwell,

PLEASES → PLEASE
1Jn 3.22 commandments and do what **p** him.

PLEASING → PLEASE
Ps 104.34 May my meditation be **p** to him,
Eph 5.10 to find out what is **p** to the Lord.
Php 4.18 a sacrifice acceptable and **p** to God.

PLOT
Ps 2. 1 and the peoples **p** in vain?
Na 1. 9 Why do you **p** against the Lord?

PLOWSHARES
Isa 2. 4 they shall beat their swords into **p,**
Joel 3.10 Beat your **p** into swords, and your

POLLUTED → POLLUTES
Ac 15.20 from things **p** by idols and from
Rev 21. 8 the cowardly, the faithless, the **p,**

POLLUTES → POLLUTED
Nu 35.33 blood **p** the land, and no expiation

POOR → POVERTY
Ex 23. 6 not pervert the justice due to your **p**
1Sa 2. 8 He raises up the **p** from the dust;
Ps 113. 7 He raises the **p** from the dust,
Mt 5. 3 "Blessed are the **p** in spirit,
Mk 10.21 own, and give the money to the **p,**
12.42 **p** widow came and put in two small
2Co 6.10 as **p,** yet making many rich;
8. 9 yet for your sakes he became **p,**
Jas 2. 5 Has not God chosen the **p** in the

PORTION
Dt 32. 9 the Lord's own **p** was his people,
Sir 17.17 Israel is the Lord's own **p.**
La 3.24 "The Lord is my **p,"** says my soul,

POSSESSED → POSSESSION
Mt 8.16 many who were **p** with demons;

POSSESSION → POSSESSED, POSSESSIONS
Ex 19. 5 treasured **p** out of all the peoples.
Ps 2. 8 and the ends of the earth your **p.**

POSSESSIONS → POSSESSION
Lk 12.15 not consist in the abundance of **p."**
1Co 13. 3 If I give away all my **p,**

POSSIBLE
Mt 19.26 but for God all things are **p."**
26.39 if it is **p,** let this cup pass from me;

POTTER
Sir 33.13 Like clay in the hand of the **p,**
Isa 64. 8 we are the clay, and you are our **p;**
Ro 9.21 Has the **p** no right over the clay,

POUR → POURED
Isa 44. 3 I will **p** my spirit upon your
Eze 39.29 I **p** out my spirit upon the house of
Joel 2.28 I will **p** out my spirit on all flesh;
Ac 2.17 I will **p** out my Spirit upon all flesh,

POURED → POUR
Mt 26.28 is **p** out for many for the forgiveness
Ac 2.33 he has **p** out this that you both see
Tit 3. 6 This Spirit he **p** out on us richly

POVERTY → POOR
Mk 12.44 out of her **p** has put in everything
2Co 8. 9 by his **p** you might become rich.

POWER → POWERFUL, POWERS
1Ch 29.11 O Lord, are the greatness, the **p,**
Jdt 9.14 the God of all **p** and might,
Sir 39.18 and none can limit his saving **p.**
Isa 40.29 He gives **p** to the faint,
Zec 4. 6 by might, nor by **p,** but by my spirit,
Mt 22.29 the scriptures nor the **p** of God.
Mk 13.26 coming in clouds' with great **p** and
1Co 1.17 might not be emptied of its **p.**
Eph 1.19 the immeasurable greatness of his **p**
Php 3.10 Christ and the **p** of his resurrection
2Pe 1. 3 divine **p** has given us everything
Rev 19. 1 and glory and **p** to our God,

20. 6   these the second death has no **p,**

POWERFUL → POWER
Mk   1. 7   one who is more **p** than I is coming

POWERS → POWER
Ro   8.38   present, nor things to come, nor **p,**
Eph   6.12   against the cosmic **p** of this present

PRACTICE → PRACTICES
Sir 50.29   For if they put them into **p,**
Mt   23. 3   for they do not **p** what they teach.

PRACTICES → PRACTICE
Ex   23.24   or worship them, or follow their **p,**
Col   3. 9   stripped off the old self with its **p**

PRAISE
Ex   15. 2   this is my God, and I will **p** him,
Dt   10.21   He is your **p;** he is your God,
Tob 12. 6   Bless and sing **p** to his name.
Ps 150. 6   that breathes **p** the Lord!
Pr   27. 2   Let another **p** you, and not your own
     31.31   let her works **p** her in the city gates.
Mt   21.16   nursing babies you have prepared **p**
Rev 19. 5   **"P** our God, all you his servants,

PRAY → PRAYED, PRAYER, PRAYERS
2Ch   7.14   humble themselves, **p,** seek my face
Ps 122. 6   **P** for the peace of Jerusalem:
Sir 37.15   But above all **p** to the Most High
Mt   5.44   and **p** for those who persecute you,
      6. 5   you **p,** do not be like the hypocrites;
Lk   11. 1   teach us to **p,** as John taught his
Ro   8.26   do not know how to **p** as we ought,
1Th   5.17   **p** without ceasing,

PRAYED → PRAY
Mk   1.35   to a deserted place, and there he **p.**
     14.35   threw himself on the ground and **p**

PRAYER → PRAY
Pr   15.29   but he hears the **p** of the righteous.
Isa 56. 7   house shall be called a house of **p**
Mt   21.13   house shall be called a house of **p';**
Mk   11.24   I tell you, whatever you ask for in **p,**
Ro   12.12   patient in suffering, persevere in **p.**
Jas   5.16   The **p** of the righteous is powerful

PRAYERS → PRAY
Heb   5. 7   Jesus offered up **p** and supplications
Rev   5. 8   which are the **p** of the saints.

PREACH → PREACHING
Tit   1. 9   able both to **p** with sound doctrine

PREACHING → PREACH
1Ti   5.17   those who labor in **p** and teaching;

PRECEPTS → PRECEPT
Ps   19. 8   the **p** of the Lord are right,
Mt   15. 9   teaching human **p** as doctrines.'"

PRECIOUS
Ps   72.14   and **p** is their blood in his sight.
Pr   3.15   She is more **p** than jewels,
Isa 28.16   a tested stone, a **p** cornerstone,
1Pe   1.19   but with the **p** blood of Christ,
      2. 6   a cornerstone chosen and **p;**
2Pe   1. 1   received a faith as **p** as ours

PREDESTINED
Ro   8.30   those whom he **p** he also called;

PREDICTION → PREDICTIONS
Isa 44.26   and fulfills the **p** of his messengers;

PREDICTIONS → PREDICT
Jude 1.17   the **p** of the apostles of our Lord

PREPARE
Ps   23. 5   You **p** a table before me in the
Mt   3. 3   **'P** the way of the Lord, make his
Jn   14. 2   I have told you that I go to **p** a place

PRESENCE → PRESENT
Ex   25.30   the bread of the **P** on the table
Ps   51.11   Do not cast me away from your **p,**
    139. 7   Or where can I flee from your **p?**
Jn   17. 5   with the glory that I had in your **p**

PRESENT → PRESENCE
Ro   6.13   but **p** yourselves to God as
1Co   3.22   or death or the **p** or the future—
Eph   5.27   **p** the church to himself in splendor,
2Ti   2.15   **p** yourself to God as one approved

PRICE
Mt   27. 9   the one on whom a **p** had been set,
1Co   6.20   For you were bought with a **p;**

PRIDE → PROUD
Ps   20. 7   our **p** is in the name of the Lord
Pr   16.18   **P** goes before destruction,
Sir 10.13   For the beginning of **p** is sin,
Mk   7.22   licentiousness, envy, slander, **p,**
1Jn   2.16   the desire of the eyes, the **p** in riches

PRIEST → PRIESTHOOD, PRIESTS
Ge   14.18   he was **p** of God Most High.
Ps 110. 4   "You are a **p** forever according to
Mk   14.63   Then the high **p** tore his clothes and
Heb   3. 1   apostle and high **p** of our confession
      7. 3   the Son of God, he remains a **p**

PRIESTHOOD → PRIEST
Ex   29. 9   the **p** shall be theirs by a perpetual
Heb   7.24   but he holds his **p** permanently,
1Pe   2. 5   a holy **p,** to offer spiritual sacrifices

PRIESTS → PRIEST
Ex   28. 1   the Israelites, to serve me as **p**—
Mk   15. 3   the chief **p** accused him of many
Heb   7.27   Unlike the other high **p,** he has no
Rev 20. 6   they will be **p** of God and of Christ,

PRINCE → PRINCES
Isa   9. 6   Everlasting Father, **P** of Peace.
Eze 37.25   David shall be their **p** forever.

PRINCES → PRINCE
1Sa   2. 8   to make them sit with **p** and inherit
Da   8.25   even rise up against the Prince of **p.**

PRISONER → PRISONERS
Mk   15. 6   at the festival he used to release a **p**
Eph   3. 1   that I Paul am a **p** for Christ Jesus

PRISONERS → PRISONER
Ps 146. 7   The Lord sets the **p** free;
Isa 61. 1   to the captives, and release to the **p;**

PRIZE
1Co 9.24 but only one receives the **p**?
Php 3.14 the **p** of the heavenly call of God in

PROMISE → PROMISED, PROMISES
Ps 105.42 For he remembered his holy **p,**
Eph 2.12 and strangers to the covenants of **p,**
2Pe 3. 9 The Lord is not slow about his **p,**

PROMISED → PROMISE
Dt 1.11 and bless you, as he has **p** you!
Ac 13.23 to Israel a Savior, Jesus, as he **p;**
Eph 1.13 with the seal of the **p** Holy Spirit;
Heb 10.23 for he who has **p** is faithful.

PROMISES → PROMISE
Jos 21.45 the good **p** that the Lᴏʀᴅ had made
2Co 1.20 every one of God's **p** is a "Yes."

PROOFS → PROVE
Ac 1. 3 to them by many convincing **p,**

PROPHECIES → PROPHESY
1Co 13. 8 as for **p,** they will come to an end;

PROPHECY → PROPHESY
Ac 21. 9 daughters who had the gift of **p.**
1Co 12.10 to another **p,** to another
2Pe 1.20 that no **p** of scripture is a matter

PROPHESY → PROPHECIES, PROPHECY, PROPHET, PROPHETS
Joel 2.28 sons and your daughters shall **p,**
Mt 7.22 Lord, did we not **p** in your name,
1Co 13. 9 only in part, and we **p** only in part;
Rev 11. 3 my two witnesses authority to **p**

PROPHET → PROPHESY
Dt 18.18 a **p** like you from among their own
1Mc 4.46 until a **p** should come to tell what
Mal 4. 5 the **p** Elijah before the great and
Lk 4.24 no **p** is accepted in the prophet's
Rev 16.13 and from the mouth of the false **p.**

PROPHETS → PROPHESY
Nu 11.29 that all the Lᴏʀᴅ's people were **p,**
1Mc 9.27 that **p** ceased to appear among them.
Mt 5.17 come to abolish the law or the **p;**
    22.40 hang all the law and the **p."**
1Co 12.28 the church first apostles, second **p,**
Eph 2.20 the foundation of the apostles and **p,**
    4.11 some **p,** some evangelists,
Rev 11.10 these two **p** had been a torment to
    18.20 you saints and apostles and **p!**

PROSPER → PROSPERITY
Ps 1. 3 In all that they do, they **p.**
Isa 53.10 the will of the Lᴏʀᴅ shall **p.**

PROSPERITY → PROSPER
Dt 30.15 have set before you today life and **p,**

PROSTITUTE → PROSTITUTES
Jos 2. 1 a **p** whose name was Rahab,
1Co 6.15 and make them members of a **p?**
Heb 11.31 By faith Rahab the **p** did not perish

PROSTITUTES → PROSTITUTE
Sir 9. 6 Do not give yourself to **p,**
Mt 21.31 the **p** are going into the kingdom of

PROUD → PRIDE
Ps 94. 2 give to the **p** what they deserve!
Pr 21. 4 Haughty eyes and a **p** heart—
Jas 4. 6 God opposes the **p,** but gives grace

PROVERBS
Pr 1. 1 The **p** of Solomon son of David,
Ecc 12. 9 and studying and arranging many **p.**
Sir 39. 3 seeks out the hidden meanings of **p**

PROVOKE → PROVOKED
Jer 25. 6 not **p** me to anger with the work of
Heb 10.24 how to **p** one another to love

PROVOKED → PROVOKE
Ps 78.41 and **p** the Holy One of Israel.

PRUNES
Jn 15. 2 he **p** to make it bear more fruit.

PSALMS
Lk 24.44 and the **p** must be fulfilled."
Eph 5.19 you sing **p** and hymns and spiritual

PUFFS
1Co 8. 1 Knowledge **p** up, but love builds up.

PUNISH → PUNISHING, PUNISHMENT
Ex 32.34 I will **p** them for their sin."
1Pe 2.14 by him to **p** those who do wrong

PUNISHING → PUNISH
Dt 5. 9 **p** children for the iniquity of parents
Joel 2.13 in steadfast love, and relents from **p.**

PUNISHMENT → PUNISH
Isa 53. 5 was the **p** that made us whole,
Mt 25.46 these will go away into eternal **p,**
1Jn 4.18 for fear has to do with **p,**

PURE → PURIFICATION, PURIFIED
2Sa 22.27 with the **p** you show yourself **p,**
Ps 19. 9 the fear of the Lᴏʀᴅ is **p,** enduring
Hab 1.13 Your eyes are too **p** to behold evil,
Mt 5. 8 "Blessed are the **p** in heart, for they
Php 4. 8 whatever is **p,** whatever is pleasing,
Tit 1.15 To the **p** all things are **p,**
1Jn 3. 3 purify themselves, just as he is **p.**

PURIFICATION → PURE
Heb 1. 3 When he had made **p** for sins,

PURIFIED → PURE
1Pe 1.22 **p** your souls by your obedience to

PURPLE
Ex 25. 4 **p,** and crimson yarns and fine linen,
Mk 15.17 And they clothed him in a **p** cloak;

PURPOSE
Isa 46.10 saying, "My **p** shall stand,
Ro 8.28 who are called according to his **p.**
2Ti 1. 9 works but according to his own **p**

Q

QUAILS
Ex 16.13 In the evening **q** came up
Nu 11.31 and it brought **q** from the sea and

QUARRELED
Ex 17. 7 the Israelites **q** and tested the Lᴏʀᴅ,

Nu   20. 3   The people **q** with Moses and said,

QUEEN
1Ki 10. 1   the **q** of Sheba heard of the fame of
Rev 18. 7   in her heart she says, 'I rule as a **q;**

QUIET
1Ti   2. 2   **q** and peaceable life in all godliness
1Pe   3. 4   beauty of a gentle and **q** spirit,

R

RABBI
Jn   1.38   **"R"** (which translated means Teacher),

RACE
Ecc   9.11   the sun the **r** is not to the swift,
1Co   9.24   that in a **r** the runners all compete,
Heb 12. 1   let us run with perseverance the **r**
1Pe   2. 9   But you are a chosen **r,** a royal

RAIN → RAINBOW
Ge   7. 4   For in seven days I will send **r** on
Isa 45. 8   let the skies **r** down righteousness;
Mt   5.45   sends **r** on the righteous and on the
Rev 11. 6   so that no **r** may fall during the days

RAINBOW → BOW
Rev   4. 3   the throne is a **r** that looks like an

RAISE → RISE
Jn   2.19   and in three days I will **r** it up."
2Co   4.14   who raised the Lord Jesus will **r** us

RAISED → RISE
Mt 17.23   and on the third day he will be **r."**
Ac   2.24   God **r** him up, having freed him
Ro   4.25   and was **r** for our justification.
1Co 15. 4   **r** on the third day in accordance

RANSOM
Ps 49. 8   For the **r** of life is costly, and can
Mt 20.28   and to give his life a **r** for many."
1Ti   2. 6   who gave himself a **r** for all

REAP
Gal   6. 7   for you **r** whatever you sow.
Rev 14.15   for the hour to **r** has come,

REBUILD → BUILD
Ezr   1. 3   and **r** the house of the LORD,
Ne   2.17   let us **r** the wall of Jerusalem,
Da   9.25   went out to restore and **r** Jerusalem
Ac 15.16   and I will **r** the dwelling of David,

REBUKE
Pr 27. 5   Better is open **r** than hidden love.
Zec   3. 2   said to Satan, "The LORD **r** you,
Mk   8.32   Peter took him aside and began to **r**
2Ti   4. 2   convince, **r,** and encourage,

RECEIVE
Jn 16.24   Ask and you will **r,** so that your joy
Ac   2.38   you will **r** the gift of the Holy Spirit.
      20.35   'It is more blessed to give than to **r.'**
Rev   4.11   to **r** glory and honor and power,

RECKONED
Ge 15. 6   LORD **r** it to him as righteousness.
Ro   4. 3   it was **r** to him as righteousness."

RECONCILIATION
Ro   5.11   whom we have now received **r.**
2Co   5.18   and has given us the ministry of **r;**

REDEEM → REDEEMER, REDEMPTION
Ex   6. 6   I will **r** you with an outstretched
Gal   4. 5   to **r** those who were under the law,

REDEEMER → REDEEM
Job 19.25   For I know that my **R** lives,
Ps 19.14   O LORD, my rock and my **r.**

REDEMPTION → REDEEM
Lk 21.28   because your **r** is drawing near."
Eph   1. 7   In him we have **r** through his blood,
Heb   9.12   own blood, thus obtaining eternal **r.**

REFINE
Jer   9. 7   I will now **r** and test them,
Zec 13. 9   **r** them as one refines silver,

REFLECTED → REFLECTION
2Co   3.18   though **r** in a mirror,

REFLECTION → REFLECTED
1Co 11. 7   since he is the image and **r** of God;
Heb   1. 3   He is the **r** of God's glory

REFUGE
Nu 35.11   select cities to be cities of **r** for you,
Ps   2.12   Happy are all who take **r** in him.

REGULATIONS
Col   2.20   Why do you submit to **r,**
Heb   9.10   **r** for the body imposed until the

REIGN
Ex 15.18   The LORD will **r** forever and ever."
Ps 146.10   The LORD will **r** forever,
1Co 15.25   **r** until he has put all his enemies
2Ti   2.12   we will also **r** with him;
Rev 11.15   and he will **r** forever and ever."
      22. 5   and they will **r** forever and ever.

REJECTED
Ps 118.22   The stone that the builders **r**
Isa 53. 3   He was despised and **r** by others;
Mt 21.42   'The stone that the builders **r**

REJOICE
Ps 118.24   let us **r** and be glad in it.
Zep   3.17   he will **r** over you with gladness,
Php   4. 4   **R** in the Lord always; again I will say, **R.**

RELENT → RELENTED
Eze 24.14   I will not spare, I will not **r.**
Joel   2.14   whether he will not turn and **r,**
Jnh   3. 9   God may **r** and change his mind;

RELENTED → RELENT
1Ch 21.15   LORD took note and **r** concerning
Jer   4.28   I have not **r** nor will I turn back.

REMEMBER → REMEMBRANCE
Ge   9.15   I will **r** my covenant that is between
Ex 20. 8   **R** the sabbath day, and keep it holy.
Dt   8.18   But **r** the LORD your God,
Sir 23.18   The Most High will not **r** sins."
2Ti   2. 8   **R** Jesus Christ, raised from the dead
Heb   8.12   and I will **r** their sins no more."

REMEMBRANCE → REMEMBER
Lk   22.19   Do this in **r** of me."

REMNANT
Isa   10.21   A **r** will return, the **r** of Jacob,
Jer   50.20   will pardon the **r** that I have spared.
Ro   9.27   only a **r** of them will be saved;

RENEW → RENEWAL, RENEWED, RENEWING
Isa   40.31   the LORD shall **r** their strength,
La   5.21   **r** our days as of old—

RENEWAL → RENEW
Mt   19.28   I tell you, at the **r** of all things,

RENEWED → RENEW
2Co   4.16   inner nature is being **r** day by day.
Eph   4.23   to be **r** in the spirit of your minds,

RENEWING → RENEW
Ro   12.2   transformed by the **r** of your minds,

REPENT → REPENTANCE
Sir   18.21   and when you have sinned, **r.**
Mt   3.2   **"R,** for the kingdom of heaven has
Ac   2.38   **"R,** and be baptized every one of

REPENTANCE → REPENT
Mk   1.4   a baptism of **r** for the forgiveness
Lk   3.8   Bear fruits worthy of **r.**
Ro   2.4   kindness is meant to lead you to **r?**
2Co   7.10   **r** that leads to salvation and brings
2Pe   3.9   any to perish, but all to come to **r.**

REPROVE
Pr   19.25   **r** the intelligent, and they will gain
Tit   2.15   exhort and **r** with all authority.
Rev   3.19   **r** and discipline those whom I love.

REQUIRE
Dt   10.12   does the LORD your God **r** of you?
Mic   6.8   the LORD **r** of you but to do justice,

RESCUE → RESCUED
Mt   6.13   but **r** us from the evil one.
2Pe   2.9   the Lord knows how to **r** the godly

RESCUED → RESCUE
Sir   51.12   and **r** me in time of trouble.
Col   1.13   has **r** us from the power of darkness

RESIST
Mt   5.39   I say to you, Do not **r** an evildoer.
Ro   9.19   For who can **r** his will?"
Jas   4.7   **R** the devil, and he will flee from

REST → RESTED
Ex   31.15   seventh day is a sabbath of solemn **r**
Ps   95.11   swore, "They shall not enter my **r."**
Mt   11.28   and I will give you **r.**
Heb   4.10   those who enter God's **r** also cease

RESTED → REST
Ge   2.2   he **r** on the seventh day from all the
Ex   20.11   all that is in them, but **r** the seventh

RESURRECTION
Mt   22.30   For in the **r** they neither marry nor
Mk   12.18   Sadducees, who say there is no **r,**
Jn   11.25   said to her, "I am the **r** and the life.
1Co   15.12   you say there is no **r** of the dead?

Php
Php   3.10   know Christ and the power of his **r**
Rev   20.5   This is the first **r.**

RETURN
Ge   3.19   you are dust, and to dust you shall **r.**
Mal   3.7   **R** to me, and I will **r** to you,

REVEAL → REVEALED, REVELATION
Mt   11.27   to whom the Son chooses to **r** him.

REVEALED → REVEAL
Isa   40.5   the glory of the LORD shall be **r,**
Mt   16.17   flesh and blood has not **r** this to you
Lk   17.30   on the day that the Son of Man is **r.**
Ro   1.17   in it the righteousness of God is **r**

REVELATION → REVEAL
1Co   14.6   some **r** or knowledge or prophecy
Eph   3.3   was made known to me by **r,**

REVERE → REVERENCE
Jos   24.14   "Now therefore **r** the LORD,
Tob   4.5   **"R** the Lord all your days,
Mal   4.2   But for you who **r** my name the sun

REVERENCE → REVERE
Eph   5.21   subject to one another out of **r** for

REVILE → REVILED
Ex   22.28   You shall not **r** God, or curse
Mt   5.11   people **r** you and persecute you

REVILED → REVILE
1Co   4.12   When **r,** we bless;
1Pe   4.14   If you are **r** for the name of Christ,

REWARD
Ps   19.11   in keeping them there is great **r.**
Isa   40.10   **r** is with him, and his recompense
Mt   6.5   I tell you, they have received their **r.**
Lk   6.23   for surely your **r** is great in heaven;
Rev   22.12   I am coming soon; my **r** is with me,

RIB
Ge   2.22   **r** that the LORD God had taken from

RICH → RICHES
Mt   19.23   hard for a **r** person to enter the
2Co   8.9   by his poverty you might become **r.**
Eph   2.4   But God, who is **r** in mercy,

RICHES → RICH
Sir   13.24   **R** are good if they are free from sin;
Lk   8.14   they are choked by the cares and **r**
Ro   11.33   O the depth of the **r** and wisdom
1Jn   2.16   the desire of the eyes, the pride in **r**

RIGHT → BIRTHRIGHT
Ex   15.6   Your **r** hand, O LORD, glorious in
Dt   6.18   Do what is **r** and good in the sight
Ps   110.1   says to my lord, "Sit at my **r** hand
Pr   14.12   a way that seems **r** to a person,
Ac   2.34   said to my Lord, "Sit at my **r** hand,
Heb   1.13   "Sit at my **r** hand until I make your

RIGHTEOUS → RIGHTEOUSNESS
Ps   11.7   For the LORD is **r;** he loves **r** deeds;
Wis   5.15   **r** live forever, and their reward
Sir   35.22   and does justice for the **r,**
Jer   23.5   I will raise up for David a **r** Branch,
Eze   3.20   if the **r** turn from their righteousness

Hab	2. 4	but the **r** live by their faith.
Mt	5.45	rain on the **r** and on the unrighteous.
Mk	2.17	come to call not the **r** but sinners."
Ro	1.17	one who is **r** will live by faith.
Heb	10.38	but my **r** one will live by faith.
1Jn	2. 1	with the Father, Jesus Christ the **r;**
Rev	19. 8	the fine linen is the **r** deeds of the

RIGHTEOUSNESS → RIGHTEOUS

Ge	15. 6	the LORD reckoned it to him as **r.**
Isa	11. 5	**R** shall be the belt around his waist,
Jer	23. 6	be called: "The LORD is our **r."**
Da	9.24	to bring in everlasting **r,**
Hos	10.12	Sow for yourselves **r;** reap steadfast
Mt	5. 6	those who hunger and thirst for **r,**
Jn	16. 8	about sin and **r** and judgment:
Ro	5.18	act of **r** leads to justification
Gal	3. 6	and it was reckoned to him as **r,"**
Eph	6.14	and put on the breastplate of **r.**
2Pe	3.13	heavens and a new earth, where **r**

RIPE

Jn	4.35	how the fields are **r** for harvesting.
Rev	14.15	the harvest of the earth is fully **r."**

RISE → ARISE, RAISE, RAISED, ROSE

Da	12.13	shall **r** for your reward at the end of
Mal	4. 2	the sun of righteousness shall **r,**
Mt	27.63	'After three days I will **r** again.'
1Th	4.16	and the dead in Christ will **r** first.

ROAD

Mt	7.13	and the **r** is easy that leads to

ROBBERS

Jer	7.11	become a den of **r** in your sight?
Mt	21.13	but you are making it a den of **r."**

ROBE

Ex	28. 4	a breastpiece, an ephod, a **r,**
Jn	19. 5	crown of thorns and the purple **r.**
Rev	6.11	They were each given a white **r** and
	19.13	He is clothed in a **r** dipped in blood,

ROCK

Ex	17. 6	Strike the **r,** and water will come
Nu	20. 8	you shall bring water out of the **r**
1Sa	2. 2	there is no **R** like our God.
Mt	16.18	and on this **r** I will build my church,
Mk	15.46	that had been hewn out of the **r.**
1Pe	2. 8	and a **r** that makes them fall."

ROD

Ps	2. 9	shall break them with a **r** of iron,
	23. 4	your **r** and your staff—they comfort
Pr	13.24	who spare the **r** hate their children,
Rev	2.27	to rule them with an iron **r,**

ROLL

Mk	16. 3	"Who will **r** away the stone for us

ROOT

Isa	11.10	On that day the **r** of Jesse
	53. 2	and like a **r** out of dry ground;
Ro	15.12	"The **r** of Jesse shall come,
1Ti	6.10	For the love of money is a **r** of all
Rev	5. 5	the tribe of Judah, the **R** of David,

ROSE → RISE

SS	2. 1	I am a **r** of Sharon, a lily
1Th	4.14	believe that Jesus died and **r** again,

RULE

Eph	1.21	far above all **r** and authority and
Col	3.15	the peace of Christ **r** in your hearts,

RUMORS

Mt	24. 6	you will hear of wars and **r** of wars;

RUN

Isa	40.31	they shall **r** and not be weary,
Heb	12. 1	let us **r** with perseverance the race

RUST

Bar	6.12	cannot save themselves from **r**
Mt	6.19	where moth and **r** consume

S

SABBATH

Ex	20. 8	Remember the **s** day, and keep it holy.
1Mc	1.43	to idols and profaned the **s.**
Mk	2.28	Son of Man is lord even of the **s."**

SACRIFICE → SACRIFICED

Ex	12.27	'It is the passover **s** to the LORD,
1Sa	15.22	Surely, to obey is better than **s,**
Ps	40. 6	**S** and offering you do not desire,
Da	9.27	he shall make **s** and offering cease;
Hos	6. 6	For I desire steadfast love and not **s,**
Mt	9.13	this means, 'I desire mercy, not **s.'**
Ro	3.25	put forward as a **s** of atonement
Heb	13.15	let us continually offer a **s** of praise
1Jn	2. 2	and he is the atoning **s** for our sins,

SACRIFICED → SACRIFICE

1Co	5. 7	our paschal lamb, Christ, has been **s.**
	8. 1	Now concerning food **s** to idols:

SADDUCEES

Mt	16. 6	the yeast of the Pharisees and **S."**
Mk	12.18	**S,** who say there is no resurrection,

SAFE → SAFETY

Ps	37.28	righteous shall be kept **s** forever,
Pr	18.10	the righteous run into it and are **s.**

SAFETY → SAFE

Dt	12.10	around so that you live in **s,**
Eze	34.28	they shall live in **s,**

SAINTS

Ps	31.23	Love the LORD, all you his **s.**
Ro	8.27	the Spirit intercedes for the **s**
1Co	6. 2	that the **s** will judge the world?
Eph	4.12	equip the **s** for the work of ministry,
Rev	5. 9	by your blood you ransomed for God **s**

SALT

Ge	19.26	back, and she became a pillar of **s.**
Mt	5.13	"You are the **s** of the earth;

SALVATION → SAVE

Ex	15. 2	and he has become my **s;**
Ps	27. 1	The LORD is my light and my **s;**
Isa	52. 7	brings good news, who announces **s,**
Bar	4.29	everlasting joy with your **s.**
Lk	3. 6	all flesh shall see the **s** of God.'"
Ac	4.12	There is **s** in no one else,
Php	2.12	work out your own **s** with fear
Heb	2. 3	escape if we neglect so great a **s?**
2Pe	3.15	regard the patience of our Lord as **s.**

SAMARITAN

Lk	10.33	But a **S** while traveling came near
Jn	4. 7	A **S** woman came to draw water,

SANCTIFICATION → SANCTIFY

Ro	6.19	as slaves to righteousness for **s.**
1Th	4. 3	For this is the will of God, your **s:**

SANCTIFIED → SANCTIFY

Jn	17.19	so that they also may be **s** in truth.
1Co	6.11	But you were washed, you were **s,**

SANCTIFY → SANCTIFICATION, SANCTIFIED

Lev	11.44	**s** yourselves therefore, and be holy,
Heb	13.12	to **s** the people by his own blood.

SANCTUARY

Ex	25. 8	And have them make me a **s,**
1Ch	22.19	build the **s** of the LORD God
1Mc	1.21	He arrogantly entered the **s**
Heb	9.24	Christ did not enter a **s** made by

SAND

Mt	7.26	foolish man who built his house on **s.**

SAT → SIT

Heb	10.12	"he **s** down at the right hand of God,
Rev	3.21	and **s** down with my Father

SATAN

1Ch	21. 1	**S** stood up against Israel,
Job	1. 6	and **S** also came among them.
Zec	3. 2	"The LORD rebuke you, O **S!**
Mt	4.10	Jesus said to him, "Away with you, **S!**
	16.23	said to Peter, "Get behind me, **S!**
2Co	11.14	**S** disguises himself as an angel of light.
Rev	12. 9	who is called the Devil and **S,**
	20. 7	**S** will be released from his prison

SAVE → SALVATION, SAVED, SAVIOR

Isa	59. 1	LORD's hand is not too short to **s,**
Jer	15.20	for I am with you to **s** you
Mt	1.21	he will **s** his people from their sins."
	16.25	who want to **s** their life will lose it,
Lk	19.10	came to seek out and to **s** the lost."

SAVED → SAVE

Isa	45.22	Turn to me and be **s,**
Joel	2.32	on the name of the LORD shall be **s;**
Mt	10.22	who endures to the end will be **s.**
Mk	15.31	He **s** others; he cannot save himself.
Ro	10.13	on the name of the Lord shall be **s."**
Eph	2. 8	For by grace you have been **s**

SAVIOR → SAVE

Isa	49.26	know that I am the LORD your **S,**
Hos	13. 4	and besides me there is no **s.**
1Ti	4.10	who is the **S** of all people,
Tit	2.13	of the glory of our great God and **S,**
2Pe	3.18	knowledge of our Lord and **S** Jesus

SCARLET

Isa	1.18	your sins are like **s,** they shall be
Mt	27.28	stripped him and put a **s** robe on him

SCEPTER

Ge	49.10	The **s** shall not depart from Judah,
Nu	24.17	and a **s** shall rise out of Israel;

SCRIBES

Mt	7.29	having authority, and not as their **s.**

	23.13	"But woe to you, **s** and Pharisees,

SCRIPTURE → SCRIPTURES

Lk	4.21	"Today this **s** has been fulfilled in
Jn	10.35	and the **s** cannot be annulled—
1Ti	4.13	attention to the public reading of **s,**
2Ti	3.16	All **s** is inspired by God and is useful

SCRIPTURES → SCRIPTURE

Mt	22.29	know neither the **s** nor the power
Lk	24.45	their minds to understand the **s,**
Jn	5.39	"You search the **s** because you think

SEA

Ps	95. 5	The **s** is his, for he made it,
Mic	7.19	all our sins into the depths of the **s.**
Rev	4. 6	there is something like a **s** of glass,
	21. 1	and the **s** was no more.

SEAL

2Co	1.22	by putting his **s** on us and giving us
Eph	1.13	the **s** of the promised Holy Spirit;
Rev	7. 3	our God with a **s** on their foreheads.

SEASON → SEASONS

Ps	1. 3	which yield their fruit in its **s,**
Ecc	3. 1	For everything there is a **s,**

SEASONS → SEASON

1Th	5. 1	Now concerning the times and the **s,**

SEAT

Ex	25.17	make a mercy **s** of pure gold;
Ro	14.10	stand before the judgment **s** of God.
2Co	5.10	must appear before the judgment **s**

SECRET

Dt	29.29	The **s** things belong to the LORD
Ro	2.16	will judge the **s** thoughts of all.

SEE → SEEN, SEES, SIGHT

Ex	33.20	for no one shall **s** me and live."
Jn	9.25	that though I was blind, now I **s."**
Rev	1. 7	the clouds; every eye will **s** him,

SEED → SEEDS, SEEDTIME

Mt	17.20	have faith the size of a mustard **s,**

SEEDS → SEED

Mt	13. 8	Other **s** fell on good soil
Mk	4.31	the smallest of all the **s** on earth;

SEEK

1Ch	28. 9	If you **s** him, he will be found by
Ps	34.10	those who **s** the LORD lack no good
Sir	2.16	who fear the Lord **s** to please him,
Isa	55. 6	**S** the LORD while he may be found,
Lk	19.10	came to **s** out and to save
Heb	11. 6	that he rewards those who **s** him.

SEEN → SEE

Jn	1.18	No one has ever **s** God.
	14. 9	Whoever has **s** me has **s** the Father.

SELF-CONTROL

2Pe	1. 6	with **s,** and **s** with endurance,

SEPARATE

Mt	19. 6	joined together, let no one **s."**
Ro	8.35	will **s** us from the love of Christ?

SERPENT
Ge   3. 1   the **s** was more crafty than any other
2Co   11. 3   the **s** deceived Eve by its cunning,
Rev   20. 2   He seized the dragon, that ancient **s,**

SERVANT
Isa   42. 1   Here is my **s,** whom I uphold,
    53.11   my **s,** shall make many righteous,
Zec   3. 8   going to bring my **s** the Branch.
Lk   1.38   "Here am I, the **s** of the Lord;
Ac   3.13   has glorified his **s** Jesus,
Heb   3. 5   faithful in all God's house as a **s,**

SERVE
Jos   24.15   my household, we will **s** the LORD."
1Sa   12.20   but **s** the LORD with all your heart;
Mt   6.24   You cannot **s** God and wealth.
Mk   10.45   Son of Man came not to be served but to **s,**
1Pe   4.10   **s** one another with whatever gift

SEVEN → SEVENTH
Ge   7. 2   with you **s** pairs of all clean animals,
Ex   25.37   You shall make the **s** lamps for it;
Jos   6. 4   march around the city **s** times,
Da   9.25   prince, there shall be **s** weeks;
Mt   18.22   "Not **s** times, but, I tell you, seventy-seven
Rev   1.12   turning I saw **s** golden lampstands,
    5. 1   and on the back, sealed with **s** seals;
    8. 2   I saw the **s** angels who stand before
    12. 3   a great red dragon, with **s** heads and
    15. 1   **s** angels with **s** plagues,

SEVENTH → SEVEN
Ge   2. 2   on the **s** day God finished the work
Ex   20.10   the **s** day is a sabbath to the LORD
Heb   4. 4   God rested on the **s** day from all his

SEVENTY → SEVENTY-SEVEN
Da   9.24   **S** weeks are decreed for your people

SEVENTY-SEVEN → SEVENTY
Mt   18.22   "Not seven times, but, I tell you, **s**

SHADOW
Ps   17. 8   hide me in the **s** of your wings,
    91. 1   who abide in the **s** of the Almighty,

SHAME → ASHAMED
Da   12. 2   some to **s** and everlasting contempt;
1Co   1.27   foolish in the world to **s** the wise;
Heb   12. 2   endured the cross, disregarding its **s,**
1Jn   2.28   be put to **s** before him at his coming.

SHARE
Col   1.12   to **s** in the inheritance of the saints
Heb   12.10   in order that we may **s** his holiness.
Jude   1. 3   to you about the salvation we **s,**

SHARPENS → SHARPER
Pr   27.17   Iron **s** iron, and one person **s**

SHARPER → SHARPENS
Heb   4.12   **s** than any two-edged sword,

SHED
Ge   9. 6   shall that person's blood be **s;**
Rev   16. 6   **s** the blood of saints and prophets,

SHEEP
Isa   53. 6   All we like **s** have gone astray;
Mt   9.36   like **s** without a shepherd.

Jn   10. 7   I am the gate for the **s.**
    10.15   And I lay down my life for the **s.**
Heb   13.20   the great shepherd of the **s,**
1Pe   2.25   For you were going astray like **s,**

SHEOL
Ps   139. 8   if I make my bed in **S,** you are there.
Hos   13.14   O **S,** where is your destruction?

SHEPHERD → SHEPHERDS
Ps   23. 1   The LORD is my **s,** I shall not want.
Isa   40.11   He will feed his flock like a **s;**
Mt   2. 6   ruler who is to **s** my people Israel.'"
Jn   10.11   "I am the good **s.**
Heb   13.20   the great **s** of the sheep,
1Pe   5. 4   And when the chief **s** appears,

SHEPHERDS → SHEPHERD
Lk   2. 8   there were **s** living in the fields,

SHIELD
Eph   6.16   With all of these, take the **s** of faith,

SHINE → SHINES
Nu   6.25   LORD make his face to **s** upon you,
Ps   4. 6   light of your face **s** on us, O LORD!"
Da   12. 3   Those who are wise shall **s** like the
Mt   5.16   let your light **s** before others,

SHINES → SHINE
Jn   1. 5   The light **s** in the darkness,

SHORT
Ro   3.23   sinned and fall **s** of the glory of God;

SHOW → SHOWED
Ex   33.18   Moses said, **"S** me your glory,
Ps   85. 7   **S** us your steadfast love, O LORD,
Jn   14. 8   said to him, "Lord, **s** us the Father,
1Co   12.31   will **s** you a still more excellent way

SHOWED → SHOW
Jn   20.20   he **s** them his hands and his side.

SICK → SICKNESS
Mt   8.16   and cured all who were **s.**
Jas   5.14   Are any among you **s?**

SICKNESS → SICK
Ex   23.25   I will take **s** away from among you.
Mt   4.23   and curing every disease and every **s**

SIDE
Jn   19.34   soldiers pierced his **s** with a spear,

SIGHT → SEE
Mt   11. 5   blind receive their **s,** the lame walk,
2Co   5. 7   for we walk by faith, not by **s.**

SIGN → SIGNS
Mt   24. 3   the **s** of your coming and of the end
Mk   8.12   does this generation ask for a **s?**

SIGNS → SIGN
Ge   1.14   be for **s** and for seasons and for days
Mt   16. 3   cannot interpret the **s** of the times.
Jn   20.30   Jesus did many other **s** in the
1Co   1.22   Jews demand **s** and Greeks desire
Rev   16.14   demonic spirits, performing **s,**

SILENT
Isa   53. 7   a sheep that before its shearers is **s,**

| Mk | 14.61 | But he was **s** and did not answer. |

SILVER
| Mt | 26.15 | They paid him thirty pieces of **s.** |
| Ac | 3. 6 | But Peter said, "I have no **s** or gold, |

SIN → SINNED, SINNER, SINNERS, SINS
Nu	32.23	and be sure your **s** will find you out.
2Ch	7.14	forgive their **s** and heal their land.
Tob	12.10	but those who commit **s**
Ps	119.11	so that I may not **s** against you.
Wis	10.13	but delivered him from **s.**
Sir	3.30	so almsgiving atones for **s.**
Isa	53.12	yet he bore the **s** of many,
Mt	5.29	If your right eye causes you to **s,**
Jn	1.29	who takes away the **s** of the world!
Ro	6.23	For the wages of **s** is death,
Heb	4.15	tested as we are, yet without **s.**
1Jn	1. 7	Jesus his Son cleanses us from all **s.**

SINAI
| Ex | 19.20 | the Lᴏʀᴅ descended upon Mount **S,** |

SING → SONG, SONGS, SUNG
Jdt	16.13	I will **s** to my God a new song:
Ps	47. 6	**S** praises to God, **s** praises;
1Co	14.15	I will **s** praise with the spirit,
Col	3.16	gratitude in your hearts **s** psalms,
Rev	5. 9	They **s** a new song:

SINNED → SIN
Ps	51. 4	Against you, you alone, have I **s,**
Sir	18.21	and when you have **s,** repent.
La	5. 7	Our ancestors **s**; they are no more,
Ro	3.23	all have **s** and fall short of the glory
1Jn	1.10	If we say that we have not **s,**

SINNER → SIN
| Lk | 15. 7 | over one **s** who repents than |
| Jas | 5.20 | that whoever brings back a **s** |

SINNERS → SIN
Pr	23.17	Do not let your heart envy **s,**
Ro	5. 8	we still were **s** Christ died for us.
1Ti	1.15	Jesus came into the world to save **s**

SINS → SIN
1Sa	2.25	if someone **s** against the Lᴏʀᴅ,
Sir	2.11	he forgives **s** and saves
Eze	18. 4	only the person who **s** that shall die.
Mt	9. 6	has authority on earth to forgive **s**"—
Lk	11. 4	forgive us our **s,** for we ourselves
Ac	3.19	to God so that your **s** may be wiped
1Co	15. 3	Christ died for our **s** in accordance
Heb	9.28	offered once to bear the **s** of many,
1Jn	1. 9	If we confess our **s,** he who is faithful
Rev	1. 5	loves us and freed us from our **s**

SISTER
| Pr | 7. 4 | Say to wisdom, "You are my **s,"** |
| Mk | 3.35 | the will of God is my brother and **s** |

SIT → SAT
Ps	110. 1	says to my lord, **"S** at my right hand
Mt	20.23	to **s** at my right hand and at my left,
Heb	1.13	**"S** at my right hand until I make

SIX
| Ex | 20. 9 | **S** days you shall labor and do all |
| Pr | 6.16 | are **s** things that the Lᴏʀᴅ hates, |

SKULL
| Mt | 27.33 | Golgotha (which means Place of a **S)** |

SLANDER → SLANDERED
Ps	15. 3	who do not **s** with their tongue,
Pr	10.18	and whoever utters **s** is a fool.
Mt	15.19	fornication, theft, false witness, **s.**
1Pe	2. 1	all guile, insincerity, envy, and all **s.**

SLANDERED → SLANDER
| 1Co | 4.13 | when **s,** we speak kindly. |

SLAUGHTER
| Isa | 53. 7 | like a lamb that is led to the **s,** |
| Ac | 8.32 | "Like a sheep he was led to the **s,** |

SLAVE → SLAVERY
Mk	10.44	first among you must be **s** of all.
Jn	8.34	who commits sin is a **s** to sin.
Gal	3.28	there is no longer **s** or free,

SLAVERY → SLAVE
| Gal | 5. 1 | do not submit again to a yoke of **s.** |

SLEEP → ASLEEP, SLEEPER, SLEEPING
| Ps | 121. 4 | keeps Israel will neither slumber nor **s.** |
| Da | 12. 2 | Many of those who **s** in the dust of |

SLEEPER → SLEEP
| Eph | 5.14 | **"S,** awake! Rise from the dead, |

SLEEPING → SLEEP
| Mt | 9.24 | for the girl is not dead but **s."** |
| | 26.40 | to the disciples and found them **s;** |

SLING
| 1Sa | 17.50 | over the Philistine with a **s** and a stone, |

SLOW → SLOWNESS
Ex	34. 6	merciful and gracious, **s** to anger,
Sir	5. 4	for the Lord is **s** to anger.
2Pe	3. 9	The Lord is not **s** about his promise,

SLOWNESS → SLOW
| 2Pe | 3. 9 | think of **s,** but is patient with you, |

SNOW
Ps	51. 7	and I shall be whiter than **s.**
Isa	1.18	sins are like scarlet, they shall be like **s;**
Da	7. 9	his clothing was white as **s,**
Rev	1.14	as white wool, white as **s;**

SOBER
| 1Th | 5. 6 | but let us keep awake and be **s;** |
| 2Ti | 4. 5 | always be **s,** endure suffering, |

SODOM
Ge	19.24	rained on **S** and Gomorrah sulfur
Lk	10.12	it will be more tolerable for **S** than
Rev	11. 8	city that is prophetically called **S**

SOLDIERS
| Mt | 28.12 | give a large sum of money to the **s,** |
| Jn | 19.23 | When the **s** had crucified Jesus, |

SON → SONS
Ex	4.23	now I will kill your firstborn **s.'"**
2Sa	7.14	and he shall be a **s** to me.
Ps	2. 7	He said to me, "You are my **s;**
Sir	4.10	be like a **s** of the Most High,
Isa	7.14	is with child and shall bear a **s,**
Mt	1.23	virgin shall conceive and bear a **s,**

3.17 from heaven said, "This is my **S,**
16.16 the Messiah, the **S** of the living God."
Mk 10.45 **S** of Man came not to be served but to
Lk 1.35 he will be called **S** of God.
Jn 3.16 loved the world that he gave his only **S,**
1Th 1.10 to wait for his **S** from heaven,
Heb 1. 2 last days he has spoken to us by a **S,**
1Jn 4. 9 God sent his only **S** into the world
Rev 12. 5 she gave birth to a **s,** a male child,
14.14 the cloud was one like the **S** of Man,

SONG → SING
Ps 40. 3 He put a new **s** in my mouth,
Rev 5. 9 They sing a new **s:** "You are worthy
15. 3 and the **s** of the Lamb:

SONGS → SING
Col 3.16 hymns, and spiritual **s** to God.

SONS → SON
Ac 2.17 **s** and your daughters shall prophesy,
2Co 6.18 you shall be my **s** and daughters,

SOON
Rev 22.20 says, "Surely I am coming **s.**"

SOUL → SOULS
Dt 6. 5 all your **s,** and with all your might.
Jos 22. 5 all your heart and with all your **s.**"
Sir 7.29 With all your **s** fear the Lord,
Mt 10.28 fear him who can destroy both **s** and
Heb 4.12 piercing until it divides **s** from spirit
Jas 5.20 will save the sinner's **s** from death
3Jn 1. 2 just as it is well with your **s.**

SOULS → SOUL
Jer 6.16 walk in it, and find rest for your **s.**
Mt 11.29 and you will find rest for your **s.**

SOWS
Jn 4.37 'One **s** and another reaps.'
2Co 9. 6 who **s** sparingly will also reap

SPARROWS
Lk 12. 7 you are of more value than many **s.**

SPEAK → SPEAKING
Ecc 3. 7 time to keep silence, and a time to **s;**
Mt 13.13 The reason I **s** to them in parables is
Ac 2. 4 began to **s** in other languages,
1Co 12.30 Do all **s** in tongues?

SPEAKING → SPEAK
1Co 14.39 and do not forbid **s** in tongues;
Eph 4.15 But **s** the truth in love,

SPEAR → SPEARS
Jn 19.34 the soldiers pierced his side with a **s,**

SPIES → SPY
Nu 13.32 we have gone through as **s**
Jos 2. 1 two men secretly from Shittim as **s,**

SPIRIT → SPIRITS, SPIRITUAL
Ge 6. 3 My **s** shall not abide in mortals forever,
Nu 11.25 **s** rested upon them, they prophesied.
Ps 31. 5 Into your hand I commit my **s;**
51.17 acceptable to God is a broken **s;**
Isa 42. 1 I have put my **s** upon him;
Eze 36.26 and a new **s** I will put within you;
Joel 2.28 I will pour out my **s** on all flesh;

Mt 1.18 to be with child from the Holy **S.**
5. 3 "Blessed are the poor in **s,**
26.41 the **s** indeed is willing, but the flesh
Mk 1. 8 will baptize you with the Holy **S.**"
Jn 3. 5 without being born of water and **S.**
4.24 God is **s,** and those who worship him must
worship in **s** and truth."
14.26 But the Advocate, the Holy **S,**
Ac 2. 4 of them were filled with the Holy **S**
Ro 8.26 the **S** helps us in our weakness;
1Co 12. 4 are varieties of gifts, but the same **S;**
2Co 3. 6 the letter kills, but the **S** gives life.
Gal 5.22 the fruit of the **S** is love, joy, peace,
Eph 1.13 the seal of the promised Holy **S;**
5.18 but be filled with the **S,**
1Th 5.19 Do not quench the **S.**
Heb 4.12 piercing until it divides soul from **s,**
1Jn 4. 1 Beloved, do not believe every **s,**

SPIRITS → SPIRIT
Lk 4.36 power he commands the unclean **s,**
Rev 1. 4 seven **s** who are before his throne,

SPIRITUAL → SPIRIT
1Co 2.13 interpreting **s** things to those who are **s.**
12. 1 Now concerning **s** gifts,
14. 1 Pursue love and strive for the **s** gifts,
Eph 1. 3 every **s** blessing in the heavenly
1Pe 2. 5 yourselves be built into a **s** house,

SPIT
Mk 14.65 began to **s** on him, to blindfold him,
Rev 3.16 am about to **s** you out of my mouth.

SPY → SPIES
Nu 13. 2 men to **s** out the land of Canaan,
Jos 6.25 whom Joshua sent to **s** out Jericho.

STAFF
Ex 4. 4 and it became a **s** in his hand—
Nu 17. 6 the **s** of Aaron was among theirs.
Ps 23. 4 your rod and your **s**—they comfort me.

STAND → STANDING
Ex 14.13 "Do not be afraid, **s** firm,
Job 19.25 at the last he will **s** upon the earth;
Ps 1. 5 wicked will not **s** in the judgment,
Mt 12.25 house divided against itself will **s.**
Ro 14.10 all **s** before the judgment seat of God.

STANDING → STAND
1Co 10.12 So if you think you are **s,**
Rev 3.20 I am **s** at the door, knocking;

STAR → STARS
Nu 24.17 a **s** shall come out of Jacob,
Isa 14.12 are fallen from heaven, O Day **S,**
Mt 2. 2 For we observed his **s** at its rising,
2Pe 1.19 day dawns and the morning **s** rises
Rev 9. 1 saw a **s** that had fallen from heaven
22.16 of David, the bright morning **s.**"

STARS → STAR
Ge 1.16 to rule the night—and the **s.**
Job 38. 7 when the morning **s** sang together
Rev 1.16 In his right hand he held seven **s,**

STATUE
Da 2.31 there was a great **s.**

STATUTE → STATUTES
Lev 16.29 This shall be a **s** to you forever:
Nu   19.21 It shall be a perpetual **s** for them.

STATUTES → STATUTE
Ge   26. 5 commandments, my **s**, and my laws.
Dt   4. 1 give heed to the **s** and ordinances
Ne   9.13 good **s** and commandments,
Ps 119. 8 I will observe your **s**;

STEADFAST
Heb   6.19 a sure and **s** anchor of the soul,
1Pe   5. 9 Resist him, **s** in your faith,

STEAL
Ex   20.15 You shall not **s**.
Mt   6.19 and where thieves break in and **s**;

STILL
Ps   46.10 "Be **s**, and know that I am God!
Mk   4.39 said to the sea, "Peace! Be **s**!"

STING
1Co 15.55 Where, O death, is your **s**?"

STONE → CORNERSTONE, MILLSTONE, STONED, STONES
Ex   31.18 tablets of **s**, written with the finger of
1Sa 17.50 the Philistine with a sling and a **s**,
Ps 118.22 The **s** that the builders rejected has
Isa 28.16 in Zion a foundation **s**, a tested **s**,
Eze 36.26 from your body the heart of **s**
Mt   4. 6 will not dash your foot against a **s**.'"
Mk   12.10 'The **s** that the builders rejected has
     16. 3 "Who will roll away the **s** for us
Ro   9.32 have stumbled over the stumbling **s**,
2Co   3. 3 not on tablets of **s** but on tablets

STONED → STONE
Ac   14.19 Then they **s** Paul and dragged him
Heb 11.37 **s** to death, they were sawn in two,

STONES → STONE
Mt   3. 9 God is able from these **s** to raise
Lk   19.40 were silent, the **s** would shout out."
1Co   3.12 precious **s**, wood, hay, straw—
1Pe   2. 5 like living **s**, let yourselves be built

STRAIGHT
Pr   3. 6 and he will make **s** your paths.
Isa 40. 3 **s** in the desert a highway for our God.
Mt   3. 3 way of the Lord, make his paths **s**.'"
Ac   9.11 Get up and go to the street called **S**,

STRANGER → STRANGERS
Dt   10.19 You shall also love the **s**,
Mt   25.35 I was a **s** and you welcomed me,

STRANGERS → STRANGER
Ro   12.13 extend hospitality to **s**.
Heb 11.13 They confessed that they were **s**

STREAMS
Ps   1. 3 like trees planted by **s** of water,
     42. 1 As a deer longs for flowing **s**,

STRENGTH → STRONG
Ex   15. 2 The Lord is my **s** and my might,
Jdt   9.11 your **s** does not depend on numbers,
1Ch 16.11 Seek the Lord and his **s**,
Ne   8.10 for the joy of the Lord is your **s**."
1Mc   3.19 but **s** comes from Heaven.

STRENGTHEN → STRONG
Ps 119.28 **s** me according to your word.
Heb 12.12 hands and **s** your weak knees,

STRENGTHENS → STRONG
Php   4.13 do all things through him who **s** me.

STRIFE
Pr   23.29 Who has sorrow? Who has **s**?
Ro   1.29 Full of envy, murder, **s**, deceit,
Gal   5.20 enmities, **s**, jealousy, anger,

STRIKE
Ge   3.15 he will **s** your head, and you will **s**
Ex   17. 6 **S** the rock, and water will come out
Mk   14.27 'I will **s** the shepherd, and the sheep

**STRONG → STRENGTH, STRENGTHEN, STRENGTHENS,
STRONGHOLD**
Dt   31. 6 Be **s** and bold; have no fear
Jos   1. 6 Be **s** and courageous; for you shall
Ecc   9.11 nor the battle to the **s**, nor bread to
Ro   15. 1 We who are **s** ought to put up with
1Co   1.27 in the world to shame the **s**;
2Co 12.10 whenever I am weak, then I am **s**.
Eph   6.10 be **s** in the Lord and in the strength

STRONGHOLD → STRONG
Ps   9. 9 The Lord is a **s** for the oppressed,
Na   1. 7 a **s** in a day of trouble;

STUDY
Ezr   7.10 Ezra had set his heart to **s** the law
Ecc 12.12 much **s** is a weariness of the flesh.

STUMBLE → STUMBLING
Mt   18. 9 And if your eye causes you to **s**,
Ro   9.33 a stone that will make people **s**,

STUMBLING → STUMBLE
Mt   16.23 You are a **s** block to me;
Ro   11. 9 a **s** block and a retribution for them;
1Co   8. 9 not somehow become a **s** block to

SUBDUE
Ge   1.28 and fill the earth and **s** it;

SUBJECT
Ro   13. 1 be **s** to the governing authorities;
Eph   5.21 **s** to one another out of reverence

SUBMISSION → SUBMIT
1Ti   2.11 a woman learn in silence with full **s**.
Heb   5. 7 was heard because of his reverent **s**.

SUBMISSIVE → SUBMIT
1Ti   3. 4 keeping his children **s** and respectful
Tit   2. 5 kind, being **s** to their husbands,

SUBMIT → SUBMISSION, SUBMISSIVE
Heb 13.17 Obey your leaders and **s** to them,

SUCCEED → SUCCESSFUL
Pr   15.22 but with many advisers they **s**.
Ecc 10.10 but wisdom helps one to **s**.

SUCCESSFUL → SUCCEED
Jos   1. 7 that you may be **s** wherever you go.

SUDDENLY
Mal 3. 1 Lord whom you seek will **s** come to
Mk 13.36 find you asleep when he comes **s.**

SUFFER → SUFFERED, SUFFERING, SUFFERINGS
Lk 22.15 this Passover with you before I **s;**
24.46 the Messiah is to **s** and to rise from
Heb 9.26 then he would have had to **s** again

SUFFERED → SUFFER
1Pe 2.21 because Christ also **s** for you,

SUFFERING → SUFFER
Isa 53. 3 a man of **s** and acquainted with
Mk 8.31 Son of Man must undergo great **s,**

SUFFERINGS → SUFFER
Ro 8.18 the **s** of this present time are not

SUFFICIENT
2Co 12. 9 "My grace is **s** for you,

SULFUR
Ge 19.24 rained on Sodom and Gomorrah **s**
Ps 11. 6 he will rain coals of fire and **s;**
Rev 21. 8 in the lake that burns with fire and **s,**

SUN
Jos 10.13 And the **s** stood still,
Ecc 1. 9 there is nothing new under the **s.**
Mt 5.45 he makes his **s** rise on the evil and
Rev 22. 5 they need no light of lamp or **s,**

SUPPER
Lk 22.20 he did the same with the cup after **s,**
Rev 19. 9 to the marriage **s** of the Lamb."

SUPPLICATION → SUPPLICATIONS
Eph 6.18 at all times in every prayer and **s.**

SUPPLICATIONS → SUPPLICATION
1Ti 2. 1 then, I urge that **s,** prayers,
Heb 5. 7 Jesus offered up prayers and **s,**

SURPASSES
Eph 3.19 the love of Christ that **s** knowledge,
Php 4. 7 the peace of God, which **s** all

SUSTAINS
Ps 3. 5 for the LORD **s** me.
Heb 1. 3 he **s** all things by his powerful word.

SWALLOW → SWALLOWED
Jnh 1.17 provided a large fish to **s** up Jonah;
Mt 23.24 You strain out a gnat but **s** a camel!

SWALLOWED → SWALLOW
1Co 15.54 "Death has been **s** up in victory."

SWEAR
Dt 10.20 and by his name you shall **s.**
Ps 24. 4 and do not **s** deceitfully.
Mt 5.34 Do not **s** at all, either by heaven,

SWEAT
Ge 3.19 By the **s** of your face you shall eat
Lk 22.44 〚**s** became like great drops of blood〛

SWINE
1Mc 1.47 sacrifice **s** and other unclean animals,
Mt 7. 6 do not throw your pearls before **s,**

SWORD → SWORDS
Ge 3.24 and a **s** flaming and turning to guard
Sir 21. 3 All lawlessness is like a two-edged **s**
Mt 10.34 not come to bring peace, but a **s.**
Eph 6.17 the **s** of the Spirit, which is the word
Heb 4.12 sharper than any two-edged **s,**
Rev 1.16 mouth came a sharp, two-edged **s,**

SWORDS → SWORD
Isa 2. 4 shall beat their **s** into plowshares,
Joel 3.10 Beat your plowshares into **s,**

SYMPATHIZE → SYMPATHY
Heb 4.15 unable to **s** with our weaknesses,

SYMPATHY → SYMPATHIZE
Php 2. 1 any compassion and **s,**
1Pe 3. 8 all of you, have unity of spirit, **s,**

SYNAGOGUE → SYNAGOGUES
Lk 4.16 he went to the **s** on the sabbath day,
Ac 18.26 He began to speak boldly in the **s;**

SYNAGOGUES → SYNAGOGUE
Mt 4.23 teaching in their **s** and proclaiming
Jn 18.20 always taught in **s** and in the temple,

T

TABERNACLE
Ex 25. 9 concerning the pattern of the **t**
40.34 the glory of the LORD filled the **t.**
1Ch 6.48 for all the service of the **t** of the house

TABLE → TABLES
Ex 25.23 You shall make a **t** of acacia wood,
Ps 23. 5 a **t** before me in the presence of my

TABLES → TABLE
Mk 11.15 overturned the **t** of the money changers

TABLETS
Ex 31.18 gave him the two **t** of the covenant,
2Co 3. 3 not on **t** of stone but on **t** of human hearts.

TALENT
Mt 25.25 and hid your **t** in the ground.

TAX → TAXES
Mt 11.19 a friend of **t** collectors and sinners!'
Lk 18.10 Pharisee and the other a **t** collector.

TAXES → TAX
Mt 22.17 Is it lawful to pay **t** to the emperor,
Ro 13. 7 **t** to whom **t** are due,

TEACH → TEACHER, TEACHERS, TEACHING
Dt 6. 1 to **t** you to observe in the land that
Jer 31.34 No longer shall they **t** one another,
Col 3.16 **t** and admonish one another in all
1Jn 2.27 so you do not need anyone to **t** you.

TEACHER → TEACH
Ecc 1. 1 words of the **T,** the son of David,
Jn 1.38 "Rabbi" (which translated means **T)**

TEACHERS → TEACH
Ps 119.99 more understanding than all my **t,**
1Co 12.28 second prophets, third **t;**
Eph 4.11 evangelists, some pastors and **t,**
Jas 3. 1 Not many of you should become **t,**

TEACHING → TEACH
Mk 1.27 A new **t**—with authority!

TEAR
Rev 7.17 God will wipe away every **t** from

TEETH → TOOTH
Mt 8.12 will be weeping and gnashing of **t."**

TEMPLE
2Ch 2.12 who will build a **t** for the Lord,
1Mc 4.48 sanctuary and the interior of the **t,**
Mt 4.5 placed him on the pinnacle of the **t,**
    12.6 something greater than the **t** is here.
1Co 3.16 you are God's **t** and that God's Spirit
Eph 2.21 and grows into a holy **t** in the Lord;
Rev 21.22 its **t** is the Lord God the Almighty and

TEMPTATION → TEMPTED
1Ti 6.9 who want to be rich into **t** and
Jas 1.12 Blessed is anyone who endures **t.**

TEMPTED → TEMPTATION
Mk 1.13 wilderness forty days, **t** by Satan;
Gal 6.1 care that you yourselves are not **t.**

TEN
Ex 34.28 the covenant, the **t** commandments.

TENT
Ex 27.21 the **t** of meeting, outside the curtain
2Co 5.1 the earthly **t** we live in is destroyed,

TEST → TESTED, TESTING
Dt 6.16 put the Lord your God to the **t,**
Sir 37.27 My child, **t** yourself while you live;
Lk 4.12 not put the Lord your God to the **t.'**
    10.25 then a lawyer stood up to **t** Jesus.
2Co 13.5 indeed, you fail to meet the **t!**
1Jn 4.1 **t** the spirits to see whether they are

TESTED → TEST
Ge 22.1 After these things God **t** Abraham.
Ps 78.41 They **t** God again and again,
Heb 4.15 been **t** as we are, yet without sin.

TESTIMONY
Mk 14.59 on this point their **t** did not agree.
Rev 1.9 the word of God and the **t** of Jesus.

TESTING → TEST
1Co 10.13 No **t** has overtaken you that is not
Jas 1.3 **t** of your faith produces endurance;

THANK → THANKS, THANKSGIVING
2Ch 29.31 bring sacrifices and **t** offerings to
Ps 52.9 I will **t** you forever,
Sir 35.4 gives alms sacrifices a **t** offering.

THANKS → THANK
1Co 11.24 and when he had given **t,**

THANKSGIVING → THANK
Ps 50.14 Offer to God a sacrifice of **t,**
Php 4.6 with **t** let your requests be made known
Rev 7.12 glory and wisdom and **t** and honor

THIEF → THIEVES
Ex 22.1 The **t** shall make restitution,
Jn 10.10 The **t** comes only to steal and kill
1Th 5.2 day of the Lord will come like a **t** in

Rev 16.15 ("See, I am coming like a **t!**

THIEVES → THIEF
Mt 6.19 and where **t** break in and steal;

THINK → THOUGHTS
Ro 12.3 not to **t** of yourself more highly than
1Co 10.12 So if you **t** you are standing,

THIRD → THREE
Mt 26.44 and prayed for the **t** time,
Lk 18.33 and on the **t** day he will rise again."

THIRST → THIRSTY
Mt 5.6 who hunger and **t** for righteousness,
Rev 7.16 will hunger no more, and **t** no more;

THIRSTY → THIRST
Mt 25.35 I was **t** and you gave me something
Jn 6.35 believes in me will never be **t.**
Rev 22.17 And let everyone who is **t** come.

THORN → THORNS
2Co 12.7 a **t** was given me in the flesh,

THORNS → THORN
Jn 19.2 the soldiers wove a crown of **t** and

THOUGHTS → THINK
Isa 55.8 For my **t** are not your **t,**
1Co 3.20 "The Lord knows the **t** of the wise,
Heb 4.12 judge the **t** and intentions of the heart.

THOUSAND
Ps 90.4 **t** years in your sight are like yesterday
2Pe 3.8 one day is like a **t** years, and a **t** years
Rev 20.4 and reigned with Christ a **t** years.

THREE → THIRD
Mt 18.20 two or **t** are gathered in my name,
    26.34 you will deny me **t** times."
Mk 8.31 be killed, and after **t** days rise again.
2Co 12.8 **T** times I appealed to the Lord
1Jn 5.7 There are **t** that testify:

THRONE
Ps 45.6 Your **t,** O God, endures forever
Isa 6.1 I saw the Lord sitting on a **t,** high
Mt 19.28 the Son of Man is seated on the **t**
Heb 4.16 approach the **t** of grace with boldness,
Rev 4.10 they cast their crowns before the **t,**
    20.11 I saw a great white **t** and the one

THUMMIM
Ex 28.30 you shall put the Urim and the **T,**

THUNDER
Ex 9.23 and the Lord sent **t** and hail,
Rev 4.5 and rumblings and peals of **t,**

TIME → TIMES
Est 4.14 dignity for just such a **t** as this."
Ecc 3.1 a **t** for every matter under heaven:
Da 7.25 for a **t,** two times, and half a **t.**
Ro 5.6 the right **t** Christ died for the ungodly.
2Co 6.2 See, now is the acceptable **t;**
Gal 4.4 when the fullness of **t** had come,
Rev 12.14 for a **t,** and times, and half a **t.**

TIMES → TIME
Sir 20.12 but pay for it seven **t** over.

Mt 16. 3 cannot interpret the signs of the **t**.
18.22 seven **t**, but, I tell you, seventy-seven **t**.
Mk 14.30 you will deny me three **t**."

TITHE
Dt 12.17 the **t** of your grain, your wine, and
Mal 3.10 Bring the full **t** into the storehouse,

TODAY
Ps 2. 7 my son; **t** I have begotten you.
Heb 1. 5 my Son; **t** I have begotten you"?
13. 8 Christ is the same yesterday and **t**

TOMB
Mk 15.46 laid it in a **t** that had been hewn out
Lk 24. 2 the stone rolled away from the **t**,

TOMORROW
Mt 6.34 "So do not worry about **t**,
Jas 4.14 do not even know what **t** will bring.

TONGUE → TONGUES
Isa 45.23 shall bow, every **t** shall swear."
Php 2.11 every **t** should confess that Jesus Christ

TONGUES → TONGUE
Ac 2. 3 Divided **t**, as of fire, appeared
1Co 12.10 **t**, to another the interpretation of **t**.

TOOTH → TEETH
Ex 21.24 **t** for **t**, hand for hand, foot for foot,
Mt 5.38 'An eye for an eye and a **t** for a **t**.'

TOWER
Ge 11. 4 and a **t** with its top in the heavens,
Pr 18.10 The name of the LORD is a strong **t**;

TRADITION
Mt 15. 2 disciples break the **t** of the elders?
Col 2. 8 empty deceit, according to human **t**,

TRAIN → TRAINING
Pr 22. 6 **T** children in the right way, and
1Ti 4. 7 **T** yourself in godliness,

TRAINING → TRAIN
1Ti 4. 8 while physical **t** is of some value,
2Ti 3.16 and for **t** in righteousness,

TRAITOR
Lk 6.16 and Judas Iscariot, who became a **t**.

TRANSFIGURED
Mt 17. 2 And he was **t** before them,

TRANSFORM → TRANSFORMED
Php 3.21 will **t** the body of our humiliation

TRANSFORMED → TRANSFORM
Ro 12. 2 be **t** by the renewing of your minds,
2Co 3.18 are being **t** into the same image

TRANSGRESSION → TRANSGRESSIONS
Ex 23.21 for he will not pardon your **t**;
Da 9.24 to finish the **t**, to put an end to sin,

TRANSGRESSIONS → TRANSGRESSION
Ps 103.12 so far he removes our **t** from us.
Isa 53. 5 But he was wounded for our **t**,

TREASURE → TREASURES
Mt 6.21 where your **t** is, there your heart

2Co 4. 7 But we have this **t** in clay jars,
2Ti 1.14 Guard the good **t** entrusted to you,

TREASURES → TREASURE
Col 2. 3 are hidden all the **t** of wisdom

TREE
Ge 3.24 to guard the way to the **t** of life.
Mt 12.33 for the **t** is known by its fruit.
Rev 22. 2 the **t** of life with its twelve kinds

TREMBLING
Ps 2.11 Serve the LORD with fear, with **t**
Php 2.12 your own salvation with fear and **t**;

TRESPASS → TRESPASSES
Ro 5.15 But the free gift is not like the **t**.

TRESPASSES → TRESPASS
Mt 6.14 For if you forgive others their **t**,
2Co 5.19 not counting their **t** against them,

TRIAL → TRIALS
Lk 11. 4 do not bring us to the time of **t**."
2Pe 2. 9 knows how to rescue the godly from **t**,
Rev 3.10 I will keep you from the hour of **t**

TRIALS → TRIAL
Jas 1. 2 whenever you face **t** of any kind,
1Pe 1. 6 you have had to suffer various **t**,

TRIBES
Ge 49.28 All these are the twelve **t** of Israel,
Ex 24. 4 to the twelve **t** of Israel.
Mt 19.28 judging the twelve **t** of Israel.
Rev 21.12 inscribed the names of the twelve **t**

TRIUMPHAL → TRIUMPHS
2Co 2.14 Christ always leads us in **t** procession,

TRIUMPHS → TRIUMPHAL
Jas 2.13 mercy **t** over judgment.

TROUBLE → TROUBLED
Ps 9. 9 a stronghold in times of **t**.
Pr 11. 8 The righteous are delivered from **t**,
Isa 33. 2 our salvation in the time of **t**.
Mt 6.34 Today's **t** is enough for today.

TROUBLED → TROUBLE
Jn 14. 1 "Do not let your hearts be **t**.

TRUE → TRUTH
Ps 119.151 and all your commandments are **t**.
Jn 1. 9 The **t** light, which enlightens
1Jn 5.20 He is the **t** God and eternal life.
Rev 3.14 the Amen, the faithful and **t** witness,
19.11 Its rider is called Faithful and **T**,

TRUMPET
1Co 15.52 twinkling of an eye, at the last **t**.
1Th 4.16 and with the sound of God's **t**,

TRUST → ENTRUSTED, TRUSTED, TRUSTWORTHY
Ps 37. 3 **T** in the LORD, and do good;
Pr 3. 5 **T** in the LORD with all your heart,
Sir 2. 6 **T** in him, and he will help you;

TRUSTED → TRUST
Da 3.28 delivered his servants who **t** in him.
6.23 because he had **t** in his God.
13.35 for her heart **t** in the Lord.

TRUSTWORTHY → TRUST
1Mc 14.41 until a **t** prophet should arise,
Ps 111. 7 and just; all his precepts are **t.**
Rev 22. 6 "These words are **t** and true,

TRUTH → TRUE
Tob 3. 2 all your ways are mercy and **t;**
Pr 23.23 Buy **t,** and do not sell it;
Jn 1.17 grace and **t** came through Jesus Christ.
4.23 worship the Father in spirit and **t,**
8.32 and the **t** will make you free."
14. 6 "I am the way, and the **t,** and the life.
14.17 This is the Spirit of **t,**
Eph 4.15 But speaking the **t** in love,
2Ti 2.15 rightly explaining the word of **t.**

TURNED → TURN
Isa 53. 6 we have all **t** to our own way,
Ro 3.12 All have **t** aside, together they have

TWELVE
Ge 49.28 All these are the **t** tribes of Israel,
Mt 10. 1 Jesus summoned his **t** disciples
Lk 9.17 **t** baskets of broken pieces.
Rev 21.12 inscribed the names of the **t** tribes
22. 2 tree of life with its **t** kinds of fruit,

TWINKLING
1Co 15.52 in the **t** of an eye, at the last trumpet

TWO → TWICE, TWO-EDGED
Ge 1.16 God made the **t** great lights—
6.19 bring **t** of every kind into the ark,
Ex 31.18 the **t** tablets of the covenant,
Dt 17. 6 of **t** or three witnesses the death
Mt 6.24 "No one can serve **t** masters;
19. 5 and the **t** shall become one flesh'?

TWO-EDGED → TWO
Heb 4.12 sharper than any **t** sword,
Rev 1.16 his mouth came a sharp, **t** sword,

U

UNBELIEF → UNBELIEVER, UNBELIEVERS
Mk 6. 6 And he was amazed at their **u.**
9.24 cried out, "I believe; help my **u!**"

UNBELIEVER → UNBELIEF
1Co 10.27 If an **u** invites you to a meal and
2Co 6.15 does a believer share with an **u?**

UNBELIEVERS → UNBELIEF
2Co 6.14 Do not be mismatched with **u.**

UNCIRCUMCISED → UNCIRCUMCISION
Ac 7.51 people, **u** in heart and ears,
Ro 4.11 he had by faith while he was still **u.**
Col 3.11 circumcised and **u,** barbarian,

UNCIRCUMCISION → UNCIRCUMCISED
1Co 7.19 Circumcision is nothing, and **u** is
Gal 5. 6 neither circumcision nor **u** counts

UNCLEAN → UNCLEANNESS
Lev 5. 2 when any of you touch any **u** thing
Isa 52.11 Touch no **u** thing;
Mk 3.11 Whenever the **u** spirits saw him,
Rev 21.27 But nothing **u** will enter it,

UNDERSTAND → UNDERSTANDING
Lk 24.45 opened their minds to **u** the scriptures,
Eph 5.17 but **u** what the will of the Lord is.

UNDERSTANDING → UNDERSTAND
Ex 36. 1 has given skill and **u** to know how
Pr 2. 6 from his mouth come knowledge and **u**
Lk 2.47 heard him were amazed at his **u**
Php 4. 7 peace of God, which surpasses all **u,**

UNGODLY
Ro 5. 6 the right time Christ died for the **u.**
2Pe 2. 6 example of what is coming to the **u;**

UNITY
Ps 133. 1 when kindred live together in **u!**
Eph 4. 3 to maintain the **u** of the Spirit

UNJUST
Ro 3. 5 That God is **u** to inflict wrath on us?
Heb 6.10 For God is not **u;** he will

UNLEAVENED
Ex 12.17 shall observe the festival of **u** bread,
Mt 26.17 first day of **U** Bread the disciples

UNRIGHTEOUS → UNRIGHTEOUSNESS
Mt 5.45 rain on the righteous and on the **u.**
2Pe 2. 9 **u** under punishment until the day

UNRIGHTEOUSNESS → UNRIGHTEOUS
Ps 92.15 and there is no **u** in him.
1Jn 1. 9 and cleanse us from all **u.**

URIM
Ex 28.30 of judgment you shall put the **U**

USEFUL
2Ti 3.16 scripture is inspired by God and is **u**

V

VAIN → VANITY
Ps 2. 1 and the peoples plot in **v?**
Mt 15. 9 in **v** do they worship me,
Php 2.16 that I did not run in **v** or labor in **v.**

VALLEY
Ps 23. 4 through the darkest **v,** I fear no evil;

VANITY → VAIN
Ecc 1. 2 **v** of vanities! All is **v.**

VEIL
Ex 34.33 he put a **v** on his face;
2Co 3.15 a **v** lies over their minds;

VENGEANCE → AVENGE, AVENGER, AVENGING
Ps 94. 1 O Lord, you God of **v,**
Isa 34. 8 For the Lord has a day of **v,**
Na 1. 2 the Lord takes **v** on his adversaries

VICTORY
Pr 21.31 but the **v** belongs to the Lord.
1Co 15.54 Death has been swallowed up in **v.**"

VINE → VINEYARD
Jn 15. 1 "I am the true **v,** and my Father is

VINEYARD → VINE
Isa 5. 1 had a **v** on a very fertile hill.
Mt 21.33 a landowner who planted a **v,**

VIOLENCE

Ge	6.11	and the earth was filled with **v.**
Isa	53. 9	although he had done no **v,**
Hab	2.17	because of human bloodshed and **v**

VIRGIN

Mt	1.23	the **v** shall conceive and bear a son,
Lk	1.34	"How can this be, since I am a **v?**"

VISION → VISIONS

Isa	22. 1	oracle concerning the valley of **v.**
Da	8.26	As for you, seal up the **v,**

VISIONS → VISION

Nu	12. 6	make myself known to them in **v;**
Eze	1. 1	were opened, and I saw **v** of God.
Da	1.17	Daniel also had insight into all **v**
Joel	2.28	and your young men shall see **v.**
Ac	2.17	and your young men shall see **v,**

VOICE

Heb	3. 7	says, "Today, if you hear his **v,**
Rev	3.20	if you hear my **v** and open the door,

VOID

Ge	1. 2	the earth was a formless **v**

VOW

Ecc	5. 4	Fulfill what you **v.**
Sir	18.23	Before making a **v,** prepare yourself

W

WAGES

Ro	6.23	For the **w** of sin is death,

WAIT

Ps	27.14	**W** for the LORD; be strong,
Sir	2. 7	fear the Lord, **w** for his mercy;
1Th	1.10	to **w** for his Son from heaven,

WALK

Dt	10.12	to **w** in all his ways, to love him,
Ps	23. 4	I **w** through the darkest valley,
Isa	40.31	they shall **w** and not faint.
2Co	5. 7	for we **w** by faith, not by sight.

WALL

Jos	6.20	shout, and the **w** fell down flat;
Ne	2.17	let us rebuild the **w** of Jerusalem,
Eph	2.14	has broken down the dividing **w,**

WANT

Ps	23. 1	LORD is my shepherd, I shall not **w.**

WAR → WARRIOR, WARS

Ecc	3. 8	a time for **w,** and a time for peace.

WARRIOR → WAR

Ex	15. 3	LORD is a **w;** the LORD

WARS → WAR

Mt	24. 6	you will hear of **w** and rumors of **w;**

WASH

Ps	51. 7	**w** me, and I shall be whiter than snow.
Jn	13. 5	and began to **w** the disciples' feet

WATER → WATERS

Jer	2.13	the fountain of living **w,**
Eze	36.25	I will sprinkle clean **w** upon you,
Mk	1. 8	I have baptized you with **w;**

Jn	2. 9	tasted the **w** that had become wine,
	3. 5	without being born of **w** and Spirit.
	4.10	he would have given you living **w.**"
1Jn	5. 6	the one who came by **w** and blood,
Rev	22. 1	showed me the river of the **w** of life,

WATERS → WATER

Ge	7. 7	the ark to escape the **w** of the flood.
Isa	55. 1	who thirsts, come to the **w;**

WAY → WAYS

Ps	1. 6	watches over the **w** of the righteous,
Pr	22. 6	Train children in the right **w,**
Mt	3. 3	'Prepare the **w** of the Lord,
Jn	14. 6	"I am the **w,** and the truth, and the life.
1Co	12.31	show you a still more excellent **w.**
Heb	10.20	the new and living **w** that he opened

WAYS → WAY

Dt	10.12	to walk in all his **w,** to love him,
Sir	2.15	who love him keep his **w.**

WEAK → WEAKNESS, WEAKNESSES

Mt	26.41	indeed is willing, but the flesh is **w.**"
1Co	1.27	God chose what is **w** in the world
2Co	12.10	whenever I am **w,** then I am strong.

WEAKNESS → WEAK

Ro	8.26	the Spirit helps us in our **w;**

WEAKNESSES → WEAK

Heb	4.15	to sympathize with our **w,**

WEALTH

Sir	5. 1	Do not rely on your **w,**
Rev	5.12	receive power and **w** and wisdom

WEARY

Isa	40.31	they shall run and not be **w,**
Heb	12. 3	you may not grow **w** or lose heart.

WEDDING

Jn	2. 1	there was a **w** in Cana of Galilee,

WEEKS

Ex	34.22	You shall observe the festival of **w,**
Lev	23.15	you shall count off seven **w;**

WEEP → WEEPING

Ecc	3. 4	a time to **w,** and a time to laugh;
Ro	12.15	**w** with those who **w.**

WEEPING → WEEP

Ps	30. 5	**W** may linger for the night,
Mt	8.12	will be **w** and gnashing of teeth."

WELL

Dt	6. 3	so that it may go **w** with you,
Mt	3.17	with whom I am **w** pleased."
	17. 5	I am **w** pleased; listen to him!"
2Pe	1.17	with whom I am **w** pleased."

WICKED → WICKEDNESS

Ps	1. 5	the **w** will not stand in the judgment,
Isa	48.22	no peace," says the LORD, "for the **w.**"
Eze	18.23	any pleasure in the death of the **w,**

WICKEDNESS → WICKED

Ps	45. 7	you love righteousness and hate **w.**
Lk	11.39	inside you are full of greed and **w.**

WIDOW → WIDOWS
Ex	22.22	shall not abuse any **w** or orphan.
Ps	146. 9	he upholds the orphan and the **w**,
1Ti	5. 4	If a **w** has children or grandchildren,

WIDOWS → WIDOW
| 1Ti | 5. 3 | Honor **w** who are really **w**. |
| Jas | 1.27 | to care for orphans and **w** in their |

WIFE → WIVES
Ge	2.24	and his mother and clings to his **w**,
Ex	20.17	shall not covet your neighbor's **w**,
Tob	8. 6	his **w** Eve as a helper and support.
Pr	18.22	who finds a **w** finds a good thing,
Sir	26. 3	A good **w** is a great blessing;
Mt	5.32	that anyone who divorces his **w**,
Eph	5.28	He who loves his **w** loves himself.
Rev	21. 9	the bride, the **w** of the Lamb."

WILDERNESS
| Isa | 40. 3 | the **w** prepare the way of the LORD, |
| Mt | 3. 3 | voice of one crying out in the **w:** |

WILL → WILLING
Ps	40. 8	I delight to do your **w**, O my God;
Mt	6.10	Your **w** be done, on earth as it is in
Lk	22.42	yet, not my **w** but yours be done."
Jn	4.34	"My food is to do the **w** of him who
Eph	6. 6	doing the **w** of God from the heart.
1Jn	5.14	if we ask anything according to his **w**,

WILLING → WILL
| Mt | 26.41 | spirit indeed is **w**, but the flesh is weak. |
| Lk | 22.42 | if you are **w**, remove this cup from |

WIND
Ecc	1.14	all is vanity and a chasing after **w**.
Jn	3. 8	The **w** blows where it chooses,
Ac	2. 2	a sound like the rush of a violent **w**,

WINE
Mt	9.17	is new **w** put into old wineskins;
Jn	2. 9	tasted the water that had become **w**,
Eph	5.18	Do not get drunk with **w**, for that is

WINGS
Ex	19. 4	and how I bore you on eagles' **w**
Ps	17. 8	hide me in the shadow of your **w**,
Mal	4. 2	shall rise, with healing in its **w**.
Lk	13.34	hen gathers her brood under her **w**,

WIPE
| Isa | 25. 8 | GOD will **w** away the tears from all |
| Rev | 21. 4 | he will **w** every tear from their eyes. |

WISDOM → WISE
1Ki	4.29	God gave Solomon very great **w**,
Pr	1.20	**W** cries out in the street;
	9.10	fear of the LORD is the beginning of **w**,
Wis	6.12	**W** is radiant and unfading,
Sir	1. 1	All **w** is from the Lord,
	24. 1	THE PRAISE OF **W**
Jer	9.23	Do not let the wise boast in their **w**,
Mt	13.54	this man get this **w** and these deeds
Lk	2.52	Jesus increased in **w** and in years,
Ro	11.33	the depth of the riches and **w** and
1Co	1.19	"I will destroy the **w** of the wise,
Col	2. 3	whom are hidden all the treasures of **w**
Jas	3.17	But the **w** from above is first pure,
Rev	5.12	wealth and **w** and might and honor

WISE → WISDOM
Ps	19. 7	are sure, making **w** the simple;
Pr	3. 7	Do not be **w** in your own eyes;
Da	12. 3	are **w** shall shine like the brightness
1Co	1.26	not many of you were **w** by human
Eph	5.15	not as unwise people but as **w**,

WITHER → WITHERS
| Ps | 1. 3 | and their leaves do not **w**. |
| Eze | 47.12 | Their leaves will not **w** nor their |

WITHERS → WITHER
| Jn | 15. 6 | is thrown away like a branch and **w**; |
| 1Pe | 1.24 | The grass **w**, and the flower falls, |

WITNESS → EYEWITNESSES, WITNESSES
| Dt | 19.15 | single **w** shall not suffice to convict |
| Rev | 1. 5 | faithful **w**, the firstborn of the dead, |

WITNESSES → WITNESS
Mt	26.60	though many false **w** came forward.
Heb	12. 1	surrounded by so great a cloud of **w**,
Rev	11. 3	my two **w** authority to prophesy

WIVES → WIFE
| Eph | 5.22 | **W**, be subject to your husbands as |
| 1Pe | 3. 1 | **W**, in the same way, accept the |

WOMAN → WOMEN
Ge	2.22	he made into a **w** and brought her to
	3.15	enmity between you and the **w**,
Jdt	16. 5	foiled them by the hand of a **w**.
Ps	113. 9	He gives the barren **w** a home,
Pr	11.16	A gracious **w** gets honor,
	31.30	**w** who fears the LORD is to be praised.
Rev	12. 1	a **w** clothed with the sun,

WOMEN → WOMAN
Lk	1.42	"Blessed are you among **w**,
	23.55	**w** who had come with him from
1Pe	3. 5	that the holy **w** who hoped in God

WONDERFUL → WONDERS
| Ge | 18.14 | Is anything too **w** for the LORD? |
| Isa | 9. 6 | named **W** Counselor, Mighty God, |

WONDERS → WONDERFUL
Ex	3.20	and strike Egypt with all my **w** that
Ps	136. 4	who alone does great **w**,
Jn	4.48	signs and **w** you will not believe."
2Th	2. 9	who uses all power, signs, lying **w**,

WORD → BYWORD, WORDS
Dt	30.14	No, the **w** is very near to you;
Ps	119.105	Your **w** is a lamp to my feet and
Pr	30. 5	Every **w** of God proves true;
Isa	40. 8	the **w** of our God will stand forever.
Jn	1. 1	In the beginning was the **W**, and the **W** was with God, and the **W** was God.
	1.14	the **W** became flesh and lived among
2Ti	2.15	rightly explaining the **w** of truth.
Jas	1.22	But be doers of the **w**,
Rev	19.13	his name is called The **W** of God.

WORDS → WORD
Ex	20. 1	Then God spoke all these **w:**
Dt	11.18	put these **w** of mine in your heart
Mt	24.35	but my **w** will not pass away.

WORK → WORKS
| Ge | 2. 2 | the seventh day God finished the **w** |

Ex   20.10 you shall not do any **w**—
Php   2.12 **w** out your own salvation with fear
2Ti   3.17 equipped for every good **w.**

WORKS → WORK
Gal   2.16 and not by doing the **w** of the law,
      5.19 the **w** of the flesh are obvious:
Eph   2. 9 not the result of **w,** so that no one may
1Ti   6.18 to do good, to be rich in good **w,**

WORLD
Mt   5.14 "You are the light of the **w.**
     16.26 gain the whole **w** but forfeit their life?
Jn   1.10 yet the **w** did not know him.
      3.16 loved the **w** that he gave his only Son,
      8.12 saying, "I am the light of the **w.**
1Jn   2.15 not love the **w** or the things in the **w.**
Rev 11.15 kingdom of the **w** has become the

WORRY
Mt   6.25 do not **w** about your life,
     10.19 not **w** about how you are to speak

WORSHIP
Ex   20. 5 not bow down to them or **w** them;
Ps 100. 2 **W** the Lord with gladness;
Mt   4. 9 if you will fall down and **w** me."
Jn   4.24 who **w** him must **w** in spirit and truth."
Ro   12. 1 which is your spiritual **w.**

WORTHY
2Sa 22. 4 Lord, who is **w** to be praised,
Eph   4. 1 to lead a life **w** of the calling
Rev   4.11 "You are **w,** our Lord and God,
      5.12 **W** is the Lamb that was slaughtered

WOUNDS
1Pe   2.24 by his **w** you have been healed.

WRAPPED
Mk   15.46 the body, **w** it in the linen cloth,
Lk   2. 7 **w** him in bands of cloth,

WRATH
Nu   16.46 For **w** has gone out from the Lord;
Ps   2. 5 Then he will speak to them in his **w,**
Pr   15. 1 A soft answer turns away **w,**
Sir 16.11 For mercy and **w** are with the Lord;
Zep   1.15 That day will be a day of **w,**
Mt   3. 7 you to flee from the **w** to come?
Ro   1.18 **w** of God is revealed from heaven
1Th   1.10 rescues us from the **w** that is coming
Rev   6.17 the great day of their **w** has come,

WRITE → WRITING, WRITTEN, WROTE
Ex   34.27 Lord said to Moses: **W** these words;
Dt   6. 9 **w** them on the doorposts of your house
Pr   7. 3 **w** them on the tablet of your heart.
Jer 31.33 and I will **w** it on their hearts;
Heb   8.10 and **w** them on their hearts,

WRITING → WRITE
Ex   32.16 and the **w** was the **w** of God,

WRITTEN → WRITE
Lk   24.44 everything **w** about me in the law
Jn   21.25 if every one of them were **w** down,
Rev 21.27 are **w** in the Lamb's book of life.

WRONG → WRONGED
Lk   23.41 but this man has done nothing **w.**"
Ac   23. 9 "We find nothing **w** with this man.

WRONGED → WRONG
1Co   6. 7 Why not rather be **w?**

WROTE → WRITE
Ex   24. 4 And Moses **w** down all the words

Y

YEAR → YEARS
Ex   23.14 Three times in the **y** you shall hold a
Heb 10. 1 continually offered **y** after **y,**

YEARS → YEAR
Ps   90. 4 For a thousand **y** in your sight are like
Jer 25.12 Then after seventy **y** are completed,
Da   9. 2 of Jerusalem, namely, seventy **y.**
2Pe   3. 8 the Lord one day is like a thousand **y,**
Rev 20. 2 and bound him for a thousand **y,**

YEAST
Mt   16. 6 beware of the **y** of the Pharisees and
Gal   5. 9 A little **y** leavens the whole batch of

YESTERDAY
Heb 13. 8 Jesus Christ is the same **y** and today

YOKE
Mt   11.30 my **y** is easy, and my burden is light."

YOUTH → YOUNG
Ecc 12. 1 Remember your creator in the days of your **y,**

Z

ZEAL
1Mc   2.26 Thus he burned with **z** for the law,
Ps   69. 9 **z** for your house that has consumed me
Jn   2.17 "**Z** for your house will consume me.
Ro   10. 2 testify that they have a **z** for God,

ZION
2Sa   5. 7 David took the stronghold of **Z,**
Ps   2. 6 I have set my king on **Z,** my holy hill.
Isa 28.16 I am laying in **Z** a foundation stone,
Mic   4. 2 For out of **Z** shall go forth instruction,
Zec   9. 9 Rejoice greatly, O daughter **Z!**
Mt   21. 5 "Tell the daughter of **Z,**
Ro   11.26 "Out of **Z** will come the Deliverer;
1Pe   2. 6 "See, I am laying in **Z** a stone,
Rev 14. 1 the Lamb, standing on Mount **Z!**

∧ ∨ CONCORDANCE